Langenscheidts
Fachwörterbücher

Langenscheidt's Dictionary of Agriculture, Forestry and Horticulture

German-English

Reprint of the first edition

Edited by
Dr. agr. Peter Mühle

Langenscheidt
Berlin · München · Wien · Zürich · New York

Langenscheidts Fachwörterbuch Landwirtschaft, Forstwirtschaft und Gartenbau

Deutsch-Englisch

Nachdruck der ersten Auflage

Herausgegeben von
Dr. agr. Peter Mühle

Langenscheidt
Berlin · München · Wien · Zürich · New York

Autoren:

Dipl.-Gärtn. *Dorothea Fritzsche*, Dr. agr. *Sabine Granda*, Dr. agr. *Peter Mühle, Wolfgang Neubert*, Dipl. phil. *Helga Schuricht*

Die Deutsche Bibliothek - CIP-Einheitsaufnahme

Langenscheidts Fachwörterbuch Landwirtschaft, Forstwirtschaft und Gartenbau / hrsg. von Peter Mühle. [Autoren: Dorothea Fritzsche ...]. - Berlin ; München ; Wien ; Zürich ; New York : Langenscheidt
Deutsch-Englisch. - Nachdr. der 1. Aufl. - 2002
ISBN 3-86117-025-6

Eingetragene (registrierte) Warenzeichen sowie Gebrauchsmuster und Patente sind in diesem Wörterbuch nicht ausdrücklich gekennzeichnet. Daraus kann nicht geschlossen werden, daß die betreffenden Bezeichnungen frei sind oder frei verwendet werden können.

Das Werk ist urheberrechtlich geschützt. Jede Verwendung außerhalb der Grenzen des Urheberrechtsgesetztes bedarf der vorherigen schriftlichen Zustimmung des Verlages. Dies gilt besonders für Übersetzungen, Vervielfältigungen, auch von Teilen des Werkes, Mikroverfilmungen, Bearbeitungen sonstiger Art sowie für die Einspeicherung in elektronische Systeme.

ISBN 3-86117-025-6

Nachdruck der 1. Auflage 2002
© Langenscheidt Fachverlag GmbH München (ehem. Verlag Alexandre Hatier) 1993
Printed in Germany
Gesamtherstellung: Druckhaus „Thomas Müntzer" GmbH, Bad Langensalza/Thüringen
Lektor: *Helga Kautz*

Vorwort

Das Wörterbuch bietet dem Nutzer mit etwa 65 000 Wortstellen die bisher umfangreichste Zusammenstellung von Begriffen der Land- und Forstwirtschaft wie auch angrenzender Fachgebiete.
Grundlage für den Wortbestand bildete der englisch-deutsche Band. Die Wortstellen wurden durch das Autorenteam anhand moderner Fachliteratur überprüft, weniger wichtige Wortstellen wurden eliminiert und zahlreiche neue Termini, u. a. aus den Bereichen Wirtschaft und besonders der Ökologie, wurden ergänzt. Neben Termini aus den naturwissenschaftlichen Grundlagenfächern werden die einschlägigen Spezies von Nutzpflanzen und Nutztieren, Nützlingen und Schädlingen geboten; Termini aus dem Landbau von der Bestellung bis zur Ernte einschließlich technischer Ausrüstungen, aus der Tierhaltung einschließlich veterinärmedizinischer Aspekte sowie aus der Forstwirtschaft bis hin zur Verarbeitung land- und forstwirtschaftlicher Produkte werden berücksichtigt.
Bei der Auswahl und Benennung der Pflanzen dienten Standardwerke wie der „Zander – Handwörterbuch der Pflanzennamen" und „Rudolf Mansfelds Kulturpflanzenverzeichnis" als Grundlage. Bei der Benennung von Enzymen wurde die EC-Nomenklatur zugrunde gelegt. Die Schreibung chemischer Verbindungen entspricht weitgehend den Empfehlungen der IUPAC. Bei der alphabetischen Einordnung wurde auch in diesem Band das bewährte Nestwortsystem angewandt. Aus Adjektiv und Substantiv bestehende Pflanzen- und Tiernamen sowie die Namen von Rassen, Viren und Virosen sind in ihrer natürlichen Wortfolge aufgenommen worden.
Ich möchte nicht versäumen, den Mitautoren für ihre Arbeit auch an diesem Band zu danken. Mein Dank gilt ferner dem Verlag für die verständnisvolle Förderung des Vorhabens sowie der Lektorin, Frau *Helga Kautz*, für ihren unverzichtbaren Beitrag zur lexikographischen Aufbereitung, Korrektur und Verbesserung des Manuskripts.
Ich hoffe, daß auch dieser Band bei den Nutzern eine gute Aufnahme finden und zur Vertiefung der Kontakte zwischen den Fachleuten der beiden Sprachgebiete beitragen wird.
Wie bei einer Erstauflage nicht anders zu erwarten, wird auch dieser Band nicht frei von Unzulänglichkeiten sein. Ich bitte darum, kritische Hinweise und Vorschläge, die einer Verbesserung weiterer Auflagen dienen können, an den Langenscheidt Fachverlag GmbH, Postfach 40 11 20, 80711 München, zu richten.

Die Autoren

Preface

The German-English Dictionary of Agriculture, Forestry and Horticulture presented here by Verlag A. Hatier is the companion volume to the English-German edition previously published by Verlag Technik.
With about 65,000 terms, the dictionary is the most comprehensive collection available on agriculture, forestry and adjacent disciplines.
The present work is based on the English-German volume. The terms were checked by the compilers with the latest literature in the field, items of minor importance omitted and a large number of new ones included for the first time, e.g. from the fields of business and ecology. Apart from the fundamental natural sciences, the dictionary includes the names of species of useful plants and animals, beneficial animals and pests. It also covers farming terms from sowing to harvesting, including the relevant machinery and equipment, the vocabulary of animal husbandry and veterinary medicine as well as forestry terms and including the processing of agricultural produce, timber, etc.
The selection and designation of plants was based on standard works like "Zander – Handwörterbuch der Pflanzennamen" and "Rudolf Mansfelds Kulturpflanzenverzeichnis", while the names of enzymes conform with the EC nomenclature. The spelling of chemical compounds largely accords with IUPAC recommendations.
In this dictionary we have used the proven key word system and listed terms consisting of a key word and a complement under the former. Where the names of plants and animals consists of adjectives and nouns they are listed in their natural written and spoken order. The same applies to the names of breeds, viruses and viroses.

I would like to thank my co-authors for their assistance with the volume. My thanks also go out to Verlag A. Hatier for their encouragement and understanding, and to publisher's reader Mrs. *Helga Kautz* for her invaluable lexicographical work, proofreading and correction of the manuscript.
I hope that the present volume will meet with a positive reception and help to further contacts between English and German-speaking experts in the field.
Any first edition ist bound to have its weaknesses, and the present volume is no exception. I would therefore be grateful for any criticisms and suggestions with might help to improve future editions. They should be addressed to Langenscheidt Fachverlag GmbH, Postfach 40 11 20, 80711 München.

Peter Mühle

Benutzungshinweise · Directions for Use

1. Beispiele für die alphabetische Ordnung · Examples of Alphabetization

Destillationsholz
detritivor
Deutsch Drahthaar
Deutsche Bunte Edelziege
~ Landrasse
Deutscher Schäferhund
Deutsches Braunvieh
~ Edelschwein
~ Schwarzbuntes Rind
DFD-Fleisch
Diallelkreuzung
Diätfuttermittel
Dibbelmaschine
dibbeln
Dibbelsaat
Dickdarmflora
dicklegen
Dickmaische
Diffusionssaft
digerieren
diploid
Dissimilation
DL
DL-Methode
DmR
DNA-Fragmentierung
DNA-Polymerase
~/RNA-abhängige
domestizieren
DoR

Jagddruck
jagen
~/Federwild
~/mit dem Beizhabicht
~/zu Pferde
Jagen
Jahreseinschlag
Jahreshiebssatz
Jahresring
Jahresringmessung
Jahreszeit
• der ~ entsprechend
• nicht der ~ entsprechend
~ erhöhter Waldbrandgefahr
~/lichtarme
~/vegetationslose
Jahreszyklus
Jährige Rispe
Jährling
Japan-B-Virus
Japanische Wachtel
Japanische-B-Enzephalitis
Japanischer Buchweizen
Jätemaschine
jäten
Jauche
Jauchedrillgerät
Jauchepumpe
Jauchetankwagen
jauchig

Kursive Symbole wie *m-, o-, p-, N-, D-, L-* in chemischen Verbindungen und griechische Buchstaben bleiben bei der alphabetischen Einordnung unberücksichtigt.
Italicized symbols like *m-, o-, p-, N-, D-, L-* in chemical compounds and Greek letters are disregarded in alphabetization.

2. Zeichen · Signs

/	Getreide/grobvermahlenes = grobvermahlenes Getreide
( )	Gefurchter Dickmaulrüßler (Lappenrüßler) = Gefurchter Dickmaulrüßler *oder* Gefurchter Lappenrüßler
	inorganic (mineral) fertilizer = inorganic fertilizer *or* mineral fertilizer
[ ]	Dreibock[pflück]leiter = Dreibockpflückleiter *oder* Dreibockleiter
	final [harvest] cut = final harvest cut *or* final cut
( )	Diese Klammern enthalten Erklärungen
	These brackets contain explanations

Abkürzungen · Abbreviations

Am	American English/amerikanisches Englisch
api	apiculture/Bienenwirtschaft
biom	biometry/Biometrie
bot	botany/Botanik
convar., convar.	convariety/Konvarietät
cv., cv.	cultivar/Sorte
dairy	dairying/Milchwirtschaft
e.g.	for example/zum Beispiel
ecol	ecology/Ökologie
ent	entomology/Entomologie
esp.	especially/besonders
f	feminine noun/Femininum
f., f.	form/Form
f.sp., f.sp.	special form/Spezialform
forest	forestry/Forstwirtschaft
gen	genetics/Genetik
hunt	hunting/Wildwirtschaft und Jagdwesen
m	masculine noun/Maskulinum
n	neuter noun/Neutrum
phyt	phytopathology and plant protection/Phytopathologie und Pflanzenschutz
pisc	ichthyology and pisciculture/Fischkunde und Fischwirtschaft
pl	plural/Plural
s.	see/siehe
s.a.	see also/siehe auch
slaught	slaughtering and carcass processing/Schlachtung und Schlachtkörperaufbereitung
spp., spp.	species plural/Arten
ssp., ssp.	subspecies/Unterart
var., var.	variety/Varietät
vet	veterinary medicine/Veterinärmedizin
x, x	hybrid/Hybride
zoo	zoology/Zoologie

A

a *s.* Ar
A *s.* 1. Adenin; 2. Aushieb
Aal *m* eel, Anguilla anguilla
Aalfangkorb *m* buck
Aalkultur *f* eel culture
Aalquappe *f* burbot, Lota lota
Aalreuse *f* pod-net
Aalstrich *m* eel stripe (back), dorsal stripe *(at animal's back)*
AAR *s.* Antigen-Antikörper-Reaktion
AAS *s.* Adaptationssyndrom/allgemeines
Aas *n* carrion
Aasblume *f* carrion flower, stapelia *(genus Stapelia)*
Aasfauna *f* carrion fauna
aasfressend necrophagous
Aasfresser *m* carrion feeder
Aasjagd *f (hunter's language)* pot-hunting
Aasjäger *m* pot-hunter
Aaskäfer *m* carrion (burying) beetle *(family Silphidae)*
Aasseite *f* flesh side *(of furs)*
Aba, ABA *s.* Abscisinsäure
Abaca *m* abaca, Manila [hemp] *(from Musa textilis)*
Abachi *n s.* Abachiholz
Abachibaum *m* obeche, Triplochiton scleroxylon
Abachiholz *n* obeche
abakteriell abacterial, abacillary
Abart *f* variety
abäsen *s.* äsen
Abasie *f (vet)* abasia
abasten *s.* asten
abbalgen to skin, to flay *(e.g. hares or wildfowl)*
Abbau *m* 1. degradation, breakdown; 2. decay, decomposition, disintegration; 3. degeneration *(yield depression of crop plants due to insufficient breeding work)*
~/**bakterieller** biodegradation, biodestruction
~/**biologischer** biodegradation, biodestruction
~/**chemischer** chemical breakdown
~/**durch Pilze bewirkter** mycogenic decomposition
~ **körpereigener Stoffe** catabolism, destructive metabolism
~/**mikrobieller** microbial degradation
~/**mykogener** mycogenic decomposition
~/**oxidativer** oxidative degradation
~/**photochemischer** photodegradation *(e.g. of wood substances)*
~ **von Inhaltsstoffen** decline *(of fruits during storage)*
abbaubar degradable, decomposable
~/**bakteriell** biodegradable
~/**biologisch** biodegradable
~/**nicht** undegradable
Abbaubarkeit *f* degradability, decomposability
~/**bakterielle** biodegradability
~/**biologische** biodegradability

abbauen 1. to degrade, to break down *(e.g. nutrients)*; 2. to decay, to decompose, to disintegrate; 3. to degenerate, to run out *(yield)*
~/**bakteriell** to biodegrade
~/**biologisch** to biodegrade
~/**chemisch** to degrade
~/**körpereigene Stoffe** to catabolize
~/**zu Dextrin** to dextrinize
~/**zu Pepton** to peptonize
Abbaukrankheit *f (phyt)* degeneration (replant) disease, decline [disease]
Abbaulage *f* degeneration area
Abbauprodukt *n* degradation (breakdown) product; decomposition product; detritus
abbeeren to [de]stem, to strip *(grapes)*
Abbeermaschine *f* stemmer, stalk separator
Abbeilen *n* rounding-up, setting-up, facing, laying-in, notching *(of root collars at tree felling)*
abbeißen to bite off; to browse
abbinden to set, to cure *(adhesive)*
abblättern to exfoliate, to peel [off]
Abblätterung *f* exfoliation, peeling
abborken to rind, to flay
abböschen to slope
abbrechen to break off, to snap off *(e.g. lateral shoots)*
~/**die Jagd** to call off, to interrupt
Abbrechen *n* **der Krone** crown break[age]
abbrennen to burn down (off)
Abbrennen *n* burning down (off), flaming
~ **der Stoppel** stubble burning
~/**flächenweises [kontrolliertes]** broadcast burning
~/**frühzeitiges gezieltes** early burning *(forest fire prevention)*
~/**gezieltes** prescribed burning *(forest fire prevention)*
~/**kontrolliertes** controlled burning
Abbrennmittel *n* deflagrating agent
abbrühen to blanch, to scald
abbrunften to cease rutting
ABC-Boden *m* ABC soil
ABC-Krankheit *f* **der Kartoffel** potato ABC disease *(virosis)*
ABC-Profil *n (soil)* ABC profile
abdämmen to dam up
abdarren to cure *(malt)*
abdecken 1. to cover *(e.g. sown seeds)*; 2. to flay, to skin
~/**mit einem Netz** to net
~/**mit Erde** to earth over; to bury *(e.g. potato clamps)*
~/**mit Fenstern (Frühbeetfenstern)** to glass up
~/**mit Glas** to glass up
~/**mit Stroh** to straw
Abdecker *m* flayer, knacker, skinner
Abdeckerei *f* flaying-house, knackery
Abdeckhaube *f* hotcap *(for single plants)*
Abdeckmaterial *n* covering material

Abdeckung

Abdeckung f **mit Polyethylenfolie** polyethylene covering
abdestillieren to distil off
Abdomen n (zoo) abdomen; hind body (of arthropods) • **im ~ liegend** intra-abdominal
abdominal abdominal
Abdominalbein n, **Abdominalfuß** m (ent) proleg
Abdominalgravidität f abdominal pregnancy
Abdominalsegment n abdominal segment
Abdominoskopie f (vet) laparoscopy
abdrängen to push aside (animal behaviour)
Abdrehen n calibration (of a seeder)
Abdrehkurbel f proof crank, hand crank
Abdrehprobe f calibration test
Abdrift f drift (e.g. in broadcasting of plant protectants)
Abdriftgefahr f drift danger
Abdriftkontrolle f drift control
Abdriftverlust m drift loss
Abduktion f abduction (of limbs)
Abduktor m abductor [muscle]
abduzieren to abduct (limbs)
Abendfütterung f evening feeding
Abendgemelk n evening milk
Abendländische Platane f American plane[-tree], buttonwood, Platanus occidentalis
Abendländischer Lebensbaum m common arbor vitae, northern white cedar, Thuja occidentalis
Abendlevkoje f night scented stock, evening stock, Matthiola [longipetala ssp.] bicornis
Abendmilch f evening milk
Abendschildlaus f soft [brown] scale, Coccus hesperidum
Abendtau m night dew
abenterisch abenteric
Aberdeen Angus n, **Aberdeenrind** n Aberdeen [Angus] (cattle breed)
abernten s. ernten
aberrant aberrant
Aberration f aberration
~/chromosomale chromosomal aberration
Abessinierkatze f Abyssinian cat (breed)
Abessiniertee m Arabian tea, Catha edulis
Abessinische Zwerghirse f Abyssinian love grass, teff [grass], Eragrostis tef (abyssinica)
Abessinischer Meerkohl m (bot) crambe, Crambe abyssinica
~ Senf m Abyssinian mustard, Brassica carinata
Abessinisches Liebesgras n s. Abessinische Zwerghirse
abfahren to cart off (away), to haul
abfährten (hunt) to track
Abfall m 1. waste, refuse, offal; garbage, cleansing; 2. s. Abfallen
~/tierischer animal waste
Abfallaufbereitung f [zur Wiederverwertung] recycling
abfallen to fall off, to drop, to shed (e.g. leaves)
~ lassen to abscise (plant organs)

Abfallen n falling off, fall, drop
~ der Blüten flower drop (fall)
~ erntereifer Früchte fruit (harvest) drop
~/vorzeitiges premature fall (of fruits)
abfallend 1. deciduous (leaves); 2. s. abholzig
~/frühzeitig (bot, zoo) caducous
Abfallenergie f waste energy
Abfallhalde f waste tip
Abfallholz n waste wood, wood waste (residues, refuse), collars
abfällig s. abholzig
Abfallkalk m waste lime (fertilizer)
Abfallkompostierung f waste composting
Abfallmaterial n waste material
Abfallmolke f whey waste
Abfallprodukt n s. Abprodukt
Abfallreisig n lop and top, loppings, lops, browst, (Am) lapwood
Abfallverwertung f waste utilization
Abfallwärme f waste heat
Abfallwolle f tailings
Abfallzerkleinerer m refuse grinder
abfangen to intercept (e.g. precipitation by tree crowns)
Abferkelbereich m farrowing area
Abferkelbox f, **Abferkelbucht** f farrowing pen, farrowing crate (stall)
Abferkelergebnis n farrowing result
abferkeln to farrow [down], to pig
Abferkelperiode f farrowing period (season)
Abferkelrate f farrowing rate
Abferkelstall m farrowing[-lactation] house, swine farrowing unit
Abferkelung f farrowing
abfischen to fish out, to harvest • **mit Netzen ~** to net
abflachen/die Krone to flatten the head (orcharding)
abflammen to flame (e.g. field plots); to singe (e.g. a carcass)
Abflammgerät n **zur Unkrautbekämpfung** flame cultivator, flame weeder
abfliegen to fly off (wildfowl)
abfließen to flow off, to drain [off], to discharge
~ lassen to discharge
abflügeln to dewing (seeds)
Abfluß m 1. flowing (draining) off, [stream] discharge, stream flow; run-off; 2. outlet, drain
~/bodeninnerer subsurface run-off, interflow
~/oberirdischer overland flow
~/unterirdischer underground run-off
Abflußbecken n drainage basin
Abflußgebiet n water catchment
Abflußgraben m drain
Abflußhydrograph m runoff hydrograph
Abflußkanal m discharge (escape) channel; outlet channel (ditch), outfall (wasteway) channel; drain
Abflußkurvenzahl f (soil) run-off curve number
Abflußleitung f discharge (outlet) line; sewer, waste line

Abflußmenge f run-off
Abflußmengenkurve f hydrograph
Abflußöffnung f outlet
Abflußparzelle f run-off plot
Abflußregulierung f stream flow control
Abflußrinne f outlet channel (ditch), outfall channel
Abflußrohr n drain pipe, run-off tube
Abflußwasser n runoff water
Abfohlbox f foaling box
abfohlen to foal [down]
Abfohlrate f foaling rate
Abfohlzeit f foaling season
Abfolge f (ecol) succession
Abformigkeit f s. Abholzigkeit
Abfräswalze f discharge beater
abfressen to eat away, to eat (bite) off, to browse (shoots, twigs)
Abfuhr f (forest) haulage, removal
~/baumweise full-tree removal
abführen s. abrichten
abführend laxative, purgative
Abfuhrentfernung f transport distance
Abführmittel n laxative, purgative
Abfuhrperiode f hauling season, removal period
Abfuhrstraße f, **Abfuhrweg** m clearing (export) road, track
Abfuhrzeit f s. Abfuhrperiode
Abfüllanlage f filling station; bottling line
abfüllen to fill [up]; to rack [off] (wine, beer)
~/in Säcke to bag, to sack
Abfüllvorrichtung f filling device, filler
Abfüllwaage f bagging scale (weigher), bagging and weighing unit
Abgabe f 1. delivery; release; 2. levy
Abgang m reject (from sorting or cleaning processes); offal (milling); waste [material]
~/natürlicher (forest) stand mortality
Abgangsrate f culling rate (breeding)
Abgangsstadium n stage of decline (declining) (of a tree)
Abgas n exhaust [gas], waste (flue) gas
Abgasanlage f exhaust [system]
Abgasturbolader m turbocharger
abgebaut worn-out (grape-vine)
abgeben/Wasserdampf to transpire
abgebissen (bot, ent) premorse
abgeblüht deflorate
abgebrochen (bot) abrupt
abgeflacht (bot) applanate
abgehärtet hardened, hardy
Abgehen n **der Nachgeburt** placental separation
abgelagert seasoned (e.g. wood); mellow, mature (wine)
abgemagert (vet) emaciated, cachectic
abgenicken (hunt) to stab
abgeschwemmt (soil) colluvial
abgesetzt firm (soil, seed-bed)
abgestorben necrotic, dead
abgestumpft (bot, zoo) obtuse, retuse

abgetragen truncate[d] (soil); cutover (peatbog)
abgetrieben worn-out, screwy (horse)
abgeworfen werden to unhorse
abgezehrt (vet) emaciated, cachectic
abgipfeln to poll[ard], to [be]head, to decapitate; to lop [off], to trim
Abgleitcontainer m sliding container
abgraben to digg off
abgrasen to graze off (down), to run; to browse
abgrenzen to demarcate, to mark off
Abgrenzung f 1. demarcation; 2. determination (developmental physiology)
Abhaaren n pelage shedding
abhacken to chop off; to cut off (down) (e.g. trees)
abhalftern to unharness
abhalsen to unleash, to uncouple (a dog)
Abhang m slope
abhären to change hair
abharken to rake off
abhärten to harden, to acclimate; to wean (nursery plants)
Abhärten n, **Abhärtung** f hardening, acclimation; weaning (of nursery plants)
abhauben to unhood (falconry)
abhäufeln to unearth
abhäuten to flay, to skin; to peel
Abhieb m felling point (between bole and stump)
abhobeln to plane [off], to dress
abholzen to deforest, to cut down (over), to clear[-cut], to fell, (Am) to log
Abholzen n deforestation, clear-cut[ting], clear felling, clearing
abholzig taper[ing], falling off
Abholzigkeit f [stem, tree] taper, taperness, fall off (timber mensuration)
Abholzigkeitskurve f taper curve
Abholzigkeitstafel f taper table
Abholzung f s. Abholzen
abhorchen (vet) to auscultate
Abhorchen n auscultation
abhüten to fold off
Abieta-7,14-dien-19-carbonsäure f, **Abietinsäure** f abieti[ni]c acid, sylvic acid (resin acid, diterpene)
Abietum n fir forest
abimpfen to subculture (microbiology)
Abimpfung f subculture
Abiose f abiosis
Abiotinose f (vet) abiotinosis, biotin deficiency
abiotisch abiotic, inanimate
abiotroph abiotrophic
Abiotrophie f abiotrophy
Abiozön n (ecol) abiocoen
Abkalbeabteilung f calving pen
Abkalbebox f calving pen
Abkalbeergebnis n percent calf crop
abkalben to calve [down], to freshen
Abkalben n calving
Abkalbeplatz m calving stall

Abkalberate

Abkalberate f calving rate
Abkalbestall m calving house; calving stall
Abkalbezeit f calving season (time)
abkanten to edge *(timber)*
abkappen to poll[ard], to [be]head, to decapitate *(trees)*; to nose *(a bole)*; to trim, to equalize, to end-butt *(sawn wood)*
abklären to clarify; to fine [down] *(beer)*
abklassifizieren to downgrade *(e.g. breeding animals)*
Abklassifizierung f downgrading
Abklatschgeschwür n *(vet)* contact ulcer
Abklopfen n **der Körperoberfläche** *(vet)* percussion
abknackend crisp *(e.g. apples)*
abknospen to disbud
abkochen to decoct
Abkochung f decoction
Abkömmling m descendant, offspring
abkoppen to nose *(a bole)*
abkoppeln s. abhalsen
Abkotverhalten n excretory behaviour
Abkühlungsperiode f cooling period *(e.g. in potato storage)*
Abkürzsäge f s. Ablängsäge
Abladegebläse- und Dosieranlage f unloading blower and batcher
abladen to unload, to offload, to discharge
Abladeschneidgebläse n unloader chopper blower
Abladevorrichtung f unloader
Ablage f **zunächst unbefruchteter Eier** *(ent)* oviparity
ablagern to age, to mellow *(wine)*
~ lassen to age; to season *(timber)*
Ablagern n ag[e]ing *(esp. food, wine)*
Ablagerung f 1. deposition, sedimentation; 2. deposit, sediment
~/äolische *(soil)* 1. aeolian deposition; 2. aeolian deposit, wind[-borne] deposit
~/eiszeitliche (glaziale) *(soil)* glacial deposit
~/organische *(soil)* organic deposit
ablaichen to spawn
Ablaktation f 1. *(bot)* ablactation, inarching, grafting by approach, approach-grafting; 2. *(zoo)* ablactation, weaning
ablaktieren 1. *(bot)* to ablactate, to inarch, to graft by approach; 2. *(zoo)* to ablactate, to wean, to spean
Ablaktieren n s. Ablaktation
Ablammbucht f lambing pen
ablammen to lamb, to yean
Ablammen n lambing
Ablammergebnis n lambing percentage (result), lamb crop
Ablammkoppel f lambing paddock
Ablammrate f lambing rate
Ablammstall m lambing shed
Ablammzeit f lambing period, time of lambing

ablängen 1. to cut into lengths, to buck, to crosscut into logs, to log; to trim; 2. to measure off, to mark off, to lay off *(felled timber)*
Ablänger m, **Ablängmaschine** f *(forest)* slasher, bucker, bucksaw
Ablängprogramm n bucking programme
Ablängreste mpl trim ends, trimmings
Ablängsäge f docking saw, docker, drag saw; cutoff saw; slasher, bucker, bucksaw; log crosscutting saw; [end-]trimmer, trimming machine
~/einfache single-end docker
Ablängsägemaschine f s. Ablängsäge
Ablängstab m measuring stick, [one-metre] measuring rod
Ablängtabelle f bucking table
Abläng- und Bündelmaschine f bucker-buncher
Ablängungsabfall m, **Ablängungsverlust** m trimming waste, trimmings
Ablängzeichen n trimming mark
ablassen to drain *(a pond)*
Ablaßventil n discharge (outlet) valve; safety valve
Ablation f ablation
Ablationsmoräne f *(soil)* ablation moraine
Ablauf m 1. course; 2. run-off, effluent
~/grüner green syrup *(sugar manufacture)*
Ablaufbrett n draining board
abläufig s. abholzig
Ablauftrennung f classification of runnings, syrup separation *(sugar manufacture)*
abläutern to lauter, to clarify
ablegen/Eier *(ent)* to oviposit, to blow
~/in Haufen to pile *(e.g. crop products)*
~/seitlich to flank *(an animal e.g. for veterinary treatment)*
Ableger m 1. scion; cutting; slip; 2. s. Absenker; 3. nucleus [honey-bee colony], subsidiary nest
Ablegerbeute f *(api)* nuc[leus] box, nucleus hive
Ablegerbildung f *(api)* making increase
Ablegerkasten m *(api)* nuc[leus] box, nucleus hive
ablehren to calliper
Ablieferungssoll n procurement obligation, delivery quota
Ablösekraft f removal force *(e.g. to separate fruits from their fruit wood)*
ablösen to peel [off] *(e.g. bark)*
Ablösung f **von Baumarten** *(forest)* succession of tree species, species conversion
Abluft f leaving (outgoing) air; spent (foul) air
Abluftschacht m flue
abmagern to emaciate, to atrophy
abmagernd atrophic
Abmagerung f emaciation, atrophy, cachexia
abmähen to mow [off], to reap, to crop
abmaischen to finish mashing *(brewing)*
Abmaischen n final mashing (mash pumping)
Abmelkbetrieb m dairy
~/städtischer town dairy
Abmelkstall m flying herd cowshed
Abmelkwirtschaft f milk-and-feed system

abmessen to measure; to scale *(timber)*
Abmoosen *n* air layering, marcottage, marcotting
AbMV *s.* Abutilonmosaikvirus
Abnabelung *f* omphalotomy
Abnahme *f (forest)* registration of felled timber, revision of felling record, coupe inventory, produce check, acceptance
abnicken *(hunt)* to stab
abnorm abnormal, anomalous
Abnormität *f* abnormality, anomaly
Abnutzung *f* wear
Abnutzungspigment *n* lipofuscin
Abnutzungssatz *m (forest)* allowable cut, prescribed cut (yield)
A-Bock *m* **[für Verladezwecke]** A-frame *(timber transport)*
abomasal abomasal
Abomasitis *f (vet)* abomasitis
Abomasum *n* abomasum, abomasus, rennet stomach (bag), fourth (true) stomach, reed, maw
aboral aboral; caudal
Abort *m (vet)* abortion • **einen ~ herbeiführen** to abort • **einen ~ herbeiführend** abortifacient
~/der Schafe enzootischer enzootic abortion in sheep
çhabitueller habitual abortion
~/wiederholt auftretender habitual abortion
Abortfliege *f* moth fly *(genus Psychoda)*
abortieren to abort, to slink
Abortin *n* brucellin *(allergen)*
Abortion *f (bot, phyt)* abortion
abortiv abortive • **~ wirkend** abortifacient
Abortivum *n* abortifacient [agent]
Abortseuche *f* contagious abortion
Abortus *m s.* Abort
Abortus-Bang-Ringprobe *f (vet)* ring test
Abpackschuppen *m* packing-house, packing-shed
abplaggen to pare off turf, to cut sods, to screef
abplatzen to peel [off]
Abposten *n s.* Abnahme
Abprodukt *n* 1. waste [product], off-product, offal; 2. *s.* ~/ verwertbares
~ der [maschinellen] Reisaufbereitung rice by-product
~/industrielles industrial waste
~/verwertbares [usable] by-product
Abproduktbeseitigung *f* disposal of waste products
Abpuffern *n* buffering
ABR *s.* Abortus-Bang-Ringprobe
abrahmen to skim, to cream [off]
abrasen *s.* abplaggen
Abrasion *f* abrasion
Abraum *m* 1. felling refuse (waste), logging residues (debris), slash, brash; brushwood; 2. mine spoil, rubbish, waste
abräumen to clear *(e.g. a harvest area)*
Abräumen *n* clearance

Abraumhalde *f,* **Abraumkippe** *f* [mine] dump, spoil heap (bank)
Abraumverbrennung *f* slash burning
Abraumwall *m* **[gegen Hangerosion]** trash bund
abraupen to clear of caterpillars
abrechen to rake off
abreiben/den Bast to fray (burnish, rub off) the antlers *(e.g. at tree-trunks)*
Abreiben *n* **des Bastes** fraying, antler burnishing, rubbing-off
abrichten to break [in], to train; to enter *(a hunting dog)*
Abrichter *m* dog-breaker
Abrichtung *f* training
Abrieb *m* abrasion
Abriebfestigkeit *f* abrasion resistance
Abriebverschleiß *m* abrasive wear
Abriß *m* stool-layer, mound-layer *(shoot from a back-cut mother plant)*
Abrißgewinnung *f* **im Mutterbeet** stoolbed harvesting *(esp. of fruitwood rootstocks)*
Abrißvermehrung *f* stool-layering, mound-layering *(esp. of fruitwood rootstocks)*
Abrollnest *n* roll-away [laying] nest *(poultry management)*
absacken to bag, to sack
Absackplattform *f,* **Absackstand** *m* bagging platform
Absackstutzen *m* bagging-off spout
Absackvorrichtung *f* bagging device, bagging-off facility, bagger
Absackwaage *f* bagging scale (weigher), bagging and weighing unit
absägen to saw off
absahnen to skim, to cream [off]
absamen to ejaculate
Absamintervall *n* semen collection interval
absatteln to unsaddle
Absatz *m* **landwirtschaftlicher Erzeugnisse** agricultural marketing
Absatzboden *m* colluvial (transported) soil
Absatzferkel *n s.* Absetzferkel
Absatzgestein *n* sedimentary rock
abschälen to decorticate, to peel; *(Am)* to ross *(stemwood)*
~/Borke to flay, to scale
abschätzen to estimate, to appraise; *(forest)* to cruise
Abschätzung *f* estimation, appraisal, appraisement; *(forest)* cruise
abscheiden to separate; to precipitate
~/Erde to de-earth
~/Wasser in Tropfenform to guttate
Abscheider *m* separator, separating device
Abscheiderotor *m* rotary separator
Abscheidung *f* 1. separation; precipitation; deposition; 2. deposit
Abscheidungsthrombose *f (vet)* thrombosis
abscheren to shear

abscheren

~/**Klunkern (Schmutzwolle)** to dag, to dod[d]
Abscheren n shear
Abscherwiderstand m shear resistance (strength) (e.g. of a soil)
Abschiebebandfütterer m, **Abschiebefutterband** n push-off belt feeder
Abschiebe[heu]gabel f push-off stacker
abschiefern to exfoliate
abschiefernd scaly, flaky (e.g. wood)
Abschieferung f exfoliation
Abschilferung f desquamation
abschirmen to screen; to shelter
abschirren to unharness, to outspan
abschlachten to slaughter, to butcher
Abschlag m cross-drain, scupper, let, grip, (Am) water-bar (road construction)
abschlämmen to elutriate
Abschleiffestigkeit f abrasion resistance
Abschluß m/**hermetischer** hermetic seal
Abschlußbegehung f (forest) concluding circuit
Abschlußhaut f tertiary wall (of plant cells)
Abschlußprotokoll n (forest) concluding record
Abschmelzung f (soil) ablation
abschmieren to lubricate, to grease
Abschmieren n lubrication
Abschmierfett n grease
abschneiden/den Schwanz to tail, to dock
Abschnitt m 1. cutting, section, (of a plant); 2. log, block, bolt
Abschnittsleiter m (Am) line boss (forest fire control)
Abschnürung f strangulation
Abschöpfvorrichtung f skimmer
abschrecken to deter (e.g. pests); to frighten off (game)
Abschreck[ungs]mittel n deterrent; repellent, repelling agent
Abschreck[ungs]wirkung f deterrent action; repellency
Abschreibung f depreciation
abschuppen to desquamate; to exfoliate
Abschuppung f desquamation; exfoliation
Abschuß m 1. shooting (of game); 2. s. Abschußquote
Abschußhirsch m deformed stag
Abschußlimit n s. Abschußquote
Abschußplanung f planning of shooting
Abschußquote f permitted hunter-kill ratio, [normal] kill ratio; bag limit, permitted bag (wildfowl)
~/**jährliche** total bag of the year
Abschußrate f release-kill ratio
abschußreif ripe [for shooting]
abschwächen to attenuate (e.g. virulent causal agents)
abschwächend attenuating; hypomorphic (allele)
abschwarten to skin, to flay; to peel; to slab (roundwood)
Abschwemmung f rain-wash (of soil)
abschwenden (forest) to assart, to burn broadcast

Abschwenden n assartment, broadcast burning
Abscisin n abscisin (phytohormone)
Abscisinsäure f abscisic acid, ABA (terpene, phytohormone)
Abscission f s. Abszission
Abseihbier n waste beer
abseihen to strain off
Absengen n **des Bodens** ground scorching
absenken to layer (offshoots)
Absenken n layering, layerage
~ **in Bodenfurchen** trench layering
~ **von Triebspitzen** tip layering (layerage)
Absenker m layer, offset, offshoot • ~ **mit Haken befestigen** to peg down
~/**bewurzelter** rooted layer
Absenkerhaken m layering peg
Absenkervermehrung f layering, layerage
Absetzalter n weaning age, age at weaning
Absetzbecken n sedimentation tank (basin), precipitation tank
Absetzcontainer m lifted container
absetzen 1. to wean, to spean, to ablactate; 2. to deposit, to sediment
~/**Kot** to defecate, to dung
~/**sich** to settle, to deposit (e.g. soil)
Absetzen n 1. weaning, ablactation; 2. deposition, sedimentation
~ **[krankhaft] großer Harnmengen** polyuria
~ **von Kot** defecation
~/**vorzeitiges** early weaning
Absetzer m 1. weaner, weanling; 2. subsider (sugar manufacture)
Absetzerstall m weaner house, weanery
Absetzferkel n weaner [pig], weanling (starter) pig
Absetzferkelbucht f weaner pen
Absetzferkelstall m weaner house, swine nursery building (house)
Absetzfohlen n weaned (grass) foal
Absetzkalb n weaning calf
Absetzleistung f weaning performance
Absetzmasse f weaning weight
Absetzregime n weaning regimen (schedule)
Absetzteer m settled tar
Absetzteich m settling pond
absicheln to reap, to sickle
absieben to screen
Absiedlung f (vet) metastasis
Absinth m 1. [common] wormwood, Artemisia absinthium; 2. absinth[e] (liqueur)
Absinthin n absinthin (bitter substance)
absitzen to dismount, to alight
absondern 1. to secrete, to excrete; 2. to isolate
~/**ein Tier von der Herde** to cast, (Am) to cut out
~/**Milch** to milk, to lactate
Absonderung f 1. secretion, excretion; 2. isolation
Absonderungsgefüge n (soil) lenticular structure
~/**kryogenes** lenticular structure
Absorbens n absorbent
Absorber m absorber; scrubber

Absorbierbarkeit *f* absorbability
absorbieren to absorb
Absorption *f* absorption
~ durch Wurzeln root absorption
Absorptionsflammenphotometrie *f* absorption flame photometry
Absorptionsgrad *m* absorptivity
Absorptionskälteanlage *f* absorption refrigeration plant
Absorptionskältemaschine *f*, **Absorptionskühlmaschine** *f* absorption refrigeration machine
Absorptionskühlung *f* absorption refrigeration
Absorptionsmittel *n* absorbent
Absorptionsspektrophotometrie *f* [absorption] spectrophotometry
Absorptionsspektrum *n* absorption spectrum
Absorptionsvermögen *n* absorptivity
Absorptionswärmepumpe *f* absorption heat pump
abspalten to split off, to cleave; to separate
Abspaltung *f* cleavage; separation
abspannen to rig [up] *(a cable logging machine)*
Abspannseil *n* guy line, guy rope *(of a cable logging machine)*
Absperrgitter *n* 1. *(api)* queen-excluder; 2. partition *(stable equipment)*
Absperrschieber *m* shutter *(e.g. of a drill)*
abspreizen to spread out, to abduct *(e.g. a limb)*
Abspreizen *n* **von Ästen** branch spreading
Abspreizer *m* abductor [muscle]
Absprengungsfraktur *f (vet)* chip fracture
Abspritzbier *n* overflow beer
Abspülung *f* wash-out
~/flächenhafte *(soil)* denudation
abspüren *(hunt)* to track
abstammen [von] to descend [from], to be descended from, to derive [from]
Abstammung *f* descent, derivation, parentage, blood; lineage, strain
Abstammungsgeschichte *f* phylogenesis, phylogeny
Abstammungskoeffizient *m* coefficient of parentage
Abstammungslehre *f* theory of descent, theory of the origin of species
Abstand *m* **in der Reihe** [with]in-row spacing, spacing with[in] the row
~/verallgemeinerter *(biom)* generalized distance
~ zwischen den Reihen between-row spacing
abständig declining, doddered, overmature *(tree)*
Abstandsbügel *m (api)* spacer [of frame]
Abstandsdurchforstung *f (forest)* stick thinning
Abstandshalter *m s.* Abstandsbügel
abstechen to stick
~/Soden to cut sods, to pare off turf, to screef
Abstechpflug *m* paring plough
Abstechschaufel *f* turf spade (spud)
abstecken to stake out
Absteckpfahl *m*, **Absteckflock** *m* picket

abstehen lassen to age *(flour)*
Abstehende Sammetblume *f* French marigold, Tagetes patula
absterben to die [off], to perish; to wither
~/basipetal *(phyt)* to die back
~/durch Überfeuchtung *(phyt)* to fog
~/infolge Pilzbefalls *(phyt)* to damp off
~/langsam to decline
absterbend *(bot, zoo)* caducous
Absterbeordnung *f* mortality
Absterbeprozeß *m* dying-off
abstocken to stock down
abstoßen *(bot, phyt)* to abort, to abscise
~/die Nachgeburt to cleanse
Abstoßungsreaktion *f* graft rejection
Abstoßungswirkung *f* repellency
Abstrahlung *f* emission
Abstrahlungswärmestrom *m* sensible heat flow (flux)
abstreichen 1. to strip; 2. to fly off, to rode *(wildfowl)*
Abstreicher *m* spade-scraper *(at the body of a disk plough)*
abstreifen to strip
~/Blüten to deflower, to deblossom
~/Samenkapseln to boll
Abstreifer *m* stripper; cleaner *(of a harvesting machine)*
Abstreifmaschine *f* stripping machine, stripper
Abstreifvorsatz *m* stripping header
Abstrich *m (vet)* swab • **einen ~ vornehmen** to swab
Abstrichpräparat *n* swab
Abstrom *m* efflux
abstumpfen 1. to dull, to blunt *(cutting tool)*; 2. to nose *(bole, roundwood)*
abstützen to prop *(e.g. fruit-bearing branches)*
absuchen *(hunt)* to track
Absud *m* decoction
Absüßen *n*, **Absüßung** *f* sweetening off *(sugar manufacture)*
Abszeß *m* abscess
Abszisin *n* abscisin *(phytohormone)*
Abszission *f* abscission *(of plant organs)*
Abszissionszone *f* abscission zone
Abtankhilfseinrichtung *f* auxiliary grain tank unloading system *(of a combine)*
Abtankschnecke *f s.* Austragschnecke
Abtankzeit *f* tank unloading time
abtastbar palpable
abtasten to palpate *(e.g. for pregnancy detection)*
Abtasten *n* palpation
Abteilung *f* 1. *(bot)* division *(taxonomy)*; *(zoo)* phylum *(taxonomy)*; 2. [forest] compartment; 3. compartment, section *(e.g. in dryers)*
Abteilungsgrenze *f* compartment boundary
Abteilungslinie *f*, **Abteilungsschneise** *f* compartment line, ride between compartments

Abteilungsstein

Abteilungsstein *m* boundary stone
abterminal *(bot, zoo)* abterminal
abtöten to kill, to deaden; to destroy *(e.g. bacteria)*
~/durch Frost to frost *(e.g. plants)*
~/durch Ringelung to girdle, to deaden *(a tree)*
Abtötung *f* kill, deadening; destruction
abtragen to train *(a hawk)*
~/flächenhaft *(soil)* to denude
Abtragung *f (soil)* erosion
~ durch Wind deflation
~/flächenhafte denudation
abtransportieren/mit dem Gespann to cart [off]
abtreiben 1. to drift, to drive away; 2. to deforest, to cut down (over), to clear[-cut], *(Am)* to log; 3. to abort
Abtreibungsmittel *n (vet)* abortifacient [agent]
Abtrennung *f* abscission *(of plant organs)*; *(vet)* ablation
Abtrieb *m (forest)* deforestation, clear-cut[ting], clear felling, clearing
Abtriebsalter *n* age at felling (cutting), removal (final) age
Abtriebsertrag *m* final [harvest] yield, net revenue from final cut
Abtriebsfläche *f* area under felling, cutover, coupe
abtriebsreif ripe for felling (cutting), mature
Abtriebsschlag *m* overstorey removal *(in case of natural regeneration)*
Abtriebswert *m* felling (realization) value, exploitation (utilization, liquidation) value
abtrocknen to dry [up, off]
Abtrocknungsperiode *f* drying period *(e.g. in potato storage)*
Abtrommeln *n* paying-out *(of a rope)*
Abtropfen *n* **der Milch** *(vet)* galactorrhoea
Abtropfgewicht *n* drained weight
Abtropfpferch *m* draining (dripping) pen, draining crush *(livestock handling facility)*
Abtropfverlust *m (slaught)* drip
Abundanz *f (ecol)* abundance
Abundanzdynamik *f* abundance dynamics
Abutilonmosaikvirus *n* abutilon mosaic virus
Abwachsteich *m* finishing (fattening, forage) pond
abwandern to emigrate; to drift *(game)*
Abwanderung *f* emigration
~ aus ländlichen Gebieten rural exodus (depopulation)
Abwärme *f* waste heat
Abwärmenutzung *f* waste-heat utilization
Abwärmerückgewinnung *f* waste-heat recovery
Abwasser *n* waste-water, sewage; foul water; effluent [liquid] • **~ verregnen** to sewage
~/städtisches urban (town) sewage
Abwasserbehandlung *f* waste-water treatment; effluent [liquid] treatment
Abwasserbelastung *f* waste-water load
Abwasserbiologie *f* sewage biology
Abwasserfischteich *m* sewage fish-pond
Abwasserkanal *m* sewer
Abwasserlagune *f* sewage lagoon
Abwasserpilz *m* sewage fungus *(comprehensive term)*
Abwasserreinigung *f* sewage purification, waste-water treatment (refining)
Abwasserschlamm *m* sewage sludge
Abwasserschmutzstoff *m* waste-water contaminant
Abwasserteich *m* waste-water pond, sewage (oxidation) pond, lagoon
Abwassertoxizität *f* sewage toxicity
Abwasserverregnung *f* sewage sprinkling (irrigation)
Abwasserverwertungsbetrieb *m* [/landwirtschaftlicher] sewage-farm
abwechselnd alternate
Abwehr *f* defence
Abwehrenzym *n* defence enzyme
Abwehrmechanismus *m* defence mechanism
Abwehrreaktion *f* defence reaction
Abwehrreflex *m* defence reflex
Abwehrstoff *m* deterrent
Abwehrstoffdrüse *f* repugnatorial gland
Abwehrsystem *n* defence mechanism
abweichend aberrant; heterologous; off-type
Abweichung *f* aberration; *(biom)* variation, deviation
~/chromosomale chromosomal aberration
~/durchschnittliche *(biom)* mean deviation
~/epistatische *(gen)* epistatic deviation
~/mittlere *(biom)* mean deviation
~/mittlere quadratische *(biom)* standard deviation, mean square deviation (error)
~/quadratische *(biom)* square deviation
Abweichungsquadrat *n/*mittleres *(biom)* mean square
abweidbar depasturable
abweiden to graze [off], to [de]pasture, to crop
~ lassen to graze, to [de]pasture
Abweiser *m* deflector
abwerfen to cast, to shed, to drop; to abscise *(plant organs)*
~/abgestorbenes Gewebe to slough
~/Blätter s. ~/Laub
~/den Reiter to unhorse
~/durch Bocken to buck [off] *(horseman or burden)*
~/Gehörn (Geweih) to moult
~/Laub to shed (drop) the leaves, to defoliate
~/Nadeln to shed (drop) the needles, to defoliate
Abwerfen *n* **der Krone** heading back the crown
~ der Unterlage heading back the rootstock
abwipfeln to [be]head, to top, to head back (down), to decapitate; to poll[ard]; to lop [off]
abwölfen to whelp
Abwurf *m* cast, shedding, drop; abscission *(of plant organs)*
Abwurfstange *f* shed antler
abyssal, abyssisch abyssal

abzapfen to bleed, to tap *(e.g. a tree)*
abzäumen to unbridle
abzäunen to fence off
~/mit Hürden to hurdle
Abzehrung *f (vet)* cachexia
abziehen 1. to rack [off] *(wine, beer)*; 2. to peel *(carcass)*
~/auf Flaschen to bottle
~/die Haut to skin, to flay
Abzieher[muskel] *m* abductor [muscle]
Abziehmesser *n* cleaning knife, cleaner *(for barking in full)*
abzopfen *(forest)* to top, to [be]head
Abzugshahn *m* cock *(of a gun)*
Abzugsloch *n* drainage hole *(e.g. in a planting pot)*
Abzweigschieber *m* by-pass valve
Acajubaum *m* cashew[-tree], Anacardium occidentale
Acajugummi *n* cashew-gum
Acardius *m (vet)* acardiac[us], acardius
Acarusräude *f (vet)* demodectic mange
AC-Boden *m* AC soil
Acca *f (bot)* feijoa *(genus Acca)*
Acealdehyd *n* acealdehyde *(fungicide)*
Acephat *n* acephate *(insecticide)*
Acervulus *m* acervulus *(cushion-shaped spore-bearing layer of certain fungi)*
Acetacetat *n* acetoacetate
Acetacetyl-CoA-Reductase *f* acetoacetyl-CoA reductase *(enzyme)*
Acetaldehyd *m* acetaldehyde, ethanal
Acetamid *n* acetamide
Acetarsol *n* acetarsol *(anthelminthic)*
Acetat *n* acetate
Acetat-Carboxy-Lyase *f* acetoacetate carboxylyase *(enzyme)*
Acetat-CoA-Ligase *f* acetate-CoA ligase *(enzyme)*
Acetatkinase *f* acetate kinase, acetokinase *(enzyme)*
Acetazolamid *n* acetazolamide *(enzyme inhibitor)*
Acetessigsäure *f* acetoacetic acid
Acetoacetyl-CoA-Thiolase *f* acetyl-CoA acetyltransferase, acetoacetyl-CoA thiolase *(enzyme)*
Acetochlor *n* acetochlor *(herbicide)*
Acetoin *n* acetoin *(microbial metabolite)*
Acetokinase *f* acetate kinase, acetokinase *(enzyme)*
Aceton *n* acetone
Acetonämie *f (vet)* acetonaemia, ketosis, ketonaemia, slow fever
Acetonkörper *m* acetone (ketone) body
Acetonurie *f (vet)* acetonuria, ketonuria
Acetsäure *f* ethanoic acid
Acetylaceton *n* acetylacetone
Acetylaminofluoren *n* acetylaminofluorene *(carcinogen)*
Acetylcellulose *f* cellulose acetate

Acetylcholin *n* acetylcholine *(amino compound, neurotransmitter)*
Acetylcholinesterase *f* acetylcholinesterase *(enzyme)*
Acetyl-CoA *n* acetyl coenzyme A
Acetyl-CoA-Acetyltransferase *f* acetyl-CoA acetyltransferase, acetoacetyl-CoA thiolase *(enzyme)*
Acetyl-CoA-Carboxylase *f* acetyl-CoA carboxylase *(enzyme)*
Acetyl-CoA-Synthetase *f* acetate-CoA ligase *(enzyme)*
Acetyl-Coenzym n A *s.* Acetyl-CoA
Acetylen *n* acetylene, ethyne
Acetylenkohlenwasserstoff *m* alkyne
Acetylenreduktion *f* acetylene reduction
Acetylessigsäure *f* acetoacetic acid
(N-)Acetyl-ß-Glucosaminidase *f* N-acetyl-ß-glucosaminidase, beta-N-acetylglucosaminidase *(enzyme)*
Acetylglutaminsäure *f* acetylglutamic acid *(amino acid)*
Acetylharnstoff *m* acetylurea
Acetylierung *f* acetylation
Acetylmethionin *n* acetylmethionine
Acetylnaphthylesterase *f* acetylnaphthyl esterase *(enzyme)*
Acetylsalicylsäure *f* acetylsalicylic acid, aspirin *(analgesic)*
Achaltekiner *m*, **Achal-Telkinsker** *m* akhal-teke *(horse breed)*
Achäne *f (bot)* achene, akene, achenium
Achillein *n* achillein, betonicine *(plant constituent)*
Achillessehne *f* Achilles tendon, hamstring
AC-Horizontfolge *f (soil)* AC horizon
Achromatin *n* achromatin *(cell nucleus constituent)*
achromatisch achromatic *(e.g. cell parts)*
Achromatose *f* achromatosis, albinism
Achromotrichie *f* achromotrichia
Achromycin *n s.* Tetracyclin
Achse *f* 1. *(bot, zoo)* [main] axis; 2. axle; arbor
• **von der ~ entfernt** *(bot, zoo)* abaxial
Achselhöhle *f* axilla *(animal anatomy)*
Achselknospe *f* axillary (lateral) bud
~ des Rosenkohls Brussels sprout
achselständig *(bot)* axillary
Achsenskelett *n* axial skeleton
achsentfernt *(bot, zoo)* abaxial
Achsenzylinder[fortsatz] *m* axon *(of nerve-cell)*
Achshalterung *f* housing
Achsschenkellenkung *f* king-pin steering assembly
Achsstand *m* wheelbase
Achstrieb *m* lead[ing] shoot, leader *(plant anatomy)*
Achtender *m*, **Achter** *m* stag of eight points (tines)
Achtsamkeit *f* obedience *(of a dog)*

Achtzähniger

Achtzähniger Zirbenborkenkäfer *m* cembra-fir bark-beetle, Ips amitinus [var. montanus]
Achylia *f*, **Achylie** *f (vet)* achylia
Acidophilin *n* acidophilin *(antibiotic)*
Acidosis *f (vet)* acidosis
Acifluorfen *n* acifluorfen *(herbicide)*
Acker *m* field, acre
Ackeranhänger *m* agricultural trailer, farm trailer
Ackeraufforstung *f* afforestation of arable (agricultural) land
Ackerbau *m* [field] husbandry, arable cropping (farming), arable crop production, [arable, tillage] farming, agriculture • ~ **treiben** to farm
~ **ohne Zusatzbewässerung** rain-fed farming, dry[-land] farming
Ackerbaubetrieb *m* arable farm
Ackerbauer *m* arable farmer, tiller
Ackerbaulehre *f* agronomy
ackerbaulich agronomic[al], agricultural
Ackerbaunebenprodukt *n* arable by-product
Ackerbausystem *n* arable farming system, cropping system
Ackerbauzone *f* farming region
Ackerboden *m* [arable] soil, field (tilled, tillage) soil; agricultural (cultivated) soil
Ackerbohne *f* 1. broad (faba, thick, Windsor) bean, fava [bean], Vicia faba; 2. broad (field, horse, tick) bean, fava [bean], Vicia faba var. minor (equina)
Ackerbohnenchlorosevirus *n* broad bean chlorosis virus
Ackerbohnengelbbandvirus *n* broad bean yellow band virus
Ackerbohnenkäfer *m* bean seed beetle, Bruchus rufimanus
Ackerbohnenrost *m* broad bean rust *(caused by Uromyces viciae-fabae)*
Ackerbohnensamenverfärbungsvirus *n* broad bean stain virus, BBSV
Ackerbohnenscheckungsvirus *n* broad bean mottle virus, BBMV
Ackerbohnenwelke *f* broad bean wilt *(virosis)*
Ackerbohnenwelkevirus *n* broad bean wilt virus, BBWV
Ackerbürste *f* field brush, weeder
Ackerdaun *m* red hemp-nettle, Galeopsis ladanum
Ackerdill *m* dill, Anethum graveolens var. graveolens
Ackerdistel *f* creeping (Canada, Canadian) thistle, corn (field) thistle, Cirsium arvense
Ackeregge *f* field (tilling, zigzag) harrow
~/schwere heavy harrow, field drag
Ackerehrenpreis *m* [green] field speedwell, procumbent speedwell, Veronica agrestis
Ackererde *f* arable earth, mould *(s.a. Ackerboden)*
Ackerfräse *f* tiller
Ackerfrauenmantel *m* parsley-piert, Aphanes (Alchemilla) arvensis
Ackerfrucht *f* arable crop
Ackerfrüchte *fpl* [arable] crops, tillage
Ackerfruchtfolge *f* arable rotation (cropping sequence)
Ackerfuchsschwanz *m* 1. green (common) amaranth, *(Am)* redroot [pigweed], Amaranthus retroflexus; 2. black grass, slender foxtail, Alopecurus myosuroides
Ackerfurche *f* furrow
Ackerfutter *n* [arable] forage, field fodder
Ackerfutterbau *m* [arable] forage cropping, forage growing
Ackerfutterfläche *f* forage area
Ackerfutterkultur *f* [arable] forage crop, feed crop
Ackerfutterpflanze *f* field-fodder plant
Ackerfuttersilage *f* arable silage
Ackergalle *f* gall[nut], damp patch
Ackergänsedistel *f* corn (field) sowthistle, creeping (perennial) sowthistle, dindle, Sonchus arvensis
Ackergare *f* [soil] tilth
Ackergauchheil *n* [scarlet] pimpernel, shepherd's clock, wink-a-peep, Anagallis arvensis
ackergenutzt/vormals old-field, old-arable *(soil)*
Ackergerät *n* field tool (implement), agricultural (farming) implement
Ackerglockenblume *f* creeping campanula, rover bell-flower, Campanula rapunculoides
Ackergrasbau *m* ley farming
Ackergrasland *n* ley, lea
Acker-Grasland-Verhältnis *n* arable land/grass ratio
Ackergrenze *f* boundary
Ackerhahnenfuß *m* corn buttercup, goldilocks, Ranunculus arvensis
Ackerhellerkraut *n* [field] penny-cress, fanweed, stinkweed, Thlaspi arvense
Ackerhohlzahn *m* red hemp-nettle, Galeopsis ladanum
Ackerhornkraut *n (bot)* starry cerastium, Cerastium arvense
Acker[hunds]kamille *f* field c[h]amomile, corn c[h]amomile, ox-eye, Anthemis arvensis
Ackerkastenschleppe *f* clod crusher (breaker)
Ackerkohl *m (Am)* hare's-ear [mustard], Conringia orientalis
Ackerknauel *m* annual knawel, Scleranthus annuus
Ackerknoblauch *m* great round-headed garlic, great-head garlic, Levant (elemi) garlic, wild leek, Allium ampeloprasum
Ackerkratzdistel *f s.* Ackerdistel
Ackerkrume *f* topsoil, tilth *(s.a. Ackererde)*
Ackerkrummhals *m* [small] bugloss, Anchusa (Lycopsis) arvensis
Ackerkultur *f* cropping standards, standards of arable farming
Ackerland *n* arable [land], plough-land, infield, *(Am)* cropland; agricultural (farm) soil, tillage [land], tilth
Ackerleinkraut *n* corn toadflax, Linaria arvensis

Ackerminze f field (corn) mint, Mentha arvensis var. arvensis
Ackern n ploughing [work], tillage
Ackernachtnelke f [night-flowering] campion, night-flowering catchfly, sticky cockle, Silene noctiflora
Ackerochsenzunge f [small] bugloss, Anchusa (Lycopsis) arvensis
Ackerpferd n farm (plough) horse, dobbin
Ackerrettich m wild radish, white charlock, Raphanus raphanistrum
Ackerringelblume f field marigold, Calendula arvensis
Ackerrittersporn m field (branching) larkspur, annual delphinium, Delphinium consolida
Ackerröte f field madder, Sherardia arvensis
Ackerschachtelhalm m common (field) horse-tail, toadpipe, Equisetum arvense
Ackerschiene f tool-bar, drawbar, tilling beam
Ackerschleppe f float, scrubber
Ackerschlepper m agricultural (farm) tractor
Ackerschmalwand f thale (mouse-ear) cress, Arabidopsis thaliana
Ackerschmiele f wind (corn) grass, [loose] silky-bent, Apera spica-venti
Ackerschnecke f 1. field slug (genus Deroceras); 2. grey field slug, Deroceras (Agrolimax) agreste
Ackerschöterich m treacle mustard, Erysimum cheiranthoides
Ackersenf m [yellow] charlock, field mustard (kale), runch, Sinapis arvensis
Ackersinau m parsley-piert, Aphanes (Alchemilla) arvensis
Ackerspark m, **Ackerspörgel** m corn-spurr[e]y, Spergula arvensis
Ackersteinsame m corn gromwell, bastard alkanet, wheat thief, Lithospermum arvense
Ackerstiefmütterchen n field (wild) pansy, kiss-me, Viola tricolor (arvensis)
Ackertaubnessel f purple dead-nettle, Lamium purpureum
Ackertraktor m agricultural (farm) tractor
Ackertrespe f field brome[-grass], Bromus arvensis
Acker- und Pflanzenbau m plant husbandry (growing), plant cropping (cultivation)
Ackerunkraut n field (arable) weed
Ackerveilchen n s. Ackerstiefmütterchen
Ackervergißmeinnicht n common (field) forget-me-not, Myosotis arvensis
Ackerwagen m farm cart (trailer), [agricultural] trailer
Ackerwagenreifen m trailer tyre
Ackerwalze f field (land) roller, farming roll[er]
Ackerweide[fläche] f arable pasture, (Am) rotation pasture
Ackerwicke f common vetch, tare, Vicia sativa ssp. sativa
Ackerwiese f arable meadow
Ackerwildpflanze f [field, arable] weed
Ackerwinde f 1. bindweed, convolvulus, (Am) morning glory (genus Convolvulus); 2. field (trailing, European) bindweed, lesser bindweed, creeping jenny, bearbine, Convolvulus arvensis
Ackerziest m field (corn) woundwort, field-nettle betony, Stachys arvensis
Acne f (vet) acne
Aconitase f, **Aconitathydratase** f aconitate hydratase (enzyme)
Aconitin n aconitin[e] (alkaloid)
Aconitsäure f aconitic acid, propen-1,2,3-tricarboxylic acid
AC-Profil n (soil) AC profile
Acre m acre (measure of land, 1 acre = 0.405 ha)
Acridin n acridine
Acridinorange n acridine orange (mutagen)
Acriflavin n acriflavine (antiparasitic, disinfectant)
acrokarp (bot) acrocarpic, acrocarpous
Acrolein n acrolein (herbicide)
acropetal (bot) acropetal
Acrosin n acrosin (enzyme)
Acrylaldehyd m acrolein (herbicide)
Acrylamid n acrylamide (soil conditioner)
Acrylsäure f acrylic acid
ACTH s. Hormon/adrenocorticotropes
Actidion n cycloheximide (antibiotic, fungicide)
Actin n actin (muscle protein)
Actinfilament n actin filament
Actinomycin n actinomycin (antibiotic)
Actinospectocin n spectomycin (antibiotic)
Actinpolymerisationsinhibitor m actin polymerization inhibitor
Actomyosin n actomyosin (protein)
Actoplanin n actoplanin (antibiotic)
ACV s. Ackerbohnenchlorosevirus
acyclisch acyclic (chemical compounds)
Acyl-CoA-Dehydrogenase f acyl-CoA dehydrogenase (enzyme)
Acyl-CoA-Desaturase f acyl-CoA desaturase, fatty acid desaturase (enzyme)
Acyl-CoA-Hydrolase f acyl-CoA hydrolase (enzyme)
Acyl-CoA-Synthetase f acyl-CoA synthetase (enzyme)
Acyltransferase f acyl transferase (enzyme)
Adaktylie f (vet) adactyly
Adamantin n [dental] enamel
Adamssche Lahmheit f Adam's lameness (of horse)
Adamycin n s. Oxytetracyclin
adaptabel adaptable, adaptive
Adaptabilität f adaptability, adaptivity, adaptation power
Adaptation f adaptation
Adaptationsimport m adaptation importation (biological control)

Adaptationssyndrom n adaptation syndrome (animal physiology)
~/[Selyesches] allgemeines [Selye's] general adaptation syndrome
adaptieren to adapt
Adaption f s. Adaptation
adaptiv adaptive, adaptable
adaxial adaxial (e.g. parenchyma)
Additionalwirt m accessory host
Additionsregel f (gen) additive theorem
Additiv n additive
Adduktion f adduction (of a limb)
Adduktor m adductor [muscle]
Adelphogamie f adelphogamy, sib (brother-sister) pollination; self-pollination
Adelphoparasitismus m adelphoparasitism
Adelphophagie f adelphophagia, cannibalism
Adenie f (bot) adenia (genus Adenia)
Adenin n adenine (nucleic acid constituent)
Adeninaminohydrolase f, **Adenindesaminase** f adenine deaminase (enzyme)
Adeninnucleotid n adenine nucleotide
Adeninphosphoribosyltransferase f adenine phosphoribosyltransferase (enzyme)
Adenitis f (vet) adenitis
Adenohypophyse f adenohypophysis
Adenokarzinom n (vet) adenocarcinoma
Adenokarzinomatose f mountain disease (of sheep)
Adenom n (vet) adenoma
Adenomatose f (vet) adenomatosis
Adenopathie f adenopathy
Adenosin n adenosine (nucleoside)
Adenosinaminohydrolase f adenosine deaminase (enzyme)
Adenosin-3',5'-cyclophosphat n s. Adenosin-3',5'-phosphat
Adenosindesaminase f s. Adenosinaminohydrolase
Adenosin-5'-diphosphat n adenosine-5'-diphosphate, ADP (nucleotide)
Adenosindiphosphorsäure f s. Adenosin-5'-diphosphat
Adenosinmethionindecarboxylase f adenosylmethionine decarboxylase (enzyme)
Adenosinmonophosphat n adenosine monophosphate, AMP
~/cyclisches s. Adenosin-3',5'-phosphat
Adenosin-5'-monophosphat n adenosine-5'-monophosphate, adenylic acid, AMP (nucleotide)
Adenosinmonophosphorsäure f s. Adenosin-5'-monophosphat
Adenosinphosphat n adenosine phosphate (nucleotide)
Adenosin-3',5'-phosphat n adenosine-3',5'-monophosphate, cyclic AMP (cyclonucleotide)
Adenosin-5'-triphosphat n adenosine-5'-triphosphate, ATP (nucleotide) (s.a. under ATP)

Adenosintriphosphatase f adenosine triphosphatase, ATPase (enzyme)
Adenosintriphosphatzyklus m adenosine triphosphate cycle
Adenosintriphosphorsäure f s. Adenosin-5'-triphosphat
Adenosylmethionin n adenosylmethionine
Adenovirus n adenovirus (family Adenoviridae)
Adenylatcyclase f adenyl[ate] cyclase, adenylylcyclase (enzyme)
Adenylatkinase f adenylate kinase (enzyme)
Adenylsäure f s. Adenosin-5'-monophosphat
Adenylsäuredesaminase f AMP deaminase (enzyme)
Adenylsuccinatlyase f adenylosuccinate lyase (enzyme)
Adenylylcyclase f s. Adenylatcyclase
Ader f (zoo) vein, blood vessel; vein, rib (of insect wings); (bot) vein, nerve; streak (in wood) • **zur ~ lassen** (vet) to bleed
Adergeflecht n [des Gehirns] choroid plexus
Aderlaß m (vet) blood-letting
Aderlaßkanüle f fleam (for bleeding of horses)
Adermin n adermin, pyridoxine, vitamin B_6
Adernaufhellung f (phyt) vein clearing, vein etch[ing]
Adernaufhellungsvirus n **der Erdbeere** strawberry vein clearing virus
Adernbänderung f (phyt) vein banding (virosis)
~ der Stachelbeere gooseberry vein banding
Adernbänderungsvirus n **der Stachelbeere** gooseberry vein banding virus
Adernbräune f (phyt) vein browning
Adernchlorose f (phyt) vein chlorosis (virosis)
Adernchlorosevirus n **der Himbeere** raspberry vein chlorosis virus
Adernende n vein ending (plant anatomy)
Adernmosaik n (phyt) vein mosaic (virosis)
Adernnekrose f (phyt) vein necrosis
Adernnetzungsvirus n **der Pelargonie** pelargonium vein netting virus
Adernscheckungsvirus n **der Nelke** carnation vein mottle virus, CVMV
Adernschwärze f (phyt) bacteriaemia (caused by Xanthomonas campestris)
~ des Kohls cabbage black rot, black rot [of crucifers] (caused by Xanthomonas campestris)
Adernschwärzung f s. Adernschwärze
Adernvergilbung f (phyt) vein yellowing (virosis)
~ der Birne pear vein yellows
Adersystem n, **Aderung** f (bot) venation, veining, nervation; (ent) venation
ADH s. Adiuretin
adhärent adherent
Adhärenz f adherence
Adhäsion f adhesion (e.g. of soil constituents)
adhäsiv adhesive
Adhäsivum n adhesive [agent]
Adhumulon n adhumulone (hop resin)

Adipinsäure f adipic acid
Adipocire f adipocere, lipocere
Adipokinin n adipokinetic hormone
adipös adipose, obese, fat
Adipositas f adiposity, obesity, fatness
Adipozyt m adipocyte, fat cell
Adiuretin n antidiuretic hormone, ADH, vasopressin
ADI-Wert m acceptable daily intake *(of an active ingredient)*
Adjuvans n adjuvant
Adjuvansvakzine f adjuvant vaccine
Adlerfarn m bracken [fern], eagle fern, Pteridium aquilinum
Adlerfarnbestand m bracken [fern]
Adlerfarnvergiftung f *(vet)* bracken poisoning
Ad-libitum-Fütterung f ad lib[itum] feeding, unrestricted (free-choice) feeding
Adlupulon n adlupulone *(hop resin)*
Adnexitis f *(vet)* adnexitis
Adobe[ton] m adobe
Adobeziegel m adobe
adoleszent adolescent
Adoleszenz f adolescence *(of animals)*
Adonisröschen n 1. adonis *(genus Adonis)*; 2. pheasant's-eye [flower], Adonis vernalis
ADP s. Adenosin-5'-diphosphat
Adramycin n methacyclin *(antibiotic)*
adrenal adrenal
Adrenalektomie f *(vet)* adrenalectomy
Adrenalin n adrenalin[e], epinephrine *(hormone)*
Adrenalinausschüttung f adrenaline discharge
Adrenalinoxidase f s. Aminoxidase (flavinhaltig)
adrenergisch adrenergic
Adrenolytikum n *(vet)* sympatholytic [agent]
Adrenomimetikum n *(vet)* sympathomimetic [agent]
Adriamycin n, **Adriblastin** n doxorubicin *(antibiotic)*
Adsorbens n adsorbent [material]
Adsorber m adsorber; scrubber
adsorbieren to adsorb
~/chemisch to chemisorb
Adsorption f adsorption
Adsorptionsapparat m adsorber
Adsorptionschromatographie f adsorption chromatography
Adsorptionsmittel n adsorbent
Adsorptionswasser n adsorption water; *(soil)* hygroscopic moisture
adult adult
Adultus m adult
Advektion f advection
Advektivfrost m advective frost
adventiv adventitious
Adventivembryo m *(bot)* adventitious embryo
Adventivembryonie f *(bot)* adventitious embryony
Adventivknospe f *(bot)* adventitious bud
Adventivpflanze f adventive, adventitious plant
Adventivsproß m adventitious shoot
Adventivwurzel f adventitious root, secondary (coronal) root
Adventsstern m poinsettia, Christmas star, Euphorbia pulcherrima
Adzukibohne f adzuki (adsuki) bean, Phaseolus angularis, Vigna angularis [var. angularis]
AE s. 1. Enzephalomyelitis/aviäre; 2. Arbeitseinheit
Aecidium n *(bot)* aeci[di]um
Aegyptianellose f **des Geflügels** fowl aegyptianellosis *(caused by Aegyptianella pullorum)*
AEMV s. Echtes Ackerbohnenmosaikvirus
Aerationszone f *(soil)* zone of aeration
Aerenchym n *(bot)* aerenchyma
Aerifizieren n aerating *(e.g. of lawns)*
Aerifizierer m lawn aerator
Aerifiziergabel f lawn aerator fork
aerob aerobic, oxybiotic
Aerobier m aerobe, aerobic bacterium
Aerobiologie f aerobiology
Aerobiont m s. Aerobier
Aerobiose f aerobiosis, oxybiosis
aerobisch s. aerob
aerogen airborne
Aerophagie f *(vet)* aerophagy
Aerophotogrammetrie f aerial photogrammetry, aerophotogrammetry
Aerophyt m epiphyte, aerophyte, air plant
aerophytisch epiphytic, epiphytal
Aeroplankton n aeroplankton, aerial plankton
Aeroponik f aeroponics *(soilless culture e.g. of ornamentals)*
Aerosacculitis f aerosacculitis, airsacculitis, air sac disease (infection) *(of fowl)*
Aerosol n aerosol
Aerosolbehandlung f aerosol therapy
Aerosolgenerator m, **Aerosolgerät** n aerosol generator *(e.g. for disinfection of animal houses)*
Aerosolsprühgerät n aerosol sprayer
Aerosoltherapie f aerosol therapy
Aerosprühmittel n aerial spray
Aerotaxis f aerotaxis
Aerothorax m *(vet)* pneumothorax, aerothorax
Aerotriangulation f aerial triangulation
Aerotropismus m *(bot)* aerotropism
Aesculin n aesculin *(glucoside)*
Aestivation f *(bot)* aestivation
af s. aschefrei
afebril afebrile
Affektion f affection
Affenblume f monkey flower, mimulus *(genus Mimulus)*
Affenbrot n monkey-bread *(fruit of Adansonia digitata)*
Affenbrotbaum m baobab, monkey-bread, calabash tree, Adansonia digitata
Affenpinscher m affenpinscher *(dog breed)*
Affenseife f Mexican walnut, Enterolobium cyclocarpum

Affentreppe

Affentreppe *f (bot)* maloo *(genus Bauhinia)*
Affinade *f* affinated (affination) sugar, washed raw sugar
Affination *f* affination *(sugar manufacture)*
Affinationszentrifuge *f* affination centrifuge
affinieren to affine, to wash *(sugar)*
Affinität *f* affinity
~/genetische genetic affinity
Affodil *m (bot)* asphodel *(genus Asphodelus)*
Afghane *m*, **Afghanischer Windhund** *m* Afghan hound *(breed)*
Aflatoxikose *f (vet)* aflatoxicosis, turkey X disease
Aflatoxin *n* aflatoxin *(mycotoxin)*
Aflatoxinvergiftung *f* s. Aflatoxikose
AFR s. Abferkelrate
Africander-Rind *n*, **Afrikander-Rind** *n* Africander, Afrikander *(cattle breed)*
Afrikanische Liebesblume *f* [blue] African lily, lily of the Nile, Agapanthus africanus (umbellatus)
~ **Pferdepest (Pferdesterbe)** *f* African horse sickness
~ **Schmucklilie** *f* s. Afrikanische Liebesblume
~ **Schweinepest** *f* African swine fever, ASF *(virosis)*
~ **Wicke** *f* Tangier pea [vine], Lathyrus tingitanus
Afrikanischer Baldrian *m* African valerian, horn of plenty, Fedia cornucopiae
~ **Butterbaum** *m* shea [butter] tree, Vitellaria paradoxa, Butyrospermum parkii
~ **Maisstengelbohrer** *m (ent)* African maize (sorghum) stem borer, Busseola fusca
~ **Rosenholzbaum** *m* African rosewood (kino tree), molompi, Pterocarpus erinaceus
~ **Wels** *m* African catfish, Clarias gariepinus
Afrikanisches Padouk *n* African padauk, barwood, Pterocarpus soyauxii
~ **Rosenholz** *n* African (Gambia) rosewood *(from Pterocarpus erinaceus and P. sieberiana)*
~ **Rotholz** *n* camwood, Baphia nitida
~ **Sandelholz** *n* 1. African kino tree, barwood, Pterocarpus erinaceus; 2. s. Afrikanisches Padouk
~ **Schweinefieber** *n* African swine fever, ASF *(virosis)*
Afrormosiabaum *m (bot)* African afrormosia, Afrormosia (Pericopsis) elata
AFS s. Raum/Scheinbar Freier
After *m* anus, vent, anal orifice • **zum ~ hin [liegend]** aboral
Afterahorn *m* Tatarian maple, Acer tataricum
Afterdrüse *f* anal (rectal) gland
Afterflosse *f* anal fin
Afterfühler *m (ent)* tail-feeler
Afterjäger *m* pot-hunter
Afterklaue *f* dew-claw *(animal anatomy)*
Afteröffnung *f* s. After
Afterpicken *n* vent-pecking *(of fowl)*
Afterraupe *f* saw-fly caterpillar, pseudocaterpillar, false caterpillar
Aftersegment *n* telson *(of arthropods)*

Afterstrich *m* s. Afterzitze
Afterweisel *f* drone layer, drone-laying queen honey-bee, laying worker honey-bee
Afterzitze *f* rear (supernumerary) teat
Agalaktie *f* agalactia, lactation failure
~/infektiöse contagious agalactia *(of goats and sheep, caused by Mycoplasma agalactiae)*
agam[isch] *(bot)* agamous, amphigamous; *(zoo)* agamic, asexual
Agamogenese *f*, **Agamogonie** *f* agamogenesis, agamy
Agamospermie *f (bot)* agamospermy
Agar[-Agar] *m(n)* agar[-agar] *(polysaccharide)*
Agargel *n* agar gel
Agargelelektrophorese *f* agar gel electrophoresis
Agargelimmunodiffusionstest *m* agar gel immunodiffusion test, AGID, Coggins test *(for detection of infectious equine anaemia)*
Agaricinsäure *f* agaric acid
Agarkeimzahl *f* plate count on agar medium
Agarnährboden *m* agar medium
Agarnährplatte *f* nutrient agar plate
Agarose *f* agarose *(polysaccharide)*
Agarplatte *f* nutrient agar plate
Agarröhrchenmethode *f* agar-tube method
Agave *f* agave, pita *(genus Agave)*
Agavenfaser *f* pita
Agens *n* agent
~/alkylierendes alkylating agent
~/kausales (ursächliches) causal agent, causative organism
Ageotropismus *m (bot)* ageotropism
Ageratum *n (bot)* ageratum, paint brush *(genus Ageratum)*
Agglomerat *n* agglomerate
Agglomeration *f* agglomeration
Agglutination *f* agglutination
Agglutinationsfaktor *m* agglutination factor
Agglutinationsreaktion *f (vet)* agglutination test
agglutinieren to agglutinate
Agglutinin *n* agglutinin
Agglutinogen *n* agglutinogen *(blood antigen)*
Aggradation *f (soil)* aggradation
Aggregat *n* [soil] aggregate, ped, crumb • **ein ~ bilden** to aggregate
Aggregatdichte *f* aggregate density
Aggregatgefüge *n* aggregate structure
Aggregatgröße *f* aggregate size
Aggregatgrößenverteilung *f* aggregate size distribution
Aggregation *f* aggregation
Aggregationspheromon *n* aggregation pheromone
Aggregatstabilität *f* aggregate (crumb) stability, stability of aggregation
aggregieren to aggregate
~/sich to aggregate
Aggression *f* aggression *(animal behaviour)*
Aggressionsverhalten *n* aggressive behaviour

Aggressivität f aggressiveness, aggressivity
Agmatin n agmatine
Agnathie f (vet) agnathia
Agonie f agony
Agrar... s. a. **Agro...**
Agrarausfuhr f agricultural export
Agraraußenhandel m foreign agricultural trade
Agrarbank f agricultural (land) bank
Agrarbetrieb m farm enterprise
Agrarbiologie f agricultural biology, agrobiology
Agrareinfuhr f agricultural import
Agrarentomologe m agricultural entomologist
Agrarentwicklung f agricultural development
Agrarerzeugnis n agricultural (farm) product, agricultural commodity
Agrarerzeugnisse npl agricultural produce, farm products
Agrarexperte m agricultural expert
Agrarexport m agricultural export
Agrarexporteur m agricultural exporter
Agrarfachmann m agricultural expert
Agrarfinanzpolitik f agricultural financial policy
Agrarflug m, **Agrarflugwesen** n agricultural aviation, ag-aviation
Agrarflugzeug n agricultural aircraft, crop-spraying plane
Agrarforscher m agricultural researcher
Agrarforschung f agricultural research
Agrargebiet n agricultural region
Agrargeographie f agricultural geography
Agrargeschichte f agricultural history
Agrargesellschaft f agricultural society
Agrargesetzgebung f agricultural legislation
Agrargüter npl agricultural produce, farm products
Agrarhandel m agricultural trade, trade in agricultural commodities
Agrarhaushalt m agricultural budget
Agrarhochschule f (Am) Aggie
Agrarhochschüler m (Am) Aggie
Agrarhydrologie f agricultural hydrology
Agrarimport m agricultural import
Agrarindustrie f agricultural industry, agri-industry; factory farming
Agrar-Industrie-Komplex m agribusiness
Agrar-Industrie-Land n agricultural-industrial country (nation)
agrarindustriell agro-industrial
Agraringenieur m technical agriculturist
agrarisch agrarian
agrarklimatisch agroclimatic
Agrarklimatologie f agricultural climatology, agroclimatology
agrarklimatologisch agroclimatologic[al]
Agrarkredit m agricultural credit
Agrarkrise f agricultural crisis
Agrarland n agricultural (agrarian) country
Agrarlandschaft f agricultural landscape • **nur in der ~ vorkommend** agrobiotic
Agrarmarkt m agricultural [products] market

Agrarmarktwirtschaft f agricultural marketing
Agrarmeteorologe m agricultural meteorologist
Agrarmeteorologie f agrometeorology, agricultural meteorology
Agrarmikrobiologie f agricultural microbiology
Agrarministerium n ministry of agriculture
Agrarnebenprodukt n agricultural by-product
Agrarökologie f agroecology, agricultural ecology
agrarökologisch agroecological
Agrarökonom m agricultural economist
Agrarökonomie f, **Agrarökonomik** f agricultural economy (economics)
agrarökonomisch agronomic-economic, agricultural economic
Agrarpädagogik f agricultural pedagogics
Agrarpilot m agricultural pilot
Agrarplanung f agricultural planning
Agrarpolitik f agrarian policy
Agrarpraxis f farming practice
Agrarpreise mpl agricultural prices
Agrarprodukt n agricultural (farm) product, agricultural commodity
Agrarproduktion f agricultural production, (Am) agriproduction
Agrarprognose f agricultural forecast
Agrarrecht n agricultural [and rural] law, farm (rural) law
Agrarreform f agrarian reform
Agrarregion f agricultural region
Agrarsektor m agricultural (rural) sector, farm sector
Agrarsozialpolitik f rural social policy
Agrarsoziologie f agricultural sociology
Agrarstadt f agro-town
Agrarstandort m agricultural site
Agrarstatistik f agricultural statistics
Agrarstruktur f agricultural structure
Agrartechnik f agricultural engineering
Agrartechniker m agricultural engineer, A.E.
Agrartechnologe f agricultural technologist
Agrartechnologie f agricultural technology
Agrarwirtschaft f agricultural economy (economics); agriculture
Agrarwirtschaftslehre f agricultural economics
Agrarwissenschaft f agricultural science, agronomy, agriculturism
Agrarwissenschaftler m agricultural scientist
Agribusineß n agribusiness
Agrikultur f agriculture (for compounds s. under Landwirtschaft)
Agrikultur... s. **Agrar...** and **Agro...**
Agro... s. a. **Agrar...**
Agrobioenergie f agrobioenergy
Agrobiologie f agrobiology, agricultural biology
agrobiologisch agrobiologic[al]
agrobiont agrobiotic
Agrobiozönose f agro[bio]coenosis
Agrobusineß n agribusiness
Agrochemie f agrochemistry, agricultural chemistry

Agrochemikalie

Agrochemikalie *f* agricultural chemical, agrochemical, farm chemical
Agrochemiker *m* agricultural chemist
agrochemisch agrochemical, agrichemical
Agrochemotaxometrie *f* agrochemotaxometry
Agroforstwirtschaft *f* agroforestry
Agrogeochemie *f* agrogeochemistry
Agrogeologie *f* agrogeology, agricultural geology
agrogeologisch agrogeologic[al]
Agrohydrologie *f* agrohydrology
Agromelioration *f* agronomic amelioration
agrometeorologisch agrometeorological
Agronom *m* agronomist
Agronomie *f* agronomy
agronomisch agronomic[al]
agroökologisch agroecological
Agroökosystem *n* agroecosystem, agricultural ecosystem
agrophil *(ecol)* agrophilous
agrophob *(ecol)* agrophobic
Agrophysik *f* agrophysics, agricultural physics
Agrophytozönose *f* agrophytocoenosis
Agropin *n* agropine *(peptide)*
Agrostemin *n* agrostemin *(growth regulator)*
Agrostographie *f* agrostography
Agrostologe *m* agrostologist
Agrostologie *f* agrostology
agrostologisch agrostological
Agrotechnik *f* agricultural technology
Agrotechniker *m* agricultural technician
agrotechnisch agrotechnical
Agrotopoklimatologie *f* agrotopoclimatology
Agrozönose *f* agro[bio]coenosis
Aguacate *f s.* Avocadobaum
Ägyptische Akazie *f* gum arabic tree, Acacia nilotica (arabica)
~ **Baumwolle** *f* Egyptian cotton *(group of cultivars belonging to Gossypium vitifolium)*
~ **Baumwollraupe** *f (ent)* Egyptian cotton caterpillar, cotton [leaf-]worm, tobacco caterpillar, Spodoptera littoralis
~ **Biene** *f* Egyptian honey-bee, Apis mellifica lamarcki *(breed)*
~ **Bohne** *f* Egyptian [black] bean, tonga bean, Dolichos lablab, Lablab niger (purpureus)
~ **Heuschrecke** *f (ent)* large brown Egyptian grasshopper, Anacridium aegyptium
~ **Lotosblume** *f (bot)* Egyptian lotus, Nymphaea lotus
~ **Lupine** *f* Egyptian lupin[e], Lupinus albus (termis)
~ **Weide** *f* Egyptian willow, Salix aegyptiaca
Ägyptischer Baumwollkapselwurm *m (ent)* Egyptian bollworm, Earias insulana
~ **Klee** *m s.* Alexandrinerklee
~ **Kümmel** *m s.* Ajowanpflanze
Ah[-Horizont] *m (soil)* humus horizon, Ao-horizon
Ahlbeere *f* black currant, Ribes nigrum

Ahlkirsche *f* bird (cluster) cherry, Prunus padus (avium)
AHLV *s.* Amerikanisches Latentes Hopfenvirus
Ahn[e] *m* progenitor, ancestor
Ahnen *mpl,* **Ahnenreihe** *f* ancestry
Ahnentafel *f* pedigree
ähnlich similar; homologous
Ähnlichkeitsmatrix *f (biom)* similarity matrix
A-Horizont *m (soil)* A-horizon, eluvial (leached) horizon
Ahorn[baum] *m* maple *(genus Acer)*
ahornblättrig maple-leaved
Ahornblättriger Schneeball *m* dockmackie, Viburnum acerifolium
Ahorneule *f* sycamore moth, Acronycta aceris
Ahornholz *n* maple
Ahornrunzelschorf *m* maple tar-spot *(caused by Rhytisma acerinum)*
Ahornsirup *m* maple syrup, maple sap
Ahornzierlaus *f* sycamore aphid, Drepanosiphum platanoidis
Ahornzucker *m* maple sugar
Ähre *f* ear, [seed-]head, spike • **Ähren [nach-] lesen** to glean • **Ähren schieben** to go (run) to ear, to ear [up]
~/körnertragende grain-bearing head
Ährenachse *f* rachilla
Ährenbildung *f* ear formation
Ährenborste *f* awn
Ährenbruch *m* chobs
Ährenchristophskraut *n* baneberry, herb Christopher, Actaea spicata
Ährendichte *f* head (spike) density
Ährendifferenzierung *f* spike differentiation
Ährendrescher *m* stripper[-harvester]
Ährenelevator *m* gleaning (tailings) elevator *(of a combine)*
Ähreneule *f* rustic shoulder knot moth, Apamea sordens
Ährenfeld *n* field in ear
ährenförmig spiciform
Ährengetreide *n* spiked cereal
Ährengrasähnliche Trespe *f* rescue brome (grass), Schrader's (prairie) grass, Bromus catharticus (unioloides)
Ährenheber *m* ear (crop) lifter, grain lifter (guard), grain-saving guard
Ährenheide *f (bot)* bruckenthalia *(genus Bruckenthalia)*
Ährenlese *f,* **Ährenlesen** *n* gleaning
Ährenleser *m* gleaner
Ährenneigungswinkel *m* spike nodding angle
Ährenrücklaufboden *m* tail-board *(of a combine)*
Ährenschieben *n* heading
Ährenschnecke *f* helical ear feeder, tailings auger *(of a combine)*
Ährenspindel *f* rachis
Ährenstripper *m s.* Ährendrescher
ährentragend ear bearing, eared, spiciferous

ährig spiked, spicate
Ährige Scheinhasel f flowering (winter) hazel, Corylopsis spicata
Ähriger Ehrenpreis m spiked speedwell, Veronica spicata ssp. spicata
~ Erdbeerspinat m strawberry blite, Chenopodium (Blitum) capitatum
Airedaleterrier m Airedale [terrier] (breed)
Aitel m (zoo) chub, Leuciscus cephalus
aitionom aitionomic
Ajanfichte f Hondo (Yezo) spruce, Picea jezoensis
Ajmalin n ajmaline (alkaloid)
Ajowan m(n) ajowan caraway (spice)
Ajowanöl n ajowan oil
Ajowanpflanze f ajowan caraway, stone-parsley, Trachyspermum ammi, Carum copticum
AK s. 1. Aujeszkysche Krankheit; 2. Austauschkapazität
Akabaneerkrankung f akabane disease (of ruminants)
Akabanevirus n akabane virus
Akaganeit m akaganeite (non-clay mineral)
Akantholyse f (vet) acantholysis
Akanthose f (vet) acanthosis
Akanthozephale m acanthocephalid, thorny-headed worm (division and class Acanthocephala)
Akanthus m (bot) 1. acanthus, brank-ursine, bear's-breech (genus Acanthus); 2. bear's-breech, Acanthus mollis
Akapnie f acapnia
Akardier m (vet) acardiac[us], acardius
Akarine f acarid, mite (order Acari)
Akarinose f 1. (phyt, vet) acariasis; 2. (phyt) acarinosis (caused by Phyllocoptes vitis)
Akariphage m acariphage
Akaripidose f acarine (Isle of Wight) disease (of honey-bees, caused by Acarapis woodi)
akarizid acaricidal
Akarizid n acaricide, miticide
Akarophilie f (bot) acarophily
Akarose f s. Akarinose 1.
Akarp-Methode f bulk method (plant breeding)
Akaryobiont m prokaryote
akaryotisch akaryotic, acaryote (cell)
Akazie f acacia, wattle (genus Acacia)
Akaziensavanne f acacia savanna[h]
Akebie f (bot) common akebia, Akebia quinata
Akee f s. Akipflaume
Akelei f 1. columbine, aquilegia (genus Aquilegia); 2. [garden] columbine, capon's feather, Aquilegia vulgaris
Akeleiwiesenraute f s. Amstelraute
Akh s. Arbeitskraftstunde
Akines[i]e f (vet) akinesia
Akipflaume f akee[-apple], ackee
Akipflaumenbaum m akee[-apple], ackee, Blighia sapida
Akita-Inu m Akita (dog breed)
Akklimation f acclimation, hardening

Akklimatisation f acclimatization, (Am) acclima[ta]tion
akklimatisieren to acclimatize, to climatize, (Am) to acclimate
~/sich to acclimatize, to climatize, (Am) to acclimate
Akklimatisierung f s. Akklimatisation
Akkommodation f accommodation
Akkumulation f accumulation, cumulation
Akkumulator m accumulator, battery
akkumulieren to accumulate, to heap [up]
Aklomid n aklomide (coccidiostat)
Akne f (vet) acne
A-Kohle f s. Aktivkohle
Akonit m (bot) wolfsbane, monkshood, aconite (genus Aconitum)
Akrodermatitis f (vet) acrodermatitis
akrokarp (bot) acrocarpic, acrocarpous
Akromegalie f (vet) acromegaly
Akronekrose f (phyt) top necrosis
Akropachie f (vet) acropachy
~ der Küken avian osteopetrosis, Paget's disease of fowl, thick leg disease
akropetal (bot) acropetal
Akrosom n acrosome (part of sperm head)
akrosomal acrosomal
Akrosomenreaktion f acrosome reaction, capacitation
Akrotonie f (bot) acrotony
akrozentrisch acrocentric (chromosome)
Aktinometer n actinometer
Aktinograph m actinograph
Aktinometrie f actinometry
aktinomorph actinomorphic, actinomorphous
Aktinomykose f (vet) actinomycosis
Aktinomyzet m actinomycete (order Actinomycetales)
Aktion f [/hohe] action (of horse's gait)
Aktionsfläche f exercise (loafing) area (free-stall housing)
Aktionskatalog m ethogram (ethology)
Aktionspotential n action potential
Aktionsradius m (Am) cruising radius (of game)
Aktionsraum m (ecol) home range
Aktionsspektrum n action spectrum, spectrum of activity (e.g. of antibiotics)
Aktivationshormon n activation hormone
Aktivator m activator; enzyme activator
Aktivität f activity
~/biologische bioactivity
Aktivitätskoeffizient m (soil) activity coefficient (ratio)
Aktivkohle f activated carbon
Aktivkohleadsorber m, Aktivkohlescrubber m activated carbon scrubber (in crop storage buildings)
Aktivsubstanz f active ingredient, active substance (principle), a.i. (e.g. of a plant protectant)

Aktomyosin

Aktomyosin *n* actomyosin *(protein)*
akut *(phyt, vet)* acute
Akzeleration *f* acceleration
Akzeptor *m* acceptor
akzident[i]ell accidental
AL *s.* Leukose/aviäre
Ala *s.* Alanin
Alachlor *n* alachlor *(herbicide)*
Alambadi *n* alambadi *(cattle breed)*
Aland *m* *(zoo)* ide, Idus idus
Alang-Alang[-Gras] *n*, **Alanggras** *n* 1. alang grass, Imperata cylindrica; 2. cogon grass, cogon satin tail, Imperata cylindrica var. major
Alanin *n* alanine, 2-aminopropionic acid
Alaninaminopeptidase *f* alanine aminopeptidase *(enzyme)*
Alaninaminotransferase *f* alanine aminotransferase (transaminase), glutamate pyruvate transaminase, GPT *(enzyme)*
Alanindehydrogenase *f* alanine dehydrogenase *(enzyme)*
Alanin-tRNA-Ligase *f* alanine-tRNA ligase *(enzyme)*
Alant *m* *(bot)* 1. inula *(genus Inula)*; 2. elecampane, Inula helenium
Alanylhistidin *n* carnosine *(amino-acid)*
Alarmpheromon *n* alarm pheromone (substance)
Alarmreaktion *f* alarm reaction *(first stage of Selye's general adaptation syndrome)*
Alarmsubstanz *f s.* Alarmpheromon
Alaskaelch *m* moose, Alces alces ssp. americanus
Alaskan Malamute *m* Alaskan malamute *(dog breed)*
Alatauer Rind *n* Ala-tau *(cattle breed)*
Alaunstein *m* alunite *(non-clay mineral)*
Albedo *f* albedo *(reflective power of the atmosphere)*
Albedometer *n* albedometer
Albendazol *n* albendazole *(anthelminthic)*
Alber *f* white (silver-leaf) poplar, abele, Populus alba
Albinismus *m* albinism • ~ **aufweisend** albin[ot]ic • **zum ~ neigend** albin[ot]ic
Albino *m* albino
Albinoratte *f* albino rat *(laboratory animal)*
albinotisch albin[ot]ic
Albit *m* albite *(non-clay mineral)*
Albizzia-Wollaus *f* lebbek mealy bug, Nipaecoccus vastator
Albumen *n* 1. albumen, egg-white; 2. *s.* Albumin
Albumin *n* albumin
albuminartig albuminous
Albuminat *n* albuminate
Albuminausscheidung *f* im Harn albuminuria, proteinuria
Albuminoid *n* albuminoid *(scleroprotein)*
albuminös albuminous
Albuminschönung *f* fining with albumin *(winemaking)*
Albuminurie *f* albuminuria, proteinuria
Älchen *n* eelworm *(order Tylenchida)*
Älchenkrankheit *f* *(phyt)* eelworm disease
Aldehyd *m* aldehyde
Aldehyddehydrogenase *f* aldehyde dehydrogenase *(enzyme)*
Aldehydoxidase *f* aldehyde oxidase *(enzyme)*
Aldehydreductase *f* aldehyde reductase *(enzyme)*
Aldehydzucker *m* aldose
Alderney[rind] *n* Alderney *(cattle breed)*
Aldicarb *n* aldicarb *(insecticide, nematicide)*
Aldimorph *n* aldimorph *(fungicide)*
Alditol *m* alditol, sugar alcohol
Aldoheptose *f* aldoheptose *(monosaccharide)*
Aldohexose *f* aldohexose *(monosaccharide)*
Aldolase *f* fructose-bisphosphate aldolase *(enzyme)*
Aldonsäure *f* aldonic acid *(polyhydroxymonocarboxylic acid)*
Aldopentose *f* aldopentose *(monosaccharide)*
Aldose *f* aldose
Aldosereductase *f* aldehyde reductase *(enzyme)*
Aldosteron *n* aldosterone *(adrenocortical hormone)*
Aldoxycarb *n* aldoxycarb *(insecticide)*
Aldrin *n* aldrin *(insecticide)*
Ale *n* ale
Aleppohirse *f* Aleppo (Johnson, Tunis) grass, Sorghum halepense
Aleppokiefer *f* Aleppo pine, Pinus halepensis
Aleuriospore *f* *(bot)* aleur[i]ospore
Aleuron *n* aleuron[e], cerealin • **zum ~ gehörend** aleuronic
Aleurongewebe *n* aleuron tissue
Aleuronkorn *n* aleuron grain
Aleuronmehl *n* aleuron flour
Aleuronprotoplast *m* aleuron protoplast
Aleuronschicht *f* aleuron layer
Aleuronzelle *f* aleuron cell
Aleutenkrankheit *f* Aleutian disease *(of minks)*
Alexanderfuß *m* *(bot)* pellitory of Spain, Anacyclus pyrethrum
Alexandrinerklee *m* berseem [clover], Egyptian (alexandrian) clover, Trifolium alexandrinum
Alexandrinischer Lorbeer *m* 1. Alexandrian laurel, Danae racemosa; 2. Alexandrian laurel, Borneo mahogany, Calophyllum inophyllum
Alexin *n* alexin[e] *(blood constituent)*
alf *s.* Alfisol
Alfa *f* esparto [grass], Stipa tenacissima
Alfacillin *n* phenethicillin *(antibiotic)*
Alfisol *m* *(Am, soil)* alfisol
algaezid *s.* algizid
Algarobaslinse *f* one-flowered vetch, monantha vetch, Vicia articulata
Alge *f* alga *(division Phycophyta)*
algenabtötend algicidal
Algenabtötungsmittel *n* algicide
algenbekämpfend algicidal

Algenbekämpfung f algae control
Algenbekämpfungsmittel n algicide
Algenblüte f algal bloom
Algendünger m seaweed fertilizer
Algeneiweiß n algal protein
Algeninokulation f algal inoculation, algalization *(rice growing)*
Algenkultur f algae culture
Algenmehl n algae meal *(feed-stuff)*
Algenpilz m phycomycete
Algenprotein n algal protein
Algiermalve f blue (Mediterranean tree) mallow, Malva sylvestris (mauritiana)
Algiersalat m African valerian, horn of plenty, Fedia cornucopiae
Alginat n alginate
Alginsäure f alginic acid
algizid algicidal
Algizid n algicide
Algologie f phycology
Aliesterase f carboxylesterase *(enzyme)*
alimentär alimentary
Alizarin n alizarin *(plant dye)*
Alizarolprobe f *(dairy)* alizarin alcohol test
Alkali n alkali
Alkalialbuminat n alkali albuminate
Alkaliboden m alkali[ne] soil; saline (halomorphic) soil
Alkalicellulose f alkali cellulose *(wood pulping)*
alkali[en]liebend alkalophilic
Alkalilignin n alkali lignin
Alkalinität f s. Alkalität
Alkalipflanze f basiphyt
Alkalireserve f alkali reserve *(for buffering of blood pH)*
alkalisch alkaline, basic
Alkalisierung f alkali[ni]zation
Alkalität f alkalinity, basicity
Alkalizellstoff m soda pulp
Alkaloid n alkaloid
alkaloidisch alkaloidal
alkalophil alkalophilic
Alkalose f *(vet)* alkalosis
~/metabolische metabolic alkalosis
~/respiratorische respiratory alkalosis
Alkamin n amino alcohol
Alkan n alkane, paraffin
Alkanna[wurzel] f [dyer's, false] alkanet, Alkanna tinctoria (tuberculata)
Alkannin n alkannin, alkanet, anchusin *(dye)*
Alkanolamin n amine alcohol
Alkaptonausscheidung f im Harn, **Alkaptonurie** f alkaptonuria
Alken n alkene
Alkin n alkyne
Alkohol m alcohol
~/absoluter absolute alcohol
Alkoholbildungsvermögen n alcohol-forming power

Alkoholdehydrogenase f alcohol dehydrogenase *(enzyme)*
Alkohol-Extrakt-Verhältnis n alcohol/extract ratio *(of wine)*
alkoholfrei non-alcoholic
Alkoholgärung f alcoholic fermentation
Alkoholgehalt m alcohol content
Alkoholgrad m alcohol strength
alkoholhaltig alcoholic; heavy *(wine)*
alkoholisch alcoholic
Alkoholkraftstoff m alcohol fuel
Alkoholmesser m alcoholometer
Alkohol[o]meter n alcoholometer
Alkoholometrie f alcoholometry
Alkoholprobe f, **Alkoholtest** m alcohol test
Alkylcellulose f alkyl cellulose
Allamande f *(bot)* common allamanda, Allamanda cathartica
Allantiasis f botulism *(feed poisoning)*
Allantochorion n chorioallantois
Allantoicase f allantoicase *(enzyme)*
allantoid *(zoo)* allantoid
Allantoin n allantoin *(urea derivative)*
Allantoinase f allantoinase *(enzyme)*
Allantoinsäure f allantoic acid
Allantois f allantois, allantoic sac
Allantoisflüssigkeit f allantoic fluid
Allantoishöhle f allantoic cavity
Allantoiskreislauf m placental circulation
Allantoissack m allantoic sac, allantois
Allantoisstiel m urachus
Allantonematode m allantonematid *(family Allantonematidae)*
Alleebaum m avenue tree
Alleinfutter[mittel] n sole food (forage), complete feed
allel *(gen)* allelic
Allel n allele, allel[omorph]
~/abschwächendes hypomorph
~/amorphes amorph
~/antimorphes antimorph
~/entgegengesetzt wirkendes antimorph
~/hypermorphes hypermorph
~/hypomorphes hypomorph
~/multiples multiple allele
~/neomorphes neomorph
~/rezessives recessive allele, allogene
~/verstärkendes hypermorph
~/wirkungslos bleibendes amorph
Alleleffekt m gene effect
Allelenpaar n allelic pair
Allelfrequenz f allele (gene) frequency
Allelie f allelism, allelomorphism
allelisch allelic
Allelochemikalie f allelochemical
Allelogenese f, **Allelogenie** f allelogenesis
allelomorph allelomorphic
Allelomorphismus m allelomorphism, allelism

Allelopathie

Allelopathie f allelopathy *(mutual influencing of plant species by way of metabolic products)*
Allelopathikum n allelopathic
Allelopathin n allelopathin
allelopathisch allelopathic
allelotrop allelotropic
Allelotyp m allelotype
Allelsymbol n gene symbol
allergen allergenic
Allergen n allergen
Allergenität f allergenicity
Allergie f allergy • **eine ~ hervorrufend** allergenic
~/alimentäre alimetary allergy
~ des Soforttyps/angeborene atopy
Allergiebereitschaft f/[erbliche] atopy, idiosyncrasy
Allergietest m allergic test
allergisch allergic
Allergose f allergosis
allesfressend omnivorous, pantophagous
Allesfresser m omnivore, panthophagist
Allesfressertum n omnivorousness, pantophagy
Alles-rein-alles-raus-Prinzip n all-in-all-out management principle (system) *(of sanitation in animal houses)*
Allethrin n allethrin *(insecticide)*
Allgäuer Rind n Allgäu *(cattle breed)*
Allgemeines Wassermelonenmosaikvirus n water-melon mosaic virus 2, WMV 2, common water-melon mosaic virus, CMMV
Allgemeinnarkose f *(vet)* general anaesthesia
Allgemeinschädling m general pest
Allianz f *(ecol)* alliance
Allicin n allicin
Allidochlor n allidochlor *(herbicide)*
Alligatorkakao m alligator cacao, Theobroma cacao ssp. cacao f. pentagonum
Alligatorkraut n alligator weed, Alternanthera philoxeroides
Alliinlyase f alliin lyase *(enzyme)*
allitisch *(soil)* allitic
alliumartig *(bot)* alliaceous
Allmendewald m common forest
Alloantigen n alloantigen
allochthon allochthonous
allogam *(bot)* allogamous, xenogamous, cross-pollinating
Allogamie f allogamy, xenogamy, cross-pollination
allogen *(gen)* allogenic, allogenous
Allogen n allogene, recessive allele
alloheteroploid *(gen)* alloheteroploid
Alloheteroploide m alloheteroploid
Alloheteroploidie f alloheteroploidy
Allokarpie f *(bot)* allocarpy
Allometrie f allometry
allometrisch allometric
Allomon n allomone *(semiochemical)*
allopatrisch *(ecol)* allopatric
Allophan m allophane *(clay mineral)*
Allophän n *(gen)* allophene
Allophanboden m allophanic soil
Alloplasma n alloplasm, paraplasm
alloplasmatisch alloplasm[at]ic, paraplasm[at]ic
alloploid *(gen)* alloploid
Alloploide m alloploid
Alloploidie f alloploidy
allopolyhaploid *(gen)* allopolyhaploid, allohaploid
Allopolyhaploide m allopolyhaploid, allohaploid
Allopolyhaploidie f allopolyhaploidy
allopolyploid *(gen)* allopolyploid, amphidiploid
Allopolyploide m allopolyploid
Allopolyploidie f allopolyploidy
Allosom n allosome, gonosome, hetero[chromo]some, sex chromosome
allosomal allosomal
Allosterie f allostery
allosterisch allosteric
allotetraploid *(gen)* allotetraploid
Allotetraploide m allotetraploid
Allotetraploidie f allotetraploidy
Allotriophagie f *(vet)* allotriophagy
allotriploid *(gen)* allotriploid
Allotriploide m allotriploid
Allotriploidie f allotriploidy
Allotyp m *(gen)* allotype
Alloxan n alloxan
Alloxydim-Natrium n alloxydim-natrium *(herbicide)*
Allozygote f *(gen)* allozygote
Allozyklie f *(gen)* allocycly
Allozym n *(gen)* allozyme
Allozympolymorphismus m allozyme polymorphism
Allradantrieb m all-wheel drive, four-wheel drive, f.w.d.
Allradlenkung f four-wheel steering
Allradschlepper m all-wheel-drive tractor, four-wheel-drive tractor
alluvial *(soil)* alluvial
Alluvialboden m alluvial soil
Alluvialton m adobe
Alluvion f *(soil)* alluvion
Alluvium n Holocene
Allwetterkabine f all-weather cab
Allwetterverdeck n all-weather cab
Allylalkohol m allyl alcohol *(herbicide)*
1-Allyl-3-methoxy-4-hydroxy-benzen n eugenol
4-Allyl-2-methoxy-phenol n eugenol
(N-)Allylnormorphin n s. Nalorphin
Allylsenföl n allyl mustard oil
Allyltrenbolon n allyl trenbolone *(synthetic progesterone)*
Allyxycarb n allyxycarb *(insecticide)*
Allzweckförderer m general-purpose elevator
Allzweckfutter[lade]wagen m all-purpose forage wagon
Allzweckgebäude n general-purpose building

Allzweckkörper *m* general-purpose body *(of a mould-board plough)*
Allzweckmehl *n* all-purpose flour
Allzweckschlepper *m* utility (general-purpose) tractor
Allzweckstreichblech *n* general-purpose mould-board
Allzwecktragrahmen *m* multi-purpose implement frame
Allzwecktraktor *m* all-purpose tractor
Alm *f* alp, Alpine range (pasture), high mountain pasture
Almend *m (bot)* terminalia *(genus Terminalia)*
Almenrausch *m* Alpine rose, hairy Alpenrose, Rhododendron hirsutum
Almwiese *f* Alpine meadow *(s.a.* Alm*)*
Almwirt *m* Alpine farmer
Alnetum *n* alder forest
Aloe *f* aloe *(genus Aloe)*
Aloeblättrige Palmlilie *f* aloe yucca, Spanish bayonet (dagger), Yucca aloifolia
Alopezie *f (vet)* alopecia; hairlessness
Alp *f s.* Alm
Alpaka *n* alpaca, Lama [guanicoe f.] pacos
Alpakavlies *n* alpaca fleece
Alpakawolle *f* alpaca
Alpakawollstoff *m* alpaca
Alpen *pl* Alps • **in den ~ entstanden** alpigenous • **in den ~ wachsend** Alpine
Alpenampfer *m* monk's rhubarb, Rumex alpinus
Alpenaster *f* Alpine aster, Aster alpinus
Alpenaugenwurz *f* candy carrot, Athamanta cretensis
Alpenaurikel *f* auricula [primrose], bear's ear, dusty miller, Primula auricula
Alpenbärentraube *f* Alpine bearberry, Arctostaphylos alpinus
Alpengänsekresse *f* Alpine (mountain) rock-cress, Arabis alpina
Alpengemswurz *f (bot)* leopard's-bane, Doronicum columnae (cordifolium)
Alpenglöckchen *n (bot)* soldanella *(genus Soldanella)*
Alpengoldregen *m (bot)* Scotch laburnum, Laburnum alpinum
Alpenhase *m* mountain (varying) hare, Lepus timidus (variabilis)
Alpenheckenkirsche *f* Alps honeysuckle, Lonicera alpigena
Alpenjohannisbeere *f* mountain (Alpine) currant, Ribes alpinum
Alpenklee *m* mountain liquorice, Trifolium alpinum
Alpenkreuzdorn *m* Alpine buckthorn, Rhamnus alpinus
Alpenlieschgras *n* mountain timothy, Phleum alpinum (commutatum)
Alpenmurmeltier *n* mountain-rat, Marmota marmota
Alpenpflanze *f* Alpine [plant]

Alpenquendel *m* Alpine savory, basil thyme, Acinos alpinus, Calamintha alpina
Alpenrebe *f (bot)* Alpine clematis, Clematis alpina
Alpenrose *f* 1. rhododendron, azalea, rose-bay *(genus Rhododendron)*; 2. Alpine (drooping) rose, rusty-leaved rhododendron, Rhododendron ferrugineum
Alpenschneehuhn *n* [common European] ptarmigan, white grouse, Lagopus mutus
Alpenschnittlauch *m* large chive[s], Allium schoenoprasum var. sibiricum
Alpenseidelbast *m (bot)* Alpine mezereon, Daphne alpina
Alpensteinquendel *m* Alpine savory, basil thyme, Acinos alpinus, Calamintha alpina
Alpenstraußgras *n* Alpine bent[-grass], Agrostis alpina
Alpenveilchen *n* 1. cyclamen, Persian (Alpine) violet *(genus Cyclamen)*; 2. sowbread, Cyclamen europaeum
Alpenvergißmeinnicht *n* forget-me-not, Myosotis alpestris
Alpenwaldrebe *f* Alpine clematis, Clematis alpina
Alpenwiese *f* Alpine meadow *(s.a.* Alm*)*
Alpenzwergbuchs *m* bastard box, Polygala chamaebuxus
Alpha-Aminobernsteinsäure *f* aspartic acid, asparagine (aminosuccinic) acid
Alpha-Aminobernsteinsäuremonoamid *n* asparagine *(amino-acid)*
Alpha-Aminoessigsäure *f* glycine, glycocoll
Alpha-Amylase *f* alpha-amylase, ptyalin *(enzyme)*
Alpha-Amyrin *n* alpha-amyrin *(terpene)*
Alpha-Caroten *n* alpha-carotene *(vegetable dye)*
Alpha-Casein *n* alpha-casein *(milk protein)*
Alpha-Cellulose *f* alpha-cellulose
Alpha-D-Mannosidmannohydrolase *f* mannosidase *(enzyme)*
Alpha-Fetoprotein *n* alpha-foetoprotein
Alpha-Galactosidase *f* alpha-galactosidase *(enzyme)*
Alpha-Glucosidase *f* alpha-glucosidase, alpha-glucosidehydrolase, maltase *(enzyme)*
Alpha-Humus *m* alpha-humus
Alpha-Lactalbumin *n* alpha-lactalbumin *(milk protein)*
Alpha-Mannosidase *f* alpha-mannosidase *(enzyme)*
Alpha-Pinen *n* alpha-pinene
Alphasäure *f* alpha-acid *(hop constituent)*
Alpha-S-Casein *n* alpha-S-casein *(milk protein)*
Alpha-S1-Casein *n* alpha-S1-casein *(milk protein)*
Alphaspektrometrie *f* alpha spectrometry
Alphastrahlung *f* alpha radiation
Alpha-Terpineol *n* alpha-terpineol
Alpha-Tomatin *n* alpha-tomatine *(alkaloid)*
Alphavirus *n (vet)* alphavirus
alpin Alpine
Alpinengewächshaus *n* Alpine house

Alpinin

Alpinin *n* alpinine *(alkaloid)*
ALSOK *(vet)* avian leucosis sarcomatosis osteopetrosis complex
Alstroemerie *f* alstroemeria, Peruvian lily *(genus Alstroemeria)*
Altaifichte *f* Siberian spruce, Picea obovata
Altaischaf *n* Altai *(sheep breed)*
Altai-Wapiti *m* Siberian red deer, Cervus elaphus sibiricus
Altai-Weißdorn *m* Altai hawthorn, Crataegus altaica
Altbestand *m s.* Altholz
Altbock *m* mature ram
Altbulle *m* old bull
Alteber *m* mature boar
Alter *n* age • **das ~ bestimmen** to age
altern to age, to senesce
~ lassen to age
Alternanz *f* alternation *(e.g. of vegetation)*
Alternaria-Blattbräune *f* **der Rübe** alternaria leaf spot of beet *(caused by Alternaria tenuis)*
Alternaria-Blattfleckenkrankheit *f* **an Senecio** alternaria leaf spot of senecio *(caused by Alternaria senecionis)*
~ und Stengelfäule *f* **der Nelke** alternaria leaf spot of dianthus *(caused by Alternaria dianthi and A. dianthicola)*
Alternaria-Fäule *f* alternaria rot, alternariosis *(caused by Alternaria spp.)*
Alternaria-Fruchtfäule *f* alternaria fruit rot *(caused by Alternaria spp.)*
~ der Tomate early blight of tomato *(caused by Alternaria solani)*
Alternaria-Knollenfäule *f* potato early blight *(caused by Alternaria solani)*
Alternariose *f s.* Alternaria-Fäule
Alternation *f* alternation *(e.g. of vegetation)*
Alternativhypothese *f (biom)* alternative hypothesis
Alternativverteilung *f* alternative distribution *(of chromosomes in meiosis)*
Alternativwirt *m (phyt)* alternative (alternate) host
alternieren to alternate
Altersaufbau *m* age structure
Altersbestimmung *f* age determination, ag[e]ing
~/radiometrische radiometric dating
Altersfleischbräune *f* senescent (internal, sleepy) breakdown *(of pome fruit)*
Altersgruppe *f* age-group
Alterskern *m* **[der Rotbuche]** red heart[wood], false heart[wood]
Altersklasse *f* age class; *(hunt)* year class • **aus allen Altersklassen bestehend** *(forest)* all-staged
Altersklassenabstufung *f* age-class gradation
Altersklassenaufbau *m* age-class composition
Altersklassenfolge *f* series of age classes (gradations)
~/normale normal series of age classes

Altersklassengliederung *f* age-class proportion
Altersklassenmethode *f (forest)* method of age classes, age-class method
Altersklassenreihe *f*, **Altersklassenstufenfolge** *f s.* Altersklassenfolge
Altersklassentafel *f*, **Altersklassenübersicht** *f* age-class table (schedule)
Altersklassenverhältnis *n* age-class proportion, ratio of age classes
Altersklassenverteilung *f* age-class distribution (structure)
Alterskorrekturfaktor *m* age correction factor
Altersresistenz *f* age resistance
Altersschwäche *f* decrepitude, senility, marasmus
Altersstadium *n* stage of age
Altersstar *m (vet)* senile cataract
Altersstruktur *f* age structure
Altersstufe *f* age class
Altersstufenverteilung *f* age-class distribution (structure)
Altersverteilung *f* age distribution
Alterswertfaktor *m (forest)* age constant, value reduction factor
Alterszusammensetzung *f* age composition
Alterung *f*, **Alterungsprozeß** *m* ag[e]ing, senescence
Altgeschmacksausbildung *f* staling *(of alcoholic beverages)*
Althee *f (bot)* althaea *(genus Althaea)*
Altholz *n*, **Altholzbestand** *m* mature [timber] stand, mature forest, old forest (stand)
Altholzrinde *f* coarse bark
Altholzschirm *m* [forest, tree] canopy, tree (canopy) cover
altimontan oreal
Altiplano *m(n) (Am)* altiplano, tableland, plateau
Altkuh *f* old cow
Altokumulus *m* altocumulus *(cloud formation)*
Altöl *n* waste (used, old motor) oil
altomontan altomontane
Altostratus *m* altostratus *(cloud formation)*
Altsau *f* breeding (brood) sow, old (aged) sow
Altschneider *m* brawner, stag *(castrated breeding boar)*
Altstreu *f* old litter
Alttier *n* old hind *(red deer, fallow deer)*
Altwasser *n* ox-bow
Altwassersee *m* ox-bow
Altweibersommer *m* 1. Indian summer, 2. gossamer *(floating cobwebs)*
Alufolie *f s.* Aluminiumfolie
Aluminium *n* aluminium
Aluminiumfolie *f* aluminium foil
Aluminiumfolienmulch *m* aluminium foil mulch *(for vector control)*
Aluminiumfosetyl *n* aluminiumfosetyl *(fungicide)*
Aluminiumhydroxid *n* aluminium hydroxide
Aluminiumoxid *n* aluminium oxide *(non-clay mineral)*

Aluminiumphosphat n aluminium phosphate
Aluminiumphosphid n aluminium phosphide *(insecticide, rodenticide)*
Aluminiumtoxizität f aluminium toxicity *(of soils)*
Alumosilicat n aluminosilicate *(primary soil-forming mineral)*
Alunit m alunite *(non-clay mineral)*
Alveogramm n alveogram
Alveograph m alveograph
alveolär alveolar
Alveolardentalmembran[e] f periodontum *(animal anatomy)*
Alveolarepithel n alveolar epithelium
Alveolarsack m alveolar sac
Alveole f 1. [pulmonary] alveolus; 2. alveolus, tooth-socket • **innerhalb der ~** intra-alveolar
Alveolengang m alveolar duct
Alveolus m alveolus
Amanitin n amanitin *(mycotoxin, oligopeptide)*
Amantadin n amantadine *(antiviral substance)*
Amarant m *(bot)* 1. amaranth *(genus Amaranthus)*; 2. edible amaranth, Chinese spinach, Amaranthus tricolor
Amaranthus-lividus-Scheckungsvirus n amaranthus lividus mottle virus
Amarelle f amarelle cherry, Prunus cerasus var. cerasus
Amaryllis f *(bot)* amaryllis *(genus Hippeastrum)*
Amateurimker m amateur bee-keeper
Amaurose f, **Amaurosis** f *(vet)* amaurosis
Amazonas-Riesenseerose f Victoria water-lily, Victoria amazonica (regia)
Ambari n kenaf, ambary, brown Indian hemp, wild stockrose, Hibiscus cannabinus
Ambatsch m *(bot)* ambatch, Aeschynomene elaphroxylon
Amberbaum m *(bot)* liquidambar *(genus Liquidambar)*
Ambercodon n *(gen)* amber codon
Amberkraut n cat thyme, Teucrium marum
Amblabaum m *(bot)* myrobalan, Phyllanthus emblica
Amblosin n ampicillin *(antibiotic)*
Ambozeptor m amboceptor *(immunology)*
Ambrosiakäfer m 1. pin-hole borer, platypodid *(family Platypodidae)*; 2. ambrosia beetle (borer) *(esp. of genera Xyloterus and Xyleborus that cultivate a fungus on which they feed)*
Ambrosie f *(Am)* ragweed, stickweed *(genus Ambrosia)*
Ameiose f ameiosis
Ameise f ant, emmet *(family Formicidae)* • **mit Ameisen vergesellschaftet [lebend]** myrmecophilous
Ameisenbuntkäfer m ant (chequer) beetle, Thanasimus formicarius
Ameisenei n ant['s] egg
Ameisengast m myrmecophile

Ameisenhaufen m, **Ameisenhügel** m antheap, anthill
Ameisenlöwe m *(ent)* ant-lion *(family Myrmeleonidae)*
Ameisennest n ant nest, formicary
Ameisensäure f formic (methanoic) acid
Ameisensäuredehydrogenase f formate dehydrogenase *(enzyme)*
Amelioration f amelioration
ameliorieren to ameliorate
Amensalismus m *(ecol)* amensalism
American Foxhound m American foxhound *(breed)*
~ Staffordshire Terrier m American Staffordshire terrier *(breed)*
~ Water Spaniel m American water spaniel *(breed)*
Amerikanische Blattkrankheit f American leaf spot [of coffee] *(caused by Mycena citricolor)*
~ Blueberry f swamp (highbush) blueberry, Vaccinium corymbosum
~ Buche f [North American] beech, Fagus grandifolia
~ Edelkastanie f [American] chestnut, *(Am)* prickly burr, Castanea dentata (americana)
~ Esche f American ash, Fraxinus americana
~ Faulbrut f *(api)* American foul brood *(caused by Bacillus larvae)*
~ Flockenblume f basket-flower, American star thistle, Centaurea americana
~ Gartenpflaume f wild-goose plum, Prunus munsoniana
~ Gleditschie f honey (sweet) locust, three-thorned acacia, Gleditsia triacanthos
~ Hainbuche f American hornbeam, blue beech, Carpinus caroliniana
~ Hasel[nuß] f American hazel (filbert), Corylus americana
~ Himbeere f red raspberry, Rubus strigosus
~ Hopfenbuche f [American] hop hornbeam, Ostrya virginiana
~ Kastanie f s. ~ Edelkastanie
~ Kermesbeere f Virginian pokeweed, Phytolacca americana
~ Kiefer f short-leaf pine, Pinus echinata
~ Kohleule f *(ent)* cabbage looper, Trichoplusia ni
~ Lebensbaumminiermotte f *(ent)* arbor vitae leaf-miner, Argyresthia thuiella
~ Linde f *(Am)* bee tree, Tilia americana
~ Lotosblume f American lotus, water chinquapin, duck acorn, Nelumbo lutea
~ Nieswurz f American hellebore, Indian poke, Veratrum viride
~ Ölpalme f American oil-palm, Corozo (Elaeis) oleifera
~ Pekingente f [White] Peking duck *(breed)*
~ Pferdeenzephalitis f **der Vögel** equine encephalitis in birds
~ Pferdeenzephalomyelitis f equine encephalomyelitis, sleeping sickness

Amerikanische

~ **Platane** f American plane[-tree], Platanus occidentalis
~ **Roteiche** f [northern] red oak, Quercus rubra (borealis)
~ **Roterle** f Oregon (red) alder, Alnus oregona (rubra)
~ **Rotkiefer** f red pine, Pinus resinosa
~ **Schabe** f American cockroach, Periplaneta americana
~ **Scheinpflaume** f American plum, Prunus americana
~ **Seide** f dodder, Cuscuta gronovii
~ **Weide** f American (heart-leaved) willow, Salix rigida, Salix x eriocephala
~ **Weißbuche** f American hornbeam, blue beech, Carpinus caroliniana
~ **Weymouthskiefer** f Californian mountain pine, Pinus monticola
~ **Wicke** f pea vine, Vicia americana
~ **Zitterpappel** f quaking asp[en], [American] aspen, asp, Populus tremuloides
Amerikanischer Aal m American eel, Anguilla rostrata
~ **Amberbaum** m sweet gum, Liquidambar styraciflua
~ **Baumwollkapselwurm** m (ent) cotton bollworm (earworm), tomato fruit worm, Heliothis zea
~ **Blumenthrips** m (ent) western (American) flower thrips, Frankliniella occidentalis
~ **Elch** m moose, Alces alces ssp. americanus
~ **Erdbeerbaum** m Pacific madrone, Arbutus menziesii
~ **Faulbaum** m cascara buckthorn, Rhamnus purshianus (purshiana)
~ **Ginseng** m [American] ginseng, (Am) tatar-root, Panax quinquefolius
~ **Holunder** m American elder, Sambucus canadensis
~ **Luzernerüßler** m alfalfa weevil, Hypera postica, Phytonomus variabilis
~ **Nerz** m mink, Mustela (Lutreola) vison
~ **Reismehlkäfer** m confused flour beetle, Tribolium confusum
~ **Riesenleberegel** m giant liver fluke, Fascioloides magna
~ **Schneeball** m [American] cranberry bush, highbush-cranberry, Viburnum trilobum
~ **Stachelbeermehltau** m American gooseberry mildew (caused by Sphaeroteca mors uvae)
~ **Storax** m American storax, sweet gum (balsam from Liquidambar styraciflua)
~ **Strauß[en]farn** m ostrich fern, Matteuccia [struthiopteris var.] pensylvanica
~ **Traber** m American trotter, Standardbred [trotter] (horse breed)
~ **Webebär** m (ent) fall web-worm, Hyphantria cunea
~ **Wisent** m [American] bison, buffalo, Bison bison

~ **Zürgelbaum** m [American] hackberry, nettle tree, Celtis occidentalis
Amerikanisches Braunvieh n Brown Swiss (cattle breed)
~ **Fleckfieber** n s. ~ Zeckenfieber
~ **Himbeerkräuselvirus** n American raspberry leaf curl virus
~ **Latentes Hopfenvirus** n American hop latent virus
~ **Oregano** n Mexican oregano (sage), Lippia graveolens
~ **Pfirsichmosaikvirus** n American peach mosaic virus
~ **Pflaumenbandmosaikvirus** n American plum line pattern virus
~ **Zeckenfieber** n (vet) Rocky Mountain spotted fever, RMS-fever
Amerikapflaume f American (red, river) plum, Prunus americana
ametabol (ent) ametabolic
Amethopterin n amethopterin, methotrexate (antimetabolite, vitamin antagonist)
Amethystblaue Edeldistel f amethyst sea holly, Eryngium amethystinum
amethystfarben amethystine
Amethystschwingel m amethyst fescue, Festuca amethystina
Ametridone n ametridone (herbicide)
Ametryn n ametryne (herbicide)
Amfostat n amphotericin B (antibiotic)
Amicarbalid n amicarbalide (antiparasitic)
Amicloral n amicloral (feed additive)
Amid n amide
Amidase f amidase (enzyme)
Amiddünger m amide fertilizer
Amidintransferase f amidine transferase (enzyme)
Amidithion n amidithion (acaricide)
Amidherbizid n amide herbicide
Amidhydrolase f amide hydrolase (enzyme)
Amidophosphoribosyltransferase f amidophosphoribosyltransferase (enzyme)
Amidoschwarzmethode f, **Amidoschwarzverfahren** n amido black method (for protein determination in milk)
Amidstickstoff m amide nitrogen
Amin n amine
Aminoacylhistidindipeptidase f aminoacyl-histidine dipeptidase, carnosinase (enzyme)
Aminoacyltransferase f aminoacyl transferase (enzyme)
Aminoacyl-tRNA-Hydrolase f aminoacyl-tRNA hydrolase (enzyme)
Aminoadamantan n amantadine (antiviral substance)
Aminoalkohol m amino alcohol
Aminoazidurie f aminoaciduria
Aminobenzoesäure f aminobenzoic acid
2-Aminobenzoesäure f anthranilic acid

Aminobutan *n* aminobutane *(fungicide)*
Aminobuttersäure *f* aminobutyric acid
Aminocarb *n* aminocarb *(acaricide, insecticide)*
Aminocarbonsäure *f s.* Aminosäure
Aminodesoxyzucker *m* amino sugar
2-Aminoethan-1-ol *n* ethanolamine
Aminoethansulfonsäure *f* taurine
2-Amino-ethanthiol *n* mercaptamine, cysteamine
Aminoethoxyvinylglycin *n* aminoethoxyvinylglycine, AVG *(growth regulator)*
Aminogruppe *f* amino group
2-Amino-4-hydroxybuttersäure *f* homoserine *(amino-acid)*
2-Amino-6-hydroxypurin *n* guanine
Aminoisobuttersäure *f* aminoisobutyric acid
Aminolävulinatdehydratase *f* porphobilinogen synthase *(enzyme)*
5-Aminolävulinatsynthase *f* 5-aminolaevulinate synthase, delta-aminolaevulinate synthase *(enzyme)*
Aminolävulinsäure *f* aminolaevulinic acid
Aminolävulinsäuredehydratase *f* aminolaevulinic dehydratase *(enzyme)*
2-Aminopentandisäure *f* glutamic (glutaminic) acid
Aminopeptidase *f* aminopeptidase *(enzyme)*
Aminopropionsäure *f* alanine, 2-aminopropionic acid
6-Amino-purin *n* dihydrozeatin *(cytokinin)*
Aminosäure *f* amino-acid
~/essentielle essential amino-acid
~/freie free amino-acid
~/lebenswichtige essential amino-acid
~/limitierende limiting amino-acid
~/nichtproteinogene non-protein amino-acid
~/schwefelhaltige sulphur amino-acid
~/verzweigtkettige branched amino-acid
Aminosäureabkömmling *m* amino-acid derivative
Aminosäureaminotransferase *f/verzweigtkettige* branched-chain amino-acid aminotransferase *(enzyme)*
Aminosäureanreicherung *f* amino-acid fortification *(of feed-stuffs)*
Aminosäurebedarf *m* amino-acid requirement
Aminosäurecode *m* genetic code
(L)-Aminosäuredecarboxylase *f/aromatische* aromatic-L-amino-acid decarboxylase, DOPA decarboxylase, [hydroxy]tryptophan decarboxylase *(enzyme)*
Aminosäurederivat *n* amino-acid derivative
Aminosäurenanalysator *m* amino-acid analyzer
Aminosäurenanalyse *f* amino-acid analysis
Aminosäurenantagonist *m* amino-acid antagonist
Aminosäurenpool *m* amino-acid pool
Aminosäurenzusammensetzung *f* amino-acid composition
Aminosäureoxidase *f* amino-acid oxidase *(enzyme)*
Aminosäuresequenz *f* amino-acid sequence

Aminosidin *n* paromomycin *(antibiotic)*
Aminostickstoff *m* aminonitrogen
Aminotriazol *n* aminotriazole *(herbicide)*
Aminotransferase *f* aminotransferase, transaminase *(enzyme)*
Aminoverbindung *f* amino compound
Aminoxidase *f* amine oxidase *(enzyme)*
~ (flavinhaltig) amine oxidase flavin-containing, adrenaline oxidase, monoamine oxidase, tyraminase *(enzyme)*
~ (kupferhaltig) amine oxidase copper-containing, diamine oxidase, histaminase *(enzyme)*
Aminozucker *m* amino sugar
Amiprofos-methyl *n* amiprofos-methyl *(herbicide)*
Amiton *n* amiton *(acaricide, insecticide)*
Amitose *f* amitosis
amitotisch amitotic
Amitraz *n* amitraz *(acaricide, insecticide)*
Amitrol *n* amitrole, aminotriazole *(herbicide)*
Amixie *f* amixia
AmLSV *s.* Amaranthus-lividus-Scheckungsvirus
Amme *f* nurse
Ammenbiene *f* nurse [honey-]bee
Ammenkrankheit *f* nursing anaemia *(of fur-bearing animals)*
Ammenkuh *f* nurse cow
Ammenpflanze *f* nurse
Ammensterilität *f* lactation anoestrus
Ammenveredelung *f* nurse-root grafting
Ammenzeugung *f* metagenesis
Ammer *m* emmer [wheat], Triticum dicoccon
Ammonchlorid *n s.* Ammoniumchlorid
Ammoniak *n* ammonia • **mit ~ behandeln** to ammoniate
~/flüssiges liquid ammonia
~/schwefelsaures *s.* Ammoniumsulfat
~/verflüssigtes liquid ammonia
~/wasserfreies anhydrous ammonia *(fertilizer)*
ammoniakalisch ammoniac[al]
Ammoniakapplikator *m* ammonia applicator
Ammoniakbegasung *f* ammonia fumigation
Ammoniakbildner *m* ammonifier, ammonifying bacterium
Ammoniakdünger *m* ammonium fertilizer
Ammoniaksalpeter *m* ammonium nitrate *(fertilizer)*
Ammoniakstickstoff *m* ammonium (ammonia) nitrogen
Ammoniaksuperphosphat *n* ammoniated superphosphate *(fertilizer)*
Ammoniaktanklager *n* ammonia tank store
Ammoniakvergiftung *f* *(vet)* ammonia poisoning
Ammoniakwasser *n* ammonia water, aqueous ammonia
Ammonifikant *m* ammonifier, ammonifying bacterium
Ammonifikation *f* ammonification
ammonifizieren to ammonify
Ammonifizierung *f* ammonification
ammonisieren to ammoniate *(e.g. feed-stuffs)*

Ammonisier-Granuliertrommel

Ammonisier-Granuliertrommel f reaction-granulation drum *(fertilizer industry)*
Ammonisierung f ammoniation
Ammonium n ammonium
Ammoniumchlorid n ammonium chloride
Ammoniumdünger m ammonium fertilizer
Ammoniumfixierung f ammonium fixation
Ammoniumhumat n ammonium humate
Ammoniumhydrogencarbonat n ammonium bicarbonate
Ammoniumnitrat n ammonium nitrate *(fertilizer)*
Ammoniumphosphat n ammonium phosphate, ammophos *(fertilizer)*
Ammoniumstickstoff m ammonium (ammonia) nitrogen
Ammoniumsulfamat n ammonium sulphamate, AMS *(herbicide)*
Ammoniumsulfat n ammonium sulphate, sulphate of ammonia *(fertilizer)*
Ammoniumverbindung f ammonium compound
~/quaternäre quaternary ammonium compound *(e.g. as disinfectant)*
Ammonnitrat n ammonium nitrate
Ammonolyse f ammonolysis *(e.g. of resin acids)*
Ammonsalpeter m ammonium nitrate
Ammonsulfat n s. Ammoniumsulfat
Ammophoska f ammophoska *(NPK fertilizer)*
Amnion n amnion, caul *(animal anatomy)*
Amnionflüssigkeit f amniotic fluid
Amnionhöhle f amniotic cavity
amniotisch amniotic
Amöbe f amoeba *(order Amoebina)*
amöbenartig amoeboid
Amöbendysenterie f amoebic dysentery *(caused by Entamoeba histolytica)*
Amöbengift n amoebicide
Amöbenkrankheit f s. Amöbenseuche der Bienen
Amöbenruhr f s. Amöbendysenterie
Amöbenseuche f der Bienen *(api)* amoeba disease *(caused by Malpighamoeba mellificae)*
Amöbizid n amoebicide
amöboid amoeboid
Amomum n cardamom, cardamon, cardamum *(genus Amomum)*
amorph[isch] amorphous, amorphic *(allele)*
Amorphismus m amorphism
Amoxil n, **Amoxycillin** n amoxicillin *(antibiotic)*
AMP s. Adenosin-5'-monophosphat
AMP-Desaminase f AMP deaminase *(enzyme)*
Ampel f hanging flowerpot
Ampelographie f ampelography
Ampelometrie f ampelometry
Ampelotherapie f ampelotherapy
Ampelpflanze f hanging plant
Ampfer m sorrel, dock *(genus Rumex)*
Ampferblattlaus f [true] dock aphid, Aphis rumicis
Ampferknöterich m *(bot)* pale persicaria, curltop lady's-thumb, Polygonum lapathifolium
Amphetamin n amphetamine *(analeptic)*

Amphiarthrose f amphiarthrosis
Amphibol m amphibole *(soil-forming rock)*
Amphibolit m amphibolite *(soil-forming rock)*
amphidiploid *(gen)* amphidiploid, allopolyploid
Amphidiploide m amphidiploid, allopolyploid
Amphidiploidie f amphidiploidy, allopolyploidy
amphigam *(bot)* amphigamous
Amphigonie f amphigenesis, amphigony
amphimiktisch amphimictic
Amphimixis f amphimixis
amphiploid *(gen)* amphiploid
Amphiploide m amphiploid
Amphiploidie f amphiploidy
amphoter amphoteric
Amphotericin n **B** amphotericin B *(antibiotic)*
Ampicillin n ampicillin *(antibiotic)*
Amprolium n amprolium *(coccidiostatic)*
Amputation f *(vet)* amputation
amputieren to amputate; to dock *(e.g. an animal's tail)*
Amstelraute f feathered (tufted) columbine, Thalictrum aquilegifolium
Am-Sup s. Ammoniaksuperphosphat
Amurflieder m Amur lilac, Syringa amurensis
Amurkarpfen m grass carp, white amur, Ctenopharyngodon idella
Amurkorkbaum m cork-tree, Phellodendron amurense
Amurliguster m Amur privet, Ligustrum amurense
Amurrebe f Amur grape, Vitis amurensis
AMV s. Atemminutenvolumen
Amygdalase f beta-glucosidase *(enzyme)*
Amygdalin n amygdalin *(glycoside)*
Amylalkohol m amyl alcohol
Amylase f amylase, diastase *(enzyme)*
amylasereich high-diastase
Amylocellulose f amylocellulose
Amylodextrin n amylodextrin[e] *(product of starch degradation)*
Amyloglucosidase f, **Amylo-1,6-glucosidase** f amyloglucosidase *(enzyme)*
Amylogramm n amylogram
Amylograph m amylograph *(milling)*
amyloid amyloid[al]
Amyloid n amyloid *(polysaccharide)*
Amyloidose f *(vet)* amyloidosis
Amylolyse f amylolysis
amylolytisch amylolytic
Amylopectin-1,6-glucosidase f amylopectin-1,6-glucosidase *(enzyme)*
Amylopektin n amylopectin *(polysaccharide)*
Amyloplast m amyloplast *(starch-forming plastid)*
Amylose f amylose *(polysaccharide)*
Amylosubtilin n amylosubtilin *(antibiotic)*
Amylum n amylum *(polysaccharide)*
Amyostenie f *(vet)* myasthenia
Amyotrophie f amyotrophia
Anaakazie f white acacia, Faidherbia (Acacia) albida

Anabasin n anabasine *(alkaloid)*
Anabasis f *(bot)* anabasis *(genus Anabasis)*
anabatisch anabatic *(e.g. air current)*
Anabiose f anabiosis
anabiotisch anabiotic
anabol anabolic
Anabolikum n anabolic [agent], metabolic stimulant
anabolisch anabolic
Anabolismus m anabolism, constructive (synthetic) metabolism
Anabolit m anabolite
anadrom *(pisc)* anadromous
anaerob anaerobic
Anaerobier m anaerobe, anaerobic bacterium
Anaerobierenterotoxämie f **des Geflügels** avian ulcerated enteritis, ulcerative enteritis of birds, quail disease
Anaerobiont m s. Anaerobier
Anaerobiose f anaerobiosis, anoxibiosis
anaerobisch s. anaerob
anal anal
Analbeutel m anal sac, para-anal sinus *(of dog and cat)*
Analdrüse f anal (rectal) gland
Analeptikum n analeptic
Analgesie f analgesia
Analgetikum n analgesic
Analkanal m anal canal
Analöffnung f anal orifice
Analsegment n telson *(of arthropods)*
Analyse f analysis; assay
~/mehrdlmensionale *(biom)* multivariate analysis
~/organoleptische organoleptic analysis (assessment, test)
~/statistische statistical analysis
Analysenmethode f analytical method; analytical operation
Analysenquarzlampe f quartz lamp
Analysentechnik f analytical technique
Analysenverfahren n analytical method
Analysenwaage f analytical balance
Analzim m analcime, analcite *(non-clay mineral)*
Anämie f *(vet)* anaemia
~/aplastische aplastic anaemia
~ der Einhufer/infektiöse equine infectious anaemia
~ der Forelle/infektiöse Egtved disease [of trout]
~/hämolytische haemolytic anaemia (disease)
~/hyperchrome hyperchromic anaemia
~/hypochrome hypochromic anaemia
~/makrozytäre macrocytic anaemia
~/mikrozytäre microcytic anaemia
~/normozytäre normocytic anaemia
~/perniziöse pernicious anaemia
~/posthämorrhagische posthaemorrhagic anaemia
anämisch anaemic
Anamnese f anamnesis

Ananas f 1. pineapple, ananas, Ananas comosus; 2. pineapple *(fruit)*
Ananaserdbeere f 1. garden (pineapple) strawberry, Fragaria x ananassa (grandiflora); 2. [garden] strawberry *(fruit)*
Ananasfaser f pineapple fibre
Ananasgalle f *(phyt, forest)* pineapple gall
Ananasgewächs n bromelia[d] *(family Bromeliaceae)*
Ananaskirsche f Cape gooseberry, Peruvian ground cherry, Physalis peruviana
Ananaskrankheit f **des Zuckerrohrs** pineapple rot of sugar-cane *(caused by Ceratocystis paradoxa)*
Ananaspflanzung f pinery
Ananastreibhaus n pinery
Anaphase f anaphase *(nuclear division)*
Anaphorese f anaphoresis
Anaphrodisie f anoestrus, silent heat (oestrus)
Anaphylaxie f anaphylaxis
Anaplasie f anaplasia
Anaplasmose f anaplasmosis, gall sickness *(esp. of cattle, caused by Anaplasma marginale)*
Anasarka f *(vet)* anasarca
Anästhesie f *(vet)* anaesthesia
~/allgemeine general anaesthesia
anästhesieren to anaesthetize
anästhesierend anaesthetic
Anästhesin n anaesthesin *(anaesthetic)*
Anästhetikum n anaesthetic
anästhetisch anaesthetic
Anastomose f anastomosis
~/arteriovenöse arterio-venous anastomosis
Anatomie f anatomy
~/angewandte (makroskopische) gross anatomy
anatomisch anatomical
anatrop *(bot)* anatropous
Anauxit m anauxite *(clay mineral)*
AnAV s. Anemonen-Alloiophyllie-Virus
anbacken to mount *(a sporting gun)*
Anbau m cropping, crop husbandry, growing, cultivation, culture
~/bodenbearbeitungsloser s. ~/pflugloser
~/geschützter protected cropping (cultivation), growing under cover
~ im Gewächshaus greenhouse cropping, glasshouse cultivation
~ in Bewässerungsrinnen flow-channel-culture *(horticulture)*
~ in Foliesäcken bag culture (growing) *(e.g. of mushrooms)*
~ in Hydrokultur hydroponic growing
~ ohne Zusatzbewässerung rain-fed culture
~/pflugloser non-plough cultivation, no-tillage system, zero tillage (cultivation)
~/praxisüblicher good agricultural practice
~ unter Glas greenhouse cropping
~ unter Holländerfenstern Dutch light growing

Anbau

~ unter natürlichen Niederschlagsbedingungen rainfed cultivation
~ unter Schirm[bestand] *(forest)* planting under shelterwood
~/vertraglich gebundener contract growing
Anbaubeetpflug *m* mounted one-way plough
Anbaubedingung *f* growing condition
Anbauberater *m* extension agent, fieldman
Anbauberatung *f* extension service
Anbauberatungsprogramm *n* extension programme
Anbaubeschränkung *f* planting (acreage) limitation
Anbaudauer *f* cropping period
Anbaudrehpflug *m* [mounted] half-turn plough, semiturning (two-way-mounted) plough
Anbaudrillmaschine *f* [tractor-]mounted drill
Anbaueigenschaft *f* cropping property
anbauen to crop, to grow, to cultivate, to farm
~/als Mischfrucht (Mischkultur) to intercrop
~/bewässerungslos to dry-farm
~/Gras zur Heugewinnung to hay
~/im Gemenge to intercrop
~/streifenweise to strip-crop
Anbauer *m* grower, cropper, cultivator
~/gewerblicher commercial grower
anbaufähig cultivable
~/nicht uncultivable
Anbaufähigkeit *f* cultivability
Anbaufederzinkengrubber *m* mounted spring-tine cultivator
Anbaufläche *f* crop[ping] area, growing (planting) area, acreage, cultivated area, land under cultivation
~ in Hektar hectar[e]age
Anbauflächenbeschränkung *f* acreage limitation
Anbaufolge *f* crop[ping] sequence, crop succession
Anbaufräse *f* tractor-mounted rotary cultivator
Anbaugebiet *n* crop[ping] area, growing (planting, cultivated) area
Anbaugerät *n* [tractor-]mounted implement, attached implement
Anbaugerätesystem *n* system of mounting implements
Anbaugewächshaus *n* lean-to glasshouse
Anbaugrenze *f* crop margin
Anbaugrubber *m* [tractor-]mounted cultivator
Anbauhacke *f,* **Anbauhackrahmen** *m* mounted [steerage] hoe
Anbaujahr *n* growing year
Anbaulenkhacke *f s.* Anbauhacke
Anbaumähbalken *m,* **Anbaumähwerk** *n* mounted mower
Anbaumaschine *f* tractor-mounted machine
Anbaumethode *f* cultural method, method of cultivation
Anbaunormativ *n* cropping standard
Anbaupause *f* cropping interval, crop-free period

Anbaupflug *m* mounted plough
Anbauplan *m* cropping plan (schedule, scheme)
Anbauperiode *f* cropping period
Anbaupraxis *f* cultural practice
Anbauprogramm *n* cropping programme
Anbauprüfung *f* cultivation test
Anbaurahmen *m* tool frame
Anbauraupe *f* half-track device (unit)
Anbaurisiko *n* planting risk
Anbauschälpflug *m* tractor-mounted skim plough
Anbauscharpflug *m* mounted mould-board plough
Anbauscheibenpflug *m* mounted disk plough
Anbauschleuderdüngerstreuer *m* mounted spinner-broadcaster for fertilizers
Anbauschleuderstreuer *m* mounted broadcaster
Anbaustäubegerät *n* tractor-mounted duster
Anbaustrohpresse *f* built-in straw baler
Anbaustufe *f* generation of authentic seed
Anbausystem *n* cropping (growing, planting) system
Anbautechnik *f* [field] cropping practice, growing (cultural, cultivation) technique, crop husbandry technique
Anbauverfahren *n* cultural method
Anbauversuch *m* cultivation test, planting trial
Anbauvertrag *m* growing contract
Anbauwechselpflug *m* mounted alternate plough
anbauwürdig worthy of cultivation
Anbauzone *f* growing zone
anbellen to bay *(game)*
Anbindeautomatik *f* self-catching device *(cattle barn equipment)*
Anbindekette *f* tying chain
~/automatische self-locking neck tie
Anbindekuhstall *m* tie-up cow-house
anbinden to tie [up], to tether
~/an einen Baumpfahl to stake
Anbindering *m* tethering ring
Anbindestall *m* tie [stall] barn, stanchion barn (stable)
Anbindestand *m* tie (tying, tether) stall
Anbindevorrichtung *f* tying [device] *(s.a.* Anbindeautomatik*)*
anbleien *s.* anschießen
anbohren to bore; to tap; *(ent)* to terebrate
Anbrechen *n* **von Trieben** brutting *(in fruit woods)*
anbrüchig *s.* angefault
AnBRV *s.* Anemonenbraunringvirus
Ancylosis *f (vet)* ankylosis
Anconschaf *n* Ancon (otter) sheep
Ancymidol *m* ancymidol *(growth regulator)*
Andalusier *m* Andalusian *(horse breed)*
Andalusierhuhn *n* Andalusian *(breed of fowl)*
Andamanen-Koko *m* lebbek [tree], chatter box tree, woman's-tongue [tree], Albizia lebbeck
Andenhimbeere *f* Andes berry (black raspberry), Rubus glaucus
Andenkartoffelscheckungsvirus *n* Andean potato mottle virus

Andenlupine f *(bot)* tarwi, Lupinus mutabilis
andersartig heterologous
Andesit m andesite *(soil-forming rock)*
Andiroba[holz] n crab wood, Carapa guianensis
Andorn m *(bot)* 1. horehound *(genus Marrubium)*; 2. horehound, Marrubium vulgare
Andosol m *(soil)* andosol
Androdiözie f *(bot)* androdioecism
androdiözisch androdioecious
Androeceum n *(bot)* androecium
Androgamet m androgamete, microgamete, sperm [cell]
Androgamie f *(bot)* androgamy
androgen androgenous
Androgen n androgen *(sex hormone)*
Androgenese f androgenesis, male parthenogenesis
androgenetisch androgenetic
Androgenwirksamkeit f androgenicity
androgyn androgynous, androgynal
Androgynie f androgyny
Androgynophor n *(bot)* androgynophore
Andromonözie f *(bot)* andromonoecism
andromonözisch andromonoecious
Androphor n androphore
Androsaemum-Hartheu n *(bot)* sweet amber, Hypericum androsaemum
Androspore f *(bot)* androspore
Androstendion n androstendione *(sex hormone)*
Androstenon n androstenone *(pheromone)*
androsteril *(bot)* androsterile
Androsterilität f androsterility, pollen sterility
Androsteron n androsterone *(sex hormone)*
Andrözeum n *(bot)* androecium
Aneinanderhaften n adherence, adhesion
aneinanderhaftend adherent
anemochor *(bot)* anemochorous, wind-dispersed
Anemochorie f anemochory, wind dispersion
anemogam *(bot)* anemophilous, anemogamous, wind-pollinated
Anemogamie f anemophily, wind pollination
Anemogramm n anemogram
Anemograph m anemograph
Anemometer n anemometer, wind-gauge
Anemone f anemone, anemony, wind-flower *(genus Anemone)*
Anemone-Japonica-Hybride f Japanese anemone, Anemone x hybrida
Anemonen-Alloiophyllie-Virus n anemone alloiophylly virus
Anemonenbraunringvirus n anemone brown ring virus
Anemonenmosaikvirus n anemone mosaic virus
Anemonenwaldrebe f mountain (anemone-flowered) clematis, Clematis montana
Anemonin n anemonin *(aromatic compound)*
anemophil s. anemogam
Anemoplankton n aeroplankton, aerial plankton
Anemotaxis f *(zoo)* anemotaxis

Anenzephalie f *(vet)* anencephaly
Anergie f habituation *(tissue culture)*
anerkannt approved, certified; source-identified *(seed)*
anerkennen to approve, to certify *(e.g. cultivars)*
Anerkennung f approval, certification, admission *(e.g. of new cultivars)*
~ **von Waldbeständen** certification of [forest] stands
Aneroid[barometer] n aneroid [barometer]
aneuploid *(gen)* aneuploid
Aneuploide m aneuploid
Aneuploidie f aneuploidy
Aneurin n aneurin, thiamine, vitamin B_1
Aneurysma n *(vet)* aneurysm, aneurism
Anfall m 1. *(vet)* attack, seizure, insult; 2. outturn *(e.g. of timber assortments)*
~/**epileptiformer** epileptiform attack
anfallen to alight *(wildfowl)*
~/**die Fährte** *(hunt)* to track (take up) the scent, to follow the track
anfällig susceptible, predisposed
~/**nicht** refractory
Anfälligkeit f susceptibility
Anfangsaufnahme f initial absorption *(e.g. of wood preservatives)*
Anfangsbelag m initial deposit *(of plant protectants)*
Anfangsertrag m initial yield
Anfangsfeuchte f, **Anfangsfeuchtigkeitsgehalt** m initial moisture content
Anfangshenne f point-of-lay pullet
Anfangsstadium n initial stage • **im ~ unterdrücken** *(vet)* to abort *(a disease)*
Anfangssymptom n initial symptom
Anfangsverband m initial spacing *(silviculture)*
Anfangsverunkrautung f initial weed infestation
Anfangswachstum n initial (early) growth
anfärben to stain
Anfärbung f staining
~/**unterschiedliche** differential staining *(microbiology)*
anfeuchten to moisten, to humidify, to wet, to damp
Anfeuchten n, **Anfeuchtung** f moistening, humidification
anfliegen to approach *(wildfowl)*
Anflug m 1. approach; 2. *(forest)* self-sown crop, natural seeding, [natural] regeneration • **durch ~ entstanden** self-grown *(timber stand)*
anfressen to begnaw; to chop
Angärung f starting fermentation
angebaut 1. grown, cultivated; 2. mounted, attached
~/**hinten** rear-mounted
~/**im eigenen Betrieb** home-grown
~/**im Freiland** field-grown
~/**in Nährlösung** solution-grown

angeboren innate, inbred, congenital, connatal, native
angedrückt *s.* angepreßt
angefault drux[e]y, punky, dosey, doty *(wood)*
angeflogen self-sown *(tree seeds)*
angegliedert adjunct
Angel *f* 1. fishing rod, angle; 2. buckle *(of frame saw)*
Angelfischerei *f* angling, line-fishing
Angelika *f (bot)* angelica *(genus Angelica)*
angeln to angle, to fish; to hook
Angeln *n* angling
Angelschnur *f* [fishing] line
angenähert approximate
angeordnet/bandartig banded
~/geradzeilig *(bot)* orthostichous
~/hintereinander tandem
~/kreisförmig (ringförmig) *(bot, zoo)* gyrate
angepaßt adapted
~/an mittlere Feuchtigkeitsbedingungen mesophytic, mesic
~/an reichliche Wasserversorgung hygromorphic
angepreßt *(bot, zoo)* appressed, adpressed
Angertrespe *f* hairy brome, Bromus commutatus
angesät/durch Samenausfall self-sown
angeschwemmt *(soil)* alluvial
angeschwollen turgid
angestammt ancestral
angestockt *s.* angefault
angetrieben driven, powered
~/hydraulisch hydraulic
angewachsen *(bot, zoo)* adnate
Angewende *n* headland, turn land
Angialgie *f s.* Angiopathie
angießen to water in
Angießen *n* watering in
Angiitis *f (vet)* angiitis
Angina *f (vet)* angina
Angiographie *f* angiography
angiokarp *(bot)* angiocarpic, angiocarpous
Angiokarp *n* cleistothecium *(of ascomycetes)*
Angiom *n (vet)* angioma
Angioparalyse *f (vet)* angioparalysis
Angiopathie *f* angiopathy, vascular disease; blood-vessel disorder
Angiosperme *f (bot)* angiosperm *(division Angiospermae)*
Angiotensin *n* angiotensin *(hormone)*
Angiotensinase *f* angiotensinase, angiotonase *(enzyme)*
Angiotensinogenase *f* renin *(enzyme)*
Angiotonase *f s.* Angiotensinase
Angleichung *f* accommodation
~ der Landwirtschaft agricultural adjustment *(agricultural economics)*
Angler Rind (Rotvieh) *n* [Red] Angeln *(cattle breed)*
~ Sattelschwein *n* Angeln [Saddleback] *(pig breed)*

Anglo-Araber *m* Anglo-Arab *(horse breed)*
Anglo-Nubier-Ziege *f* Anglo-Nubian goat *(breed)*
Angolaerbse *f* bamba[r]ra [ground]nut, Congo goober, earth pea, underground bean, Voandzeia (Vigna) subterranea
Angorakaninchen *n* angora rabbit *(breed)*
Angorakatze *f* angora cat
Angorawolle *f* angora [wool]; mohair
Angoraziege *f* angora goat
Angoraziegenwolle *f* mohair
Angosturabaum *m* angostura, Galipea officinalis
Angosturarinde *f* angostura bark
angreifen to attack *(animal behaviour)*
angrenzend adjunct *(e.g. a stand)*
~/seitlich collateral
Angriff *m* attack
~/bakterieller bacterial attack
Angriffshieb *m* preparatory (first) felling
Anguriagurke *f* [West Indian] gherkin, gooseberry gourd, Cucumis anguria
Angusrind *n* Angus *(cattle breed)*
anhaften to adhere, to cling
anhaftend adherent
anhalftern to halter [up]
anhalsen to leash *(a dog)*
Anhängebalken *m* implement beam
Anhängebeetpflug *m s.* Anhängepflug
Anhängedrillmaschine *f* tractor[-drawn seed] drill
Anhängegerät *n* drawn (trailed) implement, trailed equipment
Anhängegrubber *m* trailed cultivator
Anhängehäcksler *m* trailed chopper
Anhängemähdrescher *m* trailed (pull-type) combine
Anhängemäher *m*, **Anhängemähmaschine** *f* trailer mower
Anhängeöse *f* hitch-ring
Anhängepflug *m* pull-type plough, trailer (drawn) plough
Anhänger *m* trailer
~/landwirtschaftlicher agricultural (farm) trailer
~ mit festem Aufbau non-tipping trailer
~ mit Seitenentleerung side discharge trailer
~/zapfwellengetriebener p.t.o.-driven trailer
~/zweiachsiger full trailer
Anhängeraufbau *m* trailer body
Anhängerbremse *f* trailer brake
Anhängerreifen *m* trailer tyre
Anhängertriebachse *f* power-driven trailer axle
Anhängescharpflug *m* trailed share plough
Anhängescheibenegge *f* trailed disk harrow
Anhängescheibenpflug *m* trailed disk plough
Anhängeschiene *f* drawbar, hitch bar, drag rail
Anhängevorrichtung *f* coupling
Anhängewagen *m* trailer
Anhängezugmaul *n* clevis, yoke
anhäufeln to hill [up], to ridge [up], to earth [up], to mound [up], to base up

Anhäufelungsmaterial *n*, **Anhäufelungsmittel** *n* hilling medium
anhäufen 1. to heap [up], to accumulate; 2. to agglomerate
Anhäufung *f* 1. accumulation, cumulation; 2. agglomeration; 3. agglomerate
anheften to peg down *(layering)*
Anhidrose *f (vet)* anhydrosis, dry coat syndrome
Anhieb *m s.* Angriffshieb
anholozyklisch *(ent)* anholocyclic
Anhydrit *m* anhydrite *(non-clay mineral)*
Anhydrose *f*, **Anidrose** *f s.* Anhidrose
Anilazin *n* anilazine *(fungicide)*
Anilofos *n* anilofos *(herbicide)*
animal[isch] animal
Anionenaustausch *m (soil)* anion exchange
Anionenaustauscher *m* anion exchanger
Anionenaustauschkapazität *f* anion-exchange capacity
Anionensorption *f (soil)* anion exchange
Anis *m* 1. anise, sweet Alice, Pimpinella anisum; 2. aniseed
anisodont *(bot, zoo)* heterodont
anisogam heterogamous
Anisogamet *m* heterogamete
Anisogamie *f* heterogamy
Anisöl *n* aniseed oil
Anisophyllie *f* anisophylly
anisoploid *(gen)* anisoploid
Anisoploide *m* anisoploid
Anisoploidie *f* anisoploidy
anisotrop anisotropic
Anisotropie *f* anisotropy
Anissaat *f*, **Anissamen** *m* aniseed
Anisuron *n* anisuron *(herbicide)*
ankeimen to chit *(e.g. potatoes)*
Ankerwurzel *f* anchor[ing] root
ankirren to bait *(game)*
anklebend adhesive
ankochen to parboil
anködern to bait, to lure *(e.g. predators)*
Ankommen *n* creaming *(brewing)*
ankoppeln to leash *(a dog)*
ankuppeln to couple, to hitch *(e.g. field implements)*
Ankylose *f (vet)* ankylosis
Ankylostomatidose *f (vet)* hookworm disease
Anlage *f* 1. primordium, anlage *(of an plant organ)*; 2. landside *(at body of a mould-board plough)*; 3. amenity area (site); park, green area; 4. rig; plant; operation; 5. *s.* Anlegen
~/**faktorielle** factorial design *(experimentation)*
~/**heckenartige** hedgerow planting
~/**öffentliche** public garden, public green
~/**rollende** roller (rolling) landside *(of a mould-board plough)*
~/**systematische** systematic design *(experimentation)*
Anlagenase *f* frog nose *(of a mould-board plough)*
Anlagenbau *m*/**landtechnischer** agricultural plant construction
Anlagenträger *m (gen)* conductor
Anlageplan *m* field plan *(experimentation)*
Anlagerung *f (vet)* juxtaposition
Anlandung *f (soil)* 1. aggradation; 2. alluvium, alluvion, alluvial deposit
anlassen to ignite *(a combustion engine)*
Anlassen *n* ignition
Anlasser *m* starter
Anlaßmotor *m* starter motor
Anlauffruchtfolge *f* initial crop rotation
anlegen to establish *(e.g. a crop stand)*; to plant *(e.g. a garden)*
~/**das Halsband** to leash *(a dog)*
~/**den Geschühriemen** to jess *(falconry)*
~/**den Halfter** to halter [up]
~/**den Schrot** to notch *(tree felling)*
~/**die Kandare** to curb
~/**die Nasenbremse (Oberlippenbremse)** to twitch
~/**die Trense** to snaffle
~/**ein Vorfeuer** to backfire
~/**eine Fistel** to fistulate
~/**eine Hecke** to hedge
~/**eine Nachkultur** to subculture
~/**eine Obstanlage** to establish an orchard
~/**einen Maulkorb** to muzzle
~/**Rasen** to bottom
~/**Scheuklappen** to blinker
Anlegen *n* establishment *(e.g. of a crop stand)*
~ **einer Dickdarmfistel** *(vet)* colostomy
~ **einer Magenfistel** *(vet)* gastrostomy
~ **von Gegenfeuer** counter-firing *(forest fire control)*
~ **von Grünanlagen** planting of greenery
~ **von Waldschutzstreifen** shelter-belt establishment
anleinen to leash
anleiten to train *(a woody plant)*
anlenken to link
Anlenkpunkt *m* link point *(three-point hitch)*
Anlenkung *f* linkage
Anlieferungsmilch *f* raw milk
anliegend *(bot, zoo)* accumbent
~/**eng** appressed, adpressed
anlocken to attract; to lure; to decoy *(wildfowl)*
anlockend attractant
Anlocker *m (hunt)* lurer
Anlockstoff *m* attractant
Anlockungseigenschaft *f*, **Anlockwirkung** *f* attractancy, attractant action
anludern to bait *(predators)*
Anmoor *n* half-bog
Anmoorboden *m* half-bog soil
Anmoorgley *m* humic gley [soil], humic groundwater gley
AnMV *s.* Anemonenmosaikvirus

Annäherung

Annäherung *f* approach; approximation; convergence, convergency • **durch ~ pfropfen** to ablactate *(grafting)*
Annahmedosierer *m* [bulk] reception hopper, dump box, metering bin
Annahmeförderer *m* receiving conveyor
Annahmeplattform *f* receiving platform
Annahmetisch *m* reception table
Annatto *m(n)* annatto, arnotto, roucou *(dye)*
Annattostrauch *m* annatto[-tree], Bixa orellana
annehmen to accept; to take *(scion in grafting)*
~/den Bullen to bull
Annehmer *m* acceptor
Annelide *f* annelid[an] *(phylum Annelida)*
Annidation *f (ecol)* annidation
annuell annual
Annuelle *f* annual, therophyte
anomal anomalous, abnormal
Anomalie *f* anomaly, abnormality
Anophthalmie *f (vet)* anophthalmia
Anorchidie *f*, **Anorchie** *f* anorchism
Anordnung *f* **der Blütenkronblätter (Perianthblätter, Petalen)** aestivation
~/räumliche spatial arrangement
~/schraubenförmige helix
~/zufallsweise *(biom)* randomization
Anordnungstest *m (biom)* rank order test
Anorexie *f* anorexia, inappetence
anorganisch inorganic, mineral
Anormogenese *f* anormogenesis
Anorthit *m* anorthite
anorthoploid *(gen)* anorthoploid
Anorthoploide *m* anorthoploid
Anorthoploidie *f* anorthoploidy
Anosmie *f (vet)* anosmia
Anöstrie *f* anoestrus
anöstrisch anoestrous
anovulatorisch anovulatory
Anoxie *f* anoxia
Anoxybiose *f* anoxibiosis, anaerobiosis
anpaaren to mate [to], to pair up, to breed, to put to
Anpaarungspartner *m* mate
Anpaarungsperiode *f* breeding season
anpassen to adapt, to accommodate, to fit
Anpassung *f* adaptation, accommodation; adjustment
~/landwirtschaftliche agricultural adjustment *(agricultural economics)*
~/osmotische osmotic adjustment
anpassungsfähig adaptable, adaptive
Anpassungsfähigkeit *f* adaptability, adaptivity, adaptation power
Anpassungsschwierigkeit *f* adaptation difficulty
Anpassungsvermögen *n s.* Anpassungsfähigkeit
Anpassungswert *m* fitness *(animal breeding)*
anpfählen to stake
anpflanzen to plant; to cultivate
Anpflanzen *n* planting • **zum ~ geeignet** plantable

Anpflanzung *f* planting
Anpflegevolk *n (api)* starter colony
anpflocken to picket
Anpflügen *n* ridging *(of a field)*
anpirschen *(hunt)* to approach
Anplatten *n* veneer grafting
~ von Edelaugen chip budding
anplattieren, anplätzen *(forest)* to blaze, to spot
Anregung *f* stimulation
Anregungsmittel *n* stimulant; *(vet)* analeptic
anreichern to enrich; to fortify
~/mit Vitaminen to vitaminize
Anreicherung *f* enrichment; fortification *(e.g. of feed-stuffs by adding nutrients or vitamins)*
Anreicherungsbecken *n* recharge basin
Anreicherungshieb *m* improvement felling
Anreicherungshorizont *m (soil)* enrichment (illuvial) horizon, B-horizon
Anreicherungskalkung *f* heavy liming
Anreicherungsnährboden *m* enrichment medium *(microbiology)*
anreißen *(forest)* to scarify; to blaze, to spot
Anreißschaden *m (forest)* gouge injury
anritzen to scarify
anrücken *(forest)* to skid, to haul, *(Am)* to log, to yard
Anrücken *n* skidding, haulage, *(Am)* logging, yarding
Anrüsten *n* **des Euters** udder stimulation (massage)
Ansaat *f* initial seeding
~ unter Deckfrucht undersowing
Ansaatjahr *n* seeding year
Ansaatmischung *f* seed[s] mixture
ansäen to seed, to sow, to plant; to undersow, to underseed
~/neu to reseed, to resow
ansammeln to accumulate, to amass
Ansammlung *f* accumulation; aggregation *(e.g. of organisms)*; head *(of livestock or game)*
Ansamung *f (forest)* natural seeding
ansässig *(zoo)* sedentary
Ansatz *m* gain *(of body mass)*
Ansatzstelle *f* insertion place *(of an offshoot)*
~ des Fruchtstieles *(bot)* hilum
Ansatzvermögen *n* gainability, gaining ability, ability to gain *(of fatteners)*
ansauer acidulous, acidulent
ansäuern to acidulate, to acidify
Ansäuerung *f* acidulation, acidification
Ansäuerungsmittel *n* acidulant, acidulent
ansaugen to aspirate
Ansaugen *n* aspiration
Ansauggeräuschdämpfer *m* intake silencer
Ansaugkorb *m* suction strainer
Ansaugluft *f* ingoing air *(combustion engine)*
Ansaugstutzen *m* intake stack
anschalmen *(forest)* to blaze, to spot, to mark; to scarify

anschießen *(hunt)* to wound [by a shot]
anschirren to harness, to gear [up], to yoke, to put to, to team, *(Am)* to hitch up; to horse
Anschlag *m* plough-shoe, sidecap, wearing plate, gunnel [of share]
anschlagen 1. to choke *(tree-trunks)*; 2. to mark, to blaze
Anschlagen *n* challenge *(of hunting dogs)*
Anschläger *m* chokerman, tong hooker, tonger, pigman *(logging)*
Anschlußpunkt *m* tie point *(terrestrial photogrammetry)*
anschneiden to cut up; to chop *(hunting dogs e.g. venison)*
anschoppen *(vet)* to congest
Anschoppung *f* congestion
anschwänzen to sparge *(brewing)*
Anschwänzvorrichtung *f* sparger
Anschwänzwasser *n* sparge liquor (water)
anschweißen *s.* anschießen
Anschweiß[schar]spitze *f* welded share point
anschwellen to swell
anschwellend turgescent
Anschwellung *f* 1. swelling, turgescence, turgidity; 2. intumescence, bulb
Anschwemm[druck]filter *n* precoat filter
Anschwemmung *f (soil)* 1. alluviation; 2. alluvium, alluvion, alluvial deposit; warp
Anschwemmungsprodukt *n s.* Anschwemmung 2.
Ansehnliche Nachtkerze *f* white evening primrose, Oenothera speciosa
Ansehnliches Mannagras *n* brook grass, reed sweet grass, Glyceria maxima (aquatica)
ansengen to singe, to scorch
anserin anserine
Anserin *n* anserine *(muscle protein)*
ansetzen 1. to put on, to lay down *(e.g. fat)*; 2. to set *(e.g. a brood-hen)*
~/Ähren to ear [up]
~/Blätter to [come into] leaf, to put forth leaves
~/einen Hund *(hunt)* to hound
~/einen Kopf to head *(cabbage, lettuce)*
~/Frucht (Früchte) to set [fruit]
~/Hülsen to pod
~/Knospen to form buds
~/Kolben to ear [up]
~/Körner to kernel
~/Masse to put on weight
~/Samen to set seed
~/vorzeitig Blütentriebe to bolt, to run to seed *(beet)*
ansiedeln to settle
~/sich to settle
Ansiedeln *n* settling, settlement
Ansiedlung *f* 1. settlement; 2. *(zoo)* epoecism, epoecy
Ansiedlungsstimmung *f* settlement mood *(of aphids)*

Ansitz *m (hunt)* hide, hiding-place, [hidden] station, stand, butt, *(Am)* blind
Ansitzjagd *f* runway watching
Ansitzschirm *m s.* Ansitz
anspannen *s.* anschirren
anspitzen to snipe *(a tree-trunk)*
ansprechen to describe *(a soil)*
~/auf Düngung to respond to manuring
anspruchslos hardy, unexacting, undemanding
Anspruchslosigkeit *f* hardiness *(of plants and animals)*
anspruchsvoll fastidious, exacting
Anstand *m s.* Ansitz
Anstau *m* bank
anstauen to dam up; *(vet)* to congest
~/Flutpegel zwecks Sedimentgewinnung to warp
Anstauen *n* damming [up]
Anstauhydrokultur *f*, **Anstauhydroponik** *f* floating hydroponics
Anstauverfahren *n* flooded bench system
anstechen 1. to puncture; 2. to tap, to broach *(e.g. a cask)*
anstecken 1. to infect; 2. *s.* anstechen 2.
ansteckend infectious, contagious, virulent
~/nicht non-infectious
Ansteckraupe *f* half-track device (unit)
Ansteckung *f* infection • **gegen eine ~ gerichtet** antiinfective *(s.a. under Infektion)*
~ durch Samen seed-transmission
~/vorgeburtliche prenatal infection
ansteckungsfähig contagious
Ansteckungsfähigkeit *f*, **Ansteckungskraft** *f* contagiousness
Ansteckungsstoff *m* contagium
Anstellbottich *m s.* Anstellgefäß
anstellen to pitch *(brewing)*
Anstellen *n* pitching
Anstellgefäß *n* pitching (starting) vessel
Anstellhefe *f* pitching yeast
Anstellwürze *f* pitching (original) wort
Anstieg *m* **der Atmungsintensität** climacteric rise *(of fruit woods during fruit ripening)*
anstreichen to approach *(wildfowl)*
Antacidum *n (vet)* antacid
Antagonismus *m* antagonism
~/mutueller *(phyt, vet)* premunition, cross protection
Antagonist *m* antagonist
antagonistisch antagonistic
Anteil *m* share, portion
~ [morphologisch] anomaler Spermien abnormal/normal sperm ratio
Antemetikum *n s.* Antiemetikum
Antenne *f (ent)* antenna, feeler
Anthelminthikum *n* anthelmint[h]ic, helminthicide, worm remedy, wormer, vermifuge
anthelminthisch anthelmint[h]ic
Anthem *n (vet)* exanthema
Anthere *f (bot)* anther

Antherenbrand

Antherenbrand *m* anther smut *(of Caryophyllaceae, caused by Ustilago violaceae)*
Antherenbrandpilz *m* anther smut, Ustilago violaceae
Antherenkultur *f* anther (pollen) culture *(plant breeding)*
antherenlos anantherous
Antheridium *n (bot)* antherid[ium]
Anthese *f (bot)* anthesis, flowering [season], blossom, bloom
Anthochlor *n* anthochlor *(pigment)*
Anthocyan *n* anthocyanin[e], anthocyan *(vegetable dye)*
Anthocyanaglykon *n* anthocyanidin *(pigment)*
Anthocyanidin *n* anthocyanidin *(pigment)*
Anthocyanin *n s.* Anthocyan
Antholyse *f (phyt)* antholysis
Anthoxanthin *n* anthoxanthin *(vegetable dye)*
Anthracenöl *n* anthracene oil *(wood preservative)*
Anthrachinonaufschluß *m* anthraquinone pulping *(of wood)*
~/alkalischer soda-anthraquinone pulping
Anthraknose *f (phyt)* anthracnose
~ **der Erbse** ascochyta pod spot of pea, leaf and pod spot of pea, pea anthracnose, pea black stem *(caused esp. by Ascochyta pisi)*
~ **der Gurke** anthracnose of cucumber *(caused by Colletotrichum lagenarium)*
~ **der Himbeere** anthracnose of raspberry *(caused by Elsinoe veneta)*
~ **der Kichererbse** blight of chick-pea *(caused by Mycosphaerella rabiei and Phyllosticta rabiei)*
~ **der Rose** rose anthracnose, leaf scorch (spot) of rose *(caused by Sphaerulina rehmiana)*
~ **der Speisebohne** anthracnose of bean *(caused by Colletotrichum lindemuthianum)*
~ **des Kaffees** die back of coffee, coffee berry disease *(caused by Glomerella cingulata, conidial stage Colletotrichum coffeanum)*
Anthrakose *f (vet)* anthracosis
Anthranilatsynth[et]ase *f* anthranilate synthase *(enzyme)*
3-Anthraniloyl-alanin *n* kynurenine *(metabolite)*
Anthranilsäure *f* anthranilic acid
Anthrax *m (vet)* anthrax
Anthropochore *f (bot, ecol)* anthropochore
Anthropochorie *f* anthropochory
Anthropophyt *m* adventive, adventitious plant
Anthropozoonose *f* anthropozoonosis, zoonosis
Anthurie *f* 1. tail-flower, anthurium *(genus Anthurium)*; 2. flamingo flower (plant), Anthurium-Scherzeranum hybrid; 3. painter's palette, Anthurium-Andreanum hybrid
Anthurium-Mosaikvirus *n* anthurium mosaic virus
Antiandrogen *n* antiandrogen
Anti-Antikörper *m* anti-antibody
Antiauxin *n* antiauxin *(growth regulator)*
Antibackmittel *n* anticaking agent *(e.g. in feedstuffs and fertilizers)*
antibakteriell [wirkend] antibacterial
Antibiose *f* antibiosis
Antibiotikaresistenz *f* antibiotic resistance
Antibiotikaresistenzgen *n* antibiotic resistence gene
Antibiotikum *n* antibiotic [agent]
~/antimykotisches antifungal [agent, drug], antimycotic
antibiotisch [wirkend] antibiotic
anticandidal anticandidal
Anticoccidium *n* anticoccidial [agent]
Anticodon *n (gen)* anticodon
Antidiabetikum *n* antidiabetic [agent], hypoglycaemic agent
Antidiarrhoikum *n* antidiarrhoea agent
Antidot[on] *n* antidote
Antiemetikum *n* antiemetic [agent]
Antiepileptikum *n* anticonvulsant
Antienzym *n* antienzyme
Antifraßstoff *m* antifeedant, antifeeding compound *(for repelling insects)*
antifungal [wirkend] antifungal
antigen [wirkend] antigenic
Antigen *n* antigen
~/somatisches somatic antigen, O-antigen *(of bacteria)*
~/tumorspezifisches tumour antigen
Antigen-Antikörper-Reaktion *f* antigen-antibody-reaction *(immunology)*
Antigen-Antikörper-Wechselwirkung *f* antigen-antibody-interaction
Antigenität *f* antigenicity
Antigenkonkurrenz *f* antigenic competition
Antigenreaktion *f* antigenic reaction
Antigenwirkung *f* antigenicity
Antigibberellin *n* antigibberellin *(growth regulator)*
Antiglobulinserum *n* antiglobulin serum
Antiglobulintest *m* antiglobulin (Coombs) test *(for antibody detection)*
Antigräsermittel *n* grass herbicide (killer), gramicide
Antihistaminikum *n (vet)* antihistaminic [agent]
Antihormon *n* antihormone, hormone antagonist
Antihypertensivum *n*, **Antihypertonikum** *n (vet)* antihypertensive agent
Antiimmun[globulinanti]körper *m* anti-antibody
antiinfektiös antiinfective
antiketogen antiketogenic
antiklin *(bot)* anticlinal
Antikoagulans *n* anticoagulant
Antikokzidium *n* anticoccidial [agent]
Antikondensationsfolie *f* aus Polyethylen antifog PE film, anti-condensate polythene
Antikonvulsivum *n* anticonvulsant
Antikörper *m* antibody, immune body
~/anaphylaktischer anaphylactic antibody
~/bivalenter bivalent antibody
~/blockierender blocking (incomplete) antibody
~/fluoreszierender fluorescent antibody

~ gegen körpereigene Antigene autoantibody
~/heterogenetischer heterogenetic antibody
~/humoraler humoral antibody
~/markierter tagged antibody
~/maternaler maternal antibody
~/natürlicher natural antibody
~/neutralisierender neutralizing antibody
~/protektiver (schützender) protective antibody
~/unvollständiger incomplete (blocking) antibody
~/zellauflösender cytolysin
~/zirkulierender circulating antibody
~/zytophiler cytophilous antibody
Antikörperbildner *m* antigen
Antikörperbildung *f* antibody formation
Antikörpersynthese *f* antibody synthesis
Antikörpertechnik *f* antibody technique
~/direkte (fluoreszierende) fluorescent antibody technique
Antikörpertiter *m* antibody titre
Antillenakazie *f*, Antillenkassie *f* huisache, fragrant (sweet) acacia, Acacia farnesiana
Antillenkieselholz *n* (Am, bot) catclaw blackbead, Pithecellobium unguis-cati
Antilopengras *n* antelope grass, Echinochloa pyramidalis
Antimetabolit *m* antimetabolite
antimikrobiell antimicrobial, microbicidal, germicidal
antimorph antimorphic *(allele)*
Antimutagen *n* antimutagen
Antimycin *n* [A] antimycin A *(insecticide, antibiotic)*
Antimykotikum *n* antifungal [agent, drug], antimycotic
antimykotisch antifungal, antimycotic
Antiöstrogen *n* antioestrogen
Antioxidans *n* antioxidant
Antiparasitikum *n* antiparasitic [agent], parasiticide
Antipellagravitamin *n* pellagra-preventive factor
Antiperistaltik *f* antiperistalsis
Antiphlogistikum *n* antiphlogistic [agent], antiinflammatory agent
antiphlogistisch antiplogistic
Antipsychotikum *n* neuroleptic
Antipyretikum *n* antipyretic [agent]
Antischaummittel *n* antifoaming agent *(e.g. as feed additive)*
Antischlupfeinrichtung *f* antislip device
Antischlupfrad *n* anti-skid wheel
Antisepsis *f*, Antiseptik *f (vet)* antisepsis
Antiseptikum *n* antiseptic [agent], sanitize
antiseptisch antiseptic
Antiserum *n (vet)* antiserum
Antisomatogen *n* antigen
Antisporulans *n* antisporulant
Antistreß-Futtergemisch *n* antistress mixture
Antithiamin *n* antithiamin, thiamine antagonist

Antitoxin *n* antitoxin
antitoxisch antitoxic
Antitranspirans *n*, Antitranspirationsmittel *n* antitranspirant
Antitrypsinfaktor *m* antitrypsin [substance]
Antitussivum *n (vet)* antitussive agent
Antivenenum *n* antivenene, antivenin
antiviral antiviral
Antivitamin *n* antivitamin
Antiwuchsstoff *m* inhibitor
Antizyklon *m* anticyclone
AntMV *s.* Anthurium-Mosaikvirus
Antoniusschwein *n* Anthony pig *(smallest piglet of a farrow)*
antraben to trot on
antreiben to drive
Antrieb *m* 1. drive; 2. stimulus, drive; 3. instinct
~/hydrostatischer hydrostatic drive
~ mit [ein]stellbarer Drehzahl adjustable speed drive
Antriebsrad *n* driving wheel
Antriebsschwinge *f* driving reciprocating link
Antriebssystem *n* power system
Antriebswelle *f* drive shaft
Antwortsender *m* transponder
Anurie *f (vet)* anuria
Anus *m* anus, vent • um den ~ [herum] perianal
anvisieren to sight [at]
anwachsen 1. to strike (take) roots; to take *(a graft)*; 2. to accrete; to increase
Anwachsen *n* von Augen bud take *(in grafting)*
Anwärter *m (forest)* chosen tree, candidate
anwelken to [pre]wilt
~ lassen to [pre]wilt
Anwelksilage *f* [pre]wilted silage, low-moisture silage
Anwendung *f* vor dem Auspflanzen preplant application *(e.g. of protectants)*
~ vor dem Aussäen preplant application
Anwendungsdatum *n* application date
Anwendungsmethode *f* application method
Anwuchs *m (forest)* young (early) growth; regeneration, survival
~ durch Anflug young natural reproduction
Anwuchserfolg *m* initial survival *(of planting stock)*
Anwuchsprozent *n* tree (plant, survival) percent
~/durchschnittliches average survival [percent]
anwurzeln to take (strike) roots
Anwurzeln *n* rooting, rootage
anzapfen to tap, to broach, to box, to bleed *(e.g. a tree for resin collection)*; to tap, to broach *(casks or barrels)*
anzeichnen to mark [out], to score, to spot; to scarify, to blaze *(a tree)*
Anzeichnen *n* marking [out]
~ eines Hiebsortes *(forest)* marking out of a coupe
~ von Laßbäumen marking of trees as standards
Anzeichner *m* marker

anzeigen 44

anzeigen 1. to indicate; 2. to feather *(hunting dog's behaviour)*
Anzeigevorrichtung f indicating device, indicator
~/optische display
anziehen to rear, to raise, to nurse, to train *(plants)*
~/den Sattelgurt to girth
~/im Warmhaus to hothouse, to stove
Anziehmuskel m adductor [muscle]
Anzucht f rearing, raising, propagation
~ in Saatkisten box-raising
Anzuchtbeet n nursery (seeding) bed, plant (stool) bed
Anzuchtfrühbeet n propagating frame, propagator
Anzucht[gewächs]haus n plant nursery, propagating [glass]house, propagator
Anzuchtkäfig m breeding cage
Anzuchtkasten m forcing (force) bed, hotbed
Anzuchtmethode f method of propagation
Anzuchtphase f *(forest)* establishment phase
Anzuchtplatte f cultivating tray, [seed] flat
Anzuchtraum m growth chamber (room)
Anzuchtschale f plant tray
~ für kleine Pflanztöpfe plug tray
Anzuchtsystem n **für Jungpflanzen** plant raising system
~/standardisiertes module plant raising system
Anzuchttisch m plant growing bench
Anzuchttopf m cultivating pot
~ aus Pappe cardboard pot
anzünden to ignite; to set on fire
Anzünden n ignition
Ao-Horizont m *(soil)* Ao-horizon, O-horizon, organic surface layer
äolisch aeolian, wind-borne
Aoo-Horizont m *(soil)* Aoo-horizon, L-layer, surface litter
Aorta f aorta
aortal aortic
Aortenbogen m aortic arch
Aortenentzündung f aortitis
Aortenruptur f aorta rupture
~ der Pute dissecting aneurysm of turkey
Aortitis f aortitis
AP s. Afrikanische Pferdepest
Apathie f *(vet)* apathy
Apatit apatite *(non-clay mineral)*
Apatitgestein n phosphate rock
ApCBFV s. Chlorotisches Blattfleckungsvirus des Apfels
Apenninensonnenröschen n white rock-rose, Helianthemum apenninum
Aperistaltik f *(vet)* aperistalsis
apetal *(bot)* apetalous
Apex m apex; shoot tip
APF s. Cobalamin
Apfel m 1. apple *(genus Malus)*; 2. apple *(fruit)*
~ für den Frischverzehr dessert apple
~/grünschaliger greening

~/kantiger angular (quoining) apple, queening [apple]
Apfelanlage f apple orchard
apfelartig pomaceous
Apfelbaum m apple[-tree] *(genus Malus)*
Apfelbaumgespinstmotte f apple [ermine] moth, small apple ermine [moth], Yponomeuta (Hyponomeuta) malinella
Apfelbaumglasflügler m apple clear-wing[ed] moth, apple sesia, Synanthedon (Aegeria) myopaeformis
Apfelbeere f 1. chokeberry *(genus Aronia)*; 2. black chokeberry, Aronia melanocarpa
Apfelblattgallmücke f apple leaf curling midge, Dasyneura mali
Apfelblattminiermotte f apple leaf-miner, apple leaf mining moth, Stigmella (Nepticula) malella
Apfelblattmotte f *(ent)* apple and thorn sceletonizer, Anthophila (Simaethis) pariana
Apfelblattsauger m *(ent)* apple [leaf-]sucker, apple psylla, Psylla mali
Apfelblattzikade f *(ent)* apple leaf-hopper, Empoasca maligna
Apfelblüte f apple bloom (blossom)
Apfelblütenstecher m apple blossom weevil, Anthonomus pomorum
Apfelblutlaus f s. Blutlaus
Apfelbrand m apple blight *(caused by Erwinia amylovora)*
Apfelfaltenmotte f *(ent)* spotted tentiform leaf-miner, Lithocolletis (Phyllonorycter) blancardella
apfelförmig apple-shaped, pomiform, maliform
Apfelfrucht f pome (pomaceous, pip) fruit
Apfelfruchtfliege f apple maggot, Rhagoletis pomonella
Apfelgespinstmotte f s. Apfelbaumgespinstmotte
Apfelgraslaus f apple grain aphid, Rhopalosiphum insertum
Äpfelkrankheit f *(vet)* rumen acidosis, acid indigestion
Apfelmehltau m apple [powdery] mildew *(caused by Podosphaera leucotricha)*
Apfelminze f apple (round-leaved) mint, Mentha x rotundifolia
Apfelmosaik n apple mosaic *(virosis)*
Apfelmosaikvirus n apple mosaic virus
Apfelmost m s. Apfelsaft
Apfelmostbereitung f *(Am)* cider-making
Apfelmotte f apple fruit moth, Argyresthia conjugella
Apfelmus n apple sauce
Apfelpflücker m apple picker
Apfelplantage f apple orchard
Apfelpreßkuchen m apple press cake
Apfelproliferation f apple proliferation *(mycoplasmosis)*
Apfelquitte f apple-shaped quince
Apfelrose f apple rose, Rosa villosa (pomifera)

Apfelrostmilbe *f* apple rust mite, Aculus schlechtendali
Apfelsaft *m* apple juice (must), *(Am)* cider
Apfelsägewespe *f* [European] apple saw-fly, Hoplocampa testudinea
Apfelsauger *m s.* Apfelblattsauger
Äpfelsäure *f* malic acid
Apfelschalenwickler *m* [summer] fruit tortrix [moth], Adoxophyes reticulana (orana)
Apfelschimmel *m* dapple-grey [horse]
Apfelschorf *m* apple scab *(caused by Venturia inaequalis)*
Apfelsine *f* 1. [China, sweet] orange, Citrus sinensis; 2. orange *(fruit)*
Apfelsinenschale *f* orange peel
Apfelsinenschalenöl *n* orange oil
Apfelsirupkonzentrat *n* concentrated apple syrup
Apfelstammfurchungsvirus *n* apple stem grooving virus, ASGV
Apfelstammnarbungsvirus *n* apple stem pitting virus
apfeltragend pomiferous
Apfeltreber *pl* apple pomace
Apfelung *f*, **Äpfelung** *f* dappling *(of horses)*
Apfelwein *m* cider, *(Am)* hard cider
Apfelweinbereitung *f* cider-making
Apfelweinkellerei *f* cider mill
Apfelwickler *m* codlin[g] moth, Cydia (Laspeyresia) pomonella
Apfelwicklerraupe *f* apple (fruit) worm, codlin[g] (palmer) worm
ApFRBV *s.* Virus der Fruchtringberostung des Apfels
Aphanomyces-Krankheit *f (vet)* crayfish plague *(caused by Aphanomyces astaci)*
Aphelandra *f*, **Aphelandre** *f (bot)* 1. aphelandra *(genus Aphelandra)*; 2. zebra plant, Aphelandra squarrosa
aphidenübertragbar aphid-transmissible
aphidivor, **aphidophag** aphidivorous, aphidophagous
Aphidophage *m*, **Avidovore** *m* aphidophage, aphidivorous insect
aphizid aphicidal
Aphizid *n* aphicide, aphidocide
Apholat *n* apholate *(chemosterilant)*
Aphosphorose *f* aphosphorosis, phosphorus deficiency
Aphoxid *n* aphoxide *(chemosterilant)*
Aphrodisiakum *n* aphrodisiac
Aphrodisie *f* aphrodisia
aphrodisisch aphrodisiac
Aphthe *f (vet)* aphtha
Aphthenseuche *f* foot-and-mouth [disease], FMD
aphthös aphthous
Aphyllie *(bot)* aphylly
aphyllisch aphyllous
Apigenin *n* apigenin *(flavon)*
apikal apical

Apikaldominanz *f* apical dominance
Apikalmeristem *n* apical meristem
Apikalnekrose *f (phyt)* apical necrosis
Apikaltrieb *m* apical shoot, terminal [shoot]
Aplasie *f (vet)* aplasia
ApMV *s.* Apfelmosaikvirus
Apneumatose *f (vet)* atelectasis
Apoatropin *n* belladonnine
Apnoe *f (vet)* apnoea
apod *(zoo)* apodal, apodous, legless
Apoenzym *n* apoenzyme
Apoferritin *n* apoferritin
apogam *(bot)* apogamous
Apogam[et]ie *f* apogamy
apokarp *(bot)* apocarpous
Apokarpie *f* apocarpy
Apokrensäure *f* apocrenic acid *(a fulvic acid)*
Apomeiose *f (bot)* apomeiosis
apomiktisch *(bot)* apomictic[al]
Apomixis *f* apomixis
Apomorphin *n* apomorphine *(alkaloid)*
Aponeurose *f* aponeurosis *(animal anatomy)*
Apophyse *f (bot, zoo)* apophysis
Apophyt *m* apophyte
Apoplast *m (bot)* apoplast, apoplasm
apoplastisch apoplastic
Apoplexie *f* apoplexy
~ **der Aprikose** apricot apoplexy *(virosis)*
Aporocactus-Virus *n* aporocactus virus
Aposporie *f (bot)* apospory
aposporisch aposporic, aposporous
Apothezium *n* apothecium *(cupped fruit-body of ascomycetes)*
apotracheal apotracheal *(parenchyma)*
ApoV *s.* Aporocactus-Virus
Appaloosa *n(m)* Appaloosa *(horse breed)*
Apparent Freier Raum *m* Donnan free space *(of plant tissue)*
Appell *m* obedience *(of dog)*
Appendix *m(f)* appendage • **zum ~ gehörend** appendiculate
Appenzellerziege *f* Appenzell *(goat breed)*
Appetenzverhalten *n* appetitive behaviour *(of animals)*
Appetit *m* appetite
~ **/abnormer** pica
Appetitanreger *m* appetite stimulant
Appetitlosigkeit *f* inappetence
Appetitsstimulans *n* appetite stimulant
Appetitszügler *m* appetite suppressor (depressant, inhibitor), anorexiant [agent]
Applikation *f* application *(e.g. of fertilizers)*
~ **aus der Luft** aerial (air-to-ground) application
Applikationsgerät *n* [mechanical] applicator
Applikationsverfahren *n* application method
applizieren to apply
Applizieren *n* application *(e.g. of fertilizers)*
~ **/ganzflächiges** area-application
apport! fetch!, go! *(command to dogs)*

apportieren

apportieren (hunt) to retrieve, to fetch
Apportierhund m retriever; (Am) bird dog
Appressorium n appressorium (of parasitic fungi)
Apramycin n apramycin (antibiotic)
Aprikose f apricot, Prunus armeniaca
~ **von St. Domingo** mammee [apple], mammea, mamey, Mammea americana
Aprikosenbaum m apricot [tree], Prunus armeniaca
Aprikosenspinner m vapourer moth, Orgyia antiqua
Aprikosenwelke f apricot wilt (caused by Verticillium albo-atrum)
ApSFV s. Apfelstammfurchungsvirus
apter[ygot] (bot, zoo) apterous, wingless
Aptyalismus m (vet) aptyalism
Apyrase f apyrase (enzyme)
Apyrexie f (vet) apyrexia
Aquakultur f aquaculture, aquiculture
aquakulturell aquacultural
Aquarienfisch m aquarium fish
aquatil aquatic
Äquationsteilung f mitosis, mitotic division
aquatisch aquatic
Äquator[ial]gürtel m equatorial belt
Äquatorialplatte f equatorial (metaphase) plate (mitosis)
Äquivalentwelkepunkt m equivalent wilting point
Äquivalentwert m **der Feldkapazität** (soil) moisture equivalent
Ar n are (square measure; 1 are = 100 square metres)
A.R. s. Ahnenreihe
Araban n araban (polysaccharide)
Araber m Arabian [horse], Arab
Arabica-Kaffee m [Arabian, Arabica, common] coffee, Coffea arabica
Arabinan n araban (polysaccharide)
Arabinogalactan n arabinogalactan (polysaccharide)
Arabinose f arabinose (monosaccharide)
Arabinosidase f arabinosidase (enzyme)
Arabinoxylan n arabino-xylan (hemicellulose)
Arabischer Gummibaum m gum arabic tree, Acacia nilotica (arabica)
~ **Schneckenklee** m spotted medic[k], heart trefoil, southern bur clover, Medicago arabica
Arabisches Gummi n gum arabic (acacia) (from Acacia spp.)
~ **Vollblut[pferd]** n Arabian [horse], Arab
Arabismosaikvirus n arabis mosaic virus, ArMV
Arabit m arabitol (sugar alcohol)
Arabogalactan n s. Arabinogalactan
Arachidonsäure f arachidonic acid, eicosatetraenoic acid (fatty acid)
Arachisöl n arachis (ground-nut) oil
Arachnide f arachnid (class Arachnida)
arachnoid arachnoid
Arachnoide f s. Arachnide

Arachnoidea f arachnoid (animal anatomy)
Aradagurke f [West Indian] gherkin, gooseberry gourd, Cucumis anguria
A-Rahmen m A-frame (timber transportation)
Aralie f (bot) aralia (genus Aralia)
Aramit n aramite (insecticide)
Aräometer n areometer
Aräopyknometer n areopycnometer
Araukarie f (bot) araucaria (genus Araucaria)
Arbeiten n **im Gespann** shaft work (horse management)
Arbeiterin f (api) worker [honey-bee]
Arbeiterinnenbrut f worker brood
Arbeiterinnenfuttersaft m worker jelly
Arbeiterinnenzelle f worker cell
Arbeitsablauf m work sequence
Arbeitsaufwand m labour expenditure (input)
Arbeitsbedarf m labour requirement
Arbeitsbelastung f labour load
Arbeitsbereich m working area
Arbeitsbiene f s. Arbeiterin
Arbeitsbreite f working width
~ **des Pflugs** plough width
Arbeitsbühne f working platform
Arbeitseinheit f labour (work) unit
Arbeitsfläche f working surface (e.g. of a mouldboard)
Arbeitsgalopp m work gallop
Arbeitsgang m operation; pass (field work)
Arbeitsgasse f alley [way], aisle
~/**begrünte (mit Gras bewachsene)** grassed alley, alley sward (in orchards)
Arbeitsgeschwindigkeit f working speed (rate), operating speed
Arbeitsgruppe f working group (party), outfit
Arbeitshaltung f posture
Arbeitskondition f working condition (of horses)
Arbeitskraft f 1. working power; 2. labour, manpower
Arbeitskräfte fpl/**familieneigene** family labour
~/**landwirtschaftliche** agricultural labour
Arbeitskräftebedarf m labour requirement
Arbeitkraftstunde f man-hour [of labour]
Arbeitskraftstundenbedarf m worker-hour requirement
Arbeitsleistung f rate of work[ing], work performance, working capacity; output
Arbeitsmaschine f [work] machine
Arbeitsmessung f work measurement
Arbeitsorganisation f organization of work
Arbeitspferd n work[ing] horse
Arbeitsproduktivität f labour productivity (efficiency)
Arbeitsrinder npl draught cattle (group of breeds)
Arbeitsschutz m labour (occupational) safety
~ **in der Landwirtschaft** farm safety
Arbeitsschutz[be]kleidung f safety (protective) clothing

Arbeitsschutzmaßnahme f precaution
Arbeitsschutzstiefel mpl protective boots
Arbeitsschweiß m **des Pferdes** lather
Arbeitssicherheit f safety at work
arbeitssparend labour-saving
Arbeitsspitze f peak labour demand, peak labour (work) load
Arbeitsstichprobe f working sample
Arbeitsstudie f work study
Arbeitstiefe f working depth, depth at work
Arbeitstiefenstellspindel f depth screw gear (e.g. of a plough)
Arbeitstier n work[ing] animal
Arbeitstiere npl work stock
Arbeitsunfall m occupational accident
Arbeitsvermögen n working capacity
Arbeitsvorgang m operation
Arbeitsweise f [mode of] operation; method
Arbeitswirtschaft f labour management
Arbeitzeug n duffel, duffle (e.g. of a lumberman)
Arbeitszylinder m hydraulic cylinder, (Am) ram
~/einfachwirkender single-acting cylinder
~/wechselseitig beaufschlagter double-acting cylinder
arboreszent arborescent, arboraceous
Arboretum n arboretum, tree-garden
~/forstliches forest arboretum (garden)
arborikol arboreal, living on (in) trees
Arborizid n arboricide, silvicide, brush-killer
Arbuse f s. Dessertwassermelone
Arbutin n arbutin (glycoside)
Archegonium n (bot) archegonium
Archenteron n archenteron, primitive gut
Archespor n (bot) archespore, archesporium
Ardenner m, **Ardennerpferd** n [French] Ardennes (horse breed)
Area f s. Fläche
Areal n (ecol) area, range
~ gleicher Standortbeschaffenheit climatope
Arealkunde f chorology
arealkundlich chorological
Arealkurve f species-area curve (line)
Arealschrumpfung f regression
Arecolin n arecoline (alkaloid)
Areflexie f (vet) areflexia
Arengapalme f arenga [palm], [true] sugar palm, Arenga pinnata (saccharifera)
Arenosol n (soil) arenosol
Areole f (bot) areola
Argali m(n) (zoo) argali, Ovis aries ammon
Arganbaum m argan tree, Argania spinosa (sideroxylon)
Argentinische Ameise f Argentine ant, Iridomyrmex humilis
Argilluvisation f (soil) argilluviation, lessivage, lessivation, clay translocation (illuviation)
Arginase f arginase (enzyme)
Arginin n arginine (amino-acid)
Argininantagonist m arginine antagonist

Arginindecarboxylase f arginine decarboxylase (enzym)
Arginindeiminase f, **Argininhydrolase** f arginine deiminase (enzyme)
Arginin-Harnstoffzyklus m, **Arginin-Ornithinzyklus** m ornithine[-arginine] cycle, urea cycle, Krebs-Henseleit pathway (biochemistry)
Argininsuccinatlyase f argininosuccinate lyase (enzyme)
Argininsuccinatsynthetase f argininosuccinate synth[et]ase (enzyme)
Arhythmie f s. Arrhythmie
Ariboflavinose f (vet) ariboflavinosis
Aricin n aricin[e] (alkaloid)
arid arid, xeric, dry
Aridisol m (Am, soil) aridisol, id
Aridität f aridity, aridness
Ariditätsindex m index of aridity (meteorology)
aridophil aridophilous, xerophilous, xerophytic
Arillus m (bot) aril, seed-coat
Arista f (ent) arista
Aristoteleshirsch m sambar deer, Cervus unicolor
Arizona-Zypresse f Arizona cypress, Cupressus arizonica
Arm m arm
Armaturenbrett n instrument assembly (board)
Armbandorchidee f chain orchid (genus Dendrochilum)
armförmig (bot, zoo) brachiate
Armschwinge f pinion (of birds)
ArMV s. Arabismosaikvirus
Arnika f 1. arnica (genus Arnica); 2. [mountain] arnica, mountain tobacco, Arnica montana
Arom[a] n aroma, flavour
Aromastoff m aroma substance, flavouring [substance]
aromatisch aromatic, spiced
Aron m s. Aronstab
Aronia f, **Aronie** f 1. chokeberry (genus Aronia); 2. black chokeberry, Aronia melanocarpa; 3. chokeberry (fruit)
Aronstab m (bot) 1. arum, wake-robin (genus Arum); 2. lords and ladies, wild arum, wake-robin, cuckoo-pint, Arum maculatum
Aronstabgewächs n aroid (family Araceae)
Arracacha f 1. arracacha (genus Arracacia); 2. arracacha, Peruvian carrot (parsnip), Arracacia xanthorrhiza (esculenta)
Arrangieren n **von Blumen (Blüten)** flower arranging
Arrector m arrector [muscle], erector muscle
Arrhenotokie f (zoo) arrhenotoky (parthenogenetic production of male descendants)
arrhenotokisch arrhenotokous
Arrhythmie f (vet) arrhythmia
arrhythmisch arrhythmic
Arsanilsäure f arsanilic acid (growth regulator)
arsenhaltig arsenical
Arseninsektizid n arsenical insecticide

Arsenverbindung

Arsenverbindung f arsenical, arsenic compound
Arsenvergiftung f arsenic poisoning
Art f species, sp.; order; race • **der gleichen ~ angehörend** conspecific • **innerhalb der ~** intraspecific
~/**allopatrische** allopatric species
~/**azöne** associated (accessory, companion) species
~/**bedrohte** threatened species
~/**gefährdete** endangered species
~/**gesellschaftsfremde** strange species
~/**nicht zu bekämpfende (unterdrückende)** nontarget species
~/**säureanzeigende** acidity indicator species
~/**stellvertretende (vikariierende)** (ecol) vicarious species
~/**zu bekämpfende (unterdrückende)** target species
Artbastard m species hybrid, interspecific cross (hybrid)
Artbastardierung f interspecific hybridization
Artbildung f speciation
arteigen species-specific
Artemisia-Halbwüste f sage-b[r]ush semidesert
Artenabundanz f s. Artendichte
Artenarealkurve f (ecol) species-area curve (line)
Artendichte f species density, abundance
Artengemeinschaftsanalyse f community analysis
Artengemisch n species mixture
Artengruppe f species group, group of species
Artenreichtum m wealth of species, species richness (diversity)
Artenrückgang m species decline
Artenschutz m species protection (conservation), protection (preservation) of species
Artenschutzgesetzgebung f endangered-species legislation
Artenspektrum n species spectrum
Artenverarmung f species impoverishment
Artenvielfalt f s. Artenreichtum
Artenzentrum n floristic centre
Arterenol n noradrenalin[e] (neurotransmitter)
Arterhaltung f species perpetuation
Arterie f artery • **innerhalb der ~** intra-arterial
~/**präkapillare** arteriole
Arteriektasie f (vet) arterioectasia
arteriell arterial
Arterienentzündung f s. Arteriitis
Arterienerweiterung f (vet) arterioectasia
Arteriengeflecht n arterial plexus
Arterienverkalkung f (vet) arteriosclerosis
Arteriitis f (vet) arteritis
~ des Pferdes/infektiöse equine viral arteritis, epizootic cellulitis
Arteriole f arteriole
Arteriosklerose f (vet) arteriosclerosis
Arteritis f s. Arteriitis
Artgenosse f conspecific

Arthritis f (vet) arthritis
arthritisch arthritic
Arthrochondritis f (vet) arthrochondritis
Arthrogrypose-Hydranenzephalie-Syndrom n akabane disease (of ruminants)
Arthroplastik f (vet) arthroplasty
Arthropode m arthropod (phylum Arthropoda)
Arthropodenmull m arthropod mull
Arthrose f (vet) arthrosis
Arthrospore f (bot) arthrospore, oidium
Arthrotomie f (vet) arthrotomy
Arthybride f species hybrid, interspecific cross (hybrid)
artikulär articular
Artikulat m articulate animal (subkingdom Articulata)
Artischocke f [globe] artichoke, Cynara scolymus
Artischockenblattkräuselungsvirus n artichoke mottle crinkle virus, AMCV
Artischockenboden m artichoke bottom, choke
Artischockenmosaikvirus n cynara mosaic virus
Artkreuzung f 1. species hybrid, interspecific cross (hybrid); 2. s. Artkreuzungszüchtung
Artkreuzungszüchtung f interspecific hybridization, crossing (hybridization) of species
artrein true to type
Artreinheit f trueness to type
artspezifisch species-specific
Arve f cembra[n] pine, arolla [pine], Swiss (stone) pine, Pinus cembra
Arylaminacetyltransferase f arylamine acetyltransferase (enzyme)
Arylester[hydrol]ase f arylesterase (enzyme)
Arylsulfamat n arylsulphamate (herbicide)
Arylsulfat[sulfohydrol]ase f arylsulphatase (enzyme)
Arzneibaldrian m common valerian, all-heal, Valeriana officinalis
Arzneibuch n pharmacopoeia
Arzneikraut n officinal (medicinal) herb
arzneilich officinal
Arzneimittel n [medicinal] drug, medicine, medicament, medicant, remedy
Arzneimittelallergie f (vet) drug fever
Arzneimittelrückstand m (vet) drug residue
Arzneimohn m oriental poppy, Papaver orientale (bracteatum)
Arzneipflanze f medicinal (officinal) plant, health (healing) plant
Arzneipflanzengarten m physic garden
Arzneipflanzenkunde f medical botany
Arzneiwein m medicine wine
As m (soil) esker, eskar
AS s. 1. Aminosäure; 2. Aktivsubstanz; 3. Angler Sattelschwein; 4. Schweinelähmung/ansteckende
Asa foetida f, **Asant** m asafoetida (gum resin from Ferula asafoetida)
ASaV s. Ackerbohnensamenverfärbungsvirus

Asbestzement[drän]rohr *n* asbestos cement [drain] pipe
Ascariasis *f (vet)* ascariasis, ascaridose
Ascaridiose *f (vet)* ascarididiosis
Ascaris *f* ascarid *(family Ascarididae)*
Asche *f* ash
~/vulkanische volcanic ash
Äsche *f* grayling, Thymallus thymallus
aschearm low-ash
Aschebestandteil *m* ash constituent
Aschebestimmung *f* ash determination
~/konduktometrische conductometric ash determination
aschefrei ash-free
Aschegehalt *m* ash content • **mit niedrigem ~** low-ash
~/prozentualer ash percentage, percentage of ash
Aschegehaltsbestimmung *f* ash determination
aschenarm low-ash
Aschenblume *f s.* Gartencinerarie
aschenfrei ash-free
Äschenregion *f* grayling zone
Aschequalität *f* ash quality *(of tobacco)*
Äscherich *m* powdery mildew of grape *(caused by Uncinula necator)*
asche- und wasserfrei ash-free-[and-]dry
Aschheim-Zondek-Test *m* Aschheim-Zondek reaction (test) *(for gonadotropin detection in the blood of pregnant mares)*
Aschoff-Tawara-Knoten *m* atrioventricular node *(of the heart)*
Aschweide *f* grey willow (sallow), Salix cinerea
Ascochyta-Krankheit *f* **der Chrysantheme** ray blight [of chrysanthemum] *(caused by Mycosphaerella ligulicola)*
Ascokarp *n*, **Ascoma** *n* ascocarp *(mature fruiting body of an ascomycete)*
Ascophaeriose *f (api, vet)* chalk brood
Ascorbatoxidase *f* ascorbate oxidase *(enzyme)*
Ascorbinsäure *f* ascorbic acid, vitamin C
Ascorbinsäureoxidase *f* ascorbic acid oxidase *(enzyme)*
äsen *(hunter's language)* to browse, to graze
Äsen *n* browsing, grazing *(of game)*
Asepsis *f* asepsis
aseptisch aseptic • **~ machen** to asepticize, to sterilize
Äser *m* mouth *(of furred game)*
Asexualität *f* asexuality
asexuell asexual
Asiatische Geflügelpest *f* Newcastle disease, ND, pseudo poultry plague
~ Korkeiche *f* Chinese cork-oak, Quercus variabilis
~ Ranunkel *f (bot)* Persian (turban) buttercup, Ranunculus asiaticus
Asiatischer Büffel *m* [water] buffalo, water-ox, Bubalus arni
~ Elefant *m* Indian elephant, Elephas maximus

~ Maiszünsler *m (ent)* Asian maize borer, Ostrinia furnacalis, Pyrausta salentialis
~ Storax *m* Levant storax *(balsam from Liquidambar orientalis)*
Asiatisches Geflügelpestvirus *n* Newcastle disease virus
~ Kammhuhn *n* red jungle fowl, Gallus gallus (bankiva)
Asiderose *f (vet)* asiderosis
Askanija[schaf] *n* Askanian *(sheep breed)*
Askarididose *f s.* Ascariasis
Askogon *n* ascogonium *(gametangium of ascomycetes)*
Askomyzet *m* ascomycete *(class Ascomycetes)*
Askospore *f (bot)* ascospore
Askus *m (bot)* ascus
Asn *s.* Asparagin
Asp *s.* Asparaginsäure
ASP *s.* 1. Afrikanische Schweinepest; 2. Augenstecklingsprüfung
Asparagin *n* asparagine *(amino-acid)*
Asparaginase *f* asparaginase *(enzyme)*
Asparaginat-Aminotransferase *f* asparagine aminotransferase *(enzyme)*
Asparaginsäure *f* aspartic (asparagine, aminosuccinic) acid
Asparaginsynthetase *f* aspartate-ammonia ligase, asparagine synthetase *(enzyme)*
Asparagus *m s.* Zierspargel
Aspartase *f* aspartate ammonia-lyase *(enzyme)*
Aspartataminotransferase *f* aspartate aminotransferase, glutamate oxaloacetic transaminase, GOT *(enzyme)*
Aspartatammoniakligase *f* aspartate-ammonia ligase, asparagine synthetase *(enzyme)*
Aspartatammoniaklyase *f* aspartate ammonia-lyase *(enzyme)*
Aspartatcarbamoyltransferase *f* aspartate carbamoyltransferase *(enzyme)*
Aspe *f s.* Espe
Aspekt *m* aspect *(appearance of an ecosystem)*
Aspektwechsel *m* aspect change *(phenology)*
Aspenblattgallmücke *f* aspen gnat, Harmandia tremulae
Aspenprachtkäfer *m* aspen buprestid, *(Am)* aspen burncow, Poecilonota conspersa
Aspergillin *n* aspergillin
Aspergillose *f (vet)* aspergillosis
Aspergillsäure *f* aspergillic acid
Aspergillus *m* aspergillus *(genus Aspergillus)*
Aspergillusinfektion *f* **von Geflügeleiern** eggborne aspergillosis *(esp. caused by Aspergillus fumigatus)*
Aspermatismus *m (vet)* aspermatism, aspermia
Aspermatogenesis *f (vet)* aspermatogenesis
Aspermie *f s.* Aspermatismus
Aspirateur *m* aspirator
Aspiration *f* aspiration

Aspirationspsychrometer

Aspirationspsychrometer *n* aspirated (aspiration) psychrometer, Assmann psychrometer
aspirieren to aspirate
Asphaltklee *m* asphalt clover, bitumen trefoil, Psoralea bituminosa
Asphyxie *f (vet)* asphyxia[tion]
Assaipalme *f* assai (monkey tail) palm, Para (manicole) palm, Euterpe edulis
Assel *f* slater, wood-louse, sow[-bug], pill-bug *(order Isopoda)*
Asselkaktus *m* hatchet cactus *(genus Pelecyphora)*
Assimilat *n* assimilate, photosynthate
Assimilatakkumulation *f* photosynthate accumulation
Assimilataufteilung *f* assimilate partition[ing]
Assimilation *f* assimilation; anabolism
~/**autotrophe** autotrophy
~/**heterotrophe** heterotrophy
Assimilationsleistung *f* assimilation rate, assimilative efficiency
Assimilationsparenchym *n*/[chloroplastenhaltiges] chlorenchyma
Assimilationsprodukt *n* s. Assimilat
Assimilationsprozeß *m* assimilative process
Assimilationsquotient *m* assimilation quotient
Assimilationsrate *f* assimilation rate
Assimilationsspeicherstelle *f* sink
Assimilationsstärke *f* assimilation starch
assimilatorisch assimilative, assimilatory
Assimilattransport *m* assimilate transport
Assimilatverteilung *f* assimilate partition[ing]
assimilierbar assimilable
Assimilierbarkeit *f* assimilability
assimilieren to assimilate; to anabolize
assimilierend assimilative, assimilatory
Associes *f* associes, subclimax stage *(plant sociology)*
Assoziation *f* association
Assoziationsreflex *m* conditioned reflex
Ast *m* 1. branch, bough; 2. knot, knurl, knag (defect in wood); 3. barb, harl[e] *(of bird's feather)* • **Äste bilden** to branch
~/**abgestorbener** dead knot
~/**ausfallender** falling-out knot, loose knot
~/**durchgehender** passing knot
~/**eingeschlossener (eingewachsener)** encased knot
~ **erster Ordnung** limb, scaffold branch, leader
~/**fauler** decayed knot, rotten (punk) knot
~/**fäulnisfreier** sound knot
~/**feiner** small knot
~/**gegabelter** forked branch
~/**gesunder** sound knot
~/**kleiner** small knot
~/**leicht angefaulter** knot with incipient decay
~/**loser** loose (falling-out) knot
~/**mittlerer** medium knot
~/**nadelartiger** pin knot
~/**offener** visible knot

~/**runder** round knot
~/**seitenständiger** lateral branch
~/**überwallter** encased knot
~/**verzweigter** branch[ed] knot
Astansammlung *f* knot cluster
Astanstellwinkel *m* branch (limb) angle, axil; crotch angle
Astaxanthin *n* astaxanthin *(animal carotenoid)*
Astaxt *f* lopping axe
Astbeule *f* branch swelling; blind conk
Astbildung *f* branch formation, branching
Astbüschel *n* knot cluster
asten to prune [down], to lop [off], to [de]limb, to brush through (up), to abnodate
~/**chemisch** to prune chemically
~/**liegend** to trim
~/**stehend** to prune, to [dis]branch, to [de]limb
ästen s. asten
Astentfaltung *f* expansion of the branches
Aster *f* aster, Michaelmas daisy, starwort *(genus Aster)*
Asterazee *f* composite *(family Asteraceae = Compositae)*
Asterazeen *fpl* aster family *(family Asteraceae = Compositae)*
Asternvergilbung *f* aster yellows *(mycoplasmosis)*
Astfäule *f* branch rot
astfrei s. astrein
Astgabel *f* forked branch, fork, crotch, crutch
Astgerüst *n* main scaffold
Asthaltung *f* branch position
Asthenie *f (vet)* asthenia
Asthippe *f* pruning knife (hook)
Asthma *n* [bronchale] *(vet)* asthma
Asthöhle *f* branch hole
Astholz *n* branchwood, brushwood; lopwood
~/**abgefallenes** fallen wood
Astholzformzahl *f* branch form factor *(timber mensuration)*
Astholzvolumen *n* branchwood volume
astig, ästig *(bot, zoo)* ramose, ramate, brachiate; branched, branchy, limby, boughy; knotty, knaggy *(timber)*
Ästige Sommerwurz *f* branched (hemp) broomrape, Orobanche ramosa
Astigkeit *f* branchiness; knottiness
Astigmatismus *m (vet)* astigmatism
Astilbe *f (bot)* astilbe, false goat's-beard, false spire *(genus Astilbe)*
Ästivation *f (bot)* aestivation
Astknorren *m*, **Astknoten** *m* knot, knurl, knag
Ästling *m* eyas *(falconry)*
Astloch *n* branch hole; knot-hole
Astlochflicken *n* repair of [knot] holes
astlos branchless; doddered *(tree)*
~ **bis zum Wipfel auslaufend** excurrent *(tree-trunk)*
Astlose Graslilie *f* St.-Bernard's-lily, Anthericum liliago

Astlosigkeit f branchlessness; absence of knots, clearness
Astnarbe f branch scar
Astordnung f branch order
Astpaar n pair of branches
Astquirl m [branch] whorl
Astrachan n astrakhan, astrachan *(fleece)*
Astrachanschaf n Astrakhan *(sheep breed)*
Astragalus m astragalus, tragacanth *(genus Astragalus)*
Astrangordnung f branch order
astreich boughy, limby; knotty *(s.a. astig)*
astrein branchless, branchfree, limbless; clear-shafted, clear-boled; knot-free, clear, clean *(timber)*
Astreinheit f branchlessness; absence of knots, clearness
Astreinigung f pruning of branches
~/**natürliche** self-pruning, natural pruning
Astreisig n lopwood, branchwood, lop and top, lops
Astrichtung f branch orientation
Astrinde f branch bark
Astringelung f limb-girdling
Astrose f twig burr
Astrosphäre f centrosphere *(cell division)*
Astsäge f pruning (garden) saw
Astschere f pruning shears, pruner, clipper; averruncator
Astschneider m averruncator, branch remover
Astspreizung f limb spreading
astständig ram[e]al
Aststärke f branch base diameter
Aststellung f branch distribution
Aststreu f branch (twig) litter
Aststummel m [branch] stub, branch stump, snag; knot
~/**eingeschlossener (eingewachsener)** encased knot
~/**kaum überwallter** dead knot
~/**überwallter** encased knot
Aststumpen m, **Aststumpf** m s. Aststummel
asttragend branching
Ästuar[ium] n estuary
Astüberwallung f occlusion of a branch
Astung f pruning, brushing, abnodation
~/**erste** brushing-through, brushing-up, brashing
Astungsgerät n pruning (limbing) tool, tree pruner
Astungshaken m pruning-hook
Ästungshöhe f pruning height
Astungsroboter m robot pruner
Astungssäge f pruning saw, tree pruner
Astwerk n branchage
Astwinkel m s. Astanstellwinkel
Asulam n asulam *(herbicide)*
Äsung f browse, food *(for game)*
Äsungsgewohnheit f feed[ing] habit
Äsungspflanze f browse plant
Äsungsplatz m feeding place

ASV s. Ackerbohnenscheckungsvirus
asymbiontisch asymbiotic
Asynapsis f asynapsis, asyndesis *(meiosis)*
asynaptisch asynaptic
Aszendent m ancestor, progenitor
Aszendenztafel f pedigree
aszendierend ascendent, ascending
Aszites m *(vet)* ascites, dropsy of the belly (peritoneum)
Atactostele f *(bot)* atactostele
ataktisch *(vet)* ataxic
Ataraktikum n ataractic [agent]
Atavismus m atavism
~ **der Schwarzen Johannisbeere** black currant reversion *(mycoplasmosis)*
~/**mutativer** *(gen)* reversion, return mutation
atavistisch atavistic
Ataxie f *(vet)* ataxia, ataxy
~ **der Fohlen/spinale** equine sensory ataxia, wobbles of foals
~ **der Schaflämmer/enzootische** enzootic (neonatal) ataxia, sway-back, swingback *(of sheep lambs)*
~/**feline** feline panleukopenia, feline distemper (infectious enteritis)
Atelektase f *(vet)* atelectasis
Atem m breath
Atembewegung f breathing (respiratory) movement
Atemfrequenz f breathing frequency, respiratory rate
Atemfrequenzsteigerung f polypnoea
Atemgift n respiratory poison
Atemloch n breathing pore, respiratory opening (e.g. of slugs and snails)
Atemluft f breathing (tidal) air
Atemminutenvolumen n minute respiratory volume
Atemnot f *(vet)* dyspnoea
Atemöffnung f *(zoo)* stigma
Atemsack m breather bag *(silo equipment)*
Atemschutzgerät n, **Atemschutzmaske** f respirator
Atemweg m respiratory pathway
~/**oberer** upper airway
Atemwurzel f respiratory (aerating) root, pneumatophore
Atemzug m breath
Atemzugvolumen n tidal volume
~/**inspiratorisches** inspiratory volume
ätherisch volatile, essential *(oil)*
Atherom n *(vet)* atheroma
Atheromatose f *(vet)* atheromatosis
Atherosklerose f *(vet)* atherosclerosis
Athidathion n athidathion *(insecticide)*
Ätiologie f aetiology
ätiologisch aetiologic[al]
Atlantische Pistazie f large terebinth, Pistacia atlantica

Atlantischer

Atlantischer Lachs *m* [Atlantic] salmon, Salmo salar
Atlas *m* atlas *(animal anatomy)*
Atlasblume *f* godetia *(genus Godetia)*
Atlasspinner *m* willow (satin) moth, Leucoma (Stilpnotia) salicis
Atlaszeder *f* atlas cedar, Cedrus atlantica
atmen to breathe, to respire; to disassimilate *(plant physiology)*
Atmen *n* breathing, respiration *(for compounds s. under* Atmung)
Atmometer *n* atmometer
Atmosphäre *f* atmosphere
~/gesteuerte controlled atmosphere, CA
~ mit verringertem Sauerstoffgehalt low-oxygen atmosphere *(in storing fruit and vegetable)*
Atmosphärilien *pl* subaerial agents
atmosphärisch atmospheric[al], aerial
Atmung *f* respiration; disassimilation
~/äußere external respiration
~/cyanidresistente cyanide-resistant respiration
~/gesteigerte hyperpnoea
~/hechelnde panting
~/innere internal respiration, cell (tissue) respiration
~/rasselnde (röchelnde) stertor
~/verminderte hypopnoea
Atmungsanstieg *m* climacteric rise *(of plants during fruit ripening)*
Atmungsbewegung *f* breathing (respiratory) movement
Atmungsenzym *n* respiratory enzyme
Atmungsferment *n*/**Warburgsches** cytochrome-c oxidase *(enzyme)*
Atmungsfrequenz *f* breathing frequency, respiratory rate
Atmungsgas *n* respiratory gas
Atmungsgeräusch *n* respiratory murmur
Atmungsinhibitor *m* respiratory inhibitor *(plant physiology)*
Atmungskette *f* respiratory (oxidation) chain *(biochemistry)*
Atmungskettenphosphorylierung *f* oxidative phosphorylation
Atmungskrankheit *f* respiration disease
~ der Hühner/chronische chronic respiration disease of chickens, CRD, respiratory syndrome of chickens
Atmungslähmung *f (vet)* respiratory paralysis
Atmungsmessung *f* respirometry
Atmungsöffnung *f* respiratory opening, breathing pore *(e.g. of slugs and snails)*
Atmungsorgan *n* respiratory organ
Atmungsquotient *m* respiratory quotient
Atmungsrate *f* respiratory rate
Atmungsrhythmus *m* respiratory rhythm
Atmungsschwand *m* respiration loss *(malting)*
Atmungsstillstand *m* respiratory arrest, apnoea
Atmungsstoffwechsel *m* respiratory metabolism
Atmungsstörung *f* respiratory disorder
Atmungssystem *n* respiratory system (tract)
Atmungstiefe *f* breathing depth
Atmungstrakt *m* respiratory tract (ducts)
Atmungstrockner *m* platen dryer
Atmungsverlust *m* respiration loss *(malting)*
Atmungsvolumen *n* tidal volume
Atmungszentrum *n* respiratory centre
AtMV *s.* Artischockenmosaikvirus
Atomabsorptionsspektralphotometrie *f* atomic absorption spectrophotometry
Atomabsorptionsspektrometrie *f* atomic absorption spectrometry
Atomabsorptionsspektrophotometer *n* atomic absorption spectrophotometer
Atomabsorptionsspektrophotometrie *f* atomic absorption spectrophotometry
Atomabsorptionsspektroskopie *f* atomic absorption spectroscopy
Atomfluoreszenzspektroskopie *f* atomic fluorescence spectroscopy
Atomiseur *m* fog generator, low-volume mist blower
Atonie *f (vet)* atony
Atopie *f (vet)* atopy, idiosyncrasy
atoxisch atoxic
ATP ATP, adenosine-5'-triphosphate *(nucleotide)*
ATPase *f* ATPase, adenosine triphosphatase *(enzyme)*
ATP-Citratlyase *f*, **ATP-Citrat(pro-3S)-Lyase** *f* ATP-citrate(pro 3S)-lyase *(enzyme)*
ATP-Pyrophosphatase *f* ATP-pyrophosphatase *(enzyme)*
Atraton *n* atraton *(herbicide)*
Atrazin *n* atrazine *(herbicide)*
Atresie *f (vet)* atresia
atrial atrial
atrioventrikulär atrioventricular
Atrioventrikularklappe *f* atrioventricular valve *(of the heart)*
Atrioventrikularknoten *m* atrioventricular node *(of the heart)*
Atrium *n* atrium, auricle *(of the heart)*
Atrophie *f (phyt, vet)* atrophy
~/fetale foetal atrophy
atrophieren to atrophy
atrophisch atrophic *(tissue, organ)*
Atropin *n* atropine *(alkaloid)*
Atropinesterase *f* atropinesterase *(enzyme)*
Attacke *f* attack
Attapulgit *m* attapulgite *(clay mineral)*
Attenuierung *f* attenuation
Attest *n* certificate
Attestierung *f* certification *(e.g. of seed)*
Attich *m* danewort, ground (dwarf) elder, Sambucus ebulus
Attraktans *n* attractant *(e.g. for insect control)*
Attraktionszentrum *n* sink *(plant physiology)*
Attraktivpheromon *n* sex pheromone (attractant)

Attraktivstoff *m s.* Attraktans
Atzblock *m* hack *(falconry)*
atzen *(hunter's language)* to feed off (up) *(hawks in falconry)*
ätzen to cauterize, to etch
Ätzen *n* cauterization, cautery, etching
Ätzkalk *m* calcium oxide
Ätzmittel *n* 1. caustic; 2. contact herbicide (weed-killer)
~ **zur kalten Kauterisation** cautery
Ätzmittelemulsion *f* contact emulsion
Ätzmuster *n (phyt)* etching
Ätznatron *n* caustic soda, sodium hydroxide
Ätzschaden *m (phyt)* etching
Atzung *f (hunter's language)* food
Ätzung *f (phyt)* etching
Ätzwunde *f (phyt)* scorch
Au *f s.* Aue
Aubergine *f* 1. egg-plant, Guinea squash, Solanum melongena; 2. aubergine, brinjal, garden egg *(fruit)*
Aubrac *n* Aubrac, Laguiole *(cattle breed)*
Aubrietie *f* aubrietia, purple madwort *(genus Aubrieta)*
Aucubamosaik *n* **der Kartoffel** aucuba mosaic *(virosis)*
Aucymidol *n* aucymidol *(growth regulator)*
Aue *f* riverside, river basin (valley, meadow), flood plain
Auenboden *m* riverside soil, fluviogenic (flood-plain) soil
~/**brauner** brown warp soil
Auenbrombeere *f* dewberry, Rubus caesius
Auengrasland *n* strath
Auenlehm *m* flood-plain loam
Auenton *m* bottom clay
Auenwald *m* river-meadow forest, alluvial (lowland, flood-plain) forest
Auenwaldboden *m s.* Auenboden
Auergeflügel *n s.* Auerwild
Auerhahn *m* mountain cock
Auerhuhn *n* 1. mountain hen, hen capercaillie; 2. *s.* Auerwild
Auerochs *m* urus, Bos taurus primigenius
Auerwild *n* capercaillie, capercailzie, wood grouse, cock of the wood, Tetrao urogallus
Auf *m s.* Uhu
aufarbeiten *(forest)* 1. to trim, to clear off *(a lying trunk)*; 2. to convert, to process *(timber)*
Aufarbeitung *f* conversion, processing
Aufarbeitungsplatz *m* conversion point (site)
aufasten to prune [down], to lop [off], to [de]limb, to brush through (up), to abnodate, to set up, to trim
Aufasten *n* pruning, brushing, abnodation, setting-up
Aufbau *m* 1. construction, building-up; 2. setting-up; 3. construction, structure, arrangement, set-up; composition; 4. body *(of vehicle)*

~ **eines Blätterdachs** canopy architecture
~/**geweblicher** texture
aufbaumen *(hunt)* to tree; to perch, to alight *(wildfowl)*
aufbäumen/sich to rear, to prance
Aufbäumen *n* prance
Aufbaumittel *n* anabolic [agent]
Aufbäummoment *n* overturning torque *(e.g. of tractors)*
Aufbauschnitt *m* form pruning *(orcharding)*
Aufbaustoffwechsel *m* anabolism, constructive (synthetic) metabolism • **einen ~ vollziehen** to anabolize
aufbereiten to process; to condition; to dress; to treat
Aufbereiter *m* conditioner
Aufbereitung *f* processing; conditioning; dressing; treatment
~/**feuchte (nasse)** wet processing
Aufbereitungsanlage *f* 1. processing facility (plant); 2. packing[-house] line
Aufbereitungsindustrie *f* processing industry
Aufbereitungsmaschine *f* conditioner
Aufbereitungsstation *f* packing-house, packing-station, packing-shed *(fruit production)*
Aufbereitungsverlust *m* processing loss
Aufbereitungszentrale *f* central grading plant
aufbewahren to keep
Aufbewahrung *f* keeping
aufbinden to tie up, to stake
Aufbinden *n* **der Triebe** first tying *(viticulture)*
Aufblähung *f (vet)* emphysema
aufblocken to perch, to alight *(wildfowl)*
aufblühen to blossom, to burst (break out) into blossom, to bloom, to effloresce
Aufblühen *n* blossoming, blooming, efflorescence, inflorescence
aufblühend blossoming, blooming, [ef]florescent
Aufblühlösung *f* disbudding solution *(for cut flowers)*
Aufbodenheizung *f* floor-level heating, on-floor heating [system], up-soil heating *(in glasshouses)*
aufbrauchen to deplete, to exhaust *(e.g. stores)*
aufbrechen 1. to open, to burst *(buds)*; 2. to fallow *(soil)*; 3. *(hunt)* to disembowel, to break up, to gut, to eviscerate; to gralloch *(hoofed game)*
Aufbruch *m (hunt)* bowels; gralloch, [h]umbles
Aufeinanderfolge *f* sequence
Aufenthaltspflanze *f* dwelling plant
Auffangbecken *n* catch pit
auffangen to catch; to intercept *(e.g. precipitation)*
Auffangen *n* interception
Auffangfläche *f* catching surface
Auffanggefäß *n* cup, pot, buck, trap *(resin-tapping)*
Auffanggraben *m* **an Berghängen** *(Am)* gutter trench
Auffangplane *f* catching canvas (sheet)
Auffangrahmen *m* catching frame

Auffangtrichter

Auffangtrichter *m* cone collector
Auffangtuch *n* catching canvas (sheet)
auffliegen to fly up, to flush *(birds)*
aufforsten to [re]afforest, to [re]forest, to restock
Aufforsten *n* afforestation, [re]forestation
~ **nach dem Bifang-Verfahren** afforestation with the Bifang method
~ **trockengelegter Moore** afforestation of swamps
~ **von Halden** afforestation of [mine] dumps
~ **von Hängen** slope afforestation
~ **von Schluchten** gully afforestation
Aufforstung *f s.* Aufforsten
Aufforstungsgebiet *n* afforestation area
Aufforstungsplan *m* afforestation scheme (plan)
Aufforstungsprojekt *n* afforestation project
Aufforstungstrupp *m* planting crew
Auffrieren *n* frost lift[ing], frost heave (heaving) *(of soil)*
Auffüllreaktion *f* anaplerotic reaction *(plant physiology)*
Aufgabeende *n* green end *(of a progressive kiln)*
Aufgang *m* emergence *(of seedlings)*
aufgantern to pile [up] *(roundwood)*
aufgeben to abandon *(e.g. agricultural acreage)*
aufgehen to emerge *(seedlings)*
aufgepfropft grafted
~**/nicht** own-root[ed]
aufgeregt flighty *(fowl)*
aufgesattelt semimounted, semi-integral, semi-integrated *(agricultural implements)*
Aufgeschwollensein *n* turgescence, turgidity
Aufgewicht *n* handicap *(equestrian sport)* • **mit ~ versehen** to handicap
Aufgießverfahren *n* pour-on method *(e.g. of insecticide application in animal husbandry)*
aufhacken to hoe [up], to pick
aufhaken to perch, to alight *(wildfowl)*
aufhalten to intercept *(e.g. precipitation)*
~**/im Wachstum** to nip
Aufhalten *n* **des Schnees** snow retention *(on fields)*
~ **von Niederschlägen durch Baumkronen** crown interception
Aufhalter *m* compressor arm *(reaper-binder)*
Aufhängeapparat *m* suspensory apparatus *(animal anatomy)*
Aufhänger *m (forest)* lodged (hang-up) tree
aufhäufeln to hill [up] *(e.g. in potato-growing)*
aufhäufen to heap [up]
~**/manuell** to hand-pile *(e.g. felling refuse)*
aufhellen/sich to clear *(e.g. virus-infected plant tissue)*
Aufhellung *f* clearing, paling
~**/interkostale (zwischenaderige)** *(phyt)* interveinal paling
Aufhöhen *n* mounding *(amelioration)*
aufholzen *(hunt)* to tree; to perch, to alight *(wildfowl)*
aufjagen to rouse *(game)*; to flush *(birds)*

aufkalken to lime, to chalk
Aufkalkung *f* liming *(of soil)*
Aufkaufpreis *m* procurement price
Aufklärung *f* **aus der Luft** aerial reconnaissance
aufkochen to boil up
aufkoppeln to leash *(hounds)*
aufkratzen to scrape
aufkräusen to kra[e]usen *(brewing)*
aufladen to load
~**/mit der Gabel** to fork
Auflagen *n* loading
~ **in Querrichtung** crosshauling, *(Am)* parbuckling *(timber transport)*
Auflagehumus *m* leaf mould (soil), duff mull; raw humus
Auflagehumushorizont *m* organic surface layer, Ao-horizon, O horizon
Auflagenaßtorf *m* wet forest humus
Auflagerung *f (vet)* juxtaposition
Auflandung *f (soil)* 1. aggradation; 2. alluvium, alluvion, alluvial deposit
auflaufen to emerge *(seedlings)*
Auflaufen *n* emergence
auflichten to admit light, to open up *(a plant stand)*
Auflichtung *f* opening-up
Auflichtungshieb *m (forest)* secondary felling, *(Am)* removal cutting
auflockern to loosen [up], to mellow *(soil)*; to open up *(a stand)*
~**/Heu** to ted
Auflockern *n*, **Auflockerung** *f* loosening-up; opening-up
auflösen to dissolve; to melt *(sugar)*
Auflösung *f* dissolution • **durch ~ entstanden** lysigenous
~ **der Stachelzellenschicht** *(vet)* acantholysis
~ **von Bakterien[zellen]** bacteriolysis
Aufmaischen *n* second mashing *(brewing)*
aufmästen to feed off (up), to finish
aufmessen to mark out *(a field trial)*; to scale *(e.g. timber)*
aufnageln to nail on *(e.g. a horseshoe)*
Aufnahme *f* 1. uptake, intake; resorption; 2. appraisal, appraisement, assessment, survey *(of a plant stand)*
~**/terrestrische** terrestrial (ground) survey
~**/topographische** reconnaissance
Aufnahmebasis *f* air base *(remote sensing)*
Aufnahmebereitschaft *f* receptiveness, receptivity *(e.g. of female breeding animals)*
Aufnahmebericht *m (forest)* assessment (survey) report
Aufnahmeeinrichtung *f* pick-up [device]
Aufnahmehaspel *f* pick-up reel
Aufnahmekette *f* gathering chain
Aufnahmelinie *f (forest)* assessment (survey) line
Aufnahmemanual *n s.* Aufnahmeprotokoll
Aufnahmemasse *f* loading *(of a wood preservative)*

Aufnahmemechanismus *m* uptake mechanism
Aufnahmeprotokoll *n (forest)* enumeration sheet, survey field sheet (sketch)
Aufnahmeprozent *n (forest)* sampling percent
Aufnahmepunkt *m* pass (wing) point, minor control point *(ground survey)*
Aufnahmetrupp *m (forest)* cruising (valuation) party, estimating (survey) crew
Aufnahmevorrichtung *f* pick-up [device]
Aufnahmezinke *f* pick-up tine
aufnehmbar available *(nutrients)*
Aufnehmbarkeit *f* availability *(of nutrients)*
aufnehmen 1. to take up (in); to resorb; 2. to conceive *(female breeding animal)*
~/eine Fährte (Spur) to follow the track, to check
~/einen Forstbestand to appraise, to assess, to cruise, to enumerate, to tally, to survey
~/Futter to feed
~/Geruch to smell
~/Nahrung to ingest
~/Witterung to scent, to wind
aufnehmend receptive
Aufnehmer *m* pick-up [device]
Aufnehmertrommel *f* pick-up cylinder
aufpassen to fit, to apply *(a horseshoe)*
Aufpassen *n* **des Hufeisens** shoe application
aufpfropfen to graft
aufpicken to pick
aufplatzen to burst, to dehisce
Aufplatzen *n* bursting, dehiscence; blowing-up *(of stumps)*
aufplatzend dehiscent
~/nicht indehiscent
aufplustern to fluff, to ruffle [up] *(plumage)*
aufpoltern to pile [up] *(roundwood)*
aufpumpen to pump up
aufrahmen to cream
Aufrahmen *n* creaming
Aufrahmfähigkeit *f*, **Aufrahmungsvermögen** *n* creamability
aufrecht 1. upright, erect; 2. *s.* aufrechtwachsend
~/fast suberect
Aufrechte Sammetblume *f* African marigold, Tagetes erecta
~ Trespe *f* upright (erect) brome[-grass], meadow brome[-grass], Bromus erectus
~ Waldrebe *f* ground clematis, Clematis recta
aufrechtwachsend, aufrechtwüchsig *(bot)* orthotropic, orthotropous
Aufrechtwüchsige Erdnuß[pflanze] *f* bunch-type peanut, Arachis hypogaea ssp. fastigiata
aufreißen to rip [up], to tear open
~/den Trauf (Windmantel) *(forest)* to tear open the wind mantle
aufreutern to put on racks
aufrichtbar erectile
aufrichten 1. to erect; 2. to collect *(a horse)*
Aufrichter[muskel] *m* arrector [muscle], erector muscle

Aufrichtung *f* **der Haare** piloerection *(e.g. for body heat regulation)*
Aufrollen *n* mangling *(felling against the main wind direction)*
Aufsammelerntemaschine *f* pick-up machine
aufsammeln to pick up, to gather [up]
Aufsammelpresse *f* pick-up baler (press)
Aufsammel-Rübenvollerntemaschine *f* tank-type beet harvester
Aufsammelverlust *m* gathering loss; cutter bar loss *(combining)*
Aufsattelanhänger *m* pick-up trailer
Aufsattelbeetpflug *m* semimounted lea plough
Aufsatteldrehpflug *m* semimounted reversible plough
Aufsattelgerät *n* semimounted equipment
Aufsattelkipper *m* semimounted tipping trailer
Aufsattellast *f* linkage load; *(forest)* turn size
Aufsattelpflug *m* semimounted (unit) plough
Aufsattelscheibenegge *f* offset disk harrow
Aufsattelwinkeldrehpflug *m* semimounted quarter turn plough
Aufsaugbarkeit *f* absorbability
aufsaugen to absorb, to resorb
Aufsaugen *n*, **Aufsaugung** *f* absorption, resorption
Aufschaufelbehälter *m* ladle hopper
aufscheuchen *s.* aufschrecken
aufschichten *s.* aufstapeln
Aufschlag *m (forest)* 1. seedlings from heavy seeds; 2. seedling crop (stand), regeneration, recruitment
aufschlagen 1. to nail on *(a horseshoe)*; 2. to disintegrate, to defiberize *(cellulose)*
Aufschlaggerät *n* defibrator
Aufschlämmung *f* suspension
aufschließen 1. to digest, to macerate; to predigest *(nutrients)*; 2. to open up, to make accessible *(e.g. a forest)*
~/chemisch to digest, to cook
aufschlitzen to rip
Aufschluß *m* digestion; pulping
~/alkalischer alkaline pulping
~/chemischer digestion; chemical pulping
~/halbchemischer semichemical pulping
Aufschlußgrad *m* degree of cooking *(pulp manufacture)*
Aufschlußprodukt *n* digest
aufschobern to rick, to stack, to pile [up] *(hay)*
aufschrecken to start[le], to walk up, to flush *(birds)*
aufschulen to line out
aufsetzen/die Haube to hood *(falconry)*
~/Rundholz to pile [up]
Aufsetzen *n* **eines Dreieckstapels** crib piling (stacking), cribbing
~ eines Flachstapels flat piling (stacking)
~ eines Kastenstapels box-end piling (stacking)

Aufsetzen 56

~ **eines Scherenstapels** pole stacking, end racking
~ **eines Senkrechtstapels** end piling (stacking)
Aufsiedler *m (ecol)* epizoite
~/**auf Tieren lebender tierischer** epizoon
~/**nichtparasitärer pflanzlicher** epiphyte
Aufsiedlertum *n*, **Aufsiedlung** *f (ecol)* epoecism, epoecy
aufsitzen 1. to mount, to horse, to saddle; 2. to cover *(hoofed game)*
Aufsitz[rasen]mäher *m* riding (ride-on) mower
aufspalten to split up, to cleave; *(gen)* to segregate; to dissociate; to fission
Aufspaltung *f* splitting; *(gen)* segregation; dissociation
~/**genetische** gene segregation
aufspringen *(bot)* to dehisce *(e.g. pericarp)*; to burst *(e.g. buds)*
Aufspringen *n* **der Fruchtwand** *(bot)* dehiscence
aufspringend *(bot)* dehiscent
~/**nicht** indehiscent
Aufsprühen *n* jetting *(e.g. of ectoparasiticides)*
aufspüren *(hunt)* to hunt up, to stalk, to track, to trail
aufstaken to pitchfork
aufstallen to confine, to stall [up], to house
Aufstallungssystem *n* confinement (housing) system
aufstapeln to pile [up], to stack, to bank [up]
aufstauen to dam up
aufstecken/Rauhfutter to rack [up]
aufsteigend ascendent, ascending; anabatic *(air stream)*
aufstellen/in Puppen to shock, to stook
~/**Rundhocken** to shock, to stook
aufstöbern *(hunt)* to rouse, to start
Aufstockung *f* recruitment *(game management)*
aufstoßen to eructate, to belch
Aufstoßen *n* eructation, belching *(of ruminants)*
aufsuchen/die Sitzstange to roost, to perch
auftanken to fuel, to fill up, *(Am)* to gas up
auftauen to thaw; to defrost *(foodstuff)*
Auftaulösung *f* thawing solution
Auftausalz *n* thawing (de-icing) salt
Auftauschicht *f* active layer *(in permafrost soil)*
auftreiben to drive, to turn out *(livestock)*
Auftreiben *n* **[von Vieh]** drive [of livestock], turning out [to pasture], trailing; rodeo
Auftreibung *f* **der sternalen Rippenenden** *(vet)* enlarged costochondral junction
auftrennen/in Faserrichtung to rip *(timber)*
Auftrennen *n* rip sawing, ripping
auftretend/lokal *(phyt, vet)* endemic
Auftrieb *m s.* Auftreiben
Auftrommeln *n* paying-in *(of a cable or rope)*
aufwachsen to grow up
~/**im Schluß** *(forest)* to grow in a closed stand
Aufwandmenge *f* application (dose) rate, rate (dosage) of application

Aufwandmengenempfehlung *f* dose rate recommendation
Aufwärtsbewegung *f* upward movement *(e.g. of soil water)*
aufwärtsgerichtet up-oriented, *(bot)* antrorse
aufweichen to macerate
Aufweichung *f* maceration
Aufwind *m* thermal up-current
Aufwölbung *f* blower *(of tins)*
Aufwuchs *m* growth, *(Scotland)* braird
Aufwuchsfläche *f* growing layer *(e.g. of bacteria or algae)*
aufwühlen/den Boden to root *(game)*
Aufzählung *f (forest)* enumeration [survey]
aufzäumen to bridle, to rein, to bit
aufziehen to nurse, to rear, to raise, to breed
~/**bis zum Flüggewerden** to fledge
Aufzucht *f* rearing, raising, breeding
~/**künstliche (mutterlose)** artificial rearing
~ **unter Auslaufbedingungen** range rearing
~/**vollmilchsparende** milk replacer system *(calf rearing)*
Aufzuchtanlage *f* rearing plant
Aufzuchtbatterie *f* rearing battery
Aufzuchtbetrieb *m* rearing farm; breeding enterprise
Aufzüchter *m* raiser
Aufzuchtergebnis *n* rearage, rearing proportion
Aufzuchtfutter *n* rearing feed; creep feed *(e.g. for piglets and lambs)*
Aufzuchtfuttermischung *f* rearing mix
Aufzuchtgefäß *n* **für Insekten** insectarium, insectary
Aufzuchtkäfig *m* rearing cage
Aufzuchtleistung *f* rearing performance (efficiency); mothering performance
~ **einer Sau** number of piglets raised per sow
Aufzuchtmischung *f* rearing mix
Aufzuchtperiode *f* rearing period
Aufzuchtrate *f* rearing rate
Aufzuchtstall *m* rearing (growing) house
~/**geheizter** brooder house
Aufzuchtstation *f* rearing station
Aufzuchtteich *m (pisc)* rearing (nursery) pond
Aufzuchtvermögen *n* rearing capacity; mothering ability *(of a dam)*
Aufzug *m* 1. hoist; 2. toe clip *(of horseshoe)*
~/**seitlicher** quarter clip
Aufzugnetz *n (pisc)* lift net
Augapfel *m* eyeball
Augapfelwassersucht *f (vet)* hydrophthalmia
Auge *n* 1. eye; 2. *(bot)* bud, button, pip, burgeon
• **das ~ einsetzen** to insert the bud *(in grafting)*
~/**schlafendes** dormant (latent) bud
~/**treibendes** pushing bud
Augenannahme *f* bud take *(in grafting)*
Augenanplatten *n* chip budding

Augenbohne f cowpea, southern (black-eyed) pea, Vigna unguiculata ssp. unguiculata
Augenbutter f gum
Augende n brow antler
Augenentzündung f (vet) ophthalmia
Augenerkrankung f eye disease
Augenfleck m (phyt) eyespot
Augenfleckenkrankheit f eyespot, strawbreaker (of cereals, caused by Pseudocercosporella herpotrichoides)
~ **des Kaffeebaumes** brown eyespot of coffee (caused by Cercospora coffeicola)
~ **des Weizens** foot-rot of wheat (caused by Pseudocercosporella herpotrichoides)
~ **des Zuckerrohrs** eyespot of sugar-cane (caused by Helminthosporium sacchari)
Augenfliege f autumn (face) fly, Musca autumnalis
Augenhöhle f eyehole, eye socket, orbit
Augenkammerwasser n aqueous humour
Augenkrankheit f eye disease
Augenkrebs m ocular squamous[-cell] carcinoma, cancer eye (of cattle)
Augenlederhaut f s. Lederhaut
Augenlid n eyelid
~ /**drittes** third eyelid, nictitating membrane, haw
Augenlid... s. Lid...
Augenschätzung f ocular estimate (method)
Augensteckling m eye-cutting, cutting of single eye
Augenstecklingsprüfung f, **Augenstecklingstest** m (phyt) tuber indexing [method]
Augentrost m (bot) 1. euphrasy (genus Euphrasia); 2. euphrasy, eyebright, Euphrasia officinalis
Augenveredelung f inoculation, bud (eye) grafting, budding • **eine ~ vornehmen** to inoculate, to bud[-graft]
~ /**gewöhnliche** shield budding
Augenwinkel m canthus
Augit m augite, pyroxene (non-clay mineral)
Augsproß m brow antler
Augustakrankheit f der Tulpe augusta disease of tulip (virosis)
Aujeszkysche Krankheit f (vet) Aujeszky's disease, infectious bulbar paralysis, pseudorabies, mad itch
Aujeszky-Virus n Aujeszky virus, pseudorabies virus
Auktion f auction
Aukubamosaik n **der Kartoffel** [potato] aucuba mosaic, pseudo net necrosis (virosis)
Aukube f Japanese laurel (aucuba) (1. genus Aucuba; 2. Aucuba japonica)
Aureofungin n aureofungin (fungicide)
Aureomycin n chlortetracycline, biomycin (antibiotic)
Aurikel f auricula [primrose], Primula auricula
aurikulär auricular
ausasten to prune; to [de]limb, to disbranch

Ausbringtiefe

Ausäst- und Bündelmaschine f [de]limber-buncher, delimber-bucker-buncher
ausatmen to expire, to breathe out, to exhale
Ausatmung f expiration, exhalation
Ausatmungsluft f expired (exhaled) air
Ausbau m ag[e]ing (of wine)
Ausbauchung f bellying (e.g. of a tree-trunk)
Ausbauholz n mine timber, pitwood
ausbeinen to bone [out], to debone
Ausbeinungsvorrichtung f (slaught) meat-boning facility
ausbessern (forest) to recruit, to recondition, to beat up, to replant, to fill up
Ausbeute f yield, crop, rendiment, rendement (s.a. under Ertrag)
~ /**rentable (wirtschaftliche)** economic yield
Ausbeuteverlust m yield loss
ausbilden/Gefieder to feather
~ /**Seitentriebe** to stool, to tiller, to stock
~ /**Wundkork** to cork
~ /**Zweige** to branch [out]
Ausbildung f/**forstliche** forestry education
~ /**tierärztliche (veterinärmedizinische)** veterinary education
Ausbildungsbetrieb m/**landwirtschaftlicher** training farm
Ausbindezügel m bearing-rein, standing martingale
ausblühen to effloresce, to bloom (e.g. salt crystals)
ausbluten to bleed
~ **lassen** to bleed, to exsanguinate
Ausblutung f bleeding; (vet) exsanguination
ausbracken to cull
Ausbracken n cull[ing]
ausbrechen to break out (animals)
~ /**Geiztriebe** s. ausgeizen
~ /**Knospen** to disbud
ausbreiten to spread, to diffuse, to disseminate, to propagate; to scatter
~ /**Heu** to ted
~ /**sich** to spread, to diffuse, to propagate
ausbreitend/sich lokal (regional) (phyt, vet) endemic
Ausbreitungsgeschwindigkeit f eines Feuers rate of fire spread
ausbringen to apply, to place (fertilizers, pesticides)
~ /**bandförmig** to band
~ /**breitwürfig** to [apply] broadcast
~ /**Dung** to dung
~ /**Dünger bandförmig (reihenweise)** to sidedress
~ /**flächig** to [apply] broadcast
~ /**Mulch** to mulch
~ /**reihenweise** to drill
Ausbringen n s. Ausbringung
Ausbringmenge f application rate
Ausbringtiefe f application depth

Ausbringung

Ausbringung f application, placement (e.g. of pesticides)
~ **auf den Boden** soil application
~ **aus der Luft** aerial (air-to-ground) application
~/**aviotechnische** aeroplane (aircraft) application
~/**bandförmige** band application
~/**breitflächige (breitwürfige)** broadcast (blanket) application
~ **durch Einpflügen** plough-down application
~/**ganzflächige** overall (total) application, area-application
~/**nestweise (teilflächenweise)** spot application
~ **vom Flugzeug aus** aeroplane (aircraft) application
Ausbringungsgerät n [mechanical] applicator
Ausbringungsgeräte npl application equipment
Ausbringungsmenge f application rate
Ausbringungstermin m application date
Ausbringungstiefe f application depth
Ausbruch m outbreak
ausbrüten to hatch [out], to brood, to clutch, to cover
~/**im Brutkasten** to incubate
Ausbrüten n hatching
ausdämpfen to steam out
Ausdarrungsgrad m degree of kilning (malting)
Ausdauer f persistence, persistency; endurance, staying-power, stay, stamina
ausdauernd persistent, remontant; perennial; perpetual flowering
Ausdauernde Lupine f wild lupin[e], Lupinus perennis
Ausdauernder Lein m perennial flax, Linum perenne
Ausdauerndes Bingelkraut n dog's mercury, ground elder, Mercurialis perennis
~ **Silberblatt** n perennial honesty, Lunaria rediviva
~ **Weidelgras** n [common, perennial] rye-grass, Lolium perenne
Ausdauerritt m endurance ride
Ausdehnungsgefäß n expansion tank
ausdestillieren to distil out
ausdreschen to thresh, to thrash
ausdruckslos characterless (wine)
Ausdrucksverhalten n display (of animals)
ausdünnen to thin [out], to gap
Ausdünnen n thinning
~/**chemisches** chemical thinning
~ **durch Abflammen** flame thinning
~/**maschinelles** machine thinning
Ausdünner m, **Ausdünngerät** n thinning implement, thinner, gapper
Ausdünnmaschine f thinning machine
Ausdünnmittel n s. Ausdünnungsmittel
Ausdünnung f thinning
~/**übermäßige** overthinning
~ **von Hand** hand thinning
Ausdünnungsmittel n [chemical] thinner, thinning medium

Auseinanderpflügen n splitting, casting
auseinanderrücken to space out (e.g. pot plants)
Ausfallast m loose (falling-out) knot
ausfallen to shatter, to shell, to shed (seed grains)
ausfallfest shatter-resistant, non-shattering
Ausfallfestigkeit f shattering resistance, resistance to shattering (shedding)
Ausfallfläche f open space (e.g. in a tree nursery)
Ausfallgetreide n self-sown cereal (grain)
Ausfallgetreidepflanzen fpl volunteer cereal plants
Ausfalljahr n off-year, barren year
Ausfallneigung f liability to shattering (shedding)
Ausfällung f precipitation
Ausfallverluste mpl shattering losses (of grain)
ausfaulen 1. to smother, to asphyxiate (winter cereals); 2. to digest, to cook (sewage sludge)
Ausfaulgrube f septic tank
ausfetten to oil off (cheese)
ausfischen to fish out
~/**zu stark** to overfish
Ausflockung f flocculation, coagulation
Ausflockungsmittel n flocculant, coagulating agent
Ausflug m (ent) adult emergence
Ausflugloch n (ent) emergence hole, exit (flight) hole
Ausfluß m 1. effluence, effusion, outflow, discharge; 2. outlet (site); 3. effluent, outflow (material)
Ausflußkanal m discharge (escape) channel; outlet channel (ditch), outfall (wasteway) channel; drain
ausformen (forest) to convert, to lumber, to buck, to cut into lengths, to cross-cut [into logs], to lay off
Ausformen n, **Ausformung** f (forest) conversion, bucking, cross-cutting, assortment formation, laying off
Ausformungsstrecke f cross-cutting line
Ausformungstabelle f bucking table
ausfressen/die Königin (api) to feed the queen
Ausführungsgang m duct • **ohne** ~ ductless
~ **der Gallenblase** cystic duct
Ausgangsebene f datum level (terrestrial survey)
Ausgangsgestein n bedrock, parent (solid) rock, maternal (living) rock
Ausgangsmaterial n parent[al] material
Ausgangspflanze f stock plant
Ausgangspopulation f (biom) initial population
Ausgangsstammzahl f initial number of trees
Ausgangssubstrat n parent [soil] material
ausgebaut mature, aged (wine)
ausgebreitet (bot) effuse, patulous, patent
Ausgebreitete Flammenblume f (bot) wild sweet William, Phlox divaricata
Ausgebreitetes Flattergras n wood millet[-grass], Milium effusum
ausgebuchtet emarginate[d]

ausgedünnt/von Hand hand-thinned
ausgefranst *(bot)* laciniate[d]
ausgefüllt *(bot)* farctate
ausgehen/auf Beute to prey [up]on
ausgehöhlt cavernous
ausgeizen to pinch off (out), to nip off, to snap (pluck) off suckers, to sucker, to stop
ausgemästet in grease, in pride (prime) of grease, *(Am)* chuffy
ausgenagt *(bot)* erose
ausgerandet emarginate[d]
Ausgerandeter Buchweizen *m* Japanese buckwheat, Fagopyrum [esculentum var.] emarginatum
ausgereift 1. ripe, full-grown; 2. mellow *(wine)*
ausgeschweift *(bot)* repand
ausgestorben extinct
ausgetrocknet dry
ausgewachsen full-grown, mature, adult
ausgezehrt *(vet)* cachectic
Ausgleich *m* handicap *(in horse-races)*
Ausgleichsdüngung *f* compensating (levelling) fertilization
Ausgleichspaarung *f* corrective mating *(animal breeding)*
Ausgleichsrennen *n* handicap [race]
ausgraben to dig [out, up], to grub, to lift, to unearth
aushalten *s.* ausformen
aushärten to cure, to harden [off] *(e.g. tree resin)*
aushauen 1. to clear, to cut out *(an aisle)*; 2. *s.* durchforsten
ausheben/einen Graben to ditch, to dig a ditch; to trench
Aushieb *m (forest)* selective felling (cutting), extraction felling; prelogging
~ von Überhältern final felling (cutting), extraction of old (reserve) trees
aushülsen to shell
ausklauben to pick [out]
Ausklauben *n* picking
Auskleidung *f (bot, zoo)* tapetum
ausklengen *s.* klengen
Auskratzung *f (vet)* abrasion
Auskultation *f (vet)* auscultation
auskultieren to auscultate
Auslage *f* span *(e.g. of horns)*
Auslaß *m* outlet, exit, drain
auslassen to render [down] *(fat)*
Auslaßöffnung *f s.* Auslaß
Auslauf *m* 1. exercise; 2. range, run; paddock; yard
auslaufen lassen to run *(livestock)*
Auslaufen *n* **der Milch** *(vet)* galactorrhoea
auslaufend/astlos bis zum Wipfel excurrent *(tree-trunk)*
Ausläufer *m (bot)* runner, offshoot, stolon, stole; creeping shoot • **~ bildend** rhizomatic, rhizomatous

Ausläufergras *n* sod-forming grass, sod-type grass
ausläufertreibend stolonate, stoloniferous
Ausläufertreibender Rotschwingel *m* creeping red fescue, Festuca rubra var. rubra
Auslaufhaltung *f* free-range management
Auslaufhuhn *n* open-range chicken
auslaugen to leach [away, out], to lixiviate, to macerate, to extract; *(soil)* to eluviate
Auslaugung *f* leaching, lixiviation, maceration, extraction; *(soil)* eluviation
Auslaugungshorizont *m* [b]leached horizon, eluvial horizon, A-horizon
Auslaugungsschicht *f* [b]leached layer
auslegen to set *(seed)*
Ausleger *m* jib[-boom], [crane] boom, arm
Auslegerkran *m* jib crane
Auslegerkreissäge *f* radial[-arm] saw, universal saw
Auslese *f* 1. selection *(s.a. under* Selektion*)*; 2. choice wine
~/disruptive disruptive selection
~/gerichtete directional selection
~/indirekte indirect selection
~/künstliche artificial selection
~/lineare directional selection
~/natürliche natural selection
~/negative negative selection
~/positive positive selection
~/rückgreifende recurrent selection
~/stabilisierende stabilizing selection
~/wechselseitig rückgreifende reciprocal recurrent selection
Auslese... *s. a.* Selektions...
Auslese band *n* sorting belt, sorting conveyor (elevator)
Auslesebaum *m (forest)* elite stem (tree), choice tree (stem)
Auslesedurchforstung *f* selection thinning
auslesen to select, to pick [out], to sort [out]; to rogue, to cull
Ausleseprinzip *n* selection principle
Ausleseprogramm *n* selection programme
Auslesequalität *f* fancy grade *(e.g. of fruit)*
Auslesestamm *m s.* Auslesebaum
Auslesesystem *n* selection system
Auslesetechnik *f* selection technique
Auslesewein *m* choice wine
Auslesezüchtung *f* selection breeding
auslichten to prune; to admit light, to thin
Auslichten *n* [thinning-out] pruning, [branch] thinning
~/starkes bulk pruning
Auslösungspheromon *n* releaser pheromone
Ausmahlungsgrad *m* extraction rate *(milling)*
ausmästen to feed off (up), to finish
Ausmästungsgrad *m* degree of fattening (finish), fattening grade
ausmelken to milk out, to strip

ausmelken

~/maschinell to machine-strip
Ausmelken *n* complete (strip) milking, udder stripping [out]
ausmerzen to cull, to eliminate, to weed [out]
Ausmerzung *f* cull[ing], elimination
ausmisten to muck [out], to demanure, to clear, to clean
ausnehmen to disembowel, to eviscerate, to paunch, to gut; to draw *(fowl)*; to gill *(fish)*
~/ein Nest to nest, to rob
Ausnehmen *n* evisceration
Ausnutzungskoeffizient *m* utilization coefficient
ausölen to oil off *(butter)*
auspfählen to stake out, to pole
Auspflanzbeet *n* plantation bed
auspflanzen to plant out, to set out, to bed [out]; to prick out (off), to reset *(plantlets)*
Auspflanzen *n* planting (setting) out • **zum ~ geeignet** plantable
~ **ins Freiland** field setting
auspflücken to pick (go) over
auspflügen to plough out, to finish
Auspflügen *n* finishing, finished ploughing
Auspflugfurche *f* dead (open) furrow
ausplentern *(forest)* to log selectively
auspressen to squeeze, to press out
~/Fruchtsaft to squeeze, *(Am)* to ream
ausräuchern to fumigate, to smoke [out]
Ausreife *f* maturity
ausreifen to mature, to ripen
~ **lassen** 1. to mature; 2. to mellow *(wine)*
Ausreißer *m* *(biom)* outlier
ausreiten to go for a ride
Ausrenkung *f* *(vet)* luxation
~/teilweise subluxation
Ausrichten *n* **der Sägezähne** jointing
ausroden to grub out (up), to assart
Ausrodung *f* grubbing out (up), assartment
Ausrollgrenze *f* *(soil)* lower plastic limit
ausrotten to eradicate, to exterminate, to weed [out]
Ausrottung *f* eradication, extermination
Ausrottungsmittel *n* eradicant
Ausrückefrist *f* travel time *(forest fire control)*
ausrücken *(forest)* to skid, to remove
Ausrücken *n* [pre]skidding, removal
~ **im Seilzug** cable line thinning
Ausrüstung *f* equipment, outfit, rig
Aussaat *f* 1. sowing, seeding; planting; 2. seed • **vor der ~** preplant[ing]
~/aviotechnische aerial seeding, air-sowing, aerosowing
~/breitwürfige broadcast seeding
~/direkte sowing in situ
~/einarbeitungslose surface seeding
~ **in breitem Reihenabstand** broad drill sowing, wide-space sowing
~ **in die Radspur** wheel-track planting
~/maschinelle machine planting

~ **mit dem Flugzeug** aerial seeding, air-sowing, aerosowing
~ **ohne Deckfrucht** plain sowing
~/stellenweise *(forest)* patch (partial) sowing
~ **von Hand** hand sowing
Aussaatbeet *n* seeding bed
Aussaatbegrenzung *f* planting limitation
Aussaatdichte *f* sowing density
Aussaaterde *f* seed compost
Aussaatfläche *f* sowing area; sown area
Aussaatkiste *f* seed tray
~/standardisierte modular seed tray
Aussaatmenge *f* sowing (seed, planting) rate
Aussaatmethode *f* sowing method
Aussaatmischung *f* seeding mixture
Aussaatschale *f* seed cup (pan)
Aussaatstufe *f* generation of authentic seed
Aussaattabelle *f* sowing table
Aussaattermin *m* sowing (seeding, planting) date
Aussaattiefe *f* sowing (planting) depth, depth of sowing
Aussaatverfahren *n* sowing (planting) method
Aussaatzeit *f* sowing time (season), planting season, seed-time
Aussaatzusatzgerät *n* seeder attachment
Aussackung *f*/lokalisierte *(vet)* aneurysm *(esp. of arteries)*
aussäen to sow, to seed, to plant, to bed *(s.a. under säen)*
~/breitwürfig to sow broadcast
~/im Gemenge to intercrop
~/in Reihen to drill
Ausschälung *f* *(vet)* extirpation, enucleation
ausscheiden to excrete, to secrete, to void
~/Kot to defecate, to dung
Ausscheider *m* *(vet)* shedder
Ausscheidung *f* 1. excretion; 2. *s.* Ausscheidungsprodukt
~ **von Kot** defecation
Ausscheidungsorgan *n* excretory organ
Ausscheidungsprodukt *n* excrement, excretion
Ausscheidungsprozeß *m* excretory process
~/natürlicher *(ecol, forest)* natural suppression
Ausscheidungssystem *n* excretory system
Ausscheidungsverhalten *n* excretory behaviour
ausschirren to outspan, to unharness
ausschlachten to kill out, to cut up; to dress *(poultry)*
Ausschlachtungsprozente *npl* killing-out percentage, carcass [dressing] percentage, *(Am)* cutability; dressing-out percent[age]
Ausschlag *m* 1. *(vet)* exanthema; 2. *(forest)* regrowth, understorey, coppice
Ausschlagbestand *m* coppice [stand], copse
Ausschlagbottich *m* hot-wort receiver *(brewing)*
ausschlagen 1. to bud, to sprout; to break into leaf; 2. to kick [out], to fling [back], to hoof *(horse)*; 3. to rake out *(a fire)*
~/Bierwürze to cast, to strike out

~/vom Stock to sprout from stool
Ausschlagfähigkeit f shoot-forming capacity *(of woody plants)*
Ausschlaggefäß n hot-wort receiver *(brewing)*
Ausschlagverjüngung f coppice (sucker) regeneration
Ausschlagwald m s. **Ausschlagbestand**
Ausschlagwürze f cast (finished) wort *(brewing)*
ausschlämmen to elutriate, to outwash
Ausschlämmung f elutriation
ausschlüpfen to hatch [out], to creep out; to emerge *(insects)*
Ausschlüpfen n hatching [out]; emergence *(of insects)*
ausschmelzen to render [down] *(e.g. beeswax)*
ausschneiden 1. to excise, to cut out; 2. to prune, to lop *(a tree)*
Ausschneidung f excision
ausschoten to husk, to hull, to shell
Ausschuß m 1. reject; 2. exit hole *(caused by a bullet e.g. in killed game)*
Ausschußaushieb m *(forest)* weeding
Ausschußholz n cull timber
ausschweißen lassen *(hunt)* to bleed
Ausschwitzung f exudation
Ausschwitzungsprodukt n exudate
Aussehen n appearance
Außenabteiler m s. **Außenhalmteiler**
Außendruck m external pressure
Außenfläche f facies, face *(e.g. of an organ)*
Außenhalmteiler m outer divider
Außenhandel m **mit landwirtschaftlichen Gütern** foreign agricultural trade
Außenhaut f skin
Außenkelch m *(bot)* epicalyx, calyce • **ohne ~** acalyculate
Außenleine f **[/durchgehende]** driving rein
Außenlüftertrocknungsanlage f external fan kiln
Außenohr n [external] ear
Außenparasit m ectoparasite, ectozoon
Außenrinde f [outer, dead] bark, rhytidome, *(Am)* ross
Außenrotation f outer [crop] rotation, outer sequence
Außenschale f outer shell, hull
Außenschmarotzer m ectoparasite, ectozoon
~/tierischer epizoon
Außenschmarotzertum n ectoparasitism
Außenschuh m outer shoe *(of a mounted mower)*
Außenschuhvorlauf m cutter bar lead
Außenskelett n *(zoo)* exoskeleton, ectoskeleton
Außentemperatur f outdoor (outside) temperature
Außen[weide]zaun m boundary fence
aussetzen 1. to expose; 2. to release; to plant *(fingerlings)*
~/der Sonnenstrahlung to solarize, to insolate
Aussieben n screening
aussitzen to sit *(riding)*
aussondern to select, to cull, to rogue

Australische

aussortieren to sort [out], to grade out, to reject *(s.a. aussondern)*
ausspannen to outspan, to unharness
Ausspinnbarkeit f **nach Bradford** Bradford count *(degree of wool fineness)*
Ausspritzungsgang m **[des Samenleiters]** ejaculatory duct
ausspülen to rinse (wash) out; *(vet)* to irrigate
Ausspülung f *(vet)* irrigation
ausstecken to prick [off, out]
Ausstellungskondition f show condition (ring appearance) *(of breeding cattle)*
Ausstellungstier n show animal
aussterben to die out, to become extinct
ausstocken to grub [up stumps], to clear
ausstoßen/Brunftschreie to troat
ausstrahlen to radiate, to irradiate
Ausstrahlung f radiation, irradiation, emission
Ausstrahlungsfrost m radiation[al] frost
ausstreuen to scatter, to spread
~/Samen to seed, to disseminate
Ausstreuen n scattering, dissemination
~ des Blütenstaubs pollin[iz]ation
Austauschadsorption f exchange adsorption
Austauschazidität f *(soil)* exchange[able] acidity
Austauschbelastung f *(gen)* substitutional load
Austauschdüngung f exchange fertilization
Austauschfeuchtemenge f **[/spezifische]** drying rate, rate of drying
Austauschharz n ion exchange resin
Austauschholz n substitute timber
Austauschkalk m *(soil)* exchangeable calcium
Austauschkapazität f *(soil)* exchange capacity, e.c., EC
Austauschkomplex m *(soil)* exchange complex
Austauschmaterial n *(soil)* exchange material, ion-exchange compound
Austauschwert m *(gen)* crossing-over value
Austernschalenmehl n oyster-shell flour *(feed lime)*
Austernseitling m oyster fungus (mushroom), Pleurotus ostreatus
austopfen to pot out
Austopfen n potting out
Austrag m discharge
austragen 1. to discharge; 2. to bear *(a fruit)*
Austragschnecke f discharge (unloading) auger; grain discharge auger *(of a combine)*
Australian Silky Terrier m silky terrier, silky *(dog breed)*
Australische Fuchsie f Australian fuchsia *(genus Correa)*
~ Keulenlilie f dracaena (grass) palm, giant dracena, Cordyline australis
~ Reisblume f rice flower, Pimelea ferruginea
~ Schabe f Australian cockroach, Periplaneta australasiae
~ Seideneiche f silk[y] oak, silk-bark oak, Grevillea robusta

Australische

~ **Silberakazie** f silver[green] wattle, silvergreen acacia, Acacia dealbata
~ **Silbereiche** f s. ~ Seideneiche
~ **Wachsblume** f Geraldton wax flower, Cham[a]elaucium uncinatum
~ **Wollschildlaus** f cottony-cushion scale, Icerya purchasi
Australischer Blaustengel m Australian bluestem [grass], Bothriochloa intermedia
~ **Diebkäfer** m Australian spider beetle, Ptinus tectus
~ **Kelpie** m kelpie *(dog breed)*
~ **Terrier** m Australian terrier *(dog breed)*
Australisches Lampenputzergras n dwarf fountain grass, Pennisetum alopecuroides (compressum)
Australmerino n Australian merino *(sheep breed)*
Australorp n Australorp *(poultry breed)*
austreiben 1. *(bot)* to sprout, to burgeon, to grow out, to flush, to take; 2. to turn (run) out *(cattle)*
~/**aus der Wurzel** to ratoon
~/**Blätter** to leaf [out]
~/**wieder** to revegetate *(plant)*
Austreiben n *(bot)* sprouting, burgeoning
~/**vorzeitiges** feathering *(in fruit woods)*
Austreibung f expulsion
Austreibungsphase f, **Austreibungsstadium** n expulsion stage *(birth process)*
austreten to leave *(game for browsing)*
austrocknen to dry [out], to dehydrate, to exsiccate, to desiccate; to season *(e.g. timber)*; to wither
~ **und schrumpfen/durch Kälte** to parch *(plants)*
Austrocknen n drying [out]; seasoning *(e.g. of timber)*
Austrocknung f 1. exsiccation, desiccation; 2. *(vet)* xerosis
~ **der Mundhöhle** *(vet)* aptyalism
~/**übermäßige** drying up
Austrocknungsmittel n desiccant
Austrocknungsregime n drying regime
Austrocknungsresistenz f drought hardiness
Auswachsen n preharvest germination, preharvest (premature) sprouting *(of seeds within the ears)*
Auswahl f 1. choice, selection; 2. assortment
~/**verbesserte** *(biom)* screening method (test), screening
Auswahleinheit f sampling unit
auswählen to select, to pick, to cull
Auswahlhieb m *(forest)* selection felling
Auswahlsatz m sampling fraction
Auswanderung f *(ecol)* emigration
Auswärtsdreher m supinator [muscle]
Auswärtsdrehung f supination
~ **des Lidrandes** *(vet)* ectropion
auswärtsführen to abduct *(limb)*
Auswärtsführung f abduction
auswaschen to leach [out, away], to outwash, to elutriate, to lixiviate; *(vet)* to lavage

Auswaschung f wash-out, leaching [out, away], elutriation, lixiviation; *(soil)* eluviation; *(vet)* lavage
~ **von Nährstoffen durch Regen** rain-wash
Auswaschungshorizont m *(soil)* [b]leached horizon, eluvial horizon, A-horizon
Auswaschungsverlust m leaching (wash-out) loss
Auswaschungszone f *(soil)* zone of eluviation
Ausweichstelle f lay-by, passing place, turn-out *(logging)*
Ausweichwirt m reserve (reservoir) host
ausweiden to eviscerate, to disembowel, to gut, to break up, to paunch; to gralloch, to grallock *(wildfowl)*
Ausweidung f evisceration
auswerfen 1. to eject; 2. s. ausweiden
Auswertung f evaluation
Auswintern n winter killing *(of crops)*
Auswinterung f, **Auswinterungsschaden** m winter kill, [damages by] winterkilling
Auswitterung f efflorescence *(of salt crystals)*
Auswuchs m outgrowth, excrescence, enation, emergence
~/**seitlicher** enation
Auswuchsfestigkeit f resistance to sprouting [in the ear] *(grain crops)*
Auswuchsneigung f liability to sprouting
Auswurfbogen m delivery chute
Auswurfklappe f swivelling head, deflector *(of a forage harvester)*
Auswurfkrümmer m deflector *(e.g. of a pneumatic conveyor)*
Auswurföffnung f outlet
Auswurfrohr n ejection pipe
Auswurfschacht m chute *(of a forage harvester)*
auszählen to enumerate, to tally *(a timber stand)*
Auszählung f enumeration; *(forest)* enumeration survey
auszäunen to fence off
Auszehrung f *(vet)* cachexia
~/**hungerbedingte** inanition
Auszeichenpistole f spray-gun *(timber marking)*
auszeichnen to mark
Auszeichnen n marking
~ **eines Hiebsortes** marking out of a coupe (felling site)
~ **von Laßbäumen** marking of trees as standards
Auszeichnungsschaden m gouge injury
ausziehen 1. to pull [out], to extract, to lift; 2. to extract, to leach; 3. to gralloch, to grallock *(wildfowl)*
Ausziehtopfplatte f extension cultivating tray
Auszug m extract[ive]; leachate
Autoagglutinin n autoagglutinin *(antibody)*
Autoantigen n autoantigen
Autoantikörper m autoantibody
Autochore f autochore, autochorous plant
Autochorie f autochory *(self-spreading of fruits or seeds)*

autochthon autochthonous, autochthonal, indigenous; *(soil)* sedentary
Autochthonie f autochthony
autogam *(bot, zoo)* autogamic, autogamous, orthogamous
Autogamie f autogamy, orthogamy, self-fertilization, self-fructification; self pollin[iz]ation
Autograder m autograder
Autohaemorrhoe f *(ent)* exudation
Autoimmunisierung f auto-immunization
Autoimmunität f auto-immunity
Autoimmunkrankheit f auto-immune disease, immunologic disease
Autoinfektion f *(phyt, vet)* autoinfection
Autoinokulation f autoinoculation
Autointoxikation f *(vet)* auto-intoxication, self-poisoning
Autokarpie f autocarpy
Autokatalyse f autocatalysis
Autökie f autoecism
Autoklav m [steam] autoclave
autoklavieren to autoclave
Autökologie f autecology, physio-ecology
autökologisch autecological
Autokonservierung f sealed storage *(e.g. of cereals)*
Autolysat n autolysate
Autolyse f autolysis
autolytisch autolytic
Automatenfütterung f automatic feeding
Automatisierung f **der Ernte** harvest automation
Automixis f automixis
Automutagen n *(gen)* automutagen
Automutilation f *(vet)* self-mutilation
Autoparasitismus m autoparasitism
Autoparthenogenese f autoparthenogenesis
Autopathie f *(phyt)* autopathy
autopathisch autopathic
autophag autophagic
Autophagie f autophagy *(of starving animals)*
Autophän n *(gen)* autophene
autoploid *(gen)* autoploid
Autoploide m autoploid
Autoploidie f autoploidy
~/intraindividuelle spontane endopolyploidy
autopolyploid *(gen)* autopolyploid
Autopolyploide m autopolyploid
Autopolyploidie f autopolyploidy
Autopsie f *(vet)* autopsy, post-mortem
Autopsiebefund m autopsy findings
Autoradiographie f autoradiography, radioautography
Autoregulation f autoregulation
Autosensibilisierung f auto-immunization
Autosom n *(gen)* autosome, euchromosome
autosomal autosomal
autotetraploid *(gen)* autotetraploid
Autotetraploide m autotetraploid
Autotetraploidie f autotetraploidy

Autotomie f autotomy
Autotransplantat n *(vet)* autograft
Autotransplantation f autografting
autotroph autotrophic
Autotrophie f autotrophy
Autotropismus m *(bot)* autotropism
Autotoxikose f autotoxicosis
Autotoxin n autotoxin
autotoxisch autotoxic
Autotoxizität f autotoxicity
Autovakzine f autovaccine
Autovakzinierung f autovaccination
Autoxidation f autoxidation
Autozidverfahren n autocidal control [tactics], sterile male (release) technique *(genetical pest control)*
Autözie f autoecism
autözisch aut[o]ecious, autoicous
Auwald m s. Auenwald
Auxanogramm n auxanogram
Auxanograph m auxanograph
Auxanographie f auxanography
Auxanometer n auxanometer, auximeter
Auxin n auxin *(growth regulator)*
~/natürliches natural growth hormone *(phytohormone)*
Auxintransporthemmstoff m auxin-transport inhibitor
Auxois-Pferd n Auxois *(horse breed)*
Avaram n *(bot)* tanner's cassia, Cassia auriculata
Avenazin n avenacin *(cereal glycoside)*
Avenin n avenin *(alkaloid)*
Avermectin n avermectin *(anthelminthic)*
Avezid n avicide
aviär avian
Avidin n avidin *(egg-white constituent)*
Avidität f avidity *(immunology)*
Avifauna f avifauna *(of an area)*
aviotechnisch aerial
avirulent avirulent
Avirulenz f avirulence
A-Virus-Mosaik n *(phyt)* mild mosaic *(of potato)*
avitaminös avitaminous
Avitaminose f avitaminosis
Avitellinose f *(vet)* avitellinosis *(caused by helminths of genus Avitellina)*
Avocado f 1. avocado [pear] *(fruit)*; 2. s. Avocadobaum
Avocadobaum m 1. avocado *(genus Persea)*; 2. avocado [pear], alligator pear, Persea americana
Avocadobirne f s. Avocado 1.
Avocado[birnen]futtermehl n avocado meal
Avocato... s. Avocado...
Avoparcin n avoparcin *(antibiotic)*
Avotan n avotan *(antibiotic)*
Awassi[schaf] n Awassi *(sheep breed)*
ÄWP s. Äquivalentwelkepunkt
AWV s. Ackerbohnenwelkevirus

Axenie

Axenie f axeny *(inhospitality of an organism against parasites)*
Axerophthol n axerophthol, vitamin A
Axialdreschwerk n rotary threshing device
Axialflußmähdrescher m axial-flow combine [harvester], rotor combine
Axialflußpumpe f axial-flow pump, propeller pump
Axialgebläse n, **Axiallüfter** m axial fan, axial-flow blower
Axialpumpe f axial-flow pump, propeller pump
Axialschlag m axial knock, *(Am)* chatter *(of a circular saw-blade)*
Axialventilator m axial fan, axial-flow blower
Axilla f *(bot)* axil; axilla *(animal anatomy)*
axillar, axillär axillary
Axillarknospe f axillary (lateral) bud
Axis m *(bot, zoo)* axis; main axis
Axishirsch m axis [deer], chital, Axis axis
Axon n axon *(of the nerve cell)*
Axt f axe, ax, single-bladed axe, *(Am)* single-bitted axe
Axtauge n [axe-]eye
Axtbahn f [axe-]face, side, flat
Axtblatt n axe-blade
Axthaupt n, **Axthelm** m [axe-]head
Axtkeil m axe wedge
Axtöhr n [axe-]eye
Axtschalm m axe-blaze
Axtstiel m axe-handle, axe-helve
Aylesburyente f Aylesbury *(duck breed)*
Ayrshirerind n Ayrshire [cattle] *(breed)*
A-Zahn m peg tooth *(of a saw)*
Azalee f azalea, Rhododendron simsii, Azalea indica
Azaleengallmilbe f azalea gall-mite, Phyllocoptes azaleae
Azaleenmotte f azalea leaf miner (roller), rhododendron slender, Gracilaria azaleella
Azaleentopf m azalea pot
Azaleenwelke f cylindrocladium disease of rhododendron *(caused by Cylindrocladium scoparium)*
Azamethiphos n azamethiphos *(insecticide)*
Azarolbaum m Mexican hawthorn, Crataegus pubescens
Azaroldorn m *(bot)* azarole, Crataegus azarolus
Azauracil n azauracil *(cytostatic)*
azellulär acellular
azentrisch acentric
azephal acephalous
Azepromazin n acepromazine *(neuroleptic)*
Azetimeter n, **Azetometer** n acetometer, acetimeter
Azetometrie f acetometry, acetimetry
Azidämie f acidaemia
azidifizieren to acidify
Azidifizierung f acidification
Azidimeter n acidimeter
Azidimetrie f acidimetry
Äzidiospore f *(bot)* aeci[di]ospore

Azidität f 1. acidity; 2. sourness
~/aktive *(soil)* active (actual) acidity
~/hydrolytische *(soil)* hydrolytic acidity
~/potentielle potential acidity
Äzidium n *(bot)* aeci[di]um
azidophil acidophilic, acidophil[e], acidophilous, oxyphil[e]
Azidophilusmilch f acidophilous milk
azidophob acidophobic
Azidophyt m acidophyte
Azidose f *(vet)* acidosis
~/metabolische metabolic acidosis
azidotisch acidotic
azidotolerant acidotolerant, acid-tolerant
Azidurie f aciduria
Azimutalkreis m azimuthal (graduated) circle, protractor *(surveying)*
azinös *(bot, zoo)* acinose, acinous
Azinphos-ethyl n azinphos-ethyl *(acaricide, insecticide)*
Azinphos-methyl n azinphos-methyl *(insecticide)*
Aziprotryn n aziprotryne *(herbicide)*
Aziridin n aziridine *(chemosterilant)*
Azithiram n azithiram *(fungicide)*
Azobe f scrubby oak, Lophira lanceolata (alata)
Azocyclotin n azocyclotin *(acaricide)*
azonal *(soil, ecol)* azonal
Azoospermie f azoospermia
Azoprotein n azoprotein
Azorische Kriechheide f Azores St. Daboec's heath, Daboecia azorica
Azotämie f azotaemia
Azotobakter m(n) azotobacter *(genus Azotobacter)*
Azotobakterin n azotobacterin
Azotobakterium n azotobacter *(genus Azotobacter)*
Azoturie f *(vet)* azoturia, Monday morning disease
Azoverbindung f azo compound
Azulen n azulene *(hydrocarbon)*
azurblau sky-blue
Azurblauer Salbei m blue (Pitcher) sage, Salvia azurea [var. grandiflora]
Azygospore f azygospore
Azygote f azygote
azyklisch acyclic
azymisch azymic, azymous

B

B s. 1. Berkshire; 2. Brauner; 3. Bestockungsgrad
BA s. Benzyladenin
Babassuöl n babassu oil
Babassupalme f babassu *(genus Orbignya)*
Babcock-Test m Babcock method (test) *(for milk fat determination)*
Babesi[ell]ose f *(vet)* babesiasis, babesiosis, nuttalliosis, red-water [disease], blackwater

Bakterienauflösung

Babes-Negri-Körperchen *n* Negri body *(in the nerve cells of rabid animals)*
Babtitoxin *n* cytisine *(alkaloid)*
Babybeef *n* baby beef
Bach *m* brook, rivulet, burn, *(Am)* run
Bachbett *n* ditch
Bachbunge *f*, **Bachbungenehrenpreis** *m (bot)* brooklime, Veronica beccabunga
Bache *f* old wild sow, [wild] sow
Bachforelle *f* common (brown) trout, Salmo trutta ssp. fario
Bachminze *f* water mint, Mentha aquatica var. aquatica
Bachneunauge *n* brook lamprey, Lampetra planeri
Bachsaibling *m* brook (speckled) trout, American char, Salvelinus fontinalis
Bacitracin *n* bacitracin *(antibiotic)*
Backe *f* cheek, chap, jowl
Backeigenschaft *f* baking property
backen to bake; to cake *(e.g. fertilizers)*
Backenbremse *f* unarmed horse bot-fly, Gasterophilus inermis
Backendrüse *f*/**dorsale** zygomatic gland *(of carnivores)*
Backenstück *n* cheek [strap], cheekpiece *(of a bridle)*
Backenzahn *m* cheek tooth
~/großer (hinterer) molar [tooth]
~/kleiner (vorderer) premolar [tooth]
backfähig bakable
Backfähigkeit *f* bakability; caking power
Backfähigkeitsverlust *m* loss of caking power
Backhähnchen *n s.* Brathähnchen
Backhefe *f* bread yeast
Backobst *n* dried fruit[s]
Backobstkäfer *m* dried fruit beetle, Carpophilus hemipterus
Backobstmilbe *f* dried fruit mite, Carpoglyphus lactis
Backpflaume *f* prune, dried plum
Backqualität *f* baking quality
Backsteinkäse *m* brick cheese
Backversuch *m* baking test
Backwaren *fpl* bakery products, baker's ware
Backweizen *m* bread[making] wheat
Bacon *m* bacon
Baconschwein *n* bacon pig, baconer
Bacterium *n s.* Bakterium
Bactopen *n* cloxacillin *(antibiotic)*
Bactospein *n* bactospeine *(insecticide)*
Bacto-strip-Verfahren *n* bacto-strip method *(for bacterial count)*
baden/im Staub to dust[-bath]
Badischer Femelschlag *m s.* Femelschlag/Badischer
Baelbaum *m* bael, Bengal quince, Aegle marmelos
Bagasse *f* bagasse *(residue esp. of sugar-cane extraction)*
Bagger *m* excavator; dredger
Baggerboot *n* dredging boat
Bahiagras *n* bahia grass, Paspalum notatum
Bahia-Piassavapalme *f* piassava-palm, Attalea funifera
Bahnverladepunkt *m* railroad loading point
Baileys Akazie *f* Coatamundra wattle, Acacia baileyana
Bakteriämie *f (vet)* bacteriaemia
Bakterie *f s.* Bakterium
bakteriell bacterial
Bakterielle Blattfleckenfäule *f* der Sammetblume bacterial leaf spot of African marigold *(caused by Pseudomonas tagetes)*
~ Blattfleckenkrankheit *f* der Gurke angular leaf spot of cucumber *(caused by Pseudomonas lachrymans)*
~ Blattfleckenkrankheit *f* der Pelargonie bacterial blight of pelargonium *(caused by Xanthomonas pelargoni and Pseudomonas erodii)*
~ Blattfleckenkrankheit *f* der Tomate bacterial leaf spot of tomato *(caused by Xanthomonas vesicatoria)*
~ Blatt- und Fruchtfleckenkrankheit *f* der Tomate bacterial speck of tomato *(caused by Pseudomonas syringae tomato)*
~ Braunfäule *f* brown rot, southern bacterial wilt *(of potato, caused by Pseudomonas solanacearum)*
~ Braunflecken *mpl* des Kulturchampignons bacterial blotch of mushroom *(caused by Pseudomonas tolaasii)*
~ Fruchtfleckenkrankheit *f* der Tomate bacterial speck of tomato *(caused by Pseudomonas syringae tomato)*
~ Gurkenwelke *f* bacterial wilt of cucumber[s] *(caused by Erwinia tracheiphila)*
~ Naßfäule *f (phyt)* bacterial soft rot
~ Nierenkrankheit *f* bacterial kidney disease *(of salmonoids)*
~ Salatfäule *f* bacterial rot of lettuce *(esp. caused by Pseudomonas marginalis)*
~ Stengelgrund- und Wurzelfäule *f* der Chrysantheme bacterial blight of chrysanthemum *(caused by Erwinia chrysanthemi)*
~ Tomatenwelke *f* bacterial canker of tomato *(caused by Corynebacterium michiganense)*
~ Weichfäule *f (phyt)* bacterial soft rot
Bakterieller Bohnenbrand *m* common blight of bean[s] *(caused by Xanthomonas phaseoli)*
bakterienabtötend bactericidal
Bakterienabtötungsmittel *n* bactericide, antibacterial [agent]
Bakterienabwehrstoff *m* [/körpereigener] bacteria inhibitor
Bakterienaktivität *f* bacterial activity (action)
Bakterienantagonismus *m* bacterial antagonism
Bakterienantigen *n* bacterial antigen
bakterienauflösend bacteriolytic
Bakterienauflösung *f* bacteriolysis

Bakterienausscheidung 66

Bakterienausscheidung *f* mit dem Harn bacteriuria
Bakterienbrand *m (phyt)* 1. bacterial blight; 2. bacterial [blossom blight and] canker *(of stone fruit, caused by Pseudomonas syringae)*
Bakterienchlorophyll *n* bacteriochlorophyll
Bakteriendünger *m* bacterial fertilizer (manure)
Bakterieneiweiß *n* bacterial protein
Bakterienembolie *f (vet)* bacterial embolism
Bakterienenzym *n* bacterial enzyme
Bakterienfärbung *f* bacteria staining
Bakterienfäule *f (phyt)* bacterial rot
Bakterienfilter *n* bacteria-excluding filter
Bakterienfleckenkrankheit *f (phyt)* bacterial spot disease
Bakterienflora *f* bacterial flora
Bakteriengalle *f (phyt)* bacterial gall
Bakteriengärung *f* bacterial fermentation
Bakteriengift *n* bacteriotoxin, bacterial toxin
bakterienhemmend bacteriostatic
Bakterienhemmstoff *m* bacteriostat[ic]
Bakterienhemmung *f* bacteriostasis
Bakterienimpfstoff *m* bacterin *(a vaccine made of suspended killed or attenuated bacteria)*
Bakterieninhibitor *m* bacteria inhibitor
Bakterienkolonie *f* bacterial colony
Bakterienkrebs *m (phyt)* crown gall *(caused by Agrobacterium tumefaciens)*
Bakterienkultur *f* bacterial culture
Bakterienpräparat *n* bacterial preparation
Bakterienprotein *n* bacterial protein
Bakterienringfäule *f* der Kartoffel potato ring rot, [bacterial] ring rot of potato *(caused by Corynebacterium sepedonicum)*
Bakterientätigkeit *f* bacterial action (activity), activity of bacteria
bakterientötend bactericidal
Bakterientotimpfstoff *m s.* Bakterienimpfstoff
Bakterientransformation *f (gen)* bacterial transformation
Bakterientriebfäule *f* des Flieders lilac blight *(caused by Pseudomonas syringae)*
Bakterienwachstum *n* bacterial growth
bakterienwachstumshemmend bacteriostatic
Bakterienwachstumshemmung *f* bacteriostasis
Bakterienwelke *f (phyt)* bacterial wilt
~ **der Nelke** bacterial wilt of dianthus *(caused by Pseudomonas caryophylli)*
~ **der Tomate** bacterial canker of tomato *(caused by Corynebacterium michiganense)*
~ **des Tabaks** bacterial wilt of tobacco *(caused by Pseudomonas solanacearum)*
Bakterienwelkekrankheit *f s.* Bakterienwelke
Bakterin *n s.* Bakterienimpfstoff
Bakteriochlorophyll *n* bacteriochlorophyll
Bakterioid *n* bacteroid *(genus Bacteroides)*
bakteriologisch bacteriologic[al]
Bakteriolyse *f* bacteriolysis
Bakteriolysin *n* bacteriolysin *(antibody)*

bakteriolytisch bacteriolytic
Bakteriophag[e] *m* bacteriophage, phage
Bakteriophagie *f* bacteriophagy
Bakteriose *f* bacteriosis, bacterial disease
Bakteriostase *f* bacteriostasis
Bakteriostatikum *n* bacteriostat[ic]
bakteriostatisch bacteriostatic
Bakteriotoxin *n* bacteriotoxin
Bakteriozezidie *f (phyt)* bacterial gall
Bakteriozin *n* bacteriocin *(antibacterial protein)*
bakteriozinogen bacteriocinogenic
Bakteriozinogenie *f* bacteriocinogenicity *(hereditary ability to produce bacteriocin)*
Bakterium *n* bacterium, schizomycete *(class Bacteriophyta)*
~/**aerobes** aerobic bacterium
~/**anaerobes** anaerobic bacterium
~/**bewegliches** vibrion
~/**cellulosespaltendes** cellulose-splitting bacterium
~/**denitrifizierendes** denitrifying bacterium, denitrifier
~/**nitrifizierendes** nitrifying bacterium, nitrobacterium, nitrifier
~/**pyogenes** pyogenic bacterium
~/**säurebildendes** acid-forming bacterium, acid former (producer)
~/**stäbchenförmiges [sporenbildendes]** bacillus
~/**stickstoffbindendes** nitrogen-fixing bacterium, nitrogen-fixer
Bakteriumvirus *n* bacteriophage, phage
Bakteriurie *f* bacteriuria, bacilluria
bakterizid bactericidal
Bakterizid *n* bactericide, antibacterial [agent]
Baktofuge *f (dairy)* bactofuge
Baktofugierung *f* bactofugation
Baktrisches Kamel *n* Bactrian (two-humped) camel, Camelus bactrianus
Balanitis *f (vet)* balanitis
Balanoposthitis *f (vet)* balanoposthitis
Balantidienruhr *f*, **Balantidiose** *f (vet)* balantidiasis, balantidiosis *(caused by Balantidium coli)*
Balata *f* balata *(latex product; a polyterpene)*
Balatabaum *m* balata, bully tree, Manilkara bidentata, Mimusops balata
Balbaum *m* bael, Bengal quince, Aegle marmelos
Balbianiring *m* Balbiani ring *(of giant chromosomes)*
Baldrian *m (bot)* valerian *(genus Valeriana)*
Baldrianöl *n* valerian oil
Baldriansäure *f* valeric (pentanoic) acid
Baldrianwurzel *f* valerian [root]
Balearischer Buchsbaum *m* Balearic box [tree], Buxus balearica
Balfours Kiefer *f* Balfour's (foxtail) pine, Pinus balfouriana
Balg *m* fur, hide, skin *(esp. of small animals)*
Balggeschwulst *f (vet)* atheroma

Balkan-Forsythie f European forsythia, Forsythia europaea
Balkan-Kaschkawal m Kachkaval cheese
Bälkchen n trabecula (e.g. in muscle fibres)
bälken to rafter
Balkenbock[käfer] m s. Hausbock[käfer]
Balkenmähwerk n cutter bar mower
Balkenschröter m little stag-beetle, Dorcus parallelopipedus
Balkonkasten m balcony (window) box, flower trough
Balkonpflanze f balcony (window box) plant
Ballast[stoff] m bulky material
Ballen m 1. bale (of hay or straw); ball (of roots); 2. ball, pad (animal anatomy); heel (of the hoof) • in ~ **verpacken** to ball • **zu ~ pressen** to bale
Ballenabroller m bale unroller
Ballenauflöser m bale shredder
Ballenaufnehmer m bale pick-up
Ballenaufsammelgerät n bale collector (accumulator)
Ballenaufsammelwagen m bale pick-up wagon
Ballenausheber m ball lifter
Ballenbewässerung f ball watering
Ballendichte f bale density
Balleneinwickelmaschine f bale wrapper
Ballenförderanlage f bale handling system
Ballenförderer m bale conveyor (elevator, handler)
Ballenfördergebläse n bale blower, pneumatic bale conveyor
Ballenfördersystem n bale handling system
Ballengebläse n bale blower, pneumatic bale conveyor
Ballengeschwür n footpad dermatitis, bumble foot (of fowl)
Ballenheu n baled hay
Ballenheutrockner m baled hay dryer
Ballenladegabel f bale loading fork
Ballenladegerät n, **Ballenlader** m bale loader
Ballenladewagen m bale [pick-up] wagon
Ballenleistung f baling capacity (of a baling press)
Ballenpacker m bale packer
Ballenpflanze f root ball plant, ball[ed] plant, ball-rooted seedling
~/verkaufsfertige ball and burlap
Ballenpflanzung f ball planting
Ballenpresse f baling (pick-up) press, [pick-up] baler
Ballenrutsche f bale chute (slide)
Ballensammelgerät n s. Ballensammler
Ballensammelmaschine f s. Ballenschleppe
Ballensammelwagen m bale pick-up wagon
Ballensammler m bale collector (accumulator)
Ballenschleppe f, **Ballenschlitten** m bale sledge, sledge bale collector
Ballenschurre f bale chute (slide)
Ballenspaten m, **Ballenstecher** m circular spade

Ballenstechmaschine f circular spade machine, root balling machine
Ballenstroh n baled straw
Ballenumschlag m bale handling
Ballenwagen m bale wagon
Ballenware f ball and burlap
Ballenwerfer m bale thrower
Ballenwickler m round baler, roto-baler
Ballenzähler m bale counter
Ballenzählvorrichtung f bale counter
ballieren to ball
Balliermaschine f root balling machine
Ballon m **für die Holzrückung** logging balloon
Ballonblume f balloon flower, Chinese bell-flower, Platycodon grandiflorus
Ballonpflanze f balloon vine, heart-seed, heart-pea, Cardiospermum halicacabum
Ballonrückung f (forest) balloon yarding
Ballonzitze f balloon teat
Ballottement n (vet) ballottement
Ballungsgebiet n (ecol) agglomeration area
Balsa n balsa[-wood]
Balsabaum m balsa, Ochroma pyramidale (lagopus)
Balsaholz n balsa[-wood]
Balsam m balsam, balm, balsamic resin
Balsamapfel m balsam apple, Momordica balsamina
Balsambaum m 1. balsam torchwood, Amyris balsamifera; 2. tolu [balsam-]tree, Myroxylon balsamum [var. balsamum]
Balsambirne f bitter gourd, balsam pear, Momordica charantia
Balsamgurke f s. Balsambirne
Balsamine f balsam, snapweed, impatiens, (Am) jewelweed (genus Impatiens)
balsamisch balsamic
Balsamkraut n costmary, alecost, Chrysanthemum majus (balsamita)
balsamliefernd balsamiferous
Balsampappel f balsam poplar, balm of Gilead, tacamahac, Populus balsamifera [var. balsamifera]
Balsamtanne f balsam [fir], silver (subalpine) fir, balm of Gilead, Abies balsamea
Balsamtannenharz n Canada balsam (from Abies balsamea)
Baltischer Strandhafer m purple (hybrid) marram, Ammocalamagrostis x baltica
Balz f mating, pairing, treading (of wildfowl)
Balzflug m nuptial flight
Balzgeschrei n mating cry
Balzplatz m [bird's] mating-place, playing ground, lek
Balzruf m mating-call
Balzverhalten n courtship behaviour, display (of male birds)
Balzzeit f mating (pairing) season

Bambaraerdnuß

Bambaraerdnuß f bamba[r]ra [ground]nut, Congo goober, earth pea, underground bean, Voandzeia (Vigna) subterranea
Bambus m bamboo *(genera Bambusa, Arundinaria, Dendrocalamus)*
Bambusbohrer m *(ent)* smaller bamboo shot-hole borer, Dinoderus minutus
Bambusgras n bamboo grass, Hymenachne amplexicaulis
Bambusrohr n bamboo cane
Bambusschößling m, **Bambusspitze** f s. Bambussproß
Bambussproß m bamboo shoot *(as vegetable)*
Bambuswald m bamboo forest
BäMV s. Bärenklaumosaikvirus
Banane f 1. banana, plantain *(genus Musa)*; 2. banana, plantain, Musa x paradisiaca; 3. banana *(fruit)*
Bananenblattlaus f banana aphid, Pentalonia nigronervosa
Bananenfleckenkrankheit f banana leaf spot [disease], sigatoka disease [of bananas] *(caused by Mycosphaerella musicola)*
Bananengewächse npl banana family *(family Musaceae)* • **die ~ betreffend** musaceous
Bananenmehl n banana meal
Bananenrüßler m banana root weevil, Cosmopolites sordidus
Bananenstaude f banana tree (plant)
Bananenwelke f Panama disease *(of banana, caused by Fusarium oxysporum f.sp. cubense)*
Band n 1. band; belt; 2. ligament, taenia *(animal anatomy)*
Bandage f bandage
Bandagenverfahren n bandage (banding) treatment *(of wood impregnation)*
bandagieren to bandage
Bandanlage f conveying system
bandartig [angeordnet] banded
Bandausleser m sorting belt
~ zur Saatgutreinigung frictional seed cleaner
Bandbehandlung f band treatment *(of plant stands e.g. with protectants)*
Bandbrenner m strip burner *(for weed control)*
Bandchlorose f *(phyt)* banded chlorosis
Banddüngerstreuer m placement drill
Banddüngung f band (row) fertilization, row (side) dressing, band placement of fertilizers
Bande f band *(spectrum)*
Bandenmuster n *(gen)* banding pattern
Bänderton m *(soil)* banded (bandy) clay, ribbon (varved) clay
Bandförderer m belt (band) conveyor, conveyor belt
Bandfutterverteilungsanlage f feed distributing conveyor
Bandhaft f syndesmosis *(animal anatomy)*
Bandmaß n tape-measure
Bandmosaik n *(phyt)* line mosaic (pattern) *(virosis)*

~ der Pflaume plum line pattern
~ der Süßkirsche cherry line pattern
~ des Pfirsichs peach (apricot) line pattern
Bandmuster n line pattern *(of various plant viroses)*
Bandrechwender m belt-type side [delivery] rake
bandreich ligamental, ligamentary *(animal anatomy)*
Bandrollegge f band roller (rotary) harrow
Bandsaat f band seeding (sowing), sowing in strips
Bandsaatschar n band sowing coulter
Bandsäge f band-saw, belt (ribbon) saw
~/doppelte twin band-saw
~/einfache single[-cutting] band-saw, single-edge[d] band-saw, narrow band-saw
~/zweiseitig bezahnte double-cutting band-saw, double-edge[d] band-saw
Bandsägeblatt n band-saw blade, saw band
Bandsägemaschine f s. Bandsäge
Bandsägemühle f s. Bandsägewerk
Bandsägerät n band drill
Bandsägewerk n band sawmill
~ für Dünnholz pony mill
Bandsämaschine f strip (band) seeder
Bandsäschar n band sowing coulter
Bandscheibe f intervertebral disk
Bandspritze f s. Bandspritzgerät
Bandspritzgerät n band sprayer (applicator), [down-the-row] strip sprayer
Bandspritzung f band spraying
Bandspritzvorrichtung f s. Bandspritzgerät
Bandstreuer m, **Bandstreugerät** n band spreader, placement drill
Bandstreuvorrichtung f band spreading attachment
Bandtrockner m band (belt) dryer, conveyor (apron) dryer
Bandwaage f band weigher, weigh belt, [belt] conveyor scale
Bandweide f [common, velvet] osier, Salix viminalis
Bandwurm m tapeworm, cestode [worm], cestoid *(class Cestoda)*
Bandwurmbefall m *(vet)* cestodiasis, t[a]eniasis
Bandwurmfinne f tapeworm larva, measle
Bandwurmglied n proglottid
Bandwurmkopf m scolex
Bandwurmmittel n taeniacide
Bangsche Krankheit f *(vet)* brucellosis *(caused by Brucella spp.)*
Bank f bench *(e.g. of a plant nursery)*
Bankbeet n bench (raised, trough) bed
Bankettmäher m [ditch] bank mower, bank cutter
Bankivahuhn n [red] jungle fowl, Gallus gallus (bankiva)
Bankkalb n veal calf
Banksia f *(bot)* banksia *(genus Banksia)*
Bankskiefer f Banksian (jack) pine, Pinus banksiana

Banksrose f banksia rose, Rosa banksiae
Bankulnuß f candlenut
Bankulnußbaum m candlenut[-tree], Aleurites moluccanus
Bannforst m, **Bannwald** m closed forest
Banse f bay, mow *(of a barn)*
Bantam[huhn] n bantam *(breed of fowl)*
Banteng n *(zoo)* banteng, Bos javanicus
Banyanbaum m banian[-tree], banyan, Bengal fig, Ficus benghalensis
Baobab m baobab, monkey-bread, calabash tree, Adansonia digitata
Bär m 1. bear *(family Ursidae)*; 2. s. Bärenspinner
Barbadoskirsche f Barbados (West Indian) cherry, acerola, Malpighia glabra
Barbadosstachelbeere f Barbados gooseberry, blade apple, lemon vine, Pereskia aculeata
Barban n barban *(herbicide)*
Barbarakraut n yellow rocket, winter-cress, Barbarea vulgaris
Barbe f 1. barbel, barb *(genus Barbus)*; 2. barbel, barb, Barbus barbus
Barbenkraut n American cress *(genus Barbarea)*
Barbenregion f barbel zone
Barbet m barbet *(dog breed)*
Barbital n barbital *(anaesthetic)*
Barbiturase f barbiturase *(enzym)*
Barbiturat n barbiturate *(salt, ester or derivative of barbituric acid)*
Bärenhatz f, **Bärenhetze** f bear-baiting
Bärenhöhle f bear den
Bärenjagd f bear-hunting
Bärenjunges n cub
Bärenklau m 1. cow-parsnip, hogweed *(genus Heracleum)*; 2. cow-parsnip, hogweed, bear's-breech, Heracleum sphondylium; 3. s. Akanthus
bärenklaublättrig acanthifolious
Bärenklaumosaikvirus n cow-parsnip mosaic virus
Bärenlauch m ramson[s], bear's (wild) garlic, Allium ursinum
Bärenohr n 1. African daisy *(genus Arctotis)*; 2. bear's ear, Arctotis venusta (grandis)
Bärenraupe f s. Bärenspinnerraupe
Bärenschote f milk-vetch, Astragalus glycyphyllos
Bärenspinner m tiger-moth *(family Arctiidae)*
Bärenspinnerraupe f *(ent)* leaf-tier, leaf-tyer, webworm, woolly-bear [caterpillar]
Bärentraube f [red] bearberry, Arctostaphylos uva-ursi
Barfrost m black (soil-lifting) frost
bärig sein to be at (in, on) heat *(sow)*
Barillekraut n *(bot)* kali, Salsola kali
Bärin f sow
Barium n barium
Barkenspitz m keeshond *(dog breed)*
Bärlapp m club moss *(genus Lycopodium)*
Bärlappgewächs n club moss *(order Lycopodiales)*

Bärme f barm
Barnevelder n Barnevelder *(chicken breed)*
Barogramm n barogram
Barograph m barograph
Barometer n barometer, rainglass
barometrisch barometric
Barpflanzung f *(forest)* bar-rooted planting, open-rooting planting
Barrandit m barrandite *(non-clay mineral)*
Barred Plymouth Rock n Barred Plymouth Rock *(striped variety of the Plymouth Rock chicken breed)*
Barrierekultur f barrier crop
Barr-Körper m Barr body *(of female somatic cells)*
Barrosa-Rind n Barroso *(cattle breed)*
Barsch m 1. perch *(genus Perca)*; 2. common (river) perch, Perca fluviatilis
Barsoi m borzoi, Russian wolfhound *(dog breed)*
Bart m 1. beard, sloven, tombstone, *(Am)* barber's chair *(tree-trunk injury at the felling cut surface)*; 2. vane *(of bird's feather)*
Bartel f *(zoo)* barb[el], cirrus
Bartfaden m *(bot)* beard-tongue, pentstemon *(genus Penstemon)*
Bartflechte f beard moss *(genus Usnea)*
Bartgras n 1. beard grass *(genus Andropogon)*; 2. Gamba grass, Andropogon gayanus; 3. East Indies bluestem, Bothriochloa (Andropogon) ischaemum; 4. goat grass, Triticum vagans, Aegilops ovata; 5. [Ceylon] citronella grass, citronella, Cymbopogon nardus [var. nardus]
Bartgrasöl n citronella
Barthafer m bearded oat, slender [wild] oat, Avena barbata
Bartiris f [tall-]bearded iris, German iris, Iris germanica
Bartirismosaikvirus n bearded iris mosaic virus
Bartnelke f sweet william, London tuft, Dianthus barbatus
Bärwurz f *(bot)* baldmoney, spignel, spicknel, Meum athamanticum
Baryt m barite *(non-clay mineral)*
basal basal; basilar[y]
Basalfäule f der Gladiole scab of gladiolus *(caused by Pseudomonas gladioli)*
~ **der Narzisse** fusarium rot of narcissus *(caused by Fusarium oxysporum f.sp. narcissi)*
Basalglied n **der Antenne** *(ent)* scape
~ **des Insektenbeins** coxa
Basalknoten m *(bot)* basal node
Basalration f basal ration (diet), basic ration (diet)
Basalsteckling m basal cutting
Basalstoffwechsel m basal metabolism (energy exchange), basal (standard) metabolic rate, BMR
Basaltboden m basal soil
Basaluminit m basaluminite *(non-clay mineral)*
Base f base

Basellkartoffel 70

Basellkartoffel f *(bot)* ulluco, olluco, Ullucus tuberosus
basenarm *(soil)* base-poor, base-deficient
Basenaustauschkomplex m cation-exchange complex
Basengehalt m base content *(s.a.* Basizität*)*
basengesättigt base-saturated
basenhaltig base-containing
Basenji m Basenji *(dog breed)*
basenliebend basophilic, basophilous
basenmeidend basifugal
Basenpaaraustausch m *(gen)* base pair substitution
basenreich base-rich
Basensättigung f base saturation
Basensättigungsgrad m base saturation percentage, degree of base saturation
Basenüberschuß m base excess, BE
basenungesättigt base-unsaturated
Basenzustand m base status
Basidie f basidium
Basidiomyzet m basidiomycete, palisade fungus *(class Basidiomycetes)*
Basidiospore f basidiospore
basilar *(bot, zoo)* basilar[y]
Basilienkraut n, **Basilikum** n 1. basil *(genus Ocimum)*; 2. [European] sweet basil, basil, balm, Ocimum basilicum
Basilikumöl n basil oil
basipetal *(bot)* basipetal
Basiphyt m basiphyt
Basis f base • **zur ~ gehörend** *(bot, zoo)* basilar[y]
Basisabfluß m ground-water discharge (run-off), ground-water seepage
basisch basic, alkaline
Basisdurchmesser m butt [end] diameter *(timber mensuration)*
Basislatte f subtense bar *(terrestrial survey)*
Basisschlepper m basic tractor
Basisschutt m *(soil)* basal detritus
Basistraktor m basic tractor
Basistrieb m basal shoot
Basiszahl f *(gen)* basic number
Basiszucht f foundation breeding
Basiszuchtbetrieb m foundation breeder company
Basitonie f *(bot)* basitony
Basizität f basicity, alkalinity
~ des Bodens soil alkalinity
basophil basophilous
Basophiler m basophil[e]
Basse f solitary boar
Basset [Hound] m basset[-hound] *(breed)*
Bassie f *(bot)* mawro, Bassia latifolia
Bassin n basin
Bast m 1. bast, liber; 2. velvet *(of antlers or horns)*
• **den ~ abreiben** to fray (to burnish, to rub off) the antlers (e.g. at tree-trunks)
~/abgefegter fraying *(from antlers or horns)*
Bastard m bastard, hybrid, cross, mongrel
~/[genetisch] entfernter wide hybrid

~/intergenerischer intergeneric hybrid (cross)
~/vegetativer vegetative hybrid
Bastardamarant m smooth pigweed, prince's feather, Amaranthus hybridus (hypochondriacus)
Bastardeberesche f Finnish whitebeam, Sorbus x hybrida
Bastardfuchsschwanz m green amaranth, Amaranthus hybridus convar. hybridus
Bastardgoldregen m golden chain tree, Laburnum x watereri
bastardierbar hybridizable
bastardieren to hybridize
Bastardierung f hybridization *(s.a.* under Hybridisation*)*
~/intergenerische intergeneric hybridization
Bastardindigo m 1. amorpha *(genus Amorpha)*; 2. bastard indigo, Amorpha fruticosa
Bastardklee m alsike [clover], Trifolium hybridum
Bastardluzerne f bastard (sand) lucern[e], variegated alfalfa, Medicago sativa ssp. falcata x ssp. sativa, Medicago x varia
Bastardplatane f London plane[-tree], Platanus x hybrida (x acerifolia)
Bastardsagopalme f fish-tail palm, Caryota urens
Bastardteakbaum m Indian (Malabar) kino tree, Pterocarpus marsupium
Bastardvitalität f hybrid vigour, heterosis
Bastardweidelgras n hybrid rye-grass, Lolium hybridum (multiflorum x perenne)
Bastardwüchsigkeit f s. Bastardvitalität
Bastfaser f bast [fibre]
Bastkäfer m bast beetle
Bastpalme f raffia palm, Raphia farinifera (ruffia)
Bastpalmfaser f raffia, raphia
Bastparenchym n soft bark
Bastschäler m bast stripper
Bastteil m *(bot)* phloem
Bastverband m bast bandage (layer), raffia bandage *(in grafting)*
Batate f 1. sweet (Spanish) potato, batata, kumara, *(Am)* yam, Ipomoea batatas; 2. sweet potato, batata, *(Am)* yam *(tuberous root from 1.)*
Batatenkäfer m 1. sweet potato weevil, Cylas formicarius; 2. sweet potato weevil, Cylas brunneus
Batchkultur f batch culture
Batokopflaume f Madagascar plum, Flacourtia indica
Batterie f 1. [cage] battery; 2. [storage] battery
Batterieaufzucht f battery rearing
Batterieblock m battery block
Batteriefütterung f battery feeding
Batteriehaltung f battery husbandry (keeping), battery [cage] management
Batteriehauptschalter m battery main switch
Batterieheckenschere f battery hedge trimmer
Batteriekäfig m battery cage
Batteriekrankheit f der Hühner cage paralysis of fowls, cage layer fatigue
Batteriemast f battery fattening

Bätze f bitch
Bau m 1. building, construction; 2. burrow, earth (e.g. of fox or rabbit) • **aus dem ~ treiben** to unearth
Bauch m abdomen; belly; side (cut of meat)
Bauchatmung f abdominal respiration
Bauchbruch m (vet) abdominal hernia
Bauchdecke f abdominal wall
Bauchfell n peritoneum (animal anatomy)
Bauchfellentzündung f (vet) peritonitis
Bauchfellflüssigkeit f peritoneal fluid
Bauchfellhöhle f peritoneal cavity
Bauchfett n abdominal fat
Bauchflosse f pelvic fin
Bauchfurche f crease (of a caryopsis)
Bauchfuß m (ent) proleg
~/reduzierter abdominal appendage (of geometrids)
Bauchfüß[l]er m gastropod, gasteropod (class Gastropoda)
Bauchgurt m belly-band, surcingle (of a harness)
Bauchhernie f (vet) abdominal (ventral) hernia
Bauchhoden m abdominal testicle
Bauchhöhle f abdominal cavity • **in die ~ hinein** intraperitoneal • **innerhalb der ~** intraperitoneal
Bauchhöhleneröffnung f (vet) laparotomy
Bauchhöhlenträchtigkeit f abdominal (extrauterine) pregnancy
bauchig (bot, zoo) ventricose
Bauchluftsack m abdominal air sac (of fowl)
Bauchnervengeflecht n abdominal brain, solar plexus
Bauchplatte f sternite (of arthropods)
Bauchriemen m s. Bauchgurt
bauchseitig ventral
Bauchspeck m belly bacon
Bauchspeichel m pancreatic juice
Bauchspeichelamylase f amylopsin (enzyme)
Bauchspeicheldrüse f pancreas
Bauchspeicheldrüsenentfernung f (vet) pancreatectomy
Bauchspeicheldrüsenhauptausführungsgang m pancreatic duct
Bauchspeicheldrüsenhormon n pancreatic hormone, insulin
Bauchspeicheldrüsensaft m pancreatic juice
Bauchstäuber m chest-type hand duster
Bauchwand f abdominal wall
Bauchwandbruch m (vet) abdominal hernia
bauchwärts ventral
Bauchwassersucht f (vet) dropsy of the belly (peritoneum), ascites
~ der Karpfen/[akute, aszidide, aszitische] infektiöse infectious carp dropsy, spring viraemia of carp, SVC
Bauchwolle f belly wool
Bauen n/landwirtschaftliches farm-building construction
Bauer m farmer; peasant, countryman, hind

Bäuerin f farmerette, woman farmer; countrywoman, peasant woman
bäuerlich rustic
Bauernbank f agricultural bank
Bauernbutter f farmhouse butter
Bauernforstwirtschaft f farm forestry
Bauerngarten m cottage garden
Bauernhaus n farmhouse, farm dwelling
Bauernhof m farmstead, steading, barnyard
Bauernmarkt m farmer market
Bauernrhabarber m cypress spurge, Euphorbia cyparissias
Bauernschaft f farming community; peasantry
Bauernsenf m 1. shepherd's-purse, shovelweed, blind (case) weed, Capsella bursa-pastoris; 2. penny-cress, stinkweed, Thlaspi arvense
Bauerntabak m common tobacco, Nicotiana rustica
Bauernverband m farmer's association
Bauernvereinigung f farmer union
Bauernwald m farm forest (woodland, woodlot)
Bauersfrau f s. Bäuerin
Bauholz n [building, structural] timber, construction[al] timber
~/rundes spar (up to 20 cm diameter)
Baum m tree, arbor • **auf einen ~ klettern** to tree (game) • **einem ~ die Fällrichtung geben** to gun
~/abgestorbener (abständiger) dead[-standing] tree, snag, stub
~/aus ästhetischen Gründen wertvoller amenity tree
~/balsamliefernder balsam [tree]
~/bohnenähnliche Früchte tragender bean tree
~/dammarliefernder dammar, damar (esp. of genera Agathis and Shorea)
~/das Kronendach [weit] überragender emergent tree
~ der Reisenden traveller's tree, Ravenala madagascariensis
~/ebenholzliefernder ebony (comprehensive term)
~/fehlerhafter defective tree
~/flachwurzelnder shallow-rooted tree
~/fruchttragender fruiter
~/gefallener deadfall (due to aging or rotting)
~/geköpfter pollard
~/geringwertiger filler (silviculture)
~/gipfeldürrer rampike
~/hängengebliebener lodged (hang-up) tree, (Am) deadman
~/harzhaltiger (Am) greasewood
~ im ertragsfähigen Alter bearing-age tree
~ im Stangenholzstadium pole
~/im Wachstum zurückbleibender laggard
~/im Wachstum zurückgebliebener stunted tree
~/junger sapling, maiden tree
~/kautschukliefernder rubber (caoutchouc) tree
~/kleinkroniger compact tree
~/lackharzliefernder varnish-tree

Baum

~/**laubabwerfender** deciduous (broad-leaved) tree
~/**liegender** *(Am)* downtree
~/**lückenfüllender** filler *(silviculture)*
~ **mit niedriger Krone** low-headed tree
~ **mit Rückeschäden** bruised tree
~ **mit Stammverlängerung** central leader tree
~ **mit Zwischenveredelung** stem piece tree, tree with intermediate graft
~/**rotholzliefernder** redwood
~/**schattenliefernder (schattenspendender)** shade tree
~/**schwachwachsender** dwarf tree
~/**sommergrüner** *s.* ~/laubabwerfender
~/**stammtrockener** *s.* ~/abgestorbener
~/**terpentin[öl]liefernder** turpentine tree
~/**umgestürzter** deadfall *(due to aging or rotting)*
~/**ungeharzter** virgin tree, *(Am)* round tree
~/**untergebauter** underplant
~/**wildwachsender** wild[l]ing
~/**wipfeldürrer** rampike
Baumabtötung *f* **durch chemikalienbeschichtete Bandagen** dry packing
baumähnlich *s.* baumartig
Baumalter *n* tree age
Baumanalyse *f* tree (stem) analysis
Baumart *f* tree species
~/**bestandesbildende** forest-forming [tree] species
~/**lichtliebende** light-demanding tree species
~/**schattentragende** shade-bearing tree species, shade-bearer
~/**standortgemäße** climax tree species
~/**unerwünschte** undesirable tree species
~/**unterstandbildende** understorey species
~/**waldbaulich wertlose** secondary [tree] species
~/**waldbildende** forest-forming [tree] species
Baumartenanteil *m* percentage of tree species
Baumartenklassifikation *f* classification of tree species
Baumartenmischung *f* tree species mixture, composition of tree species
Baumartenwahl *f* choice of tree species, tree species selection
Baumartenwechsel *m* alternation (succession, change) of tree species, species conversion
baumartig tree-like, arborescent, arboraceous, arboreal, dendroid
Baumartige Hortensie *f (bot)* snowhill hydrangea, Hydrangea arborescens
~ **Lavatere** *f* tree mallow, Lavatera arborea
Baumastschüttler *m* branch shaker
Baumausheber *m* tree lifter
Baumband *n* tree wall
Baumbestand *m* [tree] stand
~/**für spätere Nutzung belassener** reserve
baumbestanden wooded, timbered
baumbewohnend arboricole, tree-dwelling
Baumblüte *f* 1. blossom [of a tree]; 2. blossoming season • **während der** ~ while the trees are in blossom
Bäumchen *n* small tree, arbuscle

bäumchenartig arbuscular
Baumchirurg *m* tree surgeon
Baumchirurgie *f* tree surgery
Baumdahlie *f* bell tree dahlia, candelabra dahlia, Dahlia imperialis
Baum-Derbholzvolumen *n* tree volume above 7 cm diameter
Baumdurchmesser *m* tree diameter
Bäume *mpl***/einer Baumklasse zugehörende** tree class
~ **[in] einer Höhenklasse** height class [of trees]
bäumeliebend dendrophilous
bäumen/sich to prance, to rear *(e.g. horse)*
Baumepiphyt *m* tree epiphyte
Baumerntemaschine *f* tree harvester (harvesting machine)
Baumerziehung *f* tree training (formation)
Baumfalke *m* hobby, Falco subbuteo
Baumfällmaschine *f* tree felling machine, feller, *(Am)* faller
Baumfällung *f* tree felling
Baumfarm *f* tree farm
Baumfarn *m* tree fern, Cyathea australis
Baumfeldwirtschaft *f* combination of forestal and agricultural crops
Baumform *f* tree shape (form)
baumförmig tree-shaped, dendriform
Baumformklasse *f (forest)* form class
Baumformzahl *f (forest)* tree form factor
Baumfreund *m* 1. philodendron, parlour ivy, sweetheart plant *(genus Philodendron)*; 2. common philodendron, Philodendron scandens
Baumfrucht *f* tree fruit
Baumgarten *m* tree-garden, arboretum
Baumgerüst *n* main scaffold, framework
Baumgestalt *f s.* Baumform
Baumgrenze *f* tree-line, timber-line; tree-limit
~/**alpine** tree-line
~/**polare** tree-limit
Baumgrün *n* tree foliage, green matter
Baumgrundfläche *f (forest)* tree basal area
Baumgruppe *f* group of trees, grove, hurst
~/**alleinstehende** clump [of trees]
Baumgurke *f* bilimbi[ng] *(fruit from Averrhoa bilimbi)*
Baumgürtel *m* belt [of trees]
Baumhackmaschine *f* tree chipper
Baumharz *n* tree resin
Baumhasel *f* Turkish filbert (hazel), tree hazel, cluster nut, Corylus colurna
Baumhecke *f* tree wall
Baumheide *f* brier, briar, tree heath, Erica arborea
Baumhöhe *f* [total] tree height, height of tree
Baumhöhenmesser *m* dendrometer
Baumhöhenwachstum *n* tree height growth
Baumhöhenzuwachs *m (forest)* accretion in height
Baumhöhle *f* tree cavity
Baumholz *n* 1. timber stand; 2. old-growth timber
Baumholzalter *n s.* Baumholzstadium

Baumschutzgebiet

Baumholzformzahl f tree-wood form factor
Baumholzstadium n tree (young timber) stage
Baumholz[volumen]tafel f tree volume table
Bauminjektion f tree injection
Baumkante f wane, rough (dull) edge, natural bevel *(of converted timber)*
baumkantig waney, rough-edged, unedged
Baumkauz m tawny (wood) owl, Strix aluco
Baumklasse f *(forest)* tree class • **einer ~ zugehörende Bäume** tree class
Baumklassifikation f classification of tree species
Baumkluppe f [tree] calliper, [tree] caliper
Baumkohl m marrow-stem kale, marrow cabbage, Brassica oleracea convar. acephala var. medullosa
Baumkrankheit f tree disease
Baumkratzer m bark (tree) scraper
Baumkrone f tree-top, [tree] crown, head of a tree *(s.a. under Krone)*
~/abgestorbene black top
Baumkronen... s. a. **Kronen...**
Baumkronenschluß m crown closure (contact)
Baumkronenumriß m canopy [cover], tree canopy
Baumkultur f arboriculture
Baumkunde f dendrology
Baumkundiger m, **Baumkundler** m dendrologist, arborist
Baumleiche f dead[-standing] tree, snag, stub
baumlos treeless, bald
Baumlupine f tree lupin[e], Lupinus arboreus
Baumluzerne f moon trefoil, Medicago arborea
Baummarder m pine marten, Martes martes
Baummeißel m pruning chisel
Baummesser m s. **Baummeßgerät**
Baummesser n pruning knife (hook)
Baummeßgerät n dendrometer
Baummeßkunde f dendrometry, forest mensuration (measurement)
Baummeßschreiber m dendrograph
Baummörder m *(bot)* bitter-sweet *(genus Celastrus)*
Baumnadel f [tree] needle
Baumobst n, **Baumobstarten** fpl tree fruit[s], top fruit[s]
Baumobsternte f tree fruit harvest
Baumökologie f dendroecology
Baumorchidee f *(bot)* dendrobium *(genus Dendrobium)*
Baumpfahl m [tree-]prop, stake, post, stick • **an einen ~ [an]binden** to stake
Baumpflanzer m tree grower
Baumpflanzung f tree plantation
Baumpflanzungstag m Arbor Day *(esp. in USA and Australia)*
Baumpflege f tree care, care of trees
Baumphysiologie f tree physiology
Baumratte f American grey squirrel, Sciurus carolinensis

baumreich silvan
Baumreife f harvest maturity *(of tree fruit)*
Baumreihe f row (strip) of trees
Baumreißer m bark blazer, scribe, scratcher, race *(marking tool)*
Baumrinde f [tree] bark
Baumrodegabel f tree lift fork
Baumrodegerät n tree extractor (uprooting device), forest devil
Baumrodemaschine f tree-dozer
Baumrodung f grub felling, assart[ment]
Baumruine f abandoned tree *(s.a. Baumleiche)*
Baumrüttelmaschine f, **Baumrüttler** m s. **Baumschüttelmaschine**
Baumsaatgutbestand m forest seed stand
Baumsaftzucker m sap sugar
Baumsäge f pruning saw, handsaw; garden saw
Baumsämling m tree seedling
Baumsavanne f tree savanna[h]
Baumschaft m s. **Baumstamm**
Baumscheibe f tree-grid
Baumscheibenplatte f tree base flagstone
Baumschere f [pruning] shears, [tree-]pruner, [pair of] secateurs, averruncator, clipper
~/einschneidige anvil pruning shears
~/zweischneidige scissor-action pruning shears
Baumschicht f tree layer (storey)
Baumschläfer m forest dormouse, Dryomys nitedula
Baumschlinge f 1. periploca *(genus Periploca)*; 2. silk vine, Periploca graeca
Baumschnitt m [tree] pruning
~/maschineller power (mechanical) pruning
~/regelmäßiger regular pruning
Baumschnittechnik f pruning technique
Baumschnittgerät n tree pruner
Baumschnittmaschine f power pruning saw
Baumschnittwerkzeug n pruning tool
Baumschnittwunde f pruning wound (cut)
Baumschulbestand m nursery stock
Baumschulbetrieb m nursery firm
Baumschule f [tree] nursery, nursery of [woody] stock, orchard
~ für Containerpflanzen container nursery
~ zur Anzucht verschulter Pflanzen transplant (lining-out) nursery
Baumschuler m nurseryman
Baumschulerzeugnisse npl nursery stock
Baumschulfachmann m nurseryman
Baumschulfruchtfolge f nursery rotation
Baumschulgehilfe m nursery hand
Baumschulgehölze npl nursery stock
~/fertige (veredelte) maiden trees
Baumschulpflanzen fpl nursery stock
Baumschulpflanzmaschine f nursery tree planter
Baumschulspaten m nursery spade
Baumschüttelmaschine f, **Baumschüttler** m tree shaker (knocker)
Baumschutzgebiet n tree sanctuary

Baumsiedlerorchidee

Baumsiedlerorchidee f buttonhole orchid *(genus Epidendrum)*
Baumspitze f s. Baumkrone
Baumstamm m tree[-trunk], trunk, [tree] stem, bole, shaft, boll
~/junger maiden tree
~/versteinerter dendrolite
Baumstamm... s. Stamm...
Baumsteiggerät n [tree] climbing device
Baumsteppe f tree steppe
Baumsterben n dying-off of trees
Baumstreifen m/**herbizidbehandelter** herbicide strip
Baumstumpf m [tree] stump, stock, stub, stob; stool
~/spitzer snag
Baumstumpfrodemaschine f stump puller (grubber, extractor), stumper, [stump] eradicator
Baumstütze f tree prop (brace, support)
Baumtabak m tree tobacco, Nicotiana glauca
Baumtomate f tree-tomato, tamarillo, Cyphomandra betacea
baumtötend arboricidal
Baumtundra f tree tundra
Baumverpflanzmaschine f tree transplanter (mover)
Baumversteinerung f dendrolite
Baumwacholder m prickly juniper (cedar), Juniperus oxycedrus [ssp. oxycedrus]
Baumwachs n grafting-wax
Baumwachstum n tree growth
Baumwanze f shieldbug, pentatomid bug *(family Pentatomidae)*
Baumweißling m *(ent)* black-veined white, Aporia crataegi
Baumwipfel m tree-top, summit, tip
Baumwipfel... s. Wipfel...
Baumwollanbau m cotton growing
Baumwollanbaugürtel m cotton belt
baumwollartig cottony
Baumwollbakteriose f bacterial blight of cotton *(caused by Xanthomonas malvacearum)*
Baumwollballen m cotton bale *(around 218 kg)*
Baumwollbaum m *(bot)* bombax *(genus Bombax)*
Baumwollblattlaus f cotton aphid, melon (orange) aphid, Aphis gossypii
Baumwollboden m cotton soil
Baumwolle f 1. cotton *(genus Gossypium)*; 2. cotton *(yarn, fabric)*
~/feldgeerntete seed cotton
~/langstapelige long-staple cotton, bony cotton
~/unaufbereitete seed cotton
baumwollen cotton
Baumwollentkernung f cotton ginning
Baumwollentkernungsmaschine f cotton gin
Baumwollerntemaschine f cotton harvester
Baumwolleule f s. 1. Ägyptische Baumwollraupe; 2. Amerikanischer Baumwollkapselwurm
Baumwollfaser f cotton fibre, cotton

Baumwollfeinheit f cotton count
Baumwollgallenälchen n cotton root-knot nematode, Meloidogyne incognita
Baumwollgin m [cotton] gin
Baumwollgürtel m cotton belt
Baumwollkapsel f cotton boll
Baumwollkapselkäfer m [cotton-]boll weevil, Anthonomus grandis
Baumwollkapselsammelmaschine f stripper-type cotton harvester, cotton stripper
Baumwollkapselwurm m cotton bollworm, [corn] earworm *(comprehensive term)*
Baumwollkuchen m cotton-cake
Baumwollöl n cotton-seed oil
Baumwollpflücker m cotton picker
Baumwollpflückmaschine f cotton picker
Baumwollsaat f cotton-seed
Baumwollsaathülse f cotton-seed hull (husk)
Baumwollsaatkuchen m cotton-cake
Baumwollsaatmehl n cotton-seed meal
Baumwollsaatöl n cotton-seed oil
Baumwollsämaschine f cotton planter
Baumwollsamen m cotton-seed • ~ **entfasern** to delint
~/gossypoldrüsenloser glandless cotton-seed
Baumwollsamenkapselschale f cotton-seed hull (husk)
Baumwollschwanzkaninchen n cottontail [rabbit] *(genus Sylvilagus)*
Baumwollstengelroder m cotton stem puller
Baumwollwanze f *(ent)* cotton stainer *(genus Dysdercus)*
Baumwollwurzelgallenälchen n cotton root-knot nematode, Meloidogyne incognita
Baumwollwurzelfäule f cotton root rot *(caused by Phymatotrichum omnivorum)*
Baumwucherer m *(bot)* dendrobium *(genus Dendrobium)*
Baumwuchs m tree growth
Baumwuchsform f tree habit
Baumwunde f tree wound
Baumwürger m bitter-sweet, staff-tree *(genus Celastrus)*
Baumwurzel f tree root *(for compounds s. under Wurzel)*
Baumzahlverteilung f tree frequency
Baumzucht f arboriculture
Baumzüchter m tree breeder, arboriculturist
Baumzüchtungsprogramm n tree-breeding programme
Baurahmen m *(api)* building frame
Bausatz m kit
Bauschnittholz n sawn structural timber, structural sawnwood, *(Am)* [yard] lumber
Baustoffwechsel m anabolism, constructive (synthetic) metabolism
Bauverhalten n building behaviour *(of animals)*
Bauwesen n/**ländliches** rural construction
Baycillin n propicillin *(antibiotic)*

Baycor *n* baycor *(fungicide)*
Bayerischer Femelschlag *m s.* Femelschlag/Bayerischer
Bayerisches Braunvieh *n* Bavarian Brown Swiss *(cattle breed)*
Bayerit *m* bayerite *(non-clay mineral)*
Baymicin *n* sisomicin *(antibiotic)*
Baypen *n* mezlocillin *(antibiotic)*
Bayrumbaum *m* bayberry, Pimenta racemosa (acris)
bazillär bacillary
Bazillariophyt *m* diatom
Bazilleninfektion *f* bacillosis
Bazillurie *f* bacteriuria
Bazillus *m* bacillus
BBH *s.* Bootsbauholz
BCG-Impfstoff *m* BCG [vaccine]
B-Chromosom *n* B chromosome
BCM *s.* Benomyl
BCPE chlorfenethol *(acaricide)*
BE *s.* Bestandeseinheit
Beagle *m* beagle *(dog breed)*
Beagle Elizabeth *m* pocket beagle *(dog breed)*
beanspruchen to stress; to strain
Beanspruchung *f* stress; strain; load[ing]
bearbeitbar workable; tillable *(soil)*
~/leicht easy-working *(soil)*
~/schwer refractory *(e.g. wood)*
Bearbeitbarkeit *f* workability
bearbeiten to work, to cultivate, to husband, to till *(a soil)*; to work *(e.g. materials)*; to treat
~/mit dem Gänsefußmesser (Gänsefußschar) to duckfoot
~/mit dem Grubber to cultivate
~/mit dem Pflanzholz to dibble
~/mit dem Rotavator to rotavate
~/mit dem Tieflockerer to chisel
~/mit dem Messeregge to scarify
~/mit der Scheibenegge to disk
~/übermäßig [mechanisch] to overcultivate
~/zwischenreihig to intertill
Bearbeitung *f* cultivation, tillage; treatment
~/bodenschonende conservation tillage
~/züchterische breeding work
~/zwischenreihige intertillage
Bearbeitungseigenschaft *f* working property
Bearbeitungsmethode *f* method of cultivation
Bearbeitungstiefe *f* working depth, depth of work
Bearded Collie *m* bearded collie *(dog breed)*
beastet branched, branchy, branching, ramose
~/schwach subramose
Beastung *f* branching, branchiness
Beaufortskala *f* Beaufort [wind] scale
bebaubar cultivable, tillable *(soil)*
Bebaubarkeit *f* cultivability
~ des Bodens land capability
bebauen to cultivate, to farm, to crop, to till
bebaut under crop, cropped
Bebauung *f* cultivation, crop, culture

bebeilen to axe, to hew
beblättert leaved, leafed, foliate
bebrüten to brood, to incubate, to hatch, to sit on
bebrütet hard set *(egg)*
Bebrütung *f* brooding, incubation
Becher *m* cup, bucket; *(bot)* scyphus, scypha
becherartig cupular, cupulate
Becherelevator *m* bucket[-type] elevator
Becherflechte *f (bot)* cladonia *(genus Cladonia)*
Becherförderer *m* cup (bucket) conveyor
becherförmig cupular, cupulate, acetabuliform; *(bot)* scyphose, cyathiform, urn-shaped
Becherkätzchen *n* silk-tassel tree, garrya *(genus Garrya)*
Becherkeim *m (zoo)* gastrula
Becherkeimbildung *f* gastrulation
Becherkette *f* cup conveyor
Becherkettenförderer *m* cup (bucket) conveyor
Becherketten[lege]mechanismus *m* chain-cup drop mechanism
Becherling *m* cup fungus, peziza *(genus Peziza)*
Bechermalve *f* tree mallow *(genus Lavatera)*
Becherpflanze *f* cup-plant, Silphium perfoliatum
Becherprimel *f* top primrose, Primula obconica
Becherradkartoffellegemaschine *f* cup-feed potato planter
Becherspore *f (bot)* aeci[di]ospore
Becherwerk *n* bucket[-type] elevator
Becherzelle *f* goblet cell *(animal anatomy)*
Becken *n* 1. basin, pool; 2. pelvis *(animal anatomy)*
Beckenausgang *m* pelvic outlet
Beckenband *n* pelvic ligament
Beckenbewässerung *f* basin irrigation
Beckenboden *m* pelvic floor
Beckenbruch *m (vet)* pelvic fracture
Beckeneingang *m* pelvic inlet
Beckenendlage *f* pelvic (posterior) presentation
Beckenfuge *f* symphysis
Beckengliedmaße *f* pelvic limb, hind limb (leg)
Beckengürtel *m* pelvic girdle
Beckenhöhle *f* pelvic cavity
Beckenlage *f s.* Beckenendlage
Beckmanngras *n* 1. Beckman's (slough) grass, Beckmannia eruciformis; 2. American slough grass, Beckmannia syzigachne
Bedarfsdränung *f* non-steady drainage, random system of drainage
bedecken 1. to cover, to coat; 2. to hood *(a falcon)*; 3. *s.* belegen
~/mit Erde to earth [up, over], to mould
~/mit Mehltau to mildew
~/mit Rasen to turf, to sod
~/mit Stroh to straw
~/sich mit neuer Haut to skin *(wound healing)*
~/sich mit Rasen to sward
~/sich mit schaumigem Schweiß to lather *(horse)*
~/sich mit Schuppen to scale

bedecktfrüchtig

bedecktfrüchtig *(bot)* angiocarpic, angiocarpous
Bedecktsamer *m (bot)* angiosperm *(division Angiospermae)*
bedecktsamig angiospermous
Bedeckung *f* covering
Bedeckungsmaterial *n* cladding material *(e.g. for glasshouses)*
Bedeckungstiefe *f* depth of covering *(in sowing)*
Bedeguar *m (phyt)* bedeguar *(of the rose-bush, caused by Rhodites roseae)*
Bedeutung *f* **des Waldes/landeskulturelle** indirect forest effect, non-wood beneficial effect, welfare function of a forest
Bedienanleitung *f* rule of operation
Bedienelement *n* control
Bedienkomfort *m* operational comfort
Bedienperson *m* operator
~ **für Landmaschinen** farm machinery operator
Bedienung *f* 1. operation, handling; 2. s. Bedienperson
Bedienungsanleitung *f*, **Bedienungsanweisung** *f* 1. rule of operation; 2. instruction book
Bedienungsstand *m* platform
Bedienungsvorschrift *f* rule of operation
bedingt/pflanzlich phytogenous
Bedingungen *fpl*/**experimentelle** experimental conditions
~/**meteorologische** meteorological conditions
Bedlingtonterrier *m* Bedlington [terrier] *(dog breed)*
bedornt thorny, thorned
Bedsonieninfektion *f* **des Geflügels** *(vet)* ornithosis *(caused by Chlamydia psittaci)*
Beef Shorthorn[rind] *n* beef shorthorn *(cattle breed)*
Beefmaster *m* Beefmaster *(cattle breed)*
beeinflussen/die Keimstimmung to vernalize
beeinträchtigen to impair, to harm; to diminish *(e.g. quality)*
beenden/die Brunftzeit to cease rutting
Beere *f* berry • **Beeren bilden** to berry
Beerenapfel *m* Siberian crab-apple, Malus baccata var. baccata, Malus sibirica
Beerenbüschel *n s.* Beerentraube
beerenförmig berry-shaped, bacciform, baccate, aciniform, acinose, acinous
Beerenhochstamm *m* standard berry tree (bush)
Beerenkräuter *npl* berry herbs
Beerenmalve *f* sleeping hibiscus, Malvaviscus arboreus
Beerenobst *n* berry fruit[s], berries, soft (small, cane) fruit
Beerenobstanlage *f* berry plantation (planting)
Beerenobstpflückmaschine *f* ground fruit picker, berry-picking machine
Beerenobstvirose *f* small fruit virosis (virus disease)
Beerenpflanze *f* berry plant
beerenreich acinose, acinous

Beerenrispe *f* panicle
Beerenstrauch *m* berry-bush, berry-bearing shrub
beerentragend berried, bacciferous, baccate
Beerentraube *f* berry cluster, cluster of berries
Beerenwanze *f* 1. shieldbug, pentatomid bug *(family Pentatomidae)*; 2. sloe bug, Carpocoris (Dolycoris) baccarum
Beet *n* 1. bed; plot patch; 2. land *(ploughing)*
Beetalziege *f* Beetal goat *(breed)*
Beetanbau *m* bed[ding] cultivation
Beetausformung *f* formation of beds *(e.g. in a nursery)*
Beetbewässerung *f* bed irrigation
Beete *f s.* Bete
Beeteinfassung *f* [bed] border
Beetformer *m* bed shaper
Beetformung *f* bed forming
Beetfüllgerät *n* bed filler
Beetfurche *f* open furrow
Beetgrabenbau *m* bedding
Beetkante *f* bed edge
Beetkultur *f* 1. bed[ding] cultivation; 2. bed crop
Beetpflanze *f* bedding plant, bedder
Beetpflug *m* conventional (one-way) plough, runround plough, on-land plough, non-reversible mould-board plough
Beetpflügen *n* ploughing in lands
Beetscharpflug *m* non-reversible mould-board plough
Beetstaude *f* flower-bed perennial
Beetsystem *n* bed system
Beettiefpflug *m* conventional deep digger plough
Beetwinde *f* bed winch
Befahrbarkeit *f* trafficability
Befall *m (phyt, vet)* infestation, affection; attack; invasion
~/**lokal begrenzter** spot infestation
befallen to infest, to affect; to attack
befallen infested, affected; attacked
~/**von Brandpilzen** smutted
~/**von Mehltau** mildewed, mildewy
~/**von Parasiten** parasitized
~/**von Phomafäule** *(phyt)* gangrenous
~/**von Ratten** ratty
~/**von Rost[pilzen]** rusty
~/**von Schmarotzern** parasitized
~ **werden/von Brand** *(phyt)* to blight
Befallsanalyse *f* infestation analysis
Befallsareal *n* infested area
Befallsflug *m* infestation (attack) flight *(e.g. of aphids)*
Befallsfrequenz *f* infestation frequency
Befallsgrad *m* degree of infestation, infestation level
Befallshäufigkeit *f* infestation frequency
Befallsherd *m* focus of infestation
Befallsintensität *f* intensity of attack
Befallskurve *f* infestation curve
Befallsprognose *f* infestation prognosis

Befallsstadium *n* infestive stage
Befallsstärke *f* intensity of attack
Befallssymptom *n* symptom of attack
befestigen 1. to fix, to fasten; 2. to consolidate *(e.g. soil)*; to stabilize *(e.g. an embankment)*; to make up *(e.g. a road)*
~/Ableger (Absenker) mit Haken to peg down
~/durch Strauchpflanzung to bush
~/mit einem Kabel (Seil) to cable
Befestigung *f* fixation
~ von Sanden sand fixation (stabilization), stabilization of sands
befeuchten to humidify, to moisten, to damp, to wet
Befeuchter *m* humidifier
Befeuchtung *f* humidification, moistening
Befeuchtungsfrontdruckhöhe *f* **nach Green-Ampt** *(soil)* GREEN-AMPT wetting front pressure head
Befeuchtungszone *f (soil)* wetting zone
befiedern to feather, to fledge
~/sich to feather, to fledge
Befiederung *f* feathering
Befiederungsgen *n* feathering gene
Befiederungsgeschwindigkeit *f* feathering rate
befördern to convey, to transport, to haul
Beförderung *f* conveyance, transport[ation], haulage
Beforstung *f* forestation
befruchtbar fertilizable, impregnable
befruchten to fertilize, to fecundate, to impregnate, to fructify
befruchtend fecund
Befruchtung *f* fertilization, fecundation, impregnation; conception • **sich ohne ~ entwickelnd** parthenogenetic, parthenogenid • **sich ohne ~ fortpflanzend** agamogenetic, agamous
~ bei geöffneter Blüte *(bot)* chasmogamy
~/künstliche artificial fertilization
~/polysperme polyspermy
~/präferentielle (selektive) preferential fertilization, selective (selection) fertilization
Befruchtungsalter *n* age at fertilization
befruchtungsbereit receptive
Befruchtungserfolg *m*, **Befruchtungsergebnis** *n* fertilization success
befruchtungsfähig fertilizable
~/gegenseitig interfertile, interfruitful
Befruchtungsfähigkeit *f* fertilizing ability (capacity)
Befruchtungshundertsatz *m* conception rate *(animal breeding)*
Befruchtungskolben *m (bot)* antherid[ium]
Befruchtungsrate *f* pregnancy rate
Befruchtungsspore *f (bot)* androspore
Befruchtungsstoff *m* gamone
Befruchtungsvermögen *n* fertilizing ability (capacity), fertility
Befüllschnecke *f* loading auger

Befüllvorrichtung *f* filler
Befund *m* findings, status
Befundeinheit *f (forest)* assessment unit
~ der Forsteinrichtungsplanung working plan area
Begang *m (forest)* ranger district, beat
Begangspfad *m* inspection path
begasen to fumigate, to gas
Begasse *f s.* Bagasse
Begasung *f* fumigation, gassing
Begasungsgerät *n* fumigator
Begasungskammer *f* fumigation chamber
Begasungsmittel *n* fumigant
Begasungsmitteltoxizität *f* fumigant toxicity
Begasungsraum *m* fumigation chamber
Begasungsrohr *n* fumigating tube
begatten to mate [with], to copulate, to couple; to cover *(bull, stallion)*
~/sich to mate, to pair
Begattung *f* mating, copulation
begattungsfähig potent
Begattungsfähigkeit *f* potence, potency, mating ability
Begattungshilfsorgan *n* accessory copulatory organ *(e.g. of nematodes)*
Begattungskästchen *n (api)* mating hive (nucleus)
Begattungsorgan *n* copulatory organ
Begattungstasche *f* copulatory pouch *(e.g. of the queen bee)*
Begattungsvermögen *n* serviceability
begehen[/ein Revier] *(forest)* to go the rounds
begeißelt flagellate
begießen to water
Begleitart *f*, **Begleiter** *m (ecol)* associate (companion, accessory) species
Begleitpflanze *f* associate plant
Begonia-Elatior-Hybride *f* elatior begonia
Begonia-Knollenbegonien-Hybride *f* tuberous[-rooted] begonia, Begonia x tuberhybrida
Begonia-Lorrainebegonien-Hybride *f* Lorraine begonia
Begonia-Rex-Hybride *f* rex (rhizomatous) begonia, Begonia rex-cultorum
Begonia-Semperflorens-Hybride *f* fibrous[-rooted] begonia, wax begonia, Begonia x semperflorens-cultorum
Begonie *f (bot)* begonia *(genus Begonia)*
begrannt *(bot)* awned, bearded, aristate
Begrannung *f* awning
Begrenzungslinie *f* **in pilzbefallenem Holz** pencil (black) line
begründen to establish *(e.g. a plant stand)*
begründet established
~/reihenweise row-planted *(a forest stand)*
~/weitständig established at wide spacing
Begründung *f* **von Forstkulturen** forest plantation establishment
~ von Waldschutzstreifen shelter-belt establishment

begrünen

begrünen to [make] green, to grass [down], to turf, to sod [down], to bottom; to plant with shrubs
~/sich to [become] green
behaart hairy, pilose, pilous, pubescent
~/fein pubescent
behaartblättrig trichophyllous
behaartblütig trichosanthous
Behaarte Alpenrose *f* hairy Alpenrose, Alpine rose, Rhododendron hirsutum
~ Lupine *f* hairy (blue) lupin[e], Lupinus varius ssp. orientalis, Lupinus pilosus
~ Segge *f* hairy sedge, Carex hirta
Behaarter Baumschwammkäfer *m* hairy fungus beetle, Typhaea stercorea
~ Samenlaufkäfer *m* strawberry seed beetle, Harpalus rufipes (pubescens)
Behaartes Liebesgras *n* India love grass, Eragrostis pilosa
~ Riedgras *n* hairy sedge, Carex hirta
behaartsamig *(bot)* trichospermous
Behaarung *f* hair coat (covering)
Behaglichkeitstemperatur *f* comfort temperature *(for farm animals)*
Behaglichkeitszone *f (ecol)* comfort zone, preferendum
Behälter *m* box, bin; container
~/blasenförmiger (sackförmiger) *(zoo)* receptacle
Behältertrocknung *f* in-bin drying *(e.g. of grain crops)*
Behälterwaage *f* bin balance, bin-type weighing machine
behandeln to treat; to process, to condition, to handle; to manage
~/durch Sonneneinstrahlung to insolate, to solarize
~/mit Ammoniak to ammoniate
~/mit Creosotöl to creosote *(wood)*
~/mit Malz[extrakt] to malt
~/mit Wasserdampf to steam
Behandlung *f* 1. treatment; processing, conditioning, handling, management; 2. treatment, variant (experimentation)
~ aus der Luft aerial treatment
~/drucklose non-pressure treatment *(wood preservation)*
~ mit Flammschutzmitteln fire-proofing
~ mit Wachstumsregulatoren height control
~ von Pflanzenkrankheiten plant-disease management
~ während der Winterruhe dormant treatment
~/waldbauliche silvicultural treatment
Behandlungsgang *m* working race, crush *(livestock handling facility)*
Behandlungsklasse *f (forest)* treatment class
Behandlungspferch *m* handling pen *(sheep husbandry)*
Behandlungsplatz *m* working pen *(livestock handling facility)*

Behandlungsstand *m* 1. cattle handler, handling chute; 2. veterinary treatment table
Behandlungswirkung *f* treatment effect
Behang *m* leather *(of dog's ears)*; lop-ears *(of dogs)*
Behängezeit *f* season for entering (training) hounds
Beharrungsration *f* maintenance ration *(animal feeding)*
behauen to hew, to hack, to axe, to adze, to chip *(timber)*; to butt off *(a tree-trunk)*
behäufeln to earth [up], to hill [up]
behavioral behavioural
beheizen *n* to heat, to fire
Behelfsentwässerung *f* provisional drainage
Behelfslandeplatz *m* für Hubschrauber *(Am)* helispot
Behelfssilo *m* stack silo
Behelfsweg *m* für Löschfahrzeuge *(Am)* fire lane
beherrschen to dominate; to overtop *(silviculture)*
behöft bordered *(pit-pair)*
~/einseitig half-bordered
behorchen *(vet)* to auscultate
Behorchen *n* auscultation
behornt horned
behost feather-legged *(bird)*
Beidellit *m* beidellite *(clay mineral)*
beifüllen to stum *(wine-making)*
Beifüllwein *m* stum
Beifuß *m* 1. wormwood, sage[-bush] *(genus Artemisia)*; 2. mugwort, motherwort, Artemisia vulgaris
Beifußambrosie *f* [common] ragweed, Ambrosia artemisifolia
Beifutter[mittel] *n* supplementary feed
Beifütterung *f* supplementary feeding
beigeordnet adjunct
Beigeschmack *m* off-flavour, taint
~ nach Eber boar taint
Beihirsch *m* unattached stag
Beiholzart *f (forest)* accessory tree species, auxiliary (ancillary) species
Beiknospe *f* accessory (secondary, stipulary) bud
~/seriale serial bud
Beil *n* hatchet, axe
beimengen to admix
Beimengen *n* admixture
Beimengung *f* 1. admixture; 2. *s.* Beimengungen
Beimengungen *fpl* foreign material, alien matter, rubbish, trash, soil, dirt *(e.g. in harvested produce)*
Beimengungstrenneinrichtung *f* soil removal equipment
beimischen to admix
Beimischen *n* admixture
Beimischung *f* 1. admixture; 2. admixture, impurity (*s.a.* Beimengungen*)*
beimpfen to inoculate, to seed *(e.g. a cell culture)*
Beimpfung *f* inoculation

Beimpfung mit Bodenalgen algal inoculation *(rice growing)*
Bein *n* leg
Beinbefiederung *f* shank feathering
Beinhaut *f* periosteum
beinig fanged, fangy *(beetroot)*
Beinigkeit *f* fanging *(of beetroots)*
Beinlaus *f* **des Schafes** sheep foot louse, Linognatus pedalis
Beinleder *n* side-flap *(of the riding saddle)*
beinlos *(zoo)* legless, apodal, apodous
Beinlosigkeit *f* leglessness
Beinpaar *n* pair of legs
Beinschwäche *f (vet)* leg weakness
Beinschwächesyndrom *n* **der Broiler** [runting and] leg weakness syndrome in broilers, infectious stunting and leg weakness in broilers
Beinstellung *f* stance
Beinwell *m (bot)* 1. comfrey *(genus Symphytum)*; 2. [common] comfrey, consound, Symphytum officinale
Beinzwinge *f* kicking (hock) strap
Beißbeernachtschatten *m* false Jerusalem cherry, winter cherry, Solanum capsicastrum
beißen to bite; to savage
Beißer *m* biter *(horse)*
Beißkohl *m* leaf (spinach) beet, Swiss chard, Beta vulgaris var. vulgaris
Beistrich *m* extra (supernumerary) teat *(of an udder)*
Beitritt *m* overreaching *(of the red deer track)*
Beiwurzel *f* adventitious root
Beize *f* 1. [seed] dressing, seed protectant (treatment); pickle, pickling solution; 2. stain *(esp. for treating wood)*; 3. *s.* Beizen; 4. *s.* Beizjagd
beizen 1. to dress, to treat *(seed)*; to pickle; to stain *(wood)*; 2. *(hunt)* to hawk
~/**mit dem Falken** to hawk
Beizen *n* dressing; pickling
Beizgerät *n* [seed] dresser, seed dressing machine, seed treater (treatment machine)
Beizjagd *f* falconry, hawking • ~ **betreiben** to hawk
Beizmaschine *f s.* Beizgerät
Beizmittel *n* [seed] dressing, seed protectant (treatment)
Beizpuder *m* [seed] dressing powder
Beizung *f s.* Beizen
Beizvogel *m* falcon • **mit dem** ~ **jagen** to hawk
~/**männlicher** t[i]ercel
~/**weiblicher** falcon
Beizvogelhaube *f* hawking hood
Beizwild *n* quarry
Bejagungsintensität *f* shooting incidence
bekämpfen to control
~/**Ratten** to rat
~/**Ungeziefer** to disinfest
Bekämpfung *f* control
~ **aus der Luft/chemische** airborne chemical attack

~/**biologische** biological control
~/**chemische** chemical control
~ **der Schluchtenbildung** *f* gully control
~/**gezielte** directed control
Bekämpfungslinie *f* control line *(forest-fire control)*
~/**gehaltene** held line
~/**verlorene** lost line
Bekämpfungsmaßnahme *f* control measure (manipulation)
Bekämpfungsmittel *n* control agent
~/**biologisches** biological control agent
Bekämpfungsschwelle *f*, **Bekämpfungsschwellenwert** *m* control [action] threshold
Bekämpfungstrupp *m* suppression squad *(forest-fire control)*
Bekassine *f* [common] snipe, Capella (Gallinago) gallinago
Beklopfen *n* **der Körperoberfläche** *(vet)* percussion
beködern to bait *(e.g. a trap)*
bekömmlich palatable, [easily] digestible
Bekömmlichkeit *f* palatability *(e.g. of feed-stuffs)*
Bekreuzter Traubenwickler *m* grape-vine moth, Lobesia (Polychrosis) botrana
Bel Paese *m* bel paese [cheese]
Belademaschine *f* loading machine, loader
Beladen *n* loading
~ **von Siebröhren** phloem loading *(plant physiology)*
Belade[seil]winde *f* hoisting (lifting) winch
Beladung *f* 1. load; 2. *s.* Beladen
Beladungsreaktion *f* priming reaction *(biochemistry)*
Belag *m* coat[ing], cover[ing] • **mit reifähnlichem** ~ *(bot)* pruinose, glaucous
~/**deckender** coverage *(e.g. of plant protectants)*
~/**dünner** film
~/**sekundärer** secondary deposit *(of plant protectants)*
Belastbarkeit *f* load (carrying) capacity; stress capacity (tolerance); endurance *(e.g. of horses)*
Belastung *f* load[ing]; stress
~/**genetische** genetic load
~/**statische** static load[ing]
Belastungsfähigkeit *f s.* Belastbarkeit
Belastungsfaktor *m* stress factor, stressor
Belastungsmyopathie *f* **des Schweines** *(vet)* porcine stress syndrome, PSS
belatscht feather-legged *(bird)*
belauben/sich to come into leaf
belaubt leafy, in leaf
~/**dicht** leafy
Belaubtheit *f* leafiness
Belaubung *f* leafing, foliation, amount of foliage
Belauf *m (forest)* ranger district, beat
belebt animate
Belebtschlamm *m* activated (biological) sludge *(sewage purification)*

Belebtschlammanlage

Belebtschlammanlage *f* activated-sludge plant
Belebtschlammbecken *n* activated-sludge tank
Belebtschlammverfahren *n* activated-sludge process
Belebung *f* animation, stimulation, invigoration
Belebungsanlage *f* activated-sludge plant
Belebungsbecken *n* activated-sludge tank
Belegeinrichtung *f (api)* mating station
belegen to cover, to serve, to impregnate, to breed, to stock *(a breeding animal)*; to tup *(sheep)*; to line *(a bitch)*
~/erneut to rebreed
Belegstand *m (api)* mating yard
Belegstation *f*, **Belegstelle** *f (api)* [queen-]mating station
Belegung *f* 1. covering, service; 2. *s.* Deckakt
Belegungserfolg *m* fertilization success
Belegungsfärse *f* bulling heifer
Belegungszeitraum *m* covering (breeding) season
beleuchten to light [up], to illuminate
Beleuchtung *f* lighting, illumination
~/künstliche artificial lighting
Beleuchtungsprogramm *n* lighting programme
Beleuchtungsregelung *f* lighting control
Beleuchtungsregime *n* lighting regime
Beleuchtungsstärke *f* light intensity, illumination [intensity], illuminance
Beleuchtungssteuerung *f* lighting control
Beleuchtungszeit *f* duration of lighting (illumination)
Belfacillin *n* methicillin *(antibiotic)*
Belgische Landrasse *f* Belgian Landrace *(pig breed)*
Belgischer Riese *m* Flemish Giant [rabbit] *(breed)*
~ Schäferhund *m* Belgian sheep-dog *(group of breeds)*
Belgisches Kaltblut[pferd] *n* Belgian *(horse breed)*
belichten *s.* beleuchten
Belladonna *f* belladonna, deadly (black) nightshade, Atropa belladonna
Belladonnalilie *f* 1. amaryllis *(genus Amaryllis)*; 2. amaryllis, belladonna [lily], bell lily, Amaryllis belladonna
Belladonnin *n* belladonnine *(alkaloid)*
bellen to bark, to bay, to give tongue *(hunter's term)*
Bellen *n* bark[ing]
Beltsvillepute *f* Beltsville Small White [turkey] *(breed)*
belüften to aerate, to air, to ventilate, to vent
Belüftung *f* aeration, airing, ventilation
Belüftungsanlage *f* aeration plant, ventilation unit
Belüftungsautomatik *f* automatic ventilation
Belüftungsbewässerung *f* aeration irrigation
Belüftungsdränung *f* aeration drainage
Belüftungsheu *n* aerated (barn-dried) hay
Belüftungskanal *m* ventilation duct
Belüftungsöffnung *f* [air-]vent, ventilation hole

Belüftungsrate *f* ventilation rate
Belüftungsregelung *f* ventilation control
Belüftungsschacht *m* flue
Belüftungstrockner *m* barn dryer
Belüftungstrocknung *f* dryeration, drieration, ventilation (forced-air) drying, aeration drying
Belüftungswinterlagerung *f* ventilated winter storage
Beluga *m* beluga *(caviar from beluga roe)*
Beluga *f* beluga, Acipenser (Huso) huso
bemoost mossy
bemuskelt muscled
Bemuskelung *f* muscling
Bemuskelungstyp *m* type of muscling
bemuttern to mother
Benadelung *f* amount of foliage
benagen to [be]gnaw
Benazolin *n* benazolin *(herbicide)*
Bendiocarb *n* bendiocarb *(insecticide)*
Benediktenkraut *n* 1. blessed thistle *(genus Cnicus)*; 2. blessed thistle, Cnicus benedictus
Benemicin *n* rifampicin *(antibiotic)*
benetzbar wettable, hydrophilic
Benetzbarkeit *f* wettability, hydrophilicity
benetzen to wet, to moisten, to bedew
Benetzungsmittel *n* wetting agent, wetter
Benfluralin *n* benfluralin *(herbicide)*
Benfuresat *n* benfuresate *(herbicide)*
Bengalenziege *f* Bengal goat *(breed)*
Bengalischer Hanf *m* 1. sunn [crotalaria, hemp], sann hemp, Crotalaria juncea; 2. sunn hemp fibre
Bengalisches Kino[gummi] *n* Bengal kino
Bengalpfeffer *m* long pepper, Piper longum
Bengalrose *f* China (Chinese, Indian, fairy) rose, rose of China, Rosa chinensis
benigne *(vet)* benign[ant]
Benignität *f* benignity
Benodanil *n* benodanil *(fungicide)*
Benommenheit *f (vet)* drowsiness
Benomyl *n* benomyl, benlate, fundazol, BCM *(fungicide)*
Benquinox *n* benquinox *(fungicide)*
Bentazon *n* bentazone *(herbicide)*
benthal benthal
Benthal *n* benthal *(bottom region of waters)*
Benthalm *n* blae grass, [purple] moor grass, molinia, Molinia caerulea
Benthiazuron *n* benthiazuron *(herbicide)*
Benthiocarb *n* benthiocarb, thiobencarb *(herbicide)*
benthisch *s.* 1. benthonisch; 2. *s.* benthal
Benthon *n s.* Benthos
benthonisch benth[on]ic
Benthos *n* benthos *(organisms on or in the bottoms of waters)*
~/tierisches zoobenthos
Bentonit *m* bentonite *(clay mineral)*
Benzacillin *n* penicillin G *(antibiotic)*

Benzadox *n* benzadox *(herbicide)*
Benzaldehyddehydrogenase *f* benzaldehyde dehydrogenase *(enzyme)*
Benzalkoniumchlorid *n* benzalkonium chloride *(herbicide, fungicide, disinfectant)*
Benzamizol *n* benzamizole *(herbicide)*
Benzen-1,3-diol *n* 1,3-benzenediol, *(m-)*dihydroxybenzene, resorcin[ol]
Benzin-Alkohol-Gemisch *n (Am)* gasohol
Benzinmotor *m* petrol engine, *(Am)* gasoline engine
Benzinmotorsäge *f* petrol-engine saw
Benzipram *n* benzipram *(herbicide)*
Benzo[b]pyridin *n s.* Benzopyridin
Benzoe *f*, **Benzoeharz** *n* benzoin, storax, styrax
Benzoe-Storaxbaum *m* storax-tree, Styrax benzoin
Benzoguanamin *n* benzoguanamine *(herbicide)*
Benzopyridin *n* quinoline
2,3-Benzopyrrol *n* indole
Benzoylcholinesterase *f* cholinesterase *(enzyme)*
Benzoylprop *n* benzoylprop *(herbicide)*
Benzoylprop-ethyl *n* benzoylprop-ethyl *(herbicide)*
Benzthiazuron *n* benzthiazuron *(herbicide)*
Benzyladenin *n*, **6-Benzylamino-purin** *n* benzyladenine, benzylaminopurine, BA, BAP *(cytokinin)*
Beobachtungsbeute *f (api)* observation hive
Beobachtungsfläche *f* monitoring plot *(in field studies)*
Beobachtungskabine *f* observatory, look-out cabin (cupola), tower cupola *(forest-fire control)*
Beobachtungsstock *m (api)* observation hive
bepflanzen to plant, to crop, to stock down
~/neu to replant; to replace [plants]
Bepflanzung *f* 1. planting; 2. plantation, planting
berankt *(bot)* cirrose, cirrous, capreolate
beräppeln to rough-bark, to rough-peel
berasen to sod, to turf
Berater *m*/**landwirtschaftlicher** agricultural adviser (advisor)
Beratungsdienst *m* advisory (extension) service
~/gartenbaulicher horticultural advisory service
~/landwirtschaftlicher agricultural advisory (extension) service
Beratungstätigkeit *f* advisory work
Berber *m* Barb *(horse breed)*
Berberitze *f* 1. barberry, berberry, berberis *(genus Berberis)*; 2. barberry *(fruit)*
Berberitzenrost *m* barberry rust *(caused by Puccinia graminis)*
beregnen to sprinkle, to irrigate
Beregner *m s.* Beregnungsanlage
Beregnung *f* sprinkling, [sprinkler, spray] irrigation
~/klimatisierende air conditioning irrigation *(e.g. in greenhouses)*
Beregnungsanlage *f* sprinkling (sprinkler) installation, [sprinkler] irrigation plant, sprinkler [system], irrigator, rainer
~/bewegliche mobile sprinkler, portable pipe sprinkler installation
~/ortsfeste permanent [set type of] sprinkler system
~/teilbewegliche semiportable sprinkler system
~/vollbewegliche fully portable sprinkler system
Beregnungsautomat *m* robot sprinkler
Beregnungsbedürftigkeit *f* irrigation requirement (need)
Beregnungsdiagramm *n* water-balance sheet
Beregnungsdüngung *f* fertilizing irrigation, ferti[rri]gation, fertilizer sprinkling, dressing by spray irrigation
Beregnungsfläche *f* irrigation area (surface)
Beregnungsfruchtfolge *f* irrigation rotation
Beregnungshäufigkeit *f* irrigation frequency
Beregnungsmaschine *f* sprinkling (irrigation) machine
~/geradeausfahrende linear-move sprinkling machine
~/selbstfahrende self-propelled irrigation system
Beregnungspumpe *f* irrigation pump
Beregnungssteuerung *f* irrigation scheduling
Beregnungssystem *n* sprinkling (irrigation) system
Beregnungswasser *n* irrigation water
Beregnungszeitraum *m* irrigation period
Bereich *m*/**agrarindustrieller** agro-industrial complex
~/fruchttragender fruiting zone
~/landwirtschaftlicher agricultural (rural, farm) sector
bereift 1. *(bot)* pruinose, glaucous; 2. tyred; 3. rimy, frosted
Bereifte Brombeere *f* dewberry, Rubus caesius
Bereiftfrüchtiger Holunder *m* blue elder, Sambucus caerulea (glauca)
Bereifung *f* 1. bloom *(on plums and grapes)*; 2. [set of] tyres; 3. frost deposit
Bereinigungshacke *f* final trimming *(e.g. in beet growing)*
bereiten to break [in], to rough *(a horse)*
~/ein Bett to bed, to lay, to table *(tree-felling)*
~/Kompost to [make] compost
~/Malz to malt
~/Wein to vinify, to vint
Bereiter *m* horse-breaker, rough-rider, [bronco]buster
Bereitschaftsmesser *m* preparedness meter *(forest-fire control)*
bereitstellen *(forest)* to log, to extract, to harvest
Bereitstellen *n* logging, extraction
~/baumweises full-tree logging
~ ganzer Stämme whole-stem logging, long-length logging
bergabrücken *(forest)* to ballhoot
Bergahorn *m* harewood, [English] sycamore, sycamore (great) maple, Acer pseudoplatanus
Bergamaskerschaf *n* Bergamo *(sheep breed)*

Bergamotte

Bergamotte[nbirne] *f* 1. bergamot [orange], Citrus aurantium ssp. bergamia; 2. bergamot *(fruit)*
Bergamottminze *f* bergamot (Eau de Cologne) mint, Mentha piperita var. citrata
Bergamottöl *n* bergamot oil
Bergapten *n* bergaptene *(vegetable fish poison)*
Bergaster *f* Italian aster, Aster amellus
Bergaufförderung *f* **mit einseitig angehobener Last** *(forest)* high-lead [cable] logging, high-lead yarding, highleading
Bergbauabraum *m* mine mill tailings
Bergbauer *m* hill farmer
Bergbauernhof *m* hill farm
Bergbauernwirtschaft *f* 1. hill farm; 2. hill farming
Bergbauhalde *f* [mine] dump, spoil heap
Bergbetrieb *m*/**landwirtschaftlicher** mountain farm
Bergblume *f* Alpine flower *(comprehensive term)*
Bergenie *f (bot)* 1. bergenia *(genus Bergenia)*; 2. giant rockfoil, Bergenia cordifolia
Berger de Brie *m* Briard *(dog breed)*
Bergeraum *m* barn, store, storage; loft
~/deckenlastiger [overhead] loft
Bergfarn *m* mountain shield fern, Thelypteris limbosperma, Dryopteris oreopteris
Bergfenchel *m* stone-parsley, stonewort *(genus Seseli)*
Bergflockenblume *f (bot)* mountain bluet, Centaurea montana
Berghemlocktanne *f* mountain hemlock, Tsuga mertensiana
Bergholunder *m* red-berried elder, Sambucus racemosa
bergig mountainous
Bergkaffee *m* [Arabian, Arabica, common] coffee, Coffea arabica
Bergkiefer *f* dwarf (mountain) pine, Pinus mugo (montana)
Bergklee *m* mountain clover, Trifolium montanum
Bergkrankheit *f (vet)* brisket disease
Berglandfarm *f* hill farm
Berglandwirtschaft *f* mountain (hill) farming, hill agriculture
Berglandzone *f* montane (highland) zone • **die ~ betreffend** altomontane
Berglauch *m* perennial welsh onion, Allium cirrhosum *(montanum)*
Berglorbeer *m* 1. mountain laurel, calico bush, Kalmia latifolia; 2. California laurel *(genus Umbellularia)*
Berglungenkraut *n* lungwort, Pulmonaria mollis
Bergmahagoni *m* mountain mahogany, cercocarpus *(genus Cercocarpus)*
Bergmischwald *m* mountain mixed forest
Bergpalme *f* 1. chamaedorea *(genus Chamaedorea)*; 2. parlour (dwarf mountain) palm, Chamaedorea elegans
Bergpapaya *f* mountain papaw, Carica pubescens
Bergpfirsich *m* David peach, Prunus davidiana

bergreich mountainous
Bergreis *m* upland (mountain, hill) rice
Bergriedgras *n* mountain sedge, Carex montana
Bergrüster *f s.* Bergulme
Bergrutsch *m* landslide, landslip
Bergsandglöckchen *n* sheep's-bit [scabious], Jasione montana
Bergschaf *n* mountain (hill) sheep
Bergschafrasse *f* hill breed
Bergschafwolle *f* mountain wool
Bergsegge *f* mountain sedge, Carex montana
Bergspirke *f* erect mountain pine, Pinus uncinata ssp. uncinata
Bergstütze *f* spud *(at forestry tractors)*
Bergtabak *m* wild tobacco, Nicotiana sylvestris
Bergulme *f* mountain (common, Scotch) elm, wych-elm, witch-hazel, Ulmus glabra
Bergungsfloß *n (forest)* catamaran, cat *(for sinkers)*
Bergwald *m* mountain (montane) forest
Bergwaldrebe *f* mountain (anemone-flowered) clematis, Clematis montana
Bergweide[fläche] *f* mountain pasture (range), Alpine range (pasture), hill grazing (pasture)
Bergweidekrankheit *f* pulpy kidney disease *(of sheep)*
Bergwiese *f* mountain (hill) meadow
Bergwind *m* mountain wind
Bergwirtschaft *f* hill farm
Bergwohlverleih *m* [mountain] arnica, mountain tobacco, Arnica montana
Bergwundklee *m (bot)* Alps anthyllis, Anthyllis montana
Bergziege *f* mountain goat
Bergziest *m* upright hedge-nettle, Stachys recta
berieseln to [be]sprinkle, to irrigate
Berieselung *f* sprinkling, [trickle, spray, flush] irrigation
berindet barked, corticate[d]
beringen to ring, to band *(birds)*
beringt ringed; *(bot, zoo)* annulate[d]
Beringung *f* ringing, banding
Beringungsversuch *m* ringing experiment
beritten mounted
Berkshire[schwein] *n* Berkshire *(pig breed)*
Berlicetin *n* chloramphenicol *(antibiotic)*
Bermespritze *f* roadside sprayer
Bermudagras *n* Bermuda [devil] grass, Bahama (scutch) grass, doob [grass], *(Am)* coastal bermudagrass, Cynodon dactylon
Berner Sennenhund *m* Bernese mountain dog *(breed)*
Bernhardiner *m* St. Bernard dog *(breed)*
Bernickelgans *f* barnacle [goose], brent [goose], Branta bernicla
Bernoulliverteilung *f (biom)* binomial distribution
Bernstein *m* amber, succinite
Bernsteincodon *n (gen)* amber codon
Bernsteinsäure *f* amber (succinic) acid

Bernsteinsäuredehydrogenase *f* succinate dehydrogenase *(enzyme)*
Bernsteinsäure-2,2-dimethylhydrazid *n* daminozide *(growth inhibitor)*
Berocillin *n* pivampicillin *(antibiotic)*
Beromycin *n* penicillin V *(antibiotic)*
Berostung *f (phyt)* russetting
Bertramsgarbe *f* sneezewort [yarrow], Achillea ptarmica
Beruf *m*/**landwirtschaftlicher** agricultural trade
Berufkraut *n* 1. fleabane, erigeron *(genus Erigeron)*; 2. Canadian fleabane, Conyza (Erigeron) canadensis
Berufsausbildung *f*/**landwirtschaftliche** vocational education in agriculture
Berufskrankheit *f* occupational disease (disorder), professional (vocational) disease
Berufskraut *n* s. Berufkraut
Berufsrennreiter *m* jockey
beruhigen to sedate, to tranquilize, to calm; to subdue *(honey-bees)*
beruhigend sedative, calming
Beruhigung *f* sedation
Beruhigungsbecken *n* stilling pond, debris basin *(torrent control)*
Beruhigungsmittel *n* sedative [agent], tranquilizer
Berührungsgift *n* contact poison
Berührungstrockner *m* contact dryer
besäen to sow, to seed, to stock down *(s.a. under säen)*
~/mit Gras to grass
besamen to inseminate
Besamer *m* s. Besamungstechniker
Besamung *f* insemination
~/künstliche (technische) artificial insemination, AI
Besamungsaufwand *m* insemination index
Besamungsbulle *m* AI bull
Besamungsdosis *f* insemination dose, inseminate
Besamungseber *m* AI boar; breeding (service) boar
Besamungserfolg *m* fertilization success
Besamungshieb *m (forest)* seeding felling, seed cut[ting]
~/lichter open seeding felling
Besamungsindex *m* insemination index
Besamungskatheter *m* insemination catheter (syringe)
Besamungspipette *f* insemination (inseminating) pipette
Besamungsschlag *m* s. Besamungshieb
Besamungsstation *f* insemination centre (station), AI centre (stud)
Besamungstechniker *m* AI operator (technician), inseminator, artificial breeding technician
Besatz *m* 1. stocking; 2. foreign (extraneous) matter, alien (foreign) material, rubbish *(e.g. in seed)*; dockage *(esp. in cereals)* • **mit zu hohem ~** overstocked

Besatzdauer *f* stocking period
Besatzdichte *f* stocking density
Besatzstärke *f* stocking rate (capacity), carrying capacity
Besatzzyklus *m* density cycle *(game management)*
Besaugen n/gegenseitiges intersucking *(behavioural disorder esp. of young animals)*
beschälen to cover, to serve, to horse *(a mare)*
Beschäler *m* [covering] stallion, stud[-horse]
Beschälseuche *f* covering disease, dourine, breeding paralysis, equine syphilis *(caused by Trypanosoma equiperdum)*
beschatten to shade
Beschattung *f* shading
beschicken to feed *(e.g. a conveyor)*; to stoke *(a furnace)*
Beschickung *f* feed[ing]
~/manuelle hand feeding
Beschickungsanlage *f* stoker *(of a furnace)*
Beschickungsschacht *m* hopper
Beschickungstank *m* working tank
Beschickungsvorrichtung *f* feeder
beschirmen to shelter
Beschirmung *f* shelter; *(forest)* canopy cover
~ der Jungwüchse *(forest)* sheltering of young plantations
Beschirmungsfläche *f (forest)* area under canopy (crown cover)
Beschirmungsgrad *m (forest)* crown density, canopy cover, canopy [cover] density
Beschlag *m* [horse]shoeing
~/orthopädischer corrective shoeing
beschlagen 1. to shoe; 2. to cover *(hoofed game) (s.a. decken)*; 3. to rough-hew, to adze *(timber)*
~/scharf to caulk *(a hoof)*
beschlagen 1. shod *(hoof)*; 2. pregnant, gravid *(hoofed game)*; 3. rough-hewn *(timber)*
~ sein to be in fawn *(red deer)*
Beschlagfehler *m* shoeing fault
Beschlaghammer *m* shoeing hammer
Beschlagschmied *m* farrier, horseshoer
Beschlagschmiede *f* farriery
Beschlagstand m horseshoeing frame, brake
Beschlagzeug *n* farrier's tools
beschneiden to trim, to clip; to cut [back]; to dock, to dub *(e.g. an animal's tail)*; to prune, to lop [off] *(a woody plant)*; to pare *(hoofs or claws)*; to round *(e.g. the ears of a dog)*
~/eine Hecke to hedge
~/heckenförmig to hedge
beschottern to metal *(road construction)*
Beschotterung *f* metalling
Beschreikraut *n (bot)* fleabane, erigeron *(genus Erigeron)*
Beschuppung *f* scaling
beseitigen/Unkraut to weed
Beseitigen *n* **der lebenden Bodendecke/platzweises** *(forest)* scalping

Besenbeifuß

Besenbeifuß *m* oriental wormwood, Artemisia scoparia
Besenbirke *f* pubescent birch, Betula pubescens
Besenginster *m* common (Scotch) broom, Cytisus scoparius
Besenheide *f* 1. heather, heath, ling *(genus Calluna)*; 2. common heather (ling), Scotch heather, moor besom, Calluna vulgaris
Besenhirse *f* broomcorn *(comprehensive term)*
Besenkrankheit *f* brooming [disease] *(of walnut)*
~ **der Rebe** acarinosis of grape-vine *(caused by Phyllocoptes vitis)*
Besenkraut *n* summer cypress, tumble-weed, Kochia (Bassia) scoparia
Besenried *n s.* Benthalm
Besensorghum *n* broomcorn *(comprehensive term)*
Besenwuchs *m* **des Apfels** apple proliferation, apple witches' broom, AWB *(mycoplasmosis)*
besetzen/mit Vieh to stock *(a pasture)*
~/wieder mit Vieh to restock
besiedeln to colonize, to settle
Besiedelung *f* colonization, settlement
Besiedelungsfähigkeit *f* colonizing ability
Besiedlung *f s.* Besiedelung
Besitzung *f* estate
besonnen to solarize, to insolate
besonnt sunlit
Besonnung *f* solarization, insolation
bespannen to horse
bespelzt husky
besprengen to sprinkle, to bedew
bespringen to mount, to cover
bespritzen to [be]sprinkle; to syringe
besprühen to spray
Besprühen *n*/**aviotechnisches** aerial spraying, aerospraying
Besseykirsche *f* western sand cherry, Prunus pumila ssp. besseyi
Bestachelter Laubkaktus *m* Barbados gooseberry, lemon vine, blade apple, Pereskia aculeata
Bestand *m* 1. crop, stand; [timber, forest] stand; 2. population; 3. stock, store
~/alter old stand
~/angerissener *(forest)* broke
~/aus Stockausschlag hervorgegangener *(forest)* coppice crop, stand originating from coppice (suckers)
~/ausgezeichneter *(forest)* broke
~ **aus natürlicher Verjüngung** *(forest)* seedling stand (crop)
~/ausscheidender *(forest)* volume (timber) to be removed, drain; thinnings
~/begründeter *(forest)* artificial stand (crop)
~/dichter dense crop
~/durch Holzeinschlag ausscheidender *(forest)* drain
~/durch Naturverjüngung entstandener *(forest)* recruitment
~/durch Substitutionsaufforstung begründeter *(forest)* compensatory planting
~/gedrungener crowded crop
~/gemischter mixed stand
~/geringwertiger low-quality stand
~/geschlossener dense crop
~/hochbevorrateter *(forest)* high-volume stand
~ **im Stangenholzstadium** *(forest)* pole[-stage] stand
~/künstlich begründeter *(forest)* artificial stand (crop)
~/licht bestockter sparse stand, stand of low density
~/lichter (lockerer) open crop
~/lückenhafter incomplete stand
~/minderbestockter incomplete stand
~/natürlicher natural stand
~/sehr dichter crowded crop
~/überalterter (überjähriger) old-growth stand
~/unbehandelter *(forest)* old growth
~/verbleibender *(forest)* remaining stand, residual (final, principal, main) crop, final felling stand
~/verjüngter *(forest)* natural regeneration, volunteer growth
Bestandesabfall *m (forest)* litterfall
Bestandesalter *n* stand (crop) age
Bestandesanalyse *f* stand analysis
Bestandesansprache *f s.* Bestandesbeschreibung
Bestandesaufbau *m* stand structure, constitution
Bestandesaufbauform *f* stand structure type
Bestandesaufnahme *f*, **Bestandesauszählung** *f (forest)* [stand] enumeration, inventory of a stand, [valuation] survey, tally, *(Am)* timber cruising
Bestandesbegründung *f* stand formation (establishment)
~/künstliche artificial formation of a stand
Bestandesbehandlung *f* stand treatment
Bestandesbeschreibung *f (forest)* description of stand (crop), mensurational description, assessment report
Bestandesbewertung *f* stand valuation
bestandesbildend stand-forming
Bestandesbildung *f* stand formation, crop establishment
Bestandesbonität *f* quality of stand
Bestandeschronik *f s.* Bestandesgeschichte
Bestandesdichte *f* crop (stand, planting) density, density of stand (crop)
Bestandesdichtekennwert *m* stand density index
bestandesdichtensensitiv population-sensitive
Bestandesdichtenversuch *m* density trial
Bestandeseinheit *f* block of trees *(e.g. in orchards)*
Bestandesentwicklung *f* stand development
Bestandeserziehung *f s.* Bestandespflege
Bestandesetablierung *f s.* Bestandesbegründung
Bestandesfläche *f* stand area
Bestandesform *f* form of stand
Bestandesführung *f* crop management

Bestandesgeschichte *(forest)* stand (compartment) history, compartment register
Bestandesgrundfläche f stand (crop, total) basal area *(forest mensuration)*
Bestandesgüteklasse f *(forest)* merchantability class
Bestandeshöhe f height of stand, stand height
Bestandeshusten m stable cough, equine influence, epizootic cough in horse
Bestandeshygiene f crop hygiene
Bestandesinventur f s. Bestandesaufnahme
Bestandeskarte f stand map
Bestandesklima n climate of a stand
Bestandeslockerung f *(forest)* thinning
~/natürliche natural thinning, self-thinning, autothinning
Bestandeslücke f blank, gap, miss, fail-place
Bestandesmerkmal n stand characteristic
Bestandesmikroklima n crop microclimate
Bestandesmittelhöhe f *(forest)* mean stand height
Bestandesmittelstamm m average tree of the stand
Bestandesparameter m stand parameter
Bestandespflege f crop cultivation (care), care of a stand, stand tending; postdrilling cultivation
Bestandesprofil n stand profile
Bestandesrand m stand border
Bestandesreife f crop (stand) maturity
Bestandesschätzung f s. Bestandesaufnahme
Bestandesschicht f *(forest)* storey, story
Bestandesschirm m leaf canopy; forest (stand) canopy, overhead cover
Bestandesschluß m canopy closure
Bestandesschutz m stand protection
Bestandesschutzholz n *(forest)* nurse (pioneer) crop
Bestandessortentafel f *(forest)* stand assortment table
Bestandesstruktur f s. Bestandesaufbau
Bestandesstrukturklasse f *(forest)* structural class
Bestandestyp[us] m stand type
Bestandesüberwachung f crop (field) inspection, scouting, stand monitoring
~ im Obstbau orchard supervision
Bestandesverbesserung f [timber] stand improvement, T.S.I.
Bestandesvitalität f stand vigour
Bestandesvolumen n *(forest)* stand volume
Bestandesvolumentafel f stand volume table
Bestandesvorrat m s. Bestandesvolumen
Bestandeswirtschaft f forest management by compartments (stands)
Bestandeszusammensetzung f stand composition
Bestandeszyklus m density cycle *(game management)*
beständig 1. constant; continuous; 2. stable; persistent *(e.g. biocides)*

Beständigkeit f 1. constancy, continuance; 2. stability; persistence, persistency
Bestands... s. Bestandes...
Bestandteil m constituent, component, part, ingredient
~/giftiger toxic ingredient (principle)
bestäuben *(bot)* to pollinate, to pollen[ize], to pollinize
~/sich selbst to self[-pollinate]
Bestäuber m *(bot)* pollinator, pollenizer, pollinizer
bestäubt/mehlig *(bot)* farinose
Bestäubung f pollination, pollinization
~ bei geöffneter Blüte chasmogamy
~ durch Insekten insect pollination
~/freie open pollination
~/künstliche artificial pollination
Bestäubungshilfe f pollination aid
Bestäubungstätigkeit f pollination activity
Bestäubungszeitraum m pollination period
~/effektiver effective pollination period, EPP
bestellbar arable, cultivable, tillable *(soil)*
Bestellbarkeit f arability
bestellen to cultivate, to till, to crop; to sow [down] *(a field)*; to dress *(a garden)*
~/einen Garten to garden, to dress (to keep) a garden
~/erneut to rework *(a field)*
~/mit Getreide to corn
Bestellkombination f, **Bestellkombine** f cultivation and sowing combination
Bestellung f cultivation, tillage; gardening
~ auf Endbestand planting to stand
Bestellzeit f seed-time
bestimmen/das Alter to age
Bestimmen n **der Brandgefahr** fire-danger rating *(forest-fire prevention)*
Bestimmtheitsmaß n *(biom)* coefficient of determination
Bestimmung f **des Ernährungszustandes** diagnosis of nutritional status
bestocken to stock, to [af]forest
~/sich to stock, to stool; to tiller *(grasses)*
bestockt stocked, forested, wooded
~/licht (locker) understocked, open[-stocked], thinly stocked (forested), sparse, clear
Bestockung f 1. *(forest)* stocking, stooling; tillering; 2. s. Bestockungsgrad
Bestockungsaufbau m growing-stock structure
Bestockungsbefund m stocking study
Bestockungsbeschreibung f assessment report
Bestockungsfähigkeit f tillering ability (capacity, potential)
Bestockungsgrad m stocking [degree, level], degree (density) of stocking, stand (degree of) density
Bestockungsknoten m tillering node, tiller (crown) bud
Bestockungsphase f tillering phase
Bestockungstrieb m tiller, side-shoot

Bestockungsverhalten

Bestockungsverhalten n tillering habit
Bestockungsvermögen n s. Bestockungsfähigkeit
Bestockungsziel n growing-stock objective (target)
Bestoßmaschine f slotting machine *(for sharpening of beet slicing knives)*
bestrahlen to [ir]radiate
Bestrahlung f [ir]radiation
Bestrahlungsstärke f irradiance
Beta-(N)-Acetylglucosaminidase f beta-N-acetylglucosaminidase, N-acetyl-beta-glucosaminidase *(enzyme)*
Beta-Amylase f beta-amylase *(enzyme)*
Beta-Amyrin n beta-amyrin *(terpene)*
Beta-Caroten n beta-carotene *(vegetable dye)*
Beta-Casein n beta-casein *(milk protein)*
Beta-Cellulose f beta cellulose
Beta-Cyanin n beta cyanin *(vegetable dye)*
Beta-Diketonase f fumarylacetoacetase *(enzyme)*
Beta-Fructofuranosidase f beta-fructofuranosidase, invertase, invertin, saccharase, sucrase *(enzyme)*
Beta-Galactosidase f beta-galactosidase, lactase *(enzyme)*
Beta-Glucan n beta-glucan *(polysaccharide)*
Beta-Glucanase f beta-glucanase *(enzyme)*
Beta-Glucosidase f beta-glucosidase, cellobiase *(enzyme)*
Betain n betaine
Beta-Lactam-Antibiotikum n beta-lactam antibiotic
Beta-Lactamase f beta-lactamase, penicillinase, cephalosporinase *(enzyme)*
Beta-Lactoglobulin n beta-lactoglobulin *(milk protein)*
Betalain n betalain *(vegetable dye)*
Beta-Mannosidase f beta-mannosidase *(enzyme)*
Betamethason n betamethasone *(glucocorticoid)*
betanken to fuel
Beta-Oxidation f beta-oxidation *(fatty acid degradation)*
Beta-Pinen n beta-pinene
Beta-Säure f beta-acid *(hop constituent)*
Beta-Sitosterol n beta sitosterol *(plant constituent)*
betätigt/pneumatisch pneumatic, [compressed-] air-operated, air-actuated
betäuben *(vet)* to anaesthetize; to stun *(slaughter animals)*
betäubend anaesthetic, narcotic
~/örtlich local anaesthetic
Betäubender Kälberkropf m rough chervil, Chaerophyllum temulum
Betäubung f anaesthesia; stunning *(of slaughter animals)*
~/elektrische electrical stunning
~/örtliche local anaesthesia
Betäubungsfalle f stunning pen
Betäubungsgewehr n *(vet)* Cap-Chur gun
Betäubungsmittel n anaesthetic

Betäubungszone f stunning area
Beta-Xylosidase f beta-xylosidase, xylan-1,4-ß-xylosidase *(enzyme)*
Bete f beet *(genus Beta)*
Betelblatt n betel *(from Piper betle)*
Betelnuß f areca (betel) nut
Betel[nuß]palme f 1. areca *(genus Areca)*; 2. areca, betel palm, Areca catechu
Betelpfefferblatt n betel
Betelpfefferpflanze f betel [pepper], Piper betle
Betonbottich m concrete vat
Betondränrohr n concrete drain-pipe
Betonfaß n concrete vat
Betonformstein m precast concrete block
Betonicin n betonicine, achillein *(plant constituent)*
Betonie f *(bot)* betony, Stachys (Betonica) officinalis
Betonpfahl m concrete post
Betonsilo m concrete silo
Betonspaltenboden m slatted concrete floor, concrete slatted floor *(in animal houses)*
Betonteich m concrete pond
Betonzaunpfahl m concrete post
betreiben/Beizjagd (Falknerei) to hawk
~/Fremdzucht to outbreed
~/Gartenbau to garden, to do gardening
~/Gemenge[an]bau to intercrop
~/Inzucht to inbreed, to self
~/Raubbau to overcrop
~/Regenfeldbau to dry-farm
~/Reinzucht to breed pure
~/Trockenfarmerei to dry-farm
~/Viehzucht to raise (rear) cattle, *(Am)* to ranch
~/Vorratshaltung to stock
~/Wadenfischerei to seine, to trawl
~/Weidwerk to hunt
Betreuungsforstamt n supervisory forest district
Betrieb m enterprise, plant • **im eigenen ~ angebaut (erzeugt)** home-grown
~/aussetzender *(forest)* irregular yield management
~/kleinbäuerlicher peasant holding
~/landwirtschaftlicher farm, *(Am)* ranch, agricultural holding (enterprise)
~/natürliches Weideland bewirtschaftender hill farm
~/ohne Bewässerung wirtschaftender dry farm
Betriebsanlage f plant
Betriebsanweisung f instruction book
Betriebsart f system of management; mode of forest management, silvicultural system
Betriebsberater m/**landwirtschaftlicher** farm adviser
betriebsbereit operable; available
Betriebsbereitschaft f operability; availability
Betriebsberufsschule f **für Waldarbeiter** forest worker school
Betriebsbremse f service brake
Betriebsdauer f life[time], life span *(of machines)*

86

Betriebseinkommen *n*/**landwirtschaftliches** farm income
Betriebserhebung *f* farm survey
Betriebsfläche *f* [/**landwirtschaftliche**] farm area; *(forest)* area under management
Betriebsform *f* type (system) of farming *(s. a.* Betriebsart*)*
Betriebsführung *f* [/**landwirtschaftliche**] farm management
Betriebsgröße *f* farm size
Betriebsgrößenklasse *f* farm-size category
Betriebsgroßversuch *m*/**landwirtschaftlicher** on-farm trial
Betriebshygiene *f* farm hygiene
Betriebskarte *f (forest)* management map
Betriebsklasse *f (forest)* management class, working circle, *(Am)* working group
Betriebskontrolle *f* process control *(e.g. in sugar manufacture)*
Betriebsleiter *m* farm manager
Betriebsmittel *npl*/**landwirtschaftliche** agricultural supplies
Betriebsmodell *n*/**landwirtschaftliches** farm model
Betriebsökonom *m*/**landwirtschaftlicher** farm economist
Betriebsökonomie *f*/**landwirtschaftliche** agricultural economy (economics), farm economy
Betriebsorganisation *f*/**landwirtschaftliche** farm [business] organization
Betriebsplanung *f*/**forstwirtschaftliche** forest regulation (production planning)
~/landwirtschaftliche farm (management) planning
Betriebsregelung *f* forest management regulation, forest [management] organization
Betriebsregelungsanweisung *f* forest management instruction
Betriebsregelungszeitraum *m* period of forest management regulation
Betriebssäurewecker *m (dairy)* bulk starter
Betriebsschätzung *f*/**landwirtschaftliche** farm appraisal
Betriebsstoffwechsel *m* energy metabolism
Betriebsstruktur *f* farm (operational) structure
Betriebsstundenzähler *m* working hours counter, proofmeter *(e.g. of a tractor engine)*
Betriebssystem *n*/**landwirtschaftliches** farming scheme (system) *(s. a.* Betriebsart*)*
Betriebstyp *m* farm type
Betriebsverband *m s.* Betriebsklasse
Betriebsvollzugsnachweis *m* records of forest operations
Betriebswerk *n* forest management records
Betriebswirt *m* farm manager
Betriebswirtschaft *f*/**landwirtschaftliche** farm management; farm [business] organization
Betriebswirtschaftler *m* farm manager

Betriebswirtschaftslehre *f*/**forstliche** science of forest management
Betriebszählung *f*/**landwirtschaftliche** farm survey
Betriebsziel *n (forest)* management (business) goal, object of [silvicultural] management
~/landwirtschaftliches farm business goal
Betriebszieltyp *m* management goal type
Betriebszusammenlegung *f* farm amalgamation
Betriebszweig *m* [eines Landwirtschaftsbetriebes] [production] branch of a farm, farm enterprise
betropft *(bot, zoo)* guttate
Bett *n* bed • **ein ~ bereiten** to bed, to lay, to table *(tree-felling)*
Bettwanze *f* bed bug, Cimex lectularius
Betuletum *n* birch forest (grove)
Betulin *n* betulin[ol] *(triterpene alcohol)*
Beugemuskel *m* flexor [muscle]
Beugemuskelreflex *m* flexor reflex
Beuger *m* flexor [muscle]
Beugesehne *f* flexor tendon
Beugesehnenentzündung *f (vet)* flexor tendinitis
Beugungsreflex *m* flexor reflex
Beule *f (phyt, vet)* bump, outgrowth, excrescence
Beulenkrankheit *f*/**endemische** *(vet)* oriental sore *(caused by Leishmania tropica)*
beulig bumpy; knobby *(tree-trunk)*
Beulprobe *f* bilging test *(in canning)*
beurteilen to estimate, to assess; to judge
Beurteilung *f* estimation, assessment; judgement, judging
~/organoleptische organoleptic assessment
~/sensorische sensory evaluation (examination)
Beurteilungsmerkmal *n* point
Beurteilungspunkt *m* point
Beute *f* 1. *(hunt)* bag, prey, quarry; 2. [bee]hive
• **auf ~ ausgehen** to prey [up]on • **in eine ~ einschlagen** to hive *(honey-bees)*
~/doppelwandige double-walled [bee]hive
Beutedichte *f* prey density
Beutel *m* bag, sack; *(zoo)* bursa
Beutelabpackmaschine *f* bag packing machine
Beutel[druck]filter *n* bag filter
Beutelgalle *f (phyt)* pouch gall
Beutelnetz *n (pisc)* bag-net, purse-seine
Beutelverschließmaschine *f* bag sealing machine
Beutenabdeckung *f (api)* hive cover
Beutenbaum *m* bee tree
Beutetier *n* game, prey
Beuteverzehr *m* prey consumption
Bevölkerung *f* population
~/in der Landwirtschaft tätige agricultural population
~/ländliche rural population
bevorraten to store, to stock
bevorzugend/regenreiche Standorte ombrophilous
Bevorzugung *f (ecol, phyt)* preference

Bevorzugung 88

~ **der Gipfelknospe** apical dominance
Bewahrung *f* **der Natur** nature preservation (protection)
bewalden to [af]forest
bewaldet forested, wooded, woody, silvan, bosky
bewaldrechten to cut off branches, to [rough-]hew, to clear, to trim
Bewaldung *f* 1. [af]forestation; 2. woodiness
Bewaldungsdichte *f* **in Prozent** *s.* Bewaldungsprozentsatz
Bewaldungskarte *f* map of forest vegetation
Bewaldungsprozentsatz *m* percentage of forested area, forest [cover] percentage
Bewässerbarkeit *f* irrigability
bewässern to irrigate, to water
Bewässerung *f* irrigation, watering
~/**anfeuchtende** moistening irrigation
~/**düngende** fertilizing irrigation, ferti[rri]gation
~/**unterirdische** subirrigation, subsurface irrigation (watering)
~/**zu reichliche** overirrigation
Bewässerungsanlage *f* irrigation plant (facility), watering equipment
Bewässerungsausrüstung *f* irrigation (watering) equipment
Bewässerungsbedürftigkeit *f* irrigation need (requirement), need for irrigation
Bewässerungsboden *m* irrigated soil
Bewässerungsbrunnen *m* irrigation well
Bewässerungsdeich *m* levee • **einen ~ anlegen** to levee
Bewässerungsdüngung *f s.* Bewässerung/düngende
Bewässerungseffektivität *f* irrigation efficiency
Bewässerungsfeldbau *m* irrigated (irrigation) farming
Bewässerungsfläche *f* irrigation area (surface)
Bewässerungsforschung *f* irrigation research
Bewässerungsfruchtfolge *f* irrigation rotation
Bewässerungsfurche *f* irrigation furrow
Bewässerungsgabe *f* irrigation application
Bewässerungsgraben *m* [irrigation, watering] ditch, catch feeder
~/**schmaler** drove
Bewässerungsintensität *f* irrigation intensity
Bewässerungskanal *m* irrigation channel (canal), flume, fiume
Bewässerungskanalsystem *n* irrigation channel system
Bewässerungslandbau *m* irrigated (irrigation) farming
Bewässerungslandwirtschaft *f* irrigated agriculture
Bewässerungsleitung *f* irrigation line
bewässerungslos unirrigated, dry
Bewässerungsmatte *f* watering mat
Bewässerungsmethode *f* irrigation method
Bewässerungsplan *m* irrigation scheme

Bewässerungsprojekt *n* irrigation project
Bewässerungspumpe *f* irrigation pump
Bewässerungsregime *n* irrigation regime
Bewässerungsrohr *n* irrigation pipe
Bewässerungsrohrleitung *f* irrigation pipeline
Bewässerungsschlauch *m* irrigation hose
Bewässerungsschlepprohr *n* irrigation trail tube
Bewässerungsschleuse *f* irrigation sluice
Bewässerungssteuerung *f* irrigation scheduling
Bewässerungssystem *n* irrigation system
Bewässerungstechnik *f* irrigation engineering
Bewässerungstechnologie *f* irrigation technology
Bewässerungstiefe *f* irrigation depth
Bewässerungsventil *n* irrigation valve
Bewässerungsverfahren *n* irrigation method
Bewässerungsversuch *m* irrigation experiment
Bewässerungsvorrichtung *f* watering device
Bewässerungswasser *n* irrigation water
Bewässerungsweide *f* irrigated pasture
Bewässerungswirksamkeit *f* irrigation efficiency
Bewässerungszeitraum *m* irrigation period
bewegen to move; to exercise *(e.g. breeding animals)*; to give an airing to *(esp. said of horses)*
beweglich movable, mobile; motile
Beweglichkeit *f* movability, mobility; motility
~ **der Spermatozoen** sperm motility
Bewegung *f*/**nastische** nastic movement *(of plants)*
~/**seismonastische** seismonasty *(of plants)*
Bewegungsanomalie *f* locomotive disorder
Bewegungsapparat *m* locomotor system
Bewegungsarmut *f (vet)* akinesia
Bewegungsenergie *f* kinetic energy
bewegungsfähig motile
Bewegungsfähigkeit *f* motility
Bewegungskoordinationsstörung *f (vet)* ataxy
Bewegungslosigkeit *f (vet)* akinesia, torpor
Bewegungsnerv *m* motor nerve
Bewegungsorgane *npl* locomotor system
Bewegungphysiologie *f* exercise physiology
Bewegungsreaktion *f* **auf Temperaturreize** *(bot)* thermonasty
Bewegungsstörung *f (vet)* movement (locomotive) disorder
Bewegungsunlust *f* hypokinesis *(of animals)*
Bewegungsunruhe *f* hyperkinesis *(of animals)*
beweidbar [de]pasturable
beweiden to pasture, to graze
Beweidung *f* grazing, pastoral use
~/**jahreszeitliche (saisonale)** seasonal grazing
Beweidungsdruck *m* grazing pressure
Beweidungsintensität *f* grazing intensity
Beweidungsschaden *m* grazing damage
Beweis *m*/**experimentell erbrachter** experimental evidence
beweiseln *(api)* to queen
Beweiseln *n (api)* adding, allocation
bewerten to [e]valuate, to appraise; to estimate
~/**nach Punkten** to score

Bewertung f [e]valuation, appraisal, appraisement; estimate, estimation
~ **der Marktfähigkeit** market evaluation (e.g. of fruit)
~/**waldbauliche** silvicultural evaluation
bewimpert (bot, zoo) ciliate[d]
bewirtschaften 1. to manage; 2. to cultivate (soil)
~/**agrarisch** to farm
Bewirtschafter m manager
Bewirtschaftung f 1. management; 2. cultivation (of soil)
~/**extensive** extensive management (husbandry)
~/**intensive** intensive management (husbandry)
~/**komplexe (unspezialisierte)** mixed farming
~ **von Wasserlebewesen** aquaculture, aquiculture
~ **von Wild** game (wildlife) management
Bewirtschaftungseinheit f (forest) management unit
Bewirtschaftungsempfehlung f management scheme
Bewirtschaftungsgruppe f (forest) treatment class
Bewirtschaftungsrichtlinie f management instruction
bewölken/sich to becloud
bewölkt cloudy
Bewölkung f cloudiness
bewollt woolly, fleeced, lanate[d]
Bewuchs m plant (vegetation, vegetable) cover
bewurzeln/sich to root, to take root[s]
bewurzelt rooted, rooty
Bewurzelung f rooting, rootage
~/**reiche** rootiness
Bewurzelungsdichte f root density (of a soil)
Bewurzelungsfähigkeit f rootability, rooting ability
Bewurzelungsförderung f rooting stimulation
Bewurzelungshormon n rooting hormone
Bewurzelungsstimulierung f rooting stimulation
Bewurzelungsvermögen n rooting capacity
Bewußtlosigkeit f (vet) coma
Beziehung f/**mutualistische (zwischenartliche)** (ecol) mutualism
Bezoar[stein] m (vet) bezoar
Bezoarziege f ibex, Capra ibex ssp. aegagrus
Bezugshöhe f, **Bezugshorizont** m datum level (terrestrial survey)
BFI s. Blattflächenindex
BG s. Braugerste
BGMV s. Bohnengelbmosaikvirus
BHD s. Brusthöhendurchmesser
B-Horizont m (soil) B-horizon, enrichment (illuvial) horizon, accumulate layer
BI s. Besamungsindex
Biber m 1. castor (genus Castor); 2. beaver, Castor fiber
Biberbau m beaver-cave, beavery
Biberfell n beaver skin
Bibergeil n castor[eum] (excretion)
Bibernelle f (bot) burnet, Sanguisorba minor

Bienenwohnung

Bibernellrose f burnet (Scotch) rose, Rosa pimpinellifolia
Biberratte f coypu, Myocastor coypus
Bidens-Scheckungsvirus n bidens mottle virus, BmoV
Biegefestigkeit f bending (flexural, transverse) strength
Biegeholz n bentwood
Biegen n bending; curvature (of fruiting laterals)
Biegesteifigkeit f flexural rigidity (e.g. of timber)
Biegsame Nevadakiefer f limber pine, Pinus flexilis
Bien m honey-bee colony, bee people, hive
Biene f 1. bee (genus Apis); 2. honey-bee, hive bee, Apis mellifica (mellifera)
~/**einäugige** cyclops honey-bee (malformation)
Bienenbotanik f bee botany
Bienenbrut f [honey-bee] brood
Bienenfresser m bee-eater (genus Merops)
Bienenfutterpflanze f bee plant
Bienengarten m bee-garden
Bienengift n bee poison, honey-bee venom
Bienenhalter m bee-keeper, bee master (farmer), apiculturist, apiarist
Bienenhaltung f bee-keeping, apiculture, bee-culture
Bienenhaus n bee house (hut), apiary
Bienenhonig m honey, hinnie
Bienenkäfer m bee beetle, Trichodes apiarius
Bienenkönigin f queen [bee]
Bienenkorb m beehive, skep
Bienenkot m bees' faeces
Bienenkrankheit f bee disease
Bienenkunde f apiology
Bienenlaus f bee louse, Braula coeca
Bienenmännchen n s. Drohn
Bienenmotte f bee moth, Galleria mellonella
Bienennahrung f honey-bee forage
Bienenpflanze f bee plant
Bienenprodukt n hive product
Bienenschleier m bee veil
Bienenschwarm m swarm, hive
Bienenstand m apiary, (Am) bee yard
Bienenstich m bee sting
Bienenstock m [bee]hive
Bienentanz m bee dance
Bienentoxizität f bee toxicity (e.g. of pesticides)
Bienentränke f drinking fountain
bienenungefährlich safe to bees (e.g. a herbicide)
Bienenvolk n honey-bee colony, bee people, hive
Bienenwachs n beeswax, wax
~/**gebleichtes (weißes)** bleached beeswax, white wax
Bienenweide f bee pasture
Bienenweidepflanze f bee plant
Bienenwirtschaft f apiculture, bee-culture, [commercial] bee-keeping
bienenwirtschaftlich apicultural
Bienenwohnung f [bee]hive

Bienenwolf

Bienenwolf m *(ent)* beewolf, Philantus triangulum
Bienenzucht f bee breeding (culture), apiculture
Bienenzüchter m [honey-]bee breeder, apiculturist, apiarist
Bienenzüchtung f s. Bienenzucht
bienn *(bot)* biennial
Bier n beer
~/**alkoholarmes** low-alcohol beer, alcohol-reduced beer
~/**alkoholfreies** alcohol-free beer, near beer
~/**dunkles** dark beer
~/**helles** pale beer
~/**kalorienarmes** low-calorie beer
~/**obergäriges** top-fermented beer
~/**untergäriges** lager [beer], bottom-fermented beer
~/**wildes** gushing beer
Bieragave f *(bot)* maguey blando of Mexico, Agave atrovirens
bierartig alish
Bierbrauerei f brewery
Bierfarbe f beer colour
Bierfaß n beer barrel, cask
~/**bauchiges** cask
Bierfehler m beer defect
Bierfiltration f beer filtration
Bierhefe f 1. brewer's (beer) yeast *(comprehensive term)*; 2. s. ~/obergärige
~/**geerntete** spent yeast
~/**getrocknete** dried brewer's yeast
~/**obergärige** top[-fermentation] yeast, English (common beer) yeast, Saccharomyces cerevisiae
~/**untergärige** bottom[-fermentation] yeast
Bierherstellung f brewing
Bierschwand m, **Bierschwund** m beer loss
Biersorghum n beer sorghum, Sorghum nigricans
Biertreber pl brewer's grains
Biertreberpreßwasser n expeller waste
Bierwürze f [beer] wort • ~ **ausschlagen** to cast, to strike out
Bierwürzeagar m [beer-]wort agar
Biesfliege f bot[t]-fly, warble fly *(family Oestridae)*
Biestmilch f colostrum, colostral (first, early) milk, beestings, biestings
Bietzkalb n suckling calf
bifacial *(bot)* bifacial
Bifang-Kultur f afforestation with the Bifang method
Bifang-Verfahren n Bifang method
Bifenox n bifenox *(herbicide)*
Bifurkation f bifurcation
Bigaradie f bigarade, bitter orange *(from Citrus aurantium ssp. aurantium)*
bikollateral *(bot)* bicollateral
Bilanz f/**energetische** energy balance
Bilanzversuch m balance trial *(animal nutrition science)*
Bilch m, **Bilchmaus** f dormouse *(family Gliridae)*
bilden/Äste to branch [out]

~/**Beeren** to berry
~/**ein Aggregat (Bodenaggregat)** *(soil)* to aggregate
~/**eine Fistel** to fistulate
~/**eine Pfahlwurzel** to taproot
~/**Grasnarbe** to sward
~/**neue Haut** to skin *(wound healing)*
~/**Schuppen** to scale
~/**Wurzeln** to root
Bildetikett n picture tag
Bildhauptpunkt m principal point *(terrestrial survey)*
Bildmeßwesen n photogrammetry
Bildspektrometrie f imaging spectrometry
Bildüberdeckung f overlap *(photogrammetry)*
Bildungsdotter m light (white) yolk, yolk layers *(of bird's egg)*
Bildungsgewebe n *(bot)* meristem • **zum ~ gehörig** meristematic
~/**primäres** primary tissue
~ **zwischen Holz und Rinde** cambium
Bildungsschicht f matrix
Bildungswesen n/**landwirtschaftliches** agricultural education
Bilharzie f bilharzia worm, schistosome *(genus Schistosoma)*
Bilharzi[ell]ose f *(vet)* bilharziasis, schistosomiasis
biliär biliary
Bilifuszin n bilifuscin *(bile pigment)*
Bilineurin n bilineurine, choline *(vitamin)*
biliös bilious
Bilirubin n bilirubin *(bile pigment)*
Bilirubinausscheidung f **im Harn, Bilirubinurie** f *(vet)* bilirubinuria
Biliverdin n biliverdin *(bile pigment)*
Bilsenkraut n *(bot)* henbane, hyoscyamus, Hyoscyamus niger
Bilsenkrautmosaikvirus n henbane mosaic virus, HeMV
Biltmorestock m Biltmore stick *(timber mensuration)*
Bimetallthermometer n bimetallic thermometer
Bimsstein m pumice
BiMV s. Bartirismosaikvirus
Binapacryl n binapacryl *(acaricide, fungicide)*
Binde f bandage
Bindeapparat m binding apparatus *(of a pick-up baler)*
Bindedraht m binding wire; florist's wire
Bindegarn n binding thread (twine), binder (baler) twine
Bindegewebe n connective tissue
~/**embryonales** mesenchyme
~/**geformtes straffes** regular dense connective tissue
~/**lockeres** loose connective tissue
~/**straffes** dense connective tissue
~/**ungeformtes straffes** irregular dense connective tissue

Bindegewebe... *s.* Bindegewebs...
Bindegewebsentzündung *f (vet)* desmitis
Bindegewebsgerüst *n* stroma *(of an organ)*
Bindegewebsgeschwulst *f (vet)* fibroma; sarcoma
~/bösartige sarcoma
Bindegewebskapsel *f* fibrous capsule *(of the kidney)*
Bindegewebsknorpel *m* fibro-cartilage
Bindegewebsvermehrung *f (vet)* fibrosis
Bindegewebszelle *f* fibrocyte
~/undifferenzierte fibroblast
Bindehaut *f* conjunctiva
Bindehautentzündung *f (vet)* conjunctivitis
Bindekette *f* binding (binder, safety) chain *(timber transport)*
Bindemäher *m* [reaper-]binder, sheaf (grain) binder, sheafer, self-binder, harvester
Bindemaschine *f* binding machine *(e.g. for cut flowers)*
Bindematerial *n* tie material *(e.g. in grafting)*
binden 1. to bind, to tie; 2. to pounce *(bird of prey)*
~/an die Raufe to rack
~/an einen Baumpfahl to stake
~/ein Bukett to make up a bouquet
~/Garben to sheafe, to sheave
Bindeprotein *n* binding protein
Binder *m s.* Bindemäher
Bindesalat *m* cos [lettuce], Roman lettuce, romaine [lettuce], Lactuca sativa var. longifolia (romana)
Bindeseil *n* choker *(logging)*
Bindetisch *m* binder deck
Bindetuch *n* binding cloth
Bindevorrichtung *f* binding apparatus, binder, tying device
bindig cohesive, tenacious, non-scouring *(soil)*
Bindigkeit *f* cohesion
Bindungsstärke *f* affinity *(e.g. of antibodies)*
Bingelkraut *n* 1. mercury *(genus Mercurialis)*; 2. annual (garden, French) mercury, Mercurialis annua
Binkelweizen *m* club wheat, Triticum aestivum ssp. compactum
Binnendruck *m s.* Turgor[druck]
Binnenentwässerung *f* surface drainage
Binnenfischerei *f* freshwater (inland) fishery
Binnengewässerkunde *f* limnology
binnengewässerkundlich limnological
Binnengraben *m* inner trench
Binnenhodigkeit *f* cryptorchidism
Binnenklima *n* continental climate
Binnenrotation *f* inner [crop] rotation, inner sequence
Binnensee *m* inland lake
Binnenseefisch *m* lake fish
Binom *n* binomial
Binomialverteilung *f (biom)* binomial distribution
Binse *f* rush *(genus Juncus)*
Binsenginster *m* Spanish broom *(genus Spartium)*
Binsenkaktus *m* wickerware cactus *(genus Rhipsalis)*
Binsenlilie *f* 1. satin-flower *(genus Sisyrinchium)*; 2. blue-eyed grass, Sisyrinchium angustifolium
Binsenmoor *n* rush marsh
Binsenquecke *f* sea wheat-grass, Agropyron junceum
Bioakkumulation *f* bioaccumulation
bioaktiv bioactive
Bioaktivität *f* bioactivity
Bioanalogon *n* bioanalogue
Biochanin *n* **A** biochanin A *(phytoestrogen)*
Biochemie *f* biochemistry
~ der Eiweiße protein biochemistry
~ des Bodens soil biochemistry
~/mikroskopische cytochemistry
Biochemikalie *f* biochemical
biochemisch biochemical
Biochorologie *f* synchorology
biodegradabel biodegradable
Biodegradation *f* biodegradation, biodestruction
biodynamisch biodynamic[al]
bioelektrisch bioelectric[al]
Bioelektrizität *f* bioelectricity
Bioelement *n* bioelement
Bioenergetik *f* bioenergetics
bioenergetisch bioenergetic
Bioenergie *f* bioenergy
Bioethanomethrin *n* bioethanomethrin *(insecticide)*
Biofeedback *n* biofeedback
Bioformation *f (ecol)* biome
Biogas *n* biogas, fermentation (sewage) gas
Biogasanlage *f* biogas plant (installation)
Biogasmilcherhitzer *m* biogas milk pasteurizer
biogen biogenic
Biogenese *f* biogenesis
biogenetisch biogenetic
Biogenie *f* biogenesis
Biogeochemie *f* biogeochemistry
biogeochemisch biogeochemical
Biogeographie *f* biogeography
Biogeozönose *f (ecol)* biogeocoenosis
Bioindikator *m* bioindicator
Bioindikatornetz *n* bioindicator network
Biokatalysator *m* biocatalyst
Biokatalyse *f* biocatalysis
Biokinetik *f* biokinetics
Bioklima *n* bioclimate
Bioklimatik *f* bioclimatics
bioklimatisch bioclimatic
Bioklimatologie *f* bioclimatology
Biokolloid *n* biocolloid
Biokraftstoff *m* biofuel
Biolith *m* biolite, biolith *(non-clay mineral)*
Biologie *f* biology
~/landwirtschaftliche agricultural biology, agrobiology
biologisch biologic[al]

biologisch

~ aktiv (wirksam) bioactive
Biolumineszenz *f* bioluminescence
biolytisch biolytic
Biom *n (ecol)* biome
Biomagnifikation *f* biological magnification (amplification) *(increase of concentration e.g. of pesticides within a food chain)*
Biomasse *f* biomass
~/forstliche forest biomass
~/pflanzliche phytomass
Biomasseakkumulation *f* biomass accumulation
Biomassebestimmung *f* biomass determination
Biomassebrennstoff *m* biomass fuel
Biomasseertrag *m* biological yield
Biomasseproduktion *f* biomass production
Biomechanik *f* biomechanics
Biomembran[e] *f* biomembrane
Biometeorologie *f* biometeorology, bioclimatology
biometeorologisch biometeorological
Biometrie *f* biometrics, biometry, biostatistics
Biometriker *m* biometrician
biometrisch biometric[al], biostatistical
Biomonitoring *n* biomonitoring
Biomycin *n* biomycin, chlortetracycline *(antibiotic)*
Bionomie *f (ecol)* bionomy
bionomisch bionomic
Bioökologe *f* bioecologist
Bioökologie *f* bioecology
bioökologisch bioecological
Biopermethrin *n* biopermethrin *(insecticide)*
biophag biophagous
Biophage *m* biophage
Biophotolyse *f* biophotolysis *(photosynthesis)*
Biophysik *f* biophysics
biophysikalisch biophysical
Biophysiker *m* biophysicist
Biopräparat *n* biopreparation
Bioproduktion *f* bioproduction
Bioproduktivität *f* bioproductivity
Bioprozeßtechnik *f* bioprocess technology
Biopsie *f (vet)* biopsy
Biopterin *n* biopterin
Bioreaktor *m* fermenter, fermentor, fermenting tub
Bioresmethrin *n* [bio]resmethrin *(insecticide)*
Bioressource *f* bioresource
Biorhythmik *f* biorhythmics
Biorhythmus *m* biorhythm
Bios *n* II biotin, coenzyme R
~ III pantothenic acid *(of the vitamin B complex)*
Bioschlamm *m* biogas slurry, activated sludge
Biosfaktor *m* biofactor
Biosphäre *f* biosphere, ecosphere
Biosstoff *m* biofactor
Biostabilität *f* biostability
Biostatistik *f* biostatistics, biometrics, biometry
Biostatistiker *m* biometrician
biostatistisch biostatistical, biometric[al]
Biostimulator *m* biostimulator
Biostrom *m* bioelectric potential

Biosynthese *f* biosynthesis
Biosynthesehemmstoff *m* biosynthesis inhibitor
Biosyntheseweg *m* biosynthetic pathway
biosynthetisch biosynthetic
Biosystem *n* biosystem
Biosystematik *f* biosystematics
Biota *f (ecol)* biota
Biotechnik *f* bioengineering, biological engineering
biotechnisch biotechnical
Biotechnologie *f* biotechnology
biotechnologisch biotechnological
Biotelemetrie *f* radiotelemetry
Biotest *m* bioassay
Biotin *n* biotin, vitamin H, coenzyme R
Biotincarboxylase *f* biotin carboxylase *(enzyme)*
Biotinidase *f* biotinidase *(enzyme)*
Biotinmangel *m (vet)* biotin deficiency, abiotinosis
biotisch biotic[al]
Biotit *m* biotite *(non-clay mineral)*
Biotop *m(n) (ecol)* biotope, habitat
Biotop... *s. a.* Habitat...
biotopeigen indigenous, autochthonal, autochthonous
biotopfremd allochthonous
Biotopgestaltung *f* habitat creation
Biotopinsel *f* habitat island
Biotopkartierung *f* habitat mapping
Biotopklima *n* bioclimate, ecoclimate
Biotopmanagement *n*, **Biotoppflege** *f* habitat management
Biotopschutz *m* biotope protection, habitat conservation
Biotronik *f* biotronics
Biotrophie *f* biotrophy
Biotropismus *m* biotropism
Biotyp[us] *m* biotype
Bioverfahrenstechnik *f* bioengineering, biological engineering
Bioverfügbarkeit *f* bioavailability
Biowirkstoff *m* hormone
Biowissenschaft *f* bioscience, life science
biozid [wirkend] biocidal
Biozid *n* biocide
Biozönologie *f* biocoenology, biocoenotics, synecology
Biozönose *f* biocoenosis
Biozönotik *f* biocoenotics
biozönotisch biocoenotic
Biozyklus *m* biocycle
Biphenyl *n* biphenyl *(fungicide)*
bipolar bipolar
Bipolarität *f* bipolarity
Birke *f* birch *(genus Betula)*
Birkenblattroller *m* birch[-tree] weevil, birch-leaf rolling weevil, Deporaus betulae, Rhynchites alni
Birkenhain *m* birch grove, birch forest
Birkenholz *n* birchwood, birch
Birkenkampfer *m* betulin[ol] *(triterpene alcohol)*

Birkenmilchling *m (bot)* shaggy milk cap, sharp agaric, Lactarius torminosus
Birkennestspinner *m (ent)* small eggar (egger), Eriogaster (Bombyx) lanestris
Birkenöl *n* birch oil
Birkenpilz *m* birch mushroom, rough-stemmed boletus, rough[-stalked] boletus, shaggy boletus, Leccinum scabrum
Birkenporling *m* birch bracket fungus, Piptoporus betulinus
Birkenreizker *m s.* Birkenmilchling
Birkenrindenöl *n* birch oil
Birkenröhrling *m s.* Birkenpilz
Birkenrost *m (phyt)* birch rust
Birkensaft *m* birch sap
Birkenspanner *m* peppered moth, Biston betularius
Birkenwald *m* birch forest (grove)
Birkhahn *m* black (heath) cock
Birkhenne *f* grey-hen
Birkhuhn *n*, **Birkwild** *n* grey (heath) hen, black grouse (game), Lyrurus tetrix
Birnbaum *m* pear[-tree] *(1. genus Pyrus; 2. Pyrus communis)*
Birnbaumnetzwanze *f* pear lace bug, Stephanitis pyri
Birnbaumprachtkäfer *m* [sinuate] pear borer, pear[-tree] borer, Agrilus sinuatus
Birnbaumprachtkäferlarve *f* [sinuate] pear borer, pear[-tree] borer
Birne *f* pear
Birnenblattfloh *m* pear psylla (sucker), Psylla pyricola
Birnenblattgallmücke *f* pear leaf curling midge, Dasineura pyri
Birnenblattwanze *f* pear lace bug, Stephanitis pyri
Birnenblattwespe *f s.* Birnengespinstwespe
Birnenblutlaus *f* woolly pear aphid, pear woolly aphis, Eriosoma pyricola, Schizoneura lanuginosa
Birnenbrand *m* pear blight *(caused by Erwinia amylovora)*
birnenförmig pyriform, piriform
Birnengallmücke *f* pear midge, Contarinia pyrivora
Birnengespinstwespe *f* social pear saw-fly, Neurotoma flaviventris
Birnengitterrost *m* pear rust *(caused by Gymnosporangium sabinae = G. fuscum)*
Birnenknospenfall *m* pear bud drop *(virosis)*
Birnenmost *m* perry
Birnenpockenmilbe *f* pear leaf blister mite, Eriophyes pyri
Birnenquitte *f* pear[-shaped] quince
Birnensägewespe *f* pear saw-fly, Hoplocampa brevis
Birnenschorf *m (phyt)* pear scab *(caused by Venturia pyrina)*

Birnensplintkäfer *m* pear bark-beetle, Scolytus rugulosus
Birnenverfall *m* pear decline [disease] *(mycoplasmosis)*
Birnenwein *m* perry
Birnessit *m* birnessite *(non-clay mineral)*
Birsch *f s.* Pirsch
Bisam *m s.* Bisamrattenfell
Bisamdistel *f (bot)* jurinea *(genus Jurinea)*
Bisamklee *m* sweet trefoil, blue (Swiss) melilot, Trigonella coerulea
Bisamkürbis *m* cushaw, China squash, winter crookneck [pumpkin], Cucurbita moschata
Bisamochse *m* musk-ox, Ovibos moschatus
Bisamratte *f* musk-rat, musquash, Ondatra zibethica
Bisamrattenfell *n* musk-rat, musquash
Bisamstrauch *m* musk mallow, Abelmoschus moschatus, Hibiscus abelmoschus
Bischofsmütze *f* star cactus *(genus Astrophytum)*
Bisexualität *f* bisexuality
bisexuell bisexual, hermaphroditic[al], hermaphrodite
Bismut-Sulfit-Agar *m* bismuth sulphite agar *(microbiology)*
Bison *m* bison *(genus Bison)*
bissig ferocious, vicious *(dog)*
Bissigkeit *f* ferocity
Bißwunde *f* bite wound
Bisystem *n (ecol)* coaction
Bitertanol *n* bitertanol *(fungicide)*
Bithionol *n* bithionol *(anthelminthic, fungicide)*
Bitoscanat *n* bitoscanate *(anthelminthic)*
Bitterdistel *f* blessed thistle, Cnicus benedictus
Bittere Schleifenblume *f* [flowered] candytuft, rock[et] candytuft, Iberis amara
Bittereinheit *f* bitterness unit *(brewing)*
Bitterer Schwefelkopf *m (bot)* sulphur tuft, Hypholoma fasciculare
Bitteres Yams *n* bitter (three-leaved) yam, Dioscorea dumetorum
Bitterfäule *f* bitter (gloeosporium) rot *(of stored fruit, caused by Gloeosporium spp.)*
Bittergeschmack *m* bitterness *(e.g. of wine)*
Bitterklee *m* buckbean, marigold trefoil, bean bog, Menyanthes trifoliata
Bitterkraut *n (bot)* French scorzonera, Reichardia picroides
Bitterlich-Gerät *n* Bitterlich's angle-gauge, angle-count gauge, sighting bar *(timber mensuration)*
Bitterlich-Methode *f* [Bitterlich] angle-count method of cruising, Bitterlich (prism-count) method, variable-radius method
Bitterlich-Stab *m s.* Bitterlich-Gerät
Bittermandelbaum *m* bitter almond, Prunis dulcis var. amara
Bittermandelöl *n* bitter almond oil
Bitternuß *f* bitternut, Carya cordiformis

Bitterorange

Bitterorange f 1. trifoliate orange, Poncirus trifoliatus; 2. bitter (sour) orange, bigarade *(fruit from Citrus aurantium ssp. aurantium)*
Bitterpeptid n bitter peptide
Bittersalz n Epsom (bitter) salt *(laxative, magnesium fertilizer)*
Bitterschopf m aloe *(genus Aloe)*
Bitterspat m magnesite *(non-clay mineral)*
Bitterstoff m bitter substance (principle)
Bitterstoffwert m bitterness value *(of hop)*
Bittersüß n, **Bittersüßer Nachtschatten** m bittersweet, bitter (woolly) nightshade, felonwood, Solanum dulcamara
Bitterwein m bitter wine
Bitterwert m bitterness value *(of hop)*
Bitumen n bitumen, pitch
Bitumenemulsion f bitumen emulsion *(soil conditioner)*
Bitumenmulch m asphalt mulch
Bitumensiegel n tar seal *(road construction)*
Biuret n biuret *(urea derivative)*
Biuretreaktion f biuret reaction *(e.g. for detecting peptid bonds in milk)*
Bivalent n *(gen)* bivalent
Bixin n 1. bixin *(carotenoic acid)*; 2. annatto, arnotto, roucou *(dye)*
BK s. Krankheit/Bornasche
BkMV s. Bilsenkrautmosaikvirus
BKMV s. Kräuselmosaikvirus der Gartenbohne
Blähsucht f *(vet)* bloat, hoven, meteorism, tympanites, tympany
blanchieren to blanch, to bleach, to etiolate *(plant parts by exclusion of light)*
Blanchieren n blanching, bleaching, etiolation
Blankaal m silver eel
Blankkochen n blank boiling *(sugar manufacture)*
Blanksaat f 1. direct seeding, open (plain, coverless) sowing; 2. pure crop
Bläschen n blister, vesicle, follicle
Bläschenausschlag m *(vet)* coital exanthema, infectious pustular vulvovaginitis
~ **des Pferdes** equine coital exanthema, horse-pox
Bläschendrüse f vesicular gland
Bläschenfollikel m Graafian follicle (vesicle)
Bläschenkeim m *(zoo)* blastocyst, blastodermic vesicle
Bläschenkrankheit f **der Schweine** swine vesicular disease, S.V.D.
Blase f 1. bladder, vesica; 2. [urinary] bladder
~/flüssigkeitsgefüllte *(zoo, vet)* cyst
Blasenbaum m 1. koelreuteria, China tree *(genus Koelreuteria)*; 2. goldenrain tree, Koelreuteria paniculata
Blasenfarn m 1. bladder fern *(genus Cystopteris)*; 2. berry bladder fern, Cystopteris bulbifera
Blasenfinne f cysticercus *(of numerous tapeworms)*
Blasenfinnenbefall m *(vet)* cysticercosis
blasenförmig vesical

Blasenfuchsschwanz m creeping foxtail, Alopecurus ventricosus (arundinaceus), Gastridium ventricosum
Blasenfuß m *(ent)* thrips *(order Thysanoptera)*
Blasenkäfer m 1. blister beetle *(family Meloidae)*; 2. Spanish fly, blister fly (beetle), Lytta (Cantharis) vesicatoria
Blasenkeim m *(zoo)* blastula
Blasenkirsche f *(bot)* 1. alkekengi, Physalis alkekengi; 2. tomatillo, Physalis ixocarpa
Blasenklee m strawberry clover, Trifolium fragiferum
Blasenkrankheit f **der Teepflanze** blister blight [of tea] *(caused by Exobasidium vexans)*
Blasenniere f polycyclic kidney [disease]
Blasenriedgras n s. Blasensegge
Blasenrost m blister rust *(caused by Cronartium spp.)*
Blasensegge f blister (bladder) sedge, Carex vesicaria
Blasensenne f s. Blasenstrauch
Blasenspeicher m bladder-type accumulator *(hydraulic equipment)*
Blasenspiere f *(bot)* ninebark *(genus Physocarpus)*
Blasenstein m *(vet)* bladder stone, urolith, cystolith
Blasenstrauch m bladder senna *(genus Colutea)*
Blasensucht f *(vet)* pemphigus
Blasenwurm[finnen]befall m *(vet)* measles, echinococcosis, cysticercosis
Blasiger Rindenkrebs m **der Birne** pear blister canker *(virosis)*
Blaskopf m deflector, outlet *(of a pneumatic conveyor)*
Blässe f *(vet)* pallor, paleness
Blasser Hahnenfuß m *(bot)* hairy buttercup, Ranunculus sardous
Blasticidin-S n blasticidin-S *(fungicide)*
Blastoderm n blastoderm, embryonic disk
Blastodiskus m blastodisk
Blastogenese f blastogenesis
Blastokinin n blastokinin *(glycoprotein)*
Blastomer n, **Blastomere** f blastomere
Blastomykose f *(vet)* blastomycosis
Blastospore f *(bot)* blastospore
Blastovariation f blastovariation
Blastoöl n *(zoo)* blastocoel[e]
Blastozyste f blastocyst, blastodermic vesicle
Blastula f blastula
Blatt n 1. *(bot)* leaf; 2. blade *(e.g. of a saw)* *(s. a. under Blätter)*
~/elektronisches electronic leaf *(in horticulture)*
~/gefiedertes feathery leaf
~/geteiltes compound leaf
~/gipfelständiges terminal leaf
~/grundständiges bottom leaf
~/ungeteiltes entire leaf
~/unpaarig (wechselständig) gefiedertes alternate pinnate leaf

~/zusammengesetztes compound leaf
Blattabszission f, Blattabwurf m s. Blattfall
Blattachsel f [leaf] axil
blattachselbürtig axillary
Blattachselsproß m sucker
blattachselständig axillary
Blattader f [leaf] vein, nerve [of leaf]
Blattaderung f veining
blattähnlich s. blattartig
Blattälchen n leaf (foliar) nematode (genus Aphelenchoides)
Blattalter n leaf age
Blattalterung f leaf senescence
Blattanalyse f leaf (foliar) analysis
Blattanatomie f leaf anatomy
Blattanlage f [leaf] primordium
Blattanordnung f leaf arrangement
~ in der Blattknospe vernation
Blattansatzstelle f leaf initiation site
Blattanstellwinkel m leaf (foliage) angle
Blattapparat m leaf apparatus
Blattapplikation f foliage application (e.g. of plant protectants)
Blattarchitektur f leaf architecture
blattartig leafy, foliate, foliaceous, phylloid
Blattatmung f leaf respiration
Blattaufhellung f leaf paling
Blattausbruch m s. Blattaustrieb
Blattausrichtung f leaf orientation
Blattaustrieb m leafing, frondescence
Blattbegonie f foliage begonia (comprehensive term)
Blattbehaarung f leaf-hairiness
Blattbehandlung f foliage application
Blattbeulenkrankheit f der Birne leaf blister of pear (caused by Taphrina bullata)
Blattbildung f foliation
Blattbrand m (phyt) leaf burn (scorch), leaf blight (necrosis); leaf smut (caused by fungi)
~ der Narzisse leaf spot of narcissus (caused by Heterosporium gracile)
Blattbräune f der Kirsche cherry leaf scorch (caused by Gnomonia erythrostoma)
Blättchen n leaflet, foliole • mit einem ~ unifoliolate
blättchentragend folioliferous
Blattchlorose f leaf chlorosis (yellowing)
Blattdach n s. Blätterdach
Blattdiagnose f foliar diagnosis
Blattdichte f foliage density
Blattdiffusionswiderstand m leaf [diffusion, diffusive] resistance
Blattdill m green dill
Blattdünger m foliar[-applied] fertilizer, foliar feed
Blattdüngung f leaf-feeding, leaf (foliage) dressing, foliar fertilization (dressing)
Blatte f (hunt) [deer-]caller
Blatteiweiß n leaf protein

Blattentfaltung f unfolding of leaves
Blätter npl leaves (s. a. under Blatt) • ~ abwerfen to abscise • ~ austreiben to leaf [out] • ~ hervorbringend phyllophorous • mit Blättern wie Achillea achilleafolious • mit drüsigen Blättern adenophyllous • mit durchwachsenen Blättern perfoliate • mit eiförmigen Blättern oval-leaved, ovalifolious, ovatifolious • mit gebogenen Blättern curvifoliate • mit gefiederten Blättern pinnately-leaved, pinnatifolious • mit gegenständigen Blättern oppositifolious • mit gesägten Blättern serratifolious • mit gestielten Blättern petiolar, petiolate, podophyllous • mit gleichen Blättern isophyllous • mit kellenförmigen Blättern trullifolious • mit kurzen Blättern brevifoliate • mit sitzenden Blättern sessifolious • mit stengelumfassenden Blättern amplexifoliate • mit stielrunden Blättern teretifolious • mit ungeteilten Blättern integrifolious • mit ungleichen Blättern anisophyllous • mit wechselständigen Blättern alternifoliate • mit wolligen Blättern eriophyllous
Blätterdach n [leaf, foliar] canopy, canopy cover
~/geschlossenes close (full) canopy
Blätterdachdichte f canopy density
blätterfressend leaf-eating, phyllophagous
Blätterkamm m leaf comb (of fowl)
Blätterkohl m winter cabbage, Brassica oleracea var. acephala
Blättermagen m omasum, third stomach (of ruminants)
Blättermagenverstopfung f omasal impaction
Blätterpilz m agaric, gill fungus, gill-bearing mushroom (order Agaricales)
Blattexplantat n leaf explant
Blattfall m leaf fall (abscission), leaf drop[ping], leaf cast[ing], defoliation
Blattfallkrankheit f der Johannis- und Stachelbeere leaf spot of currant (caused by Drepanopeziza ribis)
~ der Weinrebe downy mildew of grapes, grape [downy] mildew (caused by Plasmopara viticola)
~ des Kaffees die back of coffee, coffee berry disease (caused by Glomerella cingulata, conidial stage Colletotrichum coffeanum)
Blattfallperiode f period of leaf fall
Blattfarbstoff m leaf pigment
Blattfaser f leaf fibre
Blattfederchen n acrospire (e.g. in cereals)
Blattfilter n leaf filter
Blattfläche f leaf (foliage) area, phylloplane
Blattflächendauer f leaf area duration
Blattflächenindex m leaf area index, LAI
Blattflächenintegral n leaf area duration
Blattflächenverhältnis n leaf area ratio, LAR
Blattflächenwirkungsdauer f leaf area duration
Blattflächenzeitintegral n leaf area duration
Blattflavanoid n leaf flavanoid

Blattfleckenkrankheit 96

Blattfleckenkrankheit f *(phyt)* leaf spot[ting disease], leaf-flecking disease, leaf blotch *(comprehensive term)*
~ **der Schwarzen Johannisbeere** common leaf spot of black currant *(caused by Mycosphaerella ribis)*
~ **der Tomate** tomato leaf spot, leaf blight of tomato *(caused by Septoria lycopersici)*
~ **des Salats** anthracnose of lettuce *(caused by Marssonina panattoniana)*
~ **des Selleries** celery leaf spot, late celery blight *(caused by Septoria apii)*
Blattfleckenvirus n **der Dendrobie** dendrobium leaf spot virus
Blattfleckigkeit f, **Blattfleckung** f leaf spotting (mottle) *(s. a. Blattfleckenkrankheit)*
Blattfloh m psylla, psyllid, flea (jumping plant) louse *(family Psyllidae)*
Blattförderschnecke f leaf auger
Blattform f leaf shape
blattförmig leaf-shaped, foliiform
Blattfraß m leaf-feeding
blattfressend leaf-eating, phyllophagous
Blattfresser m foliage feeder
Blattfrucht f leaf (foliage) crop
Blattfungizid n foliage fungicide
Blattgalle f leaf gall
Blattgelb n xanthophyll, phylloxanthin
Blattgelenk n leaf joint
Blattgemüse n green vegetable[s], greens, leafy greens (vegetable)
Blattgewebe n leaf tissue
Blattgrün n chlorophyll, leaf-green • **ohne** ~ achlorophyllose, achlorophyllous
Blattgrund m leaf base
Blatthaar n leaf hair
Blatthäutchen n ligule • **ohne** ~ liguleless
Blattherbizid n leaf[-acting] herbicide, foliage herbicide
Blatthornkäfer m chafer, scarabaeid, dung beetle *(family Scarabaeidae)*
Blatthornkäferlarve f [chafer, white] grub
Blattizid n blatticide
Blattkäfer m leaf[-eating] beetle, tortoise beetle, chrysomelid *(family Chrysomelidae)* • **die** ~ **betreffend** chrysomelid
Blattkaktus m 1. phyllocactus *(comprehensive term)*; 2. Christmas (orchid) cactus, epiphyllum *(genus Epiphyllum)*
Blattkammer f leaf chamber *(for metabolic studies)*
Blattkeim m acrospire *(e.g. in cereals)* • **den** ~ **treiben** to acrospire
Blattkissen n leaf cushion (joint), pulvinus
Blattknospe f [leaf] bud
Blattknospensteckling m leaf-bud cutting
Blattkohl m kale, collard, Brassica oleracea convar. acephala var. viridis
Blattkonzentration f s. Blattnährstoffkonzentration
Blattkrankheit f foliage disease

Blattkräuselung f leaf curl[ing], curling of leaves
Blattkronenbaum m tufted tree
Blattlappung f leaf lobes
Blattlauch m scallion
Blattlaus f 1. aphid, aphis, leaf louse, greenfly (suborder Aphidina); 2. aphid, aphis, plant-louse *(family Aphididae)*
~/**gallenerzeugende** gall aphid *(comprehensive term)*
Blattlausbekämpfung f aphid control
Blattlausbekämpfungsmittel n aphi[do]cide
blattlausbürtig aphid-borne
blattlausfressend aphidivorous, aphidophagous
Blattlausfresser m aphidophage, aphidivorous insect
Blattlausgalle f aphid gall
blattlausresistent aphid-resistant
Blattlausparasit m aphid parasite
blattlausübertragbar aphid-transmissible
blattlausübertragen aphid-borne
Blattlausübertragung f aphid transmission
blattlausvernichtend aphicidal
Blattlausvernichtungsmittel n aphi[do]cide
Blattleitfähigkeit f leaf conductance
blattlos leafless, bald, aphyllous
Blattloser Igelbusch m leafless anabasis, Anabasis aphylla
Blattlosigkeit f leaflessness, aphylly
Blattmasse f herbage, herb
Blattmeristem n leaf meristem
Blattmine f *(phyt)* leaf mine
Blattminierer m *(ent)* leaf (foliage) miner
Blattmosaik n *(phyt)* leaf mosaic
Blattnager m leaf-eating weevil, brown leaf weevil *(genus Phyllobius)*
Blattnährstoffkonzentration f leaf [nutrient] concentration
~/**kritische** critical leaf concentration, CLC
Blattnarbe f leaf scar
Blattnekrose f *(phyt)* leaf necrosis (blight); leaf smut *(caused by fungi)*
Blattnekrosevirus n **des Salats** lettuce necrosis virus
Blattnematode m leaf (foliar) nematode *(genus Aphelenchoides)*
Blattnerv m s. Blattrippe
Blattoberfläche f leaf surface
Blattöhrchen n *(bot)* auricle, claw
Blattorgan n foliage organ
Blattparasit m foliar parasite
Blattpetersilie f parsley, Petroselinum crispum ssp. crispum
Blattpflanze f foliage (green) plant
Blattpigment n leaf pigment
Blattpocken[gall]milbe f leaf blister mite *(genus Phytoptus)*
Blattpolster n leaf cushion (joint), pulvinus
Blattpolymorphismus m heterophylly
Blattprimordium n [leaf] primordium

Blattprotein *n* leaf protein
Blattproteinkonzentrat *n* leaf protein concentrate, LPC
Blattquirl *m (bot)* whorl, verticil
Blattrand *m* leaf margin
Blattrandbrand *m (phyt)* edge burn
Blattrandchlorose *f (phyt)* edge chlorosis
Blattrandkäfer *m* pea and bean weevil, *(Am)* pea leaf weevil *(genus Sitona)*
Blattrandnekrose *f (phyt)* edge necrosis, marginal necrosis (scorch)
Blattrandtyp *m* leaf margin type
Blattrandverbrennung *f* leaf margin burn
Blattrandvergilbung *f* edge yellowing, yellow edge, xanthosis
Blattranke *f* leaf tendril
blattreich leafy, foliose
Blattreichtum *m* leafiness
blättrig foliate
Blattrippe *f* rib, nerve [of leaf], [leaf] vein
Blattrippennekrose *f (phyt)* rib necrosis
Blattrippenverfärbung *f (phyt)* rib discolo[u]ration
Blattrollkrankheit *f* leaf-roll disease, leaf curl[ing]
~ der Erbse pea leaf rolling
~ der Kartoffel potato phloem necrosis, potato leaf roll, tuber net necrosis
~ der Süß- und Sauerkirsche cherry leaf roll
Blattrollrosenblattwespe *f* rose leaf saw-fly, Blennocampa pusilla
Blattrollung *f* leaf rolling (curl)
Blattrollvirose *f (phyt)* leaf curl virosis
Blattrollvirus *n* leaf curl virus
~ der Erbse und Ackerbohne pea leaf roll virus, PLRV
Blattrosette *f* leaf rosette
~/trichterförmige plant vase *(e.g. of Bromeliaceae for collecting rain-water)*
Blattrosettenbildung *f* rosetted growth, rosetting *(abnormal graftage reaction)*
Blattrost *m* leaf rust [disease]
Blattröte *f* **des Hafers** barley yellow dwarf *(virosis)*
Blattsaft *m* leaf sap
Blattsäge *f* blade saw
Blattsalat *m* [loose-]leaf lettuce, curled (cut, cutting) lettuce, Lactuca sativa var. crispa
Blattsauger *m* 1. leaf-sucker *(suborder Psyllina)*; 2. flea-louse, psylla, psyllid *(family Psyllidae)*
• **die ~ betreffend** psyllid
Blattschaden *m* foliar injury
Blattschädling *m* foliar pest
Blattscheckung *f (phyt)* leaf mottle, mottle leaf
~ der Süßkirsche cherry mottle leaf *(virosis)*
Blattscheckungsvirus *n* **der Erdbeere** strawberry mottle virus
Blattscheide *f* [leaf] sheath
~/tütenartige ocrea, ochrea • **mit tütenartiger ~** ocreate[d]
Blattschmarotzer *m* foliar parasite

Blattschneiderameise *f* leaf-cutting ant, leaf cutter *(genera Atta and Acromyrmex)*
Blattschneiderbiene *f* [patchwork] leaf-cutting bee, leaf cutter *(genus Megachile)*
Blattschnittstück *n* leaf cut
Blattsikkationsmittel *n* foliage desiccant
Blattspindel *f* rachis
Blattspitze *f* leaf tip (apex)
Blattspitzenform *f* shape of leaf apex
Blattspitzenwelke *f (phyt)* leaf die back
Blattspray *m* foliar spray *(for treating ornamentals)*
Blattspreite *f* [leaf] blade, [leaf] lamina, limb
Blattspritzmittel *n* foliar spray *(for treating ornamentals)*
Blattspritzung *f* foliar spray[ing]
Blattspur *f* leaf trace
Blattspurbündel *n*, **Blattspurstrang** *f* leaf vascular bundle, leaf trace
Blattsteckling *m* leaf [bud] cutting, leafy cutting
Blattstellung *f* leaf position (pose, arrangement)
Blattstellungslehre *f* phyllotaxis, phyllotaxy
Blatt-Stengel-Verhältnis *n* leaf-[to-]stem ratio
Blattstiel *m* leaf-stalk, [leaf] petiole, footstalk, strig
Blattstielblatt *n* phyllode, phyllodium
Blattstreckung *f* leaf extension
Blattstreifenkrankheit *f*/**bakterielle** *(phyt)* bacterial stripe
Blattstreifigkeit *f* leaf stripping
Blattstück *n* leaf cut
blatttragend phyllophorous
Blattüberstand *m* saw-blade projection
Blatt- und Stengelbakteriose *f* **der Begonie** bacterial blight (leaf spot) of begonia *(caused by Xanthomonas campestris begoniae)*
Blattunterseite *f* leaf undersurface
Blattverbrennung *f (phyt)* leaf (foliage) burn, leaf scorch (firing)
Blattverdrehung *f (phyt)* leaf distortion
Blattvergilbung *f* leaf yellowing (chlorosis)
Blattverlust *m* leaf loss *(e.g. during haymaking)*
Blattverschmälerung *f (phyt)* leaf narrowing
Blattwachs *n* leaf-wax
Blattwachstum *n* leaf growth
Blattwanze *f* leaf bug *(comprehensive term)*
Blattwassergehalt *m* leaf water content
Blattwasserpotential *n* leaf water potential
Blattwerk *n* foliage, leafage, herbage
Blattwerkdichte *f* foliage density
Blattwespe *f* leaf-wasp, saw-fly *(family Tenthredinidae)*
Blattwespenlarve *f* saw-fly caterpillar, pseudocaterpillar, false caterpillar
Blattwiderstand *m* leaf resistance
Blattwinkel *m* leaf (foliage) angle
Blattwinkelverteilung *f* foliage angle distribution
Blattzeit *f (hunt)* rutting season (time), rut
Blattzisterne *f* plant vase *(e.g. of Bromeliaceae for collecting rain-water)*
blau blue, caeruleus • **~ werden** to blue *(timber)*

Blaualge

Blaualge f blue-green alga *(division Cyanophyta)*
Blaubart m *(bot)* bluebeard, Caryopteris incana
Blaubeere f s. Heidelbeere
Blaublattfunkie f plantain lily, Hosta sieboldiana
Blaubock m *(zoo)* nilg[h]ai, Boselaphus tragocamelus
Blaudolde f blue lace-flower, Didiscus caeruleus
Bläue f blue [sap] stain *(of sapwood, esp. caused by fungi of genera Ophiostoma, Ceratostomella, Penicillium or Fusarium)*
Blaue Akelei f *(bot)* columbine, Aquilegia caerulea
~ **Funkie** f blue plantain lily, Hosta ventricosa
~ **Jakobsleiter** f *(bot)* Jacob's ladder, Polemonium caeruleum
~ **Kiefernholzwespe** f *(ent)* giant horntail, Sirex juvencus
~ **Lupine** f narrow-leaved lupin[e], blue lupin[e], Lupinus angustifolius
~ **Luzerne** f alfalfa, [blue] lucern[e], [purple] medic[k], Medicago sativa [ssp. sativa]
~ **Malve** f blue mallow, Mediterranean tree mallow, Malva sylvestris (mauritiana)
~ **Passionsblume** f blue passion-flower, Passiflora caerulea
~ **Prunkwinde** f blue morning glory, Nile ipomoea, Pharbitis (Ipomoea) nil
~ **Scheinzypresse** f Lawson['s] cypress, Chamaecyparis lawsoniana
~ **Schwertlilie** f German (tall bearded) iris, Iris germanica
~ **Zecke** f 1. blue tick, Boophilus decoloratus; 2. [tropical] cattle tick, Boophilus microplus
Blaueisenerde f vivianite *(non-clay mineral)*
Bläuepilz m blue stain fungus
Blauer Brummer m bluebottle, blowfly, Calliphora vicina
~ **Eisenhut** m *(bot)* monkshood, aconite, Aconitum napellus
~ **Erlenblattkäfer** m alder leaf beetle, Agelastica alni
~ **Heinrich (Natternkopf)** m *(bot)* [viper's] bugloss, blue devil, blueweed, Echium vulgare
~ **Schattenmohn** m blue poppy, Meconopsis betonicifolia
~ **Sisal** m blue sisal, Agave amaniensis
~ **Weidenblattkäfer** m blue willow beetle *(1. Phyllodecta vitellinae; 2. Phyllodecta vulgatissima)*
~ **Wiener** m Vienna Blue [rabbit] *(breed)*
Blaues Büffelgras n blue buffalo grass, Cenchrus ciliaris
~ **Lieschen** n German (Persian) violet, exacum, Exacum affine
~ **Ordensband** n *(ent)* ash underwing, Catocala fraxini
~ **Pfeifengras** n [purple] moor grass, blae grass, flying bent, molinia, Molinia caerulea
Blauesche f blue ash, Fraxinus quadrangulata
Blaufäule f **[von Koniferen]** blue rot, blueing [of conifers] *(caused by Ceratostomella spp.)*
Blaufichte f Colorado spruce, Picea pungens
Blaufrüchtige Heckenkirsche f sweet-berry honeysuckle, Lonicera caerulea
Blaufuchs m blue fox, Alopex lagopus
Blauglockenbaum m *(bot)* 1. paulownia *(genus Paulownia)*; 2. paulownia, Paulownia tomentosa
Blaugras n moor grass *(genus Sesleria)*
blaugrau *(bot, zoo)* glaucous, caesious
blaugrün *(bot, zoo)* glaucous, caesious, blue-green
Blaugrüne Alge f blue-green alga *(class Cyanophyceae)*
~ **Binse** f hard rush, Juncus inflexus
~ **Palmlilie** f soap-weed, Spanish-bayonet, Yucca glauca
~ **Quecke** f intermediate wheat-grass, Agropyron intermedium, Elymus hispidus
Blaugummibaum m blue gum [tree], southern blue gum, Eucalyptus globulus
Blauholz n logwood, Campeachy wood
Blauholzbaum m logwood, Haematoxylum campechianum
Blauholzfarbstoff m logwood principle
Blaukammkrankheit f 1. blue comb [disease], summer disease *(of fowl)*; 2. s. ~ des Huhnes
~ **des Huhnes** avian monocytosis (infectious diarrhoea), battery nephrosis, Bright's (pullet) disease, X-disease
Blaukäse m blue cheese
Blaukissen n aubrietia, purple madwort *(genus Aubrieta)*
Blaulicht n blue light
Blaulilie f *(bot)* agapanthus *(genus Agapanthus)*
Blaumeise f blue tit, Parus caeruleus
Blauregen m *(bot)* Chinese wisteria, Wisteria sinensis
Blaurücken m sockeye [salmon], nerka, Oncorhynchus nerka
Blausäure f hydrocyanic (prussic) acid
Blausäurefreisetzung f cyanogenesis
Blausäurevergiftung f *(vet)* prussic acid poisoning
Blauschimmel m *(phyt)* blue mould
~ **des Tabaks** tobacco blue mould, blue mould [of tobacco] *(caused by Peronospora tabacina)*
Blauschimmelkäse m blue cheese
Blauschönung f blue fining *(wine-making)*
Blauschwarzfärbung f iron-tannate stain *(of wood)*
Blauschwingel m blue fescue, Festuca cinerea (glauca)
Blausieb n [wood-]leopard moth, wood-leopard, Zeuzera pyrina
Blaustern m *(bot)* squill, scilla *(genus Scilla)*
Blausternchen n *(bot)* Siberian squill, Scilla sibirica
Blautaube f stockdove, Columba oenas
Blauverfärbung f **der Haut** *(vet)* cyanosis
Blauwerden n blu[e]ing *(of sapwood)*
Blauzungenerkrankung f *(vet)* bluetongue

Blauzungenvirus n bluetongue virus
Blei m bream, Abramis brama
Blei n lead
Bleiarsenat n lead arsenate
Bleiber-Weicher-Pflanzung f modified intercrop planting (orcharding)
Bleibusch m lead plant, Amorpha canescens
bleich werden to turn pale; to bleach, to blanch
Bleiche Getreidelaus f rose grain (grass) aphid, Metopolophium (Acyrthosiphon) dirhodum
~ **Segge** f pale sedge, Carex pallescens
bleichen to bleach, to blanch, to etiolate
Bleichen n bleaching, blanching, etiolation
Bleicherde f (soil) bleaching clay (earth), podzol, podsol; fuller's earth
Bleiches Riedgras n pale sedge, Carex pallescens
Bleichfleck m (phyt) bleached spot
Bleichhorizont m (soil) [b]leached horizon, eluvial horizon, A-horizon
Bleichmoostorf m sphagnum [moss] peat
Bleichpulver n bleaching powder
Bleichschicht f (soil) bleached layer
Bleichsellerie m [blanched, salad] celery, Apium graveolens var. dulce
Bleichspargel m blanched (white) asparagus
Bleichsucht f (phyt) chlorosis, blanching, bleaching
bleichsüchtig (phyt) chlorotic
Bleichzahl f bleach figure (of flour)
Bleiglanzkrankheit f silver-leaf [disease] (of deciduous trees, caused by Stereum purpureum)
Bleivergiftung f (vet) lead-poisoning
Bleiwurz f leadwort, plumbago (genus Plumbago)
Blender... s. Plenter...
Blendzeug n (hunt) toils
Blepharitis f (vet) blepharitis
Blesse f blaze
Bleßhuhn n, **Bleßralle** f [European, bald] coot, Fulica atra
Blindbremse f breeze [fly], Chrysops coecutiens
Blinddarm m blind gut, c[a]ecum, typhlon • **den ~ [operativ] entfernen** to caecectomize
Blinddarmentzündung f (vet) typhlitis
Blinddarmkokzidiose f coccidiosis in chickens, caecal coccidiosis (caused by Eimeria tenella)
Blinddarm-Leber-Entzündung f [des Geflügels] blackhead [disease], histomoniasis (of fowl, caused by Histomonas meleagridis)
Blinde Fliege f breeze [fly], Chrysops coecutiens
Blinden[führ]hund m guide-dog
Blindheit f [/totale] (vet) blindness, amaurosis
Blindmelken n over-milking, dry milking
Blindprobe f blind experiment
Blindsack m blind pouch (animal anatomy)
Blindschleiche f slow-worm, blindworm, Anguis fragilis
Blindstrich m blind teat

Blindtrieb m (bot) blind shoot
Blindverkostung f blind tasting
Blindversuch m blind experiment
Blindwanze f capsid [bug], mirid (family Miridae)
Blinkers pl s. Scheuklappen
Blinzelhaut f nictitating membrane, third eyelid, haw (animal anatomy)
Blitz m lightning
Blitzableiter m lightning conductor, (Am) lightning rod
Blitzbeleuchtung f flash lighting (poultry keeping)
Blitzdränung f zigzag drainage system
Blitzriß m lightning (thunder) shake (in wood)
Blitzschaden m lightning damage (injury)
Blitzschlag m lightning stroke
Blitzschutz m s. Blitzableiter
Blitzwurm m (ent) sinuate pear [tree] borer, pear[-tree] borer, Agrilus sinuatus
Blizzard m blizzard
BLM s. Lipidmembran/bimolekulare
BIMV s. Blumenkohlmosaikvirus
Bloch m s. Block 2.
Block m 1. block; 2. log, block, butt, bolt
~/**abgeschwarteter** slabbed log
~ **für die Schindelherstellung** shingle bolt
~ **für Fässer** barrel (stave) log
~ **für Schwellen** sleeper log
Blockabwerfer m log ejector, [log] kicker
Blockanlage f block design (field experimentation)
~/**randomisierte** randomized block [design]
~/**unvollständige** incomplete block design
Blockaufzug m log haul[-up], log hoist (jack)
Blockaufzugkette f (Am, forest) jacker chain
Blockbandsäge f log band saw[ing machine]
Blockbutter f block butter
Blockdamm m crib dam
Blockeinspannwagen m log [saw-]carriage, butt carriage, saw[mill] carriage, log table; dogging carriage, bogie
Blockförderer m 1. log conveyor; log slide; 2. s. Blockaufzug
Blockgewächshaus n multispan (multibay) greenhouse
Blockgreifer m log grab (grapple), dog
Blockholzmaß n log scale (rule)
Blockkettenförderer m log chain conveyor
Blockkreissäge[maschine] f mit übereinanderliegenden Sägeblättern top-and-bottom saw
Blockmutation f (gen) block mutation
Blocksäge f log (breakdown) saw, head saw (rig)
Blocksahne f block cream
Blockspannzange f log dog
Blockstapel m boule
Blockwagen m s. Blockeinspannwagen
blöken to bleat, to baa (sheep); to low (calf)
Blonde d'Aquitaine n Aquitaine blond (cattle breed)
Bloodhound m bloodhound (breed)

Blöße

Blöße *f* blank, glade, denuded area; cleared (clear felled) area, clearance, clearing, non-restocked forest land
Blötwolle *f* carrion wool
Bluetick Coonhound *m* Blue Tick Hound *(breed)*
Bluetongue *f (vet)* bluetongue
Blühbeginn *m* first bloom
Blühdatum *n* flowering date
blühen to flower, to bloom, to blossom; to be in blossom *(trees)*; to silk *(maize)*; to arrow *(sugarcane)*
Blühen *n* flowering, bloom, florescence • **zum ~ bringen** to bring (get) to bloom
~/verspätetes (verzögertes) delayed flowering
blühend blooming, abloom, in blossom, [in]florescent
~/einseitig (einseitswendig) secundiflorous
~/frühzeitig precocious
~/nicht blind
~/tagsüber diurnal
~ und fruchtend/einmal monocarpic, monocarpous, hapaxanthic, hapaxanthous
~ und fruchtend/wiederholt polycarpic, polycarpous
~/wiederholt perpetually flowering
~/zur Nachtzeit night-blooming
Blüher *m* flowerer, bloomer
Blühhabitus *m* flowering habit
Blühhormon *n* flowering hormone, florigen
Blühhormonkomplex *m* florigen
Blühinduktion *f* flower[ing] induction, induction of flowering
Blühperiode *f* flowering (blooming) period
Blühperiodizität *f* flowering periodicity
Blühphase *f* flowering [stage], bloom (blossom) stage, anthesis *(s. a.* Blütezeit*)*
Blühprozeß *m* flowering process
blühreif mature, adult
Blühreife *f* maturity
Blühstadium *n s.* Blühphase
Blühstärke *f* amount of blossoms
Blühstimulierung *f* stimulation of flowering
Blühtermin *m* flowering date
Blühverhalten *n* flowering behaviour
Blühverzögerung *f* delayed flowering
Blümchen *n* flower[l]et, floret
Blume *f* 1. flower *(s. a.* Blüte*)*; 2. bouquet, aroma, flavour *(of wine)*; 3. froth *(of beer)*; 4. *(slaught)* rump; aitchbone *(of beef carcass)*; 5. tag, scut *(of game)*; 6. small star *(at horse's forehead)*
~ des Blumenkohls curd
Blume-Leiss-Baumhöhenmesser *m* Blume-Leiss altimeter
Blumenanbau *m* flower growing (cultivation)
Blumenausstellung *f* flower-show
Blumenbeet *n* flower-bed
Blumenbindedraht *m* florist's wire
Blumenbinden *n* flower arranging
Blumenbinder *m* florist

Blumenbinderei *f* floristics, floristry
Blumenbukett *n* bouquet [of flowers]
Blumenbund *n* bunch of flowers
Blumendraht *m* florist's wire
Blumenduft *m* scent of flower[s]
Blumendünger *m* flower fertilizer
Blumenerde *f* flower soil, potting compost, garden mould
Blumenesche *f* flowering (manna) ash, Fraxinus ornus
Blumenfenster *n* window garden
Blumenfliege *f* root-fly *(family Anthomyiidae)*
Blumenflor *m* flush (abundance) of flowers, flowerage
Blumenfreund *m* florist
Blumenfrischhaltemittel *n* floral preservative
Blumenfurnier *n* crotch veneer
Blumengarten *m* flower-garden
Blumengärtner *m* flower grower
Blumengeschäft *n* flower (florist's) shop
Blumengießer *m*, **Blumengießkanne** *f* flower watering can
Blumengroßhändler *m* wholesale florist
Blumenhandel *m* floral trade
Blumenhändler *m* florist
Blumenhartriegel *m* [flowering] dogwood, boxwood, flowering cornel, Cornus florida
Blumenkasten *m* flower box (trough)
Blumenknolle *f* corm
Blumenkohl *m* cauliflower, Brassica oleraceae var. botrytis
Blumenkohlerntemaschine *f* cauliflower harvester
Blumenkohlkopf *m* cauliflower, curd
Blumenkohlkrankheit *f* **der Erdbeere** cauliflower disease [of strawberry] *(caused by Aphelenchoides fragariae and Corynebacterium fascians)*
Blumenkohlmosaik *n* cauliflower mosaic *(virosis)*
Blumenkohlmosaikvirus *n* cauliflower mosaic virus, CauMV
Blumenkorso *m* flower corso
Blumenkranz *m* [floral] wreath
Blumenkrone *f* corolla
blumenkronenartig corollate[d]
Blumenmarkt *m* flower-market
Blumenproduktion *f* flower production
Blumenrabatte *f* flower-border
Blumenrohr *n* 1. canna, Indian shot [plant], flower reed *(genus Canna)*; 2. canna, Queensland arrowroot, Canna edulis
Blumenrohrgewächse *npl* canna family *(family Cannaceae)*
Blumensaatgut *n* flower seeds
Blumensamen *m* flower seed
Blumenschale *f* 1. flower bowl (dish); 2. bowl of plants
Blumenschau *f* flower-show
Blumenschilf *n* common (Virginian) spiderwort, Tradescantia virginiana

Blumenspritze f flower sprayer (for treating ornamentals)
Blumenstrauß m bunch of flowers; bouquet; nosegay
~/**duftender** nosegay
Blumenteppich m carpet of flowers
Blumentopf m flowerpot, [clay] pot
Blumentopferde f garden mould
blumentragend floriferous
Blumentreiberei f flower forcing
Blumenuhr f floral clock
Blumenvase f flower-vase
Blumenverpackungsmaschine f flower wrapper
Blumenwanze f anthocorid [bug] (family Anthocoridae)
Blumenwiese f wildflower meadow
Blumenzucht f floriculture
Blumenzüchter m floriculturist, florist
Blumenzwiebel f flowerbulb, [ornamental] bulb
~/[im Austrieb] **gehemmte** retarded bulb
Blumenzwiebelanbau m bulb growing
Blumenzwiebeldesinfektionsmaschine f flowerbulb disinfection equipment
Blumenzwiebelerntemaschine f bulb lifter
Blumenzwiebellager n bulb store
Blumenzwiebellagerschuppen m bulb shed
Blumenzwiebelpflanzmaschine f bulb planter
Blumenzwiebelrodemaschine f bulb lifter
Blumenzwiebelsortiermaschine f bulb grading machine
Blumenzwiebelzählmaschine f flowerbulb counting machine
Blumenzwiebelzucht f bulb growing
blumig 1. flowery, full of flowers; 2. flowery, with a fine bouquet (wine)
Bluncksche Regel f Blunck's rule, rule of temperature summation
BLUP-Prinzip n BLUP principle (of breeding-value appraisal)
Blut n blood • ~ **entnehmen** to bleed, to draw blood
~ **trächtiger Stuten** pregnant mare blood (for extration of serum gonadotropin)
Blutader f vein
Blutagar m blood agar
Blutalbumin n blood albumin
Blutalbuminleim m albumin glue, blood [albumin] adhesive
Blutantigen n blood antigen
Blutapfelsine f blood orange, Citrus sinensis var. sanguinea
blutarm anaemic
Blutarmut f anaemia
Blutauffrischung f refreshing of blood
Blutauge n (vet) haemophthalmus
Blutbeule f (vet) haematoma
Blutbild n blood picture, blood[-cell] count
blutbildend haemotopoietic

Blutbildung f haemato[poie]sis, haemopoiesis, blood formation
Blutbildungsgewebe n haemopoietic tissue
Blutblume f bloodflower, blood lily (genus Haemanthus)
Blutbruch m (vet) haematocele
Blutbuche f purple (copper) beech, Fagus sylvatica cv. purpurea
Blutcalcium[spiegel]erhöhung f (vet) hypercalcaemia
Blutcalcium[spiegel]verringerung f (vet) hypocalcaemia
Blütchen n floscule; floret, flower[l]et
blütchentragend floscular, flosculous
Blutdorn m redhaw hawthorn, Crategus sanguinea
Blutdruck m blood-pressure
Blutdruckherabsetzung f (vet) hypotension
Blutdruckmanometer n blood-pressure manometer
Blutdruckregulation f blood-pressure regulation
blutdrucksenkend antihypertensive
Blüte f 1. flower, bloom, blossom, inflorescence; 2. bloom[ing period], blossom, blow, flowering, florescence, anthesis (s. a. under Blüten) • **in** ~ blooming, abloom • **in** ~ **stehen** to bloom, to flower • **in voller** ~ in full bloom • **mit unregelmäßiger** ~ anomaliflorous • **zur** ~ **bringen** to flower
~/**angestochene** (phyt) punctured flower
~/**erste** king blossom
~/**gefüllte** double blossom (flower)
~/**halbgefüllte** semidouble blossom
~/**kelchförmige** chalice
~/**kräftigste** king blossom (of an inflorescence)
~/**männliche** staminate flower (inflorescence)
~/**noch nicht geöffnete** popcorn flower (in stone fruit)
~/**vor den Blättern erscheinende** precocious blossom
~/**vorzeitige** precocious blossom
~/**weibliche** pistillate flower (inflorescence)
Blutegel m leech (class Hirudinea)
Blutegelbefall m (vet) hirudiniasis
Bluteiweißkonzentrat n blood protein concentrate
Bluteiweißstoff m blood [serum] protein, serum protein, plasm[a] protein
bluten to bleed
Bluten n bleeding; [sap] bleeding (of plants)
Blüten fpl:
• ~ **abstreifen (entfernen)** to deflower, to deblossom • **auf** ~ **lebend** floricolous • ~ **hervorbringen** to blossom • **mit breiten** ~ platyanthous • **mit gestielten** ~ pedicellate, pediculate • **mit sitzenden** ~ sessiflorous • **sich von** ~ **ernährend** florivorous (esp. insects) • ~ **tragen** to bloom • ~ **treiben** to blossom, to bloom
Blütenabort m, **Blütenabstoßung** f flower abortion
Blütenabwerfen n flower abortion; bud dropping (physiological disorder e.g. in fruit-woods)

Blütenachse

Blütenachse *f* floral axis, thalamus
Blütenachsenverlängerung *f* gynophore
~/den Fruchtknoten tragende gynophore
Blütenähre *f* flower spike *(e.g. in gladiolus)*
Blütenälchen *n* flower and leaf-gall nematode *(genus Anguina)*
Blütenalterung *f* flower senescence
Blütenansatz *m* flower setting (initiation)
blütenartig blossomy
Blütenausdünnung *f* flower (blossom) thinning
Blütenbecher *m* flower cup
Blütenbestäubung *f* pollination, pollinization
Blütenbildung *f* flower formation
Blütenblatt *n* petal
Blütenblattfall *m* petal fall
Blütenboden *m* receptacle, flower cup
Blütenbrand *m* (phyt) blossom blight *(comprehensive term)*
Blütenbüschel *n* cluster (bunch) of blossoms, truss, fascicle, fasciculus
Blütendifferenzierung *f* flower (floral) differentiation
Blütenduft *m* scent of flower
Blütenduftstoffdrüse *f* osmophor
Blütenendfäule *f* blossom-end rot
Blütenentfaltung *f* flowering [display], anthesis, inflorescence
Blütenentfernung *f* deflowering, flower removal
Blütenfall *m* flower drop (fall), blossom drop, petal fall
Blütenfarbenbrechung *f (phyt)* flower colour breaking *(virosis)*
Blütenfarbenbrechungsvirus *n* der Pelargonie pelargonium flower-break virus
Blütenfäule *f* blossom rot
Blütenfleckenkrankheit *f* petal blight *(esp. of azalea, caused by Ovulinia azaleae)*
Blütenflor *m* flush (abundance) of flowers, flowerage
Blütenfrost *m s.* Frühjahrsfrost
Blütengalle *f (phyt)* flower gall
Blütenhaltbarkeit *f* vase-life
Blütenhüllboden *m* der Artischocke *s.* Artischockenboden
Blütenhülle *f* perianth, floral envelope
~ aus zwei gleichartigen Blattkreisen perigone, perigonium
~/äußere perianth, floral envelope
blütenhüllenlos achlamydeous
Blütenkalender *m* flower calendar *(phenology)*
Blütenkätzchen *n* catkin, ament
Blütenkelch *m* flower calyx (cup), chalice • ohne ~ acalycine, acalyxinous
~/haarförmiger pappus
Blütenknospe *f* [flower, floral] bud, fruit bud
Blütenknospenbildung *f* flower-bud formation, flower budding
Blütenknospendifferenzierung *f* flower-bud differentiation

Blütenknospenstadium *n* flower-bud stage
Blütenkopf *m* button *(of composites)*
Blütenköpfchen *n* flower-head, capitulum
Blütenkörbchen *n* capitulum
Blütenkronblatt *n* petal
blütenlos flowerless, ananthous, blind
Blütenmorphologie *f* flower (floral) morphology
Blütennektar *m* floral nectar
Blütennematode *m* flower and leaf-gall nematode *(genus Anguina)*
Blütenöl *n* flower (blossom) oil
Blütenorgan *n* floral organ
Blütenpflanze *f* flowering plant, flowerer, phanerogam, spermatophyte *(division Spermatophyta)*
~/bedecktsamige angiosperm
~/nacktsamige gymnosperm
~/nektarproduzierende nectar flower
~/pollenproduzierende pollen flower
blütenreich blossomy, floriferous, floribund
Blütensaft *m s.* Nektar
Blütenscheide *f* spathe, spatha
Blütenspelze *f* lemma
Blütensproß *m* floral (flower) shoot
Blütenstand *m* inflorescence, flower-head • mit gestieltem ~ pedunculate[d], peduncular
~/männlicher staminate inflorescence (flower)
~/terminaler terminal (apical) inflorescence
~/unvollständig entwickelter curd *(e.g. in cauliflower and broccoli)*
~/verzweigter spray of blooms
~/weiblicher pistillate inflorescence (flower)
~/zapfenförmiger strobile, strobilus
Blütenstandsablösung *f (phyt)* loose bud *(of hyacinth)*
Blütenstandsbasis *f* cluster base
Blütenstaub *m* pollen, farina
Blütenstengel *m s.* Blütenstiel
Blütenstiel *m* flower stalk (stem), pedicel, pedicle, peduncle, strig
~/blattloser scape
Blütenstrahl *m* ray
Blütenstrauch *m* flowering shrub
Blütentaubheit *f (phyt)* blindness
~ bei Zwiebeliris three-leaves of iris
Blütenteppich *m* carpet of flowers
blütentragend floriferous, bearing
Blütentraube *f* flower cluster, cluster (bunch) of blossoms, truss
Blütenvergrünung *f (phyt)* phyllomania; clover phyllody
~ der Erdbeere strawberry green petal *(mycoplasmosis)*
Blütenverkümmerung *f* flower blasting
Blütenvertrocknung *f* flower blasting
Blütenverwachsung *f* synanthy
Blütenwirtel *m* flower-whorl
Blütenzapfen *m* cone, conelet
Blütenzweig *m* flowering branch; flowering tip; spray of blooms

Blutenzym *n* blood enzyme
Bluterbrechen *n (vet)* haematemesis
Bluterguß *m (vet)* haematoma
Bluterkrankheit *f (vet)* haemophilia
Blutersatzmittel *n* blood substitute
Blütezeit *f* bloom[ing] period, blossom, blow, flowering [season, time, period], florescence, anthesis
Blutfarbstoff *m* blood pigment
Blutfaserstoff *m* fibrin
Blutfennich *m*, **Blutfingerhirse** *f* [hairy] finger grass, [hairy] crab-grass, Digitaria sanguinalis, Panicum sanguinale
Blutfleck *m* blood spot *(e.g. in a hen's egg)*
Blutfleckenei *n* blood-spotted egg
Blutfleckenkrankheit *f (vet)* transmissible petechial fever
Blutfluß *m* blood flow
Blutflüssigkeit *f* haemolymph
Blutfülle *f (vet)* hyperaemia
Blutgas *n* blood gas
Blutgefäß *n* blood vessel
Blutgefäßanordnung *f* vasculature
Blutgefäßerkrankung *f* blood-vessel disorder
Blutgefäßsystem *n* blood [vascular] system
Blutgerinnsel *n (vet)* blood clot, coagulum, coagulate
Blutgerinnung *f* blood-clotting, blood coagulation
Blutgerinnungsfaktor *m* blood-clotting factor
blutgerinnungshemmend anticoagulant
Blutgerinnungsstörung *f* blood-clotting disorder
Blutgerinnungszeit *f* blood-clotting time
Blutgift *n* haemotoxin
Blutglucose *f* blood glucose (sugar)
Blutgruppe *f* blood group
Blutgruppenantigen *n* blood group antigen
Blutgruppenbestimmung *f* blood typing (grouping)
Blutgruppeneinteilung *f* blood typing (group classification)
bluthaltig bloody, sanguineous
Blutharnen *n (vet)* haematuria, red-water [disease], blackwater, babesiasis, babesiosis
Blutharnstoff *m* blood urea
Blutharnstoffspiegel *m* blood urea level
~/gesteigerter hyperuricaemia
Bluthirse *f* [hairy] finger grass, [hairy] crab-grass, Digitaria sanguinalis, Panicum sanguinale
Bluthochdruck *m (vet)* hypertension, high blood pressure
Blutholzbaum *m* logwood, Haematoxylum campechianum
Bluthund *m* bloodhound *(breed)*
blutig bloody, sanguineous
Blutinsel *f* blood islet *(embryology)*
Blutkalium[spiegel]erhöhung *f (vet)* hyperkal[i]aemia
Blutkalium[spiegel]verringerung *f (vet)* hypokal[i]aemia

Blutkatalase *f* erythrocyte catalase *(enzyme)*
Blutklee *m* crimson clover, trifolium, Trifolium incarnatum
Blutkoagulation *f* blood-clotting
Blutkörperchen *n* blood-cell, blood-corpuscle, haemocyte
~/rotes red [blood-]cell, RBC, red corpuscle, erythrocyte
~/weißes white [blood-]cell, WBC, white corpuscle, leucocyte, leukocyte
Blutkörperchensenkung *f* blood sedimentation
Blutkörperchensenkungsgeschwindigkeit *f* erythrocyte sedimentation rate, ESR
Blutkörperchenverklumpung *f* haemagglutination
Blutkörperchenvolumen *n* blood corpuscular volume
Blutkörperchenzählung *f* blood[-cell] count; erythrocyte count
Blutkrankheit *f* blood disease
Blutkrankheitslehre *f* haematology
Blutkrebs *m (vet)* leukaemia, leucaemia, leucosis
Blutkreislauf *m* blood-circulation
~/kleiner (pulmonaler) pulmonary circulation
Blutkreislaufstörung *f* blood-circulation disorder
Blutkuchen *m* blood clot
Blutkultur *f* blood culture *(bacteriology)*
Blutlaus *f* woolly [apple] aphid, American blight, Eriosoma lanigerum
Blutleere *f (vet)* ischaemia
Blutlehre *f* haematology
Blutlinie *f* blood line
Blutlipid *n* blood lipid
Blutlipid[spiegel]erhöhung *f (vet)* hyperlipaemia
Blutlipid[spiegel]verringerung *f (vet)* hypolipaemia
Blutmangel *m s.* Blutleere
Blutmehl *n* blood meal, dried blood *(fertilizer, feedstuff)*
Blutmenge *f* blood volume
Blutorange *f* blood orange, Citrus sinensis var. sanguinea
Blutparasit *m* blood parasite
Blutpfropf *m (vet)* thrombus
Blutpfropfauflösung *f* thrombolysis
Blut-pH[-Wert] *m* blood pH
Blutpigment *n* blood pigment
Blutplasma *n* blood-plasma, plasm[a]
Blutplasmaenzym *n* plasm[a] enzyme
Blutplasmaprotein *n* blood-plasma protein
Blutplasmavolumen *n* blood-plasma volume
Blutplasmazerfall *m* plasmoschisis
Blutplättchen *n* blood platelet, thrombocyte
Blutprobe *f* blood sample (specimen)
Blutprobenahme *f* blood sampling
Blutprotein[spiegel]erhöhung *f (vet)* hyperproteinaemia
Blutprotein[spiegel]senkung *f (vet)* hypoproteinaemia
blutrot blood-red, sanguineous

Blutroter

Blutroter Storchschnabel *m s.* Blutstorchschnabel
Blutrotfrüchtiger Weißdorn *m* redhaw hawthorn, Crataegus sanguinea
Blutrute *f* common (bloody, bloodtwig) dogwood, bloody twig, gaiter [tree], Cornus sanguinea
Blutschwamm *m (vet)* haemangioma, angioma
Blutschwitzen *n (vet)* bracken poisoning
~ **der Pferde** parafilariosis *(caused by Parafilaria multipapillosa)*
Blutsenkung *f* blood sedimentation
Blutserum *n* [blood] serum
Blutserumalbumin *n* blood albumin
Blutstauung *f*, **Blutstillstand** *m (vet)* blood stasis, haemostasis, congestion
Blutstorchschnabel *m* blood-dock, blood-red geranium, Geranium sanguineum
Blutstrom *m* bloodstream
blutsverwandt related by blood, consanguineous, akin
Blutsverwandtschaft *f* blood relationship, consanguinity
Bluttransfusion *f (vet)* blood transfusion
Bluttröpfchen *n* pheasant's-eye [flower], Adonis aestivalis
Blutübertragung *f (vet)* blood transfusion
Blutung *f (vet)* bleeding, haemorrhage
~ **in den Pleuraraum** haemothorax
Blutungsbereitschaft *f* haemorrhagic diathesis
Blutungen *fpl*/**punktförmige** petechiae
Blutungssaft *m* bleeding sap *(of plants)* • ~ **abgeben** to bleed *(plant)*
Blutunterdruck *m (vet)* hypotension
Blutverdünnung *f* haemodilution
Blutvergiftung *f* blood-poisoning, septicaemia, sepsis, toxaemia
Blutverlust *m* blood loss
Blutversorgung *f* blood supply
Blutviskosität *f* blood viscosity
Blutvolumen *n* blood volume
Blutvolumenvergrößerung *f* hypervolaemia
Blutvolumenverminderung *f* hypovolaemia
Blutweiderich *m* [purple] loosestrife, Lythrum salicaria
Blutwurz *f (bot)* 1. bloodroot, [red] puccoon, Surmeric, Sanguinaria canadensis; 2. tormentil, Potentilla erecta
Blutzelle *f* blood-cell, blood-corpuscle, haemocyte
Blutzellenzählgerät *n* haemocytometer
Blutzucker *m* blood sugar (glucose)
Blutzucker[spiegel]erhöhung *f (vet)* hyperglycaemia
Blutzucker[spiegel]verringerung *f (vet)* hypoglycaemia
Blutzusammensetzung *f* blood composition
B-Lymphozyt *m* B cell, B lymphocyte
BML *s.* Bundesministerium für Ernährung, Landwirtschaft und Forsten
BMV *s.* Gewöhnliches Bohnenmosaikvirus

BnGSV *s.* Gelbscheckungsvirus der Großen Brennessel
Bö *f* gust, squall *(accompanied by rain or snow)*
Board-Fuß *m (Am)* board foot *(1 bd ft = 2.360 dm^3 of timber)*
Board-Fuß-Meßstab *m* board rule
Bobaum *m* bo-tree [of the Hindus], pipal (peepal, peepul) tree, Ficus religiosa
Bobtail *m* bobtail, Old English sheep-dog *(breed)*
Bock *m* 1. buck; 2. *s.* Bockkäfer; 3. trestle
Bockbeinigkeit *f* bucked-knee conformation, bucked knees *(of forelimbs)*
Bockbier *n* bock [beer]
bocken 1. to buck *(horse)*; 2. to be at (in, on) heat, to blissom *(female sheep, goat or rabbit)*
Bocken *n* 1. buck *(of a horse)*; 2. heat *(of sheep, goat or rabbit)*
Bockhuf *m (vet)* club-foot, mule-foot
bockig blissom *(female sheep, goat or rabbit)*
Bockkäfer *m* longhorn [beetle], longicorn, capricorn beetle, cerambycid, *(Am)* round-headed borer *(family Cerambycidae)*
Bockkitz *n* male fawn
Bockkran *m* gantry crane
Bocklamm *n* ram lamb
Bockmühle *f s.* Bockwindmühle
Bocksbart *m* goat's-beard, salsify, salsafy, oyster-plant, vegetable oyster, John-go-to-bed-at-noon *(genus Tragopogon)*
Bocksdorn *m* box thorn, matrimony vine *(genus Lycium)*
Bocksfeige *f* caprifig, wild fig [tree], Ficus carica var. sylvestris
Bockshauhechel *f* rest-harrow, ground furze, landwhin, petty (moor) whin, Ononis arvensis
Bockshornklee *m (bot)* 1. trigonella *(genus Trigonella)*; 2. fenugreek, Trigonella foenum-graecum
Bocksknöterich *m* goat's-wheat *(genus Atraphaxis)*
Bockwindmühle *f* post-mill, windmill on trestles
Boden *m* 1. soil; 2. land, ground, earth; 3. floor; 4. fundus *(anatomy)* • **am ~ liegend** *(bot)* decumbent • **den ~ aufwühlen** to root *(game)* • **den ~ verbessern** to ameliorate • **den ~ verbessernd** ameliorative • **gut auf alkalischem ~ wachsend** basophilous • **im ~ lebend** soil-dwelling, soil-inhabiting • ~ **lockern** to hoe, to loosen • **vom ~ abhängig** edaphic
~/**abgetragener** soil wash
~/**alkalischer** alkaline soil
~/**allochthoner** secondary (transported) soil
~/**anmooriger** muck (half-bog) soil
~/**anthropogener** anthropogenic (man-made) soil
~/**äolischer** aeolian soil
~/**autochthoner** primary (residual) soil
~/**bearbeiteter (bestellter)** tillage [land]
~/**bewaldeter** forested soil
~/**durchlässiger** pervious ground
~/**ferrallitischer** laterite

~/**fetter** rank (fat) soil
~/**flachgründiger** shallow soil
~/**fossiler** fossil soil
~/**gepflügter** ploughed land, plough, *(Am)* plow
~/**hitziger** hot (burning) soil
~ **im engeren Sinne** solum *(A- and B-horizons)*
~/**jungfräulicher** virgin soil
~/**kastanienfarbiger** chestnut soil
~/**kiesiger** flinty ground
~/**künstlicher** anthropogenic (man-made) soil
~/**landwirtschaftlich genutzter** agricultural (farm) soil
~/**leichter** light soil
~/**lockerer** loose soil, soft ground
~/**magerer** poor (hungry) soil
~ **mit Braunhorizont** cambisol
~ **mit deutlich ausgeprägtem ABC-Profil** ABC soil
~ **mit hohem Sandanteil** light soil
~ **mit hohem Tonanteil** heavy soil
~/**mittlerer** medium soil
~/**natürlich verdichteter ungepflügter** hardpan
~/**organischer** organic soil
~/**pleistozäner** diluvial soil
~/**pseudovergleyter** pseudogleyed soil
~/**saurer** acid soil
~/**schwerer** heavy (hard) soil
~/**stauvergleyter** pseudogleyed soil
~/**steiniger** stony soil
~/**terrestrischer** terrestrial soil
~/**vom Menschen geschaffener** anthropogenic (man-made) soil
~/**vulkanischer** volcanic soil
~/**windtransportierter** aeolian soil
~/**zwischenreihig gelegener** inter-row
Bodenabfolge *f* catena
Bodenablösung *f* soil detachment
Bodenabsorption *f* soil absorption
Bodenabspülung *f* soil-washing
Bodenabtrag *m* soil loss *(e.g. due to erosion)*
Bodenabtragsgleichung *f* soil loss equation
Bodenaggregat *n* soil aggregate
Bodenaggregation *f* soil aggregation
Bodenaktivität *f* soil activity
Bodenalbedo *f* soil albedo
Bodenalge *f* soil alga
Bodenalgenkultur *f* soil algal culture
Bodenalkalität *f* soil alkalinity
Bodenalter *n* soil age, age of soil
Bodenanalyse *f* soil analysis
Bodenanalytik *f* soil analytics
Bodenansprüche *mpl* soil requirements *(of crop plants)*
Bodenantrieb *m* ground drive *(e.g. of soil-working tools)*
Bodenanzeiger *m* soil (plant) indicator, indicator plant
Bodenart *f* type (kind) of soil, soil type

Bodenbegasungsmittel

Bodenatmosphäre *f* soil atmosphere
Bodenatmung *f* soil respiration (aeration)
Bodenaufnahme *f* soil survey
Bodenaufzucht *f* floor rearing *(of young animals)*
Bodenausbringung *f* soil application *(e.g. of pesticides)*
Bodenauslaugung *f* soil leaching
Bodenaustrocknung *f* soil drying
Bodenauswaschanlage *f*, **Bodenauswaschgerät** *n* soil-washing apparatus *(e.g. for recording micro-organisms in soil samples)*
Bodenauswaschung *f* soil leaching (washing)
Bodenauszug *m* soil extract
Bodenazidität *f* soil acidity (sourness)
Bodenbakteriologie *f* soil bacteriology
Bodenbakterium *n* soil bacterium
Bodenbasizität *f* soil alkalinity
Bodenbearbeitung *f* [soil] tillage, soil working (preparation), [soil] cultivation
~ **durch zapfwellengetriebene Werkzeuge** p.t.o.-driven tillage operation
~/**ganzflächige** total area tillage, general cultivation
~ **in Höhenlinie** contour tillage
~/**kombinierte** combined tillage
~/**konservierende** conservation tillage
~ **mit Seilzuggeräten** cable cultivation
~/**pfluglose** no-plough tillage, cultivation without ploughing
~/**schonende** conservation tillage
~/**teilflächige** partial area tillage
~/**tiefe** deep cultivation
~/**vollständige** full (complete) cultivation
~/**zwischenreihige** inter-row tillage
Bodenbearbeitungsgerät *n* tillage implement, implement for tillage and seedbed preparation
Bodenbearbeitungsmaßnahme *f* cultivation operation
Bodenbearbeitungsschicht *f* tillage layer
Bodenbearbeitungstiefe *f* tillage depth
Bodenbearbeitungswerkzeug *n* soil working (engaging) tool, tillage (farming, cultivation) tool
Bodenbebrütung *f* soil incubation
bodenbedeckend ground-covering
Bodenbedeckung *f* ground cover
Bodenbedeckungsmaterial *n* mulching material, mulch matter
Bodenbedeckungspflanze *f* ground cover plant
Bodenbedeckungsvermögen *n* ground covering ability *(of plants)*
bodenbedingt edaphic
Bodenbefall *m* soil infestation
Bodenbefestigung *f* soil stabilization (fixing)
Bodenbefeuchtung *f* soil moistening
Bodenbegasung *f* soil fumigation, gassing of the soil
Bodenbegasungsmittel *n* soil fumigant
~/**biozid wirkendes** soil fumigant biocide

Bodenbegutachtung

Bodenbegutachtung f soil examination
Bodenbehandlung f soil treatment
Bodenbelüftung f soil aeration (ventilation)
Bodenbelüftungsanlage f floor dryer *(e.g. for grain)*
Bodenbelüftungstrocknung f floor drying *(e.g. of grain)*
Bodenbeschaffenheit f soil condition (characteristics), nature of the soil (ground)
Bodenbeschreibung f soil description
Bodenbestandteil m soil constituent
Bodenbestellung f [soil] cultivation *(s. a.* Bodenbearbeitung*)*
Bodenbeurteilung f soil evaluation
Bodenbewegung f soil movement
Bodenbewertung f soil evaluation
Bodenbewirtschaftung f soil (land) management
bodenbewohnend soil-dwelling, soil-inhabiting
Bodenbewohner m soil dweller
Bodenbezeichnung f soil name
bodenbildend soil-forming
Bodenbildner m soil former
Bodenbildung f soil formation (building), pedogenesis
Bodenbildungsart f type of soil formation
Bodenbildungsfaktor m soil-forming factor
Bodenbildungsgestein n soil-forming rock
Bodenbildungsprimärmineral n primary soil-forming mineral
Bodenbildungsprozeß m soil-forming process
Bodenbiologie f soil biology, pedobiology
bodenbiologisch soil pedological
Bodenbiomasse f soil biomass
Bodenbiostruktur f soil biostructure
Bodenbiota f soil biota
Bodenbiovolumen n soil biovolume
Bodenbohrer m soil auger; soil sampler (tube)
Bodenbohrkern m soil core
Bodenbonitierung f land judging, evaluation of soil
Bodenbrand m s. Bodenfeuer
Bodenbrauchbarkeitsklassifikation f land-capability classification
Bodenbrett n **[der Beute]** *(api)* [hive] floor-board
bodenbürtig soil-borne
Bodenbürtiges Gelbmosaikvirus n **der Wintergerste** soil-borne barley yellow mosaic virus
~ **Hafermosaikvirus** n oat mosaic virus
~ **Weizenmosaikvirus** n wheat soil-borne mosaic virus, WSBMV
Bodencharakterisierung f soil characterization
Bodenchemie f soil chemistry
Bodendämpfung f soil steaming
Bodendecke f ground (soil) cover, pedosphere
• **die lebende ~ beseitigen** *(forest)* to screef
~/**lebende** live ground cover *(s. a.* Bewuchs*)*
~/**tote** dead ground cover
Bodendecker m ground cover plant
Bodendegradation f soil degradation

Bodendesinfektion f soil disinfection (sterilization)
Bodendesinfektionsgerät n soil sterilizer
Bodendesinfektionsmittel n soil disinfectant (sterilant)
Bodendesinfestant n soil disinfestant
Bodendiagnose f diagnosis of soil
Bodendichte f soil density (compactness)
Bodendispersibilität f soil dispersibility (detachability)
Bodendruck m ground pressure, soil pressure (load) *(e.g. of farm machinery)*
Bodendrucksonde f [soil] penetrometer
Bodendünger m soil fertilizer
Bodendüngung f soil fertilization
Bodendurchfeuchtung f soil moistening
Bodendurchlässigkeit f soil permeability (porosity)
Bodendurchlüftung f soil aeration
Bodendynamik f soil dynamics
Bodeneigenschaft f soil property
Bodeneignung f soil suitability, land [use] capability
Bodeneignungskarte f land use capability map
Bodeneindringsonde f soil cone penetrometer
Bodeneinebnung f land levelling (grading, smoothing)
Bodeneinlage f *(api)* [hive] floor-board
Bodenelement n soil element
bodeneng bandy-legged, base narrow *(limbs)*
Bodenentseuchung f soil disinfection (sterilization)
Bodenentseuchungsmittel n soil disinfectant (sterilant)
Bodenentstehung f soil genesis
Bodenentwässerung f soil drainage
Bodenentwesung f soil disinfestation
Bodenentwesungsmittel n soil disinfestant
Bodenentwicklung f soil development, pedogenesis *(s. a.* Bodenbildung*)*
Bodenentwicklungslehre f soil genetics
Bodenenzym n soil enzyme
Bodenerhaltung f soil conservation
Bodenerhärtungsmittel n soil stabilizer (stabilizing agent)
Bodenerkundung f soil survey
Bodenerosion f soil erosion
~/**beschleunigte** accelerated [soil] erosion
Bodenersatz[stoff] m soil substitute
Bodenerschöpfung f soil exhaustion (depletion, impoverishment)
Bodenertrag m yield (produce) of soil
Bodenerwärmung f soil heating (warming)
Bodenerwartungswert m [land] expectation value
Bodenextrakt m soil extract
Bodenextraktionsmittel n soil extractant
Bodenfalle f pit trap *(pest control)*
Bodenfamilie f soil family
Bodenfarbe f soil colour
Bodenfauna f soil fauna

Bodenfeingefüge *n* soil microstructure
Bodenfestigkeit *f* soil strength
Bodenfestlegung *f* soil fixing
Bodenfeuchte *f* soil moisture (humidity, wetness), ground humidity (damp)
Bodenfeuchteanzeiger *m* soil moisture indicator
Bodenfeuchtedefizit *n* soil moisture deficit, SMD
Bodenfeuchtegang *m* soil water flux
Bodenfeuchtegehalt *m* soil water content
Bodenfeuchtegradient *m* soil moisture gradient
Bodenfeuchtehaushalt *m* soil moisture budget
Bodenfeuchtemesser *m* soil wetness meter
Bodenfeuchtemessung *f* soil moisture measurement
Bodenfeuchtepotential *n* soil water potential
Bodenfeuchteprofil *n* soil moisture profile
Bodenfeuchtevorrat *m* soil moisture reserve
Bodenfeuchtigkeit *f s.* Bodenfeuchte
Bodenfeuer *n* ground (surface) fire
~/langsam laufendes creeping fire
Bodenfilter *n* soil filter
Bodenfläche *f* [land] area; ground surface
~ des Hufeisens ground surface of shoe
Bodenfließen *n* earth flow, solifluction
Bodenflora *f* soil (ground) flora, live ground cover
Bodenflüssigkeit *f s.* Bodenwasser
Bodenfonds *m* land pool
Bodenform *f* land form; soil series
Bodenformenreihe *f* [/typische] catena
Bodenforschung *f* soil research
Bodenfraktion *f* soil fraction
Bodenfräse *f* [rotary] power tiller, rototiller, [rotary] tiller (cultivator, plough)
~ mit federnden Werkzeugen rotary cultivator with coil shanks
Bodenfreiheit *f* ground clearance *(e.g. of a vehicle)*
bodenfremd allochthonous
Bodenfrost *m* ground (soil) frost
Bodenfruchtbarkeit *f* soil fertility, land productivity
Bodenfruchtbarkeitsminderung *f* soil degradation
Bodenfruchtbarkeitsschätzung *f* soil fertility appraisal
Bodenfrüchtiger Klee *m* subterranean clover, subclover, Trifolium subterraneum
Bodenfungizid *n* soil fungicide
Bodenfütterung *f* floor feeding
Bodengare *f* [soil] tilth
Bodengefrornis *f* soil freezing
Bodengefüge *n* soil structure
Bodengefügestabilisator *m* soil conditioner (ameliorant, amendment), soil improver (improving material)
Bodengefügestabilisierung *f* soil conditioning (amelioration, amendment), soil improvement
Bodengefügeverbesserung *f* soil structure improvement
Bodengekriech *n* soil creep

Bodengemisch *n* soil mixture
Bodengenese *f* soil genesis, pedogenesis
Bodengenetik *f* soil genetics
Bodengeographie *f* soil geography
Bodengerät *n* ground machine (equipment)
Bodengerüst *n* soil skeleton
Bodengesellschaft *f* soil association
Bodengesetzgebung *f* soil legislation
Bodengift *n* soil toxin
Bodengroßgruppe *f* great soil group *(US soil classification)*
Bodengruppe *f* soil group
Bodengüte *f* soil quality
Bodenhaltung *f* floor management *(e.g. of poultry)*
Bodenhärte *f* soil hardness
Bodenheizkabel *n* soil-warming cable
Bodenheizung *f* soil heating
Bodenherbizid *n* soil[-applied] herbicide, soil-acting [residual] herbicide, root herbicide
Bodenhöhe *f* ground level
Bodenhorizont *m* soil horizon
~/fossiler palaeosol
Bodenhumifizierung *f* soil humification
Bodenhumus *m* soil humus
Bodenhumusbestandteil *m* soil humic constituent
Bodenhydraulik *f* soil hydraulics
bodenhydraulisch soil-hydraulic
Bodenhygiene *f* soil hygiene
Bodenimpfung *f* soil vaccination (inoculation)
Bodeninfektion *f* soil infection
Bodeninjektion *f* soil injection *(e.g. of pesticides)*
Bodeninjektor *m* soil injector
Bodeninkubation *f* soil incubation
Bodeninsekt *n* soil insect
Bodeninsektizid *n* soil insecticide
Bodenintensivhaltung *f* complete confinement rearing *(of poultry)*
Bodenkalorimeter *n* soil calorimeter
Bodenkapillarwasserpotential *n* soil water matric potential
Bodenkarte *f* soil map
~/kleinmaßstäbliche small-scale soil map
~/mittelmaßstäbliche middle-scale soil map
Bodenkartierung *f* soil mapping
Bodenkartierungseinheit *f* soil mapping unit
Bodenkataster *m* land cadaster (cadastre, register)
Bodenkategorisierung *f* soil categorization
Bodenkern *m* soil core
Bodenkernprobenehmer *m* soil core sampler, soil corer (coring machine)
Bodenklappe *f* gate *(of a sowing unit)*
Bodenklasse *f* soil class (order)
Bodenklassifikation *f*, **Bodenklassifizierung** *f* soil (land) classification
Bodenklima *n* soil climate
Bodenkohäsion *f* soil cohesion
Bodenkolloid *n* soil colloid
Bodenkomplex *m* soil complex

Bodenkomplex

~/adsorbierender cation-exchange complex, exchange material
Bodenkonsistenz f soil consistency
Bodenkontur f ground contour
Bodenkörnung f soil texture
Bodenkörnungsart f soil textural (texture) class
Bodenkörper m soil body
Bodenkorrosion f soil corrosion
Bodenkriechen n [soil] creep
Bodenkrümel m soil crumb
Bodenkrümelung f soil aggregation
Bodenkrümler m crumbler, soil miller
Bodenkruste f soil crust (cap)
Bodenkultivierung f soil (land) cultivation
Bodenkunde f pedology, soil science
~/**forstliche** forest pedology (soil science)
~/**landwirtschaftliche** agrology
Bodenkundler m soil scientist, pedologist
~/**landwirtschaftlicher** agrologist
bodenkundlich pedologic[al]
Bodenlagerung f floor storage
Bodenleben n soil life (biota)
Bodenlebewesen n soil organism; soil animal
Bodenlockerer m soil loosener (tormentor)
Bodenlockerung f soil loosening, tormenting of soil
Bodenlockerungsgerät n s. Bodenlockerer
Bodenlösung f soil solution
Bodenluft f soil air (aerosphere)
Bodenluftpyknometer n soil air pycnometer
Bodenluftverhältnisse npl soil air relations
Bodenmächtigkeit f soil depth (thickness)
Bodenmakrofauna f soil macrofauna
Bodenmarkt m land market
Bodenmaschine f ground machine
Bodenmatrix f soil matrix
Bodenmechanik f soil mechanics
Bodenmeißel m [sub]soil (ground) chisel, subsoiler; chisel plough
Bodenmelioration f soil amelioration (amendment), land improvement
~ **durch Anlage von Schutzwaldstreifen** silvicultural (afforestation) amelioration
Bodenmerkmal n soil characteristic
Bodenmesofauna f soil mesofauna
Bodenmikrobe f soil microbe (microorganism)
Bodenmikrobiologie f soil microbiology
Bodenmikroflora f soil microflora
Bodenmikrogefüge n soil fabric
Bodenmikromorphologie f soil micromorphology
Bodenmikroorganismus m soil microorganism (microbe)
Bodenmikrostruktur f soil microstructure
Bodenmilbe f soil mite *(comprehensive term)*
Bodenmineral n soil mineral
Bodenmineralogie f soil mineralogy
Bodenmischung f soil mixture
Bodenmonolith m soil monolith (column)
Bodenmorphologie f soil morphology

bodenmorphologisch soil morphological
Bodenmosaik n soil mosaic
Bodenmüdigkeit f soil sickness (exhaustion, fatigue), soil depletion (impoverishment)
Bodenmulch m soil mulch
Bodenmykologie f soil mycology
Bodenmykoökologie f soil mycoecology
bodennah ground-proximate, near-ground, near-earth
Bodennähe f ground proximity
Bodennährstoff m soil nutrient
Bodennässe f soil wetness
Bodennässebildung f [soil] waterlogging
Bodennebel m ground fog
Bodennest n ground nest
Bodenneutralität f soil neutrality
Bodennitratstickstoff m soil nitrate-nitrogen
Bodennitrifizierung f soil nitrification
Bodennomenklatur f soil nomenclature
Bodennutzer m land user
Bodennutzung f land use (utilization, management)
Bodennutzungsaufnahme f land-use survey
Bodennutzungseignung f soil capability (suitability)
Bodennutzungseignungskarte f land use capability map
Bodennutzungsempfehlung f land-use recommendation
Bodennutzungsklasse f land-use class
Bodennutzungsordnung f regulations on land utilization
Bodennutzungsplanung f land-use planning
Bodennutzungspolitik f land-use policy
Bodennutzungssystem n cropping system
Bodennutzungstyp m land utilization type
Bodennutzungsverordnung f land-use regulation
Bodenoberfläche f soil (ground) surface
Bodenökologie f soil ecology
Bodenökosystem n soil ecosystem
Bodenorganismus m soil organism; soil animal
Bodenpacht f tenancy
Bodenpächter m tenant
Bodenpacker m land packer
Bodenparameter m soil parameter
Bodenpartikel n soil particle
Bodenpasteurisator m soil pasteurizer
Bodenpasteurisierung f soil pasteurization
Bodenpenetrometer n soil cone penetrometer
Bodenpestizid n soil pesticide
Bodenpflege f soil husbandry (conservation)
Bodenphosphat n soil phosphate
Bodenphosphor m soil phosphorus
Boden-pH-Wert m soil pH
Bodenphysik f soil physics
bodenphysikalisch soil-physical
Bodenpilz m soil fungus *(comprehensive term)*
Bodenplanierung f soil levelling
Bodenplanum n road bed, subgrade

Bodenplastizität *f* soil plasticity
Bodenplatte *f* [der Gleiskette] track plate (shoe)
Bodenpopulation *f* soil population (e.g. of pests)
Bodenpore *f* soil pore
Bodenporensystem *n* soil pore system
Bodenporosität *f* soil porosity
Bodenpreis *m* land price (cost)
Bodenprobe *f* soil sample
Bodenprobenahme *f* soil sampling
Bodenprobenahmegerät *n* soil [core] sampler, soil corer (coring machine), soil tube
Bodenprobenbohrer *m* soil auger
Bodenprobenentnahmegerät *n*, **Bodenprobenzieher** *m s.* Bodenprobenahmegerät
Bodenprobenzylinder *m* soil sampling cylinder
Bodenproduktivität *f* soil (land) productivity
Bodenproduktivitätsindex *m* soil productivity index
Bodenprofil *n* soil profile (cross section)
Bodenprovinz *f* soil province
Bodenprüfung *f* soil examination
Bodenqualität *f* soil quality
Bodenquerschnitt *m s.* Bodenprofil
Bodenradantrieb *m* ground-wheel drive
Bodenrayonierung *f* soil zonation
Bodenreaktion *f* soil reaction
Bodenreaktionsvermögen *n* soil reactivity
Bodenreaktivität *f* soil reactivity
Bodenrecht *n* land legislation
Bodenreform *f* land reform
Bodenregion *f* land region
Bodenreifung *f* soil ripening
Bodenreinertrag *m* soil rent[al] *(forest economics)*
Bodenrelief *n* soil contour
Bodenressourcen *fpl* land resources
Bodenriß *m* soil crack
Bodenroller *m* tumble-weed *(comprehensive term)*
Bodenruhe *f* rest of soil
Bodensalinität *f* soil salinity
Boden-Samen-Kontakt *m* soil-seed contact
Bodensättigung *f* soil saturation
Bodensatz *m* sediment, settlings; lees *(esp. in fermentation)*
Bodensauerstoff *m* soil oxygen
Bodensaugvermögen *n* soil suction
Bodensäule *f* soil column
Bodensäure *f* soil acid
Bodenschadinsekt *n* soil insect pest
Bodenschädling *m* soil (ground) pest
Bodenschädlingsbekämpfungsmittel *n* soil pesticide
Bodenschätzung *f* soil fertility appraisal, land evaluation
Bodenschicht *f* soil layer
~/durchwurzelte root[ing] zone, root range
Bodenscholle *f* soil clod
Bodenschurf *m* soil pit
Bodenschutz *m* soil protection
Bodenschutzbearbeitung *f* conservation tillage

Bodenschutzpflanze *f* soil-protecting plant, cover plant
Bodenschwund *m* soil shrinkage
Bodensequenz *f* soil sequence, pedosequence
Bodenserie *f* soil series
Bodenskelett *n* soil skeleton
Bodenskelettuntersuchung *f* soil fabric study
Bodensonde *f* soil probe (penetrometer)
Bodensorption *f* soil sorption
bodenspezifisch soil-specific
Bodenstabilisation *f s.* Bodenstabilisierung
Bodenstabilisator *m* soil stabilizer (stabilizing agent)
Bodenstabilisierung *f* soil stabilization; soil fastening *(road construction)*
bodenständig autochthonal, autochthonous, indigenous; rustic
Bodenständigkeit *f* autochthony
Bodenstatik *f* soil statics
Bodenstein *m* bedstone *(milling)*
Bodensterilisation *f* soil sterilization
Bodensterilisator *m* soil sterilizer
Bodenstickstoff *m* soil nitrogen
Bodenstickstoffhaushalt *m* nitrogen economy of the soil
Bodenstreu *f* ground (soil) litter
Bodenstruktur *f* soil structure
Bodenstruktureinheit *f* soil structural unit
Bodenstrukturverbesserung *f* soil conditioning, soil [structure] improvement, soil amelioration (amendment)
Bodenstrukturverbesserungsmittel *n* soil conditioner (improver, improving material), soil ameliorant (amendment)
Bodensubstanz *f* soil substance
~/organische soil organic matter, SOM
Bodensubstrat *n* soil substrate (material)
Bodensuspension *f* soil suspension
Bodensystematik *f* soil systematics (taxonomy)
Bodentauglichkeit *f* land capability
Bodentauglichkeitsklassifikation *f* land-capability classification
Bodentaxonomie *f* soil taxonomy (systematics)
Bodenteilchen *n* soil particle (grain)
Bodenteilchengröße *f* soil particle size
Bodentemperatur *f* soil temperature
Bodentermite *f* subterranean termite
Bodentest *m* soil test
Bodentextur *f* soil texture
Bodenthermometer *n* soil thermometer
Bodentiefe *f s.* Bodenmächtigkeit
Bodentier *n* soil animal
Bodentoxin *n* soil toxin
Bodentoxizität *f* soil toxicity
Bodentrieb *m* ground shoot; neck sprout *(of grape-vine)*
Bodentrockenheit *f* soil drought
Bodentrockenmasse *f* soil dry weight

bodentrocknen

bodentrocknen to field-dry, to field-cure *(e.g. hay)*
Bodentrocknis *f* soil drought
Bodentrocknung *f* 1. soil drying; 2. field drying (curing) *(forage cropping)*; floor drying *(e.g. of grain)*
~ **von Heu** field hay drying
Bodentyp *m* soil type, type (kind) of soil
Bodenübersicht *f* soil survey
bodenübertragbar *s.* bodenbürtig
Bodenunebenheit *f* **durch Windwurf** *(Am, forest)* cradle knoll
Bodenungeziefer *n* ground vermin
Bodenunterordnung *f* soil suborder
Bodenunterschied *m* soil difference
Bodenuntersuchung *f* soil test (investigation)
Bodenuntersuchungsdienst *m* soil testing (analysis) service
Bodenvariation *f* soil heterogeneity
Bodenvarietät *f* soil series
Bodenvegetation *f* ground vegetation
~/**lebende** live ground cover
Bodenverbesserer *m* soil improver
Bodenverbesserung *f* soil (land) improvement, [soil] amelioration
Bodenverbesserungsmaschine *f* soil improving machine
Bodenverbesserungsmittel *n* soil improver (improving material), soil conditioner (ameliorant, amendment)
Bodenverdichtung *f* soil compaction (cementation), soil compression (consolidation)
Bodenverdichtungszone *f* pan
Bodenverdunstung *f* soil evaporation
Bodenverfestigung *f s.* Bodenverdichtung
Bodenverformung *f* soil deformation
Bodenvergiftung *f* soil poisoning
Bodenverkleidung *f* bottom shield *(e.g. of a combine)*
Bodenverkrustung *f* soil crusting (cap)
Bodenverlust *m* soil loss
Bodenvermörtelung *f* soil grouting
Bodenvernässung *f* soil waterlogging
Bodenversalzung *f* soil salin[iz]ation
Bodenversalzungsgrad *m* soil salinity
Bodenversauerung *f* soil acidification (acidulation)
Bodenverschmierung *f* soil smear
Bodenverschmutzung *f* soil pollution (contamination)
Bodenverseuchung *f* soil infection
Bodenverunreinigung *f* soil pollution (contamination)
Bodenverwehung *f* deflation
Bodenverwundung *f* soil wounding
Bodenviskosität *f* soil viscosity
Bodenvolumen *n* soil volume
Bodenvorarbeiten *fpl s.* Bodenvorbereitung
Bodenvorbereitung *f* soil (land) preparation, preparatory soil cultivation
Bodenwalze *f* land roller

Bodenwärme *f* 1. soil heat; 2. bottom heat *(e.g. in glasshouses)*
Bodenwärmehaushalt *m* soil thermal regime
Bodenwärmestrom *m* soil heat flux
Bodenwaschanlage *f*, **Bodenwaschgerät** *n* soil-washing apparatus *(e.g. for recording microorganisms in soil samples)*
Bodenwasser *n* soil water
~/**nicht nutzbares** dead store
~/**totes** dead store
Bodenwasseraufnahme *f* soil water uptake
Bodenwasserausschöpfung *f* soil water depletion
Bodenwasserbewegung *f* soil water movement (flux)
Bodenwasserbilanz *f* soil water balance
Bodenwasserdefizit *n* soil water deficit
Bodenwasserdiffusivität *f* soil water diffusivity
Bodenwassererschöpfung *f* soil water depletion
Bodenwasserevaporation *f* soil water evaporation
Bodenwasserextrakt *m* soil water extract
Bodenwassergehalt *m* soil water content
Bodenwasserhaushalt *m* soil water budget
Bodenwasserkategorie *f* soil water category
Bodenwasserkonstante *f* soil water constant
Bodenwasserpotential *n* soil water potential
Bodenwasserprobenehmer *m* soil water sampler
Bodenwasserregime *n* soil water regime
Bodenwassersättigung *f* soil water saturation
Bodenwassersaugspannung *f* soil matric suction
Bodenwasserspeicherung *f* soil water storage
Bodenwasserstreß *m* soil water stress
Bodenwasserverdunstung *f* soil water evaporation
Bodenwasserverhältnisse *npl* soil water relations
Bodenwasservorrat *m* soil water reserve
Bodenwasserwiederauffüllung *f* soil water recharge
Bodenwasserzustand *m* soil water status
bodenweit base-wide *(limbs)*
Bodenwertzahl *f* index of land quality
Bodenwiderstand *m* soil resistance
Bodenwühler *m* soil burrowing animal *(comprehensive term)*
Bodenwurzel *f* ground root
Bodenzement *m* soil cement
Bodenzementweg *m* soil cement road
Bodenzerstörung *f* soil devastation (erosion)
Bodenzone *f* soil zone
~ **außerhalb des Pflanzenwurzelbereichs** edaphosphere
Bodenzoologie *f* soil zoology, pedozoology
Bodenzusammenlegung *f* field clearing, land consolidation, consolidation of arable land
Bodenzusammensetzung *f* soil composition
Bodenzustand *m* soil condition (status)
Böe *f s.* Bö
Boerhavie *f (bot)* spiderling *(genus Boerhavia)*
bogenförmig *(bot)* arcuate

Bogengrindel *m* beam with curved section *(plough)*
Bogenhanf *m* 1. sansevieria *(genus Sansevieria)*; 2. bowstring hemp *(some Sanseveria spp.)*
Bogenhanffaser *f* bowstring hemp
Bogenholz *n* Osage-orange, Maclura pomifera
Bogensäge *f* bow saw
Bogensieb *n* curved screen *(of a pulp separator)*
Bogensprung *m* curvet *(equitation)*
Bohea *f* bohea *(a black tea)*
Bohle *f* [thick] plank, batten, cant
Böhmit *m* boehmite *(non-clay mineral)*
Bohne *f* 1. bean *(esp. of genera Phaseolus, Dolichos and Vigna)*; 2. s. Ackerbohne; 3. mark of mouth *(of horse's incisors)*
~/gelbhülsige butter-bean
~/grüne green bean
~/grünhülsige butter-bean
~/unausgereifte green bean
bohnenähnlich, bohnenartig bean-like, fabaceous
Bohnenbrand *m* common blight of bean[s] *(caused by Xanthomonas phaseoli)*
Bohnenenthülser *m* bean-sheller
Bohnenerntemaschine *f* bean harvester
Bohnenfliege *f* bean [seed] fly, Delia (Phorbia) platura
Bohnenfliegenlarve *f* seed-corn maggot
bohnenförmig bean-shaped
Bohnengelbmosaik *n* (phyt) bean yellow mosaic
Bohnengelbmosaikvirus *n* bean yellow mosaic virus, BeYMV
Bohnenhülsenscheckungsvirus *n* bean pod mottle virus, BPMV
Bohnenkraut *n* 1. savory *(genus Satureja)*; 2. summer savory, Satureja hortensis
Bohnenlegemaschine *f* bean drill
Bohnenmähdrescher *m* bean combine
Bohnenmosaikvirus *n* bean mosaic virus
Bohnenrost *m* bean rust *(caused by Uromyces phaseoli and U. appendiculatus)*
Bohnensamen *m* bean [seed]
Bohnenschober *m* bean stack
Bohnenstange *f* beanpole
Bohnenstengel *m* beanstalk
Bohnenstroh *n* bean straw
Bohnenstrohmehl *n* bean vine meal
Bohrbrunnen *m* tube well
bohren 1. to drill, to bore; 2. *(ent)* to terebrate
Bohrer *m* drill; bit; auger
Bohrfliege *f* fruit-fly *(family Trypetidae)*
Bohrkäfer *m* 1. anobium (furniture) beetle, death-watch [beetle] *(family Anobiidae)*; 2. powder-post beetle (borer), bostrychid *(family Bostrychidae)*
Bohrkäferlarve *f* [wood]worm
Bohrkern *m* [increment, boring] core, coring *(timber mensuration)*
Bohrloch *n* 1. borehole; 2. insect (worm, grub) hole

~/kleines pin-hole
Bohrlochverfahren *n* borehole treatment *(wood preservation)*
Bohrmehl *n* bore (boring) dust, bore meal, frass *(of mining insects)*
Bohrschädling *m* wood (timber) borer *(comprehensive term)*
Bohrschneide *f* bit
Bohrspan *m* s. Bohrkern
böig gusty; squally *(with showers)*
Boisduval-Schildlaus *f* Boisduval scale, Diaspis boisduvalii
Bokharaklee *m* white sweet clover, Melilotus alba
Boletus *m* *(bot)* boletus *(genus Boletus)*
Bolle *f* onion, Allium cepa [var. cepa]
Boltonie *f* false starwort, Boltonia asteroides [var. latisquama]
Bolus *m* bolus, ball
Bolzenschußbetäubung *f* *(slaught)* captive bolt stunning
Bomarie *f* white Jerusalem artichoke, Bomarea edulis
Bombage *f* blower *(of tins)*
Bombayhanf *m* sunn [crotalaria, hemp], Crotalaria juncea
Bombay-Muskatnuß *f* Bombay nutmeg, Myristica malabarica
Bombesin *n* bombesin *(polypeptide)*
Bonität[sklasse] *f* *(forest)* site (locality) class, quality (productivity, growth, yield) class
Bonitätskurve *f* *(forest)* site index curve
Bonitätstafel *f* *(forest)* site index table
bonitieren to assess, to score, to evaluate
Bonitierung *f* assessment, scoring; *(forest)* site class determination
Boniturschema *n* scoring system
Bonsai *m* 1. bonsai *(artificially dwarfed potted tree)*; 2. s. Bonsaikultur
Bonsaikultur *f* bonsai
Bonsmara *n* Bonsmara *(cattle breed)*
Boosterimpfung *f* *(vet)* booster injection
bootförmig *(bot, zoo)* cymbiform
Bootsbauholz *n* shipbuilding timber
Boranrind *n* Boran cattle *(breed)*
Borassuspalme *f* Borassus [palm] *(genus Borassus)*
Borat *n* borate
Borax *m* borax *(boron fertilizer, larvicide)*
Borbonol *n* borbonol *(fungicide)*
Bordeaux *m* Bordeaux *(a white or red wine)*
Bordeauxbrühe *f* Bordeaux mixture *(fungicide)*
Bordeauxterpentin *n* galipot *(from Pinus pinaster)*
Bordelaiser Brühe *f* Bordeaux mixture *(fungicide)*
Border-Collie *m* Border collie *(dog breed)*
Border-Leicester *n* Border Leicester *(sheep breed)*
Border-Terrier *m* Border terrier *(dog breed)*
Bordetellose *f* *(vet)* bordetellosis *(caused by Bordetella bronchiseptica)*

Bordüngemittel

Bordüngemittel n boron fertilizer
boreal boreal
Borg m, **Bork** m hog pig, [slaughter] barrow
Borke f [rough outer] bark, dead bark, rind, cortex, rhytidome, *(Am)* ross • ~ **abschälen** to flay, to scale
Borkenflechte f *(vet)* ringworm
Borkenkäfer m bark (engraver) beetle, keyhole (shot-hole) borer, ipid [beetle], *(Am)* flag worm *(family Scolytidae = Ipidae)*
~/**bastbrütender** bast beetle
Borkenkäferbefall m bark-beetle infestation
Borkenkäferfalle f bark-beetle trap
Borkenplatte f catch bark, bark trap
Bormangel m boron deficiency
Bornavirus n *(vet)* Borna disease virus
Borneokampfer m Borneo camphor *(wood extract from Dryobalanops aromatica)*
Borneol n, **Bornylalkohol** m borneol, bornyl alcohol
Borretsch m 1. borage *(genus Borago)*; 2. [common] borage, talewort, Borago officinalis
Borretschgewächse npl borage family *(family Boraginaceae)* • **die ~ betreffend** boragin[ac]eous
Borsäure f boric acid
Borste f *(bot, zoo)* bristle, seta
borstenartig setaceous
borstenblättrig chaetophyllous
borstenförmig setaceous
Borstengras n 1. three-awn [spear grass] *(genus Aristida)*; 2. s. Borstgras
Borstenhaar n bristle
Borstenhirse f 1. bristle-grass *(genus Setaria)*; 2. foxtail (Italian, German) millet, Hungarian (Bengal) grass, Setaria italica
Borstenmehl n hog hair meal *(feed-stuff)*
Borstenschwingel m shade fescue, Festuca heterophylla
borstentragend setiferous, setigerous
Borstgras n [moor] mat-grass, small-mat-weed, nard[us], Nardus stricta
borstig bristly, setose, setaceous, hispid, strigose
Borstige Fingeraralie f Siberian (thorny) ginseng, Eleutherococcus senticosus
~ **Prunkwinde** f Brazilian morning glory, Ipomoea setosa
~ **Rinderlaus** f buffalo louse, Solenopotes capillatus
~ **Robinie** f rose acacia, bristly locust, Robinia hispida
~ **Stachelkraftwurz** f s. Borstige Fingeraralie
bösartig 1. malign[ant], pernicious *(disease)*; 2. vicious, outlaw *(animal)* • ~ **sein** to savage *(animal behaviour)*
Bösartige Faulbrut f *(api, vet)* American foul brood, AFB *(caused by Bacillus larvae)*
Bösartigkeit f 1. malignancy; 2. vice, viciousness
~ **der Sau** savage sow syndrome
Böschung f bank, embankment, slope, scarp

~/**steile** escarpment
Böschungsabschwemmung f slope wash
Böschungsbefestigung f consolidation of banks
Böschungshobel m backsloper *(road construction)*
Böschungsmäher m, **Böschungsmähwerk** n bank mower (cutter), embankment (verge) mower; ditch bank mower
Böschungswinkel m angle of repose
Boskett n boscage, boskage *(growth of trees)*
Bosnisches Gebirgspferd n Bosnian pony *(breed)*
Boston Terrier m Boston terrier (bull) *(dog breed)*
Botanik f botany, plant biology (science), phytology
~/**landwirtschaftliche** agricultural botany
Botaniker m botanist, phytologist
botanisch botanical, phytologic[al]
botanisieren to botanize, to herborize
Boten-RNA f messenger RNA
Botenstoff m semiochemical
Bothriozephalose f bothriocephalosis *(of freshwater fishes, caused by Bothriocephalus gowkongensis)*
Botryomykose f *(vet)* botryomycosis
Botrytisfäule f *(phyt)* botrytis disease (rot) *(caused by Botrytis spp.)*
~ **des Apfels** dry eye-rot of apple *(caused by Botrytis cinerea)*
Bottich m vat, tub
Bottichkühler m attemperator
Botulinustoxin n s. Botulismustoxin
Botulismus m botulism *(feed poisoning)*
Botulismustoxin n botulin, botulinal toxin
Boucherie-Verfahren n sap displacement (replacement) treatment *(wood preservation)*
Bougainvillea f *(bot)* bougainvillea *(genus Bougainvillea)*
Bougie f *(vet)* bougie
Bouillon f broth *(microbiology)*
Boulonnais-Pferd n Boulonnais *(horse breed)*
Bouquet n s. Bukett
Bourbonrose f Edward rose, Rosa x borboniana
Bouvardie f *(bot)* 1. bouvardia *(genus Bouvardia)*; 2. Bouvardia longiflora
Bouvier des Flandres m Bouvier des Flandres *(dog breed)*
bovin bovine, taurine
Bovist m puff-ball [fungus], puckball *(genus Lycoperdon)*
Bowen-Technik f Bowen technique *(in sheep breeding)*
Bowmansche Kapsel f Bowman's (glomerular) capsule *(of kidney)*
Box f pen, box, cubicle, stall
Boxenhaltung f cubicle housing
Boxen[lauf]stall m stable, pen barn, cubicle house
Boxenstallhaltung f cubicle housing
Boxentrenngitter n stanchion, partition

Boxer *m* boxer *(dog breed)*
Boxpalette *f* box pallet, pallet box (bin)
Boykin-Spaniel *m* American water spaniel *(dog breed)*
Boysenbeere *f* boysenberry, Rubus loganobaccus
Brabanter *m* Brabancon, Brabant *(horse breed)*
Brabanter Krankheit *f (vet)* stockman disease
brach fallow, uncropped, bare of crop
Brachdistel *f* 1. field eryngo, Eryngium campestre; 2. *s.* Ackerdistel
Brache *f* fallow [ground, land] *(s. a.* Brachland*)*
~/ökologische ecofallow
Brache-Anbau-System *n* fallow-cropping system
Brachefrucht *f* fallow crop
brachen to fallow
Bracherotation *f* fallow rotation
Brachfeld *n* fallow [ground], naked field
Brachfliege *f* wheat-bulb fly, Delia (Leptohylemyia) coarctata
Brachfrucht *f* fallow crop
Brachkäfer *m* june beetle (bug), summer (European) chafer, Amphimallon solstitiale, Amphimallus (Rhizotrogus) solstitialis
Brachland *n* fallow [ground, land]; former agricultural land; lea[land], ley; barren [land]
Brachlandgrubber *m* fallow cultivator
Brachlandrückgewinnung *f* fallow recovery
brachliegen to lie fallow; to lie waste (lasting)
Brachliegen *n* fallowness
brachliegend fallow, uncropped, bare of crop
Brachpflug *m* fallow plough
Brachsen *m* bream, Abramis brama
Brachsenkraut *n* quillwort *(genus Isoetes)*
Brachvogel *m* curlew *(genus Numenius)*
Brachzeit *f* fallow season
Brackschaf *n* cull sheep
Brackwasser *n* brackish water
Brackwasserteich *m* brackish-water pond
Bractee *f s.* Braktee
Bradsot *f(rh)* bradsot *(clostridial intoxication esp. of sheep)*
~/Deutsche black disease
Bradykardie *f* bradycardia
Bradykinin *n* bradykinin *(nonapeptide)*
Braford[rind] *n* Braford *(cattle breed)*
Brahma *n* brahma[putra] *(chicken breed)*
Brahman[rind] *n* Brahman *(cattle breed)*
Braktee *f (bot)* bract, wrapper leaf
Brakteole *f (bot)* bracteole
Branchiomykose *f (vet)* branchiomycosis
Brand *m* 1. *(phyt)* blight, blast, brand *(comprehensive term)*; smut; scorch; scald; 2. *(vet)* gangrene; necrosis; 3. fire *(for compounds s.* under Waldbrand*)* • **durch ~ vernichten** to blight • **von ~ befallen werden** to blight
~/durch Überspringen entstandener hopover [fire]
Brand... *s. a.* Waldbrand...
Brandader *f* crural vein *(anatomy of hoofed game)*

Brandausbreitung *f* fire spread (progress)
Brandausbreitungskarte *f* fire progress map
brandbefallen *s.* brandig
Brandbekämpfung *f* fire fighting (control), fire conservancy (suppression) *(s. a.* Waldbrandbekämpfung*)*
Brandbeobachtungs- und -löschkraft *f* look-out fireman
Brandblock *m* burning block *(forest fire control)*
Brandbutte *f (phyt)* smut (bunt) ball
Brandeisen *n* brand[ing] iron
Brandentdeckung *f* fire discovery
Branderkundung *f*, **Brandermittlung** *f* fire detection
Brandflächengrößenklasse *f* fire [size] class
brandfleckig *(bot, phyt)* sphacelate[d]
Brandfuchs *m* brant fox, Vulpes alopex
Brandgebiet *n* burned (burnt) area
Brandgefahr *f*, **Brandgefährdung** *f* fire danger (risk, hazard)
Brandgefährdungsindex *m* fire-danger index, burning (fire hazard) index
Brandgefährdungs[index]messer *m* fire-danger meter
Brandgefahrenbestimmung *f* fire danger rating
Brandgefahrenskala *f* fire-danger scale
Brandgefahrentabelle *f* fire-danger table
Brandholz *n* burnt timber
brandig *(bot, phyt)* sphacelate[d]; *(phyt)* smutted; *(vet)* gangrenous; necrotic
Brandklimax[gesellschaft] *f* fire (pyric) climax
Brandkrankheit *f s.* Brand 1.
Brandkraut *n* Jerusalem sage *(genus Phlomis)*
Brandkultur *f* fire cultivation
Brandmeldung *f* fire detection
Brandnarbe *f* fire scar
Brandortung *f s.* Branderkundung
Brandpilz *m* brand fungus; smut [fungus] *(order Ustilaginales)*
Brandrodewirtschaft *f* 1. fire cultivation; 2. *s.* **~/wandernde**
~/wandernde shifting (roving, swidden) agriculture, shag, slash-and-burn agriculture, bush fallowing (fallow system)
Brandrodung *f* fire cultivation
Brandrodungshackbau *m s.* Brandrodewirtschaft/wandernde
Brandsaum *m* fire (burning) edge, fire line (margin)
Brandschneise *f* fire break (belt), fuel break
Brandschutz *m* fire protection (control, conservancy)
~/vorbeugender fire prevention
Brandschutzakte *f* fire atlas
Brandschutzanlagen *fpl* fire control improvements
Brandschutzbeauftragter *m* fire prevention officer
Brandschutzbezirk *m* fire district
Brandschutzstreife *f* look-out patrol
Brandschutzstreifen *m s.* Brandschneise

Brandschutzverantwortlicher

Brandschutzverantwortlicher *m* fire prevention officer
Brandsicherheit *f* fire safety
Brandspore *f* brand spore
Brandstempel *m* brand[ing] iron
Brandstiftung *f* fire-raising, arson
Brandursachenklasse *f* fire cause class
Brandwache *f* fire watcher[s]
Brandwächter *m* fire (smoke) chaser, look-out patrolman
Brandwarnstufenanzeige[vorrichtung] *f* fire-danger board
Brandwart *m s.* Brandwächter
Brandwirtschaft *f* fire cultivation
Brandwunde *f* fire wound; *(phyt)* scorch
Brandzeichen *n* brand *(e.g. for animal identification)* • **mit ~ versehen** to brand
Brangus[rind] *n* Brangus *(cattle breed)*
Branntkalk *m* [burnt, anhydrous] lime, quicklime, calcium oxide, burned oyster shell lime
Branntweinbrennerei *f* alcohol plant
Brasilbohnenkäfer *m* Mexican bean weevil, Zabrotes subfasciatus
Brasilholz *n* [prickly] brazilwood, Brazil[-wood], Lima wood, *(esp.)* Caesalpinia (Guilandia) echinata
Brasilianische Araukarie *f* Parana pine, Araucaria angustifolia
~ **Futterhirse** *f* Dallis grass, Paspalum dilatatum
~ **Luzerne** *f* Brazilian (wild) lucern[e], stylo, Stylosanthes guianensis
~ **Tradeskantie** *f (bot)* wandering jew, Tradescantia fluminensis (myrtifolia)
Brasilianischer Bohnenkäfer *m s.* Brasilbohnenkäfer
~ **Pfefferbaum** *m* Christmas berry, Schinus terebinthifolius
Brasilienopuntie *f* Brazil prickly pear, Brasiliopuntia (Opuntia) brasiliensis
Brasilkiefer *f* Parana pine, Araucaria angustifolia
Brasilkirsche *f* cherry-of-the-Rio-Grande, Eugenia aggregata
Brasilnuß *f* Brazil (Para, cream) nut
Brasilnußbaum *m* Brazil (Para) nut, almendron, Bertholletia excelsa
Brassen *m* bream, Abramis brama
Brassicazee *f* crucifer *(family Cruciferae = Brassicaceae)*
Brassicazeen *fpl* mustard family *(family Cruciferae = Brassicaceae)*
Brassidinsäure *f* brassidic acid *(fatty acid)*
Brassinolid *n* brassinolide *(sterol)*
Brassinsäure *f s.* Brassidinsäure
Brathähnchen *n* broiler, *(Am)* fryer [chicken], frier
Brathähnchen... *s.* Broiler...
Bratverlust *m* shrinkage on roasting *(of meat)*
brauen to brew
~/Bier to brew
Brauer *m* brewer

Brauerei *f* brewery
Brauereiabwasser *n* brewery effluent
Brauereichemie *f* brewing chemistry
Brauereihefe *f* brewer's (beer) yeast
Brauereimalz *n* brewer's malt
Brauereinebenprodukt *n* brewery by-product
Brauereipferd *n* dray-horse
Brauereischlamm *m* brewery's sludge
Brauermalz *n* brewer's malt
Braugerste *f* brewer's (malting) barley
Braugerstenboden *m* malting barley soil
Braugerstensorte *f* malting variety
Brauindustrie *f* brewing industry
Braumaische *f* brewing-mash
braun brown; bay *(colour of a horse)*
Braunbandschabe *f* brown-banded cockroach, Supella longipalpa (supellectilium)
Braunbär *m* brown bear, Ursus arctos
Braunbeiniger Dickmaulrüßler *m* clay-coloured weevil, Otiorhynchus singularis
Bräune *f (phyt)* browning
Braune Fruchtfäule *f* fruitlet brown rot *(of pineapple, caused by Pseudomonas spp. and Erwinia spp.)*
~ **Haselwurz** *f* European wild ginger, Asarum europaeum
~ **Hühnerlaus** *f* brown chicken louse, Oulocrepis (Goniodes) dissimilis
~ **Hundezecke** *f* kennel (brown dog) tick, Rhipicephalus sanguineus
~ **Obstbaumspinnmilbe** *f* brown mite, Bryobia rubrioculus
~ **Wurzelfäule** *f* brown root disease *(e.g. of the para rubber tree, caused by Phellinus noxius)*
~ **Zecke** *f* brown ear tick, Rhipicephalus appendiculatus
Braunebenprodukt *n* brewery by-product
Braunelle *f (bot)* prunella *(genus Prunella)*
Brauner *m* bay [horse], b.
~ **Bär** *m* brown bear, Ursus arctos
~ **Jura** *m (soil)* Dogger
~ **Rosenwickler** *m* rose tortrix (twist) moth, Archips rosanus, Cacoecia rosana
~ **Rübenaaskäfer** *m* beet carrion beetle, Aclypea (Blitophaga, Silpha) opaca
~ **Senf** *m* black mustard, Brassica nigra
~ **Splintholzkäfer** *m* brown powder-post beetle, Lyctus brunneus
Braunerde *f* brown earth, *(Am)* ochrept
~/podsolige degraded brown earth
Braunes Höhenvieh *n* Brown Mountain *(cattle breed)*
~ **Leghorn** *n* Brown Leghorn *(chicken breed)*
Braunfärbung *f* browning
Braunfäule *f* 1. *(phyt)* brown rot, raan *(comprehensive term)*; 2. red rot *(esp. of pine and spruce, caused by Fomes spp.)*
Braunfleckengrind *m (phyt)* bark scab disease

Braunfleckenkrankheit f (phyt) brown spot [disease] (comprehensive term)
~ **der Erbse** mycosphaerella blight of pea (caused by Mycosphaerella pinodes)
~ **des Reises** rice brown spot, brown spot of rice (caused by Cochliobolus miyabeanus, conidial stage Helminthosporium oryzae)
~ **des Tabaks** tobacco brown spot [disease] (caused by Alternaria longipes)
Braunfleckigkeit f **der Tomate** tomato leaf mould (caused by Cladosporium fulvum)
~ **der Zwiebel** brown stain of onion (caused by Botrytis cinerea)
~ **des Weizens** glume blotch (caused by Septoria nodorum)
Braunhafer m brown oat[s], dun oat[s] (type of Avena sativa)
Braunherzigkeit f (phyt) brown heart
Braunheu n haylage
Braunhorizont m (soil) cambic B-horizon
Braunhuminsäure f (soil) brown humic acid
Braunkern m brown heart (wood defect)
Braunkohl m curly kale, Brassica oleracea convar. acephala var. sabellica
Braunkohle f brown coal
Braunlehm m brown loam
Braun[moos]moor n hypnum moss bog
Braunmoostorf m Bryophyllum peat
Braunpodsol m brown podzol[ic soil], podzolic brown earth
Braunrost m (phyt) leag rust [disease] (comprehensive term)
~ **des Roggens** brown rust of rye (caused by Puccinia dispersa)
braunrot (bot) rubiginose
Braunrückige Reiszikade f (ent) brown plant hopper, Nilaparvata lugens
braunschalig brown-shelled (e.g. an egg)
Braunschecke f(m) skewbald (esp. horse)
Braunschimmel m strawberry roan
Braunschwarzerde f brown chernozemic soil
Bräunung f browning
Braunverfärbung f browning
~ **von künstlich getrocknetem Holz** kiln burn, kiln [brown] stain
Braunvieh n Brown Mountain, European Brown Swiss (cattle breed)
Braunweizen m red wheat
Braunwerden n browning
Braunwurz f figwort (genus Scrophularia)
Braunwurzgewächse npl figwort family (family Scrophulariaceae) • **die ~ betreffend** scrophulariaceous
Braunzucker m brown sugar
Brauprozeß m brewing process, brew
Brauqualität f brewing quality
Braureis m brewer's rice
Braut f **in Haaren** (bot) love-in-a-mist, Nigella damascena

Brautmyrte f [common] myrtle, Myrtus communis
Brautprimel f annual (fairy) primrose, Primula malacoides
Brautstrauß m bridal (wedding) bouquet
Brauvorgang m brewing process, brew
Brauvorschrift f brewing instruction
Brauwasser n [brewing] liquor
Brauwissenschaft f brewing science
Brauzucker m brewer's sugar
Bravaisscher Korrelationskoeffizient m correlation coefficient
Brechbohne f [garden, French] bean, haricot [bean], (Am) snap bean, Phaseolus vulgaris var. nanus forma rotunda
brechen 1. to break; 2. to root (feeding wild boars)
Brechen n **der Winterruhe** breaking of dormancy
Brechmittel n (vet) emetic
Brechnuß f (bot) nux vomica, Strychnos nux-vomica
Brechnußsamen m nux vomica
Brechreiz m (vet) nausea
brechreizlindernd antiemetic
Brechungsindex m refractive index (e.g. of sugar solutions)
Brechungsmesser m refractometer
Brechveilchen n s. Brechwurz[el]
Brechweinstein m antimony potassium tartrate (anthelminthic)
Brechwurz[el] f (bot) ipecac[uanha], Cephaelis (Uragoga) ipecacuanha
Brechzahl f refractive index (e.g. of sugar solutions)
Brechzahlmesser m refractometer
Brei m mash; pulp
~/**dünner (dünnflüssiger)** slurry (filtration)
Breiapfel m sapodilla [plum]
Breiapfelbaum m sapodilla, Manilkara (Achras) zapota
breiartig s. breiig
breiig pulpy • ~ **werden** to pulp
Breinierenkrankheit f pulpy kidney disease, overeating disease, enterotoxaemia (of sheep)
Breitadernvirus n **des Salats** lettuce big vein virus, LBVV
Breitadrigkeit f **des Salats** big vein disease
Breitbandanthelminthikum n broad-spectrum wormer
Breitbandantibiotikum n broad-spectrum antibiotic
Breitbandherbizid n broad-spectrum herbicide
Breitbandpestizid n broad-spectrum pesticide
Breitbandsäge[maschine] f wide-band saw
Breitbandwirkung f broad-spectrum effect
Breitbeil n broad (side) axe
Breitbettfelge f wide rim, wide-base drop-centre rim with shallow well
breitblättrig broad-leaved, (Am) broadleaf, latifoliate, latifolious, platyphyllous

Breitblättrige

Breitblättrige Endivie f escarole, Cichorium endivia var. latifolium
~ **Glockenblume** f broad-leaved bell-flower, Campanula latifolia
~ **Ölweide** f bastard oleaster, Elaeagnus latifolia
~ **Platterbse** f everlasting pea, Lathyrus latifolius
Breitblättriger Lavendel m spike lavender, aspic, Lavandula latifolia (spica)
~ **Lorbeerliguster** m mock privet, Phillyrea [latifolia var.] media
~ **Merk** m water parsnip, Sium latifolium
~ **Rohrkolben** m cat's-tail, bulrush, reed-mace, water torch, *(Am)* cattail, Typha latifolia
Breitblättriges Knabenkraut n marsh orchis, Dactylorhiza majalis, Orchis latifolia
~ **Yams** n bitter (three-leaved) yam, Dioscorea dumetorum
breitblütig platyanthous
breitbrüstig broad-breasted
Breitbrüstige Bronzepute f Broad-Breasted Bronze turkey *(breed)*
~ **Weiße Pute** f Broad White Turkey *(breed)*
Breitdreschmaschine f broad thresher
Breitdüngerstreuer m fertilizer broadcaster, full-width fertilizer distributor
Breite f/therapeutische chemotherapeutic index
breitfrüchtig *(bot)* platycarpous
Breithacke f, **Breithaue** f mattock
Breitkanalwehr n broad-crested weir
breitkronig broad-crowned
Breitmilbe f broad mite, Polyphagotarsonemus (Hemitarsonemus) latus
breitringig broad-ringed, broad-zoned, fast-grown, open-grown, open-grained *(wood)*
Breitröhrige Kartoffelknollenlaus f bulb and potato aphid, Rhopalosiphoninus latysiphon
breitrund *(bot)* oblate
Breitsaat f broadcast seeding
Breitsaatschar n broad shoe coulter
Breitsäen n broadcast seeding
Breitsägerät n/**rückentragbares** knapsack seeder
Breitsämaschine f broadcast seeder, [seed] broadcaster
breitsamig *(bot)* platyspermous
Breitsäschar n broadcast coulter
Breitsaumschlagbetrieb m *(forest)* uniform strip system
Breitschar n broad share, sweep
Breitschargrubber m wide-blade sweep
Breitschwanz m 1. broadtail *(of a caracul lamb)*; 2. s. Breitschwanzfell
Breitschwanzfell n broadtail [pelt]
Breitspektrumantibiotikum n s. Breitbandantibiotikum
breitstreuen to broadcast *(e.g. fertilizer)*
Breitstreuer m broadcast distributor
Breitwegerich m [common, broad-leaved, greater] plantain, waybread, Plantago major
Breitwurf m broadcast *(e.g. in seeding)*

Bremsanlage f brake system
Bremsbacke f brake shoe
Bremsbelag m brake lining
Bremse f 1. brake; 2. horse-fly, breeze [fly], gadfly, greenhead, cleg, tabanid *(family Tabanidae)*
~/**hydraulische** hydraulic brake
~/**pneumatische** pneumatic brake, air [pressure] brake
Bremsenöl n antigadfly oil
Bremsklotz m chock
Bremsvorrichtung f brake
Bremszylinder m brake cylinder
brennbar combustible
~/**nicht** incombustible, non-combustible
Brennderbholz n firewood over 2.75 inches in diameter
Brenneisen n *(vet)* searing-iron
brennen 1. to burn; 2. to distil; 3. *(vet)* to cauterize, to sear
Brennen n 1. burning; 2. distillation; 3. *(vet)* cauterization, cautery
brennend *(bot)* urent
Brennende Liebe f Maltese-cross, scarlet lychnis, flower of Bristol (Constantinople), Lychnis chalcedonica
~ **Lilie** f scarlet Turk's cap lily, Lilium chalcedonicum
Brennerei f distillery, alcohol plant
Brennereiindustrie f distilling industry
Brennereimaische f distillery mash
Brennereischlempe f distillery slop (vinasse)
Brennessel f 1. nettle *(genus Urtica)*; 2. s. Große Brennessel
brennesselblättrig urticifolious
Brennesselgewächse npl nettle family *(family Urticaceae)* • **die** ~ **betreffend** urticaceous
Brennfleckenkrankheit f s. Anthraknose
Brennhaar n *(bot)* sting
Brennholz n burning (fuel) oil
Brennholzberechtigung f right to firewood
Brennholzeinschlag m firewood felling
Brennholzhacken n fuel wood chipping
Brennholzrecht n right to firewood
Brennholzspaltmaschine f firewood cleaving (splitting) machine
Brenninstrument n *(vet)* cautery
Brennmalz n distillery malt
Brennmittel n *(vet)* cautery
Brennöl n burning (fuel) oil
Brennpalme f *(bot)* kittul, kitool, Caryota urens
Brennrinde f bark for fuel
Brennschnitzel npl hog[ged] fuel
Brennstoff m fuel • **mit** ~ **versorgen** to fuel
~/**fossiler** fossil fuel
Brennstoffbehälter m fuel tank
Brennstoffbeschickungsschacht m fuel hopper
Brenntherapie f *(vet)* therapeutic cautery
Brenztraubensäure f pyruvic acid, 2-oxopropionic acid

Bretone m Breton *(horse breed)*
Brett n board
~/herzfreies centre board
Brettermaßstab m board measure
Brettfuß m *s.* Board-Fuß
Brettmaß n board measure
Brettsägewerk n board sawmill
Brettwurzel f buttress [root], plank buttress
Brevicid n xanthocillin *(antibiotic)*
Brewer-Fichte f Brewer's (weeping) spruce, Picea breweriana
Brianconaprikose f *(Am)* Briancon apricot, Prunus brigantina
Briard m Briard *(dog breed)*
Brieftaube f homing pigeon
Briekäse m Brie [cheese]
Bries[el] n sweetbread, thymus [gland] *(esp. of a calf)*
Brika-Ballen m *(forest)* planting block (brick)
Brikett n briquette, briquet
brikettieren to briquette
Brikettierpresse f briquetting press
Brillantgrün n brilliant green *(bacteriostat)*
Brillantgrün-Phenolrot-Agar m brilliant green/phenol red agar *(microbiology)*
Brille f spectacles *(mark esp. at horse's head)*
bring! fetch!, go! *(command to dogs)*
bringen *(forest)* to haul, to extract, to drag out, *(Am)* to log, to yard; *(hunt)* to retrieve
~/Ertrag to yield, to crop
~/über den Winter to winter; to hog *(young sheep)*
~/zum Decken to put to *(breeding animal)*
~/zum Laichen to spawn
~/zum Sprießen to flush
~/zum Welken to wilt
~/zur Blüte to flower
~/zur Reife to mature
Bringen n *s.* Bringung
Bringung f *(forest)* haulage, hauling, extraction, dragging out, *(Am)* logging, yarding
~/baumweise whole-tree logging, full-tree logging
~ mit Tieren animal hauling
~ mit Traktoren tractor hauling
Brise f breeze *(Beaufort scale)*
~/frische fresh breeze
~/leichte light breeze
~/mäßige moderate breeze
~/schwache gentle breeze
Bristopen n oxacillin *(antibiotic)*
Britische Saanen-Ziege f British Saanen *(goat breed)*
~ Toggenburg-Ziege f British Toggenburg *(goat breed)*
British Alpine f British Alpine *(goat breed)*
~ White n British White *(cattle breed)*
British-Friesian-Rind n British Friesian *(cattle breed)*
BrMV *s.* Brunnenkressemosaikvirus
Broccoli pl *s.* Brokkoli

Bröckelfutter n mash
Bröckelgefüge n *(soil)* blocky structure
bröckelnd crumbly
bröcklig crumbly; friable
Brodiaea f *(bot)* brodiaea *(genus Brodiaea)*
Brodifacoum n brodifacoum *(rodenticide)*
Broika m rabbit broiler
Broiler m broiler, *(Am)* fryer [chicken], frier
Broileraufzucht f broiler rearing
Broilerausstallung f broiler harvest
Broilerbestand m broiler stock
Broilerbetrieb m broiler farm
Broilereinstreu f broiler litter
Broilerfarm f broiler farm
Broilerfutter n broiler feed
Broilerhautpigmentation f broiler pigmentation
Broilerindustrie f broiler industry
Broilerleistung f broiler performance
Broilermastfutter n broiler mash
Broilermaststall m broiler house
Broilerpigmentation f broiler pigmentation
Broilerproduktionsbetrieb m broiler farm
Broilerpute f broiler turkey
Broilerration f broiler ration
Broilerschlachtfett n broiler carcass fat
Broilerschlachtkörper m broiler carcass
Broilerstall m broiler house
Broilerstarterfutter n broiler starter
Broiler[tief]streu f broiler litter
Broilerverarbeitungsanlage f broiler processing plant
Broilerverarbeitungsbetrieb m broiler processing plant
Broilerzuchthenne f broiler breeder
Brokkoli pl(m) broccoli [sprouts], Italian asparagus (sprouting broccoli), calabrese, Brassica oleracea convar. botrytis var. italica
Bromacil n bromacil *(herbicide)*
Bromadiolon n bromadiolone *(rodenticide)*
Brombeere f blackberry, bramble *(genus Rubus)*
~/kriechende (niedrigwachsende) trailing blackberry, dewberry
Brombeerensaummücke f raspberry (blackberry) stem gall-midge, Lasioptera rubi
Brombeerfalterchen n *(ent)* green hairstreak, Callophrys rubi
Brombeergallmilbe f blackberry mite, Aceria essigi
Brombeergallwespe f *(ent)* blackberry gall maker, Diastrophus rubi
Brombeerminierwespe f *(ent)* blackberry leafminer *(genus Metallus)*
Brombeerrute f *(Am)* floricane
Brombeerstrauch m blackberry[-bush], bramble *(genus Rubus)*
Bromelain n bromelain *(enzyme)*
Bromelie f *(bot)* bromelia[d] *(genus Bromelia)*
Bromfenvinphos n bromfenvinphos *(insecticide)*
Bromid n bromide

Bromkalium

Bromkalium n potassium bromide
Bromocriptin n bromocriptine *(alkaloid)*
Bromocyclen n bromocyclen *(acaricide, insecticide)*
Bromofenofos n, **Bromofenophos** n bromofenophos *(anthelminthic)*
Bromofenoxim n bromofenoxim *(herbicide)*
Bromomethan n bromomethane *(fumigant, insecticide)*
Bromophos n bromophos *(insecticide, acaricide)*
Bromophos-ethyl n bromophos-ethyl *(insecticide)*
Bromopropylat n bromopropylate *(acaricide)*
Bromoxynil n bromoxynil *(herbicide)*
Brompyrazon n brompyrazone *(herbicide)*
[5-]Bromurazil n bromouracil *(antimetabolite)*
Bronchialbaum m bronchial tree
Bronchialdrüse f bronchial gland
Bronchialkatarrh m *(vet)* bronchitis
Bronchie f bronchus
Bronchiole f bronchiole
Bronchiolitis f *(vet)* bronchiolitis
Bronchitis f *(vet)* bronchitis
~ des Huhnes/infektiöse avian infectious bronchitis, infectious bronchitis of chickens
~ des Rindes/enzootische cuffing pneumonia
Bronchitisvirus n **des Huhnes** [avian] infectious bronchitis virus
Bronchopneumonie f *(vet)* bronchopneumonia
Bronchoskopie f *(vet)* bronchoscopy
Bronchulitis f *(vet)* bronchiolitis
Bronchus m bronchus
Bronzeartige Blattwelke f **der Erdbeere** strawberry bronze leaf wilt *(virosis)*
Bronzefärbung f s. Bronzefleckenkrankheit
~ des Blattes leaf bronzing *(due to chlorine deficiency)*
Bronzefleckenkrankheit f *(phyt)* bronze spotting [disease], bronzing [disease] *(virosis)*
~ der Tomate spotted wilt of tomato *(virosis)*
Bronzefleckenvirus n bronze spotting virus, BSV
Bronzepute f bronze turkey, American mammoth bronze *(breed)*
Bronzierung f s. Bronzefleckenkrankheit
Brotaufstrich m **aus Milchprodukten** dairy spread
Brotbackqualität f bread-making quality
Brotfrucht f 1. bread-fruit; 2. s. Brotgetreide
Brotfruchtbaum m bread-fruit, Artocarpus altilis
Brotgetreide n bread cereal (grain), breadstuff
Brotgetreidemehl n breadstuff[s]
Brotianid n brotianide *(anthelminthic)*
Brotkäfer m bread beetle, drugstore beetle (weevil), Stegobium paniceum
Brotkäse m loaf cheese
Brotmehl n bread flour, breadstuff[s]
Brotnußbaum m bread-nut [tree], Brosimum alicastrum
Brotteig m bread dough
Brotwaren pl breadstuffs

Brotweizen m bread wheat
Brougham m brougham *(two-seated one-horse carriage)*
Browallie f *(bot)* 1. browallia, bush violet *(genus Browallia)*; 2. browallia, Andean forget-me-not, Browallia speciosa; 3. sapphire flower, Browallia speciosa var. major
Brown Swiss n Brown Swiss *(cattle breed)*
Brown-Heckenkirsche f scarlet trumpet honeysuckle, Lonicera x brownii
brr! whoa, wo *(command to horses)*
Brucellaantigen n brucella antigen
Brucellaimpfstoff m brucella vaccine
Brucellaphage m brucella phage
Brucellenabort m s. Brucellose
Brucellin n, **Brucello[hydro]lysat** n brucellin *(allergen)*
Brucellose f *(vet)* brucellosis, Bang's disease *(caused by Brucella spp.)*
~ der Schafe und Ziegen Malta fever
~ des Rindes contagious abortion in cattle *(caused by Brucella abortus)*
Brucelloseantigen n brucella antigen
brucellosefrei *(vet)* brucellosis-free
Bruch m 1. break[age]; rupture; *(vet)* fracture *(s. a. under Fraktur)*; 2. *(vet)* [intestinal] hernia, rupture; 3. s. Bruch n; 4. marsh[land], fen [forest], bog; 5. *(dairy)* curd; 6. break *(brewing)*
~/eingeklemmter (inkarzerierter) strangulated hernia
~ quer zur Faser[richtung] cross fracture *(of wood)*
Bruch n marsh[land], fen forest, bog
Bruchähren fpl chobs
Bruchbearbeitung f *(dairy)* curd treatment
Bruchbelastung f s. Bruchlast
Bruchboden m boggy soil
Bruchfestigkeit f breaking (ultimate) strength *(e.g. of wood)*
Bruch-Fusions-Hypothese f *(gen)* breakage-fusion hypothesis
Bruchhefe f flocculent yeast
brüchig brittle, brash[y], fragile *(e.g. wood)*
Brüchigkeit f brittleness, brashness, fragility
Bruchkorn n 1. broken grain; 2. *(dairy)* curd grain
Bruchlast f ultimate load[ing], failing load *(e.g. of wood)*
Bruchleiste f crest, hinge, key, hold, tipping edge, *(Am)* bridge *(tree-felling)*
Bruchmesser n *(dairy)* curd knife
Bruchmoor n wooded swamp
Bruchoperation f *(vet)* herniotomy
Bruchpunkt m rupture (breaking) point
Bruchreis m ground rice
Bruch-Reunions-Hypothese f *(gen)* breakage-reunion hypothesis
Bruchsack m *(vet)* hernial sac
Bruchsalzen n *(dairy)* curd salting
Bruchschnitt m *(vet)* herniotomy

Brustgräte

Bruchwald *m* fen (swamp) forest, fenwood
Bruchweide *f* crack (brittle, redwood) willow, Salix fragilis
Bruchwiderstand *m* fracture resistance
Brucin *n* brucine *(alkaloid)*
Brücke *f* 1. bridge; 2. pons *(part of the hindbrain)*
Brückenbildung *f* bridging *(of material being conveyed)*
Brückenhirn *n* hindbrain
Brücken[lauf]kran *m* overhead travelling crane
Brückenregner *m* bridge sprinkler
Brüdenhaube *f* air dome
Brühanlage *f* scalder *(poultry processing)*
Brühe *f* wash *(esp. in pest control)*
~/Bordelaiser Bordeaux mixture *(fungicide)*
~/Burgunder Burgundy mixture, soda bordeaux *(fungicide)*
Brüheaufwandmenge *f* mixture dosage *(plant protection)*
Brühebehälter *m* liquid tank
brühen to scald
Brühespritzgerät *n* hydraulic sprayer *(plant protection)*
Brühkessel *m* scalding vat *(poultry processing)*
Brühmalz *n* scalding malt, brumalt
Brühschnitzel *npl* pulp of scalding process, Steffen sugar pulp
Brühtrog *m* scalding trough, scald tank
Brühverfahren *n*/**Steffensches** Steffen process *(sugar manufacture)*
Brühwasser *n* scald water
brüllen to roar, to bellow; to low *(cattle)*
Brüllen *n* roar[ing]; low[ing]
Brüller *m* buller *(cow)*
Brüllerkrankheit *f* constant (continuous) oestrus, nymphomania *(of cow)*
Brummerkrankheit *f s.* Brüllerkrankheit
Brunelle *f (bot)* prunella *(genus Prunella)*
Bruneomycin *n* rufocromomycin *(antibiotic)*
Brunft *f* rut *(esp. of the male deer)*; heat *(esp. of the female deer) (s. a.* Brunst*)*
brunften to rut; to be at (in, on) heat, to go to match *(s. a.* brunsten*)*
Brunftgeruch *m* rutting smell
Brunfthirsch *m* rutting stag
brunftig ruttish
Brunftlaut *m* bell
Brunftplan *m*, **Brunftplatz** *m* rutting place
Brunftruf *m s.* Brunftschrei
Brunftrute *f* pizzle
Brunftschrei *m* troat, mating cry, bell • **Brunftschreie ausstoßen** to troat
Brunftstrang *m* pizzle
Brunftverhalten *n* courtship behaviour
Brunftwitterung *f* rutting smell
Brunftzeit *f* rutting time (season), rut, pairing season (time) • **die ~ beenden** to cease rutting
Brunisjom *m(n) (soil)* brunizem

Brunnen *m* well
~/artesischer artesian well
Brunnenkresse *f* 1. nasturtium *(genus Nasturtium)*; 2. watercress, Nasturtium officinale
Brunnenkressemosaikvirus *n* watercress mosaic virus
Brunnenschacht *m* well
Brunnenwasser *n* well water
Brunnersche Drüsen *fpl* Brunner's (duodenal) glands *(animal anatomy)*
Brunst *f* oestrus, oestrum, heat *(s. a.* Brunft*)*
~/stille (zu schwache) silent (still) heat, silent oestrus
Brunstaktivität *f* oestrous activity
Brunstbeobachtung *f* oestrus (heat) detection
Brunstbestimmung *f* oestrus (heat) detection
brunsten to be at (in, on) heat; to blissom *(female sheep) (s. a.* brunften*)*
Brunstfeststellung *f* oestrus detection
Brunsthormon *n* oestrogen, follicular hormone
brünstig oestrous, in season; blissom *(female sheep)* • **~ werden** to come on heat, to come in season; to flush *(sheep)*
~/in regelmäßigen Abständen polyoestrous
~/nicht anoestrous
Brünstigkeit *f s.* Brunst
Brunstinduktion *f* oestrus induction
Brunstkontrolle *f* oestrous cycle control, oestrus control; heat detection
Brunstlosigkeit *f* anoestrus
Brunstperiode *f s.* Brunst
Brunstschrei *m* mating cry
Brunstschwäche *f* suboestrus
Brunststeuerung *f* oestrus regulation
Brunstsynchronisation *f* oestrus (heat) synchronization
Brunstverhalten *n* oestrous (courtship) behaviour
Brunstzyklus *m* oestrous cycle
Brusonkrankheit *f* **von Reis** rice blast *(caused by Pyricularis oryzae)*
Brüsseler Kohl *m* Brussels sprouts, Brassica oleracea var. gemmifera
Brust *f* breast, chest, thorax; *(slaught)* brisket
Brustabschnitt *m (ent)* thorax
Brustbeere *f* sebasten[-plum], Cordia myxa
Brustbein *n* 1. breastbone, sternum; 2. *(ent)* thoracic leg • **hinter dem ~ befindlich** retrosternal
Brustbeinverkrümmung *f* crooked breast *(poultry)*
Brustbeule *f*, **Brustblase** *f (vet)* breast blister
Brustbuckel *m* thoracic hump
Brustbuckelzebu *n* chest-humped zebu
Brustfell *n* pleura *(animal anatomy)*
Brustfellentzündung *f (vet)* pleurisy, pleuritis
Brustfellpunktion *f (vet)* pleurocentesis
Brustfleisch *n* breast meat
Brustflosse *f* pectoral fin
Brustgliedmaße *f* foreleg, forelimb, thoracic limb
Brustgräte *f (ent)* sternal spatula, anchor process

brusthoch

brusthoch breast-high, chest-high, at breast height
Brusthöhe f breast (chest) height
Brusthöhendurchmesser m breast-height diameter, b.h.d., diameter [at] breast height *(timber mensuration)*
~ **der Spitzenhöhenstämme/mittlerer** top-height diameter
Brusthöhenformzahl f breast-height form factor *(timber mensuration)*
Brusthöhengrundfläche f, **Brusthöhenkreisfläche** f basal area at breast height *(timber mensuration)*
Brusthöhenumfang m breast-height girth, b.h.g. *(timber mensuration)*
Brusthöhle f thoracic cavity
Brusthöhleneröffnung f *(vet)* thoracotomy
Brustkorb m chest, thorax
Brustmuskel m breast (pectoral) muscle
Brustregion f chest, thorax
Brustschild m *(ent)* cors[e]let
Brustspitze f picnic [shoulder] *(of pig's carcass)*
Brusttiefe f depth of chest
Brustumfang m circumference of chest
Brustwarze f nipple, papilla
Brustwinkel m side[-plate] angle, side-edge angle *(of the chain-saw)*
Brustwirbel m thoracic vertebra
Brustzyste f *(vet)* breast blister
Brut f 1. brood, breed, progeny; hatch, nest *(of young animals)*; clutch *(of chicks)*; covey *(of birds)*; 2. s. Brüten
~/**offene** *(api)* unsealed brood
~/**verdeckelte** *(api)* sealed brood, capped brood
~/**verkühlte** *(api, vet)* chilled brood
Brutabfall m hatchery waste (offal)
Brutanlage f hatchery
Brutanstalt f hatchery
Brutapparat m incubator
Brutaufzucht f brood rearing
Brutbaum m *(ent)* brood (bug) tree
Brutdauer f incubation period (duration)
Brutei n hatching (hatchery) egg
Bruteiersortiermaschine f hatching egg grader
Bruteizüchtung f egg culture *(microbiology)*
brüten to brood, to breed, to hatch, to incubate, to sit, to clutch, to cover
Brüten n brood, hatch[ing], incubation
Brüter m incubator
Brüterei f hatchery, brooder house, hatching operation
Brütereiabfall m hatchery waste (offal)
Bruterfolg m hatching success
Brutfähigkeit f brooding ability, hatchability
Brutfaktor m hatching factor
brutfreudig broody
Brutfreudigkeit f broodiness
Brutfürsorge f s. Brutpflege
Brutgang m brood (egg) gallery *(e.g. of xylophagous insects)*

Brutgeschäft n s. Brüten
Bruthenne f brooding (sitting) hen
brütig broody
Brütigkeit f broodiness
Brutkammer f brooding chamber
Brutknöllchen n *(bot)* bulbil, bulblet, brood bud
Brutknolle f *(bot)* cormel, cormlet
Brutkrankheit f brood disease
Brutlust f broodiness
Brutnest n *(api)* brood nest
brutparasitär brood-parasitic
Brutpflege f brood (parental) care
Brutpflegeinstinkt m mothering (maternal) instinct
Brutplatz m breeding site, hatchery, nest
Brutrahmen m *(api)* brood frame
Brutraum m brood[ing] chamber; spawn running room *(mushroom culture)*
Brutrückstand m hatchery waste (offal)
Brutschrank m [cabinet] incubator
Brutsproß m *(bot)* bulbil, bulblet, brood bud
~/**oberirdischer** aerial bulbil
Brutstätte f *(ent)* brooding place
Brutstelle f breeding site
Brutstreckteich m *(pisc)* brood (hatching, hatchery) pond
Bruttauglichkeit f hatchability
Bruttemperatur f incubation temperature
Bruttoaufnahme f gross absorption *(e.g. of wood preservatives)*
Bruttoenergie f gross (total) energy, GE *(e.g. of a feed-stuff)*
Bruttophotosynthese f gross (real) photosynthesis
Bruttovolumen n **eines Baumes** tree overbark volume
Bruttozuwachs m gross increment
Brutwabe f *(api)* brood comb, honeycomb
Brutzwiebel f bulbil, bulblet, brood bud; clove; scale; offset bulb
~/**oberirdische** aerial bulbil
Brutzwiebelvermehrung f scale propagation
Bryophyllumtorf m Bryophyllum peat
Bryophyt m bryophyte *(division Bryophyta)*
BSB s. Sauerstoffbedarf/biochemischer
Bsch. s. Braunschimmel
BSE s. Enzephalopathie/bovine spongiforme
BSG s. 1. Blutkörperchensenkungsgeschwindigkeit; 2. Blutsenkung
BSMV s. Südliches Bohnenmosaikvirus
B-Spermatogonie f, **B-Spermiogonie** f B spermatogonia
BSR s. Blutkörperchensenkung
Bt-Horizont m *(soil)* argilluvic B-horizon
Bubakrankheit f **der Andenkartoffel** buba disease of Andean potato, thecaphora smut *(caused by Thecaphora solani)*
Bubiköpfchen n *(bot)* baby's tears, Soleirolia (Helxine) soleirolii

Buch *n s.* Blättermagen
Bucharamandel *f* Bucharian almond, Amygdalus bucharica
Buchdrucker *m* eight-toothed [spruce] bark-beetle, Norway spruce engraver, Ips (Tomicus) typographus
Buche *f* beech, buck *(genus Fagus)*
Buchecker *f* beech-nut, beechmast
Bucheckernöl *n* beech oil
Buchel *f s.* Buchecker
Buchelmast *f* beech mast
Buchenblattbaumlaus *f s.* Buchenzierlaus
Buchenblattgallmücke *f* beech tree leaf gallmidge, Mikiola fagi
Buchenfarn *m* beech polypody, Thelypteris (Dryopteris) phegopteris
Buchenfrostspanner *m* northern winter moth, Operophthera (Cheimatobia) fagata
Buchenholz *n* beech[wood]
Buchenholzteer *m* beech tar
Buchenkrebs *m* beech canker *(caused by Nectria ditissima)*
Buchenmast *f* beech mast
Buchenmischwald *m* beech-mixed forest
Buchenprachtkäfer *m (ent)* beech agrilus, Agrilus viridis
Buchenrotkern *m* red heart[wood], false heart[wood]
Buchenrotschwanz *m s.* Buchenspinner
Buchenspinner *m* pale tussock [moth], Dasychira pudibunda
Buchenspringrüßler *m (ent)* beech leaf-miner, Rhynchaenus (Orchestes) fagi
Buchenteer *m* beech tar
Buchenwoll[schildl]aus *f* beech scale, felted beech coccus, Cryptococcus fagi
Buchenzierlaus *f* beech tree louse, woolly beech aphid, Phyllaphis (Lachnus) fagi
Buchöl *n* beech oil
Buchs *m* 1. compression wood, redwood, tenar; 2. *s.* Buchsbaum; 3. *s.* Buchsbaumholz
Buchsbaum *m* 1. box [tree] *(genus Buxus)*; 2. common box tree, European box, Buxus sempervirens
Buchsbaumblattfloh *m (ent)* boxwood psylla (psyllid), box sucker, Psylla buxi
Buchsbaumgewächse *npl* box family *(family Buxaceae)* • **die ~ betreffend** buxeous
Buchsbaumholz *n* box[wood]
Buchsbaumsauger *m s.* Buchsbaumblattfloh
Buchsblättrige Berberitze *f* Magellan barberry, Berberis buxifolia
~ Kreuzblume *f* bastard box, Polygala chamaebuxus
Büchse *f* 1. gun, rifle; 2. *s.* Konservenbüchse
Büchsenfleisch *n* canned meat
Büchsenlicht *n* shooting light
Büchsenmacher *m* gunsmith
Büchsenmilch *f* canned milk

Buchsholz *n* box[wood]
Bucht *f* pen, box, stall *(animal house)*
Buchtenabgrenzung *f* stall division
Buchtenhieb *m (forest)* bay (wavy-fronted) felling
Buchtenstall *m* pen barn
Buchtentür *f* stall gate
buchtig *(bot, zoo)* sinuate, lacunose; *(bot)* emarginate[d]
Buchweizen *m* 1. buckwheat *(genus Fagopyrum)*; 2. common buckwheat, heath (Saracen) corn, Fagopyrum esculentum
Buchweizenausschlag *m (vet)* fagopyrism
Buchweizengrütze *f* buckwheat groats
Buchweizenhonig *m* buckwheat honey
Buchweizenmehl *n* buckwheat flour
Buckelfrüchtigkeit *f* des Apfels apple green crinkle *(virosis)*
Buckelkäfer *m* hump beetle (mite), mite beetle, Gibbium psylloides
Buckellachs *m* pink salmon, Oncorhynchus gorbuscha
Buckelrind *n* zebu, humped cattle, Indian ox, Bos indicus
Buckelstreifiger Rübenaaskäfer *m* beet carrion beetle, Aclypea (Blitophaga, Silpha) opaca
Buckelzirpe *f (ent)* buffalo tree hopper, Ceresa (Stictocephala) bubalus
bucklig bumpy *(wood)*
Buddleie *f* butterfly bush, summer lilac, buddleia *(genus Buddleja)*
Budjonnypferd *n* Budennyi *(horse breed)*
Bufencarb *n* bufencarb, metalkamate *(insecticide)*
Büffel *m* [water] buffalo, Bubalus arni (bubalis)
Büffelbeere *f* 1. buffalo berry *(genus Shepherdia)*; 2. [silver] buffalo berry, Shepherdia argentea
Büffelfleisch *n* buffalo meat
Büffelgras *n* 1. buffel grass, Rhodesian (African) foxtail, Cenchrus ciliaris, Pennisetum ciliare; 2. buffalo grass, Buchloe dactyloides
Büffelkalb *n* buffalo calf
Büffelklee *m* buffalo clover, Trifolium reflexum
Büffellaus *f* buffalo louse, Haematopinus tuberculatus (bufalieuropaei)
Büffelmast *f* buffalo fattening
Büffelmilch *f* buffalo milk
Bügel *m* bow; saw bow, saw-blade buckle
Bügelhacke *f* bow hoe
Bügelkettensäge *f* bow chain-saw
Bügelsäge *f* bow saw
Bügelzughacke *f* bow draught hoe
Buggelenk *n* shoulder-joint
Buggelenkhöcker *m* point of shoulder
Bukett *n* 1. bouquet *(of flowers)*; 2. bouquet, aroma, flavour *(of wine)* • **ein ~ binden** to make up a bouquet
Bukettnarzisse *f* bunch-flowered narcissus, French daffodil, Narcissus tazetta
bukettreich bouquet-rich *(wine)*
Bukettrieb *m* bouquet spur

Bukettzweig

Bukettzweig *m* multiple buds
Bulbille *f s.* Brutzwiebel
bulbös bulbous
Bulbosum-Technik *f* bulbosum method (technique) *(for production of haploids in barley)*
Bulbourethraldrüse *f* bulbo-urethral gland, Cowper's gland *(animal anatomy)*
Bulbus *m (zoo)* bulb
~ **glandis** bulb of glans *(anatomy of carnivores)*
Bulgarisches Latentes Weinrebenvirus *n* grapevine Bulgarian latent virus
Bulkmethode *f* bulk method *(plant breeding)*
Bulldogge *f* bulldog *(breed)*
Bulldoggkalb *n (vet)* bulldog-type calf
Bulldozer *m* bulldozer, trailbuilder
Bulle *m* bull
~/**kastrierter** bullock
~/**zuchtbewährter (zuchtwertpositiver)** proved bull
Bullenaufzucht *f* bull rearing
Bullenaufzuchtstation *f* bull rearing station
Bullenfleisch *n* bull beef
Bullenführstab *m* bull (leading) staff
Bullenfütterung *f* bull feeding
Bullenhütte *f* bull pen
Bullenindex *m* bull index *(estimation of breeding value)*
Bullenkalb *n* bull (steer) calf
Bullenkörung *f* bull licensing
Bullenleistungsprüfung *f* bull performance test
Bullenmast *f* bull fattening
Bullenmutter *f* bull mother
Bullenpfleger *m* bull attendant, bullman
Bullenprüfstation *f* bull testing station
Bullenring *m* bull holder, nosering
Bullensperma *n* bull semen, bull's ejaculate
Bullenstall *m* bull barn (pen)
Bullenverwahrstation *f* bull stud
Bullenwärter *m s.* Bullenpfleger
Bullfinch *m* bullfinch *(obstacle in horse-races)*
Bullmastiff *m* bull mastiff *(dog breed)*
Bullterrier *m* bull-terrier *(dog breed)*
Bult *m s.* Bülte
Bülte *f* hillock, tussock, hassock, *(Am)* hummock
bültendurchsetzt tussocky
Bültenfläche *f* tussock land
Bültengrasland *n* tussock grassland
Bültenmoor *n* hillock (tussock) bog, *(Am)* hummock bog
Bültenwiese *f* tussocky meadow
bültig tussocky
Bunamidin *n* bunamidine *(antiparasitic)*
Bunchy-top-Krankheit *f (phyt)* bunchy top disease *(virosis)*
Bunchy-top-Virus *n* **der Banane** banana bunchy top virus
Bund *n s.* Bündel
Bündel *n* bundle, bunch, sheaf, bottle *(of hay or straw)*; *(bot, zoo)* fascicle, fasciculus, bundle

~/**Hissches** atrioventricular bundle *(of the heart)*
Bündelgestör *n* bundle raft *(log driving)*
Bündelholz *n* bundled wood
Bündelladung *f* bundle load
Bündelmaschine *f* bundling machine, buncher, bunching mechanism
bündeln to bundle, to bunch, to package, to sheaf, to sheave
Bündeln *n* bundling, bunching; cribbing *(rafted timber)*
Bündelscheide *f (bot)* bundle sheath
Bundesernährungsministerium *n s.* Bundesministerium für Ernährung, Landwirtschaft und Forsten
Bundesforstmeister *m (Am)* chief forester
Bundesministerium *n* **für Ernährung, Landwirtschaft und Forsten** Federal Ministry of Food, Agriculture and Forestry
Bungekiefer *f* lace-bark pine, Pinus bungeana
Bunker *m* bin, bunker; accumulation tank *(e.g. of a harvester)*
Bunkerfüllstands[an]zeiger *m* bin level indicator
Bunkerselbstfütterer *m* automatic bunker feeder
Bunkskidder *m (forest)* clam [bunk] skidder, clamp tractor
bunt *(bot, zoo)* variegated
buntblättrig poecilophyllous
Buntblättrigkeit *f* variegation
Bunte Klimme *f* tapestry vine, Cissus discolor
~ **Kronwicke** *f* crown vetch, Coronilla varia
~ **Lupine** *f* western Australian blue lupin[e], Lupinus varius (cosentinii)
~ **Stockfäule** *f* mottled butt rot *(of root-stock and lower trunk)*
~ **Wicke** *f* woolly-pod vetch, Vicia dasycarpa
Bunter Erlenrüsselkäfer (Erlenrüßler) *m* alder (poplar, willow) weevil, poplar-and-willow borer, Cryptorhynchus lapathi
~ **Eschenbastkäfer** *m* [common, small] ash barkbeetle, Leperesinus (Hylesinus) fraxinus
~ **Hohlzahn** *m* large-flowered hemp-nettle, Galeopsis speciosa
~ **Nagekäfer** *m* death tick, death-watch [beetle], Xestobium rufovillosum
~ **Porling** *m (bot)* common zoned polyporus, Trametes versicolor
Buntes Getreidehähnchen *n* cereal (barley) leaf beetle, Oulema (Lema) melanopus
~ **Guineagras** *n* coloured Guinea grass, Panicum coloratum var. coloratum
Buntfäule *f* mottled rot *(of wood)*
Buntkäfer *m* checkered beetle *(family Cleridae)*
Buntlupine *f* pearl lupin[e], tarwi, Lupinus mutabilis
Buntnessel *f (bot)* coleus *(genus Coleus)*
Buntsandstein *m* bunter [sandstone], variegated (mottled) sandstone
buntschälen to rough-bark, to rough-peel
Buntstreifigkeit *f* **der Blume[n]** *(phyt)* flower colour breaking *(virosis)*

Buschwindröschen

~ **der Tulpe** tulip breaking
Buntwurz f *(bot)* caladium *(genus Caladium)*
Bunya-Bunya-Baum m *(bot)* bunya, Araucaria bidwillii
Buphthalmus m *(vet)* hydrophthalmia
Buprofezin n buprofezin *(insecticide)*
Buquinolat n buquinolate *(coccidiostatic)*
Bürde f/**genetische** genetic load
Burdizzozange f Burdizzo [castrator], Burdizzo emasculator (pincers)
Bürette f burette
Burgenahorn m Montpellier maple, Acer monspessulanum
Burgstall m hillock *(mark of red deer's track)*
Burgunder m burgundy *(wine)*
Burgunder Brühe f Burgundy mixture, soda bordeaux *(fungicide)*
Buripalme f buri palm, Corypha elata (utan)
Burley[tabak] m burley
Burma-Pony n Shan pony *(breed)*
Burmakatze f Burmese [cat] *(breed)*
Burmazimtbaum m Padang (Batavia) cassia, Cinnamomum burmanii
burnettisieren to burnettize *(wood preservation)*
Burosem m, **Burosjom** m(n) burozem, brown soil of semi-deserts
Bursa f *(zoo)* bursa, pouch
~ **copulatrix** copulatory pouch *(e.g. of the queen bee)*
~ **fabricii** bursa fabricii, bursa of Fabricius *(animal anatomy)*
Bursektomie f *(vet)* bursectomy
Bursitis f *(vet)* bursitis
~ **des Huhnes/infektiöse** avian infectious bursitis, kidney-liver-syndrome in chickens, Gumboro disease
Bursolith m *(vet)* bursolith
Bursotomie f *(vet)* bursotomy
Bürstenbesatz m s. Bürstensaum
Bürstenbinder m *(ent)* rusty [tussock] moth, Orgyia antiqua
Bürstenfichte f brush-type spruce
Bürstensärad n brush feed mechanism
Bürstensaum m brush border *(animal anatomy)*
Bürstenzelle f s. Büschelzelle
Bürstmaschine f scrubber *(potato cleaning)*
Bürzel m rump, saddle, uropygium, parson's nose *(of birds)*
Bürzeldrüse f *(zoo)* uropygial gland, preen (oil) gland
Burzelkraut n *(bot)* portulaca *(genus Portulaca)*
Busch m 1. bush, shrub, scrub; dwarf bush tree *(form of fruit-trees)*; 2. s. Buschland; 3. s. Buschwald
buschartig [wachsend] bushy
Buschbohne f bush (ground, kidney) bean, dwarf [French] bean, Phaseolus vulgaris ssp. vulgaris var. nanus
Buschbrand m bush fire

Buschegge f brush harrow
Büschel n bunch, cluster, fascicle, fasciculus; tuft *(e.g. of feathers, grass)* • **in Büscheln wachsend** c[a]espitose, caespitous • **in dichten Büscheln wachsend** iteroparous
büschelartig [wachsend] clustery
büschelförmig clustered, tassel[l]ed
Büschelglockenblume f *(bot)* Canterbury-bell[s], Campanula glomerata
Büschelgras n bunch[-type] grass *(comprehensive term)*
büschelig bunchy, bushy, fascicled, fasciculate[d], iteroparous
Büschelkraut n 1. tick clover (trefoil) *(genus Desmodium)*; 2. s. Büschelschön
Büschelnelke f spray[-type] carnation *(comprehensive term)*
Büschelpflanzung f *(forest)* bunch (nest, cluster) planting
Büschelrose f spray rose *(comprehensive term)*
Büschelschön n *(bot)* 1. phacelia *(genus Phacelia)*; 2. tansy phacelia, valley vervenia, Phacelia tanacetifolia
Büscheltriebkrankheit f **der Kartoffel** mop top *(virosis)*
Büschelwuchs m bushy growth
Büschelyams n bitter (three-leaved) yam, Dioscorea dumetorum
Büschelzelle f tuft cell *(animal anatomy)*
Büschelzweig m multiple buds
Buscherbsenstrauch m Russian pea shrub, Caragana frutex
Buschfeuer n bush fire
Buschfläche f brushfield
Buschförmiger Gemüsekürbis (Sommerkürbis) m zucchini, Cucurbita pepo ssp. pepo var. styriaca convar. giromontiina
Buschhacker m brush chopper, brushwood cutter
Buschhortensie f *(bot)* snowhill hydrangea, Hydrangea arborescens
buschig bushy, bunchy, shrubby, bosky
Buschklee m 1. lespedeza *(genus Lespedeza)*; 2. [Japanese] bush clover, Japan clover, [common, Japanese] lespedeza, kobe [lespedeza], Lespedeza striata
Buschland n bush [land], brush, scrub
~/**tropisches** bush
Buschmesser n machete
Buschobstbaum m bush tree
Buschrodung f assart[ment]
Buschschneider m bush (shrub) cutter, brush killer (buster)
Buschtomate f bush tomato, Lycopersicon lycopersicum
Buschwald m shrub wood (forest), scrub
Buschwerk n shrubbery, bushes
Buschwindröschen n wind-flower, wood anemone, Anemone nemorosa

Buserelin

Buserelin *n* buserelin *(activating analogue of gonadotropin-releasing hormone)*
Bushel *m* bushel, bu
Bussard *m* buzzard *(genus Buteo)*
Butacarb *n* butacarb *(insecticide)*
Butachlor *n* butachlor *(herbicide)*
Butam *n* butam *(herbicide)*
Butamifos *n* butamifos *(herbicide)*
Butan-2,3-dion *n* diacetyl, butane-2,3-dione
Butandisäure *f* amber (succinic) acid, butanedioic acid
Buteakino *n* Bengal kino [gum]
Buthidazol *n* buthidazole *(herbicide)*
Buthiobat *n* buthiobate *(fungicide)*
Buthiuron *n* buthiuron *(herbicide)*
Butocarboxim *n* butocarboxim *(acaricide, insecticide)*
Butonat *n* butonate *(acaricide, insecticide)*
Butopyronoxyl *n* butopyronoxyl *(repellent)*
Butoxycarboxim *n* butoxycarboxim *(insecticide)*
Butralin *n* butralin *(herbicide)*
Butte *f* hip, rose-hip *(false fruit)*
Butter *f* butter
Butterausbeute *f* butter yield
Butterbildung *f* butter formation
Butterblume *f* crowfoot [buttercup], field (meadow, tall) buttercup, Ranunculus acris
Butterbohrer *m* butter trier *(sampler)*
Buttereikultur *f* butter starter
Butterfabrik *f* creamery
Butterfarbe *f*, **Butterfarbstoff** *m* butter dye (colour)
Butterfaß *n* [butter-]churn
Butterfehler *m* butter defect
Butterfertiger *m* [butter-]churn; butter-making machine
Butterfett *n* butter fat, B.F.
~/geschmolzenes butteroil
Butterform- und -packautomat *m* butter moulding and packing machine
Buttergelb *n* butter yellow *(dye)*
Butterherstellung *f* butter-making
Butterhomogenisator *m* butter homogenizer
Butterkopfsalat *m* butterhead [lettuce], Lactuca sativa var. capitata nidus tenerrima
Butterkorn *n* butter grain
Buttermilch *f* buttermilk
~/geschlagene cultured buttermilk (skim milk)
Buttermilchpulver *n* dried buttermilk
Buttermilchquark *m* buttermilk curd
buttern to churn, to make butter
Buttern *n* butter-making
Butternuß *f* 1. [American] butter-nut, white walnut, Juglans cinerea; 2. sawari nut, Caryocar nuciferum
Butteröl *n* butteroil
~/indisches ghee, ghi
Butterpilz *m*, **Butterröhrling** *m* brown-yellow boletus, ringed (annulated) boletus, Suillus (Boletus, Ixocomus) luteus

Buttersalat *m s.* Butterkopfsalat
Buttersäure *f* butyric acid
Buttersäurebakterium *n* butyric acid bacterium
Buttersäuregärung *f* butyric fermentation
Buttersäurewecker *m* butter starter
Butterschmalz *n* clarified (rendered, run) butter, solidified butteroil
~/indisches ghee, ghi
Butterserum *n* butter serum
Butterungsmaschine *f* butter-making machine
Butterungsrahm *m* cream for butter-making
Butterungsverfahren *n* butter-making process
Butterverfälschung *f* butter adulteration
Buturon *n* buturon *(herbicide)*
Butylat *n* butylate *(herbicide)*
Butyrometer *n* butyrometer, cream gauge *(for milk fat determination)*
~/Gerbersches Gerber butyrometer
butyrometrisch butyrometric
Butyrylcholinesterase *f* butyryl cholinesterase *(enzyme)*
Butyryl-CoA-Dehydrogenase *f* butyryl-CoA dehydrogenase *(enzyme)*
Buxin *n* buxin[e] *(alkaloid)*
Bv-Horizont *m* *(soil)* cambic B-horizon
BVM *s.* Bodenverbesserungsmittel
BW *s.* Eiweißwertigkeit/biologische

C

c *s.* Wärme/spezifische
Caatinga *f* ca[a]tinga *(Brazilian dry forest)*
Cabernet *m* cabernet [sauvignon] *(kind of wine)*
Cableskidder *m* *(forest)* cable skidder
Cachou *n* catechu *(plant extract)*
Cadang-Cadang-Krankheit *f* der Kokospalme *(phyt)* [coconut] cadang cadang
Cadaverin *n* cadaverine, pentamethylenediamine
Cadmium *n* cadmium
cadmiumhaltig cadmiferous
Caecum *n s.* Blinddarm
Caesalpinie *f* *(bot)* brasiletto *(genus Caesalpinia)*
Caffeol *n* caffeol *(volatile oil of coffee beans)*
Cairn Terrier *m* cairn [terrier] *(dog breed)*
Caladium-Bicolor-Hybride *f* *(bot)* caladium, Caladium x hortilanum
CA-Lager *n* controlled-atmosphere store
CA-Lagerung *f* controlled-atmosphere storage
~/einseitig gesteuerte one-side controlled-atmosphere storage
~/zweiseitig gesteuerte two-side controlled-atmosphere storage
Calandrinie *f* rock-purslane, Calandrinia ciliata
Calcaneus *m* calcaneum *(animal anatomy)*
calcicol calcicolous, calciphile, calcipetal, lime-loving *(plant)*
Calcidiol-1-Monooxygenase *f* calcidiol-1-monooxygenase, 25-hydroxycholecalciferol 1-hydroxylase *(enzyme)*

Calciferol n calciferol *(group of vitamins)*
calcifug calcifugous, calciphobous, lime-intolerant *(plant)*
Calcit m calcite, calcspar *(non-clay mineral)*
Calcitonin n [thyro]calcitonin, TCT *(hormone)*
Calciumacetat n calcium acetate, pyrolignite of lime *(fertilizer)*
Calciumarsenat n calcium arsenate *(herbicide, insecticide)*
Calciumborogluconat n calcium borogluconate
Calciumcarbid n calcium carbide
Calciumcarbonat n calcium carbonate, ground limestone, soil sugar
Calciumcarbonatkruste f auf Trockenböden caliche
Calciumchlorat n calcium chlorate
Calciumchlorid n calcium chloride
Calciumcyanamid n [calcium] cyanamide, lime nitrogen, nitrolime
Calciumhydroxid n calcium hydroxide
Calciummangel m calcium deficiency
Calciummetaphosphat n calcium metaphosphate *(fertilizer)*
Calciumnitrat n calcium nitrate, nitrate of lime *(fertilizer)*
Calciumoxalat n calcium oxalate
Calciumoxid n calcium oxide
Calciumphosphat n calcium phosphate
~/tertiäres tricalcium phosphate
Calciumpolyphosphat n calcium polyphosphate
Calciumsilicat n calcium silicate *(fertilizer)*
Calciumstoffwechsel m calcium metabolism
Calciumsulfat n calcium sulphate, gypsum, plaster of Paris
Caliaturholz n red sandalwood *(esp. from Pterocarpus santalinus)*
Calicivirus n *(vet)* calici virus
California-Mastitis-Test m *(vet)* California mastitis test, CMT
Caliche m caliche *(raw salt)*
Calla f calla lily *(genus Zantedeschia)*
Callose f callose *(polysaccharide)*
Callosetest m *(phyt)* callose test
Calluna-Kiefernwald m heather pinery, Pinetum callunosum
Callus m *(bot, vet)* callus
Calmodulin n calmodulin *(protein)*
Calvin-Pflanze f C-3 plant *(plant physiology)*
Calvin-Zyklus m Calvin cycle, reductive pentose phosphate cycle (pathway) *(of CO_2 fixation)*
Calyptra f *(bot)* calyptra, pileorhiza
Calyptrogen n calyptrogen *(meristematic layer for developing of the root cap)*
Calyx m calyx; flower calyx (cup), hull
CAM s. 1. Chorioallantoismembran; 2. Crassulaceen[säure]stoffwechsel
Cambendazol n cambendazole *(antiparasitic, fungicide)*
Cambendichlor n cambendichlor *(herbicide)*

Cambisol m *(soil)* cambisol
Cambium[gewebe] n s. Kambium
Cambridgewalze f Cambridge roll[er] *(soil-working implement)*
Camembert m Camembert [cheese]
Camholz n camwood, barwood *(from Baphia nitida)*
cAMP s. Adenosin-3',5'-phosphat
Campbell-Ente f Khaki Campbell [duck] *(breed)*
Campeche n logwood, Campeachy wood *(from Haematoxylum campechianum)*
Campechebaum m logwood, Haematoxylum campechianum
Campesterol n campesterol *(phytosterol)*
CAM-Pflanze f CAM plant *(s. a. CAM-Weg)*
Camphechlor n camphechlor, toxaphene *(insecticide, rodenticide)*
Camphen n camphene *(constituent of volatile oils)*
Campher m camphor *(constituent of volatile oils)*
CAM-Weg m CAM pathway, crassulacean acid metabolism *(plant physiology)*
Cancer m *(phyt)* canker
Candidamykose f, **Candidose** f *(vet)* candidiasis
canin canine
Caninus m canine [tooth]
Cannabinoid n cannabinoid *(dibenzopyran from Cannabis sativa)*
Canna-Indica-Hybride f *(bot)* canna, Canna x generalis
Canna-Rost m *(phyt)* canna rust *(caused by Puccinia cannae)*
Cantalafaser[agave] f Bombay hemp, Agave cantala
Canthaxanthin n canthaxanthin *(carotenoid)*
Canthus m canthus, corner of the eye *(animal anatomy)*
CAP s. Katabolit-Aktivator-Protein
Cap-Chur-Palmer-Karabiner m *(vet)* Cap-Chur gun
Capillariasis f *(vet)* capillariasis
Capreomycindisulfat n capreomycin disulphate *(antibiotic)*
Caprinsäure f decanoic (capric) acid, *(fatty acid)*
Capronsäure f hexanoic (caproic) acid *(fatty acid)*
Caprylsäure f octanoic acid *(fatty acid)*
Capsaicin n capsaicin *(amide)*
Capsanthin n capsanthin *(xanthophyll)*
Capsidiol n capsodiol *(phytoalexin)*
Captafol n captafol *(fungicide)*
Captan n captan *(fungicide)*
Carbachol n carbachol, carbamoylcholine *(parasympathomimetic agent)*
Carbadox n carbadox *(growth regulator)*
Carbamat n carbamate, urethan[e]
Carbamatkinase f carbamate kinase *(enzyme)*
Carbamazin n diethylcarbamazine *(anthelminthic)*
Carbamid n carbamide, urea
Carbamidsäureester m carbamate, urethan[e]
Carbamoylcholin n carbachol, carbamoylcholine *(parasympathomimetic agent)*

Carbamoylphosphatsynth[et]ase

Carbamoylphosphatsynth[et]ase *f* carbamoyl-phosphate synthase, glutaminehydrolysing *(enzyme)*
Carbaryl *n* carbaryl, sevin *(insecticide)*
Carbasulam *n* carbasulam *(herbicide)*
Carbendazim *n* carbendazim *(fungicide)*
Carbendazol *n* carbendazole *(fungicide)*
Carbenicillin *n* carbenicillin *(antibiotic)*
Carbetamid *n* carbetamide *(herbicide)*
Carbid *n* [calcium] carbide
Carbidkalk *m* carbide (acetylene) lime
Carbinol *n* carbinol *(fungicide)*
Carboanhydrase *f s.* Carbonatdehydratase
Carbofuchsin *n* carbol fuchsine *(dye)*
Carbofuran *n* carbofuran *(nematicide, insecticide)*
Carbohydrase *f* carbohydrase *(enzyme)*
Carbol *n s.* Carbolsäure
Carbolineum *n* carbolineum, coal-tar creosote [solution], green (anthracene) oil *(wood preservative)*
Carbolsäure *f* carbolic acid, phenol
Carbonat *n* carbonate
Carbonatboden *m* calcareous soil
Carbonatdehydratase *f* carbonate dehydratase (hydro-lyase) *(enzyme)*
Carbonsäure *f* carboxylic acid
Carbophenothion *n* carbophenothion, nephocarb *(insecticide)*
Carbophosphonat *n* carbophosphonat *(fungicide)*
Carboxin *n* carboxin, DCMO *(fungicide)*
Carboxylase *f* carboxylase *(enzyme)*
Carboxylester[hydrol]ase *f* carboxylesterase, ali-esterase *(enzyme)*
Carboxy-Lyase *f* carboxy-lyase *(enzyme)*
Carboxypeptidase *f* carboxypeptidase *(enzyme)*
Carcinoma *n (vet)* carcinoma
Cardenolid *n* cardenolide *(glycoside)*
Cardia *f* heart
Card-Verfahren *n* Card (Rütger) process *(wood preservation)*
Cardy *m s.* Kardone
Caren *n* carene *(constituent of turpentine oil)*
Carnallit *m* carnallite *(potassium fertilizer)*
Carnaubapalme *f* carnauba [palm], Copernicia prunifera (cerifera)
Carnaubawachs *n* carnauba wax
Carnicabiene *f* carniolan honey-bee, Apis mellifica carnica
Carnitin *n* carnitine, beta-hydroxy-gamma-butyro-betain
Carnitinacetyltransferase *f* carnitine acetyltransferase *(enzyme)*
Carnitinpalmitoyltransferase *f* carnitine palmitoyltransferase *(enzyme)*
Carnosin *n* carnosine *(amino-acid)*
Carnosinase *f* aminoacyl-histidine dipeptidase *(enzyme)*
Carnosinsynthase *f* carnosine synthase *(enzyme)*
Carolina-Schneeglöckchenbaum *m* snowdrop tree, Halesia carolina (tetraptera)
Caroten *n* carotene, carotin *(provitamin A)*
Carotenoid *n* carotenoid *(natural dye)*
Carotin *n s.* Caroten
Carpitis *n (vet)* carpitis
Carpus *m* carpus *(animal anatomy)*
Carragen *m (bot)* carrag[h]een, Chondrus crispus
Carrier *m* carrier *(plant physiology, immunology, embryology)*
Cartagenakautschuk *m* Castilla rubber *(from Castilla elastica)*
Cartap *n* cartap *(insecticide)*
Cartertrieur *m* disk separator *(seed processing)*
Carvon *n* carvone *(monoterpene ketone)*
Caryophyllen *n* caryophyllene *(constituent of volatile oils)*
Casben *n* casbene *(phytoalexin)*
Casein *n* casein *(milk protein)*
~/iodiertes iodinated casein
Caseinaminosäure *f* casein amino-acid
Caseinat *n* caseinate
Caseinhydrolysat *n* casein hydrolysate
Caseinmizelle *f* casein micella
Caslicksche Operation *f (vet)* Caslick's operation
Casparyscher Streifen *m* Casparian strip *(of plant cells)*
Cassava *f* cassava, bitter cassava (manioc), tapioca plant, Manihot esculenta (utilissima)
Castasteron *n* castasterone *(growth regulator)*
Castoreum *n* castor[eum] *(glandular secretion of the beaver)*
Catawissazwiebel *f* Catawissa (tree) onion, Allium cepa var. proliferum
Catechin *n*, **Catechol** *n* catechin, catechol, 3,3',4',5,7-pentahydroxyflavan *(plant substance)*
Catecholamin *n* catecholamine
Catecholmethyltransferase *f* catechol methyltransferase *(enzyme)*
Catecholoxidase *f* catechol (polyphenol, *(o)*-di-phenol) oxidase, phenolase, tyrosinase *(enzyme)*
Catena *f (soil, ecol)* catena
Catesby's Traubenheide *f (bot)* drooping leucothoe, Leucothoe fontanesiana (catesbaei)
Cathepsin *n* cathepsin *(enzyme)*
Cathidin *n* cathidin *(alkaloid)*
Catinga *n s.* Caatinga
Catjangbohne *f* catjang [bean], cherry bean, Vigna unguiculata ssp. cylindrica
Cattalo *n* Cattalo, catalo, beefalo *(cattle breed)*
Cattleya *f*, **Cattleye** *f (bot)* cattleya *(genus Cattleya)*
Cauda *f s.* Schwanz
Caudicula *f* caudicle, caudicula *(of orchid flowers)*
cauliflor *(bot)* cauliflorous
Cauliflorie *f (bot)* cauliflory, trunciflory
Cayennepfeffer *m* 1. red pepper, Spanish (African) pepper, Capsicum frutescens; 2. cayenne [pepper], red pepper *(spice)*
Cayugaente *f* Cayuga *(duck breed)*
Cb *s.* Cumulonimbus

CBuBV s. Citrus-Buntblättrigkeitsvirus
CCBFV s. Chlorotisches Blattfleckungsvirus bei Citrus
CCC s. Chlorcholinchlorid
CCK s. Cholecystokinin
CCK-PZ s. Cholecystokinin-Pankreozymin
CCM[-Silage f] corn-cob mix
CC-Test m contemporary comparison (breeding value appraisal)
CDEC s. Sulfallat
C$_4$-Dicarbonsäureweg m Hatch-Slack pathway (of photosynthetic CO_2 fixation)
Ceara-Kautschuk m ceara rubber
Ceara-Kautschukbaum m ceara rubber, Manihot glaziovii
Cecidium n plant gall, gallnut
Cellobiose f cellobiose (disaccharide)
Cellulase f cellulase (enzyme)
Cellulosan n hemicellulose (polysaccharide)
Cellulose f cellulose (polysaccharide)
~/mikrokristalline microcrystalline cellulose
~/regenerierte regenerated cellulose
Celluloseabbau m cellulose decomposition (degradation), cellulolysis
Celluloseacetat n cellulose acetate
Celluloseaufschluß m cellulose digestion, cellulolysis
Cellulosederivat n cellulose derivative
Cellulosenitrat n nitrocellulose
Celluloseverdauung f cellulose digestion, cellulolysis
Celluloseverdaulichkeit f cellulose digestibility
Cellulosexanthat n cellulose xanthate (soil conditioner)
CELO-Virus n chicken embryo lethal orphan virus
CELO-Virusinfektion f quail bronchitis
Celosie f (bot) celosia, cockscomb (genus Celosia)
Cental m cental
Centriol n centriole (organelle)
Centromer n centromere (portion of a chromosome) • **ohne ~** acentric
Centrosom n centrosome (centriole-containing region of cytoplasm)
Cephalochromin n cephalochromin (antibiotic)
Cephalopharynxskelett n (ent) cephalopharyngeal skeleton
Cephalosporin n cephalosporin (antibiotic)
Cephalothorax m (zoo) cephalothorax
Cephapirin n cephapirin (antibiotic)
Ceratostomellawelke f der Kakaobäume cacao canker (caused by Ceratocystis fimbriata)
Cercospora-Blattfleckenkrankheit f cercospora leaf blotch (spot) (caused by Cercospora spp.)
~ der Rübe beet leaf spot (caused by Cercospora beticola)
Cercospora-Nadelkrankheit f cercospora needle disease
Cercus m (ent) tail-feeler

Cerebellum n s. Kleinhirn
Cerebron n phrenosin (lipid)
Cerebrosid n cerebroside (glycolipid)
Cerebrum n s. Großhirn
Ceroid[pigment] n ceroid
Ceruloplasmin n ferroxidase (enzyme)
cervin cervine
Cervix f uteri cervix [of the uterus]
Cestodose f (vet) cestodiasis
Cetrimid n cetrimide (disinfectant)
Cetyl-trimethyl-ammoniumbromid n cetrimide (disinfectant)
CExV s. Citrus-Exocortis-Virus
Ceylonkardamome f Ceylon (long) cardamom, Elettaria major
Ceylonzimt m Ceylon cinnamon
Ceylonzimtbaum m cinnamon tree, [Ceylon] cinnamon, Cinnamomum zeylanicum
C-Füllmasse f low-grade massecuite (sugar manufacture)
Chabaudnelke f carnation Chabaud (cultivar grouping from Dianthus caryophyllus)
Chabertiose f (vet) chabertiosis
Chablis m Chablis (kind of wine)
Chaco m chaco (dry forest in South America)
Chalaza f 1. (bot) chalaza; 2. chalaza, gallature, tread (of bird's egg)
Chalazogamie f (bot) chalazogamy
Chalcedonische Lichtnelke f Maltese-cross, scarlet lychnis, flower of Bristol (Constantinople), Lychnis chalcedonica
Chalcon n chalcone (pigment)
Chalcon-Flavanon-Isomerase f, **Chalconisomerase** f chalcone [flavanone] isomerase (enzyme)
Chamaephyt m chamaephyte
Chamäleontrichterling m (bot) deceiver, Laccaria laccata
Champagner m champagne
Champaka[baum] m (bot) champac, champak, golden champa, Michelia champaca
Champignon m 1. mushroom, agaric (genus Agaricus); 2. [cultivated] mushroom, Agaricus bisporus
Champignonanbau m mushroom growing (cultivation)
champignonartig champignous
Champignonbeet n mushroom bed
Champignonerntemaschine f mushroom harvester
Champignonfliege f mushroom phorid, Megaselia halterata
Champignonhaus n mushroom-house
~ mit Grundbeetanbau bed mushroom-house
~ mit Stellagenanbau shelf mushroom-house
Champignonkiste f mushroom-growing kit
Champignonkultur f mushroom culture
Champignonstellage f mushroom shelf
Champignonsubstrat n mushroom substrate (compost)

Champignonvirus

Champignonvirus *n* mushroom virus
Champignonweichfäule *f* soft rot of mushroom (caused by Mycogone perniciosa)
Champignonzucht *f* mushroom growing (cultivation)
chaptalisieren to chaptalize *(wine)*
Charakter *m* character *(of farm animals)*; disposition *(of pets)*
Charakterart *f (ecol)* characteristic species
Charbray *n* Charbray *(cattle breed)*
Charge *f* batch
Chargenmischer *m* batch mixer
Chargentrockner *m* batch dryer
Chargentrocknung *f* batch drying
Charmat-Verfahren *n* bulk fermentation method *(wine-making)*
Charolaisrind *n* Charol[l]ais *(cattle breed)*
chasmogam *(bot)* chasmogamic
Chasmogamie *f (bot)* chasmogamy
Chasteksche Lähme (Paralyse) *f (vet)* Chastek paralysis
ChASV *s.* Chrysanthemenadernscheckungsvirus
Chattigummi *n* gum ghatti *(from Anogeissus latifolia)*
Chaulmoograbaum *m (bot)* chaulmoogra, Hydnocarpus kurzii
Chayote[pflanze] *f (bot)* chayote, choco, mirliton, vegetable pear, Sechium edule
ChBV *s.* Chrysanthemen-B-Virus
Cheddar[käse] *m* Cheddar [cheese], store (rat) cheese
Cheiloschisis *f (vet)* cheiloschisis, cleft (hare) lip
Chelat *n* chelate *(metallo-organic complex)*
Chelatbildner *m* chelating agent
Chelatbildung *f* chelation
Chelatdünger *m* chelated fertilizer
Chelator *m* chelating (sequestering) agent
Chelicere *f* chelicera *(e.g. of mites)*
Chelidonin *n* chelidonine *(alkaloid)*
Chemie *f* **der Milch** dairy chemistry
~ **der Schädlingsbekämpfungsmittel** pesticide chemistry
~ **des Bodens** soil chemistry
~/**milchwirtschaftliche** dairy chemistry
Chemikalie *f* chemical
~/**verhaltensbeeinflussende** behavioural chemical
Chemikalienausbringung *f* **mit Beregnungsanlagen, Chemikalienverregnung** *f* chemigation
Chemilumineszenz *f* chemiluminescence
Chemisierung *f* chemicalization
chemisorbieren to chemisorb
Chemolumineszenz *f* chemiluminescence
Chemonastie *f (bot)* chemonasty
Chemoprophylaxe *f (vet)* chemoprophylaxis
Chemoresistenz *f* chemical resistance
Chemorezeptor *m* chemoreceptor
chemosensorisch chemosensory
chemosorbieren to chemisorb

Chemosorption *f* chemisorption *(wood preservation)*
Chemostat *m* chemostat
Chemosterilans *n* chemosterilant
Chemosterilisation *f* chemosterilization
Chemosterilisationsmittel *n* chemosterilant
Chemosynthese *f* chemosynthesis
Chemosystematik *f* chemosystematics
chemotaktisch chemotactic
Chemotaxis *f* chemotaxis
Chemotaxonomie *f* chemotaxonomy
chemotherapeutisch *(phyt, vet)* chemotherapeutic[al]
Chemotherapeutikum *n* chemotherapeutical, chemotherapeutant
Chemotherapie *f* chemotherapy
Chemotropismus *m* chemotropism
Chemotyp *m* chemotype
Chenodesoxycholsäure *f* chenodeoxycholic acid *(bile acid)*
Chenopodiummosaikvirus *n* sowbane mosaic virus, SoMV
Cherimoya *f (bot)* cherimoya, Annona cherimola
Chesapeake Bay Retriever *m* Chesapeake Bay retriever *(dog breed)*
Cheshire Käse *m* Cheshire cheese
Chester White *n* Chester [County] White *(pig breed)*
Cheviot *n s.* 1. Cheviotwolle; 2. Cheviotschaf
Cheviotschaf *n* [South Country] Cheviot *(sheep breed)*
Cheviotwolle *f* cheviot
Cheyne-Stokes-Atmung *f (vet)* Cheyne-Stokes breathing (respiration)
Chi-Quadrat-Test *m* chi-squared test *(statistics)*
Chi-Quadrat-Verteilung *f* chi-squared [probability] distribution
Chianinarind *n* Chians, Chianina *(cattle breed)*
Chianti[wein] *m* Chianti *(wine)*
Chiasma *n (gen)* chiasma
Chiasmenhäufigkeit *f* chiasma frequency
Chicasapflaume *f* Chikasaw plum, Prunus angustifolia
Chicken-Embryolethal-Orphan-Virus *n* chicken embryo lethal orphan virus, CELO virus
Chicle *m*, **Chiclegummi** *n* chicle *(gum esp. from Manilkara zapota)*
Chicorée *m(f)* [salad, witloof] chicory, succory, French endive, witloof, Cichorium intybus var. foliosum
Chicoréegelbscheckungsvirus *n* chicory yellow mottle virus
Chicoréesproß *m* chicon, succory, *(Am)* chic[k]ory
Chicoréetreiberei *f* chicory forcing
ChiGSV *s.* Chicoréegelbscheckungsvirus
Chihuahua *m* chihuahua *(dog breed)*
Chileerdbeere *f* Chilean strawberry, Fragaria chiloensis

Chilenische Araukarie *f* monkey-puzzle, Chile pine, Araucaria araucana (imbricata)
~ **Fabiana** *f* false heath, Fabiana imbricata
~ **Guave** *f* Chilean guava, Ugni molinae
~ **Honigpalme** *f* coquito palm, Jubaea chilensis (spectabilis)
Chilesalpeter *m* [Chile] nitre, Chile saltpetre, Chilean nitrate, caliche *(raw salt)*
Chilly *n* chilli [pepper], chili, chile *(spice from Capsicum spp.)*
chimär *s.* chimärisch
Chimäre *f (gen)* chimera, chimaera
chimärisch chimeric[al]
Chimärismus *m* chimerism
Chinacetolsulfat *n* quinacetol sulphate *(fungicide)*
Chinagras *n* 1. ramie, China grass, Chinese silkplant, Boehmeria nivea; 2. China grass, Pennisetum polystachyon
Chinahickory *m(f)* Chinese hickory, Carya cathayensis
Chinaholzöl *n* Chinese wood oil, Chinawood (tung) oil *(esp. from Aleurites fordii)*
Chinakohl *m* Chinese (celery, shantung) cabbage, pak-choi, petsai, Brassica chinensis
Chinanelke *f* Chinese (Indian) pink, Dianthus chinensis
Chinanessel *f* false nettle *(genus Boehmeria)*
Chinarinde *f* cinchona [bark], Peruvian (jesuit's) bark *(from Cinchona spp.)*
Chinarindenbaum *m* cinchona *(genus Cinchona)*
Chinasäure *f* quinic acid *(phytohormone, growth regulator)*
Chinaschilf *n* zebra grass, Miscanthus sinensis cv. zebrinus
Chinawurzel *f* China-root, Smilax china
Chinazimt *m* Chinese cinnamon
Chinazimtbaum *m* Chinese cinnamon (cassia), cassia bark tree, Cinnamomum aromaticum (cassia)
Chincherinchee *n (bot)* chincherinchee, Ornithogalum thyrsoides
Chinchilla *f* chinchilla *(genus Chinchilla)*
Chinchillakaninchen *n* chinchilla *(rabbit breed)*
Chinesenbart *m* Chinese beard (whiskers) *(timber defect)*
Chinesische Birne *f* Chinese (Japanese, sand) pear, Pyrus pyrifolia
~ **Dattelpflaume** *f* Chinese persimmon, kakee [plum], kaki, Diospyros kaki
~ **Hängeweide** *f* weeping (mourning) willow, Salix babylonica
~ **Jute** *f* China jute, Indian mallow, velvetleaf, Abutilon theophrasti (avicennae)
~ **Kartoffel** *f* Chinese yam, Chinese [sweet] potato, cinnamon vine, Dioscorea opposita (batatas)
~ **Kastanie** *f* Chinese [sweet] chestnut, Castanea mollissima
~ **Kiefer** *f* Chinese pine, Pinus tabuliformis (funebris)

Chinesisches

~ **Klettertrompete** *f* Chinese trumpet creeper (flower), Campsis grandiflora
~ **Korkeiche** *f* Chinese cork-oak, Quercus variabilis
~ **Nelke** *f* Chinese (rainbow) pink, Dianthus chinensis
~ **Päonie** *f* Chinese (fragrant) peony, Paeonia lactiflora
~ **Rose** *f* China (Chinese, fairy) rose, Rosa chinensis
~ **Schwarze Olive** *f* Chinese black olive, Canarium pimela
~ **Sommeraster** *f* [China, annual] aster, Callistephus chinensis
~ **Stachelbeere** *f* kiwi [berry, fruit], Chinese gooseberry, Actinidia chinensis
~ **Trauerweide** *f s. ~* Hängeweide
~ **Trompetenblume** *f s. ~* Klettertrompete
~ **Wassernuß** *f* water chestnut (caltrop), jesuit's nut, Trapa bicornis var. bicornis
~ **Weiße Olive** *f* Chinese white olive, Canarium album
~ **Zaubernuß** *f* Chinese wych-hazel, Hamamelis mollis
~ **Zwittertanne** *f* [common] China fir, Cunningham pine, Cunninghamia lanceolata
Chinesischer Birnbaum *m* Chinese pear, Pyrus lindleyi
~ **Bocksdorn** *m* Chinese matrimony vine, Chinese wolfberry, tea-tree, Lycium chinense
~ **Bohnenkäfer** *m* southern cowpea weevil, Callosobruchus maculatus
~ **Flieder** *m* Chinese lilac, Syringa x chinensis
~ **Hanf** *m* China jute, Indian mallow, velvetleaf, Abutilon theophrasti (avicennae)
~ **Judasbaum** *m* Chinese redbud, Cercis chinensis (japonica)
~ **Klebsame** *m (bot)* Japanese pittosporum, Pittosporum tobira
~ **Mais** *m* waxy maize, *(Am)* wax corn, Zea mays convar. ceratina
~ **Ölbaum** *m* Chinese wood-oil tree, tung-[oil-]tree, Aleurites fordii
~ **Palasthund** *m* Pekin[g]ese, peke *(dog breed)*
~ **Rhabarber** *m* medicinal rhubarb, Rheum officinale
~ **Roseneibisch** *m* Chinese hibiscus (rose), shoe flower, Hibiscus rosa-sinensis
~ **Salat** *m* Indian lettuce, Lactuca indica
~ **Schlingknöterich** *m* silver lace vine, China fleece vine, Fallopia (Polygonum) aubertii
~ **Spitz** *m* chow[-chow] *(dog breed)*
~ **Surenbaum** *m* Chinese mahogany, Toona (Cedrela) sinensis
~ **Talgbaum** *m* [Chinese] tallow-tree, Sapium sebiferum
~ **Wacholder** *m* Chinese juniper, Juniperus chinensis
Chinesisches Judasbaumblatt *n s.* Chinesischer Judasbaum

Chinesisches

~ **Maskenschwein** *n* Chinese Mask *(pig breed)*
~ **Süßholz** *n* Chinese liquorice, Glycyrrhiza uralensis
~ **Wasserreh** *n* [Chinese] water deer, Hydropotes inermis
~ **Yams** *n* 1. Chinese yam, Chinese [sweet] potato, cinnamon vine, Dioscorea opposita (batatas); 2. lesser yam, Dioscorea esculenta
~ **Zimtöl** *n* cassia oil *(from Cinnamomum aromaticum)*
Chinin *n* quinine *(alkaloid)*
Chinolin quinoline, benzopyridine
Chinolinsäure *f* quinolic acid, pyridine-2,3-dicarboxylic acid
Chinolizidin *n* quinolizidin *(alkaloid)*
Chinomethionat *n* chinomethionate, quinomethionate, oxythioquinox *(fungicide)*
Chinomethionin *n* quinomethionine *(fungicide)*
Chinon *n* quinon
Chinonamid *n* quinonamid *(herbicide)*
Chinothionat *n* chinothionat, thioquinox *(acaricide)*
Chipfraktur *f (vet)* chip fracture
Chipokulation *f* chip budding
Chips *mpl* chips, chippings
Chirurgie *f (vet)* surgery
Chitin *n* chitin
Chitinase *f* chitinase *(enzyme)*
chitinisieren to chitinize
Chitinogenschicht *f (ent)* hypodermis
chitinös chitinous
Chlamydienabort *m* enzootic abortion in sheep, kebbing
Chlamydieninfektion *f (vet)* chlamydial infection
~ **des Geflügels** ornithosis *(caused by Chlamydia psittaci)*
Chlamydospore *f (bot)* chlamydospore
Chlor *n* chlorine
Chloralhydrat *n* chloral hydrate *(herbicide)*
Chloramphenicol *n* chloramphenicol *(antibiotic)*
Chloraniformethan *n* chloraniformethan *(fungicide)*
Chloranil *n* chloranil *(fungicide)*
Chlorbensid *n* chlorbensid[e] *(acaricide)*
Chlorbenzilat *n* chlorbenzilate *(acaricide)*
Chlorbrompropen *n* chlorbrompropen *(herbicide, insecticide, fungicide, nematicide)*
Chlorcholinchlorid *n* chlorcholine chloride, CCC, chlormequat, cycocel *(growth regulator)*
Chlordan *n* chlordane *(insecticide)*
Chlordecon *n* chlordecone *(insecticide)*
Chlordiazepoxid *n* chlordiazepoxide *(fungicide)*
Chlordimephorm *n* chlordimephorm *(acaricide)*
Chlordüngemittel *n* chlorine fertilizer
Chlorella *f (bot)* chlorella
Chlorenchym *n (bot)* chlorenchyma
Chlorethan *n* ethyl chloride
2-Chlorethanol *n* 2-chlorethanol, ethylene chlorohydrin

2-Chlorethanphosphonsäure *f* 2-chlorethanephosphonic acid, ethephon *(growth regulator)*
Chloreturon *n* chloreturon *(herbicide)*
Chlorfenethol *n* chlorfenethol *(acaricide)*
Chlorfenprop-methyl *n* chlorfenprop-methyl *(herbicide)*
Chlorfenson *n* chlorfenson, difensan *(acaricide)*
Chlorfensulfid *n* chlorfensulphide *(acaricide)*
Chlorfenvinphos *n* chlorfenvinphos *(insecticide)*
Chlorflurazol *n* chlorflurazole *(fungicide)*
Chlorflurenol *n* chlorflurenol, chlorflurecol[-methyl] *(growth regulator)*
Chloridazon *n* chloridazon, pyrazone *(herbicide)*
Chlorit *m* chlorite *(clay mineral)*
Chlorkalium *n* potasssium chloride, muriate of potash
Chlorkalk *m* chloride of lime, bleaching powder
Chlorkarnallit *m* carnallite
Chlormadinon *n* chlormadinone, CAP *(sex hormone)*
Chlormephos *n* chlormephos *(insecticide)*
Chlormequat *n* chlormequat, chlorcholine chloride, cycocel, CCC *(growth regulator)*
Chlormethiuron *n* chloromethiuron *(ectoparasiticide)*
Chlornatrium *n* sodium chloride
Chlornitromycin *n* chloramphenicol *(antibiotic)*
Chloroform *n* chloroform, trichloromethane
Chlorogensäure *f* chlorogenic acid, caffeoylquinic acid
Chloroleukämie *f s.* Chloromyelose
Chloromethiuron *n* chloromethiuron *(ectoparasiticide)*
Chloromyelose *f (vet)* Aran's cancer
Chloroneb *n* chloroneb *(fungicide)*
Chloropenie *f (vet)* chloropenia
Chlorophyll *n* chlorophyll, leaf-green
Chlorophyllase *f* chlorophyllase *(enzyme)*
Chlorophyllbiosynthese *f* chlorophyll biosynthesis
chlorophyllfrei achlorophyllous, achlorophyllose
Chlorophyllid *n* chlorophyllide *(chlorophyll precursor)*
Chlorophyllkorn *n* chlorophyll grain
Chlorophyllmetabolismus *m* chlorophyll metabolism
Chlorophyllmutation *f* chlorophyll mutation
Chlorophyllstoffwechsel *m* chlorophyll metabolism
Chloroplast *m* chloroplast
Chloroplasten-DNA *f* chloroplast-DNA
Chloroplastenbiogenese *f* chloroplast biogenesis
Chloroplastengenetik *f* chloroplast genetics
Chloroplastenmatrix *f* stroma
Chloroplastenphysiologie *f* chloroplast physiology
Chlorpropylat *n* chloropropylate *(acaricide)*
Chlorose *f (phyt)* chlorosis, blanching, bleaching
Chlorosevirus *n* **des Hopfens** hop chlorotic disease virus
chlorotisch *(phyt)* chlorotic

Chlorotische Blattfleckung f chlorotic fleck *(virosis)*
~ **Blattfleckung** f **des Apfels** apple chlorotic leaf spot
~ **Fleckung** f chlorotic fleck
~ **Ringfleckenkrankheit** f chlorotic ring spot
~ **Ringfleckenkrankheit** f **der Süßkirsche** cherry chlorotic ring spot
Chlorotisches Apfelblattfleckungsvirus n apple chlorotic leaf spot virus
~ **Blattfleckungsvirus** n **bei Citrus** citrus tatter leaf virus
~ **Blattfleckungsvirus** n **des Apfels** apple chlorotic leaf spot virus
~ **Blattrollvirus** n **der Aprikose** apricot chlorotic leaf roll virus
~ **Chrysanthemenscheckungsviroid** n chrysanthemum chlorotic mottle viroid, ChCMV
~ **Fliederblattfleckungsvirus** n lilac chlorotic leaf spot virus, LCLSV
~ **Kundebohnenscheckungsvirus** n cowpea chlorotic mottle virus
~ **Maisscheckungsvirus** n maize chlorotic mottle virus
~ **Maisverzwergungsvirus** n maize chlorotic dwarf virus
~ **Ringfleckenvirus** n **der Kirsche** prune dwarf virus, PDV
Chloroxuron n chloroxuron *(herbicide, nematicide)*
Chloroxylenol n chloroxylenol *(disinfectant)*
Chlorphacinon n chlorphacinon *(rodenticide)*
Chlorphoxim n chlorphoxim *(insecticide)*
Chlorpikrin n chloropicrin, trichloronitromethane *(nematicide, insecticide)*
Chlorpromazin n chlorpromazine *(neuroleptic)*
Chlorpropham n chlorpropham, CIPC *(growth regulator, herbicide)*
Chlorpyrifos n chlorpyrifos *(insecticide)*
Chlorpyrifos-methyl n chlorpyriphos-methyl *(insecticide)*
Chlorquinox n chlorquinox *(fungicide)*
Chlorsulfuron n chlorsulfuron *(herbicide, growth regulator)*
Chlortetracyclin n chlortetracycline, CTC, biomycin, aureomycin, aurofac *(antibiotic)*
Chlorthal-[di]methyl n chlorthal-[di]methyl, DCPA *(herbicide)*
Chlorthalonil n chlor[o]thalonil *(fungicide)*
Chlorthion n chlorthion *(insecticide, acaricide)*
Chlorthiophos n chlorthiophos *(insecticide)*
Chlorwasserstoffsäure f hydrochloric acid
Chokebohrung f chokebore *(of a sporting gun)*
Chokerseil n choker *(skidding)*
Cholagogum n cholagogue
Cholangitis f *(vet)* cholangitis
Cholansäure f cholanic acid
Cholecalciferol n cholecalciferol
Cholecystokinin[-Pankreozymin] n cholecystokinin[-pancreozymin], CCK *(hormone)*

Choleinsäure f choleic acid
Cholelith m *(vet)* cholelith, biliary calculus, gallstone
Cholelithiasis f *(vet)* cholelithiasis
Cholepoesis f cholepoiesis
Choleprasin n bilifuscin *(bile pigment)*
Cholestase f *(vet)* cholestasis
Cholesterol n cholesterol
Cholesterolacyltransferase f cholesterol acyltransferase *(enzyme)*
Cholesterolesterase f cholesterol esterase *(enzyme)*
Cholesterolhydroxylase f cholesterol hydroxylase *(enzyme)*
Cholezystektomie f *(vet)* cholecystectomy, gallbladder removal
Cholezystitis f *(vet)* cholecystitis
Cholin n choline, bilineurine *(phospholipid)*
Cholinacetyl[transfer]ase f choline acetyltransferase *(enzyme)*
Cholinesterase f cholinesterase *(enzyme)*
Cholinkinase f choline kinase *(enzyme)*
Cholinoxidase f choline oxidase *(enzyme)*
Cholinphosphatcytidylyltransferase f cholinephosphate cytidylyltransferase *(enzyme)*
Cholsäure f cholic acid *(bile acid)*
Chondrifikation f chondrification
Chondriom n chondriome
Chondriosom n chondriosome, mitochondrion *(organelle)*
Chondritis f *(vet)* chondritis
Chondrodystrophie f *(vet)* chondrodystrophy
Chondrogenese f chondrogenesis
Chondroitinsulfat n chondroitin sulphate *(mucopolysaccharide)*
Chondrosamin n galactosamine
Chondrozyt m chondrocyte, cartilage cell
Chorea f *(vet)* chorea
chorikarp *(bot)* apocarpous
Chorioallantois f chorioallantois
Chorioallantoismembran f chorioallantoic membrane
Choriomeningitis f *(vet)* choriomeningitis
~/**lymphozytäre** lymphocytic choriomeningitis
Choriomeningitisvirus n lymphocytic choriomeningitis virus
Chorion n chorion *(animal anatomy)*
Choriongonadotropin n human chorionic gonadotrop[h]in, HCG *(for ovulation induction e.g. in mares)*
Chorionsack m chorionic sac
Chorioptes-Räude f **des Rindes** chorioptic mange of cattle *(caused by Chorioptes bovis)*
Chorioretinitis f **der Puten** *(vet)* turkey blindness syndrome
choripetal *(bot)* choripetalous
chorisepal *(bot)* chorisepalous
Chorismatmutase f chorismate mutase *(enzyme)*
C-Horizont m *(soil)* C-horizon

Chorologie

Chorologie *f (ecol)* chorology, science of plant species range
chorologisch chorological
Chow-Chow *m* chow[-chow] *(dog breed)*
Christbaumzucht *f* Christmas tree farming (growing)
Christdorn *m* Christ's thorn, Paliurus spina-christi
Christophskraut *n* baneberry, grapewort *(genus Actaea)*
Christrose *f* 1. hellebore *(genus Helleborus)*; 2. Christmas rose, black hellebore, Helleborus niger
Christusdorn *m* Christ's thorn, crown of thorns, Euphorbia milii (splendens)
Chromaffinozyt *m* chromaffin cell
Chromatid *n* chromatid
Chromatidenaberration *f* chromatid aberration
Chromatidenbrücke *f* chromatid bridge
Chromatidentetrade *f* chromatid tetrad
Chromatin *n* chromatin *(cell-nucleus constituent)*
Chromatinhiston *n* chromatin histone
Chromatogramm *n* chromatogram
Chromatographie *f* chromatography
chromatographisch chromatographic
Chromatophor *n* chromatophore
Chromatophorom *n (vet)* chromatophoroma
Chromobakterium *n* chromobacterium
Chromomer *n* chromomere
Chromonema *n* chromonema
Chromonemaverdickung *f* chromomere
Chromoplast *m (bot)* chromoplast
Chromoproteid *n*, **Chromoprotein** *n* chromoprotein
Chromosom *n* chromosome
~/polytänes polytene (polytenic, giant) chromosome
chromosomal chromosomal
Chromosomenaberration *f* chromosomal aberration
Chromosomenaddition *f* chromosome addition
Chromosomenanalyse *f* chromosome analysis
Chromosomenarm *m* chromosome arm
Chromosomenatlas *m* chromosome atlas
Chromosomenbande *f* chromosome band
Chromosomenbandenmuster *n* chromosome banding pattern
Chromosomenbänderung *f* chromosome banding
Chromosomenbruch *m* chromosome break
Chromosomenbrücke *f* chromosome bridge
Chromosomenchimäre *f* cytochimera
Chromosomenchimärismus *m* chromosome chimerism
Chromosomendefekt *m* chromosome defect
Chromosomenduplikation *f* chromosome doubling
Chromosomeneliminierung *f* chromosome elimination
Chromosomenfragment *n* chromosome fragment
Chromosomenfusion *f* chromosome fusion
Chromosomenglied *n* chromosome arm
Chromosomeninversion *f* chromosome inversion
Chromosomenkarte *f* chromosome map
Chromosomenkartierung *f* chromosome mapping
Chromosomenkomplement *n* chromosome complement
Chromosomenkopplungskarte *f* [chromosome] linkage map
Chromosomenmanipulation *f* chromosome manipulation (engineering)
Chromosomenmobilisierung *f* chromosome mobilization
Chromosomenmorphologie *f* chromosome morphology
Chromosomenmosaik *n* chromosome mosaic[ism]
Chromosomenmutation *f* chromosome mutation
~/numerische genome mutation
Chromosomenpaar *n* chromosome pair, pair of chromosomes
~/homologes bivalent
Chromosomenpaarung *f* chromosome pairing, conjugation of chromosomes
Chromosomenpolymorphismus *m* chromosome polymorphism
Chromosomensatellit *m* chromosome satellite
Chromosomensatz *m* chromosome set (complement), genome, karyotype • **mit achtfachem ~** octoploid, octaploid • **mit doppeltem ~** diploid • **mit dreifachem ~** triploid • **mit einfachem ~** haploid • **mit fünffachem ~** pentaploid • **mit geradzahlig vervielfachtem ~** orthoploid • **mit mehrfachem ~** polyploid • **mit sechsfachem ~** hexaploid • **mit siebenfachem ~** septaploid • **mit ungeradzahlig vervielfachtem ~** anorthoploid • **mit vierfachem ~** tetraploid
~/haploider genome
Chromosomensatzvervielfachung *f* polyploidy
Chromosomenschenkel *m* chromosome arm
Chromosomensegment *n* chromosome segment
Chromosomensegmentverdrehung *f* inversion
Chromosomenspalthälfte *f* chromatid
Chromosomenstellung *f* chromosome localization
Chromosomenstück *n* chromosome segment
Chromosomensubstitution *f* chromosome substitution
Chromosomentheorie *f* **der Vererbung** chromosome theory of [Mendelian] heredity
Chromosomentranslokation *f* chromosome translocation
Chromosomenvariation *f* chromosome variation
Chromosomenverdopplung *f* chromosome doubling
Chromosomenverteilung *f* chromosome distribution
Chromosomenzahl *f* chromosome number
Chromosomoid *n* microchromosome
Chrom(III)-oxid *n* chromic oxide
Chromozentrum *n* chromocentre
Chronaxie *f* chronaxie *(animal physiology)*

chronisch *(phyt, vet)* chronic
Chronosequenz *f (soil)* chronosequence
Chrysalis *f (ent)* chrysalis, chrysalid, pupa
Chrysantheme *f* chrysanthemum, chrysanth, Chrysanthemum indicum
~/**einfache** single chrysanthemum
~/**großblumig-ballförmige** standard chrysanthemum
~/**pomponförmige** pompon chrysanthemum
~/**strahlenförmige** spider chrysanthemum
~/**ungefüllte** single chrysanthemum
Chrysanthemenadernscheckungsvirus *n* chrysanthemum vein mottle virus, ChVMV
Chrysanthemen[blatt]älchen *n* chrysanthemum leaf eelworm, chrysanthemum nematode, Aphelenchoides ritzemabosi
Chrysanthemenblattminierfliege *f* chrysanthemum leaf-miner, Phytomyza (Agromyza) atricornis
Chrysanthemen-B-Virus *n* chrysanthemum virus B, CVB
Chrysanthemengallmücke *f* chrysanthemum [gall-]midge, Diarthronomyia chrysanthemi
Chrysanthemenringfleckenvirus *n* chrysanthemum ring spot virus
Chrysanthemenrosettenvirus *n* chrysanthemum rosette virus
Chrysanthemenrost *m* rust of chrysanthemum *(caused by Puccinia chrysanthemi)*
Chrysanthemenstauche *f (phyt)* chrysanthemum stunt
Chrysanthemenstaucheviroid *n* chrysanthemum stunt viroid, CSV
Chrysanthemenstauchevirus *n* chrysanthemum stunt virus
Chrysanthemenverkümmerung *f s.* Chrysanthemenstauche
Chrysanthemenweißrost *m* chrysanthemum white rust *(caused by Puccinia horiana)*
Chrysanthemum-Maximum-Hybride *f* Shasta daisy, Chrysanthemum x superbum
Chufa *f s.* Erdmandelgras
Chupon *m* chupon *(upright growing shoot of Theobroma cacao)*
Chylomikron *n* chylomicron *(fat digestion)*
Chylus *m* chyle *(milky lymph)*
Chymase *f* chymase *(enzyme)*
Chymosin *n* chymosin, rennin, rennet
Chymosinogen *n* chymosinogen, renninogen, prorennin
Chymotrypsin *n* chymotrypsin *(enzyme)*
Chymotrypsininhibitor *m* chymotrypsin inhibitor
Chymotrypsinogen *n* chymotrypsinogen *(chymotrypsin precursor)*
Chymus *m* chyme, digesta
Cicatrix *f* cicatrice, cicatrix, scar
Cidre *m* cider
Cinchonin *n* cinchonine *(alkaloid)*
Cineol *n* cineole *(terpene)*

Cinerarie *f* florist's cineraria, Senecio cruentus
*(trans-)***Cinnamat-4-Monooxygenase** *f (trans-)*cinnamate 4-monooxygenase *(enzyme)*
Cinnamylalkohol *m* cinnamyl alcohol *(lignin precursor)*
CIPC CIPC, chlorpropham *(growth regulator, herbicide)*
Cirrus *m* cirrus
Cisanilid *n* cisanilide *(herbicide)*
Cismethrin *n* cismethrin *(insecticide)*
Cisterna *f* cistern[a] *(animal anatomy)*
cis-trans-Test *m* cis-trans test *(for detection of mutational sites)*
Cistron *n* cistron, gene
Citratdehydratase *f* citrate dehydratase *(enzyme)*
Citrat-(si)-Synthase *f s.* Citrogenase
Citratspaltungsenzym *n* ATP-citrate(pro 3S)-lyase
Citrin *m* citrine *(non-clay mineral)*
Citrin *n* vitamin P
Citrinin *n* citrinin *(antiobiotic, mycotoxin)*
Citrogenase *f* citrate-(si)-synthase, condensing enzyme
Citronensäure *f* citric acid
Citronensäuregärung *f* citric acid fermentation
citronensäurelöslich citric soluble
Citronensäurezyklus *m* tricarboxylic (citric) acid cycle, TCA cycle, Krebs cycle *(biochemistry)*
Citrullin *n* citrulline *(amino-acid)*
Citrus *f* citrus *(genus Citrus)* • **zur Gattung ~ gehörend** citrous
Citrus-Buntblättrigkeitsvirus *n* citrus variegation virus
Citrus-Exocortis-Virus *n* citrus exocortis virus
Citrus-Tristeza-Virus *n* citrus tristeza virus
Citrusfrucht *f* citrus [fruit]
Citrusöl *n* citrus oil
Citrussaft *m* citrus juice
Citrusschorf *m* sour orange scab *(caused by Elsinoe fawcetti)*
Cladosporid *n* cladosporide *(growth regulator)*
Clan *m (ecol)* clan *(kind of climax community)*
Claret *m* claret, red wine *(esp. from Bordeaux)*
Clarkie *f (bot)* clarkia, godetia *(genus Clarkia)*
Classis *f* class *(taxonomy)*
Clavicula *f* clavicle, collar-bone
Clearance *f*, **Clearance-Wert** *m* clearance *(of blood plasma purification)*
Clementine *f* clementine, ortanique, Citrus reticulana x Citrus aurantium
Cleomycin *n* clindamycin *(antibiotic)*
Clerodendrum *n (bot)* 1. clerodendrum *(genus Clerodendrum)*; 2. bleeding-heart vine, tube-flower, glory bower, Clerodendrum thomsoniae
Climbazol *n* climbazol *(fungicide)*
Clindamycin *n* clindamycin *(antibiotic)*
Cliodinat *n* cliodinate *(herbicide)*
Clioxanid *n* clioxanide *(anthelminthic)*

Clitorie

Clitorie *f* 1. butterfly pea *(genus Clitoria)*; 2. Cordofan pea, Clitoria ternatea
Clivie *f* kaffir lily *(genus Clivia)*
Clofop-isobutyl *n* clofop-isobutyl *(herbicide)*
Clon *m* s. Klon
Clopidol *n* clopidol, meticlorpindol *(coccidiostatic)*
Cloprop *n* cloprop *(growth regulator, herbicide)*
Cloprostenol *n* cloprostenol *(prostaglandin analogue)*
Clostridien *npl* clostridia [bacteria] *(genus Clostridium)*
Clostridieninfektion *f (vet)* clostridial infection, clostridiosis
~ **des Geflügels** avian ulcerated enteritis, ulcerative enteritis of birds, quail disease
Clostridiopeptidase *f* **A** collagenase *(enzyme)*
Clostridiose *f s.* Clostridieninfektion
Clostridium-perfringens-Typ-B-Enterotoxämie *f* **der Lämmer** lamb dysentery
Clostridium-perfringens-Typ-C-Enterotoxämie *f* infectious necrotic enteritis *(of sucking pigs)*
Clostridium-tetani-Infektion *f (vet)* tetanus
Cloxacillin *n* cloxacillin *(antibiotic)*
Clumber Spaniel *m* Clumber *(dog breed)*
Clun Forest *n* Clun Forest *(sheep breed)*
Clusteranalyse *f (biom)* cluster analysis
Clydesdale *m*, **Clydesdalepferd** *n* Clydesdale *(horse breed)*
Clypeus *m (ent)* clypeus
CMA *s.* Pentanochlor
^{14}**C-Methode** *f* **der Altersbestimmung** radiocarbon dating [method]
CMU *s.* Monuron
C/N-Verhältnis *n* C/N ratio, carbon-to-nitrogen ratio
CO$_2$- ... *s.* Kohlendioxid...
CoA CoA, coenzyme A
Coagulase *f* coagulase *(enzyme)*
Coagulasetest *m* coagulase test *(for measurement of the blood-clotting time)*
CoA-Transferase *f* CoA-transferase *(enzyme)*
Cobalamin *n* cobalamin, extrinsic factor, animal protein factor, APF, vitamin B$_{12}$
Cobaltdüngemittel *n* cobalt fertilizer
Cobaltsulfat *n* cobalt sulphate
Cobra-Impfverfahren *n* Cobra process, gun-injection *(wood preservation)*
Cocain *n* cocaine *(alkaloid)*
Cocainesterase *f* cocainesterase *(enzyme)*
Cocarboxylase *f* cocarboxylase, thiamine pyrophosphate *(enzyme)*
Coccidie *f s.* Kokzidie
Cochenille *f* cochineal *(dye)*
Cochin[china] *n* Cochin [China] *(chicken breed)*
Cochlea *f* cochlea *(of the inner ear)*
cochlear *(bot, zoo)* cochlear
Cocker-Spaniel *m* cocker [spaniel], English cocker spaniel *(dog breed)*
Code *m*/**genetischer** genetic code

Codein *n* codeine *(alkaloid)*
codieren to encode
Codon *n (gen)* codon
Coecotrophe *f* caecotrophe, soft pellets *(in rabbits)*
Coecotrophie *f* caecotrophy *(of rabbits)*
Coenobium *n* coenobium
Coenzym *n* coenzyme, prosthetic group
~ **A** coenzyme A, CoA
~ **Q** coenzyme Q, CoQ, ubiquinone
~ **R** coenzyme R, biotin
Coffein *n* caffeine, theine *(alkaloid)*
coffeinhaltig caffeinic
Coffeo-3-ylchinasäure *f* chlorogenic acid
Coggins-Reaktion *f* Coggins test, agar gel immunodiffusion test, AGID *(for detection of infectious equine anaemia)*
Cohumulon *n* cohumulone *(hop resin)*
Coir *f* coir, coconut fibre
Cola *f* cola, kola *(drink)*
Colaminkephalin *n* cephalin
Colaminphosphatid *n* phosphatidylethanolamine
Colchicin *n* colchicine *(alkaloid)*
Colchicinbehandlung *f* colchicine treatment *(plant breeding)*
Colemanit *m* colemanite *(boron fertilizer)*
Colepsinstärke *f (dairy)* colepsin strength
Coleus-Blumei-Hybride *f (bot)* coleus
Colibazillus *m s.* Kolibakterium
Collagen *n* collagen *(scleroprotein)*
Collagenase *f* collagenase *(enzyme)*
College *n*/**agrarwissenschaftliches (landwirtschaftliches)** agricultural college, *(Am)* aggie
Collembole *m (ent)* collembolan *(order Collembola)*
Colletotrichum-Schalennekrose *f* **der Kartoffel** black dot of potato *(caused by Colletotrichum coccodes)*
Collie *m* Collie *(dog breed)*
Collophor *m (ent)* collophore
Collum *n (zoo)* collum, neck
Colombowurzel *f* columba root, Jateorhiza palmata
Colon *n s.* Kolon
Colorado... *s.* Kolorado...
Columbusgras *n* Columbus grass, Sorghum almum
Columna *f (bot, zoo)* column, gynandrium
Columnariskrankheit *f*, **Columnarismyxobakteriose** *f* columnaris disease *(of fishes, caused by Flexibacter columnaris)*
Columnee *f (bot)* columnea, goldfish vine *(genus Columnea)*
Colupulon *n* colupulone *(hop resin)*
Commeline *f* day-flower *(genus Commelina)*
Common Name *m* common name
Comovirus *n* comovirus
Compudose *n* compudose *(anabolic agent)*
Computerbewässerung *f* computer[-assisted] irrigation
Concanavalin *n* **A** concanavalin A *(lectin)*

Condylus *m* condyle, articular process
Coniferylalkohol *m* coniferyl alcohol *(lignin constituent)*
Coniin *n* coniine *(alkaloid)*
Conjugase *f* conjugase, gamma-glutamyl hydrolase *(enzyme)*
Connemarapony *n* Connemara pony *(breed)*
Constaphyl *n* dichloxacillin *(antibiotic)*
Containeranbau *m* container growing
Containerhubwagen *m* container lifting trailer
Containerjungpflanze *f* super seedling, speedy
Containerkultur *f* container growing
Containerkulturverfahren *n* container culture method
Containerpflanze *f* container plant; paper pot plant
Containerpflanzung *f* container planting
Containertransport *m* container transport
Containerverfahren *n s.* Containerkulturverfahren
contort *(bot, zoo)* contorted
Convallotoxin *n* convallotoxin *(glycosid)*
Coombs-Test *m* Coombs (antiglobulin) test *(for antibody detection)*
Copaibo... *s.* Kopaiva...
CoQ *s.* Coenzym Q
Coquitopalme *f* coquito palm, Jubaea chilensis (spectabilis)
Coracoid *n* coracoid bone *(animal anatomy)*
Corium *n* corium, dermis, [true] skin
Cormus *m (bot)* corm
Cormophyt *m* cormophyte
Cornea *f s.* Hornhaut
Corned Beef *n* corned beef, bully [beef]
Cornflakes *pl* cornflakes
Corniculus *m (ent)* cornicle
Cornish *n* Cornish *(chicken breed)*
Cornish Game *n* Game Cornish *(chicken breed)*
Cornishhuhn *n s.* Cornish
Cornwall *n* Large Black *(pig breed)*
Cornwallheide *f* Cornish heath, Erica vagans
Cornwallschwein *n s.* Cornwall
Corolla *f (bot)* corolla
Coronatin *n* coronatine *(phytotoxin)*
Corpora pedunculata *npl* mushroom bodies *(bee anatomy)*
Corpus luteum *n (zoo)* corpus luteum, yellow body
Corriedale-Schaf *n* Corriedale *(sheep breed)*
Cortex *f* cortex; bark; rind
Cortexon *n* deoxycorticosterone *(hormone)*
cortical cortical
Corticin *n* corticine *(alkaloid)*
Corticium-Krankheit *f* pink disease *(e.g. of fig trees, caused by Corticium salmonicolor)*
Corticoid *n s.* Corticosteroid
corticol corticole, corticoline, corticolous
Corticoliberin *n* corticoliberin *(hypophyseal hormone)*
Corticosteroid *n* cortico[stero]id, adrenal cortex hormone
Corticosteron *n* corticosterone *(corticosteroid)*

corticotrop corticotrop[h]ic
Corticotropin *n* corticotrop[h]in, adrenocorticotrop[h]in, adrenocorticotrop[h]ic hormone, ACTH
Cortische Membran *f* tectorial membrane *(of the inner ear)*
Cortisol *n* cortisol, hydrocortisone *(corticosteroid)*
Cortison *n* cortisone *(corticosteroid)*
Cortisonreductase *f* cortisone reductase *(enzyme)*
Corynebakteriose *f* bacterial kidney disease *(of salmonoids)*
Costena-Ziege *f* Malaga goat *(breed)*
Costiakrankheit *f*, **Costiosis** *f* costiasis *(of fishes, caused by Costia necatrix)*
Cotswold[schaf] *n* Cotswold [sheep] *(breed)*
Cottage Cheese *m* cottage (Dutch, pot) cheese, smearcase
Cottonöl *n* cotton-seed oil
Cottontailkaninchen *n* cottontail [rabbit] *(genus Sylvilagus)*
Cotyledone *f* 1. *(bot)* cotyledon, seed (embryonic) leaf, seed lobe; 2. *(zoo)* cotyledon
Coumachlor *n* coumachlor *(rodenticide)*
Coumafos *n* coumaphos *(anthelminthic, insecticide, nematicide)*
Coumafuryl *n* coumafuryl *(rodenticide)*
Coumaphos *n s.* Coumafos
Coumatetralyl *n* coumatetralyl *(rodenticide)*
Courbette *f* curvet *(equitation)*
courbettieren to curvet
Cowboy *m (Am)* cowboy, wrangler, cowpuncher
Cowboysattel *m* cowboy (stock, western) saddle
Cowpersche Drüse *f* Cowper's (bulbo-urethral) gland
Coxa *f* 1. *(ent)* coxa; 2. *s.* Hüfte
C_3-Pflanze *f* C-3 plant *(physiology)*
C_4-Pflanze *f* C-4 plant *(physiology)*
Crabapfel *m* 1. crab[-apple]; 2. *s.* Crabapfelbaum
Crabapfelbaum *m* crab[-apple] *(comprehensive term for varieties producing small sour fruits)*
Crabwood *n* crab wood *(from Carapa guianensis)*
Crack *m* crack *(as a superior racehorse)*
Cranberry *f* cranberry, Vaccinium macrocarpon
Cranium *n s.* Kranium
Crassulaceen[säure]stoffwechsel *m* crassulacean acid metabolism, CAM *(plant physiology)*
Creosot *n s.* Creosotöl
creosotieren to creosote *(wood)*
Creosotöl *n* creosote [oil] • **mit ~ behandeln (tränken)** to creosote *(wood)*
Cresol *n* cresol, methylphenol *(disinfectant)*
Crimidin *n* crimidine *(rodenticide)*
Crimper *m* [roller] crimper *(haymaker)*
Criollo *m* criollo *(variety of Theobroma cacao)*
Criollo *n* Criuolo, Criollo *(horse breed)*
Criollorind *n* Criollo *(cattle breed)*
Crossandre *f (Am)* firecracker flower, Crossandra infundibuliformis (undulifolia)
Cross-Bevan-Cellulose *f* Cross and Bevan cellulose

Crossing-over

Crossing-over n (gen) crossing-over
Crossing-over-Einheit f Morgan unit
Crossing-over-Ereignis n crossing-over
Crossing-over-Wert m crossing-over value
Crosskillwalze f crosskill roller (soil working implement)
Crossover n (gen) crossover
Crossresistenz f cross-resistance (e.g. of bacteria and insects)
Croton m Bombay laurel, Codiaeum variegatum
Crotonin n crotonin[e] (alkaloid)
Crotonöl n croton oil
Crotonölbaum m croton-oil plant, purging croton, Croton tiglium
Crotoxyphos n crotoxyphos (insecticide)
Croupade f croupade (equestrian sport)
Crufomat n crufomate (anthelminthic)
Crumena f (ent) crumena
Crusher m crusher
Cryolit n cryolite (insecticide)
Cryptoxanthin n cryptoxanthin (carotinoid)
CSF s. Zerebrospinalflüssigkeit
C_4-Syndrom n C-4 syndrome (plant physiology)
CTC s. Chlortetracyclin
CTP-Synthase f CTP synthase (enzyme)
CUE-Verdünner m Cornell University extender (for bull's semen)
Culpen n fluxoxacillin (antibiotic)
Cultivar f [crop] cultivar, cv, cultivated (crop plant) variety, cultigen
Cultoplant-Jungpflanzenanzuchtsystem n cultoplant [system]
Cumarin n coumarin (glycoside)
Cumarinsäure f coumarinic acid
Cumarol n s. Cumarin
[4-]Cumarsäure f coumaric (hydroxycinnamic) acid (growth inhibitor)
Cumatetralyl n cumatetralyl (rodenticide)
Cumöstrol n coumoestrol (phytoestrogen)
Cumulonimbus m cumulonimbus [cloud]
Cumulus m cumulus [cloud]
Cuprobam n cuprobam (fungicide)
Cupula f (bot, zoo) cupule
Curarin n curarine (alkaloid)
Curcumin n curcumin, tu[r]meric (dye)
Curin n curine (alkaloid)
Curly Coated Retriever m curly-coated retriever (dog breed)
Curzate n curzate (fungicide)
Cush-cush-Yams n (bot) cush-cush, Dioscorea trifida
Cush-cush-Yamswurzel f cush-cush
Cushing-Krankheit f, **Cushing-Syndrom** n (vet) Cushing's syndrome
Cuticula f 1. cuticle; 2. bloom (of hen egg)
Cutin n (bot) cutin
Cutinase f cutinase (enzyme)
Cutinhäutchen n cuticle
Cutter m [meat] cutter

C_3-Weg m reductive pentose phosphate cycle (pathway), Calvin cycle (of CO_2 fixation)
C_4-Weg m Hatch-Slack pathway (of CO_2 fixation)
Cyacetazid n cyacetazide (anthelminthic)
Cyadox n cyadox (growth regulator)
Cyalothrin n cyalothrin (insecticide)
Cyanamid n cyanamide
Cyanatryn n cyanatryn (herbicide)
Cyanazin n cyanazine (herbicide)
Cyanhydringlycosid n cyanogenic glycoside (plant physiology)
Cyanin n cyanin (plant substance)
Cyankali n potassium cyanide
Cyanobakterium n blue-green alga (division Cyanophyta)
Cyanocobalamin n cyanocobalamin, vitamin B_{12}
Cyanogenese f cyanogenesis
Cyanofenphos n cyanofenphos (insecticide)
Cyanophos n cyanophos (insecticide)
Cyanwasserstoffsäure f hydrocyanic (prussic) acid
Cyathium n (bot) cyathium
Cybride f cybrid
Cyclafuramid n cyclafuramid (fungicide)
Cyclanthere f climbing cucumber, Cyclanthera pedata
cyclo-AMP cyclic adenosine monophosphate, cyclic AMP
Cycloartenol n cycloartenol (triterpene alcohol)
Cycloat n cycloate (herbicide)
Cycloheximid n cycloheximide (antibiotic, fungicide)
Cyclophosphamid n cyclophosphamide (cytostatic)
Cyclopropensäure f cyclopropenoic acid (fatty acid)
Cycloserin n cycloserine, oxamycin (antibiotic)
Cycluron n cycluron (herbicide)
Cyd s. Cytidin
Cyhexatin n cyhexatin (acaricide)
Cylindrocladium-Stammgrundfäule (Cylindrocladium-Wurzelhalsfäule) f des Rhododendrons cylindrocladium disease of rhododendron, crown canker of rhododendron (caused by Cylindrocladium scoparium)
Cymbidienmosaikvirus n cymbidium mosaic virus, CyMV
Cymbidienringfleckenvirus n cymbidium ring spot virus
cymös (bot) cymose
CyMV s. Cymbidienmosaikvirus
Cyometrinil n cyometrinil (herbicide antidote)
Cypendazol n cypendazole (fungicide)
Cypergras n 1. cypress grass, flat sedge (genus Cyperus); 2. chufa, Cyperus esculentus
Cypermethrin n cypermethrin (insecticide)
Cypernbiene f Cyprian honey-bee, Apis mellifica cypria
Cyprazin n cyprazine (herbicide)
Cyprazol n cyprazole (herbicide)

Cyprinide *m (pisc)* cyprinoid
Cyprofuram *n* cyprofuram *(fungicide)*
Cypromid *n* cypromid *(herbicide)*
Cyproteron[acetat] *n* cyproterone *(antiandrogen)*
CyRFV *s.* Cymbidienringfleckenvirus
Cys *s.* Cystein
Cystathion *n s.* Cystathionin
Cystathionin *n* cystathionine *(dicarboxylic acid)*
Cystathionin-Gamma-Lyase *f* cystathionine-gamma-lyase, cystathionase, cystine desulfhydrase *(enzyme)*
Cystathioninsynthetase *f* cystathionine synthase *(enzyme)*
Cyste *f s.* Zyste
Cysteamin *n* cysteamine, mercaptamine
Cysteamindioxygenase *f* cysteamine dioxygenase *(enzyme)*
Cystein *n* cysteine *(amino-acid)*
Cysteinaminotransferase *f* cysteine aminotransferase *(enzyme)*
Cysteindioxygenase *f* cysteine dioxygenase *(enzyme)*
Cysteinproteinase *f* cysteine proteinase *(enzyme)*
Cysteinsäure *f* cysteic acid
Cysticercus *m* cysticercus *(in numerous tapeworms)*
Cystin *n* cystine *(amino-acid)*
Cystinausscheidung *f* **im Harn, Cystinurie** *f (vet)* cystinuria
Cyt *s.* Cytosin
Cytase *f* cytase *(enzyme)*
Cytidin *n* cytidine *(nucleoside)*
Cytisin *n* cytisine *(alkaloid)*
Cyto... *s. a.* Zyto... and Zell...
Cytochimäre *f (gen)* chimaera, chimera
Cytochrom *n* cytochrome
~ **c** cytochrome c
Cytochrom-b5-Reductase *f* cytochrome-b5 reductase *(enzyme)*
Cytochrom-c-Oxidase *f* cytochrome-c oxidase, Warburg's respiratory enzyme
Cytochrom-c-Peroxidase *f* cytochrome-c peroxidase *(enzyme)*
Cytochrom-c-Reductase *f* NADH dehydrogenase *(enzyme)*
Cytosin *n* cytosine *(nucleic acid base)*
Cytosolaminopeptidase *f* cytosol (leucine) aminopeptidase *(enzyme)*
Cytovirin *n* cytovirin *(antibiotic)*

D

Dachberegnung *f* roof sprinkling *(of greenhouses)*
Dachboden *m* loft
Dachgarten *m* roof-garden
Dachhauswurz *f* houseleek, hen and chickens, Sempervivum tectorum
dachig *(bot, zoo)* imbricated
Dachlüfter *m* roof ventilator
Dachpappe *f* tar[red] board, roofing (sarking) felt
Dachratte *f* roof rat, Rattus rattus
Dachreinigungsanlage *f* roof cleaner *(for greenhouses)*
Dachs *m* badger, brock, Meles meles
Dachsbau *m* badger's burrow, badger-earth
Dachsbeil *n* adze, *(Am)* adz
Dachschattierung *f* roof shading *(of greenhouses)*
Dachshund *m* dachshund, badger-dog *(breed)*
Dachslosung *f* billeting
Dachstroh *n* thatching [straw]
Dachstrohgras *n* thatching (jaragua) grass, Hyparrhenia rufa
Dachtrespe *f* roof brome[-grass], downy brome[-grass], cheat [grass], drooping brome[-grass], Bromus tectorum
Dachwinkel *m* face angle *(of a chain-saw tooth)*
dachziegelig *(bot, zoo)* imbricated
Dackel *m* dachshund, badger-dog *(breed)*
Dadantbeute *f (api)* Dadant hive
Dahlia-Hybride *f (bot)* dahlia
Dahlie *f (bot)* dahlia *(genus Dahlia)*
~/**einfache** single dahlia
Dahlienmosaikvirus *n* dahlia mosaic virus
Dahurische Lärche *f* Dahurian larch, Larix gmelinii (dahurica)
Daidzein *n* daidzein *(flavone)*
Dairy-Shorthorn-Rind *n* Dairy Shorthorn [cattle], Durham [cattle], Dual-Purpose Shorthorn [cattle], Milking Shorthorn *(breed)*
Dalapon[-Na] *n* dalapon[-Na], 2,2-dichlorpropionic acid *(herbicide)*
Dales-Bred *n* Dales-Bred *(sheep breed)*
Dalespony *n* Dales pony *(breed)*
Dallisgras *n* Dallis (large water) grass, Paspalum dilatatum
Dalmatiner *m* Dalmatian [dog], coach (carriage, plum-pudding) dog *(breed)*
Dalmatinische Insektenblume *f* [Dalmatian] pyrethrum, Chrysanthemum cinerariifolium
Damaszener Rose *f* damask rose, Rosa x damascena
~ **Ziege** *f* Damascus goat *(breed)*
Damensattel *m* side-saddle
Damentulpe *f* lady tulip, Tulipa clusiana
Damhirsch *m* fallow-stag, fallow buck
~ **im dritten Jahr** sorel
Daminozid *n* daminozide, succinic acid-2,2-dimethylhydrazide, SADH *(growth inhibitor)*
Damkalb *n* young [fallow] deer
Damkuhhaut *f* doeskin
Damkuhleder *n* doeskin
Damm *m* 1. ridge *(e.g. in potato growing)*; bank, embankment; 2. *s.* Deich; 3. perineum *(animal anatomy)*
Dammar *n s.* Dammarharz
Dammarabaum *m* amboyna pine, [amboyna] pitch tree, Agathis dammara (alba)

Dammaraholz

Dammaraholz n amboyna *(from Agathis dammara)*
Dammaratanne f *s.* Dammarabaum
Dammarharz n dammar [resin], damar *(esp. from Agathis spp. and Shorea spp.)*
~/Schwarzes black da[m]mar *(esp. from Balanocarpus penangianus)*
Dammaufnahme f ridge lifting
Dammdrillmaschine f ridge drill
Dammdruckwalze f ridge roller
dämmerungsaktiv *(zoo)* crepuscular
Dämmerungssehen n scotopic vision
Dammkultur f ridge culture, ridge growing (system); *(forest)* bedding
Dammpflanzung f ridge planting; *(forest)* bedding
Dammpflügen n damming
Dammriß m *(vet)* perineal tear
Dammsaat f ridge drilling (sowing)
Dammstriegel m ridge weeder, saddle-back harrow
Damozid n damozide *(growth regulator)*
Dampf m steam, vapour
~/belüfteter aerated steam *(for soil disinfection)*
Dämpfanlage f steaming plant
Dämpfapparat m steamer
dampfbehandeln to steam
Dampfbehandlung f steaming [treatment]
Dampfbiegeverfahren n steam bending *(e.g. of wood)*
Dampfbleiche f steam blanching
Dampfdarre f steam-operated kiln
Dampfdecke f steam washing *(sugar manufacture)*
Dampfdesinfektion f steam disinfection
Dampfdestillation f steam distillation
Dampfdiffusion f vapour diffusion
Dampfdruck m vapour pressure
Dampfdrucksterilisator m [steam] autoclave
Dämpfegge f steaming grid
dämpfen 1. to steam; to coddle; 2. *(vet)* to sedate
dämpfend *(vet)* sedative
Dämpfer m steamer
Dampferzeuger m steam generator
Dampfextrakt m steam extract
Dämpfglocke f steaming cover
Dampfheizung f steam heating
dämpfig *(vet)* broken-winded
Dämpfigkeit f *(vet)* broken wind, heave[s]
Dampfkessel m [steam] boiler
Dampfkesselhaus n boiler house
Dämpfkolonne f steamer column
Dampfmaschine f steam engine
Dampfphasenoxidation f vapour phase oxidation
Dampfpflugaggregat n steam ploughing set
Dampfschälen n steam peeling
Dampfspannung f vapour pressure
Dampfsterilisation f steam sterilization
Dampfsterilisationsapparat m autoclave
Dampfsterilisator m *s.* Dampfdrucksterilisator
dampfsterilisieren to steam-sterilize
Dämpfung f *(vet)* sedation

Dampfzugmaschine f steam tractor (traction engine)
Damschaufler m fallow stag (buck)
Damtier n doe
Damwild n fallow deer, Cervus dama dama, Dama dama
Dandie Dinmont Terrier m Dandie Dinmont [terrier] *(dog breed)*
Dänische Dogge f Great Dane *(dog breed)*
~ Landrasse f Danish landrace *(pig breed)*
Dänisches Blaubuntes Rind n Danish blue white cattle *(breed)*
Darcy-Fluß m Darcian flow *(of soil water)*
Darcy-Gleichung f Darcy's law *(of soil water movement)*
Darm m gut, intestine[s], bowel[s]
Darmbeinarterie f iliac artery
~/gemeinsame common iliac artery
~/innere hypogastric artery
darmbewohnend gut-dwelling
Darmblatt n entoderm, endoderm, hypoblast
Darmbruch m *(vet)* enterocele
Darm[eigen]drüsen fpl intestinal glands
Darmeinklemmung f *(vet)* intestinal incarceration
Darmeinlauf m *(vet)* enema
Darmentzündung f *(vet)* enteritis
~ der Puten/parasitäre hexamitiasis
~/geschwürige necrotic enteritis
Darmepithelzelle f enterocyte
Darmerkrankung f intestinal disease, enteropathy
• **Darmerkrankungen hervorrufend** enteropathogenic
Darmfett n intestinal fat; *(slaught)* channel fat
Darmflora f intestinal flora
Darmflüssigkeit f intestinal fluid
Darmgärung f intestinal fermentation
Darmgas n intestinal gas
Darmkatarrh m *(vet)* enteritis
Darmlänge f intestine length
Darmligaturtechnik f intestinal loop ligation technique *(for detection of the enterotoxin-forming capacity of Escherichia-coli-strains)*
Darmmikroflora f gut microflora
Darmmotilität f gut motility
Darmmotorik f intestine motility
Darmnarkose f *(vet)* rectal anaesthesia
Darmparasit m intestinal parasite
Darmpassage f intestinal passage
Darmpech n foetal dung, meconium
Darmpeptidase f intestinal peptidase *(enzyme)*
Darmresektion f *(vet)* intestine resection
Darmresorption f intestinal absorption *(e.g. of nutrients)*
Darmsaft m intestinal juice
Darmschleife f intestinal loop
Darmschleimhaut f intestinal mucosa, intestine epithelium
Darmsekret n intestinal juice

Darmseuche f *(api, vet)* nosema disease *(caused by Nosema apis)*
Darmstein m *(vet)* enterolith
Darmstreptokokkus m enterococcus
Darmtätigkeit f bowel activity
Darmverschlingung f *(vet)* volvulus
Darmverschluß m *(vet)* gut closure, ileus
Darmwand[ung] f intestinal (gut) wall
Darmwind m flatus
Darmzotte f [intestinal] villus
Darrdichte f oven-dry density *(of wood)*
Darre f 1. [seasoning, dry] kiln, [platform] dryer, drying chamber; oast, floor, crib; malt kiln; 2. *(vet)* bush sickness *(due to cobalt deficiency)*
darren to kiln, to desiccate, to cure
Darren n kilning, kiln-drying
Darrführung f kilning conditions
Darrhaus n oast-house
Darrhorde f [kiln] floor
Darrmalz n kilned (cured, dried) malt
Darrowsche Infusionslösung f *(vet)* Darrow's solution
Darrtemperatur f kilning temperature
darrtrocken oven-dry, oven-dried
Darrzeit f kilning time
Dartmoor n s. Dartmoorschaf
Dartmoorpony n Dartmoor pony *(breed)*
Dartmoorschaf n Dartmoor *(sheep breed)*
Darwinismus m Darwinism, Darwinian evolution (theory)
Darwins Berberitze f Darwin barberry, Berberis darwinii
Dasselbeule f *(vet)* warble
Dasselfliege f bot[t]-fly, warble fly *(family Oestridae)*
Dassellarve f warble [maggot], bot
Dassellarvenbefall m warble infestation
Datenerfassung f data acquisition
Dattel f date *(fruit)*
Dattelmotte f dried fig moth, chocolate (almond) moth, Ephestia (Cadra) cautella
Dattelpalme f date[-palm], Phoenix dactylifera
Dattelpflaume f 1. persimmon *(genus Diospyros)*; 2. date-plum, Diospyros lotus; 3. persimmon *(fruit)*
Daube f stave
Dauerausscheider m *(vet)* chronic carrier
Dauerbelag m permanent residue *(of plant protectants)*
Dauerbeobachtungsfläche f quadrat *(plant ecology)*
Dauerbeweidung f continuous grazing
Dauerbrunst f continuous (constant) oestrus, nymphomania
Dauerbutter f canned butter
Dauerdüngungsversuch m long-term fertilizer trial
Dauereckzahn m permanent corner incisor (tooth)
Dauererektion f *(vet)* priapism
Dauererhitzung f s. Dauerpasteurisation
Dauerfläche f s. Dauerbeobachtungsfläche
Dauerfrostboden m permafrost soil, ever frozen soil, pergelisol
Dauerfruchtfolgeversuch m permanent rotation experiment
Dauergärtank m continuous fermentation tank
Dauergesellschaft f perpetuating community, permanent association *(plant ecology)*
Dauergrasland n, **Dauergrünland** n permanent grass[land]
dauerhaft lasting *(s. a. haltbar)*
Dauerhumus m stable humus
Dauerinfusion f *(vet)* drop infusion
Dauerkatheter m *(vet)* indwelling catheter
Dauerkultur f 1. permanent crop (culture); 2. s. Dauerkulturwirtschaft
Dauerkulturwirtschaft f continuous (perennial) cropping
Dauerlagerfähigkeit f long-time keeping quality
Dauerlagertemperatur f holding (keeping) temperature
Dauerlagerung f long-term storage
Dauerleistung f continuous output *(e.g. of a tractor)*
Dauermilcherzeugnis n preserved milk product
Dauermodifikation f *(gen)* persistent modification, dauermodification
Dauermyzel n sclerotium
Dauerpasteurisation f *(dairy)* holder (holding) pasteurization
Dauerpflügeversuch m continuous ploughing test *(for testing tractors)*
Dauerregen m lasting rain
Dauerrosse f continuous (constant) oestrus, nymphomania *(of a mare)*
Dauerschneidezahn m permanent incisor
Dauersporangium n resting sporangium
Dauerspore f resting spore, hypnospore
Dauertropfinfusion f *(vet)* drop infusion
Dauertrübung f permanent haze *(of beer)*
Dauerversuchsfläche f permanent study area, permanent sample plot; *(forest)* tree increment plot, growth plot
Dauerwald m continuous (permanent, perpetual) forest, dauerwald
Dauerwaldwirtschaft f continuous forestry
Dauerweide f permanent pasture
Dauerwiese f permanent meadow
Dauerwirkung f persistence, persistency
Dauerwirt m stationary host *(parasitology)*
Dauerzahn m adult (permanent) tooth
Dauerzaun m permanent fence
Daune[n]feder f down [feather], pile
Daunomycin n daunomycin *(antibiotic)*
Davallie f ball fern, Davallia bullata
Davidmarille f David peach, Prunus davidiana
Dazomet n dazomet *(nematicide, fungicide, herbicide)*
2,4-DB 2,4-DB *(herbicide)*

DBC nemagon *(nematicide)*
DBCP DBCP, dibromochloropropane *(nematicide)*
DCS DCS *(nitrification inhibitor)*
DCU DCU, dichloralurea *(herbicide)*
DD DD *(nematicide made of dichloropropene and dichloropropane)*
DDD DDD *(insecticide)*
DdS-Extraktionsanlage f DdS-slope diffusion apparatus *(sugar manufacture)*
DDT DDT, dichlorodiphenyltrichloroethane *(insecticide, rodenticide)*
Deakklimation f deacclimation, dehardening *(plant physiology)*
Decafentin n decafentin *(fungicide)*
Decansäure f decanoic (capric) acid *(fatty acid)*
Decarboxylase f decarboxylase *(enzyme)*
Dechsel f adze, *(Am)* adz; cupping axe *(resin-tapping)*
Dechsellachte f resin channel *(resin-tapping)*
dechseln to adze
Deckablauf m [high-]wash syrup *(sugar manufacture)*
Deckakt m mating (covering) act, act of breeding (service), service, coitus, copulation, covering procedure
~ **beim Rind** bulling
~/**natürlicher** natural service
Deckbereitschaft f willingness (keenness) to serve
Deckblatt n *(bot)* bract, wrapper leaf
Deckblattabak m **für Zigarren** cigar wrapper tobacco
Deckbrettchen n *(api)* crown board
Deckbulle f bull for natural service
Decke f 1. *(bot, zoo)* involucre, tapetum; *(zoo)* tegmentum; skin *(of hoofed game)*; 2. blanket
Deckeber m service (breeding) boar
Deckel m 1. lid; 2. *(bot, zoo)* operculum
Deckelkapsel f *(bot)* pyxidium, pyxis
decken to cover, to serve, to impregnate, to breed, to stock *(a breeding animal)*; to bull *(a cow)*; to tup *(a sheep)*; to line *(a bitch)*
~/**erneut** to rebreed
Decken n covering, serving, breeding; tupping
• **zum ~ bringen** to put to *(breeding animal)*
~/**erneutes** rebreeding
deckenartig *(bot, zoo)* testaceous
Deckengebläse n s. Deckenlüfter
Deckenluftbeheizung f s. Deckenluftheizung
Deckenlüfter m ceiling fan *(e.g. in greenhouses)*
Deckenluftheizung f overhead radiation heating [system] *(e.g. in greenhouses)*
Deckenschnitt m blanket clip *(of horses)*
Deckerde f casing soil *(e.g. over cultivated mushrooms)*
deckfähig serviceable, impregnable
Deckfähigkeit f serviceability, covering capacity, mating ability
Deckfarbe f overcolour
Deckfeder f quill[-feather], contour feather

Deckflügel m *(ent)* wing case (sheath), elytron, elytrum, shard
~/**verdickter** tegmen *(of Orthopteroidea)*
Deckfrucht f cover (nurse, companion) crop
~/**reifende** companion crop
Deckfruchtabtötung f cover crop killing
Deckgebühr f service fee
Deckglas n cover slip (glass) *(microscopy)*
Deckglaspräparat n cover slip preparation
Deckhaar n cover (guard, top) hair
Deckhaut f *(zoo)* integument, tegmen
Deckhengst m [covering] stallion, stud[-horse]
Deckkondition f breeding condition
Deckmaterial n covering material
Deckpflanze f nurse [plant]
Deckphantom n [service] dummy, phantom *(for semen collection)*
Deckplatz m covering site
~/**überdachter** covering shed
Deckreflex m copulatory (mating) reflex
Decksaison f covering (breeding) season; tupping time *(of sheep)*
Decksamer m *(bot)* angiosperm *(division Angiospermae)*
Deckschicht f casing layer; soil mantle; seal *(road construction)*
Deckschutt m *(soil)* covering detritus
Deckspelze f *(bot)* lemma, inner pale
Deckstand m service pen (crate), mating box
~/**überdachter** covering shed
Deckstation f, **Deckstelle** f service (mating) station
Decktaxe f service fee
Decktermin m mating date
Deckung f 1. coverage *(e.g. attained in crop spraying)*; 2. [hiding] cover *(of game)*
Deckungsgrad m degree of coverage; dominance *(phytosociology)*
deckungsreich well-covered *(hunting-ground)*
Deckungsschutz m shelter *(for game)*
Deckverhalten n mating behaviour
Deckvermögen n covering capacity
Deckvorgang m s. Deckakt
Deckwein m blend wine
Deckzeit f covering (breeding) season
Dedifferenzierung f dedifferentiation *(of cells)*
Deerhound m deer-hound *(dog breed)*
DEET DEET, diethyltoluamid *(repellent)*
Defäkation f 1. defecation; 2. defecation, liming *(sugar manufacture)*
defäkieren to def[a]ecate, to dung
Defekt m/**genetischer** genetic defect
Defensive f defence, defensive *(animal behaviour)*
defibrieren to defiberize
Defibrillation f *(vet)* defibrillation
Defibrillator m *(vet)* defibrillator
Defibrinierung f defibrination *(of fresh blood)*
Definitivwirt m *(phyt, vet)* definitive (final) host
Deflation f *(soil)* deflation, wind erosion
Deflationskessel m blow-out *(in loose soil)*

Deflationsrückstand *m* desert pavement
Defolians *n*, **Defoliant** *n* defoliant, defoliator
Defoliation *f* defoliation
~/künstliche artificial defoliation
Defoliationsmittel *n* defoliant, defoliator
defoliieren to defoliate
Deformation *f* deformation
Deformationsmosaikvirus *n* **der Aprikose** apricot deformation mosaic virus
deformieren to deform, to distort
Deformität *f* deformity, deformation
Degeneration *f* degeneration
~/fettige *(vet)* fatty degeneration
~/hepatolentikuläre *(vet)* hepatolenticular degeneration, Wilson's disease
~/hyaline *(vet)* hyaline degeneration
~/Zenkersche *(vet)* Zenker's degeneration [of muscles]
Degenerationsvirus *n* **der Narzisse** narcissus degeneration virus
degenerativ degenerative
degenerieren to degenerate
Deglutition *f* deglutition, swallowing
Degorgieren *n* digorging process *(of sparkling wine)*
degradieren to degrade
Degradierung *f* degradation
degummieren to degum; to discharge *(raw silk)*
Degustation *f* degustation
degustieren to degust
Degustator *m* taster
Degustatorengruppe *f* taste panel
Dehiszenz *f (bot, vet)* dehiscence
dehnen to strain; to dilate
Dehnsonde *f (vet)* bougie
Dehnung *f* strain; dilatation
Dehnungsmeßgerät *n* extensometer
Dehydrase *f* dehydrogenase *(enzyme)*
Dehydratation *f s.* Dehydratisierung
dehydratisieren to dehydrate, to desiccate, to dry
Dehydratisierung *f* dehydration, desiccation, drying
Dehydroascorbinsäure *f* dehydroascorbic acid
Dehydrobilirubin *n* biliverdin *(bile pigment)*
7-Dehydrocholesterol *n* 7-dehydrocholesterol
Dehydrocholsäure *f* dehydrocholic acid
Dehydrocortisol *n* prednisolone *(antiphlogistic agent)*
Dehydroepiandrosteron *n* dehydroepiandrosterone *(sex hormone)*
Dehydroessigsäure *f* dehydroacetic acid
Dehydrogenase *f* dehydrogenase *(enzyme)*
Dehydrotestosteron *n* dehydrotestosterone
Deich *m* dike, dyke
Deichschleuse *f* bank sluice
Deichsel *f* 1. shaft, pole; 2. *s.* Dechsel
Deichselarbeit *f* shaft work *(horse keeping)*
Deichselholz *n* shaftwood

Deichselkette *f* pole chain
Deichselpferd *n* shaft (pole) horse
Deichselstütze *f* screwjack
~/zurückklappbare self-storing jack stand
Deichselstützfuß *m* [mit Hubspindel] jack stand
Deichsystem *n* dike system
Deiquat *n* deiquat, diquat dibromide *(herbicide)*
Dejarowisation *f* devernalization
Dekalzifikation *f* decalcification
Dekante[u]r *m* decanter *(sugar manufacture)*
Dekapitation *f* decapitation
dekap[i]tieren to decapitate
Dekkanhanf *m* 1. ambary, wild stockrose, Hibiscus cannabinus; 2. ambary, kenaf *(fibre from 1.)*
Dekokt *n* decoction, decoctum
Dekoktionsverfahren *n* decoction [mashing] method *(brewing)*
dekolorieren to decolo[u]rize
Dekomposition *f* decomposition
Dekontamination *f* decontamination
dekontaminieren to decontaminate
Dekortikation *f* decortication
Dekortikator *m* decorticator
Dekubitus *m (vet)* bedsore
Dekubituswunde *f (vet)* bedsore
Dekupiersäge *f* fretsaw
dekussiert *(bot, zoo)* decussate
Delachlor *n* delachlor *(herbicide)*
Delavays Incarvillea *f* Chinese trumpet-flower, Incarvillea delavayi
Deletion *f (gen)* deletion
Delignifikation *f* delignification
delignifizieren to delignify
Delnav *n* dioxathion *(insecticide, acaricide)*
Delphinidin *n* delphinidin *(anthocyanidin)*
Delphinium-Belladonna-Hybride *f (bot)* bell delphinium
Delphinium-Hybride *f (bot)* delphinium
Delta *n* delta, deltaic area
deltaförmig *(bot, zoo)* deltoid
Deltamethrin *n* deltamethrin, decamethrin *(insecticide)*
demarkieren to demarcate *(e.g. a field or forest plot)*
Demarkierung *f* demarcation
Demeton *n* demeton, mercaptophos *(insecticide)*
Demeton-S-methyl *n* demeton-S-methyl, *(Am)* methyl-demeton *(insecticide, acaricide)*
Demethon-S-methylsulfon *n* demeton-S-methylsulphone *(acaricide, insecticide)*
Demijohn *m* demijohn
Demineralisation *f* demineralization
demineralisieren to demineralize
Demodikose *f (vet)* demodectic mange
Demökologie *f* demecology, population ecology
Demonstrationsbeute *f (api)* demonstration hive
Demyelinisation *f (vet)* demyelination
denaturieren to denaturate
Denaturierung *f* denaturation

Denaturierungsmittel

Denaturierungsmittel *n* denaturant
Dendrarium *n* arboretum, tree-garden
dendrisch *s.* dendritisch
Dendrit *m* dendrite, dendron
dendritisch dendritic
Dendrobie *f (bot)* dendrobium *(genus Dendrobium)*
Dendrochronologie *f* dendrochronology
dendrochronologisch dendrochronological
Dendrograph *m* dendrograph
Dendroklimatologie *f* dendroclimatology
dendroklimatologisch dendroclimatological
Dendrolith *m* dendrolite
Dendrologe *m* dendrologist
Dendrologie *f* dendrology
dendrologisch dendrological
Dendromasse *f* dendromass
~/**nutzbare** crop
Dendrometer *n* dendrometer
Dendrometrie *f* dendrometry, forest mensuration
Dendroökologie *f* dendroecology
dendrophil dendrophilous
Denervierung *f (vet)* denervation
Dengelbank *f* scythe-sharpening bench
Dengelhammer *m* scythe hammer
dengeln to sharpen by hammering
Denitrifikant *m* denitrifying bacterium
Denitrifikation *f* denitrification
denitrifizieren to denitrify
Denitrifizierung *f* denitrification
Densimeter *n* densimeter, densitometer; pycnometer
Densimetrie *f* densimetry, densitometry
Densität *f* density
Densitometrie *f s.* Densimetrie
dental dental
Dentin *n* dentine
Dentition *f* dentition, tooth eruption, teething
Denudation *f (soil)* denudation, sheet erosion
Denudationsfläche *f* peneplain, peneplane
denudieren *(soil)* to denude, to denudate
Deodorant *n* deodorant
Depigmentierung *f* depigmentation
Depletion *f* depletion
Deponie *f* tip, tipping site, *(Am)* landfill
~/**geordnete** controlled tip[ping site], *(Am)* sanitary landfill
Deposition *f* deposition
Depotdünger *m* depot (slow-acting) fertilizer, controlled-release fertilizer, CRF
Depotfett *n* depot fat
Depravation *f* deprivation
Depression *f* depression; cyclone *(meteorology)*
Depressionsfraktur *f (vet)* depressed fracture
Depressionsimmunität *f* depression immunity
Derbholz *n* compact wood, large timber
Derbholzformzahl *f* timber form factor
Derbholzformzahltafel *f* merchantable form factor table
Derbholzvolumen *n* volume of large timber

Derbholzvolumentafel *f* merchantable volume table
Derbstange *f* [thick] pole, small roundwood
Derby *n* Derby *(equitation)*
dermal dermal
Dermatitis *f (vet)* dermatitis
~ **des Fußpolsters** footpad dermatitis, bumble foot
~ **pustulosa** contagious pustular dermatitis, CPD, sore mouth, orf *(of sheep and goats, caused by Latens paravacciniae)*
~ **solaris** solar eczema
Dermatogen *n (bot)* dermatogen, protoderm, mantle
Dermatomykose *f (vet)* dermatomycosis, mycodermatitis
Dermatophilose *f* **der Schafe** lumpy wool [of sheep] *(caused by Dermatophilus congolensis)*
Dermatophyt *m* dermatophyte
Dermatose *f (vet)* dermatosis, skin-disease
Dermatosparaxie *f (vet)* Danlos syndrome
Dermis *f* dermis, corium, [true] skin
Dermomykose *f s.* Dermatomykose
Dernopodsol[boden] *m* dernopodzolic soil
Derrickkran *m* stiff-leg [derrick], *(Am)* jill poke (pole)
Derris *f (bot)* derris *(genus Derris)*
Derrisinsektizid *n* derris
Derrispräparat *n* derris
Derriswurzel *f* derris [root], tuba root, Derris elliptica
Desaminase *f* deaminase *(enzyme)*
desaminieren to deaminate
Desaminierung *f* deamination
Descemetozele *f (vet)* keratocele, herniation of Descemet's membrane
Descemetsche Membran *f* Descemet's membrane *(animal anatomy)*
Desertifikation *f* desertification
Desikkans *n*, **Desikkant** *n* desiccant
Desikkation *f* desiccation
Desilifizierung *f (soil)* ferrallitization, laterization
Desinfektant *n s.* Desinfektionsmittel
Desinfektion *f* disinfection
Desinfektionsbad *n* **für Schafe** sheep-dip[per], sheep-wash
Desinfektionsmittel *n* disinfectant, disinfecting agent
Desinfektionswanne *f* [disinfectant] foot-bath
~ **für Fahrzeuge** drive-through sanitizing bath
Desinfektor *m* disinfector
Desinfestant *n* disinfestant
Desinfestation *f* disinfestation
Desinfiziens *n s.* Desinfektionsmittel
desinfizieren to disinfect
desinfizierend disinfectant
Desinsektion *f* insect control
Desmedipham *n* desmedipham *(herbicide)*
Desmetryn *n* desmetryne *(herbicide)*
Desmitis *f (vet)* desmitis

Desodorans *n* deodorant
Desodorierung *f* deodorizing
desorbieren to desorb
Desorption *f* desorption
Desoxycholsäure *f* deoxycholic (glycodehydroxycholic) acid
Desoxycorton *n* deoxycorticosterone, DOCA *(hormone)*
2-Desoxy-*(D)*-erythro-pentose *f* deoxyribose *(monosaccharide)*
6-Desoxygalactose *f* fucose
6-Desoxy-*(L)*-mannose *f* rhamnose *(monosaccharide)*
Desoxynorephedrin *n* amphetamine *(analeptic)*
Desoxyribonuclease *f* I deoxyribonuclease I, DNase *(enzyme)*
Desoxyribonucleinsäure *f* deoxyribonucleic acid, *(Am)* desoxyribonucleic acid, DNA
Desoxyribonucleinsäure... *s.* DNA-...
Desoxyribonucleotid *n* deoxyribonucleotide
2-Desoxyribose *f* deoxyribose *(monosaccharide)*
Desoxyribotid *n* deoxyribonucleotide
Desquamation *f* *(soil, vet)* desquamation
desquamativ desquamative
Dessertbanane *f* banana
Dessertwassermelone *f* water-melon, Citrullus lanatus var. caffer
Dessertwein *m* dessert (sweet) wine
Destillans *n* distilland
Destillat *n* distillate
Destillation *f* distillation
Destillationsgut *n* distilland
Destillationsholz *n* distillation (chemical, acid) wood
Destillationsnebenprodukt *n* distillery by-product
Destillationsprodukt *n* distillate
destillieren to distil
Destillieren *n* distillation
Destruent *m* *(ecol)* reducer
Destruktion *f* destruction
Destruktionsfäule *f* red (brown) rot, red heart, crumbling *(esp. of pine and spruce, caused by Fomes spp.)*
Desulfurikation *f* desulphurication *(plant physiology)*
Desynapsis *f* desynapsis *(meiosis)*
Deszendent *m* descendant
Deszendenztheorie *f* theory of descent, theory of the origin of species
deszendieren to descend [from]
Detailpunkt *m* detail point *(photogrammetry)*
Detergens *n* detergent, cleansing agent; soap
~/saures acid detergent
Detergent *m* detergent
Determination *f* determination
Determinationszone *f* cell enlargement area *(in shoot tips or root tips)*
Deterrent *n* deterrent *(against animal pests)*
Detomidin *n* detomidine *(analgesic, sedative agent)*

Detoxi[fi]kation *f* detoxification
Detraktion *f* *(soil)* detraction
detritivor detritivorous, detritophagous, saprophagous, saprovorous
Detritivore *m* detritivore, detritus feeder
detritophag *s.* detritivor
Detritus *m* detritus, debris
detritusfressend *s.* detritivor
Detritusfresser *m* *s.* Detritivore
Deuterogamie *f* deuterogamy
Deuteromyzet *m* imperfect fungus *(group Deuteromycetes or Fungi imperfecti)*
Deutonymphe *f* deutonymph *(developmental stage of a mite)*
Deutsch Drahthaar *n(m)* German wire-haired pointer *(dog breed)*
~ Kurzhaar *n* German short-haired pointer *(dog breed)*
Deutsche Bunte Edelziege *f* German Improved Fawn, Fawn German Improved *(goat breed)*
~ Dogge *f* Great Dane, dane *(dog breed)*
~ Galle *f* *(phyt)* marble gall *(caused by Cynips kollari)*
~ Iris *f* bearded (German, flag) iris, Iris germanica
~ Kichererbse *f* chickling [pea, vetch], chick-pea, grass pea [vine], Lathyrus sativus
~ Landrasse *f* German landrace *(pig breed)*
~ Narde *f* true lavender, Lavandula angustifolia
~ Schabe *f* German cockroach, Croton bug, Blatella germanica
~ Schwertlilie *f* *s.~* Iris
~ Tamariske *f* German tamarisk, Myricaria germanica
~ Weiße Edelziege *f* German Improved White, White German Improved *(goat breed)*
Deutscher Blasenstrauch *m* common bladder senna, Colutea arborescens
~ Boxer *m* boxer *(dog breed)*
~ Bradsot *m* *(vet)* black disease
~ Ginster *m* German broom, Genista germanica
~ Kurzhaariger Vorstehhund *m* *s.* Deutsch Kurzhaar
~ Pudel *m* poodle *(dog breed)*
~ Schäferhund *m* German shepherd [dog], Alsatian [dog] *(breed)*
~ Spitz *m* Pomeranian [dog], pom *(breed)*
~ Straußfarn *m* ostrich fern, Matteuccia struthiopteris
Deutsches Braunvieh *n* German Brown *(cattle breed)*
~ Edelschwein *n* German (White) Edelschwein, German White Prick-eared, German Short-eared *(pig breed)*
~ Fleckvieh *n* German Simment[h]al, Red Spotted Highland *(cattle breed)*
~ Gelbvieh *n* German Yellow *(cattle breed)*
~ Rotbuntes Rind *n* German Red Pied, Red Pied Lowland *(cattle breed)*

Deutsches

~ **Rotvieh** *n* [Middle] German Red, Red Hill *(cattle breed)*
~ **Sattelschwein** *n* German Saddleback *(pig breed)*
~ **Schwarzbuntes Rind** *n* German Black Pied, Black Pied Lowland, Black Spotted Cattle *(breed)*
~ **Veredeltes Landschwein** *n* German Improved Landschwein, German White Lop-eared, German Long-eared *(pig breed)*
~ **Weidelgras** *n* [perennial, common] rye-grass, red darnel, Lolium perenne
~ **Weideschwein** *n* German Pasture, Hanover-Brunswick, Hildesheim *(pig breed)*
Deutzie *f (bot)* deutzia *(genus Deutzia)*
Devastation *f* devastation
Devernalisation *f* devernalization
Devitalisation *f (vet)* devitalization
Devon *n* [North] Devon, Red Devon cattle, Red Ruby *(breed)*
devorieren to devour, to eat greedily (ravenously)
Dexamethason *n* dexamethasone *(glucocorticoid)*
Dexon *n* dexon *(fungicide)*
Dexterrind *n* dexter [cattle] *(breed)*
Dextran *n* dextran *(polysaccharide)*
Dextranase *f* dextranase *(enzyme)*
Dextrin *n* dextrin[e], starch gum *(polysaccharide)*
• **in ~ umwandeln** to dextrinize
Dextrose *f* dextrose, (D)-glucose, grape-sugar
Dextroseagar *m* dextrose agar
Dextrosepeptonagar *m* Sabouraud's glucose peptone agar
Dezitonne *f* quintal
Df. *s.* Dunkelfuchs
DFD-Fleisch *n* DFD meat *(dark, firm and dry meat from pig and beef)*
DFS *s.* Donnan-Freiraum
DGR *s.* Durchmessergruppe
DGZ *s.* Gesamtzuwachs/durchschnittlicher jährlicher
DHEA *s.* Dehydroepiandrosteron
Diabas *m* diabase *(soil-forming rock)*
diabasisch diabasic
Diabetes *m (vet)* diabetes [mellitus]
~ **insipidus** diabetes insipidus
~ **mellitus** diabetes [mellitus]
Diabetikerbier *n* diabetic beer
Diacetyl *n* diacetyl, butanedione
Diacetylcholin *n* suxamethonium *(muscle relaxant)*
Diachenium *n (bot)* diachenium
Diagnose *f* diagnosis
Diagnosefehler *m* diagnostic mistake
Diagnoseschlüssel *m* diagnostic key
Diagnostik *f* diagnostics
~/**funktionelle** functional diagnostics
diagnostisch diagnostic
diagnostizieren to diagnose
Diagonalreifen *m* diagonal (cross-ply) tyre
Diakinese *f* diakinesis *(stage of meiosis)*

Dialifos *n* dialifos *(insecticide, acaricide)*
Diallat *n* diallate *(herbicide)*
diallel diallel *(breeding)*
Diallelkreuzung *f* diallel cross[ing]
Dialyse *f* dialysis
dialysieren to dialyse
Diamantfuchsin *n* diamond fuchsine *(dye)*
Diamfenetid *n* diamfenetide *(anthelminthic)*
Diamin *n* diamine
Diaminoxidase *f* amine oxidase, copper-containing, histaminase *(enzyme)*
Diammoniumphosphat *n* diammonium phosphate
Dianabol *n* dianabol *(sex hormone)*
Diapause *f (zoo, ent)* diapause, hold-over
Diaphorase *f* dihydrolipoamide dehydrogenase *(enzyme)*
diaphoretisch sudoriferous
Diaphragma *n* diaphragm, midriff *(animal anatomy)*; *(slaught)* skirt
Diaphragmatozele *f (vet)* diaphragmatic hernia
Diaphyse *f* diaphysis *(of a long bone)*
diarch diarch *(root)*
Diarrhöe *f (vet)* diarrhoea, scour[s], loose bowels
Diarrhöevirus *n* [bovine] diarrhoea virus, mucosal disease virus
Diaspor *m* diaspore *(non-clay mineral)*
Diaspore *f (bot)* diaspore
Diasporenausbreitung *f* **durch Säugetiere** mammaliochory
Diastase *f* amylase, diastase *(enzyme)*
Diastasemalz *n* diastatic malt
diastasereich high-diastase
diastatisch diastatic, diastasic
Diastole *f* diastole
diastolisch diastolic
Diät *f* diet
Diätbier *n* dietetic beer
Diätetik *f* dietetics
Diätetikum *n* dietetic
diätetisch dietetic[al]
Diätfuttermittel *n* dietetic
Diätfütterung *f* dieting
Diathermie *f (vet)* diathermy
Diathese *f (vet)* diathesis
~/**exsudative** exudative diathesis
~/**hämorrhagische** haermorrhagic diathesis
Diatomee *f* diatom
Diatomeenerde *f*, **Diatomit** *m* diatomaceous earth, kieselguhr
Diaveridin *n* diaveridine *(coccidiostatic)*
Diazepam *n* diazepam *(tranquilizer)*
1,4-Diazin *n* 1,4-diazine, pyrazine *(hydrocarbon)*
Diazinon *n* diazinon *(insecticide, acaricide, nematicide)*
Dibbeleinrichtung *f* dibbling device
Dibbelklappe *f* seed valve
Dibbelmaschine *f* dibbling machine
dibbeln to dibble
Dibbeln *n* dibbling

Dibbelsaat f dibbling
Dibbelvorrichtung f dibbling device
Dibenzo[b,e]pyridin n acridine
1,2-Dibromethan n ethylene dibromide *(insecticide, nematicide)*
Dibutylzinndilaurat n dibutyltin dilaurate *(anthelminthic)*
Dicalciumphosphat n dicalcium phosphate
Dicamba n dicamba *(herbicide, growth regulator)*
Dicarbonsäure f dicarboxylic acid
Dichasium n *(bot)* dichasium
Dichlofenthion n dichlofenthion *(insecticide, nematicide)*
Dichlofluanid n dichlofluanid *(fungicide)*
Dichlone n dichlone *(fungicide, herbicide)*
Dichloralharnstoff m s. Dichlorharnstoff
Dichloran n dic[h]loran, DCNA *(fungicide)*
Dichlordiphenyltrichlorethan n dichlorodiphenyltrichloroethane, DDT *(insecticide, rodenticide)*
Dichloressigsäure f, **Dichlorethansäure** f dichloroacetic (dichloroethanoic) acid
Dichlorflurenol n dichlorflurenol *(herbicide, growth regulator)*
Dichlorharnstoff m dichloralurea, DCU *(herbicide)*
Dichlormethan n dichloromethan, methylene dichloride
Dichlorophen n dichlorophen *(anthelminthic)*
4-(2',4'-Dichlorphenoxybuttersäure f 4-(2',4'-dichlorophenoxy)butyric acid, 2,4-DB *(herbicide)*
2,4-Dichlorphenoxyessigsäure f 2,4-dichlorophenoxyacetic acid, 2,4-D *(herbicide)*
Dichlorphos n dichlorvos, DDVP *(insecticide, acaricide, anthelminthic)*
Dichlorprop n dichlorprop, 2,4-DP *(herbicide, growth regulator)*
Dichlorvos n s. Dichlorphos
Dichlozolin n dichlozoline *(fungicide)*
dichogam *(bot)* dichogamic, dichogamous
Dichogamie f *(bot)* dichogamy
dichotom *(bot, zoo)* dichotomous
Dichotomie f *(bot, zoo)* dichotomy
dichotomisch s. dichotom
dicht 1. dense *(e.g. a hedge)*; thick *(e.g. hair coat, moss)*; 2. dense, consistent *(structure)*; fine-grained, compact *(soil)*; 3. tight, impermeable *(e.g. to water, air)*
~ beieinanderliegend appressed, adpressed
dichtbelaubt densely leaved
dichtblättrig pleiophyllous
Dichtblättriges Laichkraut n opposite-leaved pondweed, Groenlandia densa
dichtblütig *(bot)* pycnanthus
Dichtblütige Kiefer f Japanese red pine, Pinus densiflora
Dichte f 1. density; 2. denseness; compactness
~/scheinbare apparent density
Dichtebestimmung f density determination
Dichtefunktion f probability density
Dichtegrad m consistency, consistence

Dichtegradientenzentrifugation f density gradient centrifugation
Dichtemesser m densimeter; pycnometer; areometer
Dichtemessung f densimetry
Dichternarzisse f [poet's] narcissus, Narcissus poeticus
dichtfilzig *(bot)* pannose
dichtfrüchtig *(bot)* pycnocarpous
Dichtpflanzung f high-density planting, HDP, compact planting
Dichtsaat f dense sowing
dichtstielig *(bot)* pachypod
dick 1. thick; 2. curdy *(milk)*; 3. heavy *(wine)*
• **~ werden** to curdle *(milk)*
dickbäuchig *(bot, zoo)* ventricose
Dickbeinkrankheit f **der Hühner** avian osteopetrosis, Paget's (thick leg) disease of fowl
Dickblatt n jade plant, thickleaf, crassula *(genus Crassula)*
Dickblattgewächs n *(bot)* succulent
dickblättrig thick-leaved
Dickdarm m large gut (intestine)
Dickdarmentzündung f *(vet)* colitis
~/ulzerative (ulzeröse) ulcerative colitis
Dickdarmfistel f *(vet)* colostomy • **eine ~ anlegen** to colostomize
Dickdarmflora f faecal flora
Dicke Bohne f 1. broad bean, fava [bean], Vicia faba var. major; 2. s. Ackerbohne
Dickenklasse f diameter class *(forest mensuration)*
Dickensortierer m thickness grader
Dickenwachstum n growth in thickness, thickening; radial growth, diameter growth *(of trees)*
~/primäres primary thickening
~/sekundäres secondary thickening
Dickenzuwachs m *(forest)* diameter increment (accretion) *(s. a. Dickenwachstum)*
Dickete f curdled milk, coagulum, coagulate
dickflüssig semiliquid, viscous, thick
Dickgülle f dewatered sludge, thick slurry
Dickhals n bottle-neck *(malformation of onions)*
Dickhornschaf n bighorn, Rocky Mountain sheep, Ovis canadensis
Dickicht n thick[s]et, brush[wood], boscage, boskage, brake, shaw • **in ein ~ verwandeln** to coppice
Dickit m dickite *(clay mineral)*
dicklegen *(dairy)* to curdle
Dicklegungsvermögen n coagulability *(of milk)*
Dickmaische f set mash *(brewing)*
Dickmaulrüßler m vine weevil *(genus Otiorhynchus)*
Dickmilch f fermented (sour) milk, junket
dickörtig butt end first *(logging)*
Dickrahm m clotted (Devonshire) cream
Dickrübe f fodder (feeding) beet, Beta vulgaris var. alba (crassa)

Dicksaft

Dicksaft *m* thick juice, treacle *(sugar manufacture)*
Dicksaftkocher *m* thick juice blowup
dickstämmig thick-stemmed
dickstengelig thick-stalked
Dickstoffpumpe *f* thick liquid pump
Dickung *f (forest)* 1. sapling stand (crop), dense young stand, brake; 2. *s.* Dickicht
Dickungsalter *n*, **Dickungsstadium** *n* 1. sapling stage; 2. thicket[-life] stage
Dickungspflege *f* tending of thicket
Dickwabe *f* deep comb, honeycomb
Dickwerden *n* thickening
Dickwurz *f s.* Dickrübe
Dickzuckerfrüchte *fpl* candied fruits
Diclofop[-methyl] *n* diclofop[-methyl] *(herbicide)*
Dicloxacillin *n*, **Dicloxil** *n* dicloxacillin *(antibiotic)*
Dicofol *n* dicofol, kelthane *(acaricide)*
Dicoumarol *n* dicoumarol, dicoumarin, *(Am)* dicumarol *(natural substance found in sweet clover)*
Dicrotophos *n* dicrotophos *(insecticide)*
didelphys *(zoo)* didelphic
Didymitis *f (vet)* orchitis, inflammation of a testis
Dieffenbachie *f (bot)* dieffenbachia *(genus Dieffenbachia)*
Dieldrin *n* dieldrin, HEOD *(insecticide, acaricide)*
Dielektrizitätskonstante *f* dielectric constant
Dieme *f*, **Diemen** *m* rick, stack
Diemenheu *n* hay-mow
Diemensetzen *n* ricking, stacking
Dienochlor *n* dienochlor *(acaricide)*
Dienstbezirk *m (forest)* beat
Dienzephalon *n* diencephalon, betweenbrain, thalamencephalon
Dieselaggregat *n* diesel-electric generator
Dieselfahrzeug *n* diesel
Dieselgenerator *m s.* Dieselaggregat
Dieselkraftstoff *m* diesel oil
Dieselmotor *m* diesel [engine], compression ignition engine
Dieselöl *n* diesel [oil, fuel]
Dieselschlepper *m*, **Dieseltraktor** *m* diesel tractor
diesig hazy
Diethamquat *n* diethamquat *(herbicide)*
Diethylamin *n* diethylamine
Diethylcarbamazin *n* diethylcarbamazine *(anthelminthic)*
Diethylendiamin *n* piperazine *(anthelminthic)*
Diethylentriaminpentaessigsäure *f* diethylenetriaminepentaacetic acid, DTPA *(chelating agent)*
Diethylether *m* [diethyl] ether
Diethylpyrocarbamat *n* diethyl pyrocarbamate *(fungicide)*
Diethylstilboestrol *n* [diethyl]stilboestrol, DES *(oestrogen)*
Diethylsulfat *n* diethyl sulphate
Diethylsulfid *n* diethyl sulphide
Diethyltoluamid *n* diethyltoluamid, DEET *(repellent)*
Difenacoum *n* difenacoum *(rodenticide)*
Difenoxuron *n* difenoxuron *(herbicide)*
Difenzoquat *n* difenzoquat[-methylsulphate] *(herbicide)*
Differential *n* differential [gear]
Differentialart *f (ecol)* differential (vicarious) species
Differentialblutbild *n* differential white cell count
Differentialdiagnose *f (phyt, vet)* differential diagnosis
Differentialerreger *m (phyt)* pathovar
Differentialfärbung *f* differential staining *(microbiology)*
Differentialimpulspolarographie *f* differential pulse polarography
Differentialnährboden *m* differential medium *(bacteriology)*
Differentialrente *f* differential rent *(agricultural economics)*
Differentialsperre *f* differential lock
Differentialwirt *m* indicator host *(for detection of phytopathogens)*
Differenz f/psychrometrische wet-bulb depression *(meteorology)*
Differenzierung *f* differentiation
Differenzierungsnährboden *m s.* Differentialnährboden
Differenzierungszone *f* cell maturation area *(in a shoot or root)*
Differenzmethode *f* difference method *(animal experimentation)*
Differenzversuch *m* difference trial
diffundieren to diffuse
Diffuseur *m* [beet] diffuser *(sugar manufacture)*
Diffusionsabwasser *n* beet pulp water
Diffusionsbatterie *f* diffusion battery
Diffusionsdruckdefizit *n* diffusion pressure deficit, DPD *(plant physiology)*
Diffusionsfähigkeit *f* **des Bodens** soil diffusivity
Diffusionsflux *m* diffusive flux *(plant physiology)*
Diffusionskoeffizient *m* diffusion coefficient
Diffusionspotential *n* diffusion potential
Diffusionssaft *m* diffusion juice *(sugar manufacture)*
Diffusionsschnitzel *mpl* diffusion cossettes, [wet beet] pulp
Diffusionswiderstand *m* diffusion (diffusive) resistance
Diffusivität *f* diffusivity *(e.g. of a soil)*
~/thermische temperature conductivity
Diflubenzuron *n* diflubenzuron *(insecticide)*
Diformamidindisulfid *n* diformamidindisulphide *(growth regulator)*
Digallussäure *f* digallic acid
digen *(zoo)* digenous
Digenesis *f*, **Digenie** *f* digenesis
digerieren 1. to digest, to cook *(chemically)*; 2. *s.* verdauen
Digest *n* digest
Digestion *f* 1. digestion; 2. *s.* Verdauung

Digestions... s. Verdauungs...
digestiv digestive
Digestor m digester, digestor, digestive vessel
Digilanid n lanatoside *(mixture of glycosides)*
digital *(zoo)* digital; *(zoo, bot)* digitate
Digitalis f digitalis *(drug)*
Digitonin digitonin *(glycoside)*
Digitoxin n, **Digitoxosid** n digitoxin *(glycoside)*
Digitus m digit, finger; toe
Diglycerid n diglyceride
Digoxin n digoxin *(glycoside)*
dihaploid *(gen)* dihaploid
Dihaploide m dihaploid
Dihaploidie f dihaploidy
Dihydroabietinsäure f dihydroabietic acid
Dihydrodiethylstilböstrol n hexoestrol *(synthetic oestrogen)*
Dihydrofolatreductase f, **Dihydrofolsäurereductase** f dihydrofolate reductase, tetrahydrofolate dehydrogenase *(enzyme)*
Dihydrolipoamiddehydrogenase f dihydrolipoamide dehydrogenase, diaphorase *(enzyme)*
Dihydropyrimidinase f dihydropyrimidinase, hydantoinase *(enzyme)*
Dihydroquercetin n taxifolin *(flavanol)*
Dihydrostreptomycin n dihydrostreptomycin *(antibiotic)*
Dihydrotachysterol n dihydrotachysterol
1,2-Dihydroxyanthrachinon n alizarin *(plant dye)*
(m-)Dihydroxybenzen n (m-)dihydroxybenzene, 1,3-benezenediol, resorcin[ol]
2,5-Dihydroxybenzoesäure f dihydroxybenzoic acid, DHBA, gentisic acid
3,4-Dihydroxybenzoesäure f protocatechuic acid
2,3-Dihydroxybutandisäure f tartaric acid
Dihydroxycholecalciferol n dihydroxycholecalciferol
7,4'-Dihydroxyisoflavon n daidzein
3,5-Dihydroxy-3-methylvaleriansäure f mevalonic acid *(metabolite)*
3,4-Dihydroxyphenylalanin n 3,4-dihydroxyphenylalanine, DOPA *(amino-acid)*
2,5-Dihydroxyphenylessigsäure f homogentisic acid
3,5-Dihydroxystilben n pinosylvin
3,4-Dihydroxyzimtsäure f caffeic acid
Dihydrozeatin n dihydrozeatin *(cytokinin)*
Diiodtyrosin n diiodotyrosine
Dikegulac n dikegulac *(growth regulator)*
diklin *(bot)* diclinous
Diklorofen n dichlorophen *(anthelminthic)*
dikotyl *(bot)* dicotyledonous
Dikotyledone f *(bot)* dicotyledon, dicot[yl]
Dikrozöliose f *(vet)* dicrocoeliosis *(caused by Dicrocoelium dendriticum)*
Dikumarin n s. Dicoumarol
Dilatation f dilatation, dilation, expansion
dilatieren to dilate, to expand, to widen

Dill m 1. dill *(genus Anethum)*; 2. dill, Anethum graveolens var. graveolens
Dillessig m dill vinegar
Dillsamen m dill [seed]
diluieren to dilute, to thin
Dilution f dilution, thinning
Diluvialboden m diluvial soil
Diluvium n s. Eiszeit
Dimefox n dimefox *(insecticide)*
Dimefuron n dimefuron *(herbicide)*
Dimension f dimension, size
Dimensionsholz n s. Dimensionsware
Dimensionsplenterung f selection felling (logging)
Dimensionsware f dimension stock (timber)
dimer dimerous
Dimercaprol n, **Dimercaptopropanol** n dimercaprol *(chelating agent, antidote)*
Dimetan n dimetan *(insecticide)*
Dimethachlor n dimethachlor *(herbicide)*
Dimethirimol n dimethirimol *(fungicide)*
Dimethoat n dimethoate *(insecticide, acaricide, nematicide)*
Dimethylamin n dimethylamine
Dimethylarsinsäure f dimethylarsinic (cacodylic) acid *(herbicide)*
Dimethylbenzen n, **Dimethylbenzol** n dimethylbenzene, xylene
Dimethylformamid n dimethylformamide
Dimethylhydrazid n dimethyl hydrazide
6,7-Dimethylisoalloxazin n lumichrome
Dimethylketon n acetone, propanon
Dimethylphosphat n dimethyl phosphate
Dimethylphthalat n dimethylphthalate *(repellent)*
2',2'-Dimethylsuccinohydrazid n s. Daminozid
Dimethylsulfat n dimethyl sulphate
Dimethylsulfid n dimethyl sulphide
Dimethylsulfoxid n dimethyl sulphoxide, DMSO
Dimetilan n dimetilan *(insecticide)*
Dimetridazol n dimetridazole *(antiparasitic agent)*
Dimidazon n dimidazon *(herbicide)*
dimorph *(bot, zoo)* dimorphic
Dimorphismus m dimorphism
Dinex n dinex *(acaricide)*
Dinitolmid n dinitolmide, zoalene *(coccidiostatic)*
Dinitramin n dinitramine *(herbicide)*
4,6-Dinitro-(o)-cresol n dinitro-o-cresol, DNOC *(insecticide, acaricide, herbicide)*
Dinkel m *(bot)* dinkel, spelt, Triticum spelta
Dinobuton n dinobuton *(acaricide, fungicide)*
Dinocap n dinocap *(fungicide, acaricide)*
Dinopenton n dinopenton *(fungicide)*
Dinoterb n dinoterb *(herbicide)*
Dinoterbon n dinoterbon *(fungicide)*
Dinoseb n dinoseb, DNBP *(herbicide)*
Dinosebacetat n dinoseb-acetate *(herbicide)*
Dinosulfon n dinosulfon *(fungicide)*
Dinsed n dinsed *(coccidiostatic)*
Diökie f s. Diözie

Diopter

Diopter *m* [optical] sight, peep sight *(e.g. at a sporting gun)*
Diorit *m* diorite, diabase *(soil-forming rock)*
Dioscorin *n* dioscorine *(alkaloid)*
Diosgenin *n* diosgenin *(sapogenin)*
diöstrisch *(zoo)* dioestrous, interoestrous
Diöstrus *m (zoo)* dioestrum, dioestrus
Dioxacarb *n* dioxacarb *(insecticide)*
Dioxathion *n* dioxathion, delnav *(insecticide, acaricide)*
Dioxin *n* dioxin
2,6-Dioxotetrahydropurin *n* xanthine
4,8-Dioxychinaldinsäure *f* xanthurenic acid
Diözie *f (bot)* dioecism, dioecy
diözisch *(bot)* dioecious, diecious
Dipeptid *n* dipeptide
Dipeptidase *f* dipeptidase *(enzyme)*
Diphacinon *n* diphacinone *(rodenticide)*
Diphenamid *n* diphenamid *(herbicide)*
Diphenyl *n* biphenyl *(fungicide)*
Diphenylethen *n* stilbene *(plant constituent)*
Diplodia-Fruchtfäule *f* **des Kakaobaumes** charcoal rot of cacao-tree *(caused by Botryodiplodia theobromae)*
diploid *(gen)* diploid
Diploidie *f* diploidy
Diploidisierung *f* diploidization
Diplomforstingenieur *m,* **Diplomforstwirt** *m* graduated (certificated) forester
Diplomgärtner *m* horticultural graduate, Bachelor of Science graduated in horticulture
Diplomlandwirt *m* graduate farmer
Diplont *m (gen)* diplont, diploid [organism]
Diplophase *f* diplophase
Diplosporie *f (bot)* diplospory
Diplotän *n* diplotene *(meiosis)*
Diprenorphin *n* diprenorphine *(anaesthetic)*
Dipropetryn *n* dipropetryn *(herbicide)*
Dipsopathie *f* drought injury
Diptam *m* dittany, flame flower *(genus Dictamnus)*
Diptamdost *m* dittany, Origanum dictamnus
Diptere *m* dipteran, two-winged fly *(order Diptera)*
Dipterokarpazeen-Wald *m* dipterocarp forest
Diquat *n* diquat *(herbicide)*
Direktdrillmaschine *f* no-till drill
Direktdrusch *m* direct combining
Direkteinspritzung *f* direct injection *(diesel engine)*
Direktmähdrusch *m* direct combining
Direktsaat *f* direct drilling (seeding, sowing), sod seeding (sowing)
Direktsaatgrubber *m* direct drilling cultivator
Direktsämaschine *f* sod seeder
Direktscherprüfung *f* direct shear testing
Direktstarterkultur *f (dairy)* direct-to-the-fat-starter
Direktstrahlung *f* direct radiation
Direktvermarktung *f* direct marketing
Direktverzehr *m* direct consumption

Dirofilariose *f (vet)* dirofilariasis *(caused by Dirofilaria immitis)*
Disaccharid *n* disaccharide, disaccharose, double sugar
Disaccharidase *f* disaccharidase *(enzyme)*
disjunkt disjunctive
Disklimax *f (ecol)* disclimax, plagioclimax
Diskriminanzanalyse *f (biom)* discriminant (discriminatory) analysis
Dislokation *f* dislocation
disom *(gen)* disomic
Disophenol *n* disophenol *(anthelminthic)*
Disparlure *n* disparlure *(sex hormone)*
Dispergierbarkeit *f* dispersibility
Dispergierung *f* dispersion; *(biom)* variance
Dispersion *f* dispersion
Disposition *f* disposition
Dissemination *f* dissemination
Dissimilation *f* dis[as]similation, catabolism *(plant physiology)*
dissimilatorisch dis[as]similative, catabolic
dissimilieren to dis[as]similate, to catabolize
Dissolution *f* dissolution
Dissoziation *f* dissociation
~/thermische thermal dissociation; pyrolysis
Dissoziationsfaktor *m (gen)* dissociation factor
Dissoziationsgleichgewicht *n* equilibrium of dissociation
distal distal *(anatomy)*
Distanzflug *m* dispersal (distance) flight *(e.g. of insect pests)*
Distanzmesser *m* range-finder, range-finding apparatus
Distel *f* thistle *(esp. of genera Carduus, Cirsium, Cynara, Sonchus, Onopordum)*
Distelsommerwurz *f* thistle broomrape, Orobanche reticulata
distich *(bot)* distichous
Distickstoff[mon]oxid *n* nitrous oxide, laughing gas *(anaesthetic)*
Distomatose *f (vet)* fascioliasis, fasciolosis, liver rot
Distorsion *f* distortion
Distribution *f* distribution
Distrikt *m* [forest] compartment
Distylin *n s.* Dihydroquercetin
Disulfiram *n* disulfiram *(fungicide, herbicide)*
Disulfoton *n* disulfoton *(insecticide, acaricide, nematicide)*
Ditalimfos *n* ditalimfos *(fungicide)*
ditelosom *(gen)* ditelosomic
Ditelosome *m* ditelosome
Diterpen *n* diterpene
Dithianon *n* dithianon *(fungicide)*
Dithiazanin *n* dithiazanine *(anthelminthic)*
Dithiocarbamat *n* dithiocarbamate
Dithioglycerol *n* dimercaprol *(chelating agent, antidote)*
Diurese *f* diuresis

Diuretikum *n* diuretic [agent]
diuretisch diuretic
diurnal diurnal
Diuron *n* diuron, DCMU *(herbicide)*
Diversitätsindex *m (ecol)* diversity index
Divertikulose *f (vet)* diverticulosis
Dividivi *fpl s.* Dividivihülsen
Dividivibaum *m* divi-divi, Caesalpinia coriaria, American sumac[h]
Dividivihülsen *fpl* divi-divi
Divisio *f* 1. *(bot)* division *(taxonomy)*; 2. *(zoo)* phylum *(taxonomy)*
113-Divisor *m* 113-divisor *(timber mensuration)*
dizentrisch dicentric *(e.g. a chromosome)*
dizygot dizygotic, dizygous
DK *s.* Dieselkraftstoff
DL *s.* 1. Dosis/letale; 2. Deutsche Landrasse
DL-Methode *f s.* Doppellactatmethode
DmR *s.* Durchmesser mit Rinde
DMSO *s.* Dimethylsulfoxid
DMV *s.* Dahlienmosaikvirus
DNA *f* DNA, deoxyribonucleic acid
DNA-Fragmentierung *f (gen)* restriction
DNA-Nucleotidylexotransferase *f* DNA nucleotidylexotransferase *(enzyme)*
DNA-Polymerase *f* DNA polymerase *(enzyme)*
~/RNA-abhängige reverse transcriptase
DNBP *s.* Dinoseb
DNOC *s.* 4,6-Dinitro-*(o)*-cresol
DNS *f s.* DNA
do *s.* Dominanzabweichung
Döbel *m (zoo)* chub, Leuciscus cephalus
Dobermann *m* Dobermann [pinscher] *(dog breed)*
Dochmiasis *f (vet)* uncinariasis *(caused by Uncinaria spp.)*
Dochtapplikator *m* rope-wick applicator *(plant protection)*
Docosensäure *f* docosenoic acid *(fatty acid)*
(cis)-Docos-13-ensäure *f* erucic acid *(fatty acid)*
Dodecan-1-carbonsäure *f* tridecanoic acid *(fatty acid)*
Dodecansäure *f* dodecanoic (lauric) acid *(fatty acid)*
Dodemorph *n* dodemorph *(fungicide)*
Dodemorphbenzoat *n* dodemorph benzoate *(fungicide)*
Dodicin *n* dodicine *(fungicide)*
Dodin *n* dodine, doguadin *(fungicide)*
Dogcart *m* dogcart *(two-wheeled one-horse carriage)*
Dogger *m (soil)* Dogger
Dohne *f (hunt)* springe
Doktor *m* **der Veterinärmedizin** doctor of veterinary medicine, DVM
dolchförmig *(bot)* pugioniform
Döldchen *n (bot)* umbellet
Dolde *f (bot)* umbel
~/cymöse cyme
~/kleine umbellet

doldenartig *s.* doldig
Doldenblütige Schleifenblume *f s.* Doldige Schleifenblume
doldenförmig umbelliform
Doldenfrucht *f* diachenium
Doldengewächs *n* umbellifer *(family Umbelliferae = Apiaceae)*
doldentragend umbelliferous
Doldentraube *f* corymb
doldentraubenförmig, doldentraubig corymbiform, corymbose
Doldentraubige Sonnenwende *f* [common] heliotrope, Heliotropium arborescens (peruvianum)
doldig umbellar, umbellate
Doldige Blumenbinse *f* flowering rush, Butomus umbellatus
~ Ölweide *f* autumn olive, Elaeagnus umbellata
~ Schleifenblume *f* [globe] candytuft, Iberis umbellata
Dole *f* culvert *(amelioration)*
Dolomit *m (soil)* dolomite
Dolomitkalk *m* dolomitic limestone
Dolomitkalkboden *m* dolomitic limestone soil
Dolomitkalkmehl *n* ground magnesium limestone
Dolomitkalkstein *m* dolomitic limestone
Domäne *f* domain *(structural element of proteins)*
Domestikation *f* domestication
Domestikationsgrad *m* degree of domestication
Domestikationszentrum *n* centre of domestication
domestizieren to domesticate; to reclaim *(an animal)*
dominant *(gen)* dominant
Dominanz *f* dominance
~/apikale apical dominance
~/regelmäßige complete dominance
~/unvollständige partial (incomplete) dominance, semidominance, prevalence
~/vollständige complete dominance
Dominanzabweichung *f* dominance deviation
Dominanzhypothese *f* dominance hypothesis *(heterosis research)*
dominieren to [pre]dominate
Dompfaff *m* bullfinch, Pyrrhula pyrrhula
Donator *m* donor
Donaulachs *m* huch[en], Hucho hucho
Done-Einschlußkörper *m (vet)* Done inclusion body
Donnan-Freiraum *m* Donnan free space, DFS *(of plant tissues)*
Donnan-Gleichgewicht *n* Donnan equilibrium
Donnan-Potential *n* Donnan potential
Donnan-Verteilung *f* Donnan distribution
Donpferd *m* Don [horse], Trans-Don *(breed)*
DOPA *s.* 3,4-Dihydroxyphenylalanin
DOPA-Decarboxylase *f* aromatic-L-amino-acid decarboxylase, [hydroxy-]tryptophan decarboxylase *(enzyme)*
Dopachrom *n* dopachrome
Dopamin *n* dopamine

Dopamin-Beta-Monooxygenase

Dopamin-Beta-Monooxygenase f dopamine beta-monooxygenase *(enzyme)*
Dopingkontrolle f dope testing *(e.g. in horse-racing)*
Doppelachsengelenk n biaxial joint
Doppelauslaßdüse f double outlet nozzle
Doppelaxt f double-bladed axe, *(Am)* double-bitted ax[e]
Doppelbefruchtung f double fertilization, superfecundation
Doppelbelegung f double mating *(animal breeding)*
Doppelbereifung f double tyres
Doppelbeute f *(api)* twin hive
Doppelbüchse f double-barrelled rifle, double-barrel
Doppel-Crossing-over n *(gen)* double crossing-over
Doppeldeckkäfig m double-deck cage
Doppeldiffusionsverfahren n double-diffusion treatment *(wood preservation)*
Doppeldrän m double drain
Doppellendigkeit f double muscling *(in beef)*
Doppelfederzinke f double-spring collecting finger
Doppelfinger m double finger
Doppelfingermähbalken m twin-finger cutter bar
Doppelflinte f double-barrelled gun, double-barrel
Doppelfoliengewächshaus n greenhouse with double-layer film cover
Doppelfrühbeetkasten m double[-light] span frame, spanroof frame
Doppelfüßer m millepede, millipede *(class Diplopoda)*
Doppelgespann n double harness, pair [of horses]
doppelhiebig two-storeyed, two-storied *(forest stand)*
Doppelhybride f double cross [hybrid]
Doppelkasten m s. Doppelfrühbeetkasten
Doppelkegelbutterfertiger m double-ended conical churn
Doppelkern m double pith *(wood defect)*
Doppelknoten m *(phyt)* double node *(malformation)*
Doppelkreuzung f double crossing, four-way cross *(breeding)*
Doppelkrone f double-crown *(of a stag)*
Doppelkupplung f double (two-stage) clutch
Doppellactatmethode f *(soil)* double-lactate method *(for determination of plant-available potassium and phosphorus)*
Doppelmähfinger m double finger
Doppelmessermähwerk n, **Doppelmesserschneidwerk** n double-knife cutter bar
Doppelmutante f double mutant
Doppelnase f double nose *(bulb malformation in narcissus)*
Doppelnutzungsrasse f dual-purpose breed, two-way breed
Doppelpflanzung f double planting
Doppelrad n twin wheel
Doppelrahmkäse m double-cream cheese
Doppelraufe f double manger
Doppelrauke f *(bot)* white wall rocket, Diplotaxis erucoides
Doppelreifen m dual (double) tyre
Doppelreihe f twin row
Doppelreihenpflanzung f double-row planting
Doppelsalzentsäuerung f double lime deacidification *(of wine)*
Doppelschalenvermehrung f twin-scale propagation, double-scaling *(e.g. of narcissi)*
Doppelscheibendüngerstreuer m double-spinner spreader
Doppelscheibenegge f double-disk harrow
Doppelscheibensäschar n double-disk coulter (furrow opener)
Doppelscheibenschar n double-disk share
Doppelscheibenstreuer m double-spinner spreader
Doppelschlitten m double sledge (sled, dray), bob-sleigh, bob-sled *(timber haulage)*
Doppelschnepfe f great snipe, Gallinago media
Doppelschöpfkolbenpumpe f double-piston hand pump, double-acting pump
Doppelschutztrichter m double guard cone *(of a p.t.o. shaft)*
Doppelselbsttränke f double drinking bowl
Doppelsprung m double mating *(animal breeding)*
Doppelstegplatte f dual-web plate *(e.g. for a garden path)*
Doppelstreichblechpflug m double-mould-board plough
Doppelsuperphosphat n treble superphosphate *(fertilizer)*
doppelt double, twofold, twin; *(bot, zoo)* didymous
~ **dreizählig** *(bot)* biternate
Doppeltgefiedertes Schmuckkörbchen n *(bot)* cosmos, cosmea, Cosmos bipinnatus
doppeltgezähnt *(bot)* bidentate
Doppeltreffertheorie f double hit hypothesis *(plant physiology)*
Doppeltrommeldreschwerk n double-drum thresher, two-cylinder thresher
Doppeltrommel[seil]winde f double-drum winch
doppelverglast double-glazed *(e.g. greenhouse)*
Doppelverglasung f double glazing
Doppelwulststadium n double-ridge stage *(of spike development)*
Doppelzentner m quintal
DoR s. Durchmesser ohne Rinde
Dorbar[huhn] n Dorbar *(chicken breed)*
Dorf n village
Dorfbewohner m villager
Dorfbewohnerin f villager
Dörfchen n small village, hamlet
Dorfgemeindewald m village forest
Dorkinghuhn n Dorking *(chicken breed)*
dormant dormant
Dormanz f *(bot)* [physiological] dormancy, endodormancy, [true] rest period

~/**konsekutive** quiescence
~/**sekundäre** secondary dormancy
Dormin n abscisic acid, ABA *(terpene, phytohormone)*
Dorn m *(bot, zoo)* thorn, spine, acantha
Dornapfel m thorn-apple, *(Am)* jimson [weed], Jamestown weed, Datura stramonium
Dornbaumgehölz n thorn [tree] woodland
Dornbaum-Sukkulenten-Wald m thorn forest with succulents
Dornbaumwald m thorn forest
Dornbusch m thorn-bush, brier, briar *(s. a.* Dornbaumgehölz*)*
dornenlos thornless
Dornenlosigkeit f thornlessness
Dornenranke f thorny tendril
Dornenstrauch m *s.* Dornbusch
dornförmig aculeiform
Dorngestrüpp n briers
dornig thorny, acanthoid
Dornige Cleome f spider-flower, Cleome spinosa
~ **Hauhechel** f *(bot)* rest-harrow, Ononis spinosa
Dorniger Fuchsschwanz m thorny pigweed, Amaranthus spinosus
Dornigkeit f thorniness
Dornloser Speckkäfer m leather beetle, Dermestes frischii
Dornlosigkeit f thornlessness
Dornmelde f *(bot)* mawro, Basia latifolia
Dornpolsterformation f thorn cushion plant formation
Dornpolsterpflanze f thorn cushion plant
Dornspeckkäfer m hide beetle, Dermestes maculatus (vulpinus)
Dornsteppe f scrub
Dornstrauchsavanne f thorn savanna[h]
dörren to desiccate, to dehydrate, to dry
Dörren n desiccation, dehydration, drying
Dörrfisch m dried fish
Dörrfleckenkrankheit f **[des Hafers]** dry spot [of oats], grey speck [of oats], greyleaf *(due to a lack of manganese)*
Dörrfleisch n dried meat, pemmican
Dörrgemüse n dried vegetables
Dörrobst n dried (dehydrated) fruit[s]
Dörrobstmotte f Indian meal moth, Plodia interpunctella
Dörrpflaume f prune, dried plum
dorsal *(zoo)* dorsal
Dorset Down n Dorset Down *(sheep breed)*
~ **Horn** n Dorset Horn *(sheep breed)*
dorsiventral 1. *(bot)* dorsiventral, zygomorphic; 2. *s.* dorsoventral
dorsoventral *(zoo)* dorsoventral
Dosagewein m dosage syrup
Dose f can, tin [can]
Dosenabfüllung f canning
Dosenbarometer n aneroid [barometer]
Dosenbutter f canned butter

Dosenmilch f canned milk
Dosenverschließmaschine f can closing machine
Dosieranlage f batcher
Dosierband n dispensing belt
Dosierbandwaage f balanced-weigh belt
Dosiereinrichtung f *s.* Dosiervorrichtung
dosieren to dose, to meter, to proportion; to batch
Dosierer m *s.* Dosiervorrichtung
Dosierfutterwagen m metering feed carrier
Dosiergetriebe n proportioning gear; drill gearing
Dosierpumpe f metering pump
Dosierschnecke f screw feeder
Dosierung f 1. dosage, metering, proportioning; 2. *s.* Dosis
Dosierventil n metering valve
Dosiervorrichtung f metering device, dosing (dispensing) equipment, proportioner; batcher
Dosierwaage f dosing scale; batcher
Dosimeter n dosimeter
Dosimetrie f dosimetry
dosimetrisch dosimetric
Dosis f dose, dosage
~/**letale** lethal dose, LD
~/**mittlere effektive** median effective dose
~/**mittlere letale** median lethal dose, MLD, LD50
~/**tägliche** daily dose
~/**therapeutische (therapeutisch wirksame)** average dose
~/**tödliche** lethal dose, LD
~/**toxische** toxic dose
~/**unwirksame** non-effect level
Dosis-Effekt-Kurve f, **Dosis-Wirkungs-Kurve** f dose-effect curve
Dost m 1. origan[um], marjoram *(genus Origanum)*; 2. common origanum (marjoram), wild (pot) marjoram, Origanum vulgare
DOT *s.* Dinitolmid
Dotter m(n) [egg-]yolk, vitellus
~/**gelber** dark yolk
~/**weißer** light (white) yolk
Dotterfarbe f egg-yolk colour
dotterlos yolkless
Dottermembran f vitelline membrane
Dottersackbrutfisch m alevin
Dotterweide f golden willow, Salix alba var. vitellina
Dotterzusammensetzung f egg-yolk composition
Douglasie f 1. Douglas fir, Douglas pine (spruce) *(genus Pseudotsuga)*; 2. Douglas fir (spruce), Oregon pine, Pseudotsuga menziesii (taxifolia, douglasii)
Douglas-Spiraee f *(bot)* Douglas spiraea, Spiraea douglasii
Douglastanne f *s.* Douglasie
Douglas-Weißdorn m black (Douglas) hawthorn, Crataegus douglasii
Dourine f covering disease, equine syphilis *(caused by Trypanosoma equiperdum)*
down! down! *(command to dogs)*

Doxorubicin

Doxorubicin *n* doxorubicin *(antibiotic)*
Doxocyclin *n* doxocyclin *(antibiotic)*
Doyle-Schnittholztabelle *f (Am, forest)* Doyle rule
Doyle-Scribner-Kubiktabelle *f* Doyle-Scribner rule
DP *s.* Dermatitis pustulosa
2,4-DP 2,4-DP, dichlorprop *(herbicide, growth regulator)*
Drachenapfel[baum] *m* argus pheasant tree, Dracontomelon dao
Drachenbaum *m* dragon-tree, Dracaena draco
Drachenkopf *m (bot)* dragon's-head, dragonhead *(genus Dracocephalum)*
Drachenlilie *f (bot)* dracaena *(genus Dracaena)*
Drachenwurzel *f (bot)* green dragon, Arisaema dracontium
Dragon *m s.* Estragon
Draht *m* **und Nerv** *m* temperament *(animal judging)*
Drahtgeflecht *n* woven wire, wire-netting
Drahtgitterboden *m* wire floor *(cage management)*
drahthaarig wire-haired
Drahthaarterrier *m* wire-haired terrier
Drahtkäfig *m* wire cage
Drahtleiterschiene *f (vet)* Kramer's wire splinting
Drahtrahmenabspannung *f* guy wire *(e.g. of a trellis)*
Drahtrahmenspalier *n* wire trellis
Drahtriese *f (forest)* wire gravity cable
Drahtschiene *f s.* Drahtleiterschiene
Drahtschmiele *f* wavy (wood) hair-grass, Avenella (Deschampsia) flexuosa
Drahtseil *n* wire rope, cable
Drahtseilausrüstung *f (forest)* rig, rigging
Drahtseilrutsche *f (forest)* wire slide
Drahtspalier *n* wire trellis
Drahtspanner *m* wire tightener *(fencing)*
Drahtwälzegge *f* combined rotary harrow, cage-harrow
Drahtwurm *m (ent)* wire-worm, elaterid larva
Drahtzaun *m* wire fence
Drain *m* 1. *(vet)* drain, drainage tube; 2. *s.* Drän 1.
Drainage *f* 1. *(vet)* drainage; 2. *s.* Dränage 1.
drainieren *(vet)* to drain
Dralldüse *f* swirl nozzle
Drallkammer *f* swirl chamber
Drallplättchen *n* swirl plate
Drän *m* 1. drain [line] *(for water removal)*; 2. *s.* Drain 1.
Dränabstand *m* drain spacing
Dränage *f* drainage
Dränagewasser *n* drainage water
Dränausmündung *f* drainage outlet, outfall
dränbar drainable
Dränbarkeit *f* drainability
Dränfiltermaterial *n* drainage filter material
Drängefälle *n* gradient (fall) of drains
Drängerät *n* draining implement
Drängeräte *npl* drainage equipment
Drängraben *m* drainage ditch (trench), drain

Drängrabenfräse *f* drain (rotary wheel) trencher, drainage ditcher
Drängrabenpflug *m* drain plough
Drängrabensohle *f* invert
Drängrabenverfüllgerät *n* trench filler
dränieren to drain • **mittels Gräben** ~ to ditch
Dränkopf *m* head of a drain
Dränmaschine *f* drainage (tile) machine, drainer ~ **zur grabenlosen Rohrdränung** trenchless drainer
Dränmaschinen *fpl* drainage equipment
Dränmatten[ver]legemaschine *f* drain-mat laying machine
Dränmündung *f* outfall
Dränortungsmaschine *f* drain finder
Dränpflug *m* drain plough
Dränreiniger *m* drain cleaner
Dränreinigungsgerät *n* drain cleaner
Dränrohr *n* drain pipe (tile), drainage tube
Dränrohrreinigungsgerät *n* drain cleaner
Dränspaten *m* drain (ditching) spade
Dränspülgerät *n* drain jetter
Dränspülmaschine *f* drain flushing machine
Dränstrang *m* drain [line]
Dränsystem *n* drainage system
Dräntechnik *f* drainage engineering
Dräntiefe *f* drainage depth
Dränumhüllungsmaterial *n* drain envelope material
Dränung *f* drainage
~/**grabenlose** trenchless drainage
~/**künstliche** artificial drainage
~/**systematische** systematic (full) drainage, parallel system of drainage
Dränungssystem *n* drainage [system]
Dränverleger *m* drainer *(worker)*
Dränwasser *m* drainage water
Dränzufluß *m* drain inflow
Drauflassen *n* blending of wort, doubling *(brewing)*
Drazoxolon *n* drazoxolon *(fungicide)*
Drecklähme *f (vet)* foot-rot
Drehegge *f* rotary [cross] harrow
Drehfilter *n* rotary drum [vacuum] filter
~/**zelluloses** non-cellular rotary-drum [vacuum] filter
Drehfrucht *f* Cape primrose *(genus Streptocarpus)*
Drehgefäßwaage *f* rotating-bin weighing machine
Drehhacke *f* rotary hoe
Drehhalskürbis *m* 1. *(Am)* crookneck *(cultivar grouping)*; 2. summer crookneck, Cucurbita pepo ssp. pepo var. oleifera convar. torticollis
Drehherzigkeit *f* **des Kohls** blindness of cauliflower *(caused by Contarinia nasturtii)*
Drehherzmücke *f* turnip and swede midge, Contarinia nasturtii
Drehkiefer *f* lodge-pole pine, *(Am)* shore pine, Pinus contorta
Drehkolbenmotor *m* rotary engine
Drehkolbenpumpe *f* rotary [piston] pump

Drehkran *m* slewing crane
drehkrank *(vet)* sturdied *(sheep)*
Drehkrankheit *f* **der Salmoniden** whirling disease of salmonids *(caused by Myxosoma cerebralis)*
~ **der Schafe** sturdy, coenurosis, louping (trembling) ill, circling disease, gid, goggle *(caused by Coenurus cerebralis)*
~ **des Geflügels** avian rotator disease
~/**Wendener** X disease *(of cattle after uptaking chlorated naphthalenes)*
Drehling *m* oyster fungus (mushroom), Pleurotus ostreatus
Drehmoment *n* torque
Drehmomentverstärker *m* torque amplifier
Drehmomentwandler *m* torque converter
Drehpflug *m* reversible (half-turn) plough
Drehschemel *m* bogie
Drehstrahlregner *m* revolving sprinkler head, rotating (rotary) sprinkler
Drehstrahlregnersystem *n* rotating sprinkler system
Drehtisch *m* rotating table *(e.g. in processing plants)*
Drehtrommeltrockner *m* rotary drum dryer
Drehwuchs *m* spiral grain (growth), twisted (torse) grain, twist, roe *(of wood)*
~/**sonn[enläuf]iger** counter-clockwise spiral grain, left-hand[ed] spiral grain
~/**tangentialer** tangential twist
~/**widersonniger** clockwise spiral grain, right-hand[ed] spiral grain
drehwüchsig spirally grained, gnarled, gnarly
Drehwüchsigkeit *f s.* Drehwuchs
Drehwurz *f* field (trailing, European) bindweed, wild morning glory, Convolvulus arvensis
Drehzahl *f* speed
Drehzahlmesser *m* speedometer, tachometer
Drehzahlregelung *f* speed control
~/**stufenlose** infinitely variable speed control
Drehzahlregler *m* [speed] governor
dreibeerig *(bot)* tricoccous
Dreiblatt *n* wood lily, three-leaved nightshade, *(Am)* wake-robin *(genus Trillium)*
dreiblättrig *(bot)* triphyllous, trifoliate, three-leaved
Dreiblättrige Zeichenwurz *f (bot)* jack-in-the-pulpit, Arisaema triphyllum
dreiblütig *(bot)* triflorous, trianthous
Dreibock[pflück]leiter *f* tripod (three-legged) ladder
Dreibockreuter *m* tripod
Dreieckmelkstand *m* triangle (trigon) milking parlour
Dreieckpflanzung *f* triangular planting
Dreieckschar *n* box-type share, *(Am)* shin share
Dreiecksdiagramm *n* **der Körnungsarten** *(soil)* textural triangle, triangle for textural classification
Dreieckverband *m* triangular spacing (planting)
Dreieckzahn *m* peg tooth, fleam tooth *(e.g. of a saw)*

Dreierverbindung *f* trivalent *(of meiotic paired chromosomes)*
Dreietagenbatterie *f* triple tier *(layer house installation)*
Dreifachbandsäge[maschine] *f* triple band saw
Dreifachhybride *f*, **Dreifachkreuzung** *f s.* Dreiwegkreuzung 1.
Dreifachzucker *m* trisaccharide
Dreifarbenamaranth *m* edible amaranth, Joseph's-coat, Chinese spinach, Amaranthus tricolor
Dreifarbige Winde *f* dwarf convolvulus (morning glory), Convolvulus tricolor
Dreifarbiger Fuchsschwanz *m s.* Dreifarbenamaranth
Dreifelderwirtschaft *f* three-field rotation (system)
dreiflüglig *(bot)* tripterous
dreifurchig *(bot)* trisulcate
dreigabelig *(bot)* trifurcate
Dreigattungshybride *f* trigeneric hybrid
Dreigespann *n* troika *(equitation)*
dreigestaltig trimorphic
Dreigestaltigkeit *f* trimorphism
dreigliedrig *s.* dreiteilig
dreigrannig *(bot)* triaristate
dreihäusig *(bot)* trioecious
Dreihordendarre *f* three (treble) floor kiln *(malting)*
dreihörnig *(bot)* tricornute
dreikantig *(bot)* trigonous, triquetrous
dreikeimblättrig *(bot)* tricotyledonous
dreiköpfig triceps
dreilappig *(bot, zoo)* trilobal, trilobate[d]
Dreilappige Zaunrebe *f* Boston ivy, Parthenocissus tricuspidata
Dreilappiger Flaschenbaum *m (Am)* papaw, pawpaw, Asimina triloba
Dreilappiges Leberblümchen *n* liver leaf, Hepatica nobilis, Anemone hepatica
dreimächtig *(bot)* tridynamous
Dreimaischverfahren *n* three-mash method *(brewing)*
Dreimasterblume *f* 1. spiderwort, tradescantia *(genus Tradescantia)*; 2. common (Virginian) spiderwort, Tradescantia virginiana
Dreinährstoffdünger *m* complete [mixed] fertilizer
dreinervig *(bot)* trinervate, trinerve[d]
Dreinutzungsrasse *f* triple-purpose breed
Dreiphasenernte *f* three-stage harvesting
Dreiphasenwechselstrommotor *m* three-phase a.c. motor
Dreiproduktschema *n* three-boiling system *(sugar manufacture)*
Dreipunktanbau *m* three-point hitch (linkage), three-link hitch
Dreipunktaufhängung *f* three-point suspension
Dreipunktbock *m* headstock
Dreipunktgerätekupplung *f s.* Dreipunktanbau
Dreipunktschnellkupplung *f* three-point quick coupling

Dreiradpflegeschlepper

Dreiradpflegeschlepper *m s.* Dreiradschlepper
Dreiradschlepper *m*, **Dreiradtraktor** *m* three-wheel tractor, tricycle tractor
Dreirassenkreuzung *f s.* Dreiwegkreuzung 2.
Dreirassenrotationskreuzung *f* three-breed rotational cross
Dreirippenstück *n* three-rib piece *(beef carcass)*
dreirippig *(bot)* tricostate
dreisamig *(bot)* trispermous
dreischichtig three-storeyed, three-storied *(forest stand)*
Dreischichtmineral *n (soil)* three-layer mineral
Dreiseitenkipp[anhäng]er *m* three-way tipper, three-way tipping four-wheeled trailer
dreispaltig *(bot, zoo)* trifid
Dreispaltige Malope *f* three-cleft mallow-wort, Malope trifida
dreispitzig *(bot, zoo)* tricuspid
Dreitagekrankheit *f des Rindes* bovine ephemeral (epizootic) fever, three-day sickness, lazy man's disease
dreiteilig *(bot, zoo)* trimerous, tripartite
Dreiteiliger Ehrenpreis *m* fingered speedwell, Veronica triphyllos
~ **Zweizahn** *m* bur marigold, Bidens tripartita
Dreiviertelhufeisen *n* three-quarter bar shoe
Dreiwalzenmühle *f* three-roller cane mill *(sugar cane processing)*
Dreiwegkreuzung *f* 1. three-way cross [hybrid], triple cross; 2. three-breed cross *(animal breeding)*
Dreiwegkreuzungsprogramm *n* three-breed crossing programme
Dreizack *m* arrow-grass *(genus Triglochin)*
dreizählig *(bot)* [tri]ternate
~/**doppelt** biternate
dreizähnig *(bot)* tridentate
dreizeilig *(bot)* tristichous
dreizinkig three-pronged
Dresch... *s. a.* Drusch...
dreschen to thresh, to thrash
~/**mit dem Dreschflegel** to flail
Dreschflegel *m* [threshing] flail
Dreschkanalbreite *f* width of the threshing channel
Dreschkasten *m* [harvester] threshing box
Dreschkorb *m* concave
Dreschkorbabstand *m* concave clearance
Dreschkorbeinstellskale *f* concave indicator
Dreschkorbeinstellung *f* concave adjustment (setting)
Dreschkorbeinstellvorrichtung *f* concave adjuster
Dreschkorbgitter *n* concave grate
Dreschlein *m* flax, Linum usitatissimum
Dreschmaschine *f* threshing-machine, thresher
Dreschsatz *m* threshing unit, thresher
Dreschtrommel *f* [threshing] cylinder, [threshing] drum, beater

Dreschtrommeldrehzahl *f* cylinder (threshing-drum) speed
Dreschtrommeldrehzahlvariator *m* threshing speed variator
Dreschtrommeldurchmesser *m* threshing-cylinder diameter
Dreschtrommeldurchsatz *m* dragging-in-capacity of the drum
Dreschtrommelgetriebe *n* threshing-cylinder gear
Dreschtrommelverluste *mpl* threshing-drum grain losses
Dreschwerk *n* threshing unit (gear), thresher
Dreschwerksverluste *mpl* threshing losses
Dresseur *m* [animal] trainer
dressieren 1. to train, to break [in] *(animals)*; 2. to dress, to truss [up] *(market poultry)*
Dressur *f* 1. training; 2. dressage
Dressurfähigkeit *f* dressage ability
Dressur[hunde]halsband *n* training collar
Dressurprüfung *f* dressage test (competition)
Dressurreiten *n* dressage
Dressursattel *m* dressage saddle
Drift *f* drift *(e.g. in broadcasting plant protectants)*
~/**genetische** genetic drift
~/**zufallsbedingte** *(gen)* random drift, Sewall-Wright effect
Driftnebeln *n* drift spraying
Driftsprühen *n* drift spraying
Drille *f s.* Drillmaschine
Drilleinrichtung *f* seed-feeding device
drillen to drill
~/**auf Endabstand** to drill to a stand *(e.g. beets)*
~/**kreuzweise (über Kreuz)** to cross-drill
Drillen *n* drilling, row seeding
drillfähig drillable
Drillfähigkeit *f* drillability
Drillfurche *f* drill furrow
Drilling *m* 1. triplett; 2. *(hunt)* three-barrel[led] gun
Drillingsblume *f (bot)* bougainvillaea *(genus Bougainvillea)*
Drillkasten *m* drill box, seed[ing] box
Drillmaschine *f* [seed] drill, [drill] seeder, sower
~/**mehrreihige** multiple-row drill
~ **mit Schwerkraftzuführung [des Saatguts]** gravity feed drill
~/**motorbetriebene** power-drawn drill
~/**pneumatische** pneumatic [feed] drill
Drillmaschinenbeschickungsgerät *n* drill feeder (filler)
Drillmaschineneinstellung *f* drill setting
Drillreihe *f* drill [row]
Drillreihenabstand *m* drill row distance, drill width
Drillsaat *f* drill (row) seeding, sowing in rows (lines)
Drillschar *n* [drill, seed] coulter, seed furrow opener, planter shoe, [planter] runner
Drilosphäre *f (soil)* drilosphere
Drip[verlust] *m (slaught)* drip[ping loss]
Drittfrucht[an]bau *m* triple cropping
Droge *f* drug

~/pflanzliche vegetable drug
Drogenauszug *m* tincture
Drogenpflanze *f* drug plant
Drohn *m*, **Drohne** *f* drone [honey-bee], male bee
Drohnenbrut *f* drone brood, male bee brood
Drohnenbrutwabe *f* drone comb
Drohnenfalle *f* drone trap
Drohnenmütterchen *n* drone layer, drone-laying queen honey-bee, laying worker honey-bee
Drohnenpflegevolk *n* drone-rearing colony
Drohnensammelplatz *m* drone congregation area
Drohnenvolk *n* drone-rearing colony
Drohnenwabe *f* drone comb
Drohnenzelle *f* drone cell
Dromedar *n* Arabian camel, Camelus dromedarius
Dropper *m* **der Tulpe** dropper of tulip
Drosometer *n* drosometer
Drossel *f* 1. thrush *(family Turdidae)*; 2. *s.* Drosselklappe
Drosselklappe *f* throttle
Drosselvene *f* jugular [vein]
Droughtmaster *n* Droughtmaster *(cattle breed)*
Druck *m* pressure
~/atmosphärischer atmospheric (barometric) pressure
~/kolloidosmotischer (onkotischer) oncotic pressure
~/osmotischer osmotic pressure
Druckausgleichsblase *f* breather bag *(silo)*
Druckbeanspruchung *f* compressive (bearing) stress
Druckbelüftung *f* forced ventilation
Druckbrand *m (vet)* bedsore
druckempfindlich susceptible to bruise *(fruit)*
Druckentsafter *m* compression-type juice separator
druckerhöht hypertonic
Druckfestigkeit *f* compressive strength
Druckfilter *n* pressure filter
Druckfleck *m s.* Druckstelle
Druckgärung *f* pressure fermentation *(brewing)*
Druckgeber *m* pressure transducer
Druckholz *n* compression (pressure, bull) wood, redwood, tenar
Druckkammer *f* pressure chamber
Drucklager *n* thrust bearing
Druckluftbehälter *m* compressed-air tank
druckluftbetätigt [compressed-]air-operated, air-actuated
Druckluftbremse *f* air [pressure] brake, pneumatic brake
Druckluftfilter *n* compressed-air filter
Drucklüftung *f* pressurized ventilation
Druckmeßgerät *n* pressure gauge
~/piezoelektrisches piezometer
Druckmeßwandler *m* pressure transducer
Druckplatte *f* tongue *(of self-waterer)*
Druckpotential *n* pressure potential
Druckpunkt *m* pressure point

Druckreinigungsgerät *n* pressure cleaner
Druckrezeptor *m* pressoreceptor *(in blood vessels)*
Druckrolle *f* press wheel (roller)
Drucksauglüftung *f* forced-draught ventilation
Druckschaden *m* impact bruise *(of fruit)*; *(vet)* bedsore
Druckschlauch *m* pressure hose
Druckschmierung *f* pressure lubrication
Druckspannung *f* compressive stress
Druckstange *f* pushpole, Sampson, killig *(tree-felling equipment)*
Druckstelle *f* press mark, bruise • **Druckstellen bekommen** to bruise • **Druckstellen verursachen** to bruise
Druckstoß *m* water-hammer
Drucktank *m* pressure tank, high-pressure vessel
~ für filtriertes Bier bright beer tank
Drucktränkung *f* pressure treatment (process) *(wood preservation)*
~/alternierende alternating-pressure process, oscillating-pressure process
Druckumlaufschmierung *f* pressure lubrication
druckunempfindlich bruise-resistant *(fruit)*
Druckverband *m (vet)* pressure dressing (bandage)
Druckverletzung *f* impact damage (injury) *(e.g. of fruit)*
druckvermindert hypotonic
Druckwandler *m* pressure transducer
Drumlin *m* drumlin, drum
Drusch *m* threshing
Drusch... *s. a.* Dresch...
Druscheinrichtung *f* threshing equipment
druschfähig threshable
Druschfähigkeit *f* threshability
Druschfrucht *f* grain crop
Druschgemeinschaft *f* neighbourhood threshing ring
Druschleistung *f* threshing capacity
Druschplatz *m* threshing site
Druschverluste *mpl* threshing losses
Druschvorrichtung *f* threshing aggregate
Druschzeit[spanne] *f* threshing time
Druse *f* 1. druse *(crystal in wood cells)*; 2. *(vet)* strangles, equine distemper *(caused by Streptococcus equi)*
Drüse *f* gland
~/alkalische alkaline [venom] gland *(of the honey-bee)*
~/apokrine apocrine gland
~/Bartholinische Bartholin's gland, gland of Bartholin
~/Cowpersche Cowper's (bulbo-urethral) gland
~/endokrine endocrine (ductless) gland
~/Hardersche Harder's gland *(animal anatomy)*
~/kleine glandule
~/Littrésche urethral gland

Drüse 156

~/**Meibomsche** Meibomian (tarsal) gland *(animal anatomy)*
~/**Nassanoffsche** Nasonov gland *(of worker honey-bees)*
~/**vulvovaginale** *s.* ~/**Bartholinische**
Drüsen *fpl*:
~/**Brunnersche** Brunner's (duodenal) glands *(animal anatomy)*
~/**Lieberkühnsche** intestinal glands
Drüsenentzündung *f (vet)* adenitis
Drüsenepithelkrebs *m (vet)* adenocarcinoma
Drüsenerkrankung *f (vet)* adenopathy
drüsenfrüchtig *(bot)* adenocarpous
drüsenfüßig *(bot)* adenopodous
Drüsengeschwulst *f (vet)* adenoma
~/**gutartige** adenoma
Drüsenhaar *n (bot)* glandular trichome (hair)
drüsenhaarig adenotrichous
Drüsenkelch *m* garlic shrub, Adenocalymna alliacea
Drüsenkrebs *m (vet)* adenocarcinoma
Drüsenmagen *m* glandular stomach
~ **des Geflügels** proventriculus
Drüsenteil *m* **der Milchzisterne** *s.* Drüsenzisterne
drüsentragend glanduliferous
Drüsenzelle *f* gland cell
Drüsenzisterne *f* udder cistern[a]
Drüsenzotte *f (bot)* colleter
drüsig glandular
Drüsige Strauchkirsche *f* flowering almond, Prunus glandulosa
DS *s.* Deutsches Sattelschwein
Dschungel *m(n)* jungle
Dschungelrodung *f* jungle clearing
DSR *s.* Deutsches Schwarzbuntes Rind
DTPA *s.* Diethylentriaminpentaessigsäure
dtr *s.* darrtrocken
Ductus *m* duct *(for compounds s. under* Gang*)*
Duft *m* odour, [pleasant] smell, fragrance, aroma; bouquet *(of wine)*; *(hunt)* scent
Duftblüte *f (bot)* 1. osmanthus *(genus Osmanthus)*; 2. fragrant (sweet) olive, Osmanthus fragrans
Duftbruch *m* rime break *(at trees)*
Duftdrüse *f* scent (sweat) gland; Nasonov (Nassanoff) gland *(of the worker honey-bee)*
duftend odoriferous, odorous, sweet-smelling, fragrant, sweet-scented, aromatic
~/**süß** sweet-scented, sweet smelling
Duftende Reseda *f (bot)* mignonette, peaches and cream, Reseda odorata
Duftender Himmel[s]schlüssel *m* cowslip, polyanthus, Primula veris
Duftmarke *f* scent mark *(of game)*
Duftorgan *n (zoo)* scent organ
Duftpflanze *f* aromatic plant, perfume (essential oil) plant
Duftschaden *m* glaze damage, damage by rime *(on forest trees)*
Duftspur *f* scent, drag *(of game)*
Duftsteinrich *m (bot)* [sweet] alyssum, sweet alison, Lobularia maritima, Alyssum maritimum
Duftstoff *m* smell attractant
Duftveilchen *n* sweet[-scented] violet, [garden] violet, Viola odorata
Duftwicke *f* sweet pea, Lathyrus odoratus
Düker *m* siphon *(hydrotechnical amelioration)*
Dulcit[ol] *m* galactitol *(sugar alcohol)*
Duldungsreflex *m* standing reflex *(mating behaviour)*
Dumpalme *f* doum[-palm], doom palm, Hyphaene thebaica
Dumpalmwein *m* doum-palm wine
dumpfig musty *(e.g. smell)*; damply *(hay)*
Düne *f* dune, sand-hill
Dünenaufforstung *f* afforestation of dunes
Dünenbefestigung *f* dune fixation, sand-dune stabilization
Dünenboden *m* dune soil
Dünenkäfer *m (ent)* scarred melolontha, Polyphylla fullo
Dünenpflanze *f* dune plant
Dünenrose *f* Scotch (burnet) rose, Rosa pimpinellifolia
Dünensand *m* dune sand
Dung *m* manure, dung, muck, dressing • ~ **ausbringen** to dung *(s. a.* Düngemittel*)*
Dung... *s. a.* Mist...
Dungausbringung *f* manure disposal
Dungbahn *m* overhead manure carrier, manure bucket on overhead monorail
Düngebedürfnis *n* fertilizer requirement (needs)
Dungeinarbeitung *f* **[in den Boden]** dung burial [into soil]
Dungeinleger *m* skim coulter, skim[mer], manure (mulcher) attachment, jointer *(at a mould-board plough)*
Düngekalk *m* [manuring] lime, lime (calcium) fertilizer, agricultural limestone
Düngelanze *f* lance
Düngematerial *n s.* Düngestoff
Düngemischkalk *m* compound lime fertilizer
Düngemittel *n* fertilizer, fertiliser, dressing *(s. a. under* Dünger*)*
~/**anorganisches** inorganic (mineral, commercial) fertilizer
~/**direkt wirkendes** plant fertilizer (food)
~/**halborganisches** semiorganic fertilizer
~/**indirekt wirkendes** soil fertilizer
~/**mineralisches** mineral (inorganic, commercial) fertilizer
~ **mit langsamer Nährstofffreisetzung** slow-release fertilizer, slow-acting fertilizer
~/**organisches** [natural] organic fertilizer, [organic] manure
~/**physiologisch saures** acid-forming fertilizer
Düngemittel... *s. a.* Dünger...
Düngemittelanalyse *f* fertilizer analysis

Düngemittelaufwand *m* fertilizer input
Düngemitteleinsatz *m* fertilizer usage (use)
Düngemittelfabrik *f* fertilizer factory
Düngemittelfestlegung *f* fertilizer fixation *(in the soil)*
Düngemittelgranulat *n* granulated (pelleted) fertilizer
Düngemittelhandel *m* fertilizer trade
Düngemittelindustrie *f* [chemical-]fertilizer industry
Düngemittelklasse *f* fertilizer grade
Düngemittelkombination *f* fertilizer combination
Düngemittelkonzentrat *n* concentrated fertilizer
Düngemittellager *n* fertilizer store
Düngemittellagerraum *m* fertilizer shed
Düngemittellösung *f* fertilizer solution
Düngemittelnährstoff *m* fertilizer nutrient
Düngemittelsalz *n* fertilizer salt
Düngemittelumschlag *m* fertilizer handling
düngen to fertilize, to dress, to batten; to dung, to manure
~/**durch Überfluten** to warp
~/**mit Guano** to guano
~/**mit Kalk** to lime, to chalk
~/**mit Kompost** to compost
~/**mit Mergel** to marl
~/**mit Mist** to muck
~/**organisch** to dung, to manure
~/**zu schwach** to underfertilize
Dünger *m* fertilizer, fertiliser, dressing *(s. a. under* Düngemittel*)* • ~ **neben die Pflanzenreihe eindrillen** to side-dress
~/**einzupflügender** plough-down fertilizer
~/**in Reihen ausgebrachter** row fertilizer
~/**langsamwirkender** slow-release fertilizer, slow-acting fertilizer, depot fertilizer
~/**wirtschaftseigener** [farm] manure, farmyard (barnyard) manure
Dünger... *s. a.* Düngemittel...
Düngerausbringung *f* fertilizer application, dressing
~ **in die Pflugsohle** plough-sole placement of fertilizer
Düngerbedarf *m* fertilizer requirement (needs)
Düngerbedarfsermittlung *f* fertilizer requirement determination
Düngerbruchgranulat *n* kibbled fertilizer
Düngerdrillmaschine *f* fertilizer drill
~/**kombinierte** combined fertilizer and seed drill, combined grain-fertilizer drill, combine drill
Düngereffektivität *f* fertilizer efficiency
Düngereinsatzempfehlung *f* fertilizer [use] recommendation
Düngereinspeisegerät *n* fertilizer injector
Düngererde *f* vegetable mould
Düngergabe *f* fertilizer application, [fertilizer] dressing
~/**jährliche** annual dressing
Düngergüteklasse *f* fertilizer grade

Düngerkippwagen *m* fertilizer dumping cart
Düngerlöse- und -dosiergerät *n* fertilizer dilution and injection device
Düngerlösung *f* fertilizer solution
Düngerlösungsinjektor *m* fertilizer solution injector
Düngermaterial *n s.* Düngestoff
Düngermühle *f* fertilizer mill
Düngerplazierung *f* fertilizer placement
Düngerstreuer *m* fertilizer distributor (spreader), fertilizing machine; manure spreader
Düngertablette *f* fertilizer tablet (pill)
Düngerträger[stoff] *m* fertilizer carrier
Düngertrockner *m* manure dryer
Düngerumschlag *m* fertilizer handling
Düngerverregnung *f* fertilizer sprinkling (irrigation), ferti[rri]gation
Düngerverregnungsanlage *f* manure rainer
Düngerwalze *f* fertilizer roller
Düngerwirkung *f* manure effect
Düngesalz *n* fertilizer (manuring, manurial) salt
Düngestoff *m* fertilizer material, manuring (manurial) substance, dressing *(s. a. under* Dünger*)*
~ **tierischen Ursprungs** animal manure
Düngetorf *m* peat fertilizer
Düngeversuch *m* fertilizer experiment (trial)
Düngewert *m* fertilizing (manurial) value
Düngwirkung *f* manuring effect
Dungfladen *m* dung pat
Dunggreifer *m* manure grab
Dunggrube *f* dung[ing] pit, manure pit
Dungkanal *m* dung channel
Dungkarren *m* dung-cart
Dunglader *m* dung-loader
Dunglager *n* manure store
Dunglagerteich *m* manure storage lagoon
Dunglagerung *f* manure storage
Dungplatte *f* laystall
Dungplatz *m* manure store
Dungräumer *m* dung cleaner
Dungrinne *f* dung channel
Dungschiebemulde *f* yard scraper
Dungschieber *m* dung (muck, yard) scraper, dung dozer
Dungstapel *m* muck heap, dunghill, compost pile
Dungstreuanhänger *m* trailer spreader
Dungtrockner *m* manure dryer
Düngung *f* fertilization • **auf ~ ansprechen (reagieren)** to respond to manuring
~ **aus der Luft** aerial (aeroplane) fertilization, crop-dusting
~/**aviotechnische** *s.* ~ aus der Luft
~/**harmonische** balanced fertilization
~/**mineralische** mineral fertilization
~/**organische** manure fertilization
Düngungsempfehlung *f* fertilizer [use] recommendation
Düngungsmethode *f* fertilizing practice
Düngungspflug *m* fertilizing plough

Düngungspraxis

Düngungspraxis *f* fertilizing practice
Düngungsprogramm *n* manurial programme
Düngungsversuch *m* fertilization experiment (trial), manurial experiment
Düngungswert *m* fertilizing (manurial) value
Dungverteiler *m* dung (manure) spreader
Dunkeladaptation *f* dark adaptation *(of the eye)*
Dunkelatmung *f* dark respiration *(plant physiology)*
dunkelfarbig dark-coloured, dematiaceous
Dunkelfärbung *f* dark stain, black check *(e.g. of wood)*
Dunkelfeldmikroskopie *f* dark-field microscopy
dunkelfrüchtig *(bot)* atrocarpous
Dunkelfuchs *m* dark (liver) chestnut *(horse)*
dunkelgefärbt dematiaceous
Dunkelhieb *(forest)* dark felling
Dunkelkeim *m* dark sprout
Dunkelkeimer *m* dark germinator
Dunkellagerung *f* dark storage
Dunkelperiode *f* scotoperiod *(photoperiodism)*
Dunkelphase *f* dark period *(of a lighting regime)*
dunkelpurpurrot *(bot)* atropurpureous
Dunkelreaktion *f* dark reaction (fixation) *(photosynthesis)*
Dunkelrespiration *f* dark respiration *(plant physiology)*
Dunkelschlag *m* *(forest)* dark felling
Dunkelstall *m* low-light house; windowless poultry house
Dunkelstallhaltung *f* windowless housing
Dunkelverfärbung *f* dark stain, black check *(esp. of wood)*
dunkelviolett *(bot)* atroviolaceous
Dunker *m* Norwegian Dunkerhound *(dog breed)*
Dunkle Chrysanthemenlaus *f* chrysanthemum aphid, Macrosiphoniella sanborni
Dunkler Pelzkäfer *m* black carpet beetle, Attagenus megatoma (piceus)
Dünnbier *n* weak beer
dünnblättrig *(bot)* tenuifolious
Dünndarm *m* small intestine (gut)
Dünndarmpeptidase *f* intestinal peptidase *(enzyme)*
dünnflüssig inviscid
dünnhäutig thin-skinned
Dünnholz *n* small[-sized] timber, smallwood, topwood, wood of small diameter, thinwood, thinnings
Dünnholzauslichtung *f* thinwood pruning *(orcharding)*
Dünnholzprozessor *m* small timber processor
Dünnholzsägewerk *n* pony [saw]mill
dünnörtig *(forest)* top end first
Dünnsaat *f* thin sowing
Dünnsaft *f* thin juice *(sugar manufacture)*
Dünnsafteinengung *f* thin juice evaporation
Dünnsaftendschwefelung *f* final sulphitation of thin juice
Dünnsaftfilter *n* light-liquor filter

dünnschalig thin-shell[ed]
Dünnschichtchromatographie *f* thin-layer chromatography
Dünnschichttrockner *m* thin-layer dryer
Dünnschichttrocknung *f* thin-layer drying
Dünnschnittpräparat *n* thin section preparation
Dünn- und Dickdarmentzündung *f (vet)* enterocolitis
Dünnung *f (slaught)* [thin] flank
dünnwandig thin-walled
dünnzweigig *(bot)* stenocladous
Dunst *m* 1. haze; mist, fog; 2. dunst, break middlings *(milling)*
~/atmosphärischer haze
dünsten to coddle
Dunsthaube *f* air dome
dunstig hazy
duodenal duodenal
Duodenaldrüsen *fpl* duodenal (Brunner's) glands
Duodenalflüssigkeit *f* duodenal fluid
Duodenalgeschwür *n (vet)* duodenal ulcer
Duodenalsaft *m* duodenal fluid
Duodenitis *f (vet)* duodenitis
Duodenum *n* duodenum
Duplikation *f* duplication
Duplikatprobe *f* duplicate sample
Durchblätterter Gänsefuß *m* strawberry blite, Chenopodium foliosum
Durchblutung *f* blood flow, [blood] circulation
Durchfahrsilo *m* draw-over clamp
Durchfahrt *f* bout *(e.g. of a field-working machine)*
Durchfall *m (vet)* scour[s], loose bowels, diarrhoea
• ~ **haben** to scour
~/blutiger bloody diarrhoea (flux)
Durchfallast *m* loose (falling-out) knot
durchfeuchten to moisten thoroughly
Durchfluß *m* flow, flux
Durchfluß[mengen]messer *m* flow-meter
Durchflußtrockner *m* flow dryer
durchforsten *(forest)* to thin, to clean
~/übermäßig to overthin
Durchforstung *f (forest)* thinning
~ älterer Bestände advanced thinning
~/chemische chemical (poison) thinning
~/freie free thinning
~ im Beherrschten thinning from below, thinning in the upper storey
~ im Herrschenden thinning from above
~/industrielle (kommerzielle) commercial thinning
~/ökonomisch effektive extraction thinning
~/schematische mechanical thinning
~/selektive selection (subjective) thinning
~/streifenweise strip thinning
~/unökonomische non-productive (uneconomic, non-commercial) thinning, thinning-to-waste
Durchforstungsart *f* type of thinning, thinning class
Durchforstungsbestand *m* thinned stand

Durchforstungseingriff *m* thinning operation (treatment)
Durchforstungsfläche *f* thinning area
Durchforstungsforwarder *m* forwarder for thinnings
Durchforstungsgrad *m* thinning grade
Durchforstungshäufigkeit *f* thinning frequency (periodicity)
Durchforstungsholz *n* thinning[s]
Durchforstungsintensität *f* thinning intensity
Durchforstungsintervall *n* thinning interval
Durchforstungsmaschine *f* [/tragbare] [forest] clearing saw
Durchforstungsmaßnahme *f* thinning operation (treatment)
Durchforstungsperiode *f* thinning cycle (period)
Durchforstungsprogramm *n* thinning table (schedule)
Durchforstungsprozessor *m* processor for thinnings
Durchforstungsreihe *f* thinning series
Durchforstungsschere *f* thinning shears, forest pruning shears
Durchforstungsstärke *f* intensity of thinning, thinning grade (weight)
Durchforstungstechnik *f* thinning technique
Durchforstungsumlauf *m* thinning cycle (period)
Durchforstungsversuch *m* thinning trial
Durchforstungsweise *f* thinning regime
Durchführbarkeitsstudie *f* feasibility study
durchführen/Sanitärhiebe *(forest)* to sanitize
Durchgang *m* underbeam clearance *(of plough)*
Durchgänger *m* shyer, bolter *(horse)*
Durchgangs[vieh]waage *f* walk-through weigher
Durchgangszeit *f* **durch den Verdauungskanal** intestinal transit time
durchgehen to bolt *(horse)*
Durchgehen *n* stampede *(of large animals)*
durchgezüchtet thoroughbred
Durchhang *m*, **Durchhängen** *n* sagging *(of a rope)*
Durchhau *m* *(forest)* cleared strip, lane, ride
durchhauen to cut a lane, to cut over
Durchlaß *m* 1. culvert, water transmission; 2. throughfall [through the canopy]
durchlassen 1. to let through, to be permeable to *(e.g. water)*; 2. to transmit *(e.g. radiation)*
durchlässig 1. permeable, transparent; porous; 2. open *(e.g. a protective forest strip)*; 3. leaky
Durchlässigkeit *f* 1. permeability; openness *(e.g. of a leaf canopy)*; 2. transmittance
Durchlässigkeitsfaktor *m* transmittance factor
Durchlaßkanal *m* culvert
Durchlaufkörnertrockner *m* continuous-flow grain dryer
Durchlaufmelkstand *m* tunnel milking parlour
Durchlauftrockner *m* [continuous-]flow dryer, continuous[-action] dryer

Durchlaufwanne *f* **für Schafe** sheep foot bath
durchläutern to clean, to thin *(a forest stand)*
durchleuchten to candle *(eggs)*
durchlichten to admit light, to thin
durchlüften to aerate *(e.g. soil)*
Durchlüftung *f* aeration
Durchlüftungsgewebe *n*, **Durchlüftungsparenchym** *n* *(bot)* aerenchyma
Durchlüftungszone *f* *(soil)* zone of aeration
Durchmesser *m* diameter *(e.g. in timber mensuration)*
~ **am oberen Stammende** diameter at the top, small-end diameter
~ **am stärkeren (unteren) Stammende** diameter at foot, butt [end] diameter, base diameter
~ **des Grundflächenmittelbaumes (Grundflächenzentralstammes)** diameter of median basal area tree
~/**kostendeckender** economic diameter limit *(of stems)*
~ **mit Rinde** diameter over bark, d.o.b., outside-bark diameter
~ **ohne Rinde** diameter under bark, d.u.b., inside-bark diameter
~ **über Wurzelanlauf** diameter above buttress
Durchmesserband *n* diameter tape
Durchmesserfrequenztafel *f* stand table
Durchmessergruppe *f* diameter group (category)
Durchmesserklasse *f* diameter (size) class
Durchmesserklassengrenze *f* diameter[-class] limit
Durchmesserstamm *m* mean diameter tree
Durchmesserstufe *f s.* Durchmesserklasse
Durchmesserverteilung *f* diameter distribution
Durchmesserverteilungstafel *f* stand table
Durchmesserwachstum *n* diameter growth
Durchmesserzuwachs *m* diameter increment (accretion), radial increment (growth)
durchnäßt sodden
durchpflücken to pick (go) over
durchpicken to pip *(the eggshell)*
durchplentern to cull out, to clean *(a forest stand)*
Durchplenterung *f* *(forest)* assistance felling, cleaning cutting, cull
Durchreiche *f* hatch
durchreisern *(forest)* to brush through (up), to thin a young pole wood
durchsägen to saw through
Durchsatz *m* throughput, capacity
Durchsatzleistung *f* discharge
durchscheinend 1. translucent; limpid *(wine)*; 2. *s.* durchsichtig
Durchschlag *m*, **Durchschlagskraft** *f* *(hunt)* penetrating power *(of a bullet)*
Durchschnittsalter *n* average age
Durchschnittsertrag *m* average (mean) yield
Durchschnittsfettgehalt *m* average fat content
Durchschnittszuwachs *m* *(forest)* mean annual increment

Durchschnittszuwachs

~/periodischer [jährlicher] periodic mean annual increment
durchseihen to strain
durchsichtig transparent, hyaline, pellucid
Durchsichtigkeit f transparency; limpidity
durchsickern to percolate, to seep, to soak, to trickle through, to strain; to leak
durchsieben to sieve, to sift *(e.g. flour)*; to screen *(e.g. grain)*
durchstechen to pierce, to puncture
Durchstechung f puncture; *(vet)* paracentesis
Durchstrahlung f transmission
Durchstrahlungselektronenmikroskop n transmission electron microscope
Durchströmung f perfusion *(e.g. of organs)*
Durchströmungsmoor n valley bog
durchtränken to imbibe, to impregnate, to soak, to saturate; to drench
Durchtränkung f imbibition, impregnation, soaking
durchtrittig coon-footed *(horse)*
Durchtropfen n throughfall [through the canopy] *(of precipitation)*
Durchwachsenblättrige Kompaßpflanze f cup plant, Silphium perfoliatum
~ Kresse f yellow-flower pepperweed, Lepidium perfoliatum
~ Silphie f cup plant, Silphium perfoliatum
durchwerfen to riddle *(e.g. compost)*
Durchwuchs m *(phyt)* second growth, gemmation
Durchwuchskartoffel f volunteer potato [plant]
Durchwurf m, **Durchwurfgitter** n riddle
Durchwurzelung f root penetration, rooting
Durchwurzelungskanal m root channel
Durchwurzelungstiefe f rooting depth
Durchziehwalze f snap roller, snapping roll *(of a maize header)*
Dürener Krankheit f *(vet)* stockman disease
dürftig poor *(soil)*
Durianbaum m *(bot)* durian, Durio zibethinus
Duriane f, **Duriofrucht** f durian *(fruit from Duria zibethinus)*
Duroc-Schwein n Duroc *(pig breed)*
dürr 1. dry, droughty; arid; 2. barren, jejune *(land)*; 3. thin, lean, poor *(cattle)*
Durra f durra, dhurra, dura, Indian millet, guineacorn, Sorghum durra
Dürrast m dead knot
Dürre f 1. dryness, drought, drouth, aridity, aridness; 2. *(vet)* bush sickness *(due to cobalt deficiency)*
Dürreabhärtung f drought-hardening
dürreanfällig drought-sensitive
Dürrefestigkeit f drought hardiness
Dürregebiet n drought area
Dürrejahr n drought year
Dürreperiode f drought
dürreresistent drought-resistant
Dürreresistenz f drought resistance
Dürreschaden m drought injury (damage)
Dürrestreß m drought stress

dürreverträglich drought-tolerant
Dürreverträglichkeit f drought tolerance
Dürrfleckenkrankheit f *(phyt)* alternariosis, early blight [disease] *(caused by Alternaria solani)*
~ der Tomate tomato early blight, early blight of tomato *(caused by Alternaria solani)*
Durrha f s. Durra
Dürrheu n field hay
Dürrholz n dry (dead) wood
Dürrling m, **Dürrständer** m dead-standing tree
~ ohne Wipfel stub, snag
Dürrwipfel m spike-top
Dürrwurz f cinnamon-root, inula, Inula conyza
Durst m thirst
~/übermäßiger *(vet)* polydipsia
Durumweizen m durum [wheat], Triticum durum
Düse f nozzle
~/nicht nachtropfende anti-drip nozzle
Düsengehäuse n nozzle housing
Düsenkappe f nozzle cap
Düsenklärzentrifuge f *(dairy)* bactofuge
Düsenmündung f s. Düsenöffnung
Düsenöffnung f nozzle orifice (tip)
Düsenplatte f nozzle disk
Düsenprüfstand m nozzle testing stand
Düsenrohr n nozzle bar
Düsenrohrberegnung f nozzle-line irrigation
Düsenverschmutzung f nozzle fouling
Düsenverstopfung f nozzle blockage
Dust m s. Stäubemittel
Düsterer Humusschnellkäfer m common click beetle, Agriotes obscurus
Duwock m *(bot)* marsh horse-tail, marsh-equisetum, cat-whistles, Equisetum palustre
DWE s. Deutsche Weiße Edelziege
Dy m *(soil)* dy
Dynamometer n dynamometer
Dyrehund m Norwegian elk-hound *(breed)*
Dyren n dyrene *(fungicide)*
Dyschondroplasie f *(vet)* growth disorder (disturbance)
~ des Geflügels/infektiöse leg weakness syndrome in broilers
Dysenterie f *(vet)* dysentery
Dysfunktion f dysfunction
Dysgalaktie f dysgalactia
dysgen[et]isch dysgenic
Dyskeratose f *(vet)* dyskeratosis
Dyspepsie f *(vet)* dyspepsia
dyspeptisch dyspeptic
Dysperistaltik f *(vet)* dysperistalsis
Dysphagie f *(vet)* dysphagia
Dysplasie f *(vet)* dysplasia
Dyspnoe f *(vet)* dyspnoea
Dystokie f *(vet)* dystocia, parturition complication
dystroph dystrophic
Dystrophie f dystrophy, dystrophia
dystrophisch dystrophic
Dysurie f *(vet)* dysuria
Dzierzonbeute f *(api)* Dzierzon hive

E

E *s.* Redoxpotential
EAA-Index *m* EAA (essential amino-acid) index, EAAI
EABIV *s.* Blattrollvirus der Erbse und Ackerbohne
EB *s.* Erstbesamung
EBA *s.* Erstbesamungsalter
EbAAV *s.* Adernaufhellungsvirus der Erdbeere
EbBSV *s.* Blattscheckungsvirus der Erdbeere
Ebene *f* plain, plane
~/**strauchbewachsene [sandige]** barren
~/**trophische** *(ecol)* trophic level
Ebenheit *f* levelness *(e.g. of a seed-bed)*
Ebenholz *n* ebony *(from Diospyros spp.)*
Ebenholzbaum *n* ebony, *(esp.)* Diospyros ebenum
Eber *m* boar, he-swine
~/**kastrierter** hog pig
Eberesche *f* 1. mountain ash, service [tree], sorb *(genus Sorbus)*; 2. rowan[-tree], [European] mountain-ash, quickbeam, Sorbus aucuparia
Ebereschenbeere *f* rowan[-berry], service-berry
Ebereschenblättrige Fiederspiere *f (bot)* Ural false spiraea, Sorbaria sorbifolia
Ebereschenmotte *f* apple fruit moth, Argyresthia conjugella
Eberferkel *n* boar piglet
Eberfleisch *n* boar [meat], brawn
Eberfütterung *f* boar feeding
Ebergeruch *m* boar odour
Ebermast *f* boar fattening
Ebernachkommenschaftsprüfung *f* boar (pig) progeny testing
Eberraute *f* southernwood, old-man wormwood, lad's (boy's) love, brotan, abrotanum, Artemisia abrotanum
Ebersperma *n* boar semen
Eberwurz *f* 1. carline [thistle] *(genus Carlina)*; 2. smooth carline, Carlina acaulis
EBIMV *s.* Erbsenblattrollmosaikvirus
ebnen to level
Ebo *m* tonka bean tree, coumarou, Dipteryx odorata
EC *s.* 1. Ethylcellulose; 2. Energieladung
Ecesis *f (ecol)* ecesis
Echeverie *f (bot)* echeveria, Mexican fire cracker *(genus Echeveria)*
Echinococcus *m (zoo)* echinococcus *(genus Echinococcus)*
Echinokokkose *f (vet)* echinococcosis, hydatid disease
Echinokokkus *m* 1. echinococcus, hydatid [larva]; 2. *s.* Echinococcus
Echoortung *f* echo analysis *(e.g. of fish stocks)*
Echte Bärentraube *f* [red] bearberry, Arctostaphylus uva-ursi
~ **Bastardvogelbeere** *f* Finnish whitebeam, Sorbus x hybrida
~ **Betonie** *f (bot)* betony, Stachys (Betonica) officinalis
~ **Eberesche** *f* rowan[-tree], [European] mountain-ash, quickbeam, Sorbus aucuparia
~ **Erbsenwelke** *f* pea fusarium wilt, top yellows of pea *(esp. caused by Fusarium oxysporum f. pisi)*
~ **Federnelke** *f* common garden pink, Dianthus plumaris
~ **Flacourtie** *f* Madagascar plum, Flacourtia indica
~ **Geißraute** *f* [common] goat's-rue, Galega officinalis
~ **Goldrute** *f* European golden rod, Solidago virgaurea
~ **Gräser** *npl* grass family *(family Poaceae = Gramineae)*
~ **Hickory** *f* mockernut [hickory], big-bud hickory, Carya tomentosa (alba)
~ **Hirse** *f* [common, broomcorn, true] millet, Indian (French, hog) millet, proso [millet], Panicum miliaceum
~ **Kamille** *f* [wild] c[h]amomile, scented mayweed, Chamomilla (Matricaria) recutita
~ **Kastanie** *f s.* Edelkastanie
~ **Königskerze** *f* common (great) mullein, Aaron's rod, flannel mullein (plant), Verbascum thapsus
~ **Koschenille[schild]laus** *f* cochineal [insect], Coccus cacti, Dactylopius coccus
~ **Kuhschelle** *f* daneflower, Pulsatilla vulgaris
~ **Laus** *f* sucking louse *(group Anoplura)*
~ **Mehlbeere** *f* whitebeam [tree], beam tree, Sorbus aria
~ **Mispel** *f* medlar, Mespilus germanica
~ **Motte** *f* [tineid] moth *(family Tineidae)*
~ **Nelkenwurz** *f* [herb] bennet, common avens, Geum urbanum
~ **Ochsenzunge** *f* [common] alkanet, ox-tongue, common (garden) bugloss, Anchusa officinalis
~ **Pechkiefer** *f* Georgia (American pitch) pine, Pinus palustris
~ **Pistazie** *f* pistachio, pistache, Pistacia vera
~ **Pitchpine** *s.* ~ Pechkiefer
~ **Rockenbolle** *f* rocambole, Allium sativum var. ophioscorodon, Allium scorodoprasum
~ **Sagopalme** *f* sago[-tree], Metroxylon sagu
~ **Schierlingstanne** *f* eastern (Canada) hemlock, Tsuga canadensis
~ **Schirmpalme** *f* Chinese fan palm, Livistona chinensis
~ **Schlupfwespe** *f* ichneumon[-wasp], ichneumonfly *(family Ichneumonidae)*
~ **Sisalagave** *f* sisal, Agava sisalana
~ **Stechmücke** *f (ent)* gnat *(genus Culex)*
~ **Steineiche** *f* holm[-oak], holly [oak], Quercus ilex
~ **Taube** *f* dove *(family Columbidae)*
~ **Trauerweide** *f* weeping willow, Salix babylonica
~ **Vanille** *f* vanilla, Vanilla planifolia (fragrans)
~ **Zuckerpalme** *f* true sugar palm, arenga [palm], Arenga pinnata (saccharifera)
~ **Zwergmispel** *f* dwarf medlar, Sorbus chamaemespilus

Echte

- ~ **Zypresse** *f* Italian cypress, Cupressus sempervirens
- **Echter Alant** *m (bot)* elecampane, Inula helenium
- ~ **Ammei** *m (bot)* bisnaga, Ammi visnaga
- ~ **Apfelmehltau** *m* apple [powdery] mildew *(caused by Podosphaera leucotricha)*
- ~ **Baldrian** *m* common valerian, setwall, Valeriana officinalis
- ~ **Bärenklau** *m (bot)* bear's-breech, brank-ursine, Acanthus mollis
- ~ **Baumwürger** *m (bot)* American bitter-sweet, Celastrus scandens
- ~ **Brasilholzbaum** *m* prickly brazilwood, Caesalpinia echinata
- ~ **Brotfruchtbaum** *m* jack fruit, jack [tree], Artocarpus heterophyllus (integrifolius)
- ~ **Ehrenpreis** *m (bot)* common [field] speedwell, [field, drug] speedwell, fluellen, Veronica officinalis
- ~ **Eibisch** *m* marsh mallow, Althaea officinalis
- ~ **Erdbeermehltau** *m* strawberry mildew *(caused by Sphaerotheca humuli = S. macularis)*
- ~ **Falke** *m* falcon *(family Falconicae)*
- ~ **Farn** *m* fern *(class Filicatae)*
- ~ **Feigenbaum** *m* [common] fig, Smyrna (edible) fig, Ficus caria
- ~ **Feuerschwamm** *m s.* ~ Zunderschwamm
- ~ **Fuchs** *m* fox *(genus Vulpes)*
- ~ **Gamander** *m s.* Edelgamander
- ~ **Gelber Steinklee** *m s.* ~ Steinklee
- ~ **Haarstrang** *m* sulphur-weed, sulphur-wort, Peucedanum officinale
- ~ **Hanf** *m* true hemp, Cannabis dativa
- ~ **Hausschwamm** *m* house (dry-rot) fungus, Serpula (Merulius) lacrymans
- ~ **Hickory** *m* mockernut [hickory], big-bud hickory, Carya tomentosa (alba)
- ~ **Jasmin** *m* Spanish (common) jasmin[e], Jasminum grandiflorum
- ~ **Kapernstrauch** *m* caper [bush], Capparis spinosa
- ~ **Kreuzdorn** *m* common buckthorn, Rhine berry, Rhamnus catharticus
- ~ **Kugelamarant** *m* globe amaranth, Gomphrena globosa
- ~ **Lavendel** *m* [true] lavender, Lavandula angustifolia
- ~ **Mahagonibaum** *m* mahogany [tree], Swietenia mahagoni
- ~ **Mehltau** *m (phyt)* powdery (true) mildew *(caused by fungi of order Erysiphales)*
- ~ **Mehltau** *m* **der Begonie** powdery mildew of begonia *(caused by Oidium begoniae)*
- ~ **Mehltau** *m* **der Gurke** powdery mildew of cucumber *(caused by Sphaerotheca fuliginae)*
- ~ **Mehltau** *m* **der Quitte** quince mildew *(caused by Podosphaera oxyacanthae = P. tridactyla)*
- ~ **Mehltau** *m* **der Rose** powdery mildew of rose *(caused by Sphaerotheca pannosa)*
- ~ **Mehltau** *m* **der Schwarzwurzel** courgette powdery mildew *(caused by Erysiphe cichoracearum)*
- ~ **Mehltau** *m* **der Weinrebe** powdery mildew of grape, grape mildew *(caused by Uncinula necator)*
- ~ **Mehltau** *m* **des Getreides** powdery mildew of cereals *(caused by Erysiphe graminis)*
- ~ **Mehltau** *m* **des Parakautschukbaumes** powdery mildew of Para rubber tree *(caused by Oidium heveae)*
- ~ **Mehltaupilz** *m* powdery mildew
- ~ **Pernambukholzbaum** *m* prickly brazilwood, Caesalpinia echinata
- ~ **Pfeffermilchling** *m* pepper mushroom, peppery milk cap, Lactorius piperatus
- ~ **Pfifferling** *m* [yellow] chanterelle, Cantharellus cibarius
- ~ **Pilz** *m* fungus *(division Eumycota)*
- ~ **Pistazienbaum** *m* pistachio, pistache, Pistacia vera
- ~ **Quendel** *m* calamint savory, Calamintha nepeta ssp. glandulosa
- ~ **Reizker** *m* saffron milk cap, orange agaric, Lactarius deliciosus
- ~ **Rohrkolben** *m* cat's-tail, cattail, reed-mace, Typha latifolia
- ~ **Safran** *m* saffron [crocus], Crocus sativus
- ~ **Salbei** *m* sage, Salvia officinalis
- ~ **Sandel[holz]baum** *m* sandal[wood], Santalum album
- ~ **Seidelbast** *m* mezereon, mezereum, February daphne, Daphne mezereum
- ~ **Steinklee** *m* yellow[-flowered] sweet clover, yellow (field) mellilot, Melilotus officinalis
- ~ **Steinsame** *m* gromwell, Lithospermum officinale
- ~ **Walnußbaum** *m* Persian walnut, Madeira nut, Juglans regia ssp. regia
- ~ **Ysop** *m* hyssop, Hyssopus officinalis
- ~ **Zunderschwamm** *m* [German] tinder fungus, tinder bracket, Fomes (Polyporus) fomentarius
- **Echtes Ackerbohnenmosaik** *n (phyt)* bean common mosaic
- ~ **Ackerbohnenmosaikvirus** *n* broad bean true mosaic virus, BBTMV
- ~ **Benediktenkraut** *n* blessed thistle, Cnicus benedictus
- ~ **Geißblatt** *n* Italian woodbine, Lonicera caprifolium
- ~ **Gras** *n* grass *(family Poaceae = Gramineae)*
- ~ **Herzgespann** *n* motherwort, Leonurus cardiaca
- ~ **Johanniskraut** *n* common St. John's wort, Klamath weed, hardhay, Hypericum perforatum
- ~ **Löffelkraut** *n* scurvy-grass, Cochlearia officinalis
- ~ **Mädesüß** *n* meadowsweet, queen-of-the-meadow[s], Filipendula ulmaria
- ~ **Militz[gras]** *n* reed sweet grass, brook grass, Glyceria maxima (aquatica)

~ **Pferdefleischholz** *n* beef wood, Swartzia tomentosa
~ **Sandelholz** *n* sandal[wood] *(from Santalum album)*
~ **Seifenkraut** *n* common soap-wort, Saponaria officinalis
~ **Tausendgüldenkraut** *n* common centaury, Centaurium erythraea (minus)
Eckenberegner *m* corner irrigator
Ecker *f* beech nut (mast)
Eckige Blattfleckenkrankheit *f* **der Bohne** angular leaf spot of bean *(caused by Isariopsis griseola = Phaeoisariopsis griseola)*
~ **Blattfleckenkrankheit** *f* **der Gurke** angular leaf spot of cucumber *(caused by Pseudomonas lachrymans)*
Eckschneidezahn *m* corner incisor (tooth)
Eckstrebenwinkel *m* angle of wall *(of the hoof)*
Eckzahn *m* corner tooth (incisor); canine [tooth]
Economiser *m* economizer
ED 50 *s.* Dosis/mittlere effektive
Edamer *m* Edam [cheese]
edaphisch edaphic *(of or relating to the soil)*
Edaphologie *f* edaphology
edaphologisch edaphologic[al]
Edaphon *n* edaphon
Edaphosphäre *f* edaphosphere
Eddo *f (bot)* 1. eddo, Colocasia esculenta var. antiquorum; 2. eddo *(edible tuber)*
edel noble *(e.g. a wine)*
Edelauge *n* [scion] bud
Edeldistel *f (bot)* eryngo *(genus Eryngium)*
Edeleberesche *f* rowan[-tree], Sorbus aucuparia var. edulis
Edelesche *f* narrow-leaved ash, Fraxinus angustifolia ssp. oxycarpa
Edelfäule *f* noble rot[tenness] *(of grape, caused by Botrytis cinerea)*
Edelfurnier *n* decorative veneer
Edelgamander *m (bot)* chamaedrys germander, Teucrium chamaedrys
Edelholz *n* 1. luxury (fine) wood; 2. *s.* Edelreis
Edelkamille *f* Roman (noble, sweet) camomile, Chamaemelum nobile, Anthemis nobilis
Edelkastanie *f* [sweet, edible, European] chestnut, marron, Castanea sativa (vesca)
Edelknospe *f* scion bud
Edellaubbaum *m* valuable broad-leaved tree, broad-leaved tree of high value
Edelmarder *m* pine marten, Martes martes
Edelminze *f* ginger mint, *(Am)* Scotch mint, Mentha x gentilis
Edelmist *m* fermented manure
Edelpelargonie *f (bot)* regal pelargonium, Pelargonium-Grandiflorum hybrid
Edelpelztier *n* furbearer, fur-bearing animal
Edelraute *f* Alpine wormwood, Artemisia mutellina
Edelreis *n* scion[wood], cion, grafting scion (twig), graft, fruiting scion (cane); bud stick *(inoculation)*

Edelreiser *npl* budwood
Edelreizker *m* saffron milk cap, orange agaric, Lactarius deliciosus
Edelsorte *f* top variety
Edeltanne *f* 1. noble fir, Abies procera; 2. silver fir, Abies alba
Edeltier *n (hunt)* hind
Edeltrieb *m* scion shoot
Edelweiß *n* edelweiss, Leontopodium alpinum
Edelwild *n* red deer, Cervus elaphus
Edifenphos *n* edifenphos, EDPP *(fungicide)*
Editon *n* editon *(fungicide)*
EDTA *s.* Ethylendiamintetraessigsäure
EE *s.* Amerikanische Pferdeenzephalomyelitis
EEG *s.* Elektroenzephalogramm
EF *s.* 1. Futtereinheit/Energetische; 2. Ephemeralfieber
EFA *s.* Erstferkelalter
EFBIV *s.* Falsches Blattrollvirus der Erbse
Efeu *m* 1. ivy, hedera *(genus Hedera)*; 2. [English] ivy, Hedera helix
Efeuaralie *f* 1. fatshedera *(genus x Fatshedera)*; 2. aralia (tree) ivy, x Fatshedera lizei
Efeuartiger Gundermann *m (bot)* gill-over-the-ground, Glec[h]oma hederacea
efeubewachsen ivied
Efeublattlaus *f* ivy aphid, Aphis hederae
Efeublättriger Ehrenpreis *m*, **Efeuehrenpreis** *m* ivy[-leaved] speedwell, henbit, Veronica hederaefolia
Efeupelargonie *f* ivy-leaved pelargonium, Pelargonium peltatum
Efeutute *f (bot)* 1. pothos, scindapsus *(genus Scindapsus)*; 2. devil's ivy, golden (marble Queen) pothos, Epipremnum aureum, Scindapsus aureus
Effekt *m***/maternaler** *(gen)* maternal effect
~**/zytopathischer** cytopathic effect
Effektivität *f* **des Wasserverbrauches** water-use efficiency, consumptive-use efficiency
Effektor *m* effector
effizient efficient
Effizienz *f***/photosynthetische** photosynthetic efficiency
Efflation *f* eructation, belching *(of ruminants)*
Effloreszenz *f* 1. *(bot)* efflorescence, blossoming, blooming; 2. *(vet)* efflorescence, eruption *(redness of the skin)*
Efflux *m* efflux
Effusion *f* effusion
EFVbV *s.* Virus der Frühen Verbräunung der Erbse
Egel *m* leech *(class Hirudinea)*
Egelbefall *m (vet)* hirudiniasis
Egelschnecke *f* limacid [slug] *(family Limacidae)*
Egerling *m* agaric, mushroom *(genus Agaricus)*
Egge *f* harrow
~**/leichte** light harrow
~ **mit aktiven Werkzeugen** power[-driven] harrow
~**/mittelschwere** medium harrow

Egge

~/schwere heavy harrow, brake[-harrow]
eggen to harrow
Eggenbalken *m* harrow-bar
Eggenfeld *n* harrow leaf (section)
Eggenrahmen *m* harrow frame
Eggenscheibe *f* harrow disk
Eggenschlitten *m* harrow sledge
Eggenträger *m* harrow carrier
Eggentragrahmen *m* harrow frame
Eggenzahn *m s.* Eggenzinke
Eggenzinke *f* harrow spike (tine, tooth)
Eglinazin *n* eglinazine *(herbicide)*
egrenieren to gin *(cotton)*
Egrenieren *n* ginning
Egreniermaschine *f* [cotton] gin, deseeder
EGSV *s.* Grünscheckungsvirus der Erbse
Egtved-Krankheit *f* Egtved disease *(of trouts)*
Ehlers-Danlos-Syndrom *n (vet)* Danlos syndrome
Ehrenpreis *m(n)* speedwell, veronica *(genus Veronica)*
Ehrlichiose *f (vet)* ehrlichiosis
Ei *n* egg; ovum, macrogamete; berry *(of fish or lobster)* • ein ~ legen to lay an egg • Eier [ab]legen *(ent)* to oviposit, to blow • Eier unterlegen to set [eggs]
~/grünfaules green-rot egg
~/kleines ovule
~/unverarbeitetes shell egg
Eiablage *f* egg laying; oviposition *(esp. of insects)*
~/erste point-of-lay *(of fowl)*
~ in frühem Embryonalstadium *(ent)* oviparity
Eiablagelockstoff *m* oviposition attractant
Eiablagerate *f* ovipositional rate
Eiablageverhalten *n* oviposition behaviour
Eiabnahme *f* egg collection
eiabtötend ovicidal
eiähnlich ovoid[al]
Eialbumin *n* egg albumin (albumen)
eiartig ovoid[al]
Eibe *f* 1. yew[-tree] *(genus Taxus)*; 2. common (English) yew, Taxus baccata
Eibefruchtung *f* oogamy
Eibehälter *m* oogonium, ovogonium
Eibenholz *n* yew
Eibenvergiftung *f (vet)* yew poisoning
Eibildung *f* egg formation, oogenesis, ovogenesis
Eibildungszelle *f* oogonium, ovogonium
Eibisch *m* 1. rose-mallow, hibiscus *(genus Hibiscus)*; 2. althaea *(genus Althaea)*
Eiblättriger Liguster *m* California privet, Ligustrum ovalifolium
Eichapfel *m (phyt)* oak apple (gall, berry)
Eiche *f* oak *(genus Quercus)*
~/junge (kleine) *s.* Eichenheister
Eichel *f* 1. *(bot)* acorn 2. *(zoo)* glans *(anatomy)*
Eichelbecher *m (bot)* cupule
Eichelbohrer *m* acorn weevil, Balaninus glandium
Eichelentzündung *f (vet)* balanitis
Eichelhäher *m* [European] jay, Garrulus glandarius
Eichelmast *f* mast of acorns, oak-mast
Eichelspießer *m (hunt)* knobber
Eichelwickler *m (ent)* bright marble tortrix, Cydia splendana
eichen oaken
eichen to calibrate *(e.g. measuring instruments)*; to adjust *(weighing-scales)*
Eichen *n s.* Ei/kleines
Eichenbestand *m* oakery, *(Am)* encinal
Eichenblattmosaik *n (phyt)* oak leaf mosaic
Eichenblattmuster *n (phyt)* oak-leaf pattern
Eichenblattroller *m* oak leaf-roller weevil, Attelabus curculionides
Eichenblattrollgalle *f* curved leaf (twig) gall
Eichenfarn *m* oak fern, Currania dryopteris
Eichenfaß *n* oak cask
Eichenfurnierholz *n* oak veneer wood
Eichengalle *f s.* Eichapfel
Eichengerbrinde *f* oak [tan]bark
Eichenheister *m* oaklet, oakling, oak sapling, flittern
Eichenholz *n* oak
Eichenholzfaß *n* oak cask
Eichenkernholzkäfer *m (ent)* [oak] pin-hole borer, Platypus cylindrus
Eichenknospenmotte *f* oak bud moth, Coleophora lutipennella
Eichenlohe *f* oak [tan]bark
Eichenmehltau *m* oak [powdery] mildew *(caused by Microsphaera alphitoides)*
Eichenmistel *f (bot)* loranthus *(genus Loranthus)*
Eichenniederwald *m s.* Eichenschälwald
Eichenpockenschildlaus *f* golden oak scale, Asterolecanium variolosum
Eichenprozessionsspinner *m* procession[ary] moth, oak procession moth, Thaumetopoea (Cnethocampa) processionea
Eichenrinde *f* oak [tan]bark
Eichensägeholz *n* oak saw timber
Eichenschälwald *m* oak-bark coppice (forest), oak-coppice forest
Eichenspinner *m* oak eggar moth, Lasiocampa quercus
Eichensplintkäfer *m* oak bark-beetle, Scolytus (Eccoptogaster) intricatus
Eichenstarkholz *n* large oak timber
Eichenwald *m* oak forest, oakery
Eichenwäldchen *n* oak grove, *(Am)* encinal
Eichenwaldtyp *m* oak forest type
Eichenwelke *f* oak wilt *(caused by Ceratocystis fagacearum)*
Eichenwickler *m (ent)* bright marble tortrix, Cydia splendana
Eichenwurzelfäule *f* oak roots disease
Eichhörnchen *n* 1. squirrel *(genus Sciurus)*; 2. red squirrel, Sciurus vulgaris
Eichhörnchenfell *n* squirrel [skin]
Eichkurve *f* calibration curve
Eichung *f* calibration; adjustment

Eicos-9-ensäure f eicos-9-enoic (gadoleic) acid *(fatty acid)*
Eicosansäure f eicosanoic acid *(fatty acid)*
Eicosapentaenylsäure f eicosapentanoic acid *(fatty acid)*
Eicosatetraensäure f eicosatetraenoic (arachidonic) acid *(fatty acid)*
Eiderdaune[n *fpl]* f eider[-down]
Eiderente f eider duck *(esp. genus Somateria)*
Eidotter m [egg-]yolk, vitellus
Eidottercitratverdünner m egg-yolk-citrate diluent *(for conservation of semen)*
Eierabsammeln n egg collection
Eierband n egg collector (collecting belt)
Eierbehandlung f egg handling
Eierdurchleuchter m egg candler (candling plant)
Eierdurchleuchtung f egg candling
Eiereinsammeln n egg collection
Eierelevator m egg elevator
Eiererzeugungsbetrieb m egg farm
Eierfangrost m egg groove
Eierfressen n egg-eating *(vice of fowl)*
Eierfrucht f egg-plant, aubergine, garden egg, Solanum melongena
Eierfruchtmosaikvirus n egg-plant mosaic virus
Eiergift n ovicide, egg killer
Eierherz n **des Huhns** round-heart disease of fowl, fatal syncope of fowl, toxic heart degeneration of fowl
Eierklärlampe f egg candler (candling plant)
Eierkonservierung f egg conservation
Eierkühlung f egg cooling
Eierlagerung f egg storage
Eierlegen n egg laying; oviposition *(esp. of insects)*
eierlegend oviparous
Eierpflanze f s. Eierfrucht
Eierpicken n egg pecking (picking) *(vice of fowl)*
Eierproduktion f egg production
Eierreinigung f egg cleaning
Eierreinigungsgerät n egg cleaner
Eiersack m egg sac *(of certain nematodes)*
Eiersammelband n egg collecting belt, egg collector
Eierschale f s. Eischale
Eierschwamm m *(bot)* [yellow] chanterelle, Cantharellus cibarius
Eiersortieranlage f egg grader
Eiersortierer m, **Eiersortiermaschine** f egg grader
Eierstock m *(zoo)* ovary, ovarium
Eierstockentfernung f *(vet)* ovariectomy, ovariotomy, oophorectomy
Eierstockentzündung f *(vet)* ovaritis, oophoritis
Eierstockgekröse n mesovarium
Eierstockhoden m ovotestis
Eierstocktasche f ovarian bursa
Eierstockträchtigkeit f ovarian pregnancy
Eierstockzyste f *(vet)* ovarian cyst
eiertragend berried *(fish or lobster)*

Eierverlustsyndrom n *(vet)* egg drop syndrome '76, EDS '76
Eierverpackungsschale f egg tray
Eierwaage f egg weigher
Eierwaschmaschine f egg washing machine
Eierzeugnis n egg product
Eifollikel m Graafian follicle (vesicle)
Eiform f egg shape
eiförmig ovate[d], oviform, ovoid[al]
~/verkehrt *(bot)* oboval, obovate, oblate
Eigelb n s. Eidotter
Eigelege n batch of eggs
Eigenantrieb m self-contained drive
Eigenbestäubung f *(bot)* self-pollination
eigenerzeugt home-grown
Eigenimpfstoff m autovaccine
Eigenleistung f own performance *(e.g. of a breeding animal)*
Eigenschaft f character, characteristic, property
~/angeborene innate character
~/erworbene acquired character
Eigentliche Zecke f [wood] tick *(family Ixodidae)*
Eigentum n/**genossenschaftliches** co-operative property
Eigenversorgung f self-sufficiency
Eigröße f egg size
Eigrube f *(ent)* egg niche
Eihaut f, **Eihülle** f embryonic membrane
Eikapsel f egg capsule (case), ootheca
Eikern m egg nucleus
Eiklar n egg-white, [egg] albumen, egg albumin, glair[e]
Eiklarhöhe f albumen height
Eiklarindex m egg albumen index
Eiklarprotein n egg protein
Eikokon m egg capsule (case), ootheca
Eikultur f egg culture *(microbiology)*
Eilarve f *(ent)* egg-larva, first instar [larva]
~ der Schmetterlinge first instar caterpillar
Eileiter m oviduct, uterine (Fallopian) tube *(animal anatomy)*
Eileiterentzündung f *(vet)* salpingitis
Eileiterträchtigkeit f oviductal (tubal, Fallopian) pregnancy
Eileitertrichter m oviduct pavilion
Eileitervereiterung f *(vet)* pyosalpinx
Eimasse f egg mass (weight)
Eimembran f egg (inner shell) membrane
Eimer m bucket, pail
Eimerfütterung f bucket (pail) feeding *(e.g. of calves)*
Eimerkette f **zur Kälberfütterung** bucket calf feeder
Eimerketten[drän]grabenbagger m bucket chain dredger
Eimermelkanlage f bucket milker (unit), bucket-type milking installation
Eimermelken n bucket (pail) milking
Eimermelkmaschine f bucket milking machine

Eimerspritze

Eimerspritze *f* bucket sprayer
Einachsantrieb *m* single-axle drive
einachsig 1. *(bot)* haplocaulescent; 2. single-axle[d], two-wheel[ed] *(vehicle)*
Einachskippanhänger *m*, **Einachskipper** *m* two-wheeled [rear] tipping trailer
Einachsmuldenkipper *m* dump body tipping trailer
Einachsschlepper *m*, **Einachstraktor** *m* walking (two-wheel) tractor
einährig *(bot)* single-eared, monostach[y]ous
einarbeiten to incorporate, to turn under *(e.g. fertilizer applications)*
~/Gründünger to green-manure
Einarbeitung *f* incorporation
einatmen *n* to inspire, to breathe in; to inhale
Einatmung *f* inspiration; inhalation
Einatmungsluftvolumen *n* **je Zeiteinheit** ventilation rate
einball[ier]en to ball
Einbeere *f* 1. Paris *(genus Paris)*; 2. one-berry, Paris quadrifolia
einbinden/in Sackleinen to burlap *(e.g. root balls)*
Einbinden *n* binding; cribbing, bundling *(a raft)*
Einblatt *n* spathe flower *(genus Spathiphyllum)*
einblättrig *(bot)* unifoliar, unifoliate
Einblättrige Esche *f* Utah ash, Fraxinus anomala
einblütig one-flowered, monanthous, uniflorous
Einblütige Wicke *f* one-flowered vetch, Vicia articulata
Einbohrloch *n* *(ent)* entrance hole
Einbrennen *n* cleaning by fumigation *(of wine casks)*
einbringen to [in]gather, to harvest *(a crop)*
~/Tonscherben zu Dränungszwecken to crock
Einbringung *f* incorporation
~ von Phosphordünger phosphatization
einbürgern to naturalize *(e.g. a plant species)*
eindämmen to dam *(e.g. a river) (s. a. eindeichen)*
~/ein Feuer to check (control) a fire, to bring a fire under control; to knock-down a fire
eindampfen to evaporate
Eindampfer *m* evaporator
Eindeckmaterial *n*, **Eindeckung** *f* shelter (covering) material *(e.g. for greenhouses)*
eindeichen to dike, to impolder, to empolder *(land)*
eindicken to thicken, to condense
Eindickfilter *n* thickening filter *(sugar manufacture)*
eindosen to can
eindrillen/Dünger neben die Pflanzenreihe to side-dress
Eindringfähigkeit *f* permeativity *(e.g. of plant protectants)*
Eindringling *m* *(ecol)* invader
Eindringtiefe *f* penetration depth; digging-in depth *(e.g. of a dozer blade)*
Eindringung *f* penetration
Eindringungsmeßgerät *n* penetrometer
einebnen to level
eineggen to harrow in

eineiig monozygotic, monozygous, monovular, uniovular, one-egg
einelterlich uniparental
Einengung *f* *(vet)* stenosis
einetagig *s.* einhiebig
Einfachbier *n* einfachbier
Einfachbouillon *f* broth *(microbiology)*
einfächerig *(bot, zoo)* unilocular, uniloculate
Einfachhybride *f* single cross [hybrid]
Einfachkamm *m* single (shell) comb *(of fowl)*
Einfachkreuzung *f* single (simple) crossing *(breeding)*
Einfachkreuzungshybride *f* single cross [hybrid]
Einfachschnitt *m* **parallel zur Stammlängsachse** sawing alive, through-and-through sawing
Einfachverglasung *f* single[-layer] glazing
Einfachzucker *m* simple sugar, monosaccharide
einfahren to earth, to go to earth (ground) *(fox or badger)*
einfaktoriell unifactorial
einfallen to alight *(wildfowl)*
einfarbig 1. one-coloured, unicolour[ed]; 2. monochromatic *(light)*
Einfarbig Gelbes Höhenvieh *n* German Yellow *(cattle breed)*
Einfassungspflanze *f* border (edging) plant
einfetten to grease, to dub *(leather)*
einflechten to braid *(a mane or horse-tail)*
einflößen to drench *(e.g. a veterinary drug)*
Einfluß *m*/**maternaler** *(gen)* maternal effect
Einfriedung *f* fence, fencing
einfrieren 1. to freeze, to turn to ice; 2. *s.* einfrosten
einfrosten to [deep-]freeze *(food)*
einfrüchtig monocarpous
Einfüllsieb *n* strainer
Einfülltrichter *m* [feed] hopper
Eingänger *m* *(hunt)* solitary boar
Eingangsgröße *f* input
eingattern to fence [in] *(e.g. game)*
Eingattern *n* fencing [in]
eingebaut inbuilt
eingehen to perish, to die
eingeklemmt crowded, jammed, addressed *(e.g. a tree in a stand)*
Ein-Gen-Ein-Enzym-Hypothese *f* one-gene-one enzyme hypothesis
Ein-Gen-Heterosis *f* overdominance, superdominance
eingepfercht pent-up • **~ sein** to be crammed together
eingerollt rolled-up
~/kreisförmig *(bot, zoo)* circinate
eingesäuert pickle-cured
eingeschlagen felled, cut *(a tree)*; cutover *(a forest)*
eingeschlämmt root-puddled *(a bare-rooted plant)*
eingeschlechtig *(bot)* unisexual
eingeschleppt accidentally imported *(e.g. a pest)*

Eingeschnittene Taubnessel f cut-leaved dead nettle, Lamium hybridum
eingeschoben intercalary
eingesessen indigenous, autochthonal, autochthonous
eingestaltig monomorphic, monomorphous
Eingestaltigkeit f monomorphism
eingestreut incidental *(e.g. a tree species)*
eingewachsen encased, intergrown, blind *(e.g. a knot)*
Eingeweide n intestine, gut
Eingeweide npl bowels, entrails, viscera
Eingeweidebruch m *(vet)* [intestinal] hernia, rupture
Eingeweidefett n visceral fat
Eingeweideorgan n viscus
Eingeweidesack m visceral mass (hump) *(of snails)*
Eingeweidewurm m intestinal worm, mawworm, helminth *(comprehensive term)*
eingewöhnen to [ac]climatize, *(Am)* to acclimate
~/sich to [ac]climatize, *(Am)* to acclimate
Eingewöhnung f acclimatization, *(Am)* acclimat[at]ion
Eingießung f infusion
eingraben to bury, to dig [in]
~ in einen Bau to burrow in
Eingriff m 1. *(forest)* felling operation, removal; 2. *(vet)* operation; 3. *(hunt)* slot *(of a track)*
Eingriffe mpl **in das Kronendach** *(forest)* manipulation of canopy
eingriffelig *(bot)* monogynous
Eingriffeliger Weißdorn m [one-seed, English] hawthorn, hedgerow thorn, haw, Crataegus monogyna
Eingriffsstärke f *(forest)* heaviness of felling, intensity of cut
einhalmig *(bot)* single-stalked, uniculm
Einhandpistolensprüher m one-hand pistol sprayer *(plant protection)*
Einhandsäge f handsaw
Einhandschere f secateurs
einhängen/in die Förderkette *(slaught)* to shackle
einharken to rake in
Einhauen n forging, striking *(movement disorder of horses)*
einhäusig *(bot)* monoecious, monecious
Einhäusigkeit f *(bot)* monoecism, monoecy
einheimisch native, indigenous, autochthonal, autochthonous, aboriginal, endemic
Einheit f/**infektiöse** infectious unit *(microbiology)*
~/koloniebildende colony-forming unit, CFU *(microbiology)*
~/photosynthetische photosynthetic unit
~/taxonomische taxon
Einheitserde f standard soil *(horticulture)*
Einheitsfang m sweep-net catch (sample) *(of a pest population)*
Einheitshöhenkurve f uniform height curve *(forest mensuration)*

Einheitsmembran f unit mebrane *(cytology)*
Einheitssärad n studded roller *(of seed drill)*
Einheitsvolumenkurve f uniform volume curve *(forest mensuration)*
Einhieb m *(forest)* axe damage
einhiebig single-storeyed, one-storied, monocyclic *(forest stand)*
einhöckerig *(bot, zoo)* unicuspid
Einhöckeriges Kamel n [Arabian] camel, Camelus dromedarius
einhodig monorchic, monorchid
Einhodigkeit f monorchidism
Einhordendarre f one-floor kiln, single-floor kiln *(malting)*
Einhufer m soliped, solidungulate *(family Equidae)*
einhufig soliped, solid-hoofed, solidungulate
einhürden s. einpferchen
einimpfen to inoculate
Einimpfen n inoculation
Einische f *(ent)* egg niche
Einjahrespflanze f annual, therophyte
einjährig 1. *(bot)* annual; 2. one-year-old
Einjähriger m yearling *(sport horse)*
Einjähriger Beifuß m sweet wormwood, Artemisia annua
~ Knäuel m annual knawel, Scleranthus annuus
~ Sonnenhut m gloriosa (yellow) daisy, black-eyed Susan, Rudbeckia hirta [var. hirta]
~ Ziest m hedge-nettle betony, Stachys annua
Einjähriges Bingelkraut n annual (French, garden) mercury, Mercurialis annua
~ Bohnenkraut n [summer] savory, Satureja hortensis
~ Rispengras n annual bluegrass (meadow grass), Suffolk-grass, Poa annua
~ Silberblatt n common honesty, satin-flower, Lunaria annua (biennis)
~ Weidelgras n annual (Westerwolds, Swiss) rye-grass, Lolium multiflorum var. westerwoldicum
Einjahrsphlox m annual (Drummond) phlox, Phlox drummondii
Einkeilung f *(vet)* gomphosis
einkeimblättrig *(bot)* monocotyledonous
einkeimig *(bot)* monogerm
einkerben to notch
Einkerben n notching
Einkerbung f 1. notch, indenture; 2. s. Einkerben
einkernig mononuclear, uninucleate
einkochen 1. to preserve *(s. a. konservieren)*; 2. to thicken, to boil down *(e.g. juice)*
einkolbig single-eared *(maize)*
Einkorn n s. Einkornweizen
Einkornramschmethode f single-seed descent method *(plant breeding)*
Einkornweizen m einkorn [wheat], Triticum monococcum
einkreisen *(hunt)* to track
Einkreiser m tracker
einkürzen to pinch back, to shorten *(a plant)*

einlaben

einlaben to rennet
Einlabungstemperatur f renneting temperature
einlagern to store [up], to put into store
~/**Heu im Stadel** to staddle
~/**in Lattenkisten** to crate
~/**in Mieten** to clamp
~/**in Steigen (Stiegen)** to crate
Einlagerung f storage
Einlagerungsmaschine f store conveyor
Einlagetabak m **für Zigarren** cigar filler tobacco
einlappig (bot, zoo) unilobate
Einlaß m, **Einlaßöffnung** f inlet, intake
Einlaßventil n intake valve
Einlauf m (vet) enema
einlaufen lassen (vet) to infuse
Einlaufflüssigkeit f (vet) enema
einläufig one-barrelled (sporting gun)
Einlaufseiher m suction strainer
Einlaufwette f (Am) exacta
Einlegeflüssigkeit f pickle
Einlegegurke f pickling cucumber, pickle
~/**[sehr] kleine** gherkin
einlegen[/sauer] to pickle (e.g. vegetable)
Einlegetrommel f feeding drum (of a thresher)
einmachen s. einkochen
einmaischen to mash
Einmaischeverfahren n single-mash method (brewing)
Einmann-Motor[ketten]säge f one-man power saw
Einmannsäge f one-man saw
Einmessen n **der Brandstelle** cross bearing, (Am) cross shot (forest fire control)
einmieten to clamp, to pit
Einmieter m (ecol) inquiline
Einnährstoffdünger m straight (single-constituent) fertilizer, individual (simple) fertilizer
Einnischung f (ecol) annidation
Einnistung f nidation
Einnutzungsrasse f single-purpose breed
einpaarig (bot, zoo) unijugate, unijugous
einpferchen to pen [up], to corral, to crib, to [pin]fold
einpflanzen 1. to plant, to bed; to prick [off, out] (esp. seedlings); 2. to implant (e.g. organs)
~/**Myzel** to spawn
Einpflanzung f 1. planting; 2. implantation
einpflügen to plough in [back, down, under], (Am) to plow in
Einphasenernte f single-stage working system
einpökeln to cure, to pickle, to corn (esp. by salting); to souse (esp. with brine)
Einradantrieb m single-wheel drive
Einradeinachstraktor m single-wheel walking tractor
Einradhacke f single-wheel hand hoe, hand-pushed wheeled cultivator, Dutch hoe
Einradmotorkarrenspritze f one-wheel barrow motor sprayer
einrechen to rake in

Einreibung f (vet) liniment, embrocation
einreihig single-row; (bot) uniseriate
Einreißung f (vet) laceration
einreiten to break [in] (a horse)
Einrichtung f (vet) reposition (e.g. of fractures)
~ **des Wintersitzes** (api) autumn management
Einsaat f 1. additional sowing, undersowing; 2. undercrop, catch crop
einsacken to sack, to bag
einsäen to interseed, to intersow, to overseed, to oversow, to undersow
~/**Rasen neu** to returf
einsalzen to salt, to pickle, to cure, to corn
einsamig (bot) one-seeded, monospermous, monocarpous
einsammeln to [in]gather, to collect
Einsatz m 1. application (of a machine); 2. compartment, section (e.g. in dryers)
~/**überbetrieblicher** multifarm use (e.g. of agricultural machinery)
~ **unter schwierigen Betriebsbedingungen** heavy-duty application
einsatzfähig serviceable, available
Einsatzfähigkeit f serviceability, availability
Einsatzmenge f dose, dosage
Einsatzstärke f strength of attack (forest fire control)
einsaugen to suck [in], to absorb
Einscharpflug m one-body plough, single mouldboard plough
einschätzen to appraise, to assess, to estimate, to judge
Einschätzung f appraisal, appraisement, assessment, estimation
Einscheiben[sä]schar n single-disk coulter
Einschenkelkluppe f **nach Biltmore** Biltmore stick (timber mensuration)
einschichtig s. einhiebig
Einschichtung f s. Stratifikation
Einschiebung f intussusception
Einschießen n **der Milch** milk ejection (let-down)
einschießen lassen/Milch to give down (said of a cow)
einschiffig single-bay (greenhouse)
Einschlafen n **der Nelkenblüten** sleepiness of carnation (injurious effect of ethylene)
Einschlag m 1. forest harvest[ing], timber harvest, felling [operation], fall, [wood] cutting, cut, throwing, (Am) logging (s. a. under Holzeinschlag); 2. s. Einschlagsort
~ **ab bestimmtem Mindestumfang in Brusthöhe** girth-limit cutting, diameter-limit cutting
~/**jährlicher** annual cut
~/**selektiver** selective felling
~ **unter Belassung von Überhaltbäumen** seed-tree cutting
einschlagen 1. (forest) to fell, to cut, to log, to harvest; 2. to wrap [up] (e.g. flowers); to bury, to heel in, to embed, to sheugh (young plants)

~/Bienen in eine Beute to hive
Einschlagplatz *m* rooting (plunging) bed, laying-in ground
Einschlagsfläche *f* felling area
Einschlagsgenehmigung *f* felling licence
Einschlagsmöglichkeit *f* logging chance
Einschlagsort *m* felling site (place, point)
Einschlagsplan *m* felling plan, cutting budget
Einschlagsrecht *n* timber concession (right)
Einschlagssoll *n* felling quota, calculated cut (yield)
Einschlagszeit *f* felling period (season, time)
Einschlämmen *n* puddling *(bare-rooted plants)*
Einschleppung *f* accidental importation, [unwanted] introduction *(e.g. of pests)*
einschliefen *(hunt)* to earth, to go to earth (ground)
Einschluß *m* inclusion
Einschlußkörper *m*, Einschlußkörperchen *n* inclusion body, nuclear inclusion
Einschlußkörperhepatitis *f* der Hühnerküken inclusion body hepatitis of chickens, IBH, infectious (aplastic) anaemia of chickens, hepatomyelopoetic disease of chickens
Einschlußkörperkrankheit *f* der Taube *(vet)* Smadel's disease
Einschneidemaschine *f (forest)* slasher, bucker, bucking machine
einschneiden to incise; to buck, to slash; to notch
Einschnitt *m* incision, kerf; notch *(tree-felling)*
Einschnittabelle *f (forest)* log rule (scale)
Einschnittprogramm *n* bucking programme *(roundwood conversion)*
Einschnittschema *n* sawing pattern *(roundwood conversion)*
einschnürig curved, crooked *(tree-trunk)*
Einschnürungskrankheit *f* constriction disease, blight *(of forest tree seedlings, caused by Pestalotia hartigii)*
~ der Scheinzypresse die back of chamaecyparis *(caused by Pestalotia funerea)*
Einschrittmutation *f* one-step mutation *(bacteriology)*
einschrumpfen to shrink
Einschürige Esparsette *f* giant (double-cut) sainfoin, Onobrychis viciifolia
Einschurwolle *f* single-clip wool
Einschuß *m*, Einschußstelle *f (hunt)* shooting-spot
einschwefeln to stum *(must)*
einschwemmen *(forest)* to flume, to send down a flume *(logs)*
einseitig blühend *(bot)* secundiflorous
einseitswendig *(bot)* secund
~ blühend secundiflorous
Einsendungsprobe *f* submitted sample
einsickern to seep [in], to soak in
Einsickern *n* seepage, soaking
einsilieren to [en]silage, to ensile, to silo

Einspänner *m* one-horse carriage
~/leichter zweirädriger gig
einspännig one-horse
einspeicheln[/Nahrung] to insalivate
Einspeichelung *f* insalivation
einspeisen to feed
Einspeisung *f* feeding
einsperren to pen [up]
~/in einen Käfig to cage
einspinnen/sich in einen Kokon to cocoon
einspitzen to insert *(inoculation)*
~/seitlich to side-graft
Einsporauslese *f* single-spore selection
Einsporisolat *n* single-spore isolate
Einspritzdüse *f* injection nozzle
einspritzen to inject
Einspritzmotor *m* fuel injection engine
Einspritzpumpe *f* injection pump
Einspritzung *f* injection
Einspritzvorrichtung *f* injector
Einspülung *f (soil)* illuviation
einstallen to house, to stable, to stall [up]
Einstallungszeitraum *m* housing period
Einstammstarter *m*, Einstammstarterkultur *f (dairy)* single-strain starter
Einstand *m*, Einstandsgebiet *n (hunt)* cover[t]
Einstau *m* s. Einstaubewässerung
Einstaubewässerung *f* infiltration irrigation, irrigation by infiltration
einstellbar adjustable
einstellen to adjust, to set
Einstellung *f* adjustment, setting, calibration
Einstellvorrichtung *f* adjustment
Einstellwert *m* setting
einstengelig single-stalked
Einstreu *f* litter, bedding, bed of straw • mit ~ bedecken to litter [down]
Einstreubehandlung *f* litter management
einstreuen to litter [down], to bed
Einstreuhaltung *f* litter management
einstreulos litterless
Einstromplatte *f* single-flow plate *(of a pasteurizing plant)*
einstufen to grade, to classify, to rate
~/nach Punkten to score
Einstufenkreiselpumpe *f* single-stage centrifugal pump
Einstufenselektion *f* single-stage selection
einstufig single-storeyed, one-storeyed *(a forest stand)*
Einstufung *f* grading, classification
Einstülpung *f* intussusception
einstutzen to cut back to stump
Einstutzen *n* des Sprosses shoot pruning
eintägig one-day, diurnal, ephemeral
Eintagsküken *n* day-old chick, baby chick
Eintagsweide *f* one-day grazing, single-day grazing
eintauchen to dip, to immerse

Eintauchflüssigkeit

Eintauchflüssigkeit *f* **zur Schafdesinfektion** sheep-dip
Eintauchthermometer *n* dipper thermometer
Eintauchvorrichtung *f* dipper, dipping bath (pit)
Eintauschstärke *f* (soil) replacing power
Einteilungsnetz *n* (forest) net of rides, boundaries network
eintopfen to pot [off, up]
Eintopfen *n* potting[-off]
Eintopfmaschine *f* pot [and repot] machine
Einträufelung *f* (vet) instillation
Eintrittsgang *m* (ent) entrance tunnel
Eintrittspforte *f* entrance portal *(e.g. for pathogens)*
eintrocknen to dry up; to blast, to wither *(e.g. seedlings)*
Eintrommelwinde *f* single-drum winch
eintüten to bag *(e.g. inflorescences to prevent unwanted pollination)*
Ein- und Umtopfmaschine *f* pot and repot machine
einverleiben to incorporate
Einverleibung *f* incorporation
Einwachs *m s.* Einwuchs
einwachsen to ingrow *(e.g. horns)*
Einwanderung *f* (ecol) immigration, invasion
Einwanderungspflanze *f* neophyte
Einwärtsdreher *m* pronator [muscle]
einwärtsgerollt *(bot)* involute
Einwaschung *f* (soil) illuviation
Einwaschungshorizont *m* (soil) illuvial (enrichment) horizon, B-horizon
Einwaschungszone *f* (soil) zone of illuviation
einwässern to water in
Einwässern *n* 1. watering [in]; 2. launching *(of drift-wood)*
einwecken to preserve, to conserve, to bottle *(s. a. konservieren)*
einweichen to soak, to steep, to drench; to macerate; to liquor *(malting barley, malt)*; to pickle *(seed)*
Einweiseln *n* (api) adding, allocation
Einwellentrogwäsche *f* beet washer with revolving-arm agitators
Einwerfen *n s.* Einwässern 2.
einwintern to winter *(honey-bees)*; to in-winter *(e.g. livestock)*
einwirtig monoxenous
Einwuchs *m* (forest) 1. recruitment; 2. recruits, ingrowth
einwurzeln to root
Einwurzelung *f* rooting
einzäunen to fence[in], to paddock
Einzäunen *n* fencing
Einzäunung *f* fence, fencing
Einzelauslese *f* individual selection
Einzelbauer *m* individual farmer
Einzelbaum *m* solitary (single) tree, individual stem (tree)
Einzelbaumauslese *f* individual-tree selection
Einzelbaummischung *f* (forest) single-tree mixture
Einzelbaumüberhalt *m* (forest) reserve cutting
Einzelbestand *m* single (individual) stand
Einzelblock *m* (forest) single (floating) periodic block
Einzelblüte *f* floret, flower[l]et, floscule, solitary (single) flower
Einzelbox *f* single pen
Einzelbucht *f* single (individual) pen
Einzeldünger *m* straight (single-constituent) fertilizer, simple (individual) fertilizer
Einzeleimasse *f* egg mass (weight)
Einzelflößerei *f*, **Einzelflößung** *f s.* Einzelstammflößerei
Einzelfreßstand *m* individual feeding stall *(e.g. for sows)*
Einzelfrucht *f* (bot) simple fruit
Einzelfruchtgröße *f* individual (single) fruit size
einzelfrüchtig monocarpous
Einzelfrüchtigkeit *f* monocarpy
Einzelfutterautomat *m* automatic feeder for individual feeding
Einzelfütterung *f* individual feeding
Einzelgabe *f* single application *(fertilization, irrigation)*
Einzelgenheterosis *f s.* Ein-Gen-Heterosis
Einzelgenresistenz *f* single-gene resistance
Einzelgewächshaus *n* single (free-standing) greenhouse
Einzelkäfig *m* individual cage
Einzelkornablage *f s.* Einzelkornaussaat
Einzelkornaussaat *f* single-grain sowing, precision drilling (seeding)
Einzelkorngefüge *n* (soil) single-grain[ed] structure
Einzelkornsaat *f s.* Einzelkornaussaat
Einzelkornsämaschine *f* single-seed drill, precision drill (planter), [seed-]spacing drill
~/zellenradlose plateless planter
Einzelkornstruktur *f s.* Einzelkorngefüge
Einzellähmung *f* (vet) monoplegia
Einzelleistung *f* individual performance *(breeding)*
Einzellerprotein *n* single-cell protein, SCP
Einzellerverband *m* coenobium
einzellig unicellular
Einzellkultur *f* single-cell culture, single-spore isolate
Einzelmischung *f* (forest) individual-tree mixture, single-tree mixture, tree-by-tree mixture, mixture by single trees
Einzelnährstoffdünger *m s.* Einnährstoffdünger
Einzelnest *n* individual nest *(poultry management)*
einzelnlebend solitary
einzelnstehend isolated, solitary
Einzelpfannenkarbonatation *f* batch carbonation *(sugar manufacture)*
Einzelpflanzenanzucht *f* single growing

Einzelpflanzenauslese f single-plant selection, selection of individual plants
Einzelpflanzenbestand m individual (single) stand
Einzelpflanzencontainer m single-plant container
Einzelpflanzenertrag m individual plant yield
Einzelpflanzung f individual planting; *(forest)* planting by single trees
Einzelplanung f *(forest)* yield planning on a single-stand basis, planning of particular measures
Einzelradantrieb m one-wheel drive; all-wheel drive, four-wheel drive, f.w.d.
Einzelradbremse f individual (steering, single-wheel) brake
Einzelsaat f single-grain sowing; spot seeding (sowing)
Einzelschicht f stratum *(of vegetation)*
Einzelschlupf m single hatch
Einzelsporauslese f single-spore selection
Einzelsporisolat n single-spore isolate
Einzelstamm m single (individual) stem, individual tree
Einzelstammflößerei f [loose] floating, timber (river, stream) driving
Einzelstammpflege f *(forest)* tending of individual trees
Einzelstammwirtschaft f *(forest)* single-tree system of management
Einzelstaudenkartoffelroder m single-hill potato digger
Einzeltiererkennung f animal identification
Einzeltierfütterung f individual feeding
Einzeltierleistung f individual animal performance
Einzug m pitch adjustment *(of a plough)*
Einzugsgebiet n catchment [area, basin], water catchment, watershed, gathering ground
~ **eines Flusses** drainage basin
Einzugsgut n feed liquor, *(Am)* fillmass *(sugar manufacture)*
Einzugskette f gathering chain
Einzugsschnecke f feed table auger
Einzugswalze f gathering roller
Einzweckrasse f single-purpose breed
Einzylindermotor m single-cylinder engine
Eiparasit m egg parasite
Eiprodukt n egg product
Eiprotein n egg protein
Eipulver n egg powder, powdered (dried) egg
Eiqualität f egg quality
Eiraupe f *(ent)* first instar caterpillar
Eis n ice • **mit ~ bedecken (überziehen)** to ice • **sich in ~ verwandeln** to ice • **sich mit ~ bedecken** to cover with ice, to ice, to frost [over]
Eisanhang m glazed frost (ice), *(Am)* glaze
Eisbein n knuckle of pork; forehock
Eisbergsalat m iceberg [lettuce], crisp-head lettuce, Lactuca sativa convar. incocta var. capitata nidus jaggeri
Eisbruch m ice-break[age]
Eischale f eggshell

Eischalenbildung f eggshell formation
Eischalendicke f eggshell thickness
Eischalenfehler m eggshell defect
Eischalenfestigkeit f eggshell strength
Eischalenmehl n eggshell meal
Eischalenmißbildung f eggshell deformation
Eischalenporosität f eggshell porosity
Eischalenultrastruktur f eggshell ultrastructure
Eischwiele f s. Eizahn
Eisenbahnfieber n, **Eisenbahnkrankheit** f *(vet)* transport staggers, transit tetany, *(Am)* railroad sickness
Eisenbahnschwelle f rail[way] sleeper, sleeper, *(Am)* railroad [cross]tie, tie
Eisenchlorose f *(phyt)* iron chlorosis
Eisendextran n iron dextran
Eisendüngemittel n iron fertilizer
Eisenfleckigkeit f internal heat necrosis, internal brown (rust) spot, corky ring spot *(of the potato tuber)*
Eisenglimmerschiefer m itabirite
eisenhaltig iron-containing, ferruginous, ferreous
Eisen(III)hämoglobin n methaemoglobin
Eisenharke f iron (steel) rake
Eisenholz n 1. ironwood *(comprehensive term)*; 2. iron tree, Parrotia persica; 3. horse-tail [tree], Casuarina equisetifolia
Eisenholzbaum m 1. New Zealand Christmas bush *(genus Metrosideros)*; 2. argan tree, Argania spinosa (sideroxylon)
Eisenhut m *(bot)* 1. monkshood, wolfsbane, aconite *(genus Aconitum)*; 2. monkshood, Aconitum napellus
Eisenhydroxid n iron hydroxide *(non-clay mineral)*
Eisenkraut n [garden] verbena, vervain, holy wort, Juno's tears, Verbena officinalis
Eisenkrautsalbei m wild clary, vervain, Salvia verbenaca
Eisenmangel m iron deficiency
Eisenmangelanämie f *(vet)* iron-deficiency anaemia, nutritional anaemia
Eisen(III)phosphat n ferric phosphate
Eisenphosphattrübung f ferric phosphate haze *(of beer)*
Eisenpigment n haemosiderin
Eisen(II)protoporphyrin n haem
Eisen(III)protoporphyrin n haemin
Eisensalzablagerung f [in Körpergeweben] *(vet)* siderosis
eisenschüssig *(soil)* iron-shot, ferruginous, ferreous
Eisen(III)sulfat n ferric sulphate
Eisfischerei f ice-fishing
Eisfuchs m Arctic fox, Alopex lagopus
Eishang m s. Eisanhang
Eisheiligen/die pl Icemen, Ice Saints *(meteorological phenomenon)*
Eiskluft f frost cleft, frost split (crack) *(in wood)*
eisklüftig frost-clefted, frost-split *(wood)*

Eiskraut

Eiskraut *n* ice-plant, Mesembryanthemum (Cryophytum) crystallinum
Eiskrautgewächse *npl* carpetweed family *(family Aizoaceae)*
Eisprung *m* ovulation, ovulatory surge, follicle rupture
Eissalat *m s.* Eisbergsalat
Eissproß *m*, **Eissprosse** *f* bay (bez) antler
Eiswasser-Rieselkühlanlage *f (dairy)* chilled-water cooler
Eisweg *m* ice[d] road
Eiswein *m* ice wine
Eiswolke *f* cirrus
Eiszeit[epoche] *f* glacial [epoch, period], Pleistocene
eiszeitlich glacial
Eiter *m (vet)* pus, purulence, [suppurative] matter
Eiteransammlung *f* empyema
Eiterbeule *f* abscess
Eiterbläschen *n* pustule, fester
eitererregend pyogenic
Eitererreger *m* pyogenic bacterium
eitern to matter, to fester, to suppurate
eiternd purulent, mattery
Eiternessel *f* burning (small, sting) nettle, Urtica urens
Eiterung *f* 1. purulence; 2. pus formation, festering, suppuration • **Eiterungen erzeugend** pyogenic
eitragend ovigerous
Eitransplantation *f* inovulation, ovum transfer, ova transplant
eitrig purulent, mattery • ~ **werden** to fester
Eitrockenmasse *f* egg solids
Eiübertragung *f s.* Eitransplantation
Eivakzine *f* egg vaccine
Eiweiß *n* 1. protein *(for compounds s. under* Protein*)*; 2. *s.* Eiklar
Eiweiß... *s. a.* Protein...
Eiweißbedarf *m* protein requirement
Eiweißbestandteil *m* protein constituent
Eiweißbewertung *f* protein evaluation
Eiweißbilanz *f* protein balance
Eiweißekzem *n (vet)* parakeratosis, swine dermatosis *(due to zinc deficiency)*
Eiweißenergie *f* protein energy
Eiweißergänzungsfuttermittel *n* protein supplement
Eiweißfaser *f* protein fibre
Eiweißfraktion *f* protein fraction
eiweißfrei protein-free
Eiweißfutter *n* protein feed
Eiweißfutterkonzentrat *n* protein feed concentrate
Eiweißfuttermittel *n* protein feed
Eiweißgehalt *m* protein content
Eiweißkonzentrat[futtermittel] *n* protein concentrate
Eiweißkörper *m* protein body, proteic substance
Eiweißlücke *f* protein gap
Eiweißmangel *m* protein deficiency
Eiweißminimum *n* protein minimum
Eiweißmischsilage *f* protein mixed silage
Eiweißoxidation *f* protein oxidation
Eiweißqualität *f* protein quality
eiweißreich protein-rich
~/relativ narrow *(feed, diet)*
Eiweißreserve *f* protein reserve
Eiweißschönung *f* fining with albumin *(of wine)*
eiweißspaltend proteolytic, protein-splitting
Eiweißspaltung *f* proteolysis
Eiweißspektrum *n* protein spectrum
Eiweißstabilität *f (dairy)* protein stability
Eiweißstickstoff *m* protein (albuminous) nitrogen
Eiweißstoff *m* [/einfacher] protein, proteic substance *(for compounds s. under* Protein*)*
Eiweißstoffwechsel *m* protein metabolism
Eiweißstoffwechselstörung *f* protein metabolism disorder
Eiweißtiter *m (dairy)* protein titre
Eiweißüberschuß *m* protein excess
Eiweißumsatz *m* protein turnover
Eiweißverdaulichkeit *f* protein digestibility
Eiweißverdauung *f* protein digestion, proteolysis
Eiweißverwertung *f* protein utilization
Eiweißwertigkeit *f*/**biologische** biological value, BV
Eiweißzersetzer *m* proteolytic bacterium
Eiweißzucker *m* glycoprotein
Eiweißzusammensetzung *f* protein composition
Eizahl *f* egg number
Eizahn *m* egg tooth *(of birds for breaking through the eggshell)*
Eizelle *f* egg cell, ovum, oocyte, ovocyte
~/befruchtete zygote
Eizellenbehälter *m* archegonium *(of mosses and ferns)*
Eizellenhülle *f* egg membrane
Eizellentransplantation *f*, **Eizellenübertragung** *f* inovulation, ovum transfer, ova transplant
Eizellkern *m* egg nucleus, germinal vesicle
Eizusammensetzung *f* egg composition
Ejakulat *n* ejaculate
Ejakulation *f* ejaculation
~/fehlende aspermatism, aspermia
Ejakulatvolumen *n* ejaculate volume
ejakulieren to ejaculate
ejizieren to eject
EK *s.* 1. Energiekonzentration; 2. Einschlußkörper
EKA *s.* Erstkalbealter
Ekdysis *f* ecdysis, moult *(esp. in insects and crustaceans)*; exuviation, sloughing *(esp. in snakes)*
Ekdyson *n (ent)* ecdysone, moulting hormone
EKG *s.* Elektrokardiogramm
ekkrin eccrine, exocrine
Eklampsie *f (vet)* eclampsia, lactation (puerperal) tetany
Ekraseur *m (vet)* ecraseur
Ekthyma *n (vet)* ecthyma

Ektoblast *n(m) s.* Ektoderm
Ektoderm *n (bot, zoo)* ectoderm, exoderm, ectoblast, epiblast
ektodermal ectodermal, ectodermic
Ektoenzym *n* ectoenzyme, exoenzyme
ektogen exogenous
Ektohormon *n s.* Pheromon
Ektomie *f (vet)* resection
Ektoparasit *m* ectoparasite, external parasite
~/tierischer ectozoon, epizoon
ektoparasitär ectoparasitic
Ektoparasitenbekämpfungsmittel *n* ectoparasiticide
Ektoparasitismus *m* ectoparasitism
Ektoparasitizid *n* ectoparasiticide
Ektoparasitose *f* ectoparasitosis
Ektoskelett *n* ectoskeleton, exoskeleton
Ektotoxin *n* exotoxin
ektotroph ectotrophic
Ektropium *n (vet)* ectropion
Ekzem *n (vet)* eczema
~/nässendes moist (weeping) eczema, moist scall
ekzematisch eczematous
EL *s.* Energieladung
Elaidinsäure *f* elaidic acid *(fatty acid)*
Elaioplast *m* elaioplast *(oil-storing leucoplast)*
Elaiosom *n (bot)* elaiosome
Eland *m s.* Elenantilope
Elastase *f* elastase *(enzyme)*
Elastin *n* elastin *(protein)*
Elastizität *f* elasticity, resilience
Elastizitätsgrenze *f* elastic limit
Elastizitätsmodul *m* elastic (Young's) modulus, modulus of elasticity
Elastration *f (vet)* elastration, bloodless castration (as of a lamb)
Elastrator *m (vet)* elastrator
Elatiorbegonie *f* elatior begonia
Elbspitzklette *f* sea burdock, Xanthium albinum [ssp. riparium], Xanthium italicum
Elch *m* 1. elk *(genus Alces)*; 2. elk, moose, Alces alces
Elchhund *m* elk-hound *(group of breeds)*
Elchwild *n* elk-deer
Eledoisin *n* eledoisin *(kinin)*
Elefant *m* elephant *(genus Elephas)*
Elefantenapfel *m (bot)* elephant's (wood) apple, Limonia acidissima, Feronia limonia
Elefantenfuß *m (bot)* elephant's foot, Testudinaria elephantipes
Elefantengras *n* 1. elephant grass, Typha elephantina; 2. napier grass, napier's fodder, Pennisetum purpureum
Elefantenrüssel *m* proboscis flower, unicorn plant, Proboscidea louisianica
Elefantenyams *n* elephant yam, whitespot giant arum, telinga potato, Amorphophallus campanulatus (paeoniifolius)

Eleganter Röhrling *m (bot)* elegant boletus, Boletus grevillei
Elektivfärbung *f* selective staining *(microbiology)*
Elektroanästhesie *f* electronarcosis, electrical anaesthesia
Elektroantennogramm *m (ent)* electroantennogram
Elektroantrieb *m* electric drive
Elektrobetäubung *f (slaught)* electrical stunning
Elektrobrüter *m* electric brooder (incubator)
Elektrocortin *n* aldosterone *(adrenocortical hormone)*
Elektrodialyse *f* electrodialysis
Elektroejakulation *f* electroejaculation
Elektroejakulator *m* electroejaculator
Elektroendosmose *f* electroosmosis
Elektroenzephalogramm *n (vet)* electroencephalogram, EEG
Elektroenzephalographie *f (vet)* electroencephalography
Elektrofischerei *f* electrofishing, electric fishing
Elektrofusion *f* electrofusion *(of protoplasts during somatic hybridization)*
Elektroglucke *f* electric brooder (incubator)
Elektrokardiogramm *n* electrocardiogram, ECG
Elektrokardiographie *f* electrocardiography
Elektrokauter *m (vet)* electric cautery (firing iron)
Elektrokauterisation *f (vet)* electrocauterization, electric cautery
Elektrokoagulation *f (vet)* electrocoagulation
Elektrokoagulator *m* electrocoagulator
Elektrolyse *f* electrolysis
Elektrolyt *m* electrolyte
Elektrolythaushalt *m* electrolytes balance
Elektromotorsäge *f* electric power saw
Elektromyographie *f* electromyography
Elektronarkose *f* electronarcosis, electrical anaesthesia
Elektronenmikroskop *n* electron microscope
Elektronenmikroskopie *f* electron microscopy
elektronenmikroskopisch electron microscopic
Elektronenspinresonanz *f* electron spin resonance
Elektronentransport *m* electron transport
Elektronentransportkette *f* electron-transport chain
Elektroosmose *f* electroosmosis
Elektropaletten[hub]wagen *m* electric pallet truck
Elektropflug *m* electric plough
Elektrophorese *f* electrophoresis
elekrophoretisch electrophoretic
Elektropulsator *m* electric pulsator *(milking machine)*
Elektroretinogramm *n* electroretinogram
Elektroretinographie *f* electroretinography
Elektrosaatgutreinigungsmaschine *f* electrical seed cleaner
Elektrosäge *f* electrical power saw
Elektrostabzaun *m* electric bar fence

Elektrostimulation

Elektrostimulation f electrostimulation (for semen collection)
Elektrotherapie f (vet) electrotherapy, current therapy
Elektrotod m (slaught, vet) electrocution
Elektrotraktor m electric tractor
Elektrotropismus m (bot) galvanotropism
Elektroviehtreiber m electric stock prod
Elektro[weide]zaun m electric [wire] fence
~/mobiler forward fence
Elektro[weide]zaungerät n [electric] fencer
~ mit elektronisch gesteuertem Impulsgeber electronic fencer
Element n/**chemisches** [chemical] element
~/thermoelektrisches thermocouple, thermoelectric couple
Elementarfibrille f elementary fibril, fusiform body (wood anatomy)
Elementargefüge n fabric (e.g. of a soil)
Elementarherd m (ecol) natural focus
Elementarmembran f unit membrane (cytology)
Elementgehalt m elemental content
Elemi n elemi (oleoresin)
Elen n(m) s. Elch
Elenantilope f eland, Taurotragus oryx
Elevator m elevator
Elevatorentsafter m elevator-type juice separator
Elevatorium n (vet) raspatory
Elfazepam n elfazepam (fungicide)
Elfenbeinginster m Warminster broom, Cytisus x praecox
Elfenbeinpalme f ivory palm (genus Phytelephas)
Elfenblume f 1. barrenwort, bishop's-hat (genus Epimedium); 2. large-flowered barrenwort, Epimedium grandiflorum
Elfenring m fairy ring (of fungi)
Elicitor m elicitor
Elimination f elimination (breeding)
ELISA-Test m ELISA [test], enzyme-linked immunosorbent assay
Elite f elite (breeding)
Elitebaum m (forest) elite stem (tree), plus (choice, champion) tree
Elitebestand m (forest) elite (plus) stand
Eliteherde f elite flock
Eliteklon m (gen) elite clone
Elitesaatgut n elite (selected, basic) seed
Elitesaatgutbestand m elite seed stand
Elitesorte f elite cultivar
Elitestamm m s. Elitebaum
Elk m s. Elch
Ellagsäure f ellagic acid
Elle f ulna (animal anatomy)
Ellenbogen m elbow
Ellenbogengelenk n elbow joint
Ellenbogenhöcker m point of elbow
Elongation f elongation
Elsässer m Alsace (kind of wine)

Elsbeere f wild service [tree], service [tree], (Am) chequer tree, Sorbus torminalis
Elsohacke f (vet) spastic paresis
Elster f magpie, Pica pica
Elter m(n) parent [member] • **dem mütterlichen ~ ähnelnd** matroclinal, matroclinous • **dem väterlichen ~ ähnelnd** patroclinal, patroclinous
elterlich parental
Elterngeneration f parental generation, P
Elternlinie f parent[al] line
Elternmittel n mid-parent value (animal breeding)
Eltern-Nachkommen-Regression f parent-offspring regression
Elternteil m s. Elter
Elterntierbestand m parent stock
Elternzeugung f digenesis
Eluat n eluate
eluieren to elute
Elution f elution (of adsorbed substances)
Eluvialboden m (soil) eluvium
Eluvialhorizont m (soil) eluvial (leached) horizon, A-horizon
Eluviationszone f (soil) zone of eluviation
Eluvium n (soil) eluvium
Elytron n (ent) elytron, elytrum, wing case (sheath), shard
Emaskulation f emasculation, castration
Emaskulator m emasculator
emballieren to wrap in gauze (e.g. nursery plants)
Embden-Meyerhof-Parnas-Weg m s. Glycolyse
Embolie f (phyt, vet) embolism
Embolus m (vet) embolus
Embryo m embryo
embryoähnlich, embryoartig embryoid
Embryobildung f ohne Befruchtung (bot) apomixis
Embryoentwicklung f embryogenesis
Embryoernährung f embryotrophy
embryogen embryogenic
Embryogenese f embryogenesis
Embryogewinnung f embryo recovery
embryoid embryoid
Embryoid n embryoid
Embryokultur f embryo culture, embryonic engineering
Embryolemma n embryonic membrane
Embryologie f embryology
embryonal embryonal, embryonic, embryous
Embryonalentwicklung f embryonic development
Embryonalgewebe n embryonic tissue
Embryonalhülle f embryonic membrane
Embryonalisierung f dedifferentiation (of cells)
Embryonalkreislauf m foetal circulation
Embryonalschild m embryonic shield (disk)
Embryonenverlust m embryo abort
embryonisch s. embryonal
Embryosack m (bot) embryo sac
~/einkerniger megaspore
Embryosackbasis f chalaza

Embryosackbildung f ohne Reduktionsteilung apomeiosis
Embryosackmutterzelle f megaspore mother cell
Embryosackzelle f megaspore
Embryotomie f (vet) embryotomy
Embryoträger m (bot) suspensor
Embryotransfer m embryo transfer (animal breeding)
Embryotransplantation f embryo transplantation
Embryotrophe f uterine fluid
Embryotrophie f embryotrophy
EMC-Virus n encephalomyocarditis virus
Emdener Gans f Embden, Emden (goose breed)
Emergenz f (bot) emergence
Emetikum n (vet) emetic
Emetin n emetine (alkaloid, anthelminthic)
EMG s. Elektromyographie
Emigration f (ecol) emigration
Emission f emission
Emissionsquelle f emission (emitting) source
Emissionsspektrum n emission spectrum
Emittent m s. Emissionsquelle
Emitter m [water] emitter, dripper (drip irrigation)
Emmentaler m Emment[h]al cheese
Emmer[weizen] m emmer [wheat], Triticum dicoccon
Emodikiefer f chir pine, Pinus roxburghii
Emodin n emodin (anthraquinone)
Emodirhabarber m Himalayan rhubarb, Rheum australe (emodi)
E-Modul m s. Elastizitätsmodul
Empfänger m recipient; acceptor; clonee (of a transplant)
empfänglich susceptible, predisposed; receptive
Empfänglichkeit f susceptibility, [pre]disposition; receptiveness, receptivity (e.g. of female breeding animals)
Empfänglichkeitsgrad m [pre]disposition
Empfindlicher Krempling m (bot) involute paxillus, Paxillus involutus
Empfindlichkeit f sensibility, sensitivity
~/**gesteigerte** (vet) hyperaesthesia
Empfindung f [/sinnliche] sensation
Empfindungsfähigkeit f s. Empfindungsvermögen
empfindungslos anaesthetic
Empfindungslosigkeit f anaesthesia
Empfindungsvermögen n sensitivity, perceptivity
Emphysem n (vet) emphysema
emporklettern to climb
Empyem n (vet) empyema
Emulgator m emulsifier, emulsifying agent
emulgieren to emulsify
Emulgierung f emulsification
Emulgierungsmittel n s. Emulgator
Emulsin n emulsin (enzyme)
Emulsion f emulsion
Emulsionsbildung f emulsification
EMV s. Gewöhnliches Erbsenmosikvirus
EN s. Ernährungsniveau

Enarthrose f enarthrosis (form of a ball-and-socket joint)
Enation f (phyt) enation
enchondral endochondral
Endabstand m final spacing
Endbestandesdichte f final plant population
Endblüte f apical flower
Endblütenstand m terminal inflorescence
Endblütige Pachysandra f Japanese pachysandra (spurge), Pachysandra terminalis
Endbulbus m terminal bulb, bulb of oesophagus (of nematodes)
Enddarm m hind-gut
Ende n 1. end; 2. snag, point, tine, royal (of an antler)
~/**dünnes** small[er] end (of a tree-trunk)
Endemie f endemic [disease]
endemisch endemic
Endemismus m endemicity, endemism
Endemit m endemic
Endertrag m final [harvest] yield
Endfeuchte f final moisture
Endhandlung f consummatory action (animal behaviour)
Endhieb m s. Endnutzungshieb
Endivie f [winter] endive, escarole, Cichorium endivia
Endknospe f terminal (upmost) bud
Endmast f finishing (of cattle)
~ **auf Getreidebasis** cereal finishing
Endmastfutter[mittel] n finisher
Endmastleistung f finishing performance
Endmastperiode f finishing period
Endmastration f finisher diet (ration), finishing ration
Endmaststall m finishing house
Endmelasse f final molasses (sugar manufacture)
Endmoräne f (soil) terminal moraine
Endnutzung f s. Endnutzungshieb
Endnutzungsalter m (forest) final age
Endnutzungsbestand m final felling stand, final crop
Endnutzungsertrag m final [harvest] yield
Endnutzungsetat m s. Endnutzungshiebssatz
Endnutzungsfläche f area of final felling, final cut area
Endnutzungshieb m final (principal) felling, final [harvest] cut, harvest cut[ting], clearing
Endnutzungshiebssatz m allowable final cut, allowable cut of harvesting, cut prescription
Endnutzungskarte f exploitation map
Endnutzungssatz m s. Endnutzungshiebssatz
endobiotisch endobiotic
Endocard[ium] n endocardium
endochondral endochondral
Endoderm n s. Entoderm
Endodermis f (bot) endodermis
endodynamorph (soil) endodynamorphic
Endoenzym n endoenzyme

endogen

endogen endogenous
Endokard *n* endocardium
Endokarditis *f (vet)* endocarditis
Endokarp *n (bot)* endocarp
endokrin endocrine
Endokrinium *n* endocrine system
Endokrinologie *f* endocrinology
Endo-L-Glucanase *f* endo-L-glucanase *(enzyme)*
Endolymphe *f* endolymph *(of the inner ear)*
Endolysin *n* lysozyme *(bacteriolytic enzyme)*
Endomeiose *f* endomeiosis
Endometalloskop *n (vet)* metal detector
Endometritis *f (vet)* endometritis
Endometrium *n* endometrium, endometrial area
Endomitose *f* endomitosis
Endomycorrhiza *f* endomycorrhiza, endotrophic mycorrhiza
Endonuclease *f* endonuclease *(enzyme)*
Endoparasit *m* endoparasite, entoparasite, entorganism, internal parasite
endoparasitär endoparasitic
Endoparasitismus *m* endoparasitism
Endopeptidase *f* endopeptidase, proteinase *(enzyme)*
Endophyt *m* endophyte
endophytisch endophytic
Endoplasmaretikulum *n* endoplasmic reticulum, ER *(organelle)*
Endopolyphosphatase *f* endopolyphosphatase, metaphosphatase, polyphosphate depolymerase *(enzyme)*
Endopolyploidie *f (gen)* endopolyploidy
Endorgan *n* receptor organ
Endorphin *n* endorphin *(peptide, neurotransmitter)*
Endoskelett *n* endoskeleton
Endoskop *n (vet)* endoscope
Endoskopie *f (vet)* endoscopy
Endosperm *n* endosperm
Endospermbildung *f* endosperm formation
Endospermeiweiß *n* endosperm protein
Endospermtextur *f* endosperm texture
Endospore *f*, **Endospor[ium]** *n* endospore
Endosulfan *n* endosulfan *(insecticide)*
Endothal *n* endothal *(growth regulator, herbicide)*
Endothel *n* endothelium
endothelial endothelial
Endotheliose *f*/**aviäre** T virus infection [of fowl]
Endothion *n* endothion *(insecticide, acaricide)*
Endotoxin *n* endotoxin *(bacterial toxin)*
Endotrachealtubus *m (vet)* endotracheal tube
endotroph endotrophic
endovenös intravenous
Endozoochorie *f* endozoochory
Endozyt *m* endocyte, Kupffer cell
Endozytose *f* endocytosis
Endpflanzenbestand *m* final plant population
Endprodukt *n* final (end) product
Endregner *m* end gun *(of a pivot irrigation system)*
Endrin *n* endrin *(insecticide, rodenticide)*

Endriß *m* end split (check) *(defect in timber)*
endständig terminal, apical
Endstück *n* cauda
Endtiter *m* titre, *(Am)* titer
Endverbraucher *m* final (ultimate) consumer
Endvergärungsgrad *m* attenuation limit, final attenuation *(brewing)*
Endwirt *m (phyt, vet)* final (definitive) host
Enema *n (vet)* enema
energetisch energetic[al]
Energie *f* energy; power
~/geothermische geothermal energy
~/Gibbs[sche] Freie Gibbs free energy *(plant physiology)*
~/kinetische kinetic energy
~/nutzbare metabolizable energy, ME, available energy *(animal feeding)*; power
~/thermische heat energy
~/umsetzbare *s.* ~/nutzbare
~/verdauliche digestible energy, DE
Energieanspruch *m* energy requirement
Energieaufnahme *f* energy intake
Energieaufwand *m* energy input
Energieausnutzung *f* energy utilization
Energieaustausch *m* energy exchange
Energiebalance *f* energy balance
Energiebedarf *m* energy requirement
Energiebilanz *f* energy balance (budget)
Energiebilanzgleichung *f* energy budget equation
Energiedichte *f* energy density
energieeffektiv energy-efficient
Energieerhaltung *f* energy conservation
Energieerhaltungsbedarf *m* maintenance energy requirement
Energiefluß *m* energy flow (flux)
Energiefreisetzung *f* energy release
Energiefutter *n* energy feed
Energiegehalt *m* energy content
Energiegleichgewicht *n* energy equilibrium
Energiegleichung *f* energy budget equation
Energiekonzentration *f* energy concentration (density)
Energieladung *f* energy charge
Energienutzung *f* energy utilization
energiereich energy-rich
Energiereserve *f* energy reserve
energiesparend energy-efficient
Energiespeicher *m* energy store
Energiespeicherung *f* energy storage
Energiestoffwechsel *m* energy metabolism
Energieumsatz *m* energy exchange
Energieumwandlung *f* energy conversion
Energieverdaulichkeit *f* energy digestibility
Energieverwertung *f* energy utilization
energiewirtschaftlich günstig energy-efficient
Energiezapfwelle *f* power take-off, p.t.o., power shaft
engbrüstig narrow-chested
Enge *f* **der Inzucht** level of inbreeding

Engelmann[s]fichte *f* Engelmann (silver, white) spruce, Picea engelmannii
Engel-Recklinghausensche Krankheit *f (vet)* fibrous osteodystrophy
Engelstrompete *f (bot)* angel's trumpet, Datura suaveolens
Engelsüß *n* common polypody, wood (oak, wall) fern, Polypodium vulgare
Engelwurz *f* [garden] angelica, archangel, Angelica archangelica [var. archangelica]
Engerling *m* [chafer, white] grub
Engholz *n* late (summer) wood
Englische Krankheit *f (vet)* rickets
~ **Ulme** *f* common (English, European) elm, Ulmus procera
Englischer Ginster *m* furze, common gorse, thorn broom, whin, Ulex europaeus
~ **Setter** *m* English setter *(dog breed)*
~ **Spinat** *m* patience [dock], spinach (vegetable) dock, Rumex patientia
~ **Walnußbaum** *m* English walnut, Juglans regia
~ **Windhund** *m* greyhound *(breed)*
Englisches Raygras *n* common (perennial) ryegrass, Lolium perenne
~ **Schlickgras** *n* common cord-grass, Spartina anglica
~ **Vollblut** *n* [British] Thoroughbred, English Racehorse *(breed)*
English Bulldog *m* [English] Bulldog *(breed)*
~ **Coonhound** *m* Black and Tan Coonhound *(breed)*
~ **Springer Spaniel** *m* English springer [spaniel] *(dog breed)*
engmaschig close-meshed
engporig fine-porous
Engreihensämaschine *f* close-row seed drill
engringig narrow-ringed, fine-grained, close-grained, slow-grown *(wood)*
Engsaat *f* close (narrow-row) sowing
Engzucht *f* close [in]breeding
Enkephalin *n* enkephalin *(neurotransmitter)*
Enolase *f* enolase *(enzyme)*
Enoyl-CoA-Hydratase *f*, **Enoylhydrase** *f* enoyl-CoA hydratase *(enzyme)*
EnSV *s.* Erdnußscheckungsvirus
entarten to degenerate
Entartung *f* degeneration
Entaschung *f* de-ashing
entasten, entästen to [de]limb, to disbranch, to [de]branch, to chop (cut) off branches, to lop [off], to knot, to clear, to trim
Entastungs-Einschneide-Maschine *f* delimber-bucker, delimber-slasher
Entastungsgerät *n* [de]limber, branch remover, lopper
Entastungshacker *m* processor-chipper
Entastungskopf *m* delimbing head
Entastungsmaschine *f* delimbing machine
Entastungs-Paketier-Kombine *f* [de]limber-buncher, delimber-bucker-buncher

Entastungsvorrichtung *f* delimbing device
entbasten to decorticate *(plant fibres)*; to degum, to discharge *(raw silk)*
Entbasung *f* decalcification *(of a soil)*
einbeinen to bone [out]
entbittern to debitter
entblättern to defoliate, to deleaf
~/sich to defoliate, to deleaf, to shed the leaves
Entblätterung *f* defoliation
Entblätterungsmaschine *f* stem trimmer *(ornamental production)*
Entblätterungsmittel *n* defoliant
Entblätterungsvorrichtung *f* defoliator
entblüten to deblossom
Entblutungsanämie *f (vet)* posthaemorrhagic anaemia
Entcarbonisierung *f* decarbonation
entdasseln *(vet)* to warble
entdeckeln to uncap *(honeycombs)*
Entdeckelungsgabel *f* uncapping fork
Entdeckelungsmesser *n* uncapping knife
Entdifferenzierung *f* dedifferentiation *(of cells)*
entdornen to dethorn
Ente *f* duck, teal [duck] *(genus Anas)*
Entenbroiler *m* duck broiler
Entenei *n* duck egg
Entenfalle *f* decoy
Entenfarm *f* duck farm, duckery
Entenfett *n* duck fat
Entenfleisch *n* duck [meat]
Entenflinte *f* punt gun
Entenflott *n (bot)* duckweed, Lemna minor
Entenflottrechen *m* duckweed rake *(for ditch clearing)*
Entenfütterung *f* duck feeding
Entengrütze *f* duckweed, Lemna minor
Entenhalter *m* ducker
Entenhaltung *f* duck keeping
Entenhepatitis *f (vet)* duck virus hepatitis
Entenhepatitisvirus *n* duck hepatitis virus
Enteninfluenza *f* duck flu, avian influenza
Entenjagd *f* ducking
Entenjäger *m* ducker
Entenjägerboot *n* dinkey
Entkarbonisieren *n* decarbonation
Entenküken *n* duckling
Entenleukose *f* lymphoproliferative disease in ducks, T virus infection
Entenlinse *f (bot)* water-meal, Wolffia arrhiza
Entenmast *f* duck fattening
Entenpest *f* duck plague (virus enteritis)
Entenpestvirus *n* duck plague virus
Entenproduktion *f* duck production
Entenruf *m* decoy-whistle
Entenschrot *n* duck shot
Entenstall *m* duck house
Entenvogel *m* duck *(family Anatidae)*
Entenzucht *f* duck breeding (production)
Enteramin *n* serotonin *(neurotransmitter)*

Enterich

Enterich *m* drake
Enteritis *f (vet)* enteritis
~ des Geflügels/ulzerative ulcerative enteritis of birds, avian ulcerated enteritis, quail disease
~/hämorrhagische haemorrhagic enteritis
~/infektiöse infectious enteritis
~/nekrotisierende infectious necrotic enteritis *(of sucking pigs)*
Enteritisinfektion *f s.* Salmonellose
enterobakteriell enterobacterial
Enterobakterium *n* enterobacterium *(family Enterobacteriaceae)*
Enterogastron *n* enterogastrone *(hormone)*
Enterohepatitis *f (vet)* enterohepatitis
Enterokinase *f s.* Enteropeptidase
Enterokokkus *m* enterococcus
Enterokolitis *f (vet)* enterocolitis
Enterokrinin *n* enterocrinin *(hormone)*
Enterolith *m (vet)* enterolith
Enteropathie *f* enteropathy, intestinal disease
enteropathogen enteropathogenic
Enteropeptidase *f* enteropeptidase, enterokinase *(enzyme)*
Enterotom *n (vet)* enterotome
Enterotomie *f* enterotomy
Enterotoxämie *f (vet)* enterotoxaemia *(comprehensive term for Clostridium-perfringens intoxications)*
Enterotoxin *n* enterotoxin
Enterovirus *n* enterovirus
Enterozele *f (vet)* enterocele
Enterozentese *f (vet)* enterocentesis
Enterozyt *m* enterocyte
entfahnen to detassel *(maize)*
Entfahnen *n* detasseling, tassel removal
Entfahn[ungs]maschine *f* detasseling machine
entfalten/sich to unfold, to unfurl *(e.g. leaves)*
Entfaltungsfrist *f (Am)* corral time *(forest fire control)*
entfärben to decolo[u]rize
Entfärbung *f* decolo[u]rization, discoloration
Entfärbungsharz *n* decolo[u]rizing resin *(sugar manufacture)*
entfasern/Baumwollsamen to delint
entfernen/Blüten to deflower, to deblossom
~/das Kerngehäuse to core
~/den Blinddarm [operativ] *(vet)* to caecectomize
~/die Grobrinde to remove coarse bark, to redden *(resin-tapping)*
~/die Mittelrippe to stem *(tobacco leaf)*
~/ein Tier von der Herde to cast, *(Am)* to cut out
~/Fruchtfleisch to pulp
~/Samen to seed, to remove (extract) the seeds *(esp. from fruits)*
~/Schosser to sucker
~/Triebe to deshoot
~/Wurzelsprosse to sucker
Entferntährige Segge *f* remote sedge, Carex remota

Entfernungsmesser *m* range-finder, range-finding apparatus
entfetten to defat, to degrease; to scour *(wool)*
entfeuchten to dehumify, to desiccate
Entfeuchter *m* dehumidifier
Entfeuchtung *f* dehumidification, desiccation
entflammbar inflammable
~/nicht non-flammable, uninflammable
Entflammbarkeit *f* inflammability
Entflimmerung *f (vet)* defibrillation
Entflockung *f (soil)* deflocculation
entflügeln to dewing *(seeds)*
Entflügelungsmaschine *f* dewinger, dewinging machine
entfluorieren to defluorinate
entgasen to degas
Entgasung *f* degasification; dry distillation, pyrolysis *(e.g. of wood)*
entgeizen to pinch off (out), to nip off, to pluck off suckers, to stop
entgiften to detoxify
Entgiftung *f* detoxification
Entgiftungsmittel *n* detoxicant
entgipfeln *s.* entwipfeln
Entgranner *m* awner, de-awning machine
entgräten to bone [out]
entgrünen to degreen *(e.g. citrus fruits)*
enthaaren to depilate, to grain *(skins)*
enthaart *(bot, zoo)* glabrate
Enthalpie *f* enthalpy
~/Freie Gibbs free energy *(plant physiology)*
enthärten 1. to soften *(water)*; 2. to deharden *(plants)*
Enthärtung *f* dehardening, deacclimation *(plant physiology)*
entharzen to deresinify
Entharzung *f* deresination
enthaupten to decapitate
Enthauptung *f* decapitation
enthäuten to skin, to flay
enthornen to dehorn, to dishorn, to poll
Enthornung *f* dehorning
Enthornungsgerät *n* dehorner
enthülsen to hull, to shuck, to shell, to pod *(legumes)*
Enthülser *m* huller, hulling apparatus
Entisol *m (soil)* entisol, ent
entkalken to decalcify
Entkalkung *f* decalcification
entkeimen to degerm[inate], to desprout; to sterilize
Entkeimung *f* degermination; sterilization
Entkeimungsmaschine *f* degerminator
entkelchen to plug *(strawberries)*
entkernen 1. to core, to pit; to gin *(cotton)*; 2. *(vet)* to enucleate
entknospen to disbud
Entknospen *n* disbudding, debudding
Entknospungsästung *f (forest)* bud pruning, disbudding

entkörnen to gin *(cotton)*
entkräftet prostrate
Entkräftung *f* prostration
~/hungerbedingte inanition
Entladeband *n* discharge conveyor
Entladegebläse *n* pneumatic unloading conveyor
Entladegeschwindigkeit *f* unloading speed
entladen to unload, to offload, to discharge
Entladevorrichtung *f* loading-out facility
Entladewalze *f* discharge beater
Entladezeit *f* unloading time
Entladung *f* unloading, discharge
Entlastungsdrän *m* relief drain *(amelioration)*
Entlastungsschleuse *f* relief sluice *(amelioration)*
Entlastungstakt *m* massage phase *(machine milking)*
entlauben to defoliate
entlaubt defoliated, bare
Entlaubung *f* defoliation
Entlaubungsmittel *n* defoliant
Entlaubungsspritzgerät *n* defoliator-sprayer
entlausen to [de]louse
entleeren to empty, to discharge, to exhaust; to unload; to evacuate, to void *(bowels)*
Entleerungsschnecke *f* unloading auger
Entleerungsvorrichtung *f* unloader, discharge device
entlieschen to husk *(maize)*
Entlieschkralle *f* husking pin, husker
Entlieschrolle *f*, **Entlieschwalze** *f* husking roll
entlignifizieren to delignify
entlüften to deaerate, to air out; to vent[ilate]
Entlüfter *m* deaerator, exhaust, vent
Entlüftung *f* deaeration, airing; ventilation
Entlüftungshahn *m* vent plug
Entmarkung *f (vet)* demyelination
Entmineralisation *f* demineralization
entmineralisieren to demineralize
entmisten to demanure, to muck [out]
Entmistung *f* manure removal
Entmooser *m* lawn scarifier
entnadeln to deneedle
Entnadelung *f* needle fall, shedding of needles
Entnahme *f (forest)* removal, depletion
~ in den beherrschten Baumklassen thinning from below
~ in den herrschenden Baumklassen thinning from above, crown thinning
Entnahmeende *n* dry end *(of a tunnel dryer)*
Entnahmefräse *f* silo unloader (tapping plant)
entnehmen/Blut to bleed, to draw blood
~/eine Probe to sample
Entoblast *n(m) s.* Entoderm
Entoderm *n* entoderm, endoderm, hypoblast
entodermal entodermal, entodermic
entomogam *(bot)* entomogamous, entomophilous
Entomogamie *f (bot)* entomogamy, entomophily
entomogen entomogenous
Entomologe *m* entomologist

Entomologie *f* entomology
entomologisch entomological
entomopathogen entomopathogenic
entomophag entomophagous, insectivorous
Entomophag[e] *m* insectivore
entomophil *s.* entomogam
Entomotoxin *n* entomotoxin
Entomozezidie *f (phyt)* insect gall
Entoparasit *m s.* Endoparasit
Entpulper *m* pulper, pulping machine
entrahmen *(dairy)* to cream, to skim
Entrahmung *f* cream separation, creaming, skimming
Entrahmungsschärfe *f* separating efficiency
Entrahmungsschleuder *f* skimming machine
Entrahmungsseparator *m s.* Entrahmungszentrifuge
Entrahmungszentrifuge *f* milk centrifuge, milk (cream) separator, creamer
entranken to remove tendrils, to pinch off (out)
entrappen to [de]stem *(grapes)*
Entrappungsmaschine *f* stemmer, stalk separator
entrinden to [de]bark, to disbark, to unbark, to rind, to peel, *(Am)* to ross; to decorticate, to excorticate
~/bastfrei to clean-bark
~/fleckenweise to patch-bark, to bark in patches (places)
~/grob to rough-bark, to rough-peel
~/platzweise *s.* ~/fleckenweise
~/saftfrisch to sap-peel
~/streifenweise to strip[-bark], to bark (peel) in strips
~/vollständig to clean-bark
Entrinder *m* [de]barker, barking machine, bark-peeling machine, *(Am)* rosser
~/hydraulischer hydraulic (stream) barker, hydrobarker
Entrindung *f* [de]barking, peeling, *(Am)* rossing; decortication
~/chemische chemical [de]barking, chemi-peeling
~ durch Druckeinwirkung compression debarking
~/hydraulische stream barking
~/mechanische mechanical (machine) barking
~/pneumatische pneumatic barking
Entrindungsabfälle *mpl* barking waste, bark shavings
Entrindungsbeil *n* barking axe
Entrindungshackmaschine *f* debarker chipper
Entrindungskopf *m* rosser head
Entrindungsmaschine *f s.* Entrinder
Entrindungstrommel *f* barking drum, drum barker
Entrindungswerkzeug *n* barking tool
entrippen to derib *(leaves)*
entrollen/sich *s.* entfalten/sich
Entropium *n (vet)* entropion
entsaften to sap
Entsafter *m* juice extractor (separator)
Entsaftung *f* juice extraction

Entsaftungskammer

Entsaftungskammer *f* juice-separating chamber *(wine-making)*
entsalzen to desalt, to desalinate, to desalinize
Entsalzung *f* desalin[iz]ation
entsamen to seed
entschäumen to defoam
Entschäumer *m* antifoaming agent
Entschleimen *n* desliming *(wine-making)*
Entschleimungsmaschine *f* mucus-removal machine
entschoten to shuck *(peas)*
entseuchen to disinfect, to decontaminate
Entseuchung *f* disinfection, decontamination
Entseuchungsgerät *n* disinfector
Entsorgung *f* **von Abprodukten** disposal of waste products
entspelzen to debran, to hull, to mill
entspitzen to tip, to pinch [back], to head [back, down], to top off, to stop
Entspitzen *n* **von Trieben** shoot tipping, removal of shoot tips
Entspunder *m* bung puller
entstanden/aus Stockausschlag *(forest)* of vegetative origin, originating from coppice *(suckers)*
~/durch Fusion fusogenic
~/primär *(vet)* idiopathic, primary
Entstaubung *f* dust removal
Entstaubungsanlage *f* dust extractor
Entstehung *f* genesis
entsteinen to [de]stone, to pit *(stone fruit)*
entstielen to [de]stem
entstippen to deflake *(wood)*
Entstipper *m* deflaker
Entteerer *m* tar separator
entvliesen to defleece, to dewool *(sheep)*
Entvliesung *f* dewoolling
entwalden to deforest, to dis[af]forest, to denude
entwaldet deforested, destitute of forests, bare
Entwaldung *f* deforestation, dis[af]forestation
entwässerbar drainable
Entwässerbarkeit *f* drainability
entwässern to dewater, to dehydrate; to desiccate; to drain *(land)*
~/übermäßig to overdrain
Entwässerung *f* drainage, drain of water, water removal
Entwässerungsbecken *n* drainage basin
Entwässerungsdichte *f* drainage density
Entwässerungsgebiet *n* drainage [area]
Entwässerungsgerät *n* dehydration plant, dehydrator
Entwässerungsgraben *m* drain, [drainage] ditch
~/schmaler [flacher] sheep drain
Entwässerungskanal *m* drainage channel
Entwässerungsstutzen *m* trap
Entwässerungssystem *n* drainage system
entwesen to disinfest
Entwesung *f* disinfestation

Entwesungsmittel *n* disinfestant
Entwicklung *f* development; genesis; evolution
~/stadiale stage development
~/stammesgeschichtliche evolution
Entwicklungsabschnitt *m* stadium
Entwicklungsbeschleunigung *f* acceleration
Entwicklungsbiologie *f* developmental biology
entwicklungsfähig viable
Entwicklungsfähigkeit *f* viability
entwicklungsgehemmt abortive
Entwicklungsgeschichte *f* developmental history
~/biologische biogenesis
Entwicklungshemmstoff *m* retardant
Entwicklungshemmung *f* retardation
Entwicklungsrhythmus *m* development rhythm
Entwicklungsrückschlag *m* atavism
Entwicklungsruhe *f* **mit herabgesetztem Stoffwechsel** *(zoo, ent)* diapause
Entwicklungsskala *f* growth [stage] scale *(e.g. of a cereal plant)*
Entwicklungsstadium *n* development[al] stage, stage [of development]
Entwicklungsstörung *f* developmental disorder
Entwicklungsstufe *f s.* Entwicklungsstadium
Entwicklungszyklus *m* development cycle
~ des Individuums life cycle
entwipfeln to poll[ard], to [be]head, to head back (down), to decapitate, to top; to lop [off]
Entwipfelung *f* decapitation
entwöhnen to wean, to spean, to ablactate
Entwöhnen *n* weaning, ablactation
entwurmen to [de]worm
Entwurmung *f* deworming
entwurzeln to disroot, to uproot
entziehen to withdraw
~/Gossypol to degossypolize
~/Stickstoff to denitrogenate, to denitrogenize
~/Wasser *s.* entwässern
entzuckern to desugar, to desaccharify
Entzuckerung *f* desugarization, desaccharification
entzündbar [in]flammable, ignitable
~/nicht non-flammable, incombustible
Entzündbarkeit *f* [in]flammability, ignitability
entzünden to ignite, to inflame
~/sich *(vet)* to become inflamed
Entzünden *n* ignition, firing
entzündlich 1. *s.* entzündbar; 2. *(vet)* inflammatory, phlogistic
Entzündlichkeit *f* inflammability
Entzündung *f* ignition; *(vet)* inflammation, phlogosis
~ der Gebärmutteranhänge adnexitis
~ der Gebärmutterschleimhaut endometritis
~ der grauen Rückenmarksubstanz poliomyelitis
~ der harten Hirnhaut pachymeningitis
~ des äußeren Gehörgangs external otitis
~ des die Gallenblase umgebenden Gewebes pericholecystitis
~ des drüsenumgebenden Gewebes periadenitis

Epilepsie

~ **des Gebärmutterbauchfellüberzugs** perimetritis
~ **des gelenkumgebenden Gewebes** periarthritis
~ **seröser Häute** serositis
~ **von Regenbogenhaut und Strahlenkörper** cyclitis
~ **von Zervikalkanal und äußerem Muttermund** cervicitis
entzündungserregend phlogogenic, phlogogenous
entzündungshemmend *(vet)* antiphlogistic, antiinflammatory
Entzündungstemperatur *f* ignition temperature
Entzwiebelmaschine *f* debulbing machine
Enukleation *f (vet)* enucleation
Enumeration *f (forest)* enumeration [survey]
ENV *s.* Erbsennekrosevirus
Environik *f* environmental engineering
Enzelienverbesine *f (bot)* crown-beard, Verbesina encelioides
Enzephalitis *f (vet)* encephalitis
Enzephalogramm *n* encephalogram
Enzephalom *n (vet)* encephaloma
Enzephalomalazie *f (vet)* encephalomalacia
~ **der Küken/alimentäre** crazy chick disease
Enzephalomyelitis *(vet)* encephalomyelitis
~/**aviäre** [infectious] avian encephalomyelitis, epidemic tremor, jittery
Enzephalomyelopathie *f (vet)* encephalomyelopathy
Enzephalomyokarditisvirus *n* encephalomyocarditis virus
Enzephalomyopathie *f (vet)* encephalomyelopathy
Enzephalopathie *f (vet)* encephalopathy
~/**bovine spongiforme** mad cow disease
~ **des Nerzes/infektiöse** transmissible mink encephalopathy, scrapie-like disease
Enzian *m* 1. gentian *(genus Gentiana)*; 2. *s.* Enziananschnaps
Enzianschnaps *m* gentian [bitter]
Enzootie *f (vet)* enzootic
enzootisch enzootic
Enzym *n* enzyme, ferment
~/**eiweißspaltendes** protease
~/**hydrolytisches** hydrolase
~/**metallhaltiges** metalloenzyme
~/**nukleolytisches** nuclease
~/**proteolytisches** protease
~/**stärkespaltendes** amylase, diastase
~/**tryptisches** trypsin
Enzymaktivator *m* enzyme activator
Enzymaktivität *f* enzyme (enzymatic) activity
enzymartig enzyme-like
enzymatisch enzymatic, enzymic, fermentative
Enzymausschüttung *f* enzyme discharge
Enzymgift *n s.* Enzymhemmstoff
Enzymhemmstoff *m* enzyme inhibitor (poison)
Enzymhemmung *f* enzyme inhibition

Enzymimmunoassay *n*, **Enzymimmun[o]test** *m* enzyme immunoassay
Enzyminduktion *f* enzyme induction
Enzymkinetik *f* enzyme kinetics
Enzymmarker *m* enzyme marker
Enzymnomenklatur *f* enzyme nomenclature
Enzymologie *f* enzymology
Enzympolymorphismus *m* enzyme polymorphism
Enzympräparat *n* enzyme preparation
Enzymprodukt *n* enzyme product
Enzymprotein *n* enzyme protein, apoenzyme
Enzymrepression *f* enzyme repression
Enzymsystem *n* enzyme system
Enzymvorstufe *f* enzyme precursor, proenzyme, zymogen
Enzymwirkung *f* action of enzymes
enzystieren to encyst
Enzystierung *f* encystation, encystment
Eonymphe *f (ent)* eonymph
Eosin *n* eosin *(dye)*
Eosinopenie *f (vet)* eosinopenia
Eosinopher *m s.* Eosinozyt
Eosinophilie *f (vet)* eosinophilia
Eosinozyt *m* eosinophil [leucocyte]
EP *s.* 1. Epoxidharz; 2. Punkt/isoelektrischer
Epagon *n* sex pheromone (attractant)
Ephedra *f (bot)* ephedra *(genus Ephedra)*
ephedraähnlich *(bot)* ephedroid
Ephedrin *n* ephedrine *(alkaloid)*
ephedroid *(bot)* ephedroid
ephemer ephemeral, diurnal
Ephemeralfieber *n* bovine ephemeral (epizootic) fever, stiff (three-day) thickness
ephemerisch *s.* ephemer
Epiblast *m s.* Ektoderm
Epicillin *n* epicillin *(antibiotic)*
Epicotyl *n (bot)* epicotyl
Epidemie *f* epidemic
Epidemiologie *f* epidemiology
epidemiologisch epidemiological
epidemisch epidemic
epidermal epidermal
Epidermis *f* epidermis, outer skin, scarf-skin; *(ent)* hypodermis
Epididymis *f* epididymis
Epiduralanästhesie *f (vet)* epidural anaesthesia
Epiduralraum *m* epidural space *(animal anatomy)*
epigäisch *(bot, zoo)* epigeal, epigeous
Epigastrium *n* epigastrium
Epigenese *f*, **Epigenesis** *f* epigenesis
Epigenetik *f* epigenetics
Epiglottis *f* epiglottis
epigyn *(bot)* epigynous
Epikard *n* epicardium
Epikarp *n (bot)* epicarp
Epikotyl *n (bot)* epicotyl
epikutikulär *(bot)* epicuticular
Epilepsie *f (vet)* epilepsy

Epilimnion

Epilimnion *n* epilimnion *(the water layer overlying the thermocline of a lake)*
epilimnisch epilimnetic
Epimerase *f* epimerase *(enzyme)*
Epinastie *f (bot, phyt)* epinasty
epinastisch eoinastic
Epinephrektomie *f (vet)* adrenalectomy
Epinephrin *n* adrenalin[e], epinephrine *(hormone)*
epipetal *(bot)* epipetalous
Epiphora *f (vet)* epiphora
epiphyll *(bot)* epiphyllous
Epiphyse *f (zoo)* epiphysis, pineal body *(gland, organ)*
Epiphysenablösung *f* epiphysiolysis
Epiphysenbruch *m (vet)* epiphyseal fracture
Epiphysenfugenscheibe *f*, **Epiphysen[fugen]knorpel** *m* epiphyseal cartilage, metaphyseal growth plate
Epiphysenlösung *f*, **Epiphysiolysis** *f* epiphysiolysis
Epiphyt *m* epiphyte, aerophyte, air plant
epiphytisch epiphytic, epiphytal
Epiphytologie *f* epiphytology
Epiphytose *f*, **Epiphytotie** *f* epiphytotic
epiphytotisch epiphytotic
Epiploon *n* epiploon, greater omentum *(animal anatomy)*
Episcie *f* 1. flaming violet *(genus Episcia)*; 2. flaming violet, Episcia cupreata
episepal *(bot)* episepalous
Episioplastie *f (vet)* episioplasty
Episit *m* episite, predator
Episom *n (gen)* episome
Epistas[i]e *f*, **Epistasis** *f (gen)* epistasis
epistatisch *(gen)* epistatic
Epistaxis *f (vet)* epistaxis, nasal (nose) bleeding
Epithel *n* epithelium
~/ spermatogenes (spermiogenes) spermatogenic epithelium
Epithelgeschwulst *f (vet)* epithelioma
Epithelgewebe *n* epithelium
epithelial epithelial
Epitheliom *n (vet)* epithelioma
Epithelkörperchenhormon *n* parathyroid hormone, parathormone, parathyrin
Epithelschicht *f* epithelial layer
Epithelschutzvitamin *n* retinol, axerophthol, vitamin A
Epithelzelle *f* epithelial cell
Epizoochorie *f* epizoochory
Epizoon *n* epizoon
Epizoose *f*, **Epizootie** *f (vet)* epizootic
Epizootiologie *f* epizootiology
epizootisch epizootic
Epökie *f* epoecism, epoecy
Epoxidharz *n* epoxy [resin], ethoxylene resin
Epoxidhydrase *f* epoxide hydrase *(enzyme)*
Epoxidhydrolase *f* epoxide hydrolase *(enzyme)*

Epoxidzyklus *m* xanthophyll cycle *(of photosynthesis)*
1,2-Epoxyethan *n* ethylene oxide *(fumigant)*
Eppich *m* 1. celery *(genus Apium)*; 2. [common] celery, Apium graveolens
EPR *s.* Resonanz/elektronenparamagnetische
Epronaz *n* epronaz *(herbicide)*
Eprouvette *f* culture tube
Epsom-Bittersalz *n* Epsom salt *(laxative, magnesium fertilizer)*
ept *s.* Inceptisol
Eptam *n*, **EPTC** eptam, EPTC *(herbicide)*
Epulis *f (vet)* epulis
Equestrik *f* equitation, equestrianism, horsemanship
Equiden *mpl* horse family *(family Equidae)*
Equilenin *n* equilenin *(mare oestrogen)*
Equilin *n* equilin *(mare oestrogen)*
equin equine
Equines Herpesvirus *n* **Typ 1** equine herpes virus 1
Equisetin *n* equisetine *(alkaloid)*
Equisetonin *n* equisetonine *(saponin)*
Equisetum *n (bot)* equisetum *(genus Equisetum)*
ER *s.* Retikulum/endoplasmatisches
Eradikation *f* eradication
Erbänderung *f* mutation
Erbanlage *f s.* Gen
Erbanlagen *fpl* heritage, inheritance
erbbar inheritable
Erbbild *n* genotype, idiotype, genetic constitution (make-up)
erben to inherit
erbeuten to prey [up]on
Erbfaktor *m s.* Gen
Erbfehler *m* hereditary (inherited) defect
Erbgang *m* mode of inheritance
erbgleich homozygous
Erbgrind *m (vet)* favus
~ der Hühner white comb *(of chicken)*
Erbgut *n* heritage, inheritance
Erbkrankheit *f* hereditary disease
Erblehre *f* genetics
erblich hereditary, [in]heritable
Erblichkeit *f* heritability, heredity, inheritance
~ erworbener Eigenschaften inheritance of acquired characters
Erblichkeitsanteil *m*, **Erblichkeitsgrad** *m* degree of heritability
Erblichkeitsmodus *m* mode of inheritance
Erblichkeitsschätzung *f* heritability estimation
Erblichkeitsziffer *f* coefficient of heritability, heritability estimate
erblühen to blossom, to burst (break out) into blossom, to bloom, to effloresce
Erbmangel *m* inherited (hereditary) defect
Erbon *n* erbon *(herbicide)*
erbrechen *(vet)* to vomit
~/ scheinbar to regurgitate

Erbrochenes *n* vomit
erbrüten to brood, to hatch
Erbrütung *f* hatch
Erbse *f* 1. pea *(genus Pisum)*; 2. pea vine, garden pea, Pisum sativum
Erbsen *fpl* pease
Erbsenälchen *n s.* Erbsenzystenälchen
Erbsenblasenfuß *m (ent)* pea thrips, Kakothrips robustus (pisivorus)
Erbsenblattlaus *f* pea aphid, Acyrthosiphon pisum
Erbsenblattrollmosaikvirus *n* pea leaf rolling mosaic virus, pea seed-borne mosaic virus, PSbMV
Erbsendrescher *m*, **Erbsendreschmaschine** *f* [pea] podder
Erbsenenationenmosaikvirus *n* pea enation mosaic virus, PEMV
Erbsenerntemaschine *f* pea harvester
erbsenförmig pisiform
Erbsenfrüchtige Scheinzypresse *f* Sawara cypress, Chamaecyparis pisifera
Erbsengallmücke *f* pea midge, Contarinia pisi
Erbsenheber *m* pea lifter (lifting machine)
Erbsenheu *n* pea hay
Erbsenhülse *f* pea pod, peacod
Erbsenkäfer *m* pea beetle (bug), [four-spotted] bean weevil, Spanish bean beetle, Bruchus pisorum, Callosobruchus maculatus
Erbsenkamm *m* pea (triple) comb *(of chicken)*
Erbsenkorn *n* pea corn
Erbsenkraut *n* pea haulm
Erbsenkrautsilage *f* pea haulm silage
Erbsenlaus *f s.* Erbsenblattlaus
Erbsenmähbalken *m* pea-cutter
Erbsenmehltau *m* powdery mildew of pea *(caused by Erysiphe polygoni)*
Erbsenminierfliege *f* pea leaf-miner, Phytomyza atricornis
Erbsenmosaikvirus *n* pea mosaic virus
Erbsennekrosevirus *n* pea necrosis virus, PNV
Erbsenpflückmaschine *f* [pea] viner, vining machine
Erbsenproteinkonzentrat *n* pea protein concentrate
Erbsenreinigungs- und -sortiermaschine *f* pea cleaner and grader
Erbsenrost *m* pea rust *(caused by Uromyces pisi)*
Erbsenschneidwerk *n* pea-cutter
Erbsenschote *f* pea pod, peacod
Erbsenschrot *n* pea meal
Erbsenschwader *m* pea swather
Erbsenstrauch *m* 1. pea shrub *(genus Caragana)*; 2. Siberian pea shrub, Siberian acacia, Caragana arborescens
Erbsenstrichelvirus *n* pea streak virus
Erbsenstroh *n* pea straw
erbsentragend pisiferous
Erbsenwelke *f* pea fusarium wilt, top yellows of pea *(esp. caused by Fusarium oxysporum f. pisi)*

Erbsenwickler *m* pea moth, Cydia (Laspeyresia) nigricana
Erbsenzystenälchen *n* pea cyst-nematode, pea root eelworm, Heterodera goettingiana
Erbsschrot *n* pea meal
Erbtyp[us] *m* genotype, idiotype, genetic constitution (make-up)
Erdabscheider *m* soil separator, soil removal equipment
Erdapfel *m* potato [tuber]
Erdarbeitsmaschine *f* earth-moving machine
Erdaustausch *m* resoiling
Erdbalken *m* furrow-slice *(ploughing)*
Erdbeeradernbänderungsvirus *n* strawberry vein banding virus, SVCV
Erdbeerbaum *m* 1. madrone, arbutus *(genus Arbutus)*; 2. strawberry-tree, apple of Cain, Arbutus unedo
Erdbeerblättälchen *n* strawberry leaf nematode, strawberry (fern) eelworm, Aphelenchoides fragariae
Erdbeerblattkäfer *m* strawberry leaf beetle, Galerucella tenella
Erdbeerblattrandvergilbungsvirus *n* strawberry mild yellow edge virus, SMYEV
Erdbeerblütenstecher *m* strawberry blossom (bud) weevil, Anthonomus rubi
Erdbeer-Duchesnea *f* Indian strawberry, Duchesnea indica
Erdbeere *f* 1. strawberry *(genus Fragaria)*; 2. strawberry *(fruit)*
~/**knopfartig mißgeformte** buttonberry
~/**knotenartig mißgeformte** nubbin
~/**mehrmals tragende** everbearing (remontant) strawberry
Erdbeererntemaschine *f* strawberry harvester
Erdbeerhimbeere *f* strawberry-raspberry, balloonberry, Rubus illecebrosus
Erdbeerklee *m* strawberry clover, Trifolium fragiferum
Erdbeerknotenhaarlaus *f* strawberry aphid, Pentatrichopus fragaefolii
Erdbeerkräuselvirus *n* strawberry crinkle virus, SCV
Erdbeerlaufkäfer *m* strawberry seed beetle, Harpalus rufipes (pubescens)
Erdbeermehltau *m* strawberry mildew *(caused by Sphaerotheca humuli = S. macularis)*
Erdbeermilbe *f* strawberry (cyclamen) mite, Tarsonemus (Stenotarsonemus) pallidus
Erdbeerpflanze *f* strawberry plant *(genus Fragaria)*
Erdbeerpflanzenrodemaschine *f* strawberry plant harvester
Erdbeerpflückmaschine *f* strawberry picker
Erdbeerspinat *m* strawberry blite, Chenopodium foliosum
Erdbeerstiel *m* strawberry stalk, stobb
Erdbeertomate *f s.* Erdkirsche

Erdbeerwickler

Erdbeerwickler *m (ent)* strawberry tortrix, Acleris comariana
Erdbeerwiese *f* solid strawberry bed
Erdbeerwurzelrüßler *m* strawberry root weevil, Othiorhynchus ovatus
Erdbeton *m* soil cement
Erdbetonweg *m* soil cement road
Erdbewegungsmaschine *f* earth-moving machine
Erdbirne *f* 1. ground-nut, potato bean, *(Am)* Dakota potato, Apios americana (tuberosa); 2. Jerusalem artichoke, topinambur, girosol, girasol[e], Helianthus tuberosus; 3. yacon strawberry, Polymnia sonchifolia (edulis)
Erdblock *m (forest)* butt log (block, length), bottom log (piece)
Erdboden *m* earth, ground
Erdboden... s. Boden...
Erdbohrer *m* earth drill, hole digger; post-hole auger (borer, digger)
Erddämpfung *f* soil steaming
Erddesinfektion *f* soil disinfection
Erddränung *f* mole drainage
Erde *f* earth *(s. a. Boden)* • **auf der ~ lebend** *(zoo)* epigeal, epigeous • **dicht über der ~ wachsend** *(bot)* epigeal, epigeous • **mit ~ bedecken** to earth [over, up], to mould
~/gärtnerische garden (gardener's) soil, artificial soil mix
Erdefressen *n* soil ingestion, geophagia *(animal behaviour)*
Erdeichel *f* heath pea, Lathyrus tuberosus
Erdeinschlag *m* rooting (plunging) bed *(e.g. for woody plants)*
erdelos soilless
Erderbse *f* bamba[r]ra [ground]nut, earth pea, Congo goober, underground bean, Madagascar peanut, Voandzeia (Vigna) subterranea
Erdeule *f* s. Erdraupe
Erdfließen *n* earth flow, solifluction
Erdfloh *m* flea beetle (bug) *(subfamily Halticinae)*
Erdgas *n* natural gas
~/verflüssigtes liquid petroleum gas
Erdgewächshaus *n* sunk glasshouse
Erdgrubensilo *m* pit silo
Erdhobel *m* land plane (leveller), autograder
Erdhöhle *f* earthen cell *(for certain insect larvae)*
Erdholztermite *f* subterranean termite
Erdkastanie *f* hawk nut *(genus Bunium)*
Erdkirsche *f* 1. ground cherry, strawberry tomato, dwarf Cape gooseberry, tomatillo, Physalis pruinosa; 2. tomatillo, Physalis ixocarpa
Erdklotz *m* s. Erdblock
Erdklumpen *m* clod
Erdkompost *m* [soil] compost
Erdkrebs *m* mushroom root rot *(e.g. on fruit-trees, caused esp. by Armillaria mellea)*
Erdkrümel *m* soil crumb
Erdkruste *f* earth's crust
Erdkultur *f* soil culture

Erdmandel *f* chufa, earth almond, rush nut *(from Cyperus esculentus)*
Erdmandelgras *n* yellow nutsedge, chufa, nut grass, Cyperus esculentus
Erdmarder *m* kolinsky, Mustela siberica
Erdmarderfell *n*, **Erdmarderpelz** *m* kolinsky
Erdmaus *f* field (short-tailed) vole, Microtus agrestis
Erdmeiler *m* earth (pit, country) kiln
Erdmiete *f* earth silo, clamp
Erdmischung *f* soil mixture
Erdmorchel *f* truffle *(genus Tuber)*
erdnah near-earth, near-ground, ground-proximate
Erdnuß *f* 1. peanut, ground-nut, earth-nut, goober, pinder, Arachis hypogaea; 2. peanut *(seed)*
Erdnußbutter *f* peanut butter
Erdnußerntemaschine *f* ground-nut harvester
Erdnußextraktionsschrot *n* ground-nut [oil-]meal
Erdnußgelbscheckungsvirus *n* peanut yellow mottle virus
Erdnußheu *n* peanut hay
Erdnußhülse *f* ground-nut husk (shell)
Erdnußkräuselvirus *n* ground-nut rosette virus
Erdnußkraut *n* ground-nut haulm (straw)
Erdnußkuchen *m* ground-nut cake
Erdnußkuchenmehl *n* ground-nut [oil-]meal
Erdnußkuchenschrot *n* ground-nut cake
Erdnußlaus *f* cowpea aphid, Aphis craccivora
Erdnußmehl *n* ground-nut flour
Erdnußöl *n* ground-nut oil, arachis oil
Erdnußölkuchenmehl *n* ground-nut [oil-]meal
Erdnußpflanze *f* s. Erdnuß 1.
Erdnußplattkäfer *m* merchant grain beetle, Oryzaephilus mercator
Erdnußpreßkuchen *m* ground-nut cake
Erdnußproteinisolat *n* ground-nut protein isolate
Erdnußringmosaikvirus *n* ground-nut ring mosaic virus
Erdnußrosettenvirus *n* ground-nut rosette virus
Erdnußschale *f* ground-nut husk (shell)
Erdnußscheckungsvirus *n* peanut mottle virus, PnMV
Erdnußstauchevirus *n* ground-nut stunt virus
Erdorchidee *f* terrestrial orchid *(comprehensive term)*
Erdpflanze *f* geophyte, cryptophyte
Erdpreßtopf *m* soil block, [compressed] block
Erdrauch *m (bot)* 1. fumitory *(genus Fumaria)*; 2. [common] fumitory, earth smoke, Fumaria officinalis
Erdraupe *f (ent)* cutworm, surface caterpillar *(comprehensive term)*
Erdreich *n* earth, soil *(s. a. Boden)*
~/durch Regen abgeschwemmtes rain-wash
Erdreißer *m* soil shredder
Erdriese *f* s. Erdrutsche
Erdrohrwärmetauscher *m* earth-tube heat exchanger
Erdrückungsverlust *m* crushing loss *(pig rearing)*
Erdrutsch *m* landslide, landslip, earth slide

Erdrutsche *f (forest)* earthen chute, ground slide
Erdschaufel *f* earth scoop, soil bucket
Erdschocke *f s.* Erdbirne 2.
Erdscholle *f* soil clod
Erdschürfepflanze *f* hemicryptophyte
Erdsieb *n* riddle
Erdsilo *m* pit silo, earth-walled silage clamp
Erdsproß *m* root-stock, rhizome, stem-tuber
Erdstabilisierung *f* soil stabilization
Erdstammstück *n s.* Erdblock
Erdstrahlung *f* terrestrial radiation
Erdstreifen *m* furrow-slice *(ploughing)*
Erdteich *m* earthen pond
Erdtopf *m* [soil, peat] block, [soil, peat] pot • **im ~ gezogen** block-raised
Erdtopfpflanzmaschine *f* block planter, soil-block planting machine
Erdtopfpflanzung *f* block planting
Erdtopfpflanzwagen *m* soil-block planting cart
Erdtopfpresse *f* soil-block maker (press), blocking (block-making) machine, soil-pot maker
Erd- und Feinkrautabscheider *m* soil and fine haulm remover
erdverlegt buried *(e.g. a pipeline)*
Erdwärme[energie] *f* geothermal energy
Erdwechsel *m* resoiling • **einen ~ durchführen** to resoil
Erdweg *m* earth (unmetalled) road, unmade (unsurfaced) road, *(Am)* dirt (strip) road
erdwendig *(bot)* geotropic
Erdwendigkeit *f* geotropism, gravitropism
Erdwicke *f* heath pea, Lathyrus tuberosus
Erdwirtschaft *f* soil management *(horticulture)*
erektil erectile
Erektion *f* erection
erektionsfähig erectile
Eremophyt *m* eremophyte, desert plant
Eremurus *m* eremurus, foxtail lily *(genus Eremurus)*
Erepsin *n* erepsin *(enzyme mixture)*
ererben *s.* erben
ererbt hereditary
Erfahrung *f/tierpflegerische* stockmanship
Erfahrungstafel *f (forest)* experimental table
Erfassungspreis *m* procurement price
Erfolgsorgan *n* effector *(of the reflex arc)*
erfrieren to be killed (damaged) by frost *(plant)*; to freeze [to death] *(animal)*
~ lassen to freeze
ERG *s.* 1. Elektroretinographie; 2. Elektroretinogramm
Ergänzen *n (forest)* filling up, infilling, repair planting, gapping, beating[-up], blanking; recruitment *(game management)*
~ der Naturverjüngung supplementing of natural regeneration
Ergänzungsdüngung *f* complementary fertilization
Ergänzungsfutter *n* supplementary (extra) feed, supplement

Ergänzungsfütterung *f* supplementary feeding
Ergänzungskalkung *f* maintenance liming
Ergänzungsluft *f* inspiratory reserve volume
Ergasilose *f* ergasilosis *(of fishes, caused esp. by Ergasilus sieboldii)*
Ergobasin *n s.* Ergometrin
Ergocalciferol *n* ergocalciferol, vitamin D_2
Ergograph *m* ergometer
Ergometer *n* ergometer
Ergometrin *n* ergometrine, ergonovine *(alkaloid)*
Ergonomie *f* ergonomics
Ergonovin *n s.* Ergometrin
Ergosterin *n*, **Ergosterol** *n* ergosterol *(provitamin D_2)*
Ergotamin *n* ergotamine *(ergot alkaloid)*
Ergothionein *n* ergothioneine *(histidine derivative)*
Ergotinin *n* ergotinine *(mixture of ergot alkaloids)*
Ergotismus *m (vet)* ergotism, ergot poisoning, St. Anthony's fire
Ergotoxin *n* ergotoxine *(mixture of ergot alkaloids)*
Ergotropikum *n* growth promoter (stimulant), growth-promoting agent
ergrünen to green
Erguß *m* effusion
Erhaltung *f* **der Bodenfruchtbarkeit** soil conservation (fertility management)
~ der Umwelt environmental conservation
Erhaltungsatmung *f* maintenance respiration
Erhaltungsbedarf *m* maintenance requirement *(animal nutrition)*
~/energetischer maintenance energy requirement
Erhaltungsdüngung *f* maintenance dressing
Erhaltungsfutterbedarf *m* maintenance feed requirement
Erhaltungsfutterration *f* maintenance ration
Erhaltungsfütterung *f* maintenance feeding
Erhaltungsgebiet *n (ecol)* refuge
Erhaltungsgleichgewicht *n* maintenance equilibrium (condition) *(animal nutrition)*
Erhaltungskalkung *f* maintenance liming, liming for preservation
Erhaltungsquotient *m* survival index *(breeding)*
Erhaltungsration *f* maintenance ration
Erhaltungsschnitt *m* maintenance pruning *(orcharding)*
Erhaltungszüchtung *f* maintenance (reproduction) breeding
Erhaltungszustand *m* maintenance condition *(animal physiology)*
erhärten to harden [off], to set
Erhebung *f/diagnostische* diagnostic sampling *(e.g. in silviculture)*
erhitzen to heat
Erhitzer *m* heater
Erhitzung *f* heating
Erhitzungsnachweis *m (dairy)* test for the control of heat treatment
erhöhen/die Luftfeuchte to damp

Erholung

Erholung *f* recreation; recovery *(e.g. from a disease)*
Erholungsfunktion *f* recreational function *(e.g. of forests)*
Erholungsgebiet *n* recreation area (ground)
Erholungsnutzung *f* recreational use *(e.g. of forests)*
Erholungswald *m* amenity (recreational) forest
Erholungswert *m* recreational value *(e.g. of a landscape)*
erigibel erectile
Erika *f* erica, heath[er] *(genus Erica)*
Erikaaster *f* heath aster, Aster ericoides (multiflorus)
Erimado *m (bot)* mugongo, Ricinodendron heudelotii (africanum)
erkalten to cool [down, off], to grow cold
Erkältung *f* chilling injury (damage) *(of plants)*; chill, cold *(of animals)*
Erkältungsresistenz *f* chilling resistance *(of plants)*
Erkrankung *f* disease, disorder, illness, sickness, ailment, affection *(s. a. under* Krankheit*)*
~/ansteckende infectious (transmissible) disease
~/bakterielle bacterial disease, bacteriosis
~ der Atmungsorgane respiratory disease
~ der Bauchspeicheldrüse pancreatic disease
~ durch Pilze mycosis
~/geschwürige canker
~ infolge Bandwurmbefalls cestodiasis
~/protozoäre protozoal infection
~/ulzeröse canker
~/virusbedingte virosis
Erkrankungshäufigkeit *f* morbidity, morbidness
Erkrankungswahrscheinlichkeit *f* morbidity, morbidness
Erkrankungsziffer *f* morbidity rate
Erkundung *f* reconnaissance
~ aus der Luft aerial reconnaissance
Erle *f* alder *(genus Alnus)*
erlegen *(hunt)* to kill, to shoot
~/mit dem Spieß to stick
Erlegerprämie *f* bounty
Erlegungsrate *f* release-kill ratio
erlenblättrig alder-leaved
Erlenblättrige Felsenbirne *f* western service-berry, saskatoon [service-berry], western shadbush, Amelanchier alnifolia
~ Scheineller *f* sweet pepperbush, Clethra alnifolia
Erlenblättriger Zwergapfel *m* Korean mountain ash, Sorbus alnifolia
Erlenbruch[wald] *m*, **Erlenmoor** *n* alder swamp [forest], [alder] carr
Erlenrüßler *m* alder (poplar, willow) weevil, poplar-and-willow borer, Cryptorhynchus lapathi
Erlenwald *m* alder forest
ErLV *s.* Latentes Erysimum-Virus
ermahlen *s.* mahlen
ermatten to exhaust; to fatigue

Ermattung *f* fatigue
ermüden to fatigue, to tire
Ermüdung *f* fatigue
ernähren to nourish, to feed
~/sich to live [on]
Ernährung *f* nutrition, nutriture, nourishment, diet
~ [höherer Pflanzen] durch Mykorrhiza mycotrophy
~/mineralische mineral nutrition
~ von lebenden Organismen/parasitäre biotrophy
Ernährungsbedarf *m* nutritional requirements
Ernährungsbiologie *f* feeding biology
Ernährungschemiker *m* nutrition chemist
Ernährungsdiagnose *f* diagnosis of nutritional status
Ernährungsfehler *m* nutritional error
Ernährungsforschung *f* nutrition research
Ernährungsfraß *m (ent)* after-eating *(of caterpillars)*
ernährungsgestört dystrophic
Ernährungslehre *f* dietetics
Ernährungsmangel *m* innutrition
Ernährungsniveau *n* plane (level) of nutrition, nutritional level
Ernährungsökologie *f* feeding ecology
Ernährungsphysiologie *f* nutrition[al] physiology
Ernährungsprogramm *n* nutrition programme
Ernährungsregime *n* nutritional (dietary) regime
Ernährungsschaden *m s.* Ernährungsstörung
Ernährungsstörung *f* nutritional disorder (disturbance), dystrophy
Ernährungsstreß *m* nutritional stress
Ernährungsstufe *f (ecol)* trophic level
Ernährungswissenschaft *f* nutritional science
Ernährungswissenschaftler *m* nutritionist
Ernährungszustand *m* nutritional state (status), nutritive condition, nutrient status, trophy • **den ~ betreffend** trophic
erneuern to renew, to regenerate, to recondition, to re-establish
~/sich to be renewed, to regenerate
Erneuerung *f* renewal, regeneration
~ der Waldressourcen forest regeneration
~ des Pflanzen[be]wuchses revegetation
Erneuerungsschnitt *m* renewal pruning *(orcharding)*
Erneuerungstrieb *m* renewal spur
erntbar harvestable, ready for harvest
Erntbarkeit *f* harvestability
Ernte *f* 1. harvest[ing], crop[ping]; 2. *s.* Erntegut; 3. *s.* Erntezeit • **~ einbringen** *s.* ernten • **~ tragen** to crop
~ auf dem Halm standing crop
~/beschädigungsarme low-damage harvesting *(e.g. of root crops)*
~/geringe light crop
~ in [mehreren] Durchgängen repeated harvest[ing]

~/kontinuierliche continuous harvest[ing]
~/mechanisierte machine harvest[ing]
~/reiche heavy crop
~/schlechte poor crop
~/stehende standing crop
~/vollmechanisierte combine harvesting, machine harvest[ing]
~/wiederholte repeated harvest[ing]
~/zweiphasige two-phase harvest[ing]
Erntearbeit f harvest work
Erntearbeiter m harvester, cropper
Ernteaufbereitung f crop processing
Ernteausfall m crop failure
Ernteausrüstung f harvesting equipment
Ernteaussichten fpl crop (harvest) prospects
Ernteband n harvest belt
Erntebericht m crop report
Erntedankfest n harvest home (festival), *(Am)* Thanksgiving [Day]
Erntedatum n harvest date
Ernteermittlung f harvest statistics
Ernteertrag m crop [yield], harvest
Ernteerzeugnis n harvest product
erntefähig harvestable, ready for harvest
Erntefähigkeit f harvestability
Erntefeld n harvest field
Erntefest n s. Erntedankfest
Erntefeuchte f harvest moisture
Erntefläche f harvest area, *(Am)* harvested cropland
Erntegerät n cropper
Erntegut n crop, harvested produce
~/stehendes standing crop
Erntegutaufbereitung f crop processing
~ **auf dem Feld** field processing
Erntegutlagerhalle f crop storage building
Erntegutlagerung f crop storage
Erntegutqualität f crop quality
Erntegutrückstand m crop residue, [post]harvest residue
Erntegutschädigung f crop damage (injury)
Ernteguttrockner m crop dryer
Ernteguttrocknung f crop drying
Erntegutverarbeitung f crop processing
Erntegutverlust m crop (harvesting) loss
Erntegutversicherung f crop insurance
Erntegutverwertung f crop utilization
Erntegutzeile f swath[e], windrow
Erntehäufigkeit f harvesting frequency
Erntehelfer m [volunteer] harvester
Erntehieb m *(forest)* harvest cut[ting]
Erntehilfsmittel n harvest aid
Ernteindex m harvest index, HI, crop [yield] index
Erntejahr n harvest (crop) year
Erntekampagne f harvesting campaign
Erntekranz m harvest wreath
Erntekrätze f trombidiasis *(anthropozoonosis)*
Ernteleiter f harvest ladder

Erntemaschine f harvest[ing] machine, harvester, cropper
~/kontinuierlich arbeitende continuous harvester
~/reihengebundene row cropper
~/selbstfahrende self-propelled harvester
Erntemaschinen fpl **und -geräte** npl harvesting equipment
Erntemaschinenkomplex m group of harvesters
Erntemechanisierung f harvest mechanization
Erntemenge f crop [load]
Erntemethode f harvest method
Erntemilbe f harvest mite, Neotrombicula (Trombicula) autumnalis
ernten to harvest, to crop, to reap, to [in]gather; to pick; to cut
~/Hopfen to hop
~/mit dem Mähdrescher to combine
~/übermäßig to overharvest
Ernten n harvesting, cropping, gathering; picking
~/streifenweises strip harvesting (cutting)
Erntenebenprodukt n crop by-product
Ernteperiode f harvest period
~/ausgedehnte long-season cropping
Ernteplattform f picking platform
Ernteprodukt n harvest product
Ernterechen m harvesting rake
erntereif harvest ripe, ready for harvest, ripe for cutting
Erntereife f harvest maturity
Erntereihe f harvest row
Ernterückstand m crop residue, [post]harvest residue
Ernterückstände mpl crop remains, rubbish
Ernterückstandsbehandlung f crop residue management
Ernteschätzung f crop estimation
Ernteschätzwert m crop estimate
Erntestatistik f harvest statistics
Erntetechnik f harvest technique
Erntetermin m harvest date
Erntetuch n canvas liner
Ernteverfahren n harvest method (technique)
Ernteverfrühung f cropping (harvest) advancement
Ernteverlust m crop (harvesting) loss; *(forest)* logging waste
Ernteverspätung f, **Ernteverzögerung** f cropping (harvest) delay
Erntevoranschlag m crop estimate
Erntewagen m harvest van (wagon); frame cart *(in greenhouses)*
Erntewelle f cropping cycle, flush *(e.g. in mushroom growing)*
Erntewetter n harvest weather
Erntezeit f harvest [time, season]
Erntezeitpunkt m harvest date
Erntezeitspanne f harvest period
Erntezyklus m cropping (harvest) cycle
erodierbar erodible *(soil)*

Erodierbarkeit

Erodierbarkeit f erodibility, erosivity
erodieren to erode
Eröffnungsphase f dilatation stage *(parturition)*
Eröffnungsschnitt m face (slab) cut *(timber conversion)*
Eröffnungsstadium n dilatation stage *(parturition)*
Erosion f erosion
~/beschleunigte accelerated erosion
erosionsanfällig erosion-sensitive, erodible
Erosionsbekämpfung f erosion control
Erosionsgefahr f erosion hazard
erosionsgefährdet erosion-sensitive
Erosionsgefährdung f erosivity
Erosionslandschaft f erosional landscape
Erosionsneigung f erosivity, erodibility, susceptibility to erosion
Erosionsschutzstreifen m buffer strip
erosionsverhütend erosion-preventive
erosiv erosive
Erpel m drake
Erregbarkeit f excitability, irritability
erregen 1. to excite; 2. to cause, to produce *(diseases)*
~/die Bildung von Pflanzengallen *(phyt)* to gall
Erreger m 1. excitant *(physiology)*; causal agent; 2. causative organism, invader; pathogen, germ
Erregung f excitation
Ersatz m/**isomorpher** *(soil)* isomorphous replacement *(of central ions in silicate crystal lattices)*
Ersatzbaumart f substitute tree species
Ersatzdüngemittel n, **Ersatzdünger** m substitute fertilizer
Ersatzfaser f substitute fibre *(wood anatomy)*
Ersatzfrucht f catch crop
Ersatzholz n *s.* Ersatzzapfen
Ersatzholzart f substitute tree species
Ersatzteil n spare part, renewal (repair, component) part
Ersatzwirt m reserve (reservoir) host
Ersatzzapfen m renewal cane (spur) *(of grapevine)*
Erscheinung f 1. phenomenon; 2. *s.* Erscheinungsbild
~/meteorologische meteorological occurrence
Erscheinungsbild n appearance, habit; phenotype; physiognomy; facies *(e.g. of an organ)*
~ der verkaufsfähigen Frucht fruit finish
Erscheinungslehre f phenology
Erscheinungstyp m phenotype
erschließbar accessible *(e.g. nutrients)*
~/nicht inaccessible
Erschließbarkeit f accessibility
erschließen to make accessible *(e.g. a region)*; to tap *(e.g. reserves)*
Erschließung f [land] reclamation
erschöpfen to impoverish, to deplete, to exhaust, to prostrate *(e.g. a nutrient reserve)*
~/[Boden] durch Raubbau to overcrop, to rack

Erschöpfung f impoverishment, depletion, exhaust[ion], prostration
Erschöpfungstest m exhaustion test *(for determining the ability of semen reproduction in breeding animals)*
Erstarrungsgestein n igneous rock
Erstaufnahme f *(forest)* initial survey (inventory)
Erstausformung f initial (primary, rough) conversion *(of timber)*
Erstbelegungsfärse f first-service heifer
Erstbesamung f first insemination
Erstbesamungsalter n age at first insemination, age for first service
Erstdurchforstung f *(forest)* first thinning
Ersteinrichtung f *s.* Erstaufnahme
Erstferkelalter n age at first farrowing
erstgebärend primiparous
ersticken to suffocate, to smother, to stifle, to choke, to asphyxiate
Erstickung f suffocation, asphyxiation
Erstickungskrankheit f suffocation disease, bronzing [disease] *(of rice on swamp soils too rich in nitrates)*
Erstickungssyndrom n *(vet)* choke syndrome
Erstickungszustand m *(vet)* asphyxia[tion]
Erstkalbabsetzmasse f first-calf weaning weight
Erstkalbealter n age at first calving
Erstkalbung f first calving
Erstlaktation f first lactation
Erstlegealter n age at first egg *(poultry breeding)*
Erstlingskuh f first-calf heifer
Erstlingssau f first-litter sow
Erstmilch f colostrum, colostral (first, early) milk, beestings
Erstprobe f primary sample
Ertrag m yield, crop, outturn, output, fruit
 • **~ [er]bringen (geben)** to yield, to crop • **im ~ übertreffen** to outyield
~/aussetzender *(forest)* intermittent yield
~/biologischer biological yield
~/forstlicher forest yield
~/geringer light crop (yield)
~/hoher heavy crop
~/jährlicher annual yield
~ je Hektar yield per hectare, per-hectare yield
~/kumulativer cumulative yield
~/mittlerer average yield
~/nachhaltiger *(forest)* sustained yield
~/periodischer *(forest)* periodic yield (cut)
~/potentieller potential yield
~/rentabler economic yield
~/vom Wiederaustrieb erzielter ratoon [crop], rattoon *(e.g. of sugar-cane)*
~/wirtschaftlicher economic yield
ertragarm low-yielding
ertragreich high-yielding, heavy yielding, productive; rich, fat *(soil)*
Ertragsalternanz f alternate (biennial) bearing, alternation *(orcharding)*

Ertragsaufbau *m* yield structure
Ertragsausfall *m* crop failure
Ertragsaussichten *fpl* yield (crop, harvest) prospects
Ertragsberechnung *f s.* Ertragsbestimmung
Ertragsbestimmung *f* yield determination (calculation), determination (assessment) of yield
Ertragsbildung *f* yield formation
~ **an den Triebspitzen** terminal bearing *(of fruit)*
Ertragsbildungsvermögen *n* yielding ability (capacity), crop potential[ity], cropping potential
Ertragsbiologie *f* yield biology
ertragschwach low-yielding
Ertragsdaten *pl* yield data
Ertragseigenschaft *f* cropping property
Ertragseinbuße *f* yield reduction (penalty)
Ertragseinschätzung *f* yield estimation
Ertragsermittlung *f* assessment of yield; yield measurement
Ertragserwartung *f* yield expectation
Ertragsfähigkeit *f* yielding ability (capacity), cropping (productive) capacity, [crop] productivity
Ertragsfaktor *m* yield factor
Ertragsfeststellung *f s.* Ertragsermittlung
Ertragsfortschritt *m* yield progress
Ertragsfunktion *f* yield function
Ertragsgesetz *n* law of yields
Ertragsgleichung *f* yield equation
Ertragsgrenze *f* yield limit
Ertragshöhe *f* yield level
Ertragsjahr *n* crop (marketing) year, on-year
Ertragskapazität *f* yield capacity
Ertragsklasse *f* yield (productivity) class; *(forest)* growth class, quality (locality) class
Ertragskomponente *f* yield component
Ertragskorrelation *f* yield correlation
Ertragskultur *f* crop, yielder
~/**landwirtschaftliche** agricultural crop
Ertragskunde *f/forstliche* science of forest yield, forest yield science
Ertragskurve *f* yield curve
Ertragsleistung *f* yield (cropping) performance, productivity
ertragslos unproductive *(e.g. soil)*
Ertragsmenge *f* crop load
Ertragsmerkmal *n* yield characteristic (trait)
Ertragsmeßgerät *n* yield meter
Ertragsmessung *f* yield measurement
Ertragsminderung *f* yield reduction (depression, penalty)
Ertragsmodell *n* yield model
Ertragsmodellierung *f* yield modelling
Ertragsniveau *n* yield level
Ertragsparameter *m* yield parameter
Ertragsperiode *f* bearing period *(orcharding)*
Ertragsphysiologie *f* crop physiology
Ertragspotential *n* yield[ing] potential, crop potential[ity], cropping potential

Ertragsprobefläche *f* experimental plot for yield studies; *(forest)* yield-table sample plot
Ertragsprüfung *f* yield test[ing]
~/**mehrortige** multisite yield test[ing]
Ertragsqualität *f* yield (crop) quality
Ertragsreaktion *f* yield response
Ertragsregelung *f (forest)* yield regulation (control), regulating of fellings, cut regulation
Ertragsrübe *f* E-type sugar-beet
Ertragsrückgang *m* yield decline
Ertragsrute *f (Am)* floricane *(of brambles)*
Ertragsschädigung *f* crop damage
Ertragsschätzung *f* yield estimation
Ertragsschätzwert *m* yield estimate
Ertragsschwankung *f* yield variation (fluctuation)
Ertragssicherheit *f* crop safety, safety (certainty) of yield, yield stability
Ertragssorte *f* yielder
Ertragsstabilität *f* yield stability
Ertragsstadium *n* yielding stage; bearing stage, stage of maturity *(of fruit-tree)*
Ertragsstagnation *f* yield stagnation
ertragsstark *s.* ertragreich
Ertragssteigerung *f* yield increase
Ertragsstruktur *f* yield structure
Ertragsstrukturanalyse *f* yield structure analysis
Ertragstabelle *f (forest)* yield table
~ **für mehrere Vornutzungseingriffe** multiple-yield table
~ **für unterschiedliche Bestockungsdichte** variable-density yield table
Ertragstafel *f s.* Ertragstabelle
Ertragstrend *m* yield trend
Ertragstreue *f* yield stability
Ertragsüberlegenheit *f* yielding superiority
Ertragsüberschuß *m* crop surplus
Ertragsübersicht *f* crop survey
Ertragsunterschied *m* yield difference
Ertragsvariabilität *f* yield variability
Ertragsvariation *f* yield variation
Ertragsverbesserung *f* yield improvement
Ertragsvergleich *m* yield comparison
Ertragsverlust *m* yield (crop) loss
Ertragsverlustschätzung *f* crop loss appraisal
Ertragsvermögen *n* yielding ability (capacity), potential, cropping capacity (power, potential), crop-producing power
Ertragsversuch *m* yield trial
Ertragsvorausschätzung *f*, **Ertragsvorhersage** *f* [crop] yield forecasting, yield prediction
Ertragswirkung *f* effect on yield *(e.g. of fertilizers)*
Ertragsziel *n* yield target
Ertragszüchtung *f* breeding for yield
Ertragszunahme *f* yield increase
Ertragszuverlässigkeit *f* crop safety, safety (certainty) of yield, yield stability
Ertragszuwachs *m* yield increase
E-Rübe *f s.* Ertragsrübe
Eruca *f (ent)* caterpillar

Erucasäure

Erucasäure f erucic acid *(fatty acid)*
Eruktation f eructation, belching *(of ruminants)*
eruktieren to eructate, to belch
Eruptivgestein n igneous rock
Erve[nwicke] f bitter (lentil) vetch, Vicia ervilia
erwachsen adult, full-grown
erwärmen to heat, to warm
Erwärmung f heating, warming
~ **nach feuchtkalten Umschlägen** *(vet)* fomentation
Erwärmungsbewässerung f warming irrigation
erwartungstreu accurate; unbiased *(estimator)*
Erwartungstreue f *(biom)* accuracy
Erwartungswert m *(biom)* expected (expectation) value; *(gen)* population mean
erweichen to macerate, to soften
Erweichung f 1. maceration, softening; 2. *(vet)* malacia
~ **der grauen Hirnsubstanz** *(vet)* polioencephalomalacia
erweitern to dilate; to enlarge
erweitert *(bot, zoo)* ampliate
Erweiterung f dila[ta]tion; enlargement
Erwerbsforstwirtschaft f commercial forestry
Erwerbsgarten m market garden
Erwerbsgartenbau m market gardening, commercial gardening (horticulture)
Erwerbsgärtner m market gardener, *(Am)* trucker
Erwerbsgemüsebau m commercial vegetable growing, *(Am)* truck farming
Erwerbsimkerei f commercial bee-keeping
Erwerbsobstanlage f commercial orchard (planting)
Erwerbsobstbau m commercial orcharding (fruit growing)
Erwerbsobstbauer m commercial orchardist
Erwerbswald m commercial forest
Erycen n erythromycin *(antibiotic)*
Erysipel n *(vet)* erysipelas, diamond skin disease *(caused by Erysipelothrix rhusiopathiae)*
erysipelartig erysipelatous
Erysipelas n s. Erysipel
Erythem n *(vet)* erythema
Erythrämie f *(vet)* polycythaemia
~/**erbliche** polycythaemia vera
Erythroagglutination f haemagglutination
Erythroblast m erythroblast
erythroblastisch erythroblastic
Erythroblastose f *(vet)* erythroblastosis
~/**aviäre** avian erythroblastosis *(erythroblastic form of transmissible fowl leucosis)*
Erythrodermatitis f *(vet)* erythrodermatitis
Erythroleukose f des Geflügels s. Erythroblastose/aviäre
Erythromycin n erythromycin *(antibiotic)*
Erythropoese f erythropoiesis, production of red blood cells
Erythropoetin n erythropoietin, erythropoietic stimulating factor *(polypeptid)*

erythropoetisch erythropoietic
Erythrose f erythrose *(monosaccharide)*
Erythrozyt m erythrocyte, red [blood] cell, RBC, red corpuscle
Erythrozytenauflösung f haemolysis
erythrozytenbildend erythropoietic
Erythrozytenbildung f erythropoiesis
Erythrozytencatalase f erythrocyte catalase *(enzyme)*
Erythrozytenenzym n erythrocyte enzyme
Erythrozytenmangel m im Blut hypoglobulia
Erythrozytenvermehrung f im Blut hyperglobulia
Erythrozytenzählung f erythrocyte count
Erythrozytose f *(vet)* polycythaemia
Erzengelwurz f *(bot)* [garden] angelica, archangel, Angelica archangelica [var. archangelica]
Erzeugerabfüllung f estate bottling *(of wine)*
Erzeugerwert m farm value *(of agricultural produce)*
Erzeugnis n product
~/**jagd[wirtschaft]liches** product of hunting and shooting
~/**landwirtschaftliches** agricultural (farm) product, agricultural commodity
~/**pflanzliches** crop product
~/**tierisches** animal product
Erzeugnisse npl zweiter Qualität seconds
Erzeugung f production; generation
~/**landwirtschaftliche** agricultural production, *(Am)* agriproduction
~ **von künstlichem Regen** rain-making
Erzeugungsfähigkeit f des Bodens land productivity
erziehen to train *(e.g. woody plants)*
~/**im Spalier** to espalier, to trellis
Erziehung f training
~/**niedrige** low-training *(e.g. of grape-vines)*
Erziehungshieb m *(forest)* tending felling, improvement thinning
Erziehungsschnitt m form (shape) pruning, training
Erziehungssystem n training system *(orcharding)*
Erzwespe f chalcid wasp *(family Chalcididae)*
ESAMV s. Scharfes Adernmosaikvirus der Erbse
Esche f 1. ash *(genus Fraxinus)*; 2. common (European) ash, Fraxinus excelsior
Eschenahorn m ash-leaved maple, box elder, Acer negundo
Eschenblättrige Jasmintrompete f yellow-elder, yellow bells (bignonia), Tecoma stans
Escheneule f *(ent)* ash underwing, Catocala fraxini
Eschenfrucht f ash-key
Eschenholz n ash
Eschensamen m ash-key
Eschenzwieselmotte f ash bud moth, Prays curtisellus
Escherichia-coli-Infektion f *(vet)* coliform septicaemia

~ des Geflügels coligranulomatosis, Hjärre's disease
Esel *m* 1. ass *(genus Equus)*; 2. donkey, [domestic] ass, cuddy, Equus asinus
Eselhengst *m* jack[ass]
Eselin *f* she-ass, jennet
Eselsdistel *f* cotton thistle *(genus Onopordum)*
Eselsfeige *f* sycamore (sycomore, mulberry) fig, Ficus sycomorus
Eselsgurke *f* squirting cucumber, Ecballium elaterium
Eselskerbel *m* royal chervil, Chaerophyllum temulum
Eselsmilch *f* donkey milk
Eselsohren *npl (bot)* lamb's ear, Stachys byzantina (lanata)
Eselsrücken *m* carp back *(of horses)*
Eselstute *f* she-ass, jennet
Eselswolfsmilch *f (bot)* leafy spurge, Euphorbia esula
Eserin *n* physostigmine *(alkaloid)*
ESF *s.* Erythropoetin
ESiV *s.* Erbsenstrichelvirus
Eskariol *m (bot)* escarole, endive, Cichorium endivia var. latifolium
Esker *m (soil)* esker, eskar
Eskimohund *m* Husky, Eskimo [dog] *(breed)*
Esparsette *f* [common, double-cut] sainfoin, saintfoin, esparcet, cockshead, French grass, Onobrychis viciifolia
Esparsetteheu *n* sainfoin hay
Esparsettenblütengallmücke *f* sainfoin flower midge, Contarinia onobrychidis
Esparto[gras] *n* alfa [grass], Spanish grass, Stipa tenacissima
Espe *f* asp[en], trembling poplar, Populus tremula
Espenblattkäfer *m* unspotted aspen leaf-beetle, Melasoma tremulae
Espenlaub *n* aspen-leaves
ESR *s.* Elektronenspinresonanz
eßbar edible, esculent
~/nicht inedible
Eßbare Arracacha *f* Peruvian carrot (parsnip), arracacha, Arracacia xanthorrhiza (esculenta)
~ **Eberesche** *f* rowan[-tree], Sorbus aucuparia var. edulis
~ **Klettenwurzel** *f* edible burdock, Arctium lappa var. edule
~ **Nandine** *f* heavenly bamboo, [Chinese] sacred bamboo, nandina, Nandina domestica
~ **Pestwurz** *f* butterbur, Petasites japonicus
Eßbares Blumenrohr *n* [edible] canna, Australian (Queensland) arrowroot, Canna edulis
essentiell essential *(e.g. an amino-acid)*
Essentiellität *f* essentiality
Essig *m* vinegar
Essigbakterium *n s.* Essigsäurebakterium
Essigbaum *m* stag-horn sumac[h], American sumac[h], Rhus typhina

Essigfliege *f* fruit (vinegar, ferment) fly, drosophila *(genus Drosophila)*
Essigfrüchte *fpl* pickled fruits
Essiggemüse *n* [mixed] pickles
Essiggurke *f* pickling cucumber, pickle; pickled cucumber, gherkin
Essiggurkenerntemaschine *f* pickle harvester
Essigherstellung *f* acetification
Essigmesser *m* acetimeter
Essigmessung *f* acetimetry
Essigrose *f* French rose, Rosa gallica
essigsauer acetic, acetous
Essigsäure *f* acetic (ethanoic) acid
~/aktivierte acetyl coenzyme A
Essigsäureamid *n* acetamide
Essigsäurebakterium *n* acetic-acid bacterium, vinegar bacterium
Essigsäurebildung *f* acetification
Essigsäuregärung *f* acetic[-acid] fermentation, acetous (vinegar) fermentation
Essigsäuremesser *m* acetimeter
Essigsäuremessung *f* acetimetry
Essigzwiebel *f* pickled onion
Eßkastanie *f* edible (sweet) chestnut, marron, [Spanish, Italian, European] chestnut, Castanea sativa (vesca)
Eßmandel *f* sweet almond *(from Prunus dulcis var. dulcis)*
Eßqualität *f s.* Verzehrqualität
Eßreife *f* eating maturity
Eßtraube *f* table grape
Ester *m* ester
Esterase *f* esterase *(enzyme)*
Esterzahl *f* ester value
Estnische Baconrasse *f* Estonian bacon *(pig breed)*
Estragon *m* tarragon, estragon, Artemisia dracunculus
Estrogen *n s.* Östrogen
etablieren to establish *(e.g. a plant stand)*
Etablierung *f* eines Pflanzenbestandes crop establishment
Etacelasil *n* etacelasil *(growth regulator)*
Etage *f* tier *(of a cage battery)*
Etagenanbau-Champignonhaus *n* shelf mushroom house
Etagenbatterie *f* multideck battery, battery in tiers *(animal housing)*
Etagenbaum *m* India-almond, Terminalia catappa
Etagenbodenmeißel *m* terrace subsoiler
Etagenlachte *f* two-storey face *(resin-tapping)*
Etagenlagerung *f* floor storage *(e.g. of corn)*
Etagenprimel *f* candelabra primula *(grouping of cultivars)*
Etagenstellage *f* stage shelving *(glasshouse installation)*
Etagenwagen *m* trolley *(glasshouse installation)*
Etat *m s.* Hiebssatz
ETEM ETEM *(fungicide)*

Ethalfluralin

Ethalfluralin n ethalfluralin *(herbicide)*
Ethan n ethane
Ethanal n ethanal, acetaldehyde
Ethan-1,2-diol n ethane-1,2-diol, ethylene glycol
Ethandisäure f ethanedioic (oxalic) acid
Ethanol n ethanol, [ethyl] alcohol
Ethanolamin n ethanolamine
Ethanolaminkinase f ethanolamine kinase *(enzyme)*
Ethansäure f ethanoic (acetic) acid
Ethazol n ethazol *(fungicide)*
Ethen n eth[yl]ene *(growth regulator)*
Ethephon n ethephon, 2-chloroethanephosphonic acid, CEPA *(growth regulator)*
Ether m ether
Etherextrakt m ether extract
Ethidinuron n ethidinuron *(herbicide)*
Ethin n ethine, ethyne, acetylene
Ethinylöstradiol n ethinyl oestradiol *(oestrogen)*
Ethiofencarb n ethiofencarb *(insecticide)*
Ethiolat n ethiolate *(herbicide)*
Ethion n ethion *(insecticide, acaricide)*
Ethionin n ethionine *(antimetabolite)*
Ethirimol n ethirimol *(fungicide)*
Ethnobotanik f ethnobotany
Ethofumesat n ethofumesate *(herbicide)*
Ethogramm n ethogram *(ethology)*
Ethologe m ethologist
Ethologie f ethology
ethologisch ethological
Ethophyon n epideictic pheromone
Ethoprophos n ethoprophos, ethoprop *(nematicide, insecticide)*
Ethoxychin n, **Ethoxyquin** n ethoxyquin, EQ, santoquin *(antioxidant)*
Ethrel n ethrel *(growth regulator)*
Ethylalkohol m [ethyl] alcohol, ethanol
Ethylcellulose f ethylcellulose
Ethylchlorid n ethyl chloride
Ethyl-DDD n ethyl-DDD *(insecticide)*
Ethylen n ethylene *(growth regulator)*
Ethylenchlorhydrin n ethylene chlorohydrin
Ethylendiamintetraessigsäure f ethylenediaminetetraacetic acid, EDTA *(chelating agent)*
Ethylendibromid n ethylene dibromide, EDB *(insecticide, nematicide)*
Ethylendinitrilotetraessigsäure f s. Ethylendiamintetraessigsäure
Ethylenglycol n [ethylene] glycol
Ethylenkohlenwasserstoff m alkene
Ethylenoxid n ethylene oxide *(fumigant)*
Ethylhexandiol n ethyl hexanediol *(insect repellent)*
Ethylquecksilberphosphat n ethyl mercury phosphate, EMP *(fungicide)*
Ethylurethan n [ethyl]urethane *(anaesthetic)*
Etikett n label
etikettieren to label
Etikettiermaschine f labelling machine

Etiolement n etiolation *(yellowing or whitening of green plants due to darkness)*
etiolieren to etiolate
Etiolierung f s. Etiolement
Etioplast m *(bot)* etioplast
Etnipromid n etnipromid *(herbicide)*
ETR s. Embryotransfer
Etridiazol n etridiazol, echlomezol *(nitrification inhibitor, fungicide)*
Etrimfos n, **Etrimphos** n etrimfos, etrimphos *(insecticide)*
EU s. Extrauteringravidität
Eucalyptus m s. Eukalyptus
eucephal *(ent)* eucephalous
Euchromatin n euchromatin *(nucleoprotein)*
Euchromosom n *(gen)* autosome, euchromosome
Eugen[et]ik f eugenics
eugen[et]isch eugenic
Eugenol n eugenol *(constituent of essential oils)*
Euglobulin n euglobulin
Eukalyptol n cineole *(terpene)*
Eukalyptus[baum] m eucalypt[us], box [tree], gum-tree *(genus Eucalyptus)*
Eukalyptusöl n eucalyptus oil
Eukaryo[n]t m eukaryote
eukaryo[n]tisch eukaryotic
Euklimax f euclimax
Eulaliagras n *(bot)* eulalia, Miscanthus sinensis, Eulalis japonica
Eule f s. Eulenschmetterling
Eulenkopf m *(zoo)* muffcock, Burhinus oedicnemus
Eulenraupe f *(ent)* cutworm
Eulenschmetterling m noctuid [moth], owlet moth *(family Noctuidae)*
Eumitose f eumitosis
Eupatorin n eupatorine *(alkaloid)*
Eupepsie f eupepsia
Euphorbienmosaikvirus n poinsettia mosaic virus
euploid *(gen)* euploid
Euploidie f euploidy
Europäische Edeltanne f silver fir, Abies alba
~ **Faulbrut** f *(api, vet)* European foul brood, EFB *(caused by Streptococcus pluton)*
~ **Geflügelpest** f fowl pest (plague)
~ **Haselwurz** f *(bot)* asarabacca, asarum, Asarum europaeum
~ **Himbeere** f [red] raspberry, Rubus idaeus
~ **Lärche** f common (European) larch, Larix decidua
~ **Napfschildlaus** f European fruit lecanium (scale), European peach scale, brown elm scale, Parthenolecanium (Eulecanium, Lecanium) corni
~ **Rauhblättrigkeit** f der Süßkirsche cherry rasp leaf *(virosis)*
~ **Rinderbabesiose** f babesiasis, babesiosis, redwater [disease] *(of cattle)*
~ **Rostfleckung** f der Süßkirsche cherry European rusty mottle *(virosis)*

~ **Seide** f great (large) dodder, Cuscuta europaea
~ **Trollblume** f globe-flower, Trollius europaeus
~ **Zwergpalme** f European (dwarf) fan palm, Chamaerops humilis
Europäischer Biber m beaver, Castor fiber
~ **Feuerdorn** m firethorn, Pyracantha coccinea
~ **Flußaal** m eel, Anguilla anguilla
~ **Iltis** m polecat, fitch[et], fitchew, Mustela putorius
~ **Kiefern[knospen]triebwickler** m [European] pine-shoot moth, Rhyacionia (Evetria) buoliana
~ **Lärchenkrebs** m European larch canker *(caused by Lachnellula willkommii)*
~ **Maulwurf** m mole, Talpa europaea
~ **Mufflon** m mou[f]flon, Ovis aries ssp. musimon
~ **Nerz** m European mink, Mustela (Lutreola) lutreola
~ **Ölbaumborkenkäfer** m olive bark-beetle, Phloeotribus scarabaeoides
~ **Stachelbeermehltau** m European gooseberry mildew *(caused by Microsphaera grossulariae)*
~ **Stechginster** m [common] gorse, Ulex europaeus
~ **Wisent** m wisent, [European] bison, aurochs, Bison bonasus
Europäisches Kohlhernie-Testsortiment n European club-root differential set
~ **Maismosaikvirus** n European maize mosaic virus, maize dwarf mosaic virus, MDMV
~ **Streifiges Mosaik** n **des Weizens** striate mosaic [of wheat]
~ **Streifiges Mosaikvirus** n **des Weizens** European wheat striate mosaic virus
~ **Wildschwein** n [European] wild boar (hog), Sus scrofa
Europiumchelat n europium chelate *(dye)*
eurytherm eurythermal, eurythermic
Eurytrematose f *(vet)* eurytrematosis
euryxen euryxenous *(parasite)*
Eustachysche Röhre f auditory (Eustachian) tube *(animal anatomy)*
Eustoma f prairie gentian, Texas blue bell, Eustoma russelianum
Euter n udder, dug, mammary (milk) gland, mamma
Euterabschnitt m section of the udder
Euterbeurteilung f, **Euterbonitur** f udder evaluation
Euterdusche f udder douche
Euterentzündung f *(vet)* udder inflammation (clap), mastitis, garget
Eutererkältung f udder chill
Euterform f udder shape
Euterformindex m udder index
Eutergesundheit f udder (mammary) health, udder soundness
Euterhygiene f udder sanitation
Euterinfektion f udder infection
Euterkapazität f udder capacity

Euterkongestion f *(vet)* udder congestion
Euterkrankheit f udder disease
Eutermassage f udder stimulation (massage, preparation)
Eutermessung f udder measurement
Euterödem n *(vet)* udder oedema
Euterpocken pl **des Rindes** false (natural) cowpox, pseudocowpox
Euterreinigung f udder cleaning
Euterrückbildung f udder involution
Euterseuche f/**Holsteinische** *(vet)* summer mastitis *(caused by Corynebacterium pyogenes)*
Eutertuberkulose f udder tuberculosis
Eutertuch n udder-cloth
Euterviertel n udder quarter, quarter [of the udder]
Eutervolumen n udder volume
Euthanasie f euthanasia
euthanasieren to euthanize
Eutokie f eutocia *(obstetrics)*
eutroph eutrophic
Eutrophie f eutrophy
Eutrophierung f eutrophication
Evaluierung f, **Evalvation** f evaluation
Evaporation f evaporation
~/**potentielle** s. Evaporationsvermögen
Evaporationsrate f evaporation rate
Evaporationsverlust m evaporation loss
Evaporationsvermögen n evaporating capacity, potential evaporation, evaporitivity
evaporativ evaporative
evaporieren to evaporate
Evaporimeter n evaporimeter, evaporometer
Evaporograph m evaporograph
Evapotranspiration f evapotranspiration, water loss
~/**potentielle** potential evapotranspiration, P.E.
Evapotranspirationsrate f evapotranspiration rate
Eventration f *(vet)* evisceration
Evertebrat m invertebrate
Evolution f evolution
~/**infraspezifische** microevolution
~/**interspezifische** macroevolution
~/**koordinierte** coevolution
~/**Nichtdarwinsche** non-Darwinian evolution
~/**transspezifische (zwischenartliche)** macroevolution
evolutionär evolutional, evolutionary
Evolutionsökologie f evolutionary ecology
Evolutionsrichtungsregel f Szidat's rule *(parasitology)*
Evolutionstheorie f theory of descent, theory of the origin of species
Ewiger Kohl m thousand-head[ed] kale, Brassica oleracea convar. oleracea var. ramosa
~ **Spinat** m patience [dock], spinach (vegetable) dock, Rumex patientia
Exaktfeldhäcksler m s. Exakthäcksler
Exakthäcksel m precision (exact) chop
Exakthäckselsilage f precision-chopped silage

Exakthäcksler

Exakthäcksler *m* precision chopper (cut forager), precision-chop [forage] harvester, metered-chop forage harvester
Exaktsaat *f* precision seeding (drilling)
Exanthem *n (vet)* exanthema
~/flüchtiges rash
Exazerbation *f* exacerbation *(recrudescence of a disease)*
EXD EXD *(herbicide)*
Exemplar *n* specimen
Exenteration *f* evisceration
Exfoliation *f (soil, phyt, vet)* exfoliation, onion-skin weathering
exfoliieren to exfoliate
Exhaustion *f* exhaust[ion]
Exhaustor *m* exhaust[er]
Exkavator *m* excavator
Exkrement *n* excrement
Exkremente *npl* f[a]eces, faecal matter, dung, droppings *(s. a. under* Kot*)*
~/[zur Düngung verwendete] menschliche night-soil
Exkreszenz *f (phyt, vet)* excrescence
Exkret *n* excretion
Exkretion *f* excretion
Exkretionsporus *m* excretory pore *(of nematodes)*
Exkretionsverhalten *n* excretory behaviour
exkretorisch excretory, excretive
Exmoor Horn *n* Exmoor Horn, Porlock *(sheep breed)*
Exmoorpony *n* Exmoor pony *(breed)*
Exocortis[krankheit] *f* citrus exocortis [disease]
Exocortisvirus *n* **von Citrus** citrus exocortis virus
Exoderm *n (bot, zoo)* exoderm, ectoderm, ectoblast, epiblast
Exodermis *f (bot)* exoderm[is]
Exoenzym *n* ectoenzyme, exoenzyme
exogen exogenous
Exokarp *n (bot)* exocarp
exokrin exocrine, eccrine
Exopeptidase *f* exopeptidase, peptidase *(enzyme)*
Exopolyphosphatase *f* exopolyphosphatase, metaphosphatase *(enzyme)*
Exoskelett *n* ectoskeleton, exoskeleton
Exostose *f* exostosis *(a spur or small bony outgrowth from a bone)*
Exoten[anbau]versuch *m (forest)* trial of exotics
exotherm exothermal
Exotoxin *n* exotoxin
Expeditionskorken *m* final cork *(bottling of wine)*
Expektorans *n (vet)* expectorant
Expeller[kuchen] *m* expeller [cake], seed-cake
Experiment *n* experiment, test
Experimentator *m* experimentalist, experimenter
Explantat *n* explant
Explantation *f* explantation
Exploitationshieb *m (forest)* exploitation felling (cutting)
Exploration *f* exploration, reconnaissance

Exponentialphase *f* log[arithmic] phase
Exposition *f* 1. exposure, aspect; 2. exposure *(as to radiation)*
Expression *f* expression
Expressivität *f* expressivity
Expulsion *f* expulsion
Exsikkation *f* exsiccation
Exsikkose *f* exsiccation
Exspiration *f* expiration
Exspirationsluft *f* expired (exhaled) air
exspirieren to expire
Exstirpation *f (vet)* extirpation
Exsudat *n* exudate
Exsudation *f* exudation
exsudieren to exude
Extensivhaltung *f* extensive husbandry (management), free-range management
Extensivweide *f* extensive pasture
Extensograph *m* extensograph
Extensometer *n* extensometer
Extensor *m* extensor [muscle]
Exterieur *n* habit, [body] conformation *(livestock judging)*
Extero[re]zeptor *m* exteroceptor
Extraduralanästhesie *f (vet)* epidural anaesthesia
Extraduralraum *m* epidural space *(animal anatomy)*
extraembryonal extraembryonic
extrahierbar extractable
Extrahierbarkeit *f* extractability
extrahieren to extract
extraintestinal abenteric
Extrakt *m* extract[ive]; diffusion juice *(sugar manufacture)*
Extraktabnahme *f* attenuation *(brewing)*
Extraktabzug *m* draw-off *(sugar manufacture)*
Extraktans *n* extractant
Extraktausbeute *f* extract yield
Extraktdifferenz *f* extract difference *(malting)*
Extraktgehalt *m* potential extract *(of malt)*
Extraktion *f* extraction
Extraktionsanlage *f* extraction plant
Extraktionsholz *n* extract wood
Extraktionskolophonium *n (Am)* wood rosin
Extraktionsmittel *n* extractant
Extraktionsschrot *n* seed-cake, extracted meal
Extraktionsstockholz *n* resinous stumpwood
Extraktivstoff *m s.* Extraktstoff
Extraktor *m (vet)* extractor
Extraktreinigung *f* extract purification; juice purification, clarification *(sugar manufacture)*
Extraktschwand *m* extract loss *(brewing)*
Extraktstoff *m* extractive [material]
~/N-freier (stickstofffreier) nitrogen-free extract[ive], NFE
Extraktumwandlung *f* attenuation *(brewing)*
extraosmotisch extraosmotic
extrauterin extrauterine
Extrauteringravidität *f* extrauterine (ectopic) pregnancy

extrazellulär extracellular
Extremität f extremity, limb
Extremitäten fpl extremities; points (of horse or dog)
Extremwert m (biom) extreme value
Extrinsic factor m extrinsic (animal protein) factor, APF, cobalamin, vitamin B_{12}
extrors (bot) extrorse, extrorsal
Extruder m extruder
Extrusion f extrusion
Extrusionskocher m extruder cooker
Exuvie f (zoo) exuvia, exuvium
Exzeß m (biom) excess
exzidieren to excise
Exzision f excision
Exzitans n (vet) analeptic

F

F s. 1. Inzuchtkoeffizient; 2. Feuchteindex; 3. Fleckvieh 1.; 4. Femelschlag
Fa s. 1. Falbe; 2. Faschinenholz
FA s. Futteraufwand
FÄ s. Feuchteäquivalent
Fabrikabgas n factory fume
Fabrikhufeisen n ready made [horse]shoe, machine-made horse[shoe]
Fabrikrauch m factory fume
Facettenauge n (ent) compound eye
fächeln to fan (honey-bees)
Fächer m fan (trained form of fruit trees)
Fächerahorn m Japanese maple, Acer palmatum
fächerartig flabellate
Fächer[blatt]baum m ginkgo, gingko, maidenhair tree, Ginkgo biloba
Fächerblattbildung f (phyt) fan-leaf formation
fächerblättrig fan-leaved
Fächerblättrigkeit f [der Weinrebe] grape-vine fan leaf, fan leaf disease of grape-vine
Fächerblättrigkeitsvirus n [der Weinrebe] grape-vine fan leaf virus
fächerförmig flabelliform
Fächerpalme f fan palm (comprehensive term)
Fächerzwergmispel f (bot) rock (herring-bone) cotoneaster, Cotoneaster horizontalis
Fachkapselfrauenschuh m (bot) Lady's slipper (genus Phragmipedium)
fachspaltig (bot) loculicidal
Fachwerksmethode f (forest) allotment method, method of periods
~/kombinierte periodic method by area and volume
Facies f facies, face (of mammalians)
Fackellilie f (bot) 1. red-hot poker, kniphofia, tritoma (genus Kniphofia); 2. torch lily, Kniphofia uvaria
FAD s. Flavinadenindinucleotid
Faden m 1. thread; filament; string (of bean pod); 2. ridge (of stag's track)

Fadenblättrigkeit f (phyt) shoe-string [disease], shoe-stringing, shoe-lacing
~ der Tomate s. Farnblättrigkeit der Tomate
Fadenfeder f pin (stub) feather, filoplume
Fadenfingerhirse f smooth crab-grass, Digitaria ischaemum (linearis)
fadenförmig (bot, zoo) thread-shaped, filiform
Fadenhalter m thread holder (of pick-up baler)
Fadenhirse f s. Fadenfingerhirse
Fadenkasten m thread box (of pick-up baler)
Fadenkeimigkeit f (phyt) hair sprout[ing]
Fadenklee m small hop clover, lesser (slender) yellow trefoil, lesser clover, Trifolium dubium
Fadenkreuz n cross spider (wire) (e.g. of a sporting gun)
fadenlos stringless (bean pod)
Fadenpalmlilie f (bot) Adam's needle, Yucca filamentosa
Fadenpilz m filamentous fungus
Fadenwurm m nematode [worm], roundworm (class Nematoda)
~/pflanzenparasitischer plant[-parasitic] nematode
Fadenwurminfestation f nematodiasis
fadenziehend rop[e]y
fädig filamentary, filamented, stringy
Fädlein n ridge (of red deer's track)
Fagopyrismus m (vet) fagopyrism
Fähe f she-fox, vixen, bitch fox
Fahlerde f (soil) fahlerde
fahlgelb (bot) lurid
Fahlwild n rock-goat, [Alpine] ibex, Capra ibex (hircus)
Fahne f 1. (bot) flag, vexillum; tassel (of maize plant); standard (of papilionaceous flower); 2. feather[ing] (fringe of hair on the legs or tail of a dog); 3. vane (of bird's feather)
fahnenartig vexillary
Fahnenblatt n (bot) flag [leaf], top (uppermost) leaf
Fahnenblattscheide f boot
Fahnenblattstadium n flag leaf stage
Fahnenerscheinen n s. Fahnenschieben
fahnenförmig flag-shaped
Fahnenhafer m side oat[s], Avena orientalis
Fahnenrispe f one-sided panicle (of oats)
Fahnenschieben n tasseling, tassel emergence (of maize)
Fahrantrieb m travelling drive
~/hydrostatischer hydrostatic travelling drive
Fahren n s. Fahrsport
Fahrerhaus n, **Fahrerkabine** f [driver's] cab
Fahrerplatz m, **Fahrersitz** f driver's seat
Fahrerstand m operator's platform
Fahrgasse f tramline
Fahrgeschwindigkeit f travel speed
Fahrgeschwindigkeitsmesser m speedometer, tachometer
Fahrgestell n carriage, bogie
Fahrhebel m speed governor

Fahrkupplung

Fahrkupplung *f* master clutch
Fahrpferd *n* driving horse
fahrrücken *(forest)* to forward
Fahrschiene *f* rail
Fahrsilo *m* horizontal (clamp) silo, draw-over clamp
Fahrsport *m* coaching sport *(equestrian sport)*
Fahrspur *f* tramline; wheel track
Fahrspurmarkierung *f* tramline marking
Fahrt *f* drive *(floating)*
Fährte *f* track, trail, spoor, trace, foil[ing]; slot *(esp. of a deer)*; scent • **auf der ~ sein** to be on the trail • **die ~ anfallen (aufnehmen)** to track (take up) the scent • **die ~ verlieren** to lose the trail (scent) • **eine ~ verfolgen** *s.* fährten
~/kranke red track
fährten to track, to trail, to spoor, to scent
Fährtenfinder *m* tracker, spoorer
Fahrtrense *f* driving bit
Fahrvariator *m* speed variator
Fahrwerk *n* undercarriage
Fahrzeit *f* travel time
Fahrzeug *n* vehicle
~/geländegängiges cross-country vehicle
Fahrzeugwaage *f* vehicle weighing platform
fäkal faecal
Fäkaldünger *m* poudrette
Fäkalien *pl* f[a]eces, faecal matter
Fäkalstreptokokkus *m* enterococcus
Faktor *m* factor
~/abiotischer abiotic factor
~/biotischer biotic factor
~/erythropoesestimulierender erythropoietic stimulating factor, erythropoietin *(polypeptid)*
~/fertilitätsrestaurierender fertility restoring factor *(plant breeding)*
~/lipotroper lipotropic factor
~/mutationsauslösender mutagen
~/physiographischer abiotic factor
Faktorenanalyse *f* factor analysis
Faktoren[aus]tausch *m (gen)* crossing-over
Faktoren[aus]tauschprodukt *n* crossover
Fäkulom *n (vet)* coproma
Fakultät *f*/**veterinärmedizinische** veterinary college
falb dun
Falbe *m* dun *(horse)*
Falbschecke *f(m)* skewbald *(horse)*
Falerner *m* Falernian *(kind of wine)*
Falke *m* falcon *(genus Falco)*
Falkenbeize *f* falconry
Falkenier *m s.* Falkner
Falkenkappe *f* hawking hood
Falkner *m* falconer, hawker
Falknerei *f* falconry • **~ betreiben** to hawk
Falknerhandschuh *m* gauntlet
Falknertasche *f* hawking bag
Fäll... *s. a.* Hiebs..
Falläpfel *mpl* drop apples, cullage

Fallaub *n* fallen leaves
Fäll-Aufarbeitungskombine *f* feller-processor
Fäll-Aufarbeitungsmaschine *f* feller-delimber-slasher-forwarder
Fällaxt *f* felling axe, axe for felling
fällbar fellable
Fällbruch *m* felling break (fracture) *(wood defect)*
Fäll-Bündel-Maschine *f* feller-buncher, felling-bunching machine
Falle *f* trap, gin
~/chemotropische chemotropic trap *(e.g. for insect pest control)*
fällen to fell, to cut [down], to hew, *(Am)* to log
Fällen *n* felling, cutting, logging, throwing
~ in der vorgeschriebenen Richtung directional felling
Fallenfang *m* 1. [live-]trapping; 2. trap catch
Fallensteig *m s.* Fallenstrecke
Fallensteller *m* trapper
Fallenstrecke *f (hunt)* trap-line
Fäll-Entastungs-Bündel-Maschine *f* feller-delimber-buncher
Fäll-Entastung-Maschine *f* feller-delimber, felling-limbing machine, tree-harvesting delimbing unit
Fäller *m s.* Holzfäller
Fallfilmverdampfer *m* falling-film evaporator
Fallgatter *n* guillotine gate
Fällgerät *n* felling (woodcutting) tool
Fallgrube *f* pitfall
Fällhieb *m s.* Fallkerb
Fallholz *n* fallen logs
Fällkeil *m* felling wedge
~/hydraulischer hydraulic felling wedge
~ mit Holzeinsatz socket wedge
Fallkerb *m*, **Fällkerb** *m* [felling, stem] notch, kerf, mouth, bate, undercut, belly cut, throat, round-up, *(Am)* box • **den ~ anlegen** to notch, to undercut, to box
Fallkerbdach *n* scarf
Fallkerbsohle *f* bed [of the undercut]
Fällkopf *m* felling head
Fallkorb *m* gullet
Fallkrankheit *f (vet)* epilepsy
Fällmaschine *f* felling machine, feller, cutter, *(Am)* logger, faller
~ zum Fällen in vorgegebene Richtung feller director
Fallmeister *m* flayer, skinner
Fällmethode *f* felling (logging) method
Fallnest *n* trap-nest [unit]
Fallobst *n* dropped crop, drop-fruit, windfall, cullage
Fallobstsammelmaschine *f* pick-up machine
Fallobstsammler *m* fallen fruit collector
Fällort *m* felling site (place, point)
Fallout *m* [radioactive] fall-out
Fäll-Paketier-Kombine *f* feller-buncher, felling-bunching machine
Fällperiode *f s.* Fällzeit

Fällrichtung f, **Fallrichtung** f felling direction, lie, front [side] • **einem Baum die ~ geben** to gun
Fällrichtungsanzeiger m gunning stick, [shot]gun, timber compass
Fällriß m felling shake, felling break *(wood defect)*
Fallrohr n drop tube *(of a potato harvester)*
Fäll-Rückemannschaft f cut-and-skid crew
Fäll-Rücke-Maschine f feller-forwarder; feller-skidder, felling-skidding machine
Fäll- Rücke- und Verladekosten pl stump-to-truck costs
Fällsäge f felling saw
Fallschachttrockner m fallshaft dryer
Fällschnitt m felling (back) cut
Fällseite f s. Fällrichtung
Fallstromeindampfanlage f falling-film evaporator
Fallstromverdampfapparat m falling-film evaporator
Fallsucht f *(vet)* epilepsy
Fälltisch m jigger[-board], staging
Falltrockner m fallshaft dryer
Fällung f felling, cutting, logging, throwing
Fällungs... s. a. Hiebs...
Fällungskompaß m s. Fällrichtungsanzeiger
Fällungsschaden m logging damage
Fällungstechnik f felling technique
Fällungsverlust m loss in felling, logging waste
Fällungsvorschrift f felling instruction (rule)
Fällungswerkzeug n felling (woodcutting) tool
Fallwind m gradient wind
Fallzahl f falling number
~ **nach Hagberg** Hagberg falling number
Fällzeit f felling (cutting) period, felling time (season)
Falsche Akazie f false acacia, common robinia, Robinia pseudoacacia
~ **Hirse** f rice (smilo) grass, Oryzopsis miliacea
~ **Kamille** f horse daisy, scentless mayweed, Matricaria perforata (maritima ssp. inodora), Tripleurospermum maritimum
~ **Melde** f white goose-foot, fat-hen, *(Am)* lamb's-quarters, Chenopodium album
fälschen to adulterate
Falscher Eierschwamm m false chanterelle, Cantharellus aurantiacus
~ **Feuerschwamm** m false tinder fungus, male agaric, Phellinus (Fomes, Polyporus) igniarius
~ **Hopfenmehltau** m hop downy mildew *(caused by Pseudoperonospora humuli)*
~ **Jasmin** m philadelphus, mock orange *(genus Philadelphus)*
~ **Mehltau** m *(phyt)* downy (false) mildew
~ **Mehltau der Kohlgewächse** brassica downy mildew, downy mildew of cabbage *(caused by Peronospora parasitica = P. brassicae)*
~ **Mehltau der Weinrebe** downy mildew of grapes (vine), grape [downy] mildew *(caused by Plasmopara viticola)*
~ **Mehltau** m **der Zuckerrübe** downy mildew of sugar-beet *(caused by Peronospora schachtii)*
~ **Mehltau** m **der Zwiebel** onion downy mildew *(caused by Peronospora destructor = P. schleidenii)*
~ **Mehltau** m **des Kopfsalats** downy mildew of lettuce, lettuce [downy] mildew *(caused by Bremia lactucae)*
~ **Mehltaupilz** m downy (false) mildew *(family Peronosporaceae)*
~ **Pfifferling** m s. Falscher Eierschwamm
Falsches Blattrollvirus n **der Erbse** pea false leaf roll virus
Falschkern m false heart[wood], abnormal (pathological) heartwood *(wood defect)*
faltenreich *(bot, zoo)* rugose
Faltenwespe f wasp *(family Vespidae)*
Faltgrubber m folding cultivator, cultivator with folding sections
Falz m **des Hufeisens** fullering, swedging
Falzhufeisen n full-swedged shoe
Familie f 1. family *(taxonomy)*; 2. lineage *(animal breeding)*
Familienanalyse f pedigree analysis *(animal breeding)*
Familienauslese f family selection
Familienbetrieb m family[-type] farm, family holding
Familienkäfig m group cage
Familienleistung f family performance
Familienselektion f family selection
Familienzucht f family breeding
Famphur n famphur *(insecticide)*
Fang m 1. catch, take; haul, draught *(esp. of fishes)*; 2. catching, capture; trapping; 3. claw *(of a predatory bird)*; 4. s. Fangzahn
Fanganalyse f catch analysis
Fangbaum m 1. trap (decoy) tree; 2. [trap] boom *(rafting)*
Fangbucht f catching pen *(sheep husbandry)*
Fangdamm m checking dam
Fangdrän m catch (intercepting, curtain) drain
Fangdränung f intercepting (cut-off) drainage system, curtain drainage
Fangeisen n *(hunt)* spring-trap, steel-trap
fangen to catch, to capture; to trap
~/**Feuer** to ignite
~/**mit dem Netz** to net
~/**mit dem Stellnetz** to gill
Fangergebnis n, **Fangertrag** m s. Fang 1.
Fanggerät n catch device
Fanggitter n catching rack
Fanggraben m interception ditch *(drainage)*; trap trench *(pest control)*
Fanggrube f pitfall, pit trap *(pest control)*
Fangheuschrecke f [praying] mantis, mantid *(order Dictyoptera = Mantodea)*
Fanghof m catch pen *(paddock)*

Fangkegel

Fangkegel *m* malaise trap *(for determining the density of insect pest populations)*
Fangklappe *f* check flap (plate); deflector *(combine)*
Fanglampe *f* light trap *(for determining the density of insect pest populations)*
Fangnetz *n* [fishing] net; *(hunt)* gin
Fangpflanze *f* bait (trap) plant
Fangpflanzenanbau *m* trap-cropping
Fangpflanzenkultur *f* trap crop
Fangprämie *f (hunt)* bounty
Fangrate *f* catch rate
Fangrechen *m* [trap] boom *(rafting)*
~ **von Schwimmern** catch boom
Fangrechenarbeiter *m* boom man (worker)
Fangrinde *f* catch (trap) bark, bark trap
Fangring *m* trap ring
Fangschrecke *f s.* Fangheuschrecke
Fangschuß *m (hunt)* coup de grâce
Fangstand *m* handling chute *(livestock handling facility)*
Fangtechnik *f* trapping technique
Fangtopf *m* trap pot
Fangtuch *n* grain-catching cloth cover *(of a thresher)*
Fangvorrichtung *f* catch device
Fangzahn *m* canine [tooth], fang
Fangzusammensetzung *f* catch composition
FAPP-System *n* filtered air positive pressure [system] *(ventilation system in keeping of specific pathogen-free animals)*
färbbar colourable, dyeable; stainable *(esp. wood)*
~/mit basischen Farbstoffen leicht basophilous
~/mit sauren Farbstoffen leicht acidophil[e], acidophilic
Farbbindung *f* dye binding
Farbbindungskapazität *f* dye-binding capacity
Färbemittel *n* colouring [agent, matter]; stain
färben to colour, to dye, to tint; to stain
färbend tinctorial
Farbensehen *n* colour vision
Färbepflanze *f* dye plant
Färberdistel *f* safflower, saffron thistle, Carthamus tinctorius
Färberdorn *m* rock buckthorn, Rhamnus saxatilis ssp. saxatilis
Färbereiche *f* black oak, Quercus velutina (tinctoria)
Färberflechte *f* orchil[la] weed, orchal, Roccella tinctoria
Färberginster *m* dyer's (base, green) broom, dyer's [green]weed, greenweed, woodwaxen, woadwaxen, waxen woad, Genista tinctoria
Färberhülse *f* 1. wild indigo *(genus Baptisia)*; 2. blue wild indigo, Baptisia australis
Färber[hunds]kamille *f* dyer's camomile, golden camomile (marguerite), Anthemis tinctoria
Färberkrapp *m* madder, Rubia tinctorum
Färberpflanze *f* dye plant

Färberresede *f* dyer's rocket (weed), weld [mignonette], Reseda luteola
Färberröte *f* madder, Rubia tinctorum
Färbersaflor *m s.* Färberdistel
Färberscharte *f* [dyer's] saw-wort, Serratula tinctoria
Färbersumach *m* Venetian (elm-leaved) sumac[h], Cotinus coggygria
Färberwaid *m (bot)* woad, Isatis tinctoria
Farbewechselnde Lupine *f* pearl lupin[e], Lupinus mutabilis
Farbholz dyewood
Farbindex *m* colour index *(sugar manufacture)*
Farbkarte *f* colour card
Farbkern *m* [dis]coloured heartwood
Farbkernholz *n* [dis]coloured heartwood
Farbluftbild *n* colour aerial photograph
Farbmalz *n* colour (black) malt
Farbmutante *f* colour strain
Farbpflanze *f* dye plant
Farbschlag *m* colour strain
Farbsortierer *m* colour sorter
Farbspritzpistole *f* paint gun
Farbstoff *m* dye[stuff], colouring [agent, matter]
Farbstoffbindung *f* dye binding
Farbstoffmarkierung *f* dye tracing
Farbstoffmischung *f/Greifswalder* gentian violet *(anthelminthic, fungicide)*
Farbstoffpflanze *f* dye plant
Farbtafeln *fpl* **nach Munsell** *(soil)* Munsell colour charts
Färbung *f* colouring, staining
~ **nach Giemsa** Giemsa staining *(microbiology)*
~ **nach Gram** Gram method *(microbiology)*
Färbungstyp *m* colour pattern *(e.g. of fruits)*
Farbveränderung *f* discolo[u]ration
Farbwert *m* chromaticity value *(e.g. of fruits)*
Farbzeichnung *f* colour pattern *(e.g. of animals)*
Farbzellengeschwulst *f (vet)* chromatophoroma
Farin *m* brown sugar
Farinograph *m* farinograph *(kneading machine for testing baking quality)*
farinographisch farinographic
Farinzucker *m* brown sugar
Farm *f* farm, homestead
Farmberater *m* farm adviser
Farmer *m* farmer
Farmerlunge[nerkrankung] *f* farmer lung [disease]
Farmersfrau *f* farmerette
Farmervereinigung *f* farmer's association
Farmnerz *m* mink, Mustela (Lutreola) vison
Farmverschuldung *f* farm indebtedness
Farmwald *m* farm forest (woodland, woodlot)
Farn *m* fern *(class Filicatae)* • **mit ~ bedeckt** ferny
Farnblattlaus *f* fern aphid, Idiopterus nephrelepidis
Farnblättrigkeit *f* **der Tomate** fern leaf of tomato *(virosis)*
Farnesen *n* farnesene *(insect attractant)*

Farnesol *n* farnesol *(plant substance)*
Farnheide *f* fern heath
Farnkraut *n s.* Farn
Farnpflanze *f* fern *(division Pteridophyta)*
Farnpflanzung *f* fernery
Farnwedel *m* fern frond
Farrenkalb *n* bull-calf
Färse *f* heifer, stirk, quey
~/**hochtragende** down-calving heifer
~/**noch unbelegte** maiden heifer
~/**trächtige (tragende)** in-calf heifer
~/**vorgenutzte** once-bred heifer
Färsenaufzucht *f* heifer rearing
Färsenaufzuchtanlage *f* heifer rearing plant
Färsenhaut *f* heifer hide
Färsenkalb *n* [dairy] heifer calf, cow-calf
Fasan *m* pheasant *(genus Phasianus)*
Fasanengelege *n* nide
Fasanenschutzgehölz *n* protective woodland for pheasants
Fasanerie *f* pheasantry
Faschine *f* fascine, bavin, bundled brushwood
Faschinenbau *m* fascine-work
Faschinendamm *m* fascine dike
Faschinendrän *m* fascine drain
Faschinendränung *f* fascine drainage
Faschinenholz *n* fascine wood
Faschinenweg *m* fascine (brushwood) road
Faschinenwerk *n* fascine-work
Faselbohne *f* Egyptian (black) bean, tonga (hyacinth) bean, Dolichos lablab, Lablab niger (purpureus)
Faser *f* 1. fibre; 2. *s.* Faserrichtung
~/**argyrophile** reticular fibre
~/**elastische** elastic fibre
~/**pflanzliche** plant fibre
~/**tierische** animal fibre
faserartig fibrous, fibred
Faserbanane *f (bot)* abaca, Musa textilis
Faserbündel *n* fibre bundle
Fäserchen *n* fibril
Faserfeinheitsmeßgerät *n* micronaire *(cotton testing)*
Faserfestigkeitsmeßgerät *n* stilometer *(cotton testing)*
faserförmig fibriform
Fasergehalt *m* fibre content
Fasergeschwulst *f (vet)* fibroma
Fasergewebe *n* fibrous tissue
faserhaltig fibrous, fibred
Faserholz *n* pulpwood, paper wood
Faserholzrolle *f* pulpwood bolt
faserig fibrous, fibred; stringy
Faserknorpel *m* fibro-cartilage
Faserknorpelring *m* meniscus
Faserkohlenhydrat *n* fibre carbohydrate
Faserlänge *f* fibre length
Faserlängenmeßgerät *n* fibrograph
Faserlein *m* fibre flax

Faserneigung *f* slope of grain *(wood structure)*
Faserneigungswinkel *m* grain angle *(wood structure)*
Faserpflanze *f* fibre (textile) plant
~/**hanfähnliche** hemp
Faserpflanzenkultur *f* fibre crop
Faserplatte *f* fibreboard, fibre building-board, fibrous felted board
Faserprotein *n* fibrous protein
Faserqualität *f* fibre quality
faserreich fibrous, fibred
Faserrichtung *f* fibre direction, grain [of timber]
 • **in ~ auftrennen** to rip • **längs der ~** along (parallel to) the grain • **quer zur ~** across the grain
~/**verdrehte** crotch [grain] *(of wood)*
Fasersättigungspunkt *f* fibre-saturation point
Faserstauchung *f* compression failure *(tree injury)*
~ **am stehenden Stamm** upsets
Faserstoff *m* fibrous material, fibre
Fasertorf *m* fibrous peat
Fasertracheide *f* fibre tracheid *(wood anatomy)*
Faserverlauf *m* **im Holz** grain of timber
Faserwurzel *f* fibrous root, hair[-like] root
Faserwurzelsystem *n* fibrous root system
faß! take it!, sick him! *(command to dogs)*
Faß *n* cask, barrel; vat, tun, butt
Faßabfüllmaschine *f* cask filling machine
Faßabfüllorgan *n* racker arm *(brewing)*
Faßabfüllung *f* cask filling, kegging
Fassadenbegrünung *f* facade greening
faßbeinig bandy-legged
Faßbier *n* draught (keg) beer
Faßbutter *f* cask butter
Fäßchen *n* keg, firkin
Faßdaube *f* stave, shook
fassen/Wurzeln to root, to strike (take) roots
Faßfüller *m* cask filling machine
Faßgärung *f* cask fermentation
Faßgeschmack *m* mouldy taste *(wine defect)*
Faßhahn *m* spigot
Faßholz *n* cask (stave) wood
Faßpech *n* brewer's pitch
Faßpumpe *f* barrel pump
Faßreifen *m* hoop
Fassungsvermögen *n* capacity; *(ecol)* carrying capacity
~ **eines Teiches** pondage
Faßwaschmaschine cask (keg) washing machine
Faßwein *m* cask (bulk) wine
Faßzapfen *m* spigot
Fastebene *f* peneplain, peneplane
fasten to fast
~ **lassen** to fast, to starve
Fasziation *f (bot, phyt)* fasciation
Faszie *f (zoo)* fascia • **mit einer ~ versehen** fasciate[d]
Faszikel *m (bot, zoo)* fascicle, fascicule, fasciculus, bundle

Fasziolose

Fasziolose f *(vet)* fascioliasis, fasciolosis, distomatosis, liver rot
~ **der Schafe** core *(caused by Fasciola spp.)*
Fathom n fathom *(quantity of wood)*
faul putrid; rotten; punky; addle[d] *(egg)* • ~ **werden** to addle *(egg)* (s. a. faulen)
Faulast m decayed (unsound) knot, rotten (punk) knot
~/**überwallter** blind conk *(wood defect)*
Faulbaum m alder (glossy) buckthorn, black dogwood, Persian bark, berry-bearing alder, Rhamnus frangula
Faulbehälter m septic tank
Faulbrut f *(api, vet)* foul brood
~/**Bösartige** American foul brood, AFB *(caused by Bacillus larvae)*
~/**Gutartige** European foul brood, EFB *(caused by Streptococcus pluton)*
Fäule f s. Fäulnis
faulen to rot, to turn rotten, to foul, to decay, to spoil, to decompose *(esp. plant matter)*; to putrefy, to become putrid, to fester *(meat, fish)*; to ret[t] *(hay)*
faulend putrescent
Faulfleck m speck, fleck, rotten spot *(in plant tissue)*
Faulgas n biogas, sewage gas
faulig putrid
Faulkern m rotten heart *(wood defect)*
Fäulnis f rot[tenness], decay, spoilage, decomposition *(esp. of plant matter)*; putrefaction, putrescence, putridity *(of meat)*; dote *(of timber)*
• **durch ~ verfärbt** doty *(wood)* • ~ **hervorrufen** to decay • **in ~ übergehen** to rot; to putrefy • **in ~ übergehen lassen** to putrefy
~/**bakterielle** bacterial rot
Fäulnisbakterium n putrefactive bacterium
fäulnisbeständig rotproof, decay-resistant
Fäulnisbeständigkeit f rotproofness, decay resistance
fäulnisbewohnend saprophytic
Fäulnisbewohner m saprophyte, saprophytic organism
fäulniserregend putrefactive, saprogenic
Fäulniserreger m saprogen, septic agent
fäulnisfrei sound, clean *(e.g. wood)*
Fäulnisgärung f putrefactive fermentation
fäulnishemmend, fäulnishindernd antirot, rotproofing
Fäulnishumus m rotten humus
fäulnisliebend saprophilous
Fäulnisschaden m decay damage
Fäulnisschutz m rot protection
fäulnisverhindernd antirot, rotproofing
Fäulnisverhütungsmittel n rotproofing agent
fäulniswidrig rotproof, decay-resistant
Fäulniswidrigkeit f decay resistance
Faulschlamm m 1. sewage (digested, foul) sludge, putrid mud, biogas slurry; 2. sapropel

Faulstelle f fleck, rotten spot *(in plant tissue)*
Faulung f [anaerobic] digestion *(of sewage sludge)*
Fauna f fauna
Faunenzählung f faunal census
Faunist m faunist
faunistisch faunistic[al]
Fausten n dry fist milking
Favus m *(vet)* favus
~ **der Vögel** fowl favus
Fäzes pl s. Fäkalien
Faziation f, **Fazies** f facies *(phytosociology)*
FBG s. Forstbetriebsgemeinschaft
FE s. Futtereinheit
Febantel n febantel *(anthelmintic)*
febril febrile
Fechser m root cutting, runner, seed piece *(for vegetative propagation esp. of hop, grape-vine or sugar-cane)*
Feder f 1. feather; 2. spring
federähnlich plumose, plumate
Federbaum m silk tree, Albizia julibrissin
Federbuschcelosie f *(bot)* [feathered] celosia, Celosia argentea var. plumosa
Federfahne f vane
Federflur f feather tract, pteryla *(of bird's skin)*
Federfollikel m feather follicle
Federfressen n feather-pecking *(vice of fowl)*
federfüßig feather-legged *(bird)*
Federgras n feather (needle) grass *(genus Stipa)*
Federkiel m scape, shaft
Federkleid n feathering, plumage • **das ~ wechseln** to moult
federlos featherless, bald
Federlosigkeit f featherlessness, baldness
Federmehl n feather meal *(feed)*
Federmilbe f feather mite *(superfamilies Analgoidea and Pterolichoidea)*
Federmohn m 1. plume poppy *(genus Macleaya)*; 2. plume poppy, Macleaya cordata
Federnelke f common garden pink, cottage pink, *(Am)* pheasant's-eye, Dianthus plumarius
Federpicken n feather-pecking *(vice of fowl)*
Federrastsicherheitskupplung f bevel-jaw-type safety clutch
Federspiel n lure *(falconry)*
Federspule f quill
Federstrahl m barbule
Federvieh n fowl, poultry
Federwechsel m moult, *(Am)* molt
Federweißer m green wine
Federwild n wildfowl, feathered game, wing[ed] game, game-birds • ~ **jagen (schießen)** to fowl, to grass
Federwolke f cirrus
Federzahnstriegel m finger weeder
Federzupfen n s. Federpicken
fedrig plumose, plumate
Feedback n feedback

Feekes-Skala *f* Feekes' scale *(of developmental stages in cereals)*
fegen to fray, to burnish, to rub [off] *(game)*
Fegen *n* fraying, antler burnishing, rubbing-off
Fegeschaden *m (forest)* fraying damage, damage due to fraying
Fegeschutz *m (forest)* fraying damage protection
Fegestelle *f* velvet mark *(on tree-trunks)*
Feh *n s.* Eichhörnchen
Fehlbildung *f* malformation, abnormality
Fehldiagnose *f* misdiagnosis, diagnostic mistake
fehlen to miss *(in shooting)*
Fehlentwicklung *f* 1. defective development; 2. dysplasia, malfunction
Fehler *m*/**zufälliger** *(biom)* random error
~/zulässiger allowable (permissible) defect
Fehlerabzug *m* defect deduction, allowance for defect, cull *(timber mensuration)*
fehlernährt malnourished
Fehlernährung *f* malnutrition
Fehlerquadrat *n*/**mittleres** *(biom)* error mean square
Fehlervarianz *f (biom)* residual (error) variance
Fehlfarbenfotografie *f* near-infrared photography
fehlfarbig blotchy *(blossom)*
Fehlfunktion *f* malfunction
Fehlgärung *f* faulty fermentation
fehlgebären *(vet)* to abort
Fehlgeburt *f (vet)* abortion
Fehljahr *n* fail year; *(forest)* non-seed year
Fehlkante *f* wane, rough (dull) edge, natural bevel *(of conversed timber)*
Fehllage *f* malpresentation, malposition *(obstetrics)*
Fehlregulation *f* dysregulation
Fehlrippe *f* rib, ribs *(beef carcass)*
fehlschießen to miss *(in shooting)*
Fehlschuß *m* miss
Fehlsinnmutation *f (gen)* missense codon (mutation)
Fehlstart *m* breakaway *(e.g. in horse-races)*
Fehlstelle *f* miss, skip, blank, fail-place, gap
Fehlwirt *m* atypical host
Fehn *n* fen [soil]
Feiertagskrankheit *f (vet)* lumbago *(of horses)*
Feige *f* fig
Feigenbaum *m* fig[-tree] *(genus Ficus)*
Feigenblattkürbis *m* fig-leaved gourd, Malabar gourd, Cucurbita ficifolia
Feigengallwespe *f* fig (blastophaga) wasp, Blastophaga psenes
Feigengänsefuß *m* fig-leaved goose-foot, Chenopodium ficifolium
Feigenkäfer *m* fig beetle, Cotinis texana
Feigenkaktus *m (bot)* prickly pear, opuntia, nopal *(genus Opuntia)*
Feigenmotte *f* raisin moth, Ephestia (Cadra) figulilella

Feigenopuntie *f* Indian fig, Opuntia megacantha (ficus-indica)
Feigenrost *m* fig rust *(caused by Physopella fici = Kuehneola fici)*
Feigwurz *f* pilewort, Ranunculus ficaria
Feijoa *f (bot)* feijoa *(genus Acca)*
Feilwinkel *m* filing (top-plate) angle *(of a chain-saw tooth)*
Feime *f*, **Feimen** *m* rick, stack
fein fine
Feinanteile *mpl* fines
feinästig finely branched
Feinastschüttler *m* twig vibrator
Feinblättriges Hasenohr *n (bot)* slender hare's-ear, Bupleurum tenuissimum
Feinboden *m* fine earth (soil)
Feinbrause *f* mist rose *(of a watering-can)*
Feind *m*/**natürlicher** natural enemy
Feinegge *f* extra-light seed harrow
Feineinstellung *f* micrometer rate control *(of a seed drill)*
Feinerde *f* fine earth (soil)
Feines Hasenohr *n s.* Feinblättriges Hasenohr
~ Nadelgras *n* fine needle grass, Aristida mutabilis
feinfaserig fine-fibred; close-grained, fine-textured, fine-grown *(wood)*
Feinfaserigkeit *f* close grain, fine texture *(of wood)*
feinfilzig *(bot)* tomentulose
Feinfraktion *f* fine fraction
Feinfrostobst *n* deep-frozen fruit[s]
feingehäckselt finely chopped
feingemahlen finely ground
feingeschlitzt *(bot)* dissected
Feingrubber *m* Danish cultivator
Feingut *n* fines
Feinheit *f* fineness
Feinjährigkeit *f s.* Feinringigkeit
feinkörnig fine-grained, fine-textured *(soil)*
Feinkrümelschleppe *f* fine clod crusher
feinmahlen to grind finely
Feinmull *m (soil)* fine mull
Feinpore *f (soil)* micropore, fine pore
feinporig fine-porous, fine-pored
Feinporigkeit *f* microporosity
Feinreisig *n* twigs
Feinringigkeit *f* close grain, close (fine) texture, fineness *(of wood)*
Feinsämereien *fpl* fine (miniature) seeds
feinsamig small-seeded
Feinsand *m* fine sand
Feinsärad *n* fine seed cell wheel
Feinschluff *m (soil)* fine silt
Feinseide *f* clover dodder, ailweed, Cuscuta epithymum ssp. trifolii
Feinsprühen *n* fine-droplet spraying, ULV (ultra-low volume) spraying *(plant protection)*
~ mit extrem geringer Aufwandmenge UULV (ultra-ultra-low volume) spraying

Feinsprühgerät 202

Feinsprühgerät *n* microsprayer, ultra-low volume sprayer
Feinstgut *n* fines
Feinstrahl *m (bot)* erigeron *(genus Erigeron)*
Feinstrahlberuf[s]kraut *n* daisy-fleabane, Erigeron annuus
Feinstrahldüse *f* microjet nozzle
Feinststoff *m* fines
Feinstufengetriebe *n* multistep transmission
Feintalg *m* rendered tallow
Feinton *m* fine clay
Feintrub *m* fine coagulum, fine (cold) trub *(brewing)*
feinvermahlen finely ground
Feinwolle *f* fine wool, pick
feinwollig fine-woolled
Feinwollrasse *f* fine-wool breed
Feinwollschaf *n* fine-wool sheep
Feinwollschafrasse *f* fine-wool breed
Feinwurzel *f* fine root, rootlet
feist adipose, obese, fat; in grease, in pride (prime) of grease *(game)*
Feist *n* [deer-]grease, fat
Feisthirsch *m* fat stag
Feiung *f s.* Immunisierung
fekund *s.* fruchtbar 1.
Fekundation *f s.* Befruchtung
Fekundität *f s.* Fruchtbarkeit 1.
Felber[baum] *m s.* Silberweide
Felberich *m (bot)* loosestrife *(genus Lysimachia)*
Feld *n* field, acre • **auf dem ~ gereift** field-ripened • **das ~ bestellen** to till the field
~/eingezäuntes paddock
Feldahorn *m* common (hedge) maple, [English] field maple, Acer campestre
Feldanbau *m* field (outdoor) cropping
Felderkennung *f* field approbation (testing) *(of seed-producing areas)*
Feldarbeit *f* field work
Feldarbeiter *m* farm (field) hand, farm labourer
Feldarbeitsgang *m* field operation
Feldarbeitsmaschine *f* field machine
Feldarbeitsstellung *f* position for field operation *(of agricultural machinery)*
Feldarbeitstag *m* field working day
Feldarbeitszeit *f* field time
Feldaufgang *m* field emergence (germination)
Feldaussaat *f* field seeding
Feldbau *m* arable agriculture, field cropping, arable farming, field husbandry (crop production)
Feldbedingungen *fpl* field conditions
Feldbegehung *f* field observation
Feldbeifuß *m* field (sagewort) wormwood, Artemisia campestris
Feldberegnung *f* field [sprinkler] irrigation, outdoor irrigation
Feldbesichtigung *f* field inspection
Feldbestand *m* field crop, stand
Feldbestellung *f* field cultivation

Feldbestimmung *f* field identification *(e.g. of pests)*
Feldbewirtschaftung *f* field management
Feldboden *m* field soil
Feldbohne *f* broad (field, faba) bean, fava [bean], Vicia faba var. minor (equina)
Feldchampignon *m* common field mushroom, [meadow] mushroom, champignon, Agaricus campester (campestris, arvensis)
Felddistel *f* creeping (Canada) thistle, corn (field) thistle, Cirsium arvense
Felddränung *f* field drainage
Felddrusch *m* field threshing
Felddüngungsversuch *m* field fertilization test
Feldehrenpreis *m* corn (wall) speedwell, Veronica arvensis
Feldentwässerung *f* field drainage
Felderbse *f* field (Australian winter) pea, Pisum sativum ssp. sativum convar. speciosum
Feldflur *f* field
Feldfrucht *f* [field, arable] crop
~/einjährige annual field crop
Feldfruchtbestand *m* crop
Feldfruchtfolge *f* arable rotation (cropping sequence)
Feldfutter *n* [field, arable] forage
Feldfutter... *s. a.* Futter...
Feldfutterbau *m* [arable] forage cropping, [field] forage growing
Feldfuttererntemaschine *f* field forage harvester
Feldfutterfrucht *f* [arable] forage crop, arable feed crop
Feldfutterschneidwerk *n* field-forage cutter
Feldfuttersilage *f* arable silage
Feldgemüse *n* field vegetable
Feldgemüse[an]bau *m* field vegetable farming (growing), outdoor vegetable growing, farm-scale vegetable production
feldgereift field-ripened
Feldgraswirtschaft *f* alternate husbandry
Feldgrenze *f* field boundary
Feldgrille *f* field cricket, Acheta (Gryllus) campestris
Feldhäcksler *m* chopper-type forage harvester, [field] chopper, forage harvester
~ mit Nachzerkleinerung double-chop forage harvester
~ mit Schneidegebläse pick-up chopper blower
Feldhahn *m* cock-partridge *(Perdix perdix)*
Feldhamster *m* hamster, Cricetus cricetus
Feldhase *m* brown hare, Lepus europaeus [occidentalis]
Feldhecke *f* field hedge
Feldheuschrecke *f* 1. short-horned grasshopper *(superfamily Acridioidea)*; 2. locust *(family Acrididae)*
Feldheutrocknung *f* field hay drying
Feldhuhn *n* common (grey) partridge, Perdix perdix

Feldhygiene f field sanitation
Feldkäfig m field cage
Feldkapazität f s. Feldwasserkapazität
Feldkeimfähigkeit f field germination (emergence)
Feldklee m [large] hop clover, yellow suckling clover, trefoil hop, Trifolium campestre (procumbens)
Feldkultur f field (arable) crop
Feldlader m crop loader
Feldlagerung f field storage
Feldlauch m field (wild) garlic, crow garlic (onion), Allium vineale
Feldleistung f field performance *(of plant protectants)*
Feldmaikäfer m cockchafer, may-bug, May beetle, Melolontha melolontha (vulgaris)
Feldmännertreu f, **Feldmannstreu** f *(bot)* common eryngo, Eryngium campestre
Feldmaß n land measure, measure of land
Feldmaus f [common] vole, [continental] fieldmouse, harvest-mouse, Microtus arvalis
Feldmesser m [land] surveyor
Feldnachreife f field curing *(e.g. of onions)*
Feldnagetier n field rodent
Feldparzelle f field plot
Feldpopulation f field population *(of pests)*
Feldproduktion f field production
Feldprüfung f field testing *(of seed-producing areas)*
Feldrand m field edge (margin), balk
Feldrandmiete f field clamp
Feldraute f herb of grace, herb-grace, Ruta graveolens var. vulgaris
feldreif field-ripe
Feldreife f field-ripeness
Feldresistenz f field resistance *(against a pest)*
Feldrittersporn m field (forking) larkspur, Delphinium consolida
Feldrose f field (Ayrshire) rose, Rosa arvensis
Feldsaat f field seeding
Feldsalat m [common] corn-salad, field salad, lamb's-lettuce, fetticus, Valerianella locusta (olitoria)
Feldschädling m field pest
Feldscheune f field barn; Dutch barn
Feldschicht f field layer, festratum *(phytosociology)*
Feldschmiede f field forage
Feldschutzstreifen m field (farm) shelter-belt, windbelt
Feldschwindling m fairy-ring mushroom, Scotch bonnet, Marasmius oreades
Feldspat m fel[d]spar *(soil-forming rock)*
Feldsperling m tree sparrow, Passer montanus
Feldspritzdüse f field sprayer nozzle
Feldspritzeinrichtung f rig sprayer
Feldspritzgestänge n s. Feldspritzrohr
Feldspritzmaschine f field [crop] sprayer
Feldspritzrohr n field sprayer boom, crop boom

Feldspritzung f field spraying
Feldstecher m field glass[es]
Feldstein m fieldstone
Feldstiefmütterchen n pansy, *(Am)* Johnny-jump-up, Viola tricolor
Feldstrohhäcksler m field straw chopper
Feldstück n croft
Feldtensiometer n field tensiometer
Feldthymian m creeping (wild) thyme, mother-of-thyme, serpolet, Thymus serpyllum
Feldtreiben n *(hunt)* field drive
Feldtrocknung f field drying (curing)
Feldüberwachung f field observation
Feldüberwinterung f field overwintering
Feldulme f field (common) elm, smooth-leaved elm, *(Am)* French elm, Ulmus minor (carpinifolia)
Feldverluste mpl field losses *(of harvested crops)*
Feldvermessung f land survey[ing]
Feldversuch m field test (trial) • einen ~ vornehmen to field-test
Feldversuchsarbeit f field experimental (trials) work
Feldversuchsfläche f field trials area
Feldversuchsschema n plot design
Feldversuchsserie f series of field tests
Feldversuchstechnik f field-plot technique
Feldversuchswesen n field experimentation
Feldwalze f field (land) roller, farming roll[er]
Feldwasserkapazität f field [moisture] capacity, FC, field [capillary, carrying] capacity, field maximum, moisture [retention] capacity, water capacity, specific retention
~/nutzbare available field [moisture] capacity
Feldwerkstatt f field workshop
Feldwicke f narrow-leaved vetch, Vicia sativa ssp. nigra
Feldwirksamkeit f field performance *(of plant protectants)*
Feldwirt m arable farmer
Feldwirtschaft f field husbandry (cropping), arable farming (agriculture)
Feldwirtschaftssystem n cropping system
Feldysop m [common] rock-rose, Helianthemum nummularium
Felge f rim
Felgenbett n well
Felicie f kingfisher daisy, Felicia bergerana
Felide f feline *(family Felidae)*
felin feline
Felines Panleukopenievirus n [feline] panleucopenia virus
Fell n hide, coat; skin *(esp. of small animals)*; fell; fur; pelage *(of mammals)*
~/unzugerichtetes pelt *(of furbearers)*
~/zugerichtetes fur
Fellbeißen n fur chewing *(vice of animals)*
Fellfressen n fur-eating, trichophagy *(vice of animals)*
Fellkaninchen n fur-producing rabbit

Fellpony n Fell pony *(breed)*
Fellrassekaninchen n fur-producing rabbit
Fellzurichtung f fur dressing
Fels m rock • **auf ~ wachsend** saxatile, saxicoline, saxicolous • **in ~ lebend** saxatile, saxicoline, saxicolous
Felsenbirne f 1. service-berry *(genus Amelanchier)*; 2. snowy mespilus, Amelanchier ovalis (vulgaris); 3. service-berry *(fruit from Amelanchier spp.)*; 4. Juneberry *(fruit from Amelanchier canadensis)*
Felsengebirgsdickhornschaf n Rocky Mountain sheep, bighorn, Ovis canadensis ssp. canadensis
Felsengebirgsfieber n *(vet)* Rocky Mountain spotted fever, RMS-fever
Felsengebirgsheuschrecke f Rocky Mountain grasshopper, Melanoplus [mexicanus] spretus
Felsengebirgswacholder m Rocky Mountain juniper, Juniperus scopulorum
Felsenhimbeere f stone bramble, stoneberry, Rubus saxatilis
Felsenjohannisbeere f rock [red] currant, Ribes petraeum
Felsenkirsche f mahaleb [cherry], rock (St. Lucie) cherry, Prunus (Cerasus) mahaleb
Felsenkohl m saxatile cabbage, Brassica rupestris [ssp. rupestris]
Felsenröschen n trailing azalea, Loiseleuria procumbens
Felsensteinkraut n goldentuft [madwort], madwort, gold-dust, basket-of-gold, Alyssum saxatile
Felsentaube f rock pigeon (dove), wild pigeon, blue rock[-pigeon], Columba livia
Felsenulme f rock elm, Ulmus thomasii
Felsenwalnuß f little walnut, Juglans microcarpa (rupestris)
Felsfetthenne f *(bot)* tripmadam, Sedum reflexum
Felsheide f stone heath
felsig rocky
Felswüste f stony desert
Femelbetrieb m *(forest)* femel system, group-selection [system]
Femelhieb m s. Femelschlag
Femelsaumschlagfläche f femel strip coupe
Femelschlag m 1. femel (gap, group-selection) felling ; 2. s. Femelschlagfläche
~/Badischer irregular shelterwood system
~/Bayerischer Bavarian femel felling
Femelschlagfläche f femel coupe
~/Badische Baden femel coupe
~/Bayerische Bavarian femel coupe
Femel[schlag]wald m selection forest
feminin feminine
Feminisierung f *(vet)* feminization
~/testikuläre testicular feminization
Femur m femur
Fen n fen [soil]
Fenac n fenac, chlorfenac *(herbicide)*

Fenaminsulf n fenamin[o]sulf *(fungicide)*
Fenamiphos fenamiphos, phenamiphos *(nematicide)*
Fenarimol n fenarimol *(fungicide)*
Fenazaflor n fenazaflor, fenofluorazol *(acaricide)*
Fenazox n fenazox *(acaricide, insecticide)*
Fenbendazol n fenbendazole *(anthelminthic, fungicide)*
Fenbutatinoxid n fenbutatinoxid *(acaricide)*
Fenchel m 1. fennel, Foeniculum vulgare; 2. fennel *(drug, spice)*
Fenchelöl n fennel [seed] oil
Fenchelsamen m fennel seed
Fenchlorphos n, **Fenclofos** n fenchlorphos, ronnel, nankor *(insecticide, acaricide)*
fenestrat *(bot, zoo)* fenestrate
Fenfuram n fenfuram *(fungicide)*
Fenitrothion n fenitrothion *(insecticide)*
Fenmull n *(soil)* fenmull
Fenn n fen [soil]
Fennich m pigeon-grass *(genus Setaria)*
Fennmull n *(soil)* fenmull
Fenoprop n fenoprop, silvex, 2,4,5-TP *(growth regulator, herbicide)*
Fenpropimorph n fenpropimorph *(fungicide)*
Fenridazon n fenridazon *(growth regulator)*
Fenson n fenson *(acaricide)*
fensterartig *(bot, zoo)* fenestrate
Fensterbankkultur f window garden
Fensterblatt n s. Monstera
fensterförmig *(bot, zoo)* fenestriform
Fenstergarten m window garden
Fensterhalterung f s. Fensterisicherung
Fenstersicherung f light securing *(in greenhouses)*
Fensulfothion n fensulfothion *(nematicide, insecticide)*
Fenteracol n fenteracol *(herbicide)*
Fenthion n fenthion *(insecticide)*
Fenthiuram n fenthiuram *(fungicide)*
Fentinacetat n fentin-acetate, triphenyltin acetate *(fungicide)*
Fentinhydroxid n fentin hydroxide, TPTH *(fungicide)*
Fenuron n fenuron *(herbicide)*
Fenvalerat n fenvalerate *(insecticide, acaricide)*
Fenz f fence, fencing
Ferbam n ferbam *(fungicide)*
Ferien-Streckenreiten n pony-trekking
Ferkel n piglet, pigling, piggy, farrow, porkling, *(Am)* pig
~/mutterloses orphan piglet
~/zitterkrampfbefallenes *(vet)* shaker, trembler
Ferkelanämie f *(vet)* baby-pig anaemia
Ferkelaufzuchtanlage f swine nursery
Ferkelaufzuchtbetrieb m swine nursery
Ferkelaufzuchtfutter n piglet starter
Ferkelaufzuchtstall m swine nursery building (house)

Ferkelbatterie f piglet battery
Ferkelenteritis f s. Ferkelruhr
Ferkelfütterung f piglet feeding
Ferkelgrippe f swine enzootic pneumonia
Ferkelkäfigbatterie f piglet battery
Ferkelliegebereich m piglets lying area
Ferkelliegefläche f hover box
Ferkelliegeplatz m creep [area] *(in a farrowing crate)*
Ferkelmast f piglet fattening
ferkeln to farrow [down], to pig
Ferkeln n farrowing
Ferkelnest n s. Ferkelliegeplatz
Ferkelnuß f, **Ferkelnußbaum** m pignut [hickory], Carya glabra (porcina)
Ferkelruhr f *(vet)* coliform scour[s] in piglets
Ferkelselbsttränkebecken n piglet drinking bowl
Ferkelstall m piglet house
Ferkelsterblichkeit f piglet mortality
Ferkeltränke f piglet drinker
Ferment n ferment, enzyme *(for compounds s. under* Enzym*)*
~/gelbes s. Flavinenzym
Fermentation f fermentation
Fermentationshorizont m *(soil)* fermentation layer, F-layer
Fermentationsprodukt n fermentation product
Fermentationswärme f heat of fermentation
fermentativ fermentative
Fermenter m fermenter, fermentor, fermenting tub, fermentation vessel
fermentieren to ferment
Fermentierung f fermentation
Fernambuk[holz] n Brazil-wood *(esp. from Caesalpinia echinata)*
Fernanzeige f remote indication (signalling, display)
Fernbedienung f remote control
Fernerkundung f remote sensing
~/satellitengestützte satellite remote sensing
Fernerkundungsdaten pl remotely sensed data
Fernglas n field glass[es]
Fernmessung f telemetry
Fernöstliche Pflaume f Ussurian plum, Prunus ussuriensis
Fernrezeptor m teleceptor
Fernsteuerung f remote control
Ferntransport m long-distance transport
Fernwechsel m migration route *(of game)*
Fernweidewirtschaft f transhumance
Fernzeugung f telegony *(breeding)*
Ferrallitisation f *(soil)* ferrallitization, laterization
• **durch ~ gebildet** ferrallitic
ferrallitisch ferrallitic
Ferralsol n *(soil)* latosol, *(Am)* oxisol, ox
Ferredoxin n ferredoxin *(proteide)*
Ferredoxin-NADP⁺-Reductase f ferredoxin-NADP⁺ reductase *(enzyme)*
Ferrihydrit m *(soil)* ferrihydrite

Ferritin n ferritin *(iron-containing protein)*
Ferrochelatase f ferrochelatase *(enzyme)*
Ferroskop n *(vet)* metal detector
Ferrugination f *(soil)* ferruginization, rubefaction
Fersenbein n heel-bone, calcaneum
Fersenbürste f pollen brush, scopa, scopula *(of honey-bees)*
Fersenkrankheit f perosis *(of growing birds due to manganese deficiency)*
fersiallitisch *(soil)* fersiallitic
Fertigerde f artificial soil mix
Fertigfutter n 1. mess *(e.g. for dogs)*; 2. s. Fertigfuttermittel
Fertigfuttergemisch n ready-to-feed mixture
Fertigfuttermittel n finished (formulated, compound) feed
Fertigfutter[mittel]ration f ready-mixed animal ration
Fertignahrung f convenience food
Fertigrasen m ready sawn lawn carpet
fertil s. fruchtbar
Fertilitätsrate f s. Fruchtbarkeitsrate
Ferulasäure f ferulic acid
Fervin n fervin *(herbicide)*
Fervinal n fervinal *(herbicide)*
Fessel f pastern, ankle *(animal anatomy)*
Fesselbehang m fetlock, feather *(of a horse)*
Fesselbein n long pastern, first phalanx *(animal anatomy)*
Fesselbeinachse f pastern foot axis
Fesselbeuge f ankle
Fesselgelenk n ankle, metacarpophalangeal joint; hock joint *(of hoofed animals)*
Fesselgelenkgalle f *(vet)* wind gall (puff)
Fesselkopf m fetlock
Fessellinie f der Gliedmaße pastern axis
Fesselmanschette f ring boot *(for jumping horses)*
fesseln to hobble, to fetter *(e.g. a horse)*
Fesselseil n hobble
Fesselstand m foot and pastern axis
Festbetttrockner m static bed dryer
festbinden/am Stallplatz to stanchion, to tether
Festdüngerstreuer m solid fertilizer distributor
festfleischig firm-fleshed
Fest-Flüssig-Trennung f solid-liquid separation *(e.g. of slurry)*
Festgehalt m s. Festmaß
Festigkeit f 1. strength, stability; 2. strength, resistance *(to influences)*
Festigkeitseigenschaft f strength property *(e.g. of timber)*
Festigungsgewebe n strengthening tissue, sclerenchyma
festkleben to stick
festlegen to fix, to immobilize
Festlegung f fixation, immobilization *(e.g. of nutrients)*
Festliegen n *(vet)* parturient paresis

Festmaß

Festmaß *n* solid measure (volume) *(timber mensuration)*
Festmaßermittlung *f* cubing, calculation of volume *(of timber)*
Festmeter *m(n)* solid [cubic] metre, cubic metre solid
Festmist *m* solid manure
Festpunkt *m* 1. station *(surveying)*; 2. fixed point
Festsetzung *f s.* Ecesis
festsitzend *(bot, zoo)* sessile
Feststellbremse *f* hand (stop, parking) brake
Feststoffe *mpl* solids
Feststoffkonzentration *f* solids concentration
Feststoffreduktion *f* solids reduction *(slurry treatment)*
Festuca-Nekrosevirus *n* festuca necrosis virus
Festvolumen *n s.* Festmaß
fetal foetal, embryonic
Fetalflüssigkeit *f* foetal (amniotic) fluid
Fetalkreislauf *m* foetal circulation
Fetalmedizin *f (vet)* foetal medicine
Fetalmembran[e] *f* foetal membrane
Fetalphysiologie *f* foetal physiology
Fetaltod *m* foetal death
Feterita[hirse] *f (bot)* feterita, *(Am)* hegari, Sorghum caudatum var. feterita
Fetotomie *f (vet)* embryotomy
fett 1. fat, adipose, obese, *(Am)* chuffy; in grease, in pride (prime) of grease *(game)*; 2. rank *(soil)*; 3. heavy *(wine)* • ~ **werden** to fat[ten], to batten
~/übermäßig overfat
Fett *n* fat
~/pflanzliches vegetable fat
~/subkutanes subcutaneous fat
~/tierisches animal fat, grease, adipose
Fettabbau *m* fat breakdown
Fettabsorption *f* fat absorption
Fettalkohol *m* fatty alcohol
Fettanreicherung *f* **im Blutplasma** *(vet)* lipaemia
Fettansatz *m* fat deposition
~/zu starker overfatness
Fettanteil *m* fat content
fettarm 1. low in fat, low-fat ; 2. lean
Fettauflage *f* fat cover *(of a carcass)*
Fettausbeute *f* fat yield
fettbedingt lipogenic, lipogenous
Fettbestimmung *f* determination of fat content
Fettbildung *f* fat development, lipid formation, lipogenesis
Fettbildungsvermögen *n* fat-forming capacity
Fettbohne *f* soya (soja) bean, soybean, Glycine max
Fettdepot *n* fat depot
Fettdurchfall *m (vet)* steatorrhoea
Fetteinheit *f* fat unit, *(Am)* fat standard
Fettembolie *f (vet)* fat embolism
Fettemulsion *f* fat emulsion
fetten to grease, to lubricate

Fettfleckenkrankheit *f* **[der Bohne]** bean halo blight, grease spot disease *(caused by Pseudomonas phaseolicola)*
Fettflosse *f* adipose fin
fettfrei fat-free, non-fat[ty]
Fettgehalt *n* fat content
~/prozentualer fat percentage
Fettgehaltsbestimmung *f* determination of fat content
Fettgeruch *m* fat odour
Fettgeschwulst *f* **[/gutartige]** *(vet)* lipoma
Fettgewebe *n* fatty (adipose) tissue
Fettgewebelipid *n* adipose tissue lipid
Fettgräserei *f* range fattening, fattening by grazing
fetthaltig fatty
Fetthenne *f (bot)* stonecrop, sedum *(genus Sedum)*
fettig fatty, greasy
Fettkäse *m* fat (rich) cheese
Fettkügelchen *n* fat globule *(of milk)*
Fettkügelchenhülle *f* [fat] globule membrane *(of milk)*
Fettleber *f (vet)* fatty liver, liver steatosis
Fettleberkrankheit *f*, **Fettlebersyndrom** *n* fatty liver disease *(of chicken)*
fettlöslich fat-soluble
Fettmark *n* fatty (yellow) marrow *(of bones)*
Fettmobilisierung *f* fat mobilization
Fettmobilisierungshormon *n* fat mobilization hormone
Fettöl *n* fatty (fixed) oil
Fettoxidation *f* fat oxidation
Fettpolster *n* fat deposit (pad)
Fettpresse *f* grease-gun
Fettprozente *npl* fat percentage
fettreich 1. rich in fat; 2. *s.* fett 1.
Fettsättigung *f* fat saturation
Fettsäure *f* fatty acid
~/essentielle essential fatty acid
~/flüchtige volatile fatty acid, VFA
~/freie free fatty acid, FFA
~/gesättigte saturated fatty acid
~/höhere long-chain fatty acid
~/kurzkettige short-chain fatty acid
~/langkettige long-chain fatty acid
~/mehrfach ungesättigte polyunsaturated fatty acid
~ mit mehreren Doppelbindungen polyenoic fatty acid
~/ungesättigte unsaturated fatty acid
~/verzweigtkettige branched-chain fatty acid
Fettsäuredesaturase *f* acyl-CoA desaturase *(enzyme)*
Fettsäureester *m* fatty acid ester
Fettsäurestoffwechsel *m* fatty acid metabolism
Fettsäuresynthase *f* fatty acid synthase *(enzyme)*
Fettschwanz *m* fat tail
Fettschwanzschaf *n* fat-tailed sheep
Fettschwein *n* lard pig, lard-type hog

Fettschweiß *m* grease, yolk, suint, wool oil
fettspaltend fat-splitting, lipolytic
Fettspaltung *f* lipolysis
Fettsteißschaf *n* fat-tailed sheep
Fettstoff *m* lipid[e], lipine, lipoid
Fettstoffwechsel *m* lipid (fat, adipose) metabolism
Fettstoffwechselstörung *f* lipid metabolism disorder
Fettsucht *f* adiposity, obesity
Fettviehweide *f* fattening pasture
Fettwachs *n* adipocere, lipocere
Fettwiese *f* fertile meadow
Fettzelle *f* fat cell, adipocyte
Fettzersetzung *f* fat breakdown
Fetus *m* foetus, conceptus
Fetusatrophie *f (vet)* foetal atrophy
Fetuswachstum *n* foetal growth
feucht moist, damp, wet; humid; unseasoned, green *(wood)* • **~ werden** to moisten
Feuchtbeizung *f* wet dressing (treatment)
Feuchte *f* moisture, moistness, dampness; humidity
~/absolute absolute humidity, vapour concentration
~/gebundene bound moisture
~ lufttrockener Substanz air-dried moisture
~/relative percentage humidity
Feuchte... *s. a.* Feuchtigkeits...
Feuchteanteil *m* moisture content
Feuchteäquivalent *n (soil)* moisture equivalent, m.e.
Feuchteaufnahme *f* moisture absorption (pick-up)
Feuchteaufnahmevermögen *n* moisture-carrying capacity
Feuchteentzug *m* moisture extraction [rate]
Feuchtegehalt *m* moisture content, m.c, MC, humidity, moistness
Feuchtegrad *m* degree of moistness
Feuchtegradient *m* moisture gradient
Feuchteindex *m (soil)* humidity index
feuchteliebend moisture-loving, hygrophilous, hydrophilic
Feuchtemesser *m* moisture meter, humidity gauge; hygrometer, hygroscope
~/dielektrischer electric-capacity moisture meter
~/elektrischer electrical moisture meter
~ nach dem Widerstandsmeßverfahren/elektrischer electric-resistance moisture meter
Feuchtemeßstab *m* fuel-moisture indicator stick *(for monitoring the ignitability of woodlands)*
Feuchter Brand *m* **des Flieders** lilac blight, bacterial blight of syringa *(caused by Pseudomonas syringae syringae)*
Feuchtgebiet *n* wetland
Feuchtgetreide *n* high-moisture grain (corn), wet (damp, moist) grain
Feuchtgetreidebelüftung *f* wet-grain aeration
Feuchtgetreidelagerung *f* moist (high-moisture) grain storage
Feuchtgetreidesilage *f* moist grain silage
Feuchtgut *n* wet product
Feuchtgutmasse *f* fresh (wet) weight
Feuchtigkeit *f* moisture, moistness, humidity *(s. a. under Feuchte)* • **~ entziehen** to desiccate
Feuchtigkeits... *s. a.* Feuchte...
Feuchtigkeitsanzeiger *m* hygroscope
Feuchtigkeitsbedarf *m* moisture requirement
Feuchtigkeitsbedingungen *fpl* hygrometric conditions • **an mittlere ~ angepaßt** mesophytic • **mit durchschnittlichen ~** mesic *(site)*
feuchtigkeitsempfindlich hygroscopic
Feuchtigkeitsgefälle *n* moisture gradient
feuchtigkeitsgesättigt soggy
Feuchtigkeitsgleichgewicht *n* moisture equilibrium
Feuchtigkeitsmangel *m* moisture deficiency
Feuchtigkeitsmeßgerät *n s.* Feuchtemesser
Feuchtigkeitsprüfung *f* moisture test
Feuchtigkeitsschutz *m* moisture proofing *(e.g. for timber)*
Feuchtigkeitsverhältnisse *npl* moisture relations
Feuchtkorn *n s.* Feuchtgetreide
Feuchtlagerbeständigkeit *f* resistance to damp storing
Feuchtmais *m (Am)* high-moisture corn
Feuchtpflanze *f* hygrophyte
Feuchtraumschalter *m* moisture-proof switch
Feuchtrohdichte *f (soil)* bulk volume
Feuchtsavanne *f* moist savanna[h]
Feuchtsilage *f* wet silage
Feuchtverarbeitung *f* wet processing
Feuchtvermahlung *f* wet milling [process]
feuchtwarm sultry, sweltering, muggy
Feuchtwiese *f* moist (wet) meadow
Feuer *n* fire • **ein ~ eindämmen** to check (control) a fire, to bring a fire under control; to knock-down a fire • **ein ~ lokalisieren (umzingeln)** to contain (to corral) a fire • **~ fangen** to ignite
~ gegen den Wind/kontrolliertes backfire, backburn *(forest fire control)*
~/ruhendes sleeper (hangover, hold-over) fire
~/unbekämpftes uncontrolled (free-burning) fire
Feuerahorn *m* Amur maple, Acer ginnala
Feuerbohne *f* [scarlet] runner bean, scarlet runner, kidney bean, Phaseolus coccineus
Feuerbrand *m (phyt)* fire-blight *(caused by Erwinia amylovora)*
~ der Birne pear blight *(caused by Erwinia amylovora)*
~ des Apfels apple blight *(caused by Erwinia amylovora)*
Feuerbrücke *f* flue bridge
feuerdämmend fire-retardant
Feuerdorn *m* 1. firethorn, pyracantha *(genus Pyracantha)*; 2. scarlet firethorn, Pyracantha coccinea
Feuereinmeßgerät *n (forest)* fire-finder

Feuerfront

Feuerfront *f* firefront, head
~/die Bekämpfungslinie überschreitende breakaway, breakover, slopover
Feuergefahr *f* fire hazard (risk, danger)
feuergefährlich inflammable, combustible
Feuergestell *n s.* Feuerschutzstreifen
feuergetrocknet fire-cured *(tobacco)*
Feuergrenze *f (forest)* fire perimeter
feuerhemmend fire-retardant
Feuerkolben *m (bot)* dragon arum, jack-in-the-pulpit *(genus Arisaema)*
Feuerlilie *f* 1. orange lily, Lilium bulbiferum ssp. croceum; 2. orange lily, Lilium bulbiferum ssp. bulbiferum
Feuerlöschausrüstung *f* fire-fighting equipment
Feuerlöscher *m*, **Feuerlöschgerät** *n* fire extinguisher
Feuerlöschteich *m* fire pond
Feuermarder *m* kolinsky, Mustela siberica
Feuermeldung *f* fire detection
Feuernarbe *f* fire scar, catface *(on timber)*
Feuerortung *f* fire detection
Feuerpatsche *f* fire beater (flail)
Feuerraum *m* furnace
Feuersaum *m* fire edge (margin, line)
Feuerscheinzypresse *f* Japanese cypress, hinoki [cypress], tree of the sun, Chamaecyparis obtusa
Feuerschutzbehandlung *f* fire-proofing *(e.g. of wood)*
Feuerschutzmittel *n* fire retardant
Feuerschutzstreifen *m* fire-break, fire belt, safety-strip
~/aufgeforsteter evergreen fire-break
Feuerschröter *m s.* Hirschkäfer
Feuerschwamm *m* false tinder fungus, male agaric, Phellinus (Fomes, Polyporus) igniarius
Feuersturm *m* fire-storm
Feuertrocknen *n* fire-curing *(of tobacco)*
Feuerung *f* 1. firing; 2. furnace; 3. fuel
Feuerungsanlage *f* furnace
Feuerungsmaterial *n* fuel
Feuerungsraum *m* furnace, stokehold
Feuerverhütung *f* fire prevention
Feuerversicherung *f* fire insurance
~/betriebliche farm fire insurance
Feuerwachmann *m*, **Feuerwächter** *m* fire-watcher, fire-guard, fire-spotter
Feuerwach[t]turm *m* fire tower, watch (look-out) tower
~/bewohnter tower cabin, look-out house
Feuerwehrmann *m* fireman, fire-fighter
Feuerzypresse *f s.* Feuerscheinzypresse
Feulgenreaktion *f* Feulgen staining *(for DNA detection)*
FFM *s.* Fertigfuttermittel
FG *s.* Freiheitsgrad
F1-Generation *f* first filial generation *(breeding)*
fh *s.* Formhöhe
Fiber *f* fibre *(for compounds s. under Faser)*

fibrillär fibrillar[y]
Fibrille *f* fibril, fibrilla
Fibrillenwinkel *m* fibril angle *(wood anatomy)*
Fibrillierung *f* fibrillation
Fibrin *n* fibrin
Fibrinabbau *m* fibrinolysis
Fibrinentfernung *f* defibrination
Fibrinhydrolysat *n* fibrin hydrolysate
Fibrinogen fibrinogen *(blood-plasma protein)*
Fibrinolyse *f* fibrinolysis
fibrinös fibrinous
Fibroadenom *n (vet)* fibroadenoma
Fibroblast *m* fibroblast
Fibroepitheliom *n (vet)* fibroepithelioma
Fibrom[a] *n (vet)* fibroma
Fibronektin *n* fibronectin *(blood-plasma protein)*
fibrös fibrous, fibrose, fibred
Fibrosarkom *n (vet)* fibrosarcoma
Fibrose *f (vet)* fibrosis
Fibrozyt *m* fibrocyte
Fibula *f* fibula *(animal anatomy)*
Fichte *f* spruce *(genus Picea)*
Fichtenaltholz *n* mature spruce stand
Fichtenblattwespe *f* European spruce saw-fly, Diprion (Gilpinia) hercyniae
Fichtenbock *m s.* Fichtensplintbock
Fichtenbruchholz *n* windbroken spruce
Fichtenfaserholz *n* spruce pulpwood
Fichtengallaus *f (Am)* eastern spruce gall aphid, Adelges (Sacchiphantes) abietis
Fichtenharz *n* spruce resin
~/weißes barras *(from southern France)*
Fichtenharzrüßler *m* Norway spruce weevil, Pissodes hercyniae
Fichtenholz *n* spruce[-wood], white deal, whitewood
Fichtenkreuzschnabel *m* red crossbill, Loxia curvirostra
Fichtenmischwald *m* compound spruce forest
Fichtennadelritzenschorf *m s.* Fichtennadelröte
Fichtennadelröte *f*, **Fichtennadelschütte** *f* Norway spruce leaf blight *(caused by Lophodermium macrosporum)*
Fichtenspinnmilbe *f* spruce spider mite, Oligonychus ununguis
Fichtensplintbock *m (ent)* spruce longhorn, Tetropium luridum (castaneum)
Fichtentriebsterben *n* shoot disease of Norway spruce, *(Am)* [seedling] twig blight
Fichtentriebwickler *m (ent)* Norway spruce leafroller, Cacoecia histrionana
Fichtenwald *m* spruce forest
Fichtenzapfenwickler *m (ent)* [spruce] cone tortrix, Cydia (Laspeyresia) strobilella
Fichtenzapfenzünsler *m (ent)* spruce cone pyralid, Dioryctria abietella (mutatella)
Ficin *n* ficin *(enzyme)*
Fidschikrankheit *f* Fiji disease *(of sugar-cane)*
Fidschivirus *n* Fiji disease virus

Fieber *n (vet)* fever, pyrexia, hyperthermia • **nach dem ~ [auftretend]** postfebrile
~/Krim-zentralasiatisches hämorrhagisches Crimean-Congo haemorrhagic fever
~/undulierendes (wellenartig verlaufendes) undulant fever
fiebererzeugend pyrogenic, pyrogenous
fieberfrei afebrile
fieberhaft febrile
Fieberheilbaum *m* [southern] blue gum-tree, Eucalyptus globulus
Fieberkurve *f* fever curve
fieberlos afebrile
Fieberlosigkeit *f* apyrexia
Fiebermittel *n* antipyretic [agent]
fiebernd febrile
fiebersenkend antipyretic, antifebrile
Fieberstrauch *f (bot)* benzoin *(genus Lindera)*
Fieberthermometer *n* clinical thermometer
Fieberwurz *f* horse gentian *(genus Triosteum)*
Fiederberberitze *f* trailing mahonia, Oregon [holly] grape, Mahonia aquifolium
Fiederblatt *n* feathery leaf
Fiederblättchen *n* pinnule
fiederblättrig pinnately-leaved, pinnatifolious
fiederförmig *(bot)* penniform
fiederlappig pinnatilobed, pinnately-lobed
fiedern to feather
fiedernervig *(bot)* feather-veined
fiederspaltig *(bot)* pinnatifid
~/doppelt bipinnatifid
~/handförmig palmatifid
fiederteilig *(bot)* pinnatipartite
Fiederteiliger Weißdorn *m* Chinese hawthorn, Crataegus pinnatifida
Fiederzwenke *f* tor-grass, Japanese (heath) false brome, Brachypodium pinnatum
Field Spaniel *m* field spaniel *(dog breed)*
Fijoa *f* tree-tomato, tamarillo, Cyphomandra betacea
Filament *n* 1. *(bot)* filament; 2. *s.* Faden
Filariasis *f (vet)* filariasis
Filarie *f* filaria *(order Filariidea, superfamily Filarioidea)*
Filarieninfektion *f s.* Filariose
Filariide *f s.* Filarie
Filariose *f (vet)* filariasis
Filet *n* fillet
filetieren to fillet
Filetkotelett[stück] *n* sirloin [chop]
Filialgeneration *f* filial generation, F *(breeding)*
filiform *(bot, zoo)* filiform
Film *m* film
Filmwasser *n (soil)* film water
Filopluma *f* filoplume, pin (stub) feather
Filter *n(m)* filter
Filterbett *n* filter bed
Filtereinsatz *m* filter element
Filterhilfsmittel *n*, **Filterhilfsstoff** *m* filter aid

Filterkuchen *m* filter cake
Filtermasse *f* filter mass, filter pulp
Filtermassekuchen *m* filter pad *(brewing)*
Filtermelkkreuz *n* filter milk claw
filtern to filter, to filtrate
Filterpapier *n* filter-paper
Filterpresse *f* filter press
Filterrückstand *m* filtration residue (waste)
Filterschicht *f* filter bed
Filterstoff *m* filter aid
Filtertuch *n* filter (straining) cloth
Filterung *f* filtration
Filtrat *n* filtrate
Filtration *f* filtration; straining
Filtrationsrate *f* filtration rate
Filtrationsrückstand *m* filtration residue (waste)
filtrierbar filterable
Filtrierbarkeit *f* filterability
filtrieren to filter, to filtrate; to strain
Filtrierpapier *n* filter-paper
Filz *m* felt
Filzblättrige Jujube *f (bot)* Indian jujube, Ziziphus mauritiana
~ Strauchkirsche *f* Nanking cherry, Prunus (Cerasus) tomentosa
Filzfähigkeit *f* felting quality *(of wool)*
Filzhaare *npl* linters *(of cotton seeds)*
filzig *(bot)* tomentose, tomentous
Filzige Königskerze *f* clasping[-leaved] mullein, Verbascum phlomoides
Filzkirsche *f* Nanking cherry, Prunus (Cerasus) tomentosa
Filzkissen *n (api)* felt pad *(for hive isolation)*
Filzrose *f* downy-leaved dog rose, tomentose rose, Rosa tomentosa
Finalprodukt *n* final (end) product
Finanzwesen *n*/**forstliches** forest finance
Findling *m (soil)* [erratic] boulder
Findlingsroder *m* boulder picker
Finger *m* 1. finger, digit; 2. finger, guard *(of a cutter bar)*
Fingeraralie *f (bot)* dizygotheca *(genus Dizygotheca)*
Fingerbalken *m* finger bar *(of a cutter bar)*
Fingerbolzen *m* finger bolt
Fingerehrenpreis *m* fingered speedwell, Veronica triphyllos
fingerförmig *(bot, zoo)* digitate
Fingergras *n* finger (windmill) grass *(genus Chloris)*
Fingerhirse *f* 1. finger (coracan) millet, African (South Indian) millet, ragee, ragi, Eleusine coracan [ssp. coracan]; 2. finger grass, *(Am)* digitgrass *(genus Digitaria)*
Fingerhut *m* foxglove, digitalis *(genus Digitalis)*
Fingerknochen *m* phalanx
Fingerkraut *n (bot)* cinq[ue]foil, five-finger, potentilla *(genus Potentilla)*
Fingerplatte *f* cutting finger plate, [cutting] ledger plate, guard ledger, finger liner *(of a cutter bar)*

Fingerplatte

~/gerippte serrated ledger plate
Fingerrechen *m* [grain] finger
Fingerriedgras *n s.* Fingersegge
Fingerschneidwerk *n* finger[-type] cutter bar
Fingersegge *f* fingered sedge, Carex digitata
Fingerstrauch *m* bush (shrubby) cinquefoil, Potentilla fruticosa
Fingerteilung *f* cutting finger spacing *(of a cutter bar)*
Finne *f* measle, cysticercoid, bladder worm *(tapeworm cysticercus larva) (s. a.* Blasenfinne*)*
Finnenbefall *m (vet)* measles
Finnenkrankheit *f (vet)* cysticercosis
finnig *(vet)* measly
Finnische Landrasse *f* Finnish Landrace *(sheep breed)*
Finnisches Rind *n* Finnish [cattle] *(breed)*
Finnschaf *n* Finnish Landrace *(sheep breed)*
Fioringras *n* fiorin[-grass], white bent[-grass], herd's-grass, *(Am)* redtop, Agrostis gigantea
FIP *s.* Peritonitis der Katze/infektiöse
firnisglänzend *(bot)* vernicose
Firstfenster *n* top light
Firstlüftung *f* ridge (top) ventilation
Firstlüftungsklappe *f* top vent[ilation]
Firstschlitzlüftung *f* centre-ridge opening ventilation *(in animal houses)*
Fisch *m* fish *(group Pisces)*
Fischabfall *m* fish offal
Fischadler *m* osprey, Pandion haliaetus
Fischaufzucht *f* fish rearing
~/künstliche pisciculture
Fischbesatz *m* stock of fish
Fischbestand *m* fish stock
Fischbrut *f* fry
Fischbrutanstalt *f* fish hatchery
Fischbrutfalle *f* fry trap
Fischei *n* roe-corn, fish-egg
Fischeier *npl* [fish, hard] roe, spawn
Fischeingeweidesilage *f* fish viscera silage
Fischeiweißkonzentrat *n* fish protein concentrate
fischen to fish [for]
~/mit dem Ledderingsnetz to trammel
~/mit dem Schleppnetz to trawl
~/mit dem Stellnetz to gill
~/mit der Schleppangel to troll, to trail
~/mit der Wade to seine
~/mit Netzen to net
Fischen *n* fishing
~/gewerbliches artisanal fishing
Fischer *m* fisherman
Fischerei *f* fishery
Fischereibiologie *f* fishery biology
Fischereiforschung *f* fisheries research
Fischereitechnologie *f* fishing technology
Fischereiwirtschaft *f* fisheries management
Fischereiwissenschaft *f* fisheries science
Fischernährung *f* fish nutrition
Fischertrag *m* fish yield
Fischextrakt *m* fish extract

Fischfalle *f* fish trap
Fischfarm *m* fish-farm
Fischfauna *f* fish fauna
Fischfleisch *n* fish [meat]
Fischfuttermehl *n* fish-meal
Fischfütterung *f* fish feeding
Fischgemeinschaft *f* fish community
Fischgeschmack *m* fishiness *(e.g. of milk)*
Fischgewässer *n* fish water
Fischgiftpflanze *f* fish-poison plant, piscicidal plant
Fischgrätenmelkstand *m* herring-bone milking parlour
Fischguano *m* fish guano
Fischhoden *m* milt *(esp. during the spawning season)*
fischig fishy
Fischigkeit *f* fishiness *(e.g. of milk)*
Fischkrankheit *f* fish disease
Fischkraut *n* opposite-leaved pondweed, frog's lettuce, Groenlandia densa
Fischkultur *f* fish culture
Fischkunde *f* ichthyology
Fischkundler *m* ichthyologist
Fischlaich *m* [fish, hard] roe, spawn
Fischlarve *f* alevin
Fischleber *f* fish liver
Fischmehl *n* fish-meal; fish tankage *(as fertilizer)*
Fischmehlkrankheit *f (vet)* parakeratosis, swine dermatosis *(due to zinc deficiency)*
Fischmilch *f* soft roe, milt, semen, seed
Fischnetz *n* [fishing] net, fish-net
Fischöl *n* fish oil
Fischotter *m* common otter, Lutra lutra
Fischpaß *m* fish-way, pass
~/treppenförmiger fish ladder
Fischpreßsaft *m* fish solubles *(feed)*
~/eingedickter condensed fish solubles
Fischpreßwasser *n* fish solubles *(feed)*
Fischproteinhydrolysat *n* fish protein hydrolysate
Fischproteinkonzentrat *n* fish protein concentrate, FPC
Fischreiher *m* [common] heron, Ardea cinerea
Fischreuse *f* fish trap, creel
Fischrogen *m s.* Fischlaich
Fischschuppe *f* [fish] scale
Fischschuppenkrankheit *f (vet)* hyperkeratosis
Fischschwanzpalme *f* fish-tail palm, Indian (bastard) sago palm *(genus Caryota)*
Fischsilage *f* fish silage
Fischsterben *n (ecol)* fish kill (mortality)
Fischteich *m* fish pond (pool), piscina
~/kleiner stew
fischtoxisch piscicidal
Fischtoxizität *f* fish toxicity
Fischverarbeitung *f* fish processing
Fischwasser *n* fish water
Fischwirt *m* fish farmer (breeder), fish-culturist
Fischwirtschaft *f* pisciculture, fisheries management

fischwirtschaftlich piscicultural
Fischzucht f fish farming (breeding, culture), pisciculture
Fischzüchter m fish breeder, pisciculturist
Fisettholz n s. Färbersumach
Fisole f garden (common, French) bean, Phaseolus vulgaris
Fission f fission
fissipar fissiparous
Fistel f (vet) fistula • **eine ~ anlegen** to fistulate
• **eine ~ bilden** to fistulate
fistelig fistulous, fistular
fisteln to fistulate
fistelnd fistulous, fistular
Fitness f fitness (animal breeding)
Fixation f 1. fixation, immobilization (e.g. of fractures); 2. s. Fixierung
Fixationstisch m veterinary treatment table
fixieren to fix
Fixierung f fixation
~ von Luftstickstoff/bakterielle azofication
Fixierungsmittel n fixative
Fjordpferd n fjord (horse breed)
FK s. Feldwasserkapazität
Flachästigkeit f (phyt) branch flattening
~ des Apfels [apple] flat limb (virosis)
Flachbandförderer m flat-belt conveyor
Flachbatterie f flat deck battery
Flachbeet n flat bed
Flachbetttrockner m shallow bed dryer
flachblättrig (bot) planifolious
Flachbodenbearbeitung f surface (shallow) tillage, shallow cultivation
Flachbrause f flat rose (of a watering can)
Fläche f 1. area; 2. flat, plain; 3. face; surface
~/abgeholzte (abgetriebene) cleared (clearfelled) area
~/angeschliffene flat
~/bebaute s. ~/bestellte
~/bepflanzte planted area
~/beschirmte (forest) area under canopy
~/bestellte crop area; planted area
~/bestockte (forest) overgrowth
~/direkt einsehbare directly visible area, seen area (forest fire control)
~/eingezäunte (gegatterte) exclosure
~ in Acre acreage
~/indirekt einsehbare indirectly visible area (forest fire control)
~/landwirtschaftlich genutzte farm land
~/unvollkommen bestockte (forest) poorly stocked area
Flächenbehandlung f broadcast treatment (e.g. with fertilizers)
Flächenbuch n (forest) area register
Flächeneinheit f unit area
Flächenerosion f (soil) surface (sheet) erosion
Flächenfachwerk n (forest) yield regulation (rotation) by area, periodic method by area, equal-area regulation system

Flächenfachwerkmethode f (forest) periodic area allotment method, method of allotting woods by area
Flächenhiebssatz m/**jährlicher** (forest) annual yield (possibility) by area
Flächenkühler m (dairy) surface cooler
Flächenleistung f area capacity, output per unit area, rate of work[ing] (of field-working machinery)
Flächennutzungssatz m (forest) annual yield (possibility) by area
Flächenproduktivität f output per unit area
Flächenräumung f (forest) ground clearing (clearance)
Flächenregister n, **Flächentabelle** f (forest) area register
Flächentrockner m platform dryer, kiln
Flächenverzeichnis n s. Flächenregister
Flachfolientunnel m low tunnel
flachgliedrig flat-jointed (cactus)
Flachgurt m flat belt
Flachhuf m flat hoof (foot)
Flachkäfig m flat-deck cage
Flachkäfigbatterie f flat-deck battery
Flachkäfigstall m flat deck
Flachkorb m flat
Flachkrone f flattened head
flachkronig broad-crowned (tree)
Flachlagerung f shallow storage (e.g. of potatoes)
Flachland n lowland, flat (plain) country
Flachmoor n low[land] moor, flat (low-level) bog
Flachmoortorf m low-moor peat, basin peat
Flachpalette f seedling tray, flat
Flachpflug m shim
Flachpolsterpflanze f flat cushion plant
Flachrennen n flat race (equestrian sport)
Flachrennsaison f flat
Flachriemen m flat belt
Flachriemenscheibe f pulley
Flachriementrieb m flat-belt drive
Flachs m flax, Linum usitatissimum
Flachsanbau m flax growing
Flachsaufstellmaschine f flax stooker
Flachsbinder m flax binder
Flachsdotter m false flax, gold of pleasure, Camelina sativa
Flachsee m shallow lake
Flachsegreniermaschine f, **Flachsentsamungsmaschine** f flax deseeder
Flachserdfloh m flax flea-beetle, Aphthona euphorbiae
Flachsernte f flax harvest[ing]
Flachserntemaschine f, **Flachsernter** m flax harvester
Flachsfaser f flax (linen) fibre, flax, harl[e]
Flachshechel f flax comb, hackle, hatchel
Flachshechelgerät n flax comber, flax-hackling machine
Flachshocke f flax stack

Flachsiebmaschine

Flachsiebmaschine *f* flat-sieve seed cleaner
Flachsilo *m* bunker (clamp) silo
Flachsmüdigkeit *f s.* Flachswelke
Flachsnäher *m* flax sewer
Flachsproß *m (bot)* cladode, cladophyll
Flachsraufmaschine *f* flax puller (lifter)
Flachsriffelmaschine *f*, **Flachsriffler** *m* flax ripper
Flachsrost *m* flax rust *(caused by Melampsora lini)*
Flachsröste *f* 1. retting; 2. *s.* Flachsrösterei
Flachsrösterei *f* rettery
Flachssamen *m* linseed
Flachsseide *f* flax dodder, Cuscuta epilinum
Flachsstroh *n* flax straw
flachstellen to bend [down], to incline *(fruit-trees)*
Flachstrahlberegnung *f* flat-spray irrigation
Flachstrahldüse *f* flat[-pattern] spray nozzle, slot nozzle
Flachstrahlregner *m* flat-jet sprinkler
Flachstreu *f* shallow litter
Flachswelke *f* flax wilt, fusarium wilt of flax *(caused by Fusarium lini)*
Flachswender *m* flax turner
Flachtunnel *m s.* Flachfolientunnel
Flachwendepflug *m* light-duty plough
Flachwurzel *f* surface (horizontal) root
flachwurzelnd shallow-rooted
Flachwurzelsystem *n* lateral root system
Flachwurzler *m* surface rooter; shallow-rooted tree
Fladenverteiler *m* cow-pat spreader
Fladenverteilschleppe *f* dung-spreading float (harrow)
Fladerzeichnung *f* quilted figure; bastard grain [of wood]
F-Lage *f* F-layer *(of the humus profile)*
Flagellat *m* flagellate *(class Flagellata)*
Flagellose *f (vet)* flagellosis
Flagellum *n* flagellum
Flaggenbaum *m* flag-shaped tree
flaggenförmig flag-shaped *(e.g. a tree-crown)*
Flamingoblume *f* tail-flower, anthurium *(genus Anthurium)*
Flämische Rasse *f* Flemish *(cattle breed)*
Flämischer Ziehhund *m* matin *(dog breed)*
Flämisches Rind *n* Flemish *(cattle breed)*
Flammbirke *f* flamy birch
Flämmen *n (forest)* prescribed burning
Flammenblume *f (bot)* 1. phlox *(genus Phlox)*; 2. annual (Drummond) phlox, Phlox drummondii
Flammendes Käthchen *n (bot)* flaming Katy, Kalanchoe blossfeldiana
Flammenphotometer *n* flame photometer
Flammenphotometrie *f* flame photometry
Flammenspritzgerät *n*, **Flammenwerfer** *m* flamethrower, flame (fire) gun *(e.g. for controlling weeds)*; *(forest)* backfire torch
Flammrohr *n* flue
Flammrohrkessel *m* flue (fire tube) boiler
Flammschutzmittel *n* fire retardant, fire-proofing agent

Flamprop-ethyl *n* flamprop-ethyl *(herbicide)*
Flamprop-isopropyl *n* flamprop-isopropyl *(herbicide)*
Flamprop-methyl *n* flamprop-methyl *(herbicide)*
Flanke *f* flank, side
Flankenfeuer *n (forest)* flank fire
Flankierbaum *m* bail *(stable installation)*
Flaschenabfüllanlage *f* bottling plant
Flaschenabfüllmaschine *f* bottling machine
Flaschenabfüllung *f* bottling, bottle filling
Flaschenbier *n* bottled beer
Flaschenbürstengras *n* bottle-brush grass, Hystrix patula, Asperella hystrix
Flaschenfütterung *f* bottle feeding *(of suckers)*
Flaschengärverfahren fermentation in the bottle *(sparkling wine production)*
Flaschengestell *n* bottle rack
Flaschenkork *m* cork [stopper]
Flaschenkürbis *m* [bottle] gourd, calabash, Lagenaria siceraria
Flaschenlager *n* bottle rack
Flaschenmilch *f* bottled milk
Flaschenpfropfung *f* bottle-grafting
Flaschenspülmaschine *f* bottle rinsing machine
Flaschenverkorkmaschine *f* bottle corker, [bottle] corking machine
Flaschenwaschmaschine *f* bottle washer
Flaschenwein *m* bottle[d] wine, bottling
Flaschenzug *m* pulley, hoist
Flat Coated Retriever *m* flat-coated retriever *(dog breed)*
Flat-Deck-Käfig *m* flat-deck cage
Flatterbinse *f* soft (common) rush, Juncus effusus
Flattergras *n* millet-grass, wood millet[-grass], Milium effusum
Flattertrespe *f* Japanese brome[-grass], Bromus japonicus
Flatterulme *f* European white elm, Ulmus laevis
Flatus *m* flatus
Flaum *m (bot, zoo)* fluff, down, pile, pubescence
flaumbildend *(bot)* pubigerous
Flaumeiche *f* downy oak, Quercus pubescens
Flaumfeder *f* down feather, plumule [feather]
Flaumhaar *n* fluff, pile; fur hair *(of mammals)*
flaumhaarig fluffy, downy
Flaumhafer *m* downy oat-grass, hairy oat, Avenula (Helictotrichon) pubescens
flaumig fluffy, pubescent, downy
~/schwach *(bot)* puberulous, puberulent
Flaumlaus *f* fluff louse, Goniocotes gallinae (hologaster)
Flaumquecke *f* pubescent (stiff-hair) wheat-grass, Elymus hispidus barbulatus, Agropyron trichophorum
flaumtragend *(bot)* pubigerous
Flavanoid *n* flavonoid *(plant substance)*
Flavanol *n* flavanol *(plant substance)*
Flavin *n* flavin *(pigment)*

Flavinadenindinucleotid *n* flavin adenine dinucleotide, FAD
Flavinenzym *n* flavin enzyme, flavoprotein
Flavinmononucleotid *n* flavin mononucleotide, FMN
Flavinmononucleotidoxidoreductase *f* flavin mononucleotide oxireductase *(enzyme)*
Flavivirus *n* flavivirus
Flavobakterium *n* flavobacterium
Flavomycin *n* bambermycin *(antibiotic)*
Flavon *n* flavon[e] *(pigment)*
Flavonoid *n* flavonoid *(plant substance)*
Flavonol *n* flavonol *(pigment)*
Flavoprotein *n s.* Flavinenzym
Flavour *n* flavour
Flechse *f s.* Sehne
Flechte *f* 1. *(bot)* lichen *(group Lichenes)*; 2. *(vet)* lichen, eczema
~/farbstoffliefernde orchil[la], archil *(esp. of genera Roccella and Lecanora)*
~/nässende *(vet)* moist eczema (scall)
flechten to braid *(a mane or horse-tail)*
flechtenartig lichenous
Flechtendecke *f* lichen cover
Flechtenheide *f* lichen heath
Flechten-Kiefernwald *m* lichen pine forest
Flechtentundra *f* lichen tundra
Flechtgewebe *n (bot)* plectenchyma
Flechtstraußgras *n* creeping bent[-grass], marsh bent[-grass], carpet bent[-grass], water-grass, Agrostis stolonifera (palustris)
Fleck *m* 1. blotch, blur, fleck, spot, stain; macula *(esp. in skin)*; 2. plot *(of land)*
~/kleiner speck[le]
flecken *s.* fleckentrinden
Fleckenbildung *f (phyt)* spotting, flecking, dappling
Fleckenfäule *f* mottled (marble) rot *(of wood)*
Fleckenkrankheit *f (phyt)* blotch[ing]
fleckentrinden to patch-bark, to scorch, *(Am)* to spot-bark
fleckig blotched, variegated; pitted • ~ **werden** to stain
Fleckige Hainblume *f (bot)* five-spot, Nemophila maculata
Fleckschierling *m* [poison] hemlock, Conium maculatum
Flecksucht *f* pebrine [disease of silkworms] *(caused by Nosema bombycis)*
Fleckung *f (phyt)* spottiness, flecking, freckling, blot[ching], mottling, mottle, rash, dappling
Fleckvieh *n* 1. German Simment[h]al, Red Spotted Highland *(cattle breed)*; 2. Simmental *(cattle breed)*
Fledermaustollwut *f* vampire bat rabies
Fleisch *n* 1. flesh; 2. meat; 3. *s.* Fruchtfleisch
~ **des Wildes** game [meat]
~ **eines abortierten Kalbes** slink
~/exsudatives exudative meat

~/[kalt]geräuchertes smoke meat
~/mageres lean
fleischartig fleshy, carneous
Fleischaufbereitungsanlage *f* meat [processing] plant
Fleischausbeute *f* meat yield
Fleischbeschau *f* meat inspection
Fleischbeschauer *m* [official] meat inspector
Fleischbeschaugesetz *n* meat inspection law
Fleischbeschaurecht *n* meat inspection law
Fleischbildungsvermögen *n* fleshing ability
Fleischbräune *f* brown core, flesh browning, [low-temperature] breakdown *(of stored fruits)*
Fleischdüngemehl *n* animal tankage
Fleischeiweiß *n* meat protein
Fleischerei *f* butchery
Fleischersatz[stoff] *m* meat substitute
Fleischertrag *m* meat yield
Fleischerzeugnis *n* meat product
Fleischextrakt *m* meat extract
~/Liebigs beef extract
Fleischfarbe *f* meat colour
fleischfarben meat-coloured
Fleischfaser *f* meat fibre
Fleischfläche *f* **im Kotelettanschnitt** loin eye area
Fleischfleck *m* meat spot *(in hen's egg)*
Fleischfleckenei *n* meat-spotted egg
Fleischfliege *f* 1. flesh-fly *(family Sarcophagidae)*; 2. flesh-fly *(genus Sarcophaga)*; 3. blowfly, greenbottle, meat-fly, Sarcophaga (Musca) carnaria
fleischfressend flesh-eating, meat-eating, carnivorous
Fleischfresser *m* flesh-eater, carnivore
Fleischfülle *f* meatiness
Fleischfuttermehl *n* meat meal
Fleischgefrierung *f* meat freezing
Fleischgeruch *m* meat odour
Fleischgeschwulst *f (vet)* sarcoma
Fleischhandel *m* meat trade
Fleischhygiene *f* meat hygiene
fleischig 1. fleshy, meaty, carneous; beefy; 2. pulpy, pulpous; succulent
Fleischigkeit *f* meatiness; beefiness
Fleischindustrie *f* meat industry
Fleischkalb *n* veal calf
Fleischkaninchen *n* meat rabbit
Fleisch-Knochen-Verhältnis *n* meat-bone ratio
Fleischkonserve *f* canned (preserved) meat, tin of meat
Fleischkonservierung *f* meat packing
Fleischkonservierungsnebenprodukt *n* meat packing by-product
Fleischkuh *f* beef cow
Fleischlauch *m* perennial welsh onion, Allium cirrhosum (montanum)
fleischliefernd meat-yielding
Fleischmast *f* meat fattening
Fleischmehl *n* meat meal (flour), animal tankage

Fleischnebenprodukt

Fleischnebenprodukt *n* meat by-product
Fleisch-Pepton-Agar *m* meat-and-peptone agar
Fleischpferd *n* meat horse
Fleischprodukt *n* meat product
Fleischproduktion *f* meat production
Fleischprotein *n* meat protein
Fleischqualitätsmerkmal *n* meat quality characteristic
Fleischrasse *f* meat breed
Fleischreifung *f* meat maturing
Fleischrind *n* beef ox
Fleischrindbulle *m* beef bull (sire)
Fleischrinderrasse *f* beef[-type] breed
Fleischrindfärse *f* beef heifer
Fleischrindochse *m* beef steer
Fleischrindvieh *n* beef (black) cattle
Fleischrippe *f* floating rib *(animal anatomy)*
Fleischschaf *n* mutton sheep
Fleischschafbock *m* mutton-type ram
Fleischschafrasse *f* mutton breed
Fleischschwein *n* meat-type hog, pork[-type] pig, porker, lean-type swine
~/leichtes light porker *(55 to 65 kg live weight)*
Fleischschweinrasse *f* pork breed
Fleisch-Shorthorn[rind] *n* beef shorthorn [cattle] *(breed)*
Fleischtechnologie *f* meat technology
Fleischteilstück *n* meat cut
~/knochenreiches scrag
Fleischtier *n* meat animal
Fleischtomate *f* flesh[y] tomato
Fleischtyp *m* meat type *(of livestock)*
Fleisch- und Knochenmehl *n* meat and bone meal, tankage
Fleischuntersucher *m* meat inspector
Fleischuntersuchung *f* meat inspection
Fleischuntersuchungsanordnung *f* meat inspection law
Fleischverarbeitung *f* meat processing
Fleischverarbeitungsanlage *f* meat [processing] plant
Fleischverwertungsindustrie *f* meat processing industry
Fleischvieh *n* beef (black) cattle
Fleischwärzchen *n*, **Fleischwarze** *f* caruncle
Fleischwasser *n* meat water
Fleischwolf *m* mincer, meat grinder
Fleischzapfen *m* snood *(fleshy projection at forehead of turkeys)*
Fleischzerlegung *f* meat cutting
Fleischzusammensetzung *f* meat composition
Fleißiges Lieschen *n* patience plant, busy Lizzie, Impatiens wallerana
Flexor *m* flexor [muscle]
Flieder *m* 1. lilac *(genus Syringa)*; 2. [common] lilac, pipe tree, Syringa vulgaris
Fliedermotte *f (ent)* lilac leaf-miner, Gracilaria (Xanthospilapterix) syringella

Fliederprimel *f* annual (fairy) primrose, Primula malacoides
Fliederringscheckungsvirus *n* lilac ring mottle virus, LRMV
Fliederseuche *f* lilac blight, bacterial blight of syringa (forsythia) *(caused by Pseudomonas syringae)*
Fliege *f* fly *(suborder Brachycera)*
Fliegenbekämpfung *f* fly control
Fliegenbekämpfungsmittel *n* antifly preparation, fly poison
Fliegenblume *f (bot)* caralluma *(genus Caralluma)*
Fliegenkraut *n* mugwort, motherwort, Artemisia vulgaris
Fliegenlarve *f* [fly] maggot, grub
Fliegenlarvenbefall *m (vet)* fly-strike, myiasis
Fliegennetz *n* fly-net
Fliegenpilz *m* fly (deadly) agaric, fly toadstool (amanita), scarlet flycap, Amanita muscaria
Fliegenschmutzfleckenkrankheit *f* fly speck *(of apple, caused by Schizothyrium pomi)*
Flieger *m* flyer, flier *(horse-racing)*
Fliehkraftabscheider *m* centrifugal separator, cyclone
Fliehkraftregler *m* centrifugal governor
Fließbettgranulierung *f* fluid-bed granulation *(e.g. of fertilizers)*
Fließbetttrockner *m* fluid[ized]-bed dryer
Fließei *n* soft-shelled egg, shell-less egg, wind-egg, mole
Fließernte *f* continuous harvesting
fließfähig flowable
Fließfähigkeit *f* flowability *(e.g. of fertilizers)*
Fließförderer *m* conveyor
Fließgewässer *n* running water
Fließgleichgewicht *n* steady state
Fließgrenze *f (soil)* liquid (upper plastic) limit
Fließgrenzen *fpl* **nach Atterberg** *(soil)* Atterberg limits
Fließkanal *m (pisc)* raceway
Fließlawine *f* flowing avalanche
Fließrinnenkultur *f* flow-channel culture *(gardening)*
Fließschicht *f* active layer *(in a permafrost soil)*
Fließvermögen *n* flowability *(e.g. of fertilizers)*
Fließwasser *n* flowing water
Flinte *f* smooth-bore, gun
Flissigkeit *f (phyt)* silver-top[s]
Flocke *f* 1. floccule, flock *(esp. of wool)*; flake; 2. small star *(marking esp. at horse's forehead)*
Flockenblume *f* 1. knapweed, cropweed, hardhead, centaurea *(genus Centaurea)*; 2. sweet sultan, Centaurea imperialis
Flockenflachs *m* cottonized flax
flockig *(bot)* floccose; flaky
Flockung *f* flocculation
Flockungsmittel *n* flocculant
Floh *m* flea *(order Siphonaptera)*
Flohkäfer *m* flea-beetle, *(Am)* flea-bug *(subfamily Halticinae)*

Flohknöterich *m* peachwort, redshank, common persicaria, *(Am)* Lady's-thumb, Polygonum persicaria
Flohkraut *n s.* Flohknöterich
Flohwegerich *m* flea-wort, Plantago afra (psyllium)
Flom[en] *m* leaf [fat] *(of pig)*
Flor *m* flowerage, flush (abundance) of flowers
Flora *f* flora
Florenatlas *m* floral atlas
Florenbereich *m (ecol)* floristic kingdom
Florenkunde *f* floristics, floristry
Florenkundler *m* florist
Florenverarmung *f* depletion of floral diversity
Floreszenz *f* florescence, flowering *(for compounds s. under* Blühen*)*
Florfliege *f* 1. lacewing [fly] *(family Chrysopidae)*; 2. lacewing [fly], green lacewing, Chrysop[erl]a carnea
Floribundarose *f* floribunda [rose]
Floridaklee *m* Florida clover, beggarweed, Desmodium tortuosum
florieren to flourish
Florigen *n* florigen, flowering hormone
florikol floricolous *(living on blossoms)*
Florist *m* florist
Floristik *f* floristics, floristry
floristisch floristic
florivor florivorous *(feeding on flowers, esp. said of insects)*
Floß *n* raft, float; *(Am)* crib
flößbar floatable
Floßbindemaschine *f* bundle binder, bundling installation
Floßbindestätte *f* raft-construction point
Floßbrücke *f* raft bridge
Flosse *f* fin
flößen to float, to raft, to drive, *(Am)* to crib [logs]
~/loses Holz to drift, to drive
Flossenfäule *f (vet)* fin rot
Flossenstrahl *m* fin-ray
Flößer *m* rafter, raftsman, boom man (worker); wood (timber) floater, floating operator, river driver
Flößerei *f* [timber] rafting, wood (timber) floating, log driving
Flößereiarbeiter *m s.* Flößer
Flößereirecht *n* rafting (floating) right
Flößereistange *f* floating hook, pike pole, clip
Flößereistatut *n* floating (driving) regulation
Floßgasse *f* **im Wehr** dam sluiceway for rafts
Floßhaken *m s.* Flößereistange
Floßholz *n* raftwood, rafted wood, floated timber
Floßlände *f s.* Floßplatz
Flößordnung *f s.* Flößereistatut
Floßplatz *m* floating (water transport) depot
Floßrechen *m* [trap] boom
Flößrecht *n* rafting (floating) right
Floßreede *f s.* Floßplatz
Floßsektion *f* brail, *(Am)* crib

Flößung *f* **in Einzelstämmen** loose floating, drifting
Flotation *f* flo[a]tation
Flotzmaul *n* muzzle
Floury-2-Mais *m* floury-2 maize *(mutant)*
Floxapen *n* flucloxacillin *(antibiotic)*
Fluazifop *n* fluazifop *(herbicide)*
Flubendazol *n* flubendazole *(anthelminthic, fungicide)*
Fluchloralin *n* fluchloralin *(herbicide)*
flüchtig 1. volatile; 2. fleeing *(game)*
Flüchtigkeit *f* volatility
Flucloxacillin *n* flucloxacillin *(antibiotic)*
Flucythrinat *n* flucythrinate *(insecticide)*
Flugaktivität *f (ent)* flight activity
Flugasche *f* fly ash
flugbar *s.* flügge
Flugbiene *f* flying [honey-]bee, harvesting (foraging, field) bee, forager
Flugbrand *m (phyt)* loose (common) smut
Flugbrett[chen] *n (api)* alighting (flight) board
Flügel *m* 1. *(bot, zoo)* wing, ala; 2. blade, vane *(e.g. of an agitator)* • **zum ~ gehörend** alar
Flügeladerung *f (ent)* [wing] venation, nervation
flügelartig wing-like, alar[y]
Flügelast *m* splay (spike) knot, horn (slash) knot
Flügeldecke *f (ent)* wing case (sheath), elytron, elytrum, shard
Flügelfeder *f* pen-feather, flag[-feather]
flügelförmig wing-shaped, aliform
Flügelfrucht *f (bot)* key (winged) fruit, key, samara
Flügelgeäder *n s.* Flügeladerung
Flügellaus *f* **der Taube** slender pigeon louse, Columbicola columbae [columbae]
~ des Huhnes depluming (wing) louse, Lipeurus caponis
Flügelleiste *f* wing bar *(animal anatomy)*
flügellos *(bot, zoo)* wingless, apterous
Flügelmarke *f* wing tag
Flügelmauer *f* wing wall *(erosion control)*
Flügelnuß *f* wing-nut *(genus Pterocarya)*
Flügelpumpe *f* vane pump
Flügelsamen *m* winged seed
flügelsamig *(bot)* pterospermous
Flügelschar *n* wing share
Flügelschuppe *f (zoo)* scale
Flügelschwimmer *m* fin boom *(rafting)*
Flügelsech *n* wing coulter
Flügelspannhaut *f* wing web
Flügelspannweite *f* wing span (spread, expanse)
Flügelzeichnung *f* wing marking
Flugente *f* flying duck, Cairina moschata
Flugestonacetat *n* flugestone, fluorogestone acetate *(sex hormone)*
Flugfeder *f* flight (primary) feather, quill[-feather], flag[-feather]
~/abgenutzte fray feather
flügge [full-]fledged • **~ werden** to fledge
~/noch nicht unfledged, callow

flügge

~/seit kurzem new-fledged
Flughafer m [common] wild oat[s], oat-grass, Avena fatua
Fluginsekt n flying (winged) insect *(group Pterygota)*
Flugloch n *(ent)* flight hole, exit (emergence) hole; hive entrance
Fluglochklappe f hive entrance closing device
Fluglochschieber m *(api)* adjustable entrance
Flugsand m drift (shifting) sand, blowing (travelling) sand, quicksand
Flugsandbefestigung f, **Flugsandbindung** f fixation of shifting sands
Flugsanddüne f travelling (mobile) dune
Flugschopf m *(bot)* pappus • **mit einem ~ versehen** pappose, pappous
Flugstaub m fly (airborne) dust
Flugstunde f flying hour *(agricultural aviation)*
Flugtransport m air transport[ation]
Flugweite f distance of dissemination *(e.g. of seeds)*
Flugwild n wildfowl, feathered game, wing[ed] game, game-birds • **~ jagen** to fowl, to grass
Flugwildjagd f wildfowling
Flugzeit f *(ent)* flight time, emergence period
Flugzeugausbringung f aeroplane (aircraft) application *(e.g. of pesticides)*
Flugzeugaussaat f aerial seeding, aerosowing, air-sowing
Flugzeugsprühgerät n aerial sprayer, aviasprayer
Flugzeugverstäubungsgerät n aeroduster, aviaduster
fluid fluid
Fluktuation f fluctuation
Flumetason n flumethasone *(antiphlogistic agent)*
Fluometuron n fluometuron *(herbicide)*
Fluor n fluorine
Fluorapatit m fluorapatite, phosphate of lime *(non-clay mineral)*
Fluorescein n fluorescein, resorcinolphthalein *(dye)*
Fluoresceinisothiocyanat n fluorescein isothiocyanate *(dye)*
Fluoressigsäure f fluoroacetic acid
Fluoreszenz f fluoroscence
Fluoreszenzanalyse f fluorescence analysis
Fluoreszenzantikörpertest m fluorescent antibody technique
Fluoreszenzemissionsspektroskopie f fluorescence emission spectroscopy
Fluoreszenzfarbstoff m fluorescent dye
Fluoreszenzfärbung f fluorescence staining
Fluoreszenzmikroskop n fluorescence microscope
Fluoreszenzmikroskopie f fluorescence microscopy
Fluoreszenzphotometrie f s. Fluorimetrie
Fluoreszenztest m fluorescent antibody technique
fluoreszierend fluorescent

Fluorhektorit m fluorhectorite *(clay mineral)*
Fluorid n fluoride
Fluorimetrie f s. Fluorometrie
Fluorochrom n fluorescent dye
Fluorodifen n fluorodifen *(herbicide)*
Fluorometrie f fluorometry, fluorimetry
Fluoronitrofen n fluoronitrofen *(herbicide)*
Fluorose f, **Fluorvergiftung** f *(vet)* fluorosis
Fluorwasserstoffsäure f hydrofluoric acid
Fluothiuron n fluothiuron, thiochlormethyl *(herbicide)*
Flutrimazol n flutrimazole *(fungicide)*
Fluprostenol n fluprostenol *(prostaglandin analogue)*
Flur f field[s]
Fluraufnahme f land survey
Flurbereinigung f field clearing, land consolidation, consolidation of arable land
Flurbuch n [land] cadaster, cadastre, terrier
Flurenol n flurenol, flurecol[-butyl] *(herbicide)*
Flurholz n hedgerow trees
Flurholzanbau m extension forestry, timber growing outside the forest
Fluridon n fluridone *(herbicide)*
Flurkarte f field (cadastral) map
Flurmelioration f land amelioration
Flurneuordnung f reallotment (reparcelling) of land
Fluromidin n fluromidine *(herbicide)*
Flurschaden m damage to crops
Flurstück n plot, lot, parcel
Flushing-Ernährung f flushing *(animal nutrition)*
Fluß m 1. river; 2. flux
Flußaal m eel, Anguilla anguilla
Flußablagerungsboden m fluviogenic soil
Flußampfer m great water dock, Rumex hydrolapathum
Flußanstau m river damming
Flußausbau m river regulation (training)
Flußbarbe f barbel, barb, Barbus barbus
Flußbarsch m [common, river] perch, bass, Perca fluviatilis
flußbedingt fluvial, fluviatile
flußbegleitend riverain
Flüßchen n rivulet, brook, *(Am)* creek
Flußdelta n delta
Flußfisch m river (stream) fish
Flußfischerei f river fishery
flüssig liquid
Flüssigaussaat f fluid drilling, liquid seed application
Flüssigbeizmittel n liquid dressing
Flüssigbettverbrennung f fluidized-bed combustion
Flüssigchromatographie f liquid chromatography
Flüssigdrillen n s. Flüssigaussaat
Flüssigdrillmaschine f fluid drill
Flüssigdung m liquid manure, slurry
Flüssigdüngemittel n s. Flüssigdünger

Flüssigdünger *m* liquid (fluid) fertilizer; liquid manure
~/tierischer animal (livestock waste) slurry
Flüssigdüngerinjektor *m* liquid fertilizer (manure) injector
Flüssigdüngung *f* liquid fertilization
Flüssigdüngungsanlage *f* liquid fertilization system
Flüssigerdgas *n* liquid petroleum gas
Flüssig-fest-Chromatographie *f* liquid-solid chromatography
Flüssig-flüssig-Chromatographie *f* liquid-liquid chromatography
Flüssigfutter *n* liquid feed
Flüssigfütterung *f* liquid feeding
Flüssigfütterungsanlage *f* liquid feed installation
Flüssigfutterverteiler *m* liquid feed dispenser
Flüssiggas *n* liquefied gas
Flüssiggasdüngegerät *n* liquid fertilizer distributor; [anhydrous] ammonia applicator
Flüssiggutcontainer *m* tank container
Flüssigkeit *f* liquid; liquor
~/gefilterte filtrate
~/Newtonsche Newtonian liquid
~/nicht-Newtonsche non-Newtonian liquid
Flüssigkeitsaufnahme *f einer Zelle* pinocytosis
Flüssigkeitsbehälter *m* tank [container]; cistern
Flüssigkeitschromatographie *f* liquid chromatography
Flüssigkeitskühlung *f* liquid cooling
Flüssigkeitskultur *f* liquid culture *(microbiology)*
Flüssigkeitsmeßstab *m* dip-stick
Flüssigkompostierung *f* liquid composting
Flüssigkultur *f* liquid culture *(microbiology)*
Flüssigmist *m* liquid manure, slurry
Flüssigmistabscheider *m* slurry separator
Flüssigration *f* liquid diet *(animal nutrition)*
Flüssigsämaschine *f* fluid seeding machine
Flüssigzucker *m* liquid sugar
Flußkanalisierung *f s.* Flußregulierung
Flußmergel *m* river clay
Flußmorphologie *f* river morphology
Flußmündung *f* river mouth, outfall
~/der Gezeitenwirkung ausgesetzte estuary
Flußniederung *f* river basin (valley)
Flußregulierung *f* river regulation (training)
Flußsäure *f* hydrofluoric acid
Flußschleife *f*, **Flußschlinge** *f s.* Flußwindung
Flußsediment *n* stream sediment
Flußtal *n* riverside, river basin (valley)
~/breites strath
Flußterrasse *f* flood-plain terrace
Flußufer *n* bank [of river], riverbank, riverside
~/abfallendes bank [of river], riverbank
Flußuferwald *m* riverbank forest
Flußverbauung *f* river damming
Flußversalzung *f* stream salinity
Flußverschmutzung *f*, **Flußverunreinigung** *f* river pollution

Flußwasser *n* river water
Flußwiese *f* water-meadow
Flußwindung *f* meander [of a river], ox-bow
Flußzeder *f* incense-cedar, Calocedrus (Libocedrus) decurrens
Flut *f* flood
Flutender Schwaden *m*, **Flutendes Mannagras** *n* [water] manna grass, floating [sweet] grass, Glyceria fluitans
Fluvalinat *n* fluvalinate *(insecticide)*
fluvial, fluviatil fluvial, fluviatile
fluvioglazial fluvio-glacial, glaciofluvial
Fluvisol *m* fluvisol, marsh soil
Flux[us] *m* flux
FLV *s.* Felines Panleukopenievirus
fm *s.* Festmeter
FMN *s.* Flavinmononucleotid
FNV *s.* Festuca-Nekrosevirus
fohlen to foal [down]
Fohlen *n* foal
~/abgesetztes weaned (grass) foal
Fohlenfell *n* foalskin
Fohlenkrankheit *f* foal disease
Fohlenlähme *f* joint ill
Fohlenrosse *f* foal (nine-day) heat
Föhn *m* foehn, föhn *(a warm descending wind)*
Föhre *f* 1. pine *(genus Pinus)*; 2. common pine, Scotch pine (fir), Pinus sylvestris
Föhren... *s. a.* Kiefern...
Föhreneule *f (ent)* pine noctuid (beauty), Panolis flammea
Föhrenholz *n* red (yellow) deal, redwood *(from Pinus sylvestris)*
Föhrenmistel *f* mistletoe, Viscum album ssp. austriacum
Föhrenschütte *f* pine needle cast, fir leaf cast *(caused by Lophodermium pinastri)*
Föhrenwald *m* pine forest, pinewood, pinery
Fokalinfektion *f* focal infection
Foley-Katheter *m (vet)* indwelling catheter
Folgeeinrichtung *f (forest)* second inventory
Folgeerscheinung *f* sequela *(e.g. of a disease)*
Folgefrucht *f* follower (succeeding, successive) crop
Folgekultur *f s.* Folgefrucht
folgen/einer Witterung to road *(hunting dog)*
Folie *f* 1. [plastic] film; 2. foil *(thin sheet of metal)*
~/bedampfte vapour-plated [plastic] film
~/dünne film
~/durch Licht abbauare photodegradable film
~/langlebige long-life film
~/UV-stabilisierte ultraviolet (UV) film
~/verstärkte reinforced [plastic] film
Folienabdeckung *f* vinyl covering
Folienbeutel *m* film (plastic) bag, poly[ethylene] bag
Foliengewächshaus *n* polyethylene greenhouse, plastic [film] greenhouse, film-greenhouse
Folienhaube *f* plastic cloche *(for covering plantlets)*

Folienlegegerät 218

Folienlegegerät *n* plastic film (mulch) layer
Folienlege-Pflanzmaschine *f* mulcher-transplanter
Folienmulch *m* polyethylene (plastic) mulch
Folienmulchgeräte *npl* plastic mulch machinery
Folienringkultur *f* ring culture *(vegetable growing)*
Folienschlauch *m* plastic tube
~/**luftgefüllter** air-inflated plastic tube *(greenhouse installation)*
Folienschlauchheizung *f* plastic tube heating [system]
Foliensilo *m* plastic[-sheeting] silo
Folientunnel *m* plastic tunnel (film cold frame)
~/**doppelwandiger** twin-skin tunnel
Folienzelt *n s.* Foliengewächshaus
Folinsäure *f* folinic acid, 5-formyltetrahydrofolic acid
Follikel *m* follicle
~/**Graafscher** Graafian follicle (vesicle), ovarian follicle
Follikelepithelzelle *f*/**ovariale** granulosa cell
Follikelflüssigkeit *f* follicular fluid
Follikelhormon *n* follicular hormone, oestrogen
Follikelreifungshormon *n* follicle-stimulating hormone, FSH
Follikelsprung *m* ovulation, ovulatory surge, follicle rupture • **ohne ~** anovulatory
Follikelzyste *f (vet)* follicular cyst
follikulär follicular
Follikulitis *f (vet)* folliculitis
Follitropin *n s.* Follikelreifungshormon
Folpet *n* folpet *(fungicide)*
Folsäure *f* folic (pteroglutamic) acid
Fomentation *f (vet)* fomentation
Fomesafen *n* fomesafen *(herbicide)*
Fonds *m*/**metabolischer** metabolic pool
Fonofos *n* fonofos *(insecticide)*
Förderanlage *f* conveying system
Förderband *n* conveyor (feed) belt, belt (band) conveyor, apron
Förderbandtrockner *m* band (apron) dryer
Förderer *m* conveyor; feeder
~/**pneumatischer** pneumatic (air) conveyor
Fördergebläse *n* blower, pneumatic conveyor
Fördergurt *m* belt
Fördergut *n* material being conveyed; material to be conveyed
Förderhöhe *f* lift
Förderkette *f* chain conveyor, conveyor chain • **in die ~ einhängen** *(slaught)* to shackle
Förderleistung *f* discharge, output
Fördermenge *f* discharge [rate]
Fördermittel *n* conveyor
Fördermittel *npl* handling machinery (equipment)
fördern 1. to convey; to haul, to transport; 2. to deliver, to discharge *(e.g. a pump)*; 3. to promote, to stimulate *(e.g. the growth)*
~/**aufwärts** to lift
~/**durch Luftstrom** to blow

~/**mittels Riesbahn** to chute *(timber)*
~/**mittels Schwemmrinne** to flume
Förderrinne *f* conveyor chute
Förderrohr *n* delivery tube
Förderrutsche *f* [conveyor] chute
Förderschnecke *f* conveyor screw, screw [conveyor], auger (helix) conveyor
Förderung *f* conveying; haulage, transport, handling
~/**pneumatische** pneumatic (air) conveying
Förderverlust *m* handling loss
Förderwerk *n* elevator
Forelle *f* trout *(genus Salmo)* • **Forellen fischen** to trout
Forellenaufzucht *f* trout rearing
Forellenbach *m* trout-stream
Forellenseuche *f* Egtved disease [of trouts]
Forellenzucht *f* trout breeding (culture)
Forestiere *f* swamp-privet, Forestiera acuminata
Forke *f* [pitch]fork, prong, graip
~/**dreizinkige** three-pronged fork
forkeln to butt *(to strike with the head or horns)*
Forle *f s.* Föhre
Form *f* shape, form; conformation *(livestock judging)*
Forma *f* form *(taxonomy)*
Formabweichung *f* deformity
Formaldehyd *m* formaldehyde
Formaldehyddehydrogenase *f* formaldehyde dehydrogenase *(enzyme)*
Formaldehydlösung *f s.* Formalin
Formalin *n* formalin *(disinfectant)*
Formamidase *f* formamidase *(enzyme)*
Formänderung *f* deformation
Formänderungsrest *m* unrecovered strain *(e.g. of wood)*; residual deformation
Formation *f* formation *(plant ecology)*
Formbarkeit *f* formability; plasticity
Formbaum *m* topiary
Formbildung *f* morphogenesis
~ **durch Licht** *(bot)* photomorphogenesis
Formelmethode *f (forest)* formula method
Formenmannigfaltigkeit *f*, **Formenvielfalt** *f* diversity of shape
Formetanat *n* formetanat *(acaricide)*
Formhöhe *f* form-height [quotient] *(timber mensuration)*
Formhöhenreihe *f* form-height curve
Formhöhentafel *f* form-height table
Formhöhentarif *m* form-height tariff
Formhöhenzuwachs *m* form-height increment
Formhöhenzuwachsprozent *n* form-height increment percent
Formiat *n* formate, formiate
Formiatdehydrogenase *f* formate dehydrogenase *(enzyme)*
Formiattetrahydrofolatligase *f* formate-tetrahydrofolate ligase, formyltetrahydrofolate synthetase *(enzyme)*

Formicarium *n* formicary, ant nest
formieren to form, to train; to prune *(e.g. fruit-trees)*
Formiminoglutamase *f* formiminoglutamase *(enzyme)*
Formiminoglutaminsäure *f* formiminoglutamic acid
Formindex *m* shape index *(of hen's egg)*
Formklasse *f* *(forest)* form class
Formlinie *f* form line *(terrestrial survey)*
Formobstbaum *m* espalier [fruit tree]
Formol *n* formalin *(disinfectant)*
Formoltitration *f* formol titration [method]
Formolvakzine *f* *(vet)* formalinized (formolated) vaccine
Formononetin *n* formononetin *(phytoestrogen)*
Formothion *n* formothion *(insecticide, acaricide)*
Formplatte *f* **für Jungpflanzen** cell tray, seed flat
~ für kleine Pflanztöpfe plug tray
Formquotient *m* form (girth) quotient, form ratio *(timber mensuration)*
~/absoluter absolute form quotient
~/echter true (normal) form quotient
~/unechter artificial form quotient
Formschnitt *m* [form] pruning, shearing, topiary
Formulierung *f* formulation *(e.g. of plant protectants)*
Formyltetrahydrofolatsynthetase *f* formate-tetrahydrofolate ligase *(enzyme)*
5-Formyltetrahydrofolsäure *f s.* Folinsäure
Formzahl *f* form factor (number) *(timber mensuration)*
~/absolute absolute form factor
~/echte normal form factor
~/unechte artificial form factor
Formzahltafel *f* form factor table
Formzuwachs *m* form increment (growth) *(timber mensuration)*
Formzuwachsprozent *n* form increment percent
Förna *f* [wood, forest] litter, litterfall
Förnahorizont *m* *(soil)* L-layer, Aoo-horizon
Fornix *m* vault *(animal anatomy)*
Forschung *f*/**forstwirtschaftliche** forestry research
~/landwirtschaftliche agricultural research
Forst *m* forest *(for compounds s. under* Wald*)*
Forst... *s. a.* Wald...
Forstakademie *f* forest academy, forestry college
Forstamt *n* forestry field office
Forstarbeit *f* forest labour
Forstarbeiter *mpl* forest[ry] worker, forester, lumberman, lumberjack
Forstassessor *m* junior (assistant) forester
Forstästhetik *f* forest aesthetics
Forstaufseher *m* forest warden (guard, overseer), *(Am)* forest ranger
Forstausbildung *f* forestry education
Forstbaumschule *f* forest[-tree] nursery
Forstbeamter *m* forest officer

~/höherer senior forest officer
~/leitender chief district officer
Forstbetrieb *m* forest enterprise, forestry operation
Forstbetriebsfläche *f* productive forest area
Forstbetriebsgemeinschaft *f* forestry partnership
Forstbetriebskarte *f* forest management map
Forstbezirk *m* forest ranger district
Forstbodenmeißel *m* forestry subsoiler
Forstbodenmelioration *f* amelioration of forest sites
Forstbotanik *f* forest botany
Forstbüro *n* forest office (agency)
Forstdelikt *n s.* Forstfrevel
Forstdünger *m* forest fertilizer
Forsteinrichter *m* forest manager, working plan officer, cruiser
~/leitender working plan conservator
Forsteinrichtung *f* forest management [planning], forest regulation
Forsteinrichtungsamt *n*, **Forsteinrichtungsanstalt** *f* board of forest management
Forsteinrichtungsanweisung *f* working plans code
Forsteinrichtungsgruppe *f* cruising party
Forsteinrichtungsgruppen-Einsatzbereich *m* working plans circle
Forsteinrichtungsplan *m* forest management plan
Forsteinrichtungsverfahren *n* mode of forest management
Forstentomologie *f* forest entomology
Förster *m* 1. forester; 2. *s.* Forstaufseher
Försterei *f* forester's house
Forsterzeugnis *n* forest product
Forstfacharbeiter *m* skilled forest worker
Forstfachschule *f* technical forestry school, forest ranger school
Forstflugwesen *n* forestry aviation
Forstfrevel *m* forest offence (trespass), infringement of forest regulations, offence against forest laws
Forstgarten *m* forest arboretum, woodland garden
Forstgerät *n* forest implement
Forstgesetz *n* forestry act (law)
Forstgesetzbuch *n* forest code
Forstgesetzgebung *f* forestry legislation
Forstgesetzsammlung *f* forest code
Forstgrund *m* woodland
Forstgrundbesitz *m* forest ownership
Forstgrundkarte *f* basic forest map
Forsthaus *n s.* Försterei
Forsthochschule *f* forestry college (academy)
Forstingenieur *m* forest engineer, senior forestry official
Forstingenieurwesen *n* forest engineering
Forstinsekt *n* forest insect
Forstinsektenbekämpfung *f* forest insect control
Forstinspektion *f* forest inspection
Forstinventur *f* forest inventory (survey)
Forstklimatologie *f* forest climatology

Forstkrankheit

Forstkrankheit *f* forest disease (disorder)
Forstkultur *f* 1. silviculture; 2. forest plantation (culture)
Forstkunde *f* science of forestry
Forstlehrling *m* forest apprentice
Forstlehrpfad *m* forest demonstration path
forstlich forestal
Forstmann *m* forester, silviculturist
Forstmaschine *f* forest machine
Forstmaschinen *fpl* forestry machinery
Forstmelioration *f* forest amelioration (reclamation), silvicultural melioration
Forstmeteorologie *f* forest meteorology
Forstnutzungsfläche *f* forest land
Forstökonom *m* forest economist
Forstökonomie *f* forest economics
Forstordnung *f* forest regulation (law)
Forstorganisation *f* forest organization
Forstort *m* block *(forest management)*
Forstpathologie *f* forest pathology
Forstpflanze *f* forest plant
Forstpflanzenanzucht *f* forest plant raising (rearing)
Forstpflanzenzüchtung *f* forest plant breeding
Forstpflanzmaschine *f* forestry planting machine, [mechanical] tree planter
Forstpflanzung *f* forest plantation
Forstpflug *m* forest (woodland) plough
Forstpflugkarren *m* forest plough carriage
Forstplanung *f* forestry planning
Forstpolitik *f* forest policy
Forstprodukt *n* forest product
Forstrecht *n* forest right (law)
Forstreservat *n* forest reserve (protection area), reserved forest
Forstrevier *n* [forest, ranger] district, [forest] range, forest division
Forstsaatgut *n* forest seed
Forstsaatgutproduktion *f* forest seed production
Forstsamenkatalog *m* forest seed directory
Forstsamenkunde *f* forest seed science
Forstsamenzuchtbetrieb *m* forest seed establishment
Forstschädenausgleichsgesetz *n* forest damage compensation law
forstschädigend, forstschädlich injurious to forests
Forstschädling *m* forest pest (destroyer)
Forstschätzer *m* forest estimator, enumeration officer, *(Am)* cruiser
Forstschätzung *f* forest estimation
Forstschlepper *m* forestry tractor
Forstschutz *m* forest protection (conservation, preservation)
Forstschutzmittel *n* forest protection agent
Forstspezialtraktor *m* forestry tractor
Forststatistik *f* forest statistics
Forststraße *f* forest road

Forstraßenbau *m* forest road construction, forest roading
Forsttechnik *f* forest engineering (technology)
Forsttechniker *m* technical forester, forestry technician *(s. a.* Forstingenieur*)*
Forsttechnologe *m* forest technologist
Forsttechnologie *f* forest technology
Forstterminologie *f* forestry terminology
Forsttraktor *m* forestry tractor
Forsttypologie *f* forest typology
Forstunkraut *n* forest weed
Forstuntergrundlockerer *m* forestry subsoiler
Forstverbesserung *f* forest improvement
Forstvergehen *n s.* Forstfrevel
Forstvermessung *f* forest surveying
Forstverwalter *m* forest superintendent, administrator of forests
Forstverwaltung *f* forest administration
Forstverwaltungschef *m* chief forester
Forstverwaltungskosten *pl* administrative costs of forestry
Forstwart *m s.* Forstaufseher
Forstwerkzeug *n* forest tool
Forstwesen *n* forestry
Forstwirt *m* forester
Forstwirtschaft *f* 1. forestry; 2. forest economy
~/naturgemäße natural forestry
Forstwirtschaftsbetrieb *m* forestry operation
~/staatlicher governmental (state) forest enterprise
Forstwirtschaftsjahr *n* forest year
Forstwissenschaft *f* forest science, [science of] forestry
Forstwissenschaftler *m* scientific forester
Forstzoologie *f* forest zoology
Forsythie *f* 1. golden bell, forsythia *(genus Forsythia)*; 2. golden bell, Forsythia x intermedia
Fortbestehen *n* persistence, persistency
Fortbewegung *f* locomotion
fortdauern to persist
fortdauernd persistent
Fortluft *f* leaving air
fortpflanzen to propagate, to reproduce, to multiply *(s. a. under* vermehren*)*
~/sich to reproduce, to breed
Fortpflanzung *f* propagation, reproduction, multiplication *(s. a. under* Vermehrung*)*
~/generative (geschlechtliche) sexual (generative) reproduction, amphigenesis, amphigony
~/ungeschlechtliche (vegetative) asexual (vegetative) reproduction, non-sexual propagation, monogenesis, monogony
~/zweigeschlechtliche digenesis
Fortpflanzungsfähigkeit *f* reproductivity, reproductiveness, reproductive ability
Fortpflanzungsgemeinschaft *f* population
Fortpflanzungsleistung *f* reproductive performance

Fortpflanzungsorgan *n* reproductive (sex) organ
Fortpflanzungsphysiologie *f* reproductive physiology
Fortpflanzungspotential *n* breeding potential, reproductive potential (capacity)
Fortpflanzungsrate *f* reproductive (breeding) rate
Fortpflanzungsstörung *f* reproductive disorder (disturbance)
Fortpflanzungssystem *n* reproductive system, genital tract
Fortpflanzungsverhalten *n* reproductive behaviour
Fortpflanzungsvermögen *n s.* Fortpflanzungsfähigkeit
Fortpflanzungszyklus *m* reproductive cycle
Fortsatz *m* process
~/**schnabelartiger** rostrum
Fortschritt *m*/**genetischer** genetic advance, selection progress (response)
Fortune-Pfaffenhütchen *n (bot)* winter-creeper [euonymus], Euonymus fortunei
Forwarder *m (forest)* forwarder, forwarding machine
Forzeps *m(f) (vet)* forceps
Fosamin *n* fosamin[-ammonium] *(herbicide)*
Fosetyl *n* fosetyl *(fungicide)*
fossil fossil
Fossil *n* fossil
Fossilfestkalk *m* biolite, biolith *(non-clay mineral)*
fötal *s.* fetal
Foto... *s.* Photo...
Fötus *m s.* Fetus
Fourage *f* forage, fodder
Foxhound *m* foxhound *(dog breed)*
Foxterrier *m* fox-terrier *(dog breed)*
FPV *s.* Klassisches Geflügelpestvirus
Fragarin *n* pelargonidin *(vegetable dye)*
Fragilin *n* fragilin *(glycoside)*
Fragmentation *f* fragmentation
Fragmentgefüge *n (soil)* fragmental structure
Fraktionierung *f* fractionation
Fraktion-I-Protein *n* ribulose-bisphosphate carboxylase *(enzyme)*
Fraktur *f (vet)* [bone] fracture *(s. a. under* Bruch*)*
~/**gedeckte** closed fracture
~/**komplizierte** complicated fracture
Frameshiftmutation *f (gen)* frame-shift mutation
Framycetin *n* framycetin, neomycin *(antibiotic)*
Frangipani *f (bot)* frangipani *(genus Plumeria)*
Fransenflügler *m (ent)* thrips *(order Thysanoptera)*
Fransenschwertel *n* wand (harlequin) flower *(genus Sparaxis)*
Französische Bulldogge *f* [French] bulldog *(dog breed)*
~ **Trüffel** *f* earth ball, [Périgord] truffle, Tuber melanosporum
~ **Wicke** *f* Narbonne vetch, Vicia narbonensis
Französischer Ahorn *m* Montpellier maple, Acer monspessulanum

~ **Stechginster** *m* Welsh (western) gorse, Ulex gallii
~ **Traber** *m* French (Norman) Trotter *(horse breed)*
~ **Widder** *m* French Lop [rabbit] *(breed)*
Französisches Raygras *n* tall oat[-grass], bulbous oat-grass, onion grass, Arrhenaterum elatius
Fräsbeetformer *m* rotary bed shaper
Fräsbodenbearbeitung *f* rotary tillage (cultivation), roto[culti]vation, gyrotillage
fräsen to rotavate, to rototill
Fraser's Balsamtanne *f* Fraser fir, Abies fraseri
Fräsgrubber *m* rotary [power] tiller, rototiller, rotary cultivator
Fräskette *f* cutter chain *(of a silo)*
Fräspflug *m* rotary plough
Fraß *m* feeding, feed *(of animal pests)*
Fraßabschreckung[swirkung] *f* phagodeterrency
Frässämaschine *f* rotary cultivation seeder
Fraßbild *n*, **Fraßfigur** *f* feed mark *(of animal pests)*; *(ent)* gallery design, gallery pattern
Fräßschnecke *f* gathering auger
Fraßgang *m* [feeding] tunnel, [feeding] gallery, mine, bore[hole], burrow[ing passage]
Fraßgift *n* food (stomach, internal) poison; stomach insecticide
Fraßhemmstoff *m* feeding inhibitor
Fraßhemmung *f* feeding inhibition
Fraßloch *n* insect hole
~/**kleines** pin-hole
Fraßmehl *n* bore (boring) dust, bore meal, frass *(of mining insects)*
Fraßschaden *m* feeding damage
Fraßstelle *f* feeding-site *(of pests)*
Fraßstimulation *f* phagostimulation
Fraßtätigkeit *f* voracity
Frauendistel *f* blessed milk thistle, St. Mary thistle, Silybum marianum
Frauenfarn *m* lady (female shield) fern, Athyrium (Asplenium) filix-femina
Frauenflachs *m* flaxweed, common toadflax, butter-and-eggs, ramstead, Linaria vulgaris
Frauenhaarfarn *m* 1. maidenhair [fern], adiantum *(genus Adiantum)*; 2. fragrant maidenhair, Adiantum raddianum
Frauenmantel *m (bot)* Lady's mantle *(genus Alchemilla)*
Frauenminze *f (bot)* costmary, Chrysanthemum majus (balsamita)
Frauenschuh *m* Lady's (Venus's) slipper, slipper orchid (plant), cypripedium *(genus Cypripedium)*
Frederiksborger *m* Frederiksborg *(horse breed)*
Freemartinismus *m s.* Zwickenbildung
Freesie *f (bot)* freesia *(genus Freesia)*
Freesienmosaikvirus *n* freesia mosaic virus, FMV
freiabblühend open-pollinated
Freiberger Pferd *n* Freiberg *(horse breed)*
Freier Raum *m* free space *(of plant tissue)*
Freifläche *f* open field [site] • **auf der ~ wachsend** open-growing

Freifläche

~/gestaltete amenity area (site)
freifließend free-flowing *(e.g. fertilizer)*
Freigärhaufen *m* stack silo
freihauen *s.* freistellen
Freiheitsgrad *m (biom)* degree of freedom
Freihieb *m (forest)* liberation felling, release cutting; opening up *(of a stand)*
Freilagerung *f* outdoor storage
Freiland *n* open [ground], field • **im** ~ outdoors • **im** ~ **angebaut (gezogen)** field-grown • **im** ~ **wachsend** free-growing • **ins** ~ **versetzen** to reset *(plantlets)*
Freilandanbau *m* outdoor cropping (growing), growing in the open, field production
Freilandaufzucht *f* outdoor rearing *(of animals)*
Freilandaussaat *f* outdoor sowing, sowing in situ
Freilandbedingungen *fpl* field conditions
Freilandbewässerung *f* outdoor (field) irrigation
Freilandbonsai *m* outdoor bonsai
Freilandbuschtomate *f* field-grown bush tomato
Freilanderzeugung *f* field production
Freilandgemüse *n* field (outdoor) vegetable
Freilandgemüseanbau *m* field vegetable farming (growing)
Freilandgewächs *n* outdoor plant
Freilandgloxinie *f* trumpet-flower *(genus Incarvillea)*
Freilandisolat *n (phyt)* field isolate
Freilandkompostierung *f* outdoor-composting
Freilandkultur *f* field (outdoor) crop, open-air culture, open-soil culture
Freilandniederschlag *m* precipitation in the open
Freilandparzelle *f* field plot
Freilandpflanze *f* outdoor plant; garden plant
Freilandpflanzung *f* outdoor planting
Freilandsaat *f* field seeding, sowing in situ
Freilandsalat *m* outdoor lettuce
Freilandschädling *m* field (outdoor) pest
Freilandterrarium *n* open-air vivarium
Freilandtomate *f* outdoor tomato
Freilanduntersuchung *f* field investigation (study)
Freilandveredelung *f* field grafting
Freilandversuch *m* field trial (test), outdoor trial
Freilandversuchsparzelle *f* field plot
Freilaufkupplung *f* overrun[ning] clutch
freilebend free-living
Freipolter *m (Am, forest)* bucking ladder
Freiraumgestaltung *f* open space design
Freiraumplaner *m* open space planner
Freischneidegerät *n* bush cutter, brush cutter (buster)
freisetzen to release
Freisetzungshormon *n* releasing hormone, releaser
Freistand *m* 1. *(forest)* open position; 2. *s.* ~/überdachter • **im** ~ **wachsend** open-growing, free-growing
~/**überdachter** *(api)* bee hut
freistehend detached, isolated, solitary *(e.g. a forest-tree)*

freistellen to set free, to release, to isolate *(a forest-tree)*; to open up *(a forest stand)*
Freistellung *f (forest)* setting free, liberation felling, release cutting
~ **der Krone** setting free of the crown
Freiwasserzone *f* open water zone, pelagial
Freiwinkel *m* clearance (back) angle *(of cutting tools)*
Freizeitgarten *m* leisure garden
Freizeitgärtner *m* leisure (amateur) gardener
Freizeitimker *m* amateur (hobbyist) bee-keeper
Freizeitpferd *n* pleasure horse
Freizeitreiten *n* recreational riding, leisure[-time] riding
Fremdart *f (ecol)* invader species
fremdbefruchten *(bot)* to cross-fertilize
fremdbefruchtend cross-fertile
Fremdbefruchtung *f* cross-fertilization
Fremdbesatz *m* extraneous matter, foreign material (matter), dockage; moits *(in sheep's wool)*
Fremdbestandteil *m* extraneous substance
fremdbestäuben *(bot)* to cross-pollinate, to cross-pollinize
fremdbestäubend allogamous, xenogamous
Fremdbestäubung *f* cross-pollination, allogamy, xenogamy
fremdbürtig allochthonous
Fremder Ehrenpreis *m* purslane speedwell, neckweed, Veronica peregrina
Fremdgeruch *m* foreign odour, taint
Fremdgeschmack *m* off-flavour, foreign taste
Fremdkörper *m* foreign body
Fremdkörperabscheider *m* foreign-body separator
Fremdkörpererkrankung *f (vet)* hardware disease
~ **der Wiederkäuer** traumatic reticuloperitonitis
Fremdkörperpneumonie *f (vet)* foreign-body pneumonia
Fremdpaarung *f* disassortative (negative assortative) mating, compensatory mating *(animal breeding)*
Fremdstoff *m* foreign material (matter), contaminant
Fremdzucht *f* outbreeding • ~ **betreiben** to outbreed
Fremitus *m (vet)* fremitus
French Alpine *f* French Alpine *(goat breed)*
Freßbeutel *m* nosebag *(for horses)*
fressen to eat, to feed [on]
~/**einen Köder** to bait
~/**hastig** to eat greedily, to devour
Fressen *n* **der Einstreu** bed-eating
~ **der Nachgeburt** placentophagia
Freßfläche *f* grazing area
Freßgeschwindigkeit *f* feeding rate
Freßgewohnheit *f* feeding habit
Freßgitter *n* feedgate, feeding rack, feed fence
~ **mit Gleitkette** manger with sliding chain
Freßlust *f* feeding drive

Freßplatz *m* feeding site (stall); feeding table; crib
Freßplatzbreite *f* trough space
Freßrepellenz *f* phagodeterrency
Freßunlust *f* inappetence, anorexia
Freßverhalten *n* feeding (eating) behaviour
Freßfertigkeit *f* feeding (eating) time
Freßzelle *f* phagocyte
Frett *n s.* Frettchen
Frettchen *n* ferret, Mustela putorius f. domesticus (furo), Putorius furo
~/männliches hob
frettieren to ferret
Freund Gräwing *(huner's language) s.* Dachs
Freundsches Adjuvans *n* Freund's adjuvant *(immunology)*
friedfertig docile
Friedfertigkeit *f* docility *(animal behaviour)*
Friedhofsbagger *m* grave digging equipment
Friedhofsgärtnerei *f* cemetery gardening
Friedhofskranz *m* [funeral] wreath
Frieren *n* 1. freezing; 2. *s.* Gefrieren
Friesenrind *n* Friesian *(cattle breed)*
Friesischer Klee *m* strawberry clover, Trifolium fragiferum
Friesisches Pferd *n* Friesian *(horse breed)*
Frigidität *f* frigidity
frigophil psychrophilic
Friktion *f* friction, attrition
Friktionsbewegung *f* thrust *(in mating)*
frisch 1. fresh *(e.g. meat, fruit)*; green, fresh *(e.g. vegetables)*; fresh, new-laid *(eggs)*; 2. hot *(scent or track)*
Frischei *n* fresh (shell) egg
frischen to farrow [down], to pig *(female wild boar)*
Frischfleisch *n* fresh meat
Frischfutter *n* fresh feed (fodder)
frischgefällt freshly cut, new-fallen *(tree)*
frischgelegt new-laid *(egg)*
frischgemäht new-mown
Frischgemüse *n* fresh vegetable
frischgeschlagen *s.* frischgefällt
Frischhäcksel[futter] *n* green chop, soilage
Frischhaltelagerung *f* fresh storage
Frischkäse *m* fresh (uncured) cheese
Frischlagerung *f* fresh storage
Frischling *m* wild piglet, young wild boar
~/überlaufener singler
Frischluftgebläse *n* fresh-air fan
Frischmarkt *m* fresh market
Frischmasse *f* fresh weight
Frischmilch *f* fresh milk
~/entrahmte skim[med] milk, skim, non-fat milk
Frischmist *m* fresh (green) manure, long dung
Frischobst *n* fresh fruit[s], dessert fruit
Frischrohdichte *f* green density *(of wood)*
Frischschlamm *m* raw sludge *(sewage treatment)*
Frischsilagebereitung *f* direct-cut method of silage preparation
Frischverfütterung *f* fresh feeding, soiling

Frischvermarktung *f* fresh marketing
Frischverzehr *m* fresh consumption
Frischverzehrqualität *f* dessert quality *(of fruit)*
Frischzustand *m* freshness
Fritfliege *f* frit-fly, wheat pest, Oscinella frit
Fritte *f* frit
FRM *s.* Fäll-Rücke-Maschine
FrMV *s.* Freesienmosaikvirus
frohwüchsig vigorous, thrifty, rapid-growing, fast-growing, quick-growing
Frohwüchsigkeit *f* thriftiness
fromm *s.* friedfertig
Frondeszenz *f (bot)* frondescence *(the process or period of putting forth leaves)*
frondos *(bot)* frondose, frond-bearing
Frontanbau *m* front-mounted linkage *(at a tractor)*
Frontanbaugerät *n* front-mounted equipment
Frontanbaupflug *m* front plough
Frontantrieb *m* front-wheel drive
Frontensystem *n* frontal system *(meteorology)*
Fronthydraulik *f* front power (hydraulic) lift
Frontkraftheber *m s.* Fronthydraulik
Frontlader *m* fore-loader, front[-mounted tractor] loader, loading shovel, skid-steer loader
Frontpflug *m* front plough
Frontschaufellader *m s.* Frontlader
Frontschieber *m* front-mounted tractor scraper
Frontschneidwerk *n* front-mounted cutter bar
Frontschnittmähdrescher *m* front-cut combine, push-type combine
Frontseilwinde *f* front-mounted winch
Frontsitzkabine *f* front seat cab
Frontwinkel *m* side[-plate] angle, side-edge angle *(of a chain-saw tooth)*
Frontzapfwelle *f* front power take-off, front p.t.o.
Froschaugenblattflecken *mpl*, **Froschaugenkrankheit** *f* frog-eye *(of tobacco plants, caused by Cercospora nicotianae)*
Froschbiß *m (bot)* frog-bit, Hydrocharis morsus-ranae
Froschlöffel *m* great water plantain, Alisma plantago-aquatica
Frost *m* frost, freeze • **durch ~ abtöten** to frost *(e.g. plants)* • **durch ~ schädigen** to frost *(e.g. plants)*
Frostakklimation *f* frost acclimation (hardening)
Frostaufbruch *m* frost heave (heaving)
Frostaussaat *f* frost seeding
frostbeständig frost-proof
Frostbeule *f (vet)* chilblain
frostempfindlich frost-susceptible, frost-sensitive, frost-tender
Frostempfindlichkeit *f* frost susceptibility (sensitivity)
frosten to frost, to freeze
Frostfront *f (soil)* freezing front
Frostgare *f* frost mould, natural tilth
Frostgefahr *f* frost hazard (danger)
Frostgraupeln *fpl s.* Graupeln

frosthart

frosthart frost-hardy, frost-proof, frost-resistant, winter-hardy
Frosthärte f frost (winter) hardiness, resistance to freezing
Frosthärtung f chill-hardening, frost acclimation
Frosthebung f, **Frosthub** m frost lift[ing] (of soil)
frostig frosty
Frostkern m frost heart (wood defect)
Frostkluft f s. Frostriß
Frostlage f frost locality (site)
Frostleiste f frost rib (callus, scar) (wood defect)
Frostloch n frost hole (hollow), frost pocket (spot)
Frostmusterboden m patterned ground
Frostperiode f frost period
Frostplatte f frost lesion [of bark]
frostresistent s. frosthart
Frostring m frost ring
Frostriß m frost crack (cleft), chap (in timber)
frostrissig frost-cracked, split by frost
Frostsaat f frost seeding
Frostschaden m frost (freezing) injury, chilling damage (in plants)
Frostschutz m frost protection
Frostschutzbakterium n frost-preventing bacterium
Frostschutzberegnung f frost [protection] sprinkling, blanketing
Frostschutzbewässerung f frost protection irrigation
Frostschutzthermostat m antifrost thermostat
frostsicher frost-proof
Frostsicherheit f resistance to freezing
Frostspalt m s. Frostriß
Frostsprengung f (soil) frost weathering, congelifraction
Froststrukturboden m patterned ground
Frosttag m frost day
Frosttiefe f frost level (in the soil)
Frosttoleranz f frost tolerance
Frosttrocknis f frost drought, parch blight, winter drought (burn, killing) (plant physiology)
Frostverwitterung f (soil) frost weathering, congelifraction
Frostwarnung f frost warning
Frostwiderstandsfähigkeit f frost (freezing) resistance
Frostwirkung f frost action
Fru s. Fructose
Frucht f 1. (bot) fruit (s. a. under Früchte); [field] crop; 2. (zoo) foetus, conceptus • **[aus]bilden** to fructify, to fruit • **~ tragen** to crop, to fruit • **keine ~ erzeugend** (bot) acarpous • **keine ~ tragend** fruitless
~/**abgeplattete** flat globose fruit
~/**aus einer zweiten Blüte angelegte** secondary fruit
~/**aussortierte** low-grade fruit, cull
~/**fleischige** berry
~/**garefördernde (garemehrende)** renovating crop
~/**garezehrende** exhausting crop
~/**geflügelte** winged fruit
~/**minderwertige** low-grade fruit, cull
~/**mißgebildete** misshapen fruit
~/**nicht steinlösende** clingstone [fruit]
~/**steinlösende** freestone [fruit]
Fruchtablösekraft f fruit removal force (orcharding)
Fruchtablösung f separation of fruit
Fruchtansatz m fruit set[ting], fruit development
Fruchtansatzperiode f fruiting period
Fruchtart f crop
Fruchtartengemisch n crop mixture
fruchtartig fruitlike
Fruchtast m fruiting branch
Fruchtauge n fruit (blossom, flower) bud
Fruchtausbreitung f **durch Fische** ichthyochory
~ durch Reptilien saurochory
~ durch Vögel ornithochory
Fruchtausdünnung f fruit thinning (orcharding)
~/**chemische** chemical thinning
Fruchtausfärbung f fruit colouring
fruchtbar 1. fertile, fecund, breedy; fruitful, prolific, productive; 2. fertile, fat, rich, rank (soil)
• **~ machen** to fertilize, to fat[ten], to batten (soil)
Fruchtbare Rispe f fowl (swamp) meadow-grass, Poa palustris
Fruchtbarkeit f 1. fertility, fecundity; fruitfulness, prolificacy, productivity; 2. [natural] fertility, rankness (of soil)
Fruchtbarkeitsindex m fertility index
Fruchtbarkeitskennziffer f indicator of fertility
Fruchtbarkeitsleistung f reproductive performance
Fruchtbarkeitsparameter m fertility index
Fruchtbarkeitsprüfung f fertility testing
Fruchtbarkeitsrate f fertility rate
Fruchtbaum m fruit-tree
Fruchtbecher m (bot) cupule; acorn cup
Fruchtbehang m fruit (crop) load
Fruchtberostung f (phyt) fruit russet[ing], russeting (virosis)
~ des Apfels apple russet ring, apple leaf pucker
Fruchtbildung f (bot) fruit formation, fructification
~ nach Fremdbestäubung allocarpy
~ nach Selbstbestäubung autocarpy
~ ohne Befruchtung apomixis
Fruchtblase f chorionic sac (animal anatomy)
Fruchtblatt n (bot) carpel • **Fruchtblätter entfernen** to decap (e.g. of strawberries) • **mit einem ~** monocarpellary • **ohne ~** acarpe[l]lous
Fruchtblattroller m s. Fruchtschalenwickler
Fruchtblütenstand m female inflorescence
Fruchtboden m (bot) receptacle
Fruchtbrand m fruit blight (of stone fruit, caused by Erwinia amylovora)
Fruchtbrei m fruit pulp
~/**dünner** fruit slurry
Fruchtbrücke f bridge graft

Fruchtbüschel *n* fruit[ing] truss, fruit cluster
Früchtchen *n* fruitlet, drupel[et]
Früchte *fpl* fruits *(s. a. under* Frucht*)* • **gestielte ~ tragend** podocarpous • **kurze ~ tragend** brachycarpous • **schöne ~ tragend** callicarpous • **stachlige ~ tragend** acanthocarpous • **wenig ~ tragend** oligocarpous
~/kandierte candied fruits
~/minderwertige low-grade fruits
~/nicht standardgerechte cullage
fruchten to fruit, to fructify
fruchtend fruiting
Fruchtentwicklung *f* fruit development
Fruchtentwicklungsperiode *f* fruiting period
Frucht[ernte]ertrag *m* fruitage
Fruchtessig *m* fruit vinegar
Früchtetraube *f* bunch of fruit[s], fruit cluster
Fruchtfall *m* fruit drop
~ im Juni June drop
Fruchtfärbung *f* fruit colouring
Fruchtfäule *f* fruit rot
~ der Tomate late blight of tomato *(caused by Phytophthora infestans)*
Fruchtfestigkeit *f* fruit firmness
Fruchtfleisch *n* [fruit] pulp, [fruit] flesh, *(Am also)* meat • **~ entfernen** to pulp
~/inneres core flesh, marrow
Fruchtfleischfarbe *f* [fruit] flesh colour
Fruchtfleischfestigkeit *f* [fruit] flesh firmness
Fruchtfleischverfall *m* **der Birne** core breakdown [of pear]
Fruchtfliege *f* fruit-fly *(family Trypetidae)*
Fruchtfolge *f* crop rotation (succession), crop[ping] sequence, rotation [of crops]
~/enge short rotation
~/vierfeldrige four-course rotation
~/wissenschaftlich begründete science-based crop rotation
Fruchtfolgegestaltung *f* organization of crop rotation
Fruchtfolgestellung *f* position in rotation
Fruchtfolgeglied *n* crop rotation link; rotation period
Fruchtfolgekombination *f* rotation combination
Fruchtfolgekrankheit *f* rotation disease
Fruchtfolgeschema *n* crop rotation pattern
Fruchtfolgeversuch *m* crop rotation experiment
Fruchtfolgewirkung *f* rotation effect
Fruchtform *f* fruit shape
fruchtfressend frugivorous, carpophagous
Fruchtgemüse *n* fruit[ing] vegetable
Fruchtgestalt *f* fruit shape
Fruchtgröße *f* fruit size
Fruchthalter *m* *(bot)* carpophore
Fruchthälterbruch *m* *(vet)* hysterocele
Fruchtholz *n* fruit[ing] wood, fruit-bearing wood
Fruchtholzrotation *f* rejuvenation of fruiting wood
Fruchtholzschnitt *m* fruit-wood pruning, renewal pruning, pruning for fruiting

Fruchtholzumtrieb *m*, **Fruchtholzverjüngung** *f* rejuvenation of fruiting wood
Fruchthülle *f s.* 1. Fruchtwand; 2. Embryonalhülle
fruchtig fruity
Fruchtigkeit *f* fruitiness
Fruchtinneres *n* [fruit] core
Fruchtkern *m* kernel
Fruchtklimakterium *n* fruit climacteric *(plant physiology)*
Fruchtknospe *f* fruit (flower, blossom) bud
Fruchtknoten *m* *(bot)* ovary, ovarium, gynobase, gynopodium, button, germen • **über dem ~ stehend** epigynous *(blossom)* • **um den ~ herum angeordnet** perigynous *(blossom)* • **unter dem ~ stehend** hypogynous *(blossom)*
Fruchtknotenfach *n* *(bot)* locule
Fruchtkörper *m* fruit[ing]-body, fruiting structure *(of fungi)*
~/konsolenförmiger bracket, corbel, conk
Fruchtkörperbildung *f s.* Fruchtbildung
Fruchtkuchen *m* 1. *(zoo)* placenta; 2. *(bot)* knob, bourse *(of pome fruit)*
fruchtlos fruitless, acarpous
Fruchtlosigkeit *f* fruitlessness
Fruchtmark *n* [fruit] pulp • **~ entfernen** to pulp
Fruchtmarkierungspheromon *n* fruit marking pheromone
Fruchtmißbildung *f* misshapen fruit
Fruchtmumie *f (phyt, vet)* mummy
Fruchtmus *n* pomace
Fruchtnaht *f (bot)* suture
Fruchtnekrose *f (phyt)* fruit necrosis
Fruchtplatzen *n* fruit cracking
~ vor der Reife premature [fruit] cracking
Fruchtpulpe *f* fruit pulp
Fruchtreife *f* fruit ripeness (maturity)
Fruchtreifung *f* fruit ripening (maturation)
Fruchtringberostung *f* **des Apfels** apple russet ring, apple leaf pucker *(virosis)*
Fruchtringfleckigkeit *f* **des Apfels** apple ring spot *(virosis)*
Fruchtsack *m* chorionic sac *(animal anatomy)*
Fruchtsaft *m* [fruit] juice
Fruchtsaftgetränk *n* fruit beverage
Fruchtsaftpresse *f* fruit juice extractor, *(Am)* reamer
Fruchtsäure *f* fruit acid
Fruchtschale *f* fruit coat, rind, [fruit] peel
~/stachelige bur[r]
Fruchtschalenwickler *m (ent)* [summer] fruit tortrix [moth], fruit leaf-roller, Adoxophyes reticulana (orana)
Fruchtschaumwein *m* fruit champagne, sparkling fruit wine
Fruchtscheckung *f* **des Apfels** dapple apple *(virosis)*
Fruchtschicht *f* hymenium *(of fungi)*
Fruchtsekt *m s.* Fruchtschaumwein
Fruchtspieß *m*, **Fruchtsproß** *m* spur, dart

Fruchtstand

Fruchtstand *m (bot)* infructescence
Fruchtstandsbasis *f* cluster base
Fruchtstiel *m* fruit stem, footstalk, peduncle, strig
Fruchttod *m* foetal death
~/embryonaler [early] embryonic death
Fruchttragen *n* [fruit] bearing, fruitage
~/zweijährliches biennial bearing (fruiting), bienniality *(orcharding)*
fruchttragend [fruit-]bearing, frugiferous, fructiferous, fruiting
Fruchttrieb *m* fruiting cane *(of grape-vine)*
Fruchtumriß *m* fruit shape
Fruchtungsverhalten *n* fruiting habit
Fruchtverfall *m (phyt)* fruit decay
Fruchtwand *f* seed case (vessel), pericarp [of a fruit]
~/äußere exocarp, epicarp
~/innere endocarp
~/mittlere mesocarp
Fruchtwandoberhaut *f s.* Fruchtwand/äußere
Fruchtwasser *n* amniotic (foetal) fluid
Fruchtwechselwirtschaft *f* rotation[al] cropping, convertible husbandry
Fruchtwein *m* fruit (berry) wine
Fruchtzucker *m s.* Fructose
Fructan *n* polyfructosan *(polysaccharide)*
Fructofuranosidase *f* fructofuranosidase *(enzyme)*
Fructolyse *f* fructolysis
Fructosan *n* fructosan *(polysaccharide)*
Fructose *f* fructose, fruit sugar, laevulose
Fructoseabbau *m* fructolysis
Fructosebisphosphataldolase *f* [fructose-bisphosphate] aldolase *(enzyme)*
Fructosebisphosphatase *f* fructose-bisphosphatase, hexosediphosphatase *(enzyme)*
Fructosediphosphataldolase *f* [fructose-bisphosphate] aldolase *(enzyme)*
Fructose-1,6-diphosphatase fructose-1,6-diphosphatase *(enzyme)*
Fructose-6-phosphat *n* fructose-6-phosphate
Fructosylraffinose *f* fructosylraffinose *(oligosaccharide)*
Frühabort *m* early abortion
~/embryonaler embryo abort
Frühabsetzen *m* early weaning *(of sucklings)*
Frühabsetzer *m* early weaner
Frühbast *m s.* Frühjahrsrinde
Frühbeet *n* forcing (force) bed; hotbed *(s. a.* Frühbeetkasten*)* • **im ~ getrieben** hotbed-forced • **im ~ ziehen** to hotbed
~/beheiztes hotbed
~/verglastes glass bed
Frühbeetdrillmaschine *f* hotbed seeder
Frühbeetfenster *n* hotbed sash, frame light
Frühbeetkasten *m* [forcing] frame, garden-frame, forcing pit *(s. a.* Frühbeet*)*
~/beweglicher mobile frame
~/einseitiger single-light span frame
~/kalter (ungeheizter) cold frame
~/warmer heated frame
~/zweiseitiger double[-light] span frame
Frühbeettreiberei *f* hotbed-forcing
Frühblähung *f* early blowing *(in cheese)*
frühblühend early flowering (blossoming)
Frühblühende Winterblume *f* winter flower, Chimonanthus praecox
Frühblüher *m* **bei Blumenkohl** button *(of cauliflower)*
Frühdiagnose *f* early diagnosis
Frühe Bräune *f* **der Erbse,** ~ **Erbsenverbräunung** *f* pea early browning *(virosis)*
~ **Haferschmiele** *f* early hair grass, Aira praecox
~ **Winterkresse** *f* [up]land cress, Barbarea verna (praecox)
Frühentwöhnung *f* early weaning *(of sucklings)*
Frühes Barbarakraut *n s.* Frühe Winterkresse
Frühfrost *m* autumn frost, early [fall] frost
Frühgeburt *f (vet)* premature birth, abortion
Frühgemüse *n* early vegetable[s]
Frühgravidität *f* early pregnancy
Frühherbst *m* early autumn
Frühholz *n* early (spring) wood
Frühholzanteil *m* share of early wood
Frühholztracheide *f* early-wood tracheid, thin-walled tracheid
Frühjahrsapfel[blatt]sauger *m (ent)* apple [leaf-] sucker, apple psylla, Psylla mali
Frühjahrsbestellung *f* spring cultivation
Frühjahrsfrost *m* spring frost *(s.a.* Spätfrost*)*
Frühjahrsfrühweide *f* early spring grazing, early bite
Frühjahrskohl *m* spring cabbage
Frühjahrsrinde *f* early bark
Frühjahrsschwindsucht *f* nosema disease *(of honey-bees, caused by Nosema apis)*
Frühjahrsvirämie *f* **der Karpfen** spring viraemia of carp, SVC, infectious carp dropsy
Frühjahrsvorweide *f* early spring grazing, early bite
Frühkartoffel *f* early potato
Frühklee *m* broad[-leaved] red clover, medium (early-flowering) red clover, double-cut cowgrass, Trifolium pratense var. sativum subvar. praecox
Frühkohl *m* spring cabbage
Frühlähme *f* **der Fohlen** sleepy foal disease
Frühlaktation *f* early lactation
Frühlingsahorn *m* Italian maple, Acer opalus
Frühlingsbraunwurz *f* yellow figwort, Scrophularia vernalis
Frühlings-Gedenkemein *n (bot)* blue-eyed Mary, Omphalodes verna
Frühlingsgrün *n* spring (vernal) foliage
Frühlingsholz *n s.* Frühholz
Frühlingskrokus *m* Dutch crocus, Crocus neapolitanus (vernus)
Frühlingsscharbockskraut *n* [lesser] celandine, pilewort, Ranunculus ficaria

Frühlingssteinrich *m* goldentuft [madwort], golddust, basket-of-gold, Alyssum saxatile
Frühlingsstern *m* California hyacinth *(genus Brodiaea)*
Frühphase *f* early stage
frühreif early-maturing, quick-maturing, precocious
Frühreife *f* early maturity (maturation), earliness in (of) ripening, precociousness, precocity
~/geschlechtliche neoteny
frühreifend early-maturing
Frührinde *f* early bark
Frührodung *f* early lifting *(of root crops)*
Frühsaat *f* early seeding
Frühselektion *f* early selection
Frühsommer *m* early summer
Frühstadium *n* early stage
Frühtod *m*/**embryonaler** *(vet)* early embryonic death
Frühträchtigkeit *f* early pregnancy
Frühwarnsystem *n* early warning system *(e.g. in pest control)*
Frühweide *f* early grazing
frühzeitig precocious, early • **~ abfallend** *(bot)* caducous • **~ blühend** precocious
Frühzeitigkeit *f* precociousness, precocity, earliness
Fruktifikation *f* fructification
Fruktifikationsalter *n (forest)* age of seed production
fruktifizieren to fructify, to fruit
Fruktifizierung *f* fructification
fruktivor frugivorous, carpophagous
F/S *s.* Femelsaumschlagfläche
Fsch. *s.* Fuchsschimmel
FSH *s.* Follikelreifungshormon
FSH-Freisetzungshormon *n* FSH releasing hormone, FSHRH
F-Test *m* F-test, variance-ratio test *(statistics)*
Fuberidazol *n* fuberidazole *(fungicide)*
Fuc *s.* Fucose
Fuchs *m* 1. fox *(genus Vulpes)*; 2. fox, reynard, Vulpes vulpes; 3. chestnut *(horse)*
Fuchsbau *m* fox-earth, fox-hole
Fuchsbeere *f (bot)* paris *(genus Paris)*
Fuchsbrücke *f* flue bridge
Fuchsenzephalitis *f* canine viral (virus) hepatitis
Fuchsfährte *f* track of fox, ball
Fuchsfell *n* fox
Fuchsie *f (bot)* lady's-eardrops, fuchsia *(genus Fuchsia)*
fuchsig chestnut, rufous
Füchsin *f* vixen, bitch fox, she-fox
Fuchsin *n* fuchsin[e] *(dye)*
~/saures acid fuchsin[e]
Fuchsinfärbung *f* fuchsin[e] staining
Fuchsjagd *f* fox-hunting, hunt • **auf ~ gehen** to hunt, to go fox-hunting, to ride to hounds
Fuchslosung *f* billeting
Fuchspelz *m* fox

Fuchsrebe *f* fox (labrusca) grape, Isabel[la] grape, *(Am)* skunk grape, Vitis labrusca
Fuchsriedgras *n* fox sedge, Carex vulpina
Fuchsrose *f* Austrian brier, yellow rose, Rosa foetida
fuchsrot chestnut, rufous • **~ werdend** *(bot, zoo)* rufescent
Fuchsschecke *m(f)* skewbald *(horse)*
Fuchsschimmel *m* [red] roan *(horse)*
Fuchsschwanz *m* 1. *(bot)* amaranth *(genus Amaranthus)*; 2. prince's feather, Amaranthus caudatus (cruentus); 3. black grass, slender foxtail, Alopecurus myosuroides; 4. foxtail, brush; 5. handsaw, one-man cross-cut saw
Fuchsschwanzgewächse *npl* amaranth family *(family Amaranthaceae)* • **die ~ betreffend** amaranthaceous
Fuchsschwanzgras *n* foxtail[-grass] *(genus Alopecurus)*
Fuchsschwanzkiefer *f* Balfour's (foxtail) pine, Pinus balfouriana
Fuchsschwanzsägemaschine *f* reciprocating log cross-cut saw
Fuchssegge *f* fox sedge, Carex vulpina
Fuchsstute *f* alezan
Fucose *f* fucose *(aldose sugar)*
Fucoxanthin *n* fucoxanthin *(pigment)*
Fuder *n* [cart-]load
~ Heu/ein a load of hay
Fuderlader *m* hay loader
fühlbar palpable
Fühler *m (zoo)* palpus, palp; *(ent)* antenna, feeler
Fühlerborste *f (ent)* arista
Fühlerkontakt *m* antennal contact
Fühlerputzapparat *m* antenna cleaner
Fuhre *f* cart-load
führen/ein Kalb to freshen *(cow)*
Führ[ungs]pferd *n* pace-maker, pace-setter *(horse-racing)*
Führungsplatte *f* knife guide, clip of the mower-sickle *(of a finger cutter bar)*
Führungsrolle *f* fairlead *(of a winch)*
Führungsschiene *f* chain bar (blade, guide), cutter bar, guide bar (plate) *(of a chain-saw)*
Fuhrwerk *n* cart, wheeled vehicle; horse-drawn vehicle
Fuhrwerkswaage *f* vehicle weighing platform, weigh-bridge
Führzügel *m* leading-rein
Fulani-Rind *n* Fulani *(cattle breed)*
Füllbestand *m (forest)* auxiliary stand
Füllen *n s.* Fohlen
Fullererde *f* fuller's earth
Füllgerät *n* filling device, filler
Füllmaschine *f* filling machine, filler
Füllmasse *f* massecuite, *(Am)* fillmass *(sugar manufacture)*
Füllmaterial *n* load, feed material
Füllmittel *n* filler, bulking agent

Füllschlauch

Füllschlauch *m* filling (filler) hose
Füllstand *m* level [of filling]
Füllstandsanzeiger *m* level indicator
Füllstoff *m* filler, bulking agent
Fülltrichter *m* feed chute, storage hopper
Füllung *f* 1. filling; loading; 2. *s.* Füllmaterial
Füllventil *n* fill valve
Füllwein *m* stum
Fulvosäure *f (soil)* fulvic acid
Fumagillin *n* fumagillin *(antibiotic)*
Fumarsäure *f* fumaric acid
Fumarylacetoacetase *f* fumarylacetoacetase *(enzyme)*
Fumigant *n* fumigant
Fumigation *f* fumigation, gassing
Fundament *n* foundation
Fundatrigenia *f* fundatrigenia *(of aphids)*
Fundatrix *f* fundatrix *(of aphids)*
Fundort *m (ecol)* natural habitat
Fundus *m* fundus *(animal anatomy)*
Fundusdrüse *f* fundic gland
fünfblättrig *(bot)* quinquefoliate, pentaphyllous
fünfblütig *(bot)* quinqueflorous
fünffächerig *(bot)* quinquelocular
fünffeldrig five-course, five-crop *(rotation)*
fünffingerig pentadactyl
fünffrüchtig *(bot)* pentacarpous
fünfgliedrig *(bot)* pentamerous
fünfgriffelig *(bot)* pentagynous
Fünfgriffeliger Weißdorn *m* pentagynous (Chinese) hawthorn, Crataegus pentagyna
fünfnervig *(bot)* quinquenerved
fünfteilig *(bot)* pentamerous
fünfzählig *(bot)* quinate
Fungicidin *n* nystatin *(antibiotic)*
Fungistase *f*, **Fungistasis** *f* fungistasis, fungistatic action
fungistatisch fungistatic, mycostatic
Fungistatikum *n* fungistat, mycostat
fungitoxisch fungitoxic
Fungitoxizität *f* fungitoxicity
fungivor fungivorous, myc[et]ophagous
fungizid [wirkend] fungicidal, antifungal
Fungizid *n* fungicide
~/kupferhaltiges copper fungicide
~/protektives protective (protectant) fungicide
~/sporentötendes antisporulant fungicide
~/vorbeugend wirkendes *s.* ~/protektives
fungizidresistent fungicide-resistant
Fungizidresistenz *f* fungicide resistance
Fungizidrückstand *m* fungicide residue
fungös fungous
Fungus *m* fungus *(kingdom Mycota)*
Funkie *f* plantain lily, funkia, hosta *(genus Hosta)*
Funktion *f* function
~/erzeugende *(biom)* generating function
Funktionsschwäche *f (vet)* insufficiency
Funktionsstörung *f* dysfunction, malfunction, functional disorder

Furadan *n* furadan *(insecticide)*
Furage *f* forage, fodder
Fural *n s.* Furfural
Furalaxyl *n* furalaxyl *(fungicide)*
Furanose *f* furanose *(monosaccharide)*
Furazolidon *n* furazolidone *(chemotherapeutical)*
Furca *f* forked springing organ *(of collembolans)*
Furcarbanil *n* furcarbanil *(fungicide)*
Furche *f* furrow • **Furchen ziehen** to furrow, to list
~/tiefe trench
Furchenanbau *m* trough culture *(horticulture)*
Furchenberieselung *f*, **Furchenbewässerung** *f* furrow irrigation
Furchendrillmaschine *f* furrow drill
Furchendüngung *f* furrow fertilization
Furchenegge *f* drill harrow
Furchenentwässerung *f* furrow drainage
Furchenerosion *f (soil)* rill (shoe-string) erosion
Furchenflügeliger Fichtenborkenkäfer *m* micrographer bark-beetle, Pityophthorus micrographus
Furchenkamm *m* furrow crest, ridge, comb of the furrow, bund
Furchenpflanzung *f* furrow planting
Furchenrad *n* furrow wheel
Furchenrain *m* box-ridge, tie-ridge, balk *(ploughing)*
Furchensaat *f* sowing in furrows
Furchenschar *n* furrow press
Furchensohle *f* furrow sole (bottom)
Furchenstreifen *m* furrow-slice *(ploughing)*
Furchenwand *f* furrow wall
Furchenziehen *n* furrowing, listing
Furchenzieher *m* furrow opener (drawer), moulder, marker; *(forest)* trencher
~/verstellbarer adjustable marker
Furcht *f* fright, fear *(animal behaviour)*
Furchtkrankheit *f (vet)* fright disease
Furchung *f* blastogenesis *(embryogenesis)*
Furchungshöhle *f* blastocoel[e]
Furchungszelle *f* blastomere
Furcula *f s.* Furca
Furfural *n*, **Furfurol** *n* furfural, 2-furylaldehyde
6-Furfurylamino-purin *n* 6-furfurylaminopurine, kinetin *(phytohormone)*
Furnier *n* veneer
Furnierband *n* band of veneer, veneer ribbon
Furnierbild *n* matched veneer
Furnierblatt *n* veneering sheet
Furnierblock *m s.* Furnierrolle
furnieren to veneer
Furnierholz *n* veneering wood
Furnierholzzucht *f* veneer timber growing
Furnierplatte *f* veneer panel
Furnierrolle *f*, **Furnierschälklotz** *m* veneer log (block, bolt), peeler log
Furnierschälmaschine *f* rotary veneer machine
Furnierwerk *n* veneer mill
Furophanat *n* furophanate *(fungicide)*
Furt *f* ford, Irish bridge, water-splash

Furunkulose f (vet) furunculosis
~ **der Salmoniden** fish furunculosis (caused by Aeromonas salmonicida)
Fusarientoxin n fusariotoxin (mycotoxin)
Fusariose f (phyt) fusariose
Fusariotoxikose f (vet) fusariotoxicosis
Fusariumfäule f (phyt) fusarium rot
Fusarium-Fußkrankheit f **der Gladiole** fusarium corm rot of gladiolus (caused by Fusarium oxysporum f.sp. gladioli)
Fusariumtoxin n fusariotoxin (mycotoxin)
Fusariumtrockenfäule f fusarium dry (storage) rot (of potato tubers, caused by Fusarium spp.)
Fusariumwelke f (phyt) fusarium (eumartii) wilt, (Am) fusarium yellows (caused by Fusarium spp.)
~ **der Gurke** fusarium wilt (root rot) of cucumber (caused by Fusarium reticulatum)
~ **der Melone** melon wilt (caused by Fusarium oxysporum f.sp. melonis)
~ **der Nelke** carnation wilt (caused by Fusarium dianthi)
Fusicoccin n fusicoccin (mycotoxin)
Fusion f fusion • **durch** ~ **entstanden** fusogenic
Fusionshybride f fusion hybrid
Fusionstranslokation f (gen) fusion translocation
fusogen fusogenic
Fuß m foot
~/**laufender** foot run (timber mensuration)
Fußballen m footpad
Fußballengeschwulst f footpad dermatitis, bumble foot (of fowl)
Fußblatt n may-apple, podophyllum (genus Podophyllum)
Fußbodenheizung f floor heating
Fußbodenheizvorrichtung f floor-warming unit
Fußdüngung f side dressing
Fußdurchmesser m diameter at foot (timber mensuration)
Fußenderodemaschine f mushroom stump lifter
Fußfäule f (phyt) stalk (foot) rot, stalk decay; (vet) foot rot
fußförmig (bot) pedatiform, pedate
Fußgeschwulst f s. Fußballengeschwulst
Fußgift n tarsal poison
Fußkrankheit f (phyt) foot-rot, blackleg [disease]
~ **von Zwiebeln** bulb basal rot (caused by Fusarium oxysporum f. cepae)
fußlos (zoo) apodal, apodous
Fußpolster n s. Fußballen
Fußräude f (vet) foot mange, barn itch; itchy leg (of horses)
~ **des Geflügels** scaly leg of fowl (caused by Knemidokoptes spp.)
Fußrodemaschine f mushroom stump lifter
Fußrohrberegnung f lay-flat tube [watering] system, on-floor sprinkling (in greenhouses)
Fußrohrheizung f on-floor heating [system], floor-level heating (in greenhouses)

Fußrollenentzündung f navicular disease (of horses)
Fußungsreibung f stumbling (of hoof or claw)
Fußwurzel f tarsus (animal anatomy)
Fußwurzelknochen m tarsal (navicular) bone
Fußzelle f/**Sertolische** Sertoli cell (animal anatomy)
Fustik m fustic (wood from Chlorophora spp.)
Futter n forage, food, feed[ing], feed-stuff, fodder, provender; diet • ~ **suchen** to forage • ~ **verabreichen** s. füttern
~/**energiereiches** energy feed
~/**pelletiertes** pelleted feed[-stuff]
~/**wiedergekäutes** rumen
~/**wiederzukäuendes** cud
~/**wirtschaftseigenes** farm-produced fodder, home-grown feed
~/**zugeteiltes** mess
Futter... s. a. Futtermittel...
Futterabbaurate f feed digestion rate
Futterabfall m waste feed
Futteranbaufläche f forage area, fodder acreage
Futteranhänger m forage trailer (wagon)
Futteraufbereitung f feed processing
Futteraufbereitungsanlage f feed-processing plant
Futteraufbereitungsmaschinen fpl forage handling equipment
Futteraufnahme f feed intake, feeding
~/**übermäßige** hyperphagia
Futteraufnahmeverhalten n feeding behaviour
Futteraufnahmevermögen n feed intake capacity
Futteraufwand m feed input
Futterausnutzung f feed conversion (efficiency)
Futterautomat m self-feeder, self-feed facility, automatic feed dispenser
Futterbahn f overhead feed carrier
Futterband n feed distributing conveyor
Futterbandförderer m feed conveyor
Futterbasis f forage base
Futterbau m forage cropping (growing)
Futterbedarf m feed requirement
Futterbehälter m forage container
Futterbeinwell m (bot) rough comfrey, Symphytum asperum
Futterbereitstellung f allocation of feed
Futterbereitung f feed preparation
Futterbergeraum m fodder store
Futterbestandteil m feed ingredient, dietary constituent
Futterbeutel m nosebag (for horses)
Futterbewertung f feed evaluation
Futterbilanz f feed balance
Futterbissen m bolus
Futterblattfrucht f leafy fodder crop
Futterblock m feed block
Futterbrei m mash
Futtercellulose f fodder cellulose

Futterdämpfanlage

Futterdämpfanlage f, **Futterdämpfer** m fodder (feed) steamer
futterdankbar thrifty
Futterdarbietung f, **Futterdarreichung** f feed presentation
Futterdosierer m feed proportioner (metering hopper), metering feeder (feed dispenser)
Futterdosierwagen m metering feed carrier
Futtereinheit f feed unit
~/Energetische energetic feed unit
Futtereinsatz m feed use (supply)
Futtereinsparung f feed saving
Futtereiweiß n forage (dietary) protein
Futterenergie f feed energy
Futterenergiekonzentration f feed energy concentration
Futtererbse f field (forage) pea, Dun (Australian winter) pea, Pisum sativum ssp. sativum convar. speciosum
Futterergänzungsstoff m feed supplement
Futtererte f forage harvest[ing]
Futtererntemaschine f forage harvester, forager
~/selbstfahrende self-propelled forage harvester
Futtererntemaschinen fpl forage-harvesting machinery
Futterertrag m forage yield
Futterfett n dietary fat
Futterfisch m forage fish
Futterfläche f 1. forage area, fodder acreage; 2. feeding area *(in animal houses)*
Futterfonds m feed fund[s]
Futterfruchtfolge f fodder crop rotation
Futtergang m feed pass[age], feed[ing] alley, feedway *(in animal houses)*
Futtergebläse n forage blower
Futtergemisch n feed mix, fodder mixture; mess *(e.g. for dogs)*
Futtergerste f feed[ing] barley, winter (rowed) barley
Futtergeschmack m **der Milch** weed taint of milk
Futtergestell n rack, hack
Futtergetreide n feed grain (cereal), coarse grain
Futterglas n *(api)* feeder, bottle
Futtergras n fodder (forage) grass
Futtergrasland n forage grassland
Futtergrobmehl n feed[ing] meal
Futtergrundlage f forage base
Futtergrünland n forage grassland
Futterhackfrucht f fodder root [crop], feed[ing] root
Futterhafer m feeding oat[s]
Futterhängebahn f [monorail] overhead feed carrier
Futterharnstoff m dietary urea
Futterhauptfrucht f forage main crop
Futterhefe f fodder (food, mineral) yeast
Futterhirse f forage sorghum, Sorghum bicolor (vulgare)
Futterhülsenfrucht f s. Futterleguminose
Futterkalk m feed lime

Futterkammer f forage shed
Futterkarre f feed barrow
Futterkartoffel f fodder (cull, stock-feed) potato, chat
Futterkasten m corn-chest
Futterkette f chain feeder
Futterkleie f beeswing
Futterknappheit f food shortage, scarcity of feed
Futterknochenschrot n bone-meal
Futterkohl m 1. fodder kale *(comprehensive term)*; 2. kale, collard, Brassica oleracea convar. acephala var. viridis
Futterkonservierung f forage preservation (conservation)
Futterkonzentrat n concentrate [food], feed concentrate
Futterkraut n [forage] herb, forb
Futterkrippe f crib, manger, feeding rack, trough
Futterküche f forage kitchen
Futterkultur f forage crop, fodder (feed) crop
Futterlader m forage (green-crop) loader
Futterladewagen m self-loading forage wagon, *(Am)* chuck-wagon
Futterlager n food store
Futterlagerraum m food store, feed room
Futterlaub n leaf fodder
Futterleguminose f forage legume, leguminous forage crop, fodder pulse crop
Futterloch n *(api)* feed-hole
Futtermehl n feed[ing] meal, bran shorts
Futtermischer m feed mixer
Futtermischmühle f feed grinder-mixer
Futtermischung f feed mix[ture]
Futtermischwagen m feeder mixer wagon
Futtermittel n feed[-stuff], food *(for compounds s. under Futter)*
Futtermittel... s. a. Futter...
Futtermittelanalyse f feed analysis
~/Weender Weende [feed] analysis
Futtermittelantibiotikum n fodder (feed-additive) antibiotic
Futtermittelattestierung f feed attestation
Futtermittelhygiene f food hygiene
Futtermittelindustrie f feed (food) industry
Futtermittelintoxikation f food (feed) poisoning
Futtermittelionisation f radicidation
Futtermittelkunde f feed science
Futtermittelmikrobiologie f feed microbiology
Futtermittelprobe f feed sample
Futtermittelprüfstelle f feed analysis laboratory
Futtermittelprüfung f feed testing
Futtermitteltabelle f feed [composition] table
Futtermitteltoxikologie f feed toxicology
Futtermittelvergiftung f food (feed) poisoning
Futtermittelvollanalyse f complete feed analysis
Futtermittelzusammensetzung f feed composition
Futtermittelzusatz[stoff] m feed additive, animal feed supplement

Fütterungsperiode

~/**antibiotischer** fodder antibiotic
Futtermöhre f cattle-feeding carrot
Futtermühle f feed mill
Futtermühlenmischer m feed grinder-mixer
Futtermuser m feed masher
füttern to feed, to forage, to fodder, to provender
~/**ad libitum** to feed (to give) to appetite
~/**diätetisch** to diet
~/**[frischgemähtes] Grünfutter** to soil
~/**im Stall** to stall[-feed]
~/**mit Getreide** to corn
~/**mit Heu** to hay
~/**reichlich** to flush
~/**ungenügend** to underfeed
Futternährstoff m dietary nutrient
Futternährstoffration f dietary nutrient allowance
Futternährstoffzuteilung f dietary nutrient allowance
Futternapf m feed pan, feeding bowl
Futterneuansaat f new forage seeding
Futternorm f feeding standard
Futterökonomie f feed use efficiency, feed economics
Futterparzellenerntemaschine f forage plot harvester
Futterpelletierung f forage pelleting
Futterpflanze f forage (herbage) plant, fodder plant (crop)
~/**mehrschnittige** multicut forage plant, forage plant for repeated cutting
Futterpflanzen[an]bau m fodder cultivation
Futterpflanzenernte f fodder crop harvest
Futterpflanzenkultur f feed (forage, fodder) crop
Futterpflanzensaatgut n forage [crop] seed, herbage seed
Futterpflanzensamenbau m herbage seed growing
Futterpflanzentrockner m forage crop dryer
Futterplan m feeding plan
Futterplanung f feed planning
Futterplatz m feeding site (area); haunt (of game)
Futterportion f mess
Futterproduktion f forage production
Futterprotein n forage (dietary) protein
Futterqualität f feed quality
Futterquetscher m grater
Futterquotient m feed conversion ratio
Futterraps m [swede] forage rape, Brassica napus var. napus
Futterration f [feed] ration, diet, dietary [allowance], feed [allowance]
Futterrationierung f feed rationing
Futterraum m food store, feed room
Futterrehe f (vet) grain founder
Futterreinigungsmaschine f feed cleaning machine
Futterreißer m forage shredder, [husker] shredder, feed masher

Futterreserve f forage reserve
Futterrinne f (api) glossal groove
Futterroggen m forage (feeding, green) rye
Futterrübe f 1. feeding beet (comprehensive term); 2. fodder (feeding) beet, mangel[-wurzel], Beta vulgaris var. alba (crassa)
~/**walzenförmige** tankard mangel
Futtersaatgut n forage seed
Futtersack m feed bag
Futtersaft m (api) brood (larval) food
~ **der Ammenbienen** bee-bread
Futtersaftdrüse f brood food gland
Futtersammelverhalten n foraging behaviour
Futterschale f feed pan, feeding bowl
Futterschneidebank f fodder chopping bench
Futterschneidemaschine f forage (feed) cutter
Futterschnitt m herbage cut
Futterschrot n feed[ing] meal
Futterschrotmühle f feed grain crusher
Futterspender m feed dispenser (distributor), feeder
Futterstapel m s. Futterstock
Futterstaudenkohl m cow (tree) cabbage, Brassica oleracea var. acephala subvar. plana
Futterstelle f feeding place
Futterstickstoff m dietary nitrogen
Futterstock m feed stock (pile)
Futterstoff m feed-stuff
Futterstroh n feeding straw, stover
Futterstruktur f feed structure
Futtersuche f search for food, forage
Futterteig m (api) candy
Futtertisch m feeding table
Futtertrockner m forage dryer
Futtertrog m feed trough (pan), manger, (Am) [feed]bunk
Futterturm m forage tower
Futterumschlag m feed-handling
Futterumstellung f change in feeding
Fütterung f feeding, feed • **nach der** ~ postprandial • **vor der** ~ preprandial
~ **auf Leistung** feeding to yield
~/**ausgewogene** balanced feeding
~/**automatische** automatic feeding
~ **im Freien** outdoor feeding
~ **im Stall** indoor feeding, stall-feeding
~/**manuelle** hand feeding
~/**rationierte** rationed feeding
~/**restriktive (verhaltene)** restricted (limited) feeding
Fütterungsautomat m automatic feed dispenser
Fütterungsdauer f feeding time
Fütterungsempfehlung f feeding recommendation
Fütterungsfrequenz f feeding frequency
Fütterungshäufigkeit f feeding frequency
Fütterungshygiene f feeding hygiene
Fütterungsniveau n feed[ing] level
Fütterungsnorm f feeding standard
Fütterungsperiode f feeding period

Fütterungsplan

Fütterungsplan *m* feeding plan
Fütterungsplatz *m* feeding place
Fütterungspraxis *f* feeding practice
Fütterungsregime *n* feeding regime[n], feeding management (pattern), diet
Fütterungssequenz *f* feeding sequence
Fütterungssystem *n* feeding system
Fütterungstechnik *f* feeding technique
Fütterungstechnologie *f* feeding technology
Fütterungsverfahren *n* feeding practice
Fütterungsversuch *m* feeding experiment (trial)
Fütterungszeit *f* feeding time
Futterverabreichung *f s.* Fütterung
Futterverbrauch *m* feed consumption
Futterverdaulichkeit *f* feed digestibility
Futterverfügbarkeit *f* forage availability
Futtervergiftung *f* forage (feed) poisoning
Futterversorgung *f* feed supply, keep
Futterverteilanlage *f* feed distribution plant
Futterverteilautomat *m* automatic feed dispenser
Futterverteilband *n* feed distributing conveyor
Futterverteiler *m* feed dispenser (distributor), feeder
~ **mit Volumendosierung** metering feeder (feed dispenser)
Futterverteilschnecke *f* feeding auger
Futterverteil[ungs]wagen *m* feed [dispenser] wagon, food trolley
Futterverwerter *m* feed converter
Futterverwertung *f* 1. feed conversion; 2. feed efficiency
Futterverwertungsfaktor *m* feed conversion factor, FCF
Futterverwertungsrate *f* feed conversion rate, FCR
Futterverzehr *m* feed consumption
Futtervorrat *m* feed supply
Futterwagen *m* forage trailer (wagon), *(Am)* chuckwagon; hay trailer
~ **mit seitlicher Entleerung** side-delivery forage trailer
Futterwanze *f* common green capsid, Lygocoris (Lygus) pabulinus
Futterwechsel *m* change in feeding
Futterweg *m s.* Futtergang
Futterweizen *m* feed wheat
Futterwert *m* feed value
Futterwerteinheit *f* feed value unit
Futterwerttabelle *f* feed value (composition) table
Futterwicke *f* tare, Vicia sativa ssp. sativa
Futterwirtschaft *f* feed management
Futterzubereitung *f* feed preparation
Futterzucker *m* feeding sugar (syrup)
Futterzuckerrohr *n* forage cane
Futterzuckerrübe *f* fodder sugar-beet, Beta vulgaris var. alba (crassa)
Futterzusatz[stoff] *m* feed additive
~/**milchsäureerzeugender** probiotic
Futterzuteilung *f* allocation of feed

Futterzuteilvorrichtung *f* **im Melkstand** in-parlour feeder
Futterzweitfrucht *f* secondary forage crop
Futterzwischenfrucht *f* forage catch crop
F-Verteilung *f (biom)* variance-ratio distribution

G

G *s.* 1. G-Horizont; 2. Energie/Gibbs[sche] Freie
GA *s.* Grubenholz
GäAVV *s.* Gänsedisteladernvergilbungsvirus
Gabanholz *n* camwood *(from Baphia nitida)*
Gabbro *m (soil)* gabbro
Gabe *f* application *(e.g. of fertilizers)*
Gabel *f* 1. fork, prong; 2. frog *(of the hoof)* • **mit der** ~ **aufladen** to fork
~/**dreizinkige** three-pronged fork
Gabelantilope *f* prong-horn [antelope], prong-buck, Antilocapra americana
gabelartig *(bot, zoo)* dichotomous, bifurcate, forked
Gabelbaum *m* forked tree
Gabelbock *m s.* Gabelantilope
Gabeldeichsel *f* forked shaft, thill
gabelförmig forked, furcate
Gabelgang *m* forked (branching) gallery *(of mining pests)*
Gabelheuwender *m* fork-type hay tedder
Gabelhornantilope *f s.* Gabelantilope
gabelig *s.* gabelartig
Gabelleine *f* **mit Halsungen** leash
gabeln to [pitch]fork, to butt
~/**sich** to bifurcate
Gabelrückeschlitten *m (forest)* alligator
Gabelstamm *m* forked stem
Gabelstapler *m* fork-lift [truck], lift truck
Gabelsteinsammler *m* fork-type stone picker
Gabelstreifenfarn *m* forked spleenwort, Asplenium septentrionale
Gabelung *f* 1. [bi]furcation, dichotomy; 2. *s.* Gabelzweig
Gabelwelle *f* fork shaft
Gabelwender *m* fork-type hay tedder
Gabelwuchs *m* forked growth, bifurcation, crotch
Gabelzweig *m* double leader *(of young trees)*
gackern to cackle, to clack
Gackern *n* cackle
Gadoleinsäure *f* gadoleic (eicos-9-enoic) acid *(fatty acid)*
Gadolensäure *f* gadolenic acid *(fatty acid)*
Gagel[strauch] *m* 1. bayberry *(genus Myrica)*; 2. bog (moor) myrtle, [sweet] gale, Myrica gale
Gagnepain-Berberitze *f* black barberry, Berberis gagnepainii
gähnen to yawn
Gal *s.* Galactose
Galactan *n* galactan *(polysaccharide)*
Galactitol *m* galactitol, dulcitol *(sugar alcohol)*
Galactokinase *f* galactokinase *(enzyme)*

Galactolipid *n* galactolipid
Galactosamin *n* galactosamine
Galactose *f* galactose *(monosaccharide)*
Galactoseakkumulation *f* im Blut *(vet)* galactosaemia
Galactose-1-Phosphaturidylyltransferase *f* UTP-hexose-1-phosphate uridylyltransferase *(enzyme)*
Galactosidase *f* galactosidase *(enzyme)*
Galactoskop *n* milk poise
(D)-Galacturonsäure *f* galacturonic acid
Galaktagogum *n* [ga]lactagogue
Galaktämie *f (vet)* galactaemia
galaktogen galactogenic
Galaktometer *n* lactometer
Galaktophoritis *f (vet)* galactophoritis
Galaktopoese *f* galactopoiesis, lactogenesis
galaktopoetisch galactopoietic, lactogenic
Galaktorrhoe *f (vet)* galactorrhoea
Galaktosämie *f (vet)* galactosaemia
galaktosämisch galactosaemic
Galaktostase *f (vet)* galactostasis
Galaktosurie *f (vet)* galactosuria
Galaktozele *f*, **Galaktozystis** *f (vet)* [ga]lactocele
Galakturie *f s.* Galaktosurie
Galambutter *f* shea-butter *(from Vitellaria paradoxa)*
Galban[um] *n* galban[um] *(gum resin)*
Galecron *n* galecron *(insecticide)*
Galeriewald *m* gallery (fringing) forest
Galgant *m (bot)* lesser galangal, Alpinia officinarum
Galiceno *n* Galician Pony *(breed)*
Galipot *m* gal[l]ipot, barras *(hardened turpentine from Pinus pinaster)*
Gallapfel *m (phyt)* nut gall
Gallapfeleiche *f s.* Galleiche
Galle *f* 1. gall[-bladder]; 2. bile, gall; 3. *(phyt)* gall[nut]; *(vet)* gall
Galleiche *f* gall oak, Quercus infectoria
Gallenbildung *f* 1. cholepoiesis; 2. *(phyt)* galling
Gallenblase *f* gall-bladder
Gallenblasenentfernung *f (vet)* gall-bladder removal, cholecystectomy
Gallenblasenentzündung *f (vet)* cholecystitis
Gallenblasengang *m* cystic duct
Gallenfarbstoff *m* bile pigment
Gallenfett *n* cholesterol
Gallenfieber *n (vet)* piroplasmosis
Gallenflüssigkeit *f* bile, gall
Gallengang *m* bile-duct
~/gemeinsamer common bile-duct
Gallengangentzündung *f (vet)* cholangitis
Gallenmittel *n* cholagogue
Gallenpilz *m s.* Gallenröhrling
gallenreich bilious
Gallenröhrling *m* bitter boletus, Boletus felleus
Gallensaft *m* bile, gall
Gallensaftsekretion *f* bile secretion
Gallensalz *n* bile salt
Gallensäure *f* bile acid
Gallenseuche *f* benign bovine gonderiosis (theileriasis), tzaneen disease
Gallenstein *m (vet)* gallstone, biliary calculus, cholelith
Gallensteinleiden *n (vet)* cholelithiasis
Gallensumach *m* Chinese sumac[h], Rhus chinensis
Gallenweg *m s.* Gallengang
gallertartig gelatinous
Gallestauung *f (vet)* cholestasis
galletreibend cholagogue, choleretic
gallig biliary, bilious
Gallknoten *m* knopper *(of the fruits of Quercus robur)*
Gallmilbe *f* gall-mite, eriophyid [mite] *(family Eriophyidae)*
Gallmücke *f* gall-midge, gall-gnat, cecidomyid *(family Cecidomyidae)*
~/wurzelschädigende root gall-midge *(comprehensive term)*
~/zapfenbefallende cone midge *(comprehensive term)*
Gallocatechin *n* gallocatechin *(tannin)*
Gallotannin *n* gallotannin, gallotannic acid
Gallowaypony *n* Galloway [Pony] *(breed)*
Gallowayrind *n* Galloway, Southern Scots Polled *(cattle breed)*
gallus-adeno-like-Virus *n* gallus adeno-like virus, GAL virus
Gallusgerbsäure *f* [gallo]tannic acid
Gallussäure *f* gallic acid, 3,4,5-trihydroxybenzoic acid
Gallwespe *f* gall-wasp, gall-fly, cynipid *(family Cynipidae)*
GalN *s.* Galactosamin
Galopp *m* gallop • **im ~** at a gallop • **in ~ fallen** to break into a gallop • **in ~ versetzen** to gallop
~/abgekürzter short gallop
~/gestreckter extended gallop, career
~/starker racing gallop
galoppieren to gallop
~/gestreckt to career
Galvanotropismus *m (bot)* galvanotropism
GAL-Virus *n* GAL virus, gallus adeno-like virus
Gamagras *n* gama [grass], Tripsacum dyctyloides (pilosum)
Gamander *m* germander *(genus Teucrium)*
Gamanderehrenpreis *m* germander speedwell, Veronica chamaedrys
Gamanderspierstrauch *m* germander spiraea, Spiraea chamaedryfolia
Gambade *f* gambade, gambado *(equitation)*
Gambagras *n* Gamba grass, Andropogon gayanus
Gambir *m* 1. gambi[e]r, pale catechu *(tannin extract)*; 2. *s.* Gambirpflanze
Gambirpflanze *f*, **Gambirstrauch** *m* gambi[e]r, Uncaria gambir

Gambohanf

Gambohanf *m (bot)* okra, bhendi, bhindi, Abelmoschus (Hibiscus) esculentus
Gamet *m* gamete, germ-cell, sex cell
Gametangium *n (bot)* gametangium
~/weibliches oogonium, ovogonium
Gametenbildung *f* gametogenesis
Gametenhormon *n* gamone
Gametenverschmelzung *f* amphimixis
gametisch gametic
Gametobiont *m s.* Gametophyt
Gametogenese *f* gametogenesis
Gametophyt *m (bot)* gametophyte, prothallium, prothallus
gametophytisch gametophytic
gametozid gametocidal
Gametozid *n* gametocide
gamisch gamic
Gammabestrahlung *f* gamma irradiation
Gamma-Casein *n* gamma-casein
Gammacellulose *f* gamma cellulose
Gammaeule *f* gamma [moth], silver Y moth, Autographa (Phytometra, Plusia) gamma
Gammaglobulin *n* gamma-globulin
Gamma-Glutamylcyclotransferase *f* gamma-glutamylcyclotransferase *(enzyme)*
Gamma-Glutamylhydrolase *f* gamma-glutamyl hydrolase, [folate] conjugase *(enzyme)*
Gamma-Glutamyltransferase *f* [gamma-]glutamyltransferase *(enzyme)*
Gammastrahl *m* gamma ray
Gammastrahlen-Dickenmeßgerät *n* gamma[-ray] thickness gauge
Gammastrahlung *f* gamma radiation
Gamogonie *f* gamogony, gamogenesis
Gamon *n* gamone
Gamswild *n* chamois, Rupicapra rupicapra
Ganasche *f* cheek, chap *(of a horse)*
Gang *m* 1. duct; 2. gait, air *(e.g. of a horse)*; 3. gear
~/bügelnder paddling *(of a horse)*
~/Müllerscher Muellerian duct *(animal anatomy)*
~/unterirdischer burrow, gallery *(of animals)*
~/Wolffscher Wolffian (mesonephric) duct *(animal anatomy)*
Ganganomalie *f* anomaly of gait
Gangart *f* gait, air *(e.g. of a horse)*
Ganglien[zell]blocker *m (vet)* ganglionic blocker (blocking agent)
Ganglienzelle *f* ganglion-cell, gangliocyte
Ganglion *n* ganglion, nerve-knot
Gangliosid *n* ganglioside
ganglos ductless
Gangmanier *f* action *(of a horse)*
Gangrän *f(n) (vet)* gangrene
gangränös gangrenous
Ganiterbaum *m* bead tree of India, Elaeocarpus ganitrus
Gans *f* goose *(genus Anser)*
gänseartig anserine

Gänseblümchen *n* [English, true] daisy, Bellis perennis
Gänsedistel *f* sowthistle, milk thistle *(genus Sonchus)*
Gänsedisteladernvergilbungsvirus *n* sowthistle yellow vein [mosaic] virus
Gänsedistellaus *f* currant-sowthistle aphid, Hyperomyzus lactucae
Gänseei *n* goose egg
Gänsefett *n* goose fat
Gänsefingerkraut *n* goose tansy (grass), silverweed, Potentilla anserina
Gänsefleisch *n* goose [meat]
Gänsefuß *m* 1. *(bot)* goose-foot *(genus Chenopodium)*; 2. *s.* Gänsefußschar
Gänsefußgewächs *n* chenopod *(family Chenopodiaceae)*
Gänsefußmesser[blatt] *n* A-blade, A-hoe *(s. a. Gänsefußschar)*
Gänsefußmosaikvirus *n* sowbane mosaic virus, SoMV
Gänsefußschar *n* duck-foot share (shovel), A-share • **mit dem ~ bearbeiten** to duckfoot
~/halbes half shovel (sweep)
Gänsefußschönwanze *f* alfalfa plant bug, Adelphocoris lineolatus
Gänsegang *m* goose-stepping *(of pigs with pantothenic acid deficiency)*
Gänsegonorrhoe *f* epidemic venereal disease in geese
Gänsegras *n* yard grass, Eleusine indica (africana)
Gänsehalsstadium *n* goose-neck stage *(harvest date of narcissus flowers)*
Gänseherde *f* flock of geese, gaggle
Gänseklein *n* [goose] giblets
Gänsekresse *f* rock (wall) cress, arabis *(genus Arabis)*
Gänseküken *n* gosling
Gänseleber *f* goose liver
Gänseleberpastete *f* goose-liver paste, foie gras
Gänsemast *f* goose fattening
Gänsemiere *f* chick[en]weed, Stellaria media
Gänserich *m* gander
Gänseschar *f s.* Gänseherde
Ganter *m* gander
gantern to bank [up], to bunch *(longwood)*
Ganzbaum *m (forest)* whole tree
Ganzbaumbereitstellung *f* whole-tree logging
Ganzbaumernte *f* whole-tree harvest[ing]
Ganzbaumhackung *f* full-tree chipping
Ganzbaumnutzung *f* whole-tree utilization
Ganzbaumrückung *f* full-tree skidding
Ganzbaumtransport *m* full-tree removal
Ganzblättrige Weißtanne *f* Manchurian fir, Abies holophylla
Ganzflächenapplikation *f s.* Ganzflächenausbringung
Ganzflächenausbringung *f* area-application, overall (total) application *(e.g. of fertilizers)*

Ganzflächenbehandlung f overall treatment
Ganzflächenbesprühung f overall spraying
Ganzflächenspritzung f overall spraying
ganzfrüchtig (bot) holocarpous
Ganzjahreskultur f all-year-round crop, ayr crop, year-round culture
Ganzkornreis m whole rice
Ganzkörperstoffwechsel m whole-body metabolism
Ganzkörpervibration f whole-body vibration
Ganzpflanzenernte f whole-crop harvest[ing]
Ganzpflanzensilage f whole-crop silage
ganzrandig entire (leaf)
Ganzspaltenboden m fully-slatted floor (in animal houses)
Ganzstammrückung f (forest) tree-length skidding
Gaolao-Rind n Gaolao [cattle] (breed)
gar mellow[y], of good tilth, unctuous (soil)
Gär... s. a. Gärungs...
Garbe f 1. sheaf; 2. yarrow (genus Achillea) • **Garben binden** to sheafe, to sheave
Gärbehälter m digester (s. a. Gärbottich)
Garbenaufstellen n **auf dem Felde** field shocking, windrowing
Garbenbinden n sheafing
Garbenbinder m [sheaf] binder, sheafer
Garbenförderer m, **Garbenfördervorrichtung** f sheaf elevator
Garbenhalter m packer
Garbenhaufen m mow, pile
Garbenreihe f windrow
Garbensammler m sheaf carrier
Garbentrenner m sheaf separator
Garbenwagen m bundle wagon
Gärbottich m fermenting vat (cask), fermentation tub, [open] fermenter, [open] fermentor
Gardenie f 1. gardenia (genus Gardenia); 2. Cape jasmin[e], [garden] gardenia, Gardenia jasminoides
Gare f mellowness, [good] tilth, unctuousness (of a soil) • **~ mehren** to mellow
~/natürliche natural tilth
Gareförderer m renovating crop
gären to ferment
Gären n fermentation
gärend fermentative
Garezehrer m exhausting crop
gärfähig fermentable
Gärfaß n s. Gärbottich
Gärfaulverfahren n fermentation septization process
Gärflüssigkeit f fermentable liquid
Gärführung f fermentation method (e.g. in wine-making)
Gärfutter n silage, ensilage (for compounds s. under Silage)
Gärfutter... s. a. Silage...
Gärfutterbehälter m silo
Gärfutterbereitung f silage-making, [en]silage

Gärfutterbewertung f silage evaluation
Gärfutterhochsilo m forage tower
Gärfuttermiete f silage clamp
~ mit Selbstfütterungsvorrichtung self-feed silage clamp
Gärfuttersilo m silage (forage) silo
Gärfutterverabreichung f silage feeding
Gärgebinde n, **Gärgefäß** n fermentation tank (vat, cask), wine-making vat
Gärheu n haylage
Garigue f garigue (mediterranean shrub heath formation)
Gärkeller m fermenting cellar (room), starting cellar
Garnelenblume f 1. beloperone (genus Beloperone); 2. shrimp plant, Beloperone guttata
Gärniederschlag m lees
Garnier n s. Stauhölzer
Gärprozeß m fermentation process
Garrigue f s. Garigue
Garron n Highland pony (breed)
Garryeiche f Garry (Oregon white) oak, Quercus garryana
Gärtank m fermentation tank (wine-making)
Gärtemperatur f fermentation temperature
Garten m garden
~/architektonisch gestalteter formal garden
~/botanischer botanical garden
~/englischer landscape garden
~/forstbotanischer forest-botanical garden
~ mit dekorativ verschnittenen Bäumen topiary
~/regelmäßiger formal garden
~/unregelmäßiger informal garden
~/zoologischer zoological garden, zoo
Gartenabfall m garden waste (refuse)
Gartenabfälle mpl garden refuse
Gartenabfallzerkleinerer m garden waste chipper (shredder)
Gartenampfer m 1. patience [dock], spinach (vegetable) dock, garden (herb) patience, Rumex patientia; 2. s. Gartensauerampfer
Gartenanemone f crown (poppy) anemone, Anemone coronaria
Gartenanlage f gardens; park
Gartenarbeit f gardening
Gartenarchitekt m garden architect, landscape gardener
Gartenartikel mpl garden sundries
Gartenausrüstung f gardening equipment
Gartenbalsamine f garden (common) balsam, balsam[ine], Lady's slipper, Impatiens balsamina
Gartenbank f garden seat
Gartenbau m 1. horticulture, gardening; 2. horticulture industry • **~ betreiben** to garden, to do gardening
~/alternativer (organischer) organic gardening
Gartenbauarchitekt m landscape gardener
Gartenbauausstellung f garden (horticultural) show

Gartenbauberater

Gartenbauberater *m* horticultural adviser
Gartenbaubetrieb *m* horticultural enterprise (farm), market garden
Gartenbaudrillmaschine *f* gardening seed drill
Gartenbauer *m* horticulturist
Gartenbaufacharbeiter *m* horticultural graduate
Gartenbaufachschule *f* horticultural technical school
Gartenbauforschung *f* horticultural research
Gartenbaugehilfe *m* nursery hand
Gartenbaugesellschaft *f* horticultural society
Gartenbaukultur *f* horticultural crop
Gartenbaukunst *f* horticulture, science of gardening
gartenbaulich horticultural, garden
Gartenbaum *m* garden tree
Gartenbaumschule *f* tree nursery
Gartenbauökonomik *f* horticultural economics
Gartenbaupraxis *f* horticultural practice
Gartenbautechnik *f* horticultural engineering
Gartenbauverein *m* garden club
Gartenbauversuchsstation *f* experimental horticultural station
Gartenbauwissenschaft *f* horticultural science, science of gardening
Gartenbedarfsartikel *mpl* garden sundries
Gartenbeet *n* [garden] bed
Gartenbeet... *s.* Beet...
Gartenbesen *m* wire-tooth rake
Gartenblume *f* garden flower
Gartenboden *m* hortisol
Gartenbohne *f* French (garden) bean, common (green) bean, snap (kidney) bean, haricot [bean], flageolet, *(Am)* navy bean, Phaseolus vulgaris
Gartencenter *n* garden centre
Gartencinerarie *f (bot)* cineraria *(Senecio-cruentus hybrid)*
Gartendill *m* green dill, Anethum graveolens var. hortorum
Gartendünger *m* garden fertilizer
Gartenerbse *f* garden (green) pea, Pisum sativum
Gartenerdbeere *f* [pineapple] strawberry, dessert strawberry, Fragaria x ananassa (grandiflora)
Gartenerde *f* garden earth, [garden] mould
Gartenfenchel *m s.* Gemüsefenchel
Gartenfräse *f* horticultural rotary cultivator
Gartenfuchsschwanz *m* love-lies-bleeding, prince's feather, velvet flower, Amaranthus caudatus (cruentus)
Gartengänsedistel *f* annual (common) sowthistle, Sonchus oleraceus
Gartengänsekresse *f* wall rock-cress, Arabis caucasica (albida)
Gartengehölze *npl* woody plants for gardens
Gartengerät *n* garden[ing] tool, garden implement; garden[ing] implements, gardening equipment
Gartengestalter *m* landscape gardener
Gartengestaltung *f* landscape gardening (horticulture)

Gartengloxinie *f* florist's gloxinia, Sinningia hybrid
Gartengrubber *m* garden cultivator
Gartenhaarmücke *f* March fly, Bibio hortulanus
Gartenhacke *f* [combined] garden hoe
Gartenhäcksler *m* garden waste chipper (shredder)
Gartenhippe *f s.* Gartenmesser
Gartenhof *m* courtyard garden, back-garden, atrium
Gartenhortensie *f* hortensia, French (common) hydrangea, florist's hydrangea, Hydrangea macrophylla
Gartenkerbel *m* [garden] chervil, salad chervil, Anthriscus cerefolium ssp. cerefolium
Gartenklarglas *n* horticultural glass
Gartenkompost *m* garden compost
Gartenkresse *f* garden [pepper]cress, pepperwort, peppergrass, Lepidium sativum
Gartenkultivator *m* garden cultivator
Gartenkulturpflanze *f* horticultural plant
Gartenkunst *f* horticulture
Gartenkürbis *m s.* Gemüsekürbis
Gartenland *n* garden land
Gartenlaube *f* summer-house, arbour
Gartenlaubkäfer *m* garden chafer, Phyllopertha horticola
Gartenleimkraut *n (bot)* sweet william campion (catchfly, silene), Silene armeria
Gartenlevkoje *f (bot)* [florist's, ten-week] stock, Matthiola incana
Gartenlöwenmaul *n (bot)* [common] snapdragon, snap, dragon's mouth, Antirrhinum majus
Gartenmajoran *m* sweet marjoram, Majorana hortensis
Gartenmargerite *f* Shasta (max) daisy, Chrysanthemum maximum
Gartenmarkt *m* garden centre
Gartenmauer *f* garden wall
Gartenmelde *f* [garden, purple] orach[e], mountain spinach, saltbush, Atriplex hortensis
Gartenmelisse *f* lemon (common) balm, Melissa officinalis
Gartenmelone *f* honeydew (musk, sweet) melon, cantaloup[e], Cucumis melo
Gartenmesser *n* hedge-bill, pruning-knife, pruning-hook, bill[hook]
Gartenmöhre *f* carrot, Daucus carota ssp. sativus
Gartenmontbretie *f (bot)* montbretia, Crocosmia x crocosmiiflora
Gartenmorchel *f* garden morel, Morchella hortensis
Gartennelke *f* [mediterranean] carnation, clove-scented pink, clove [pink], [clove] gillyflower, Dianthus caryophyllus
Gartenparzelle *f* allotment garden
Gartenpfahl *m* horticultural post
Gartenpflanze *f* garden (horticultural) plant
~/verwilderte escape
Gartenpflege *f* garden maintenance

Gartenpflug *m* hand plough
Gartenpimpinelle *f* fodder burnet, Sanguisorba minor ssp. muricata
Gartenraute *f* herb [of] grace, Ruta graveolens var. vulgaris
Gartenregner *m* garden sprinkler
Gartenreseda *f* mignonette, Reseda odorata
Gartenringelblume *f* pot (English) marigold, yellow gold, Calendula officinalis
Gartenrittersporn *m* [rocket] larkspur, lark-heel, [annual] delphinium, Delphinium ajacis
Gartensäge *f* pruning saw
Gartensalbei *m* [garden] sage, Salvia officinalis
Gartensalvie *f* scarlet sage, salvia, Salvia splendens
Gartensämaschine *f* horticultural seeder
Gartensauerampfer *m* garden sorrel, sour dock, Rumex acetosa [var. hortensis], Rumex rugosus
Gartenschere *f* pruning shears, pruner, secateur
~/einschneidige anvil pruning shears
~/zweischneidige scissor-action pruning shears
Gartenschlauch *m* garden hose
Gartenschlepper *m* garden tractor
Gartenschnecke *f* garden snail, Helix aspersa (hortensis)
Gartenschnur *f* marking line
Gartenschuppen *m* garden shed
Gartenschwarzerde *f* hortisol
Gartenspargel *m* [garden] asparagus, Asparagus officinalis
Gartensparte *f* garden club
Gartenspringkraut *n s.* Gartenbalsamine
Gartenspritze *f* syringe
Gartenspritzmittel *n* horticultural spray
Gartenstadt *f* garden city
Gartensteig *m s.* Gartenweg
Gartenstiefmütterchen *n* pansy, heart's-ease, Viola-Wittrockiana-hybrid
Gartenstrauch *m* garden shrub
Gartenstrohblume *f* everlasting flower, strawflower, Helichrysum bracteatum
Gartenteich *m* garden pond
Gartenthymian *m* [garden, common] thyme, Thymus vulgaris
Gartentithonie *f (bot)* tithonia, Tithonia rotundifolia (tagetiflora)
Gartentorf *m* garden peat
Gartentraktor *m* garden tractor
Gartenverein *m* garden club
Gartenweg *m* garden path (walkway)
Gartenwegschnecke *f* garden (black field) slug, Arion hortensis
Gartenwolfsmilch *f* petty spurge, Euphorbia peplus
Gartenzaun *m* garden fence
Gartenzinnie *f (bot)* youth-and-old-age, Zinnia elegans
Gärtner *m* gardener, horticulturist, *(Am)* yard-man
~/halbkommerzieller semicommercial gardener

~ mit Kleinverkauf retail grower
Gärtnerei *f* 1. market garden, horticultural enterprise (farm), *(Am)* truck farm; 2. gardening, horticulture
Gärtnereierzeugnisse *npl* garden-stuff
gärtnerisch horticultural, garden
Gärtnerlehrling *m* gardener's apprentice
Gärtnermeister *m* gardener
gärtnern to garden, to do gardening
Gärtnern *n* gardening
Gärtnerpflaume *f* hortulan plum, Prunus hortulana
Gärung *f* fermentation
~/aerobe aerobic fermentation
~/alkoholische alcoholic fermentation
~/anaerobe anaerobic fermentation
~/bakterielle bacterial fermentation
~/beschleunigte accelerated fermentation
~/gelenkte (gezügelte) pressure-controlled fermentation
~/kochende boiling (fretting) fermentation *(of young beer)*
~/mikrobielle microbial fermentation
~/milchsaure lactic-acid fermentation
~/oxidative aerobic fermentation
Gärungs... *s. a.* Gär...
Gärungsabprodukt *n* fermentation waste
Gärungsbakterium *n* fermenting bacterium
Gärungschemie *f* fermentation chemistry
Gärungsenzym *n* fermentation enzyme
gärungserregend fermentative, zymogenic, zymogenous
Gärungserreger *m* fermenter
Gärungserzeugnis *n* fermentation product
gärungsfördernd zymogenic, zymogenous
Gärungshilfsmittel *n* fermentation aid
Gärungsindustrie *f* fermentation industry
Gärungsrückstand *m* fermentation residue
Gärungstätigkeit *f* fermentation activity
Gärungstechnik *f* zymotechnology
Gärungstechnologie *f* fermentation technology, zymotechnology
Gärungsvorgang *m* fermentation process
gasartig gaseous
Gasaustausch *m* gas exchange (interchange)
Gasbehandlung *f* fumigation
Gasbrand *m (vet)* gas gangrene
Gasbrust *f (vet)* pneumothorax, aerothorax
Gaschromatographie *f* gas chromatography
Gascogner[rind] *n* Gascony *(cattle breed)*
gasdicht gas-tight
Gas-flüssig-Chromatographie *f* gas-liquid chromatography
gasförmig gaseous
Gasgangrän *f (vet)* gas gangrene
Gashaut *f* boundary layer *(e.g. of an animal body)*
Gaslagerung *f* gas storage, controlled (modified) atmosphere storage *(of agricultural produce)*
Gas-Lufterhitzer *m* gas-air heater
Gasnarkose *f (vet)* gas anaesthesia

Gasödemerkrankung

Gasödemerkrankung f *(vet)* gas gangrene
Gasohol n gasohol
Gaspatrone f gas cartridge *(pest control)*
Gaspeldorn m s. Englischer Ginster
Gasstoffwechsel m gas exchange (interchange)
Gasstoffwechselanalyse f gas exchange analysis
Gasstoffwechselbilanz f gas exchange balance
Gastbaumart f exotic tree species
Gastrektasie f gastromegaly
Gastrektomie f *(vet)* gastrectomy
Gastrin n gastrin *(hormone)*
gastrisch gastric
Gastritis f *(vet)* gastritis
gastroenteral gastro-enteric
Gastroenteritis f *(vet)* gastro-enteritis, gastro-enteropathy
gastrointestinal gastro-intestinal
Gastrointestinaltrakt m gastro-intestinal tract, GI tract
Gastrolith m gastrolith
Gastromegalie f gastromegaly
Gastron n gastrone *(hormone)*
Gastropode m gast[e]ropod *(class Gastropoda)*
Gastrostomie f *(vet)* gastrostomy
Gastrula f *(zoo)* gastrula
Gastrulation f gastrulation
Gaswechsel m s. Gasstoffwechsel
Gaswäscher m gas washer
gatten s. begatten
Gatter n 1. fencing; enclosure, holding paddock; deer fence; 2. saw gate
Gatterführer m sawyer, frame-saw operator
Gatterführung f saw frame guide
Gatterrahmen m sash, gate, frame
Gatterriegel m frame crossbar (cross beam)
Gattersäge[maschine] f log frame [saw], frame saw[ing machine], gate (gang) saw
Gattersägemühle f gang [saw]mill, frame sawmill, Swedish gang mill
~ **mit mehreren Gatterstraßen** multiple-frame sawmill
Gatterschneider m s. Gatterführer
Gatterwagen m saw[mill] carriage, log [saw-]carriage, bogie
Gattung f genus *(taxonomy)*
Gattungsbastard m intergeneric cross (hybrid)
Gattungsbastardierung f intergeneric hybridization
Gattungsgruppe f tribe *(taxonomy)*
Gattungskreuzung f intergeneric hybridization
Gattungskreuzungsprodukt n intergeneric cross (hybrid)
Gattungsname m generic (genus) name
Gattungsverwandter m congener
Gauchheil m pimpernel, poor man's weather-glass *(genus Anagallis)*
Gauklerblume f monkey flower, mimulus *(genus Mimulus)*
Gaultheriaöl n sweet birch oil *(fungicide)*

Gaumen m palate
~/**harter** hard palate
~/**weicher** soft palate
Gaumenbein n palatine bone
Gaumenmandel f palatine tonsil
Gaumenplatte f dental pad *(of ruminants)*
Gaumensegel n soft palate, velum, veil
Gaumenspalte f *(vet)* cleft (fissured) palate
Gaumenzäpfchen n uvula
Gaur m gaur, Bos gaurus
Gaußverteilung f *(biom)* Gaussian distribution, normal [frequency] distribution
Gayal m gayal, Bos [gaurus] frontalis
Gazanie f treasure flower, Gazania rigens (splendens)
GD s. Grenzdifferenz
GE s. Getreideeinheit
geadert, geädert veined, venated, venose
Geäse n mouth *(of game)*
Geäst n branchage
Gebäckweizen m biscuit wheat
gebändert *(bot, zoo)* banded, fasciate[d], vittate, taeniate
Gebänderter Eichenprachtkäfer m *(Am, ent)* oak burncow, Coraebus (Agrilus) bifasciatus
~ **Gewächshausblasenfuß** m palm thrips, Parthenothrips dracaenae
gebären to give birth to, to bring forth, to breed, to bear; to drop *(esp. lambs)*
~/**vorzeitig** to cast
~/**Zwillinge** to twin
Gebärkoma n *(vet)* parturient hypocalcaemia (paralysis), milk fever
Gebärmutter f womb, uterus • **außerhalb der** ~ extra-uterine • **innerhalb der** ~ intra-uterine • **mit doppelter** ~ didelphic
Gebärmutter... s. a. Uterus...
Gebärmutterarterie f uterine artery
Gebärmutterbesamung f uterine insemination
Gebärmutterdrall m, **Gebärmutterdrehung** f uterine torsion
Gebärmutterentfernung f *(vet)* hysterectomy, metrectomy
Gebärmutterentzündung f *(vet)* uterine inflammation, metritis
~/**eitrige** pyometra
~/**puerperale** puerperal metritis
Gebärmutterhalskanal m cervical canal
Gebärmutterhernie f *(vet)* hysterocele
Gebärmutterkatarrh m *(vet)* endometritis
Gebärmuttermuskulatur f myometrium
Gebärmutterschleimhaut f endometrium, endometrial area
Gebärmuttervorfall m *(vet)* uterine prolapse
Gebärparalyse f s. Gebärkoma
Gebärparese f *(vet)* parturient (puerperal) paresis, parturient fever
Gebäude n/**landwirtschaftliches** farm building
Gebäudeerhaltung f upkeep of buildings

Gebell *n* bark[ing], bay • **mit tiefem ~** deep-mouthed
geben/Milch to milk
Geber *m* donor
Gebiet *n* area, tract [of land]
~ mit hoher Lichteinstrahlung high-light area
Gebietsvorhersage *f* area forecast *(e.g. in pest control)*
Gebirge *n* mountains
gebirgig mountainous
Gebirgsbach *m* torrent, burn
Gebirgsboden *m* mountain soil
Gebirgsklima *n* mountain climate
Gebirgspaß *m* pass
Gebirgspflanze *f* orophyte
Gebirgsregenwald *m* mountain rain forest
Gebirgsstrobe *f* Californian mountain pine, Pinus monticola
Gebirgsstufe *f* oreal belt
Gebirgstaigawald *m* mountain taiga forest
Gebirgstundra *f* mountain (Alpine) tundra
Gebirgsvorland *n* piedmont
Gebirgswald *m* montane forest
Gebirgswaldbau *m* montane silviculture
Gebiß *n* 1. dentition, set of teeth; 2. bit, mouthpiece *(of a bridle)*
~/bleibendes permanent dentition
Gebißformel *f* dental formula
Gebläse *n* blower, [air] fan, ventilator
Gebläsebelüftung *f* blower aeration
Gebläseflügel *m* fan blade
Gebläsehäcksler *m* chopper-blower, blower-chopper
Gebläsezerstäuber *m* aerosol generator
Geblök *n* baa
Geblüt *n* blood
gebogen *(bot, zoo)* flexuous
~/hakig *(bot)* aduncate
Gebräch *n* rooting-place *(of game)*
Gebräu *n* brew
Gebräuchlicher Baldrian *m* garden heliotrope (valerian), Valeriana officinalis
~ Himmel[s]schlüssel *m* cowslip, polyanthus, Primula veris
Gebrauchsherde *f* commercial herd; commercial flock *(of sheep or poultry)*
Gebrauchshund *m* utility (all-round) dog
Gebrauchskondition *f* working condition *(of horses)*
Gebrauchskreuzung *f* 1. commercial cross-breeding; 2. commercial breed
Gebrauchskreuzungsprodukt *n* commercial breed
Gebrauchsrasen *m* amenity turf
Gebrauchswerteigenschaft *f* functional value characteristic
Gebrauchszucht *f* commercial breeding
Gebrauchszüchter *m* commercial (farmer) breeder

Gebrech *n* snout, mouth *(of wild boar)*
Gebrüll *n* low, bellow *(esp. of cattle)*
Gebuchteter Birnbaumprachtkäfer *m* sinuate pear [tree] borer, pear [tree] borer, Agrilus sinuatus
Gebuckelte Tramete *f (bot)* gibbous trametes, Trametes gibbosa
Gebund *n* bundle *(rafting)*
Geburt *f* 1. birth; 2. birth process, parturition, labour; 3. *s.* Abstammung • **nach der ~** postnatal, post-partum • **vor der ~ [auftretend]** prenatal, prepartal • **während der ~** intrapartal
~ beim Rind/erschwerte calving difficulty
~/leichte (streßarme) eutocia
Geburtenfolge *f* birth sequence
Geburtenhäufigkeit *f*, **Geburtenrate** *f* birth rate, natality
Geburtensynchronisation *f* birth synchronization
Geburtsbox *f* foaling box
Geburtserschwerung *f* parturition complication, dystocia
Geburtshilfe *f* obstetrics
geburtshilflich obstetric[al]
Geburtskunde *f* obstetrics
geburtskundlich obstetric[al]
Geburtsmasse *f* birth weight
Geburtsrehe *f (vet)* postparturient laminitis
Geburtsschmerz *m* labour, pains
Geburtsstörung *f* parturition complication, dystocia
Geburtstermin *m* **[nach normaler Trächtigkeitsdauer]** [full] term
Geburtstetanie *f (vet)* puerperal (lactation) tetany, eclampsia
Geburtsvorgang *m s.* Geburt 2.
Geburtsweg *m* birth canal (passage)
Gebüsch *n* bush, shrub[bery]
Gebüschgesellschaft *f* shrub association
Gebüschsavanne *f* shrub savanna[h]
Gedächtnis *n* memory
Gedächtniszelle *f* memory cell
Gedärm *n* intestine, guts, bowels
gedarrt kiln-dried, KD, k.d., kiln-seasoned
Gedeckter Brand *m (phyt)* covered smut *(comprehensive term)*
~ Brand *m* **des Hafers** covered smut of oat[s] *(caused by Ustilago kolleri)*
~ Hirsebrand *m* covered kernel smut *(caused by Sphacelotheca sorghi)*
gedeihen to thrive, to grow (do) well
~/üppig to flourish
gedeihend vigorous
~/üppig luxuriant, lush, flourishing *(vegetation)*
gedeihlich thrifty
Gedeihlichkeit *f* thriftiness
Gedenkemein *n (bot)* blue-eyed Mary, Omphalodes verna
Gedränge *n* crowding *(animal behaviour)*
gedrängt *(bot, zoo)* aggregate

gedreht

gedreht *(bot, zoo)* contorted
gedrehtblättrig *(bot)* streptophyllous
gedrungen stocky, squat *(plant, animal)*
Geest *f*, **Geestland** *n* sandy upland
Gefahrenindex *m* **nach Wright** Wright danger index *(of forest fire control in Canada)*
gefährlich dangerous, hazardous; *(vet)* malign[ant]
Gefälle *n* descent, [downward] slope, grade, incline, fall *(e.g. of land)*; gradient, drop *(e.g. of temperature)*
Gefällewinkelmesser *m* clinometer
gefaltet *(bot, zoo)* plicate[d]
~/**doppelt** biplicate[d]
Gefäß *n* 1. *(zoo)* vessel, vas; *(bot)* trachea; receptacle; 2. vessel, container
~/**Malpighisches** Malpighian tubule (tube) *(e.g. of insects)*
gefäßartig cymbiform
Gefäßbesiedelung *f* vascular colonization *(by pests)*
Gefäßbündel *n* vascular bundle (strand)
Gefäßdurchbrechung *f* vessel perforation
Gefäßentzündung *f (vet)* vasculitis, angiitis
Gefäßerkrankung *f (vet)* vascular disease, angiopathy
gefäßerweiternd vasodilating
Gefäßerweiterung *f* vasodilation
Gefäßfarbstoff *m* vascular dye *(biochemistry)*
Gefäßgeschwulst *f (vet)* angioma
Gefäßglied *n (bot)* vessel element (member), tracheal element
Gefäßknäuel *n* glomerulus *(e.g. of the kidney)*
Gefäßkrampf *m (vet)* vasospasm
Gefäßkultur *f* pot culture
Gefäßlähmung *f (vet)* angioparalysis
Gefäßmykose *f (phyt)* vascular mycosis, tracheomycosis
Gefäßnervensystem *n* vasomotor system
Gefäßpflanze *f* vascular plant
Gefäßring *m* vascular ring
Gefäßsaft *m (bot)* xylem sap
Gefäßschwamm *m (vet)* angioma
Gefäßstrang *m* vascular strand (bundle); *(bot)* xylem ray
Gefäßsystem *n* vascular system
Gefäßteil *m s.* Xylem
Gefäßtracheide *f (bot)* vascular tracheid, imperfect vessel member
Gefäßunterbindung *f (vet)* ligation, ligatur
gefäßverengend vasoconstrictive
Gefäßvereng[er]ung *f* vasoconstriction
Gefäßversorgung *f* vascularization
Gefäßverstopfung *f (phyt, vet)* embolism
Gefäßversuch *m* pot experiment (trial)
Gefäßversuchswesen *n* pot experimentation
Gefäßverteilung *f* vasculature
Gefege *n* fraying *(of game)*
gefeldert *(bot, zoo)* areolate[d]

Gefieder *n* plumage, feathering • ~ **ausbilden** to feather
Gefiederfärbung *f* plumage colour
gefiedert 1. *(bot)* pinnate[d]; 2. *(zoo)* feathered, plumaged *(birds)*; plumate *(as antennae)*
~/**abgebrochen** abruptly pinnate[d]
~/**doppelt** bipinnate[d]
~/**dreifach** tripinnate[d], tripennate
~/**paarig** paripinnate[d], even pinnate[d]
~/**unpaarig** imparipinnate[d], odd-pinnate[d], unequally pinnate[d]
~/**wechselständig** alternate pinnate[d]
Gefiederte Zwenke *f* Japanese false brome, torgrass, Brachypodium pinnatum
Gefiederwechsel *m* moult
Gefiederzeichnung *f* plumage pattern
gefingert *(bot, zoo)* digitate
Geflecht *n* plexus *(animal anatomy)*
gefleckt *(bot, zoo)* maculate[d], mottled, blotched
Gefleckte Gewächshauslaus *f* mottled arum aphid, lily aphid, Aulacorthum circumflexum
~ **Kartoffellaus** *f* glasshouse [and] potato aphid, solanum (foxglove) aphid, Aulacorthum solani
~ **Kleezierlaus** *f s.* ~ Luzerneblattlaus
~ **Luzerneblattlaus** *f* spotted alfalfa aphid, yellow clover aphid, Therioaphis trifolii (maculata)
~ **Schach[brett]blume** *f* fritillary, guinea-hen flower, snake's-head, Fritillaria meleagris
~ **Taubnessel** *f* spotted dead nettle, Lamium maculatum
~ **Wolfsmilch** *f (bot)* milkweed, Euphorbia maculata
Gefleckter Aron[stab] *m (bot)* spotted (wild) arum, lords and ladies, cuckoo-pint, Arum maculatum
~ **Kohltriebrüßler** *m* cabbage stem weevil, *(Am)* cabbage seed-stalk curculio, Ceutorhynchus pallidactylus (quadridens)
~ **Schierling** *m* [poison] hemlock, [spotted] cowbane, Conium maculatum
Geflecktes Knabenkraut *n* spotted orchis, Dactylorhiza (Orchis) maculata
Geflügel *n* poultry, fowl
Geflügelaufzucht *f* poultry rearing
Geflügelaufzuchtstation *f* poultry rearing station
Geflügelauslauf *m* poultry (fowl) run
Geflügelauslaufhaltung *f* free-range poultry farming
Geflügelausstellung *f* poultry show (fair)
Geflügelbotulismus *m (vet)* limberneck, western duck sickness
Geflügelbrutanlage *f* poultry incubator
Geflügelcholera *f (vet)* fowl cholera
Geflügeldiphtherie *f (vet)* fowl (avian) diphtheria
Geflügeldung *m* poultry manure
Geflügeleinstreu *f* poultry[-house] litter
Geflügelernährung *f* poultry nutrition
Geflügelfarm *f* poultry-farm
Geflügelfett *n* poultry fat
Geflügelfleisch *n* poultry meat, fowl
Geflügelfleischkonserve *f* canned poultry meat

Geflügelfutter *n* poultry feed
Geflügelfutterration *f* poultry ration (diet)
Geflügelfütterung *f* poultry feeding
Geflügelgülle *f* poultry waste slurry
Geflügelhalter *m* poultryman
Geflügelhaltung *f* poultry farming (keeping, management)
Geflügelhändler *m* poultryman, poulterer
Geflügelhelminthose *f (vet)* ascaridiosis
Geflügelhof *m* poultry yard
Geflügeljungtier *n* poult
Geflügelklein *n* giblets
Geflügelkonserve *f* canned poultry meat
Geflügelkot *m* poultry droppings
Geflügelkotband *n* poultry droppings belt
Geflügelkrankheit *f* avian disease, poultry (fowl) disease
Geflügelkunde *f* poultry science
Geflügellähme *f*, **Geflügellähmung** *f s.* Krankheit/Mareksche
Geflügelleukose *f (vet)* avian leucosis (lymphomatosis), big liver disease of fowl
Geflügellisteriose *f (vet)* listeriosis (tiger river disease) of birds
Geflügelmast *f* poultry fattening
Geflügelmist *m* poultry manure
Geflügelpasteurellose *f (vet)* fowl cholera
Geflügelpest *f (vet)* fowl pest, poultry plague *(comprehensive term)*
~/atypische Newcastle disease, ND, pseudo poultry plague
~/Europäische (klassische) fowl pest, poultry plague
Geflügelpestvirus *n* Newcastle disease virus
Geflügelpocken *pl (vet)* roup, fowl (bird, pigeon) pox • **an ~ erkrankt** roupy
Geflügelproduktion *f* poultry production
Geflügelproduktionsanlage *f* poultry production unit, poultry operation
Geflügelproduzent *m* poultryman
Geflügelrasse *f* poultry breed
Geflügelration *f* poultry ration (diet)
Geflügelrupfmaschine *f* poultry picker, roughing machine
Geflügelschlachtabwasser *n* poultry processing waste-water
Geflügelschlachtbetrieb *m*, **Geflügelschlachterei** *f s.* Geflügelschlachthof
Geflügelschlachtgerät *n* poultry slaughtering tool
Geflügelschlachthof *m* poultry slaughterhouse (slaughtering plant), poultry abbatoir, poultry processing (dressing) plant
Geflügelschnupfen *m (vet)* coryza of chickens (poultry)
Geflügelsperma *n* chicken semen
Geflügelspirochätose *f (vet)* avian spirochaetosis *(caused by Borrelia anserina)*
Geflügelstall *m* poultry house
~/fensterloser windowless poultry house

Geflügelstaphylokokkose *f (vet)* avian staphylococcal arthritis
Geflügelstarterfutter *n* poultry starter
geflügelt winged, alate, pterygote
Geflügelte Thunbergie *f (bot)* black-eyed Susan, Thunbergia alata
Geflügelter Spindelstrauch *m (bot)* winged euonymus, Euonymus alatus
~ Tabak *m* flowering (Persian) tobacco, Nicotiana alata
Geflügeltes Pfaffenhütchen *n s.* Geflügelter Spindelstrauch
Geflügeltuberkulose *f (vet)* avian tuberculosis
Geflügeltyphus *m (vet)* fowl typhoid
Geflügelverarbeitungsanlage *f* poultry processing (dressing) plant
Geflügelweide *f* poultry pasture
Geflügelwirtschaft *f* poultry farming (management, industry)
Geflügelzecke *f* fowl tick (tampan), blue bug, Argas persicus
Geflügelzucht *f* poultry breeding
Geflügelzüchter *m* poultry farmer
gefranst *(bot, zoo)* fimbriate[d]
gefräßig voracious
Gefräßigkeit *f* voracity
Gefrierätztechnik *f* freeze-etching
Gefrierätzung *f* freeze-etching
Gefrierbrand *m* 1. freeze brand *(for marking of animals)*; 2. freezer burn *(of foodstuffs due to incorrect frozen storage)*
Gefrierei *n* frozen egg
Gefriereignung *f* freezability
gefrieren to freeze, to congeal *(esp. liquids)*
~ lassen/schnell to quick-freeze
~/zu Eis to freeze
Gefrieren *n* freeze, freezing, congelation
Gefrierfleisch *n* frozen (chilled) meat
Gefrierfrakturelektronenmikroskopie *f* freeze-fracture electron microscopy
Gefriergemüse *n* frozen vegetable
Gefrierkonservierung *f* freezing preservation, cryopreservation
~ von Sperma semen freezing
Gefrierlagerung *f* frozen (freezer) storage
Gefriermilch *f* frozen milk
Gefrierobst *n* frozen (chilled) fruit
Gefrierpaillette *f* freeze straw *(for semen preservation)*
Gefrierpunkt *m* freezing-point, FP
Gefrierpunkterniedrigung *f* freezing-point depression
Gefrierröhrchen *n s.* Gefrierpaillette
Gefrierschutzmittel *n* cryoprotectant
Gefriersperma *n* frozen semen
Gefriersubstitution *f* freeze substitution *(microscopy)*
Gefriertechnik *f* freezing technique
gefriertrocken freeze-dry

gefriertrocknen

gefriertrocknen to freeze-dry, to lyophilize
Gefriertrocknung *f* freeze drying (dehydration), lyophilization
Gefrier- und Auftauwirkung *f* freeze-and-thaw action
Gefrorensein *n* freeze
Gefüge *n* structure; texture
Gefügebildner *m (soil)* structure-former; *(dairy)* texturator
Gefügekörper *m* [soil] aggregate, ped, crumb
Gefügeschaden *m (soil)* structural damage
Gefügestabilität *f (soil)* structural stability
Gefügezerstörung *f* aggregate destruction
gefüllt double *(e.g. a blossom)*
gefurcht furrowy; *(bot, zoo)* sulcate
Gefurchter Dickmaulrüßler (Lappenrüßler) *m* black vine weevil, Otiorhynchus sulcatus
gegabelt *(bot, zoo)* forked, bifurcate, dichotomous
Gegendruckfüller *m* isobarometric filler *(beer bottling)*
Gegenfeuer *n* counterfire *(forest fire control)*
Gegengift *n* antidote, antivenene, antivenin
Gegenhypothese *f (biom)* alternative hypothesis
Gegenmittel *n* antidote
Gegenschneide *f* opposite cutting edge; shear plate *(of a mower)*
Gegenspieler *m* antagonist
gegenständig opposite
Gegenstrahlung *f* counter (back) radiation *(of the atmosphere)*
Gegenstromtrockner *m* counterflow dryer
Gegenstromwärmeaustausch *m* counter-current heat exchange
gegittert *(bot, zoo)* cancellate[d]
geglättet *(bot, zoo)* glabrate, laevigate
gegliedert articulate
Gegrunze *n* grunt
GeGSMV *s.* Virus des Gelben Streifenmosaiks der Gerste
GeGVzV *s.* Gerstengelbverzwergungsvirus
Gehalt *m* **an löslichen Feststoffen** soluble solids content
Gehaltsanalysentabelle *f* ingredient analysis table
Gehaltsrübe *f* medium dry-matter mangel
Gehängemoor *n* hanging bog
geharzt *(Am, forest)* worked-out
gehäuft *(bot, zoo)* aggregate; *(bot)* [co]acervate
Gehäuseschnecke *f* snail *(esp. of genus Helix)*
Gehege *n* enclosure, fence, pen; [holding] paddock, corral; [game] preserve[s]; cote
Gehegekaninchen *n* warren rabbit
gehen:
~/**auf die Jagd** to hunt
~/**auf Fuchsjagd** to go fox-hunting, to hunt
~/**auf Pirschjagd (Schleichjagd)** to stalk, to hunt
~/**auf Schnepfenjagd** to snipe
~/**im Schritt** to walk
~/**zur Tränke** to water *(game)*

242

Gehirn *n* brain, encephalon
Gehirn... *s. a.* Hirn...
Gehirnanhang *m* hypophysis, pituitary [gland]
Gehirnbasisarterie *f* basilar[y] artery
Gehirnentzündung *f (vet)* encephalitis
Gehirnerkrankung *f (vet)* brain disease, encephalopathy
Gehirnerweichung *f (vet)* encephalomalacia
Gehirngeschwulst *f (vet)* encephaloma
Gehirnmarksentzündung *f (vet)* encephalomyelitis
Gehirn-Rückenmark-Entzündung *f* **des Geflügels** avian encephalomyelitis
Gehirnschlag *m (vet)* apoplexy
Gehirnventrikel *m* cerebral ventricle
Gehlchen *n s.* Pfifferling
Gehöft *n* farm[stead], homestead, steading
Gehölz *n* 1. [small] wood, copse, timber; 2. woody (ligneous) plant
~/**bodendeckendes** low-bush
~/**edelreislieferndes** grafter
~/**immergrünes** indeciduous shrub
~/**laubabwerfendes** deciduous shrub
~/**strauchiges** frutex
Gehölzansiedlung *f* establishment of woody plants
Gehölzgarten *m* arboretum, tree-garden
Gehölzgesellschaft *f* woody plant community
Gehölzgruppe *f* boscage, boskage
Gehölzkunde *f* dendrology
Gehölzkundler *m* dendrologist
gehölzkundlich dendrological
Gehölzpflanzung *f*, **Gehölzplantage** *f* wood (tree) plantation
Gehölzvernichtungsmittel *n* silvicide, arboricide, brush-killer
Gehör *n* [sense of] hearing, ear, audition
gehorchen to obey *(horse, dog)*
Gehörgang *m* ear canal
~/**äußerer** external acoustic meatus
~/**innerer** internal acoustic meatus
Gehörknöchelchen *n* auditory ossicle
Gehörn *n* attire, horns, antlers • **ohne** ~ poll[ed]
~/**schädelechtes** attire
Gehörnende *n*, **Gehörnsproß** *m* tine
gehörnt cornute[d], cornigerous
gehorsam obedient • ~ **sein** to obey *(horse, dog)*
Gehorsam *m* obedience
Gehörsinn *m s.* Gehör
Gehunfähigkeit *f (vet)* abasia
geigenförmig *(bot)* pandurate, panduriform
geil rank *(plant growth)*
Geilstelle *f* [rank] patch
Geiß *f* she-goat, nanny[-goat], goat doe
Geißbaum *m* common (European) ash, Fraxinus excelsior
Geißblatt *n* honeysuckle, bindweed, lonicera *(genus Lonicera)*

Geißel f flagellum • **mit einer ~** monotrichous • **mit mehreren Geißeln** polytrichous • **ringsum mit Geißeln besetzt** peritrichous
Geißeltierchen n flagellate *(superclass Mastigophora)*
Geißeltierchenbefall m *(vet)* flagellosis
geißeltragend flagellate
Geißfuß m goutweed, goutwort, bishop's-weed, goat's-foot, garden plaque, ground elder, herb Gerard, Aegopodium podagraria
Geißfußpfropfen n, **Geißfußveredelung** f notch (cleft, stump, wedge) grafting, triangulation, crown grafting by inlaying
Geißkitz n female fawn
Geißklee m 1. broom *(genus Cytisus)*; 2. s. Geißraute
Geißraute f 1. goat's-rue *(genus Galega)*; 2. [common] goat's-rue, Galega officinalis
Geisterflecken mpl, **Geisterfleckenkrankheit** f *(phyt)* ghost spot[ting]
Geitonogamie f s. Selbstbestäubung
geizen to pluck off suckers, to pinch off (out), to nip (snap) off, to sucker, to stop
Geiztrieb m lateral shoot, sucker
gekerbt *(bot, zoo)* crenate[d]
~/fein crenulate[d]
gekielt *(bot, zoo)* carinate[d]
geknäuelt *(bot, zoo)* glomerate
gekniet *(bot, zoo)* geniculate
Geknieter Fuchsschwanz m marsh (floating, water) foxtail, float grass, Alopecurus geniculatus
geköpft *(soil)* truncate[d]
gekörnt granular, granulated, grainy
gekraust *(bot, zoo)* crispate
gekreuzt *(bot, zoo)* cruciate, decussate
Gekröse n mesentery *(animal anatomy)*; *(slaught)* crow
Gekröseentzündung f *(vet)* mesenteritis
gekrümmt *(bot)* repand, anfractuous, gyrate, crooked
~/hakig aduncate
~/in zwei oder mehr Ebenen many-sided *(tree-trunk)*
~/querliegend campylotropous
gekrümmtnervig *(bot, zoo)* curvinervate, curvinerved
Gel n gel • **ein ~ in ein Sol umwandeln** to peptize
Gelach n wallow, soiling pool *(of game)*
Geläger n lees, deposit from must, sediment *(winemaking)*
Gelägerbier n waste beer
gelähmt *(vet)* paralyzed
~/vollständig [motorisch] paralytic
Gelände n ground, terrain
~/durchschnittenes broken ground
~/hügeliges (welliges) rolling land
~/zerschnittenes broken ground
Geländeauffüllung f filling-in of land
Geländeaufnahme f [ground] survey

Geländeausformung f s. Geländegestaltung
Geländeerkundung f ground (terrain) reconnaissance
Geländefahrzeug n off-road vehicle, cross-country vehicle, [rough] terrain vehicle
Geländefaktor m terrain factor
Geländeform f land form, relief
Geländegabelstapler m all-ground lift truck, rough terrain fork-lift truck
Geländegängigkeit f cross-country properties, [cross-country] mobility *(of vehicles)*
Geländegestaltung f configuration (conformation) of the ground
Geländehindernis n cross-country obstacle *(equestrian sport)*
Geländehöhe f [ground] level
Geländeklassifikation f terrain classification
Geländeklima n topoclimate
Geländeoberfläche f ground surface (level)
Geländepatrouille f ground patrol *(e.g. for forest fire prevention)*
Geländereifen m off-road tyre, lug base tyre, ground-grip tyre
Geländerelief n ground relief
Geländestapler m s. Geländegabelstapler
Geländeunebenheit f terrain roughness
Geländevermessung f field (topographical) survey
gelappt *(bot, zoo)* lobate[d], lobed
~/handförmig palmatilobate[d], palmatilobed
~/klein lobular
Gelatine f gelatin[e]
Gelatineagar m gelatin agar
Gelatinierung f gelatinization *(of starch grains)*
gelatinös gelatinous
Geläuf n course; trace, track *(of wildfowl)*
Geläut[e] n barking, bay *(of a hunting dog)* • **mit tiefem ~** deep-mouthed
gelb yellow • **~ werden** to yellow • **~ werdend** flavescent • **sich ~ färben** to yellow
Gelbaal m yellow eel
Gelbadrigkeit f *(phyt)* vein yellowing
~ der Weinrebe grape-vine yellow vein *(virosis)*
Gelbbirke f yellow (gold) birch, Quebec (curly) birch, Betula alleghaniensis (lutea)
Gelbblühende Taubnessel f s. Goldnessel
Gelbblütige Heckenkirsche f coralline honeysuckle, Lonicera chrysantha
Gelbbrauner Dieb[s]käfer m brown spider beetle, Ptinus clavipes
Gelbe Alpenrose f yellow-flowered rhododendron, Rhododendron luteum
~ Bete s. ~ Rübe
~ Borstenhirse f yellow foxtail (bristle-grass), yellow pigeon-grass, bottle grass, Setaria pumila (glauca, lutescens)
~ Calla f golden calla, Zantedeschia elliottiana
~ Kellerschnecke f yellow slug, Limax flavus
~ Lupine f yellow lupin[e], Lupinus luteus

Gelbe

~ **Mombinpflaume** *f* yellow mombin, hog (Jamaica) plum, golden apple, Spondias mombin
~ **Narzisse** *f s.* Gemeine Narzisse
~ **Osterblume** *f* yellow wood anemone, Anemone ranunculoides
~ **Pflaumensägewespe** *f* plum saw-fly, Hoplocampa flava
~ **Roßkastanie** *f* sweet buckeye, Aesculus octandra
~ **Rübe** *f* yellow beet, Beta vulgaris var. lutea
~ **Stachelbeerblattwespe** *f* gooseberry (currant) saw-fly, imported currant worm, Nematus (Pteronidea) ribesii
~ **Taglilie** *f* yellow day lily, Hemerocallis lilio-asphodelus, Hemerocallis flava
~ **Teichrose** *f (bot)* brandy bottle, Nuphar lutea
~ **Weizengallmücke** *f* wheat (lemon wheat blossom) midge, Contarinia (Diplosis) tritici
~ **Weizenhalmfliege** *f* gout-fly, Chlorops pumilionis
~ **Wicke** *f* yellow vetch, Vicia lutea
~ **Wiesenraute** *f* yellow meadow rue, Thalictrum flavum ssp. flavum
Gelbei *n* [egg-]yolk *(for compounds s. under* Dotter*)*
Gelber Enzian *m* yellow gentian, Gentiana lutea
~ **Fingerhut** *m* yellow (straw) foxglove, Digitalis lutea
~ **Fuchsschwanz** *m s.* Gelbe Borstenhirse
~ **Gamander** *m* yellow germander, Teucrium flavum
~ **Günsel** *m* yellow bugle, ground pine, Ajuga chamaepitys
~ **Hartriegel** *m* cornelian cherry, cornel, Cornus mas
~ **Hornmohn** *m* horned poppy, Glaucium flavum
~ **Kartoffelnematode** *m s.* Gelbes Kartoffelzystenälchen
~ **Kiefernblattkäfer** *m* yellow pine leaf beetle, Cryptocephalus pini
~ **Köstlicher** *m* Golden Delicious *(apple cultivar)*
~ **Reisbohrer** *m (ent)* paddy borer, Schoenobius bipunctifer
~ **Rotz** *m* **der Hyazinthe** *s.* Gelbfäule der Hyazinthe
~ **Steinklee** *m* field melilot, yellow[-flowered] sweet clover, Melilotus officinalis
~ **Wau** *m* wild (yellow, cut-leaved) mignonette, Reseda lutea
~ **Weidenblattkäfer** *m* willow (sallow) leaf beetle, Lochmaea capraea
Gelbes Ageratum *n* African daisy, Lonas annua (inodora)
~ **Engelsüß** *n (bot)* golden polypody, Polypodium (Phlebodium) aureum
~ **Guinesisches Yams** *n s.* ~ Yams
~ **Kartoffelzystenälchen** *n* [yellow] potato cyst-nematode, potato root eelworm, golden nematode [of potato], golden eelworm, Globodera (Heterodera) rostochiensis

~ **Verzwergungsmosaik** *n* **der Zwiebel** yellow dwarf of onion *(virosis)*
~ **Windröschen** *n s.* Gelbe Osterblume
~ **Yams** *n* twelve-months yam, yellow Guinea yam, cut-and-come-again yam, Dioscorea cayenensis
Gelbfärbung *f* yellow-stain *(esp. of oak, caused by Paecilonyces variota)*
Gelbfäule *f* **der Hyazinthe** yellow disease of hyacinth, yellows of hyacinth *(caused by Xanthomonas campestris hyacinthi)*
Gelbfettkrankheit *f (vet)* yellow fat disease, fatty degeneration
Gelbfiebermücke *f* yellow fever mosquito, Aedes aegypti
Gelbfleckigkeit *f*, **Gelbfleckung** *f (phyt)* yellow blotch [disease], YBD
gelbfleischig yellow-fleshed
gelbfrüchtig *(bot)* xanthocarpous
Gelbhaariger Fennich *m s.* Gelbe Borstenhirse
Gelbhafer *m* yellow oat *(type of cultivated oats)*
Gelbhalsmaus *f* yellow-necked field mouse, Apodemus flavicollis
Gelbherzigkeit *f (phyt)* dead heart [condition]
~ **des Kohls** yellow heart of cabbage *(caused by Phytomyza rufipes)*
Gelbholz *n* 1. prickly-ash, Japan pepper *(genus Zanthoxylum)*; 2. Osage-orange, Maclura pomifera; 3. fustic *(wood from Chlorophora tinctoria)*
gelbhülsig yellow-podded
Gelbkiefer *f* 1. yellow (hard) pine *(comprehensive term)*; 2. ponderosa [pine], western yellow pine, bull (heavy-wooded) pine, Pinus ponderosa
Gelbklee *m* hop clover, black medic[k], [yellow] trefoil, non[e]such, Medicago lupulina
Gelbkörper *m (zoo)* yellow body, corpus luteum
• ~ **bilden** to luteinize
gelbkörperauflösend luteolytic
Gelbkörperauflösung *f* luteolysis
Gelbkörperbildung *f* luteinization
Gelbkörperbildungsphase *f* metoestrus
Gelbkörperhormon *n* progesterone
Gelbkörperreifungshormon *n* luteinizing hormone, lutropin
Gelbkraut *n* dyer's rocket (weed), weld [mignonette], Reseda luteola
gelblich flavescent
Gelblichweißer Klee *m* sulphur clover, Trifolium ochroleucum
Gelbmais *m* yellow maize *(comprehensive term)*
Gelbmosaik *n* **der Wasser- und Kohlrübe** turnip yellow mosaic *(virosis)*
gelbnervig *(bot)* xanthoneurous
Gelbpflaume *f s.* Gelbe Mombinpflaume
Gelbreife *f* yellow ripeness *(of cereals)*
Gelbrost *m* yellow (stripe) rust *(of cereals, caused by Puccinia glumarum = P. striiformis)*
gelbschalig yellow-podded
Gelbscheckung *f (phyt)* yellow blotch [disease]

Gelbscheckungsvirus n der Großen Brennessel large nettle yellow mottle virus
Gelbschimmel m [an Champignons] yellow mould [of mushrooms] *(caused by Myceliophthora lutea)*
Gelbschwänziger Goldafter m gold-tail[ed] moth, Euproctis similis
Gelbstreifiger Kohlerdfloh m turnip flea beetle, fly, Phyllotreta nemorum
Gelbsucht f *(vet)* jaundice, icterus, yellows, hyperbilirubinaemia
~ **der Rübe** *(phyt)* beet yellows *(virosis)*
~/**infektiöse** *(vet)* infectious icterus, leptospiral jaundice, Weil's disease
Gelbverzwergung f *(phyt)* yellow dwarf *(virosis)*
~ **der Gerste** barley yellow dwarf, BYD
~ **der Johannisbeere** currant yellow dwarf
Gelbverzwergungsvirus n der Gerste barley yellow dwarf virus
Gelbvieh n German Yellow *(cattle breed)*
Gelbwerden n yellowing
Gelbwurz[el] f *(bot)* 1. yellow zedoary, wild tu[r]meric, Curcuma aromatica; 2. tu[r]meric, curcuma, Curcuma longa
Gelbzwergigkeit f der Kartoffel potato yellow dwarf *(virosis)*
Gelchromatographie f gel [permeation, filtration] chromatography
Gelderland m Gelderland *(horse breed)*
Geldertragstafel f *(forest)* money (financial) yield table
Geldiffusion f s. Gelpräzipitation
Gelee n jelly
~ **Royal** royal (queen bee's nutrient) jelly
geleeartig gelatinous
Geleefrucht f jelly fruit
Gelege n clutch [of eggs], nest, set[ting]
Gelegenheitserreger m opportunist invader
Gelegenheitsparasit m facultative parasite
Gelegenheitsschädling m occasional pest
Gelegenheitsweide f opportunist grazing
Gelegenheitswirt m *(phyt, vet)* casual (accidental, optional) host
Geleitzelle f [phloem] companion cell
Gelelektrophorese f gel electrophoresis
Gelenk n joint
~/**biaxiales** biaxial joint
~/**multiaxiales** multiaxial joint
gelenkartig articulated
Gelenkband n ligament *(animal anatomy)*
Gelenkblume f 1. false dragonhead *(genus Physostegia)*; 2. obedient plant, obedience, false dragonhead, Physostegia virginiana
Gelenkdauerwinkel m permanent joint angle *(of a cardan shaft)*
Gelenkegge f peg-tooth harrow
Gelenkende n [des Röhrenknochens] epiphysis *(an end of a long bone)*
Gelenkentzündung f *(vet)* arthritis

Gelenkerkrankung f *(vet)* joint disease
Gelenkeröffnung f *(vet)* arthrotomy
Gelenkflüssigkeit f synovia, synovial fluid
Gelenkfortsatz m articular process, condyle
Gelenkgalle f *(vet)* gall
Gelenkhöcker m s. Gelenkfortsatz
Gelenkhöhle f articular cavity
gelenkig articulated
Gelenkkapsel f articular capsule • **innerhalb der** ~ intracapsular
Gelenkknorpel m articular cartilage
Gelenkknorpelentzündung f *(vet)* arthrochondritis
Gelenkleiden n/degeneratives *(vet)* arthrosis
Gelenkmeniskus m articular meniscus
Gelenkneubildung f nearthrosis
Gelenkrahmenpflug m *(Am)* flex-frame plow
Gelenkscheibe f articular disk
Gelenkschleimhautentzündung f *(vet)* synovitis
Gelenkschmiere f s. Gelenkflüssigkeit
Gelenkversteifung f *(vet)* ankylosis
Gelenkwelle f cardan shaft, p.t.o. (power take-off) shaft, coupling (drive) shaft
Gelenkwellenanschluß m power intake connection, PIC
Gelenkwellenschutz m p.t.o. shaft guard, drive shaft safety guard
Gelfiltration f gel filtration
Gelierprobe f jelly test
Geliersaft m jellying juice
Gelose f gelose *(polysaccharide)*
Gelpermeationschromatographie f s. Gelchromatographie
Gelpräzipitation f gel precipitation (diffusion)
Gelpräzipitationstest m gel precipitation (diffusion) test
Gel-Sol-Umwandlung f peptization
gelt farrow, non-pregnant, barren
Geltschaf n non-pregnant ewe, eild, yeld
Gelttier n barren (yeld) hind
gelzen to geld, to castrate, to emasculate
Gemarkung f area of a community
gemasert figured, veined, curly, burly *(wood)*
gemäßigt temperate *(e.g. climate)*
gemästet fat *(cattle)*
gemein *(bot, zoo)* common
Gemeindeforst m, **Gemeindewald** m communal (community, village) forest
Gemeine... s. a. Gewöhnliche...
Gemeine Ackerröte f field madder, Sherardia arvensis
~ **Akelei** f [garden] columbine, capon's feather, Aquilegia vulgaris
~ **Bärentraube** f [red] bearberry, Arctostaphylos uva-ursi
~ **Berberitze** f European barberry, Berberia vulgaris
~ **Besenheide** f [common] heather, moor besom, [common] ling, Calluna vulgaris

Gemeine

- **Blasenkirsche** f Chinese-lantern [plant], Physalis alkekengi
- **Braunelle** f (bot) self-heal, prunella, Prunella vulgaris
- **Brunnenkresse** f watercress, Nasturtium officinale
- **Buchwinde** f wild buckwheat, field bindweed, Fallopia (Polygonum) convolvulus
- **Eberesche** f rowan[-tree], [European] mountain ash, quickbeam, Sorbus aucuparia
- **Eibe** f common (English) yew, ground hemlock, Taxus baccata
- **Esche** f common (European) ash, Fraxinus excelsior
- **Felsenbirne** f snowy mespilus, Amelanchier ovalis (vulgaris)
- **Fichte** f Norway (European) spruce, Picea abies (excelsa)
- **Fichtengespinstblattwespe** f (Am) false spruce web-worm, Cephaleia abietis
- **Fichtenholzwespe** f s. ~ Stahlblaue Fichtenholzwespe
- **Flockenblume** f black (meadow) knapweed, Centaurea jacea
- **Getreidewanze** f cereal (pale green) bug, Eurygaster maura
- **Goldrute** f European golden rod, Solidago virgaurea
- **Haferschmiele** f silver[y] hair grass, Aira caryophyllea
- **Hainbuche** f European hornbeam, yoke elm, Carpinus betulus
- **Haselwurz** f European wild ginger, Asarum europaeum
- **Hundszunge** f hound's-tongue, Cynoglossum officinale
- **Irische Heide** f heather (genus Daboecia)
- **Karausche** f crucian [carp], Prussian carp, Carassius carassius (vulgaris)
- **Kiefer** f common pine, Scotch pine (fir), Pinus sylvestris
- **Kiefernbuschhornblattwespe** f pine saw-fly, Diprion pini
- **Kommaschildlaus** f mussel (oyster-shell) scale, Lepidosaphes ulmi
- **Kratzdistel** f common (spear, bull) thistle, Cirsium vulgare (lanceolatum)
- **Kriebelmücke** f ornate blackfly, Simulium ornatum
- **Küchenschelle (Kuhschelle)** f pasque-flower, daneflower, pulsatilla, Pulsatilla vulgaris
- **Lärche** f common (European) larch, Larix decidua
- **Lobelie** f great lobelia, Lobelia siphilitica
- **Mahonie** f [trailing] mahonia, Oregon [holly] grape, holly-leaved barberry, Mahonia aquifolium
- **Melde** f common orach[e], lamb's-quarters, Atriplex patula
- **Moosbeere** f mossberry, [small] cranberry, (Am) European cranberry, Vaccinium oxycoccos
- **Nachtviole** f dame's violet, sweet (garden) rocket, Hesperis matronalis
- **Napfschildlaus** f European fruit lecanium (scale), European peach scale, brown elm scale, Parthenolecanium (Lecanium, Eulecanium) corni
- **Narzisse** f trumpet narcissus, Narcissus pseudonarcissus
- **Ochsenzunge** f (bot) ox-tongue, [common] alkanet, common bugloss, Anchusa officinalis
- **Opuntie** f Barbary fig, drooping prickly pear, Opuntia vulgaris
- **Osterluzei** f birthwort, Aristolochia clematis
- **Pestwurz** f pestilenceweed, butterbur, flea-dock, Petasites hybridus (officinalis)
- **Quecke** f common couch [grass], couch (quack, twitch, quitch) grass, quick, creeping wheatgrass, Agropyron repens
- **Rauke** f rocket, Eruca vesicaria ssp. sativa
- **Rispe** f rough-stalked meadow grass, rough blue grass, Poa trivialis
- **Roßkastanie** f [horse-]chestnut, Aesculus hippocastanum
- **Ruke** f s. ~ Rauke
- **Schafgarbe** f [common] yarrow, milfoil, Achillea millefolium
- **Schlammfliege** f drone fly, Eristalis tenax
- **Schneebeere** f snow-berry, Symphoricarpos albus
- **Spinnmilbe** f red [glasshouse] spider mite, red spider (mite), two-spotted [spider] mite, Tetranychus urticae (telarius)
- **Stahlblaue Fichtenholzwespe** f steel-blue wood-wasp, Sirex (Paururus) juvencus
- **Stechmücke** f northern house mosquito, Culex pipiens
- **Stechpalme** f English holly, European (Christmas) holly, Ilex aquifolium
- **Strandnelke** f sea-pink, [common, sea] thrift, Armeria maritima
- **Traubenkirsche** f [European] bird cherry, cluster cherry, Prunus padus, Padus avium
- **Wachtel** f quail, Coturnix coturnix
- **Waldrebe** f (bot) old man's beard, traveller's joy, Clematis vitalba
- **Wiesenwanze** f tarnish[ed] plant bug, Lygus pratensis
- **Wildtaube** f wood-pigeon, Columba palumbus
- **Wunderblume** f (bot) four-o'clock, marvel of Peru, Mirabilis jalapa

Gemeiner Baldrian m [common] valerian, setwall, all-heal, Valeriana officinalis
- **Bastardindigo** m bastard indigo, Amorpha fruticosa
- **Beifuß** m 1. mugwort, motherwort, Artemisia vulgaris; 2. sweet wormwood, Artemisia annua
- **Beinwell** m (bot) [common] comfrey, consound, Symphytum officinale
- **Birnenblattsauger** m pear louse, Psylla pyri
- **Blasenstrauch** m [common] bladder senna, Colutea arborescens

- **Blattrüßler** *m* leaf-eating weevil, Phyllobius oblongus
- **Borretsch** *m* [common] borage, talewort, Borago officinalis
- **Efeu** *m* [English] ivy, hedera, Hedera helix
- **Erbsenstrauch** *m* Siberian pea shrub, Siberian acacia, Caragana arborescens
- **Erdbeerlaufkäfer** *m* strawberry ground beetle, Pterostichus vulgaris
- **Erdrauch** *m (bot)* [common] fumitory, earth-smoke, Fumaria officinalis
- **Eschenbastkäfer** *m* [common, small] ash bark-beetle, Leperesinus (Hylesinus) fraxinus
- **Fasan** *m* pheasant, Phasianus colchicus
- **Feldsalat** *m* [common] corn-salad, Valerianella locusta
- **Fischotter** *m* common otter, Lutra lutra
- **Flieder** *m* [common] lilac, pipe tree, Syringa vulgaris
- **Frauenfarn** *m* lady (female shield) fern, Athyrium (Asplenium) filix-femina
- **Frostspanner** *m* [common] winter moth, geometer [moth], Operophthera (Cheimatobia) brumata
- **Hamster** *m* [European] hamster, Cricetus cricetus
- **Hase** *m* common hare, Lepus europaeus
- **Holunder** *m* [common] elder, Sambucus nigra
- **Holzbock** *m* sheep (castor-bean) tick, Ixodes ricinus
- **Hopfen** *m* [common] hop, climber (European) hop, Humulus lupulus
- **Hornklee** *m* 1. [common] bird's-foot trefoil, Lotus corniculatus; 2. wild trefoil, Trigonella corniculata
- **Kiefernspanner** *m* pine looper [moth], bordered white moth, Bupalus piniarius
- **Krähenfuß** *m (bot)* swine (wart) cress, Coronopus squamatus
- **Kreuzdorn** *m* purging (common) buckthorn, Rhamnus catharticus
- **Leberbalsam** *m* goatweed, floss flower, Ageratum conyzoides
- **Lederstrauch** *m* [common] hop-tree, Ptelea trifoliata
- **Löwenzahn** *m (bot)* dandelion, horse gowan, Taraxacum officinale
- **Luchs** *m* lynx, Lynx lynx
- **Maiapfel** *m* common may-apple, Podophyllum peltatum
- **Ohrwurm** *m* common (European) earwig, Forficula auricularia
- **Oleander** *m* oleander, nerium, Nerium oleander
- **Pfeifenstrauch** *m* mock orange, syringa, Philadelphus coronarius
- **Regenwurm** *m* [common] earthworm, rain-worm, Lumbricus terrestris
- **Reiherschnabel** *m* common stork's-bill, pin clover (grass), red stem filaree, alfilaria, alfilerilla, Erodium cicutarium
- **Sanddorn** *m* sea buckthorn, sallow thorn, Hippophae rhamnoides
- **Sauerdorn** *m* barberry, Berberis vulgaris
- **Sauerklee** *m* wood sorrel, stubwort, Oxalis acetosella
- **Schneeball** *m* snowball[-tree], guelder rose, cranberry bush, water elder, Viburnum opulus
- **Schwammspinner** *m* gypsy (gipsy) moth, Lymantria (Porthetria) dispar
- **Seidelbast** *m (bot)* February daphne, mezereon, mezereum, Daphne mezereum
- **Stachelmohn** *m* prickly (Mexican) poppy, Argemone mexicana
- **Stechapfel** *m* thorn-apple, *(Am)* jimson [weed], Jamestown weed, Datura stramonium
- **Stinkstrauch** *m* bean trefoil, Anagyris foetida
- **Tüpfelfarn** *m* oak (wall) fern, Polypodium vulgare
- **Wacholder** *m* [common] juniper, Juniperus communis
- **Wasserdost** *m* water hemp, hemp agrimony, hempweed, Eupatorium cannabinum
- **Wildemmer** *m* [common] wild emmer, Triticum dicoccoides
- **Windhalm** *m* wind-grass, corn-grass, [loose] silky-bent, Apera spica-venti
- **Wundklee** *m* woundwort, kidney-vetch, Anthyllis vulneraria
- **Wurmfarn** *m* male [shield] fern, Dryopteris filix-mas
- **Ysop** *m (bot)* hyssop, Hyssopus officinalis

Gemeines Eichhörnchen *n* red squirrel, Sciurus vulgaris
- **Ferkelkraut** *n (bot)* cat's-ear, Hypochoeris radicata
- **Fettkraut** *n* butterwort, Pinguicula vulgaris
- **Hornblatt** *n* hornwort, Ceratophyllum demersum
- **Hornkraut** *n* 1. mouse-ear chickweed, Cerastium holosteoides (vulgatum); 2. field cerastium, Cerastium caespitosum
- **Johanniskraut** *n* common St. John's wort, Klamath weed, hardhay, Hypericum perforatum
- **Kammgras** *n (bot)* crested dog's-tail, Cynosurus cristatus
- **Katzenpfötchen** *n (bot)* [common] pussy-toes, Antennaria dioica
- **Kreuzkraut** *n* [common] groundsel, birdseed, Senecio vulgaris
- **Leimkraut** *n* bladder campion, maiden's-tears, Silene vulgaris (cucubalus)
- **Leinkraut** *n* [common] toadflax, flaxweed, butter-and-eggs, ramstead, Linaria vulgaris
- **Maßliebchen** *n s.* Gänseblümchen
- **Rispengras** *n* rough-stalked meadow grass, rough blue grass, Poa trivialis
- **Rohr** *n* reed, common reed [grass], Phragmites australis (communis)
- **Seifenkraut** *n* [common] soap-wort, bouncing bet, Saponaria officinalis
- **Sonnenröschen** *n* common rock-rose, Helianthemum nummularium
- **Sophienkraut** *n* flixweed, Descurainia (Sisymbrium) sophia

Gemeines

~ **Straußgras** *n* colonial bent[-grass], common bent[-grass], astoria bent[-grass], *(Am)* brown top, Agrostis capellaris (tenuis)
~ **Zittergras** *n* common quaking-grass, Briza media
Gemeinkosten *pl* overhead [charges, costs]
Gemeinschaft *f (ecol)* community, coenosis
~/**edaphische** edaphic community
Gemeinschaftskoeffizient *m (ecol)* coefficient of community, Jaccard's index
Gemeinschaftsnest *n* community (communal) nest *(fowl keeping)*
Gemeinschaftstreue *f* fidelity *(animal ecology)*
Gemeinschaftswald *m* communal (community, common) forest
Gemeinschaftsweide *f* communal grazing
Gemeinwald *m s.* Gemeinschaftswald
Gemelk *n* milking, meal
Gemenge *n* 1. mixture, blend *(esp. from solids)*; 2. *s.* Gemengesaat
Gemenge[an]bau *m* intercropping, interplanting, mixed cropping, polyculture, multicropping
• ~ **betreiben** to intercrop
Gemengesaat *f* mixed sowing, intercrop
Geminivirus *n* gemini virus
Gemisch *n* mixture, mix
gemischterbig heterozygous
Gemme *f (bot)* chlamydospore
Gemse *f* Alpine goat, chamois, Rupicapra rupicapra
Gemshorn *n (bot)* 1. night scented stock, Matthiola [longipetala ssp.] bicornis; 2. proboscis flower, unicorn plant, Proboscidea louisianica
Gemswurz *f* leopard's-bane *(genus Doronicum)*
Gemüse *n* vegetable[s], greens, veg
~/**[anbautechnisch] kleingehaltenes** *(Am)* baby-veg
Gemüseampfer *m* patience [dock], spinach (vegetable) dock, Rumex patientia
Gemüseanbau *m s.* Gemüsebau
Gemüseanzucht *f* vegetable growing
Gemüseartischocke *f (bot)* cardoon, Cynara cardunculus
Gemüsebankbeet *n* vegetable bank bed
Gemüsebau *m* vegetable growing (cropping, farming), olericulture
~ **im Garten** vegetable gardening
Gemüsebaubetrieb *m* vegetable farm (holding), truck farm, olericultural operation
Gemüsebauer *m* vegetable grower (planter), olericulturist
Gemüsebaufläche *f* vegetable growing area, area under vegetables
Gemüsebeet *n* vegetable bed
Gemüsebestand *m* vegetable culture
Gemüsebohne *f* haricot [bean], garden (French) bean
~/**fädige [grünhülsige]** string bean
Gemüsedrillmaschine *f* vegetable drill (seed planter)

Gemüseerbse *f* green (vining) pea, green corn
Gemüseernte *f* 1. vegetable harvest[ing]; 2. vegetable crop
Gemüseerntemaschine *f* vegetable harvester
Gemüseertrag *m* vegetable crop
Gemüseerzeuger *m* vegetable producer
Gemüseerzeugnis *n* vegetable product
Gemüseeule *f* tomato moth, bright-line brown-eye moth, Lacanobia (Diataraxia, Mamestra) oleracea
Gemüsefenchel *m* sweet fennel, Foeniculum vulgare var. azoricum
Gemüsefruchtfolge *f* vegetable crop rotation
Gemüsegarten *m* vegetable garden, market garden, kitchen garden (ground)
Gemüsehochbeet *n* vegetable bank bed
Gemüsejungpflanze *f* vegetable seedling
Gemüsekonserve *f* canned (preserved, tinned) vegetable
Gemüsekonservenfabrik *f* vegetable cannery
Gemüsekultur *f* vegetable culture (crop)
Gemüsekürbis *m* vegetable marrow, [marrow-type] pumpkin, marrow (summer) squash, gourd, courgette, Cucurbita pepo
~/**krummhalsiger** *(Am)* crookneck *(group of cultivars)*
Gemüsemaiskolben *mpl (Am)* green corn
Gemüsemarkt *m* vegetable market
Gemüsemelone *f* oriental pickling melon, Cucumis melo ssp. conomon
Gemüsepaprika *m* eating capsicum, sweet (bell) pepper, pim[i]ento
~/**gelber** yellow pepper
~/**grüner** green pepper
~/**roter** red pepper
Gemüsepflanze *f* 1. vegetable [crop] plant, vegetable, vegetal; 2. *s.* Gemüsejungpflanze
Gemüsepflanzenzüchtung *f* vegetable breeding
Gemüsepflanzgerät *n* vegetable planter
Gemüsepflanzmaschine *f* vegetable planter (planting machine)
Gemüseproduktion *f* vegetable production
Gemüseproduzent *m* vegetable producer
Gemüserhabarber *m* rhubarb, Rheum rhabarbarum
Gemüsesaatgut *n* vegetable seed[s]
Gemüsesaatschutz *m* vegetable-seed protection
Gemüsesaft *m* [vegetable] juice
Gemüsesamen *m* vegetable seed
Gemüsesämereien *pl* vegetable seed[s]
Gemüsesetzling *m* vegetable seedling
Gemüsesortiment *n* vegetable variety collection
Gemüsespargel *m* asparagus, Asparagus officinalis
Gemüseverarbeitungsindustrie *f* vegetable industry
Gemüsezucht *f* vegetable growing
Gemüsezüchter *m* 1. vegetable breeder; 2. *s.* Gemüsebauer
Gemüsezüchtung *f* vegetable breeding

Gemüsezwiebel f salad (Spanish) onion
Gen n gene, [hereditary] factor, hereditary determinant • **durch ein einziges ~ kontrolliert** monogenic
~/allelomorphes allele, allel[omorph]
~/epistatisches epistatic gene
~/geschlechtsgebundenes sex-linked gene
~/komplementäres complementary gene
~/modifizierendes modifier [gene]
~/nitrogenasecodierendes nif gene
~/prozessiertes processed gene
Genaktivität f gene activity
Genamplifikation f gene amplification
Genanzahl f gene number
Genaufspaltung f gene segregation
Genauigkeit f accuracy
Genaustausch m gene exchange, crossing-over
Genbank f gene (germ-plasm) bank
~/genomische genomic library
Genbestand m gene[tic] pool
Genbibliothek f s. Genbank
Genchirurgie f genetic engineering
Genealogie f genealogy
Geneffekt m gene effect
Generalisierung f generalization (e.g. of a disease)
~ eines Sarkoms (vet) sarcomatosis
Generation f generation
Generationenwechsel m alternation of generations
Generationsdauer f generation time
Generationsintervall n generation interval (length)
Generationswechsel m alternation of generations
Generationszyklus m life cycle • **mit unvollständigem ~** anholocyclic (development of aphids)
Generator m dynamo
generativ generative
Generativsproß m (bot) generative (reproductive) shoot
generisch generic
Generosion f gene erosion
Genese f genesis
Genesung f recovery, convalescence
Genetik f genetics
~/angewandte applied genetics
~/biochemische biochemical genetics
~/faktorielle (qualitative) Mendelian genetics
~/quantitative quantitative genetics
Genetiker m geneticist
genetisch genetic[al]
Genetzte Ackerschnecke f netted (grey field) slug, Deroceras reticulatum
Genevolution f gene evolution
Genexpression f [gene] expression
Genfluß m gene flow, migration
~ zwischen den Arten introgression, introgressive hybridization
Genfonds m gene[tic] pool

Genfrequenz f gene (allele) frequency
Gen-für-Gen-Konzept n gene-for-gene concept (theory) (plant breeding)
Genick n neck, scruff, poll
Genickbeule f s. Genickfistel
genicken (hunt) to stab
Genickfänger m (hunt) hanger
Genickfistel f (vet) fistulous withers
genießbar esculent, edible
Geninaktivierung f gene repression
Geninteraktion f gene interaction
genisch genic
Genistein n genistein (phytoestrogen)
genital genital
Genitale n reproductive organ
Genitalien pl genitals, genitalia
Genitalinfektion f genital infection
Genitalöffnung f genital opening (aperture); genital pore (e.g. of fishes)
Genitaltrakt[us] m genital (reproductive) tract
Genkarte f gene map
Genkartierung f gene mapping
Genklonung f gene cloning
Genkombination f gene combination
Genkomplex m gene complex
Genkonversion f gene conversion
Genlocus m s. Genort
Genlokalisierung f gene localization
Genmanipulation f gene[tic] manipulation
Genmechanismus m gene mechanism
Genmutation f gene (intragenic, point) mutation
Genmutationsrate f [gene] mutation rate
Genökologie f genecology
Genom n genome
Genomanalyse f genome analysis
Genomer n chromomere
genomisch genomic
Genommutation f genome mutation
Genort m [gene] locus
Genortung f gene localization
Genossenschaft f co-operative, co-op
~/bäuerliche farmer co-operative, collective farm
~/landwirtschaftliche agricultural co-operative
genossenschaftlich co-operative, co-op
Genossenschaftsbauer m co-operative farmer, collective farmer
Genossenschaftsforst m, **Genossenschaftswald** m co-operative forest, association forest
Genotyp m genotype, genetic constitution (make-up)
genotypisch genotypic[al]
Genotyp-Umwelt-Wechselwirkung f genotype-environment interaction
Genotypus m s. Genotyp
Genpaar n gene pair
Genpool m gene[tic] pool
Genprodukt n gene product
Genrepression f gene repression
Genreservoir n gene[tic] pool

Gensymbol

Gensymbol *n* gene symbol
Gentamycin *n* gentamicin *(antibiotic)*
Gentechnik *f* genetic engineering, gene technology
Gentechniker *m* genetic engineer
Gentechnologie *f s.* Gentechnik
Gentianaviolett *n* gentian violet *(anthelminthic, fungicide)*
Gentiobiase *f* beta-glucosidase *(enzyme)*
Gentiobiose *f* gentiobiose *(disaccharide)*
Gentisinsäure *f* dihydroxybenzoic acid
Gentransfer *m* gene transfer
Gentransfertechnik *f s.* Gentechnik
Genübertragung *f* gene transfer
Genügsamer Hafer *m* winter wild oat, Avena sterilis [ssp. ludoviciana]
Genus *n* genus *(taxonomy)*
Genußmittelpflanze *f* stimulant plant
genußreif [eating-]ripe
Genußreife *f* eating maturity, ripeness
genußtauglich edible, esculent, wholesome
Genußtauglichkeit *f* edibility, wholesomeness
genußuntauglich inedible
Genußuntauglichkeit *f* inedibility
Genverstärkung *f* gene amplification
Genwechselwirkung *f* gene interaction
Genwirkung *f* gene action
~/gleichsinnig additive polymery
~/vielseitige pleiotropism, pleiotropy, polypheny
Genzentrum *n* gene centre, centre of origin (domestication)
Geobiozönologie *f* landscape ecology
Geobotanik *f* geobotany, plant geography, phytogeography
~/floristische floristics, floristry, vegetation chorology
~/zönologische vegetation science
Geobotaniker *m* geobotanist, plant geographer
geobotanisch geobotanic[al], phytogeographic[al]
Geochemie *f* geochemistry
~/landwirtschaftliche agrogeochemistry
Geomorphologie *f* geomorphology, physiography
Geomycin *n* gentamicin *(antibiotic)*
Geoökologie *f* landscape ecology
Geophagie *f* geophagia
Geophyt *m* geophyte, cryptophyte
Georgine *f* 1. dahlia *(genus Dahlia)*; 2. common dahlia, Dahlia pinnata
Geotaxis *f* geotaxis
Geothermalwasser *n* geothermal water
geotrop[isch] *(bot)* geotropic
Geotropismus *m* geotropism, gravitropism
Geozoologie *f* animal geography
gepaart *(bot, zoo)* conjugate, twin
gepunktet *(bot, zoo)* punctate[d]; pitted *(skin of pome fruits)*
Gepunktete Gewächshauslaus *f* ornate aphid, Myzus ornatus

Geradezugfeinstriegel *m* non-tracking spiked chain harrow
geradfaserig straight-grained *(timber)*
Geradfaserigkeit *f* straight grain
geradschaftig straight-boled, straight-stemmed
Geradschaftigkeit *f* straightness of bole (stem)
Geradschubkolbenpresse *f* ram baler
geradstämmig *s.* geradschaftig
geradzeilig [angeordnet] *(bot)* orthostichous
Geradzeiligkeit *f* orthostichy
Geradzinkenegge *f* straight-tined harrow
gerändert *(bot, zoo)* marginate[d]
Geränderter Porling *m* red belt fungus, Fomes marginatus
gerandet *(bot, zoo)* marginate[d]
Geranie *f (bot)* geranium *(genus Geranium)*
Geraniol *n* geraniol *(terpenoid)*
Gerät *n* implement, tool
~/bodengebundenes ground equipment *(e.g. in plant protection)*
~/landwirtschaftliches field implement (tool), agricultural (farming) implement
~ zur humanen (schmerzlosen) Tötung *(slaught)* humane killer
Geräteabstellraum *m s.* Geräteschuppen
Geräteanbauvorrichtung *f* implement coupler
Geräteanschluß *m* **zwischen den Achsen** mid-mounted pad *(of a tractor)*
Gerätekopplung *f* [implement] coupling
Gerätekopplungsvorrichtung *f* implement coupler
Gerätescheinwerfer *m* adjustable rear working light
Geräteschuppen *m* implement shed (store), tool shed
Geräteträger *m* [implement, tool] carrier, mounted-implement tractor
Gerätewagen *m* trolley
Geräteüberwachungssystem *n* implement control system
geräumig spacious
gerben to tan
Gerbera *f* 1. gerbera *(genus Gerbera)*; 2. Barberton-daisy, Transvaal-daisy, gerbera, Gerbera jamesonii
Gerberakazie *f* 1. black wattle, Acacia mearnsii; 2. catechu acacia, Acacia catechu
Gerbereiabfall *m* tannery waste
Gerber-Methode *f* Gerber method *(of milk fat determination)*
Gerberstrauch *m (bot)* coriaria *(genus Coriaria)*
Gerbersumach *m* tanning (tanner's, hide) sumac[h], Rhus coriaria
Gerbmittel *n* tan-stuff, tanning material *(s. a. Gerbstoff)*
Gerbrinde *f* tan[bark]
Gerbsäure *f* tannic acid
Gerbstoff *m* tanning agent, tannin
gerbstoffhaltig tannic
Gerbstoffpflanze *f* tan[nin] plant

gereift ripened, ripe, mature; mellow *(wine)*
~/auf dem Feld field-ripened
Gerfalke *m* gyrfalcon, Falco rusticolus gyrfalco
~/männlicher jerkin
gerichtet/horizontal *(bot)* plagiotropic
~/spitzenwärts *(bot, zoo)* acropetal
gerieft, gerillt fluted *(tree-trunk)*
Gerinnbarkeit *f s.* Gerinnungsfähigkeit
Gerinne *n* channel, race
gerinnen to coagulate, to clot *(e.g. blood)*; to curdle, to sour *(esp. milk)*
~ lassen to coagulate, to clot; to curdle
Gerinnsel *n* coagulum, coagulate, clot
Gerinnung *f* coagulation, clotting *(e.g. of blood)*; curdling, souring *(esp. of milk)*
Gerinnungsfähigkeit *f* coagulability; curdling ability
Gerinnungsfaktor *m* coagulation (clotting) factor *(immunology)*
~ Xa coagulation factor Xa, thrombokinase *(enzyme)*
Gerinnungspunkt *n* coagulation point; setting (curdling) point *(esp. of milk)*
Gerinnungszeit *f* clotting time
Gerippe *n* skeleton
gerippt *(bot, zoo)* costate, ribbed
Germer *m* [false] hellebore *(genus Veratrum)*
germerblättrig verbascifolious
germinal germinal
Germinalaplasie *f (vet)* aspermatogenesis
Germination *f* germination
germinativ germinative, germinating
germizid germicidal, microbicidal
Germizid *n* germicide
Gernebcin *n s.* Tobramycin
Geröll *n* detritus, scree
Geröllhalde *f* scree
geronnen coagulated, clotted; curdy, curdled
Gerste *f* 1. barley *(genus Hordeum)*; 2. [common] barley, Hordeum vulgare
~/bespelzte husky barley
~/milde mealy barley
Gerstenenzym *n* barley enzyme
Gerstenflocken *fpl* barley flakes
Gerstenflugbrand *m* loose smut of barley, brown loose smut *(caused by Ustilago nuda)*
Gerstenfuttermehl *n* barley feed meal
Gerstengelbmosaikvirus *n* barley yellow mosaic virus, BaYMV
Gerstengelbverzwergungsvirus *n* barley yellow dwarf virus, BYDV
Gerstengraupen *fpl* barley groats
~/grobe pot barley
Gerstengrieß *m* barley grits
Gerstengrütze *f* barley groats
Gerstengummi *n*, **Gerstengummistoff** *m* barley gum
Gerstenhartbrand *m* covered smut of barley *(caused by Ustilago hordei)*

Gerstenheu *n* barley hay
Gerstenkleie *f* barley bran
Gerstenmalz *n* barley malt, malted barley
Gerstenmehl *n* barley flour, patent barley
Gerstenprolamin *n* hordein
Gerstenputzanlage *f*, **Gerstenreinigungsanlage** *f* barley cleaning equipment *(malting)*
Gersten-Roggen-Bastard *m* hordecale
Gerstenschrot *n* barley meal
Gerstenschwarzbrand *m* black loose smut *(caused by Ustilago avenae)*
Gerstensilage *f* barley silage
Gerstenstärke *f* barley starch
Gerstenstreifenkrankheit *f* barley stripe disease, leaf stripe of barley *(caused by Pyrenophora graminea)*
Gerstenstreifenmosaikvirus *n* barley stripe mosaic virus, BSMV
Gerstenstroh *n* barley straw (shag)
Gerstentrockner *m* barley dryer
Gerstenweichwasser *n* barley steep water
Gerstenzucker *m* barley sugar
Gerstenzwergrost *m* dwarf leaf rust [of barley], barley brown rust *(caused by Puccinia hordei)*
Gerte *f* 1. twig, rod, switch, wand; sapling; 2. riding crop
Geruch *m* odour, smell; scent, fragrance • **dem ~ nachspüren** to road (hunting dog) • **~ nehmen** *(hunt)* to scent • **~ wahrnehmen** to smell
~/staubgetragener dust-borne odour
geruchlich olfactory
geruchlos odourless, inodorous, non-odorous, scentless
Geruchlose Kamille *f* scentless mayweed, horse daisy, Matricaria perforata (maritima ssp. inodora), Tripleurospermum maritimum
Geruchsbekämpfung *f* odour control
Geruchsbelästigung *f* odour (smell) nuisance
Geruchsbeseitigung *f* odour abatement, deodorizing
Geruchsemission *f* odour emission
Geruchsfehler *m* taint
Geruchsintensitätsindex *m* odour intensity index
Geruchsorgan *n* olfactory organ, organ of smell
Geruchsrezeptor *m* olfactory receptor
Geruchsschwelle *f* odour threshold
Geruchssinn *m* olfaction, olfactory sense, [sense of] smell
Geruchsstoff *m* odorant, odorous substance *(s. a. Duftstoff)*
Geruchsverbesserung *f* odour improvement
Geruchsverringerung *f* odour abatement
Geruchszentrum *n* olfactory centre
Gerüst *n* frame[work]; scaffold, trestle, rack *(e.g. for tobacco drying)*; trellis
Gerüstachse *f* central leader *(of a fruit-tree)*
Gerüstast *m* scaffold (framework) branch, limb; arm *(of the grape-vine)*

Gerüsteiweiß

Gerüsteiweiß *n*, **Gerüsteiweißstoff** *m* scleroprotein
Gerüstsilicat *n* *(soil)* framework silicate
Gerüstsubstanz *f* skeleton substance
~ **in modifizierter saurer Detergentienlösung** modified acid detergent fibre, MADF *(feed analysis)*
~ **in neutraler Detergentienlösung** neutral detergent fibre, NDF *(feed analysis)*
~ **in saurer Detergentienlösung** acid detergent fibre, ADF *(feed analysis)*
Gerüsttrocknung *f* rack drying
Gerüstveredelung *f* topworking, top grafting *(orcharding)*
gesägt *(bot, zoo)* serrated, saw-toothed
~/**doppelt** biserrate
~/**fein** serrulate
Gesamtabflußmenge *f* total runoff
Gesamtaminosäureindex *m* total amino-acid value, TAAV
Gesamtarbeitsbreite *f* overall working width *(e.g. of field implements)*
Gesamtastholz[volumen] *n* total branchwood
Gesamtausbeute *f* total yield
Gesamtazidität *f* total acidity *(e.g. of soil)*
Gesamtblattfläche *f* total leaf area
Gesamtblutvolumen *n* [total] blood volume, TBV
Gesamteinschlagmenge *f* s. Gesamtnutzung
Gesamtenergie *f* total (gross) energy *(e.g. of a feedstuff)*
Gesamtertrag *m* total yield
~ **mehrerer Jahre** cumulative yield
Gesamtgehalt *m* **an austauschbaren Basen** *(soil)* total exchange bases
Gesamtheit *f* *(biom)* universe
Gesamtholzaufkommen *n*, **Gesamtholzeinschlag** *m* overall timber yield, total cut (wood availability)
Gesamtholzvorrat *m* *(forest)* total growing stock
Gesamtkeimzahl *f* total bacterial count, TBC, total number of germs
Gesamtmasse *f* total weight
Gesamtmassenleistung *f* s. Gesamtvolumenleistung
Gesamtniederschlag *m* total precipitation
Gesamtnutzung *f* *(forest)* total cut
Gesamtnutzungsetat *m* *(forest)* total allowable cut
Gesamtprodukt *n***/landwirtschaftliches** agricultural (farm) produce
Gesamtschaftholz[volumen] *n* total stemwood
Gesamtschwindung *f* total shrinkage *(timber drying)*
Gesamtstickstoff *m* total nitrogen
Gesamtstrahlung *f* total radiation
Gesamtverdaulichkeit *f* total digestibility
Gesamtverdunstung *f* total evaporation
Gesamtvolumen *n* **stehenden Holzes** *(forest)* total standing volume

~ **eines Baumes über dem Boden** total tree volume
Gesamtvolumenleistung *f* *(forest)* total volume production
Gesamtwaldbestand *m* forest fund
Gesamtwaldfläche *f* total forest area
Gesamtwuchsleistung *f* s. Gesamtzuwachs
Gesamtzuchtwert *m* aggregate genotype
Gesamtzuwachs *m* *(forest)* total increment (growth, yield)
~/**durchschnittlicher** total mean increment
~/**durchschnittlicher jährlicher** mean annual increment, m.a.i.
~/**laufender** total current increment
Gesäuge *n* dug, udder; teat
~ **der Sau** sow's teats
gescheckt mottled, blotched; piebald, dappled, mealy, *(Am)* pinto *(horse)*; tabby *(cat)*
Gescheide *n* *(hunt)* gralloch, [h]umbles, pluck, viscera, guts, bowels
Geschiebe *n* *(soil)* drift, detritus, shingle
Geschiebelehm *m*, **Geschiebemergel** *m* boulder clay [soil], [clay, glacial] till
Geschirr *n* harness, gear
Geschirrhalter *m* harness frame
Geschirrkette *f* harness chain
Geschirrleine *f* line
Geschlängelte Schmiele *f* wavy (wood) hairgrass, Avenella (Deschampsia) flexuosa
Geschlecht *n* sex • **das ~ bestimmen** to sex • **von männlichem ~** male, masculine • **von weiblichem ~** female, feminine
Geschlechterverhältnis *n* sex ratio
geschlechtlich sexual
Geschlechtlichkeit *f* sexuality
Geschlechtsaktivität *f* sexual activity
Geschlechtsausdruck *m* sex expression
Geschlechtsbestimmung *f* sex determination
~/**diplogenotypische** diplogenotypic sex determination
~/**haplogenotypische** haplogenotypic sex determination
Geschlechtscharakter *m* sex expression
Geschlechtschromatin *n* sex chromatin
Geschlechtschromosom *n* sex chromosome, hetero[chromo]some, allosome, gonosome
Geschlechtsdetermination *f* sex determination
Geschlechtsdiagnose *f* sex diagnosis
Geschlechtsdifferenzierung *f* sex differentiation
Geschlechtsdimorphismus *m* sex dimorphism
Geschlechtsdrüse *f* sex gland, gonad
~/**akzessorische (zusätzliche)** accessory [sex] gland
Geschlechtsdrüsenunterfunktion *f* hypogenitalism
Geschlechtsgang *m* gonoduct, gonaduct
~/**embryonaler** Muellerian duct
Geschlechtsgeruch *m* sex odour
~ **des Ebers** boar odour

Geschlechtsgeschmack *m* **von Eberfleisch** boar taint
Geschlechtshormon *n* sex hormone
Geschlechtskopplung *f (gen)* sex linkage
Geschlechtskrankheit *f (vet)* venereal disease
geschlechtslos asexual
Geschlechtsmerkmal *n* sex[ual] characteristic
~/primäres primary sex[ual] characteristic
~/sekundäres secondary sex[ual] characteristic
Geschlechtsmutterzelle *f (bot)* gametangium
Geschlechtsöffnung *f* genital opening (aperture)
Geschlechtsorgan *n* sex (reproductive) organ
Geschlechtsorgane *npl* genitals, genitalia • **die ~ betreffend** genital • **ohne ausgeprägte ~** agamous, amphigamous
Geschlechtspheromon *n* sex pheromone (attractant)
Geschlechtsphysiologie *f* sex physiology
Geschlechtsrealisator *m (gen)* sex realizator (realizer)
geschlechtsreif sexually mature, adult • **~ werdend** pubescent
Geschlechtsreife *f* sexual maturity • **vor der ~** prepubertal
Geschlechtssortierung *f* sexing
~ durch Kloakenuntersuchung vent sexing *(of chicks)*
Geschlechtstiere *npl* sexuales *(members of the bisexual generation in aphids)*
Geschlechtstrennung *f (zoo)* gonochorism
Geschlechtstrieb *m* sexual drive (urge), libido • **den ~ anregend** aphrodisiac
~/krankhaft gesteigerter aphrodisia
Geschlechtstyp *m* sex expression
Geschlechtsumkehrung *f*, **Geschlechtsumwandlung** *f* sex reversal (change)
Geschlechtsunterschied *m* sex difference
Geschlechtsvererbung *f* sex inheritance
Geschlechtsverhalten *n* sexual behaviour
Geschlechtsverhältnis *n* sex ratio
Geschlechtszelle *f* sex (reproductive) cell, germcell, gamete
~/männliche microgamete, androgamete
~/weibliche macrogamete
Geschlechtszyklus *m* sexual (oestrous) cycle
Geschlitzter Grünkohl *m* [curly] kale, curled [kitchen] kale, green cabbage, Brassica oleracea convar. acephala var. sabellica
geschlüpft out *(chick)*
Geschmack *m* taste, flavour
geschmacklos flavourless, insipid
Geschmacksbeeinträchtigung *f* taint
Geschmackseigenschaft *f* flavour
Geschmacksempfindlichkeit *f* taste sensitivity
Geschmacksknospe *f* taste bud (corpuscle) *(animal anatomy)*
Geschmacksqualität *f* gustatory quality
Geschmacksrezeptor *m* gustatory receptor
Geschmackssinn *m* [sense of] taste

Geschmacksstoff *m* flavouring [substance], flavour
Geschmacksverbesserung *f* improvement of flavour
geschnäbelt *(bot, zoo)* rostrate
Geschnatter *n* gaggle
geschränkt spring-set, *(Am)* brier-dressed *(saw)*
Geschröte *n* testicles *(of dog and furred game)*
Geschüh[e] *n s.* Geschühriemen
Geschühriemen *m* leash, jess *(falconry)* • **den ~ anlegen** to jess
geschult aged *(wine)*
geschuppt 1. *(bot, zoo)* scaly, squamate[d], squamous; 2. [de]scaled *(fish)*
geschwänzt *(bot, zoo)* caudate
Geschwister *n* sib[ling]
Geschwisterbestäubung *f (bot)* sib (brother-sister) pollination, adelphogamy
Geschwisterkreuzung *f* sib crossing
Geschwisterleistung *f* sib performance
Geschwisterpaarung *f* sib-mating
Geschwisterprüfung *f* sib-test[ing]
Geschwisterteil *m* sib[ling]
geschwollen *(bot)* turgid
Geschwulst *f* 1. *(phyt, vet)* tumour, neoplasm, growth; 2. *s.* Anschwellung 1.
~/bösartige malignant growth
~/gutartige benign growth
Geschwulstentstehung *f (vet)* oncogenesis
geschwulsterzeugend oncogenic, oncogenous
Geschwür *n (vet)* ulcer, sore, canker • **ein ~ bilden** to ulcerate
~/peptisches peptic ulcer
Geschwürbildung *f* ulceration, ulcer formation
Geschwürhämophilose *f* ulcer disease *(of trouts and brook trouts, caused by Haemophilus piscium)*
geschwürig ulcerous • **~ zerfallen** to ulcerate, to undergo ulceration • **~ zerfallend** ulcerative, ulcerous
gesellig *(zoo)* gregarious, sociable
Gesellige Fichtengespinstblattwespe *f (Am, ent)* false spruce web-worm, Cephaleia abietis
Gesellschaft *f (ecol)* society
~ laubabwerfender Gehölze deciduligniosa
gesellschaftsfest selective
gesellschaftsfremd accidental
gesellschaftshold preferential
gesellschaftstreu exclusive
Gesellschaftstreue *f* fidelity
gesellschaftsvag[e] indifferent
Gesetz *n* **der homologen Reihen** law of homologous series *(plant breeding)*
~/Ficksches *(soil)* Fick's law *(of diffusion)*
~/Stokessches Stokes' law *(soil physics)*
~ vom abnehmenden Ertragszuwachs law of diminishing returns, law of effectivity of growth factors

Gesetz 254

~ vom Minimum law of limiting factors *(plant nutrition)*
~ von Darcy Darcy's law *(of soil water movement)*
gesichert/statistisch *(biom)* significant
~/statistisch nicht insignificant, non-significant
Gesicht *n* face, facies *(of mammals)* • **mit unbewolltem ~** open-faced *(sheep)*
Gesichtsarterie *f* facial artery
Gesichtsausdruck *m* face
Gesichtsfeld *n* visual field
Gesichtsmaske *f* face screen
Gesichtsnerv *m* facial nerve
Gesichtsschutzmaske *f* face screen
Gesichtssinn *m* sense of sight
GeSMV *s*. Gerstenstreifenmosaikvirus
gespalten *(bot, zoo)* fissured, multifid; cleft, riven *(wood)*
Gespann *n* team, pair [of horses], rig, cart, span • **mit dem ~ [ab]transportieren** to cart [off]
Gespannegge *f* harrow for animal traction
Gespannführer *m* teamster, coachman, carter, *(Am)* reinsman
gespanngezogen horse-drawn
Gespannhacke *f* horse[-pulled] hoe
Gespannhäufelpflug *m* horse ridger
Gespannmähmaschine *f* horse mower
Gespannpferd *n* harness horse
Gespannpflug *m* walking (horse) plough
Gespannrückung *f (forest)* horse (animal) skidding
Gespanntier *n* draught animal
Gespanntransport *m* carting
Gespannzug *m* horse (animal) traction
Gespenstheuschrecke *f* stick-insect *(family Phasmidae)*
Gespinst *n* web[bing]
Gespinstblattwespe *f* web-spinning saw-fly *(family Pamphiliidae)*
Gespinstkokon *m* web-like cocoon
Gespinstmotte *f* small ermine [moth], ermine moth *(family Yponomeutidae)*
Gespinstpflanze *f* fibre plant
gespornt *(bot, zoo)* calcarate[d]
Gespornte Bohne *f* rice (climbing mountain) bean, Vigna umbellata, Phaseolus umbellatus
gesprenkelt mottled, speckled; pitted *(skin of pome fruits)*; merle *(hair coat)*
Gestalt *f* shape, form
~/äußere appearance, facies
gestalten/landschaftsgärtnerisch to landscape
Gestaltentwicklung *f* morphogenesis
Gestaltlehre *f* morphology
gestaltlos amorphous, amorphic
Gestaltlosigkeit *f* amorphism
Gestaltmodifikation *f* morphosis
Gestaltwandel *m* metamorphosis
Gestation *f* gestation, pregnancy, gravidity
Gestations... *s. a.* Trächtigkeits...

Gestationskörper *m (zoo)* yellow body, corpus luteum
gestaucht swage-set, swaged, square-dressed *(saw-tooth)*
Gestein *n* rock, stone
~/metamorphes metamorphic rock
~/unverwittertes primary rock
Gesteinsboden *m* mineral soil, lithosol
Gesteinskunde *f* petrology
Gesteinsmantel *m* **der Erde** lithosphere
Gesteinsrohboden *m (soil)* syrozem
Gesteinsschicht *f* stratum
Gesteinsschutt *m* scree, detritus
Gesteinswelt *f* lithosphere
Gestell *n* 1. shelf, frame, rack; 2. cradle *(of a scythe)*; 3. *(forest)* ride
Gestellwagen *m* frame cart *(glasshouse installation)*
gestielt *(bot, zoo)* pedunculate[d], peduncular, stalked; *(bot)* petiolar, petiolate, stipitate
Gestose *f (vet)* gestational toxicosis
Gesträuch *n s.* Gestrüpp
Gestreckter Ehrenpreis *m* harebell Hungarian speedwell, Veronica prostrata
gestreift *(bot, zoo)* fasciate[d], striate[d], striped; banded, zonate[d]; *(ent)* strigose
Gestreifte Kartoffellaus *f* potato aphid, Macrosiphum euphorbiae
~ Luzernewanze *f* alfalfa plant bug, Adelphocoris lineolatus
Gestreifter Geißklee *m* striped broom, Cytisus striatus
~ Graurüßler *m* sand weevil, Philopedon plagiatus
~ Gurkenkäfer *m* striped cucumber beetle, squash beetle, Diabrotica vittata
~ Nutzholzborkenkäfer *m* lineate bark-beetle, Trypodendron (Xyloterus) lineatus
Gestrenge Herren *pl s.* Eisheiligen/die
Gestrüpp *n* brush[wood], scrub, coppice[-wood], shrubbery, copsewood, brake, tangled growth
Gestrüppmäher *m* brush cutter (buster), scrub cutter
Gestrüppschläger *m* brush (wood) shredder
Gestüt *n* stud[-farm]
~/staatliches state stud[-farm]
Gestütsarbeiter *m* stud hand
gestutzt *(bot)* truncate[d]; *(bot)* abrupt; polled *(tree)*
gesund healthy, sound
gesundheitlich sanitary
Gesundheitslehre *f* hygiene
Gesundheitspaß *m* health passport (certificate) *(e.g. for breeding animals)*
Gesundheitspflege *f* hygiene, sanitation
Gesundheitsschutz *m* health care
Gesundheitsstörung *f* health upset
Gesundheitszustand *m* health condition (status), state of health
gesundschneiden to cut prime *(a woody plant)*; to butt off, to jump butt *(a tree-trunk)*

Gesundungsfrucht f break crop *(in a rotation)*
Get-away-Käfig m get-away cage *(fowl keeping)*
getigert merle *(hair coat)*
Getränk n drink, beverage
~/alkoholisches alcoholic beverage, spirit, liquor
Getreide n cereal[s], corn, grain, breadstuff *(s. a. under* Korn*)* • **mit ~ bestellen** to corn • **mit ~ füttern** to corn
~/eigenerzeugtes home-grown corn (cereal), locally grown grain
~/gemahlenes milled grain
~/grobvermahlenes kibble
~/kleinkörniges small-grain cereal
~/lagerndes lodged corn (grain)
Getreide... *s. a.* Korn...
Getreideabfall m dockage
Getreideabfallprodukt n cereal by-product
Getreideanbau m *s.* Getreidebau
Getreideart f cereal [species]
Getreideaufbereitungsanlage f corn dresser
Getreidebau m corn (grain) growing
Getreidebaubetrieb m grain farm
Getreidebauer m grain grower
Getreidebaufläche f cereal area (acreage), area under cereals
Getreidebaugebiet n grain-growing area
Getreidebaugrenzlage f marginal cereal land
Getreidebestand m cereal stand
Getreidebestimmung f **[im blütenlosen Zustand]** recognition of cereals
Getreideblasenfuß m *(ent)* grain thrips *(Limothrips spp.)*
Getreideblattlaus f 1. cereal aphid *(comprehensive term)*; 2. wheat aphid, *(Am)* greenbug, Schizaphis (Toxoptera) graminum; 3. *s.* Große Getreideblattlaus
Getreideboden m cereal soil
Getreidebörse f corn exchange, *(Am)* [grain] pit
Getreidebrand m *(phyt)* smut
Getreidechemie f cereal chemistry
Getreidedrillmaschine f grain drill, corn (cereal) drill
Getreidedrusch m grain threshing
Getreidedurchlaufregulierung f grain flow regulation
Getreideeinheit f cereal equivalent
Getreideeiweiß n cereal protein
Getreideendmast f cereal finishing
Getreideerdfloh m striped flea-beetle, Phyllotreta vittula
Getreideernte f grain harvest
Getreideerntemaschine f grain harvester
Getreideersatzfuttermittel n cereal substitute
Getreideertrag m cereal yield
Getreideerzeugnis n cereal product
Getreideerzeugung f cereal production
Getreidefarm f grain farm
Getreidefeldbestand m cereal stand
Getreidefläche f cereal area

Getreideförderer m grain conveyor
Getreidefruchtfolge f cereal rotation
Getreidefütterung f grain feeding
Getreideganzpflanzenernte f whole-crop cereal harvest[ing]
Getreideganzpflanzensilage f whole-crop cereal silage
Getreidegarbe f corn-sheaf
Getreidegranne f grain awn
Getreidegrobmehl n corn meal
Getreidehähnchen n cereal (barley) leaf beetle, Oulema (Lema) melanopus
Getreidehalm m corn stalk
Getreidehalmfliege f gout-fly, Chlorops pumilionis
Getreidehalmwespe f wheat stem saw-fly, Cephus pygmaeus
Getreidehändler m corn-chandler, *(Am)* grain broker
Getreidehauptanbaugebiet n granary
Getreide-Hülsenfrucht-Gemenge n mashlum, grain-legume mixture
Getreidekaltbelüftungsanlage f ambient-temperature grain dryer
Getreidekapuziner m lesser grain borer, Australian wheat weevil, Rhyzopertha dominica
Getreidekeim m cereal germ
Getreidekonservierung f grain conservation (preservation)
Getreidekonzentrat[futtermittel] n grain mixture concentrate
Getreidekorn n [cereal] grain, kernel, berry
Getreidekrankheit f cereal disease
Getreidekühlung f grain chilling
Getreidekultur f grain (cereal) crop
Getreidelager[haus] n grain store, granary
Getreidelagerraum m grain-elevator
Getreidelagerung f grain storage
Getreidelagerungsbetrieb m cereal storage firm
Getreidelaus f *s.* Getreideblattlaus
Getreide-Leguminosen-Gemisch n grain-legume mixture, mashlum
Getreidemähmaschine f corn cutter, reaper[-binder], reaping-machine
Getreidemalzbier n malt beer
Getreidemehl n cereal flour, cornflour, farina, breadstuff[s]
Getreidemehltau m cereal mildew, powdery mildew of cereals *(caused by Erysiphe graminis)*
Getreidemotte f angoumois grain moth, Sitotroga cerealella
Getreidemühle f [grain] mill, corn (flour) mill
Getreidemüller m miller
Getreidenährmittel n cereal
Getreidenebenprodukt n cereal by-product
Getreidepflanze f cereal [plant]
Getreideplattkäfer m saw-toothed grain beetle, Oryzaephilus surinamensis
Getreideprobenzieher m grain sampler
Getreideprodukt n cereal product, breadstuff
Getreideproduktion f cereal production

Getreideproduktionsforschung 256

Getreideproduktionsforschung *f* cereal production research
Getreideproduktionssystem *n* cereal production system
Getreidequalität *f* cereal quality
Getreidereiniger *m* grain cleaner
Getreidereinigungsanlage *f* corn dresser, scourer
Getreiderohfrucht *f* cereal adjunct *(brewing)*
Getreiderost *m*, **Getreiderostkrankheit** *f (phyt)* cereal rust
Getreidesaatgut *n* cereal seed
Getreidesaftkäfer *m* corn sap beetle, Carpophilus dimidiatus
Getreideschädling *m* cereal pest
Getreidescheune *f* corn barn
Getreideschlag *m* cornfield
Getreideschlempe *f* grain stillage, distiller's spent grains
Getreideschmalkäfer *m* saw-toothed grain beetle, Oryzaephilus surinamensis
Getreideschott *n* grain bulkhead
Getreideschrot *m* crushed (bruised) grain
Getreideschwarzrost *m* barberry rust *(caused by Puccinia graminis)*
Getreidesilo *m* grain silo (elevator)
Getreidesorte *f* cereal cultivar (variety)
Getreidesortenversuch *m* cereal cultivar trial
Getreidespeicher *m* granary, grain loft
Getreidesproß *m* cereal sprout
Getreidestärke *f* cereal starch
Getreidestaub *m* grain dust
Getreidestecher *m* grain sampler
Getreidestetigförderer *m* grain conveyor
Getreidestoppel *f* corn (cereal) stubble
Getreidestroh *n* cereal straw
Getreidesubstitut *n* cereal substitute
Getreidethrips *m*, **Getreidethysanoptere** *m (ent)* grain thrips *(Limothrips spp.)*
Getreidetrockner *m* grain dryer
Getreidetrocknung *f* grain drying
Getreidetrocknungsanlage *f* grain-drying plant, grain dryer
Getreidetrocknungseinrichtung *f* **mit schubweiser Behälterbeschickung** batch-in-bin corn drying system
Getreideunkraut *n* corn-weed
Getreideverarbeitung *f* grain processing
Getreideverarbeitungsrückstand *m* cereal by-product
Getreideverteileinrichtung *f* grain spreader
Getreidevorrat *m* grain stock
Getreidevorratsschädling *m* stored-grain pest, pest of stored grain
Getreidevorreinigungsmaschine *f* boby cleaner
Getreidewechselform *f* facultative cereal
Getreidewirtschaft *f* grain husbandry; grain industry (sector)
Getreidewirtschaftler *m* cerealist
Getreidezüchter *m* cereal breeder
Getreidezüchtung *f* cereal breeding
Getreidezystenälchen *n* 1. cereal cyst nematode, cereal stem eelworm *(genus Heterodera)*; 2. oat cyst (root) eelworm *(Heterodera avenae)*
getrenntgeschlechtlich *(bot)* heteroecious, diclinous; *(zoo)* gonochoristic, gonochoric
Getrenntgeschlechtlichkeit *f (bot)* heteroecism; *(zoo)* gonochorism
getrenntkelchblättrig *(bot)* chorisepalous
getrenntkronblättrig *(bot)* choripetalous
Getriebe *n* transmission; gear
~/hydraulisches hydraulic transmission
~/hydrostatisches hydrostatic transmission
~/stufenloses infinitely variable speed transmission, variator
Getriebegehäuse *n*, **Getriebekasten** *m* gearbox, gearcase
getrieben/im Frühbeet hotbed-forced
Getriebeöl *n* transmission oil
Getrieberegner *m* geared sprinkler
Getriebezapfwelle *f* transmission-driven p.t.o. (power take-off) shaft
getrocknet dried; seasoned *(timber)*
~/künstlich (technisch) kiln-dried; kiln-seasoned
getüpfelt *(bot, zoo)* guttate, guttulate, spotted, speckled
Getüpfelter Tausendfuß *m* spotted (snake) millepede, Blaniulus guttulatus
getupft/rotbaun flea-bitten *(horse)*
Gewächs *n* 1. plant; 2. [out]growth
Gewächshaus *n* greenhouse, glasshouse, plant (growing) house; hothouse • **im ~ gewachsen** greenhouse-grown • **im ~ gezogen** greenhouse-grown
~ aus Holländerfenstern Dutch light structure
~/doppelwandiges twin-walled greenhouse
~/fahrbares mobile greenhouse
~/freistehendes single greenhouse
~/freitragendes wide-span greenhouse
~ für Ausstellungszwecke conservatory
~ für Rebstöcke vinery
~ in Blockbauweise block greenhouse
~/mehrschiffiges multispan (multibay) greenhouse
~ mit doppelter Eindeckung double-clad greenhouse
~/nicht beheizbares unheated greenhouse
~/temperiertes cool[-temperate] glasshouse, temperate glasshouse
~/vollklimatisiertes phytotron
Gewächshausanbau *m* greenhouse (glasshouse) culture
Gewächshausanlage *f* greenhouse complex (farm)
Gewächshausbauer *m* greenhouse grower
Gewächshausbedingungen *fpl* greenhouse conditions
Gewächshausbeet *n* bench

Gewächshausbeleuchtung f glasshouse illumination
Gewächshausbetrieb m greenhouse farm
Gewächshausbewirtschaftung f greenhouse management (farming)
Gewächshausblasenfuß m (ent) greenhouse thrips, Heliothrips haemorrhoidalis
Gewächshausblock m multispan (multibay) greenhouse
Gewächshausboden m greenhouse soil
Gewächshauseffekt m greenhouse effect
Gewächshausetagenwagen m glasshouse trolley
Gewächshausform f glasshouse shape
Gewächshausgärtner m greenhouse grower
Gewächshausgärtnerei f greenhouse gardening
Gewächshausgefäßversuch m greenhouse (indoor) pot experiment
Gewächshausgemüse n greenhouse vegetable[s]
Gewächshausgießkanne f greenhouse watering can
Gewächshausgrundfläche f greenhouse floor space
Gewächshausgurke f greenhouse cucumber
Gewächshausheizung f greenhouse heating
Gewächshaushülle f greenhouse cover
Gewächshausinneneinrichtung f interior equipment of a greenhouse
Gewächshauskanne f greenhouse watering can
Gewächshausklima n greenhouse climate
Gewächshauskultur f greenhouse (glass-raised) crop, greenhouse culture
Gewächshausluft f greenhouse air
Gewächshausmottenschildlaus f glasshouse white fly, Trialeurodes vaporariorum
Gewächshausnutzfläche f effective area of a greenhouse
Gewächshauspflanze f greenhouse (glass-raised) plant
Gewächshausreinigung f greenhouse cleaning
Gewächshausröhrenschildlaus f greenhouse orthezia, lantana bug, Orthezia insignis
Gewächshausschädling m glasshouse pest
Gewächshausschattierung f greenhouse shading
Gewächshausschiff n greenhouse aisle, span
Gewächshausschmierlaus f citrus (common) mealy-bug, Pseudococcus (Planococcus) citri
Gewächshaustisch m staging [bench]
Gewächshausversuch m greenhouse experiment
Gewächshausversuchswesen n greenhouse experimentation
Gewächshauswagen m glasshouse trolley
Gewächshauswirtschaft f greenhouse management (farming), glasshouse industry
Gewächshauszikade f (ent) glasshouse leaf-hopper, Erythroneura pallidifrons
Gewaff n tusks (of wild boar)
Gewalteinwirkung f trauma • durch ~ entstanden traumatic
Gewässer n water[s], water body

~/stehendes standing (stagnant) water
Gewässerkunde f hydrology
gewässerkundlich hydrologic[al]
Gewässerschutz m water conservation
Gewässerschutzwald m water-regulating forest
Gewebe n 1. (bot, zoo) tissue; 2. textile [fabric]
~/abgestoßenes [totes] slough
~/interstitielles interstitial tissue
~/knochenähnliches osteoid tissue
~/lymphatisches lymphatic (lymphoid) tissue
~/osteoides osteoid tissue
~/pflanzliches plant tissue
~/retikuläres reticular tissue
~/subkutanes subcutaneous (superficial) tissue
~/textiles textile [fabric]
Gewebe... s. a. Gewebs...
Gewebeauflösung f histolysis
Gewebeaustrocknung f exsiccation
Gewebedifferenzierung f tissue differentiation, histogenesis
Gewebeeinlage f fabric ply (of a tyre)
Gewebeextrakt m tissue extract
Gewebefleck m (phyt) blotch
Gewebekultur f tissue culture
Gewebekulturmedium n tissue-culture medium
Gewebekulturmethode f tissue-culture method
Gewebelage f s. Gewebeeinlage
Gewebelehre f histology
Gewebeprotein n tissue protein
Gewebeschicht f lamina; (bot, zoo) tunic
Gewebeschwund m atrophy
Gewebestoffwechsel m tissue metabolism
Gewebetransplantat n graft
Gewebeumwandlung f metaplasia
Gewebeunverträglichkeit f tissue incompatibility
Gewebeverpflanzung f graft[ing]
Gewebeverträglichkeit f histocompatibility
Gewebewucherung f tissue proliferation
Gewebezerstörung f (phyt, vet) histolysis, lesion
Gewebs... s. a. Gewebe...
Gewebsbildung f histogenesis
~/übermäßige hypermorphosis, overgrowth
Gewebseiweiß n tissue protein
Gewebsflüssigkeit f tissue fluid; (zoo) lymph
Gewebshormon n tissue hormone
Gewebsinkompatibilität f tissue incompatibility
Gewebsneubildung f (vet) neoplasm, tumour
Gewebsparasit m tissue parasite
Gewebsreaktion f tissue response
Gewebstod m necro[bio]sis
Gewebstrümmer pl detritus
Gewebswanderzelle f histiocyte
Gewebswassersucht f (vet) oedema
Gewehr n 1. gun, rifle; 2. tusk (of wild boar)
Gewehrkolben m [rifle] butt
Gewehrmündung f muzzle
Gewehrschaft m gun-stock
Geweih n attire, antlers, horns, head • **ohne ~** poll[ed] • **~ tragend** antlered, branching

Geweih 258

~/schädelechtes attire
Geweihbast *m* velvet • den ~ abreiben to fray (to burnish, to rub off) the antlers *(e.g. at tree-trunks)*
~/abgefegter fraying *(from antlers or horns)*
Geweihbaum *m* coffee tree *(genus Gymnocladus)*
Geweihende *n* antler, branch, royal, tine
Geweihfarn *m* 1. stag-horn fern *(genus Platycerium)*; 2. common stag-horn fern, Platycerium bifurcatum [var. bifurcatum]
Geweihkamm *m* antler (V-shaped) comb *(of chicken)*
Geweihsproß *m s.* Geweihende
Geweihstange *f* horn, beam
geweiht antlered, branching
Gewelltstreifiger Kohlerdfloh *m* striped flea-beetle, Phyllotreta undulata
Gewichtsanalyse *f* gravimetry
Gewichtsfunktion *f (biom)* weight function
Gewichtshufeisen *n* weighted shoe
Gewieher *n* 1. neigh, nicker; 2. neighing
gewimpert *(bot, zoo)* ciliate[d]
Gewinde *n* thread
Gewinn *m/genetischer* genetic gain (improvement)
Gewitter *n* thunderstorm
Gewitterschauer *m* thunder-shower
Gewitterwolke *f* thunder-cloud, cumulonimbus [cloud]
Gewohnheit *f* habit
Gewohnheitsmaß *n* customary measure *(timber mensuration)*
gewohnheitsmäßig habitual
gewöhnlich *(bot, zoo)* common
Gewöhnliche... *s. a.* Gemeine...
~ **Grüne Schmeißfliege** *f* sheep blowfly (maggot fly), Lucilia sericata
~ **Karausche** *f* crucian [carp], Prussian carp, Carassius carassius (vulgaris)
~ **Platane** *f* London plane[-tree], Platanus x hybrida (x acerifolia)
~ **Robinie** *f* falsa acacia, common robinia, [honey] locust, Robinia pseudoacacia
~ **Traubenkirsche** *f* [European] bird cherry, cluster cherry, Prunus padus, Padus avium
Gewöhnlicher Ackerfrauenmantel *m* parsley-piert, Aphanes (Alchemilla) arvensis
~ **Buchsbaum** *m* common box tree, European box, Buxus sempervirens
~ **Hohlzahn** *m* day nettle, Galeopsis tetrahit
~ **Kartoffelschorf** *m* common scab [of potato], [potato common] scab *(caused by Streptomyces scabies)*
~ **Klettenkerbel** *m* hedge parsley, Torilis japonica
~ **Nagekäfer** *m* [common] furniture beetle, death-watch [beetle], Anobium punctatum (striatum)
~ **Rainkohl** *m* nipple-wort, Lapsana communis
~ **Trompetenbaum** *m (bot)* southern catalpa, Catalpa bignonioides

Gewöhnliches Bohnenmosaik *n* bean common mosaic
~ **Bohnenmosaikvirus** *n* bean common mosaic virus, BCMV
~ **Erbsenmosaik** *n* common pea mosaic
~ **Erbsenmosaikvirus** *n* pea common mosaic virus, PCMV
~ **Greiskraut** *n* common groundsel, birdseed, Senecio vulgaris
~ **Kundebohnenmosaikvirus** *n* cowpea aphid-borne mosaic virus, CAbMV
Gewöhnung *f* habituation
Gewölbe *n* vault *(animal anatomy)*
Gewölle *n* cast, pellet, vomits *(of predatory birds)*
gewunden *(bot, zoo)* contorted; *(bot)* anfractuous, tortuous
Gewürz *n* spice, seasoning
Gewürze *npl* spice[ry]
Gewürzextrakt *m* spice extract
Gewürzfenchel *m* Florence fennel, finnochio, Foeniculum vulgare var. dulce
Gewürzgurke *f* [pickled] gherkin
Gewürzkultur *f* spice crop
Gewürzkraut *n* [pot-]herb, aromatic herb
Gewürznelke *f* clove
Gewürznelkenbaum *m* clove [tree], Syzygium aromaticum, Eugenia aromatica (caryophyllus)
Gewürznelkenöl *n* oil of cloves
Gewürzpaprika *m* red (hot) pepper, cayenne [pepper]
Gewürzpflanze *f* spice plant
Gewürzpflanzenkultur *f* spice crop
Gewürzrinde *f* cassia *(genus Cassia)*
Gewürzstrauch *m* 1. Carolina-allspice, strawberry shrub *(genus Calycanthus)*; 2. Carolina-allspice, sweetshrub, Calycanthus floridus
Gewürztraminer *m* gewürztraminer *(wine)*
Gezähnelter Himmel[s]schlüssel *m* drumstick primrose, Primula denticulata
gezahnt, gezähnt *(bot, zoo)* toothed, dentate; *(bot)* rucinate
~/fein *(bot)* denticulate
Gezähnter Lavendel *m* toothed lavender, Lavandula dentata
~ **Schneeball** *m* arrow-wood, Viburnum dentatum
Gezähntes Kreuzkraut *n* golden groundsel, Ligularia dentata
gezapft *s.* geharzt
Gezeitenkraftwerk *n* tidal power station
Gezeitenmarsch *f* tidal marsh
Gezeitenwald *m* tidal forest
gezogen 1. trained, nursed *(e.g. plants)*; raised, reared *(esp. animals)*; 2. rifled *(barrel)*
~/aus Samen maiden *(plant)*
~/im Freiland field-grown
~/im Gewächshaus greenhouse-grown
gezüchtet/auf Milchproduktion milk, milch
GGSMV *s.* Gurkengrünscheckungsmosaikvirus
Ghee *n (dairy)* ghee, ghi

G-Horizont m *(soil)* gleyic horizon
Giardiasis f *(vet)* giardiasis
Gibberellin n gibberellin *(phytohormone)*
~ **A3** s. Gibberellinsäure
Gibberellinsäure f gibberellic acid, GA *(phytohormone)*
Gibbsit m gibbsite *(non-clay mineral)*
Gibbssches Potential n Gibbs free energy *(plant physiology)*
Gicht f *(vet)* gout
Gichtknoten m *(vet)* tophus
Gichtkorn n *(phyt)* cockle
Gidran n Gidran *(horse breed)*
Giebel m 1. gibel, Prussian (German) carp, Carassius auratus ssp. gibelio; 2. gable
Giebellüftung f gable ventilation
Giemsa-Färbung f Giemsa staining
Gierfalke f gyrfalcon, Falco rusticolus gyrfalco
Giersch m herb Gerard, goutweed, goutwort, goat's-foot, bishop's-weed, ground elder, Aegopodium podagraria
Gierschblattlaus f parsnip (willow-carrot) aphid, Cavariella aegopodii
gießen 1. to water; 2. to pour
~/**mit dem Schlauch ~** to hose
~/**übermäßig ~** to overwater
Gießkanne f watering can (pot)
Gießkannenbrause f rose
Gießkannenschimmel[pilz] m aspergillus *(genus Aspergillus)*
Gießmittel n gravity-fed spray
Gießschlitten m watering sledge
Gießwagen m gantry *(greenhouse installation)*
Gießwasser n irrigation water
GIF s. Wachstumshormon-Releaser-Hemmfaktor
Gift n poison, toxicant; toxin
~/**pflanzliches** plant poison, phytotoxin
~/**pilzliches** fungal toxin, mycotoxin
~/**sich im Organismus anreicherndes** cumulative poison
~/**tierisches** animal poison, zootoxin; venom
~/**zellauflösendes** cytolysin
giftbedingt toxi[co]genic
Giftbeere f apple of Peru, Nicandra physalodes
giftbildend toxi[co]genic
Giftbildungsvermögen n toxigenicity
Giftblase f venom sac *(e.g. of honey-bee)*
Giftdrüse f poison gland
Giftfangbaum m poisoned trap tree
Giftganggerät n, **Giftgangleger** m poison passage maker *(water-vole eradication)*
Giftgetreide n poisoned grain
Gifthahnenfuß m blister (celery-leaved) buttercup, Ranunculus sceleratus
gifthaltig toxiferous
giftig poisonous, toxic[al], virulent; venenate
~/**nicht** non-toxic
Giftigkeit f toxicity, poisonousness *(for compounds s. under* Toxizität*)*

Giftköder m poison[ed] bait, toxic bait
~ **gegen Nagetiere** rodent bait
Giftkunde f toxicology
Giftlattich m hemlock-lettuce, bitter (acrid, prickly) lettuce, Lactuca virosa
giftliefernd toxiferous
giftmeidend s. giftscheu
Giftpflanze f poisonous plant
Giftpilz m poisonous fungus, toadstool, deadly agaric
Giftringeln n *(forest)* poison girdling
Giftsalat m s. Giftlattich
giftscheu poison-shy *(e.g. rodents)*
Giftstoff m toxicant, toxic substance
~/**von Lebewesen erzeugter** toxin
Giftsumach m 1. poison sumac[h], poison elder, Toxicodendron (Rhus) vernix; 2. poison ivy, Toxicodendron quercifolium, Rhus toxicodendron
Giftunkraut n poisonous weed
Giftwicke f crown vetch, Coronilla varia
giftwidrig antidotal
Giftwirkung f toxic effect (action)
Giftzahn m [poison] fang
Gig n gig *(one-horse carriage)*
Gigantismus m gigantism
Gigantregner m giant rainer (irrigator), extra-large rainer
Gigasintoxikation f *(vet)* black disease
Gigaswuchs m gigas *(growth anomaly of autopolyploid plants)*
Giglisäge f *(vet)* Gigli saw
Gilbkraut n s. Großes Schöllkraut
Gilchristsche Krankheit f *(vet)* North American blastomycosis
Gilie f *(bot)* gilia *(genus Gilia)*
Gimpel m bullfinch, Pyrrhula pyrrhula
Gin m gin
Gingellikraut m niger seed, Guizotia abyssinica
Gingiva f gingiva, gum[s]
gingival gingival
Gingivitis f *(vet)* gingivitis
Ginkgo[baum] m 1. ginkgo, gingko *(genus Ginkgo)*; 2. ginkgo, gingko, maidenhair tree, Ginkgo biloba
Ginseng m [false] ginseng, Chinese herb, Panax [pseudo]ginseng
Ginsengwurzel f ginseng, Chinese herb
Ginster m broom, genista *(genus Genista)*
Gipfelblüte f apical flower
Gipfelbohrkäfer m top bark-beetle, Ips acuminatus
gipfeldürr s. wipfeldürr
gipfelfrüchtig *(bot)* acrocarpic, acrocarpous
Gipfelknospe f terminal (upmost) bud
Gipfelsproß m apical shoot, terminal [shoot]
gipfelständig apical, terminal
Gipfeltrieb m s. Gipfelsproß
Gips m gypsum, calcium sulphate, plaster of Paris
Gipsdüngung f gypsuming
gipsen to plaster *(e.g. in wine-making)*

Gipsverband

Gipsverband *m (vet)* plaster bandage
Gipszuführung *f* gypsuming
Gir *n* gir *(cattle breed)*
Girlandenbaum *m* cordon
girren to coo *(ring-dove)*
Gitoxin *n* gitoxine *(glycoside)*
Gitter *n* lattice, grating, grate, grid
Gitteranlage *f* lattice design *(experimentation)*
Gitterbau *m* lattice structure *(of crystals)*
Gitterboden *m* grid floor
Gitterdüngerstreuer *m* reciprocating plate fertilizer distributor
Gitterfaser *f* reticular fibre
gitterförmig *(bot, zoo)* reticulate[d], candellate[d]; latticed
Gitterfußboden *m* grid floor
Gitternetz *n* map grid *(photogrammetry)*
Gitterpflanze *f* lattice plant, Aponogeton madagascariensis
Gitterrad *n* skeleton (cage) wheel *(for ground pressure reduction)*
Gitterrost *m s.* Kotrost
Gitterrostzapfen *m* cedar apple *(of certain juniper species)*
Gitterstreuer *m s.* Gitterdüngerstreuer
Gittertopf *m* lattice pot *(for ornamentals)*
Gittertrommelrübenschneider *m* spiked-drum-type root cutter
Gitterwalze *f* grid roller
Gladiole *f* sword lily (grass), gladiolus *(genus Gladiolus)*
Gladiolenblasenfuß *m (ent)* gladiolus thrips, Taeniothrips simplex (gladioli)
Glandula *f* gland *(for compounds s. under* Drüse*)*
glandulär glandular
Glans *f* clitoridis glans *(animal anatomy)*
~ **penis** glans
Glanz *m* 1. lustre, brilliancy *(e.g. of a hair coat)*; 2. canary grass, Phalaris canariensis
Glanzehrenpreis *m* wayside speedwell, Veronica polita
glänzend *(bot, zoo)* nitid, glossy, shiny
Glänzende Sammetblume *f* sweet-scented marigold, sweet mace, Tagetes lucida
Glänzender Ehrenpreis *m s.* Glanzehrenpreis
~ **Getreideschimmelkäfer** *m* lesser mealworm, Alphitobius diaperinus
~ **Salbei** *m* scarlet sage, salvia, Salvia splendens
Glanzfiltration *f* polishing filtration *(brewing)*
Glanzfliege *f* black blowfly, wool maggot, Phormia regina
Glanzfrüchtige Binse *f* jointed rush, Juncus articulatus
Glanzgras *n* reed grass *(genus Phalaris)*
Glanzkäfer *m* blossom (pollen, sap) beetle *(family Nitidulidae)*
Glanzkölbchen *n (bot)* 1. aphelandra *(genus Aphelandra)*; 2. zebra plant, Aphelandra squarrosa
glanzlos dull, staring

Glanzmispel *f (bot)* 1. photinia *(genus Photinia)*; 2. tollon, Photinia arbutifolia
Glanzrinde *f* smooth bark
Glanzstrauch *m* rice flower, Pimelea ferruginea
Glanzstreifiger Schildkäfer *m* small tortoise beetle, Cassida nobilis
Glanzwolle *f* lustre (bright) wool
~ **erster Schur** roller *(with broad staple, 30 to 38 cm long)*
Glas *n* **mit geringer Abstrahlung** low emissivity glass
Glasaal *m* elver
Glasabdeckung *f* glass cover
glasartig hyaline
Glasauge *n* glass eye *(absence of iridic pigments in domestic animals)*
Glasdecke *f* glass cover
Glasflügler *m* 1. clearwing, clear-winged moth *(family Aegeriidae)*; 2. sesiid *(family Sesiidae)*
glasgedeckt glass-covered
Glasgewächshaus *n s.* Glashaus
Glasglocke *f*, **Glashaube** *f* cloche, bell-jar, garden-glass
~/**fest installierte** continuous cloche
Glashaus *n* glasshouse, glass greenhouse *(for compounds s. under* Gewächshaus*)*
glasig glassy, vitreous, hyaline, steely, flinty *(malt or maize endosperm)*
Glasigkeit *f* 1. glassiness, vitreousness; steeliness, flintiness; 2. water core *(of pome fruit)*; 3. *(phyt)* jelly end rot *(esp. of tubers)*
Glasigwerden *n* vitrification
Glaskirsche *f* 1. duke [cherry] *(group of cultivars)*; 2. amarelle cherry, Prunus cerasus var. cerasus
Glasknorpel *m* hyaline cartilage
Glaskörperflüssigkeit *f* vitreous humour *(of the eye)*
Glaskraut *n* 1. pellitory [of the wall], wall pellitory *(genus Parietaria)*; 2. pellitory [of the wall], hammerwort, Parietaria erecta (officinalis)
Glasmalz *n* glassy (flinty, vitreous) malt
Glasschmelz *m* glasswort *(genus Salicornia)*
Glasschwärmer *m (ent)* sesiid *(family Sesiidae)*
Glässersche Krankheit *f* Glasser's disease *(of pigs, caused by Haemophilus parasuis)*
Glasüberbauung *f* glass casing
Glasweide *f* brittle (redwood) willow, Salix fragilis
Glasweizen *m* 1. vitreous wheat *(comprehensive term)*; 2. durum [wheat], Triticum durum
glatt smooth, even; *(bot)* laevigate; sleek *(hair coat)*
Glattblattaster *f* New York aster, Aster novi-belgii
Glatte Bougainvillea *f* paper flower, Bougainvillea glabra
Glatthaarvorstehhund *m* pointer *(dog breed)*
Glatthafer *m* 1. tall oat[-grass], Arrhenaterum elatius; 2. false oat-grass, Arrhenaterum elatius ssp. elatius
glatthäutig *(bot, zoo)* glabrous

glattrindig smooth-barked
glattsamig smooth-seeded
glattschalig smooth-shelled
Glattwalze f smooth roll[er], flat roll[er], plain roll[er]
Glattwasser m last runnings (wort) *(brewing)*
Glatzflechte f *(vet)* ringworm
Glaubersalz n *(vet)* Glauber's salt *(laxative)*
Glaukom n *(vet)* glaucoma, hydrophthalmia
Glaukonit m glauconite *(clay mineral)*
glazial glacial
Glazial n glacial
Glazialgeschiebe n glacial drift
Glazialperiode f Pleistocene
Glaziärsediment n, **Glaziärsubstrat** n [glacial] till
Glc s. (D)-Glucose
GLC s. Gas-flüssig-Chromatographie
Gleba f *(bot)* gleba
Gleditschie f honey (sweet) locust, three-thorned acacia, Gleditsia triacanthos
gleichaltrig even-aged
gleichartig homogeneous, conspecific, of the same species
Gleichartigkeit f homogeneity
Gleichbein n sesamoid bone *(animal anatomy)*
Gleichblättrige Glockenblume f bell flower, falling stars, Italian bell[-flower], star-of-Bethlehem, Campanula isophylla
Gleichfarbige Lilie f star lily, Lilium concolor
~ Tanne f Colorado (white) fir, Abies concolor
Gleichflügler m *(ent)* plant sap feeder, homopteran *(order Homoptera)*
gleichgerichtet isotropic
gleichgestaltig isomorphous
Gleichgestaltigkeit f isomorphism
Gleichgewicht n equilibrium, balance
~/dynamisches steady state
~/genetisches genetic equilibrium
~/natürliches natural balance
~/ökologisches ecological balance (equilibrium)
~/physiologisches physiological balance
~/populares population balance
Gleichgewichtsdichte f *(ecol)* equilibrium density
Gleichgewichtsfeuchte f equilibrium moisture [content], e.m.c.
Gleichgewichtsorgan n organ of equilibrium (balance) *(animal anatomy)*
Gleichgewichtspopulation f equilibrium population
Gleichgewichtssteinchen n *(zoo)* statolith
Gleichgewichtsstörung f *(vet)* equilibrium disorder, vertigo
Gleichgewichtszustand m 1. equilibrium level (position); 2. *(ecol)* population balance, characteristic abundance
gleichgriff[e]lig *(bot)* homostyled, homostylous
Gleichgriff[e]ligkeit f *(bot)* homostyly
gleichmäßig 1. regular, even; 2. constant *(e.g. temperature)*

Gleichmäßigkeit f der Pflanzenstandraumzumessung plant-spacing uniformity
Gleichsaum m tree gloxinia *(genus Koehleria)*
gleichsporig *(bot)* isosporic
Gleichstanddrillmaschine f seed-spacing drill, check-row drill
Gleichstromgetreidetrockner m concurrent flow grain dryer
Gleichstromtrockner m concurrent flow dryer
gleichwarm homoiothermic, warm-blooded
Gleiskette f Caterpillar [track, tread], [chain] track
Gleiskettenanhänger m track-laying trailer
Gleiskettenfahrzeug n tracked vehicle, Caterpillar
Gleiskettenglied n track plate (shoe)
Gleiskettenlaufwerk n track-laying assembly
Gleiskettenmähdrescher m Caterpillar combine, chain-track combine
Gleiskettentraktor m Caterpillar (track-laying) tractor, track-layer, crawler [tractor]
Gleitbahn f slide
gleiten to slide, to glide; to chute *(e.g. timber)*
Gleitkolben[ballen]presse f push plunger baler
Gleitkufe f glide shoe
Gleitlager n sliding bearing
Gleitmuffe f sliding coupling
Gleitreibung f sliding friction
Gleitschlupf m slip[page]
Gleitschutzkette f skid chain
Gley[boden] m gley [soil], *(Am)* glei, meadow soil
Gleyhorizont m gleyic horizon
Gleylöß m gley loess
Gleypodsol m gley (peaty gleyed) podzol
Gleywaldboden m forest gley soil
Glia f neuroglia
Gliadin n gliadin, glutin *(cereal protein)*
Glied n limb, extremity; link
Gliederbandförderer m apron conveyor
Gliederegge f chain harrow
Gliederfüß[l]er m arthropod *(phylum Arthropoda)*
• **die ~ betreffend** arthropodal
Gliedergefüge n *(soil)* aggregate structure
Gliederheizkessel m sectional heating boiler
Gliederhülse f *(bot)* loment
gliederhülsig lomentaceous
Gliederkette f strobile, strobila *(of tapeworms)*
Gliederschote f *(bot)* loment
Gliederspore f *(bot)* arthrospore, oidium
Gliedertier n articulate animal *(subkingdom Articulata)*
Gliederungshieb m preparatory felling (cutting)
Gliederwalze f articulated roller
Gliederwurm m annelid[an] *(phylum Annelida)*
Gliedkraut n ironwort *(genus Sideritis)*
Gliedmaße f limb, extremity
Gliedmaßen fpl limbs, extremities; points *(of horse or dog)*
Gliedmaßenknochen m limb bone
Gliedmaßenskelett n appendicular skeleton
glimmen to smoulder

Glimmer

Glimmer *m* mica *(non-clay mineral)*
Glimmerboden *m* micaceous soil
Glimmerschiefer *m* mica-schist, mica-slate
Glimmfeuer *n* smouldering fire
Gliom *n (vet)* glioma
Globalstrahlung *f* global (total) radiation
Globalstrahlungsmeßgerät *n* solarimeter
Globin *n* globin
Globulin *n* globulin
~/Sexualhormone bindendes sex steroid binding protein, SBP
Glochid[i]e *f (bot)* glochidium
Glocke *f* 1. bell; 2. ring boot *(for jumping horses)*; 3. *s.* Glasglocke
Glockenblume *f* bell flower, campanula *(genus Campanula)*
glockenförmig *(bot, zoo)* campanulate
Glockenförmiger Scheidenkelch *m* African tulip-tree, Spathodea campanulata
Glockenförmiges Büschelschön *n* scorpion weed, Phacelia campanularia
Glockenheide *f* 1. heath[er], erica *(genus Erica)*; 2. bell-heather, heather-bell, cross-leaved heath, Erica tetralix
Glockenkurve *f*/**Gaußsche** *(biom)* Gaussian curve, Gauss's bell curve
Glockenrebe *f* 1. cathedral bells *(genus Cobaea)*; 2. monastery (cathedral) bells, Mexican ivy, cup and saucer, Cobaea scandens
Glockenwinde *f* Chilean bell-flower, Nolana paradoxa (atriplicifolia)
Glockenwurz *f (bot)* elecampane, Inula helenium
Gloeosporium-Fäule *f* **des Apfels** watchglass-mould [of apple]
Glomerulonephritis *f (vet)* glomerulonephritis
Glomerulum *n* glomerulus *(e.g. of the kidney)*
Glomerulumkapsel *f* glomerular capsule *(of kidney)*
Glomerulus *m s.* Glomerulum
Glossitis *f (vet)* glossitis
Glottis *f* glottis *(animal anatomy)*
Gloucester *m* Gloucester [cheese]
Gloxinie *f (bot)* 1. gloxinia *(genus Gloxinia)*; 2. gloxinia, sinningia, Sinningia (Gloxinia) speciosa
Glu *s.* Glutaminsäure
Glucagon *n* glucagon *(polypeptide)*
Glucan *n* glucan *(polysaccharide)*
Glucanase *f* glucanase *(enzyme)*
Glucarsäure *f* glucaric acid
Glucke *f* brood-hen, broody, cluck
~/künstliche brooder, foster-mother, artificial mother
glucken to cluck
Gluckenraupe *f (ent)* tent caterpillar, leaf-tier, *(Am)* web-worm *(family Lasiocampidae)*
Gluckhenne *f s.* Glucke
Glückskäfer *m* coccinellid [beetle] *(family Coccinellidae)*

Glücksklee *m* redwood sorrel, Irish shamrock, good luck plant, Oxalis deppei
Glucobrassicin *n* glucobrassin *(glucosinolate)*
Glucocortico[stero]id *n* glucocorticoid *(hormone)*
Glucogenese *f* gluco[neo]genesis
Glucoinvertase *f* alpha-glucosidase, alpha-glucosidehydrolase, maltase *(enzyme)*
Glucokinase *f* glucokinase *(enzyme)*
Glucomannan *n* glucomannan *(hemicellulose)*
Gluconapin *n* gluconapin *(glucosinolate)*
Gluconeogenese *f s.* Glucogenese
(D)-Gluconsäure *f* (D)-gluconic acid
(D)-Glucosamin *n* glucosamine *(amino sugar)*
(D)-Glucose *f* (D)-glucose, dextrose, grape-sugar
Glucoseabbau *m* glycolysis, glucose metabolism
Glucoseagar *m* glucose agar
Glucoseausscheidung *f* **im Harn** *(vet)* glucosuria, glycosuria
Glucoseisomerase *f* glucose isomerase *(enzyme)*
Glucoseoxidase *f* glucose oxidase *(enzyme)*
Glucosephosphat *n* glucose phosphate
Glucose-1-phosphat *n* glucose-1-phosphate
Glucose-6-phosphat *n* glucose-6-phosphate
Glucose-6-phosphatase *f* glucose-6-phosphatase *(enzyme)*
Glucose-6-phosphatdehydrogenase *f* glucose-6-phosphate dehydrogenase *(enzyme)*
Glucose-6-phosphatisomerase *f* glucose-6-phosphate isomerase, phosphosaccharomutase, oxo-isomerase *(enzyme)*
Glucosesynthese *f* gluco[neo]genesis
Glucosetoleranz *f* glucose (blood sugar) tolerance
Glucosetoleranztest *m (vet)* glucose tolerance test
Glucosid *n* glucoside
Glucosinolat *n* glucosinolate *(plant substance)*
Glucosteroid *n* glucocorticoid
Glucosurie *f (vet)* glucosuria, glycosuria
Glucovanillin *n* avenin *(alkaloid)*
Glucuronidase *f* glucuronidase *(enzyme)*
(D)-Glucuronsäure *f* glucuronic acid
Glufosinat *n* glufosinate *(herbicide)*
Glühanlaßschalter *m* heater starter switch *(diesel engine)*
Glühkerzenzündung *f* glow plug ignition
Glühphosphat *n* fused (calcined) phosphate *(fertilizer)*
glukoplastisch antiketonic
Glutamat *n* glutamate
Glutamatammoniakligase *f* glutamate-ammonia ligase, glutamine synthetase *(enzyme)*
Glutamatdecarboxylase *f* glutamate decarboxylase *(enzyme)*
Glutamatdehydrogenase *f* glutamate (glutamic) dehydrogenase *(enzyme)*
~, NAD(P)$^+$ glutamate dehydrogenase, NAD(P)$^+$ *(enzyme)*
~, NADP$^+$ glutamate dehydrogenase, NADP$^+$ *(enzyme)*

Glutamatsynthase f glutamate synthase *(enzyme)*
Glutamin n glutamine *(amino-acid)*
Glutaminase f glutaminase *(enzyme)*
Glutamin-Carbamoylphosphatsynthetase f carbamoyl-phosphate synthase, glutamine-hydrolysing *(enzyme)*
Glutaminsäure f glutami[ni]c acid, 1-aminopropane-1,3-dicarboxylic acid
Glutaminsäureamid n glutamine *(amino-acid)*
Glutaminsäuredecarboxylase f glutamic acid decarboxylase *(enzyme)*
Glutaminsäuremonoamid n glutamine *(amino-acid)*
Glutaminsynthetase f glutamate-ammonia ligase, glutamine synthetase *(enzyme)*
Glutamyltransferase f glutamyltransferase *(enzyme)*
Glutamyltranspeptidase f [gamma-]glutamyltransferase *(enzyme)*
Glutarsäure f glutaric acid, propane-1,3-dicarboxylic acid
Glutaryl-CoA-Dehydrogenase f glutaryl-CoA-dehydrogenase *(enzyme)*
Glutathion n glutathione *(tripeptide)*
Glutathionperoxidase f glutathione peroxidase *(enzyme)*
Glutathionreductase, NAD(P)H f glutathione reductase, NAD(P)H *(enzyme)*
Glutathionsynth[et]ase f glutathione synthase *(enzyme)*
Glutelin n glutelin *(cereal protein)*
Gluten n gluten *(flour substance)*
Glutenfeed n gluten feed
glutenhaltig glutenous
Glutenin n glutenin *(storage protein)*
Glutenparenchym n gluten parenchyma
Glutin n glutin *(bone glue)*
Gly s. Glycin
Glycan n glycan, polysaccharide
(D)-Glyceraldehyd m glyceraldehyde *(triose)*
Glyceraldehydphosphatdehydrogenase f glyceraldehyde-3-phosphate dehydrogenase *(enzyme)*
Glycerid n glyceride
Glyceridstoffwechsel m glyceride metabolism
Glycerokinase f glycerokinase *(enzyme)*
Glycerol n glycerol, glycerin[e], propane-1,2,3-triol
Glycerolagar m glycerol agar
Glyceroldehydrogenase f glycerol dehydrogenase *(enzyme)*
Glycerolkinase f glycerol kinase *(enzyme)*
Glycerol-1-phosphat n glycerophosphate
Glycerol-1-phosphatacyltransferase f glycerophosphate acyltransferase *(enzyme)*
Glycerol-3-phosphatdehydrogenase f glycerol-3-phosphate dehydrogenase *(enzyme)*
Glycerolphosphatid n glycerophosphatide
Glycerophosphat n glycerophosphate
Glycerophosphatid n glycerophosphatide

Glycin n glycine, glycocoll, aminoacetic acid
Glycinbetain n [glycine]betaine
Glycoalkaloid n glycoalkaloid
Glycocholsäure f glycocholic acid *(bile acid)*
Glycogen n glycogen, animal starch
Glycogenabbau m glycogenolysis
Glycogenase f alpha-amylase *(enzyme)*
Glycogenese f glycogen synthesis, glycogenesis
Glycogenkörper m glycogen body *(in the spinal cord of fowl)*
Glycogenolyse f glycogenolysis
Glycogenose f s. Glycogenspeicherkrankheit
Glycogenphosphorylase f glycogen phosphorylase *(enzyme)*
Glycogenspeicherkrankheit f *(vet)* glycogen storage disease, glycogenosis
Glycogensynthase f glycogen synthase *(enzyme)*
Glycogensynthese f glycogen synthesis, glycogenesis
Glycol n [ethylene] glycol
Glycolat n glycollate
Glycolatoxidase f glycollate oxidase, (s)-2-hydroxy-acid oxidase *(enzyme)*
Glycolatreaktionsweg m glycollate pathway *(plant physiology)*
Glycolipid n glycolipid
Glycolprolin n glycolproline *(dipeptide)*
Glycolsäure f glycolic (hydroxyacetic) acid
Glycolyse f glycolysis
Glycopeptid n glycopeptide
Glycoproteid n glycoproteid[e]
Glycoprotein n glycoprotein
Glycoproteinhormon n glycoprotein hormone
Glycosid n glycoside
~/cyanogenes cyanogenic glycoside
~/herzwirksames cardiac glycoside
Glycosidase f glycosidase *(enzyme)*
Glycosphingolipid n glycosphingolipid
Glycosylierung f glycosylation
Glycosyltransferase f glycosyl transferase *(enzyme)*
Glycylglycin n glycylglycine *(dipeptide)*
Glycylphenylalanin n glycylphenylalanine *(dipeptide)*
Glykämie f glycaemia
Glykokoll n s. Glycin
Glyodin n glyodin *(fungicide)*
Glyoxalin n imidazole
Glyoxim n glyoxime *(growth regulator)*
Glyoxylat n glyoxylate
Glyoxylattransacetase f malate synthase *(enzyme)*
Glyoxylatzyklus m glyoxylate cycle *(plant physiology)*
Glyoxylsäure f glyoxylic acid
Glyoxylsäurezyklus m s. Glyoxylatzyklus
Glyphosin n glyphosine *(growth regulator)*
Glyphosat n glyphosate *(herbicide)*
Glyzerin n s. Glycerol

Glyzine

Glyzine *f (bot)* 1. wisteria *(genus Wisteria)*; 2. Japanese wisteria, Wisteria floribunda; 3. Chinese wisteria, Wisteria sinensis
GMV *s.* Gurkenmosaikvirus
Gnadenkraut *n* hedge hyssop *(genus Gratiola)*
Gneisboden *m* gneiss soil
Gnitze *f* biting midge *(genus Culicoides)*
Gnomonia[frucht]fäule *f* **der Erdbeere** stem-end rot of strawberry *(caused by Gnomonia fruticola)*
gnotobiotisch gnotobiotic, gnotophoric
GnRH *s.* Gonadotropinreleasinghormon
Goabohne *f* goa (winged) bean, asparagus (four-angled) bean, Psophocarpus tetragonolobus
Gobeleterziehung *f* goblet training *(of fruit trees)*
Godetie *f (bot)* godetia *(genus Godetia)*
Goethit *m* goethite, limonite *(non-clay mineral)*
Goggelschaf *n* Zackel [sheep], Prong (Twisted) Horn *(breed)*
Goitrin *n* goitrin, vinylthiooxazolidone *(goitrogenic substance)*
Goldafter *m (ent)* brown-tail [moth], Euproctis chrysorrhoea
Goldakazie *f* golden wattle, Acacia pycnantha
Goldauge *n* 1. lacewing [fly] *(family Chrysopidae)*; 2. green lacewing, Chrysop[erl]a carnea
Goldbandleistengras *n* cord-grass, Spartina pectinata (michauxiana)
Goldbandlilie *f* golden-rayed lily [of Japan], gold band lily, Lilium auratum
Goldbart *m*, **Goldbartgras** *n* 1. scented grass *(genus Chrysopogon)*; 2. scented grass, cricket rhaphis, Chrysopogon (Andropogon) gryllus
Goldblatt *n s.* Goldorange
Goldblume *f* garland chrysanthemum, Chrysanthemum coronarium
Golddistel *f* golden thistle, scolymus *(genus Scolymus)*
Golden Retriever *m* golden retriever *(dog breed)*
Goldene Dostwolfsmilch *f (bot)* cushion euphorbia, Euphorbia polychroma (epithymoides)
Goldfaden *m (bot)* goldthread *(genus Coptis)*
Goldfarbiger Lauch *m s.* Goldlauch
Goldfarn *m* gold fern *(genus Pityrogramma)*
Goldfisch *m* goldfish, Carassius auratus
Goldflieder *m* European forsythia, Forsythia europaea
Goldfruchtpalme *f (bot)* areca, Chrysalidocarpus lutescens
Goldfuchs *m* golden-chestnut *(horse)*
Goldgarbe *f* fern-leaf yarrow, Achillea filipendulina
Goldgelbe Blattfärbung (Vergilbung) *f* **der Weinrebe** grape-vine golden flavescence, flavescence doree *(virosis)*
Goldglöckchen *n* 1. golden bell, forsythia *(genus Forsythia)*; 2. golden bell, Forsythia x intermedia
Goldhaar *n* goldilocks, Aster linosyris, Linosyris vulgaris
Goldhafer *m* golden (yellow) oat-grass, Trisetum flavescens

Goldhamster *m* golden (Syrian) hamster, Mesocricetus auratus
Goldhirse *f* golden millet, Setaria sphacelata
Goldjohannisbeere *f* golden (flowering, buffalo) currant, American black currant, Ribes aureum
Goldkäfer *m* rose chafer, Cetonia aurata
Goldkiefer *f s.* Gelbkiefer
Goldklee *m* yellow clover, Trifolium agrarium (aureum)
Goldkugelkaktus *m* barrel cactus, Echinocactus grusonii
Goldlack *m* 1. wallflower *(genus Cheiranthus)*; 2. wallflower, Cheiranthus cheiri
Goldlärche *f* 1. Chinese larch *(genus Pseudolarix)*; 2. golden (Chinese, false) larch, Pseudolarix kaempferi (amabilis)
Goldlauch *m* yellow (golden) garlic, moly, Allium moly
Goldlaufkäfer *m* gilt ground beetle, golden carabid, Carabus auratus
Goldleistengras *n* cord-grass, Spartina pectinata (michauxiana)
Goldmohn *m* California poppy, eschscholtzia *(genus Eschscholzia)*
Goldnessel *f (bot)* yellow archangel, Galeobdolon luteum, Lamium galeobdolon
Goldopuntie *f (bot)* bunny-ears, Opuntia microdasys
Goldorange *f* Japanese laurel (aucuba), Aucuba japonica
Goldpflaume *f* otaheite apple, Spondias dulcis (cytherea)
Goldrandblume *f* creeping zinnia, Sanvitalia procumbens
Goldranunkel *f (bot)* goldilocks, gold knots, Ranunculus acris
Goldregen *m (bot)* 1. golden chain (rain), laburnum *(genus Laburnum)*; 2. golden chain (rain), laburnum, Laburnum anagyroides
Goldregengelbadernvirus *n* laburnum yellow vein virus
Goldröhrling *m (bot)* elegant boletus, Boletus grevillei
Goldröschen *n (bot)* kerria *(genus Kerria)*
Goldrute *f* golden rod, flower of gold, solidago *(genus Solidago)*
Goldschimmernde Lamarchie *f (bot)* golden-top, Lamarchia aurea
Goldschmied *m s.* Goldlaufkäfer
Goldstreifiger Schildkäfer *m* small tortoise beetle, Cassida nobilis
Goldweide *f* golden willow, Salix alba var. vitellina
Goldweiderich *m (bot)* yellow loosestrife, Lysimachia vulgaris
Goldwespe *f* ruby wasp *(family Chrysididae)*
Goldwurzel *f* golden thistle, Spanish salsify (oyster-plant), Scolymus hispanicus
Golfplatz *m* golf-course, golf-links, golf putting green

Golgi-Apparat *m*, **Golgi-Komplex** *m* Golgi apparatus (body) *(organelle)*
Goltix *n* goltix *(herbicide)*
Gommer *m* Polish wheat, Triticum polonicum
Gomphosis *f (vet)* gomphosis
Gomutipalme *f* [true] sugar palm, Arenga pinnata (saccharifera)
gonadal gonadal
Gonade *f* gonad
Gonadektomie *f (vet)* gonadectomy
Gonadoliberin *n s.* Gonadotropinreleasinghormon
gonadotrop gonadotrop[h]ic
Gonadotropin *n* gonadotrop[h]in, luliberin *(sex hormone)*
Gonadotropinfreisetzung *f* gonadotrop[h]in release
Gonadotropinreleasinghormon *n* gonadoliberin, gonadotrop[h]in releasing hormone, GnRH
Gonarthritis *f*, **Gonitis** *f (vet)* gonitis
Gonderiose *f (vet)* theileriasis
Gonochorismus *m (zoo)* gonochorism
gonochoristisch gonochoristic, gonochoric
Gonochromosom *n s.* Gonosom
Gonodukt *m* gonoduct, gonaduct
Gonosom *n* gonosome, hetero[chromo]some, sex chromosome, allosome
gonosomal gonosomal
Gonozyt *m* gonocyte
Göpel *m* whim, gin
Göpeldreschmaschine *f* threshing gin
Gordon Setter *m* Gordon [setter] *(dog breed)*
Gorgonzola *m* Gorgonzola [cheese]
Gössel *n* gosling
Gossyplure *n* gossyplure *(pheromone)*
Gossypol *n* gossypol *(toxic pigment in cottonseed)*
• ~ **entziehen** to degossypolize
Götterbaum *m* 1. ailanthus *(genus Ailanthus)*; 2. tree of heaven, Ailanthus altissima
götterbaumblättrig ailanthus-leaved
Götterblume *f (bot)* 1. shooting star *(genus Dodecatheon)*; 2. American cowslip, Dodecatheon meadia
Gottesanbeterin *f (ent)* mantis, mantid, Mantis religiosa
Gottvergeß *n (bot)* bastard horehound *(genus Ballota)*
Gouda *m* Gouda [cheese]
Goyazit *m* goyazite *(non-clay mineral)*
GPx *s.* Glutathionperoxidase
Grabbepflanzung *f* grave planting
Grabegabel *f* spading (digging) fork
Grabemaschine *f* excavator
graben to dig
~/flach to grub
~/mit dem Spaten to spade
Graben *m* ditch; trench; dike, dyke; gullet • **einen ~ ausheben** to ditch, to dig a ditch; to trench • **Gräben unterhalten** to ditch • **mittels Gräben dränieren** to ditch

Grabenabstand *m* trench spacing
Grabenausheben *n* ditching
Grabenbagger *m* ditch (trench) digger, ditcher, ditching machine, trencher, excavator
Grabenbau *m* ditching
Grabenboden *m s.* Grabensohle
Grabenböschung *f* ditch bank, bank of ditch
grabend *(zoo)* fossorial
Grabendränung *f* dig drainage
Grabeneinstau *m* infiltration irrigation
Grabenentkrautung *f* ditch weeding
Grabenentwässerung *f* surface (open ditch) drainage • **eine ~ vornehmen** to dike
Grabenerosion *f (soil)* gully (stream) erosion, gullying
Grabenfräse *f* trench cutter (cutting machine)
Grabenfüller *m*, **Grabenfüllgerät** *n* trench filler
Grabenlöffel *m* ditch bucket
grabenlos trenchless
Grabenpflanzung *f (forest)* trench planting
Grabenpflug *m* ditch[ing] plough, trench[ing] plough
Grabenrandfräse *f* ditch side rotary cutter
Grabenräumgerät *n* ditch cleaning implement
Grabenräumlöffel *m* ditch cleaning bucket, dredge scoop
Grabenräummaschine *f* ditch cleaner, ditcher
Grabenräumung *f* ditch cleaning (clearing)
Grabensaat *f (forest)* sowing in trenches
Grabensilo *m* trench silo
Grabensohle *f* ditch bottom (floor), invert
Grabensohlenfräser *m* ditch bottom cutter
Grabensprengung *f* trench blasting
Grabensystem *n* dike system
Grabenüberstau *m* submergence
Grabenunkraut *n* ditch-weed
Grabenunterhaltung *f* ditch maintenance
Grabenverfüllung *f* trench backfill
Grabenziehgerät *n*, **Grabenziehmaschine** *f* ditcher, trencher
Grabenzieh- und Dränverlegemaschine *f* trench drain layer
Grabkranz *m* [funeral] wreath
Grablader *m* digger-loader
Grabmaschine *f* excavator
Grabmilbe *f* burrowing mite *(genus Sarcoptes)*
Grabschmuck *m* grave decoration
Grabstock *m* digging stick
Grabvase *f* grave vase
Grabzypresse *f* southernwood, lad's (boy's) love, old-man wormwood, abrotanum, Artemisia abrotanum
Gradation *f (ecol)* gradation
Gradtag *m* degree day
graduieren to grade, to scale, to calibrate
Graft-versus-host-Reaktion *f* graft-versus-host reaction
Gramagras *n* grama [grass], gramma [grass], buffalo grass *(genus Bouteloua)*

Gram-Färbemittel

Gram-Färbemittel n, **Gram-Farbstoff** m Gram stain *(microbiology)*
Gramfärbung f Gram method *(microbiology)*
Gramicidin n gramicidin *(antibiotic)*
Gramin n gramine *(alkaloid)*
graminivor graminivorous
Grami[ni]zid n gramicide, grass herbicide (killer)
Grammagras n s. Gramagras
gramnegativ Gram-negative
grampositiv Gram-positive
Granadilla f 1. passion-fruit *(of Passiflora spp.)*; 2. sweet granadilla, Passiflora ligularis
Granadina-Ziege f Granada goat *(breed)*
Granalie f granule
Granatapfel m pomegranate
Granat[apfel]baum m pomegranate, Punica granatum
Grandlure n grandlure *(pheromone)*
Granegillin n aspergillic acid
Granitporphyr m granite-prophyry
Gränke f *(bot)* wild rosemary, andromeda *(genus Andromeda)*
Granne f *(bot)* awn, beard, arista • **Grannen tragend** awned, bearded, aristate
Grannenhaar n *(bot, zoo)* awn, bristle; tectrix barbed hair
Grannenhirse f smilo grass, rice-grass, Orytopsis miliacea
Grannenkiefer f bristle cone pine, foxtail pine, Pinus aristata
Grannenkokardenblume f blanket flower, Gaillardia x aristata
Grannenzähnige Kirsche f Japanese [flowering] cherry, Prunus (Cerasus) serrulata
grannig awny
granulär granular
Granulat n granulate, granules, granular material
Granulation f granulation
Granulationsanlage f granulation plant
Granulationsgewebe n granulation tissue *(animal anatomy)*
Granulatmehl n agglomerated flour *(milling)*
Granulator m granulator *(sugar manufacture)*
Granulatstreuer m, **Granulatstreuvorrichtung** f granule distributor, granulate (granular) applicator, granules placer
granulieren to granulate, to grain, to corn
Granulierung f granulation
Granuloblastose f **des Geflügels** avian myeloblastosis (granuloblastosis)
Granulom n *(vet)* granuloma
granulomatös *(vet)* granulomatous
Granulomatosis f *(vet)* granulomatosis
Granulopoese f granulopoiesis
granulös granular
Granulosazelle f granulosa cell
Granulosevirus n *(phyt)* granulosis virus
Granulozyt m granulocyte
~/basophiler basophil[e]

~/neutrophiler neutrophil
Granulozytenbildung f granulopoiesis
Grapefruit f grapefruit
Grapefruitbaum m grapefruit, pomelo, pummelo, Citrus paradisi
Grappleskidder m *(forest)* grapple skidder
Gras n grass
~/ausdauerndes strong grass
~/ausläufertreibendes sod-forming grass, sod-type grass
~/bültenbildendes tussock (tufted) grass *(comprehensive term)*
~/horstbildendes bunch[-type] grass
Grasansaat f grass seeding
grasartig grassy, gramin[ac]eous
Grasauffangvorrichtung f grass catcher *(at a lawn mower)*
Grasbestand m grass stand
grasblättrig graminifolious
Grasblättrige Goldrute f grass-leaved golden rod, Solidago graminifolia
Grasblütenälchen n flower gall nematode, seed nematode, Anguina agrostis
Grasbrache f grass fallow
grasen to graze, to [de]pasture, to run, to browse
~ lassen to graze, to pasture, to run, to stock, *(Am)* to grass
Grasen n grazing, graze
Gräserbeschreibung f agrostography
Gräserbestimmung f grass identification
Gräserblasenfuß m s. Gräserthrips
Gräsergemisch n grass mixture
Gräserherbizid n grass herbicide (killer), gramicide
Gräserhirse f grass sorghum *(comprehensive term)*
Gräserkunde f agrostology
Gräserkundler m agrostologist
gräserkundlich agrostological
Gräserthrips m, **Gräserthysanoptere** m grass thrips *(esp. Aptinothrips rufus and A. obscurus)*
Grasezeit f grazing time
Grasfangvorrichtung f grass catcher *(at a lawn mower)*
Grasfilz m matting of grass
grasfressend graminivorous
Grasfrucht f caryopsis
Grashalm m grass culm (stem)
~/grober bent, bennet
Grasheide f grass heath
Grashorst m tuft
grasig 1. grassy, grass-covered; 2. s. grasartig; 3. green *(wine)*
Graskalb n runner calf
Graskarpfen m grass carp, white amur, Ctenopharyngodon idella
Graskrankheit f grass sickness *(of horses)*
Grasland n grassland, ley, lea
~/absolutes absolute grassland

Graugrüne

~/**fakultatives** optional grassland
~/**natürliches** natural (native) grassland
~/**nicht eingezäuntes** bent
~/**überständiges** fog
~/**unbedingtes** s. ~/**natürliches**
Graslandaufbesserung f grassland improvement
Graslandbestand m grassland sward
Graslandbetrieb m all-grass farm
Graslandbewässerung f grassland irrigation
Graslandbewirtschaftung f grassland management
Graslandboden m grassland (pasture) soil
Graslanddüngung f manuring of grassland
Graslanderneuerung f grassland renewal (renovation)
Graslandfläche f meadow
Graslandflora f grassland flora
Graslandfräse f grassland rotary cultivator
Graslandgemeinschaft f grassland community
Graslandkarte f grassland map
Graslandkartierung f grassland mapping
Graslandklassifikation f grassland classification
Graslandkunde f grassland science
Graslandleguminose f pasture legume
Graslandnarbe f grassland sward
Graslandneuansaat f grassland establishment
Graslandnutzung f grassland utilization
Graslandökologie f grassland ecology
Graslandpflege f pasture maintenance
Graslandpflügen n grassland ploughing
Graslandschar n grassland ripper share
Graslandschätzung f grassland survey
Graslandtiefenmeißel m grassland subsoiler
Graslandumbruch m ploughing-up of grassland
Graslandunkraut n grassland weed
Graslandunterbodenlockerer m grassland subsoiler
Graslandverbesserung f grassland improvement
Graslandwirt m grassland farmer
Graslandwirtschaft f all-grass farming, grassland farming (husbandry)
Graslaus f grass aphid, Metopolophium (Acyrthosiphon) festucae
Gras-Leguminosen-Gemisch n grass-legume mixture
Grasmähen n grass cutting
Grasmäher m grass (hay) mower
Grasmüdigkeit f grass sickness *(of a soil)*
Grasmulch f grass mulch
Grasmulchsystem n sod culture *(in orchards)*
Grasnachsämaschine f grass reseeder
Grasnarbe f turf, [grass] sward, [grass] sod, grass cover • ~ **bilden** to sward
~/**verfilzte** matted turf
Grasnarbenbelüfter m turf aerator
Grasnarbennachwuchs m sward regrowth
Grasnarbensammelkehrmaschine f turf sweeper-collector
Grasnelke f *(bot)* thrift *(genus Armeria)*

Graspflanze f grass
Graspreßsaft m grass juice
Grasrechen m lawn rake
Grasreihensämaschine f grass drill
Grassaat f grass seeding
Grassaatguterzeugung f grass seed production
Grassaft m grass juice
Grassämaschine f grass [seed] drill
Grassamen m grass seed
Grassamenälchen n flower gall nematode, seed nematode, Anguina agrostis
Grassamenbau m grass seed cropping
Grassamenbestand m grass seed crop
Grassamenernte f grass seed harvest
Grassamengemisch n grass seed mixture
Grassavanne f grass savanna[h]
Grasschere f grass shears
Grassilage f grass silage
Grassodenschneider m sod cutter
Grasstengel m grass culm (stem)
Grassteppe f grass steppe
~/**nordamerikanische** prairie
~/**südafrikanische** veld[t]
Grastetanie f *(vet)* grass tetany (staggers) *(of ruminants)*
Grasweide f grass pasture
Graszetter m [hay-]tedder, tedding machine
Graszystenälchen n, **Graszystennematode** m grass cyst-nematode, Punctodera punctata
Grat m *(bot)* rib
Gräte f fish-bone
grätenlos boneless, bone-free
grätig bony
Graubär m s. Grislybär
Graubraunes Höhenvieh n Brown Mountain *(cattle breed)*
Graue Ackerschnecke f grey field slug, Deroceras (Agriolimax) agreste
~ **Bartblume** f *(bot)* bluebeard, Caryopteris incana
~ **Bruchweide** f grey willow (sallow), Salix cinerea
~ **Fleischfliege** f grey flesh-fly, Sarcophaga carnaria
Grauer Ehrenpreis m woolly speedwell, Veronica spicata ssp. incana
~ **Gänsefuß** m oak-leaf goose-foot, Chenopodium glaucum
~ **Lärchenwickler** m grey larch tortrioid, larch [tree] tortrix, Zeiraphera (Semasia) diniana
Grauerde f grey soil, serozem, sierozem [soil]
Grauerle f grey (speckled, European) alder, Alnus incana
Graues Eichhörnchen n American grey squirrel, Sciurus carolinensis
~ **Liebesgras** n grey love grass, stink grass, Eragrostis cilianensis
Graugans f greylag [goose], grey (wild) goose, Anser anser
graugrün *(bot, zoo)* glaucous, caesious
Graugrüne Binse f hard rush, Juncus inflexus

Graugrüne

~ **Borstenhirse** *f s.* Gelbe Borstenhirse
~ **Quecke** *f* intermediate wheat-grass, Agropyron intermedium, Elymus hispidus
Grauheide *f* bell-heather, heather-bell, Erica cinerea
Grauhuminsäure *f (soil)* grey humic acid
Graukern *m* grey heart *(wood defect)*
Graukresse *f (bot)* hoary alyssum, Berteroa incana
Graupappel *f* grey poplar, Populus canescens
graupeln to sleet
Graupeln *fpl* graupel, sleet
Graupelregen *m* sleet, soft hail, granular snow
Graupen *fpl* pearl barley • **zu ~ verarbeiten** to pearl
Graureiher *m* [common] heron, Ardea cinerea
Grauschimmel *m* 1. *(phyt)* grey mould, botrytis blight *(caused by Botrytis spp.)*; 2. grey horse
~ **an Cyclamenblüten** grey mould of cyclamen *(caused by Botrytis cinerea)*
~ **der Chrysantheme** grey mould of chrysanthemum *(caused by Botrytis cinerea)*
~ **der Hyazinthe** fire of hyacinthus *(caused by Botrytis hyacinthi)*
~ **der Lilie** lily disease *(caused by Botrytis elliptica)*
~ **der Tomate** tomato grey mould *(caused by Botrytis cinerea)*
~ **der Tulpe** fire (botrytis blight) of tulip *(caused by Botrytis tulipae)*
Grautanne *f* Colorado fir, Abies concolor
Grauvieh *n* Brown Mountain *(cattle breed)*
Grauwacke *f (soil)* greywacke, grauwacke
gravid gravid, pregnant
Gravidität *f* gravidity, pregnancy, gestation
~/ektopische extrauterine pregnancy
Gravimetrie *f* gravimetry
gravimetrisch gravimetric
Graviperzeption *f* graviperception *(plant physiology)*
Gravitationspotential *n* gravitational potential *(e.g. of soil water)*
Gravitationsrücken *n (forest)* gravity cable logging
Gravitationswasser *n (soil)* gravitational (surplus) water
Gravitropismus *m* gravitropism, geotropism *(of plant growth)*
GrCh *s.* Großchinchillakaninchen
gregär *(bot, zoo)* gregarious *(growing in a cluster or colony)*
Greifarm *m* grapple [loader]
greifen 1. to strike, to interfere, to click, to forge *(a horse having movement disorder)*; 2. to pounce *(bird of prey)*; 3. to grasp, to grip
Greifenbart *m* long-stem moss, Tillandsia usneoides
Greifer *m* grapple [loader]; grab, bucket *(of excavators)*; *(forest)* log grab
Greiferaufzug *m* barn hoist
Greiferrad *n* 1. gripwheel, strake (anti-skid) wheel; 2. picker wheel *(e.g. of a potato planter)*

Greifhufeisen *n* anti-forging shoe
Greifnetz *n (pisc)* cast-net
Greifswalder Farbstoffmischung *f* gentian violet *(anthelminthic, fungicide)*
Greifvogel *m* predatory (raptorial) bird, bird of prey, raptor
Greifvogelnest *n* eyrie, aerie
Greifwerkzeug *n s.* Greifer
Greisenhaupt *n* old man cactus, Cephalocereus senilis
Greiskraut *n* 1. groundsel, ragwort, ragweed *(genus Senecio)*; 2. common groundsel, Senecio vulgaris
Grenadille *f* passion-fruit *(of Passiflora spp.)*
Grenzabmarkung *f s.* Grenzregulierung
Grenzbaum *m* boundary (border) tree
Grenzbeetpflug *m* headland (end-rig) plough
Grenzbegang *m*, **Grenzbegehung** *f (forest)* boundary inspection, visitation of boundaries
Grenzbetrieb *m* marginal farm *(agricultural economics)*
Grenzboden *m* marginal soil
Grenzdifferenz *f (biom)* least significant difference, LSD
Grenzertragsboden *m* marginal soil
Grenzertragsstandort *m* marginal site (land)
grenzflächenaktiv surface-active
Grenzflächenwiderstand *m* boundary layer resistance *(plant physiology)*
Grenzfurche *f* outside furrow *(ploughing)*
Grenzintensität *f (forest)* marginal intensity
Grenzkrankheit *f* border disease *(of new-born lambs)*
Grenzlinie *f* pencil (black) line, pencilling *(between sound and decayed wood)*
Grenzmesser *m s.* Feldmesser
Grenznutzungsdauer *f* longevity *(e.g. of machines)*
Grenzpflug *m s.* Grenzbeetpflug
Grenzregulierung *f (forest)* marking of boundaries, boundary settlement
Grenzschicht *f* boundary layer
Grenzschichtwiderstand *m* boundary layer resistance
Grenzstamm *m* boundary tree *(timber mensuration)*
Grenzstandort *m* marginal site (land)
Grenzstein *m* land-mark, boundary stone
Grenzvermarkung *f s.* Grenzregulierung
Grenzwahrscheinlichkeit *f* probability level
Grenzwert *m* **der [ab]tötenden Wirkung** toxic limit
Greyerzer Käse *m* gruyere [cheese]
Greyfaceschaf *n* Greyface *(sheep cross-breed of Border Leicester and Scottish Blackface)*
Greyhound *m* greyhound *(breed)*
Gribbel *m* beet-lifting fork
Gricin *n* griseofulvin *(antibiotic, fungicide)*

Großblumige

Griechisch-Heu n *(bot)* fenugreek, Trigonella foenum-graecum
Griechisch-lateinisches Quadrat n *(biom)* Graeco-Latin square
Griechische Strobe f Macedonian [white] pine, Pinus peuce
~ **Tanne** f Greek fir, Abies cephalonica
Griechischer Salbei m Greek sage, Salvia triloba
Griechisches Blaukissen n purple rock-cress, Aubrieta deltoidea
Griesbeil n floating hook, pike pole, clip
Grieß m semolina
Griessäule f [plough-]beam, plough-shaft, leg, *(Am)* standard
Grießig n bees' faeces
Grießigkeit f riciness *(of cauliflower)*
~ **des Fruchtfleisches** grittiness of fruit flesh
Grießkörnchenkrankheit f ichthyophthiriasis *(of fishes, caused by Ichthyophthirius multifiliis)*
Griff m 1. nib *(of sickle or scythe)*; handle, helve, haft *(of tool)*; 2. toe grab *(of horseshoe)*
Griffel m *(bot)* style
Griffelfuß m, **Griffelpolster** n *(bot)* style-foot
Griffon m griffon *(dog breed)*
~ **Bruxellois** [Brussels] griffon *(dog breed)*
Grifulvin n s. Griseofulvin
Grille f cricket *(family Gryllidae)*
Grillverlust m shrinkage on roasting *(of meat)*
Grimmdarm m colon
~/**absteigender** descending colon
~/**aufsteigender** ascending colon
Grimmdarmarterie f colic artery
Grimmen n s. Burgstall
Grind m *(phyt, vet)* scab, scurf
Grindel m s. Griessäule
Grindkraut n *(bot)* devil's bit *(genus Scabiosa)*
Grindwurz f common (bitter, broad-leaved) dock, blood-wort, Rumex obtusifolius
Griseofulvin n griseofulvin *(antibiotic, fungicide)*
Grislybär m grizzly [bear], Ursus arctos horribilis
Grit m grit, oyster-shell
Grizzlybär m s. Grislybär
grob 1. coarse, rough; 2. capital *(e.g. a wild boar)*
grobästig limby, coarsely branched
Grobegge f brake[-harrow], field drag
grobfaserig coarse-fibred, coarse fibrous; coarse-grained, coarse-textured *(wood)*
Grobfiltration f coarse filtration
Grobfraktion f coarse fraction
Grobfutter n roughage, forage, [coarse, bulk] fodder, bulk feed
Grobfutterdosierer m roughage batcher, bulk feed hopper
Grobfutterhäcksler m roughage chopper
Grobfutterration f bulk ration
Grobfutterschneider m roughage cutter
Grobfutterstoff m s. Grobfutter
Grobheit f coarseness *(e.g. of flour)*

grobjährig broad-ringed, broad-zoned, open-grown, open-grained, fast-grown *(wood)*
Grobkies m coarse gravel
Grobkleie f bran
grobknochig heavy-boned
grobkörnig coarse-grained; coarse-textured *(soil)*
Grobkörnigkeit f coarse texture, coarseness *(of a soil)*
grobmaschig wide-meshed
Grobmehl n coarse meal
Grobmoder m *(soil)* duff
Grobmull m *(soil)* coarse mull
Grobpore f *(soil)* macropore, large pore
Grobporenvolumen n *(soil)* large pore volume
grobreinigen to preclean
Grobreiniger m precleaner
Grobrinde f coarse bark, *(Am)* ross • **die ~ entfernen** to remove coarse bark, to redden *(resin-tapping)*
grobringig s. grobjährig
Grobsämereien fpl coarse seeds
Grobsand m coarse sand, grit
Grobschluff m *(soil)* coarse silt
Grobschmied m blacksmith
Grobschrot m kibble
Grobschutt m *(soil)* coarse gravel
Grobsieb n riddle
Grobtrub m coarse coagulum *(brewing)*
grobvermahlen coarse-milled
Grobwolle f coarse[-bred] wool, shag
grobwollig coarse-woolled
Grobwoll[schaf]rasse f
Groenendael m Belgian sheep-dog *(breed)*
Groninger m Groningen *(horse breed)*
Groningerrind n Groningen [Whiteheaded] *(cattle breed)*
Grönlandfalke m, **Grönländischer Jagdfalke** m Greenland falcon, Falco rusticolus candicane
Groom m groom, [h]ostler
Großballen m big (large) bale *(hay, straw)*
Großballenpresse f big baler
Großballensilage f big bale silage
Großbauer m large farmer
Großbaumschule f large nursery
Großbekämpfung f large-scale control
Großbetrieb m/**landwirtschaftlicher** large (big) farm
Großblattahorn m broad-leaved maple, Acer macrophyllum
großblättrig large-leaved, grandifolious
Großblättrige Linde f broad-leaved lime[-tree], large-leaved lime[-tree], *(Am)* bigleaf linden, Tilia platyphyllos
Großblumige Gartenmargerite f Shasta (max) daisy, Chrysanthemum maximum
~ **Königskerze** f wool mullein, Verbascum densiflorum (thapsiforme)
~ **Wucherblume** f Shasta (max) daisy, Chrysanthemum maximum

Großblumiger

Großblumiger Portulak *m* garden portulaca, rose-moss, sun plant, Portulaca grandiflora
~ **Rittersporn** *m* larkspur, lark-heel, Delphinium grandiflorum
Großblumiges Heliotrop *n* common heliotrope, Heliotropium arborescens (peruvianum)
~ **Mädchenauge** *n* large-flowered tickseed, Coreopsis grandiflora
~ **Wollkraut** *n s.* Großblumige Königskerze
großblütig large-flowered, grandiflorous
Großblütige Magnolie *f* southern magnolia, Magnolia grandiflora
~ **Wicke** *f* showy (big-flower) vetch, Vicia grandiflora
Großblütiger Eibisch *m* mallow marvel, Hibiscus grandiflorous
~ **Fingerhut** *m* yellow foxglove, Digitalis grandiflora (ambigua)
~ **Herzenkelch** *m* Amazon (eucharis) lily, Eucharis grandiflora (amazonica)
~ **Lein** *m* flowering flax, Linum grandiflorum
Großblütiges Portulakröschen *n s.* Großblumiger Portulak
Großchinchilla[kaninchen] *n* Giant Chinchilla *(rabbit breed)*
Große Bekassine *f* great snipe, Gallinago media
~ **Bibernelle** *f* 1. greater burnet saxifrage, Pimpinella major; 2. *s.* Großer Wiesenknopf
~ **Brennessel** *f* common [stinging-]nettle, sting (greater) nettle, Urtica dioica
~ **Brombeerlaus** *f* European raspberry aphid, Amphorophora (Nectarosiphon) rubi
~ **Eberwurz** *f (bot)* smooth carline, Carlina acaulis
~ **Egelschnecke** *f* great house-slug, Limax maximus
~ **Fetthenne** *f* orpin[e], live-forever [stonecrop], Sedum telephium
~ **Flamingoblume** *f* painter's palette, Anthurium-Andreanum hybrid
~ **Getreide[blatt]laus** *f* grain (cereal) aphid, Macrosiphum (Sitobion) avenae
~ **Holzameise** *f* large carpenter ant, Camponotus herculeanus
~ **Hühnerlaus** *f* large chicken louse, Stenocrotaphus (Goniodes) gigas
~ **Kapuzinerkresse** *f* [garden] nasturtium, Tropaeolum majus
~ **Klette** *f* great bur[dock], greater burdock, Arctium lappa
~ **Knorpelmöhre** *f* bullwort, bishop's-weed, Ammi majus
~ **Kohlfliege** *f* turnip root fly, Delia (Hylemyia) floralis
~ **Kugeldistel** *f* great globe thistle, Echinops sphaerocephalus
~ **Kugelige Napfschildlaus** *f* nut scale, Eulecanium tiliae, Lecanium coryli
~ **Küstentanne** *f* white fir, Abies grandis

~ **Lärchenblattwespe** *f* [large] larch saw-fly, Pristiphora erichsonii
~ **Meise** *f* great tit, Parus major
~ **Nacktschnecke** *f* great house slug, Limax maximus
~ **Narzissenfliege** *f* narcissus bulb-fly, large narcissus fly, Merodon (Lampetia) equestris
~ **Pimpinelle** *f* greater burnet saxifrage, Pimpinella major
~ **Rinderdasselfliege** *f* warble fly, Hypoderma bovis
~ **Rohrdommel** *f* bittern, Botaurus stellaris
~ **Rosenblattlaus** *f* rose aphid Macrosiphum rosae
~ **Sapote** *f* marmalade tree (plum), sapote, Pouteria sapota, Calocarpum mammosum
~ **Sommerwurz** *f* greater broomrape, Orobanche major
~ **Sterndolde** *f* great masterwort, Astrantia major
~ **Sumpfschnepfe** *f* great snipe, Gallinago media
~ **Wachsmotte** *f* bee moth, greater (larger) wax moth, Galleria mellonella
~ **Wallwurz** *f* [common] comfrey, consound, Symphytum officinale
~ **Wegschnecke** *f* red slug, Arion rufus (empiricorum)
~ **Wolfsmilchwanze** *f* large milkweed bug, Oncopeltus fasciatus
~ **Wühlmaus** *f* [water-]vole, black water rat, Arvicola terrestris (amphibius)
~ **Zwiebelfliege** *f* narcissus bulb-fly, Merodon (Lampetia) equestris
Großelter *m* grandparent *(animal breeding)*
Größensortiereinrichtung *f* [size] grader, grading (sizing) equipment, [dimension] sizer *(e.g. for fruits)*
Großer Achtzähniger Fichtenborkenkäfer *m* eight-toothed [spruce] bark-beetle, large spruce bark-beetle, Norway spruce engraver, Ips (Tomicus) typographus
~ **Baldrian** *m* common valerian, Valeriana officinalis
~ **Birkensplintkäfer** *m* birch bark (sapwood) beetle, birch scolytus, Scolytus ratzeburgi
~ **Birnenblattsauger** *m (ent)* pear sucker, Psylla pirisuga
~ **Brauner Kiefernrüsselkäfer (Nadelholzrüßler, Rüsselkäfer)** *m* [large] pine weevil, Hylobius abietis
~ **Buchdrucker** *m s.* Großer Achtzähniger Fichtenborkenkäfer
~ **Buntspecht** *m* [northern] great spotted woodpecker, Dendrocopus major
~ **Eichelbohrer** *m* acorn weevil, Balaninus glandium
~ **Eichenbock[käfer]** *m* great capricorn beetle, oak cerambyx, Cerambyx cerdo
~ **Erbsenstrauch** *m* pea-tree, Siberian pea shrub, Caragana arborescens

~ **Fichtenborkenkäfer** *m s.* Großer Achtzähniger Fichtenborkenkäfer
~ **Frostspanner** *m* great winter moth, mottled umber moth, Hibernia (Erannis) defoliaria
~ **Gabelschwanz** *m* puss moth, Cerura vinula
~ **Galgant** *m* greater galanga[l], Alpinia galanga
~ **Geweihfarn** *m* elk's horn fern, Platycerium grande
~ **Hahn** *m s.* Auerhahn
~ **Heldbock** *m s.* ~ Eichenbock[käfer]
~ **Kiefernborkenkäfer** *m* stenograph bark-beetle, pine tree beetle, Ips sexdentatus
~ **Kiefernmarkkäfer** *m* larger pine-shoot beetle, larger pine pith-borer, pine beetle, Tomicus (Blastophagus) piniperda
~ **Knorpellattich** *m* skeleton weed, Chondrilla juncea
~ **Kohltriebrüßler** *m* rape stem weevil, Ceutorhynchus napi
~ **Kohlweißling** *m* large white butterfly, cabbage butterfly, garden white, Pieris brassicae
~ **Kornbohrer** *m (ent)* larger grain borer, Prostephanus (Dinoderus) truncatus
~ **Krallenklee** *m* serradella, serradilla, Ornithopus sativus
~ **Lärchenborkenkäfer** *m* larch bark-beetle, Ips cembrae
~ **Leberegel** *m* [common] liver fluke, Fasciola hepatica
~ **Macawbaum** *m* macaw, gru-gru palm, Acrocomia sclerocarpa (aculeata)
~ **Magenwurm** *m* barber's pole worm, Haemonchus contortus
~ **Pappelbock[käfer]** *m (ent)* large poplar [and willow] borer, Saperda carcharias
~ **Pfeifenstrauch** *m* mock orange, Philadelphus coronarius
~ **Rapsstengelrüßler** *m* rape stem weevil, Ceutorhynchus napi
~ **Schaflungenwurm** *m* sheep lungworm, Dictyocaulus filaria
~ **Schwarzer Eschenbastkäfer** *m* large [black] ash bark-beetle, Hylesinus crenatus
~ **Speik** *m* spike lavender, Lavandula latifolia (spica)
~ **Ulmensplintkäfer** *m* [large] elm bark-beetle, Scolytus destructor (scolytus)
~ **Waldgärtner** *m s.* ~ Kiefernmarkkäfer
~ **Wiesenknopf** *m* [great, garden] burnet, Sanguisorba officinalis
Großerholungsgebiet *n* large recreational zone
Großes Asiatisches Yams *n* greater (water) yam, ten-months yam, Dioscorea alata
~ **Flohkraut** *n* [common] fleabane, Pulicaria dysenterica
~ **Liebesgras** *n s.* Graues Liebesgras
~ **Riedgras** *n* pendulous sedge, Carex pendula
~ **Schöllkraut** *n* [greater] celandine, tetterwort, swallow-wort, Chelidonium majus
~ **Singrün** *n* large periwinkle, band-plant, cut-finger, Vinca major
~ **Wiesel** *n* ermine, stoat, Mustela erminea
~ **Zittergras** *n* great (big) quaking-grass, Briza maxima
Großfarm *f* large (big) farm
Großflächen *fpl* broadacres
Großflächenanbau *m* large-scale growing
Großflächenbehandlung *f* large-scale treatment
Großflächenbewässerung *f* large-scale irrigation
Großflächenbewirtschaftung *f* large-area farming
Großflächenlandwirtschaft *f* large-area farming, large-scale agriculture
Großflächenmähdrescher *m* giant combine
Großflächenmähwerk *n* gang mower
Großflächenmelioration *f* large-area amelioration
Großflächenstreuer *m* bulk spreader
Großflächenstreuversuch *m* farm-scale scattered trial
großfrüchtig large-fruited
Großfrüchtige Douglasie *f* big-cone Douglas fir, Pseudotsuga macrocarpa
~ **Eiche** *f* bur oak, Quercus macrocarpa
~ **Moosbeere** *f* [American] cranberry, fen-berry, Vaccinium macrocarpon
~ **Zypresse** *f* Monterey cypress, Cupressus macrocarpa
Großfrüchtiger Kohl *m* big-fruited cabbage, Brassica macrocarpa
Großgrundbesitz *m* large landed property; ownership of large estates
Großgrundbesitzer *m* big landowner
Großhirn *n* cerebrum
Großhirnrinde *f* cerebral cortex
großhülsig large-podded
Großkahlschlag *m* extensive clear felling
Großkamp *n* (forest) large nursery
Großkiste *f* bulk bin, pallet box (bin), box pallet
Großkistenfüller *m* bulk-bin filling machine
Großkistenkippgerät *n* bulk-bin tipper, tipping device for pallet boxes
Großkistenlager *n* pallet box store
Großklima *n* macroclimate
großklimatisch macroclimatic
Großkopf *m s.* Streifenmeeräsche
großkörnig large-seeded
Großkörnige Ackerbohne *f* large-seeded bean, Vicia faba ssp. major
Großmähdrescher *m* giant combine
Großmutation *f* large-scale mutation
Großmutter *f*, **Großmuttertier** *n* grand dam *(animal breeding)*
Großohrhirsch *m* mule deer, Odocoileus hemionus, Cariacus macrotis
großörtig butt end first *(timber transportation)*
Großproduktion *f*/**landwirtschaftliche** large-area farming
Großpudel *m* Standard Poodle *(dog breed)*

großrahmig

großrahmig large-framed, large-bodied *(animal body)*
Großraumbelegstelle *f (api)* mating yard
Großraumgewächshaus *n* hangar hothouse, wide-span greenhouse
Großrauminventur *f (forest)* large-scale inventory
Großraumlandwirtschaft *f* large-scale agriculture (farming)
Großraumreaktor *m* **in Freibauweise** large-scale outdoor reactor *(brewing)*
Großraumwirtschaft *f* large-scale husbandry
Großregner *m* large (giant) rainer
großsamig large-seeded
Großschirmschlagsystem *n (forest)* shelterwood compartment system, uniform [shelterwood] system
Großschlächterei *f* large slaughterhouse
Großsilo *m* giant store
Großsortieranlage *f* potato storage sorter
Größte Margerite (Wucherblume) *f* Shasta (max) daisy, Chrysanthemum maximum
Großteilstück *n* main (whole) plot *(field experimentation)*
Großtier *n* large animal
Großtierchirurgie *f* large-animal surgery
Großtiermedizin *f* large-animal medicine
Großtierzucht *f* large-animal breeding
Großtraktor *m* large tractor
Großtrappe *f* great (giant) bustard, Otis tarda
Großunternehmen *n* [large-scale] enterprise
~/agrarindustrielles agribusiness enterprise
Großvater *m*, **Großvatertier** *n* grandsire *(animal breeding)*
Großversuch *m* large-scale experiment (trial)
~/pflanzenbaulicher field-scale test
Großvieh *n* large cattle, large (heavy) livestock
Großvieheinheit *f* large-cattle unit, livestock (animal) unit
Großviehhaltung *f* large livestock husbandry
Großwaldbesitz *m* large forest property
Großwild *n* big game
Großwildjagd *f* big game hunting
großzapfig large-coned
Groznyi-Feinwollrasse *f*, **Groznyischaf** *n* Grozny (sheep breed)
grubben *s.* grubbern
Grubber *m* cultivator, chisel plough, grubber, tiller, scarifier
~/schwerer heavy[-duty] cultivator, ripper
Grubberdrillmaschine *f* cultivator drill
Grubberegge *f* drag-harrow
grubbern to cultivate, to grub
Grube *f* 1. pit; 2. *(bot, zoo)* fovea; 3. *s.* Fallgrube
Grubenhalde *f s.* Halde
Grubenholz *n* mine (pit) timber, pitwood
Grubenkurzholz *n* short pitwood
Grubenlangholz *n* long pitwood
Grubenrundholz *n* round pitwood, chockwood
Grubensilo *m* pit silo

Grubenstempel *m* mine prop, [pit-]prop, stull, durn, stemple
grubig *(bot, zoo)* lacunose
Grummet *n*, **Grumt** *n* aftermath, aftergrass, aftercrop, second[-cut] hay, fog, eddish, eadish, *(Am)* rowen
grün 1. green, verdant; 2. fresh, alive, unseasoned *(wood)* • **~ werdend** virescent, viridescent
Grün *n* green, greenery, verdure
Grünablauf *m* green syrup *(sugar manufacture)*
Grünalge *f* green alga *(division Chlorophyta)*
Grünanlage *f* green area (space), amenity planting, verdure plantation, pleasure-ground; park
~/öffentliche public garden (green), park[s]
~/städtische town verdure, urban green[ery]
Grünanlagenunterhaltung *f* maintenance of urban amenity land
Grünanpflanzung *f* planting of greenery
Grünastung *f* green (branch) pruning, pruning of live branches
Grünbesatz *m* green-stain, greenstuff
grünblättrig viridifolious
Grünblättriger Schwefelkopf *m (bot)* sulphur tuft, Hypholoma fasciculare
grünblütig viridiflorous
Grund *m* 1. ground; land; 2. fundus *(anatomy)*
Grundbeet *n* ground [level] bed *(in glasshouses)*
~/erhöhtes raised [ground] bed
Grundbegehung *f (forest)* primary circuit
Grundbesitz *m* 1. real estate, land tenure, landed property, ground; 2. land ownership
~/landwirtschaftlicher farm real estate
Grundbesitzer *m* landowner, landholder
Grundbodenbearbeitung *f* basic tillage, primary tillage (cultivation)
Grundbuch *n* [land] cadaster, cadastre, land register, register of landed property, terrier
Grunddünger *m* basic (basal, preplant) fertilizer
Grunddüngergabe *f* 1. basic fertilizer application; 2. *s.* Grunddüngung
Grunddüngung *f* basal dressing (fertilization), basic fertilizer application
Grundebene *f* datum level *(terrestrial survey)*
Gründeckfrucht *f* green cover crop
Grundeigentum *n s.* Grundbesitz
Grundenergiewechsel *m s.* Grundumsatz
Gründereffekt *m*, **Gründerprinzip** *n (gen)* founder effect
Grundfarbe *f* base (ground) colour, undercolour *(e.g. of a horse)*
Grundfläche *f (forest)* basal area, b.a. *(of a stand)*
~ eines Baumes tree basal area
~/mittlere mean basal area
Grundflächenhaltung *f (forest)* basal-area density
Grundflächenmittelstamm *m (forest)* mean basal area tree
Grundflächenregulierung *f (forest)* basal-area regulation (control)

Grundflächensumme f *(forest)* basal area of a whole crop, total basal area
Grundflächentafel f *(forest)* table of basal areas
Grundflächenzentralstamm m *(forest)* median basal area tree
Grundflächenzuwachs m *(forest)* basal-area increment
Grundflächenzuwachsprozent n *(forest)* basal-area increment percent[age]
Grundfutter n basal feed, basic diet
Grundfutterration f basal (basic) ration, basal (basic) diet
Grundgesamtheit f *(biom)* [parent] population, universe
Grundgesetz n/**biogenetisches** biogenetic law
Grundgewebe n *(bot, zoo)* fundamental (ground) tissue; *(bot)* parenchyma [tissue]; stroma *(of an animal organ)*
Grundgley m *(soil)* ground-water gley
Gründigkeit f soil depth
Grundmaschine f basic machine
Grundmoräne f *(soil)* ground (basal) moraine
Grundmoränenrücken m drumlin
Grundnahrungsmittel n staple food, basic food[stuff]
Grundpächter m landholder
Grundplasma n ground substance, hyaloplasm
Grundrahmen m basic frame
Grundration f s. Grundfutterration
Grundregel f/**biogenetische** biogenetic law
grundständig *(bot, zoo)* basilar[y]
Grundsteuer f land tax
Grundstück n plot [of land], lot; [real] estate
Grundstückspacht f land tenure
Grundstücksumlegung f field clearing
Grundstücksverzeichnis n [land] cadaster, [land] cadastre
Grundsubstanz f ground substance
Grundtraktor m basic tractor
Grundumsatz m basal (standard) metabolic rate, BMR, basal metabolism, basal (resting) energy exchange
Gründung f foundation, fill *(road construction)*
gründüngen to green-manure
Gründünger m green manure • ~ **einarbeiten** to green-manure
Gründüngung f green manuring
Gründüngungskultur f green manure crop
Gründüngungspflanze f green manure plant
Grundverbesserung f land (soil) improvement, [soil] amelioration
Grundwasser n ground water, GW, phreatic (subsoil) water
Grundwasserabfluß m ground-water discharge (seepage, run-off)
Grundwasserabsenkung f ground-water lowering, water-table drawdown
Grundwasseranhebung f, **Grundwasseraufhöhung** f ground-water mounting

Grundwasserbeobachtungsrohr n ground-water observation gauge
Grundwasserbewegung f ground-water flow
Grundwasserboden m ground-water soil
Grundwasserbrunnen m ground-water well
Grundwasserentnahme f ground-water withdrawal
Grundwasserentzug m ground-water extraction
Grundwassergrasland n hydromorphic grassland
Grundwasserhorizont m ground-water table (level), phreatic surface
Grundwasserlaterit m *(soil)* ground-water laterite
Grundwasserleiter m aquifer, aquafer
Grundwassermeßrohr n ground-water observation gauge
grundwassernah close to ground water
Grundwasserneubildung f ground-water recharge
Grundwasseroberfläche f s. Grundwasserspiegel
Grundwasserpflanze f phreatophyte
Grundwasserregulierung f ground-water regulation
Grundwasserschutz m ground-water protection
Grundwassersohle f confining layer (stratum)
Grundwasserspiegel m ground-water table (level), water-table, phreatic surface
Grundwasserverschmutzung f, **Grundwasserverseuchung** f ground-water pollution, water-table contamination
Grundwasserwärmepumpe f ground-water heat pump
Grundwasserwiese f water-meadow
Grundwolle f linters *(of cottonseed)*
Grundzahl f *(gen)* basic number
Grundzytoplasma n ground substance, hyaloplasm
Grüne Apfel[blatt]laus f [green] apple aphid, Aphis pomi
~ **Bananenschabe** f green banana roach, Panchlora exoleta
~ **Blattwanze** f lygus bug, tarnish[ed] plant bug *(genus Lygus)*
~ **Bohne** f haricot [bean], French (garden) bean
~ **Borstenhirse** f green bristle-grass, green pigeon-grass, bottle grass, *(Am)* green foxtail, Setaria viridis
~ **Chrysanthemenlaus** f green chrysanthemum aphid, Coloradoa rufomaculata
~ **Eidechse** f European green lizard, Lacerta viridis
~ **Erbsen[blatt]laus** f pea aphid, Acyrtosiphon pisum
~ **Fruchtscheckung** f **des Apfels** apple green dimple, green mottle *(virosis)*
~ **Kaffeeschildlaus** f green coffee scale, green bug, Coccus viridis
~ **Minze** f spearmint, Mentha spicata var. spicata
~ **Nieswurz** f green hellebore, bear's-foot, Helleborus viridis

Grüne

~ **Pfirsichblattlaus** f green peach aphid, peach-potato aphid (aphis), tobacco aphid, Myzus persicae
~ **Reiswanze** f southern green stink-bug, Nazara viridula
~ **Revolution** f green revolution *(agrarian policy)*
~ **Ringscheckung** f *(phyt)* green ring mottle
~ **Ringscheckung** f **der Sauerkirsche** cherry green ring mottle *(virosis)*
~ **Roßminze** f s. ~ Minze
~ **Schmeißfliege** f greenbottle, [sheep] blowfly, sheep maggot fly, Lucilia sericata
~ **Tannenhoniglaus** f green fir honey aphid, Buchneria pectinatae
grünen 1. to green, to turn (become) green; 2. to be green
Grüner Drachen m *(bot)* green dragon, dragon arum, Arisaema dracontium
~ **Eichenwickler** m green tortrix (oak-roller) moth, oak leaf-roller, Tortrix viridana
~ **Fennich** s. Grüne Borstenhirse
~ **Fruchtkäfer** m fig beetle, Cotinis texana
~ **Knollenblätterpilz** m death cap (cup), deadly agaric, *(Am)* destroying angel, Amanita phalloides
~ **Laubholzprachtkäfer** m *(ent)* beech agrilus, Agrilus viridis
~ **Pippau** m *(bot)* smooth hawk's-beard, Crepis capillaris
~ **Streifenfarn** m green spleenwort, Asplenium viride
~ **Tannentriebwickler** m *(ent)* silver fir shoot tortricid, silver fir leaf-roller, Cacoecia murinana
Grünerbse f green (vining) pea, green corn
Grünerbsendreschmaschine f [mobile] pea viner, vining machine
Grünerbsenvollerntemaschine f pod picker
Grünerde f celadonite *(clay mineral)*
Grünerle f green alder, Alnus viridis [ssp. viridis]
Grünesche f green ash, Fraxinus pennsylvanica [var. subintegerrima]
Grünfärbung f greening
Grünfäule f *(phyt)* green rot
Grünfläche f park (grassed) area, green [area]
Grünflächenplaner m open-space planner
Grünfleckigkeit f **der Johannisbeere** s. Grünscheckung der Johannisbeere
Grünfüßiges Teichhuhn n [common] gallinule, moorhen, water-hen, Gallinula chloropus
Grünfutter n green fodder (forage, crop), soilage
• [frischgemähtes] ~ **verfüttern** to soil
Grünfutterernte f green-crop harvest
Grünfutterkette f green forage chain *(machinery)*
Grünfutterlader m green-crop loader
Grünfuttermais m forage maize
Grünfutterpflanze f green fodder [plant]
Grünfutterroggen m forage rye
Grünfutterschneider m green-fodder cutter
Grünfutterschnitt m herbage cut
Grünfutterstoff m green roughage
Grünfuttertrockner m green-crop dryer, grass (forage crop) dryer
Grünfuttertrocknung f green-crop drying, grass drying
Grünfütterung f green feeding, soiling
Grüngestaltung f planting of greenery
Grüngürtel m green (forest) belt
~ **an Wasserläufen** waterfront zone
Grüngut n green forage; *(forest)* tree foliage
Grünguthäckselkette f green forage-chopping chain
Grünhäcksel n green chop
Grünhafer m green oat[s], forage oat[s], feeding oat[s]
Grünholz n green cutting
Grünholzfraktur f *(vet)* greenstick fracture
Grünkohl m [curly] kale, curled [kitchen] kale, green (winter) cabbage, Brassica oleracea convar. acephala var. sabellica
Grünkragen m green shoulder *(of tomatoes due to disturbed maturation)*
Grünland n grassland, meadow land *(for compounds s. under* Grasland*)*
Grünlandbetrieb m grassland farm
Grünlandfläche f meadow
Grünlandkraut n grassland herb
Grünlandumbruch m ploughing-up of grassland
Grünlilie f spider plant, Chlorophytum comosum
Grünmais m green (forage) maize
Grünmalz n green malt
Grünmasse f 1. green crop (material), foliage; tree foliage; 2. green weight
Grünmasseertrag m green crop
Grünmehl n grass (hay) meal
Grünmulch m green mulch
Grünpellet n moist pellet
Grünpflanze f foliage (green) plant
Grünplaner m open-space planner
Grünplanung f planning of green areas
grünreif mature-green
Grünreife f green (milk) ripeness *(of cereals)*
Grünroggen m green (forage, feeding) rye
Grünrüßler m green leaf weevil *(genus Phyllobius)*
grünschalig green-podded
Grünscheckung f **der Johannisbeere** red currant green mottle *(virosis)*
Grünscheckungsvirus n **der Erbse** pea green mottle virus
Grünschimmel m 1. green mould *(genus Penicillium)*; 2. blue mould *(of stored fruit, caused esp. by Penicillium expansum)*
Grünschimmelkrankheit f *(phyt)* green mould
Grünschmuck m greens
Grünschnitt m summer pruning *(of fruit-trees)*
Grünsirup m green syrup *(sugar manufacture)*
Grünspargel m green asparagus (spears)

Grünspecht *m* green woodpecker, *(Am)* popinjay, Picus viridis
Grünsteckling *m* herbaceous (softwood, summer) cutting
Grünstreifige Kartoffellaus *f* potato aphid, Macrosiphum euphorbiae
Grünverbauung *f* biological engineering
Grünverfärbung *f* greening *(e.g. of meat)*; greenstain *(of certain hardwoods due to fungal attack)*
grunzen to grunt
Grunzen *n* grunt
Grünzeug *n* greens
Grunzochse *m* yak, grunting ox, Bos grunniens
Grünzone *f* green belt (space)
Gruppe f/prosthetische prosthetic group, coenzyme
~/sexuell aktive sexually active group, SAG *(of female grazing animals)*
Gruppenaufzuchtkäfig *m* group rearing cage
Gruppenauslese *f* group selection
Gruppenbucht *f* group pen
Gruppenbuchthaltung *f* group penning
Gruppeneffekt *m* group effect *(animal behaviour)*
Gruppenfütterungsversuch *m* group-feeding experiment (trial)
Gruppenhaltung *f* group housing
Gruppenimmunität *f* group immunity
Gruppenkäfig *m* group cage
Gruppenklassierung *f* group grading
Gruppenpaarung *f* group mating
Gruppenpflanzung *f* group planting, planting in groups
Gruppenplenterung *f* group-selection felling
Gruppenresistenz *f* group resistance
Gruppenselektion *f* group selection
Gruppenstallhaltung *f* group housing
Gruppensterilität *f* intersterility
Gruppenstichprobenahme *f* cluster sampling
Gruppenverhalten *n* group behaviour *(e.g. of animals)*
Gruppenzucht *f* group breeding
Grütze *f* groats
Gruyère *m* gruyere [cheese]
GS *s.* Glutaminsynthetase
GSH *s.* Glutathion
GtBKV *s.* Virus der Getreidebestockungskrankheit
Gua *s.* Guanin
Guajacyleinheit *f* guaiacyl unit *(structural unit of lignin)*
Guajakbaum *m (bot)* guaiacum *(genus Guajacum)*
Guajakharz *n* guaiac[um]
Guajakholz *n* guaiac[um]
Guajakol *n* guaiacol, guaifenesin *(expectorant)*
Guajave *f (bot)* guava, Psidium guajava
Guanidin *n* guanidine
4-Guanidinobutylamin *n* agmatine
Guanin *n* guanine
Guanindesaminase *f* guanine deaminase *(enzyme)*

Guaninribonucleosid *n* guanosine
Guano *m* guano *(fertilizer chiefly from faeces of seafowl)*
~/phosphathaltiger phosphatic guano
Guanosin *n* guanosine
Guanosindiphosphat *n* guanosine diphosphate
Guanosin[mono]phosphat *n* guanosine monophosphate, GMP
Guanosintriphosphat *n* guanosine triphosphate
Guanostreuer *m* guano drill
Guanosuperphosphat *n* superphosphate of guano
Guanylatcyclase *f* guanylate cyclase, guanyl[yl] cyclase *(enzyme)*
Guarpflanze *f* cluster bean, Cyamopsis tetragonoloba (psoraloides)
Guatemalagras *n* Guatemala grass, Tripsacum laxum
Guave *f*, **Guayave** *f s.* Guajave
Guayulekautschuk *m* guayule rubber
Guayulestrauch *m (bot)* guayule, Parthenium argentatum
Guazatin *n* guazatine *(fungicide)*
Gubernakulum *n* gubernaculum *(of nematodes)*
Guernsey-Rind *n* Guernsey [cattle] *(breed)*
Guernseylilie *f* Guernsey lily, Nerine sarniensis
Guesathion *n* guesathion *(insecticide)*
Guinea corn *n* guinea-corn, Sorghum guineense
Guineagras *n* guinea grass, green panic, Panicum maximum
Guineapfeffer *m* African pepper *(spice)*
Guinesisches Yams *n* eight months Guinea yam, Dioscorea rotundata
Guldenbaum *m* sweet gum, gum-tree, Liquidambar styraciflua
Gülle *f* [animal] slurry, farm (livestock waste) slurry, [semi]liquid manure, sludge, muck
~/eingedickte dewatered sludge
Gülle[bearbeitungs]anlage *f* slurry treatment (handling and storing) plant
Güllebecken *n* slurry lagoon
Güllebehälter *m* slurry store
Güllebelüfter *m* slurry aerator
Güllebelüftung *f* slurry aeration
Güllebeseitigung *f* slurry disposal
Güllebewirtschaftung *f* slurry management
Gülleerdbecken *n* slurry lagoon
Güllefeststoff *m* slurry solid, solid slurry fraction
Gülleflachbehälter *m* slurry lagoon
Güllegrube *f* slurry pit, [liquid] manure pit, liquid manure cistern
Güllegrubenbelüftungssystem *n* manure pit ventilation system
Güllehochbehälter *m* above ground slurry store
Gülleinjektor *m* liquid manure injector
Güllelager *n*, **Güllelagerbehälter** *m* slurry store
Güllemischer *m* slurry mixer
Güllepumpe *f* [manure] slurry pump, [liquid] manure pump

Gülleregner

Gülleregner *m s.* Gülleverregner
Güllerohr *n* liquid manure pipe
Güllerührer *m* slurry (manure) agitator
Güllesammelbehälter *m* slurry store; liquid manure tank
Gülletankwagen *m* slurry tanker, liquid manure tank
Güllevergärung *f* muck digestion
Gülleverregner *m* slurry thrower, manure sprinkler (gun)
Gülleverregnung *f* slurry sprinkling, organic irrigation, slurry application by rain gun
Gülleverteiler *m*, **Gülleverteilwagen** *m* slurry spreader
Güllewirtschaft *f* semiliquid manure management
(L)-Gulunolactonoxidase *f* (L)-gulunolactone oxidase *(enzyme)*
Gumar-Teakbaum *m*, **Gumaribaum** *m* goomar teak, Gmelina arborea
Gummi *n* gum
~/Arabisches gum arabic (acacia) *(from Acacia spp.)*
~/pflanzliches [plant, vegetable] gum
Gummi *m(n)* [India] rubber, india rubber *(s. a. Kautschuk)*
Gummiakazie *f* gum arabic acacia, Acacia senegal
Gummiarabikum *n s.* Gummi/Arabisches
Gummiarabikumbaum *m s.* Gummiakazie
gummiartig gummy
Gummibaum *m* 1. gum tree *(comprehensive term)*; 2. rubber plant, India[n] rubber fig, Ficus elastica
gummibereift rubber-tyred
Gummifluß *m (phyt)* gummosis
~ der Gurke *s.* Gurkenkrätze
Gummigebiß *n* India rubber snaffle
Gummigeschmack *m* rubber taste *(defect of wine)*
Gummigleisband *n* rubber crawler
Gummigurtbandförderer *m* rubber belt conveyor
Gummigutt *n* gamboge *(gum resin esp. from Garcinia hanburyi)*
Gummi-Guttibaum *m (bot)* Siam gamboge, Garcinia hanburyi
Gummiharz *n* gum resin
Gummihecke *f* milk bush, Euphorbia tirucalli
Gummiholz *n s.* Gummiholzkrankheit
Gummiholzkrankheit *f* rubbery wood [disease] *(fruit-tree virosis)*
~ des Apfels apple rubbery wood
Gummikraut *n* curly-cup gumweed, Grindelia squarrosa
Gummilack *m* lac [resin]
gummiliefernd gummy
Gummilücke *f (bot)* gum cyst
Gummimatte *f* rubber mat
Gummirutsche *f* rubber chute
Gummischürze *f* rubber apron
Gummistallmatte *f* rubber stable mat
Gummistiefel *m* rubber boot, gumboot
Gummistoff *m* gum
~ der Gerste barley gum
Gummitrensengebiß *n* India rubber snaffle
Gummose *f (phyt)* gummosis
Gundelrebe *f*, **Gundermann** *m* ground ivy, alehoof, Glec[h]oma hederacea
Gunnera *f* prickly rhubarb, gunnera *(genus Gunnera)*
Günsel *m* bugle[weed], ajuga *(genus Ajuga)*
Gur *f s.* Kieselgur
Gurjunbalsam *m* gurjun [balsam]
Gurjunbalsamöl *n* gurjun balsam oil
Gurjunbaum *m (bot)* gurjun, Dipterocarpus alatus
Gurke *f* 1. cucumber *(fruit)*; 2. *s.* Gurkenpflanze
~/eingelegte preserved cucumber, gherkin
Gurkenbaum *m* cucumber-tree, blimbing, Averrhoa bilimbi
Gurkenblattfleckenvirus *n* cucumber leaf spot virus, CuLSV
Gurkenblattlaus *f* cotton aphid, Aphis gossypii
Gurkenerdfloh *m* cucumber flea beetle, Epitrix cucumeris
gurkenförmig cucumiform
Gurkenfrucht *f* pepo
Gurkengrünscheckungsmosaikvirus *n* cucumber green mottle mosaic virus, CGMMV
Gurkenkäfer *m* cucumber beetle, *(Am)* cucumber bug *(Diabrotica spp.)*
Gurkenkrätze *f* cucumber scab (gummosis) *(caused by Cladosporium cucumerinum)*
Gurkenkraut *n* [common] borage, talewort, Borago officinalis
Gurkenkürbis *m s.* Gemüsekürbis
Gurkenmagnolie *f* cucumber-tree, Magnolia acuminata
Gurkenmehltau *m* cucumber mildew *(caused by Erysiphe cichoriacearum)*
Gurkenmosaik *n* cucumber mosaic *(virosis)*
Gurkenmosaikvirus *n* cucumber (cucumis) mosaic virus, CMV
Gurkennekrose *f* cucumber necrosis *(virosis)*
Gurkenpflanze *f* cucumber [plant], Cucumis sativus
Gurkenspinnmilbe *f* red spider [mite], red [glasshouse spider] mite, two-spotted [spider] mite, Tetranychus urticae (telarius)
Gurkenwelke *f* 1. cucumber wilt *(comprehensive term)*; 2. [bacterial] cucumber wilt *(caused by Erwinia tracheiphila)*
gurren to coo *(pigeon)*
Gurt *m* belt, band; tether
Gurtbandförderer *m* belt (band) conveyor, conveyor belt
Gurtbecherwerk *n* belt elevator
Gürtel *m* belt; zone
gürtelartig *(bot)* zonate[d]
Gürtelplazenta *f* zonary placenta *(of carnivores)*
Gürtelreifen *m* radial[-ply] tyre

Gürtelschorf *m* **der Rübe** girth scab of beet *(caused by Streptomyces spp.)*
Gürtelung *f* zonation, zonality *(geobotany)*
~/vertikale vertical (altitudinal) zonation
Gurtförderer *m* s. Gurtbandförderer
Gurtscheibe *f* belt pulley
Gurtzeug *n* belting
Gurtschar *n* cast-iron share
güst barren, farrow, non-pregnant, empty, open *(female animal)*; fallow *(sow)*
Güstzeit *f* **bei Hase und Kaninchen** kindling-to-mating interval
Gut *n* farm, landed estate
gutartig *(vet)* benign[ant]
Gutartige Faulbrut *f (api)* European foul brood, EFB *(caused by Streptococcus pluton)*
Gutartigkeit *f (vet)* benignity
Güteansprache *f (forest)* quality rating
Güteklasse *f* grade [of quality]
Güteklassensortierung *f* quality grading
Güteminderung *f* quality loss
Guter Heinrich *m* Good King Henry, allgood, fathen, Chenopodium bonus-henricus
Güterkraftwagen *m* van, [goods] truck
~ für den Tiertransport livestock van
~/selbstladender self-loading truck, self-loader
Güterumschlag *m* goods handling (transshipment)
Güterwagen *m* wagon, waggon
Gütevorschrift *f* quality specification
Gutfeuchte *f* product moisture
Guthacke *f* final trimming *(esp. in beet growing)*
Gutsverwalter *m* [farm] bailiff
Guttapercha *f(n)* gutta-percha *(latex product esp. from Palaquium gutta)*
Guttaperchabaum *m* gutta-percha tree, Palaquium gutta
Guttation *f (bot)* guttation
guttieren to guttate
Gutverlust *m* product loss
GV *s.* 1. Großvieheinheit; 2. Geschlechterverhältnis
GWL *(Gesamtwuchsleistung)* s. Gesamtzuwachs
gymnokarp *(bot)* gymnocarpous, naked-fruited
gymnosperm *(bot)* gymnospermous
Gymnosperme *f* gymnosperm *(division Gymnospermae)*
gymnospermisch gymnospermous
gynandrisch *(bot, zoo)* gynandrous
gynandromorph *(bot, zoo)* gynandromorphic
Gynandromorphie *f*, **Gynandromorphismus** *m* gynandromorphism
Gynogenese *f (zoo)* gynogenesis
gynogenetisch gynogenetic
Gynophor *m (bot)* gynophore
~ der Erdnußpflanze peg
Gynospore *f (bot)* megaspore
Gynostegium *n (bot)* gynostegium
Gynostemium *n* gynostemium *(of orchid flowers)*

Gynözeum *n (bot)* gynoecium
Gyplure *n* gyplure *(insect attractant)*
Gyttia *f*, **Gyttja** *f (soil)* gyttja

H

ha *s.* Hektar
Haar *n* hair • **das ~ wechseln** to change hair *(game)* • **durch den Haarwechsel verlorene Haare** moult
~/borstenartiges *(bot, zoo)* seta
~/widerhakiges glochidium
Haaranalyse *f* hair analysis
Haarausfall *m* loss of hair; *(vet)* alopecia
~ beim Schwein/iodmangelbedingter hairless pig malady
Haarbalgentzündung *f (vet)* folliculitis
Haarbalgmilbe *f* 1. follicular mite *(genus Demodex)*; 2. demodectic mange mite, Demodex phylloides (suis)
Haarbalgmilbenbefall *m (vet)* demodectic mange
Haarbalgmuskel *m* arrector pili muscle
Haarballen *m (vet)* trichobezoar
Haarbirke *f* pubescent birch, Betula pubescens
Haarborstenbüschel *n (bot)* glochidium
Haarbüschel *n* tuft of hair; beard *(of turkeycock's breast)*
haaren to moult, to lose the hair
~/sich to moult
Haarfarbe *f* hair colour
Haarfeder *f* pin (stub) feather, filoplume
Haarfollikel *m* hair follicle
Haarfressen *n* trichophagy
Haarfrüchtige Balsampappel *f* black cottonwood, Populus trichocarpa
Haargefäß *n* capillary [tube]
Haargerste *f* lyme-grass, wild rye *(genus Elymus)*
Haargeschwulst *f* s. Haarballen
Haargurke *f* bur cucumber, Sicyos angulatus
Haarhainsimse *f* hairy woodrush, Luzula pilosa
Haarhygrometer *n* hair hygrometer
Haarigkeit *f* medullation *(of a fleece)*
Haarkegel *m* hair cone
Haarkleid *n* hair coat (covering), pelage *(of mammals)*
Haarlänge *f* hair length
haarlos hairless, bald
Haarlosigkeit *f* hairlessness, baldness; furlessness *(genetic defect)*
Haarmark *n* hair marrow
Haarmoos *n* haircap moss *(genus Polytrichum)*
Haarmücke *f* bibionid [fly] *(family Bibionidae)*
Haarmuskel *m* arrector pili muscle
Haarpapille *f* hair papilla
Haarpolster *n (bot)* areola
Haarriß *m* hair check (crack), hairline crack
Haarröhrchen *n* s. Kapillare
Haarsaum *m* hair fringe

Haarschaf

Haarschaf *n* hair sheep
Haarschaft *m* hair shaft
Haarschneidemaschine *f* clipper
Haarschotengras *n* mosquito grass, Bouteloua gracilis (oligostachya)
Haarseil *n (vet)* seton
haartragend *(bot, zoo)* piliferous
Haarwechsel *m* moult, pelage shedding
Haarwild *n* furred game, fur
Haarwildtier *n* game mammal
Haarwuchs *m* growth of hair • **mit vermindertem** ~ *(vet)* hypotrichotic
~/verminderter *(vet)* hypotrichosis
Haarwurm *m* hairworm *(genera Capillaria, Gordius and Mermis)*
Haarwurmbefall *m (vet)* capillariasis
Haarwurzel *f* hair root; hair-like root
Haarwurzelkrankheit *f* hairy root disease, woolly knot *(of apple-trees, caused by Agrobacterium rhizogenes)*
Habicht *m* 1. hawk *(genus Accipiter)*; 2. goshawk, Accipiter gentilis
Habichtskraut *n* hawkweed, dindle *(genus Hieracium)*
Habichtsmännchen *n* t[i]ercel
Habitat *n (ecol)* habitat
Habitat... *s. a.* Biotop...
Habitatdestruktion *f* habitat destruction
Habitaterhaltung *f* habitat conservation
Habitatinsel *f* habitat island
Habitatselektion *f*, **Habitatspezialisation** *f* habitat selection
Habitatverbesserung *f* habitat improvement
Habitatzerstörung *f* habitat destruction
Habituation *f* habituation
habituell habitual
Habitus *m* habit, appearance, life form
Hachse *f (slaught)* hock; knuckle (shank) of veal
Hackamore *f (Am)* hackamore *(bridle)*
Hackbau *m* hoe farming (culture)
Hackbauer *m* hoe farmer
Hackbeil *n* chopper
Hackblatt *n* hoe[ing] blade, hoe
Hacke *f* hoe, mattock; pick
~ **mit Zacken** prong hoe
~/zweizinkige forked hoe
hacken 1. to hoe, to hack *(soil)*; 2. to chop, to chip, to hog *(e.g. vegetables, wood)*; 3. to peck, to pick
~/manuell to hand-hoe
~/mit der Ziehhacke to scuffle
~/von Hand to hand-hoe
Hacken *n* 1. hoeing; 2. chopping; chipping, hogging; 3. pecking
~/zwischenreihiges inter-row hoeing
Hackenstiel *m* pick handle
Hacker *m* chopper, chipper, chipping machine, hog[ger], hogging machine, hammer hog
Hackfräse *f* motor (rotary) hoe
Hackfrucht *f* root [crop], row (tilled) crop
Hackfrucht[an]bau *m* row crop husbandry
Hackfruchtdrillmaschine *f* root drill, row [crop] seeder
Hackfruchternte *f* root harvest
Hackfruchterntemaschine *f* root [crop] harvester, rooter
Hackfruchtmuser *m* root and tuber crop masher
Hackfruchtreißer *m* root chopper
Hackfruchtsämaschine *f s.* Hackfruchtdrillmaschine
Hackfruchtstriegel *m* saddle-back harrow, ridge weeder
Hackfruchtvereinzelungsgerät *n* row crop thinner
Hackfruchtwaschmaschine *f* root crop washer
Hackkultur *f s.* Hackbau
Hackmaschine *f* 1. hoeing machine, mechanical hoe, tillivator; 2. *s.* Hacker
Hackmesser *n* 1. hoe blade; 2. chopping knife, chopper
Hackney *m* Hackney, Hack *(horse breed)*
Hackordnung *f* peck[ing] order *(animal behaviour)*
Hackrahmen *m* hoeing tool bar
~/lenkbarer steerage hoe
Hackschnitzel *n* chip
Hackschnitzel *npl* chips, chippings
Hackschnitzelentrindung *f* chip debarking
Hackschnitzelfahrzeug *n* chip truck (van)
Hackschnitzelherstellung *f* chipping
Hackschnitzelmaschine *f* chipping (hogging) machine, chipper
Hackschnitzelrohrleitung *f* chip pipeline
Hackschnitzelvollerntemaschine *f* feller-chipper
Häcksel *n(m)* chop, chaff
Häckselaggregat *n* chopping assembly
häckselartig chaffy
Häckselauswerfer *m* chaff ejector
Häckselbank *f* straw-cutting bench
Häckseldrusch *m* chop threshing
Häckseldruschanlage *f* chop-thresher plant
Häckselgebläse *n* chaff blower
Häckselgut *n* chopped material, chop, chaff
Häckselheu *n* chopped hay
Häckselladewagen *m* pick-up chopping trailer
Häcksellänge *f* chop length
Häckselmaschine *f* chopper, [chaff-]cutter, chaff-cutting machine; forage cutter; shredder; straw-cutting machine
Häckselmesser *n* [chaff-]chopping knife
häckseln to chop, to chaff
Häckselstroh *n* chopped straw
Häckseltrommel *f* chopping (shredding) cylinder
Häckselverteiler *m* chaff distributor
Häcksler *m s.* Häckselmaschine
Hackspäne *mpl* chips, chippings
Hackspänezerkleinerer *m* chip disintegrator
Hackstreu *f (forest)* chat litter
Hackwald *m* coppice with field crops
Hackwaldbetrieb *m*, **Hackwaldwirtschaft** *f* system of coppice with field crops

Hackwirtschaft *f s.* Hackbau
Hadenvirus *n* bovine parvovirus
Haematokrit *m* haematocrit
Haemophilus-gallinarum-Infektion *f* infectious coryza of chickens (poultry)
Haemophthalmus *m (vet)* haemophthalmos
Hafer *m* 1. oat, oats *(genus Avena)*; 2. [common, cultivated] oat, corn *(in Scotland and Ireland)*, Avena sativa
Haferabspitzmaschine *f* oat clipper
Haferälchen *n s.* Haferzystenälchen
Haferflocken *fpl* oat flakes, rolled (flail) oats
Haferflugbrand *m* loose smut of oat[s] *(caused by Ustilago avenae)*
Hafergrobmehl *n* round meal, grits, corn meal *(Scotland, Ireland)*
Hafergrütze *f* oat groats, grits
Haferhäcksel *m* oat chaff
Haferheu *n* oat hay
Haferkasten *m* oat bin
Haferkirschenlaus *f* bird cherry[-oat] aphid, apple bud aphid, oat aphis, Rhopalosiphum padi
Haferkleie *f* oat bran
Haferkorn *n* oat [grain]
Haferkronenrost *m* crown rust of oat[s], oat crown rust *(caused by Puccinia coronata)*
Haferlaus *f s.* Haferkirschenlaus
Hafermalz *n* oat malt, malted oat
Hafermehl *n* oatmeal, oat flour, ground oats, meal *(Scotland)*
Haferpflaume *f* [wild] damson, damask plum, bullace, Prunus domestica ssp. insititia
Haferprotein *n* oat protein
Haferquetsche *f* oat crusher
Haferrispe *f* oat panicle
Haferschälgang *m* oat huller
Haferschrot *n s.* Hafergrobmehl
Haferschwarzrost *m* oat stem rust *(caused by Puccinia graminis f.sp. avenae)*
Hafersilage *f* oat silage
Haferspreu *f* oat chaff
Haferstärke *f* oat starch
Haferstroh *n* oat-straw
Haferstrohhäcksel *m* oat-straw chaff
Haferwildart *f* wild oat[s] *(comprehensive term)*
Haferwurz[el] *f* salsify, salsafy, vegetable oyster, Tragopogon porrifolius
Haferzystenälchen *n* cereal cyst nematode, oat cyst (root) eelworm, Heterodera avenae
Haflinger *m* Hafling [mountain Pony] *(breed)*
haften to stick, to adhere
Haften *n* **der Frucht [am Baum]** persistence of fruit
Haftfähigkeit *f* adhesiveness
~/anfängliche initial retention *(of plant protectants)*
Haftmittel *n* adhesive [agent], sticker
Haftscheibe *f* appressorium *(of parasitic fungi)*
Haftung *f* adhesion *(e.g. of soil constituents)*
Haftwasser *n (soil)* imbibition[al] moisture, imbibed (retained) water

Hagebuche *f s.* Hainbuche
Hagebutte *f* [rose-]hip *(false fruit of Rosaceae)*
Hagebuttenstachelbeere *f* prickly gooseberry, Ribes cynosbati
Hagel *m* hail
Hagelbekämpfung *f* hail control
Hagelkorn *n* hail-stone
hageln to hail
Hagelschaden *m* hail damage (injury)
Hagelschauer *m* hail shower (squall)
Hagelschlag *m* hail[-storm]
Hagelschnur *f* chalaza, gallature, tread *(of bird's egg)*
Hagelsturm *m* hail-storm
Hagelversicherung *f* hail insurance
~ für Ernteerzeugnisse crop insurance against hail
HAH *s.* Hämagglutinationshemmungstest
Hahn *m* 1. cock, *(Am)* rooster; 2. *s.* Feldhahn
~/Kleiner *s.* Birkhahn
Hähnchen *n* cock[erel]
Hähnchenküken *n* cockerel chick
Hahnendorn *m s.* Hahnenspornweißdorn
Hahnenfuß *m* crowfoot, crow's-foot, buttercup, kingcup, ranunculus *(genus Ranunculus)*
Hahnenfußgewächse *npl* crowfoot family *(family Ranunculaceae)* **die ~ betreffend** ranunculaceous
Hahnenkamm *m* 1. *(zoo)* [cocks]comb; 2. *(bot)* [common] cockscomb, [crested] celosia, Celosia argentea var. cristata; 3. esparcet, [common, double-cut] sainfoin, saintfoin, cockshead, Onobrychis viciifolia
~ des Hornstrahls (Strahls) frog stay *(of hoof)*
Hahnenschritt *m s.* Hahnentritt 2.
Hahnenspornweißdorn *m* cockspur [hawthorn], Crataegus crus-galli
Hahnentritt *m* 1. tread, cicatricle, blastodisk *(of bird's egg)*; 2. *(vet)* spring-halt, string-halt *(of horse)*
HAHT *s.* Hämagglutinationshemmungstest
Hain *m* grove, small wood
Hainblume *f* baby-blue-eyes, Nemophila menziesii
Hainbuche *f* 1. hornbeam *(genus Carpinus)*; 2. [European] hornbeam, hornbeech, horse (hurst) beech, hardbeam, yoke elm, Carpinus betulus
Hainbuchenahorn *m* hornbeam maple, Acer carpinifolium
Hainbuchenholz *n* hornbeam
Hainrispe *f*, **Hainrispengras** *n* wood meadow-grass, Poa nemoralis
Hainschnecke *f* banded snail, Cepaea (Helix) nemoralis
Hainsimse *f* 1. woodrush *(genus Luzula)*; 2. field woodrush, Luzula campestris
Häkchen *n (bot, zoo)* hamulus
Haken *m* 1. hook; *(bot, zoo)* uncus, hook; 2. hack *(for resin-tapping)* • **~ schlagen** to double [back] *(hare, rabbit)* • **mit dem ~ angeln** to hook

hakenförmig

hakenförmig *(bot, zoo)* hamate[d], uncinate
Hakenfortsatz *m (bot, zoo)* hamulus
Hakenkaktus *m* strawberry cactus, Hamatocactus setispinus
Hakenkiefer *f* 1. Spanish pine, Pinus uncinata; 2. erect mountain pine, Pinus uncinata ssp. uncinata
Hakenkopf *m (bot)* dshusgun *(genus Calligonum)*
Hakenkugel *f* onc[h]osphere *(of true tapeworms)*
Hakenpflug *m* stick plough
Hakenstange *f* floating hook, pike pole, clip
Hakenwurm *m* hookworm *(family Ancylostomatidae)*
Hakenwurmbefall *m*, **Hakenwurmkrankheit** *f (vet)* hookworm [disease]
Hakenzahn *m* 1. canine [tooth]; tush *(horse's dentition)*; 2. s. Hauer
Hakenzange *f (vet)* hook forceps
hakig *(bot, zoo)* uncate, uncinate
Halacrinat *n* halacrinate *(fungicide)*
Halbantigen *n* hapten
Halbblütenstadium *n* half-bloom stage *(forage cropping)*
Halbblutpferd *n* half-breed [horse], cocktail
~/kleines cob
Halbbrache *f* half-fallow
Halbbruder *m* half-brother *(animal breeding)*
Halbdaune *f* semiplume
Halbdecken *fpl (ent)* hemelytra
halbdurchlässig semipermeable
Halbdurchlässigkeit *f* semipermeability
halbentrinden to bark partially
halbentrindet half-barked
halbessentiell semiessential *(e.g. an amino-acid)*
Halbfaulschlamm *m (soil)* gyttja
Halbfenster *n* half-light
halbfeucht semimoist, semihumid
Halbflügler *m (ent)* hemipteran, bug *(order Hemiptera)*
halbflüssig semiliquid
Halbfußschar *n* half shovel (sweep)
halbgefiedert *(bot)* semipinnate
halbgeflügelt *(bot)* semialate
halbgeschält half-barked
Halbgeschwister *n* half-sib[ling] *(animal breeding)*
Halbgeschwisterkorrelation *f* half-sib correlation
Halbgeschwisterkreuzung *f* half-sib mating
Halbgeschwisterselektion *f* half-sib selection
Halbheu *n* haylage
Halbholz *n* half-round wood
halbimmergrün semi-evergreen, semideciduous
Halbkettentraktor *m* half-track tractor
Halbkonserve *f* preserve
Halbkugelpolsterpflanze *f* hemispheric cushion plant
halbmondförmig *(bot, zoo)* lunate
halbnomadisch seminomadic
Halbparasit *m* s. Halbschmarotzer
halbpflügen to rafter, to rib

Halbraupe *f* half-track
Halbraupenmähdrescher *m* half-track combine, semicrawler combine
Halbraupenschlepper *m*, **Halbraupentraktor** *m* half-track tractor
halbreif half-ripe, semimature
halbringporig semiring-porous *(wood)*
Halbschatten *m* half shade
Halbschattenbaumart *f* semitolerant timber tree species
Halbschattenkamp *m (forest)* bush nursery
Halbschattenpflanze *f* semishade plant
halbschmarotzend semiparasitic, hemiparasitic, parasitoid
Halbschmarotzer *m* semiparasite, hemiparasite, parasitoid
Halbschur *f* twice-yearly shearing
Halbschurwolle *f* double-clip wool
Halbschwester *f* half-sister *(animal breeding)*
Halbseitenlähmung *f (vet)* hemiplegia
halbseitig *(bot, zoo)* semilateral
Halbstamm *m* half-standard [fruit-]tree
halbstationär semipermanent
Halbstrauch *m* subshrub, half-shrub, semishrub, suffrutex
halbstrauchartig suffrutescent
halbstrauchig suffruticose, suffruticous
halbtrocken semidry; semiarid *(climate)*
halbtropisch semitropical
halbverdaut semidigested
Halbwert[s]zeit *f* half-life
halbwild semiwild
Halbwüste *f* semidesert
Halbwüstenboden *m* semidesert soil
~/brauner burozem, brown soil of semideserts
~/grauer serozem
Halbzellstoff *m* semichemical pulp
Halbzellstoffaufschluß *m* semichemical pulping
Halbzwerg *m* semidwarf *(plant breeding)*
Halbzwergsommerweizen *m* semidwarf spring wheat
Halbzwergsorte *f* semidwarf cultivar
Halbzwergwinterweizen *m* semidwarf winter wheat
Haldane-Regel *(gen)* Haldane's rule
Halde *f* dump, tip, heap
Haldenaufforstung *f* tip afforestation
Haldenbegrünung *f* tip afforestation
Halfa *f* alfa [grass], esparto [grass], Stipa tenacissima
Halfbred[schaf] *n* Halfbred *(sheep cross-breed of Border Leicester and Cheviot)*
Halfter *m(n)* halter, headstall • **~ anlegen** to halter [up]
halftern to halter [up]
Halfterriemen *m* halter-rope
Halisterese *f (vet)* halisteresis, decalcification of bones
Halit *m* halite, rock-salt

Hallentrocknung f barn curing *(e.g. of tobacco)*
Hallimasch[pilz] m honey (shoe-string) fungus, honey agaric, *(Am)* oak fungus, Armillariella (Armillariella) mellea
Halloysit m halloysite *(clay mineral)*
Halm m culm, ha[u]lm, stalk, stem *(of grasses)* • **auf dem ~** in the blade • **einen ~ bilden** to culm • **Getreide auf dem ~ verkaufen** to sell the standing crop
~/blütentragender culm
Halmbrecher m [hay] crusher, hay bruiser
Halmbruch m stalk breakage
Halmbruchkrankheit f eyespot, strawbreaker, stem break *(of cereals, caused by Pseudocercosporella herpotrichoides)*
~ des Weizens foot-rot of wheat *(caused by Pseudocercosporella herpotrichoides)*
Halmfestigkeit f stem solidness, strength of culm
Halmfliege f 1. gout-fly *(family Chloropidae)*; 2. grass stem-fly, yellow swarming fly, Thaumatomyia notata
Halmförderschnecke f table auger
Halmfrucht f grain (cereal, straw) crop
Halmfutter n grass
Halmfuttersilage f stalk silage
Halmheber m 1. crop lifter; 2. hypocotyl, rhizome *(of a cereal plant)*
Halmhöhe f culm height
Halmknoten m stem node
Halmpflanze f culmiferous plant
Halmquetscher m crimper *(hay processing equipment)*
Halmrost m *(phyt)* stem rust *(caused by Puccinia graminis)*
Halmschnecke f s. Halmförderschnecke
Halmstreckung f culm elongation, stem extension
Halmteiler m [crop] divider, haulm-parting device, stalk deflector *(of grain harvesters)*
Halmteilerspitze f divider head (tip), dial
halmtragend culmiferous
Halmverkürzer m retardant, culm stabilizer
Halmwespe f stem-boring saw-fly *(family Cephidae)*
Halmwuchshöhe f culm height
Halokortin n mineralcorticoid
halomorph *(soil)* halomorphic
halophil halophilous
Halophyt m halophyte
Halophytenvegetation f halophytic vegetation
Haloserie f halosere, halarch succession *(plant ecology)*
Halostachin n halostachine *(alkaloid)*
Halosteroid n mineralcorticoid
Halothan n halothane *(anaesthetic)*
Halothantest m halothane test *(for examining the stress-susceptibility of pigs)*
Halothrin n halothrin *(insecticide)*
Haloxon n haloxon *(anthelminthic)*
Haloxydin n haloxydine *(herbicide)*

Hals m neck, cervix, collum; scrag *(of sheep carcass)* • **~ geben** to give tongue *(hunter's language)*
~/verkehrter ewe neck *(growth anomaly of horses and dogs)*
Halsarterie f cervical artery
Halsband n collar; neck band *(animal marking)* • **das ~ anlegen** to leash *(a dog)*
halsbandförmig *(bot, zoo)* moniliform
Halsbandsender m radiocollar
Halsbogen m ox-bow *(of an ox-yoke)*
Halsbuckel m neck (cervico-thoracic) hump *(of the zebu)*
Halsbuckelzebu n neck-humped zebu
Halsbügel m neck bow (collar)
Halsfangrahmen m catching yoke *(cowshed installation)*
Halsfäule f *(phyt)* neck rot
~ der Zwiebel onion neck rot, neck rot of onion *(caused by Botrytis allii)*
~ des Salates lettuce drop *(caused by Sclerotinia sclerotiorum)*
Halsfeder f neck feather, hackle
Halskranz m **für Hunde** *(vet)* Elizabethan collar
Halsmarke f neck tag *(animal marking)*
Halsrahmen m 1. neck bow (collar), yoke; bail *(parlour installation)*; 2. s. Halsfangrahmen
Halsschlagader f carotid [artery]
Halsstück n *(slaught)* neck
Halsung f dog-collar *(hunter's language)*
Halswirbel m cervical vertebra *(animal anatomy)*
~/erster atlas
~/zweiter axis
Halsverkrümmung f *(vet)* torticollis
haltbar 1. lasting, durable; strong, solid; 2. non-perishable *(food)* • **~ machen** to preserve, to conserve; to cure
Haltbarkeit f durability; keeping quality, keepability, storage stability (resistance) *(of food)*
Haltbarkeitsdauer f shelf-life
Haltbarmachung f preservation
~/begrenzte short-term preservation
Halteapparat m stay apparatus *(animal anatomy)*
Haltekraft retention force (strength)
~ zwischen Frucht und Fruchtstiel fruit retention
halten to keep, to rear *(livestock)*
~/im Käfig to cage
~/im Stall to house, to stable
~/im Zwinger to kennel *(dog)*
~/in Bewegung to exercise *(e.g. a breeding animal)*
~/in teilweiser Freiheit to hack *(falcon)*
~/sich to keep *(e.g. food, flowers)*
~/Sommerruhe to aestivate
~/Winterschlaf to hibernate
Halter m keeper
Hälter m *(pisc)* stew
Haltere f *(ent)* haltere, balancer
Haltezahn m canine [tooth]

Haltung

Haltung f keep, keeping, management (of livestock)
~ in Gruppenbuchten group penning
Haltungsbedingungen fpl housing conditions
Häm n haem, protohaem
Hämadsorptionsreaktion f haemadsorption reaction
Hämagglutination f haemagglutination
Hämagglutinationshemmungstest m haemagglutination inhibition test
Hämagglutinationsreaktion f haemagglutination test
~/indirekte (passive) passive haemagglutination test
Hämagglutinationstest m haemagglutination test
Hämagglutinin n haemagglutinin
Hämalaun m haematoxylin (plant dye)
Hämatemesis f (vet) haematemesis
Hämatit m haematite (non-clay mineral)
Hämato... s. a. Hämo...
Hämatokrit m 1. haematocrit (instrument); 2. s. Hämatokritwert
Hämatokritbestimmung f packed cell method
Hämatokritwert m haematocrit, packed cell volume, PCV
Hämatologie f haematology
hämatologisch haematological
Hämatom n (vet) haematoma
Hämatopoese f haemato[poie]sis, haemopoiesis, blood formation
hämatopoetisch haematopoietic
Hämatose f s. Hämatopoese
Hämatothorax m (vet) haemothorax
Hämatoxylin n haematoxylin (plant dye)
Hämatozele f (vet) haematocele
Hämaturie f (vet) haematuria
Hamburger Huhn n Hamburg (chicken breed)
Hämiglobin n methaemoglobin
Hämiglobinämie f (vet) methaemoglobinaemia
Hämin n haemin, protohaemin
Hammel m 1. wether, wedder; 2. s. Hammelfleisch
~ vor der ersten Schur f hogg[et]
hammelbeinig calf-kneed (anomalous position of forelegs)
Hammelfleisch n [wether] mutton
Hammelherde f wether flock
Hammelkeule f leg of mutton, gigot
Hammellamm n wether lamb
Hammelmast f wether fattening
Hammelrücken m saddle of mutton
Hammeltalg m mutton tallow (fat)
Hammer m 1. hammer; 2. malleus (animal anatomy)
Hammermühle f hammer mill
Hammerstrauch m bastard jasmin[e] (genus Cestrum)
Hämo... s. a. Hämato...
Hämoangiom n (vet) haemoangioma

hämochemisch haemochemical
Hämodilution f (vet) haemodilution
Hämodynamometer n blood-pressure manometer
Hämoglobin n haemoglobin, (Am) hemoglobin, Hb
Hämoglobinausscheidung f im Harn s. Hämoglobinurie
Hämoglobinurie f (vet) haemoglobinuria
~/bazilläre (seuchenhafte) babesiasis, babesiosis, red-water [disease]
Hämokultur f blood culture (bacteriology)
Hämolymphe f haemolymph
Hämolyse f haemolysis
Hämolysin n haemolysin
hämolytisch haemolytic
Hämonchose f (vet) haemonchosis
Hämopexin n haemopexin (globulin)
Hämophilie f (vet) haemophilia
Hämopoetin n intrinsic factor (enzyme, mucoprotein)
Hämoptoe f (vet) pulmonary haemorrhage
Hämorrhagie f (vet) haemorrhage, bleeding
Hämorrhoide f (vet) haemorrhoid
Hämosiderin n haemosiderin
Hämosit m blood parasite
Hämostase f haemostasis
Hämothorax m (vet) haemothorax
Hämotoxin n haemotoxin
Hämozyt m haemocyte, blood-cell, blood corpuscle
Hämozytometer n haemocytometer
Hampshire n s. 1. Hampshireschwein; 2. Hampshireschaf
Hampshireschaf n Hampshire [Down] (sheep breed)
Hampshireschwein n Hampshire (pig breed)
Hamster m [European] hamster, Cricetus cricetus
Hamulus m (bot, zoo) hamulus
Hand f hand • **von ~** by hand
Handabfüllung f hand filling
Handarbeit f handiwork, manual work
Handbeil n hatchet
Handbestäubung f hand-pollination (plant breeding)
Handbetätigung f actuation by hand (of controls)
Handbodensonde f hand-held soil penetrometer
Handbremse f hand (parking) brake
Handdibbelmaschine f, **Handdrillmaschine** f hand seed drill, hand seeder
Handeinlage f hand feeding (e.g. of a planting machine)
Handelsdünger m [commercial, artificial] fertilizer, artificial manure
Handelshybridsaatgut n hybrid seed of commerce, commercial hybrid seed
Handelsmilch f market milk
Handelspflanzgut n commercial seed
Handelssaatgut n commercial seed
Handelssorte f commercial variety

Handelssortiment *n* merchantable assortment *(of timber)*
handelsüblich merchantable, saleable *(e.g. standing timber)*
Handelsweizen *m* commercial wheat
Handentfahnung *f* hand detasseling *(maize breeding)*
Handernte *f* hand picking
Handfangnetz *n (pisc)* landing-net
Handfettpresse *f* hand-push grease gun
handförmig *(bot)* palmate[d], palmatiform
~/geteilt palmatipartite, palmately parted
Handfütterung *f* hand feeding
Handgalopp *m* hand-gallop
Handgas *n*, **Handgashebel** *m* hand engine speed control
Handgegenzugsäge *f* double-handed saw, two-man handsaw
Handgerät *n* hand tool
Handgrubber *m* hand cultivator
Handhabe *f* nib *(of a sickle or scythe)*
Handhabung *f* handling
Handhacke *f* hand hoe
Handhäufler *m* hand ridger
Handhubwagen *m* hand lift [platform] truck
Handicap *n*, **Handikap** *n* 1. handicap *(equestrian sport)*; 2. handicap [race]
handikapen to handicap
Handikapper *m* handicapper
Handkarre *f*, **Handkarren** *m* hand cart, barrow
Handkäse *m* hand cheese
Handkiste *f* flat
Handkontrolle *f* **auf Glut** feeling for fire *(forest fire control)*
Handkrümler *m* crumbling tool *(gardening equipment)*
Handkultivator *m* hand cultivator
Handlenkung *f* hand steering
Handmelken *n* hand milking
Handnachgemelk *n* hand strippings
handnervig *(bot)* palmate[d], palmatiform
Handpalettenwagen *m* hand pallet truck
Handpflücke *f* hand picking
Handpflug *m* hand plough
Handpumpe *f* hand pump
Handrasenmäher *m* hand mower
Handrechen *m* hand rake
Handrefraktometer *n* hand refractometer
Handsaat *f* hand sowing, sowing by hand
Handsäge *f* handsaw
Handsägerät *n* hand seed drill, hand seeder
Handsämaschine *f* hand sowing machine
~/geschobene drill barrow
Handschere *f* hand shear, clipper[s] *(for sheepshearing)*
Handschleifmaschine *f* hand grinder
Handschur *f* hand shearing, shearing by hand
Handselektion *f* roguing
Handsichel *f* hand sickle

Handspritze *f* hand[-operated] sprayer
Handsprühgerät *n* hand-[operated] sprayer
Handstäubegerät *n* hand duster
Handveredelung *f* bench grafting
Handwerk *n*/**ländliches** rural craft
Handwerkerbock[käfer] *m (ent)* sawyer *(genus Monochamus)*
Handwerkszeug *n* hand tool
Handwinde *f* monkey winch
Handwurzel *f* wrist, carpus
Handwurzelgelenk *n* wrist
Handwurzelknochen *m* carpal bone
Handzerstäuber *m* s. Handsprühgerät
Hanf *m* 1. hemp, cannabis *(genus Cannabis)*; 2. s. Echter Hanf
Hanfanbau *m* hemp farming
Hanferntemaschine *f* hemp harvester
Hanffaser *f* hemp, harl[e]
Hanfnessel *f* 1. hemp-nettle *(genus Galeopsis)*; 2. [dawny] hemp-nettle, day (flowering) nettle, Galeopsis tetrahit
Hanfsamen *m* hempseed
Hanfschrot *m* coarse hemp meal
Hanfseide *f (bot)* great dodder, Cuscuta europaea
Hanfstreifenvirus *n* hemp streak virus
Hanftod *m (bot)* hemp (branched) broomrape, Orobanche ramosa
Hanfweide *f* common (velvet) osier, basket willow (osier), Salix viminalis
Hanfzopf *m* twisted hemp
Hang *m* slope
Hangarbeit *f* operation on slopes, hillside operation
Hangausgleichsvorrichtung *f* slope compensation, hillside conversion kit
Hangbearbeitungsgrenze *f* limit to cultivation of slopes
Hangberieselung *f* contour flooding, surface irrigation of slopes
Hangcatena *f (soil)* toposequence
Hängebahn *f* overhead rail conveyor, overhead carrier (runway); monorail trolley *(esp. in glasshouses)*
Hängebahnförderer *m* overhead rail conveyor
Hängebirke *f* European [white] birch, weeping birch, Swedish (white, silver) birch, Betula pendula (alba, verrucosa)
Hängebrett *n* hanging board (shelf) *(in glasshouses)*
Hängebuche *f* [green] weeping beech, Fagus sylvatica cv. pendula
Hängeetikett *n* hang-along
Hängeeuter *n* pendulous udder
Hängefichte *f* weeping spruce, Picea abies cv. viminalis
Hängeflieder *m* nodding lilac, Syringa reflexa
Hängeforsythie *f* weeping forsythia, Forsythia suspensa

Hängeglockenprimel 284

Hängeglockenprimel f *(bot)* moonlight sikkimensis, Primula sikkimensis
Hängegoldglocke f *(bot)* big merrybells, Uvularia grandiflora
Hängegurt m *(vet)* hammock
Hängekorb m hanging basket
Hängekropf m *(vet)* crop-bound
Hängende Segge f pendulous sedge, Carex pendula
Hängendes Ampelkraut n wandering jew, inch plant, Zebrina pendula, Tradescantia zebrina
~ **Leimkraut** n *(bot)* nodding (drooping) catchfly, Silene pendula
Hängeohr n lop-ear, drooping ear
hängeohrig lop-eared
Hängepflanze f hanging plant
Hänger m 1. *(forest)* hang-up tree, lodged tree, widow-maker; 2. s. Anhänger
Hangerosion f slope erosion
Hängetopfpflanze f hanging plant
Hängezeug n *(vet)* hammock, sling
Hanggraben m contour (hillside) ditch
Hanggrabenbewässerung f contour ditch irrigation
Hanggrasland n slope pasture
Hangklima n slope climate
Hanglage f sloping (slopy) site, exposure, aspect
Hangmähdrescher m hillside combine [harvester]
Hangmoor n hanging bog
Hangneigung f slope gradient
Hangneigungsgruppe f, **Hangneigungsklasse** f *(soil)* slope class
Hangneigungswinkel m angle of slope
Hangrieselung f s. Hangberieselung
Hangrutsch m landslip, landslide, earth slide
Hangschlepper m slope (hillside) tractor, self-levelling tractor
Hangtauglichkeit f permissible hillside slope
Hangüberstauung f mountain flooding
Hangweide f slope pasture
Hannover-Braunschweigisches Landschwein n German Pasture *(pig breed)*
Hannoveraner m, **Hannoversches Pferd** n Hanover *(horse breed)*
H-Antigen n H-antigen *(bacteriology)*
hapaxanth *(bot)* hapaxanthic, hapaxanthous, monocarpic
haploid *(gen)* haploid, monoploid
Haploide m s. Haplont
Haploidie f haploidy
haplokaulisch *(bot)* haplocaulescent
Haplont m *(gen)* haploid, haplont
Haplophase f haplophase
Haplosomie f haplosomy
haplostemon *(bot)* haplostemonous
Hapten n hapten
Haptogenmembran f fat globule membrane *(of milk)*
Haptoglobin n haptoglobin *(protein)*

Haptonastie f *(bot)* thigmonasty, haptonasty
Haptotropismus m *(bot)* thigmotropism
Hardersche Drüse f Harder's gland *(animal anatomy)*
Hardy-Weinberg-Gleichgewicht n *(gen)* Hardy-Weinberg equilibrium [principle]
Harfenstrauch m Swedish ivy *(genus Plectanthus)*
Hariana[rind] n Hariana [cattle] *(breed)*
Harke f [garden] rake, hand (garden) fork
harken to rake
Harmalan n, **Harmalin** n harmaline *(alkaloid)*
Harmelraute f harmala shrub, Peganum harmala
Harmin n harmin[e] *(alkaloid)*
harmlos harmless, innocuous *(e.g. a disease)*
harmonisch 1. harmonic *(e.g. a mean value)*; 2. harmonious *(wine)*
Harn m urine; stale *(esp. of beef and horse)*
• ~ **lassen** s. harnen
~/**embryonaler** allantoic fluid
Harnausscheidung f diuresis
~/**verminderte** oliguria
Harnbildung f uropoiesis
Harnblase f [urinary] bladder, vesica
Harnblasenentzündung f *(vet)* cystitis
Harnblasenhaarwurm m bladder worm, Capillaria plica
harnen to urinate, to micturate; to stale *(esp. horse, beef)*
Harnen n urination, micturition
Harnenergie f urine (urinary) energy
Harnflut f *(vet)* diabetes insipidus
Harngang m urachus
Harnlassen n s. Harnen
Harnleiter m ureter
Harnröhre f urethra
Harnröhrenöffnung f urethral orifice
Harnröhrenschleimdrüse f urethral gland
Harnröhrenzwiebeldrüse f bulbo-urethral gland, Cowper's gland
Harnsack m allantois, allantoic sac
Harnsäure f uric acid
Harnsperre f *(vet)* anuria
Harnstein m *(vet)* urolith, urinary calculus, bladder stone
Harnsteinkrankheit f *(vet)* urolithiasis
Harnstoff m urea, carbamide
~/**schwefelumhüllter** sulphur-coated urea, SCU
Harnstoffagar m urea agar
Harnstoffammoniumphosphat n urea ammonium phosphate
harnstoffausscheidend urosecretory
Harnstoffausscheidung f urea excretion
Harnstoffbiosynthese f urea biosynthesis
Harnstoffderivat n urea derivative
Harnstoffdosierer m urea applicator
Harnstoff-Formaldehyd-Kombinationsdüngemittel n urea-form *(fertilizer)*
Harnstoffherbizid n urea herbicide
Harnstoffkonzentrat n urea concentrate

Harnstoffphosphat *n* urea phosphate
harnstoffspaltend ureolytic
Harnstoffspaltung *f* ureolysis
Harnstoffstickstoff *m* urea nitrogen
Harnstoffsynthese *f* urea synthesis
Harnstofftoxizität *f* urea toxicity
Harnstoffzyklus *m* urea cycle, ornithine[-arginine] cycle, Krebs-Henseleit pathway *(biochemistry)*
Harnsystem *n*, **Harntrakt** *m* urinary tract (system)
harntreibend diuretic
Harnuntersuchung *f* urinalysis
Harnvergiftung *f* uraemia
Harnwinde *f (vet)* lumbago *(of horses)*
Harnzucker *m (vet)* glucosuria, glycosuria
Harnzwang *m (vet)* strangury, dysuria
~/schmerzhafter tenesmus
Harrier *m* harrier *(dog breed)*
Harringtons Kopfeibe *f* 1. Harrington plum yew, Cephalotaxus harringtonia; 2. cow's-tail pine, Cephalotaxus harringtonia var. drupacea
Harsch[schnee] *m* crusted snow, frozen snow crust
hart 1. hard *(as materials)*; 2. hardy *(e.g. plants)*
• **~ werden** to harden [off], to cure *(e.g. resin)*
Hartballenkrankheit *f* hard pad [disease] *(of dogs)*
Hartbast *m* hard bast
hartblättrig hard-leaved, sclerophyllous
Hartblättrigkeit *f* sclerophylly
Hartbrand *m (phyt)* covered smut *(comprehensive term)*
Härte *f* 1. hardness *(e.g. of materials)*; 2. hardiness *(of plants and animals)*
Härtegrad *m* **des Wassers** degree of water hardness
härten 1. to cure *(e.g. tree resin)*; to hydrogenate *(oils and fats)*; 2. s. abhärten
Hartfaser *f* hard fibre
Hartfäule *f (phyt)* hard (dry) rot
~ der Kartoffel potato early blight, early blight [disease] *(caused by Alternaria solani)*
Hartgrieß *m* semolina
Hartgrießmühle *f* semolina mill
Hartgußschar *n* chilled [cast-iron] share
Hartholz *n* hardwood
Hartkalkhorizont *m (soil)* lime pan
Hartkäse *m* hard cheese
Hartlaubbaum *m* hardwood [tree]
Hartlaubgebüschformation *f* sclerophyllous shrub formation; maquis *(of mediterranean areas)*
Hartlaubgewächs *n*, **Hartlaubpflanze** *f* sclerophyll, sclerophyte
Hartlaubwald *m* sclerophyllous (hard-leaved) forest
Hartmais *m* flint (yankee) maize, *(Am)* flint corn, Zea mays convar. vulgaris
hartmetallbestückt [hard-]tipped *(e.g. a sawtooth)*
Hartpolstervegetation *f* hard cushion vegetation

Hartriegel *m* dogwood, cornel *(genus Cornus)*
Hartriegelgewächse *npl* dogwood family *(family Cornaceae)*
hartsamig hard-seeded
Hartsamigkeit *f* hard-seededness
hartschalig *(bot, zoo)* testaceous, hard-coated, hard-shell[ed]; thick-skinned *(e.g. apples)*
Hartschaligkeit *f* hard-coatedness
hartschlägig *(vet)* broken-winded
Hartschlägigkeit *f (vet)* broken wind, heave[s], roaring
hartschnaufig s. hartschlägig
Hartstrahl *m* fish-spine *(of a fin)*
Härtung *f* 1. hydrogenation *(of oils and fats)*; 2. s. Abhärten
Hartweizen *m* durum [wheat], hard (flint, macaroni) wheat, Triticum durum
Hartweizengrieß *m* [hard] semolina
Hartweizenmittelmehl *n (Am)* semolina
Hartweizenstärke *f (Am)* semolina
Harvester *m (forest)* harvester, harvesting machine, *(Am)* logger
Harz *n* resin, gum; rosin
Harzabscheider *m* resin separator, fractionator
Harzabscheidung *f* s. Harzfluß
Harzarbeiter *m* s. Harzer 1.
harzartig resinous
harzbildend resiniferous
Harzbildung *f* resin formation, resinification, resinosis
Harzbeule *f* s. Harzgalle
Harzdestillation *f* resin distillation
Harzeisen *n* barking-iron
harzen to tap [for resin], to bleed, to box, to broach
Harzen *n* 1. [resin] tapping, resin collecting (boxing), bleeding, broaching, *(Am)* chipping; 2. waxing up *(colostrum secretion of mares prior foaling)*
~ mit Doppellachten back cupping
Harzer *m* 1. resin tapper, resin collector (gatherer), dipper; 2. s. Harzer Rind
Harzer Rind (Rotvieh) *n* Harz *(cattle breed)*
Harzertrag *m* resin yield (productivity)
Harzerzeugnis *n* resin product
Harzfluß *m (phyt)* resinosis, resin bleeding (exudation), resin flow (flux)
Harzgalle *f* resin (gum) gall, resin (pitch) pocket, resiniferous cavity; black check *(esp. in Tsuga heterophylla)*
~/streifige resin streak, *(Am)* pitch streak
Harzgang *m* resin canal, resin (gum) duct
Harzgehalt *m* resin content
Harzgewinnung *f* s. Harzen
harzhaltig resinous, resiniferous, fat
Harzhaltigkeit *f* resinousness
harzig resinous, resiny
Harzkanal *m* s. Harzgang
Harzklee *m* asphalt clover, Psoralea bituminosa

Harzlachte

Harzlachte f resin blaze, face, streak *(for compounds s. under Lachte)*
harzliefernd resiniferous
Harzlücke f resin cyst
Harzöl n resin (tall, tar) oil; rosin oil
Harzprodukt n resin product
Harzproduktivität f resin productivity
harzreich resinous, rich in resin
Harzriß m 1. resin seam, pitch seam (shake) *(wood defect)*; 2. *s.* Harzungsriß
Harzrüsselkäfer m Norway spruce weevil, Pissodes harcyniae
Harzsammelgefäß n gum cup
Harzsammler m *s.* Harzer 1.
Harzsäure f resin (rosin) acid
Harzscharrer m *s.* Harzer 1.
Harzschöpfspachtel m dipper, dip iron
Harztasche f *s.* Harzgalle
Harztrichter m resin tube *(at the boreholes of bark-beetles)*
Harzung f *s.* Harzen
Harzungsriß m streak
Hase m 1. hare *(genus Lepus)*; 2. [common, brown] hare, Lepus europaeus [occidentalis]
~/männlicher buck hare
Hasel f 1. hazel, *(Am)* hazelbush tree *(genus Corylus)*; 2. [European] hazel, filbert, cob[-nut], Corylus avellana
Haselblattroller m *(ent)* hazel leaf-roller, Apoderus coryli
Haselbusch m *s.* Hasel
Haselgehölz n hazel wood
Haselhahn m hazel-cock
Haselholz n hazel, cob
Haselhuhn n 1. hazel-hen; 2. *s.* Haselwild
Haselnuß f 1. hazel[-nut], filbert; 2. *s.* Hasel
Haselnußbohrer m hazel-nut borer (weevil), nut weevil, Balaninus (Curculio) nucum
Haselnußdickkopfroller m *s.* Haselblattroller
Haselnußmilbe f filbert rust mite, Aculus comatus
Haselnußstrauch m *s.* Hasel
Haselnußzierlaus f hazel (filbert) aphid, Myzocallis coryli
Haselschildlaus f nut scale, Eulecanium tiliae, Lecanium coryli
Haselwild n hazel-grouse, Tetrastes (Bonasia) bonasia
Haselwurz f 1. asarabacca, asarum, wild ginger *(genus Asarum)*; 2. hazelwort, asarabacca, asarum, European wild ginger, Asarum europaeum
Hasenbalg m hare-skin
Hasenfleisch n hare meat
Hasenfußfarn m 1. hare's-foot fern *(genus Davallia)*; 2. hare's-foot fern, Davallia canariensis
Hasenglöckchen n wild (wood) hyacinth, Scilla non-scripta
Hasenhacke f *(vet)* curb
Hasenjagd f hare-hunting
Hasenkaninchen n Belgian hare *(breed)*

Hasenklee m hare's-foot [clover], harefoot, puss (stone, rabbit-foot) clover, Trifolium arvense
Hasenkot m crottels
Hasenlager n hare's lair, lair of hare, form
Hasenlosung f crottels
Hasenmeutenhund m harrier
Hasenohr n *(bot)* hare's-ear, thoroughwax *(genus Bupleurum)*
Hasenpest f rabbit fever, tularaemia *(caused by Francisella tularensis)*
Hasenscharte f *(vet)* hare (cleft) lip
Hasenschwanzgras n hare's-tail [grass], Lagurus ovatus
Hasenspat m *(vet)* curb
Hasenwechsel m hare run
HaSeV s. Hanfstreifenvirus
Häsin f doe[-hare]
~/tragende in-kindle rabbit
Haspel f 1. reel *(e.g. of a combine)*; 2. winch, windlass, capstan
Haspelantrieb m reel drive
Haspeldrehzahl f reel speed
Haspeldrehzahlvariator m reel speed variator
Haspelfinger m reel finger
Haspelhorizontalverstellung f reel for-and-aft adjuster
Haspelleiste f reel slat (bat), rake bar
Haspelspeiche f arm
Haspelumfangsgeschwindigkeit f reel speed
Haspelvariator m reel speed variator
Haspelverluste mpl reel losses *(combining)*
Haspelvertikalverstellung f reel adjuster
Haspelwelle f reel and line
Haspelzinke f reel tine
hassen to pounce, to swoop [down] *(raptorial bird)*
Hatch-Slack-Weg m Hatch-Slack pathway *(photosynthesis)*
haubar *(forest)* ripe for felling (cutting), mature
Haubarkeitsalter n *(forest)* felling age, [age of] maturity, exploitable (rotation) age
~/biologisches (physiologisches) physiological exploitability (maturity), physical maturity
~/physisches physical exploitability (maturity)
~/technisches technical maturity
Haubarkeitsdurchschnittszuwachs m final mean annual increment, mean annual increment at the age of rotation *(timber mensuration)*
Haubarkeitsertrag m final [harvest] yield
Haube f 1. hood; 2. *(zoo)* tegmentum; reticulum *(of ruminants)* • die ~ **aufsetzen** to hood *(falconry)*
Hauben-Pansen-Zyklus m reticulo-ruminal cycle
Haubenrinne f reticular groove *(of the ruminant stomach)*
Hauberge f *s.* Hackwald
hauen *s.* fällen
Hauer m tusk *(of wild boar's dentition)*
Häufelfräse f ridging (ridge forming) rotary cultivator

Häufelgerät *n* ridging implement, ridger, bedder, potato cultivator
Häufelhacke *f* hand ridger, Dutch (thrust) hoe
Häufelkörper *m* ridging body, ridger
häufeln to ridge [up], to hill [up], to earth [up], to mound [up]
Häufelpflug *m* ridging (ridge) plough, [cultivating] ridger, bouting (earthing-up) plough, middlebreaker, middlebuster, double-breasted plough
Häufelschar *n* ridging (hilling) share
Häufelscheibe *f* ridgiog (ridger) disk
häufen to heap [up]
Haufen *m* heap, pile, hill; couch *(floor malting)* • **in ~ ablegen** to pile *(e.g. crop products)* • **in ~ wachsend** *(bot)* acervate
~/kleiner cock, pike
Haufenführung *f* germination conditions *(malting)*
Haufensilo *m* stack silo
Haufenverteiler *m*, **Haufenverteilmaschine** *f* heap-spreading machine *(manure application)*
Haufenwolke *f* cumulus [cloud]
~/mittelhohe altocumulus
Häufige Sumpfkresse *f* marsh yellow cress, Rorippa islandica
Häufigkeit *f (biom)* frequency; incidence *(e.g. of a disease)*
~/absolute absolute frequency
~/erwartete expected frequency
~/prozentuale percentage frequency
~/relative relative frequency
Häufigkeitspolygon *n (biom)* frequency polygon
Häufigkeitstabelle *f (biom)* frequency table
Häufigkeitsverteilung *f (biom)* frequency distribution
Häufler *m s.* 1. Häufelkörper; 2. Häufelgerät
Häufung *f* [ac]cumulation
Häufungsweise *f (ecol)* sociability
Haugh-Einheit *f* Haugh unit *(determination of egg quality)*
Hauhechel *f (bot)* 1. rest-harrow, *(Am)* stay plow *(genus Ononis)*; 2. rest-harrow, Ononis spinosa
Haukerb *m s.* Fällkerb
Haumeister *m* felling (logging) foreman
Haumesser *n* machete, matchet
Haupt *n* head
Hauptabfuhrweg *m* arterial road *(timber transport)*
Hauptalkaloid *n* principal alkaloid
Hauptanbaukultur *f s.* Hauptkultur
Hauptast *m* [main] branch, limb, leader, bough
~/zentraler central leader
Hauptastringelung *f* limb-girdling
Hauptbaumart *f* main (chief) tree species, leading (ruling, principal) tree species
Hauptbestand *m* dominant crop; *(forest)* main (principal) stand
Hauptbestandteil *m* basic component
Hauptblühzeit *f*, **Hauptblüte** *f* king bloom
Hauptbodenform *f* principal soil form
Haupteffekt *m (biom)* main effect

Hauptentwässerung *f* arterial drainage
Hauptertragsperiode *f* prime
Hauptertragsstadium *n* main bearing stage *(of orchard crops)*
Haupterzeugnisse *npl*/**forstliche** major forest produce
Hauptfrucht[art] *f* 1. full-season crop; 2. *s.* Hauptkultur
Hauptfruchtform *f* perfect (sexual) stage, perfect (sexual) state *(of fungi)*
Hauptfutter *n* basal feed, basic diet
Hauptfutterfläche *f* main forage area
Hauptgallengang *m* common bile duct
Hauptgärung *f* main (primary) fermentation
Hauptgen *n* major gene, oligogene
Hauptgestell *n (forest)* main ride
Hauptgetreideart *f* main cereal
Hauptholzart *f s.* Hauptbaumart
Hauptkalkung *f* main defecation *(sugar manufacture)*
Hauptkalkungstrübe *f* defecated juice
Hauptknospe *f* main bud
Hauptkomponentenanalyse *f* principal-component analysis *(e.g. of feedstuffs)*
Hauptkörperschlagader *f* aorta
Hauptkultur *f* major (main, dominant) crop, staple crop
Hauptkupplung *f* master (drive) clutch
Hauptmaschine *f* log (head, breakdown) saw, headrig *(of a sawmill)*
Hauptmasse *f* bulk
Hauptnährstoff *m* major (primary) nutrient
Hauptnahrungsmittel *n* staple food
Hauptnutzungssatz *m (forest)* allowable final cut, allowable cut of harvesting
Hauptpunkt *m* principal point *(remote sensing)*
Hauptrad *n* master wheel *(of a sowing machine)*
Hauptreihe *f*/**Schimper-Braunsche** *(bot)* Schimper and Braun series, Fibonacci series
Hauptrippe *f* midrib, mid-vein *(of a leaf)*
Hauptschaderreger *m* major (key) pest
Hauptscheidung *f s.* Hauptkalkung
Hauptschlagader *f* aorta
Hauptschneise *f (forest)* main ride
Hauptschönung *f* main fining *(wine-making)*
Hauptschwein *m* capital wild boar, tusker
Hauptsproß *m (bot)* main shoot, lead[ing] shoot, leader
Hauptstengel *m* main stem
Hauptstrang *m* main drain
Haupttracht *f (api)* main [honey, nectar] flow
Haupttrieb *m s.* Hauptsproß
Hauptwirkung *f (biom)* main effect
Hauptwirt *m (phyt, vet)* principal (primary) host
Hauptwurzel *f* primary (main) root, tap-root
Hauptzapfwelle *f* main power take-off
Hausbock[käfer] *m* house longhorn beetle, European house-borer, oldhouse borer, Hylotrupes bajulus

Hausbüffel

Hausbüffel *m* domestic buffalo
Hausen *m (pisc)* beluga, huso, Acipenser (Huso) huso
Hausenblasenschönung *f* isinglass fining *(of wine)*
Hausente *f* [domestic] duck, Anas domestica
Hausesel *m* donkey, cuddy *(Scotland)*, Equus asinus
Hausgans *f* goose, Anser domesticus
Hausgarten *m* [home, household, domestic] garden, back-garden, yard
Hausgärtner *m* home gardener
Hausgeflügel *n* [domestic] poultry, domestic fowl
Haushaltsabfall *m* domestic waste, household refuse
Haushaltskonserve *f* domestic preserve
Haushaltskonservierung *f* home-canning
Haushaltsschädling *m* household pest
Haushuhn *n* [domestic, barnyard] fowl, [domestic] chicken, Gallus gallus [domesticus]
Haushund *m* [domestic] dog, Canis familiaris
Hauskaninchen *n* domestic rabbit
Hauskatze *f* [domestic] cat, Felis domestica
Hauskuh *f* house cow
Hausmarder *m* rock marten, Martes foina
Hausmaus *f* house (domestic) mouse, Mus musculus [domesticus]
Hausmilbe *f* furniture mite, Glycyphagus domesticus
Hausmüll *m* garbage
Hauspferd *n* horse, Equus caballus
Hauspflaume *f* garden plum, Prunus domestica
Hauspute *f* turkey, Meleagris domesticus
Hausratte *f* black (house) rat, roof (ship) rat, Rattus rattus
Hausrind *n* ox, neat, Bos taurus
Haussäugetier *n* domestic mammal
Hausschaf *n* [domestic] sheep, Ovis aries
Hausschlachtung *f* home slaughter[ing]
Hausschwein *n* [domestic] pig, hog, swine, Sus scrofa domestica
Haussperling *m* house (English) sparrow, Passer domesticus
Haustaube *f* [domestic] pigeon, Columba domestica
Haustier *n* 1. domestic[ated] animal; 2. pet [animal]
~/**bovines** beast, shin
~/**streunendes** stray
Haustierfutter *n* pet feed (food)
Haustierhandlung *f* pet shop
Haustierkot *m* mess
Haustierwerdung *f* domestication
Haustorium *n* haustorium *(of parasitic plants)*
Haustrunk *m* rape (marc) wine
Hausungeziefer *n* indoor pest
Hausveredelung *f* indoor (winter) grafting
Hauswachtel *f* [European] quail, Coturnix coturnix
Hauswirtschaft *f* housekeeping

Hauswurz *f* houseleek, joubard, sempervivum *(genus Sempervivum)*
Hausziege *f* goat, Capra hircus
Haut *f* skin, dermis; hide *(coat esp. of larger animals)*; peel *(skin esp. of fruit)* • **die ~ abziehen** to skin, to flay • **durch die ~ hindurch** percutaneous, transcutaneous • **in der ~ gelegen** intracutaneous • **in die ~ hinein** intracutaneous • **mit faltiger ~** hidebound *(store cattle)* • **neue ~ bilden** to skin *(wound healing)* • **sich mit neuer ~ bedecken** to skin *(wound healing)* • **unter der ~ [befindlich]** subcutaneous, hypodermic • **unter die ~ [erfolgend]** subcutaneous, hypodermic
~/**abgestreifte (abgeworfene)** *(zoo)* exuvia, exuvium, slough
~ **des Schwarzwildes** boar skin
~/**seröse** serosa *(animal anatomy)*
Hautabstrich *m (vet)* skin scraping
Hautausschlag *m (vet)* exanthema
Hautbindegewebegeschwulst *f (vet)* fibroepithelioma
Hautbläschen *n (vet)* blister
Hautblüte *f (vet)* efflorescence
Hautbrand *m (vet)* gangrenous dermatitis
Hautbräune *f (phyt)* [superficial] scald
Hautbremse *f* cattle grub *(genus Hypoderma)*
Häutchen *n* cuticle, membrane, film
~ **auf altem Wein** beeswing
Hautdassel *f* 1. warble [maggot], bot; cattle grub; 2. *s.* Hautdasselfliege
Hautdasselfliege *f* 1. bot[t]-fly, warble fly *(family Oestridae)*; 2. warble fly *(genus Hypoderma)*
~ **des Rentiers** reindeer warble fly, Hypoderma (Oedemagena) tarandi
Hautdrüse *f* skin (dermal) gland
Hautdurchblutung *f* skin blood flow
Hauteiterung *f* [mit Geschwürbildung] *(vet)* ecthyma
häuten to skin, to flay, to peel
~/**sich** to moult *(esp. insects)*; to slough, to exuviate *(esp. snakes)*
Hautentzündung *f (vet)* dermatitis
Hautfalte *f* skin fold
Hautfaltendicke *f* skin fold thickness
Hautfarbe *f*, **Hautfärbung** *f* skin colour
Hautflügler *m (ent)* hymenopteran *(order Hymenoptera)* • **die ~ betreffend** hymenopterous
Hautfollikelentzündung *f (vet)* folliculitis
Hautgeschabsel *n (vet)* skin scrapings
Hautgeschwulst *f (vet)* epithelioma
häutig *(bot, zoo)* tunicate[d]
Hautjucken *n (vet)* pruritus
Hautklammer *f (vet)* wound clip
Hautknötchen *n (vet)* papule
Hautkrankheit *f (vet)* skin-disease, dermatosis
Hautleishmaniose *f (vet)* oriental sore *(caused by Leishmania tropica)*
Hautmuskel *m* cutaneous (dermal) muscle
Hautödem *n (vet)* anasarca

Hautparasit *m* skin parasite
Hautpigment *n* skin pigment
Hautpilz *m* dermatophyte
Hautpilzerkrankung *f (vet)* dermatomycosis, mycodermatitis
Hautprobe *f (vet)* skin test
Hautrötung *f (vet)* erythema
Hautrotz *m (vet)* farcy
Hautschaden *m* hide damage
Hautschleim *m* skin mucus *(e.g. of fish)*
Hautschmarotzer *m* skin parasite
Hautschorfigkeit *f (vet)* scabby hip *(of chicken broilers)*
Hautschuppen *fpl (vet)* scurf
Hautschwiele *f* callosity
Hauttalg *m* skin grease, sebum [grease]
Hauttest *m (vet)* skin test
Hauttransplantation *f (vet)* skin grafting
Hauttuberkulose *f (vet)* skin tuberculosis
Haut- und Hautanhangsystem *n* integumentary system
Haut- und Kiementrübung *f*/**ansteckende** costiasis *(of fish, caused by Costia necatrix)*
Häutung *f (zoo)* moult, sloughing, skinning, exuviation, ecdysis
Häutungshormon *n* moulting hormone, ecdysone
Häutungsrest *m* slough
Hautverhärtung *f* callosity; *(vet)* scleroderma
Hautverhornung *f (vet)* hyperkeratosis
Hautwassersucht *f (vet)* anasarca
Hautwolle *f* skin (dead) wool
Hauung *f* felling operation, cutting, logging
Hauungs... *s. a.* **Fällungs...**
Hauungsanweisung *f* felling instruction (rule)
Hauungsplan *m* felling plan, plan of cuttings
Hatz *f s.* Hetzjagd
Havelmilitz *n* reed canary grass, Phalaris arundinacea
Haversscher Kanal *m* Haversian canal *(of lamellar bone)*
Haversches System *n* Haversian system, osteone *(of lamellar bone)*
Haxe *f s.* Hachse
Hb *s.* Hämoglobin
HB *s.* Holzboden
HBVzV *s.* Virus der Blauverzwergung des Hafers
HCB *s.* Hexachlorbenzen
HCC *s.* Hepatitis contagiosa canis
HCC-Virus *n* canine hepatitis virus
HCG *s.* Choriongonadotropin
HCH *s.* Hexachlorcyclohexan
Hds *s.* Handelssaatgut
Hebebock *m* lifting jack
Hebebühne *f* extension platform
Hebenetz *n (pisc)* lift net
Heber *m* siphon *(furrow irrigation)*
Heber-Überlauf *m* siphon spillway
Hebewinde *f* lifting jack
Hebezeug *n* joist

Hebezeugmast *m* standing derrick, gin pole
Hechel[maschine] *f* hackle, hatchel
hecheln 1. to hackle, to heckle, to hatchel *(flax, hemp)*; 2. to pant
Hecheln *n* [thermal] panting, thermal polypnoea
Hecht *m* 1. pike *(family Esocidae)*; 2. pike, Esox lucius
~/ausgewachsener luce
Hechtgebiß *n (vet)* parrot mouth
Hechtkopf *m* dished face *(e.g. of a horse)*
Heckanbaudrillmaschine *f* rear-mounted seed drill
Heckanbaugerät *n* rear-mounted implement
Heckanbauscheibenpflug *m* rear-mounted disk plough
Heckanbauvielfachgerät *n* rear-mounted hoe
Heckantrieb *m* rear drive
Hecke *f* 1. hedge[row]; 2. brood, hatch *(of young animals)*; covey *(of birds)* • **eine ~ anlegen** to hedge • **eine ~ [be]schneiden** to hedge • **mit einer ~ umgeben** to hedge
~ mit Graben bullfinch *(obstacle)*
~ zur Steckholzgewinnung hardwood cutting hedge
hecken to breed, to hatch
Heckenanlage *f* hedgerow planting
Heckenkälberkropf *m (bot)* rough chervil, Chaerophyllum temulum
Heckenkirsche *f* honeysuckle, bindweed, lonicera *(genus Lonicera)*
Heckenpflanze *f* hedgerow (hedging) plant, quickset
Heckenpflanzensteckling *m* quickset
Heckenpflanzung *f* hedgerow planting
Heckenrose *f* 1. hedge-rose *(comprehensive term)*; 2. dogrose, brier-rose, Rosa canina; 3. shrubby rose, Rosa corymbifera (dumetorum)
Heckenschere *f* hedge shears (trimmer), [hedge, garden] clipper
~/batteriegetriebene battery hedge trimmer
~/elektrische electric hedge trimmer
Heckenschneidemaschine *f* hedge cutter
Heckenschnitt *m* hedging
Heckensichel *f* pruning-hook
Heckenstrauch *m* hedge shrub
Heckenwickler *m* hedge (filbert) leaf-roller, oblique-banded leaf-roller, rose tortrix (twist) moth, Archips rosanus, Cacoecia rosana
Heckenwicklerlarve *f* rose worm
Heckenzwiebel *f* Welsh onion, Japanese [bunching] onion, stone (Japan) leek, Allium fistulosum
Heckklappe *f* tail gate *(of combine harvester)*
Hecklader *m* rear-loader
Heckmähwerk *n* rear-mounted mower
Heckmotor *m* rear engine
Heckschaufel *f* rear bucket
Heckschieber *m* rear-mounted dozer blade
Heckschiebesammler *m* rear-mounted buck-rake

Hederich

Hederich *m* wild radish, white charlock, runch, Raphanus raphanistrum
Heerwurm *m (ent)* beet army-worm, Spodoptera (Laphygma) exigua
Hefe *f* yeast, barm
hefeartig yeasty, yeast-like
Hefeaufziehapparat *m* yeast rousing apparatus *(brewing)*
Hefebier *n* barm beer
Hefedecke *f* yeast head *(brewing)*
Hefeeiweiß *n* yeast protein
Hefeernte *f* yeast crop
Hefeextrakt *m* yeast extract
Hefefermentation *f*, **Hefegärung** *f* yeast fermentation
Hefehydrolysat *n* yeast hydrolyzate
Hefekeller *m* yeast store
Hefekultur *f* yeast culture
Hefemykose *f (vet)* candidiasis
Hefepilz *m* yeast [fungus] *(order Saccharomycetales)*
Hefeprotein *n* yeast protein
Hefeproteinase *f* B yeast proteinase B *(enzyme)*
Heferasse *f* strain of yeast, yeast strain
Hefereinzuchtapparat *m* yeast propagator (propagating plant)
Heferibonuclease *f* yeast ribonuclease *(enzyme)*
Hefeschönung *f* yeast fining
Hefestamm *m s.* Heferasse
Hefevermehrung *f* yeast propagation
Hefewasser *n* yeast water
Hefewein *m* yeast wine
Hefezelle *f* yeast cell
hefig *s.* hefeartig
Heft *n* helve, handle *(of hand tools)*
Heften *n* tying[-up] *(wine-growing)*
~/erstes first tying
Heftende *n* butt end *(of a saw)*
Hege *f* gamekeeping, game preserving (conservation), wildlife preservation
hegen to preserve, to foster
Heger *m* gamekeeper
Hegewald *m* forest reserve, reserved forest
Hegezeit *f* close[d] season, close time, fence season, fence-month *(game management)*
Heide *f* 1. heath[land], moor[land], bent; 2. *s.* Heidekraut
Heideboden *m* heath soil
Heidegarten *m* heather (moorland) garden
Heidehonig *m* heather honey
Heidekorn *n* common buckwheat, Fagopyrum esculentum
Heidekraut *n* 1. heather, heath, ling *(genus Calluna)*; 2. [common, Scotch] heather, [common] ling, Calluna vulgaris
Heidekrautgewächse *npl* heather family *(family Ericaceae)* • **die ~ betreffend** ericaceous
Heidekraut-Kiefernwald *m* heather pinery
Heidekultur *f* heath cultivation

Heideland *n* heath[land], moor[land], bent
heidelbeerblättrig vaccinifolious
Heidelbeere *f* 1. blueberry, windberry, whortleberry, *(Am)* hucklebery *(genus Vaccinium)*; 2. bilberry, blaeberry, whortleberry, hurtleberry, Vaccinium myrtillus
Heidelbeer-Fichtenwald *m* bilberry spruce forest
Heidelbeerheide *f* bilberry heath
Heidelbeerstrauch *m* bilberry-bush
Heidelerche *f* wood-lark, Lullula arborea
Heidemoorkrankheit *f* reclamation disease, yellow (wither) tip *(of cereals due to copper deficiency)*
Heidenelke *f* meadow (maiden) pink, Dianthus deltoides
Heidenkorn *n* Tatary buckwheat, Fagopyrum tataricum
Heidepodsol *m (soil)* heath podzol
Heidschnucke *f* [German] Heath *(sheep breed)*
heilbar curable
heilen to cure, to heal [over, up]
heilend curative
Heiligenkraut *n* 1. santolina *(genus Santolina)*; 2. lavender cotton, cotton lavender, Santolina chamaecyparissus
Heiliger Feigenbaum *m* bo-tree [of the Hindus], pipal, peepul tree, Ficus religiosa
~ Sternanis *m* Japanese sacred anise tree, poison bay, Illicium anisatum
Heilimpfung *f (vet)* emergency vaccination
Heilkraut *n* [officinal, medicinal] herb
Heilkräutergarten *m* physic garden
Heilmittel *n* curative, remedy, therapeutic
Heilpflanze *f* officinal (medicinal) plant
Heilziest *m (bot)* betony, Stachys (Betonica) officinalis
Heimbereich *m (ecol)* home range
Heimchen *n* house cricket, Acheta domestica, Gryllus domesticus
Heimgarten *m s.* Hausgarten
heimisch domestic, indigenous, autochthonal, autochthonous, endemic
Heimische Seekanne *f* fringed water lily, yellow floating heart, Nymphoides peltata
Heimpflanze *f* house (indoor) plant
Heimrevier *n (ecol)* territory
Heimtier *n s.* Haustier 2.
Heinz-Ehrlich-Innenkörper *m* Heinz body *(of erythrocytes)*
Heinze *f* drying monopod
heiß sein to be at (in, on) heat *(bitch)*
Heißbelüftung *f* dryeration
Heißeisenbrand *m* hot iron brand *(for marking of livestock)*
Heißluft *f* hot air
Heißluftbehandlung *f* hot-air treatment
Heißluftsterilisator *m* hot-air sterilizer
Heißlufttrockner *m* hot-air dryer, high-temperature dryer

Heißlufttrocknung f hot-air drying, high-temperature drying
Heißmist m fermented manure
Heißmistverfahren n hot fermentation of manure
Heißnebeln n thermal spraying *(plant protection)*
Heißtrub m hot sludge (break) *(brewing)*
Heißvergärung f hot fermentation
Heißwasserbehandlung f hot-water treatment *(e.g. of seed)*
Heißwasserbeize f hot-water dressing
Heißwasserheizung f hot-water boiler system
Heißwasserspeicher m boiler
Heißwürze f hot wort *(brewing)*
Heister m(f) sapling, staddle
heizen to heat; to fire, to stoke
Heizen n **von Obstanlagen** orchard heating *(frost protection measure)*
Heizgerät n heater
Heizhaus n boiler house
Heizkanal m flue
Heizkörper m heater
Heizöl n fuel oil
Heizperiode f heating period
Heizrohr n heating pipe (tube)
Heizrohr[schienen]bahn f pipe rail system *(in greenhouses)*
Heizrohr[schienen]wagen m pipe rail trolley
Heizschlauch m heating hose
Heizstrahler m radiant heater
Heizsystem n heating system
Heizung f heating
Heizungsanlage f heating plant
Heizungsausrüstung f firing equipment
Heizungsrohr n heating pipe (tube)
Heizungssystem n heating system
Heizvorrichtung f **für Obstanlagen** orchard heater
Heizwert m calorific value
Hektar n(m) hectare, ha
Hektarertrag m per-hectare yield, yield per hectare
Hektarzähler m hectar[e]meter
Hektolitergewicht n s. Hektolitermasse
Hektolitermasse f hectolitre weight
Hektorit m hectorite *(clay mineral)*
Heldbock[käfer] m great capricorn beetle, Cerambyx cerdo
Helenenkraut n elecampane, Inula helenium
Helfervirus n *(phyt, vet)* helper virus
Heliomycin n heliomycin *(antibiotic)*
heliophil heliophilous
heliophob heliophobic
Heliophobie f photophobia
Heliophyt m heliophyte, heliophile, sun[-loving] plant
Heliosis f *(vet)* sunstroke
heliotrop s. heliotropisch
Heliotrop m *(bot)* 1. heliotrope, turnsole *(genus Heliotropium)*; 2. common heliotrope, Heliotropium arborescens (peruvianum)

heliotropisch heliotropic, phototropic
Heliotropismus m heliotropism, phototropism
Helix f 1. helix; 2. *(zoo)* helix *(genus Helix)*
Helixstruktur f helix
hell bright; light; *(bot, zoo)* lucid
Hell-Dunkel-Adaptation f dark adaptation *(of the eye)*
Helleborein n helleborein *(glycoside)*
Helleborin n helleborin *(glycoside)*
Hellfuchs m sorrel *(horse)*
Hellgrüne Zwergikade f *(ent)* potato leaf-hopper, Empoasca (Chlorita) flavescens
Helligkeit f brightness; luminosity [level] *(e.g. in a greenhouse)*
Helligkeitssehen n photopic vision *(animal physiology)*
Hellwerden n **von Holz** whitening of wood
Helmbohne f Egyptian (black) bean, dolichos (hyacinth, tonga) bean, lablab [bean], bonavist [bean], Dolichos lablab, Lablab niger (purpureus)
Helmert-Pearson-Verteilung f chi-squared [probability] distribution *(statistics)*
Helmgras n beach grass, reed *(genus Ammophila)*
Helminthe f helminth, intestinal worm, mawworm *(comprehensive term)*
Helminthiasis f s. Helminthose
Helminthizid n helminthicide, anthelmint[h]ic
Helminthologie f helminthology
Helminthose f *(vet)* helminthiasis, helminthosis
Helminthosporium-Blattfleckenkrankheit f helminthosporium leaf blotch *(of cereals, esp. caused by Cochliobolus sativus = Helminthosporium sativum)*
~ **von Mais** *(Am)* corn leaf spot *(caused by Helminthosporium carbonum)*
Helminthosporium-Fußkrankheit f common root rot *(of cereals)*
Helminthozoonose f helminthozoonosis
Helmkraut n *(bot)* skull-cap *(genus Scutellaria)*
Helophyt m helophyte, bog plant
Hemeralopie f *(vet)* hemeralopia
Hemerophyt m hemerophyte
Hemicellulase f cytase *(enzyme)*
Hemicellulose f hemicellulose, pseudocellulose, wood poly[sacchar]ose
hemicephal *(ent)* hemicephalous
Hemielytren fpl *(ent)* hemelytra
Hemikryptophyt m hemicryptophyte
hemimetabol *(ent)* hemimetabolous
Hemiparasit m hemiparasite, semiparasite, parasitoid
hemiparasitär hemiparasitic, semiparasitic, parasitoid
Hemiparese f *(vet)* hemiparesis
Hemiplegie f *(vet)* hemiplegia
Hemiptere m *(ent)* hemipteran, bug *(order Hemiptera)*
hemizygot *(gen)* hemizygous
Hemizygotie f *(gen)* hemizygosity

Hemlocktanne

Hemlocktanne *f* hemlock [fir], hemlock spruce *(genus Tsuga)*
Hemmeffekt *m* retarding effect
hemmen to inhibit, to retard
~/im Wachstum to check (to reduce) in growth, to stunt
Hemmkonzentration *f* inhibition concentration *(of an active substance)*
~/minimale minimal inhibition concentration
Hemmstoff *m* inhibitor, retardant
Hemmtest *m* inhibition assay *(microbiology)*
Hemmung *f* inhibition
~/kompetitive (konkurrierende) competition *(of enzyme reactions)*
~/korrelative correlated inhibition *(plant physiology)*
Hemmwirkung *f* inhibitory effect
Henequen[agave] *f* [white] henequen, Yucatan sisal, Agave fourcroydes
Henequenfaser *f* henequen
Hengst *m* stallion, [he-]horse, sire
~/kryptorchider cryptorchid stallion
Hengstanwärter *m* stallion-candidate
Hengstfohlen *n* colt, [male] foal
~ nach dem ersten Jahr hogget
Hengstsperma *n* stallion semen
Henlesche Schleife *f* Henle's loop *(of the nephron)*
Henna *f* henna *(dye)*
Hennastrauch *m* henna [plant], true alkanet, Lawsonia inermis (alba)
Henne *f* hen
Henne mit Küken *(bot)* piggyback plant, Tolmiea menziesii
Hennen[käfig]batterie *f* hen-battery
Hennenküken *n* pullet chick
HEOD *s.* Dieldrin
Hepar *n s.* Leber
Heparin *n* heparin
Heparinase *f* heparinase *(enzyme)*
Heparinozyt *m* mast cell
Hepatektomie *f (vet)* hepatectomy, liver removal
Hepatika *f (bot)* hepatica *(genus Hepatica)*
hepatisch hepatic
Hepatitis *f (vet)* hepatitis *(s. a. under* Leberentzündung*)*
~ contagiosa canis canine viral (virus) hepatitis, CVH
hepatogen hepatogenic
hepatolentikulär hepatolenticular
Hepatolith *m (vet)* hepatolith, hepatic calculus
Hepatom *n (vet)* hepatoma
Hepatomegalie *f (vet)* hepatomegaly, liver enlargement
Hepatopathie *f* hepatopathy, liver disease
Hepatotoxin *n* hepatotoxin
Hepatozyt *m* hepatocyte, liver cell
Heptachlor *n* heptachlor *(insecticide)*
Heptenophos *n* heptenophos *(insecticide)*
Heptose *f* heptose *(monosaccharide)*
herabhängend/welk to flag
herablaufend *(bot)* decurrent
herabstoßen *s.* hassen
heranbringen *s.* apportieren
heranfliegen to approach *(wildfowl)*
heranpirschen/sich *(hunt)* to stalk up, to approach
heranreifen to ripen, to mature
heranwachsen to grow up
heranwachsend adolescent, pubescent
heranziehen to raise, to grow *(e.g. plants)*
herausdestillieren to distil out
Herausforderung *f* challenge *(immunology)*
heraushacken to hack *(e.g. roots)*
herausheben to lift [out]
herauslösen to elute, to extract
herauspflügen to plough out
Herauspressen *n* expression *(e.g. of the afterbirth)*
Herausschneiden *n* **von Intronen** gene splicing *(genetic engineering)*
heraustretend *(bot)* excurrent
herauszüchten to breed out
herb acerb[ic], acrid, austere; harsh, sec, rough, dry *(wine)*
Herba *f* herb *(drug)*
Herbar *n* herbarium
Herbarbeleg *m* specimen
Herbarium *n* herbarium
Herbe *f*, **Herbheit** *f* acerbity, acridity, harshness; roughness, dryness *(of wine)*
herbiphag, herbivor herbivorous, phytophagic, phytophagous, plant-eating
Herbivore *m* herbivore, plant eater (feeder)
herbizid herbicidal
Herbizid *n* herbicide, [chemical] weed-killer
~/innertherapeutisches *s.* ~/translokales
~/nichtselektives total (non-selective) herbicide, soil sterilant
~/selektives selective herbicide
~/staubförmiges herbicidal dust
~/translokales translocated (translocatory, non-contact) herbicide
Herbizidantidot[on] *n* herbicide antidote (safener)
Herbizidanwendung *f*, **Herbizideinsatz** *m* herbicide application (usage), herbigation
Herbizid[einsatz]empfehlung *f* herbicide [application] recommendation
Herbizidfolge *f* herbicide rotation
Herbizidformulierung *f* herbicide formulation
Herbizidforschung *f* herbicide research
Herbizidgegenmittel *n* herbicide antidote (safener)
Herbizidmetabolismus *m* herbicide metabolism
Herbizidmischung *f* herbicide mixture
Herbizidresistenz *f* herbicide resistance
Herbizidrotation *f* herbicide rotation
Herbizidrückstand *m* herbicide residue

Herbizidschaden *m* herbicidal injury
Herbizidselektivität *f* herbicide selectivity
Herbizidstreifen *m* herbicide strip
Herbizidtoleranz *f* herbicide tolerance
Herbizidtoxizität *f* herbicidal toxicity
Herbizidwirkung *f* herbicidal effect
Herbologie *f* weed science
Herbst *m* autumn, *(Am)* fall
Herbstabkalbung *f* autumn calving
Herbstanbau *m* autumn culture *(of greenhouse tomatoes)*
Herbstanemone *f* 1. Japanese anemone, Anemone x hybrida; 2. Japanese anemone, Anemone hupehensis
Herbstaster *f* Michaelmas daisy, perennial (fall-flowering) aster *(comprehensive term)*
Herbstaussaat *f* autumn seeding (drilling)
Herbstbestellung *f* autumn cultivation
Herbstbestockung *f* fall tillering
Herbstbewässerung *f* fall irrigation
Herbstblüher *m* autumn-flowering plant, autumnal
Herbstbodenbearbeitung *f* fall tillage
Herbstdüngung *f* autumn fertilization
Herbstfärbung *f* autumn tints, autumnal colours
Herbstfeldarbeit *f* autumn field work
Herbstfeuerröschen *n* pheasant's-eye [flower], red morocco, Adonis annua
Herbstflieder *m* summer [perennial] phlox, Phlox paniculata
Herbstfrost *m* autumn frost, early [fall] frost
Herbstfurche *f* 1. winter furrow; 2. autumn ploughing
Herbstfutter *n* fall forage
Herbstgrasmilbe *f* harvest mite, Neotrombicula (Trombicula) autumnalis
Herbstgrünfutter *n* fall forage
Herbstholz *n s.* Spätholz
Herbstkalbung *f* autumn calving
Herbstkalkung *f* autumn liming
Herbstkultur *f* autumn culture *(as of greenhouse tomatoes or cucumbers)*
Herbstlaichung *f* fall spawning
Herbstlammung *f* autumn lambing
Herbstlaub *n* autumnal foliage, autumn leaves
herbstlich autumnal
Herbstlöwenzahn *m* autumn hawkbit, fall dandelion, Leontodon autumnalis
Herbstmilbe *f s.* Herbstgrasmilbe
Herbstpflanzung *f* autumn planting, *(Am)* fall planting
Herbstpflugfurche *f* autumn ploughing
Herbstrübe *f* [stubble] turnip, Brassica campestris ssp. rapifera
Herbstsaat *f* autumn seeding (drilling)
Herbstsches Körperchen *n* Herbst corpuscle *(pressoreceptor in birds)*
Herbststschurwolle *f* fall wool
Herbststoppel *f* fall stubble
Herbst-Tagundnachtgleiche *f* autumnal equinox

Herbstwaldrebe *f* sweet autumn clematis, Clematis maximowicziana (paniculata)
Herbstweide *f*, **Herbstweidegang** *m* fall grazing
Herbstzeitlose *f* meadow saffron, autumn crocus, Colchicum autumnale
Herd *m (phyt, vet)* focus
Herdbuch *n* herd-book *(esp. of cattle or swine)*; stud-book *(esp. of horses and dogs)*; flock-book *(esp. of sheep)* • **im ~ verzeichnet** pedigree
~/geschlossenes closed herd-book
Herdbuchtier *n* pedigree (registered) animal
Herdbuchvieh *n* registered breeding stock
Herdbuchzucht *f* pedigree breeding (method)
Herdbuchzuchtarbeit *f* pedigree work
Herdbuchzuchtbetrieb *m* pedigree breeding farm
Herdbuchzüchter *m* pedigree breeder
Herdbuchzüchtung *f* pedigree breeding (method)
Herde *f* herd *(esp. of larger animals), (Am)* pod; flock • **ein Tier von der ~ entfernen** to cast, *(Am)* to cut out • **in der ~ lebend** gregarious
~/durch Eigenreproduktion ergänzte self-replacing flock, self-contained flock *(e.g. of sheep)*
~/durch Tierzukauf ergänzte flying flock *(e.g. of sheep)*
~/geschlossene closed herd
~/getriebene drove
Herdenaufzeichnung *f* flock record *(sheep breeding)*
Herdenauslese *f* herd selection
Herdenbesitzer *m* herdsman, herder
Herdenbulle *m* herd bull
Herdendurchschnitt *m* herd average
Herdenfruchtbarkeit *f* herd fertility
Herdengebrauchshund *m* herding dog
Herdengesundheit *f* herd health
Herdengesundheitskalender *m* herd health calendar
Herdengesundheitsüberwachung *f* herd health control
Herdengröße *f* herd size
Herdenhalter *m* herd manager
Herdenhaltung *f* herd management
Herdenhierarchie *f* herd hierarchy
Herdenhund *m* herding dog
Herdenhygiene *f* herd hygiene; flock hygiene
Herdenimmunität *f* herd immunity
Herdenleistung *f* herd productivity
Herdenmilch *f* herd [bulk] milk
Herdenpaarung *f* lot (flock) mating
Herdenproduktivität *f* herd productivity; flock productivity
Herdenselektion *f* herd selection
Herdensterilität *f* herd sterility
Herdenstruktur *f* herd structure
Herdentier *n* gregaripus animal
Herdentrieb *m* herd[ing] instinct; flocking instinct
Herdenüberwachung *f* herd monitoring
Herdenumfang *m* herd size
Herdenvatertier *n* herd sire

Herdenverhalten

Herdenverhalten *n* herding behaviour; flocking behaviour
Herdenvieh *n* drove cattle
Herderscheinung *f s.* Herdsymptom
Herdinfekt *m (phyt, vet)* focal infection
Herdsymptom *n (phyt, vet)* focal symptom
Herdwick[schaf] *n* Herdwick *(sheep breed)*
hereditär hereditary, inheritable
Heredität *f* heredity, inheritance
Herefordrind *n* Hereford *(cattle breed)*
Heringsmehl *n* herring meal *(feed)*
Heritabilität *f* heritability
~ **im engeren Sinne** narrow-sense heritability
~ **im weiteren Sinne** broad-sense heritability, gross heritability
~/**realisierte** realized heritability *(animal breeding)*
Heritabilitätsgrad *m* degree of heritability
Heritabilitätskoeffizient *m* coefficient of heritability, heritability estimate
Heritabilitätsschätzung *f* heritability estimation
Herkogamie *f (bot)* hercogamy
Herkuleskraut 1. cow-parsnip, hogweed *(genus Heracleum)*; 2. cow-parsnip, hogweed, bear's-breech, Heracleum sphondylium
Herkunft *f* provenance, *(Am)* provenience, origin, derivation, strain; introduction *(esp. of seed)*
• **[von] pflanzlicher** ~ phytogenous
~ **von Saatgut/verbürgte** original seed source
Herkunftsgebiet *n* area of origin
herkunftsgeprüft source-identified *(seed)*
Herkunftsversuch *m* provenance trial
Herkunftswert *m* value of origin
Herlitze *f* cornelian cherry, cornel, Cornus mas
Hermaphrodismus *m s.* Hermaphroditismus
hermaphrodit hermaphroditic[al], bisexual, monoecious, autoecious
Hermaphrodit *m* hermaphrodite, bisexual, intersex
hermaphroditisch *s.* hermaphrodit
Hermaphroditismus *m* hermaphroditism, androgyny, bisexuality, monoecism, monoecy
Hermelin *n* ermine, stoat, Mustela erminea
hermetisch hermetic
Hernie *f (vet)* hernia, rupture
Herniotomie *f (vet)* herniotomy
Heroin *n* heroin *(alkaloid, narcotic)*
Herpes *m(f) (vet)* herpes
Herpesvirus *n* herpes virus
~ **der Marekschen Krankheit** avian herpes virus, Marek's disease virus
~ **Typ 1/bovines** IBR/IPV virus
~ **Typ 1/equines** equine herpes virus 1
Herpesvirus-B-Infektion *f des Huhns (vet)* Marek's disease
Herpesvirusinfektion *f der Taube (vet)* Smadel's disease
Herrenpilz *m* edible boletus, cep[e], Boletus edulis
herstammen to descend [from], to originate
herumgedreht *(bot)* resupinate
herunterbinden to bend [down]

heruntereggen to harrow down
herunterhängen to trail *(twigs or branches)*
herunterkühlen to cool [down]
heruntertrocknen to dry down
herunterwirtschaften to farm out
hervorbringen/Blüten to blossom
hervorrufen/Fäulnis to decay
hervorschwellend *(bot, zoo)* protuberant
hervorstehend *(bot)* exserted
Hervortreten *n* protrusion
Herz *n* 1. heart; 2. *(bot)* heart, pith, core • **in das** ~ **hinein** intracardiac, intracardial
~/**mürbes** brittle heart, spongy (soft) heart *(wood defect)*
~/**schlängeliges** wandering heart *(wood defect)*
~/**schwammiges** *s.* ~/mürbes
Herzaußenhaut *f* epicardium
Herzbeutel *m* heart (pericardial) sac, pericardium
Herzbeutelentzündung *f (vet)* pericarditis
Herzbeutelflüssigkeit *f* pericardial fluid
Herzbeutelhöhle *f* pericardial cavity
Herzbeutelwassersucht *f (vet)* hydropericardium
Herzblatt *n* heart leaf
Herzblättrige Bergenie *f* heart-leaf begonia, Bergenia cordifolia
~ **Gemswurz** *f* leopard's-bane, Doronicum columnae (cordifolium)
~ **Mittagsblume** *f* dew-plant, Aptenia cordifolia
Herzblattvergilbung *f (phyt)* dead heart [condition, symptom]
Herzblattverkrümmung *f* crumpled leaf *(of cabbage due to larval attack of Contarinia nasturtii)*
Herzblume *f* 1. bleeding heart, lyre-flower *(genus Dicentra)*; 2. fringed bleeding heart, Dicentra eximina
Herzbräune *f* core browning (flush) *(storage disorder e.g. of apples)*
Herzdilatation *f s.* Herzerweiterung
Herzenkelch *m (bot)* eucharis *(genus Eucharis)*
Herzerkrankung *f (vet)* heart-disease
Herzerschlaffung[sphase] *f* diastole
Herzerweiterung *f (vet)* cardiac dila[ta]tion
Herzfäule *f (phyt)* heart (core) rot
~ **des Selleries** celery heart rot *(caused by Bacterium carotovorum)*
herzförmig *(bot, zoo)* heart-shaped, cordate
~/**verkehrt** obcordate
Herzfrequenz *f* heart rate
~/**beschleunigte** tachycardia
Herzgeräusch *n* heart sound
Herzgespann *n (bot)* motherwort, Leonurus cardiaca
Herzglycosid *n* cardiac glycoside
Herzhemmungszentrum *n* cardioinhibitory centre
Herzinfarkt *m (vet)* myocardial infarction
Herzinnenhaut *f* endocardium
Herzinnenhautentzündung *f (vet)* endocarditis
Herzkammer *f* ventricle

Herzkirsche f heart-cherry, Prunus avium var. juliana
Herzklappe f heart valve
Herzkontraktion[sphase] f systole
Herzkrankheit f *(vet)* heart-disease
Herzkranzgefäß n coronary vessel
Herz-Kreislauf-System n cardio-vascular system
Herzlosigkeit f *(bot)* blindness
Herzmassage f *(vet)* cardiac massage
Herzminutenvolumen n cardiac output
Herzmuskel m heart muscle, myocardium
Herzmuskelentzündung f *(vet)* myocarditis
Herzmuskelerkrankung f *(vet)* cardiomyopathy
Herzmuskelgewebe n myocardium
Herzmuskelversagen n s. Herzversagen
Herznekrose f *(phyt)* blackheart
Herzohr n auricle *(animal anatomy)*
Herzrate f s. Herzfrequenz
Herzsame m 1. heart-seed, heart-pea *(genus Cardiospermum)*; 2. heart-seed, heart-pea, balloon-vine, Cardiospermum halicacabum
Herzschall m heart sound
Herzschlag m heartbeat
Herzschlagfrequenz f s. Herzfrequenz
Herzschlagvolumen n stroke volume
Herzstillstand m *(vet)* cardiac arrest
Herzstromkurve f electrocardiogram
Herztod m *(vet)* acute heart failure
~ **des Huhns/enzootischer** round-heart disease of fowl, fatal syncope of fowl, toxic heart degeneration of fowl
Herztöne mpl heart sound
Herz- und Trockenfäule f **der Zuckerrübe** heart rot of sugar-beet, brown-heart of sugar-beet *(due to boron deficiency)*
Herzvergrößerung f *(vet)* cardiomegaly
Herzversagen n *(vet)* heart *(cardiac)* failure
~/akutes acute heart failure
Herzvorhof m, **Herzvorkammer** f atrium, auricle
Herzwasser n *(vet)* heart water disease
Herzwassererreger m heart water agent, Cowdria ruminantium
Herzwurm m 1. heartworm, Dirofilaria immitis; 2. cabbage moth, Mamestra brassicae
Herzwurmkrankheit f *(vet)* dirofilariasis *(caused by Dirofilaria immitis)*
Herzynische Fichtenblattwespe f European spruce saw-fly, Diprion (Gilpinia) hercyniae
Hesperidin n hesperidin *(flavonoid)*
Hesse f *(slaught)* shank, shin of beef
Hessenfliege f, **Hessenmücke** f Hessian fly, Mayetiola destructor
Hessian n Hessian [cloth]
Heterakiasis f, **Heterakidose** f *(vet)* heterakidosis *(helminthosis)*
heteroallel *(gen)* heteroallelic
Heteroallel n *(gen)* heteroallele
Heteroauxin n heteroauxin, indolacetic acid, IAA *(phytohormone)*

heterochrom heterochromatic
Heterochromatin n heterochromatin
heterochromatisch heterochromatic
Heterochromosom n hetero[chromo]some, gonosome, allosome, sex chromosome
heterodont *(bot, zoo)* heterodont
Heteroduplexstruktur f *(gen)* heteroduplex
Heterofermentation f heterofermentation
heterofermentativ heterofermentative
heterogam heterogamous
Heterogamet m heterogamete
heterogametisch heterogametic
Heterogamie f heterogamy
heterogen heterogenous
Heterogenese f heterogenesis
heterogenetisch heterogenetic
Heterogenität f heterogeneity
Heterogonie f heterogony
heterokarp *(bot)* heterocarpous
Heterokaryon n *(gen)* heterokaryon
Heterokaryose f *(gen)* heterokaryosis
heterolog heterologous
Heterolysin n heterolysin
heteromer *(bot)* heteromerous
Heteromerie f heteromery
heterometabol heterometabolous
heteromorph heteromorphic
Heteromorphie f, **Heteromorphismus** m heteromorphism
Heterophyllie f *(bot)* heterophylly
heteroploid *(gen)* heteroploid
Heteroploide m heteroploid
Heteroploidie f heteroploidy
Heteroptere m *(ent)* heteropteran *(order Heteroptera)*
Heterosis f heterosis
~/positive hybrid vigour
heterosisbedingt heterotic
Heterosiseffekt m heterosis
Heterosissorte f hybrid variety (cultivar)
Heterosiszüchtung f heterosis breeding
Heterosom n s. Heterochromosom
Heterosperma n mixed semen
heterospor *(bot)* heterosporous
Heterosporie f heterospory
heterostyl *(bot)* heterostyled, heterostylous
Heterostylie f heterostyly
Heterotaxie f heterotaxy
Heterothallie f *(bot)* heterothallism
heterotisch heterotic
heterotroph heterotrophic
Heterotrophie f heterotrophy
heterotypisch heterologous
heteroxen heteroxenous
Heteroxenie f heteroxenia
heterozellulär heterocellular
Heterözie f *(bot, zoo)* heteroecism
heterözisch heteroecious
heterozygot *(gen)* heterozygous

Heterozygote

Heterozygote *m* heterozygote
Heterozygotie *f* heterozygosis, heterozygosity
heterozyklisch heterocyclic
hetzen to chase, to hunt *(esp. foxes)*; to course *(esp. hares)*
~/mit Hunden to hound, to bait
Hetzjagd *f* chase, hunt[ing]; course, coursing, run
• **an einer ~ teilnehmen** to take part in a hunt, to course
Hetzkrankheit *f* Jaagsiekte *(of horses)*
Hetzpeitsche *f* hunting-crop
Hetzseuche *f* pulmonary adenomatosis, mountain disease *(of sheep)*
Heu *n* hay • **~ auflockern (ausbreiten)** to ted
• **~ in Stadel einlagern** to staddle • **~ machen (werben)** to [make] hay • **zu ~ machen** to hay
~/bodengetrocknetes field hay
~/geerntetes hay-crop
~/gehäckseltes chopped hay
~/scheunengelagertes hay-mow
Heuabfälle *mpl* hayseed
Heuaufbereiter *m* hay conditioner
Heuballenpresse *f* hay baler (baling press)
Heubanse *f* hay-bay
Heubelüftung *f* hay ventilation
Heubelüftungsanlage *f* barn hay dryer
Heubelüftungstrocknung *f* barn (mow) hay drying
Heubergung *f* hay harvest[ing], hay-crop, haymaking
Heubergungsmaschine *f* hay harvesting machine
Heublume *f* hayseed
Heuboden *m* hay-loft
Heubrikett *n* hay cube
Heubündel *n* truss [of hay]
Heudebolin *n* heudebolin *(terpene)*
Heudieme *f*, **Heudiemen** *m* haystack, hay-rick, haycock
Heudrehmaschine *f* hay-band machine (twister)
Heuei *n* hay egg
heuen to [make] hay
Heuernte *f* hay harvest[ing], haymaking, hay-crop
Heuerntemaschine *f* hay harvesting machine
Heuertrag *m* **einer Wiese** sweepage
Heufeime *f s.* Heudieme
Heufieber *n* hay fever *(pollen allergy)*
Heugabel *f* hay-fork, pitchfork
Heugebläse *f* hay blower
Heugewinnung *f* haymaking, hay production, wilting
Heugreifer *m* hay grab (sweep)
Heuhäcksel *n* chopped hay
Heuhaufen *m* haycock, mow
Heuhütte *f* quadpod
Heukonservierungsmittel *n* hay preservative
Heuladegerät *n*, **Heulader** *m* hay loader
Heuladewagen *m* haystacking wagon
Heulagerung *f* hay storage
Heumehl *n* hay meal, ground hay
Heumesser *n* hay-knife

Heumotte *f* cacao[-bean] moth, tobacco (chocolate, walnut) moth, red-streaked knothorn, Ephestia elutella
Heumühle *f* hay tub grinder
Heupellet *n* hay pellet
Heupelletierung *f* hay pelleting
Heuproduktion *f* hay production
Heuraufe *f* hay-rack
Heurechen *m* hay rake
Heuriger *m* this year's wine, wine of the latest vintage
Heuroller *m* round baler, roto-baler
Heusamen *m* hayseed
Heusammelpresse *f* pick-up hay baler
Heuschiebesammler *m* hay sweep
Heuschnupfen *m (vet)* summer snuffles
Heuschober *m* haystack, hay-rick, haycock
Heuschrecke *f* grasshopper *(order Saltatoria)*
Heuschreckenbaum *m* locust tree, anime resin, Hymenaea courbaril
Heuschuppen *m* hay-barn
Heuschwaden *m* hay swath
Heuschwanz *m s.* Heuschiebesammler
Heuseil *n* hay-band
Heuseildrehmaschine *f* hay-band machine (twister)
Heustadel *m* staddle
Heutrockner *m* hay dryer
Heutrocknung *f* hay drying
Heuturm *m* hay tower
Heuwaffelpresse *f* hay waferer
Heuwagen *m* hay-cart, hay-trailer
Heuwender *m* hay turner (turning machine), turner
Heuwerbung *f* haymaking, hay production, wilting; hay harvest[ing], hay-crop
Heuwerbungsmaschine *f* haymaker, haymaking machine
Heuwerbungsverlust *m* haymaking loss
Heuwert *m* hay equivalent
Heuwiese *f* hay meadow, hayfield
Heuwürfel *m* hay cube
Hexachlorbenzen *n* hexachlorobenzene, HCB *(fungicide)*
Hexachlorcyclohexan *n* hexachloran[e], HCH, benzene hexachloride, BHC *(insecticide)*
Hexachlorobutadien *n* hexachlorobutadiene *(fungicide)*
Hexachloroethan *n* hexachloroethane *(anthelminthic, nematicide)*
Hexachlorophen *n* hexachlorophene *(bacteriostatic, anthelminthic)*
Hexadecansäure *f* hexadecanoic (palmitic) acid *(fatty acid)*
Hexa-2,4-diensäure *f* sorbic (hexa-2,4-dienoic) acid *(fatty acid)*
Hexaflurat *n* hexaflurate *(herbicide)*
Hexahydropyrazin *n* piperazine *(anthelminthic)*
Hexahydropyrin *n* piperidine

Hilfsbaumart

Hexamethylentetramin *n* methenamine, hexamine, hexamethylenetetramine
Hexamethylmelamin *n* hexamethylmelamine *(chemosterilant)*
Hexamin *s*. Hexamethylentetramin
Hexamitakrankheit *f*, **Hexamitiasis** *f (vet)* hexamitiasis *(esp. of trouts)*
Hexansäure *f* hexanoic (caproic) acid *(fatty acid)*
Hexapode *m* hexapod, insect *(class Hexapoda) (for compounds s. under* Insekt*)*
hexaploid *(gen)* hexaploid
Hexaploidie *f* hexaploidy
Hexathirium *n* hexathirium *(fungicide)*
Hexazinon *n* hexazinone *(herbicide)*
Hexenbesen *m (phyt)* witches' broom, fasciculation *(mycoplasmosis)*
~ **bei Weißtanne** witches' broom fir rust
~ **der Erdnuß** ground-nut witches' broom
~ **der Kartoffel** potato witches' broom
Hexenkraut *n* enchanter's nightshade *(genus Circaea)*
Hexenmilch *f* witches' (sorcerer's) milk *(of newborn mammals)*
Hexenring *m* fairy ring *(of mushrooms)*
Hexenzwirn *m (bot)* dodder *(genus Cuscuta)*
Hexit *m* hexitol *(hexavalent alcohol)*
Hexokinase *f* hexokinase *(enzyme)*
Hexosan *n* hexosan *(polysaccharide)*
Hexose *f* hexose, six-carbon sugar *(monosaccharide)*
Hexosediphosphatase *f* fructose-bisphosphatase *(enzyme)*
Hexosemonophosphatweg *m* pentose phosphate cycle, phosphogluconate pathway *(of glucose degradation)*
Hexöstrol *n* hexoestrol *(synthetic oestrogen)*
Hexylresorcin *n* hexylresorcinol *(anthelminthic, disinfestant)*
Hexylthiofos *n* hexylthiofos *(fungicide)*
HfSV *s*. Hirschzungenfarnscheckungsvirus
Hibalebensbaum *m* hiba [arbor vitae], thujopsis, Thujopsis dolabrata
Hibbertie *f (bot)* snake vine, Hibbertia scandens
Hibernakel *n (bot, zoo)* hibernacle, hibernaculum
hibernal hibernal
Hibernation *f* hibernation, winter sleep (survival), overwintering
Hibiskus *m* rose-mallow, hibiscus *(genus Hibiscus)*
Hickory *m(f)*, **Hickorybaum** *m* hickory *(genus Carya)*
Hickoryholz *n* hickory
Hickorynuß *f* 1. hickory-nut, *(Am)* pignut; mockernut *(from Carya tomentosa)*; 2. *s*. Hickory
Hieb *m (forest)* felling, cutting
~ **auf den besten Stamm** selection felling, highgrading
Hiebs... *s. a*. Fäll... und Fällungs...

Hiebsalter *n* age at felling (cutting), felling (rotation) age, age of maturity, exploitable (removal, final) age
Hiebsanweisung *f* felling instruction (rule)
Hiebsart *f* method (type) of felling
Hiebsatz *m s*. Hiebssatz
Hiebseingriff *m* felling (cutting) operation • **den ersten ~ vornehmen** to make a first felling
Hiebsergebnis *n*, **Hiebsertrag** *m* felling yield (outturn)
Hiebsfigur *f* felling unit
Hiebsfonds *m* harvest cut fund
Hiebsfortschritt *m* felling sequence (rotation), felling cycle (interval)
Hiebsführung *f* management of cuttings
Hiebskarte *f* exploitation map
Hiebsklasse *f* felling class
Hiebsmethode *f* felling method
Hiebsordnung *f* order of felling
Hiebsort *m* felling site (place, point)
Hiebsplan *m* felling plan, plan of cuttings
Hiebsplanung *f* planning of fellings
hiebsreif ripe [for felling], mature
Hiebsreife *f* [stand, crop] maturity
~ **des höchsten Geldertrages** maturity of highest cash return
~ **des höchsten Mengenertrages** maturity of highest volume yield
~/**finanzielle** financial maturity
~/**ökologische** ecological maturity
~/**ökonomische** *s*. ~/wirtschaftliche
~/**physiologische** physiological maturity
~/**physische (waldbauliche)** silvicultural maturity
~/**wirtschaftliche** economic (merchantable, financial) maturity
Hiebsreihe *f* felling series *(s. a*. Hiebsfolge*)*
Hiebsrichtung *f* felling direction
Hiebssatz *m* prescribed yield, prescribed (allowable) cut; planned (calculated) yield; felling volume
~/**jährlicher** annual yield
~/**normaler** normal yield, normal allowable cut
~/**periodischer** periodic yield (cut)
Hiebssatzbestimmung *f*, **Hiebssatzherleitung** *f* assessment of annual or periodic yield, yield determination
Hiebssatzweiser *m* formula for the calculation of prescribed yield, yield indicator
Hiebsumlauf *m* felling cycle
Hiebszeit *f* felling time (season, period)
Hiebszug *m* felling series
~ **mit Traufbildung** order of felling areas
Higankirsche *f* higan cherry, Prunus subhirtella
Highlandpony *n* Highland pony *(breed)*
Highlandrind *n* Highland [cattle] *(breed)*
Hilfe *f* cue, aid *(equestrian sport)*
Hilfsausrüstung *f* auxiliary (ancillary) equipment
Hilfsbaumart *f (forest)* auxiliary (accessory) tree species, ancillary [tree] species

Hilfsförster

Hilfsförster *m* associate forester, assistant ranger
Hilfsstoff *m* adjuvant *(esp. in preparations)*
Hilfszeit *f* unproductive time *(time study)*
Hilfszelle *f (bot)* synergid
Hill-Reaktion *f* Hill reaction *(photosynthesis)*
Hilum *n (bot)* hilum, cicatrice, scar *(e.g. on bean seed)*
Hilus *m (zoo)* hilus, hilum *(recess or opening, where vessels or nerves enter an organ)*
Himalajakiefer *f* Himalayan (blue) pine, Pinus wallichiana
Himalajatanne *f* Himalayan silver fir, Abies spectabilis
Himalajatraubenkirsche *f* Himalayan bird cherry, Padus cornuta
Himalajazeder *f* deodar [cedar], true cedar, Cedrus deodara
Himbeeradernchlorosevirus *n* raspberry vein chlorosis virus, RVCV
Himbeerblattfleckenvirus *n* raspberry leaf spot virus, RLSV
Himbeerblattscheckungsvirus *n* raspberry leaf mottle virus, RLMV
Himbeerblütenstecher *m* strawberry blossom weevil, Anthonomus rubi
Himbeere *f* 1. raspberry, bramble *(genus Rubus)*; 2. [red] raspberry, Rubus idaeus; 3. red raspberry, Rubus strigosus; 4. raspberry, bramble *(fruit)*
~/rote [purple] raspberry *(fruit)*
Himbeererntemaschine *f* raspberry harvester
Himbeergallmilbe *f* leaf and bud mite, Phyllocoptes (Eriophyes) gracilis
Himbeergallmücke *f* raspberry (blackberry) stem gall-midge, Lasioptera rubi
Himbeerglasflügler *m (ent)* raspberry root borer, Bembecia hylaeiformis
Himbeerkäfer *m* raspberry beetle, Byturus tomentosus (unicolor)
Himbeerkäferlarve *f* raspberry fruit worm, Byturus tomentosus (unicolor)
Himbeerkräuselvirus *n* raspberry leaf curl virus, RLCV
Himbeerlaus *f* raspberry aphid, Aphis idaei
Himbeermade *f s.* Himbeerkäferlarve
Himbeermotte *f* raspberry bright moth, Incurvaria rubiella
Himbeerpflanze *f s.* Himbeere 1.
Himbeerringfleckenvirus *n* raspberry ring spot virus, RRV
Himbeerrute *f* raspberry-cane
Himbeerrutenfliege *f* raspberry-cane maggot, Pegomia rubivora
Himbeerstauche *f (phyt)* rubus (raspberry) stunt *(mycoplasmosis)*
Himbeerstrauch *m s.* Himbeere 1.
Himbeer-52-V-Virus *n* raspberry virus 52 V
Himbeerzwergbuschvirus *n* raspberry bushy dwarf virus, RBDV

Himmelblaue Mostie *f* blue plantain lily, Mosta ventricosa
Himmelblaues Bitterkraut *n* German (Persian) violet, exacum, Exacum affine
Himmelschlüssel *m(n)* 1. primrose, primula, polyanthus *(genus Primula)*; 2. cowslip, Primula veris
Himmelsröschen *n* rose of heaven, Silene coelirosa
Himmelsschlüssel *m(n) s.* Himmelschlüssel
Himmelsstrahlung *f* sky (diffuse) radiation
hinaustreiben to run out *(cattle)*
Hindernis *n* jump, obstacle *(equestrian sport)*
Hindernisrennen *n* obstacle-race
hinken to limp, to [go] lame, to walk lamely
Hinken *n* limp[ing], claudication
Hinmutation *f (gen)* forward mutation
Hinoki-Scheinzypresse *f* hinoki [cypress], Chamaecyparis obtusa
Hinschkrankheit *f (vet)* bush sickness *(due to cobalt deficiency)*
Hinterbacke *f* buttock
Hinterbehandlungsbeute *f (api)* back-opening hive
Hinterbeinmittelstück *n (slaught)* round of beef
Hinterbrust *f (ent)* metathorax
hintereinander [angeordnet] tandem
Hinterendlage *f* posterior (pelvic) presentation *(obstetrics)*
Hinterextremität *f s.* Hintergliedmaße
Hinterflanke *f* hind (rear) flank *(of the animal body)*
Hinterflügel *m (ent)* hind-wing
Hintergliedmaße *f* rear (hind) leg, hindlimb, pelvic limb
Hinterhand *f* hindquarters *(s. a. Hintergliedmaße)*
Hinterhaupt *n* occiput
Hinterhauptsbein *n* occipital bone
Hinterhachse *f (slaught)* shank end, hind foot
Hinterhesse *f (slaught)* leg of beef
Hinterhirn *n* hindbrain, metencephalon
Hinterkeule *f* ham *(of pig)*
Hinterkipper *m* rear tipping trailer
Hinterkorn *n* shrivelled grain, tail corn
Hinterleib *m* hind body *(of arthropods)*; abdomen *(of hexapods)*
Hintermast *m* tail spar (tree), back spar *(of a cable logging machine)*
Hintermittelfuß *m* instep *(of the horse)*
Hinterrad *n* rear wheel; depth wheel *(of a plough)*
Hinterradantrieb *m* rear[-wheel] drive
Hinterradbremse *f* rear[-wheel] brake
Hinterradlenkung *f* rear-wheel steering
Hinterröhre *f s.* Hintermittelfuß
Hinterschinken *m* ham *(of pig)*
Hinterseite *f* back, rear
hinterständig camped behind *(hindlimb position)*
Hinterviertel *n* hindquarter *(carcass)*
Hinterwälder Rind *n* Hinterwald [cattle] *(breed)*
Hiobsträne *f (bot)* Job's tears, adlay, Coix lacryma-jobi

H-Ionenkonzentration f hydrogen-ion concentration
Hippe f pruning knife, bill[hook]; brush hook
Hippiatrie f, **Hippiatrik** f hippiatry, equine medicine
Hippodrom m(n) hippodrome
Hippologie f hippology
Hippursäure f hippuric acid
Hiproly-Gerste f hiproly barley
hircin hircine
HiRFV s. Himbeerringfleckenvirus
Hirn n brain, encephalon
Hirn... s. a. Gehirn...
Hirnanhangsdrüse f hypophysis, pituitary [gland]
Hirnfläche f cross-cut end, end face *(of timber)*
Hirnhaut f meninx
~/harte dura mater
Hirnhautbruch m *(vet)* menigocele
Hirnhautentzündung f *(vet)* meningitis
Hirnkammer f [cerebral] ventricle
Hirnmarkflüssigkeit f neurolymph
Hirnnerv m cranial nerve
Hirnrinde f cerebral cortex
Hirnrückenmarkentzündung f **der Pferde** *(vet)* equine encephalomyelitis
Hirnrückenmarkflüssigkeit f cerebrospinal fluid
Hirnschädel m cranium, skull
Hirnschnitt m 1. end-grain cutting *(of timber)*; 2. s. Hirnschnitt[ober]fläche
Hirnschnitt[ober]fläche f end-grain surface, cross-cut [end], transverse (cross) section *(of timber)*
Hirnstamm m brain stem
Hirn- und Rückenmarksentzündung f **des Rindes/sporadische** *(vet)* sporadic bovine encephalomyelitis
Hirsch m deer *(family Cervidae)*
~ im fünften Jahr stag
~ im sechsten Jahr hart
~ im vierten Jahr staggard, staggart
~ im zweiten Jahr brocket, knobber
~/kapitaler royal
Hirsch tot! mort *(note sounded on a hunting-horn at death of deer)*
hirschähnlich cervine
Hirschfährte f [deer] slot
Hirschfänger m hunting-knife, hanger
Hirschfleisch n venison
Hirschgeweih n antlers, attire
Hirschhals m ewe neck *(of horse or dog)*
Hirschhaut f deerskin; buckskin
Hirschholunder m red-berried elder, Sambucus racemosa
Hirschhorn n hartshorn, stag-horn
Hirschhornsalat m buck's horn [plantain], Plantago coronopus
Hirschhund m 1. staghound *(breed)*; 2. buckhound *(variety of staghound)*
Hirschkäfer m stag-beetle, Lucanus cervus

Hirschkalb n [male] fawn, stag calf, young deer; male calf of red deer
Hirschkolbensumach m stag-horn sumac[h], American sumac[h], Rhus typhina
Hirschkuh f hind, doe, female deer
Hirschlausfliege f deer fly (ked), Lipoptena cervi
Hirschleder n buckskin
Hirschlosung f deer droppings
Hirschmaus f deer mouse, Peromyscus maniculatus
Hirschpark m deer park
Hirschzunge f hart's-tongue [fern], scolopendrium, Phyllitis scolopendrium
Hirschzungenfarnscheckungsvirus n hart's-tongue fern mottle virus
Hirse f 1. millet *(comprehensive term)*; 2. panic[-grass] *(genus Panicum)*
Hirsebrand m head smut of millet *(caused by Sphacelotheca destruens)*
Hirsekorn n millet [seed]
hirsekornartig miliary
Hirseschößlingsfliege f, **Hirsetriebfliege** f sorghum shoot fly, Atherigona varia
Hirt m herdsman, herd[er]
Hirtenhund m herding dog
Hirtennomadismus m nomadism
Hirtenpferd n stock horse
Hirtenstab m sheep-hook, shepherd's crook
Hirtentäschel n shepherd's-purse, shovelweed, case (blind) weed, Capsella bursa-pastoris
Hirudiniasis f, **Hirudinose** f *(vet)* hirudiniasis
His s. Histidin
Hissar[schaf] n Hissar, Uzbek *(sheep breed)*
Hissches Bündel n atrioventricular bundle *(of the heart)*
Histaminase f histaminase, amine oxidase, copper containing *(enzyme)*
Histidase f histidase, histidine ammonia lyase *(enzyme)*
Histidin n histidine *(amino-acid)*
Histidinammoniaklyase f histidine ammonia lyase, histidase *(enzyme)*
Histogenese f s. Histogenese
Histiozymatose f s. Histiozytose
Histiozyt m histiocyte
Histiozytose f *(vet)* histiocytosis
Histochemie f histochemistry
histochemisch histochemical
Histoenzymologie f histoenzymology
Histogenese f histogenesis, tissue differentiation
Histogramm n histogram
Histohämin n cytochrome
Histokompatibilität f histocompatibility
Histologie f histology
histologisch histological
Histolyse f histolysis
Histomonasinfektion (Histomoniasis) f **des Geflügels** histomoniasis, blackhead [disease] *(of fowl, caused by Histomonas meleagridis)*

Histon

Histon *n* histone *(chromosome protein)*
Histonkinase *f* histone kinase *(enzyme)*
Histopathologie *f* histopathology
histopathologisch histopathologic[al]
Histoplasmose *f (vet)* histoplasmosis
Histosol *m (Am, soil)* histosol, ist
Hitzdrahtanemometer *n* hot-wire anemometer
Hitze *f* heat
Hitzebehandlung *f* heat treatment
Hitzebeständigkeit *f s.* Hitzeresistenz
hitzefest *s.* hitzeresistent
Hitzekoagulation *f* heat coagulation
Hitzekollaps *m* heat shock
hitzeresistent heat-resistant, resistant to heat, thermostable, thermoduric
Hitzeresistenz *f* heat resistance, resistance to heat, thermostability
Hitzeresistenzzüchtung *f* heat-resistance breeding
Hitzeriß *m* drought (sun) crack *(of timber)*
Hitzeschaden *m* heat damage (injury)
Hitzeschock *m* heat shock
Hitzespaltung *f* pyrolysis
Hitzestreß *m* heat stress
hitzeverträglich heat-tolerant
Hitzeverträglichkeit *f* heat tolerance
Hitzewelle *f* heat wave
Hitzschlag *m (vet)* heat stroke (apoplexy)
Hi52VV *s.* Himbeer-52-V-Virus
HiZBV *s.* Himbeerzwergbuschvirus
Hjärre's Krankheit *f* Hjärre's disease *(of fowl)*
H-Kette *f* heavy chain *(of the immunoglobulin molecule)*
H-Lage *f* H-layer *(of a humus profile)*
Hlf. *s.* Hellfuchs
H-Meromyosin *n* heavy meromyosin *(muscle protein)*
HMF *s.* Hydroxymethylfurfural
H-Milch *f* sterile (long keeping) milk, ultra-high temperature milk
HMV *s.* 1. Bodenbürtiges Hafermosaikvirus; 2. Herzminutenvolumen
Hobbygarten *m* leisure garden
Hobbygärtner *m* leisure (amateur) gardener
Hobelkettensäge *f* chipper chain-saw
Hobelspäne *mpl* wood shavings
Hobelzahn *m* chipper chain-saw cutter link, cutter [link]
Hobelzahnkette *f* chipper chain *(of a chain-saw)*
Hobelzahnkettensäge *f* chipper chain-saw
Hoch *n s.* Hochdruckgebiet
Hochastung *f (forest)* high (carry-up) pruning
~/selektive selective high pruning
Hochbeet *n* raised bed
hochbeinig leggy *(e.g. a hunting dog)*
Hochbinden *n* tying-up *(orcharding)*
Hochblatt *n (bot)* terminal leaf; spathe, spatha
• **mit blütenumhüllendem ~** spathaceous, spathal, spathose, spathous

~/blütenumhüllendes spathe, spatha
Hochbusch-Kulturheidelbeere *f* southeastern highbush-blueberry, Vaccinium australe
Hochdruckballenpresse *f* high-density baler, high-pressure baler
Hochdruckdüngelanze *f* high-pressure soil injector
Hochdruckdüse *f* high-pressure nozzle
Hochdruckgebiet *n* high-pressure zone, anticyclone *(climatology)*
Hochdruckgürtel *m* high-pressure belt *(climatology)*
Hochdruckkrankheit *f (vet)* hypertension
Hochdruckpresse *f s.* Hochdruckballenpresse
Hochdruckquecksilberdampflampe *f* high-pressure mercury-vapour lamp
Hochdruckreifen *m* high-pressure tyre
Hochdrucksammelpresse *f* high-density pick-up baler
Hochdruckschlauch *m* high-pressure hose
Hochdruckspritze *f* high-pressure sprayer
Hochdrucksprühgerät *n* high-pressure sprayer
Hochdrucksterilisator *m* autoclave
Hochdruckwascheinrichtung *f* high-pressure washer, big-pressure washer
Hochdruckwasch- und -desinfektionsgerät *n* high-pressure washing and disinfecting unit
Hochdruckzone *f s.* Hochdruckgebiet
Hochdurchforstung *f (forest)* high (crown) thinning, above treatment, thinning from above
Hochebene *f* [high] plateau, tableland, *(Am)* altiplano *(s. a.* Hochland*)*
Hochenergiereaktion *f* high-irradiance reaction *(plant physiology)*
Hochertragskultur *f* bumper crop
Hochertragssorte *f* high-yielding variety, HYV
Hochgebirgspflanze *f* Alpine [plant]
Hochgebirgsschaf *n* mountain (hill) sheep
Hochgebirgswald *m* high montane forest
Hochgebirgsweide *f* Alpine pasture (range), high mountain pasture, alp
Hochgeschwindigkeitsdrillmaschine *f* high-speed drill
hochgewachsen tall
hochgezüchtet highly-bred *(animal)*; specially selected *(plant)*
Hochgrasgesellschaft *f* tall-grass community
Hochgrasprärie *f* tall-grass prairie
Hochgrassavanne *f* tall-grass savanna[h]
hochhäufeln to earth [up]
Hochintensitätsreaktion *f s.* Hochenergiereaktion
Hochkippbehälter *m* high-level tipping hopper
Hochkräusen *pl* high (rocky) heads *(brewing)*
Hochlachte *f* high (pulling) face *(resin-tapping)*
Hochlagenaufforstung *f* high-altitude afforestation
Hochland *n* upland, highland, *(Am)* altiplano
Hochlandboden *m* hill (upland) soil
Hochlandschaf *n* upland sheep
Hochlandweide *f* upland pasture

Hochleistungsfütterung f feeding for high yields
Hochleistungsgel[permeations]chromatographie f high-performance gel permeation chromatography
Hochleistungs[milch]kuh f high milking cow, high-yielding dairy cow
Hochleistungsrasse f high-performance breed
Hochleistungssorte f high-yielding variety
Hochleistungstier n high-performance animal
Hochleistungszapfwelle f heavy-duty p.t.o. (power take-off)
Hochleistungszuchttier n high-performance breeding animal
Hochlysinmais m high-lysine maize
hochmontan oreal
Hochmoor n high[land] moor, high (raised) bog, rain-water bog (moor), hill (upland) moor, sphagnum bog
~/ombrogenes ombrogenous moor
Hochmoorboden m high-moor soil
Hochmoortorf m high-moor peat, white (raised bog) peat
Hochschirm m s. Hochsitz
Hochschlagen n kick, kickback (tree-felling)
Hochschleppwerk n (forest) overhead (aerator) cableway
Hochschnellen n s. Hochschlagen
Hochschnitt m high-cut (in grain harvesting)
Hochschnittbalken m high-cut cutter bar
Hochschnittkopf m snow comb (of a shearing machine)
Hochschule f/**forsttechnische** forestry technical college
~/landwirtschaftliche agricultural college (high school), (Am) aggie
Hochsilo m overground (upright) silo, tower silo
Hochsitz m (hunt) high stand (seat), raised hide, station
Hochsommer m midsummer
Hochsommertrockenheit f midsummer drought
Hochstamm m high-stem, high-stemmed tree; standard [fruit-tree]
Hochstammheidelbeere f highbush-blueberry
hochstämmig long-boled
Hochstämmige Hanfpalme f windmill palm, Trachycarpus fortunei
Hochstammrose f tree rose
Hochstaudengesellschaft f tall-forb community, tall-herb community
Höchstertrag m top (maximum, record) yield
Hochstollenreifen m lug base tyre
Hochtemperaturdrehtrommeltrockner m high-temperature rotary drum dryer
Hochtemperaturkompostierung f high-temperature composting, peak-heat composting
Hochtemperaturkurzzeitpasteurisation f high-temperature short-time pasteurization, HTST pasteurization, ultra-high temperature preservation (sterilization)

Hochtemperaturtrockner m high-temperature dryer
Hochtemperaturtrocknung f high-temperature drying
Hochtemperaturtrommeltrockner m high-temperature rotary drum dryer
hochtrabend high-stepping (horse)
Hochträchtigkeit f late pregnancy
hochtragend late-pregnant, big; to be heavy in calf (cow)
Hochumladekipp[anhäng]er m high-lift trailer, high-tipping trailer, elevating-tipping trailer
Hochveredelung f high graft
Hochwald m high [timber] forest
~/schlagweiser clear-felling high forest
Hochwaldbetrieb m, **Hochwaldsystem** n high-forest system
Hochwasser n high water; flood
Hochwasserbekämpfung f flood control
Hochwassermarke f flood mark
Hochwasserschutz m flood protection
Hochwassertoleranz f flood tolerance (e.g. of trees in flood-plain forests)
Hochweide f upland pasture; high mountain pasture
Hochwild n 1. big game; 2. [red] deer
Hochwildbestand m stock of deer
Hochwildjagd f big game hunting (shooting)
Hochwildrevier n deer forest
Hochwildwechsel m deer path
Hochzeitsflug m (ent) mating (nuptial) flight
Hochzeitskammer f brood chamber (mass-rearing of insects)
Hochzeitskleid n nuptial plumage (of birds)
Hochzwiesel f schoolmarm
Hocke f heap, pile
Hockendrusch m heap (pile) threshing
Höckerbildung f beading (in apples)
Höckerchen n tubercle
höckerig knobby, tuberous, tuberose
Höckerkiefer f knob-cone pine, Pinus attenuata
Höckerpappe f egg tray
HoCV s. Chlorosevirus des Hopfens
Hoden m testicle, testis, spermary
Hodenabstieg m testicular descent
Hodenarterie f spermatic artery
Hodenatrophie f testicular atrophy
Hodendegeneration f testicular degeneration
Hodenentfernung f (vet) orchidectomy
Hodenentzündung f (vet) orchitis
Hodenheber m external cremaster muscle
Hodenhochstand m cryptorchidism
Hodenhüllenentzündung f (vet) periorchitis
Hodenkanälchen n testicular (seminiferous) tubule
Hodenkarzinom n (vet) seminoma
Hodennetz n rete testis
Hodensack m scrotum, scrotal sac, cod
Hodensackbruch m (vet) scrotal hernia, scrotocele

Hodensackentzündung

Hodensackentzündung f *(vet)* scrotitis
Hodensackform f scrotal shape
Hodensackumfang m scrotal circumference
Hodenzwischenzelle f Leydig cell
Hodgkinsche Krankheit f *(vet)* lymphogranuloma[tosis]
Hof m 1. yard; 2. pit border *(wood anatomy)*
Hofarbeiten fpl farmyard work
Hofhund m house-dog
Hofmeistersche Ionenreihe f Hofmeister (lyotropic) series
Hofnekrosevirus n **der Tulpe** tulip halo necrosis virus
Hofraum m farmyard
Hofstatt f farmstead, steading
Hoftüpfel m bordered pit *(wood anatomy)*
Hof- und Stalltraktor m tractor for use in livestock houses
HoGV s. Hopfengelbnetzvirus
Hohe Schule f haute école *(equitation)*
~ **Sommerwurz** f greater broomrape, Orobanche major
~ **Zackenschote** f hill mustard, Turkish rocket, Bunias orientalis
Höhe f height, altitude; latitude *(geography)*
~ **des geometrischen Kronenmittelpunktes** form-point height *(of a tree)*
~/**mittlere** mean (average) height *(e.g. of a forest stand)*
Höhenanpassung f altitude adaptation
Höhenbonität f *(forest)* [height] site index
Höhenfeuchtsavanne f upland moist savanna[h]
Höhenfleckvieh n German Simment[h]al *(cattle breed)*
Höhenförderer m elevator
Höhenkiefer f upland [form of] Scotch pine
Höhenklasse f height class *(timber mensuration)*
Höhenklima n mountain climate
Höhenkrankheit f *(vet)* brisket disease
Höhenkurve f *(forest)* height curve
Höhenlinie f contour [line], level
Höhenmarke f datum level
Höhenmesser m altimeter
Höhenmessung f/**trigonometrische** trigonometrical levelling
Höhenparallaxe f Y-parallax, vertical parallax *(remote sensing)*
Höhenrasse f mountain breed
Höhenrind n mountain cattle
Höhenschichtlinie f s. Höhenlinie
Höhenstufe f altitudinal zone *(geobotany)*
Höhenstufung f altitudinal (vertical) zonation
Höhentrockensavanne f upland dry savanna[h]
Höhenviehrasse f mountain breed
Höhenwachstum n height growth, growth in height *(s. a. Höhenzuwachs)*
Höhenwiese f mountain meadow
Höhenwuchs m s. Höhenwachstum

Höhenzuwachs m height increment (accretion) *(e.g. of trees)*
Höhenzuwachskurve f height increment curve
Hoher Ampfer m great water dock, Rumex hydrolapathum
~ **Glatthafer** m tall oat[-grass], Arrhenaterum elatius
~ **Staudenrittersporn** m *(bot)* [candle] larkspur, lark-heel, Delphinium elatum
~ **Steinklee** m *(bot)* tall melilot, Melilotus altissima
~ **Wacholder** m Grecian juniper, Juniperus excelsa
Hohes Franzosengras n s. Hoher Glatthafer
Hohlast m hollow knot, pith knot
hohlblütig *(bot)* tubuliflorous
Höhle f 1. cavern, cavity, hole *(esp. anatomy)*; 2. cave; burrow, hole, den *(s. a. Bau)* • **innerhalb einer ~ [liegend]** intracavitary
Höhlenbrüter m hole nester
Hohlfäule f pipe [rot] *(of wood)*
Hohlherzigkeit f *(phyt)* hollow heart
Hohlkammerreifen m semipneumatic tyre
Hohlkegeldüse f hollow-cone nozzle
Hohlkehle f flute *(e.g. in a tree-trunk)*
hohlkehlig fluted
Hohlkrone f open-centre crown, vase-shaped crown
Hohlkronenbaum m open-centre tree
Hohlraum m hollow [space], cavity; void
Hohlraumvolumen n void volume *(e.g. of a timber stack)*
Hohlschutzscheibe f concave protecting disk *(e.g. of a planting machine)*
Hohlsein n **in der Spargelstangen** hollow stem of asparagus *(due to extreme cold in winter)*
Hohlspaten m semicircular spade
Hohltaube f stockdove, Columba oenas
Höhlung f s. Hohlraum
Hohlwurz f hollowwort *(genus Corydalis)*
Hohlzahn m hemp-nettle *(genus Galeopsis)*
Holländerblock m Dutch light structure *(greenhouse)*
Holländerfenster n Dutch light *(of a cold frame)*
Holländergewächshaus n Dutch-type greenhouse
Holländerhacke f Dutch (thrust) hoe, hand ridger
Holländerhaus n s. Holländergewächshaus
Holländerkasten m Dutch light frame
Holländern n bastard trenching, double digging
Holländische Iris f Dutch iris, Iris-hollandica hybrid
~ **Linde** f lime, Tilia vulgaris
Holländisches Rotbuntes Rind n Meuse-Rhine-Yssel *(cattle breed)*
Holländisch-Friesisches Rind n Friesian *(cattle breed)*
HolLV s. Latentes Holundervirus
Holm m spar
Holocellulose f holocellulose
holokarp *(bot)* holocarpous
holokrin holocrine *(gland)*
holometabol *(ent)* holometabolous

Holzbegleitstoff

Holometabolie f *(ent)* holometabolism
Holoparasit m holoparasite, true parasite
Holosulf n holosulf *(growth regulator)*
Holozän n Holocene
Holozänsediment n Holocene sediment
Holozön n ecosystem, biogeocoenosis
holozönotisch ecosystemic, holocoenotic
holozyklisch *(ent)* holocyclic
Holstein-Friesian-Rind n Holstein-Friesian *(cattle breed)*
Holsteiner m Holstein *(horse breed)*
Holsteinische Euterseuche f *(vet)* summer mastitis *(caused by Corynebacterium pyogenes)*
Holunder m elder[-berry] *(genus Sambucus)*
Holunderbeere f elder-berry
Holunderbeerenwein m elder[-berry] wine
Holunderblattlaus f elder aphid, Aphis sambuci
Holunderblättrige Vogelbeere f mountain ash, Sorbus sambucifolia
Holundercarlavirus n elder-berry carlavirus, ECV
Holunderlaus f s. Holunderblattlaus
Holunderschwamm m Jew's-ear [fungus], Hirneola (Auricularia) auricula-Judae
Holunderwein m elder[-berry] wine
HoLV s. Latentes Hopfenvirus
Holz n wood; timber, *(Am)* lumber • **auf ~ wachsend** lignicole, lignicolous • **aus ~** wooden, ligneous • **~ ausformen (aushalten)** to convert, to lumber, to buck, to cut into lengths, to cross-cut [into logs], to lay off • **~ fällen** to fell, to cut [down], to hew, *(Am)* to log • **loses ~ flößen** to drift, to drive
~/**abgestorbenes (abständiges)** dead wood
~/**astfreies (astreines)** clean timber
~ auf dem Stamm (Stock) s. ~/stehendes
~/**behauenes** hewn timber
~/**brandgeschädigtes** burnt timber
~/**buchsbaumartiges** boxwood
~/**eingeschlagenes** felled timber, fall
~/**exotisches** exotic timber
~/**farbstoffliefernds** dyewood
~/**faules** rotten wood, touchwood, conk, punk
~/**fehlerhaftes** cull [timcer], wrack
~/**gefälltes** felled timber, fall
~/**gefäßreiches** pored (porous) wood
~/**geflößtes** drive
~/**geharztes (gezapftes)** bled (tapped-out) timber
~/**harzgetränktes** superwood
~/**jugendliches (juveniles)** juvenile (pith, core) wood
~/**marknahes** heart [centre], pith stock
~/**morsches** s. ~/faules
~/**poriges** pored (porous) wood
~/**reifes** adult (mature) wood
~/**Reizstoffe enthaltendes** irritant timber
~/**roten Farbstoff lieferndes** redwood
~/**sekundäres** secondary xylem
~/**stehendes** [standing] timber, growing stock, standing crop
~/**triftendes** drift[wood]
~/**verblautes** blue timber
~/**verfaultes** s. ~/faules
~/**verkientes** resinous wood, fatwood, lightwood, stumpwood
Holzabfall m wood waste (residues), waste wood
Holzabfuhr f timber transport[ation], haulage
Holzabfuhrfahrzeug n timber truck, timber (wood) transport vehicle
Holzabfuhrschlitten m timber transport sledge
Holzabfuhrweg m clearing (timber transport) road, *(Am)* lumber road
~/**mit Lkw befahrbarer** lorry road
Holzablage f **am Fluß** riverside landing
Holzalkohol m wood alcohol, wood spirit[s] (naphtha), crude (natural) methanol
Holzameise f carpenter ant *(genus Camponotus)*
Holzanatomie f wood anatomy
Holzapfel[baum] m wild apple, crab[-apple], Malus sylvestris ssp. sylvestris
Holzart f wood (tree) species
~/**nutzholzliefernde** timber species
Holzartenanteil m percentage of tree species
Holzartengruppe f [tree] species group
Holzartenmischung f tree species mixture (composition)
Holzartenwahl f choice of tree species
Holzartenwechsel m change in tree species, alternation (succession) of tree species, species conversion
holzartig wood-like, woody, ligneous
Holzasche f wood ash
Holzaufarbeitung f timber conversion, assortment formation
Holzaufarbeitungskombine f multioperational logging machine, processor
Holzaufbereitung f wood processing
Holzaufkommen n timber crop, volume of timber cut
Holzaufkommensgebiet n timbershed
Holzaufmesser m scaler, culler
Holzaufschluß m wood pulping (digestion)
~ nach dem Sulfatverfahren sulphate cooking (pulping)
~ nach dem Sulfitverfahren sulphite cooking (pulping)
~/**schwefelfreier** non-sulphur pulping, alkali-peroxide pulping
Holzauktion f auction of timber
Holzausformung f timber conversion, assortment formation
Holzausformungsplatz m timber conversion yard, conversion point (site), final landing
~/**zentraler** central processing yard, industrial log depot, lower depot (landing)
Holzauszeichnung f wood marking
Holzbearbeitung f woodworking
Holzbegleitstoff m extraneous component of wood

Holzbeize

Holzbeize f stain
Holzbereitstellung f **in Abschnitten** log-length logging
Holzbeschaffungsindustrie f logging industry
Holzbestandteil m wood component
~/akzessorischer s. Holzbegleitstoff
holzbewohnend lignicole, lignicolous
Holzbiene f 1. carpenter bee (family Xylocopidae; esp. genus Xylocopa); 2. carpenter bee, Xylocopa violacea
Holzbild n wood texture, wood grain [figure]
Holzbirne f wild pear, Pyrus pyraster ssp. achras
Holzblock m log
Holzbock m (ent) sheep (castor-bean) tick, Ixodes ricinus
Holzboden m forest soil (land), timber[land], [productive] wooded area
~/absoluter absolute forest soil
Holzbodenfläche f s. Holzboden
Holzbohrer m 1. wood borer (comprehensive term); 2. carpenter moth (family Cossidae)
Holzbohrerlarve f (ent) carpenter worm
Holzbohrkäfer m wood-boring beetle (comprehensive term)
Holzbringung f logging, hauling, haulage, extraction
~ mit der Waldeisenbahn railway logging, (Am) railroad logging
~ mit Luftfahrzeugen aerial logging
~ mit Schleppern (Traktoren) tractor logging (hauling)
~ mittels Sapinen brutting (in Alpine regions)
holzbrütend timber-breeding (e.g. bark-beetle)
Holzcellulose f wood cellulose, lignocellulose
Holzdestillation f wood distillation
~/trockene wood carbonization (pyrolysis)
Holzdichte f wood density
Holzdiebstahl m theft of timber (wood)
Holzeinschlag m timber harvest, forest harvest[ing], felling, fall, [wood] cutting, cut, throwing, (Am) logging (s. a. under Einschlag)
~ auf überfluteten Schlagflächen underwater logging
~ durch Lohnunternehmen contract-felling
~/exploitativer timber mining
~ gegen den Wind mangling
~ im Sommer summer felling
~ mit Kraftbetrieb power (powered cable) logging
Holzeinschlagsbetrieb m logging enterprise
Holzeinschlagsgebiet n logging region, chance
Holzeinschlagsindustrie f logging industry
Holzeinschlagskonzession f timber concession, logging (cutting) right
Holzeinschlagsmaschinensystem n complete logging system
Holzeinschlagstrupp m logging crew
Holzeinschlagunternehmer m lumberman, logger
Holzeinzugsgebiet n timbershed
Holzelement n wood element

Holzentnahme f **aus dem Bestand** stand depletion
Holzentrindung f s. Entrindung
hölzern 1. wooden, made of wood, timber; 2. s. holzig
Holzernte f timber harvest, forest harvest[ing] (s. a. Holzeinschlag)
Holzerntekombine f s. Holzerntemaschine
Holzerntekosten pl logging (cutting) expenses
Holzerntemaschine f [timber, tree] harvester, tree harvesting machine
Holzertrag m timber yield (crop)
~/erntekostenfreier stumpage [value]
Holzerzeugung f timber production (growing), wood production
Holzessig m wood vinegar, pyroligneous vinegar (acid)
Holzextrakt[iv]stoff m wood extractive
Holzfäller m woodcutter, wood hewer, feller, (Am) faller, logger, chopper, lumberman, lumberer, lumberjack, axe-man
Holzfälleraxt f woodcutter's axe, axe for felliog
Holzfällermeister m logging foreman
Holzfällerpodest n staging
Holzfällerrotte f logging crew
Holzfällerunterkunft f logging camp
Holzfällung f s. Holzeinschlag
Holzfaser f wood (ligneous) fibre, libriform [wood-]fibre
Holzfaserplatte f wood fibreboard
Holzfaß n wooden cask
Holzfäule f wood rot, timber decay
Holzfehler m wood defect, fault in timber
~/geringfügiger flaw in wood
Holzfläche f s. Holzboden
Holzfloß n (Am) crib; raft, float
Holzflößen n s. Flößerei
holzfressend xylophagous, lignivorous, wood-eating, wood-feeding
Holzfresser m xylophage, lignivore, wood-eater
Holzfrevel m s. Holzdiebstahl
holzfrüchtig xylocarpous
Holzfuhre f s. Holzladung
Holzgasgenerator m wood-gas engine
Holzgefäß n (bot) wood vessel (tube)
Holzgeist m s. Holzalkohol
Holzgerüst n scaffold (e.g. for tobacco drying)
Holzgewächs n woody (ligneous) plant
Holzgewebe n s. Holzparenchym
Holzgummi n wood gum, xylan (polysaccharide)
Holzhackschnitzel n wood chip
Holzhandel m timber (lumber) trade, wood marketing
Holzharke f wooden rake
Holzhauer m s. Holzfäller
Holzhof m s. Holzlager
Holzhydrolyse f wood [pulp] hydrolysis, wood saccharification
holzig woody, ligneous, xyloid

Holzigkeit f woodiness
Holzimprägnieranstalt f wood impregnation plant
Holzimprägnierung f wood impregnation (steeping)
Holzimprägnierungsmittel n wood preservative
Holzindustrie f wood industry (s. a. Holzwirtschaft)
Holzknospe f wood bud
Holzkohle f [wood-]charcoal, char[coal]
Holzkohlenbrenner m charcoal-burner, wood collier
Holzkohlenteer m charcoal tar
Holzkonservierung f wood preservation
Holzkonservierungsmittel n wood preservative
Holzkropf m (phyt) rind gall
Holzkunde f wood science
Holzladebaum m timber tosser
Holzladekran m log loader
Holzladevorrichtung f wood loading equipment
Holzladung f cart-load of wood, drag, turn
Holzlager n, **Holzlagerplatz** m wood (log) storage place, forest depot, sawmill (lumber) yard, timber yard (stock), bank, ramp[site]
Holzlagerung f timber (wood) storage
Holzleber f (vet) amyloidosis
Holzlos n parcel (timber trade)
Holzmarkstrahl m wood ray
Holzmarkt m timber market
Holzmaserung f wood grain [figure]
Holzmasse f 1. wood weight, weight of wood; 2. s. Holzschliff
Holzmehl n wood flour (meal)
Holzmeßanlage f [timber] volume calculator
Holzmeßanweisung f mensurational instruction
Holzmeßkunde f timber mensuration; forest (tree) mensuration, dendrometry
holzmeßkundlich mensurational
Holzmessung f in Boardfuß (Brettfuß) board measure[ment]
Holzmilz f (vet) amyloidosis
Holznutzung f forest cropping
Holznutzungsabgabe f tax on wood exploitation
Holznutzungsgebiet n forest economic region
Holznutzungsrecht n timber concession, logging (cutting) right
Holzöl n Chinese wood oil, Chinawood (tung) oil
Holzölbaum m Chinese wood-oil tree, tung-[oil-]tree, Aleurites fordii
Holzparenchym n wood (xylem) parenchyma, wood[-parenchyma] tissue, woody tissue
Holzpfahl m wood (timber) pile, pale, paling; wood[en] post
Holzpflanze f woody (ligneous) plant
Holzpflug m wooden plough
Holzplantage f timber plantation
Holzplatz m s. Holzlager
Holzpolyose f wood poly[sacchar]ose, hemicellulose, pseudocellulose
Holzposten m parcel (timber trade)

Holzprobensammlung f wood [sample] collection, collection of wood specimens, xylarium
Holzprüfgerät n wood testing apparatus
Holzpyrolyse f wood pyrolysis (distillation)
Holzrechen m wooden rake
Holzressourcen fpl timber resources
Holzreste mpl s. Holzabfall
Holzriese f log chute, [timber, log] slide, slip, channel
Holzrohdichte f wood density
Holzrückekarren m bogie, bummer
Holzrückung f skidding, snigging
~ **mit Pferden** horse skidding
~ **mit Schleppern** tractor skidding
~ **mit tierischer Kraft** animal skidding
~ **ohne Chokerseil** chokerless skidding
Holzrutsche f s. Holzriese
Holzsammelplatz m [im Wald] [forest] log depot, bank[ing ground], upper landing
Holzsäure f wood acid
Holzschädling m wood (timber) pest, wood destroyer (fretter)
Holzschälmaschine f wood-peeling machine
Holzscheit n billet [of wood], log, shide
Holzschild m shield (in bud grafting)
Holzschleifen n wood grinding
Holzschleifer m wood grinder
Holzschliff m [mechanical] wood pulp, groundwood [pulp]
Holzschnitzel n wood chip
Holzschutz m wood preservation (protection), preservation of timber
Holzschutzmittel n wood preservative
~/**öl[art]iges** tar-oil-type preservative
Holzschwemmteich m rafting reservoir
Holzsirup m wood molasses
Holzsortiment n timber assortment
Holzspaltmaschine f wood-splitting machine, cleaving machine
Holzspan m wood chip; [wood] sliver
Holzspanplatte f wood particle board, wood chipboard
Holzsplitter m wood splinter
Holzstapel m timber stack, stack of wood, woodpile
Holzstapler m wood stacker
Holzstärke f wood starch
Holzstau m [log-]jam
Holzstaub m wood dust
Holzstoff m 1. lignin, encrusting (incrusting) ingredient; 2. s. Holzschliff
Holzstrahl m wood ray, vascular (xylem) ray
Holzstrahlzelle f [wood] ray cell
Holzsubstanz f wood (ligneous) substance, lignified tissue
Holztannin n wood tannin
Holztaxe f statutory stumpage price
Holztechnologie f wood technology
Holzteer m wood tar

Holzteerkreosot

Holzteerkreosot *n* wood-tar creosote
Holzteerphenol *n* wood-tar phenol
Holzteil *m* wood vessels, xylem
Holzterpentinöl *n* wood [spirits of] turpentine, wood spirit[s]
Holztextur *f* wood texture, wood grain [figure]
Holztorf *m* woody peat
Holztränkung *f* timber (wood) impregnation, wood steeping
Holztränkungsanlage *f* timber (wood) impregnation plant
Holztransportfahrzeug *n* timber transport vehicle
Holztrieb *m* long shoot
Holztrift *f* wood floating, log driving
Holztrocknungsanlage *f* timber dryer, wood-drying plant, seasoning (timber-drying) kiln
Holzüberschußgebiet *n* timber-surplus region
Holzung *f* 1. forest, wood[land]; 2. *s.* Holzeinschlag
Holzverarbeitung *f* wood processing
Holzverarbeitungsprodukt *n* wood processing product
Holzverbrennungsanlage *f* wood burner
Holzveredelung *f* wood processing
Holzveredelungsprodukt *n* wood processing product
Holzverkohlung *f* charcoal burning, wood charring (carbonization)
Holzverladevorrichtung *f* wood loading equipment
Holzvermesser *m* scaler, culler
Holzversteigerung *f* auction of timber, timber auction
Holzverzuckerung *f* wood saccharification, wood [pulp] hydrolysis
Holzvolumen *n* timber volume
~ in Kubikfuß footage
~ mit Rinde tree overbark volume
Holzvorrat *m* timber stock
~/lebender (stehender) growing stock, *(Am)* stumpage
Holzvorratsaufnahme *f*, Holzvorratsinventur *f* growing-stock inventory, timber survey (inventory), cruise, tally
Holzwerbung *f s.* Holzernte
Holzwespe *f* wood-wasp, horn-tail *(family Siricidae)*
Holzwespenlarve *f* horn-tail
Holzwirtschaft *f* timber trade and industry, forest [products] industry
Holzwolle *f* wood-wool, excelsior
Holzwolle-Leichtbauplatte *f* wood-wool building slab
Holzwurm *m* [common, European] furniture beetle, death-watch [beetle], woodworm, worm, Anobium punctatum (striatum)
Holzzeichnung *f* wood grain [figure], wood grain pattern[ing]
Holzzelle *f* wood cell (element)
Holzzellstoff *m* 1. [chemical] wood pulp; 2. *s.* Holzcellulose
Holzzersetzung *f* wood decay (decomposition)
holzzerstörend wood-destroying, ligniperdous
Holzzerstörer *m* wood destroyer
Holzzerstörung *f* wood destruction
Holzzucht *f s.* Holzerzeugung
Holzzucker *m* wood sugar, xylose *(pentose)*
Holzzunge *f (vet)* wooden tongue
Holzzuschußgebiet *n* timber-deficit region
Homa *s.* Holzmeßanweisung
HoMCV *s.* Hopfenmosaikchlorosevirus
Homocyst[e]in *n* homocysteine
Homocyst[e]insäure *f* homocysteic acid *(amino-acid)*
Homofermentation *f* homofermentation
homofermentativ homofermentative
homogam *(bot)* homogamous
Homogamet *m* homogamete • **Homogameten bildend** homogametic
homogametisch homogametic
Homogamie *f (bot)* homogamy
homogen homogeneous; regular, uniform *(a tree stand)*
Homogenisat *n* homogenate
Homogenisator *m* homogenizer
homogenisieren to homogenize
Homogenisierung *f* homogenization
Homogenisierzentrifuge *f (dairy)* clarifixator
Homogenität *f* homogeneity
Homogenitätstest *m* chi-squared test *(statistics)*
Homogentisinsäure *f* homogentisic acid
Homoglucan *n* polysaccharide
homoiotherm homoiothermic, homo[eo]thermal
Homoiotherme *m* homoiotherm, endotherm
Homoiothermie *f* homoiothermy
homolog homologous
Homolyse *f* homolysis
Homomerie *f (gen)* homomery
Homöokinese *f* homoeokinesis
homöolog homoeologous *(chromosome)*
Homöostas[i]e *f* homoeostasis *(biocybernetics)*
homöotherm *s.* homoiotherm
homoploid *(gen)* homoploid
Homoploide *m* homoploid
Homoploidie *f* homoploidy
Homoptere *m (ent)* homopteran, plant sap feeder *(order Homoptera)*
Homoserin *n* homoserine *(amino-acid)*
Homoserindehydratase *f* homoserine dehydratase *(enzyme)*
homospor *(bot)* homosporous, isosporic
Homospore *f* homospore, isospore
Homosporie *f* homospory, isospory
homostyl *(bot)* homostyled, homostylous
Homostylie *f* homostyly
Homothallie *f (bot)* homothallism
homozygot homozygous, pure
Homozygote *m* homozygote

Homozygotie *f* homozygosis, homozygosity, purity
HoMV *s.* Hopfenmosaikvirus
Honig *m* honey, hinnie, hinny *(Scotland)*
~/[aus]geschleuderter extracted honey
~/reifer ripe honey
Honigausbeute *f* honey crop
Honigbeere *f* Spanish-lime, kinnup tree, Melicoccus bijugatus
Honigbiene *f* honey-bee, [hive] bee, Apis mellifica (mellifera)
Honigbienenhaltung *f s.* Bienenhaltung
Honigblase *f* honey sac, honey stomach (bag) *(of the honey-bee)*
Honigdrüse *f (bot)* nectary
honigend *(bot)* melliferous
Honigernte *f* honey harvest
Honigertrag *m* honey crop
honigerzeugend *(bot, zoo)* melliferous
Honigglas *n* honey jar
Honigklee *m* white[-flowered] sweet clover, white melilot, Melilotus alba
Honigkleekrankheit *f* sweet clover poisoning *(of cattle)*
Honigmagen *m s.* Honigblase
Honigmelone *f* honeydew melon, Cucumis melo
Honigpalme *f* honey palm *(genus Jubaea)*
Honigpresse *f* honey press
Honigraumzarge *f* honey super
Honigsaft *m s.* Nektar
Honigschleuder *f* honey extractor (centrifuge)
Honigschwamm *m* honey-fungus, shoe-string fungus, Armillaria (Armillariella) mellea
Honigsieb *n* honey strainer
Honigtau *m* honeydew, melligo
Honigtauhonig *m* honeydew honey
Honigwabe *f* honeycomb, deep comb
Honigwein *m* mead
hopfen to hop *(beer)*
Hopfen *m* 1. hop *(genus Humulus)*; 2. [common, climber] hop, Humulus lupulus • **~ ernten** to hop • **~ erzeugen** to hop • **mit ~ würzen** to hop *(beer)*
Hopfenanbau *m* hop growing
Hopfenanbaugebiet *n* hop-growing district
Hopfenanlage *f* hop-garden, hop-yard
Hopfenaroma *n* hop aroma
Hopfenbau *m* hop growing
Hopfenbauer *m* hop grower
Hopfenbauschlepper *m*, **Hopfenbautraktor** *m* hop-garden tractor
Hopfenbestandteil *m* hop constituent
Hopfenbitter *m s.* Hopfenbitterstoff
Hopfenbittersäure *f* [hop] bitter acid *(comprehensive term)*
Hopfenbitterstoff *m* hop bitter [substance]
Hopfenblattlaus *f* [damson-]hop aphid, hop fly, Phorodon humuli
Hopfenblattrollvirus *n* hop leaf roll virus
Hopfenblüten *fpl* hop

Hopfenbuche *f* hop hornbeam *(genus Ostrya)*
Hopfendarre *f* hop dryer, hop[-drying] kiln, oast, cockle
Hopfendrüse *f* hop gland
Hopfeneiweiß *n* hop protein
Hopfenerdfloh *m* hop flea-beetle, Psylliodes punctulata
Hopfenernte *f* hopping
Hopfenerntemaschine *f* hop harvester
Hopfenextrakt *m* hop extract
Hopfenfeld *n* hop field *(s. a.* Hopfenanlage*)*
Hopfenfräse *f* rotary hop cultivator
Hopfengabe *f* hop addition *(brewing)*
Hopfengarten *m s.* Hopfenanlage
Hopfengelbfleckenvirus *n* hop yellow leaf spot virus, HYLV
Hopfengelbnetzvirus *n* hop yellow net virus
Hopfengerüst *n* hop wirework
Hopfengranulat *n* hop granules
Hopfenharz *n* hop resin
Hopfeninhaltsstoff *m* hop constituent
Hopfenklee *m* hop clover, black medic[k], yellow trefoil, nonesuch, Medicago lupulina
Hopfenkonzentrat *n* hop concentrate
Hopfenlagerung *f* hop storage
Hopfenlaus *f s.* Hopfenblattlaus
Hopfenluzerne *f s.* Hopfenklee
Hopfenmehl *n* lupulin
Hopfenmehltau *m* hop mould
Hopfenmosaikchlorosevirus *n* hop mosaic chlorosis virus
Hopfenmosaikvirus *n* hop mosaic virus, HMV
Hopfenöl *n* hop oil
Hopfenpellet *n* hop pellet
Hopfenpflanze *f* hop plant
Hopfenpflücker *m* hop-picker, hopper
Hopfenpflückmaschine *f* hop picking machine, hop-picker
Hopfenpflug *m* hop plough
Hopfenpreßwasser *n* hop press liquor
Hopfenpulver *n* hop powder (dust)
Hopfenqualität *f* hop quality
Hopfenrebe *f* [hop-]bine, hop-bind, hop vine
Hopfenrebenmehl *n* hop-bine meal *(feed-stuff)*
Hopfenrebenpellet *n* hop-bine pellet *(feed-stuff)*
Hopfenseide *f (bot)* large dodder, Cuscuta europaea
Hopfenseiher *m* hop back, *(Am)* hop jack
Hopfenseparator *m* hop separator (strainer)
Hopfenspinner *m* ghost [swift] moth, Hepialus humuli (lupulinus)
Hopfenspinnerlarve *f (ent)* otter
Hopfenstange *f* hop-pole
Hopfenstauchviroid *n* hop stunt viroid
Hopfentreber *pl* spent hops
Hopfentrocknung *f* hop drying
Hopfenwurzelspinner *m s.* Hopfenspinner
Hopfenzapfen *m* hop cone
Hopfenzapfenschuppe *f* hop cone scale

Hopfenzerreißmaschine

Hopfenzerreißmaschine f hop shredder
Hopfung f hopping *(brewing)*
Hoppegartener Husten m equine influenza, epizootic cough in horse
Hoppus[kubik]fuß m Hoppus [cubic] foot
Hoppus-Messung f Hoppus (quarter-girth) measure *(timber mensuration)*
Horde f 1. feeding rack; 2. *s.* Hürde 1.; 3. *s.* Hordendarre
Hordecale m hordecale, barley-rye bastard
Hordein n hordein *(prolamine of barley)*
Hordendarre f floor, flake, screen dryer
Hordenin n hordenine *(alkaloid)*
Hordenschlag m sheep-cote, hurdle fold
Hordenschüttler m [oscillating] straw rack, multiple-section shaker *(of a thresher)*
Hordentrockner m tray (deep-bed) dryer
Horizont m *(soil)* horizon, level
Horizontabfolge f horizon sequence
horizontal gerichtet *(bot)* plagiotropic
Horizontaldarre f horizontal kiln
Horizontalgattersägewerk n horizontal-frame [saw]mill
Horizontalkelter f horizontal press
Horizontalparallaxe f X-parallax, absolute parallax *(surveying)*
Horizontalschnitt m undercutting *(of nursery transplants)*
Horizontalsilo m horizontal (clamp) silo, silage clamp
~/ebenerdiger bunker silo
~/überdachter Dutch barn silo
Horizontalversetzung f **von Luftmassen** advection
Horizontalwurzel f horizontal (surface) root
Horizontalzellenraddrillmaschine f horizontal-plate planter
Horizontfolge f *(soil)* horizon sequence
Horizontierung f *(soil)* horizonation
Horizontprofil n *(soil)* horizon sequence
Hormon n hormone
~/adrenocorticotropes corticotrop[h]in, adrenocorticotrop[h]ic hormone, ACTH
~/aglanduläres tissue hormone
~/antidiuretisches antidiuretic hormone, vasopressin
~/follikelstimulierendes follicle-stimulating hormone, FSH
~/gastrointestinales gastro-intestinal hormone
~/laktogenes (laktotropes) lactogenic hormone, luteotrop[h]ic hormone, LTH, luteotrop[h]in, prolactin, mammotropin
~/luteinisierendes luteining hormone, LH, lutropin, interstitial-cell stimulating hormone, ICSH
~/luteotropes (mammotropes) *s.* ~/laktogenes
~/melanozytenstimulierendes melanocyte-stimulating hormone, melanotropin, intermedin
~/östrogenes oestrogen
~/pflanzliches phytohormone

~/somatotropes somatotropin, STH, growth hormone, GW
~/thyreotropes thyrotropin, thyrotropic (thyroid-stimulating) hormone, TSH
~/wachstumsförderndes growth-promoting hormone
hormonal hormonal
Hormonantagonist m hormone antagonist
hormonbedingt, hormonell hormonal
Hormonfalle f hormone trap *(biological pest control)*
Hormonimitation f hormone mimic
Hormoninhibitor m hormone inhibitor
Hormonsekretion f hormone secretion
Hormonwirkung f hormonal activity
Horn n 1. horn *(of horned animals)*; 2. *s.* Hornstoff
hornähnlich corneous
hornartig corneous
hornig corneous
Hornast m horn knot
Hornballen m bulb of the heel *(hoof anatomy)*
Hornbaum m hornbeam, hornbeech, horse (hurst, white) beech, yoke elm, Carpinus betulus
Hornbildungsanomalie f, **Hornbildungsstörung** f dyskeratosis
Hornblatt n hornwort *(genus Ceratophyllum)*
Hornblende f hornblende, amphibole *(soil-forming rock)*
Hörnchen n squirrel *(family Sciuridae)*
Hornentfernung f dehorning
Hörnerkamm m horn[ed] comb *(of fowl)*
hörnertragend cornute[d], cornigerous
Hörnerv m auditory (acoustic) nerve
Hornfaser f horn fibre
Hornfleck m *(vet)* quittor, quitter
Hornfliege f horn fly, Haematobia irritans
Hornführer m horn trainer
Hornhaut f [eye] cornea
Hornhautbruch m *(vet)* keratocele, herniation of Descemet's membrane
Hornhauteinschmelzung f *(vet)* keratomalacia
Hornhautentzündung f *(vet)* keratitis
Hornhautnarbe f *(vet)* leucoma
Hornhauttrübung f *(vet)* corneal opacity
Hornisse f [giant] hornet, Vespa crabro
Hornissenschwärmer m hornet moth (clear-wing), Aegeria apiformis
Hornkauter m electric dehorner
Hornklee m 1. bird's-foot, lotus *(genus Lotus)*; 2. common bird's-foot trefoil, *(Am)* broadleaf birds-foot trefoil, Lotus corniculatus
Hornkluft f *s.* Hornspalte
Hornknospe f horn bud (button) *(e.g. of calves)*
• **die ~ zerstören** to disbud, to dishorn
Hornknospenzerstörung f dishorning
Hornkraut n 1. chick[en]weed, mouse-ear [chickweed], cerastium *(genus Cerastium)*; 2. snow-in-summer, snow-in-harvest, Cerastium tomentosum

Hornleiter *m* horn trainer
hornlos hornless, poll[ed], hummel
Hornlosigkeit *f* hornlessness, polledness
Hornmehl *n* horn meal
Hornmelde *f (Am, bot)* winter fat *(genus Krascheninnikovia)*
Hornmilbe *f* wood mite *(family Oribatidae)*
Hornrichteapparat *m* horn trainer
Hornring *m* horn ring
Hornsauerklee *m* creeping oxalis, yellow sorrel, Oxalis corniculata
Hornschale *f* parchment skin *(of coffee berry)*
Hornschicht *f* horny layer *(of epidermis)*
Hornschotenklee *m s.* Hornklee
Hornsohle *f* sole [of hoof]
Hornspalte *f (vet)* sand-crack
~/durchlaufende complete sand-crack, false quarter
Hornstoff *m* keratin, horn *(scleroprotein)*
Hornstrahl *m* frog *(of hoof)*
Hornstrauchgewächse *npl* dogwood family *(family Cornaceae)*
Horntrespe *f* prairie grass, Bromus catharticus (unioloides)
Hornveilchen *n* horned violet, tufted pansy, Viola cornuta
Hornvieh *n* [horned] cattle, bovine animals
Hornwand *f* wall of the hoof
Hornwurm *m (vet)* panaritium
Hornzange *f* horn-removal nippers
Hornzapfen *m* core *(of ruminants)*
HorRFV *s.* Hortensienringfleckenvirus
Horst *m* 1. eyrie, aerie *(nest of raptorial birds)*; 2. hurst, clump *(of plants)*; tuft *(of grass)*
horstbildend *(bot)* c[a]espitose, caespitous, tufted
Horstgras *n* bunch[-type] grass, tussock (tufted) grass
Horstsaat *f* dibbling
Hortensie *f* 1. hydrangea *(genus Hydrangea)*; 2. hortensia, common (florist's, French) hydrangea, Hydrangea macrophylla
Hortensienringfleckenvirus *n* hydrangea ring spot virus, HRSV
Hortikultur *f s.* Gartenbau
Hortisol *m* hortisol, horticultural soil
hott!, hottehü! gee[-ho], gee-up, giddap *(command to draught animals)*
Hottentottenfeige *f* hottentot fig, Carpobrotus edulis
Houdan *n* Houdan *(breed of fowl)*
HS-CoA *s.* Coenzym A
HSV *s.* Hopfenstaucheviroid
HSVzV *s.* Virus der sterilen Verzwergung des Hafers
hü! *s.* hott!
Hub *m* lift
Hubarm *m* lift arm
Hubgabel *f* fork-lift, lifting prong; push-off buck-rake

Hubhöhe *f* [height of] lift, hoisting height
Hubkarren *m* lift truck
Hubkupplung *f* [pick-up] hitch *(of a tractor)*
Hublader *m* push-off buck-rake
Hubleistung *f* lifting power
Hubrad *n* lifting (lifter) wheel, wheel elevator
Hubraum *m s.* Motorhubraum
Hubschrauberlandeplatz *m* heliport
Hubschraubertank *m* helitank *(forest fire control)*
Hubstange *f* lift rod (link) *(of a three-point hitch)*
Hubstapler *m* stacker
Hubwelle *f* rockshaft *(of a three-point hitch)*
Huchen *m (zoo)* huch[en], Hucho hucho
hudern to dust[-bath] *(fowl)*
Huderplatz *m* dusting place
Huf *m* 1. hoof, foot; 2. *s.* Hufkapsel
~ des Schalenwilds cloven hoof
~/krummer twisted foot
~/regelmäßiger normal foot
~/spitzer (spitz gewinkelter) sloping (oblique) foot
~/stumpfer (stumpf gewinkelter) upright (steep front wall) hoof
Hufballen *m* hoof-pad, footpad, frog pad, digital cushion
Hufbein *n* pedal (coffin) bone, third phalanx
Hufbeinbeugesehne *f* deep digital flexor tendon
Hufbeschlag *m* [horse]shoeing
~/aufklebbarer glue-on shoe *(esp. made of epoxy)*
~/orthopädischer corrective shoeing
Hufbeschlaghammer *m* shoeing hammer
Hufbeschlagschmied *m s.* Hufschmied
Hufbeschlagstand *m* brake
Hufbeschlagvorrichtung *f* horseshoeing frame
Hufbeschlagzange *f* farrier's pincers
Hufe *f* old German unit of land area, 1 Hufe = 8 to 15 hectares
Hufeisen *n* horseshoe, shoe • **mit Stollen versehen** to rough • **ein ~ verlieren** to cast
~ mit durchlaufendem Falz full-swedged shoe
~/eiförmig geschlossenes egg-bar shoe
~/geschlossenes full-bar shoe
~/offenes open shoe
~/orthopädisches surgical shoe
Hufeisenklee *m* horseshoe vetch, Hippocrepis comosa (multisiliquosa)
Hufeisenschenkelbreite *f* web [of shoe]
Hufeisenvorderteil *m* toe
Huferkrankung *f* hoof disease
Hufflache *f* bearing surface [of the shoe]
Hufgelenk *n* coffin-joint, corono-pedal joint, distal interphalangeal joint
Hufgeschwür *n (vet)* fetlow
Hufgesundheit *f* hoof health
Hufkapsel *f* coffin
Hufknorpelentzündung *f*, **Hufknorpelfistel** *f (vet)* quittor, quitter
Hufknorpelverknöcherung *f (vet)* sidebone disease
Hufkrone *f* coronet, coronamen

Huflattich

Huflattich *m (bot)* coltsfoot, foalfoot, horse-foot, Tussilago farfara
Huflederhautnekrose *f (vet)* necrotic pododermatitis
Hufmesser *n* hoof knife (cutter)
Hufnagel *m* horseshoe nail, hobnail
Huföl *n* hoof oil
Hufpflege *f* hoof (foot) care, care of hoofs, hoof trimming
Hufpflegeöl *n* hoof oil
Hufraspel *f* hoof rasp
Hufräumer *m* hoof-pick
Hufrehe *f (vet)* founder, laminitis
Hufrollenentzündung *f* navicular disease *(of horses)*
Hufscher Klemmspaten *m (forest)* planting bar, notching spade
Hufschlag *m* hoofbeat
Hufschmied *m* farrier, horseshoer, shoeing smith
Hufschmiede *f* farriery
Hufschneidezange *f* hoof cutting pincers
Hufsohle *f* sole [of hoof]
Hufstrahl *m* frog, footpad
Hüftbein *n* 1. hip-bone, innominate bone; 2. *s.* Hüftstück
Hüftbeugehaltung *f* breech position (presentation)
Hüftdarm *m* ileum
Hüftdarmentzündung *f (vet)* ileitis
Hüftdarmverdaulichkeit *f* ileal digestibility *(of nutrients)*
Hüfte *f* hip, hep, coxa
Hüftgelenk *n* hip-joint; thurl *(of cattle)*
Hüftgelenkdysplasie *f (vet)* hip dysplasia
~ der Puten shaky-leg syndrome of turkeys, leg weakness condition of turkeys
Hüfthöcker *m* point of hip, hook *(animal anatomy)*
Hüfthöhe *f* hip-height
Huftier *n* hoofed animal, ungulate *(group Ungulata)* • **zu den Huftieren gehörend** ungulate
~/paarzehiges cloven-hoofed animal (ungulate), artiodactyl *(order Artiodactyla)*
~/unpaarzehiges odd-toed animal (ungulate), perissodactyl[e] *(order Perissodactyla)*
hüftig hippy *(livestock judging)*
Hüftknochen *m s.* Hüftbein 1.
Hüftstück *n (slaught)* aitchbone, edgebone, rump
Huf- und Hornmehl *n* hoof and horn [meal] *(nitrogen fertilizer)*
Hufuntersuchungszange *f* hoof tester
Hufverschlag *m s.* Hufrehe
Hufwand *f* wall of the hoof
Hufzange *f* farrier's pincers
hufzwängig *(vet)* hoof-bound
Hügel *m* hill
~/kleiner hillock
Hügelameise *f* hill (wood) ant, Formica rufa
Hügelbeet *n* raised bed, ridge
Hügelerdbeere *f* green strawberry, Fragaria viridis

Hügelgelände *n*, **Hügelland** *n* hill[y] country, rolling (undulating) land
Hügellandstufe *f* hill belt
Hügelmeier *m (Am, bot)* quinsywort, Asperula cynanchica
Hügelpflanzung *f (forest)* mound (hillock) planting, mounding, planting on mounds
Hügelsaat *f (forest)* sowing on ridges
Hügelstufe *f* hill belt • **zur ~ gehörend** *(ecol)* colline
Huhn *n* 1. fowl, chicken, Gallus gallus domesticus; 2. hen; 3. common partridge, Perdix perdix
Hühnchen *n* chicken
Hühnerauslauf *m* fowl-run, hen-run
Hühnerbroiler *m* chicken broiler
Hühnercholera *f (vet)* fowl cholera
Hühnerei *n* [chicken, hen] egg
Hühnerfarm *f* fowl farm, hennery
Hühnerfavus *m (vet)* fowl favus
Hühnerfleisch *n* chicken [meat]
Hühnerfloh *m* [European] chicken flea, hen flea, Ceratophyllus gallinae
Hühnerfutter *n* chicken-feed
Hühnerhabicht *m* goshawk, Accipiter gentilis
Hühnerhaltung *f* fowl farming
Hühnerhaus *n* henhouse
Hühnerhirse *f* water-grass, Echinochloa crus-galli
Hühnerhof *m* hen-yard, hennery, fowl-run
Hühnerkammfloh *m* sticktight flea of poultry, Echidnophaga gallinacea
Hühnerkopflaus *f* chicken head louse, Cuclotogaster (Gallipeurus) heterographus
Hühnerkorb *m* coop
Hühnerkot *m* chicken faeces
Hühnerkrankheit *f* fowl disease
Hühnermast *f* chicken fattening
Hühnerpest *f (vet)* fowl pest (plague)
Hühnerpocken *pl (vet)* roup • **an ~ erkrankt (leidend)** roupy
Hühnerrasse *f* chicken breed, breed of fowl
Hühnerschnupfen *m* infectious coryza of chickens (poultry)
Hühnerseuche *f*/**Nigerianische (Palästinensische)** avian cell inclusion disease
Hühnersperma *n* chicken semen
Hühnerstall *m* henhouse, chicken (fowl) house, chicken coop, [chicken-]roost, [hen-]coop
Hühnerstange *f* hen-roost, perch
Hühnerzucht *f* chicken breeding
Hulebaum *m* Castilla rubber, Castilla elastica
Hüllblatt *n (bot)* wrapper leaf, bract
Hülle *f (bot, zoo)* hull, husk; coat; sheath; involucre, velum, veil, theca • **mit häutiger (häutchenartiger) ~** tunicarte
~/becherförmige *(zoo)* cupule
~ der Samenanlage *(bot)* integument, tegument
~ der Samenanlage/innere tegmen
~/innere partial veil *(of gill fungi)*
hüllfrüchtig *(bot)* angiocarpic, angiocarpous

Hüllprotein *n* coat protein *(of viruses)*
Hüllschicht *f* peridium *(of fungal fruiting bodies)*
Hüllspelze *f (bot)* glume
~/obere upper glume
Hülse *f (bot)* 1. capsule; pod, cod, siliqua, *(Am)* shuck; legume; skin *(of fruits)*; 2. [English, Christmas] holly, Ilex aquifolium • **Hülsen ansetzen** to pod • **Hülsen bilden** to pod
Hülsenabwurf *m* pod abortion
Hülsenfäule *f (phyt)* pod rot
Hülsenfrucht *f* legume, pulse [crop], black straw crop
hülsenfruchtartig leguminous
Hülsenfruchtdreschmaschine *f* podder
Hülsenfruchter *m s.* Hülsenfrüchtler
Hülsenfrüchtler *m* legume, leguminous plant *(family Leguminosae)* • **die ~ betreffend** leguminous
Hülsennaht *f* pod seam
Hülsensammelvorrichtung *f* pods gathering device
hülsig husky
Humat *n (soil)* humate
Humatdünger *m* humate fertilizer
Humerus *m* humerus *(animal anatomy)*
humid[e] humid, damp, moist
Humidität *f* humidity, dampness, moisture
Humifikation *f s.* Humifizierung
humifizieren to humify
Humifizierung *f* humification, humus formation
humikol humicolous
Humin *n* humin
Huminsäure *f* humic acid
Huminsäurefraktion *f* humic acid fraction
Huminstoff *m* humic material (substance) • **Huminstoffe bilden** to humify
Huminstoffentstehung *f* humification
Hummel *f* bumble-bee, humble-bee *(genus Bombus)*
humos, humös humic, humous, humus-rich
[α-]Humulen *n* α-humulene *(constituent of essential oils)*
Humulon *n* humulon[e] *(hop resin)*
Humus *m* humus, soil organic matter, SOM; mould, detritus
~/milder mild (soft) humus
Humusabbau *m* humus decomposition
Humusakkumulation *f*, **Humusanreicherung** *f* humus accumulation, accumulation of humus
Humusanteil *m* humus portion
Humusauflage *f* ectohumus; forest floor
Humusbedarf *m* humus requirement
humusbewohnend humicolous
Humusbildung *f* humus formation
Humusbiochemie *f* humus biochemistry
Humusboden *m* humus (vegetable) soil, vegetable (ulmous) earth, mould
Humuscarbonatboden *m* humus (humic) carbonate soil, rendzina
Humuschemie *f* humus chemistry

Humusdünger *m* humic fertilizer
Humusdynamik *f* humus dynamics
Humuserde *f s.* Humusboden
Humusform *f* humus form
Humusfraktionierung *f* humus fractionation
Humusgley[boden] *m* humic gley [soil], humic ground-water gley
Humushandelsdünger *m* humic fertilizer
Humushorizont *m* humus horizon, Ao-horizon
Humuskohle *f* humic coal
Humusortstein *m* humic ortstein
Humusprofil *n* humus profile
humusreich humus-rich, humous, humic
Humussäure *f* humic acid
Humusschicht *f* humus layer
Humussilicatboden *m* ranker
Humusspiegel *m* humus level
Humusstaugley *m* stagnohumic gley
Humusstoff *m* humus substance
Humusstoffschicht *f* humic matter layer
Humussubstanz *f* humus substance
Humusverbindung *f* humus compound
Humusvorrat *m* **des Bodens** soil's store of humus
Humuszersetzung *f* humus decomposition
Hund *m* 1. dog, hound *(family Canidae)*; 2. [domestic] dog, hound, Canis familiaris • **einen ~ ansetzen** *(hunt)* to hound • **mit dem ~ hetzen** to hound, to bait
~/rattenjagender ratter
Hundebandwurmfinne *f* hydatid, echinococcus
Hundebesitzer *m* dog owner
Hundeblume *f* dandelion, horse gowan, Taraxacum officinale
Hundedresseur *m* dog-breaker
Hundefloh *m* dog flea, Ctenocephalides canis
Hundefutter *n* dog-food
Hundefütterung *f* dog feeding
Hundehaarling *m* dog-biting louse, Trichodectes canis
Hundehalsband *n* dog collar
Hundehalter *m* dog owner
Hundehütte *f* [dog's] kennel, *(Am)* doghouse
Hundejunges *n* hound-puppy
Hundekorb *m* dognest
Hundekuchen *m* dog-biscuit
Hundelaus *f* dog-sucking louse, Linognathus setosus
Hundeleine *f* [dog] lead, leash
Hundeleistungsschau *f* **im Freien** field trial (test)
Hundemarke *f* dog tag
Hundemilch *f* dog milk
Hunderasse *f* dog breed
Hunderennen *n* coursing
Hundertfüßer *m* centipede *(class Chilopoda)*
Hundertjährige Aloe *f* century plant [agave], American aloe, agave, pita, Agave americana
Hundeschlitten *m* dog sledge
Hundestaupe *f (vet)* canine distemper
Hundezüchter *m* dog breeder

Hundezüchterverein

Hundezüchterverein *m* kennel club
Hundezwinger *m* kennel
Hündin *f* bitch
Hündinnenmilch *f* dog milk
Hundskamille *f* c[h]amomile *(genus Anthemis)*
Hundskirsche *f* fly honeysuckle, Lonicera xylosteum
Hundslauch *m* field (wild) garlic, crow garlic (onion), Allium vineale
Hundspetersilie *f* dog parsley (poison), fool's parsley, lesser hemlock, Aethusa cynapium
Hundsquecke *f* bearded (awned) couch grass, awned wheat grass, Agropyron caninum, Elymus caninus
Hundsrose *f* dogrose, hedge-rose, brier-rose, Rosa canina
Hundsstraußgras *n* brown bent[-grass], velvet bent[-grass], Agrostis canina
Hundstage *mpl* dog days *(meteorological phenomenon)*
Hundsveilchen *n* dog-violet, Viola canina
Hundswürger *m (bot)* mosquito trap *(genus Cynanchum)*
Hundswut *f s.* Tollwut
Hundszahn *m* 1. dog's-tooth violet, fawn lily, trout lily (flower), erythronium *(genus Erythronium)*; 2. dog's-tooth violet, Erythronium dens-canis
Hundszahngras *n* 1. dog-tooth grass *(genus Cynodon)*; 2. scutch grass, coastal bermudagrass, Bermuda [devil] grass, Cynodon dactylon
Hundszunge *f (bot)* hound's-tongue, cynoglossum *(genus Cynoglossum)*
Hunger *m* hunger
Hungeratrophie *f (vet)* inanition atrophy
Hungerblümchen *n (bot)* 1. draba *(genus Draba)*; 2. *s.* Hungerblume
Hungerblume *f (bot)* faverel, Erophila verna
Hungergrube *f* hunger hollow *(of animal's body)*
Hungerkondition *f* fasting (starving) condition
Hungerkontraktion *f* hunger contraction *(of gastric wall)*
Hungerkot *m* starvation excrement
Hungerkraut *n* corn-spurr[e]y, Spergula arvensis
hungern to hunger, to starve, to famish
~ lasssen to hunger, to famish
Hungern *n* starvation
Hungerödem *n (vet)* nutritional (famine) oedema
Hungerreis *m* hungry rice, fonio millet, acha, Digitaria exilis
Hungersterilität *f* fasting sterility
Hungerstoffwechsel *m* fasting (standard) metabolic rate, fasting metabolism (catabolism), resting energy exchange
Hungertod *m* [death of] starvation
Hungerumsatz *m s.* Hungerstoffwechsel
Hungerwolle *f* hungry wool
Hungerzustand *m* fasting state
hungrig hungry
Hunter *m* hunter *(horse)*

Hüpfer[ling] *m (ent)* hopper
Hürde *f* 1. crib, pen, fold; 2. hurdle
Hürdenrennen *n* hurdle-race
Hurrikan *m* hurricane
Hurrikangras *n* hurricane (pitted blue) grass, Bothriochloa pertusa
Husarenknopf *m (bot)* creeping zinnia, Sanvitalia procumbens
Huskie *m* Husky, Eskimo [dog] *(breed)*
husten to cough
Husten *m (vet)* cough
~/Hoppegartener (seuchenhafter) equine influenza, epizootic cough in horse
Hustenmittel *n* antitussive agent, cough suppressant
Hut *m* cap, pileus *(of mushrooms)* • **mit ~** *(bot)* pileate
Hütehund *m* herding (shepherd) dog, sheep-dog
hüten to herd, to fold, to tend, to graze; to shepherd, to tend
Hüten *n* herding, folding, shepherding
~/gespanntes close folding
~ im weiten Gehüt open herding
Hütepferd *n* stock horse
Hütewald *m* grazed forest
Hüteweide *f* hirsel *(of a shepherd)*
Hutöffnungsphase *f* cap-opening *(of mushrooms)*
Hutpilz *m* mushroom, pileate fungus, agaric *(order Agaricales)*
Hütte *f* 1. cottage, shack; 2. *s.* Hundehütte; 3. *s.* Jagdhütte
Hüttenkalk *m* smelting (converter) lime *(fertilizer)*
Hüttenrauch *m* fly ash
Hutung *f* rough grazing, sheep-walk, fold[ing] crop
Hutwald *m* grazed forest
Hutweide *f s.* Hutung
Huzule *m* Hutsul, Carpathian Pony *(breed)*
HVL *s.* Hypophysenvorderlappen
HWZ *s.* Halbwertszeit
Hy *s.* Hygroskopizität
hyalin hyaline
Hyalinose *f (vet)* hyaline degeneration
Hyalodendrin *n* hyalodendrin *(antibiotic, fungicide)*
Hyaloplasma *n* hyaloplasm, ground substance
Hyalospore *f (bot)* hyalospore
Hyaluronidase *f* hyaluronidase *(enzyme)*
Hyaluronsäure *f* hyaluronic acid *(mucopolysaccharide)*
Hyazinthe *f* 1. hyacinth *(genus Hyacinthus)*; 2. hyacinth, Hyacinthus orientalis
Hyazinthenmosaikvirus *n* hyacinth mosaic virus
hybrid hybrid
Hybrid *m s.* Hybride
Hybride *f* hybrid, bastard, cross *(s. a. under* Bastard*)*
~/vegetative vegetative hybrid
Hybrideffekt *m* heterosis
Hybridgetreide *n* hybrid cereal (corn)
Hybrid-Handelssaatgut *n* hybrid seed of commerce

Hybridhenne f hybrid layer
Hybridisation f hybridization
~/interspezifische interspecific hybridization, vicinism
~/somatische (vegetative) somatic (vegetative) hybridization
~/zwischenartliche s. ~/interspezifische
hybridisch hybrid
hybridisierbar hybridizable
hybridisieren to hybridize, to cross-breed
Hybridisierung f s. Hybridisation
Hybridkirsche f duke [cherry] *(group of cultivars)*
Hybridmais m *(Am)* hybrid corn
Hybridom[a] n hybridoma *(cell hybrid of an antibody-producing lymphocyte and a tumour cell)*
Hybridpappel f hybrid poplar *(comprehensive term)*
Hybridpopulation f hybrid population
Hybridsaatgut n hybrid seed
Hybridschwarm m hybrid swarm
Hybridschwein n hybrid (cross-bred) pig
Hybridsorte f hybrid cultivar (variety)
Hybridstamm m hybrid strain
Hybridzüchtung f hybrid (heterosis) breeding
Hydantoinase f dihydropyrimidinase *(enzyme)*
Hydathode f *(bot)* hydathode
Hydatide f hydatid, echinococcus
Hydatidose f *(vet)* hydatid disease
Hydragogum n diuretic
Hydramnion n *(vet)* hydramnios
Hydrant m hydrant
Hydrargillit m gibbsite *(non-clay mineral)*
Hydrargosis f *(vet)* mercury poisoning
Hydrastin n hydrastine *(alkaloid)*
Hydratation f hydration, aquatization
Hydratationswasser n *(soil)* hydration water of exchangeable ions, water of hydration
Hydration f, **Hydratisierung** f s. Hydratation
Hydratwasser n s. Hydratationswasser
Hydraulik[anlage] f hydraulic equipment (system)
Hydraulikflüssigkeit f hydraulic fluid
Hydraulikkolben m hydraulic ram
Hydraulikkran m hydraulic crane
Hydraulikkreislauf m hydraulic circuit
~/geschlossener closed-centre hydraulic system
~/offener open-centre hydraulic system
Hydraulikmotor m hydraulic motor
Hydrauliköl n hydraulic oil
Hydraulikpresse f hydraulic press
Hydraulikschlauch m hydraulic hose
Hydraulikschnellkupplung f quick release hydraulic coupling
Hydraulikzapfwelle f hydraulic p.t.o. (power take-off)
Hydraulikzylinder m hydraulic cylinder (ram)
~/doppeltwirkender double-acting cylinder (hydraulic ram)
~/einfachwirkender single-acting cylinder (hydraulic ram)

hydraulisch [angetrieben] hydraulic
hydrieren to hydrogenate
Hydrierung f hydrogenation
Hydrobiologie f hydrobiology, aquatic biology
hydrobiologisch hydrobiological
Hydrochorie f *(bot)* hydrochory
Hydrocortison n cortisol *(hormone)*
Hydroentrindungsmaschine f hydraulic (stream) barker, hydrobarker
Hydrogenase f hydrogenase *(enzyme)*
Hydrogenisation f hydrogenation
Hydrogenium n hydrogen
Hydroglimmer m *(soil)* hydromica, hydrous mica
Hydrokardie f *(vet)* hydropericardium
Hydroklimatologie f hydroclimatology
Hydrokultur f s. Hydroponik
Hydrokupplung f hydraulic coupling
Hydrolase f hydrolase, hydrolytic enzyme
Hydrolenkung f hydrostatic steering
Hydrologie f hydrology
~/forstliche forest hydrology
hydrologisch hydrologic[al]
Hydrolyse f hydrolysis
~/saure acid hydrolysis
hydrolysieren to hydrolyze
hydrolytisch hydrolytic
Hydromelioration f hydrotechnical amelioration
Hydrometeorologie f hydrometeorology
hydromorph *(soil)* hydromorphic, hydrogenetic
Hydromorphie f hydromorphy
Hydromorphose f *(bot)* hydromorphosis
Hydromotor m hydraulic motor
Hydronephrose f *(vet)* hydronephrosis
Hydropedologie f hydropedology
Hydroperikard n *(vet)* hydropericardium
hydrophil hydrophilic, hydrophile, hydrophilous, moisture-loving
Hydrophilie f hydrophilicity
hydrophob hydrophobic, hydrophobe, water-repellent
Hydrophobie f hydrophobicity, hydrophobia
Hydrophobieren water-repellent treatment
Hydrophobier[ungs]mittel n hydrophobing agent
Hydrophthalmus m *(vet)* hydrophthalmia
Hydrophyt m hydrophyte, hygrophyte, hydrophil, aquatic [plant], water plant
Hydropneumothorax m *(vet)* hydropneumothorax
Hydroponik f hydroponics, water (soilless) culture, water-tank gardening, tray agriculture, tank farming
~ mit zirkulierender Nährlösung recirculating water culture
Hydroponikverfahren n hydroponic technique
hydroponisch hydroponical
Hydropren n hydroprene *(insecticide)*
Hydrops m *(vet)* hydrops, dropsy
Hydropumpe f hydraulic pump
~/verstellbare variable-displacement pump

Hydroreiniger

Hydroreiniger *m* hydrocleaner
Hydrosalpinx *f (vet)* hydrosalpinx
Hydroserie *f* hydrosere *(plant sociology)*
Hydrosolgewächshaus *n* hydrosol greenhouse
Hydrosphäre *f* hydrosphere
Hydrotaxis *f (bot)* hydrotaxis
Hydrothorax *m (vet)* hydrothorax
hydrotrop[isch] hydrotropic
Hydrotropismus *m* hydrotropismus
Hydroxamat *n* hydroxamate
Hydroxamsäure *f* hydroxamic acid
Hydroxid *n* hydroxide
Hydroxinon *n* hydroxinone *(growth regulator)*
3-Hydroxyacyl-CoA-Dehydrogenase *f*, **ß-Hydroxyacyldehydrogenase** *f* 3-hydroxyacyl-CoA dehydrogenase, beta-hydroxyacyl dehydrogenase *(enzyme)*
3-Hydroxyanthranilatoxidase *f* 3-hydroxyanthranilate oxidase *(enzyme)*
(o)-Hydroxybenzoesäure *f* salicylic acid
Hydroxybernsteinsäure *f*, **Hydroxybutandisäure** *f* hydroxybutanedioic acid, hydroxysuccinic (malic) acid
3-Hydroxybuttersäure *f* hydroxybutyric acid
Hydroxybutyrat *n* hydroxybutyrate *(ketone body)*
8-Hydroxychinolincitrat *n* 8-hydroxyquinoline citrate, 8-HQC *(for preserving cut flowers)*
3-Hydroxycholansäure *f* 3-hydroxy-cholanic acid, lithocholic acid *(bile acid)*
25-Hydroxy-cholecalciferol-1-Hydroxylase *f* calcidiol-1-monooxygenase *(enzyme)*
Hydroxycobalamin *n* hydroxycobalamin, aquocobalamin
4-Hydroxy-3,5-dimethoxyzimtsäure *f* sinapic acid
Hydroxyethansäure *f* hydroxyethanoic acid, hydroxyacetic (glycolic) acid
Hydroxyethylethylendiamintetraessigsäure *f* hydroxyethylethylenediaminetetraacetic acid, HEDTA *(chelating agent)*
Hydroxyethylhydrazin *n* hydroxyethylhydrazine *(growth regulator)*
2-Hydroxyethyl-trimethyl-ammoniumhydroxid *n* choline *(phospholipid)*
Hydroxyfettsäure *f* hydroxy fatty acid
Hydroxyisoxazol *n* hydroxyisoxazole *(fungicide)*
Hydroxylamin *n* hydroxylamine *(mutagen)*
Hydroxylapatit *m* hydroxylapatite
Hydroxylase *f* hydroxylase *(enzyme)*
Hydroxylysin *n* hydroxylysine *(amino-acid)*
4-Hydroxy-2-mercapto-6-methylpyrimidin *n* methylthiouracil *(thyreostatic)*
4-Hydroxy-3-methoxybenzaldehyd *m* vanillin
4-Hydroxy-3-methoxy-benzoesäure *f* vanillic acid
4-Hydroxy-3-methyl-butylamino-purin *n* dihydrozeatin *(cytokinin)*
Hydroxymethylfurfural *n* hydroxymethylfurfural, HMF *(fungicide)*
Hydroxymethylglutaryl-CoA-Lyase *f* hydroxymethylglutaryl-CoA lyase *(enzyme)*
Hydroxymethylglutaryl-CoA-Reductase, NADPH *f* hydroxymethylglutaryl-CoA reductase, NADPH *(enzyme)*
Hydroxynaphthalin *n* naphthol
Hydroxyprolin *n* hydroxyproline, oxyproline *(amino-acid)*
2-Hydroxypropansäure *f* 2-hydroxypropionic (lactic) acid
1-Hydroxy-propan-1,2,3-tricarbonsäure *f* isocitric acid
6-Hydroxypurin *n* 6-hydroxypurine, hypoxanthine
6-Hydroxypurinribonucleosid *n* inosine
3-ß-Hydroxy- 5-Steroiddehydrogenase *f* 3-ß-hydroxy-5-steroid dehydrogenase *(enzyme)*
Hydroxytoluen *n* hydroxytoluene, cresol
~/butyliertes butylated hydroxytoluene, BHT *(antioxidant)*
5-Hydroxytryptamin *n* serotonin, 5-hydroxytryptamine *(neurotransmitter)*
Hydroxytryptophandecarboxylase *f* aromatic-L-amino-acid-decarboxylase, tryptophan decarboxylase *(enzyme)*
Hydroxytyramin *n* dopamine
Hydrozele *f (vet)* hydrocele
Hydrozephalus *m (vet)* hydrocephalus
Hygiene *f* hygiene
Hygienemaßnahme *f* hygienic measure, sanitation
Hygienestandard *m* standard of hygiene
Hygienevorschrift *f* hygiene regulation
hygienisch hygienic, sanitary
Hygrogramm *n* hygrogram, hygrograph
Hygrograph *m* hygrograph, self-recording hygrometer
Hygrom *n (vet)* hygroma
Hygrometer *n* hygrometer
Hygrometrie *f* hygrometry
hygromorph hygromorphic
Hygromull *m* hygroscopic plastic soil
Hygromycin *n* hygromycin *(anthelminthic)*
hygrophil hygrophilous
Hygrophyt *m* hygrophyte
Hygroskop *n* hygroscope
hygroskopisch hygroscopic, water-attractant; deliquescent
Hygroskopizität *f* hygroscopicity; hygroscopic coefficient
Hygrothermogramm *n* hygrothermogram, hygrothermograph
Hygrothermograph *m* hygrothermograph
Hyläa *f*, **Hylaea** *f* hylaea *(type of tropical rain forests esp. in the Amazon region)*
Hy-line *f* hy-line, hybrid line
Hymatomelansäure *f (soil)* hymatomelanic acid
Hymen *n(m)* hymen
Hymenium *n* hymenium *(a spore-bearing layer of ascomycetes and basidiomycetes)*

Hymeniumträger m, **Hymenophor** n(m) hymenophore
Hymenoptere m (ent) hymenopteran (order Hymenoptera) • **die Hymenopteren betreffend** hymenopterous
Hymexazol n hymexazol (fungicide)
HyMV s. Hyazinthenmosaikvirus
Hyoscin n hyoscine, scopolamine (alkaloid)
Hyoscyamin n hyoscyamine (alkaloid)
Hyp s. Hydroxyprolin
Hyperadrenokortizismus m (vet) Cushing's syndrome
Hyperalimentation f hyperalimentation
Hyperämie f (vet) hyperaemia
Hyperästhesie f (vet) hyperaesthesia
Hyperazidität f superacidity
Hyperazotämie f azotaemia
Hyperbilirubinämie f (vet) hyperbilirubinaemia
Hypercalcitoninismus m (vet) hypercalcitoninism
Hypercholesterinämie f, **Hypercholesterose** f (vet) hypercholesterolaemia
Hyperchromämie f (vet) hyperchromic anaemia
Hyperdaktylie f polydactylism, polydactyly
Hyperfunktion f hyperfunction
Hyperglobulie f hyperglobulia
Hyperglykämie f (vet) hyperglycaemia, glycaemia
Hyperimmunisierung f hyperimmunization
Hyperimmunserum n (vet) hyperimmune serum
Hyperinsulinismus m (vet) hyperinsulinism
Hyperkaliämie f (vet) hyperkal[i]aemia
Hyperkalzämie f (vet) hypercalcaemia
Hyperkapnie f (vet) hypercapnia
Hyperkeratose f (vet) hyperkeratosis
Hyperketonämie f (vet) hyperketonaemia
Hyperkinese f hyperkinesis, overactivity
Hyperlipämie f (vet) hyperlipaemia
Hypermagnesämie f (vet) hypermagnesaemia
Hypermetamorphose f (ent) hypermetamorphosis
hypermorph hypermorphic
Hypermorphose f hypermorphosis, overgrowth
Hypermotilität f s. Hyperkinese
Hypernatriämie f (vet) hypernatraemia
Hypernephritis f (vet) hypernephritis
Hyperostose f (vet) hyperostosis
Hyperoxie f (vet) hyperoxia
Hyperparasit m hyperparasite, secondary (tertiary) parasite
Hyperparasitismus m hyperparasitism, secondary parasitism
Hyperphagie f hyperphagia
Hyperphos[phat] n hyperphosphate (fertilizer)
Hyperphosphatämie f (vet) hyperphosphataemia
Hyperpituitarismus m (vet) hyperpituitarism
Hyperplasie f hyperplasia (e.g. of tissues)
Hyperploidie f (gen) hyperploidy
Hyperpnoe f hyperpnoea
Hyperproteinämie f (vet) hyperproteinaemia
Hypersekretion f hypersecretion
hypersensibel hypersensitive

Hypersensibilität f hypersensitivity
hypersensitiv s. hypersensibel
Hypertension f s. Hypertonie
Hyperthermie f (vet) hyperthermia
Hyperthermiesyndrom n/**malignes** malignant hyperthermia syndrome, MHS
Hyperthyreoidismus m, **Hyperthyreose** f (vet) hyperthyroidism, thyrotoxicosis
Hypertonie f (vet) hypertension, hypertonia, hypertonicity
Hypertonin n angiotensin
hypertonisch hypertonic
Hypertonus m s. Hypertonie
hypertroph hypertrophic
Hypertrophie f hypertrophy
hypertrophieren to hypertrophy
Hyperurikämie f, **Hyperurinämie** f (vet) hyperuricaemia
Hypervitaminose f hypervitaminosis
Hypervolämie f hypervolaemia
Hyphe f hypha, fungal thread, fungus filament
Hyphenbrücke f clamp, buckle (esp. of basidiomycetes)
Hyphenfusion f hyphal fusion
Hyphengeflecht n mycelium, [mushroom] spawn
Hyphidie f paraphysis (of fungal fruit-bodies)
Hyphomyzet m filamentous fungus
Hypnospore f (bot) hypnospore, hypnosperm
Hypnozygote f (bot) zygospore
Hypoazidität f subacidity
Hypoblast n hypoblast, entoderm, endoderm
Hypochlorämie f chloropenia
Hypochlorit n hypochlorite (disinfectant)
Hypocholesterinämie f, **Hypocholesterose** f (vet) hypocholesterolaemia
Hypochromämie f (vet) hypochromic anaemia
Hypoderm n (bot) hypodermis
hypodermatisch hypodermic
Hypodermis f hypodermis, hypoderma, subcutaneous tissue, superficial fascia
hypodermoid hypodermoid
Hypodermose f (vet) hypodermosis
Hypoestes f (bot) freckleface (genus Hypoestes)
Hypofunktion f hypofunction
hypogäisch (bot) hypogeal, hypogean, hypogeous
Hypogalaktie f hypogalactia
Hypogammaglobulinämie f (vet) hypogammaglobulinaemia
hypogastrisch hypogastric
Hypogastrium n hypogastrium
Hypogenitalismus m (vet) hypogenitalism, hypogonadism
Hypoglobulie f hypoglobulia
Hypoglykämie f (vet) hypoglycaemia
~ [**und Unterkühlung** f] **der Ferkel** baby-pig disease
Hypogonadismus m s. Hypogenitalismus
hypogyn (bot) hypogynous
Hypoinsulinismus m (vet) hypoinsulinism

Hypokaliämie

Hypokaliämie f (vet) hypokal[i]aemia
Hypokalzämie f (vet) hypocalcaemia
Hypokinese f hypokinesis
Hypokotyl n (bot) hypocotyl
Hypokotylstreckung f (bot) hypocotyl elongation
Hypokuprose f (vet) hypocupraemia; neonatal (enzootic) ataxia, sway-back, swingback (of lambs)
Hypolimnion n hypolimnion
Hypolipämie f (vet) hypolipaemia
Hypomagnesämie f (vet) hypomagnesaemia
hypomorph hypomorphic
Hypomotilität f hypokinesis
Hyponastie f (bot) hyponasty
Hyponatriämie f (vet) hyponatraemia
Hypoparathyreoidismus m, **Hypoparathyreose** f (vet) hypoparathyroidism
Hypophosphatämie f (vet) hypophosphataemia
hypophysär pituitary
Hypophyse f pituitary [gland], hypophysis
Hypophysektomie f (vet) hypophysectomy, pituitary removal
Hypophysenbehandlung f (pisc) pituitary treatment, hypophysation
Hypophysenhinterlappen m neurohypophysis
Hypophysenhinterlappenhormon n posterior pituitary hormone
Hypophysenhormon n pituitary hormone
Hypophysentasche f Rathke's pouch
Hypophysenüberfunktion f (vet) hyperpituitarism
Hypophysenunterfunktion f (vet) hypopituitarism
Hypophysenvorderlappen m adenohypophysis, anterior pituitary [gland]
Hypophysenvorderlappenhormon n anterior pituitary hormone
Hypophysenvorderlappenüberfunktion f (vet) hyperpituitarism
Hypophysenvorderlappenunterfunktion f, **Hypopituitarismus** m (vet) hypopituitarism
Hypophysen-Zwischenhirn-System n hypothalamo-hypophysial portal system
Hypophysierung f s. Hypophysenbehandlung
Hypoplasie f hypoplasia (e.g. of tissues)
Hypoploidie f (gen) hypoploidy
Hypopnoe f hypopnoea
Hypoproteinämie f (vet) hypoproteinaemia
Hypoprothrombinämie f (vet) hypoprothrombinaemia
Hypopus n hypopus, hypopial stage (of numerous acarids)
Hyposekretion f hyposecretion
hyposensibel hyposensitive
Hyposensibilität f hyposensitivity
hyposensitiv s. hyposensibel
Hypospadie f (vet) hypospadias
Hypostas[i]e f, **Hypostasis** f (gen) hypostasis
hypostatisch hypostatic
Hypotension f s. Hypotonie
Hypothalamus m hypothalamus

Hypothalamus-Hypophysen-System n hypothalamo-hypophysial portal system
Hypothermie f (vet) hypothermia
Hypothese f hypothesis
~/**statistische** statistical hypothesis
Hypothyreoidismus m, **Hypothyreose** f (vet) hypothyroidism
Hypotonie f (vet) hypotension, hypotonia, hypotonicity
hypotonisch hypotonic
Hypotonus m s. Hypotonie
Hypotrichose f, **Hypotrichosis** f (vet) hypotrichosis
hypotroph hypotrophic
Hypotrophie f hypotrophy
Hypovitaminose f hypovitaminosis
Hypovolämie f hypovolaemia
Hypoxämie f (vet) hypoxia
Hypoxanthin n hypoxanthine
Hypoxanthinoxidase f [hypo]xanthine oxidase (enzyme)
Hypoxie f (vet) hypoxia
Hypso[thermo]meter n hypsometer
Hysterektomie f (vet) hysterectomy, metrectomy
Hysterese f, **Hysteresis** f hysteresis
Hysterie f (vet) hysteria
Hysterophyt m hysterophyte
Hysterotomie f (vet) hysterotomy, Caesarean operation (section)
Hysterozele f (vet) hysterocele, hernia of uterus
Hystiozytenwucherung f (vet) histiocytosis

I

I s. Infiltrationsrate
IAA s. Indolyl-3-essigsäure
IAA-Oxidase f indoleacetic oxidase (enzyme)
IB s. Bronchitis des Huhnes/infektiöse
IBA s. Indolyl-3-buttersäure
Ibaraki-Krankheit f Ibaraki disease (of oxen)
Iberia-Wärmetoleranztest m Iberia heat-tolerance test
IBH s. Bursitis des Huhnes/infektiöse
I-Biene f Italian honey-bee, Apis mellifica ligustica
IBR s. Rhinotracheitis/infektiöse bovine
IBR/IPV-Virus n IBR/IPV virus
IBV s. Virus der Infektiösen Bursitis des Huhnes
IB-Virus n infectious bronchitis virus
IBW s. Bauchwassersucht der Karpfen/infektiöse
ICBN s. Internationaler Code der Botanischen Nomenklatur
ICF-Säurewecker m (dairy) direct-to-the-fat-starter
ichörös (vet) ichorous
Ichthyochorie f ichthyochory
Ichthyofauna f fish fauna
Ichthyologe m ichthyologist
Ichthyologie f ichthyology

ichthyologisch ichthyological
Ichthyophthiriose f (vet) ichthyophthiriasis (caused by Ichthyophthirius multifiliis)
ICNCP s. Internationaler Code der Nomenklatur der Kulturpflanzen
Icosansäure f s. Eicosansäure
Idation f (gen) mutation (for compounds s. under Mutation)
Idioblast m (bot) idioblast, idiosome
Idiogamie f (bot) idiogamy, self-pollination
Idiogramm m idiogram (schematic diagram of chromosome sets)
Idiopathie f (vet) idiopathy, autopathy
idiopathisch idiopathic, autopathic
Idioplasma n (gen) idioplasm, germ-plasm
Idiosynkrasie f (vet) idiosyncrasy, atopy
Idiotyp[us] m idiotype
Idiovariation f (gen) mutation (for compounds s. under Mutation)
IE s. Internationale Einheit
I.E. s. Einheit/infektiöse
IEP s. Punkt/isoelektrischer
IES s. Indolyl-3-essigsäure
IES-Oxidase f indoleacetic oxidase (enzyme)
Ig s. Immunglobulin
Igel m hedgehog (genus Erinaceus)
Igelbusch m (bot) anabasis (genus Anabasis)
Igelginster m hedgehog broom, branch thorn, Erinacea anthyllis (pungens)
Igelgurke f wild balsam apple, Echinocystis lobata
Igelkopf m purple coneflower (genus Echinacea)
Igel-Lange-Test m [nach Hofferbert] (phyt) callose test
Igelsäulenkaktus m hedgehog cactus (genus Echinocereus)
igelstachelig (bot) echinate[d]
IGMV s. Irisgelbmosaikvirus
Ignatiusbohne f St. Ignatius bean, Strychnos ignatii
IHN s. Nekrose/infektiöse hämatopoetische
IHR s. Hämagglutinationsreaktion/indirekte
IK s. Ibaraki-Krankheit
Ikterus m (vet) icterus, jaundice, yellows, hyperbilirubinaemia
Ile s. Isoleucin
Ile de France n Ile-de-France (sheep breed)
Ileitis f (vet) ileitis
Ileum n ileum
Ileumverdaulichkeit f ileal digestibility (of nutrients)
Ileus m (vet) ileus, gut closure
I-Linie f inbred [line]
Illimerisation f (soil) clay translocation (illuviation), lessivage, lessivation, argilluviation
Illini-Verdünner m Illini variable temperature medium, IVT (for liquid preservation of bull's semen)
Illit m illite (clay mineral)
Illuvialhorizont m (soil) illuvial horizon, B-horizon

Illuviation f (soil) illuviation
Illuviationszone f zone of illuviation
ILT s. Laryngotracheitis des Geflügels/infektiöse
Iltis m polecat, fitch[et], fitchew, foumart, Mustela putorius
i.m. s. intramuskulär
imaginal (ent) imaginal
Imaginalphase f (ent) adult phase
Imaginalstadium n (ent) adult instar
Imago f (ent) imago, adult
Imanin n imanin (antibiotic)
Imazalil n imazalil (fungicide)
imbibieren to imbibe
Imbibition f imbibition
imbricat (bot, zoo) imbricated
Imidazol n imidazole
Imidocarb n imidocarb (antiparasitic)
IMiMV s. Mildes Irismosaikvirus
Iminoharnstoff m iminourea, guanidine
Imker m bee-keeper, bee-master, bee farmer, apiculturist, apiarist
Imkerei f 1. bee-keeping, apiculture; 2. bee-garden
Imkereierzeugnis n hive product
Imkereigeräte npl bee-keeping equipment, bee appliances
imkereilich apicultural
Imkergeräte npl s. Imkereigeräte
Imkerhandschuh m bee glove
Imkerpfeife f bee blower, smoker
immatur immature, unripe
Imme f honey-bee, hive bee, Apis mellifica (mellifera)
Immenblatt n bastard balm, Melittis melissophylum
immergrün (bot) evergreen, sempervirent
Immergrün n 1. periwinkle (genus Vinca); 2. [common, lesser] periwinkle, creeping myrtle, Vinca minor
Immergrüne Bärentraube f [red] bearberry, Arctostaphylos uva-ursi
~ Schleifenblume f evergreen (edging, hardy) candytuft, Iberis sempervirens
~ Trespe f rescue brome (grass), Schrader's (prairie) grass, Bromus catharticus (unioloides)
Immergrüner Schneeball m laurustinus, Viburnum tinus
~ Wegerich m shrubby plantain, Plantago sempervirens
Immigration f (ecol) immigration, invasion
Immission f immission (sending or thrusting in, esp. said of environmental pollutants)
immissionsbedingt pollution-induced
Immissionsbelastung f contamination by air pollution
immissionsempfindlich sensitive to atmospheric pollution
immissionsexponiert pollution-exposed (e.g. a site)
Immissionsgebiet n immission region
immissionsgeschädigt pollution-damaged

Immissionsökologie f atmospheric pollution ecology
immissionsresistent pollution-resistant *(e.g. a tree species)*
Immissionsresistenz f resistance to air pollution
Immissionsschaden m air pollution damage, immission; emission damage (injury)
immobil immobile
Immobilisans n *(vet)* immobilizing agent
Immobilisation f immobilization
immobilisieren to immobilize, to fix *(e.g. nutrients)*
Immobilisierung f immobilization
Immortelle f *(bot)* everlasting, immortelle *(comprehensive term)*
immun immune
Immunadhärenz f immune adherence
Immunadsorbens n immunoadsorbent
Immunantikörper m immune antibody
Immunbiologie f immunology
immunbiologisch immunobiological
Immunchemie f immunochemistry
immunchemisch immunochemical
immundefekt immune-deficient
Immundefizienz f immunodeficiency
Immundepression f immunodepression
Immundiagnose f immunodiagnosis
Immundiffusion f immunodiffusion
Immunelektronenmikroskopie f immune (immunospecific) electron microscopy
Immunelektrophorese f immunoelectrophoresis
Immunferritin n immunoferritin
Immunfluoreszenz f immunofluorescence
Immunfluoreszenzmikroskopie f immunofluorescence microscopy
Immunfluoreszenztechnik f fluorescent antibody technique
Immungenetik f immunogenetics
Immunglobulin n immunoglobulin, immune globulin, Ig
Immunglobulinallotyp m immunoglobulin allotype *(antibody)*
Immunhämatologie f immunohaematology
Immunhämolyse f immunohaemolysis
Immunisation f s. Immunisierung
immunisieren to immunize
Immunisierung f immunization
~/**aktive** active immunization
~/**passive** passive immunization
~/**pränatale** prenatal immunization
Immunisierungsstärke f immunogenicity
Immunität f immunity • ~ **erzeugend** immunogenic
~/**adaptiv erworbene** adaptively acquired immunity
~/**aktive** active immunity
~/**erworbene** acquired immunity
~/**humorale** humoral immunity
~/**infektionsgebundene** premunition, cross protection
~/**laktogene** lactogenic immunity
~/**passive** passive immunity
~/**relative** relative immunity
~/**übergreifende** cross-immunity
~/**zelluläre** cellular immunity
~/**zellvermittelte** cell-mediated immunity, CMI
immunitätsunterdrückend immunosuppressive
Immunitätsunterdrückung f immunosuppression
Immunkompetenz f immunocompetence
Immunkonglutinin n immunoconglutinin
Immunkörper m immune body, antibody
Immunmangel m immunodeficiency
Immunmechanismus m immune mechanism
Immunmodulation f immunomodulation
Immunoassay immunoassay
immunogen immunogenic
Immunogen n immunogen
Immunogenese f immunogenesis
immunogenetisch immunogenetic[al]
Immunogenität f immunogenicity
Immunologe m immunologist
Immunologie f immunology
immunologisch immunologic[al]
Immunosom n virosome
immunosupprimieren to immunosuppress
Immunozyt m immunocyte
Immunpathologie f immunopathology
Immunperoxidase f immunoperoxidase *(enzyme)*
Immunpräzipitation f immunoprecipitation
Immunprobe f immunoassay
Immunprophylaxe f immunoprophylaxis
Immunreaktion f immune reaction (response)
• **Immunreaktionen unterdrücken** to immunosuppress
Immunserum n immune serum
Immunstatus m immune status
Immunstimulation f immunostimulation
Immunsuppression f immunosuppression
immunsuppressiv immunosuppressive
Immunsuppressivum n immunosuppressive [agent], immunosuppressant
Immunsystem n immune system
Immuntherapie f immunotherapy
Immunthyreoiditis f *(vet)* thyroiditis
Immuntoleranz f immune tolerance
Imogolit m imogolite *(clay mineral)*
Impaktdüse f impinging-stream nozzle
Impatiens f *(bot)* busy Lizzie, Impatiens wallerana
Impatiens-Neu-Guinea-Hybride f New Guinea impatiens
Imperfektstadium n imperfect stage (state), conidial (asexual) stage *(of fungi)*
impermeabel impermeable
impfen 1. to inoculate *(microbiology)*; 2. *(vet)* to vaccinate; 3. to seed *(e.g. sugar solutions in sugar manufacture)*
Impfkalender m *(vet)* vaccination programme (schedule)
Impfkompost m inoculated compost
Impfkultur f inoculum

Impfmaterial *n* inoculum
Impfnadel *f* inoculating wire *(microbiology)*
Impföse *f* inoculation loop *(microbiology)*
Impfstoff *m* 1. inoculum; 2. *(vet)* vaccine *(s. a. under* Vakzine*)*
~/bakterieller bacterial preparation
Impfsuspension *f* inoculum
Impfung *f* inoculation, vaccination; seeding
~ mit Autovakzine autovaccination
Impfzucker *m* seed sugar
Implantation *f* 1. *(vet)* implantation; 2. *s.* Nidation
impotent impotent
Impotenz *f* impotence, impotency
Imprägnation *f s.* Imprägnierung
imprägnieren to impregnate
Imprägnierung *f* impregnation; artificial carbonation *(of sparkling wine)*
Impressionsfraktur *f (vet)* depressed fracture
Impuls *m* pulse
Impulsberegnung *f* pulse irrigation
Impulsschwallbewässerung *f* pulse-spate irrigation
Impulssteuervorrichtung *f* controller *(of an electronic fencer)*
in vitro in vitro
in vivo in vivo
Inaktivierungspunkt *m* inactivation point
~/thermaler thermal inactivation point *(of viruses)*
Inanition *f* inanition
Inanitionsatrophie *f (vet)* inanition atrophy
Inanitionsödem *n (vet)* nutritional oedema
Inappetenz *f* inappetence, anorexia
Inceptisol *m (soil)* inceptisol, ept
Index *m* index
~/bioklimatischer bioclimatic index
~/chemotherapeutischer chemotherapeutic index
~/panmiktischer panmictic index
indexieren to index
Indexselektion *f* index selection *(animal breeding)*
Indianerfeige *f* Indian fig, Opuntia ficus-indica
Indianernessel *f (bot)* monarda *(genus Monarda)*
Indianischer Tabak *m* Indian tobacco, Lobelia inflata
Indifferenztemperatur *f* thermal-indifference zone
indigen indigenous, autochthonal, autochthonous
Indigestion *f* indigestion
Indigo *m(n)* 1. indigo *(dye)*; 2. *s.* Indigostrauch
Indigostrauch *m (bot)* 1. indigo *(genus Indigofera)*; 2. Indian (common, true) indigo, Indigofera tinctoria
Indikator *m* indicator; [radioactive] tracer
Indikatormethode *f* tracer technique
Indikatornährboden *m* identification medium *(bacteriology)*
Indikatororganismus *m* bioindicator, indicator organism
Indikatorpapier *n* indicator (test) paper
Indikatorpflanze *f* indicator (test) plant, soil (plant) indicator, phytometer

Indikatorwirtspflanze *f (phyt)* indicator host
Indische Azalee *f* azalea, Rhododendron simsii, Azalea indica
~ Baumwolle *f* [Asiatic] tree cotton, Gossypium arboreum
~ Biene *f* Indian bee, Apis cerana (indica)
~ Erdbeere *f* Indian strawberry, Duchesnea indica
~ Fadenröhre *f (bot)* Rangoon creeper, Quisqualis indica
~ Honigbiene *f s.* ~ Biene
~ Lagerstroemie *f* crape myrtle, Lagerstroemia indica
~ Laufente *f* White Runner [duck] *(breed)*
~ Lotosblume *f* [Indian, East Indian, sacred] lotus, Nelumbo nucifera
~ Sandklette *f* Indian sandbur, Cenchrus biflorus
Indischer Elefant *m* Indian elephant, Elephas maximus
~ Hanf *m* [Indian] hemp, Cannabis sativa ssp. indica
~ Korallenbaum *m* sandal bead tree, Adenanthera pavonina
~ Kugelweizen *m s.* ~ Zwergweizen
~ Lotos *m s.* Indische Lotosblume
~ Mandelbaum *m* India-almond, Terminalia catappa
~ Sandoribaum *m* sandal-tree, Sandoricum koetjape (indicum)
~ Senf *m* Indian (Chinese, brown) mustard, Brassica juncea [ssp. juncea]
~ Spinat *m* Malabar spinach (nightshade), Indian spinach, Basella alba (rubra)
~ Steinklee *m* Indian (yellow annual sweet) clover, Melilotus indica
~ Traganth *m* karaya (sterculia) gum *(esp. from Sterculia urens)*
~ Zedrachbaum *m* China tree, Persian lilac, chinaberry, Melia azedarach
~ Zwergweizen *m* Indian dwarf wheat, shot wheat, Triticum sphaerococcum
Indisches Blumenrohr *n* Indian shot [plant], Indian reed, African turmeric, Canna indica
~ Mahagoni *n* Ceylon cedar, Melia dubia (composita)
Individualauslese *f* individual (phenotypic, mass) selection
Individualdistanz *f* individual distance *(animal behaviour)*
Individualentwicklung *f* ontogenesis, ontogeny
Individualleistung *f* individual performance *(breeding)*
Individualselektion *f s.* Individualauslese
Individuendichte *f (ecol)* abundance
Individuum *n* individual
~/adultes adult
~/ausgewachsenes (geschlechtsreifes) *s.* ~/adultes
~/männliches male
~/weibliches female

Individuum

~/zwischengeschlechtliches intersex
Indol *n* indole
Indol-3-acetonitril indole-3-acetonitrile *(auxin)*
Indolalkaloid *n* indole alkaloid
Indol-3-carbinol *n* indole-3-carbinol *(auxin)*
Indolyl-3-buttersäure *f* indolebutyric (indolylbutyric) acid, IBA *(growth regulator)*
Indolyl-3-essigsäure *f* 3-indolylacetic acid, indoleacetic acid, heteroauxin, IAA *(phytohormone)*
Indolyl-3-essigsäureoxidase *f* indoleacetic oxidase *(enzyme)*
Indolylethylamin *n* tryptamine
Indomethacin *n* indomethacin *(inhibitor of prostaglandin synthase)*
Induktion *f* induction
Industrie *f* **der chemischen Holzverarbeitung** wood chemical industry
~/fleischverarbeitende meat processing industry
~/Forsterzeugnisse verarbeitende forest products industry
~/holzverarbeitende wood [processing] industry
~/lebensmittelverarbeitende food[-processing] industry
~/lederverarbeitende leather industry
~/wollverarbeitende wool industry
Industrieabfall *m* industrial waste
Industriekartoffel *f* industrial (cull) potato
Industriepflanze *f* non-food plant, industrial crop, plant for technical use
Industriepute *f* commercial (market) turkey
Industriestaub *m* industrial dust
Industrietomate *f* canning tomato
inert inert
Infantilismus *m (vet)* infantilism
Infekt *m s.* Infektion
Infektion *f (phyt, vet)* infection
~/aerogene airborne (aerator) infection
~/bodenbürtige soil-borne infection
~ durch Saatgutübertragung seed-borne infection
~/kryptogene[tische] cryptogenic infection
~/latente latent infection
~/lokale (lokalisierte) localized infection
~/pränatale prenatal infection
~/protozoäre protozoal infection
~/puerperale puerperal infection
~/pyogene pyogenic infection
~/ruhende (stille) quiescent infection
~ unklarer Genese cryptogenic infection
Infektionsdichte *f* infection density
Infektionsdruck *m* infection pressure
Infektionserreger *m* infectious agent
Infektionsherd *m* [infective] focus
Infektionskrankheit *f* infectious disease
Infektionsmultiplizität *f* multiplicity of infection *(virology)*
Infektionspforte *f* infection court
Infektionspotential *n* infection potential
Infektionsprozeß *m* infection process

Infektionsquelle *f* infection source
Infektionsstelle *f* infection court
Infektionsverlauf *m* infection process
infektiös infectious, infective, contagious
Infektiosität *f* infectiousness, infectivity
inferior inferior
infertil infertile, unfertile, sterile
Infertilität *f* infertility, sterility
Infestation *f* infestation *(parasitology)*
Infiltrationsanästhesie *f (vet)* infiltration anaesthesia
Infiltrationsflux *m*, **Infiltrationsgeschwindigkeit** *f s.* Infiltrationsrate
Infiltrationsgleichung *f (soil)* infiltration equation
Infiltrationsrate *f* infiltration rate (capacity) *(of soil water)*
Infiltrometer *n* infiltrometer
infizieren to infect
inflammabel inflammable
Inflammation *f (vet)* inflammation
In-Flaschen-Sterilisation *f* in-bottle sterilization *(e.g. of milk)*
Infloreszenz *f* inflorescence, flower-head *(for compounds s. under* Blütenstand*)*
Influenza *f (vet)* influenza, flu
~/aviäre avian influenza, duck flu
Influenzavirus *n* influenza virus
Information *f/genetische* genetic information
Informationstanz *m (api)* directional dance
infrarot infra-red
Infrarot-Farbluftbild *n* infra-red colour photograph
Infrarot-Farb-Orthophotokarte *f* infra-red colour orthophoto map
Infrarotfeuchtemesser *m* infra-red moisture meter
Infrarotfotografie *f* infra-red photography
Infrarotheizkörper *m*, **Infrarotlampenstrahler** *m s.* Infrarotstrahler
Infrarotlicht *n* infra-red light, far red light
Infrarotluftaufnahme *f* aerial infra-red photograph
Infrarotspektralphotometrie *f* infra-red spectrophotometry
Infrarotspektroskopie *f* infra-red spectroscopy
Infrarotstrahler *m* infra-red heater (lamp), heat lamp, hover
Infrarotstrahlung *f* infra-red radiation
Infrarottrockner *m* infra-red dryer
Infrastruktur *f* infrastructure
Infundibulum *n* **des Eileiters** oviduct pavilion
infundieren *(vet)* to infuse
Infusion *f* infusion
Infusionslösung *f/Darrowsche (vet)* Darrow's solution
Infusions[maisch]verfahren *n* infusion mashing (method) *(brewing)*
Infusorium *n* ciliate *(class Ciliata)*
Ingenieuragronom *m* technical agriculturist
Ingenieurtechnik *f/biochemische* biochemical engineering

Ingenieurwesen *n*/**genetisches** genetic engineering
Ingesta *pl* ingesta
ingestieren to ingest *(to take in for digestion)*
Ingestion *f* ingestion
Inguinalring *m* inguinal ring *(animal anatomy)*
Ingwer *m* 1. ginger *(genus Zingiber)*; 2. [common] ginger, Zingiber officinale; 3. ginger *(spice)*
Ingweröl *n* ginger oil
Ingwerwein *m* ginger wine
Ingwerwurzel *f* ginger root, race
INH *s.* Isoniazid
Inhalationsnarkose *f (vet)* inhalation anaesthesia
Inhalationsnarkotikum *n* inhalation anaesthetic
Inhambanekaffee *m* inhambane coffee, Coffea racemosa
inhibieren to inhibit
inhibierend inhibitory, inhibitive
Inhibition *f* inhibition
Inhibitor *m* inhibitor, retardant
Inhibitorgen *n* inhibitor gene
Initialfruchtansatz *m (bot)* initial fruit set
Initialinokulum *n (phyt)* initial (primary) inoculum, initial pathogen population
Initialphase *f* lag period *(of bacterial growth)*
Initialsymptom *n* initial symptom
Initiationskodon *n (gen)* initiation codon
Initiatorgen *n* initiator gene
Injektion *f* injection
~/subkutane *(vet)* hypodermic
~ von flüssigem Ammoniak nitrojection
Injektionsgerät *n* injection apparatus *(e.g. for liquid fertilizers)*
Injektionspflugschar *n* injection ploughshare *(for liquid fertilizers)*
Injektionsspritze *f* syringe
Injektor *m* injector
injizieren to inject
Inkalilie *f* 1. Peruvian (Chilean, herb) lily, lily-of-the-Incas, alstroemeria *(genus Alstroemeria)*; 2. Peruvian lily, lily-of-the-Incas, Alstroemeria pelegrina
Inkarnatklee *m* crimson (Italian) clover, incarnate (scarious) clover, trifolium, Trifolium incarnatum
Inkarzeration *f (vet)* incarceration
Inklinometer *n* inclinometer
inkompatibel incompatible
Inkompatibilität *f* incompatibility
Inkontinenz *f (vet)* incontinence
Inkorporation *f* incorporation
inkorporieren to incorporate
Inkrement *n* increment
Inkretdrüse *f* endocrine gland
Inkretin *n* incretin *(gastro-intestinal hormone)*
inkretorisch endocrine
Inkrustation *f s.* Inkrustierung
Inkrustierapparat *m* [seed] coater
Inkrustierung *f* incrustation, encrustation
Inkubation *f* incubation

Inkubationsdauer *f* incubation duration
Inkubationszeit *f* incubation (latent) period • **die ~ durchlaufen** to incubate
Inkubator *m* incubator
inkubieren to incubate
inkurabel incurable
Inlandsmarkt *m* home market
Inlandtraubenwein *m* domestic grape wine
Innenabteiler *m s.* Innenhalmteiler
Innenfäule *f* internal rot *(e.g. of softwood due to fungal attack)*
Innenhalmteiler *m* inner divider
Innenkork *m* internal cork *(esp. of apples due to boron deficiency)*
Innenkörper *m* [**/Heinz'**] Heinz body *(of erythrocytes)*
Innenleine *f* [**der Deutschen Kreuzleine**] check (branch) rein
Innenlüftertrocknungsanlage *f* internal-fan kiln
Innenohr *n* inner (internal) ear
Innenohrentzündung *f (vet)* internal otitis
Innenphloem *n (bot)* internal phloem, intraxylary (perimedullary) phloem
Innenraumgestaltung *f* **mit großen Pflanzen** interiorscaping
Innenrinde *f* inner bark
Innenriß *m* internal shake (check) *(wood defect)*
Innenrotation *f* inner [crop] rotation, inner sequence
Innenschale *f* inner shell
Innenschmarotzer *m* endoparasite, entoparasite, entorganism, internal parasite
Innenschmarotzertum *n* endoparasitism
Innenschuh *m* inner shoe *(of a mounted mower)*
Innenseite *f* [**von Fellen**] flesh side
Innenskelett *n (zoo)* endoskeleton
Innenspannung *f* internal stress *(e.g. in timber)*
Innentemperatur *f* indoor temperature
Innenwirtschaft *f* farmyard work
innerartlich intraspecific
Innereien *pl* entrails, pluck, umbles, offal
Innergruppenschätzung *f (biom)* within-groups estimation
innersekretorisch endocrine
innertherapeutisch systemic
Inner-Väter-Regression *f (gen, biom)* intra-sire regression
Inokulation *f* inoculation
inokulativ inoculative
inokulieren to inoculate
Inokulum *n (phyt, vet)* inoculum, inoculant, inoculation
Inokulumpotential *n (phyt)* inoculum potential
Inosin *n* inosine
Inosit[ol] *n* inosite, inositol
Inovulation *f* inovulation; ovum transfer, ova transplant
Input *m* input
Inquilin *m (ecol)* inquiline

Insalivation

Insalivation *f* insalivation
Insekt *n* insect, hexapod *(class Hexapoda)*
~/**blattfressendes** leaf-chewing insect
~/**blattminierendes** leaf-miner
~/**blütenschädigendes** flower-damaging insect
~/**hüpfendes** hopper
~/**kriechendes** crawler
~/**minierendes** miner
~/**soziales (staatenbildendes)** social insect
~/**wurzelminierendes** root-miner
~/**zapfenfressendes** cone insect
Insektarium *n* insectarium, insectary
Insektenabwehrmittel *n* insect repellent
Insektenanlockmittel *n s.* Insektenlockstoff
Insektenbefall *m* insect infestation (invasion, attack)
insektenbefruchtet insect-pollinated
Insektenbein *n* insect's leg
Insektenbekämpfung *f* insect control
Insektenbekämpfungsmittel *n* insecticide
insektenbestäubt *(bot)* insect-pollinated
Insektenbestäubung *f* insect pollination, entomophily
Insektenbiß *m* insect bite
insektenblütig *(bot)* entomophilous, entomogamous
Insektenblütigkeit *f* entomophily, entomogamy
Insektenentwicklungsinhibitor *m* insect developmental inhibitor
Insektenfalle *f* insect trap
Insektenfraß *m* insect feeding *(s. a.* Insektenschaden*)*
Insektenfraßgang *m* bore[hole], borer hole, burrow
Insektenfraßgift *n* stomach insecticide
insektenfressend insectivorous, entomophagous
Insektenfresser *m* insectivore
Insektengalle *f (phyt)* insect gall
Insektenhaus *n* insectarium, insectary
Insektenhormon *n* insect hormone
Insektenkalamität *f* excessive insect multiplication
Insektenkunde *f* entomology
Insektenkundler *m* entomologist
insektenkundlich entomological
Insektenlarve *f* [insect] larva
~/**blattlausfressende** aphis lion (wolf), aphid lion
~/**minierende** miner, borer
~/**wurmförmige** worm
~/**wurzelschädigende** root worm
Insektenlockstoff *m* insect attractant
~/**geschlechtsselektiver** insect sex attractant
Insektenökologie *f* insect ecology
Insektenpathogen *n* insect pathogen
Insektenpathologie *f* insect pathology
Insektenplage *f* insect pest
Insektenpopulation *f* insect population
Insektenpulver *n* insect-powder
Insektenrepellens *n* insect repellent, insectifuge
Insektenresistenz *f* insect resistance
Insektensaugfalle *f* insect suction trap
Insektenschaden *m* insect injury (damage), damage by insects
Insektenstich *m* insect bite
insektentötend *s.* insektizid
insektenübertragbar insect-transmissible
insektenvernichtend insecticidal
Insektenvertilgungsmittel *n s.* Insektizid
Insektenvirus *n* insect virus
Insektenwachstumsregulator *m* insect growth regulator, IGR
Insektistatikum *n* insectistatic
insektivor insectivorous, entomophagous
Insektivor[e] *m* insectivore
Insektivore *f* insectivorous (carnivorous) plant
insektizid insecticidal
Insektizid *n* insecticide, insect-killer
~/**biogenes** *s.* ~/pflanzliches
~/**mikrobielles** microbial insecticide
~/**pflanzliches** botanical (plant-derived, vegetable) insecticide
~/**protektives** protective insecticide
~/**sofortwirkendes** knock-down agent (poison)
~/**vorbeugend wirkendes** protective insecticide
Insektizidaktivität *f* insecticidal power
Insektizidanwendung *f* insecticide application
Insektizidnebel *m* insecticidal fog
Insektizidprüfung *f* insecticide evaluation
Insektizidrauch *m* insecticidal smoke
Insektizidresistenz *f* insecticide resistance
Insektizidrückstand *m* insecticide residue
Insektizidwirkung *f* insecticidal action
Inselhormon *s.* Insulin
Inseln *fpl/***Langerhanssche** islets [of Langerhans], pancreas islets
Inseminat *n* inseminate
Insemination *f* [artificial] insemination, AI
~/**intrazervikale** deep cervical insemination
~/**wiederholte** repeat insemination
inseminieren to inseminate
inserieren to insert
Insertionsstelle *f* insertion place
insipid[e] insipid
Insolation *f* insolation, solarization
insolubel insoluble
Inspiration *f*, **Inspirium** *n s.* Einatmung
Instabilität *f* instability, lability *(e.g. of an ecological system)*
instandhalten to maintain, to service, to keep in order
Instandhaltung *f* maintenance, servicing
~/**vorbeugende** preventive maintenance
Instandhaltungsmechaniker *m* maintenance worker
Instandhaltungsschnitt *m* containment (maintenance) pruning, regulated pruning *(orcharding)*
instandsetzen to recondition
Instantizer *m* instantizer, spray drying appliance
Instantmilch *f* instant milk

Instantmilchpulver *n* instant milk powder
Instillatio[n] *f (vet)* instillation
Instinkt *m* instinct
instinktiv instinctive, instinctual
Insuffizienz *f (vet)* insufficiency
Insufflationsnarkose *f (vet)* insufflation anaesthesia
Insulin *n* insulin *(hormone)*
Insulinmangel *m (vet)* hypoinsulinism
Insulinsekretion *f* insulin secretion
Insulinüberschuß *m (vet)* hyperinsulinism
Insult *m (vet)* insult
Integration *f*/**harmonische** *(gen)* coadaptation
Integrator *m (gen)* integrator
Integument[um] *n (bot, zoo)* [in]tegument, tegmen
~/inneres *(bot)* tegmen
Intensitätskategorie *f (forest)* management type
Intensivanbau *m* intensive cropping (crop cultivation)
Intensivanlage *f* intensive-type plantation (orcharding)
Intensivbodenbearbeitung *f* intensive tillage
Intensivfruchtfolge *f* high-intensity crop rotation
Intensivhaltung *f* **von Nutztieren** *s.* Intensivtierhaltung
intensivieren to intensify
Intensivierung *f* intensification
Intensivkultur *f* **[/pflanzenbauliche]** intensive crop
Intensivmast *f* intensive fattening
Intensivtierhaltung *f* intensive livestock farming, intensive breeding (management)
Intensivweide *f* intensive pasture (grazing)
Intensivwirtschaft *f* intensive farming
Intentionsbewegung *f* intention movement *(animal behaviour)*
Interaktion *f* interaction, coaction
interallel *(gen)* interallelic
Interglazial *n* interglacial
Interferenzmikroskop *n* interference microscope
Interferenzphänomen *n* interference phenomenon *(virology)*
Interferon *n* interferon *(glycoprotein)*
interkalar *(bot)* intercalary
Interkalarmeristem *n (bot)* intercalary meristem
Interkinese *f,* **Interkinesestadium** *n* interkinesis *(of meiosis)*
interkostal *(bot)* intercostal, interveinal; *(zoo)* intercostal *(situated between the ribs)*
Interkostalchlorose *f (phyt)* interveinal chlorosis
Interkostalmuskel *m* intercostal muscle
intermediär intermediate, intermediary
Intermediärprodukt *n* intermediate [product]
Intermediärstoffwechsel *m* intermediate metabolism
Intermediärwirt *m* intermediate (bridging) host
Intermediat *n s.* Intermediärprodukt
Intermedin *n* intermedin, melanocyte-stimulating hormone, melanotropin
Intermitosezelle *f* interphase cell

Intermitosezellkern *m* interphase nucleus
Internationale Einheit *f* international unit, IU *(standard quantity of a biological)*
Internationaler Code *m* **der Botanischen Nomenklatur** International Code of Biological Nomenclature, ICBN
~ Code *m* **der Nomenklatur der Kulturpflanzen** International Code of Nomenclature of Cultivated Plants, ICNCP
Interneuron *n* interneuron
Internodienstreckung *f (bot)* internode elongation (extension)
Internodienverkürzung *f (bot)* internode shortening
Internodium *n (bot)* internode, merithal; *(zoo)* internode
Interorezeptor *m* proprioceptor, interoceptor *(animal physiology)*
interöstrisch *(zoo)* dioestrous
Interöstrus *m (zoo)* dioestrum, dioestrus
Interozeptor *m s.* Interorezeptor
Interphase *f* interphase *(of cell division)*
Interphasekern *m* interphase nucleus
Interphasenzelle *f* interphase cell
Interphasezellkern *m* interphase nucleus
Intersex *n* intersex
interspezifisch interspecific
intersteril intersterile, intrasterile
Intersterilität *f* intersterility
Intersterilitätsgruppe *f* intersterility group
interstitiell interstitial
Intervallbeleuchtung *f* interval lighting
intervaskulär intervascular, intervessel
intervenös intervenous, interveinal
interzellulär, interzellular intercellular
Interzellularflüssigkeit *f* intercellular fluid
Interzellularkanal *m* intercellular canal (duct)
Interzellularraum *m* intercellular space
~/gummigefüllter *(bot)* gum cyst
~/harzgefüllter *(bot)* resin cyst
~/sekretfreier non-secretory intercellular space *(of wood)*
Interzellularsubstanz *f* intercellular substance
Interzeption *f* interception
Interzeptionsverdunstung *f* evaporation of intercepted water
intestinal intestinal
Intestinal... *s. a.* Darm... *and* Eingeweide...
Intestinalmucosa *f* intestinal mucosa, intestine epithelium
Intestinalpeptid *n* intestinal peptide
~/vasoaktives vaso-active intestinal peptide, VIP *(hormone)*
Intestinalstase *f* intestinal stasis
Intestinum *n* intestine, bowel, gut
intolerant intolerant
Intoleranz *f* intolerance
Intoxikation *f* intoxication, poisoning
~/alimentäre alimentary intoxication

Intra

intra partum intrapartal
intraabdominal, intraabdominell intra-abdominal
intraalveolar intra-alveolar
intraarteriell intra-arterial
intraartikulär intra-articular
intradermal intradermal
intraepithelial intra-epithelial
intragastrisch intragastric
intrakapsulär intracapsular
intrakardial intracardiac, intracardial
intrakavitär intracavitary
intrakranial intracranial
intrakutan inracutaneous
intramembranös intramembranous
intramural intramural
intramuskulär intramuscular, IM
intraoral intra-oral
intrapelvin intrapelvic
intraperitoneal intraperitoneal
intraruminal intraruminal
intraspezifisch intraspecific *(e.g. a cross)*
intrathorakal intrathoracic
Intratrachealnarkose *f (vet)* intubation anaesthesia
intrauterin intra-uterine
intravaginal intravaginal
intravasal, intravaskulär intravascular
intravenös intravenous, IV
intrazellulär intracellular
intrazisternal intracisternal
intrazonal *(soil)* intrazonal
Intrinsic factor *m* intrinsic factor, apoerythein *(enzyme, mucoprotein)*
Introgression *f* introgression, introgressive hybridization
introgressiv introgressive
Intromission *f* intromission *(esp. of penis during copulation)*
Intron *n (gen)* intron, intervening sequence
intrors *(bot)* introrse
Intubationsnarkose *f (vet)* intubation anaesthesia
Intumeszenz *f (bot, zoo)* intumescence
Intussuszeption *f (bot, zoo)* intussusception
Inulase *f* inulase *(enzyme)*
Inulin *n* inulin *(reserve carbohydrate)*
Inundation *f (soil)* inundation
Invagination *f s.* Intussuszeption
Invasion *f (phyt, vet, ecol)* invasion
Invasionskrankheit *f* invasion disease
Inventar *n*/**lebendes** livestock
Inversion *f* inversion
Inventurverfahren *n (forest)* inventory technique
Invertase *f* beta-fructofuranosidase, invertase, sucrase *(enzyme)*
Invertebrat *m* invertebrate
Invertemulsion *f* invert emulsion *(e.g. of herbicides)*
Invertzucker *m* invert sugar
Invertzuckersirup *m* invert syrup

In-vitro-Befruchtung *f* in vitro fertilization, IVF
In-vitro-Kultur *f* in vitro culture
In-vitro-Verdaulichkeit *f* in vitro digestibility
In-vitro-Verklonung *f* in vitro cloning
Involucrum *n (bot, zoo)* involucre
Involution *f* involution
Inzestprüfung *f* incest test *(animal breeding)*
Inzidenz *f* incidence
inzidieren to incise
inzipient incipient
Inzision *f* incision
Inzisiv[us] *m* incisor [tooth]
Inzucht *f* inbreeding • ~ **betreiben** to inbreed, to self • **durch ~ erzeugt** inbred
~/**enge** close [in]breeding
~/**mäßige (milde)** mild inbreeding
Inzuchtdepression *f* inbreeding degeneration (depression)
Inzuchteignung *f* inbred suitability
Inzuchtgrad *m* degree (level) of inbreeding
Inzuchtkoeffizient *m* coefficient of inbreeding, inbreeding coefficient
Inzuchtlinie *f* inbred [line]
Inzuchtschaden *m s.* Inzuchtdepression
Iod *n* iodine
~/**proteingebundenes** protein-bound iodine, PBI
Iodaminosäure *f* iodo amino-acid
Iodcasein *n* iodinated casein
Iodgorgosäure *f* iodogorgoic acid, 3,5-diiodotyrosine
iodieren to iodinate
Iodierung *f* iodination
Iodinin *n* iodinin *(antibiotic)*
Iodismus *m (vet)* iodism
Iodkali *n* potassium iodide
Iodmangel *m* iodine deficiency
Iodophor *n* iodophor *(disinfectant)*
Iodopsin *n* iodopsin *(photosensitive pigment in the retinal cones)*
Iodprobe *f* iodine test *(e.g. in brewing)*
Iodprotein *n* iodoprotein, iodinated protein
Iodthyronin *n* [tetra]iodothyronine, thyroxine *(thyroid hormone)*
Iodtinktur *f* tincture of iodine
Iodtyrosin *n* iodotyrosine *(iodo amino-acid)*
Iodvergiftung *f* iodine poisoning
~/**chronische** *(vet)* iodism
Iodzahl *f* iodine number (value)
Iomud-Pferd *n* lomut *(horse breed)*
Ionenantagonismus *m* ion antagonism
Ionenaufnahme *f* ion uptake
Ionenaustausch *m* ion exchange
Ionenaustauschchromatographie *f* ion-exchange chromatography
Ionenaustauscher *m* ion exchanger
Ionenaustauscherharz *n* ion exchange resin
Ionenaustauschkapazität *f* ion exchange capacity
Ionenreihe *f*/**Hofmistersche** Hofmeister (lyotropic) series

Ionenstärke f ionic strength
Ionentransport m ion transport
Ionenumtausch m ion exchange
Ionisation f, **Ionisierung** f ionization
Ionophor n ionophore
Iowa-Kronenapfel m Iowa crab-apple, Malus coronaria ssp. ioensis
Ioxynil n ioxynil (herbicide)
i.p. s. intraperitoneal
IP s. Punkt/isoelektrischer
Ipazin n ipazine (herbicide, nitrification inhibitor)
IPC s. Propham
Ipekakuanha f (bot) ipecac[uanha], Cephaelis (Uragoga) ipecacuanha
IPN s. Pankreasnekrose der Salmoniden/infektiöse
IPN-Virus n trout infectious pancreatitis virus
Iprodion n iprodione, glycophene (fungicide)
Iprondazol n iprondazole (antiparasitic)
Ipronidazol n ipronidazole (growth regulator)
Iprymidam n iprymidam (herbicide)
IPV s. Vulvovaginitis/infektiöse pustulöse
IPV-Virus n infectious pustular vulvovaginitis virus
Iridochorioiditis f (vet) iridochoroiditis
Iridoid n iridoid (alkaloid, monoterpene)
Iridozyklitis f (vet) cyclitis
Iridozyklochorioiditis f (vet) iridochoroiditis
Iris f 1. (bot) iris, flag (genus Iris); 2. (zoo) iris (of the eye)
Irische Heide f 1. St.-Daboec's-heath, heather (genus Daboecia); 2. Irish heath, St.-Daboec's-heath, Daboecia cantabrica
Irischer Setter m Irish setter (dog breed)
Irisgelbmosaikvirus n iris yellow mosaic virus
Irisgewächse npl iris family (family Iridaceae) • die ~ **betreffend** iridaceous
Irish Setter m Irish setter (dog breed)
~ **Terrier** m Irish terrier (dog breed)
~ **Water Spaniel** m Irish water spaniel (dog breed)
~ **Wolfhound** m Irish wolfhound (dog breed)
Irish-Blue-Terrier m Kerry blue (dog breed)
Iritis f (vet) iritis
Iroko[baum] m (bot) iroko, Chlorophora excelsa
Irokoholz n iroko
irregulär irregular
Irritabilität f irritability
Irrigation f (vet) irrigation
Irrigationspumpe f irrigation pump
Irrigator m irrigator
Irrtumswahrscheinlichkeit f (biom) level of significance, probability level, significance probability
Isabelle f Isabel[la] (horse)
isabellfarben, isabellfarbig isabelline
Isazophus n isazophus (nematicide)
Ischämie f (vet) ischaemia
Isländer m s. Islandpony
Isländische Rasse f Icelandic (cattle breed)
Isländischer Mohn m Iceland poppy, Papaver nudicaule

Isländisches Moos n Iceland lichen (moos), Cetraria islandica
Islandmohn m s. Isländischer Mohn
Islandpony n Iceland Pony (breed)
Isoadhumulon n isoadhumulon[e] (hop resin)
Isoallel n (gen) isoallele
Isoamylase f isoamylase (enzyme)
Isoantigen n isoantigen
Isoantikörper m isoantibody
isobar isobaric
Isobare f isobar
Isobarometer n isobarometric filler
Isobenzan n isobenzan (insecticide)
Isobuttersäure f isobutyric acid, 2-methylpropionic acid
Isocarbamid n isocarbamid (herbicide)
Isochromosom n isochromosome
Isocil n isocil (herbicide)
Isocitratdehydrogenase f isocitrate dehydrogenase (enzyme)
Isocitratlyase f isocitrate lyase (enzyme)
Isocitronensäure f isocitric acid
Isocitronensäuredehydrogenase f isocitrate dehydrogenase (enzyme)
Isocohumulon n isocohumulon[e] (hop resin)
Isocumarin n isocoumarin (plant substance)
isoelektrisch isoelectric
Isoenzym n isoenzyme, isozyme
isoenzymatisch isoenzymatic
Isofenphos n isofenphos (insecticide)
Isoflavan n isoflavan
Isoflavon n isoflavone
isogam isogamous
Isogamet m isogamete
Isogametenvereinigung f, **Isogamie** f isogamy
isogen (gen) isogenic
Isohumulon n isohumulon[e] (hop resin)
Isohyete f isohyet, isohyetal line (connecting areas of equal rainfall)
Isohypse f isohypse, contour [line]
Isolan n isolan (insecticide)
Isolat n isolate (microbiology)
Isolation f isolation
Isoleucin n isoleucine
Isolierbucht f isolation box
isolieren 1. (phyt, vet) to isolate; to quarantine; 2. to isolate, to separate (e.g. substances); 3. to insulate
Isolierfolie f insulating film
Isoliermaterial n insulating material
Isolierschicht f/termitensichere termite shield, termite-proof course
Isolierstreifen m fire line (forest fire control)
Isoliertüte f pollination bag (plant breeding)
Isolierverglasung f insulating glass covering (e.g. of greenhouses)
Isolinie f isopleth, isogram
Isomaltase f isomaltase, oligo-1,6-glucosidase (enzyme)

Isomaltose

Isomaltose *f* isomaltose *(disaccharide)*
Isomerase *f* isomerase *(enzyme)*
Isomethiozin *n* isomethiozin *(herbicide)*
isomorph isomorphous
Isomorphismus *m* isomorphism
Isoniazid *n*, **Isonicotinsäurehydrazid** *n* isoniazid, isonicotinic acid hydrazide, INAH *(tuberculostatic)*
Isonoruron *n* isonoruron *(herbicide)*
Isoosmie *f s.* Isotonie
Isop *m (bot)* 1. hyssop *(genus Hyssopus)*; 2. hyssop, Hyssopus officinalis
Isopentenyladenin *n*, **6-Isopentenylamino-purin** *n* isopentenyladenine *(cytokinin)*
Isophane *f*, **Isophäne** *f* isophane, isophene *(phenology)*
Isoplethe *f* isopleth, isogram
Isopren *n* isoprene
Isoprenalin *n s.* Isoproterenol
Isoprenoid *n* isoprenoid *(natural substance)*
Isoprocarb *n* isoprocarb *(insecticide)*
Isopropalin *n* isopropalin *(herbicide)*
Isopropylalkohol *m* isopropyl alcohol *(disinfectant)*
Isoproterenol *n* isoproterenol, isoprenaline *(sympathomimetic)*
Isoprothiolan *n* isoprothiolane *(fungicide)*
Isoproturon *n* isoproturon *(herbicide)*
Isoptere *f* white ant, termite *(order Isoptera)*
Isopteren... *s.* Termiten....
Isopyrimol *n* isopyrimol *(growth regulator)*
Isosmie *f s.* Isotonie
isospor *(bot)* homosporous, isosporic
Isospore *f* isospore, homospore
Isosporie *f* isospory, homospory
Isotherme *f* isotherm, isothermal line
Isothiocyanat *n* isothiocyanate
~/organisches mustard oil
Isotonie *f* isotonicity
isotonisch isotonic
Isotop *n* isotope
~/radioaktives radioisotope, radioactive isotope
isotrop isotropic
Isotropie *f* isotropy
Isouron *n* isouron *(herbicide)*
Isovaleriansäure *f* isovaleric acid *(plant substance)*
Isoxathion *n* isoxathion *(insecticide)*
Isozym *n s.* Isoenzym
ist *s.* Histosol
Isthmus *m* isthmus *(animal anatomy)*
Istmaß *n* actual measure (size) *(e.g. of timber)*
~ nach dem Sägen green size
Itabirit *m* itabirite *(iron-containing mineral)*
Itaconsäure *f* itaconic acid
Italienische Biene *f* Italian honey-bee, Apis mellifica ligustica
~ Distel *f* Italian thistle, Carduus pycnocephalus

~ Strohblume *f* white-leaf everlasting, Helichrysum italicum
~ Waldrebe *f* blue clematis, Clematis viticella
~ Zypresse *f* Italian cypress, Cupressus sempervirens
Italienischer Ahorn *m* Italian maple, Acer opalus
~ Hahnenkamm (Hahnenkopf) *m* Spanish esparcet, cockshead, French honeysuckle, sulla [sweet-vetch], Hedysarum coronarium
~ Kohl *m* palm cabbage, Brassica oleracea var. palmifolia
Italienisches Latentes Artischockenvirus *n* artichoke Italian latent virus
~ Nelkenringfleckenvirus *n* carnation Italian ring spot virus, CIRV
~ Raygras *n* [Italian] ryegrass, Lolium multiflorum
ITME *s.* Meningoenzephalitis der Puten/infektiöse
i.v. *s.* intravenös
Ivermectin *n* ivermectin *(antiparasitic)*
I.V.T.-Verdünner *m* Illini variable temperature medium *(for liquid preservation of bull's semen)*
Ixie *f (bot)* ixia *(genus Ixia)*
IZ *s.* Iodzahl

J

J *s.* Joule
Jaagsiekte *f (vet)* 1. Jaagsiekte *(of horses)*; 2. mountain disease *(of sheep)*
Jaccardsche Zahl *f (ecol)* Jaccard's index, coefficient of community
Jack Russell *m* Jack Russell *(kind of terrier)*
Jackbohne *f* [common] jack bean, horse bean, Canavalia ensiformis
Jackfrucht *f* jack [fruit]
Jackfruchtbaum *m* jack [fruit] tree, Artocarpus heterophyllus (integrifolius)
Jagd *f* hunt[ing], chase, shooting • **auf die ~ gehen** to go hunting (shooting) • **~ machen auf** to prey [up]on • **zur ~ aufbrechen** to set off
~ auf Federwild [wild]fowling
~/gewerbliche commercial hunting
~/hohe big game hunting
~ im Dickicht cover-shooting
~ mit Gewehr [game-]shooting
~/niedere small game shooting
~ und Fischfang *m* field sports
~/unweidmännische pot-hunting
Jagdaufseher *m* game-warden
Jagdausrüstung *f* hunting equipment
jagdbar runnable, huntable
Jagdberechtigung *f s.* Jagderlaubnis
Jagdbeschränkung *f* hunting limitation
Jagdbeute *f* [hunter] kill, bag
~/jährliche sportsman toll, hunter kill
Jagdbezirk *m* shooting-district, chase
Jagdbüchse *f* sporting-rifle
Jagddruck *m* shooting incidence, hunting pressure

Jagderlaubnis f game (hunting) licence
Jagdfasan m pheasant, Phasianus colchicus
Jagdgebiet n hunting ground (territory), shooting, range
Jagdgebrauchshund m s. Jagdhund
Jagdgeflügel n wildfowl, feathered game, wing[ed] game, game-birds
Jagdgesellschaft f hunt, chase, shooting party
Jagdgesetz n game (hunting) law, game act
Jagdgesetzgebung f game legislation
Jagdgetier n game [animals], venery
Jagdgewehr n sporting-gun
Jagdhelfer m gillie
~ **der seitensichernden Treiberwehr** flanker
Jagdhorn n hunting-horn, bugle
Jagdhund m hunting (gun) dog, hound, hunter
Jagdhütte f hunting-lodge, hunting-box, shooting-box
Jagdkrankheit f (vet) Jaagsiekte (of horses)
Jagdkultur f hunting culture
Jagdkundler m wildlife scientist
Jagdland n, **Jagdländereien** pl hunting lands
Jagdmesser n hunting-knife, hanger
Jagdordnung f sporting regulations
Jagdpacht f hunting-lease
Jagdpächter m game (shooting) tenant, lessee of a shooting
Jagdpferd n hunter
Jagdrecht n hunt[ing] right, game acts
Jagdrennen n steeplechase
Jagdrennpferd n steeplechaser
Jagdrennreiter m steeplechaser
Jagdrevier n hunting-ground, shooting-district, hunt, chase
Jagdsafari f safari
Jagdsattel m hunting saddle
Jagdschein m game (hunting) licence
Jagdschnitt m hunter clip (of a horse)
Jagdschutz m game protection
Jagdschütze m gunner
Jagdsitz m hunting-lodge
Jagdtasche f gamebag; fowling bag
Jagdteilnehmer n hunt member
Jagdtrophäe f [hunting-]trophy
Jagdwaffe f hunting weapon (arm)
Jagdwild n beast [of chase], game [animals]
Jagdwirtschaft f game (wildlife) management
Jagdwissenschaftler m wildlife scientist
Jagdzeit f hunting-season, open season
Jagdzeug n toils
jagen to hunt, to chase, to shoot, to go shooting, to gun
~/**Federwild (Flugwild)** to fowl, to grass
~/**mit dem Beizhabicht (Beizvogel)** to hawk
~/**mit dem Frettchen** to ferret
~/**mit dem Gewehr** to gun
~/**mit Hunden** to course, to hunt; to follow the hounds, to hound (with horses)
~/**zu Pferde** to hunt

~/**zu Pferde mit Hunden** to follow the hounds
Jagen n 1. [forest] compartment; 2. s. Jagd
Jagenstein m boundary stone
Jäger m hunter, huntsman, sportsman, nimrod
~/**unweidmännischer** pot-hunter, poacher
Jägerin f huntress
Jägerlatein n hunter's cant, nimrod's yarn
Jägersprache f hunter's language (slang)
Jagsiekte f s. Jaagsiekte
Jahr n/**ertragsloses** off-year, barren year
Jahreseinfluß m s. Jahreswirkung
Jahreseinschlag m (forest) annual cut
~/**planmäßiger** annual allowable cut
Jahresertrag m annual yield, crop
Jahresetat m s. Jahreshiebssatz
Jahreshiebssatz m (forest) annual yield (allowable cut)
~ **nach Stammzahl** annual yield by number of trees
Jahresmittelniederschlag m average annual precipitation
Jahresmitteltemperatur f yearly mean temperature
Jahresniederschlag m annual precipitation
Jahresperiodizität f annual periodicity
Jahresrhythmik f annual periodicity
Jahresrhythmus m annual rhythm
~/**endogener** circa-annual rhythm
Jahresring m annual (growth, tree) ring, annual growth layer (of wood)
~/**falscher** false annual (growth) ring
Jahresringanalyse f tree-ring analysis, analysis of annual rings
Jahresring[auf]bau m annual (growth) ring structure • **mit breitem** ~ coarse-grained, coarse-ringed, coarse-textured • **mit engem** ~ slow-grown
Jahresringbildung f annual ring formation
Jahresringbreite f ring width
Jahresringchronologie f growth ring chronology, dendrochronology
Jahresringmessung f measurement of growth rings
Jahresringstärke f ring width
Jahresschlagfläche f (forest) annual felling area, annual cut
Jahresschoß m, **Jahrestrieb** m annual shoot, current twig
Jahreswasserbilanz f annual water balance (e.g. of a soil)
Jahreswirkung f year effect (e.g. on field trial results)
Jahreszeit f season • **der** ~ **entsprechend** seasonable • **nicht der** ~ **entsprechend** unseasonable
~ **erhöhter Waldbrandgefahr** fire season
~/**frostfreie** frost-free season
~/**lichtarme** season wanting in light

Jahreszeit

~ **mit durchschnittlichem Waldbrandgeschehen** normal fire season
~/vegetationslose non-growing season
jahreszeitgemäß seasonable
jahreszeitlich seasonal
Jahreszeitlichkeit *f* seasonality
Jahreszyklus *m (ecol)* annual cycle
Jahrgang *m* 1. age group; year class *(of game)*; 2. vintage
Jahrgangswein *m* vintage [wine]
Jahrhundertpflanze *f* century plant [agave], Agave americana
jährig annual
Jährige Rispe *f* annual meadow grass, *(Am)* annual bluegrass, spear grass, Poa annua
Jährling *m* yearling, hogget
Jährlingsbock *m* yearling ram
Jährlingsbulle *m* yearling bull, stirk
Jährlingsfärse *f* yearling heifer, stirk
Jährlingsmasse *f* yearling weight
Jährlingspflanze *f* yearling
Jährlingsrind *n s.* 1. Jährlingsbulle; 2. Jährlingsfärse
Jährlingsschaf *n* yearling [sheep], hogget
~/weibliches *s.* Jährlingszibbe
Jährlingsstute *f* yearling mare
Jährlingswolle *f* yearling's wool
Jährlingszibbe *f* yearling (maiden) ewe, gimmer, gimber, theave
Jahrring *m s.* Jahresring
Jak *m* grunting ox, Bos grunniens
Jakarandaholz *n* rosewood *(from Dalbergia nigra)*
Jakobs[kreuz]kraut *n* [common, tansy] ragwort, Senecio jacobaea
Jakobsleiter *f (bot)* Jacob's ladder *(genus Polemonium)*
Jakobslilie *f* jacobaea (jacobean) lily, Sprekelia formosissima
Jalape *f (bot)* jalap [convolvulus], Ipomoea (Exogonium) purga
Jalousiesichter *m* louvre deduster
Jalousiesieb *n* louvre screen, frog-mouth sieve
Jamaica-Hope *n* Jamaica hope *(cattle breed)*
Jambolanapflaume *f* jambolan plum, jambolana, rose-apple, Syzygium cumini, Eugenia jambolana
Jambuse *f* rose-apple, Syzygium (Eugenia) jambos
Jamnapari-Ziege *f* Jamnapari goat *(breed)*
Jams *n s.* Yams
Japan-B-Virus *n* Japanese encephalitis virus
Japan-Himmel[s]schlüssel *m* primrose, Primula japonica
Japan-Ingwer *m* mioga ginger, Zingiber mioga
Japanische Aprikose *f* Japanese apricot, Prunus (Armeniaca) mume
~ **Blütenkirsche** *f* Japanese [flowering] cherry, Prunus (Cerasus) serrulata
~ **Buche** *f* Japanese beech, buna, Fagus crenata
~ **Eibe** *f* Japanese yew, Taxus cuspidata
~ **Erle** *f* Japanese alder, Alnus japonica
~ **Faserbanane** *f* Japanese banana, Musa basjoo
~ **Hasel[nuß]** *f* Siebold filbert, Corylus sieboldiana var. sieboldiana
~ **Heckenkirsche** *f* Japanese honeysuckle, Lonicera japonica var. japonica
~ **Hirse** *f* Japanese [barnyard] millet, water-grass, Echinochloa [crus-galli var.] frumentacea
~ **Kaisereiche** *f* daimyo oak, Quercus dentata
~ **Kartoffel** *f* Chinese artichoke, Stachys sieboldii (affinis)
~ **Kastanie** *f* Japanese chestnut, Castanea crenata
~ **Kirsche** *f s.* ~ Blütenkirsche
~ **Klettenwurzel** *f* edible burdock, Arctium lappa var. edule
~ **Kopfeibe** *f* Harrington plum yew, Cephalotaxus harringtonia
~ **Kornelkirsche** *f* Japanese cornel (dogwood), Cornus officinalis
~ **Lärche** *f* Japanese larch, Larix kaempferi (leptolepis)
~ **Lavendelheide** *f (bot)* Japanese pieris (andromeda), Pieris (Andromeda) japonica
~ **Mandelkirsche** *f* Japanese flowering almond, Japanese cherry, Prunus (Cerasus) japonica
~ **Marille** *f s.* Japanische Aprikose
~ **Minze** *f* Japanese [pepper]mint, Mentha arvensis var. piperascens
~ **Mispel** *f* Japan[ese] medlar, loquat, Eriobotrya japonica
~ **Pferdeenzephalitis** *f (vet)* Japanese B-encephalomyelitis
~ **Pflaume** *f* Japanese (willow-shaped) plum, Prunus salicina [var. salicina]
~ **Prachtschwertlilie** *f* Japanese iris, Iris kaempferi
~ **Quitte** *f s.* ~ Scheinquitte
~ **Rinne** *f (pisc)* Japanese-style keeper channel
~ **Rotkiefer** *f* Japanese red pine, Pinus densiflora
~ **Scheinquitte** *f* [dwarf] Japanese quince, flowering (Maule's) quince, japonica, Chaenomeles japonica
~ **Schönfrucht** *f* beautyberry, Callicarpa japonica
~ **Schwarzkiefer** *f* [Japanese] black pine, Pinus thunbergii
~ **Sicheltanne** *f* Japanese cedar, sugi, cryptomeria, Cryptomeria japonica
~ **Stachelbeere** *f (bot)* bower actinidia, Actinidia arguta
~ **Stieleiche** *f* Japanese oak, Quercus glandulifera (serrata)
~ **Thuja** *f* hiba [arbor vitae], Thujopsis dolabrata
~ **Trespe** *f* Japanese brome[-grass], Bromus japonicus
~ **Wachtel** *f* Japanese quail, Coturnix coturnix japonica
~ **Weinbeere** *f* wine raspberry, Rubus phoenicolasius

~ **Zaubernuß** *f* Japanese wych-hazel, Hamamelis japonica
~ **Zeder** *f s.* ~ Sicheltanne
~ **Zierquitte** *f s.* ~ Scheinquitte
Japanische-B-Enzephalitis *f (vet)* Japanese B-encephalomyelitis
Japanischer Aal *m* Japanese eel, Anguilla japonica
~ **Ahorn** *m* 1. Japanese maple, Acer japonicum; 2. Japanese maple, Acer palmatum
~ **Blütenhartriegel** *m* kousa dogwood, Cornus kousa
~ **Buchweizen** *m* Japanese buckwheat, Fagopyrum [esculentum var.] emarginatum
~ **Chrysanthemenrost** *m* white rust of chrysanthemum *(caused by Puccinia horiana)*
~ **Hopfen** *m* Japanese hop, Humulus scandens
~ **Ingwer** *m* mioga ginger, Zingiber mioga
~ **Klee** *m* Japan [bush] clover, bush clover, common (Japanese) lespedeza, kobe [lespedeza], Lespedeza striata
~ **Ölbaum** *m* Japanese wood oil tree, Japanese tung, Aleurites cordatus
~ **Pfeffer** *m* Japan pepper, Japanese prickly ash, Zanthoxylum piperitum
~ **Rosinenbaum** *m* Japanese raisin tree, Hovenia dulcis
~ **Schlangenbart** *m* Japanese snake's beard, mondo grass, Ophiopogon japonicus
~ **Schneeball** *m* Japanese snowball, double-fire viburnum, Viburnum plicatum
~ **Schnurbaum** *m* Japanese pagoda tree, umbrella tree, Sophora japonica
~ **Sommerflieder** *m* Japanese butterfly bush, Buddleja japonica
~ **Spindelstrauch** *m (bot)* Japanese euonymus, Euonymus japonicus
~ **Staudenknöterich** *m* Japanese fleece-flower, Reynnoutria japonica
~ **Sternanis** *m* Japanese sacred anise tree, poison bay, Illicium anisatum
~ **Trompetenbaum** *m (bot)* Chinese catalpa, Catalpa ovata
~ **Wurm** *m* epizootic lymphangitis *(of solidungulates, caused by Histoplasma farciminosum)*
Japanisches Geißblatt *n* Japanese honeysuckle, Lonicera japonica var. japonica
~ **Goldröschen** *n (bot)* kerria, Kerria japonica
~ **Mahagoni** *n* Japanese raisin tree, Hovenia dulcis
~ **Schwarzbuntes Rind** *n* Japanese black cattle *(breed)*
~ **Seidenhuhn** *n* silk-fowl *(breed)*
~ **Zuckerrohr** *n* Japanese (Chinese sweet) cane, Saccharum sinense
Japankäfer *m* Japanese beetle, Popillia japonica
Japanrose *f* bramble (pillar) rose, Rosa multiflora
Jarosit *m* jarosite *(non-clay mineral)*
Jarowisation *f* vernalization
Jarowisationsstadium *n* vernalization stage
jarowisieren to vernalize
Jarrah[baum] *m (bot)* jarrah, Eucalyptus marginata
Jasmin *m* jasmin[e], jessamin[e] *(genus Jasminum)*
Jasminartiger Nachtschatten *m* potato vine, Solanum jasminoides
Jasmonsäure *f* jasmonic acid *(growth regulator)*
Jätehäckchen *n* weeding-hook, small double hoe
Jätehacke *f* weeding hoe
Jätekralle *f* weeding claw (fork)
Jätemaschine *f* weeding machine
jäten to [hand-]weed, to eradicate • **mit der Hacke** ~ to hoe
Jäter *m* weeding machine
Jäthacke *f* weeding hoe
Jauche *f* liquid manure, muck, dung-water *(s. a. Gülle)*
Jauchedrillgerät *n* manure drill
Jauche[n]grube *f* cesspit, cesspool, liquid manure pit (cistern), dung-water cistern
Jauchepumpe *f* liquid manure pump, manure [slurry] pump
Jauchetank *m* liquid manure tank
Jauchetankwagen *m* liquid manure tanker
jauchig *(vet)* ichorous
jaulen to yowl
Javanische Himbeere *f* Mauritius raspberry, bramble of the Cape, Rubus rosaefolius
Javanischer Langer Pfeffer *m* Javanese long pepper, Piper retrofractum
Jeffrey-Kiefer *f* Jeffrey pine, Pinus jeffreyi
Jehovablümchen *n (bot)* London pride, Saxifraga umbrosa
Jejunitis *f (vet)* jejunitis
Jejunum *n* jejunum
Jelängerjelieber *n* Italian woodbine, [sweet] honeysuckle, Lonicera caprifolium
Jerba *f* maté, mate *(tealike beverage)*
Jerseykiefer *f* Jersey (Virginia) pine, Pinus virginiana
Jerseyrind *n* Jersey *(cattle breed)*
Jerusalembohne *f* mung bean, Phaseolus aureus
Jerusalemdorn *m* Jerusalem thorn, prickly broom, Parkinsonia aculeata
Jervin *n* jervin[e] *(alkaloid)*
Jesuitentee *m* Mexican tea, Chenopodium ambrosioides var. ambrosioides
JH *s.* Juvenilhormon
Jiffytopf *m* Jiffy pot *(for raising of plantlets)*
Jingganmycin *n* jingganmycin *(antibiotic)*
Joch *n* yoke
Jochbein *n* cheek-bone, zygomatic (jugal, malar) bone
Joch[bein]bogen *m* zygomatic arch
Jockei *m*, **Jockey** *m* jockey
Jod *n s.* Iod
Jodhpur-Reithose *f* jodhpurs
Joghurt *m(n)* yoghurt, joghurt, yaourt, mazun

Joghurtstarter

Joghurtstarter *m*, **Joghurtstarterkultur** *f* yoghurt starter
Johannisbeerblasenlaus *f* red currant aphid, Cryptomyzus ribis
Johannisbeerblattgallmücke *f* black currant leaf-midge, Dasyneura tetensi
Johannisbeere *f* currant *(genus Ribes)*
Johannisbeergallmilbe *f (ent)* [black] currant gallmite, currant bud mite, Cecidophyopsis (Eriophyes, Phytoptus) ribis
Johannisbeerglasflügler *m (ent)* currant clearwing, Aegeria (Ramosia) tipuliformis
Johannisbeerglasflüglerlarve *f* currant borer, Aegeria (Ramosia) tipuliformis
Johannisbeerknospengallmilbe *f s.* Johannisbeergallmilbe
Johannisbeermotte *f (ent)* currant shoot borer, Incurvaria capitella
Johannisbeertomate *f* currant tomato, Lycopersicon pimpinellifolium
Johannisberger *m* Johannisberger *(a kind of grape-wine)*
Johannisbrache *f* clover fallow
Johannisbrot *n* carob, St. John's bread
Johannisbrotbaum *m* carob[-tree], locust [tree], bean tree, Ceratonia siliqua
Johannisbrotmehl *n* carob meal
Johannisbrotmotte *f (ent)* blunt-winged knot-horn, Ectomyelois (Myelois) ceratoniae
Johannisbrotsamen *m* carob seed
Johanniskraut *n* 1. St. John's wort, Klamath weed, hypericum *(genus Hypericum)*; 2. common (perforated) St. John's wort, hardhay *(Hypericum perforatum)*
Johannistrieb *m (bot)* Lammas-shoot, secondary shoot (growth)
Johimbin *n* yohimbine *(alkaloid)*
Johnesche Krankheit *f (vet)* Johne's disease, chronic specific enteritis, paratuberculosis *(caused by Mycobacterium paratuberculosis)*
JoMiMV *s.* Mildes Jonquillenmosaikvirus
Jonathanflecken *mpl* Jonathan spot *(damage of stored fruit)*
Jonquille[nnarzisse] *f (bot)* jonquil, Narcissus jonquilla
Jorquette *f* jorquette *(branch bifurcation in Theobroma cacao)*
Josuabaum *m* Joshua-tree, Yucca brevifolia
Joule *n* joule, J *(SI unit of work, energy and heat)*
Juckbohne *f*, **Juckfasel** *f (bot)* cowage, cowitch, Mucuna pruriens
Juckreiz *m (vet)* pruritus
Juckseuche *f (vet)* Aujeszky's disease
Judasbaum *m* 1. Judas-tree, *(Am)* redbud *(genus Cercis)*; 2. Judas-tree, Cercis siliquastrum
Judasohr *n* Jew's-ear [fungus], Juda's ear, Hirneola (Auricularia) auricula-Judae
Judassilberling *m (bot)* [common] honesty, satinpod, moonwort, Lunaria annua (biennis)
Judenbart *m* Aaron's beard, strawberry geranium (saxifrage), Saxifraga stolonifera (sarmentosa)
Judenkirsche *f* Jerusalem (Christmas) cherry, Solanum pseudocapsicum
Jugendentwicklung *f* juvenile development
Jugendholz *n* juvenile (pith) wood, core [wood]
jugendlich juvenile
Jugendphase *f*, **Jugendstadium** *n* juvenile (early) stage, juvenility, stage of youth
Jugendwachstum *n*, **Jugendwuchsleistung** *f* juvenile (early) growth
jugular[is] jugular
Jujube *f (bot)* 1. jujube *(genus Ziziphus)*; 2. jujube, Ziziphus jujuba
Juliana-Berberitze *f* winter barberry, Berberis julianae
Juliaprimel *f* primrose, Primula juliae
Jundzills Rose *f* large-leaved rose, Rosa jundzilli
Jungaal *m* elver
Jungbär *m* [bear-]cub
Jungbauer *m* young farmer
Jungbaum *m* maiden tree, sapling
Jungbestand *m* young stand
~ aus Kernwuchs *(forest)* young stand of seedling origin
Jungbestandespflege *f (forest)* tending of young stands
Jungbiene *f* young bee
Jungbier *n* young (green) beer
Jungbiergeschmack *m* green beer flavour
Jungbierüberleitung *f* green beer transfer
Jungbulle *m* young bull, steerling, stirk
Jungeber *m* young boar
Jungente *f* duckling
Jungerpel *m* drakerel
Junges *n* young[ling]; cub *(of game) (s. a.* Jungtier*)* • **Junge werfen** to cub, to drop
Jungfärse *f* young heifer, stirk
Jungfasan *m* poult
Jungfer *f (ent)* virgin
~ im Grünen *(bot)* love-in-a-mist, Nigella damascena
Jungfernbau *m (api)* virgin comb
jungfernfrüchtig *(bot)* parthenocarpic
Jungfernfrüchtigkeit *f* parthenocarpy
Jungfernhäutchen *n* hymen
Jungfernöl *n* virgin [olive] oil
Jungfernzeugung *f* virgin birth, parthenogenesis
jungfräulich virgin
Jungfuchs *m* young fox, fox-cub, kit[ten]
Junggans *f* green goose
Junghahn *m* cockerel
~/hormonell kastrierter caponette
Junghammel *m* young wether
Junghase *m* leveret *(esp. in the first year)*
Junghecht *m* pickerel
Junghengst *m* young stallion, stag
Junghenne *f* pullet *(esp. in the first year)*
Junghennen[allein]futter *n* pullet developer, growing mash

Junghennenkrankheit f pullet disease, avian monocytosis (infectious diarrhoea), battery nephrosis, X disease
Junghennenstall m pullet growing house
Jungholz n 1. juvenile wood; 2. *(forest)* seedling stand (crop), second growth
Junghuhn n poult
~/verschnittenes poulard[e]
Junghund m puppy, pup
Jungkalbfleisch n bob veal
Jungkaninchen n young rabbit
Jungkatze f kitten, kit
Jungkräusen pl young heads, low krausen *(brewing)*
Junglachs m pink
~ **nach dem ersten Meeraufenthalt** grilse, peal
Junglarve f *(ent)* first instar [larva], egg-larva
Jungmastgans f fattened gosling
Jungmasthuhn n *(Am)* fryer [chicken], broiler, roaster
Jungmasthuhn... s. Broiler...
Jungmastkaninchen n fryer (young fattening) rabbit, rabbit broiler
Jungnerz m kit, kitten
Jungochse m [young] bullock, steer
Jungpelztier n kit, kitten
Jungpferd n young horse, stag
~/12 bis 30 Monate altes young horse I
~/2 1/2 bis 4 1/2 Jahre altes young horse II
Jungpflanze f young plant, plantlet, set[t], seedling [plant]
~ **aus der Mikrovermehrung** microplant, microcutting
~/im Container angezogene super seedling
~/in standardisierten Aussaatkisten angezogene module-raised plant, modular transplant
~ **mit stöpselförmigem Topfballen** miniplug
~/verpflanzbare transplant
~/verpflanzte transplant
Jungpflanzen fpl planting stock (material) *(for compounds s. under* Jungpflanze*)*
Jungpflanzenanzucht f seedling production, [trans]plant growing, transplant raising
Jungpflanzenanzuchthaus n nursery greenhouse
Jungpflanzenbestand m young stand
Jungpflanzenentwicklung f **nach dem Sämlingsalter** post-seedling development
Jungpflanzenrodegerät n mechanical seedling harvester
Jungpilz m button
Jungpute f poult
Jungrinder npl young cattle
Jungrinderaufzucht f young cattle raising
Jungrute f primocane *(esp. of currants)*
Jungsau f gilt
Jungschaf n young sheep, lamb, maiden (yearling) ewe, gimmer, gimber, theave
Jungschwein n young pig (swine), porkling, runner, *(Am)* hog, shoat, shote
~ **nach dem Absetzen** growing pig

Jungschweinfleisch n pig
Jungstute f maiden
Jungtier n young animal, young[ling], juvenile
~/abgesetztes weaner, weanling
~/abortiertes slink
~/mutterloses poddy
~/saugendes suck[l]er
~/vorzeitig geborenes slink
Jungtiere npl young stock
Jungtierhaut f kip
Jungtierkrankheit f young animal disease
Jungvieh n young cattle (stock)
Jungviehaufzucht f young stock rearing
Jungviehbestand m young stock
Jungviehstall m young stock barn
Jungvogel m fledg[e]ling
Jungwein m young wine
~ **im ersten Jahr** this year's wine
Jungweisel f virgin queen [honey-bee]
Jungwuchs n young (early) growth *(e.g. of trees)*
Jungwuchspflege f *(forest)* young growth tending; first cleaning (weeding)
Jungziege f kid
Jungziegenleder n kid [leather]
Junifruchtfall m June drop
Junikäfer m june-beetle, june-bug, [mid]summer (European) chafer, Amphimallus (Rhizotrogus) solstitialis
Junkerlilie f *(bot)* asphodel *(genus Asphodeline)*
Jupiterblume f flower of Jove, Lychnis flos-jovis
Jupiters Bart m *(bot)* Jupiter's-beard, Anthyllis barba-jovis
Jura m/**Brauner** *(soil)* Dogger
Jute f [white] jute, gunny fibre, Corchorus capsularis • **aus ~** [**hergestellt**] jute
Juteerntemaschine f jute harvester
Jutefaser f jute [fibre], gunny fibre
Jutesack m jute sack
Jütisches Pferd n, **Jütländer** m Jutland, Danish *(horse breed)*
Juvabion n juvabione *(juvenile hormone)*
juvenil juvenile
Juvenilhormon n juvenile hormone, neotenin
Juvenilhormonanalogon n juvenile hormone analogue, juvenoid
Juvenilität f juvenility
Juvenoid n *s.* Juvenilhormonanalogon
Juxtaposition f juxtaposition

K

k *s.* 1. Selektivitätskoeffizient; 2. Formquotient
K *s.* 1. Leitfähigkeit/hydraulische; 2. Klangholz
Ka *s.* Kahlschlag 1.
Kabardiner m Kabarda *(horse breed)*
Kabel n cable • **mittels Kabels befestigen** to cable
Kabelkran m cable-crane
Kabelleiter m *s.* Kabelträger

Kabelsuchgerät

Kabelsuchgerät *n* cable detection equipment
Kabelträger *m* fairlead *(cableway)*
Kabeltrommel *f* cable drum
Kabelwinde *f* cable winch
Kabine *f* cab
~/klimatisierte air conditioned cab
Kabinenheizanlage *f*, **Kabinenheizung** *f* cabin heater
kachektisch *(vet)* cachectic
Kachexie *f (vet)* cachexia
Kadamölpflanze *f* kadam seed, Hodgonsonia macrocarpa
Kadaver *m* cadaver, carcass, carcase
Kadavermehl *n* animal tankage
Kadaverwolle *f* carrion wool
Kadethrin *n* kadethrin *(insecticide)*
Kaempferol *n* kaempferol *(plant dye)*
Käfer *m* beetle, coleopteran *(order Coleoptera)*
• **die ~ betreffend** coleopterous, coleopteran
~/kohlfressender cabbage beetle *(comprehensive term)*
käferbefallen weevil[l]ed, weevil[l]y
Käferfraß *m* beetle damage
Käferlarve *f* [beetle] grub
~/minierende borer
Käferschaden *m* beetle damage
Kaff *n s*. Spreu
Kaffee *m* 1. coffee *(roasted and ground coffee beans; beverage)*; 2. *s*. Kaffeestrauch
~/ungerösteter green coffee
Kaffeebaum *m s*. Kaffeestrauch
Kaffeebohne *f* coffee [bean], berry
Kaffeebohnen *fpl*/**enthülste (geschälte)** nibs
Kaffeebohnenkäfer *m* coffee bean weevil, arecanut weevil, Araecerus fasciculatus
Kaffee-Erbse *f* asparagus (winged) pea, Tetragonolobus purpureus
Kaffee-Erntemaschine *f* coffee harvester
Kaffeekirsche *f* coffee berry, cherry
Kaffeekirschenkäfer *m (ent)* coffee berry borer, Hypothenemus (Stephanoderes) hampei
Kaffeekirschenkrankheit *f* coffee berry disease, die back of coffee *(caused by Glomerella cingulata, conidial stage: Colletotrichum coffeanum)*
3-Kaffeeoylchinasäure *f* caffeoylquinic acid
Kaffeepflanzung *f*, **Kaffeeplantage** *f* coffee plantation
Kaffeerost *m* coffe leaf rust *(caused by Hemileia vastatrix)*
Kaffeesäure *f* caffeic acid
Kaffeestrauch *m* 1. coffee [tree] *(genus Coffea)*; 2. [Arabian, Arabica, common] coffee, coffee tree, Coffea arabica
Kaffeewanze *f* Antestia bug *(genus Antestiopsis)*
Kaffeewicke *f* Swedish coffee, Astragalus boeticus
Kaffeezichorie *f* common (coffee) chicory, Cichorium intybus var. sativum
Kaffernbrot *n* kaffir (Kafir) bread, Encephalartos caffer

Kaffernbüffel *m* [African, Cape] buffalo, Bubalus (Syncerus) caffer
Kaffernhirse *f* sorghum, sorgo *(genus Sorghum)*
Kaffernpflaume *f* 1. African dovyalis, Dovyalis (Doryalis) abyssinica; 2. Ceylon gooseberry, Dovyalis (Doryalis) hebecarpa
Käfig *m* cage
Käfiganordnung *f* cage arrangement
Käfigaufzucht *f* cage rearing
Käfigbatterie *f* [cage, rearing] battery
Käfigdichte *f* cage density
Käfigeinheit *f* cage unit
Käfigfalle *f* cage trap
Käfighaltung *f* cage housing (keeping, management)
Käfighenne *f* cage layer
Käfigintensivhaltung *f* laying-cage system
Käfigkultur *f (pisc)* cage culture
Käfiglähmung *f* **der Hühner** cage paralysis of fowls, cage layer fatigue
Käfiglegehenne *f* cage layer
Käfigmüdigkeit (Käfigparalyse) *f* **der Hühner** *s*. Käfiglähmung der Hühner
Käfigvogel *m* cage-bird
Kafirsorghum *n* kaffir [corn], kafir, Sorghum caffrorum
kahl *(bot, zoo)* denudate[d], glabrous, bare, bald; hairless
Kahle Felsenbirne *f* service-berry, Amelanchier laevis
Kahler Krempling *m (bot)* involute paxillus, brown roll-rim, Paxillus involutus
~ Sumach *m* smooth sumac[h], Rhus glabra
Kahles Bruchkraut *n* rupture-wort, Herniaria glabra
~ Ferkelkraut *n (bot)* smooth cat's ear, Hypochoeris glabra
Kahlfläche *f s*. Kahlschlagfläche
kahlgeworden *(bot, zoo)* glabrate
Kahlheit *f* hairlessness, baldness
Kahlhieb *m s*. Kahlschlag 1.
Kahlhirsch *m* pollard, hummel
Kahlschlag *m (forest)* 1. clear (clean) felling, complete felling (exploitation), cutting clear, clearing; 2. *s*. Kahlschlagfläche
Kahlschlagbetrieb *m* clear-felling system
kahlschlagen to clear[-cut]
Kahlschlagfläche *f* clear-cut area, cleared (denuded, clear-felled) area; non-restocked forest land
Kahlschlagmethode *f*, **Kahlschlagsystem** *n* clear-felling system
Kahlschlagvegetation *f* clear-felling vegetation
Kahlschlagwirtschaft *f* clear-felling system
Kahlstreifenschlag *m* clear-strip felling
Kahlstreifen[schlag]system *n* clear-strip system
Kahlstreifen- und Kahlsaumschlagsystem *n* progressive clear-strip system
kahlwerdend *(bot, zoo)* glabrescent
Kahmhaut *f* pellicle

kahmig rop[e]y *(wine)*
Kahnbein *n* central tarsal bone, navicular bone
kahnförmig *(bot, zoo)* navicular, cymbiform
Kahnlippe *f*, **Kahnorche** *f (bot)* cymbidium *(genus Cymbidium)*
Kaimastrauch *m (bot)* jet-bead, Rhodotypos scandens
Kainit *n* kainit[e] *(fertilizer)*
Kairomon *n (ent)* kairomone *(messenger substance)*
Kaiserdahlie *f* bell tree dahlia, Dahlia imperialis
Kaisereiche *f* daimyo oak, Quercus dentata
Kaisergras *n* imperial grass, Axonopus scoparius
Kaiserkrone *f (bot)* crown imperial, Fritillaria imperialis
Kaiserlingsche Lösung *f* Kaiserling's solution *(for preservation of anatomical preparations)*
Kaiserschnitt *m (vet)* Caesarean operation (section), hysterotomy
Kajeputbaum *m* cajeput [tree], swamp tea tree, paperbark, Melaleuca leucadendra
KAK *s.* Kationenaustauschkapazität
Kakao *m* 1. cocoa *(powder from crushed cacao seeds; beverage)*; 2. *s.* Kakaobaum
Kakaobaum *m* cacao[-tree], chocolate tree, Theobroma cacao
Kakaoblasenfuß *m (ent)* cacao (red-banded) thrips, Selenothrips rubrocinetus
Kakaobohne *f* cacao bean
Kakaobutter *f*, **Kakaofett** *n* cocoa (cacao) butter
Kakaofrucht *f* cocoa pod
Kakaofruchtschale *f* cocoa husk
Kakaokrebs *m (phyt)* cacao canker *(caused by Ceratocystis fimbriata)*
Kakaomalve *f* perennial Indian hemp, devil's-cotton, Abroma augusta
Kakaomotte *f* cacao[-bean] moth, tobacco (walnut, warehouse) moth, chocolate (currant) moth, Ephestia elutella
Kakaoschalen *fpl* cacao shells
Kakaoschote *f* cocoa pod
Kakaosproßschwellungsvirus *n* cacao swollen shoot virus
Kakaotrunk *m* chocolate milk
Kakerlak *m (ent)* cockroach, *(Am)* roach *(order Blattariae)*
Kakipflaume *f* kakee [plum], kaki, [Chinese] persimmon, Diospyros kaki
Kakodylsäure *f* cacodylic acid *(herbicide)*
Kaktee *f* cactus *(family Cactaceae)*
Kakteenschildlaus *f* prickly pear scale, Diaspis echinocacti
Kakteen-X-Virus *n* cactus virus X
Kaktus *m* cactus *(family Cactaceae)*
Kaktusdahlie *f* cactus dahlia, Dahlia juarezii
Kal *s.* Kalifornier
Kala-Azar *f (vet)* kala-azar *(caused by Leishmania donovani)*

Kalabarbohne *f* Calabar (ordeal) bean, Physostigma venenosum
Kalabasse *f s.* Kalebasse
Kalabrische Kiefer *f* Calabrian pine, Pinus nigra ssp. laricio
Kaladie *f (bot)* caladium *(genus Caladium)*
Kalamität *f (phyt)* calamity
Kalamitätsholz *n* calamity wood
Kalamitätsnutzung *f* salvage (extraordinary) felling, salvaging
Kalanchoe *f (bot)* kalanchoe *(genus Kalanchoe)*
Kalb *n* calf, boss; deer calf *(of Cervidae)*; fawn *(of red deer)* • ein ~ führen to freshen *(cow)*
~/abortiertes slink
~/angebundenes *(Am)* necked calf
~/mutterlos aufgezogenes poddy *(esp. Australia)*
~/mutterloses (vernachlässigtes) *(Am)* maverick, dogie
~/vor dem Absetzen geschlachtetes bobby [calf]
~/vorzeitig geborenes slink
Kalbe *f s.* Färse
Kalbeabteil *n* calving pen *(in a cowshed)*
Kalbefieber *n* parturient hypocalcaemia (paralysis)
Kalbeleichtigkeit *f* calving ease
Kalbeleistung *f* calving performance
kalben to calve [down], to freshen
Kalbepause *f* calving interval (index)
Kälberaufzucht *f* calf rearing
Kälberaufzuchtfutter *n* calf starter, calf-rearing concentrate
Kälberaufzuchtstall *m* calf nursery
Kälberbox *f*, **Kälberbucht** *f* calf pen, calf-raising quarter
Kälberdiphtheroid *n* calf diphtheria *(mainly caused by Fusobacterium necrophorum)*
Kälberdurchfall *m* calf (white) scours
Kälbereinzelbucht *f s.* Kälberbox
Kälberenteritis *f* coliform scour[s] in calves
Kälbererstlingsfutter *n s.* Kälberaufzuchtfutter
Kälberflechte *f (vet)* ringworm, trichophytosis, tinea *(mainly caused by Trichophyton verrucosum)*
Kälberfütterung *f* calf feeding
Kälberkropf *m* chervil *(genus Chaerophyllum)*
Kälberlähme *f (vet)* joint ill
Kälbermagenlab *n* rennet
Kälbermilchbereiter *m* milk replacer mixer for calf feeding
Kälbermilchwärmer *m* milk heater for calf feeding
Kälberpneumonie *f (vet)* calf pneumonia
Kälberrheumatismus *m* stiff calf disease
Kälberruhr *f* coliform scour[s] in calves
Kälberschutzhütte *f* calf shelter
Kälberschwächesyndrom *n (vet)* weak-calf syndrome
Kälberstall *m* calf house (barn)
Kälberstand *m s.* Kälberbox
Kälberstarterfutter *n* calf starter, calf-rearing concentrate

Kälbersterblichkeit

Kälbersterblichkeit *f* calf mortality
Kälbertränkautomat *m* calf milk dispenser, teat-type milk feeder, automatic wet nurse
Kälberverluste *mpl* calf losses
Kalbestall *m* calving house
Kalbezeit *f* calving season (time)
Kalbfleisch *n* veal
kalbfleischartig vealy
Kalbsbries *n* thymus [gland], sweetbread
Kalbsfell *n* calfskin
Kalbshachse *f* knuckle (shank) of veal
Kalbskeule *f* leg of veal
Kalbsleder *n* calf-leather
Kalbsmilch *f s.* Kalbsbries
Kalbung *f* calving
Kalebasse *f* 1. [bottle] gourd, calabash, Lagenaria siceraria; 2. *s.* Kalebassenbaum
Kalebassenbaum *m* 1. calabash [tree] *(genus Crescentia)*; 2. [common] calabash tree, calabash, Crescentia cujete
Kalebassenmuskat *m* calabash (Jamaica) nutmeg, Monodora myristica
Kali *n s.* 1. Kalisalz; 2. Kalidüngemittel
~/schwefelsaures *s.* Kaliumsulfat
~/übermangansaures *s.* Kaliumpermanganat
kalibrieren to calibrate, to size
Kalibrieren *n* calibration
Kalibriermaschine *f* calibrator, [dimension] sizer, grader
Kalibrierung *f* calibration
Kalidüngemittel *n* potash (potassium, potassic) fertilizer
~/stickstoffhaltiges nitrogen-potassium fertilizer
Kalidüngesalz *n*/**50er** muriate of potash
~/60er pink floatation potash, muriate of potash
Kalifeldspat *m* orthoclase *(non-clay mineral)*
Kalifornier *m*, **Kalifornierkaninchen** *n* Californian rabbit *(breed)*
Kalifornische Brodiäe *f (bot)* Ithuriel's spear, Triteleia (Brodiaea) laxa
~ Eschscholzie *f s.* Kalifornischer Mohn
~ Fächerpalme *f (bot)* California washingtonia, Washingtonia filifera
~ Flußzeder *f* California incense cedar, Calocedrus decurrens
~ Nußeibe *f (bot)* California torreya, Torreya californica
~ Steineiche *f (bot)* encina, Quercus agrifolia
~ Tanne *f* grand (white) fir, Abies grandis
Kalifornischer Kiefernborkenkäfer *m (ent)* California pine engraver, Ips plastographus
~ Mohn *m* California poppy, Noah's nightcap, Eschscholzia californica
Kaliglimmer *m* muscovite *(non-clay mineral)*
Kaliko *n (phyt)* calico
kaliliebend potash-loving *(plant)*
Kalimagnesia *f* [sulphate of] potash-magnesia *(fertilizer)*

Kalimangel *m* potassium deficiency
Kalirohsalz *n* mine-run salt
Kalisalpeter *m* 1. saltpetre, saltpeter, nitre, *(Am)* niter; 2. *s.* Kaliumnitrat
Kalisalz *n* potash [salt]
Kalisulfat *n s.* Kaliumsulfat
Kaliumantimonyltartrat *n* antimony potassium tartrate *(anthelminthic)*
Kaliumazid *n* potassium azide *(nitrification inhibitor)*
Kaliumbromid *n* potassium bromide
Kaliumcarbonat *n* potassium carbonate, potash
Kaliumchlorid *n* potassium chloride, muriate of potash
Kaliumcyanid *n* potassium cyanide
Kaliumfixierung *f* potassium fixation
Kaliumhydrogentartrat *n* potassium hydrogentartrate, wine-stone, tartar
Kaliumiodid *n* potassium iodide
kaliumliebend potash-loving *(plant)*
Kaliumnatriumtartrat *n* potassium sodium tartrate, Rochelle salt
Kaliumnitrat *n* potassium nitrate
Kaliumoxid *n* potassium oxide, potash
Kaliumperchlorat *n* potassium perchlorate
Kaliumpermanganat *n* potassium permanganate *(disinfectant)*
Kaliumsulfat *n* potassium sulphate, sulphate of potash *(fertilizer)*
Kalk *m* lime • **mit ~ düngen** to lime
~/gebrannter burnt (anhydrous) lime, burned oyster shell lime, quicklime
~/gelöschter slaked (hydrated) lime, hydroxide of lime, agricultural hydrate *(fertilizer)*
~/kohlensaurer calcium carbonate, ground limestone
~/ungelöschter *s.* **~/gebrannter**
Kalkablagerung *f* incrustation; *(vet)* calcinosis
Kalkammonsalpeter *m* calcium ammonium nitrate, CAN, ammonium nitrate lime, nitrochalk *(fertilizer)*
Kalkanreicherungshorizont *m (soil)* lime accumulation horizon, lime pan
Kalkanstrich *m* whitewash
kalkarm lime-deficient, short of lime
kalkartig limy
Kalkbedarf *m* lime requirement
kalkbedürftig in need of lime
Kalkbeinkrankheit *f* **des Geflügels** *(vet)* scaly leg *(caused by Knemidokoptes ssp.)*
Kalkbeinmilbe *f* scaly leg mite, Knemidokoptes mutans
Kalkbilanz *f* lime balance
Kalkboden *m* lime (limy, calcareous) soil • **auf ~ gedeihend** calcipetal
Kalkbraunerde *f* brown calcareous soil
Kalkbrut *f (api, vet)* chalk (calcified) brood
Kalkchlorose *f* lime-induced chlorosis

Kalkdüngemittel *n* lime[stone] fertilizer, agricultural limestone, lime, calcium fertilizer
Kalkdüngergabe *f* lime dressing
Kalkdüngung *f* lime fertilization (dressing)
Kalkdüngungsversuch *m* lime [fertilizer] treatment trial
Kalkeinlagerung *f* calcification *(e.g. in tissues)*
kalken 1. to lime, to chalk *(soil)*; 2. to lime, to defecate *(sugar manufacture)*; 3. to whitewash • **zu stark ~** to overlime *(soil)*
Kalkentsäuerung *f* lime deacidification *(of wine)*
Kalkfeldspat *m* anorthite
Kalkflieher *m* calcifuge
Kalkgestein *n* limerock
Kalkgicht *f* calcium gout *(of young dogs)*
Kalkgrit *m* oyster-shell
kalkhaltig calcareous, limy
kalkhold *s.* kalkliebend
Kalkhydrat *n* calcium hydroxide
kalkig limy, calcareous
Kalk-Kohlensäure-Verfahren *n* carbonation process *(sugar manufacture)*
kalkliebend lime-loving, calcicolous, calcipetal, calciphile *(plant)*
Kalklöschtrommel *f* lime slaking drum, rotary lime slaker *(sugar manufacture)*
Kalkmangel *m* lime deficiency
kalkmeidend lime-intolerant, calcifugous, calciphobous *(plant)*
Kalkmergel *m* lime (calcareous) marl
Kalkmilch *f* milk of lime, lime milk; whitewash
Kalkmilchgrießabscheider *m*, **Kalkmilchklassierer** *m* lime-milk classifier *(sugar manufacture)*
Kalkmilchpumpe *f* milk of lime pump
Kalkmilchscheidung *f* wet liming *(sugar manufacture)*
Kalkmoorboden *m* calcareous peat soil
Kalknatronfeldspat *m* lime-soda feldspar, plagioclase *(non-clay mineral)*
Kalkofen *m* lime kiln *(sugar manufacture)*
Kalkofengas *n* lime-kiln gas
Kalkpflanze *f* calcicole
kalkreich calcareous
Kalksaccharat *n* saccharate of lime
Kalksalpeter *m* calcium nitrate, nitrate of lime, Norge nitre *(fertilizer)*
Kalkschwarzerde *f* calcareous chernozem
Kalkspat *m* calcspar, calcite *(non-clay mineral)*
Kalkstein *m* limestone
~/dolomitischer dolomitic limestone
~/magnesiahaltiger magnesian limestone
Kalksteinboden *m* limestone soil
Kalksteinbraunlehm *m (soil)* terra fusca
Kalksteinmehl *n* ground limestone, agricultural meal *(fertilizer)*
Kalksteinrotlehm *m (soil)* terra rossa
Kalkstickstoff *m* lime nitrogen, nitrolime
Kalkstreuer *m* lime spreader (broadcaster, sower)
Kalktonboden *m (soil)* malm

Kalkung *f* 1. liming, lime treatment *(of soil)*; 2. liming, defecation *(sugar manufacture)*
Kalkungscarbonatation *f* defecocarbonatation *(sugar manufacture)*
Kalkungsstoff *m* liming material
Kalkversorgungsgrad *m s.* Kalkzustand
Kalkvorrat *m* lime reserve *(e.g. of a soil)*
Kalkwasser *n* lime water
Kalkzustand *m* lime status *(of a soil)*
Kalla *f s.* Calla
Kallikrein *n* kallikrein *(enzyme)*
kallös callous, callose
Kallose *f* callose *(polysaccharide)*
Kallositas *f* callosity
Kallus *m (bot, vet)* callus
Kallusgewebe *n* callus tissue
Kalluskultur *f* callus culture
Kallusproliferation *f*, **Kalluswucherung** *f* callus proliferation
kalmieren to calm, to sedate, to tranquilize
Kalmodulin *n* calmodulin *(protein)*
Kalmückenrind *n* Kalmyk *(cattle breed)*
Kalmus *m (bot)* sweet flag (rush, sedge), Acorus calamus
Kalorie *f* calorie *(non-SI unit of heat energy; 1 cal = 4,1868 J)*
Kalorimeter *n* calorimeter
Kalorimetrie *f* calorimetry
kalorimetrisch calorimetric
kalorisch caloric, calorific
Kaltauszug *m* maceration
Kaltbau *m (api)* cold-way hive
Kaltbelüftung *f* cold-air ventilation
Kaltbelüftungsanlage *f* cold-air ventilation system
Kaltbelüftungstrocknung *f* barn hay storage drying
Kaltbeschlag *m* cold shoeing *(of hoofs or claws)*
Kaltblut *n s.* Kaltblutpferd
Kaltblüter *m (zoo)* poikilotherm
kaltblütig cold-blooded, poikilothermic
Kaltblutpferd *n* cold-blooded horse, heavy horse
Kaltbodenpflanze *f* psychrophyte
Kälte *f* cold, chill; frost • **bei ~ gedeihend (wachsend)** psychrotrophic
~/[strenge] trockene black frost
Kälteabhärtung *f* cold hardening (acclimation), chill-hardening *(e.g. of plants)*
Kälteagglutination *f* cold agglutination
Kälteakklimation *f s.* Kälteabhärtung
Kälteanästhesie *f (vet)* refrigeration anaesthesia
Kältebedarf *m*, **Kältebedürfnis** *n* cold (chilling) requirement *(of plants)*; cooling requirement *(e.g. of stored fruit)*
kältebedürftig cold-requiring
Kältebedürftigkeit *f s.* Kältebedarf
Kältebeständigkeit *f s.* Kälteresistenz
kälteempfindlich cold-sensitive, sensitive to cold
Kälteempfindlichkeit *f* chilling sensitivity, sensitivity to cold

kältefest

kältefest s. kälteresistent
Kältefleischbräune f brown core *(damage of stored fruit)*
Kältehämagglutination f cold agglutination
Kältehärtung f s. Kälteabhärtung
kälteliebend cool-loving, cryophilic
Kältemittel n coolant, cooling agent, refrigerant [agent]
kälteresistent cold-resistant, cold hardy
Kälteresistenz f cold (chilling) resistance, resistance to cold
Kälterezeptor m cold receptor
Kälteschaden m cold damage (injury), chilling injury (damage)
Kälteschock m cold shock
Kälteschutz m cryoprotection
Kälteschutzmittel n cryoprotectant
Kältestabilität f chill stability
Kältestreß m cold stress
Kältetod m cold death
kältetolerant cold-tolerant
Kältetoleranz f cold tolerance
kältetrocknen to lyophilize
Kältetrocknung f lyophilization
Kältetrub m cold sludge (break) *(brewing)*
Kältetrübung f chill haze *(e.g. of beer)*
kälteverträglich cold-tolerant
Kälteverträglichkeit f cold tolerance
Kälteverkürzung f *(slaught)* cold shortening
Kältevorbehandlung f prechilling
Kältezittern n [/reflektorisches] shivering *(animal physiology)*
Kaltgärhefe f cold fermentation yeast
Kaltgärung f cold (cool) fermentation
Kaltgärverfahren n cold fermentation method
kalt-gemäßigt boreal *(climate)*
Kalthaus n coldhouse, cold (unheated) greenhouse
Kaltlagerung f cold (cool) storage
Kaltluft f cold air
Kaltluftbelüftung f cold-air drying
Kaltluftfluß m cold-air flow
Kaltluftinversion f cold-air inversion *(meteorology)*
Kaltluftsee m, **Kaltluftstau** m cold-air lake, frost pool
Kaltluftstrom m cold-air flow
Kaltlufttrockner m cold-air dryer
Kaltlufttrocknung f cold-air drying
Kaltmasse f **des Schlachtkörpers** cold carcass weight
Kaltnebeldüse f cold-fogging nozzle
Kaltnebelmaschine f power air blast sprayer, atomizer for cold fogging *(plant protection)*
Kaltsilage f cold silage
Kaltsilierung f cold (cool) fermentation
Kaltstall m cold animal house, cold confinement
Kaltstarteinrichtung f, **Kaltstarthilfe** f cold weather starting aid *(of a tractor)*

Kaltstratifizierung f cold stratification, prechilling *(of seed)*
Kalttreiben n cold forcing *(e.g. of vegetable plants)*
Kaltwasserbehandlung f hydrocooling *(e.g. of vegetable)*
Kaltwasserdruckreinigungsgerät n cold-water pressure cleaner (washer)
Kaltwasserkrankheit f peduncle disease *(of salmonoids, caused by Cytophaga psychrophila)*
Kaltwassersee m cold-water lake
Kaltzeit f glacial
kaltzeitlich glacial
Kalumbawurzel f columba root, Jateorhiza palmata
Kalyptra f *(bot)* calyptra, root cap, pileorhiza
Kalzeolarie f slipperwort, pocket-book plant, calceolaria *(genus Calceolaria)*
Kalzifikation f, **Kalzifizierung** f calcification
kalzifug calcifuge, calcifugous, calciphobous, lime-intolerant *(plant)*
kalzikol calcicolous, calcipetal, calciphile, lime-loving *(plant)*
Kalzinose f *(vet)* calcinosis
Kalziphylaxie f *(vet)* calciphylaxis
Kamala n kamala *(anthelminthic)*
Kamassie f *(bot)* camas[s] *(genus Camassia)*
Kamaxin n kanamycin *(antibiotic)*
Kambial... s. Kambium...
Kambium n *(bot)* cambium
Kambiumgalle f *(phyt)* nodosity *(on grape-vine roots)*
Kambiumgewebe n cambium
Kambiuminitiale f cambial initial (element)
Kambiumkultur f cambium culture
Kambiumring m arc of the cambium
Kambiumschicht f cambium layer
Kambiumzelle f cambium cell
Kambiumzone f cambial zone
Kamel n camel, oont *(family Camelus)*
Kameldorn m camel thorn, Alhagi pseudalhagi (camelorum)
Kamelhaar n camel['s]-hair
Kamelfleisch n camel meat
Kamelie f *(bot)* 1. camellia *(genus Camellia)*; 2. [common] camellia, camelia, Camellia japonica
Kamelmilch f camel milk
Kameltrab m pace *(horse's gait)*
Kamille f c[h]amomile *(genus Chamomila)*
Kamm m 1. *(bot, zoo)* crista; *(zoo)* pecten; comb, crest *(e.g. of fowl)*; 2. ridge, crest *(e.g. of a plough furrow)*; 3. crest, crease *(of horse's back)*; 4. *(slaught)* chine, neck; Boston butt *(of pig's carcass)*; chuck *(beef carcass)*; 5. beard, sloven, barber's chair, tombstone *(tree felling)* • **den ~ kupieren** to decomb
~/V-förmiger V-shaped comb
~/Weißer s. Kammgrind
kammartig *(bot, zoo)* pectinate[d]
Kammblatt n comb blade

Kammer f chamber; *(bot)* locule
Kammerfilterpresse f chamber filter press *(sugar manufacture)*
Kammertrockner m compartment (charge) kiln
Kammertrocknung f kiln-drying
Kammerwasser n aqueous humour
Kammfahne f comb blade
Kammfichte f comb spruce *(growth form)*
Kammform f comb shape
kammförmig *(bot, zoo)* pectinate[d], cristate, crested
Kammförmiges Laichkraut n pond-grass, Potamogeton pectinatus
Kammgras n *(bot)* 1. dog['s]-tail *(genus Cynosurus)*; 2. crested dog['s]-tail, Cynosurus cristatus
Kammgrind m *(vet)* fowl favus, white comb *(caused by Trichophyton spp.)*
Kammhuhn n red jungle fowl, Gallus gallus (bankiva)
Kammkupierung f decombing
Kämmling m noil *(wool)*
Kammpflanzung f ridge planting
Kammschmiele f *(bot)* koeleria *(genus Koeleria)*
Kammstück n *(slaught)* chine, neck
Kammwolle f combed (combing) wool
Kammzacke f point
Kamp m(n) [forest] nursery
~/fliegender field (flying) nursery
~/ständiger permanent nursery
Kampagne f campaign
Kampbetrieb m *(forest)* nursery practice
Kampescheholz n logwood, Campeachy wood *(from Haematoxylum campechianum)*
Kampf m/zwischenartlicher *(ecol)* competition between species
Kampfer m camphor *(constituent of volatile oils)*
Kampferbasilikum n 1. hoary basil, Ocimum canum; 2. camphor basil, Ocimum kilimandscharicum
Kampferbaum m camphor tree (laurel), camel's-tree, Cinnamomum camphora
Kampferöl n camphor oil
Kampfhahn m fighting cock, gamecock
Kampfläufer m ruff, Philomachus pugnax
Kampfstier m fighting bull
Kampfzone f *(ecol)* struggle zone
kampylotrop *(bot)* campylotropous
Kamycin n s. Kanamycin
Kanadabalsam m Canada balsam (turpentine) *(from Abies balsamea)*
Kanadagans f Canada (wild) goose, Branta canadensis
Kanadaterpentin n s. Kanadabalsam
Kanadische Akelei f *(bot)* columbine, Aquilegia canadensis
~ **Eibe** f Canada yew, Taxus canadensis
~ **Felsenbirne** f service-berry, Juneberry, grape pear, Amelanchier canadensis

~ **Hanfnessel** f Canadian (wood) nettle, Laportea canadensis
~ **Hemlocktanne** f Canada (eastern) hemlock, Tsuga canadensis
~ **Lilie** f Canada (meadow) lily, Lilium canadense
~ **Orangenwurzel** f *(bot)* golden seal, Hydrastis canadensis
~ **Pappel** f Canadian (Carolina) poplar, Populus canadensis (euramericana)
~ **Scheinpflaume** f Canada plum, Prunus nigra
Kanadischer Biber m southern beaver, Castor canadensis
~ **Ginseng** m [American] ginseng, *(Am)* tatar-root, Panax quinquefolius
~ **Hartriegel** m bunchberry, Cornus canadensis
~ **Holunder** m American elder, Sambucus canadensis
~ **Rhododendron** m *(bot)* rhodora, Rhododendron canadense
~ **Schneeball** m sheepberry, Viburnum lentago
~ **Zander** m sauger, Stizostedion canadense
Kanadisches Beruf[s]kraut n Canadian fleabane, horseweed, bitterweed, colt's-tail, Conyza (Erigeron) canadensis
Kanal m 1. canal, duct *(anatomy)*; 2. channel, ditch, watercourse; race; drain
~/Haversscher Haversian canal *(of lamellar bone)*
kanalartig *(bot, zoo)* caniculate[d]
Kanaltrockner m, **Kanaltrocknungsanlage** f tunnel dryer (kiln), progressive kiln
Kanalwels m channel cat[fish], Ictalurus punctatus
Kanalwelsvirose f channel catfish virus disease
Kanamycin n kanamycin *(antibiotic)*
Kanariengras n canary grass, Phalaris canariensis
Kanarinuß f Java almond, Canarium commune (indicum)
Kanarische Banane f dwarf [Cavendish] banana, Musa acuminata (cavendishii)
~ **Eiche** f Algerian oak, Quercus canariensis
Kandare f curb • **an die ~ nehmen** to curb • **die ~ anlegen** to curb
Kandarengebiß n curb-bit
Kandarenzaum m curb
Kandarenzügel m gag-rein; curb
Kandelaberprimel f candelabra primula *(group of cultivars)*
Kandidamycose (Kandidose) f des Geflügels *(vet)* avian candidiasis (moniliasis)
Kandis[zucker] m [sugar-]candy
Känguruhbaum m casuarina, horse-tail [tree] *(genus Casuarina)*
Känguruhblume f kangaroo plant (paw's) *(genus Anigozanthos)*
Känguruhdorn m kangaroo thorn, Acacia armata
Känguruhgras n red [oat] grass, rooi grass, Themeda triandra (hispida)
Känguruhklimme f kangaroo vine, Cissus antarctica
Känguruhpfote[n] f[fpl] s. Känguruhblume

Kaninchen

Kaninchen *n* [wild] rabbit, con[e]y, Oryctolagus cuniculus
~/hängeohriges lop[-ear]
~/weibliches rabbit doe
Kaninchenbroiler *m* rabbit broiler
Kaninchenbucht *f* hutch
Kaninchenfell *n* rabbit fur, con[e]y
Kaninchenfett *n* rabbit fat
Kaninchenfieber *n (vet)* tularaemia *(caused by Francisella tularensis)*
Kaninchenfleisch *n* rabbit meat
Kaninchenfloh *m* rabbit flea, Spilopsyllus cuniculi
Kaninchenfütterung *f* rabbit feeding
Kaninchengehege *n* [rabbit-]warren
Kaninchenhaar *n* rabbit hair
Kaninchenhaltung *f* rabbit farming
Kaninchenhaut *f* rabbit skin
Kaninchenkrankheit *f* rabbit disease
Kaninchenlaus *f* rabbit louse, Haemodipsus ventricosus
Kaninchenmast *f* rabbit fattening
Kaninchenmilch *f* rabbit milk
Kaninchenmyxomvirus *n* myxoma virus
Kaninchenpapillomvirus *n* rabbit papilloma virus
Kaninchenpest *f* myxomatosis
Kaninchenpocken *pl (vet)* rabbit variola
Kaninchenpockenvirus *n* rabbit [ortho]pox virus
Kaninchenrasse *f* rabbit breed
Kaninchensperma *n* rabbit semen
Kaninchenspirochätose *f s.* Kaninchensyphilis
Kaninchenstall *m* [rabbit-]hutch, rabbitry, coop
Kaninchensyphilis *f,* **Kaninchentreponemose** *f* rabbit syphilis, vent disease *(caused by Treponema paraluis-cuniculi)*
Kaninchenwolle *f* rabbit wool
Kaninchenzucht *f* rabbit breeding
Kaninchenzuchtbetrieb *m* rabbitry
Kaninchenzüchtung *f* rabbit breeding
Kaninhaar *n* rabbit hair
Kanne *f* can; milk-can, churn; watering can
Kannenberieselungskühler *m* can sprinkling cooler
Kannenmelkanlage *f* bucket milker, bucket-type milking installation, cow-to-can milker, in-churn milking installation (plant)
Kannenmelken *n* bucket milking
Kannenmelkmaschine *f* bucket milking machine
Kannenmilchkühler *m* in-can milk cooler
Kannenstrauch *m* pitcher plant *(genus Nepenthes)*
Kannenwaschanlage *f* churn washer
Kannenwaschmaschine *f* can washing machine, churn washer
kannibalisch cannibalistic
Kannibalismus *m* cannibalism, adelphophagia
Kanonierblume *f* 1. pilea *(genus Pilea)*; 2. artillery plant, Pilea microphylla; 3. creeping charlie, Pilea nummulariifolia
Kantala *f (bot)* Bombay hemp, Agave cantala
Kantalupe *f (bot)* cantaloup[e], Cucumis melo ssp. melo
Kantenast *m* edge (corner) knot *(timber conversion)*
Kantenblatthaargurke *f* bur-cucumber, Sicyos angulatus
Kantenmäher *m* edge (verge) mower, edger
Kanter *m* canter, lope *(horse's gait)*
kantern to canter
~ lassen to canter
Kanthaken *m (forest)* cant-hook, cant-dog, *(Am)* peav[e]y
Kantholz *n* scantling, cant, balk, beam, square log, squared timber
K-Antigen *n* K-antigen *(bacteriology)*
Kanüle *f (vet)* cannula
Kanülengewehr *n (vet)* Cap-Chur gun
Kanzel *f (hunt)* high stand (set), station
kanzerogen *(vet)* carcinogen[et]ic
Kanzerogen *n (vet)* carcinogen
kanzerös *(vet)* cancerous
Kaolin *m(n)* kaolin[e]
kaolinhaltig kaolinitic
Kaolinit *m* kaolinite *(clay mineral)*
kaolinitisch kaolinitic
Kaori *m* amboyna pine (pitch tree), Agathis dammara (alba)
Kapaun *m* capon
kapaunen, kapaunisieren to caponize
Kapaunisierung *f* caponization
Kapazität *f* capacity
Kapazitation *f* capacitation, acrosome reaction
Kapazitätsausnutzung *f* **von Feldarbeitsmaschinen** field efficiency
Kapbiene *f* Cape honey-bee, Apis mellifica capensis
Kaper *f* caper *(flower bud from Capparis spinosa, used as seasoning)*
Kapernstrauch *m* 1. caper [bush] *(genus Capparis)*; 2. caper [bush], Capparis spinosa
Kaphyazinthe *f* Cape cowslip, leopard lily *(genus Lachenalia)*
kapillar, kapillär capillary
Kapillaranziehung *f* capillary attraction, capillarity
Kapillaraufstieg *m* capillary rise
Kapillarbewässerung *f* capillary irrigation (watering)
~ auf Tischbeeten capillary benching
Kapillare *f* capillary [tube]
Kapillargaschromatographie *f* capillary gas chromatography
Kapillariose *f (vet)* capillariasis
Kapillarität *f* capillarity
Kapillarkraft *f* capillary force
Kapillarnetz *n* capillary network
Kapillarporosität *f (soil)* capillary porosity
Kapillarröhrchen *n* capillary [tube]
Kapillarrohrviskosimeter *n* capillary tube viscometer

Kapillarsaum *m (soil)* capillary fringe, zone of capillarity
~/offener zone of aeration
Kapillarschlauch *m* capillary hose
Kapillarstrom *m* capillary flow
Kapillarviskosimeter *n* capillary viscometer
Kapillarwasser *n* capillary water (moisture)
Kapillarwasserkapazität *f* capillary water capacity
Kapillarwassersaum *m s.* Kapillarsaum
Kapillarwirkung *f* capillarity, capillary attraction
kapital capital *(e.g. antlers)*
Kapitalhirsch *m* royal
Kapkörbchen *n* 1. Cape marigold *(genus Dimorphotheca)*; 2. Cape marigold, Dimorphotheca sinuata (aurantiaca)
Kapmaiblume *f* freesia *(genus Freesia)*
Kapok *m s.* Kapokfaser
Kapokbaum *m* kapok (silk cotton) tree, ceiba [tree], Ceiba pentandra
Kapokfaser *f* kapok fibre, silk (Java) cotton
Kapoköl *n* kapok oil
Kappe *f* 1. hood *(e.g. for a hawk)*; 2. toe clip *(of horseshoe)*; 3. stemple, stempel, stull *(pitwood assortment)* • **die ~ aufsetzen** to hood
kappen to cut back, to head [back, down], to poll[ard], to decap, to equalize
Kapper *m s.* Kappsäge
Kapphahn *m* capon
Kappmesser *n* brush hook
Kappriß *m* felling shake (break) *(wood defect)*
Kappsäge *f* cross-cutting saw, bucksaw, docking saw
Kaprifikation *f* caprification *(suspending flowering male branches of the caprifig in cultivated fig trees for improved pollination by insects)*
Kapschotendorn *m* allthorn acacia, Acacia karoo (horrida)
Kapsel *f* capsule; *(zoo)* theca
~/Bowmansche Bowman's (glomerular) capsule
Kapselantigen *n* K-antigen *(bacteriology)*
Kapselfrucht *f (bot)* capsular fruit
Kapselfruchtsegment *n* valve
Kapsikum *m* pepper *(genus Capsicum)*
Kapstachelbeere *f* Cape gooseberry, Peruvian ground cherry, Physalis peruviana
kapuzenförmig *(bot)* cucullate[d]
Kapuzenkäfer *m (ent)* bostrychid *(family Bostrychidae)*
Kapuzinerkresse *f* 1. Indian cress, tropaeolum, nasturtium *(genus Tropaeolum)*; 2. Indian cress, [common, garden] nasturtium, Tropaeolum majus
Karabach-Pferd *n* Karabakh *(horse breed)*
Karabaier *m* Karabair *(horse breed)*
Karakul *n* caracul, karakul, broadtail *(sheep breed)*
Karakullamm *n* caracul lamb, Persian lamb
Karakullammfell *n* Persian lamb
Karakulschaf *n s.* Karakul
Karambolabaum *m (bot)* carambola, Averrhoa carambola

Karambolafrucht *f*, **Karambole** *f* carambola *(fruit from Averrhoa carambola)*
Karamel *m(n) s.* Karamelzucker
Karamelbier *n* malt beer
karamelisieren to caramelize
Karamelisierung *f* caramelization
Karamelmalz *n* caramel (crystal) malt
Karamelzucker *m* caramelized sugar, caramel
Karausche *f* crucian [carp], Prussian carp, Carassius carassius (vulgaris)
Karayagummi *n* karaya (sterculia) gum *(esp. from Sterculia urens)*
Karbolineum *n* carbolineum, coal-tar creosote [solution], green oil *(wood preservative)*
Karbonatation *f* carbonation, saturation *(sugar manufacture)*
~/periodische batch carbonation
Karbonatationsschlamm *m* carbonation mud (scum), saturation mud, lime sludge, defecation scum
Karbonatationstrübe *f* [first] carbonation juice
Karbonisierung *f* carbonation *(e.g. of food)*
Karbutilat *n* karbutilate *(herbicide)*
Kardamom *m(n)* 1. *(bot)* cardamom, cardamon, cardamum, Elettaria cardamomum; 2. cardamom *(condiment)*
Kardangelenkkupplung *f* cardan joint coupler *(of irrigation tubes)*
Kardanwelle *f* cardan shaft
Kardätsche *f* body brush, dandy-brush
kardätschen 1. to card *(plant fibre processing)*; 2. *s.* striegeln 1.
Karde *f (bot)* teasel, teasle, teazel *(genus Dipsacus)*
kardial cardiac, cardial
Kardia *f* cardia *(animal anatomy)*
Kardinalslobelie *f* cardinal flower, Lobelia cardinalis
Kardiolipin *n* cardiolipin
Kardiomegalie *f (vet)* cardiomegaly
Kardiomyopathie *f (vet)* cardiomyopathy
kardiorespiratorisch cardiorespiratory
Kardiosklerose *f (vet)* cardiosclerosis
kardiovaskulär cardio-vascular
Kardone *f* cardoon, artichoke thistle, Cynara cardunculus
Karenzzeit *f* waiting period (time); preharvest interval *(between agrochemical treatment and harvest of field products)*
Karfiol *m s.* Blumenkohl
Karibische Kiefer *f* Caribbean pitch-pine, slash (Cuba) pine, Pinus caribaea
Karibu *m(n) (zoo)* caribou, Rangifer tarandus
Karies *f (vet)* [teeth, dental] caries
karminrot crimson
Karminspinnmilbe *f* carmine [spider] mite, Tetranychus cinnabarinus (cucubitacearum)
Karnallit *m* carnallite *(potassic mineral)*

Karnaubapalme

Karnaubapalme f carnauba [palm], Copernicia prunifera (cerifera)
Karnaubawachs n carnauba wax
karnivor carnivorous, flesh-eating, meat-eating
Karnivore m carnivore, flesh-eater, flesh-eating animal
Karnivore f carnivore, insectivorous plant
Kärntner Biene f carniolan honey-bee, Apis mellifica carnica
Karobe f s. Karube
Karotisdrüse f, **Karotiskörper** m carotid body *(animal anatomy)*
Karotissinus m carotid sinus *(animal anatomy)*
Karotte f s. Möhre
Karpalballen m carpal pad *(animal anatomy)*
karpaleng knock-kneed
Karpalknochen m carpal bone
Karpatenglockenblume f tussock bell-flower, Campanula carpatica
Karpell n *(bot)* carpel • ohne ~ acarpe[l]lous
Karpfen m 1. carp *(genus Cyprinus)*; 2. [pond] carp, Cyprinus carpio
Karpfenbrut f carp fry
Karpfenfisch m cyprinid, white fish *(family Cyprinidae)*
Karpfenfischartiger m cyprinoid *(order Cypriniformes)*
Karpfenfütterung f carp feeding
Karpfengebiß n *(vet)* undershot jaw, fish face
Karpfengewässer n cyprinid lake
Karpfenlaus f carp louse *(genus Argulus)*
Karpfenlende f high loin *(e.g. of a horse)*
Karpfenpocken pl *(vet)* fish pox, hyperplastic epidermal disease, cutaneous warts
Karpfenrücken m carp back *(esp. of horse)*; roach back *(e.g. of a dog)*
Karpfensee m cyprinid lake
Karpfenteich m carp-pond
Karpologie f carpology
karpophag carpophagous, frugivorous
Karpophor m *(bot)* carpophore
~ **der Erdnußpflanze** peg
Karpoxenie f carpoxenia *(of fruit woods)*
Karpus m carpus, wrist *(animal anatomy)*
Karpusentzündung f carpitis *(esp. of trotters)*
Karrageen n *(bot)* carrag[h]een, Chondrus crispus
Karre f barrow, cart
Karreepflügen n round-and-round ploughing, ploughing round and round, roundabout ploughing
Karren m s. Karre
Karrenmotorstäuber m barrow motor duster
Karrenpflug m cart (gallows) plough
Karrenspritze f cart (barrow-mounted) sprayer, hand-operated sprayer barrow, wheelbarrow (hand-propelled) sprayer
Karrensprühgerät n, **Karrenzerstäuber** m s. Karrenspritze
Karribaum m *(bot)* karri, Eucalyptus diversicolor

Karriere f career
Karst m 1. *(soil)* karst; 2. prong hoe
Karstboden m karst soil
Kartäusernelke f Carthusian pink, Dianthus carthusianorum
Kartenhausstruktur f *(soil)* cardhouse effect
Kartennetz n map grid
kartieren to map
Kartierung f/**genetische** genetic mapping
Kartierungseinheit f 1. *(soil)* mapping unit; 2. *(gen)* Morgan unit, crossover (crossing-over) unit
kartilaginär cartilaginoid, cartilaginous
Kartoffel f 1. potato; 2. s. Kartoffelpflanze
Kartoffelabfallmehl n potato waste meal
Kartoffeladernvergilbungsvirus n potato vein-yellowing virus
Kartoffelagar m potato agar
Kartoffelanbau m potato growing
Kartoffelanbauer m potato grower
Kartoffelanbaugebiet n potato-growing area
Kartoffelaukubamosaikvirus n potato aucuba mosaic virus, PAMV
Kartoffelaukubavirus n potato aucuba virus
Kartoffelausschlag m *(vet)* potato eczema
Kartoffel-A-Virus n potato virus A, PVA
Kartoffelbau m s. Kartoffelanbau
Kartoffelbeizautomat m automatic potato dipper (dresser)
Kartoffelblattrollvirus n potato leaf roll virus, PLRV
Kartoffelbüscheltriebvirus n potato mop-top virus, yellow mottling virus, PMTV
Kartoffelchip m potato chip
Kartoffeldammschar n sweep for ridged potatoes
Kartoffeldämpfer m potato steamer
Kartoffelerdfloh m potato flea-beetle, Psylliodes affinis
Kartoffelerntemaschine f potato harvester
Kartoffelerntemaschinen fpl potato crop machinery
Kartoffelerzeugnis n potato product
Kartoffelfäule f tuber rot *(comprehensive term)*
Kartoffelflachsiebsortierer m potato grader with flat sieves
Kartoffelflocken fpl potato flakes
Kartoffelförderer m potato conveyor
Kartoffelfruchtfolge f potato rotation
Kartoffelgärfutter n potato silage
Kartoffelgelbverzwergungsvirus n potato yellow dwarf virus
Kartoffelhacke f potato fork
Kartoffelhäufler m potato ridger
Kartoffelhöhenförderer m potato elevator
Kartoffelkäfer m Colorado [potato] beetle, potato beetle (bug), Leptinotarsa decemlineata
Kartoffelknolle f potato [tuber]
Kartoffelkrankheit f potato disease
Kartoffelkrätzeälchen n potato [tuber-]rot nematode, Ditylenchus destructor

Kartoffelkraut n potato tops (vine, haulm)
Kartoffelkrautschläger m haulm slasher (stripper)
Kartoffelkrautsilage f potato vine silage
Kartoffelkrautzieher m haulm extractor
Kartoffelkrebs m potato wart [disease], [black] wart *(caused by Synchytrium endobioticum)*
Kartoffellagereinrichtung f potato storage facility
Kartoffellagerhaus n potato store[house], indoor (bulk) potato store
Kartoffellagerung f potato storage
Kartoffellegeautomat m automatic potato planter
Kartoffellegemaschine f potato planter
~ **mit Handeinlage** hand-fed potato planter
~ **nach dem Becherradprinzip** cup-feed potato planter
Kartoffelmehl n potato flour *(s. a. Kartoffelstärke)*
Kartoffelmiete f potato clamp (pit)
Kartoffelmilbe f bulb mite, Rhizoglyphus echinopus
Kartoffelmotte f potato [tuber] moth, Phthorimaea (Gnorimoschema) operculella
Kartoffelmüdigkeit f potato fatigue *(of a soil)*
Kartoffel-M-Virus n potato virus M, PVM
Kartoffelpflanze f [Irish, white] potato, potato vine, Solanum tuberosum
Kartoffelpflanzlochstern m potato dibbler
Kartoffelpreßschrot m crushed potato
Kartoffelprodukt n potato product
Kartoffelproteinkonzentrat n potato protein concentrate
Kartoffelpülpe f potato pulp
Kartoffelquetsche f potato masher (crusher)
Kartoffelringfäule f potato ring rot *(caused by Corynebacterium sepedonicum)*
Kartoffelrodekörper m potato-raising body
Kartoffelrodemaschine f s. Kartoffelroder
Kartoffelrodepflug m potato[-raising] plough, blade-type potato digger
Kartoffelroder m potato lifter (grubber), [potato] digger
Kartoffelrose f ramanas (rugosa) rose, Rosa rugosa
Kartoffelsammelroder m complete potato harvester
Kartoffelschale f potato skin
Kartoffelschalen fpl potato peelings
Kartoffelschlempe f potato slop (stillage)
Kartoffelschleuderradroder m potato spinner
Kartoffelschorf m common scab [of potato], [potato] scab *(caused by Streptomyces scabies)*
Kartoffelschosser m volunteer potato [plant]
Kartoffelschrägförderer m potato elevator
Kartoffelschwarzringfleckenvirus n potato black ring spot virus
Kartoffelsetzmaschine f potato planter
Kartoffelsilage f potato silage
Kartoffelsortieranlage f potato grading plant, potato storage sorter

Kartoffelsortierer m, **Kartoffelsortiermaschine** f potato sorter (grader, sizer)
Kartoffelspindelknollenviroid n potato spindle tuber viroid, PSTV
Kartoffelspiritus m, **Kartoffelsprit** m potato alcohol (spirits)
Kartoffelstampfer m potato masher
Kartoffelstärke f potato starch, farina
Kartoffelstauchevirus n potato stunt virus, PSV
Kartoffelstaudenzieher m pulling-type potato harvester, potato puller
Kartoffelsteckmaschine f potato planter
Kartoffel-S-Virus n potato virus S, PVS
Kartoffeltrockenfäule f potato dry rot *(comprehensive term)*
Kartoffeltrockenschnitzel n dried potato chip
Kartoffelverladeband n potato elevator
Kartoffelverleseband n potato picking conveyor
Kartoffelvollerntemaschine f complete potato harvester, potato combine
Kartoffelvorratsroder m elevator-type potato digger
Kartoffelwalzmehl n drum-dried whole potatoes
Kartoffelwanze f (ent) potato capsid, Calocoris norvegicus
Kartoffel-X-Virus n potato virus X, PVX
Kartoffel-Y-Virus n potato virus Y, PVY
Karube f carob, locust bean, St. John's bread *(from Ceratonia siliqua)*
Karunkel f *(bot, zoo)* caruncle
Karussellmelkstand m rotary milker (milking parlour), rotary parlour, rotolactor
Karyogamie f karyogamy
Karyogramm n karyogram
Karyokinese f mitosis, mitotic division
karyokinetisch mitotic
Karyologie f karyology
Karyolymphe f karyolymph, nuclear sap
Karyolyse f karyolysis
Karyon n s. Kern 1.
Karyoplasma n karyoplasm, nucleoplasm
Karyoplasmaverdichtung f pycnosis
Karyopse f caryopsis, grain, kernel
Karyosom n, **Karyosphäre** f karyosome
Karyotyp m karyotype, chromosome set
karzinogen *(vet)* carcinogen[et]ic
Karzinogen n carcinogen
Karzinogenese f carcinogenesis
Karzinom n *(vet)* carcinoma, canker
~/**verhärtetes** scirrhus
karzinomatös cancerous
KAS s. Kalkammonsalpeter
Kasachisches Weißköpfiges Rind n Kazakh whiteheaded *(cattle breed)*
Kaschkawal[käse] m Kachkaval cheese
Kaschmirwolle f cashmere
Kaschmirziege f Kashmir[i] goat, cashmere goat *(breed)*

Kaschubaum

Kaschubaum *m* cashew [tree], Anacardium occidentale
Kaschumandel *f* cashew-nut kernel
Kaschumehl *n* cashew meal
Kaschunuß *f* cashew-nut
Kaschuschalenöl *n* cashew-nut shell liquid
Käse *m* cheese
~/gereifter ripened cheese
~/geriebener grated cheese
~/nichtreifender fresh (uncured) cheese
~/salzkonservierter pickled cheese
~/un[aus]gereifter green cheese
käseartig caseous
Käseausbeute *f* cheese yield
Käsebereiter *m* cheese-maker
Käsebereitung *f* cheese-making
Käseblähung *f* cheese blowing
Käsebohrer *m* cheese borer *(sampler)*
Käsebruch *m* [cheese] curd
Käsebruchkorn *n* curd grain
Käsebruchmühle *f* cheese mill
Käseeiweiß *n* cheese protein
Käseerzeugnis *n* cheese product
Käsefabrik *f* cheese factory (dairy)
Käsefehler *m* cheese defect
Käsefertiger *m* cheese-making machine
Käsefliege *f* cheese [and bacon] fly, cheese skipper, Piophila casei
Käseform *f* cheese mould, chessel
Käseharfe *f* cheese harp
Käseherstellung *f* cheese-making
Käsehorde *f* cheese grate
Käsekorn *n* cheese grain
Käsekrebs *m s.* Käserindenkrebs
Käsekühlraum *m* cheese cooling room
Käselager *n* cheese store
Käselaib *m* cheese loaf
Käsemilbe *f* cheese mite, Tyrophagus casei
Käsemolke *f* cheese whey
Käsepappel *f* common mallow, Malva neglecta
Käsepresse *f* cheese press
Käseprodukt *n* cheese product
Käsepulver *n* cheese powder
Käser *m* cheese-maker
Käserei *f* 1. cheese factory (dairy); 2. cheese-making
Käsereierzeugnis *n* cheese product
Käsereifung *f* cheese ripening (maturation)
Käsereifungslager *n* cheese store
Käsereimilch *f* cheese milk
Käsereimolke *f* cheese whey
Käsereiprodukt *n* cheese product
Käsereitauglichkeit *f* **der Milch** suitability of milk for cheese-making
Käserinde *f* [cheese] rind
Käserindenkrebs *m* cheese rind rot *(caused by Penicillium brevicaule)*
Käsesäbel *m* cheese sword
Käsesorte *f* cheese variety
Käsestaub *m* cheese dust
Käsestoff *m* casein *(milk protein)*
Käseteig *m* cheese body, body of cheese
Käsewanne *f* cheese vat
Käsewasser *n s.* Molke
käsig caseous
Kaskadenmilchkühler *m* cascade milk cooler
Kaskadentrockner *m* cascade dryer
Kaskarillabaum *m (bot)* 1. cascarilla, Croton cascarilla; 2. cascarilla, Croton eluteria
Kaspische Weide *f* pussy willow, Salix acutifolia
Kassave *f* [bitter] cassava, bitter manioc, tapioca plant, Manihot esculenta (utilissima)
Kassia *f (bot)* cassia, senna *(genus Cassia)*
Kassiaöl *n* cassia oil
Kassiarinde *f*, **Kassiazimt** *m* cassia [bark], Chinese cinnamon *(from Cinnamomum aromaticum)*
Kassie *f s.* Kassia
Kastanie *f* 1. chestnut *(genus Castanea)*; 2. chestnut *(fruit)*; 3. chestnut *(callosity at horse's leg)*
Kastanienblättrige Eiche *f* chestnut-leaved oak, Quercus castaneifolia
Kastanienboden *m* chestnut soil
Kastanieneiche *f* chestnut oak, Quercus prinus
Kastanienholz *n* chestnut[-wood]
Kastanienrindenkrebs *m* chestnut (endothia) blight *(caused by Endothia parasitica)*
Kastanosjom *m(n) (soil)* kastanozem
Kasten *m* 1. box, case; 2. frame *(horticulture)*
~/beweglicher mobile frame
~/einseitiger single-light span frame
~/kalter cold frame
~/warmer heated frame
~/zweiseitiger double-light span frame
Kastenbeet *n* frame bed
Kastenbeute *f (api)* box hive
Kastendrän *m* box drain
Kastenfalle *f* box trap
Kastenglucke *f* foster-mother
Kastengurke *f* hotbed cucumber
Kastenkarren *m* box cart
Kastenmälzerei *f* box (compartment) malting, Saladin [box] malting [system]
Kastenstand *m* crate stall *(sow keeping)*
Kastentrockner *m* bin dryer
Kastoröl *n* castor[-bean] oil
Kastorzucker *m* castor sugar
Kastrat *m* castrate, gelding, g., neuter
Kastration *f* castration, emasculation
~/chemische chemical castration
~/unblutige bloodless castration
kastrieren to castrate, to emasculate, to geld, to doctor, to cut, *(Am)* to alter; to steer *(a bull-calf)*
Kastriermesser *n* castration (castrating) knife
Kastrierzange *f* emasculator
Kasuarine *f* 1. casuarina, horse-tail [tree] *(genus Casuarina)*; 2. coast she-oak, Casuarina stricta
Kasugamycin *n* kasugamycin *(antibiotic)*
katabatisch katabatic *(wind)*

Katabäumchen n *(bot)* mayteno *(genus Maytenus)*
katabol[isch] catabolic, disassimilative
katabolisieren to catabolize, to disassimilate *(plant physiology)*
Katabolismus m catabolism, katabolism, disassimilation, destructive metabolism
Katabolit-Aktivator-Protein n catabolite activator protein, CAP
katadrom *(pisc)* catadromous
Katalase f catalase *(enzyme)*
Katalaseprobe f *(dairy, vet)* catalase test
Katalpe f *(bot)* catalpa *(genus Catalpa)*
Katalysator m catalyst
Katalyse f catalysis
katalytisch catalytic
Katappenbaum m India-almond, Terminalia catappa
Katarakt f *(vet)* cataract
Katarrh m *(vet)* catarrh
Katarrhalfieber n catarrhal fever
~/**bösartiges** malignant catarrhal fever, MCF
katarrhalisch catarrhal
Kataster m(n) cadastre, cadaster
Katasterkarte f cadastral map
Katathermometer n katathermometer
Kate f cottage, shack, hut
Katechu n catechu, cutch, kath[a] *(plant extract esp. from Acacia catechu)*
~/**braunes (dunkles)** [dark] cutch, Pegu cutch
~/**gelbes (helles)** pale cutch
Katechuakazie f catechu acacia, Acacia catechu
Kater m tom[-cat]
Kathabäumchen n *(bot)* mayteno *(genus Maytenus)*
Katharometer n katharometer *(for controlling the atmospheric conditions in storehouses)*
Katheter m *(vet)* catheter
Kathstrauch m flower of paradise, Arabian tea, khat, Catha edulis
Kationenaustausch m *(soil)* cation (base) exchange
Kationenaustauscher m cation exchanger
Kationenaustauschkapazität f cation (total) exchange capacity, CEC
Kätner m cottager
Katsurabaum m katsura tree, Cercidiophyllum japonicum
Kattunkatze f calico cat *(colour variant of domestic cat)*
Kätzchen n *(bot)* catkin, chat, ament
kätzchenblütig amentiferous
kätzchentragend amentiferous
Katze f 1. cat, feline *(family Felidae)*; 2. [domestic] cat, Felis domestica
~/**ausgewachsene weibliche** queen [cat]
~/**rattenjagende** ratter
katzenartig feline
Katzenenteritis f *(vet)* cat distemper (enteritis), infectious feline viral enteritis, panleucopenia

Katzenfloh m cat flea, Ctenocephalides felis
Katzenhaarling m cat louse, Felicola subrostratus
Katzenkraut n cat thyme, Teucrium marum
Katzenleberegel m cat fluke, Opistorchis felineus (tenuicollis)
Katzenleberegelkrankheit f *(vet)* opistorchiasis
Katzenleukosevirus n feline leukaemia virus, FeLV
Katzenlungenwurm m feline lungworm, Aelurostrongylus abstrusus
Katzenmelisse f s. Katzenminze
Katzenminze f 1. catmint, catnip *(genus Nepeta)*; 2. catmint, catnip, Nepeta cataria
Katzenpanleukopenie f s. Katzenenteritis
Katzenpfötchen n cat-claw, everlasting flower *(genus Antennaria)*
Katzenschwanz m *(bot)* chenille plant, red-hot cat's-tail, Acalypha hispida
Katzenstaupe f s. Katzenenteritis
Katzentoilette f sanitary tray for cats
Katzentyphus m s. Katzenenteritis
Katzenzucht f cat breeding
Katzenzwinger m cattery
Kauarbeit f mastication
kaudal *(zoo)* caudal, aboral, inferior
Kaudophagie f tail-biting *(vice e.g. of pigs)*
kauen to masticate, to chew
Kauen n mastication; champ *(of horses on the bit)*
Kaufläche f masticatory (grinding) surface, table *(of a tooth)*
Kaukasische Biene f Caucasian [honey-]bee, Apis mellifica caucasica
~ **Lallemantie** f s. Kaukasischer Ölziest
Kaukasischer Birnbaum m Caucasian pear, Pyrus caucasica
~ **Ölziest** m *(bot)* lallemantia, Lallemantia iberica
Kaukasusfichte f oriental spruce, Picea orientalis
Kaukasusskabiose f *(bot)* scabious, Scabiosa caucasica
Kaukasustanne f Caucasian fir, Abies nordmanniana
Kauliflorie f *(bot)* cauliflory, trunciflory
Kaumagen m gizzard *(of chewing insects)*
Kaumuskel m muscle of mastication, masseter
Kaumuskelschlagader f masseteric artery
KAuMV s. Kartoffelaukubamosaikvirus
Kauren[ol] n kaurene *(terpene)*
Kaurensäure f kaurenoic acid *(terpene)*
Kaurifichte f 1. pitch tree, wax pine *(genus Agathis)*; 2. kauri, Agathis australis
Kaurikopal m kauri-gum
Kausche f [dead-]eye
Kauschring m eye ring
Kaustik f *(vet)* cauterization, cautery
Kaustikum n *(vet)* caustic
~ **zur kalten Kauterisation** cautery
Kauter m cauter, cautery [knife]
Kauterisation f 1. *(phyt)* scorch; 2. *(vet)* cauterization, cautery, firing

kauterisieren

kauterisieren to cauterize, to burn *(tissue)*
Kautschuk *m(n)* caoutchouc, rubber
Kautschukbaum *m* caoutchouc (rubber) tree, Hevea brasiliensis
Kautschukbaumpflanzung *f* rubber plantation
Kautschuklöwenzahn *m (bot)* kok-sag[h]yz, Taraxacum kok-saghyz
Kautschukmilch *f* [rubber] latex, rubber milk
Kautschukpflanze *f* rubber (gum) plant *(comprehensive term)*
Kautschukpflanzung *f*, **Kautschukplantage** *f* rubber plantation
Kautschuksammelgefäß *n* gum cup
KAuV *s.* Kartoffelaukubavirus
KAV *s.* Kartoffel-A-Virus
Kaverne *f (vet)* cavern
kavernös cavernous
Kaviar *m* caviar[e]
~ vom Hausen beluga
Kaviarersatz *m* caviar[e] substitute
Kavität *f* cavity
Kawapfeffer[strauch] *m* kava, kawa pepper, Piper methysticum
KaXV *s.* Kakteen-X-Virus
Kayennepfeffer *m s.* Cayennepfeffer
KB *s.* Besamung/künstliche
KBE *s.* Einheit/koloniebildende
K-Biene *f s.* Kärntner Biene
KBMV *s.* Kundebohnenmosaikvirus
KBR *s.* Komplementbindungsreaktion
KBRV *s.* Kartoffelblattrollvirus
KBSMV *s.* Schweres Kundebohnenmosaikvirus
KBTV *s.* Kartoffelbüscheltriebvirus
KD-Effekt *m s.* Knockdown-Effekt
KE *s.* Kartierungseinheit
Keeshond *m* keeshond *(dog breed)*
Kefir *m* kefir *(beverage of fermented milk)*
Keg *n* keg *(standardized metal barrel esp. for beer)*
Kegbier *n* keg beer
kegelartig conoid
Kegelblume *f* purple coneflower *(genus Echinacea)*
kegelförmig *(bot, zoo)* conical
~/verkehrt obconical
Kegelpflanze *f* cone plant *(genus Conophytum)*
Kegelrad *n* bevel gear
Kegelradgetriebe *n* bevel gear
Kegelrollenlager *n* tapered roller-bearing
Kegelstrahldüse *f* [hollow-]cone nozzle
kegelstumpfförmig truncate conical
Kegelwiderstand *m (soil)* cone resistance
Kegelzahnrad *n* bevel gear
Kehldeckel *m* epiglottis *(animal anatomy)*
Kehldeckelreflex *m* epiglottic reflex
Kehle *f*, **Kehlgang** *m* throat[latch], throttle
Kehlgangsbremse *f* Linnaeus' horse bot-fly, Gasterophilus nasalis (veterinus)
Kehlkopf *m* larynx
Kehlkopfentzündung *f (vet)* laryngitis

Kehlkopfpfeifen *n (vet)* heave[s], roaring, broken wind *(of horses)*
Kehlkopfpfeifer *m* roarer, piper *(horse)*
Kehlkopfspiegel *m* laryngoscope
Kehllappen *m* wattle, gill *(of fowl)* • **die ~ kupieren** to dewattle
Kehlriemen *m* throatlatch, throatband
Kehrmaschine *f* sweeper
Kehrpflug *m* reversible plough, one-way (flip-over) plough, *(Am)* two-way plow
Keiapfel *m* Kei apple, Kai apple, Dovyalis (Doryalis) caffra
Keil *m* wedge
Keilangel *f* key buckle *(of frame saw)*
Keilbein *n* sphenoid, sphenoidal bone *(animal anatomy)*
keilblättrig *(bot)* sphenophyllous
Keiler *m* [solitary] boar
~ mit Hauern tusker
keilförmig *(bot, zoo)* sphenoid[al], cuneate, cuneiform
Keilförmiger Buschklee *m* Chinese lespedeza, Lespedeza cuneara (sericea)
Keilostektomie *f (vet)* wedge ostectomy
Keilriemen *m* V-belt, vee belt
Keilriemenscheibe *f* sheave
Keilriementrieb *m* V-belt drive
Keilriemenvariator *m* V-belt variator
Keilschirmschlag *m (forest)* wedge system felling, wedge shelterwood cutting
Keilschirmschlagsystem *n* wedge system
Keilschnitt *m* wedge-shaped notch *(grafting)*
Keilspaten *m (forest)* notching (wedge-shaped) spade
Keilwinkel *m* tooth (sharpening, sharpness) angle *(of a saw-tooth)*
Keim *m* 1. germ, embryo [of seed] *(s. a.* Keimling*)*; sprout, burgeon, chit, bud; eye *(e.g. of a potato tuber)*; 2. germ, microorganism, microbe *(esp. pathogenic)* • **dem ~ abgewandt** abgerminal
keimabtötend germicidal, microbicidal
Keimachse *f (bot)* hypocotyl
Keimapparat *m* germinating apparatus, germinator *(for determination of germinative capacity)*
Keimbahn *f* germ line (track)
Keimbereitschaft *f* readiness for germination
Keimbett *n* germination bed
Keimbläschen *n s.* Eizellkern
Keimblase *f (zoo)* blastocyst, blastodermic vesicle
Keimblasenwand *f* trophoblast
Keimblatt *n (bot)* cotyledon, seed leaf (lobe), embryonic leaf; *(zoo)* cotyledon, germ layer
~ ohne ~ acotyledonous
~/äußeres *(zoo)* ectoderm, ectoblast, epiblast
~/inneres *(zoo)* entoderm, endoderm, hypoblast
~/mittleres *(zoo)* mesoderm, mesoblast
Keimblattbildung *f* gastrulation
keimblattlos *(bot)* acotyledonous
Keimblattscheide *f* coleoptile *(of grasses)*

Keimblattstadium *n* cotyledon stage
Keimdrüse *f* gonad, sex gland
Keimdrüsenentfernung *f (vet)* gonadectomy
Keimdrüsenhormon *n* sex hormone
keimdrüsenstimulierend gonadotrop[h]ic
Keimdrüsenunterfunktion *f (vet)* hypogenitalism
Keimdurchwuchs *m (phyt)* internal sprouting *(of potato tubers)*
keimen to germ[inate], to sprout, to chit, to bud, to burgeon, to pullulate, to acrospire, to braird
Keimen *n* germination, pullulation, sprouting • **zum ~ bringen** to germinate
~/vorzeitiges preharvest germinating, preharvest (premature) sprouting
Keimenergie *f* germination (germinative) energy, germinative (seed) vigour
Keimenergieprüfung *f* seed viability test
keimentwicklungsfähig *s.* keimfähig
Keimepithel *n* germinal (seminiferous, spermatogenic) epithelium
Keimesentwicklung *f*, **Keimesgeschichte** *f* ontogenesis, ontogeny
keimesgeschichtlich ontogenetic
keimfähig germinable, germinative, germinating, viable
Keimfähigkeit *f* germinability, germination ability, germinative capacity (activity), viability
Keimfähigkeitsnachuntersuchung *f* germination recheck
Keimfleck *m* germ spot
keimfrei germ free, sterile, aseptic; axenic *(gnotobiotics)* • **~ machen** to sterilize, to asepticize
~/nicht aseptic
Keimfreiheit *f* sterility, asepsis
Keimfreimachung *f* sterilization
Keimhaut *f (zoo)* blastoderm
Keimhemmung *f* germination inhibition; seed dormancy
Keimhemmungsmittel *n* germination inhibitor, anti-sprouting chemical
Keimhöhle *f (zoo)* blastocoel[e], segmentation cavity
Keimkammer *f* germination chamber
Keimkasten *m* germinator *(for seedling production)*; malting (germination) box
Keimkastenraum *m* malting (germination) room
Keimkraft *f* seed vigour, germination power *(s. a. Keimenergie)*
Keimling *m* [germinating, young] seedling *(s. a. Keim)*
Keimlings... *s. a.* Keimpflanzen...
Keimlingsbrand *m (phyt)* seedling blight, damping-off [disease] *(mycosis)*
Keimlingskrankheit *f (phyt)* seedling disease
keimlos *(zoo)* ablastous
Keimmedium *n* germination bed
Keimmund *m (bot)* micropyle
Keimöl *n* germ oil

Keimpflanze *f* germinal plant, [germinating] seedling
Keimpflanzen... *s. a.* Keimlings...
Keimpflanzenanlage *f (bot)* embryo
Keimpflanzenaufgang *m* seedling emergence
Keimpflanzenbeschädigung *f* seedling injury
Keimpflanzenbestand *m* seedling stand (crop)
Keimpflanzenkonkurrenz *f* seedling competition
Keimpflanzenkultur *f* seedling culture
Keimpflanzenmethode *f* **nach Neubauer-Schneider** *(soil)* Neubauer's method
Keimpflanzenschädigung *f* seedling injury
Keimpflanzenschädling *m* seedling pest
Keimpflanzenstadium *n* seedling stage
Keimpflanzentod *m* seedling death
Keimpflanzenverlust *m* seedling loss
Keimpflanzenwachstum *m* seedling growth
Keimpflanzenwurzel *f* seedling root
Keimplasma *n* germ-plasm
Keimpotenz *f s.* Keimkraft
Keimprobe *f* germination test
Keimprozentsatz *m* total germinability
Keimprüfung *f* germination test
Keimringtest *m (vet)* ring test
Keimruhe *f* [seed] dormancy • **~ haltend** dormant
~/erzwungene ectodormancy, quiescence
~/natürliche endodormancy
~/thermisch bedingte thermodormancy
Keimschale *f* germination dish
Keimscheibe *f* blastodisk, germinal (embryonic) disk, cicatricle, tread *(of bird's egg)*
Keimscheide *f* coleoptile *(of grasses)*
Keimschicht *f* matrix; germinative layer *(of epidermis)*
Keimschlauch *m* germ tube
Keimschnelligkeit *f* germination speed
Keimstadium *n* germination stage
Keimstimmen *n* partial (mini) chitting *(potato seed)*
Keimstimmung *f* readiness for germination • **die ~ beeinflussen** to vernalize
Keimtemperatur *f* germination temperature
Keimtest *m* germination test
keimtötend germicidal, microbicidal
Keimtrommel *f* germination drum *(malting)*
Keimung *f* germination
~ unter Labor[atoriums]bedingungen laboratory germination
~/verspätete (verzögerte) delayed germination
Keimungsapparat *m* seed germinator
Keimungsphase *f* germination stage
Keimungsschädigung *f* germination damage (injury) *(e.g. caused by seed dressings or fertilizers)*
Keimungstemperatur *f* germination temperature
Keimungsverzögerung *f* delayed germination
Keimvermögen *n s.* Keimfähigkeit
Keimversuch *m* germination test
Keimwurzel *f* seed[ling] root, seminal (embryonic) root, radicle

Keimzahl

Keimzahl f bacterial count
Keimzahlbestimmung f bacterial count
Keimzelle f germ (sex) cell, gamete
keimzellenabtötend gametocidal
Keimzellenbildung f gametogenesis
keimzellentötend gametocidal
Keith-Flackscher Knoten m sinuatrial node *(of the heart)*
Kelch m *(bot)* calyx; eye *(of pome fruit)*; *(zoo)* calyx
Kelchblatt n *(bot)* sepal; calyx lobe • **mit einem ~ monosepalous**
Kelchblüte f chalice
Kelchende n calyx (eye) end *(of pome fruit)*
Kelchgrube f calyx basin (cavity), eye cavity
Kelchhöcker m [eye] bead *(of pome fruit)*
Kelchhöhle f calyx hole, core cavity
kelchlos acalycine, acalycinous
Kelchmelde f *(bot)* sea blite *(genus Suaeda)*
Kelchröhre f calyx tube
Kelevan kelevan *(insecticide)*
Kelle f 1. *(dairy)* curd scoop; 2. beaver's tail
Keller m cellar
Kellerassel f scaby slater, Porcellio scaber
Kellerhals m *(bot)* [February] daphne, mezereon, Daphne mezereum
Kellerlaus f bulb and potato aphid, Rhopalosiphoninus latysiphon
Kellermeister m cellarmaster, cellarer, cellarman, wine master
Kellerschnecke f yellow slug, Limax flavus
Kellerschwamm m cellar fungus, Coniophora puteana (cerebella)
Kellerwirtschaft f cellarage
Kelotomie f *(vet)* herniotomy
Kelpie m kelpie *(dog breed)*
Kelter f winepress, winefat, [grape] press
Kelterbütte f press tub (vat)
Kelterei f winery
Kelterhaus n press room
keltern to vinify
Keltern n vinification, wine-making
Kelthan m dicofol *(acaricide)*
Kenaf n 1. kenaf, deccan hemp, wild stockrose, Hibiscus cannabinus; 2. kenaf, ambary *(fibre from 1.)*
Keniaschafgras n Kenya sheep grass, Surinam grass, Brachiaria decumbens
Kennart f *(ecol)* characteristic species
Kennel m s. Hundezwinger
Kennreiz m key stimulus
Kennwert m parameter
kennzeichnen to mark, to tag
Kennzeit f chronaxie, chronaxy *(animal physiology)*
Kent n s. Kentschaf
Kentiapalme f, **Kentie** f Kentia palm, Howeia (Kentia) belmoreana
Kentschaf n Kent, Romney Marsh *(sheep breed)*
Kephalin n cephalin, phosphatidylethanolamine

Keramik[drän]rohr n ceramic drain-pipe, clay pipe, clayware field drain-pipe
Keratin n keratin, horn [matter] *(scleroprotein)*
Keratinisation f keratinization
Keratitis f *(vet)* keratitis
Keratokonjunktivitis f *(vet)* keratoconjunctivitis
Keratomalazie f *(vet)* keratomalacia
Keratose f keratosis
Keratozele f *(vet)* keratocele, herniation of Descemet's membrane
Kerb m, **Kerbe** f kerf, notch
Kerbel m chervil *(genus Anthriscus)*
Kerbelrübe f bulbous-rooted chervil, parsnip (turnip-rooted) chervil, Chaerophyllum bulbosum
kerben to notch
Kerben n [über einer Knospe] bud notching *(orcharding)*
Kerbschlüssel m notching scheme *(animal identification)*
Kerbtier n insect, hexapod *(class Hexapoda)* (for compounds s. under Insekt)
Kerbzange f notcher *(animal identification)*
Kerf m s. Kerbtier
Kermesbeere f 1. pokeweed, poke[berry], pokeroot, *(Am)* garget *(genus Phytolacca)*; 2. [Virginian] pokeweed, poke[berry], pokeroot, Phytolacca americana
Kermeseiche f kermes oak, Quercus coccifera
Kern m 1. nucleus [of cell], karyon *(s. a. under Zellkern)*; 2. kernel *(of nut or stone-fruit)*; pip, [small] fruit seed; 3. core *(e.g. of pome-fruits)*; 4. s. Kernholz 1.; 5. s. Steinkern
~/generativer generative nucleus
~/weicher brittle (spongy) heart *(wood defect)*
Kernauflösung f karyolysis
Kernfaden m chromosome
Kernfäule f *(phyt)* heart rot; heartwood decay; central rot *(of black alder esp. caused by Polyporus radiata)*
Kernfragmentation f amitosis
Kernfrüchte fpl s. Kernobst
Kerngehäuse n core, seed pocket • **das ~ entfernen** to core
Kerngen n nuclear gene
Kerngene npl genome
kernhaltig *(bot)* acinaceous, seeded
Kernhaus n s. Kerngehäuse
Kernhausbräune f core browning, brown heart, [core] flush *(of stored fruit)*
Kernhausfäule f core rot, mouldy core *(of stored fruit, caused by Fusarium spp.)*
Kernholz n 1. heartwood, heart, core [wood], truewood, duramen, pith; 2. seedling forest
~/pathologisches pathological (false) heartwood
Kernholzbildung f heartwood formation, duramin[iz]ation
Kern[holz]käfer m pin-hole borer, ambrosia (timber) beetle, platypodid *(family Platypodidae)*
Kernkammer f locule *(of pome fruit)*

Kernkörperchen *n* nucleolus
Kernlohdenbestand *m (forest)* seedling crop (stand)
kernlos 1. akaryotic, acaryote *(cell)*; 2. seedless, pipless
Kernlosigkeit *f* seedlessness
kernmagnetisch nuclear-magnetic
Kernmatrix-DNA *f* nuclear matrix DNA
Kernmembran *f* nuclear membrane
Kernnährstoff *m* primary nutrient
Kernobst *n* pome [fruit], pomiferous (pomaceous) fruit, hard (pip) fruit
Kernobsternte *f* pome fruit harvest
Kernplasma *n* nucleoplasm, karyoplasm
Kernpolyhedrosevirus *n* nuclear polyhedrosis virus
Kernprobe *f (soil)* core sample
Kernriß *m* [heart] shake, rift crack, *(Am)* heart check *(wood defect)*
~/einfacher simple shake
~/gekreuzter crossed heart shake
~/sternförmiger [mehrfacher] star shake (check)
kernrissig heartshaken
Kernrissigkeit *f* quagginess
Kernschäle *f* ring (round) shake *(wood defect)*
Kernschleife *f* chromosome
Kernteilung *f* nuclear division
~/direkte amitosis
~/indirekte mitosis
Kerntemperatur *f* body core temperature
Kernverlagerung *f* eccentric growth *(wood defect)*
Kernverschmelzung *f* karyogamy
Kernwertigkeitsgrad *m (gen)* ploidy
Kernwuchs *m* forest of seedling origin
Kerrie *f* Jew's mallow, kerria *(genus Kerria)*
Kerry *n s.* Kerryrind
~ Hill *n* Kerry Hill *(sheep breed)*
Kerry-Blue-Terrier *m* Kerry blue *(dog breed)*
Kerryrind *n* Kerry [Longhorn] *(cattle breed)*
Kerzenbaum *m* Panama candle tree, Parmentiera cerifera
Kescher *m (pisc)* landing-net; sweep-net
Kessel *m* 1. kettle; boiler; vat; 2. couch *(of game)*; wild boar clearing
Kesselfilter *n* pressure leaf filter
Kesselhaus *n* boiler house
Kesseljagd *f s.* Kesseltreiben
Kesselmilch *f* vat milk *(cheese-making)*
Kesselmoor *n* watershed moor
kesseln to dust-bath *(fowl)*
Kesselspeisewasser *n* boiler feed water
Kesselstein *m* scale, fur
Kesseltreiben *n (hunt)* circular beat (drive)
Ketalachs *m* chum [salmon], Oncorhynchus keta
Ketembilla *f* Ceylon gooseberry, Dovyalis (Doryalis) hebecarpa
Ketocarbonsäure *f* keto [carboxylic] acid
ketogen ketogenic
Ketogenese *f* ketogenesis

Ketoglutarsäure *f* ketoglutaric (oxoglutaric) acid, oxopentanedioic acid
Ketokörper *m s.* Ketonkörper
Ketolyse *f* ketolysis
Keton *n* ketone
Ketonämie *f (vet)* ketosis, ketonaemia, acetonaemia
Ketonkörper *m* ketone (acetone) body
Ketonkörperabbau *m* ketolysis
Ketonkörperbiosynthese *f* ketogenesis
Ketonurie *f (vet)* ketonuria, acetonuria
ketoplastisch ketogenic
ß-Ketoreductase *f* ß-keto reductase, beta-hydroxyl dehydrogenase, 3-hydroxyacyl-CoA dehydrogenase *(enzyme)*
Ketosäure *f* keto [carboxylic] acid
Ketosäuredehydrogenase *f* keto acid dehydrogenase *(enzyme)*
Ketose *f* 1. *(vet)* ketosis, acetonaemia, ketonaemia, slow fever; 2. ketose, ketonic sugar *(monosaccharide)*
~ des Schafes *(vet)* pregnancy toxaemia (disease), twin-lamb disease
17-Ketosteroid *n* 17-ketosteroid
ketotisch *(vet)* ketotic
Ketovaleriansäure *f* laevulinic acid *(metabolite)*
Ketozucker *m s.* Ketose 2.
Kette *f* 1. chain; tether; track *(of a crawler-type vehicle)*; 2. hessian warp *(kind of jute fibre)*; 3. covey *(of partridges)*
~ für die Holzrückung *(forest)* drag (skid) chain
Kettenantrieb *m* chain[-and-sprocket] drive
Kettenbecherwerk *n* chain-and-bucket elevator
Kettenblockanlage *f* linked block design *(experimentation)*
Kettenbolzen *m* master pin *(of the crawler drive)*
Kettenbremse *f* chain brake *(of a chain-saw)*
Kettendüngerstreuer *m* endless-chain [fertilizer] distributor
Kettenentrinder *m* chain [flail] barker
Kettenfahrzeug *n* tracked (crawler-type) vehicle
Kettenfangvorrichtung *f* chain catcher *(of a chain-saw)*
Kettenförderer *m* chain conveyor
kettenförmig *(bot, zoo)* catenulate
Kettenfutterverteileinrichtung *f* chain feeder
Kettenkokke *f s.* Streptokokke
Kettenlaufwerk *n* track
Kettenmitnehmer *m* chain dog *(timber transport)*
Kettenrechwender *m* chain-type side [delivery] rake
Kettenreflex *m* chain reflex
Kettenrücketraktor *m* tracked log skidder
Kettensäge *f* chain-saw
Kettenschälmaschine *f* chain [flail] barker
Kettenschärfmaschine *f* chain sharpening machine
Kettenschiene *f* chain rail *(of the chain-saw)*
Kettenschleppe *f* diamond-link chain harrow

Kettensilicat

Kettensilicat *n (soil)* chain silicate
Kettenspanner *m* chain tightener
Kettenspannrolle *f* chain idler
Kettentraktor *m* crawler (Caterpillar) tractor, track-laying tractor, track-layer
Kettentrieb *m s.* Kettenantrieb
Kettenwuchs *m (phyt)* gemmation, second growth (e.g. of potatoes)
keuchen to pant
Keule *f (slaught)* haunch, buttock; round (of beef carcass); leg (of sheep's carcass)
keulen *(vet)* to cull
Keulenbärlapp *m* stag-horn, Lycopodium clavatum
Keulenbaum *m* horse-tail [tree], Casuarina equisetifolia
keulenblättrig club-leaved
keulenförmig *(bot, zoo)* clavate, claviform
Keulenlilie *f (bot)* 1. ti *(genus Cordyline)*; 2. ti, common dracaena, Cordyline fruticosa (terminalis)
Keulenpilz *m* club fungus, coral mushroom (family Clavariaceae)
Keulung *f (vet)* culling, stamping out
Keuper *m (soil)* Keuper
Keuperton *m* Keuper marl
Khaki-Campbell-Ente *f* Khaki Campbell [duck] (breed)
Khapräkäfer *m* khapra beetle, Trogoderma granarium (khapra)
Khorassanweizen *m* Khorasan wheat, Triticum turanicum
KiBRV *s.* Kirschenblattrollvirus
Kichererbse *f* chick (dwarf) pea, [Indian, Bengal] gram, *(Am)* garbanzo [bean], Cicer arietinum
Kichertragant *m* cicer milk-vetch, mountain chickpea, Astragalus cicer
KiCRFV *s.* Chlorotisches Ringfleckenvirus der Kirsche
Kid *n s.* Jungziegenleder
Kiebitz *m* plover, Vanellus vanellus
Kiebitzblume *f* chequered lily, guinea-hen flower, fritillary, Fritillaria meleagris
Kiefer *m* jaw[-bone], mandible
Kiefer *f* pine *(genus Pinus)*
~/harzliefernde pitch-pine *(comprehensive term)*
Kieferfühler *m* chelicera (e.g. of mites)
Kieferfuß *m* maxilliped (of a crustacean)
Kieferhöhle *f* maxillary sinus
Kieferklaue *f s.* Kieferfühler
Kieferknochen *m* jaw-bone, mandible
Kieferlaus *f* biting louse (order Mallophaga)
Kieferlosigkeit *f (vet)* agnathia
kiefern piny
kiefernähnlich piny
Kiefernaltstöcke *mpl* pine stumpwood
Kiefernblasenrost *m s.* Kiefernrindenblasenrost
Kiefernbruch *m* wet mossy pine forest
Kiefernbuschhornblattwespe *f* common pine saw-fly, Diprion pini

Kieferndreher *m,* **Kieferndrehrost** *m* pine twist[ing] rust, pine branch twist *(caused by Melampsora pinitorqua)*
Kiefernharz *n* pine-resin
Kiefernharzgallenwickler *m* pine-resin gall-moth, Rhyacionia resinella
Kiefernharzgallmücke *f* European pine resin midge, Cecidomyia pini
Kiefernholz *n* 1. pine[wood]; 2. *s.* Kiefernschnittholz
Kiefernholzteer *m* pine tar
Kiefernholzwespe *f* giant horntail, steel-blue wood-wasp, Sirex (Paururus) juvencus
Kiefernknospentriebwickler *m* [European] pine-shoot moth, Rhyacionia (Evetria) buoliana
Kiefernknospenwickler *m (ent)* pale orange-spotted tortrix, Rhyacionia (Evetria) turionana
Kiefernkotsackblattwespe *f s.* Kiefernkulturgespinstblattwespe
Kiefernkreuzschnabel *m* parrot-crossbill, Loxia pityopsittacus
Kiefernkulturgespinstblattwespe *f* web-spinning pine saw-fly, Acantholyda hieroglyphica
Kiefernkulturrüsselkäfer *m,* **Kiefernkulturrüßler** *m* banded (small) pine weevil, Pissodes castaneus (notatus)
Kiefernmischwald *m* compound pine forest
Kiefernnadelblasenrost *m* pine leaf rust
Kiefernnadelöl *n* pine [needle] oil
Kiefernpflanzung *f* pinetum
Kiefernprozessionsspinner *m* pine procession[ary] moth, Cnethocampa (Thaumetopoea) pinivora
kiefernreich piny
Kiefernrindenblasenrost *m* pine blister rust (caused by Cronartium flaccidum = Peridermium pini)
Kiefernrindensubstrat *n* pine bark medium (substrate)
Kiefernrindenwanze *f* pine bark bug, Aradus cinnamomeus
Kiefernritzenschorf *m s.* Kiefernschütte
Kiefernsaateule *f (ent)* archer's dart, Rhyacia (Agrotis) vestigialis
Kiefernscharrharz *n* pine scrape
Kiefernschnittholz *n* red (yellow) deal, European (Baltic, Kara) redwood
Kiefernschütte *f* pine (fir) leaf cast, pine needle cast (caused by Lophodermium pinastri)
Kiefernschwärmer *m* pine hawk-moth, *(Am)* pine tree sphinx, Hyloicus pinastri
Kiefernspanner *m* pine looper [moth], bordered white moth, Bupalus piniarius
Kiefernspinner *m* pine moth, pine lappet [moth], Dendrolimus pini
Kiefernstockfäule *f* pine butt rot, butt rot in Scotch fir (esp. caused by Polyporus sistotremoides)
Kiefernstockholz *n* pine stumpwood
Kiefernteer *m* pine tar

Kieferntriebwickler *m* [European] pine-shoot moth, Rhyacionia (Evetria) duplana
Kiefernwald *m* pine forest, pinewood, pinery, pineland
~/flechtenreicher moss-lichen pinery
Kiefernzapfen *m* pine cone (nut)
Kiefernzapfenrüßler *m (Am)* pine-cone weevil, Pissodes validirostris
Ki-Eiche *f (bot)* Allegheny chinkapin, chinquapin, Castanea pumila
kielförmig *(bot, zoo)* carinate[d]
Kielwucherblume *f* tricolour chrysanthemum, Chrysanthemum carinatum
Kieme *f* gill
Kiemendeckel *m* gill-cover, flap *(of fishes)*
Kiemenfäule *f (pisc, vet)* branchiomycosis
Kiemennekrose *f (pisc, vet)* branchionecrosis
Kiemennetz *n (pisc)* gill-net
Kien *m s.* Kienholz
Kienharz *n* pine-resin
Kienholz *n* resinous wood, fatwood, lightwood, stumpwood
kienig resinous
Kienöl *n* pine oil
Kienspan *m* splinter
Kienteer *m* pine tar
Kienteerpech *n* pine pitch
Kienzopf *m s.* Kiefernrindenblasenrost
Kiepe *f* pannier, dosser
Kies *m* gravel; grit
Kiesbett *n* gravel bed
Kiesboden *m* gravelly soil
Kieselalge *f* diatom
Kieselerde *f* silica *(non-clay mineral)*
Kieselgel *n* silica gel
Kieselgur *f* kieselguhr, diatomaceous earth
Kieselgurfilter *n* kieselguhr filter
Kieselgurfiltration *f* diatomite filtration
Kieselpflanze *f* acidophyte
Kieselsäure *f* silicic acid
Kieselsäuregel *n* silica gel
Kieserit *m (soil)* kieserite
Kiesgrube *f* gravel-pit
Kiesgrund *m* flinty ground
kiesig gravelly
Kieskultur *f* gravel culture
Kiessand *m* grit
Kiesschicht *f* gravel layer
Kieviton *n* kievitone *(phytoalexin)*
KiGRSV *s.* Kirschengrünringscheckungsvirus
Kikeriki *n* cock-a-doodle-doo
Kikuyugras *n* kikuyu grass, Pennisetum clandestinum
Kinase *f* kinase, phosphokinase *(enzyme)*
Kindelbildung *f (phyt)* second growth
Kindermilch *f* humanized milk
Kindernährmittel *n* infant food
Kinese *f*, **Kinesis** *f* kinesis
Kinetin *n* kinetin, 6-furfurylaminopurine *(phytohormone)*

Kinetochor *n* centromere
King Charles [Spaniel] *m* King Charles spaniel *(dog breed)*
~ Orange *f* king orange, Citrus x nobilis
Kinin *n* kinin
Kinn *n* chin *(animal anatomy)*
Kinnkette *f* curb
Kinnriemen *m* chin strap *(of the halter)*
Kino[gummi] *n*, **Kinoharz** *n* kino [gum], gum kino
~/Bengalisches Bengal kino, butea gum
Kinopren *n* kinoprene *(insecticide)*
KiNRFV *s.* Nekrotisches Ringfleckenvirus der Kirsche
KiNRoFV *s.* Virus der Nekrotischen Rostfleckigkeit der Kirsche
Kippanhänger *m* dump (tipping, tilt-deck) trailer, [trailer] tipper
Kippbunker *m* tipping hopper
Kippdämpfer *m* tipping steamer
Kippdarre *f s.* Kipphorde
Kippe *f* [mine] dump, spoil heap; [waste] tip
Kippenaufforstung *f* post mining reforestation
Kippenboden *m* mine soil (spoil)
Kippenbodenrekultivierung *f* mined-land reclamation
Kippenböschung *f* slope of mine dump
Kippenrekultivierung *f* mined-land reclamation
Kipper *m*, **Kipperfahrzeug** *n* tipper
Kipper-Lastzug *m* dump truck
Kippgefäßwaage *f* tilting-bin weighing machine
Kipphorde *f* tipping (dumping, tilting) floor *(malting)*
Kippmoment *n* overturning torque *(e.g. of a tractor)*
Kipppflug *m* balance plough
Kippung *f* tilt
Kippvorrichtung *f* tipping device, tipp[l]er
Kippwagen *m* tipping lorry, dump truck
kirnen to churn, to make butter
Kirrung *f (hunt)* bait
Kirschapfel *m* Siberian crab-apple, Malus baccata var. baccata, Malus sibirica
Kirschbaum *m* cherry[-tree] *(genus Prunus)*
Kirschbaumholz *n* cherry[-wood]
Kirschblattwespe *f* pear slugworm saw-fly, Caliroa cerasi (limacina)
Kirschblattwespenlarve *f* pear-slug, Caliroa cerasi (limacina)
Kirsche *f* cherry
Kirschenblattrollvirus *n* cherry leaf roll virus, CLRV
Kirschengrünringscheckungsvirus *n* cherry green ring mottle virus, CGRMV
Kirschenrauhblättrigkeit *f (phyt)* cherry rasp leaf
Kirschenrauhblättrigkeitsvirus *n* cherry rasp leaf virus
Kirschenschorf *m* cherry scab *(caused by Venturia cerasi)*
Kirschentsteiner *m* cherry pitter

Kirschfruchtfliege 350

Kirschfruchtfliege *f* cherry fruit-fly, Rhagoletis cerasi
Kirschholz *n* cherry[-wood]
Kirschlorbeer *m* [common] cherry laurel, Prunus laurocerasus
Kirschmyrtenbaum *m* rose-apple, stopper *(genus Eugenia)*
Kirschpflaume *f* cherry-plum, myrobalan[-plum], Prunus cerasifera (myrobalana)
Kirschtomate *f* cherry tomato, Lycopersicon esculentum var. cerasiforme
Kissenaster *f* bushy aster, Aster dumosus
Kissenprimel *f* [common, English] primrose, Primula vulgaris
Kiste *f* box, [packing] case; crate
Kistenanbausystem *n* für Champignons champignon tray system
Kisten[aus]kippvorrichtung *f* box tippler; tipping device for pallet boxes
Kistenlager *n* pallet box store
Kistenwagen *m* trolley
Kitazin *n* kitazin *(fungicide)*
Kittharz *n* propolis, bee-glue, balm
Kittharzpflanze *f* propolis plant *(comprehensive term)*
Kitulfaser *f* kittul, kitool *(fibre from Caryota urens)*
Kitulpalme *f (bot)* kittul, kitool, Caryota urens
Kitz *n* fawn; deer calf
Kitzler *m* clitoris
kitzlig skittish, flighty *(horse)*
Kiwi[frucht] *f* kiwi [berry, fruit]
Kiwipflanze *f* Chinese gooseberry, kiwi [bush], Actinidia chinensis
Kjeldahl-Methode *f* Kjeldahl determination, Kjeldahl procedure *(of nitrogen determination)*
KkMV *s.* Königskerzenmosaikvirus
Kladodium *n (bot)* cladode, cladophyll
klaffen *(vet)* to dehisce *(wound edges)*
Klaffen *n* **[des Wundrandes]** *(vet)* dehiscence
Klafter *m(n)* cord *(measure of cut wood; 1 Klafter ≈ 3,6 m^3)*
Klafterholz *n* cordwood, corded timber, stacked cubic wood
Klamm *f* gorge, ravine
Klan *m (ecol)* clan *(kind of climax community)*
Klangholz *n* resonance (resonant, tonal) wood, wood for musical instruments
Klappenschorf *m* **der Luzerne** common leaf spot of alfalfa *(caused by Pseudopeziza medicaginis)*
Klappensieb *n* louvre screen, Peterson (frog-mouth) sieve
Klapperhülse *f*, **Klapperschote** *f (bot)* rattle-box *(genus Crotalaria)*
Klappgreifer *m* gripwheel *(of a tractor)*
klappig *(bot)* valvate
Klapptür *f* sorting gate *(in a livestock handling facility)*
klar clear, lipid *(e.g. wine)* • **~ werden** to [become] clear, to clarify, to fine *(liquid)*

Kläranlage *f* sewage (waste-water treatment) plant
Klärbehälter *m* septic tank
Kläre *f* [clearing, sugar] liquor *(sugar manufacture)*
klären to clarify, to clear, to fine [down], to candle
~/sich to clarify, to [become] clear, to fine
Klärgrube *f* catch pit
Klarheit *f* limpidity
Klarifikator *m* clarifier
Klarifixator *m (dairy)* clarifixator
Klärmittel *n* clarifying agent, clarifier
Klarmost *m* clear must
Klarsaft *m* clarified juice *(sugar manufacture)*
Klärschlamm *m* [sewage] sludge; digested sludge
~ als Düngemittel sludge fertilizer
~/städtischer municipal sludge
Klärschlammbestrahlung *f* sludge irradiation
Klärschlammkompost *m* composted sewage sludge
Klärschleuder *f* clarifying machine, clarifier
Klärtank *m* sedimentation basin, clarifying tank
Klärteich *m* settling pond
Klärung *f* clarification *(of liquids)*; fining, cleansing *(e.g. of beer)*
Klarwein *m* clear wine
Klärzentrifuge *f (dairy)* centrifugal clarifier
Klasse *f* class *(taxonomy, biometry)*
Klassenhäufigkeit *f (biom)* class frequency
Klassensprung *m* natural service *(animal breeding)*
Klassieranlage *f* grading plant
klassieren to grade, to size, to class[ify]
Klassierung *f* grading, sizing, [size] classification
Klassifikation *f* classification, assortment
klassifizieren to classify, to assort
Klassifizierung *f* classification, assortment
Klassisches Geflügelpestvirus *n* fowl plague virus, FPV
Klatschmohn *m*, **Klatschrose** *f* corn (field, common) poppy, corn rose, red weed, ponceau, Papaver rhoeas
klauben to pick [out]
Klauben *n* picking
Klaue *f* claw, unguis; pounce, talon *(of a raptorial bird)*
Klauenbad *n* foot-bath
Klauenbeschädigung *f* claw injury
Klauenbeschlag *m* shoeing
Klauenentzündung *f*/**infektiöse** *(vet)* foot-rot
Klauenfarn *m* 1. claw fern *(genus Onychium)*; 2. claw fern, Onychium japonicum
Klauenfäule *f (vet)* foot-rot
Klauenfett *n* neat's-foot oil
klauenförmig *(bot, zoo)* unguiculate
Klauengelenk *n* corono-pedal (distal interphalangeal) joint
Klauengeschwür *n (vet)* fetlow
Klauenkrankheit *f* claw disease
Klauenkupplung *f* positive (dog) clutch

Klauenlederhautnekrose f *(vet)* necrotic pododermatitis
Klauenmesser n hoof knife (cutter)
Klauenöl n neat's-foot oil
Klauenpflege f care of claws, claw trimming, foot paring
Klauenraspel f claw (hoof) rasp
Klauenschädigung f claw injury
Klauenseuche f foot-and-mouth [disease], hoof-and-mouth disease, murrain *(virosis)*
Klauensohle f sole of claw
Klauensohlengeschwür n ulcer (prolapse) of the sole
klauentragend unguiculate[d]
Klauenverschlag m *(vet)* laminitis, founder
Klauenzange f claw pincers
Klavikula f clavicle, collar-bone
klavikular clavicular
Klebast m epicormic [branch], bole sprout, secondary growth *(wood defect)*
Klebefalle f sticky trap
Kleber m, **Klebereiweiß** n gluten
Kleberfestigkeit f gluten strength
Kleberparenchym n gluten parenchyma
klebfähig adhesive
Klebgras n bur grass, sandbur[r] *(genus Cenchrus)*
Klebgrenze f *(soil)* sticky point
Klebkörper m rostellum *(of an orchid)*
Klebkraut n cleavers, clivers, bedstraw, goose-grass, Galium aparine
klebrig glutinous, gummy, viscid; rop[e]y *(wine)*
Klebriger Gänsefuß m Jerusalem-oak, Chenopodium botrys
Klebriges Kreuzkraut n *(bot)* stinking groundsel, Senecio viscosus
Klebsame m *(bot)* pittosporum *(genus Pittosporum)*
Klebschwertel n African corn lily, ixia *(genus Ixia)*
Klebstoff m adhesive [agent]
Klee m clover, trefoil, trifolium *(genus Trifolium)* *(s. a. Rotklee and Weißklee)*
Kleeälchen n clover cyst-nematode, Heterodera trifolii
Kleeanteil m clover part *(in a field forage mixture)*
Kleeblasenfuß m *(ent)* red clover thrips, Haplothrips niger
Kleeblattgallmücke f clover leaf midge, Dasineura trifolii
Kleebrache f clover fallow
Kleebreitsämaschine f clover seed broadcaster
Kleedrescher m clover thresher
Klee-Eule f *(ent)* clover cutworm [moth], nutmeg moth, Scotogramma (Dicestra) trifolii
Kleefarngewächs n pepperwort *(family Marsileaceae)*
Kleegärheu n clover haylage
Kleegelbadrigkeitsvirus n clover yellow vein virus, CYVV

Kleegelbmosaikvirus n clover yellow mosaic virus
Kleegras[gemenge] n, **Kleegrasgemisch** n grass-clover mixture
Kleegrasnarbe f grass-clover sward
Kleeheu n clover hay
Kleehonig m clover honey
Kleekarre f clover seed barrow
Kleekrankheit f *(vet)* clover disease, trifoliosis
Kleekrebs m clover rot, crown rot of clover *(caused by Sclerotinia trifoliorum)*
Kleemosaik n *(phyt)* clover mosaic
kleemüde clover-sick *(soil)*
Kleemüdigkeit f clover sickness *(of a soil)*
Kleereibegewebe n friction canvas for clover
Kleereiber m clover huller (rasper)
Kleerotblättrigkeitsvirose f subterranean clover red leaf virus disease
Kleesägerät n clover seeder
Kleesamen m clover seed
Kleesamenbau m clover seed cropping
Kleesamenwespe f chalcid fly, Bruchophagus gibbus
Kleesäure f oxalic (ethanedioic) acid
Kleeseide f common (clover) dodder, ailweed, Cuscuta [epithymum ssp.] trifolii
Kleesilage f clover silage
Kleeteufel m lesser (clover) broomrape, Orobanche minor
Kleeulme f common hop-tree, Ptelea trifoliata
Kleevergilbungsvirus n clover yellows virus
Kleeverlaubung f *(phyt)* clover phyllody
Kleewurzel[borken]käfer m clover root bark-beetle, clover root borer, Hylastinus obscurus
Kleezystenälchen n clover cyst-nematode, Heterodera trifolii
Kleidermotte f common clothes moth, Tineola bisselliella
Kleie f bran, pollard, offal
kleieartig branny, furfuraceous
Kleiebürste f bran brush
kleiehaltig branny
Kleietränke f bran mash
kleinästig *(bot)* ramulose
Kleinäugiger Reismehlkäfer m small-eyed flour beetle, Palorus ratzeburgi
Kleinbauer m smallholder [farmer], small farmer, peasant, crofter, cottager
Kleinbauernhaus n cottage, cot[e]
Kleinbauernhof m steading
Kleinbauernwirtschaft f smallholding, small farm, peasant holding
kleinblättrig small-leaved, microphyllous, parvifoliate
Kleinblättrige Linde f small-leaved lime (linden), Tilia cordata
~ **Zwergmispel** f small-leaved cotoneaster, Cotoneaster microphyllus
Kleinblättriges Sonnenröschen n common rock-rose, Helianthemum nummularium

Kleinblumenzwiebel 352

Kleinblumenzwiebel *f* minor [flower]bulb
Kleinblumiges Wollkraut *n s.* Kleinblütige Königskerze
kleinblütig parviflorous
Kleinblütige Kiefer *f* Japanese white pine, Pinus parviflora
~ **Königskerze** *f* common (great) mullein, flannel mullein (plant), shepherd's-club, Aaron's [beard] rod, Verbascum thapsus
~ **Malve** *f* dwarf mallow, Malva rotundifolia
~ **Roßkastanie** *f* bottle-brush buckeye, Aesculus parviflora
Kleinblütiger Steinklee *m* small-flowered melilot, *(Am)* sour clover, Melilotus indica (parviflora)
Kleinblütiges Franzosenkraut (Knopfkraut) *n (bot)* gallant soldier, Galinsoga parviflora
Kleinborstige Opuntie *f (bot)* bunny-ears, Opuntia microdasys
kleindoldig *(bot)* umbellulate
Kleine Bekassine *f* jack-snipe, Lymnocryptes minima
~ **Bibernelle** *f (bot)* common saxifrage, Pimpinella saxifraga
~ **Blaue Rinderlaus** *f* little blue cattle louse, blue louse, Solenopotes capillatus
~ **Braunelle** *f (bot)* self-heal, prunella, Prunella vulgaris
~ **Brennessel** *f* small (burning, sting) nettle, annual (dog) nettle, Urtica urens
~ **Fichtenblattwespe** *f* spruce saw-fly, Pristiphora abietina
~ **Flamingoblume** *f* flamingo flower (plant), Anthurium scherzeranum
~ **Gerste** *f* little barley, Hordeum pusillum
~ **Himbeerlaus** *f* raspberry aphid, Aphis idaei
~ **Klette** *f* common (smaller, lesser) burdock, Arctium minus
~ **Kohlfliege** *f* [cabbage] root-fly, cabbage fly, Chortophila (Hylemyia, Phorbia) brassicae, Delia brassicae (radicum)
~ **Maräne** *f (zoo)* vendace, Coregonus albula
~ **Narzissenfliege** *f* [small] narcissus fly, lesser bulb fly, Eumerus strigatus
~ **Nelkenbasilie** *f* bush basil, Ocimum minimum
~ **Pflaumenlaus** *f* leaf-curling plum aphid, Brachycaudus helichrysi
~ **Pimpinelle** *f s.* ~ Bibernelle
~ **Pricke** *f s.* Kleines Flußneunauge
~ **Rebschildlaus** *f* European fruit lecanium (scale), European peach scale, brown elm scale, Parthenolecanium (Eulecanium) corni
~ **Rinderdasselfliege** *f* common cattle grub, heel fly, Hypoderma lineatum
~ **Sommerwurz** *f* lesser (clover) broomrape, Orobanche minor
~ **Stachelbeer[blatt]laus** *f* gooseberry aphid, Aphis grossulariae
~ **Stechfliege** *f* horn fly, Haematobia irritans
~ **Stubenfliege** *f* lesser (little) house fly, Fannia canicularis
~ **Sumpfschnepfe** *f s.* Kleine Bekassine
~ **Taglilie** *f* dwarf yellow day lily, Hemerocallis minor
~ **Wachsmotte** *f* small (lesser) wax moth, Achroea grisella
~ **Wasserlinse** *f* duckweed, Lemna minor
~ **Weiße Rosenschildlaus** *f* rose scale, Aulacaspis rosae
~ **Wolfsmilch** *f* dwarf spurge, Euphorbia exigua
~ **Zwiebelfliege** *f s.* ~ Narzissenfliege
~ **Zwiebeliris** *f* dwarf (species) iris, Iris reticulata
Kleiner Ampfer *m* sheep['s] sorrel, field (red) sorrel, sour dock, Rumex acetosella
~ **Birnenblattsauger** *m (ent)* pear psylla (sucker), Psylla pyricola
~ **Buntspecht** *m* lesser spotted woodpecker, Dendrocopos minor
~ **Eschenbastkäfer** *m* [small, common] ash bark-beetle, Leperesinus (Hylesinus) fraxinus
~ **Fichtenborkenkäfer** *m* micrographer bark-beetle, Pityophthorus micrographus
~ **Frauenspiegel** *m s.* ~ Venusspiegel
~ **Frostspanner** *m* [common, small] winter moth, geometer [moth], Operophthera (Cheimatobia) brumata
~ **Gelbstreifiger Getreideerdfloh** *m* barley (striped) flea beetle, Phyllotreta vittula
~ **Hahn** *m s.* Birkhahn
~ **Kieferborkenkäfer** *m* small (two-toothed) pine tree bark-beetle, Pityogenes bidentatus
~ **Kiefernrüsselkäfer** *m* small pine weevil, Pissodes notatus
~ **Klappertopf** *m (bot)* yellow rattle, Rhinanthus minor
~ **Klee** *m* small hop clover, slender (lesser) yellow trefoil, lesser (suckling) clover, Trifolium dubium
~ **Kohlweißling** *m* cabbage (small white) butterfly, turnip white butterfly, Pieris (Artigeia) rapae
~ **Leberegel** *m* lancet fluke, Dicrocoelium dendriticum (lanceolatum)
~ **Leistenkopfplattkäfer** *m* flat grain beetle, biscuit beetle, Cryptolestes pusillus
~ **Obstbaumsplintkäfer** *m* fruit (pear) bark-beetle, shot-hole borer, Scolytus rugulosus (mediterraneus)
~ **Odermennig** *m (bot)* [common] agrimony, Agrimonia eupatoria
~ **Pappelbock** *m (ent)* small poplar longicorn, small poplar and willow longhorn, small poplar borer, Saperda populnea
~ **Tabakkäfer** *m* tobacco (cigarette) beetle, Lasioderma serricorne
~ **Tannenborkenkäfer** *m* white spruce [bark-]beetle, silver fir bark-beetle, Cryphalus piceae
~ **Ulmensplintkäfer** *m* [smaller] European elm bark-beetle, small elm bark-beetle, Scolytus multistriatus

Klemmen

~ **Venusspiegel** *m (bot)* Venus's-looking-glass, Legousia hybrida
~ **Waldgärtner** *m* lesser pine-shoot beetle, Blastophagus (Tomicus) minor
~ **Wiesenknopf** *m* 1. burnet, Sanguisorba minor; 2. salad burnet, Sanguisorba minor ssp. minor; 3. fodder burnet, Sanguisorba [minor ssp.] muricata
Kleineres [Chinesisches] Yams *n* lesser (Chinese) yam, cinnamon vine, Dioscorea esculenta
Kleinerzeuger *m* small-scale producer
Kleines Flußneunauge *n* brook lamprey, Lampetra planeri
~ **Habichtskraut** *n* mouse-ear [hawkweed], Hieracium pilosella
~ **Immergrün** *n* [common, lesser] periwinkle, creeping myrtle, Vinca minor
~ **Liebesgras** *n* little love-grass, Eragrostis minor
~ **Löwenmaul** *n (bot)* lesser snapdragon, Antirrhinum orontium
~ **Mädesüß** *n* dropwort, Filipendula vulgaris
~ **Schneeglöckchen** *n* snowdrop, snow (purification) flower, Galanthus nivalis
~ **Singrün** *n s.* ~ **Immergrün**
~ **Springkraut** *n* small balsam, Impatiens parviflora
~ **Timotheegras** *n* small timothy, smaller cat's-tail, Phleum bertolonii
~ **Wiesel** *n* weasel, Mustela nivalis
~ **Zittergras** *n* lesser quaking-grass, Briza minor
kleinfrüchtig small-fruited
Kleinfrüchtigkeit *f* small-fruitedness
~ **der Kirsche** little cherry [disease], cherry little cherry *(virosis)*
~ **des Apfels** apple chat fruit *(virosis)*
Kleingarten *m* family garden, allotment [garden], small plot (space) garden, *(Am)* garden-patch
Kleingartenarbeit *f* allotmenteering
Kleingärtner *m* allotment (small) gardener, domestic gardener
Kleingerät *n* small implement
Kleinhirn *n* cerebellum
Kleinhirnrinde *f* cerebellar cortex
Kleinkläranlage *f* septic tank
Kleinklima *n* microclimate
Kleinköpfiger Pippau *m (bot)* smooth hawk's-beard, Crepis capillaris
kleinkörnig miliary
kleinkronenblättrig *(bot)* micropetalous
Kleinpächter *m* crofter
Kleinparzelle *f* small plot, microplot
Kleinparzellenspritzgerät *n* small plot sprayer
Kleinparzellensprühgerät *n* small plot sprayer
Kleinparzellenversuch *m* small-plot trial
Kleinpferd *n* pony, nag; galloway
Kleinproduzent *m* small-scale producer
Kleinpudel *m* toy poodle *(breed)*
kleinrahmig small-framed *(animal body)*
Kleinregner *m* small irrigator
kleinsamig *(bot)* small-seeded, microspermous

Kleinsäugetier *n* small mammal
Kleinschlepper *m* small (low-powered, midget) tractor, mini-tractor, microtractor
~ **zur Dünnholzrückung** *(forest)* thinnings tractor
Kleinschuppiger Waldchampignon *m* wood mushroom, Agaricus sylvaticus
Kleinsiedler *m* smallholder [farmer]
kleinstachelig *(bot)* aculeolate
Kleinstandort *m* microsite
Kleinstbetrieb *m* [/landwirtschaftlicher/] very small farm
Kleinstblumentopf *m* thumb-pot
Kleinste Rosenblattrollwespe *f* rose leaf saw-fly, Blennocampa pusilla
kleinsternig *(bot)* stellular
Kleinstlebewesen *n* microorganism, microbe
• **von Kleinstlebewesen frei** axenic *(gnotobiotics)*
Kleinstparzelle *f* microplot
Kleinstparzellensägerät *n* microplot seeder
Kleinstschlepper *m*, **Kleinsttraktor** *m s.* **Kleinschlepper**
Kleinteich *m* small pond
Kleinteilstück *n* subplot *(field experimentation)*
Kleintier *n* small animal
Kleintierarzt *m* small animal clinician
Kleintierhaltung *f* small animal rearing (keeping)
Kleintierhaut *f* kip
Kleintierherde *f* flock
Kleintierklinik *f* small animal veterinary practice
Kleintierkunde *f* small animal science
Kleintierstall *m* animal pen, cot[e]
Kleintierwelt *f* microfauna
Kleintierzucht *f*, **Kleintierzüchtung** *f* small animal breeding
Kleintraktor *m s.* **Kleinschlepper**
Kleinverstäuber *m* hand duster
Kleinversuch *m* small-scale trial (experiment)
Kleinvieh *n* small animals, small [live]stock
Kleinviehtransportanhänger *m* small livestock trailer
Kleinwiederkäuer *m* small ruminant
kleinwüchsig small-growing
kleinwulstig *(bot)* torulose
Kleinzapfige Lärche *f* tamarack, Larix laricina (americana)
Kleistermotte *f* white-shouldered house moth, Endrosis sarcitrella
Kleistertrübung *f* starch haze (turbidity) *(of beer)*
kleistogam *(bot)* cleistogamic, cleistogamous
Kleistogamie *f* cleistogamy
Kleistokarp *n*, **Kleistothezium** *n* cleistothecium *(spore-bearing structure in ascomycetes)*
Klematis *f (bot)* clematis *(genus Clematis)*
Klemmband *f* lifting belt *(vegetable harvester)*
Klemmbank *f (forest)* clam bunk
Klemmbanktraktor *m (forest)* clam [bunk] skidder, clamp tractor
Klemmen *n* **der Säge** saw binding

Klemmfingermechanismus

Klemmfingermechanismus *m* clamp feed mechanism *(e.g. of a potato planter)*
Klemmfingerpflanzensetzmaschine *f* clamp transplanter
Klemmfingerrad *n* gripper wheel
Klemmfingersystem *n* gripping finger system
Klemmgreiferpflanzmaschine *f* clamp transplanter
Klemmgrifflastenträger *m (forest)* straddle carrier (truck), timber carrier (cart)
Klemmpflanzung *f (forest)* slit planting, notch (wedge) planting
Klemmscheibenpflanzensetzmaschine *f* flexible disk transplanter
Klemmspaten *m* **[/Hufscher]** *(forest)* planting bar, notching spade
Klenganstalt *f*, **Klenge** *f (forest)* seed-extraction plant, seed extractory, [seed] kiln, cone-dryer
klengen to extract [tree seed], to kiln [conifer seeds]
Klengen *n* seed extraction
Klepper *m* jade, rip, screw
Klette *f* 1. burdock *(genus Arctium)*; 2. bur[r] *(infructescence)*
Klettenlabkraut *n (bot)* cleavers, clivers, bedstone, Galium aparine
Kletterbohne *f* pole [snap] bean, climbing (stick) bean, Phaseolus vulgaris ssp. vulgaris var. vulgaris
Klettereisen *n* climbing iron
Kletterer *m s.* Kletterpflanze
Kletterfarn *m* climbing fern *(genus Lygodium)*
Kletterfeige *f*, **Kletter-Ficus** *f* creeping ficus (fig), climbing fig, Ficus pumila
Klettergerüst *n* climbing frame *(for plants)*
Kletterhortensie *f (bot)* climbing hydrangea, Hydrangea anomala ssp. petiolaris
Kletterkraut *n (Am)* vine
klettern to climb, to run, *(Am)* to vine *(plant)*
~/auf einen Baum to tree *(game)*
kletternd *(bot)* scandent, climbing
Kletternder Giftsumach *m* poison ivy, Toxicodendron (Rhus) radicans
Kletterpflanze *f* climbing plant, climber, liana, liane, *(Am)* vine
Kletterpflanzenstamm *m (Am)* vine
Kletter-Spindelstrauch *m* winter-creeper [euonymus], Euonymus fortunei
Klettersproß *m* climbing stem
Kletterstaude *f* climbing shrub
Kletterstrauch *m* climbing shrub
Klettertrompete *f* 1. Cape honeysuckle, [red] trumpet flower, Tecomaria (Tecoma) capensis; 2. trumpet-creeper, trumpet-vine, Campsis (Tecoma) radicans
Klettervorrichtung *f* climbing frame *(for plants)*
Kletterwein *m* Boston ivy, Parthenocissus tricuspidata
Kletterwurzel *f* climbing root

KIGAV *s.* Kleegelbadrigkeitsvirus
Klima *n* climate
~/gemäßigtes temperate (moderate) climate
~/maritimes maritime climate
~/ozeanisches oceanic climate
~/polares polar climate
Klimaänderung *f* climatic change
Klimaanlage *f* [air] conditioner, air conditioning system (equipment)
Klimaatlas *m* climatic atlas
Klimabeeinflussung *f* climate control
Klimadiagramm *n* climate diagram
Klimaelement *n* climatic element
Klimafaktor *m* climatic factor
Klimahaus *n* phytotron
Klimakammer *f* [plant-]growth chamber, climate (environmentally controlled) chamber *(phytotron)*
Klimakarte *f* climatic map
Klimaklassifikation *f* **nach Köppen** Köppen classification (system) of climates
Klimakterium *n* climacteric *(plant physiology)*
Klimakunde *f* climatology
klimakundlich climatological
Klimalenkung *f* climate control
Klimameßverfahren *n* climate measuring procedure
Klimaregelung *f* air conditioning, climate control
Klimaregion *f* climatic region
Klimaschwankung *f* climate fluctuation
Klimatabelle *f* climatic table
klimatisch climatic
klimatisieren to climatize, to [air-]condition
Klimatisierung *f* [air] conditioning
Klimatisierungsanlage *f s.* Klimaanlage
Klimatogramm *n* clima[to]gram, climograph, hyther[o]graph
Klimatologe *m* climatologist
Klimatologie *f* climatology
~/landwirtschaftliche agricultural climatology, agroclimatology
~/phänologische phenological climatology
klimatologisch climatological
Klimatop *n (ecol)* climatope
Klimaverwerfung *f* climatic change
Klimax *f (ecol)* climax [community]
~/echte euclimax
~/edaphische edaphic climax
~/klimatische euclimax
~/pyrogene fire climax
Klimaxbaumart *f* climax tree species
Klimaxkomplex *m* climax complex
Klimaxvegetation *f* climax vegetation
Klimaxwald *m* climax forest
Klimazone *f* climatic zone (area)
Klimmendes Pfeffergesicht *n (bot)* Cupid peperomia, Peperomia serpens (scandens)
Klimogramm *n s.* Klimatogramm
Klingstein *m* phonolite *(non-clay mineral)*

Klinkengesperr *n*, **Klinkensperrkupplung** *f* pawl-and-ratchet overrunning clutch
Klinometer *n* clinometer
Klinomycin *n* minocyclin *(antibiotic)*
Klinoptilolit *m* clinoptilolite *(non-clay mineral)*
Klinotropismus *m* plagiotropism
Klistier *n*, **Klistierspritze** *f (vet)* enema
Klitoris *f* clitoris
Klivie *f* kaffir lily *(genus Clivia)*
Kloake *f* cloaca *(e.g. of fowl)*
Kloakenentzündung *f (vet)* cloacitis ~/**diphtheroid-ulzerierende** vent gleet
Kloakenöffnung *f* vent
Kloakenuntersuchung *f* cloacal examination
Kloazitis *f s.* Kloakenentzündung
Kloben *m* [split] log
Klobsäge *f* frame (web) saw, whip-saw
Klon *m* clone, cl.
klonal clonal
Klonauslese *f* clonal selection
klonen, klonieren to clone
Klonkultur *f* clonal culture
Klonmaterial *n* clonal material
Klonprüfung *f* clone testing
Klonselektion *f* clonal selection
Klonsorte *f* clonal variety
Klonunterlage *f* clonal rootstock
Klonvermehrung *f* clonal propagation
Klonversuch *m* clone trial
Klopfkäfer *m* anobium beetle, death-watch [beetle] *(family Anobiidae)*
Klopfkäferlarve *f* woodworm, worm
Klopphengst *m* cryptorchid stallion
Klostridien *npl s.* Clostridien
Klotz *m* block, bolt, butt, chock; log, stem section
Klotzförderbahn *f*, **Klotzförderer** *m (forest)* log conveyor (chute, slide), log-way; log haul[up], log hoist (jack)
Klotzteich *m* log (mill) pond, boom
Kluft *f s.* Kernriß
klumpen to lump, to clot
Klumpenporling *m* stone fungus, Polyporellus tuberaster
Klumpenseparator *s.* Klutenabscheider
klumpig lumpy • ~ **werden** *s.* klumpen
Klunkern *fpl* cots, dag *(in a hair coat)*
Kluppbuch *n (forest)* enumeration sheet, tally
Kluppe *f (forest)* [tree] calliper, [tree] caliper, diameter gauge • **[Holz] mit der ~ messen** *s.* kluppen
kluppen to calliper, to caliper, to tally
Klupp[en]führer *m* calliper man
kluppieren *s.* kluppen
Kluppierer *m* calliper man
Kluppmanual *n s.* Kluppbuch
Kluppmeßstock *m* calliper stick
Kluppschiene *f* calliper (graduated) rule
Kluppstock *m* calliper stick
Kluppung *f* tally
Klute *f* clod

Klutenabscheider *m* clod separator
Klutenabweiser *m* clod deflector (clearer)
Klutenbrecher *m* clod crusher (breaker)
klutenfrei clodfree
Klutenräumer *m* clod remover
Klutenrost *m* clod separator
klutig cloddy
Klutigkeit *f* cloddiness *(of a soil)*
Klysma *n (vet)* enema
KM *s.* Körpermasse
KmGSV *s.* Kümmelgelbscheckungsvirus
Knabenkraut *n (bot)* orchis *(genus Orchis)*
Knäckebrot *n* crispbread, hard bread
knackig crisp *(e.g. apples)*
Knackigkeit *f* crispness
Knackweide *f* crack-willow, brittle (redwood) willow, Salix fragilis
Knagge *f* stay
Knäkente *f* garganey, Anas querquedula
Knappheit *f* shortage
Knäuel *m (bot)* knawel *(genus Scleranthus)*
Knäuel *n* cluster, [beet] seed ball ~/**polygermes (polykarpes)** multigerm cluster
Knäuelampfer *m* sharp dock, Rumex conglomeratus
Knäueldrüse *f* sweat gland
Knäuelgras *n s.* Knaulgras
Knäuelkapsel *f* Bowman's capsule *(of kidney)*
Knaulblütige Glockenblume *f* clustered bell-flower, Campanula glomerata
Knaulgras *n* cocksfoot [grass], *(Am)* orchard grass, Dactylis glomerata
Knaulgrascheckungsvirus *n* cocksfoot mottle virus, CfMoV
Knaulgrasstrichelvirus *n* cocksfoot streak virus
Knebeln *n* pinch milking *(umwanted practice of hand-milking)*
Kneter *m*, **Knetmaschine** *f* kneading machine *(butter-making)*
Knickei *n* cracked egg
Knicker *m s.* Knickzetter
Knickerkrankheit *f* **der Tulpe** stem topple of tulip *(non-parasitic disease)*
Knickfuchsschwanz *m* water foxtail, Alopecurus geniculatus
Knickgelenkrückertraktor *m (forest)* articulated skidder
Knick[rahmen]lenkung *f* articulated steering [system], articulated frame steering
Knickrücken *m* kinky back *(of broiler chicken)*
Knickschwänzigkeit *f (vet)* kinky tail
Knickwuchs *m* crooked (bent) growth
Knickzetter *m* crimper; roller crimper (conditioner) *(haymaker)*
Knie *n* knee; *(slaught)* hock *(s. a. Kniegelenk)*
Knieaktion *f* action *(of horse's gait)*
Kniebug *m (slaught)* hock
knieeng knock-kneed
Kniefalte *f* grip *(of animal's body)*

kniefömig

kniefömig *(bot, zoo)* geniculate
Kniegelenk *n* knee-joint, stifle[-joint]
Kniegelenkentzündung *f (vet)* gonitis
Kniegelenksband *n*/**gekreuztes** cruciate ligament
kniehängig over in the knees *(forelimb conformation)*
Kniehängigkeit *f* bucked-knee conformation, bucked knees *(of forelimbs)*
Knieholz *n* knee timber
Knieholzflur *f* elfin woodland (forest)
Knieholzformation *f* elfin-wood formation
Knieholzstufe *f* elfin-wood belt *(plant ecology)*
Kniekehlgelenk *n* femorotibial joint
Kniescheibe *f* kneecap, knee-pan, stifle-bone, patella
Kniescheibengelenk *n* femoropatellar joint
Kniescheibenverrenkung *f (vet)* patella luxation
Knippmaschine *f* chipping machine, chipper *(lump sugar manufacture)*
KnMMV *s.* Mildes Knaulgrasmosaikvirus
Knob *m* knob *(knobby structure of maize chromosomes)*
Knoblauch *m* [common] garlic, Allium sativum
• **nach ~ riechend** garlicky
knoblauchartig garlicky
Knoblauchknolle *f* bulb of garlic
Knoblauchmosaikvirus *n* garlic mosaic virus, GMV
Knoblauchöl *n* garlic oil
Knoblauchskraut *n* garlic wort (mustard), hedge garlic, jack-by-the-hedge, Alliaria petiolata (officinalis)
Knoblauchzehe *f* garlic [clove], clove of garlic, button
Knoblauchzopf *m* garlic string
Knoblauchzwiebel *f* garlic [bulb]
Knöchelbinde *f* ankle boot *(for horses)*
Knöchelchen *n* ossicle
Knochen *m* bone
~/kurzer short bone
~/langer long bone
~/lufthaltiger pneumatic bone
~/platter flat bone
~/pneumatischer pneumatic bone
Knochenaktinomykose *f (vet)* lumpy jaw *(of cattle and pigs)*
Knochenasche *f* bone-ash
Knochenauswuchs *m* apophysis
knochenbildend bone-forming, skeletogenous
Knochenbildung *f* bone formation, ossification, osteogenesis
Knochenbildungszelle *f* osteoblast
Knochenbruch *m (vet)* [bone] fracture *(for compounds s. under* Fraktur*)*
Knochenbrüchigkeit *f (vet)* brittle bones
Knochendüngemittel *n* bone fertilizer
Knochenende *n* epiphysis
Knochenentzündung *f (vet)* osteitis

Knochenerkrankung *f (vet)* bone disease, osteopathy; osteodystrophy *(caused by disturbed mineralization)*
Knochenerweichung *f (vet)* osteomalacia
Knochenfestigkeit *f* bone strength
Knochenfett *n* bone fat
Knochenfortsatz *m* apophysis, process
Knochenfraß *m (vet)* caries
Knochenfuge *f* synarthrosis
Knochenfuttermehl *n* [steamed] bone flour
Knochenfutterschrot *m* bone-meal
Knochengerüst *n* skeleton
Knochengeschwulst *f (vet)* osteoma
Knochengewebe *n* bone [tissue]
Knochenhaft *f* synostosis
Knochenhasenhacke *f (vet)* curb
Knochenhaut *f* periosteum
Knochenhautentzündung *f (vet)* periostitis
Knochenkeimgewebe *n* callus
Knochenkohle *f* bone char[coal], animal char[coal]
knochenlos boneless, bone-free
Knochenmark *n* [bone] marrow, medulla
~/gelbes fatty (yellow) marrow
~/rotes red marrow
~/weißes fatty (yellow) marrow
knochenmarkartig myeloid
Knochenmarkentzündung *f (vet)* osteomyelitis
Knochenmarkerschöpfung *f (vet)* pancytopenia
Knochenmarkfibrose *f (vet)* osteofibrosis
Knochenmarkkeimzelle *f* myeloblast
Knochenmarkriesenzelle *f* megakaryocyte
Knochenmarkzelle *f* bone marrow cell
Knochenmatrix *f* bone matrix
Knochenmehl *n* bone-meal *(fertilizer)*; bone flour (dust)
Knochenmineralisierung *f* bone mineralization
Knochenmühle *f* bone grinder
Knochennaht *f* [bone] suture
Knochennekrose *f (vet)* osteonecrosis
Knochenöl *n* bone-oil
Knochenreiben *n (vet)* crepitus
Knochenresorption *f* bone resorption
Knochensarkom *n (vet)* osteosarcoma
Knochenschaft *m* diaphysis
Knochenschrot *m* bone-meal *(fertilizer)*
Knochenschwiele *f* callus
Knochenschwund *m (vet)* osteoporosis
Knochensubstanz *f* bone
Knochensubstanzwucherung *f (vet)* hyperostosis
Knochensucher *m (vet)* bone seeker (seeking element) *(radionuclide)*
Knochensuperphosphat *n* bone superphosphate
knochentrocken bone-dry
Knochentuberkulose *f (vet)* tuberculosis of bone
Knochen- und Gelenkentzündung *f (vet)* osteoarthritis
~ des Geflügels/ansteckende avian staphylococcal arthritis

Knochen- und Gelenkerkrankung f *(vet)* osteoarthropathy
Knochen- und Knorpelentzündung f *(vet)* osteochondritis
Knochenverbindung f durch straffes Bindegewebe fibrous joint, Junctura fibrosa
Knochenverdichtung f *(vet)* osteosclerosis
Knochenvereinigung f *(vet)* osteosynthesis
Knochenverkalkung f bone calcification
Knochenvorsprung m apophysis
~/kleiner tubercle
Knochenweiche f *(vet)* osteomalacia
Knochenzelle f bone cell, osteocyte
Knochenzubildung f exostosis; *(vet)* osteophyte
~/entzündliche *(vet)* osteophyte
knöchern bony, osseous
knochig bony, raw-boned
Knockdown-Effekt m knock-down effect *(of a pesticide)*
Knockdown-Mittel n knock-down agent (poison)
Knödelbirne f wild pear, Pyrus pyraster ssp. pyraster
Knöllchen n nodule • ~ **bilden** to nodulate • **sich mit ~ besetzen** to nodulate *(e.g. leguminous roots)*
Knöllchenbakterium n nodule[-forming] bacterium, legume bacterium *(genus Rhizobium)*
Knöllchenbildung f nodulation
Knöllchensucht f *(phyt)* premature tuber formation, secondary tubers, little potato[es], no-top
Knolle f tuber *(e.g. potato)*; corm, bulb *(of iridaceous plants)* • **Knollen bilden** to tuberize
knollenartig tuberous
Knollenbegonie f [hybrid] tuberous begonia, Begonia x tuberhybrida
Knollenbildung f tuberization
Knollenblätterpilz m s. Grüner Knollenblätterpilz
Knollenbohne f African yam bean, Sphenostylis stenocarpa
Knollenbraunfäule f der Kartoffel late blight of potato *(caused by Phytophthora infestans)*
Knollenfäule f tuber rot *(comprehensive term)*
Knollenfenchel m Florence fennel, finnochio, Foeniculum vulgare var. dulce
Knollenfrucht f tuber crop
Knollengewächs n tuberous plant
Knollenglatthafer m onion couch, Arrhenaterum elatius ssp. bulbosum
Knollenhahnenfuß m bulbous buttercup, cuckoo buds, Ranunculus bulbosus
Knolleninfektion f *(phyt)* tuber infection
Knollenkälberkropf m, **Knollenkerbel** m bulbous-rooted chervil, parsnip chervil, Chaerophyllum bulbosum
Knollenkerbel m s. Kerbelrübe
Knollenlegemaschine f tuber planter
Knollennaßfäule f der Kartoffel potato soft rot, bacterial soft rot of potato *(caused by Erwinia carotovora var. atroseptica)*

Knollenpetersilie f Hamburg (turnip-rooted) parsley, Petroselinum crispum ssp. tuberosum
Knollenpflanze f tuber[ous] plant
Knollenpflanzmaschine f tuber planter
Knollenplatterbse f heath pea, Lathyrus tuberosus
Knollenprotein n tuber protein
Knollenrettich m [black, winter] radish, Raphanus sativus var. niger
Knollensellerie m(f) celeriac, knob (turnip-rooted, German) celery, Apium graveolens var. rapaceum
Knollenspierstaude f dropwort, Filipendula vulgaris
Knollensteinbrech m meadow saxifrage, Saxifraga granulata
knollentragend tuber-bearing, tuberiferous, tuberous
knollenübertragen tuber-borne *(e.g. a plant disease)*
Knollenziest m Chinese (Japanese) artichoke, crosne[s], Stachys sieboldii (affinis)
Knollenzwiebel f bulb onion, bulbo tuber
knollig bulbous; tuberous, tubercular, tuberculate[d]
Knollige Seidenpflanze f butterfly weed, pleurisy root, Asclepias tuberosa
Knolliger Hahnenfuß m bulbous buttercup, Ranunculus bulbosus
Knolliges Rispengras n bulbous blue grass, Poa bulbosa
Knopfblume f scabious, devil's bit *(genus Scabiosa)*
Knopfbusch m button bush
Knopfgalle f *(phyt)* button gall
Knopfpflanze f cone plant *(genus Conophytum)*
Knopfspießer m knobber *(roe deer, red deer)*
Knopper m knopper *(a gall on acorns and leaves of various oaks)*
Knorpel m cartilage, gristle • **im ~ gelegen** endochondral
~/elastischer elastic cartilage
~/hyaliner hyaline cartilage
Knorpelbildung f chondrogenesis
Knorpelentzündung f *(vet)* chondritis
Knorpelgeschwulst f *(vet)* chondroma
Knorpelgewebe n cartilage, gristle
Knorpelhaft f cartilaginous joint
Knorpelhaut f perichondrium
knorpelig cartilaginous, cartilaginoid, gristly
Knorpelkallus m provisional callus
Knorpelkirsche f hard-fleshed cherry, bigaroon, bigarreau, Prunus avium var. duracina
Knorpelzelle f chondrocyte
Knorren m knag, gnarl, knob *(in wood)*
knorrig knaggy, gnarled, gnarly, knobby *(wood)*
Knospe f *(bot)* bud, burgeon, button, gemma; eye *(e.g. of a potato tuber)*
~/akzessorische accessory bud

Knospe

~/**gemischte** mixed (multiple) bud
~/**korrelativ gehemmte** latent bud
~/**ruhende (schlafende)** dormant (resting) bud
~/**zusätzliche** accessory bud
knospen to bud, to burgeon, to pullulate, to shoot
Knospen n budding, burgeoning, pullulation, gemmation • **zum ~ bringen** to bud
Knospenannahme f bud take (in grafting)
Knospenastung f (forest) bud pruning, disbudding
Knospenaufbruch m bud break[ing], bud bursting
~/**beginnender** silver tip
Knospenausdünnung f durch Abreiben bud-rubbing
Knospenauslese f bud selection (plant breeding)
Knospenaustrieb m s. Knospenaufbruch
Knospenbestäubung f bud pollination
Knospenbildung f bud formation
knospenbohrend (ent) bud-boring
Knospendecke f s. Knospenschuppe
Knospendeckung f aestivation
Knospenentfernung f durch Abreiben bud-rubbing
Knospenentwicklung f bud formation
Knospenfäule f (phyt) bud rot
Knospenförderung f an den Zweigspitzen acrotony
Knospengalle f (phyt) bud gall
~/**tütenartige** oc[h]rea • **mit tütenartiger ~** ocreate[d]
Knospenhemmung f/korrelative apical dominance
Knospenkrankheit f **des Flieders** phytophthora disease of lilac (caused by Phythophthora syringae)
Knospenlage f vernation
knospenlos ablastous
Knospenmilbengalle f big bud (esp. of black currant, caused by Cecidophyopsis ribis)
Knospenminierer m (ent) bud-miner
Knospenmutation f bud (somatic) mutation
Knospenöffnung f bud break (bursting)
Knospenruhe f rest of buds
~/**durch Apikaldominanz bedingte** paradormancy
~/**echte (endogene)** bud dormancy
Knospenschuppe f [bud] scale, bud cover, tegmentum
Knospenschwellen n bud swelling
Knospenselektion f bud selection (plant breeding)
Knospenspringen n s. Knospenaufbruch
Knospenspur f bud trace
Knospenstadium n bud stage
Knospenstellung f bud position
~/**abstehende** held-out bud position
Knospentreiben n s. Knospenaufbruch
Knospenwulst m bud support
Knospung f s. Knospen
Knötchen n nodule, tubercle
Knötchenausschlag m lumpy skin disease (of cattle)

358

Knötchenausschlagvirus n lumpy skin disease virus
Knötchenbildung f nodulation
knötchenförmig nodulose, nodulous
Knötchenwurm m nodular worm (genus Oesophagostomum)
knoten to knot
Knoten m 1. knot; node; 2. s. Knorren
~/**Keith-Flackscher** sinuatrial node (of the heart)
knotenartig nodose, nodular, tuberous
Knotenausschlag m s. Knötchenausschlag
Knotenblume f (bot) snowflake (genus Leucojum)
knotenförmig nodose, nodular
knotenreich nodose, nodular
Knotenschwanz m (vet) kinky tail
Knoter m s. Knüpfapparat
Knöterich m knotweed, persicaria (genus Polygonum)
Knöterichflöh m mangel (beet) flea beetle, Chaetocnema concinna
Knöterichgewächse npl buckwheat family, dock family (family Polygonaceae) • **die ~ betreffend** polygonaceous
knotig 1. knotty; nodose, nodular; 2. s. knorrig; 3. s. knollig
Knotige Braunwurz f knotted figwort, Scrophularia nodosa
KnSiV s. Knaulgrasstrichelvirus
KnSV s. Knaulgrascheckungsvirus
Knüpfapparat m knotting apparatus, knotter (of a pick-up baler)
knüpfen to knot
Knüppel m billet (chunky piece of wood)
Knüppeldamm m, **Knüppelweg** m corduroy (plank) road
Koadaptation f (gen) coadaptation
Koagulat n coagulum, coagulate
Koagulation f coagulation
Koagulierbarkeit f coagulability
koagulieren to coagulate
~ **lassen** to coagulate
Koagulum n coagulum, coagulate
Koben m pen; pigsty
Kochapfel m cooking (stewing, culinary) apple
Kochapparat m boiling apparatus (sugar manufacture)
Kochbanane f plantain (Musa x paradisiaca)
Kochbutter f butter for cooking
kochen to cook; to boil
~/**auf Korn** to boil to grain, to sugar off
Kochen n **auf Korn** crystal boiling (sugar manufacture)
Köcherblümchen n cigar flower, cuphea (genus Cuphea)
Köcherfliege f caddis-fly (order Trichoptera)
kochfertig pot-ready
Kochie f summer cypress (genus Kochia)
Kochkäse m cooked cheese
Kochmaische f decoction (cooker) mash (brewing)

Kochmaischeverfahren n decoction [mashing] method *(brewing)*
Kochqualität f cooking (culinary) quality, quality for cooking *(e.g. of potatoes)*
Kochsalz n [common, cooking] salt, sodium chloride
Kochsalzfieber n *(vet)* salt fever
Kochsalzlösung f saline solution
~/physiologische physiological salt solution
Kochsalzmangelsyndrom n *(vet)* low salt syndrome *(of ruminants)*
Kochsalzvergiftung f *(vet)* salt poisoning syndrome
Kochschinken m cooked ham
Kochtrub m hot sludge (break) *(brewing)*
Kodahirse f koda (kodo, ditch) millet, Paspalum scrobiculatum [var. scrobiculatum]
Köder m bait, lure
Köderfalle f bait[-lure] trap *(pest control)*
Köderfisch m live bait, bait fish
Ködermittel n bait
ködern to bait, to lure
Köderpflanze f bait (trap) plant
Köderpflanzenkultur f trap crop
Köderscheu f bait shyness
Köderspritzmittel n bait spray
Kodetriplett n *(gen)* codon
Kodohirse f s. Kodahirse
kodominant codominant
Kodominanz f codominance
Kodon n *(gen)* codon
Koeffizient m/**osmotischer** osmotic coefficient
Koenzym n s. Coenzym
Koevolution f coevolution
Koexistenz f coexistence
Kofaktor m co-factor *(enzymology)*
Kofloreszenz f *(bot)* coflorescence
Kog m s. Koog
kohärent coherent
Kohärentgefüge n *(soil)* coherent structure, massive condition (structure)
Kohäsion f cohesion
kohäsiv cohesive
Kohl m 1. cabbage, brassica *(genus Brassica)*; 2. kale, kail, [bore]cole *(comprehensive term)*
~/ovalköpfiger oval cabbage
Kohlanämie f *(vet)* kale anaemia
Kohlbaum m tree lettuce, Pisonia alba
Kohlblattlaus f cabbage aphid, Brevicoryne brassicae
Kohlblattwanze f pentatomid rape bug, Eurydema oleraceum
Kohldistel f cabbage (garden) thistle, Cirsium oleraceum
Kohldrehherz[gall]mücke f [turnip and] swede midge, Contarinia nasturtii
Kohlehydrat n s. Kohlenhydrat
kohlen to char

Kohlenbrenner m charcoal burner, woodcollier
Kohlendioxid n carbon dioxide
Kohlendioxidanreicherung f carbon dioxide enrichment (supplementation) *(e.g. of greenhouse atmosphere)*
Kohlendioxidassimilation f carbon dioxide assimilation
Kohlendioxiddüngung f carbon dioxide fertilization
Kohlendioxidkompensationspunkt m carbon dioxide compensation point *(photosynthesis)*
Kohlendioxidmangel m **im Blutplasma** acapnia
Kohlenhydrat n carbohydrate
kohlenhydratreich rich in carbohydrates, wide
Kohlenhydratstoffwechsel m carbohydrate metabolism
Kohlenhydratstoffwechselstörung f carbohydrate metabolism disorder
Kohlenhydratsynthese f carbohydrate synthesis
Kohlenmeiler m [charcoal] pile, charcoal kiln, heap
~/stehender earth kiln
Kohlen[mon]oxid n carbon monoxide
Kohlensäure f carbonic acid
Kohlensäureanhydratase f carbonate dehydratase (hydro-lyase), carbonic acid dehydratase *(enzyme)*
Kohlenstaublunge f *(vet)* anthracnosis
Kohlenstoff m carbon
Kohlenstoffassimilation f carbon assimilation
Kohlenstoffbilanz f carbon balance
Kohlenstoffkreislauf m carbon cycle (metabolism)
Kohlenstoff-Stickstoff-Verhältnis n carbon-to-nitrogen ratio, C/N ratio
Kohlenstoffturnover m s. Kohlenstoffumsatz
Kohlenstoffumsatz m carbon turnover
Kohlenwasserstoff m hydrocarbon
~/chlorierter chlorinated hydrocarbon, organochlorine [compound]
Köhler m charcoal burner, woodcollier
Kohlerdfloh m 1. flea beetle (bug) *(genus Phyllotreta)*; 2. cabbage flea [beetle], cabbage beetle, Phyllotreta vittata
Köhlerei f charcoal burning
Köhlereiholz n charcoal wood
köhlern to char
Kohlerntemaschine f cabbage harvester
Kohleule f cabbage moth, Mamestra brassicae
Kohleulenlarve f cabbage worm
Kohlfeld n cabbage patch
Kohlfliege f cabbage [root-]fly, root-fly, Chortophila (Hylemyia) brassicae, Delia brassicae (radicum)
Kohlfliegenlarve f cabbage (turnip) maggot
Kohlfuchs m brant fox, Vulpes alopex
Kohlgallenrüßler m turnip (cabbage) gall (seed) weevil, Ceutorhynchus pleurostigma
Kohlgänsedistel f annual (common) sowthistle, hare thistle, hare's-lettuce, Sonchus oleraceus
Kohlgemüse n brassica vegetable

Kohlhernie

Kohlhernie f *(phyt)* [cabbage] club-root, club foots, ambury, anbury *(caused by Plasmodiophora brassicae)*
Kohlkistenwagen n cabbage box cart
Kohlkopf m cabbage [head]
Kohlkratzdistel f cabbage (garden) thistle, Cirsium oleraceum
Kohlmeise f great tit, Parus major
Kohlmotte f diamond-back moth, Plutella maculipennis (xylostella)
Kohlmottenschildlaus f cabbage white fly, Aleyrodes brassicae (proletella)
Kohlpalme f 1. cabbage palm (tree), pina-palm, Euterpe oleracea; 2. cabbage palm (tree), Roystonea oleracea
Kohlportulak m [common, garden] purslane, *(Am)* pusley [weed], pussl[e]y, Portulaca oleracea
Kohlrabi n kohlrabi, kale (Hungarian) turnip, turnip[-rooted] cabbage, Brassica oleracea var. gongylodes
Kohlrabierntemaschine f kohlrabi harvester
Kohlrappe m coal-black *(horse)*
Kohlraupe f s. Kohlweißlingsraupe
Kohlrose f [moss] cabbage-rose, Rosa centifolia
Kohlrübe f swede [turnip], rooted (Swedish, yellow) turnip, *(Am)* rutabaga, Brassica napus var. napobrassica, Brassica napus ssp. rapifera
Kohlrübenblattwespe f turnip saw-fly, Athalia rosae
Kohlsaat f, **Kohlsamen** m winter [oil-seed] rape, cole[-seed], Brassica napus var. napus
Kohlschabe f s. Kohlmotte
Kohlschnake f common crane-fly, Tipula oleracea
Kohlschotenmücke f brassica (bladder) pod midge, Dasyneura brassicae
Kohlschotenrüßler m cabbage seed [pod] weevil, [swede] seed weevil, Ceutorhynchus assimilis
Kohlschotenschwärze f *(phyt)* dark pod spot *(caused by Alternaria brassicae and A. brassicicola)*
Kohlschwärze f alternaria leaf spot of cabbage, dark leaf spot, brown rot of cauliflower *(caused by Alternaria brassicae and A. brassicicola)*
Kohlschwarzringvirus n cabbage black ring virus, CBRV, cabbage ring spot virus
Kohlstrunk m cabbage stalk (stump), runt
Kohlwanze f pentatomid rape bug, Eurydema oleraceum
Kohlweißling m cabbage butterfly, cabbage white [butterfly] *(genus Pieris)*
Kohlweißlingsraupe f cabbage worm (caterpillar)
Kohlzünsler m garden pebble moth, Evergestis (Phlyctaenia) forficalis
Kohlzystenälchen n brassica cyst-nematode, Heterodera cruciferae
Koir f s. Kokosfaser
koital coital
Koitalexanthem n *(vet)* coital exanthema, infectious pustular vulvovaginitis

~ des Pferdes equine coital exanthema, ECE, horse-pox
Koitus m coitus
Kojisäure f kojic acid *(antibiotic)*
Koka f s. Kokastrauch
Kokablätter npl coca
Kokain n cocaine *(alkaloid)*
Kokardenblume f blanket flower, gaillardia *(genus Gaillardia)*
Kokardenblumenhybride f blanket flower, Gaillardia x aristata
Kokardenzelle f *(vet)* target cell
Kokastrauch m [Amazonian, Bolivian] coca, Erythroxylum coca
Kokke f, **Kokkus** m coccus
Kokon m *(zoo, ent)* cocoon, pod • **sich in einen ~ einspinnen** to cocoon
Kokosexpeller m coconut expeller
Kokosfaser f coconut fibre, coir
Kokosfett n s. Kokosöl
Kokoskuchen m coconut cake, palm kernel cake (meal), poonac *(extraction residue)*
Kokosmilch f coconut milk
Kokosnuß f coco[nut], cocoa[nut]
Kokosnußnashornkäfer m coconut (rhinoceros) beetle, Oryctes rhinoceros
Kokosnußöl n s. Kokosöl
Kokosnußschalenmehl n coconut shell flour
Kokosöl n coconut (copra) oil, coconut butter
Kokospalme f coconut palm, coco [palm], cocoa, Cocos nucifera
Kokospreßkuchen m, **Kokosschrot** m s. Kokoskuchen
Kokoswasser n coconut water
Kokroduabaum m *(bot)* African afrormosia, Afrormosia elata
Kok-Saghys m kok-sag[h]yz, Russian dandelion, Taraxacum kok-saghyz
Kok-Saghys-Kautschuk m kok-sag[h]yz rubber
Kokzidie f coccidium *(order Coccidia)*
Kokzidienbefall m *(vet)* coccidiosis
Kokzidienbekämpfungsmittel n anticoccidial [agent]
kokzidienhemmend coccidiostatic
Kokzidienruhr f *(vet)* coccidiosis
Kokzidioidomykose f *(vet)* coccidio[ido]mycosis *(caused by Coccioides immitis)*
Kokzidiose f *(vet)* coccidiosis
Kokzidiostatikum n coccidiostat, coccidiostatic agent
kokzidiostatisch coccidiostatic
Kolabaum m kola [tree], cola [tree], Cola acuminata
Kolanuß f kola [nut], cola [nut]
Kolben m 1. piston; 2. *(bot)* spadix; ear *(e.g. of maize)* • **~ schieben** to ear [up]
kolbenartig *(bot)* spadiceous, spadicose
Kolbenblatt n ear leaf *(of maize)*

Kolbenfaden *m (bot)* 1. aglaonema *(genus Aglaonema)*; 2. Chinese evergreen, Aglaonema modestum
Kolbenfäule *f (phyt)* ear rot
Kolbenhirse *f* Italian (foxtail) millet, Hungarian grass (millet), Bengal grass, Setaria italica
Kolbenpumpe *f* piston pump
Kolbenspindel *f (Am)* cob *(of maize)*
kolbentragend ear-bearing
Kolchische Stechpalme *f* Colchis holly, Ilex colchica
Kolchischer Emmer *m* Colchic (Georgian) emmer, Triticum georgicum (karamyschevii)
Kolchos *m* kolkhoz, collective farm *(of the former U.S.S.R.)*
Kolchosbauer *m* kolkhoznik, collective farmer
Kolchose *f s.* Kolchos
Koleoptile *f* coleoptile *(of grasses)*
Koleor[r]hiza *f (bot)* coleorhiza, root sheath
Kolibakterium *n* colibacillus, Escherichia coli
Kolibazillose *f (vet)* colibacillosis, colibacteriosis *(caused by Escherichia coli)*
Kolienteritis *f s.* Koliruhr
Kolienterotoxämie *f (vet)* oedema disease *(caused by Escherichia coli)*
koliform coliform
Koliformenindex *m* coli index *(microbiology)*
Koliinfektion *f (vet)* colibacillus, colibacteriosis *(caused by Escherichia coli)*
Kolik *f (vet)* colic
~/spastische spasmodic colic
kolikartig *(vet)* colicky
Kolimastitis *f (vet)* coliform mastitis
Kolinski *m*, **Kolinsky** *m (zoo)* kolinsky, Mustela siberica
Koliruhr *f (vet)* coliform scour[s], enteric colibacillosis *(caused by Escherichia coli)*
~ der Ferkel coliform scour[s] in pigs
~ der Kälber coliform scour[s] in calves
~ der Küken Hjärre's disease
~ der Lämmer coliform scour[s] in lambs
Kolisepsis *f*, **Koliseptikämie** *f (vet)* coliform septicaemia
Kolitis *f (vet)* colitis
~/ulzerative (ulzeröse) ulcerative colitis
Kolititer *m* coli titre
Kolitoxikose *f (vet)* oedema disease *(caused by Escherichia coli)*
Kolkrabe *f* raven, Corvus corax
Kolkschutzsperre *f* dam
Kolkwitzie *f* beauty bush, Kolkwitzia amabilis
kollabieren to collapse, to break down
kollagen collagenous
Kollagen *n* collagen *(scleroprotein)*
Kollagenfaser *f* collagenous fibre
Kollaps *m* collapse, breakdown
kollateral collateral
Kölle *f (bot)* 1. calamint *(genus Satureja)*; 2. summer savory, Satureja hortensis

Kollenchym *n (bot)* collenchyma
kollenchymatös collenchymatous
Koller *m (vet)* stagger[s]
kollern to gobble *(turkey)*
Kollerwuchs *m (forest)* stunted growth, stunt
Kolletere *f (bot)* colleter
kollin *(ecol)* colline
kolloid colloid[al]
Kolloid *n* colloid
kolloidal colloid[al]
Kolloidmühle *f* colloid mill, *(Am)* viscolizer
Kollonema *n (vet)* myxoma
kolluvial *(soil)* colluvial
Kolluvialboden *m* colluvial (transported) soil
Kolluviallehm *m* colluvial loam
Kolluvialprofil *n* colluvial profile
Kolluvium *n* colluvium
Kolokasie *f (bot)* taro, coco yam, dasheen, Colocasia esculenta
Kolon *n (animal anatomy)*
~/absteigendes descending colon
~/aufsteigendes ascending colon
Kolonie *f* colony *(e.g. of bacteria)*
koloniebildend colony-forming *(microbiology)*
Koloniehybridisation *f (gen)* colony hybridization
Koloniezahl *f* bacterial count
Kolonisierung *f* colonization
Kolonnenspundung *f* section bunging *(beer storage)*
Kolophonium *n* colophony, [pine] rosin, gum resin
Koloquint[h]e *f* colocynth, bitter apple (cucumber), Citrullus colocynthis
Koloradodouglasie *f* [Rocky Mountain, blue] Douglas fir, Pseudotsuga menziesii var. glauca
Koloradokäfer *m* Colorado [potato] beetle, potato bug, Leptinarsa decemlineata
Koloradotanne *f* Colorado fir, Abies concolor
Kolorimeter *n* colorimeter
Kolorimetrie *f* colorimetry
Kolostomie *f (vet)* colostomy
kolostomieren *(vet)* to colostomize
kolostral colostral
Kolostralimmunität *f* colostral immunity
Kolostralmilch *f*, **Kolostrum** *n* colostral (first, early) milk, colostrum, beastings, beestings, biestings
Kolostrumantikörper *m* colostral antibody
Kolpitis *f (vet)* colpitis, vaginitis
Kolpoptose *f (vet)* colpoptosis, vaginal prolapse
Kolposkop *n (vet)* colposcope
Kolter *n s.* Messersech
Kolumbusgras *n* Columbus grass, Sorghum almum
Koma *n (vet)* coma
Kombihacke *f* combined hoe and fork
Kombinationsdrillmaschine *f* combine drill, combined grain-fertilizer drill
Kombinationsdünger *m* compound fertilizer

Kombinationseignung

Kombinationseignung f combining ability *(breeding)* • **gute ~ aufweisen** to nick
~/allgemeine general combining ability
~/spezielle (spezifische) specific combining ability
Kombinationsimpfstoff m combined vaccine
Kombinationspflegegerät n multipurpose equipment (implement)
Kombine f s. Mähdrescher
kombustibel combustible, burnable
Kombustion f combustion
Komfortsitz m comfort seat *(e.g. in tractors)*
Komfortzone f comfort zone
Komfrey m *(bot)* rough comfrey, Symphytum asperum
Kommabazillus m vibrio[n] *(genus Vibrio)*
Kommaschildlaus f oyster-shell scale, mussel scale, Lepidosaphes ulmi
kommensal commensal
Kommensale m commensal
Kommensalismus m commensalism, commensality
Kommunalwald m communal (community) forest
Komondor m komondor *(dog breed)*
Kompaktheit f compactness *(e.g. of a soil)*
kompaktieren to compact
Kompaktierung f compaction
Kompaktknochen m compact bone
Kompaktschlepper m, **Kompakttraktor** m compact tractor
Kompartimentsanalyse f compartmental analysis *(for determination of cell contents)*
Kompaßpflanze f 1. compass plant; 2. common wild lettuce, prickly lettuce, Lactuca serriola (scariola); 3. compass plant, Silphium laciniatum
kompatibel compatible
Kompatibilität f compatibility
Kompensationspunkt m light compensation point, compensating point *(plant physiology)*
Kompetition f competition *(of enzyme reactions)*
Komplement n complement *(haematology)*
Komplementaktivität f complement activity
Komplementärgen n complementary (multiple) gene
Komplementarität f complementarity
Komplementärluft f inspiratory reserve volume
Komplementärstrang m complementary strand *(of a nucleic acid)*
Komplementation f *(gen)* complementation
Komplementbindung f complement fixation
Komplementbindungsreaktion f complement fixation test
Komplementfixation f complement fixation
Komplettierung f *(forest)* filling up, infilling, recruitment
Komplex m/**lichterntender** light-harvesting complex, LHC *(photosynthesis)*
~/organomineralischer organomineral (colloidal) complex, organo-clay complex, clay-humus complex

Komplexauge n *(ent)* compound eye
Komplexdünger m complex fertilizer
Komplexeinsatz m complex deployment *(e.g. of field machinery)*
Komplexmechanisierung f full (complete) mechanization
Komplextumor m *(phyt)* teratoma
Komponente f component, constituent; ingredient
Komposite f *(bot)* composite
Kompositen fpl s. Korbblütler
Kompositprobe f composite sample
Kompost m compost, mould • **~ bereiten** to [make] compost • **mit ~ düngen** to compost
~/gespickter spawned (spawn-run) compost *(mushroom production)*
Kompostaufträger m potting soil loader
Kompostbereitung f s. Kompostierung
Komposterde f [soil] compost, vegetable mould, muck
Komposthaufen m compost heap (pile)
Kompostieranlage f compost preparation facility (plant), composter
kompostieren to [make] compost
Kompostierfläche f s. Kompostplatz
Kompostiermaschine f composting machine
Kompostierung f composting, compost making (preparing)
~ in geschlossenen Räumen indoor-composting
Kompostierungsbetrieb m composting enterprise
Kompostierungsmittel n composting additive
Kompostierungsplatz m s. Kompostplatz
Kompostierungsprozeß m composting process
Kompostierungszusatz m composting additive
Kompostmaterial n compost material
Kompostmiete f compost heap (pile)
Kompostmischer m compost mixer, composting machine, soil shredder
Kompostpflanze f compost crop
Kompostplatz m compost yard (site), composting area, *(Am)* batch ground
Kompostsilo m compost silo
Kompostwender m compost turner
Kompott n stewed fruit, compote
Kompottfrüchte fpl stewing fruit[s]
Kompressibilität f compressibility *(e.g. of a soil)*
Kompressionsentrindung f compression debarking
Kompressionswärmepumpe f compression heat pump
Kompressorstation f compressor station
Konalbumin n conalbumin *(glycoproteide, egg protein fraction)*
Kondensationshygrometer n dew-point hygrometer
Kondensationswärme f condensation heat
Kondensator m/**barometrischer** barometric condenser *(sugar manufacture)*
kondensieren 1. to condense *(gas or vapour)*; 2. to condense, to thicken [by evaporation], to evaporate, to concentrate

Kondensmagermilch f condensed skim milk
Kondensmilch f condensed milk, evaporated (concentrated) milk
~/gesüßte Swiss milk
Kondensvollmilch f condensed whole milk
Kondenswasser n condensation water
Kondition f condition
konditionieren to condition; to air-condition; to age *(flour after milling)*
Konditionierung f conditioning [treatment]
Konduktor m *(gen)* conductor
Kondurangostrauch m *(bot)* cundurango, Marsdenia cundurango
Konfidenzbereich m *(biom)* confidence interval
Konfidenzgrenze f *(biom)* confidence limit
Konfidenintervall n *(biom)* confidence interval
Konfidenzschätzung f *(biom)* confidence estimation
Konfiskat n *(slaught, vet)* confiscation
Konfitüre f jam
Kongelifraktion f *(soil)* congelifraction
kongenital congenital, connatal
Kongestion f *(vet)* congestion
Konglomerat n *(soil)* conglomerate
Konglutination f conglutination
Kongoakazie f owala oil tree, oil-bean tree, Pentaclethra macrophylla
Kongogras n Congo (Ruzizi) grass, Brachiaria ruziziensis
Kongorot n Congo-red *(diazo dye)*
Kongreßwürze f congress wort *(brewing)*
Konidie f s. Konidiospore
Konidienträger m, **Konidiophor** m conidiophore
Konidiospore f *(bot)* conidiospore, conidium, fungal spore
Konifere f conifer, needle-leaved tree *(order or subclass Coniferae = Pinidae)*
Koniferenpflanzung f pinetum
Koniferenwald m coniferous forest
Koniferenzapfen m conifer cone
König-Boris-Tanne f King Boris's fir, Abies borisii-regis
Königin f queen [bee], [colony] queen • **die ~ ausfressen** to feed the queen
~ der Nacht queen of the night, night-blooming cereus, night-flowering cactus, Selenicereus grandiflorus
Königinnenaufzucht f queen rearing
Königinnenfuttersaft m queen bee's nutrient jelly, royal jelly
Königinnensubstanz f queen substance *(pheromone)*
Königinnenzucht f queen rearing
Königsfarn m 1. royal (flowering) fern, water fern, osmund *(genus Osmunda)*; 2. royal (flowering) fern, water fern, osmund, Osmunda regalis
Königsfelder Messer (Schnitzelmesser) n Koenigsfeld (Koenigsfelder-type) knife *(sugar-beet processing)*

Königsgranadille f *(bot)* giant granadilla, marquesa, Passiflora quadrangularis
Königskerze f *(bot)* mullein, mullen *(genus Verbascum)*
Königskerzenmosaikvirus n mullein mosaic virus
Königskrabbenmehl n king crab meal *(feed-stuff)*
Königslachs m king (chinook) salmon, Oncorhynchus tshawytscha
Königslilie f regal lily, Lilium regale
Königsnuß f big shellbark, Carya laciniosa
Königspalme f [Cuban] royal palm, royal wine palm, Roystonea regia
Königswein m grape ivy, Cissus rhombifolia
Konik m Konik *(horse breed)*
Koniose f *(vet)* koniosis
Konjunktiva f conjunctiva
konjunktival conjunctival
Konjunktivitis f *(vet)* conjunctivitis
Konkrement n *(vet)* concrement, stone
Konkreszenz f concrescence
Konkretion f *(soil)* concretion
Konkurrent m *(ecol)* competitor
Konkurrenz f competition
~/pflanzliche plant competition
~/zwischenartliche competition between species
Konkurrenzfähigkeit f, **Konkurrenzvermögen** n competitive ability (capacity), competitiveness
konkurrieren to compete
konnatal congenital, connatal
Konsanguinität f consanguinity, blood relationship
Konserve f preserve, conserve, preserved food
~/im Haushalt hergestellte domestic preserve
Konservenaufkommen n pack
Konservenbüchse f, **Konservendose** f can, tin [can]
Konservenfabrik f cannery, preserving (canning) plant
Konservengemüse n canned (tinned, processed) vegetable
Konservenglas n [packing] jar, preserving bottle
Konservenglasfüllmaschine f bottling machine
Konservenherstellung f canning
Konservenindustrie f canning (canned food) industry
Konservenobst n processed fruit[s], preserved (canned) fruit
Konservenpfirsich m cling peach
Konservierbarkeit f preservability
konservieren to preserve, to conserve; to cure *(esp. by drying, salting or smoking)*
~/in Büchsen (Dosen) to can, to tin
Konservierung f preservation, conservation; canning, tinning
Konservierungsindustrie f s. Konservenindustrie
Konservierungsmethode f pack
Konservierungsmittel n preservative [agent]; curing agent
Konservierungsreife f canning maturity
Konservierungsstoff m s. Konservierungsmittel

konsistent

konsistent consistent
Konsistenz f consistency, consistence
Konsistometer n consistometer
Konsole f corbel, bracket, conk, shelf *(of a tree-colonizing basidiomycete)*
konsolidieren to consolidate
Konsoziation f consociation *(plant sociology)*
Konsozies f consocies *(plant sociology)*
Konstanz f *(ecol)* constancy
Konstanzklasse f constancy class
Konstipation f *(vet)* constipation, obstipation
Konstitution f constitution, habit
Konstitutionsanomalie f, **Konstitutionsfehler** m *(vet)* constitutional abnormality
Konstitutionsschwäche f constitutional weakness
Konsultationsbetrieb m [/**landwirtschaftlicher**] consulting farm
Konsumtionskrankheit f *(vet)* wasting disease
Konsumwein m beverage wine, vin ordinaire
kontagiös *(phyt, vet)* contagious
Kontagiosität f contagiousness
Kontagium n contagium
Kontaktausbreitung f contact spread *(e.g. of causative agents)*
Kontaktdermatitis f *(vet)* contact dermatitis
Kontaktdüngung f contact fertilization
Kontaktemulsion f contact emulsion
Kontaktgift n contact poison
Kontaktgiftwirkung f contact toxicity
Kontakthemmung f contact inhibition *(microbiology)*
Kontaktherbizid n contact herbicide (weed-killer)
Kontaktherbizidemulsion f contact emulsion
Kontaktinfektion f contact infection
Kontaktinsektizid n contact insecticide
~ mit Dauerwirkung residual contact insecticide
~/protektives protective contact insecticide
Kontaktpestizid n contact pesticide
Kontakttoxizität f contact toxicity
Kontakttrockner m contact dryer
Kontakttrocknung f contact drying
Kontaktulkus n *(vet)* contact ulcer
Kontaktwirkung f contact activity *(e.g. of an insecticide)*
Kontaminant m contaminant
Kontamination f contamination
Kontinentalklima n continental climate
Kontingent n share, quota
Kontingenz f *(biom)* contingency
~/mittlere quadratische mean square contingency
Kontingenztafel f contingency table
Kontinuum n *(ecol)* continuum
kontraktil contractile
Kontraktion f contraction
kontraktionsfähig contractile
Kontraktionsfaktor m contraction factor *(brewing)*
Kontrastfärbung f contrastive staining *(microbiology)*

Kontrollampe f indicator lamp
Kontrolle f control, check
Kontrollfläche f check area, control plot
kontrollieren to control, to check
Kontrollmethode f/**Biolley's** *(forest)* Biolley's continuous inventory system
Kontrollparzelle f check (control) plot *(field experimentation)*
Kontrollschlachtungsversuch m control slaughtering trial
Kontrollsorte f check (control) cultivar
Kontrollteilstück n s. Kontrollparzelle
Kontrolltier n control animal *(experimentation)*
Kontrollvariante f control
Kontur[boden]bearbeitung f contour tillage
Konturenschnitt m contour (cutter bar) pruning *(orcharding)*
Konturenschnittmaschine f trimmer, trimming machine
Konturfeder f contour feather, quill[-feather]
Konturfurche f contour furrow
Kontur[linien]pflanzung f contour planting
Konturpflügen n contour ploughing
Kontusion f *(vet)* contusion, bruise
Konuszentrifuge f continuous conical screen centrifuge *(sugar manufacture)*
Konvarietät f convariety *(taxonomy)*
Konvektion f convection
Konvektionsregen m convectional (convective) rain
Konvektionstrockner m convective dryer
Konvektionstrocknung f convection drying
Konvektionswärmestrom m convective heat flow
Konvektorheizung f convector heating
Konvergenz f convergence, convergency
Konvulsion f *(vet)* convulsion
Konzentrat n 1. concentrate; 2. s. Konzentratfutter
~/emulgierbares emulsifiable concentrate, e,c, EC
Konzentratdüngemittel n concentrated fertilizer
Konzentratfutter n [feed] concentrate, concentrate food
Konzentratfütterung f concentrate feeding
Konzentratfutterverteiler m concentrate dispenser
Konzentration f concentration
~/molare molarity, molar concentration
Konzentrationsprofil n *(soil)* concentration profile
Konzentrator m cream separator
Konzentrieren n concentration
Konzeption f conception
Konzeptionserfolg m, **Konzeptionsrate** f conception rate
Koog m polder, dikeland *(low-lying land reclaimed from sea)*
Kooperation f co-operation
kooperativ co-operative, co-op
Kooperative f co-operative, co-op
~/landwirtschaftliche agricultural co-operative

Kopaivabalsam *m* 1. copaiba *(oleoresin)*; 2. *s.* Kopaivabaum 2.
Kopaivabaum *m* 1. copaiba *(genus Copaifera)*; 2. [balsam of] copaiba, Copaifera officinalis
Kopal *m*, **Kopalharz** *n* copal [resin]
Kopallsumach *m* shining sumac[h], dwarf sumac[h], Rhus copallina (copallinum)
Koparasitismus *m* multiparasitism, multiparasitization
Kopf *m* head • **einen ~ ansetzen (bilden)** to head *(cabbage, salad)* • **mit ~ [versehen]** *(bot, zoo)* capitate • **mit unbewolltem ~** open-faced *(sheep)* • **ohne ~** *(bot, zoo)* acephalous
Kopfabzeichen/mit weißem bald[-faced] *(e.g. a horse)*
Köpfaggregat *n* topping unit
Kopfbaum *m* pollard [tree]
Kopfbewollung *f* head wool
Kopfbildung *f* heading, hearting *(of cabbage)*
Kopfbrand *m* **der Mohrenhirse und des Maises** head smut of sorghum and corn *(caused by Sphacelotheca reiliana)*
Kopfbruststück *n (zoo)* cephalothorax
Köpfchen *n* çapitulum
köpfchenförmig capitellate
Köpfchenschimmel[pilz] *m* bread mould, Mucor mucedo
kopfdüngen to top-dress
Kopfdünger *m* top-dressing
Kopfdüngergabe *f* top-dressing
Kopfdüngung *f* top-dressing, top fertilization
Köpfeinheit *f* topping unit
köpfen to head, to decapitate, to top, to stop *(esp. plants)*; to poll[ard] *(esp. trees)*; to behead *(e.g. poultry)*
Köpfen *n* heading, topping; pollarding; *(forest)* coppicing
Kopfendlage *f* cephalic (normal) presentation *(obstetrics)*
Kopffalte *f* head fold *(embryology)*
Kopffäule *f (phyt)* head rot
~ **der Zwiebel** onion neck rot, neck rot of onion *(caused by Botrytis allii)*
Kopffliege *f* head fly, Hydrotaea irritans
Kopffliegenkrankheit *f* [**der Schafe**] wounded heads [of sheep]
kopfförmig capitate
Kopfförmige Marante *f* Guinea arrowroot, sweet corn tuber, Calathea allouia
Kopfgeschwulst *f (vet)* poll evil *(of horses)*
Kopfgestell *n* halter
Kopfgrind *m (vet)* favus
Kopfhirn *m* brain
Kopfhochverfahren *n (forest)* high-lead [cable] logging, high-lead yarding, high leading
Kopfhöhe *f* **des Sägezahns** addendum of tooth
Kopfholz *n*, **Kopfholzausschlag** *m* pollard shoot
Kopfholzbetrieb *m s.* Kopfholzwirtschaft
Kopfholzschoß *m* pollard shoot

Koppelungsgruppe

Kopfholzstamm *m* pollard
Kopfholzwirtschaft *f*, **Kopfholzzucht** *f (forest)* branch coppice method, pollard[ing] system, lopping system
Kopfkalkung *f* top liming
Kopfkapsel *f (ent)* head capsule • **mit normal entwickelter ~** eucephalous • **mit nur teilweise sklerotisierter ~** hemicephalous • **ohne [sklerotisierte]** ~ acephalous
Kopfkohl *m* [headed, drumhead] cabbage, Brassica oleracea convar. capitata var. capitata
Kopfkrankheit *f (vet)* Borna disease
~/bösartige malignant catarrhal fever
Köpflader *m* top saver
Kopflänge *f* neck *(racing)*
Kopflaus *f* **des Huhnes** chicken head louse, Cuclotogaster (Gallipeurus) heterographus
~ **des Schafes** sucking body louse, Linognathus ovillus
kopflos *(bot, zoo)* acephalous
Köpfmaschine *f* topper
Köpfmesser *n* topping knife
Kopfrahmen *m* bail *(parlour installation)*
Kopfrasen *m* head turf
Kopfräude *f (vet)* head mange
~ **des Geflügels** scaly face *(caused by Knemidokoptes spp.)*
Kopfsalat *m* round-headed garden lettuce, head (cabbage) lettuce, Lactuca sativa var. capitata
Kopfschild *m (ent)* clypeus
Köpfschlitten *m* topper
Köpfschwader *m* windrowing [beet] topper, topper windrower
Kopfskelett *n* skull, cranium
Kopfspaltmaschine *f (slaught)* head splitting machine
Kopfsteckling *m* tip (top, terminal) cutting
Kopfstück *n* poll piece, crownpiece *(bridle)*
Kopfthymian *m* cone-head thyme, Thymus capitatus
Kopftier *n* leading hind *(of red deer's herd)*
Kopfwärme *f* overhead heat *(in greenhouses)*
kopfwärts *(zoo)* cranial
Kopfweide *f* pollard[ed] willow
Kopfweidenstamm *m* pollard
Köpfwerkzeug *n* topper
Kopfwolle *f* head wool • ~ **scheren** to face
Kopfzeug *n* headgear, head harness, headcollar
Kopoubohne *f* kudzu [bean], Pueraria lobata (thunbergiana)
Koppel *f* 1. paddock, enclosure; 2. pack, leash *(of hounds)*; 3. *s.* Koppelriemen
koppeln 1. to couple, to link; 2. to leash, to couple *(hounds)*
Koppelpunkt *m* hitch point *(three-point linkage)*
Koppelriemen *m* leash
Koppelung *f* linkage, coupling
Koppelungsanalyse *f (gen)* linkage analysis
Koppelungsgruppe *f (gen)* linkage group

Koppelungspunkt

Koppelungspunkt *m s.* Koppelpunkt
Koppelungswagen *m* implement carriage
Koppelweide *f* paddock grazing, controlled (field) grazing
Kopplung *f s.* Koppelung
Kopra *f* copra *(dried meat of coconuts)*
Koprakäfer *m* red-legged ham beetle, Necrobia rufipes
Koprämie *f (vet)* copraemia
Kopraschrot *n* copra meal
Kopräzipitat *n (dairy)* coprecipitate
koprogen coprogenic *(e.g. humus)*
Koprolith *m (vet)* coprolith
Koprologie *f (vet)* coprology
Koprom *n (vet)* coproma
koprophag coprophagous
Koprophagie *f* coprophagy
Koprostanol *n*, **Koprosterin** *n* coprostanol
Kopulation *f* 1. *(zoo)* copulation, mating; 2. splice grafting *(orcharding)*
~ **mit Gegenzunge[n]** [whip-and-]tongue grafting
Kopulationsreflex *m* mating reflex
kopulieren 1. to copulate, to couple, to mate; 2. to splice-graft *(orcharding)*
Kopulierhippe *f*, **Kopuliermesser** *n* grafting knife, bill[hook]
Korakan *f* coracan (finger, African) millet, rag[g]ee, ragi, Eleusine coracan [ssp. coracan]
Korallenbaum *m* 1. coral-tree, Erythrina corallodendron; 2. *s.* Korallenstrauch
Korallenbeere *f* coral-berry, Symphoricarpos orbiculatus
Korallenlilie *f* coral lily, Lilium pumilum
Korallenpilz *m* coral mushroom, club fungus *(family Clavariaceae)*
Korallenraute *f (bot)* boronia *(genus Boronia)*
Korallenstrauch *m* 1. Jerusalem (Christmas) cherry, Solanum pseudocapsicum; 2. coral-bean, coral-tree *(genus Erythrina)*; 3. cockspur coralbean, Brazilian cockspur coral tree, Erythrina crista-galli; 4. coral-tree, Erythrina humanea
Korallentröpfchen *n (bot)* coral-drops, Bessera elegans
Korb *m* 1. basket *(s. a.* Spankorb, Tragkorb*)*; 2. concave, cage *(of a harvester)*; 3. cradle *(of a scythe)*
Korbabstand *m* concave clearance
Korbblütengewächse *npl s.* Korbblütler
Korbblütler *mpl* composite (sunflower) family, aster (daisy) family *(family Compositae = Asteraceae)* • **die ~ betreffend** asteraceous
Korbeinstellskale *f* concave indicator
Korbflasche *f* demijohn
Korbflechten *n* basket weaving
Korbmarante *f* peacock (rattle snake) plant, calathea *(genus Calathea)*
Korbschleuder *f (api)* tangential extractor
Korbsense *f* cradle scythe • **mit der ~ mähen** to cradle

Korbweide *f* basket willow, [basket, common, velvet] osier, Salix viminalis
Kord[gewebe]lage *f* cord ply *(of tyres)*
Kordon *m* cordon *(orcharding)*
~ **/ einarmiger waagerechter** horizontal cordon
~ **/ senkrechter** vertical cordon
~ **/ zweiarmiger waagerechter** double horizontal cordon
Kordonerziehung *f* cordon training
~ **/ niedrige** low cordon training
Koreakiefer *f* Korean pine, Pinus koraiensis
Koreanischer Klee *m* Korean lespedeza, Lespedeza stipulacea
~ **Schneeball** *m* fragrant viburnum, Viburnum carlesii
kören to license *(breeding animals)*
Koriander *m* coriander, Coriandrum sativum
Korianderfrucht *f* coriander [seed]
Koriandrol *m* linalool *(terpene alcohol)*
Korinthe *f* currant
Korium *n* corium, dermis, true skin
Kork *m* 1. *(bot)* cork, phellem; 2. *s.* Korken
korkartig corky, suberose
Korkbaum *m* 1. cork-tree *(genus Phellodendron)*; 2. cork-tree, Phellodendron amurense
Korkbildung *f* cork formation
Korkbildungsgewebe *n* cork cambium, phellogen
Korkeiche *f* cork-oak, cork[-tree], Quercus suber
korken to cork *(a bottle)*
Korken *m* cork [stopper]
Korkenmaschine *f* corking machine
Korkfleck *m (phyt)* cork spot
Korkfleckigkeit *f* corky (drought) spot *(of stored fruit)*
~ **/ innere und äußere** internal and external cork[y spots] *(of apples due to boron deficiency)*
Korkgewebe *n* cork[y] tissue
korkig corky, corked *(wine)*
Korkkambium *n* cork cambium, phellogen
Korkkrankheit *f* **der Weinrebe** woody cork *(virosis of grape-vine)*
Korkrinde *f* cork [bark], phelloderm
Korksäure *f* suberic acid
Korkschaligkeit *f* **des Apfels** apple rough skin, apple star crack *(virosis)*
Korkschicht *f (bot)* phellem
Korkstoff *m* suberin
Korkstopfen *m* cork [stopper]
Korktanne *f* cork-bark fir, Abies lasiocarpa var. arizonica
Korkwarze *f (bot)* lenticel
Korkwurzelkrankheit *f* **der Tomate** corky root of tomato, tomato brown and corky root rot *(caused by Pyrenochaeta lycopersici)*
Korkzelle *f* cork cell
Kormophyt *m* cormophyte
Kormus *m (bot)* corm
Korn *n* 1. grain, kernel; 2. grain, cereal[s], corn *(s. a. under* Getreide*)* • **auf ~ [ver]kochen** to boil to grain, to sugar off • **Körner ansetzen** to kernel

~/vermahlenes milled grain
Korn... *s. a.* Getreide...
Kornabscheidung *f* grain separation
Kornähre *f* [cereal] ear, grain spike
Kornährenverband *m* (vet) spica
Kornansatz *m* grain set
Kornausbildung *f* grain [con]formation
Kornaustragschnecke *f* grain discharge auger *(combine)*
Kornauszählung *f* kernel count
Kornbeschädigung *f* grain damage
Kornbildung *f* grain [con]formation
Kornblume *f* cornflower, bluebottle, bachelor's button[s], Centaurea cyanus
Kornblumenaster *f* 1. Stoke's aster *(genus Stokesia)*; 2. Stoke's aster, cornflower aster, Stokesia laevis
Kornboden *m* grain loft *(of a barn)*
Kornbunker *m* grain tank *(combine)*
Körnchen *n* [small] grain, granule
Körnchenbildung *f* granulation
Körnchenröhrling *m* (bot) granulated boletus, Boletus (Suillus) granulatus
Kornea *f* s. Hornhaut
Kornelevator *m* vertical grain elevator
Kornelkirsche *f*, **Kornelkirschbaum** *m* cornelian cherry, cornel, Cornus mas
Kornelkirschgewächse *npl* dogwood family *(family Cornacea)*
körnen to grain, to granulate, to corn
Körnerbelüftung *f* grain ventilation
Körnerbruch *m* 1. grain breakage (damage); 2. *s.* Bruchkorn.
Körnerbrut *f* grain spawn *(mushroom production)*
Körnerbunker *m* grain bin
körnerdicht grain-tight
Körnerdrillmaschine *f* grain drill
~ **mit Düngevorrichtung** fertilizer grain drill
Körnerdrusch *m* grain threshing
Körnerdurchsatz *m* grain feed rate
Körnereinfülltrichter *m* grain hopper
Körnerelevator *m* [grain-]elevator
Körnerfeuchtemeßgerät *n* grain moisture tester
körnerfressend granivorous
Körnerfrucht *f* grain crop
Körnerfrüchte *fpl* grain, corn
Körnerfutter *n* grain feed
Körnergebläse *n* grain blower, pneumatic grain conveyor
Körnerhaufwerk *n* granular bed
Körnerhirse *f* grain sorghum, millet *(comprehensive term)*
Körnerhülsenfrucht *f* s. Körnerleguminose
Körnerlack *m* seed-lac
Körnerleguminose *f* grain (seed) legume, pulse [crop], black straw crop
Körnermais *m* grain maize, *(Am)* grain corn
Körnerquetscher *m* grain crusher
Körnerreife *f* grain maturity

Körnersämaschine *f* grain drill
Körnerschleuse *f* grain sluice
Körnerschnecke *f* grain auger; horizontal grain auger *(combine)*
Körnerschüttung *f* granular bed
Kornertrag *m* grain yield
körnertragend graniferous
Kornertragsbildung *f* grain yield formation
Kornertragskomponente *f* grain yield component
Körnertransportfahrzeug *n* grain truck
Körnertransportwagen *m* grain trailer, trailed grain hopper
Körnerverlustanzeigegerät *n* grain loss indicator (monitor) *(of a combine)*
Körnerverluste *mpl* grain losses
Körnerverunreinigungen *fpl* grain impurities
Körnerzählgerät *n* grain (kernel) counter
Kornfeld *n* cornfield
Kornfeuchte *f*, **Kornfeuchtegehalt** *m* grain moisture [content]
Kornfeuchtegleichgewicht *n* grain moisture equilibrium
Kornförderschnecke *f* auger-type grain conveyor
Kornform *f* grain conformation
Kornfraktion *f* soil fraction
Kornfüllung *f* grain fill[ing]
Kornfüllungsdauer *f* grain filling duration
Kornfüllungsperiode *f*, **Kornfüllungsphase** *f* grain filling period
Kornfüllungsrate *f* grain filling rate
Korngröße *f* grain size
Korngrößenklasse *f* soil fraction
Korngrößenzusammensetzung *f* granulometric composition; soil texture
Kornhärte *f* grain hardness
körnig granular, granulated • ~ **werden** to grain
Kornkäfer *m* grain (granary) weevil, Sitophilus granarius, Calandra granaria
Kornkammer *f* granary
Kornkochen *n* crystal boiling *(sugar manufacture)*
Kornmasse *f* kernel weight
Kornmotte *f* mottled (European) grain moth, wolf moth, Nemapogon granellus, Tinea granella
Kornphysiologie *f* grain physiology
Kornpigment *n* grain pigment
Kornprotein *n* grain protein
Kornqualität *f* grain quality
Kornqualitätsmerkmal *n* grain quality character
Kornquetsche *f* [grain, seed] crusher
Kornrade *f* [corn-]cockle, corn rose, cornflower, Agrostemma githago
Kornreifungsprozeß *m* grain maturation process
Kornschnecke *f* grain auger
Kornschrumpfung *f* grain shrivelling
Kornsollabstand *m* preset spacing interval *(beet growing)*
Kornspeicher *m* [mit Umschlags- und Aufbereitungsanlage] grain-elevator
Korn-Spelzen-Verhältnis *n* kernel-to-husk ratio

Korn-Stroh-Verhältnis

Korn-Stroh-Verhältnis *n* grain-to-straw ratio, harvest index
Korntank *m* grain tank *(combine)*
Korntankabdeckung *f* grain tank cover
Korntankvolumen *n* grain tank capacity
Korntrespe *f* rye[like] brome, common chess, chess [brome], cheat [grass], wheat thief, Bromus secalinus
Korntrockenmasse *f* grain dry weight
Körnung *f* 1. grain [size]; 2. granulometric composition, soil texture
Körnungsart *f* [soil] textural class
Körnungsartendreieck *n* [soil] textural triangle, triangle for textural classification
Kornvolumen *n* grain volume
Kornzählung *f* kernel count
Korolle *f (bot)* corolla
Koronararterie *f* coronary artery
Koronargefäß *n* coronary vessel
Körper *m* body • **mit schwerem** ~ full-bodied *(wine)*
~/**Heinz'** Heinz body *(of erythrocytes)*
~/**tierischer** animal body
Körper *mpl*/**pilzhutförmige** mushroom bodies *(of honey-bees)*
Körperanhängsel *n* appendage
Körperbau *m* [body-]build
Körperbehaarung *f* body hair
Körperbeschaffenheit *f* habit
Körperbestandteil *m* body component
Körperbewegung *f* exercise
Körperchen *n*/**Barrsches** Barr body *(of female somatic cells)*
~/**Herbstsches** Herbst corpuscle *(pressoreceptor in birds)*
Körperdecke *f (zoo)* integument • **durch die ~ hindurch** percutaneous, transcutaneous
Körperdichte *f* body density
Körpereiweiß *n* body protein
Körperenergie *f* body energy
Körperenergiebilanz *f* body energy balance
Körperfarbe *f*, **Körperfärbung** *f* body colour
Körperfett *n* body fat
Körperfettsynthese *f* body fat synthesis
körperfern distal
Körperflüssigkeit *f* body fluid
Körperform *f* body form, [body] conformation
körperfremd [wirkend] xenobiotic
Körpergegend *f* body region
Körpergestalt *f* body shape
Körpergewebe *n* body tissue
Körpergewicht *n* body weight
Körpergröße *f* body size
~/**metabolische** metabolic [body] size, MBS
Körperhaar *n* body hair
Körperhaltung *f* posture, stance
Körperhöhle *f* body cavity
Körperkapazität *f* body capacity *(livestock judging)*
Körperkern *m* body core

Körperkerntemperatur *f* body core temperature
Körperkomponente *f* body component
Körperkondition *f* body condition
Körperlähmung *f*/**halbseitige** *(vet)* hemiparesis
Körperlänge *f* body length
Körperlaus *f* **des Huhnes** chicken body louse, Menacanthus (Eomenacanthus) stramineus
körperlich bodily, somatic
Körpermasse *f* body mass (weight)
Körpermassezunahme *f*, **Körpermassezuwachs** *m* body[-weight] gain
Körpermerkmal *n* bodily characteristic
Körperoberfläche *f* body surface [area]
~/**effektive** effective body-surface area
Körperproportion *f* body proportion
Körperräude *f (vet)* psoroptic mange (scab) *(caused by Psoroptes spp.)*
Körperreserve *f* body reserve
Körperschaftswald *m* corporate (corporation) forest
Körperschale *f* body shell
Körpersegment *n* [body] segment
Körperstellung *f s.* Körperhaltung
Körperstoffwechsel *m* body metabolism
Körperteil *m* body part
Körpertemperatur *f* body temperature
Körpertemperaturregulierung *f* body temperature regulation
Körpertyp *m* body type, somatotype
Körperverfassung *f* bodily condition, constitution
Körperwachstum *n* body growth
Körperwärme *f* body heat
Körperwasser *n* body water
Körperzusammensetzung *f* body composition
Korrasion *f (soil)* corrasion *(erosion process)*
Korrekturfaktor *m* correction factor
Korrelation *f* correlation
~/**genetische (genotypische)** genetic correlation
~/**mehrfache (multiple)** multiple correlation
~/**phänotypische** phenotypic correlation
Korrelationsanalyse *f* correlation analysis (calculation)
Korrelationskoeffizient *m* **[/Bravaisscher]** correlation coefficient, coefficient of correlation
Korrelationsmatrix *f* correlation matrix
Korrelationsstörung *f* correlation disturbance
Korrelationstabelle *f* correlation table
korrelieren to correlate
Korridorkrankheit *f* corridor (buffalo) disease *(of bovine animals, caused by Theileria lawrencei)*
Korrosion *f* corrosion
Korrosionsbeständigkeit *f*, **Korrosionsfestigkeit** *f* corrosion resistance
Korrosionsschutz *m* corrosion protection
Korrosionsschutzmittel *n* corrosion preventative (protective)
Korsische Schwarzkiefer *f* Calabrian pine, Pinus nigra ssp. laricio
Kortex *m* cortex; bark; rind

kortikal cortical
Koryza f (vet) coryza, rhinitis
Koschenille f cochineal (dye)
Koschenillelaus f s. Koschenilleschildlaus
Koschenillerot n cochineal (dye)
Koschenilleschildlaus f cochineal [insect] (comprehensive term)
Kosmee f cosmos, cosmea, Mexican daisy (genus Cosmos)
Kosmopolit m (ecol) cosmopolite
Kosobaum m (bot) cuso, Hagenia abyssinica, Brayera anthelminthica
KoSRV s. Kohlschwarzringvirus
Kossäte m cottager
kostal costal
Kostalatmung f costal respiration
kosten to degust, to taste
Kostiasis f (vet) costiasis (of fish, caused by Costia necatrix)
Kostromaer Rind n, **Kostromarind** n Kostroma [cattle] (breed)
Kot m faecal matter, f[a]eces, dung, droppings
 • ~ **absetzen (ausscheiden)** to dung, to defecate
 • **aus ~ entstanden** coprogenic (e.g. humus)
Kotanfall m faecal output
Kotbunker m dung pit
Kotelett n chop (pig carcass)
Kotelettfläche f eye muscle area
Kotenergie f faecal energy
Kötenschopf m fetlock, feather (of a horse)
Kotentleerung f defecation
Kotfang m (ent) frass sheet
Kotfläche f dung area
Kotflora f faecal flora
Kotfressen n coprophagia
kotfressend coprophagous
Kotgang m dung passage
Kotgeschwulst f (vet) coproma
Kotgrube f dung (droppings) pit
kothaltig, kotig stercoraceous, stercoral
Kotindexmethode f faecal index method (for determining the digestibility of amino-acids)
Kotplatte f dung area (channel)
Kotprobe f faecal sample
Kotrinne f [manure] gutter
Kotrost m dung grid
Kotsackblattwespe f s. Gespinstblattwespe
Kotschieber m dung dozer (scraper)
Kotstein m (vet) coprolith
Köttsdorfer Zahl f saponification number (value) (fatty acid determination)
Kotwanne f droppings tray (of a cage battery)
Kotyledone f 1. (bot) cotyledon, seed (embryonic) leaf, seed lobe; 2. (zoo) cotyledon
Kotyledonarknoten m cotyledonary node
Kotzusammensetzung f faeces composition
Kotzwang m tenesmus
Kovacs' Reagens n Kovacs reagent (microbiology)

Kovarianz f (biom) covariance
Kovarianzanalyse f covariance analysis
Kovarianzmatrix f variance-covariance matrix
Koxa f 1. (ent) coxa; 2. s. Hüfte
KPV s. Klassisches Geflügelpestvirus
Krabbenkaktus m Christmas cactus, Schlumbergera truncata, Zygocactus truncatus
Krachsalat m iceberg [lettuce], crisp-head lettuce, Lactuca sativa convar. incocta var. capitata nidus jaggeri
Kraft f power, force
~/**"alte"** residual fertility (of a soil)
~/**diastatische** diastatic (diastasic) power (of malt)
~/**osmotische** osmotic force
Kraftdynamometer n force dynamometer
Kraftegge f power[-driven] harrow
Kräfteverfall m (vet) marasmus, prostration
Kraftfahrzeugversicherung f für die Land- und Forstwirtschaft agriculture and forestry vehicles insurance
Kraftfutter n feed (grain mixture) concentrate, concentrate [food]
Kraftfutterbehälter m concentrate hopper
Kraftfuttergemisch n, **Kraftfuttermischung** f concentrate mix[ture]
Kraftfuttermischwerk n mixed-feed plant
Kraftfuttermittel n s. Kraftfutter
kraftgetrieben power-driven
Kraftheber m power lift
~/**hydraulischer** hydraulic [power] lift
kräftig strong, vigorous
Kräftigungsmittel n (vet) roborant
Kraftlenkung f power[-assisted] steering
kraftlos (vet) asthenic; flaccid
Kraftlosigkeit f (vet) asthenia
Kraftmesser m dynamometer
Kraftsteckdose f power plug socket
Kraftstecker m power plug
Kraftstoff m fuel • **mit ~ versorgen** to fuel
Kraftstoffbehälter m fuel tank
Kraftstoffeinspritzung f fuel injection
Kraftstofffilter m fuel filter
Kraftstoffpumpe f fuel pump
Kraftstoffverbrauch m fuel consumption
~/**spezifischer** specific fuel consumption
Kraftwerksabwärme f power plant waste heat
Kraftwurz f 1. ginseng (genus Panax); 2. s. Kanadischer Ginseng
Kraftzellstoff m kraft (sulphate) pulp
Kragenblume f (bot) carpesium (genus Carpesium)
Kragenfäule f collar rot (girdle), [apple] crown rot (of pome fruit, caused by Phytophthora cactorum)
Krähe f crow (genus Corvus)
krähen to crow
Krähen n crow
Krähenbeere f crowberry, crakeberry, Empetrum nigrum

Krähenfußgras

Krähenfußgras *n* 1. crowfoot grass, Dactyloctenium aegyptium, Eleusine aegyptiaca; 2. crowfoot grass, Eleusine indica
Krähenfußwegerich *m* buck's horn [plantain], Plantago coronopus
Krähenhorst *m* rookery
Krainer Biene *f* carniolan honey-bee, Apis mellifica carnica
Kralle *f* claw, unguis; pounce, talon *(esp. of raptorial birds)*
Krallenbett *n* quick
Krallengelenk *n* corono-pedal joint, distal interphalangeal joint
Krallenklee *m* [French] serradella, serradilla, Ornithopus sativus
Krallenwinde *f (bot)* cathedral bells, cup and saucer, Cobaea scandens
Krambe *f (bot)* crambe, Crambe abyssinica
Kramerschiene *f (vet)* Kramer's wire splinting
Krammetsvogel *m* fieldfare, *(Am)* fieldpore, Turdus pilaris
Krampf *m (vet)* spasm, cramp
~/**epileptiformer** epileptiform attack
~/**klonischer** clonic spasm
~/**tonischer** tonic spasm
Krampfaderbruch *m (vet)* varicocele
krampfartig, krampfhaft *(vet)* spastic, spasmodic, tetanic
Krampfkolik *f (vet)* spasmodic colic
krampflösend *(vet)* spasmolytic
Krampfseuche *f (vet)* ergotism, ergot poisoning, St. Anthony's fire
krampfstillend *(vet)* spasmolytic
Krampfzittern *n (vet)* tremor
Kran *m* crane
~/**hydraulischer** hydraulic crane
Kranarm *m*, **Kranausleger** *m* [crane] boom, jib[-boom]
kranial *(zoo)* cranial
Kranialnerv *m* cranial nerve
Kranium *n* cranium, head capsule, skull
kranken/an Wipfeldürre *(phyt)* to die back
Krankenabteil *n* sick (hospital) pen *(of an animal house)*
Krankenbucht *f* isolation box
Krankenstall *m* hospital barn
krankhaft pathologic[al]
Krankheit *f* disease, disorder, illness, sickness, ailment, affection *(s. a. under* Erkrankung*)*
~/**allergische** *(vet)* allergosis
~/**anzeigepflichtige** notifiable disease
~/**Aujeszkysche** *(vet)* Aujeszky's disease, infectious bulbar paralysis, pseudorabies, mad itch
~/**auszehrende** *(vet)* wasting disease
~/**Bangsche** *(vet)* Bangs, Bang's disease, brucellosis *(caused by Brucella spp.)*
~/**Bornasche** *(vet)* Borna disease
~/**Brabanter** *(vet)* stockman disease
~ **der Schattenmorelle/Stecklenberger** Stecklenberger disease of cherry *(virosis)*
~ **der Weinrebe/Piercesche** Pierce's disease of vine *(bacteriosis)*
~/**durch Milben hervorgerufene** *(vet)* acariasis
~/**Dürener** *(vet)* stockman disease
~/**endemisch auftretende** endemic
~/**Engel-Recklinghausensche** *(vet)* fibrous osteodystrophy
~/**Englische** *(vet)* rickets
~/**Gilchristsche** *(vet)* North American blastomycosis
~/**Glässersche** Glasser's disease *(of pigs, caused by Haemophilus parasuis)*
~/**Hjärre's** Hjärre's disease *(of fowl)*
~/**Hodgkinsche** *(vet)* lymphogranuloma[tosis]
~/**Johnesche** *(vet)* Johne's disease, chronic specific enteritis, paratuberculosis *(caused by Mycobacterium paratuberculosis)*
~/**knollenübertragene** tuber-borne disease
~/**Mareksche** *(vet)* Marek's disease, MD, fowl (range) paralysis, acute avian leucosis
~/**Mathieusche** *(vet)* infectious icterus
~/**meldepflichtige** notifiable disease
~/**nichtparasitäre** non-parasitic disease
~/**Pfeffinger** cherry rasp leaf *(virosis)*
~/**saatgutbürtige** seed-borne disease
~/**Schweinsberger** straining disease *(of horses)*
~/**Teschener** Teschen (talfan) disease *(virosis of swine)*
~/**Weilsche** *(vet)* Weil's disease, leptospiral jaundice, infectious icterus
~/**Wilsonsche** *(vet)* Wilson's disease, hepatolenticular degeneration
Krankheitsabwehr *f* disease defence
Krankheitsanfälligkeit *f* disease susceptibility
Krankheitsausbreitung *f* disease spread (distribution)
Krankheitsbekämpfung *f* disease control
Krankheitsbereitschaft *f* [pre]disposition, diathesis
Krankheitsbeschreibung *f* nosography
Krankheitsentstehung *f* pathogenesis
krankheitserregend pathogenous, pathogenic, morbific
Krankheitserreger *m* pathogen, disease agent (excitant), disease-causing organism, invader
~/**mikrobieller** microbial pathogen, germ
~/**pilzlicher** fungal pathogen
Krankheitserscheinung *f* symptom
krankheitsfrei disease-free, clean
Krankheitsherd *m* focus
Krankheitslehre *f* pathology, pathobiology, nosology
krankheitsresistent disease-resistant
Krankheitsresistenz *f* disease resistance
Krankheitsträger *m* disease carrier
krankheitsübertragend morbiphor, pestiferous
Krankheitsüberträger *m* disease transmitter (vector); disease carrier
Krankheitsübertragung *f* disease transmission

Krankheitsursache f cause of a disease • **die ~ betreffend** aetiologic[al]
krankheitsverhütend prophylactic
Krankheitsverhütung f prophylaxis, disease prevention
krankheitsverursachend morbific
Krankheitszeichen n symptom, diagnostic
Krankheitszyklus m disease cycle
kränklich sickly, unthrifty
krankmachend pathogenous, pathogenic
krankschießen (hunt) to wound [by a shot]
Kranz m wreath
Kranz-Anatomie f Kranz anatomy (plant physiology)
Kranzarterie f coronary artery (animal anatomy)
kranzförmig (zoo) coronal
Kranzgefäß n coronary vessel
Kranzreißer m wreath shredder
Kranzschlinge f 1. stephanotis (genus Stephanotis); 2. Madagascar jasmin[e], wax flower, Stephanotis floribunda
Krapp m madder (genus Rubia)
Krapprot n madder (dye)
Krappwurzel f madder root
Kraterkrankheit f (phyt) crater disease (caused by Periconia macrospinosa and Rhizoctonia solani)
Kraterzitze f inverted nipple
Kratzband n scraper-chain conveyor
Kratzbeere f 1. dewberry, Rubus caesius; 2. s. Brombeere
Kratzboden m s. Kratzerboden
Kratzdistel f common thistle (genus Cirsium)
Krätze f (vet) sarcoptic mange (scab) (caused esp. by Sarcoptes scabiei)
Krätzemilbe f sarcoptic mange mite, Sarcoptes scabiei
kratzen to scratch, to scrape, to paw
Kratzer m acanthocephalid, thorny-headed worm (division and class Acanthocephala)
Krätzer m rough wine
Kratzerband n scraper belt
Kratzerboden m scraper floor, floor conveyor (of a muck spreader)
Kratzerförderer m s. Kratzerkettenförderer
Kratzerkette f scraper (scraping, gathering) chain
Kratzerkettenentmistungsanlage f dung scraper, scraper-chain dung cleaning plant, (Am) scraper barn cleaner
Kratzerkettenförderer m chain-and-flight conveyor (elevator), scraper[-chain] conveyor
Kratz-Wasch-Anlage f (slaught) brush-wash unit
kraus (bot, zoo) crispate, crisped, curled
Krausblättriger Ampfer m s. Krauser Ampfer
~ Grünkohl m s. Krauskohl
Krause Distel f curly bristle thistle, Carduus crispus
~ Malve f curled mallow, Malva verticillata
~ Winterendivie f curled (curly) endive, Cichorium endivia var. crispum
Kräuselblättrigkeit f crinkle leaf

Kräuselkrankheit f (phyt) leaf curl[ing], curl[ing], curly-leaf disease; beet curly top [disease]
~ der Rebe acarinosis (caused by Phyllocoptes vitis)
~ des Pfirsichs leaf curl of peach, peach [leaf] curl (caused by Taphrina deformans)
Kräuselmilbe f rust mite, Phyllocoptes (Calepitrimerus) vitis
Kräuselmosaikvirus n **der Gartenbohne** garden bean crinkle mosaic virus
kräuseln/sich to crinkle, to curl, to wrinkle, to crumple
Kräuselnekrose f (phyt) crinkle necrosis
~ der Roten Johannisbeere red currant crinkle necrosis, RCCN
Kräuselschopf m [der Rübe], **Kräuselschopfkrankheit** f [beet] curly top [disease]
Kräuselschopfvirus n [beet] curly top virus
Kräuselung f crinkle, crinkling, curl[ing], wrinkling, crimp, crumpling, waviness
Kräuselungsbogen m crimp (of the wool fibre)
Kräuselungsgrad m [der Wolle] degree of crimp
Krauseminze f [German] spearmint, garden mint, Mentha spicata var. crispa
kräusen to krausen, to kraeusen (brewing)
Krauser Ampfer m curled (yellow) dock, cure (sour) dock, Rumex crispus
~ Rhabarber m rhubarb, Rheum rhabarberum
Krauskohl m [curly] kale, curled [kitchen] kale, green cabbage, Brassica oleracea convar. acephala var. sabellica
Kraut n 1. herb, herbaceous (herbage) plant; 2. herbage, foliage; haulm (esp. of beans, peas, potatoes); (Am) vine (esp. of climbers)
~/duftstofflieferndes aromatic herb
Krautabblättermaschine f cabbage stripper
Krautabflammgerät n foliage burner
Krautabscheider m trash catcher
Krautabscheidung f haulm removal (potato harvest)
Krautabtötung f haulm destruction, vine killing
Krautabtötungsmittel n haulm destroyer
Krautabweiser m vine deflector
krautartig herbaceous, herby
Krautbrenner m foliage burner, flame cultivator (weeder)
Krautdroge f herb
Kräuter npl herbage • **~ sammeln** to herborize
Kräuterdecke f herb cover
~/artenreiche mixed herb cover
Kräutergarten m herb garden
Kräuterkäse m spiced cheese
Kräuterkenner m herbalist
Kräutersaft m juice of herbs
Kräutersammeln n herborization
Kräutersammler m herbalist
Kräuterwein m aromatized wine
Kräuterwiese f herb meadow
Krautfang m weeds screen

Krautfänger

Krautfänger *m* leaf (trash) catcher *(sugar beet processing)*
Krautfäule *f (phyt)* foliar blight
~ **der Tomate** late blight of tomato *(caused by Phytopthora infestans)*
Krautfläche *f* haulm area
Krauthäcksler *m* haulm chopper
Krauthaken *m* weed-hook
krautig herbaceous, herby
Kräutlein-rühr-mich-nicht-an *n (bot)* touch-me-not, Impatiens noli-tangere
Krautmäher *m* haulm cutter, foliage mower
Krautpflanze *f* herb, herbaceous (herbage) plant, forb
krautreich herby
Krautschicht *f* herbaceous (field) layer, ground cover, festratum *(plant sociology)*
Krautschläger *m* root topper, haulm stripper (pulverizer)
Krautschneideboot *n* boat-mower, weed-cutting launch, water-weed mowing vessel
Krautschneider *m* weed cutter
Krauttrennung *f* haulm removal *(potato harvest)*
Kraut- und Knollen[braun]fäule *f* **der Kartoffel** potato [late] blight, late blight of potato, potato mildew (mould) *(caused by Phytophthora infestans)*
Krautungsboot *n s.* Krautschneideboot
Krautwerk *n* herb, haulm
Krautziehen *n* haulm pulling
Krautzieher *m*, **Krautziehmaschine** *f* haulm puller (extractor)
Kreatin *n* creatine *(amino-acid)*
Kreatinase *f* creatinase *(enzyme)*
Kreatinin *n* creatinine
Kreatinkinase *f* creatine [phospho]kinase *(enzyme)*
Kreatinphosphat *n* creatine phosphate, phosphocreatine
Kreatinurie *f (vet)* creatinuria
Krebapfel[baum] *m* crab[-apple] *(comprehensive term)*
Krebs *m* 1. *(phyt)* canker; *(vet)* cancer, carcinoma; 2. crayfish
~/**bakterieller** *(phyt)* bacterial canker
~ **des Apfelbaumes** apple [tree] canker *(caused by Nectria galligena)*
krebsartig *(phyt)* cankerous; *(vet)* cancerous
Krebsauge *n* cancer eye, ocular squamous[-cell] carcinoma *(of cattle)*
Krebsbildung *f (vet)* carcinogenesis
krebserzeugend *(vet)* carcinogen[et]ic
Krebsgalle *f (phyt)* cankerous excrescence
Krebsgeschwulst *f (phyt)* canker; *(vet)* cancer, carcinoma
Krebs-Henseleit-Reaktionsweg *m* Krebs-Henseleit pathway, ornithine[-arginine] cycle, urea cycle *(biochemistry)*
krebsig *s.* krebsartig

Krebs-Kronberg-Zyklus *m* glyoxylate cycle *(plant physiology)*
Krebsotter *m s.* Europäischer Nerz
Krebspest *f* crayfish plague *(caused by Aphanomyces astaci)*
Krebstier *n* crustacean *(class Crustacea)*
Krebsvirus *n* oncogenic virus
Krebsweide *f* purple willow, Salix purpurea
Krebs-Zyklus *m* Krebs cycle, tricarboxylic (citric) acid cycle, TCA cycle *(biochemistry)*
Kreide *f* chalk
Kreideboden *m* chalk soil
Kreidemergel *m* chalk marl
Kreisberegnung *f* [centre-]pivot irrigation, circle watering
Kreisberegnungsanlage *f* rotating sprinkler system, revolving irrigation system
Kreiselegge *f* rotary [cross] harrow, circular [spike] harrow
kreiselförmig *(bot)* turbinate[d]
Kreiselgebläse *n* centrifugal fan
Kreiselheuer *m* rotary tedder
Kreiselmäher *m* rotary (drum) mower, rotary scythe
Kreiselpflug *m* rotary plough
Kreiselpumpe *f* centrifugal pump
Kreiselrechwender *m* rotary rake tedder
Kreiselschwader *m* rotary wind-rower
Kreiseltaster *m* sensing wheel, rotary feeler
Kreiselzetter *m* rotary tedder
Kreiselzettwender *m* rotary tedder and turner
Kreisfläche *f (forest)* [tree] basal area, b.a., sectional area [of a single tree]
~/**mittlere** mean basal area
Kreisflächenhaltung *f* basal-area density
Kreisflächenmitteldurchmesser *m* [quadratic] mean diameter, average diameter
Kreisflächenmittelstamm *m* mean basal area tree, stem of mean basal area
Kreisflächenregner *m* rotating (circle) sprinkler
Kreisflächensumme *f* basal area of a whole crop, crop basal area *(timber mensuration)*
Kreisflächenzuwachs *m* basal-area increment *(timber mensuration)*
Kreisflächenzuwachsprozent *n* basal-area increment percent[age]
kreisförmig circular, round; *(bot, zoo)* orbicular, orbiculate[d]
~/**annähernd (fast)** suborbicular
kreisfrüchtig *(bot)* cyclocarpous
Kreiskolbenverdichter *m* Roots blower
Kreislauf *m* 1. cycle; 2. circulation; 3. *s.* Blutkreislauf
~/**biogeochemischer** *(ecol)* biogeochemical cycle
~/**fetaler** foetal circulation
~/**hydrologischer** hydrologic cycle
Kreislaufkollaps *m*, **Kreislaufschock** *m (vet)* [circulatory] shock
Kreislaufstörung *f (vet)* circulatory disorder

Kreuzwirbel

Kreislaufsystem n circulatory system
Kreislaufversagen n, **Kreislaufzusammenbruch** m s. Kreislaufkollaps
Kreisprobefläche f (forest) circular sample plot, radius plot
Kreisregner m s. Kreisflächenregner
Kreisritt m volt[e] (equitation)
Kreissäge f circular (plate, round) saw, (Am) buzzsaw • **mit der ~ geschnitten** rotary-sawn, rotary-cut
~ mit eingesetzten Zähnen inserted-tooth saw
Kreissägeblatt n circular saw-blade, saw disk
Kreissägenschärfautomat m automatic circular saw sharpener
Kreissägewerk circular sawmill, scrag mill
~ mit Mehrblattsägemaschinen gang [saw]mill
krempeln to card (fibre processing)
Krempling m (bot) paxillus (genus Paxillus)
Kren m horse-radish (root vegetable)
Krensäure f crenic acid (a fulvic acid)
Kreolenrind n Criollo (cattle breed)
Kreophage m s. Karnivore
Kreosot n [wood-tar] creosote
Kreosotstrauch m creosote bush (plant), Larrea tridentata (divaricata)
Krepitation f (vet) crepitus
Kresse f 1. cress (comprehensive term); 2. pepperwort, peppergrass (genus Lepidium)
Kressenfeige f (bot) common papaw, Carica papaya
Kressetest m cress test[ing] (bioassay)
Kreta-Berberitze f Cretan barberry, Berberis cretica
Kretische Augenwurz f candy carrot, Athamanta cretensis
Kretischer Saumfarn m table (ribbon) fern, Pteris cretica
Kreuz n haunch, rump (animal body)
Kreuzband n cruciate ligament (animal anatomy)
kreuzbar crossable, hybridizable
Kreuzbarkeit f crossability
Kreuzbein n sacrum (animal anatomy)
Kreuzbeinschlagader f sacral artery
Kreuzbeinwirbel m sacral vertebra
Kreuzbestäubung f (bot) cross-pollination, allogamy, xenogamy
Kreuzblättrige Wolfsmilch f mole (gopher) plant, mole weed, caper euphorbia (spurge), Euphorbia lathyris
Kreuzblume f milkwort (genus Polygala)
kreuzblütig cruciferous
Kreuzblütler m crucifer (family Cruciferae = Brassicaceae)
Kreuzblütler mpl mustard family (family Cruciferae = Brassicaceae) • **die ~ betreffend** cruciferous
Kreuzdarmbeingelenk n sacroiliac articulation (joint)
Kreuzdorn m 1. buckthorn (genus Rhamnus); 2. purging (common) buckthorn, Rhine berry, Rhamnus catharticus

Kreuzdornlaus f buckthorn[-potato] aphid, Aphis nasturtii
kreuzen to cross[-breed], to hybridize, to interbreed
~/nichtverwandte Individuen to outbreed
~/verwandte Individuen to inbreed
~/Zuchttiere erfolgreich to nick
Kreuzen n crossing, cross-breeding, interbreeding
~/diskontinuierliches discontinuous crossing
kreuzförmig cruciate
Kreuzfuchs m cross fox (colour variant of fox)
Kreuzfuchsfell n, **Kreuzfuchspelz** m cross fox
Kreuzgalopp m cross-legged gallop
kreuzgegenständig (bot, zoo) decussate
Kreuzimmunität f (vet) cross-immunity
Kreuzinfektion f (vet) cross-infection
Kreuzkraut n 1. groundsel, ragwort, ragweed (genus Senecio); 2. [common] groundsel, Senecio vulgaris
Kreuzkümmel m cum[m]in, Cuminum cyminum
Kreuzotter f [common] viper, adder, Vipera berus
Kreuzpflanzung f (forest) quincuncial (quincunx) planting
Kreuzreaktion f cross-reaction (immunology)
Kreuzrebe f cross vine, Bignonia capreolata
Kreuzresistenz f cross-resistance
Kreuzsalbei m Greek sage, Salvia triloba
Kreuzung f 1. cross, crossbreed, interbreed; 2. s. Kreuzen
~/diallele diallel crossing
~ nichtverwandter Individuen outcrossing, outbreeding
~/reziproke reciprocal crossing
~ verwandter Individuen inbreeding
Kreuzungsbeutel m pollination bag (plant breeding)
Kreuzungseltern pl crossing parents
Kreuzungsfeld n crossfield (wood anatomy)
Kreuzungsmaterial n crossing material
Kreuzungsmutterschaf n cross-bred ewe
Kreuzungsnachkommenschaft f cross-bred progeny
Kreuzungsprodukt n s. Kreuzung 1.
Kreuzungsprogramm n cross-breeding programme, crossing programme
Kreuzungsrasse f cross-breed
Kreuzungstier n cross animal
kreuzungsunverträglich intersterile
Kreuzungsunverträglichkeit f intersterility, cross-incompatibility
Kreuzungsverfahren n/**diskontinuierliches** discontinuous crossing
Kreuzungsverhalten n crossing behaviour
Kreuzungswolle f cross-bred wool
Kreuzungszüchtung f cross-breeding, amphimixis
Kreuzverschlag m (vet) lumbago (of horses)
kreuzweise diallel (breeding)
Kreuzwinkel m posting square (of a frame saw)
Kreuzwirbel m sacral vertebra

Kreuzzuchtwolle

Kreuzzuchtwolle *f* cross-bred wool
Krickelwild *n s.* Gamswild
Krickente *f* common teal, teal [duck], Anas crecca
Kriebelkorn *n* ergot, Claviceps purpurea
Kriebelkrankheit *f (vet)* ergotism, ergot poisoning, St. Anthony's fire
Kriebelmücke *f* blackfly *(family Simuliidae)*
kriechen to creep; *(bot)* to trail
kriechend *(bot, zoo)* repent, reptant
Kriechende Hauhechel *f* [common, twining] restharrow, Ononis repens
Kriechender Hahnenfuß *m* butter daisy, creeping buttercup, Ranunculus repens
~ Klee *m* white (Dutch, honeysuckle) clover, shamrock, Trifolium repens
Kriechenpflaume *f* [wild] damson, bullace, Prunus domestica ssp. insititia
Kriechgang *m* creep speed *(e.g. of a tractor)*
Kriechganggetriebe *n* creep speed gear
Kriechgatter *n* creep gate
Kriechgünsel *m* bugle, [carpet] bugleweed, Ajuga reptans
Kriechpflanze *f* creeping (trailing) plant, creeper, trailer
Kriechrose *f* field (Ayrshire) rose, Rosa arvensis
Kriechsproß *m* creeping stem
Kriechtier *n* reptile *(class Reptilia)*
Kriechtrieb *m* creeping shoot, runner
Kriechwacholder *m* creeping juniper, Juniperus horizontalis
Kriechweide *f* 1. creeping (dwarf) willow, Salix repens; 2. [forward-]creep grazing *(for lambs)*
Kriechwüchsige Erdnuß *f* runner-type peanut, Arachis hypogaea ssp. hypogaea
Kriechwurzel *f* creeper
Kriechzaun *m* creep fence
Kriging-Technik *f* kriging *(of soil-physical examinations)*
Krilium *n* krilium *(soil conditioner)*
Krillmehl *n* krill meal *(feed)*
Krimmer *m* krimmer *(sheep pelt)*
Krippe *f* crib, manger, feeding rack, trough
Krippenbeißen *n* crib-biting *(vice of horses)*
Krippenbeißer *n* crib biter, cribber
Krippenfläche *f* trough space
Krippenlänge *f* manger length
Kristallbildner *m* crystallizer *(sugar manufacture)*
kristallführend crystalliferous *(wood call)*
Kristallgehalt *m* crystal content *(e.g. of sugar)*
Kristallgröße *f* crystal size *(e.g. of sugar)*
Kristallisation *f* crystallization
Kristallisationsschema *n* boiling system *(sugar manufacture)*
Kristallisator *m* crystallizer
Kristallisierung *f* crystallization
Kristallit *m* crystallite, micelle, micell[a] *(of cellulose)*
Kristallkeimbildner *m s.* Kristallbildner

374

Kristallsuspension *f* massecuite *(sugar manufacture)*
Kristalltrübung *f* crystal turbidity *(defect of wine)*
Kristallviolettvakzine *f (vet)* crystal violet vaccine
Kristallzucker *m* crystal (table) sugar
Kroatzbeere *f s.* Brombeere
Krokus *m (bot)* crocus *(genus Crocus)*
Kronbein *n* short pastern, second phalanx *(animal anatomy)*
Kronblatt *n (bot)* petal • **mit einem ~** monopetalous
kronblattähnlich petaloid
kronblattlos apetalous
Krone *f* 1. crown, head *(e.g. of a tree)*; 2. corolla *(of flowers)*; 3. coronet *(of a horse's pastern)*; 4. *s.* Kronenende 2. • **die ~ abflachen** to flatten the head *(orcharding)* • **mit abgestorbener ~** black-topped *(tree)* • **mit freier ~ wachsend** open-growing, free-growing *(tree)*
~/naturgemäße semicultured crown
~ über Zwischenveredelung/veredelte varietal top
~/überbaute imbalanced head
Kronenabflachung *f* flattening of the head
Kronenanemone *f* crown (poppy) anemone, Anemone coronaria
Kronenansatz *m* crown base
Kronenapfel *m* American (sweet) crab-apple, sweet-scented crab, Malus coronaria [ssp. coronaria]
kronenartig coronal, coronary
Kronenaufbau *m* crown (tree) structure, structure of the head
~/naturbeschränkter semiformal structure of the head
~/naturentfernter formal structure of the head
~/naturgemäßer seminatural structure of the head
~/naturnaher nearly natural structure of the head
Kronenauffang *m s.* Kroneninterzeption
Kronenausrichtung *f* canopy position
Kronenbau *m s.* Kronenaufbau
Kronenbruch *m* crown break[age]
Kronendach *n* canopy [cover], tree canopy, forest (leaf) canopy, shelter • **das ~ überragend** predominant
~/durchbrochenes broken canopy
~/offenes open canopy
Kronendichte *f* crown density
Kronendurchforstung *f (forest)* crown thinning
Kronendurchlaß *m* throughfall [through the canopy]
Kronendurchmesser *m* crown diameter
~/mittlerer crown mean diameter (width)
Kronendurchmesserverhältnis *n* crown diameter ratio *(tree mensuration)*
Kronenende *n* 1. bud end *(of the potato tuber)*; 2. sur-royal antler, crown antler *(of red deer)*
Kronenentwicklung *f*/**einseitige** lop development *(of a tree)*

Kronenerneuerungsschnitt m renewal pruning *(orcharding)*
Kronenfäule f der Erdbeere vascular collapse of strawberries *(caused by Phytophthora cactorum)*
Kronenfeuer n *(forest)* crown[ing] fire
Kronenfläche f crown area
Kronenflächenindex m crown-area index *(tree mensuration)*
Kronenform f crown form, head shape, form of the head; tree form
Kronengelenk n pastern-joint, fetlock[-joint], proximal interphalangeal joint *(animal anatomy)*
Kronengerüst n head structure, framework *(e.g. of a fruit-tree)*
Kronengestaltung f formation of [the] crown
Kronengrundfläche f crown projection area, foliage area *(tree mensuration)*
Kronengrundriß m plan view of the head
Kronengüteklasse f crown quality class
Kronenhöhe f crown height *(tree mensuration)*
~/**mittlere** mean crown height
~/**obere** upper crown height
~/**untere** lower crown height
Kroneninterzeption f crown interception, interception by canopy *(e.g. of precipitations)*
Kronenkamm m buttercup comb *(of fowl)*
Kronenkarte f crown map
Kronenklasse f *(forest)* crown class (status), social position
Kronenlage f canopy position, position of the head
Kronenlänge f crown length (depth)
~/**mittlere** mean crown length
Kronenlängenprozent n crown length ratio, crown percent
Kronenlichtnelke f rose campion, mullein pink, Lychnis coronaria
Kronenmantelfläche f crown surface area
Kronenmasse f crown weight
Kronenmittelpunkt m/**geometrischer** form point *(tree mensuration)*
Kronennaht f coronary suture *(animal anatomy)*
Kronenprojektion f crown projection
Kronenprojektionsfläche f crown projection area, crown cover (spread, plan)
Kronenprozent n crown ratio
Kronenrand m s. Kronrand
Kronenrückschnitt m heading
Kronenschirm m s. Kronendach
Kronenschluß m canopy closure, crown closure (contact)
~/**dichter** close canopy
~/**horizontaler** horizontal [crown] closure
~/**vertikaler** vertical [crown] closure
~/**vollständiger** complete (closed, continuous) canopy
Kronenschlußgrad m canopy cover [density], canopy density
Kronenschnitt m crown reduction; paring of crowns

Kronensüßklee m Spanish esparcet, cockshead, Hedysarum coronarium
Kronenüberbauung f imbalanced head *(orcharding)*
Kronenveredelung f topworking, top grafting
Kronenvolumen n crown volume
Kronenwachstum n crown growth
Kronenwinkel m angle at the crown apex *(of woody plants)*
Kronenwucherblume f garland chrysanthemum, crown daisy, Chrysanthemum coronarium
Kronenwurzel f crown root *(e.g. of grasses)*
Krone-Wurzel-Verhältnis n crown-root ratio
Krongelenk n s. Kronengelenk
Kronismus m infanticide
Kronlederhaut f coronary corium *(of hoof or claw)*
Kronrand m coronary band *(of hoof or claw)*
Kronrand[horn]spalte f *(vet)* sand-crack
Kronrinne f coronary sulcus *(of hoof or claw)*
Kronsbeere f red bilberry (whortleberry), cowberry, Vaccinium vitis-idaea
Kronwicke f crown vetch *(genus Coronilla)*
Kropf m 1. *(zoo)* crop, craw, maw *(of birds)*; 2. honey sac (stomach) *(of bee)*; 3. *(vet)* goitre, struma
kropfartig strumose
Kröpfer m s. Kropftaube
Kropferweiterung f *(vet)* crop-bound
kropferzeugend goitrogenic, goitrogenous
kropfig strumose
Kropfkrankheit f s. Kohlhernie
Kropfleimkraut n bladder campion, maiden's-tears, Silene vulgaris (cucubalus)
Kropfmilch f [**der Tauben**] pigeon's milk, pigeon crop milk
Kropftaube f pouter [pigeon], cropper *(group of breeds)*
Kropftympanie f *(vet)* sour crop
Kropfverstopfung f *(vet)* impacted crop, crop-bound
Kröte f toad *(genus Bufo)*
Krötenbinse f *(bot)* toad rush, Juncus bufonius
Krötenhautkrankheit f valsa *(of pome and stone fruit, caused by Leucostoma cincta = Valsa leucostoma)*
Krötenlilie f toad lily *(genus Tricyrtis)*
Krotonöl n croton oil
Krotowine f *(soil)* crotovina, crotovine
Krugfarn m rabbit's-foot fern, Davallia fejeensis
krugförmig *(bot)* olliform, urceolate
Krukenbaum m *(bot)* monkey pot, sapucaia, sapucaya, Lecythis urnigera (ollaria)
Krume f topsoil, surface soil, tilth
Krümel m(n) crumb *(e.g. of soil)*
Krümelbildner m aggregating agent
Krümelbildung f crumb formation
Krümelegge f crumbling (pulverizing) harrow, pulverizer
Krümelfutter n fines

Krümelfütterung

Krümelfütterung *f* crumb feeding
Krümelgefüge *n* crumb structure
krümelig crumbly, friable
Krümeligkeit *f* crumbliness, friability, friableness
krümeln to crumble
Krümelpflug *m* pulverizer plough
Krümelrechen *m* crumbling rake
Krümelstabilität *f* crumb (aggregate) stability, stability of aggregation
Krümelstruktur *f* crumb structure
Krümelungsbereitschaft *f* friability
Krümelwalze *f* crumbling roller, clod crusher (breaker)
Krumenbasislockerer *m* pan breaker
Krumenbasislockerung *f* plough pan loosening
Krumenbasisverdichtung *f* plough pan (sole)
Krumendünger *m* plough-down fertilizer
Krumenpacker *m* land packer, furrow press, compactor
Krumenvertiefung *f* topsoil deepening
Krümler *m* crumbler
Krummdarm *m* ileum
Krummdarmentzündung *f (vet)* ileitis
krummgewachsen crooked-grown
Krummhals *m (bot)* bugloss *(genus Lycopsis)*
Krummhalskürbis *m (bot)* summer crookneck, Cucurbita pepo ssp. pepo var. oleifera convar. torticollis
Krummholz *n* curved (knee) timber, krummholz
Krummholzbestand *m* elfin woodland (forest)
Krummholzformation *f* elfin-wood formation
Krummholzkiefer *f* mountain (dwarf) pine, Pinus mugo (montana)
Krummholzstufe *f* elfin-wood belt *(plant ecology)*
krummschaftig crooked-stemmed
Krummschaftigkeit *f* crookedness of stem
Krummschwanz *m (vet)* kinky tail
krummstämmig crooked-stemmed
Krummstämmigkeit *f* crookedness of stem
Krümmungsbewegung *f (bot)* tropism
~/lichtreizbedingte photonastic movement
krummzähnig *(bot, zoo)* curvidentate
Krummzähniger Tannenborkenkäfer *m* fir bark-beetle, Pityokteines (Ips) curvidens
Kruppade *f* croupade *(equestrian sport)*
Kruppbohne *f* bush bean, Phaseolus vulgaris var. nanus
Kruppe *f* croup *(of animal's body)*; crupper *(of horse)*
Krüppelbestand *m (forest)* scrub stand
Krüppelgurke *f* nubbin
Krüppelholz *n* scrub
krüppelig *s.* krüppelwüchsig
Krüppelwuchs *m* crooked (stunted) growth, stunt; bent growth *(of timber)*
krüppelwüchsig crooked-grown *(timber)*
Kruskal-Wallis-Test *m (biom)* Kruskal-Wallis test
Krustazee *f s.* Krustentier
Kruste *f* crust; incrustation

Krustenbildung *f* incrustation
Krustentier *n* crustacean *(class Crustacea)*
kruzifer *(bot)* cruciferous
Kruzifere *f* crucifer *(family Cruciferae = Brassicaceae)*
Kruziferen *fpl* mustard family *(family Cruciferae = Brassicaceae)* • **die ~ betreffend** cruciferous
kryobiochemisch cryobiochemical
Kryobiologie *f* cryobiology
Kryochirurgie *f (vet)* cryosurgery
Kryodesikkation *f s.* Gefriertrocknung
Kryoelektronenmikroskopie *f* cryoelectron microscopy
Kryomikroskopie *f* cryomicroscopy
kryophil cryophilic
Kryophyt *m* cryophyte
Kryoprotektivum *n*, **Kryoprotektor** *m* cryoprotectant
Krypten *fpl/Lieberkühnsche* intestinal glands
kryptogam *(bot)* cryptogamic, cryptogamous
Kryptogame *f* cryptogam
Kryptogramm *n* cryptogram *(virology)*
Kryptokokkose *f (vet)* cryptococcosis, European blastomycosis *(caused by Cryptococcus neoformans)*
Kryptomerie *f (gen)* cryptomerism, latency
Kryptomull *m (soil)* crypto-mull
Kryptophyt *m* cryptophyte, geophyte
Kryptopodsol[boden] *m (soil)* latent podzol
kryptorchid cryptorchid
Kryptorchide *m* cryptorchid, ridgeling, rig[g]
Kryptorchismus *m* cryptorch[id]ism
Kryptosporidieninfektion *f*, **Kryptosporidiose** *f (vet)* cryptosporidiosis
KSpKV *s.* Kartoffelspindelknollenviroid
KTP *s.* Kurztagpflanze
Kubagras *n* Tunis grass, Sorghum halepense
Kubajute *f* Queensland hemp, Cuba jute, Sida rhombifolia
Kubaspinat *m* winter purslane, *(Am)* miners lettuce, Montia perfoliata
Kubatur *f s.* Kubikinhalt
Kubebe *f* cubeb *(fruit)*
Kubebenpfeffer *m* Java (tailed) pepper, Piper cubeba
Kübel *m* bucket *(e.g. of an elevator)*; tub *(as for flowers)*
Kübelpflanze *f* tub plant
kubieren to cube, to scale *(timber)*
Kubierung *f* cubing, calculation of cubic content, scaling *(of timber)*
Kubierungsformel *f* cubing (volume) formula
Kubierungstafel *f* cubic scale, log volume table, log rule, outturn table
Kubikfuß *m* **[Schichtholz, Stapelholz]** stacked cubic foot
Kubikinhalt *m* cubic content
~/wirklicher true volume *(timber mensuration)*

Kubikmeter *m* **feste Holzsubstanz** cubic metre solid, solid metre
~ **Stapelvolumen** cubic metre of piled wood, stacked cubic metre, stere
Kubiktabelle *f*, **Kubiktafel** *f s.* Kubierungstafel
kubizieren *s.* kubieren
Küchenabfall *m* kitchen waste, garbage, pig's wash, [pig]swill
Küchenapfel *m* cooking (culinary) apple
Küchengarten *m* kitchen garden (ground), vegetable (pot) garden, kaleyard
Küchengemüse *f* bread-and-butter-vegetable
Küchenkraut *n* kitchen (culinary) herb, pot-herb
Küchenkräuter *npl* small salads
Küchenkerbel *m* [garden, salad] chervil, Anthriscus cerefolium ssp. cerefolium
Kuchenmehl *n* pastry (biscuit) flour
Küchenobstsorte *f* culinary (cooking) variety
Küchenschabe *f* common (oriental, black) cockroach, black-beetle, Blatta orientalis
Küchenschelle *f s.* Kuhschelle
Küchensorte *f s.* Küchenobstsorte
Küchenzwiebel *f* onion, Allium cepa [var. cepa]
Kücken *n s.* Küken
Kuckucksblume *f*, **Kuckucksnelke** *f* meadow pink, ragged robin, Lychnis flos-cuculi
Kuckucksspeichel *m* cuckoo spit[tle]
Kudzu *f* 1. kudzu [bean], Pueraria lobata (thunbergiana); 2. tropical kudzu, Pueraria phaseoloides
Kufe *f* 1. skid (for sliding); 2. brewing vat
Kufentaster *m* skid feeler (of a beet harvester)
Küfer *m* cellarer, cellarman, cellarmaster, wine dresser
Kugel *f*/**Nissensche** milk globule
Kugelamarant *m* 1. globe amaranth (genus Gomphrena); 2. globe amaranth, bachelor's button[s], Gomphrena globosa
Kugelbakterium *n* coccus
Kugelblume *f* globe daisy, globularia (genus Globularia)
Kugelbrause *f* ball rose (of a watering can)
Kugeldistel *f* 1. globe thistle (genus Echinops); 2. globe thistle, Echinops sphaerocephalus
Kugelfangprofil *n* ball guide cone (of the p.t.o. shaft)
Kugelfichte *f* ball-shaped spruce
kugelförmig globose, globular
Kugelgelenk *n* ball[-and-socket] joint, multiaxial joint (animal anatomy)
Kugelherz *n* **des Huhns** round-heart disease of fowl, fatal syncope of fowl, toxic heart degeneration of fowl
Kugelhülse *f* ball bush (of the p.t.o. shaft)
kugelig globose, globular
Kugelkäfer *m* hump (mite) beetle, hump mite, Gibbium psylloides
kugelköpfig sphaerocephalous
Kugellager *n* ball-bearing
Kugellagerung *f* ball-bearing

Kugelmalve *f* globe mallow (genus Sphaeralcea)
Kugelmühle *f* ball mill (crusher), jar mill
Kugelmühlenvermahlung *f* ball-mill grinding
Kugelprimel *f* [drumstick] primrose, denticulate primula, Primula denticulata
Kugelratschenkupplung *f* ball-type safety clutch
kugelrund globose, globular
Kuh *f* cow
~/**frischmelkende** fresh cow
~/**geprüfte** recorded cow
~/**hartmelkende** hard milker
~/**hornlose** mulley
~/**kalbende** calver
~/**milchleistungsgeprüfte** [milk-]recorded cow
~/**rindernde** buller, bulling
~/**schwer melkbare** hard milker
~/**stierige (stiersüchtige)** *s.* ~/rindernde
~/**trächtige** calver
~/**umbullende (umrindernde)** repeat-breeder cow
Kuhaylan-Stamm *m* Keheilan (of Arabian horse)
Kuhbaum *m* cow (milk) tree, Brosimum galactodendron (utile)
Kuhbehandlungsbox *f* cow treatment box
Kuhbehandlungskipptisch *m* cow treatment tipping table
Kuhbehandlungskissen *n* cow treatment air cushion
Kuhbehandlungsstand *m* cow treatment box
Kuhblume *f* dandelion, horse gowan, Taraxacum officinale
Kuhbohne *f* cowpea, southern (black-eyed) pea, Vigna unguiculata ssp. unguiculata
Kuhbutter *f* cow butter
Kuhbutterfett *n* cow milk fat
Kuhdung *m* cow dung (manure)
Kuherbse *f s.* Kuhbohne
Kuhfladen *m* cow-pat
Kuhfleisch *n* cow beef
Kuhgeruch *m* cowiness (milk defect) • ~ **aufweisend** cowy (milk)
Kuhgeschmack *m* cowiness (milk defect) • ~ **aufweisend** cowy (milk)
Kuhglocke *f* cowbell
Kuhgülle *f* cow[-dung] slurry
Kuhhaut *f* cowhide
Kuhherde *f* cow herd
kuhhessig cow-hocked (hindlimb conformation)
Kuhhessigkeit *f* cow-hocked conformation, cow hocks (of hindlimbs)
Kuhhirt *m* cowman, cowherd, cowboy, neatherd, (Am) cowpoke, cowpuncher, cowhand
Kuhindex *m* cow index
Kuhkalb *n* heifer (cow) calf
Kuhkäse *m* cow's-milk cheese, cow cheese
Kuhkohl *m* cow (tree) cabbage, Jersey kale, Brassica oleracea var. acephala subvar. plana
Kuhkraut *n* cow cockle, soap-wort, Vaccaria hispanica (pyramidata)

Kühlanlage

Kühlanlage *f* refrigerating plant, cooling plant (system)
Kuhleder *m* cowhide
kühlen to cool [down], to chill; to refrigerate *(esp. food)*
~/**mit Eis** to ice
~/**mit Luft** to air
Kühler *m* cooler, radiator *(s. a. Kühlvorrichtung)*
Kühlfleisch *n s.* Gefrierfleisch
Kühlflüssigkeit *f* refrigeration fluid
Kühlhaus *n* cold store
Kühlhausbutter *f* cold-stored butter
Kühlhausei *n* [cold-]storage egg, refrigerated (refrigerator) egg
Kühlkonservierung *f* chilling (freezing) preservation
Kühllager *n* cold store
Kühllagerung *f* cold (cool, refrigerator) storage
Kühlluft *f* cooling air
Kühlmittel *n* cooling agent, coolant, refrigerant
Kühlschiff *n* coolship *(brewing)*
Kühlschirm *m* water wall *(sugar manufacture)*
Kühlschlange *f* attemperator, cooling coil
Kühlsole *f* [refrigerating] brine
Kühlsystem *n* cooling (refrigeration) system
Kühltank *m* cooling (refrigerating) tank
Kühltoleranz *f* chilling tolerance
Kühlturm *m* cooling tower
Kühlung *f* cooling, refrigeration *(esp. of food)*
Kühlungskristallisation *f* cooling crystallization *(sugar manufacture)*
Kühlungskristallisator *m* cooler-crystallizer
Kühlvorrichtung *f* cooler, chilling device; refrigerator *(esp for food)*
Kühlwasserpumpe *f* cooling-water circulating pump
Kuhmilch *f* [cow] milk, milch
Kuhmilchbaum *m* cow (milk) tree, Brosimum galactodendron (utile)
Kuhmilchfett *n* cow milk fat
Kuhmilchkäse *m* cow's-milk cheese, cow cheese
Kuhmist *m s.* Kuhdung
Kuhpocken *pl (vet)* cowpox
~/**falsche (unechte)** false cowpox *(virosis)*
Kuhschelle *f* pulsatilla, pasque (paschal) flower *(genus Pulsatilla)*
Kuhstall *m* cowshed, cow barn, cow (dairy cattle) house, byre, shippen, shippon
Küken *n* chick
Kükenaufzucht *f* chick rearing, brooding
Kükenaufzuchtfutter *n* chick mash (starter)
Kükenaufzuchtstall *m* brooder house
Kükenbehandlung *f* chick handling
Kükenei *n* pullet egg
Kükenenzephalomalazie *f (vet)* crazy chick disease
Kükenkarussell *n* chick carrousel
Kükenmasse *f* chick weight

Kükenödemkrankheit *f (vet)* chick oedema disease, CED, congestive heart failure, toxic fat disease, water belly
Kükenring *m* confinement ring, hoverguard
Kükenruhr *f* [/**Rote**] *(vet)* coccidiosis in chickens
Kükensortierer *m* chick sexer *(worker)*
Kükensortiertisch *m* chick-sorting table
Kükensortierung *f* chick sorting
~ **nach Geschlecht** chick sexing
Kükenstall *m* brooder house
Kükenzählgerät *n* chick counter
Kulisse *f (forest)* coulisse, belt of trees, *(Am)* leave strip
Kulissenschlagbetrieb *m* alternate clear-strip system
Kultivar *f s.* Kulturpflanzensorte
Kultivator *m s.* Grubber
kultivierbar 1. cultiva[ta]ble, arable, tillable, reclaimable *(soil)*; 2. cultivable, growable *(crop)*
~/**nicht** non-arable, irreclaimable *(soil)*
Kultivierbarkeit *f* cultivability, arability, land capability
kultivieren 1. to cultivate, to farm, to till, to subdue *(a soil)*; 2. to grow, to rear, to husband, *(Am)* to tame *(a crop)*; to culture *(bacteria)*
Kultivierung *f* cultivation
kultiviert cultivated, *(Am)* tame
~/**in Nährlösung** solution-grown
Kultosol *m* anthropogenic soil
Kultur *f* 1. culture; crop; 2. *(forest)* young plantation; 3. *s.* Kultivierung
~/**abzuhütende** fold[ing] crop
~/**bodenunabhängige** soilless culture
~/**einjährige** one-year crop, annual [field] crop
~/**erdelose** soilless culture
~/**ertragreiche** good cropper
~/**geschützte** protected crop
~/**getränkeliefernde [pflanzliche]** beverage crop
~/**kontinuierliche** continuous culture *(microbiology)*
~/**landwirtschaftliche** [agricultural] crop
~/**nahrungsmittelliefernde** food crop
~/**pflanzenbauliche** crop
~/**stärkeliefernde** starch crop
~/**stationäre** batch culture
~/**technische** industrial crop
~/**überbaute** cloched crop *(horticulture)*
~/**unkrautunterdrückende** smother crop
~ **unter Glas** cultivation under glass
~/**unter Glas angezogene** glass-raised crop
~/**zuckerliefernde** sugar crop
~/**zwischengepflanzte** intercrop
Kulturarbeiten *fpl s.* Kulturpflege
Kulturbanane *f* banana, plantain, Musa x paradisiaca (sapientum)
Kulturbaumwolle *f* cotton *(genus Gossypium)*
Kulturbegründung *f (forest)* plantation establishment
Kulturbiotop *n* cultivation biotope

Kulturbiozönose f *(ecol)* agrobiocoenosis, agrocoenosis
Kulturboden m cultivated (agricultural) soil, tilth
Kulturchampignon m cultivated mushroom, Agaricus bisporus
~/weißhütiger (weißköpfiger) white button mushroom *(strain of Agaricus bisporus)*
Kulturensammlung f culture collection
kulturfähig s. kultivierbar
Kulturfiltrat n culture filtrate
Kulturfläche f cultivated area
Kulturflora f cultivated flora
Kulturforst m cultivated (man-made) forest
Kulturgefäß n pot
Kulturgrasland n cultivated grassland
Kulturhefe f industrial yeast, culture[d] yeast
Kulturkartoffel m [Irish, white] potato, Solanum tuberosum
Kulturkasten m frame *(horticulture)*
Kulturland n *(Am)* cropland *(s. a.* Kulturboden*)*
• ~ **aufsuchend** *(ecol)* synanthropic
Kulturlandschaft f cultural (man-made) landscape
Kulturlösung f culture solution (liquid), [nutrient] broth *(biotechnology)*
Kulturmedium n [culture] medium
Kulturpflanze f crop [plant], cultivated (economic) plant *(s. a. under* Pflanze*)*
~/garefördernde renovating crop
~/garezehrende exhausting crop
Kulturpflanzenanbau m crop husbandry *(for compounds s. under* Pflanzenbau*)*
Kulturpflanzenart f crop species
Kulturpflanzenbestand m crop stand
Kulturpflanzenbewässerung f crop irrigation
Kulturpflanzenernährung f crop nutrition
Kulturpflanzenertrag m crop yield
Kulturpflanzenforschung f crop science
Kulturpflanzengeographie f crop geography
Kulturpflanzenkrankheit f crop disease
Kulturpflanzenmimikry f crop mimicry *(e.g. of weeds)*
Kulturpflanzenökologie f crop ecology
Kulturpflanzenphysiologie f crop physiology
Kulturpflanzenschädling m crop pest
Kulturpflanzensorte f [crop] cultivar, cv., cultivated (crop plant) variety, cultigen
Kulturpflanzenzüchtung f crop breeding
Kulturpflege f crop cultivation, cultural operations; *(forest)* tending of young plantations, weeding
Kulturplan m planting plan
Kulturpreiselbeere f [American, large] cranberry, crowberry, fen-berry, Vaccinium macrocarpon
Kulturrasse f [improved] breed
Kulturröhrchen n culture tube
Kultursorte f select cultivar *(s. a.* Kulturpflanzensorte*)*
Kultursteppe f *(ecol)* artificial steppe, man-made prairie

Kultursubstrat n culture substrate, [growth, growing] medium
Kulturtechnik f culture (culturing) technique
Kultur- und Jungwuchspflegemaßnahmen fpl cultural operations
Kulturverfahren n culture method
Kulturwachstum n *(forest)* growth of young plantations
Kulturwald m cultivated (man-made, artificial) forest
Kulturweide f [cultivated, improved, sown] pasture
Kulturzustand m **des Bodens** [soil] tilth
Kumachlor n coumachlor *(rodenticide)*
Kumbapfeffer m African pepper, Xylopia aethiopica
Kumis m s. Kumys
Kümmel m 1. caraway, Carum carvi; 2. caraway [seed], cumin
Kümmelgelbscheckungsvirus n caraway yellow mottle virus
Kümmelkorn n s. Kümmel 2.
Kümmelmotte f carrot moth, Depressaria nervosa
Kümmerer m weakling, scallywag, scal[l]awag, starveling, runt, scrub; shott *(esp. said of sheep)*
Kümmerform f scrub *(plant)*
Kümmerfrucht f *(bot)* button
kümmern to grow sickly
Kümmerwuchs m stunted growth, dwarfism, dwarfishness, nanism; unthriftiness
~ **mit korkartigen Gewebewucherungen** *(phyt)* corky stunt
kümmerwüchsig dwarfed, dwarfish
Kummet n [horse-]collar
Kummetdeckel m housing
Kummetgeschirr n collar harness
Kummetkissen n sweat pad
Kumquat[pflanze] f *(bot)* kumquat, cumquat *(genus Fortunella)*
Kumt n s. Kummet
Kumulation f cumulation
Kumulationsgift n cumulative poison
Kumulonimbus m cumulonimbus [cloud]
Kumulus m cumulus [cloud]
Kumys m, **Kumyß** m koumiss, kumis[s] *(fermented mare's milk)*
Kunde f mark of mouth *(of horse's incisors)*
Kundebohne f cowpea, southern (black-eyed) pea, Vigna unguiculata ssp. unguiculata
Kundebohnenmosaikvirus n cowpea mosaic virus, CpMV
Kundebohnenringfleckenvirus n cowpea ring spot virus
Kundekäfer m cowpea weevil, Callosobruchus (Bruchus) chinensis
Kunigundenkraut n water hemp, hemp agrimony, hempweed, Eupatorium cannabinum
Kunstbestand m *(forest)* artificial stand (crop)
Kunstbiene f buzzle *(pollinating device)*

Kunstdünger

Kunstdünger *m* artificial fertilizer (manure), commercial fertilizer
Kunstforst *m s.* Kulturwald
Kunstglucke *f* artificial mother, brooder
Kunstlicht *n* artificial light
Kunstlichtregime *n* light regime
Kunstmist *m* artificial manure
Kunstschwarm *m (api)* artificial (shook) swarm
Kunststoff... *s. a.* Plastik...
Kunststoffbeute *(api)* plastic hive
Kunststoffmulch *m* plastic mulch
Kunststoffolie *f* plastic film (foil)
Kunstverjüngung *f (forest)* artificial regeneration (reproduction)
Kunstwabe *f (api)* [comb] foundation
Kupferacetarsenit *n*, **Kupferarsenitacetat** *n* copper acetoarsenite, Paris green *(insecticide, anthelminthic)*
Kupferbrühe *f* copper spray
Kupferdüngemittel *n* copper fertilizer
kupferfarbig cupreous, coppery
Kupferfungizid *n* copper fungicide
Kupferhydroxidlösung *f*/**ammoniakalische** *s.* Kupferoxidammoniak
Kupferkalkbrühe *f* Bordeaux mixture *(fungicide)*
Kupfermangel *m* copper deficiency; *(vet)* hypocupraemia
Kupfermangelkrankheit *f* neonatal (enzootic) ataxia, sway-back, swingback *(of sheep lambs)*
Kupferoxid *n* cuprous oxide *(fungicide)*
Kupferoxidammoniak *n* ammoniacal copper hydroxide, cuprammonium [solution], cuoxam, Schweizer's reagent *(solvent)*
Kupferrote Dörrobstmotte *f* Indian meal moth, Plodia interpunctella
Kupfersodabrühe *f* Burgundy mixture, soda bordeaux *(fungicide)*
Kupferspritzbrühe *f* copper spray
Kupferstaub *m* copper dust *(fungicide)*
Kupferstecher *m* six-toothed spruce bark-beetle, six-dentated engraver beetle, Pityogenes (Ips) chalcographus
Kupfersulfat *n* copper sulphate
Kupfertoxizität *f* copper toxicity
Kupfervergiftung *f (vet)* copper poisoning
Kupfervitriol *n* copper vitriol
Kupfervitriolkalkbrühe *f* Bordeaux mixture *(fungicide)*
Kupffersche Sternzelle *f* Kupffer cell
Kupiereisen *n* docking (tailing) iron
kupieren to dock, to round
~/**den Schnabel** to debeak
~/**den Schwanz** to tail, to dock
~/**die Kehllappen** to dewattle *(fowl)*
~/**die Zehenkrallen** to detoe *(young fowl)*
Kupiermesser *n* docking knife
kupiert *(soil)* truncate[d]
Kuppel *f (zoo)* cupule

kuppeln 1. to couple, to hitch *(e.g. field implements)*; 2. to clutch
Kupplung *f* 1. coupling; 2. clutch
~/**ausrückbare (formschlüssige)** positive clutch
~/**hydraulische** hydraulic coupling
~/**hydrostatische** hydrostatic clutch
Kupplungsbremslenkung *f s.* Kupplungslenkung
Kupplungseinrichtung *f* coupling
Kupplungslenkung *f* clutch steering *(of crawler tractors)*
Kupplungswelle *f* coupling shaft
Kupula *f (bot, zoo)* cupule
Kurbe *f (vet)* curb
Kurbelstange *f* pitman
Kurbelstangenantrieb *m* pitman drive
Kurbelwelle *f* crankshaft
Kürbis *m* 1. pumpkin, squash *(genus Cucurbita)*; 2. *s.* Kürbisfrucht
kürbisartig cucurbitaceous
Kürbisbaum *m* 1. calabash [tree] *(genus Crescentia)*; 2. common calabash tree, Crescentia cujete
Kürbisbohrer *m (ent)* squash borer, Melittia cucurbitae
Kürbisfrucht *f* pumpkin, gourd, pepo
Kürbisgewächs *n* gourd, melon, cucurbit *(family Cucurbitaceae)*
~/**buschförmiges** bush-type vegetable marrow *(comprehensive term)*
Kürbismosaik *n (phyt)* pumpkin (squash) mosaic
Kürbismosaikvirus *n* pumpkin mosaic virus
Kürbissamen *m* pumpkinseed
Kürbiswanze *f* squash bug, Anasa tristis
kurabel curable
kurativ curative
Kürettage *f (vet)* curettage, abrasion
Kurganser Rind *n* Kurgan *(cattle breed)*
Kurkuma *f (bot)* curcuma, tu[r]meric, Curcuma longa
Kurkumagelb *n s.* Kurkumin
Kurkumapapier *n* tu[r]meric paper *(indicator)*
Kurkumin *n* curcumin, tu[r]meric *(dye)*
Kürschner *m* furrier
kurzästig short-branched
kurzblättrig brevifoliate
Kurzblättrige Eibe *f* Pacific yew, Taxus brevifolia
kurzborstig *(bot)* hirtellous
Kurzdecken-käfer *m* rove-beetle, staphylinid [beetle] *(family Staphylinidae)* • **zu den Kurzdeckenkäfern gehörend** staphylinid
kürzen to shorten, to pinch back, to stop *(e.g. plants)*
Kurzfessel *f* short leash *(falconry)*
kurzfilzig *(bot)* tomentulose
kurzflügelig *(ent)* short-winged, brachypterous
Kurzflügler *m s.* Kurzdeckenkäfer
kurzfrüchtig *(bot)* brachycarpous
Kurzfühlerschrecke *f (ent)* short-horned grasshopper *(suborder Caelifera)*

kurzgeflügelt s. kurzflügelig
kurzgehäckselt finely chopped
Kurzgrasprärie f short-grass prairie
Kurzgrassavanne f short-grass savanna[h]
Kurzgrassteppe f short-grass steppe
Kurzgrasweide f short-grass range
kurzgriffelig (bot) short-styled
Kurzhäcksel[gut] n short chop
Kurzhäckselvorrichtung f short-cutting device
kurzhalmig short-stemmed
Kurzhocherhitzung f short-time high-temperature method (e.g. of wine)
Kurzholz n shortwood, short timber
Kurzholzanhänger m shortwood trailer
Kurzholzgreifer m log grab
Kurzholzlademaschine f (Am) logger
Kurzholzverfahren n shortwood method (logging)
Kurzholzvollerntemaschine f shortwood harvester, feller-delimber-slasher-buncher
Kurzholzwagen m short timber truck
Kurzknoten m (phyt) double node (malformation)
Kurzkompostierungsverfahren n peak-heat-composting
kurzköpfig brachycephalic
Kurzköpfige Rinderlaus f s. Kurznasige Rinderlaus
Kurzkornreis m short-grain rice, pearl rice
kurzkronig small-cupped (narcissus flower)
Kurzkupplung f clutch
Kurzlangtagpflanze f short-long-day plant
kurzlebig short-lived, ephemeral, hapaxanthic, hapaxanthous
Kurzmaischverfahren n abridged mash method (brewing)
Kurzmalz n short-grown malt, chit malt
Kurznasige Rinderlaus f short-nosed cattle louse, cattle sucking louse, bull-nosed louse, ox louse, Haematopinus eurysternus
Kurznaßbeizung f instant (instable) dip
kurzschädelig brachycephalic
kurzschäftig s. kurzstämmig
Kurzschnabelgans f pink-footed goose, Anser brachyrhynchus
Kurzschnittladewagen m short chopping self-loading wagon
Kurzschwanzschaf n short-tailed sheep
Kurzsproß m s. Kurztrieb
kurzstämmig short-stemmed, short-boled
kurzstengelig, kurzstielig short-stalked, short-stemmed
Kurzstrahlregner m short-range sprinkler
Kurzstroh n short straw
kurzstrohig short-strawed
Kurzstrohigkeit f shortness of straw
Kurzstrohweizen m short-strawed wheat, dwarf wheat
Kurztag m short-day
Kurztagbedingungen fpl short-day conditions

Kurztagbehandlung f short-day treatment
Kurztagpflanze f short-day plant, SDP
Kurztagreaktion f short-day reaction
Kurztrieb m short shoot, brachyblast; spur [shoot], bourse shoot (of fruit woods)
~/blattähnlicher phylloclade
Kurztriebrückschnitt m spur shortening
Kurzumtrieb m (forest) short rotation
Kurzwildbret n testicles (of game)
kurzwollig short-woolled
Kurzzeitanbau m short-term growing
Kurzzeiterhitzung f (dairy) flash-pasteurization, higth-temperature short-time pasteurization; short-time high-temperature method (e.g. in wine-making)
~/schonende thermization
Kurzzeitlagerung f short-term storage, short period storage
Kuschel f, **Kussel** f bushy tree
Kussobaum m (bot) cusso, Hagenia abyssinica, Brayera anthelminthica
Kustanaier Pferd n Kustanai (horse breed)
Küstendünenvegetation f coast dune vegetation
Küstenfieber n [/Ostafrikanisches] (vet) African (east) coast fever, Rhodesian red-water, Rhodesian tick fever, theileriasis of cattle (caused by Theileria parva)
Küstenklima n coast climate
Küstenmammutbaum m [coast, Californian] redwood, sequoia, Sequoia sempervirens
Küstensand m coast sand
Küstenschutzstreifen m coast shelter-belt
Küstenschutzwald m coast protection wood
Küstenschutzwaldstreifen m coast shelter-belt
Küstensequoie f s. Küstenmammutbaum
Küstensteppe f littoral steppe
Küstentanne f grand (lowland, white) fir, Abies grandis
Küstenwald m coast (shore, littoral) forest
kutan cutaneous
Kutikula f 1. cuticle; 2. bloom (of hen egg)
kutikular cuticular
Kutin n (bot) cutin
kutinisieren to cutinize
Kutinisierung f cutinization
Kutkihirse f little (Indian) millet, Panicum sumatrense (miliare)
Kutscher m coachman, teamster
Kutschpferd n coach horse
Kutter m [meat] cutter
kuttern to dust-bath (fowl)
Kutterplatz m dusting place
Kwaß m kvass (alcoholic beverage)
k-Wert m heat transfer value
kyanisieren to kyanize (wood preservation)
Kynurenin n kynurenine, 3-anthraniloyl-(L)-alanine (metabolite)
Kynurensäure f kynurenic acid

L

l *s.* Liter
L *s.* 1. Lehmboden; 2. Generationsintervall; 3. Deutsche Landrasse
Lab *n* rennin, rennet, chymosin • **mit ~ behandeln** to rennet *(milk)*
Labcasein *n* rennet casein
Labenzym *n s.* Lab
Labfähigkeit *f* rennetability, rennet coagulability *(of milk)*
Labfähigkeitskonstante *f* rennetability constant
Labferment *n s.* Lab
Labgallerte *f* rennet coagulum
Labgärprobe *f* rennet fermentation test
Labgerinnung *f* rennet coagulation
Labialtaster *m (ent)* labial palp
Labiate *f s.* Lippenblütler
Labilität *f* lability *(e.g. of an ecological system)*
Labkäse *f* rennet cheese
Labkraut *n* bedstraw, galium *(genus Galium)*
Labkrautgewächse *npl* madder family *(family Rubiaceae)* • **die ~ betreffend** rubiaceous
Labmagen *m* rennet stomach (bag), fourth (true) stomach, abomasum, abomasus, reed, maw *(of ruminants)*
Labmagenentzündung *f (vet)* abomasitis
Labmagenflüssigkeit *f* abomasal fluid
Labmagenhaut *f* rennet
Labmagenpararauschbrand *m (vet)* braxy *(caused by Clostridium septicum)*
Labmagensaft *m* abomasal fluid
Labmagenschleimhaut *f* rennet
Labmagenverlagerung *f (vet)* displaced abomasum
Labor[atorium] *n* laboratory
Laborausrüstung *f* laboratory equipment
Laborfütterungsversuch *m* laboratory feeding test
Laborkeimung *f* laboratory germination
Labormaus *f* laboratory mouse
Labormethode *f* laboratory method
Laborprobe *f* laboratory sample
Labortier *n* laboratory animal
Laborverfahren *n* laboratory method
Laborversuch *m* laboratory test
Labproenzym *n* reninogen, chymosinogen *(enzyme)*
Labquark *m* rennet curd
Labrador Retriever *m* Labrador [dog, retriever] *(breed)*
Labrum *n (ent)* labrum
Labstärke *f* rennet strength
labträge slow-renneting *(milk)*
Labyrinth *n* labyrinth *(animal anatomy)*
Labyrinthgefüge *n (soil)* labyrinthine structure
Lacaune[schaf] *n* Lacaune *(sheep breed)*
Laccase *f* laccase, urishiol oxidase *(enzyme)*

Lache *f s.* Lachte
Lachenalie *f (bot)* Cape cowslip *(genus Lachenalia)*
Lachgas *n* laughing gas, nitrous oxide, nitrogen(I) oxide *(anaesthetic)*
Lachs *m* [Atlantic] salmon, Salmo salar
~ im dritten Jahr mort
~ in der Laichzeit/männlicher kipper
Lachsähnliche *m s.* Lachsartige
lachsartig salmon[o]id
Lachsartige *m* salmon[o]id *(family Salmonidae)*
Lachsforelle *f* salmon trout *(comprehensive term)*
Lachsmilchner *m* kipper
Lachszucht *f* salmon culture
Lachtaube *f* stockdove, Columba oenas
Lachte *f (forest)* [resin] blaze, face, streak
~ der fallenden Harzung descending face
~ der steigenden Harzung ascending face
~ / erste front (virgin) face
~ / glatte smooth face
~ im ersten Nutzungsjahr first-year face
~ im zweiten Nutzungsjahr second-year face, yearling face
~ mit V-förmigen Rissen herring-bone face
~ / trockene dry (dead) face
Lachtenausarbeitung *f* [face] delimitation
Lachtenbeil *n* cupping axe
Lachtenbreite-Stammumfang-Verhältnis *n* tapping intensity
Lachtenreißer *m* chipper for resin tapping
Lack *m* 1. lacquer; varnish; 2. lac *(esp. from Coccus lacca)*; 3. *s.* Goldlack
Lackharz *n* lac (varnish) resin, elemi
Lackinsekt *n* lac insect *(comprehensive term)*
Lack[schild]laus *f* [Indian] lac insect, Kerria (Coccus, Laccifer) lacca, Lakshadia indica
Lackschorf *m* **der Gladiole** scab of gladiolus *(caused by Pseudomonas gladioli)*
Lacksumach *m* lacquer-tree, [Japan] varnish-tree, Toxicodendron vernicifiua, Rhus vernicifera
Lacktrichterling *m (bot)* deceiver, Laccaria laccata
Lacombe *f*, **Lacombeschwein** *n* Lacombe *(pig breed)*
Lacrimae Christi *m* lachryma Christi *(kind of wine)*
Lactalbumin *n* lactalbumin, milk albumin
ß-Lactamantibiotikum *n* beta-lactam antibiotic
ß-Lactamase *f* beta-lactamase, penicillinase, cephalosporinase *(enzyme)*
Lactase *f* beta-galactosidase *(enzyme)*
Lactat *n* lactate
Lactatdehydrogenase *f* lactate dehydrogenase *(enzyme)*
Lactobakterium *n*, **Lactobazillus** *m* lactobacillus *(genus Lactobacillus)*
Lactobiose *f* lactose, milk sugar
Lactoferrin *n* lactoferrin *(milk protein)*
Lactoflavin *n* lactoflavin, riboflavin, vitamin B_2, vitamin G
Lactoglobulin *n* lactoglobulin, milk globulin

Lagerung

Lacton *n* lactone *(cyclic ester of hydroxy acids)*
Lactoprotein *n* milk protein
Lactose *f* lactose, milk sugar, sugar of milk
Lactoseausscheidung *f* **im Harn** lactosuria
Lactosesynthetase *f* lactose synthase *(enzyme)*
Lactosurie *f* lactosuria
Lactotransferrin *n* lactoferrin *(milk protein)*
Lactotropin *n* prolactin *(hormone)*
Lactulose *f* lactulose *(disaccharide)*
Ladebrücke *f* loading bridge
Ladedreibaum *m* [loading] tripod, gin
Ladefähigkeit *f* carrying capacity
Ladegerät *n* 1. loader; 2. [battery] charger
Ladehöhe *f* loading height
Lademaschine *f s.* Lader
Lademasse *f* load weight
laden to load
~/bündelweise (paketweise) to bunch-load, to bundle-load, to sling-load
Ladeplatte *f* pallet
Ladepritsche *f* loading body
Lader *m* loader, loading device
~ mit Radfahrwerk wheel loader
Laderampe *f* loading platform (ramp, dock)
Laderzange *f* grapple [loader]
Ladeschaufel *f* bucket
Ladewagen *m* loader wagon, self-loader, self-[un]loading trailer, pick-up trailer
Ladinoklee *m* ladino [clover], giant (large-leaved) white clover, white Dutch clover, *Trifolium repens* f. *lodigense*
Ladung *f* 1. load; 2. [electric] charge *(as of a lightning)*
Ladungsdichte *f* charge density *(soil physics)*
Laevoglucosan *n* laevoglucosan *(sugar anhydride)*
Laevopimarsäure *f* laevopimaric acid *(resin acid)*
Lage *f* 1. position; 2. layer; ply; 3. site; 4. presentation, position *(obstetrics)*
Lageanomalie *f* malpresentation, malposition *(obstetrics)*
Lageeffekt *m* *(gen)* position effect
Lagenkennziffer *f* ply rating
lagenweise stratiform
Lageplan *m* field plan *(experimentation)*
Lager *n* 1. store, storage, stock *(s. a.* Lagerhalle*)*; 2. lair, couch, holt *(of game)*; 3. bearing *(as of a shaft)*; 4. *s.* Lagergetreide
~ mit gesteuerter Atmosphäre controlled-atmosphere store
Lagerapfel *m* keeping (winter) apple
lagerbar *s.* lagerfähig
Lagerbehälter *m* storage bin (container)
lagerbeständig *s.* lagerfähig
Lagerbier *n* lager [beer], bottom-fermented beer, stock beer
Lagerbräune *f* storage scald *(of pome fruit)*
Lagerbuchse *f* bearing bush[ing]
Lagerdauer *f* storage duration

Lagereignung *f s.* Lagerfähigkeit
lagerfähig storable, stable in storage
Lagerfähigkeit *f* storability, keepability, keeping quality, storage stability (resistance, performance), shelf-life
Lagerfaß *n s.* Lagergebinde
Lagerfäule *f* storage rot (decay)
Lagerfestigkeit *f* storage stability
Lagerfrucht *f* laid grain (crop)
Lagerfruchthaspel *f* laid-grain (pick-up) reel, grain-saving reel
Lagergebinde *n* ag[e]ing (storage) cask, lagering vat *(wine-making)*
Lagergefahr *f* risk of [grain] lodging
Lagergemüse *n* **zur Winterversorgung** winter vegetable
Lagergetreide *n* laid grain, lodged corn (grain), ley, lea
Lagerhalle *f* crop storage building, storage structure
~ mit Unterflurbelüftung floor-ventilated bin
Lagerhaus *n* storehouse, store; warehouse *(s. a.* Lagerhalle*)*
Lagerholz *n* fallen dead wood
Lagerkeller *m* storage cellar
Lagerkrankheit *f* storage disease (disorder), postharvest disorder (plant disease), market disease
lagern 1. to store, to keep; to warehouse; 2. to age, to mellow *(e.g. wine)*
~/in Mieten to clamp
~/sich to lodge *(e.g. grain crops)*
Lagern *n* 1. *s.* Lagerung; 2. lodging, laying flat, falling over *(e.g. of grain crops)*
Lagerobst *n* storable fruit[s], fruit for keeping
Lagerobstschaden *m* postharvest disorder, market disease
Lagerpflanze *f* thallophyte, thallogen
Lagerraum *m* store[-room], storage [space]
Lagerraumklima *n* storage climate
Lagerschädling *m* stored-product[s] pest, storage pest
Lagerschädlingsbekämpfung *f* stored-product[s] pest control
Lagerschale *f* bearing bush[ing]
Lagerschorf *m* storage scab *(of apples, caused by* Venturia inaequalis*)*
Lagerschwund *m s.* Lagerungsverlust
Lagerspund *m* cellar plug *(of a wine cask)*
Lagertank *m* storage (lagering) tank
Lagertemperatur *f* storage temperature
Lagerung *f* storage, keeping; stockpiling
~ bei geringem Sauerstoffgehalt low-oxygen storage
~ im Freien outdoor storage
~ in frischem Zustand fresh storage
~ in gesteuerter (kontrollierter) Atmosphäre controlled atmosphere storage, CA storage
~ unter inerten Gasen controlled atmosphere storage, CA storage

Lagerung

~ **unter Luftabschluß** airtight storage
Lagerungsatmosphäre f storage atmosphere
~/zweiseitig gesteuerte two-sided controlled storage atmosphere
Lagerungsmöglichkeit f storage capacity
Lagerungsschaden m storage damage
Lagerungstemperatur f s. Lagertemperatur
Lagerungsverhalten n storage behaviour
Lagerungsverlust m storage loss
Lagerweißkohl m white storage cabbage
Lagerzeit f storage period
Lageveränderung f tropism (of sessile organisms)
Lagg n lagg (of raised bogs)
Lagune f lagoon
lahm 1. lame; 2. musty (wine)
Lähme f/Chasteksche (vet) Chastek paralysis
~ **der Jungtiere** (vet) joint ill
lahmen to lame, to limp, to founder, to cripple
Lahmen n, **Lahmgehen** n limp, claudication
Lahmheit f lameness
~/Adamssche Adam's lameness (of horse)
Lahmkrankheit f (vet) botulism
Lahmseuche f carrion poisoning (of cattle)
Lähmung f (vet) paralysis, palsy
~ **sämtlicher Gliedmaßen** quadriplegia
~/unvollkommene paresis
~/vollständige [motorische] paralysis, palsy
Lähmungsseuche f s. Lahmseuche
Lähmungswut f (vet) paralytic (dumb) rabies
Laibkäse m loaf cheese
Laibvolumen n loaf volume (baking test)
Laich m (pisc) spawn
Laichbereitschaft f spawning readiness
laichen to spawn
Laichen n spawning • **zum ~ bringen** to spawn
Laicher m s. Laichfisch
Laicherfolg m spawning success
Laichfisch m spawner, brood (seed) fish, seeder
Laichfische mpl broodstock
Laichfresser m spawn-eater
Laichkraut n pondweed (genus Potamogeton)
Laichnest n, **Laichplatz** m spawning ground (place), redd[-site], nest
Laichteich m spawning (breeding) pond
Laichtrieb m spawning instinct
Laichzeit f spawning season (time)
Lake f brine
Lakeland Terrier m Lakeland terrier (dog breed)
Lakritze f s. 1. Lakritzestaude; 2. Lakritzensaft
Lakritzensaft m liquorice, licorice
Lakritzenwurzel f liquorice, licorice, sweet-root
Lakritzestaude f liquorice, licorice, sweet-root, Glycyrrhiza glabra
Lakt... s. a. Lact...
Laktagogum n [ga]lactagogue
Laktation f 1. lactation, milk secretion; 2. s. Laktationsperiode • **in die ~ eintreten** to freshen (dairy cattle)

Laktationsanöstrie f lactation anoestrus
Laktationsbeständigkeit f lactation persistency
Laktationsdauer f lactation duration
Laktationshöhepunkt m peak of lactation
Laktationshormon n prolactin, lactogenic hormone
Laktationsinduktion f lactation induction
Laktationskurve f lactation curve
Laktationslänge f lactation duration
Laktationsleistung f lactation[al] performance, lactation yield
Laktationsmitte f midlactation
Laktationsperiode f lactation period, milking cycle
Laktationsstadium n lactation stage, stage of lactation
Laktationsstörung f lactation disorder
Laktationszahl f lactation period number
Laktazidämie f (vet) lactacidaemia
laktieren to lactate, to milk
laktierend lactating, in milk
~/nicht dry (dairy cattle)
Lakto... s. a. Lacto...
Laktodensimeter n lactodensimeter, milk areometer
laktogen lactogenic, galactopoietic
Laktogenese f lactogenesis, galactopoiesis, milk formation
Laktologie f dairy science
Laktometer n [ga]lactometer
Laktoprotein n lactoprotein
Laktorrhoe f (vet) galactorrhoea
Laktoskop n lactoscope (for milk fat determination)
laktotrop s. laktogen
lakunär (bot, zoo) lacunose
lakustrisch lacustrine
Lama n llama (genus Lama)
Lamavlies n llama fleece
Lamawolle f llama [wool]
Lamawollstoff m llama
Lambdamycin n lambdamycin (antibiotic)
Lambertsnuß f [giant] filbert, Corylus maxima
Lambliasis f, **Lamblienkrankheit** f (vet) giardiasis
Lamelle f lamella, gill (of fungi)
lamellenartig (bot, zoo) lamellate
Lamellengefüge n (soil) lamellar structure
Lamellenknochen m lamellar bone
Lamellenkörperchen n/**Pacinisches** Pacinian corpuscle (animal physiology)
Lamellenkupplung f multiplate clutch
Lamellenpilz m gill fungus, gill-bearing mushroom (order Agaricales)
Lamellenreibkupplung f multiplate clutch
lamellenreich (bot, zoo) lamellose
Lamellensieb n frog-mouth sieve
Lamiazee f s. Lippenblütler
Lamina f (bot) [leaf] lamina, [leaf] blade
Laminarase f lichenanase (enzyme)
Laminitis f (vet) laminitis, founder

Lamium-Mosaikvirus *n* lamium mild mosaic virus
Lamm *n* lamb
~ **vor der ersten Schur** hogg[et], hog
~ **vor der ersten Schur/weibliches** ewe hogg[et], gimmer hog
~ **zur Weitermast** feeder (store) lamb
Lammbock *m* ram lamb
lammen to lamb, to yean, to drop
Lammen *n* lambing
Lämmeraufzucht *f* lamb rearing
Lämmerdysenterie *f s.* Lämmerruhr
Lämmerendmast *f* lamb finishing
Lämmerenteritis *f s.* Lämmerruhr
Lämmerfrühmast *f* lamb fattening
Lämmerfütterung *f* lamb feeding
Lämmergrind *m (vet)* trichophytosis, ringworm
Lämmerintensivmast *f* intensive fat lamb system, early fat lamb production
Lämmerintensivmastbetrieb *m* intensive meat lamb producing unit
Lämmermast *f* lamb fattening (finishing)
Lämmermaststall *m* lamb fattening house
Lämmerproduktion *f* lamb production
Lämmerruhr *f (vet)* lamb dysentery, coliform scour[s] in lambs
Lämmerschlupf *m* lamb creep *(in a pasture fencing)*
Lämmerstall *m* lamb house
Lämmersteifkrankheit *f* stiff lamb disease
Lämmersterblichkeit *f* lamb mortality
Lämmertränke *f* lamb drinker
Lämmertränkvorrichtung *f* lamb drinker
Lämmerwolle *f s.* Lammwolle
Lammfell *n* lambskin, lamb pelt
~ **des Astrachanschafes** astrakhan, astrachan
Lammfleisch *n* lamb [meat]
Lammkeule *f* gigot
Lammpelz *m* budge
Lammwolle *f* lamb's-wool, shearling; hogget-wool, hog[g]
~ **von Feinwollrassen** teg
Lammzeit *f* lambing period (season), time of lambing
Lammzibbe *f* ewe lamb
Lampe *m (hunter's language) s.* Hase
Lampenbürstenchromosom *n* lampbrush chromosome
Lampionblume *f* 1. ground-cherry, husk-tomato *(genus Physalis)*; 2. alkekengi, Physalis alkekengi
Lamprete *f* lamprey *(genus Lampetra)*
Lamziekte *f* carrion (forage) poisoning *(of oxen)*
Lanatosid *n* lanatoside *(glycoside mixture)*
Land *n* 1. land, ground *(s. a. under Boden)*; 2. countryside
~/**bebaubares (bestellbares)** arable [land]
~/**eingedeichtes** dikeland
~/**fruchtbares** fat land
~/**trockengelegtes** intake
~/**unbebautes (unbestelltes)** fallow [ground], lealand
Landarbeit *f* farm (land) work, agricultural work (labour)
Landarbeiter *m* farm worker (hand), agricultural worker (labourer), peasant, hind, cottager
Landarbeitergewerkschaft *f* agricultural trade union
Landarbeiterhütte *f* cottage
Landassel *f* wood-louse *(family Oniscoidea)*
Landbau *m* farming, husbandry
~/**alternativer (ökologischer)** alternative (ecological) farming, ecofarming, eco-agriculture
Landbausystem *n* agricultural system, farming scheme (system)
Landbesitz *m* land ownership (tenure); estate
Landbesitzer *m* landowner, landlord
Landbevölkerung *f* rural (agricultural) population
Landbewirtschaftung *f* land-use management
Landboden *m* terrestrial soil
Landbutter *f* farm butter
Landei *n* farm egg
Landesforstverwaltung *f* state forest service
Landeskultur *f* countryside improvement
Landespflege *f s.* Landschaftspflege
Landfernsprechnetz *n* rural telephone system
Landflucht *f* rural exodus (depopulation)
Landforstmeister *m* chief forest officer
Landfrau *f* countrywoman
Landgeflügel *n* landfowl
Landgewinnung *f* reclamation [of land]
Landgut *n* manor, country estate
Landhaus *n* country house; cottage, bower
Landhausgarten *m* cottage garden
Landhuhn *n* Mediterranean chicken
Landjugend *f* rural youth
Landklassifikation *f* land classification
Landklima *n* continental climate
ländlich rural, rustic
Landlosigkeit *f* landlessness
Landmaschine *f* agricultural (farm, field) machine
Landmaschinen *fpl s.* Landmaschinenpark
Landmaschinenbau *m* agricultural engineering
Landmaschinenhersteller *m* farm-equipment manufacturer
Landmaschinenindustrie *f* agricultural machinery industry, farm-equipment industry
Landmaschinenpark *m* agricultural (farm) machinery, farm equipment, deadstock
Landomycin *n* oleandomycin *(antibiotic)*
Landpflanze *f* land (terrestrial) plant
Landrace *f s.* Landrasse 2.
Landrad *n* landwheel
Landrasse *f* 1. local (native) breed, land-race; 2. Landrace *(pig breed)*; 3. German landrace *(pig breed)*

Landrohrgras

Landrohrgras *n* feather-top grass, wood reed [grass], chee reed grass, Calamagrostis epigejos
Landschaft *f* landscape; countryside
Landschaftsarchitekt *m* landscape architect
Landschaftsarchitektur *f* landscape architecture (design), landscaping
Landschaftsästhetik *f* landscape aesthetics
Landschaftsgarten *m* landscape garden
Landschaftsgärtner *m* landscape gardener
Landschaftsgärtnerei *f* landscape gardening (horticulture)
Landschaftsgestalter *m* landscape architect
Landschaftsgestaltung *f* landscape architecture (design), landscaping
Landschaftsökologie *f* landscape ecology
Landschaftspflege *f* landscape care (tending, management), conservation of landscape
Landschaftspfleger *m* environmentalist
Landschaftsplanung *f* landscape planning
Landschaftsschutz *m* [landscape] conservation, landscape preservation (protection)
Landschaftsschutzgebiet *n* [landscape] conservation area, landscape conservancy reserve, protected landscape
Landschnecke *f* land snail *(comprehensive term)*
Landseite *f* landside *(ploughing)*
Landsitz *m* residential farm
Landsorte *f* native (home-grown) variety
Landstrich *m* tract [of land], region
Landstufe *f* escarpment
Landtechnik *f* agricultural engineering
Landtechniker *m* agricultural engineer, A.E.
Landvermessung *f* land survey[ing]
Landwein *m* local wine
Landwirt *m* farmer, agricultur[al]ist, husbandman, cultivator
~/staatlich geprüfter *(Am)* graduate farmer
Landwirtschaft *f* agriculture, farming, husbandry, rural economy
~ der gemäßigten Zonen temperate agriculture
~/industriemäßige agricultural industry, agri-industry; factory farming
~/mechanisierte power farming
~/praktische practical agriculture, farming
~/tropische tropical agriculture
landwirtschaftlich agricultural, farm, agrarian, rural
Landwirtschafts... s. a. Agrar... and Agro...
Landwirtschaftsattaché *m* agricultural attaché
Landwirtschaftsausstellung *f* agricultural show (exhibition), country fair
Landwirtschaftsbank *f* agricultural (land) bank
Landwirtschaftsbauten *pl* agricultural buildings
Landwirtschaftsbetrieb *m* farm [enterprise], agricultural enterprise (holding)
~/industriemäßig produzierender factory farm
~/staatlicher state farm
Landwirtschaftschemie *f* agricultural chemistry, agrochemistry

Landwirtschaftschemiker *m* agricultural chemist
Landwirtschaftsexperte *m* agricultural expert
Landwirtschaftsgeologie *f* agricultural geology, agrogeology
Landwirtschaftsgeschichte *f* agricultural history
Landwirtschaftshochschule *f* agricultural college (high school), *(Am)* aggie
Landwirtschaftsjahr *n* farming year
Landwirtschaftskunde *f* agriculturism
Landwirtschaftslader *m* farm loader
Landwirtschafts-Lkw *m* farm truck
Landwirtschaftsminister *m* agriculture (farm) minister, minister of agriculture, *(Am)* secretary of agriculture
Landwirtschaftsministerium *n* ministry of agriculture
Landwirtschaftsökologie *f* agricultural ecology, agroecology
Landwirtschaftsprognose *f* agricultural forecast
Landwirtschaftsroboter *m* agricultural robot
Landwirtschaftssachverständiger *m* agricultural expert
Landwirtschaftsschädling *m* agricultural pest
Landwirtschaftsstatistik *f* agricultural statistics (census)
Landwirtschaftraktor *m* agricultural tractor
Landwirtschafts- und Nahrungsgüterhandel *m* agro-alimentary trade
Landwirtschaftswissenschaft *f* agricultural science, agronomy, agriculturism
Landwirtschaftswissenschaftler *m* agricultural scientist
Landwirtschaftszählung *f* agricultural census
Langährige Quecke *f* tall wheat-grass, Agropyron elongatum, Elymus elongatus
Langarm[baum]schere *f* lopper
Langbartshasel *f (bot)* filbert, Corylus maxima
Langblattehrenpreis *m* clump speedwell, Veronica longifolia
Langblättrige Akazie *f* Sydney acacia, Acacia longifolia var. floribunda
~ Rauke *f (bot)* London rocket, Sisymbrium irio
Langblütige Lilie *f* Easter lily, Lilium longiflorum
Langbohne *f* asparagus bean, yard-long bean (cowpea), Vigna unguiculata ssp. sesquipedalis
Langbrand *m* **der Mohrenhirse** long smut of sorghum *(caused by Tolyposporium ehrenbergii)*
Langdorniger Orangenbaum *m* Mauritius papeda, porcupine orange, Citrus hystrix
Länge *f*/**astreine** clear length *(of a tree-trunk)*
~/handelsübliche (verkäufliche) merchantable (saleable) height, commercial height *(of standing timber)*
Lange Muskatnuß *f* Papua nutmeg, Myristica argentea
Längenwachstum *n* longitudinal (length, height) growth, elongation
Längenwachstumszone *f* **des Röhrenknochens** metaphysis

Langer Pfeffer m long pepper, Piper longum
Langerhanssche Inseln fpl islets [of Langerhans], pancreas islets
langfaserig long-fibre
Langfessel f long leash *(falconry)*
langflügelig long-winged
langhaarig long-haired
Langhäcksel n long chop
Langheu n loose (long) hay
Langholz n longwood, stemwood, long (tree-length) logs
Langholzabfuhr f log-hauling, bole removal
Langholzausformungstrupp m longwood crew
Langholzbereitstellung f, **Langholzbringung** f tree-length logging, long[-length] logging, whole-stem logging
Langholzentladeeinrichtung f log unloader
Langholzfahrzeug n timber lorry, lumber carrier, log truck
Langholzförderbahn f log haul[-up], log conveyor (chute), log slide (way)
Langholzladung f sett of timber
Langholzlastzug m log truck
Langholznachläufersystem n timber drag
Langholzriese f timber slide (slip)
Langholztransport m log transport[ation], log-hauling
Langholzverfahren n tree-length method
Langholzvollerntemaschine f longwood harvester, feller-delimber-buncher
Langholzwagen m lumber wagon
Langhornbock[käfer] m *(ent)* sawyer *(genus Monochamus)*
Langkapseljute f [long-fruited] jute, West African sorrel, Corchorus olitorius
langköpfig *(zoo)* dolichocephalic
Langköpfige Rinderlaus f s. Langnasige Rinderlaus
Langkornreis m long-grain rice, Patna rice
Langkurztagpflanze f long-short-day plant
Langlebiger Spätklee m late-flowering red clover, American mammoth red clover, single-cut red clover, Trifolium pratense var. sativum subvar. serotinum
Langlebigkeit f longevity
länglich rund *(bot, zoo)* terete
Langlochsieb n oblong-hole screen
Langmalz n long-grown malt
Langnasige Rinderlaus f long-nosed cattle louse, cattle sucking louse, Linognathus vituli
Langnutzholz n long timber
Langparzellenanlage f [nach Zade] long-plot design *(field experimentation)*
Langrohholz n s. Langholz
Längsachsrotorkrümler m rotary tiller with longitudinal shafts
Längsbau m *(api)* cold-way hive
Längsbruch m longitudinal fracture

Lanosterol

langschädelig *(zoo)* dolichocephalic
langschäftig long-boled, long-stemmed
Langschan n Langshan *(breed of fowl)*
Langschnabel m woodcock, Scolopax rusticola
Langschwanzmaus f murid *(family Muridae)*
Längsdränung f longitudinal drainage
Längsflußmähdrescher m axial-flow combine [harvester], long-flow combine harvester, straight-through combine
~/selbstfahrender self-propelled axial-flow combine
Längsförderer m longitudinal conveyor
Längsfraktur f *(vet)* longitudinal fracture
Längsfurchenberieselung f, **Längsfurchenbewässerung** f long line furrow method
Längsneigung f tip *(terrestrial survey)*
Längsreihenausdünner m down-the-row thinner *(beet growing)*
längssägen to rip [down]
Längssägen n, **Längsschneiden** n rip sawing
Längsschnitt[schrot]säge f rip-saw, ripper
Längsschwadköpfroder m windrow-topper-lifter, windrowing sugar-beet harvester
Längsstabilität f longitudinal stability
Längsstromtrockner m longitudinal-shaft kiln *(timber drying)*
langstämmig long-stemmed, long-boled
langstielig long-stalked, long-stemmed
Langstreckentransport m long-distance transport[ation]
Langstroh n long straw
Langstroth-Beute f *(api)* Langstroth hive
Langtag m long day
~/eingeschobener intercalated long day *(in photoperiodic treatment of plants)*
Langtagbedingungen fpl long-day conditions
Langtagbehandlung f long-day treatment
Langtagpflanze f long-day plant, LDP
Langtagreaktion f long-day reaction
Langtrieb m long (elongated, extension) shoot
langwollig long-woolled
Langwolliges Devonschaf n Devon longwool[led] *(sheep breed)*
Langzeitanbau m long-term growing
Langzeitbekämpfung f long-term control
Langzeitdünger m slow-release fertilizer, slow-acting fertilizer, controlled-release fertilizer
Langzeitfeldversuch m long-term field experiment
Langzeitfruchtfolgeversuch m long-term crop rotation study
Langzeitkultur f long-term crop
Langzeitlagerung f long-term storage, prolonged storage
Langzeitmelioration f long-term amelioration
Langzeitversuch m long-term experiment
langzeitwirksam persistent
Lanolin n lanolin *(wool grease preparation)*
Lanosterin n, **Lanosterol** n lanosterol

Lansabaum

Lansabaum *m*, **Lansibaum** *m (bot)* langsat, Lansium domesticum, Aglaia domestica
Lanzengras *n* spear grass, tangle head, Heteropogon contortus
Lanzenrosette *f* living vase, urn plant, aechmea *(genus Aechmea)*
Lanzenzahn *m* lance tooth *(of a saw)*
lanzettähnlich *s.* lanzettlich
Lanzettegel *m* lancet fluke, Dicrocoelium dendriticum (lanceolatum)
Lanzettegelkrankheit *f (vet)* dicrocoeliosis *(caused by Dicrocoelium dendriticum)*
lanzettförmig *s.* lanzettlich
Lanzettkratzdistel *f* common (spear) thistle, bull (fuller's) thistle, Cirsium vulgare (lanceolatum)
Lanzettleberegel *m s.* Lanzettegel
lanzettlich *(bot, zoo)* lanceolar, lanceolate[d], lance-shaped
~/verkehrt oblanceolate[d]
Laparoskopie *f (vet)* laparoscopy
Laparotomie *f (vet)* laparotomy
Laparozele *f (vet)* abdominal hernia
Läppchenkrankheit *f* wattle disease *(of fowl)*
Lappen *m (bot, zoo)* lobe
Lappenrüßler *m* vine weevil *(genus Otiorhynchus)*
Lappjagd *f* hunting with toils
Lärche *f* larch *(genus Larix)*
Lärchenbock[käfer] *m s.* Lärchensplintbock[käfer]
Lärchenholz *n* larch[wood]
Lärchenknospengalle *f* larch bud-gall
Lärchenknospengallmücke *f* larch bud-gall-midge, Dasyneura laricis
Lärchenminiermotte *f* larch leaf-miner [moth], larch miner (mining moth), larch case-bearer [moth], Coleophora laricella
Lärchenrüsselkäfer *m* larch weevil, Hylobius piceus
Lärchensplintbock[käfer] *m (ent)* larch longhorn (longicorn), Tetropium gabrieli
Lärchentriebmotte *f* larch shoot[-borer] moth, Argyresthia laevigatella (atmoriella)
Lärchenwald *m* larch forest
Large Black *n* Large Black, Cornwall, Devon *(pig breed)*
~ White *n* Large White [English, Yorkshire], Large York, [Grand] Yorkshire *(pig breed)*
Laricetum *n* larch forest
Lärmbekämpfung *f* noise abatement (control)
Lärmschutzwand *f* acoustic screen wall, sound-insulating wall
larval *(ent)* larval
Larvalhormon *n* juvenile hormone
Larve *f* 1. [insect-]larva, grub, worm; maggot *(esp. of flies and midges)*; slug *(esp. of hymenopterans)* 2. alevin *(of fishes)* • **Larven ablegen** to blow *(insects)* • **mit einer ~** *(bot, zoo)* personate
~/pflanzenschädigende canker[-worm]
larvenabtötend larvicidal

larvenbekämpfend larvicidal
Larvenbekämpfungsmittel *n* larvicide
Larven[fraß]gang *m* larval gallery (tunnel, mine)
Larvengeneration *f s.* Larvenstadium
Larvenparasit *m* larval parasite
Larvenstadium *n* larval stage, [larval] instar
larvipar *(ent)* larviparous
larvizid larvicial
Larvizid *n* larvicide
Laryngitis *f (vet)* laryngitis
Laryngoskop *n* laryngoscope
Laryngotracheitis *f (vet)* laryngotracheitis
~ des Geflügels/infektiöse infectious laryngotracheitis of poultry
~ des Hundes/infektiöse contagious respiratory disease of dogs, kennel cough
Larynx *m* larynx
Lasalocid *n* lasalocid *(antibiotic, feed additive)*
Laserfluoreszenzspektroskopie *f* laser fluorescence spectroscopy
Lasersondenmassenspektrographie *f* laser probe mass spectrography
Laserstrahlung *f* laser radiation
Läsion *f (phyt, vet)* lesion
Lasso *n(m)* lasso, lariat
Laßreiser *m*, **Laßreitel** *m (forest)* maiden [tree]
Last *f* load
~/genetische genetic load
Lastkraftwagen *m* lorry, *(Am)* truck
~/selbstbeladender self-loading truck, self-loader
Lastkraftwagen-Anhänger *m* truck trailer
Lasttier *n* pack-animal, beast of burden
Lateinisches Quadrat *n* latin square *(experimentation)*
~ Rechteck *n* latin rectangle *(experimentation)*
latent latent, hidden, dormant *(e.g. a disease)*
Latente Rosettenkrankheit *f* **der Rübe** beet latent rosette disease
Latentes Andenkartoffelvirus *n* Andean potato latent virus, APLV
~ Anemonenvirus *n* anemone latent virus, AnLV
~ Artischockenvirus *n* artichoke latent virus, AtLV
~ Brombeervirus *n* black raspberry latent virus, BRLV
~ Chrysanthemenvirus *n* chrysanthemum latent virus
~ Erdbeerringfleckenvirus *n* strawberry latent ring spot virus, SLRV
~ Erysimum-Virus *n* erysimum latent virus
~ Geißblattvirus *n* lonicera latent virus, LLV
~ Holundervirus *n* elder-berry latent virus, ELV
~ Hopfenvirus *n* hop latent virus, HLV
~ Lilienvirus *n* lily symptomless virus
~ Myrobalanenringfleckenvirus *n* myrobalan latent ring spot virus
~ Narzissenvirus *n* narcissus latent virus
~ Nelkenvirus *n* carnation latent virus, CLV
~ Nerinevirus *n* nerine latent virus

~ **Passiflora-Virus** n, ~ **Passionsblumenvirus** n passiflora latent virus, PaLV
~ **Ringfleckenvirus** n **der Erdbeere** strawberry latent ring spot virus, SLRV
~ **Schalottenvirus** n shallot latent virus, SLV
~ **Sellerievirus** n celery latent virus, CeLV
Latentwärmespeicher m latent heat store
Latenz f latency, dormancy; *(gen)* cryptomerism
Latenzphase f lag period *(of bacterial growth)*
Latenzzeit f *(phyt, vet)* incubation period
lateral lateral
Lateralblüte f lateral flower
Lateralknospe f lateral (axillary) bud
~ **am fruchtenden Kurztrieb** bourse bud
Lateraltrieb m lateral shoot
Laterisation f *(soil)* laterization, ferrallitization
Laterit m laterite
Lateritboden m lateritic soil
Laterne f white face *(marking esp. on horse's head)*
Laternenpflanze f *(bot)* alkekengi, Physalis algekengi
Latex m latex, milky sap, vegetable milk • ~ **ausscheidend** laticiferous
latexerzeugend laticiferous
latexhaltig laticiferous
Latexkanal m latex canal (channel) *(wood anatomy)*
Lathyrismus m *(vet)* lathyrism
Latosol m *(soil)* latosol, *(Am)* oxisol, ox
Latrinenfliege f latrine fly, Fannia scalaris
Latsche[nkiefer] f dwarf pine, Pinus mugo ssp. pumilio
Lattenkiste f crate • **in Lattenkisten einlagern** to crate
Lattenrost m slatted grate
Lattenzaun m pale (slat) fence, paling [fence]
Lattich m 1. lettuce *(genus Lactuca)*; 2. lettuce, salad, Lactuca sativa
Lattierbaum m bail *(in a stable)*
Laub n foliage, leafage, leaves • ~ **abwerfen** to shed (drop) the leaves, to defoliate
~/**abgefallenes** dry (dead) leaves
~/**dichtes** thick leaves
~/**junges** young leaves
laubabwerfend deciduous
Laubaustrocknungsmittel n foliage desiccant
Laubbaum m deciduous (broad-leaved, leaf) tree, hardwood [tree]
~/**junger** staddle
Laubbaumart f deciduous tree species
Laubbereich m phyllosphere
Laubbesen m leaf (fan-shaped) sweep
Laubbildung f leafing
Laubblatt n foliage leaf
Laubdach n foliar canopy
Laubdichte f foliage density
Laube f summer-house, arbour, bower
Laubengang m pergola, arcade

Laubentfaltung f frondescence, unfolding of leaves
Lauberde f leaf mould (soil)
Laubfall m leaf fall (abscission), leaf drop[ping], leaf cast[ing], defoliation
Laubgebläse n leaf blower
Laubgehölz n deciduous shrub
Laubholz n hardwood, pored (porous, angiospermous) wood
Laubholzbaum m s. Laubbaum
Laubholzbeimischung f *(forest)* admixture of broad-leaved species
Laubholzmistel f [European] mistletoe, Viscum album ssp. album
Laubholzschüppling m *(bot)* changeable agaric, Pholiota (Kuehneromyces) mutabilis
Laubholzstamm[abschnitt] m, **Laubholzstammstück** n hardwood log
Laubholzwirtschaft f broad-leaf silviculture
laubig leafy, frondose
Laubkaktus m Barbados gooseberry, blade apple *(genus Pereskia)*
Laubmoos n, **Laubmoospflanze** f moss *(class Bryatae)*
Laubmulm m leaf-mould
Laub-Nadelmischwald m broad-leaved and conifer mixed forest
Laubreißer m leaf shredder (mill)
Laubrundholz n round hardwood
Laubsauger m, **Laubsaugmaschine** f leaf-and-refuse aspirator, vacuum sweeper
Laubschnittholz n sawn hardwood
Laubschnittling m leaf bud cutting
Laubstammholz n round hardwood
Laubstreu f leaf litter (debris)
Laubwald m deciduous (broad-leaved) forest, hardwood (foliage) forest
~/**kleinblättriger** forest of small-leaved deciduous species
~/**sommergrüner** deciduous summer forest
Laubwaldzone f broad-leaved forest zone
Laubwechsel m leaf change
Laubwerk n leafage, foliage, herbage
~/**grünes** greens, verdure
Lauch m 1. allium, onion *(genus Allium)*; 2. s. Porree
lauchartig *(bot)* alliaceous
Lauchblättriger Bocksbart m salsify, salsafy, vegetable oyster, Tragopogon porrifolius
Lauchbohrer m *(ent)* bulb maggot, Dyspessa ulula
Lauchgamander m water germander, Teucrium scordium
Lauchkraut n garlic mustard *(genus Alliaria)*
Lauchmotte f leek moth, Acrolepia (Acrolepiopsis) assectella
Lauchzwiebel f green onion, shallot
Laudanin n laudanine *(alkaloid)*
Laufband n treadmill, tread-wheel *(e.g. for exercising horses)*

Laufbereich

Laufbereich *m* loafing area, paddock *(in a loose-housing barn)*
Laufbucht *f* loose box
laufen 1. to run; 2. to work, to operate *(machine)*
~ lassen/ein Pferd to run a horse
~ lassen/im Rechtsgalopp to canter
Laufente *f* White Runner [duck] *(breed)*
Läufer *m s.* Jungschwein
Läuferstein *m* running millstone
Lauffeuer *n* running fire
Lauffläche *f s.* Laufbereich
Laufgewichtswaage *f* steelyard
läufig sein to be at (in, on) heat *(bitch)*
Läufigkeit *f* heat
Laufkäfer *m* carabid [beetle], ground beetle *(family Carabidae)* • **die ~ betreffend** carabid
Laufkatze *f (forest)* [skyline] carriage, trolley, buggy, bicycle *(of a cableway)*
Laufkran *m* [overhead] travelling crane
Lauflänge *f* runnage *(e.g. of twine)*
Laufmilbe *f* harvest mite *(family Trombiculidae)*
Laufmilbenlarve *f* harvest (red) bug, chigger *(family Trombiculidae)*
Laufrolle *f* pulley
Laufstall *m* loose[-housing] barn, pen barn, free stall, loafing shed, yard
Laufstallhaltung *f* loose-housing system, free-stall housing
Lauftragseil *n* running skyline
Laufvogel *m* cursorial bird
Laufwagen *m s.* Laufkatze
Laufwurzel *f* creeper
Laufzeit *f* heat *(of a bitch)*
~ der Kultur *(forest)* establishment (formation) period
Lauge *f* 1. lye, alkaline solution; 2. brine
Laumontit *m* leonardite (non-clay mineral)
Laurinsäure *f* lauric (dodecanoic) acid *(fatty acid)*
Laurustinus *m (bot)* laurustinus, Viburnum tinus
Laus *f* louse *(order Anoplura)* • **Läuse bekämpfen** to delouse
Läusebefall *m* pediculosis
läusebefallen lousy, pedicular, pediculous
Läuseei *n* nit
Läusekraut *n* lousewort *(genus Pedicularis)*
lausen to louse
Läusesamen *m* 1. sabadilla seed *(from Schoenocaulon officinale)*; 2. *(bot)* stavesacre, Delphinium staphisagria
Lausfliege *f* louse fly *(family Hippoboscidae)*
Laut geben to give tongue *(dog)*
Lautäußerung *f* vocalization *(animal behaviour)*
Läuterbatterie *f* lauter battery *(brewing)*
Läuterboden *m* false bottom *(of a brewery)*
Läuterbottich *m* lauter-tub, lauter-tun
läutern 1. to lauter, to clarify *(brewing)*; to affine *(raw sugar)*; 2. to thin, to clean *(a forest stand)*
Läutertemperatur *f* mash separation temperature *(brewing)*

Läuterung *f* 1. clarification *(of liquids)*; 2. *(forest)* thinning, cleaning, release cutting
Läuterungshieb *m (forest)* release cutting
Lauwasser *n (dairy)* tepid water
Lavandin *n (bot)* lavandin, Lavandula x intermedia (x hybrida)
Lavatere *f* tree mallow *(genus Lavatera)*
Lavendel *m* 1. lavender *(genus Lavandula)*; 2. true lavender, Lavandula angustifolia
Lavendelheide *f* 1. wild rosemary, andromeda *(genus Andromeda)*; 2. marsh (bog) rosemary, marsh andromeda, moorwort, Andromeda polifolia
Lavendelöl *n* lavender [flower] oil
Lävulinsäure *f* l[a]evulinic acid *(metabolite)*
Lävulose *f* l[a]evulose, fructose *(monosaccharide)*
Lawine *f* avalanche, snow-slip
lawinengefährdet liable to damage by avalanches
Lawinenverbauung *f* anti-avalanche defence work, damming of avalanches, avalanche control operations
Lawsons Scheinzypresse *f* Port-Orford-cedar, Lawson['s] cypress, Oregon-cedar, Chamaecyparis lawsoniana
Laxans *n*, **Laxativ[um]** *n* laxative, purgative
laxieren to scour
laxierend laxative, purgative
Layia *f (bot)* tidy tips, Layia elegans
Lazeration *f (vet)* laceration
LCM lymphocytic choriomeningitis
LCM-Virus *n* lymphocytic choriomeningitis virus
LD *s.* Letaldosis
LD 50 *s.* Dosis/mittlere letale
LDH *s.* Lactatdehydrogenase
Lebediner Braunvieh *n* Lebedin [cattle] *(breed)*
Leben *n* life
~/latentes anabiosis
lebend [a]live, living, animate; on the hoof *(cattle)*
~/auf Bäumen arboreal, dendrophilous
~/auf der Erde *(zoo)* epigeal, epigeous
~/einzeln solitary
~/gesellig *(bot, zoo)* gregarious, sociable
~/im Boden soil-dwelling, soil-inhabiting
~/im Nadelwald conophorophilous
~/im [stehenden] Süßwasser limnic
~/im Wasser aquatic
~/in Bäumen arboreal, dendrophilous
~/in Seen lacustrine
~/in verschiedenen geographischen Gebieten allopatric
~/mit Ameisen vergesellschaftet myrmecophilous
~/räuberisch predatory, predacious
~/unter Luftabschluß anaerobic
~/unter Luftzutritt aerobic
Lebendbeschau *f (slaught)* ante-mortem inspection
Lebendbeurteilung *f (slaught)* live estimation

Lebende Steine *mpl (bot)* living-stones *(genus Lithops)*
Lebendendmasse *f* preslaughter weight
Lebender Granit *m (bot)* living rock *(genus Pleiospilos)*
Lebendfang *m* live-trapping
Lebendfisch *m* live fish
Lebendgebären *n (zoo)* viviparity, viviparousness
lebendgebärend viviparous, live-bearing
lebendgeboren live-born
Lebendgeburt *f* live birth
Lebendgeflügel *n* live poultry
Lebendgewicht *n s.* Lebend[körper]masse
lebendig 1. lively *(wine)*; 2. *s.* lebend
Lebendimpfstoff *m* live vaccine
Lebend[körper]masse *f* live [body] weight
Lebendmasseausbeute *f*, **Lebendmasseertrag** *m* live weight yield
Lebendmassezunahme *f* live weight gain, L.W.G.
~/tägliche daily live weight gain
Lebendmassezuwachs *m s.* Lebendmassezunahme
Lebendmulch *m* live mulch
Lebendstreifen *m* interface, interspace, *(Am)* bark (life) bar *(resin-tapping)*
Lebendtierausstellung *f* live animal show
Lebendtierbeurteilung *f* live animal evaluation
Lebendtiervermarktung *f* live auction [marketing]
Lebenduntersuchung *f s.* Lebendbeschau
Lebendvakzine *f* live vaccine
Lebendverbauung *f* biological engineering; stabilization of banks by planting
Lebendvermarktung *f* live auction [marketing]
Lebendvieh *n* live cattle
Lebendvirusimpfstoff *m*, **Lebendvirusvakzine** *f* live viral (virus) vaccine
Lebendzaun *m* hedge[row]
Lebensbaum *m* arbor vitae, thuja, thuya, tree of life *(genus Thuja)*
Lebensbaumlichtwald *m* thuja light forest
Lebensdauer *f* 1. life duration, life [span], lifetime; 2. service (working) life *(of a machine)*
~/lange longevity
~ von Samen seed longevity
Lebenserwartung *f* life expectancy
lebensfähig viable, livable
~/innerhalb großer Temperaturbereiche eurythermal, eurythermic
Lebensfähigkeit *f* viability, livability
Lebensform *f* life-form, growth form
Lebensformenspektrum *n (ecol)* life-form spectrum, biological spectrum
Lebensgemeinschaft *f (ecol)* life community, biocoenosis
Lebenskraft *f* vitality, vigour
Lebenskreis *m* biocycle
Lebensleistung *f* lifetime productivity *(of a farm animal)*
Lebensmittel *n* food[stuff]

~ auf Milchbasis milk-based food
~/leichtverderbliches perishable food
~/tiefgefrorenes deep-frozen food
Lebensmittelbedarf *m* food requirement
Lebensmittelchemie *f* food chemistry
Lebensmittelforschung *f* food research
Lebensmittelhygiene *f* food hygiene
Lebensmittelindustrie *f* food[-processing] industry
Lebensmittelkonservierung *f* food preservation
Lebensmittelkonservierungsstoff *m* food preservative
Lebensmittelkunde *f* food science
Lebensmitteltechnologie *f* food technology
Lebensmitteltoxikologie *f* food toxicology
Lebensmittelüberwachung *f* food inspection
Lebensmittelverarbeitung *f* food processing
Lebensmittelverarbeitungsanlage *f* food processing plant
Lebensmittelvergiftung *f* food poisoning
Lebensmittelversorgung *f* food supply
Lebensmittelvorrat *m* food supply
Lebensmittelzusatz[stoff] *m* food additive
Lebensraum *m (ecol)* biotope, habitat
~/blattnaher [mikrobieller] phyllosphere
~/wurzelnaher rhizosphere
Lebensraum... *s.* Biotop... *and* Habitat...
Lebensstätte *f s.* Lebensraum
lebensunfähig abiotrophic, inviable
Lebensunfähigkeit *f* abiotrophy, inviability
Lebensverein *m* synusia, synusium *(plant ecology)*
lebenswichtig essential *(e.g. an amino-acid)*
~/nicht non-essential
Lebenswurzel *f (bot)* ginseng, Panax pseudoginseng (ginseng)
Lebenszeit *f s.* Lebensdauer
Lebenszone *f (ecol)* life zone
Lebenszyklus *m* life cycle
Leber *f* liver, hepar • **von der ~ ausgehend** hepatogenic
Leberabszeß *m (vet)* liver abscess
Leberarterie *f* hepatic artery
Leberbalsam *m* floss flower, ageratum, paint brush *(genus Ageratum)*
Leberbalsamschafgarbe *f (bot)* sweet Nancy (yarrow), Achillea ageratum
Leberblümchen *n* liverwort, liver leaf, hepatica *(genus Hepatica)*
Leberegel *m* liver fluke *(comprehensive term)*
leberegelbefallen fluky
Leberegelkrankheit *f (vet)* liver rot, fascioliasis, fasciolosis, distomatosis *(caused by Fasciola spp.)*
~ der Schafe core *(caused by Fasciola spp.)*
Leberegelseuche *f s.* Leberegelkrankheit
Leberentfernung *f [/operative] (vet)* hepatectomy
Leberentzündung *f (vet)* hepatitis *(s. a. under* Hepatitis*)*

Leberentzündung

~ des Huhns/infektiöse avian vibrionic (infectious) hepatitis
~ des Hundes/ansteckende canine viral (virus) hepatitis
~/enzootische enzootic hepatitis, Rift valley fever *(of ruminants)*
Lebererkrankung *f (vet)* liver disease, hepatopathy
Leberextrakt *m* liver extract
Leberfäule *f (vet)* liver rot, bane
Leberfunktion *f* liver function
Lebergang *m* hepatic duct
~/gemeinsamer common hepatic duct
Lebergeschwulst *f (vet)* hepatoma
Lebergewebe *n* liver parenchyma
Lebergift *n* hepatotoxin
Leberkapselentzündung *f (vet)* perihepatitis
Leberkrankheit *f s.* Lebererkrankung
Lebermoos *n* liverwort *(class Hepaticae)*
Leberparenchym *n* liver parenchyma
Leberpilz *m* beefsteak fungus, Fistulina hepatica
Leberprotein *n* liver protein
Leberruptur *f (vet)* liver rupture
Leberschwamm *m s.* Leberpilz
Leberstärke *f* glycogen, animal starch
Lebersteatose *f (vet)* liver steatosis, fatty liver
Leberstein *m (vet)* hepatic calculus, hepatolith
Lebertran *m* cod-liver oil
Lebervergrößerung *f (vet)* hepatomegaly, liver enlargement
Leberwurstbaum *m* liver (African) sausage tree, Kigelia africana
Leberzelle *f* liver cell, hepatocyte
Leberzerreißung *f (vet)* liver rupture
Leberzirrhose *f (vet)* liver cirrhosis
Lebewelt *f (ecol)* biota
~ des Bodens soil biota
Lebewesen *n* [living] being, living organism
• **~ fressend** biophagous
~/gnotobiotisches gnotobiote
~/männliches he
~ mit bekannter Keimflora gnotobiote
~/weibliches she
Lebhaftigkeit *f* alertness *(animal behaviour)*
leblos lifeless, abiotic
Leblosigkeit *f* lifelessness, abiosis
Lecithin *n* lecithin, phosphatidylcholine
Lecithincholesterolacyltransferase *f* lecithin[cholesterol] acyltransferase *(enzyme)*
Lecke *f*, **Leckstein** *m* salt-lick
Ledderingnetz *n (pisc)* trammel • **mit dem ~ fischen** to trammel
Leder *n* leather
~/ungegerbtes rawhide, raw skin
Lederabfall *m* leather refuse (waste) *(fertilizer)*
lederartig leathery, coriaceous
Lederbirne *f* snow pear, Pyrus nivalis
Lederfarn *m* leather fern, Arachniodes (Rumohra) adiantiformis

Lederfäule *f* **der Erdbeere** leather rot of strawberry *(caused by Phytophthora cactorum)*
Lederhaut *f* 1. corium, dermis, true (inner) skin; 2. sclera *(of the eye)* • **die ~ betreffend** dermal
Lederhautentzündung *f (vet)* scleritis
Lederholz *n* leather-wood, Dirca palustris
Lederhülsenbaum *m* honey locust *(genus Gleditsia)*
lederig leathery, coriaceous
Lederindustrie *f* leather industry
Lederkarpfen *m* leather (scaleless) carp
Ledermehl *n* leather meal *(fertilizer)*
Lederstrauch *m* 1. hop-tree *(genus Ptelea)*; 2. common hop-tree, Ptelea trifoliata
Lederzecke *f* soft tick *(family Argasidae)*
Leerdarm *m* jejunum
Leerdarmentzündung *f (vet)* jejunitis
leerfischen to fish out
Leergang *m* idle gear
Leerlauf *m* idle running, idling
Leerlaufdrehzahleinstellung *f* idle speed adjuster
Leermelken *n* over-milking, dry milking
Leerseillinie *f (forest)* unloaded cable profile
Lefzen *fpl* flews *(of dogs)*
Legeabfallsyndrom *n (vet)* egg drop syndrome '76, EDS'76, egg production decrease
Legeapparat *m s.* Legebohrer
Legebatterie *f* laying battery
Legebeginn *m* point-of-lay *(of fowl)*
Legebohrer *m (ent)* ovipositor, terebra, egg-laying mechanism
Legedarm *m* oviduct *(of birds)*
Legegeschwindigkeit *f* speed of planting *(potato growing)*
Legehaken *m* tile-hook *(draining implement)*
Legehenne *f* laying hen, layer
Legehennenalleinfutter *n* laying mash
Legehennenhaltung *f* laying hen husbandry
Legehennenherde *f* laying flock
Legehennenintensivhaltung *f* complete confinement of laying chickens
Legehennenkäfig *m* laying cage
Legehennenküken *n* layer chick
Legehennenration *f* layer diet
Legehennenstall *m* layer (laying) house, henhouse
Legehuhn *n s.* Legehenne
Legehybride *f*, **Legehybridhuhn** *n* hybrid layer, hy-line
Legeintensität *f* rate of lay, percentage lay
Legejahr *n* laying year, [egg-]laying season
Legejunghenne *f* laying pullet
Legekäfig *m* laying cage
Legekäfigparalyse *f* cage paralysis of fowls, cage layer fatigue
Legeleistung *f* laying performance, egg yield
legen 1. to lay *(eggs)*; 2. to set, to plant *(as potatoes)*; to sow, to plant *(e.g. beans)*
~/sich 1. to lay down *(animals)*

Legenest *n* laying nest, nest[ing] box
Legenot *f* **des Geflügels** *(vet)* egg-bound
Legepause *f* laying pause
Legeperiode *f* s. Legejahr
Legerate *f* rate of lay, percentage lay
Legeration *f* layer diet
Legerohr *n* drop tube *(of a potato planter)*
Legeserie *f* egg-laying sequence, set, clutch
Legestachel *m* *(ent)* spicule
Legestall *m* laying house
Legetermin *m* planting date *(potato growing)*
Legetiefe *f* planting depth, depth of planting *(potato growing)*
Legetier *n* laying bird
Legewespe *f* *(ent)* terebrant *(superfamily Terebrantes)*
Legföhre *f* dwarf pine, Pinus mugo ssp. pumilio
Leghämoglobin *n* leghaemoglobin *(chromoproteide of leguminous root nodules)*
Leghorn *n* [White] Leghorn *(chicken breed)*
Legumelin *n* legumelin *(reserve protein)*
Legumen *n* s. Leguminose
Legumin *n* legumin *(reserve protein)*
Leguminose *f* leguminous plant, legume *(family Leguminosae)*
leguminosenartig leguminous, fabaceous
Leguminosengärheu *n* legume haylage
Leguminosenheu *n* legume hay
Leguminosenimpfung *f* legume inoculation
Leguminosenprotein *n* legume protein
Leguminosensilage *f* legume silage
Leguminosenweide *f* legume pasture
Lehm *m* loam
~/sandiger sandy loam
~/toniger clay loam
Lehmboden *m* loam soil, loamy ground
lehmhaltig loamy
lehmig loamy
Lehne *f* s. Leinbaum
Lehrforst *m* demonstration (training) forest
Lehrforstrevier *n* training forest district
Lehrgarten *m* school garden
Lehr- und Versuchsgut *n* instructional and experimental farm
Lehrwald *m* s. Lehrforst
Leibesfrucht *f* s. Embryo
Leicester[schaf] *n* Leicester [sheep], English Leicester *(breed)*
Leichenalkaloid *n*, **Leichengift** *n* ptomaine
Leichenschau *f* *(vet)* autopsy
Leichenstarre *f* rigor mortis
Leichenwachs *n* adipocere
Leichtbautraktor *m* lightweight tractor
Leichtbauweise *f* light construction
Leichtbier *n* light (low-gravity, near) beer
Leichttraben *n* posting, rocking a trot *(equestrian sport)*
leichtverderblich perishable
Leichtwein *m* light wine

leierförmig *(bot)* lyrate
Leimkraut *n* *(bot)* campion, catchfly *(genus Silene)*
Leimring *m* glue (grease, sticky) band, trap ring *(plant protection)* • **[Bäume] mit einem ~ versehen** to band
Leimstoff *m* collagen *(scleroprotein)*
Leimtafel *f* lime plate *(for catching insects)*
Leimzotte *f* *(bot)* colleter
Lein *m* 1. flax *(genus Linum)*; 2. flax, Linum usitatissimum
Leinacker *m* flax field
Leinbaum *m* plane maple, Acer platanoides
Leinblasenfuß *m* *(ent)* field (cabbage) thrips, Thrips angusticeps
Leindotter *m* false flax, Camelina sativa
Leine *f* line; driving rein *(of harness)*; lead, leash *(esp. for dogs)* • **an der ~ führen** to leash
Leinen *n* linen
Leinenfischerei *f* line-fishing
Leinenzwang *m* lead and muzzle order
Leinerdfloh *m* linseed flea beetle, Longitarsus parvulus
Leinernte *f* flax harvest[ing]
Leineschaf *n* Leine [sheep] *(breed)*
Leinextraktionsschrot *n* linseed oil meal
Leingewächse *npl* flax family *(family Linaceae)* • **die ~ betreffend** linaceous
Leinkraut *n* 1. toadflax *(genus Linaria)*; 2. [common] toadflax, flaxweed, butter-and-eggs, ramstead, Linaria vulgaris
Leinkuchen *m* linseed cake
Leinlolch *m* hardy ryegrass, Lolium remotum
Leinöl *n* linseed (flax-seed) oil
Leinölhydrolysat *n* linseed oil hydrolysate
Leinölsäure *f* linoleic acid *(fatty acid)*
Leinraufmaschine *f* flax puller (lifter)
Leinrost *m* *(phyt)* flax rust *(caused by Melampsora lini)*
Leinsaatexpeller *m* linseed expeller cake
Leinsamen *m* linseed, flax-seed
Leinsamenöl *n* linseed (flax-seed) oil
Leinsamenprotein *n* linseed protein
Leinsamenschleim *m* linseed mucilage
Lein[samen]schrot *n* linseed meal
Leinseide *f* flax dodder, Cuscuta epilinum
Leishmania *f* *(zoo)* leishmania *(genus Leishmania)*
Leishmaniose *f* *(vet)* leishmaniasis
~/viszerale kala-azar
Leisten *pl* s. Kopfwolle
Leistenelevator *m* ledge elevator
Leistenhaspel *f* slat reel
Leistenkanal *m* inguinal canal *(animal anatomy)*
Leistenkopfplattkäfer *m* flat grain beetle, Cryptolestes pusillus
Leistenring *m* inguinal ring *(animal anatomy)*
~/oberflächlicher superficial inguinal ring
Leistung *f* 1. performance *(e.g. of farm animals)*; 2. power *(e.g. of an engine)*; 3. capacity; efficiency

Leistung

~/abgegebene output
~ am Zughaken drawbar power
~ des Waldes/landeskulturelle indirect forest effect, non-wood beneficial effect, welfare function of a forest
~/zugeführte input
Leistungsaufzeichnung f performance record[ing] *(animal breeding)*
Leistungsbedarf m power requirement
Leistungsbonität f yield class
Leistungsdüngung f output fertilization
Leistungsfähigkeit f performance ability; capacity; efficiency; power
Leistungsfutterration f production ration
Leistungsfütterung f feeding for performance, feeding to yield
leistungsgeprüft performance-tested
Leistungsindex m performance index
Leistungskarte f für Kühe cow record
Leistungskennwert m performance parameter
Leistungsklasse f *(forest)* production (quality) class
Leistungsmerkmal n performance characteristic (trait), production trait
Leistungsparameter m performance parameter
Leistungspferd n performance horse
Leistungsprüfung f performance test
Leistungsprüfungsstation f performance test station
Leistungsration f s. Leistungsfutterration
Leistungsstufe f yield class
Leistungstafel f für Bestände *(forest)* performance table
Leistungstemperatur f temperature for production *(animal physiology)*
Leistungstier n yielder
Leistungsvermögen n s. Leistungsfähigkeit
Leistungszüchtung f breeding for production, efficiency breeding
Leitast m [branch] leader
Leitastenfaltung f expansion of the leaders (branches)
Leitasthaltung f leader (branch) position
Leitaststellung f leader (branch) distribution
Leitastwinkel m crotch [angle]
Leitblech n deflector, baffle; gutter, tin, lip, apron *(in resin-tapping)*; trashboard *(of mould-board plough body)*
Leitbündel n *(bot)* vascular bundle
Leitbündelanordnung f/zerstreute atactostele
Leitbündelkambium n vascular cambium
Leitbündelpflanze f vascular plant
Leitbündelscheide f bundle sheath
Leitenzym n marker enzyme
Leiter f ladder
leiterförmig *(bot, zoo)* scalariform
Leitfähigkeit f/elektrische electric conductivity
~/hydraulische hydraulic conductivity

Leitfähigkeitsmesser m conductivity meter, conductometer
Leitgatter n cattle-grid, cattle-guard
Leitgewebe n s. Phloem
Leithaar n guard hair
Leithammel m bell-wether
Leitkuh f lead cow
Leitpferd n saddle-horse, leader
Leitpflanze f indicator plant
Leitrohr n delivery tube
Leitstab m leading-staff
Leittier n boss (lead) animal, leader; leading hind *(of red deer's herd)*
Leittrieb m lead[ing] shoot, leader *(plant anatomy)*
Leittrommel f stripper drum, straw stripper [beater]
Leitung f 1. duct; pipe[line]; 2. conduction *(e.g. of heat)*
Leitungsanästhesie f *(vet)* conduction anaesthesia
Leitungsgewebe n s. Phloem
Leitungskabel n cable
Leitungsmast m mast
Leitungsrohr n pipe
Leitungswasser n tap (mains) water
Leitzelle f *(bot)* tracheid
Lektin n lectin, phytomitogen *(glycoprotein)*
Lemming m lemming *(genus Lemmus)*
Lemongras n lemon grass, Cymbopogon citratus
Lenacil n lenacil *(herbicide)*
Lende f loin
~/hohe high loin
Lendenendstück n chump *(of sheep carcass)*
Lendengegend f lumbar area (region)
Lendenstück n loin
Lendenwirbel m lumbar vertebra
Lenkachse f steering axle
Lenkautomatik f automatic steering [system]
Lenkbarkeit f steerability
Lenkbremse f steering brake
Lenker m link *(of a three-point hitch)*
~/oberer upper (top, centre) link
~/unterer lower [draft] link
Lenkerhaltekette f linkage check chain
Lenkgetriebe n steering gear
Lenkhacke f steerage hoe
Lenkkupplung f steering clutch
Lenkrad n steering wheel
Lenksäule f steering column
Lenkschemel m steering bolster
Lenksystem n steering system
Lenkung f steering
~ mit Lenkkraftunterstützung power[-assisted] steering
Lenkungskontrollvorrichtung f steering controller
Lenkungsventil n steering valve
lentikulär lenticular, lens-shaped
Lentizelle f *(bot)* lenticel
Lentizellenfleckenkrankheit f, **Lentizellenröte** f lenticel blotch (spotting) *(of pome fruit)*

Lentizellenwucherung f lenticel *(esp. of potato tubers)*
Lepidokrokit m lepidocrocite *(non-clay mineral)*
Lepidoptere m lepidopteran, butterfly *(order Lepidoptera)*
Leptophos n leptophos *(insecticide)*
Leptospireninfektion f, **Leptospirose** f *(vet)* leptospirosis
Leptotän[stadium] n leptotene *(of meiosis)*
Lerchensporn m hollowwort, holewort *(genus Corydalis)*
Lernen n learning *(animal behaviour)*
~/assoziatives associative learning
~/einsichtiges insight learning
~/latentes latent learning
Lernfähigkeit f learning ability
Lernverhalten n learning behaviour
Lese f picking; grape picking, vintage
lesen 1. to pick *(berries, fruit)*; 2. *s.* verlesen
~/Ähren to glean
Leserahmen m *(gen)* reading frame
Lessivé m leached brown soil
Lessivierung f *(soil)* lessivage, lessivation, clay translocation (illuviation), argilluviation
letal lethal, deadly
Letaläquivalent n *(gen)* lethal equivalent
Letaldefekt m lethal defect
Letaldosis f lethal dose, LD
Letalfaktor m lethal factor, lethal [gene]
Letalfehler m lethal defect
Letalität f lethality
Letalitätsrate f lethality rate
Letalmutation f lethal mutation
Letaltemperatur f lethal temperature
Lethargie f *(vet)* lethargy
lethargisch lethargic
Leu *s.* Leucin
Leuchtbakterium n photobacterium
Leuchte f *s.* Laterne
leuchtend *(bot, zoo)* lucid
Leuchtende Wolfsmilch f *(bot)* scarlet plume, Euphorbia fulgens
Leuchterblume f 1. *(bot)* ceropegia *(genus Ceropegia)*; 2. rosary vine, string of hearts, Ceropegia woodii
Leuchtkäfer m glow-worm *(family Lampyridae)*
Leuchtröhre f fluorescent tube (lamp)
Leuchtstofflampe f fluorescent (gas-discharge) lamp
Leucin n leucin *(amino-acid)*
Leucinaminopeptidase f leucine [aryl]aminopeptidase, cytosol aminopeptidase *(enzyme)*
Leucinaminotransferase f leucine aminotransferase *(enzyme)*
Leucosin n leucosin *(vegetable albumin)*
Leukämie f *s.* Leukose
Leukom n *(vet)* leucoma
Leukomyelose f **des Geflügels** *(vet)* avian myeloblastosis (granuloblastosis)

Leukopenie f *(vet)* leucopenia, leukopenia
Leukophosphit m leucophosphite *(non-clay mineral)*
Leukoplast m *(bot)* leucoplast
Leukopoese f leucopoiesis
Leukose f *(vet)* leucosis, leukaemia
~/aviäre avian leucosis
~/aviäre lymphoide avian lymphomatosis, [avian] lymphoid leucosis, visceral lymphomatosis of fowl, big liver disease of fowl
~ der Katze feline leukaemia
~ des Huhnes *s.* ~/aviäre
~/extravaskuläre lymphatische *s.* ~/aviäre lymphoide
Leukose-Sarkomatose-Osteopetrose-Komplex m/aviärer avian leucosis sarcomatosis osteopetrosis complex
Leukotaxis f chemotaxis
Leukotoxin n leucotoxin
Leukozidin n leucocidin *(leucocyte-damaging substance)*
Leukozyt m leucocyte, leukocyte, white [blood-]cell, WBC, white corpuscle
~/azidophiler eosinophil [leucocyte], acidophilic leucocyte
~/basophiler basophil[e]
~/eosinophiler *s.* ~/azidophiler
~/neutrophiler neutrophil
~/polymorphkerniger polymorph
Leukozytämie f **des Geflügels** *(vet)* avian myeloblastosis (granuloblastosis)
Leukozytenmangel m *(vet)* leucopenia, leukopenia
leukozytenschädigend leucotoxic
Leukozytenzählung f leucocyte count
Leukozythämie f *s.* Leukose
Leuzit m leucite *(non-clay mineral)*
Levantebaumwolle f Levant (Asiatic) cotton, Gossypium herbaceum
Levantiner Storax m Levant storax *(balsam from Liquidambar orientalis)*
Levenshtein-Metrik f Levenshtein metric *(of soil classification)*
Levkoje f 1. stock *(genus Matthiola)*; 2. [common, florist's, ten-week] stock, gillyflower, Matthiola incana
Leydigsche Zwischenzelle f Leydig cell *(of testicles)*
Leylandzypresse f Leyland cypress, Cupressocyparis leylandii
L-Flußmähdrescher m side-cut[ting] combine [harvester]
LH *s.* Luteninisierungshormon
Lhasa Apso m Lhasa [apso] *(dog breed)*
L-Horizont m *(soil)* L-layer, litter horizon (layer), Aoo-horizon, surface litter
LHS *s.* System/lichterntendes
Liane f liana, liane, climbing plant, climber, vine
Lianenwald m vine forest

Liatris

Liatris *f (bot)* liatris *(genus Liatris)*
Libanonzeder *f* cedar of Lebanon, Cedrus libani
Libelle *f* dragon-fly *(order Odonata)*
Liberi[c]akaffee *m* Liberian (Liberica) coffee, Coffea liberica
Liberin *n* releasing hormone, releaser
Libido *f* libido, sexual drive (urge)
Libriformfaser *f* libriform wood-fibre
Lichen *m (vet)* lichen, eczema
Lichenase *f* lichenanase *(enzym)*
Lichenin *n* lichenan *(polysaccharide of numerous lichens)*
licht open[-stocked], sparse, clear, thinly stocked *(plant stand)*
Licht *n* light
~/fluoreszierendes fluorescent light
~/künstliches artificial light
~/natürliches natural light
lichtabsorbierend light-absorbing
Lichtabsorption *f* light absorption
lichtaktiv photoactive
Lichtatmung *f* photorespiration *(plant physiology)*
Lichtaufnahme *f* light interception (gathering)
Lichtausnutzung *f* light utilization
Lichtbaumart *f* light-demanding tree species, light demander
Lichtbedarf *m* light demand (requirement)
Lichtbedürfnis *n* love of light *(of plants)*
lichtbedürftig light-demanding, shade-intolerant, intolerant of shade
Lichtbedürftigkeit *f* shade intolerance
Lichtdermatose *f (vet)* photodermatitis
Lichtdurchlässigkeit *f* light permeability (transmission)
Lichtdurchlässigkeitskoeffizient *m* light transmission coefficient *(e.g. of a plant stand)*
Lichteinfall *m* light entry
lichtempfindlich photosensitive
Lichtempfindlichkeit *f* photosensitivity
lichten to thin out, to clear, to prune, to admit light
Lichtenergie *f* light energy
Lichtfalle *f* light trap *(pest control)*
Lichtfallenfang *m* light-trap catch *(plant protection)*
Lichtfischerei *f* light fishing
Lichtfluß *m* light flux
Lichtholzart *f s.* Lichtbaumart
Lichtintensität *f* light intensity
Lichtkeim *m* pigmented sprout
Lichtkompensationspunkt *m* [light] compensation point *(plant physiology)*
Lichtkonkurrenz *f* light competition
lichtkronig thin-crowned
lichtliebend light-loving, photophilous
Lichtmangel *m* light deficiency (stress)
lichtmangeltolerant shade-tolerant
Lichtmangeltoleranz *f* shade tolerance
Lichtmaschine *f* dynamo
lichtmeidend photophobic

Lichtmikroskop *n* optical (light) microscope
Lichtmikroskopie *f* optical microscopy
Lichtnelke *f (bot)* catchfly, campion, lychnis *(genus Lychnis)*
Lichtnuß *f* candlenut
Lichtnußbaum *m* candlenut[-tree], lumbang (varnish) tree, Indian walnut, Aleurites moluccanus
Lichtperiode *f* light period
Lichtpflanze *f* light-demanding plant, light demander
Lichtreaktion *f* light reaction, photophase, photoreaction *(photosynthesis)*
Lichtregime *n* light regime
Lichtreiz *m* light (photic) stimulus
Lichtröschen *n* rose of heaven, Silene coeli-rosa
Lichtsättigung *f* light saturation *(plant physiology)*
Lichtsättigungspunkt *m* light saturation point
lichtscheu photophobic
Lichtscheu *f* photophobia
Lichtschlag *m (forest)* secondary felling
lichtschluckend light-absorbing
Lichtstadium *n* light stage, photostage
Lichtstand *m (forest)* 1. open position; 2. open stand (crop)
lichtstellen to admit light, to open up, to thin [out] *(esp. a forest stand)*
Lichtstellung *f* admitting of light, opening up, thinning [out]
~/natürliche *(forest)* natural thinning, autothinning, self-thinning
Lichtstrahlung *f* photic radiation
Lichtstreß *m* light stress
Lichtstrom *m* light flux
Lichtstromdichte *f* light flux density
Lichtung *f (forest)* clearance, clearing, glade, open space
Lichtungshieb *m (forest)* accretion felling (cutting)
Lichtungszuwachs *m (forest)* open stand increment, light increment
~ vor dem Abtrieb accretion
Lichtversorgung *f* light supply
Lichtverteilung *f* light distribution
Lichtverteilungskurve *f* light distribution curve
Lichtverträglichkeit *f* light tolerance
Lichtwald *m* open woodland
Lichtwaldsavanne *f* woodland savanna[h]
lichtwendig *(bot)* heliotropic, phototropic
Lichtwendigkeit *f* heliotropism, phototropism
Lichtwuchsbetrieb *m (forest)* open stand system
Lichtwuchsdurchforstung *f (forest)* accretion thinning
Lichtzufuhr *f* light supply
Lichtzuwachs *m s.* Lichtungszuwachs
Lid *n* eyelid
Lidbindehaut *f* conjunctiva
Lideinwärtsdrehung *f (vet)* entropion
Lidentzündung *f (vet)* blepharitis
Lidocain *n* lidocaine, lignocaine *(anaesthetic)*
Lidrandeinwärtsdrehung *f (vet)* entropion

Lidrandverdickung f (vet) tylosis
Liebesblume f [blue] African lily, [blue] lily of the Nile, Agapanthus africanus (umbellatus)
Liebesgras n 1. love-grass (genus Eragrostis); 2. veld love-grass, Eragrostis superba
Liebfrauenmilch f Liebfraumilch (wine)
Liebhaberobstbau m amateur fruit growing
Liebhaberzucht f home-breeding
Liebliche Hundszunge f (bot) Chinese-forget-me-not, Cynoglossum amabile
Liebstöckel n(m) [garden] lovage, Levisticum officinale
Liefergenossenschaft f/landwirtschaftliche farm supply co-operative
Liegebox f lying (resting) box, cubicle
Liegeboxenabtrennung f resting box partition
Liegeboxenhaltung f cubicle housing
Liegeboxenlaufstall m lying box loose housing
Liegeboxentrennbügel m cubicle division
Liegefläche f nesting (sleeping) area; bedded area, standing (in a loose-housing barn)
Liegendkubikmeter m felled solid meter (timber)
Liegendmessung f [von Holz] log measurement
Liegeplatz m lair
Lien m s. Milz
Lieschblatt n husk leaf, shuck (of maize)
Lieschblätter npl, **Lieschen** pl (Am) husk
Lieschgras n (bot) cat's-tail, cattail (genus Phleum)
Lieschgrasscheckungsvirus n phleum mottle virus
Liesen pl (Am) leaf [fat] (of pig)
LieSV s. Lieschgrasscheckungsvirus
Ligament[um] n ligament (animal anatomy)
Ligase f ligase, synthetase (enzyme)
Ligatur f (vet) ligation, ligatur
Lignan n lignan (plant substance)
lignifizieren to lignify, to run to wood
Lignifizierung f lignification
lignikol lignicole, lignicolous
Lignin n lignin
~ **in saurer Detergentienlösung** acid detergent lignin, ADL (feed analysis)
~/**technisches** technical lignin
Lignin-Eiweiß-Komplex m lignin-protein complex (of humus)
Ligninentfernung f delignification
ligninreich rich in lignin
Lignintrübung f lignin turbidity (defect of wine)
lignivor lignivorous, xylophagous, wood-eating, wood-feeding
Lignivore m lignivore, xylophage, wood-eater
Lignocain n s. Lidocain
Lignocellulose f lignocellulose
Lignocerinsäure f lignoceric (tetracosanoic) acid (fatty acid)
Lignol n lignol (lignin precursor)
Lignosulfonsäure f lignosulphonic acid

Lignotuber m lignotuber
Ligula f (bot) ligule
Liguster m 1. privet (genus Ligustrum); 2. [common] privet, Ligustrum vulgare
Ligusterschwärmer m privet-hawk [moth], Sphinx ligustri
Likör m liqueur
Likörwein m dessert (appetizer) wine
lila lilac, amethystine
Lilie f lily (genus Lilium)
lilienartig liliaceous
Lilienblütige Tulpe f lily-flowered tulip (group of cultivars)
Liliendolde f lily asphodel (genus Crinum)
Liliengewächse npl lily family (family Liliaceae)
• **die ~ betreffend** liliaceous
Liliengrün n spider plant, Chlorophytum comosum
Lilienhähnchen n lily beetle, Crioceris lilii
Lilienmagnolie f yulan, lily tree, Magnolia denudata
Lilienmosaikvirus n lily mosaic virus
Lilienringfleckenvirus n lily ring spot virus
Lilienrosettenvirus n lily yellow-flat virus
Lilienschweif m desert-candle, foxtail lily, eremurus (genus Eremurus)
Liliensimse f false asphodel (genus Tofieldia)
Lilientraube f lilyturf, Liriope (Ophiopogon) muscari
Lilienzwiebelpflanzmaschine f lilybulb planter
LiLV s. Latentes Lilienvirus
Limabohne f lima [bean], moon (sugar) bean, Phaseolus lunatus [var. lunatus]
Limberneck m s. Geflügelbotulismus
Limburger [Käse] m Limburg cheese, Limburger
Limette f [sour, common] lime (fruit from Citrus aurantiifolia)
Limettenöl n lime oil
Limettensaft m lime-juice
limnisch limnic
Limnologie f limnology
limnologisch limnological
Limnoplankton n limnoplankton
Limone f s. 1. Limette; 2. Zitrone
Limonen n limonene (monoterpene)
Limousin-Rind n Limousin (cattle breed)
limpid limpid, clear (esp. wine)
Limpidität f limpidity
LiMV s. Lilienmosaikvirus
Lin. s. Liniment[um]
Linalool m linalool (terpene alcohol)
Linalylacetat n linalyl acetate
Linamarin n linamarin (linseed glycoside)
Lincoln n s. Lincolnlangwollschaf
Lincoln Red n Lincoln Red [Shorthorn] (cattle breed)
Lincolnensin n s. Lincomycin
Lincolnlangwollschaf n Lincoln Longwool (sheep breed)
Lincomycin n lincomycin, lincocin (antibiotic)

Lindan

Lindan *n* lindane, gamma-HCH, gamma-BCH *(acaricide, insecticide)*
Linde *f* lime[-tree], linden, *(Am)* basswood *(genus Tilia)*
Lindenbast *m* [lime] bast, bass; Russian bast *(esp. used in grafting)*
Lindenholz *n* lime, basswood
Lindenprachtkäfer *m (Am, ent)* linden burncow, Poecilonota rutilans
Lindenwald *m* lime wood
Lindenzierlaus *f* lime aphid, Eucallipterus tiliae
lindern *(vet)* to calm
Linie *f* 1. line; 2. [breeding] line, strain
~ **gleichen Luftdrucks** isobar
~ **gleicher Lufttemperatur** isotherm
~ **gleicher Niederschlagsmenge** isohyete
~/**isogene** isogenic line, isoline
~/**reine** pure line *(breeding)*
~/**weiße** white line *(of hoof)*
Linienbestandsaufnahme *f s.* Linientaxation
Linienhybride *f* line cross
Linienkreuzung *f*, **Linienkreuzungsprodukt** *n* line cross
Linienmosaik *n (phyt)* line mosaic
~ **der Pflaume** plum narrow striped variegation, plum pseudo pox *(virosis)*
Linienmuster *n (phyt)* line pattern *(of viroses)*
Linientaxation *f (forest)* line[ar] survey, strip survey (cruising), line-intercept method
~ **der Naturverjüngung** linear regeneration sampling
Linienzucht *f* line breeding
Linienzuchtherde *f* line-bred herd
Linienzuchtsorte *f* strain variety
Linienzüchtung *f* line breeding
Liniierter Nutzholzborkenkäfer *m* lineate bark-beetle, Trypodendron (Xyloterus) lineatus
Liniment[um] *n (vet)* liniment, embrocation
Linin *n* achromatin *(cell nucleus constituent)*
links near, nigh *(side of animal or vehicle)*
linksdrehend 1. laevorotatory, laevogyrate, *(optical activity of molecules)*; 2. *s.* linkswindend
linkswindend *(bot)* sinistrorse, sinistrorsal
Linolensäure *f* linolenic acid *(fatty acid)*
Linolsäure *f* linoleic acid *(fatty acid)*
Linse *f* 1. lentil, Lens culinaris (esculenta); 2. eye lens
Linsenbaum *m* bladder senna, Colutea arborescens
linsenförmig lenticular
Linsenkäfer *m* lentil weevil, Bruchus lentis
Linsenwicke *f* bitter (lentil) vetch, ervil, Vicia ervilia
Lint *m* lint *(of cotton seeds)*
Linters *pl* linters, fuzz [fibre] *(of cotton seeds)*
Lintersentfernungsmaschine *f* linter
Linuron *n* linuron *(herbicide)*
Liothyronin *n* triiodothyronine *(hormone)*
Lipämie *f (vet)* lipaemia
lipämisch *(vet)* lipaemic

Lipase *f* [triacylglycerol] lipase, tributyrase *(enzyme)*
Lipid *n* lipid[e], lipin; lipoid
Lipidabsorption *f* lipid absorption
Lipidgehalt *m* lipid content
Lipidkörper *m* lipid body
Lipidmembran *f* lipid membrane
~/**bimolekulare (doppelschichtige)** bilayer lipid membrane *(plant physiology)*
Lipidose *f s.* Lipidspeicherkrankheit
Lipidperoxid *n* lipid peroxide
Lipidperoxidation *f* lipid peroxidation
Lipidspeicherkrankheit *f (vet)* lipidosis, lipoidosis
Lipidstoffwechsel *m* lipid (adipose, fat) metabolism
Lipidstoffwechselstörung *f* lipid metabolism disorder
Lipidüberschuß *m* lipid excess
Lipidvakuole *f (bot)* oleosome, sphaerosome
Lipizzaner *m* lippizaner, Lipitsa, Lipizzaner *(horse breed)*
Lipoamidreductase *f* dihydrolipoamide dehydrogenase *(enzyme)*
Lipoblast *m* lipoblast
Lipochrom *n* lipochrome *(natural dye)*
Lipodystrophie *f (vet)* lipodystrophy
Lipofuszin *n* lipofuscin *(pigment of animal tissues)*
lipogen lipogenic, lipogenous
Lipogenese *f* lipogenesis, lipid formation
Lipoidose *f s.* Lipidspeicherkrankheit
Lipolyse *f* lipolysis, fat breakdown
lipolytisch lipolytic, fat-splitting
Lipom *n (vet)* lipoma
Lipomatose *f (vet)* lipomatosis
Liponsäure *f* lipoic acid *(coenzyme)*
Lipophilie *f* lipophilia
Lipopigment *n s.* Lipofuszin
Lipopolysaccharid *n* lipopolysaccharide
Lipoproteid *n* lipoproteid[e]
Lipoprotein *n* lipoprotein
~ **sehr geringer Dichte** very-low-density lipoprotein
~ **sehr hoher Dichte** very-high-density lipoprotein
Lipoproteinesterase *f* lipoprotein esterase *(enzyme)*
Lipoproteinlipase *f* lipoprotein (diacylglycerol) lipase *(enzyme)*
Liposaccharid *n* lipopolysaccharide
Liposarkomatose *f (vet)* liposarcomatosis
lipotrop lipotropic
Lipotropin *n* lipotropin *(hormone)*
Lipovitellin *n* lipovitellin *(constituent of egg-yolk protein)*
Lipoxydase *f*, **Lipoxygenase** *f* lipoxygenase *(enzyme)*
Lipozyt *m* adipocyte, fat cell
Lippe *f* lip
lippenähnlich, lippenartig labiate

löffelförmig

Lippenblütler m labiate *(family Lamiaceae = Labiatae)*
Lippenblütler mpl mint family *(family Lamiaceae = Labiatae)*
Lippendrüse f labial gland *(animal anatomy)*
Lippengrind m sore mouth, contagious pustular dermatitis, contagious ecthyma *(of sheep and goats, caused by Latens paravacciniae)*
Lippenrinne f philtrum *(animal anatomy)*
Lippenspalte f *(vet)* cleft (hare) lip
Lippentaster m *(ent)* labial palp
Liquor m 1. liquor; 2. *s.* Flüssigkeit
LiRFV *s.* Lilienringfleckenvirus
LiRoV *s.* Lilienrosettenvirus
Lissapol n lissapol *(emulsifier)*
Listeriose f *(vet)* listeriosis, listerellosis *(caused by Listeria monocytogenes)*
~ **des Geflügels** listeriosis of birds, tiger river disease
Litauisches Kaltblut n Lithuanian Draft *(horse breed)*
Litchibaum m *(bot)* li[t]chi, lichee, lychee, Litchi chinensis
Litchipflaume f 1. litchi [nut]; 2. *s.* Litchibaum
Liter m(n) litre
Lithium n lithium
Lithocholsäure f lithocholic acid *(bile acid)*
lithomorph *(soil)* lithomorphic
Lithoserie f lithosere *(plant sociology)*
Lithosol m lithosol, skeletal soil
Lithosphäre f lithosphere
Litlur[e] n litlure *(sex pheromone)*
litoral littoral
Litoral n littoral
Litoralwald m littoral forest
Littrésche Drüse f urethral gland
Liverpoolkandare f Liverpool driving bit
Livetin n livetin *(constituent of egg-yolk protein)*
Livistonie f fountain palm, livistona *(genus Livistona)*
LKTP *s.* Langkurztagpflanze
Lkw *s.* Lastkraftwagen
L-Meromyosin n light meromyosin *(muscle protein)*
LmMV *s.* Lamium-Mosaikvirus
LMV *s.* Luzernemosaikvirus
LN *s.* Nutzfläche/landwirtschaftliche
Lobelanin n lobelanin[e] *(alkaloid)*
Lobelie f *(bot)* lobelia *(genus Lobelia)*
Lobelin n lobelin[e] *(alkaloid)*
Lobivie f cob cactus *(genus Lobivia)*
lobulär *(bot, zoo)* lobular
Lobus m *(bot, zoo)* lobe
Lochbanddrillmaschine f belt [feed] drill
Lochbandeinzelkornsämaschine f perforated belt spacing drill
Lochbildung f **[im Käse]** eye formation [in cheese]
Lochbrett n **für Anzuchtplatten** marker for plant trays

Lochdüngung f hole dressing
Löcherpflanzung f *s.* Lochpflanzung
Löcherverjüngung f *(forest)* gap regeneration
Lochfolie f perforated [plastic] film
Lochhügelpflanzung f *(forest)* pit-mound planting
lochial *(vet)* lochial
Lochialfluß m, **Lochien** pl *(vet)* lochia
Lochpflanzung f hole (peg, pit) planting, pitting, dibbling
Lochsaat f hole seeding, dibbling
Lochscheibe f perforated (seed) plate
Lochscheibendrillmaschine f plate planter (seeder)
Lochspaten m drill spade
Lochzange f nose plier
Locke f 1. *(hunt)* bird (decoy) whistle, bird-call; 2. tag *(wool)*
~/**lebende** decoy
locken to lure; to decoy
Locken fpl britch [wool], duggings
Lockenfeder f curly feather
Lockenfell n *s.* Krimmer
Lockente f decoy-duck
locker *(bot, zoo)* sparse
Lockerährigkeit f spike laxness
lockerblättrig sparsifolious
lockerblütig *(bot)* laxiflorous
Lockerboden m loose soil, mantle rock, rock mantle, regolith
Lockermaterial n *(soil)* detritus
lockern 1. to loosen, to mellow, to rip, to hoe, to break up *(soil)*; 2. to open up *(a plant stand)*
lockernervig *(bot)* vaginervose, vaginervous
Lockerpflug m tormentor
Lockersediment n *(soil)* loose sediment
Lockerwerden n **von Holz** mellowing of wood
Lockmittel n attractant, lure
Lockpfeife f *s.* Locke 1.
Lockruf m call of a decoy-bird
Lockspeise f food lure *(pest control)*
Lockstoff m attractant, lure
Lockstoffalle f attractant trap, pheromone[-containing] trap
Lockverhalten n calling behaviour
Lockvogel m decoy
Lockwirkung f attractancy, attractant action
Locus m *s.* Genort
Lode f *(bot)* shoot, deciduous transplant; sapling, staddle
Lodicula f lodicule *(of gramineous flower)*
Lodigiano m, **Lodiklee** m *s.* Ladinoklee
Löffel m bucket *(of excavators)*
löffelartig *(bot, zoo)* cochlear
Löffelblättrigkeit f **der Johannisbeere** red currant ring spot *(virosis)*
Löffelegge f scuffler, Canadian (blade, acme) harrow
löffelförmig *(bot, zoo)* cochlear

Löffelkrankheit

Löffelkrankheit *f* der Topfazalee azalea leaf gall *(caused by Exobasidium vaccinii)*
Löffelkraut *n* 1. spoonwort *(genus Cochlearia)*; 2. scurvy-grass, Cochlearia officinalis
Löffelraddrillmaschine *f*, **Löffelradsämaschine** *f* cup[-feed] drill
Löffelsärad *n* cup-feed wheel, cup [wheel] feed mechanism
Löffelstör *m* paddlefish, Polyodon spathula
log-Phase *f s.* Wachstumsphase/logarithmische
Loganbeere *f* loganberry, boysenberry, Rubus loganobaccus
logarithmisch logarithmic
Logarithmus *m* logarithm
lohbraun black and tan
Lohe *f*, **Lohrinde** *f* tan[bark]
Lohnunternehmer *m*/**forstwirtschaftlicher** forest work contractor
Lohschälen *n (forest)* barking in period of sap flow
Lokaier Pferd *n* Lokai *(horse breed)*
lokal auftretend *(phyt, vet)* endemic
~ **ausbreitend/sich** *(phyt, vet)* endemic
~ **begrenzt vorkommend** *(ecol)* endemic
Lokalanästhesie *f (vet)* local anaesthesia
Lokalanästhetikum *n* local anaesthetic
lokalanästhetisch local anaesthetic
Lokalertragstafel *f (forest)* regional (local) volume table, local yield table
Lokalhormon *n* tissue hormone
Lokalklima *n* local climate, topoclimate
Lokalläsion *f (phyt, vet)* local lesion
Lokalsorte *f* local (indigenous) variety
Lokomobile *f* steam traction engine, steam tractor
Lokomotion *f* locomotion *(progressive movement)*
lokulizid *(bot)* loculicidal
Lolch *m* rye-grass, darnel *(genus Lolium)*
Lombardische Geflügelpest *f* fowl pest (plague)
Lompenzucker *m* lump sugar
LöMV *s.* Löwenzahnmosaikvirus
Longanbaum *m (bot)* longan, longyen, linkeng, dragon's eye, Dimocarpus longan, Nephelium longana
Longane *f* 1. longan *(fruit from Dimocarpus longan)*; 2. *s.* Longanbaum
Longävität *f* longevity
Longe *f* longe, lunge *(equestrian sport)*
Longhorn[rind] *n* longhorn *(cattle breed)*
longieren to lunge *(a horse)*
Longierpeitsche *f* lunging whip
Lontaropalme *f* palmyra [palm], Borassus flabellifer
Loofah *f (bot)* loofah *(genus Luffa)*
Looplure *n* looplure *(insect attractant)*
Loquate *f (bot)* Japan[ese] medlar, loquat, Eriobotrya japonica
Lorbeerbaum *m* 1. laurel, laurus *(genus Laurus)*; 2. bay[-tree], bay laurel, sweet bay (laurel), Laurus nobilis
Lorbeerblatt *n* laurel (bay) leaf
Lorbeerblattfloh *m* bay psyllid (flea louse), Trioza alacris
Lorbeerblättrige Zistrose *f* laurel-leaved rockrose, Cistus laurifolius
Lorbeerblättriger Flachsbaum *m* Chinese laurel, Antidesma bunius
Lorbeereiche *f* laurel oak, Quercus laurifolia
Lorbeeren *fpl* deer droppings
Lorbeerfrucht *f* bayberry
Lorbeerkirsche *f* [common] cherry laurel, Prunus laurocerasus
Lorbeerlaub *n* laurel
Lorbeerrose *f* American laurel, kalmia *(genus Kalmia)*
Lorbeerseidelbast *m* wood laurel, Daphne laureola
Lorbeerwald *m* laurel forest
Lorbeerweide *f* bay (laurel-leaved) willow, Salix pentandra
Lorchel *f* saddle fungus, turban top *(genus Gyromitra)*
Lord-Howe-Palme *f* sentry palm *(genus Howeia)*
Lordose *f* lordosis
Lorrainebegonie *f* Lorraine begonia
Lorrainebegonien-Hybride *f* Christmas begonia, *(Am)* Scandinavian begonia
Losbaum *m (bot)* 1. clerodendrum *(genus Clerodendrum)*; 2. bleeding-heart vine, tube flower, Clerodendrum thomsoniae
Löschausrüstung *f* fire-fighting equipment, fire-extinguishing apparatus
~/tragbare fire pack
Löschfahrzeug *n* fire-fighting vehicle, fire-engine
Löschflugzeug *n* air tanker
Löschhubschrauber *m (Am)* helitanker
Löschkalk *m* slaked lime, slacklime, agricultural hydrate, calcium hydroxide *(fertilizer)*
Löschmannschaft *f* fire-fighting team, fire squad (brigade)
~/aus Hubschraubern abspringende helitack crew
Löschpatsche *f* fire beater (flail, swatter), fire-flap[per]
Löschtechnik *f* fire-fighting equipment
Löschtrupp *m s.* Löschmannschaft
lose 1. loose; 2. in bulk
Löseapparat *m* melter *(sugar manufacture)*
Losedünger *m* bulk fertilizer
Lösegut *n* melted sugar
Lösepfanne *f* melting pan *(sugar manufacture)*
Löser *m* omasum, third stomach *(of ruminants)*
Löserdürre *f (vet)* omasal impaction
losfas[e]rig flaky, scaly *(wood)*
Loshieb *m (forest)* severance felling (cutting)
loskoppeln to unleash, to uncouple *(hounds)*
Löslichkeit *f* solubility
Löslichkeitseigenschaften *fpl* solubility properties
Löslichkeitsverhalten *n* solubility behaviour
Löß *m (soil)* loess, löss

Lößablagerung f loess deposit
lößähnlich loessial, loessic
Lößboden m loess soil
Losschaligkeit f der Kartoffel feathering
lößig s. lößähnlich
Lößkindel n loess doll (nodule) *(calcareous concretion)*
Lößlehm m loess loam (clay)
Lößmergel m loess, löss
Lößpuppe f s. Lößkindel
Losstall m s. Laufstall
Losung f droppings, pellets *(of game)*
~ **des kleinen Raubwildes** fuants
~/**kugelförmige** pellet
Lösung f 1. solution; 2. dissolution
~/**äquimolare** equimolar solution
~/**Kaiserlingsche** Kaiserling's solution *(for preservation of anatomical preparations)*
~/**Knopsche** Knop's solution
~/**Lugolsche** *(vet)* Lugol's [iodine] solution
~/**Ringersche** *(vet)* Ringer's solution
Lösungsmittel n solvent
Lösungsmittelextraktion f solvent extraction
Lösungsmitteltrocknung f solvent drying
Lösungspotential n osmotic potential
Lösungsverdrängung f solution displacement
Lösungsverwitterung f *(soil)* disintegration by solution
Lotbaum m s. Lottbaum
lotisch lotic *(climatology)*
Lotos m, **Lotosblume** f *(bot)* lotus, nelumbo, nelumbium *(genus Nelumbo)*
Lotospflaume f date-plum, Diospyros lotus
Lottbaum m *(forest)* slip
Lotus m 1. *(bot)* lotus *(genus Lotus)*; 2. s. Lotos
Louisianamoos n Spanish (long-stem) moss, vegetable horsehair, Tillandsia usneoides
Louping-ill-Virus n louping ill virus
Löwenmaul n 1. snap[dragon], flapdragon, antirrhinum *(genus Antirrhinum)*; 2. s. Gartenlöwenmaul
Löwenohr n *(bot)* 1. lion's ear *(genus Leonotis)*; 2. lion's-ear, Leonotis nepetaefolia
Löwenzahn m 1. dandelion, horse gowan, Taraxacum officinale; 2. hawkbit *(genus Leontodon)*
Löwenzahngelbmosaikvirus n dandelion yellow mosaic virus
Löwenzahnkautschuk m kok-sag[h]yz rubber
Löwenzahnmosaikvirus n taraxacum mosaic virus
Lowicz[schaf] n Lowicz *(sheep breed)*
LSVzV s. Virus der scheckigen Verzwergung der Luzerne
LTH s. Hormon/laktogenes
LTP s. Langtagpflanze
Lubomycin n erythromycin *(antibiotic)*
Lubpresse f hand-push grease gun
Lucanthon n lucanthone *(anthelminthic)*
Luchs m 1. lynx *(genus Lynx)*; 2. lynx, Lynx lynx

Luciferase f luciferase *(enzyme)*
Luciferin n luciferin *(light-emitting substance)*
Lücke f gap
~ **im Kronendach** canopy gap
Lückenausbesserung f, **Lückenauspflanzung** f *(forest)* filling up, infilling, gapping, beating[-up], blanking, afterculture, after-planting, reinforcement planting
Lückenzahn m wolf-tooth *(of horses)*
lückig gappy, open *(crop stand)*; *(bot, zoo)* lacunose
Lucopenin n methicillin *(antibiotic)*
Ludwig-Effekt m *(ecol)* annidation
Luffa f 1. loofah, luffa *(genus Luffa)*; 2. ridge gourd, Luffa acutangula
Luft f air • **aus der** ~ aerial • **durch die** ~ **übertragen** airborne • **in der** ~ aerial
Luftableger m air layer
Luftabscheider m air sifter (sifting machine), air separator
Luftabschluß m air exclusion • **unter** ~ **[lebend]** anaerobic, under anaerobic conditions
Luftabzug m air discharge
Luftansaugschlauch m air suction hose
Luftaufnahme f 1. air (aerovisual, aerial) survey; 2. s. Luftbild
Luftaufnahmekammer f s. Luftbildkamera
Luftaustausch m air exchange
Luftbefeuchter m [air] humidifier
Luftbefeuchtung f air moistening (humidifying), damping-down
Luftbeobachtung f aerial observation
luftbereift tyred
luftbetätigt air-operated
Luftbewegung f air movement
Luftbild n aerial photograph, air photo, airscope
Luftbildauswertung f, **Luftbildinterpretation** f aerial photographic evaluation, aerial photointerpretation
Luftbildkamera f aerial (air) camera, aerial survey[ing] camera
Luftbildkarte f air [survey] map
Luftbildmessung f aerial photogrammetry, aerophotogrammetry
Luftbildmosaik n air-photo mosaic
Luftbildskizze f [aerial] mosaic
Luftbildtechnik f aerial photography
Luftbildumzeichner m sketchmaster
Luftbildvermessung f air (aerovisual, aerial) survey
Luftbildvolumentafel f *(forest)* aerial volume table
Luftbildwesen n aerial photography
Luftblase f air cell (space) *(of bird's egg)*
luftbürtig airborne
luftdicht airtight, air-proof
Luftdruck m air pressure; atmospheric (barometric) pressure • **bei gleichem** ~ isobaric
Luftdruckbaumschere f pneumatic clipper

Luftdruckmesser

Luftdruckmesser *m* air-pressure gauge, manometer; barometer
Luftdruckschreiber *m* barograph
lüften to aerate, to air, to ventilate, to vent
Lüfter *m* aerator, air (aeration) fan, ventilator
Lüfterheizung *f* fan heating
Lufterhitzer *m* [hot-]air heater
Lufterkundung *f* aerial reconnaissance
Luftfeuchte *f* atmospheric humidity (moisture), humidity of [the] air, air moisture (humidity) • **die ~ erhöhen** to damp
~/absolute absolute humidity, vapour concentration
~/relative relative humidity, rh
~/spezifische specific humidity
Luftfeuchtemesser *m* hygrometer
~/elektrischer [electric] psychrometer
Luftfeuchtemessung *f* hygrometry
Luftfeuchteschreiber *m* hygrograph
Luftfeuchtigkeit *f* s. Luftfeuchte
Luftfilter *n* air filter (cleaner)
Luftförderer *m* air conveyor
luftgekühlt air-cooled *(e.g. an engine)*
luftgetragen airborne
luftgetrocknet air-seasoned, air-dried
Lufthaltigkeit *f* pneumaticity *(e.g. of bones)*
Luftheizung *f* [hot-]air heating
Luftinfektion *f (vet)* airborne (aerator, droplet) infection
Luftkammer *f* air cell (space) *(of bird's egg)*
Luftkapazität *f (soil)* air capacity
Luftkissen[rasen]mäher *m* air-cushion [lawn] mower, hover mower
Luftknolle *f* aerial tuber; bud tuber *(of potato)*
Luftknollenyams *n* air potato, Dioscorea bulbifera
Luftkoppen *n* wind-sucking *(vice of horses)*
Luftkopper *m* wind-sucker *(horse)*
Luftkropf *m (vet)* sour crop
Luftkugelkissen *n* hemispheric cushion plant
Luftkühlung *f* air cooling
Luftloch *n s.* Lüftungsöffnung
Luft-Luft-Wärmepumpe *f* air-to-air heat pump *(e.g. in greenhouses)*
Luftmassenaustausch *m*/**horizontaler** advection
~/vertikaler convection
Luftpflanze *f* air plant, epiphyte, aerophyte
Luftplankton *n* aeroplankton, aerial plankton
Luftpolsterfolie *f* air-cushion plastic film, nap-finish plastic film
Luftporenvolumen *n (soil)* air-filled porosity
Luftreinhaltung *f* air conservation
Luftriß *m* check, sun-crack *(in wood)*
Luftröhre *f* trachea, windpipe
Luftröhren... *s. a.* Tracheo...
Luftröhrenast *m* bronchus
Luftröhrenentzündung *f (vet)* tracheitis
Luftröhreneröffnung *f (vet)* tracheotomy
Luftröhrengabelung *f* tracheal bifurcation
Luftröhrenknorpel[ring] *m* tracheal cartilage

Luftröhrenwurm *m* gapeworm *(genus Syngamus)*
Luftsack *m* air sac (cell) *(animal anatomy)*
~/klavikulärer interclavicular air sac *(of fowl)*
Luftsackentzündung *f* air sac disease (infection), aerosacculitis, airsacculitis *(of fowl)*
Luftsauerstoff *m* atmospheric oxygen
luftsauerstoffabhängig aerobic
luftsauerstoffunabhängig anaerobic
Luftschacht *m* air shaft, chimney
Luftschadstoff *m* air pollutant (contaminant)
Luftschlucken *n (vet)* aerophagy
Luftsieb *n* mit automatischem Staubaustrag rotary discharge screen
Luftsprung *m* gambade, gambado *(equestrian sport)*
Luftstaub *m* aerial dust
Luftstickstoff *m* atmospheric nitrogen
Luftstrom *m* air flow (stream) • **mittels Luftstroms fördern** to blow
Luftstromgefrieren *n* blast freezing
Lufttemperatur *f* air temperature
Lufttransport *m* air transport[ation]
Lufttriangulation *f (forest)* aerial triangulation
lufttrocken air-seasoned, air-dry
Lufttrockenfeuchte *f* air-dried moisture
Lufttrockenheit *f* air drought
lufttrocknen to air-dry, to air-cure; to win *(hay)*
Lufttrockner *m* air dryer
Lufttrocknung *f* air (atmospheric) drying, air-curing, air (natural) seasoning
Luftumwälzung *f* air circulation
Lüftung *f* aeration, airing, ventilation
~/freie natural ventilation
Lüftungsklappe *f* vent, half-light
Lüftungsöffnung *f* [air] vent, ventilation hole
Lüftungssteuerung *f* ventilation control
Luftvermessung *f s.* Luftbildvermessung
Luftverschmutzung *f,* **Luftverunreinigung** *f* air (atmospheric) pollution
Luftverunreinigungsstoff *m* air pollutant (contaminant)
Luftvolumen *n s.* Luftporenvolumen
Luftvorwärmer *m* economizer
Luftwechsel *m* air [ex]change, air changing *(e.g in greenhouses)*
Luftweg *m* airway
~/oberer upper airway
Luftwege *mpl* respiratory system (tract)
Luftweiche *f* air steeping (resting) *(malting)*
Luftwurzel *f* aerial (air) root
Luftziegel *m* adobe
Luftzirkulation *f* air circulation
Luftzufuhr *f* air supply, admission of air
Luftzuführung *f* aeration
Luftzutritt *m* access of air • **unter ~ [lebend]** aerobic, under aerobic conditions
Luftzwiebel *f* Egyptian (top, tree) onion, Allium cepa var. viviparum
Luingrind *n* Luing [cattle] *(breed)*

Luzerneprotein

Luke f hatch; skylight *(e.g. in a greenhouse)*
Lukenband n door band *(of a silo)*
Luliberin n gonadoliberin, gonadotrop[h]in releasing hormone, GnRH
Lumbago f *(vet)* lumbago *(of horses)*
lumbal lumbar
Lumen n lumen
Lumichrom n lumichrome
Lumiflavin n lumiflavine
Lumpenzucker m lump sugar
Lunge f lung
Lungenabszeß m *(vet)* lung abscess
Lungenadenomatose f *(vet)* pulmonary adenomatosis, mountain disease, Montana progressive pneumonia *(of sheep)*
Lungenarterie f pulmonary artery
Lungenatmung f pulmonary respiration
Lungenblähung f s. Lungenemphysem
Lungenbläschen n [pulmonary] alveolus
Lungenblutung f *(vet)* pulmonary haemorrhage
Lungen-Brustfell-Entzündung f *(vet)* pleuropneumonia
Lungenembolie f *(vet)* pulmonary embolism
Lungenemphysem n *(vet)* pulmonary emphysema
Lungenentzündung f *(vet)* pneumonia *(for compounds s. under Pneumonie)*
Lungenenzian m *(bot)* harvest (autumn) bells, Gentiana pneumonanthe
Lungenfell n pulmonary (visceral) pleura
Lungenflügel m lung
Lungenhaarwurm m tracheal worm, Capillaria aerophila
Lungenkollaps m *(vet)* atelectasis
Lungenkraut n 1. lungwort *(genus Pulmonaria)*; 2. [common] lungwort, Jerusalem cowslip, Pulmonaria officinalis (obscura)
Lungenkreislauf m pulmonary circulation
Lungenlappen m pulmonary lobe
Lungenödem n *(vet)* lung oedema
Lungenpfeifer m *(vet)* piper *(horse)*
Lungenschwindsucht f s. Lungentuberkulose
Lungenseuche f **der Rinder** *(vet)* contagious bovine pleuropneumonia
Lungentuberkulose f *(vet)* pulmonary tuberculosis
Lungenvene f pulmonary vein
Lungenwurm m lung worm *(family Protostrongylidae)*
Lungenwurzel f root of the lung
Lunte f foxtail, brush
Lupanin n lupanin[e] *(alkaloid)*
Lupine f lupin, lupine *(genus Lupinus)*
Lupinenalkaloid n lupin alkaloid
Lupinenheu n lupin hay
Lupinenklee m bastard lupin, lupinaster, Trifolium lupinaster
Lupinensamen m lupin, lupine
Lupinenschrot n lupin [seed] meal
Lupinidin n lupinidin *(alkaloid)*
Lupinin n lupinin *(alkaloid)*

Lupinose f *(vet)* lupinosis
Lupulin n lupulin
Lupulindrüse f lupulin gland
Lupulon n lupulone *(hop resin)*
Lupus m **vulgaris** *(vet)* lupus, skin tuberculosis
Lurcher m lurcher *(dog breed)*
Lutein n lutein, luteol *(yellow natural dye)*
luteinisieren to luteinize
Luteinisierung f luteinization
Luteinisierungshormon n luteinizing hormone, LH, lutropin, interstitial-cell stimulating hormone, ICSH, prolan
Luteolin n luteolin, weld *(dye from Reseda luteola)*
Luteolyse f luteolysis
luteolytisch luteolytic
Luteoskyrin n luteoskyrin *(toxin from Penicillum islandicum)*
Luteotropin n luteotrop[h]ic, hormone, LTH, luteotrop[h]in, prolactin
Lutropin n s. Luteinisierungshormon
Lutropinfreisetzungsfaktor m luteinizing-hormone releasing factor, LH-RF
Luvisol m luvisol *(great unit of FAO soil classification)*
Luvseite f windward, weather side
Luxation f *(vet)* luxation, dislocation
Luxurianz f luxuriance *(e.g. of plant growth)*
Luxurieren n **der Bastarde** hybrid vigour, heterosis
Luxusaufnahme f, **Luxuskonsumption** f luxury consumption *(e.g. of nutrients)*
Luxushund m toy dog
Luzerne f alfalfa, [blue] lucerne, lucern, purple medic[k], Medicago sativa [ssp. sativa]
Luzerneblattkonzentrat n lucerne leaf concentrate
Luzerneblattmehl n lucerne leaf meal
Luzerneblattnager m alfalfa weevil, Hypera postica, Phytonomus variabilis
Luzerneblütengallmücke f lucerne flower midge, Contarinia medicaginis
Luzernefalter m alfalfa caterpillar, Colias chrysotheme (eurytheme)
Luzernefloh m lucerne flea, Sminthurus viridis
Luzernegärheu n lucerne haylage
Luzernegrasanbau m lucerne-grass cropping
Luzernegrasgemisch n lucerne-grass mixture
Luzernegrünmehl n lucerne meal, dried lucerne
Luzerneheu n lucerne hay
Luzernemarienkäfer m alfalfa ladybird [beetle], Subcoccinella vigintiquattuorpuncta (24-punctata)
Luzernemehl n lucerne meal, dried lucerne
Luzernemosaik n alfalfa mosaic *(virosis)*
Luzernemosaikvirus n alfalfa mosaic virus, AlMV, AMV
Luzernepellet n lucerne pellet
Luzernepreßwürfel m lucerne cube
Luzerneprotein n lucerne protein

Luzerneproteinkonzentrat

Luzerneproteinkonzentrat *n* lucerne protein concentrate
Luzernerüßler *m* alfalfa snout beetle, root weevil (borer), Otiorhynchus (Brachyrhinus) ligustici
Luzernesaatgut *n* lucerne seed
Luzernesaft *m* lucerne juice
Luzernesamen *m* lucerne seed
Luzernesilage *f* lucerne silage
Luzernewanze *f* alfalfa plant bug, Adelphocoris lineolatus
Luzernewelke *f* wilt of lucern[e] *(caused by Corynebacterium insidiosum)*
luzid 1. lucid, luminous, bright; *(bot, zoo)* lucid, translucent
L-Winkelmesserblatt *n* L-blade, L-hoe
LWKV *s.* Warzenkrankheitsvirus der Luzerne
Ly *s.* Lysin
Lyase *f* lyase *(enzyme)*
Lycopen *n* lycopene *(plant dye)*
Lycorin *n* lycorine *(alkaloid)*
Lymphadenitis *f (vet)* lymphadenitis
lymphähnlich lymphoid
Lymphangitis *f s.* Lymphgefäßentzündung
Lymphansammlung *f (vet)* lymphoma
Lymphapparat *m* lymphatic system
lymphatisch lymphatic
Lymphbildung *f* lymphopoiesis
Lymphdrüse *f s.* Lymphknoten
Lymphe *f* lymph, serum
Lymphgefäß *n* lymph vessel, lymphatic [vessel]
~ der Darmzotte/zentrales lacteal
Lymphgefäßentzündung *f (vet)* lymphangitis
~/epizootische epizootic lymphangitis *(of solipeds, caused by Histoplasma farciminosum)*
Lymphgefäßsystem *n* lymph vascular system
Lymphgewebe *n* lymphatic (lymphoid) tissue
Lymphkapillare *f* lymph capillary
Lymphknötchenaggregationen *fpl* Peyer patches *(in the last division of the small intestine)*
Lymphknoten *m* lymph node (gland)
Lymphknotenentzündung *f (vet)* lymphadenitis
Lymphkörperchen *n s.* Lymphozyt
Lymphocystisvirus *n* lymphocystis virus
Lymphogranulomatose *f (vet)* lymphogranuloma[tosis], Hodgkin's disease
lymphoid lymphoid
Lymphokin *n* lymphokine
Lymphom *n (vet)* lymphoma
Lymphomatose *f (vet)* lymphomatosis
Lymphopoese *f* lymphopoiesis
Lymphosarkom *n (vet)* lymphosarcoma
Lymphozyt *m* lymphocyte
~/thymusabhängiger thymus-derived lymphocyte, T lymphocyte (cell)
Lymphozytenstimulation *f,* **Lymphozytentransformation** *f* lymphocyte transformation
Lymphsystem *n* lymphatic system
Lymphtumor *m (vet)* lymphoma
Lymphzelle *f s.* Lymphozyt

Lyophilisation *f* lyophilization, freeze drying (dehydration)
lyophilisieren to lyophilize, to freeze-dry
lyotrop lyotropic
Lysergsäure *f* lysergic acid *(basic substance of ergot alkaloids)*
lysigen lysigenous
Lysimeter *n* lysimeter
Lysimetrie *f* lysimetry
lysimetrisch lysimetric
Lysin *n* lysine, 2,6-diaminohexanoic acid *(amino-acid)*
Lysinbedarf *m* lysine requirement
Lysinmangel *m* lysine deficiency
Lysocithin *n s.* Lysolecithin
Lysogenie *f* lysogeny
Lysogenisierung *f* lysogenization
Lysolecithin *n* lysolecithin, lysophosphatidylcholine *(phospholipid)*
Lysosom *n* lysosome *(organelle)*
lysosomal lysosomal
Lysotyp *m* lysotype *(bacteriology)*
Lysotypie *f* phage typing
Lysozym *n* lysozyme *(bacteriolytic enzyme)*
Lyssa *f s.* Tollwut
Lyxose *f* lyxose *(monosaccharide)*
LZ *s.* Zuwachs/laufender jährlicher

M

M *s.* Malling-Unterlage
Maack-Heckenkirsche *f* Amur honeysuckle, Lonicera maackii
Mäander *m* meander, ox-bow
Maas-Rhein-Ijssel-Rind *n* Meuse-Rhine-Yssel, MRY *(cattle breed)*
Macahubapalme *f s.* Macawbaum
Macajabutter *f* macaw butter (fat)
Macassaröl *n* Macassar [oil] *(from Schleichera oleosa)*
Macawbaum *m,* **Macawpalme** *f (bot)* 1. macaw *(genus Acrocomia)*; 2. macaw, Acrocomia sclerocarpa (aculeata)
Macchia *f,* **Macchie** *f* maquis *(brushwood of mediterranean regions)*
Machaweizen *m* macha wheat, Triticum macha
Machete *f* machete, matchet
Mächtigkeitsspringen *n* puissance *(equestrian sport)*
Mädchenauge *n (bot)* 1. coreopsis, tickseed *(genus Coreopsis)*; 2. golden-wave, Coreopsis basalis
Mädchenkiefer *f* Japanese white pine, Pinus parviflora
Made *f* grub, worm, [insect] larva; maggot *(esp. of flies and midgets)*; slug *(esp. of hymenopterans)*
Madeira *m* Madeira, malmsey, malvoisie *(wine)*

Madeiraschabe f Madeira roach, Leucophaea maderae
Madenfraß m (vet) myiasis
Mädesüß n 1. meadowsweet, goat's-beard (genus Filipendula); 2. goat's-beard, maid of the meadow, Filipendula (Spiraea) ulmaria; 3. dropwort, Filipendula vulgaris
Madie f [Chile] tarweed, Media sativa
madig maggoty, wormy, worm-eaten
Madiöl n madia oil (from Madia sativa)
Madonnenlilie f madonna lily, Juno's rose, Lilium candidum
Maedi f (vet) maedivisna (of sheep)
Maedi-Virus n visna maedi virus
Magazinheizkessel m magazine boiler
Magen m stomach, maw, ventriculus • mit einhöhligem ~ monogastric • mit mehrhöhligem ~ polygastric, multistomached
~/einhöhliger one-compartment stomach
~/mehrhöhliger multichambered stomach
Magenausgang m pylorus, pyloric opening
Magen-Darm-Entzündung f (vet) gastro-enteritis, gastro-enteropathy
Magen-Darm-Kanal m gastro-intestinal tract, GI-tract, digestive tract
Magendarmwurmkrankheit f (vet) trichostrongylosis
Magendassel f s. Magenfliege
Magendrüse f gastric gland
Mageneingang m cardia
Magenentfernung f (vet) gastrectomy
Magenentleerung f gastric emptying
Magenerweiterung f gastromegaly
Magenfaktor m intrinsic factor (enzyme, mucoprotein)
Magenfliege f 1. horse bot-fly (genus Gasterophilus); 2. horse bot-fly, Gasterophilus intestinalis
Magengekröse n/dorsales epiploon, greater omentum
Magengeschwür n (vet) gastric ulcer
Magengift n stomach poison
Magenhormon n gastric hormone
Magen-Leber-Arterie f coeliac artery
Magenleerung f gastric emptying
Magenmotilität f gastric motility
Magenmund m cardia
Magensaft m gastric juice
Magensäure f gastric acid
Magenschleimhaut f gastric mucosa
Magenschleimhautentzündung f (vet) gastritis
Magensekretin n gastrin (hormone)
Magensonde f (vet) stomach tube
Magenstase f, **Magenstauung** f (vet) gastric stasis
Magenstein m (vet) gastrolith
Magentotalentfernung f (vet) gastrectomy
Magenulkus n (vet) gastric ulcer
Magenverdauung f gastric digestion
Magenwurm m stomach worm (comprehensive term)

mager 1. lean, meagre, poor, scraggy; fatless (food); 2. poor, hungry (soil)
Magerfleisch n lean
Magerkäse m skim-milk cheese
Magerkeit f leanness, meagreness; poorness (of a soil)
Magerkrankheit f der Pferde straining disease [of horses]
Magermilch f skim [milk], skimmed (non-fat) milk
~/eingedickte condensed skim milk
Magermilchpulver n skim-milk powder, dried skim milk
Magerrindvieh n store cattle
Magerweide f rough grazing
Magerwiese f dry meadow
Maggikraut n [garden] lovage, Levisticum officinale
Maghemit m maghaemite (non-clay mineral)
Magmatit m igneous rock
Magnesia f magnesium oxide
Magnesiaglimmer m phlogopite (non-clay mineral)
Magnesiakalk m magnesian limestone
Magnesiamergel m magnesium marl (fertilizer)
Magnesit m magnesite (non-clay mineral)
Magnesiumammoniumphosphat n magnesium ammonium phosphate (fertilizer)
Magnesiumbranntkalk m burnt magnesian lime
Magnesiumcarbonat n magnesium carbonate
Magnesiumdüngemittel n magnesium fertilizer
Magnesiumlöschkalk m hydrated magnesium lime
Magnesiumoxid n magnesium oxide
Magnesiumsilicat n magnesium silicate
Magnesiumspiegelerhöhung f im Blut (vet) hypermagnesaemia
Magnesiumspiegelverringerung f im Blut (vet) hypomagnesaemia
Magnesiumsulfat n magnesium sulphate; (soil) kieserite
Magnetabscheider m magnetic separator
Magnetabscheidung f magnetic separation
Magnetausleser m electromagnetic seed cleaner
Magneteisenstein m s. Magnetit
Magnetfutterverteiler m magnet feeder
Magnetit m magnetite, magnetic iron [ore]
magnetotrop (bot) magnetotropic
Magnetotropismus m (bot) magnetotropism
Magnetspritzventil n solenoid spray valve
Magnetzünder m magneto
Magnifikation f/**biologische** biological magnification (amplification) (increase of concentration e.g. of pesticides within a food chain)
Magnolie f (bot) magnolia (genus Magnolia)
Magnum n magnum (protein-forming part of the oviduct)
Magnumflasche f magnum (a large bottle holding about 1.5 litres of wine or spirits)
Magyar Vizsla m vizsla (dog breed)
Mahagoni n mahogany

Mahagonibaum

Mahagonibaum *m* mahogany [tree] *(genus Swietenia)*
Mahagoniholz *n* mahogany
Mahagonitriebminierer *m (ent)* mahogany shootborer *(genus Hypsipyla)*
Mähbalken *m* cutter (cutting, sickle) bar, reaping beam
Mähbalkenfinger *m* knife finger
Mähbinder *m* [reaper-]binder, grain (harvester, sheaf) binder, sheafer
~ **mit Handbindung** hand-tie reaper
Mahd *f* 1. mowing, cutting; 2. cut; [cut] grass
Mähdreschbinder *m* combine with binder attachment
Mähdrescher *m* combine harvester [thresher], grain combine (harvester), [field] combine, harvester-thresher • **mit dem ~ ernten** to combine
~ **mit Absackvorrichtung** bagger-type combine, sack-type combine
~ **mit Einmannbedienung** one-man combine
~ **mit Hangausgleich** hillside combine [harvester]
~ **mit seitlichem Schneidwerk** side-cut[ting] combine [harvester]
~ **mit vollem Hangausgleich** full-levelling combine
~/**selbstfahrender** self-propelled combine harvester
Mähdrescherfahrer *m* combine operator
Mähdrescherreinigung *f* cleaning shoe
Mähdrusch *m* combine harvesting, combining
mähdruschfähig threshable
Mähdruschfähigkeit *f* threshability
Mähdruschfrucht *f* combined-harvested crop, combinable (grain) crop
mähen to mow, to cut; to reap, to crop *(esp corn)*
~/**mit der Korbsense** to cradle
~/**mit der Sense** to scythe
~/**mit der Sichel** to sickle
Mäher *m* reaper *(worker)*
Mähhäckselladen *n* mowing-chopping loading
Mähhäcksler *m* chopper harvester, harvester-chopper, chaff-cutting combine [harvester]
Mähknicker *m* mower conditioner (crimper), mower with roller conditioner, crusher-mower
Mählader *m* cutter-loader, loader combine (harvester)
Mähladewagen *m* mower-loader wagon, cutter-forage wagon
mahlbar *s.* mahlfähig
mahlen to mill, to grind; to flour; to disintegrate
~/**grob** to kibble, to crush
Mahlen *n* milling; disintegration
~/**maschinelles** machine milling
mahlfähig millable
Mahlfähigkeit *f* millability, milling ability
Mahlgut *n* grist *(milling)*
Mahlstein *m* millstone
Mahlwerk *n* mill
Mahlzahn *m* molar [tooth], cheek tooth

Mähmaschine *f* mower, mowing machine, reaper, reaping-machine; corn cutter
~ **mit Doppelmesserschneidwerk** double-knife mower
Mähmesser *n* [mower, mowing] knife; mower-sickle
Mähmesserhub *m* lift of mowing knives
Mähmesserklinge *f* knife section
Mähmesserschleifmaschine *f* mower knife grinder
Mähne *f* mane
Mähnengerste *f* foxtail barley, Hordeum jubatum
Mähnenhaar *n* mane hair
Mähnenkamm *n* mane comb, crest
Mähnenschaf *n* aoudad, Barbary sheep, Ammotragus lervia
Mähnutzung *f* **von Grasland (Grünland)** soilage, zero grazing
Mahonie *f (bot)* mahonia *(genus Mahonia)*
Mähquetscher *m* mower crusher, crusher-mower
Mähre *f* jade, screw, rip
Mähweide *f* hay (mowing, temporary) pasture, grazing ley
Mähwender *m* mower conditioner
Mähwerk *n* mower, header
~/**kombiniertes** gang mower
~ **mit Scherenschneidwerk** cutter bar mower
Mähwerk[s]antrieb *m* mower drive
Mähwiese *f* hay meadow
Mähzetter *m* mower tedder
Maiapfel *m* 1. may-apple, podophyllum *(genus Podophyllum)*; 2. [common] may-apple, Podophyllum peltatum
Maiblume *f s.* Maiglöckchen
Maiden *n*, **Maidenstute** *f* maiden *(horse racing)*
Maiglöckchen *n* lily of the valley, wood lily, Convallaria majalis
Maiglöckchenbaum *m* snowdrop tree, snowbell *(genus Halesia)*
Maikäfer *m* may-bug, May beetle, [cock]chafer *(genus Melolontha)*
Maikälte *f* Icemen *(meteorological phenomenon)*
Maikrankheit *f* May sickness *(of honey-bees)*
Maillard-Reaktion *f* Maillard (browning) reaction
Mairose *f* cinnamon rose, Rosa majalis (cinnamomea)
Mais *m* maize, *(Am)* [Indian] corn, mealie[s] *(South Africa)*, Zea mays
~/**bodenbearbeitungslos angebauter** no-till corn
~/**geschälter** hominy
~/**in Selbstfolge angebauter** continuous corn
~/**lysinreicher** high-lysine maize
Maisanbau *m* maize growing, *(Am)* corn growing
Maisanbaugürtel *m* corn belt *(of the USA)*
Maisbeulenbrand *m* common smut [of maize], blister (boil) smut, *(Am)* corn smut *(caused by Ustilago maydis)*
Maisblattfleckenvirus *n* maize leaf fleck virus

Maiszünsler

Maisblattlaus *f* corn (cereal) leaf aphid, Rhopalosiphum maidis
Maisbrei *m* hominy
Maisch *m s.* Maische
Maischapparat *m* masher
Maischbottich *m* mash-tub, mash-tun, mash vat (copper)
Maische *f* 1. mash; crushed grape; 2. mixer, crystallizer *(sugar manufacture)*
Maischefertiger *m* masher
Maischefilter *n* mash filter
Maischekochen *n* mash boiling
maischen to mash
Maischepumpe *f* mash pump
Maischesäuerung *f* mash acidification
Maischgefäß *n*, **Maischkessel** *m s.* Maischbottich
Maischharke *f* oar
Maischpfanne *f s.* Maischbottich
Maischverfahren *n* mashing method
Maisdrillmaschine *f* maize drill, *(Am)* corn planter
Maisentlieschmaschine *f* [maize] husker, husking machine
Maiserntemaschine *f (Am)* corn harvester
Maiserntevorsatz *m s.* Maispflückvorsatz
Maisfeldhäcksler *m* maize forage harvester
Maisflocken *fpl* flaked maize
~/geröstete *(Am)* cornflakes
Maisfuttermehl *n* maize meal, *(Am)* corn meal
Maisganzpflanzensilage *f* full crop maize silage, *(Am)* whole-plant corn silage
Maisgärfutter *n* maize silage
Maisgebiß *n s.* Maispflückvorsatz
Maisgürtel *m* corn belt *(of the USA)*
Maishäcksler *m* maize chopper (forage harvester)
Maiskäfer *m* maize weevil, *(Am)* corn billbug, Sitophilus zeamais
Maiskeim *m* maize germ
Maiskeimöl *n* maize [germ] oil
Maiskeimschrot *n* maize germ meal
Maiskleber *m* maize gluten
Maiskleberfutter[mittel] *n* maize gluten feed
Maiskleie *f* maize bran
Maiskolben *m* maize ear (cob), *(Am)* [corn-]cob, mealie[s] *(South Africa)*
Maiskolbenernte *f* maize husking
Maiskolbenfäule *f (phyt)* ear rot
Maiskolbenpflücker *m* maize picker (snapper); picker sheller
Maiskolbenpflückhäcksler *m* maize cob snapper chopper
Maiskolbenrebbelmaschine *f* [maize] picker sheller
Maiskolbenschrot *m* maize ear meal, *(Am)* corn and cob meal, ground-ear corn
Maiskolbensilage *f* maize ear silage, ensiled maize ears, whole maize cob silage
Maiskolbensilo *m* maize ear silo
Maiskolbenspindel *f (Am)* cob
Maiskombine *f* maize combine
Maiskorn *n (Am)* corn kernel
Maiskorn-Spindel-Gemisch *n (Am)* corn-cob mix, CCM
Maiskrankheit *f*/**Stewartsche** *(Am)* Stewart's disease of sweet corn *(caused by Bacterium stewartii)*
Maislegemaschine *f* maize drill, *(Am)* corn planter
Maismehl *n* maize (Indian) meal, maize flour, *(Am)* cornflour, [corn] meal
Maismelasse *f (Am)* corn sugar molasses
Maismosaikvirus *n* maize mosaic virus
Maisnebenprodukt *n* maize by-product
Maisöl *n* maize oil
Maisolin *n* gluten feed
Maispflückdrescher *m* maize combine
Maispflücker *m* maize picker (snapper)
Maispflückvorsatz *m* maize [picker] head, maize header (attachment)
Maisprotein *n* maize protein
Maisquellwasser *n* corn-steep liquor
Maisrauhverzwergungsvirus *n* maize rough-dwarf virus, MRDV
Maisrebbelmaschine *f*, **Maisrebbler** *m* [maize] sheller
Maissämaschine *f* maize drill, *(Am)* corn planter
Maisschlempe *f* maize stillage
Maisschneidwerk *n* maize cutter
Maisschrot *m* maize meal, hominy, *(Am)* corn meal
Maissilage *f* maize silage
Maissirup *n* corn syrup
Maisspindel *f* maize cob, *(Am)* [corn-]cob
Maisstärke *f* maize starch
Maisstengel *m (Am)* corn stalk
Maisstengelbohrer *m* African maize (sorghum) stem borer, Busseola fusca
Maisstoppel *f (Am)* corn stubble
Maisstrichelvirus *n* maize streak virus
Maisstroh *n* maize straw (trash), *(Am)* corn stover (plant residue)
Maisstroheinleger *m* maize straw skimmer
Maistrockenschuppen *m* maize crib, *(Am)* corn drying shed
Maisverzwergung *f (phyt, Am)* corn stunt
Maisverzwergungsmosaik *n* maize dwarf mosaic [disease], MDM
Maisverzwergungsmosaikvirus *n* maize dwarf mosaic virus
Maisvollerntemaschine *f* maize combine
Maiswärmeeinheit *f (Am)* corn heat unit *(phenology)*
Maisweißlinienmosaikvirus *n* maize white line mosaic virus
Maiszüchtung *f* maize breeding
Maiszucker *m (Am)* corn sugar
Maiszuckermelasse *f (Am)* corn sugar molasses
Maiszünsler *m (ent)* [European] corn borer, Ostrinia (Pyrausta) nubilalis

Maiszystennematode

Maiszystennematode *m* corn cyst-nematode, Heterodera zeae
Maizenafutter *n* gluten feed
Majoran *m* [sweet, annual, knotted] marjoram, Origanum majorana, Majorana hortensis
Makadamnuß *f* macadamia nut
Makadamnußbaum *m* macadamia nut, Macadamia ternifolia
Makel *m* blemish *(e.g. of fruits)*
Makkaroniweizen *m* macaroni wheat, durum [wheat], Triticum durum
Makroaggregat *n (soil)* macroaggregate
Makroarthropode *m* macroarthropod
Makrobiose *f* longevity
Makroelement *n* macroelement
Makroevolution *f* macroevolution
Makrofauna *f* macrofauna
Makroflora *f* macroflora
Makrogamet *m* macrogamete
Makrogefüge *n (soil)* macrostructure
Makroinvertebrat *m* macroinvertebrate
Makroklima *n* macroclimate
makroklimatisch macroclimate
Makroklimatologie *f* macroclimatology
Makromutation *f (gen)* macromutation
Makronährelement *n*, **Makronährstoff** *m* macronutrient, basic nutrient
Makroökosystem *(ecol)* biome
Makroparasit *m* macroparasite
Makropeptid *n* macropeptid[e]
Makrophag[e] *m* macrophage *(blood cell)*
Makrorelief *n (soil)* macrorelief
makroskopisch macroscopic
Makrosomie *f* gigantism
Makrospore *f (bot)* megaspore
Makroumwelt *f (ecol)* macroenvironment
Makrovermehrung *f* macropropagation
Makrozytose *f (vet)* macrocytosis
Malabargras *n* Malabar (East Indian) lemon grass, Cochin grass, Cymbopogon flexuosus
Malabarkardamome *f (bot)* cardamom, cardamon, cardamum, Elettaria cardamomum
Malabarspinat *m* 1. Malabar spinach (nightshade), [East] Indian spinach, Basella alba (rubra); 2. *s.* Dorniger Fuchsschwanz
Malabsorption *f* malabsorption
Malabsorptionssyndrom *n (vet)* malabsorption syndrome
Malachitgrün *n* malachite green *(dye, inhibitor)*
Malaga-Ziege *f* Malaga goat *(breed)*
Malaguetapfeffer[baum] *m* African (Guinea) pepper, spice tree, Xylopia aethiopica
Malaienblume *f* moth orchid, phalaenopsis *(genus Phalaenopsis)*
Malakkaapfel *m* malay apple, Eugenia malaccensis
Malakkarohr *n* Malacca cane *(from Calamus rotang)*
Malaria *f (vet)* malaria

Malat *n* malate
Malatdehydrogenase *f* malate (malic) dehydrogenase *(enzyme)*
Malatenzym *n* malic enzyme *(comprehensive term)*
Malathion *n* malathion, mercaptothion *(insecticide, acaricide)*
Malatoxidase *f* malate oxidase *(enzyme)*
Malatsynth[et]ase *f* malate synthase, glyoxylate transacetylase *(enzyme)*
Malazie *f (vet)* malacia
Malbaum *m* boundary tree; rubbed tree
Maldigestion *f* maldigestion
Maldivische Nuß *f* double coco-nut [palm], Lodoicea maldivica
Maleinsäure *f* maleic acid *(fatty acid)*
Maleinsäurehydrazid *n*, **Maleinylhydrazin** *n* maleic hydrazide, MH *(growth regulator, herbicide)*
maligne *(vet)* malign[ant]
Malignität *f (vet)* malignancy
Malinois *m* [Belgian] Malinois *(dog breed)*
Mallein *n (vet)* mallein *(cultural filtrate for detection of glanders)*
Malleus *m* malleus *(of the mammalian ear)*
Malling-Merton-Unterlage *f* Malling Merton rootstock, MM *(standardized name for an apple rootstock, resistant to Eriosoma lanigerum)*
Malling-Unterlage *f* Malling rootstock, M
Malm *m (soil)* malm
Malmsey *m s.* Malvasier
Malnutrition *f* malnutrition
Malonaldehyd *m* malonaldehyde
Malonat-CoA-Transferase *f* malonate CoA-transferase *(enzyme)*
Malonyl-CoA *n* malonyl-CoA
Malonyl-CoA-Carboxy-Lyase *f*, **Malonyl-CoA-Decarboxylase** *f* malonyl-CoA decarboxylase, malonyl-CoA carboxy-lyase *(enzyme)*
Malonyl-Reaktionsweg *m* malonyl pathway *(of fatty acid synthesis in mammary glands)*
Malonsäure *f* malonic acid
~/aktivierte malonyl-CoA
Malonsäurealdehyd *m* malonaldehyde
Malope *f s.* Trichtermalve
Malpighisches Gefäß *n* Malpighian tubule (tube) *(e.g. of insects)*
~ Nierenkörperchen *n* renal corpuscle
Malresorptionssyndrom *n (vet)* malabsorption syndrome
Maltase *f* maltase, alpha-glucosidase, alpha-glucosidehydrolase *(enzyme)*
Malteser *m* Maltese dog (terrier) *(breed)*
Maltodextrin *n* maltodextrin *(starch degradation product)*
Maltose *f* maltose, malt sugar *(disaccharide)*
Maltosedextrin *n s.* Maltodextrin
Maltosezahl *f* maltose figure

Malvasier *m* 1. malvasia *(grape)*; 2. Madeira, malmsey, malvoisie *(wine)*
Malve *f* mallow *(genus Malva)*
Malvengewächse *npl* mallow family *(family Malvaceae)* • **die ~ betreffend** malvaceous
Malvenmosaikvirus *n* malva vein clearing virus
Malvenrost *m* hollyhock rust *(caused by Puccinia malvacearum)*
Malz *n* malt • **~ bereiten** to malt • **mit ~ behandeln** to malt • **zu ~ werden** to malt
~/dunkles dark malt
~/helles pale (ordinary) malt
~/Münchner Munich malt
~/Pils[e]ner Pils[e]ner malt
Malzagar *m* malt agar
Malzamylase *f* malt amylase
Malzanalyse *f* malt analysis
malzartig malty
Malzbehandlung *f* malt handling
Malzbereitung *f* malting
Malzbier *n* malt beer
Mälzeigenschaft *f* malting property
mälzen to malt
Mälzen *n* malting
Mälzer *m* maltster, maltman
Mälzerei *f* 1. malt-house, malting [house]; 2. *s.* Mälzen
Mälzereiabwasser *n* malt-house effluent
Malzessig *m* malt vinegar, alegar
Malzextrakt *m* malt extract
Malzfabrik *f* malt-house, malting [house]
malzhaltig malty
Malzhärte *f* malt hardness
Malzhaus *n* malt-house, malting [house]
Malzherstellung *f* malting
~/kontinuierliche continuous malting
malzig malty
Mälzindustrie *f* malting industry
Malzkeim *m* malt rootlet (sprout)
Malzlagerhaus *n s.* Malzhaus
Malzmehl *n* malt flour
Malzmilch *f* malted milk
Malzpolierabfall *m* malt culms
Malzreinigung *f* malt cleaning
Malzreinigungsabfall *m* malt culms
Malzschrot *m* malt grind (meal), grist
Malzstärke *f* malt starch
Malztenne *f* [malting] floor
Mälzung *f* malting
Mälzungsausbeute *f* outcast
Mälzungsschwand *m* malting loss
Malzwender *m* oar
Malzwürze *f* malt wort
Malzzucker *m* malt sugar, maltose *(disaccharide)*
Mamey-Sapote *f* marmalade tree (plum), Pouteria sapota, Calocarpum mammosum, Lucuma mammosa
Mamillarkegelschicht *f* mamillary cone layer *(of bird's-egg)*

Mammatumor *m (vet)* mammary tumour (gland neoplasm)
Mammiapfel *m* mammee [apple], mamey, mammea, Santo Domingo apricot, Mammea americana
Mammutbaum *m* 1. sequoia, wellingtonia *(genus Sequoia)*; 2. [giant] sequoia, mammoth (big) tree, Sequoiadendron giganteum, Sequoia gigantea
Mammutpumpe *f* mammoth pump *(sugar-beet processing)*
MaMV *s.* Malvenmosaikvirus
Manchester Terrier *m* Manchester terrier *(dog breed)*
Mancozeb *n* mancozeb *(fungicide)*
Mandarine *f* mandarin [orange], mandarine, Citrus reticulata
Mandel *f* 1. almond; 2. *s.* Mandelbaum; 3. tonsil *(animal anatomy)*
~/bittere bitter almond
~/süße sweet almond
mandelähnlich, mandelartig amygdaloid
Mandelbaum *m* [sweet] almond, Prunus dulcis var. dulcis
Mandelbäumchen *n* flowering almond, Prunus triloba
Mandelblättriger Birnbaum *m* almond-leaved pear, long-leaf pear, Pyrus spinosa (amygdaliformis)
Mandelentzündung *f (vet)* tonsillitis
Mandelkern *m* almond
Mandelöl *n* [sweet] almond oil
Mandelweide *f* almond-leaved willow, French (peach-leaf) willow, Salix triandra
Mandibel *f*, **Mandibula** *f* mandible, jaw; lower jaw *(of mammals)*; upper jaw *(of arthropods)*
Mandibulardrüse *f* mandibular gland *(of arthropods)*
Mandioka *f s.* Maniok
Mandschurische Hasel[nuß] *f* 1. Manchurian filbert (hazel), Corylus sieboldiana var. mandshurica; 2. Japanese hazel, Corylus heterophylla
~ Marille *f* Manchurian apricot, Prunus (Armeniaca) mandshurica
~ Tanne *f* Amur (Siberian white) fir, Abies nephrolepis
~ Walnuß *f* Manchurian walnut, Juglans mandshurica
Mandschurischer Ahorn *m* Amur maple, Acer ginnala
~ Kirschapfel *m* Manchurian crab-apple, Malus baccata var. mandshurica
Maneb *n* maneb *(fungicide)*
Manech[schaf] *n* Manech *(sheep breed)*
Manet *n* manet *(fungicide)*
Mangalitzaschwein *n* Mangalitsa *(pig breed)*
Mangandüngemittel *n* manganese fertilizer
Manganit *m* manganite *(non-clay mineral)*
Manganmangel *m* manganese deficiency
Mangansulfat *n* manganese sulphate *(fertilizer)*

Mangantoxizität

Mangantoxizität *f* manganese toxicity
Mangel *m* shortage, deficiency
Mangelanämie *f (vet)* nutritional anaemia
Mangelelement *n* missing element
Mangelerkrankung *f* deficiency disease
mangelernährt malnourished
Mangelernährung *f* malnutrition, nutritional stress, innutrition
Mangelerscheinung *f* deficiency symptom
Mangelkorn *n* shrivelled grain
Mangelkrankheit *f* deficiency disease
Mangelsterilität *f* fasting sterility
Mangelsymptom *n* deficiency symptom
Mangelversuch *m* missing element trial
Mangelzustand *m* deficiency state
Mango[baum] *m* mango[-tree], Mangifera indica
Mango[frucht] *f* mango
Mangoingwer *m* mango-ginger, Curcuma amada
Mangold *m* spinach (leaf) beet, [Swiss] chard, Beta vulgaris var. vulgaris (cicla)
Mangopflaume *f* hog plum, Spondias pinnata (mangifera)
Mangosamen *m* mango seed
Mangostanbaum *m (bot)* mangosteen, Garcinia mangostana
Mangostane *f*, **Mangostanfrucht** *f* mangosteen
Mangrove *f*, **Mangrovebaum** *m (bot)* mangrove *(genus Rhizophora)*
Mangrovenannone *f* alligator (pond) apple, Annona glabra
Mangrovenwald *m* mangrove-forest
Mangrovenwaldgesellschaft *f* avicennietum
Mangrovenrindenextrakt *m* [mangrove-]cutch *(tanning material)*
Mangue *f*, **Manguebaum** *m* mangrove, Rhizophora mangle
Manihot *m* cassava *(genus Manihot)*
Manilahanf *m* Manila [hemp], abaca, Musa textilis
Manilapapier *n* Manila paper
Maniok *m* [bitter] cassava, manioc, mandioc[a], tapioca plant, Manihot esculenta (utilissima)
Maniokbrot *n* cassava
Manioknolle *f* cassava [tuber]
Maniokmehl *n* cassava [meal]
Maniokmosaikvirus *n* cassava mosaic virus
Maniokstärke *f* cassava [starch]
Manipulation *f* manipulation, handling
manipuliert/genetisch genetically manipulated
Mankatze *f s.* Manxkatze
Manna *n(f)* manna *(sugar-containing dried exudate esp. from Fraxinus ornus)*
Mannabaum *m* manna tree, Alhagi maurorum
Mannaeiche *f* manna oak, Quercus brantii
Mannaesche *f* manna (flowering) ash, Fraxinus ornus
Mannagras *n* manna (sweet) grass *(genus Glyceria)*
Mannan *n* mannan *(polysaccharide)*
Mannanase *f* beta-mannosidase *(enzyme)*
Mannaschwaden *m* water manna grass, Glyceria fluitans
Mannase *f s.* Mannanase
Männchen *n* male, jack, tom, he; cock *(of domestic fowl)*
Männertreu *n* blue lobelia of gardens, Lobelia erinus
Mannigfaltigkeitszentrum *n* centre of origin (domestication), gene centre
Mannit *m* mannite, mannitol *(sugar alcohol)*
männlich male, masculine, bull
männlich-fertil male-fertile
Männlichkeit *f* masculinity
männlich-steril male-sterile
(D)-Mannose *f* mannose *(monosaccharide)*
(D)-Mannosemannohydrolase *f* mannosidase *(enzyme)*
Mannosephosphatisomerase *f* mannosephosphate isomerase *(enzyme)*
Mannosidase *f* mannosidase *(enzyme)*
Mannsblut *n (bot)* sweet amber, Hypericum androsaemum
Mannskraft *f* herb bennet, common avens, Geum urbanum
Mannsschild *m* 1. rock jasmin[e] *(genus Androsace)*; 2. rock jasmin[e], Androsace septentrionalis
Mannstreu *f (bot)* field eryngo, Eryngium campestre
(D)-Mannuronsäure *f* mannuronic acid
Manometer *n* manometer, pressure gauge
Manövrierfähigkeit *f* mobility, *(Am)* maneuverability *(of vehicles)*
Mantel *m* 1. mantle *(e.g. of snails)*; 2. casing, cover; jacket *(e.g. of a cooler)*
Mantelhöhle *f* mantle cavity *(of snails)*
Mantelkühlraum *m* jacketed cold store
Mantelriß *m* radial shake (check) *(timber defect)*
~/radialer ray shake
Manxkatze *f* Manx cat, rumpy *(breed)*
Manzanitastrauch *m* manzanita, Arctostaphylos manzanita
MAP *s.* Mikroangiopathie
Maquis *m s.* Macchia
Maradi-Ziege *f* Red Sokoto goat *(breed)*
Maral *m s.* Sibirischer Rothirsch
Maräne *f* whitefish *(genus Coregonus)*
Marante *f* 1. [West Indian] arrowroot, Maranta arundinacea; 2. red-veined prayer plant, Maranta lenconeura var. erythroneura; 3. green-veined prayer plant, Maranta leuconeura var. kerchoviana
marantisch *s.* marastisch
Marasmus *m* marasmus
marastisch marasmic, marantic
Marbel *f* woodrush *(genus Luzula)*
Marchigiana[rind] *n* [Improved] Marche *(cattle breed)*
Marder *m* marten *(genus Martes)*

Marderfell *n* marten
Mareksche Geflügellähme (Krankheit) *f* Marek's disease, MD, fowl (range) paralysis, paralysis of domestic fowl, acute avian leucosis
Marekvakzine *f* Marek's vaccine
Marekvirus *n* Marek's disease virus, avian herpes virus
Maremmana[rind] *n* Maremma *(cattle breed)*
Margarine *f* margarine
marginal marginal
Marienblatt *n (bot)* costmary, alecost, Chrysanthemum majus (balsamita)
Mariendistel *f* 1. holy thistle *(genus Silybum)*; 2. [blessed] milk thistle, St. Mary thistle, Silybum marianum
Marienglockenblume *f (bot)* Canterbury-bell[s], Campanula medium
Marienkäfer *m* ladybird [beetle], ladybug, coccinellid [beetle] *(family Coccinellidae)* • **die ~ betreffend** coccinellid
Marienkraut *n* pennyroyal germander, Teucrium polium
Marille *f s.* Aprikose
Mark *n (bot, zoo)* pith, marrow, marc, medulla, core; pulp *(of fruit)*; centre *(esp. said of a tree)*
Markbaum *m (bot)* ambatch, Aeschynomene elaphroxylon
Markberaubungsanämie *f (vet)* aplastic anaemia
Markbildung *f* medullation, myelination
Markbräune *f* core browning (flush) *(of stored fruit)*
Marke *f* 1. mark, tag *(e.g. for animal identification)*; 2. *s.* Kunde
Markenbutter *f* branded butter
Markenwein *m* branded wine
Marker *m* 1. marker [substance]; 2. *s.* Markergen
Markerbse *f* marrow (wrinkled) pea, marrowfat, Pisum sativum convar. medullare
Markerenzym *n* marker enzyme
Markergen *n* marker [gene]
Markerlinie *f* marker line
Märkerwald *m s.* Markwald
Marketing *n* marketing
Markeur *m* marker
Markfäule *f (phyt)* heart rot
Markfleck *m* medullary spot, pith fleck
Markfleckchen *n* medullary blemish
markgefüllt pithy
markhaltig medullated
Markhöhle *f* medullary cavity *(of long bones)*
markieren 1. to mark; to label, to tag; 2. *(hunt)* to feather
~/**mittels Stangen** to pole
Markierhammer *m (forest)* marking hammer
Markierrolle *f* marking roller
Markierung *f* 1. mark[ing], demarcation; 2. mark
Markierungsgen *n* marker [gene]
Markierungspheromon *n* marking pheromone
Markierungsschnur *f* marking line
Markierungssubstanz *f* marker [substance]

Markierungszeichen *n* mark
Markierwalze *f* marking roller
Markierzange *f* tag plyers (puncher)
markig *(bot, zoo)* pithy, pulpy, pulpous, marrowy
Markigkeit *f* pithiness, pulpiness
Markknochen *m* marrowbone
Markkohl *m s.* Markstammkohl
marklos pithless, marrowless
Markottieren *n* marcotting, marcottage, air layering
Markröhre *f (bot)* pith; heart centre *(of wood)*
Markscheide *f* medullary (myelin) sheath
Markscheidenbildung *f* medullation, myelination
Markstammkohl *m* marrow-stem kale, marrow cabbage, Brassica oleracea convar. acephala var. medullosa
Markstrahl *m (bot)* [medullary, pith] ray
~/**falscher** aggregate ray
~/**primärer** primary ray
~/**sekundärer** secondary ray
Markstrahlgefäß *n* ray-vessel
Markstrahlgefäßtüpfelung *f* ray-vessel pitting
Markstrahlparenchym *n* ray parenchyma
Markstrahltracheide *f* ray tracheid
Markstrahlzelle *f* ray cell
~/**liegende** procumbent ray cell
Markstrang *m* heart centre *(of wood)*
marktfähig marketable, merchantable, sal[e]able
Marktfähigkeit *f* marketability
Marktfrucht *f* commercial (cash, sale) crop
Marktfruchtanbau *m* cash cropping
Marktfruchtbetrieb *m* cash crop farm
Marktfruchtertrag *m* ware yield
marktgängig *s.* marktfähig
Marktgemüse *n (Am)* truck
Marktgemüse[an]bau *m (Am)* truck gardening
Marktgetreide *n* cash grain
Marktproduktion *f*/**landwirtschaftliche** sale cropping
Marktqualität *f* market quality
Marktschwein *n* market hog
Markttier *n* market animal
Markushaarmücke *f* St. Mark's fly, Bibio marci
Markverlagerung *f* eccentric growth *(timber defect)*
Markwald *m*, **Markwaldung** *f* border (undivided association) forest
Markzone *f* core flesh *(of a fruit)*
Marmelade *f* jam • **zu ~ verarbeiten** to jam
Marmeladenpflaume *f* marmalade plum (fruit, tree) Pouteria sapota, Calocarpum mammosum, Lucuma mammosa
marmoriert marbled, mottled
Marmorierung *f* marbling *(e.g. of leaves or slaughtering products)*
Marmorknochenkrankheit *f (vet)* osteopetrosis, Paget's disease
Marmorkrankheit *f* fruitlet brown rot *(of pineapple, caused by Pseudomonas spp. and Erwinia spp.)*
Marmorlilie *f s.* Kiebitzblume

Marmormilzkrankheit

Marmormilzkrankheit f **der Fasane** *(vet)* marble spleen disease
Marmorwels m channel cat[fish], Ictalurus punctatus
Marmorwelsvirose f channel catfish virus disease, CCVD
Marone f 1. sweet (edible) chestnut, marron *(from Castanea sativa)*; 2. s. Maronenröhrling
Maronenröhrling m *(bot)* bay-coloured bolete, Xerocomus badius
Marsala m Marsala *(wine)*
Marsch f marsh[land]
Marschboden m marsh soil
Marschland n marsh[land]
Marssonina-Blattfallkrankheit f **an Daphne** leaf spot of daphne *(caused by Marssonina daphnes)*
Marssoninafäule f anthracnose of lettuce, shothole disease of lettuce *(caused by Marssonina panattoniana)*
Martingal n martingale *(auxiliary rein)*
~/gleitendes (laufendes) running martingale
~/stehendes standing martingale, bearing-rein
Marumikumquat f *(bot)* Marumi (round) kumquat, Fortunella japonica
März[en]becher m *(bot)* snowflake, Leucojum vernum
Märzente f mallard, stock (wild) duck, Anas platyrhynchos
Märzfliege f 1. bibionid [fly] *(family Bibionidae)*; 2. s. Markushaarmücke
Maschendraht m mesh (chicken) wire, wire-netting
Maschinenausfall m machinery failure
Maschinenauslastung f machinery utilization
Maschinenausleihring m machine ring
Maschinenausleihstation f machinery hire station
Maschinenbedarf m machinery requirement
Maschineneinsatz m machinery usage
Maschinenernte f machine harvest[ing]
maschinengeerntet machine-harvested
Maschinenhof m machine yard
Maschinenmelken n machine milking
Maschinenmüllerei f machine milling
Maschinennachgemelk n machine strippings
Maschinenpark m [stock of] machinery
Maschinenpflug m ploughing machine
Maschinenring m machine ring
Maschinensäge f power saw
Maschinensatz m compound machinery
Maschinenschaden m breakdown
Maschinenschuppen m machinery shed
Maschinenschur f machine shearing
Maschinenstunde f machine hour
Maschinensystem n machinery system
Maschinenteil n component part
Maschinenträger m self-propelled tool-carrying tractor
Maser f 1. vein, streak *(in wood)*; 2. s. Maserknolle

Maserbirke f curly birch
Maserholz n curled (burr) wood
maserig figured, veined, curly, burly *(wood)*
Maserknolle f burr, burl *(in wood)*
Maserung f figure, grain [pattern], veining, crotch *(of wood)*
~/streifige stripe [figure], ribbon grain
Mash m s. Futterbrei
Maskenschwein n Chinese [Mask] *(pig breed)*
maskiert *(bot, zoo)* personate
Maskierung f *(phyt)* masking; masking *(animal behaviour)*
maskulin masculine; male
Maskulinisierung f masculinization
Maskulinität f masculinity
Maß n measure
~/wirkliches true measure *(timber mensuration)*
Massage f *(vet)* massage
Masseanalyse f gravimetry
masseanalytisch gravimetric
Massefilter n pulp filter
Maßeinteilung f scale
Massenanzucht f, **Massenaufzucht** f mass-rearing
Massenauslese f mass (phenotypic) selection
Massenaustausch m mass exchange
Massenbefall m mass infestation
Massenfachwerk n *(forest)* yield regulation by volume, allotment by volume
Massenfachwerkmethode f *(forest)* periodic method by volume
Massenfang m mass trapping *(e.g. of bark-beetles)*
Massenflucht f stampede
Massenfluß m mass flow
Massenförderer m mass conveyor
Massenfusion f mass fusion
Massengut n bulk
Massengutlagerung f bulk storage
Massengutumschlag m bulk handling
Massenkastration f mass castration *(plant breeding)*
Massenlagerung f bulk storage
Massenrübe f low dry-matter mangel
Massenselektion f s. Massenauslese
Massenspektrometer n mass spectrometer
Massenspektrometrie f mass spectrometry
Massensterben n mass die-off, mass mortality
Massenstrom m, **Massenströmung** f mass flow
Massentafel f *(forest)* log volume table, outturn table, log rule
Massenvermehrung f mass propagation, [mass] outbreak, gradation *(e.g. of pests)*
~ von Insekten excessive insect multiplication
Massenwechsel m *(ecol)* population change
Massenzuckerrübe f gross sugar-beet
Massepreßapparat m, **Massepresse** f pulp press *(beer filtration)*

Masseprozent *n* weight percent, percentage by weight
Masseter *m* masseter *(muscle)*
Masseverlust *m* weight loss
~ **durch Körperausscheidungen** *(slaught)* excretory shrink
Massezunahme *f*, **Massezuwachs** *m* weight gain
~ **nach dem Absetzen** post-weaning gain
Maßholder *m* common (hedge) maple, [English] field maple, mazer tree, Acer campestre
Maßnahme *f*/**agrotechnische (pflanzenbauliche)** cultural practice
~/**waldbauliche** silvicultural measure
Massivgefüge *n (soil)* coherent structure, massive condition (structure)
Maßvergütung *f* **für Rinde** *(forest)* allowance for bark, a.f.b., bark allowance
Maßzugabe *f* overlength, overmeasure *(timber mensuration)*
Mast *m* pole, mast
Mast *f* 1. fattening; 2. *(forest)* mast *(tree seed yield)*
~/**industrielle** commercial fattening
Mastanlage *f* fattening unit
~ **im Freien** feedlot
Mastbatterie *f* fattening (feeding) battery
Mastbetrieb *m* feedlot
Mastbucht *f* fattening pen
Mastbulle *m* fattening bullock, beefling [bull], [beef, feeder] steer
Mastdarm *m* rectum
Mastdarmvorfall *m (vet)* rectal prolapse
Mastdauer *f* feeding period
mästen to fat[ten], to batten, to put to mast, to feed; to beef, to tallow *(oxen)*; to cram *(poultry)*
~/**durch Trockenfütterung** to stall[-feed]
~/**im Stall** to stall[-feed]
Mastendmasse *f* finished weight
Mastenholz *n* mast timber
Mastfähigkeit *f* fleshing ability
Mastfärse *f* feeder (cull) heifer
Mastforelle *f* farmed trout
Mastfutter *n* fattening feed (food), mast
Mastfuttergemisch *n*, **Mastfuttermischung** *f* fattening mixture
Mastfuttermittel *n s.* Mastfutter
Mastgrad *m* degree of fattening, fattening grade
Mastherde *f* fattening herd
Masthuhn *n* poulard[e]
Masthybridküken *n s.* Mastküken
Mastiff *m* mastiff *(dog breed)*
Mastigophore *m (zoo)* flagellate *(superclass Mastigophora)*
Mastikation *f* mastication, chewing
Mastitis *f (vet)* mastitis, mammitis, udder inflammation
~/**chronische** garget, udder clap
~ **der Schafe** bluebag
Mastitis-Metritis-Agalaktie-Syndrom *n* MMA syndrome *(of pigs)*

Mastitismilch *f* mastitis (mastitic, garget) milk
Mastitisresistenz *f* mastitis resistance
Mastitis-Schnelltest [Bernburg] *m* California mastitis test
Mastix *m* mastic [gum], mastix
Mastixstrauch *m* mastic [tree], lentisk, Pistacia lentiscus
Mastixthymian *m* mastic thyme, Spanish marjoram, Thymus mastichina
Mastjahr *n (forest)* mast (seed, cone) year
Mastjungbulle *m s.* Mastbulle
Mastjunghuhn *n* poussin *(5 to 7 weeks old)*
Mastjungochse *m s.* Mastbulle
Mastjungschwein *n* finishing pig *(in general with more than 70 kg liveweight)*
Mastkäfig *m* fattening cage
Mastkalb *n* veal (feeder, store) calf, baby beef; stocker *(between weaning and start of fattening)*
Mastkälberproduktion *f* baby beef production
Mastkalbfell *n* veal skin
Mastkalbfleisch *n* baby beef
Mastkondition *f* fattening condition
Mastküken *n* fattening (meat-type) chicken, broiler [chick, chicken], fryer [chicken]
Mastlamm *n* fattening (meat) lamb
Mastleistung *f* fattening (feedlot) performance
Mastleistungsprüfung *f* fattening performance testing
Mastmethode *f* fattening method
Mastochse *f* fattening ox (bullock), beef steer
Mastperiode *f* fattening period
Mastprüfstation *f* performance test station
Mastpute *f* market turkey
Mastrasse *f* meat breed
Mastration *f* fattening ration
Mastrinder *npl* beef [fattening] cattle, beef, feeder (black) cattle, store stock
Mastrinderfütterung *f* beef cattle feeding
Mastrindrasse *f* beef[-type] breed
Mastrindvieh *n s.* Mastrinder
Mastschwein *n* fattening (growing-finishing) pig, feeder (pork-type) pig, porker
Mastschweinebucht *f* fattening pen
Maststall *m* fattening house
Mastteich *m (pisc)* fattening (finishing, forage) pond
Mastier *n* fattener, feeder
~/**junges** fatling
Mästung *f* fattening
Mastverfahren *n* fattening method
Mastversuch *m* fattening trial (experiment)
Mastvieh *n* fattening (store) stock, fatstock *(s. a.* Mastrinder*)*
Mastviehherde *f* fattening herd
Mastviehlaufhofanlage *f* feedlot, drylot
Mastweideland *n* fattening pasture
Mastzelle *f (zoo)* mast cell
Masulachs *m* masu (cherry) salmon, Oncorhynchus masou

MAT

MAT *s.* Milchaustauscher
Mate *m* maté, mate *(tea, beverage)*
Mate *f s.* Mate[tee]strauch
Material *n*/**brennbares** *(forest)* fuel, firebrand
~/**schattenspendendes** shading material
Materialwagen *m* trolley
matern[al] maternal
Maternaleffekt *m (gen)* maternal effect
Maternität *f* maternity
Mate[tee]strauch *m* [yerba] maté, mate, Paraguayan tea, Ilex paraguariensis (paraguayensis)
Mathieusche Krankheit *f (vet)* infectious icterus
Matin belge *m* matin *(dog breed)*
Matrix *f* matrix
Matrixdruckpotential *n* **des Bodens** soil matric potential
Matrixflußpotential *n* matric (matrix) flux potential *(soil physics)*
Matrixpotential *n* matric potential
matroklin matroclinal, matroclinous
Matroklinie *f* matrocliny, matromorphy *(breeding)*
matt exhausted, weak, faint *(with hunger)*; flaccid *(e.g. a plant part)*; dull, lustreless *(fur)*; faint *(wine)*
Mattenabdeckung *f* matting *(e.g. of greenhouses)*
Mattenbewässerung *f* ; capillary watering *(in greenhouses)*; mat watering *(of pot plants)*
~ **auf Tischbeeten** capillary benching
Mattenbohne *f* moth [bean], mat bean, aconite[-leaved kidney] bean, Vigna aconitifolia, Phaseolus aconitifolius
Mattenkühlung *f* pad cooling *(of greenhouses)*
Mattschwarzer Getreideschimmelkäfer *m* black fungus beetle, Alphitobius laevigatus
~ **Orchideenrüßler** *m (ent)* acythopeus, Acythopeus aterrimus
matur mature, ripe
Maturität *f s.* Reife
Mauerassel *f (Am)* dooryard sow-bug, Oniscus asellus
mauerförmig *(bot)* muriform
Mauergänsefuß *m (bot)* nettle-leaf goose-foot, Chenopodium murale
Mauergänsefußmosaikvirus *n* sowbane mosaic virus, SoMV
Mauerlattich *m* wall lettuce, Lactuca muralis
Mauerpfeffer *m* wall-pepper, [biting, gold moss] stonecrop, Sedum acre
Mauerraute *f* wall rue, Asplenium ruta-muraria
mauerwerkförmig *(bot)* muriform
Mauke *f (vet)* scratches, grease (cracked) heels *(of horses)*
maukebefallen scratchy
Maul *n* mouth, muzzle, neb
Maulbeerbaum *m* mulberry *(genus Morus)*
Maulbeere *f* mulberry
Maulbeerherzkrankheit *f* mulberry heart disease, microangiopathy *(of pigs)*
Maulbeerkeim *m (zoo)* morula

Maulbeerringfleckenvirus *n* mulberry ring spot virus, MRV
Maulbeerseidenspinner *m* silk moth, Bombyx mori
Maulbeerseidenspinnerraupe *f* silkworm
Maulbeerspinner *m s.* Maulbeerseidenspinner
Maulesel *m* mule, hinny, jennet
Maulhöhle *f* mouth (oral) cavity • **innerhalb der** ~ intra-oral
~ **mit lückigem Gebiß** broken mouth *(esp. of sheep)*
Maulhöhlenentzündung *f (vet)* stomatitis
Maulkorb *m* muzzle • **einen** ~ **anlegen** to muzzle
Maulkorbzwang *m* lead and muzzle order
Maulsonde *f (vet)* oesophageal tube
Maultier *n* mule
Maultierhirsch *m* mule deer, Odocoileus hemionus, Cariacus macrotis
Maultierhuf *m* mule-foot
Maul- und Klauenseuche *f* foot-and-mouth [disease], hoof-and-mouth disease, murrain *(virosis)*
Maulwinkelentzündung *f (vet)* angular stomatitis
Maulwurf *m* 1. mole *(genus Talpa)*; 2. mole, Talpa europaea; 3. mole cartridge *(of mole plough)*; 4. *s.* Maulwurfspelz
Maulwurfdrän *m* mole drain
Maulwurfdränkanal *m* mole drainage channel
Maulwurfdränmaschine *f* mole drainer, moling machine
Maulwurf[erd]dränung *f* mole drainage
Maulwurfpflug *m* mole plough
Maulwurfrohrdränung *f* mole-cum-tile drainage
Maulfwurfsfalle *f* mole trap
Maulwurfsgang *m* mole passage
Maulwurfsgrille *f* 1. mole-cricket *(family Gryllotalpidae)*; 2. mole-cricket, churrworm, Gryllotalpa gryllotalpa
Maulwurfshaufen *m*, **Maulwurfshügel** *m* molehill
Maulwurfspelz *m* moleskin
Mauritiusgras *n* Mauritius (Para) grass, Brachiaria (Panicum) purpurascens
Mauritiushanf *m* Mauritius hemp, Furcraea foetida (gigantea)
Maus *f* 1. mouse *(genus Mus)*; 2. house (domestic) mouse, Mus musculus [domesticus]
Mäusebussard *m* common buzzard, Buteo buteo
Mäusedorn *m* 1. butcher's-broom *(genus Ruscus)*; 2. butcher's-broom, Ruscus aculeatus
Mäuseeinheit *f* mouse unit *(hormone examination)*
Mäusefuchsschwingel *m* rat-tail fescue, Festuca (Vulpia) myuros
Mäusegerste *f* mouse barley, wall-barley [grass], way-bent, Hordeum murinum
Mauser *f* moult[ing] • **in der** ~ **sein** to be moulting
~/**künstlich ausgelöste** induced moulting
mausern/sich to moult, to shed (cast off) feathers, to mew

Mäuseschwanzfederschwingel m s. Mäusefuchsschwingel
Mausohrstadium n mouse-ear [stage], half-inch-green (of bud development in fruit-trees)
Mauswicke f Narbonne vetch, Vicia narbonensis
Mauswiesel n s. Kleines Wiesel
Maxilla f (zoo) maxilla
Maxillartaster m (ent) maxillary palp, mouth-feeler
Maxilliped[e] m maxilliped (of slaters)
Maximalertrag m maximum yield
Maximumthermometer n maximum thermometer
Mazeration f maceration
mazerieren to macerate
Mazerierung f maceration
Mazis m mace (spice)
MBFV s. Maisblattfleckenvirus
MCPA 4-chloro-2-methylphenoxyacetic acid (herbicide)
MCPP s. Mecoprop
MEA s. Cysteamin
Mecarphon n mecarphon (insecticide, nematicide)
Mechanisator m farm machinery operator, mechanizer
mechanisieren to mechanize
Mechanisierung f mechanization
~ **der Ernte[arbeiten]** harvest mechanization
~ **der Landwirtschaft** farm mechanization
~/**komplexe** full (complete) mechanization
Mechanisierungsgrad m level (degree) of mechanization
Mechanorezeptor m mechanoreceptor
meckern to bleat
Mecoprop n mecoprop, MCPP, CMPP (herbicide)
Mebendazol n mebendazole (anthelminthic, fungicide)
Medaillonkrankheit f eyespot, strawbreaker (of cereals, caused by Pseudocercosporella herpotrichoides)
mediastinal mediastinal
Mediastinitis f (vet) mediastinitis
Mediastinum n mediastinum (animal anatomy)
Mediator m transmitter substance
Medicarpin n medicarpin (phytoalexin)
Medikament n medicament, medicant, remedy, drug
Medinoterb n medinoterb (herbicide)
Medium n [culture] medium
~/**abfließendes** effluent [liquid]
Medizinalfuttermittel n (vet) medicated feed
Medizinalpflanze f medicinal (officinal) plant
Medizinalrhabarber m East Indian rhubarb, Rheum palmatum ssp. palmatum
Medoc m Medoc (wine)
Medroxyprogesteron n medroxyprogesterone (sex hormone)
Medulla f medulla
Medullation f medullation
Meeh-Formel f Meeh equation (for calculating the body surface of farm animals)

Meeresalgen fpl seaweed (feed)
Meeresfischzucht f sea farming
Meereskultur f mariculture
Meerfenchel m samphire, sea fennel, Crithmum maritimum
Meerforelle f [European] sea trout, salmon (river) trout, bulltrout, Salmo trutta
meergrün sea green
Meerkirsche f Greek strawberry tree, Arbutus andrachne
Meerkohl m 1. crambe (genus Crambe); 2. seakale, sea cabbage, Crambe maritima
Meerlavendel m 1. statice (genus Limonium); 2. sea lavender, Limonium sinuatum
Meerrettich m horse-radish, Armoracia rusticana
Meerrettichblattkäfer m mustard beetle, Phaedon cochleariae
Meerschaum m sepiolite (clay mineral)
Meerschwein[chen] n guinea-pig, cavy, Cavia porcellus
Meerstrandlevkoje f Virginian (Malcolm) stock, Malcolmia maritima
Meerträubchen n sea grape, Russian joint fir, Ephedra distachya
Meertraube f sea[side] grape, Coccoloba uvifera
Meerträubel n (bot) ephedra (genus Ephedra)
Meerwermut m sea (maritime) wormwood, Artemisia maritima
Meerzwiebel f sea onion, Urginea maritima
Mefluidid n mefluidide (growth regulator)
Megajoule npl **je kg Trockensubstanz** M/D value (feed analytics)
Megakaryozyt m megakaryocyte
Megaloblast m megaloblast
Megaloblastenanämie f (vet) megaloblastic anaemia
Megalosplenie f (vet) megalosplenia
Megalozyt m megalocyte
Megaspore f (bot) megaspore, macrospore
Megasporenbildung f, **Megasporogenese** f megasporogenesis
Megestrol n megestrol (sex hormone)
Megestrolacetat n megestrol acetate (sex hormone)
Mehl n flour; meal (coarsely ground)
~/**grobes** meal
~/**mittelfeines** middlings, sharps
mehlartig floury, farinaceous, mealy
Mehlausbeute f flour yield
Mehlbanane f plantain (from Musa x paradisiaca)
Mehlbeerbaum m, **Mehlbeere** f, **Mehlbirne** f whitebeam [tree], beam tree, Sorbus aria
Mehlfäßchen n haw (fruit from Crataegus spp.)
mehlig 1. mealy (e.g. fruit, potatoes); 2. s. mehlartig
~ **bestäubt** (bot) farinose
Mehlige Apfel[blatt]laus f [rosy] apple aphid, Dysaphis plantaginea

Mehlige

~ **Kohlblattlaus** *f* [mealy] cabbage aphid, turnip aphid, Breviocoryne brassicae
~ **Meldenlaus** *f* chenopod aphid, Hayhurstia atriplicis
~ **Pfirsichlaus (Pflaumenlaus)** *f* mealy plum aphid, Hyalopterus pruni ssp. amygdali, H. arundinis
Mehligkeit *f* mealiness
Mehligwerden *n* **von Früchten** mealy breakdown [of fruits], internal breakdown [of fruits]
Mehlkäfer *m* 1. bran bug *(comprehensive term)*; 2. flour (meal) beetle, Tenebrio molitor
Mehlkäferlarve *f s.* Mehlwurm
Mehlkörper *m* endosperm, floury portion *(of cereal grain)*
Mehlkrankheit *f* **der Speisezwiebel** onion (bulb) white rot, white rot of onion *(caused by Sclerotium cepivorum)*
Mehlmaul *n* mealy-coloured muzzle *(marking e.g. of horses)*
Mehlmilbe *f* flour (forage) mite, Acarus siro
Mehlmotte *f* Mediterranean flour moth, Anagasta (Ephestia) kuehniella
Mehlmüllerei *f* flour-milling
Mehlprotein *n* flour protein
Mehlprüfer *m*, **Mehlprüfgerät** *n* aleurometer
Mehl-Schrot-Differenz *f* extract difference *(malting)*
Mehlstaubhimmel[s]schlüssel *m* bird's-eye primrose, Primula farinosa
Mehltankwagen *m* bulk flour tanker
Mehltau *m (phyt)* mildew, leaf-mould *(s. a.* Echter Mehltau *and* Falscher Mehltau *)* • **mit ~ bedecken** to mildew
~ **der Weinrebe** grape mildew, powdery mildew of grape *(caused by Uncinula necator = Oidium tuckeri)*
mehltauartig mildewed, mildewy
mehltaubefallen mildewed, mildewy
Mehltaupilz *m* mildew *(comprehensive term)*
mehltauresistent mildew-resistant, mildew-proof
Mehltauresistenz *f* mildew resistance
Mehlwurm *m (ent)* [yellow] meal-worm, Tenebrio molitor
Mehlzünsler *m* meal moth, Pyralis farinalis
Mehrachsanhänger *m* multiaxle trailer
mehrährig multiple-eared *(maize)*
Mehrebenenbatterie *f* multideck battery *(animal husbandry)*
Mehreinschlag *m (forest)* excessive felling, overcut[ting]
mehren/Gare *(soil)* to mellow
Mehrertrag *m* additional (extra) yield
Mehretagenkultur *f* cultivation on different levels *(in greenhouses)*
Mehrfach[an]bau *m* multiple cropping
Mehrfachbefruchtung *f (zoo)* superfecundation
Mehrfachbelegung *f* multiple *(planting, seeding)*
Mehrfachkappsägemaschine *f* multiple cross-cut saw, trimming machine, trimmer

Mehrfachnutzung *f* 1. multiple use; 2. *s.* Mehrfachanbau
Mehrfachnutzungssystem *n* multiple-cropping system
Mehrfachovulation *f* multiple ovulation • **eine ~ provozieren** to superovulate
Mehrfachvakzine *f (vet)* multiple vaccine
mehrfaktoriell multifactorial, polyfactorial
mehrfarbig multicoloured, varicoloured
mehrfrüchtig polycarpic, polycarpous
Mehrfurchenpflug *m* multifurrow (multiple-furrow) plough
mehrgliedrig multinodal *(conifer)*
Mehrhieb *m (forest)* excessive felling, overcut[ting]
mehrhiebig polycyclic
mehrjährig *(bot)* perennial, polycarpic, sychnocarpous
Mehrjährige Teosinte *f* perennial teosinte, Euchlaena (Zea) perennis [ssp. perennis]
Mehrjährigkeit *f (bot)* perenniality
mehrkeimblättrig *(bot)* polycotyledonous
mehrkeimig *(bot)* multigerm, multiple-germ
mehrknotig multinodal
mehrkolbig multiple-eared *(maize)*
Mehrkolbigkeit *f* multiple cobbing
Mehrlingsgeburt *f* multiple birth
Mehrnährstoffdünger *m* multinutrient (compound) fertilizer, blended (mixed) fertilizer
Mehrnutzungsrasse *f* multipurpose breed
Mehroperationsmaschine *f (forest)* multiprocessor, multifunction (multiple-function) machine
mehrortig multilocational *(e.g. a cultivar testing)*
Mehrphasenernte *f* multistage working system
mehrrassig multibreed
Mehrscharpflug *m* multifurrow (multiple-furrow) plough, *(Am)* gangplow
mehrschichtig multilayer[ed], [multi]storeyed *(e.g. a forest stand)*
Mehrschrittmutation *f* multiple-step mutation
Mehrstammschnitt *m* multiple-stem pruning system *(of coffee trees)*
mehrstufig *v.* mehrschichtig
Mehrungsmist *m* artificial manure, straw compost
Mehrzuwachstabelle *f (forest)* increment increase table
Mehrzweckanhänger *m* multipurpose trailer
Mehrzweckdüngerstreuer *m* vari-spreader
Mehrzweckfahrzeug *n* multipurpose (utility) vehicle
Mehrzweckforstwirtschaft *f* multiple-use forestry, multiple-purpose forestry
Mehrzweckgebäude *n* multipurpose building
Mehrzweckrasse *f* multipurpose breed
Mehrzuwachstabelle *f (forest)* increment increase table
Meibomsche Drüse *f* Meibomian (tarsal) gland *(animal anatomy)*
Meidereaktion *f (ecol)* avoidance response
Meidung *f (ecol)* avoidance

Meilenpferd *n* miler
Meiler *m* [charcoal, wood] pile, charcoal kiln, heap, stack
Meilerholz *n* charcoal wood
Meilerkohle *f s.* Holzkohle
Meilerverkohlung *f* charcoal burning
Meiofauna *f* mesofauna, meiofauna
Meiose *f* meiosis, meiotic (reduction) division
Meiospore *f (bot)* meiospore
meiotisch meiotic
Meißelpflug *m* chisel plough
Meißelschar *n* chisel share, bar-point[ed] share
Meister *m (bot)* woodruff *(genus Asperula)*
"**Meister Braun**" *m (hunter's language) s.* Bär
"**Meister Grimbart**" *m (hunter's language) s.* Dachs
"**Meister Petz**" *m (hunter's language) s.* Bär
Mekkabalsam *m* balm of Gilead
Mekkabalsambaum *m* balm of Gilead, balsam tree, Commiphora opobalsamum
Mekonium *n* meconium, foetal dung
Melanin *n* melanin *(pigment)*
Melaninbildungszelle *f* melanoblast
melanisieren to melanize
Melanismus *m* melanism, melanosis
Melanoblast *n* melanoblast
Melanoidin *n*, **Melanoidinfarbstoff** *m* melanoidin[e] *(condensation product of amino-acids and reducing sugars)*
Melanom *n (vet)* melanoma
Melanophorenhormon *n s.* Melanotropin
Melanose *f* 1. *(zoo)* melanism, melanosis; 2. *(phyt)* melanose *(of citrus plants, caused by Diaporthe citri)*
Melanotropin *n* melanotropin, intermedin, melanocyte-stimulating hormone
Melanozyt *m* melanocyte
Melaphyr *m (soil)* melaphyre
Melasse *f* molasses, treacle
Melassefuttermittel *n* molasses fodder
Melassegras *n* molasses grass, Melinis minutiflora
Melasseschlempe *f* molasses stillage, vinasse
Melasseschnitzel *npl* dried molassed beet pulp
Melassetank *m* molasses tank
Melatonin *n* melatonin *(hormone)*
Melde *f* 1. orach[e], saltbush, French spinach *(genus Atriplex)*; 2. common orach[e], Atriplex patula
melden *s.* röhren
Meldewanze *f* lace bug *(family Piesmidae)*
Melecitose *f* melezitose *(trisaccharide)*
Melengestrol *n* melengestrol *(sex hormone)*
Melengestrolacetat *n* melengestrol acetate *(sex hormone)*
Melibiase *f* alpha-galactosidase *(enzyme)*
Melibiose *f* melibiose *(disaccharide)*
Melilotosid *n* coumarinic acid
Melioidose *f (vet)* melioidosis *(caused by Pseudomonas pseudomallei)*

Melioration *f* [a]melioration, soil (land) improvement, reclamation, amendment
~/**forstliche** forest (silvicultural) amelioration, forest improvement
~/**großflächige** large-area amelioration
Meliorationsbaumart *f* ameliorating [tree] species
Meliorationsgebiet *n* amelioration area
Meliorationsgenossenschaft *f* land improvement co-operative
Meliorationsholzart *f* ameliorating [tree] species
Meliorationsingenieur *n* reclamation (drainage) engineer
Meliorationslanze *f* amelioration injector *(for liquid fertilizer)*
Meliorationsmaschine *f* amelioration machine
Meliorationspflug *m* reclamation (double-deck) plough
Meliorationsprojekt *n* amelioration project
meliorativ ameliorative
meliorieren to ameliorate
Melisse *f* balm *(genus Melissa)*
Melissinsäure *f* melissic acid
Melitose *f* melitose, raffinose *(trisaccharide)*
Melkanlage *f* milking[-machine] installation, milking plant (premise, facility)
Melkausrüstung *f* milking equipment
Melkbarkeit *f* milkability, milking ability (ease)
Melkbecher *m*, **Melkbecherhülse** *f* milking [teat] cup
Melkbox *f* milking stall
Melkeimer *m* milking bucket
melken to milk
Melken *n* milking
~/**maschinelles** machine milking
Melker *m* milker, milkman, dairyman, cowman
Melkerin *f* milkmaid
Melkerknoten *m* milker's nodule
Melkermeister *m* milker master
Melkerschwiele *f* milker's nodule
Melkerzugang *m* operator access *(of a rotary milker)*
Melkfett *n* milking grease (salve)
Melkflur *m* cowman's pit *(of a tandem parlour)*
Melkgerät *n*, **Melkgerätschaften** *pl* milking equipment
Melkgeschwindigkeit *f* milking rate
Melkhaus *n* milking house (shed)
Melkkarussell *n* rotary milker, rotary (revolving) milking parlour, rotolactor, milking carousel
~ **mit Tandemanordnung** rotary tandem milking parlour
Melkmaschine *f* milking-machine, milker
~/**elektrische** electric milker
Melkmaschinenluftleitung *f* milking air pipe
Melkmethode *f* milking method
Melkplattform *f* milking platform
Melkpumpe *f* milk pump
Melkraum *m* milking barn
Melkrohrsystem *n* cowshed pipeline milkers

Melkschemel 418

Melkschemel *m* milking stool
Melkstand *m* [milking, dairy] parlour, milking stand (shed), bail
~/fahrbarer milking trolley, mobile milking parlour
Melkstandanlage *f s.* Melkanlage
Melkstand[einzel]box *f* milking stall
Melkstandfutterautomat *m* milking parlour feeder
Melkstandwagen *m s.* Melkstand/fahrbarer
Melkstrumpf *m* teat [cup] liner
Melktaktfolge *f* pulsation sequence
Melktechnik *f* milking technique
Melktuch *n* udder-cloth
Melkunterdruck *m*, **Melkvakuum** *n* milking vacuum
Melkvakuumleitung *f* vacuum line
Melkvorgang *m* milking operation (routine)
Melkzeit *f* milking [time]
Melkzeug *n* milking unit, milking[-machine] cluster, [teat cup] cluster
Melkzeugabnahme *f* cluster removal
~/automatische automatic cluster removal
Melkzeugabnahmeroboter *m* cluster-removing robot
Mellitin *n* melittin *(polypeptide)*
Melone *f* 1. melon *(comprehensive term)*; 2. musk (sweet) melon, musky gourd (pumpkin), honeydew melon, cantaloup[e], Cucumis melo
Melonenauflesemaschine *f* melon pick-up machine
Melonenbaum *m (bot)* common papaya (papaw), Carica papaya
Melonenblattlaus *f* cotton aphid, Aphis gossypii
Melonenerntemaschine *f* melon harvester
Melonenfliege *f* melon fly, gourd fruit-fly, Dacus (Strumeta) cucurbitae
Melonensamenöl *n* melon seed oil
Melonensammelmaschine *f* melon pick-up machine
Melophagose *f (vet)* sheep scab
Membran *f* membrane, diaphragm
~/Cortische tectorial membrane *(of the inner ear)*
~/Descemetsche Descemet's membrane *(animal anatomy)*
~/fetale foetal membrane
~/hyaline hyaline layer *(in the periderm of cereal grains)*
membranartig membran[e]ous, membranaceous
Membranfilter *n* membrane filter, ultrafilter
Membranfiltermethode *f*, **Membranfiltration** *f* membrane filtration
membranös *s.* membranartig
Membranpotential *n* membrane potential
Membranpumpe *f* diaphragm pump
Memphishufeisen *n* Memphis-bar shoe *(for trotters)*
MEMV *s.* Europäisches Maismosaikvirus
Menadion *n* menadione, menaquinone, vitamine K_3
Menazon *n* menazon *(insecticide)*

Mendel-Genetik *f* Mendelian genetics
Mendelgesetze *npl* Mendel's laws of inheritance, Mendel laws
Mendelismus *m* Mendel[ian]ism, Mendelian (particulate) inheritance
mendeln to segregate
mendelnd Mendelian segregating
Mendelpopulation *f* Mendelian population
Menge *f*/**duldbare** permissible level *(e.g. of herbicide residues)*
~/geduldete permitted level
~/[toxikologisch] zulässige *s.* Menge/duldbare
mengen to blend
Mengenelement *n* macroelement
Mengenleistung *f* output
Menggetreide *n*, **Mengkorn** *n* mixed (dredge) corn, maslin
Menichlopholan *n* niclofolan *(anthelminthic)*
meningeal meningeal
Meningitis *f (vet)* meningitis
Meningoenzephalitis *f* **der Puten[/infektiöse]** *(vet)* Israel turkey meningo-encephalitis, ITME
Meningozele *f (vet)* meningocele
Meninx *f* meninx
Meniskus *m* meniscus
mennigrot miniate
Menotaxis *f* menotaxis *(animal behaviour)*
Menschenfloh *m* human flea, Pulex irritans
Menschenfressertomate *f* cannibal's tomato, Solanum uporo
Menthol *n* menthol *(terpene alcohol)*
Mentorpollen *m* mentor pollen
Mephenesin *n* mephenesin *(muscle relaxant)*
Mephosfolan *n* mephosfolan *(insecticide)*
Mepiquat *n* mepiquat *(growth regulator)*
Mepiquatchlorid *n* mepiquat chloride *(growth regulator)*
Merbau *m (bot)* Bajam teak, Intsia bijuga
Mercaptodimethur *n* mercaptodimethur, methiocarb *(acaricide, insecticide, molluscicide)*
Mercaptogruppe *f* mercapto (sulphydryl) group
Mercaptophos *n* demeton *(insecticide)*
Mergelboden *m* marl soil
mergelig marly
mergeln to marl, to fertilize with marl
Mergeln *n* marling
Mergelschiefer *m* marl slate
Mergelton *m* marl (chalky) clay, argillaceous marl
Meridianpflanze *f* compass plant
Merikarp *n (bot)* mericarp
Merino *m s.* Merinowollstoff
Merinofleischschaf *n* [German] Mutton Merino, Merino Meat *(sheep breed)*
Merinolandschaf *n* German Improved Land, German Whiteheaded Land, Improved German Farm *(sheep breed)*
Merinorasse *f* merino [sheep] breed
Merinoschaf *n* merino [sheep], Spanish sheep
Merinoschafrasse *f* merino [sheep] breed

Merinowolle f merino [wool], Botany [wool] (esp. in Australia)
Merinowollstoff m merino
Meristem n (bot) meristem
meristematisch meristematic
Meristemkultur f mericloning
Meristemvermehrung f tissue culture propagation
Merkmal n characteristic, feature; (gen) character, trait
~/**diagnostisches** diagnostic character
~/**qualitatives** qualitative character
~/**quantitatives (umweltlabiles)** quantitative character
~/**umweltstabiles** qualitative character
~/**unterscheidendes** diagnostic character
Merkmalsänderung f/**korrelative** correlated response
Merkmalsanlage f hereditary factor (determinant)
Merkmalsausbildung f expression
Merkmalsdivergenz f character divergence
Merkmalskorrelation f character correlation
Merkmalspaar n pair of characters
Merkmalsvariation f character variation
Merkmalträger m carrier
Merlefaktor m merle factor (defective gene in dogs)
Merlesyndrom n (vet) merle syndrome
Merlinfalke m merlin, Falco columbarius [aesalon]
Merlot m merlot (wine)
Merlottraube f merlot (grape)
Merogonie f androgenesis, male parthenogenesis
merokrin merocrine (gland)
meromiktisch meromictic (limnology)
Meromyosin n meromyosin (muscle protein)
Merthiolat n thiomersal (preservative, fungicide)
merzen to cull
Merzen n culling
Merzschaf n cull sheep, cast; cull (cast) ewe
Merztier n cull
Merzung f cull
Merzungsgrenze f selection limit
Merzungsrate f culling rate
Merzvieh n culled stock, cull
Mescalin n mescalin[e] (alkaloid)
Mesenchym n mesenchyme
mesenchymal mesenchymal
mesenterial mesenteric
Mesenteritis f (vet) mesenteritis
Mesenterium n mesentery (animal anatomy)
Mesenzephalon n mesencephalon, midbrain
Mesoblast n(m), **Mesoderm** n (zoo) mesoblast
Mesofauna f mesofauna, meiofauna
Mesoinosit n myoinositol
Mesokarp n (bot) mesocarp
Mesoklima n local climate, topoclimate
Mesokotyl n (bot) mesocotyl
Mesometrium n mesometrium, broad ligament (animal anatomy)
mesophil mesophile, mesophilic

Mesophyll n (bot) mesophyll
Mesophyllzelle f mesophyll cell
Mesophyt m mesophyte
mesophytisch mesophytic, mesic
Mesoprazin n mesoprazine (herbicide)
Mesothorax m (ent) mesothorax, medithorax
mesotroph mesotrophic
Mesovarium n mesovarium
Mesoxalylharnstoff m alloxan
Mesquitebaum m s. Mesquitestrauch
Mesquitebohne f mesquite bean, screw-bean
Mesquitestrauch m mesquite tree, mesquit (genus Prosopis)
Meßband n tape-measure
Meßbildverfahren n photogrammetry
messen/[Holz] mit der Kluppe (forest) to calliper, to caliper, to tally
Messenger-RNA f messenger RNA (ribonucleic acid), mRNA
Messer n knife; cutter; [mower-]sickle
~/**Königsfelder** Koenigsfeld knife, Koenigsfelder-type knife (sugar-beet processing)
Messeraufhängung f knife suspension (assembly) (of a mower)
Messerbestoßmaschine f slotting machine (for sharpening of beet-slicing knives)
Messeregge f knife harrow, scarifier
Messerfräsmaschine f fraising machine (for beet-slicing knives)
Messerführungsplatte f clip of the mower-sickle, wear plate
Messergeschwindigkeit f knife speed (of a mower)
Messerhalter m knife clip
Messerholz n slicewood
Messerhub m knife stroke (register)
Messerkasten m knife box (e.g. of a slicer)
Messerklinge f blade, knife; knife section (mower)
~/**gerippte** serrated knife section
Messerkopf m knife head
Messerradgebläsehäcksler m flywheel chopper blower
Messerradhäcksler m flywheel chopper (forager)
Messersatz m bank of knives (of a mower)
Messerrücken m knife back
Messerschleifmaschine f knife grinder
Messerschutz m knife guard
Messersech n [knife] coulter
Messersechstiel m coulter arm
Messerwalzenmäher m cylinder mower
Messerwinkel m knife angle (pitch)
Messerzinke f knife tine
Messingkäfer m golden spider beetle, Niptus hololeucus
Meßkluppe f (forest) [tree] calliper, [tree] caliper
Meßkolonne f, **Meßmannschaft** f (forest) measuring party
Meßpunkt m s. Meßstelle
Meßrad n metering wheel

Meßschiene

Meßschiene f calliper (graduated) rule
Meßstab m log scale (rule)
Meßstelle f 1. measuring point; 2. station *(surveying)*
Meßstock m measuring (scale) stick, calliper-scale
Meßtrupp m s. Meßkolonne
Messung f **mit Schnurmaß** *(forest)* string measure
~ **nach Hoppusfuß** Hoppus (quarter-girth) measure *(timber mensuration)*
Mestranol n mestranol *(sex hormone)*
Met s. Methionin
Met m mead, metheglin *(fermented beverage)*
Metabenzthiazuron n metabenzthiazuron *(herbicide)*
Metabiose f metabiosis
metabol 1. *(ent)* metabolous, metabolic *(undergoing metamorphosis)*; 2. s. metabolisch
Metabolie f *(zoo, ent)* metamorphosis
metabolisch metabolic
metabolisieren to metabolize
Metabolismus m metabolism
Metabolismus... s. Stoffwechsel...
Metabolit m metabolite, product of metabolism
Metacil n metacil *(insecticide)*
Metagenese f metagenesis
metagenetisch metagenetic
Metahalloysit m metahalloysite *(clay mineral)*
metakarpal metacarpal
Metakarpalballen m metacarpal pad
Metakarpus m metacarpus
Metalaxyl n metalaxyl *(fungicide)*
Metalcaptase f penicillamine *(chelating agent)*
Metaldehyd m metaldehyde *(molluscicide)*
Metalimnion n metalimnion, discontinuity layer *(of a water)*
Metallenzym n metalloenzyme
Metallgeschmack m metallic taste *(e.g. of wine)*
Metallion n metal ion
Metalloenzym n metalloenzyme
Metallosat n metalosate *(plant nutrient)*
Metallproteid n metalloproteid[e]
Metallprotein n metalloprotein
Metallsuchgerät n *(vet)* metal detector
Metallthionin n metallothionein
Metalltrübung f metal turbidity *(defect of wine)*
Metamitron n metamitron *(herbicide)*
Metamorphit m metamorphic rock
Metamorphose f metamorphosis
~/unvollständige incomplete metamorphosis
Metamorphosehormon n *(ent)* moulting hormone, ecdysone
Metanaxin n metanaxin *(fungicide)*
Metandienon n dianabol *(sex hormone)*
Metaphase f metaphase *(of nuclear division)*
Metaphloem n *(bot)* metaphloem
Metaphyse f metaphysis *(of the long bone)*
Metaplasie f metaplasia, tissue transformation
Metaplasma n metaplasm
Metarteriole f metarteriole *(animal anatomy)*

Metastase f *(phyt, vet)* metastasis
metastasieren to metastasize
metatarsal metatarsal
Metatarsalballen m metatarsal pad
Metatarsus m metatarsus
Metathorax m *(ent)* metathorax
metatracheal metatracheal *(parenchyma)*
Metawein[stein]säure f metatartaric acid
Metaxenienbildung f carpoxenia *(of fruit woods)*
Metaxylem n *(bot)* metaxylem
Metazachlor n metazachlor *(herbicide)*
metazentrisch metacentric *(chromosome)*
Metazerkarie f metacercaria *(larval stage of flukes)*
Metazoxolon n metazoxolon *(fungicide)*
Metencephalon n metencephalon, hindbrain
Meteorismus m *(vet)* meteorism, tympanites, tympany, bloat, hoven
Meteorologe m meteorologist
Meteorologie f meteorology
meteorologisch meteorological
Metepa n metepa *(chemosterilant)*
Meterholz n cordwood
Meterstock m *(forest)* one-metre measuring rod
Metflurazon n metflurazone *(herbicide)*
Methacyclin n methacyclin *(antibiotic)*
Metham n metham, carbathion *(fungicide, herbicide)*
Methamidophos n methamidophos *(insecticide)*
Metham-Natrium n metham-sodium *(fungicide, herbicide, nematicide)*
Methämoglobin n methaemoglobin
Methämoglobinämie f *(vet)* methaemoglobinaemia
Methan n methane, marsh gas
Methanal n methanal, formaldehyde
Methanbildung f methanogenesis
Methangewinnung f, **Methanisierung** f methane fermentation, methanization
Methanol n s. Methylalkohol
Methansäure f methanoic (formic) acid
Methazol n methazole *(herbicide)*
Methenamin n methenamine, hexamethylenetetramine
Methfuroxam n methfuroxam *(fungicide)*
Methicillin n methicillin *(antibiotic)*
Methidathion n methidathion *(insecticide)*
Methionin n methionine *(amino-acid)*
Methioninadenosyltransferase f methionine adenosyltransferase *(enzyme)*
Methitural n methitural *(anaesthetic)*
Methiuron n methiuron *(herbicide)*
Methode f **der kleinsten Quadrate** *(biom)* least squares method
~ **der multiplen unvollständigen Erfassung** *(gen, biom)* multiple incomplete selection of affected individuals
~ **der systematischen Variationen nach Homès** Homès' method of systematic variations *(in fertilizer experiments)*

Methometon *n* methometon *(herbicide)*
Methomyl *n* methomyl *(insecticide)*
Methoprotryn *n* methoprotryne *(herbicide)*
Methoxychlor *n* methoxychlor *(insecticide)*
Methoxyfluran *n* methoxyflurane *(anaesthetic)*
3-Methoxy-4-hydroxymandelsäure *f* vanillomandelic acid
Methylacetoxyprogesteron *n* methylacetoxyprogesterone *(sex hormone)*
Methylalkohol *m* methyl alcohol, methanol
~/unreiner wood alcohol, wood spirit[s]
Methylamin *n* methylamine
Methylase *f* methylase *(enzyme)*
Methylbenzen *n* methylbenzene, toluene
Methylbromid *n* methyl bromide *(fungicide, insecticide, herbicide)*
3-Methylbutansäure *f* 3-methylbutane (isovaleric) acid *(plant substance)*
Methyl-carbophenothion *n* methylcarbophenothion *(insecticide)*
Methylcoffein *n* methylcaffeine *(mutagen)*
Methylcystein *n* methylcysteine
Methylcysteinsulfoxid *n* S-methylcysteine sulphoxide, kale anaemia factor *(feed ingredient)*
Methylenblau *n* methylene blue *(dye)*
Methylenblauprobe *f*, **Methylenblautest** *m* methylene blue test
(cis)-Methylen-butandisäure *f* itaconic acid
Methylenchlorid *n* dichloromethane, methylene dichloride
Methylentetrahydrofolatcyclohydrolase *f* methylenetetrahydrofolate cyclohydrolase *(enzyme)*
Methylentetrahydrofolatreductase *f* methylenetetrahydrofolate reductase *(enzyme)*
Methyleugenol *n* methyl eugenol *(attractant)*
Methylglucose *f* methylglucose
Methylglucosid *n* methylglucoside
(N-)Methylglycin *n* sarcosine *(amino-acid)*
Methylglycocoll *n* sarcosine *(amino-acid)*
Methylierung *f* methylation
Methylindol *n* skatol[e]
Methylisothiocyanat *n* methyl isothiocyanate, MIT *(fumigant, nematicide)*
Methylmalonyl-CoA-Mutase *f* methylmalonyl-CoA mutase *(enzyme)*
Methylmethansulfonat *n* methyl methanesulphonate *(mutagen)*
Methylmetiram *n* methylmetiram *(fungicide)*
Methylmorphin *n* codeine *(alkaloid)*
Methylphenol *n* methylphenol, cresol *(disinfectant)*
2-Methylpropionsäure *f* 2-methylpropionic acid, isobutyric acid
Methylquecksilber *n* methylmercury
Methyltestosteron *n* methyltestosterone *(anabolic)*
Methylthiouracil *n* methylthiouracil *(thyreostatic)*
Methyltransferase *f* methyltransferase *(enzyme)*
(N-)Methyltryptophan *n* abrine *(amino-acid)*
5-Methyluracil *n* thymine *(pyrimidine base)*

Methylviolett *n s.* Gentianaviolett
Methyridin *n* methyridine *(anthelminthic)*
Meticlorpindol *n* clopidol *(coccidiostatic)*
Metiram *n* metiram *(fungicide)*
Metmercapturon *n* metmercapturon *(insecticide)*
Metobromuron *n* metobromuron *(herbicide)*
Metolachlor *n* metolachlor *(herbicide)*
Metöstrus *m* metoestrus
Metoxuron *n* metoxuron *(herbicide)*
Metrektomie *f (vet)* metrectomy, hysterectomy
Metribuzin *n* metribuzin *(herbicide)*
Metritis *f (vet)* metritis, uterine inflammation
~/kontagiöse equine contagious equine metritis, CEM *(caused by Haemophilus equigenitalis)*
~/puerperale puerperal metritis
Meute *f* pack *(of hounds)*
Mevalonat *n* mevalonate
Mevalonsäure *f* mevalonic acid *(metabolite)*
Mevinphos *n* mevinphos, phosdrin *(insecticide, acaricide, nematicide)*
Mexacarbat *n* mexacarbate *(acaricide, insecticide, molluscicide)*
Mexican Hairless *m* Mexican hairless *(dog breed)*
Mexikanische Distel *f* prickly (Mexican) poppy, Argemone mexicana
~ Fruchtfliege *f* Mexican fruit-fly, Anastrepha ludens
~ Zypresse *f* Portuguese cypress, Cupressus lusitanica
Mexikanischer Baumwollkapselkäfer *m* [cotton-]boll weevil, Anthonomus grandis
~ Bohnenkäfer *m* Mexican bean beetle, Epilachna varivestis (corrupta)
~ Holunder *m* Mexican elder[berry], Sambucus mexicana
~ Leberbalsam *m* goatweed, Ageratum houstonianum (mexicana)
~ Weißdorn *m* Mexican hawthorn, Crataegus pubescens
Mexikanisches Teekraut *n* Mexican tea, Chenopodium ambrosioides var. ambrosioides
Mexikogras *n* Mexican grass, Ixophorus unisetus
Mezcalin *n* mescalin[e] *(alkaloid)*
Mezlocillin *n* mezlocillin *(antibiotic)*
M-Faktor *m (gen)* M factor
MGA *s.* Megestrolacetat
MgMV *s.* Mauergänsefußmosaikvirus
MH *s.* Maleinsäurehydrazid
MHK *s.* Hemmkonzentration/minimale
MHS *s.* Hyperthermiesyndrom/malignes
Miacin *n* pyrimidine *(heterocyclic nitrogen compound)*
Micell *n s.* Micelle
Micellarstrang *m* crystallite *(of cellulose)*
Micelle *f* micelle, micell[a]
Michaelis-Menten-Gleichung *f* Michaelis-Menten equation
Michaelis-Menten-Konstante *f* Michaelis-Menten constant *(of enzymatic reactions)*

Miere

Miere f chick[en]weed *(genus Minuartia)*
Miesmuschelschildlaus f poplar (willow) scale, Chionaspis (Aspidiotus) salicis
Miete f clamp, pit; stack • **in Mieten einlagern** to clamp
mieten to clamp
Mietenabdeckgerät n clamp coverer
Mietenabdeckung f, **Mietendecke** f clamp cover
Mietenfäule f clamp (pit-storage) rot *(comprehensive term)*
Mietenhof m rick yard
Mietenhygiene f clamp hygiene
Mietenlagerung f clamp (pit) storage
Mietenplatz m clamp site
Mietensetzgerät n, **Mietenstapelgerät** n clamp stacker, push-off buck-rake
Mietenzudeckgerät n clamp coverer
Migrans m *(zoo)* migrant
Migration f 1. *(ecol)* migration; 2. gene flow
Migrationsdruck m migration pressure
migratorisch migratory
migrieren to migrate
Mikanie f plush vine, Mikania ternata
Mikroaggregat n *(soil)* microaggregate
Mikroangiopathie f microangiopathy, mulberry heart disease *(of pigs)*
Mikrobe f microbe, micro-organism *(for compounds s. under Mikroorganismus)*
Mikroben... *s.* Mikroorganismen...
Mikrobestandteil m microingredient
Mikrobewässerung f microirrigation
mikrobiell microbial, microbic
Mikrobiologe m microbiologist
Mikrobiologie f microbiology
mikrobiologisch microbiological
Mikrobiotop n *(ecol)* microhabitat
mikrobivor microbivorous
mikrobizid microbicidal, germicidal
Mikrobronchitis f *(vet)* bronchiolitis
Mikrobürette f microburette
Mikrochromosom n microchromosome
Mikrodiffusion f microdiffusion
Mikroelement n microelement
Mikroertragsversuch m microyield trial
Mikroevolution f microevolution
Mikrofauna f microfauna
Mikrofibrille f microfibril, fusiform body *(wood anatomy)*
Mikrofilarienpityriasis f sweet itch, summer sores *(of horses)*
Mikroflora f microflora
Mikrofortpflanzung f micropropagation
Mikrogamet m microgamete, androgamete, sperm [cell]
Mikrogefüge n microstructure, fabric
Mikrohabitat n *(ecol)* microhabitat
Mikroingrediens n microingredient
Mikrokalorimetrie f microcalorimetry
Mikrokapsel f microcapsule *(e.g. of pesticides)*

Mikroklima n microclimate
~ **in Pflanzenbeständen** plant climate, phytoclimate
mikroklimatisch microclimatic
Mikroklimatologie f microclimatology
Mikrokonidie f *(bot)* spermatium, pycnospore
Mikrokultur f microculture *(microbiology)*
Mikrolin m microline *(non-clay mineral)*
mikromälzen to micromalt
Mikromälzung f micromalting
Mikromälzversuch m micromalting laboratory test
Mikrometeorologie f micrometeorology
mikrometeorologisch micrometeorological
Mikromorphologie f micromorphology *(e.g. of a soil)*
mikromorphologisch micromorphological
Mikromorphometrie f *(soil)* micromorphometry
Mikromutation f *(gen)* micromutation
Mikronährelement n, **Mikronährstoff** m microelement, micronutrient, minor (trace) nutrient, minor (trace) mineral
Mikronährstoffdünger m micronutrient (trace element) fertilizer
Mikronährstoffmangel m micronutrient (trace element) deficiency
Mikroökologie f microecology
Mikroökosystem n microecosystem
mikroorganismenabtötend microbicidal, antimicrobial
Mikroorganismeneiweiß n microbial protein
mikroorganismenfressend microbivorous
Mikroorganismenkultur f microbial culture
Mikroorganismenpopulation f microbial population
Mikroorganismenprotein n microbial protein
Mikroorganismenstamm m microbial strain
Mikroorganismus m micro-organism, microorganism, microbe
~/**abbauender** decomposer
~/**gärungserregender** fermenter
~/**genetisch (gentechnologisch) veränderter** genetically engineered micro-organism
~/**krankheitserregender** germ
~/**ligninabbauender** lignin decomposer
~/**milchsäurebildender** lactic-acid micro-organism, lactic-acid producer
~/**psychrotropher** psychrotroph
Mikrophthalmie f *(vet)* microphthalmia
Mikrophytozönose f microphytocoenosis
Mikropilz m microfungus
Mikropräzipitationstest m microprecipitin test *(serology)*
Mikropsychrometer n micropsychrometer
Mikropyle f *(bot, zoo)* micropyle
Mikroradiographie f microradiography
Mikrorelief n *(soil)* microrelief
Mikroröntgenographie f microradiography
Mikroschadstoff m micropollutant
Mikroschnittling m microcutting *(tissue culture)*
Mikroskop n microscope

Mikroskopie f microscopy
mikroskopisch microscopic
Mikrosom n microsome
Mikrospore f (bot) microspore
Mikrosporenbildung f microsporogenesis
Mikrosporie f, **Mikrosporose** f (vet) microsporosis (caused by Microsporum spp.)
Mikrostandort m microsite
Mikrosteckling m microcutting (tissue culture)
Mikrotom n microtome
Mikrotubulus m microtubule (organelle)
Mikroumwelt f (ecol) microenvironment
Mikroveredelung f micrografting
Mikrovermehrung f micropropagation
Mikrowellentrockner m microwave dryer
Mikrozentrum n (gen) microcentrum
mikrozid microbicidal, germicidal
Miktion f micturition, urination
Milbe f mite, acarid (order Acari)
milbenabtötend acaricidal
Milbenbefall m (phyt, vet) acariasis
Milbenbekämpfung f mite control
Milbenbekämpfungsmittel n acaricide, miticide
Milbenfresser m acariphage
Milbengalle f big bud (esp. on black currant, caused by Cecidophyopsis ribis)
Milbenseuche f acarine (Isle of Wight) disease (of honey-bees, caused by Acarapis woodi)
milbentötend acaricidal
Milbenvernichtungsmittel n acaricide, miticide
Milch f 1. milk, milch; 2. (pisc) soft roe, milt, semen
• ~ **absondern** to milk, to lactate • ~ **einschießen lassen** to give down (said of a cow)
• ~ **geben** to milk • ~ **gerinnen lassen** to curd[le]
• ~ **saugen** to suck, to milk
~/**adaptierte** humanized milk
~/**ansaure** slightly sour milk
~/**blaue** blue milk (milk defect)
~/**blutige** bloody milk (milk defect)
~/**dickgelegte** curdled milk
~/**dysgenetische** dysgenic milk
~/**eingedampfte** evaporated milk
~/**eingedickte** concentrated milk
~ **einschießen lassen** to give down (said of a cow)
~/**energiekorrigierte** energy-corrected milk
~/**enteiweißte** milk serum
~/**evaporierte** evaporated (condensed) milk
~/**fadenziehende** ropy (slimy, lacy) milk
~/**fettangereicherte** fat-filled milk
~/**fettarme** low-fat milk
~/**fettkorrigierte** fat-corrected milk, FCM
~/**fettreduzierte** low-fat milk
~/**garantiert tuberkulosefreie** certified milk
~/**geronnene** curdled milk, curds and whey
~/**gesäuerte** acidified milk
~/**haltbare** long-keeping milk
~/**homogenisierte** homogenized milk
~/**humanisierte** humanized milk
~/**mit Säureweckern versetzte** fermented milk
~ **mit zugesicherten Eigenschaften** attested (certified) milk
~/**pasteurisierte** pasteurized milk
~/**ranzige** rancid milk
~/**rekonstituierte** reconstituted milk
~/**rote** red milk (milk defect)
~/**salzige** salty milk (milk defect)
~/**spontan gesäuerte** naturally soured milk
~/**standardisierte** standardized milk
~/**sterile (sterilisierte)** sterile (sterilized) milk
~/**teilentrahmte** partly skimmed milk
~/**tuberkulosefreie** certified milk
~/**ultrahocherhitzte** ultra-high temperature milk
~/**ungesüßte eingedampfte** evaporated milk
~/**verfälschte** adulterated milk
Milchabfallprodukt n dairy waste
Milchabscheider m air separating jar
milchabsondernd lactating
Milchabsonderung f milk secretion, lactation
Milchader f milk (lacteal) vein
Milchalbumin n milk albumin, lactalbumin
Milchannahme f milk reception (in a dairy)
Milchannahmebehälter m milk storage vessel
Milchapolactoferrin n milk apo-lactoferrin
milchartig milky
Milchaustauscher m, **Milchaustauschfuttermittel** n milk replacer (equivalent, substitute), calf milk substitute
Milchbehälter m milk container (vessel)
Milchbehandlung f milk treatment
Milchbestandteil m milk constituent
Milchbestrahlung f milk irradiation
Milchbetrieb m s. Milcherzeugungsbetrieb
Milchbezahlung f milk payment
milchbildend [ga]lactogenic, galactopoietic
Milchbildung f milk formation, lactogenesis, galactopoiesis • **die ~ anregend** galactogenic
Milchbrustgang m thoracic duct
Milchbusch m milk bush, Euphorbia tirucalli
Milchcontainer m milk container
Milchdauerware f milk preserve
Milchdrüse f mammary (milk, lactiferous) gland, mamma, udder
Milchdrüsenerkrankung f mammary gland disease
Milchdurchflußmeßgerät n milk flow-meter
Milcheckzahn m milk corner [incisor, tooth] (animal anatomy)
Milcheimer m milk pail
Milcheinzugsgebiet n milk shed
Milcheis n frozen milk
Milcheiweiß n milk protein, lactoprotein
Milcheiweißbestimmung f milk protein determination
Milcheiweißgehalt m milk protein content
Milcheiweißpolymorphismus m milk protein polymorphism
Milchejektion f milk ejection (let-down)
milchen to milk, to lactate

Milchentzug

Milchentzug *m* milk withdrawal
Milchenzym *n* milk enzyme
Milcher *m (pisc)* milter
Milcherfassung *f* milk collection
Milcherhitzer *m* milk heater, pasteurizer
Milcherhitzung *f* milk heating
Milcherhitzungsapparat *m s.* Milcherhitzer
Milchersatzpräparat *n* milk replacer
Milchertrag *m* milk yield
milcherzeugend milk-producing; [ga]lactogenic
Milcherzeuger *m* milk producer
Milcherzeugnis *n* milk product
Milcherzeugung *f* milk production
Milcherzeugungsbetrieb *m* dairy (milk producing) farm
Milchfahrer *m* milk haul[i]er
Milchfarbe *f* milk colour
Milchfarm *f* dairy farm
Milchfehler *m* milk defect (taint)
Milchferment *n* milk enzyme
Milchfernleitung *f* milk pipeline
Milchfett *n* milk fat
Milchfettausbeute *f* milk fat yield
Milchfettdepression *f* milk fat depression
Milchfettertrag *m* milk fat yield
Milchfetterzeugung *f* milk fat production
Milchfettgehalt *m* milk fat percentage
Milchfettproduktion *f* milk fat production
Milchfettprozente *npl* milk fat percentage
Milchfettrefraktometer *n* milk fat refractometer
Milchfettsynthese *f* milk fat synthesis
Milchfieber *n (vet)* milk fever, parturient hypocalcaemia (paralysis), lambing sickness
Milchfilter *n* milk filter
Milchflasche *f* milk bottle
Milchflecken *mpl* **[der Leber]** *(vet)* milk spots
Milchfluß *m* milk flow
Milchflußmeßgerät *n* milk flow-meter
Milchforschung *f* dairy research
milchführend lactiferous, galactophorous
Milchgang *m* milk duct, galactophore *(of the udder)*
Milchgang[wand]entzündung *f (vet)* galactophoritis
Milchgärung *f* milk fermentation
milchgebend in milk, milky, lactating, lactic
Milchgebiß *n* milk dentition
Milchgefäß *n* milk vessel
Milchgerinnungsenzym *n* milk clotting enzyme
Milchgeschmack *m* milk flavour
Milchgesetz *n* milk code
Milchgesetzgebung *f* dairy legislation
Milchgetränk *n* milk drink, lactic beverage
Milchglanz *m* silver-leaf [disease] *(of deciduous trees, caused by Stereum purpureum)*
Milchglobulin *n* milk globulin
Milchgrind *m (vet)* trichophytosis, ringworm, tinea
Milchhahn *m* milk cock
milchhaltig milky, lactiferous
Milchhaus *n* milk house (room), dairy

Milchhaut *f* milk skin
Milchhof *m* dairy *(s. a.* Molkerei*)*
Milchhygiene *f* milk sanitation, dairy (milk) hygiene
Milchindustrie *f* dairy industry
Milchinhaltsstoff *m* milk constituent
Milchkalb *n* suckling calf
Milchkanal *m* milk duct *(of the udder)*
Milchkanne *f* milk-can, [milk] churn
Milchkannen... *s.* Kannen...
Milchkatalase *f* milk catalase *(enzyme)*
Milchkonservierung *f* milk preservation
Milchkontrolle *f* 1. milk control; 2. milk [yield] recording
Milchkontrollgefäß *n* milk recording jar *(of a parlour)*
Milchkrankheit *f* milky disease *(e.g. of the larvae of Popillia japonica; bacterial insect pest control)*
Milchkügelchen *n* milk globule
Milchkuh *f* dairy (milk) cow, milker
Milchkühlanlage *f* milk cooling plant
Milchkühler *m* milk cooler
Milchkühlung *f* milk cooling
Milchkühlwanne *f* [static refrigerated] bulk-milk tank, milk cooling basin
Milchkunde *f* dairy science
Milchlagerraum *m* milk room (house)
Milchlamm *n* milk-fed lamb
Milchleiste *f* milk ridge *(animal anatomy)*
Milchleistung *f* dairy (milk) performance, milk yield (productivity, production)
~/geringe hypogalactia
Milchleistungskontrolle *f*, **Milchleistungsprüfung** *f* milk [yield] recording
Milchleistungsvermögen *n* milkiness
Milchleitung *f* milk[ing] pipeline, milk tube (line)
Milchling *m* milk fungus, lactarius *(genus Lactarius)*
Milchlipase *f* milk lipase *(enzyme)*
milchlos barren *(cow)*
Milchmangel *m* **nach der Geburt** dysgalactia
Milchmastlamm *n* milk-fed lamb
Milchmengenkontrollgefäß *n* milk recording jar, recorder jar *(of a parlour)*
Milchmengenleistung *f s.* Milchleistung
Milchmengenmesser *m*, **Milchmengenmeßgerät** *n* milkmeter
Milchmischgetränk *n* milk drink
Milchnahrung *f* all-milk diet
Milchnäpfchen *n* milk well *(animal anatomy)*
Milchner *m (pisc)* milter
Milchpasteurisation *f* milk pasteurization
Milchprobe *f* milk sample
Milchprobenahme *f* milk sampling
Milchprobenahmerohr *n* milk thief
Milchprodukt *n* milk product
Milchprodukte *npl* dairy produce
Milchproduktion *f* milk production, dairying • **auf ~ gezüchtet** milk, milch • **für ~ geeignet** milk, milch

~/übermäßige polygalactia
Milchproduktionsbetrieb *m* dairy (milk producing) farm
Milchproduzent *m* milk producer, dairy farmer
Milchprotein *n* milk protein, lactoprotein
Milchprüfer *m* milk poise
Milchprüfgerät *n* milk tester
Milchprüfung *f* milk testing
Milchpulver *n* [whole] milk-powder, powdered (dried) milk
Milchpumpe *f* milk pump
Milchqualität *f* milk quality
Milchquotierung *f* dairy termination
Milchrasse *f* dairy breed
Milchraum *m* milk room (house), dairy
milchreif *(bot)* milk ripe, in [the] milk
Milchreife *f (bot)* milk ripeness; green ripeness *(of cereals)*
Milchreifestadium *n (bot)* milk[-ripe] stage, milky stage
Milchreinigungsseparator *m* clarifier
Milchretentionszyste *f (vet)* [ga]lactocele
Milchrindbulle *m* dairy bull
Milchrinder *npl* dairy cattle
Milchrinderbestand *m* dairy cattle stock
Milchrindkalb *n* dairy calf
Milchrindrasse *f* dairy breed
Milchrindzüchtung *f* dairy cattle breeding
Milchröhre *f (bot)* latex canal (trace)
Milchrohrleitung *f* milk pipeline (tube)
Milchrückstand *m* milk deposit
Milchsaft *m* 1. *(bot)* milky sap, latex, [vegetable] milk, milch; 2. chyle *(of intestinal lymph vessels)* • **~ absondernd** laticiferous • **~ enthaltend** laticiferous • **~ führend** laticiferous
Milchsaftschlauch *m s.* Milchröhre
Milchsaftzelle *f* laticifer
Milchsalz *n* milk salt
Milchsammelstelle *f* milk collecting (receiving) station, milk-gathering place
Milchsammelstück *n der Zentrale* milk claw, claw-piece
Milchsammeltour *f* milk collecting route
Milchsammlung *f* milk collection
~ **in Tanks** bulk-milk collection
Milchsäure *f* lactic (milk) acid, hydroxypropionic acid
Milchsäurebakterium *n* lactic-acid bacterium
Milchsäurebildner *m* lactic-acid [micro-]organism, lactic-acid producer
Milchsäuredehydrogenase *f* lactate dehydrogenase *(enzyme)*
Milchsäureerzeuger *m s.* Milchsäurebildner
Milchsäuregärung *f* lactic-acid fermentation
~/**reine** homofermentation
~/**unreine** heterofermentation
Milchsäuremikrobe *f s.* Milchsäurebildner
Milchschaf *n* milk (dairy) sheep

Milchschlauch *m* milk hose; long milk tube *(of a parlour)*
Milchschleuder *f* milk (cream) separator, milk centrifuge, skimming machine
Milchschleuse *f* milk sluice, sanitary trap
Milchschneidezahn *m* milk incisor *(animal anatomy)*
~/**erster (innerer, vorderer)** milk pincer
Milchsediment *n* milk sediment
Milchsekretion *f* milk (mammary) secretion, lactation
~/**fehlende** *(vet)* lactation failure, agalactia
Milchseparator *m s.* Milchschleuder
Milchserum *n s.* Molke
Milch-Shorthorn-Rind *n* Dairy Shorthorn [cattle] (breed)
Milchsieb *n* milk strainer
milchspendend milk, milch
Milchspiegel *m* milk mirror
Milchspindel *f* lactodensimeter
Milchstauung *f (vet)* galactostasis
Milchstechheber *m* milk thief
Milchstein *m* milk-stone
Milchsteinentferner *m* milk-stone remover
Milchsterilisation *f* milk sterilization
Milchstern *m (bot)* star-of-Bethlehem, ornithogalum *(genus Ornithogalum)*
Milchsternmosaikvirus *n* ornithogalum mosaic virus
Milchsynthese *f* milk synthesis
Milchtank *m* milk tank
Milchtankwagen *m* [bulk-]milk tanker
Milchtauchkühler *m* immersion [milk] cooler
Milchtechnologie *f* dairy (milk) technology
Milchtransport *m* milk transport
Milchtransportfahrzeug *n* bulk-milk tanker
Milchtransporttank *m* [bulk-]milk transport tank
milchtreibend [ga]lactogenic, lactagogue
Milchtrockenmasse *f* milk solids
~/**fettfreie** non-fat milk solids
Milchtrocknungsanlage *f* milk drying plant
Milchtuch *n* straining cloth
Milchtyp *m* dairy type *(as breeding objective)*
Milchüberwachung *f* milk control
Milchuntersuchung *f* milk testing
Milchvene *f* milk vein *(animal anatomy)*
Milchverarbeiter *m* milk processor
Milchverarbeitung *f* milk processing
Milchverarbeitungsanlage *f* milk processing plant
Milchverarbeitungsindustrie *f* dairy industry
Milchverbrauch *m* milk consumption
Milchverdauung *f* milk digestion
Milchverdünner *m* milk diluent *(for semen preservation)*
Milchverfälschung *f* milk adulteration
Milchvermarktung *f* milk marketing
Milchversorgung *f* milk supply
Milchvieh *n* dairy cattle
Milchviehanlage *f* dairy unit

Milchviehbestand

Milchviehbestand *m* dairy cattle stock
Milchviehbetrieb *m*, **Milchviehfarm** *f* dairy [farm], milk-farm
Milchviehgroßanlage *f* large dairy unit
Milchviehgülle *f* dairy slurry
Milchviehhalter *m* dairy farmer, dairyman
Milchviehhaltung *f* dairy farming, dairying
Milchviehherde *f* dairy herd
Milchviehpfleger *m* cowman
Milchviehstall *m* dairy cattle house
Milchviehweide *f* dairy pasture
Milchviehwirtschaft *f* dairy husbandry
Milchviehzucht *f* dairy cattle breeding
Milchvitaminisierung *f* milk vitaminization
Milchvorratstank *m* milk storage vessel
Milchwaage *f* milk balance
Milchwachsreife *f*, **Milchwachsreifestadium** *n* soft dough stage *(e.g. of a corn grain)*
Milchwicke *f* Chinese clover, Astragalus sinicus
Milchwirtschaft *f* dairy husbandry, dairying
Milchwissenschaft *f* dairy science
Milchzahn *m* milk (deciduous) tooth
Milchzange *f* milk pincers *(animal anatomy)*
Milchzeichen *n* dairy trait *(bodily characteristic)*
Milchzeit *f* lactation period
Milchzentrale *f s.* Milchsammelstück der Zentrale
Milchzentrifuge *f* milk centrifuge, milk (cream) separator, skimming machine
Milchzentrifugenschlamm *m* separator slime
Milchziege *f* dairy (milk) goat
Milchzisterne *f* milk cistern
Milchzucker *m* milk sugar, lactose, sugar of milk
Milchzusammensetzung *f* milk composition
Milchzyste *f (vet)* [ga]lactocele
mild mild; benign *(climate)*; mellow *(wine)*
mildern to attenuate *(e.g. the virulence of causative organisms)*
Mildes Irismosaikvirus *n* iris mild mosaic virus
~ **Jonquillenmosaikvirus** *n* jonquil mild mosaic virus
~ **Knaulgrasmosaikvirus** *n* cocksfoot mild mosaic virus
~ **Kuhbohnenscheckungsvirus** *n* cowpea mild mottle virus
~ **Rübenvergilbungsvirus** *n* beet mild yellowing virus, BMYV
~ **Sojabohnenmosaikvirus** *n* soya bean mild mosaic virus, SMMV
~ **Tollkirschenmosaikvirus** *n* belladonna mild mosaic virus
~ **Wasserrübenvergilbungsvirus** *n* turnip mild yellows virus
miliar miliary
Miliartuberkulose *f (vet)* miliary tuberculosis
Milieu *n* environment
Militz[gras] *n* reed canary grass, Phalaris arundinacea
Milneb *n* milneb *(fungicide)*
Milz *f* spleen, milt, lien
Milzbrand *m (vet)* anthrax
Milzvergrößerung *f (vet)* megalosplenia
Mimese *f (bot, zoo)* mimesis
Mimetikum *n* mimic
Mimikry *f (bot, zoo)* mimicry
Mimose *f* mimosa *(genus Mimosa)*
Mimosengewächse *npl* mimosa family *(family Mimosaceae)* • **die ~ betreffend** mimosaceous
Mimosin *n* mimosine *(alkaloid, amino-acid)*
MiMV *s.* Milchsternmosaikvirus
Mindereinschlag *m (forest)* undercut
Minderertrag *m* reduced yield
Mindestfettgehalt *m* minimal fat content
Mindesttemperatur *f* minimal temperature
Mindestumfang *m* minimal girth *(e.g. of a tree-trunk)*
Mine *f* mine, tunnel *(in plant tissues)* • **Minen [in Pflanzengewebe] anlegen** to mine, to tunnel
Mineral *n* mineral
~/tonfreies *(soil)* non-clay mineral
~/tonhaltiges clay mineral
Mineralboden *m* mineral soil
Mineraldünger *m* [mineral, inorganic, artificial] fertilizer, fertiliser *(for compounds s. under Dünger)*
Mineraldüngermischer *m* fertilizer blender (mixer)
Mineraldüngerstreuer *m* fertilizer (mineral) spreader, [solid] fertilizer distributor, dry applicator
Mineraldüngerverregnung *f* fert[irr]igation, fertilizer irrigation (sprinkling)
Mineraldüngung *f* inorganic (mineral) fertilization
Mineralernährung *f* mineral nutrition
Mineralfutter[mittel] *n* mineral feed, mineral mix[ture]
Mineralhaushalt *m* mineral balance
Mineralhefe *f* mineral yeast
Mineralisation *f* mineralization
Mineralisationsstörung *f* mineralization disturbance
mineralisch mineral, inorganic
mineralisieren to mineralize
Mineralisation *f* mineralization
Mineralkortikoid *n* mineralcorticoid
Mineralkunde *f* mineralogy
Mineralnährstoff *m* mineral nutrient
Mineralnährstoffmangel *m* mineral deficiency
Mineralneubildung *f* secondary mineral
Mineralogie *f* mineralogy
Mineralöl *n* mineral oil
Mineralphosphat *n* mineral phosphate
Mineralsalz *n* mineral [salt]
Mineralsalzernährung *f* mineral nutrition
Mineralstoff *m* mineral [matter], mineral element (nutrient)
Mineralstoffbedarf *m* mineral requirement
Mineralstoffbilanz *f* mineral balance
Mineralstoffdüngung *f* inorganic (mineral) fertilization
Mineralstoffgehalt *m* mineral content

Mineralstoffgemisch *n* mineral mix[ture], mineral feed
Mineralstoffhaushalt *m* mineral balance
Mineralstoffkreislauf *m* mineral cycle
Mineralstoffmangel *m* mineral deficiency
Mineralstoffmangelkrankheit *f* mineral deficiency disease
Mineralstoffüberschuß *m* mineral excess
Mineralstoffwechsel *m* mineral metabolism
Mineralstoffwechselstörung *f* mineral metabolism disorder
Mineralwolle *f* mineral (rock) wool
Mineralwollkultur *f* mineral wool culture
Mineralwollmatte *f* mineral wool mat
Miniaturbaum *m* bonsai
Miniaturschwein *n* miniature pig
minieren to mine, to tunnel
Minierer *m (ent)* miner, borer
Minierfliege *f* leaf-mining fly, agromyzid *(family Agromyzidae)*
Miniermotte *f* leaf-miner moth *(family Lyonetiidae and Lithocolletidae)*
Minigemüse *n (Am)* babyveg
Minihuhn *n* miniature chicken
Minimal[boden]bearbeitung *f* minimal (minimum) tillage
Minimal[boden]bearbeitungssystem *n* minimal tillage system
Minimalfläche *f (ecol)* minimal area
Minimaltemperatur *f* minimal temperature
Minimumareal *n (ecol)* minimal area
Minimumgesetz *n* **[nach Liebig]** law of limiting factors, Liebig's law of the minimum *(plant nutrition)*
Minimumthermometer *n* minimal thermometer
Mininelke *f* miniature carnation; spray[-type] carnation
Minirhizotron *n* mini-rhizotron
Minirose *f* miniature rose
Minitraktor *m* mini-tractor, microtractor
Minivirus *n* viroid
Minizellplatte *f* plug tray *(for raising plantlets)*
Minocin *n* s. Minocyclin
Minocyclin *n* minocyclin *(antibiotic)*
Minorka[huhn] *n* Minorca [fowl] *(breed)*
Minortranquilizer *m* ataractic [agent]
Minusbaum *m (forest)* minus tree
Minusbestand *m (forest)* minus stand
Minutengemelk *n* milk per minute
Minutenvolumen *n* minute volume
Minze *f* 1. mint *(genus Mentha)*; 2. peppermint, Mentha x piperita
Miombowald *m* miombo
Mirabelle *f* mirabelle, Syrian plum, Prunus domestica ssp. syriaca
Mirabellenlikör *m* mirabelle
Mirandarind *n* Miranda *(cattle breed)*
Mirazidium *n* miracidium *(of flukes)*
Mirex *n* mirex *(insecticide)*
Miride *f (ent)* mirid *(family Miridae)*

Mischanbau *m* mixed cropping, intercropping, interplanting • **~ betreiben** to intercrop
mischbar miscible, mixable
~/beliebig (in jedem Verhältnis) miscible in all proportions
~/nicht immiscible, non-miscible
Mischbarkeit *f* miscibility, mixability
Mischbaumart *f (forest)* admixture [tree] species
Mischbestand *m* mixed stand (crop); *(forest)* multi-species stand
Mischbrot *n* mixed (brown) bread
Mischdecke *f* mixed road surface
Mischdünger *m* mixed (blended) fertilizer
mischen to mix, to blend
Mischen *n***/phänotypisches** phenotypic mixing *(virology)*
Mischer *m* mixer, blender
mischerbig heterozygous
Mischerbigkeit *f* heterozygosis, heterozygosity
Mischflußgetreidetrockner *m* mixed-flow grain dryer
Mischfrucht *f* mixed crop, intercrop; mixed grain
Mischfruchtanbau *m* intercropping, interplanting, mixed cropping
Mischfutter *n* compound feed, feed mix, mixed feed (fodder), fodder mixture
Mischfutteranlage *f* mixed-feed plant
Mischfutterindustrie *f* compound-feed industry
Mischfuttermittel *n s.* Mischfutter
Mischfuttersilo *m* mixed-feed silo
Mischfutterwerk *n* feed mill
Mischgefüge *n (soil)* composite structure
Mischgeschwulst *f (vet)* mixed tumour
Mischgrasbestand *m* mixed sward
Mischinfektion *f* mixed infection
Mischkalk *m* compound lime fertilizer
Mischkondensator *m* jet condenser *(sugar manufacture)*
Mischkultur *f* 1. mixed culture; 2. *s.* Mischfruchtanbau; 3. *s.* Mischfrucht
Mischling *m* hybrid, bastard, mongrel
Mischluft *f* mixed air
Mischlüfter *m* blending fan *(e.g. in animal houses)*
Mischmaschine *f* mixer, blender
Mischmehl *n* blended (blender) flour
Mischpopulation *f (ecol)* mixed population
Mischprobe *f* composite sample
Mischrasse *f* cross-breed
Mischration *f* mixed ration *(animal feeding)*
Mischsaat *f* mixed sowing
Mischsilage *f* mixed silage
Mischsperma *n* mixed semen
Mischtank *m* mixing tank
Mischtumor *m (vet)* mixed tumour
Misch- und Futterverteilungswagen *m* mixer-feeder wagon
Mischung *f* 1. mix[ture], blend; 2. mixing, blending
~/reihenweise *(forest)* row-by-row mixture, line-by-line mixture, mixture by lines

Mischungsform

Mischungsform f form of mixture
Mischungsgut n s. Mischung 1.
Mischungsverhältnis n mixing proportion (ratio), formula, proportion of mixture
~ **von Mischdüngern** fertilizer formula
Mischwald m mixed (composite) forest
mischwollig mixed-woolled
Mispel f medlar (genus Mespilus)
Mißbildung f 1. malformation, abnormality; 2. s. Mißgeburt • **Mißbildungen erzeugend** teratogenic
Mißernte f crop failure, bad crop, disastrous harvest
Mißgeburt f monster, monstrosity
mißgeformt, mißgestaltet misshapen, monstrous; amorphous, amorphic
Mißgestaltung f amorphism; (vet) dysplasia
Mißwuchs m misgrowth, anomalous growth
Mist m dung, manure, muck
Mist... s. a. Dung...
Mistbeet n [manure, open] hotbed, manure bed, garden-frame
Mistbeeterde f dung earth
Mistbiene f drone fly, Eristalis tenax
Mistel f 1. mistletoe, glue, (Am) golden bough (genus Viscum); 2. s. Laubholzmistel
misten to muck [out]
Misterde f dung earth
Mistgabel f dung (muck) fork, pitchfork, graip
Mistgang m dung[ing] passage, gutter
Misthaufen m dunghill, manure (muck) heap, compost heap (pile), laystall, mixen
Mistjauche f dung liquor
Mistkäfer m dung beetle, Thyphaeus typhoeis
Mistkippwagen m manure dumping cart
Mistreißer m manure shredder (at a dung spreader)
Mistschwamm m (bot) inky cap (genus Coprinus)
Mistsickersaft m dung liquor
Miststreueregge f manure spreader harrow
MIT s. Monoiodtyrosin
mitessend (ecol) commensal
Mitesser m (ecol) commensal
Mitessertum n (ecol) commensalism, commensality
mitherrschend (ecol) co-dominant, subdominant
mitochondrial mitochondrial
Mitochondrie f mitochondrion, chondriosome (organelle)
Mitochondrienmembran f mitochondrial membrane
Mitochondrion n s. Mitochondrie
mitochondrisch mitochondrial
Mitogen n mitogen
Mitomycin n **C** mitomycin C (antibiotic)
Mitose f mitosis, mitotic division, equation[al] division, karyokinesis
Mitoseapparat m mitotic apparatus
Mitosegift n mitotic poison

Mitosezyklus m mitotic cycle
Mitostatikum n cytostatic
mitotisch mitotic
Mitralklappe f mitral valve (of the heart)
Mitscherlichanlage f Mitscherlich design (experimentation)
Mitscherlichgefäß n Mitscherlich pot
Mitscherlichgesetz n law of diminishing returns, law of effectivity of growth factors
Mittagsblume f 1. fig marigold, mesembryanthemum (genus Mesembryanthemum); 2. Livingstone daisy, Dorotheanthus bellidiformis, Mesembryanthemum criniflorum; 3. s. Mittagsgold
Mittagsgold n (bot) gazania (genus Gazania)
Mittel n 1. agent (s. a. under Stoff and Substanz); 2. s. Medikament; 3. s. Mittelwert
~/**antibakterielles** antibacterial [agent], bactericide
~/**antiinfektiöses** antiinfective agent
~/**antiphlogistisches** antiphlogistic [agent], antiinflammatory agent
~/**antiseptisches** antiseptic [agent]
~/**arithmetisches** arithmetic mean
~/**baumtötendes** arboricide, silvicide, brush killer
~/**blutdrucksenkendes** antihypertensive agent
~/**brechreizlinderndes** antiemetic [agent]
~/**entzündungshemmendes** antiphlogistic [agent], antiinflammatory agent
~/**feuerhemmendes** fire retardant
~/**fiebersenkendes** antipyretic [agent]
~/**fraßanregendes** phagostimulant
~/**freßlustminderndes** anorexiant [agent], appetite suppressor (depressant, inhibitor)
~/**freßluststeigerndes** appetite stimulant
~/**galletreibendes** cholagogue
~ **gegen Insekten und Milben** insectoacaricide
~ **gegen Insekten und Pilze** insectofungicide
~/**gerinnungshemmendes** anticoagulant
~/**geruchsbeseitigendes** deodorant
~/**harntreibendes** diuretic [agent]
~/**hustenhemmendes** antitussive agent, cough suppressant
~/**immunitätsunterdrückendes** immunosuppressive [agent]
~/**insektenabschreckendes** insect repellent
~/**keimhemmendes** sanitizer
~/**keimtötendes** germicide
~/**keimzellen[ab]tötendes** gametocide, sterilant
~/**krampflösendes** spasmolytic [agent]
~/**krankheitsverhütendes** prophylactic [agent]
~/**mikrobizides** microbicide, germicide
~/**milchtreibendes** [ga]lactagogue
~/**parasitenreduzierendes** sanitizer
~/**parasitentötendes** parasiticide
~/**pflanzen[ab]tötendes** phytocide
~/**pilz[ab]tötendes** fungicide
~/**pilzwachstumshemmendes** fungistat, mycostat
~/**säurebindendes** antacid [agent]
~/**schleimlösendes** (vet) expectorant

~/tonisierendes tonic
~/transpirationsminderndes antitranspirant
~/unterstützendes adjuvant
~/zellwachstumshemmendes cytostatic [agent]
Mittelachse f central axis *(e.g. of a leaf)*
Mittelährchen n *(bot)* middle floret
mittelalt middle-aged *(e.g. a tree-stand)*
Mittelast m central leader
Mittelbetrieb m/**landwirtschaftlicher** medium-sized farm
Mittelblume f [des Brokkoli] central head
Mittelblütchen n *(bot)* central floret
Mittelboden m medium class of soil
Mittelbrust f *(ent)* mesothorax, medithorax
Mittelbulbus m medium bulb *(of nematodes)*
Mitteldarm m mid-gut
Mitteldurchmesser m mean diameter *(timber mensuration)*
Mittelfarm f medium-sized farm
Mittelfell n mediastinum *(animal anatomy)*
Mittelfellentzündung f *(vet)* mediastinitis
Mittelfleisch n perineum *(animal anatomy)*
Mittelfleischplastik f *(vet)* episioplasty
mittelfrüh medium-early, mid-season *(maturity group)*; second early *(potato variety)*
Mittelfurche f centre (open, dead) furrow
Mittelfuß m metatarsus
Mittelfußgelenk n hock joint *(of poultry)*
Mittelfußknochen m metatarsal bone; cannon bone *(of hoofed animals)*; knuckle *(of sheep)*
Mittelgalopp m middle gallop
Mittelhand f metacarpus, coupling *(of animal body)*
 • **mit kurzer ~** short-coupled *(livestock judgement)*
Mittelhandknochen m metacarpal bone
mittelhart medium hardy *(crop plant)*
Mittelhirn n midbrain, mesencephalon
Mittelhöhe f average (mean) height
Mittelklee m zigzag clover, cow-grass, Trifolium medium
Mittelknospe f main bud
Mittellamelle f middle lamella *(of a plant cell)*
Mittellangkornreis m medium-grain rice
Mittelmeerbrombeere f *(Am)* Burbank's thornless blackberry, Rubus ulmifolius
Mittelmeerfieber n *(vet)* Mediterranean [coast] fever, Egyptian fever, tropical piroplasmosis (gonderiosis) *(caused by Theileria annulata)*
Mittelmeerfruchtfliege f Mediterranean fruit-fly, medfly, Ceratitis capitata
Mittelmeerhafer m Mediterranean oat[s], red oat, Avena byzantina
Mittelmeerhuhn n Mediterranean chicken
Mittelmeertheileriose f s. Mittelmeerfieber
Mittelmeertrespe f Spanish brome[-grass], Bromus madritensis
Mittelmehl n middlings, sharps *(milling)*
Mittelohr n middle ear
Mittelohrentzündung f *(vet)* otitis media

Mittelpore f *(soil)* medium-sized pore
Mittelprodukt n intermediate [product], intermediary
mittelrahmig medium-framed *(animal body)*
Mittelrippe f midrib, mid-vein *(of a leaf)* • **die ~ entfernen** to stem *(tobacco leaf)*
Mittelrücken m back furrow, crown *(ploughing in lands)*
Mittelsäger m red-breasted merganser, Mergus serrator
Mittelsand m *(soil)* medium sand
Mittelschutt m *(soil)* medial detritus
mittelschwer semiheavy *(e.g. a horse breed)*
mittelspät medium-late *(maturity group)*
Mittelsproß m 1. *(bot)* central head; 2. royal antler, tres-tine
Mittelsprosse f s. Mittelsproß 2.
Mittelstamm m mean (average, sample) tree, average stem; half-standard tree *(orcharding)*
Mittelstammethode f mean-tree method *(timber mensuration)*
Mittelstarkregner m medium-application sprinkler, medium-rate sprinkler
Mittelstrahlregner m medium-range sprinkler
Mittelstück n middle piece
Mittelteilstück n subplot *(field experimentation)*
Mitteltrab m middle trot
Mittelwald m coppice with standards, middle forest, *(Am)* composite forest
Mittelwaldbetrieb m, **Mittelwaldwirtschaft** f coppice-with-standards system, stored coppice
Mittelwand f *(api)* [comb] foundation
Mittelware f middlings *(timber trade)*
Mittelwert m average, mean
 ~/**arithmetischer** arithmetic mean
 ~ der Elternleistung mid-parent value *(animal breeding)*
 ~ der Stichprobe sample mean
 ~ der summierten Umfänge/arithmetischer mean girth *(timber mensuration)*
 ~ einer Verteilung expected value
 ~/**geometrischer** geometric mean
 ~/**harmonischer** *(biom)* harmonic mean
Mittendurchmesser m, **Mittenstärke** f mid-diameter, half-height diameter, diameter at half tree height *(timber mensuration)*
Mittenumfang m mid girth, circumference at the middle *(timber mensuration)*
Mittlerer Klee m cow grass (clover), Trifolium medium
~ Wegerich m hoary plantain, Plantago media
Mittleres Zittergras n common quaking-grass, doddering dillies (grass), Briza media
Mittsommerheide f Cornish heath, Erica vagans
Mixed Pickles pl mixed pickles
Mixer m mixer; centrifuge mixer (feeding trough) *(sugar manufacture)*
mixoploid *(gen)* mixoploid
Mixoploidie f *(gen)* mixoploidy

Mizell

Mizell *n*, **Mizelle** *f s.* Micelle
MK *s.* Krankheit/Mareksche
MKS *s.* 1. Maul- und Klauenseuche; 2. Motorkettensäge
MKS-Virus *n* foot-and-mouth disease virus, aphthovirus
MKV *s.* Marekvirus
MM *s.* Malling-Merton-Unterlage
MMA-Syndrom *n* MMA syndrome, mastitis-metritis-agalactia syndrome *(of pigs)*
MMV *s.* Maismosaikvirus
Mobilbau *m (api)* movable-comb hive
Mobildrehkran *m* mobile (vehicle-mounted) crane
Mobilhacker *m (forest)* mobile chipper
Mobilität *f* mobility
Mobilkran *m s.* Mobildrehkran
Mobilregner *m* mobile sprinkler
Mobiltrockner *m* mobile dryer
Mobolapflaumenbaum *m* mabo cork-tree, grysapple, Parinari curatellifolia
Mocimycin *n* mocimycin *(antibiotic)*
Modell *n*/**genetisches (genetisch-statistisches)** genetic model
~/mathematisches mathematical model
Modellbetrieb *m* **[/landwirtschaftlicher]** model (demonstration) farm
Modellierung *f*/**ökologische** ecological modelling
Modellstamm *m* sample tree, average stem (tree) *(forest estimation)*
Moder *m (soil)* mould, moder, duff, must
Moderboden *m* moder soil
Moderhinke *f (vet)* [sheep] foot-rot, foul-of-the-foot, loure
moderig mouldy, musty
Modermilbe *f* copra mite, Tyrophagus (Tyroglyphus) putrescentiae
modern to mould[er], to rot, to decay
Modifikation *f* modification
Modifikationsfaktor *m* modifying factor
Modifikationsgen *n*, **Modifikatorgen** *n* modifier [gene]
Modifizierbarkeit *f* modifiability, modificability
modifizieren to modify
Modiulus *m* modiulus *(animal anatomy)*
Modulation *f* modulation
Mohair *m*, **Mohär** *m* mohair
Mohn *m* poppy *(genus Papaver)*
mohnartig papaverous
Mohnblume *f* corn (field) poppy, Papaver rhoeas
Mohnextrakt *m* poppy
Mohnextraktionsschrot *n* poppy-seed meal
Mohngewächse *npl* poppy family *(family Papaveraceae)* • **die ~ betreffend** papaveraceous
Mohnkapsel *f* poppy-head, poppy capsule
Mohnöl *n* poppy[-seed] oil
Mohnsamen *m* poppy (maw) seed, mohnseed
Mohnsamenextraktionsschrot *m* poppy-seed meal
Mohnsamenöl *n* poppy[-seed] oil

Möhre *f* 1. carrot *(genus Daucus)*; 2. carrot, Daucus carota ssp. sativus; 3. carrot *(root vegetable)*
Möhrenblattfloh *m*, **Möhrenblattsauger** *m (ent)* 1. carrot psyllid, Trioza viridula; 2. Japanese silverfire sucker, Trioza apicalis
Möhrenbuntscheckungs- und -verzwergungsvirus *n* carrot motley dwarf virus, CMDV
Möhrenerntemaschine *f*, **Möhrenernter** *m* carrot harvester (lifter)
Möhrenfliege *f* carrot [rust] fly, Psila rosae
Mohrenhirse *f* sorghum, sorgo, great millet, milo [maize], negro corn, cush *(genus Sorghum)*
Möhrenköpfgerät *n* carrot topper
Möhrenkraut *n* carrot foliage
Möhrennaßfäule *f* carrot [bacterial] soft rot *(caused by Erwinia carotovora)*
Möhrenrodemaschine *f* carrot lifter
Möhrenrotblättrigkeitsvirus *n* carrot red leaf virus, CaRLV
Möhrensaft *m* carrot juice
Möhrenschabe *f* carrot moth, Depressaria nervosa
Möhrenscheckungsvirus *n* carrot mottle virus, CaMV
Möhrenschwärze *f* black rot of carrot *(caused by Alternaria porri f.sp. dauci)*
Möhrenwurzellaus *f* hawthorn-carrot aphid, Dysaphis crataegi
Möhrenzystenälchen *n* carrot cyst-nematode, Heterodera carotae
Mohrrübe *f s.* Möhre
Molar *m* molar [tooth], cheek tooth
Molarität *f* molarity
Molassesgras *n* molasses grass, Melinis minutiflora
Moldamin *n* penicillin G *(antibiotic)*
Mole *f (vet)* mole
Molekularbiologie *f* molecular biology
Molekulargenetik *f* molecular genetics
Molekülmasse *f* molecular weight
Molinat *n* molinate *(herbicide)*
Molke *f*, **Molken** *m* whey, [milk] serum, lactoserum
Molkenablaufbrett *n* cheese draining board
Molkenablaufsieb *n* cheese drainer
Molkenablauftrommel *f* whey draining drum
Molkenboden *m* clay-loam soil with a gley-like horizon
Molkenbutter *f* whey (serum) butter
Molkeneiweiß *n* whey (milk serum) protein
Molkeneiweißkäse *m* whey protein cheese
Molkenglobulin *n* whey globulin
Molkenhefe *f* whey yeast
Molkenkäse *m* whey (green) cheese
Molkennest *n* whey pocket *(in cheese)*
Molkenpaste *f* whey paste
Molkenpermeat *n* whey permeate
Molkenprotein *n s.* Molkeneiweiß
Molkenpulver *n* whey powder, powdered (dried) whey
Molkenrahm *m* whey cream

Molkensirup *m* condensed whey
Molkenwein *m* whey wine
Molkerei *f* dairy [factory], creamery
Molkereiabprodukt *n* dairy waste
Molkereiabwasser *n* dairy waste-water, dairy effluent
Molkereiausrüstung *f* dairy equipment
Molkereibutter *f* dairy butter
Molkereieinrichtung *f* dairy equipment
Molkereierzeugnisse *npl* dairy produce
Molkereigenossenschaft *f* dairy co-operative
Molkereihilfsstoffe *mpl* dairy aids (ancillaries)
Molkereihygiene *f* dairy hygiene
Molkereimaschinen *fpl* dairy machinery
Molkereimaschinenwesen *n* dairy engineering
Molkereinebenprodukt *n* dairy by-product
Molkereitechnik *f* dairy engineering
Molkereiwesen *n* dairying
Mollisol *m (soil)* mollisol, oll
Molluske *f* mollusc *(phylum Mollusca)*
Molluskenbekämpfung *f* mollusc control
molluskizid molluscicidal, molluscacidal
Molluskizid *n* molluscicide, molluscacide
Moltebeere *f* cloudberry, Rubus chamaemorus
Molybdändüngemittel *n* molybdenum fertilizer
Molybdänmangel *m* molybdenum deficiency
Molybdänose *f (vet)* molybdenosis
~ **der Wiederkäuer** peat scours, teart
molybdänreich teart, excessively rich in molybdenum *(soil or plants)*
Molybdänsäure *f* molybdic acid
Molybdänüberschuß *m* teartness *(of soil or plants)*
Molybdänvergiftung *f (vet)* molybdenosis
Moment *n s.* Drehmoment
Monalide *n* monalide *(herbicide)*
Monarch *m (ent)* monarda, Danaus plexippus
Monarde *f (bot)* monarda *(genus Monarda)*
Monatserdbeere *f* everbearing (remontant) strawberry
Monatsrose *f* monthly rose *(varietal group of Rosa chinensis)*
Mönch *m s.* Kahlhirsch
Mönchspfeffer *m* [common] chaste-tree, Vitex agnus-castus
Mönchsrhabarber *m* monk's rhubarb, Rumex alpinus
Mondbohne *f* lima [bean], moon (sugar) bean, curry (butter, Madagascar) bean, sieva [bean], Phaseolus lunatus [var. lunatus]
Mondfäule *f s.* Mondringe
Mondfleck *m* buff-tip[ped] moth, Phalera bucephala
Mondfleckenbürstenspinner *m* larch tussock moth, Dasychira selenitica
mondförmig *(bot, zoo)* lunate
Mondorchidee *f* moth orchid, phalaenopsis *(genus Phalaenopsis)*

Mondraute *f* 1. moonwort *(genus Botrychium)*; 2. [common] moonwort, Botrychium lunaria
Mondringe *mpl*, **Mondringigkeit** *f* included (internal) sapwood, ring rot, blown *(of timber)*
Mondsame *m (bot)* moonseed *(genus Menispermum)*
Mondwinde *f* moon-flower, Calonyction album (aculeatum)
Monensin *n* monensin [sodium], rumensin *(antibiotic)*
Mongolische Eiche *f* Mongolian oak, Quercus mongolica
Moniliafäule *f s.* Moniliakrankheit
Moniliainfektion *f (vet)* moniliasis
Moniliakrankheit *f (phyt)* monilia [disease], brown rot
~ **des Kernobstes** brown rot of pome fruits *(caused by Monilinia fructigena)*
~ **des Steinobstes** brown rot of stone fruits *(caused by Monilinia fructicola)*
Moniliasis *f (vet)* moniliasis
Monoamin *n* monoamine
Monoaminoxidase *f* amine oxidase, flavin-containing, adrenaline (tyramine) oxidase, tyraminase *(enzyme)*
Monoammoniumphosphat *n* monoammonium phosphate
Monocalciumphosphat *n* monocalcium phosphate
Monocarbonsäure *f* monocarboxylic acid
monochromatisch monochromatic
Monocrotophos *n* monocrotophos *(insecticide)*
monogastrisch monogastric
monogen monogenic
Monogen *n* monogene
Monogenese *f s.* Monogonie
Monogenie *f* monogenism
monogerm *(bot)* monogerm
Monogermsaatgut *n* monogerm (segmented) seed
Monoglycerid *n* monoglyceride
Monogonie *f* monogony, monogenesis, asexual (vegetative) reproduction, non-sexual propagation
monohaploid *(gen)* monohaploid
monohybrid monohybrid
Monohybride *f* monohybrid, single cross [hybrid]
Monohydroxybenzol *n s.* Phenol
Monoiodtyrosin *n* monoidotyrosine
monokarp *(bot)* monocarpic, hapaxanthic, hapaxanthous
Monokarpie *f (bot)* monocarpy
monoklin *(bot)* monoclinous
monoklonal monoclonal
monokotyl *(bot)* monocotyledonous
Monokotyle[done] *f (bot)* monocotyledon, monocot[yl]
Monokultur *f* monoculture, monocropping sequence, single cropping, pure crop (plantation)

Monokulturwirtschaft

Monokulturwirtschaft *f* single-crop farming, one-crop agriculture *(economy)*
Monolinuron *n* monolinuron *(herbicide)*
Monolithlysimeter *n* monolith lysimeter
monomorph monomorphic, monomorphous
Monomorphie *f*, **Monomorphismus** *m* monomorphism
mononukleär mononuclear
monophag *(ecol)* monophagous
Monophagie *f (ecol)* monophagy
Monophenolmonooxygenase *f* monophenol monooxygenase, tyrosinase *(enzyme)*
monophyletisch monophyletic
Monoplegie *f (vet)* monoplegia
monopodial *(bot)* monopodial
monorchid monorchic, monorchid
Monorchie *f*, **Monorchismus** *m* monorchidism
Monosaccharid *n*, **Monose** *f* monosaccharide, simple sugar
monosom *(gen)* monosomic
Monosomie *f (gen)* monosomics
monöstrisch *(zoo)* monoestrous
monosymmetrisch *(bot)* dorsiventral, zygomorphic
Monoterpen *n* monoterpene
monotrich monotrichous
monovoltin *(ent)* univoltine
monoxen monoxenous
Monoxybenzol *n* phenol
Monoxygenase *f* monoxygenase *(enzyme)*
Monözie *f (bot)* monoecism, monoecy
monözisch *(bot)* monoecious
Monozönose *f (ecol)* monocoenosis
monozygot monozygotic, monozygous, monoval, monovular, one-egg
monozyklisch-hapaxanth *(bot)* annual
Monozyt *m* monocyte *(kind of leucocyte)*
Monozytose *f (vet)* monocytosis
~ **der Puten** mud fever of turkeys, contagious indigestion of turkeys
~ **des Huhnes** avian monocytosis (infectious diarrhoea), battery nephrosis, pullet (Bright's) disease, X disease
Monstera *f (bot)* windowleaf philodendron, ceriman, Monstera deliciosa, Philodendron pertusum
monströs monstrous
Monstrosität *f*, **Monstrum** *n s.* Mißgeburt
Monsunbergwald *m* moist mountain forest
Monsunklima *n* monsoon climate
Monsunwald *m* monsoon[al] forest
~/**regengrüner** deciduous moist forest
Montagemast *m* standing derrick
montan *(ecol)* montane
Montbretie *f (bot)* 1. montbretia *(genus Crocosmia)*; 2. montbretia, Crocosmia x crocosmiiflora
Montebrasit *m* montebrasite *(clay mineral)*
Monte-Carlo-Methode *f* Monte Carlo method *(statistics)*
Montereykiefer *f* Monterey pine, Pinus radiata
Montereyzypresse *f* Monterey cypress, Cupressus macrocarpa
Montgomery'-Krankheit *f* African swine fever *(virosis)*
Montmorillonit *m* montmorillonite, smectite *(clay mineral)*
montmorillonitisch montmorillonitic
Monuron *n* monuron, CMU *(herbicide)*
Moor *n* moor, [quaking] bog, swamp, fen [soil], quag[mire]
~/**oligotrophes** oligotrophic moor
~/**ombrogenes** ombrogenous (hill) moor, high[land] moor, high bog, rain-water bog (moor)
Moorbirke *f* white (silver, pubescent) birch, Betula pubescens
Moorboden *m* moor soil, bog[gy] soil, histosol
Moorentwässerung *f* bog drainage
Moorfarn *m* crested shield fern, Dryopteris cristata
Moorheide *f* heather-bell, bell-heather, cross-leaved heath, Erica tetralix
moorig boggy, swampy, fenny
Moorkultur *f* muck farming
Moorland *n* moorland, bogland, fen [soil]
moorliebend uliginose, uliginous
Moorloch *n* hag
Moorpflanze *f* bog-plant
Moorpflug *m* bog[land] plough, swamp plough
Moorrandwald *m* peatbog-margin forest
Moorreitgras *n* slim-stem reed grass, Calamagrostis neglecta
Moorschneehuhn *n* [willow] ptarmigan, willow grouse, Lagopus lagopus
Moortorf *m* bog peat
Moor- und Torfkunde *f* peat land science
Moorwald *m* bog (swamp) forest
Moorwalze *f* bogland roller
Moorweide *f* 1. creeping willow, Salix repens; 2. whortleberry willow, Salix myrtilloides
Moos *n* moss, bryophyte *(division Bryophyta)*
moosbedeckt mossy, moss-clad, moss-covered, moss-grown
Moosbeere *f* 1. mossberry, *(Am)* European (small) cranberry, Vaccinium oxycoccos; 2. *s.* Rauschbeere 1
moosbewachsen *s.* moosbedeckt
Moosdecke *f* moss cover
Moosglöckchen *n* twinflower, Linnaea borealis
Moosheide *f* mossy heath
Moos-Kiefernwald *m* mossy pinery, Pinetum hylocomiosum
Moosknopfkäfer *m* pygmy mangel beetle, beet beetle, Atomaria linearis
Mooskraut *n* [little] club moss *(genus Selaginella)*
Moosmoor *n* dystrophic peat
Moospflanze *f* moss, bryophyte *(division Bryophyta)*
Moosphlox *m* moss pink, Phlox subulata
Moosrechen *m* moss rake
Moosschicht *f* moss layer

Moossteinbrech m *(bot)* mossy saxifrage, lady's-cushion, Saxifraga hypnoides
Moostorf m moss peat
~/älterer older peat
Moostundra f moss tundra
Mooswand f vertical garden
Mops m pug[-dog] *(breed)*
Mor m mor [humus] *(raw humus)*
Moräne f *(soil)* moraine
Moränenboden m moraine soil
Moränengürtel m morainic belt
Moränenschutt m moraine
Morantel[tartrat] n morantel *(anthelminthic)*
Morast m morass, swamp, marsh
morastig morassy, swampy, marshy; miry, muddy *(e.g. roads)*
Morbidität f morbidity, morbidness
Morbiditätsrate f morbidity rate
Morbilität f s. Morbidität
morbiphor morbiphor, morbiferous, disease-conveying
MöRBV s. Möhrenrotblättrigkeitsvirus
Morchel f morel *(genus Morchella)*
Mordenit m mordenite *(non-clay mineral)*
Mörder m s. Schadhirsch
Mordfliege f robber fly *(family Asilidae)*
Morelle f morello [cherry], Prunus cerasus ssp. cerasus var. austera
Morfamquat n morfamquat *(herbicide)*
Morgan Horse n Morgan [horse] *(breed)*
Morgan-Einheit f *(gen)* Morgan (map) unit, crossover (crossing-over) unit
Morgen m 1. morgen *(old unit of land area varying from 0.25 ha to 0.38 ha)*; 2. s. Acre
Morgenfütterung f morning feeding
Morgengemelk n morning milk
Morgengrauen n daybreak
Morgenländische Platane f oriental plane-tree, Platanus orientalis
~ Zackenschote f hill mustard, Turkish rocket, Bunias orientalis
Morgenländischer Lebensbaum m oriental (Chinese) arbor vitae, Thuja orientalis
~ Mohn m oriental poppy, Papaver orientale (bracteatum)
Morgenmilch f morning milk
Morgenröschen n sweet william campion (catchfly, silene), Silene armeria
Morgentau m morning dew
Mormonentulpe f mariposa [lily, tulip] *(genus Calochortus)*
Morphaktin n morphactin *(growth inhibitor)*
Morphin n, **Morphium** n morphine, morphia *(alkaloid)*
Morphogenese f, **Morphogenie** f morphogenesis
Morphologie f morphology
~/ökologische ecomorphology
morphologisch morphological
Morphometrie f morphometry

morphometrisch morphometric
Morphose f morphosis
morsch decayed, rotten *(e.g. wood)*; brittle
Mörser m mortar
mortal mortal
Mortalität f mortality
~/embryonale embryonic mortality
Mortalitätsrate f mortality (death) rate
Morula f *(zoo)* morula
Mosaik n 1. *(gen, soil, ecol)* mosaic; 2. *(phyt)* mosaic [disease]; 3. [aerial] mosaic *(surveying)*
Mosaikchlorosevirus n **des Hopfens** hop mosaic chlorosis virus
Mosaikgesellschaft f mosaic (pattern) community
Mosaikkrankheit f *(phyt)* mosaic [disease]
Mosaiklebensgemeinschaft f s. Mosaikgesellschaft
Moschus m musk
Moschusbock[käfer] m European beetle, Aromia moschata
Moschusente f Muscovy (musk, flying) duck, Cairina moschata
Moschuserdbeere f hautbois strawberry, Fragaria moschata (elatior)
Moschusgauklerblume f musk [plant], Mimulus moschatus
Moschuskraut n moschatel, hollow root, Adoxa moschatellina
Moschuskürbis m cushaw, China squash, winter crookneck [pumpkin], Cucurbita moschata
Moschusmalve f musk mallow, Malva moschata
Moschusochse m musk-ox, Ovibos moschatus
Moschusratte f musk-rat, musquash, Ondatra zibethica
Moschusreiherschnabel m musky heron's-bill, musk clover, white stem filaree, Erodium moschatum
Moschusrose f musk-rose, Rosa moschata
Moschustier n musk-deer, Moschus moschiferus
Moselwein m moselle *(wine)*
Moskito m mosquito, gnat *(family Culcidae)*
Moskitogras n mosquito grass, Bouteloua gracilis *(oligostachya)*
Most m [fruit] must, stum
Mostapfel m cider apple
Mostbereitung f cider-making
Mosterei f cider mill
Mostgewicht n density of wine
Mosthersteller m ciderist
Mostklärung f must clarification (clarifying)
Mostobst n cider fruit
Mostrich m mustard
Mosttank m must tank
Mostverdicker m must concentrator
Mostwaage f **nach Öchsle** must gauge, must[i]meter, mustometer
MöSV s. Möhrenscheckungsvirus
Motilin n motilin *(hormone)*
Motilität f motility

Motor

Motor *m*/**luftgekühlter** air-cooled engine
Motoraltöl *n* old motor oil
Motorbaumspritze *f* power tree sprayer
Motorbremse *f* engine brake
Motordrehzahl *f* engine speed
Motordumper *m* motor dumper
Motorentastungssäge *f* motorized pruning saw
Motorfräse *f* motor tiller
motorgetrieben power-driven
Motorhacke *f* motor hoe (tiller)
Motorheckenschere *f* motor hedge trimmer
Motorhubraum *m* engine (cubic) capacity, stroke volume
Motorkarren *m* motorized barrow
Motorkettensäge *f* [power] chain-saw
Motorkipplader *m* motor dumper
Motorkraftstoff *m* engine fuel
Motorkreissäge *f*/**handgeführte** [forest] clearing saw
Motorleistung *f* engine output
Motormäher *m* power mower, motor mower (scythe)
Motormuldenkipper *m* motor dumper
Motornenndrehzahl *f* rated engine speed
Motorpflug *m* motor-plough
Motorrasenmäher *m* power lawn mower (s. a. Motormäher)
Motorrechen *m* power rake
Motorrückensprühgerät *n* power-driven knapsack mist blower
Motorrückenstäuber *m* power-driven knapsack duster
Motorsäge *f* power (machine) saw
Motorsägenführer *m* power saw operator, sawyer
Motorschlitten *m* motor sled[ge], snowmobile
Motorseilwinde *f* motor-driven winch
Motorspritze *f* motor (power) sprayer
Motorsprühgerät *n* self-propelled motor atomizer
Motorstäuber *m* power (motor) duster
~/rückentragbarer engine-driven knapsack duster
Motorstraßenhobel *m* autograder
Motorwinde *f* motor-driven winch
Motorzapfwelle *f* live power take-off [shaft], continuous-running p.t.o.
Motte *f* [tineid] moth (family Tineidae)
Mottenfalle *f* moth trap
Mottenkraut *n* (bot) moth mullein, Verbascum blattaria
Mottenschildlaus *f* white fly (family Aleurodidae)
Mozzarella[käse] *m* mozzarella [cheese]
MQ *s.* Quadrat/mittleres
mR, m.R. *s.* Rinde/mit
mRNA mRNA, messenger RNA (ribonucleic acid)
mRNA-Reifung *f* [mRNA] processing
MRVzV *s.* Maisrauhverzwergungsvirus
M.R.Y. *s.* Maas-Rhein-Ijssel-Rind
M-Saatgut *n* segmented seed
MSH *s.* Hormon/melanozytenstimulierendes
MTU *s.* Methylthiourazil

Mücke *f* midge (suborder Nematocera)
Mückenlarve *f* midge larva
Mudde *f* (soil) mud
müde musty (wine)
Muehlenbeckie *f* wire vine (genus Muehlenbeckia)
Muffel *n s.* Muffelwild
Muffelkäfer *m* seed (pulse) beetle, bruchid (family Bruchidae) • **die Muffelkäfer betreffend** bruchid
Muffelwild *n* mouf[f]lon, musmon, Ovis aries (musimon)
muffig musty
Mufflon *m s.* Muffelwild
muhen to low, to moo, to boo
Muhen *n* low
Mühle *f* 1. mill; flour mill; 2. grinder, [grinding] mill
Mühlenarbeiter *m* mill-hand
Mühlenindustrie *f* milling industry
Mühlennachprodukt *n* mill[ing] residue
Mühlenprodukt *n* mill product
Mühlenschädling *m* mill pest
Mühlgraben *m* mill-race, lead
Mühlstein *m* millstone, grindstone
Mukoglobulin *n* mucoglobulin
mukolytisch mucolytic
Mukopolysaccharid *n* mucopolysaccharide
Mukoproteid *n* mucoproteid[e]
Mukoprotein *n* mucoprotein
mukos, mukös mucous
Mukosa *f* mucosa, mucous membrane
Mukositis *f* (vet) mucositis
Mukus *m* mucus, slime
Mulch *m* mulch
Mulchbalken *m* mulch bar (of a lawn mower)
Mulchdecke *f* mulch cover
mulchen to mulch
Mulchfolie *f* mulch film
Mulchgerät *n* mulching machine
Mulchmähwerk *n* mulching lawn mower
Mulchmaterial *n* mulching material, mulch matter
Mulchrasenmäher *m* mulching lawn mower
Mulchrückstand *m* mulch residue
Mulchschicht *f* mulch
Mulde *f* 1. tray, trough; 2. hollow, basin, syncline
Muldenschar *n* concave (incurved) share
Mule *n s.* Muleschaf
Muleschaf *n* Mule (sheep breed)
Mules-Operation *f* (vet) Mules operation
Mulga *f* (bot) mulga, Acacia aneura
Mulga-Strauchformation *f* mulga scrub (in Australia)
Mull *m* mull [earth], mull (mild) humus
~/moderartiger detritomull, modermull
Müll *m* refuse, garbage, waste [material], rubbish
Mullboden *m* mull soil
Mülldeponie *f* waste (refuse) tip
~/städtische municipal refuse disposal
Müller *m* miller
Müllerei *f* 1. milling; 2. mill
Müllereiabfall *m*, **Müllereiabgang** *m* mill offal

Müllereierzeugnis *n* milling product
Müllereimaschine *f* miller, milling machine
Müllergaze *f* bolting (bolter) cloth
Müllhumus *m* *(soil)* soft humus
Müllkippe *f* s. Mülldeponie
Müllkompost *m* [town] refuse compost, municipal [refuse, waste] compost
Müllverträglichkeit *f* tolerance to garbage
Mulm *m*, **Mulmfen[n]** *n* *(soil)* fenmull, mould
Multicell-Jungpflanze *f* multicell plant
Multielementanalyse *f* multielement analysis *(e.g. of soil samples)*
Multienzym *n* multienzyme
multigen multigenic
Multikanaldurchfluß-Injektionsanalyse *f* multichannel flow-injection analysis *(e.g. of feeds)*
multinukleär multinuclear, multinucleate
Multinuklearität *f* multinuclearity
Multiparasitismus *m* multiparasitism, multiparasitization
Multispektralanalyse *f* multispectral analysis
Multisporauslese *f* multispore selection
Multitopf *m* multipot *(for plantlets)*
Multitopfpalette *f* flat
multitrich polytrichous
Multivorie *f* *(zoo, ecol)* polyphagy
multizellulär multicellular
Mumie *f* *(phyt, vet)* mummy
Mumienpuppe *f* *(ent)* mummia, mummy
Mumienweizen *m* mummy wheat, Triticum compositum
Mumifikation *f*, **Mumifizierung** *f* mummification
Mummel *f* *(bot)* brandy bottle, Nuphar lutea
Mümmelmann *m* *(hunter's language)* s. Hase
Mund *m* mouth, stoma[te], orifice
Mundhaken *m* *(ent)* mouth hook
Mundhöhle *f* mouth (oral) cavity • **innerhalb der ~** intra-oral
Mundnarbe *f* *(bot)* micropyle
Mundöffnung *f* oral aperture
Mundstachel *m* mouth spear *(e.g. of plant-parasitic nematodes)*
~/dolchartiger stylet
Mundstück *n* 1. nozzle; 2. mouthpiece *(of bridle)*
Mündung *f* 1. *(bot, zoo)* ostium; 2. mouth *(e.g. of a stream)*; 3. muzzle *(of a rifle)*
~/kleine *(bot, zoo)* ostiole
Mundwerkzeuge *npl* *(ent)* mouth-parts
~/beißende biting mouth-parts
~/kauende chewing mouth-parts
~/kauend-leckende chewing-lapping mouth-parts
~/raspelnd-saugende rasping-sucking mouth-parts
~/saugende sucking mouth-parts
~/stechend-saugende piercing-sucking mouth-parts
Mundwinkelentzündung *f* *(vet)* angular stomatitis
Mungbohne *f* mung bean, green gram [bean], golden gram [bean], Phaseolus aureus

Mungo *m* mongoose, mungoos *(genus Herpestes)*
Muniqui-Stamm *m* Maneghi *(strain of the Arabian horse)*
Munsell-Farbtafeln *fpl* *(soil)* Munsell colour charts
Münster[käse] *m* Muenster [cheese], Munster [cheese]
Mur *f* s. Murbruch
mürbe *f* 1. friable, crumbly; 2. mellow[y] • **~ werden** to mellow
Mürbe *f*, **Mürbheit** *f* 1. friability, crumbliness *(e.g. of a soil)*; 2. mellowness *(e.g. of fruit)*
Murbruch *m* mud flow *(in high mountains)*
Murciana-[Granadina-]Ziege *f* Murcian (Granada) goat *(breed)*
Mure *f*, **Murgang** *m* s. Murbruch
Murgeser Pferd *n* Murge *(horse breed)*
Murmeltier *n* mountain-rat, Marmota marmota
Murnau-Werdenfelser Rind *n* Murnau-Werdenfels *(cattle breed)*
Murray-Grey-Rind *n* Murray Grey *(cattle breed)*
Musafaser *f* abaca, Manila [hemp] *(from Musa textilis)*
Muscadinerebe *f* muscadine [grape], southern fox grape, Vitis rotundifolia
Muscarin *n* muscarin[e] *(alkaloid)*
Muschelblümchen *n* *(bot)* isopyrum *(genus Isopyrum)*
Muschelblume *f* shell-flower, bells of Ireland, Moluccella laevis
Muschelgrit *m* shell grit, oyster-shell
Muschelkalk *m* shell lime[stone]
Muschelpilz *m* oyster fungus (mushroom), Pleurotus ostreatus
musen to pulp, to mash
Muser *m* pulper, pulping machine, masher
Muskat *m* nutmeg *(spice)*
Muskatblüte *f* mace *(spice)*
Muskatellersalbei *m* s. Muskatsalbei
Muskatellertraube *f*, **Muskatellerwein** *m* muscat
Muskatfrucht *f* nutmeg-apple
Muskatnuß *f* nutmeg
Muskatnußbaum *m* nutmeg[-tree], Myristica fragrans
Muskatsalbei *m* clary [sage], Salvia sclarea
Muskel *m* muscle
~/dreiköpfiger triceps [muscle]
~/glatter smooth (unstriated) muscle
~/quergestreifter striated muscle
~/unwillkürlicher involuntary muscle
~/viszeraler visceral (organic) muscle
~/willkürlicher voluntary muscle
Muskel... s. a. Myo...
Muskelarbeit *f* muscular work
Muskelatrophie *f* *(vet)* muscular atrophy, amyotrophia
Muskelbinde *f* fascia
~/tiefe deep fascia
Muskelbindegewebegeschwulst *f* *(vet)* myofibroma

Muskeldegeneration

Muskeldegeneration f *(vet)* muscular degeneration, myodegeneration
~/Zenkersche Zenker's degeneration [of muscles]
Muskeldurchschneidung f *(vet)* myotomy
Muskeldystrophie f *(vet)* muscular dystrophy, myodystrophy
~ **der Kälber/enzootische** stiff calf disease
~ **der Lämmer/enzootische** stiff lamb disease
~/diätetische (enzootische) nutritional muscular dystrophy, NMD, white muscle disease
Muskelenergie f muscular energy
Muskelentartung f s. Muskeldegeneration
Muskelentzündung f *(vet)* myositis, inflammation of the muscles
Muskelerkrankung f *(vet)* muscular disease, myopathy
Muskelermüdung f muscular fatigue
Muskelerschlaffung f muscle relaxation
Muskelfaser f [skeletal] muscle fibre, myofibre
Muskelfaserbildungszelle f myoblast
Muskelfett n intramuscular (intermuscular) fat
Muskelfleisch n brawn
Muskelfülle f muscularity
Muskelgeschwulst f *(vet)* myoma
Muskelgewebe n muscle tissue
Muskelgewebegeschwulst f *(vet)* myoma
Muskelglycogen n muscle glycogen
Muskelhämoglobin n s. Myoglobin
Muskelhypertrophie f muscular hypertrophy
Muskelkontraktion f muscular contraction
Muskelkraft f muscle power (force)
Muskelkrampf m *(vet)* muscular spasm
Muskelmagen m muscular stomach, gizzard *(of poultry)*
Muskelmagenerosion f gizzard erosion
Muskelmasse f muscle weight
Muskelprotein n muscle protein, myoprotein
Muskelrelaxans n muscle relaxant
Muskelriß m, **Muskelruptur** f *(vet)* muscle rupture, myorrhexis, tearing
Muskelscheide f [muscle] sheath
Muskelschlaffheit f myatonia
Muskelschmerz m *(vet)* myalgia
Muskelschwäche f *(vet)* myasthenia, muscular debility
Muskelschwund m *(vet)* muscular atrophy, myodystrophy, amyotrophia
Muskelspasmus m *(vet)* muscular spasm
Muskelsteifigkeit f *(vet)* muscular stiffness, rigor
Muskelstoffwechsel m muscle metabolism
Muskeltätigkeit f muscular action
Muskeltonus m muscular tone
~/fehlender *(vet)* atony
Muskeltremor m *(vet)* muscular tremor
Muskeltyp m meat type *(of farm animals)*
Muskelwachstum n muscular growth
Muskelzerreißung f s. Muskelriß
Muskelzerrung f *(vet)* strain

Muskelzittern n 1. muscular shivers, shivering *(animal physiology)*; 2. s. Muskeltremor
Muskelzucker m inosite, inositol
Muskelzytoplasma n sarcoplasm
Muskovit m muscovite *(non-clay mineral)*
muskulär muscular
Muskulatur f musculature, flesh
muskulös muscular, brawny, beefy
Mussins Katzenkraut n violet catmint, Nepeta mussinii
Mustang m mustang, bronco, bronc
Musterbestand m *(forest)* indicator stand
Musterbetrieb m model (demonstration) farm
Musterration f specimen ration *(animal nutrition)*
Musterstamm m sample tree *(forest estimation)*
Musterwald m demonstration forest
mutabel mutable
Mutabilität f mutability
mutagen mutagenic, mutagenous, mutative
Mutagen n mutagen
Mutagenantagonist m antimutagen
Mutagenese f mutagenesis
Mutagenität f mutagenicity
Mutante f mutant
~/nichtreifende non-ripening mutant, nor-mutant *(of tomatoes)*
~/reifegehemmte ripening inhibitor mutant, rin-mutant *(of tomatoes)*
Mutase f mutase *(enzyme)*
Mutation f mutation, blastovariation
~/gametische gametic mutation
~/induzierte induced mutation
~/intragene intragenic (gene, point) mutation
~/schweigende silent mutation
~/somatische somatic mutation
~/stille silent mutation
mutationsauslösend mutagenic, mutagenous, mutative
Mutationsauslösung f mutation induction (initiation)
Mutationsbelastung f mutational load
Mutationschimäre f bud mutation
Mutationsdruck m mutation pressure
Mutationseinheit f mutation unit
~/kleinste muton
Mutationsentstehung f mutagenesis
mutationsfähig mutable
Mutationsfähigkeit f mutability
Mutationsfrequenz f mutation frequency
Mutationsgenetik f mutation genetics
Mutationshäufigkeit f mutation frequency
Mutationsinduktion f mutation induction (initiation)
Mutationslast f mutational load
Mutationsort m [mutational] site
Mutationsspektrum n mutation spectrum
Mutationsrate f mutation rate
Mutationszucht f, **Mutationszüchtung** f mutation breeding

Mykologie

Mutatorgen *n* mutator gene
mutativ *s.* mutationsauslösend
mutieren to mutate
Muton *n* muton
Mutter *f* 1. mother *(s. a.* Muttertier*);* 2. ewe
Mutterbaum *m (forest)* seed tree (bearer), mother (parent) tree; grafter
Mutterbeet *n* stool[ing] bed • **im ~ vermehren** to stool
Mutterbeetvermehrung *f* stool layering
Mutterbestand *m (forest)* parent stand
Mutterboden *m* 1. topsoil, surface (tilled) soil, tilth; 2. *s.* Muttererde
Mutterbodenandeckung *f* deposit of humus soil
Muttererde *f* parent (native) soil, substratum
Muttergestein *n* bedrock, parent (maternal) rock, solid (living) rock
Mutterhefe *f* seed yeast
Mutterinstinkt *m* mothering (maternal) instinct
Mutter-Kind-Bindung *f* mother-young bond *(animal behaviour)*
Mutter-Kind-Verhältnis *n* mother-offspring interaction (relationship)
Mutterknolle *f* mother tuber
Mutterkorn *n* ergot [body] *(sclerotium of Claviceps purpurea growing on and replacing seeds esp. of rye)*
Mutterkornalkaloid *n* ergot [alkaloid]
mutterkornbefallen, mutterkorninfiziert *(phyt)* ergotized, ergoted
Mutterkornkrankheit *f (phyt)* ergot
Mutterkornpilz *m* ergot [fungus], Claviceps purpurea
mutterkornvergiftet *(vet)* ergotized, ergoted
Mutterkornvergiftung *f (vet)* ergotism, ergot poisoning, St. Anthony's fire
Mutterkraut *n* 1. c[h]amomile, mayweed, matricaria *(genus Matricaria);* 2. *s.* Mutterkrautwucherblume
Mutterkrautwucherblume *f* feverfew [chrysanthemum], Chrysanthemum parthenium
Mutterkuchen *m (zoo)* afterbirth, placenta • **durch den ~ [hindurch]** transplacental
Mutterkuh *f* suckler cow
Mutterkultur *f* mother culture
Mutterlamm *n* ewe lamb
Mutterlauge *f* mother syrup *(sugar manufacture)*
mütterlich maternal
Mutternherde *f* ewe flock, flock of ewes
Mutterpflanze *f* mother (stock, parent) plant; mother stool; *(gen)* ortet • **auf (in) der ~ keimend** viviparous
~ mit Kindel mother plant with lateral shoot
Mutterpflanzenanlage *f* mother planting
Mutterpflanzenbeet *n* stool[ing] bed
Mutterpflanzenkultur *f* stock plant culture
Mutterpflanzenmaterial *n* parent stock
Mutterpflanzung *f* mother planting

Mutterrasse *f* dam breed
Muttersaft *m* mother juice *(sugar manufacture)*
Muttersau *f* sow
Mutterschaf *n* ewe
~/trächtiges (tragendes) in-lamb ewe
Mutterschafherde *f* ewe flock, flock of ewes
Mutterschaft *f* maternity
Mutterschwein *n* sow
Muttersirup *m* mother syrup *(sugar manufacture);* high-test molasses *(sugar-cane processing)*
Muttertier *n* dam • **beim ~** at side *(young animal)*
~/säugendes suckler
Mutter-Tochter-Korrelation *f* dam daughter correlation *(breeding value appraisal)*
Mutterverhalten *n* maternal behaviour
Mutterwolle *f* ewe's wool
Mutterwurz *f* [Scotch] lovage, Ligusticum scoticum
Mutterzelle *f* mother cell
Mutterzwiebel *f* mother (parent) bulb
Mutualismus *m (ecol)* mutualism
muzigen mucigenous, muciparous
Muzin *n* mucin
Muzinsäure *f* mucic acid
MVA *s.* Milchviehanlage
M-Virus-Mosaik *n* **der Kartoffel** *(phyt)* potato leaf rolling mosaic, interveinal mosaic, paracrinkle
MWV *s.* Marmorwelsvirose
Myalgie *f (vet)* myalgia
Myasthenie *f (vet)* myasthenia, muscular debility
Myatonie *f (vet)* myatonia
Mycobacterium-avium-Infektion *f (vet)* avian tuberculosis
Mycostatin *n* nystatin *(antibiotic)*
Mydriase *f,* **Mydriasis** *f (vet)* mydriasis, pupil dilat[at]ion
Myelin *n* myelin
Myelinisation *f* myelination
Myelinscheide *f* myelin (medullary) sheath
Myelitis *f (vet)* myelitis
Myeloblast *m* myeloblast
Myeloblastom *n (vet)* myeloma
Myeloblastose *f (vet)* myeloblastosis
~/aviäre avian myeloblastosis (granuloblastosis)
myeloid, myeloisch myeloid
Myelom *n (vet)* myeloma
Myelose *f (vet)* myelosis
Myelozyt *m* myelocyte
Myelozytose *f (vet)* myelocytosis
Myiase *f,* **Myiasis** *f (vet)* myiasis
Myitis *f s.* Myositis
Myko... *s. a.* Pilz...
Mykobakterin *n (vet)* mycobactin
Mykobakteriose *f (vet)* mycobacteriosis
Mykobaktin *n (vet)* mycobactin
Mykoflora *f* mycoflora, fungus flora
Mykoherbizid *n* mycoherbicide
Mykologe *m* mycologist
Mykologie *f* mycology, fungology

mykologisch 438

mykologisch mycologic[al]
Mykoparasit *m* mycoparasite, parasitic fungus
Mykoparasitismus *m* mycoparasitism
mykophag myc[et]ophagous, fungivorous
Mykoplasma *n* mycoplasm[a], pleuropneumonia-like organism *(genus Mycoplasma)*
mykoplasmaähnlich mycoplasm[a]-like
Mykoplasmainfektion *f* **des Geflügels** chronic respiration disease of chickens
Mykoplasmenpneumonie *f (vet)* mycoplasm[a] pneumonia
Mykoplasmose *f (phyt, vet)* mycoplasmosis
Mykorrhiza *f* mycorrhiza
~/**ektotrophe** ectotrophic (exotrophic) mycorrhiza, ectomycorrhiza
~/**endotrophe** endotrophic mycorrhiza, endomycorrhiza
~/**epiphytische** *s.* ~/ektotrophe
~/**vesikulär-arbuskuläre** vesicular-arbuscular mycorrhiza, VAM
Mykorrhizapilz *m* mycorrhizal fungus
Mykose *f* mycosis, fungal disease
Mykostatikum *n* mycostat, fungistat
mykostatisch mycostatic, fungistatic
mykotisch mycotic
Mykotoxikose *f* mycotoxicosis, mycetism
Mykotoxin *n* mycotoxin, fungal toxin
Mykotrophie *f* mycotrophy
Mykozezidie *f* fungal gall
MyLRFV *s.* Latentes Myrobalanenringfleckenvirus
Myo... *s. a.* Muskel...
Myoblast *m* myoblast
Myodynie *f (vet)* myalgia
Myoepithel *n* myoepithelium
myoepithelial myoepithelial
Myoepithelzelle *f* myoepithelial cell
myofibrillär myofibrillar
Myofibrille *f* myofibril
Myofibrom *n (vet)* myofibroma
Myofilament *n* myofilament *(substructure of a myofibril)*
Myogen *n* myogen *(muscle protein)*
Myoglobin *n* myoglobin, myohaemoglobin
Myoglobinämie *f (vet)* myo[haemo]globinaemia
Myoglobinurie *f (vet)* myoglobinuria
~/**paralytische** paralytic myoglobinuria
Myohämatin *n s.* Myoglobin
Myoinositol *n* myoinositol, mesoinositol
Myokard *n* myocardium, heart muscle
myokardial myocardial
Myokardinfarkt *m (vet)* myocardial infarction
Myokarditis *f (vet)* myocarditis
Myom *n (vet)* myoma
Myometrium *n* myometrium
Myoneuraljunktion *f* myoneural junction
Myopathie *f (vet)* myopathy, muscular disease
Myorrhexis *f s.* Muskelriß
Myosin *n* myosin *(muscle protein)*

Myosin-ATPase *f* myosin ATPase *(enzyme)*
Myosinfilament *n* myosin filament
Myositis *f (vet)* myositis, inflammation of the muscles
Myotomie *f (vet)* myotomy
Myrcen *n* myrcene *(monoterpene)*
Myriapode *m*, **Myriopode** *m* myriapod, myriopod *(group Myriapoda)*
Myristinsäure *f* myristic (tetradecanoic) acid *(fatty acid)*
Myrmekochorie *f (bot)* myrmecochory *(dispersion as of seeds by ants)*
myrmekophil myrmecophilous
Myrmekophile *m* myrmecophile
Myrmekophilie *f* myrmecophilism
Myrobalane *f* 1. cherry-plum, myrobalan[-plum], Prunus cerasifera (myrobalana); 2. myrobalan *(fruit from Terminalia spp.)*
Myrobalanenbaum *m (bot)* myrobalan, Phyllanthus emblica
Myrosinase *f* thioglucosidase *(enzyme)*
Myrrhe *f*, **Myrrhenharz** *n* myrrh, balm, bdellium *(gum resin from Commiphora spp.)*
Myrrhenkerbel *m* sweet cicely, myrrh, Myrrhis odorata
Myrrhenstrauch *m (bot)* bdellium *(genus Commiphora)*
Myrte *f* myrtle *(genus Myrtus)*
Myrtenblättriger Gerberstrauch *m* Mediterranean coriaria, ink plant, Coriaria myrtifolia
Myrtengewächse *npl* myrtle family *(family Myrtaceae)* • **die ~ betreffend** myrtaceous
Myrtenheide *f (bot)* melaleuca *(genus Melaleuca)*
Myrtillus-Heide *f* bilberry heath
Mysore-Himbeere *f* Mysore raspberry, Rubus niveus
Myxoblastom *n (vet)* myxoma
Myxödem *n (vet)* myxoedema
Myxom *n (vet)* myxoma
Myxomatose *f (vet)* myxomatosis
Myxomatosevirus *n* myxoma virus
Myxomyosin *n* myxomyosin *(protein)*
Myxomyzet *m* myxomycete, slime fungus (mould) *(order Myxomycotina)*
Myxosomatose *f* **der Salmoniden** whirling disease of salmonids *(caused by Myxosoma cerebralis)*
Myxovirus *n* myxovirus
Myzel *n (bot)* mycelium, [mushroom] spawn • **~ pflanzen** to spawn
Myzelausbreitungsphase *f*, **Myzelentwicklungsphase** *f* spawn-run phase
Myzelium *n s.* Myzel
Myzelstrang *m* rhizomorph
Myzetismus *m s.* Mykotoxikose
Myzetom *n (phyt, ent)* mycetoma
myzetomatös mycetomatous
myzetophag myc[et]ophagous, fungivorous

N

N s. Niederstamm
Nabam n nabam *(fungicide)*
Nabel m navel, umbilicus; *(bot)* hilum, scar • **mit ~ versehen** umbilicate
Nabelarterie f umbilical artery
Nabelblut n cord blood
Nabelbruch m *(vet)* umbilical hernia
Nabelende n stem end *(of potato tuber)*
Nabelentzündung f *(vet)* omphalitis
nabelförmig umbilicate
Nabelinfektion f *(vet)* navel infection
Nabelschnur f, **Nabelstrang** m navel-string, navel (umbilical) cord
Nabel- und Gelenkentzündung f *(vet)* joint ill, navel ill
nachaltern to afterage
Nachauflaufbehandlung f postemergence application
Nachauflaufherbizid n postemergence herbicide
Nachauflaufspritzung f postemergence spraying
Nachaussaat f reseed
Nachbarbestäubung f *(bot)* self-pollination
Nachbarschaftshilfe f neighbouring, neighbourly help
Nachbarschaftswirkung f effect of neighbouring plants *(in crop stands)*
Nachbau m replanting
nachbauen to replant, to replace [plants]
Nachbaukrankheit f *(phyt)* replant disease
Nachbaukultur f replacement crop
Nachbauschaden m *(phyt)* damage by replant diseases
Nachbefruchtung f superfoetation
nachbehandeln to aftertreat, to retreat
Nachbehandlung f aftertreatment, retreatment
Nachbesamung f repeat insemination
nachbessern to replant, to replace [plants]; to beat up, to recruit *(silviculture)*
Nachbessern n, **Nachbesserung** f *(forest)* recruitment, beating[-up], infilling, filling up, gapping
Nachbesserungspflanzung f *(forest)* auxiliary planting, interplanting, afterculture
Nachblütespritzung f postblossom spray
Nachblütestadium n postfloral (postflowering) stage
Nachbrunft f after-rut *(of game)*
Nachbrunst f metoestrus
Nachbrunstblutung f bleeding *(of cows)*
Nachdrehschleuder f afterworker *(sugar manufacture)*
Nachdrescheinrichtung f rethresher
Nachdreschgitter n beater grate
Nachdreschhilfe f rear beater
Nachdrusch m rethreshing
nachdüngen to refertilize
Nachdüngung f complementary fertilization
nachdunkeln to darken
Nacheiszeit f Holocene
nacheiszeitlich postglacial
Nacherntebehandlung f postharvest treatment
Nacherntefäule f postharvest decay *(e.g. of strawberries)*
Nacherntephysiologie f postharvest physiology
Nacherntetrocknung f postharvest drying
Nachernteverlust m postharvest loss
Nachfolge f *(ecol)* succession
Nachfolgebaumart f, **Nachfolgeholzart** f successor [tree] species
Nachfrucht f aftercrop, follower crop
Nachgärung f secondary fermentation, afterfermentation, postfermentation
Nachgeburt f 1. afterbirth, cleansing; 2. afterbirth, placenta • **die ~ abstoßen** to cleanse
Nachgeburtsperiode f, **Nachgeburtsstadium** n cleansing
Nachgeburtsverhaltung f *(vet)* placental retention, retention of the afterbirth
Nachgemelk n afterings, strippings
Nachgeschmack m after-taste *(e.g. of a wine)*
Nachguß m second wort, afterwort, sparging *(brewing)*
Nachhaltigkeit f *(forest)* susten[ta]tion
Nachhaltigkeitsbetrieb m sustained-yield [forest] management, sustained management
Nachhaltigkeitsprinzip n principle of sustained yield
Nachhaltseinheit f sustained-yield unit
Nachhaltsertrag m sustained yield
Nachhaltsetat m allowable sustained cut
Nachhaltshiebssatz m sustained yield
Nachhaltsregelung f sustained-yield regulation
Nachhaltswirtschaft f s. Nachhaltigkeitsbetrieb
Nachhand f hindquarters, hind leg, hindlimb
Nachhandlähmung f, **Nachhandparalyse** f *(vet)* hind leg paralysis
nachharken to rake off
nachhetzen to course
Nachhieb m *(forest)* secondary felling
Nachhirn n medulla oblongata
Nachkomme m offspring, descendant
Nachkommen mpl progeny, offspring, get; strain • **~ zeugen** to generate, to sire • **männliche ~ erzeugend** androgenous • **nur männliche ~ habend** arrhenotokous • **nur weibliche ~ habend** thelytokous
~/erbrütete brood
Nachkommenleistung f progeny performance
Nachkommenprüfstation f progeny testing station
Nachkommenprüfung f progeny-test[ing], offspring testing
Nachkommenschaft f s. Nachkommen
Nachkultur f subculture *(microbiology)* • **eine ~ anlegen** to subculture
Nachlauf m 1. castor action *(vehicle steering)*; 2. afterrunnings *(wine-making)*

Nachläufer

Nachläufer m [semi]trailer, bolster, runner *(timber transportation)*
Nachläuferzug m sett
Nachlaufrad n end-wheel
Nachlese f 1. gleaning *(esp. ears)*; 2. gleanings *(yield)*
nachlesen to glean
Nachlöscharbeiten fpl, **Nachlöschen** n mopping up, cold trailing *(forest fire control)*
Nachmahd f aftermath, aftergrass, aftercrop, lattergrass, lattermath, *(Am)* rowen
Nachmahdvorrichtung f für Weideflächen pasture topper
Nachmehl n bran shorts
nachmelken to strip [out], to milk out
~/maschinell to machine-strip
Nachmelken n udder stripping [out], complete milking
Nachmelk- und Abnahmeroboter m [automatic] cluster-removing robot
Nachpflanzbehandlung f postplanting treatment
nachpflanzen to replant, to replace [plants], to fill up by planting
Nachpflanzen n replanting, replacement, interplanting; *(forest)* auxiliary planting
nachprellen to course *(retriever)*
Nachprodukt n offal *(milling)*; afterproduct *(sugar manufacture)*
Nachproduktfüllmasse f low-grade massecuite *(sugar manufacture)*
Nachproduktzucker m low-grade sugar, low[-raw] sugar
Nachreife f after-ripening
Nachreifedauer f after-ripening period
nachreifen to after-ripen; to age
~ lassen to cure; to age
Nachreifen n after-ripening, postharvest maturation; ag[e]ing
Nachreifeperiode f after-ripening period
Nachreiferaum m conditioning room *(for fruits)*
nachreinigen to reclean *(e.g. corn)*
Nachreiniger m secondary cleaner
Nachreinigung f afterpurification
Nachreinigungsmaschine f final dresser
Nachreinigungsvorrichtung f secondary cleaner
nachröten to freshen *(a face in resin-tapping)*
Nachsaat f reseed, replanting
nachsäen to reseed, to resow, to replant
Nachscheidung f postdefecation *(sugar manufacture)*
Nachschieber m *(ent)* abdominal appendage *(of Geometridae)*
nachschleppen to drag *(timber)*
Nachschneiden n double clipping *(sheep-shearing)*
Nachschnittwolle f double-clip wool
Nachschönung f secondary fining *(wine-making)*
Nachschubstraße f *(forest)* tote road
Nachschwarm m *(api)* afterswarm, cast

Nachsekret n post-sperm fraction *(of the ejaculate)*
Nachsommer m Indian summer
nachsüßen to sugar *(wine)*
Nachsüßen n chaptalization *(of wine)*
Nachtabsenkung f night lowering *(of temperature in greenhouses)*
Nachtberegnung f night irrigation
Nachtblindheit f *(vet)* night-blindness, nyctalopia
nachtblütig night-blooming, night-flowering, noctiflorous
Nachtfalterorchidee f moth orchid, phalaenopsis *(genus Phalaenopsis)*
Nachtfrost m night frost
Nachtgreifvogel m night-bird of prey
Nachtjasmin m night jasmin[e], tree of sadness, Nyctanthes arbor-tristis
Nachtkerze f evening primrose *(genus Oenothera)*
Nachtphase f dark period *(of a lighting regime)*
Nachtrocknung f secondary drying, redrying
Nachtschatten m nightshade, morel, solanum *(genus Solanum)*
nachtschattenartig solanaceous
Nachtschattengewächse npl nightshade family *(family Solanaceae)* • **die ~ betreffend** solanaceous
Nachtsichtigkeit f hemeralopia
Nachttau m night dew
Nachttemperatur f night temperature
Nachtviole f 1. rocket, hesperis *(genus Hesperis)*; 2. dame's violet, sweet (garden) rocket, Hesperis matronalis
Nachverjüngung f *(forest)* afterregeneration
nachwachsen to regrow
Nachwehen fpl *(vet)* afterpains
Nachweis m test
Nachwirkung f after-effect, afteraction
Nachwuchs m 1. regrowth, after-growth, second growth (crop); 2. s. Wiederaustrieb
~/unterdrückter *(forest)* stunted growth
Nachwürze f second wort, afterwort *(brewing)*
Nachzucht[jung]sau f [replacement] gilt
Nacken m 1. nape, neck, poll, scruff; 2. back, poll, pole *(of an axe)*
Nackenbügel m neck bow (collar)
Nackenriegel m neck yoke
Nackenschiene f bail *(of a parlour)*
nackt naked, denudate[d]; hull-less
Nacktamöbe f amoeba *(order Amoebina)*
nacktblättrig naked-leaved
nacktblumig, nacktblütig naked-flowered, nudiflorous
Nackter Ritterling m *(bot)* amethyst agaric, wood blewits, Lepista nuda
nacktflügelig naked-winged
nacktfrüchtig *(bot)* naked-fruited, gymnocarpous
Nacktgerste f naked (hull-less) barley *(comprehensive term)*

Nackthafer *m* [small] naked oat, bristle[-pointed] oat, black (hull-less) oat, pill corn, Avena nuda [ssp. nuda], Avena strigosa
Nackthals *m* naked neck *(of chicken)*
Nacktkarpfen *m* leather (scaleless) carp
Nacktkorn *n* naked grain
Nacktsamer *m (bot)* gymnosperm *(division Gymnospermae)*
nacktsamig gymnospermous
Nacktschnecke *f* slug *(family Limacidae)*
nacktstengelig *(bot)* nudicaulous
NAD *s.* Nicotinsäureamid-adenin-dinucleotid
Nadel *f (bot)* needle, needle-shaped leaf *(as of a larch)*
Nadelabfall *m s.* Nadelschütte
Nadelälchen *n* needle nematode *(genera Longidorus and Paralongidorus)*
Nadelanalyse *f* needle (foliar) analysis
nadelartig acicular
Nadelast *m* pin knot
Nadelbaum *m* needle-leaved tree, conifer, coniferous (softwood) tree *(order or subclass Pinidae = Coniferae)*
Nadelbaumart *f* coniferous species
Nadelbaumbestand *m* coniferous stand
nadelblättrig needle-leaved, coniferous
Nadelblättrigkeit *f (phyt)* shoe-stringing, shoestring [disease], shoe-lacing
Nadeleisenerz *n* goethite *(non-clay mineral)*
Nadelerde *f* forest floor, coniferous (pine) litter, pine needle carpet
Nadelextrakt *m* needle extract
Nadelfall *m s.* Nadelschütte
nadelförmig acerate, aci[culi]form
nadelfressend needle-eating
Nadelhalter *m (vet)* needle forceps
Nadelholz *n* softwood, coniferous wood (timber), soft timber, deal
~/geringwertiges wrack
Nadelholzart *f* coniferous species
Nadelholzbestand *m* coniferous stand
Nadelholzmistel *f* mistletoe, Viscum album ssp. austriacum
Nadelholzverschulpflanze *f* conifer transplant
Nadelholzwirtschaft *f* conifer silviculture
Nadeljahrgang *m* annual needle whorl
Nadeljahrgänge *mpl* needles of various ages
Nadelkerbel *m (bot)* shepherd's needle, Venus's comb, Scandix pecten-veneris
Nadelknickende Kieferngallmücke *f* needle-bending pine gall midge, Cecidomyia baeri
Nadelkraut *n (bot)* New Zealand cowage, black fellows, Bidens pilosa
Nadelmischwald *m* mixed conifer forest
Nadelpalme *f* needle palm, Rhapidophyllum hystrix
Nadelpenetrometer *n* pin penetrometer
Nadelrundholz *n* round softwood
Nadelsämling *m* conifer seedling

nadelscharf *(bot)* acerose, acerous
Nadelschichtholz *n* softwood cordwood
Nadelschnittholz *n* sawn softwood, coniferous sawn timber, softwood lumber
Nadelschütte *f (phyt)* shedding of needles, needle shedding (fall, cast), needle blight
Nadelschwachholz *n* small-diameter softwood, small-dimension softwood
nadelspitz[ig] acicular
Nadelstammholz *n* round softwood, whole-stem softwood logs
Nadelstreu *f* needle (coniferous) litter, forest floor
Nadelverfärbung *f* needle discolo[u]ration
Nadelwald *m* softwood (coniferous) forest, pinery
• im ~ lebend (wohnend) conophorophilous
~/verkrüppelter lichter conifer scrub
Nadelwaldphytozönose *f* conophorium
Nadelwaldzone *f* coniferous forest zone
Nadelwerk *n* foliage
Nadelwickler *m* needle roller *(e.g. a caterpillar of Archips spp.)*
NADH *s.* Nicotinsäureamid-adenin-dinucleotid/reduziertes
NADH-Dehydrogenase *f* NADH dehydrogenase, cytochrome-c reductase *(enzyme)*
Nadi-Blaugras *n* nadi bluegrass, Dichanthium caricosum
NADP *s.* Nicotinsäureamid-adenin-dinucleotidphosphat
NADPH-Cytochrom-c2-Reductase *f* NADPH-cytochrome-c2 reductase *(enzyme)*
NADPH-Cytochromreductase *f* NADPH-ferrihaemoprotein reductase *(enzyme)*
NADPH-Ferrihämoproteinreductase *f* NADPH-ferrihaemoprotein reductase *(enzyme)*
NADP-Oxidoreductase *f* glucose-6-phosphate dehydrogenase *(enzyme)*
NAD$^+$-Pyrophosphorylase *f* nicotinamide-nucleotide adenylyltransferase *(enzyme)*
NaDV *s.* Narzissendegenerationsvirus
Naftalofos *n* naphthalophos *(anthelminthic)*
Nagana *f (vet)* trypanosomiasis, nagana
Naganabaum *m* Indian rose chestnut, Ceylon ironwood, Mesua ferrea
Nagekäfer *m* 1. furniture (anobium) beetle *(family Anobiidae)*; 2. death-watch [beetle], Anobium punctatum (striatum)
Nagekäferlarve *f* woodworm, worm
Nagel *m* 1. *(bot, zoo)* nail, unguis; 2. nail; pin
Nagelbett *n* quick *(animal anatomy)*
Nageldruck *m (vet)* nail bound
Nagelfalz *m* **des Hufeisens** fullering, swedging
nagelförmig *(bot)* unguiculate
Nagelkraut *n* salad burnet, Sanguisorba minor ssp. minor
Nagelloch *n* nail-hole *(e.g. of a horseshoe)*
Nagelstich *m* nail bind (puncture) *(shoeing defect)*
nägeltragend *(zoo)* unguiculated
Nageltritt *m (vet)* nail puncture

Nagemilbe

Nagemilbe *f* chorioptic mite *(genus Chorioptes)*
nagen to gnaw, to prey [up]on
Nager *m s.* Nagetier
Nagerbekämpfung *f* rodent control
Nagertuberkulose *f (vet)* pseudotuberculosis
Nagetier *n* rodent, gnawer, gnawing animal *(order Rodentia)*
nagetierbekämpfend rodenticidal
Nagetierbekämpfer *m* rodent officer
Nagetierbekämpfungsmittel *n*, **Nagetiergift** *n* rodenticide
NaGSV *s.* Narzissengelbstreifenvirus
nähen *(vet)* to suture
Naherholungsgebiet *n* local (nearby) recreation area
Näherungsmasseanzeiger *m* near-weight indicator
Nähragar *m* nutrient agar
Nährboden *m* nutritive medium, substrate, matrix
• **vom gleichen ~ lebend** commensal
Nährbouillon *f* nutrient broth *(microbiology)*
Nährdotter *m* food yolk
Nährelement *n* nutrient element
Nährelementauswaschung *f* nutrient leaching
Nährelementmobilität *f* nutrient mobility
nähren to nourish, to feed
~ **von/sich** to live (feed) on
nährend nourishing, nutritive, nutritious, nutrient
~/**nicht** innutritious
Nährfilmtechnik *f* nutrient film technique, NFT *(of ornamental production)*
Nährgewebe *n* nutritive tissue; endosperm *(of seed)*
nahrhaft *s.* nährend
Nährhefe *f* nutrient (fodder, food) yeast
Nährhumus *m* nutritive (nutrient, friable) humus
Nährlösung *f* nutrient (culture) solution, liquid medium • **in ~ angebaut (kultiviert)** solution-grown
~ **nach Hoagland** Hoagland solution *(for pot trials)*
~ **nach Knop** Knop's solution
Nährlösungsbehälter *m* nutrient solution container
Nährlösungskultur *f* [nutrient] solution culture
Nährmedium *n* nutritive (nutrient) medium, growth (growing) medium, [culture] medium
~/**flüssiges** *s.* Nährlösung
Nährmittel *n* nutritive; cereal product
Nährpflanze *f* food plant
Nährsalz *n* nutrient (nutritive) salt
Nährstoff *m* nutrient, food
~/**isolierter (reiner)** pure nutrient
Nährstoffabsorption *f* nutrient absorption
Nährstoffanreicherung *f* nutrient enrichment, eutrophication
nährstoffarm oligotrophic *(e.g. a soil)*
~/**extrem** dystrophic
Nährstoffarmut *f* nutrient deficiency
Nährstoffaufnahme *f* nutrient uptake (intake)
~/**direkte** *(soil)* solid-phase feeding
Nährstoffaufnahmevermögen *n* feeding capacity
Nährstoffauswaschung *f* nutrient leaching (elution), leaching of nutrients
Nährstoffbedarf *m*, **Nährstoffbedürfnis** *n* nutrient requirement (demand, need)
Nährstoffbereitstellung *f* nutrient supply
Nährstoffbereitstellungsvermögen *n* nutrient supplying power
Nährstoffbestandteil *m* **einer Futterration** feedstuff
Nährstoffbeweglichkeit *f* nutrient mobility
Nährstoffbilanz *f* nutrient balance
~/**unausgeglichene (unausgewogene)** nutrient imbalance
Nährstoffdünger *m* plant fertilizer (food)
Nährstoffdynamik *f* nutrient dynamics *(e.g. in a soil)*
Nährstoffelement *n* nutrient element
Nährstoffentzug *m* drain of nutrients, nutrient removal (withdrawal)
Nährstofffestlegung *f* nutrient fixation
Nährstofffreisetzung *f* nutrient release
~ **aus körpereigenem Gewebe** autophagy *(in starving animals)*
Nährstoffgehalt *m* nutrient content • **mit über 20prozentigem ~** high analysis *(fertilizer)* • **von mittlerem ~** mesotrophic
Nährstoffhaltevermögen *n* nutrient-holding capacity *(of a soil)*
Nährstoffhaushalt *m* nutrient balance (budget)
Nährstofffilm *m* nutrient film
Nährstofffilmkultur *f* nutrient film technique, NFT *(in ornamental production)*
Nährstoffimbalance *f* nutrient imbalance
Nährstofffixierung *f* nutrient fixation
Nährstoffkonzentration *f* nutrient concentration
nährstoffkonzentriert nutrient-dense
Nährstoffkreislauf *m* nutrient cycle (cycling)
Nährstofflösung *f s.* Nährlösung
Nährstoffmangel *m* nutrient (nutritional) deficiency, nutrient lack (shortage)
Nährstoffmangelanämie *f (vet)* nutritional anaemia
Nährstoffmangelerscheinung *f*, **Nährstoffmangelsymptom** *n* nutrient deficiency symptom, hunger sign
Nährstoffmangelversuch *m* missing element trial
Nährstoffmetabolismus *m* nutrient metabolism
Nährstoffnachlieferungsvermögen *n* plant-nutrient-supplying power *(of a soil)*
Nährstoffpotential *n* nutrient potential
Nährstoffration *f* nutrient allowance
nährstoffreich nutritious, eutrophic
~/**mäßig** mesotrophic
Nährstoffreichtum *m* eutrophy
Nährstoffreserve *f* nutrient reserve
Nährstoffresorption *f* nutrient resorption
~/**mangelhafte** malabsorption

Nährstoffrückführung *f* recycling of nutrients
Nährstoffrückwanderung *f* nutrient remigration
Nährstoffträger *m* nutrient carrier
Nährstofftransport *m* nutrient transport
Nährstoffüberschuß *m* nutrient excess
Nährstoffverfügbarkeit *f* nutrient availability
Nährstoffverhältnis *n* nutrient (nutritive) ratio; fertilizer ratio
Nährstoffverlagerung *f* nutrient displacement, translocation of nutrients
Nährstoffversorgung *f* nutrient supply
Nährstoffverwertung *f* nutrient utilization
Nährstoffvorrat *m* nutrient reserve, store of nutrients
Nährstoffzustand *m* nutrient status
Nährstoffzuteilung *f* nutrient allowance
Nährsubstrat *n* nutrient (nutritive) medium, [culture] substrate
Nahrung *f* food, diet, nourishment • ~ **aufnehmen** to ingest • ~ **einspeicheln** to insalivate
~/**aufgenommene** ingesta
Nahrungsaufnahme *f* ingestion
Nahrungsbedarf *m* dietary (food) requirement
Nahrungsbrei *m* digesta, chyme
~/**abzuschluckender** bolus
Nahrungsdotter *m* food yolk
Nahrungseiweiß *n* food protein
Nahrungsenergie *f* dietary energy
Nahrungserzeugungsgrundlage *f* food production base
Nahrungsfaktor *m*/**lipotroper** lipotropic factor
Nahrungsfaser *f* dietary fibre
Nahrungsgüterbedarf *m* food requirement
Nahrungsgütererzeugung *f* food production
Nahrungsgüterforschung *f* food research
Nahrungsgüterindustrie *f* food industry
Nahrungsgüterverarbeitung *f* food processing
Nahrungsgüterwirtschaft *f* food economy (industry)
Nahrungskette *f (ecol)* food-chain
Nahrungskreislauf *m (ecol)* food-cycle
Nahrungskultur *f* food crop
Nahrungslockstoff *m* feed attractant; food lure *(pest control)*
Nahrungsmittel *n* food[stuff], nourishment, victual
~/**landwirtschaftliches** agricultural food product
Nahrungsmittelknappheit *f* food shortage
Nahrungsmittelkonsument *m* food consumer
Nahrungsmittelkultur *f* food crop
Nahrungsmittelproduktion *f* food production
Nahrungsmittelquelle *f* food source
Nahrungsmittelüberwachung *f* food inspection
Nahrungsmittelverbraucher *m* food consumer
Nahrungsnetz *n (ecol)* food-web
Nahrungsnutznießer *m*/**nichtparasitärer** *(ecol)* commensal
Nahrungspflanze *f* food plant
Nahrungsprotein *n* food protein

Nahrungsqualität *f* nutritional quality
Nahrungsquelle *f* food source • **auf eine einzige ~ angewiesen** *(ecol)* monophagous
Nahrungsreflex *m* food reflex
Nahrungsreichtum *n* eutrophy
Nahrungssuche *f* search of food • **auf ~ gehen** to search for food, to go in search of food
Nahrungssystem *n (ecol)* food-cycle
Nährwert *m* nutritive (nutritional, food) value • **ohne ~** non-nutritious
Nährwurzel *f* feeding root
Nährzustand *m* nutritive condition, nutritional state (status)
Naht *f (bot, zoo)* suture, raphe; rib *(esp. of a fruit)*; *(vet)* [surgical] suture
~/**versenkte** buried suture
Nahtmaterial *n* suture material
Nairobi-Schafkrankheit *f* Nairobi sheep disease, NSD *(virosis)*
Naled *n* naled *(insecticide, acaricide)*
Nalidixinsäure *f* nalidixic acid
Nalorphin *n* nalorphine, lethidrone *(alkaloid)*
NaLV *s.* Latentes Narzissenvirus
NaMV *s.* Narzissenmosaikvirus
Nandrolon *n* nandrolone, nortestosterone *(sex hormone, anabolic)*
Nanismus *m* nanism, nanosomia, dwarfism
Nankinglilie *f* Nankeen lily, Lilium x testaceum
Nanophanerophyt *m* nanophanerophyte
Nanoplankton *n* nanoplankton
napfförmig acetabuliform
Napffütterung *f* bowl feeding
Napfgalle *f (phyt)* cup gall
Napfkamm *m* cup comb *(of fowl)*
Napfschildlaus *f* soft scale, scale [insect, bug], coccid *(family Lecaniidae = Coccidae)*
Naphthalen *n*, Naphthalin *n* naphthalene *(aromatic hydrocarbon)*
Naphthalophos *n* naphthalophos *(anthelminthic)*
Naphthenacetamid *n* naphthene acetamide
Naphthensäure *f* naphthenic acid
Naphthochinon *n* naphthoquinone *(disinfectant)*
Naphthol *n* naphthol, hydroxynaphthalene
Naphthylessigsäure *f* naphthaleneacetic acid, naphthoxyacetic (naphthylacetic) acid, NAA *(growth regulator)*
Napropamid *n* napropamide *(herbicide)*
NAR *s.* Nettoassimilationsrate
Narasin *n* narasin *(antibiotic)*
Naraspflanze *f*, Narasstrauch *m* naras-plant, Acanthosicyos horridus
Narbe *f* 1. *(bot)* stigma; 2. cicatrice, cicatrix, scar; 3. turf, [grass] sward, [grass] sod • **eine ~ bilden** to scar
~/**verfilzte** matted turf
Narbenbildner *m* sward-builder
Narbenbildung *f* swarding
Narbenfaden *m* silk *(of maize)*

Narbenfädenerscheinen

Narbenfädenerscheinen n silk emergence
Narbengewebe n scar tissue
Narbonner Wicke f Narbonne vetch, Vicia narbonensis
Narcein n narceine (alkaloid)
Narde f (bot) jatamansi, spikenard, [Indian] nard, Nardostachys jatamansi
Naringenin n naringenin
Naringenin-Chalconsynthase f [naringenin-]chalcone synthase (enzyme)
Naringenin-7-Rhamnoglucosid n, **Naringin** n naringin, aurantin (flavonoid)
Narkose f (vet) narcosis, anaesthesia
~/rektale rectal anaesthesia
Narkosemittel n, **Narkotikum** n narcotic, anaesthetic
narkotisch narcotic
narkotisieren to narcotize, to anaesthetize
narkotisierend narcotic, anaesthetic
Narren[taschen]krankheit f **der Pflaume** plumpocket disease (caused by Taphrina pruni)
NÄRV s. Nelkenätzringvirus
Narzisse f daffodil, narcissus (genus Narcissus)
narzissenblütig narcissiflorous
Narzissenbrand m (phyt) narcissus fire (caused by Botryotinia polyblastis)
Narzissendegenerationsvirus n narcissus degeneration virus
Narzissengelbstreifenvirus n narcissus yellow stripe virus
Narzissenmosaikvirus n narcissus mosaic virus
Narzissenweißstreifenvirus n narcissus white streak (stripe) virus
nasal nasal
Nase f nose
Nasenausfluß m s. Nasenkatarrh
Nasenbein n nasal bone
Nasenblatt n nosepiece (of bridle)
Nasenbluten n (vet) nose (nasal) bleeding, epistaxis
Nasenbremse f 1. rectal horse bot-fly, Gasterophilus haemorrhoidalis; 2. twitch (for fixing horses)
• **die ~ anlegen** to twitch
Nasendassel f sheep nostril fly, sheep [nasal] botfly, nasal bot-fly of sheep, Oestrus ovis
Nasendassellarve f nose (sheep) bot
Nasenentzündung f (vet) coryza, rhinitis
Nasengang m nasal passage
Nasenhaare npl vibrissae
Nasenhöhle f nasal cavity • **neben der ~ liegend** paranasal
Nasenkatarrh m (vet) nasal catarrh, coryza, rhinitis
Nasen-Luftröhren-Entzündung f (vet) rhinotracheitis
Nasenmagensonde f (vet) nasopharyngeal probe
Nasennebenhöhle f paranasal sinus
Nasenöffnung f nostril
Nasen-Rachen-Fliege f bot[t]-fly (family Oestridae)
Nasenriemen m nose band (of harness)

Nasenring m nosering; bull-holder, cattle leader
• **mit ~ rung** (e.g. a bull)
Nasenrücken m bridge of nose
Nasenscheidewand f nasal septum
Nasenschleimhautentzündung f s. Nasenkatarrh
Nasenschlundsonde f (vet) nasopharyngeal probe
Nasenweg m nasal passage
Nasenwurm m tongue worm, Linguatula serrata
Nasenzange f bull leader, bulldog
Nashornkäfer m rhinoceros (coconut) beetle, Oryctes rhinoceros
naß wet, humid, moist; soggy, alive (timber)
Naßabscheider m scrubber (controlled atmosphere storage)
Nassanoffsche Drüse f Nasonov gland (of worker honey-bees)
Naßaufschluß m wet digestion
Naßbeize f wet (liquid) dressing
Naßbeizlösung f seed pickler
Naßbeizmittel n liquid dressing
Naßboden m wet soil, wetland
Naßdesinfektion f wet disinfection
Nässe f wetness, moisture
Naßfäule f (phyt) soft (wet) rot
Naßfeuerlöscher m liquid extinguisher
Naßfütterung f wet feeding
Naßgalle f wet patch (site), damp patch, gall[nut]
naßgepökelt pickle-cured
Naßgut n wet product
Naßkern m wetwood, water core, wet heart[wood] (wood defect)
Naßkernbereich m wetwood zone
Naßkot m wet manure
Naßlöscher m liquid extinguisher
Naßmuser m wet masher
naßpökeln to brine
Naßreismähdrescher m wet rice combine harvester
Naßriese f (forest) wet chute, water slide (flume)
Naßrupfer m, **Naßrupfmaschine** f wet plucker (poultry processing); drum picking machine
Naßscheidung f wet liming (sugar manufacture)
Naßschlempe f stillage
Naßschnee m wet snow
Naßschnitzel npl diffusion cossettes, wet beet pulp (sugar manufacture)
Naßschroten n wet milling
Naßschrotmühle f wet mill
Naßsieben n wet screening (sugar-beet processing)
Naßsilage f wet silage
Naßsilagebereitung f direct-cut method of silage preparation
Naßstäuben n wet feeding
Naßstelle f s. Naßgalle
Naßtreber pl wet [brewer's] grains
Naßverarbeitung f wet processing
Naßverbesserung f s. Naßzuckerung

Naßwiese f wet (moist) meadow
Naßzuckerung f liquid chaptalization, gallization (wine-making)
Nastie f (bot) nastic movement
NASV s. Nelkenadernscheckungsvirus
Natalindigo[strauch] m Natal (Java) indigo, Indigofera arrecta
Natalität[srate] f natality, birth rate
Nataljute f [long-fruited] jute, West African sorrel, Jew's mallow, Corchorus olitorius
Natalorange f kaffir orange, monkey ball, Strychnos spinosa
Nathansystem n, **Nathanverfahren** n Nathan system (of pressure fermentation in brewing)
Nationalpark m national park
nativ native
Natriumacetat n sodium acetate
Natriumarsenit n sodium arsenite (herbicide)
Natriumazid n sodium azide
Natriumbedarf m sodium requirement
Natriumbenzoat n sodium benzoate
Natriumbicarbonat n s. Natriumhydrogencarbonat
Natriumboden m black alkali soil, solonets, solonetz
Natriumcarbonat n sodium carbonate
Natriumchlorat n sodium chlorate
Natriumchlorid n sodium chloride, [common] salt
Natriumcitrat n sodium citrate
Natriumdampf-Hochdrucklampe f sodium vapour high-pressure lamp
Natriumdiphosphat n sodium diphosphate (pyrophosphate)
Natriumdisulfit n sodium disulphite (metabisulphite)
Natriumdüngemittel n sodium fertilizer
Natriumgehalt m sodicity (e.g. of a soil)
Natriumhumat n sodium humate
Natriumhydrogencarbonat n sodium hydrogencarbonate (bicarbonate)
Natriumhydroxid n sodium hydroxide, caustic soda (disinfectant)
Natriumhypochlorit n sodium hypochlorite
Natriummetaphosphat n sodium phosphate
Natriumnitrat n sodium nitrate
Natriumnitrit n sodium nitrite
Natriumpentachlorphenolat n sodium pentachlorophenate (molluscicide)
Natriumphosphat n sodium phosphate
Natriumpropionat n sodium propionate
Natriumpyrophosphat n s. Natriumdiphosphat
Natriumpyrosulfit n s. Natriumdisulfit
Natriumsalicylat n sodium salicylate
Natriumsilicat n sodium silicate
Natriumspiegelerhöhung f im Blut (vet) hypernatraemia
Natriumspiegelverringerung f im Blut (vet) hyponatraemia
Natriumsulfat n sodium sulphate; Glauber's salt (laxative)
Natriumsulfid n sodium sulphide
Natriumsulfit n sodium sulphite
Natriumtrichloracetat n sodium trichloroacetate (herbicide)
Natriumtriphosphat n sodium triphosphate
Natrojarosit m natrojarosite (non-clay mineral)
Natron n s. Natriumhydrogencarbonat
Natronfeldspat m albite (non-clay mineral)
Natronkalk m soda lime
Natronsalpeter m soda nitre, Chile nitre (saltpetre), Chilean nitrate, nitrate of soda, agricultural salt
Natronweinstein m Rochelle salt, potassium sodium tartrate
Natterkopfartiges Bitterkraut n (bot) bristly oxtongue, Picris echioides
Natternkopf m blue thistle, Echium vulgare
Naturalpächter m (Am) sharecropper
Naturbesamung f (forest) natural seeding
Naturbimsstein m pumice
Naturboden m natural soil
Naturdenkmal n natural monument
Naturell n character, disposition (e.g. of domestic animals)
Naturerhaltung f nature preservation (protection)
Naturfarbstoff m natural dye
~/pflanzlicher vegetable dye
Naturfaser f natural fibre
Naturgarten m informal garden
naturgemäß naturalistic (e.g. silviculture)
Naturgeschichte f natural history
Naturgesetz n natural law, law of nature
Naturgrasland n, **Naturgrünland** n natural grassland
Naturgummi n natural rubber
Naturharz n natural (vegetable) resin, pitch
Naturhaushaltslehre f ecology
Naturherd m (ecol) natural focus
Naturkäse m rennet cheese
Naturkatastrophe f natural disaster (calamity)
Naturkautschuk m natural rubber
Naturkraft f natural force
Naturkrone f natural head (of a tree)
Naturlandschaft f natural landscape, wilderness
Naturlehrpfad m nature trail
natürlich natural • **~ vorkommend** native
Naturlicht n natural light
naturnah near-natural, seminatural (e.g. silviculture)
Naturnahrung f natural food
Naturpark m [nature] park
Naturparkaufseher m [park] ranger
Naturphosphat n phosphorite (non-clay mineral)
Naturprodukt n natural product
Naturrasse f primitive (primary) breed
Naturreichtümer mpl natural resources
Naturreservat n s. Naturschutzgebiet
Naturressourcen pl natural resources
Naturrohstoff m natural raw material

Naturschutz

Naturschutz *m* nature preservation (protection), [nature] conservation • **unter ~ stehen** to be protected by law • **unter ~ stellen** to protect by law
Naturschutzbeauftragter *m* conservation commissioner, conservationist, nature conservation trustee
Naturschützer *m* conservationist
Naturschutzgebiet *n* nature reservation [area], [protected] natural area, nature reserve, conservation area, sanctuary
Natursprung *m* natural service (mating)
Naturstoff *m* natural substance
~/insektizider botanical (plant-derived) insecticide
Naturteich *m* natural pond
Naturverjüngung *f (forest)* natural regeneration (reproduction), volunteer growth
Naturwald *m* natural forest
Naturwaldbewirtschaftung *f* management of natural forests
Naturwalderhaltung *f* conservation of natural forests
Naturwaldreservat *n* natural forest reserve
Naturweide[fläche] *f* natural pasture, range
Naturwiese *f* native (natural) meadow
Naturwolle *f* shorn (shearing) wool
Nausea *f (vet)* nausea
Navelorange *f* navel orange *(comprehensive term)*
NaWSV *s.* Narzissenweißstreifenvirus
N-Bilanz *f* nitrogen balance, nitrogen equilibrium
N'Dama *n* N'Dama, Fouta Longhorn (Malinke) *(cattle breed)*
ND-Virus *n* Newcastle disease virus
Nearthrose *f* nearthrosis
Nebacitin *n* nebacitin *(antibiotic)*
Nebel *m* fog, mist
~/künstlicher artificial fog *(frost protection)*
Nebelblaser *m s.* Nebelgerät
Nebeldüse *f* fogging (mist) nozzle
Nebeldüsenregner *m* mist nozzle sprinkler
Nebelfieber *n* fog fever *(of range cattle)*
Nebelfrostschaden *m* glaze damage, rime break, damage by rime *(in trees)*
Nebelgerät *n* 1. fog generator, fogger, mist blower (sprayer), mister; 2. nebulizer, atomizer
~/tragbares knapsack mist blower
Nebelgras *n* cloud bent[-grass], cloud grass, Agrostis nebulosa
Nebelkrähe *f* hooded (grey, carrier) crow, hoodie [crow], Corvus corone ssp. cornix
Nebelmaschine *f s.* Nebelgerät
Nebelmittel *n* atomizing agent
nebeln 1. to fog, to mist; 2. to nebulize, to atomize
Nebeln *n* fog application
Nebelsprühgerät *n* aero-mist sprayer
Nebeltropfen *m* fog-drip
Nebelwald *m* cloud (mist) forest
Nebelwüste *f* fog desert
Nebenbaumart *f (forest)* ancillary [tree] species, accessory (auxiliary, subsidiary) tree species

Nebenbestandteil *m* minor constituent
Nebenblatt *n (bot)* stipule • **mit Nebenblättern** stipulate[d]
nebenblattartig stipulaceous, stipular
nebenblattförmig stipuliform
nebenblattlos exstipulate
Nebeneinanderstellung *f* juxtaposition *(e.g. of trees)*
Nebenerwerbsbetrieb *m* part-time farm
Nebenerwerbsgärtner *m* semicommercial gardener
Nebenerwerbslandwirt *m* part-time farmer, peasant worker
Nebenerwerbslandwirtschaft *f* part-time farming
Nebenerzeugnis *n/***forstliches** minor forest product
Nebenfruchtform *f* imperfect stage (state), conidial stage *(of fungi)*
Nebengärung *f* secondary fermentation
Nebengen *n* minor gene
Nebengestell *n (forest)* secondary ride
Nebenhoden *m* epididymis
Nebenholzart *f s.* Nebenbaumart
Nebenknospe *f* secondary (accessory, stipulary) bud
Nebenkrone *f (bot)* corona
nebenkronenartig *(bot)* coronal
Nebenkultur *f* [/**pflanzenbauliche**] minor crop
Nebenlager *n* side camp *(forest fire control)*
Nebenniere *f* adrenal [gland], suprarenal gland
Nebennierenentfernung *f* [/**operative**] *(vet)* adrenalectomy
Nebennierenentzündung *f (vet)* hypernephritis
Nebennierenerkrankung *f (vet)* adrenal gland disease
Nebennierenmark *n* adrenal medulla
Nebennierenrinde *f* adrenal cortex
Nebennierenrindenhormon *n* adrenal cortex hormone, corticosteroid
nebennierenrindenstimulierend corticotrop[h]ic
Nebennutzungserzeugnis *n (forest)* minor produce
Nebenprodukt *n* by-product, side product
~/wertloses *s.* Abfall 1.
Nebenschilddrüse *f* parathyroid [gland]
Nebenschilddrüsenextrakt *m* parathyroid extract
Nebenschilddrüsenhormon *n* parathyroid hormone, parathormone, parathyrin
Nebenschneise *f (forest)* secondary ride
Nebensproß *m* **des Brokkoli** side head
Nebenstrang *m* side (collecting) drain, [lateral] field drain
Nebenwirkung *f* side-effect
Nebenwirt *m* secondary host
Nebenwurzel *f* secondary (adventitious) root
Nebenzapfwelle *f* secondary power take-off
Nebenzitze *f* extra teat *(of the udder)*
Nebenzwiebel *f* bulbil, bulbel, bulblet, daughter bulb

neblig foggy, misty • ~ **sein** to mist • ~ **werden** to fog, to mist, to become misty
Nebliger Schildkäfer *m* clouded tortoise beetle, beet leaf (tortoise) beetle, Cassida nebulosa
Neburon *n* neburon *(herbicide)*
negativ/serologisch seronegative
Negerhirse *f* pearl (bulrush) millet, Egyptian (East Indian) millet, bajra *(India)*, Pennisetum glaucum (americanum), Penicillaria spicata
Negri-Körperchen *n* Negri body *(in nerve cells of rabid animals)*
Neiger *m* pronator *(muscle)*
Neigungs[winkel]messer *m* [in]clinometer
Nekrobazillose *f (vet)* necrobacillosis *(caused by Fusobacterium necrophorum)*
Nekrobiose *f* necrobiosis
nekrobiotisch necrobiotic
Nekrohormon *n* necrohormone, wound hormone
nekrophag necrophagous
Nekrophagie *f* necrophagy
Nekrophyt *m* necrophyte
Nekrose *f (phyt, vet)* necrosis
~/infektiöse hämatopoetische *(vet)* infectious haematopoietic necrosis, chinook (sockeye) salmon disease
Nekrosevirus *n* **der Schwarzen Himbeere** black raspberry necrosis virus, BRNV
Nekrospermie *f (vet)* necrospermia
nekrotisch necrotic
Nekrotische Ringfleckenkrankheit *f* **der Kirsche** cherry (prunus) necrotic ring spot, [cherry] tatter leaf *(virosis)*
~ **Rübenvergilbung** *f* beet yellows *(virosis)*
~ **Spitzenkräuselung** *f* **der Tomate** apical crinkling of tomato *(virosis)*
~ **Stauchung** *f* **der Erbse** pea necrotic stunting *(virosis)*
~ **Vergilbung** *f* **von Brokkoli** broccoli necrotic yellows *(virosis)*
Nekrotisches Fleckenvirus *n* **der Zuckermelone** musk-melon necrotic spot virus, MNSV
~ **Kirschringfleckenvirus** *n* prunus necrotic ring spot virus
~ **Nelkenfleckungsvirus** *n* carnation necrotic fleck virus, CNFV
~ **Ringfleckenvirus** *n* necrotic ring spot virus
~ **Ringfleckenvirus** *n* **der Kirsche** prunus necrotic ring spot virus
~ **Rotkleemosaikvirus** *n* red clover necrotic mosaic virus
~ **Rübenvergilbungsvirus** *n* beet yellows virus, BYV
~ **Salatvergilbungsvirus** *n* lettuce necrotic yellows virus
~ **Steinkleemosaikvirus** *n* sweet clover necrotic mosaic virus
~ **Vergilbungsvirus** *n* **von Brokkoli** broccoli necrotic yellows virus, BNYV
nekrotroph necrotrophic

Nekrotrophie *f* necrotrophy
Nektar *m (bot)* nectar
Nektarblume *f* nectar flower *(comprehensive term)*
Nektardrüse *f* nectar gland
nektarerzeugend *s.* nektarliefernd
Nektarine *f*, **Nektarinenpfirsich** *m* 1. nectarine, Prunus persica var. nectarina; 2. nectarine *(fruit)*
Nektarium *n (bot)* nectary • **zum ~ gehörend** nectarial
nektarliefernd, nektarspendend nectariferous, nectar-bearing, melliferous
Nektarspender *m* nectar plant
Nektartoxikose *f (api)* nectar toxicosis
Nelke *f* 1. pink, dianthus *(genus Dianthus)*; 2. carnation, clove[-scented] pink, clove [gillyflower], Dianthus caryophyllus; 3. *s.* Gewürznelke
Nelkenadernscheckungsvirus *n* carnation vein mottle virus
nelkenartig caryophyllaceous
Nelkenätzringvirus *n* carnation etched ring virus, CERV
Nelkenblätteröl *n* oil of clove leaf *(from Syzygium aromaticum)*
Nelkengelbfleckenvirus *n* carnation yellow fleck virus, CYFV
Nelkengewächse *npl* pink family *(family Caryophyllaceae)* • **die ~ betreffend** caryophyllaceous
Nelkenleimkraut *n* sweet william campion (catchfly, silene), Silene armeria
Nelkenöl *n* clove oil
Nelkenpfeffer *m* allspice, pimento
Nelkenpfefferbaum *m* allspice [tree], pimento, Pimenta dioica (officinalis)
Nelkenringfleckenvirus *n* carnation ring spot virus, CRV
Nelkenrost *m* carnation rust *(caused by Uromyces dianthi)*
Nelkenscheckungsvirus *n* carnation mottle virus, CMoV
Nelkenschmielenhafer *m* silver[y] hair grass, Aira caryophyllea
Nelkenschwärze *f* [fairy-]ring [leaf] spot of dianthus *(caused by Heterosporium echinulatum)*
Nelkenschwindling *m* fairy-ring mushroom, Scotch bonnet, Marasmius oreades
Nelkensommerwurz *f* clove-scented broomrape, Orobanche caryophylacea
Nelkenstrichelvirus *n* carnation streak virus
Nelkenwickler *m (ent)* carnation tortrix, Cacoecimorpha (Tortrix) pronubana
Nelkenwurz *f* 1. avens, geum *(genus Geum)*; 2. [herb] bennet, common (wood) avens, Geum urbanum
Nemagon *n* nemagon, DBC *(nematicide)*
nematizid nematicidal
Nematizid *n* nematicide, nematocide
Nematode *m* 1. nematode, nema, roundworm *(class Nematoda)*; 2. *s.* ~/pflanzenparasitärer
~/**freilebender** free-living nematode

Nematode 448

~/pflanzenparasitärer (pflanzenschädigender) plant[-parasitic] nematode, eelworm *(order Tylenchida)*
~/wandernder free-living nematode
Nematodenbefall *m* nemato[dia]sis, nematodosis
Nematodenbekämpfung *f* nematode control
Nematodenbekämpfungsmittel *n* nematicide, nematocide
Nematodeninfektion *f* nematode infection
nematodenresistent nematode-resistant, eelworm-resistant
Nematodenresistenz *f* nematode (eelworm) resistance
Nematodenvektor *m* nematode vector
nematodenvernichtend nematicidal
Nematodiasis *f s.* Nematose
Nematodirus[wurm] *m* nematodirus *(genus Nematodirus)*
Nematologe *m* nematologist
Nematologie *f* nematology
nematologisch nematological
nematophag nematophagous
Nematose *f* nemato[dia]sis, nematodosis, nematode disease
Nematozid *n* nematicide, nematocide
Nemesie *f (bot)* nemesia *(genus Nemesia)*
Neomelie *f* brood care
neomorph neomorphic
Neomycin *n* neomycin *(antibiotic)*
neonatal neonatal, new-born
Neophyt *m* neophyte
Neopin *n* neopine *(alkaloid)*
Neoplasie *f (vet)* neoplasia
Neoplasma *n* neoplasm
Neoregelie *f* fingernail plant *(genus Neoregelia)*
Neotenie *f* neoteny
Neotenin *n s.* Juvenilhormon
neotenisch neotenic, neotenous
neotropisch neotropical
Nephelometer *n* nephelometer
Nephelometrie *f* nephelometry
Nephocarb *n* nephocarb, carbophenothion *(insecticide)*
Nephrektomie *f (vet)* nephrectomy
Nephritis *f (vet)* nephritis
Nephritis-Nephrose-Syndrom *n* **des Huhnes** infectious avian nephrosis
Nephrokalzinose *f (vet)* nephrocalcinosis
Nephrolith *m (vet)* nephrolith, renal stone (calculus)
Nephrolithiasis *f* nephrolithiasis
Nephron *n* nephron, kidney unit
Nephropathie *f* nephropathy, kidney disease
Nephroptose *f (vet)* nephroptosis
Nephrose *f (vet)* nephrosis
~ des Huhnes/ansteckende infectious bronchitis of chickens
Nepovirus *n* nepovirus
Nera Verzasca *f* Verzasca goat *(breed)*

Nerine *f (bot)* nerine *(genus Nerine)*
NerLV *s.* Latentes Nerinevirus
Nerol *n* nerol *(monoterpene alcohol)*
Nerolidol *n* nerolidol *(plant substance)*
Neroliöl *n* neroli [oil], orange-flower oil *(from Citrus aurantium ssp. aurantium)*
Nerv *m* nerve • **vom ~ ausgehend** neurogenic
~/afferenter afferent (sensory) nerve
~/efferenter efferent (motor) nerve
~/heranführender *s.* ~/afferenter
~/herausführender (motorischer) *s.* ~/efferenter
~/sensorischer *s.* ~/afferenter
~/vasomotorischer vasomotor
nerval nervous
Nervatur *f (bot, ent)* nervation, venation
Nerven... *s. a.* Neuro...
Nervendurchschneidung *f*, **Nervendurchtrennung** *f (vet)* neurotomy, denervation
Nervenendigung *f (zoo)* nerve ending; *(bot)* vein ending
Nervenentfernung *f (vet)* neurectomy, denervation
Nervenentzündung *f (vet)* neuritis
Nervenfaser *f* nerve fibre
Nerven[faser]geschwulst *f (vet)* neuroma
Nervengewebe *n* nerve tissue
Nervengift *n* neurotoxin
Nervenimpuls *m* nerve impulse
Nervenknoten *m* nerve-knot, ganglion
Nervenmark *n* myelin
Nervenphysiologie *f* neurophysiology
Nervenring *m* nerve ring *(of nematodes)*
Nervensegment *n* neuromere
Nervenstückentfernung *f (vet)* neurectomy
Nervenstützgewebe *n*/**ektodermales** neuroglia
Nervensystem *n* nervous system • **auf das ~ wirkend** neurotropic • **vom ~ ausgehend** neurogenic, neurogenous
~/autonomes autonomic (involuntary) nervous system
~/peripheres peripheral nervous system
~/vegetatives (viszerales) *s.* ~/autonomes
~/zentrales central nervous system, CNS
Nerventätigkeit *f* higher nervous activity
Nervenverbindungsstelle *f* nerve junction, synapse, synapsis
Nervenzelle *f* nerve (ganglion) cell, neuron[e], neurocyte
~/embryonale neuroblast
Nervenzellfortsatz *m* nerve fibre
Nervenzentrum *n* nerve-centre
nervig *(bot)* nervate
Nervonsäure *f* nervonic acid *(fatty acid)*
nervös nervous; skittish, flighty *(e.g. a horse)*
Nervosität *f* nervousness
Nerz *m* 1. mink *(family Mustelidae)*; 2. European mink, Mustela (Lutreola) lutreola; 3. mink, Mustela (Lutreola) vison
Nerzfarm *f* mink farm (ranch)
Nerzfell *n* mink [skin]

Nerzpelz *m* mink
NES *s.* Naphthylessigsäure
Nesselausschlag *m (vet)* nettle-rash, urticaria
Nesselblatt *n (bot)* acalypha *(genus Acalypha)*
Nesselglockenblume *f* nettle-leaved bell-flower, Campanula trachelium
Nest *n* nest, nidus *(s. a. Horst 1.)*
~ **mit Eiern** clutch [of eggs], set, setting
Nestbau *m* nest-building, building of nest[s], nidification • ~ **betreiben** to nest, to nidificate, to nidify
Nestbauverhalten *n* nesting behaviour
Nestdüngung *f* nest fertilization
Nestei *n* china egg
Nesterdüngung *f* nest fertilization
Nestfarn *m* bird's nest fern, Asplenium nidus
Nestflüchter *m* nidifugous animal
Nestkasten *m* nest box *(s. a. Nistkasten)*
Nestling *m* nestling, fledg[e]ling, youngling; eyas *(falconry)*
Nestmotte *f* brown-dotted clothes moth, Niditinea fuscipunctella
Nestparasitismus *m* nest parasitism
Nestpflanzmaschine *f* hill planter
Nestpflanzung *f* nest planting, hill[-dropped] planting
Nestprobenverfahren *n* cluster sampling
Nestsaat *f* nest seeding (sowing), pocket drilling *(s. a. Nestpflanzung)*
Nestsämaschine *f* hill planter
Nestvogel *m* nestling, fledg[e]ling, youngling
Nestwurz *f (bot)* bird's nest *(genus Neottia)*
Nettoassimilation *f* net assimilation, net (apparent) photosynthesis
Nettoassimilationsrate *f* net assimilation rate, NAR
Nettoenergie *f* net energy, NE *(animal nutrition)*
Nettoenergiebedarf *m* net energy requirement
Nettogaswechsel *m* net gas exchange *(photosynthesis)*
Nettogewinn *m* net gain
Nettophotosynthese *f s.* Nettoassimilation
Nettoproteinausnutzung *f* net protein utilization, NPU *(animal nutrition)*
Nettostrahlung *f* net radiation, radiation balance (regime) *(of the atmosphere)*
Nettovolumen *n* **eines Baumes** tree underbark volume
Nettozuwachs *m* net growth
Netz *n (bot, zoo)* net, reticulum; omentum, caul *(animal anatomy)*; 2. [fishing] net • **mit einem ~ abdecken** to net • **mit Netzen abfischen** to net
~/**großes** greater (gastrocolic) omentum, epiploon
~/**kleines** lesser (gastrohepatic) omentum
netzad[e]rig *(bot)* net-veined
Netzannone *f (bot)* 1. bullock's heart, Annona reticulata; 2. custard-apple *(fruit from 1.)*
netzartig *(bot, zoo)* reticulate[d], reticular
Netzbarkeit *f* wettability
Netzbeutel *m* net (mesh) bag *(e.g. for ball plants)*

Neulandgewinnung

Netzbeuteltechnik *f* mesh bag technique *(in root growth experiments)*
Netzegge *f* chain (network, spike-tooth) harrow, flexible [tine] harrow, weed[er] harrow
netzen to moisten, to wet
Netzfischerei *f* net fishing
Netzfleckenkrankheit *f* **der Gerste** net blotch [disease] of barley, barley net *(caused by Pyrenophora teres)*
Netzfleckung *f (phyt)* net blotching
netzförmig *(bot, zoo)* reticular, cancellate[d]
Netzhaut *f* retina *(of the eye)*
Netzhautatrophie *f s.* Netzhautschwund
Netzhautentzündung *f (vet)* retinitis
Netzhauterkrankung *f (vet)* retinopathy
Netzhautschwund *m (vet)* retinal atrophy
Netzhautstäbchen *n* retinal rod
Netzhautzapfen *n* [retinal] cone
Netzkäfig *m (pisc)* net cage
Netzmagen *m* reticulum *(of ruminants)*
Netzmelone *f* net[ted] melon, nutmeg melon, Cucumis melo ssp. agrestis var. reticulatus
Netzmittel *n* 1. wetting agent, wetter, moistening substance; 2. detergent
Netzmosaik *n (phyt)* net mosaic
Netznekrose *f (phyt)* net necrosis *(e.g. of potatoes)*
netznervig *(bot)* net-veined
Netzplankton *n* net plankton
Netzschorf *m* netted scab *(of potato, caused by Streptomyces spp.)*
Netzweide *f* netleaf willow, Salix reticulata
Netzwerk *n (bot, zoo)* reticulum
Neuansaat *f* reseed, new (initial) seeding, maiden seed
Neuaufforstung *f* afforestation
Neubauer *m* new peasant
Neubauernstelle *f* new peasant holding
Neubelgische Aster *f* New York aster, Aster novi-belgii
Neubepflanzung *f* replanting
Neuberg-Ester *m* glucose-6-phosphate
Neubildung *f* 1. regeneration *(as of tissues)*; 2. *(vet)* neoplasia; 3. *(vet)* neoplasm, tumour
Neue *f s.* Neuschnee
Neuenglische Aster *f* New England aster, Aster novae-angliae
Neufchateler Käse *m* Neufchatel [cheese]
Neufundländer *m* Newfoundland [dog] *(breed)*
neugeboren new-born, neonatal
Neugeborene *n* neonate
Neugeborenendiarrhoe *f* **des Kalbes** neonatal calf diarrhoea
Neuguinea-Holz *n* Bajam teak, Intsia bijuga
Neuguinea-Impatiens *f (bot)* New Guinea impatiens
Neuland *n* reclaimed land (soil), virgin (wild) land • ~ **gewinnen** to reclaim
Neulandgewinnung *f* reclamation [of land]

Neulandpflug

Neulandpflug *m* brush plough
Neunauge *n* lamprey *(genus Lampetra)*
Neupflanzung *f* replanting
Neuraminidase *f* neuraminidase *(enzyme)*
Neuraminsäure *f* neuraminic acid
Neuraxon *n* axon *(of nerve-cell)*
Neurektomie *f (vet)* neurectomy
Neuritis *f (vet)* neuritis
Neuro... *s. a.* Nerven...
Neuroanatomie *f* neuroanatomy
Neurobiologie *f* neurobiology
Neuroblast *m* neuroblast
neuroendokrin neuroendocrine, neurosecretory
Neuroendokrinologie *f* neuroendocrinology
neurogen neurogenic, neurogenous
Neuroglia *f* neuroglia
Neurohormon *n* neurohormone
neurohormonal, neurohormonell neurohormonal
Neurohypophyse *f* neurohypophysis
Neuroleptikum *n* neuroleptic
Neurologie *f* neurology
neurologisch neurologic[al]
Neurolymphe *f* neurolymph
Neurolymphomatose *f (vet)* neurolymphomatosis
Neurom *n (vet)* neuroma
Neuromer *n* neuromere
neuromotorisch neuromotor
neuromuskulär neuromuscular
Neuron *n s.* Nervenzelle
Neuropathie *f (vet)* neuropathy, nervous system disease
Neuropathologie *f (vet)* neuropathology
Neurophysin *n* neurophysin *(animal carrier protein)*
Neurophysiologie *f* neurophysiology
Neuroplasma *n* neuroplasm
Neurose *f (vet)* neurosis
neurosekretorisch neurosecretory, neuroendocrine
neurotisch *(vet)* neurotic
Neurotomie *f (vet)* neurotomy
Neurotoxin *n* neurotoxin
Neurotransmitter *m* neurotransmitter
neurotrop neurotropic
Neurotropismus *m* neurotropism
Neurozyt *m s.* Nervenzelle
Neuschnee *m* new-fallen snow
Neuseeländer Flachs *m* 1. phormium *(genus Phormium)*; 2. New Zealand flax, flax-lily, phormium, Phormium tenax
Neuseeländerkaninchen *n* New Zealand rabbit *(breed)*
Neuseelandspinat *m* New Zealand spinach, prolific spinach, Tetragonia tetragonioides (expansa)
Neuston *n (ecol)* neuston
Neutralfett *n* neutral fat
Neutralisation *f* neutralization
Neutralisationstest *m* [serum] neutralization test *(virology)*

neutralisieren to neutralize
Neutralisierung *f* neutralization
Neutralisierungswert *m* neutralizing value *(of a lime fertilizer)*
Neutralität *f* neutrality *(e.g. of a soil)*
Neutronenaktivierungsanalyse *f* neutron activation analysis
Neutronenfeuchtemeßgerät *n* neutron moisture meter
Neutronensonde *f* neutron probe
Neutronenstrahlung *f* neutron radiation
Neutrophiler *m* neutrophil
Neuzuchtstamm *m* new breeding line
Newcastle-Krankheit *f (vet)* Newcastle disease, ND, pseudo poultry plague
New-Forest-Pony *n* New Forest pony, Forester *(breed)*
New-Hampshire *n* New Hampshire *(chicken breed)*
Newtonsche Flüssigkeit *f* Newtonian liquid
NfE *s.* Extraktstoff/N-freier
N$_2$-Fixierung *f* dinitrogen fixation
nFK *s.* Feldwasserkapazität/nutzbare
N-frei nitrogen-free
NFT-Verfahren *n* nutrient film technique *(of ornamental production)*
Ngana *f s.* Nagana
N-Gehalt *m* nitrogen content
NHB *s.* Nichtholzboden
Niacin *n s.* Nicotinsäure
Niacytin *n* niacytin
Nicaragua-Kiefer *f* Nicaraguan [pitch] pine, Pinus oocarpa
Nicarbazin *n* nicarbazin *(coccidiostatic)*
nichtallel *(gen)* non-allelic
nichtbakteriell abacterial
nichtbestellbar non-arable
Nichtderbholz *n* smallwood, wood of small diameter, small-diameter trees
Nichteiweißaminosäure *f* non-protein amino-acid
Nichteiweißstickstoff *m* non-protein nitrogen
nichterodierbar non-erodible
nichtessentiell non-essential *(e.g. an amino-acid)*
nichtgeschlechtlich non-sexual, asexual, vegetative
Nichtholzboden *m*, **Nichtholzbodenfläche** *f* non-forest area (land), non-timber land, unproductive area
Nichthuminstoff *m* non-humic compound
nichtinfektiös non-infectious
Nichtkahl[schlag]hieb *m (forest)* non-clear cutting
Nichtlandwirt *m* non-farmer
Nichtmischbarkeit *f* immiscibility
Nichtnahrungspflanze *f* non-food plant
Nichtnewtonsche Flüssigkeit *f* non-Newtonian liquid
nichtparametrisch *(biom)* non-parametric
nichtparasitär non-parasitic
nichtpathogen avirulent

nichtpersistent non-persistent
Nichtproteinstickstoff m non-protein nitrogen, N-PN
nichtriechend odourless
nichtrostend rust-resistant, incorrodible
Nichtsaccharosestoff m s. Nichtzuckerstoff
nichtschossend non-bolting
Nichtschwarzerdegürtel m non-chernozem belt
Nichtschwesterchromatid n non-sister chromatid
nichtsignifikant *(biom)* non-significant, insignificant
Nichtsinn... s. Nonsens...
Nichtsterilitätsnachweis m *(dairy)* detection of non-sterility
nichtsystemisch non-systemic
nichttoxisch non-toxic, non-poisonous
nichttragend non-bearing
Nichttrennen n non-disjunction *(of chromosomes)*
Nichtverfügbarkeit f non-availability *(e.g. of nutrients)*
Nichtwiederkäuer m non-ruminant *(suborder Nonruminantia)*
Nichtwirtspflanze f *(phyt)* non-host plant
Nichtzuckerstoff m non-sucrose substance, non-sugar [substance]
nichtzyklisch acyclic
Nickel n nickel
nickend *(bot)* nutant
Nickende Distel f nodding (musk) thistle, Carduus nutans
~ **Mohrenhirse** f Egyptian corn, white durra, Sorghum cernuum
Nickendes Perlgras n mountain melick, nodding melick grass, Melica nutans
Nicker m hunting-knife, hanger
Nickhaut f nictitating membrane, third eyelid, haw *(of birds)*
Niclofolan n niclofolan *(anthelminthic)*
Niclosamid n niclosamide, mansonil, phenasal, yomesan *(anthelminthic, molluscicide)*
Nicolieren n Nicolin budding *(method of grafting)*
Nicotin n nicotine *(alkaloid)*
Nicotinamid n s. Nicotinsäureamid
Nicotinsäure f nicotinic acid, niacin, pyridine-3-carboxylic acid
Nicotinsäureamid n nicotinamide, nicotinic acid amide, niacin amide, pyridine-3-carboxyamide, pellagra-preventive factor *(B vitamin)*
Nicotinsäureamid-adenin-dinucleotid n nicotinamide adenine dinucleotide, NAD, coenzyme I
~ **/reduziertes** nicotinamide adenine dinucleotide r, NADH
Nicotinsäureamid-adenin-dinucleotidphosphat n nicotinamide adenine dinucleotide phosphate, NADP, coenzyme II
Nicotinsäureamidavitaminose f *(vet)* pellagra
Nicotinsäureamidnucleotidadenylyltransferase f nicotinamide-nucleotide adenylyltransferase, NAD^+ pyrophosphorylase *(enzyme)*

Nicotinsulfat n nicotine sulphate *(insecticide)*
Nidation f nidation, implantation [of eggs] *(into the endometrium)*
nidicol nidicolous
nieder! down! *(command to dogs)*
Niederbinden n bending [down] *(orcharding)*
Niederblatt n *(bot)* bottom leaf
~ **/schuppenförmiges** scale-leaf
Niederdruckballenpresse f low-density baler
Niederdruckberegnung f low-pressure irrigation
Niederdruckdüse f low-pressure nozzle
niederdrücken to lay *(e.g. a crop stand)*
Niederdrucklagerung f hypobaric (low-pressure) storage, LPS *(of fruit and vegetables)*
Niederdruckpresse f low-density baler
Niederdruckregner m low-pressure sprinkler
Niederdruckreifen m low-pressure tyre
Niederdrucksammelpresse f low-density pick-up baler
Niederdruckspritze f low-pressure sprayer
Niederdrucksprühgerät n low-pressure sprayer
Niederdurchforstung f *(forest)* low (ordinary) thinning, below-treatment, thinning from below
niederfahren to swoop [down] *(raptorial bird)*
Niederglas n low glass *(greenhouse management)*
Niedergrassavanne f short-grass savanna[h]
Niederholz n undergrowth, under-shrub, boscage, boskage, bush
Niederjagd f small game shooting
Niederkräusen pl young heads, low krausen *(brewing)*
Niederländische Landrasse f Dutch Landrace *(pig breed)*
Niederländisches Kaltblut n Dutch (Netherlands) Draft, Holland Heavy *(horse breed)*
~ **Rotbuntes Rind** n Dutch red and white *(cattle breed)*
~ **Schwarzbuntes Rind** n Dutch Friesian (Black Pied), Black-and-White Holland *(cattle breed)*
niederlegen to lodge, to lay *(a crop stand)*; to cast *(livestock handling)*
~ **/seitlich** to flank *(an animal e.g. for veterinary treatment)*
~ **/sich** to bed *(animal)*
Niederliegen n lodging *(e.g. of cereals)*
niederliegend *(bot)* procumbent, decumbent, prostrate
Niederliegende Kochie (Radmelde) f prostrate summer cypress, Kochia (Bassia) prostrata
~ **Sanvitalie** f *(bot)* sanvitalia, Sanvitalia procumbens
Niederliegender Klee m yellow clover, Trifolium procumbens
Niederliegendes Mastkraut n seal-wort, pearl-wort, Sagina procumbens
Niedermoor n low[land] moor, flat (low-level) bog
Niedermoorboden m low-moor soil
Niedermoorbruchwald m fen-woodland

Niedermoortorf

Niedermoortorf[boden] *m* low-moor peat, fen peat
Niederquerschnittreifen *m* low-section tyre
Niederschlag *m* 1. precipitation; rainfall; 2. deposit
~/**als Regen fallender** rainfall
~/**als Schnee fallender** snowfall
~/**atmosphärischer** precipitation
~/**radioaktiver** [radioactive] fall-out
niederschlagsarm low-rainfall
niederschlagsbedingt ombrogenous
niederschlagsfrei free of precipitation, arid, dry
Niederschlagshäufigkeit *f* rain frequency
Niederschlagsmenge *f* precipitation; [amount of] rainfall, fall
~/**jährliche** annual precipitation
Niederschlagsmesser *m* precipitation gauge, pluviometer; rain-gauge, ombrometer, udometer
Niederschlagsmessung *f* precipitation measurement, pluviometry
niederschlagsreich high-rainfall, humid
Niederschlags-Sättigungs-Quotient *m* N/S quotient, Meyer ratio *(meteorology)*
Niederschlagsschreiber *m* rain recorder
Niederschlagssicherheit *f* rain reliability
Niederschlags-Verdunstungs-Verhältnis *n* precipitation-evaporation ratio, P/E ratio
Niederschlagsverteilung *f* rainfall distribution
Niederschlagswasser *n* atmospheric water
• **durch ~ entstanden** ombrogenic, ombrogenous
niederschnüren to cast *(livestock handling)*
Niederstamm *m* bush (quarter-standard) tree, dwarf fruit-tree *(orcharding)*
~ als Busch dwarf bush tree
Niedertemperaturfließbetttrockner *m* low-temperature conveyor-type dryer
Niedertemperaturheizung *f* low-temperature heating
Niedertemperaturtrockner *m* low-temperature dryer
Niedertemperaturtrocknung *f* low-temperature drying
Niedertemperaturwärme *f* low-grade heat
niedertragend early-pregnant
niedertreten to trample, to trail *(e.g. grass)*
Niederung *f* lowland, bottomland
Niederungsboden *m* bottomland soil
Niederungsmoor *n* s. Niedermoor
Niederungsrasse *f* lowland (low ground) breed
Niederungsrind[vieh] *n* lowland cattle
Niederungsweide *f* lowland pasture
Niederungswiese *f* low-lying meadow
Niedervolumenbelüftung *f* low-volume aeration *(e.g. of grain)*
Niederwald *m* coppice [forest], copse, low (sprout) forest, shrub-wood • **~ bilden** to coppice
~/**geplenterter** selection coppice
~ mit Schutzschleier shelterwood coppice
Niederwaldbetrieb *m* coppice system, sprout method

~/**reiner** simple coppice system
Niederwaldplenterung *f* coppice selection system
Niederwaldüberhaltbetrieb *m* two-rotation coppice [system], coppice of two rotations (systems)
Niederwild *n* small (ground) game
niederwüchsig low-growing
Niedrigtemperatur-Langzeitpasteurisation *f* low-temperature long-time pasteurization, LTLT pasteurization
Niere *f* kidney
Nierembergie *f* 1. cup flower *(genus Nierembergia)*; 2. cup flower, Nierembergia hippomanica var. violacea, Nierembergia caerulea
Nierenarterie *f* renal artery
Nierenbecken *n* renal pelvis
Nierenbeckenentzündung *f (vet)* pyelitis
Nierendegeneration *f*/**polyzystische** polycystic kidney [disease]
Nierenentfernung *f (vet)* nephrectomy
Nierenentzündung *f (vet)* nephritis
Nierenerkrankung *f (vet)* kidney disease, nephropathy
~/**degenerative** nephrosis
Nierenfarn *m* sword fern *(genus Nephrolepis)*
Nierenfett *n (slaught)* kidney fat, suet
nierenförmig kidney-shaped, reniform
Nierenfunktion *f* renal function
Nierenhormon *n* renal hormone
Niereninsuffizienz *f* renal insufficiency
Nierenkanälchen *n* renal tubule
Nierenkapselentzündung *f (vet)* perinephritis
Nierenkonkrement *n* s. Nierenstein
Nierenkörperchen *n* [/**Malpighisches**] renal corpuscle
Nierenpapille *f* renal papilla
Nierenschmalz *n (Am, slaught)* leaf-lard
Nierenschuppenfarn *m* s. Nierenfarn
Nierenschuppige Tanne *f* Amur (Siberian white) fir, Abies nephrolepis
Nierensinus *m* renal sinus
Nierenstein *m (vet)* renal calculus, nephrolith
Nierensteinerkrankung *f (vet)* nephrolithiasis
Nierentalg *m (slaught)* kidney fat, suet
Nierenteepflanze *f* Java tea, kidney tea plant, Orthosiphon aristatus (grandifloris)
Nierentubulus *m* renal tubule
Nierenvene *f* renal vein
Nierenversagen *n (vet)* renal failure
Nierenverschlag *m (vet)* lumbago *(of horses)*
Nierenwassersucht *f (vet)* renal dropsy
Niersteiner *m* Niersteiner *(wine)*
nieseln to drizzle
Nieseln *n* drizzling
Nieselregen *m* drizzle
Nieswurz *f* hellebore *(genus Helleborus)*
nif-Gen *n* nif gene, nitrogen-fixation gene
Nifurazolidon *n* furazolidone *(chemotherapeutical)*
Nigrosin-Eosin-Färbung *f* nigrosin-eosin [live-dead] staining *(semen examination)*

Nikkotanne f Nikko fir, Abies homolepis
Nilgauantilope f nilg[h]ai, Bosephalus tragocamelus
Nilgirinessel f Himalayan nettle, Girardinia diversifolia
Nilgras n Nile grass, Acroceras macrum
Nimbaum m neem [tree], nim, margosa, Antelaea (Melia) azadirachta, Azadirachta indica
Nimbostratus m nimbostratus [cloud]
Nimbus m nimbus
Nimorazol n nimorazole *(antiparasitic)*
Nimrod m Nimrod, pot-hunter
Ninhydrinreaktion f, **Ninhydrintest** m ninhydrin test *(amino-acid detection)*
Nipapalme f nipa [palm], Nypa (Nipa) fruticans
Nipf m *(vet)* pip *(of poultry)*
Nippel m nipple
Nippeltränke f nipple (bite) drinker
Niridazol n niridazole *(anthelminthic)*
Nische f *(ecol)* niche
~/**natürliche (ökologische)** natural (ecological) niche
Nisin n nisin *(antibiotic)*
Nisse f nit
nissenbefallen nitty
Nissensche Kugel f milk globule
nissig nitty
nisten to nest, to breed
Nisthöhle f nest cavity
Nistkasten m nest[ing] box, bird box (house)
Nistplatz m, **Niststelle** f nesting place, nesting (breeding) site
Nitralin n nitralin *(herbicide)*
Nitrapyrin n nitrapyrin, n-serve *(nitrification inhibitor)*
Nitrat n nitrate
Nitratassimilation f nitrate assimilation
Nitratatmung f dissimilatory nitrate reduction *(plant physiology)*
Nitratbakterium n, **Nitratbildner** m nitrate (nitric) bacterium *(genus Nitrobacter)*
Nitratbildung f nitrification
Nitratcyanose f *(vet)* methaemoglobinaemia
Nitratdünger m nitrate fertilizer
Nitratreductase f nitrate reductase *(enzyme)*
Nitratreductaseinhibitor m nitrate reductase inhibitor
Nitratreduktion f nitrate reduction
~/**dissimilatorische** s. Nitratatmung
Nitratreduktionstest m nitrate reduction test *(bacteriology)*
Nitratstickstoff m nitrate nitrogen
Nitrattoxizität f nitrate toxicity
Nitratvergiftung f *(vet)* nitrate poisoning
Nitrifikant m nitrifier, nitrifying bacterium, nitrobacterium
Nitrifikation f nitrification
Nitrifikationshemmer m, **Nitrifizid** n nitrification inhibitor (suppressant)

nitrifizieren to nitrify
Nitrifizierung f nitrification
Nitrit n nitrite
Nitritbakterium n, **Nitritbildner** m nitrite-forming bacterium, nitrous bacterium, nitrosobacterium
Nitritdünger m nitrite fertilizer
Nitritreductase f nitrite reductase *(enzyme)*
Nitritvergiftung f *(vet)* nitrite poisoning
Nitrobakterium n s. Nitrifikant
Nitrofen n nitrofen *(herbicide)*
Nitrofluorfen n nitrofluorfen *(herbicide)*
Nitrogenase f nitrogenase *(complex of enzymes)*
Nitrojektion f nitrojection
nitrophil nitrophile, nitrophilous
Nitrophoska f nitrophoska, ammophoska *(fertilizer)*
Nitrophosphat n nitrophosphate
Nitrosamin n nitrosamine
Nitroscanat n nitroscanate *(anthelminthic)*
Nitrothalisopropyl n nitrothal-isopropyl *(fungicide)*
Nitrovin n nitrovin, payzone *(growth regulator)*
Nitroxynil n nitroxynil *(anthelminthic)*
nival nival
Nivalbiotop m nival habitat
Niveau n level, plane
nivellieren to level
Nivelliergerät n, **Nivellierinstrument** n levelling instrument, level
Nivellierlatte f levelling staff
NLV s. Latentes Nelkenvirus
N-Metabolit m nitrogen metabolite
N-Mineralisierung f nitrogen mineralization
nobel noble *(wine)*
Nocardiose f *(vet)* nocardiosis, streptotrichosis
Nockenraddosiereinrichtung f studded-wheel metering mechanism
Nockenraddrillmaschine f studded roller drill
Nockenreibkupplung f inwardly acting pin-type safety clutch
Nockensärad n studded roller
Nockensäradsystem n studded roller feed
Nockenschar n cam-share *(of a plough)*
Nockenwelle f camshaft
Nodienkultur f node culture
Nodium n node, knot
nodös nodose, nodous, nodal, nodular
Nodosität f *(phyt)* nodosity
Nodum n nodum *(phytocoenology)*
Nodulation f nodulation
nodulieren to nodulate *(leguminous roots)*
nodulös nodulose, nodulous
Nodulus m nodule
Nodus m [stem] node, knot
Noisetterose f bramble rose, Rosa multiflora
Nomade m nomad
Nomadismus m nomadism
Nomenklatur f nomenclature
~/**binäre** binomial nomenclature *(of organisms)*
Nomie f mine, tunnel *(in plant tissue)*

Nonansäure

Nonansäure f nonanoic (pelargonic) acid *(monocarboxylic acid)*
Non-Disjunktion f non-disjunction *(of chromosomes)*
Nonius m Nonius *(horse breed)*
Nonne f nun moth, Lymantria (Ocneria) monacha
Non-return-Methode f non-return method *(animal production)*
Non-return-Rate f non-return rate
Nonsenskodon m *(gen)* nonsense codon, termination (terminator) codon
Nonsensmutation f nonsense mutation
Nontronit m nontronite *(clay mineral)*
Nopadien n nopadiene *(terpene)*
Nopalin n nopaline *(amino-acid)*
Noppenfolie f nap-finish plastic film
Noradrenalin n noradrenalin[e], norepinephrine *(neurotransmitter)*
Norandrostenolon n s. Nandrolon
Norbormid n norbormide *(rodenticide)*
Nordamerikanische Blastomykose f *(vet)* North American blastomycosis
~ **Jasmintrompete** f trumpet creeper (flower), Campsis (Tecoma) radicans
~ **Pfeifente** f wi[d]geon, Anas americana
~ **Rotfichte** f red spruce, Picea rubens (rubra)
~ **Stechpalme** f [common] winterberry, Ilex verticillata
Nordamerikanischer Biber m southern beaver, Castor canadensis
Nordamerikanisches Rentier n caribou, Rangifer tarandus
Nordbiene f German (dark) bee, Apis mellifica mellifica
Nordeuropäischer Rübenerdfloh m mangel (beet) flea beetle, Chaetocnema concinna
Nordische Apfelwanze f apple capsid [bug], Plesiocoris rugicollis
~ **Johannisbeere** f northern red currant, forest currant, Ribes spicatum
~ **Mehlbeere** f Swedish beam-tree (whitebeam), Sorbus intermedia
~ **Vogelmilbe** f northern fowl mite, Ornithonyssus sylviarum
Nordischer Bradsot m *(vet)* braxy *(caused by Clostridium septicum)*
Nordkaukasisches Fleischwollschaf n North Caucasus Mutton-Wool *(sheep breed)*
Nördliches Wurzelgallenälchen n nothern root-knot nematode, Meloidogyne hapla
Nordmannstanne f Caucasian fir, Abies nordmanniana
Norepinephrin n s. Noradrenalin
Norethisteron n norethisterone *(sex hormone)*
Norflurazon n norflurazon *(herbicide)*
Norfolk Terrier m Norfolk terrier *(dog breed)*
Norfolktraber m Norfolk trotter *(horse breed)*
Norgesalpeter m Norge nitre
Norgestrel n norgestrel *(synthetic hormone)*

Noriker m, **Norisches Pferd** n Noric, Oberland, South German coldblood *(horse breed)*
Norm f standard
Normalallel n *(gen)* wild-type allele
Normalballenpresse f rectangular baler
Normalertrag m normal yield
Normalertragstafel f *(forest)* normal yield table
Normaletat m *(forest)* normal yield
Normalformzahl f normal form factor *(timber mensuration)*
Normalitätstest m *(biom)* test of normality
Normallage f normal [anterior] presentation, cephalic presentation *(obstetrics)*
Normalrübe f normal beet
Normalsitz m pleasure seat *(equestrian sport)*
Normalverdauung f eupepsia
normalverteilt *(biom)* normally distributed
Normalverteilung f [/**Gaußsche**] *(biom)* Gaussian distribution, normal [frequency] distribution
Normalvorrat m *(forest)* normal growing stock
Normalvorratsmethode f *(forest)* normal growing stock method, regulation of yield based on increment and growing stock
Normalwald m normal (ideal) forest
Normalzuwachs m *(forest)* normal increment
Normoglykämie f glycaemia
Normozytenanämie f *(vet)* normocytic anaemia
Normzeit f standard time *(time study)*
Nornicotin n nornicotine *(alkaloid)*
Nortestosteron n nortestosterone *(sex hormone)*
North Country Cheviot n North Country Cheviot, Sutherland Cheviot, Caithness *(sheep breed)*
~ **Devon** n North Devon [cattle], Devon *(breed)*
Nortron n nortron *(herbicide)*
Noruron n noruron *(herbicide)*
Norwegisches Fjordpferd n fjord *(horse breed)*
~ **Rotvieh** n Norwegian Red *(cattle breed)*
Norwich Terrier m Norwich terrier *(dog breed)*
Nosema f s. Nosematose
Nosemaseuche f pebrine [disease] *(of silkworms, caused by Nosema bombycis)*
Nosematose f nosema disease *(of honey-bees, caused by Nosema apis)*
Nosographie f nosography
Nosologie f nosology
Notäsung f *(Am)* stuffing *(for game)*
Notatin n glucose oxidase *(enzyme)*
Notbelüftung f emergency aeration *(e.g. of fish ponds)*
Notimpfung f *(vet)* emergency vaccination
Notoedres-Räude f *(vet)* notoedric mange *(caused by Notoedres spp.)*
notreif premature
notschlachten to slaughter out of necessity
Notschlachtung f emergency (compulsory, forced) slaughter
Notstand m *(vet)* bale
Notstromaggregat n, **Notstromgenerator** m stand-by generator

Nottötung f s. Notschlachtung
Novain n carnitine, ß-hydroxy-γ-butyrobetain
Novobiocin n novobiocin (antibiotic)
Novocain n novocaine (anaesthetic)
Novyi-Ödem n (vet) malignant oedema
Nozirezeptor m nocireceptor
NPK-Dünger m NPK fertilizer, complete [mixed] fertilizer
NPK-Düngung f NPK fertilization
NPN s. Nichtproteinstickstoff
NR s. Non-return-Methode
NRFV s. Nelkenringfleckenvirus
N-Rübe f s. Normalrübe
NSiV s. Nelkenstrichelvirus
N/S-Quotient m N/S quotient, Meyer ratio (meteorology)
NSV s. Nelkenscheckungsvirus
N-Tritylmorpholin n N-tritylmorpholine (molluscicide)
Nuarimol n nuarimol (fungicide)
Nucellus m (bot) nucellus
Nucellusepidermis f nucellar epidermis (layer)
Nucellusrest m hyaline layer (of a caryopsis)
nüchtern to fast, to starve
Nüchternlebendmasse f fasted (true) live weight
Nüchternumsatz m fasting metabolic rate, fasting metabolism (catabolism)
Nüchterung f starvation
Nüchterungsverlust m (slaught) excretory shrink
nudeln to cram (poultry)
Nuklease f nuclease (enzyme)
Nucleinsäure f s. Nukleinsäure
Nukleinsäure f nucleic acid
Nukleinsäurestoffwechsel m nucleic acid metabolism
Nukleinsäuresynthese f nucleic acid synthesis
Nukleinverbindung f nucleic compound
Nukleolus n nucleolus
Nukleoplasma n nucleoplasm, karyoplasm
Nukleoprotein n nucleo-protein
Nukleosid n nucleoside
Nukleosidase f nucleosidase (enzyme)
Nukleosidphosphorylase f nucleoside phosphorylase (enzyme)
Nukleosom n nucleosome
Nukleotid n nucleotide
Nukleotidase f nucleotidase (enzyme)
Nukleotidkinase f nucleotide kinase (enzyme)
Nukleotidsequenz f nucleotide sequence
Nukleotidtriplett n (gen) codon
Nukleus m nucleus (s. a. Kern)
Nukleusherde f nucleus herd (animal breeding)
Nuklid n nuclide
~/radioaktives radioactive nuclide, radionuclide
Nullbehandlung f zero treatment (experimentation)
Nullbodenbearbeitung f no-tillage system, no-till agriculture, non-plough cultivation, zero-tillage, zero-cultivation

Nullhypothese f (biom) null hypothesis
nullipar nulliparous
nulliplex (gen) nulliplex
Nullparzelle f nil (in field trials)
Nullvariante f nil (experimentation)
Numerierschlägel m, **Numerierungshammer** m (forest) numbering hammer, die-hammer
Nuß f 1. nut [fruit], caryopsis; 2. s. Walnuß; 3. s. Haselnuß
Nußbaum m 1. nut-tree (comprehensive term); 2. walnut[-tree] (genus Juglans); 3. English (European) walnut, Juglans regia
Nußbaumholz n walnut
Nußbohrer m hazel-nut borer (weevil), Curculio (Balaninus) nucum
Nüßchen n nutlet (fruit)
Nußeibe f (bot) 1. torreya (genus Torreya); 2. Chinese torreya, Torreya grandis
Nußerntemaschine f nut harvester
nußförmig nuciform
Nußfrucht f s. Nuß 1.
nußfrüchtig caryocarpous
Nußgelenk n enarthrosis
Nußgras n nut grass, purple nutsedge, Cyperus rotundus
Nußkern m nut [kernel], (Am) nut-meat
Nußkernmehl n nut meal
Nußkiefer f single-leaf pinyon, Pinus momophylla
Nußöl n nut-oil
Nußschale f nutshell
Nußschote f nut
nußtragend nuciferous
Nüster f nostril
Nutation[sbewegung] f (bot) nutation
Nutkascheinzypresse f Nootka [false] cypress, yellow cedar (cypress), Alaska-cedar, Alaska (Sitka) cypress, Chamaecyparis nootkatensis
Nutria f coypu, Myocaster coypus
Nutria m nutria (fur)
Nutriafarm f coypu farm
nutrieren s. ernähren
Nutrition f s. Ernährung
nutritiv s. nährend
Nuttalliose f (vet) nutalliosis, red-water [disease], blackwater, babesiasis, babesiosis
Nutzdauer f service life
Nutzfläche f useful area
~/aufgegebene (brachliegende) landwirtschaftliche abandoned farm land
~/hofnahe landwirtschaftliche infield
~/landwirtschaftliche cropland area, farm (agricultural) land, utilizable agricultural area, UAA, agricultural acreage
Nutzflächendichte f (ecol) utilized area density
Nutzgarten m household garden
Nutzgeflügel n poultry
Nutzholz n [converted, commercial] timber, lumber
~ mittlerer Qualität middlings
~/schwaches small[-sized] timber

Nutzholz

~/starkes large timber
Nutzholzprozent n utilization percent *(timber conversion)*
Nutzholzvorrat m utilizable timber volume
Nutzinsekt n beneficial (useful) insect
Nutzleistung f useful power
Nützling m *(ecol)* beneficial [animal], beneficial organism (species)
Nutzpflanze f crop (economic, useful) plant
~/landwirtschaftliche agricultural crop [plant]
Nutzpflanzenart f crop species
Nutzpflanzenertrag m crop yield
Nutzpflanzenkunde f crop science
Nutzpflanzensorte f crop [plant] variety
Nutzschaf n commercial sheep
Nutzscheitholz n split log
Nutzschnittholz n factory lumber
Nutztier n [economically] useful animal; farm (agricultural) animal
~/bovines beast
~/der Nahrungsgewinnung dienendes food animal
~/im Saisonzyklus brünstiges seasonal breeder
~/landwirtschaftliches farm (agricultural) animal
~/polyöstrisches continuous breeder
Nutztierverhalten n livestock behaviour
Nutzung f 1. *(forest)* felling operation, exploitation; 2. *s.* Bodennutzung
~ ab bestimmtem Mindestdurchmesser diameter-limit cutting
~ ab bestimmtem Mindestumfang in Brusthöhe girth-limit cutting
~/außerordentliche extraordinary (unregulated, unclassed) felling
~/exploitative forest exploitation
~/nachhaltige sustained use
~ über den Etat overcut[ting]
~/übermäßige overexploitation, over-use, over-utilization
Nutzungsalter n *(forest)* age of yield, exploitable age
Nutzungsdauer f service life *(e.g. of a farm machine)*
Nutzungsentgelt n royalty *(forest economics)*
Nutzungsfaktor m *s.* Nutzungsprozent
Nutzungsfläche f *(forest)* coupe
Nutzungshieb m ohne Kahlschlag *(forest)* non-clear cutting
Nutzungsjahr n harvest year
Nutzungskarte f *(forest)* logging map
Nutzungsmenge f/jährliche *(forest)* felling volume
Nutzungsmöglichkeit f *(forest)* logging chance
Nutzungsplan m *(forest)* felling (cutting) plan, plan of cuttings
Nutzungsplanung f *(forest)* planning of fellings (harvesting)
Nutzungspotential n use potential
Nutzungsprozent n *(forest)* exploitation (utilization) percent, relative thinning intensity
Nutzungsrecht n right of use

Nutzungssatz m *(forest)* planned (prescribed) cut, prescribed yield
~/jährlicher annual allowable cut
Nutzvieh n **[/landwirtschaftliches]** [utility] livestock, farm stock
Nutzwald m commercial timberland
Nutzwild n edible game
N-Virose f der Pflaume N-virus disease [of plum]
nWK *s.* Wasserkapazität/nutzbare
Nyktalopie f *(vet)* nyctalopia, night-blindness
Nyktinastie f *(bot)* nyctinasty
nyktinastisch *(bot)* nyctinastic
Nymphe f *(ent)* nymph
Nymphenstadium n *(ent)* nymphal stage
Nymphomanie f nymphomania, continuous (constant, persistent) oestrus
Nystatin n nystatin, ceratocide *(antibiotic)*

O

O-Antigen n O-antigen, somatic antigen *(of bacteria)*
Oase f oasis
Oasenboden m oasis soil
Oasenlandwirtschaft f oasis agriculture
Obduktion f *(vet)* autopsy
Obeche[baum] m *(bot)* obeche, Triplochiton scleroxylon
O-beinig base-narrow, bandy-legged *(limb position)*
Obenentnahme f top unloading
Obenentnahmefräse f, **Obenentnahmevorrichtung** f top [silo] unloader
Oberarm m upper (true) arm
Oberarmarterie f brachial artery
Oberarmbein n, **Oberarmknochen** m humerus
Oberbauch m epigastrium
Oberbehandlungsbeute f *(api)* top-opening hive
Oberbestand m *s.* Oberholz
oberblattständig *(bot)* epiphyllous
Oberboden m 1. topsoil, surface soil, epipedon, soil proper; 2. *s.* Oberbodenhorizont
~/lockerer mould
Oberbodenhorizont m A-horizon, leached (eluvial) horizon
Oberfläche f 1. surface; 2. surface area • **senkrecht zur ~** *(bot)* anticlinal
~/phreatische ground-water surface
Oberflächenabfluß m surface (immediate) runoff, overland (surface) flow *(of rain-water)*
oberflächenaggregiert *(soil)* surface-aggregated
oberflächenaktiv surface-active
Oberflächenanästhesie f *(vet)* surface anaesthesia
Oberflächenantigen n surface antigen
Oberflächenbearbeitung f surface cultivation
Oberflächenbehandlung f surface treatment; surface dressing, surfacing *(road construction)*

Oberflächenbewässerung f surface irrigation
Oberflächendränung f surface drainage
Oberflächengestaltung f topography
Oberflächenpflanze f hemicryptophyte, chamaephyte
Oberflächenprofilmeßgerät n (soil) surface profile meter
Oberflächenrauhigkeit f surface roughness (e.g. of a soil)
Oberflächenriß m surface check (timber defect)
Oberflächenrückstand m extrasurface residue (of plant protectants)
Oberflächenschicht f stehender Gewässer epilimnion
Oberflächenschutzschicht f surface dressing (road construction)
Oberflächensediment n (soil) alluvial deposit
Oberflächenspannung f surface tension
Oberflächentemperatur f surface temperature
oberflächentrocken surface-dry (timber)
Oberflächenverdichtung f surface compaction
Oberflächenverkrustung f surface crusting (of soil)
Oberflächenwasser n (soil) surface water
~/stehendes standing (stagnant) water
Oberflurbelüftung f above-ground ventilation
Oberflurtrockner m on-the-floor dryer
Oberflurtrocknung f on-[the-]floor drying
Oberflußmeisterei f Regional Water Resources Management Authority
Oberförster m divisional (district) forest officer, chief ranger, head-forester, head forest ranger, territorial conservator
Oberförsterei f forestry field office; forest circle (district), [territorial] division
Oberforstmeister m forest conservator, head (chief) forest officer
Obergärung f top fermentation (brewing)
Obergras n top grass
Oberhaar n guard (top) hair
Oberhaut f epidermis, scarf-skin
Oberhefe f top[-fermentation] yeast (brewing)
Oberhöhe f [mean] top height, dominant (stand) height (timber mensuration)
Oberholz n (forest) upper (main) storey, overstorey, overwood
Oberholzhieb m liberation felling (cutting)
Oberholzmusterung f selecting of standards
oberirdisch above ground; (bot) epigeal, epigeous
• **~ lebend (vorkommend)** superterranean
Oberkiefer m upper jaw, maxilla (of vertebrates); mandible (of arthropods)
Oberkieferdrüse f mandibular gland (of arthropods)
Oberkohlrabi m kohlrabi, turnip[-rooted] cabbage, Brassica oleracea var. gongylodes
Oberländer Kaltblut n Oberland (horse breed)
Oberlandesforstmeister m chief forester of a state
Oberlenker m upper (top) link (of three-point hitch)

Oberlenkerhaken m top link hook
Oberlenkerregelung f, **Oberlenkerverstellung** f upper link control
Oberlippe f upper lip; (ent) labrum
Oberlippenbremse f twitch (for fixing horses) • **die ~ anlegen** to twitch
Oberrücken m dew-claw (animal anatomy)
Oberschenkel m femur, thigh
Oberschenkelarterie f femoral artery
Oberschenkelbein n, **Oberschenkelknochen** m femur, thigh-bone
oberschlächtig overshot
Oberseite f top
Obersieb n chaffer [sieve], chaff riddle, top sieve (of a thresher)
Obersiebverlängerung f top sieve extension
Oberstand m s. Oberholz
oberständig (bot, zoo) superior
Oberstärke f top diameter, diameter at the top (smaller end) (timber mensuration)
Oberteil n top
Oberträgerzwiebel f top (tree) onion, Allium cepa var. viviparum
Oberwärme f overhead heat (in greenhouses)
Obesität f obesity, adiposity, fatness
Objektglas n, **Objektträger** m specimen slide (holder), [microscopic] slide
Objektträger[schnell]agglutination f slide agglutination (microbiology)
oboval (bot) oboval, obovate
Obst n fruit, fruits
~/aussortiertes cullage, degraded fruit
~/entsteintes pitted fruit
~ für den Frischverzehr dessert fruit
~/getrocknetes dried (dehydrated) fruit
~/verkaufsfähiges marketable fruit
Obstbau m fruit growing (cultivation, farming), orcharding
Obstbaugürtel m fruit belt
Obstbausystem n orchard system
Obstanlage f orchard, fruit-tree planting, fruit grove (plantation) • **eine ~ anlegen** to establish an orchard • **eine ~ betreiben** to operate an orchard
~/heckenförmige hedgerow planting
~ im Beetsystem bed orchard
~ im Hauptertragsstadium mature orchard
Obstanlagenheizgerät n orchard heater (stove)
Obstanlagenheizung f orchard heating
Obstart f fruit species (crop)
~ der gemäßigten Zonen temperate fruit
~/mehrjährige perennial fruit crop
~ mit klimakterischem Atmungsanstieg climacteric fruit
~ ohne klimakterischen Atmungsanstieg non-climacteric fruit
Obstaufbereitung f fruit handling; packing of fruit (s. a. Obstbehandlung)
Obstauffangvorrichtung f fruit catching device
Obstbanane f banana

Obstbau

Obstbau *m* fruit growing (cultivation), orcharding, pomology
Obstbaubetrieb *m* fruit farm, commercial orchard
Obstbauboden *m* orchard soil
Obstbauer *m* fruit grower (cultivator, farmer), orchardist, orchardman
Obstbaufachmann *m* pomologist *(s. a.* Obstbauer*)*
Obstbaugebiet *n* fruit growing area
Obstbaugenossenschaft *f* fruit co-operative
Obstbaugürtel *m* fruit belt
Obstbaukunde *f* pomology, fruit science
Obstbaukundiger *m* pomologist
obstbaukundlich pomological
Obstbaum *m* fruit-tree; fruiter
~ **im Hauptertragsstadium** mature fruit-tree
~/**kleiner** compact tree, dwarf [fruit-]tree
~ **mit Hohlkrone** open-centre [fruit-]tree
~ **mit modifizierter Hohlkrone (Trichterkrone)** delayed open-centre tree
~ **mit Trichterkrone** open-centre [fruit-]tree
~/**tragender** fruiter
Obstbaumbrand *m* blight *(s. a.* Feuerbrand*)*
Obstbaumgewächshaus *n* orchard house
Obstbaumkrebs *m* fruit canker, apple[-tree] canker *(caused by Nectria galligena)*
Obstbaumkultur *f* pomiculture
Obstbaumminiermotte *f* pear leaf blister moth, Cemiostoma scitella, Leucoptera malifoliella
Obstbaumschnitt *m* pruning [of fruit-trees]
~ **mit Konturenschnittmaschine** hedging, trimming
~ **zur Förderung der Apikaldominanz** subordination pruning
Obstbaumspinnmilbe *f* fruit-tree red spider mite, European red mite, Panonychus (Metatetranychus) ulmi
Obstbaumspritze *f* orchard (stem) sprayer
Obstbaumspritzmittel *n* fruit-tree spray
Obstbaumunterlagenroder *m* fruit-tree rootstock digger
Obstbaumvibrator *m* tree shaker (knocker)
Obstbaumzucht *f* pomiculture
Obstbaumzüchter *m* pomiculturist
Obstbauschädling *m* fruit (orchard) pest
Obstbautraktor *m* orchard tractor
Obstbauwissenschaft *f s.* Obstbaukunde
Obstbehandlung *f* fruit treatment
Obst-Dauerware *f* lasting fruit product
Obsteinzelhandel *m* fruit retail trade
Obsternte *f* fruit harvest (crop)
Obsterntemaschine *f* fruit harvesting machine, mechanical fruit harvester; fruit-picking machine
Obsterntewagen *m* fruit collecting (picking) cart
Obstetrik *f (vet)* obstetrics
Obstfliege *f* fruit (pomace) fly *(family Drosophilidae)*
Obstgarten *m* orchard
Obstgehölz *n* [woody] fruit plant, fruit wood
• **Obstgehölze erziehen** to train [fruit plant], to form

~/**laubabwerfendes** deciduous fruit plant
Obstgetränk *n* fruit beverage
Obstgewächs *n* fruit plant
Obstgroßhandel *m* fruit wholesale trade
Obstgroßhändler *m* fruit wholesaler
Obsthändler *m* fruiterer, fruit retailer
Obsthorde *f* crate
Obstipation *f (vet)* constipation
Obstkalibriermaschine *f* fruit grader
Obstkalibrierung *f* fruit grading
Obstkenner *m* pomologist
Obstkern *m* pip
Obstkistenwagen *m* fruit box cart
Obstkonserve *f* tinned (canned) fruit, preserved (processed) fruit
Obstkonservenaufkommen *n* fruit pack
Obstkonservenherstellung *f*, **Obstkonservierung** *f* fruit canning (processing)
Obstkonservierungsanlage *f* fruit packing facility
Obstkultur *f* fruit (orchard) crop
Obstkunde *f* pomology, fruit science
obstkundlich pomological
Obstlagerung *f* fruit storage
~ **in kontrollierter Atmosphäre** CA (controlled atmosphere) storage
Obstmade *f* 1. fruit-worm *(comprehensive term)*; 2. apple (worm) worm, codlin[g] (palmer) worm, Cydia (Laspeyresia) pomonella
Obstmost *m* fruit must
Obstmühle *f* fruit crusher
Obstpflanze *f* fruit plant
Obstpflanzung *f* orchard
Obstpflücker *m* 1. fruit picker; 2. fruit picking machine, fruit gatherer
Obstplantage *f* orchard, fruit plantation *(for compounds s. under* Obstanlage*)*
Obstproduktion *f* fruit production
Obstproduzent *m* orchardist, orchardman
Obstsaft *m* fruit juice
Obstschädling *m* fruit (orchard) pest
Obstschälmaschine *f* fruit peeling machine, mechanical fruit peeler
Obstschaumwein *m* fruit champagne
Obstsorte *f* fruit cultivar (variety)
Obstsortenkunde *f* pomology
Obstsortieranlage *f* fruit grader
Obstsortierung *f* fruit grading
Obstsüßmost *m* unfermented fruit must (juice)
Obsttransportschiff *n* fruiter
Obsttrockner *m* fruit kiln
Obstunterlage *f s.* Unterlage 1.
Obstverarbeitung *f* fruit processing
Obstverkäufer *m* fruiterer, fruit retailer
Obstverpackungseinrichtung *f* fruit packing facility
Obstverwertung *f* fruit utilization
Obstwein *m* fruit wine, cider
Obstweinbereitung *f* cider-making
Obstwiese *f* meadow orchard
Obstzüchter *m s.* Obstbauer

Ocelle f (ent) simple eye
Ochratoxikose f (vet) ochratoxicosis
Ochratoxin n ochratoxin (mycotoxin)
Ochratoxinvergiftung f (vet) ochratoxicosis
Ochrea f (bot) ocrea, ochrea
Ochse m ox, bullock
~ **unter vier Jahren** steer
Ochsenauge n 1. (bot) ox-eye (genus Buphthalmum); 2. (vet) hydrophthalmia
Ochsengalle f ox-gall
Ochsengespann n ox team, span (South Africa)
Ochsenhaut f oxhide
Ochsenherz n (bot) bullock's heart, Annona reticulata
Ochsenhufeisen n oxshoe
Ochsenjoch n ox-yoke
Ochsenkarren m bullock-cart, hackery
Ochsenkopf m bullhead (floral malformation of roses)
Ochsentreibstock m oxgoad
Ochsenwagen m ox-wagon, ox-cart
Ochsenziemer m pizzle
Ochsenzunge f (bot) 1. bugloss, ox-tongue, anchusa (genus Anchusa); 2. s. Leberpilz
Öchsle[grad] n Oechsle degree (unit of measurement for the density of must)
Öchslewaage f must gauge, must[i]meter, mustometer (for measuring the density of must)
Ocimen n ocimene (terpene)
ockerfarben ochre
Ockermosaik n **der Pflaume** plum ochre mosaic (virosis)
Octadeca-9,12-diensäure f linoleic (octadeca-9,12-dienoic) acid (fatty acid)
Octadecansäure f octadecanoic (stearic) acid (fatty acid)
Octadeca-9,12,15-triensäure f linolenic acid (fatty acid)
(cis)-Octadec-9-ensäure f oleic acid (fatty acid)
Octahydrochinolizin n quinolizidin (alkaloid)
Octansäure f octanoic (caprylic) acid (fatty acid)
Octomitiasis f (pisc, vet) hexamitiasis
Octopin n octopine (amino-acid)
octoploid (gen) octoploid, octaploid
Octoploide m octoploid, octaploid
Octoploidie f octoploidy
Octose f octose (monosaccharide)
öde barren, jejune (land)
Ödem n (vet) oedema
~ **der Schafböcke/malignes** swelled head
~/**malignes** malignant oedema
ödematös (vet) oedematose, oedematous
Ödemkrankheit f (vet) oedema disease (caused by Escherichia coli)
Odermennig m (bot) agrimony (genus Agrimonia)
Ödland n waste land (ground), barren [land], badland, idle (wild) land
Ödlandaufforstung f waste land afforestation, afforestation of barren land, afforestation of waste areas

Ödlandrückgewinnung f waste land recovery
Odmichnion n trail pheromone
Odontoglossum-Ringfleckenvirus n odontoglossum ring spot virus, ORV
Odor m s. Geruch
Odorans n odorant
OdRFV s. Odontoglossum-Ringfleckenvirus
Ofenfischchen n firebrat, Lepismodes inquilinus, Thermobia domestica
offenblütig (bot) chasmogamic
Offenblütiger Salbei m gentian sage, Salvia patens
Offenmelkstand m open milking parlour
Offenscheune f Dutch barn
Offenstall m poll barn, open[-type] shelter, open stable
Offenstallhaltung f open housing
offizinell officinal
Öffnung f 1. opening, aperture; orifice (e.g. of a nozzle); (bot, zoo) ostium, stoma[te]; 2. lumen (the cavity of a tubular or hollow organ)
~/**kleine** (bot, zoo) ostiole, foramen
Öffnungsschnitt m bar cut (poultry slaughtering)
Of-Horizont m (soil) fermentation layer, F-layer
O-Fläche f s. Kontrollfläche
Ohio-Roßkastanie f Ohio buckeye, Aesculus glabra
O-Horizont m (soil) O-horizon, Ao-horizon, organic surface layer
Ohr n ear
~/**äußeres** external (outer) ear, auricle
~/**hängendes** lop-ear
~/**inneres** inner ear
Ohrbeißen n ear biting (vice of pigs)
Ohrenentzündung f (vet) otitis
Ohrenkrankheit f (vet) ear disease
Ohrenschmalz n cerumen
Ohrenspiegelung f (vet) otoscopy
Ohrenzecke f ear tick, Otobius megnini
Ohrenzwang m (vet) external otitis
ohrförmig auriculate
Ohrkerbe f ear notch
Ohrkerbzange f ear notcher
Ohrläppchenkrankheit f **der Topfazalee** azalea leaf gall (caused by Exobasidium vaccini)
Ohrmarke f ear tag, earmark • **eine ~ anlegen** to earmark
Ohrmarkierung f earmarking
Ohrmarkierungszange f earmarker
Ohrmuschel f concha, auricle
Ohrräude f (vet) ear mange, psoroptic mange (scab) (caused by Psoroptes spp.)
Ohrscheibe f ear lobe (of fowl)
Ohrspeicheldrüse f parotid [gland]
Ohrspeicheldrüsenentzündung f (vet) parotitis
Ohrspiegel m otoscope
Ohrspiegelung f (vet) otoscopy
Ohrtätowierung f ear tattoo

Ohrtrompete

Ohrtrompete f auditory (Eustachian) tube *(animal anatomy)*
Ohrweide f roundear willow, Salix aurita
Ohrwurm m *(ent)* earwig *(order Dermaptera)*
Oidie f, **Oidiospore** f *(bot)* oidium
Okazaki-Fragment n Okazaki piece *(of DNA)*
Ökobrache f *(Am)* ecofallow
Ökokatastrophe f ecocatastrophe, environmental catastrophe
Ökoklima n ecoclimate, bioclimate
ökoklimatisch ecoclimatic[al]
Ökolandbau m, **Ökolandwirtschaft** f eco-agriculture, ecofarming, ecological (organic, alternative) farming, biological husbandry
Ökologe m ecologist
Ökologie f ecology, oikology, bionomics, bionomy
~/angewandte applied ecology
~ der Biozönosen und Ökosysteme synecology
~ der einzelnen Arten autecology
~/physiologische autecology
ökologisch ecologic[al]
Ökomon n allelochemical
Ökomorphologie f ecomorphology
ökonomisch economic
Ökophysiologie f ecophysiology
ökophysiologisch ecophysiological
Ökospezies f ecospecies
Ökosphäre f ecosphere, biosphere
Ökosystem n ecosystem
ökosystematisch ecosystemic, holocoenotic
Ökoton n(m) ecotone
Ökotop n(m) ecotope
Ökotoxikologie f ecotoxicology
ökotoxikologisch ecotoxicological
Ökotyp m ecotype
Ökozid m(n) ecocide
Okra f *(bot)* okra, gumbo, Lady's finger, bhendi, Abelmoschus (Hibiscus) esculentus
Oktoberfetthenne f October plant, Sedum sieboldii
Okularerkundung f *(forest)* visual reconnaissance
Okularschätzung f, **Okulartaxation** f *(forest)* ocular estimate (method), visual examination, estimate by eye
Okulat n budling *(orcharding)*
Okulation f inoculation, bud grafting, budding
~ auf schlafendes Auge dormant budding
~/gewöhnliche shield budding
~ mit T-Schnitt/gewöhnliche T-budding
okulieren to inoculate, to bud[-graft]
Okulieren n s. Okulation
Okuliermesser n budding knife
Okziput n occiput
Öl n oil
~/ätherisches essential (volatile) oil, ethereal (etherial) oil
~/fettes fatty oil
~/pflanzliches plant oil
~/tierisches animal oil
~/trocknendes drying oil

Ölbadgetriebe n oil-bath gearbox
Ölbadluftfilter n oil-bath air filter
Ölbaum m 1. olive [tree] *(genus Olea)*; 2. olive [tree], Olea europaea
Ölbaumgewächse npl olive family *(family Oleaceae)* • **die ~ betreffend** oleaceous
Ölbaumharz n elemi
Ölbehälter n oil vessel *(e.g. in plant tissues)*
Ölbohne f s. Sojabohne
Oldenburger Schweineseuche f *(vet)* transmissible gastroenteritis, TGE
~ Warmblutpferd n Oldenburg *(horse breed)*
Oldenburgisches Weidelgras n short-rotation ryegrass, Lolium x hybridum
Öldruckbremse f hydraulic brake
Öldrüse f *(bot)* oil gland
Oleander m 1. rose-bay, nerium *(genus Nerium)*; 2. rose-bay, oleander, nerium, Nerium oleander
Oleanderschildlaus f oleander scale, Aspidiotus nerii
Oleandomycin n oleandomycin *(antibiotic)*
Oleanolsäure f oleanolic acid *(carboxylic acid)*
Öleinfüllstutzen m oil filler [neck]
Oleoresin n oleoresin
Oleoresinat n balsamic resin, balsam, balm
Oleosom n *(bot)* oleosome, sphaerosome, lipid body
ölerzeugend oleiferous
Ölextraktion f oil extraction
Ölextraktionsschrot m oil-meal
Olfaktometer n olfactometer
olfaktorisch olfactory
Olfaktus m olfactometer
Ölfilter n oil filter
Ölfleckenkrankheit f **der Begonie** bacterial blight (leaf spot) of begonia *(caused by Xanthomonas campestris begoniae)*
~ der Pelargonie bacterial blight of pelargonium *(caused by Xanthomonas pelargoni and Pseudomonas erodii)*
Ölfrucht f oil[-seed] crop, oil-seed
Ölgang m *(bot)* vitta
ölhaltig oily, oleaginous, oleiferous
Ölharz n oleoresin
Ölheizung f oil firing equipment
Ol-Horizont m *(soil)* Aoo-horizon, surface litter, L-layer
Olibanum n olibanum, frankincense *(gum resin from Boswellia spp.)*
ölig 1. oily, oleagineous; 2. silk, rop[e]y, unctuous *(wine)*
Oligodendrogliazelle f, **Oligodendrozyt** m oligodendrocyte
Oligogen n oligogene, major gene
Oligo-1,6-Glucosidase f oligo-1,6-glucosidase, isomaltase *(enzyme)*
Oligokardie f bradycardia
Oligomycin n oligomycin *(antibiotic)*
Oligopeptid n oligopeptide

oligophag *(zoo, ecol)* oligophagous
Oligophagie *f (zoo, ecol)* oligophagy
Oligosaccharid *n* oligosaccharide
Oligospermie *f* oligospermia
oligotroph oligotrophic
Oligozythämie *f (vet)* oligocythaemia
Oligurie *f (vet)* oliguria
Öl-in-Wasser-Emulsion *f* oil-[in-]water emulsion
Olive *f* olive
Olivenbaum *m* 1. olive [tree] *(genus Olea)*; 2. olive [tree], Olea europaea
Olivenblasenfuß *m (ent)* olive thrips, Liothrips oleae
Olivenbrei *m* olive pulp
Olivenfliege *f* olive [fruit-]fly, Dacus oleae
Olivenhain *m* olive grove
Olivenholz *n* olive-wood
Olivenmotte *f* olive moth, Prays oleae (oleellus)
Olivenöl *n* olive oil
~ **erster Pressung** virgin [olive] oil
Olivenpreßkuchen *m* olive cake
Olivin *m* olivine *(non-clay mineral)*
Ölkanal *m s.* Ölgang
Ölkreislauf *m* oil circuit
Ölkuchen *m* oilcake, oil-seed cake, seed (mill) cake
Ölkuchenbrecher *m* oilcake crusher
Ölkuchenmehl *n* oil-meal
Ölkühler *m* oil cooler
ölliefernd oleagineous
Ölmadie *f* [Chile] tarweed, Madia sativa
Ölmeßstab *m* oil dip-stick
Ölmohn *m* opium poppy, Papaver somniferum ssp. somniferum
Ölmühle *f* oil mill
Ölnußbaum *m* [American] butter-nut, Juglans cinerea
Ölpalme *f* [African] oil-palm, Elaeis guineensis
Ölperilla *f (bot)* perilla, Perilla frutescens (ocimoides)
Ölpflanze *f* oil-plant; oil crop (seed)
~/**ätherische** essential oil plant
Ölpresse *f* oil-press
Ölpreßkuchen *m* mill cake
Ölpumpe *f* oil pump
Ölraps *m* winter [oil-seed] rape, cole[-seed], swede [oil-seed] rape, Brassica napus var. napus
Ölrauke *f* [garden, Roman] rocket, rocket-salad, roquette, rugola, Eruca vesicaria ssp. sativa
Ölrettich *m* oil (fodder) radish, Raphanus sativus [var. oleiformis]
Ölrübsen *m* navew, [summer, turnip, bird] rape, Brassica rapa var. silvestris
Ölsaat *f* oil[-seed] crop, oil-seed
Ölsaatprotein *n* oil-seed protein
Ölsaatkraftstoff *m* oil-seed fuel
Ölsaatkultur *f s.* Ölsaat
Ölsaatrückstand *m* oil-seed residue
Ölsamen *m* oil-seed
Ölsäure *f* oleic (rapic) acid *(fatty acid)*

Ölsenf *m s.* Ölrettich
Ölsprühmittel *n* oil spray *(plant protection)*
Ölstand *m* oil level
Ölsumpf *m* oil sump
Ölverbrauch *m* oil consumption
Ölwanne *f* oil pan *(engine)*
Ölwechsel *m* oil change
Ölweide *f* 1. oleaster *(genus Elaeagnus)*; 2. oleaster, Russian olive, Elaeagnus angustifolia
Ölweidenblättriger Birnbaum *m* olive-leaved pear, Pyrus elaeagrifolia
Ölzelle *f (bot)* oil cell
omasal omasal
Omasum *n* omasum, psalterium, manyplies, third stomach *(of ruminants)*
ombrogen ombrogenous
ombriophil ombrophilous
Ombrograph *m* ombrograph
Ombrometer *n* ombrometer, pluviometer, rain-gauge
ombrophil ombrophilous
Omentum *n* omentum, caul *(animal anatomy)*
~ **minus** lesser omentum
Omethoat *n* omethoate *(insecticide)*
Ommatidium *n* facet *(of insect's eye)*
omnipotent omnipotent
Omnipotenz *f* omnipotence
omnivor omnivorous, pantophagous
Omnivore *m* omnivore
Omnivorie *f* omnivorousness, pantophagy
Omorikafichte *f* Serbian spruce, Picea omorika
Omphalitis *f (vet)* omphalitis
Omphalotomie *f (vet)* omphalotomy
Onager *m* onager, Equus hemionus onager
Onchozerkose *f (vet)* onchocerciasis *(caused by Onchocerca spp.)*
Oncornavirus *n* oncornavirus, oncogenic RNA virus *(subfamily Oncovirinae)*
Oncovirus *n* **Typ B** oncovirus type B
~ **Typ C** oncovirus type C
Ondiriitis *f* Ondiri disease *(of bovine animals)*
Önidin *n*, **Önin** *n* oenin, oenolin *(plant dye)*
onkogen *(vet)* oncogenic, oncogenous
Onkogenese *f (vet)* oncogenesis
Onkosphäre *f* onc[h]osphere *(of true cestodes)*
Onkovirus *n s.* Oncovirus
Önologe *m* oenologist
Önologie *f* oenology
önologisch oenological
Önometer *n* oenometer, wine gauge
Önotannin *n* grape tannin
Ontogenese *f* ontogenesis, ontogeny
ontogenetisch ontogenetic
Ontogenie *f s.* Ontogenese
ontogenisch ontogenetic
Oogamie *f* oogamy
Oogenese *f s.* Oozytogenese
Oogon *n (bot, zoo)* oogonium, ovogonium
Oolongtee *m* oolong *(a tea)*

Oophoritis

Oophoritis f (vet) oophoritis, ovaritis
Ooporphyrin n protoporphyrin
Oosphäre f s. Oozyt
Oospore f (bot) oospore
Oothek f ootheca, egg capsule (case)
Oozyste f oocyst
Oozyt m oocyte, ovocyte, egg cell
Oozytenreifung f oocyte maturation
Oozytogenese f oogenesis, ovogenesis, egg formation
Opal m opal (non-clay mineral)
Opaque-2-Mais m opaque-2 maize (mutant with increased content of lysine and tryptophan)
Operateur m (vet) operator, operating surgeon
Operation f operation
~/Caslicksche (vet) Caslick's operation
Operator m, **Operatorgen** n operator [gene]
Operculum n (bot, zoo) operculum
Operon n (gen) operon
Ophthalmie f (vet) ophthalmia
Ophthalmoskopie f ophthalmoscopy
Opin n opine (amino-acid)
Opisthotonus m (vet) opisthotonus
Opistorchose f (vet) opistorchiasis
Opium n opium (alkaloid)
Opobalsambaum m balm of Gilead, balsam tree, Commiphora opobalsamum
Opsonin n opsonin (blood protein)
Opsoninindex m (vet) opsonin index
Opsonisierung f opsonization (of bacteria)
Opuntie f prickly pear, Indian (barberry) fig, nopal, opuntia (genus Opuntia)
oR s. Rinde/ohne
ÖR s. Östrusrate
oral 1. oral; 2. orally, by mouth (e.g. application of medicants)
Orange f [China, sweet] orange, Citrus sinensis
Orange Pekoe m orange pekoe (tea)
orangefleischig orange-fleshed
Orangenblütenöl n orange-flower oil, neroli [oil] (from Citrus aurantium ssp. aurantium)
Orangenhain m orange grove
Orangenmarmelade f marmalade
Orangenplantage f orange grove
Orangenschale f orange peel
Orangenschalenöl n orange[-peel] oil
Orangerie f orangery
Orangerote Weizengallmücke f orange wheat blossom midge, red maggot, Sitodiplosis mosellana
Orbencarp n orbencarp (herbicide)
Orbita f eyehole, eye socket
Orbitaldrüse f zygomatic gland (of carnivores)
Orchidee f orchid, orchis (family Orchidaceae)
Orchideengewächse npl orchid family (family Orchidaceae) • **die ~ betreffend** orchidaceous
Orchideenkunde f orchidology
Orchideenlaus f orchid aphid, Sitobium luteum
Orchideenschildlaus f orchid scale, Furcaspis biformis
Orchidektomie f (vet) orchidectomy
Orchitis f (vet) orchitis, didymitis
Orchitomie f (vet) orchidectomy
Ordensstern m carrion flower, stapelia (genus Stapelia)
Ordnung f order (taxonomy)
~/räumliche (forest) spatial arrangement
Ordo f s. Ordnung
oreal oreal
Oregano m s. Dost
Oregonerle f red alder, Alnus oregona (rubra)
Oregonzeder f Port-Orford-cedar, Chamaecyparis lawsoniana
Orfe f (zoo) ide, Idus idus
Organ n (bot, zoo) organ
~/blutbildendes blood-forming organ
~/exkretorisches excretory organ
~/oberirdisches aerial organ (of plants)
~/pflanzliches plant organ
Organbildung f organogenesis
Organeinschmelzung f (ent) histolysis
Organell n, **Organelle** f organelle
Organellenübertragung f, **Organelltransfer** m organelle transfer
Organentwicklung f organ development
organisch organic
organismenabtötend biocidal
Organismenreste mpl detritus
Organismenwelt f **des Bodens** edaphon
Organismus m organism • **im lebenden ~** in vivo • **im ~ vorkommend** native • **in einem anderen ~ lebend** endobiotic • **zum ~ gehörig** native
~/alloheteroploider alloheteroploid
~/alloploider alloploid
~/allopolyhaploider allo[poly]haploid
~/allopolyploider allopolyploid
~/allotetraploider allotetraploid
~/allotriploider allotriploid
~/amphiploider amphiploid
~/aneuploider aneuploid
~/anisoploider anisoploid
~/anorthoploider anorthoploid
~/autoploider autoploid
~/autopolyploider autopolyploid
~/autotetraploider autotetraploid
~/autotropher autotroph
~/bisexueller bisexual, hermaphrodite
~/calcicoler calcicole
~/calcifuger calcifuge
~/dihaploider dihaploid
~/diploider diplont
~/ditelosomer ditelosome
~/endemisch vorkommender endemic
~/fäulniserregender saprogen
~/gleichwarmer homoiotherm, endotherm
~/haploider haploid, haplont
~/heteroploider heteroploid

Orthotropismus

~/heterotropher heterotroph
~/heterozygoter heterozygote
~/homoploider homoploid
~/homozygoter homozygote
~/im Pflanzeninneren lebender endophyte
~/kalkliebender calcicole
~/kalkmeidender calcifuge
~/mischerbiger heterozygote
~ mit echtem Zellkern eukaryote
~ mit sechsfachem Chromosomensatz hexaploid
~/mykoplasmaähnlicher mycoplasm[a]-like organism, MLO
~ ohne echten Zellkern prokaryote
~/orthoploider orthoploid
~/parasitoider parasitoid
~/pentaploider pentaploid
~/pflanzenschädigender plant pest
~/polyhaploider polyhaploid
~/polymorpher polymorph
~/polyploider polyploid
~/reinerbiger homozygote
~/sauerstoffabhängiger aerobe
~/sauerstoffunabhängiger anaerobe
~/tierischer the system
~/warmblütiger endotherm, homoiotherm
~/wechselwarm[blütig]er poikilotherm
~/zweigeschlechtlicher bisexual
Organkultur *f* organ (tissue) culture
Organneubildung *f* organogenesis
Organochlorverbindung *f* organochlorine [compound]
organogen organogenic
Organogenese *f* organogenesis
organoleptisch organoleptic
organomineralisch organomineral
Organophosphat *n* organophosphate, organophosphorous compound
Organoquecksilberverbindung *f* organomercurial
Organozinnverbindung *f* organotin compound
Organschrumpfung *f* (vet) cirrhosis
Organumbildung *f* anaplasia
Orgasmus *m* orgasm (animal physiology)
Orientalische Buche *f* oriental beech, Fagus orientalis
~ **Fichte** *f* oriental spruce, Picea orientalis
~ **Fruchtfliege** *f* oriental fruit-fly, Dacus dorsalis (ferrugineus)
~ **Hainbuche** *f* oriental hornbeam, Carpinus orientalis
~ **Schabe** *f* common (oriental, black) cockroach, black-beetle, Blatta orientalis
~ **Weißbuche** *f s.* ~ Hainbuche
Orientalischer Mohn *m* oriental poppy, Papaver orientale (bracteatum)
~ **Pfirsichwickler** *m* oriental peach (fruit) moth, Cydia (Laspeyresia) molesta
~ **Rattenfloh** *m* [tropical] rat flea, Xenopsylla cheopsis
~ **Weißdorn** *m* oriental hawthorn, Crataegus laciniata (orientalis)
Orientbeule *f* (vet) oriental sore (caused by Leishmania tropica)
Orientierungsflug *m* (api) orientation (exploratory) flight
Orientknöterich *m* (bot) prince's feather, Polygonum orientale
Orienttabak *m* oriental tobacco
Orientwaldrebe *f* oriental clematis, Clematis orientalis
Orifiziumbesamung *f* cervical insemination
Origano *m s.* Dost
Originalabfüllung *f* original (estate) bottling (of wine)
Orkan *m* hurricane
Orlean *n* annatto, arnotto, roucou (dye)
Orleansstrauch *m* annatto[-tree], Bixa orellana
Orlowtraber *m* Orlov Trotter (horse breed)
Ornithin *n* ornithine (amino-acid)
Ornithincarbamoyltransferase *f* ornithine carbamoyltransferase (transcarbamylase) (enzyme)
Ornithindecarboxylase *f* ornithine decarboxylase (enzyme)
Ornithinoxosäureaminotransferase *f* ornithine-oxo-acid aminotransferase (enzyme)
Ornithintranscarbamylase *f s.* Ornithincarbamoyltransferase
Ornithinzyklus *m* ornithine[-arginine] cycle, urea cycle, Krebs-Henseleit pathway (biochemistry)
Ornithochorie *f* (bot) ornithochory
Ornithologe *m* ornithologist
Ornithologie *f* ornithology
ornithologisch ornithologic[al]
ornithophil (bot) ornithophilous
Ornithose *f* (vet) ornithosis, psittacosis, parrot fever (caused by Chlamydia psittaci)
Orophyt *m* orophyte
Orotsäure *f* orotic (uracil-4-carboxylic) acid
Orpington[huhn] *n* Orpington (breed of fowl)
Orseille *f,* **Orseillefarbstoff** *m* orchil[la], orchal, orchel (dye esp. from Roccella tinctoria)
Orterde *f* (soil) orterde
Orthoborsäure *f* boric acid
Orthoklas *m* orthoclase (non-clay mineral)
Orthomyxovirus *n* myxovirus
Orthonil *n* orthonil (growth regulator)
Orthopädie *f* (vet) orthopaedics
Orthophosphat *n* orthophosphate
Orthophosphorsäure *f* [ortho]phosphoric acid
Orthophotokarte *f* orthophoto map
orthoploid (gen) orthoploid
Orthoploide *m* orthoploid
Orthoploidie *f* orthoploidy
Orthopoxvirus *n* orthopoxvirus
orthostich (bot) orthostichous
Orthostichie *f* orthostichy
orthotrop (bot) orthotropic, orthotropous
Orthotropismus *m* orthotropism

Ortsboden

Ortsboden *m* autochthonal (sedentary) soil, residual (primary) soil
Ortscheit *n* swingletree, swingle-bar, whippletree, *(Am)* whiffletree, double tree
ortsfest stationary, non-mobile
ortsfremd *(ecol)* allochthonous
Ortstein *m (soil)* iron pan, hardpan, ortstein, boundary stone
ortsveränderlich mobile
Ortswechsel *m (ecol)* change of locality
Oryzalin *n* oryzalin *(herbicide)*
Oryzenin *n* oryzenin *(reserve protein of rice)*
Os *m (soil)* esker, eskar
Osagedorn *m* 1. Osage-orange *(genus Maclura)*; 2. Osage-orange, bowwood, Maclura pomifera
Oscheozele *f (vet)* scrotocele, scrotal hernia
Osmiumsäure *f* osmic acid
Osmiumtetroxid *n* osmic acid
Osmol *n* osmole
osmolal osmolal
Osmolalität *f* osmolality
osmolar osmolar
Osmolarität *f* osmolarity
Osmometer *n* osmometer
Osmometrie *f* osmometry
osmometrisch osmometric
Osmophor *n* osmophor
Osmoregulation *f* osmoregulation
osmoregulatorisch osmoregulatory
Osmose *f* osmosis
~/negative reverse osmosis
osmotisch osmotic
Osmundafaser *f* osmunda fibre *(growth medium for orchids)*
Ösophagitis *f* **der Taube** *(vet)* Smadel's disease
Ösophagus *m* oesophagus, gullet
Ösophagusfistel *f (vet)* oesophageal fistula
Ossein *n* ossein *(collagen of bones)*
Ossifikation *f* ossification
ossifizieren to ossify
Ostafrikanischer Hochlandklee *m* African highland clover, Trifolium steudneri
Ostafrikanisches Küstenfieber *n (vet)* African (east) coast fever, Rhodesian red-water, Rhodesian tick fever, theileriasis of cattle *(caused by Theileria parva)*
Ostamerikanische Lärche *f* tamarack, Larix laricina (americana)
~ Strobe *f* Weymouth (pumpkin) pine, [eastern] white pine, Pinus strobus
Ostamerikanischer Judasbaum *m* eastern redbud, Cercis canadensis
Osteoarthritis *f (vet)* osteoarthritis
Osteoarthropathie *f*, **Osteoarthrose** *f (vet)* osteoarthropathy
Osteoblast *m* osteoblast, bone-forming cell
Osteochondritis *f (vet)* osteochondritis
Osteochondrose *f (vet)* osteochondrosis
Osteodystrophie *f (vet)* osteodystrophy

~ des Geflügels/fokale leg weakness syndrome in broilers
Osteofibrose *f (vet)* osteofibrosis
Osteogenese *f* osteogenesis, bone formation
Osteoklas[i]e *f (vet)* osteoclasis
Osteoklast *m* osteoclast
Osteom *n (vet)* osteoma
Osteomalazie *f (vet)* osteomalacia
Osteomyelitis *f (vet)* osteomyelitis
Osteon *n* osteone, Haversian system *(of lamellar bone)*
Osteonekrose *f (vet)* osteonecrosis
Osteopathie *f (vet)* osteopathy, bone disease
Osteopetrose *f (vet)* osteopetrosis
~/aviäre avian osteopetrosis, Paget's disease of fowl
Osteophyt *m (vet)* osteophyte
Osteoporose *f (vet)* osteoporosis
Osteosarkom *n (vet)* osteosarcoma, osteogenic sarcoma
Osteosklerose *f (vet)* osteosclerosis
Osteosynthese *f (vet)* osteosynthesis
Osteotom *n (vet)* osteotome
Osteotomie *f (vet)* osteotomy
Osteozyt *m* osteocyte, bone cell
Osterglocke *f* daffodil, Lent lily, trumpet narcissus, Narcissus pseudonarcissus
Osterkaktus *m* Easter cactus, Rhipsalidopsis gaertneri
Osterlamm *n* Easter lamb
Osterluzeiblättrige Stechwinde *f (bot)* Mexican sarsaparilla, Smilax aristolochiifolia
Osterluzeigewächse *npl* birthwort family *(family Aristolochiaceae)* • **die ~ betreffend** aristolochiaceous
Österreichische Galle *f (phyt)* marble gall, *(Am)* Devonshire gall *(caused by Cynips kollari)*
~ Schwarzkiefer *f* Austrian pine, Pinus nigra ssp. austriaca
Österreichischer Zwerginster *m* Austrian broom, Cytisus (Chamaecytisus) austriacus
Ostfriese *m* East Friesian *(horse breed)*
Ostfriesisches Milchschaf *n* East Friesland [milk sheep] *(breed)*
Ostindische Brennpalme *f* fish-tail palm, Caryota urens
Ostindischer Hanf *m* sunn [hemp], sann hemp, crotalaria, Crotalaria juncea
~ Krapp *m (bot)* Indian madder, Rubia cordifolia
~ Merkfruchtbaum *m* Indian marking-nut tree, Semecarpus anacardium
~ Nußbaum *m* chatter box tree, lebbek [tree], woman's-tongue [tree], Albizia lebbeck
~ Rhabarber *m* medicinal rhubarb, Rheum officinale
~ Rosenholzbaum *m* black wood, Dalbergia latifolia
~ Rotholzbaum *m (bot)* sappan caesalpinia, Caesalpinia sappan

~ **Tintenbaum** *m* kidney bean of Malacca, Semecarpus anacardium
Ostindisches Satin[holz] *n* satinwood *(esp. from Chloroxylon swietenia)*
Ostiolum *n (bot, zoo)* ostiole
Ostitis *f (vet)* osteitis
Ostküstenfieber *n s.* Ostafrikanisches Küstenfieber
Östlicher Erdbeerbaum *m* Greek strawberry tree, Arbutus andrachne
Östradiol *n* oestradiol *(sex hormone)*
Östriol *n* oestriol *(sex hormone)*
östrisch oestrous
östrogen oestrogenic
Östrogen *n* oestrogen, follicular hormone
~/pflanzliches plant oestrogen, phytoestrogen
Östrogenexkretion *f* oestrogen excretion
Östrogenrezeptor *m* oestrogen receptor
Östrogensekretion *f* oestrogen secretion
Östrogensynthese *f* oestrogen synthesis
Östron *n* oestrone *(follicular hormone)*
Östrophilin *n* oestrogen receptor
Östrose *f (vet)* oestrosis *(of sheep, caused by Oestrus ovis)*
Östrus *m* oestrus, oestrum
Östrusrate *f* oestrus rate
Oszillation *f (ecol)* oscillation
OT *s.* Ökoton
Otakariasis *f s.* Otodektesräude
OTC *s.* Oxytetracyclin
Otholith *m s.* Otokonie
Otitis *f (vet)* otitis
Otodektesräude *f (vet)* ear mange
Otokonie *f (zoo)* statolith, otolith
Otosklerose *f (vet)* ostosclerosis
Otoskop *n (vet)* otoscope
Otoskopie *f (vet)* otoscopy
Otter *m* otter *(a mammal of the genus Lutra)*
Otter *f* viper, adder *(a snake of the family Viperidae)*
Otter Hound *m* otter hound (dog) *(breed)*
Otterfell *n* otter
Otterpelz *m* otter
Otterschaf *n (vet)* Ancon sheep
Ottomotor *m* Otto (petrol) engine
Ouabain *n* ouabain *(glycoside)*
Ovalbumin *n* ovalbumin, egg albumen (albumin)
ovalblättrig *(bot)* oval-leaved, ovalifolious, ovatifolious
Ovalkrone *f* oval head (crown) *(of a tree)*
Ovar *n (zoo)* ovary, ovarium; *(bot)* gynobase, gynopodium
ovarial *(zoo)* ovarian, ovarial
Ovarialgravidität *f* ovarian pregnancy
Ovarialhormon *n* ovarian hormone
Ovarialzyklus *m* ovarian (ovulatory) cycle
Ovarialzyste *f (vet)* ovarian cyst
Ovarektomie *f (vet)* ovariectomy, oophorectomy, ovariotomy

ovarektomieren *(vet)* to ovariectomize, to spay, to doctor, *(Am)* to alter
Ovariektomie *f s.* Ovarektomie
Ovariotestis *m* ovotestis
Ovariotomie *f s.* Ovarektomie
Ovariozele *f (vet)* ovariocele
Ovarium *n s.* Ovar
Overheadförderer *m* overhead conveyor
Ovidukt *m s.* Eileiter
oviduktal oviductal, oviducal
oviger ovigerous
ovin ovine, ovile
Ovination *f (vet)* ovination
ovipar *(zoo)* oviparous
Oviparie *f (ent)* oviparity
Ovipositor *m (ent)* ovipositor, egg-laying mechanism
ovizid ovicidal
Ovizid *n* ovicide, egg killer
Ovoglobulin *n* ovoglobulin *(egg protein fraction)*
ovoid ovoid[al]
Ovomucin *n* ovomucin *(glycoproteid, egg protein fraction)*
Ovomucoid *n* ovomucoid *(glycoproteid, egg protein fraction)*
Ovoskop *n* egg candler (candling plant)
Ovotestis *m* ovotestis
Ovotransferrin *n* conalbumin *(glycoproteid, egg protein fraction)*
ovovivipar *(zoo)* ovoviviparous
Ovoviviparie *f* ovoviviparity, ovoviviparousness
Ovozyt *m* oocyte, ovocyte, egg cell
Ovulation *f* ovulation, ovulatory surge, follicle rupture
~/parazyklische paracyclic ovulation
Ovulationsgröße *f* ovulation rate
Ovulationshormon *n* ovulation hormone
Ovulationsinduktion *f* ovulation induction
Ovulationssynchronisation *f* ovulation synchronization
ovulieren to ovulate
~/erneut to superovulate
Ovulum *n (bot)* ovulum, seed bud
Ovum *n* ovum, egg
ox *s.* Oxisol
Oxacillin *n* oxacillin *(antibiotic)*
Oxadiazon *n* oxadiazon *(herbicide)*
Oxadixyl *n* oxadixyl *(fungicide)*
Oxalaldehydsäure *f* glyoxylic (oxoethanoic) acid
Oxalat *n* oxalate
Oxalbernsteinsäure *f* oxalosuccinic acid
Oxalessigsäure *f* oxal[o]acetic acid
Oxalis-Kiefernwald *m* shamrock pinery
Oxalsäure *f* oxalic (ethanedioic) acid
Oxalsäurevergiftung *f (vet)* oxalic poisoning
Oxalurie *f (vet)* oxaluria
Oxamniquin *n* oxamniquine *(anthelminthic)*
Oxamyl *n* oxamyl *(insecticide, nematicide)*
Oxantel *n* oxantel *(anthelminthic)*

Oxathiin

Oxathiin *n* oxathiin *(growth regulator)*
Oxelbeere *f* Swedish beam-tree, Swedish whitebeam, Sorbus intermedia
Oxfendazol *n* oxfendazole *(anthelminthic)*
Oxford Down *n* Oxford Down *(sheep breed)*
Oxhoft *n* hogshead *(old liquid measure e.g. for wine; 1 hogshead = 286,4 l in UK, 238,4 l in USA)*
Oxhoftfaß *n* hogshead *(containing from 300 to 600 litres)*
Oxibendazol *n* oxibendazole *(anthelminthic, fungicide)*
oxibiontisch oxybiotic, aerobic
Oxibiose *f* oxybiosis, aerobiosis
Oxid *n* oxide
Oxidans *n* oxidant, oxidizing agent
Oxidase *f* oxidase *(enzyme)*
~/**achromatische** achromatic oxidase
Oxidation *f* oxidation
~/**biologische** biological oxidation
Oxidationsgärung *f* oxybiosis
Oxidationsgraben *m*, **Oxidationskanal** *m* oxidation ditch *(sewage purification)*
oxidationshemmend antioxidant
Oxidationsmittel *n s.* Oxidans
Oxidationsteich *m* oxidation pond, sewage (waste-water) pond
Oxidationstrübung *f* oxidation haze *(of beer)*
oxidativ oxidative
Oxidoreductase *f* oxidoreductase, oxidase *(enzyme)*
Oxim *n* oxime *(organic nitrogen compound)*
Oximcarbamat *n* oximecarbamate *(nematicide)*
Oxin-Kupfer *n* oxine-copper *(fungicide)*
Oxiran *n* ethylene oxide *(fumigant)*
Oxisol *m (Am, soil)* oxisol, ox, latosol
Oxoglutarsäure *f*, **2-Oxopentandisäure** *f* oxoglutaric (ketoglutaric) acid, oxopentanedioic acid
17-Oxosteroid *n* 17-ketosteroid
OXT *s.* Oxytocin
Oxycarboxin *n* oxycarboxin *n (fungicide)*
Oxyclozanid *n* oxyclozanide *(anthelminthic)*
Oxydation *f s.* Oxidation
Oxyfluorfen *n* oxyfluorfen *(herbicide)*
Oxygenase *f* oxygenase *(enzyme)*
Oxyhämoglobin *n* oxyhaemoglobin
Oxymyoglobin *n* oxymyoglobin
oxyphil acidophilic, acidophilous, oxyphil[e]
Oxytetracyclin *n* oxytetracycline, OTC, terramycin *(antibiotic)*
Oxytocin *n* oxytocin *(hormone)*
Oxytocinausschüttung *f* oxytocin discharge
Oxyuriasis *f*, **Oxyuridose** *f (vet)* oxyuriasis *(caused by nematodes of family Oxyuridae)*
Ozelot *m* ocelot, Felis (Leopardus) pardalis
Ozelotfell *n* ocelot
Ozon *n(m)* ozone • **[Sauerstoff] in ~ umwandeln** to ozonize
Ozonempfindlichkeit *f* ozone sensitivity

ozonisieren 1. to ozonize, to convert into ozone; 2. to ozonize, to treat with ozone
Ozonschaden *m (phyt)* ozone damage (injury)
Ozonschicht *f* ozone layer, ozonosphere

P

P *s.* 1. Phosphor; 2. Parentalgeneration; 3. Probabilität f; 4. Index/panmiktischer; 5. Pekoe
paarblumig geminiflorous
paaren to mate, to pair, to breed
~/**nichtverwandte Individuen** to outbreed
~/**sich** to mate, to pair, to conjugate; to synapse *(homologous chromosomes)*
~/**verwandte Individuen** to inbreed
Paarhufer *m* cloven-hoofed animal, even-toed animal (ungulate), artiodactyl[e] *(order Artiodactyla)*
paarhufig cloven-hoofed, even-toed, artiodactyl[ous], bisulcate
paarig conjugate
~ **gefiedert** *(bot)* even pinnate[d], paripinnate[d]
Paarung *f* mating, pairing, coupling; conjugation *(e.g. of chromosomes)*
~ **ähnlicher Individuen** assortative mating
~/**assortative** assortative mating
~/**diallele** diallel cross[ing]
~ **homologer Chromosomen** synapsis, syndesis
~/**natürliche** natural mating
~ **nichtverwandter Individuen** outbreeding, outcrossing
~ **unähnlicher Individuen** disassortative mating
~ **verwandter Individuen** inbreeding
~/**zu verbesserten Eigenschaften führende** nick
Paarungsflug *m (api)* mating (nuptial) flight
Paarungskombination *f* mating combination
Paarungskonkurrenz *f* mating competition
Paarungspartner *m* mate
Paarungsreflex *m* mating (copulatory) reflex
Paarungssystem *n* mating system
Paarungsverhalten *n* mating (courtship, oestrous) behaviour
Paarungszeit *f* mating season, pairing season (time)
PAB *s.* Aminobenzoesäure
Pace *f* pace *(esp. an ambling or racking gait of a horse)*
Pacemaker *m* pace-maker, pace-setter *(racing)*
Pacer *m* pacer, pacing horse
Pacerrennen *n* pacing
Pacht *f* tenancy, lease
Pachtbauer *m* tenant farmer, *(Am)* sharecropper
Pachtbesitz *m* tenancy
Pachtdauer *f* tenancy
pachten to [take on] lease, to rent
Pächter *m* tenant, lessee
Pachtgarten *m* allotment [garden]
Pachtgut *n* agricultural holding
Pachtland *n* rented (leased) land, lease

Pachtverhältnis *n* tenancy, lease
Pachtvertrag *m* tenancy contract (agreement), lease
Pachtwirtschaft *f* tenant farm, croft
Pachyakrie *f (vet)* acromegaly
Pachymeningitis *f (vet)* pachymeningitis
Pachytän *n* pachytene *(meiotic stage)*
Pacini-Körperchen *n* Pacinian corpuscle *(animal physiology)*
Packblatt *n* [für Obst] [fruit] tray
Packhalle *f* packing house (shed, station)
Packlage *f* sub-base reinforcement, hard core *(road construction)*
Packleinen *n* packing cloth, burlap
Packpferd *n* pack horse
Packsattel *m* pack-saddle
Packtier *n* pack-animal
Paclobutrazol *n* paclobutrazol *(growth regulator)*
Paddelförderer *m* paddle elevator
Paddelrührwerk *n* paddle mixer
Paddock *m* paddock
Paddy *m* paddy [rice], padi
Pädogenese *f (ent)* paedogenesis
pädogenetisch *(ent)* paedogenetic
Padouk[holz] *n* padouk *(timber from Pterocarpus spp.)*
Padutin *n* kallikrein *(enzyme)*
PaGFV *s.* Pastinakengelbfleckenvirus
Pagodenbaum *m* Japanese pagoda tree, umbrella-tree, Sophora japonica
Pagodenprimel *f* candelabra primula *(group of cultivars)*
Pailette *f* straw *(for semen conservation)*
paketieren to package
Pako *m* alpaca, Lama [guanicoe f.] pacos
PAL *s.* Phenylalaninammoniumlyase
Paläopädologie *f* palaeopedology
Palasokino *n* Bengal kino *(esp. from Butea monosperma)*
Palästinalimette *f* common (sour) lime, Citrus aurantiifolia
Palästinensische Hühnerseuche *f* avian cell inclusion disease
Palatoschisis *f (vet)* cleft palate, fissured palate
Palatum *n* palate *(animal anatomy)*
Palea *f (bot)* palea
~ **inferior** inner palea
Palerbse *f* shelling (smooth-seeded) pea, Pisum sativum convar. sativum
Palette *f* pallet
~ **zum Ballenpflanzentransport** [trans]plant box
Paletten[hub]gabel *f* pallet fork
Palettenlagerung *f* box storage *(e.g. of potatoes)*
Palettenstapler *m* pallet stacker
Palettenwagen *m* pallet truck (wagon)
Palisadenparenchym *n (bot)* palisade parenchyma
Palisadenschicht *f (bot)* palisade layer

Palisadenwurm *m* palisade worm, strongyle *(family Strongylidae)*
Palisadenwurmbefall *m (vet)* strongylosis
Palisadenzelle *f (bot)* palisade cell
Palisanderholz *n* rosewood *(from Dalbergia nigra)*
Pallor *m (vet)* pallor, paleness
palmar palmar
Palmbaum *m s.* Palme
Palmblatt *n* palm leaf
Palme *f* palm[-tree] *(family Palmae)*
Palmenbast *m* bass, bast
Palmenhain *m* palm grove
Palmenhaus *n* palm house
Palmensaft *m* palm-sap
Palmenstärke *f*, **Palmenstärkemehl** *n* sago [flour]
Palmentopf *m* palm pot
palmenzweigähnlich palmate[d]
Palmette *f* palmette *(form of orchard trees)*
Palmettopalme *f* [cabbage] palmetto, Sabal palmetto
Palmfarn *m (bot)* cycad *(genus Cycas)*
Palmhonig *m* palm-honey
Palmitat *n* palmitate
Palmitin *n* palmitin
Palmitinsäure *f* palmitic (hexadecanoic) acid *(fatty acid)*
Palmitinsäureglycerylester *m* palmitin
Palmitoyl-Coenzym-A-Hydrolase *f* palmitoyl coenzyme A hydrolase *(enzyme)*
Palmkern *m* palm kernel
Palmkernöl *n* palm kernel (nut) oil
Palmkohl *m* palm cabbage, Brassica oleracea var. palmifolia
Palmlilie *f (bot)* yucca *(genus Yucca)*
Palmöl *n* palm[-husk] oil
Palmwein *m* palm wine
Palmyrapalme *f* palmyra [palm], brab[-tree], borassus [palm], pummelo, Citrus maxima
Palmzucker *m* palm sugar
Palomino[pferd] *n* palomino *(horse breed)*
palpabel *(vet)* palpable
Palpation *f (vet)* palpation
~/**rektale** rectal palpation
palpieren to palpate *(e.g. for pregnancy detection)*
Palpus *m (zoo)* palp[us]
Palustrin *n* palustrin *(alkaloid)*
Palygorskit *m* palygorskite *(clay mineral)*
Palynologie *f* palynology, pollen analysis
Pampa *f* pampas, pampa
Pampaboden *m* pampas soil
Pampasgras *n* pampas-grass, Cortaderia selloana
Pampelmuse *f* shaddock
Pampelmusenbaum *m* shaddock, pompelmous, pom[p]elo, pummelo, Citrus maxima
PaMV *s.* Pastinakenmosaikvirus
PAN *s.* Peroxiacetylnitrat
Panagglutinin *n* panagglutinin
Panamakautschuk *m* Castilla rubber *(from Castilla elastica)*

Panamakrankheit

Panamakrankheit f Panama disease (of banana, caused by Fusarium oxysporum f. sp. cubense)
Panamapalme f (bot) toquilla, Carludovica palmata
Panamapalmfaser f toquilla
Panaritium n (vet) panaritium
Pandanuspalme f textile (thatch) screw pine, Pandanus tectorius
Pandemie f (vet) panzooty, pandemia
Pangolagras n pangola grass, Digitaria decumbens
Pangonyl n paromomycin (antibiotic)
Panhämozytopenie f (vet) pancytopenia
Panik f stampede, breakaway (animal behaviour)
Pankreas n pancreas
Pankreasamylase f pancreatic amylase, amylopsin (enzyme)
Pankreasentzündung f (vet) pancreatitis
Pankreashormon n pancreatic hormone
Pankreasinseln fpl pancreas islets
Pankreaslipase f pancreatic lipase, steapsin (enzyme)
Pankreasnekrose f der Salmoniden/infektiöse infectious pancreatitis of trouts
Pankreaspeptidase f E elastase (enzyme)
Pankreaspolypeptid n pancreatic polypeptide
Pankreasproteinase f pancreatic proteinase (enzyme)
Pankreassaft m pancreatic juice
Pankreatektomie f (vet) pancreatectomy
Pankreatin n pancreatin (enzyme)
Pankreatitis f (vet) pancreatitis
Pankreopathie f (vet) pancreatic disease
Pankreozymin n pancreozymin (hormone)
Panleukopenie f (vet) panleucopenia
~ der Katze [feline] panleucopenia, cat distemper (enteritis), feline infectious [viral] enteritis
panmiktisch (gen) panmictic
Panmixie f panmixia, panmixis, random mating
Pannonische Wicke f Hungarian vetch, Vicia pannonica
Pannonischer Klee m Hungarian clover, Trifolium pannonicum
Panophthalmie f (vet) panophthalmia
panschen s. verschneiden 3.
Pansen m rumen, paunch, farding bag, first stomach (of ruminants) • **in den ~ hinein** intraruminal
~/künstlicher artificial rumen
Pansenazidose f (vet) rumen acidosis, acid indigestion
Pansenbakterien npl rumen flora
Pansenbakterium n rumen bacterium
Pansenbreibissen m cud, quid
Pansenegel m barrel fluke (genus Paramphistomum)
Pansenegelkrankheit f (vet) paramphistomatosis
Pansenepithel n rumen epithelium
Pansenfassungsvermögen n rumen capacity
Pansenfauna f rumen fauna • **die ~ zerstören** to defaunate

Pansenfermentation f rumen fermentation
Pansenflora f rumen flora
Pansenflüssigkeit f rumen fluid (liquor)
Pansengärgas n rumen gas
Pansengärung f rumen fermentation
Pansengas n rumen gas
Panseninhalt m rumen content
Pansenlähmung f (vet) indigestion
Pansenmetabolismus m rumen metabolism
Pansenmikrofauna f rumen microfauna
Pansenmikroflora f rumen microflora
Pansenmikroorganismus m rumen micro-organism
Pansenmotorik f rumen motility
Pansenprotozoen npl rumen protozoa
Pansensaft m rumen fluid (liquor)
Pansenschleimhaut f rumen mucosa
Pansenschleimhautentzündung f (vet) rumenitis
Pansenschnitt m (vet) rumenotomy
Pansentätigkeit f ruminal activity • **vor Eintreten der ~** preruminant
Pansenumsatz m rumen turnover
pansenverdaulich rumen-digestible
Pansenverdauung f rumen digestion
Pansenwärmeerzeugung f ruminal heat production
Pantherpilz m panther agaric (amanita), Amanita pantherina
Pantoffelblume f slipperwort, pocket-book plant, calceolaria (genus Calceolaria)
Pantoffelstrauch m jew-bush, Pedilanthus tithymaloides
pantophag pantophagous, omnivorous
Pantophage m pantophagist, omnivore
Pantophagie f pantophagy, omnivorousness
Pantothenat n pantothenate
Pantothensäure f pantothenic acid (B vitamin)
Panuveitis f (vet) iridochoroiditis
Panzerbeere f pepo
Panzerkiefer f Balkan pine, Pinus heldreichii
Panzootie f (vet) panzooty, pandemia
panzootisch panzootic
Panzytopenie f (vet) pancytopenia
Päonie f paeony, peony (genus Paeonia)
Papageienfeder f (bot) parrot's-feather, Myriophyllum brasiliense (aquaticum)
Papageienkrankheit f (vet) ornithosis, psittacosis (caused by Chlamydia psittaci)
Papageitulpe f parrot tulip (group of cultivars)
Papain n papain (enzyme)
Papaubaum m (Am, bot) papaw, pawpaw, Asimina triloba
Papaverin n papaverin[e] (alkaloid)
Papawbaum m s. Papaubaum
Papaya f (bot) common papaw, papaya, Carica papaya
Papel f (vet) papule
papierartig (bot) chartaceous

Papierbirke *f* paper (canoe, white) birch, Betula papyrifera
Papierblume *f (bot)* 1. xeranthemum *(genus Xeranthemum)*; 2. immortelle, Xerantheum annuum
Papierchromatographie *f* paper chromatography
Papierelektrophorese *f* paper electrophoresis
Papierholz *n* pulpwood, paper wood
Papierknöpfchen *n (bot)* winged everlasting, Ammobium alatum
Papiermaulbeerbaum *m* paper-mulberry [tree], Broussonetia papyrifera
Papiermulch *m* paper mulch
Papierrindenahorn *m* paperbark maple, Acer griseum
Papiersack *m* paper bag
Papiertopf *m* paper pot *(for plantlet raising)*
Papiertopfnetz *n* paper pot net
Papiertopfpflanze *f* paper pot plant
Papilla *f s.* Papille
papillar, papillär papillary, papillate, papillose
Papille *f (bot, zoo)* papilla
Papillom *n (vet)* papilloma
Papillomatose *f (vet)* papillomatosis
Papillomvirus *n* papilloma virus
Papillon *m* papillon *(dog breed)*
Pappel *f* poplar *(genus Populus)*
~ "**Balm-of-Gilead**" balm of Gilead, Populus gileadensis
Pappelblattkäfer *m* poplar leaf beetle, Melasoma (Chrysomela) populi
Pappelholz *n* poplar
Pappelmosaikvirus *n* poplar mosaic virus, PoMV
Pappelrost *m* poplar tree rust *(caused by Melampsora populnea)*
Pappelspinner *m* willow moth, Leucoma (Stilpnotia) salicis
Pappelspringrüßler *m (ent)* poplar (willow) leafminer, Rhynchaenus (Orchestes) populi
Pappelwollaus *f* poplar (lettuce root) aphid, Pemphigus bursarius
Papptopf *m* cardboard pot
Pappus *m (bot)* pappus • **mit einem ~ versehen** pappose, pappous
Paprika *m* 1. [Spanish] pepper, capsicum *(genus Capsicum)*; 2. [common] red pepper, pepper, paprika, Capsicum annuum; 3. hot pepper *(capsaicin-rich cultivars of Capsicum annuum)*; 4. paprika *(condiment)*
~/**edelsüßer** *s.* ~/milder
~/**halbscharfer** semihot pepper
~/**milder** sweet pepper
Paprikaadernbänderungsvirus *n* pepper vein banding virus, PVBV
Paprikaadernscheckungsvirus *n* pepper veinal mottle virus, PeVeMoV, PVMV
Paprikapilz *m (bot)* rufous milk-cap, Lactarius rufus

Paprikascheckungsvirus *n* pepper mottle virus, PMV
Paprikaschote *f* pepper pod, capsicum, red (Spanish) pepper, paprika
~/**gelbe** yellow pepper
Papua-Muskatnuß *m* Papua (Macassar) nutmeg, Myristica argentea
Papula *f (vet)* papule
Papyrus *n* papyrus, paper reed
Papyrusstaude *f* papyrus, [Egyptian] paper reed, bulrush, Cyperus papyrus
PAR *s.* Strahlung/photosynthetische aktive
Parabiose *f* parabiosis
parabiotisch parabiotic
Parabraunerde *f* leached brown soil, parabraunerde, grey brown podzolic soil
Paracasein *n* paracasein
Paracladium *n (bot)* paraclade
Paradepferd *n* parade horse
Paradeschritt *m* goose-stepping *(of pigs due to pantothenic acid deficiency)*
Paradichlorbenzol *n* paradichlorobenzene, PDB *(insecticide, disinfectant)*
Paradiesapfel *m* paradise apple, Malus sylvestris ssp. mitis var. paradisiaca
Paradiesfeigenbaum *m (bot)* plantain, Musa x paradisiaca (sapientum)
Paradieskörner *npl* grains of Paradise *(seed capsules from Aframomum melegueta)*
Paradieskörnerpflanze *f* grains of Paradise, Guinea grains, alligator pepper, Aframomum melegueta
Paradiesvogelblume *f* bird-of paradise [flower], Strelitzia reginae
Paraffin *n* paraffin, wax
Paraffinkohlenwasserstoff *m* alkane, paraffin (saturated) hydrocarbon
Parafilariose *f (vet)* parafilariosis *(of horses, caused by Parafilaria multipapillosa)*
Paraformaldehyd *m* paraformaldehyde *(disinfectant)*
Paragonimose *f (vet)* paragonimiasis *(caused by Paragonimus spp.)*
Parahormon *n* parahormone
Parainfluenza *f (vet)* parainfluenza
Parainfluenza-3-Virusinfektion *f* **des Rindes** crowding disease
Parakautschukbaum *m* 1. hevea *(genus Hevea)*; 2. [Brazilian] rubber tree, caoutchouc tree, seringa, Hevea brasiliensis
Parakeratose *f (vet)* parakeratosis, swine dermatosis *(due to zinc deficiency)*
Parallaxenunterschied *m* parallax difference *(surveying)*
Parallelbetrieb *m* parallel operation *(e.g. in harvesting)*
Paralleldränung *f* parallel system of drainage
Parallelentrinder *m* bag (pocket) barker

Parallelmelkstand

Parallelmelkstand *m* abreast [milking] parlour, walk-through [milking] parlour
Parallelmutation *f* parallel mutation
parallelnervig *(bot)* parallel-veined
Parallelogramm-Aufhängung *f* parallelogram-type suspension
Parallelotropismus *m (bot)* orthotropism
Parallelprobe *f* duplicate sample
Parallelresistenz *f* cross-resistance
Parallelvariation *f* parallel variation *(plant breeding)*
Paralyse *f (vet)* paralysis, palsy
~/**Chasteksche** Chastek paralysis
~ **der Bienen/akute** acute bee paralysis *(virosis)*
~ **der Bienen/chronische** chronic bee paralysis *(virosis)*
paralytisch *(vet)* paralytic
Parameter *m* **der Grundgesamtheit** population parameter
parametrisch parametric
Paramo *m* paramo *(treeless high plateau in tropical South America)*
Paramorphin *n* thebaine *(alkaloid)*
Paramphistomose *f (vet)* paramphistomatosis
Paramyxovirus *n* paramyxovirus
paranasal paranasal
Paranephritis *f (vet)* paranephritis
Paranuß *f* 1. Brazil-nut; 2. *s.* Paranußbaum
Paranußbaum *m* Brazil-nut [tree], almendron, Bertholletia excelsa
Parapflug *m* paraplough
Paraphimose *f (vet)* paraphimosis
Paraphyse *f* paraphysis *(of fungal fruit-bodies)*
Paraplasma *n* paraplasm, alloplasm
paraplasmatisch paraplasm[at]ic, alloplasm[at]ic
Paraplegie *f (vet)* paraplegia
Paraquat *n* paraquat *(herbicide)*
Pararauschbrand *m (vet)* braxy *(caused by Clostridium septicum)* • **an** ~ **erkrankt** braxy
Pararendzina *f (soil)* pararendzina
Parasexualität *f* parasexuality
parasexuell parasexual
Parasit *m* parasite
~/**fakultativer** facultative parasite
~/**obligater** obligate parasite
~/**permanenter** permanent parasite
~/**pilzlicher** mycoparasite, parasitic fungus
Parasitämie *f* parasitaemia
parasitär parasitic[al]
Parasitenbefall *m* parasite infestation
Parasitenbekämpfung *f* parasite control
parasitenfrei clean
Parasitenkunde *f* parasitology
Parasitenprävention *f*, **Parasitenvorbeuge** *f* parasite prevention
parasitieren to parasitize
Parasitierung *f* parasitization
parasitisch parasitic[al]
Parasitismus *m* parasitism

parasitoid parasitoid
Parasitoide *m* parasitoid
Parasitoidismus *m* parasitoidism
Parasitologie *f* parasitology
Parasitose *f* parasitosis, parasitic disease
Parasol[pilz] *m* parasol mushroom, Macrolepiota procera
Parasterilität *f* parasterility
Parastichie *f (bot)* parastichy
Parasympath[ik]olytikum *n (vet)* parasympatholytic [agent]
Parasympath[ik]omimetikum *n (vet)* parasympathomimetic [agent]
Parathion[-ethyl] *n* [ethyl-]parathion, thiophos *(insecticide, acaricide)*
Parathion-methyl *n* parathion-methyl *(insecticide, acaricide)*
Parathormon *n* parathormone, parathyrin, parathyroid hormone, PTH
parathyreoid parathyroid
Parathyroidea *f* parathyroid [gland]
Parathyreoidektomie *f (vet)* parathyroidectomy
Parathyrin *n s.* Parathormon
paratracheal *(bot)* paratracheal
Paratuberkulose *f (vet)* paratuberculosis, chronic specific enteritis, Johne's disease *(caused by Mycobacterium paratuberculosis)*
Paratyphoidkrankheit *f* **des Geflügels** paratyphoid infection of poultry
Paratyphus *m (vet)* paratyphoid, salmonellosis, keel disease
Paravariation *f (gen)* modification
Parazentese *f (vet)* paracentesis
Parbendazol *n* parbendazole *(anthelminthic)*
Pärchenegel *m* bilharzia worm, schistosome *(genus Schistosoma)*
Pärchenegelkrankheit *f (vet)* schistosomiasis
Pärchenkreuzung *f* brother-sister crossing *(plant breeding)*
Pardelkatze *f* ocelot, Felis (Leopardus) pardalis
Parenchym[gewebe] *n (bot, zoo)* parenchyma [tissue], soft tissue, pith
~/**diffus-aggregiertes** diffuse-zonate parenchyma, diffuse-in-aggregate parenchyma
~/**diffuses** diffuse parenchyma
Parenchymscheide *f* parenchyma sheath
Parenchymstrang *m* parenchyma strand
Parenchymzelle *f* parenchyma cell
Parentalgeneration *f* parental generation
Parese *f (vet)* paresis
~/**gutartige enzootische** Teschen disease *(virosis of pigs)*
~/**spastische** spastic paresis
Parforcejagd *f* hunt, coursing • ~ **betreiben** to hunt, to follow the hounds
Parfümöl *n* perfume oil
Parfümpflanze *f* perfume plant
parieren to halt *(a horse)*
Parimol *n* parimol *(fungicide)*

Pariser Grün *n* Paris green, copper acetoarsenite *(insecticide, anthelminthic)*
Park *m* park
~/öffentlicher public park
~/städtischer urban park
Parkanlage *f*/**ländliche** countryside park
Parkgelände *n* parkland
Parklandschaft *f* park-like landscape
Parkrose *f* bush rose *(comprehensive term)*
Parkstreifen *m* passing place *(road construction)*
Parkwaldsavanne *f* parkland savanna[h]
Parmäne *f* pearmain *(apple cultivar)*
Parmaveilchen *n* Parma violet, Viola suavis
Parmesan[käse] *m* Parmesan [cheese]
Paromomycin *n* paromomycin *(antibiotic)*
Parotis *f* parotid [gland] *(animal anatomy)*
Parotitis *f (vet)* parotitis
Parrlachs *m* parr, fingerling
Pars *f* **longa glandis** long part of glans *(anatomy of carnivores)*
Parteneser [Rind] *n* Parthenay *(cattle breed)*
Parthenogenese *f* parthenogenesis, virgin birth
~/männliche androgenesis
~/zyklische heterogony
parthenogenetisch parthenogenetic, parthenogenid
parthenokarp *(bot)* parthenocarpic
Parthenokarpie *f (bot)* parthenocarpy
Parthenospore *f (bot)* parthenospore
Partialdruck *m* partial pressure
Partialvelum *n* partial veil *(of gill fungi)*
Parvovirose *f* **der Katze** *s.* Panleukopenie der Katze
Parvovirus *n* **der Gänse** goose parvovirus
Parzelle *f* parcel, plot, lot
Parzellenboden *m* plot soil
Parzellendreschmaschine *f* parcel thresher
Parzellendrillmaschine *f* plot drill
Parzellenetikett *n* plot label
Parzellenfeldversuch *m* field-plot experiment, plot trial
Parzellenmähdrescher *m* parcel thresher, plot harvester, plot combine [harvester]
Parzellensämaschine *f* plot seeder
Parzellenspritzmaschine *f* plot sprayer
Parzellensprüher *m* plot sprayer
Parzellenversuch *m s.* Parzellenfeldversuch
parzellieren to parcel, to lot [out]
Pasaniapilz *m* pasania (shiitake) mushroom, Japanese black mushroom, Lentinus edodes
Paspalum-Taumeln *n* paspalum staggers *(of cattle, caused by Claviceps paspali)*
Paß *m s.* Paßgang
Passagerate *f* rate of passage *(animal nutrition)*
Passerpaarung *f* assortative mating *(animal breeding)*
Paßgang *m* amble, pace, running walk *(horse's gait)* • **im ~** at a jog • **im ~ gehen** to amble

~/gebrochener rack, single trot (foot) • **in gebrochenem ~ gehen** to rack
Paßgänger *m* ambler, pacer
Passionsblume *f* passion-flower *(genus Passiflora)*
Passionsblumenverholzungsvirus *n* passion-fruit woodiness virus
Passionsfrucht *f* passion-fruit *(of Passiflora spp.)*
Paßpunkt *m* pass (wing) point, minor control point *(ground survey)*
Pasteureffekt *m* Pasteur effect *(plant physiology)*
Pasteurellose *f (vet)* pasteurellosis, haemorrhagic septicaemia
Pasteurisation *f* pasteurization
Pasteurisator *m* pasteurizer
pasteurisieren to pasteurize
Pasteurisierung *f* pasteurizing, pasteurization
Pasteurisierungsanlage *f* pasteurizing plant
Pasteurisierungsapparat *m* pasteurizer
Pastinak *m*, **Pastinake** *f* parsnip, Pastinaca sativa
Pastinakengelbfleckenvirus *n* parsnip yellow fleck virus
Pastinakenmosaikvirus *n* parsnip mosaic virus
Pastinakenscheckungsvirus *n* parsnip mottle virus
PaSV *s.* Pastinakenscheckungsvirus
Patella *f* patella, kneecap, knee-pan
Patellaluxation *f (vet)* patella luxation
Patellar[sehnen]reflex *m* patellar reflex
Patentkali *n* sulphate of potash-magnesia *(fertilizer)*
Paternität *f* paternity
Paternostererbse *f* jequirity, rosary pea, crab-eyes, lucky bean, Indian liquorice, Abrus precatorius
Paternosterstrauch *m* [European] bladdernut, Staphylea pinnata
Pathobiologie *f s.* Pathologie
pathogen pathogenic, pathogenous
Pathogen *n* pathogen
~/monozyklisches *(phyt)* monocyclic pathogen
~/pilzliches fungal pathogen
Pathogenese *f* pathogenesis
pathogenetisch pathogenetic
pathogenfrei pathogen-free
~/spezifisch specific pathogen-free, SPF
Pathogenität *f* pathogen[ic]ity
Pathologie *f* pathology, pathobiology
pathologisch pathologic[al]
Pathometabolismus *m* pathometabolismus
Pathomycin *n* sisomicin *(antibiotic)*
Pathophysiologie *f* pathophysiology
Pathosystem *n (ecol)* pathosystem
Pathothesaurose *f (vet)* storage disease
Pathotoxin *n (phyt)* pathotoxin
Pathotyp *m* pathotype
~/vertikaler *(phyt)* pathovar
Patisson[kürbis] *m* scalloped squash, Cucurbita pepo convar. patissonia

Patnareis

Patnareis *m* Patna rice *(variety of long-grain rice)*
patroklin patroclinal, patroclinous
Patroklinie *f* patrocliny *(breeding)*
Patrone *f* cartridge
Patronenfilter *n* cartridge filter
Patronenhülse *f* cartridge-case
Patschuli *n* patchouli, patchouly *(fragrance)*
Patschulipflanze *f (bot)* patchouli, patchouly, Pogostemon cablin
Patulin *n* patulin *(mycotoxin)*
Paulownie *f (bot)* 1. paulownia *(genus Paulownia)*; 2. paulownia, Paulownia tomentosa
Pazifiklachs *m* salmon *(genus Oncorhynchus)*
PC, Pc *s.* Plastocyanin
PCNB *s.* Pentachlornitrobenzen
PCP *s.* Pentachlorphenol
Pebrine *f* pebrine [disease] *(of silkworms, caused by Nosema bombycis)*
Pebulate *n* pebulate *(herbicide)*
Pech *n* pitch
Pechkiefer *f* pitch-pine, Pinus rigida
Pechlarse *f s.* Pechriß
Pechnelke *f (bot)* German catchfly, Lychnis viscaria ssp. viscaria
Pechöl *n* tar (resin) oil
Pechpinie *f* loblolly pine, Pinus taeda
Pechriß *m* pitch (resin) seam, pitch shake (streak) *(timber defect)*
Pechsiederei *f* tar works
Pectase *f* pectinesterase *(enzyme)*
Pectin *n* pectin *(polysaccharide)*
Pedigree *n* pedigree
Pedigreeanalyse *f* pedigree analysis
Pedigreezüchter *m* pedigree breeder
Pedigreezüchtung *f* pedigree breeding (selection, method)
Pedikulose *f* pediculosis
Pedobiologie *f* pedobiology, soil biology
pedobiologisch soil-biological
Pedochore *f* soil mosaic
Pedogenese *f* pedogenesis, soil development (genesis)
pedogenetisch pedogenic
Pedologe *m* pedologist, soil scientist
Pedologie *f* pedology, soil science
pedologisch pedologic[al]
Pedon *m* pedon, soil body
Pedosequenz *f* pedosequence
Pedosphäre *f* pedosphere
Pedotechnik *f* pedotechnique
Pedozoologie *f* pedozoology, soil zoology
Pedunculus *m (zoo)* peduncle
Pegel *m* level
Peileinrichtung *f eines Feuerwachturmes (forest)* fire-finder
Peitsche *f* whip, lash
peitschen to whip, to flog
peitschenartig, peitschenförmig *(bot, zoo)* flagellar, flagelliform

Peitschengriff *m* crop
Peitschenhieb *m* lash
Peitschenkaktus *m* rat-tail cactus, Aporocactus (Cereus) flagelliformis
Peitschenstiel *m* crop
Peitschenstielerkrankung *f* whip tail *(of cabbage species due to molybdenum deficiency)*
Peitschenwurm *m* whipworm *(genus Trichuris)*
Peitschenwurmbefall *m (vet)* trichuriasis, trichocephaliasis
Peitscher *m* whip, whipper *(tree)*
Pekannuß *f* pecan[-nut]
Pekannußbaum *m* pecan[-nut], Carya illinoensis (pecan)
Pekingente *f* [White] Peking duck *(breed)*
Pekingpalasthund *m* Pekingese [dog], peke, Pekinese *(breed)*
Pekoe *m* pekoe *(kind of tea)*
Pektat *n* pectate
Pektatlyase *f*, **Pektattranseliminase** *f* pectate lyase *(enzyme)*
Pektin *n* pectin *(polysaccharide)*
Pektinabbau *m* pectin breakdown
Pektinase *f* pectinase, polygalacturonase *(enzyme)*
Pektinat *n* pectate
Pektinesterase *f* pectinesterase *(enzyme)*
Pektingewinnung *f* pectin extraction
Pektinmethylesterase *f* pectinesterase *(enzyme)*
pektinolytisch pectolytic
Pektinsäure *f* pectic (polygalacturonic) acid
pektinspaltend pectolytic
Pektinstoff *m*, **Pektinsubstanz** *f* pectic substance
Pektisation *f* coagulation
pektolytisch pectolytic
pelagial pelagic
Pelagial *n* pelagial, open water zone
pelagisch pelagic
Pelargonidin *n* pelargonidin *(plant dye)*
Pelargonie *f* pelargonium, geranium *(genus Pelargonium)*
Pelargonienaderngelbnetzvirus *n* pelargonium yellow net vein virus, PYNVV
Pelargonienblattkräuselvirus *n* pelargonium leaf curl virus, PLCV
Pelargonienlaus *f* geranium aphid, Acyrthosiphon pelargonii
Pelargonienmosaikvirus *n* pelargonium mosaic virus, PIMV
Pelargonienringfleckenvirus *n* pelargonium ring spot virus
Pelargonienwelke *f* geranium wilt *(caused by Xanthomonas campestris pelargonii)*
Pelargonium-Grandiflorum-Hybride *f* regal pelargonium
Pelargonium-Zonale-Hybride *f* fish geranium
Pelargonsäure *f* pelargonic (nonanoic) acid *(monocarboxylic acid)*

Pelham *m*, **Pelhamgebiß** *n* pelham *(part of a bridle)*
Pelit *m (soil)* mudstone
Pellagra *f (vet)* pellagra
Pellefarn *m (bot)* rock (cliff) brake *(genus Pellaea)*
Pellet *n* pellet
Pelletfutter[mittel] *n* pelleted feed[-stuff]
Pelletfütterung *f* pellet feeding
Pelletgefrierkonservierung *f* pellet-freezing technique *(semen preservation)*
Pelletieranlage *f* pellet production plant, pelleting mill (machine)
Pelletiereinrichtung *f* balling device
pelletieren to pellet[ize], to ball
Pelletierin *n* pelletierine *(alkaloid)*
Pelletierpresse *f* pelleting press, pelleter
Pelletierteller *m* balling disk
Pelletiertrommel *f* balling drum
Pelletierung *f* pelleting
Pellote *m* dumpling cactus, mescal button, Lophophora williamsii
Pelosol *m* pelosol, clay soil
peltat *(bot)* peltate
Peluschke *f s.* Futtererbse
pelvin pelvic
Pelvis *f* pelvis *(animal anatomy)*
Pelz *m* fur; skin *(esp. of small animals)*; pelage *(of mammals)*
Pelzauktion *f* fur auction
Pelzdichte *f* fur density
Pelzhandel *m* furriery
Pelzhändler *m* furrier
Pelzmotte *f* case-bearing clothes moth, Tinea pillionella
Pelztier *n* fur[-bearing] animal, furbearer, furred animal
Pelztierfarm *f* fur [breeding] farm
Pelztierjäger *m* trapper
Pelztierhaltung *f* fur farming
Pelztierzucht *f* fur farming
Pelztierzüchter *m* fur breeder
Pelzwaren *fpl* peltry
Pelzwerk *n* furriery, furs
Pemphigus *m (vet)* pemphigus
Pendeldüngerstreuer *m* pendulum [fertilizer] broadcaster
Pendelsäge *f* pendulum (swing) saw
Pendimethalin *n* pendimethalin, penoxalin *(herbicide)*
Penektomie *f (vet)* penectomy
Peneplain *f (soil)* peneplain, peneplane
Penetranz *f (gen)* penetrance
Penetration *f* penetration
Penetrometer *n* penetrometer
Penicillamin *n* penicillamine *(chelating agent)*
Penicillin *n* penicillin *(antibiotic)*
Penicillinase *f* beta-lactamase *(enzyme)*
Penicillinsäure *f* penicillic acid
penil penile, penial

Penis *m* penis, pizzle *(animal anatomy)*
Penisamputation *f (vet)* penectomy
Penis-Kloaken-Entzündung *f*/**ansteckende** epidemic venereal disease in geese
Penisknochen *m* penile bone
Peniskörper *m* body of the penis
Penisruptur *f (vet)* penile rupture
Penisschleife *f* flexure of the penis
Penis- und Vorhautentzündung *f (vet)* balanoposthitis
Peniswurzel *f* root of penis
Penman-Gleichung *f* Penman equation *(for estimation of evapotranspiration)*
Pennsylvanischer Gagel[strauch] *m* candleberry (wax) myrtle, southern bayberry, Myrica pensylvanica (cerifera)
Pensions[pferde]stall *m* livery stable
Pensionstierhaltung *f* agistment
Pensionsweide *f* agistment • **[Vieh, Jungvieh] in ~ nehmen** to agist
Pensionsweidenutzer *m* agister
Pentachlornitrobenzen *n* pentachloronitrobenzene, PCNB *(fungicide)*
Pentachlorphenol *n* pentachlor[o]phenol, PCP *(herbicide, insecticide)*
Pentachlorphenolnatrium *n* sodium pentachlorophenate *(molluscicide)*
Pentagastrin *n* pentagastrin *(hormone)*
Pentamethylendiamin *n* pentamethylenediamine, cadaverine
Pentamidin *n* pentamidine *(antiparasitic)*
Pentanochlor *n* pentanochlor, CMA *(fungicide, herbicide)*
Pentansäure *f* pentanoic (valeric) acid
pentaploid *(gen)* pentaploid
Pentaploide *m* pentaploid
Pentaploidie *f* pentaploidy
Pentobarbital *n* pentobarbitone *(anaesthetic)*
Pentosan *n* pentosan *(polysaccharide)*
Pentose *f* pentose *(monosaccharide)*
Pentosephosphatzyklus *m* pentose phosphate cycle, phosphogluconate pathway, Calvin cycle *(biochemistry)*
~/reduktiver reductive pentose phosphate cycle
Pentothal *n* thiopental *(anaesthetic)*
PEP-Carboxykinase *f* phosphoenolpyruvate carboxykinase *(enzyme)*
PEP-Carboxylase *f* phosphoenolpyruvate carboxylase *(enzyme)*
Peperomie *f (bot)* peperomia *(genus Peperomia)*
Pepsin *n* pepsin *(enzyme)*
Pepsinogen *n* pepsinogen *(pepsin precursor)*
Pepsinogen- und Pepsinsekretion *f*/**normale** eupepsia
Pepsinverdauung *f* peptic digestion
Peptid *n* peptide
Peptidase *f* peptidase, exopeptidase *(enzyme)*
Peptidhydrolase *f* protease *(enzyme)*
Peptidyltransferase *f* peptidyltransferase *(enzyme)*

Peptisation

Peptisation f peptization; *(soil)* deflocculation
peptisch peptic
peptisieren to peptize
Pepulbaum m **der Inder** bo-tree [of the Hindus], pipal, peepul [tree], Ficus religiosa
Pepton n peptone
peptonisieren to peptonize
Peptonwasser n peptone water *(microbiology)*
Percheron m, **Percheronpferd** n percheron *(horse breed)*
Perchlorethan n hexachloroethane *(anthelminthic, nematicide)*
perennierend *(bot)* perennial
Perennierende Lupine f perennial (wild) lupin[e], Lupinus perennis
Perennität f *(bot)* perenniality
Pereskie f Barbados gooseberry, blade apple *(genus Pereskia)*
Peressigsäure f per[oxy]acetic acid *(fatty acid, disinfectant)*
Perfektstadium n perfect stage, sexual state *(of fungi)*
Perfluidon n perfluidone *(herbicide)*
Perfusion f perfusion *(e.g. of organs)*
Pergamentschale f **[der Kaffeekirsche]** parchment skin [of coffee berry]
Pergola f pergola
Periadenitis f *(vet)* periadenitis
perianal perianal
Perianth n perianth, floral envelope *(for compounds s. under* Blütenhülle*)*
Periarthritis f *(vet)* periarthritis
Pericholezystitis f *(vet)* pericholecystitis
Perichondrium n perichondrium
Periderm n periderm, outer bark
peridial peridial
Peridie f, **Peridium** n peridium *(of fungal fruiting bodies)*
Periduralraum m epidural space *(animal anatomy)*
Perigon n *(bot)* perigone, perigonium
Perigonblatt n *(bot)* tepal
Périgord-Trüffel f [Périgord] truffle, earth ball, Tuber melanosporum
perigyn *(bot)* perigynous
Perihepatitis f *(vet)* perihepatitis
Perikard n pericardium, heart sac *(animal anatomy)*
perikardial pericardial
Perikarditis f *(vet)* pericarditis
Perikarp n *(bot)* pericarp, fruit coat, seed vessel (case), ovary wall
periklin *(bot)* periclinal
Perillaöl n perilla oil *(from Perilla frutescens)*
Perilymphe f perilymph *(of the inner ear)*
Perimeningitis f *(vet)* pachymeningitis
Perimetritis f *(vet)* perimetritis
perinatal perinatal
Perinephritis f *(vet)* perinephritis
Perineum n perineum *(animal anatomy)*
Periodenblock m *(forest)* periodic block

Periodenertrag m *(forest)* periodic yield (cut)
Periodenfläche f *(forest)* periodic block
Periodenzuwachs m *(forest)* periodic increment
Periodik f, **Periodizität** f 1. periodicity; 2. alternate bearing, alternation *(orcharding)*
Periodontium n periodontium *(animal anatomy)*
Perioplum n periople *(of hoof or claw)*
Periorchitis f *(vet)* periorchitis
Periost n periosteum
Periostitis f *(vet)* periostitis
Periostschaber m *(vet)* raspatory
Peripankreatitis f *(vet)* peripancreatitis
Periplasma n periplasma
Perisperm n *(bot)* perisperm
Peristaltik f peristalsis, gut motility
~/fehlende *(vet)* aperistalsis
peristaltisch peristaltic
Perithezium n perithecium *(of ascomycetes)*
peritoneal peritoneal
Peritonealflüssigkeit f peritoneal fluid
Peritonealhöhle f peritoneal cavity
Peritoneum n peritoneum *(animal anatomy)*
Peritonitis f *(vet)* peritonitis
~ der Katze/infektiöse feline infectious peritonitis, FIP
peritrich peritrichous
Perizykel m *(bot)* pericycle
Perkolat n leachate
Perkolation f percolation
Perkolationsrate f percolation rate
perkolieren to percolate
Perkussion f *(vet)* percussion
Perkussionshammer m *(vet)* percussion hammer, plexor
perkutan percutaneous, transcutaneous
Perlen fpl pearls *(of antlers)*
Perlenbildung f beading *(in apples)*
Perlenkastanie f Henry chestnut, Castanea henryi
Perlfarn m sensitive fern, Onoclea sensibilis
Perlgras n melic[-grass] *(genus Melica)*
Perlgraupen fpl pearl[ed] barley, barley groats • **zu ~ verarbeiten** to pearl
Perlhenne f guinea-hen
Perlhirse f pearl (bulrush) millet, Egyptian (East Indian) millet, bajra *(India)*, Pennisetum glaucum (americanum), Penicillaria spicata
Perlhuhn n 1. guinea fowl (hen) *(genus Numida)*; 2. guinea fowl (hen), Numida meleagris
~/junges keet, keat
Perlhuhnfütterung f guinea-fowl feeding
Perlhuhnmast f guinea-fowl fattening
Perlit n(m) perlite *(medium for potting plants)*
Perlmais m *(Am)* popcorn, Zea mays convar. microsperma
Perlmaisstärke f *(Am)* pearl corn starch
Perlolin n perloline *(alkaloid)*
Perlpfötchen n everlasting flower *(genus Anaphalis)*
Perlreis m short-grain rice

perlschnurartig *(bot, zoo)* moniliform
Perlsucht *f (vet)* pearl disease
Perlwein *m* semisparkling (carbonated) wine
Perlzwiebel *f* pearl onion
Permafrost *m* permafrost
Permafrostboden *m* permafrost (ever frozen) soil, pergelisol
Permanganat *n* permanganate
permeabel permeable
Permeabilität *f* permeability
Permeation *f* permeation
permeieren *n* to permeate
Permethrin *n* permethrin *(insecticide)*
Pernambukholzbaum *m* prickly brazilwood, Caesalpinia echinata
perniziös pernicious
Perodermie *f (vet)* epitheliogenesis imperfecta
Peronospora[krankheit] *f* downy mildew of grapes, grape mildew *(caused by Plasmopara viticola)*
Perosis *f* perosis, slipped tendon, hock disorder *(of growing poultry due to manganese deficiency)*
Peroxiacetylnitrat *n* peroxyacetyl nitrate, PAN *(smog constituent)*
Peroxid *n* peroxide
Peroxidase *f* peroxidase *(enzyme)*
Peroxidasereaktion *f (dairy)* peroxidase test
Peroxidation *f*, **Peroxidbildung** *f* peroxidation
Peroxidzahl *f* peroxide value *(measure of fat oxidation)*
Peroxipropionylnitrat *n* peroxypropionyl nitrate, PPN *(smog constituent)*
Peroxisom *n*, **Peroxysom** *n* peroxisome *(organelle)*
Perserkatze *f* Persian [cat] *(breed)*
Persianer *m* Persian lamb
Persianerfell *n* caracul, broadtail [pelt]
Persianerschaf *n* caracul, broadtail *(sheep breed)*
Persimone *f* persimmon
Persimonenbaum *m* [common] persimmon tree, Diospyros virginiana
Persische Akazie *f* silk tree, Albizia julibrissin
~ **Melone** *f* winter melon, Cucumis melo convar. zard
~ **Ranunkel** *f* Persian buttercup, Ranunculus asiaticus
Persischer Ehrenpreis *m* common field speedwell, garden (Tournefort) speedwell, Veronica persica
~ **Flieder** *m* Persian lilac, Syringa x persica
~ **Klee** *m* Persian (reversed) clover, Trifolium resupinatum
~ **Weizen** *m* Persian wheat, Triticum carthlicum
persistent persistent
Persistenz *f* persistence, persistency
~ **der Milchleistung** lactation persistency
persistieren to persist
Personenstunde *f* man-hour [of labour]
Perspiration *f* perspiration
perspirieren to perspire
Perthophyt *m* perthophyte, facultative saprophyte
Peruanischer Pfefferbaum *m* pepper-tree, Spanish pepper, Schinus molle
Perubalsam *m (bot)* balsam of Peru, Myroxylon balsamum var. pereirae
Perückenbock *m* peruke buck *(of roe deer)*
Perückenstrauch *m* 1. smoke plant (tree) *(genus Cotinus)*; 2. Venetian (elm-leaved) sumac[h], smoke plant, [European] smoke tree, young fustic, zantewood, wig tree, Cotinus coggygria, Rhus cotinus
Perzeption *f* perception
Pessar *n (vet)* pessary
Pestbakterium *n* plague bacterium, Yersinia pestis
Pestfloh *m* tropical rat flea, Xenopsylla cheopis
pestizid pesticidal
Pestizid *n* pesticide, pest killer
~**/organisches** organic
~**/sofortwirkendes** knock-down agent (poison)
Pestizidanwendung *f* pesticide application
Pestizidchemie *f* pesticide chemistry
Pestizideinsatz *m* pesticide application
Pestizidmißbrauch *m* pesticide abuse
Pestizidökologie *f* pesticide ecology
Pestizidpersistenz *f* pesticide persistence
pestizidresistent pesticide-resistant
Pestizidresistenz *f* pesticide resistance
Pestizidrückstand *m* pesticide residue
~**/zulässiger** pesticide tolerance
Pestizidspezifität *f* pesticide specificity
Pestizidsprühgerät *n* pesticide atomizer (dusting apparatus)
Pestizidsynergist *m* pesticide synergist
Pestizidvergiftung *f* pesticide poisoning
Pestizidverträglichkeit *f* pesticide compatibility
Pestizidwirkung *f* pesticide action
Pestizidzerstäuber *m* pesticide atomizer (dusting apparatus)
Pestmanagement *n* pest management
Pestvirus *n* pestivirus
Pestwurz *f* butterbur, pestilenceweed, flea-dock, Petasites hybridus (officinalis)
Petal *n (bot)* petal
Petalodie *f (bot)* petalody
petaloid *(bot)* petaloid
Petalum *n (bot)* petal
petechial *(vet)* petechial
Petechialfieber *n*/**infektiöses** Ondiri disease *(of cattle)*
Petechien *pl (vet)* petechiae
Petersilie *f* parsley, Petroselinum crispum
Petersilienwurzel *f* Hamburg (turnip-rooted) parsley, Petroselinum crispum ssp. tuberosum
Petiolus *m (bot)* [leaf] petiole, leaf-stalk, strig; *(zoo)* petiole, footstalk
Petitgrainöl *n* oil of bitter orange petitgrain *(from twigs, leaves and unripe fruits of Citrus aurantium ssp. aurantium)*

Petri-Oberschale

Petri-Oberschale f Petri dish top
Petri-Unterschale f Petri dish bottom
Petrifikation f petrifaction
Petrischale f Petri dish (plate)
Petrischalenbüchse f Petri dish box
Petrographie f petrography
Petroleumemulsion f white-oil spray *(pest control)*
Petrologie f petrology
Petunie f petunia *(genus Petunia)*
Petunienadernaufhellungsvirus n petunia vein clearing virus
Petuniengelbscheckungsvirus n petunia yellow mottle virus
Petuniensternmosaikvirus n petunia asteroid mosaic virus
Peyersche Platten fpl Peyer patches *(in the last division of the small intestine)*
Peyote m peyote, peyotl *(drug)*
Peyotekaktus m 1. peyote, peyotl *(genus Lophophora)*; 2. dumpling cactus, Lophophora williamsii
Peyotl m s. Peyote
Pf s. Pflegehieb
Pfaddiagramm n arrow diagram *(e.g. in breeding schemes)*
Pfadkoeffizient m *(biom)* path coefficient
Pfahl m pole, pile, post, stake, prop, stob
pfählen to stake, to prop [up], to train *(e.g. trees)*
Pfahlpilz m *(bot)* paxillus *(genus Paxillus)*
Pfahlrohr n 1. reed *(genus Arundo)*; 2. giant (great) reed, Spanish (bamboo) reed, Arundo donax
Pfahlwurzel f tap (main) root • eine ~ [aus]bilden to taproot
Pfälzisches Warmblut n Zweibrucken *(horse breed)*
Pfau m peafowl *(genus Pavo)*
~/männlicher peacock
~/weiblicher peahen
pfauenartig pavonine
Pfauenblume f [Mexican] tiger flower, tiger iris, Tigridia pavonia
Pfauenküken n pea-chick
Pfauenradfarn m American maidenhair fern, Adiantum pedatum
Pfeffer m 1. pepper *(genus Piper)*; 2. pepper *(spice)*
Pfefferbaum m pepper-tree *(genus Schinus)*
Pfefferfenchel m bitter fennel, Foeniculum vulgare ssp. piperitum
Pfefferfrucht f s. Paprika
Pfeffergurke f gherkin
Pfefferkraut n 1. savory *(genus Satureja)*; 2. summer savory, Satureja hortensis
Pfefferminze f peppermint, Mentha x piperita
Pfefferminzöl n peppermint oil
Pfefferminzrost m mint rust *(caused by Puccinia menthae)*
Pfefferschote f pepper pod

Pfefferstrauch m pepper plant *(genus Piper)*
Pfeffinger-Krankheit f cherry rasp leaf *(virosis)*
pfeifen *(vet)* to roar
Pfeifenblume f 1. birthwort *(genus Aristolochia)*; 2. [common] Dutchman's pipe, Aristolochia macrophylla (durior)
Pfeifengras n 1. molinia *(genus Molinia)*; 2. flying bent, [purple] moor grass, blae grass, molinia, Molinia caerulea
Pfeifenstrauch m mock orange, philadelphus *(genus Philadelphus)*
Pfeifentabak m pipe tobacco
Pfeifente f wi[d]geon, Anas penelope
Pfeifenwinde f s. Pfeifenblume
Pfeifferella-anatipester-Infektion f, **Pfeifferellose** f der Ente *(vet)* duck septicaemia, new duck disease (syndrome)
pfeilartig *(bot, zoo)* sagittal
Pfeilblatt n elephant's ear plant *(genus Alocasia)*
Pfeilblättrige Emilie f Flora's paint-brush, tassel flower, Emilia coccinea (flammea)
pfeilförmig *(bot, zoo)* sagittate[d], sagittiform
Pfeilkraut n arrowhead *(genus Sagittaria)*
Pfeilkresse f hoary cress (pepperwort), Cardaria draba
pfeilspitzig spicular, spiculate
Pfeilwurz f 1. arrowroot *(genus Maranta)*; 2. [West Indian] arrowroot, Maranta arundinacea
Pfeilwurzgewächse npl arrowroot family *(family Marantaceae)* • **die ~ betreffend** marantaceous
Pfeilwurzstärke f arrowroot
Pfenniggilbweiderich m s. Pfennigkraut 2.
Pfennigkraut n 1. penny-cress, stinkweed, Thlaspi arvense; 2. moneywort, creeping jenny, wandering sailor, Lysimachia nummularia
Pfennigminiermotte f pear leaf blister moth, Cemiostoma scitella, Leucoptera malifoliella
Pferch m [hurdle] fold, [sheep-]pen, crib, [sheep-]cote, pound, corral
pferchen to [pin]fold, to pen [up], to crib, to corral
Pferd n horse, Equus caballus • **vom ~ stürzen** to dismount, to alight
~/abgetriebenes jade, screw, rip
~/ausgebildetes broken horse
~/ausschlagendes kicker
~/bösartiges outlaw
~/geschecktes piebald [horse], pinto
~/leicht scheuendes shyer, shier
~/leichtes light horse
~ mit gestutztem Schwanz cocktail
~ mit hoher Aktion high-stepper
~/scheuendes shyer, shier
~/schnelles spanker, clipper
~/siegloses also-ran *(racing)*
~/stätiges (störrisches) jibber, buck-jumper
~/ungezähmtes bronc[o], brumby, warrigal *(Australia)*
~/widersetzliches s. ~/stätiges
~/zugerittenes broken horse

Pferdeabortvirus *n* equine abortion virus, equine rhinovirus
pferdeähnlich equine
Pferdeanämie *f (vet)* equine anaemia
~/infektiöse infectious equine anaemia, swamp fever
Pferdeanhänger *m* horse trailer
Pferdeäpfel *mpl* horse droppings
Pferdeartige *mpl* horse family *(family Equidae)*
Pferdeausstellung *f* horse show
Pferdebohne *f* broad (field) bean, fava [bean], Vicia faba var. minor (equina)
Pferdebohnenkäfer *m* broad bean weevil, Bruchus rufimanus
Pferdebürste *f* dandy-brush
Pferdedecke *f* horse blanket (cloth), shabrack
~/wollene rug
Pferdedoktor *m* horse-doctor
Pferdedressur *f* equitation, equestrianism
Pferdedung *m* horse manure (dung)
Pferdeenzephalomyelitis *f (vet)* equine encephalomyelitis
~/westliche western equine encephalomyelitis
Pferdeenzaphalomyelitisvirus *n* equine encephalomyelitis virus
Pferdeeppich *m (bot)* alexanders, alisander, Smyrnium olusatrum
Pferdefeige *f* hottentot fig, Carpobrotus edulis
Pferdefett *n* horse fat
Pferdefleisch *n* horseflesh, horse meat
Pferdefleischholz *n* beef wood, brown ebony, Swartzia tomentosa
Pferdefutter *n* horse feed (fodder), forage
Pferdefütterung *f* horse feeding
Pferdegeschirr *n* harness
~/verziertes trappings
Pferdegespann *n* horse team, pair of horses, pair, rig, *(Am)* span of horses
pferdegezogen horse-drawn
Pferdegöpel *m* horse-capstan, horse-gin
Pferdegrippe *f s.* Pferdeinfluenza
Pferdehaarling *m* horse-biting louse, Werneckiella equi
Pferdehacke *f* horse[-pulled] hoe, grape hoe
Pferdehalter *m* horse-keeper
Pferdehaltung *f* horse keeping (management)
Pferdehändler *m* horse trader (dealer), coper
Pferdeheilkunde *f* equine medicine, hippiatry
Pferdehuf *m* coffin
Pferdeinfluenza *f (vet)* equine influenza, stable cough, epizootic cough in horse
Pferdeinfluenzavirus *n* equine influenza virus
Pferdekrankheit *f* horse disease
Pferdekunde *f* hippology
Pferdelaus *f* horse[-sucking] louse, blood-sucking horse louse, Haematopinus asini [macrocephalus]
Pferdelausfliege *f* horse [louse] fly, forest fly, Hippobosca equina

Pferdeleistungsschau *f* horse show
Pferdemäher *m* horse mower
Pferdemist *m* horse manure (dung)
Pferdepeitsche *f* horsewhip
Pferdepest *f* African horse sickness
Pferdepestvirus *n* African horse sickness virus
Pferdepfleger *m* groom, ostler
Pferdepocken *pl (vet)* horse-pox, grease disease
Pferdepolo *n* polo
Pferderasse *f* horse breed, breed of horse
Pferderechen *m* horse rake
Pferderennbahn *f* race course, track, the turf
Pferderennen *n* horse-race
Pferderennsport *m* horse-racing, the turf
Pferderettichbaum *m* horse-radish tree, Moringa oleifera (pterygosperma)
Pferdeschau *f* horse show
Pferdeschwanz *m*, **Pferdeschweif** *m* horse-tail
Pferdeschwemme *f* horse-pond
Pferdesport *m* equestrian sport, horse riding
Pferdestall *m* [horse] stable
Pferdestallmist *m* horse manure (dung)
Pferdestärke *f* horsepower
Pferdestaupe *f (vet)* equine viral arteritis, epizootic cellulitis
Pferdesterbe *f (vet)* African horse sickness
Pferdesterbevirus *n* African horse sickness virus
Pferdetransportanhänger *m* horse trailer
Pferdetransportwagen *m* horse-box
Pferdewagen *m* wa[g]gon
Pferdeweide *f* horse grazing
Pferdezahnmais *m* dent maize, Zea mays convar. dentiformis
Pferdezucht *f* horse breeding
Pferdezuchtbetrieb *m* stud (horse breeding) farm
Pferdezüchter *m* horse breeder
Pferdezug *m* horse traction
Pferdezughacke *f* horse[-pulled] hoe
Pfifferling *m (bot)* [yellow] chanterelle, Cantharellus cibarius
Pfingstnelke *f* cheddar pink, Dianthus gratianopolitanus
Pfingstrose *f (bot)* peony *(genus Paeonia)*
PfiRoMV *s.* Pfirsichrosettenmosaikvirus
Pfirsich *m* peach
~/nicht steinlösender clingstone [peach]
~/steinlösender freestone [peach]
Pfirsich-Bandmosaik *n (phyt)* peach line pattern *(virosis)*
Pfirsichbaum *m* peach[-tree], Prunus persica
Pfirsichblattlaus *f* green peach aphid, peach-potato aphid (aphis), tobacco aphid, Myzus persicae
Pfirsichblättriger Knöterich *m* peachwort, redshank, Polygonum persicaria
Pfirsichflaum *m* peach fuzz
Pfirsichmehltau *m* peach mildew *(caused by Phaerotheca pannosa persicae)*
Pfirsichmosaikvirus *n* peach mosaic virus, PMV

Pfirsichmotte

Pfirsichmotte f s. Pfirsichzweigbohrer
Pfirsichpalme f peach palm, Bactris gasipaes
Pfirsichpflaume f s. Nektarine
Pfirsichrosettenmosaikvirus n peach rosette mosaic virus
Pfirsichschildlaus f oblong scale, Eulecanium persicae
Pfirsichschorf m (phyt) peach (plum) scab (caused by Venturia carpophila)
Pfirsichtriebbohrer m (ent) 1. lesser peach-tree borer, Synanthedon pictipes; 2. s. Pfirsichwickler
Pfirsichweide f almond-leaved willow, French willow, Salix triandra
Pfirsichwickler m oriental fruit (peach) moth, Cydia (Laspeyresia) molesta
Pfirsich-X-Krankheit f (phyt) peach X-disease (virosis)
Pfirsichzweigbohrer m (ent) peach twig borer, Anarsia lineatella
Pflanzabstand m planting distance (width), planting space (pitch), field spacing • **mit engem** ~ closely spaced • **mit weitem** ~ widely spaced
Pflanzarbeit f planting work
pflanzbar plantable
Pflanzbeet n plant[ation] bed; nursery line
Pflanzbeetvorbereitung f plant-bed preparation
Pflanzbehälter m plant box
Pflanzbeil n (forest) planting hatchet
Pflanzbestand m plantation, planting, artificial stand (crop)
Pflanzbett n plant bed
Pflanzbettbereitung f secondary tillage
Pflanzbreite f planting width
Pflanzbrett n transplanting (lining-out) board
Pflänzchen n plantlet (s. a. Pflanze/junge)
Pflanzdatum n planting date
Pflanzdichte f planting density, density of planting
Pflanzdolch m planting dagger (iron)
Pflanze f plant; vegetable
~/**anemogame (anemophile)** anemophile
~/**annuelle** annual
~/**äsung[s]spendende** browse plant
~/**ätherisches Öl liefernde** essential oil plant
~/**ausdauernde** perennial
~/**ausläuferbildende** runner
~/**bienne** biennial
~/**blühende** flowerer, bloomer
~/**blütenlose** cryptogam
~/**blütentragende** bearer
~/**bodenaufschließende** soil builder
~/**bodenbedeckende** ground cover plant
~/**bodenbefestigende** soil binder
~/**bodennah knospende** chamaephyte
~/**bodenverbessernde** soil improver
~/**buchsbaumartiges Holz liefernde** boxwood
~/**calcicole** s. ~/kalkliebende
~/**calcifuge** s. ~/kalkmeidende
~/**drogenliefernde** drug plant

~/**durch den Menschen verbreitete** anthropochore
~/**einheimische** apophyte
~/**einjährige** annual
~/**einkeimblättrige** monocotyledon, monocot[yl]
~/**einzellige** protophyte
~/**erkrankte** rogue (in a field crop)
~/**erosionsmindernde** soil binder
~/**ertragliefernde** cropper
~/**ertragreiche** good cropper
~/**farbstoffliefernde** dye plant
~/**feuerbegünstigte** pyrophyte
~/**feuerresistente** pyrophyte
~/**fischgiftliefernde** fish-poison plant, piscicidal plant
~/**fleischfressende** s. ~/insektenfressende
~/**fruchttragende** bearer
~/**genußmittelliefernde** stimulant plant
~/**gepfropfte** graft
~/**gerbstoffliefernde** tan[ning] plant
~/**getopfte** pot[ted] plant
~/**gummiliefernde** gum plant
~/**herbstblühende** autumnal
~/**honigliefernde** s. ~/nektarliefernde
~/**im Container erzogene** containerized seedling
~/**im Innern eines Wirtes lebende** endophyte
~/**immergrüne** evergreen [plant]
~/**insektenfressende (insektivore)** insectivorous (carnivorous) plant
~/**junge** young plant, plantlet, youngling
~/**kalkliebende** basiphyte, calcicole
~/**kalkmeidende** acidophyte, calcifuge
~/**kautschukliefernde** rubber (gum) plant
~/**kleeartige** clover
~/**krautige** herbaceous (herbage) plant, herb, vegetable
~/**kulturfreundliche** hemerophyte
~/**lichtbedürftige (lichtliebende)** light-damanding plant, light demander
~/**mehrjährige** perennial [plant]
~ **mit mittlerem Feuchtigkeitsbedarf** mesophyte
~/**monozyklisch-hapaxanthe** annual [plant]
~/**moosähnliche** moss
~/**nektarliefernde (nektarspendende)** nectar (honey) plant
~/**ölliefernde** oil-plant
~/**perennierende** perennial [plant]
~/**pollenliefernde** pollen plant
~/**salatähnliche** lettuce
~/**samentragende** seed-bearing plant, seed bearer
~/**sandbindende** sand-binding plant, sand-stabilizing plant
~/**säureanzeigende (säureliebende)** acidophilic plant, acidophyte, acidity indicator species
~/**schattenspendende** shade plant
~/**schwarzwurzelige** black root (e.g. Symphytum officinale)
~/**selbststerile (selbstunfruchtbare)** mule

Pflanzendecke

~/**sich rasch bewurzelnde** rooter
~/**sommerannuelle (sommereinjährige)** summer annual
~/**sortenuntypische** rogue
~/**stärkeliefernde** starch-yielding plant
~/**stickstoffsammelnde** nitrogen-collecting plant, nitrogen collector
~/**stickstoffzehrende** nitrogen consumer
~/**tagneutrale** day-neutral plant
~/**teppichbildende** carpet plant
~/**tierfangende** s. ~/insektenfressende
~/**unter Glas angezogene** glass-raised plant
~/**unterernährte** scrag
~/**unveredelte** wild[l]ing, wild stock
~/**veredelte** graft
~/**wachsende** grower
~/**wachsliefernde** wax plant
~/**wildwachsende** volunteer
~/**windbestäubte (windblütige)** anemophile
~/**winterannuelle (wintereinjährige)** winter (hardy) annual
~/**zuckerliefernde** sugar plant (crop)
~/**zweijährige** biennial [plant]
~/**zweikeimblättrige** dicotyledon, dicot[yl]
~/**zwergwüchsige** dwarf plant
Pflanzeisen n planting iron (dagger)
pflanzen to plant, to bed; to prick [off, out]; to set out (esp. seedlings)
~/**gruppenweise** to clump
~/**im Quadratnestverband** to check-row
~/**in einen Topf** to pot
~/**in einen zu großen Topf** to overpot
~/**in Kästen** to box
~/**in Kübel** to box
~/**in Reihe** to row
~/**in Saatkisten** to flat
~/**mit dem Pflanzholz (Setzholz)** to dibble
~/**Myzel** to spawn
~/**neu** to replant, to replace [plants]
~/**reihenweise** to drill
Pflanzen fpl/**nachgebesserte** (forest) recruitment
Pflanzen n planting
~ **auf den Pflugdamm** (forest) planting on the furrow-slice
~ **im Fünfeckverband** (forest) quincuncial (quincunx) planting
~ **in Höhenlinie** contour planting
~ **in röhrenförmige Klein[st]container** tube planting, tubing
~/**maschinelles** mechanized (machine) planting
~ **mit dem Pflanzgewehr** (forest) buller planting
~ **mit dem Pflanzholz** peg (pit) planting
~ **unter Schirm[bestand]** (forest) planting under shelterwood
~ **zwischen Reisigwällen** (forest) windrow (stroll) planting
Pflanzabstand m [plant] spacing • **mit engem** ~ closely spaced • **mit weitem** ~ widely spaced
~ **in der Reihe** spacing [with]in the row

pflanzenabtötend phytocidal, herbicidal
Pflanzenabtötungsmittel n phytocide, herbicide
Pflanzenampel f hanging basket
Pflanzenanalyse f plant tissue analysis (test), plant analysis
Pflanzenanatomie f plant anatomy, phytotomy
Pflanzenanbauer m plant grower
Pflanzenanordnung f arrangement of plants; plant spacing
Pflanzenanzucht f plant raising (rearing); seedling production
~ **in der Verkaufspackung** pack growing
Pflanzenanzuchtbetrieb m nursery
Pflanzenanzuchtkammer f plant-growth chamber
Pflanzenarchitektur f plant architecture
Pflanzenarrangement n arrangement of plants
Pflanzenart f plant species
Pflanzenasche f plant ash
Pflanzenaufgang m plant emergence
Pflanzenaufzucht f plant raising (rearing)
Pflanzenaushebegerät n plant lifter
Pflanzenauszug m plant extract
Pflanzenbakteriologie f phytobacteriology
Pflanzenbau m plant (crop) husbandry, crop growing (farming), plant growing (cropping, cultivation), plant agriculture, field-crop production
~/**bewässerungsloser** dry farming
~/**erdeloser** soilless cultivation, hydroponics, tray agriculture, tank farming
~/**landwirtschaftlicher** plant agriculture
~ **unter Folie** plasticulture
Pflanzenbaubetrieb m crop enterprise
Pflanzenbauer m plant grower, planter, crop producer, agronomist
Pflanzenbauforschung f field crops research
pflanzenbaulich agronomic[al]
Pflanzenbausystem n crop husbandry system
Pflanzenbeschreibung f phytography
Pflanzenbestand m plant stand (population), crop [stand], stand
~/**angebauter** culture
~/**geschützter** protected crop
~/**lagernder** laid crop
Pflanzenbestandesdichte f plant [population] density, crop (stand) density
Pflanzenbestandesentwicklung f stand development
Pflanzenbestimmung f plant identification
Pflanzenbiochemie f plant biochemistry
Pflanzenbiologie f plant biology
Pflanzenbiotechnologie f plant biotechnology
Pflanzenblindwert m plant blank value (residue analytics)
Pflanzenbutter f vegetable (green) butter
Pflanzenchemie f phytochemistry
Pflanzenchemiker m phytochemist
pflanzenchemisch phytochemical
Pflanzendecke f plant (vegetation) cover, crop canopy

Pflanzendemographie

Pflanzendemographie *f* plant demography
Pflanzendichte *f* plant density
Pflanzendünger *m* plant fertilizer (food)
Pflanzenendabstand *m* final spacing
~/mittlerer final average distance apart of plants (e.g. in beet growing)
Pflanzenentstehung *f* phytogenesis, phytogeny
Pflanzenentwicklung *f* plant development
Pflanzenentwicklungsstadium *n* plant development stage
Pflanzenernährung *f* plant nutrition
Pflanzenertrag *m* plant yield
Pflanzenertragsanteil *m*/**wirtschaftlich wichtiger** economic yield
Pflanzenextrakt *m* plant extract
Pflanzenfamilie *f* plant family
Pflanzenfarbstoff *m* plant pigment, plant (vegetable) dye
Pflanzenfaser *f* plant (vegetable) fibre
~/hanfähnliche hemp
Pflanzenfaserknäuel *n* [im Verdauungstrakt] phytobezoar
Pflanzenfett *n* vegetable fat
~/gehärtetes hydrogenated plant fat, vegetable shortening
Pflanzenformation *f (ecol)* plant formation
pflanzenfressend plant-eating, herbivorous, phytophagic, phytophagous
Pflanzenfresser *m* plant eater (feeder), herbivore
Pflanzengalle *f (phyt)* plant gall, gall[nut]
Pflanzengemeinschaft *f* plant community, phytocoenosis
~/abhängige synusia, synusium
Pflanzengenetik *f* plant genetics, phytogenetics
Pflanzengenetiker *m* plant geneticist
Pflanzengeograph *m* plant geographer, geobotanist
Pflanzengeographie *f* plant geography, phytogeography, geobotany
pflanzengeographisch phytogeographic[al], geobotanic[al]
Pflanzengesellschaft *f* [plant] association, plant community
~/räumlich abwechselnde alterne
Pflanzengesellschaftssystematik *f* systematic plant sociology
Pflanzengesundheitszeugnis *n* phytosanitary certificate
Pflanzengewebe *n* plant tissue
Pflanzengewebekultur *f* plant tissue culture
Pflanzengewebsanalyse *f* plant tissue analysis (test)
Pflanzengift *n* plant poison, phytotoxin
Pflanzengruppe *f* clump
~/blühende flourishing clump
~/gehäufelte hill
Pflanzengummi *n* [plant] gum
Pflanzengummitasche *f*/**streifenförmige** gum streak (vein)

Pflanzenhaar *n* plant hair, trichome
Pflanzenhabitus *m* plant habit
Pflanzenharz *n* vegetable resin
Pflanzenheilkunde *f* phytomedicine
Pflanzenhöhe *f* plant height
Pflanzenhormon *n* plant hormone, phytohormone
Pflanzenhorst *m* hurst
Pflanzenhygiene *f* plant (crop) hygiene
Pflanzenimmunität *f* plant immunity
Pflanzeninterferon *n* plant interferon
Pflanzenklassifikation *f* plant classification
Pflanzenklimatologie *f* plant climatology, phytoclimatology
Pflanzenkollektion *f* plant collection
Pflanzenkonkurrenz *f (ecol)* plant competition
Pflanzenkörper *m* plant-body
Pflanzenkrankheit *f* plant disease
pflanzenkrankheitserregend phytopathogenic
Pflanzenkrankheitserreger *m* plant pathogen, phytopathogen
Pflanzenkrankheitslehre *f* plant pathology, phytopathology
Pflanzenkrebs *m (phyt)* plant tumour, canker
Pflanzenkübel *m* [plant] tub
Pflanzenkunde *f* plant science, botany
Pflanzenlaus *f* plant-louse (family group Sternorrhyncha)
Pflanzenlecithin *n* vegetable lecithin
Pflanzenleim *m* vegetable glue (adhesive)
Pflanzenmaterial *n* plant material, plant matter
Pflanzenmißbildung *f* plant abnormality
Pflanzenmorphologie *f* plant morphology, phytomorphology
Pflanzenmutante *f* plant mutant
Pflanzennährelement *n* plant food element
Pflanzennährstoff *m* plant nutrient (food)
Pflanzennährstoffelement *n* plant food element
Pflanzennährstoffverhältnis *n* plant food ratio
Pflanzenökologe *m* plant ecologist
Pflanzenökologie *f* plant ecology
Pflanzenöl *n* plant (vegetable) oil
Pflanzenölbrennstoff *m*, **Pflanzenölkraftstoff** *m* plant oil fuel
Pflanzenorgan *n* plant organ
~/becherförmiges cup
pflanzenparasitär plant-parasitic
Pflanzenpatent *n* plant patent
pflanzenpathogen phytopathogenic
Pflanzenpathogen *n* plant pathogen, phytopathogen
Pflanzenpathogenese *f* plant pathogenesis
Pflanzenpathosystem *n* plant pathosystem
Pflanzenpech *n* vegetable pitch
Pflanzenpflege *f* plant care
Pflanzenphänologie *f* [plant] phenology, phytophenology
Pflanzenphysiologe *m* plant physiologist
Pflanzenphysiologie *f* plant physiology
Pflanzenprodukt *n* plant (crop) product

Pflanzenproduktion f plant (crop) production, arable farming (agriculture)
Pflanzenproduktionsbetrieb m crop enterprise
Pflanzenproduktionsforschung f crop production research
Pflanzenproduktionsgenossenschaft f co-operative farm for crop production
Pflanzenproduktionssystem n cropping system
Pflanzenproduktivität f plant (crop) productivity
Pflanzenproduzent m crop producer
Pflanzenprotein n plant protein
Pflanzenquarantäne f plant quarantine
Pflanzenregeneration f plant regeneration
Pflanzenreich n plant (vegetable) kingdom
Pflanzenresistenz f plant resistance
Pflanzenreste mpl s. Pflanzenrückstände
Pflanzenrodepflug m plant lift plough
Pflanzenrotor m plant rotor *(greenhouse installation)*
Pflanzenrückstände mpl plant remains (debris), plant residues, trash, rubbish
Pflanzensaft m [plant] sap
pflanzensaftsaugend plant sap feeding
Pflanzensaftsauger m *(ent)* homopteran, plant sap feeder *(order Homoptera)*
pflanzensaftübertragbar sap-transmissible *(virus)*
Pflanzensammeln n herborization
Pflanzensammlung f plant collection, herbarium
pflanzensaugend s. pflanzensaftsaugend
Pflanzensäure f plant acid
pflanzenschädigend phytotoxic
Pflanzenschädigung f **durch Überdüngung** fertilizer injury
Pflanzenschädling m plant (crop) pest
Pflanzenschale f flower bowl (dish)
Pflanzenschleim m [plant] mucilage
Pflanzenschutz m plant protection (conservation), crop protection
~/**gezielter** directed plant protection
~/**integrierter** integrated plant protection, integrated control
Pflanzenschutzausrüstung f crop protection equipment
Pflanzenschützer m plant protectionist
Pflanzenschutzerzeugnis n crop-protection product
Pflanzenschutzgebiet n plant sanctuary
Pflanzenschutzgerät n crop protection equipment, [mechanical] applicator
Pflanzenschutzgesetzgebung f plant protection legislation
Pflanzenschutzinspektor m plant health inspector
Pflanzenschutzmaschine f [/**bodengebundene**] field[-crop] sprayer, ground [crop] sprayer
~ **mit Feldspritzrohr** boom sprayer
Pflanzenschutzmaßnahme f plant protection measure
Pflanzenschutzmittel n plant (crop) protectant, plant protective, [crop] pesticide, control agent

~/**chemisches** crop protection chemical, agricultural control chemical
~/**flüssiges** plant spray
~/**staubförmiges [chemisches]** dust
Pflanzenschutzmittelverzeichnis n pesticide index
Pflanzenschutzspezialist m crop protection specialist
Pflanzenschutztechnik f crop protection equipment
Pflanzenschutzwart m plant protectionist
Pflanzensetzmaschine f plant-setting machine, planting machine, [vegetable] planter, transplanter
Pflanzenseuche f epiphytotic
Pflanzenseuchenlehre f epiphytology
Pflanzensoziologe m phytosociologist
Pflanzensoziologie f phytosociology, vegetation science
~/**forstliche** forest sociology
pflanzensoziologisch phytosociological
Pflanzenspezies f plant species
Pflanzenstab m prop, stick, stake
Pflanzenstamm m stock
Pflanzenstärke f plant starch
Pflanzenstreu f plant litter
Pflanzenstütznetz n crop support netting
Pflanzenstützvorrichtung f plant support
Pflanzensystematik f, **Pflanzentaxonomie** f plant systematics (taxonomy)
Pflanzenteer m vegetable tar
Pflanzenteil n plant part
~/**oberirdisches** above ground plant part, aerial part of a plant
~/**samentragendes** seed stalk
Pflanzenteile npl/**oberirdische** tops *(esp. of root crops)*
Pflanzentherapie f phytotherapy
pflanzentötend phytocidal; herbicidal
Pflanzentoxikologie f plant toxicology
Pflanzentumor m *(phyt)* plant tumour
Pflanzenüberreste mpl s. Pflanzenrückstände
Pflanzen- und Tierquarantäneinspektor m plant and animal quarantine inspector
Pflanzenverband m plant spacing; *(forest)* tree spacing
~/**weiter** wide [plant] spacing
Pflanzenverbreitung f distribution of plants
~ **durch den Menschen** anthropochory
Pflanzenverbrennung f **durch Düngemittel** fertilizer burn (scorch)
pflanzenverfügbar plant-available
Pflanzenverfügbarkeit f plant availability, availability for plants *(e.g. of nutrients)*
Pflanzenvermehrung f plant propagation, plant multiplication (reproduction)
~ **durch Luftableger** marcottage, marcotting, air layering
~ **durch Stecklinge** cuttage

Pflanzenverträglichkeit

Pflanzenverträglichkeit *f* plant compatibility, compatibility for plants
Pflanzenvirologe *m* plant virologist
Pflanzenvirologie *f* plant virology
Pflanzenvirus *n* plant virus
Pflanzenvorrat *m* [in Baumschulen] nursery stock
Pflanzenwachs *n* plant wax
Pflanzenwachstum *n* plant growth
~/**geiles** rankness
~/**überwucherndes** overgrowth
~/**üppiges** lushness, luxuriance
Pflanzenwachstumshemmstoff *m* plant growth retardant
Pflanzenwachstumsmeßgerät *n* auxanometer, auximeter
Pflanzenwachstumsphase *f* plant growth phase
Pflanzenwachstumsregulator *m* plant [growth] regulator, plant growth substance
Pflanzenwachstumsretardans *n* plant growth retardant
Pflanzenwasserzustand *m* plant water status
Pflanzenwelt *f* [eines Gebietes] flora
Pflanzenwuchs *m* vegetation
~/**üppiger** verdure
Pflanzenwuchshöhe *f* plant height
Pflanzenwuchskammer *f* plant-growth chamber
Pflanzenwurzel *f* plant-root
Pflanzenzelle *f* plant cell
Pflanzenzellensuspensionskultur *f* plant cell suspension culture
Pflanzenzellkultur *f* plant cell culture
Pflanzenzüchter *m* plant breeder
Pflanzenzüchtung *f* plant (crop) breeding
Pflanzenzüchtungsinstitut *n* plant breeding institute
Pflanzenzüchtungsmethode *f* plant breeding method
Pflanzenzusammensetzung *f* plant composition
Pflanzer *m* planter, grower
Pflanzgefäß *n* plant pot
Pflanzgerät *n* planting tool
Pflanzgewehr *n* (forest) planting gun
Pflanzgut *n* planting stock (material); seed [stock], seeds
~/**anerkanntes** certified seed
~/**eigenerzeugtes** home-saved seed
Pflanzgutanerkennung *f* seed certification
Pflanzgutaufbereitung *f* seed processing
Pflanzgutaufbereitungsanlage *f* seed processing plant
Pflanzgutaufwand *m* seed rate
Pflanzgutbehandlung *f* seed treatment
Pflanzgutbereitung *f s.* Pflanzgutaufbereitung
Pflanzgutertrag *m* seed yield
Pflanzguterzeuger *m* seed producer
Pflanzguterzeugung *f* seed production
Pflanzguthandel *m* seed trade
Pflanzguthändler *m* seedsman, seed's merchant

Pflanzgutherkunft *f* seed source, seed origin (provenance), source of seed
Pflanzgutinfektion *f* seed infection
Pflanzgutknolle *f* seed tuber
Pflanzgutkontrolle *f* seed control
Pflanzgutlagerung *f* seed storage
Pflanzgutpartie *f* seed lot
Pflanzgutprobe *f* seed sample
pflanzgutübertragen seed-borne *(causal agents, pests)*
Pflanzgutuntersuchung *f* seed test[ing]
Pflanzgutvermehrer *m* seed grower (producer)
Pflanzgutvermehrung *f* seed propagation (multiplication), seed growing (agriculture)
Pflanzgutwahl *f* choice of seed
Pflanzhacke *f* planting hoe (mattock); *(forest)* planting bar
Pflanzholz *n* planting dagger (peg, pin), dibble, dibbling tool, dibber, planter
Pflanzkartoffel *f* seed-potato
Pflanzkartoffelbau *m* seed-potato growing
Pflanzkartoffelfraktionierer *m* seed-potato dividing unit
Pflanzkartoffelschnittstück *n* seed-potato piece
Pflanzkelle *f* [garden] trowel
Pflanzkette *f* planting cord
Pflanzkistenwagen *m* trolley *(in greenhouses)*
Pflanzknolle *f* seed tuber
Pflanzknollen[schnitt]stück *n* seed-potato piece
Pflanzkübel *m* [plant] tub
Pflanzleine *f* planting cord
pflanzlich vegetable
~ **bedingt** phytogenous
Pflanzling *m* steckling
Pflanzloch *n* plant[ing] hole, dibble • **ein ~ ausheben** to hole
Pflanzlochbohrer *m* planting auger (drill, borer), [plant] hole digger
Pflanzlochbohrmaschine *f* plant hole drilling machine, dibbler
Pflanzlochbohrwagen *m* plant hole drilling cart
Pflanzlocher *m s.* Pflanzlochbohrer
Pflanzlochgerät *n* plant dibber, plant hole borer (digger), dibbler
Pflanzlochstern *m* star-wheeled dibbler
Pflanzlochvorbereitung *f* preholing
Pflanzlochwalze *f* plant hole roller
Pflanzmaschine *f* planting machine, planter
~/**halbautomatische** semiautomatic planter
~ **mit Klemmeinlegescheiben** flexible-disk transplanter
Pflanzmaterial *n* planting stock (material)
Pflanzmechanismus *m* planting apparatus
Pflanzmedium *n* substrate
Pflanzmesser *n* planting knife
Pflanznest *n* hill
Pflanzplan *m* planting plan
Pflanzreihe *f* [planting] row
Pflanzrohr *n* plant cane

Pflanzschale *f* plant bowl
Pflanzschar *n* planting coulter
Pflanzschaufel *f* [garden] trowel
Pflanzscheibe *f* spacing disk *(of a planter)*
Pflanzschnitt *m* pruning after planting
Pflanzschnur *f* planting line (cord), garden line, reel and line
Pflanzschulbeet *n* nursery bed
Pflanzschulbetrieb *m* nursery practice
Pflanzschule *f* nursery
Pflanzspaten *m* planting spade
Pflanzstelle *f* planting point
Pflanzstock *m* planting stick, planter; *(forest)* planting bar
Pflanzsystem *n* planting system
Pflanztermin *m* planting date
Pflanztiefe *f* planting depth, depth of planting
Pflanztisch *m* potting table; planting platform
~/fahrbarer movable potting table
Pflanztopf *m* planting pot
~/kleiner plug
Pflanztopfpresse *f* soil-block maker (making machine), soil-block press (pressing machine)
Pflanzung *f* 1. plantation, planting; 2. *s.* Pflanzen
~/heckenartige hedgerow planting
~/wertsteigernde *(forest)* improvement (enrichment) planting
Pflanzverband *m* planting arrangement, plant spacing
Pflanzverfahren *n* planting method
Pflanzversuch *m* planting trial
Pflanzwagen *m* planting cart
Pflanzweite *f* plant spacing, planting distance (pitch)
Pflanzwerkzeug *n* planting tool
Pflanzzeit *f* planting time (season)
Pflaume *f* 1. plum *(genus Prunus)*; 2. garden (common) plum, Prunus domestica [ssp. domestica]; 3. plum, prune *(fruit)*
Pflaumenbandmosaik *n (phyt)* plum line pattern *(virosis)*
Pflaumenbandmosaikvirus *n* plum line pattern virus
Pflaumenbaum *m* plum[-tree] *(genus Prunus)*
Pflaumenblättrige Spiraee *f (bot)* bridal wreath, Spiraea prunifolia
Pflaumenblättriger Apfel *m* Chinese apple, Malus prunifolia [var. rinkii]
~ Schneeball *m (bot)* blackhaw, Viburnum prunifolium
Pflaumenbohrer *m s.* Pflaumenstecher
pflaumenförmig pruniform
Pflaumenmus *n* plum sauce
Pflaumen-N-Virus *n* plum N virus
Pflaumenrüßler *m (ent)* plum curculio, Conotrachelus nenuphar
Pflaumenstecher *m* plum snout beetle, Rhynchites cupreus
pflaumentragend pruniferous
Pflaumenwickler *m* plum fruit moth, Grapholita (Cydia) funebrana
Pflaumenwicklerraupe *f* red plum maggot
PflBMV *s.* Pflaumenbandmosaikvirus
Pflege *f*/**zwischenreihige** inter-row cultivation
Pflegearbeitsgang *m*[/**pflanzenbaulicher**] cultivation operation
Pflegebaumart *f (forest)* nurse-tree species
pflegebedürftig in need of care, needing care
Pflegegeräte *npl* maintenance equipment
Pflegehieb *m (forest)* improvement (tending) felling
Pflegehinweis *m* [**für Zierpflanzen**] green thumb tip
pflegen 1. to care for (of), to tend, to look after *(e.g. plants, lawn)*; to attend, to dress *(animals)*, to groom *(esp. horses)*; to nurse *(sick animals)*; 2. to maintain *(machinery)*
~/mechanisch to cultivate *(a plant stand)*
Pflegevolk *n (api)* builder colony
Pflegeziel *n (forest)* tending objective
Pflichtablieferung *f* levy
Pflichtschutzimpfung *f (vet)* compulsory vaccination
PflNV *s.* Pflaumen-N-Virus
Pflock *m* stake
PflSV *s.* Scharkavirus der Pflaume
Pflückbeutel *m* picking bag, bin
~ mit Bodenentleerung bottom-dump picking bag
Pflückdruschaggregat *n* picker[-sheller] combine *(maize harvesting machine)*
Pflückdurchgang *m* pick[ing]
Pflücke *f* pick[ing], pluck
Pflückeimer *m* picking bucket
pflücken to pick, to pluck, to gather, to crop, to cull
Pflücker *m* picker, plucker
Pflückerbse *f* pick (vining) pea, cut (green) pea
Pflückernte *f* pick[ing]
Pflückerntedurchgang *m* pick[ing]
Pflückgefäß *n* picking receptacle, bin
Pflückgerät *n* picking device
Pflückhilfsmittel *n* picking aid
Pflückkarren *m* fruit picking cart
Pflückkorb *m* picking basket
Pflücklore *f* picking lorry
Pflückmaschine *f* mechanical picker
Pflückplattform *f* picking platform
pflückreif mature [for picking]
Pflückreife *f* picking maturity
Pflücksalat *m* curled (cut) lettuce, Lactuca sativa var. crispa
Pflückschroter *m* picker-grinder *(maize harvesting machine)*
Pflückvorsatz *m* picking attachment, pluck-head
Pflückwalze *f* picking roller
Pflückzeitraum *m* picking season
Pflug *m* plough, *(Am)* plow, buster • **unterm ~** under crop
~ mit kurzem Streichblech digger plough

Pflug

~ **mit langgezogenem Streichblech** ley (long plate) plough
~ **mit Rollenpflugkörpern** roller plough
~/**streichblechloser** mouldboardless plough
Pflugarbeit f ploughing [work]
Pflugarbeitstiefe f depth of ploughing
Pflugarbeitszone f plough zone (of soil)
pflügbar ploughable, arable
~/**nicht** unploughable, non-arable
Pflügbarkeit f ploughability, arability
Pflugbodenbearbeitung f plough-based tillage
Pflugbrust f [plough] breast, mould-board shin, front portion mould-board
Pflügegeschwindigkeit f speed of ploughing
Pflugeinstellung f plough setting
pflügen to plough, to furrow, (Am) to plow, to cut [a field]
~/**Brachland** to fallow
Pflügen n ploughing
~/**chemisches** chemical ploughing
~ **in Fallinie** ploughing up and down the slope, up- and-downhill ploughing
~ **in Höhenlinie** contour ploughing
~/**streichblechloses** boardless ploughing
Pflüger m plougher, ploughman, tiller
Pflügetiefe f plough[ing] depth
Pflugfurche f plough furrow
Pfluggeschwindigkeit f speed of ploughing
Pflughorizont m plough horizon
Pflugkarren m plough carriage, transport
Pflugkörper m [plough] body, [plough] bottom, box
~/**linkswendender** left-handed body
~ **mit mittelsteilem Streichblech** semidigger body
~/**rechtswendender** right-handed body
Pflugnachläufer m plough following unit
Pflugrahmen m plough frame
Pflugschar n [plough]share, plough blade (for compounds s. under Schar)
Pflugschar... s. a. Schar...
Pflugscharbein n vomer (animal anatomy)
Pflugsech n coulter, plough sock
Pflugsohle f 1. sole-shoe of plough; 2. s. Pflugsohlenverdichtung
Pflugsohlenlockerer m pan breaker
Pflugsohlenverdichtung f plough (furrow) sole, plough pan (layer), furrow bottom, pan
Pflugsterz m plough-tail, plough handle (neck)
Pflugtiefe f depth of ploughing
Pflugwiderstand m ploughing resistance
Pflugzone f plough zone (of soil)
Pfortader f portal vein (animal anatomy)
Pfortaderkreislauf m portal circulation
Pfortadernentzündung f (vet) pylephlebitis
Pförtner m pylorus, pyloric opening (animal anatomy)
Pfosten m post, pole, stanchion, stob, stake
Pfote f paw
pfriemartig (bot, zoo) subulate
Pfriemenginster m Spanish (weaver's) broom, Spartium junceum

Pfriemengras n needle (feather) grass (genus Stipa)
pfriemförmig (bot, zoo) subuliform
pfriemlich s. pfriemartig
Pfropfbastard m graft-hybrid
Pfropfchimäre f graft chim[a]era
Pfropfeisen n grafting chisel
pfropfen to [en]graft, to ingraft, to inoculate
~/**durch Annäherung** to ablactate
~/**hinter die Rinde** to crown-graft
~/**in den Spalt** to cleft-graft
~/**in die Krone** to top-work, to top-graft
Pfropfer m grafter
Pfropfhybride f graft-hybrid
Pfröpfling m s. Pfropfreis
Pfropfmesser n grafting knife, grafter
Pfropfpartner m graft partner
Propfrebe f grafted vine
Propfreis n graft, grafting scion (twig), scion, stick, cutting, slip (s. a. Edelauge)
Pfropfschnitt m, **Pfropfspalt** m grafting slit
Pfropfstelle f graft [union], union
Pfropfung f graftage, inoculation
Pfropfunverträglichkeit f graft incompatibility
Pfropfverfahren n grafting [method]
Pfropfversuch m grafting trial
Pfropfwachs n grafting-wax
PGSV s. Petuniengelbscheckungsvirus
Phaeophytin n phaeophytin
Phage m [bacterio]phage
Phagendiagnostik f phage typing
Phagostimulans n phagostimulant
Phagozyt m phagocyte
phagozytisch phagocytic
Phagozytose f (vet) phagocytosis
Phagtyp m lysotype (bacteriology)
Phalanx f phalanx
Phaltan n phaltan (fungicide)
Phän n (gen) phene
phanerogam (bot) phanerogamic, phanerogamous
Phanerogame f phanerogam
Phanerophyt m phanerophyte
Phänogenese f phenogenesis
Phänogenetik f phenogenetics
Phänoklimatographie f phenoclimatography
Phänokopie f (gen) phenocopy
Phänologe m phenologist
Phänologie f phenology
phänologisch phenological
Phänomen n phenomenon
~/**Recknagelsches** (dairy) Recknagel's phenomenon
Phänometrie f phenometry
Phänophase f phenophase
Phänotyp m phenotype
phänotypisch phenotypic[al]
Phantasiename m fancy name (e.g. of a plant cultivar)
Phantom n phantom, service dummy (for semen collection)

PhAR *s.* Strahlung/photosynthetisch aktive
Pharaoameise *f* Pharaoh's (red Egyptian) ant, Monomorium pharaonis
Pharmakologie *f* pharmacology
Pharmakopöe *f* pharmacopoeia
pharyngeal pharyng[e]al
Pharyngitis *f (vet)* pharyngitis
Pharyngoskopie *f (vet)* pharyngoscopy
Pharyngozele *f* pharyngocele
Pharynx *m* pharynx, oesophagus, throat, gullet, throttle
Pharynxdrüse *f* brood food gland *(of honey-bee)*
Phaseinsäure *f* phaseic acid *(growth regulator)*
Phase *f* phase
~/**diploide** diplophase
~/**juvenile** juvenile period
~/**vegetative** vegetative phase
Phasenfütterung *f* phase feeding
Phasenkontrastmikroskopie *f* phase-contrast microscopy
Phaseolamin *n* phaseolamin *(phytotoxin)*
Phaseollidin *n* phaseollidin *(phytoalexin)*
Phaseollin *n* phaseollin *(phytoalexin)*
Phaseollinisoflavan *n* phaseollinisoflavan *(phytoalexin)*
Phazelie *f (bot)* 1. phacelia *(genus Phacelia)*; 2. tansy phacelia, valley vervenia, Phacelia tanacetifolia
pH-Bereich *m* pH range
Phe *s.* Phenylalanin
Phellem *n (bot)* phellem
Phelloderm *n (bot)* phelloderm
Phellogen *n (bot)* phellogen, cork cambium
Phenanthren *n* phenanthrene *(hydrocarbon)*
Phenazetin *n* phenacetin *(antipyretic agent)*
Phenazon *n* phenazone, antipyrine *(analgesic)*
Phenethicillin *n* phenethicillin *(antibiotic)*
Phenisopham *n* phenisopham *(herbicide)*
Phenkapton *n* phenkapton *(acaricide)*
Phenmedipham *n* phenmedipham *(herbicide)*
Phenobarbital *n* phenobarbital *(anaesthetic)*
Phenobenzuron *n* phenobenzuron *(herbicide)*
Phenocillin *n* penicillin V *(antibiotic)*
Phenol *n* phenol
Phenol-ß-Glucosyltransferase *f* phenol-ß-glucosyltransferase *(enzyme)*
phenolisch phenolic
Phenoloxidase *f* phenol oxidase *(enzyme)*
Phenolphthalein *n* phenolphthalein *(indicator)*
Phenolrot *n*, **Phenolsulfonphthalein** *n* phenol red, phenolsulphon[e]phthalein *(indicator)*
Phenoltest *m* phenol test[ing]
Phenothiazin *n* phenothiazine, PTZ *(anthelminthic, insecticide)*
Phenthiuram *n* phenthiuram *(fungicide)*
Phenthoat *n* phenthoat *(insecticide)*
Phenylalanin *n* phenylalanine *(amino-acid)*
Phenylalaninammoniumlyase *f* phenylalanine ammonia lyase *(enzyme)*

Phenylalanindesaminase *f* phenylalanine ammonia lyase *(enzyme)*
Phenylalanin-4-Hydroxylase *f*, **Phenylalanin-4-Monoxygenase** *f* phenylalanine 4-hydroxylase, phenylalanine 4-monooxygenase *(enzyme)*
Phenylbutazon *n* phenylbutazone *(analgesic)*
Phenylessigsäure *f* phenylacetic acid
Phenylquecksilberacetat *n* phenylmercury acetate, PMA *(fungicide, herbicide, disinfectant)*
Phenylquecksilberchlorid *n* phenylmercury chloride, PMC *(fungicide)*
Phenylquecksilbernitrat *n* phenylmercury nitrate *(fungicide)*
Pheromon *n* pheromone, ectohormone
Pheromonfalle *f* pheromone[-containing] trap
Pheromonfallenfang *m* pheromone-trap catch
Pheromonverteiler *m* pheromone dispenser
Pherothrin *n* pherothrin *(insecticide)*
Philodendron *m (bot)* 1. philodendron, sweetheart plant, parlour ivy *(genus Philodendron)*; 2. common philodendron, Philodendron scandens
Philometrosis *f (vet)* philometrosis *(of carps, caused by Philometra lusiana)*
Philtrum *n* philtrum *(animal anatomy)*
Phimose *f (vet)* phimosis
Phlebitis *f (vet)* phlebitis
Phlebothrombose *f (vet)* phlebothrombosis
Phlebotomie *f (vet)* phlebotomy
Phlegmone *f (vet)* phlegmon
phlegmonös *(vet)* phlegmonous
Phlobaphen *n* phlobaphene *(pigment)*
Phloem *n (bot)* phloem, conducting tissue, [fibro-]vascular tissue, vascular system, sieve tube member, bast
~/**intraxyläres** internal phloem
~/**sekundäres** secondary phloem
Phloembeladung *f* phloem loading *(plant physiology)*
Phloemdegeneration *f (phyt)* phloem degeneration
Phloemgeleitzelle *f* phloem companion cell
Phloemmutterzelle *f* phloem mother cell
Phloemmarkstrahl *m* phloem ray
Phloemnekrose *f (phyt)* phloem necrosis
Phloemparenchym *n* phloem parenchyma
Phloemprotein *n* phloem protein
Phloemsaft *m* phloem sap
phlogistisch *(vet)* phlogistic
phlogogen *(vet)* phlogogenic, phlogogenous
Phlogopit *m* phlogopite *(non-clay mineral)*
Phlogosis *f (vet)* phlogosis
Phloridzin *n* phlorhizin, phlori[d]zin *(glucoside)*
Phloroglucin *n* phloroglucin[ol]
Phlox *m(f) (bot)* phlox *(genus Phlox)*
phobisch phobic
Phobotaxis *f* motor reflex (response)
Phoma[trocken]fäule *f* [der Kartoffel] [potato] gangrene *(caused by Phoma exigua var. foveata and P. exigua var. exigua)* • **von ~ befallen** gangrenous

Phomopsis

Phomopsis f dead-arm disease *(of grape-vine, caused by Phomopsis viticola)*
Phönizischer Wacholder m Phoenician juniper, Juniperus phoenica
Phonolith m phonolite *(non-clay mineral)*
Phorat n phorate *(insecticide, nematicide)*
Phorent m migratory host
Phoresie f *(ecol)* phoresia
Phosalon n phosalone *(insecticide)*
Phosdrin n mevinphos *(insecticide, acaricide, nematicide)*
Phosfolan n phosfolan *(insecticide)*
Phosphamidon n phosphamidon *(insecticide, acaricide)*
Phosphat n phosphate
Phosphatacetyltransferase f phosphate acetyltransferase *(enzyme)*
Phosphatase f phosphatase *(enzyme)*
~/**alkalische** alkaline phosphatase
~/**saure** acid phosphatase
Phosphatasecarboxylase f phosphatase carboxylase *(enzyme)*
Phosphatasenachweis m, **Phosphataseprobe** f *(dairy)* phosphatase test
Phosphatdüngemittel n phosphorus (phosphatic) fertilizer, phosphate [fertilizer]
~/**stickstoffhaltiges** nitrogen-phosphorus fertilizer
Phosphaterz n, **Phosphatgestein** n phosphate rock
Phosphatid n phosphatide, phospholipid, phospholipin
Phosphatidsäure f phosphatidic acid
Phosphatidylcholin n phosphatidylcholine, lecithin
Phosphatidylcolamin n s. Phosphatidylethanolamin
Phosphatidylethanolamin n phosphatidylethanolamine, cephalin
Phosphatidylinositol n phosphatidylinositol
Phosphatlöslichkeit f phosphate solubility
Phosphatpotential n phosphate potential
Phosphatpuffer m phosphate buffer
Phosphatspiegelerhöhung f im Blut *(vet)* hyperphosphataemia
Phosphatspiegelverringerung f im Blut *(vet)* hypophosphataemia
Phosphatträger m phosphate carrier
Phosphaturie f *(vet)* phosphaturia
Phosphin n phosphine, phosphorus hydride *(insecticide, rodenticide)*
Phosphobakterin n phosphobacterin
Phosphodiesterase f phosphodiesterase *(enzyme)*
Phosphoenolpyruvatcarboxykinase f phosphoenolpyruvate carboxykinase *(enzyme)*
Phosphoenolpyruvatcarboxylase f phosphoenolpyruvate carboxylase *(enzyme)*
Phosphofructokinase f phosphofructokinase *(enzyme)*

Phosphoglucoisomerase f glucose-6-phosphate isomerase *(enzyme)*
Phosphoglucomutase f phosphoglucomutase *(enzyme)*
Phosphogluconat n phosphogluconate
Phosphogluconatdehydrogenase f phosphogluconate dehydrogenase *(enzyme)*
Phosphogluconatweg m phosphogluconate pathway, pentose phosphate cycle *(of glucose degradation)*
Phosphoglyceratkinase f phosphoglycerate kinase *(enzyme)*
Phosphoglycer[ol]säure f phosphoglyceric acid, PGA
Phosphohexoseisomerase f glucose-6-phosphate isomerase *(enzyme)*
Phosphoketolase f phosphoketolase *(enzyme)*
Phosphokinase f phosphokinase *(enzyme)*
Phosphokreatin n phosphocreatine, creatine phosphate
Phospholipid n phospholipid, phospholipin, phosphatide
Phosphomannoisomerase f mannosephosphate isomerase *(enzyme)*
Phosphomonoesterase f phosphomonoesterase *(enzyme)*
Phosphon n phosphon *(growth regulator)*
Phosphonomycin n bambermycin, flavophospholipol, flavomycin *(antibiotic)*
Phosphopeptid n phosphopeptide
Phosphoprotein n phosphoproteid[e]
Phosphoprotein n phosphoprotein
Phosphoproteinphosphatase f phosphoprotein phosphatase *(enzyme)*
Phosphopyruvathydratase f enolase *(enzyme)*
Phosphor m phosphorus
Phosphoraufnahme f phosphorus uptake
Phosphorbedarf m phosphorus requirement
Phosphordünger m phosphorus (phosphatic) fertilizer, phosphate [fertilizer]
Phosphordüngung f phosphatization
Phosphoreszenz f phosphorescence
Phosphorfestlegung f phosphorus fixation
Phosphoribulokinase f phosphoribulokinase *(enzyme)*
Phosphoribuloseepimerase f ribulose-phosphate 3-epimerase *(enzyme)*
Phosphorit m phosphorite *(non-clay mineral)*
Phosphor-Kali[um]-Düngemittel n phosphorus potassium fertilizer
Phosphormangel m aphosphorosis
phosphororganisch organophosphorous
Phosphorproteid n phosphoproteid[e]
Phosphorprotein n phosphoprotein
Phosphorsäure f [ortho]phosphoric acid
Phosphorsäuredünger m s. Phosphordünger
Phosphorverbindung f/**organische** organophosphate, organophosphorous compound
Phosphorwasserstoff m s. Phosphin

Phyllosphäre

Phosphorylase f phosphorylase *(enzyme)*
Phosphorylasekinase f phosphorylase kinase *(enzyme)*
phosphorylieren to phosphorylate
Phosphorylierung f phosphorylation
~/aerobe (oxidative) oxidative phosphorylation
Phosvitin n vitellin *(egg-yolk constituent)*
photoaktiv photoactive
photoautotroph *(bot)* photoautotrophic
Photoautotrophie f *(bot)* photoautotrophy
Photobakterium n photobacterium
Photobiologie f photobiology
photobiologisch photobiologic
Photochemie f photochemistry
photochemisch photochemical
Photodermatitis f *(vet)* photodermatitis
Photogrammetrie f photogrammetry
~/forstliche forest photogrammetry
Photokinese f, **Photokinesis** f photokinesis
photokinetisch photokinetic
Photolyse f photolysis, photolytic degradation
Photometer n photometer
Photometrie f photometry
Photomigration f photomigration *(e.g. of insect larvae)*
Photomorphogenese f *(bot)* photomorphogenesis
Photomorphose f photomorphosis
Photonastie f *(bot)* photonastic movement
photonastisch *(bot)* photonastic
Photoperiode f photoperiod
photoperiodisch photoperiodic
~ unempfindlich *(bot)* day-neutral
Photoperiodismus m, **Photoperiodizität** f photoperiodicity, photoperiodism, photoperiodic behaviour
photophil photophilous
Photophilie f
photophob photophobic
Photophobie f photophobia
Photophosphorylierung f photophosphorylation *(photosynthesis)*
photopisch photopic *(relating to vision with light-adapted eyes)*
Photorespiration f photoresoiration *(plant physiology)*
photorespiratorisch photorespiratory
Photorezeptor m photoreceptor
Photosensibilisationskrankheit f *(vet)* photodermatitis
Photosensibilisierung f photosensitization
Photosensibilität f photosensitivity
photosensitiv photosensitive
Photosensitivität f photosensitivity
Photostadium n photostage, light stage
Photosynthese f photosynthesis • **durch ~ erzeugt** photosynthesized
~/apparente apparent photosynthesis, net assimilation
~/reelle (reine) real (gross) photosynthesis

Photosyntheseeffektivität f photosynthetic efficiency
Photosyntheseeinheit f photosynthetic unit
Photosyntheseintensität f s. Photosyntheserate
Photosynthesekapazität f photosynthetic capacity
Photosynthesepotential n photosynthetic potential
Photosyntheseprodukt n photosynthate
Photosynthesequotient m assimilation quotient
Photosyntheserate f photosynthetic rate, rate of photosynthesis
Photosynthesevermögen n photosynthetic capacity
Photosyntheseweg m photosynthetic pathway
Photosynthesewirkungsgrad m photosynthetic efficiency
photosynthetisch photosynthetic
photosynthetisieren to photosynthesize
Photosystem n photosystem, pigment system, PS
~ I photosystem I
~ II photosystem II
Phototaxis f phototaxis
Phototherapie f *(vet)* phototherapy
phototrop[isch] *(bot)* phototropic, heliotropic
Phototropismus m *(bot)* phototropism, heliotropism
~/positiver prophototropism
Phoxim n phoxim *(insecticide)*
PHR s. Hämagglutinationsreaktion/passive
phreatisch phreatic
Phreatophyt m phreatophyte
Phrenikus m phrenic nerve
Phrenosin n phrenosin *(lipid)*
Phthise f, **Phthisis** f *(vet)* phthisis
pH-Wert m pH [value], hydrogen-ion concentration
~ des Blutes blood pH
~ des Bodens soil pH
Phygma n *(vet)* efflorescence
Phykologie f phycology
Phykomykose f *(phyt, vet)* phycomycosis
Phykomyzet m phycomycete
Phylaxis f *(vet)* phylaxis
phyletisch s. phylogenetisch
Phyllit m *(soil)* phyllite
Phyllochinon n phylloquinone, coagulation vitamin
Phyllociad-16-en-19-säure f kaurenoic acid *(terpene)*
Phyllodie f *(phyt)* phyllody
Phyllodium n phyllode, phyllodium
Phylloerythrin n phylloerythrin *(dye)*
Phylloidie f *(phyt)* phyllody
Phyllokaktus m phyllocactus *(comprehensive term)*
Phyllokladium n *(bot)* phylloclade
Phyllomanie f *(phyt)* phyllomania
Phyllomorphie f *(phyt)* phyllody
phyllophag phyllophagous, leaf-eating
Phyllosilicat n phyllosilicate
Phyllosphäre f phyllosphere

Phyllotaxis

Phyllotaxis *f* phyllotaxis, phyllotaxy
Phylogenese *f* phylogenesis, phylogeny
phylogenetisch phylogenetic
Phylum *n* 1. phylum *(taxonomy)*; 2. division *(taxonomy)*
Physiogeographie *f* physiography
Physiognomie *f* physiognomy
Physiographie *f* physiography
Physiologe *m* physiologist
Physiologie *f* physiology
~ **der Ertragsbildung** production physiology
~ **der Fortpflanzung** reproductive physiology
~ **der Kulturpflanzen** crop physiology
~ **der Zelle** cell physiology
physiologisch physiological
Physostigmin *n* physostigmine *(alkaloid)*
Phytagglutinin *n* lectin *(glycoprotein)*
Phytalid *n* phytalide *(fungicide)*
6-Phytase *f* 6-phytase *(enzyme)*
Phytat *n s.* Phytin
Phythämagglutinin *n* lectin, phytomitogen *(glycoprotein)*
Phytiatrie *f* phytomedicine
Phytin *n* phytin, inosite hexaphosphate
Phytinphosphor *m* phytin phosphorus
Phytinsäure *f* phytic acid
Phytoalexin *n* phytoalexin
Phytoantibiotikum *n* phytoncide
Phytobakteriologie *f* phytobacteriology
Phytobezoar *m* phytobezoar
Phytochemie *f* phytochemistry
Phytochemiker *m* phytochemist
phytochemisch phytochemical
Phytochrom *n* phytochrome *(chromoprotein)*
Phytoen *n* phytoene *(carotene precursor)*
phytogen phytogenic, phytogenous
Phytogenese *f* phytogenesis, phytogeny
Phytogenetik *f* phytogenetics, plant genetics
Phytogenetiker *m* plant geneticist
phytogenetisch phytogenetic[al], phytogenic
Phytogeographie *f* phytogeography, plant geography, geobotany
phytogeographisch phytogeographic[al]
Phytogerontologie *f* phytogerontology
Phytoglycogen *n* phytoglycogen *(polysaccharide)*
Phytographie *f* phytography
Phytohämagglutinin *n* phytohaemagglutinin
Phytohormon *n* phytohormone, plant hormone
Phytoimmunologie *f* phytoimmunology
Phytokinin *n* cytokinin *(phytohormone)*
Phytoklima *n* phytoclimate, plant climate
Phytoklimatologie *f* phytoclimatology, plant climatology
Phytol *n* phytol *(diterpene)*
Phytologe *m* phytologist
Phytologie *f* phytology, plant biology (science), botany
phytologisch phytologic[al]
Phytomasse *f* phytomass

Phytomedizin *f* phytomedicine
Phytomon *n* phytomone
Phytomorphologie *f* phytomorphology, plant morphology
Phytonematode *m* plant [parasitic] nematode
Phytonematologie *f* plant nematology
Phytonose *f* plant disease
Phytonzid *n* phytoncide
Phytoparasit *m* phytoparasite
phytoparasitär plant parasitic
phytopathogen phytopathogenic
Phytopathogen *n* phytopathogen, plant pathogen
Phytopathogenese *f* plant pathogenesis
Phytopathologe *m* plant pathologist
Phytopathologie *f* phytopathology, plant pathology
phytopathologisch phytopathological
phytophag phytophagic, phytophagous, plant-eating, herbivorous
Phytophag[e] *m* plant eater (feeder)
Phytophagie *f* phytophagy
Phytophänologie *f* phytophenology, plant phenology
Phytopharmakon *n* phytopharmaceutical [agent]
phytopharmazeutisch phytopharmaceutical
Phytopharmazie *f* phytopharmaceutics, phytopharmacy
Phytophthora-Braunfleckenkrankheit *f* **des Tabaks** tobacco brown spot [disease], black shank of tobacco *(caused by Phytophthora nicotianae var. parasitica)*
Phytoplankton *n* phytoplankton, plant plankton
phytosanitär phytosanitary
Phytosanitation *f* phytosanitation
Phytosoziologie *f* phytosociology, plant sociology
Phytosterin *n*, **Phytosterol** *n* phytosterol, plant sterol
Phytöstrogen *n* phytoestrogen, plant oestrogen, phytohormone
Phytotherapie *f* phytotherapy
Phytotoxin *n* phytotoxin, plant poison
phytotoxisch phytotoxic
Phytotoxizität *f* phytotoxicity
Phytotron *n* phytotron
Phytozid *n* phytoncide
Phytozönogenese *f* phytocoenogenesis
Phytozönologie *f* phytocoenology, phytosociology
phytozönologisch phytosociological
Phytozönose *f* phytocoenosis, plant community
phytozönotisch phytocoenotic
Phytozönotyp *m* phytocoenotype
Phytuberin *n* phytuberin *(phytoalexin)*
Phytuberol *n* phytuberol *(phytoalexin)*
pH-Zahl *f s.* pH-Wert
Piaffe *f* piaffer *(equestrian sport)*
Piassavafaser *f* piassava [fibre] *(from Attalea funifera)*
Pica *f (vet)* pica
Piceetum *n* spruce forest

~ **compositum** compound spruce forest
~ **myrtillosum** bilberry spruce forest
picken to pick
Pick-up-Presse f pick-up baler (press)
Pick-up-Vorrichtung f pick-up [device]
Picloram n picloram (herbicide)
Picolinsäure f picolinic acid, pyridine-2-carboxylic acid
Piedmontfläche f piedmont
Piemontese[r] n Piedmont (cattle breed)
piep[s]en to pip, to peep, to peek, to cheep
Piercesche Krankheit f der Weinrebe Pierce's disease of vine (bacteriosis)
Piétrain[schwein] n Piétrain (pig breed)
Piezometer n piezometer
Pigment n pigment
~/**pflanzliches** plant pigment
~/**tierisches** animal pigment
Pigmentanomalie f s. Pigmentationsstörung
Pigmentation f pigmentation
Pigmentationsstörung f (vet) pigmentation disorder
Pigmentepithel n **der Netzhaut** tapetum [of the retina]
Pigmentgeschwulst f (vet) melanoma, chromatophoroma
Pigmentierung f pigmentation
Pigmentierungsmittel n pigmenter, pigmenting agent
Pigmentlosigkeit f **der Haare** achromotrichia
Pigmentschwund m depigmentation
Pigmentzelle f/**melaninhaltige** melanocyte
Pignole f pine nut (from Pinus cembra)
Pike-fry-Rhabdovirus-Krankheit f (pisc, vet) pike fry rhabdovirus disease
pikieren to prick [out, off], to line out
pikiergesät spaced-sown
Pikierholz n pricking wood
Pikierkasten m, **Pikierkiste** f pricking-out box (tray), [planting-out] tray, flat
Pikiermaschine f transplanting machine
Pikör m huntsman
Piliganin n piliganin[e] (alkaloid)
Pilinuß f pili-nut, Canarium ovatum
Pillarbaum m pillar tree (orcharding)
Pillar[kronen]form f pillar form (of orchard trees)
Pillenfarn m pillwort (genus Pilularia)
Pillenriedgras n, **Pillensegge** f pill-headed sedge, Carex pilulifera
Pillieranlage f pelleter
pillieren to pellet[ize]
Pillierung f pelleting
Pilobezoar m (vet) trichobezoar
Pilocarpin n pilocarpine (alkaloid)
Piloerektion f piloerection
Pils[e]ner n Pils[e]ner (kind of beer)
Pilz m fungus (kingdom Mycota)
~/**eßbarer** [edible] mushroom, edible fungus, champignon

~/**giftiger** poisonous fungus, toadstool
~/**holzverfärbender** [wood-]staining fungus
~/**imperfekter** imperfect fungus (group Deuteromycetes = Fungi imperfecti)
~/**parasitärer** parasitic fungus
~/**stark giftiger** deadly agaric
Pilz... s. a. Myko...
pilzabtötend fungicidal
pilzähnlich s. pilzartig
Pilzanbau m mushroom growing (cultivation)
pilzartig fungous, mushroom-like
Pilzausbruch m fungus outbreak
pilzbedingt mycotic
Pilzbefall m fungal attack (infection)
Pilzbekämpfungsmittel n fungicide
Pilzbrut f [mushroom] spawn, mycelium
~/**fruchtkörpertragende** stroma
~/**granulierte** grain spawn
Pilzbrutentwicklung f spawning
Pilzbruthersteller m spawn maker
Pilzbrutherstellung f spawn-making
Pilzbrutproduktionsanlage f spawning line
Pilzbrutziegel m spawn-brick
Pilzeiweiß n fungal protein
Pilzerkrankung f fungal disease, mycosis
Pilzfaden m s. Hyphe
Pilzfäule f (phyt) fungus rot, fungal decay
pilzfest fungus-proof
Pilzfliege f mushroom fly (genus Megaselia)
pilzförmig mushroom-shaped
pilzfressend fungivorous, myc[et]ophagous
Pilzgalle f (phyt) fungal gall
Pilzgeflecht n mycelium, [mushroom] spawn (for compounds s. under Pilzbrut)
Pilzgift n mycotoxin
pilzhemmend fungistatic, mycostatic
Pilzhut m mushroom cap
~/**geschlossener** button
Pilzkappe f s. Pilzhut
Pilzkolonie f fungus colony
Pilzkrankheit f fungal disease, mycosis
Pilzkunde f mycology, fungology
Pilzkundler m mycologist
pilzkundlich mycologic[al]
Pilzkultur f mushroom (fungal) culture
Pilzlager n s. Pilzgeflecht
Pilzlamelle f mushroom gill
pilzlich fungal, fungous
Pilzrasen m s. Pilzgeflecht
Pilzspore f fungal (fungus) spore
Pilzsubstrat n mushroom substrate (compost)
pilztötend fungicidal
Pilzvergiftung f mycotoxicosis
Pilzwachstum n fungal growth
pilzwachstumshemmend fungistatic, mycostatic
Pilzwachstumshemmung f fungistasis
Pilzwelke f (phyt) fungal wilt
Pilzzucht f mushroom growing (cultivation); cultivation of fungi (biotechnology)

Pilzzucker

Pilzzucker *m* trehalose *(disaccharide)*
Pimarsäure *f* pimaric acid *(wood extractive)*
Piment *m(n)* allspice, pimento
Pimentbaum *m* allspice [tree], pimento, Jamaica pepper, Pimenta dioica
Pimentöl *n* allspice (pimento) oil
Pimpernuß *f* 1. bladdernut *(genus Staphylea)*; 2. [European] bladdernut, Staphylea pinnata
Pimpinelle *f (bot)* pimpinella *(genus Pimpinella)*
Pindon *n* pindone, pival[dione] *(rodenticide)*
Pinealorgan *n (zoo)* pineal body (gland, organ)
Pinen *n* pinene *(monoterpene)*
Pinetum *n* pinetum, pine forest
~ **cladinosum** lichen pine forest
~ **compositum** compound pine forest
~ **sphagnosum** sphagnum pinery
Pineyharz *n* white da[m]mar *(from Vateria indica)*
Pinguinente *f* White Runner [duck] *(breed)*
Pinie *f* [Italian] stone pine, umbrella (parasol) pine, Tuscan tree, Pinus pinea
Piniole *f s.* Pignole
Pinna *f* pinna *(of the external ear)*
Pinosylvin *n* pinosylvin
Pinozytose *f* pinocytosis
Pinsel *m* tuft of hair *(on antlers)*
Pinselfeder *f* pin feather, filoplume
Pintopferd *n (Am)* pinto *(horse breed)*
Pinzette *f (vet)* forceps
Pinzgauer [Rind] *n* Pinzgau, Noric *(cattle breed)*
pinzieren to pinch [back], to head [back, down], to top [off], to tip, to stop
Pionierbaumart *f*, **Pionierholzart** *f* pioneer [tree] species
Pionierpflanze *f* pioneer [plant], soil builder
Pionierwaldfläche *f* regenerating forest land
Pioskop *n (dairy)* pioscope
Pipeline *f* pipeline
Piperazin *n* piperazine *(anthelminthic)*
Piperidin *n* piperidine
Piperin *n* piperine *(alkaloid)*
Piperophos *n* piperophos *(herbicide)*
Pipette *f* pipette
Pippau *f(m) (bot)* hawk's-beard *(genus Crepis)*
Piproctanyl *n* piproctanyl *(growth regulator)*
Piprotal *n* piprotal *(insecticide)*
Pips *m (vet)* pip *(of poultry)*
Piqueur *m* huntsman
Pirimetaphos *n* pirimetaphos *(insecticide)*
Pirimicarb *n* pirimicarb *(insecticide)*
Pirimiphos-methyl *n* pirimiphos-methyl *(insecticide)*
Piroplasmeninfektion *f*, **Piroplasmose** *f (vet)* piroplasmosis
Pirsch *f* [deer-]stalking, stalk, *(Am)* still-hunt
pirschen to stalk, to go [deer-]stalking, to hunt, *(Am)* to still-hunt
Pirschführer *m* stalker
Pirschjagd *f s.* Pirsch
Pirschjäger *m* deer-stalker, *(Am)* still-hunter

Pirschsteig *m*, **Pirschweg** *m* stalking path
Pisang[baum] *m (bot)* plantain, Musa x paradisiaca (sapientum)
Pisanghanf *m* Manila [hemp], abaca
Pisatin *n* pisatin *(phytoalexin)*
Pistazie *f* 1. pistachio, pistache *(genus Pistacia)*; 2. pistachio[-nut]
Pistaziengehölz *n*, **Pistazienlichtwald** *m* pistachio woodland
Pistazienmandel *f* pistachio[-nut]
Pistill[um] *n s.* Stempel 1.
Piszikultur *f* pisciculture, fish culture
piszizid piscicidal
Pitchpine *f* pitch-pine, Pinus rigida
Pitocin *n*, **Pituisan** *n* oxytocin *(hormone)*
Pituitrin *n* pituitrin *(hormone)*
Pityriasis *f (vet)* pityriasis
Pival *n* pindone, pival[dione] *(rodenticide)*
Pivampicillin *n* pivampicillin *(antibiotic)*
PK-Dünger *m* phosphorus potassium fertilizer
PL *s.* Panleukopenie
Pl *s.* Plenterhieb
Placenta *f s.* Plazenta
Plagge *f* sod
Plaggenboden *m* plaggen soil
Plaggenpflanzung *f* turf planting
Plaggenpflug *m* turfing plough
Plagiogeotropismus *m (bot)* plagiogeotropism
Plagioklas *m* plagioclase, lime-soda feldspar *(non-clay mineral)*
plagiotrop *(bot)* plagiotropic
Plagiotropismus *m (bot)* plagiotropism
Plane *f* canvas
~/**geteerte** tarpaulin, tarp
Planetengetriebe *n* planetary gear
planieren to level, to grade
Planiergerät *n* land leveller
Planierraupe *f* [bull]dozer, *(Am)* trailbuilder
~ **mit winkelverstellbarem Schild** angledozer
Planierschild *m* [bulldozer] blade
planktisch planktonic
Plankton *n* plankton
planktonisch planktonic
Planosol *m (soil)* planosol
Planospore *f (bot)* zoospore, swarm spore (cell)
Plansichter *m*, **Plansiebmaschine** *f* plane sifter
Plantage *f* plantation, planting
Plantagenarbeiter *m* plantation worker
Plantagenbaum *m* orchard tree
Plantagenbesitzer *m* plantation owner, planter
Plantagengrubber *m* orchard cultivator
Plantagenlandwirtschaft *f* plantation agriculture
Plantagenobstbau *m* orcharding
Plantagenpflug *m* orchard plough
plantar plantar
Plantlet *n* plantlet *(tissue culture)*
Planungszeitraum *m (forest)* felling cycle
PlANV *s.* Adernnetzvirus der Pelargonie
Plaques *npl*/**Peyersche** Peyer patches *(in the last division of the small intestine)*

Plasma n plasma, plasm
Plasmaemissionsspektroskopie f plasma emission spectroscopy
Plasmaenzym n plasma enzyme
Plasmafaktor m clotting factor *(immunology)*
Plasmagen n plasmagene
Plasmalemm[a] n plasmalemma, plasma (cell) membrane
Plasmalemmasom n *(phyt)* paramural body
Plasmalogen n plasmalogen *(phospholipid)*
Plasmalogensynthase f plasmalogen synthase *(enzyme)*
Plasmamembran n s. Plasmalemm[a]
Plasma-5'-Nucleotidase plasma 5'-nucleotidase *(enzyme)*
Plasmaphorese f plasmapheresis
Plasmaprotein n plasma protein
Plasmaströmung f protoplasmic streaming *(in a plant cell)*
plasmatisch plasmatic
Plasmavererbung f plasmatic (extrachromosomal) inheritance, extranuclear heredity (inheritance)
Plasmazelle f plasma cell
Plasmid n *(gen)* plasmid
~/tumorinduzierendes tumour-inducing plasmid
Plasmidvektor m plasmid vector
Plasmin n plasmin *(enzyme)*
Plasminogen n plasminogen
Plasminogenaktivator m plasminogen activator
Plasminvorstufe f plasminogen
Plasmodesmus m *(bot)* plasmodesm[a]
Plasmodienkrankheit f *(vet)* malaria
Plasmodium n 1. plasmodium *(multinucleate mass of protoplasm e.g. of a slime mould)*; 2. plasmodium *(blood protozoon of genus Plasmodium)*
Plasmogamie f plasmogamy
Plasmolyse f *(bot)* plasmolysis
plasmolytisch plasmolytic
Plasmon n plasmotype
Plasmoschise f plasmoschisis
Plasmotyp[us] m plasmotype
Plasmozym n s. Prothrombin
Plasmozytom n *(vet)* myeloma
Plasmozytose f Aleutian disease *(of minks)*
Plast... s. Kunststoff... and Plastik...
Plastein n plastein *(protein)*
Plastid m plastid *(organelle)*
~/pigmenthaltiger chromatophore
Plastide f s. Plastid
Plastidgen n plastid gene
Plastidmutation f plastid mutation
Plastidom n *(gen)* plastidome
Plastidotyp[us] m *(gen)* plastidotype
Plastik... s. a. Kunststoff...
Plastikdränrohrleitung f plastic drainage tubing
Plastikfolie f plastic film (foil)
Plastikfolienleger m plastic film layer
Plastikgittertopf m lattice pot *(for ornamentals)*

Plastikmull m/**hygroskopischer** hygroscopic plastic soil *(in gardening)*
Plastikschlauch m plastic hose
Plastiktopf m plastic pot
Plastizität f plasticity
~ des Bodens soil plasticity
Plastizitätsgrenze f *(soil)* plastic limit
~/obere upper plastic limit
~/untere lower plastic limit
Plastizitätsindex m, **Plastizitätszahl** f *(soil)* plastic index (number)
Plastochinon n plastoquinone *(plant substance)*
Plastocyanin n plastocyanin *(copper proteid, plant pigment)*
Plastogen n plasmagene
Plastom n *(gen)* plastom
Plastosol m *(soil)* plastosol
Plastrohrdränung f plastic drainage
Plastwelldränrohr n corrugated plastic drain-pipe
Platane f plane[-tree], platan[e], buttonwood, button-tree, *(Am)* sycamore *(genus Platanus)*
Platanenholz n buttonwood, lacewood, *(Am)* sycamore
Plateautemperatur f *(vet)* continued fever
Platinfuchs m platina fox
Plattährengras n union grass *(genus Uniola)*
Plattenbandförderer m apron conveyor
Plattenbandtrockner m apron-conveyor dryer
Plattenelevator m slat elevator
Plattenerhitzer m *(dairy)* plate pasteurizer, plate (baffle feed) heater
Plattenfichte f plate spruce *(growth habit)*
Plattenfilter n plate filter
Plattenförderer m apron conveyor
Plattengefüge n *(soil)* platy structure
Plattengefügekörper m *(soil)* platelike aggregate
Plattenkiefer f plate pine *(growth habit)*
Plattenkühlapparat m, **Plattenkühler** m plate cooler
Plattenkultur f plate culture *(microbiology)*
Plattensaat f *(forest)* patch sowing, sowing in patches
Plattenschar n slab share
Plattentrockner m platen dryer
Plattenwärme[aus]tauscher m plate heat exchanger, paraflow
Plattenwärmeübertrager m s. Plattenerhitzer
Plattenweg m flagstone path
Platterbse f chickling vetch, vetchling, meadow pea *(genus Lathyrus)*
Plattform f platform
Platthalmrispe f flattened poa, wire (Canada blue) grass, Poa compressa
Platthuf m flat hoof (foot)
Plattierungseffizienz f, **Plattierungswahrscheinlichkeit** f efficiency of plating *(virology)*
Plattkopf m pollard, hummel *(of red deer)*
Plattwurm m flatworm, platyhelminth *(phylum Plathelminthes)*

platz

platz! down! *(command to dogs)*
platzen to burst, to dehisce; to crack
Platzen *n* **der Fruchtwand** *(bot)* dehiscence
~ **des Kelches** calyx splitting *(of carnations)*
~ **von Früchten** fruit cracking
Plätzen *n (forest)* partial barking
platzend dehiscent
Plätzepflanzung *f (forest)* patch planting
Plätzesaat *f (forest)* patch sowing, sowing in patches
Platzneigung *f* cracking tendency *(e.g. of fruit peels)*
Platzregen *m* rain shower, downpour
Plazenta *f* 1. *(zoo)* placenta, afterbirth; 2. *(bot)* placenta *(esp. the ovule-bearing part of the carpel)*
Plazentahormon *n* placental hormone
plazental, plazentar placental
Plazentarkreislauf *m* placental circulation
Plazentarzotte *f (zoo)* cotyledon
Plazentatier *n* eutherian *(major division Eutheria)*
Plazentation *f* placentation
Plazentitis *f (vet)* placentitis
Plazentophagie *f* placentophagia
PIBFV *s.* Blütenfarbenbrechungsvirus der Pelargonie
Plectenchym *n (bot)* plectenchyma
Pleiochasium *n (bot)* pleiochasium
pleiotrop *(gen)* pleiotropic
Pleiotropie *f* pleiotropism, pleiotrop[h]y, polypheny
pleistozän Pleistocene
Pleistozän *n* Pleistocene, glacial epoch (period)
Plektenchym *n (bot)* plectenchyma
Plenterbestand *m (forest)* selection stand
Plenterbetrieb *m* selection system (method), plenter system, stem-by-stem selection
Plenterdurchforstung *f* selection (plenter) thinning
~ **nach Borggreve** Borggreve thinning
Plenterhieb *m* selection felling (logging), plenter felling
~**/baumweiser (einzelstammweiser)** selection felling of individual trees
~ **mit Entnahme der stärksten Durchmesserstufen** obligatory selection felling
plentern to log selectively, to cull [out]
Plentersaumschlag *m* strip selection felling (cutting), selection felling in marginal (narrow) strips
Plenterschlag *m s.* Plenterhieb
Plenterwald *m* selection (culled) forest
Plenterwirtschaft *f s.* Plenterbetrieb
pleomorph *s.* polymorph
pleophag *s.* polyphag
Plerozerkoid *n* plerocercoid *(effective larva of tapeworms)*
Plesiasmie *f (phyt)* rosetting
Plethysmogramm *n (vet)* plethysmogram
Plethysmograph *m* plethysmograph *(an instrument for measuring and registering volume variations of organs or limbs)*

Plethysmographie *f* plethysmography
plethysmographisch plethysmographic
Plethysmometrie *f* plethysmometry
plethysmometrisch plethysmometric
Pleura *f* pleura *(animal anatomy)*
Pleurahöhle *f* pleural cavity
pleural pleural, pleuric
Pleuritis *f (vet)* pleurisy, pleuritis
pleuritisch pleuritic[al]
Pleuromutilin *n* tiamulin *(antibiotic)*
Pleuropneumonie *f (vet)* pleuropneumonia
~ **der Rinder/infektiöse** contagious bovine pleuropneumonia
Pleurozentese *f (vet)* pleurocentesis
Pleuston *n (ecol)* pleuston
Plexor *m (vet)* plexor, percussion hammer
Plexus *n* plexus *(animal anatomy)*
Plicatinsäure *f* plicatic acid *(lignan constituent)*
plikat *(bot, zoo)* plicate[d]
Plinthit *m (soil)* laterite
Plinthitbildung *f* laterization, ferrallitization
Plinthitboden *m* laterite (lateritic) soil
Ploidie *f (gen)* ploidy
Ploidieeffekt *m* ploidy effect
Ploidiegrad *m* ploidy
Ploidiemutation *f* genome mutation
Ploidiestufe *f* ploidy level
Plossobaum *m* palas (dhak) tree, Butea superba (monosperma, frondosa)
Plott Hound *m* plott *(dog breed)*
Plötze *f* roach, Rutilus rutilus
PIRFV *s.* Pelargonienringfleckenvirus
Plumage *f* plumage
Plumbogummit *m* plumbogummite *(non-clay mineral)*
Plumula *f* 1. *(bot)* plumule, primary shoot; 2. *(zoo)* plumule [feather]
Plundermilch *f* naturally soured milk
Plungerpumpe *f* plunger pump
plurivoltin *(ent)* polyvoltine, multivoltine
Plusbaum *m (forest)* plus (crop) tree, choice (select) tree, choice stem (log), champion (superior) tree, phenotypic elite tree
Plusbaumauswahl *f* plus tree selection
Plusbestand *m* plus stand
plustern/sich to ruffle up *(a bird)*; to fluff *(plumage)*
Pluviograph *m* pluviograph
Pluviometer *n* pluviometer, rain-gauge, ombrometer, udometer
~**/registrierendes** pluviograph
Pluviometrie *f* pluviometry
pluviometrisch pluviometric[al]
Plymouth Rock *n* Plymouth Rock *(breed of fowl)*
p.m. *s.* postmortal
PMA *s.* Phenylquecksilberacetat
PMC *s.* Phenylquecksilberchlorid
PMR-Analyse *f* proton magnetic resonance analysis
PMSG *s.* Stutenserumgonadotropin

pneumatisch 1. pneumatic; 2. s. ~ betätigt
~ betätigt pneumatic, air-operated, air-powered
Pneumatizität f pneumaticity (e.g. of bones)
Pneumatophor n (bot) pneumatophore, respiratory (aerating) root
Pneumoenzephalogramm n encephalogram
Pneumonie f (vet) pneumonia
~ der Kälber/enzootische calf pneumonia
~ des Schweines/enzootische swine enzootic pneumonia, SEP
~/enzootische enzootic pneumonia
~/[interstitielle] progressive maedivisna (of sheep)
Pneumothorax m (vet) pneumothorax, aerothorax
Pneumovagina f (vet) pneumovagina, vaginal wind-sucking
PnMV s. Prunellamosaikvirus
Pochkäfer m death-watch [beetle] (family Anobiidae)
Pockenepitheliom n (vet) fish pox, hyperplastic epidemical disease, cutaneous warts
Pockenerkrankung f (vet) pox disease
Pockenkrankheit f der Cyclamenblüten grey mould of cyclamen (caused by Botrytis cinerea)
~ der Kartoffel rhizoctonia canker (disease), black scurf (speck), potato black scurf (caused by Rhizoctonia solani)
Pockenmilbe f leaf blister mite (genus Phytoptus)
Pockenpapillom n s. Pockenepitheliom
Pockenvirus n poxvirus (family Poxviridae)
Pocket Beagle m pocket beagle (dog breed)
Pockholz n guaiac[um]
Pockholzbaum m (bot) guaiacum (genus Guajacum)
Podagra n des Weizens s. Weizengicht
Pododermatitis f (vet) pododermatitis
podokarp (bot) podocarpous
Podophyllin n podophyllin (toxicant from Podophyllum peltatum)
Podotrochlitis f navicular disease (of horses)
Podsol m (soil) podzol, podsol
~/verborgener latent podzol
podsolig podzolic
podsolieren to podzolize
podsoliert podzolic
Podsolierung f podzolization, podzol formation
poikilotherm poikilothermic
Poikilotherme m poikilotherm
Poikilothermie f poikilothermy
Poinsettie f poinsettia, Christmas star, Euphorbia pulcherrima
Pointer m pointer (dog breed)
Poissonverteilung f Poisson distribution (statistics)
Poitevine-Ziege f Poitou goat (breed)
Poitou-Esel m Poitou (ass breed)
Pökel m pickle
Pökellake f pickling solution, souse, brine

pökeln to cure, to corn, to salt; to pickle, to souse, to brine
Pökelrindfleisch n corned beef, bully [beef]
Polaräsche f Arctic grayling, Thymallus arcticus
Polarfuchs m Arctic fox, Alopex lagopus
Polarimeter n polarimeter, polariscope
Polarimetrie f polarimetry
Polarität f polarity
Polarklima n polar climate
Polarluft f polar air
Polder m polder, dikeland (low-lying land reclaimed from sea)
Polderboden m polder soil
Poleigamander m (bot) pennyroyal germander, Teucrium polium
Poleiminze f pennyroyal, pudding grass, Mentha pulegium
polieren to polish
Poliermaschine f polishing machine, polisher
Polioenzephalomalazie f (vet) polioencephalomalacia
Poliomyelitis f (vet) poliomyelitis
Polkörperchen n pole cell (of bird's egg)
pollakanth s. polykarp
Polled Dorset n Polled Dorset (sheep breed)
Polled-Hereford n Poll[ed] Hereford (cattle breed)
Pollen m (bot) pollen, dust, farina
Pollenabortion f (phyt) pollen abortion
Pollenallergen n pollen allergen
Pollenanalyse f pollen analysis
Pollenbestrahlung f pollen irradiation
Pollenblume f pollen flower
Pollenbürste f pollen brush (of bees)
Pollendegeneration f pollen degeneration
Pollendiagramm n pollen diagram
Pollendimorphismus m pollen dimorphism
Pollenersatz[stoff] m (api) pollen substitute
Pollenfalle f (api) pollen trap
pollenfertil male-fertile
Pollenfertilität f pollen fertility
Pollenfresser m (ent) pollen feeder
Pollenfruchtbarkeit f pollen fertility
Pollengen n pollen gen
Pollengewinnung f mittels Pollenfalle pollen trapping
Pollenhöschen n (api) pollen load
Pollenkallus m pollen callus
Pollenkamm m (api) pollen trap
Pollenkeimung f pollen germination
Pollenkörbchen n pollen basket (plate), corbicula (at the hindlegs of honey-bees)
Pollenkorn n pollen grain
~/einkerniges microspore
Pollenladung f (api) pollen load
pollenlos pollenless
Pollenmitose f pollen mitosis
Pollenmutterzelle f pollen mother cell
Pollennahrung f bee-bread
Pollenpaket n pollinium

Pollenpflanze

Pollenpflanze *f* pollen plant
Pollenpigment *n* pollen pigment
Pollensack *m* pollen sac
Pollenschlauch *m* pollen tube
Pollenschlauchbefruchtung *f* siphonogamy
Pollenschlauchkeimung *f* pollen tube germination
Pollenschütten *n* pollin[iz]ation
Pollenspender *m (api)* pollen dispenser (supplier)
Pollenspendersorte *f* pollinizer
pollensteril androsterile, male-sterile
~/zytoplasmatisch cytoplasmic male-sterile, cms
Pollensterilität *f* pollen (male) sterility, androsterility
~/zytoplasmatische cytoplasmic male sterility
Pollentoxikose *f (api)* pollen toxicosis
Pollentracht *f* bee-bread
pollentragend pollinic, polliniferous
Pollenüberträger *m* pollinator, pollenizer
Pollenübertragung *f* pollen transfer (transmission)
Pollen- und Sporenkunde *f* palyngology
Pollenzelle *f* microspore
Pollination *f* pollin[iz]ation
Pollinium *n* pollinium
Pollution *f s.* Verschmutzung
Polnischer Weizen *m* Polish wheat, Triticum polonicum
Polnisches Niederungsrind *n* Polish lowland cattle *(breed)*
~ Weißes Schlappohrschwein *n* Polish White Lop-Eared *(pig breed)*
Polopferd *n*, **Polopony** *n* polo pony
Polozyt *m s.* Polzelle
Polsterformation *f* cushion plant formation
Polsterheide *f* cushion plant heath
Polsterpflanze *f* cushion plant
Polsterstaude *f* cushion plant
Polsterwucherung *f (bot)* intumescence
Polter *m(n) (forest)* log deck (dump), mill deck, rollway
Polterschild *m* logging blade
Polyacrylamid-Gel-Elektrophorese *f* polyacrylamide gel electrophoresis
Polyalkohol *m* polyalcohol, polyol
Polyandrie *f (bot, zoo)* polyandry
Polyantha-Rose *f* polyantha rose
Polyarthritis *f* **der Jungtiere** *(vet)* joint ill
Polycarbacin *n* polycarbacin *(fungicide)*
Polycarbamat *n* polycarbamate *(fungicide)*
Polychlorpinen *n* polychloropinene
polychrom polychromatic, many-coloured
Polycrossmethode *f*, **Polycrosstest** *m* polycross method *(plant breeding)*
Polydaktylie *f* polydactylism, polydactyly
Polydesoxyribonucleotidsynthase *f* polydeoxyribonucleotide synthase, DNA joinase (ligase) *(enzyme)*
Polydipsie *f (vet)* polydipsia
Polyedergefüge *n (soil)* prismatic structure
Polyederkrankheit *f s.* Polyedrose

Polyedrose *f* polyhedral (wilt) disease, polyhedrosis *(insect virosis)*
polyembryonal polyembryonic
Polyembryonie *f* polyembryony
polyembryonisch polyembryonic
Polyenfett *n* polyenoic fat
Polyenfettsäure *f* polyenoic fatty acid
Polyethylenfolie *f* polyethylene film
Polyethylenfolienmulch *m* polyethylene mulch
Polyethylenglycol *n* polyethylene glycol, PEG
Polyethylenmulch *m* polyethylene mulch
polyfaktoriell polyfactorial, multifactorial *(experimentation)*
Polyfructosan *n* polyfructosan *(polysaccharide)*
Polygalaktie *f* polygalactia
Polygalacturonase *f* polygalacturonase, pectinase *(enzyme)*
Polygalacturonsäure *f* polygalacturonic (pectic) acid
polygam *(bot, zoo)* polygamous
Polygamie *f* polygamy
polygastrisch polygastric, multistomached
polygen polygenic
Polygen *n* polygene
Polygenblock *m* supergene
Polygenie *f* polygeny, polygenic inheritance
polygenisch polygenic
polygerm *(bot)* multigerm, multiple-germ
Polygon[al]boden *m* polygonal soil
Polygonmelkstand *m* polygon [milking] parlour, diamond-shaped milking parlour
Polygonzug *m* traverse *(terrestrial surveying)*
Polygynie *f (zoo)* polygyny
polyhaploid *(gen)* polyhaploid
Polyhaploide *m* polyhaploid
Polyhaploidie *f* polyhaploidy
Polyhyalit *m* polyhyalite *(non-clay mineral)*
Polyhybride *f* polyhybrid
Polyhydramnie *f (vet)* hydramnios
polykarp *(bot)* polycarpic, polycarpous, sychnocarpous
Polykarpie *f (bot)* polycarpy
polykarpisch *s.* polykarp
Polyklimax *f (ecol)* polyclimax
Polyklimaxkonzept *n*, **Polyklimaxtheorie** *f (ecol)* polyclimax theory
polykotyl *(bot)* polycotyledonous
Polykultur *f (pisc)* polyculture
Polykulturteich *m* polyculture pond
Polymerase *f* polymerase *(enzyme)*
Polymerie *f (gen)* polymery
Polymerisationsgrad *m* degree of polymerization
polymorph polymorphous, polymorphic, ple[i]omorphic
Polymorphie *f s.* Polymorphismus
Polymorphismus *m* polymorphism, ple[i]omorphism
~/balancierter *(gen)* balanced polymorphism
~/genetischer genetic polymorphism

~/**transitiver** transient polymorphism
polymorphkernig polymorphonuclear
Polymyxin n polymyxin (antibiotic)
Polyneuritis f (vet) polyneuritis
polynukleär polynuclear
Polyol n s. Polyalkohol
Polyose f s. Polysaccharid
polyöstrisch polyoestrous
~/**saisonal** seasonally polyoestrous
Polyovulation f multiple ovulation
Polyoxin n polyoxin (fungicide)
Polypedon n (soil) polypedon
Polypeptid n polypeptide
polyphag (zoo, ecol) polyphagous
Polyphagie f (zoo, ecol) polyphagy, hyperphagia
polyphän (gen) pleiotropic
Polyphänie f (gen) pleiotropism, pleiotrop[h]y, polypheny
Polyphenol n polyphenol
Polyphenolsäure f polyphenolic acid
Polyphosphat n polyphosphate (feed additive)
Polyphosphatase f, **Polyphosphatdepolymerase** f endopolyphosphatase (enzyme)
polyphyletisch polyphyletic
Polyphyllie f (bot) polyphylly
polyploid (gen) polyploid
~/**somatisch** autopolyploid
Polyploide m polyploid
Polyploidie f polyploidy
~/**induzierte** induced polyploidy
~/**somatische** autopolyploidy
Polyploidiezüchtung f polyploid breeding
Polyploidisierung f polyploidization
Polypnoe f polypnoea
Polyram n polyram (fungicide)
Polyribosom n polyribosome, polysome
polyribosomal polyribosomal, polysomal
Polysaccharid n polysaccharide, polyose, polysaccharose
Polyserositis f (vet) polyserositis
Polysom n s. Polyribosom
Polysomatie f, **Polysomie** f (gen) polysomaty
Polyspermie f polyspermy
Polytänchromosom n polytene (polytenic, giant) chromosome
Polytänie f (gen) polyteny
polytrich polytrichous
Polyurie f polyuria
Polyuronid n polyuronid[e] (polysaccharide)
Polyvinylacetat n polyvinyl acetate
Polyvinylalkohol m polyvinyl alcohol
Polyvinylchlorid n polyvinyl chloride, PVC
polyvoltin (ent) polyvoltine, multivoltine
polyzyklisch polycyclic
polyzystisch (vet) polycystic
Polyzythämie f (vet) polycythaemia
~/**erbliche** polycythaemia vera
Polzelle f pole cell (of bird's egg)
Pomeranian m Pomeranian [dog], pom (breed)

Pomeranze f bitter (sour) orange, bigarade (fruit)
Pomeranzenbaum m bitter (sour, Seville) orange, Citrus aurantium ssp. aurantium
Pomeranzenblütenöl n orange-flower oil
Pomeranzenschalenöl n bitter-orange oil
Pommes frites pl French fried potatoes, French fries
Pomologe m pomologist
Pomologie f pomology (science of fruit cultivation) (s. a. Obstbau)
pomologisch pomological
Pompondahlie f pompon dahlia (comprehensive term)
Pondocillin n pivampicillin (antibiotic)
Pons m pons (part of the hindbrain)
Pontische Azalee f yellow-flowered rhododendron, Rhododendron luteum
Pontischer Beifuß m Roman wormwood, Artemisia pontica
Pony n pony, nag
Ponyhengst m pony stallion
Pony-Trekking n pony-trekking
Pool m/**metabolischer** metabolic pool
Population f (ecol, gen, biom) population
~/**geschlossene** closed herd
~/**panmiktische (zufallsgepaarte)** panmictic population
Populationsbekämpfung f population control
Populationsbewegung f population movement
Populationsbiologie f population biology
Populationsdichte f population density
Populationsdruck m population pressure
Populationsdynamik f population dynamics
Populationsgenetik f population genetics
Populationsgleichgewicht n population (genetic) equilibrium, population balance
Populationsindex m population index
Populationsmittel n (gen) population mean
Populationsmodell n population model
Populationsniveau n population level
Populationsökologie f population ecology, demecology
Populationsparameter m population parameter
Populationsschätzung f population estimation (assessment)
Populationssteuerung f population management
Populationsstruktur f population structure
Populationsverbesserung f population improvement (breeding)
Populationsverteilung f population distribution
Populationswachstum n population growth
Populationswelle f population wave
Populationszüchtung f bulk method (plant breeding)
Populationszyklus m population cycle
Populnetion n kaempferol (plant dye)
Populus-Canadensis-Hybride f Canadian (Carolina) poplar, Populus canadensis (euramericana)
porcin porcine
Pore f pore

Porendruck

Porendruck *m* pore pressure
Porendurchmesser *m* pore diameter
Porengröße *f* pore size
Porengrößenverteilung *f* pore size distribution
Porenkontinuität *f (soil)* continuity of the pore space
Porenluft *f* pore[-filling] air *(e.g. of soil)*
Porenpilz *m s.* Porling
Porenraum *m* pore space
Porensaugwasser *n (soil)* water of capillarity
Porensystem *n* pore system
~ **des Bodens** soil pore system
Porenvolumen *n* pore (void) volume, pore space
Porenwasser *n (soil)* pore water
Porenwassergeschwindigkeit *f* pore water velocity
Porenwinkelwasser *n (soil)* pore angle water
Porenzahl *f* pore number, porosity
Porling *m* pore fungus *(order Polyporales)*
Porometer *n* porometer
Porosität *f* porosity
Porphobilinogen *n* porphobilinogen *(dicarboxylic acid)*
Porphobilinogensynthase *f* porphobilinogen synthase, aminolaevulinate dehydratase *(enzyme)*
Porphyrin *n* porphyrin
Porree *m* leek, scallion, Allium porrum
Porree-Erntemaschine *f* leek harvester
Porreegelbstreifenvirus *n* leek yellow strike virus
Porreeputzer *m* leek trimmer
Porst *m (bot)* wild rosemary, ledum *(genus Ledum)*
Portalachse *f* portal (high-clearance) axle
Portalerntemaschine *f* straddle (over-the-row) harvester
Portalkran *m* gantry crane
Portalraupe *f* high-clearance track-layer
Portalregner *m* portal irrigation system
Portalrodepflug *m* over-the-row lifting plough
Portalschlepper *m*, **Portaltraktor** *m* high-clearance [straddle-type] tractor, field gantry
Porter *m(n)* porter *(kind of beer)*
Portionsweide *f* rotation[al] grazing, rotation pasture, cyclic grazing
Portugiesische Lorbeerkirsche *f* Portugal laurel, Portuguese laurel cherry, Prunus lusitanica
Portugiesischer Kohl *m* Portuguese cabbage (kale), Brassica oleracea convar. capitata var. costata
Portulak *m* 1. portulaca *(genus Portulaca)*; 2. [common, garden] purslane, pusley [weed], pussl[e]y, Portulaca oleracea
Portulakblattwespe *f* purslane saw-fly, Schizocorella plicorius
Portulakgewächse *npl* purslane family *(family Portulaceae)* • **die ~ betreffend** portulaceous
Portwein *m* port [wine]
Porus *m s.* Tüpfelöffnung
Porzellanblümchen *n (bot)* London pride, none-so-pretty, Saxifraga umbrosa
Porzellanei *n* china egg
Porzellanerde *f* kaolin, porcelain clay (earth)
Porzellansternchen *n (Am, bot)* bluet, quaking-ladies *(genus Houstonia)*
Positionseffekt *m (gen)* position effect
positiv/serologisch seropositive
post mortem *s.* postmortal
~ **partum** *s.* postpartal
Postalbumin *n* postalbumin *(serum protein fraction)*
Posten *m (hunt)* coarse (buck) shot
postfebril *(vet)* postfebrile
postglazial postglacial
Posthitis *f (vet)* posthitis
Postklimax *f* postclimax *(plant ecology)*
postmeiotisch postmeiotic
postmortal post-mortem, after death
Postöstrus *m* metoestrus
postpartal post-partum, post-natal, following parturition
Postpartalintervall *n* post-partum interval
Postreplikationsreparatur *f (gen)* post-replication repair
Postsynthesephase *f* G_2 phase *(of cell cycle)*
potent potent
Potential *n* potential
~**/bioelektrisches** bioelectric potential
~**/biotisches** *(ecol)* biotic potential, [gross] reproductive capacity, gross biological capacity
~**/Gibbssches** Gibbs free energy *(plant physiology)*
~**/hydraulisches** *(soil)* hydraulic potential
~**/osmotisches** osmotic potential *(e.g. of soil water)*
Potentialgradient *m* potential gradient *(e.g. of soil water)*
Potentille *f* bush cinquefoil, Potentilla fruticosa
Potentiometer *n* potentiometer
Potenz *f* potence, potency
Potenzierung *f* potentiation
Pot[et]ometer *n* potometer
Pottasche *f* potash, potassium carbonate
Potyvirus *n* poty virus
Poudrette *f* poudrette
Poulard *n*, **Poularde** *f* poulard[e]
Poxvirus *n* **ovis** ovine poxvirus
POZ *s.* Peroxidzahl
p.p. *s.* postpartal
PpMV *s.* Pappelmosaikvirus
PPN *s.* Peroxipropionylnitrat
P-Protein *n* phloem protein
PQ *s.* 1. Photosynthesequotient; 2. Plastochinon
Präadap[ta]tion *f (gen)* preadaptation
Präalbumin *n* prealbumin *(serum protein fraction)*
Prachthimbeere *f* salmon-berry, Rubus spectabilis
prächtig *s.* kapital
Prächtiges Mannagras *n* brook (reed sweet) grass, Glyceria maxima (aquatica)

Prachtkäfer *m* buprestid[an], flat-head beetle, flat-headed borer *(family Buprestidae)*
Prachtnelke *f* fringed pink, Dianthus superbus
Prachtscharte *f* 1. gay-feather, blazing star, button snake-root, liatris *(genus Liatris)*; 2. blazing star, devil's bit, Liatris spicata
Prachtspiere *f (bot)* astilbe, false spire *(genus Astilbe)*
Prädation *f*, **Prädatismus** *m (ecol)* predation, predatism, episitism
Prädator *m (ecol)* predator
prädatorisch *(ecol)* predatory, predacious
Prädetermination *f* predetermination
prädisponiert predisposed
Prädisposition *f* predisposition; susceptibility
prädominieren to predominate
Praecocität *f* precociousness, precocity
Präferendum *n (ecol)* preferendum
Präferenz *f (ecol, phyt)* preference
Prägepheromon *n* imprinting pheromone
Prägung *f* imprinting
Präimmunität *f (phyt, vet)* premunition, cross protection
Präkapillare *f* metarteriole *(animal anatomy)*
Präklimax *f* preclimax *(plant ecology)*
Präkollagenfaser *f* reticular fibre
Praktik *f/pflanzenbauliche* cropping practice
Präkursor *m* precursor
Prallbelastung *f* rebound stress *(e.g. of fruits)*
Prallblech *n* baffle
Pralldüse *f* deflector (deflection-type) nozzle
prämatur premature, early-maturing
Prämaturität *f* prematurity, early maturity
Prämedikationsmittel *n (vet)* premedicant
Prämolar *m* premolar [tooth]
Prämunität *f* s. Präimmunität
pränatal prenatal
Präöstrus *m* s. Proöstrus
Präovulator *m* Graafian follicle (vesicle)
präparasitär preparasitic
Präparat *n/biologisches* biopreparation
Präparierbesteck *n* dissecting set
präparieren to dissect
präpartal prepartal
Präpotenz *f (gen)* prepotency
präpuberal prepubertal
präpupal prepupal
präputial preputial
Präputialschlauch *m* sheath
Präputium *n* s. Vorhaut
Prärie *f* prairie
Prärieboden *m* prairie soil, brunizem
Prärielilie *f (bot)* camas[s], quamash *(genus Camassia)*
Präriemalve *f* prairie mallow *(genus Sidalcea)*
Präriepferd *n* mustang
Prärierose *f* prairie (Michigan) rose, Rosa setigera
Prärierübe *f* Indian bread-root, Indian turnip, Psoralea esculenta

präruminant preruminant
Präservation *f* preservation
Präserve *f* preserve
Präservierung *f* [short-term] preservation
Präservierungsmittel *n* preservative [agent]
Präsperm[at]ide *f* spermatocyte, sperm cell
Präsynthesephase *f* G_1 phase *(of cell cycle)*
Präsystole *f* presystole *(of the heart)*
prävalent prevalent
Prävalenz *f (gen)* prevalence, semidominance, partial (incomplete) dominance
Prävention *f* prevention
präventiv preventive
Präventivimpfung *f (vet)* preventive vaccination
Präventivknospe *f* s. Proventivknospe
Praxis *f/gärtnerische* horticultural practice
Praxiserprobung *f* [/landwirtschaftliche] farm-scale testing
Praxisversuch *m* [/pflanzenbaulicher] on-farm trial, field-scale test, grower trial
Präzipitation *f* precipitation
Präzipitationsprobe *f*, **Präzipitationsreaktion** *f* s. Präzipitinreaktion
Präzipitin *n* precipitin *(antibody)*
Präzipitinogen *n* precipitinogen *(antigen)*
Präzipitinoid *n* precipitinoid
Präzipitinreaktion *f* precipitin test *(serology)*
Praziquantel *n* praziquantel *(anthelminthic)*
Präzisionsdrillmaschine *f* precision drill (planter), [seed-]spacing drill
Präzisionssaat *f* precision drilling (seeding)
Predation *f (ecol)* predation, predatism
Prednisolon *n* prednisolone *(antiphlogistic)*
Pregnan *n* pregnane *(steroid)*
Preiselbeer-Kiefernwald *m* cowberry pinery
Preiselbeere *f* cowberry, red bilberry (whortleberry), *(Am)* mountain cranberry, lingonberry, Vaccinium vitis-idaea
Prellholz *n (forest)* fender [skid], glancer
Premier jus *m (slaught)* premier jus
Preßbrei *m* fruit slurry
Preßdichteverstellung *f* bale density control *(pick-up baler)*
Presse *f* press
~/hydraulische hydraulic press
Preßeinleger *m* press charger *(of a chaff cutter)*
pressen to press; to compress, to compact; to squeeze [out], to press *(fruit)*
~/zu Ballen to bale
~/zu Waffeln to wafer *(e.g. hay)*
~/zu Würfeln to cube
Preßgut *n* baling material, material being compacted; material to be pressed
Preßhefe *f* [com]pressed yeast
Preßhonig *m* pressed honey
Preßkammer *f*, **Preßkanal** *m* compression (baling, bale) chamber
Preßkocher *m* extruder cooker
Preßkolben *m* plunger *(of pick-up baler)*

Preßkörper

Preßkörper *m* follower, trailing bob *(of mole drainer)*
Preßkuchen *m* [press, mill] cake
Preßling *m* pellet
Preßmost *m* pressed must
Pressorezeptor *m* pressoreceptor *(in blood vessels)*
Preßrückstand *m* pomace, marc
Preßsaft *m* pressed must
Preßschnitzel *npl* pressed pulp *(sugar manufacture)*
Preßschutzschalter *m* safety stop pressure pad
Preßstroh *n* pressed straw
Preßtopf *m* soil block
preßverdichten to compact
Preßwasser *n* [pulp] press water *(sugar manufacture)*
Preßzetter *m* roller crusher *(haymaker)*
Pretilachlor *n* pretilachlor *(herbicide)*
Priapismus *m (vet)* priapism
primär entstanden *(vet)* idiopathic
Primäranschwemmung *f*, **Primärbelag** *m* precoat *(filtration)*
Primärbestand *m (forest)* virgin stand
Primärblatt *n (bot)* primary leaf
Primärfollikel *m* primary follicle
Primärfruchtansatz *m* initial fruit set
Primärgestein *n* primary rock
Primärhalm *m* primary culm
Primärinfektion *f* primary infection
Primärkonsument *m (ecol)* primary consumer
Primärlarve *f (ent)* egg-larva, first instar [larva]
Primärmineral *n (soil)* primary mineral
Primärparasit *m* primary parasite
Primärpathogen *n* primary pathogen
Primärproduktion *f* primary production
Primärproduzent *m* primary producer
Primärschädling *m* primary pest; primary insect
Primärsymptom *n* primary (initial) symptom
Primärwald *m* primeval (primary, virgin) forest, original (natural, undisturbed) forest
Primärwand *f* primary wall *(of plant cell)*
Primärwirt *m (phyt, vet)* primary (principal) host
Primärwurzel *f* primary (main) root
Primärxylem *n* primary xylem (wood)
Primel *f* 1. primrose, primula *(genus Primula)*; 2. *s.* Primula-Hybride
Primidophos *n* primidophos *(insecticide)*
primipar primiparous
Primipara *f* primipara
Primitivform *f s.* Primitivsorte
Primitivrasse *f* primitive (primary) breed
Primitivrinne *f* primitive groove *(embryology)*
Primitivsorte *f* primitive cultivar (form)
Primitivweizen *m* primitive wheat
primordial primordial
Primordialmembran *f*, **Primordialwand** *f* middle lamella *(of plant cell)*
Primordium *n* primordium, anlage

Primula-Hybride *f (bot)* polyanthus *(comprehensive term)*
Primula-Juliae-Hybride *f* miniature primula
Prion *n* prion *(infectious protein-containing particle)*
Prisma *n* prism; cruising prism *(forest appraisal)*
Prismengefüge *n (soil)* prismatic structure
Prismengefügekörper *m* prism-like aggregate
Pritsche *f* platform *(of a trailer)*
Pritschenanhänger *m* platform trailer
Privatwald *m* private forest
Privatwaldbetreuung *f* private forest supervision
Privatzucht *f* home-breeding
Privatzüchtung *f* home-bred variety
PRL *s.* Prolactin
Pro *s.* Prolin
Proanthocyanidin *n* proanthocyanidin *(plant substance)*
Probabilität *f (biom)* probability
Proband *m* proband
Probandenmethode *f* single ascertainment *(breeding)*
Probasidium *n (bot)* brand spore
Probe *f* 1. [test] specimen, sample; 2. test, assay *(s. a. under Prüfung)* • **eine ~ [ent]nehmen** to sample
~/Hayessche *(vet)* Hayes test
~/ungestörte undisturbed sample *(e.g. of soil)*
Probeeinheit *f* sampling unit
Probefläche *f* sample plot
~ der Linientaxation *(forest)* linear sample plot
~/permanente *(forest)* permanent sample (growth) plot
Probekörper *m* [test] specimen, test piece
Probekreis *m (forest)* circular sample plot, radius plot
Probenahme *f* sampling
~/diagnostische diagnostic sampling
Probenahmegerät *n s.* Probenehmer
Probenahmetechnik *f* sampling technique
Probenaufbereitung *f* sample processing
Probenaufbewahrung *f* sample storage
Probenbohrer *m* trier
Probenehmen *n* sampling
Probenehmer *m* sampler, sampling device
Probenentnahmestelle *f* sampling spot
Probenhalter *m* sample holder
Probenlagerung *f* sample storage
Probenmaterial *n* test material; assay
Probenstecher *m* sampling spear, trier
Probenteiler *m* sample splitter (divider)
Probentrocknung *f* sample drying
Probenvermahlung *f* sample grinding
Probenzieher *m* sampler, trier
Probestamm *m (forest)* sample (test) tree
Probestelle *f* sampling spot
Probestreifen *m* sample strip
~ der Vegetationsanalyse transect
Probestück *n* [test] specimen, test piece
Probierhengst *m* teaser stallion

Probierwand f teasing board *(horse breeding)*
Probiotikum n probiotic
Probitanalyse f *(biom)* probit analysis
Problemboden m problem soil
Problemunkraut n troublesome (problematic) weed
Proboscis m *(zoo)* proboscis
Procain n procaine *(anaesthetic)*
Procarpil n procarpil *(growth regulator)*
Processing n processing, mRNA ripening
Processus m *(zoo)* process
Prochloraz n prochloraz *(fungicide)*
Procollagenprolin-2-Oxoglutarat-4-Dioxygenase f s. Prolinhydroxylase
Procymidon n procymidone *(fungicide)*
Prodiamin n prodiamine *(herbicide)*
Prodromalstadium n prodromal period (stage) *(of a disease)*
Produkt n/**drittes** low-grade sugar, low [raw] sugar
~/**pflanzliches** plant product
Produktion f **je Flächeneinheit** output per unit area
~/**mehrzweigige** mixed farming
~/**pflanzliche** s. Pflanzenproduktion
~/**tierische** s. Tierproduktion
Produktionsfaktoren mpl/**landwirtschaftliche** agricultural inputs (supplies)
Produktionsfunktion f production function
Produktionsgebäude n/**landwirtschaftliches** agricultural (farm) building
Produktionsgenossenschaft f/**gärtnerische** gardening (horticultural production) co-operative
~/**landwirtschaftliche** co-operative farm, agricultural co-operative
Produktionskraft f productive capacity
Produktionslehre f/**forstliche** forest production studies
Produktionsleiter m farm manager
Produktionsmittel npl/**landwirtschaftliche** agricultural inputs (supplies)
Produktionsökologie f production ecology
Produktionsweise f/**landwirtschaftliche** farming practice
Produktionsweiser m *(forest)* production index
Produktionszweig m **eines Landwirtschaftsbetriebes** farm enterprise
produktiv productive
Produktivität f productivity
~/**aktuelle** actual productivity *(e.g. of a forest)*
~/**biologische** bioproductivity
~/**pflanzliche** plant productivity
Produktlagerung f product storage
Produktregel f reciprocity law *(plant physiology)*
Produzent m producer; grower
Proembryo m *(bot)* proembryo
Proenzym n proenzyme, enzyme precursor, zymogen
Profil n profile *(e.g. of a soil)*
Profilentwicklung f profile development

Profilgrube f soil pit
Profiliergerät n planer *(road construction)*
Profilstollen m caulk[in]
Profilwasser n profile water
Profluralin n profluralin *(herbicide)*
Progenitur f s. Nachkommen
progestagen [wirkend] progestogenic
Progestagen n progestogen, progestational hormone *(sex hormone)*
Progesteron n progesterone
Progesteronbestimmung f s. Progesterontest
progesteronfreisetzend progesterone-releasing
Progesteronfreisetzung f progesterone release
Progesterontest m progesterone test *(for pregnancy detection)*
Progestogen n s. Progestagen
Proglinazin n proglinazine *(herbicide)*
Proglottid m, **Proglottis** f proglottid
Progoitrin n progoitrin *(glucosinolate)*
Progressive Zwergwüchsigkeit f **des Pfirsichs** phony peach *(virosis)*
Prohibitin n phytoncide
Proinsulin n proinsulin
Prokain n procaine *(anaesthetic)*
Prokambium n *(bot)* procambium
Prokaryo[n]t m prokaryote
prokaryo[n]tisch prokaryotic
Pro-Kopf-Produktion f per capita production
Prolactin n, **Prolaktin** n prolactin, mammotropin, luteotrop[h]in, luteotrop[h]ic (lactogenic) hormone, LTH
Prolaktinfreisetzung f prolactin release
Prolamin n prolamin[e] *(storage protein)*
Prolan n 1. prolan, follicle-stimulating hormone; 2. prolan, luteinizing hormone
Prolaps m *(vet)* prolapse
Prolepsis f *(bot)* prolepsis
Prolidase f s. Prolindipeptidase
proliferieren to proliferate *(s. a. wuchern)*
Proliferation f proliferation
proliferativ proliferative
Prolifikation f *(bot, phyt)* prolification
Prolin n prolin[e], pyrrolidine-2-carboxylic acid
Prolindipeptidase f proline dipeptidase, iminodipeptidase *(enzyme)*
Prolinhydroxylase f procollagen-proline-2-oxoglutarate 4-dioxygenase *(enzyme)*
Prolinmangel m prolin[e] deficiency
Prolyldipeptidase f prolyl dipeptidase *(enzyme)*
Promecarb n promecarb *(insecticide)*
Promeristem n *(bot)* promeristem
Prometon n prometon *(herbicide)*
Prometryn n prometryne *(herbicide)*
Promyzel n promycelium *(basidium of Ustilaginales and Uredinales)*
Pronator m pronator [muscle]
Pronukleus m pronucleus
Pronymphe f *(ent)* pronymph, prepupa
Proöstrus m prooestrus

Propachlor

Propachlor *n* propachlor *(herbicide)*
Propagation *f* s. Fortpflanzung
Propagel *n* *(bot)* propagule, propagulum
Propamocarb *n* propamocarb *(fungicide)*
Propandi[carbon]säure *f* malonic acid
Propandiol *n* propane-1,2-diol, propylene glycol *(disinfectant)*
Propangasmotor *m* propane gas engine
Propangastrockner *m* propane dryer
Propanil *n* propanil *(herbicide)*
Propan-2-ol *n* propane-2-ol, isopropyl alcohol *(disinfectant)*
Propanrückenspritze *f* propane knapsack sprayer
Propansäure *f* s. Propionsäure
Propargit *n* propargite *(acaricide)*
Propazin *n* propazine *(herbicide)*
Propellerpumpe *f* propeller (axial-flow) pump
Propenal *n* acrolein *(herbicide)*
Prop-2-enthiosulfinsäure-S-allylester *m* allicin
Propen-1,2,3-tricarbonsäure *f* propene-1,2,3-tricarboxylic acid, aconitic acid
Propepsin *n* pepsinogen *(pepsin precursor)*
Properdin *n* properdin *(serum globulin)*
Propetamphos *n* propetamphos *(insecticide)*
Propham *n* propham, IPC *(herbicide)*
Prophase *f* prophase *(nuclear division)*
Prophetenblume *f* prophet flower, Arnebia pulchra (echioides)
Prophylaktikum *n* prophylactic
prophylaktisch prophylactic
Prophylaxe *f* prophylaxis, disease prevention
Propicillin *n* propicillin *(antibiotic)*
Propiconazol *n* propiconazol[e] *(fungicide)*
Propineb *n* propineb *(fungicide)*
Propionat *n* propionate
Propionsäure *f* propionic (propanoic) acid
Propionyl-CoA-Carboxylase *f* propionyl-CoA carboxylase *(enzyme)*
Propolis *f* propolis, bee-glue, balm • **mit ~ überziehen** to propolize • **mit ~ verstopfen** to propolize
Propolispflanze *f* propolis plant *(comprehensive term)*
Propositus *m* s. Proband
Propoxur *n* propoxur, arprocarb *(insecticide)*
Propriorezeptor *m* proprioreceptor *(animal physiology)*
Propupa *f* *(ent)* pseudochrysalis, pseudopupa
Propylenglycol *n* s. Propandiol
Propylgallat *n* propyl gallate *(antioxidant)*
Propylthiourazil *n* propylthiouracil *(antimetabolite)*
Propyzamid *n* propyzamide, pronamide *(herbicide)*
Prorennin *n* prorennin, renninogen, chymosinogen
ProRFV s. Ringfleckenvirus der Pfingstrose
Prosenchym *n* *(bot)* prosenchyma, fibrous tissue
prosenchymatisch *(bot)* prosenchymatous
Prosenzephalon *n* prosencephalon, forebrain
Prostaglandin *n* prostaglandin, PG *(fatty acid)*
Prostaglandinsynthase *f* prostaglandin synthase *(enzyme)*
Prostata *f* prostata [gland]
Prostatitis *f* *(vet)* prostatitis
Prostration *f* prostration
Prosulfalin *n* prosulfalin *(herbicide)*
Protamin *n* protamine *(polypeptide)*
Protandrie *f* *(bot, zoo)* proterandry
protandrisch *(bot, zoo)* prot[er]androus
Protea *f* *(bot)* protea *(genus Protea)*
Protease *f* protease *(enzyme)*
Proteaseinhibitor *m* protease inhibitor
Proteid *n* proteid[e], conjugated protein
Protein *n* protein
~/bakterielles bacterial protein
~/fibrilläres fibrous protein
~/konjugiertes s. ~/zusammengesetztes
~/mikrobielles microbial protein
~/pflanzliches plant protein
~/pilzliches fungal protein
~/texturiertes pflanzliches textured vegetable protein, TVP
~/tierisches animal protein
~/verdauliches digestible protein
~/zusammengesetztes conjugated protein, proteid[e]
Protein... s. a. Eiweiß...
Proteinabbau *m* protein breakdown (degradation), proteolysis
Proteinabsorption *f* protein absorption
Proteinanalyse *f* protein analysis
Proteinantigen *n* protein antigen
proteinartig proteinaceous, protein
Proteinase *f* proteinase, endopeptidase *(enzyme)*
Proteinbiochemie *f* protein biochemistry
Proteinbiosynthese *f* protein biosynthesis
Proteinextraktion *f* protein extraction
proteinhaltig proteinaceous, protein
Proteinhormon *n* protein hormone, proteohormone
Proteinhydrolysat *n* protein hydrolysate
Proteinkinase *f* protein kinase *(enzyme)*
Proteinkomplex *m* protein complex
Proteinkonzentration *f* protein concentration
Proteinmatrix *f* protein matrix
Proteinmehl *n* protein meal
Proteinmetabolismus *m* protein metabolism
Proteinpolymorphismus *m* protein polymorphism
Proteinquelle *f* protein source
Proteinschutzstoff *m* protein protectant
Proteinsekretion *f* protein secretion
Proteinsynthese *f* protein synthesis
Proteintoxin *n* protein toxin
Proteinurie *f* proteinuria, albuminuria
Proteinwirkungsverhältnis *n* protein efficiency ratio, PER *(animal nutrition)*
Protektans *n* protectant, protection agent, protective toxicant
protektiv protective

Proteohormon n proteohormone, protein hormone
Proteolyse f proteolysis
Proteolyten mpl proteolytic bacteria
proteolytisch proteolytic, protein-splitting
Proteolytmalz n proteolytic malt
Proterandrie f s. Protandrie
proterogyn s. protogyn
Prothallium n (bot) prothallium, prothallus
Prothiocarb n prothiocarb (fungicide)
Prothiophos n prothiophos (insecticide)
Prothorax m (ent) prothorax
Prothrombin n prothrombin (thrombin precursor)
Prothrombinbestimmung f nach Quick, **Prothrombinzeit** f (vet) prothrombin time
Protocatechusäure f protocatechuic acid, 3,4-dihydroxybenzoic acid
Protochlorophyll n protochlorophyll
Protocollagenhydroxylase f procollagen-proline-2-oxoglutarate 4-dioxygenase (enzyme)
Protoderm n (bot) protoderm, dermatogen
protogyn (bot, zoo) proterogynous, protogynous
Protogynie f proterogyny, metandry
Protohäm n s. Häm
protoklonal protoclonal
Protokormus m (bot) protocorm
Protolignin n protolignin, native lignin
Protolyse f hydrolysis
Protonenaktivitätsexponent m s. pH-Wert
Protonenpumpe f proton pump (plant physiology)
Protonenresonanzspektroskopie f proton resonance spectroscopy
Protonymphe f protonymph (of mites)
Protopektin n protopectin (polysaccharide)
Protopektinase f protopectinase (enzyme)
Protophloem n (bot) protophloem
Protophyt m protophyte
Protoplasma n protoplasm, plasm[a]
Protoplasmapermeabilität f protoplasm permeability
Protoplasmaströmung f protoplasmic streaming (in plant cells)
protoplasmatisch protoplasmic, protoplasmal, protoplasmatic
Protoplasmaverschmelzung f **der Gameten** plasmogamy
Protoplast m protoplast
Protoplastenfusion f protoplast fusion
Protoplastenkultur f protoplast culture
Protoplastenverschmelzung f protoplast fusion
protoplastisch protoplastic
Protoporphyrin n protoporphyrin
Protospore f s. Sommerspore
Protostele f (bot) protostele
Protoxin n protoxin (toxin precursor)
Protoxylem n (bot) protoxylem
protozoär protozoal
Protozoologie f protozoology
Protozoon n protozoon, protozoan (subkingdom Protozoa)

Protrusion f protrusion
Protrypsin n trypsinogen (trypsin precursor)
Protz m, **Protze** f (forest) weed tree
Provencerose f [moss] cabbage-rose, Rosa centifolia
Provenienz f provenance, origin
Provenienzfläche f provenance plot
Provenienzversuch m provenance trial
Proventivknospe f latent (resting) bud • **aus einer ~ hervorgegangen** epicormic
Proventriculus m proventriculus; gizzard (of chewing insects)
Provirus n provirus
Provitamin n provitamin, vitamin precursor
~ D₃ 7-dehydrocholesterol
Provokation f challenge (immunology)
Provolone m provolone [cheese]
provozieren/eine Mehrfachovulation to superovulate
proximal proximal
Proximpham n proximpham (herbicide)
Prozerkoid n procercoid (of Cestoda)
Prozeßkäse m processed cheese
Prozessor m (forest) processor, delimber-bucker
Prudel m wallow, soiling pool (of game)
prüfen to examine, to investigate; to assay, to prove; to test (esp. for a substance); to check, to control
~/im Feldversuch to field-test
Prüfglied n treatment (experimentation)
Prüfkörper m s. Probekörper
Prüfling m 1. proband; 2. s. Probekörper
Prüfstand m test bench
Prüfstation f test station
Prüfsubstanz f assay
Prüfung f examination, investigation; assay; test[ing]; check, control
~ auf dominante Letalität dominant lethal assay (mutation research)
~/biologische bioassay
~/organoleptische (sensorische) organoleptic analysis (assessment)
~/wirtsvermittelte host-mediated assay (microbiology)
Prüfverfahren n test procedure; test[ing] method
Prüfversuch m proving trial (variety testing)
Prunellamosaikvirus n prunella mosaic virus
Prunelle f sloe, Prunus spinosa
Prünelle f prunelle, prunello (a yellow dried plum)
Prunkbohne f scarlet runner [bean], kidney bean, Phaseolus coccineus
Prunkwinde f (bot) 1. morning glory, ipomoea (genus Ipomoea); 2. tall morning glory, Ipomoea (Pharbitis) purpurea
pruritisch (vet) pruritic
Pruritus m (vet) pruritus
Prynachlor n prynachlor (herbicide)
PR-Zahl f ply rating

Przewalskipferd *n* Przewalski's horse, Equus caballus przewalskii
PS *s.* Photosystem
Psalter *m* omasum, third stomach *(of ruminants)*
Psalterparese *f (vet)* omasal impaction, dry bible
Psammophyt *m* psammophyte
Psammoserie *f* psammosere *(plant sociology)*
PSE-Fleisch *n* PSE (watery) pork, [pale soft] exudative meat
Pseudanthium *n (bot)* pseudanthium
Pseudo... *s. a.* Schein...
Pseudoallel *n (gen)* pseudoallele
Pseudoböhmit *m* pseudoboehmite *(non-clay mineral)*
Pseudobulbus *m (bot)* pseudobulb
Pseudocaatinga *f (forest)* pseudo-caatinga
Pseudocercus *m (ent)* cornicle
Pseudochrysalis *f (ent)* pseudochrysalis, pseudopupa
Pseudodominanz *f (gen)* pseudodominance
Pseudogamie *f (bot, zoo)* pseudogamy
Pseudogley *m (soil)* pseudogley, stagnogley, surface-water gley
Pseudogleyhorizont *m* pseudogley horizon
Pseudogleypodsol *m* pseudogleyed podzol
Pseudogravidität *f (vet)* pseudopregnancy, pseudocyesis, false pregnancy
Pseudohermaphrodit *m s.* Scheinzwitter
pseudokarp *(bot)* pseudocarpic, pseudocarpous
Pseudoklimax *f* pseudoclimax *(plant sociology)*
Pseudokuhpocken *pl (vet)* false cowpox, pseudocowpox
Pseudoküstenfieber *n (vet)* tzaneen disease, benign bovine gonderiosis (theileriasis)
Pseudo-MKS *f der Schafe (vet)* bluetongue
Pseudomonas-fluorescens-Befall *m der Kartoffelknolle* bruise infection [of potato tuber], brown eye
Pseudomykorrhiza *f* pseudomycorrhiza
Pseudomyzel *n* pseudomycelium *(of certain yeast species)*
Pseudoparasit *m* pseudoparasite
Pseudoparenchym *n (bot)* pseudoparenchyma
Pseudophyse *f* paraphysis *(of fungal fructifications)*
Pseudopodium *n (zoo)* pseudopod[ium], false leg
Pseudopodsolierung *f (soil)* pseudopodzolization
Pseudorabies *f (vet)* pseudorabies, Aujeszky's disease, infectious bulbar paralysis, mad itch
Pseudorabiesvirus *n* pseudorabies (Aujeszky) virus
Pseudorotz *m (vet)* melioidosis *(caused by Pseudomonas pseudomallei)*
Pseudorutil *m* pseudorutile *(non-clay mineral)*
Pseudosalatvergilbungsvirus *n* lettuce pseudo yellows virus, LPYV, LYV
Pseudoselbstverträglichkeit *f (bot)* pseudo-self-compatibility
Pseudotuberkulose *f (vet)* pseudotuberculosis
Pseudovergleyung *f (soil)* pseudogleyification
Pseudowut *f s.* Pseudorabies
Pseudozirrhose *f (vet)* pseudocirrhosis
Pseudozwiebel *f (bot)* pseudobulb
Psittakose *f (vet)* psittacosis, ornithosis *(caused by Chlamydia psittaci)*
PsLV *s.* Latentes Passiflora-Virus
PSM *s.* Pflanzenschutzmittel
Psoriasis *f (vet)* psoriasis
Psorose *f bei Citrus (phyt)* psorosis [of citrus]
Psorosevirus *n* citrus psorosis virus
PSS *s.* Belastungsmyopathie des Schweines
Psychrometer *n* psychrometer
~/elektrisches electric psychrometer
psychrophil psychrophilic
Psychrophila-Krankheit *f,* **Psychrophilose** *f* peduncle disease *(of salmonoids, caused by Cytophaga psychrophila)*
Psychrophyt *m* psychrophyte
psychrotroph psychrotrophic
Psychrotrophe *pl* psychrotrophs
Pteridiose *f (vet)* bracken poisoning
Pteridophyt *m* fern *(division Pteridophyta)*
Pteroylglutaminsäure *f* pteroglutamic (folic) acid, folate, folacin *(vitamin)*
pterygot pterygote, winged
Pteryla *f* pteryla, feather tract *(of bird's skin)*
Ptomain *n* ptomaine
Ptyalin *n* ptyalin, alpha-amylase *(enzyme)*
Ptyalinmangel *m (vet)* aptyalism
puberal pubertal
Pubertät *f* puberty
Pubertätsalter *n* puberty
Pubertätsinduktion *f [/biotechnische]* puberty induction
Pubertätsstimulation *f* puberty stimulation
pubeszent pubescent
Pudel *m* poodle *(dog breed)*
Pudelpointer *m* poodle-pointer *(dog breed)*
Pudermühle *f* grinding mill for powdered sugar
Puderzucker *m* powdered sugar, icing (castor) sugar
puerperal puerperal
Puerperalsepsis *f,* **Puerperalseptikämie** *f (vet)* puerperal septicaemia
Puerperalstörung *f (vet)* puerperal disorder
Puerperaltetanie *f (vet)* puerperal tetany
Puerperium *n* puerperium
Puff *n (gen)* puff
Puffbohne *f* broad (thick) bean, [Scotch] bean, faba [bean], fava [bean], Windsor bean, Vicia faba [var. major]
puffen to parch, *(Am)* to pop *(cereal grains)*
Puffer *m* buffer
Pufferkapazität *f* buffering capacity *(e.g. of a soil)*
Pufferkurve *f* buffer curve
Pufferlösung *f* buffer solution
puffern to buffer
Puffern *n* buffering

Pufferstoff m, **Puffersubstanz** f buffer [agent, substance]
Puffersystem n buffer system
Pufferung f buffering
Puffer[ungs]vermögen n s. Pufferkapazität
Puffmais m (Am) popcorn, Zea mays convar. microsperma
Pulawy-Schwein n Pulawy (pig breed)
Pullorumseuche f pullorum disease, bacillary white diarrhoea (of chicken, caused by Salmonella pullorum)
pulmonal pulmonary, pulmonic
Pulmonalnarkose f (vet) inhalation anaesthesia
Pulmonalnarkotikum n (vet) inhalation anaesthetic
Pulmonarlappen m pulmonary lobe
Pulp m s. Pulpe
Pulpa f [tooth] pulpa
Pulpahöhle f dental cavity
Pulpe f, **Pülpe** f [fruit] pulp, pomace
Pülpeabscheider m, **Pülpefänger** m pulp separator (catcher) (sugar manufacture)
Pulper m pulper, pulping machine
Pulpitis f (vet) pulpitis
pulpös pulpous, pulpy
Pulque f pulque (alcoholic beverage)
Pulqueagave f (bot) maguey blando of Mexico, Agave atrovirens
Puls m pulse
Pulsatillaextrakt m pulsatilla (extract from Pulsatilla spp.)
Pulsation f pulsation
Pulsator m pulsator, pulsation system
~/elektrischer (elektromagnetischer) electric pulsator
pulsatorisch pulsatory
Pulsfolge f pulsation sequence
pulsförmig pulsatory
Pulsfrequenz f 1. pulse rate (animal physiology); 2. pulsation speed (of a milking machine)
pulsieren to pulsate, to pulse
Pulsschlag m pulse
Pulsschlauch m pulse tube (of a milking machine)
Pulsschreiber m (vet) sphygmograph
Pulsstrahlzerstäuber m pulsed-jet atomizer
Pulverholz n Persian bark, alder (glossy) buckthorn, berry-bearing alder, Rhamnus frangula
pulverisieren to pulverize, to powder
Pulverschnee m powder snow
Pulverschorf m **der Kartoffel** powdery (corky) scab of potato (caused by Spongospora subterranea)
Pulvinus m (bot) pulvinus
Pulwan m s. Lockvogel
Pumpaggregat n, **Pumpanlage** f pump plant
Pumpe f pump
~/halbaxiale turbo pump
~ mit konstantem Förderstrom fixed-displacement pump
~ mit variablem Förderstrom variable-displacement pump
pumpen to pump
Pumpenhub m pump lift
Pumpenkopf m head
Pumpenleistung f pump capacity
Pumpernickel m pumpernickel
Pumpspeicheranlage f, **Pumpspeicherwerk** n pump-storage plant
Pumpstation f pump station
Punkt m/**isoelektrischer** isoelectric point
~/trigonometrischer trigonometrical (triangulation) point
Punktast m pin knot
Punktauge n (ent) simple eye
Punktbewässerung f point irrigation
Punktfarn m Christmas fern, Polystichum acrostichoides
punktförmig (vet) petechial
punktieren to puncture
punktiert (bot, zoo) punctate[d]
~/fein punctulate[d]
Punktierverfahren n point scoring (e.g. in livestock judging)
Punktion f (vet) puncture, paracentesis
~ mittels Trokars trocarization
Punktmutation f point (gene, intragenic) mutation
Punktschätzung f (biom) point estimation
Punktstichprobenahme f (forest) point sampling (cruising), variable-plot sampling
Punktstichprobendichte f point density (timber mensuration)
Punktwolke f (biom) point cloud
Punnett-Schema n (gen) Punnett square
Pupa f s. Puppe 1.
Puparium n (ent) puparium, pupal case
Pupille f pupil
Pupillenerweiterung f (vet) pupil dilat[at]ion, mydriasis
Pupillenreaktion f, **Pupillenreflex** m pupillary reflex
pupipar (ent) pupiparous
Puppe f 1. (zoo, ent) pupa, chrysalis, chrysalid; mummia; 2. shock (grain harvesting) • **in Puppen aufstellen** to shock, to stook
Puppenauge n pupal eye
puppengebärend (ent) pupiparous
Puppenhemd n pupal shell (e.g. of the honey-bee)
Puppenparasit m pupal parasite
Puppenräuber m European ground beetle, (Am) forest caterpillar hunter, Calosoma sycophanta
Puppenstadium n pupal instar (stage)
Puppenwiege f larval cradle, pupal chamber, pupation cell
Purgans n purgative, laxative
purgativ purgative, laxative
Purgierbeere f, **Purgierkreuzdorn** m common (purging) buckthorn, Rhamnus catharticus
Purgiernuß f purging nut, Jatropha curcas

Purin

Purin *n* purine
Purinbase *f* purine base
Purinnucleosidphosphorylase *f* purine-nucleoside phosphorylase *(enzyme)*
Purinstoffwechsel *m* purine metabolism
Puromycin *n* puromycin *(antibiotic)*
Purpurfarbener Sonnenhut *m s.* Purpurigelkopf
Purpurfärbung *f (phyt)* purpling
Purpurglöckchen *n* 1. alum root, heuchera *(genus Heuchera)*; 2. coral bells, Heuchera sanguinea
Purpurgranadilla *f* [purple] granadilla, grenadilla, passion-fruit, Passiflora edulis
Purpurigelkopf *m* purple coneflower, Echinacea purpurea
Purpurklee *m* purple clover, Trifolium purpureum
Purpurkranz *m (bot)* purple wreath, Petrea volubilis
Purpurskabiose *f (bot)* mourning bride, sweet scabious, Scabiosa atropurpurea
Purpurtanne *f* Pacific silver fir, Abies amabilis
Purpurtute *f (bot)* syngonium *(genus Syngonium)*
Purpurviolettes Federborstengras *n* fountain grass, Pennisetum setaceum
Purpurwasserdost *m* sweet Joe-Pye-weed, Eupatorium purpureum
Purpurweide *f* purple willow (osier), Salix purpurea
Purpurwicke *f* purple vetch, Vicia benghalensis
Purpurwinde *f (bot)* [annual] morning glory, Ipomoea purpurea
Purpurzwergginster *m* scarlet dwarf broom, Cytisus (Chamaecytisus) purpureus
Pürsch *f s.* Pirsch
purulent *(vet)* purulent, mattery
Purulenz *f (vet)* purulence
Pus *n s.* Eiter
Pushball *m* push-ball *(equestrian sport)*
Pustel *f (phyt, vet)* pustule, fester
pustelartig pustulate
Pustelschorf *m (phyt)* pitted scab
Pute *f* 1. turkey *(genus Meleagris)*; 2. turkey, Meleagris domesticus; 3. [turkey] hen
Putenbroiler *m* turkey broiler
Putenei *n* turkey egg
Putenenteritis *f*/**infektiöse (transmissible)** mud fever of turkeys, contagious indigestion of turkeys
Putenfarm *f* turkey farm
Putenfleisch *n* turkey meat
Putenküken *n* turkey chick (poult)
Putenleukose *f (vet)* T virus infection
Putenmast *f* turkey fattening
Putensperma *n* turkey semen
Putenstall *m* turkey house
Putenstarterfutter *n* turkey poult starter mash
Putenveranda *f* turkey veranda[h]
Puter *m* turkeycock, gobbler, tom turkey, bubblyjock *(Scotland)*
Putrefaktion *f* putrefaction, putrescence
Putrescin *n*, **Putreszin** *n* putrescine

Putreszenz *f s.* Putrefaktion
putrid putrid
Putrid *n* putrefactive bacterium
Putzabfälle *mpl* dressing offals, trimmings
Putzapparat *m (ent)* antenna cleaner
putzen 1. to clean, to polish; to brush; to trim; 2. to dress *(animals)*; to groom, to scour *(a horse)*; 3. to excorticate *(grain)*
~/sich to preen [itself], to groom
Putzmaschine *f* polishing machine, polisher
Putzschleuder *f* crown cleaner *(of a sugar-beet harvester)*
Putztisch *m* peeling table
Putzverlust *m* trim loss
Putzzeug *n* grooming equipment (kit)
PV *s.* 1. Porenvolumen; 2. Papillomvirus
PVA *s.* Polyvinylalkohol
PVAC *s.* Polyvinylacetat
PVC *s.* Polyvinylchlorid
PWP *s.* Welkepunkt/permanenter
Pyämie *f (vet)* pyaemia
pyämisch *(vet)* pyaemic
Pydanon *n* pydanon *(herbicide)*
Pyelitis *f (vet)* pyelitis
Pyelonephritis *f (vet)* pyelonephritis
Pyelozystitis *f (vet)* pyelocystitis
Pygidium *n* telson *(of arthropods)*
Pygostyl *n* tail bone *(of fowl)*
Pyknidie *f (bot)* pycnid[ium], pycnium, spermogone, spermogonium, spermagone
Pyknidiospore *f (bot)* pycniospore, pycnidiospore, spermatium
Pyknidium *n s.* Pyknidie
Pyknometer *n* pycnometer *(for density measurement)*
Pyknose *f* pycnosis
Pyknospore *f s.* Pyknidiospore
Pylephlebitis *f (vet)* pylephlebitis
Pylorus *m* pylorus, pyloric opening *(animal anatomy)*
Pyloruskreismuskel *m* pyloric sphincter
Pyodermie *f (vet)* pyoderma
pyogen *(vet)* pyogenic, pus-producing
Pyogenesmastitis *f (vet)* summer mastitis *(caused by Corynebacterium pyogenes)*
Pyohämie *f (vet)* pyaemia
Pyometra *f (vet)* pyometra
Pyosalpinx *f (vet)* pyosalpinx
Pyracarbolid *n* pyracarbolid *(fungicide)*
Pyramidenform *f* pyramid form *(of fruit-trees)*
Pyramidenglockenblume *f (bot)* chimney, Campanula pyramidalis
Pyramidenmaser *f* curly grain (figure) *(of wood)*
Pyramidenpappel *f* Lombardy poplar, Populus nigra var. italica, Populus pyramidalis
Pyramidenzeichnung *f s.* Pyramidenmaser
Pyranocumarin *n* pyranocumarin *(rodenticide)*
Pyranometer *n* pyranometer
Pyrantel[tartrat] *n* pyrantel *(anthelminthic)*

Pyrazin *n* pyrazine *(hydrocarbon)*
Pyrazophos *n* pyrazophos *(fungicide)*
Pyrenäen-Doppelbeere *f* Pyrenean honeysuckle, Lonicera pyrenaica
Pyrenäenhund *m* Great Pyrenees *(dog breed)*
Pyrethrin *n* pyrethrine *(insecticidal plant substance)*
Pyrethrineinsatz *m* pyrethrinization *(pest control)*
Pyrethrum *n* 1. common (florist's) pyrethrum, painted daisy, Chrysanthemum coccineum; 2. pyrethrum, Persian insect powder
Pyrethrumextrakt *m* pyrethrum extract *(insecticide)*
Pyrexie *f (vet)* pyrexia, fever *(for compounds s. under* Fieber*)*
Pyrheliometer *n* pyrheliometer
Pyriclor *n* pyriclor *(herbicide)*
Pyridat *n* pyridate *(herbicide)*
Pyridin *n* pyridine *(heterocyclic nitrogen compound)*
Pyridin-2-carbonsäure *f* pyridine-2-carboxylic acid, picolinic acid
Pyridin-3-carbonsäure *f* pyridine-3-carboxylic acid, nicotinic acid, niacin
Pyridin-2,3-dicarbonsäure *f* pyridine-2,3-dicarboxylic acid, quinolic acid
Pyridinitril *n* pyridinitril *(fungicide)*
Pyridinnucleotidtranshydrogenase *f* NAD(P)$^+$ transhydrogenase *(enzyme)*
Pyridoxal *n* pyridoxal *(pyridine derivative)*
Pyridoxalphosphat *n* pyridoxal phosphate *(coenzyme)*
Pyridoxamin *n* pyridoxamine *(pyridine derivative)*
Pyridoxaminphosphatoxidase *f* pyridoxaminephosphate oxidase *(enzyme)*
Pyridoxin *n* pyridoxine, adermin, vitamin B$_6$
pyriform pyriform, pear-shaped
Pyrimethamin *n* pyrimethamine *(antiparasitic)*
Pyrimidin *n* pyrimidine *(heterocyclic nitrogen compound)*
Pyrimidinbase *f* pyrimidine base
Pyrimidinnucleotid *n* pyrimidine nucleotide
Pyrimit[h]at *n* pyrimit[h]ate *(acaricide, insecticide)*
Pyrit *m* pyrite *(non-clay mineral)*
Pyrithiamin *n* pyrithiamin *(heterocyclic nitrogen compound)*
Pyrogallol *n*, **Pyrogallussäure** *f* pyrogallol, pyrogallic acid
pyrogen *(vet)* pyrogenic, pyrogenous
Pyrogen *n (vet)* pyrogen
Pyroligninsäure *f* pyroligneous acid
Pyrologie *f* pyrology
Pyrolusit *m* pyrolusite *(non-clay mineral)*
Pyrolyse *f* pyrolysis
Pyrophosphat *n* pyrophosphate
Pyrophosphatase *f* pyrophosphatase *(enzyme)*
Pyrophyllit *m* pyrophyllite *(non-clay mineral)*
Pyrophyte *m* pyrophyte
Pyroxen *n* pyroxene, augite *(non-clay mineral)*

Pyrrolase *f* pyrrolase *(enzyme)*
3-Pyrrolidin-2-ylpyridin *n* nornicotine *(alkaloid)*
Pyrrolizidinalkaloid *n* pyrrolizidine alkaloid
Pyruvat *n* pyruvate
Pyruvatcarboxylase *f* pyruvate carboxylase *(enzyme)*
Pyruvatdecarboxylase *f* pyruvate decarboxylase *(enzyme)*
Pyruvatdehydrogenase *f* pyruvate dehydrogenase *(enzyme)*
Pyruvatkinase *f* pyruvate (pyruvic) kinase *(enzyme)*
Pyruvinsäure *f* pyruvic acid, 2-oxopropionic acid
Pyrviniumpamoat *n* pyrvinium pamoate *(anthelminthic)*
Pyurie *f (vet)* pyuria
Pyxidium *n (bot)* pyxidium, pyxis

Q

Q *s.* 1. Strahlungsbilanz; 2. Ubichinon
Q-Fieber *n s.* Query-Fieber
QMV *s.* Queckenmosaikvirus
Quaddelausschlag *m (vet)* nettle-rash, urticaria
Quaderballenpresse *f* rectangular baler
Quadrat *n*/**Griechisch-lateinisches** Graeco-Latin square *(experimental design)*
~/Lateinisches Latin square
~/mittleres *(biom)* mean square
Quadratdibbelmaschine *f* check-row drill
quadratisch square
Quadratnestpflanzmaschine *f* check-row planter
Quadratnestpflanzung *f* check-row planting
Quadratnestsaat *f (forest)* square-pocket sowing
Quadratpflanzung *f (forest)* square planting
Quadratregner *m* square-area sprinkler
Quadriplegie *f (vet)* quadriplegia
Quadrivalent *n* quadrivalent *(of meiotically paired chromosomes)*
Quadrupede *m* quadruped, tetrapod
quaken to quack *(a duck)*; to croak *(a frog)*
Qualitätsabbau *m* **bei Früchten** fruit deterioration
Qualitätsbestimmung *f* quality specification
Qualitätsholz *n* quality (high-grade) timber
Qualitätsindex *m*, **Qualitätskennziffer** *f* quality index
Qualitätsklasse *f* grade
Qualitätsmerkmal *n* quality characteristic
Qualitätsmilch *f* quality milk
Qualitätssaatgut *n* quality (high-standard) seed
Qualitätssilage *f* [top-]quality silage
Qualitätsverbesserung *f* upgrading
Qualitätsverlust *m* quality loss, decay
Qualitätsverschlechterung *f* downgrading, deterioration
Qualitätswein *m* vintage wine, supernaculum
Qualitätszüchtung *f* breeding for quality
Qualitätszuwachs *m (forest)* quality increment

Quantil

Quantil *n (biom)* quantile
Quantimeter *n* dosimeter
Quappe *f* burbot, eel-pout, Lota lota
Quarantäne *f* quarantine
Quarantänebehörde *f* quarantine authority
Quarantänedienst *m* quarantine service
Quarantäneinspektion *f* quarantine inspection
Quarantänekrankheit *f* quarantine disease
Quarantänemaßnahme *f* quarantine measure
Quarantäneschädling *m* quarantine pest
Quarantäneteich *m (pisc)* quarantine pond
Quarantänevorschrift *f* quarantine regulation
Quark *m* curd [cheese], junket, quarg
~/gekörnter (granulierter) cottage cheese
Quarkkäse *m* curd cheese
Quarkseparator *m* quarg separator
Quartier *n* block of trees *(orcharding)*
Quartierschnitt *m* quarter cut *(timber conversion)*
• **im ~ hergestellt** quarter-sawn, sawn on the quarter
Quartil *n (biom)* quartile
Quarz *m* quartz *(non-clay mineral)*
Quarzfilter *n* quartz filter
Quarzit *m (soil)* quartzite
Quarzlampe *f* quartz lamp *(a mercury vapour lamp)*
Quarzporphyrboden *m* quartz porphyry soil
Quarzsand *m* quartz sand
Quarzschiefer *m* quartz schist
Quasiklimax *f* quasiclimax *(plant ecology)*
Quassia *n*, **Quassiabrühe** *f*, **Quassiaextrakt** *m* quassia *(insecticide)*
Quassiaholzbaum *m*, **Quassie** *f (bot)* 1. quassia *(genus Quassia)*; 2. quassia, Quassia amara
Quebrachobaum *m* common white quebracho, Aspidosperma quebracho-blanco
Quecke *f* 1. couch [grass], cutch, wheat-grass, [t]witch-grass *(genus Agropyron)*; 2. common couch [grass], quack grass, [t]witch-grass, quitch [grass], quick, [creeping] wheat-grass, Agropyron repens
Queckeneule *f* rustic shoulder knot moth, Apamea sordens
Queckenmosaikvirus *n* agropyron mosaic virus
Queckentrespe *f* smooth brome[-grass], Bromus inermis
Quecksilber *n* mercury
Quecksilber(II)-chlorid *n* mercuric chloride *(disinfestant)*
Quecksilberdampflampe *f* mercury vapour lamp; quartz lamp
Quecksilberhochdrucklampe *f* high-pressure mercury-vapour lamp
Quecksilbertauchbeize *f (phyt)* mercury steep
Quecksilbertensiometer *n* mercury tensiometer
Quecksilberthermometer *n* mercury thermometer
Quecksilbervergiftung *f (vet)* mercury poisoning
Queenslandfieber *n s.* Query-Fieber
Queenslandhanf *m* Queensland hemp, Cuba jute, Sida rhombifolia
Queenslandkauri *m(f) (bot)* Queensland kauri, Agathis brownii (robusta)
Queenslandnuß *f* macadamia nut, Macadamia ternifolia
Quellbezirk *m s.* Quellgebiet
Quelle *f* 1. source; 2. spring; well
quellen to swell, to imbibe; to steep, to soak *(e.g. seeds)*
Quellenschutzwald *m* water-source protection forest
Quellenstreifenfarn *m* rock spleenwort, Asplenium fontanum
Queller *m* 1. glasswort *(genus Salicornia)*; 2. samphire, Salicornia europaea (herbacea)
Quellgebiet *n* water catchment, gathering ground, collecting area
Quellgras *n* brook grass, Catabrosa aquatica
Quellmerk *m* narrow-leaved water parsnip, Sium erectum, Berula erecta
Quellmiere *f* bog stitchwort, Stellaria alsine
Quellmittel *n* swelling agent
Quellung *f* swelling, imbibition
Quellungsreihe *f* lyotropic series, Hofmeister series
Quellwasser *n* spring water; well water
Quendel *m* wild (creeping) thyme, mother-of-thyme, serpolet, Thymus serpyllum
Quendelblättriger Ehrenpreis *m* thyme-leaved speedwell, Veronica serpyllifolia
Quendelsandkraut *n* lesser thyme, leaved sandwort, Arenaria leptoclados
Querableiter *m* cross drain, let, grip, scupper, *(Am)* water-bar *(road construction)*
~ aus Rundholz pole drain
Querbahn *f (forest)* secondary ride
Querbeet *n* headland, turn land
Querbruch *m (vet)* transverse fracture
Quercetin *n* quercetin *(plant dye)*
Quercitrin *n* quercitrin *(plant dye)*
Quercitrinase *f* quercitrinase *(enzyme)*
Querdrän *m* cross drain
Querdränung *f* cross (transverse) drainage
Querflußmähdrescher *m* cross-flow combine harvester
Querförderband *n*, **Querförderer** *m* cross (transverse) conveyor, cross-elevator
Querförderschnecke *f* cross[-feed] auger, [feed] table auger
~ des Schneidwerkes header auger
Querfortsatz *m* transverse process *(animal anatomy)*
Quergang *m (ent)* transverse feed mark
Quergestell *n (forest)* cross ride
Querheizung *f* transverse heating, perpendicular bonding [heating]
Querholz *n s.* Stapellatte
Querkolon *n* transverse colon *(animal anatomy)*

Querlage *f* transverse (trunk) presentation *(animal birth)*
Querlufttrockner *m s.* Querstromtrockner
Quermelkstand *m* abreast milking parlour, walk-through [milking] parlour
Querneigung *f* tilt
Querrinne *f* drainage dip *(road construction)*
Querrippe *f (slaught)* chuck rib[s]
Querscheibenmuster *n (gen)* banding pattern
querschneiden to cross-cut, to log, to trim *(hewn timber)*
Querschneise *f (forest)* cross ride
Querschnitt *m* cross-section, transverse section
Querschnittsfläche *f* transverse section
Querschwad[en] *m* cross wind-row
Querstromgebläse *n* cross-flow fan
Querstromkörnertrockner *m* cross-flow grain dryer
Querstromtrockner *m* cross-flow dryer, cross-shaft kiln
Querüberlappung *f* side lap *(surveying)*
Querwand *f (bot, zoo)* septum
querwandlos non-septate, coenocytic
Query-Fieber *n (vet)* query fever, Q fever *(caused by Coxiella burnetii)*
Querzelle *f* cross cell
Quesenbandwurmfinne *f* coenurus
Quetsche *f s.* Quetschmühle
quetschen to crush, to mash *(e.g. potatoes for feeding)*; to roll *(feed grain)*; to squeeze [out], to press *(e.g. juice)*; to bruise *(e.g. fruit in transport)*; to contuse *(e.g. limbs)*
Quetschmühle *f* crushing mill, [roller] crusher, masher
Quetschung *f (vet)* contusion • **durch ~ verletzen** to bruise
Quetschwalze *f* crushing roller
Quetschwunde *f (vet)* contused wound
Quetschzetter *m* semicrusher *(haymaking machine)*
Quick-pot-Anzuchtplatte *f* quick-pot *(for raising of plantlets)*
Quieszenz *f* quiescence, ectodormancy, imposed dormancy *(physiology)*
Quinalphos[-Methyl] *n* quinalphos[-methyl] *(insecticide)*
Quinazamid *n* quinazamid *(fungicide)*
Quinonamid *n* quinonamid *(herbicide)*
Quintal *n* quintal
Quintozen *n* quintozene *(fungicide)*
Quirl *m (bot)* whorl, verticil
quirlblättrig verticillate
Quirlblättrige Malve *f* whorled (curled) mallow, Malva verticillata
Quirlblättriges Mädchenauge *n* thread-leaved tickseed, Coreopsis verticillata
Quirlholz *n* compound spur, spur system *(wood anatomy)*
Quirliger Tannenwedel *m (bot)* mare's-tail, Hippuris vulgaris
Quirlsalbei *m* lilac sage, Salvia verticillata
quirlständig *(bot)* whorled, verticillate
Quirlwäsche *f* beet washer with revolving arm agitators
Quitte *f* quince
~/apfelförmige apple-shaped quince
~/birnenförmige pear[-shaped] quince
Quittenbaum *m* quince[-tree], Cydonia oblonga
Quittenstauche *f* quince stunt *(virosis)*
Quote *f* quota, share; proportion
Quotient *m*/**assimilatorischer (photosynthetischer)** assimilation quotient

R

R. *s.* 1. Rappe; 2. Räumung
Rabatte *f* [flower] border
Rabattenberegnung *f* border irrigation
Rabattenpflanze *f* border-plant
Rabattenpflanzung *f (forest)* ridge planting, planting on ridges
Rabattensaat *f (forest)* ridge sowing, sowing on ridges
rabatzen to scrape *(hides)*
Rabenkrähe *f* carrion crow, Corvus corone ssp. corone
Rabenschnabelbein *n* coracoid bone *(animal anatomy)*
Rabies *f s.* Tollwut
Rabon *n* rabon *(insecticide)*
racemös *(bot, zoo)* racemose, racemiform, botryose
Rachen *m* pharynx, throat, gullet, throttle
Rachenblütler *mpl* figwort family *(family Scrophulariaceae)* • **die ~ betreffend** scrophulariaceous
rachenförmig *(bot)* ringent
Rachenförmige Gazanie *f* treasure flower, Gazania ringens (splendens)
Rachenmandel *f* [pharyngeal] tonsil
Rachenrebe *f* goldfish vine *(genus Columnea)*
Rachenschleimhautentzündung *f (vet)* pharyngitis
Rachilla *f (bot)* rachilla
Rachis *f* 1. *(bot)* rachis; 2. *s.* Wirbelsäule
Rachitis *f (vet)* rickets
~/hypophosphatämische hypophosphataemic rickets
rachitisch rickety
Rackelhuhn *n* hybrid-capercaillie, hybrid-grouse
Rad *n*/**antriebsfreies (antriebsloses)** non-driven wheel
~/bodengeführtes landwheel
Radblättrige Seekanne *f* fringed water lily, yellow floating heart, Nymphoides peltata
Raddruck *m* wheel pressure

Raddruckschaden

Raddruckschaden *m* wheel-induced compaction, traffic pan
Raddruckverstärker *m* weight transfer unit
Rade *f* [corn-]cockle, corn rose, Agrostemma githago
Radekorn *n* (phyt) cockle
Radekrankheit *f* ear cockles, cockle *(esp. of wheat, caused by Anguina tritici)*
radförmig *(bot)* rotate
Radhacke *f* wheel [hand] hoe, Dutch (thrust) hoe
Radhaft[reib]ung *f* wheel adhesion
Radi *m s.* Rettich
Radialgebläse *n* radial (centrifugal) fan
Radialimmundiffusionstest *m (phyt)* radial immunodiffusion test
Radiallüfter *m s.* Radialgebläse
Radialmelkkarussell *n* rotary abreast milking system
Radialreifen *m* radial[-ply] tyre
Radialschleuder *f (api)* radial extractor
Radialtriangulation *f (forest)* radial (minor-control) plotting
radiär *(bot, zoo)* radiate
Radiation *f* radiation
Radiator *m* radiator
Radies[chen] *n* [small, little, garden] radish, Raphanus sativus var. sativus
Radikula *f* radicle, seminal (seed, embryonic) root
radikulär radicular
Radioaktivität *f* radioactivity
Radioautographie *f* autoradiography
Radiobiologie *f* radiobiology
radiobiologisch radiobiological
Radiocarbonmethode *f* radiocarbon dating [method]
Radiographie *f* radiography
Radioimmunoassay *m* radioimmunoassay
Radioisotop *n* radioisotope, radioactive isotope
Radiometer *n* radiometer
Radiometrie *f* radiometry
Radionuklid *n* radionuclide, radioactive nuclide
Radioprotektor *m* radiation protection agent
Radioskopie *f* radioscopy
Radiosterilisation *f* radiosterilization, radiation sterilization *(e.g. of insect pests)*
Radiotelemetrie *f* radiotelemetry
Radiotherapie *f (phyt, vet)* radiotherapy
Radius *m* radius
Radkultivator *m* wheeled cultivator
~/handgeschobener hand-pushed wheeled cultivator
Radlader *m* wheel loader
Radnor[schaf] *n* Radnor *(sheep breed)*
Radrechwender *m* spider (finger wheel) rake, spider wheel turner
Radschlepper *m* wheel[ed] tractor
Radschlupf *m* wheel slip, slip[page], wheelspin
Radspur *f* [wheel] track, wheelway
Radspurlockerer *m* track loosener
Radspurlockerung *f* track loosening
Radspurverdichtung *f s.* Raddruckschaden
Radstand *m* wheelbase
Radsturz *m* wheel lean
Radsturzwinkel *m* wheel lean angle
Radtaster *m* rotary feeler, sensing wheel
Radtraktor *m* wheel[ed] tractor
Radula *f* radula *(of snails)*
Radzusatzmasse *f* wheel weight
Raffiabast *m* raffia, raphia
Raffiabastverband *m* raffia bandage *(in grafting)*
Raffiapalme *f* raffia [palm], Raphia farinifera (ruffia)
Raffiapalmfaser *f* raffia, raphia
Raffinade *f* refined sugar, raffinade
Raffinat *n* raffinate
Raffinerie *f* refinery, refining plant
Raffinerieabwasser *n* refinery waste-water
Raffineriemelasse *f* refinery molasses, barrel syrup
raffinieren to refine
Raffinose *f* raffinose, melitose *(trisaccharide)*
Rafoxanid *n* rafoxanide *(anthelminthic)*
Ragibrand *m (phyt)* ragee smut *(caused by Melanopsichium eleusinis)*
Rahm *m* cream, head • **~ ansetzen lassen** to cream
~/saurer sour (cultured) cream
Rahmapfel *m* sweet-sop, sugar apple, Annona squamosa
Rahmbutter *f* farm butter
Rähmchen *n (api)* frame
Rähmchenzange *f* frame tongs
Rahmen *n (dairy)* creaming, skimming [off]
Rahmen *m* 1. frame; 2. frame, body, skeletal size *(livestock judging)*
Rahmenbeurteilung *f* frame evaluation *(livestock judging)*
Rahmenfilterpresse *f* frame filter press *(sugar manufacture)*
Rahmengröße *f* frame size *(livestock judging)*
Rahmenhöhe *f* underbeam clearance *(of a plough)*
Rahmenmarke *f* fiducial (collimating) mark *(aerial photogrammetry)*
Rahmenpflug *m* framed plough
Rahmkäse *m* cream cheese
Rahmpulver *n* dried cream
Rahmreifer *m* cream ripening vat, ag[e]ing vat, milk ripener
Rahmreifung *f* cream ripening
Rahmsäuerungskultur *f* butter starter
Rahmschleuder *f* cream separator
Rahnwerden *n* browning *(of wine)*
Raigras *n s.* Raygras
Rain *m* field edge (margin), border, boundary
Rainfarn *m (bot)* tansy, Tanacetum (Chrysanthemum) vulgare
Rainkohl *m* nipple-wort, Lapsana communis
Rainspritze *f* roadside sprayer
Rainweide *f* privet *(genus Ligustrum)*

Ralle f rail *(family Rallidae)*
Rama f Jamaica sorrel, Hibiscus sabdariffa
Rambouillet[schaf] n Rambouillet *(sheep breed)*
Rambutan m *(bot)* rambutan, rambootan, Nephelium lappaceum
Ramie f 1. false nettle *(genus Boehmeria)*; 2. ramie, rhea, China grass, Chinese silk-plant, Boehmeria nivea
Ramiefaser f ramie
Ramifikation f *(bot, zoo)* ramification
ramifizieren to ramify
Rammelkammer f mating chamber *(of bark-beetles)*
Rammler m buck [hare], jack hare; buck rabbit
Rammpfahl m ram pile
Rammskopf m roman-nosed head
Rampe f ramp; platform
Ramsch m/**zusammengesetzter** composite cross *(plant breeding)*
Ramschpopulation f bulk population *(plant breeding)*
Ramschzüchtung f bulk method
Ramskopf m s. Rammskopf
Ramularia-Blattfleckenkrankheit f ramularia leaf spot *(of beet, caused by Ramularia beticola)*
RaMV s. Raygrasmosaikvirus
Ranch f *(Am)* ranch
Rancharbeiter m *(Am)* rancher
Rancher m *(Am)* rancher
Randbaum m border (edge, marginal) tree
Randbeet n border
Randbesamung f *(forest)* border (marginal) seeding
Randbewässerung f ribbon check[s] irrigation
Randblüte f margin (ray) flower
Randchlorose f *(phyt)* edge chlorosis
Randeffekt m *(ecol)* edge effect
Randhämatom n *(vet)* marginal haematoma
Randhieb m *(forest)* border felling, felling affording marginal shelter
randlich *(bot, zoo)* marginal
Randnekrose f marginal (edge) necrosis
Randomanspannung f randem *(equestrian sport)*
Randomisation f randomization *(experimentation)*
randomisieren to randomize
Randreihe f border row
Randschutz m *(forest)* border protection
randschweifig *(bot)* repand
Randstamm m s. Randbaum
randständig *(bot, zoo)* marginal
Randstreifen m verge, border strip
Randsumpf m lagg *(of a high moor)*
Randvergilbung f *(phyt)* edge yellowing
Randverjüngung f *(forest)* marginal (border) regeneration, regeneration by strip fellings
Randwirkung f *(ecol)* border (edge) effect
Rangkorrelationskoeffizient m *(biom)* rank correlation coefficient
Rangordnung f order

~/soziale social rank (dominance order)
Rangsummentest m *(biom)* rank sum test
Rangtest m *(biom)* rank order test
Ranke f *(bot)* tendril, cirrus; bine *(as of the hop)*; vine [shoot] *(esp. of grape-vine)* • **Ranken ausbilden** *(Am)* to vine
ranken/sich to climb, to wind, to twine, to creep, to run, *(Am)* to vine
rankenförmig cirriform, pampiniform
Rankengewächs n, **Rankenpflanze** f tendril-climber plant, climber, creeper, twiner [plant], twining plant, *(Am)* vine [runner]
Rankenpflanzenkraut n vine
Rankenplatterbse f yellow vetchling, Lathyrus aphaca
Rankenschaumblüte f foam-flower, Tiarella cordifolia
Ranker m *(soil)* ranker
Rankgerüst n trelliswork
Ranunkel f *(bot)* Persian (turban) buttercup, Ranunculus asiaticus
Ranunkelstrauch m 1. Jew's mallow, kerria *(genus Kerria)*; 2. Japanese rose, Kerria japonica
Ranz f s. Ranzzeit
Ranzidität f s. Ranzigkeit
ranzig rancid • **~ werden** to rancidify
Ranzigkeit f rancidity, rancidness
Ranzzeit f heat *(of predatory game)*
Rapfen m rapacious carp, Aspius aspius
Raphe f *(bot, zoo)* raphe
Raphiabast m s. Raffiabast
Raphide f *(bot)* raphide
Rapontikawurzel f evening primrose, Oenothera (Onagra) biennis
Rappe m black [horse]
Rappengeschmack m stem-like taste *(defect of wine)*
Rappschecke m piebald [horse], pinto
Rappschimmel m blue roan *(horse)*
Raps m [oil-seed] rape, winter (swede, Argentina) rape, cole[-seed], Brassica napus var. napus
Rapsdrusch m rape threshing
Rapserdfloh m cabbage stem flea beetle, Psylliodes chrysocephala
Rapsextraktionsschrot m rape-seed [oil] meal
Rapsglanzkäfer m 1. flower beetle *(genus Meligethes)*; 2. [bronzed] blossom beetle, Meligethes aeneus
Rapskuchen m rape-cake
Rapsöl n rape[-seed] oil, cole-seed oil, colza-oil
Rapsprotein n rape-seed protein
Rapsproteinkonzentrat n rape-seed protein concentrate
Rapssamen m rape-seed, cole[-seed], colza
Rapssamenöl n s. Rapsöl
Raps[samen]schrot m rape-seed [oil] meal
Rapsschwadmäher m rape swather
Rapssilage f rape silage
Rapsstroh n rape straw

Rapsweißling

Rapsweißling *m* green-veined white butterfly, Pieris (Artogeia) napi
Rapünzchen *n s.* Rapunze[l] 1.
Rapunze[l] *f* 1. lamb's-lettuce, [common] corn-salad, field salad, fetticus, Valerianella locusta (olitoria); 2. rampion, Campanula rapunculus
raschwüchsig rapid-growing
Rasen *m* lawn, grass; turf, sward, sod • **einen ~ anlegen** to bottom • **mit ~ bedecken** to turf, to sod • **~ neu einsäen** to returf • **sich mit ~ bedecken** to sward
~/gärtnerischer horticultural turf
Rasenameise *f* pavement ant, Tetramorium caespitum
Rasenansaat *f* lawn sowing (making)
Rasenbaumaschine *f* lawn-maker
Rasenbesen *m* lawn broom, sweep
rasenbildend c[a]espitose, c[a]espitous
Rasenbildendes Liebesgras *n* love-grass, Eragrostis caespitosa
Rasenbildung *f* swarding
Rasenboden *m* lawn soil
Rasenbordstein *m* lawn kerb
Rasendecke *f* turf, sward, sod
Raseneisenerz *n*, **Raseneisenstein** *m (soil)* bog iron ore
Rasenerneuerung *f* lawn renovation
Rasenfalle *f (hunt)* turf trap
Rasenfläche *f* turf, greens, grass plot
~/öffentliche amenity turf
Rasengitterplatte *f*, **Rasengitterstein** *m* grating brick
Rasengley[boden] *m* soddy gley soil
Rasengras *n* lawn (turf) grass
Rasengrasmischung *f* lawn mixture
Rasenhaue *f* sod-mattock
Rasenheber *m* sod-lifter
Rasenkante *f* verge, lawn edge (side)
Rasenkantenbearbeitung *f* lawn edge trimming
Rasenkantenmäher *m* lawn side cutter, verge mower (trimmer), edge mower, edger
Rasenkantenschere *f* edging shears
Rasenkantenschneider *m s.* Rasenkantenmäher
Rasenkantenstecher *m* edging knife
Rasenkehren *n* lawn raking
Rasenkehrmaschine *f* lawn-sweeping machine
Rasenkratzer *m* lawn scarifier
Rasenlieschgras *n (bot)* small timothy, smaller cat's-tail, Phleum bertolonii
Rasenlüfter *m* lawn aerator, aerator rake
Rasenlüftergabel *f* lawn aerator fork
Rasenlüfterrechen *m* aerator rake
Rasenmähen *n* lawn mowing, grass cutting
Rasenmäher *m* lawn-mower
Rasenmähermotor *m* lawn-mower engine
Rasenmischung *f* lawn mixture
Rasenpflege *f* lawn maintenance (care)
Rasenpflug *m* turfing plough, turf cutter
Rasenplatz *m s.* Rasenfläche

Rasenprofil *n* lawn profile *(of tractor tyres)*
Rasenrechen *m* lawn rake
Rasenriedgras *n* tufted sedge, Carex caespitosa
Rasensaat *f* lawn seed
Rasensämaschine *f* lawn seeder (planter)
Rasensamen *m* lawn seed
Rasenschädling *m* lawn pest
Rasenschmiele *f* tussock (hassock) grass, tufted[-hair] grass, *(Am)* bull poll, Deschampsia caespitosa
Rasenschneidemaschine *f* lawn-mower
Rasensimse *f* deer sedge, Scirpus caespitosus
Rasensode *f s.* Sode
Rasensprenger *m* lawn sprinkler (waterer)
Rasenstück *n s.* 1. Sode; 2. Rasenfläche
Rasentraktor *m* lawn tractor
Rasenunkraut *n* lawn weed
Rasenwalze *f* lawn-roller
Rash *m (vet)* rash
Rasierklingenschar *n* sword blade share
Rasige Haarsimse *f s.* Rasensimse
~ Segge *f s.* Rasenriedgras
Rasiges Hornkraut *n (bot)* field cerastium, Cerastium caespitosum
Raspatorium *n (vet)* raspatory
Raspe *f (vet)* sallenders, sellanders
Rasse *f* breed, race, blood, strain, variety
~/gekreuzte cross-breed
~/geographische geographic breed, geographical race
~/leichte light breed
~/ökologische ecotype
~/schwere heavy breed
Rasselblume *f (bot)* Cupid's dart, catananche *(genus Catananche)*
rasselnd stertorous *(breathing)*
Rassemerkmal *n* breed character[istic], point
Rassenanerkennung *f* breed approbation
Rassenbildung *f* race formation
Rassendynamik *f* race dynamics *(e.g. of pests)*
Rassengruppe *f* breed group
Rassenhygiene *f* eugenics
Rassenkreuzung *f* breed cross[ing]
Rassenkreuzungsprodukt *n* breed cross
Rassenreinzucht *f* pure breeding
rassenspezifisch race-specific
Rassenspezifität *f* race specifity
rassenunspezifisch race-non-specific
Rassenunterschied *m* breed difference
Rassenvergleich *m* breed comparison
Rassenversuch *m* race trial
Rassenzucht *f* pure breeding
Rassepferd *n* thoroughbred [horse]
Rassepferde *npl* bloodstock
rasserein *s.* reinrassig
Rassestandard *m* breeding standard
Rassetyp *m* breed type
rassig 1. thoroughbred; 2. fiery *(wine)*
rassisch racial

Rasterelektronenmikroskop *n* scanning electron microscope
Rasterelektronenmikroskopie *f* scanning electron microscopy
Rasterkarte *f* grid map *(e.g. in soil mapping)*
Rastermikrodensitometrie *f* scanning microdensitometry
Rasterverschiebung[smutation] *f (gen)* frameshift mutation
Ratanhia *f (bot)* rhatany, Krameria triandra
Ratanhiawurzel *f* rhatany *(astringent drug)*
Rate *f* **des nachhaltigen Geldertrages** *(forest)* financial yield
Ration *f* ration, allowance, diet *(animal nutrition)*
~/gemischte mixed ration
~/nährstoffkonzentrierte high nutrient density ration, HND ration
Rationsbestandteil *m* ration ingredient
Rationsgeber *m* feed metering hopper
Rationstyp *m* specimen ration
Rationsweide *f* cyclic grazing, rotation[al] grazing
Rationszusammenstellung *f* ration (diet) formulation
Ratoon-Rohr *n* ratoon [cane, crop]
Ratschenkupplung *f* ratchet (clatter) clutch
Ratte *f* rat *(genus Rattus)* • **Ratten bekämpfen (vernichten)** to rat
~/weiße albino rat *(laboratory animal)*
rattenbekämpfend raticidal
Rattenbekämpfung *f* rat destruction
Rattenbekämpfungsmittel *n* raticide, rat killer (destroyer)
Rattengift *n* rat poison
Rattenschwanz *m (vet)* rat-tail
Rattenschwanzlarve *f (ent)* rat-tailed maggot *(from Eristalix tenax)*
rattenvernichtend raticidal
Rattenvernichtung *f* rat destruction
Rattenvernichtungsmittel *n* raticide, rat killer (destroyer)
rattenverseucht ratty
Rattler *m* ratter, rat-catching dog
Ratz *m s.* Stinkmarder
Raubbau *m* exploitive farming, exhaustive cultivation • **~ treiben** to overcrop • **durch ~ erschöpfen** to overcrop, to rack *(soil)*
Raubbiene *f* robber bee
Räuber *m (ecol, ent)* predator, episite
Räuber-Beute-Beziehung *f* predator-prey-relationship
Räuberei *f* predation, predatism; *(api)* robbing
räuberisch [lebend] predatory, predacious
räubern *(api)* to rob
Räubern *n* 1. *(api)* robbing; 2. deshooting of the rootstock *(grafting)*
Räubertum *n* predation, predatism
Raubfisch *m* predatory fish
Raubfliege *f* robber fly *(family Asilidae)*
Raubinsekt *n* predatory insect
Raubkäfer *m* rove-beetle, staphylinid [beetle] *(family Staphylinidae)*
Raubmilbe *f* predatory mite, phytoseiid [mite] *(family Phytoseiidae)*
Raubparasit *m* parasitoid
Raubparasitismus *m* parasitoidism
Raubschütze *m (hunt)* poacher
Raubtier *n* carnivore, beast of prey (ravin), predator *(order Carnivora)*
Raubvogel *m* predatory (raptorial) bird, bird of prey, raptor
Raubvogelnest *n* eyrie
Raubwanze *f* reduviid [bug] *(family Reduviidae)*
Raubwild *n* predatory game, vermin
Raubwildbekämpfungsmittel *n* predacide
Raubzeug *n* vermin, varmint
Raubzeugbefall *m* attack by vermin
raubzeugsicher predator-proof
Raubzeugvernichtungsmittel *n* predacide
Rauchdunst *m* smoke haze *(e.g. of a forest fire)*
Räucherapparat *m* fumigator
Räucherfisch *m* smoke fish
Raucherinsel *f (Am)* fag station
Räucherkäse *m* smoked cheese
Räuchermittel *n* [dry] fumigant *(pest control)*
Räuchermitteltoxizität *f* fumigant toxicity
räuchern 1. to smoke, to cure *(as meat, fish)*; 2. to fumigate *(for pest control)*; 3. to smudge *(as to repel insects or to prevent frost)*
Räuchern *n* 1. smoking, curing; 2. fumigation; 3. smudging
Räucherpatrone *f* fumigating cartridge
Räucherspeck *m* bacon
~/durchwachsener (magerer) streaky bacon
Räucherspeckseite *f* flitch
Räucherware *f* smoke product
Rauchfleisch *n* smoked meat
Rauchgas *n* smoke (flue) gas
Rauchgaskondensator *m* flue gas condenser
Rauchgasresistenz *f* resistance to fumes
Rauchgerät *n (api)* bee blower, smoker
Rauchgrauer Porling *m (bot)* scorched conk, Polyporus adustus
rauchhart fume-hardy
Rauchhärte *f* fume-hardiness, resistance to fumes
Rauchkerze *f* smoke candle *(forest fire control)*
rauchresistent *s.* rauchhart
Rauchschaden *m* fume damage, smoke damage (injury)
Rauchschadengebiet *n* smoke-damaged area
Rauchschwaden *m* drift smoke
Rauchschwalbe *f* swallow, Hirundo rustica
Rauchtabak *m* [smoking] tobacco
Rauchwaren *pl* furs, furriery, peltry
Rauchwarenhandel *m* furriery
Räude *f (vet)* scab[ies], mange; rubbers *(of sheep)*
räudeähnlich scabby, scabietic, scabious, scabrous
Räudemilbe *f* mange mite *(comprehensive term)*

räudig

räudig scabby, scabietic, scabious, scabrous
Raufe *f* [feeding, stable] rack, crib, hay bunk; trough • **an die ~ binden** to rack
~ im Freien cratch
raufen to pull *(e.g. flax)*
Raufenfläche *f* trough space
Raufriemen *m* pulling belt
rauh 1. *(bot, zoo)* rough, coarse, rugged, scabrous, asperous; 2. harsh, raw *(climate)*
Rauhblattaster *f* New England aster, Aster novae-angliae
rauhblättrig asperifolious, trachyphyllous
Rauhblättrige Alpenrose *f* hairy Alpenrose, Alpine rose, Rhododendron hirsutum
~ Rose *f* large-leaved rose, Rosa jundzillii
Rauhblättrigkeit *f* **der Süßkirsche** *(phyt)* cherry rasp leaf *(virosis)*
Rauhe Gänsekresse *f* hairy rock-cress, Arabis hirsuta
~ Nelke *f* Deptford pink, Dianthus armeria
Rauheis *n* glazed frost (ice), glaze
Rauheit *f* 1. *(bot, zoo)* roughness, coarseness, ruggedness; 2. harshness, rawness *(of climate)*
Rauher Beinwell *m (bot)* Russian comfrey, Symphytum peregrinum
~ Hahnenfuß *m (bot)* hairy buttercup, Ranunculus sardous
~ Löwenzahn *m (bot)* rough hawkbit, Leontodon hispidus
~ Schneckenklee *m* 1. bur clover, Medicago polymorpha; 2. toothed medic[k], California (toothed) bur clover, Medicago nigra
Rauhes Hornblatt *n* hornwort, Ceratophyllum demersum
Rauhfrost *m s.* Rauhreif
rauhfrüchtig *(bot)* rough-fruited, dasycarpous, trachycarpous
Rauhfußbussard *m* rough-legged buzzard, Buteo lagopus
Rauhfußhuhn *n* grouse *(family Tetraonidae)*
rauhfüßig feather-legged *(bird)*
Rauhfutter *n* roughage, fodder, forage • **~ aufstecken** to rack [up]
Rauhfutterschieber *m* roughage scraper
Rauhfutterverteiler *m* roughage spreader
Rauhfutterverwertung *f* utilization of roughage
rauhhaarig *(bot, zoo)* hirsute; rough-haired, shaggy, wire-haired *(esp. a dog)*
Rauhhaarige Platterbse *f* rough pea, Lathyrus hirsutus
~ Wicke *f* [hairy] tare, Vicia hirsuta
Rauhhaariger Fuchsschwanz *m* common amaranth, *(Am)* redroot [pigweed], Amaranthus retroflexus
~ Sonnenhut *m* yellow daisy, black-eyed Susan, Rudbeckia hirta [var. hirta]
Rauhhaarigkeit *f* shagginess
Rauhhafer *m* sand oat[s], bristle[-pointed] oat, lopside[d] oat, black oat, Avena nuda [ssp. nuda], Avena strigosa

Rauhmaß *n* nominal measure (size) *(of timber)*
Rauhmosaik *n (phyt)* mild mosaic *(of potato)*
Rauhreif *m* hoar[-frost], rime, white frost
Rauhreifschaden *m (forest)* rime break, glaze damage
Rauhrindigkeit *f* **der Birne** *(phyt)* pear rough bark *(virosis)*
rauhsamig *(bot)* trachyspermous
Rauhsamige Vogelwicke *f* woolly-pod vetch, Vicia dasycarpa
rauhschalig rough-skinned, rough-shelled
Rauhschaligkeit *f* rough skin
~ des Apfels *(phyt)* apple rough skin, apple star crack *(virosis)*
Rauhwalze *f* ribbed roll[er], corrugated roller
Rauhware *f* rough timber
Rauhweizen *m* turgid (poulard) wheat, rivet [wheat], cone (English) wheat, Triticum turgidum
Rauke *f* [salad] rocket, Eruca vesicaria ssp. sativa
raukenblättrig *(bot)* sisymbrifolious
raukenförmig *(bot, zoo)* eruciform
Raukenförmige Beckmannie *f* Beckman's (slough) grass, Beckmannia eruciformis
Raum *m*/**Freier** free space *(of plant tissue)*
~/ländlicher rural area, countryside
~/Scheinbar Freier [apparent] free space, AFS Donnan free space *(of plant tissue)*
~/toter dead space *(animal physiology)*
Räumaggregat *n (forest)* rakedozer
Raumbedarf *m* space requirement
Raumbrüter *m* brooding chamber *(poultry production)*
Räumde *f (forest)* sparse stand, poorly stocked area, stand og low density, gap
Raumdichte *f* [basic] density
räumdig *(forest)* sparse, open-stocked, gappy
räumen 1. to clear, to remove; 2. to bottom out *(a ditch)*
Räumer[zahn] *m* raker [tooth], clearer tooth *(of a chain saw)*
Raumgehalt *m s.* Schichtmaß
Räumgerät *n s.* Schwergrubber
raumgreifend spacious *(e.g. horse's gait)*
Raumheizung *f* space heating
Raumhüten *n* open herding
räumig *s.* räumdig
Rauminhalt *m* volume, cubic content
Rauminhaltsermittlung *f* volume determination
Raumkühlung *f* space cooling
Raummarke *f* floating mark *(remote sensing)*
Raummasse *f* volume weight, bulk density
Raummeter *m* stacked cubic metre, cubic metre of piled wood, stere
Raumplanung *f* regional planning
Räumpresse *f* pick-up baler (press), baling press, baler
Raumprozent *n* percentage by volume
Räumraupe *f* pusher tractor
Räumschild *m* bulldozer blade
~/gezahnter rake (rock, stump) blade, root rake

Räumspieß *m* emptying poker
Räumung *f (forest)* removal, clearing, final felling, final [harvest] cut
~ des Oberbestands overstorey removal
Räumungshieb *m*, **Räumungsschlag** *m s.* Räumung
raumzeitlich spatio-temporal
Raunze *f* heat *(of cat)*
Raupe *f* 1. *(ent)* caterpillar, grub, worm; 2. *s.* Raupenkette
~/pflanzenschädigende canker[-worm]
Raupenbefall *m* attack by caterpillars
Raupenfahrwerk *n* track
Raupenfahrzeug *n* Caterpillar
Raupenfliege *f* tachina (tachinid) fly, larvaevorid fly *(family Tachinidae = Larvaevoridae)*
Raupenfraß *m* caterpillar damage
Raupengespinst *n* cocoon
Raupenkette *f* Caterpillar [track, tread], track
Raupenleim *m* insect paste
Raupenleimpapier *n* gluepaper
Raupenschaden *m* caterpillar damage
Raupenschlepper *m* Caterpillar (crawler, track-laying) tractor, track-layer
Rauschbeere *f* 1. bog bilberry (whortleberry), moorberry, Vaccinium uliginosum; 2. [black] crowberry, Empetrum nigrum
Rauschbrand *m (vet)* blackleg [disease], black quarter, quarter ill
Rausche *f* heat *(of a sow)*
rauschen to be at (in, on) heat *(sow)*
Rauschpfeffer[strauch] *m* kava, kawa pepper, Piper methysticum
Raute *f* 1. rue *(genus Ruta)*; 2. [common, garden] rue, herb [of] grace, countryman's treacle, Ruta graveolens var. vulgaris
rautenähnlich rhomboid
rautenblättrig rhomb-leaved
rautenförmig rhomboid
Rautenmelkstand *m* polygon [milking] parlour, diamond-shaped milking parlour
Rautenpflug *m* lozenge plough
Rauwolfia *f (bot)* rauwolfia *(genus Rauvolfia)*
Rauwolfiaalkaloid *n* rauwolfia alkaloid
Rayanagras *n* [Mexican] teosinte, Guatemala grass, Euchlaena mexicana
Raygras *n* 1. rye-grass *(genus Lolium)*; 2. [perennial] rye-grass, Lolium perenne
Raygras-Cryptic-Virus *n* rye-grass cryptic virus
Raygrasmosaikvirus *n* rye-grass mosaic virus, RgMV
Rayonierung *f* zonation
razemös racemose, racemiform
RbEMV *s.* Robinienmosaikvirus
RDM *s.* Rotes Dänisches Milchvieh
RE *s.* Restriktionsenzym
Reabsorption *f* reabsorption
Reagens *n*/**kristallisationsförderndes** crystallizer
~ nach Kovacs Kovacs reagent *(microbiology)*

Reaktion *f* reaction, response
~/anamnestische anamnestic reaction *(immunology)*
~/anaplerotische anaplerotic reaction *(plant physiology)*
~/morphogenetische morphosis
~/phobische motor reflex (response)
Reaktions[ab]folge *f s.* Reaktionsweg
Reaktionsgeschwindigkeits-Temperatur-Regel *f* van't Hoff effect (rule)
Reaktionsholz *n* reaction wood
~ aus dem unteren Stammteil sway wood (grain)
Reaktionskurve *f* response curve
reaktionslos reactionless; inert
Reaktionsnorm *f* norm of reaction
Reaktionsschwelle *f* threshold of response
Reaktionsweg *m* pathway *(biochemistry)*
Reaktionszeit *f* reaction time
Reaktorgefäß *n* fermenting tub, fermenter, fermentor
Rebbelmaschine *f* sheller
rebbeln to shell
Rebbler *m* sheller
Rebe *f* 1. [grape] vine, grape tree *(genus Vitis)*; 2. *s.* Hopfenrebe
Rebelmaschine *f s.* Rebbelmaschine
rebenblättrig *(bot)* vitifolious
Rebenertrag *m* vintage
Rebengewächshaus *n* vinery
Rebenkrankheit *f* vine disease
Rebenkräuselmilbe *f* rust mite, Phyllocoptes (Calepitrimerus) vitis
Rebenmehltau *m* grape mildew *(caused by Uncinula necator = Oidium tuckeri)*
Rebensäge *f* Grecian saw
Rebenschädling *m* vine pest
Rebenschildlaus *f* grape scale, Aspidiotus uvae
Rebenspritze *f* vineyard sprayer
Rebenstecher *m s.* Rebstichler
Rebenzikade *f (ent)* grape leaf-hopper *(Erythroneura spp.)*
Rebfläche *f* grape acreage, vineyard
Rebhahn *m* cock-partridge
Rebhuhn *n* 1. partridge *(genus Perdix)*; 2. [grey, common] partridge, Perdix perdix
Rebhuhnbeere *f* wintergreen, Gaultheria procumbens
Rebkultur *f* viticulture
Reblaus *f* grape (vine) louse, [grape] phylloxera, vine fretter, Phylloxera vitifoliae, Viteus vitifolii
Rebmesser *n* vine-knife
Rebpfahl *m* grape-stake, vineyard pole
Rebpfählung *f* staking
Rebschere *f* pruning shears, pruner
Rebschoß *m* vine branch
Rebschule *f* grape nursery
Rebsorte *f* grape cultivar
Rebsortenkunde *f* ampelography
Rebstecken *m s.* Rebpfahl

Rebstichler

Rebstichler *m (ent)* vine (pear) leaf-roller, Byctiscus betulae
Rebveredelungsmaschine *f* grafting machine
Receptaculum *n s.* Rezeptakel
rechen to rake
Rechen *m* [garden] rake, hand (garden) fork
Rechenblume *f* sweetleaf *(genus Symplocos)*
Rechenhof *m* **für geflößtes Holz** log pond
Rechenklassierer *m* rake classifier
Rechenprobit *m (biom)* working probit
Rechteck *n*/**Lateinisches** Latin rectangle *(experimental design)*
Rechteckverband *m* planting in lines (rows)
rechts off *(side of animal or vehicle)*
rechtsdrehend 1. dextrorotatory, dextrogyrate, *(optical activity of molecules)*; 2. *s.* rechtswindend
Rechtsgalopp *m* canter, lope • **im ~ laufen lassen** to canter
rechtswindend *(bot)* dextrorse, dextrorsal
rechtzeitig timely
Rechtzeitigkeit *f* timeliness *(e.g. of field operations)*
Rechwender *m* rake tedder
Recon *n (gen)* recon
Recorder *m* milk recording jar, recorder jar
Recycling *n* recycling
Red Poll *n* Red Poll *(cattle breed)*
~ Sindhi *n* Red Sindhi *(cattle breed)*
Redbone Hound *m* redbone hound *(dog breed)*
Redie *f* redia *(developmental stage of trematodes)*
Redoxenzym *n* redox enzyme
Redoxpaar *n (soil)* redox couple
Redoxpotential *n* redox potential
Redoxsystem *n* redox (oxidation-reduction) system
Reductase *f* reductase *(enzyme)*
Reduktion *f* reduction
Reduktionsteilung *f* meiosis, meiotic division
Redukton *n* reductone *(brewing)*
Reduplikation *f (gen)* reduplication, replication
Reduzent *m (ecol)* reducer, decomposer
Reduzierung *f* **des Lichteinfalls** light reduction
Redwood *n* redwood *(from Sequoia sempervirens)*
Redwood-Chips *npl* tree fern chips *(as planting medium for orchids)*
Reff *n* cradle *(of a scythe)*
reflektorisch reflexly, by means of reflexes
Reflex *m* reflex
~/bedingter conditioned reflex
Reflexbewegung *f* reflex movement
Reflexbluten *n (ent)* exudation
Reflexbogen *m* reflex arc
Reflexhemmung *f* reflex inhibition
Reflexionskolorimeter *n* reflectance colorimeter
Reflexlosigkeit *f (vet)* areflexia
Reflexovulation *f* reflex ovulation
Reflexverhalten *n* reflex behaviour
Reflexzahl *f* albedo *(of the atmosphere)*
Reflexzentrum *n* reflex centre
Reformjoghurt *m* acidophilous milk
refraktär refractory
Refraktometer *n* refractometer
Refraktometrie *f* refractometry
Refrigerans *n* refrigerant
Refrigeration *f* refrigeration
Refugialgebiet *n*, **Refugium** *n (ecol)* refuge, shelter
rege machen *(hunt)* to rouse, to startle
Regel *f* **der unabhängigen Kombination** *s.* ~/Dritte Mendelsche
~/Dritte Mendelsche *(gen)* Mendel's third law, law of independent assortment
~/Erste Mendelsche *(gen)* Mendel's first law, law of dominance
~ nach Hopkins/bioklimatische Hopkin's bioclimatic law
~/Szidatsche Szidat's rule *(parasitology)*
~/van't Hoff[-Arrhenius]sche van't Hoff effect (rule), reaction-rate/temperature effect
~/Zweite Mendelsche *(gen)* Mendel's second law, law of segregation
Regelhydraulik *f* automatic hydraulic lift unit
Regelkraftheber *m* regulating power lift
Regelkreis *m* control loop *(animal physiology)*
Regen *n* rain
~/orographischer orographic rain
~/saurer acid rain *(precipitation)*
Regenabflußmenge *f* run-off
regenarm low-rainfall; with (of) little rainfall *(a region)*
Regenauswaschung *f* rainwash
Regenbaum *m (bot)* genisaro, Pithecellobium saman
Regenbogenforelle *f* rainbow (speckled) trout, Salmo gairdneri (irideus)
Regenbogenhaut *f* iris *(of the eye)*
Regenbogenhautentzündung *f (vet)* iritis
Regenbogenkaktus *m* rainbow cactus, Echinocereus pectinatus var. pectinatus f. rigidissimus
Regenbogenschwingel *m* amethyst fescue, Festuca amethystina
Regenbremse *f* rain breeze fly, Haematopota (Chrysozona) pluvialis
Regendichte *f* rainfall intensity
Regeneratfolie *f* regenerated plastic film
Regeneration *f* regeneration
Regenerationsfähigkeit *f* regenerative ability
Regenerationsfraß *m (ent)* regeneration feeding, after-eating
Regenerationsvermögen *n* regenerative ability
regenerieren to regenerate
Regenerierung *f* regeneration
Regenfall *m* rain[fall]
Regenfälle *mpl*/**anhaltende** continuous rain
~/heftige heavy rains, heavy [falls of] rain
Regenfeldbau *m* rain-fed farming, dry[-land] farming • **~ betreiben** to dry-farm

Regenfeldbaubetrieb *m* dry farm
Regengabe *f* irrigation application
Regengleiche *f* isohyet, isohyetal [line] *(of equal rainfall)*
Regengrasland *n*, **Regengrünland** *n* rain-fed grassland
Regenhäufigkeit *f* rain frequency
Regenkanone *f* rain gun, gun sprinkler
Regenmangel *m* lack of rain, dryness, drought
Regenmenge *f* **in der Vegetationsperiode** growing-season rainfall
Regenmesser *m* rain-gauge, ombrometer, pluviometer, hyetometer, udometer
Regenmoor *n* rain-water bog (moor)
regenreich high-rainfall; with high rainfall *(a region)*
Regenschaden *m* rain damage
Regenschatten *m* rain-shadow
Regenschauer *m* [rain] shower, gust, flurry, rainfall
Regenschreiber *m* rain recorder, ombrograph, pluviograph, hyetograph
Regentag *m* rainy day
Regentonne *f* water-butt
Regentropfen *m* raindrop
Regenwald *m* rain forest
~/subtropischer subtropical rain forest
Regenwaldklima *n* rain forest climate
Regenwasser *n* rain-water
Regenwetter *n* rainy weather
Regenwolke *f* rain-cloud, nimbus
~/schichtförmige [tiefe] nimbostratus
Regenwurm *m* 1. earthworm *(family Lumbricidae)*; 2. [common] earthworm, rain-worm, Lumbricus terrestris
Regenwurmgang *m* earthworm channel
Regenwurmkultur *f* vermiculture
Regenwurmlosung *f* [worm] cast
Regenwurmmull *m* earthworm mull
Regenwurmröhre *f* worm burrow
Regenzeit *f* rainy season, the rains
regional regional, regionary
~ begrenzt vorkommend *(ecol)* endemic
Regionalplanung *f* regional planning
Regionalvermessung *f* reconnaissance
registrieren to register *(e.g. breeding animals)*
Regner *m* rainer, sprinkler, irrigation sprayer, irrigator
~/fahrbarer (mobiler, ortsbeweglicher) travelling (mobile) sprinkler
~/selbstfahrender self-propelled sprinkler, self-travelling irrigator
Regnerbewässerung *f* sprinkler irrigation
regnerisch rainy, pluvious
Regnerleitung *f***/rollbare** roll-line irrigator, power-moved pipeline with sprinklers
Regnerrohr *n* irrigation pipe
Regnerschlauch *m* irrigation hose
Regnerstrang *m* spray line
~/selbstfahrender self-propelled spray line

Regnersystem *n* sprinkler system
~/handverlegtes hand-set type of sprinkler system
~/rollbares wheel line system of sprinkler irrigation
~/stationäres permanent[-set type of] sprinkler system
Regnum *n* kingdom *(taxonomy)*
Regolith *m* *(soil)* regolith
Regosol *m* *(soil)* regosol, rhegosol
Regression *f* *(biom)* regression, retrogression
~/lineare linear (straight-line) regression
~/mehrfache (multiple) multiple regression
~/nichtlineare non-linear regression
~/schrittweise stepwise regression
Regressionsanalyse *f* regression analysis
Regressionsfunktion *f* regression function (equation)
Regressionsgerade *f* regression line
Regressionsgleichung *f* regression equation (function)
Regressionskoeffizient *m* regression coefficient, coefficient of regression
Regressionskurve *f* regression curve
Regressionstabelle *f* regression table
Regulationsstörung *f* dysregulation
Regulatorgen *n* regulator[y] gene
Regulon *n* *(gen)* regulon
Regur *m* regur, black cotton soil
Regurgitation *f* *(vet)* regurgitation
regurgitieren *(vet)* to regurgitate
Reh *n* roe[-deer], deer, Capreolus capreolus
~/männliches *s.* Rehbock
~/weibliches *s.* Ricke
Rehbein *n* *(vet)* curb
Rehblatte[r] *f* *(hunt)* deer-caller
Rehbock *m* roebuck
Rehe *f* *(vet)* founder, laminitis
Rehehuf *m* foundered foot (hoof)
Rehkitz *n* fawn, young deer
Rehling *m* *s.* Pfifferling
Rehpinscher *m* miniature pinscher *(dog breed)*
Rehposten *m*, **Rehschrot** *m* *(hunt)* buck-shot
Rehwild *n* roe[-deer]
Reibefläche *f* **des Zahns** dental table
Reibkäse *m* grating cheese
Reibkeule *f* pestle
Reibkupplung *f* friction[-type safety] clutch, slip clutch
Reibplatte *f s.* Radula
Reibschale *f* mortar
Reibung *f* friction
~/gleitende sliding friction
Reibungsentrindung *f* friction debarking, barking by attrition
reibungskohäsiv frictional-cohesive *(soil)*
Reibungskupplung *f s.* Reibkupplung
Reibungsschaden *m* friction marking *(on fruits)*
Reibverschleiß *m* sliding wear
Reich *n* kingdom *(taxonomy)*
reichblühend floribund, floriferous, free flowering

Reichblühender Apfelbaum *m* showy (Japanese flowering) crab-apple, Malus floribunda
Reichblühendes Habichtskraut *n (bot)* king devil, Hieracium floribundum
reichblütig *s.* reichblühend
Reichert-Meißl-Zahl *f* Reichert-Meissl number (value) *(for determination of fatty acids)*
reif 1. ripe, mature *(e.g. fruit)*; 2. adult, sexually mature • ~ **werden** to ripen, to become ripe (mature)
~/**fast** subadult
Reif *m* hoar[-frost], rime
Reife *f* 1. ripeness, maturity; mellowness *(of wine)*; 2. *s.* Reifung • **vor Erreichung der** ~ premature • **zur** ~ **bringen** to ripen, to mature • **zur** ~ **kommen** *s.* reifen 1.
~/**fleckige** blotchy ripening, grey wall *(of tomatoes)*
~/**körperliche** physical maturity
~/**natürliche** natural maturity
~/**physiologische** physiological maturity
~/**physische** physical maturity
~/**unvollständige** incomplete ripeness
Reifealter *n* age of maturity
Reifebeschleuniger *m* ripening agent
Reifegrad *m* degree (stage) of maturity, maturity stage
Reifegruppe *f* maturity group
Reifeindex *m* maturity index
reifen 1. to ripen, to mature, to mellow *(e.g. fruit, cheese)*; 2. to age, to mellow *(wine)*
~ **lassen** to ripen, to mature; to age, to mellow, to season *(wine)*
Reifen *m* tyre
Reifen *n s.* Reifung
Reifenauflagefläche *f* tread
Reifenbesohlung *f* tyre soling
Reifenbodendruck *m* tyre ground pressure
Reifen[füll]druck *m*, **Reifeninnendruck** *m* [tyre] inflation pressure
Reifenprofil *n* tread
Reifentragfähigkeit *f* tyre load capacity
Reifenunterbaubewertung *f* ply rating
Reifenwechsel *m* tyre changing
Reifenwechselvorrichtung *f* tyre changer
Reifeperiode *f* maturation period
Reifeprozeß *m* ripening process
Reifestadium *n s.* Reifegrad
Reifeteilung *f* meiosis, meiotic division
Reifeüberwachung *f* maturity monitoring
Reifeverhalten *n* ripening behaviour
Reifezeit *f* ripening time
Reifezustand *m* state of maturity
Reifgraupeln *fpl* graupel
Reifholz *n* ripewood, adult (outer) wood
Reifholzbaum *m* sapwood tree
Reifholzzone *f* ripewood layer
Reifung *f* maturation; ag[e]ing, seasoning *(of wine)*
~/**geschmackliche** staling *(esp. of alcoholic beverages)*
Reifungsfraß *m (ent)* after-eating
Reifungssalz *n* ripening salt *(cheese-making)*
Reifweide *f* mezereon (violet, Mexican) willow, Salix daphnoides
Reihe *f* 1. row; 2. series; 3. order • ~ **für Reihe** by the row • **in Reihen pflanzen** to row
~/**beetartig verwachsene** matted row *(e.g. in strawberry plantations)*
~/**lyotrope** lyotropic (Hofmeister) series
~/**ökologische** ecological sequence (series)
~/**verwachsene** matted row *(e.g. in strawberry plantations)*
Reihenabdeckung *f* row cover
Reihenabstand *m* [between-]row-spacing, row (planting) width
Reihenausrichtung *f* row orientation
Reihenbearbeitung *f* row tillage, row crop work
Reihenbegasung *f* row fumigation
Reihenberegnung *f* row sprinkling
Reihenbreite *f s.* Reihenabstand
Reihendüngerstreuer *m* row fertilizer distributor, fertilizer drill, row spreader
Reihendüngung *f* row (band) fertilization, band placement of fertilizers, side (row) dressing
Reihendurchforstung *f (forest)* row (line) thinning
Reihenentfernung *f s.* Reihenabstand
Reihenfräse *f* row tiller, inter-row rotary cultivator
Reihenhausgarten *m* home garden
Reihenkalkstreuer *m* lime row spreader
Reihenkultur *f* row crop (culture)
Reihenkulturschlepper *m* row crop tractor
Reihenpflanzung *f* row (line) planting
Reihensaat *f* drill sowing, row seeding, sowing in rows (lines)
Reihensämaschine *f* [seed] drill
Reihenschluß *m* row closing
Reihenspritzvorrichtung *f* row-spraying attachment
Reihenstreuer *m s.* Reihendüngerstreuer
reihenweise in rows; by the row
Reihenzieher *m* [row] marker
~/**verstellbarer** adjustable marker
Reiher *m* heron *(genus Ardea)*
Reiherschnabel *m (bot)* 1. heron's-bill, stork's-bill, filaree *(genus Erodium)*; 2. common stork's-bill, pin clover (grass), alfilaria, Erodium cicutarium
rein pure, clear
reinanlagig *(gen)* isogenic
Reinasche *f* true ash
Reinbestand *m* pure (clear) stand, single-species stand
reinblütig pure
Reineclaude *f s.* Reneklode
Reineke *m (hunter's language) s.* Fuchs 1.
reinerbig homozygous, pure
Reinerbigkeit *f* homozygosis, homozygosity, purity
Reinertrag *m* clean yield, net gain
Reinette *f* reinette, rennet *(apple cultivar)*
Reinfektion *f (phyt, vet)* reinfection

reinfizieren *(phyt, vet)* to reinfect
Reingewinn *m* net gain
Reinhaltung *f* **der Luft** air conservation
Reinheit *f* 1. purity; 2. cleanliness
Reinheitsgrad *m* degree of purity
Reinheitsprüfung *f* purity analysis *(e.g. of seed)*
Reinheitsquotient *m* quotient (coefficient) of purity *(e.g. of sugar-beet juice)*
reinigen to clean[se], to purge; to dress, to scour *(e.g. seed)*; to purify *(e.g. substances, waste-water)*
~/im Luftstrom to fan, to winnow *(e.g. grain)*
~/von Kletten to bur *(wool)*
Reinigender Geißklee *m* purge broom, Cytisus purgans
Reinigung *f* cleaning, purging; dressing, scouring *(e.g. seed)*; purification
Reinigungsabgänge *mpl* scourings
Reinigungsanlage *f* cleaner
Reinigungs[aus]flug *m* *(api)* cleansing flight
Reinigungsfrucht *f* cleaning (break) crop *(in a rotation)*
Reinigungsgebläse *n* [cleaning] fan
Reinigungshieb *m* *(forest)* assistance (sanitation, sanitary) felling, release cutting
Reinigungslader *m* cleaner-loader
Reinigungsmaschine *f* cleaning machine, cleaner
Reinigungsmittel *n* cleansing agent, cleaner, detergent, abstergent
Reinigungsschnitt *m* aftermath, aftergrass, aftercrop
Reinigungsseparator *m* *(dairy)* centrifugal clarifier
Reinigungstrommel *f* cleaning drum
Reinigungsverluste *mpl* sieve (separation) losses *(threshing)*
Reinigungsvorrichtung *f* cleaning shoe *(thresher)*
Reinigungszentrifuge *f* *(dairy)* centrifugal clarifier
Reinkultur *f* 1. pure culture, monoculture; 2. s. Monokultur
Reinnährstoff *m* pure nutrient
Reinprotein *n* pure (true) protein
reinrassig straight-bred, pure-blooded, pure[-bred], thoroughbred, pedigree[d], genuine
Reinrassigkeit *f* genuineness
Reinsaat *f* 1. single-crop sowing; 2. pure crop (stand)
reintönig clear *(wine)*
Reinwolleanteil *m*, **Reinwollgehalt** *m* clean wool yield, rendiment, rendement
Reinzucht *f* pure breeding • ~ **betreiben** *s.* reinzüchten
reinzüchten to breed pure
Reinzüchter *m* pure-bred breeder
Reinzuchthefe *f* pure culture yeast
Reinzuchtherde *f* pure-bred flock *(esp. of sheep)*
Reinzuchtrasse *f* pure-breed
Reinzuchttier *n* thoroughbred
Reis *m* 1. rice *(genus Oryza)*; 2. [oriental] rice, Oryza sativa

~/geschälter brown rice
~/polierter polished rice
~/ungeschälter paddy [rice], rough rice
Reis *n* 1. twig, sprig, small shoot; 2. *s.* Pfropfreis
Reisagar *m* rice agar
Reisanbau *m* rice growing (culture)
Reisanbaugebiet *n* rice-bowl
Reisanzucht *f* rice nursery
Reisbau *m s.* Reisanbau
Reisbier *n* rice beer
Reisboden *m* rice soil
Reisbohne *f* rice (oriental) bean, mambi (climbing mountain) bean, Vigna umbellata, Phaseolus umbellatus
Reisbräune *f* *(phyt)* rice blast *(caused by Pyricularis oryzae)*
Reisdreschmaschine *f* rice thresher
Reisefieber *n* railroad sickness *(esp. of pregnant cows)*
Reisernte *f* rice harvest
Reiserntemaschine *f* rice harvester
Reserveredelung *f s.* Reisveredelung
Reisetaube *f* homing (carrier) pigeon, homer
Reisfasan *m* ring-neck[ed] pheasant, Phasianus colchicus torquatus
Reisfeld *n* rice field, paddy[-field]
Reisfeldboden *m* paddy soil
Reisflocken *fpl* rice flakes
Reisfuttermehl *n* rice meal
Reisgelbscheckungsvirus *n* rice yellow mottle virus
Reisgelbverzwergungsvirus *n* rice yellow dwarf virus
Reisgrieß *m* rice grits
Reishauptanbaugebiet *n* rice-bowl
Reisholz *n* 1. smallwood, topwood; 2. *s.* Reisig
Reisholzformzahl *f* smallwood form factor *(timber mensuration)*
Reisig *n* brush[wood], faggot wood
Reisigbündel *n* faggot, bavin, bundle of copse (twigs)
Reisighaufen *m* brush pile
Reisigkrankheit *f* **der Weinrebe** grape-vine fan leaf *(virosis)*
Reisigstreu *f* branch litter
Reisigverbrennung *f* burning of brushwood
Reisigwall *m* drift, windrow
Reisigwelle *f s.* Reisigbündel
Reiskäfer *m* rice (black) weevil, Sitophilus oryzae
Reiskeimmehl *n* rice germ meal
Reiskleie *f* rice polishings
Reiskorn *n* rice grain
Reismähdrescher *m* rice combine
Reismais *m* *(Am)* popcorn, Zea mays convar. microsperma
Reismehl *n* rice flour
Reismehlkäfer *m* flour beetle *(genus Tribolium)*
Reismelde *f* *(bot)* quinoa, Chenopodium quinoa
Reismotte *f* rice moth, Corcyra cephalonica

Reismühle f rice mill
Reismüllerei f rice milling
Reisnebenprodukt n rice by-product
Reisöl n rice oil
Reispapierbaum m rice paper tree, Tetrapanax papyriferum
Reispflug m riceland plough
Reisprotein n rice protein
Reisquecke f rice cut-grass, marsh grass, Leersia oryzoides
Reisschalen fpl rice hulls (husks)
Reisschälmaschine f rice sheller
Reisschleifmehl n rice dust (polish) *(processing offal)*
"**Reisschüssel**" f s. Reisanbaugebiet
reißen 1. to rupture, to tear *(e.g. a tendon)*; 2. to streak *(resin tapping)*
Reißer m *(forest)* 1. blazer; 2. hack operator
Reißhaken m, **Reißmesser** n *(forest)* bark blazer, hack, scribe, risser, race
Reisspinat m s. Reismelde
Reisspelzen fpl s. Reisschalen
Reißpunkt m rupture point *(e.g. of a fruit peel)*
Reisstärke f rice starch
Reisstaub m s. Reisschleifmehl
Reisstengelbohrer m *(ent)* rice stem borer, Chilo suppressalis
Reisstreifenvirus n rice stripe virus
Reisstroh n rice straw
Reisstrohpilz m paddy (rice) straw mushroom, Chinese mushroom, Volvariella diplasis (volvacea)
Reißwerk n macerator
Reißwolle f shoddy
Reißzahn m carnassial [tooth]
Reis-Tungrovirus n rice tungro virus
Reisumpflanzmaschine f rice transplanter
Reisveredelung f graftage • **eine ~ vornehmen** to [en]graft, to ingraft
Reisverzwergungsvirus n rice dwarf virus
Reiswanze f rice bug *(genus Leptocorisa)*
Reiswein m rice wine, saké
Reisweißblättrigkeitsvirus n rice hoja blanca virus
Reitbahn f riding school
Reitel m maiden [tree]
reiten to ride
~/im Paßgang to amble
~/im Rechtsgalopp to canter
Reiter m rider, horseman, reinsman
Reiterhof m equestrian enterprise on the farm
Reiterin f horsewoman
Reitgerte f [riding] crop
Reitgras n reed [bent] grass, small reed *(genus Calamagrostis)*
Reithalle f riding arena (hall), hippodrome
Reitjagd f hunting on horseback • **auf ~ gehen** to ride to hounds

Reitkunst f horsemanship, equitation, equestrianism; equestrian skills
Reitpferd n riding (saddle) horse
Reitsattel m riding (hacking, flat) saddle
Reitschule f riding school
Reitsport m equestrian sport, [horse-]riding
Reittier n riding animal
Reittouristik f leisure[-time] riding, recreational riding
Reittrense f riding bit
Reittrensengebiß n jointed snaffle
Reitunternehmen n riding establishment, equestrian enterprise
Reiturlaub m equestrian holiday[s]
Reitweg m ride, bridle path (way)
Reitzaum m tack
ReiVzV s. Reisverzwergungsvirus
Reiz m stimulus
Reizaufnahme f perception
Reizbarkeit f irritability
Reizker m *(bot)* lactarius *(genus Lactarius)*
Reizmengengesetz n reciprocity law *(plant physiology)*
Reizung f excitation, stimulation; *(phyt, vet)* irritation
~/elektrische electrostimulation *(semen collection)*
rekombinant *(gen)* recombinant
Rekombination f *(gen)* recombination
~/nichtreziproke gene conversion
Rekombinationseinheit f *(gen)* recon
Rekombinationsgenetik f Mendelian genetics
Rekombinationswert m, **Rekombinationszahl** f recombination value
rekombinieren to recombine
Rekon n s. Rekombinationseinheit
Rekonvaleszenz f convalescence, recovery
Rekordernte f record crop, bumper harvest (crop)
Rekordertrag m record yield
Rektaldrüse f rectal gland *(animal anatomy)*
Rektalnarkose f *(vet)* rectal anaesthesia
Rektaltemperatur f rectal temperature
Rektum n rectum
Rektumprolaps m *(vet)* rectal prolapse
rekultivierbar reclaimable *(soil)*
rekultivieren to reclaim, to recultivate, to restore
Rekultivierung f [land] reclamation, recultivation, restoration, rehabilitation
Relaskop n relascope *(for forest inventory)*
Relaxin n relaxin *(hormone)*
Releasinghormon n releasing hormone, releaser
Relief n relief
Reliefkarte f relief map
Reliefmelioration f land levelling
Reliktboden m relict soil
Remanenz f remanence *(e.g. of a plant protectant)*
Remedium n *(vet)* remedy, medicament
Remeristem[at]isierung f dedifferentiation *(of cells)*

Remissionsspektroskopie f im infrarotnahen Bereich near-infrared reflectance spectroscopy
remontant remontant, perpetual flowering; everbearing
Remonte f remount *(untrained young horse)*
remontierend s. remontant
Remote sensing n s. Fernerkundung
ReMV s. Rettichmosaikvirus
Ren n s. Rentier
renal renal
Rendement n rendiment, rendement, clean wool yield
Rendzina f rendzina, humic (humus) carbonate soil
Reneklode f *(bot)* [green]gage, Reine Claude, Prunus domestica ssp. italica
Renette f reinette, rennet *(apple cultivar)*
Renin n renin, angiotensinogenase, angiotensinforming enzyme
Renin-Angiotensin-System n renin-angiotensin system *(animal physiology)*
Renke f white fish *(genus Coregonus)*
Rennbahn f race-track, [race]course
Rennen n race; horse-race
~ für Zweijährige nursery [stakes]
~/klassisches classic race
Renner m s. Rennpferd
Renngalopp m racing (extended) gallop, career
Renngeschwindigkeit f racing speed
Rennhürde f hurdle
Rennin n rennin, rennet, chymosin *(enzyme)*
Rennkondition f racing condition
Rennleistung f racing (track) performance
Rennpferd n racehorse, racer, runner, clipper, spanker
~ für lange Strecken stayer
~/[sehr] gutes crack
Rennsaison f racing season
Rennsattel m racing saddle
Rennsitz m race seat
Rennsport m [horse-]racing
Rennstall m racing stable
Renntempo n pace
Rennvermögen n racing ability
Rennwesen n the turf
Rentier n reindeer, caribou, Rangifer tarandus
Rentierflechte f reindeer moss, Cladonia rangiferina
Rentierschlitten m reindeer sledge
R-Enzym n amylopectin-1,6-glucosidase *(enzyme)*
Repellent n repellent, repelling agent
Repellenz f repellency
Replikation f replication *(e.g. of DNA molecules)*
Replikon n *(gen)* replicon
Reposition f *(vet)* reposition
Reppelrinde f bark in strips
Repressor m *(gen)* repressor
Repressorgen n repressor gene
Reproduktion f reproduction *(s. a. under Fortpflanzung and Vermehrung)*

~ der Waldressourcen forest regeneration
Reproduktionsfähigkeit f reproductive ability (power)
Reproduktionsfärse f replacement heifer, stocker
Reproduktionsherde f seed stock herd
Reproduktionsimmunologie f reproductive immunology
Reproduktionsjungsau f replacement gilt
Reproduktionsleistung f reproductive performance (efficiency)
Reproduktionsphase f reproductive phase
Reproduktionsrate f reproduction (replacement) rate
Reproduktionssau f replacement gilt
Reproduktionsvermögen n reproductive ability (power)
Reproduktionswert m replacement value
Reproduktionszyklus m reproductive cycle
reproduktiv reproductive
Reproduktivität f reproductivity
reproduzierbar reproducible, renewable
Reproduzierbarkeit f reproducibility
Reptil n reptile *(class Reptilia)*
Repulsivstoff m s. Repellent
RES s. System/retikuloendotheliales
Resazurinprobe f, **Resazurintest** m *(dairy)* resazurin [reduction] test
Reseda f *(bot)* mignonette, reseda *(genus Reseda)*
Resedaweinrebe f frost grape, Vitis riparia
Resektion f *(vet)* resection
Reserpin n reserpine *(alkaloid)*
Reservat n reservation, sanctuary, preserve, park
Reserveaufbau m reserve build-up
Reserveblut n s. Residualblut
Reserveeiweiß n reserve (storage) protein
~/pflanzliches aleuron[e]
Reservefläche f spare area
Reservekohlenhydrat n reserve carbohydrate
Reserveluft f functional residual [air] capacity *(animal physiology)*
Reservenährstoff m reserve nutrient (food)
Reservepflanze f spare plant
Reservestoff m reserve [material]
Reservestoffaufbau m reserve build-up
Reservestoffmobilisierung f reserve mobilization
Reservevolumen n/**exspiratorisches** functional residual [air] capacity
~/inspiratorisches inspiratory reserve volume
Reservewirt m reserve (reservoir) host
Reservoir n reservoir
resezieren *(vet)* to resect
Residualblut[volumen] n residual blood volume (of ventricle)
Residualharn m residual urine
Residualluft f residual air *(in lungs)*
Residualmilch f residual milk
Residualstickstoff m residual nitrogen
Residualvolumen n residual volume

Residualwirkung

Residualwirkung f residual action; residual effect, persistence, persistency *(e.g. of agrochemicals)*
Residuum n residue
Resinose f *(phyt)* resinosis, resin flow (flux, bleeding)
resistent resistant
Resistenz f resistance
~/**aktive** induced resistance
~/**chemische** chemical resistance
~/**erworbene** acquired resistance
~ **gegenüber Parasiten** resistance to parasites
~ **gegenüber Schadfaktoren** resistance to injurious factors
~/**horizontale** horizontal (durable) resistance
~/**induzierte** induced resistance
~/**mikrobiologische** microbiological resistance
~/**natürliche** natural resistance
~/**passive** passive resistance
~/**pflanzliche** plant resistance
~/**polygene** s. ~/horizontale
~/**präinfektionelle** s. ~/passive
~/**primäre** natural resistance
~/**rassenspezifische** s. ~/vertikale
~/**rassenunspezifische** s. ~/horizontale
~/**sekundäre** acquired resistance
~ **unter natürlichen Feldbedingungen** field resistance
~/**vertikale** vertical resistance
Resistenzdynamik f resistance dynamics
Resistenzgen n resistance gene
Resistenzgenetik f genetics of resistance
Resistenzgrad m degree of resistance
Resistenzzucht f, **Resistenzzüchtung** f resistance breeding
Resistenzzusammenbruch m resistance breakdown
Resistomycin n kanamycin *(antibiotic)*
Resmethrin n [bio]resmethrin *(insecticide)*
Resonanz f/**elektronenparamagnetische** electron spin resonance, esr, paramagnetic [electronic] resonance, p.m.r.
Resonanzanalyse f/**protonenmagnetische** proton magnetic resonance analysis
Resonanzholz n resonance (resonant, tonal) wood
Resonanzspektroskopie f/**kernmagnetische** nmr (nuclear magnetic resonance) spectroscopy
Resonanzspektrum n/**kernmagnetisches** nuclear magnetic resonance spectrum
Resorantel n resorantel *(anthelminthic)*
resorbieren to resorb
Resorcinol n resorcinol, *(m-)*dihydroxybenzene, 1,3-benzenediol
Resorcin[ol]phthalein n resorcinolphthalein, fluorescein *(dye)*
Resorcintest m resorcin test *(virus detection)*
Resorption f resorption
Ressourcenaufteilung f resource partitioning
Ressourcenklasse f resource class
Ressourcenklassifikation f resource classification

Respiration f respiration
~/**äußere** external respiration
~/**innere** internal (tissue) respiration
Respirations... s. a. Atmungs...
Respirationsanstieg m climacteric rise *(plant physiology)*
Respirationskalorimeter n respiration calorimeter
Respirationskalorimetrie f respiration calorimetry
Respirationskrankheit f *(vet)* respiratory disease
Respirationsquotient m respiratory quotient, R.Q.
Respirationsrate f respiratory rate
Respirationstrakt m respiratory system (tract)
Respirationsversuch m respiration trial
respiratorisch respiratory
respirieren to respire, to breathe
Respirometer n respirometer
Respirometrie f respirometry
Restaurationsgen n restorer gene
Restbaum m *(forest)* cull tree
Restbier n overflow beer
Restblut[volumen] n residual blood volume *(of ventricle)*
Reste mpl/**pflanzliche** plant remains (residues), plant debris
Restenthäutung f finish-skinning
Restfeuchte f, **Restfeuchtigkeit** f residual moisture
Restfurche f rest-balk *(ploughing)*
Restfutter n waste feed
Restharn m residual urine
Resthärte f residual hardness *(e.g. of brewing liquor)*
Restitution f restitution
Restlignin n residual lignin
Restluft f residual air *(in lungs)*
Restmais m maize trash, *(Am)* corn stover (plant residue)
Restorergen n restorer gene
Restriktase f s. Restriktionsendonuclease
Restriktion f restriction
Restriktionsendonuclease f, **Restriktionsenzym** n [restriction] endonuclease, restriction enzyme
Restriktionsfütterung f restricted feeding
Restrolle f peeler (veneer) core
Reststickstoff m residual nitrogen
Restsüße f residual sugar *(of wine)*
Restvarianz f *(biom)* residual variance
Restvolumen n residual volume
Restwirkung f remanence *(e.g. of a plant protectant)*
Restzucker m s. Restsüße
Retardans n retardant, retarder
Retardation f retardation
Rete n **testis** rete testis *(animal anatomy)*
Retentat n retent *(that which is retained)*
Retention f retention
Retentionszyste f *(vet)* retention cyst
retikulär reticular

Retikulin *n* reticulin *(protein)*
Retikulinfaser *f* reticular fibre
Retikulitis *f (vet)* reticulitis
retikuloendothelial reticulo-endothelial
Retikuloendotheliose *f (vet)* reticulosis
~ **des Geflügels** T virus infection
Retikuloperitonitis *f (vet)* reticuloperitonitis
Retikulose *f (vet)* reticulosis
Retikulozyt *n* reticulocyte
Retikulozytose *f (vet)* reticulocytosis
Retikulum *n* 1. *(bot, zoo)* reticulum *(a netlike structure)*; 2. reticulum, second stomach, honeycomb [stomach, tripe] *(of ruminants)*
~/**endoplasmatisches** endoplasmic reticulum, ER *(organelle)*
~/**granuläres (rauhes) endoplasmatisches** endoplasmic reticulum with associated ribosomes
~/**sarkoplasmatisches** *(zoo)* sarcoplasmic reticulum
Retina *f* retina *(of the eye)*
Retina... *s.* Netzhaut...
retinal retinal
Retinal *n* retinal[dehyde], retinene, vitamin A aldehyde
Retinen *n*, **Retinin** *n s.* Retinal
Retininsäure *f* retinoic acid, vitamin A acid
Retinitis *f (vet)* retinitis
Retinol *n* retinol, vitamin A$_1$
Retinopathie *f (vet)* retinopathy
Retinylpalmitatesterase *f* retinyl-palmitate esterase *(enzyme)*
Retraktion *f (vet)* retraction *(e.g. of a tendon)*
Retriever *m* retriever; *(Am)* bird dog
Retrogradation *f*, **Retrogradierung** *f (soil)* retrogradation
retrosternal retrosternal
Retrovirus *n* retrovirus, oncogenic RNA virus, oncornavirus *(family Retroviridae)*
Retsina *m* retsina *(wine)*
Rettich *m* 1. radish *(genus Raphanus)*; 2. [black, Spanish, winter] radish, Raphanus sativus var. niger
Retticherntemaschine *f* radish harvester
Rettichmosaik *n (phyt)* radish mosaic
Rettichmosaikvirus *n* radish mosaic virus, RaMV
Rettichschwärze *f* black root of radish *(caused by Aphanomyces raphani)*
Reuse *f* fish-basket, fish-trap
Reuter *m* rack
Reutertrocknung *f* rack drying, hay curing on racks, tripoding [of hay]
Reuthaue *f s.* Rodehacke
Revakzination *f (vet)* revaccination
Reversion *f* reversion; *(gen)* reversion, return mutation
~ **der Schwarzen Johannisbeere** black currant reversion *(mycoplasmosis)*
Revertase *f* reverse transcriptase *(enzyme)*

Revier *n* 1. forest district (division, range), range, ranger district; 2. *s.* Jagdrevier; 3. *(ecol)* territory
• **ein ~ begehen** to go the rounds
Revierförster *m* [forest] ranger
Revierteil *n* beat *(of a ranger)*
Revierverhalten *n* territoriality
Rex-Begonie *f* rex (rhizomatous) begonia, Begonia rex-cultorum
Rexkaninchen *n* Rex rabbit *(breed)*
Rezept *n* recipe, formula
Rezeptakel *n (bot)* receptacle, flower cup
rezeptiv receptive
Rezeptivität *f* receptiveness, receptivity *(e.g. of female breeding animals)*
Rezeptor *m* receptor
~/**adrenergischer** adrenergic receptor, adrenoceptor
Rezeptororgan *n* receptor organ
rezessiv *(gen)* recessive
Rezessivität *f (gen)* recessiveness, recessivity
Rezidiv *n (phyt, vet)* recurrence, recurrency, relapse
rezidivieren *(phyt, vet)* to recur, to relapse
Rezipient *m* recipient
Reziprozitätsgesetz *n* reciprocity law *(plant physiology)*
RGNV *s.* Rübengelbnetzvirus
Rhabarber *m* 1. rhubarb, *(Am)* pieplant *(genus Rheum)*; 2. rhubarb, Rheum rhaponticum; 3. rhubarb, Rheum rhabarbarum
rhabarberartig rhubarby
Rhabarberblattstiel *m* rhubarb
Rhabarbererntemaschine *f* rhubarb harvester
Rhabarberpflanzmaschine *f* rhubarb planting machine
Rhabarberwurzel *f* rhubarb *(drug)*
Rhabdion *m* mouth spear *(of plant-parasitic nematodes)*
Rhabdovirose *f* **der Hechtbrut** pike fry rhabdovirus disease
Rhachis *f s.* Rachis
(L-)Rhamnose *f* rhamnose *(monosaccharide)*
Rhaphe *f (bot, zoo)* raphe
Rhapontik *m* rhubarb, Rheum rhaponticum
Rhein *n* rhein *(plant substance)*
Rheinisch-Deutsches Kaltblut[pferd] *n* Rhenish[-German], Rhineland *(horse breed)*
Rheinwein *m* Rhine wine, Rhenish
Rhenaniaphosphat *n* rhenania phosphate *(fertilizer)*
Rheumatismus *m (vet)* rheumatism
Rhinitis *f (vet)* rhinitis, coryza
~/**atrophische** atrophic rhinitis
Rhinopneumonitis *f (vet)* rhinopneumonitis
~ **des Pferdes** equine virus abortion
Rhinosporidiose *f (vet)* rhinosporidiosis
Rhinotracheitis *f (vet)* rhinotracheitis
~/**infektiöse bovine** infectious bovine rhinotracheitis, red nose disease of cattle

Rhinovirus

Rhinovirus *n* rhinovirus
Rhizobin *n* rhizobin *(peptide)*
Rhizoctoniafäule *f* **der Möhre** rhizoctonia heart rot of carrot *(caused by Rhizoctonia carotae)*
Rhizoctoniapocken *pl* black scurf (speck), rhizoctonia canker *(e.g. of potato, caused by Rhizoctonia solani)*
rhizodermal *(bot)* rhizodermal
Rhizogenese *f (bot)* rhizogenesis, root formation
Rhizoid *n (bot)* rhizoid
Rhizom *n (bot)* rhizome, root-stock, stem-tuber
rhizomartig rhizomatic, rhizomatous
rhizombildend rhizomatic, rhizomatous
Rhizomfäule *f* **der Erdbeere** vascular collapse of strawberries *(caused by Phytophthora cactorum)*
rhizomorph rhizomorphous
Rhizomorph *m (bot)* rhizomorph
Rhizomunkraut *n* rhizomatous weed
Rhizoplan *m* rhizoplane
Rhizopus-Weichfäule *f* rhizopus soft rot *(e.g. of potato, caused by Rhizopus spp.)*
Rhizosphere *f* rhizosphere, root[ing] zone
Rhizotron *n* rhizotron
Rhodamin *n* **B** rhodamine B *(dye)*
Rhodeländer *n* Rhode Island Red *(breed of fowl)*
Rhodesian Ridgeback *m* Rhodesian Ridgeback *(dog breed)*
Rhodesiengras *n* Rhodes grass, Chloris gayana
Rhododendron *m(n)* rhododendron, azalea, rosebay *(genus Rhododendron)*
Rhododendronhautwanze *f* rhododendron lace bug, Stephanitis rhododendri
Rhododendronsterben *n* die back of rhododendron *(caused by Phythophthora parasitica)*
Rhodopsin *n* rhodopsin, visual purple
rhomboid rhomboid
Rhönschaf *n* Rhon *(sheep breed)*
R-Horizont *m (soil)* R horizon
Rhynchosporium-Blattfleckenkrankheit *f* rhynchosporium leaf blotch [of barley and rye], barley scald *(caused by Rhynchosporium secalis)*
Rhynchote *m (ent)* hemipteran, bug *(order Hemiptera)*
Rhyodazit *m (soil)* rhyodacite
Rhythmik *f* rhythmics, periodicity
Rhythmus *m* rhythm
~/biologischer biorhythm
~/zirkaannueller circa-annual rhythm
~/zirkadianer (zirkadischer) circadian rhythm
Rhytidom *n* rhytidome, [outer] bark
RIA radioimmunoassay
Riboflavin *n* riboflavin, lactoflavin, vitamin B_2, vitamin G
Riboflavinantagonist *m* riboflavin antagonist
Riboflavinase *f* riboflavinase *(enzyme)*
Riboflavindiphosphoadenosin *n* flavin adenine dinucleotide, FAD *(coenzyme)*
Riboflavinkinase *f* riboflavin kinase *(enzyme)*
Riboflavinmangel *m* riboflavin deficiency
Ribokinase *f* ribokinase *(enzyme)*
Ribonuclease *f* ribonuclease *(enzyme)*
Ribonucleinsäure *f* ribonucleic acid, RNA *(for compounds s. under RNA)*
Ribonucleinsäure... *s.* RNA...
Ribonucleo-Protein-Granulum *n s.* Ribosom
Ribonucleosid *n* ribonucleoside
Ribonucleotidreductase *f* ribonucleotide reductase *(enzyme)*
Ribose *f* ribose *(monosaccharide)*
Ribosom *n* ribosome *(organelle)*
ribosomal ribosomal
(D)-Ribulose *f* ribose *(monosaccharide)*
(D)-Ribulose-1,5-biphosphat *n* ribulose 1,5-diphosphate
Ribulosebisphosphatcarboxylase *f* ribulose-bisphosphate carboxylase[/oxygenase], fraction-I protein *(enzyme)*
Ribulosephosphat-3-Epimerase *f* ribulosephosphate 3-epimerase, phsophoribulose epimerase *(enzyme)*
Ribulosephosphatkinase *f* phosphoribulokinase *(enzyme)*
richtungsabhängig anisotropic
Richtungsabhängigkeit *f* anisotropy
Richtungstanz *m (api)* directional dance
richtungsunabhängig isotropic
Richtungsunabhängigkeit *f* isotropy
Ricin *n* ricin *(seed protein from Ricinus communis)*
Ricinin *n* ricinin[e] *(alkaloid)*
Ricinol[ein]säure *f* ricinol[e]ic acid
Ricke *f* doe
Rickenkitz *n* female fawn
Rickettsie *f (zoo)* rickettsia *(order Rickettsiales, family Rickettsiaceae)*
Rickettsieninfektion *f*, **Rickettsiose** *f (vet)* rickettsial disease
riechen to smell
Riechen *n* smelling, olfaction
Riechkolben *m*, **Riechlappen** *m* olfactory bulb (lobe)
Riechnerv *m* olfactory nerve
Riechorgan *n* olfactory organ
Riechschleimhaut *f* olfactory region
Riechschwelle *f* olfactory threshold
Riechzentrum *n* olfactory centre
Ried *n s.* Schilf 1.
Riedgras *n* reed grass, bent *(comprehensive term)*
Riedgrasgewächse *npl* sedge family *(family Cyperaceae)* • **die ~ betreffend** cyperaceous
Riedgrastorf *m* sedge peat
Riedsumpf *m* reed swamp
Riedtorf *m* reed peat
Riemenantrieb *m* belt drive
Riemenblatt *n* kaffir lily *(genus Clivia)*
Riemenblume *f (bot)* loranthus *(genus Loranthus)*
Riemenlippe *f* rein orchis *(genus Habenaria)*
Riemenscheibe *f* [belt] pulley
Riementrieb *m* belt drive

Riesbahn f, **Riese** f (forest) [log] slide, log chute, slip
Rieselbewässerung f flush (trickle) irrigation
Rieselfeld n sewage field (area), irrigation[al] field
Rieselhang m irrigation slope
Rieselkühler m dripping cooling plant
rieseln to trickle
Rieselrinne f water furrow
Rieselrinnenpflug m water furrow plough
Rieselschlauch m irrigation (trickle) hose
Rieseltrockner m counterflow dryer
Rieselung f s. Rieselbewässerung
Rieselwiese f [over]flow meadow, inundated (water) meadow
riesen (forest) to chute, to slide
Riesenameise f large (red) carpenter ant, Camponotus herculeanus
Riesenbambus m giant bamboo (genus Dendrocalamus)
Riesenbastkäfer m s. Riesenfichtenbastkäfer
Riesenbiene f s. Riesenhonigbiene
Riesenbohne f [common] jack bean, Canavalia ensiformis
Riesenchromosom n giant chromosome, polytene (polytenic) chromosome
Riesenfenchel m giant fennel, ferula, Ferula communis
Riesenfichtenbastkäfer m great [European] spruce bark-beetle, Dendroctonus micans
Riesenfuchsschwanz m (bot) giant foxtail, Setaria faberi
Riesengranadille f (bot) giant granadilla, Passiflora quadrangularis
Riesenholzwespe f large wood-wasp, pinewood-wasp, Urocerus (Sirex) gigas
Riesenhonigbiene f giant bee, Apis dorsata
Riesenhülse f sword bean, Entada phaseoloides (scandens)
Riesenhyazinthe f summer hyacinth, Galtonia candicans
Riesenkaktus m saguaro [cactus], Carnegiea gigantea
Riesenkürbis m winter (vining) squash, Cucurbita maxima
Riesenlebensbaum m giant arbor vitae, western red cedar, canoe-cedar, Thuja plicata (gigantea)
Riesenlilie f giant lily, Cardiocrinum giganteum
Riesenorange f shaddock, Citrus maxima
Riesenscheinagave f Mauritius hemp, Furcraea foetida (gigantea)
Riesenschierlingstanne f western hemlock, Tsuga heterophylla
Riesenschilf n giant reed, Arundo donax
Riesenschirmpilz m parasol mushroom, Macrolepiota procera
Riesenschnauzer m giant schnauzer (dog breed)
Riesenschwingel m giant fescue, Festuca gigantea

Riesensequoie f [giant] sequoia, mammoth tree, Sequoiadendron giganteum, Sequoia gigantea
Riesensüßgras n brook (reed sweet) grass, water poa, Glyceria maxima (aquatica)
Riesentanne f grand fir, lowland (white) fir, Abies grandis
Riesenthuja f s. Riesenlebensbaum
Riesenvallisnerie f tape grass, wild celery, Vallisneria gigantea
Riesenwuchs m gigantism; (bot) gigas
Riesenzelle f giant cell
~/**knochengewebeabbauende** osteoclast
Riesling m Riesling (wine)
Rieslingrebe f Riesling (grape-vine)
Riesweg m (forest) road slide
Rifampicin n rifampicin (antibiotic)
Rifamycin n SV rifamycin SV (antibiotic)
Riffeldränrohr n corrugated [plastic] drain-pipe
Riffelmaschine f fluting machine
riffeln to ripple, to seed (flax)
Riffel[plastik]rohr n corrugated plastic pipe
Riffelwalze f fluted roll[er]
Riffelzelle f s. Stachelzelle
Rifocin n s. Rifamycin SV
Rifttalfieber n Rift valley fever, enzootic hepatitis (of ruminants)
Rifttalfiebervirus n Rift valley fever virus
rigid[e] rigid, strict, stiff
rigolen to trench[-plough], to subsoil
Rigolen n deep digging; deep ploughing
Rigolhacke f trenching hoe
Rigolpflug m trench[ing] plough, deep-digger plough
Rigor m (vet) rigor, muscular stiffness
~ **mortis** rigor mortis
Rillenbewässerung f corrugation irrigation
Rillenbrett n (forest) sowing board
Rillenerosion f (soil) rill erosion
Rillenkrankheit f **des Apfels** apple flat limb (virosis)
Rillenscheibe f sheave
Rillenzieher m, **Rillenziehhacke** f drill hoe
Rimactan n s. Rifamycin SV
Rind n ox, bovine [animal], neat (genus Bos)
~/**ausgewachsenes** beef
~/**hornloses** poll
Rinde f (bot) cortex, bark, rind (e.g. of a tree); peel[ing], skin, rind (of fruit); (zoo) cortex (of an organ) • **auf** ~ **wachsend** corticole, corticoline, corticolous • **mit** ~ over (outside) bark (timber mensuration) • **ohne** ~ under (inside) bark, bare (timber mensuration)
~/**äußere** s. Außenrinde
~/**innere** s. Innenrinde
~/**offizinelle** medicinal bark
~/**sekundäre** (bot) secondary phloem, bast, liber
Rindenabfälle mpl bark shavings, barking refuse
Rindenabschlag m (forest) bark allowance (deduction), allowance for bark, a.f.b.

Rindenabschuppung

Rindenabschuppung f *(phyt)* bark scaling
Rindenabzug m s. Rindenabschlag
Rindenanteil m **[in Prozent]** bark percent[age]
rindenbewohnend corticol[in]e, corticolous
Rindenbrand m *(phyt)* bark blister (burn), bark scorch[ing], sun-scald
~ **/im Winter verursachter** winter bark scorch, winter sun-scald
rindenbrütend bark-breeding *(e.g. beetles)*
Rindenbündel n bark bundle
Rindendicke f bark thickness
Rindendickenmesser m bark gauge
Rindeneinschluß m s. Rindentasche
Rindeneinschnitt m bark incision
Rindenextraktstoff m bark extractive
Rindenfaserstoff m bark-fibre product
Rindenfäule f *(phyt)* bark (rind) rot
Rindengalle f *(phyt)* rind gall
Rindengebund n bark bundle
Rindengerbstoff m bark tannin
Rindenhumus m bark humus
Rindenkompost m bark [shaving] compost
Rindenkratzer m bark (tree) scraper
Rindenkrebs m *(phyt)* bark canker
~ **von Käse** cheese rind rot *(caused by Penicillium brevicaule)*
Rindennekrose f *(phyt)* bark (rind) necrosis
~ **des Apfels** apple bark necrosis *(virosis)*
~ **/innere** internal bark necrosis *(of apple trees due to manganese toxicity)*
Rindenpfropfen n bark (rind) grafting
Rindenpore f *(bot)* lenticel
Rindenprozent m s. Rindenanteil
Rindenpyrolyse f bark pyrolysis
Rindenriß m **[durch Sonnenbestrahlung]** sun crack
Rindenrissigkeit f bark split
~ **der Birne** pear bark split *(virosis)*
Rindenrösten n bark burning *(bark-beetle control)*
Rindenschäler m [bark] peeler, barker, barking-iron, rosser
Rindenschälmaschine f barking (bark-peeling) machine, [de]barker, rosser
Rindenschälmesser n barking spud
Rindenschälung f barking, flaying
~ **in der Saftzeit** barking in sap-flow period
Rindenschild m shield *(bud grafting)*
Rindenschuppigkeit f s. Rindenschuppung
Rindenschuppung f *(phyt)* bark scaling, scaly bark *(virosis)*
~ **des Apfels** apple scaly bark
Rindensegment n **der Ananas** pip
Rindenstärke f bark thickness
Rindensubstrat n bark substrate (medium)
Rindentannin n bark tannin
Rindentasche f bark pocket (inclusion), ingrown bark, inbark
rindentragend corticate[d], rinded
Rindenveredelung f bark (rind) grafting

Rindenzuwachs m bark increment
Rinder npl [horned] cattle, oxen, bovine animals, horned stock • ~ **treiben** *(Am)* to wrangle
rinderartig bovine, taurine
Rinderaufzucht f cattle rearing
Rinderausstellung f cattle-show
Rinderbabesiose f/**Europäische** babesiasis, babesiosis, red-water [disease] *(of cattle)*
Rinderbehandlungsstand m cattle [treatment] crate
Rinderbeurteilung f cattle evaluation
Rinderdung m cattle manure (dung), cow-dung
Rinderdungsilage f cattle manure silage
Rinderfarm f cattle farm
Rinderfeintalg m premier jus
Rinderfußöl n s. Rinderklauenöl
Rinderfütterung f cattle feeding
Rindergrippe f *(vet)* cuffing pneumonia
Rindergülle f cattle slurry
Rinderhaarling m cattle biting louse, Bovicola (Damalinia) bovis
Rinderhalter m cattle farmer, *(Am)* cattleman, pastoralist
Rinderhaltung f cattle farming (husbandry, management), keeping of cattle
Rinderherde f beef (cattle) herd, herd of cattle
Rinderhirt m oxherd
~ **/berittener** cowboy, wrangler
Rinderklauenöl n neat's-foot oil, cattle foot oil
Rinderlaufstall m cattle-yard, free stall
Rinderlausfliege f cattle louse fly, Hippobosca rufipes
Rinderleukose f *(vet)* [enzootic] bovine leucosis
Rindermast f cattle fattening (feeding)
Rindermastanlage f cattle fattening unit, cattle-feeding operation, beef lot
Rindermastbetrieb m, **Rindermastfarm** f cattle fattening farm
rindern to be at (in, on) heat *(cow)*
Rinderoffenstall m open-front cattle barn
Rinderpapillomvirus n bovine papilloma virus
Rinderpeitsche f stock-whip
Rinderpest f rinderpest, cattle-plague, steppe murrain
Rinderpestvirus n rinderpest virus
Rinderpocken pl cowpox
Rinderrasse f cattle breed, breed of cattle
Rinderschlachtkörper m beef [carcass]
Rinderschußbolzen m cattle killer cartridge
Rinderspreize f *(slaught)* beef tree spreader
Rinderstall m cattle building (barn), cattle shed (shelter), cattle (neat) house, cowshed, stall
Rinderstallanlage f cattle-yard
Rindertalg m [beef] tallow, beef fat
Rindertuberkulose f bovine tuberculosis, grapes *(esp. caused by Mycobacterium bovis)*
Rinderwahnsinn m *(vet)* mad cow disease
Rinderweideland n cattle range (run)
Rinderweidezaun m cattle (ox) fence, oxer

Rinderzucht *f* cattle breeding
Rinderzüchter *m* cattle breeder, *(Am)* cattleman, pastoralist
Rindfleisch *n* beef, bovine meat
~/durch Gerstenmast erzeugtes barley beef
rindfleischartig beefy
Rindfleischextrakt *m* beef extract
Rindite *n* rindite, ethylene chlorohydrin
Rindshaut *f* oxhide, neat's hide
~/ungegerbte rawhide, raw skin
Rindsleder *n* neat's leather, oxhide, cowhide
Rindvieh *n s.* Rinder
Ringanalyse *f* ring test, interlaboratory study
Ringbein *n (vet)* ring-bone *(of horse)*
Ringchromosom *n* ring chromosome
Ringelblume *f (bot)* marigold, calendula *(genus Calendula)*
Ringelgans *f* barnacle [goose], brent [goose], Branta bernicla
Ringelkette *f* tree girdler
ringeln to girdle, to ring[-bark], to strip *(a tree)*
~/durch senkrecht geführte Axteinhiebe to frill[-girdle], to hack-girdle
Ringelnatter *f* ring[ed] snake, grass-snake, Natrix natrix
Ringelröschen *n* pot marigold, Calendula officinalis
Ringelspieß *m* short shoot, spur [shoot] *(of fruit-trees)*
Ringelspinner *m* lackey moth, Malacosoma neustria
Ringelspinnerraupe *f* tent caterpillar
Ringeltaube *f* ring-dove, wood-pigeon, cushat, queest, Columba palumbus
Ringelung *f* [band, ring] girdling, ring-barking, ringing, stripping *(of trees)*
~ mit Giftanwendung poison girdling
~ ohne Giftanwendung mechanical girdling
Ringelwalze *f* corrugated roller, ring roll[er]
Ringelwurm *m (zoo)* annelid *(phylum annelida)*
Ringelzunge *f (vet)* curled tongue
Ringentwässerung *f* annular drainage pattern
Ringfäule *f* 1. ring rot *(comprehensive term)*; 2. [bacterial] ring rot *(of potato tubers, caused by Corynebacterium sepedonicum)*
Ringfleckenbildung *f (phyt)* ring spotting
Ringfleckenkrankheit *f* ring spot *(of cabbage, caused by Mycosphaerella brassicicola)*
Ringfleckenmosaik *n* **der Birne** pear ring pattern mosaic *(virosis)*
Ringfleckenvirus *n* **der Pfingstrose** peony ring spot virus
Ringfleckigkeit *f (phyt)* ring spot *(comprehensive term)*
~ der Johannisbeere red currant ring spot *(virosis)*
Ringfleckung *f s.* Ringfleckigkeit
Ringfloß *n (Am)* crib
ringförmig circular, annular; cyclic *(chemical compounds)*

~ angeordnet gyrate
Ringgefäß *n (bot)* annular vessel
Ringimpfung *f (vet)* ring vaccination
Ringkluft *f s.* Ringschäle
Ringkultur *f* ring culture *(vegetable growing)*
Ringlochzange *f* nose plier
Ringmartingal *n* running martingale
Ringmuskel *m* sphincter
Ringnetz *n (pisc)* pod-net
Ringokulation *f* patch budding
Ringpilz *m (bot)* brown-yellow boletus, Ixocomus (Suillus) luteus
ringporig ring-porous *(wood)*
Ringprobe *f (vet)* ring test
Ringriß *m* ring shake, ring (burst) check *(wood defect)*
Ringschäle *f* ring (annular) delamination, round shake *(wood defect)*
Ringschwimmer *m* bag (towing) boom *(rafting)*
Ringspülung *f* circulation cleaning *(of milking installations)*
Ringversuch *m (vet)* ring test
Ringwade *f (pisc)* bag-net
Rinne *f* 1. channel, gutter, trench; 2. *(zoo)* stria, groove
~/kunststoffausgekleidete plastic-lined channel *(plantlet rearing)*
Rinnenerosion *f (soil)* rill erosion
Rinnenkultur *f* flow-channel culture *(in greenhouses)*
Rinnenrutsche *f* trough-type chute
Rinnenstausee *m* riverine reservoir
Rinnentränke *f* automatic water trough
Rinnhufmesser *n* hoof knife (cutter)
rinnig *(bot, zoo)* canaliculate[d]
Rio-Grande-Schönmalve *f (bot)* weeping Chinese lantern, Abutilon megapotamicum
Rio-Tradeskantie *f (bot)* wandering Jew, Tradescantia fluminensis (myrtifolia)
Rippe *f* 1. rib, costa; 2. *s.* Blattrippe
~/dünne chuck rib[s] *(beef carcass)*
~/falsche false (asternal) rib
~/hohe prime rib[s] *(beef carcass)*
~/sternale *s.* ~/wahre
~/wahre true (sternal) rib
Rippenanzahl *f* rib number
Rippenatmung *f* costal respiration
Rippenbogen *m* costal arch, rib-cage
Rippenbräune *f (phyt)* vein necrosis
Rippenfarn *m* 1. saw fern *(genus Blechnum)*; 2. hard fern, Blechnum spicant
Rippenfell *n* costal (parietal) pleura
Rippenfellentzündung *f (vet)* pleurisy, pleuritis
rippenfrüchtig *(bot)* cladocarpous, cladogenous
Rippenknorpel *m* rib cartilage
Rippenkohl *m* Portuguese cabbage (kale), Brassica oleracea convar. capitata var. costata
rippenlos ribless, ecostate

Rippensäraddrillmaschine

Rippensäraddrillmaschine f external force-feed drill
Rippenschlagleiste f rasp bar (of thresher)
Rippenzahl f rib number
Rishitin n rishitin (phytoalexin)
Rispe f (bot) 1. panicle; 2. s. Rispengras • **Rispen schieben** to go (run) to ear
Rispelstrauch m German tamarisk, Myricaria germanica
Rispenamarant m (bot) purple amaranth, Amaranthus paniculatus
rispenförmig (bot) paniculiform
Rispenfuchsschwanz m s. Rispenamarant
Rispengras n meadow-grass, poa (genus Poa)
Rispenhirse f [common, panicled, true, hog] millet, Indian (French, broomcorn) millet, proso [millet], Panicum miliaceum
Rispenschieben n panicle earing, heading
Rispenstiel m cluster stem (of berry fruits)
rispig (bot) panicled, paniculate
Rispige Segge f, **Rispiges Riedgras** n panicled sedge, Carex paniculata
Riß m crack, check; split, shake, chink (esp. in wood); streak (resin-tapping)
~/durchgehender through check (shake) (in wood)
Rißbildung f **im Stamm** popping (tree-felling)
Risser m (forest) scribe, scratcher, risser
Risser[zahn]kettensäge f scratcher chain saw
rissig (bot) rimose, rimous; cracked, chinked (e.g. bark, wood); fissured (e.g. skin)
Rißwinkel m angle of streak (freshening) (resin-tapping)
Ritt m ride [on a horse]
Ritterling m (bot) tricholoma (genus Tricholoma)
Rittersporn m (bot) [annual] larkspur, lark-heel, delphinium (genus Delphinium)
Ritterstern m (bot) hippeastrum, amaryllis (genus Hippeastrum)
Rittigkeit f comfort for (of) the rider
Ritzdrillmaschine f slot seeder
ritzen to scarify (e.g. hard-shelled seeds)
Ritzen n scarification
Ritzmaschine f scarifier
Ritzsaat f slot-seeding
Rivieranelke f Mediterranean carnation, Dianthus caryophyllus
Rizinusöl n castor[-bean] oil
Rizinuspflanze f castor-oil plant, castor bean [plant], palma Christi, Ricinus communis
Rizinussamen m castor bean
Rizinussamenschrot m castor-oil meal
Rizinussamenvergiftung f (vet) castor-bean poisoning
RkAMV s. Rotkleeadernmosaikvirus
RkNMV s. Nekrotisches Rotkleemosaikvirus
RkSV s. Rotkleescheckungsvirus
RKV s. Rübenkräuselvirus
RL 50 s. Rückstandshalbwertzeit
rm s. Raummeter

RMiVV s. Mildes Rübenvergilbungsvirus
RMV s. Rübenmosaikvirus
RN s. Reststickstoff
RNA RNA, ribonucleic acid
~/chromosomale chromosomal RNA
~/infektiöse pathogenic (infectious) RNA, viroid
~/lösliche transfer RNA
~/ribosomale ribosomal RNA
RNA-Nucleotidyltransferase f RNA nucleotidyltransferase (enzyme)
RNA-Spleißen n gene splicing (genetic engineering)
RNA-Tumorvirus n oncogenic RNA virus, oncornavirus (subfamily Oncovirinae)
RNS s. RNA
RNVV s. Nekrotisches Rübenvergilbungsvirus
Robertson-Translokation f (gen) fusion translocation
Robigenin n kaempferol (plant dye)
Robinie f 1. robinia (genus Robinia); 2. false acacia, common robinia, honey (black) locust, Robinia pseudoacacia
Robinienmosaikvirus n robinia mosaic virus, RoMV
Roborans n (vet) roborant
Robustakaffee m robusta coffee, Coffea canephora (robusta)
Rochellesalz n Rochelle (Seignette) salt, potassium-sodium tartrate
röchelnd stertorous (breathing)
Rockenbolle f rocambole, sand leek, giant garlic, Allium sativum var. ophioscorodon, Allium scorodoprasum
Rodeaggregat n lifting unit, digger section (of a root crop harvester)
Rodearbeit f bush and bog work
Rodeaxt f grub-axe
Rodebock m (forest) tripod stump-puller
Rodegabel f graip
Rodegerät n lifting implement, lifter; eradicator, extractor, uprooter, puller
Rodehacke f, **Rodehaue** f grub-hoe, grubbing mattock; trenching hoe
Rodekörper m lifting body
Rodelader m lifter loader
Rodeland n s. Rodungsfläche
Rodemaschine f s. Rodegerät
roden 1. to clear [land], to grub [out, up], to assart; 2. to dig [out], to plough out, to lift (root crops); 3. to eradicate, to uproot, to extract (e.g. trees)
~/Gestrüpp to brush
~/Stöcke (Stubben) to stub [out], to grub up stumps
~/Unterholz to brush
Roden n 1. [land] clearing, land clearance, assart[ment]; 2. digging [out], lifting; 3. eradication, extraction
Rodentier m rodent, gnawer, gnawing animal (order Rodentia)
Rodentiose f (vet) pseudotuberculosis

rodentizid rodenticidal
Rodentizid *n* rodenticide
Rodeo *m(n)* rodeo
Rodepflug *m* lifting plough, lifter
Roder *m s.* 1. Rodegerät; 2. Rodepflug
Roderad *n* lifting (lifter) wheel
Röderwaldbetrieb *m* alternation of agricultural and forestal crops
Rodeschar *n* lifting (digging) share
Rodescheibe *f* lifting (digging) disk
Rodespaten *m* lifting spade
Rodetiefe *f* digging depth
Rodetrennlader *m* lifter loader
Rodewerkzeug *n* lifting implement
Rodewinde *f (forest)* windlass stump-puller
Rodezinke *f* lifting tine
Rodung *f s.* 1. Roden; 2. *s.* Rodungsfläche
Rodungsfläche *f* clearing, cleared land, assart
Rogen *m* [fish, hard] roe
Rogener *m* spawner
rogentragend berried *(fish)*
Roggen *m* 1. rye *(genus Secale)*; 2. rye, Secale cereale
Roggenbraunrost *m* brown rust of rye *(caused by Puccinia dispersa)*
Roggenbrot *n* rye [bread]
Roggengerste *f* meadow barley grass, Hordeum secalinum
Roggengrobmehl *n* rye meal
Roggenkleber *m* rye gluten
Roggenkleie *f* rye middlings (bran)
Roggenknäckebrot *n* Scandinavian rye crispbread
Roggenkörner *npl* rye
Roggenmehl *n* rye flour
~/**grobes** rye meal
Roggenmutter *f* ergot [fungus], Claviceps purpurea
Roggenmutterkorn *n* *(phyt)* rye ergot *(caused by Claviceps purpurea)*
Roggenprotein *n* rye protein
Roggenschwarzbrot *n* black bread
Roggenschwarzrost *m* leaf rust of rye *(caused by Puccinia graminis f.sp. secalis)*
Roggensilage *f* rye silage
Roggenstärke *f* rye starch
Roggensteinbrand *m* rye bunt *(caused by Tilletia secalis)*
Roggenstroh *n* rye straw
Roggentrespe *f* rye[like] brome, chess [brome], common chess, cheat [grass], wheat thief, Bromus secalinus
Roggenwhisky *m* rye [whisky]
Rogner *m (pisc)* spawner
roh 1. raw, unprocessed, untreated *(as materials)*; crude *(esp. substances)*; 2. raw, uncooked *(vegetable, fruit)*; 3. raw, untanned, undressed *(hides)*; 4. in the grease *(wool, fur)*
Rohasche *f* crude ash *(feed analysis)*
Rohbaumwolle *f* raw (seed) cotton, cotton wool

Rohboden *m* raw (virgin) soil
~ **aus Festgestein** lithosol
Rohcasein *n* crude casein
Rohdichte *f* [bulk, crude] density
Rohdichtebestimmung *f* density determination
Rohfaser *f* crude fibre
Rohfasergehalt *m* fibre content
Rohfett *n* raw (crude) fat
Rohfrucht *f* raw (unmalted) grain *(brewing)*
Rohfruchtkocher *m* cereal cooker *(brewing)*
Rohfruchtmaische *f* adjunct mash *(brewing)*
Rohharz *n* dip
Rohhaut *f* rawhide, raw (untanned) skin, green hide
~/**geschorene** pelt *(e.g. of sheep)*
Rohholz *n* [undressed, forest, unhewn] timber, [raw]wood, *(Am)* lumber
Rohholzbereitstellung *f* forest harvest[ing], *(Am)* logging
Rohholzerzeugung *f* timber production (growing), wood production
Rohholzfestmeter *m* cubic metre round timber
Rohholzgeist *m* crude methanol
Rohholzkubikmeter *m s.* Rohholzfestmeter
Rohholzsortiment *n* timber assortment
Rohhumus *m* raw humus, duff
~/**moderartiger** modermor
~/**unter sauren Bedingungen entstandener** mor [humus]
Rohkaffee *m* green coffee
Rohkompost *m* crude compost
Rohmaß *n* gross (full) scale, bigness scale *(timber mensuration)*
Rohmaterial *n* raw material (stuff)
Rohmethanol *n* crude methanol
Rohmilch *f* raw milk
Rohmost *m* crude must
Rohnährstoff *m* crude nutrient
Rohphosphat *n* rock (mineral) phosphate
~/**vermahlenes** ground rock phosphate
Rohphosphatmehl *n* ground rock phosphate
Rohprodukt *n* raw product
Rohprotein *n* crude protein, C.P.
~/**verdauliches** digestible crude protein, D.C.P.
Rohr *n* 1. tube; pipe; 2. cane *(s. a. Zuckerrohr)*; 3. reed [grass] *(genus Phragmites)*; 4. [common] reed, Phragmites australis (communis)
Rohrartiges Silbergras *n* cogon grass (satin tail), Imperata cylindrica var. major
Röhrbein *n* shank *(animal anatomy)*; cannon-bone *(of hoofed animals)*
Rohrbewässerungssystem *n* pipe irrigation system
Rohrbrunnen *m* tube well
Rohrbrunnenbewässerung *f* tube well irrigation
Rohrbündelwärmeübertrager *m* [shell-and-]tube exchanger
röhrchenblütig *s.* röhrenblütig
Röhrchenhorn *n* tubular horn *(of hoof or claw)*

Röhrchentest

Röhrchentest *m* **nach Wright** *(vet)* Wright's test
Rohrdommel *f* bittern, Botaurus stellaris
Rohrdrän *m* pipe (tile) drain
Rohrdränung *f* pipe drainage
Röhre *f* 1. tube; pipe; 2. *(bot, zoo)* fistula; 3. *s.* Röhrbein
~/Eustachysche auditory (Eustachian) tube *(animal anatomy)*
röhren to bell, to roar, to troat
Rohren *n s.* Kehlkopfpfeifen
Röhrenblüte *f* tubular floret
röhrenblütig tub[ul]iflorous
röhrenförmig tubular, tubate
röhrengetrocknet flue-cured *(tobacco)*
Röhrenkassie *f* Indian laburnum, purging cassia, drumstick tree, Cassia fistula
Röhrenknochen *m* long bone
Röhrenlaus *f* aphis, plant-louse *(family Aphididae)*
Röhrenpflanzung *f (forest)* sleeve (tube) planting, tubing
Röhrenpilz *m* 1. tube[-bearing] fungus *(order Boletales)*; 2. bolete, boletus *(genus Boletus)*
Röhrentrocknung *f* flue-curing *(of tobacco)*
Rohrerntemäher *m* reed harvester (mower)
Rohrförderanlage *f* pipe conveyor equipment
Rohrförderer *m* pipe conveyor
Rohrfuchsschwanz *m (bot)* creeping foxtail, Alopecurus ventricosus (arundinaceus), Gastridium ventricosum
Rohrfütterungsanlage *f* pipeline (tube) feeder, pipe feeding plant
Rohrglanzgras *n* reed canary grass, ribbon-grass, painted grass, gardener's garters, Phalaris arundinacea
Rohrheizung *f* pipe heating
Röhricht *n* reed[s], reed bank
röhrig *(bot, zoo)* fistulous, fistular, tubulose
Rohrkolben *m (bot)* bul[l]rush *(genus Typha)*
Rohrkupplung *f* pipe coupling
Rohrlegemaschine *f* pipe layer, pipe-laying machine, tubing-burying machine *(drainage)*
Rohrleitung *f* pipeline, line of tubing
Rohrleitungsfütterung *f* pipeline feeding
Röhrling *m s.* Röhrenpilz
Rohrmäher *m* reed mower (harvester)
Rohrmatte *f* reed mat
Rohrmelasse *f* cane molasses
Rohrmelkanlage *f* pipeline milking installation (plant), milking pipeline installation
Rohrmühle *f* cane mill *(sugar-cane processing)*
Rohrnetzberegnungssystem *n* grid sprinkler system
Rohrrohzucker *m*, **Rohrrohzucker** *m* cane raw sugar, muscovado
Rohrsaturation *f* tube saturation *(sugar manufacture)*
Rohr-Schlauch-Beregnung *f* combined pipe and hose irrigation

Rohr-Schlauch-Beregnungsanlage *f* pipe-hose installation
Rohrschleifenbelüfter *m* tubular loop aerator
Rohrschneckenförderer *m* tubular screw conveyor
Rohrschwingel *m* tall (reed) fescue, randall grass, Festuca arundinacea
Rohrsolarimeter *n* tube solarimeter
Rohrstrang *m* line of pipes
Rohrtorf *m* reed peat
Rohrtransportwagen *m* pipe trailer
Rohrverbindung *f* pipe coupling
Rohrverlegemaschine *f s.* Rohrlegemaschine
Rohrzucker *m* cane-sugar, saccharose, sucrose *(from Saccharum officinale)*
Rohrzuckerfabrik *f* cane-sugar mill
Rohrzuckersirup *m* cane-sugar syrup
Rohsaft *m* crude juice; extract[ive] *(sugar manufacture)*
Rohsalz *n* mine-run salt
Rohschellack *m* lac
Rohstoff *m* raw material (stuff)
~/pflanzlicher raw material of plant origin, plant material (matter, source)
~/tierischer raw material of animal origin
Rohstoffpflanze *f* industrial crop, plant for technical use
Rohstoffrückgewinnung *f* recycling
Rohterpentin *n* crude terpentine
Rohtorf *m* raw peat
Rohwein *m* crude wine
Rohwolle *f* raw (crude) wool, wool in the grease
Rohzucker *m* raw (crude) sugar; brown sugar
Rollballen[sammel]presse *f* roll baler
rollbar rollable
Rollboden *m* floor conveyor, moving (endless) floor *(e.g. of a manure spreader)*
Rollboden[an]hänger *m* endless-floor trailer, movement floor trailer
Rollegge *f* rolling harrow
Rollenförderer *m* roller conveyor
Rollengesperr *n s.* Rollensperrkupplung
Rollenklinkenautomat *m* self-lift [mechanism] *(of plough)*
Rollenpumpe *f* roller pump
Rollenrost *m* roller table screen *(sugar-beet processing)*
Rollensortierer *m* roller grader
Rollensperrkupplung *f* roller-type overrunning clutch
Rollenunterlage *f* apron *(timber transport)*
Roller *m* roller *(pigeon breed)*
Rollhacke *f* roller-type hand hoe
Rollhaus *n* mobile greenhouse
Rollhügel *m* trochanter *(of long bone)*
Rolligsein *n* heat *(of cat)*
Rollkrümler *m* soil miller
Rollmosaik *n* **der Kartoffel** *(phyt)* potato leaf rolling mosaic, interveinal mosaic, paracrinkle

Rollnest *n* roll-away [laying] nest *(poultry management)*
Rollstabilität *f* roll stiffness
Rollstrangregner *m* roll-line irrigator, power-moved pipeline with sprinklers
~/wasserdruckgetriebener water-driven roll-line irrigator
Rolltafel *f*, **Rolltisch** *m* rolling (movable) bench *(greenhouse installation)*
Rollwiderstand *m* rolling resistance
Romadur *m* Romadur cheese
Romagnola *n s*. 1. Romagnolarind; 2. Romagnolaschwein
Romagnolarind *n* Romagna *(cattle breed)*
Romagnolaschwein *n* Romagna *(pig breed)*
Romano[käse] *m* Romano cheese
Romanowschaf *n* Romanov *(sheep breed)*
Romilan *n* romilan *(fungicide)*
Römische Kamille *f* [common, Roman, sweet] camomile, noble (English) camomile, Chamaemelum nobile, Anthemis nobilis
Römischer Ampfer *m* French sorrel, Rumex scutatus
~ Beifuß *m* Roman wormwood, small absinth, Artemisia pontica
~ Bertram *m (bot)* pellitory of Spain, Anacyclus pyrethrum
~ Kümmel *m* cumin, Cuminum cyminum
~ Salat *m* Roman (romaine, celery) lettuce, cos [lettuce], Lactuca sativa var. longifolia (romana)
Romney Marsh *n* Romney Marsh, Kent *(sheep breed)*
RoMV *s*. Rosenmosaikvirus
Romycil *n* oleandomycin *(antibiotic)*
Rondell *n* circular (round) flower-bed
Rondomycin *n* methacyclin *(antibiotic)*
Röntgendarstellung *f (vet)* roentgenography, radiography
Röntgendurchleuchtung *f* roentgenoscopy, radioscopy
Röntgenkontrastdarstellung *f* contrast[-medium] roentgenography, contrast radiography
~ von Gefäßen angiography
Röntgenmikroanalyse *f*/**energiedisperse** energy-dispersive X-ray microanalysis
Röntgensortiergerät *n* X-ray sorter
Röntgenspektrometrie *f* X-ray spectrometry
Röntgenstrahlen *mpl* X-rays, roentgen rays
Röntgenstrahlung *f* X-radiation
Röntgenuntersuchung *f* radiography, X-ray examination
Rooibos *m* [red] bush tea, Aspalathus linearis
Roots-Verdichter *m* Roots blower
Roquefort *m* Roquefort [cheese]
Rosa Fruchtfäule *f* pink disease *(of pineapple, caused by Pseudomonas spp. and Erwinia spp.)*
Rosa-Noisettiana-Hybride *f* noisette rose, Rosa x noisettiana
Rosa-Polyantha *f* polyantha rose

Rosarium *n s*. Rosengarten
Röschen *n* **[des Blumenkohls]** flower cluster [of cauliflower]
Rose *f* 1. rose *(genus Rosa)*; 2. burr *(of antler)*
~ des Rosenkohls Brussels sprout
~ von Jericho rose of Jericho, Anastatica hierochuntica
~ von Sharon *(bot)* Aaron's beard, Hypericum calycinum
Rosé *m s*. Roséwein
Röse-Gottlieb-Methode *f* Roese-Gottlieb method *(of milk fat determination)*
Rosella *f*, **Roselle** *f* roselle [hemp], Jamaica sorrel, Hibiscus sabdariffa [var. altissima]
Rosenapfel *m* rose-apple, Syzygium (Eugenia) jambos
Rosenbeet *n* rosary, rosery
Rosenblattlaus *f* rose aphid, Macrosiphum rosae
Rosenbusch *m* rose-bush
Rosenbuschhornblattwespe *f* large rose saw-fly, Arge rosae
Roseneibisch *m* 1. [shrubby] althaea, rose-of-Sharon, Hibiscus syriacus; 2. Chinese hibiscus (rose), shoe flower, Hibiscus rosa-sinensis
Rosengalle *f (phyt)* rose-gall, bedeguar *(of rose-bush, caused by Rhodites roseae)*
Rosengallwespe *f* bedeguar gall-wasp, mossy rose-gall wasp, Rhodites roseae
Rosengarten *m* rose-garden, rosarium, rosary, rosery, rosetum
Rosengärtner *m* rosarian
Rosengeranium *n s*. Rosenpelargonie
Rosengewächse *npl* rose family *(family Rosaceae)* • **die ~ betreffend** rosaceous
Rosenholz *n* rosewood *(from Dalbergia variabilis or D. frutescens)*
Rosenkäfer *m* rose chafer, Cetonia aurata
Rosenkamm *m* rose comb *(of fowl)*
Rosenknospe *f* rose-bud
Rosenkohl *m* Brussels sprouts, Brassica oleracea var. gemmifera
Rosenkranz *m*/**rachitischer** *(vet)* enlarged costochondral junction, beading
Rosenkranzpappel *f* eastern cottonwood, Populus deltoides
Rosenlaubkäfer *m* rose beetle, Adoretus versutus (vestitus)
Rosenliebhaber *m* rosarian, rose-fancier
Rosenmosaikvirus *n* rose mosaic virus, RMV
Rosenohr *n* rose ear *(of certain dog breeds)*
Rosenöl *n* rose oil, attar [of roses], otto [of roses]
Rosenpappel *f* okra, Abelmoschus (Hibiscus) esculentus
Rosenpelargonie *f* rose (sweet-scented) geranium, Pelargonium graveolens
Rosenrost *m (phyt)* rose rust *(caused by Phragmidium spp.)*
Rosenrote Wucherblume *f* common pyrethrum, painted daisy, Chrysanthemum coccineum

Rosenrotes

Rosenrotes Immergrün (Singrün) *n* [Madagascar] periwinkle, old maid, Vinca rosea, Catharanthus roseus
Rosenstämmchen *n* tree rose
Rosenstock *m* rose tree
Rosenstrauch *m* rose-bush
Rosentopf *m* rose pot
Rosentriebbohrer *m* rose tip-infesting saw-fly, Ardis brunniventris
Rosenwasser *n* rose-water *(perfume)*
Rosenwelkevirus *n* rose wilt virus
Rosenwickler *m (ent)* filbert (hedge) leaf-roller, Archips rosanus, Cacoecia rosana
Rosenwurz *f* rose-root, Rhodiola (Sedum) rosea
Rosenzikade *f (ent)* rose leaf-hopper, Typhlocyba rosae
Rosenzucht *f* rose growing
Rosenzüchter *m* rosarian, rose grower, rose-fancier
Rosette *f* rosette
rosettenbildend *(bot)* rosulate
Rosettenbildung *f (phyt)* rosetting
Rosettenkrankheit *f (phyt)* rosette virus disease
~ **des Apfels** apple rosette *(virosis)*
Rosettenmosaikvirus *n* **des Pfirsichs** peach rosette mosaic virus
Rosettenstadium *n* rosette stage *(of plant development)*
Roséwein *m* pink (rose, pale) wine
Rosine *f* raisin, plum
Rosinenwein *m* raisin wine
Rosmarin *n (bot)* rosemary, Rosmarinus officinalis
Rosmarinheide *f* wild rosemary, andromeda *(genus Andromeda)*
Rosmarinseidelbast *m* garland flower, Daphne cneorum
Roß *n* horse, Equus caballus
Roßameise *f* carpenter ant *(genus Camponotus)*
Rosse *f* heat *(of mare)*
rossen to be at (in, on) heat, to horse *(mare)*
Roßhaar *n* horsehair
Roßhaut *f* horsehide
rossig sein *s.* rossen
Rossigkeit *f s.* Rosse
Roßkastanie *f* 1. buckeye *(genus Aesculus)*; 2. horse-chestnut, Aesculus hippocastanum; 3. buckeye, horse-chestnut, conker *(fruit)*
Roßkastanienbohrer *m* leopard moth, wood leopard [moth], Zeuzera pyrina
Roßkastanienspanner *m* March moth, Anisopteryx (Alsophila) aescularia
Roßminze *f* horse-mint, Mentha longifolia var. longifolia
Roßschlächterei *f* knackery
Rost *m* 1. *(phyt)* rust; 2. grate, grid *(for firing or screening)*; 3. rust *(corrosion product)* • **von ~ befallen werden** to rust
Rostblättrige Alpenrose *f* Alpine (drooping) rose, rusty-leaved rhododendron, Rhododendron ferrugineum
Röste *f* retting *(of flax)*
Rostellum *n* 1. *(bot)* rostellum *(the apex of the pistils of an orchid flower)*; 2. *(zoo)* rostellum *(anterior projection at the head of certain tapeworms)*
rosten to rust, to get rusty
rösten to roast, to parch, to kiln, *(Am)* to pop; to ret[t], to rot *(flax, hemp)*
Rostfarbiger Fingerhut *m* rusty foxglove, Digitalis ferruginea
Rostfleckigkeit *f* [necrotic] rusty mottle *(virosis of woody fruit plants)*
~ **des Pfirsichs** peach red suture *(virosis)*
Rostfleckung *f s.* Rostfleckigkeit
Rostgelbes Fuchsschwanzgras *n (bot)* orange foxtail, Alopecurus aequalis
rostig rusty • ~ **werden** to rust, to get rusty
Rostkrankheit *f (phyt)* rust [disease], leaf rust [disease]
Rostmilbe *f* 1. rust mite *(family Phytoptidae)*; 2. *s.* Rostrote Zitrusmilbe
Rostpilz *m* rust [fungus] *(order Uredinales)*
rostral *(zoo)* rostral
Röstreife *f* retting ripeness *(of flax)*
rostresistent rust-resistant *(plant)*
Rostresistenz *f* rust resistance
Rostrote Alpenrose *f s.* Rostblättrige Alpenrose
~ **Zitrusmilbe** *f* citrus rust mite, Phyllocoptruta oleivora
Rostrum *n (zoo)* rostrum
Rostschutzmittel *n* antirust[ing] agent, rust preventive (inhibitor)
Röstung *f* roast, kilning, *(Am)* popping; retting *(flax, hemp)*
Rotahorn *m* red (swamp) maple, Acer rubrum
Rotalge *f* red alga *(class Rhodophyceae)*
Rotangpalme *f (bot)* 1. rattan *(genus Calamus)*; 2. rotang, Calamus rotang
Rotation *f* 1. rotation; 2. *s.* Fruchtfolge
Rotations... *s. a.* Rotor...
Rotationsdungstreuer *m* rotary muck spreader
Rotationsextruder *m* rotary extrusion device
Rotationskannenwaschanlage *f* rotary churn washer
Rotationskolbenmotor *m* rotary engine
Rotationskreuzung *f* rotational cross-breeding, rotational crossing
Rotationsmähdrescher *m* rotary combine [harvester]
Rotationsmäher *m* disk mower
Rotationspumpe *f* rotary [piston] pump
Rotationssiebtrommel *f* rubble reel *(of a seed cleaner)*
Rotationsspatenmaschine *f* rotary spading machine
Rotationsverteiler *m* rotaspreader
Rotationszeit *f (forest)* rotation (circulation) period
Rotationszerkleinerer *m* rotary cutter
Rotationszerstäuber *m* rotary atomizer (duster)
~/handgetriebener rotary hand duster
Rotationszerstäubung *f* rotary atomization

Rotauge n (zoo) roach, Rutilus rutilus
Rotavator m Rotavator (trade mark of a tiller-like implement)
Rotbeiniger Schinkenkäfer m red-legged ham beetle, Necrobia rufipes
Rotblättrige Rose f milky-green rose, Rosa glauca (rubrifolia)
Rotblättriger Fächerahorn m purple Japanese maple, Acer palmatum cv. Atropurpureum
Rotblättrigkeit f (phyt) red leaf
~ **des Hafers** barley yellow dwarf
Rotblauverfärbung f der Haut (vet) cyanosis, blue jaundice
Rotblühende (Rotblütige) Roßkastanie f red horse-chestnut, Aesculus x carnea
Rotborstige Himbeere f wine raspberry, Rubus phoenicolasius
Rotbrauner Getreideerdfloh m wheat flea beetle, Crepidodera ferruginea
~ **Leistenkopfplattkäfer** m rust-red grain beetle, Cryptolestes ferrugineus
~ **Milchling** m (bot) rufous milk-cap, Lactarius rufus
~ **Reismehlkäfer** m [rust-]red flour beetle, Tribolium castaneum
Rotbuche f [European] beech, Fagus sylvatica
Rotbuntes Niederungsrind (Rind) n Red and White Holstein [cattle] (breed)
Röte f (phyt) redding
Rote Beete (Bete) f red (garden) beet, beetroot, Beta vulgaris ssp. vulgaris var. conditiva
~ **Calla** f pink (red) calla, Zantedeschia (Calla) rehmanii
~ **Heckenkirsche** f fly honeysuckle, Lonicera xylosteum
~ **Hornlose Rasse** f Red Poll (cattle breed)
~ **Johannisbeere** f red (garden) currant, Ribes rubrum
~ **Kicher[erbse]** f s. ~ Platterbse
~ **Miere** f [scarlet] pimpernel, wink-a-peep, Anagallis arvensis
~ **Mombinpflaume** f red (purple) mombin, Spanish plum, Spondias purpurea
~ **Pestwurz** f pestilenceweed, butterbur, flea-dock, Petasites hybridus (officinalis)
~ **Platterbse** f chickling vetch, flat pod pea, Lathyrus cicera
~ **Rhizomfäule** f der Erdbeere red stele [root rot] of strawberry, red core [disease] of strawberries, Lanarkshire disease (caused by Phytophthora cactorum and P. fragariae)
~ **Rübe** f s. Rote Beete
~ **Schildblume** f (bot) turtle head, Chelone obliqua
~ **Sokoto-Ziege** f Red Sokoto goat (breed)
~ **Spinne** f red spider [mite], red mite, carmine (two-spotted) spider mite, Tetranychus urticae (telarius)
~ **Spornblume** f (bot) red valerian, Jupiter's-beard, Centranthus ruber

~ **Stachelbeermilbe** f gooseberry red spider [mite], clover mite, Bryobia ribis (praetiosa)
~ **Taubnessel** f purple dead-nettle, Lamium purpureum
~ **Traubenkirsche** f [common] choke-cherry, Prunus (Padus) virginiana
~ **Vogelmilbe** f poultry (chicken) mite, bird mite, Dermanyssus gallinae
~ **Waldameise** f hill (wood) ant, Formica rufa
~ **Wegschnecke** f red slug, Arion rufus (empiricorum)
~ **Winterbeere** f [common] winterberry, Ilex verticillata
~ **Wurzelfäule** f 1. red root disease (esp. of Hevea brasiliensis, caused by Ganoderma philippii); 2. brick-red root rot (of tea plant, caused by Poria hypolateritia)
~ **Wurzelfäule** f der Erdbeere s. ~ Rhizomfäule der Erdbeere
~ **Zaunrübe** f red[-berry] bryony, snake bryony, Bryonia [cretica ssp.] dioica
~ **Zeder** f western red cedar, Thuja plicata (gigantea)
Röteeisen n (forest) bark shave, freshening tool, hogal, puller (resin-tapping)
Roteiche f northern red oak, Quercus rubra (borealis)
Roteisenstein m (soil) haematite
Rötelmaus f bank (wood) vole, Clethrionomys glareolus
röten to redden, to remove coarse bark (resin-tapping)
Röten n reddening, [face] delimitation, bark scraping
Rötender Schirmpilz m shaggy parasol, Macrolepiota rhacodes
Rotenoid n rotenoid (isoflavan)
Rotenon n rotenon[e] (insecticide)
Roter Aspenblattkäfer m aspen leaf beetle, Melasoma (Chrysomela) tremulae
~ **Baumwollkapselwurm** m (ent) pink bollworm, Pectinophora gossypiella
~ **Busch** m s. Rooibos
~ **Fingerhut** m [purple, common] foxglove, digitalis, Digitalis purpurea
~ **Fliegenpilz** m fly (deadly) agaric, fly amanita (toadstool), scarlet flycap, Amanita muscaria
~ **Gänsefuß** m red goose-foot, (Am) red coast blite, Chenopodium rubrum
~ **Getreideblasenfuß** m (ent) flower thrips, Frankliniella (Haplothrips) tritici
~ **Hafer** m Mediterranean oat[s], Avena byzantina
~ **Hartriegel** m [red, common] dogwood, bloodtwig dogwood, gaiter [tree], Cornus sanguinea
~ **Hickory** m sweet pignut, Carya ovalis
~ **Ingwer** m red ginger, Alpinia purpurata
~ **Knospenwickler** m eye-spotted bud moth, Spilonota ocellana
~ **Luftröhrenwurm** m gapeworm, Syngamus trachea

Roter

- **Maulbeerbaum** *m* red mulberry, Morus rubra
- **Neuseeländer** *m* New-Zealand Red *(rabbit breed)*
- **Rapsblattkäfer** *m* red turnip beetle, rape leaf beetle, Entomoscelis adonidis
- **Reismehlkäfer** *m* [rust-]red flour beetle, Tribolium castaneum
- **Sandelbaum** *m* red sandalwood, ruby wood, sanders, Pterocarpus santalinus
- **Sandelholzbaum** *m* sandal bead tree, Adenanthera pavonina
- **Sommerhartweizen** *m* hard red spring wheat *(type of cultivated wheat)*
- **Wasserhanf** *m* sweet Joe-Pye-weed, queen-of-the-meadow-root, Eupatorium purpureum
- **Winterhartweizen** *m* hard red winter wheat *(type of cultivated wheat)*
- **Winterweichweizen** *m* soft red winter wheat *(type of cultivated wheat)*
- **Ziest** *m* field (corn) woundwort, field-nettle betony, Stachys arvensis

Roterde *f* red soil (earth), kraznozem
Roterle *f* 1. [common, black] alder, aller, Alnus glutinosa; 2. Oregon (red, western) alder, Alnus oregona (rubra)
Rotes Dänisches Milchvieh *n* Red Dane (Danish), Fünen *(cattle breed)*
- **Dschungelhuhn** *n* jungle fowl, Gallus gallus (bankiva)
- **Hafergras** *n* red [oat] grass, Themeda triandra (hispida)
- **Höhenvieh** *n* German Red *(cattle breed)*
- **Hornloses Ostlandvieh** *n* Red Polled [Ostland], Ostland, Norfolk (Suffolk Red) Polled *(cattle breed)*
- **Kammhuhn** *n s.* ~ Dschungelhuhn
- **Rhodeländer** *n* Rhode Island Red *(breed of fowl)*
- **Sandelholz** *n* red sandalwood, caliatur wood *(esp. from Pterocarpus santalinus)*
- **Straußgras** *n* colonial bent[-grass], common bent[-grass], Agrostis capellaris (tenuis)
- **Wollkraut** *n* purple mullein, Verbascum phoenicum

Rotesche *f* red ash, Fraxinus pubescens var. pennsylvanica
Rotfährte *f (hunt)* red track
Rotfärbung *f* 1. *(phyt)* redding; red stain *(of wood)*; 2. blush *(of fruit surfaces)*
rotfaul foxy *(of wood)*
Rotfäule *f (phyt)* red rot (heart) *(comprehensive term)*
~/**beginnende** marginal (advance) rot *(of woody plants)*
Rotfeder *f* rudd, red-eye, Scardinius erythrophthalmus
Rotfichte *f* 1. [European, Norway] spruce, European whitewood, Picea abies (excelsa); 2. red spruce, Picea rubens (rubra)
Rotfichtenholz *n* white deal

Rotfleckenkrankheit *f* **der Erdbeere** leaf scorch of strawberry *(caused by Diplocarpon earliana)*
Rotfleckigkeit (Rotfleckung) *f* **der Birne** [pear] red mottle *(virosis)*
Rotfuchs *m* [red] fox, Vulpes vulpes
Rotgelbe Kiefernbuschhornblattwespe *f* European pine saw-fly, fox-coloured saw-fly, Neodiprion (Diprion) sertifer
Rothalsente *f* [common] pochard, Aythya ferina
Rothalsiges Getreidehähnchen *n* cereal (barley) leaf beetle, Oulema (Lema) melanopus
Rothändiger Samenkäfer *m* bean seed beetle, bean beetle (weevil), Bruchus rufimanus
Rothautröhrling *m s.* Rotkappe
Rothirsch *m* [red] deer, Cervus elaphus
Rotholz *n* 1. redwood *(comprehensive term)*; 2. compression (pressure, glassy) wood, tenar; 3. brazilwood, *(esp.)* Caesalpinia (Guilandina) echinata
Rothuhn *n* hazel-hen
Rotkappe *f (bot)* orange-cap boletus, Leccinum aurantiacum
Rotkern *m* false (pathological) heartwood, red heart[wood]
Rotkiefer *f* red pine, Pinus resinosa
Rotklee *m* red (purple) clover, cow-grass, Trifolium pratense
Rotkleeadernmosaikvirus *n* red clover vein mosaic virus, RCVMV
Rotkleescheckungsvirus *n* red clover mottle virus
Rotkohl *m*, **Rotkraut** *n* red cabbage, Brassica oleracea [convar. capitata] var. capitata f. rubra
Rotlachs *m* sockeye [salmon], red salmon, nerka, Oncorhynchus nerka
Rotlauf *m (vet)* erysipelas, red murrain, St. Anthony's fire *(caused by Erysipelothrix rhusiopathiae)*
Rotlaufseuche *f (vet)* equine viral arteritis, epizootic cellulitis
Rotlehm *m* red loam
Rötlichbraune Erdeule *f (ent)* variegated cutworm, Peridroma (Agrotis) saucia
Rötliche Schuppenwurz *f* toothwort, Lathraea squamaria
Rotlicht *n* red light
Rotmaulkrankheit *f*, **Rotmaulseuche** *f* enteric red-mouth disease *(esp. of rainbow trouts)*
Rotnervige Fittonie *f* red-nerved plant, Fittonia verschaffeltii
Rotolaktor *m* rotary milker (milking parlour), rotary parlour, rotolactor
Rotor... *s. a.* Rotations...
Rotorabscheider *m* rotary separator
Rotoregge *f* rotary [cross] harrow
Rotorentrindungsanlage *f* rotary (ring) barker
Rotorentrindungsmaschine *f* rotary (ring) barker
Rotorfräse *f* power tiller
Rotorhacke *f* rotary hoe

Rübenkopf

Rotorkrümler *m* rotary [power] tiller, rototiller, rotary cultivator
Rotormähwerk *n* rotary mower (scythe)
Rotorpflug *m* rotary plough
Rotorrasenmäher *m* rotary lawn-mower
Rotorscheibenmähwerk *n* rotor disk mower
Rotorschneidwerk *n* rotary cutter
Rotorschwader *m* rotary swather
Rotorschwadwender *m* rotary swath turner
Rotorspatenfräse *f* spading rotary cultivator
Rotorstriegel *m* rotary weeder
~/handgeführter rotary hand weeder
Rotorteiler *m* rotary (corkscrew) divider, revolving spiral divider
Rotorwender *m* rotary swath turner
Rototandem *n* rotary tandem milking parlour
Rotpustelkrankheit *f* coral spot *(of woody plants, caused by Nectria cinnabarina)*
Rotrind *n* banteng, Bos javanicus
Rotrock *m* *(hunter's language) s.* Rotfuchs
Rotscheckiger Klopfkäfer *m* death tick, deathwatch [beetle], Xestobium rufovillosum
Rotschwingel *m* red (fine) fescue, Festuca rubra
Rotseuche *f* **der Hechte** pike fry rhabdovirus disease
Rotsprenkelung *f* **der Birne** [pear] red mottle *(virosis)*
Rotstraußgras *n* colonial bent[-grass], common bent[-grass], Agrostis capellaris (tenuis)
rotstreifig red-striped *(e.g. wood)*
Rottaler [Pferd] *n*, **Rottaler Warmblut** *n* Rottal *(horse breed)*
Rotte *f* rot, rotting
Rottemist *m* short dung
rotten to rot, to ret *(flax, hemp)*
Rotteprozeß *m* rotting process
Rottier *n* female deer, hind, [red-deer] doe
Rottweiler *m* Rottweiler *(dog breed)*
Rotulme *f* red (slippery, moose) elm, Ulmus rubra
Rotulmenrinde *f* slippery elm
Rotverfärbung *f* red stain *(of wood)*
Rotvieh *n* 1. Angeln *(cattle breed)*; 2. [Middle] German Red, Red Hill *(cattle breed)*
Rotwanze *f* *(ent)* cotton stainer *(genus Dysdercus)*
Rotwasser *n* *(vet)* red-water [disease], bacillary haemoglobinuria, babesiasis, babesiosis, blackwater
Rotwasserbaum *m* sassy [bark], sassywood, Erythrophleum guineense
Rotwein *m* red wine, claret
Rotwild *n* [red] deer, Cervus elaphus
~/weibliches *s.* Rottier
Rotwildhaltung *f* deer farming
Rotwildrevier *n* deer-forest
Rotwurm *m* gapeworm, Syngamus trachea
Rotz *m* *(vet)* farcy *(caused by Pseudomonas mallei)*
Rotzeder *f*, **Rotzederwacholder** *m* [eastern] red cedar, red juniper, savin[e], Juniperus virginiana

Rotzknoten *m*, **Rotzpustel** *f (vet)* farcy bud (button)
Rouenente *f* Rouen (Rhone) duck *(breed)*
Rouge del' Ouest *n* Eastern Red Pied *(cattle breed)*
Rough Fell *n* Rough Fell, Kendal Rough Sheep *(breed)*
Rous-Sarkom *n (vet)* Rous sarcoma
Rous-Sarkomvirus *n* Rous sarcoma virus
RoWV *s.* Rosenwelkevirus
RPW *s.* Reproduktionswert
RQ *s.* Respirationsquotient
RR *s.* Rollstrangregner
rRNA *s.* RNA/ribosomale
Rsch. *s.* Rappschimmel
RSV *s.* Rous-Sarkomvirus
Rübe *f* 1. beet *(genus Beta)*; 2. beet[root]
Rubefizierung *f (soil)* rubefaction, ferruginization
Rüben... *s. a.* Zuckerrüben...
Rübenälchen *n* beet [cyst] eelworm, Heterodera schachtii
Rübenanbau *m* beet growing
Rübenbauer *m* beet-grower
Rübenausdünngerät *n* beet row thinner
Rübenausdünnmaschine *f* thinning machine
Rübenbestand *m* beet stand
Rübenblätter *npl* beet leaves
Rübenblattlader *m* beet foliage loader, beet top [pick-up] loader
Rübenblattlaus *f* beet aphid, Aphis fabae
Rübenblattschwader *m* beet-top windrower
Rübenblattverteiler *m* beet foliage spreader
Rübenblattwanze *f* beet leaf (lace) bug, Piesma quadratum
Rübenblattzerkleinerer *m* beet-top crusher
Rüben-Cryptic-Virus *n* beet cryptic virus, BCV
Rübenderbrüßler *m* beetroot weevil, Bothynoderes punctiventris
Rübenelevator *m* beet elevator
Rübenerdfloh *m* mangel (mangold) flea beetle, Chaetocnema concinna
Rübenerntemaschine *f* beet harvester
Rübenextraktionsschnitzel *npl* beet pulp, leached cossettes
Rübenfliege *f* beet fly, mangel (mangold) fly, Pegomya betae (hyoscyami)
Rübenfliegenlarve *f* beet (spinach) leaf-miner, Pegomya betae (hyoscyami)
rübenförmig *(bot)* napiform
Rübengabel *f* root crop bucket
Rübengelbnetzvirus *n* beet yellow net virus
Rübengreifer *m* beet grab
Rübenheben *n* lifting of beets
Rübenkerbel *m* bulbous-rooted chervil, parsnip (turnip-rooted) chervil, Chaerophyllum bulbosum
Rübenkern *m*, **Rübenknäuel** *n* beet seed ball
Rübenkopf *m* beet crown
~ mit Blättern beet top

Rübenkopfälchen

Rübenkopfälchen *n* stem eelworm, stem [and bulb] nematode, Ditylenchus dipsaci
Rübenköpflader *m* beet topper-loader
Rübenköpfwerkzeug *n* beet topper
Rübenkörper *m* beet[root]
Rübenkräuselvirus *n* beet leaf curl virus, BLCV, [beet] curly top virus, BCTV, beet kräuselkrankheit virus
Rübenkraut *n* beet leaves
Rübenkrautfänger *m* beet leaf catcher, trash catcher
Rübenladegerät *n*, **Rübenlader** *m* beet loader
Rübenmangold *m s.* Futterrrübe 2.
Rübenmark *n* marc
Rübenmelasse *f* beet molasses
Rübenmosaik *n (phyt)* beet mosaic *(virosis)*
Rübenmosaikvirus *n* beet mosaic virus, BMV
Rübenmotte *f* beet moth, Scrobipalpa (Gnorimoschema, Phthorimaea) ocellatella
Rübenmüdigkeit *f* beet sickness (weariness) *(of soil)*
Rübenmuser *m* beet (root) pulper
Rübennematode *m* beet [cyst] eelworm, Heterodera schachtii
Rübenpektin *n* beet pectin
Rübenpflug *m* beet plough
Rübenprobenehmer *m*, **Rübenprobestecher** *m* beet sampler
Rübenpumpe *f* beet pump *(sugar manufacture)*
Rübenreinigung *f* beet cleaning
Rübenreinigungsgerät *n* beet (root) cleaner
Rübenreps *m s.* Rübsen
Rübenrodegabel *f* beet-lifting fork
Rübenrodegerät *n* beet lifter
Rübenrodelader *m* beet harvester-loader, loading beet lifter
Rübenrodemaschine *f* beet lifter
Rübenrodepflug *m* beet plough
Rübenroder *m* beet lifter
Rübenrohsaft *m* crude beet juice
Rübenrohzucker *m* raw beet sugar, beet raw sugar
Rübenrost *m* [mangold and] beet rust *(caused by Uromyces betae)*
Rübensaatgut *n* beet seed
Rübensamen *m* beet seed
Rübensamenträgerbestand *m* beet seed crop
Rübensammellader *m* beet [pick-up] loader
Rübenschildkäfer *m* tortoise beetle *(genus Cassida)*
Rübenschnecke *f* beet screw
Rübenschneider *m s.* Rübenschnitzelmaschine
Rübenschnitzel *npl* beet slices (chips, pulp), shreds
Rübenschnitzelmaschine *f* beet slicing machine, beet slicer (cutter)
Rübenschnitzelmesser *n* beet slicing knife
Rübenschorf *m (phyt)* beet scab *(caused by Streptomyces scabies)*

Rübenschwanz *m* beet tail
Rübenschwänzeabscheider *m*, **Rübenschwanzfänger** *m* beet tail catcher
Rübenschwemmwasser *n* flume-water
Rübensilage *f* beet silage
Rübenspaten *m s.* Rübenrodegabel
Rübenstapelgerät *n* beet stacker
Rübentrocknung *f* beet drying
Rübenvergilbung *f* beet yellows, yellow virosis of beet
Rübenvollerntemaschine *f* complete beet harvester
Rübenwanze *f* lace bug *(family Piesmidae)*
Rübenwäsche *f* 1. beet cleaning; 2. beet washer
Rübenwaschmaschine *f* beet washer
Rübenweißling *m* cabbage (turnip white) butterfly, Pieris rapae
Rübenwurzelbärtigkeitsvirus *n* beet necrotic yellow vein virus, BNYVV
Rübenzucker *m* beet-sugar, saccharose, sucrose *(from Beta vulgaris var. altissima)*
Rübenzuckerfabrik *f* beet-sugar factory, sugar-beet factory, sugar-beet mill
Rübenzuckerproduktion *f* beet-sugar production
Rübenzünsler *m (ent)* beet web-worm, Loxostege sticticalis
Rübenzystenälchen *n* beet [cyst] eelworm, Heterodera schachtii
Rubidium *n* rubidium
Rubinglimmer *m* lepidocrocite *(non-clay mineral)*
Rüböl *n* rape[-seed] oil, colza-oil
Rubratoxin *n* rubratoxin *(mycotoxin)*
Rübsamen *m* rape-seed, cole[-seed], colza
Rübsen *m* [turnip, summer, bird] rape, navew, wild turnip, Brassica rapa var. sylvestris
Rübsenblattwespe *f* turnip saw-fly, Athalia rosae
Rübsenextraktionsschrot *m* rape-seed [oil] meal
Rübsenöl *n* rape[-seed] oil, colza-oil
Rubus-Gelbnetz *n (phyt)* rubus yellow-net *(virosis)*
Rubus-Stauche *f* rubus stunt *(mycoplasmosis)*
Ruchgras *n* [scented, sweet] vernal grass, Anthoxanthum odoratum
Ruchgrasmosaikvirus *n* anthoxanthum mosaic virus
rückbiegig calf-kneed *(forelimb position)*
Rückbiegigkeit *f* calf-knee conformation, sheep-knee conformation
Rückbildung *f* regression, involution
Rückebogen *m (forest)* [logging, wheeled] arch
Rückeentfernung *f (forest)* skidding distance (length)
Rückefläche *f (forest)* setting
Rückegabel *f (forest)* lizard
Rückegasse *f s.* Rückeweg
Rückehaube *f (forest)* skidding cap, Baptist cone
Rückekapazität *f (forest)* loadsize
Rückekarren *m (forest)* bogie, drag cart, dolly, bummer, jinker
Rückekette *f (forest)* skid[ding] chain, drag chain

Rückelinie f s. Rückeweg
Rückemaschine f **für Drahtseilzug** *(forest)* yarder
Rückemast m *(forest)* spar
Rückemastanlage f *(forest)* high lead
Rückemastverfahren n *(forest)* high-lead [cable] logging, high-lead yarding, highleading
rücken 1. *(forest)* to skid, to remove *(timber)*; 2. to space out *(potted plants)*
~/**mit Seilzug** to cable
Rücken m back, saddle *(animal body)*; saddle *(carcass)* • **mit kurzem** ~ short-coupled *(livestock judging)*
~/**aufgezogener** acute (arched) back
~/**gespaltener** double back
Rücken n *(forest)* skidding, removal
~/**baumweises** full-tree skidding, whole-tree skidding
~/**dickörtiges** butt-end-first skidding
~/**dünnörtiges** top-end-first skidding
~ **ganzer Stämme** tree-length skidding
~ **in aufgesatteltem Zustand** semisuspended skidding
~ **in der Kette** chaining
~/**manuelles** hand skidding
~ **mit Drahtseilzug** yarding
~ **mit Pferden** horse skidding
~ **mit Schleppern** tractor skidding
~ **mit Tieren** animal skidding
~ **ohne Anschlingen der Stämme** chokerless skidding
Rückenfeder f hackle
Rückenfett n back fat *(s. a. Rückenspeck)*
Rückenfettdicke f back fat thickness
Rückenflosse f dorsal fin
Rückenmark n spinal cord (marrow), medulla
Rückenmarkanästhesie f *(vet)* epidural anaesthesia
Rückenmarkentzündung f *(vet)* myelitis
Rückenmarkflüssigkeit f neurolymph
Rückenmarkhaut f meninx
~/**harte** dura mater
Rückenmarkhautentzündung f *(vet)* meningitis
Rückenmoräne f *(soil)* ablation moraine
Rückenmuskel m eye muscle *(of carcass)*
Rückenmuskelfläche f eye muscle area
Rückenplatte f tergite *(of arthropods)*
Rückenriemen m crupper turnback *(of harness)*
Rückenröhrchen n *(ent)* siphuncle, cornicle
Rückensaat f *(forest)* ridge sowing, sowing on ridges
Rückenschwefelgerät n knapsack sulphur duster
Rückenspeck m back fat; fat back *(pork carcass)*
Rückenspeckdicke f [back] fat thickness
Rückenspeckmessung f back fat probe
Rückenspecksonde f back fat probe
Rückenspritze f knapsack sprayer (pump), backpack pump
Rückensprühgerät n knapsack atomizer

Rückenstäubegerät n knapsack (shoulder-mounted) duster
Rückenstück n saddle *(of carcass)*
Rückenverstäuber m s. Rückenstäubegerät
Rückenwinkel m clearance angle *(of cutting tool)*; back angle *(of saw-tooth)*
Rückepfanne f *(forest)* skidding pan (shoe), skidding dish
Rückeschaden m *(forest)* skidding (logging) damage
Rückeschild m *(forest)* [logging] blade • **mit dem** ~ **arbeiten** to blade
Rückeschlepper m *(forest)* skidding tractor, [logging] skidder, wheel[ed] skidder
~/**knickgelenkter** frame-steer[ed] wheeled skidder
~/**selbstladender** self-loading skidder
Rückeschlitten m *(forest)* log-sled[ge], drag sled, bob-sleigh, lizard, dray, scoot, sloop, cat[amaran], travoy
Rückeschneise f s. Rückeweg
Rücketraktor m s. Rückeschlepper
Rückewagen m s. Rückekarren
Rückewanne f s. Rückepfanne
Rückeweg m *(forest)* skid[ding] road, log trail, [skidding] track, logging [chain] road, drag[ging] road, rack[way], travois road
Rückewinde f *(forest)* [skidding] winch, skidder
~/**tragbare** donkey [engine]
Rückezange f *(forest)* skidding grapple (tongs)
Rückfall m *(phyt, vet)* recurrence, recurrency, relapse
Rückfeuchtung f rewetting
rückführen to return, to recycle, to feed back *(e.g. in circulation processes)*
rückgebildet abortive
Rückgewinnung f recovery, reclaim
Rückgrat n backbone, chine
Rückhaltebecken n [detention] reservoir, laying-up basin
Rückholseil n haul-back line, snubbing (receding) line, back (return, trip) line, tail rope *(logging)*
Rückkopplung f feedback
~/**biologische** biofeedback
rückkreuzen to back-cross
Rückkreuzen n back-crossing
Rückkreuzungselter m recurrent parent
Rückkreuzungsnachkommenschaft f back-cross progeny
Rückkreuzungsprodukt n back-cross
Rückkreuzungszüchtung f back-cross breeding
Rücklaufboden m chaffer board, grain pan *(of a thresher)*
Rückmutation f *(gen)* back (return) mutation, reversion
Rückresorption f reabsorption
Rückschlag m 1. kick[back] *(e.g. of a combustion engine)*; 2. s. Rückstoß
rückschneiden to prune (cut) back, to pollard *(e.g. fruit-trees)*

Rückschnitt

Rückschnitt *m* pruning back, pollarding; renewal pruning *(of grape-vines)*
~/schwacher long pruning
~/starker short pruning
Rückschnittpflanze *f* stump [trans]plant, root-and-shoot cutting • **eine ~ setzen** to stump-plant
rucksen to coo *(ring-dove)*
Rücksetzpflug *m* reset plough
Rückstand *m* residue; reject[ion] *(of a grading or sorting process)*
rückständig camped behind *(hindlimb conformation)*
Rückstandsbehandlung *f* residue treatment
rückstandsfrei non-residual
Rückstandshalbwertzeit *f* residue half-life [time] *(of plant protectants)*
rückstandslos non-residual
Rückstandsmenge *f/duldbare* residual tolerance
Rückstandsproblem *n* residue problem
Rückstandssubstrat *n* waste substrate
Rückstandstoxikologie *f* residue toxicology
Rückstandstoxizität *f* residual toxicity
Rückstandswert *m* residual value
Rückstandswirkung *f* residual effect; residual action
Rückstoß *m* kick, backlash, recoil *(e.g. of a sporting gun)*
Rücktrocknung *f* redrying
Rückung *f s.* Rücken *n*
rückwärts gekehrt *(bot)* retrorse
rückwiegen to reweigh
Rückzugsgebiet *n (ecol)* refuge
Rudbeckie *f* coneflower, rudbeckia *(genus Rudbeckia)*
Rüde *m* 1. [male] dog; 2. *(hunt)* boar hound
Rudel *n* herd *(red deer)*; party *(wild boars)*; pack *(hounds or wolves)*
ruderal *(ecol)* ruderal
Ruderalboden *m* ruderal soil
Ruderalpflanze *f* ruderal [plant]
Ruderalstelle *f* ruderal place
Rüdesheimer *m* Rüdesheimer *(wine)*
Rudiment *n* rudiment, vestige
rudimentär rudimentary, vestigial, abortive
Rufocromomycin *n* rufocromomycin *(antibiotic)*
Rufzeicheneule *f* heart and dart moth, Agrotis (Scotia) exclamationis
Ruhe *f* rest *(e.g. of plants)*
~/aitionome *s.* ~/erzwungene
~/echte (endogene) dormancy, true rest
~/erzwungene (exogene) imposed dormancy, quiescence
~/innere *s.* ~/echte
Ruhekern *m* interphase nucleus
Ruheknospe *f* resting (dormant) bud • **aus einer ~ hervorgegangen** epicormic
Ruheperiode *f* rest period, dormant period (season)
Ruhepotential *n* resting potential

Ruhepulsfrequenz *f*, **Ruhepulsrate** *f* resting pulse rate
Ruhespore *f (bot)* hypnospore
Ruhestadium *n* resting stage, dormant period
Ruhestimmung *f* resting mood *(e.g. of aphids)*
Ruhestoffwechsel *m* resting energy exchange, resting metabolic rate; basal metabolism (metabolic rate), basal energy exchange, standard metabolic rate, SMR
Ruhestrom *m* resting potential
Ruhetakt *m* rest (release) phase *(machine milking)*
Ruhezeit *f* resting period
Ruhezustand *m* rest, dormancy
Ruhmesblume *f* 1. glory pea, lobster's claw, clianthus *(genus Clianthus)*; 2. glory pea, Clianthus speciosus (formosus)
Ruhmeskrone *f* gloriosa (glory) lily *(genus Gloriosa)*
Rühmliche Palmlilie *f* moundlily yucca, Spanish-bayonet, Yucca gloriosa
Ruhr *f (vet)* dysentery
Rührdüse *f* agitator nozzle
Rührer *m* agitator, stirrer
Ruhrflohkraut *n* common fleabane, Pulicaria dysenterica
Ruhrkraut *n* everlasting flower, cudweed *(genus Gnaphalium)*
Rührlüfter *m* stirring fan
Rührschneckenförderer *m* paddle screw conveyor
Rührstock *m* oar
Rührwelle *f* agitating (rotating) shaft
Rührwerk *n* agitator, stirrer
Ruke *f (bot)* rocket, Eruca vesicaria ssp. sativa
Ruktus *m* eructation, belching *(of ruminants)*
Rumelische Kiefer (Weymouthskiefer) *f* Macedonian [white] pine, Balkan spruce, Pinus peuce
Rumen *m s.* Pansen
Rumenitis *f (vet)* rumenitis
Rumenotomie *f (vet)* rumenotomy
ruminal ruminal
Rumination *f* rumination, cudding
ruminieren to ruminate, to chew the cud
Ruminitis *f (vet)* rumenitis
Ruminograph *m* rumenograph
Rumpf *m* 1. trunk, barrel, body *(animal anatomy)*; thorax *(of insects)*; 2. [plough-]beam, ploughshaft, leg, frog • **vom ~ entfernt** distal
~/ausgeweideter *(slaught)* carcass, carcase
Rumpfebene *f* penepla[i]n
Rumpflänge *f* body length
Rumpfskelett *n* axial skeleton
Rumpsteak *n* sirloin, *(Am)* rump steak
RuMV *s.* Ruchgrasmosaikvirus
rund round, circular; *(bot, zoo)* orbicular
Rundast *m* round knot
Rundballen *m* round bale
Rundballenabrollgerät *n* bale unroller
Rundballenpresse *f* round (roll) baler, roto-baler

Rundballenschneider *m* round bale cutter
Rundbeet *n* round flower-bed
Rundblattahorn *m* vine maple, Acer circinatum
rundblättrig rotundifolious
Rundblättrige Glockenblume *f (bot)* harebell, bluebell, Campanula rotundifolia
~ **Minze** *f* round-leaved mint, apple mint, Mentha x rotundifolia
Rundblättriger Baumwürger *m* staff-tree, [oriental] bitter-sweet, Celastrus orbiculatus
~ **Sonnentau** *m* common sundew, Drosera rotundifolia
Rundblättriges Hasenohr *n (bot)* round-leaved hare's-ear, Bupleurum rotundifolium
Rundes Cypergras (Nußgras) *n* purple nutsedge, nut grass, *(Am)* coco grass, Cyperus rotundus
Rundfilterchromatographie *f* circular [paper] chromatography
Rundfutterautomat *m* circular self-feeder
Rundherzkrankheit *f* **des Huhns** round-heart disease of fowl, fatal syncope of fowl, toxic heart degeneration of fowl
Rundhocke *f* shock • **Rundhocken aufstellen** to shock, to stook
Rundholz *n* roundwood, round timber, saw logs, *(Am)* lumber
~/**nicht entrindetes** rough timber, timber in the rough
~/**schwaches** small roundwood
Rundholzabwerfer *m* log ejector, [log] kicker
Rundholz-Boardfuß *m* log-scale board foot *(timber mensuration)*
Rundholzbündel *n* bundle of logs
Rundholzbündelung *f* roundwood packaging
Rundholzgreifer *m* timber grab
Rundholzkettenförderer *m* chain logway, log chain conveyor
Rundholzkubiktabelle *f* log rule (scale)
Rundholzlader *m* log loader
Rundholzlagerplatz *m s.* Rundholzplatz
Rundholzmeßanlage *f* volume calculator
Rundholzmeßstab *m* log scale (rule)
Rundholzmessung *f* log scale
Rundholzmeßwert *m* **laut Einschnittabelle** log scale
Rundholzplatz *m* roundwood (log) yard, mill-yard
Rundholzpolter *m* log deck (dump)
~ **am Sägewerk** mill deck
Rundholzsortierung *f* log sorting
Rundholzsortiment *n* roundwood assortment
Rundholzstück *n* billet
Rundholztabelle *f* log rule (scale)
Rundkammpflügen *n* round ridge ploughing
Rundkapseljute *f* [white] jute, Corchorus capsularis
Rundköpfiger Reismehlkäfer *m* long-headed flour beetle, Latheticus oryzae
Rundkrone *f* round head (crown) *(e.g. of fruit-trees)*

Rundlauch *m* round garlic, Allium rotundum
rundlich suborbicular
Rundling *m* billet
Rundlochsieb *n* round-hole screen
Rundmorchel *f* common (true) morel, Morchella esculenta
Rundpflügen *n* roundabout (round-and-round) ploughing, ploughing round and round
Rundraufe *f* round rack
Rundstall *m* round house
Rundtanz *m (api)* round-dance
Rundtischmaschine *f* roundabout *(vegetable processing)*
Rundum[blink]leuchte *f* flashing beacon, rotating light
Rundwurm *m* roundworm, nematode *(class Nematoda)*
Runge *f* stanchion, stay, stake, pin bar
Runkel[rübe] *f* fodder (feeding) beet, mangel[-wurzel], mangold[-wurzel], Beta vulgaris var. alba (crassa)
~/**walzenförmige** tankard mangel
runzelig *(bot, zoo)* rugose
Runzelige Rose *f* ramanas rose, Rosa rugosa
Runzeliger Obstbaumsplintkäfer *m* [fruit-tree] shot-hole borer, fruit[-tree] bark-beetle, Scolytus rugulosus (mediterraneus)
~ **Rübenaaskäfer** *m* black carrion beetle, Aclypea (Blitophaga, Silpha) undata
Runzeligkeit *f* rugosity
rupfen to pluck, to pick, to deplume *(fowl)*
Rupfen *m* burlap, sackcloth, gunny
Rupfen *n* plucking, deplumation
Rupfer *m* plucker
Rupfmaschine *f* [feather-]picking machine, roughing machine, plucker
Ruprechtskraut *n* herb Robert, Geranium robertianum
Ruptur *f (vet)* rupture, rhexis
rural rural, rustic
Ruscusblättrige Sarcococca *f (bot)* fragrant sweet box, Sarcococca ruscifolia
Rußbrand *m (phyt)* burnt ear
Rüssel *m* proboscis *(esp. of insects)*; snout *(of a swine)*
Rüsselbremse *f* pig snare
Rüsselkäfer *m* weevil, snout-beetle, curculio *(family Curculionidae)*
~/**blattminierender** leaf-mining beetle *(comprehensive term)*
Rüsselscheibe *f* disk of snout
Rußfleckenkrankheit *f* sooty blotch *(of apple, caused by Gloeodes pomigena)*
Rußfleckigkeit *f* **der Quitte** quince sooty ring spot *(virosis)*
rußig *(bot)* fuliginous, sooty
Russische Distel *f (bot)* kali, Salsola kali
Russischer Birnbaum *m* Russian pear, Pyrus rossica

Russischer

~ **Traber** *m* Russian Trotter *(horse breed)*
~ **Wein** *m* kangaroo vine, Cissus antarctica
Russisches Winterweizenmosaikvirus *n* winter wheat mosaic virus
Rüßler *m s.* Rüsselkäfer
Rußtau *m (phyt)* sooty mould, dark mildew
Rüster *f* elm *(genus Ulmus)*
Rusterholzsches Sohlengeschwür *n (vet)* ulcer of the sole
Rüsternblasenlaus *f* elm leaf aphid, woolly elm aphid, Byrsocrypta (Tetraneura) ulmi
rustikal rustic, rural
Rute *f* 1. *(bot)* switch, cane, wand, twig; 2. tail; brush, foxtail; 3. *s.* Penis
rutenbildend *(bot)* vimineous
rutenförmig *(bot)* virgate, vimineous
Rutenhirse *f* switch-grass, Panicum virgatum
Rutenkaktus *m* 1. wickerware cactus *(genus Rhipsalis)*; 2. old man's head, Rhipsalis capilliformis
Rutenkrankheit *f* **der Himbeere** spur blight of raspberry *(caused esp. by Didymella applanata)*
Rutenmelde *f* common orach[e], Atriplex patula
Rutensterben *n (phyt)* cane blight *(caused by Leptosphaeria coniothyrium)*
Rutil *m* rutile *(non-clay mineral)*
Rutin *n* rutin *(glycoside)*
Rutsche *f* chute, slide, slip, shoot
Rutschkupplung *f* friction (slip, safety) clutch
Rutschungsschaden *m* landslide damage
Rutte *f (zoo)* burbot, Lota lota
Rüttelboden *m* shaker tray
Rüttelegge *f* reciprocating harrow, power[-driven] harrow, vibrating cultivator
Rüttelkette *f* riddle chain
Rüttelpult *n* special rack for the remuage *(manufacture of sparkling wine)*
Rüttelschaden *m* vibration bruise *(of fruits)*
Rüttelsieb *n* reciprocating sieve, vibrating screen, [oscillating] riddle
Rüttelsiebkette *f* riddle chain
Rüttelsiebroder *m* shaker digger, digger-shaker
Rüttel- und Auffangmaschine *f* shake-and-catch harvester
Rüttelzetter *m* oscillating hay tedder, reciprocating-tine tedder
Rüttelzinkengrubber *m* oscillating tine cultivator
RVFV *s.* Virus der Virösen Fleckigkeit der Rübe
RWC *s.* Wassergehalt/relativer
Ryania *n* ryania *(insecticide)*
Ryeland[schaf] *n* Ryeland *(sheep breed)*

S

S *s.* Sand
Sääggregat *n* seed unit
Saanenziege *f* Saanen *(goat breed)*
Sääpparat *m* seeder
Saat *f* 1. crop[s]; 2. *s.* Aussaat; 3. *s.* Saatgut

~/**auflaufende** emerging (shooting) crop
~/**sprießende** growing crop
Saatband *n* seed tape (band)
Saatbandeinzelkornsämaschine *f* seed tape spacing drill
Saatbandlegemaschine *f* seed tape planter
Saatbauberater *m* fieldman
Saatbeet *n* [nursery] seed-bed, seed-plot
Saatbeetpflanze *f* bedding plant
Saatbett *n* seed[ing]-bed
Saatbettbereitung *f* seed-bed preparation, secondary tillage
Saatbettbereitungsgerät *n* seed-bed conditioner
Saatbettbereitungskombination *f s.* Saatbettkombination
Saatbettbewässerung *f* seed-bed watering
Saatbettfräse *f* full-width rotary cultivator
Saatbettkombination *f* seed-bed preparing combination, seed-bed combination [implement]
Saatbettverdichtung *f*, **Saatbettverfestigung** *f* seed-bed compaction
Saatbettvorbereitung *f s.* Saatbettbereitung
Saatbrett *n (forest)* sowing board
Saatcontainer *m* seedling (plant) tray, flat
Saatdichte *f* sowing density
Saategge *f* drill harrow, [extra-light] seed-harrow, seed-bed harrow
Saatenanerkennung *f* seed certification
Saatenfliege *f* bean [seed] fly, Delia (Phorbia) platura
Saatenfliegenlarve *f* seed-corn maggot
Saaterbse *f* pea, Pisum sativum ssp. sativum convar. sativum
Saatfurche *f* seed furrow
Saatgans *f* bean goose, Anser fabalis
Saatgemisch *n* seed[s] mixture
Saatgerste *f* [common] barley, Hordeum vulgare
Saatgetreide *n* seed[ing] grain, seed-corn, cereal seed
Saatgetreideproduktion *f* seed grain production
Saatgrasland *n* sown grassland, ley, lea
Saatgrasheu *n* seeds (hard) hay
Saatgrasweide *f* sown (seeded) pasture
Saatgut *n* seed[s], seed stock *(s. a.* Saatgetreide*)*
• ~ **erzeugen** to grow seed
~/**anerkanntes** certified seed
~/**depelliertes** rubbed seed
~/**eigenerzeugtes** home-saved seed
~/**forstliches** forest seed
~/**inkrustiertes** coated seed
~/**kalibriertes** calibrated seed [stock], graded seed
~/**keimfähiges** viable seed
~/**keimunfähiges** dead seed, non-viable seed[s]
~/**monogermes** monogerm seed
~/**osmosekonditioniertes** osmoconditioned seed
~/**pilliertes** pelleted (pilled) seed; coated seed
~/**poliertes** rubbed seed
~/**segmentiertes** segmented seed
~/**sortiertes** *s.* ~/kalibriertes

Saatluzerne

~/umhülltes coated seed
~/unaufbereitetes raw seed[s], natural seed
Saatgutalter *n* seed age
Saatgutanerkennung *f*, **Saatgutattestierung** *f* seed certification
Saatgutaufbereitung *f* seed processing
Saatgutaufbereitungsanlage *f* seed processing plant
Saatgutbegasung *f* seed fumigation
Saatgutbehälter *m* seed[ing] box, grain box
Saatgutbehandlung *f* 1. seed treatment; 2. *s.* Saatgutbeizung
~/osmotische osmotic pretreatment (priming) of seed, seed priming
Saatgutbeize *f s.* 1. Saatgutbeizmittel; 2. Saatgutbeizung
Saatgutbeizer *m* [seed] dresser, seed dressing machine, seed treater (treating machine)
Saatgutbeizmittel *n* [seed] dressing, seed disinfectant (protectant)
~ aus organischen Quecksilberverbindungen organomercury seed dressing
~/pulverförmiges seed dressing powder
Saatgutbeizung *f* [seed] dressing, seed disinfection
Saatgutbereiter *m s.* Saatgutreiniger
Saatgutbereitstellung *f* seed procurement
Saatgutbeschaffung *f* seed procurement
Saatgutbestand *m* seed[-producing] stand
Saatgutdesinfektion *f* seed disinfection
Saatgutdesinfektionsmittel *n* seed disinfectant
Saatgutdesinfestation *f* seed disinfestation
Saatgutdosierer *m*, **Saatgutdosiervorrichtung** *f* seed-meter[ing device]
Saatgutdrillmaschine *f* seed drill
Saatguteinbettungsvorrichtung *f* seed burying device
Saatguteinweichung *f* seed soaking
Saatgutentseuchung *f* seed disinfection
Saatgutentwesung *f* seed disinfestation
Saatgutertrag *m* seed yield
Saatguterzeuger *m* seed producer
Saatguterzeugung *f* seed production
Saatguterzeugungsfläche *f* seed-producing area, seed-production area
Saatgutfonds *m* seed fund
Saatgutgesundheitsprüfung *f* seed health testing
Saatgutgewinnung *f* seed collection (harvest)
Saatguthandel *m* seed trade
Saatguthändler *m* seed's merchant, seedsman
Saatgutherkunft *f* seed source, seed origin (provenance), source of seed
Saatgutimpfung *f* seed inoculation
~ mit Bakterien seed bacterization
Saatgutinfektion *f* seed infection
Saatgutinkrustiermittel *n* seed coating
Saatgutinkrustierung *f* seed coating [treatment]
Saatgutkalibrierer *m* seed grader
Saatgutkalibrierung *f* seed grading

Saatgutkonditionierung *f*/**osmotische** osmoconditioning of seed
Saatgutkontrolle *f* seed control
Saatgutlagerung *f* seed storage
Saatgutlieferant *m* seed dealer
Saatgutmischung *f* seed[s] mixture
Saatgutpartie *f* seed lot
Saatgutpelletierung *f s.* Saatgutpillierung
Saatgutpille *f* pelleted seed
Saatgutpilliermittel *n* seed coating
Saatgutpillierung *f* pelleting (coating) of seeds, seed pelleting [treatment]
Saatgutprobe *f* seed sample
Saatgutprüfer *m* seed inspector
Saatgutprüfung *f* seed test[ing]
Saatgutqualität *f* seed quality
Saatgutreiber *m* seeding grain rasper; clover huller (rasper)
Saatgutreinheit *f* seed purity
Saatgutreiniger *m* seed cleaner, seed-cleaning machine (plant)
~/elektrischer electrical seed cleaner
~/elektromagnetischer [electro]magnetic seed cleaner
~/elektrostatischer electrostatic seed cleaner
Saatgutreinigung *f* seed cleaning
Saatgutreinigungsmaschine *f s.* Saatgutreiniger
Saatgut[rüttel]sieb *n* seed riddle
Saatgutsortierer *m*, **Saatgutsortiermaschine** *f* seed sorter (grader)
Saatgutsortierung *f* seed sorting
Saatguttrockenbeizmittel *n* dry seed dressing
Saatguttrockenbeizung *f* dry seed dressing (treatment), dust treatment
saatgutübertragen seed-borne (*e.g.* pests)
Saatgutuntersuchung *f* seed test[ing]
Saatgutvermehrer *m* seed grower (producer)
Saatgutvermehrung *f* seed growing (agriculture), seed propagation (multiplication)
Saatgutwahl *f* choice of seed
Saatgutwirtschaft *f* seed industry
~/forstliche forest seed production
Saatgutzertifikation *f* seed certification
Saathafer *m* common oat[s], [cultivated] oat', Avena sativa
Saatkamp *m* (*forest*) seedling nursery
Saatkartoffel *f* seed potato
Saatkasten *m* [seed] hopper, seed[ing] box, drill (grain) box
Saatkiste *f* seed tray, [seed] flat
Saatkistenfüllmaschine *f* flat filler
Saatkistenwagen *m* seed tray trolley
Saatkorn *n* seed-corn
Saatkrähe *f* rook, crow, Corvus frugilegus
Saatlatte *f* (*forest*) sowing lath
Saatleitung *f*, **Saatleitungsrohr** *n* seed[-drill] tube, grain-tube, coulter (seed-drop) tube
Saatluzerne *f* alfalfa, [blue] lucern[e], purple medic[k], Medicago sativa [ssp. sativa]

Saatmais

Saatmais *m (Am)* seed-corn
Saatmenge *f* sowing (planting) rate
Saatmethode *f* sowing method
Saatmischung *f* seed[s] mixture
Saatpflug *m* seeding plough
Saatplatterbse *f* chickling [pea, vetch], chick-pea, grass pea [vine], Spanish pea, Lathyrus sativus
Saatplatz *m (forest)* seed spot, sowing point
Saatquartier *n (forest)* seedling section
Saatreihe *f* seed row
Saatreis *m* rice, Oryza sativa
Saatrille *f* drill [furrow]
Saatroggen *m* rye, Secale cereale
Saatschale *f* seed pan (cup)
Saatschnur *f* seed tape
Saatschnureinzelkornsämaschine *f* seed tape spacing drill
Saatschutzmittel *n* seed protectant
~ **gegen Vögel** bird repellent
Saatstärke *f* sowing (planting) rate
Saattechnik *f* sowing technique
Saattermin *m* seeding date, sowing (planting) date
Saattiefe *f* sowing (drilling) depth, planting depth, depth of sowing
Saattrichter *m* seed port
Saatverfahren *n* sowing method
Saatweide *f* sown pasture
Saatweizen *m* [common, bread] wheat, soft wheat, Triticum aestivum (vulgare)
Saatwicke *f* common vetch, tare, Vicia sativa ssp. sativa
Saatwucherblume *f* corn marigold (chrysanthemum), yellow boy (ox-eye), Chrysanthemum segetum
Saatzeit *f* seed-time, sowing period (time, season), planting season (time)
Saatzeitversuch *m* sowing time trial
Saatzucht *f* seed growing (agriculture), seed improvement
Saatzuchtanstalt *f* seed cultivation station
Saatzuchtbetrieb *m* seed breeding enterprise
~/**forstlicher** forest seed establishment
Saatzuchtstation *f* seed breeding station
Sabadill *m*, **Sabadille** *f (bot)* sabadilla, Schoenocaulon officinale
Sabadillsamen *m* sabadilla seed
Sabaigras *n* sabai grass, Eulaliopsis binata
säbelbeinig sickle-hocked *(hindlimb conformation)*
Säbelbeinigkeit *f* sickle hocks, curby conformation
säbelblättrig acinacifolious
Säbelschar *n* stub runner [shoe], subopener
Säbelwuchs *m* sweep (of a tree-trunk)
Sabinen *n* sabinene *(terpenoid)*
Sabin-Feldman-Test *m* Sabin-Feldman dye test *(for toxoplasmosis)*
Sabouraud-[Glucose-]Agar *m* Sabouraud's glucose peptone agar
Saccharase *f* beta-fructofuranosidase, sucrase *(enzyme)*
Saccharid *n* saccharide, carbohydrate

Saccharifikation *f* saccharification, saccharization
saccharifizieren to saccharify, to saccharize
Saccharifizierung *f s.* Saccharifikation
Saccharimeter *n* saccharimeter, saccharometer
Saccharimetrie *f* saccharimetry
saccharimetrisch saccharimetric
Saccharin *n* saccharin, benzoic sulphimide *(artificial sweetener)*
saccharolytisch saccharolytic
Saccharomyzet *m* yeast fungus *(order Saccharomycetales)*
Saccharopindehydrogenase *f* saccharopine dehydrogenase *(enzyme)*
Saccharose *f* saccharose, sucrose; beet-sugar; cane-sugar *(for compounds s. under Zucker)*
Saccharosealphaglucosidase *f* sucrose alpha-glucosidase, sucrase *(enzyme)*
Saccharoseglucosyltransferase *f s.* Saccharosephosphorylase
Saccharosephosphatsynthase *f*, **Saccharosephosphat-UDP-Glucosyltransferase** *f* sucrose-phosphate synthase, sucrosephosphate-UDP glucosyltransferase *(enzyme)*
Saccharosephosphorylase *f* sucrose phosphorylase (glucosyltransferase) *(enzyme)*
Saccharosesynthase *f*, **Saccharose-UDP-Glucosyltransferase** *f* sucrose synthase *(enzyme)*
Saccharum *n s.* Zucker
Sack *m* sack, bag; pocket *(esp. for hop)*
sackartig saccate, testicular, testiculate[d]
Sackaufhalter *m* bag holder
Sackaufzug *m* sack hoist, bag[ger] elevator
Sackbegasung *f* sack fumigation
Sackbrut *f (api, vet)* sac brood *(caused by Morator aetatulae)*
Säckelblume *f* Californian lilac, ceanothus *(genus Ceanothus)*
Sackentleerungsgerät *n* bag-emptier
sackförmig *(bot, zoo)* sacciform
Sackgut *n* bag cargo
Sackhalter *m* bag holder
Sackheber *m* sack lifter
Sackkarre *f* sack barrow
Sackkultur *f* bag culture *(esp. of mushrooms)*
Sackladung *f* bag cargo
Sacklagerung *f* sack storage
Sackleinen *n* sackcloth, burlap, gunny • **in** ~ **einbinden** to burlap *(e.g. root balls)*
Sackniere *f (vet)* hydronephrosis
Sackrutsche *f* sack chute
Sackschildlaus *f (ent)* greenhouse orthezia, lantana bug, Orthezia insignis
Sacksilage *f* bagged silage
Sackspinner *m* bagworm moth *(family Coleophoridae)*
Sackspinnerlarve *f* bagworm, basket worm
Sackstapler *m* bag piler
Sackstoffkette *f* sacking warp *(kind of jute)*
Sackstoffschuß *m* sack weft *(kind of jute)*

Sackträgermotte f *(ent)* 1. case-bearer *(genus Coleophora)*; 2. s. Sackspinner
Sacktrockner m [in-]sack dryer
Sacktuch n [aus Jute] tarpaulin, tarp *(s. a.* Sackleinen*)*
sackweise by bags; in sacks
Sackzunähmaschine f bag closure sewing machine
Saddle Horse n American saddle horse *(breed)*
Sadebaum m *(bot)* savin[e], Juniperus sabina
Säeinheit f sowing unit, seed[er] unit
säen to sow, to seed, to plant, to bed *(s. a.* under aussäen*)*
~/auf Endpflanzenbestand to sow to stand
~/im Quadratnestverband to check-row
~/in Rillen to drill
~/reihenweise to drill
~/zu dicht to oversow, to overseed
Säen n sowing, seeding
~ in breitem Reihenabstand broad drill sowing
~ in Reihen drilling
Safari f safari
Saflor m *(bot)* 1. safflower *(genus Carthamus)*; 2. safflower, Carthamus tinctorius
Safloröl n safflower oil
Saflorölextraktionsschrot m, **Saflorölkuchenmehl** n safflower oil-meal
Saflorsamen m safflower seed
Saflorsamenöl n safflower oil
Safran m 1. saffron *(flavouring, dyestuff)*; 2. s. Safrankrokus
Safranblütennarbe f saffron
Safranin n safranin[e] *(dyestuff)*
Safrankrokus m saffron [crocus], Crocus sativus
Safranschirmpilz m shaggy parasol, Macrolepiota rhacodes
Safranwurz f *(bot)* curcuma *(genus Curcuma)*
Safrol n safrole *(phenolic ether)*
Saft m sap *(of plants)*; juice *(of fruits, vegetable)*
~/geschiedener limed juice *(sugar manufacture)*
~/vorgeschiedener prelimed juice *(sugar manufacture)*
Saftabfluß m seepage *(of a dunghill)*
Saftabscheider m juice separator (extractor)
Saftaufstieg m sap ascent *(in plants)*
Saftausfluß m s. Saftbluten
Saftbildung f sap production
Saftbluten n sap bleeding, exudation of sap
Saftdrüse f *(bot)* nectary
Saftextraktion f juice extraction
Saftfaden m paraphysis *(of fungal fructifications)*
Saftfluß m s. Saftbluten
saftfrisch green, verdant *(wood)*
Saftfutter[mittel] n forage (succulent) feed, succulence
Saftgewinnung f sap extraction
saftgrün green *(wood)*
saftig 1. sappy *(e.g. a stem)*; 2. juicy, succulent *(e.g. fruit)*; 3. lush, succulent *(grass, meadow)*

Saftigkeit f juiciness, succulence, succulency
saftreich s. saftig 2.
Saftreinigung f juice purification
Saftstrom m sap flow, circulation (flow) of sap *(in plants)*
~/absteigender descending sap
~/aufsteigender ascending sap
Saftzeit f sap-flow period
Säge f saw
~/Giglische *(vet)* Gigli saw
~/hin- und hergehende reciprocating saw
Sägeaufwärtsgang m upstroke of saw
Sägeblatt n [saw-]blade; saw disk
Sägeblättling m *(bot)* scaly lentinus, Lentinus squamosus
sägeblättrig *(bot)* serratifolious
Sägeblattspannen n und -richten n stretch rolling
Sägeblattspannung f saw-blade tension
Sägeblattüberstand m saw-blade projection
Sägebloch m, **Sägeblock** m saw (head rig) log
Sägebock m saw[ing]-horse, [saw]buck, saw[ing] stool, trestle
Sägedraht m **des Fetotoms** *(vet)* embryotomy wire
Sägefeilmaschine f saw filing machine
Sägegatter n log frame [saw], sash gang [saw], saw-frame, saw-gate, mill saw
Sägegin m saw gin *(cotton processing)*
Sägegrube f saw-pit
Sägeholz n sawmill wood, saw logs
Sägeindustrie f saw[mill]ing industry, *(Am)* lumber industry
Sägekette f saw chain
Sägeleistung f saw output
Sägemaschine f sawing machine
Sägemehl n sawdust, sawings, saw swarf
Sägemehlsubstrat n sawdust substrate
Sägemühle f s. Sägewerk
sägen to saw
Sägengestell n saw rack (bench)
Sägenpfleger m, **Sägenschärfer** m saw-doctor
Sägerahmen m [saw-]frame, sash, gate
sägerauh rough[-sawn], unwrought, straight from the saw *(timber)*
Sägerundholz n saw timber (logs)
Sägeschärffeile f saw [sharpening] file
Sägeschienenspitze f [bar] nose
Sägeschuffel f saw-edged push and pull hoe
Sägeschwert n [guide] bar, guide plate, sword *(of a chain-saw)*
Sägespäne mpl sawdust, sawings, saw swarf
Sägespänebrikett n sawdust briquette
Sägespäneleber f sawdust liver *(of fattening cattle due to malnutrition)*
Sägewerk n sawmill, mill, *(Am)* lumber mill
~/fliegendes [trans]portable [saw]mill
~ mit Anlagen zur Holzverschiffung cargo sawmill

Sägewerk

~ mit zwei **Blockbandsägemaschinen** double-band sawmill
~ /**mobiles** mobile [saw]mill
~ ohne **Klotzteich** dry sawmill
~ /**ortsfestes (stationäres)** stationary [saw]mill
~ /**umsetzbares** s. ~/fliegendes
Sägewerker m, **Sägewerksarbeiter** m saw[y]er, sawmill operator
Sägewespe f saw-fly (genus Hoplocampa)
Sägewespenlarve f saw-fly caterpillar
Sägezahn m [saw] tooth
~/**auswechselbarer** bit
~/**gestauchter** swaged (swage-set) tooth
sägezahnartig (bot, zoo) saw-toothed, serrated
Sägezahnrücken m heel
Sägezahnteilung f saw pitch
Saginatus-Zystizerkose f des Rindes (vet) bovine cysticercosis (caused by Cysticercus bovis)
Sago m(n) sago [flour]
Sagobaum m, **Sagopalme** f sago[-tree], common sago-palm, Metroxylon sagu
Saguarokaktus m saguaro [cactus], organ-pipe cactus, Carnegiea gigante
Sahne f [dairy] cream
~/**saure** sour (cultured) cream
Sahnepulver n cream powder
sahnig creamy
Saibling m 1. char[r] (genus Salvelinus); 2. brook trout, Salvelinus fontinalis
Saigonzimtbaum m Saigon cassia (cinnamon), Cinnamomum loureirii
Saint Leger n St. Leger (horse racing)
Saintpaulie f African violet, saintpaulia, Saintpaulia ionantha
Saisonalität f seasonality
Saisonarbeiter m casual worker, migrant [worker]
Saisonarbeitskräfte fpl migrant labour
Saisongebundenheit f seasonality
Saisonwald m seasonal forest
Saisonweide f seasonal pasture
Sake m sake, saki, rice wine
Sakerfalke m s. Würgfalke
Sakije f sakieh, sakiyeh (water-wheel for irrigation purposes, esp. in Egypt)
Sakroiliakalgelenk n (zoo) sacroiliac articulation (joint)
Saksaul m (bot) saxaul (genus Haloxylon)
Saktosalpinx f (vet) hydrosalpinx
Sal m s. Salbaum
Saladin[kasten]mälzerei f Saladin [box] malting, box (compartment) malting
Saladinweiche f Saladin steep
Salai[baum] m Indian frankincense, Boswellia serrata
Salamanderbaum m Chinese laurel, Antidesma bunius
Salat m lettuce, salad, Lactuca sativa
Salatblätter npl lettuce

Salatbreitadernvirus n lettuce big vein virus, LBVV
Salaterntemaschine f lettuce harvester
Salatfäule f lettuce rot
Salatgemüse n salad vegetable (crop)
Salatgurke f slicing cucumber
Salatkopf m lettuce head
Salatlaus f [currant-]lettuce aphid, Nasonovia ribisnigri
Salatmosaik n lettuce mosaic (virosis)
Salatmosaikvirus n lettuce mosaic virus, LMV
Salatpflanze f salad plant (crop)
Salatpflanzmaschine f mit **Handeinlage** hand-fed lettuce seedling block transplanter
Salatrapünzchen n corn (field) salad, Valerianella locusta
Salatrübe f s. Rote Beete
Salatvergilbungsvirus n lettuce yellows virus
Salatwurzellaus f lettuce root aphid, poplar aphid, Pemphigus bursarius
Salatzichorie f chic[k]ory, witloof [chicory], succory, Cichorium intybus var. foliosum
Salatzwiebel f salad onion
Salbaum m (bot) sal, Shorea robusta
Salbe f (vet) ointment, unguent, salve
Salbei m(f) 1. sage, clary, salvia (genus Salvia); 2. [garden] sage, Salvia officinalis; 3. sage (flavouring, drug)
Salbeiblättriger Birnbaum m sage-leaved pear, Pyrus salvifolia
Salbeigamander m wood germander, Teucrium scorodonia
Salharz n sal resin (from Shorea robusta)
Salicin n salicin (glycoside)
Salicylat n salicylate
Salicylsäure f salicylic acid, (o-)hydroxybenzoic acid
Salicylsäuremethylester m methyl salicylate, sweet birch oil (fungicide)
salin[ar], salinisch saline
Salinität f salinity (e.g. of a soil)
Salinomycin n salinomycin (antibiotic)
Saliva f s. Speichel
Salivation f salivation, slobbers
Salmiak m salmiac, ammonium chloride
Salmiakgeist m ammonia [water], aqueous ammonia
Salmling m s. Smolt
Salmonellaerkrankung f s. Salmonellose
Salmonella-gallinarum-Infektion f (vet) fowl typhoid (caused by Salmonella gallinarum)
Salmonella-pullorum-Infektion f (vet) pullorum disease (caused by Salmonella pullorum)
Salmonelle f salmonella (genus Salmonella)
Salmonellose f (vet) salmonellosis, salmonella disease (infection), keel disease
salmonoid salmonoid
Salmonide m salmonoid (family Salmonidae)
Salmonidenregion f salmonoid region

Salomon[s]siegel *n(m)* 1. Solomon's seal, seal-wort *(genus Polygonatum)*; 2. Solomon's seal, seal-wort, Polygonatum odoratum (officinale)
Salpeter *m* saltpetre
Salpetersäure *f* nitric acid
Salpeterstrauch *m* nitre bush *(genus Nitraria)*
Salpingitis *f (vet)* salpingitis
Salsamenschrot *m* sal seed meal
Salsolin *n* salsoline *(alkaloid)*
Saluki *m* saluki, Arabian gazelle-hound *(breed)*
Saluretikum *n (vet)* diuretic
Salweide *f* [common, goat, great] sallow, goat (hedge) willow, Salix caprea
Salz *n* 1. salt; 2. *s.* Kochsalz
~/kohlensaures carbonate
Salzanreicherung *f* salt accumulation
Salzausscheidung *f* salt excretion
Salzbad *n* brine bath *(e.g. in cheese-making)*
Salzbadsalzen *n* brine salting
Salzbaum *m* mangrove *(genus Avicennia)*
Salzbinse *f* arrow-grass *(genus Triglochin)*
Salzboden *m* halomorphic (saline) soil; alkali[ne] soil
Salzbodenpflanze *f* halophyte
Salzbodenvegetation *f* halophytic vegetation
Salzburger Steinschaf *n* [Salzburg] Steinschaf *(sheep breed)*
Salzdrüse *f* salt gland
salzempfindlich salt-sensitive
Salzempfindlichkeit *f* salt sensitivity
salzen to salt, to cure, to corn
Salzexkretion *f* salt excretion
Salzfieber *n (vet)* salt fever
Salzflora *f* halophytic vegetation
salzführend saliferous, saline
Salzgleichgewicht *n* salt balance *(e.g. of milk)*
Salzhaltigkeit *f* salinity
~ des Bodens soil salinity
Salzhaushalt *m* mineral balance
Salzhunger *m (vet)* salt hunger
salzig salty, saline
Salziger Igelbusch *m (bot)* salt anabasis, Anabasis salsa
Salzigkeit *f* salinity *(e.g. of a soil)*
Salzkraut *n* 1. glasswort *(genus Salsola)*; 2. Russian thistle (tumbleweed), Salsola australis, Salsola iberica (kali var. tenuifolia); 3. kali, Salsola kali
Salzlake *f* brine, pickle
Salzlakenkäse *m* brine-ripened cheese
Salzlecke *f* salt (deer) lick
Salzleckstein *m* cattle (salt) lick
salzliebend halophilous
Salzlösung *f* salt (saline) solution
Salzmarsch *f* salt[-marsh]
Salzpflanze *f* halophyte
salzresistent salt-resistant
Salzresistenz *f* salt resistance
Salzsäure *f* hydrochloric acid

Salzsäureauszug *m* hydrochloric acid extract
Salzsäuresekretion *f* hydrochloric acid secretion
Salzsteppenboden *m* white alkali soil, solonchak
Salzstreß *m* salt stress
salztolerant salt-tolerant
Salztoleranz *f* salt tolerance
salzverträglich *s.* salztolerant
Salzwasser *n* salt (saline) water
Salzwassermarsch *f* salt[-marsh]
Salzwermut *m* maritime wormwood, Artemisia maritima
Salzwüste *f* saline desert
Sämaschine *f* seeding (planting) machine, seeder, sower, planter
~/pneumatische pneumatic seeder (planter), air seeder (planter), vacuum seeder
Sambar *m* sambar deer, Cervus unicolor
Same *m s.* Samen
Sämechanismus *m* seeding mechanism
Samen *m* 1. *(bot)* seed; 2. *s.* Sperma • **aus ~ gezogen** maiden *(plant)* • **~ bilden** to seed • **~ entfernen** to seed *(fruits)* • **~ enthaltend** seeded • **~ erzeugen** to seed • **in ~ schießen** to go (run) to seed • **mit glattschaligem ~** smooth-seeded • **mit runzligem ~** wrinkle-seeded
~/nicht keimfähiger dead seed
~/ölhaltiger oil-seed
~/tauber empty (dead) seed
~/vollkörniger full seed
Samenabfall *m* seed fall
Samenalter *n* seed age
Samenanalyse *f* analysis of seeds
Samenanlage *f (bot)* ovule; seed bud
Samenansatz *m* seed set[ting]
Samenansatzvermögen *n* seed-setting capacity
Samenatlas *m* seed atlas
Samenauffangvorrichtung *f* seed trap
Samenausbreitung *f* seed dispersal (spreading)
~ durch Fische ichthyochory
~ durch Reptilien saurochory
~ durch Vögel ornithochory
Samenausfall *m* seed shedding • **durch ~ angesät** self-sown
Samenband *n* seed tape (band)
Samenbank *f* sperm bank
Samenbau *m* seed growing (agriculture)
Samenbaum *m (forest)* seed (mother) tree, seed bearer
Samenbaumwolle *f* seed cotton
Samenbehälter *m (zoo)* receptacle
Samenbeize *f* seed dressing
Samenbestand *m* seed stand
Samenbildung *f* seed formation
Samenblase *f (zoo)* seminal vesicle
Samenblasendrüse *f* vesicular gland
Samenblasenflüssigkeit *f* seminal (testicular) fluid
Samenblatt *n* seed (seminal, embryonic) leaf, seed-lobe, cotyledon
Samenbruch *m (vet)* spermatocele

samenbürtig

samenbürtig seed-borne
Samendarre f (forest) seed-extraction plant, seed extractory (kiln); cone dryer
samenecht true from seed, straight
Sameneiweiß n seed protein
Samenentflüg[e]ler m dewinger, dewinging machine
Samenentnahme f semen collection
Samenepithel n (zoo) seminiferous (spermatogenic, germinal) epithelium
Samenerguß m ejaculation
Samenernte f seed harvest (collection)
Samenertrag m seed yield
Samenfall m seed fall
Samenfaser f seed fibre
Samenfehljahr n (forest) non-seed year
Samenfett n seed fat
Samenfrucht f seed crop
Samenfüllung f seed filling (plant physiology)
Samengewinnung f seed production (collection)
Samenhaar n seed hair
Samenhändler m seed dealer
Samenherkunft f seed source (origin, provenance)
Samenhülle f s. Hülle der Samenanlage
Samenhülse f seed (pod, hull, husk) (s. a. Samenkapsel)
Samenimpfung f seed inoculation
Samenjahr n (forest) seed (mast, cone) year
Samenkäfer m seed (pulse) beetle, bruchid, weevil (family Bruchidae)
Samenkanälchen n testicular tubule, seminiferous tube
Samenkapsel f seed (seminal) capsule; [seed] boll (e.g. of cotton) • **Samenkapseln abstreifen** to boll
Samenkeimung f seed germination
~ **auf (in) der Mutterpflanze** viviparity, viviparousness
Samenkeimungsapparat m seed germinator
Samenkern m [seed] kernel, pip (of fruits) • **Samenkerne enthaltend** acinaceous
Samenklee m seed[-bearing] clover
Samenklengung f (forest) seed extraction
Samenknäuel n seed cluster (ball)
Samenkorn n seed [grain], corn
Samenkultur f seed crop
Samenlack m seed-lac
Samenlänge f seed length
Samenleiste f (bot) placenta
Samenleiter m spermaduct, deferent duct (animal anatomy)
Samenleiterdurchtrennung f (vet) vasotomy
samenlos seedless
Samenlosigkeit f seedlessness
Samenmantel m (bot) seed-coat, aril • **von einem ~ umgeben** arillate[d]
Samenmasse f seed weight
Samenmotte f seed (brown house) moth, Hofmannophila pseudospretella

Samenmuster n seed sample
Samennaht f (bot) raphe
Samenöl n seed oil
Samenpathologie f seed pathology
Samenpelargonie f seed[-propagated] geranium
Samenpflanze f seed[-bearing] plant, seed bearer, flowering plant, flowerer, spermatophyte, phanerogam (division Spermatophyta)
Samenphysiologie f seed physiology
Samenplantage f [forest] seed orchard, tree seed plantation (garden)
Samenplasma n seminal plasma
Samenprobe f seed sample
Samenproduktion f seed production
Samenprotein n seed protein
Samenprüfung f seed test[ing], analysis of seeds
Samenqualität f seed quality
Samenreife f seed ripeness (maturity)
Samenreifung f seed maturation
Samenreproduktion f s. Samenvermehrung
Samenruhe f [seed, embryo] dormancy • ~ **haltend** dormant
Samensammlung f seed collection
Samenschale f (bot) seed-coat, testa
~/**fleischige** sarcotesta
~/**stachelige** bur[r]
Samenschalenwucherung f (bot) strophiole
Samenschlag m (forest) seeding felling, seed cut[ting]
Samenschrumpfung f seed shrivelling
Samenschuppe f seed scale
Samenschutz m seed protection
Samenspeicherprotein n seed storage protein
Samenstauung f (vet) spermiostasis
Samenstickstoff m seed nitrogen
Samenstrang m spermatic cord
Samentasche f (zoo) spermatheca, receptacle
samentragend seed-bearing, seminiferous
Samenträger m seed-bearing plant, seed bearer (s. a. Samenpflanze)
Samenträgerkultur f seed crop
Samenüberdauerung f seed survival
samenübertragbar seed-transmissible
Samenübertragbares Erbsenmosaikvirus n pea seed-borne mosaic virus, PSbMV
samenübertragen seed-borne (e.g. pests)
samenübertragend seminiferous
Samenübertragung f seed-transmission
Samenunkraut n seedling weed
Samenverbreiter m seed disperser
Samenverbreitung f seed dispersal (spreading)
Samenverdünner m semen diluent [additive], semen extender
Samenverfärbungsvirus n **der Ackerbohne** broad bean stain virus
Samenvermehrung f seed propagation (multiplication), seedage
Samenzählgerät n seed counter

Samenzelle f sperm [cell], spermatozoon, spermatozoan, androgamete, microgamete
Samenzellenbildung f spermatogenesis, spermiogenesis, sperm formation
Samenzucht f seed improvement
Samenzünsler m Japanese grain moth, Paralispa gularis
Samenzwiebel f seed onion
Sämerei f seed
Sämereien fpl [fine] seeds, seed stock
Sämling m seedling, plant
~/**einjähriger** yearling
~ **mit verzweigtem Wurzelsystem** branch-rooted seedling
~/**unverschulter** seedling plant
Sämlingsalter n seedling age
Sämlingsausbeute f seedling percent[age]
Sämlingsbeet n seedling bed
Sämlingsfäule f seedling rot
Sämlingsjahr n seedling year (of Shorea robusta)
Sämlingspalette f plant tray
Sämlingsunterlage f seedling rootstock (tree stock)
Sammelbalgfrucht f pome (pomaceous) fruit
Sammelbehälter m bin, collecting vessel
Sammelbiene f foraging (harvesting) bee, forager
Sammelboden m collecting (receiving) board, grain pan (of a thresher)
Sammelbucht f collecting pen (sheep husbandry)
Sammelbunker m bulk hopper
Sammelexpedition f collecting expedition
Sammelfrucht f (bot) compound (collective, aggregate) fruit, etaerio
Sammelgebiet n 1. gathering ground; 2. s. Wassereinzugsgebiet
Sammelgraben m collecting trench
Sammelhieb m (forest) salvage felling, salvaging, sanitation (sanitary) felling
Sammellader m pick-up loader
Sammelmilch f bulk milk
Sammelmilchbehandlung f bulk-milk handling
Sammelmilchtank m bulk-milk tank
sammeln to collect, to [in]gather, to pick
~/**Beeren** to berry
~ **gehen/Pilze** to go mushrooming (mushroom-picking)
~/**Kräuter** to herborize
~/**Pflanzen** to botanize
~/**Pilze** to mushroom
Sammelpferch m collecting (gathering) pen
Sammelpresse f pick-up press, [pick-up] baler, baling press
Sammelrinne f gutter
Sammelroder m pick-up grubber
Sammelrohr n collecting duct (of kidney)
Sammelschlegel[rasen]mäher m collecting flail cutter
Sammelschwimmer m catch (receiving) boom (rafting)

Sammelstrang m carrier drain (amelioration)
Sammeltank m accumulation tank (of a harvester)
Sammelverhalten n (api) foraging behaviour
Sammelwirt m paratenic host
Sammetblume f marigold, tagetes (genus Tagetes)
Sammetmalve f 1. flowering maple, abutilon (genus Abutilon); 2. Indian mallow, velvetleaf, Abutilon theophrasti (avicennae)
Sammler m 1. accumulator, battery; 2. main drain; lateral [field] drain
~ **niederer Ordnung** sub-main [drain]
Samoaklee m Samoan clover, Desmodium scorpiurus
Samojede m Samoyed (dog breed)
samtartig (bot) velutinous
Samtbohne f velvet bean, Mucuna deeringiana
Samtesche f velvet (Arizona) ash, Fraxinus velutina
Samtfleckenkrankheit f der Tomate (phyt) tomato leaf mould (caused by Cladosporium fulvum)
Samtfußrübling m velvet-stemmed agaric, winter mushroom, Flammulina velutipes
samtig 1. (bot) velutinous; 2. velvety (e.g. wine)
Samtlaufmilbe f harvest mite (family Trombidiidae)
Samtmalve f s. Sammetmalve
Samtpappel f marsh mallow, Althaea officinalis
Samtrose f French rose, Rosa gallica
Samttamarinde f tamarind plum, Dialium indum
Samttrespe f soft brome[-grass], tender brome[-grass], soft chess, Bromus hordaceus ssp. hordaceus
Sand m sand
~/**lehmiger** loamy sand
Sandabscheider m sand catcher (sugar-beet processing)
sandähnlich arenaceous
Sandapfel m Chinese apple, Malus prunifolia [var. rinkii]
Sandarach m, **Sandarak** m sandarac[h], gum juniper (from Tetraclinis articulata)
Sandarakbaum m sandarac[h] tree, Tetraclinis articulata, Callitris quadrivalvis
Sandbad n dust-bath
Sandbank f sandbank, flat
Sandbeere f apple of Cain, Arbutus unedo
Sandbefestigung f sand stabilization, sand binding (fixation)
Sandbinder m sand-binding plant, sand-stabilizing plant
Sandbirke f white (silver, weeping) birch, European [white] birch, Betula pendula (verrucosa, alba)
Sandbirne f sand pear, oriental (Chinese) pear, Pyrus pyrifolia
Sandblatt n sand leaf (tobacco)
Sandboden m sandy soil, sandland • **auf ~ wachsend** (bot) arenaceous
Sandbrombeere f knee-high blackberry, sand blackberry, Rubus cuneifolius

Sandbüchsenbaum

Sandbüchsenbaum *m* sand-box tree, Hura crepitans
Sanddorn *m* 1. sea buckthorn, *(Am)* sallow thorn *(genus Hippophae)*; 2. sea buckthorn, Hippophae rhamnoides
Sanddornbeere *f* sea buckthorn berry
Sanddornöl *n* sea buckthorn oil
Sanddüne *f* sand-dune
Sandelholz *n* sandal[wood], sanders *(esp. from Santalum album)*
Sandelholzbaum *m* sandal-tree *(genus Santalum)*
Sandelholzöl *n* sandalwood oil
Sandfang *m*, **Sandfänger** *m* sand catcher *(sugar-beet processing)*
Sandfilter *n* sand filter
Sandfliege *f* 1. sand-fly *(subfamily Phlebotominae)*; 2. sand-fly *(genus Phlebotomus)*
Sandfraktion *f* sand fraction
Sandgraurüßler *m* sand weevil, Philopedon plagiatus
Sandhafer *m* 1. bristle[-pointed] oat, naked (black) oat, small (greys) oat, Avena nuda [ssp. nuda], Avena strigosa; 2. marram [grass], European beach grass, Ammophila arenaria
sandhaltig, sandig sandy, arenaceous, psammous
Sandimmortelle *f (bot)* winged everlasting, Ammobium alatum
Sandkirsche *f* sand cherry, Prunus pumila
Sandkolik *f (vet)* sand colic
Sandkorn *n* sand grain
Sandkraut *n* sandwort, chick[en]weed *(genus Arenaria)*
Sandkultur *f* sand culture
Sandlaufkäfer *m* tiger-beetle *(family Cicindelidae)*
Sandlieschgras *n (bot)* sand cat's-tail, Phleum arenarium
Sandlöß *m* sandy loess
Sandluzerne *f* sand (bastard) lucern[e], variegated alfalfa, Medicago sativa ssp. falcata x ssp. sativa, Medicago x varia
Sandmergel *m* sandy marl, marly sandstone, clay grit
Sandpflanze *f* psammophyte
Sandpflaume *f* eastern sand plum, Prunus pumila ssp. pumila
Sandrebe *f* sand grape, Vitis rupestris
Sandreitgras *n* feather-top grass, wood reed [grass], chee reed grass, Calamagrostis epigejos
Sandroggen *m* sea lyme grass, European dune wild rye, Elymus (Leymus) arenarius
Sandschliff *m (soil)* corrasion
Sandschluff *m (soil)* sand-silt
Sandsegge *f* sand sedge, Carex arenaria
Sandserie *f* psammosere *(plant sociology)*
Sandstein *m* sandstone
Sandstrohblume *f (bot)* yellow everlasting, Helichrysum arenarium
Sandsturm *m* sandstorm
Sanduriweizen *m* timopheevi wheat, Triticum timopheevi
Sandwicke *f* hairy vetch, Vicia villosa
Sandwüste *f* sandy desert
sanieren to sanitize
Sanierung *f* sanitation
Sanikel *m (bot)* 1. sanicle *(genus Sanicula)*; 2. wood sanicle, Sanicula europaea
sanitär sanitary
Sanitärhieb *m (forest)* sanitation (sanitary) felling, prelogging • **Sanitärhiebe durchführen** to sanitize
San-José-Schildlaus *f* San José scale, Quadraspidiotus perniciosus
Sankt-Bernhards-Hund *m* St. Bernard dog *(breed)*
Sansevieria *f (bot)* sansevieria *(genus Sansevieria)*
Sansibarkopal *m* Zanzibar copal *(from Trachylobium verrucosum)*
Santa Gertrudis *f*, **Santa-Gertrudis-Rind** *n* Santa Gertrudis *(cattle breed)*
Santal *m* sandal-tree, Sandoricum koetjapa (indicum)
Santalin *n* santalin *(flavonoid)*
Santolacton *n*, **Santonin[säurelacton]** *n* santonin *(anthelminthic)*
Sanvitalie *f (bot)* 1. sanvitalia *(genus Sanvitalia)*; 2. sanvitalia, Sanvitalia procumbens
Säorgan *n* seed-feeding device
Sapelibaum *m (bot)* sapele *(genus Entandrophragma)*
Säpflug *m* drill plough
Saphubaum *m* bush butter tree, Dacryodes edulis
Sapin *m s.* Sapine
Sapindusfichte *f* oriental spruce, Picea orientalis
Sapine *f (forest)* cant-hook, cant-dog, peav[e]y
Sapogenin *n* sapogenin
Saponifikation *f* saponification
Saponin *n* saponin *(plant glycoside)*
Saponinaglykon *n* sapogenin
Saponit *m* saponite *(non-clay mineral)*
Sapote *f (bot)* white sapote, Casimiroa edulis
Sapotillbaum *m* sapodilla, naseberry, Manilkara (Achras) zapota
Sappanholzbaum *m (bot)* sappan caesalpinia, Caesalpinia sappan
saprogen saprogenic
Saprolegniabefall *m (vet)* saprolegniosis *(of fishes)*
Sapropel *n(m)* sapropel, putrid mud
saprophag saprophagous, saprovorous
saprophil saprophilous
Saprophyt *m* saprophyte, saprophytic organism
~/fakultativer facultative saprophyte, perthophyte
~/obligater obligate saprophyte
saprophytär, saprophytisch saprophytic
saprovor *s.* saprophag
Sar *s.* Sarcosin

Särad *n* sowing roller
Sarcoptesräude *f (vet)* sarcoptic mange (scab) *(caused esp. by Sarcoptes scabiei)*
Sarcosin *n* sarcosine, methylaminoacetic acid *(amino-acid)*
Sarcotesta *f (bot)* sarcotesta
Sareptasenf *m* Indian (Chinese) mustard, brown (green, leaf) mustard, Brassica juncea [ssp. juncea]
Sargents-Kirsche *f* Sargent cherry, Prunus sargentii
Sarkin *n* hypoxanthine
Sarkoblast *m* myoblast
Sarkoid *n (vet)* sarcoid
Sarkolemm *n* sarcolemma
Sarkom *n (vet)* sarcoma
~/**osteoplastisches** osteosarcoma
Sarkomatose *f (vet)* sarcomatosis
Sarkomere *f* sarcomere *(structural unit of a myofibril)*
Sarkoplasma *n* sarcoplasm
Sarkoplasmaprotein *n* muscle protein
Sarkosporidiose *f (vet)* sarcosporidiosis
Sarsaparilla[wurzel] *f (bot)* [Jamaica] sarsaparilla, Smilax regelii (ornata)
Säschar *n* planter shoe, seed [drill] coulter, [drill] coulter, seed furrow opener
Säschareinstellung *f* coulter setting
Säscharhebel *m* coulter arm
Sassafras[baum] *m (bot)* sassafras, Sassafras albidum
Sassafrasöl *n* sassafras oil
Sasse *f* hare's lare, lair of hare, form
Satanspilz *m*, **Satansröhrling** *m* satan toadstool, devil's boletus, Boletus satanas
Satellitenbild *n* satellite image
Satelliten-DNA *f* satellite DNA (deoxyribonucleic acid)
Satellitenfernerkundung *f* satellite remote sensing
Satellitvirus *n (phyt)* satellite virus
Satinnußbaum *m* sweet gum, Liquidambar styraciflua
Satsuma *f* satsuma *(fruit)*
Satsumabaum *m (bot)* satsuma, Citrus reticulata var. unshiu
Sattdampf *m* saturated steam
Sattel *m* saddle • **aus dem ~ geworfen werden** to unhorse
Sattelanhänger *m*, **Sattelauflieger** *m* semitrailer, semimounted trailer
Sattelbaum *m* 1. saddle-tree; 2. spar-tree *(timber transport)*
Sattelblatt *n* saddle flap, skirt
Satteldach[gewächs]haus *n* even-span [green]house
Satteldecke *f* saddle (body) cloth, shabrack, housing
Satteldruck *m (vet)* saddle sore

Sattelgurt *m* saddle-girth, belly-band, surcingle, cinch • **den ~ anziehen** to girth
Sattelkammer *f* tack-room
Sattelknopf *m* pommel
Sattellage *f* saddle area (site) *(of horse's body)*
Sattelmücke *f* saddle gall-midge, Haplodiplosis equestris (marginata)
satteln to saddle
Sattelpferd *n* saddle-horse
Sattelpfropfen *n s.* Sattelschäften
Sattelplatz *m* paddock
Sattelrahmen *m* saddle-tree
Sattelschäften *n* saddle[-type] grafting, saddling
Sattelschlepper *m* lorry (truck) tractor, semitrailer
Sattelschwein *n* saddleback *(pig breed)*
Sattelzeug *n* saddle and harness, saddlery, tack
Sattelzugmaschine *f s.* Sattelschlepper
Sattfutter *n* basal feed, basic diet
sättigen to saturate
Sättigung *f* 1. saturation; 2. *s.* Sättigungszustand
Sättigungsdampfdruck *m* saturation [vapour] pressure
Sättigungsdefizit *n* saturation deficit
Sättigungsdruck *m* saturation [vapour] pressure
Sättigungsgrad *m (soil)* degree of base saturation, base saturation percentage
~ **des Bodens/natürlicher** field moisture equivalent
Sättigungswert *m (soil)* saturation value, S value
Sättigungszentrum *n* satiety centre *(animal physiology)*
Sättigungszone *f (soil)* zone of saturation
Sättigungszustand *m* satiety
Sattler *m* saddler, harness-maker
Sattlerei *f* saddlery
Sätuch *n* seed cloth (bag)
Saturation *f* 1. carbonation, saturation *(sugar manufacture)*; 2. *s.* Sättigung
~/**periodische** batch carbonation
Saturationsgefäß *n* carbonation tank
Saturationspfanne *f* saturation pan
Saturationssaft *m* [first] carbonation juice
Saturationsschlamm *m* carbonation mud (scum)
saturieren to carbonate, to saturate
Saturnismus *m (vet)* lead-poisoning
Saturnmälzerei *f* Saturne malting system
SatV *s.* Satellitvirus
Satz *m* 1. litter *(the offspring at one birth e.g. of hares or rabbits)*; 2. batch, charge; 3. *s.* Bodensatz
Satzfisch *m* fingerling
Satzforelle *f* troutlet, troutling
Satzhecht *m* pickerel
Satzkarpfen *m* fingerling carp
Satztrockner *m* batch (floor) dryer, deep-bed dryer
Satztrocknung *f* batch drying
Sau *f* sow; wild sow
~/**ferkelführende** nursing sow
~/**grobe** capital wild boar

Sau

~/laktierende nursing sow
~/produktive aged (old) sow, breeding (brood) sow
~/trächtige (tragende) in-pig sow
Sauberbrennen *n (forest)* clean (clear) burning
Saubohne *f* broad (thick) bean, faba (fava, Windsor) bean, Vicia faba [var. major]
Saubruch *m* rooting-place *(of wild boars)*
Saudistel *f* 1. sowthistle, milk thistle *(genus Sonchus)*; 2. corn sowthistle, creeping (field, perennial) sowthistle, dindle, Sonchus arvensis
Sauenbucht *f* sow pen
Sauenbügel *m* farrowing rail
Sauenfütterung *f* sow feeding
Sauenherde *f* sow herd
Sauenkolostrum *n* sow colostrum
Sauenmelkmaschine *f* sow milking machine
Sauenmilch *f* sow milk
Sauenreproduktion *f* sow reproduction
Sauenträchtigkeit *f* sow pregnancy
sauer 1. acid[ic] *(esp. solutions, soil)*; sour, tart, acid *(e.g. fruit)*; acerb[ic] *(esp. apple)*; sour, sharp *(wine)*; 2. *s.* essigsauer; 3. pickled *(vegetable)*
• ~ machen to sour, to acidify, to acidulate
• ~ schmecken tarty • ~ werden to acidify *(soil)*; to [become, turn] sour *(as milk, wine)*
~/schwach *s.* säuerlich
~/stark superacid
Sauerale *n* alegar
Sauerampfer *m* [garden] sorrel, Rumex acetosa [var. hortensis], Rumex rugosus
Sauerbaum *m* sorrel tree, sourwood, Oxydendrum arboreum
Sauerbier *n* sour beer
Sauerbodenvegetation *f* acidophilic vegetation
Sauerbrut *f (api, vet)* European foul brood *(caused by Streptococcus pluton)*
Sauerdorn *m* 1. barberry, berberry, berberis *(genus Berberis)*; 2. [common, European] barberry, Berberia vulgaris
Sauerdorngewächse *npl* barberry family *(family Berberidaceae)* • die ~ betreffend berberidaceous
Sauerfäule *f (phyt)* 1. sour rot *(comprehensive term)*; 2. summer rot of [grape] clusters *(caused by Botrytis cinerea)*
Sauerfutter *n* silage, ensilage
Sauergras *n* reed grass *(family Cyperaceae)*
Sauerkartoffeln *fpl* potato silage
Sauerkirschbaum *m*, Sauerkirsche *f* sour (tart) cherry, Prunus cerasus
Sauerklee *m* 1. sour clover, wood sorrel, stubwort, oxalis *(genus Oxalis)*; 2. *s.* Gemeiner Sauerklee
Sauerklee-Kiefernwald *m* shamrock pinery
Sauerkohl *m*, Sauerkraut *n* [sauer]kraut
säuerlich sourish, slightly sour, subacid, acidulous, acidulent
Sauermalz *n* acid (proteolytic) malt
Sauermilch *f* sour (set) milk, naturally soured milk

~/mit Starterkultur behandelte cultured (fermented) milk
Sauermilchkäse *m* [acid] curd cheese
Sauermilchquark *m* acid curd from skim milk, dry quarg
Sauermolke *f* cultured whey
säuern 1. to sour, to acidify, to acidulate; 2. *(dairy)* to culture, to ripen; 3. to [become, turn] sour *(as milk, wine)*
Saueorange *f s.* Pomeranze
Sauerrahm *m* sour (ripened) cream
Sauerrahmbutter *f* ripened cream butter
Sauersack *m (bot)* sour-sop, Annona muricata
Sauerschaligkeit *f der Zwiebel* sour skin disease of onion *(caused by Pseudomonas cepacia)*
Sauerstoff *m* oxygen • ~ in Ozon umwandeln to ozonize
Sauerstoffaufnahme *f* oxygen uptake
Sauerstoffbedarf *m* oxygen requirement (demand)
~/biochemischer biochemical (biological) oxygen demand, BOD
Sauerstoffdefizit *n* oxygen debt *(animal physiology)*
Sauerstoffflußdichte *f* oxygen flux density
Sauerstoffhämoglobin *n* oxyhaemoglobin
Sauerstoffkreislauf *m* oxygen cycle
Sauerstofflosigkeit *f* anoxia
Sauerstoffmangel *m* oxygen deficiency; *(vet)* hypoxia
~/atmungsbehindernder suboxidation
Sauerstoffsättigung *f* oxygen saturation
Sauerstoffschuld *f s.* Sauerstoffdefizit
Sauerstoffverbrauch *m* oxygen consumption
Säuerung *f* 1. acidification, acidulation; 2. *(dairy)* culturing
Säuerungsbakterium *n s.* Säurebildner
Säuerungsgefäß *n (dairy)* souring (ripening) vat, ag[e]ing vat
Säuerungsmittel *n* acidulant, acidulent
Säuerungswanne *f s.* Säuerungsgefäß
Säuerungszusatz *m s.* Säuerungsmittel
Sauerzitrone *f s.* Zitrone
Saufeder *f (hunt)* boar (hog) spear
Saugakt *m* act of sucking
Saugbagger *m* suction dredger
saugen to suck, to draw; to absorb, to soak [up]
~/Milch to milk
säugen to nurse, to give suck, to suckle
säugend lactating
Säugeperiode *f* nursing (suckling) period
Sauger *m* field drain; lateral [field] drain, collecting drain
Säuger *m*, Säugetier *n* mammal, suckler *(class Mammalia)*
Säugezeit *f s.* Säugeperiode
Saugfalle *f* suction trap *(e.g. for determining insect pest populations)*
Saugferkel *n* piglet, pigling, piggy, sucking (baby) pig; roaster

Saugferkelanämie *f (vet)* baby-pig anaemia
Saugfilter *n* vacuum (suction) filter
Saugfohlen *n* milk (sucking) foal
Saugförderer *m* suction conveyor
Saugfortsatz *m* haustorium *(of parasitic plants)*
Sauggebläse *n* suction (extractor) fan
Sauggraben *m* collecting ditch
Sauggrube *f s.* Saugnapf
Saughäufigkeit *f* suckling frequency
Saugkalb *n* suckling (suckler) calf, bob
Saugkraft *f* suction force
Sauglamm *n* suckling (baby, milk-fed) lamb, yeanling
Sauglüfter *m s.* Sauggebläse
Saugmilbe *f* psoroptic mite *(genus Psoroptes)*
~ **des Schafes** sheep scab mite, psoroptic mite of sheep, Psoroptes ovis
Saugmilbenräude *f (vet)* psoroptic mange (scab)
Saugnapf *m* acetabulum, sucker *(e.g. of trematodes)*
saugnapfförmig acetabuliform
Saugpumpe *f* suction pump
Saugreflex *m* sucking reflex, suckling instinct
Saugrohr *n* suction pipe
Saugrüssel *m (ent)* sucking beak, proboscis, rostrum
Saugsichter *m* suction fan cleaner
Saugspannung *f* diffusion pressure deficit *(plant physiology)*
~ **des Bodenwassers** soil water tension, moisture tension
Saugspannungskurve *f (soil)* water retention curve, moisture characteristic
Saugtakt *m* suction phase (stroke, cycle), milking phase *(machine milking)*
Saug- und Schluckbrunnen *m* suction-and-injection well
Saugverhalten *n* suckling behaviour
Saugwarze *f s.* Zitze
Saugwelpe *m* suckling pup
Saugwert *n* osmotic value
Saugwurm *m* trematode [worm], fluke *(class Trematoda)*
~/**digener (zweigeschlechtlicher)** fluke *(order Digenea)*
saugwurmbefallen fluky
Saugwurmbekämpfungsmittel *n* flukicide
Saugwurzel *f* absorbing (sucking) root
Saugzuggebläse *n* included draught fan
Säulenchromatographie *f* column chromatography
Säulendiagramm *n* histogram
Säuleneibe *f* common yew, Taxus baccata
Säulengefüge *n (soil)* columnar structure
Säulenrost *m* **der Schwarzen Johannisbeere** blister rust of black currant *(caused by Cronartium ribicola)*
Saum *m* edging, edge, border; *(bot, zoo)* limb, stria

Saumbesamung *f (forest)* border (marginal) seeding
saumblättrig *(bot)* lomatophyllous
Saumdurchforstung *f (forest)* strip thinning
Saumfarn *m* 1. dish fern *(genus Pteris)*; 2. [Cretan] brake, table (ribbon) fern, Pteris cretica
Saumfemelschlagsystem *n (forest)* strip-and-group system
saumfrüchtig *(bot)* lomatocarpous
Saumhieb *m s.* Saumschlag
Saumhorn *n* periople *(of hoof or claw)*
Saumkahlschlag *m* clear strip felling
Saumlederhaut *f* perioplic corium *(of hoof)*
Saumrinne *f* perioplic sulcus *(of hoof or claw)*
Saumschlag *m (forest)* border (strip) felling, staggering
Saumschlagbetrieb *m* strip system (method)
Saumverjüngung *f* border regeneration, regeneration by strip fellings
Saumzecke *f* fowl tick, Argas reflexus
Säure *f* 1. acid; 2. sourness, acidity *(e.g. of wine)*; sourness, tartness, acerbity *(esp. of fruit)*
~/**schweflige** sulphurous acid
Saure Limette *f* [sour] lime, common lime, Citrus aurantiifolia
Säureamid *n* [acid] amide
Säureanzeiger *m* acidophilic plant, acidophyte, acidity indicator species
Säureausscheidung *f* **im Harn** aciduria
Säure-Base-Gleichgewicht *n* acid-base balance (equilibrium)
Säurebehandlung *f* acid treatment
säurebeständig *s.* säurefest
säurebildend acid-forming, acidic
Säurebildner *m* acid former (producer), acid-forming bacterium
Säuredetergens *n* acid detergent
Säureentfaserung *f* acid delinting *(of cotton seeds)*
säureertragend *s.* säuretolerant
säurefest acid-proof, acid-resistant, acid-resisting
Säurefestigkeit *f* acid resistance (stability)
säurefrei acid-free
Säurefuchsin *n* acid fuchsine
Säuregehalt *m* acid content; acidity, sourness
~ **des Bodens** soil acidity (sourness)
Säuregehaltsbestimmung *f* acidity test
Säuregrad *m* [degree of] acidity
Säuregradbestimmung *f* acidity test
säurehaltig acid[-containing], acidic
säureliebend acid-loving, acid-preferring, acidophilic, acidophilous, oxyphil[e]
Säurelignin *n* acid lignin
Säuremangel *m* subacidity
säuremeidend acidophobic
Säuremesser *m* acidimeter
Säure-Polyacrylamidgel-Elektrophorese *f* acid polyacrylamide gel electrophoresis
säureresistent *s.* säurefest

Säurerhythmus

Säurerhythmus *m* acid rhythm *(plant physiology)*
säuretolerant acid-tolerant, acidotolerant
Säureüberschuß *m* superacidity
~ im Blut *(vet)* acidaemia
Säurezeiger *m s.* Säureanzeiger
Saurochorie *f (bot)* saurochory
Sauternes *m* Sauterne[s] *(wine)*
Savanne *f* savannah, savanna, wooded grassland
~/anthropogene (sekundäre) derived savannah
Savannenboden *m* savannah soil
Savannengras *n* savannah grass, Axonopus compressus
Savannen[licht]wald *m* savannah woodland (forest)
Savarie *f* sawari (butter) nut, Caryocar nuciferum
Savoy-Krankheit *f* **der Zuckerrübe** *(Am)* savoy disease of sugar-beet *(virosis)*
Sawahirse *f* barnyard millet (grass), billion dollar grass, Echinochloa crus-galli
Sawara-Scheinzypresse *f* Sawara cypress, Chamaecyparis pisifera
Saxaul *m (bot)* saxaul *(genus Haloxylon)*
Säzeit *f* sowing time (season, period)
Säzwiebel *f* annual onion
SBAV *s.* Salatbreitadernvirus
SBE *s.* Schwimmblasenentzündung
SBM *s.* Schädlingsbekämpfungsmittel
SbMV *s.* Sojabohnenmosaikvirus
SBNV *s.* Blattnekrosevirus des Salats
Scale-butt-Krankheit *f* **von Citrus** *(phyt)* citrus exocortis [disease]
Scanning-Elektronenmikroskopie *f* scanning electron microscopy
Scapula *f s.* Schulterblatt
Scapus *m (zoo)* scape
Sch. *s.* 1. Schimmel 2.; 2. Schirmhieb
Schabe *f (ent)* cockroach, *(Am)* roach *(order Blattariae)*
Schabenbekämpfungsmittel *n* blatticide
Schaben[woll]kraut *n (bot)* moth mullein, Verbascum blattaria
Schaber *m* scraper
Schabracke *f* shabrack, saddle (body) cloth, housing
Schabzieger *m* sapsago [cheese]
Schabziger Klee *m* blue (Swiss) melilot, sweet trefoil, Trigonella coerulea
Schachblume *f s.* Schachbrettblume
schachbrettartig *(bot)* tesselated
Schachbrettblume *f* 1. fritillary *(genus Fritillaria)*; 2. chequered lily, snake's-head, guinea-hen flower, Fritillaria meleagris
Schacht *m* grain conveyor housing, channel *(of combine harvester)*
Schachtbrunnen *m* dug well
Schachtelhalm *m (bot)* horse-tail, toadpipe, equisetum *(genus Equisetum)*
Schächten *n* kosher killing (slaughter)
Schachttrockner *m* bin (tower, column) dryer, [fall]shaft dryer
Schadbild *n* pattern of damage
Schädel *m* skull, cranium • **in den ~ hinein** intracranial
Schädeleröffnung *f (vet)* trepanation
Schädelhöhle *f* cranial cavity
Schädelkalotte *f* cranium
Schaden *m* damage, injury
Schadensschwelle *f* damage (damaging) threshold, injury level
~/ästhetische aesthetic injury threshold
~/ökonomische economic threshold, ET, economic injury level
Schadensumfang *m* extent of damage
Schaderreger *m* harmful organism, pest
~/euryxener general pest
Schaderregerbekämpfung *f* control of noxious animals and pests
schaderregerfrei clean
Schaderregerpopulation *f* pest population
Schaderregerüberwachung *f* pest monitoring, monitoring of pest populations, scouting
Schadfaktor *m* injurious factor, damaging agent
Schadgras *n* obnoxious grass
Schadhirsch *m* damager, switch-horn
Schadholz *n* damaged timber
schädigen/durch Frost to frost *(e.g. plants)*
schädigend injurious
Schädigung *f* damage, injury; impairment; lesion
~ durch Strahlungseinwirkung radiation injury
Schadinsekt *n* insect pest, harmful (destructive, pest) insect, injurious (noxious, pernicious) insect
~/blattfressendes insect defoliator
~/nissenablegendes nitter
Schadinsektenunterdrückung *f* insect pest suppression
schädlich harmful, injurious, noxious, pernicious; pestiferous
Schädling *m* pest
~/pflanzlicher *s.* Schadpflanze
~/tierischer harmful (noxious) animal, animal pest
Schädlingsausbruch *m* pest outbreak
Schädlingsausrottung *f* pest eradication
Schädlingsausrottungsprogramm *n* pest eradication programme
Schädlingsbefall *m* pest infestation
~/massenhafter calamity
Schädlingsbekämpfer *m* pest control operator
Schädlingsbekämpfung *f* pest control (destruction)
~/biologische biological [pest] control
~/chemische chemical pest control
~/integrierte integrated pest management, IPM, integrated control
~/übermäßige overkill of pests
Schädlingsbekämpfungsmittel *n* pesticide, pest killer (destruction agent), control agent
~/biologisches biological control agent

~/**chemisches** pest control chemical, pesticide [chemical]
~/**eiabtötendes** egg killer, ovicide
Schädlingsökologie f pest ecology
Schädlingspopulation f pest population
Schädlingsregulierung f pest management
schädlingsresistent pest-resistant
Schädlingsresistenz f pest resistance
Schädlingsunterdrückung f pest suppression
Schadmilbe f pest mite *(comprehensive term)*
Schadnagerbekämpfung f rodent control
Schadorganismus m s. Schädling
Schadpflanze f harmful (noxious) plant
Schadpilz m weed mould
Schadschwelle f s. Schadensschwelle
Schadstoff m pollutant, contaminant, harmful (injurious) substance, noxious substance (material), damaging agent
Schadstoffbelastung f pollutant (contaminant) loading, load of pollution
Schadstoffemission f noxious [material] emission
Schadstoffkonzentration f pollutant concentration, concentration of pollutants
Schaduf m shadoof, shaduf *(ancient esp. Egyptian water-raising device)*
Schadvogel m noxious bird, bird pest
Schadvogelabwehr f bird control
Schadwirkung f injurious effect
Schaf n 1. sheep *(genus Ovis)*; 2. sheep, jumbuck *(Australia)*, Ovis aries
~/**erstmals geschorenes** shearling
~/**güstes** non-pregnant ewe, eild, yeld
~ **im zweiten Jahr** hoggerel, teg
~/**schneidezahnloses** gummer, gummy
~ **vor dem Ablammen/weibliches** lamber
Schafbeere f sheepberry, Viburnum lentago
Schafbehandlungsanlage f sheep handling shed
Schafbestand m sheep stock
Schafbiesfliege f sheep nostril fly, sheep [nasal] bot-fly, Oestrus ovis
Schafbiesfliegenlarve f sheep (nose) bot
Schafbock m ram, tup
~/**vasektomierter** vasectomized ram
Schafbocksperma n ram semen
Schäfchenwolke f fleecy cloud
~/**feine** cirrocumulus
~/**grobe** altocumulus
~/**hohe** cirrocumulus
Schafdesinfektionsanlage f sheep-wash
Schafdung m sheep manure
Schafe npl sheep
Schäfer m shepherd, sheep-herder
Schäferhund m sheep-dog, shepherd dog
Schäferhütte f shieling
Schäferin f shepherdess
Schäferstab m sheep-hook, [shepherd's] crook, shepherd's staff
Schaffarmer m flock-master
Schaffell n sheepskin, sheep pelt, [sheep] fleece

~/**entwolltes** dewoolled sheepskin
~/**kurzwolliges** [sheep] pelt
Schaffleisch n sheepmeat, mutton
Schaffußwalze f sheep's-foot roller *(road construction)*
Schaffutter n sheep feed
~/**absolutes (unbedingtes)** absolute sheep feed
Schaffütterung f sheep feeding
Schafgarbe f milfoil, [common] yarrow, Achillea millefolium
Schafhaarling m sheep [body] louse, Bovicola (Damalinia) ovis
Schafhalter m sheep keeper, flock-master, pastoralist *(Australia)*
Schafhaltung f sheep farming (rearing), sheep husbandry (management)
~ **in Ackerbaugebieten** arable sheep farming
Schafhaut f amnion, caul *(animal anatomy)*
Schafherde f flock of sheep, sheep flock, fold
Schafhirt m s. Schäfer
Schafhürde f [sheep-]fold, sheep pen (cote), pinfold
Schafkäse m sheep cheese, sheep's (ewe) milk cheese
Schafkopf m roman-nosed head *(of horse)*
Schafkrankheit f sheep-disease
Schaflausfliege f [sheep] ked, *(Am)* sheep tick, Melophagus ovinus
Schaflausfliegenbefall m sheep scab
Schafleder n sheepskin leather, sheep; lambskin
~/**weiches** doeskin
Schaflinse f crown vetch, Coronilla varia
Schaflisteriose f *(vet)* listeriosis, listerellosis *(caused by Listeria monocytogenes)*
Schafmast f sheep fattening
Schafmilch f sheep (ewe) milk
Schafmilchkäse m s. Schafkäse
Schafmilchverarbeitung f sheep dairying
Schafmist m sheep manure
schafmüde sheep sick *(range land)*
Schafpocken pl *(vet)* sheep-pox
Schafrasse f sheep breed, breed of sheep
~/**schlichtwollige** long wool breed
Schafsandlaus f s. Schafhaarling
Schafscheranlage f sheep-shearing unit
Schafscherer m [sheep] shearer
Schafschermaschine f sheep-shearing machine, sheep shearer
Schafscherstand m sheep-shearing crate
Schafschertisch m sheep-shearing table
Schafschur f [sheep-]shearing, [sheep-]clip, clipping
~/**chemische** chemical shearing
~/**maschinelle** machine shearing
Schafschwingel m *(bot)* sheep['s] fescue, Festuca ovina
Schafskabiose f *(bot)* sheep's-bit [scabious], Jasione montana
Schafskäse m s. Schafkäse

Schafstall

Schafstall *m* sheep barn (house), sheppey
Schaft *m* 1. *(bot)* scape; [tree-]trunk, stem, shaft, bole, boll; cane *(of certain palm species)*; 2. *(zoo)* scape, shaft *(e.g. of a feather)*
Schaft... *s. a.* Stamm...
Schaftauchbad *n* sheep-dip[per]
Schaftderbholz *n* stem wood above 7 cm diameter
Schaftgüte *f* stem quality
Schaftholz *n* bole (stem) wood, bodywood
Schaftholzformzahl *f* stem wood form factor
Schaftholzvolumen *n*, **Schaftinhalt** *m* stem volume
Schaftkreisfläche *f* bole area *(timber mensuration)*
Schaftkurve *f* stem curve
Schaftlaus *f* **des Huhnes** shaft (fowl, poultry-biting) louse, Menopon gallinae
Schaftlose Schlüsselblume *f* common (English) primrose, Primula vulgaris
schaftrein clear-shafted, clear-boled
Schaftreinheit *f* clearness [of bole]
Schaftreinigung *f* self-pruning, natural pruning
schafttragend scapigerous, scapose
Schaftvermessung *f* measurement of stems
Schafweide *f*, **Schafweideland** *n* sheep keep (walk, run)
Schafwiege *f* sheep cradle
Schafwolle *f* sheep['s] wool, pile
Schafwollproduktion *f* sheep wool production
Schafzecke *f s.* Schafausfliege
Schafzucht *f* sheep breeding (farming)
Schafzuchtbetrieb *m* sheep farm
Schafzüchter *m* sheep breeder (farmer, master), grazier, pastoralist *(Australia)*
schal stale, flat *(beverage)*; musty *(wine)*
schälbar peelable
Schälbeil *n (forest)* barking axe
Schale *f* 1. *(bot)* peel, rind, cortex; testa *(of seed)*; skin *(of fruits, potatoes)*; shell *(of nuts)*; husk, hull *(dried)*; 2. *(zoo)* shell *(of eggs)*; shell, crust *(of snails)*; 3. bowl, tray • **mit brüchiger ~** broken-shelled *(e.g. seeds)*
~/**berostete** *(phyt)* russeted skin
~/**grüne** shuck *(e.g. of nuts)*
~/**harte** shell
Schäleinleger *m* husking (shelling) feeder, peeling device
Schäleisen *n (forest)* barking-iron
schälen to excorticate, to decorticate *(e.g. cereals)*; to shell, to peel, to pare *(esp. fruit)*; to [de]hull, to husk, to shuck *(esp. legumes)*; to [de]bark, to ross *(timber)*
~/**die Stoppel** to return the stubble
~/**sich** to peel
~/**zur Saftzeit** to sap-peel
Schälen *n* 1. decortication; shelling, peeling, paring; hulling, husking; barking; 2. stubble cleaning (clearing), autumn cleaning, stubbling
~/**chemisches** chemical peeling, chemi-peeling
~ **der Hülsenfrüchte** husking of legumes

~/**streifenweises** barking in strips
Schalenanteil *m* bran content *(of cereals)*
schalenartig *(bot, zoo)* testaceous
Schalenbereifung *f* bloom of skin
Schalenberostung *f (phyt)* fruit russet[ing], skin russeting
Schalenbeschaffenheit *f* skin finish
Schalenbeschichtung *f* skin coating *(for storing fruits)*
Schalenbräune *f (phyt)* skin browning, [superficial, storage] scald *(of pome fruits)*
~/**weiche** soft scald, deep (ribbon) scald
Schalendicke *f* shell thickness
Schalenei *n* shell egg
Schalenfarbe *f* shell colour
Schalenfestigkeit *f* shell strength, firmness of the skin
Schalenfilter *n* section filter
Schalenflaumigkeit *f* skin downiness *(of peaches)*
Schalenfleckenkrankheit *f* **der Zwiebel** onion smudge [disease] *(caused by Colletotrichum circinans)*
Schalenfrüchte *fpl* shell fruit[s], nut fruit[s]
Schalenfütterung *f* bowl feeding
Schalenhaut *f* shell membrane, putamen *(of bird's egg)*
~/**äußere** outer shell membrane
~/**innere** inner shell membrane
Schalenkreuzanemometer *n* windmill with cups
schalenlos decorticate
Schalenmembran *f s.* Schalenhaut
Schalennaht *f* suture
Schalennekrose *f (phyt)* rind necrosis
Schalenobst *n s.* Schalenfrüchte
Schalenöl *n* peel oil
Schalenrissigkeit *f (phyt)* skin cracking
Schalenrost *m s.* Schalenberostung
Schalenschnecke *f* snail *(esp. of genus Helix)*
Schalentemperatur *f* shell temperature
Schalenüberzug *m* skin coat *(for storing fruits)*
Schalenwild *n* [cloven-]hoofed game
Schäler *m* peeler, peeling device
Schalerbse *f* [shelling] pea, smooth (round-seeded) pea, Pisum sativum ssp. sativum convar. sativum
Schälholz *n* barked wood
schalig husky
Schälkleie *f* bran
Schälklotz *m* billet, block
Schalm *m (forest)* blaze, mark
Schälmaschine *f* peeling machine, peeler, hulling apparatus, huller, sheller, decorticator; bark-peeling machine, barking machine, barker
Schalmaxt *f*, **Schalmbeil** *n (forest)* blazer, marking hatchet
schalmen *(forest)* to blaze, to mark
Schälmesser *n (forest)* barking-iron
Schalmtest *m s.* California-Mastitis-Test

Schalotte *f* shallot, eschalot, scallion, Allium ascalonicum
Schälpflug *m* stubble cleaner (plough), paring (skim) plough; sod-plough
Schälschaden *m (forest)* bark-peeling damage, fraying damage *(by game)*
Schälschar *n* stubble share
Schälschutz *m (forest)* protection from fraying
Schaltgen *n* switch gene
Schältisch *m* peeling table
Schaltneuron *n* intercalated (connector) neuron, interneuron
Schaltrad *n s.* Zackenrad
Schälung *f s.* Schälen
Schälverlust *m* peeling loss
Schälwald *m* tanbark coppice
Scham *f s.* Schamspalte
Schamahirse *f* shama millet, jungle rice, Echinochloa (Panicum) colonum
Schamarterie *f* pudic artery *(animal anatomy)*
Schambein *n* pubic bone *(animal anatomy)*
Schamblume *f* 1. pigeonwings, butterfly pea *(genus Clitoria)*; 2. butterfly pea, Clitoria ternata
Schamentzündung *f (vet)* vulvitis
Schamhafte Sinnpflanze *f* sensitive (humble) plant, Mimosa pudica
Schamlippe *f* vulvar lip *(animal anatomy)*
Schamschlagader *f s.* Schamarterie
Schamspalte *f* vulva *(animal anatomy)*
Schankbier *n* light (low-gravity) beer, schenk (winter) beer; beer on tap
Schar *n* [plough]share, [plough] blade
~/einfaches razor (trapezoidal) share
~ mit auswechselbarer Spitze removable-point share
~/selbstschärfendes self-sharpening share
~/trapezförmiges *s. ~/einfaches*
Scharbockskraut *n* [lesser] celandine, pilewort, Ranunculus ficaria
scharf sharp; *(bot, zoo)* acute
scharfborstig *(bot)* exasperate
schärfen to sharpen, to grind
~/mit dem Wetzstein to stone
Scharfer Augenfleck *m* sharp eyespot *(of cereals, caused by Tanathephorus cucumeris = Rhizoctonia solani)*
~ Hahnenfuß *m (bot)* goldilocks, gold knots, crowfoot, tall buttercup, Ranunculus acris
Scharfes Adernmosaik *n* **der Erbse** pea enation mosaic *(virosis)*
~ Adernmosaikvirus *n* **der Erbse** pea enation mosaic virus
scharfkantig *(bot)* acute-angled
Scharfführung *f* guiding of share
Schärfwinkel *m* top-plate [filing] angle *(of a chainsaw tooth)*
Scharkakrankheit *f (phyt)* sharka *(virosis)*
~ der Pflaume plum pox
Scharkavirus *n* **der Pflaume** plum pox virus, PPV

Scharlachbeere *f* scarlet firethorn, Pyracantha coccinea
Scharlacheiche *f* scarlet oak, Quercus coccinea
Scharlacherdbeere *f* scarlet strawberry, Fragaria virginiana
Scharlachmonarde *f* bee (mountain) balm, Oswego tea, Monarda didyma
Scharlachquitte *f* Maule's quince, Chaenomeles japonica
Scharlachranke *f* ivy (scarlet) gourd, Coccinia grandis
Scharlachsalbei *m* bluebeard, Salvia viridis (horminum)
Scharlachschildlaus *f* cochineal [insect], Coccus cacti, Dactylopius coccus
Scharlachsumach *m* smooth sumac[h], scarlet sumac[h], Rhus glabra
Scharlachtürkenbund *m* scarlet Turk's cap lily, Lilium chalcedonicum
Scharniergelenk *n* hinge joint
Scharpflug *m* share (mould-board) plough
scharren to scratch, to paw
Scharrharz *n* scrape
Scharrharzhacke *f* iron scrape
Scharschälpflug *m* share skim (till) plough, mould-board stubble plough
Scharschleifmaschine *f* share grinder
Scharschmied *m* ploughshare smith
Scharschneide *f* share throat
Scharschneidewinkel *m* landside clearance
Scharspitze *f* share (plough) tip, share point
Schattenbaum *m* shade tree
Schattenbaumart *f* shade-bearing tree species, shade-bearer
schattenbedürftig shade-demanding, shade-requiring
Schattenblatt *n* shade-leaf *(plant physiology)*
Schattendach *n* shade roof
Schattendecke *f s.* Schattenmatte
schattenertragend shade-enduring, shade-tolerant
Schattenerträglichkeit *f* shade endurance, endurance of shade
Schattenerträgnis *f*, **Schattenfestigkeit** *f s.* Schattenerträglichkeit
Schattenhalle *f* lathhouse; shade roof
Schattenholzart *f s.* Schattenbaumart
schattenintolerant *s.* schattenunverträglich
Schattenleinen *n* shadecloth
schattenliebend shade-loving, umbrose
Schattenmatte *f* shading mat, blind *(greenhouse installation)*
Schattenmorelle *f* morello [cherry], Prunus cerasus ssp. acida
Schattenpflanze *f* shade plant, sciophyte
Schattenresistenz *f* shade resistance
Schattenröhre *f* flame violet *(genus Episcia)*
schattenspendend shading, umbriferous
schattentolerant shade-tolerant

Schattentoleranz

Schattentoleranz f shade tolerance
schattenunverträglich shade-intolerant
Schattenunverträglichkeit f shade intolerance
schattenverträglich s. schattentolerant
Schattenwickler m flat tortrix moth, Cnephasia interjectana (longana)
Schattieranlage f shading installation
schattieren to shade
Schattierung f shading
Schattierungsmaterial n shading material
schattig shady
Schätzfunktion f (biom) estimating function, estimator
~/unverzerrte unbiased estimator
Schätzgerade f regression line
Schätzung f estimation
~ innerhalb von Gruppen within groups estimation
Schätzwert m estimate, estimated value
Schauer m shower [of rain], squall
Schauerwolke f cumulonimbus [cloud]
Schaufel f 1. shovel; scoop; 2. broad tooth (of ruminant's dentition)
Schaufelgeweih n shovel antlers
Schaufellader m bucket-loader; skid-steer loader
Schaufelpflug m scoop plough
Schaufelrad n scoop (bucket) wheel
Schauglas n sight glass (e.g. of milking machine)
Schauhaus n conservatory
Schaum m foam, froth; head (of beer)
Schaumbeständigkeit f foam stability
Schaumbildung f foaming
Schaumdämpfungsmittel n antifoaming agent (e.g. as feed additive)
schäumen n to foam, to froth; to fizzle (beverages); to sparkle (wine)
Schaumerde f foam soil
Schaumfeuerlöschausrüstung f foam fire fighting equipment
Schaumkraut n bitter cress (genus Cardamine)
Schaum[lösch]mittel n fire foam, foam fire retardant
Schaumspiere f (bot) ocean-spray, Holodiscus discolor var. ariifolius
Schaumstoff m [plastic] foam (e.g. as soil conditioner)
Schaumstoffmatte f foam mat
Schaumwein m sparkling (effervescent, effervescing) wine
Schaumzikade f 1. cuckoo-spit [insect], cuckoo spittle, spittle bug (insect), froghopper (family Cercopidae); 2. common froghopper, cuckoo-spit insect, Philaenus spumarius
Schecke m(f) dappled horse, piebald [horse], pinto
scheckig mottled, blotched; piebald, dappled, mealy, (Am) pinto (horse); tabby (cat)
Scheckung f (phyt) mottling, mottle, blotch[ing]
Scheckungsvirus n mottle virus
Scheffel m bushel, bu

Schefflera f (bot) 1. schefflera (genus Schefflera); 2. umbrella-tree, Schefflera venulosa
Scheibe f 1. disk, disc; 2. escutcheon, white patch (of red deer and fallow deer)
Scheibenblüte f disk floret
Scheibenbremse f disk brake
Scheibendrillmaschine f disk-type seeder, disk drill
Scheibenegge f disk harrow • **mit der ~ bearbeiten** to disk
Scheibenfahrpflug m sulky disk plough
Scheibenfilter n leaf filter
scheibenförmig (bot, zoo) disciform
Scheibenfreilaufkupplung f friction disk freewheel clutch
Scheibenfuttermühle f [grinding] plate mill
Scheibengrubber m disk cultivator
Scheibenhackmaschine f disk chipper (for wood)
Scheibenhäufelpflug m disk bedder
Scheibenhäufler m disk ridger
Scheibenhonig m comb (virgin) honey
Scheibenkupplung f disk clutch
Scheibenmäher m, **Scheibenmähwerk** n [rotor] disk mower
Scheibenmatrize f disk matrix
Scheibenmühle f attrition mill
Scheibenneigungswinkel m angle of disk inclination
Scheibenpacker m disk landpacker
Scheibenpflug m disk plough
Scheibenradgebläsehäcksler m flywheel chopper blower
Scheibenradhäcksler m flywheel chopper (forager)
Scheibenrutschkupplung f slip clutch
~/stirnverzahnte dog-type slip clutch
Scheibenschälpflug m disk tiller (cultivator), disk stubble cleaner (plough), stubble disk [plough], polydisk (harrow) plough
Scheibenschälpflügen n disk plough scuffling
Scheibenschar n disk share (coulter)
Scheibenschardrillmaschine f disk drill
Scheibenschwenkpflug m reversible disk plough
Scheibensech n disk (rolling) coulter
~/gewelltes wavy-edge disk coulter
~/gezahntes notched coulter
Scheibentrieur m disk separator
Scheide f sheath; vagina • **in die ~ hinein** intravaginal • **innerhalb der ~** intravaginal
Scheidekalk m lime sludge (sugar manufacture)
scheiden to defecate, to lime (sugar manufacture)
Scheiden... s. a. Vaginal...
Scheidenarterie f vaginal artery
Scheidenbesamung f vaginal insemination
Scheideneingang m vaginal orifice
Scheidenentzündung f (vet) vaginitis, colpitis
Scheidenhalter m (vet) vaginal prolapse retainer
Scheidenöffnung f vaginal orifice
Scheidenpessar n pessary

Scheidenschleim *m* vaginal mucus
Scheidenschleimhaut *f* vaginal mucosa (mucous membrane)
Scheidenschleimhautentzündung *f (vet)* vaginitis, colpitis
Scheidenschwamm *m (vet)* [intra]vaginal sponge
Scheidensekret *n* vaginal smear
Scheidenspekulum *n (vet)* [vaginal] speculum
Scheidenvorfall *m (vet)* vaginal prolapse, colpoptosis
Scheidepfanne *f* liming (defecation) tank, limer *(sugar manufacture)*
Scheidesaft *m* defecated (limed) juice
Scheidesaturation *f* carbonation process
Scheideschlamm *m* carbonation mud (scum), saturation sludge
Scheidewand *f* diaphragm; *(bot, zoo)* septum • **mit ~ septate**
~/falsche false septum
scheidig vaginate
Scheidige Platterbse *f* Cyprus vetch, Lathyrus ochrus
Scheidung *f* defecation, liming *(sugar manufacture)*
~/kalte cold defecation
~/nasse wet liming
Schein... *s. a.* Pseudo...
Scheinachse *f (bot)* false axis, sympodium, sympode
Scheinähre *f* false spike
Scheinakazie *f* common robinia, false acacia, black locust, Robinia pseudoacacia
Scheinbeere *f* 1. wintergreen *(genus Gaultheria)*; 2. checkerberry, teaberry, boxberry, Gaultheria procumbens; 3. lemon leaf, Gaultheria shallon
Scheinbock[käfer] *m (ent)* wharf borer, Nacerda melanura
Scheinbuche *f* evergreen beech *(genus Nothofagus)*
Scheindolde *f (bot)* cyme
Scheinfrucht *f (bot)* false (accessory, spurious) fruit, pseudocarp; sorosis *(of pineapple)*
scheinfrüchtig pseudocarpic, pseudocarpous
Scheinfüßchen *n* pseudopod[ium], false leg
Scheingeißbart *m (bot)* false spire (goat's-beard), astilbe *(genus Astilbe)*
Scheingewebe *n (bot)* pseudoparenchyma
Scheinhanf *m* bastard hemp, Datisca cannabina
Scheinhasel *f* [spike] winter hazel, Corylopsis spicata
Scheinkerrie *f (bot)* jet-bead, Rhodotypus scandens
Scheinlärche *f* golden (false, Chinese) larch, Pseudolarix kaempferi (amabilis)
Scheinmohn *m* 1. Himalayan poppy *(genus Meconopsis)*; 2. harebell poppy, Meconopsis quintuplinervia
Scheinparthenokarpie *f (bot)* pseudoparthenocarpy

Scheinpuppe *f (ent)* pseudochrysalis, pseudopupa
Scheinquirl *m (bot)* false (apparent) whorl, verticillaster
Scheinquitte *f* Japanese quince, japonica, Chaenomeles japonica
Scheinring *m* traumatic ring (zone) *(wood anatomy)*
Scheintod *m* anabiosis
scheintot anabiotic
Scheinträchtigkeit *f (vet)* false pregnancy, pseudopregnancy, pseudocyesis
Scheinzwitter *m (vet)* pseudohermaphrodite
scheinzwitterhaft *(bot, zoo)* gynandrous
scheinzwittrig *(zoo)* androgynous
Scheinzwittrigkeit *f (zoo)* pseudohermaphroditism, androgyny
Scheinzypresse *f* false cypress *(genus Chamaecyparis)*
Scheit *n* billet
Scheitel *m* 1. *(bot, zoo)* apex, tip; 2. crest, crown *(road construction)*
Scheitelblüte *f* apical flower
Scheitelmeristem *n* apical meristem
Scheitelwachstum *n* apical growth
Scheitelzelle *f* apical cell
Schellack *m* shellac, lac
Schemel *m* bunk *(timber transport)*
Schemelrunge *f* bunk spike
Schenkel *m* femur *(animal anatomy)*
~ des Hufeisens branch
Schenkelende *n* **des Hufeisens** heel
Schenkelring *m* trochanter *(of insect's leg)*
Scherbolzen *m* shear bolt (pin)
Scherbruch *m* shear failure
Schere *f* [pair of] scissors, shears
scheren to shear, to clip, to crop, to [de]fleece *(sheep)*; to trim *(esp. dogs)*
~/Kopfwolle to face
Scherenkluppe *f (forest)* tree compass
Scherenkran *m (forest)* shear-legs, sheers, stiffleg [derrick]
Scherenzahn *m* scissor-tooth *(carnivore's dentition)*
Scherfestigkeit *f* shear strength (resistance) *(e.g. of a soil)*
Scherkopf *m* shearing head
Schermaschine *f* shearing machine, clipper, cropper
Schermaus *f* [water] vole, [black] water rat, Arvicola terrestris (amphibius)
Schermodul *m* shear modulus
Scherspannungsverformung *f* shear stress displacement *(e.g. of a soil)*
Scherstift *m* shear pin (bolt)
Scherung *f* shear[ing]
Scherverformung *f* shear strain *(e.g. of a soil)*
Scherwiderstand *m s.* Scherfestigkeit
Scheuchmittel *n* bird repellent
scheuen to shy, to balk *(horse)*

Scheuer

Scheuer f s. Scheune
Scheuerstelle f abrasion bruise (e.g. on fruits)
Scheuklappen fpl blinkers, blinders, winkers
• ~ **anlegen** to blinker
Scheuleder npl s. Scheuklappen
Scheune f barn, corn-house, grange
Scheunendrusch m threshing in the barn
scheunengetrocknet barn-dried
Scheunenhof m barnyard
Scheunentenne f threshing-floor
Scheunentor n barn-door
Schibutter f shea-butter (from Vitellaria paradoxa)
Schicht f layer, ply; stratum
~/**einlagige** monolayer (e.g. of cells)
~/**wasserführende** aquifer, aquafer
schichten to pile [up], to stack, to bank [up]
Schichtenfilter n sheet filter
Schichtfestmeter m stacked cubic metre
Schichtfilter n sediment filter
schichtförmig stratiform
Schichtgesellschaft f layer community (plant sociology)
Schichtholz n piled (stacked) wood, cordwood, corded (short) timber, shortwood
Schichtholzgreifer m timber grab
Schichtholzkipper m tilting cordwood trailer
Schichtholzmethode f shortwood (short-length) logging
Schichtholzrückeschlepper m forwarder
Schichtholzsattelzug m short logger
Schichtholzsortiment n (forest) stacked products
Schichtholzspaltmaschine f log splitter
Schichtkäse m layered white cheese
Schichtlinie f contour line
Schichtmaß n stacked measure (volume) (timber mensuration)
Schichtnutzholz n s. Schichtholz
Schichtsilicat n (soil) layer (sheet) silicate, phyllosilicate
Schichtung f layering, stratification
Schichtwolke f stratus [cloud]
~/**mittelhohe [geschlossene, strukturlose]** altostratus [cloud]
~/**tiefe** stratus [cloud]
Schicksalsbaum m 1. clerodendrum (genus Clerodendrum); 2. bleeding-heart vine, glory bower, tube flower, Clerodendrum thomsonae
schieben/Ähren (Rispen) to ear [up], to go (run) to ear
Schieberdüngerstreuer m reciprocating plate fertilizer distributor
Schieberechen m haystacker
Schieberpumpe f sliding pump
Schiebesammler m buck-rake
~ **mit Ausschubmechanismus** push-off buck-rake
Schiebeschild m [pusher, scraper] blade
Schied m rapacious carp, Aspius aspius
Schiedsanalyse f arbitration analysis
Schiedsmethode f reference method

Schiefblatt n begonia (genus Begonia)
Schiefe f (biom) skewness
Schiefer m (soil) slate
~/**kristalliner** schist
Schiefergestein n slate
Schieferton m (soil) shale
Schiefhals m (vet) torticollis
Schiefheitsmaß n (biom) measure of skewness
Schiefteller m 1. monkey-faced pansy, Cupid's bow, nut orchid, achimenes (genus Achimenes); 2. widow's tears (Achimenes hybrids)
Schielen n (vet) strabismus, squint
Schienbein n shin-bone, tibia, shank; instep (of horse)
Schienbeinbeule f tibial tuberosity
schieren to candle (eggs)
Schierling m cowbane (genus Conium)
Schierlingsreiherschnabel m (bot) alfilaria, alfilerilla, Erodium cicutarium
Schierlingstanne f hemlock fir (spruce) (genus Tsuga)
schießen to shoot
~/**Federwild** to grass
~/**in Samen** to go (run) to seed
~/**Wild** to hunt
Schießer m pot-hunter
Schiffbauholz n shipbuilding timber
Schiffchen n (bot) keel
Schiffswerftkäfer m ship-timber beetle, Lymexylon navale
Schild m plough breast, mould-board shin
Schildchen n (bot, ent) scutellum
Schilddrüse f thyroid [gland]
schilddrüsenaktiv thyrotrop[h]ic
Schilddrüsenarterie f thyroid artery
Schilddrüsenentfernung f (vet) thyroidectomy
Schilddrüsenentzündung f (vet) thyroiditis
Schilddrüsenextrakt m thyroid extract
Schilddrüsenfunktion f thyroid function
Schilddrüsenhormon n thyroid hormone
schilddrüsenstimulierend thyrotrop[h]ic
Schilddrüsenüberfunktion f (vet) hyperthyroidism, thyrotoxicosis
Schilddrüsenunterfunktion f (vet) hypothyroidism
Schildfarn m 1. buckler [fern] (genus Polystichum); 2. Christmas fern, Polystichum acrostichoides; 3. holly fern, Cyrtomium falcatum
schildförmig (bot, zoo) scutiform, peltate, thyroid
Schildkäfer m tortoise beetle (genus Cassida)
Schildknorpel m thyroid [cartilage] (animal anatomy)
Schildlaus f scale[-insect], scale-bug, armoured scale (suborder Coccina)
~/**cochenilleliefernde** cochineal [insect] (comprehensive term)
Schildlausabtötungsmittel n, **Schildlausbekämpfungsmittel** n scalicide
Schildlauslack m lac (esp. from Coccus lacca)
Schildträger m (bot) skull-cap (genus Scutellaria)

Schildwanze f shieldbug *(family Pentatomidae)*
Schildzecke f [hard, wood] tick *(family Ixodidae)*
Schilf n 1. reed[s], reed bank; 2. s. Schilfrohr
schilfartig arundinaceous
Schilfdecke f reed mat
Schilfer m expeller [cake]
Schilferntemäher m reed harvester (mower)
Schilfhalm m reed
Schilfmäher m reed mower (cutter)
Schilfrohr n 1. reed *(genus Phragmites)*; 2. common reed [grass], reed, Phragmites australis (communis)
Schilfschneidemaschine f s. Schilfmäher
Schilftorf m reed (phragmites) peat
Schillergras n *(bot)* koeleria *(genus Koeleria)*
Schillerwein m pink wine
Schimmel m 1. mould, must, mildew; 2. white horse
Schimmelbelag m **auf Blattwerk** leaf-mould
Schimmelbildung f mould formation
Schimmelfäule f mouldy rot *(of Hevea brasiliensis, caused by Ceratocystis fimbriata)*
Schimmelfichte f [eastern] Canadian spruce, white spruce, Picea glauca (alba)
Schimmelgeschmack m mouldy taste *(of wine)*
Schimmelhaut f mycoderma
schimmelig mouldy, mildewed, mildewy, musty, fusty
schimmeln to mould, to mildew
Schimmeln n moulding
Schimmelpilz m mould [fungus]
Schimmelpilzabort m **des Rindes** mycotic abortion in cattle
Schimmelschicht f mycoderma
Schimper-Braunsche Hauptreihe f *(bot)* Schimper and Braun series, Fibonacci series
Schindeleiche f shingle oak, Quercus imbricaria
Schinken m ham
Schinkenfliege f cheese [and bacon] fly, cheese skipper, Piophila casei
Schinkenkern m lean in the ham
Schinkenkraut n evening primrose, Oenothera (Onagra) biennis
Schinkenmasse f ham weight
Schippe f shovel *(s. a. Spaten)*
Schipperke m schipperke *(dog breed)*
Schirm m 1. screen; 2. [forest, leaf] canopy, [crown] cover; shelter
Schirmbaum m 1. umbrella-tree; 2. shelter tree
Schirmbestand m shelterwood, overstorey, overwood, parent stand
Schirmfläche f area under canopy (crown cover)
Schirmglucke f [canopy] brooder, chick-rearing hood, hover
Schirmhieb m shelterwood felling (cutting)
Schirmkeilschlagbetrieb m shelterwood wedge system
Schirmmagnolie f umbrella magnolia (tree), Magnolia tripetala (umbrella)

Schirmpalme f European (dwarf) fan palm, Chamaerops humilis
Schirmsaumschlag m shelterwood strip felling
Schirmsaumschlagsystem n shelterwood-strip system, strip cutting [method]
Schirmschlag m shelterwood felling
Schirmschlagbetrieb m, **Schirmschlagmethode** f shelterwood (compartment) system
Schirmstreifenhieb m s. Schirmsaumschlag
Schirmtanne f umbrella pine (plant), Sciadopitys verticillata
schirmtragend *(bot)* umbraculiferous
Schirmverjüngung f regeneration under shelterwood
schirren to harness, to yoke
Schirrkammer f harness (tack) room
Schirrkette f pole chain
Schistosomat[id]ose f, **Schistosomiasis** f *(vet)* schistosomiasis, bilharziasis, snail fever
schizogen schizogenous
Schizogonie f schizogony
Schizomyzet m s. Bakterium
Schlachtabfall m slaughter waste
Schlachtabschnitt m slaughter cut
Schlachtabwasser n slaughter effluent
Schlachtalter n slaughter[ing] age, age at killing (slaughter)
Schlachtausbeute f slaughter (carcass) yield, *(Am)* cutability
~/prozentuale killing-out percentage, carcass [dressing] percentage
Schlachtbetrieb m s. Schlachthof
Schlachtblut n slaughter blood
Schlachtbulle m slaughter steer
schlachten to slaughter, to butcher, to kill; to dress *(poultry)*
~/Rindvieh to beef
Schlachten n slaughter
Schlächterei f butchery *(s. a. Schlachthof)*
Schlachtergebnis n, **Schlachtertrag** m s. Schlachtausbeute
Schlachterzeugnis n slaughter product
Schlachtfähigkeit f slaughter ability
Schlachtfärse f beef heifer
Schlachtfett n slaughter fat
Schlachtgerät n slaughtering tool
Schlachthälfte f half-carcass
Schlachthaus n s. Schlachthof
Schlachthof m slaughterhouse, slaughtery, slaughter plant, abattoir
Schlachthofmasse f preslaughter weight *(of a slaughter animal)*
Schlachtkalb n slaughter (killing, market) calf, *(Am)* vealer
Schlachtkette f slaughter-line
Schlachtklasse f slaughter grade
Schlachtkörper m carcass, carcase
Schlachtkörperabfall m carcass waste
Schlachtkörperbeschau f carcass inspection

Schlachtkörperbeurteilung

Schlachtkörperbeurteilung f, **Schlachtkörperbewertung** f carcass evaluation (classification), carcass grading (judging)
Schlachtkörperbewertungsmuster n carcass classification scheme
Schlachtkörperfettgehalt m carcass fatness
Schlachtkörperhälfte f carcass side
Schlachtkörperkaltmasse f cold carcass weight
Schlachtkörperklassifizierung f s. Schlachtkörperbewertung
Schlachtkörperlänge f carcass length
Schlachtkörpermasse f carcass weight
Schlachtkörperqualität f carcass quality (grade)
Schlachtkörperuntersuchung f carcass inspection
Schlachtkörpervermarktung f carcass marketing
Schlachtkörperwanddicke f carcass wall thickness
Schlachtkörperwarmmasse f hot carcass weight
Schlachtkörperwert m carcass value
Schlachtkörperzusammensetzung f carcass composition
Schlachtkuh f beef (cull) cow
Schlachtlamm n slaughter (killing) lamb
Schlachtlinie f slaughter-line • **an die ~ anhängen** to shackle
Schlachtmasse f slaughter weight
Schlachtmassetabelle f slaughter weight table
Schlachtmethode f slaughter technique
Schlachtnebenprodukt n abattoir by-product
Schlachtochse m [slaughter] steer
Schlachtpferd n meat horse
Schlachtprämie f slaughter premium
Schlachtprodukt n slaughter product
Schlachtqualität f slaughter quality (grade)
schlachtreif ready for slaughter; in grease, in pride (prime) of grease
Schlachtreife f readiness for slaughter
Schlachtrinder npl, **Schlachtrindvieh** n slaughter (beef) cattle
Schlachtschaf n slaughter sheep
Schlachtschwein n slaughter pig, [market] hog
Schlachttechnik f slaughter technique
Schlachttechnologie f slaughter technology
Schlachtteilstück n slaughter cut; joint
Schlachttier n slaughter (market) animal, animal for slaughter
Schlachttierblut n slaughter blood
Schlachttierklasse f slaughter grade
Schlachttierlunge f lights
Schlachttierversicherung f slaughter stock insurance
Schlacht- und Schlachtkörperkühlbetrieb m freezing works
Schlachtung f slaughter[ing]
Schlachtvieh n slaughter (fat) stock, butcher livestock (s. a. Schlachtrinder)
Schlachtwert m slaughter value
Schlachtwertklasse f carcass grade

Schlachtwolle f skin wool
Schlacke f/basische basic slag (fertilizer)
Schlafapfel m (phyt) bedeguar (of rose-bush, caused by Rhodites roseae)
Schlafbaum m silk tree, Albizia julibrissin
Schlafbewegung f (bot) nyctinasty
Schläfe f temple
Schläfenbein n temporal bone
Schläfengrube f temporal fossa
Schläfer m dormouse (family Gliridae)
schlaff flabby; flaccid
Schlaffsägeblatt n web saw
Schlaffsucht f s. Polyedrose
Schlafmittelnarkose f (vet) thiobarbiturate anaesthesia
Schlafmohn m 1. garden poppy, Papaver somniferum; 2. opium poppy, Papaver somniferum ssp. somniferum
Schlafmützchen n California poppy, Noah's nightcap, Eschscholtzia californica
Schläfrigkeit f drowsiness
Schlafsucht f (vet) lethargy
Schlag m 1. stroke, blow; shock; 2. field, acre; (forest) coupe; 3. strain, variety; 4. s. Schlagfläche
Schlag... s. a. Hiebs...
Schlagabnahme f registration of felled timber, revision of felling record, coupe inventory, produce check, acceptance
Schlagabraum m felling refuse (waste), logging residues (debris), slash, brash, brush[wood]
Schlagabraumbeseitigung f slash clearance (removal), brush disposal
Schlagabraumhacker m brash chopper, brushwood cutter
Schlagabraumsammelmaschine f slash collector
Schlagabraumwall m windrow
Schlagader f artery
~/mediane median artery
Schlaganfall m (vet) [fit of] apoplexy, [apoplectic] stroke
Schlaganschluß m arrangement of the coupes in clear fellings
Schlaganweisung f felling permit (licence)
Schlagaufnahme f s. Schlagabnahme
Schlagauszeichnung f tree (timber) marking
schlagbar ripe for felling (cutting), mature
Schlagegge f shock harrow
schlagen 1. to savage (animal behaviour); to kick, to hoof (horse); 2. to strike, to pounce (bird of prey); 3. s. fällen; 4. to beat, to whip (cream)
~/aus der Decke (hunt) to skin
~/Haken to double, to dodge (hare)
~/Wurzel[n] to root, to strike (take) roots
Schläger m kicker (horse)
Schlagfähigkeit f whippability (of cream)
Schlagfalle f break-back trap
Schlagfestigkeit f shock resistance
Schlagfläche f (forest) felling (felled) area, coupe, area to be cut, cutover, cutting

~/unberäumte slash area, slashing
Schlagflächenflora *f* felled-area flora
Schlagflächenräumung *f* slash disposal (removal)
Schlagflächenvegetation *f* vegetation of clearings
Schlagfolge *f* order (succession) of fellings, felling sequence (cycle, rotation)
Schlagform *f* field shape
Schlagfront *f* felling face
Schlaggrenze *f* field boundary
Schlaggröße *f* field size
Schlagkarte *f* 1. field card; 2. *s.* Hiebskarte
Schlagkartei *f* field file (card index)
Schlagkraft *f* strength
Schlagkräutlein *n* yellow bugle, ground pine, Ajuga chamaepitys
Schlagleiste *f* beater (rasp) bar *(of a threshing-drum)*
Schlagleistentrommel *f* beater bar [threshing] drum, beater drum, rasp-bar cylinder
Schlagloch *n* pot-hole
Schlaglos *n s.* Schlagfläche
Schlagmühle *f* impact mill
Schlagrand *m* field margin (edge)
Schlagräumbrigade *f (forest)* clean-up crew
Schlagregen *m* wind-driven rain
Schlagreihe *f* felling series
Schlagreisig *n* lop and top, lip[ping]s, browst, *(Am)* lapwood
Schlagreisigschiebegabel *f* tree lippings shovel
Schlagreste *mpl s.* Schlagabraum
Schlagsahne *f* whipping-cream
~/geschlagene whipped cream
Schlagschnittverhalten *n* impact cutting behaviour
Schlagsystem *n s.* Waldbausystem
Schlagvolumen *n* stroke volume *(of the heart)*
Schlagzusammenlegung *f* field pooling
Schlamm *m* sludge, slurry; mud, mire, silt; bog
~/aktivierter (biologischer) activated sludge
Schlammasche *f* sludge ash
Schlammbehandlung *f* sludge treatment
Schlammbeize *f* slurry treatment *(of seeds)*
Schlammbelebung *f* bioaeration, sludge activation
Schlammbelebungsverfahren *n* activated-sludge process
schlämmen to outwash, to elutriate
Schlammfliege *f* drone fly, Eristalix tenax
Schlammfliegenlarve *f* rat-tailed maggot
schlammig muddy, silty; boggy
Schlammkonzentrat *n* thickened mud *(sugar manufacture)*
Schlammsaft *m s.* Saturationssaft
Schlammschnecke *f* mud snail *(family Lymnaeidae)*
Schlammstrom *m* mud flow
Schlammteich *m* mud settling pond *(of a sugar mill)*
Schlange *f* snake, serpent *(group Ophidia)*
schlangenartig *(bot)* anguine[ous]

Schlangenbart *m* lilyturf *(genus Ophiopogon)*
Schlangenbiß *m* snake bite
Schlangencereus *m* night-blooming cereus *(genus Selenicereus)*
Schlangengegengift *n* antivenene, antivenin
Schlangengift *n* snake venom
Schlangengurke *f*, **Schlangenhaarblume** *f s.* Schlangenhaargurke
Schlangenhaargurke *f* snake (serpent) gourd, long tomato, Trichosanthes cucumerina var. anguina
Schlangenkaktus *m* rat-tail cactus, Aporocactus (Cereus) flagelliformis
Schlangen[knob]lauch *m* rocambole, sand leek, giant garlic, Allium sativum var. ophioscorodon, Allium scorodoprasum
Schlangenlilie *f* tree dracaena, Dracaena arborea
Schlangenmelone *f* snake (serpent) melon, Cucumis melo convar. flexuosus
Schlangenminiermotte *f (ent)* apple leaf-miner, Lyonetia clerckella
Schlangenrettich *m* serpent radish, snake-like (rat-tailed) radish, Raphanus sativus var. mougri
Schlangenwurz *f (bot)* calla *(genus Calla)*
Schlanke Deutzie *f (bot)* slender deutzia, Deutzia gracilis
Schlankheitsgrad *m* slenderness *(timber mensuration)*
Schlappeuter *n* pendulous udder
Schlappohr *n* drooping ear
Schlauch *m* 1. hose; 2. *s.* Präputialschlauch • **mit dem ~ wässern** to hose
Schlauchanschluß *m* hose connection
schlauchartig *(bot, zoo)* utricular, utriculate
Schlauchberegnung *f* hose irrigation
Schlauchbewässerung *f* hose irrigation, cablegation
Schlauchbinder *m* hose clip
Schlauchdüse *f* hose nozzle
Schlauchen *n* green beer transfer
Schlaucherdecke *f* yeast head *(brewing)*
Schlauchfolie *f* tubular [plastic] film
schlauch[förm]ig *(bot, zoo)* utricular, utriculate, tubular
Schlauchklemme *f* hose clip
Schlauchkupplung *f* mit Abreißsicherung quick-disconnect coupler [with ball check valve]
Schlauchläufer *m* hose walker
Schlauchpflanze *f* pitcher plant *(genus Sarracenia)*
Schlauchpilz *m* ascomycete *(class Ascomycetes)*
Schlauchrolle *f* hose reel
Schlauchrollen[beregnungs]anlage *f* hose-reel irrigation system
Schlauchrollenregner *m* hose-reel irrigator (sprinkler)
Schlauchrollenwagen *m* hose reel cart
Schlauch-Schlauch-Beregnungsanlage *f* hose-hose installation

Schlauchschutzrolle

Schlauchschutzrolle f hose protection drum
Schlauchspore f (bot) ascospore
Schlauchtrommel f s. Schlauchrolle
Schlauchverbindung f hose connection
Schlauchwagen m hose reel cart
Schlauchzelle f (bot) tube cell
Schlechtseite f worse face (timber sorting)
schlechtwüchsig unthrifty
Schlegelernter m, **Schlegel[feld]häcksler** m flail chopper, flail [forage] harvester
Schlegelkrautschläger m flail haulm pulverizer
Schlegelmäher m, **Schlegelmähwerk** n flail mower (cutter)
Schlegeltrommel f flail rotor
Schlehdorn m, **Schlehe** f sloe, blackthorn, (Am) wild plum, Prunus spinosa
Schlehenfrostspanner m (ent) pale brindled beauty, Phigalia pedaria
Schlehenpflaume f s. Schlehdorn
Schlehenspinner m rusty [tussock] moth, vapourer moth, Orgyia antiqua
Schlei m s. Schleie
Schleichjagd f stalk, deer-stalking, (Am) still-hunt
Schleie f [green] tench, Tinca tinca
Schleier m (bot, zoo) velum, veil
Schleier[gips]kraut n 1. chalk plant, babies' (baby's) breath, gyp[sophila] (genus Gypsophila); 2. babies' (baby's) breath, Gypsophila paniculata
Schleier[schicht]wolke f cirrostratus [cloud]
Schleife f/Henlesche Henle's loop (of the nephron)
Schleifen n s. Schleifrücken
Schleifenbildung f der Chromosomen chromosome coiling
Schleifenblume f (bot) candytuft (genus Iberis)
Schleiffahren n (forest) high-lead skidding
Schleifholz n pulpwood
Schleifholzknüppel m, **Schleifholzrundling** m pulpwood bolt
Schleifrückekette f skid[ding] chain
Schleifrücken n (forest) ground skidding (yarding), dragging, bob-tailing, snaking
~ **mittels Seilkrans** ground-lead [cable] logging, ground hauling
Schleifschuh m **am Mähbalken** cutter bar shoe
Schleifsohle f [landside] heel, slade, runner (of a plough)
Schleifstein m grindstone, whetstone
Schleiftaster m sleeve feeler (of a beet harvester)
Schleifweg m (forest) skidding lane (track), logging (extraction, drag) road, snig [track]
Schleifwirkung f abrasion
Schleim m slime, mucus; mucilage (esp. obtained from plant seeds)
schleimabsondernd muciferous, mucous; mucilaginous
Schleimapfel m (bot) mountain sour-sop, Annona montana

Schleimapfelbaum m Bengal quince, bael, Aegle marmelos
schleimausscheidend s. schleimabsondernd
Schleimbeutel m bursa
Schleimbeutelentfernung f (vet) bursectomy
Schleimbeutelentzündung f (vet) bursitis
Schleimbeuteleröffnung f (vet) bursotomy
Schleimbeutelkonkrement n (vet) bursolith
schleimbildend mucigenous, muciparous
Schleimdrüse f mucus gland
Schleimfluß m slime flux
schleimgefüllt muciferous, mucilaginous
Schleimgewebegeschwulst f (vet) myxoma
schleimhaltig muciferous, mucilaginous
Schleimhaut f mucosa, mucous membrane
Schleimhautentzündung f (vet) mucositis
Schleimhautkrankheit f (vet) mucosal disease; bovine mucosal disease
schleimig slimy, mucous, mucilaginous, rop[e]y
Schleimkrankheit f southern bacterial wilt, brown rot (of potato, caused by Pseudomonas solanacearum)
schleimlösend mucolytic, expectorant
Schleimpilz m slime fungus (mould), myxomycete (order Myxomycotina)
Schleimsäure f mucic acid
Schleimstoff m mucin
Schleimzelle f (bot) mucilage cell
schleißen to strip (feathers, hemp)
Schlempe f distiller's solubles (wash), pot ale, spent liquor, stillage, vinasse, swill
Schlempemauke f (vet) potato eczema
Schleppboot n tug[boat] (rafting)
Schleppdach n Dutch barn
Schleppdreieck n drag triangle
Schleppe f 1. float, scrubber (field equipment); 2. break (for exercising young horses)
schleppen to trail
Schlepper m 1. tractor (for compounds s. under Traktor); 2. carrier (physiology, immunology)
Schlepper... s. Traktor...
Schleppkettenentladevorrichtung f drag-chain unloader
Schleppleine f drag-line
Schleppnetz n trail (drag) net, trawl[-net], seine[-net] • **mit dem ~ fischen** to trawl
Schlepp-Pflug m drag plough
Schlepprechen m drag rake
Schleppschar n shoe coulter
Schleppschardrillmaschine f runner planter
Schleppschaufelentmistungsanlage f push-type dung channel cleaner, winch-drawn dung channel cleaner
Schleppschlauchregner m hose-towed irrigator
Schleswiger Kaltblut[pferd] n Schleswig (horse breed)
Schleuder f (api) extractor
Schleuderdüngerstreuer m centrifugal [fertilizer] distributor, fertilizer broadcaster, rotary spreader

Schleudergrubberegge *f* drag-harrow
Schleuderhonig *m* extracted (strained) honey, centrifugal (run) honey
Schleuderkrankheit *f* false gid (sturdy) *(of sheep due to nose bot infestation)*
Schleuderkreissäge *f* wobble saw
Schleuderradroder *m* potato spinner, rotary digger, spading machine
Schleuderraum *m (api)* honey house
Schleuderstreuer *m s.* Schleuderdüngerstreuer
Schleudertrommel *f (dairy)* separator bowl
Schleuse *f* sluice
Schleusengebläse *n* pneumatic conveyor with intake hopper
Schleusenmotte *f* cork moth, Nemapogon cloacellus
Schlichtwalze *f* flat roll[er]
Schlick *m* silt, mud; warp
schliefen *(hunt)* to earth
Schließen *n* **des Jungwuchses** *(forest)* canopy closure of young stand
~ **des Pflanzenbestandes** meeting of the plants in the row
Schließfrucht *f* indehiscent fruit
~ **der Gräser** caryopsis
~/**[trockene] geflügelte** key [fruit], samara, chat
Schließmuskel *m* sphincter
Schließzelle *f (bot)* guard cell
Schlinge *f* 1. *(hunt)* snare, springe; 2. *s.* Schneeball
Schlingpflanze *f* climbing (twining) plant, climber, twiner [plant]
Schlingstörung *f (vet)* dysphagia
Schlippermilch *f* naturally soured milk
Schlitten *m* sledge, sleigh
Schlittenführer *m* sledger
Schlittenhund *m* sledge dog
Schlittenkufe *f* sledge (sleigh) runner
Schlittweg *m* sledge-way
schlitzblättrig *(bot)* schizophyllous
Schlitzblättriger Nachtschatten *m (bot)* poroporo, Solanum aviculare (laciniatum)
~ **Sonnenhut** *m* coneflower, Rudbeckia laciniata
Schlitzdränung *f* slot drainage
Schlitzdüse *f* slot (fan) nozzle
Schlitzlochsieb *n* slotted screen
Schlitzmulch *m* slot mulch
Schlitzschablone *f* slotted template (templet)
Schlotterkamm *m* lopped comb *(of fowl)*
Schlucht *f* ravine, gorge, gully, dean
Schluchtenwald *m* ravine (gorge) forest
Schluchtenwaldanbau *m* gully afforestation
Schluckakt *m* deglutition
schlucken to swallow
Schluckreflex *m* swallowing reflex
Schluckstörung *f (vet)* dysphagia
Schluff *m* silt
schluffartig silty
Schluffboden *m* silty soil, silt

schluffhaltig, schluffig silty
Schlufflehm *m* silt loam
Schlufffraktion *f* silt fraction
Schluffton *m* silty clay
Schluffverdichtungszone *f* silt pan
Schlund *m* gullet, throat, throttle, oesophagus, pharynx
Schlundfistel *f (vet)* oesophageal fistula
Schlundgerüst *n (ent)* cephalopharyngeal skeleton
Schlundhaken *m (ent)* mouth hook
Schlundkopf *m* pharynx
Schlundrinne *f* oesophageal groove
Schlundrohr *n*, **Schlundsonde** *f (vet)* oesophageal tube
Schlundspiegelung *f (vet)* pharyngoscopy
Schlupf *m* 1. [wheel] slip, slippage; 2. hatching; emergence *(of insects)*
Schlupfbrüter *m* hatcher
Schlupfdatum *n* hatching date (time)
schlüpfen to hatch, to creep out; to emerge *(insects)*
Schlupfergebnis *n* hatching rate (percentage)
Schlupffähigkeit *f* hatchability
Schlupffaktor *m* hatching factor
Schlupfhorde *f* hatching tray
Schlupfküken *n* baby chick
Schlupfloch *n* emergence (exit) hole
Schlupfmonitor *m* slip monitor
Schlüpföffnung *f* **für Melker** operator squeeze gap *(of a rotary milking parlour)*
Schlupfperiode *f* emergence period
Schlupfrate *f* hatching rate (percentage)
Schlupfregelung *f* slip control
Schlupfsynchronisation *f* hatching synchronization
Schlupftermin *m* hatching date
Schlupfwespe *f* parasitic wasp *(family Ichneumonidae)*
Schlüsselart *f (ecol)* key species
Schlüsselbein *n* collar-bone, clavicle
Schlüsselblume *f* cowslip, English primrose, polyanthus, Primula veris
Schlüsselenzym *n* key enzyme
Schlüsselfaktor *m (ecol)* key factor
Schlüsselfaktorenanalyse *f (ecol)* key factor analysis
Schlüsselgen *n* switch gene
Schlüsselreiz *m* key stimulus
Schlußfurche *f* sole furrow *(ploughing)*
Schlußgesellschaft *f (ecol)* terminal community; mature plant community
~/**[groß]klimabedingte** climax [community]
Schlußgrad *m (forest)* canopy cover [density] • **mit niedrigem** ~ open-growing, free-growing *(stand)*
Schlußhäufeln *n* final earthing-up *(potato growing)*
Schlußhufeisen *n* full-bar shoe
Schlußklasse *f (forest)* canopy cover class

Schlußunterbrechung

Schlußunterbrechung *f (forest)* interruption of canopy
Schmachtkorn *n* shrivelled grain
schmackhaft palatable, tasty, delicate
Schmackhaftigkeit *f* palatability, tastiness
schmalährig *(bot)* stenostachyous
schmalblättrig narrow-leaved, angustifolious, stenophyllous
Schmalblättrige Esche *f* narrow-leaved ash, Fraxinus angustifolia ssp. oxycarpa
~ **Lorbeerrose** *f* sheep laurel, lambkill, Kalmia angustifolia
~ **Lupine** *f* narrow-leaved lupin[e], blue lupin[e], Lupinus angustifolius
~ **Ölweide** *f* Russian olive, oleaster, Elaeagnus angustifolia
~ **Pflaume** *f* Chickasaw plum, Prunus angustifolia
~ **Rampe** *f* perennial wall rocket, Diplotaxis tenuifolia
~ **Wicke** *f* summer (narrow-leaved) vetch, Vicia sativa ssp. nigra
Schmalblättriger Hornklee *m* slender (narrow-leaved) trefoil, Lotus tenuis
Schmalblättriges Weidenröschen *n* blooming willow, Epilobium (Chamaenerion) angustifolium
Schmalblättrigkeit *f (phyt)* leaf narrowing, shoe-stringing, shoe-lacing, shoe-string [disease]
schmalblumig narrow-flowered
schmalbrüstig narrow-chested
schmalflügelig *(bot, zoo)* stenopterous
schmalfrüchtig *(bot)* stenocarpous
Schmalhornkäfer *m* slender-horned flour beetle, Echocerus maxillosus
schmalköpfig *(bot, zoo)* stenocephalous
schmalkronblättrig narrow-peta[l]led
schmalkronig narrow-crowned *(tree)*
~ **und vollholzig** drawn-up *(tree)*
Schmalreh *n* two-years-old doe
Schmalsaumschlag *m (forest)* narrow-edge coupe
Schmalspießer *m* brocket *(male red deer two years old)*
Schmalspurschlepper *m*, **Schmalspurtraktor** *m* narrow-track tractor
Schmaltier *n* two-years-old doe
Schmalz *n* lard
schmarotzen to parasitize
schmarotzend parasitic[al]
Schmarotzer *m* parasite
~/**an Pflanzen lebender** phytoparasite
~/**fakultativer** facultative parasite
~/**obligater** obligate parasite
~/**permanenter** permanent parasite
~/**pilzlicher** mycoparasite, parasitic fungus
Schmarotzerbefall *m* parasite infestation
Schmarotzerfliege *f* tachina-fly, tachinid [fly] *(family Tachinidae)*
schmarotzerhaft parasitic[al]
Schmarotzerkunde *f* parasitology

Schmarotzerpflanze *f* parasitic [higher] plant, hysterophyte
Schmarotzertum *n* parasitism
Schmasche *f* birth coat *(of lambs)*
Schmeerbirne *f* sorb[-apple], Sorbus domestica
schmeißen to kick, to savage *(animal behaviour)*
Schmeißfliege *f* bluebottle, blowfly, Calliphora vicina
Schmelz *m* [dental] enamel
schmelzen to melt; to thaw; to render [down] *(fat, beeswax)*
schmelzend melting; deliquescent
Schmelzkäse *m* processed cheese
Schmelzpunkt *m* melting point
Schmelzsalz *n* emulsifying salt *(cheese-making)*
Schmelzwärme *f* melting heat
Schmelzwasser *n* melt-water, thaw water • **von eiszeitlichem ~ gebildet** fluvio-glacial, glaciofluvial
Schmer *m(n)* leaf fat
Schmerbauchrüßler *m* sand weevil, Philopedon plagiatus
Schmerling *m (bot)* granulated boletus, Boletus (Suillus) granulatus
Schmerz *m* pain
Schmerzempfindungsrezeptor *m* nociceptor
Schmerzmittel *n (vet)* analgesic
Schmerzpunkt *m*, **Schmerzrezeptor** *m* nociceptor
schmerzunempfindlich anaesthetic
Schmerzunempfindlichkeit *f* anaesthesia
Schmerzwurz *f* black bryony, Tamus communis
Schmerzwurzbeere *f* murrain berry *(from Tamus communis)*
Schmetterling *m* butterfly, lepidopteran *(order Lepidoptera)*
schmetterlingsartig *(bot)* papilionaceous
Schmetterlingsblütler *mpl* pea family *(family Fabaceae = Papilionaceae)*
Schmetterlingshündchen *n* papillon *(dog breed)*
Schmetterlingskamm *m* leaf comb *(of fowl)*
Schmetterlingslarve *f* caterpillar
Schmetterlingsorchidee *f* 1. oncidium *(genus Oncidium)*; 2. butterfly plant, Oncidium papilio
Schmetterlingsporling *m (bot)* common zoned polyporus, Trametes versicolor
Schmetterlingsstrauch *m* 1. buddleia *(genus Buddleja)*; 2. butterfly bush, summer lilac, Buddleja davidii
Schmied *m* smith
Schmiegeegge *f* chain harrow, flexible [tine] harrow
Schmiele *f* hair-grass *(genus Deschampsia)*
Schmielenhafer *m* hair-grass *(genus Aira)*
schmieren to lubricate, to grease
Schmierfett *n* [lubricating] grease
schmierig greasy
Schmierkopf *m s.* Schmiernippel
Schmierlaus *f* mealy-bug, mealbug *(family Pseudococcidae)*

Schmiermittel *n* lubricant
Schmiernippel *m* grease nipple (fitting), fitting [for lubrication]
Schmieröl *n* lubricating oil
Schmierpresse *f* grease-gun
Schmierstoff *m* lubricant
Schmierung *f* lubrication
Schminkbeere *f* [Virginian] pokeweed, poke[berry], pokeroot, Phytolacca americana
Schminkwurz *f* [dyer's] alkanet, false alkanet, Alkanna tinctoria (tuberculata)
Schmirgel *m* corn buttercup, goldilocks, Ranunculus arvensis
Schmuckbaum *m* ornamental tree
Schmuckkörbchen *n* cosmos, cosmea, Mexican daisy *(genus Cosmos)*
Schmucklilie *f* 1. agapanthus *(genus Agapanthus)*; 2. [blue] African lily, blue lily of the Nile, Agapanthus africanus (umbellatus)
Schmuckreisig *n* ornamental branches
Schmuckwanze *f* cabbage bug, Murgantia histrionica
Schmutz *m* dirt, trash
Schmutzabscheider *m* trash eliminator
Schmutzanteil *m* dirt percentage
Schmutzbesatz *m* dirt tare
Schmutzei *n* dirty (soiled) egg
schmutzigbraun *(bot)* fuliginous, lurid
Schmutzprozente *npl* dirt percentage
Schmutzrübe *f* dirty beet
Schmutzstoff *m* contaminant, pollutant
Schmutzwasser *n* sewage; foul water
Schmutzwolle *f* raw wool, wool in the grease; dag • **~ abscheren** to tag
Schnabel *m* beak *(esp. of raptorial birds)*; bill, nab; rostrum • **den ~ kupieren** to debeak
~/flacher bill
~/gekrümmter beak
Schnabelhiebmal *n* bird peck
Schnabelhöhle *f* bill cavity
Schnabelkerf *m* [plant] bug, hemipteran *(order Hemiptera)*
Schnabelschar *n* general share *(of plough body)*
Schnabelspitze *f* beak point
Schnabelstutzer *m*, **Schnabelstutzgerät** *n* debeaker
schnabelwärts rostral
Schnake *f* crane-fly, daddy-long-legs, carter *(family Tipulidae)*
Schnakenlarve *f* crane-fly grub, leather-jacket
Schnalle *f* buckle, clamp
Schnapsagave *f* *(bot)* tequila mescal, Agave tequilana
Schnatterente *f* gadwall, Anas strepera
schnattern to cackle, to gaggle, to clack, to quack
Schnattern *n* cackle
schnauben to snort
Schnauben *n* snort
Schnauze *f* muzzle, neb; snout *(esp. of a pig)*

schnäuzen to snipe, to nose *(a tree)*
schnauzenwärts rostral
Schnauzer *m* schnauzer *(dog breed)*
Schnecke *f* 1. gast[e]ropod, snail *(class Gastropoda)*; 2. cochlea *(of the inner ear)*; 3. s. Schneckenförderer
schneckenabtötend molluscicidal
Schneckenbekämpfung *f* mollusc control
Schneckenbohne *f* snail flower, Phaseolus caracalla
Schneckenentsafter *m* auger-type juice separator
Schneckenförderer *m* auger elevator (feeder), auger (helix, screw) conveyor, conveyor screw
schneckenförmig *(bot, zoo)* cochleate[d]
Schneckengang *m* cochlear duct *(of the inner ear)*
Schneckengetriebe *n* worm-and-wheel gear
Schneckenklee *m* medic[k], snail-clover *(genus Medicago)*
Schneckenpflug *m* auger plough
Schneckenpresse *f* screw (auger-type) press, extruder, expeller
Schneckenrührwerk *n* screw mixer
Schneckenstreuer *m* auger distributor
Schneckentrogpumpe *f* screw-auger pump
Schneckenvernichtungsmittel *n* molluscicide
Schnee-auf-dem-Berge *m* *(bot)* snow-on-the-mountain, Euphorbia marginata
Schneeball *m* snowball[-tree], arrow-wood, viburnum *(genus Viburnum)*
Schneeballblattkäfer *m* cranberry tree leaf beetle, Galerucella viburni
schneebedeckt snowy
Schneebeere *f* snow-berry, St. Peter's wort *(genus Symphoricarpus)*
Schneebirne *f* snow pear, Pyrus nivalis
Schneebruch *m* *(forest)* snowbreak[age]
Schneebruchanfälligkeit *f* susceptibility to snowbreak[age]
Schneebruchbestand *m* snowbreakage stand
Schneebruchgefährdung *f* risk of snow damage
Schneebruchschaden *m* snowbreakage damage
Schneedecke *f* snow cover (blanket)
~/hohe snow pack
Schnee-Einschlag *m* snow bedding *(of forest plants)*
Schneefall *m* snowfall
Schneeflocke *f* *(bot)* snowflake *(genus Leucojum)*
Schneeflockenstrauch *m* fringe tree, Chionanthus virginicus
Schneefräse *f* snow blower (propeller)
Schneeglöckchenbaum *m* snowdrop tree, snowbell, silver-bell [tree] *(genus Halesia)*
Schneegrenze *f* snow-line • **oberhalb der [klimatischen] ~** nival
Schneehase *m* mountain (varying) hare, Lepus timidus (variabilis)
Schneeheide *f* spring heath, Erica herbacea (carnea)

Schneehuhn

Schneehuhn *n* ptarmigan, snow-grouse, white grouse *(genus Lagopus)*
Schneehürde *f* snow fence
Schneelast *f* snow load (pressure)
Schneematsch *m* slush
Schneepflug *m* snow-plough
Schneeräumgeräte *npl* snow clearing equipment
Schneeregen *m* sleet
schneereich snowy
Schneeruhm *m (bot)* glory-of-the-snow, chionodoxa *(genus Chionodoxa)*
Schneerutsch *m* snow-slip, avalanche
Schneesaat *f (forest)* snow sowing
Schneeschaden *m* snow damage
Schneeschimmel *m* 1. [pink] snow mould, fusarium leaf blotch *(of cereals, caused by Fusarium = Griphosphaeria nivalis)*; 2. snow blight *(esp. of conifers)*
Schneeschütte *f (phyt)* snow cast *(caused by Phacidium infestans)*
Schneeschutzstreifen *m* snow-retaining strip, snowbreak
Schneeschutzzaun *m* snow fence
Schneestolz *m s.* Schneeruhm
Schneesturm *m* snowstorm
~/schwerer blizzard
Schneeverwehung *f* snow-drift
Schneeweg *m* snow road
Schneewehe *f* snow-drift
Schneewein *m* snow wine
Schneezaun *m* snow fence
Schneeziege *f (Am)* mountain goat, Oreamnos americanus
Schneidabfälle *mpl* clippings
Schneidbogen *m* arrow cutter
Schneidebühne *f* pruning platform *(orcharding)*
Schneidel... *s.* Schneitel...
Schneidemaschine *f* cutter, cropper
schneiden to cut; to trim, to clip; to reap *(corn)*; to prune *(woody plants)*
Schneidermuskel *m* sartorius muscle
Schneidermuskelfett *n* sartorial fat
Schneidewurftrommel *f* cut-and-throw cylinder
Schneidezahn *m* incisor [tooth]; nipper *(of horse)*
~/erster (innerer, vorderer) pincers
Schneidgebläse *n* cutter (chopper) blower, blower-chopper
Schneidkante *f* [cutting] edge
Schneidlader *m* cutter-loader
Schneidscheibe *f* knife disk *(of a chipper)*
Schneidwerk *n* cutter [bar, section], sickle bar; cutting assembly, [cutting] table, header, mower
~/bodenkopierendes floating cutter bar
Schneidwerkrücklauf *m* table feed reverse, cutting assembly return
Schneidwerksantrieb *m* cutter bar drive, cutting table drive
Schneidwerksbreite *f* table width
Schneidwerkskupplung *f* cutter bar clutch
Schneidwerksverluste *mpl* cutter bar losses, header losses
Schneidwerkswagen *m* table (header) trailer, table transport trolley
Schneidwerkvertikalverstellung *f* header control
Schneidzahn *m* cutter tooth *(of a saw)*
schneien to snow
Schneise *f (forest)* ride, aisle, glade
Schneisennetz *n* net of rides
Schneitelbetrieb *m (forest)* lopping system, pollard[ing] system
Schneitelholz *n* pruning offal, prunings, lop and top *(crop)*, loppings, lops
schneiteln to prune [down], to lop [off], to [de]limb, to brush through (up), to abnodate
Schneitelstamm *m* lopped tree
Schneitelstreu *f* chat litter
Schneitelwirtschaft *f s.* Schneitelbetrieb
Schnellbestimmung *f* rapid determination
Schnellbodenbearbeitung *f* high-speed tillage
Schnellgärung *f* accelerated fermentation
Schnellgefrieren *n* quick-freezing
Schnellkäfer *m* click (snapping) beetle, elater[id], skipjack *(family Elateridae)* • **die ~ betreffend** elaterid
Schnellkäferlarve *f* elaterid larva, wire-worm
Schnellkompostierung *f* high-rapid composting
Schnellkühler *m* quick chiller
Schnellkuppler *m*, **Schnellkupplung** *f* quick coupling mechanism, quick-action coupler, rapid coupling device, quick release coupling system
Schnellkupplungsrohr *n* quick-coupling pipe, pipe with quick coupling
Schnellmälzung *f* accelerated malting
Schnellmast *f* rapid fattening (finishing), immediate fattening, fast finish
Schnellpflug *m* high-speed plough
Schnellpflugkörper *m* high-speed plough body
schnellreifend quick-maturing
Schnelltiefkühlverfahren *n* quick-freezing
Schnellverschluß *m s.* Schnellkuppler
Schnellwaage *f* high-speed balance
schnellwachsend fast-growing, quick-growing
Schnellwechselschar *f* quick-mounting share
schnellwirkend quick-acting *(e.g. fertilizer)*
Schnellwuchsbetrieb *m (forest)* accelerative system
schnellwüchsig *s.* schnellwachsend
Schnellwuchsplantage *f (forest)* fast-growing species plantation
Schnepfe *f* snipe, long-bill *(genus Capella)*
Schnepfendreck *m* roast giblets of snipe
Schnepfenfliege *f* ash-fly, Leptis scolopacea
Schnepfengescheide *n s.* Schnepfendreck
Schnepfenjagd *f* snipe-shooting • **auf ~ gehen** to snipe
Schnepfenstrich *m* flight (passage) of woodcocks
Schnepfenvogel *m* snipe *(family Charadriidae)*

Schnippe f snip *(white marking e.g. on a horse's head)*
Schnipperling m shearing wound
Schnitt m 1. cut, cutting; pruning *(orcharding)*; section; 2. cut, clip, crop *(esp. of grass)*
~/formgebender shearing
~ in der Vegetationsruhe dormant pruning
~/kurzer short pruning
~/langer long pruning
~/selektiver detail pruning
Schnittabfall m pruning offal[s], pruning wood, prunings
Schnittbalken m cutter (sickle) bar
Schnittblume f cut flower
Schnittblumenerzeugung f cut flower production
Schnittblumenhaltbarkeit f vase-life
Schnittblumensortiermaschine f cut flower grader
Schnittbreite f cutting width; kerf, curf *(in sawing)*
~ des Scharpflugkörpers plough size
Schnittebene f pruning level
Schnittechnik f pruning technique
Schnittentbindung f *(vet)* Caesarean birth
Schnitter m scytheman, reaper
Schnittermin m cutting date
schnittfähig millable *(undressed timber)*
Schnittfuge f notch *(tree-felling)*; [saw] kerf, curf
Schnittfugengrund m kerf bottom
Schnittführung f cutting management *(forage production)*
Schnittgeräte npl pruning equipment
Schnittgrün n cut foliage, cut [florist's] green, greens, ornamental foliage (verdure)
Schnittgüte f saw kerf quality
Schnitthäufigkeit f cutting frequency; clipping frequency
Schnitthöhe f cutting height, height of cutting
Schnitthöhenanzeige f cutting height indicator
Schnitthöhenregulierung f cutting height control
Schnittholz n 1. [sawn] timber, sawtimber, sawnwood, *(Am)* lumber; 2. pruning wood (offal), lop and top (crop), loppings, lops, brush[wood]
Schnittholzberäumung f brush disposal *(in orchards)*
Schnittholzhäcksler m wood (brush) shredder
Schnittholzindustrie f sawmilling industry
Schnittholzliste f tally sheet
Schnittholzplatz m sawnwood (timber) yard, *(Am)* lumber yard
Schnittholzsortentabelle f timber (mill) tally, *(Am)* lumber tally
Schnittkäse m [semi]hard cheese
Schnittlauch m chive, Allium schoenoprasum
Schnittling m cutting, set[t], slip
Schnittlingsvermehrung f propagation by cutting[s], cuttage
Schnittmangold m spinach (leaf) beet, silver (seakale) beet, [Swiss] chard, Beta vulgaris var. vulgaris (cicla)

Schnittnelke f cut carnation
Schnittpetersilie f parsley, Petroselinum crispum ssp. crispum
schnittreif ripe (ready) for cutting
Schnittreisigschiebegabel f tree lopping shovel
Schnittsalat m curled (cut, leaf) lettuce, Lactuca sativa var. crispa
Schnittseite f flesh side *(of a fleece)*
Schnittsellerie m cutting (curled, soup) celery, smallage, Apium graveolens var. secalinum
Schnittsenf m mustard green
Schnittsystem n pruning system
~/mehrstämmiges multiple-stem pruning system
Schnittware f s. Schnittholz 1.
Schnittwerkzeug n pruning tool
Schnittwiderstand m cutting resistance
Schnittwinkel m cutting angle
~ des Zahndaches top-plate cutting angle, [top-] face angle *(of chain-saw)*
Schnittwunde f pruning wound (cut)
Schnittzeit f cutting time
Schnittzeitpunkt m cutting date
Schnittzeitspanne f cutting period
Schnittzwiebel f green onion
Schnitzel n chop *(of pork carcass)*
Schnitzel npl(mpl) chips, chippings; cossettes, pulp, shreds *(of sugar-beets)*
Schnitzelmaschine f [beet] slicing machine, [beet] slicer
~/hängende suspended beet slicer
~ mit horizontal drehender Schneidscheibe horizontal beet slicer
Schnitzelmesser n beet knife
~/Königsfelder Koenigsfeld knife, Koenigsfelder-type knife
schnitzeln to chip; to slice *(e.g. beets)*
Schnitzelpresse f pulp press
Schnitzelpreßwasser n pulp press water
Schnitzelpumpe f pulp pump
Schnitzeltrockner m [beet] pulp dryer
Schnitzeltrocknung f [beet] pulp drying
schnitzen to carve, to whittle
Schnitzler m shredder *(s. a. Häckselmaschine)*
Schnüffelkrankheit f atrophic rhinitis *(of pigs)*
Schnupfen m *(vet)* coryza, rhinitis
Schnurbaum m 1. kowhai, locust, sophora *(genus Sophora)*; 2. Japanese pagoda tree, umbrella-tree, Sophora japonica; 3. s. Schnurspalierbaum
Schnurspalierbaum m cordon *(orcharding)*
~/einarmiger waagerechter horizontal cordon
~/senkrechter vertical cordon
~/zweiarmiger waagerechter double horizontal cordon
Schnurweide f strip grazing
Schober m rick, stack, mow
Schoberabdecktuch n rick-cloth
Schoberbau m ricking, stacking
Schoberdach n stack guard
Schoberheu n hay-mow

schobern

schobern to rick, to stack, to pile [up]
Schoberrechen *m* buck-rake
Schobersetzer *m*, **Schobersetzvorrichtung** *f* [hay]stacker; stack wagon
Schoberunterbau *m* rick stand
Schock *m* (vet) shock
~/anaphylaktischer anaphylactic (allergic) shock, anaphylaxis
Schockbeleuchtung *f* flash lighting *(poultry farming)*
schockfrosten to quick-freeze
Schockfrosten *n* quick-freezing, rapid-freezing
schockgefrieren to quick-freeze
Schockholz *n* brushwood in bundles
Schokoladen[blut]agar *m* chocolate agar
Schokoladenfleckenkrankheit *f* **der Ackerbohne** chocolate spot of broad bean *(caused by Botrytis fabae)*
Schokomilch *f* chocolate milk
Scholle *f* clod
Schöllkraut *n* [greater] celandine, swallow-wort, tetterwort, Chelidonium majus
schönen to fine *(e.g. a wine)*
Schönen *n* fining
Schöner Ampfer *m* fiddle dock, Rumex pulcher
Schönfaden *m* (bot) bottle-brush *(genus Callistemon)*
Schonforst *m* protected forest, reserve[d] forest
schönfrüchtig (bot) callicarpous
Schongebiet *n* sanctuary, closed area
Schönhäutchen *n* spider lily *(genus Hymenocallis)*
Schönknöterich *m* (bot) dshusgun *(genus Calligonum)*
Schönmalve *f* flowering maple, abutilon *(genus Abutilon)*
Schönranke *f* glory flower, Chilean glory vine, Eccremocarpus scaber
Schonung *f* (forest) nursery of young trees, young plantation
Schönung *f* fining *(e.g. of wine)*
Schönungsmittel *n* fining agent
Schonwald *m* *s.* Schonforst
Schönwetterhaufenwolke *f* cumulus [cloud]
Schonzeit *f* fence-month, fence-season, close[d] season (time), sanctuary *(game management)*
Schopf *m* forelock *(of the mane)*
Schopfbaum *m* tufted tree
Schopfbaumformation *f* mop-headed tree formation
Schöpfeimer *m* bailer
Schopfhirsch *m* tufted deer, Elaphodus cephalophus
schopfig (bot) comose, comate
Schopflavendel *m* Arabian (French) lavender, Lavandula stoechas
Schopflilie *f* pineapple lily *(genus Eucomis)*
Schöpfspachtel *m(f)* iron dip, dipper *(resin-tapping)*

Schopftintling *m* maned agaric, shaggy [ink-]cap fungus, shaggy mane, horse-tail fungus, Coprinus comatus
Schopfträubel *n* tassel hyacinth, Muscari comosum
Schöps *m* *s.* Hammel 1.
Schorf *m* (phyt) scab, scurf; (vet) scab, slough • **an ~ erkrankt** scabby
schorfbedeckt scabby
Schorffleck *m* (phyt, vet) scab
schorffleckig scabby
schorfig scabby
Schoß *m* (bot) shoot
schossen to shoot; to bolt, to run to seed *(beet)*
Schossen *n* shooting, jointing *(of cereals)*; bolting, premature seeding *(of beets)* • **zum ~ neigend** bolting-prone
Schosser *m* bolter, tiller, sucker • **~ bildend** surculose, surculous • **~ entfernen** to sucker • **~ treiben** to tiller, to sucker
Schosserbildung *f* bolting, premature seeding *(of beets)*
schoßfest bolting-resistant
~/nicht bolting-prone
Schoßfestigkeit *f* bolt[ing]-resistance
Schoßhund *m* lap (toy) dog
Schößling *m* [young] shoot, offshoot, sprout, sprig, sucker
~/wilder straggler
Schoßneigung *f* bolting propensity
schoßresistent bolting-resistant
Schoßrübe *f* [sugar-beet] bolter
Schötchen *n* (bot) silicula, silicule, silicle
schötchenartig silicular
schötchenförmig siliculose, siliculous, silicular
schötchentragend siliculose, siliculous
Schote *f* 1. siliqua, silique, pod, cod, husk, hull, boll, *(Am)* shuck; pea pod, peacod; 2. *s.* Gemüseerbse
~/aufgetriebene (vergallte) (phyt) bladder pod *(caused by larvae of Dasyneura brassicae)*
Schotenabstreifer *m* pod stripper *(of green pea harvester)*
Schotenansatz *m* pod set
Schotenansetzen *n* pod setting
schotenartig siliquose, siliquous
Schotendorn *m* acacia *(genus Acacia)*
Schotenerbsen *fpl* pulling peas
schotenförmig siliquiform
Schotenklee *m* 1. bird's-foot trefoil, Lotus corniculatus; 2. wild trefoil, Trigonella corniculata
Schotennaht *f* pod seam
Schotter *m* [road-]metal
schottern to metal
Schotterung *f* metalling
Schottische Moorschneehenne *f* moorhen
~ Schafenzephalitis *f* (vet) louping (trembling) ill
~ Zaunrose *f* eglantine, sweet-brier, Rosa rubiginosa (eglanteria)

Schubstangenentmistungsanlage

Schottischer Liebstock *m* [Scotch] lovage, Ligusticum scoticum
~ **Moorschneehahn** *m* moor-cock, gorcock
~ **Schäferhund** *m* Collie *(dog breed)*
~ **Terrier** *m* Scotch terrier, Scottie, Aberdeen *(dog breed)*
Schottisches Moorschneehuhn *n* [red] grouse, moorfowl, moor game, Lagopus lagopus ssp. scoticus
Schrägagar *m* slant (slope) agar
Schrägbruch *m s.* Schrägfraktur
Schrägförderband *n*, **Schrägförderer** *m* inclined conveyor; feed conveyor *(of a combine)*
Schrägförderkette *f* elevator
Schrägfraktur *f (vet)* oblique fracture
Schrägfurchenberieselung *f*, **Schrägfurchenbewässerung** *f* herring-bone furrow method
schräggerichtet *(bot)* plagiotropic
Schrägpflanzung *f (forest)* slant (oblique) planting
Schrägrollenlager *n* tapered roller bearing
Schrägstabköpfer *m* skew bar topper *(of beet harvester)*
Schrägstellung *f* inclination
Schrägzeiligkeit *f (bot)* parastichy
Schrägzinkengrubber *m* slope (slanting) tine cultivator
Schrank *m* saw set (wrest), lateral set [of saw-teeth]
Schränkamboß *m* setting anvil
Schränkeisen *n* saw set (wrest), setting key
schränken to set *(saw-teeth)*
~ **und schärfen** to fit *(a saw)*
Schränkhammer *m* setting hammer
Schränk[meß]lehre *f* saw set gauge
Schränkung *f s.* Schrank
Schränkzange *f* saw-setting pliers, spring saw set
Schrapper *m* scraper
Schraube *f/archimedische s.* Schraubenpumpe
Schraubel *f (bot)* bostryx, helicoid cyme
schraubelartig bostrychoid[al]
Schraubenbaum *m* screw pine *(genus Pandanus)*
Schraubenbohne *f* mesquite bean *(from Prosopis juliflora)*
Schraubenpflug *m* auger plough, helical digger
Schraubenpresse *f* screw press
Schraubenpumpe *f* Archimedean screw *(for field irrigation)*
Schraubenquirlpflug *m* helical tiller
Schraubenvallisnerie *f* tape grass, eel-grass, wild celery, Vallisneria spiralis
Schraubenwelle *f s.* Schraubenpumpe
Schraubenwurmfliege *f (ent)* screwworm, Cochliomyia hominivorax
schraubig [gebaut] *(bot)* acyclic
Schraubstollen *m* caulk[in] *(of horseshoe)*
Schrebergarten *m* allotment [garden]
Schreinerholz *n* cabinet wood
Schreitwanze *f* reduviid [bug] *(family Reduviidae)*

Schrenks Fichte *f* Schrenk spruce, Picea schrenkiana
Schriftfarn *m* 1. scale-fern, ceterach *(genus Ceterach)*; 2. rusty back, Ceterach officinarum
Schritt *m* 1. step; 2. pace, walk *(gait)* • **im ~ gehen** to walk
Schrittpferd *n* draught-horse, dobbin
schröpfen 1. to tap, to incise *(woody fruit plants)*; 2. *(api)* to rob
Schröpfen *n* 1. incision; 2. *(api)* robbing
Schrot *m* 1. [coarse] meal, crushed grain; grist; 2. [small] shot; 3. notch *(tree felling)* • **den ~ anlegen** to notch *(tree felling)*
~ **/grober** coarse shot
Schrotaxt *f* felling axe, axe for felling
schroten to [rough-]grind, to crush, to bruise, to kibble
~ **/grob** to crack
Schrotflinte *f* shotgun, fowling piece
Schrotgarbe *f (hunt)* cone of small shot
Schrotkörnchen *n* grain of small shot
Schrotkugel *f* [shot] pellet
Schrotmehl *n* meal, coarse (break) flour
Schrotmühle *f* grain (seed) crusher, kibbler, kibbling (grinding, bruising) mill; malt-mill
Schrotnummer *f* size (number) of shot
Schrotsäge *f* cross-cut saw, twart saw; pit-saw
Schrotschußeffekt *m (phyt)* shot-hole
Schrotschußkrankheit *f* shot-hole disease, leaf (gum) spot disease *(of stone fruit, caused by Clasterosporium carpophilum = Stigmina carpophila)*
Schrotvergiftung *f (vet)* rumen acidosis, acid indigestion
schrumpfen to shrink; to shrivel
Schrumpfen *n s.* Schrumpfung
Schrumpffolie *f* shrink film (foil), shrinkage film
schrumpffolienverpackt shrink-wrapped
Schrumpfgrenze *f (soil)* shrinkage limit
Schrumpfkorn *n* shrivelled grain, shrunken kernel, tail corn
Schrumpfleber *f (vet)* liver cirrhosis
Schrumpfriß *m* [shrinkage] crack
Schrumpfung *f* shrinkage; syneresis *(of gels)*
Schub *m* thrust
Schubelastizitätsmodul *m* modulus of rigidity, modulus of elasticity in shear
Schubkarre *f* [wheel]barrow
~ **/seitenwandlose** jib barrow
Schubkolben *m* plunger, ram *(of a pick-up baler)*
Schubkraft *f* thrust
Schubmodul *m s.* Schubelastizitätsmodul
Schubraddrillmaschine *f* fluted feed drill
Schubsärad *n* forced-feed wheel
Schubsäraddrillmaschine *f* external force-feed drill
Schubstangenentmistungsanlage *f* push-rod barn cleaner, pushing-bar dung channel cleaner

Schubzentrifuge

Schubzentrifuge f pusher centrifuge *(sugar manufacture)*
Schuffe f curd scoop *(cheese-making tool)*
Schuffel f(n) scuffle, push hoe, push and pull
schuffeln to scuffle
Schuft m blade-bone, blade *(of pork carcass)*
Schuhblüte f slipper plant (spurge) *(genus Pedilanthus)*
Schuhu m s. Uhu
Schule f/**Hohe** haute école *(equitation)*
Schulgalopp m ordinary (short) gallop
Schulgarten m school garden
Schulmilch f school milk
Schulreiten n equitation, equestrianism
Schulter f shoulder
Schulterblatt n shoulder-blade, blade[-bone], scapula
Schulterblattknorpel m scapular cartilage
Schultergelenk n shoulder-joint
Schultergelenkhöcker m point of shoulder
Schultergliedmaße f foreleg, forelimb, thoracic limb, arm
Schultergürtel m shoulder (pectoral) girdle
Schultermuskelschwund m **beim Pferd** *(Am, vet)* sweeny, swinney
Schulternebelgerät n knapsack mist blower
Schuppe f *(bot, zoo)* scale, squama • **Schuppen bilden** to scale • **sich mit Schuppen bedecken** to scale
Schuppen m shed
Schuppenanalyse f scale analysis
Schuppenblatt n *(bot)* scale[-leaf]
Schuppenborke f scaly (scale) bark, flaked (shell) bark
Schuppenflechte f *(vet)* psoriasis
schuppenflügelig *(ent)* scale-winged, lepidopterous, lepidopteran
Schuppenflügler m lepidopteran, butterfly *(order Lepidoptera)*
Schuppenfressende Milbe f chorioptic mite *(genus Chorioptes)*
Schuppenkarpfen m scale (scaly) carp
Schuppenkiefer f scale pine
Schuppenkopf m *(bot)* cephalaria *(genus Cephalaria)*
Schuppenlosigkeit f scalelessness
Schuppenrindenhickory m scalebark, shagbark [hickory], shellbark, Carya ovata (alba)
Schuppenschwamm m *(bot)* scaly lentinus, Lentinus squamosus
Schuppenstall m animal shelter
Schuppentrocknung f barn curing *(e.g. of tobacco)*
Schuppenwacholder m s. Schuppiger Wacholder
schuppig scaly, lepidote; desquamative
Schuppiger Wacholder m single-seed juniper, Juniperus squamata
Schüppling m *(bot)* pholiota *(genus Pholiota)*

Schur f [sheep-]shearing, sheep-clip, clip[ping], sheep cropping, cut
~/chemische chemical shearing
~/maschinelle machine shearing
Schurbank f shear board
Schurboden m shearing floor
schüren to stoke
Schurertrag m wool crop, [wool] clip
Schürfkübel m scraper
Schürfverletzung f abrasion bruise *(e.g. on fruits)*
Schurmaschine f shearing machine
Schurplatz m shearing place
Schurraum m shearing shed
Schurre f chute, shoot
Schurtisch m sheep-shearing table
Schurverletzung f shearing wound
Schurwolle f shearing (shorn, live) wool, fleece
Schurwunde f shearing wound
Schürze f apron
Schurzeit f shearing season (time), clipping time
Schuß m 1. shot; 2. hessian weft *(kind of jute)*
Schußlicht n *(hunt)* shooting light
Schußnähe f *(hunt)* shooting range
schußscheu gun-shy *(hunting dog)*
Schußzeit f hunting-season, open season
Schusterbock[käfer] m pine sawyer [beetle], Monochamus sutor
Schusterpalme f 1. aspidistra *(genus Aspidistra)*; 2. cast-iron plant, Aspidistra elatior
Schutt m *(soil)* detritus, scree, talus, rubble • **auf ~ wachsend** *(bot)* ruderal
Schuttbingelkraut n annual mercury, Mercurialis annua
Schüttbunker m hopper *(of a drill)*
Schüttdichte f bulk density, BD, apparent density; bushel weight
Schütte[krankheit] f *(phyt, forest)* needle cast
Schüttelförderer m shaker conveyor
Schüttelkrampf m *(vet)* convulsion
Schüttelkultur f shaking culture *(microbiology)*
Schüttelrinne f, **Schüttelrutsche** f shaker conveyor, jog (oscillating) conveyor
Schüttelsieb n shaking screen
Schüttgetreide n bulk grain
Schüttgut n bulk [material, goods], bed material • **als ~** in bulk
Schüttgutanhänger m bulk trailer
Schüttgutbehälter m bulk container, hopper
Schüttgutbunker m bulk bin
Schüttgutförderung f bulk handling
Schüttguthänger m bulk trailer
Schüttgutlagerung f bulk storage
Schüttgutschaufel f bucket fork *(tractor attachment)*
Schutthalde f scree, talus; dump
Schuttkresse f narrow-leaved pepperwort, Lepidium ruderale
Schüttler m shaker, [straw] walker, dressing shoe *(of thresher)*

Schütttlerfläche f shaking area
Schüttlerreiter m straw walker projection
Schüttlerverluste mpl straw walker losses, shaker (rack) losses
Schüttlerwelle f shaker shoe shaft
Schuttpflanze f ruderal [plant]
Schüttstroh n long straw
Schütttrichter m feed (discharge) hopper
Schüttung f grist *(brewing)*
Schüttvolumen n bulk volume
Schüttwinkel m angle of repose
Schutz m protection; shelter
~ **der Züchterrechte** protection of breeders
Schütz n sluice
Schutzanpassung f *(bot, zoo)* mimesis
Schutzanzug m protective suit
Schutzaufbau m **gegen herabfallende Gegenstände** falling-object protective structure, FOPS
Schutzbandage f bandage
Schutzbaum m shelter tree
Schutzbauten pl protective works *(e.g. against avalanches)*
Schutzbekleidung f s. Schutzkleidung
Schutzbestand m s. Schutzwaldbestand
Schutzdach n shed, shelter; field shelter *(for grazing animals)*
Schütze m game-shooter, gunner, gun
Schütze f s. Schütz
schützen to protect; to shelter
Schützenstand m *(hunt)* station
Schutzfärbung f protective colo[u]ration
Schutzfrucht f nurse (cover) crop
Schutzfungizid n protectant fungicide
Schutzgebiet n protected area, sanctuary
Schutzgitter n guard grille, fence
Schutzhelm m protective hat (helmet)
Schutzholz n wound wood
Schutzhund m guard (watch) dog
Schutzhütte f hut
Schutzimpfung f *(vet)* preventive vaccination
Schutzkleidung f protective (safety) clothing
Schutzkolloid n protective colloid
Schutzmittel n protectant, protective agent; protective toxicant
Schutznetz n **[gegen Vögel]** bird-net
Schutzpflanzung f shelter planting, protective plantation (planting)
Schutzraum m shelter
Schutzschirm m screen
Schutzschwelle f protective threshold
Schutzserum n immune serum
Schutzstiefel mpl protective boots
Schutzstreifen m s. Schutzwaldstreifen
Schutztuch n apron
Schutzwald m protection (protective) forest
Schutzwaldanbau m protective (field-protecting) afforestation, agricultural afforestation
Schutzwaldbau m protection forestry

Schutzwaldbestand m protective [forest] stand
Schutzwaldstreifen m shelter-belt, protective forest strip
~/**Kienitzscher** green belt, evergreen fire-break
Schutzwirkung f protective effect (action)
Schutzzone f *(ecol)* buffer zone
Schwabenkorn n *(bot)* dinkel, spelt, Triticum spelta
Schwäbisch-Hällisches Schwein n Swabian-Hall[e] *(pig breed)*
Schwäche f weakness; *(vet)* asthenia
~/**motorische** *(vet)* paresis
schwächen to weaken, to impair, to attenuate
Schwächeparasit m secondary parasite
Schwachholz n smallwood, small[-sized] timber, topwood
Schwachholzaufarbeitung f conversion of small timber
Schwachholzernte f small-timber harvesting
Schwachholzprozessor m small-timber processor
Schwachregner m slow-application sprinkler, slow-rate sprinkler
schwachwüchsig dwarfed
Schwad m(n) swath, swathe, windrow
Schwadaufnehmer m pick-up table (cylinder), swath (windrow) pick-up
Schwadbrett n swath board
Schwaddrescher m pick-up combine
Schwaddrusch m windrow combining, two-stage threshing
Schwade f s. Schwad
schwaden to swath[e], to windrow
Schwaden m s. 1. Schwad; 2. Schwadengras
Schwadengras n manna (sweet, reed) grass *(genus Glyceria)*
Schwader m swather
Schwadleger m s. Schwadrechen
Schwadleitblech n swath board
Schwadlüfter m swath aerator
schwadmähen to swath[e]
Schwadmäher m [mower-]swather, swath mower
Schwadpresse f swath press
Schwadräumer m swath clearing machine
Schwadrechen m rake swather, swath rake (lifter), side[-delivery] rake, windrower
Schwadschüttler m windrow shaker
Schwadstock m swath stick
Schwadverleger m s. Schwadrechen
Schwadwender m swath turner
Schwadzetter m **und -lüfter** m combined tedder and swath aerator
Schwalbe f swallow *(family Hirundinidae)*
Schwalbenwurz f *(bot)* 1. mosquito trap *(genus Cynanchum)*; 2. tame poison, Vincetoxicum hirundinaria, Cynanchum vincetoxicum
Schwalbenwurzenzian m willow gentian, Gentiana asclepiadea
Schwallbewässerung f surge (spate) irrigation
Schwamm m fungus *(division Eumycota)*

Schwammbaum

Schwammbaum *m* huisache, sweet acacia, Acacia farnesiana
Schwammgurke *f* loofah, vegetable sponge, dishcloth [gourd], towel gourd, Luffa aegyptiaca
schwammig spongy, conky, punky; fungous
Schwammparenchym *n* spongy (lacunose) parenchyma
Schwammspinner *m* gypsy moth, Lymantria (Porthetria) dispar
Schwand *m* loss *(brewing)*
Schwanenhals *m* 1. swan-neck, drain scoop, drainage hoe; 2. swan-neck *(of horse)*
Schwanenorchis *f (bot)* swan-neck *(genus Cycnoches)*
schwanken/jahreszeitlich to vary with (according to) the season
Schwanz *m* tail, cauda • **den ~ abschneiden (amputieren, kupieren)** to tail, to dock • **mit amputiertem ~** dock-tailed • **mit gestutztem ~** nag-tailed *(horse)* • **mit kupiertem ~** dock-tailed
Schwanzansatz *m* tail head
Schwanzbeißen *n* tail-biting *(vice esp. of pigs)*
Schwanzborste *f (ent)* tail-feeler
Schwänzelstrecke *f (api)* waggle-run
Schwänzeltanz *m (api)* waggle-dance, wag-tail dance
Schwanzfalte *f* tail fold *(embryology)*
Schwanzfeder *f* tail feather
Schwanzflosse *f* tail (caudal) fin
Schwanzlarve *f* cercaria *(of trematodes)*
schwanzlos tailless, acaudal, acaudate
Schwanzlosigkeit *f* taillessness
Schwanzmarke *f* tail tag *(livestock marking)*
Schwanzmarkierungstechnik *f* tail painting technique
Schwanzquaste *f* switch, floccus
Schwanzriemen *m* crupper *(of harness)*
Schwanzspitze *f* tag
Schwanzstummel *m* dock
schwanzwärts caudal
Schwanzwirbel *m* coccygeal vertebra
Schwanzwurzel *f* tail root, root of tail, dock
Schwanzzittern *n (vet)* tail tremor
schwären *(vet)* to fester
Schwarm *m* swarm *(of insects)*; flight, flock *(of birds)*; shoal *(of fishes)*
schwärmen to swarm
Schwärmer *m* hawk-moth, sphingid, sphinx *(family Sphingidae)*
Schwarmfangkasten *m*, **Schwarmfangkiste** *f (api)* swarm box (catcher)
Schwarmflug *m (api)* swarm flight
Schwarmperiode *f (api)* swarming period (season)
Schwärmspore *f (bot)* swarm spore (cell), zoospore
Schwarmtrieb *m (api)* swarming impulse
Schwarmtrieblenkung *f* swarm control
Schwarmwasser *n (soil)* hydration water of exchangeable ions, water of hydration

Schwarmweiselzelle *f (api)* swarm-cell
Schwärmzeit *f (api)* swarming (flight) time
Schwarte *f* 1. rind, [boar] skin; 2. *s.* Schwartenbrett
Schwartenbrett *n* slab [board]
Schwartenholz *n* slabwood
Schwarzadrigkeit *f* **des Kohls** black rot of crucifers *(caused by Xanthomonas campestris)*
Schwarzalkaliboden *m* black alkali soil, solonets, solonetz
Schwarzast *m* black knot
schwarzästig black-knotty
Schwarzäugige Susanne *f (bot)* black-eyed Susan, Thunbergia alata
Schwarzbeinigkeit *f (phyt)* blackleg [disease], take-all
~ **des Hafers** take-all of oat[s] *(caused by Gaeumannomyces graminis var. avenae)*
~ **des Weizens** take-all of wheat *(caused by Gaeumannomyces graminis var. tritici)*
Schwarzbesatz *m* black dockage *(e.g. in cereals)*
Schwarzbirke *f* river birch, Betula nigra
Schwarzblättrigkeit *f* **des Kaffeebaumes** American leaf spot of coffee *(caused by Mycena citricolor)*
Schwarzbrache *f* [black, dead, bare] fallow, fallow ground
Schwarzbraune Ameise *f* common black ant, Formica fusca (japonica)
Schwarzbrauner Kiefernblattkäfer *m* pine leaf beetle, Luperus pinicola
~ **Reismehlkäfer** *m* black flour beetle, Tribolium madens
Schwarzbrot *n* black bread
Schwarzbunte *pl* white-and-black cattle *(group of breeds)*
Schwarzbuntes Rind *n* German Black Pied, Black Spotted Cattle, Black Pied Lowland *(breed)*
Schwarzdecke *f* blacktop *(road construction)*
Schwarzdorn *m s.* Schlehdorn
Schwärze *f (phyt)* alternaria rot *(caused by Alternaria spp.)*
Schwarze Akazie *f* black (Sydney) wattle, Acacia decurrens
~ **Anatolische Ziege** *f* Anatolian black goat *(breed)*
~ **Apfelbeere** *f* black chokeberry, Aronia melanocarpa
~ **Bohne** *f* Egyptian (tonga) bean, Dolichos lablab, Lablab niger (purpureus)
~ **Bohnen[blatt]laus** *f* black [bean] aphid, black fly, Aphis (Doralis) fabae
~ **Flockenblume** *f* knapweed, hard-head, bullweed, Centaurea nigra
~ **Fruchtfäule** *f* fruitlet black rot *(of pineapple, caused by Pseudomonas spp. and Erwinia spp.)*
~ **Harnwinde** *f (vet)* lumbago *(of horses)*
~ **Heckenkirsche** *f* black honeysuckle, Lonicera nigra
~ **Himbeere** *f* black[cap] raspberry, American black raspberry, thimble berry, Rubus occidentalis

~ **Johannisbeere** *f* black currant, Ribes nigrum
~ **Kirsch[en]blattwespe** *f* pear-slug, pear slugworm saw-fly, Caliroa cerasi (limacina)
~ **Kirschenlaus** *f* black cherry aphid, Myzus cerasi
~ **Königskerze** *f* dark mullein, Verbascum nigrum
~ **Krähenbeere** *f* crowberry, crakeberry, Empetrum nigrum
~ **Nieswurz** *f* black hellebore, Christmas rose, Helleborus niger
~ **Pflaume** *f* Canada plum, Prunus nigra
~ **Pflaumensägewespe** *f* black plum saw-fly, Hoplocampa minuta
~ **Platterbse** *f* black vetchling, Lathyrus niger
~ **Rübenblattlaus** *f* s. ~ Bohnen[blatt]laus
~ **Susanne** *f* s. Schwarzäugige Susanne
~ **Verzascaziege** *f* Verzasca goat *(breed)*
~ **Wurzelfäule** *f* **der Gurke** cucumber black root rot, black root of cucumber *(caused by Phomopsis sclerotioides)*
~ **Zwiebelfliege** *f* black onion fly, Tritoxa flexa
Schwärzekrankheit *f* s. Schwärze
Schwarzer Baumwollboden *m* black cotton soil
~ **Birkenstecher** *m* birch[-tree] weevil, birch leaf rolling weevil, Deporaus betulae, Rhynchites alni
~ **Brenner** *m (phyt)* grape anthracnose *(caused by Elsinoe ampelina)*
~ **Geißklee** *m (bot)* spike broom, Cytisus nigricans
~ **Getreidenager** *m* wheat beetle, cadelle [beetle], *(Am)* bolting-cloth beetle, Tenebroides mauritanicus
~ **Gewächshausblasenfuß** *m (ent)* greenhouse thrips, Heliothrips haemorrhoidalis
~ **Gottvergeß** *m (bot)* black horehound, Ballota nigra
~ **Holunder** *m* black elder[berry], [common, black-fruited] elder, Judas's-tree, bourtree, Sambucus nigra
~ **Iltis** *m* polecat, fitch[et], fitchew, Mustela putorius
~ **Kiefernblattkäfer** *m* black pine leaf beetle, Luperus pinicola
~ **Kiefernwurzelbrüter** *m* black pine bark (bast) beetle, Hylastes ater
~ **Kohlerdfloh** *m* black flea beetle, Phyllotreta atra
~ **Maulbeerbaum** *m* black mulberry, Morus nigra
~ **Milan** *m* black kite, Milvus migrans
~ **Nachtschatten** *m* [black] nightshade, morel, Solanum nigrum
~ **Pfeffer** *m* black pepper, Piper nigrum
~ **Pelzkäfer** *m* black carpet beetle, Attagenus megatoma (piceus)
~ **Rübenaaskäfer** *m* black carrion beetle, Aclypea (Blitophaga, Silpha) undata
~ **Saxaul** *m (bot)* black saxaul, Haloxylon aphyllum
~ **Senf** *m* black (brown) mustard, Brassica nigra
~ **Streifenfarn** *m* black spleenwort, Asplenium adiantum-nigrum
~ **Wurzelbrüter** *m* s. ~ Kiefernwurzelbrüter
~ **Zweigkrebs** *m* **der Süßkirsche** *(phyt)* cherry black canker *(virosis)*

Schwarzerde *f* chernozem, black earth (soil)
Schwarzerle *f* black (common) alder, European [black] alder, aller, Alnus glutinosa
Schwarzes Bilsenkraut *n (bot)* henbane, hyoscyamus, Hyoscyamus niger
~ **Dammarharz** *n* black dammar (damar) *(resin esp. from Balanocarpus penangianus)*
~ **Gemüse** *n* alexanders, alisander, Smyrnium olusatrum
~ **Wasserhuhn** *n* [bald] coot, Fulica atra
Schwarzesche *f* black ash, Fraxinus nigra
Schwarzfärbung *f (phyt)* blackening
Schwarzfäule *f (phyt)* black rot *(comprehensive term)*
~ **der Möhre** black rot of carrot *(caused by Stemphylium radicinum)*
~ **der Rebstöcke** black rot of grapes *(caused by Guignardia bidwellii)*
~ **des Zuckerrohrs** pineapple rot of sugar-cane *(caused by Ceratocystis paradoxa)*
Schwarzfichte *f* black spruce, *(Am)* eastern spruce, Picea mariana (nigra)
Schwarzfleckenkrankheit *f,* **Schwarzfleckigkeit** *f (phyt)* black spot [disease], black blotch *(comprehensive term)*
~ **der Christrose** leaf spot of helleborus *(caused by Coniothyrium hellebori)*
~ **des Weinstocks** dead-arm disease [of grapevine] *(caused by Phomopsis viticola)*
Schwarzfleckvieh *n* black and white cattle *(group of breeds)*
Schwarzfolienabdeckung *f,* **Schwarzfolienmulch** *m* black plastic [film] mulch
schwarzfrüchtig *(bot)* atrocarpous
Schwarzfrüchtiger Himbeerstrauch *m* black[cap] raspberry, Rubus occidentalis
~ **Kürbis** *m* Malabar gourd, Cucurbita ficifolia
Schwarzfuchs *m* black fox
Schwarzgefleckte Pfirsichlaus *f* peach curl aphid, Brachycaudus prunicola ssp. schwartzi
Schwarzgraue Wegameise *f* garden ant, Lasius niger
Schwarzhafer *m* black oat *(type of cultivars)*
Schwarzherzigkeit *f (phyt)* blackheart
Schwarzholzakazie *f* blackwood [acacia], lightwood, Acacia melanoxylon
Schwarzkäfer *m* meal-worm, darkling beetle, miller, tenebrionid [beetle] *(family Tenebrionidae)*
Schwarzkern *m* black heart *(of timber)*
Schwarzkiefer *f* European black pine, Austrian pine, Pinus nigra
Schwarzköpfiger Bohrer *m (ent)* sugar-cane [shoot] borer, Diatraea saccharalis
Schwarzköpfiges Fleischschaf *n* German Black-headed Mutton, Improved Black-face Mutton *(sheep breed)*
Schwarzkopfkrankheit *f* blackhead [disease] *(of turkeys)*

Schwarzkümmel

Schwarzkümmel *m* 1. fennel-flower, devil-in-the-bush *(genus Nigella)*; 2. black cu[m]min, small fennel, nutmeg flower, Nigella sativa
Schwarzlinde *f (Am)* bee tree, Tilia americana
schwarzmähnig black-maned
Schwarznessel *f (bot)* 1. perilla, Perilla frutescens (ocimoides); 2. black horehound, Ballota nigra
Schwarznuß *f*, **Schwarznußbaum** *m* [American] black walnut, Juglans nigra
Schwarzpappel *f* [European] black poplar, willow poplar, Populus nigra
Schwarzpech *n* black pitch
Schwarzringfleckigkeit *f (phyt)* black ring [spot] *(virosis)*
Schwarzrost *m (phyt)* black rust *(caused by Puccinia graminis)*
Schwarzsamengras *n* black seed grass, Chloris virgata
Schwarzschimmel[pilz] *m* black mould, Aspergillus niger
Schwarzspecht *m* [great] black woodpecker, Dryocopus martius
Schwarzstorch *m* black stork, Ciconia nigra
Schwarzstreifiger Scheidling *m* paddy straw mushroom, Volvariella diplasis (volvacea)
Schwarztorf *m* black peat
Schwarztrockenfäule *f* [der Sojabohne] pustule disease [of soya bean] *(caused by Xanthomonas campestris glycines)*
Schwarzwerdender Geißklee *m* spike broom, Cytisus nigricans
Schwarzwild *n* wild boars • **kapitales Stück** ~ capital wild boar
Schwarzwildjunges *n* young wild boar, wild piglet
Schwarzwildlager *n* wild boar clearing
Schwarzwurzel *f (bot)* 1. scorzonera, viper's grass *(genus Scorzonera)*; 2. black salsify, scorzonera, Scorzonera hispanica
Schwarzzungenkrankheit *f* black tongue [disease] *(of dogs)*
Schwebeförderer *m* overhead conveyor
Schweberückung *f (forest)* aerial skidding, overhead skidding, (logging)
Schwebetrockner *m* fluid[ized]-bed dryer
Schwebfliege *f* syrphid, syrphus (hover) fly *(family Syrphidae)* • **die Schwebfliegen betreffend** syrphid
Schwebstaub *m* airborne dust
Schwebstaubniederschlag *m* particulate precipitation
Schwebstoff *m* suspended matter
Schwebstofffracht *f*, **Schwebstoffführung** *f* sediment charge
Schwedenklee *m* alsike [clover], Trifolium hybridum
Schwedenkleeadernmosaikvirus *n* alsike clover vein mosaic virus
Schwedenkleevergiftung *f (vet)* trifoliosis, clover disease

Schwedische Landrasse *f* 1. Swedish Landrace *(pig breed)*; 2. Swedish Landrace (Native) *(sheep breed)*
~ **Mehlbeere** *f* Swedish beam-tree (whitebeam), Sorbus intermedia
Schwedischer Hartriegel *m* dwarf cornel, Cornus suecica
~ **Kaffee** *m* Swedish coffee, Astragalus boeticus
Schwedisches Hornloses Rind *n* Swedish Polled, North Swedish *(cattle breed)*
Schwefelblume *f* sulphur smell *(of wine)*
Schwefeldioxidbegasung *f* fumigation with sulphur dioxide
Schwefeldioxidresistenz *f* sulphur dioxide resistance
Schwefeldosierer *m* sulphur doser *(wine making)*
Schwefeldüngemittel *n* sulphur fertilizer
Schwefelfestlegung *f* sulphofixation
Schwefelgelbes Schmuckkörbchen *n (bot)* yellow cosmos, Cosmos sulphureus
Schwefelkalk *m* lime sulphur *(fungicide)*
Schwefelkalkbrühe *f* lime sulphur spray
Schwefelkies *m* pyrite *(non-clay mineral)*
schwefeln to sulphurate, to sulphurize; to sulphite; to stum *(must)*
~/**übermäßig** to oversulphur
Schwefelporling *m* sulphur fungus (polypore), chicken mushroom, Polyporus (Laetiporus) sulphureus
Schwefelsäure *f* sulphuric acid
Schwefelsäurefirne *f* sulphur taste *(of wine)*
schwefelscheu sulphur-shy
Schwefelung *f* sulphuration
Schwefelverdampfer *m* sulphurator, sulphur evaporator
Schwefelzerstäuber *m* sulphur duster
Schweif *m* tail
Schweifbiber *m* coypu, Myocastor coypus
Schweifbinde *f* tail bandage
schweiffrüchtig *(bot)* urocarpous
Schweifkamm *m* tail comb
Schweifriemen *m* turnback strap, dock *(of harness)*
Schweifrübe *f*, **Schweifwurzel** *f* tail root, dock
Schwein *n* 1. swine, pig, hog *(family Suidae)*; 2. [domestic] pig, swine, hog, grunter, Sus scrofa domestica
~/**kastriertes** *(Am)* barrow
~/**spezifisch pathogenfreies** specific pathogen free pig
Schweinebauch *m (slaught)* pork belly
Schweinebehandlungsstand *m* pig treatment crate
Schweinebremse *f* pig snare
Schweinebucht *f* pig tub
Schweinedung *m* pig manure
Schweinedunggärfutter *n* pig manure fermentation feed, PMFF

Schweinedysenterie f (vet) swine (bloody, vibrionic) dysentery, bloody (black) scours, mucohaemorrhagic diarrhoea (caused by Borellia hyodysenteriae)
Schweinefett n pig fat
Schweinefieber n s. Schweinepest
Schweinefleisch n pork, pig-meat
Schweinefutter n pig feed (food, swill)
Schweinefütterung f pig feeding
Schweinegrippe f s. Schweineinfluenza
Schweinegülle f pig[gery] slurry, swine wastewater
Schweinehaarmehl n hog hair meal
Schweinehalter m pigman, pig keeper, swine manager
Schweinehaltung f pig keeping (farming, husbandry)
Schweinehaut f pigskin
Schweineherde f swine herd
Schweineinfluenza f (vet) swine influenza, hog flu (caused by myxovirus influenza-A suis)
Schweinekoben m [pig]sty
Schweinekotelett n pork loin chop
Schweinekrankheit f/vesikuläre swine vesicular disease, S.V.D.
Schweinelähmung f/ansteckende Teschen (talfan) disease
Schweinelaus f pig[-sucking] louse, Haematopinus suis
Schweineleber f pork liver
Schweinelungenwurm m lung-worm of pigs (genus Metastrongylus)
Schweinemast f pig fattening
Schweinemastanlage f pig fattening unit, swine finishing operation (s. a. Schweinestall)
Schweinemästerei f piggery
Schweinemaststall m pig fattening house, commercial pig house, piggery
~ in Dänischer Aufstallung Danish (Scandinavian-type) piggery
~ in Schleißheimer Aufstallung Suffolk house
Schweinemist m pig manure
Schweinepest f (vet) [classical] swine fever, hog cholera, red soldier
Schweinepestvirus n swine-fever virus, hog cholera virus
Schweinepfleger m pigman
Schweinepocken pl (vet) swine (pig) pox
Schweinepockenvirus n swine pox virus
Schweinerasse f pig breed
Schweinerotlauf m (vet) swine erysipelas (caused by Erysipelothrix rhusiopathiae)
Schweineruhr f (vet) coliform scour[s] in pigs
Schweineschlächterei f pork abattoir
Schweineschlachtkörper m pork carcass
Schweineschmalz n lard
Schweineseuche f/Oldenburger (vet) transmissible gastroenteritis, TGE
Schweinestall m [pig]sty, piggery, swine house (barn), (Am) pigpen, hog-pen, hoggery (s. a. Schweinemaststall)
Schweinetrog m pig tub (trough)
Schweineverladebox f pig loading pen
Schweinevermarktung f hog marketing
Schweinewaage f pig weigher
Schweineweide f pannage
Schweinezucht f pig breeding, hog raising
Schweinezuchtanlage f swine breeding facility
Schweinezuchtbetrieb m piggery
Schweinezüchter m pig breeder (farmer), swine breeder, hog raiser (grower)
Schweinezucht- und -mastbetrieb m farrow-to-finish swine farm
Schweinfurter Grün n copper acetoarsenite, Paris green (insecticide, anthelminthic)
Schweinsberger Krankheit f s. Seneziose
Schweinsborste f hog's (boar) bristle
Schweinseisen n (hunt) boar (hog) spear
Schweinsleder n pigskin, hogskin
Schweinslende f (slaught) pork loin
Schweiß m 1. sweat; 2. (hunt) blood • **sich mit schaumigem ~ bedecken** to lather (horse)
Schweißabsonderung f s. Schweißsekretion
Schweißbett n couch (of game)
Schweißdrüse f sweat (sudoriferous) gland
Schweißfährte f (hunt) red (blood) track
Schweißhund m slot-hound
Schweißsekretion f sweat secretion, perspiration, sweating
~/fehlende (vet) anhydrosis, dry coat syndrome
schweißtreibend sudoriferous
Schweißwolle f greasy (raw) wool, grease [wool], wool in the grease
Schweißwollvlies n greasy fleece
Schweizer m dairyman
Schweizer Braunvieh n Swiss Brown (cattle breed)
~ Käse m Swiss cheese
~ Simmentaler Fleckvieh n Simmental (cattle breed)
Schweizerischer Femelschlag m s. Femelschlag/Badischer
Schwelbrand m smouldering fire, smoulder
schwelen to smoulder
schwellen to swell
schwellend swelling, turgescent
Schwellenwert m threshold [value]
~/ökonomischer economic threshold, economic injury level (threshold)
schwellfähig erectile
Schwellkörper m s. Lodicula
Schwellung f swelling
Schwelteer m settled tar
Schwemme f watering place; horse-pond
schwemmen to wash; to flume (e.g. logs)
Schwemmmist m liquid manure, slurry
Schwemmistabscheider m slurry separator

Schwemmkanal

Schwemmkanal *m* 1. channel, wash; 2. *s.* Schwemmrinne
Schwemmland *n* alluvium, alluvion; flood plain, bottomland; reclaimed land (soil), warp
Schwemmlandbebauung *f* flood-plain cropping
Schwemmlandbewässerung *f* flood-plain irrigation
Schwemmlandboden *m* alluvial soil
Schwemmlandkultur *f* flood-plain cropping
Schwemmrinne *f* flume *(e.g. for transportation of logs)*
Schwemmsand *m* alluvium, alluvion
Schwemmwasser *n* flume-water
Schwende *f (forest)* burn
schwenden *(forest)* to burn broadcast, to assart
Schwenkfächerregner *m* oscillating fan sprinkler
Schwenkkran *m* slewing crane
Schwenklader *m* slewing loader
Schwenkregner *m* oscillating sprinkler (spray line), swing-arm sprinkler
Schwenkschildplanierraupe *f* angledozer, tilt dozer
Schwenktor *n* sorting gate *(of a livestock handling facility)*
Schwere *f* gravity
Schweres Kundebohnenmosaikvirus *n* cowpea severe mosaic virus
~ Mosaik *n* severe mosaic *(secondary symptoms of potato Y-mosaic)*
Schwergeburtsneigung *f beim Rind* calving difficulty *(as characteristic of certain cattle breeds)*
Schwergrubber *m* heavy[-duty] cultivator, ripper
Schwergutgabel *f* heavy-duty fork *(tractor attachment)*
Schwerholzkiefer *f (Am)* ponderosa [pine], Pinus ponderosa
Schwerkraft *f* gravity
Schwerkraftbewässerung *f* gravity irrigation
Schwerkraftdränung *f*, **Schwerkraftentwässerung** *f* gravity drainage
Schwerkraftlüftung *f* gravity (natural) ventilation
Schwerkraftseilbringung *f (forest)* gravity cable logging
Schwerlastpferd *n* heavy draught (harness) horse
Schwermetall *n* heavy metal
Schwermetallbelastung *f* heavy-metal contamination
schwersamig heavy-seeded
schwerspaltig difficult to cleave *(wood)*
Schwerspat *m* barite *(non-clay mineral)*
Schwert *n s.* Sägeschwert
schwertähnlich *(bot)* xiphoid
Schwertbohne *f* sword [jack] bean, Canavalia gladiata
Schwertfarn *m* 1. sword fern *(genus Nephrolepis)*; 2. [western] sword fern, giant holly fern, Polystichum munitum
schwertförmig *(bot, zoo)* gladiated, ensiform

Schwertgrubber *m* chisel cultivator
Schwertlilie *f* flag, fleur-de-lis, iris *(genus Iris)*
Schwertliliengewächse *npl* iris family *(family Iridaceae)* • **die ~ betreffend** iridaceous
Schwertspitze *f* bar nose *(of a chain-saw)*
Schwesterchromosom *n* sister chromosome
Schwiele *f* callus
Schwielenbildung *f (vet)* t[h]ylosis
Schwielenbrand *m* **der Veilchen** smut of viola *(caused by Tuburcinia violae)*
Schwielenlilie *f* spider lily *(genus Hymenocallis)*
Schwielenorche *f* dancing lady orchid, oncidium *(genus Oncidium)*
schwielig callous, callose
Schwimmblase *f* swim[ming]-bladder, air-bladder, [fish-]sound, maw
Schwimmblasenentzündung *f (vet)* swim-bladder inflammation, SBI
Schwimmendes Laichkraut *n* broad pondweed, Potamogeton natans
Schwimmente *f* teal [duck] *(comprehensive term)*
Schwimmer *m s.* Schwimmkette
Schwimmerventiltränke *f* float-valve drinking bowl
Schwimmfarn *m* 1. salvinia *(genus Salvinia)*; 2. water fern, Salvinia molesta
Schwimmgerste *f* skimmings, floaters *(malting)*
Schwimmkette *f* catch (towing, bag) boom *(log driving)*
Schwimmstellung *f* floating position *(e.g. of a three-point hitch)*
Schwimmvogel *m* swimming-bird
Schwindel *m (vet)* vertigo
Schwindelkorn *n* coriander, Coriandrum sativum
schwinden 1. to shrink *(e.g. wood)*; 2. *(vet)* to atrophy *(as of muscles)*
Schwinden *n* shrinkage
schwindend atrophic
Schwindmaß *n* volume (volumetric) shrinkage, shrinkage ratio *(e.g. of wood)*
Schwindling *m (bot)* marasmius *(genus Marasmius = Crinipellis)*
Schwindsucht *f s.* Tuberkulose
Schwinge *f* 1. winnow *(seed cleaner)*; 2. *s.* Schwungfeder
Schwingel *m*, **Schwingelgras** *n* fescue *(genus Festuca)*
Schwingelgraslahmheit *f (vet)* fescue foot [syndrome] *(of cattle)*
schwingen to win[now], to fan *(grain)*
Schwingfeuer[nebel]gerät *n* swingfog *(plant protection)*
Schwingförderer *m*, **Schwingförderrinne** *f* oscillating (vibrating) conveyor, jog [through] conveyor
Schwinghebel *m* pitman
Schwinghebelantrieb *m* pitman drive
Schwinghebelregner[kopf] *m* impact sprinkler head, swing-arm sprinkler

Schwingkölbchen *n (ent)* haltere
Schwingmoor *n* quag[mire], trembling (quaking) bog, swing moor
Schwingpflug *m* swing (turn-about) plough
Schwingrahmen *m* swing frame
Schwingrinne *f s.* Schwingförderer
Schwingschar *n* oscillating share
Schwingsieb *n* vibrating screen
Schwingsiebroder *m* shaker [sieve] digger, [potato] digger-shaker, oscillating sieve digger
Schwingstangenschüttler *m* sway-bar shaker *(orcharding)*
Schwingung *f* vibration, oscillation
Schwingzetter *m* oscillating hay tedder
Schwirren *n (vet)* fremitus
Schwirrfliege *f s.* Schwebfliege
schwitzen to sweat, to perspire, to transpire
Schwitzen *n* sweating, perspiration, transpiration
Schwitzkrankheit *f (vet)* sweating sickness
Schwitzwasser *n* condensation water
Schwitzwasserabscheider *m* interceptor *(of a milking installation)*
schwül sultry
Schwundriß *m* shrinkage crack *(e.g. in timber)*
Schwundverlust *m* shrinkage loss
Schwundzugabe *f* [extra] allowance for shrinkage *(timber mensuration)*
Schwungfeder *f* pen (wing) feather, pinion *(of birds)*
Sclerotiniafäule *f (phyt)* 1. sclerotinia rot *(caused by Sclerotinia spp.)*; 2. cottony rot *(caused by Sclerotinia sclerotiorum)*
~ des Salates sclerotinia rot of lettuce, lettuce drop *(caused by Sclerotinia sclerotiorum)*
Sclerotinia-Lagerfäule *f* **der Möhre** storage rot of carrot *(caused by Sclerotinia sclerotiorum)*
Sclerotiniawelke *f (phyt)* sclerotinia wilt
Sclerotium-Fäule *f (phyt)* sclerotium wilt, southern blight *(caused by Sclerotium spp.)*
Sclerotium-Knollenfäule *f* southern blight [of potato] *(caused by Corticum = Sclerotium rolfsii)*
Scopolamin *n* scopolamine, hyoscine *(alkaloid)*
Scotchterrier *m* Scotch terrier, Scottie *(dog breed)*
Scottish Blackface *n* Scottish Blackface *(sheep breed)*
scrapen to scrape *(hides)*
Scrapie-Agens *n (vet)* scrapie agent
screenen *(biom)* to screen
Screening *n (biom)* screening [method, test] • **einem ~ unterziehen** to screen
Scribner Rule *f* Scribner rule *(timber mensuration)*
Scribner-Dezimal-C-Kubiktabelle *f (Am)* Scribner Decimal C Rule *(timber mensuration)*
Scrub *m* scrub
Scrubber *m* scrubber
Scutellum *n (bot, ent)* scutellum
SE *s.* Superelitesaatgut

Sea-Island-Baumwolle *f* sea-island [cotton], pima cotton, Gossypium vitifolium var. vitifolium (peruvianum, barbadense)
Sealydale Terrier *m* Sealydale [terrier] *(dog breed)*
Sealyham Terrier *m* Sealyham [terrier] *(dog breed)*
Seborrhoe *f (vet)* seborrhoea
Sebuthylazin *n* sebuthylazine *(herbicide)*
Secalin *n* secalin *(storage protein)*
Secbumeton *n* secbumeton *(herbicide)*
Sech *n* coulter, *(Am)* colter
Secheinstellung *f* coulter setting
sechsbeinig, sechsfüßig hexapod
Sechshakenlarve *f* onc[h]osphere *(of certain tapeworms)*
Sechswalzenmühle *f* six roll[er] mill
Sechszähniger Fichtenborkenkäfer *m* six-toothed spruce bark-beetle, six-dentated engraver beetle, Pityogenes (Ips) chalcographus
~ Kiefernborkenkäfer *m* top bark-beetle, Ips acuminatus
sechszeilig *(bot)* hexastichous
Sechszeilige Gerste *f* six-rowd barley, bear, bere, Hordeum vulgare convar. hexastichon
Sectio *f* section *(taxonomy)*
Sedation *f (vet)* sedation
sedativ sedative
Sedativum *n* sedative [agent]
sedentär *(zoo, soil)* sedentary
sedieren to sedate
Sedierung *f* sedation
Sediment *n* 1. *(soil)* sediment, deposit; 2. lees, dregs *(brewing)*
~/biogenes organic deposit
~/nacheiszeitliches Holocene sediment
~/organogenes organic deposit
Sedimentablagerung *f (soil)* sedimentary deposit
Sedimentation *f* sedimentation, deposition
~/äolische aeolian (wind-borne) deposition
Sedimentationsfilter *n* sedimentation filter
Sedimentationskonstante *f* sedimentation constant
Sedimentboden *m* sedimentary soil
Sedimentgestein *n*, **Sedimentit** *m* sedimentary rock
Sedoheptulose *f* sedoheptulose *(monosaccharide)*
See m zum Angeln (Fischen) gegen Gebühr pay fishing lake, fee-lake
Seebinse *f* [great] bulrush, bullrush, Scirpus lacustris
Seefenchel *m* samphire, sea fennel, Crithmum maritimum
Seefisch *m* lake-fish
Seeforelle *f* lake trout, Salmo trutta f. lacustris
Seegras *n* eel-grass, grass-wrack, Zostera marina
Seegrüne Quecke *f* intermediate wheat-grass, Agropyron intermedium, Elymus hispidus

Seeigelkaktus

Seeigelkaktus *m* sea-urchin cactus *(genus Echinopsis)*
Seekandel *f (bot)* brandy bottle, Nuphar lutea
Seekanne *f (bot)* floating heart *(genus Nymphoides)*
Seekiefer *f s.* Seestrandkiefer
Seeklima *n* maritime (oceanic) climate
seekundlich limnological
Seele *f* pith *(of a feather)*
Seemangold *m* sea beet, Beta vulgaris ssp. maritima
Seenfisch *m* lake-fish
Seenfischerei *f* lake fishery
Seenkunde *f* limnology
Seerose *f* water (pond) lily, lotus *(genus Nymphaea)*
Seerosengewächse *npl* water-lily family *(family Nymphaeaceae)*
Seesediment *n* lacustrine deposit
Seestrandkiefer *f* 1. maritime (cluster) pine, pinaster [pine], Pinus pinaster (maritima); 2. Jerusalem (Aleppo) pine, Cyprus pine, Pinus halepensis
Seetanne *f (bot)* mare's-tail, Hippuris vulgaris
Seetraube *f* sea[side] grape, Coccoloba uvifera
Segel *n (bot, zoo)* velum, veil
Segelklappe *f* atrioventricular valve *(of the heart)*
segeltragend *(bot)* veliferous
Segeltuchrutsche *f* canvas chute
Segetalpflanze *f* weed [plant], rogue
SeGFV *s.* Selleriegelbfleckenvirus
Segge *f* sedge, carex *(genus Carex)*
Seggenmoor *n*, **Seggenried** *n* sedge fen (moor)
Seggentorf *m* sedge peat
Seggenwiese *f* sedge meadow
Segment *n* segment
segmentieren to segment
Segmentpumpe *f* rotary segment pump
SeGNV *s.* Selleriegelbnetzvirus
Segregation *f (gen)* segregation
Sehen *n*/**photopisches** photopic vision *(animal physiology)*
~/skotopisches scotopic vision
Sehfeld *n* visual field
Sehhügel *m* thalamus *(animal anatomy)*
Sehkeil *m* facet *(of insect's eye)*
Sehloch *n* pupil
Sehne *f* tendon, sinew
Sehnenentfernung *f (vet)* tenectomy
Sehnenentzündung *f (vet)* tendinitis, desmitis
Sehnenhaut *f* aponeurosis
Sehnenmehl *n* tendon meal
Sehnennaht *f (vet)* tendon suture
Sehnenplatte *f* aponeurosis
Sehnenreflex *m* tendon reflex
Sehnenscheide *f* tendon (synovial) sheath
Sehnenscheidenentzündung *f (vet)* tenosynovitis, tendovaginitis
Sehnenscheidengalle *f (vet)* hygroma

Sehnerv *m* optic nerve
sehnig tendinous
Sehpigment *n* visual pigment
Sehpurpur *m* visual purple, rhodopsin
Sehschärfe *f* visual acuity
Sehstoff *m s.* Sehpigment
Sehstörung *f* vision disorder
Seide *f* 1. silk; 2. dodder, hell-weed *(genus Cuscuta)* • **wie ~ schimmernd** *(bot, zoo)* sericeous
Seidelbast *m* 1. daphne *(genus Daphne)*; 2. mezereon, mezereum, February daphne, Daphne mezereum
Seidelbastweide *f* mezereon (violet, Mexican) willow, Salix daphnoides
Seidelbast-X-Virus *n* daphne virus X, DVX
Seidelbast-Y-Virus *n* daphne virus Y, DVY
Seidenbau *m* sericulture
seidenblütig *(bot)* sericanthous
Seidendrüse *f (zoo)* silk gland
Seidenfaden *m* silk
Seidengespinst *n* silk
Seidengras *n* plume grass *(genus Erianthus)*
Seidenhaariger Hartriegel *m* swamp dogwood, Cornus amomum
Seidenhuhn *n* silk-fowl *(breed)*
Seidenpapier *n* tissue paper, wrapping tissue
Seidenpflanze *f* 1. milkweed, swallow-wort *(genus Asclepias)*; 2. common milkweed, milkweed vine, Asclepias syriaca
Seidenraupe *f* silkworm, Bombyx mori
Seidenraupenzucht *f* silk culture, silkworm-breeding, sericulture
Seidenraupenzuchtbetrieb *m* silkworm farm
Seidenraupenzüchter *m* sericulturist, silk grower
Seidenspinner *m* silk moth, Bombyx mori
seidig *(bot, zoo)* sericeous
Seifenbaum *m* [wing-leaf] soap-berry, soap-nut, Sapinus saponaria
Seifenfluß *m* soapstock *(feed)*
Seifenkraut *n* 1. soap-wort *(genus Saponaria)*; 2. [common] soap-wort, Saponaria officinalis
Seifenstein *m* soapstone, steatite, saponite *(nonclay mineral)*
Seifenstoff *m s.* Saponin
Seignettesalz *n* Seignette (Rochelle) salt, potassium sodium tartrate 4-water
seihen to strain
Seiher *m* strainer
Seihtuch *n* straining cloth
Seil *n* rope; cable • **mit einem ~ befestigen** to cable
~ zum Anbinden von Tieren tether, lariat
Seilbahn *f s.* Seilbringungsanlage
Seilblock *m* pulley block
Seilbringung *f (forest)* cable logging (hauling), cableway logging (skidding)
~/motorkraftgetriebene powered cable logging, power logging (skidding), hauler logging
~ nach dem Zweimastverfahren two-spar logging

Seilbringungsanlage f *(forest)* cableway, overhead ropeway (line), skyline cableway, wire ropeway, aerial skidder
Seilförderer m cable conveyor
Seilkran m, **Seilkrananlage** f cable-crane, skyline crane *(s. a. Seilbringungsanlage)*
Seilpflug m cable[-drawn] plough
Seilriese f *(forest)* cable slide
Seilrolle f pulley, block, sheave
Seilrollenblock m pulley block
Seilrückung f s. Seilbringung
Seilschloß n rope clamp (clip)
Seilschwebebahn f s. Seilbringungsanlage
Seiltrommel f cable drum
Seilwinde f rope (cable) winch, capstan
Seilwindenrückeschlepper m *(forest)* cable skidder
Seilwindenrückung f *(forest)* winch skidding, drum logging
Seilzug m cable (winch) traction, cable-pull
Seilzugaggregat n wire rope haulage unit, cable cultivation outfit
Seilzugbagger m drag-line [excavator]
Seilzug[boden]bearbeitung f cable cultivation
Seilzugentmistungsanlage f s. Schleppschaufelentmistungsanlage
Seilzuggerät n s. Seilzugaggregat
Seilzugmaschine f cable engine
Seilzugpflug m winch-powered plough
Seilzugrücketraktor m *(forest)* cable skidder
Seimhonig m virgin honey
Seismonastie f *(bot)* seismonasty
Seitenast m 1. lateral branch; 2. margin (face) knot *(timber defect)*
Seitenblüte f lateral flower
Seitendeckung f *(forest)* side cover
Seitenfäule f **der Ananas** *(phyt)* pineapple side rot, pineapple yellow spot, yellow spot disease of pineapple *(virosis)*
Seitengabelstapler m side loader
Seitengriff m lead to land, landing, side (horizontal) suction *(of ploughshare)*
Seitengriffverstellung f offsetting adjuster
Seitenknospe f lateral (axillary) bud
Seitenknospenhemmung f paradormancy
Seitenkrone f branch crown
Seitenlinie f lateral line *(of fishes)*
Seitenmähbalken m s. Seitenschneidwerk
Seitenräumer m side dozer
Seitenschneidwerk n mid-mounted cutter [bar], side-cut mower
Seitenschnittmähdrescher m side-cut[ting] combine [harvester]
Seitenschub m side thrust *(e.g. of soil-working tools)*
Seitenschutz m *(forest)* side cover
Seitenschwimmer m fin boom *(rafting of timber)*
Seitenspeckdicke f side-fat thickness

Seitensproß m s. Seitentrieb
Seitenstabilität f lateral stability
seitenständig lateral
Seitenstapler m side loader
Seitenstrang m lateral
Seitentrieb m side (lateral) shoot; stool [shoot]; offshoot, tiller, sucker, branch; fan *(of Theobroma cacao)* • **Seitentriebe [aus]bilden** to stool, to tiller, to stock
~ **des Brokkoli** side head
~/**dreijähriger** swinger, tri-lat *(of fruit-trees)*
~/**steriler** stool [shoot]
Seitentriebbildung f stooling, tillering
Seitenverjüngung f lateral regeneration
Seitenwachstum n lateral growth
Seitenwurzel f lateral (branch) root
Seitenzweig m lateral branch
seitlich lateral
~ **ablegen** to flank *(an animal e.g. for veterinary treatment)*
~ **gelegen** lateral
Sejepalme f patana palm, Cenocarpus (Jessenia) bataua
Sekakulpastinake f Arabian hartwort, Malabaila secacul
Sekret n secrete
Sekretin n secretin *(hormone)*
Sekretion f secretion
Sekretions[ver]minderung f hyposecretion
sekretorisch secretory
Sekt m champagne; sparkling wine
Sektgrundwein m sparkling wine stock, base wine for champagnization
Sektion f section
Sektorenregner m sector sprinkler
Sekundärdolde f *(bot)* umbellet
Sekundärfollikel m secondary follicle
Sekundärinfektion f secondary infection
Sekundärkrone f branch crown
Sekundärmineral n secondary mineral
Sekundärparasit m secondary parasite, hyperparasite
Sekundärparasitismus m secondary parasitism
Sekundärrinde f liber, bast
Sekundärruhe f secondary dormancy *(plant physiology)*
Sekundärschädling m secondary [insect] pest
Sekundärstoffwechsel m secondary metabolism
Sekundärsymptom n secondary symptom
Sekundärtumor m metastasis
Sekundärversalzung f *(soil)* secondary salinity
Sekundärwald m secondary forest (growth)
Sekundärwand f secondary wall *(of plant cell)*
Sekundärwirt m secondary host
Sekundärwurzel f secondary (coronal, adventitious) root
Sekundärxylem n secondary xylem (wood)
Seladonit m celadonite *(clay mineral)*
selbstangetrieben self-propelled, self-driven

Selbstansteckung

Selbstansteckung f *(phyt, vet)* autoinfection
selbstauflösend autolytic
Selbstauflösung f autolysis
Selbstausbreitung f s. Selbstverbreitung
Selbstbedeckung f mit Mulch *(soil)* self-mulching
selbstbefruchtend *(bot, zoo)* autogamic, autogamous, orthogamous; *(bot)* cleistogamic, cleistogamous *(pertaining to small closed flowers)*
Selbstbefruchtung f autogamy, orthogamy, automixis, self-fertilization, self-fructification
Selbstbefruchtungsvermögen n self-fertility
Selbstbeschattung f self-shading *(of plants)*
selbstbestäubend *(bot)* autogamic, autogamous; cleistogamic, cleistogamous *(pertaining to small closed flowers)*
Selbstbestäubung f autogamy, self-pollination
~ **in der [geschlossenen] Blütenknospe** cleistogamy
selbstentladend self-unloading, self-discharging
Selbstentladetank m self-unloading tank
Selbstentladevorrichtung f self-discharging device
Selbstentladewagen m self-unloading trailer (wagon), movement floor trailer
Selbstentzündung f self-ignition, auto-ignition
Selbstentzündungstemperatur f self-ignition temperature
Selbsterhitzung f self-heating
selbstfahrend self-propelled, self-driven
Selbstfangfreßgitter n self-locking yoke, self-tethering feeding gate, self-catching manger
selbstfertil *(bot)* self-fertile, auto-fertile
Selbstfertilität f self-fertility
Selbstfolgeanbau m continuous cropping
Selbstfolgemais m *(Am)* continuous corn
Selbstfruchtbarkeit f *(bot)* self-fertility
Selbstfütterer m s. Selbstfütterungsanlage
Selbstfuttersilo m self-feed silo
Selbstfütterung f self-feeding
Selbstfütterungsanlage f, **Selbstfütterungsvorrichtung** f self-feed facility, self-feeder
Selbstfütterungswagen m mobile self-feeder
selbstgetrieben self-propelled, self-driven
Selbsthemmfaktor m self-inhibitor
selbstinkompatibel *(bot)* self-incompatible
Selbstinkompatibilität f self-incompatibility, parasterility
selbstkompatibel *(bot)* self-compatible
Selbstkompatibilität f self-compatibility, self-tolerance
Selbstladewagen m self-loading trailer, self-loader
Selbstläuterung f *(forest)* self-thinning, natural thinning, autothinning
Selbstmulcheffekt m *(soil)* self-mulching effect
Selbstoxidation f autoxidation
Selbstpaarung f autogamy, orthogamy
Selbstpflücker-Absatzmarkt m pick-your-own outlet, PYO outlet

Selbstreinigung f self-purification, self-cure
Selbstregulation f, **Selbstregulierung** f self-regulation
Selbstschärfung f self-sharpening
selbststeril *(bot)* self-sterile, self-infertile, autosterile
Selbststerilität f self-sterility, autosterility
Selbsttränke f automatic drinker (waterer), self-waterer, autodrinker
Selbsttränkebecken n automatic drinking bowl, bowl drinker
Selbsttränkrinne f automatic water trough
selbstunfruchtbar s. selbststeril
Selbstung f selfing *(plant breeding)* • **eine ~ vornehmen** to self
Selbstungsgeneration f generation of selfing
Selbstungsnachkommenschaft f self-progeny
selbstunverträglich s. selbstinkompatibel
Selbstverbreiter m autochore, autochorous plant
Selbstverbreitung f *(bot)* autochory
Selbstverdauung f autodigestion
Selbstvergiftung f self-poisoning, auto-intoxication
Selbstvermehrung f self-propagation
Selbstvermischung f automixis
Selbstvernichtungsverfahren n autocidal control [tactics] *(genetical pest control)*
Selbstversorgung f self-sufficiency
Selbstversorgungslandwirtschaft f subsistence agriculture (farming)
Selbstverstümmelung f *(vet)* self-mutilation, autotomy
Selbstverträglichkeit f s. Selbstkompatibilität
Selbstwahlfutterautomat m self-choice feeder
Selbstzündung f self-ignition
selektieren to select, to pick [out], to sort [out]; to rogue, to cull
Selektion f selection *(s. a. under Auslese)*
~ **in zwei Richtungen** disruptive selection
~/**kombinierte** combined selection
~/**mechanische** roguing *(e.g. in propagation stands)*
~/**rekurrente** recurrent selection
~/**reziproke rekurrente** reciprocal recurrent selection
selektionieren s. selektieren
Selektions... s. a. Auslese...
Selektionsdifferenz f selection differential
~/**gewogene** weighted selection differential
Selektionsdruck m selection pressure
Selektionseffekt m selection effect
Selektionsentscheid m, **Selektionsentscheidung** f selection decision
Selektionserfolg m selection gain (progress, response), genetic gain (improvement)
~/**partieller** partial response to selection
Selektionsfortschritt m s. Selektionserfolg
Selektionsgrenze f selection limit
Selektionsindex m selection index
Selektionsintensität f selection intensity

Selektionskoeffizient *m* selection coefficient, coefficient of selection
Selektionskriterium *n*, **Selektionsmerkmal** *n* selection criterion (trait)
Selektionsmethode *f* selection method
Selektionsmodell *n* selection model
Selektionsparameter *m* selection parameter
Selektionsplateau *n* selection plateau
Selektionspotential *n* selection potential
Selektionsschema *n* selection scheme
Selektionsverfahren *n* selection method
Selektionswert *m* selection value
Selektionswirkung *f* selection response
Selektionsziel *n* selection objective (goal)
selektiv selective
Selektivfärbung *f* selection staining *(microbiology)*
Selektivherbizid *n* selection herbicide
Selektivität *f* selectivity *(e.g. of plant protectants)*
Selektivitätskoeffizient *m* selectivity coefficient *(e.g. of a soil solution)*
Selektivmedium *n*, **Selektivnährboden** *m* selection medium *(microbiology)*
Selenboden *m* selenium soil
Selendüngemittel *n* selenium fertilizer
Selenose *f (vet)* selenosis
~/**akute** blind staggers
~/**chronische** alkali disease
Selenvergiftung *f (vet)* selenosis
Sellerie *m(f)* [common] celery, Apium graveolens
sellerieblättrig *(bot)* apiifolious
Selleriefliege *f* celery fly, Philophylla (Euleia) heraclei
Selleriefliegenlarve *f* celery leaf-miner, Philophylla (Euleia) heraclei
Selleriegelbfleckenvirus *n* celery yellow spot virus
Selleriegelbnetzvirus *n* celery yellow net virus
Selleriemosaikvirus *n* celery mosaic virus, CeMV
Sellerieringfleckenvirus *n* celery ring spot virus
Sellerieschorf *m* root rot of celery *(caused by Phoma apiicola)*
SeLV *s*. Latentes Sellerievirus
Semen *n s*. Sperma
semiarid semiarid, semidry *(climate)*
Semicillin *n* ampicillin *(antibiotic)*
semidwarf semidwarf
Semidwarf *m* semidwarf *(plant breeding)*
semiessentiell semiessential *(e.g. an amino-acid)*
semihumid semihumid, semimoist *(climate)*
Semikastration *f (vet)* hemicastration
Semiletalfaktor *m* semilethal [factor, gene]
Semikaktusdahlie *f* semicactus dahlia
semiletal *(gen)* semilethal
semimatur semimature
Seminalplasma *n* seminal plasma
Seminom *n* seminoma
Seminurie *f* seminuria, spermaturia
Semiochemikalie *f* semiochemical
semipermeabel semipermeable

Semipermeabilität *f* semipermeability
semipersistent semipersistent
semiproliferierend semiprolific
Semispezies *f* semispecies
semisteril semisterile
Semisterilität *f* semisterility
semitropisch semitropical
Semivariogramm *n (soil)* semivariogram
Semperflorensbegonie *f* fibrous-rooted begonia, wax begonia, Begonia x semperflorens-cultorum
Semperkrankheit *f s*. Stallkrankheit
SeMV *s*. Selleriemosaikvirus
Senecio-Cruentus-Hybride *f (bot)* cineraria
Senegalakazie *f* gum arabic acacia, Acacia senegal
Seneszenz *f* senescence
Seneziose *f* straining disease *(of horses)*
Senf *m* mustard *(genus Sinapis)*
Senfblätter *npl* mustard green
Senfblattlaus *f* mustard (turnip, false cabbage) aphid, Lipaphis erysimi pseudobrassicae
Senfextraktionsschrot *m* mustard-oil meal
Senfkohl *m* black mustard, Brassica nigra
Senfkörneröl *n* mustard[-seed] oil
Senflaus *f s*. Senfblattlaus
Senfmehl *n* mustard flour
Senföl *n* 1. isothiocyanate *(plant substance)*; 2. *s*. Senfkörneröl
Senfölglucosid *n* glucosinolate, mustard glycoside *(plant substance)*
Senfsamen *m* mustard-seed
Senfschrot *m* mustard-oil meal
sengen to singe, to scorch *(e.g. a carcass)*
Senilität *f* senility
Senkboden *m* false bottom *(of brewery)*
Senke *f* sink, depression, hollow
~/**nasse** swale
Senker *m (bot)* sinker
Senkgrube *f* cesspit, cesspool, catch pit, sink, waste well
Senkholz *n* sunken (stranded) timber, sinker, deadhead, snag; bobber *(log driving)*
Senkrücken *m* sway-back, lordosis *(of mammals)*
• **mit** ~ sway-backed
Senkung *f* subsidence *(e.g. of ground)*
Senkwaage *f* areometer
Senkwasser *n* seepage water
Senn[e] *m* Alpine dairyman
Sennerin *f* Alpine dairymaid
Sennesblätter *npl* senna
Sennes[blätter]strauch *m (bot)* 1. senna, cassia *(genus Cassia)*; 2. Alexandrian senna, Cassia senna (acutifolia)
Sennhütte *f* Alpine dairy
Sense *f* scythe • **mit der ~ mähen** to scythe
~ **mit Gestell (Korb, Reff)** cradle scythe
sensen to scythe
Sensenbaum *m (Am)* snath[e]
Sensenblatt *n* scythe blade

Sensenwurf

Sensenwurf *m (Am)* snath[e]
Sensibilisierung *f (phyt, vet)* sensitization
Sensibilität *f* sensibility
Sensitivität *f* sensitivity
Sensor *m* sensor
sensorisch sensory, sensorial
Sepalum *n (bot)* sepal, calyx lobe
Separation *f* separation
Separator *m* separator, separating device; clarifier, clarifying machine
Separator[en]schlamm *m* separator slime; clarifier slime
Separatortrommel *f* separator bowl
Sepiolith *m* sepiolite *(clay mineral)*
Sepsis *f s.* Septikämie
septaploid *(gen)* septaploid
Septaploidie *f* septaploidy
septiert septate
Septikämie *f (vet)* septicaemia, sepsis, blood-poisoning
~ der Forelle/virale hämorrhagische Egtved disease
~/hämorrhagische haemorrhagic septicaemia, pasteurellosis
~/metastasierende pyaemia
septisch septic
Septoria-Blattfallkrankheit *f* **der Topfazalee** azalea leaf scorch *(caused by Septoria azalea)*
Septoria-Blattfleckenkrankheit *f* septoria leaf spot
~ der Gladiole leaf spot of gladiolus *(caused by Septoria gladioli)*
~ der Tomate tomato leaf spot *(caused by Septoria lycopersici)*
Septoria-Braunfleckenkrankheit *f* **des Sellerie** celery leaf spot *(caused by Septoria apii)*
Septoria-Hartfäule *f* **der Gladiolenknollen** hard rot of gladiolus *(caused by Septoria gladioli)*
Septum *n* septum • **ohne ~** non-septate, coenocytic
Sequenz *f* sequence
Sequenzanalyse *f (biom)* sequential analysis
Sequoie *f (bot)* sequoia, wellingtonia *(genus Sequoia)*
Sequoienholz *n* redwood *(esp. from Sequoia sempervirens)*
Ser *s.* Serin
Seralstufe *f* seral stage *(plant ecology)*
Serbische Fichte *f* Serbian spruce, Picea omorika
Serendipitybeere *f* serendipity berry, Dioscoreophyllum cumminsii
SeRFV *s.* Sellerieringfleckenvirus
serial serial
Serialknospe *f* serial bud
Serie *f* 1. series *(taxonomy)*; 2. sere *(plant ecology)*
Serikterium *n (zoo)* silk gland
Serin *n* serine *(amino-acid)*

Serindehydratase *f*, **Serindesaminase** *f* serine dehydratase (deaminase) *(enzyme)*
Serodiagnose *f* serodiagnosis
Serodiagnostik *f* serodiagnostics
Serofarbtest *m s.* Sabin-Feldman-Test
serofibrinös serofibrinous
Serologie *f* serology
serologisch serological
seronegativ seronegative
seropositiv seropositive
seropurulent seropurulent
serös serous
Serosa *f* serosa, serous membrane
serös-eitrig seropurulent
Serositis *f (vet)* serositis
Serosjom *m(n)* s[i]erozem, grey soil
Serotherapie *f (vet)* serotherapy
serotinal serotinal
serotonerg serotonergic
Serotonin *n* serotonin, 5-hydroxytryptamine *(neutrotransmitter)*
Serotyp *m* serotype
Serovakzination *f (vet)* simultaneous vaccination
Serozem *m(n) s.* Serosjom
Serpentin *m* serpentine *(non-clay mineral)*
Serpentinboden *m* serpentine soil
Serradella *f (bot)* [French] serradella, serradilla, Ornithopus sativus
Sertolische Fußzelle (Stützzelle, Zelle) *f* Sertoli cell *(animal anatomy)*
Serum *n* [blood] serum
~/antiretikuläres zytotoxisches antireticular cytotoxic serum
~/diagnostisches diagnostic serum
~/hämolytisches haemolytic serum
~/polyvalentes polyvalent serum
~ trächtiger Stuten pregnant mare serum, PMS
Serumagar *m* serum agar
Serumagglutination *f* **nach Wright** *(vet)* Wright's test
Serumalbumin *n* serum albumen
serumartig serous
serumbildend serous
Serumdiagnose *f* serodiagnosis
Serumenzym *n* serum enzyme
Serumferritin *n* serum ferritin
Serumglobulin *n* serum globulin
Serum-Glutamat-Oxalacetat-Transaminase *f* asparagine aminotransferase *(enzyme)*
Serumgonadotropin *n* serum gonadotrop[h]in
Serumlipid *n* serum lipid
Serumlipoprotein *n* serum lipoprotein
Serumneutralisationstest *m* serum neutralization test *(virology)*
Serumpferd *n* serum horse
Serumprolactin *n* serum prolactin *(hormone)*
Serumprotein *n* [blood] serum protein, blood protein
serumreich serous

Serumschock *m (vet)* serum shock
Serumtiter *m* titre
Serviceperiode *f* sanitation break *(in commercial livestock operations)*
Servobremse *f* servo break
Servolenkung *f* power[-assisted] steering
Sesam *m (bot)* sesame, benni, gingili, Sesamum indicum
Sesambein *n* sesamoid bone *(animal anatomy)*
Sesamextraktionsschrot *m* sesame-oil meal
Sesamkuchen *m* sesame cake *(feed)*
Sesamöl *n* sesame oil, gingili
Sesamsaat *f*, **Sesamsamen** *m* sesame [seed], benniseed
Sesamschrot *m* sesame meal
Sesel *m* stone-parsley, stonewort *(genus Seseli)*
Sesquioxid *n (soil)* sesquioxide
Sesquiterpen *n* sesquiterpene *(isoprenoid)*
seßhaft *(zoo)* sedentary, settled
sessil *(bot, zoo)* sessile
Seta *f (bot, zoo)* seta, bristle
Sethoxydim *n* sethoxydim *(herbicide)*
Setter *m* setter *(dog breed)*
Setzbottich *m* settling tank, settler *(e.g. in brewing)*
setzen 1. to set *(e.g. plantlets)*; 2. to give birth *(game)*; to fawn *(red deer)*; to kindle *(hare, rabbit)*
~/**eine Rückschnittpflanze** to stump-plant
~/**sich** to settle *(e.g. a soil)*
~/**Stecklinge** to strike
Setzholz *n* dibble
Setzling *m* 1. seedling; cutting, layer; plantlet, set[t], nursery plant, transplant; 2. *(pisc)* fingerling
Setzlingsbeet *n* nursery bed
Setzlingskrankheit *f (phyt)* seedling disease
Setzlingspflanzmaschine *f* seedling planter
Setzmaschine *f* transplanter
Setzmilch *f* curdled (set) milk, naturally soured milk
Setzzwiebel *f* seed onion, set[t]
Seuche *f* epidemic, blast
~ **im Pflanzenbestand** epiphytotic
seuchenartig epidemic, epizootic
Seuchengefahr *f* danger of [an] epidemic
seuchenhaft [auftretend] epidemic
Seuchenherd *m* centre of [an] epidemic
Seuchenlehre *f* epidemiology
Sevin *n* carbaryl *(insecticide)*
Sewall-Wright-Effekt *m (gen)* Sewall-Wright effect, random drift
Sexchromatin *n* sex chromatin
Sexduktion *f (gen)* sex duction
Sexen *n* chick (Japanese) sexing
~ **durch Kloakenuntersuchung** vent sexing *(of chicks)*
Sexpheromon *n* sex pheromone

Sexualaktivität *f* sexual activity • **keine ~ aufweisend** agamic, asexual, parthenogenetic
Sexualdifferenzierung *f* sex differentiation
Sexualdimorphismus *m* sex dimorphism
Sexuales *npl* sexuales *(of aphids)*
Sexualfalle *f* sex trap *(pest control)*
Sexualhormon *n* sex hormone
Sexualität *f* sexuality
Sexuallockstoff *m* sex attractant (lure); sex pheromone
Sexualphysiologie *f* sex physiology
Sexualreflex *m* sexual reflex
Sexualsteroid *n* sexual steroid
Sexualtrieb *m* sexual drive (urge)
Sexualverhalten *n* sexual (reproductive) behaviour
Sexualzelle *f* sex cell, gamete
Sexualzyklus *m* sexual (oestrous) cycle
sexuell sexual
Seychellennuß[palme] *f* 1. double coco-nut [palm] *(genus Lodoicea)*; 2. double coco-nut [palm], Lodoicea maldivica
sezieren to dissect
SF *s.* Schlagfolge
SFT *s.* Sabin-Feldman-Test
Sh *s.* Traktorstunde
Shag[tabak] *m* shag
Shallu *f (bot)* shallu, Sorghum roxburghii
Shami-Ziege *f* Damascus goat *(breed)*
Shan-Pony *n* Shan pony *(breed)*
SHBG *s.* Globulin/Sexualhormone bindendes
Sheltie *m s.* Shetland-Zwergschäferhund
Sherry *m* sherry *(wine)*
Shetlandpony *n* Shetland pony, sheltie, shelty *(breed)*
Shetlandwolle *f* Shetland wool
Shetland-Zwergschäferhund *m* Shetland sheepdog, sheltie, shelty *(breed)*
Shiba-Inu *m* Shiba Ina *(dog breed)*
Shih-Tzu *m* shih-tzu *(dog breed)*
Shikimatdehydrogenase *f* shikimate dehydrogenase *(enzyme)*
Shikimatkinase *f* shikimate kinase *(enzyme)*
Shikimisäure *f* shikimic acid *(phytohormone, growth regulator)*
Shikimisäure-[Chorisminsäure-]Weg *m* shikimic acid pathway *(biochemistry)*
Shire[pferd] *n* shire[-horse] *(breed)*
Shoddy *n(m)* shoddy *(wool-processing offal)*
Shorthornrind *n* shorthorn *(cattle breed)*
Shropshire[schaf] *n* Shropshire *(sheep breed)*
SHZ *s.* Soxhlet-Henkel-Zahl
Sialadenitis *f s.* Speicheldrüsenentzündung
Sialinsäure *f* sialic acid
siallitisch *(soil)* siallitic
Sialolith *m s.* Speichelstein
Siamingwer *m (bot)* lesser galangal, Alpinia officinarum
Siamkatze *f* Siamese [cat] *(breed)*

Siberian

Siberian Husky *m* Siberian husky (dog) *(breed)*
Sibirische Aprikose *f* Siberian (Russian) apricot, Prunus (Armeniaca) sibirica
~ **Aster** *f* Siberian aster, Aster sibiricus
~ **Fichte** *f* Siberian spruce, Picea obovata
~ **Haselnuß** *f* Japanese hazel, Corylus heterophylla
~ **Hundswolle** *f* prairie dogbane, Trachomitum (Apocynum) venetum
~ **Iris** *f* Siberian iris, Iris sibirica
~ **Lärche** *f* Siberian larch, Larix sibirica
~ **Marille** *f s.* Sibirische Aprikose
~ **Tanne** *f* Siberian fir, Abies sibirica
~ **Ulme** *f* Siberian elm, Ulmus pumila
~ **Zirbel[kiefer]** *f* Siberian [stone] pine, Siberian cedar, Pinus [cembra var.] sibirica
Sibirischer Kiefernspinner *m (ent)* Siberian bombyx, Dendrolimus superans (sibiricus)
~ **Rothirsch** *m* Siberian red deer, Cervus elaphus sibiricus
~ **Schnittlauch** *m* large chive[s], Allium schoenoprasum var. sibiricum
Sichel *f* [hand] sickle, [reaping-]hook
Sicheleiche *f* southern red oak, Quercus falcata
Sichelfeder *f* sickle-feather *(of a cock)*
sichelförmig sickle-shaped, falciform, falcate
Sichelhasenohr *n (bot)* falcate hare's-ear, Bupleurum falcatum
Sichelklee *m s.* Sichelluzerne
Sichelluzerne *f* sickle medic[k], sickle (yellow) lucern[e], yellow alfalfa, Medicago [sativa ssp.] falcata
sicheln to sickle, to reap, to cut with a sickle
Sichelrasenmäher *m* rotary lawn-mower, roto scythe
Sicheltanne *f* Japanese cedar, sugi, cryptomeria, Cryptomeria japonica
Sicherheit *f*/statistische *(biom)* significance, confidence level
Sicherheitsanhängekupplung *f* safety hitch
Sicherheitsbügel *m* safety (security) bow, safety arc *(e.g. on tractors)*
Sicherheitskabine *f* safety cab
Sicherheitskupplung *f* safety clutch
Sicherheitsschwelle *f* confidence level *(statistics)*
Sicherheitsstreifen *m* safety belt (strip) *(e.g. in forest fire prevention)*
Sicherheitsventil *n* safety valve
Sicherheitswahrscheinlichkeit *f* probability level *(statistics)*
sichern to wind, to be on the alert *(game)*
Sicherungszusatz *m* silage additive
sichten to bolt *(flour)*
Sichter *m* sifter, separator
Sicht[igkeits]messer *m* visibility (haze) meter
Sickerauszug *m (soil)* leachate
Sickergrube *f* cesspit, cesspool; seepage pit
Sickerkanal *m* catch-water drain
sickern to seep, to trickle, to ooze, to percolate

Sickerrate *f (soil)* percolation rate
Sickersaft *m* seepage, effluent [liquid]
Sickersaftgrube *f* seepage pit
Sickerschlitzdränung *f* slot drainage
Sickersperre *f* seepage barrier
Sickerstrang *m* seepage drain
Sickerverlust *m* seepage loss, leakage
Sickerwasser *n* seepage (percolating, leakage) water; *(soil)* gravitational (surplus) water
Sickerwassermeßanlage *f* lysimeter
Siderit *m* siderite, spathic iron ore
Siderophilin *n* siderophilin, transferrin *(blood-plasma protein)*
Siderophor *n* siderophore
Siderosis *f (vet)* siderosis
Sidney-Silky *m* silky [terrier] *(dog breed)*
Siduron *n* siduron *(herbicide)*
Sieb *n* sieve, screen; bolter *(milling)*
Siebabgang *m* waste of sieves
Siebanalyse *f* screen analysis
Siebbein *n* ethmoid bone
Siebblech *n* sieve plate (disk)
Siebboden *m* screen deck, perforated floor
Siebdurchgang *m* [sieve] fines, undersize material
Siebeinstellung *f* sieve adjustment
sieben to sieve, to sift, to screen; to bolt *(flour)*
Siebenfachvakzine *f (vet)* seven-in-once vaccine
siebenlappig *(bot)* septemlobate
Siebenpunkt *m* seven-spotted lady beetle, Coccinella septempunctata
Siebenschläfer *m* fat dormouse, Glis (Myoxus) glis
Siebenstern *m* star flower *(genus Trientalis)*
siebenteilig *(bot)* septenate
Siebfeld *n (bot)* sieve area (field)
Siebfläche *f* sieving (screen) area
siebförmig *(bot, zoo)* cribriform
Siebkasten *m* sieve (cleaning) shoe *(of a thresher)*
Siebkette *f* chain web (sifter)
Siebkettenelevator *m*, **Siebkettenförderer** *m* rod link elevator, open-web elevator, rod-chain conveyor
Siebkettenroder *m* elevator digger *(potato harvester)*
Siebkettensteinsammellader *m* open-web elevator stone picker
siebklassieren to screen, to size
Siebklassierung *f* screening, screen classification
Siebmaschine *f* flat-sieve seed cleaner; bolter *(milling)*
Siebnutzfläche *f* active screen area
Siebolds Apfel *m* toringo crab-apple, Malus sieboldii
~ **Hasel** *f* Siebold filbert, Corylus sieboldiana var. sieboldiana
~ **Walnuß** *f* Japanese walnut, Juglans ailantifolia [var. ailantifolia]
Siebparenchym *n (bot)* phloem parenchyma
Siebplatte *f (bot)* sieve plate (disk), perforation plate

Siebradroder *m* reel digger
Siebrahmen *m s.* Siebkasten
Siebreiniger *m* sieve cleaner
Siebroder *m* sieve digger
Siebröhre *f (bot)* sieve tube
Siebröhrenglied *n* sieve-tube element
Siebröhrensaft *m* phloem sap
Siebrost *m* grate *(of a combine harvester)*
Siebrostroder *m* shaker digger, digger-shaker *(potato harvester)*
Siebrückstand *m* screenings, cavings
Siebsatz *m* set of sieves (screens)
Siebsichter *m* air-screen cleaner, fanning mill
Siebsortierer *m* sieve cleaner
Siebstrang *m (bot)* phloem ray
Siebteil *m (bot)* sieve tube member, phloem
Siebtest *m (biom)* screening method (test), screening • **einem ~ unterziehen** to screen
Siebtrommel *f* cleaning drum
Siebtuch *n* bolting (bolter) cloth *(milling)*
Siebtüpfelung *f (bot)* sieve pitting
Siebverluste *mpl* sieve losses; [shaker] shoe losses *(threshing)*
Siebvorrichtung *f* screening device, screen
Siebzelle *f (bot)* sieve cell
Siedebarometer *n* hypsometer
siedeln to settle
Siedepunkterhöhung *f* boiling-point elevation
Siedler *m* settler
Siedlergarten *m* settlement garden, allotment [garden], garden plot
Siedlerwirtschaft *f* smallholding
Siedlungsabfälle *mpl* garbage
Siedlungsabwasser *n* urban sewage
Siedlungsgebiet *n (ecol)* range, area
Siedlungskompost *m* garbage compost
Siedlungsmüll *m* municipal waste
Siedlungsmüllkompost *m* municipal [refuse, waste] compost
Siedlungsstruktur *f* settlement structure *(landscaping)*
Siegwurz *f* sword lily (grass), gladiolus *(genus Gladiolus)*
Siel *n* bank sluice
Siele *f* trace
Sielengeschirr *n* breast (trace) harness
Sielscheit *n* swingletree, swingle-bar, whipple tree, *(Am)* whiffletree
Sigatoka[krankheit] *f der Banane* sigatoka disease [of bananas], banana leaf spot [disease] *(caused by Mycosphaerella musicola)*
Signalgen *n* marker [gene] *(plant breeding)*
Signalgenträger *m* marker line
Signalgras *n* bread (palisade) grass, Brachiaria brizantha
Signalleuchte *f* indicator lamp
Signalreiz *m* key stimulus
signifikant *(biom)* significant
Signifikanz *f* significance

Signifikanzniveau *n* significance level, level of significance
Signifikanztest *m* significance test, test of significance
Signifikanzwahrscheinlichkeit *f* significance probability
Sika[hirsch] *m* sika, Japanese deer, Cervus sika (nippon)
Sikkant *n s.* Sikkationsmittel
Sikkation *f* desiccation; preharvest desiccation
Sikkationsmittel *n* desiccant, drying (dehydrating) agent
Silage *f* silage, ensilage
~ aus nichtangewelktem Gras direct-cut grass silage
~/trockensubstanzreiche high dry-matter silage
Silage... *s. a.* Gärfutter...
Silagebereitung *f* silage-making
Silagebeurteilung *f* silage evaluation (appraisal)
Silageblockschneider *m* silage cutter
Silagebreitverteiler *m* silage spreader
Silageentnahme *f* silage removal *(from a silo)*
Silage[entnahme]fräse *f* silage unloading cutter, silage unloader
Silagefütterung *f* silage feeding
Silagegabel *f* silage fork
Silagegebläse *n* silage blower
Silagekrankheit *f (vet)* listeriosis, listerellosis *(caused by Listeria monocytogenes)*
Silagequalität *f* silage quality
Silageschneidedosiergabelwagen *m* silage cutting trailer with dispensing equipment
Silageschneider *m* silage cutter
Silagesickersaft *m* silage effluent
Silageverfütterung *f* silage feeding
Silageverlust *m* silage (ensiling) loss
Silageverteiler *m* silage spreader
Silagewagen *m* silage trailer
Silagezusatz *m* silage additive
Silau *m* pepper saxifrage, Silaum silaus
Silberagave *f* [white] henequen, Yucatan sisal, Agave fourcroydes
Silberahorn *m* silver maple, Acer saccharinum
Silberakazie *f* silver[green] wattle, Acacia dealbata
Silberaspe *f s.* Silberpappel
Silberbaum *m* 1. silver tree, varay cotton, Leucadendron argenteum; 2. cajeput [tree], paperbark, swamp tea-tree, Melaleuca leucadendra
Silberblatt *n* 1. honesty, satin-flower *(genus Lunaria)*; 2. perennial honesty, Lunaria rediviva; 3. Mediterranean sage, Salvia aethiopis
Silberblattgreiskraut *n (bot)* dusty miller, Senecio bicolor
silberblättrig *(bot)* argyrophyllous
Silbereiche *f s.* Silberblattgreiskraut
Silberfarn *m* gold fern *(genus Pityrogramma)*
Silberfaser *f s.* Retikulinfaser
Silberfischchen *n (ent)* silver fish, slicker, Lepisma saccharina

Silberfuchs

Silberfuchs *m* silver fox, Vulpes fulva argentata
Silberglanzbrandschopf *m (bot)* celosia, Celosia argentea
Silberhaargras *n* sungrass *(genus Imperata)*
Silberimmortelle *f* pearly everlasting, Anaphalis margaritacea var. margaritacea
Silberkarpfen *m* silver carp, Hypophalmichthys molitrix
Silberkerze *f (bot)* bugbane *(genus Cimicifuga)*
Silberkraut *n* 1. silverweed *(genus Argyreia)*; 2. *s.* Duftsteinrich
Silberlachs *m* silver salmon, coho [salmon], cohoe, Oncorhynchus kisutch
Silberlinde *f* silver linden, Tilia tomentosa (argentea)
Silberling *m* satin-flower, honesty, money plant, moonwort *(genus Lunaria)*
Silbernervige Fittonie *f* nerve (mosaic) plant, silver-nerved fittonia, silver threads, Fittonia verschaffeltii var. argyroneura
Silberölweide *f* silverberry, Elaeagnus commutata (argentea)
Silberpappel *f* abele, white (silver-leaf) poplar, Populus alba
Silberscharte *f (bot)* jurinea *(genus Jurinea)*
Silberschorf *m* silver scurf *(of potato, caused by Helminthosporium solani)*
Silberthiosulfat *n* silver thiosulphate *(for preserving cut flowers)*
Silberweide *f* common (white) willow, Salix alba
Silberwurz *f (bot)* mountain avens, Dryas octopetala
silbrig argenteous
Silicagel *n* silica gel
Silicat *n* silicate
Silicatgestein *n* silicate rock
Silicatmineral *n* silicate mineral
Silicium *n* silicon
Siliciumdioxid-Sesquioxid-Verhältnis *n (soil)* silica-sesquioxide ratio
Silierbarkeit *f* ensilability
silieren to [en]silage, to ensile, to silo
Silierhilfe *f* silage additive
Silierprozeß *m* ensiling process
Siliertechnik *f* silage-making technique
Silier- und Formpresse *f* stack-silo former and consolidator
Silierung *f* silage-making, [en]silage
Silierungsverlust *m* silage (in-silo) loss
Silierverfahren *n s.* Siliertechnik
Silifikation *f (soil)* silication
Silikat *n s.* Silicat
Silikose *f (vet)* silicosis
Silky Terrier *m* silky [terrier] *(dog breed)*
Silo *m(n)* silo, bin
~/luftdicht abschließender vacuum silo
Siloabdeckung *f* silo cover
Siloentleerung *f* silo emptying

Siloentnahmevorrichtung *f* silo unloader (tapping plant)
Siloentrinder *m (forest)* silo barker
Silofuttererntemaschine *f* silage harvester
Silofuttermais *m* forage maize
Silofutterpflanze *f* silage plant
Silogas *n* silo gas
Silomais *m* silage (forage) maize, *(Am)* silage corn
Siloobenentnahmefräse *f* silo top unloader
Silosickersaft *m* silo seepage, silage effluent
Silosohle *f* silo floor
Silountenentnahmefräse *f* silo bottom unloader
Siloverfestiger *m* silo consolidator
Silowasser *n s.* Silosickersaft
Silt *m* silt
silvikol silvicolous
Simazin *n* simazine *(herbicide)*
Simeton *n* simeton *(herbicide)*
Simetryn *n* simetryne *(herbicide)*
Simmentaler Fleckvieh (Rind) *n* Simmental *(cattle breed)*
Simons [Rote] Pflaume *f* apricot plum, Prunus simonii
Simse *f* bul[l]rush, [club] rush, deer grass *(genus Scirpus)*
Simultanimpfung *f (vet)* simultaneous vaccination
Simultaninfektion *f* mixed infection
Sinalbin *n* sinalbin *(glucoside)*
Sinapin *n* sinapine
Sinapinsäure *f* sinapic acid
Sinapylalkohol *m* sinapyl alcohol *(lignin precursor)*
Sinciput *n* sinciput *(animal anatomy)*
Sindhi-Rind *n* Sindhi [cattle] *(breed)*
Singharanuß *f* singhara nut, water chestnut (caltrop), Trapa bicornis var. bispinosa
Singrün *n (bot)* 1. periwinkle *(genus Vinca)*; 2. periwinkle, Vinca minor
Singvogel *m* songbird
Singzikade *f* cicada, cicala, cigala *(family Cicadidae)*
Sinigrin *n* sinigrin *(glucosinolate)*
Sinigrinase *f* thioglucosidase *(enzyme)*
Sinker *m* **der Tulpe** dropper of tulip
Sinkholz *n* sunken (stranded) timber, sinker, snag; bobber *(timber floating)*
Sink-Source-Beziehung *f* sink-source relationship *(plant physiology)*
Sinkwasser *n (soil)* gravitational (surplus) water
Sinn *m* sense
Sinneshaar *n* sensory (tactile) hair
Sinnesnerv *m* sensory (afferent) nerve
Sinnesorgan *n* sense (sensory) organ
Sinnesphysiologie *f* sensory physiology
Sinnesprüfung *f* sensory evaluation (examination), organoleptic analysis (assessment, test)
Sinneswahrnehmung *f* sensation, perception
Sinningia-Hybride *f (bot)* florist's gloxinia
Sinnmutation *f (gen)* sense (silent) mutation
Sinnpflanze *f (bot)* mimosa *(genus Mimosa)*

Sinoatrialknoten *m* sinuatrial node *(of the heart)*
Sinuitis *f s.* Sinusitis
Sinus *m* sinus *(animal anatomy)*
Sinusarrhythmie *f (vet)* sinus arrhythmia
Sinusitis *f (vet)* sinusitis
~ **der Enten/infektiöse** duck flu, avian influenza
Sinusknoten *m s.* Sinoatrialknoten
Sipho *m* siphuncle, cornicle *(of aphids)*
Siphon *m* siphon
Siphonogamie *f (bot)* siphonogamy
Siphunculus *m s.* Sipho
Sippe *f* taxon
Sirup *m* syrup, molasses
Sisal *m* sisal[-hemp]
Sisalagave *f* sisal, Agave sisalana
Sisalbagasse *f* sisal bagasse
Sisalfaser *f* agave fibre, sisal[-hemp]
Sisalhanf *m* sisal[-hemp]
Siskiyoufichte *f* Brewer's (creeping) spruce, Picea breweriana
Sisomicin *n*, **Sisomin** *n* sisomicin *(antibiotic)*
Sissu[baum] *m* sissoo[-tree], Dalbergia sissoo
Sitkafichte *f* Sitka (tideland) spruce, Picea sitchensis
Sitosterin *n*, **Sitosterol** *n* sitosterol *(plant substance)*
Sitter *f (bot)* helleborine *(genus Epipactis)*
Sitzbeinausschnitt *m* ischial arch
Sitzbeinhöcker *m* point of rump
sitzend *(bot, zoo)* sessile
~/**fast** subsessile
Sitz[rasen]mäher *m* riding (ride-on) mower
Sitzstange *f* perch • **die** ~ **aufsuchen** to perch, to roost
Sitzstock *m* seat-stick *(of a hunter)*
Sizilianische Tanne *f* Sicilian fir, Abies nebrodensis
Sizilianischer Kapernstrauch *m* Sicilian caper, Capparis ovata
Skabiose *f* pincushion flower, gypsy rose, devil's bit, scabious *(genus Scabiosa)*
Skammoniaharz *n* scammony [resin] *(from Convolvulus scammonia)*
SkaMV *s.* Schwedenkleeadernmosaikvirus
Skapula *f* scapula, shoulder-blade, blade[-bone]
Skarifikation *f* scarification *(e.g. of hard-shelled seeds)*
Skarifikator *m* scarifier
skarifizieren to scarify
Skatol *n* skatol[e]
skatophag coprophagous
Skedastizität *f (biom)* scedasticity
skeletal skeletal
skeletogen skeletogenous
Skelett *n* skeleton
Skelettalter *n* skeletal age
Skelettboden *m* skeletal soil
Skelettentwicklung *f* skeleton development
Skelettgröße *f* skeletal size
skelettieren to skeletinize
Skelettmuskel *m* skeletal (striated) muscle
Skelettmuskelanomalie *f* musculoskeletal anomaly
Skelettmuskelfaser *f* [skeletal] muscle fibre, myofibre
Skelettmuskelfaserhülle *f* sarcolemma
Skelettmuskulatur *f* skeletal musculature, musculoskeletal apparatus (system)
Skelettsubstrat *n (soil)* skeletal substratum
Skidder *m (forest)* skidder, skidding tractor *(for compounds s. under Rückeschlepper)*
Skiophyt *m* sciophyte, shade plant
Sklera *f* sclera *(of the eye)*
skleral scleral
Sklereide *f (bot)* sclereid, brachysclereid, stone (sclerotic, grit) cell
Sklerenchym *n (bot)* sclerenchyma
Sklerenchymscheide *f* bundle sheath
Skleritis *f (vet)* scleritis
Sklerodermie *f (vet)* scleroderma
Skleroprotein *n* scleroprotein, albuminoid
Sklerophylle *f (bot)* sclerophyll, sclerophyte
Sklerophyllie *f* sclerophylly
sklerös sclerous
Sklerose *f* sclerosis
Sklerotienkrankheit *f (phyt)* sclerotial disease
~ **der Tulpe** grey bulb rot of tulip *(caused by Rhizoctonia tuliparum)*
sklerotisch sclerotic, sclerous
Sklerotium *n* sclerotium *(hardened mycelium of certain higher fungi)*
Skolex *m* scolex, head *(of tapeworms)*
skorpionähnlich *(bot)* scorpioid
Skrotalhernie *f (vet)* scrotal hernia, scrotocele
Skrotalreflex *m* scrotal reflex
Skrotum *n* scrotum, scrotal sac, cod
Skuddeschaf *n* Skudde *(sheep breed)*
Skunk *m* 1. skunk *(esp. genus Mephitis)*; 2. skunk, Mephitis mephitis
Skunkfell *n*, **Skunkpelz** *m* skunk
Skyeterrier *m* Skye [terrier] *(dog breed)*
SL *s.* Sexualockstoff
Slow-Virus-Infektion *f (vet)* slow virus disease (infection)
Smaragdeidechse *f* European green lizard, Lacerta viridis
smaragdgrün emerald green
Smectit *m* smectite, montmorillonite *(clay mineral)*
Smegma *n* smegma
Smog *m* smog
Smoker *m* smoker, bee blower
Smolt *m (pisc)* smolt, salmlet
Smoltbildung *f*, **Smoltifizierung** *f* smoltification
Smonitza *f (soil)* smonitza
Smudisch *m* Zemaitukai *(horse breed)*
SMV *s.* Salatmosaikvirus
SO₂... *s.* Schwefeldioxid...
Soapstock *m s.* Seifenfluß

Sobelin

Sobelin n clindamycin *(antibiotic)*
Sockelerosion f pedestal erosion
Sockenblume f 1. barrenwort *(genus Epimedium)*; 2. large-flowered barrenwort, Epimedium grandiflorum
Soda f(n) soda, sodium carbonate
Sodaboden m s. Solonez
Sode f 1. [lawn] sod, turf; 2. *(bot)* sea blite *(genus Suaeda)* • **Soden abheben (abstechen)** to cut sods, to pare off turf, to screef
Sodenpflanzung f turf planting
Sodenreißer m [lawn] sod shredder
Sofortwirkung f eines Pestizids knock-down effect
Soframycin n neomycin *(antibiotic)*
Sohle f sole
Sohlendurchbruch m *(vet)* dropped sole *(of horse's foundered hoof)*
Sohlengeschwür n/Rusterholzsches *(vet)* ulcer of the sole
Sohlenkörpervollhuf m *(vet)* dropped sole
Sohlenquetschung f *(vet)* corn
Sohlenschlagader f plantar artery
Soja[bohne] f soya [bean], soy[bean], soja [bean], Chinese bean, Glycine max
Sojabohnenblattkäfer m bean leaf beetle, Plagiodera inclusa
Sojabohnenblattkräuselkrankheit f *(phyt)* soya bean crinkle leaf
Sojabohnenextraktionsschrot m s. Sojaextraktionsschrot
Sojabohnengelbmosaikvirus n soya bean yellow mosaic virus, SYMV
Sojabohnenkuchen m soya bean cake, soycake *(feed)*
Sojabohnenmehl n soya bean flour
Sojabohnenmosaikvirus n soya bean mosaic virus, SMV
Sojabohnenöl n soya bean oil
Sojabohnenprotein n soya [bean] protein
Sojabohnenseifenstock m soya bean soapstock
Sojabohnenstauchevirus n soya bean stunt virus
Sojaeiweiß n soya [bean] protein
Sojaeiweißfaser f soya bean fibre
Sojaextraktionsschrot m soya bean [oil-]meal, extracted soya bean meal
Sojaheu n soya hay
Sojalecithin n soya bean lecithin
Sojamilch f soya [bean] milk
Sojaöl n soya oil
Sojaölkraftstoff m soya bean oil-fuel
Sojaschrot m s. Sojaextraktionsschrot
Sojasilage f soya silage
Sojasoapstock m soya bean soapstock
Sojastroh n soya straw
Solanidin n solanidine *(alkaloid)*
Solanin n solanine *(alkaloid)*
solar solar
Solarenergie f solar energy
Solargewächshaus n solar greenhouse
Solarheizung f solar heating
Solarimeter n solarimeter
Solarisation f solarization, solar pasteurization (heating) *(esp. of soils)*
solarisch solar
solarisieren to solarize
Solarkonstante f solar constant
Solarplexus m solar plexus, abdominal brain *(animal anatomy)*
Solarstrahlung f solar radiation
Solarteich m solar pond
Solarzelle f solar collector
Sole f [salt] brine
Solekühler m brine cooler
Solekühlung f brine cooling
Solifluktion f solifluction, earth flow
solitär solitary
Solitärbaum m solitary (single) tree
Solitärparasitismus m simple parasitism
Solitärstand m *(forest)* open position
Solitärstaude f individual perennial plant
Solleinschlag m *(forest)* volume to be cut
Solod m *(soil)* solod, soloth, soloti
solodartig solodic
solodieren to solodize
solodiert solodic
Solodierung f solodization
Solone[t]z m solonets, solonetz, soda (black alkali) soil
~ /degradierter s. Solod
~ /toniger szik soil
solonetzartig solonetzic
Solonisation f *(soil)* solonization
Solontschak m solonchak, white alkali soil
Solum n *(soil)* solum (A and B horizons)
Solution f solution *(for compounds s. under Lösung)*
Solventtrocknung f solvent drying
somaklonal *(gen)* somaclonal
somatisch somatic
~ **polyploid** *(gen)* autopolyploid
~ **zwittrig** *(bot, zoo)* gynandromorphic
Somatoliberin n somatoliberin *(hormone)*
Somatomedin n somatomedin, sulphation factor *(hormone)*
Somatostatin n somatostatin, growth-hormone release inhibiting factor
Somatotropin n somatotropin, somatotropic hormone, STH
Somatotropin-Releasinghormon n somatoliberin
Somatotyp m somatotype, body-build
Somazelle f somatic cell
Sommelier m sommelier, wine steward
Sommer m summer
Sommerabkalbung f summer calving
Sommeradonisröschen n s. Sommersblutströpfchen
Sommeranbauzeit f kharif *(in India)*

Sommerannuelle f (bot) summer annual
Sommeraster f [China] aster, Callistephus chinensis
Sommerazalee f (bot) godetia (genus Godetia)
Sommerblüher m summer-flowering plant, summer-blooming plant
Sommerblutströpfchen n pheasant's-eye [flower], Adonis aestivalis
Sommerbrache f summer fallow
Sommerbutter f summer butter
Sommerefeu m German ivy, Senecio mikanioides
Sommereiche f common (pedunculate, English) oak, Quercus robur (pedunculata)
Sommereinstand m summer range (of game)
Sommerekzem n (vet) sweet (Queensland) itch, summer sores (of horses)
Sommerendivie f cos [lettuce], Lactuca sativa var. longifolia
Sommerfällung f summer felling
Sommerflieder m 1. butterfly bush, summer lilac, buddleia (genus Buddleja); 2. [orange-eye] butterfly bush, summer lilac, Buddleja davidii
Sommerfrucht f summer crop
Sommerfuchsie f (bot) 1. clarkia (genus Clarkia); 2. clarkia, Clarkia unguiculata (elegans)
Sommerfütterung f summer feeding
sommergrün (bot) [cold-]deciduous
Sommergrüne Winterbeere f (bot) possumhaw, Ilex decidua
Sommerhaarkleid n summer [hair] coat
Sommerholz n s. Spätholz
Sommerhyazinthe f summer hyacinth, Galtonia candicans
Sommerknoblauch m great round-headed garlic, summer (great-head) garlic, wild leek, Allium ampeloprasum
Sommerknotenblume f (bot) summer snowflake, Leucojum aestivum
Sommerkronenschnitt m summer topping (orcharding)
Sommerkultur f summer crop
Sommerlammung f summer lambing
Sommerlavatere f (bot) three-monthly lavatera, Lavatera trimestris
Sommerlinde f broad-leaved lime[-tree], [large-leaved] lime, (Am) bigleaf linden, Tilia platyphyllos
Sommermast f summer fattening
Sommermastitis f (vet) summer mastitis, August bag (caused by Corynebacterium pyogenes)
Sommerpferdedecke f fly sheet
Sommerpflanze f summer plant
Sommerrahm m summer cream
Sommerraps m summer rape
Sommerräude f der Pferde parafilariosis [of horses] (caused by Parafilaria multipapillosa)
Sommerrebe f summer grape (bunch), Vitis aestivalis
Sommerrinde f late bark

Sommerruhe f, **Sommerschlaf** m summer dormancy (rest), aestivation • ~ **halten** to aestivate
Sommerschnitt m summer (green) pruning (e.g. of woody ornamentals)
Sommersonnenwende f midsummer
Sommerspore f (bot) summer spore, ured[i]ospore (of Uredinales)
Sommerspritzung f summer spraying
sommersprossig (bot) lentiginous
Sommersteckling m green cutting
Sommertrieb m (bot) secondary shoot (growth), Lammas-shoot
Sommertrockenheit f summer drought
Sommervergißmeinnicht n (bot) Chinese forget-me-not, Cynoglossum amabile
Sommerweide f, **Sommerweidegang** m sommer pasture (grazing)
Sommerwirt m summer host
Sommerwurz f broomrape (genus Orobanche)
Sommerziest m hedge-nettle betony, Stachys annua
Sommerzwiebel f onion, Allium cepa [var. cepa]
Sommerzwischenfrucht f summer catch crop
Sommerzypresse f 1. summer cypress (genus Kochia); 2. summer (mock) cypress, burning bush, Kochia (Bassia) scoparia
Somnolenz f drowsiness
Sonde f probe
Sonderkultur f special[ty] crop, specialist crop
Sonnenaufgang m sunrise
Sonnenauge n 1. orange sunflower, ox-eye (genus Heliopsis); 2. ox-eye, Heliopsis helianthoides
Sonnenbestrahlung f solar irradiation
sonnenbetrieben solar-powered
Sonnenblatt n sun-leaf (plant physiology)
Sonnenblume f 1. sunflower, helianthus (genus Helianthus); 2. common (annual) sunflower, Helianthus annuus
Sonnenblumenextraktionsschrot m sunflower [oil] meal
Sonnenblumenkuchen m sunflower cake
Sonnenblumenöl n sunflower oil
Sonnenblumenprotein n sunflower protein
Sonnenblumenrost m sunflower rust (caused by Puccinia helianthi)
Sonnenblumenschneidwerk n sunflower cutter bar, sunflower attachment
Sonnenblumensilage f sunflower silage
Sonnenbrand m (phyt, vet) sunburn, sun-scald, sun-scorch
Sonnenbrandschaden m sunburn damage
Sonnenbraut f sneezeweed (genus Helenium)
Sonneneinstrahlung f solar radiation, insolation • **durch ~ behandeln** to insolate, to solarize
Sonnenekzem n (vet) solar eczema
Sonnenenergie f solar energy (power)
Sonnenenergieverstärker m solar energy intensifier

Sonnenflügel

Sonnenflügel *m (bot)* sunray, everlasting *(genus Helipterum)*
Sonnengeflecht *n* solar plexus, abdominal brain *(animal anatomy)*
Sonnenhut *m* coneflower, rudbeckia *(genus Rudbeckia)*
Sonnenkleid *n (vet)* sun-suit *(anomaly of plumage)*
Sonnenkollektor *m* solar collector
Sonnenkollektorpumpe *f* solar collector pump
Sonnenlage *f* sun-exposed site
Sonnenlicht *n* sunlight
sonnenliebend heliophilous
sonnenmeidend heliophobic
Sonnenpflanze *f* sun[-loving] plant, heliophyte, heliophile
Sonnenröschen *n* rock (sun) rose *(genus Helianthemum)*
Sonnenscheindauer *f* sunshine duration, insolation
Sonnenscheinstunde *f* hour of sunshine
Sonnenstich *m (vet)* sunstroke
Sonnenstrahlung *f* solar radiation • **der ~ aussetzen** to insolate, to solarize
~/diffuse diffuse (sky) radiation
~/direkte direct solar radiation
Sonnenstrahlungs[wärme]messer *m* pyrheliometer
Sonnentätigkeit *f* solar activity
Sonnentau *m* sundew, youthwort *(genus Drosera)*
Sonnentrocknung *f* solar drying
Sonnenuntergang *m* sunset, sundown
Sonnenwachsschmelzer *m* solar [bees]wax extractor
Sonnenwärme *f* solar heat
Sonnenwende *f* 1. *(bot)* heliotrope, turnsole *(genus Heliotropium)*; 2. solstice *(s. a. Sommersonnenwende and Wintersonnenwende)*
sonnenwendig *(bot)* heliotropic
Sonnenwendigkeit *f* heliotropism, phototropism
Sonnenwendkäfer *m* june beetle (bug), summer (European) chafer, Amphimallus (Rhizotrogus) solstitialis
Sonnen[wend]wolfsmilch *f* sun spurge, wart grass (weed), Euphorbia helioscopia
Sophienkraut *n* flixweed, Descurainia (Sisymbrium) sophia
Sophorin *n* cystisine *(alkaloid)*
Sorbinsäure *f* sorbic acid *(fatty acid)*
Sorbit *m*, **Sorbitol** *n* sorbitol, sorbite *(sugar alcohol)*
Sorbitoldehydrogenase *f* sorbitol dehydrogenase *(enzyme)*
Sorbose *f* sorbose *(monosaccharide)*
Sorgho *m s.* Sorghum
Sorghum *n* sorghum, sorgo *(genus Sorghum)*
Sorghumeiweiß *n* sorghum protein
Sorghumheu *n* sorghum hay
Sorghumsilage *f* sorghum silage
Sorghumstroh *n* sorghum stover

Sorption *f* sorption
Sorptionseigenschaft *f* sorptional property
Sorptionskapazität *f (soil)* [cation, total] exchange capacity
Sorptionskomplex *m (soil)* adsorption (absorbing) complex
Sorte *f* 1. variety, cultivar; 2. grade, quality *(as of foods, fruit)*; 3. brand *(e.g. of tobacco)*
~/aufgepfropfte top variety
~ aus Privatzüchtung home-bred variety
~/einheimische native variety
~/synthetische synthetic [cultivar, variety]
sortenabhängig variety-dependent, varietal
Sortenanbauversuch *m* variety test[ing]
Sortenanerkennung *f* varietal certification
Sortenanfall *m (forest)* assortment yield
Sortenauswahl *f* cultivar selection
sortenbedingt varietal
Sortenbeschreibung *f* varietal description
Sortenbestimmung *f* cultivar identification
sortenecht genuine, true from seed, true to variety, true-bred *(s. a. sortenrein)*
Sortenechtheit *f* varietal trueness (identity), trueness of (to) variety, genuineness
Sortenechtheitsprüfung *f* cultivar verification testing
Sorteneffekt *m* varietal effect
sorteneigen varietal
Sortenempfehlung *f* cultivar recommendation
Sortenerkennung *f* cultivar identification
Sortenertragstafel *f (forest)* assortment [yield, volume] table
~ für den Einzelstamm single-tree assortment table
~ für frisches Schnittholz green-chain tally, mill tally
Sortenfreigabe *f s.* Sortenzulassung
Sortengemisch *n* variety mixture, mixture of cultivars
Sortengliederung *f (forest)* assortment structure
Sortengruppe *f* group of cultivars
Sortengruppierung *f* cultivar grouping
Sortenhieb *m (forest)* clear felling
Sortenhybride *f* intervarietal cross (hybrid)
Sortenidentifikation *f* cultivar identification
Sortenklassifikation *f* variety classification
Sortenkreuzung *f* intervarietal crossing
Sortenkreuzungsprodukt *n* intervarietal cross (hybrid)
Sortenliste *f* list of varieties
Sortenmerkmal *n* varietal characteristic
Sortenneuzüchtung *f* new-variety breeding
Sortenpaß *m* plant patent
Sortenprüfung *f* variety testing
Sortenprüfungsamt *n* authority for the testing and admission of new cultivars
Sortenrayonierung *f* variety zonation
Sortenreaktion *f* varietal reaction
Sortenregistrierung *f* cultivar registration

sortenrein varietally pure
Sortenreinheit *f* cultivar (varietal) purity, purity of variety
Sortenschutz *m* cultivar protection
Sortenschutzverordnung *f* plant variety protection act
sortenspezifisch cultivar-specific, varietal
Sortenstruktur *f (forest)* assortment structure
Sortentafel *f s.* Sortenertragstafel
Sortentarif *m (forest)* assortment piece rate
Sorten-Unterlagen-Kombination *f* [root]stock-scion combination, stion
Sorten-Unterlagen-Reaktion *f* stock-scion response, stion response
Sortenunterschied *m* varietal difference
Sortenvergleichsversuch *m* competitive variety trial
Sortenversuch *m* cultivar [evaluation] trial
Sortenvorvermehrung *f* preliminary variety seed multiplication
Sortenwahl *f* choice of cultivar (variety), cultivar selection
Sortenwein *m* brand wine
Sortenwert *m* value of variety
Sortenzulassung *f* cultivar release, admission of new cultivars
Sortex-Separator *m* colour sorter
Sortieranlage *f* grading plant
Sortierband *n* band separator, belt grader, sorting belt (conveyor)
Sortiereinrichtung *f* sorter, grader
sortieren to sort [out], to assort, to grade, to calibrate
~/nach dem Geschlecht to sex *(chicks)*
~/nach Größe to size, to grade by size
Sortierer *m* sorter, grader
~/elektrostatischer electrostatic seed cleaner
Sortierlinie *f* grader line
Sortiermaschine *f* sorter, grader
Sortierpferch *m* shedder
Sortierraum *m* grading room
Sortierrollen *fpl* sorting rolls
Sortiersieb *n* assorting screen
Sortiertisch *m* sorting table, grading bench
~/pneumatischer specific-gravity separator *(seed processing)*
Sortierung *f* sorting, grading; classification
Sortierungsvorschrift *f (forest)* grading rule
Sortierwasserplatz *m (forest)* sorting boom (jack)
Sortierzylinder *m* cylinder grader *(malting)*
Sortiment *n* assortment
Sortimentsanfall *m (forest)* assortment yield
Sortimentshieb *m (forest)* selective (exploitation, clear) felling, culling
~/kostendeckender (wirtschaftlicher) economic selective felling
Sortimentsmethode *f* shortwood (short-length) logging
Sortimentstafel *f s.* Sortenertragstafel

Sortimenttraktor *m (forest)* forwarder
Sorus *m* sorus *(clump of sporangia of ferns)*
Source-Sink-Beziehung *f* source-sink relation *(plant physiology)*
South-Devon-Rind *n* South Devon *(cattle breed)*
Southdown[schaf] *n* Southdown *(sheep breed)*
Southern-Hybridisierung *f*, **Southern-Technik** *f (gen)* Southern blotting
Soxhletapparatur *f (dairy)* Soxhlet apparatus (extractor)
Soxhlet-Henkel-Zahl *f (dairy)* Soxhlet-Henkel value, SHV
Soziabilität *f (ecol)* sociability
Sozialbrache *f* idle (abandoned) land
Soziallockstoff *m* [aggregation] pheromone
Sozialverhalten *n* social behaviour
Soziation *f* facies *(plant sociology)*
Sozietät *f (ecol)* society
Soziohormon *n s.* Soziallockstoff
Soziometrie *f* sociometry *(behavioural research)*
sp. *s.* Spezies
SP *s.* Schweinepest
Spadix *m (bot)* spadix
Spalier *n* espalier, trellis, treillage • **im ~ [er]ziehen** to espalier, to trellis • **mit einem ~ versehen** to espalier, to trellis
~/strenges formal (trained) espalier
~/zwangloses free espalier
Spalierbaum *m* espalier; wall fruit tree
Spalierbaumreihe *f* espalier
Spalierbogen *m* trellis arch
spalieren to espalier, to trellis
Spaliergerüst *n* espalier
Spalierobst *n* espalier (trellis, wall) fruit
Spalierobstbaum *m* espalier (trellis) fruit-tree
Spaltalge *f* blue-green alga *(class Cyanophyceae)*
Spaltaxt *f* cleaving axe, cleaver, [break] axe
spaltbar cleavable
~/schwer difficult to cleave *(wood)*
Spaltbarkeit *f* cleavability
Spaltblume *f* 1. butterfly flower, poor man's orchid, schizanthus *(genus Schizanthus)*; 2. poor man's orchid, Schizanthus pinnatus
spalten to split, to cleave, to rift *(e.g. wood)*; to segregate
Spaltenboden *m* slatted (slotted) floor
Spaltenfrost *m (soil)* congelifraction
Spaltensieb *n* grid, grate
Spalter *m (slaught)* cleaver
spalterbig heterozygous
Spalterbigkeit *f* heterozygosis, heterozygosity
spaltfähig cleavable
Spaltfähigkeit *f* cleavability
Spaltfrucht *f (bot)* schizocarp
Spaltglöckchen *n* Indian tobacco, Lobelia inflata
Spalthammer *m* splitting (cleaving) hammer
Spaltholz *n* splitwood, cleft wood (timber)
Spaltholzsortiment *n* split-up assortment

Spalthügelpflanzung

Spalthügelpflanzung f *(forest)* notch-mound planting
Spaltkeil m splitting (cleaving) wedge; riving knife
~/eiserner froe[-knife], frow[-knife]
Spaltmaschine f splitting (cleaving, riving) machine
Spaltöffnung f *(bot)* stoma, stomate
Spaltöffnungsverhalten n stomatal response
Spaltpflanzung f *(forest)* slit (wedge) planting, notch (bar, trench) planting, notching
Spaltpfropfen n cleft grafting
Spaltpilz m s. Bakterium
Spaltsaat f slot-seeding
Spaltsämaschine f slot seeder
Spaltsehne f cleavage face
Spaltung f *(gen)* segregation • **durch ~ entstanden** schizogenous
Spaltungsgärung f anaerobiosis, anoxibiosis
Spaltungsregel f *(gen)* law of segregation, Mendel's second law
Span m chip, shaving; splinter
spänen 1. to spean, to wean, to ablactate; 2. s. säugen
Spanferkel n sucking pig, piglet
Spanholzplatte f wood chipboard
Spaniel m spaniel *(dog breed)*
Spanische Esparsette f Spanish esparcet, cockshead, Hedysarum coronarium
~ Fliege f Spanish (blister) fly, Lytta (Cantharis) vesicatoria
~ Golddistel f Spanish oyster-plant, Spanish salsify, golden thistle, Scolymus hispanicus
~ Haferwurzel f s. Schwarzwurzel
~ Kresse f garden (common) nasturtium, Tropaeolum majus
~ Schwertlilie f Spanish iris, Iris xiphium
~ Tanne f Spanish fir, Abies pinsapo
~ Zistrose f ladanum [resin tree], gum cistus, Cistus ladanifer
Spanischer Ginster m Spanish (weaver's) broom, Spartium junceum
~ Klee m Spanish clover, silver-leaf desmodium, Desmodium uncinatum
~ Kragen m *(vet)* paraphimosis
~ Pfeffer m 1. [Spanish] pepper, capsicum *(genus Capsicum)*; 2. [common] red pepper, pepper, paprika, Capsicum annuum; 3. hot pepper *(varieties of Capsicum annuum with high content of capsaicin)*
~ Tragant m Swedish coffee, Astragalus boeticus
Spanisches Löwenmaul n Spanish snapdragon, Antirrhinum hispanicum ssp. hispanicum, Antirrhinum mollissimum
~ Rohr n *(bot)* rattan *(genus Calamus)*
Spanish-Erdnuß f Spanish peanut, Arachis hypogaea ssp. fastigiata var. vulgaris *(group of cultivars)*
Spankorb m chip basket, trug, prickle

spannen 1. to strain, to stress *(mechanically)*; 2. to put [up], to string *(e.g. a line)*; to stretch *(esp. in length)*; 3. to tighten, to draw tight *(e.g. a rope)*; 4. s. fesseln
Spannen n **von Netzen im Pflanzenbestand** crop support netting
Spanner m geometer [moth], geometrid *(family Geometridae)*
Spannerraupe f looper [caterpillar], inch worm, measuring-worm, *(Am)* span-worm
Spannkette f chuck (tension) chain; toggle chain *(timber transport)*
Spannknorpel m s. Schildknorpel
Spannpfahl m straining post *(fencing)*
Spannrippe f chuck rib[s] *(of beef carcass)*
spannrückig buttressed, grooved *(timber)*
Spannrückigkeit f buttressing
Spannsäge f span-saw
Spannseil n guy line (rope) *(of a cableway)*
Spannung f 1. stress, strain *(mechanical)*; 2. tension, tightness *(e.g. of a rope)*; 3. voltage
~/innere internal stress, strain *(e.g. in timber)*
Spannungsholz n tension wood
Spannungszustand m s. Tonus
Spannvorrichtung f tensioner
Spannweite f span; *(biom)* range
Spannweitetest m *(biom)* range test, G-test
~/multipler multiple range test
Spanokulation f chip budding
Sparei n yolkless egg
Spargel m asparagus *(genus Asparagus)* • **~ stechen** to cut asparagus
spargelähnlich, spargelartig asparagus-like, asparaginous
Spargelbeet n asparagus bed
Spargelbohne f 1. asparagus bean, yard-long bean (cowpea), Vigna unguiculata ssp. sesquipedalis; 2. s. Spargelerbse
Spargeldammpflug m asparagus ridging plough
Spargelerbse f asparagus (winged) pea, Tetragonolobus purpureus
Spargelerntemaschine f asparagus harvester
Spargelerntemesser n asparagus knife
Spargelfliege f asparagus fly, Platyparea poeciloptera
Spargelfliegenmade f asparagus maggot, Platyparea poeciloptera
Spargelhacke f asparagus hoe
Spargelhähnchen n asparagus beetle, Crioceris asparagi
Spargelklee m asparagus trefoil, Tetragonolobus maritimus
Spargelkohl m [sprouting] broccoli, Brassica oleracea convar. botrytis var. italica
Spargelkopf m asparagus tip
Spargelmesser n asparagus knife
Spargelpfeife f s. Spargelstange
Spargelpilz m s. Schopftintling

Spargelrost m asparagus rust *(caused by Puccinia asparagi)*
Spargelsortiertisch m asparagus hand grading table
Spargelspitze f asparagus tip
Spargelstange f spear of asparagus, asparagus spear (stalk), asparagus [shoot]
Spargelstechen n cutting of asparagus
Spargelvirus n **1** asparagus virus 1, AV1
~ **2** asparagus virus 2, AV2
Spargelwurzelfäule f asparagus root rot
Sparmischung f *(forest)* sparse mixture
Sparren m dew-claw *(animal anatomy)*
Sparrige Binse f heath rush, Juncus squarrosus
Sparriger Schüppling m *(bot)* shaggy pholiota, Pholiota squarrosa
Spartalupin n spartalupine *(alkaloid)*
Spartein n sparteine, lupinidin *(alkaloid)*
Spasmoanalgetikum n *(vet)* spasmolytic
spasmodisch *(vet)* spasmodic
Spasmolytikum n *(vet)* spasmolytic
spasmolytisch spasmolytic
Spasmus m *(vet)* spasm, cramp
spastisch spastic, spasmodic
Spat m *(vet)* spavin, bog (bone) spavin disease
spät *s.* spätblühend
Spätbefall m *(phyt)* late infestation
Spätblähung f late blowing *(in cheese)*
spätblühend late-flowering, tardiflorous, serotine, serotinous
Spätblüher m late flowerer
Spätdüngung f late top dressing
Späte Traubenkirsche f black (rum) cherry, Prunus (Padus) serotina
Spateisenstein m spathic iron ore, siderite
spatelförmig, spatelig *(bot)* spatulate
Spaten m spade • **mit dem ~ umgraben** to spade [the soil], to dig up with a spade
Spatenegge f spader
Spatenfräse f spading [rotary] cultivator, rotadigger, spader
Spatenmaschine f [rotary] spading machine
Spatenpflug m spade plough
Spatenrollegge f [Scandinavian] rotary spade harrow
Spatenstich m spit
Spaten[stich]tiefe f spade-depth, spit
Spätfrost m late [spring] frost, early season frost
Spätfrostschaden m late frost damage
Spätgärung f delayed fermentation
Spatha f *(bot)* spathe, spatha
Spätherbst m late autumn, *(Am)* late fall
Spätheu n second[-cut] hay
Spätholz n late wood, summer (autumn) wood
Spätholzanteil m share of late wood
Spätholztracheide f late-wood tracheid
Späthopfen m late hop
Spathufeisen n shoe for bone spavin disease
spatig *(vet)* spaved

Spätkartoffel f late potato
Spätkastration f late castration
Spätklee m late-flowering red clover, Trifolium pratense var. sativum subvar. serotinum
Spätkopfdüngung f late top dressing
Spätkultur f late crop
Spätlaktation f late lactation
Spätlese f late vintage (gathering)
Spätlesetrauben fpl late-gathered grapes
Spätlichtungshieb m *(forest)* increment (accretion) felling
Spätmast f late fattening
Spatoperation f/Wambergsche *(vet)* Wamberg modification of cunean tenectomy for bone spavin
spätreif late-maturing, late-ripening, backward
Spätreife f late maturity, lateness in ripening
spätreifend *s.* spätreif
Spätrinde f late bark
Spätsaat f late seeding (sowing)
Spätsaatverträglichkeit f suitability for late sowing
Spätschneider m stag *(pig)*
Spätsommer m late (Indian) summer
Spätsommerblanksaat f late summer direct sowing *(grassland farming)*
spätsommerlich serotinal
Spatula *(ent)* sternal spatula, anchor process
Spatz m 1. sparrow *(genus Passer)*; 2. house sparrow, Passer domesticus
Specht m woodpecker *(family Picidae)*
Spechthöhle f, **Spechtloch** n woodpecker hole
Species f *s.* Spezies
Speck m bacon
Speckbaum m purslane tree, Portulacaria afra
Speckdicke f fat thickness
Speckdickenmeßgerät n back fat thickness tester, fat meter
Speckkäfer m bacon (larder) beetle, Dermestes lardarius
Speckmesser m *s.* Speckdickenmeßgerät
Speckseite f flitch
Spectacillin n epicillin *(antibiotic)*
Spect[in]omycin n spectinomycin *(antibiotic)*
Speiche f radius *(animal anatomy)*
Speichel m saliva
Speichelamylase f, **Speicheldiastase** f salivary amylase *(enzyme)*
Speicheldrüse f salivary gland
Speicheldrüsenentzündung f *(vet)* sial[o]adenitis
Speicheldrüsenvirus n cytomegalovirus
Speicheleiweiß n sialoprotein
Speichelfluß m *(vet)* salivation, slobbers
Speichelreflex m salivary reflex
Speichelsekretion f salivary secretion
~/gesteigerte *(vet)* salivation
Speichelstein m *(vet)* sialolith
Speicheltest m saliva test
Speichelzentrum n salivary centre *(animal anatomy)*

Speichenarterie

Speichenarterie f radial artery
Speicher m store[house], warehouse, storage; loft; reservoir *(esp. for water)*
Speicherbecken n storage basin (impoundment), reservoir
Speicherfett[gewebe] n depot fat
Speichergebäude n storage structure
Speichergewebe n storage tissue
Speicherkapazität f storage capacity
Speicherkohlenhydrat n storage carbohydrate
Speichermotte f cacao[-bean] moth, chocolate (currant) moth, tobacco (warehouse) moth, Ephestia elutella
speichern to store, to warehouse
Speicherorgan n storage organ
Speicherparenchym n storage parenchyma, soft tissue
Speicherprotein n storage protein
Speicherraum m storage space
Speicherstoff m reserve [material]
Speicherstoffmobilisierung f reserve mobilization
Speichertrocknung f on-[the-]floor drying
Speicherung f storage
Speicherungskrankheit f *(vet)* storage disease
Speicherwurzel f storage root
Speierling m 1. service [tree], sorb, Sorbus domestica; 2. sorb[-apple] *(fruit)*
Speisebohnenkäfer m [common] bean weevil, dried bean beetle, bean seed beetle, Acanthoscelides obtectus
Speisebrei m digesta, chyme
Speiseerbse f [culinary] pea, haricot (canning) pea, Pisum sativum ssp. sativum convar. sativum
Speisefett n edible (food, cooking) fat
Speisefisch m food (table, eating) fish
Speiseforelle f table trout
Speisegeflügel n table poultry
Speisehülsenfrucht f pulse [crop], food (edible, vegetable) legume
Speisehülsenfrüchtler m food (edible) legume
Speisekartoffel f food (table) potato, ware (sale) potato
Speiseleguminose f s. Speisehülsenfrucht
Speiselinse f lentil, Lens culinaris (esculenta)
Speisemorchel f [common, true] morel, Morchella esculenta
Speiseöl n edible oil
Speiseölfabrik f edible-oil factory
Speiseölhersteller m seed crusher
Speisepaprika m eating capsicum
Speisepilz m [edible] mushroom, edible fungus, champignon
Speisequalität f culinary quality
Speisequark m quarg
Speiseröhre f gullet, oesophagus
Speiserübe f table beet
Speisescheidling m paddy straw mushroom, Chinese mushroom, Volvariella diplasis (volvacea)
Speisesenf m [table] mustard
Speisewalze f feed roll *(milling)*
~/hintere back feed roll
Speisewasser n feed water *(sugar manufacture)*
Speisezwiebel f [annual] onion, Allium cepa [var. cepa]
Spektralanalyse f spectral analysis
Spektralphotometer n spectrophotometer
Spektralradiometer n spectroradiometer
Spektralradiometrie f spectroradiometry
Spektrometer n spectrometer
Spektrometrie f spectrometry
spektrometrisch spectrometric
Spektrophotometer n spectrophotometer
Spektrophotometrie f spectrophotometry
spektrophotometrisch spectrophotometric
Spektroradiometer n spectroradiometer
Spektroradiometrie f spectroradiometry
spektroradiometrisch spectroradiometric
Spektroskop n spectroscope
Spektroskopie f spectroscopy
spektroskopisch spectroscopic
Spektrum n spectrum
~/biologisches *(ecol)* biological (life-form) spectrum
Spekulum n *(vet)* speculum
Spelz m dinkel, spelt, Triticum spelta
Spelze f *(bot)* glume, husk, hull
spelzenartig glumaceous
Spelzenbehaarung f glume pubescence
Spelzenbräune f **des Weizens** glume blotch [of wheat] *(caused by Septoria nodorum)*
spelzentragend glumiferous
Spelzmais m *(Am)* pod corn, Zea mays convar. tunicata
Spender m donor
Spendergewebe n donor tissue
Spenderkuh f donor cow *(embryo transfer)*
Sperbe f s. Speierling
Sperber m sparrow-hawk, Accipiter nisus
Sperbereule f European hawk-owl, Surnia ulula
Sperling m s. Spatz
Sperma n semen, sperm, seed
spermaabführend spermatic
Spermaantigen n semen antigen
Spermaaufbereitung f processing of semen
Spermaauffanggefäß n semen collecting vessel
Spermadepot n frozen-semen bank
Spermagefrierkonservierung f semen freezing
Spermagewinnung f semen production (collection)
Spermakonservierung f semen preservation
Spermalabor n semen-freezing station
Spermalagerung f semen storage
Spermapellet n sperm pellet
Spermaplasma n seminal plasma
Spermaplasmaantigen n semen antigen
Spermaproduktion f semen production
Spermarium n s. Hoden
Spermatheca f spermatheca *(of lower animals)*

Spermatide f spermatid
Spermatiefgefrierung f semen freezing
spermatisch spermatic
Spermatium n (bot) spermatium, pycni[di]ospore
Spermatogenese f spermatogenesis, spermiogenesis, sperm formation
~/fehlende (vet) aspermatogenesis
Spermatogonie f, **Spermatogonium** n (zoo) spermatogonium
Spermatophyt m spermatophyte, seed[-bearing] plant, seed bearer, flowering plant, flowerer (division Spermatophyta)
spermatopoietic spermatopoietic
Spermatozele f (vet) spermatocele
Spermatozoid m spermatozoid
Spermatozoidbefruchtung f (bot) zoidiogamy
Spermatozoon n s. Spermie
Spermatozyt m spermatocyte, sperm cell
~ **erster Ordnung** s. ~/primärer
~/primärer primary spermatocyte
~ **zweiter Ordnung** s. ~/sekundärer
~/sekundärer secondary spermatocyte
Spermaturia f (vet) spermaturia, seminuria
Spermauntersuchung f semen examination
Spermaverdünner m semen diluent [additive], semen extender
Spermaverdünnung f semen dilution
Spermide f s. Spermatide
Spermidin n spermidine (polyamine)
Spermie f sperm [cell], spermatozoon, spermatozoan
spermienabtötend spermicidal
Spermienausscheidung f **im Harn** s. Spermaturia
spermienbildend spermatopoietic
Spermiengesamtzahl f **im Ejakulat** total sperm per ejaculate
Spermienkonkurrenz f sperm competition
Spermienkonzentration f sperm concentration (count, density)
Spermienkopf m sperm head
Spermienmotilität f sperm motility
spermientötend spermicidal
Spermin n spermine (polyamine)
Spermiogenese f s. Spermatogenese
Spermiogonie f s. Spermatogonie
Spermiogramm n spermiogram
Spermiohistogenese f s. Spermatogenese
Spermiostasis f (vet) spermiostasis
Spermium n s. Spermie
spermizid spermicidal
Spermogonium n (bot) spermogone, spermogonium, spermagone, pycnid[ium], pycnium
Sperrfrist f **[zwischen Behandlung und Ernte von Feldprodukten]** preharvest interval
Sperrige Grindelie f curly-cup gumweed, Grindelia squarrosa
Sperrkraut n (bot) Jacob's ladder (genus Polemonium)

Sperrschicht f 1. barrier layer; 2. inversion (meteorology)
Sperrschieber m valve; shutter (e.g. of a drill)
Sperrwuchs m (forest) weed tree
sperrwüchsig crooked-grown (timber)
Spezialbeschlag m special shoeing (of hoofs or claws)
Spezialdrillmaschine f single-purpose drill
Spezialpflug m special plough
Spezialradschlepper m special-purpose tractor
Spezialrückeschlepper m (forest) skidder
Speziation f speciation
Spezies f species, sp. (taxonomy)
~/allopatrische allopatric species
~/gefährdete endangered species
SPF-Schwein n specific pathogen free pig
Sphagnion n s. Sphagnumhochmoor
Sphagnum n sphagnum [moss], peatmoss, bog moss (genus Sphagnum)
Sphagnumheide f sphagnum pinery
Sphagnumhochmoor n sphagniopratum
Sphagnumkiefernwald m sphagnum pinery
Sphagnummoor n sphagnum bog
~ **mit Niederwald** muskeg
Sphagnum[moos]torf m sphagnum [moss] peat
Sphalerit m sphalerite, zinc blende (non-clay mineral)
Sphäridium n nuclear body
Sphäroblast m sphaeroblast
Sphäroidgelenk n ball[-and-socket] joint, multiaxial joint (animal anatomy)
Sphärosom n sphaerosome, oleosome
S-Phase f s. Synthesephase
4-Sphingenin n s. Sphingosin
Sphingolipid n sphingolipid
Sphingolipidose f (vet) sphingolipidosis
Sphingomyelin n sphingomyelin (phospholipid)
Sphingosin n sphingosine (amino alcohol)
Sphinkter m sphincter (animal anatomy)
Sphygmograph m (vet) sphygmograph
Spica f 1. s. Ähre; 2. (vet) spica (a bandage)
Spickmaschine f spawning machine (mushroom production)
Spicula f (ent) spicule
Spiegel m escutcheon, white patch (of deer); 2. (ent) caterpillar brood
Spiegelkarpfen m mirror carp
Spiegelrelaskop n (forest) mirror relascope
Spiegelrinde f smooth bark
Spielhuhn n grey hen, Lyrurus tetrix
Spierstrauch m meadowsweet, queen of the meadows (genus Spiraea)
Spieß m pricket, spike, dag (of antler)
Spießbock m pricket
spießen to butt (deer)
Spießer m s. Spießbock
spießförmig (bot) hastate
Spießmelde f (bot) hastate orach[e], Atriplex hastata

Spießtanne

Spießtanne f [common] China fir, Cunningham pine, Cunninghamia lanceolata
Spießweide f apple-leaved willow, Salix hastata
Spik m (bot) aspic, Lavandula latifolia
Spikulum n (ent) spicule
Spilling m [wild] damson, bullace, Prunus domestica ssp. insititia
Spillwinde f (Am, forest) spool donkey, gypsy yarder
Spinat m spinach, Spinacia oleracea
Spindel f 1. (bot, zoo) [main] axis; 2. spindle (cell division); 3. areometer; 4. spindle (form of fruit-tree); 5. arbor, axle (of machinery)
~/freie free spindle (of a fruit-tree)
~/schlanke slender spindle (of a fruit-tree)
Spindelansatzstelle f centromere (of a chromosome)
Spindelbaumschildlaus f euonymus scale, Unaspis euonymi
Spindelbusch m spindle bush (form of fruit-tree)
spindelförmig (bot, zoo) fusiform
Spindelkelter f arbor (screw) press
Spindelknollenkrankheit f der Kartoffel potato spindle tuber (virosis)
Spindelobstbaum m spindle (for compounds s. under Spindel)
Spindelrasenmäher m reel (hand) mower
Spindelstrauch m burning bush, prickwood, euonymus (genus Euonymus)
Spindelstrauchringfleckenvirus n euonymus ring spot virus
Spinndrüse f (zoo) silk gland
Spinne f spider (order Araneida)
Spinnenchrysantheme f spider chrysanthemum (group of cultivars)
Spinnenfäden fpl spider's threads; gossamer (floating cobwebs)
Spinnengewebe n cobweb, spider's web
Spinnengewebehaut f arachnoid (animal anatomy)
Spinnengewebekrankheit f (phyt) cobweb (caused by Hypomyces rosellus)
Spinnenpflanze f spider-flower, Cleome spinosa
Spinnentier n arachnid (class Arachnida)
spinnentierähnlich arachnoid
Spinnfäden mpl s. Seidengespinst
Spinnmilbe f spider (red) mite, red spider [mite], RSM (family Tetranychidae)
Spinnrechwender m rotating head swath turner and windrower
Spinnwebe f s. Spinnengewebe
Spiralfederzinke f whorl-shaped spring tine
Spiralkrümler m tandem spiral crumbling roller
Spiralstruktur f helix (of viral protein units)
Spiritus m spirit
Spiritusbrennerei f distillery, alcohol plant
Spirke f erect mountain pine, Pinus uncinata ssp. uncinata
Spirofulvin n griseofulvin (antibiotic, fungicide)
Spirometer n spirometer, respiration chamber

Spirsäure f s. Salicylsäure
spitz pointed, peaked, sharp; (bot, zoo) acute, acuminate, cuspidate
Spitzahorn m plane (Norway, Bosnian) maple, Acer platanoides
Spitzbein n pig foot (pork carcass)
Spitzbeine npl pettitoes (pork carcass)
spitzblättrig (bot) acutifoliate
Spitzblättrige Spiraee f garland spiraea, Spiraea x arguta
~ Weide f pussy willow, Salix acutifolia
Spitzblume f coral-berry, Ardisia crenata
spitzblütig (bot) acutiflorous
spitzdornig (bot) oxyacanthous
Spitzdorniger Weißdorn m s. Stumpfblättriger Weißdorn
Spitze f tip, top, point; (bot, zoo) apex, cusp • mit einer ~ versehen (bot, zoo) mucronate[d]
~/umgeschlagene clench (of hobnail)
Spitzenchlorose f (phyt) tip burn
Spitzendürre f (phyt) die back, wither tip
Spitzenertrag m top yield
Spitzenfleckung f (phyt) top spotting
spitzenfrüchtig (bot) acrocarpic, acrocarpous
Spitzenhöhe f top (stand) height (timber mensuration)
Spitzennekrose f (phyt) top necrosis
Spitzentier n grade animal (livestock judging)
Spitzentrieb m (bot) apical shoot, terminal [shoot]
Spitzenwachstum m (bot) apical growth
spitzenwärts apical
~ gerichtet acropetal
Spitzenwein m vintage wine, supernaculum
Spitzenwinkel m s. Zahnspitzenwinkel
Spitzenzelle f (bot) apical cell
Spitzer Augenfleck m s. Scharfer Augenfleck
spitzfrüchtig (bot) sharp-fruited, oxycarpous
Spitzgraben m cutting (road construction)
Spitzgras n [moor] mat-grass, mat-weed, nardus, Nardus stricta
Spitzhacke f pick
Spitzhengst m cryptorchid stallion
spitzig (bot, zoo) spicular, spiculate, muricate[d], fastigiate[d]
Spitzkiel m [white] loco-weed (genus Oxytropis)
Spitzklette f cocklebur (genus Xanthium)
Spitzkohl m spring (oxheart) cabbage
spitzkronblättrig (bot) sharp-petaled, oxypetalous
spitzlappig (bot) acutilobate
Spitzmalz n chit malt
Spitzmaus f shrew[-mouse] (family Soricidae)
Spitzmausrüßler m (ent) [clover] seed weevil (genus Apion)
Spitzpocken pl des Rindes false cowpox (virosis)
Spitzsamen m canary grass, Phalaris canariensis
Spitzschar n sharp-pointed share, razor (plain, trapezoidal) share (of plough body)
Spitzsteißrüßler m (ent) beet [leaf] weevil, Tanymecus palliatus

Spitzwegerich *m* ribwort [plantain], [narrow-leaved] plantain, rib-grass, hen plant, Plantago lanceolata
spitzwinklig acute-angled
Spitzzahnkrümler *m* spike-tooth rotary harrow
Splint *m* 1. sapwood, sap, alburnum; 2. peg
~/falscher (innerer) internal (included) sapwood, false sap[wood], blea
Splintblaufärbung *f* blue [sap] stain *(of timber, caused esp. by fungi of genera Ophiostoma, Ceratostomella, Penicillium or Fusarium)*
Splintfäule *f* sap rot
Splintfleck *m* sap stain
splintfrei sap-clear, all-heart *(timber)*
Splintholz *n* sapwood, sap, alburnum
Splintholzkäfer *m* 1. powder-post beetle (borer) *(family Lyctidae)*; 2. lyctus beetle *(genus Lyctus)*
Splintholzkäferlarve *f* woodworm, worm
Splintholzverfärbung *f* sap stain
Splintkäfer *m* bark (engraver) beetle, shot-hole borer *(family Scolytidae = Ipidae)*
Splintschnitt *m* side notching (cutting), cornering *(tree felling)*
Splitter *m* splinter, split, sliver, chip
splittern to splinter
Splitterzahn *m* sliver tooth *(of a saw)*
Spodosol *m* *(Am, soil)* spodosol, od
Spondylolisthese *f* *(vet)* kinky back *(of broiler chicks)*
Spontangärung *f* spontaneous (tumultuous) fermentation
sporadisch sporadic
Sporangienhäufchen *n* sorus *(of ferns)*
Sporangiospore *f* *(bot)* sporangiospore
Spore *f* spore
Sporen *mpl* spurs
sporenartig sporal
Sporenbecher *m* *(bot)* aecium, aecidium
Sporenbildung *f* sporogenesis
Sporenblatt *n s.* Sporophyll
Sporenkapselhaube *f* calyptra *(of mosses)*
Sporenlager *n* hymenium *(of ascomycetes and basidiomycetes)*
~/kissenförmiges acervulus
Sporenpflanze *f* cryptogam
Sporenschlauch *m* ascus
Sporenständer *m* basidium
sporentragend sporiferous
Sporenträger *m s.* Sporophor
Spörgel *m* corn-spurr[e]y, Spergula arvensis
Sporn *m* spur
Spornblume *f* *(bot)* centranth *(genus Centranthus)*
Spornbüchschen *n* *(bot)* 1. beloperone *(genus Beloperone)*; 2. shrimp plant, Beloperone guttata
spornlos *(bot)* ecalcarate
sporntragend *(bot, zoo)* calciferous
Spornzikade *f* *(ent)* 1. plant hopper, delphacid *(family Delphacidae)*; 2. cereal plant hopper, Javesella pellucida

Sporophor *n(m)* *(bot)* sporophore, fructification *(of a fungus)*
Sporophyll *n* sporophyll, spore-bearing leaf
Sport *n(m)* bud mutation
Sportfisch *m* game fish
Sportrasen *m* turf
Sportsattel *m* riding (hacking, flat) saddle
Sporttaube *f* homing (racing, carrier) pigeon, homer
Sporulation *f* sporulation, spore formation
sporulieren to sporulate
Spottnuß *f* mockernut [hickory] *(fruit)*
Spottnußbaum *m* mockernut [hickory], big-bud hickory, Carya tomentosa (alba)
Spranz *m* *(forest)* nose, snipe, snape, snout
spranzen *(forest)* to nose, to snipe, to snape
Spraybehandlung *f* **von Vieh** cattle spraying
Spraynelke *f* spray[-type] carnation
Spreite *f* leaf blade (lamina)
Spreizholz *n*, **Spreizvorrichtung** *f* spreader *(e.g. for fruit-trees)*
sprengen 1. to [be]sprinkle, to spray, to water; 2. to blast *(e.g. stumps)*
Sprengkeil *m* *(forest)* explosive wedge, splitting gun
Sprengmast *f* *(forest)* partial (quartered) mast, scattered mast *(esp. of oak and beech)*
Sprengroden *n* stump blasting, blowing-up [of stumps]
Sprengspaltkeil *m s.* Sprengkeil
Sprenkelung *f* speck[l]ing, stippling, dotting, mottle, mottling
Spreu *f* chaff • **voll ~** chaffy
spreuartig *(bot)* paleaceous
Spreubehälter *m* chaff bunker
Spreublatt *n* *(bot)* palea
spreublattförmig paleiform
Spreublume *f* rough chaff tree, Achyranthes aspera
Spreugebläse *n* chaff blower
Spreurohr *n* chaff-blowing pipe
Spreuschlauch *m* chaff hose
Spreusichter *m* chaff sifter
sprießen to sprout, to shoot, to chit *(as leaves)*; to bud, to burgeon, to pullulate, to germinate *(as buds)*; to flush, to spring up, to shoot up *(seedlings)*
Sprießen *n* sprouting, shooting, chitting; burgeoning, pullulation, germination; flush[ing] • **zum ~ bringen** to flush
Springfeuer *n* *(forest)* jump (spot) fire
Springfrucht *f* *(bot)* dehiscent fruit
Springgabel *f* [forked] springing organ *(of collembolans)*
Springkrankheit *f* **der Schafe** *(vet)* louping (trembling) ill *(of sheep)*
Springkraut *n* snapweed, balsam, impatiens, impatience, *(Am)* jewelweed *(genus Impatiens)*

Springlaus

Springlaus *f* jumping plant-louse, psylla, psyllid *(family Psyllidae)*
Springmaischverfahren *n* jump-mash method *(brewing)*
Springpferd *n* jumping horse, jumper
Springreiter *m* jumping rider
Springrüßler *m* leaf-miner beetle *(genus Orchestes)*
Springsattel *m* jumping saddle
Springschlag *m* emergency field *(in a rotation)*
Springschlagbetrieb *m* *(forest)* alternate clear-strip system
Springschrecke *f (ent)* grasshopper *(order Saltatoria)*
Springschwanz *m (ent)* springtail, collembolan *(order Collembola)*
Springsitz *m* hunt seat *(equitation)*
Springwolfsmilch *f* caper euphorbia (spurge), mole plant (weed), gopher plant, Euphorbia lathyris
Spritzbalken *m* spray bar, rig sprayer, boom *(plant protection)*
Spritzbelag *m* spray coating
Spritzbrett *n* catch-board *(of a thresher)*
Spritzbrühe *f* plant spray, mixture for spraying; wash *(esp. in pest control)*
Spritze *f* 1. sprayer *(s. a.* Spritzgerät*)*; 2. syringe
spritzen 1. to spray *(e.g. crop plants with an insecticide)*; 2. to inject, to syringe *(e.g. medicaments)*; 3. *s.* sprengen 1.; 4. to splash, to spatter *(water, mud)*
Spritzen *n* spraying
~/bodengebundenes ground spraying
~ mit hohem Brüheaufwand high-volume spraying
Spritzflüssigkeit *f s.* Spritzbrühe
Spritzgerät *n* spraying apparatus (equipment); [crop] sprayer, hydraulic sprayer
~/bodengebundenes ground [crop] sprayer
~ mit variierender Ausbringmenge variable dosage sprayer
Spritzgestänge *n* folding boom
Spritzgurke *f* squirting cucumber, Ecballium elaterium
Spritzkanal *m* ejaculatory duct *(of drone)*
Spritzkopf *m* water gun head *(e.g. for unloading sugar-beets)*
Spritzleinwand *f* spatter cloth *(of a thresher)*
Spritzmaschine *f* field [crop] sprayer, crop sprayer
Spritzmittel *n* [plant] spray
~/fungizides fungicide spray
Spritzmittelbelag *m* spray coating
Spritzmittelrückstand *m* spray residue
Spritzpulver *n* wettable powder, w.p., WP
Spritzrohr *n* lance
Spritzung *f* spray application
Sproß *m* 1. *(bot)* sprout, shoot, chit; tiller *(esp. from the base of a plant)*; 2. *s.* Sprosse
~/blattbürtiger leaf sprout

~/wilder straggler
Sproßachse *f* shoot axis
Sproßbüschel *n* shoot cluster
Sproßdekapitierung *f* shoot tipping
Sproßdorn *m* stem spine
Sproßdrehung *f* shoot distortion
Sprosse *f* royal, snag, shoot, branch, tine, outgrowth *(of antlers)*
sprossen to sprout, to shoot, to chit; to tiller
Sprossenbrokkoli *pl* broccoli [sprouts], calabrese, Brassica oleracea convar. botrytis var. italica
Sprossenkohl *m* Brussels sprouts, Brassica oleracea var. gemmifera
Sproßentfernung *f* sprout-rubbing
Sproßentwicklung *f* shoot development
Sprosser *m* thrush nightingale, Luscinia luscinia
Sproßglied *n* joint
Sproßknolle *f* corm
Sproßknospe *f s.* Sproßspitzenmeristem
Sproßlänge *f* top length *(of seedling)*
Sprossler *m* pricket *(a two-year-old buck of fallow deer)*
Sprößling *m (bot)* offshoot
Sproßmeristem *n* shoot meristem
Sproßmyzel *n* pseudomycelium *(of some yeasts)*
Sproßpflanze *f* cormophyte
Sproßranke *f* stem tendril
Sproßrübe *f s.* Weiße Kohlrübe
Sproßscheitel *m s.* Sproßspitze
Sproßschwellkrankheit *f (phyt)* swollen shoot *(of Theobroma cacao)*
Sproßsegment *n* shoot segment
Sproßspitze *f* shoot tip (apex), stem apex
Sproßspitzenabort *m* shoot-tip abortion
Sproßspitzenkultur *f* shoot-tip culture, meristem-tip culture, mericloning
Sproßspitzenmeristem *n* shoot apical meristem, plumule
Sproßsteckling *m* stem cutting
Sproßstreckung *f* shoot elongation
Sproßtrockensubstanz *f* shoot dry material
Sproßtuff *m* shoot cluster
Sproßverdrehung *f* shoot distortion
Sproßverholzung *f* shoot lignification
Sproßvermehrung *f* shoot multiplication, tip layerage (layering)
Sproßwachstum *n* shoot growth
Sproßwucherung *f* shoot proliferation
Sproß-Wurzel-Verhältnis *n* shoot/root ratio
Sproßzelle *f* bud cell
Sprue *f/idiopathische (vet)* steatorrhoea
Sprühausleger *m*, **Sprühbalken** *m* spray bar
Sprühbehandlung *f* spray application
Sprühblaser *m s.* Sprühgerät
Sprühdüse *f* sprayer nozzle, atomizing jet (nozzle), atomizer
sprühen to spray
Sprühen *n* spraying, jetting; spray application

~/aviotechnisches aeroplane (aerial) spraying, aerospraying
~ mit geringem Brüheaufwand low-volume spraying
~ vom Boden aus ground spraying
~ vom Flugzeug aus s. ~/aviotechnisches
Sprühfleckenkrankheit f **der Kirsche** spot disease [of cherry] *(caused by Phloeosporella padi)*
Sprühgebläse n air-blast sprayer
Sprühgerät n [low-volume] sprayer, atomizer, [low-volume] mist blower, [pneumatic] mist sprayer, mister
~/aviotechnisches aviasprayer, aerial sprayer
~/bodengebundenes ground [crop] sprayer
Sprühkristallisationsanlage f prilling plant
Sprühmaschine f s. Sprühgerät
Sprühmittel n [plant] spray, atomizing agent
Sprühnebel m mist
Sprühnebelbewässerung f mist irrigation
Sprühnebelkühlung f air dropping by mist *(in greenhouses)*
Sprühnebelregler m electronic leaf *(gardening)*
Sprühnebelvermehrung f mist propagation *(of plants)*
Sprühnebler m [low-volume] mist blower
Sprühregen m drizzle, mizzle
Sprührohr n s. Sprühausleger
Sprung m 1. jump, leap; 2. service, mating (covering) act, act of breeding (service), coitus, copulation
~ aus der Hand hand service, hand mating (breeding)
~/wilder lot mating
Sprunggelenk n hock
Sprunggelenklahmheit f *(vet)* hock lameness
sprunggelenksweit bandy-legged
Sprunggelenkswinkel m hock angle
Sprungkraft f jumping ability *(e.g. of horses)*
Sprungpartner m mate
Sprungschicht f [stehender Gewässer] metalimnion
Sprungvermögen n s. Sprungkraft
Spülanschluß m flushing nozzle *(of a milking parlour)*
Spule f quill *(of a feather)*
Spüleinrichtung f *(vet)* irrigator
spülen to rinse, to flush; *(vet)* to lavage, to irrigate
Spülicht n pig's wash, [pig]swill, pigwash
Spülmilch f rinsed milk
Spülung f *(vet)* lavage
Spulwurm m ascarid *(family Ascaridiae)*
Spulwurmbefall m *(vet)* ascariasis, ascaridose
Spund m plug, bung, stopper, faucet; cellar plug *(of wine cask)*
Spundapparat m bunging apparatus
Spundbohrer m cooper's auger
spunden to bung
Spundheber m bung puller
Spundloch n bung-hole

Spundzieher m bung puller
Spur f trace, track, spoor; trail, print, foil, slot *(of game)* • **eine ~ verfolgen** to quest
Spurbiene f scout [honey-]bee, searcher bee
Spurbohlenbahn f *(forest)* strip road, trackway
Spurbreite f track width
Spurenanalyse f trace analysis
Spurenelement n trace element (mineral), microelement, bioelement
Spurenelementbelastung f trace element pollution
Spurenelementdüngemittel n trace element fertilizer, micronutrient fertilizer
Spurenelementkonzentration f trace element concentration
Spurenelementmangel m trace element deficiency, micronutrient deficiency
Spurenelementstoffwechsel m trace element metabolism
Spurenelementüberschuß m trace element excess
Spurenmenge f trace amount
Spurenmetall n trace metal
Spurfinder m tracer, tracker
Spürhund m [slot-]hound, tracker [dog]
Spurlockerer m track loosener (eradicator)
Spurlockerung f track loosening
Spurmutante f spur strain *(of apple)*
Spurpheromon n trail pheromone
Spurreißer m [row] marker
Spurschnee m new-fallen snow
Spurtafelbahn f s. Spurbohlenbahn
Spurtyp m spur type *(of woody fruit plants)*
Spurweite f track [width], tread
Spurweitenverstellung f track width adjustment; tread changing
Spy-Epinastie f **und Spy-Verfall** m **des Apfels** apple spy epinasty and decline *(virosis)*
Spy-Verfallvirus n **[des Apfels]** [apple] spy decline virus, SDV
SQ s. Summe der Abweichungsquadrate
Squama f *(zoo)* scale
SR s. Schwarzbuntes Rind
SRH s. Somatotropin-Releasinghormon
SSE s. Supersuperelitesaatgut
St s. Stratus
St. Augustine-Gras n St. Augustine grass, *Stenotaphrum secundatum*
StaABV s. Stachelbeeradernbänderungsvirus
Staatsfarm f state farm
Staatsforst m state (national) forest
Staatsforstbetrieb m state forest enterprise
Staatsgestüt n state stud[-farm]
Staatswald m s. Staatsforst
Stäbchen n s. 1. Stäbchenbakterium; 2. Stäbchenzelle
Stäbchenbakterium n rod-shaped bacterium
stäbchenförmig rod-like, bacilliform, bacillary
Stäbchenzelle f [retinal] rod

stäbe[l]n

stäbe[l]n to stake
Stabhaspel *f* rod-type reel
Stabheuschrecke *f* stick-insect *(family Phasmidae)*
Stabilbau *m (api)* fixed-comb hive
Stabilisator *m*, **Stabilisierungsmittel** *n* stabilizer
Stabilität *f* stability
~/biologische biostability
Stabkettenelevator *m* rod-chain conveyor
Stabkrümler *m* cage roller
Stabsichtigkeit *f (vet)* astigmatism
Stabspritze *f* hand lance
Stabwalze *f*, **Stabwalzegge** *f* cage roller
Stabwurz *f* southernwood, lad's (boy's) love, brotan, Artemisia abrotanum
Stachel *m (bot)* prickle, spine, acantha; thorn; *(zoo)* sting[er]
Stachelannone *f (bot)* sour-sop, Annona muricata
Stachelapparat *m* sting apparatus
stachelästig *(bot)* acanthocladous
Stachelbeeradernbänderungsvirus *n* gooseberry vein banding virus
Stachelbeere *f* 1. gooseberry *(genus Ribes)*; 2. gooseberry, feaberry, Ribes uva-crispa
Stachelbeerguave *f (bot)* Brazilian guava, Psidium guineense
Stachelbeerspanner *m* gooseberry (currant, magpie) moth, Abraxas grossulariata
Stachelbeerspinnmilbe *f* gooseberry red spider [mite], clover mite, Bryobia ribis (praetiosa)
Stachelbeerzünsler *m (ent)* gooseberry fruitworm, Zophodia convolutella
stachelblättrig *(bot)* acanthophyllous
Stacheldraht *m* barbed wire, *(Am)* barbwire
stachelförmig *(bot)* aculeiform
stachelfrüchtig *(bot)* acanthocarpous
Stachelgras *n* bur grass, sandbur[r] *(genus Cenchrus)*
stachelig *(bot)* prickly, thorny, spiny *(e.g. shrubs, cactus)*; acanthoid, aculeate, muricate[d]
Stachelige Mondwinde *f* moon-flower, Calonyction album (aculeatum)
Stacheliges Kammgras *n (bot)* hedgehog dog's-tail, Cynosurus echinatus
Stacheligkeit *f (bot)* prickliness, thorniness, spininess; *(zoo)* stinginess
Stachelkammer *f* sting chamber *(of honey-bee)*
stachellos prickless, thornless; stingless *(honey-bee)*
Stachellosigkeit *f* thornlessness
Stachelmohn *m* prickly poppy, flowering thistle *(genus Argemone)*
Stachelnüßchen *n (bot)* piripiri, Acaena anserinifolia
Stachelpanax *m* Siberian (thorny) ginseng, Eleutherococcus senticosus
Stachelpilz *m* 1. teeth fungus *(family Hydnaceae)*; 2. satyr's beard *(genus Hydnum)*

598

Stachelsalat *m* prickly (common wild) lettuce, Lactuca serriola (scariola)
Stachelscheide *f* sting sheath *(of honey-bee)*
stachelspitzig *(bot, zoo)* cuspidate
Stachelstrahl *m* fin-spine
stacheltragend *(zoo)* aculeate
Stachelwalze *f* spike-tooth roller
Stachelzelle *f* prickle cell
Stachelzellenschicht *f* prickle[-cell] layer *(of epidermis)*
Stachybotryotoxikose *f (vet)* stachybotryotoxicosis *(caused by Stachybotrys alternans)*
Stachyose *f* stachyose *(oligosaccharide)*
Stadel *m* staddle
Stadiendüngung *f* fertilization in stages
Stadienentwicklung *f* stage development
Stadium *n* stage, stadium
~ der Vorboten *(phyt, vet)* prodromal period (stage)
~/ertragloses stage of youth *(of fruit-trees)*
~/juveniles juvenile stage, stage of youth
Stadtbegrünung *f* town gardening, amenity planting
Stadtgrün *n* urban green[ery], town verdure
Stadtmüll *m* town refuse, municipal waste
Stadtmüllkompost *m* town refuse (waste) compost, municipal [waste] compost
Stadtpark *m* city (town, urban) park
Stadtwald *m* city (urban, amenity) forest
Staffordshire Bull Terrier Staffordshire bull terrier *(dog breed)*
Staghound *m* staghound *(dog breed)*
stagnierend stagnant *(e.g. water)*
Stagnogley *m s.* Staugley
Stahlblaue Fichtenholzwespe *f* steel-blue woodwasp, Sirex (Paururus) juvencus
~ Kiefern[schonungs]gespinstblattwespe *f* pine-plantation web-spinning saw-fly, *(Am)* false pine web-worm, Acantholyda erythrocephala
Stahlblauer Nerz *m* steel-blue mink *(mutation)*
Stahlgewächshaus *n* steel structure greenhouse
Staketenzaun *m* pale (paling) fence
Staknetz *n (pisc)* stake-net
Stall *m* [animal] house, stable, stall, crib, *(Am)* barn
• **im ~ füttern** to stall[-feed] • **im ~ halten** to house, to stable • **im ~ stehen** to stall • **in den ~ treiben** to cot *(esp. sheep)*
~/kleiner pen
Stallablammung *f*, **Stallammung** *f* indoor lambing
Stallapotheke *f* breeder's medical chest
Stallarbeit *f* stable work, *(Am)* barn work
Stallaufzucht *f* indoor rearing
Stallbandage *f* stable bandage *(for horses)*
Stallbedingungen *fpl* housing conditions
Stallbeleuchtung *f* stable lighting
Stallbelüfter *m (Am)* barn fan
Stallbestand *m* stable *(of horses)*
Stallboden *m* stable floor
Stallbuch *n (Am)* barn book

Stallbursche *m* [stable] lad, stableman
Stalldach *n* stable roof
Stalldienst *m s.* Stallarbeit
Stalldung *m* [stable, farmyard, barnyard] manure, [farm, pen] manure, dung, muck
~/verrotteter short dung
Stalldung... *s. a.* Dung... *and* Mist...
Stalldünger *m s.* Stalldung
Stalldungseitenstreuer *m* side-delivery manure spreader
Stalldungstreuer *m* manure (dung, muck) spreader, trailer spreader
~ mit Heckstreuwerk rear-delivery manure spreader
Stalldungwirtschaft *f* muck management
stallen to stale, to urinate
Stallendmast *f* confinement finishing
Stallfenster *n* stable window
Stallfliege *f* autumn (face) fly, Musca autumnalis
Stallfütterung *f* house-feeding, indoor (stable) feeding, stall (confinement) feeding, *(Am)* barn feeding
Stallgang *m* alley
Stallgebäude *n* livestock building
Stallgefährte *m* stable-mate, stable-companion
Stallgefährtinnenvergleich *m* herdmate (contemporary) comparison *(breeding)*
Stallhaltung *f* [livestock] housing, stable keeping (management), indoor stock keeping
~/fensterlose windowless housing
Stallhaltungsbedingungen *fpl* housing conditions
Stallhaltungsperiode *f* housing period
Stallheizung *f* stall heating
Stalljunge *m* stable-boy
Stallkalender *m* stable calendar
Stallknecht *m* ostler, groom
Stallkrankheit *f (vet)* bush sickness *(due to cobalt deficiency)*
Stallmast *f* indoor (stable, stall) fattening
Stallmeister *m* stable manager
Stallmelkanlage *f* cowshed milking installation
Stallmist *m s.* Stalldung
Stallmistdüngung *f* manure fertilization
Stallplatz *m* cubicle • **am ~ festbinden** to stanchion
Stallreinigungsgerät *n (Am)* barn cleaner
Stallreinigungsmaschine *f (Am)* barn cleaner
Stallstaub *m* stable dust
Stallstreu *f* litter
Stalltafel *f (Am)* barn chart
Stalltor *n* stable-door
Stalltraktor *m* tractor for use in livestock houses
Stalltür *f* stable-door
Stallüberwachungsgerät *n* stable monitoring equipment
Stallung *f* animal house, [animal] housing, stable yard, stalling
Stallventilator *m (Am)* barn fan

Stallvieh *n* housed livestock, captive animals, stabled cattle
Stallwagen *m* horse-box
Stamen *n (bot)* stamen
Stamina *f s.* Stehvermögen
staminal *(bot)* staminal
Staminodium *n (bot)* staminodium
Stamm *m* 1. [tree] trunk, stem, stock, bole, boll; shaft; 2. *(zoo)* phylum; *(bot)* division *(taxonomy)*; strain; 3. stock *(of plants or animals)*
Stamm... *s. a.* Schaft...
Stammabkürzsäge *f* log cross-cutting saw, log cut-off saw
Stammablauf *m* stem flow *(of precipitation)*
Stammabschnitt *m* log, block, bolt, butt, chump
Stammachse *f (bot)* hypocotyl
Stammanalyse *f* stem analysis
Stammanlauf *m* root collar, root crown (swelling)
• **mit starkem ~** swell-butted, barrel-butted, bottle-butted, churn-butted
~/spannrückiger root buttress, buttress [flare]
~/starker butt swelling
Stammassentafel *f* log volume table, log rule
Stammaustrieb *m* stem sucker
Stammbasis *f* butt [end], bottom end, base
Stammbaum *m* genealogical tree, pedigree, lineage • **mit eingetragenem ~** registered
Stammbaumzüchtung *f* pedigree breeding, pedigree selection (method)
Stammbeschädigung *f* stem damage
Stammbildner *m* stem-builder, interstock, interstem, intermediate stem piece *(orcharding)*
Stammbläue *f* log blue stain
stammblütig *(bot)* cauliflorous
Stammblütigkeit *f* cauliflory, trunciflory
Stammbohrer *m (ent)* stem-borer, stem-miner *(comprehensive term)*
Stammbrand *m (forest)* stem fire
Stammbuch *n* stud-book
Stammbulle *m* pedigree bull
Stämmchen *n* tree-form plant
Stammdreher *m* log turner
Stammelitesaatgut *f* foundation seed
Stammende *n s.* Stammfuß
Stammesgeschichte *f* phylogenesis, phylogeny
stammesgeschichtlich phylogenetic
Stammfäule *f* stem (bole) rot
Stammfeuer *n s.* Stammbrand
Stammförderer *m* log conveyor, log haul[-up], log hoist (jack)
Stammform *f* 1. stem (bole) form, tree form (shape); 2. original *(of a breed)*
Stammformfaktor *m*, **Stammformzahl** *f* stem-form factor *(timber mensuration)*
Stammfurchung *f* **des Apfels** apple stem grooving
Stammfurchungsvirus *n* **des Apfels** apple stem grooving virus, ASGV

Stammfuß

Stammfuß *m* butt [end], bottom end, [stem] base
• **mit dem ~ nach vorn** butt end first
Stammfußbehandlung *f* butt treatment, basal stem spraying, basal bark treatment
Stammfußfäule *f (phyt)* butt rot *(esp. caused by Polyporus sistrotremoides)*
Stammheber *m* log lever
Stammherde *f* stud herd; foundation (nucleus) herd; bull mother herd
Stammholz *n* stem wood (timber), round timber, roundwood, bodywood; bole wood, longwood, tree-length logs
Stammholzabfuhr *f* bole removal
Stammholzlänge *f* timber height
Stammholzrücken *n* bole skidding
Stammholztransport *m* log transport
Stamminierer *m* s. Stammbohrer
Stamminjektion *f* trunk (tree) injection
Stammklasse *f (forest)* dominance class; stem (size) class *(timber mensuration)*
~ **nach Kraft** Kraft dominance class
Stammklaue *f* trunk clamp *(of fruit-harvesting machines)*
Stammknospe *f (bot)* plume
Stammkreuzung *f* strain cross
Stammkrümmung *f* sweep
Stammkubierungsformel *f* stem volume formula *(timber mensuration)*
Stammkuhherde *f* pedigree herd
Stammkulturensammlung *f* culture collection
Stammlänge *f/astreine* clear length
Stammlösung *f* stock (principal) solution
Stammnarbung *f (phyt)* stem pitting
Stammnarbungsvirus *n* stem pitting virus
Stammquerschnittsfläche *f* trunk cross-sectional area
Stammriese *f* timber (log) slide, log chute
Stammrinde *f* stem bark
Stammringelung *f* trunk scoring, stem girdling (ringing)
Stammriß *m* stem crack
Stammrotfäule *f des Zuckerrohrs* red rot of sugar-cane *(caused by Glomerella tucumanensis)*
Stammrüttler *m* trunk shaker
Stammsaatgut *n* stock (pedigree) seed
Stammscheibe *f* stem disk
Stammschlupf *m* single hatch
Stammschüttler *m* trunk shaker
Stammselektion *f* strain selection
Stammspritze *f* stem sprayer
Stammsteckling *m* cutting with heel
Stammstück *n* log, block, bolt, butt chump
Stammumfang *m* stem girth, trunk circumference
~ **in der Mitte des Nutzholzteiles** mid-girth, average girth *(timber mensuration)*
Stammutter *f* stem mother; fundatrix *(of aphids)*
Stammvater *m* ancestor, progenitor
Stammvergrößerung *f* trunk enlargement

Stammverladebühne *f (forest)* loading jack, jack works
Stammverlängerung *f* prolongation of the trunk; central leader
Stammvolumen *n* stem volume
Stammwender *m* log-turner, cant-hook, cant-dog
Stammwirt *m* original host *(of a parasite)*
Stammwirtschaft *f (forest)* stemwise management
Stammwürze *f* original wort *(brewing)*
Stammwürzegehalt *m* original extract (gravity)
Stammzahl *f* stem number, number of trees
Stammzähler *m* enumeration counter *(timber mensuration)*
Stammzeichen *n* log mark (brand)
Stammzelle *f* stem cell
Stammzuchtbetrieb *m* stud-farm
stampfen to paw *(horse)*
Stand *m* 1. standing; box, stall, crib *(in animal houses)*; 2. status
~**/räumiger** *(forest)* open position
Standard *m* 1. standard; 2. check cultivar *(field experimentation)*
Standardabweichung *f (biom)* standard deviation, S
~**/relative** coefficient of variation
Standardallel *n (gen)* wild-type allele
Standardanlage *f* standard design *(field experimentation)*
Standardbred *m* Standardbred [trotter], American trotter *(horse breed)*
Standardfehler *m (biom)* standard error, SE
standardgerecht on-grade
~**/nicht** off-grade, substandard
Standardlaktation *f* standard lactation
Standardparzelle *f* control plot *(field experimentation)*
Standardphänotyp *m* wild type
Standardration *f* standard ration *(animal nutrition)*
Standardredoxpotential *n* standard redox potential *(biochemistry)*
Standardsämlingsausbeute *f (forest)* seedling percent
Standardschlepper *m*, **Standardtraktor** *m* utility (general-purpose) tractor
Standarte *f (hunter's language)* brush, foxtail
Ständer *f* shank *(of wildfowl)*
Ständerpilz *m* basidiomycete, toadstool *(class Basidiomycetes)*
~**/konsolenförmige Fruchtkörper ausbildender** bracket fungus
Ständerspore *f* basidiospore
Ständerung *f* station, carriage *(fowl judgement)*
Ständerzelle *f* basidium
standfest lodging-resistant *(grain crops)*; well-anchored *(trees)*
Standfestigkeit *f* standability, standing ability (power), stability; lodging (lodge) resistance, resistance to lodging; anchorage *(of trees)*

Staphylokokkose

Standfestigkeitszüchtung *f* breeding for lodging resistance
Standfläche *f* standing
Standhüten *n* close folding *(of sheep)*
Standjahr *n* year after planting *(e.g. of orchards)*
• **bis zum achten ~** to the eighth leaf
Standmast *m* standing derrick
Standmelkanlage *f* [milking] parlour, milking stand
Standort *m* site, locality, location; *(ecol)* habitat
• **auf feuchtem ~ wachsend** hygrophilous • **auf trockenem ~ wachsend** xerophilous
~/ackerfähiger arable land
~/charakteristischer *(ecol)* habitat
~/forstlicher forest site
~/natürlicher [natural] habitat
~/pflanzenbaulicher cropping site
Standortansprache *f s.* Standortbeschreibung
Standortanspruch *m* site requirement
Standortbedingungen *fpl* site conditions
Standortbeschreibung *f* site description, description of site
~/forstliche forest site diagnosis
Standortbeurteilung *f* site assessment
Standortbonität *f* site quality; *(forest)* locality (growth) class
Standortbonitierung *f* site quality assessment, site class determination
Standorteignung *f* **von Baumarten** suitability of tree species to site
Standorteinheit *f* site (land) unit
Standorterkundung *f* site reconnaissance, site investigation (survey)
~/forst[wirtschaft]liche forest site investigation
Standortfaktor *m* site (location) factor
standortgerecht site-related, adapted to the site
Standortindex *m* site index
Standortkarte *f* site map
~/forstliche forest stand map
Standortkartierung *f* site (soil) mapping
~/landwirtschaftliche mapping of agricultural land units
Standortklasse *f* site [quality] class, productivity class; *(forest)* locality (growth) class
Standortklassifikation *f*, **Standortklassifizierung** *f* site classification
Standortklima *n* local climate, topoclimate
Standortqualität *f* site quality
Standortreihe *f (ecol)* catena
Standortslokaltarif *m (forest)* simple tariff
Standortsrasse *f* site race *(forest plant breeding)*
Standorttyp *m* site type
Standorttypengruppe *f* site type group
Standraum *m* growing space, spacing
Standraum[feld]versuch *m* spacing experiment
Standraumzumessung *f* space allocation, [crop] spacing
~ in der Reihe [with]in-row spacing
Standreihe *f* range *(in animal houses)*
Standweide *f* set stocking *(grazing method)*

standweitenempfindlich population-sensitive
Standweitenversuch *m* spacing experiment
Standwild *n* standing (sedentary) game
Stange *f* 1. pole, bar, staff; 2. end, beam *(of antlers)*
~/endenlose switch-horn
~/nicht vereckte pricket, dag *(of antlers)*
~/schwache thin pole
Stangenbohne *f* pole [snap] bean, stick (climbing) bean, Phaseolus vulgaris ssp. vulgaris var. vulgaris
Stangendrän *m* pole drain
Stangenholz *n* 1. pole timber (wood); 2. *s.* Stangenholzbestand
Stangenholzbestand *m* pole-sized stand, pole forest
Stangenholzstadium *n* pole stage *(of trees)*
Stangenpferd *n* pole horse
Stangenzaun *m* pole-fence
Stangler *m* pricket *(a two-year-old buck of fallow deer)*
Stanzlochmaschine *f* hole punching machine
Stapel *m* 1. stack, pile, *(Am)* bank; 2. staple *(of wool)*
Stapelarbeiter *m* stacker
Stapelbläue *f* pile discolo[u]ration, bridging-blue *(of timber)*
Stapeldichte *f* staple density *(of wool)*
Stapelfaden *m* piled fathom *(ancient measure of stacked wood)*
Stapelförderer *m* stacking elevator
Stapelholz *n* stacked wood (timber), piled wood, cordwood
Stapelkran *m* stacker crane
Stapellänge *f* staple length *(of wool)*
Stapellatte *f* sticker, [piling] stick, stacking strip, crosser
Stapellattenabstand *m* sticker spacing
Stapelleiste *f s.* Stapellatte
Stapelmaschine *f* stacker
Stapelmist *m* solid manure
stapeln to stack [up], to pile [up], *(Am)* to bank [up]
Stapelplatte *f* pallet
Stapelschnittholz *n (Am)* yard lumber
Stapelvolumen *n* stacked volume, stacked content[s]
Stapelwagen *m* stack wagon
Stapelwirt *m* paratenic host
Stapenor *n* oxacillin *(antibiotic)*
Stapes *m* stapes *(animal anatomy)*
Staphobristol *n* cloxacillin *(antibiotic)*
Staphylokokkeninfektion *f s.* Staphylokokkose
Staphylokokkenmastitis *f (vet)* staphylococcal mastitis
Staphylokokkentoxin *n* staphylococcal toxin
Staphylokokkose *f (vet)* staphylococcosis, staphylococcal infection
~ des Geflügels avian staphylococcal arthritis, vesicular dermatitis in chickens

Staphylokokkus

Staphylokokkus *m* staphylococcus, staph *(genus Staphylococcus)*
Stapler *m* stacker
Star *m* 1. starling, Sturnus vulgaris; 2. *(vet)* cataract
~/grauer cataract
~/grüner glaucoma
stark strong, heavy *(as beverages, acids)*; heavy, severe *(as rain, frost)*; thick *(e.g. a cross section)*; capital *(e.g. a wild boar)*
Starkasten *m* [nesting] box for starlings
Starkbier *n* strong (heavy, high-gravity) beer, strong ale, barley wine
starkblättrig thick-leaved
Stärke *f* 1. starch, amylum, farina *(polysaccharide)*; 2. strength; power; vigour • **~ in Zucker umwandeln** to saccharify
~/pflanzliche plant starch
~/primäre assimilation starch
Stärkeabbau *m* starch breakdown (degradation)
stärkeähnlich, stärkeartig starchy, amyloid, amylaceous
Stärkebildung *f* amylogenesis
Stärkeeinheit *f* starch unit
Stärkeerzeugnis *n* starch product
Stärkegehalt *m* starch content
Stärkegelelektrophorese *f* starch-gel electrophoresis
stärkehaltig starch-containing, starchy, amyliferous, farinaceous
Stärkehydrolysat *n* starch hydrolysate
Stärkeindustrie *f* starch industry
Stärkekartoffel *f* starch potato
Stärkekorn *n*, **Stärkekörnchen** *n* starch grain (granule)
Stärkelieferant *m* starch-yielding plant
Stärkemais *m* soft maize, *(Am)* flour corn, Zea mays convar. amylacea
Stärkemehl *n* farina, starch [flour]
Stärkenklasse *f* size class *(timber mensuration)*
Stärkephosphorylase *f* starch phosphorylase *(enzyme)*
Stärkeprodukt *n* starch product
stärkereich starch-rich, starchy
stärkespaltend amylolytic, diastatic
Stärkespaltung *f* amylolysis
Stärkespeicherung *f* starch storage
Stärkesynthase *f* starch synthase *(enzyme)*
Stärkeverdauung *f* starch digestion
Stärkewert *m* starch equivalent, SE
~/theoretischer theoretical (ideal) starch equivalent
Stärkezucker *m* starch sugar, D-glucose
Starkholz *n* large timber
starkknochig heavy-boned
Starklichtpflanze *f* s. Sonnenpflanze
Starkregen *m* torrential rain
Starkregner *m* high-rate sprinkler, heavy-application sprinkler

Stärkungsmittel *n (vet)* roborant
starkwüchsig vigorous
starr rigid, strict, stiff
Starregge *f* rigid [tine] harrow
~/schwere drag[-harrow], duck-foot harrow
Starrer Feigenkaktus *m* common prickly pear, [common] pest pear, Opuntia stricta (inermis)
Starrkrampf *m (vet)* tetanus
starrkrampfartig tetanic
Starrzinkengrubber *m* rigid tine cultivator
Startbox *f* [starting] stall *(racing)*
Starter *m* 1. primer *(genetic engineering)*; 2. starter motor
Starterdünger *m* starter [fertilizer, dressing], pop-up fertilizer
Starterdüngergabe *f* starter dressing
Starterdüngerlösung *f* starter solution
Starterdüngung *f* starter dressing
Starterfutter *n* starter; creep feed *(e.g for piglets and lambs)*
Starterfütterung *f* creep feeding
Starterkultur *f* starter culture
Starterration *f* starter ration (diet)
Startervolk *n (api)* starter colony
Startvorrichtung *f* start[ing]-gate *(racing)*
starzen to nose *(round timber)*
Stätigkeit *f* restiveness, obstreperousness, vice *(animal behaviour)*
Station *f*/**meteorologische** weather station
stationär stationary, non-mobile
Stationärbetttrockner *m* static bed dryer
Stationärkran *m* stationary crane
Stationärparasit *m* stationary parasite
stätisch restive, obstreperous, intractable, vicious *(animal behaviour)*
Statistik *f* statistics
statistisch gesichert *(biom)* significant
~ nicht gesichert insignificant, non-significant
Statolith *m* 1. *(zoo)* statolith, otolith; 2. *s.* Statolithenstärkekorn
Statolithenstärkekorn *n (bot)* statolith
Statur *f* stature
Status *m* status
Stau *m* impounding, damming up *(of water)*
Stauanlage *f* dam, weir *(s. a.* Staudamm*)*
Staub *m* dust • **im ~ baden** to dust[-bath]
Staubabsaugevorrichtung *f* dust exhaust system
Staubabscheider *m* dust extractor
Staubauflage *f* dust deposit *(e.g. on leaves)*
Staubbad *n* dust-bath
Staubbekämpfung *f* dust control
Staubbelastung *f* dust exposure
Staubbeutel *m (bot)* anther
staubbeutellos antherless, ananthrous
Staubblatt *n (bot)* stamen • **mit einem ~** monandrous • **mit vier Staubblättern** tetrandrous
~/steriles staminodium
staubblattlos anandrous
staubblatttragend staminate

Staubblattträger *m* androphore
Staubbrand *m* **der Gräser** head smut of grasses *(caused by Ustilago bullata)*
~ **der Kolbenhirse** *f* millet kernel smut *(caused by Ustilago crameri)*
~ **der Mohrenhirse** loose kernel smut *(caused by Sphacelotheca cruenta)*
Staubecken *n* reservoir
Stäubegerät *n* [powder] duster, dusting appliance (machine)
~/**aviotechnisches** aeroduster, aviaduster
Stäubemittel *n* dusting powder (preparation), dust
~/**herbizides** herbicidal dust
~/**insektizides** insecticidal dust
Stäubemittelverteiler *m s.* Stäubegerät
stäuben to dust *(e.g. with pesticides)*
Stäuben *n* [crop-]dusting
~/**aviotechnisches** aerator dusting
Stäube- und Spritzgerät *n* duster-sprayer
Staubewässerung *f* border (ebb-and-flow) irrigation, flooding from ditches
Staubexplosion *f* dust explosion
Staubfaden *m (bot)* filament
Staubgefäß *n s.* Staubblatt
Staubhefe[rasse] *f* powdery (non-flocculent) yeast
Staubinfektion *f (vet)* dust-borne infection
Staubkrankheit *f (vet)* koniosis
Stäubling *m* puff-ball [fungus], fuzz-ball, puckball *(order Lycoperdales)*
Staubmaske *f* dust mask
Staubmilbe *f* tydeid [mite] *(family Tydeidae)*
Staubniederschlag *m* particulate precipitation
Staubschutz *m* dust protection
Staubschutzmaske *f* dust mask
Staubsturm *m* dust storm
Staubzucker *m* powdered sugar, castor (icing) sugar
Stauchbruch *m s.* Stauchungsbruch 1.
Stauche[krankheit] *f (phyt)* stunt
~ **der Himbeere** rubus stunt *(mycoplasmosis)*
~ **der Quitte** quince stunt *(virosis)*
~ **der Zyklamen** stunt of cyclamen *(caused by Ramularia cyclaminicola)*
stauchen 1. to stunt *(e.g. plant growth)*; 2. to swage *(saw teeth)*
Stauchsproß *m* short shoot
Stauchung *f (phyt)* stunt[ing], rosetting; *(vet)* distortion
Stauchungsbruch *m* 1. compression failure, upset *(of a tree)*; 2. *s.* Stauchungsfraktur
Stauchungsfraktur *f (vet)* impacted fracture
Stauchvorrichtung *f* [für Sägezähne] swager, *(Am)* upset
Staudamm *m* [checking, storage] dam, barrage
Staude *f* [herbaceous] perennial plant, hardy perennial, shrub, forb, herb
~/**winterharte** herbaceous hardy perennial
Staudenaster *f* perennial aster
Staudengewächs *n s.* Staude

Staudenkante *f s.* Staudenrabatte
Staudenkohl *m* collard, kale, Brassica oleracea convar. acephala var. viridis
Staudenlupine *f* large-leaved lupin[e], Lupinus polyphyllus
Staudenphlox *m (bot)* summer [perennial] phlox, Phlox paniculata
Staudenrabatte *f* perennial (herbaceous) border
Staudensetzer *m*, **Staudensetzmaschine** *f* shrub planter
Staudenwicke *f* everlasting pea, Lathyrus latifolius
Staudenziehroder *m* potato (plant) puller
staudig shrubby
stauen 1. to impound, to dam; 2. *(vet)* to congest
Staufferfett *n* cup grease
Staugewässer *n s.* Stausee
Staugley *m* pseudogley, stagnogley, surface-water gley [soil]
Staugleyhorizont *m* pseudogley horizon
Staugleypodsol *m* pseudogleyed podzol
Staugrabenbewässerung *f* flooding from ditches
Stauhölzer *npl* dunnage
staunaß waterlogged, poorly-drained, soggy, stagnant *(soil)*
Staunässe *f* stagnant moisture
Staunässebildung *f* [soil] waterlogging
Staupe *f (vet)* [dog, canine] distemper
Stauschütz *m* jack-gate
Stausee *m* reservoir, artificial (obstruction) lake
Stauung *f* 1. *(vet)* congestion, stasis; 2. *s.* Stau
~ **von Darminhalt** intestinal stasis
Stauungsinduration *f* **der Leber** *(vet)* pseudocirrhosis
Stauvergleyung *f (soil)* pseudogleyification
Stauwasser *n (soil)* perched [ground] water, impound water, backwater
Stauwasseroberfläche *f*, **Stauwasserspiegel** *m* perched water-table
Stauwiese *f* overflow (inundated) meadow
Stavropol[-Feinwollschaf] *n* Stavropol *(sheep breed)*
StE *s.* 1. Stammelitsaatgut; 2. Stärkeeinheit
Steak *n* steak
Stearin *n* stearin
Stearinsäure *f* stearic (octadecanoic) acid *(fatty acid)*
Stea[to]rrhoe *f (vet)* steatorrhoea
Steatose *f* steatosis
Stechapfel *m* 1. thorn-apple, datura, stramonium, stinkweed *(genus Datura)*; 2. thorn-apple, jimson [weed], Jamestown weed, Datura stramonium
Stechborste *f (ent)* [piercing] stylet
Stechborstentasche *f (ent)* crumena
stechborstenübertragbar stylet-borne *(virus)*
Stechbremse *f* horse-fly, breeze [fly], cleg, greenhead, tabanid *(family Tabanidae)*
Stechdorn *m* common (purging) buckthorn, Rhamnus catharticus
Stecheiche *f (bot)* encina, Quercus agrifolia

stechen

stechen to sting *(insects)*
~/Spargel to cut asparagus
Stechen *n* jump-off *(equitation)*
stechend pungent *(e.g. smell)*
Stechfichte *f* blue (Colorado) spruce, Picea pungens
Stechfliege *f* biting fly *(subfamily Stomoxyinae)*
Stechginster *m* 1. gorse, furze, whin *(genus Ulex)*; 2. common gorse, furze, thorn broom, whin, Ulex europaeus
Stechlaus *f* sucking louse *(group Anoplura)*
Stechmesser *n (slaught)* killing knife
Stechmücke *f* mosquito, culicid *(family Culicidae)*
Stechpalme *f* 1. holly, ilex *(genus Ilex)*; 2. Chinese holly, Ilex cornuta
Stechwinde *f (bot)* green briar, smilax *(genus Smilax)*
Stechzylinder *m* soil sampling cylinder
Stechzylinderprobe *f (soil)* core sample
Steckenkraut *n (bot)* ferula *(genus Ferula)*
Stecketikett *n* label
~/hölzernes wooden label
Steckholz *n* dormant (leafless winter) cutting, [hardwood] cutting, propagation wood
~ mit Astring cutting with heel
~/nicht voll ausgereiftes semihardwood cutting
Stecklenberger Krankheit *f* der Schattenmorelle Stecklenberger disease of cherry *(virosis)*
Steckling *m* 1. cutting, slip; nursery plant; seed piece *(e.g. of hop or sugar-cane)*; 2. steckling *(a beet or carrot plant for seed production)* • **Stecklinge setzen** to strike
~/bewurzelter sett, set
~/krautiger herbaceous (softwood) cutting
~/langer dicker truncheon
Stecklingsanzucht *f* raising by cuttings
Stecklingsbeet *n* nursery bed
Stecklingsbewurzelung *f* rooting of cuttings
Stecklingsfäule *f* seed rot *(esp. of sugar-cane)*
Stecklingsfeld *n* steckling field
Stecklingsholz *n* propagation wood
Stecklingsmesser *n* cutting dibber
Stecklingsmiete *f* steckling bed
Stecklingspflanzung *f* layering
Stecklingsrübe *f* steckling
Stecklingsvermehrung *f* propagation by cuttings, cuttage, layering
Steckreis *n* nursery plant
Steckrübe *f* swede [turnip], yellow (Swedish) turnip, *(Am)* rutabaga, Brassica napus var. napobrassica, Brassica napus ssp. rapifera
Steckzwiebel *f* [seed] bulb, seed (planting, choice) onion, onion set[t], multiplier
Steckzwiebelbeizgerät *n* seed-bulb dresser
Steeplechase *f* steeplechase *(equestrian sport)*
Steepler *m* steeplechaser *(a racehorse)*
Steffenschnitzel *npl* Steffen sugar pulp
Steghufeisen *n* bar shoe
~/geschlossenes full-bar shoe

Stegkettenförderer *m* drag (scraper-chain) conveyor
stehen/im Stall to stall
Stehendasten *n (forest)* delimbing
Stehendfestmeter *m* standing solid metre *(timber mensuration)*
Stehendzopfen *n (forest)* topping in advance of felling
Steher *m* stayer *(racing horse)*
Stehkamm *m* shell (single) comb *(of fowl)*
Stehmähne *f* upright mane
Stehohr *n* prick-ear, upright ear
stehohrig prick-eared
Stehvermögen *n* stamina, staying-power, stay *(of a sport horse)*
Stehzügel *m* check-rein
steif stiff, rigid, strict
steifblättrig hard-leaved, sclerophyllous
Steifblättriger Wacholder *m* temple juniper, Juniperus rigida
Steifblättrigkeit *f* sclerophylly
Steife Luzerne *f* tifton bur clover, Medicago rigidula
Steifer Sauerklee *m* yellow wood sorrel, Oxalis dillendii
steifhaarig hispid
Steifheit *f* stiffness
Steigbügel *m* 1. stirrup[-iron]; 2. stapes *(animal anatomy)*
Steigbügelriemen *m* stirrup leather (strap)
Steigbügelstange *f* stirrup bar
Steige *f* crate • **in Steigen einlagern** to crate
Steigeisen *n* climbing iron
Steiggebiß *n* tow snaffle[s]
steil *s.* stuhlbeinig
Steilabbruch *m*, **Steilabfall** *m* escarp[ment], precipice
Steilförderer *m* steeply inclined elevator
Steilhang *m* steep slope; scarp
Stein *m* 1. *(bot)* stone, pit; *(vet)* stone, concrement; 2. *s.* Steinschale; 3. stone, rock • **mit am Fleisch haftenden ~** clingstone *(said e.g. of peaches)*
Steinbeere *f* stone bramble, stoneberry, Rubus saxatilis
Steinbibernelle *f (bot)* common saxifrage, Pimpinella saxifraga
Steinbock *m* rock-goat, [Alpine] ibex, Capra ibex (hircus)
Steinboden *m* stony soil
Steinbrand *m (phyt)* covered smut *(comprehensive term)*
~ des Weizens covered smut of wheat, [common] wheat bunt *(caused by Tilletia spp.)*
Steinbrech *m (bot)* stone-break, saxifrage *(genus Saxifraga)*
Steinbruch *m* stone-pit, quarry
Steinbrut *f (api, vet)* stone brood *(caused by Aspergillus flavus)*
Steindrän *m* stone (rock) drain

Steindränung f stone drainage
Steineiche f 1. holm[-oak], evergreen oak, holly [oak], Quercus ilex; 2. encina, Quercus agrifolia; 3. durmast oak, Quercus petraea (sessiliflora)
Steinfänger m, **Steinfangmulde** f stone catcher (trap)
Steinfeder f maidenhair spleenwort, Asplenium trichomanes
Steinfraktion f (soil) stone fraction
steinfrei stoneless
Steinfrucht f (bot) stone fruit, drupe
steinfruchtartig, steinfrüchtig drupaceous
Steinfrüchtigkeit f der Birne pear stony pit (virosis)
Steingabel f stone fork
Steingalle f (vet) quittor
Steingarten m rock-garden, rockery
Steingartenpflanze f rock[-garden] plant
Steingeröll n shingle, scree
Steinhirse f (bot) gromwell, Lithospermum officinale
Steinholzschliff m stone groundwood
Steinhund m s. Sumpfotter
steinig stony, rocky
Steinigkeit f stoniness
Steinkastendamm m crib dam
Steinkern m (bot) stone
Steinklee m sweet clover, melilot, lotus (genus Melilotus)
Steinkohlen[teer]kreosot n creosote oil
Steinkraut n madwort, alyssum (genus Alyssum)
Steinlawine f stone (rock, debris) avalanche
Steinlinde f mock privet (genus Phillyrea)
steinlösend freestone (e.g. peach)
~/nicht clingstone
Steinlöslichkeit f stone separability
Steinmais m flint (yankee) maize, (Am) flint corn, Zea mays convar. vulgaris
Steinmarder m stone (rock, beech) marten, Martes foina
Steinmühle f stone grinder
Steinnetzboden m polygonal soil
Steinnuß f corozo-nut (from Phytelephas macrocarpa)
Steinnußpalme f ivory palm, Phytelephas macrocarpa
Steinobst n stone fruit
Steinobstbaum m drupaceous plant
Steinobsterntemaschine f stone-fruit harvester
Steinobstfrucht f stone fruit
Steinobstgespinstwespe f stone-fruit leaf saw-fly, Neurotoma nemoralis
Steinpflaster n s. Wüstenpflaster
Steinpilz m (bot) edible boletus, cep[e], Boletus edulis
Steinquendel m (bot) calamint (genus Calamintha)
Steinrechen m stone rake
Steinrodepflug m rock digger (eradicator), heavy rocker plough, stone lifter

Steinsalz n rock-salt, halite
Steinsame m stoneweed, gromwell (genus Lithospermum)
Steinsammellader m elevator stone picker
Steinsammelmaschine f, **Steinsammler** m stone (rock) picker (s. a. Steinfänger)
Steinschale f putamen (of drupaceous fruits)
Steinsicherung f **von Pflugkörpern** safeguard of plough bodies, trip bottom
Steinstaublunge f (vet) silicosis
Steintäschel n stone-cress (genus Aethionema)
Steinthylle f sclerotic tylosis (of wood)
Stein- und Klutentrennanlage f stones and clods separator
Steinweichsel f mahaleb [cherry], St. Lucie cherry, Prunus (Cerasus) mahaleb
Steinweide f purple willow, Salix purpurea
Steinwild n rock-goat, ibex, Capra ibex (hircus)
Steinwollblock m rock-wool cube
Steinwolle f rock-wool, stonewool
Steinwollplatte f rock-wool slab
Steinwüste f stony desert
Steinzelle f (bot) stone (grit) cell, sclereid, sclerotic cell
Steißlage f breech position (presentation) (obstetrics)
Stele f (bot) stele
Stellagenträger m shelving support (in greenhouses)
stellbar adjustable
stellen 1. to adjust; 2. (hunt) to bay
Stellmacher m cart-wright, wheelwright
Stellnetz n (pisc) gill-net
Stellung f**/hammelbeinige** sheep-knee, calf-knee conformation (of forelimbs)
~/kniehängige bucked knees, bucked-knee conformation (of forelimbs)
~/kuhhessige cow hocks, cow-hocked conformation (of hindlimbs)
~/rückbiegige s. Stellung/hammelbeinige
~/säbelbeinige sickle hocks, curby conformation (of hindlimbs)
stellvertretend (ecol) vicarious
Stelzpflug m Belgian (shoe) plough
Stelzradschlepper m high-clearance [straddle-type] tractor
Stelzwurzel f stilt (prop, brace) root
Stempel m 1. (bot) pistil; 2. stemple, [pit, mine] prop
Stempelfuß m (bot) gynobase
Stempelholz n prop wood, short pitwood, [short] props
stempellos (bot) agynary, agynous
stempeltragend (bot) pistillate
Stengel m (bot) stalk, stem; culm, ha[u]lm, shank, stipe (s. a. under Stiel) • **einen ~ bilden** to culm • **mit fädigem ~** filicauline • **mit weißem ~** albicaulis
~/hohler cane (of certain grasses)

Stengelälchen

Stengelälchen *n s.* Stockälchen
stengelartig stalky
Stengelbasis *f* stem base
Stengel-Blatt-Verhältnis *n* stalk-to-leaf ratio
Stengelbohrer *m (ent)* stalk borer, stem borer (miner) *(comprehensive term)*
Stengelbruch *m* stalk breakage
Stengelbuntkrankheit *f* stem mottle, corky ring spot *(virosis of potato)*
Stengelchen *n* stalklet, caulicle
Stengelexplantat *n* stem explant
Stengelfaserpflanze *f* stem fibre crop
Stengelfäule *f (phyt)* stalk (stem) rot, stalk decay
~ **des Salats** bottom rot of lettuce *(caused by Rhizoctonia solani)*
Stengelfestigkeit *f* stalk strength, stem solidness
Stengelglied *n* internode, merithal
Stengelgrund *m* stem base
stengelhaltig stemmy *(e.g. green fodder)*
stengelig 1. caulescent, cauliferous; 2. *s.* stengelhaltig
Stengelknicker *m* forage crimper
Stengelknoten *m* [stem] node
~/**kleiner** nodule
Stengelkrebs *m (phyt)* stem canker
stengellos stalkless, stemless, acaulescent, acauline, apodal, apodous
~/**fast** subcaulescent
Stengelloser Himmel[s]schlüssel *m* English primrose, Primula vulgaris
Stengelminierer *m s.* Stengelbohrer
Stengelnematode *m* stem eelworm *(esp. Ditylenchus spp.)*
Stengelquetscher *m* stalk (forage) crusher, roller conditioner
Stengelranke *f* stem tendril
Stengelrost *m (phyt)* stem rust *(caused by Puccinia graminis)*
Stengelschnittstück *n* stem cutting
Stengelschwader *m* stalk windrower
Stengelspitze *f* stem tip
stengelständig cauline
Stengelstreckung *f* stem elongation (extension)
stengelumfassend stem-clasping, stem-embracing, amplexicaul
Stengelumfassende Taubnessel *f (bot)* henbit, Lamium amplexicaule
Stengelwachstum *n* stem growth
Stengelzerkleinerer *m* stalk chopper
stenglig *s.* stengelig
Stenograph *m* twelve-toothed bark-beetle, Ips sexdentatus
Stenose *f (vet)* stenosis *(narrowing of an hollow organ)*
stenotherm *(bot, zoo)* stenothermal, stenothermic
Stenten *n* stenting *(practice in propagating roses)*
Stephanofilariose *f (vet)* stephanofilariasis
Stephanskörner *npl (bot)* stavesacre, Delphinium staphisagria

Steppe *f* steppe
Steppenbildung *f* steppization
Steppenboden *m* steppe soil
Steppenbrand *m* steppe fire
Steppenfauna *f* steppe fauna
Steppengraslandboden *m* steppe grassland soil
Steppenhain *m* forest outlier in the steppe
Steppenhexe *f s.* Steppenroller
Steppenkerze *f* desert-candle, eremurus, foxtail lily *(genus Eremurus)*
Steppenkirsche *f* European dwarf cherry, *(Am)* ground-cherry, Prunus (Cerasus) fruticosa
Steppenklima *n* steppe climate
Steppenroller *m* tumble-weed *(comprehensive term)*
Steppensalbei *m* violet sage, Salvia nemorosa
Steppenschwarzerde *f* [steppe] chernozem, black earth
Steppenwaldbau *m* steppic silviculture, forest cultivation in steppes
Ster *m* stere, stacked cubic metre *(timber mensuration)*
Sterberate *f*, **Sterbeziffer** *f* death (mortality) rate
sterblich mortal
Sterblichkeit *f* mortality, lethality
~/**perinatale** perinatal mortality
Sterblingswolle *f* carrion (skinner's, pelt) wool, mor[t]ling
Stereobildpaar *n*, **Stereogramm** *n* stereogram, stereoscopic pair *(surveying)*
Stereometer *n* stereometer, parallax bar
Stereorasterelektronenmikroskopie *f* stereoscan electron microscopy
Stereoselektivität *f* stereoselectivity *(e.g. of pesticides)*
Sterigma *n (bot)* sterigma
steril 1. sterile, infertile, unfertile, barren *(organism; soil)*; 2. sterile, aseptic
~/**zytoplasmatisch [bedingt] männlich** *(bot)* cytoplasmic male-sterile, cms
Sterilans *n* sterilant
sterile-Männchen-Methode *f s.* Sterilpartnermethode
Sterilfiltration *f* sterile filtration
Sterilisans *n*, **Sterilisant** *n* sterilant
Sterilisation *f* sterilization
Sterilisator *m* sterilizer
Sterilisierbüchse *f* Petri dish box
sterilisieren 1. to sterilize; to aseptisize; 2. to neuter, to castrate, to spay
~/**durch Dampf** to steam-sterilize
~/**im Autoklaven** to autoclave
Sterilität *f* 1. sterility, infertility, barrenness; 2. sterility, asepsis
~/**durch Chemosterilantien hervorgerufene** chemosterility
~/**männliche** male sterility; *(vet)* impotence, impotency
~/**temporäre (zeitweilige)** temporary sterility

~/zytoplasmatisch bedingte männliche *(bot)* cytoplasmic male sterility
Sterilitätsgen *n* sterility gene
Sterilmilch *f* sterilized milk
Sterilpartnermethode *f* autocidal control [tactics], sterile male (release) technique *(of genetical pest control)*
Sterin *n s.* Sterol
Sterke *f* heifer, stirk, quey *(for compounds s. under Färse)*
Sterkolith *m (vet)* coprolith
sterkoral stercoraceous, stercoral
Sterkorämie *f (vet)* copraemia
Sterlet *m* sterlet, Acipenser ruthenus
Stern *m* star *(marking e.g. on horse's head)*
~ von Bethlehem *(bot)* star-of-Bethlehem, Ornithogalum umbellatum
Sternanis *m* 1. anise-tree, aniseed tree *(genus Illicium)*; 2. star anise, Illicium verum
Sternapfel[strauch] *m* star-apple, Chrysophyllum cainito
Sternblümchen *n (bot)* swan river daisy, Brachycome iberidifolia
Sterndolde *f* masterwort, Astrantia minor
Sternfilter *n* star filter
Sternfleckenkrankheit *f* asteroid spot *(virosis e.g. of peaches)*
sternförmig star-shaped, stellate
Stern[fraß]gang *m (ent)* stellate gallery, star-shaped feed mark
Sterngliederegge *f* star-toothed harrow
Sterngras *n* star grass, Cynodon plectostachyum
Sterngucker *m* star-gazing horse
Sternit *m* sternite *(of arthropods)*
Sternjasmin *m* star jasmin[e], Trachelospermum jasminoides
Sternkaktus *m* star cactus *(genus Astrophytum)*
Sternkiefer *f* maritime pine, Pinus pinaster
Sternkrümler *m* star-wheel harrow, toothed roller
Sternmagnolie *f* star magnolia, Magnolia stellata
Sternmiere *f* chick[en]weed, stitchwort, satin-flower, starwort *(genus Stellaria)*
Sternmoos *n* 1. pearlwort, seal-wort *(genus Sagina)*; 2. pearlwort, Irish moss, Sagina subulata
Sternmosaik *n (phyt)* asteroid mosaic *(virosis)*
Sternnußpalme *f (bot)* tucum *(genus Astrocaryum)*
Sternraddüngerstreuer *m* star-wheel fertilizer distributor
Sternradrechen *m*, **Sternradrechwender** *m* spider (finger wheel) rake, spider wheel turner
Sternradrübenausdünner *m* rotary beet thinner
Sternratschenkupplung *f* outwardly acting pin-type safety clutch
Sternrechwender *m s.* Sternradrechen
Sternringelwalze *f* Cambridge roll[er] *(soil-working tool)*
Sternrissigkeit *f (phyt)* star crack[ing]
~ des Apfels apple star crack *(virosis)*

Sternrußtau *m* **der Rose** black rot (spot) of rose *(caused by Marssonia rosae)*
Sternschild *m* 1. aspidistra *(genus Aspidistra)*; 2. cast-iron plant, Aspidistra elatior
Sternschleuder *f (api)* radial extractor
Sternstachelbeerbaum *m* [otaheite] gooseberry-tree, Phyllanthus acidus
Sternum *n* sternum, breastbone, keel bone • **hinter dem ~ befindlich** retrosternal
Sternwalze *f* star (Norwegian) roller *(soil-working tool)*
Sternzelle *f*/**Kupffersche** Kupffer cell
Steroid *n* steroid *(triterpene)*
~/anabol[isch]es anabolic steroid
Steroidbildung *f*, **Steroidbiosynthese** *f* steroidogenesis
steroidogen steroidogenic
Steroidstoffwechsel *m* steroid metabolism
Sterol *n* sterol *(unsaturated alcohol)*
Stertor *m (vet)* stertor
Sterz *m* 1. short tail, parson's nose *(of birds)*; 2. plough handle
Sterzpflug *m* walking plough
Stethoskop *n (vet)* stethoscope
Stetigförderer *m* [continuous] conveyor
~/pneumatischer pneumatic conveyor
Stetigkeit *f (ecol)* constancy, stability
Steuerbarkeit *f* steerability
Steuerfeder *f* tail feather, rectrix *(of birds)*
steuern 1. to steer; 2. to control
Steuerung *f* 1. steering; 2. control
Steuerventil *n* steering valve
Steviol *n* steviol *(diterpene)*
Stewart'sche Maiskrankheit *f (Am)* Stewart's disease of sweet corn *(caused by Bacterium stewartii)*
STH *s.* Somatotropin
Stibophen *n* stibophen *(anthelminthic)*
Stich *m* sting *(e.g. of an insect)*
Stichfahrt *f* heat *(equitation)*
Stichfleisch *n* sticking-piece *(of beef carcass)*
Stichling *m* stickleback *(family Gasteroidae)*
Stichprobe *f* [random] sample
~/geschichtete stratified sample
~/systematische systematic sample
Stichprobenahme *f* [random] sampling
Stichprobenanteil *m* sampling fraction
Stichprobenaufnahme *f (forest)* sample plot inventory
Stichprobeneinheit *f* sampling unit
Stichprobenentnahme *f* [random] sampling
Stichprobenfehler *m* sampling error
Stichprobenleistungsprüfung *f* random sample performance test *(animal breeding)*
Stichprobenmittel *n* sample mean
Stichprobentaxation *f (forest)* point sampling (cruising)
Stichprobentest *m* random [sample] test, sampling [test]

Stichprobenumfang

Stichprobenumfang *m* sample size, population
Stichprobenverfahren *n* sampling method
Stichrennen *n* heat *(equitation)*
Stickoxid *n* nitric oxide, nitrogen monoxide
Stickstoff *m* nitrogen • ~ **entziehen** to denitrogenate, to denitrogenize
~/aktiver active nitrogen
~/atmosphärischer atmospheric nitrogen
~/schädlicher noxious nitrogen *(e.g. of sugarbeet)*
stickstoffarm low-N, poor in nitrogen
Stickstoffassimilation *f* nitrogen assimilation
Stickstoffaufnahme *f* nitrogen uptake
Stickstoffbalance *f* nitrogen equilibrium
Stickstoffbedarf *m* nitrogen requirement
Stickstoffbestimmung *f* nitrogen determination (estimation)
~ **nach Kjeldahl** Kjeldahl determination, Kjeldahl procedure *(of nitrogen determination)*
Stickstoffbestimmungsapparat *m* nitrogen determination apparatus
Stickstoffbinder *m* nitrogen-fixer, nitrogen-fixing bacterium
Stickstoffbindung *f s.* Stickstoff-Fixierung
Stickstoffdioxid *n* nitrogen dioxide
Stickstoffdüngemittel *n*, **Stickstoffdünger** *m* nitrogen fertilizer, nitrogenous fertilizer (manure)
Stickstoffdüngung *f* nitrogen fertilization
Stickstoffentzug *m* denitrogenation
Stickstoffestlegung *f s.* Stickstoff-Fixierung
Stickstoff-Fixierung *f* nitrogen fixation
~ **durch Bakterien** *(soil)* non-symbiotic nitrogen fixation, azofication
~/nichtsymbiotische non-symbiotic nitrogen fixation
stickstofffrei nitrogen-free, non-nitrogenous
Stickstofffreisetzung *f* nitrogen release
Stickstoffgabe *f* nitrogen dressing
Stickstoffgehalt *m* nitrogen content
Stickstoffgleichgewicht *n* nitrogen equilibrium
stickstoffhaltig nitrogenous, nitrogen-containing
Stickstoffhaushalt *m* nitrogen economy
Stickstoffhunger *m* nitrogen deficiency
Stickstoffkreislauf *m* nitrogen cycle
stickstoffliebend nitrophile, nitrophilous
Stickstoffmangel *m* nitrogen deficiency
Stickstoffmehrer *m s.* Stickstoffsammler
Stickstoffmetabolismus *m* nitrogen metabolism
Stickstoffmetabolit *m* nitrogen metabolite
Stickstoffmineralisation *f*, **Stickstoffmobilisation** *f* nitrogen mineralization
Stickstoffmonoxid *n* nitrogen monoxide, nitric oxide
Stickstoffoxid *n* nitrogen oxide
Stickstoffquelle *f* nitrogen reservoir
stickstoffreich high-N, rich in nitrogen
Stickstoffreservoir *n* nitrogen reservoir
Stickstoffretention *f* nitrogen retention
Stickstoffsammler *m* nitrogen-collecting plant, nitrogen collector (gatherer)
Stickstoffspätdüngung *f* late application of nitrogen
Stickstoffspätgabe *f* late application of nitrogen
Stickstoffträger *m* nitrogen carrier
Stickstofftranslokation *f*, **Stickstoffumlagerung** *f* nitrogen transfer
Stickstoffumsatz *m* nitrogen metabolism
Stickstoffverbindung *f* nitrogenous compound
~/organische organic nitrogen compound
Stickstoffverfügbarkeit *f* nitrogen availability
Stickstoffwirkungsverhältnis *n* nitrogen efficiency ratio, NER
Stickstoffzehrer *m* nitrogen consumer
Stiefelbohne *f s.* Stangenbohne
Stiefmütterchen *n* 1. field pansy, kiss-me, Viola tricolor (arvensis); 2. pansy, heart's-ease, Viola-Wittrockiana-hybrid
Stiefmütterchenorchidee *f* pansy orchid *(genus Miltonia)*
Stiege *f* crate • **in Stiegen einlagern** to crate
Stiel *m* 1. *(bot, zoo)* stalk, stem, scape, stipe; petiole; trunk *(e.g. of mushrooms)*; ha[u]lm, shank *(s. a. under* Stengel*)*; 2. helve *(of hand tools)*
~ **des Blütenstandes** peduncle, footstalk
stielblättrig podophyllous
Stielchen *n* stalk, sterigma; caudicle, caudicula *(e.g. of an orchid flower)*
Stieleiche *f* common (pedunculate) oak, English (Austrian) oak, Quercus robur (pedunculata)
Stielende *n* stalk end
stielförmig stipi[ti]form
Stielgemüse *n* stem vegetable
Stielgrube *f* stalk (stem) cavity *(of fruits)*
Stiellähme *f* tendril atrophy *(of grape-vine)*
Stiellösbarkeit *f* stalk-loosening behaviour *(of fruit)*
Stielpfeffer *m* Java (tailed) pepper, Piper cubeba
stielrund *(bot)* terete
Stielsellerie *m* [blanched] celery, Apium graveolens var. dulce
Stier *m* bull • **den ~ annehmen** to bull
stierig sein to be at (in, on) heat *(cow)*
Stierigkeit *f* heat *(of a cow)*
Stierkalb *n* bull-calf
Stiersucht *f* nymphomania, constant (continuous) oestrus *(of cow)*
Stiftentrommel *f* peg [threshing] drum, spike-tooth cylinder
Stiftentrommeldreschmaschine *f* peg drum thresher
Stiftfreilauf *m* pin free-wheel clutch
Stigma *n (bot, zoo)* stigma
Stigmasterol *n* stigmasterol *(phytosterol)*
Stilben *n* stilbene *(plant substance)*
Stilböstrol *n* [diethyl]stilboestrol *(growth stimulant)*
Stilett *n* stylet *(of ectoparasitic nematodes)*
Stilettälchen *n* dagger nematode *(genus Xiphinema)*

Stillgewässer *n* still water
Stillstandszeit *f* unproductive time
stillstehend stagnant *(water)*
Stillwein *m* still wine
Stiltonkäse *m* Stilton [cheese]
Stimmband *n* vocal ligament
Stimmfalte *f* vocal fold
Stimmkopf *m* syrinx *(of birds)*
Stimmlippe *f s.* Stimmfalte
Stimmritze *f* glottis *(animal anatomy)*
Stimulans *n* stimulant; stimulatory drug
Stimulation *f* stimulation, invigoration
Stimulator *m*/**biogener** biostimulator
Stimuliereber *m s.* Sucheber
Stimulus *m s.* Reiz
Stinkbrand *m* **des Weizens** covered (stinking) smut of wheat, [common] wheat bunt *(caused by Tilletia spp.)*
Stinkende Hundskamille *f s.* Stinkhundskamille
~ **Nieswurz** *f* stinking hellebore, setterwort, bear's-foot, Helleborus foetidus
Stinkender Gänsefuß *m* stinking goose-foot, notchweed, Chenopodium vulvaria
~ **Moderkäfer** *m (ent)* devil's coach-horse, Ocypus olens
Stinkhundskamille *f* [stinking] mayweed, stinking (dog's) camomile, dog-fennel, Anthemis cotula
Stinkkohl *m* skunk (swamp) cabbage *(genus Symplocarpus)*
Stinkmarder *m* polecat, fitch[et], fitchew, Mustela putorius
Stinkstrauch *m* bean trefoil, Anagyris foetida
Stinktier *n* skunk *(esp. genus Nephitis)*
Stinkwacholder *m* 1. stinking juniper, Juniperus foetidissima; 2. savin[e], Juniperus sabina
Stipel *f (bot)* stipule
Stippe *f*, **Stippigkeit** *f* bitter (crinkle) pit, stippen, Baldwin spot *(damage of stored fruit)*
Stipula *f s.* Nebenblatt
Stirn *f* forehead, brow
Stirnbein *n* frontal bone
Stirnhöhle *f* frontal sinus
Stirnriemen *m* headband, brow-band *(of bridle)*
Stirnrind *n* gayal, Bos [gaurus] frontalis
Stirnschopf *m* forelock *(of mane)*
Stirnwaffe *f* horn
Stirnwulst *m* poll
Stirnzapfen *m* core *(of ruminants)*
stöbern *(hunt)* to rouse, to start
stochastisch stochastic *(e.g. a model)*
Stock *m* 1. [tree-]stump, stub, stob, stock; 2. stick; 3. *s.* Bienenstock • **vom ~ ausschlagen** to sprout from stool • **Stöcke roden** *s.* stockroden
~ **im Niederwaldbetrieb** stool
Stock... *s. a.* Stubben...
Stockälchen *n* stem (bulb) eelworm, bulb and stem nematode, Ditylenchus dipsaci
Stockanalyse *f* stump analysis *(timber mensuration)*

Stockausschlag *m (forest)* coppice (sap) shoot, stool [shoot], stump sprout, sucker • **aus ~ entstanden** of vegetative origin, originating from coppice (suckers)
Stockbiene *f* house honey-bee
Stockdurchmesser *m* stump (base) diameter, diameter at stump height (level) *(timber mensuration)*
stocken/im Wachstum to arrest in growth, to check
Stockente *f* mallard, stock (wild) duck, Anas platyrhynchos
Stockfäule *f* stump (butt) rot *(esp. caused by Polyporus sistotremoides)*
Stockhöhe *f* stump height
Stockhöhendurchmesser *m s.* Stockdurchmesser
Stockholz *n* stump[wood]
~/**verkientes** resinous stumpwood
Stockholznutzung *f* stump utilization
Stockholzspaltmaschine *f* stump splitter
stockig mouldy, mildewy; musty *(smell, taste)*; do[a]ty, dotted, dos[e]y, rusty, pecky *(wood)*
Stocklack *m* stick-lac *(esp. from Coccus lacca)*
Stocklo[h]de *f s.* Stockausschlag
Stockmalve *f* hollyhock, rose-mallow, Alcea (Althaea) rosea
Stockmutter *f (api)* colony queen, queen [bee]
Stockpreis *m s.* Stocktaxe
Stockräumpflug *m* French plough
Stockrodegerät *n* [stump] eradicator, stump puller (grubber, extractor)
stockroden to stump [out], to stub [out], to extract (grub up) stumps
Stockroden *n* stump pulling (grubbing, extraction), stumping, [tree-]stump removal
Stockrose *f s.* Stockmalve
Stockrübe *f* sugar-beet bolter
Stocksäge *f* pole saw
Stockschere *f* pole pruner
Stockschwämmchen *n (bot)* changeable agaric, Pholiota (Kuehneromyces) mutabilis
Stocksprengung *f* stump blasting
Stockstärke *f s.* Stockdurchmesser
Stocktaxe *f (forest)* stumpage [value], statutory stumpage price
Stockverkauf *m (forest)* sale on the stump, sale of standing trees, stumpage (standing) sale
Stockvollerntemaschine *f* stump harvesting machine
stockwerkartig storeyed *(e.g. cambium)*
Stoddard-Solvent *n* Stoddard solvent *(herbicide, insecticide)*
Stoff *m* substance, matter *(s. a. under* Substanz*)*
~/**blutgerinnungshemmender** anticoagulant
~/**fiebererzeugender** pyrogen
~/**gelöster** solute
~/**reduzierender** reductone *(brewing)*
~/**wachstumsfördernder** growth promoter (stimulant), growth-promoting agent

Stoffausscheidung

Stoffausscheidung f excretion
Stoffaustausch f durch die Haut perspiration
Stoffmengenkonzentration f molarity
Stoffumsatz m turnover
~/mikrobieller microbial conversion
Stoffwechsel m metabolism • **im ~ umsetzen** to metabolize
Stoffwechselallergie f (vet) alimentary allergy
Stoffwechselazidose f (vet) metabolic acidosis
Stoffwechselbilanz f metabolic balance
Stoffwechselendprodukt n metabolic waste product, metabolite
Stoffwechselenergie f metabolic energy
Stoffwechselgleichgewicht n metabolic equilibrium
Stoffwechselhemmer m metabolic inhibitor
Stoffwechselhormon n metabolic hormone
Stoffwechselintensität f metabolic rate
Stoffwechselkäfig m metabolism cage (crate, stall)
Stoffwechselkette f metabolic chain
Stoffwechselkrankheit f (vet) metabolic disease
Stoffwechselpool m metabolic pool
Stoffwechselprodukt n metabolite, metabolic product, product of metabolism
Stoffwechselprozeß m metabolic process
Stoffwechselreaktion f metabolic reaction
Stoffwechselstörung f metabolic disorder (disturbance)
Stoffwechselüberwachung f metabolic control
Stoffwechseluntersuchung f metabolism study
Stoffwechselversuch m metabolism trial
Stoffwechselvorgang m metabolic process
Stoffwechselzustand m metabolic status
Stoffwechselzwischenprodukt n metabolite, metabolic intermediate
Stokesie f Stoke's aster (genus Stokesia)
Stolburkrankheit f [an] der Kartoffel stolbur, purple top roll (wilt) (mycoplasmosis of potatoes)
Stollen m lug (of a tyre)
~ des Hufeisens caulk[in]
Stollenwinkel m lug angle
Stolo[n] m (bot) stolon, stole, offshoot, runner
Stolonenbildung f stolonization
Stolze Lilie f American Turk's cap lily, Lilium superbum
stolzieren to strut
Stoma n (bot, zoo) stoma, stomate
Stomaapertur f stomatal aperture
stomachal stomachal
Stomatabewegung f stomatal movement
stomatär stomatal, stomatic, stomate
Stomatastoffwechsel m stomatal metabolism
Stomatawiderstand m stomatal resistance
Stomatitis f (vet) stomatitis
Stop m stop (depression in the face esp. of a dog between forehead and muzzle)
stopfen to cram (esp. geese)
Stopfen m bung, faucet, stopper
Stoppel f stubble [field] • **~ stürzen** to return the stubble
Stoppelabbrennen n stubble burning
Stoppelabdeckung f s. Stoppelmulch
Stoppelbearbeitung f stubble cultivation (tillage)
Stoppeldrillmaschine f chisel planter
Stoppelfeld n stubble [field], harvest field
Stoppelfrucht f stubble crop (fruit)
Stoppelfrucht[an]bau m stubble [catch] cropping
Stoppelhöhe f stubble height
Stoppelmulch m stubble mulch
Stoppelmulchverfahren n stubble mulching system
Stoppelpflug m stubble cleaner (plough)
Stoppelrübe f [stubble] turnip, Brassica rapa var. rapa, Brassica campestris ssp. rapifera
~/walzenförmige tankard turnip
Stoppelrückstand m stubble residue
Stoppelsaat f stubble seed
Stoppelsturz m, **Stoppelumbruch** m stubble cleaning (clearing), stubbling, autumn cleaning
Stoppelunkraut n stubble weed
Stoppelverstellung f stubble cutting adjustement (of a cutter bar)
Stoppelweide f (Am) rowen
Stoppelwurzelälchen n stubby root nematode (genera Trichodorus and Paratrichodorus)
Stoppelzwischenfruchtanbau m stubble catch cropping
Stoppkodon n (gen) termination (terminator, nonsense) codon
Stör m sturgeon (genus Acipenser)
Storax m [liquid] storax, styrax, liquidambar (balsam from Liquidambar spp.); Levant storax (styrax) (balsam from Liquidambar orientalis)
Storaxbaum m storax-tree (genus Styrax)
Storch m stork (family Ciconiidae)
Storchschnabel m (bot) 1. crane's-bill, cranesbill, geranium (genus Geranium); 2. pelargonium (genus Pelargonium)
störrisch restive, intractable, obstreperous, vicious (e.g. a horse)
Störung f disturbance, disorder
~ der Mutter-Kind-Beziehung mis-mothering (esp. in sheep flocks)
~ der Peristaltik (vet) dysperistalsis
~ des Harnlassens (vet) dysuria
~/funktionelle functional disorder
~/physiologische physiological disorder
Stoß m 1. shock; impulse, impact; 2. thrust (in mating); 3. s. Stapel 1.
Stoßbaumschüttler m impulse trunk shaker
Stoßbeschädigung f impact damage (injury) (e.g. of fruits)
Stoßbutterfaß n plunger-dasher churn
Stoßeisen n s. Pflanzeisen
stoßen to swoop [down], to pounce (raptorial bird)
~/mit dem Gehörn (Geweih) to butt

Stößer *m s.* Sperber
Stoßfestigkeit *f* shock resistance
Stoßhacke *f* push hoe, push and pull
Stoßheber *m* hydraulic ram
stößig sein *s.* stierig sein
Stoßschaden *m* impact bruise *(e.g. on fruits)*
Stoßzahn *m* tusk *(of wild boar's dentition)*
Stout *m* stout *(beer)*
Strabismus *m (vet)* strabismus, squint
straff *(bot, zoo)* strict; tight, taut *(e.g. a rope, rein)*
Strahl *m* 1. ray, beam; jet; 2. frog *(of hoof)*; 3. barbule *(of bird's feather)*
Strahlbein *n* navicular (distal sesamoid) bone *(animal anatomy)*
Strahlblüte *f* ray floret
Strahlenbiologie *f* radiobiology
strahlenbiologisch radiobiological
strahlenblättrig *(bot)* actinophyllous
Strahlenbotanik *f* radiation botany
Strahlenbündel *n* beam
strahlend radiant
Strahlenempfindlichkeit *f* radiosensitivity
strahlenförmig radiate, radial; actinomorphic, actinomorphous
Strahlengenetik *f* radiation genetics
Strahlenkörper *m* ciliary body *(of the eye)*
Strahlenkrankheit *f* radiation sickness
Strahlenkranz *m s.* Strahlenkörper
Strahlenlose Kamille *f* pineapple weed, Chamomilla suaveolens
Strahlenpilz *m (bot)* actinomycete *(order Actinomycetales)*
~ der Rose *(phyt)* black rot (spot) of rose *(caused by Marssonia rosae)*
Strahlenpilzerkrankung *f (vet)* actinomycosis
Strahlenresistenz *f* radioresistance
Strahlenschaden *m* radiation injury
Strahlenschutz *m* radiation (radiant) protection
Strahlenschutzstoff *m* radiation protection agent
Strahlensicherheit *f* radiological safety
Strahlensterilisation *f* radiation sterilization, radiosterilization *(e.g. of insect pests)*
Strahlensyndrom *n s.* Strahlenkrankheit
Strahlentherapie *f (phyt, vet)* radiotherapy
Strahlfäule *f (vet)* thrush
Strahlfurche *f* sulcus of frog, cleft *(of hoof)*
~/mittlere central sulcus of frog, central cleft
~/seitliche lateral sulcus of frog, lateral cleft
strahlig actinomorphic, actinomorphous
Strahlkissen *n* frog (hoof) pad, digital cushion
Strahlkörper *m* frog *(of hoof)*
Strahlleiste *f* frog stay
Strahlpolster *n s.* Strahlkissen
Strahlpumpe *f* jet pump
Strahlregner *m* rain gun
Strahlspitze *f* apex of frog *(of hoof)*
Strahlstörer *m* jet disturber *(of a sprinkler)*
Strahlung *f* radiation
~/infrarote infra-red radiation
~/ionisierende ionizing radiation
~/kurzwellige short-wave[length] radiation
~/langwellige long-wave[length] radiation
~/photosynthetisch aktive photosynthetic[ally] active radiation, PhAR, PAR
~/ultraviolette ultraviolet radiation
Strahlungsabsorptionsanalyse *f* radiation absorption analysis
Strahlungsbilanz *f* radiation balance (regime), net radiation *(of atmosphere)*
Strahlungsbilanzmesser *m* net radiation meter
Strahlungsdosis *f* radiation dose
Strahlungsenergie *f* radiation (radiant) energy
Strahlungsfrost *m* radiation[al] frost
Strahlungsheizkörper *m* radiator
Strahlungsintensität *f* radiation intensity
Strahlungsmenge *f* amount of radiation *(meteorology)*
Strahlungsmesser *m*, **Strahlungsmeßgerät** *n* radiation meter, radiometer; actinometer *(for measuring the direct heating power of the sun's rays)*
Strahlungsmeßschreiber *m* actinograph
Strahlungsmessung *f* radiation measurement, radiometry
Strahlungsreflexion *f* radiation reflectance
Strahlungsreflexionsvermögen *n* albedo *(of the atmosphere)*
Strahlungsschutz *m* radiation (radiant) protection; radiological safety
Strahlungssumme *f s.* Strahlungsmenge
Strahlungstemperatur *f* radiant temperature
Strahlungswärme *f* radiant heat, heat of radiation
Strahlunterbrecher *m* jet disturber *(of a sprinkler)*
Strandaster *f* sea starwort, Aster tripolium
Strandbereich *m* li[t]toral
Stranddistel *f* sea holly, Eryngium maritimum
Stranddorn *m* sea buckthorn, Hippophaë rhamnoides
Stranderbse *f* beach pea, Lathyrus japonicus ssp. maritimus
Strandflieder *m* 1. statice *(genus Limonium)*; 2. common sea lavender, Limonium vulgare
Strandgerste *f* sea barley, Hordeum marinum
Strandhafer *m* 1. sea lyme grass, European dune wild rye, Elymus (Leymus) arenarius; 2. European beach grass, marram [grass], Ammophila arenaria
Strandholz *n* stranded timber
Strandkasuarine *f* horse-tail [tree], Casuarina equisetifolia
Strandkiefer *f* maritime (cluster) pine, pinaster, Pinus pinaster (maritima)
Strandkohl *m* sea kale (cabbage), Crambe maritima
Strandkresse *f s.* Duftsteinrich
Strandling *m* shoreweed, Littorella uniflora
Strandnelke *f* common lavender, Limonium vulgare

Strandpflaume

Strandpflaume f beach plum, Prunus maritima
Strandsalde f ditch grass, Ruppia maritima
Strandweizen m sea wheat-grass, Agropyron junceum
Strandwinde f sea bindweed, Calystegia soldanella
Strang m cord, strand; trace *(of a harness)*
~/kodogener *(gen)* codogenic strand
Strangmoor n string (patterned) bog
Strangulation f strangulation
Strangurie f *(vet)* strangury, dysuria
Straße f/**befestigte** hard (made-up) road
~/unbefestigte earth road
Straßenbau m road building, road construction
Straßenbaum m street (roadside) tree
Straßenbaumart f roadside tree species
Straßenbepflanzung f roadside planting
Straßendecke f road surface, veneer
Straßenfahrgeschwindigkeit f road speed *(e.g. of tractors)*
Straßengraben m road ditch, cutting
Straßenhobel m grader
Straßennetz n road network
~/ländliches rural roads
Straßenrecht n right-of-way
Straßenschotter m road-metal
Straßentransportstellung f road travel condition *(of a field machine)*
Stratifikation f stratification
stratifizieren to stratify
Stratifizierung f stratification
stratiform stratiform
Stratokumulus m stratocumulus [cloud]
Stratus m stratus [cloud]
Strauch m bush, shrub, frutex
~/baumartiger arbuscle
~/kleiner shrublet
strauchartig shrubby, bushlike, bosky, fruticose, frutescent • **~ wachsen** to bush
Strauchbeerenobst n bush fruit
Strauchbeerenobstkultur f bush berry culture
Strauchbohne f 1. bush bean, Phaseolus vulgaris var. nanus; 2. s. Straucherbse
Strauchegge f brush harrow
Straucheibisch m rose of Sharon, shrub[by] althaea, Hibiscus syriacus
Straucherbse f pigeon (dwarf) pea, Angola (Congo) pea, d[h]al, red gram, Cajanus cajan (indicus)
Straucherbsenmosaikvirus n pigeon pea mosaic virus
Strauchformation f shrub formation
Strauchgesellschaft f shrub association
~/laubabwerfende aestifructicetum
Strauchheide f shrub heath
strauchig s. strauchartig
Strauchige Pfingstrose f s. Strauchpäonie
~ Wucherblume f s. Strauchmargerite

Strauchiger Gamander m *(bot)* shrubby germander, Teucrium fruticans
~ Papiermaulbeerbaum m paper-mulberry [tree], Broussonetia kazinoki
~ Wegerich m shrubby plantain, Plantago sempervirens
Strauchmargerite f marguerite, Paris daisy, Chrysanthemum frutescens
Strauchmelde f shrubby orach[e], sea-orach[e], sea purslane, Atriplex halimus
Strauchobst n bush fruit
Strauchpäonie f tree p[a]eony, Paeonia suffruticosa
Strauchpappel f tree mallow *(genus Lavatera)*
Strauchpflanzgerät n bush planter
Strauchportulak m purslane tree *(genus Portulacaria)*
Strauchrodung f shrub clearing
Strauchrose f bush rose *(comprehensive term)*
Strauchsavanne f shrub savanna[h]
Strauchschicht f shrub layer
Strauchschneidegerät n, **Strauchschneidemaschine** f brush buster (cutter), shrub cutter
Strauchschutzstreifen m shrub barrier
Strauchtundra f shrub tundra
Strauchvegetation f brush, scrub vegetation
Strauchveronika f *(bot)* veronica *(genus Hebe)*
Strauchwerk n shrubbery, bushes; coppice[wood], copsewood
~/dorniges briers
Strauchwerksichel f brush scythe
Strauchwüste f shrub desert
straußähnlich *(bot)* thyrsoid
straußblütig *(bot)* thyrsiflorous
Straußfarn m ostrich fern, Matteuccia struthiopteris
Straußgras n bent[-grass], agrostis *(genus Agrostis)*
Straußgras-Schwingel-Weide f agrostis-fescue pasture
Strecke f *(hunt)* kill, bag
strecken *(hunt)* to kill
Streckenpfahl m intermediate post *(fencing)*
Strecker m extensor [muscle]
Streckmetall[fuß]boden m expanded metal floor[ing]
Streckmittel n diluent
Streckmuskel m extensor [muscle]
Streckteich m *(pisc)* growing (nursery) pond
Streckung f, **Streckungswachstum** n extension growth, [cell] elongation
Streichblech n mould (breast) board, earthboard *(of a plough)*
Streichblechflügel m mould-board wing
Streichblechstrebe f mould-board stay
Streichblechstütze f mould-board brace
Streichblechteil n/**landseitiges** breast
streichen to card *(fibres)*; 2. to fly off, to rode *(wildfowl)*

streichend near-legged *(horse's gait)*
Streichkäse *m* processed cheese, cheese spread
Streichkraut *n* bastard hemp, Datisca cannabina
Streichschiene *f* mould-board extension, tailpiece
Streichwolle *f* carding-wool
streifen 1. to skin *(esp. hares or wildfowl)*; 2. s. entrinden/streifenweise
Streifen *m* strip; stripe, stria *(e.g. in tissue)*
~/Casparyscher Casparian strip *(of plant cells)*
Streifenanbau *m* strip-cropping
~ in Höhenlinie contour strip-cropping
Streifenaussaat *f s.* Streifensaat
Streifenbarsch *m* *(zoo)* striped bass, Morone saxatilis
Streifenbearbeitung *f* **des Bodens** strip (slot) tillage
Streifenbeet *n* strip [garden] bed
Streifenbehandlung *f* band treatment *(of a crop esp. with plant protectants)*
Streifenberegnung *f*, **Streifenbewässerung** *f* ribbon check[s] irrigation, border [strip] irrigation, strip sprinkler irrigation
Streifenborke *f* bark in strips
Streifenbrand *m* **des Wasserschwadens** *(phyt)* brown stripe smut *(caused by Ustilago longissima)*
~ des Weizens stripe (flag) smut of wheat *(caused by Urocystis agropyri)*
Streifendiagramm *n* histogram
Streifendurchforstung *f* *(forest)* strip thinning
Streifenfäule *f* streaked rot *(of softwoods)*
Streifengänger *m* *(forest)* patrolman
Streifenhieb *m s.* Streifenschlag
Streifenkahlschlagsystem *n* *(forest)* alternate clear-strip system
Streifenklee *m* soft trefoil, knotted (striated) clover, Trifolium striatum
Streifenkrankheit *f* **der Gerste** barley stripe disease, leaf stripe of barley *(caused by Pyrenophora graminea)*
Streifenkultur *f* strip crop
Streifenmeeräsche *f* *(zoo)* mullet, Mugil cephalus
Streifenmosaik *n* *(phyt)* stripe mosaic
Streifenmosaikvirus *n* **der Gerste** barley stripe mosaic virus
Streifenpflanzung *f* *(forest)* strip (line) planting
Streifenpflugkörper *m* slat-type mould-board, skeleton-type mould-board
Streifenrost *m* stripe (yellow) rust *(of cereals, caused by Puccinia glumarum = P. striiformis)*
Streifensaat *f* strip sowing (seeding, drilling), sowing in stripes
Streifenschlag *m* strip felling (cutting)
Streifenschnitt *m* trace clip *(horse grooming)*
Streifenweide *f* strip grazing
Streifenzeichnung *f* stripe [figure] *(of wood)*
Streifgebiet *n* *(ecol)* home range
Streifigkeit *f s.* Streifung
Streifnetz *n* sweep-net

Streifschuß *m* *(hunt)* grazing shot
Streifung *f* striping, striation, zonation
Strelitzie *f* bird-of-paradise [flower], Strelitzia reginae
streng austere *(wine)*
Strengit *m* strengite *(non-clay mineral)*
Strenze *f s.* Sterndolde
Streptancil *n s.* Streptomycin
Streptocyclin *n* streptocycline *(antibiotic)*
Streptokokke *f* streptococcus, chain coccus (genus Streptococcus)
Streptokokkeninfektion *f* *(vet)* streptococcal infection (poisoning)
Streptokokkenseptikämie *f* *(vet)* streptococcal septicaemia
Streptokokkose *f s.* Streptokokkeninfektion
Streptokokkus *m s.* Streptokokke
Streptomycin *n* streptomycin *(antibiotic)*
Streptonigrin *n* rufocromomycin *(antibiotic)*
Streptotrichose *f* *(vet)* streptotrichosis, nocardiosis
~ der Schafe lumpy wool *(of sheep, caused by Dermatophilus congolensis)*
Streß *m* stress
~/sozialer *(ecol)* social stress (strife)
streßanfällig stress-prone
Streßempfindlichkeit *f* stress-susceptibility
Streßfaktor *m* stress factor, stressor
Streßhormon *n* stress hormone
Stressor *m s.* Streßfaktor
Streßreaktion *f* stress response
streßresistent stress-resistant
Streßresistenz *f* stress resistance
Streß-Syndrom *n* stress syndrome
Streßtoleranz *f* stress tolerance
Streu *f* litter; short straw; bed of straw, bedding
• **mit ~ bedecken** to litter [down]
Streuabbau *m* litter decomposition
Streuaggregat *n* distributor mechanism
Streuberechtigung *f* *(forest)* right to litter
Streubild *n* distribution (spread) pattern *(e.g. of fertilizer distributors)*
Streubreite *f* width of spread
Streudecke *f* litter cover
streuen to scatter, to spread; to strew
Streuer *m* distributor, spreader
Streufall *m* *(forest)* litterfall
Streufinger *m* flicker *(of fertilizer distributor)*
Streufrucht *f* *(bot)* dehiscent fruit
Streugerät *n* distributor, spreader
Streukrampf *m* *(vet)* spring-halt, string-halt *(of cattle)*
Streumenge *f* rate of spread *(e.g. of a fertilizer distributor)*
Streumengenregulierhebel *m* rate control lever
Streumengenregulierschieber *m* feed gate
streunen to stray
Streuner *m* stray [animal]

Streunutzungsrecht *n (forest)* right to litter
Streuplattensystem *n* scatter plate system *(of fertilizer distributors)*
Streupuder *m* dusting powder (preparation)
Streusalz *n* de-icing salt, thawing (antifrost) salt
Streusalzschaden *m* damage due to road salting *(to roadside trees)*
Streuschicht *f (soil)* Aoo-horizon, L-layer, surface litter
Streustern *m* flicker *(of fertilizer distributor)*
Streustroh *n* bedding straw
Streuung *f (biom)* dispersion, variance, variation
Streuungsmaß *n* measure of dispersion
Streuungsursache *f* source of variation
Streuungsverhalten *n* scedasticity
Streuwalze *f* beater *(of manure spreader)*
Streuwiese *f* litter meadow
Stria *f (bot, zoo)* stria, stripe, line
striär *(bot, zoo)* striate[d]
Strich *m* 1. stripe *(marking e.g. at horse's forehead)*; 2. teat *(of the udder)*; nipple *(esp. of sow's udder)*
~ **der Tierkörperbehaarung** lie of the coat (hair)
~/**glockenförmiger** balloon teat
Strichelkrankheit *f (phyt)* streak *(virosis)*
~ **der Kartoffel** rugose mosaic of potato, stipple (leaf drop) streak of potato
~ **der Tomate** streak of tomato
Strichelmosaik *n (phyt)* streak mosaic
Strichelmosaikvirus *n* **des Weizens** wheat streak mosaic virus, WSkMV
Strichelung *f (phyt)* streaking
Strichkanal *m* teat canal
Strichöffnung *f* teat orifice
Strichverletzung *f* teat lesion
stridulieren to stridulate, to chirp
Striegel *m* [curry-]comb
striegeln 1. to curry, to comb, to groom, to scour, to rub *(esp. a horse)*; 2. to harrow down *(potato ridges)*
Striktur *f* stricture *(abnormal narrowing)*
Strippen *n* strip milking
Strobe *f* Weymouth (pumpkin) pine, [eastern] white pine, Pinus strobus
Strobenwollaus *f* pine bark adelges (aphid), Pineus strobi
Strobila *f* strobile, strobila *(of trematodes)*
Stroh *n* straw • **mit ~ abdecken (bedecken)** to straw • **mit ~ versorgen** to straw
~/**gehäckseltes** chopped straw
Strohabweiser *m* straw deflector
strohartig strawy, stramineous
Strohasche *f* straw ash
Strohaufschluß *m* pulping of cereal straw, cooking of straw
Strohballen *m* straw bale
Strohballenhäcksler *m* straw bale chopper
Strohballenkultur *f* straw bale culture
Strohballenpresse *f* straw baler
Strohbergung *f* straw collection
Strohbeseitigung *f* straw disposal
Strohbeseitigungsverfahren *n* straw disposal method
Strohblume *f (bot)* 1. everlasting, immortelle *(comprehensive term)*; 2. helichrysum *(genus Helichrysum)*; 3. everlasting [flower], Helichrysum bracteatum
Strohbündel *n* truss
Strohdecke *f* straw mat
Strohdieme *f* straw stack
Strohdüngung *f* straw manuring
Stroheinarbeitung *f* straw incorporation
Stroheinleger *m* straw charger
Strohelevator *m* straw lifter (carrier)
Strohertrag *m* straw yield
Strohfeime *f* straw stack
Strohfestigkeit *f* straw strength
Strohgabel *f* straw fork
strohgelb stramineous
Strohhäcksel *m* chopped straw
Strohhäckselmaschine *f,* **Strohhäcksler** *m* straw-cutting machine, straw chopper
Strohhalm *m* straw
strohig strawy
Strohkompost *m* straw compost
Strohleitblech *n* straw deflector
Strohleittrommel *f* straw stripper [beater], straw (rear) beater, stripper drum, beater behind cylinder
strohlos strawless *(e.g. animal housing)*
Strohmatte *f* straw mat
Strohmulch *m* straw mulch
Strohmulcher *m* straw mulcher
Strohpellet *n* straw pellet
Strohpelletieranlage *f* straw pelleting press
Strohpresse *f* straw press
Strohpreßling *m* straw pellet
Strohquetscher *m* straw crusher
Strohreißer *m* straw shredder (chopper)
Strohsammler *m* straw collector
Strohscheune *f* straw barn
Strohschneider *m* straw chopper
Strohschober *m* straw stack
Strohschüttler *m* straw shaker (walker, rack), dressing shoe *(of thresher)*
Strohverbrennung *f* straw burning (combustion)
Strohverbrennungsofen *m* straw burning furnace
Strohverteiler *m,* **Strohverteilvorrichtung** *f* straw spreader
Strohverwertung *f* straw utilization
Strohwein *m* straw wine
Strohwisch *m* straw wisp (whisk)
Strom *m*/**faradischer** *(vet)* faradic current
Stroma *n (bot, zoo)* stroma
Strömung *f*/**laminare** laminar flow
Strömungsleiter *m* aquifer, aquafer
Strömungszentrifuge *f* continuous conical screen centrifuge *(sugar manufacture)*

Strongylide *m* palisade worm, strongyle *(family Strongylidae)*
Strongylidose *f (vet)* strongylosis, strongylidosis
Strongyloidose *f (vet)* strongyloidiasis, strongyloidosis, redworm infestation
Strontium *n* strontium
Strophantin *n* strophantin *(glycosid)*
Strophiole *f*, **Strophiolum** *n (bot)* strophiole
Strukturbildner *m (soil)* structure-former
Strukturboden *m* polygonal soil, patterned ground
Strukturfestigkeit *f (soil)* aggregate stability
Strukturgen *n* structural gene
Strukturklasse *f (forest)* structural class
strukturlos structureless, amorphous
Strukturlosigkeit *f* amorphism
Strukturprotein *n* structural protein
Strukturschaden *m (soil)* structural damage
Strukturstabilität *f (soil)* structural stability
Strukturuntereinheit *f* subunit *(of virion's covering protein)*
Struma *f (vet)* goitre, struma, *(Am)* goiter
strumigen *(vet)* goitrogenic, goitrogenous
strumös *(vet, bot)* strumose
Strunk *m* stem, stalk, stock; runt
Struppfiedrigkeit *f* frizzle
Struppgefieder *n* frizzle
struppig shaggy; staring
Strychnin *n* strychnin[e] *(alkaloid)*
Strychninbaum *m (bot)* nux vomica, Strychnos nux-vomica
StS *s.* Stammsaatgut
Stubben *m* [tree-]stump, stub, stock *(for compounds s. under* Stock*)*
Stubben... *s. a.* Stock...
Stubbenkluppfläche *f (forest)* stump enumeration plot
Stubbenspalter *m* stump splitter
Stubbling *m s.* Stockschwämmchen
Stubendressur *f* indoor-training *(of a hunting dog)*
Stubenfliege *f* house (domestic) fly, Musca domestica
stubenrein house-trained, clean
Stück *n* Schwarzwild/kapitales capital wild boar
Studentenblume *f (bot)* French marigold, tagetes, Tagetes patula
Student-Test *m (biom)* Student's [t-]test
Student-Verteilung *f (biom)* [Student's] t distribution
Stufe *f*/hochmontane oreal belt
~/**kolline** hill belt
~/**oreale** oreal belt
Stufenboden *m* grain pan
stuhlbeinig straight behind *(hindlimb conformation)*
Stuhlrohr *n* rattan
Stülpzitze *f* inverted nipple
stummeln to stump, to cut back to stump
Stümmeln *n s.* Stehendzopfen
Stummelpflanze *f* stump [plant]

Stummelschwanz *m* dock, bob
stummelschwänzig dock-tailed
stumpf 1. blunt; dull *(e.g. a cutter)*; *(bot, zoo)* obtuse, round; 3. lustreless *(e.g. a fur)*; 4. torpid, apathetic, dull *(e.g. an animal)* • ~ **werden** to dull
stumpfblättrig obtusifolious, amblyophyllous, broad-leaved, *(Am)* broadleaf
Stumpfblättrige Sonnenzypresse *f* Japanese cypress, tree of the sun, Chamaecyparis obtusa
Stumpfblättriger Ampfer *m* common (broad-leaved) dock, bitter (red-veined) dock, bloodwort, Rumex obtusifolius
~ **Weißdorn** *m* quickthorn, [common, midland] hawthorn, Crataegus laevigata (oxyacantha)
Stumpfes Silberblatt *n* common honesty, satinflower, Lunaria annua (biennis)
stumpfgelappt *s.* stumpflappig
Stumpfheit *f* 1. bluntness, dullness; 2. lustrelessness; 3. torpor, apathy
stumpflappig *(bot)* obtusilobus
Stumpfschwarzer Getreideschimmelkäfer *m* black fungus beetle, Alphitobius laevigatus
Stundeneibisch *m* bladder ketmia, Venice mallow, flower-of-an-hour, Hibiscus trionum
Stundenleistung *f* hourly output
Stupor *m (vet)* stupor
stuporös stuporous
Sturm *m* storm, gale, strong wind
~/**orkanartiger** tempest, violent storm
~/**schwerer** whole gale
sturmfest wind-resistant, windfirm, stormproof
sturmgefährdet liable to injuries from storm
Sturmhut *m (bot)* monkshood, aconite, Aconitum napellus
Sturmschaden *m* storm damage, damage by storm, wind damage (blast)
Sturmschadenfläche *f* storm-damaged area
Sturzacker *m* new-ploughed field
stürzen/Stoppel to return the stubble
~/**vom Pferd** to dismount, to alight
Stutbuch *n* stud-book
Stute *f* mare, she-horse
~/**trächtige (tragende)** in-foal mare
Stutenabortvirus *n* equine rhinovirus (abortion virus)
Stutenbiestmilch *f* mare colostrum
Stutenfohlen *n*, **Stutenfüllen** *n* filly [foal]
Stutenfütterung *f* mare feeding
Stutenkolostrum *n* mare colostrum
Stutenmilch *f* mare's (horse) milk
Stutenserumgonadotropin *n* pregnant mare serum gonadotropin, PMSG, PMG *(sex hormone)*
Stützbaum *m* support tree *(e.g. for epiphytes)*
Stützbock *m* trestle
stutzen to cut (pinch) back, to clip, to crop, to trim, to shorten, to head [back] *(plants)*; to stump; to prune down, to poll[ard] *(a tree)*; to dub *(a hedge)*; to poll *(horns)*; to pare *(e.g. hoofs)*; to roach, to hog *(a mane)*; to dock, to bob *(a tail)*

Stutzen 616

Stutzen *m* short rifle
Stutzen *n*/**chemisches** chemical pruning; chemical pinching
Stützgewebe *n* supporting (supportive) tissue
Stützmast *m* supporting mast, trestle *(e.g. of an aerial skidder)*
Stutzpflanze *f* stump [trans]plant
Stützrad *n* landwheel, rear furrow wheel, depth wheel *(of a conventional plough)*
Stützrolle *f* track idler
Stutzschwanz *m* bob, dock; scut *(of hare or rabbit)*
Stützstab *m*, **Stützstange** *f* stake, prop
Stützvorrichtung *f* support
Stützwurzel *f* anchor[ing] root, supporting (prop, brace) root
Stützzelle *f* supporting cell
~/**Sertolische** Sertolic cell *(animal anatomy)*
St.W. *s.* Stärkewert
Stylospore *f (bot)* stylospore
subadult subadult
subakut *(vet)* subacute
Subaleuronschicht *f (bot)* subaleuron[e] layer
subalpin subalpine
subarktisch subarctic
Subassoziation *f* subassociation *(plant ecology)*
Subazidität *f* subacidity
Subclassis *f* subclass *(taxonomy)*
Subdivisio *f (zoo)* subphylum; *(bot)* subdivision *(taxonomy)*
subdominant subdominant
Suberin *n (bot)* suberin
Suberi[ni]sation *f (bot)* suberization, suberification
Subfamilia *f* subfamily *(taxonomy)*
Subforma *f* subform *(taxonomy)*
Subgenus *n* subgenus *(taxonomy)*
subhumid subhumid
Subimago *f (ent)* subimago
Subklimax *f (ecol)* subclimax
subklinisch *(vet)* subclinical
subkonjunktival subconjunctival
Subkultur *f* subculture *(microbiology)* • **eine ~ anlegen** to subculture
subkutan subcutaneous, hypodermic
Subkutangewebe *n* subcutaneous tissue, hypodermis
Subkutaninjektion *f (vet)* hypodermic [injection]
Subkutanspritze *f (vet)* hypodermic [syringe]
subkutikulär subcuticular
Subkutis *f* subcutis, subcutaneous, superficial fascia
Subletalfaktor *m* sublethal factor (gene)
Sublimat *n* mercuric chloride *(disinfectant)*
Subluxation *f (vet)* subluxation
submers submerse[d]
Submerskultur *f*, **Submersverfahren** *n* submerged culture *(microbiology)*
submikroskopisch submicroscopic
submontan submontane
submukös submucous

Submukosa *f* submucosa, submucous coat (membrane) *(animal anatomy)*
Submukosadrüsen *fpl* Brunner's glands
subnival subnival
subnormal subnormal
Subokzipitalpunktion *f (vet)* cisternal puncture
Subordo *f* suborder *(taxonomy)*
Subregnum *n* subkingdom *(taxonomy)*
Subsectio *f* subsection *(taxonomy)*
Subserie *f* subsere *(plant ecology)*
Subseries *f* subseries *(taxonomy)*
subserös subserous
Subsistenzlandwirt *m* subsistence farmer
Subsistenzlandwirtschaft *f* subsistence agriculture (farming)
subskapulär subscapular
Subspezies *f* subspecies
Substanz *f* substance, matter *(s. a. under* Mittel and Stoff*)*
~/**allelochemische** allelochemical
~/**antimikrobielle** microbicide, germicide
~/**arsenhaltige** arsenical, arsenic compound
~/**aufgelöste** solute
~/**färbende (farbgebende)** colouring [agent, matter]
~/**graue** grey matter *(of brain and spinal cord)*
~/**grenzflächenaktive** surfactant
~/**inkrustierende** encrusting (incrusting) substance
~/**körperfremde [chemische]** xenobiotic
~/**krebserzeugende** carcinogen
~/**kropferzeugende** goitrogen
~/**leukozytenschädigende** leucotoxin
~/**mineralische** mineral matter
~/**oberflächenaktive** surface-active agent (substance), surfactant
~/**organische** organic matter, OM
~ **P substance** P *(hormone)*
~/**pflanzliche** plant material (matter)
~/**strumigene** goitrogen
~/**teratogene** teratogenic [agent]
~/**vegetabilische** plant material (matter)
~/**weiße** white matter *(of brain and spinal cord)*
Substanzeinlagerung *f* **in Zellwandschichten** *(bot)* intussusception
Substanzverlust *m (slaught)* tissue loss (shrink)
substeril substerile
Substitutionsrückkreuzung *f* substitution backcrossing *(plant breeding)*
Substrat *n* substrate, substratum, matrix; medium *(esp. in microbiology)* • **in einem anderen ~ lebend** endobiotic
Substratbereitung *f* substrate preparation
Substratbrut *f* spawned (spawn-run) compost *(mushroom production)*
substratfrei bare-root[ed] *(plant)*
Substratkultur *f* substrate culture
Substratpflanze *f* plug seedling

Substratpolster *n* für mehrere Pflanzen multiplant bolster
Substratstapel *m* substrate rick
Substratvorbereitung *f* substrate preparation
subterminal subterminal
Subthalamus *m* hypothalamus *(of diencephalon)*
Subtribus *m* subtribe *(taxonomy)*
Subtropen *pl* subtropics
Subtropengürtel *m* subtropical belt
subtropisch subtropic[al], semitropical
Subtyp *m* *(soil)* subtype
Subvarietas *f* subvariety *(taxonomy)*
Subvitalfaktor *m* *(gen)* subvital factor
subzellular subcellular
Succinat *n* succinate
Succinat-CoA-Ligase, ADP-bildend *f* succinate-CoA ligase (ADP-forming)
Succinat-CoA-Ligase, GDP-bildend *f* succinate-CoA ligase (GDP-forming)
Succinatdehydrogenase *f* succinate dehydrogenase *(enzyme)*
Succinit *m* amber
Succinsäure *f* succinic (amber) acid, butanedioic acid
Succinyl[bi]cholin *n s.* Suxamethonium
such! [hie] seek! *(command to dog)*
Suchbock *m* teaser (vasectomized) ram
Suche *f (hunt)* tracking
Sucheber *m* teaser boar
suchen/Futter to forage
Suchhengst *m* teaser stallion
Suchtest *m* *(biom)* screening [method, test]
Sucrose *f s.* Saccharose
Sud *m* brew, gyle
Südamerikanischer Frauenschuh *m* *(bot)* Lady's (Venus's) slipper *(genus Phragmipedium)*
Sudangras *n* Sudan grass, Sorghum sudanense
Süddeutsches Kaltblut *n* Noric, South German coldblood *(horse breed)*
Südfrucht *f* tropical fruit
Südhang *m* southern (south-facing) slope
Sudhaus *n* brew-house
Sudhausausbeute *f* brew-house yield
Südländischer Hornbaum *m* oriental hornbeam, Carpinus orientalis
Südliche Rinderdasselfliege *f* common cattle grub, heel fly, Hypoderma lineatum
Südlicher Erdbeerwickler *m* *(ent)* strawberry leafroller, Ancylis comptana
~ **Schüppling** *m* poplar mushroom, Agrocybe aegerita
~ **Zürgelbaum** *m* nettle tree, Mediterranean hackberry, Celtis australis
Südliches Bohnenmosaikvirus *n* southern bean mosaic virus, SBMV
~ **Wurzelgallenälchen** *n* southern root-knot nematode, Meloidogyne incognita
Südsee-Eisenholz *n* Alexandrian laurel, Calophyllum inophyllum

Südseemyrte *f* tea-tree, Leptospermum scoparium
Suffokation *f* suffocation, asphyxiation
Suffolkpferd *n* Suffolk horse (punch) *(breed)*
Suffolkschaf *n* Suffolk *(sheep breed)*
Suhle *f* wallow, soiling pool
suhlen/sich to wallow, to welter
sukkulent succulent
Sukkulente *f (bot)* succulent
Sukkulentensavanne *f* succulent savanna[h]
Sukkulentenwüste *f* succulent desert
Sukkulenz *f* succulence, succulency
Sukzession *f (ecol)* succession
Sukzessionsabfolge *f* sere
Sukzessionslehre *f* syndynamics
Sukzessionsstadium *n* seral stage
Sukzinat *n s.* Succinat
Sulfachinoxalin *n* 1. sulphaquinoxaline *(sulphonamide)*; 2. sulfachinoxalin *(rodenticide)*
Sulfachlorpyrazidin *n* sulphachlorpyrazidine *(sulphonamide)*
Sulfadiazin *n* sulphadiazine *(sulphonamide)*
Sulfadimethoxin *n* sulphadimethoxine *(sulphonamide)*
Sulfadimidin *n* sulphadimidine *(sulphonamide)*
Sulfadoxin *n* sulphadoxine *(sulphonamide)*
Sulfafurazol *n* sulphafurazole *(sulphonamide)*
Sulfallat *n* sulfallate *(herbicide)*
Sulfamerazin *n* sulphamerazine *(sulphonamide)*
Sulfamethazin *n s.* Sulfadimidin
Sulfamethoxazol *n* sulphomethoxazole *(sulphonamide)*
Sulfamethoxypyridazin *n* sulphamethoxypyridazine *(sulphonamide)*
Sulfamethylpyrimidin *n s.* Sulfamerazin
Sulfamonomethoxin *n* sulphamonomethoxine *(sulphonamide)*
Sulfanilamid *n* sulphanilamide *(sulphonamide)*
2-Sulfanilamidopyridin *n s.* Sulfapyridin
2-Sulfanilamidothiazol *n s.* Sulfathiazol
Sulfanitran *n* sulphanitran *(coccidiostatic)*
Sulfapyrazol *n* sulphapyrazole *(sulphonamide)*
Sulfapyridin *n* sulphapyridine *(sulphonamide)*
Sulfapyrimidin *n s.* Sulfadiazin
Sulfatase *f* sulphatase *(enzyme)*
Sulfataufschluß *m* sulphate cooking (pulping) *(of wood)*
Sulfathiazol *n* sulphathiazole, 2-sulphanilamidothiazole *(sulphonamide)*
Sulfatkochlauge *f* sulphate liquor
Sulfatlignin *n* sulphate lignin, thiolignin
Sulfatterpentin *n* sulphate turpentine
Sulfatzellstoff *m* sulphate pulp
Sulfhydrylgruppe *f* sulphydryl (thiol) group, mercapto group
Sulfhydryloxidase *f* sulphydryl oxidase *(enzyme)*
Sulfid *n* sulphide
Sulfisoxazol *n s.* Sulfafurazol
Sulfitablauge *f* sulphite [waste] liquor, sulphite pulp mill waste, sulphite lye

Sulfitation

Sulfitation f sulphitation *(sugar manufacture)*
Sulfitaufschluß m sulphite cooking (pulping) *(of wood)*
Sulfitlauge f s. Sulfitablauge
Sulfitoxidase f sulphite oxidase *(enzyme)*
Sulfitzellstoff m sulphite pulp
Sulfonamid n sulphonamide
Sulfonamidpräparat n sulpha drug
Sulfonat n sulphonate
Sulfonierung f sulphonation
Sulfosalicylsäureprobe f sulphosalicylic acid test *(for detecting urinary protein)*
Sulfotep[p] n sulfotep[p] *(insecticide)*
Sulfurierung f s. Sulfonierung
Sulglycapin n sulglycapin *(herbicide)*
Sulky n sulky; *(forest)* logging (high, big) wheels, slip-tongue cart, katydid
Sulmycin n gentamicin *(antibiotic)*
Sulprofos n sulprofos *(insecticide)*
Sultanine f sultana, plum
Sumach m *(bot)* sumac[h] *(genus Rhus)*
Sumachblätter npl sumac[h]
Sumatra f Sumatra *(breed of fowl)*
Summe f **der Abweichungsquadrate** *(biom)* sum of squares
Sumpf m swamp, marsh[land], [quaking] bog, quag[mire], slough
Sumpfbärlapp m marsh club-moss, Lycopodium inundatum
Sumpfbiber m coypu, coypou, nutria, Myocastor coypus
Sumpfbiberfarm f coypu farm
Sumpfbiberfell n, **Sumpfbiberpelz** m nutria
Sumpfboden m s. Sumpf
Sumpfbrachsenkraut n quillwort, Isoetes lacustris
Sumpfdotterblume f marsh marigold, kingcup, *(Am)* cowslip, Caltha palustris
Sumpfeibe f 1. swamp cypress *(genus Taxodium)*; 2. bald cypress, Taxodium distichum var. distichum; 3. bald cypress, Taxodium distichum var. nutans
Sumpfeibisch m 1. common rose mallow, Hibiscus moscheutos; 2. musk mallow, Abelmoschus moschatus, Hibiscus abelmoschus
Sumpfeiche f swamp Spanish oak, pin (water) oak, Quercus palustris
Sumpfgas n marsh gas, methane
Sumpfgarbe f sneezewort [yarrow], Achillea ptarmica
Sumpfhimbeere f Lucretia dewberry, Rubus flagellaris
Sumpfhornklee m marsh (large) bird's-foot trefoil, big trefoil, wetland deer vetch, Lotus uliginosus
Sumpfhuhn n rail *(family Rallidae)*
sumpfig swampy, marshy, boggy, sloughy, uliginose, uliginous
Sumpfigkeit f poachiness *(of a soil)*
Sumpfiris f yellow[flag] iris, sword-flag, Iris pseudacorus
Sumpfkalla f *(bot)* 1. calla *(genus Calla)*; 2. wild calla, Calla palustris
Sumpfkiefer f swamp (long-leaf) pine, American pitch-pine, Georgia (southern yellow) pine, Pinus palustris
Sumpfkratzdistel f marsh thistle, Cirsium palustre
Sumpfland n bogland, swampland, marsh[land], fen [soil]
Sumpflärche f tamarack [larch], eastern larch, hackmatack, Larix laricina (americana)
sumpfliebend uliginose, uliginous
Sumpfmoosbeere f mossberry, *(Am)* European cranberry, Vaccinium oxycoccos
Sumpfmyrte f sweet gale, bog myrtle, Myrica gale
Sumpfohreule f short-eared owl, Asio flammeus
Sumpfotter m European mink, Mustela (Lutreola) lutreola
Sumpfpflanze f bog (marsh, paludal) plant, helophyte
Sumpfporst m marsh (Labrador) tea, crystal tea [ledum], wild rosemary, Ledum palustre
Sumpfried n 1. spike-rush *(genus Eleocharis)*; 2. water chestnut, Eleocharis dulcis
Sumpfriedgras n s. Sumpfsegge
Sumpfrispengras n fowl meadow (blue) grass, swamp meadow-grass, Poa palustris
Sumpfschachtelhalm m marsh horse-tail, marsh equisetum, cat-whistles, pewter grass, Equisetum palustre
Sumpfschlangenwurz f s. Sumpfkalla
Sumpfschnake f [common, marsh] crane-fly, *(Am)* European crane-fly, Tipula paludosa
Sumpfschnepfe f common snipe, Capella (Gallingo) gallingo
Sumpfschotenklee m s. Sumpfhornklee
Sumpfsegge f marsh sedge, Carex acutiformis
Sumpfsimse f s. Sumpfried
Sumpfstraußgras n brown bent[-grass], dog (velvet) bent, Agrostis canina
Sumpfvergißmeinnicht n *(bot)* water forget-me-not, Myosotis palustris
Sumpfwald m bog (swamp) forest
Sumpfwiese f swamp meadow
Sumpfwurz f *(bot)* helleborine *(genus Epipactis)*
Sumpfziest m marsh (clown's) woundwort, Stachys palustris
Sumpfzypresse f s. Sumpfeibe
Sunnhanf m sunn [crotalaria, hemp], Crotalaria juncea
Superazidität f superacidity
superdominant *(gen)* superdominant, overdominant
Superdominanz f *(gen)* superdominance, overdominance
Superelite f superelite
Superelitesaatgut n certified seed
Superfamilia f superfamily *(taxonomy)*
Superfekundation f *(zoo)* superfecundation
Superfetation f superfoetation

Supergen n supergene
Superinfektion f (phyt, vet) superinfection, reinfection
Superordo f superorder (taxonomy)
Superovulation f superovulation
Superoxiddismutase f superoxide dismutase (enzyme)
Superparasit m superparasite
Superparasitismus m superparasitism
Superphosphat n superphosphate (fertilizer)
~ **aus Knochenmehl** bone superphosphate
Supersekretion f hypersecretion
Supersuperelitesaatgut n registered seed
Supination f supination
Supinator[muskel] m supinator [muscle]
Supp. s. Suppositorium
Suppengemüse n pot-herb
Suppengrün n vegetables for soup-making
Suppenhuhn n stewing chicken (hen)
Suppenkraut n pot-herb
Suppositorium n (vet) suppository
Suppressor m (gen) suppressor
Suppressormutation f suppressor mutation
Suppuration f (vet) suppuration, purulence
Supravitalfärbung f supravital staining (e.g. of cells)
Suramin n suramin (anthelminthic)
Suratikäse m surati cheese
Surenbaum m toon [tree], moulmein (Burma, red) cedar, Toona ciliata, Cedrela toona
Surfaktant m surfactant, surface-active agent (compound)
Surra f (vet) surra (caused by Trypanosoma evansi)
Surveillance f s. Überwachung 1.
Survey m survey
Suspension f suspension
Suspensions[flüssig]konzentrat n flowable (plant protectant formulation)
Suspensionskultur f suspension culture
Suspensionsspritzmittel n wettable powder, w.p., WP
Suspensor m (bot) suspensor
süß sweet, sugary (esp. taste); sweet, fragrant (smell esp. of flowers)
~ **und saftig** mellow (fruit) • ~ **und saftig werden** to mellow (fruit)
Süßdolde f [garden] myrrh, sweet cicely, Myrrhis odorata
Süße Balsampflaume f otaheite apple, Spondias dulcis (cytherea)
~ **Cassava** f s. Süßer Maniok
~ **Kalabasch** f purple granadilla, Passiflora edulis
~ **Zitrone** f sweet lemon (lime), Citrus limetta
Süßer Maniok m (bot) sweet cassava (manioc), Manihot dulcis var. multifida
~ **Tragant** m milk-vetch, Astragalus glycyphyllos
Süßes Besenkraut n sweetweed, sweet broomweed, Scoparia dulcis

~ **Hohlgras** n sweet pitted grass, Bothriochloa insculpta
Sussex n 1. Sussex (breed of fowl); 2. s. Sussexrind
~ **Spaniel** m Sussex spaniel (dog breed)
Sussexrind n Sussex [cattle] (breed)
Süßgerinnung f sweet curdling (of milk)
Süßgras n grass (family Poaceae = Gramineae)
Süßgräser npl grass family (family Poaceae = Gramineae) • **die ~ betreffend** gramin[ac]eous
Süßholz n 1. liquorice, licorice (genus Glycyrrhiza); 2. liquorice, licorice, sweet-root, Glycyrrhiza glabra
Süßholzwurzel f liquorice, sweet-root
Süßkartoffel f sweet potato, batata, (Am) yam, Ipomoea batatas
Süßkirsche f sweet (wild) cherry, mazard [cherry], mazzard, gean, Prunus avium
Süßklee m esparcet, common sainfoin, cockshead, Onobrychis viciifolia
Süßkrätzer m green wine
Süßlupine f sweet lupin[e]
Süßmais m (Am) sweet (sugar) corn, Zea mays convar. saccharata
Süßmolke f sweet whey
Süßmolkenpulver n sweet whey powder
Süßmost m [unfermented] fruit juice
Süßrahmbutter f sweet-cream butter
Süßsack m s. Rahmapfel
Süßstoff m sweetener
Süßwasser n freshwater
Süßwasseraalseuche f (vet, pisc) red disease
Süßwasserablagerung f lacustrine deposit
Süßwasserfisch m freshwater fish
Süßwasserfischkultur f freshwater fish culture
Süßwasserkrebs m crayfish (comprehensive term)
Süßwassermuschel f freshwater mussel (comprehensive term)
Süßwasserökologie f freshwater ecology
Süßwasserplankton n limnoplankton
Süßwassersee m freshwater lake
Süßweichsel f morello [cherry], Prunus cerasus ssp. var. austera
Süßwein m sweet wine, dessert (appetizer) wine
Süßwurzel f (bot) skirret, chervin, Sium sisarum
suszeptibel susceptible
Suszeptibilität f susceptibility
Sutur[a] f 1. (vet) [surgical] suture; 2. [bone] suture
Suxamethonium n suxamethonium (muscle relaxant)
Svedbergzentrifuge f ultracentrifuge
S-Viruskrankheit f der Kartoffel potato mild (simple) mosaic (virosis)
Swaledale[schaf] n Swaledale, Swaddle (sheep breed)
Swartziol n kaempferol (plant dye)
S-Wert m (soil) S value, saturation value
Syenit m (soil) syenite

Sykomore

Sykomore f sycamore [fig], sycomore [fig], mulberry (Pharaoh's) fig, wild fig [tree], Ficus sycomorus
Sylvinit m sylvinite *(potassium fertilizer)*
Sylvinsäure f abiet[in]ic acid, sylvic acid *(resin acid, diterpene)*
Symbiont m symbiont, symbiote
symbiontisch symbiontic
Symbiose f symbiosis
Symbiosepartner m, **Symbiot** m s. Symbiont
Sympathikolytikum n sympatholytic [agent]
Sympathikomimetikum n sympathomimetic [agent]
sympatrisch *(ecol)* sympatric
sympetal *(bot)* sympetalous
Symphyle m s. Zwergfüßer
Symphyse f symphysis *(animal anatomy)*
Symplast m *(bot)* symplast
Sympodium n *(bot)* sympodium, sympode, false axis
Symptom n symptom, diagnostic
Symptomatik f s. Symptomatologie
symptomatisch symptomatic
Symptomatologie f symptomatology
Symptomkomplex m s. Syndrom
symptomlos symptomless
Symptomlosigkeit f symptomlessness
Symptomrückbildung f *(phyt)* masking
Synanthie f *(bot)* synanthy
synanthrop *(ecol)* synanthropic
Synapse f nerve junction, synapse, synapsis
~/neuromuskuläre myoneural junction
Synapsenbläschen n synaptic vesicle
Synapsis f synapsis, synapse, syndesis *(meiosis)*
synaptisch synaptic
Synärese f syneresis, shrinkage *(e.g. of gels)*
Synarthrose f synarthrosis
Synchondrosis f cartilaginous joint
Synchorologie f synchorology
Syndesmose f syndesmosis
Syndrom n *(phyt, vet)* syndrome
~/nephrotisches nephrotic syndrome
Syndynamik f syndynamics
synergetisch s. synergistisch
Synergide f *(bot)* synergid
Synergismus m synergism, synergy
Synergist m synergist
synergistisch synergistic, synerg[et]ic
Synfloreszenz f *(bot)* synflorescence
Syngamie f *(bot)* syngamy
Syngamose f the gapes *(of poultry, caused by Syngamus trachea)*
syngenetisch syngenetic
synkarp *(bot)* syncarpous
Synkarpie f syncarpy
Synkaryon m *(gen)* synkaryon
Synökologie f synecology, biocoenology, biocoenotics
synökologisch synecological
Synostose f synostosis
Synovex n synovex *(anabolic)*

Synovia f synovia, synovial fluid
Synovialgelenk n synovial joint
Synovialitis f s. Synovitis
Synovialmembran f synovial membrane
Synovitis f *(vet)* synovitis
Synphänologie f synphenology
synsepal *(bot)* synsepalous
Synthase f synthase *(enzyme)*
Synthese f synthesis
~/biologische biosynthesis
Synthesephase f S phase *(of cell cycle)*
Synthetase f synthetase, ligase *(enzyme)*
synthetisieren to synthesize
Synusie f synusia, synusium, layer *(plant ecology)*
Synzytium n syncytium
Syringaldehyd m syringaldehyde *(lignin precursor)*
Syrinx f syrinx *(vocal organ of birds)*
Syrische Biene f Syrian bee, Apis mellifica syriaca
Syrischer Rosenbisch m rose-of-Sharon, Hibiscus syriacus
~ Schuppenkopf m *(bot)* Syrian cephalaria, Cephalaria syriaca
Syrosem m, **Syrosjom** m *(soil)* syrozem
System n/**endokrines** endocrine system
~/exkretorisches excretory system
~/hämolytisches haemolytic system
~/Haverssches Haversian system, osteone *(of lamellar bone)*
~/inkretorisches endocrine system
~/kardiovaskuläres cardio-vascular system
~/lichterntendes light-harvesting system, LHS *(photosynthesis)*
~/lymphatisches lymphatic system
~/retikuloendotheliales reticulo-endothelial system
Systemanalyse f system analysis
Systematik f systematics, taxonomy
Systematiker m systematist, taxonomist
systematisch systematic, taxonomic
Systembiozid n systemic
Systemfungizid n systemic fungicide
Systemherbizid n systemic herbicide
systemisch systemic
Systeminsektizid n systemic insecticide
Systemnematizid n systemic nematicide
Systemwirkung f systemic property *(of a plant protectant)*
Systole f systole *(of the heart)*
systolisch systolic
Szikboden m szik soil
Szintigraphie f *(vet)* scintigraphy
Szirrhus m *(vet)* scirrhus

T

T. s. 1. Trockensubstanz; 2. Drehmoment
Tabak m 1. tobacco[-plant], Indian weed, nicotiana *(genus Nicotiana)*; 2. Virginian (common) tobacco, Nicotiana tabacum

Tabakalkaloid n tobacco alkaloid
Tabakanbau m tobacco growing
Tabakätz[mosaik]virus n tobacco etch virus, TEV
Tabakblasenfuß m onion thrips (louse), Thrips tabaci
Tabakblatt n tobacco-leaf
Tabakerntemaschine f tobacco harvester
Tabakkäfer m tobacco (cigarette) beetle, Lasioderma serricorne
Tabaklauge f tobacco liquor
Tabakmauchevirus n tobacco rattle virus, TRV
Tabakmosaik n (phyt) tobacco mosaic, calico disease
Tabakmosaikvirus n tobacco mosaic virus, TMV
Tabakmotte f tobacco (walnut) moth, Ephestia elutella
Tabaknekrose f (phyt) tobacco necrosis
Tabaknekrosevirus n tobacco necrosis virus, TNV
Tabakpflanze f s. Tabak 1.
Tabakpflanzmaschine f tobacco planter
Tabakrattlevirus n s. Tabakmauchevirus
Tabakringfleckenvirus n tobacco ring spot virus, TRSV
Tabaksamen m tobacco seed
Tabaksamenöl n tobacco seed oil
Tabaksetzling m tobacco seedling
Tabakstrichelvirus n tobacco streak virus, TSV
Tabaktrockenschuppen m tobacco curing shed
Tabakwürger m (bot) branched (hemp) broomrape, Orobanche ramosa
Tablette f tablet
Tachometer n speedometer, tachometer
Tachykardie f (vet) tachycardia
~/paroxysmale paroxysmal tachycardia
Tachymetrie f tacheometry (geodesy)
Tachypnoe f (vet) polypnoea
Tachysterol n tachysterol
Taedaföhre f loblolly (foxtail) pine, slash (old-field) pine, Pinus taeda
Taenia f 1. taenia, band (of nervous or muscular tissue); 2. tapeworm (esp. of genus Taenia) (s. a. Bandwurm)
Taeniasis f, **Taeniosis** f (vet) taeniasis, teniasis
Tafel f der Standortbonität (forest) soil-site index table
Tafelapfel m eating (dessert) apple
Tafelbutter f table butter
Tafelente f [common] pochard, Aythya ferina
Tafelgeflügel n table poultry
Tafelgemüse n table vegetable
Tafellack m shellac, lac
Tafelnuß f table nut
Tafelobst n dessert fruit
Tafelqualität f eating (dessert) quality (of fruit)
Tafelrübe f table beet
Tafelsalz n cooking salt
Tafeltraube f table grape
Tafelwein m 1. table wine; 2. table grape
Tafelweintraube f table grape

Tafelzucker m table sugar
Tag m day • **am ~ blühend** diurnal • **nur einen ~ dauernd** ephemeral
~ des Baumes Arbor Day (esp. in USA and Australia)
tagaktiv (zoo) diurnal
Tagblindheit f day blindness, hemeralopia
Tagebaukippe f strip-mine spoil
Tagelöhner m cottager
Tagesanbruch m daybreak
Tagesaufnahme f daily intake (esp. of an agent)
~/annehmbare (duldbare) acceptable daily intake, ADI
Tagesdosis f daily dose (s. a. Tagesaufnahme)
Tagesernte[menge] f daily pick (orcharding)
Tagesfutteraufnahme f daily feed intake
Tagesfuttermenge f daily [feed] ration, daily amount of feed, allowance
Tagesfutterverzehr m daily feed consumption
Tageslänge f day length
Tageslicht n daylight
Tageslichtverkürzung f shortening of daylight
Tageslichtverlängerung f lengthening of daylight
Tagesmitteltemperatur f mean daily temperature, daily mean temperature
Tagesration f s. Tagesfuttermenge
Tagesrhythmus m diurnal rhythm
~/endogener circadian rhythm
Tagessichtigkeit f night-blindness; photopia, nyctalopia
Tageszunahme f daily [rate of] gain (esp. of fattening stock)
~ an Lebendmasse daily live weight gain
~/durchschnittliche (mittlere) average daily gain
Tagewerk n man-day
Taggreifvogel m day-bird of prey, diurnal bird of prey
Taglilie f day lily, hemerocallis (genus Hemerocallis)
Tag-Nacht-Rhythmus m day-night rhythm
tagneutral day-neutral (plant)
Tagperiode f light period (of a lighting regime)
Tagverkürzung f shortening of daylight
Tagverlängerung f lengthening of daylight
Tagwasser n (soil) surface water
Tahitiapfel m otaheite apple, Spondias dulcis (cytherea)
Tahitikastanie f Tahiti (Polynesian) chestnut, Inocarpus edulis
Tahitipfeilwurz f East Indian arrowroot, Tacca leontopetaloides
Taiga f taiga
Taigawald m taiga forest
Takadiastase f takadiastase (mixture of enzymes)
Ta-Koshie-Baum m s. Zahnbürstenbaum
taktil tactile, tangible
Takyr[boden] m takyr [soil]
TAL s. Tyrosinammoniumlyase
Tal n valley

Tal

~/enges glen
Talboden m 1. alluvial soil; 2. s. Talsohle
Talerfleck m (vet) dollar spot
Talerkürbis m oyster-nut, Telfairia pedata
Talfahrt f drive (rafting)
Talfanerkrankung f Teschen (talfan) disease (virosis of swine)
Talg m 1. tallow (rendered fat of cattle and sheep); 2. sebum [grease] (secretion of specialized glands of the skin)
Talgdrüse f sebaceous gland
Talgdrüsenretentionszyste f (vet) atheroma
Talgfluß m (vet) seborrhoea
talgig tallowy
Talgigkeit f tallowiness (e.g. of milk)
talgliefernd sebiferous
Talgsumach m (bot) Japan wax, Toxicodendron succedaneum, Rhus succedanea
Talipotpalme f talipot [palm], Corypha umbraculifera
Talipotpalmenstroh n buntal
Talk m s. Talkum
Talkessel m valley basin, corrie, cirque
Talkum n talc[um] (non-clay mineral)
Talkumpuder m talc[um] powder
Tallharz n tall-oil resin
Tallöl n tall oil
Tallölkolophonium n tall-oil rosin
Tallpech n tall-oil pitch
Tallseife f tall-oil soap
Talmoor n valley bog
Talpa f s. Widerristfistel
Talsohle f valley bottom (floor)
Talsperre f dam, barrage, impoundment
Talweg m valley line
Talwind m valley wind
Tamarak n tamarack (wood from Larix laricina)
Tamarinde f, **Tamarindenbaum** m (bot) tamarind, Tamarindus indica
Tamarindenfrucht f tamarind
Tamarindenöl n tamarind oil
Tamariske f tamarisk, flowering cypress (genus Tamarix)
TÄMV s. Tabakätz[mosaik]virus
Tamworthschwein n Tamworth (pig breed)
Tandem n s. Tandemgespann
Tandemachsanhänger m tandem axle trailer
Tandemachse f tandem axle
Tandemanordnung f tandem
Tandemanspannung f tandem
Tandemantrieb m tandem drive
Tandemduplikation f (gen) tandem duplication
Tandemfusion f, **Tandem-Fusions-Translokation** f (gen) tandem fusion
Tandemgespann n tandem [cart]
Tandemmelkstand m, **Tandemmelkstandanlage** f tandem [milking] parlour
Tandemräder npl tandem wheels
Tandemscheibenegge f tandem (double-action) disk harrow

Tandemschlepper m tandem tractor
Tandemselektion f tandem selection (culling)
Tandemtraktor m tandem tractor
Tandemwaage f tandem weighing machine
Tandemwalzenmähquetscher m tandem roll mower conditioner
Tang m seaweed (feed)
Tangelo f tangelo (cross of mandarin and grapefruit)
Tangelrendzina f (soil) subalpine rendzina
Tangentialschleuder f (api) tangential extractor
Tangentialschnitt m flat (plain) sawing, tangential (through and through) cutting (timber conversion)
Tangerine f, **Tangerorange** f tangerine, kid-glove orange, Citrus [reticulata var.] deliciosa
Tanghinin n tanghinin (glycoside)
Tangkonzentrat n seaweed concentrate
Tangmehl n seaweed (feed)
Tangor f tangor (cross of mandarin and orange)
Tania f yautia[s], tannia, coco yam, American taro, Xanthosoma sagittifolium
Täniose f s. Taeniasis
Tank m tank; fuel tank; cistern
Tankanhänger m tank trailer, trailed tanker
Tankbehandlung f bulk handling (e.g. of milk)
Tankfahrzeug n [road] tanker
Tankfülleinrichtung f tank filling device
Tankfüllschnecke f tank delivery auger
Tankgärverfahren n bulk fermentation method (wine-making)
Tankkultur f tank-farming
Tankmilch f bulk milk
Tankmilchbehandlung f bulk-milk handling
Tankmilchkühler m bulk-milk cooler
Tankmischmethode f tank-mix method
Tankmischung f tank mix[ture]
Tankwagen m [road] tanker; bulk lorry
Tannase f tannase (enzyme)
Tanne f fir [tree] (genus Abies)
tannenartig abietineous
Tannenborkenkäfer m silver fir bark-beetle, white spruce [bark-]beetle, Cryphalus piceae
Tannengallaus f gall aphid (family Adelgidae = Chermesidae)
Tannenhäher m nutcracker, nutbreaker, Nucifraga caryocatactes
Tannenholz n fir
Tannenklee m woundwort, kidney-vetch, Anthyllis vulneraria
Tannenknospenlaus f s. Tannenstammrindenlaus
Tannenkrebs m witches' broom fir rust
Tannenlaus f s. Tannengallaus
Tannenmistel f mistletoe, Viscum album ssp. abietis
Tannennaßkern m wetwood of fir
Tannensamengallmücke f fir seed gall-midge, Resseliella piceae
Tannenstammrindenlaus f fir bark-louse, balsam woolly aphid, Adelges (Dreyfusia) piceae

Tannensterben n [silver] fir die back
Tannentriebwickler m (ent) silver fir shoot tortricid, silver fir leaf-roller, Cacoecia murinana
Tannenwald m fir forest
Tannia f s. Tania
Tannin n tannin; gallotannic acid, gallotannin
Tanninfärbung f tannic discolo[u]ration (of beech and oak)
Tanningerbstoff m s. Tannin
tänzeln to prance
Tanzmeisterstellung f knock knees, knee-narrow (toe-out) conformation (of forelimbs)
Tapetum n (bot, zoo) tapetum
Tapioka f tapioca (starch product from cassava tubers)
Tapiokamehl n tapioca meal
Tarentaise n Tarentaise (cattle breed)
Tarif m tariff
~/mehrere Standortklassen zusammenfassender (forest) compound tariff
Tarntracht f (bot, zoo) mimesis
Taro m (bot) taro, dasheen, elephant's-ear, cocoyam, Colocasia esculenta
Taromosaikvirus n dasheen mosaic virus
Tarpan m (zoo) tarpan
Tarpaulin m tarpaulin, tarp
Tarragona m Tarragona (wine)
Tarsaldrüse f tarsal (Meibomian) gland (animal anatomy)
Tarsenglied n tarsal segment (of insect's leg)
Tarsus m tarsus (animal anatomy)
Tasche f bag; pocket; (zoo) bursa, pouch
Taschenklappe f atrioventricular valve (of the heart)
Taschenkrankheit f der Pflaume (phyt) plum-pocket disease (caused by Taphrina pruni)
Taschenratte f pocket gopher (family Geomyidae)
tastbar palpable, tangible, tactile
tastend tactile
Taster m feeler; (zoo) palp[us]; (ent) antenna
Tasthaar n tactile (sensory) hair
Tastkörperchen n touch body (corpuscle)
Tastrad n sensing (feeler) wheel, roller feeler
Tastradköpfer m feeler [wheel] topper
Tastsinn m tactile sense, sense of touch
Tastvorrichtung f feeler
Tatarenahorn m Tatarian maple, Acer tataricum
Tatarenhafer m bristle[-pointed] oat, black oat, Avena nuda [ssp. nuda], Avena strigosa
Tatarische Heckenkirsche f Tatarian (bush) honeysuckle, garden fly honeysuckle, Lonicera tatarica
Tatarischer Ahorn[baum] m s. Tatarenahorn
~ Buchweizen m Tatary buckwheat, India-wheat, Fagopyrum tataricum
~ Hartriegel m Tatarian dogwood, Cornus alba
Tatarkorn n s. Tatarischer Buchweizen
tatauieren s. tätowieren
tätowieren to tattoo

Tätowierung f tattoo
Tätowierzange f tattoo forceps, tattooing pliers
Tau m dew
Tau n rope
taub (bot) barren; empty, blind (seed)
taubblühend sterile-flowered
Taube f pigeon, dove (family Columbidae; genus Columba)
Taube Trespe f sterile (barren) brome, poverty brome[-grass], Bromus sterilis
Taubenbaum m pocket handkerchief tree, Davidia involucrata
Taubenerbse f pigeon (dwarf) pea, Congo pea (bean), Cajanus cajan (indicus)
Taubenflugloch n pigeon-hole
Taubenfütterung f pigeon feeding
Taubenhalter m pigeon-fancier
Taubenhaus n pigeon-house
Taubenkerbel m (bot) [common] fumitory, Fumaria officinalis
Taubenkot m pigeon dung
Taubenkropf m bladder campion, spattling poppy, Silene vulgaris (inflata)
Taubenmist m pigeon dung
Taubenpocken pl (vet) pigeon pox
Taubenschlag m pigeonry, dovecot[e], loft
Taubenstall m pigeon-house
Taubenzecke f fowl tick, Argas reflexus
Taubenzüchter m pigeon-fancier
Tauber m, **Täuberich** m cock pigeon
Taubheit f 1. (vet) deafness; 2. s. Blütentaubheit
Taubildung f dew formation
Täubling m (bot) russula (genus Russula)
Taubnessel f dead nettle (genus Lamium)
Tauchbad n dip, dipper
Tauchbadlösung f dip [solution]
Tauchbehandlung f dip treatment
~ von Blumenzwiebeln bulb dip [treatment]
Tauchdesinfektionspräparat n dip
~ für Schafe sheep-dip
Tauchentleerung f water flo[a]tation (fruit handling)
Taucher m bobber (rafting)
Tauchflüssigkeit f dip [solution]
Tauchkolbenpumpe f plunger pump
Tauchkühler m immersion cooler
Tauchlösung f s. Tauchbadlösung
Tauchmilchkühler m immersion milk cooler
Tauchpumpe f immersion (submersible) pump
Tauchtränkung f steeping [treatment] (wood preservation)
Tauchverfahren n pickling method (of seed treatment)
Tauchvogel m diving bird
Tauchwanne f dipper
tauen to thaw
Taufliege f fruit (vinegar, ferment) fly, drosophila (genus Drosophila)
Tauglichkeit f fitness (animal breeding)

Tauhimbeere

Tauhimbeere *f* Lucretia dewberry, Rubus flagellaris
Taumelkerbel *m* rough (royal) chervil, Chaerophyllum temulum
Taumelkrankheit *f* **des Geflügels** avian rotator disease
Taumelkreissäge *f* wobble saw
Taumellager *n* wobble (tumbler) bearing
Taumellolch *m* (bot) [bearded] darnel, cockle, Lolium temulentum
Taumelsägeblatt *n* wobble saw
Taumelsternrotoregge *f* swash-star rotary harrow
Taumesser *m* drosometer
Taumessung *f* dew measurement
Taungya-Plantage *f* taungya plantation
Taungya-System *n* taungya system (method), agri-silviculture (in the tropics)
Taupunkt *m* dew-point
Taupunkthygrometer *n* dew-point hygrometer
Taupunkttemperatur *f* dew-point temperature
Taurocholsäure *f* taurocholic acid
Taurodesoxycholsäure *f* taurodeoxycholic acid
Tausalz *n* thawing (de-icing) salt
Tausalzschaden *m* damage due to road salting
Tausendfüß[l]er *m* 1. millepede, millipede (class Diplopoda); 2. myriapod, myriopod (group Myriapoda)
Tausendgüldenkraut *n* (bot) 1. centaury (genus Centaurium); 2. [common] centaury, Centaurium erythraea (minus)
Tausendkern *m* rupture-wort, Herniaria glabra
Tausendkopfkohl *m* thousand-head[ed] kale, Brassica oleracea convar. oleracea var. ramosa
Tausendkornmasse *f* thousand grain (kernel, corn) weight, test weight
Tausendschön[chen] *n* [English, true] daisy, Bellis perennis
Tauwaage *f* electronic leaf (gardening)
Tauwetter *n* thaw
Tauwurm *m* dew worm, night crawler, Lumbricus terrestris
Taxation *f* (forest) appraisal, appraisement, assessment, estimate, timber cruising
~ **mittels Winkelzählprobe** angle count cruising
Taxationslinie *f* assessment line
Taxator *m* appraiser, cruiser, enumeration officer
Taxidermie *f* taxidermy
taxieren (forest) to appraise, to assess, to cruise, to estimate
Taxifolin *n* taxifolin (flavonoid)
Taxin *n* taxine (alkaloid)
Taxis *f* taxis (reflex or orientational movement by motile and esp. simple organisms)
Taxon *n* taxon (taxonomic group or entity)
Taxonom *m* taxonomist, systematist
Taxonomie *f* taxonomy, systematics
taxonomisch taxonomic, systematic
Tazette[nnarzisse] *f* French daffodil, bunch-flowered narcissus, polyanthus [narcissus], paperwhite [narcissus], Narcissus tazetta

TB, Tbk *s.* Tuberkulose
TC *s.* Tetracyclin
TCA 1. TCA (herbicide, growth inhibitor); 2. *s.* Natriumtrichloracetat; 3. *s.* Trichloressigsäure
TCE-Styren *n* TCE-styrene (herbicide)
Teak[holz]baum *m* (bot) teak, Tectona grandis
Technik *f* 1. technique, method; 2. technology
technisch technical; technological
Technologe *m* technologist
Technologie *f* **der Milchverarbeitung** dairy (milk) technology
technologisch technological
Teckel *m* dachshund (dog breed)
Tecnazen *n* tecnazene, TCNB (fungicide)
Tecomarie *f* Cape honeysuckle, red trumpet flower, Tecomaria capensis
Tecoram *n* tecoram (fungicide)
Tee *m* 1. tea; 2. *s.* Teestrauch
~/**grüner** green tea
Teeblatt *n* tea-leaf
Teeblattknospe *f* tip
Tee-Erntemaschine *f* tea harvester
Teepflanzung *f* tea plantation
Teepflückmaschine *f* tea plucking machine
Teeplantage *f* tea plantation
Teepol *n* teepol (emulsifier)
Teer *m* tar
~/**Stockholmer** Stockholm (Archangel) tar
Teerabscheider *m* tar separator
Teerkessel *m*, **Teerkocher** *m* tar boiler
Teeröl *n* tar oil
Teerose *f* tea-rose, Rosa odorata
Teerpappe *f* tar[red] board
Teersäure *f* tar acid
Teerschwelerei *f* tar distillation (distilling)
Teestrauch *m* tea[-plant], Camellia sinensis
Teeswater[schaf] *n* Teeswater (sheep breed)
Tef *n* *s.* Zwerghirse
Tegmen *n* (ent) tegmen
Tegment *n* (bot) tegmentum, bud scale (cover)
Tegmentum *n* (zoo) tegmentum
Teich *m* pond, pool
Teichbelüfter *m* pond aerator
Teichbelüftung *f* pond aeration
Teichbinse *f* (bot) [great] bulrush, bullrush, Scirpus lacustris
Teichboden *m* pond bottom
Teichdesinfektion *f* pond disinfection
Teichdüngung *f* pond fertilization
Teichfauna *f* pond fauna
Teichfisch *m* pond fish
Teichflora *f* pond flora
Teichkarpfen *m* [pond] carp, Cyprinus carpio
Teichralle *f* [common] gallinule, moorhen, waterhen, Gallinula chloropus
Teichunkraut *n* pond weed
Teichwirtschaft *f* pond [fish] culture, fish-pond management
Teichzooplankton *n* pond zooplankton

Teigigwerden n von Früchten *(phyt)* core breakdown, brown heart *(of fruits)*
Teigreife f yellow ripeness *(of cereals)*
Teilaufarbeitungskombine f *(forest)* semiprocessor
~/am Stock arbeitende stump semiprocessor
Teilbiozönose f *(ecol)* synusia, synusium
Teilblättchen n *(bot)* leaflet
Teilbrache f half (bastard) fallow
Teilchen n particle
~/abschlämmbares *(soil)* washable particle
Teilchendichte f particle density
Teilchengestalt f particle shape
Teilchengröße f particle size
Teilchengrößenanalyse f particle-size analysis
Teilchengrößenbestimmung f particle-size determination
Teilchengrößenfraktion f particle-size fraction
Teilchengrößenverteilung f particle-size distribution
Teilchengrößenzusammensetzung f particle-size composition
Teildiallelkreuzung f partial diallel cross
Teildränung f non-steady drainage, random system of drainage
Teilentschlammung f partial silt clearance
Teiler m divider *(at cutter bar)*
Teilerbügel m divider bow
Teilerspitze f divider head (tip), dial
Teilfertigfuttermittel n semifinished feed
Teilfrucht f *(bot)* mericarp
Teilkastration f hemicastration
Teilkreisregner m sector sprinkler
Teilmantelgeschoß n *(hunt)* soft-nose
Teilnahmslosigkeit f apathy, lethargy, stupor
Teilpächter m *(Am)* [share]cropper
Teilprobe f subsample
Teilsaat f *(forest)* partial sowing (seeding)
Teilspaltenboden m partially (partly) slatted floor
Teilstichprobe f subsample
Teilstück n 1. *(slaught)* cut; 2. plot, parcel *(field experimentation)*
~ **des Industriefeinsortiments** commercial cut
~ **des Industriegrobsortiments** wholesale cut
~ **des Verbrauchersortiments** commercial cut
Teilstücketikett n plot label
Teilstückform f plot shape
Teilstückgröße f plot size
Teilung f division *(as of cells)*, fission *(as of bacteria)* • durch ~ **entstanden** schizogenous
~/dichotome *(bot, zoo)* dichotomy
Teilungsgewebe n *(bot)* meristem
Teilungsruhe f interphase *(of cell division)*
Teilungswachstum n embryonic growth
Tein n s. Thein
Telamon m telemon *(auxiliary copulatory organ of certain nematodes)*
Telegonie f telegony *(breeding)*
Telegrafenpflanze f moving plant, Desmodium motorium (gyrans)

Telemarkvieh n Telemark [cattle] *(breed)*
Telemeter n range-finder, range-finding apparatus
Telemetrie f telemetry
Telerezeptor m teleceptor
Teleskopachse f telescopic axle
Teleskopähenheber m telescopic lifter
Teleskopförderband n telescopic belt elevator
Teleskopförderer m telescopic conveyor
Teleutospore f *(bot)* teliospore, teleutospore
Teleutosporenlager n telium, teleutosorus *(of rust fungi)*
Teliospore f s. Teleutospore
Telium n s. Teleutosporenlager
Tellerdüngerstreuer m disk-type fertilizer sprayer, plate and flicker [fertilizer] distributor
Telleregge f disk harrow
Tellereisen n plate (spring) trap
Tellerfräse f disk-type rotary cultivator
Tellertrockner m disk dryer
Tellur n tellurium
Telochromosom n telochromosome
Telophase f telophase *(of cell division)*
Telson n telson *(of arthropods)*
Temephos n temephos *(insecticide)*
Tempelbaum m temple tree, Plumeria acuminata
Temperament n temperament, nerve *(esp. of horse)*
Temperatur f temperature
~/kritische critical temperature
~/thermisch neutrale thermoneutral (thermal-comfort) zone
Temperaturabfall m fall of temperature, temperature drop
temperaturabhängig temperature-dependent
Temperaturanpassung f thermal adaptation
Temperaturanstieg m rise of temperature, increase in temperature
Temperaturbelastung f heat load
Temperaturführung f temperature management *(e.g. in greenhouses)*
Temperaturgefälle n s. Temperaturgradient
Temperaturgleiche f isotherm
Temperaturgradient m temperaturgradient
~/vertikaler lapse rate *(meteorology)*
Temperaturgrenzwertregler m temperature limiter
Temperaturinversion f temperature inversion
Temperaturleitfähigkeit f, **Temperaturleitzahl** f temperature conductivity
Temperaturmeßgerät n temperature gauge, thermometer
Temperaturmessung f temperature measurement, thermometry
Temperaturminimum n **am Erdboden** grass minimum temperature
Temperaturprofil n temperature profile
Temperaturregelung f, **Temperaturregulation** f temperature regulation (control), thermoregulation
Temperaturregulationszentrum n thermoregulatory centre

Temperaturrezeptor 626

Temperaturrezeptor *m* thermoreceptor
Temperaturschreiber *m* thermograph
Temperaturschwankung *f* temperature variation
Temperatursturz *m* sudden drop in temperature; heat shock
Temperatursumme *f* heat (temperature) sum, accumulated temperature
Temperatursummenregel *f* rule of temperature summation, Blunck's rule
Temperaturüberwachung *f* temperature control
Temperaturverträglichkeit *f* temperature tolerance
Temperaturwarngerät *n* temperature alarm
Temperaturzunahme *f s.* Temperaturanstieg
Temperierbehälter *m*, **Temperierkessel** *m* tempering vessel *(butter-making)*
Temple *f* temple orange, Citrus sinensis x Citrus reticulata
Temporärparasit *m* temporary parasite
Temulin *n* temulin[e] *(alkaloid)*
Temulinvergiftung *f*, **Temulismus** *m (vet)* temulism
Tenazität *f* tenaciousness, tenacity *(e.g. of microbes)*
Tenderometer *n* tenderometer *(for determining the ripeness of green pease)*
Tendinitis *f (vet)* tendinitis, bowed tendon
Tendo *m* tendon, sinew
~ **gastrocnemius** hamstring *(animal anatomy)*
Tendo... *s. a.* Sehnen...
Tendosynovitis *f*, **Tendovaginitis** *f (vet)* tenosynovitis, tendovaginitis
Tenektomie *f (vet)* tenectomy
Tenesmus *m (vet)* tenesmus
Tenne *f* [barn, threshing] floor; malting room
Tennenmälzerei *f* floor malting
Tennessee Walking Horse *n* Tennessee (Plantation) Walking Horse, Tennessee Walker *(breed)*
Tenosynovitis *f* **des Huhns/infektiöse** viral arthritis of chickens
Tensid *n* surfactant, surface-active agent (compound)
Tensiometer *n* tensiometer *(for measuring the soil water tension)*
Teosinte *f* [Mexican] teosinte, Guatemala grass, Euchlaena mexicana
Tepa *n* tepa *(chemosterilant)*
Tepalum *n (bot)* tepal
Teparybohne *f* tepary [bean], Phaseolus acutifolius
Tephromyelitis *f s.* Poliomyelitis
Tephrosie *f* hoary pea, Tephrosia candida
Teppichbeet *n* carpet-bed[ding]
Teppichgras *n* [tall] carpet grass, Axonopus affinis
Teppichpflanze *f* carpet plant
Teppichwolle *f* carpet wool
Tequilaagave *f (bot)* tequila mescal, Agave tequilana

teratogen teratogenic
Teratogenese *f* teratogenesis
Teratogenität *f* teratogenicity
Teratogonie *f s.* Teratogenese
Teratoid *n (vet)* embryoid
Teratologie *f* teratology *(the study of vegetable or animal monstrosities)*
teratologisch teratologic[al]
Teratom *n (phyt, vet)* teratoma *(tumour made up of heterogeneous tissues)*
teratopathologisch teratopathologic
Terbacil *n* terbacil *(herbicide)*
Terbucarb *n* terbucarb, terbutol *(herbicide)*
Terbutryn *n* terbutryn[e] *(herbicide)*
Terbutylazin *n* terbutylazin *(herbicide)*
Terebinthe *f* terebinth [pistacio, tree], turpentine tree, Pistacia terebinthus
Terebra *f (ent)* terebra
Tereker *m* Tersk *(horse breed)*
Tergit *m* tergite *(of arthropods)*
Termin m/agrotechnischer agrotechnical deadline
terminal *(bot, zoo)* terminal
Terminalblüte *f* apical flower
Terminalknospe *f* terminal (upmost) bud
Terminalparenchym *n* terminal parenchyma
Terminaltrieb *m* terminal [shoot]
Terminationskodon *n (gen)* termination (terminator, nonsense) codon
Terminologie *f***/forstwirtschaftliche** forestry terminology
~ **/landwirtschaftliche** agricultural terminology
Termite *f* termite, white ant *(order Isoptera)*
Termitenresistenz *f* termite resistance
Termitenschild *m* termite shield, termite-proof course
Termitentunnel *m* termite runway
Terpen *n* terpene
Terpenoid *n* terpenoid
Terpentin *n(m)* [gum] turpentine • ~ **gewinnen** to turpentine
Terpentinharzöl *n* rosin oil
Terpentinöl *n* turpentine oil, oil (spirits) of turpentine, turps
Terpentinpistazie *f s.* Terebinthe
Terpineol *n* terpineol
Terra *f* **fusca** *(soil)* terra fusca
~ **rossa** terra rossa
Terrain *n* terrain
terrakottafarben *(bot, zoo)* testaceous
Terrasse *f* terrace
Terrassenanbau *m* storey cropping (farming)
Terrassenbewässerung *f* bench border irrigation
Terrassenkultur *f* storey culture, terracing
Terrassenpflug *m* terracer
terrassieren to terrace
Terrassierpflug *m* terracer
Terrassierung *f* terracing

terrestrisch terrestrial; ground-based *(forest taxation)*
Terrier *m* terrier *(dog breed)*
Territorialität *f* territoriality
Territorialverhalten *n* territorial behaviour, territoriality
Territorium *n* territory
Tertiär *n s.* Tertiärperiode
Tertiärparasit *m* tertiary parasite
Tertiärperiode *f* Tertiary *(geology)*
Tertiärstruktur *f* tertiary structure *(of proteins)*
Tertiärwand *f* tertiary wall *(of plant cells)*
Tervueren *m* Belgian Tervuren *(dog breed)*
Terzel *m* tercel, tiercel
Test *m* test; assay
~/einseitiger *(biom)* one-sided test, single-tail test
~/zweiseitiger *(biom)* two-sided test
*Testa *f (bot)* testa, seed-coat
testen to test *(s. a.* prüfen*)*
Tester *m* tester *(plant breeding)*
Testerhebung *f (forest)* reconnaissance
Testerlinie *f* tester line *(plant breeding)*
Testhypothese *f (biom)* null hypothesis
Testikel *m s.* Hoden
testikulär testicular
Testkreuzung *f* test crossing
Testkreuzungsprodukt *n* test cross
Testosteron *n* testosterone *(sex hormone)*
Testpaarung *f* test mating
Testpflanze *f* test (indicator) plant
Testserum *n* test serum
Testverfahren *n* test procedure
Tetanie *f (vet)* tetany
~/hypomagnesämische hypomagnesaemic tetany
~/puerperale lactation tetany, eclampsia
Tetanolysin *n* tetanolysin *(haemotoxin)*
Tetanus *m (vet)* tetanus *(caused by Clostridium tetani)*
Tetanustoxin *n* tetanotoxin
2,3,6,7-Tetrachlorbenzdioxin *n* dioxin
Tetrachlorkohlenstoff *m s.* Tetrachlormethan
Tetrachlormethan *n* tetrachloromethane, carbon tetrachloride
Tetrachlorvinfos *n* tetrachlorvinfos, tetrachlorvonphos *(insecticide)*
Tetracyclin *n* tetracycline *(antibiotic)*
Tetrade *f* tetrad *(meiosis)*
Tetradecansäure *f* myrisitc (tetradecanoic) acid *(fatty acid)*
Tetradifon *n* tetradifon *(acaricide)*
Tetraethylpyrophosphat *n* TEPP *(insecticide)*
Tetrafluron *n* tetrafluron *(herbicide)*
Tetragastrin *n* tetragastrin *(hormone)*
tetragonal tetragonal
Tetrahydrofolatdehydrogenase *f* dihydrofolate reductase, tetrahydrofolate dehydrogenase *(enzyme)*

1,3,4,5-Tetrahydroxycyclohexancarbonsäure *f* quinic acid *(phytohormone, growth regulator)*
tetramer *(bot)* tetramerous
Tetramethrin *n* tetramethrin, phthaltrin *(insecticide)*
Tetramisol *n* tetramisole *(anthelminthic)*
Tetranactin *n* tetranactin *(acaricide)*
Tetraplegie *f (vet)* quadriplegia
tetraploid *(gen)* tetraploid
Tetraploide *m* tetraploid
Tetraploidie *f* tetraploidy
Tetrapode *m* tetrapod, quadruped
Tetrasul *n* tetrasul *(acaricide)*
Tetravakzine *f* tetravaccine
Tetrazoliummethode *f* tetrazolium test *(for germinability determination)*
Tetrose *f* tetrose *(monosaccharide)*
Teufelsabbiß *m (bot)* devil's bit scabious, Succisa pratensis, Scabiosa succisa
Teufelsbrunst *f (vet)* mole
Teufelsdreck *m* asafoetida *(gum resin from Ferula asafoetida)*
Teufelsfarn *m* interrupted fern, Osmunda claytoniana
Teufelsklaue *f (Am)* Gregg catclaw, cat's claw [acacia], Acacia greggii
Teufelskralle *f (bot)* horned rampion *(genus Phyteuma)*
Teufelszwirn *m* 1. dodder *(genus Cuscuta)*; 2. matrimony vine, box thorn *(genus Lycium)*
Texas Longhorn *n* Texas Longhorn *(cattle breed)*
Texasfieber *n [der Rinder]* Texas (cattle-tick) fever, southern cattle fever *(caused by Babesia bigemina)*
Texasgambuse *f* mosquito fish, Gambusia affinis
Texas[zyto]plasma *n* Texas cytoplasm, T cytoplasm *(maize breeding)*
Texelschaf *n* Texel [sheep] *(breed)*
Textilfaser *f* textile fibre
Textur *f* texture, grain [pattern], figure *(of wood)*
~/geriegelte fiddleback [figure]
~/gestreifte ribbon figure (grain), stripe figure
~/gleichmäßige even (uniform) grain
~/grobe open grain, coarse texture
~/ungleichmäßige uneven grain (texture)
Texturator *m (dairy)* texturator
T-Flußmähdrescher *m* front-cut combine, push-type combine
TGE-Virus *n* transmissible gastroenteritis virus
Thalamus *m* 1. [optical] thalamus *(animal anatomy)*; 2. *s.* Blütenboden
thallös *(bot)* thalloid
Thallium *n* thallium
Thallophyt *m (bot)* thallophyte, thallogen
Thallus *m (bot)* thallus
Thalluspflanze *f s.* Thallophyt
Thebain *n* thebaine *(alkaloid)*
Theca *f s.* Theka

Theileriose

Theileriose f (vet) theileriasis, gonderiosis
~ **der Schafe und Ziegen/bösartige** malignant ovine and caprine gonderiosis (theileriasis)
~ **der Schafe und Ziegen/gutartige** benign ovine and caprine gonderiosis (theileriasis)
Thein n caffeine, theine (alkaloid)
Theka f 1. (bot) theca (receptacular part esp. in cryptogamic plants); 2. (zoo) theca (an enveloping sheath or case)
Thekaluteinzelle f theca lutein cell (of corpus luteum)
Thekazelle f thecal cell
Thekazelltumor m, **Thekom** n (vet) thecoma
Thelitis f (vet) thelitis, teat inflammation
Thelygenie f (zoo) thelygeny
Thelytokie f (zoo) thelytoky, thelytokous parthenogenesis
thelytokisch thelytokous
Theobromin n theobromine, cacain (alkaloid)
Theodolit m theodolite
Theophyllin n theophylline (alkaloid)
Therapeutik f therapeutics
Therapeutikum n therapeutic [agent]
therapeutisch therapeutic[al]
Therapie f therapy
~/**tierärztliche** veterinary therapy
Theriogenologie f (vet) theriogenology
thermal thermal, thermic
Thermalquelle f thermal spring
Thermalquellwasser n thermal spring water
Thermik f thermal up-current
Thermisation f (dairy) thermization
thermisch s. thermal
Thermistorthermometer n thermistor thermometer
Thermodormanz f thermodormancy
Thermodure pl thermodurics (bacteriology)
Thermodynamik f thermodynamics
Thermoelement n thermocouple, thermoelectric couple
Thermogenese f thermogenesis, heat production
~/**zitterfreie** non-shivering thermogenesis (animal physiology)
Thermogramm n thermogram, thermograph
Thermograph m thermograph
Thermographie f thermography
thermolabil thermolabile
Thermolyse f thermolysis
Thermometer n thermometer, temperature gauge
Thermometrie f thermometry
Thermonastie f (bot) thermonasty
Thermoperiodismus m thermoperiodism, thermoperiodic behaviour
thermophil thermophile, thermophilic
Thermophosphat n calcined phosphate (fertilizer)
Thermopluviogramm n hyther[o]graph
Thermopsychrometer n thermocouple psychrometer
Thermoregulation f thermoregulation
Thermoregulator m thermoregulatory centre (animal physiology)
thermoregulatorisch thermoregulatory
Thermorelais n thermal relay
Thermorezeptor m thermoreceptor
thermostabil thermostable
Thermostabilität f thermostability
Thermostat m thermostat
Thermotaxis f thermotaxis
Thermotherapie f (phyt, vet) thermotherapy
Thermotropismus m thermotropism
Thermoverglasung f thermoglazing (e.g. of greenhouses)
Thermoweinherstellung f thermovinification
Therophyt m (bot) therophyte, annual
Thesaurismose f (vet) storage disease
Thiabendazol n t[h]iabendazole, TBZ (anthelminthic, fungicide)
Thiacetarsamid n thiacetarsamide (anthelminthic)
Thiamin n thiamine, aneurin, vitamin B_1
Thiaminantagonist m thiamine antagonist, antithiamine
Thiaminase f thiaminase (enzyme)
Thiaminkinase f thiamine kinase (enzyme)
Thiaminphosphat n thiamine phosphate
Thiaminpyrophosphat n thiamine pyrophosphate, cocarboxylase
Thiaminpyrophosphatase f thiamine pyrophosphatase (enzyme)
Thiaminpyrophosphokinase f thiamine pyrophosphokinase (enzyme)
Thiazafluron n thiazafluron (herbicide)
Thigmonastie f thigmonasty, haptonasty (plant physiology)
Thigmotropismus m thigmotropism (plant physiology)
Thimet n thimet (insecticide)
Thiobarbituratnarkose f (vet) thiobarbiturate anaesthesia
Thiochlorofenphim n thiochlorofenphim (fungicide)
Thiochrom n thiochrome (dye)
Thioctansäure f lipoic acid (coenzyme)
Thiocyanat n thiocyanate
Thiocyclam[-hydrogenoxalat] n thiocyclam[hydrogenoxalate] (insecticide)
Thiodan n endosulfan (insecticide)
Thiodicarb n thiodicarb (insecticide)
Thiodiphenylamin n phenothiazine (anthelminthic, insecticide)
Thiofanox n thiofanox (insecticide, nematicide)
Thiofuraden n thiofuradene (anthelminthic)
Thioglucosidase f thioglucosidase, myrosinase, sinigr[in]ase (enzyme)
Thioharnstoff m thiourea
Thiolgruppe f thiol (sulphydryl) group, mercapto group
Thiolignin n thiolignin
Thiomersal n thiomersal (preservative, fungicide)

Thiometon *n* thiometon *(insecticide)*
Thionazin *n* thionazin *(nematicide, insecticide)*
Thiopental *n* thiopental *(anaesthetic)*
Thiopeptin *n* thiopeptin *(antibiotic)*
Thiophanat *n* thiophanate *(anthelminthic, fungicide)*
Thiophanat-amin *n* thiophanate-amine *(fungicide)*
Thiophanat-methyl *n* thiophanate-methyl, methyl thiophanate *(fungicide)*
Thiophen *n* thiophene *(solvent)*
Thiophosphat *n* thiophosphate
Thiosäure *f* thio acid
Thiosemikarbazon *n* thiosemicarbazone *(tuberculostatic)*
Thiosin *n* thiosin *(fungicide)*
Thiosulfat *n* thiosulphate
Thiosulfatcyanidtranssulfurase *f*, **Thiosulfat-S-Transferase** *f* thiosulphate sulphurtransferase, thiosulphate cyanide transsulphurase, rhodanase *(enzyme)*
Thiotepa *n* thiotepa *(chemosterilant)*
[2-]Thiourazil *n* thiouracil *(fattening agent)*
Thioverbindung *f* thio compound
Thi[u]ram *n* thiram, TMTD *(fungicide)*
thixotrop thixotropic
Thixotropie *f* thixotropy
Thomasmehl *n*, **Thomasphosphat** *n* Thomas meal (phosphate) *(fertilizer)*
Thomasschlacke *f* Thomas (basic) slag
thorakal thoracic
Thorakalbein *n (ent)* thoracic leg
Thorakoskop *n (vet)* thoracoscope
Thorakotomie *f (vet)* thoracotomy
Thorax *m* thorax, chest
Thorax... *s.* Brust...
T-Horizont *m (soil)* peat horizon
Thr *s.* Threonin
Threonin *n* threonine *(amino-acid)*
Threoninaldolase *f* threonine aldolase *(enzyme)*
Threonindehydratase *f* threonine dehydratase *(enzyme)*
Threonin-tRNA-Ligase *f* threonine-tRNA ligase *(enzyme)*
Threose *f s.* Tetrose
Thrips *m (ent)* thrips *(order Thysanoptera)*
Thrombin *n* thrombin *(enzyme)*
Thrombokinase *f* thrombokinase, coagulation factor Xa *(enzyme)*
Thrombolyse *f*, **Thrombomalazie** *f* thrombolysis
Thromboplastin *n* thromboplastin
Thromboplastinzeit *f*, **Thromboplastinzeitbestimmung** *f* [nach Quick] *(vet)* prothrombin time
Thrombose *f (vet)* thrombosis
Thromboxan *n* thromboxane *(fatty acid)*
Thromboxansynthase *f* thromboxane synthase *(enzyme)*
Thrombozyt *m* thrombocyte, blood platelet
Thrombozytopenie *f (vet)* thrombocytopenia
Thrombus *m (vet)* thrombus

Thryptophyt *m* facultative saprophyte, perthophyte
Thuja *f* thuja, thuya, arbor vitae, tree of life *(genus Thuja)*
Thunbergs Berberitze *f* Japanese barberry, Berberis thunbergii
Thunberg-Spierstrauch *m (bot)* Thunberg spiraea, Spiraea thunbergii
Thüringer-Wald-Ziege *f* Thuringian, German Toggenburg *(goat breed)*
Thylakoid *n* thylakoid *(photosynthetically active membrane structure)*
Thylakoidmembran *f* thylakoid membrane
Thylaxovirus *n*/**bovines** bovine syncytial virus
Thylle *f* t[h]ylosis *(wood anatomy)*
Thymektomie *f (vet)* thymectomy
Thymian *m* 1. thyme *(genus Thymus)*; 2. [garden, common] thyme, Thymus vulgaris
thymianblättrig thymifolious
Thymidin *n* thymidine *(nucleoside)*
Thymidinkinase *f* thymidine kinase *(enzyme)*
Thymin *n* thymine *(pyrimidine base)*
Thymitis *f (vet)* thymitis
Thymol *n* thymol *(monoterpene)*
Thymus *m* thymus [gland], sweetbread
Thymusentzündung *f s.* Thymitis
Thyreoglobulin *n* thyroglobulin
thyreoidal thyroid
Thyreoideahormon *n* thyroid hormone
Thyreoidektomie *f (vet)* thyreoidectomy
Thyreoiditis *f (vet)* thyroiditis
Thyreoparathyreoidektomie *f (vet)* thyroparathyroidectomy
Thyreoprotein *n* thyroprotein
Thyreostatikum *n* thyrostatic [agent], thyroid antagonist
thyreostatisch thyrostatic
Thyreotoxikose *f (vet)* thyrotoxicosis, hyperthyroidism
thyreotrop thyrotrop[h]ic
Thyreotropin *n* thyrotropin, thyroid-stimulating hormone, TSH, thyrotropic hormone
Thyreotropin-Releasinghormon *n* thyrotropin releasing hormone, TRH, thyroliberin
Thyrocalcitonin *n* calcitonin, thyrocalcitonin, TCT *(hormone)*
Thyroliberin *n s.* Thyreotropin-Releasinghormon
Thyronin *n* thyronine *(amino-acid)*
Thyrosinphenollyase *f* tyrosine phenol-lyase, beta-tyrosinase *(enzyme)*
Thyroxin *n* thyroxine, [tetra]iodothyronine *(hormone)*
Thyrsus *m* thyrsus, thyrse *(an inflorescence as in the lilac)*
Tiabendazol *n s.* Thiabendazol
Tiamulin *n* tiamulin *(antibiotic)*
Tibet-Sommerprimel *f (bot)* giant cowslip, Primula florindae
Tibet-Terrier *m* Tibetan terrier *(dog breed)*
Tibia *f (zoo)* tibia

tibial

tibial tibial
Tibiotarsus *m* tibiotarsus, tibia *(greatest bone of bird's leg)*
Tief *n s.* Tiefdruckgebiet
Tiefadrigkeit *f (phyt)* rugosity
Tiefbettfelge *f* wide-base drop-centre rim with deep well
Tiefbetttrockner *m* deep-bed dryer
Tiefbrunnen *m* deep well
Tiefbrunnenpumpe *f* deep well pump
Tiefdruckgebiet *n* low-pressure zone, low, depression, cyclone *(climatology)*
Tiefdruckgürtel *m* low-pressure belt *(climatology)*
Tiefenbegrenzer *m* 1. depth gauge; 2. raker *(of a chain-saw)*
Tiefenbegrenzerabstand *m* raker clearance
Tiefenbegrenzungsrolle *f* depth-control roller
Tiefendüngegerät *n*, **Tiefendüngerstreuer** *m* deep-down fertilizer distributor, deep placement fertilizer distributor
Tiefeneinstellung *f*, **Tiefeneinstellvorrichtung** *f* [landwheel] depth control *(of a plough)*
Tiefenmeißel *m s.* Tieflockerer
Tiefenschicht *f* subsurface layer *(e.g. of a soil)*
Tiefensensibilität *f* deep sensibility
Tiefentherapie *f (phyt, vet)* deep therapy, radiotherapy
Tiefenzone *f* **stehender Gewässer** hypolimnion
Tiefflug *m* low-level flight, low-altitude flight; low flying
Tieffräsen *n* deep rotary tillage
Tieffurchensaat *f* deep-furrow sowing
Tiefgefrieranlage *f* deep-freezer
tiefgefrieren *n* to deep-freeze, to quick-freeze
tiefgestellt low set *(animal body)*
Tiefgrubber *m s.* Tieflockerer
tiefgründig deep *(soil)*
Tiefkühlgemüse *n* deep-frozen vegetable[s]
Tiefkühllagerung *f* subfreezing storage
Tiefkühltruhe *f* deep-freezer
Tiefkühlung *f* deep cooling, deep freezing
Tiefkultivierung *f* deep cultivation *(microbiology)*
Tiefkultur *f* deep tillage
Tiefkulturpflug *m s.* Tiefpflug
Tiefladeanhänger *m*, **Tieflader** *m* low-loading trailer
Tiefland *n* lowland
Tieflandmoor *n* low[land] moor, lowland bog
Tieflandrind[vieh] *n* lowland cattle
Tieflockerer *m* subsoiler, subsoil (chisel, depth) cultivator, heavy[-duty] cultivator, deep digger, depth tormentor
tieflockern to subsoil, to chisel
Tieflockerung *f* deep loosening (cultivation), chisel[l]ing *(of soil)*
Tieflöffelbagger *m* backdigger
Tiefpflug *m* trench[ing] plough, deep[-digger] plough, deep-digging plough
tiefpflügen to trench-plough

Tiefpflugkörper *m* [deep]digger body
Tiefpflugkultur *f* deep cultivation
Tiefsaat *f* deep-furrow sowing
Tiefstall *m* deep-pit house
Tiefstreu *f* deep (built-up) litter
Tiefstreuhaltung *f* deep-litter housing
Tiefstreustall *m* deep litter (pit) house
Tieftemperaturbeständigkeit *f* resistance to cold, low-temperature resistance
Tieftemperaturkonservierung *f* cryopreservation
Tieftemperaturschaden *m* low-temperature injury *(e.g. on stored fruits)*
Tiefwasserreis *m* floating (deep-water) rice
tiefwurzelnd deep-rooting, deep-rooted
Tiefwurzelsystem *n* deep-root system
Tier *n* 1. animal; 2. female deer, roe, hind, doe
~/am Wobblersyndrom leidendes *(vet)* wobbler
~/ausgestopftes stuffed animal
~/brütendes brooder
~/einjähriges yearling
~/empfängliches *(vet)* susceptible animal
~/erstgebärendes weibliches primipara
~/festliegendes *(vet)* downer
~/hornloses pollard
~/im Saisonzyklus brünstiges seasonal breeder
~ im Vorreifestadium *(ent)* preadult
~/induziert ovulierendes reflex ovulator
~/jagdbares game animal
~/junge Triebe (Zweige) fressendes browser
~/kastriertes castrate, neuter, gelding
~/keimfreies germ free animal *(gnotobiotics)*
~/konventionelles conventional animal
~/mageres scrag
~/männliches male, jack
~/milcherzeugendes (milchgebendes, milchlieferndes) milk-yielding animal, milker
~/mit vielerlei Kleinlebewesen besiedeltes conventional animal
~/nicht reinrassiges runt
~/pathogenfreies pathogen free animal
~/polyöstrisches continuous breeder
~/provoziert ovulierendes reflex ovulator
~/rassereines *s.* ~/reinrassiges
~/räuberisch lebendes predator; episite
~/reinrassiges pure-bred, pure-blooded animal
~/streunendes stray
~/unkastriertes entire
~/unterernährtes scrag
~/weibliches female, jenny
~/wildes wild animal, wild[l]ing, beast, brute
~/zur Mast bestimmtes feeder, store
Tier... *s. a.* Vieh...
Tierabfall *m* animal waste
Tieranatomie *f* animal anatomy, zootomy
Tierarzneimittel *n* veterinary drug (pharmaceutical, medicine), drench, stock remedy
Tierarzneimitteldosis *f* drench
Tierarzt *m* animal doctor, veterinary [surgeon], VS, vet[erinarian], doctor of veterinary medicine

~/operierender operator
~/praktischer veterinary practitioner
tierärztlich veterinary
Tierarztpraxis f veterinary practice
Tierbau m earth, burrow
Tierbehandlungsanlage f livestock handling facility
Tierbeurteiler m livestock judge
Tierbeurteilung f livestock judging
Tierblut n animal blood
Tierblütigkeit f (bot) zoophily
Tierdung m animal manure
Tiereiweiß n animal protein
Tiereiweißfaktor m animal protein factor, APF, extrinsic factor, cobalamin, vitamin B_{12}
Tiereiweißkonzentrat n animal protein concentrate
Tierernährung f animal nutrition (feeding)
Tierernährungswissenschaftler m animal nutritionist
Tierexperiment n animal experiment
Tierfanggrube f pit
Tierfarbstoff m animal pigment
Tierfaser f animal fibre
Tierfett n animal fat, grease, adipose
~/festes tallow
~/halbfestes lard
Tierforschung f animal research
Tierfürsorge f animal welfare
Tierfutterration f animal ration
Tierfütterung f animal feeding
Tierfütterungsversuch m animal feeding experiment (trial)
Tiergeburtshilfe f veterinary obstetrics
Tiergemeinschaft f animal community
Tiergenetik f animal genetics
Tiergeographie f animal geography, zoogeography
Tiergesundheit f animal health
Tiergesundheitsdienst m veterinary (animal health) service
Tiergesundheitspflege f animal welfare
Tiergift n animal poison, zootoxin
Tiergülle f animal (livestock waste) slurry
Tierhaar n animal hair
Tierhabitat n animal habitat
Tierhalter m keeper, husbandman, breeder
Tierhaltung f [animal] husbandry
~/landwirtschaftliche animal agriculture
Tierhandel m animal trade
Tierhandlung f pet shop
Tierhaut f hide, fell
~/[ganze] gegerbte crop
Tierhygiene f animal hygiene (sanitation)
Tieridentifikation f, Tieridentifizierung f animal identification
tierisch animal
Tierkalb n young deer
Tierkalorimeter n animal calorimeter

Tierkennzeichnung f animal identification
Tierklinik f animal hospital, veterinary clinic (practice)
Tierkohle f animal char[coal]
Tierkörper m animal body, the system
~/toter cadaver; carcass, carcase
Tierkörperbeseitigung f carcass disposal, carrion removal, destruction of animal carcasses
Tierkörperbeseitigungsanstalt f carcass disposal (destructor) plant, rendering plant, flaying-house, knackery
Tierkörpermehl n [animal] tankage, carcass meal
Tierkörperpräparation f taxidermy
Tierkörperverwertung f s. Tierkörperbeseitigung
Tierkörperwärme f animal heat
Tierkot m s. Kot
Tierkrankheit f animal disease, livestock disorder
Tierkunde f animal science, zoology
Tierlaufstall m deep-pit house
Tierlaus f animal louse
Tierlebensversicherung f animal insurance
Tierleiche f cadaver, carcass, carcase
Tierleim m animal glue (gelatine)
Tierlunge f lights
Tiermagen m s. Magen
Tiermast f fattening
Tiermedizin f veterinary (animal) medicine
~/forensische forensic veterinary medicine
Tierökologie f animal ecology, zooecology
Tieröl n animal oil
Tierparasit m animal parasite
Tierpark m zoo[logical garden]; game-preserve
Tierpathologie f animal (veterinary) pathology
Tierpflege f animal care
Tierpfleger m [animal-]keeper, animal caretaker; (vet) animal nursing auxiliary, ANA
Tierphänologie f animal phenology
Tierphysiologie f animal physiology, zoodynamics
Tierpräparation f taxidermy
Tierprodukt n animal product
Tierproduktion f animal production, stock farming
Tierproduktionsanlage f livestock operation (enterprise), animal-production operation (plant), animal facility (unit)
~/industriemäßige large-scale livestock enterprise, industry-type animal (livestock) production unit
Tierproduktionsbetrieb m s. Tierproduktionsanlage
Tierproduktionsforschung f animal research, animal production science
Tierproduktionsgenossenschaft f co-operative farm for animal production
Tierproduktionssystem n animal production system
Tierpsychologie f animal psychology
Tierquälerei f animal cruelty, cruelty to animals
Tierrasse f animal breed
Tierration f animal ration

Tierreich 632

Tierreich n animal kingdom
Tierschädling m animal pest
Tierschmarotzer m animal parasite
Tierschutz m animal protection
Tierschutzanhänger m, **Tierschützer** m animal welfare enthusiast
Tierschutzgebiet n wildlife sanctuary
Tierschutzverein m animal protection society
Tierseuche f animal epidemic, epizootic, blast, murrain
Tiersoziologie f animal sociology
Tierstamm m stock
Tiertauchbad n animal dip (for pest control)
Tiertaxonomie f animal taxonomy
Tiertransport m transport of animals
Tiertransportfahrzeug n livestock transporter
Tiertreibstock m electric stock prod, electric animal coaxer, goad
Tierunterkunft f [animal] house, animal shelter, livestock accommodation
Tierverbreitung f [von Früchten oder Samen] (bot) zoochory
Tiervergiftung f animal poisoning
Tierverhalten n animal behaviour • **das ~ betreffend** ethological
Tierverhaltensforscher m ethologist
Tierverhaltensforschung f ethology
Tierversicherung f animal insurance
Tierversuch m animal experiment, test on animals
Tierversuchswesen n animal experimentation
Tierwachs n animal wax
Tierwärme f animal heat
Tierwärter m s. Tierpfleger
Tierwelt f [eines Gebietes] fauna, animal world
Tierzucht f animal breeding
Tierzuchtbetrieb m animal breeding farm
Tierzüchter m animal (livestock) breeder
Tierzuchtforschung f animal research
Tierzüchtung f animal breeding
Tierzüchtungsmethode f, **Tierzuchtverfahren** n animal breeding method
Tiffe f bitch fox, she-fox, vixen
Tigerblume f [Mexican] tiger flower, tiger iris, Tigridia pavonia
Tigerlilie f tiger-lily, Lilium lancifolium
Tigernuß f (bot) chufa, Cyperus esculentus
Tigerrachen m (bot) tiger-jaws (genus Faucaria)
Tiglibaum m croton-oil plant, Croton tiglium
Tikkakrankheit f **der Erdnuß** peanut leaf spot (caused by Cercosporidium personatum)
Tilietum n lime wood
Tilsiter [Käse] m Tilsit cheese
Timotheegras n timothy [grass], Phleum pratense
tinktoriell tinctorial
Tinktur f tincture
Tintenbeere f gallberry, Ilex glabra
Tintenfleckenkrankheit f **an Iris** ink spot disease of iris (caused by Mystrosporum adustum and Drechslera iridis)

Tintling m inky cap, ink mushroom, coprinus [mushroom] (genus Coprinus)
Ti-Plasmid n tumour-inducing plasmid
Tisch m table; staging (in greenhouses)
Tischannahmeförderer m conveyor table
Tischbeet n [staging] bench, staging (in greenhouses)
Tischbeetheizung f bench heating
Tischbeetrollwagen m bench trolley
Tischgemeinschaft f (ecol) commensalism, commensality
Tischlerholz n joinery timber (wood)
Tischveredelung f bench grafting
Tischwein m table (beverage) wine, vin ordinaire
Titer m titre
Tithonie f 1. tithonia, Mexican sunflower (genus Tithonia); 2. tithonia, Tithonia rotundifolia (tagetiflora)
Titration f titration
Titrationsazidität f titratable acidity
Titrationskurve f titration curve; (soil) buffer curve
titrieren to titrate
TKM s. Tausendkornmasse
TkMiMV s. Mildes Tollkirschenmosaikvirus
TKS s. Torfkultursubstrat
TkSV s. Tollkirschencheckungsvirus
T-Lymphozyt m thymus-derived lymphocyte, T lymphocyte (cell)
~/antigenstimulierter immunocyte
TMaV s. Tabakmauchevirus
TMTD s. Thi[u]ram
TMV s. 1. Töchter-Mütter-Vergleich; 2. Tabakmosaikvirus
TNT s. Temperatur/thermisch neutrale
TNV s. Tabaknekrosevirus
ToAV s. Tomatenaspermievirus
ToBFV s. Tomatenbronzefleckenvirus
Tobramycin n tobramycin (antibiotic)
Tochterchromosom n daughter chromosome, chromatid
Tochtergeneration f filial generation, F
Tochtergeschwulst f (vet, phyt) metastasis
• **Tochtergeschwülste bilden** to metastasize
Töchter-Mütter-Vergleich m daughter-dam comparison (animal breeding)
Tochterpflanze f daughter plant
Tochterzelle f daughter cell (mitosis)
Tochterzwiebel f daughter bulb
~/nicht blühfähige small offset
Toclofos-Methyl n toclofos-methyl (fungicide)
[α-]Tocopherol n [α-]tocopherol, vitamin E
Tod m death
~/thermaler heat (thermal) death
Toddy m toody (fresh or fermented sap esp. of some East Indian palms)
Todeskampf m agony
Todesrate f death (mortality) rate
Todeszeichen npl signs of death
tödlich lethal, fatal

~ verlaufend pernicious
~ wirkend lethal
Todorokit *m* todorokite *(non-clay mineral)*
Toggenburger Ziege *f* Toggenburg *(goat breed)*
Tokaier *m*, **Tokajer** *m* Tokay *(wine)*
tolerant tolerant
Toleranz *f* tolerance
Toleranzbereich *m* tolerance range
~/thermischer *(ecol)* survival zone
Toleranzdosis *f* permissible dose
Toleranzgrenze *f* tolerance limit
~/wirtschaftliche economic threshold (injury level)
Toleranzvererbung *f* tolerance inheritance
Toleranzwert *m* tolerance level
Tolldocke *f (bot)* isopyrum *(genus Isopyrum)*
Tollkirsche *f* [deadly, black] nightshade, death's herb, dwale, belladonna, Atropa bella-donna
Tollkirschenscheckungsvirus *n* belladonna mottle virus
Tollwut *f (vet)* rabies, lyssa, hydrophobia, canine madness • **~ erregend** rabigenic, rabific
~ der Fledermäuse vampire bat rabies
~/rasende raving madness
~/stille sullen rabies
tollwütig rabid
Tollwutvakzine *f* antirabic vaccine
Tollwutvirus *n* lyssa virus
Tolstolob *m* silver carp, Hypophthalmichthys molitrix
Tolubalsam *m* tolu [balsam]
Tolubalsambaum *m* tolu [balsam-]tree, Myroxylon balsamum [var. balsamum]
Toluidinblau *n* toluidine blue *(dye)*
Tolylfluanid *n* tolylfluanid *(fungicide)*
Toluen *n*, **Toluol** *n* toluene *(hydrocarbon)*
Tomate *f* tomato, Lycopersicon lycopersicum
Tomatenaspermievirus *n* tomato aspermy virus, TAV
Tomatenblattminierer *m (ent)* tomato leaf-miner, Liriomyza bryoniae
Tomatenblattrollvirus *n* tomato leaf curl virus, TLCV
Tomatenbraunwurzelfäule *f* tomato brown [root] rot *(caused by Pyrenochaeta lycopersici)*
Tomatenbronzefleckenvirus *n* tomato spotted wilt virus, TSWV
Tomatenerntemaschine *f* tomato harvester
Tomatenkonzentrat *n* tomato concentrate
Tomatenmark *n* tomato pulp (puree)
Tomatenmosaik *n (phyt)* tomato mosaic
Tomatenmosaikvirus *n* tomato mosaic virus, ToMV
Tomatenpflanze *f* **mit nur einem Blütenstand** single-truss tomato
Tomatenringfleckenvirus *n* tomato ring spot virus, T[o]RSV
Tomatenrüttler *m* tomato truss vibrator
Tomatensaft *m* tomato juice

Tomatenschwarzringvirus *n* tomato black ring virus, TBRV
Tomatenstengelfäule *f* stem and fruit rot of tomato, black rot of tomato *(caused by Didymella lycopersici)*
Tomatenvergilbungsvirus *n* tomato yellows virus, TYV
Tomatenzwergbuschvirus *n* tomato bushy stunt virus, TBSV
Tomatin *n* tomatine *(alkaloid)*
Ton *m* 1. *(soil)* clay, argil; 2. sound
tonartig clayey, argillaceous
Tonbildung *f* argillization, argillification
Tonboden *m* clay soil, pelosol
~/montmorillonitischer montmorillonitic clay
Tondränrohr *n* clayware field drain-pipe, clay pipe
Tondurchschlämmung *f s.* Tonverlagerung
Tonephin *n* vasopressin, antidiuretic hormone, ADH
Tonerde *f* argillaceous earth
Tonfraktion *f* clay fraction
Tongapflanze *f* tonga plant, Epipremnum mirabile
Tongefäß *n* crock
tonhaltig clayey, argillaceous, argilliferous
Tonhäutchen *n (soil)* clay cutan
Tonhäutchenhorizont *m (soil)* argilluvic B-horizon, Bt
Tonholz *n* tonal wood, resonance (resonant) wood
Ton-Humus-Komplex *m* clay-humus complex, organo-clay complex, organomineral (colloidal) complex
tonig *s.* tonhaltig
Tonikum *n* tonic
tonisch tonic
Tonizität *f* tone, tonus
Tonkabohne *f* tonka [bean], tonquin bean
Tonkabohnenbaum *m* tonka bean tree, coumarou, Dipteryx odorata
Tonkalk *m* argillaceous limestone
Tonkolloid *n* clay colloid
Tonlehm *m* clay loam
Tonmergel *m* clay marl, marl clay
Tonmineral *n* clay mineral
Tonmineralogie *f* clay mineralogy
Tonnage *f* tonnage
Tönnchen *n (ent)* puparium, pupal case
Tonne *f* cask, tun
Tonoplast *m (bot)* tonoplast
Tonrohr *n* clay pipe, clayware field drain-pipe
Tonrohrdrän *m* tile drain
Tonrohrdränung *f* tile drainage
Tonsandstein *m* argillaceous sandstone
Tonscherbe *f* crock *(e.g. for drainage)* • **Tonscherben [zu Dränungszwecken] einbringen** to crock
Tonschicht *f* clay layer
~/verdichtete clay pan
Tonschichtteilchen *n* micelle, micell[a]
Tonschwarzerde *f* black clay soil

Tonsille 634

Tonsille f tonsil (animal anatomy)
Tonsillitis f (vet) tonsillitis
Tontopf m clay pot, crock
Tonus m tone, tonus
Tonverlagerung f (soil) clay translocation (illuviation), argilluviation, lessivage, lessivation
Top-cross n s. Top-cross-Prüfung
Top-cross-Hybride f top cross
Top-cross-Produkt n top cross
Top-cross-Prüfung f top cross[ing]
Topf m pot
Topfballen m pot (root) ball
Topfballenpflanze f pot ball plant
Topfblume f pot[ted] plant
Topfbürste f pot cleaning brush
Topfchrysantheme f pot mum
topfen to pot
Topferde f potting soil (compost)
Topferdelader m potting soil loader
Topferdeverarbeitungsmaschine f potting soil handling equipment
Topffüllmaschine f potting machine, [plant] pot filling machine, potter
Topfgießgerät n pot watering lance
Topfmaschine f s. Topffüllmaschine
Topfpalette f plant tray
Topfpflanze f pot[ted] plant
~/blühende flowering pot plant
Topfpflanzenanbau m pot plant culture
Topfpflanzenkultur f pot growing
Topfpflanzen-Verkaufseinheit f cell pack
Topfpflanzenwagen m pot plant trolley
Topfpflanzung f pot planting
Topfreinigungsbürste f pot cleaning brush
Topfrose f pot (miniature) rose
Topfsubstrat n potting substrate (medium)
Topfzierpflanze f ornamental pot[ted] plant
Topinambur m(f) Jerusalem artichoke, girasol[e], girosol, topinambur, Helianthus tuberosus
Topochemie f histochemistry
topochemisch histochemical
Topographie f topography
topographisch topographical
Topoklima n topoclimate, mesoclimate
Topoklimatologie f topoclimatology
topoklimatologisch topoclimatological
Toposequenz f (soil) toposequence
Torenie f wishbone flower, torenia, Torenia fournieri
Torf m peat, turf, bog
~/sekundär abgelagerter allochthonous peat
Torfanmoor n peat anmoor
torfartig peaty
torfbildend peat-forming
Torfbildung f peatification
Torfbinse f (bot) heath rush, Juncus squarrosus
Torfblock m peat block, turf
Torfboden m peat[bog] soil, bog[gy] soil
Torfbrand m peat fire

Torfbrikett n peat briquette
Torfbrombeere f cloudberry, Rubus chamaemorus
Torfdünger m peat fertilizer
Torferde f peat soil
Torferdekultur f muck farming
torfhaltig peaty
Torfhorizont m peat horizon
Torfhumus m peat humus
torfig peaty, boggy
Torfklein n crumbling peat
Torfkompost m peat compost
Torfkultur f 1. peat culture; 2. muck farming
Torfkultursubstrat n peat culture substrate
Torflager n peat bed (deposit)
Torfmoor n peatbog, peat moor, peatery
Torfmoorboden m peatbog soil
Torfmoos n peatmoss, bog moss, sphagnum [moss] (genus Sphagnum)
Torfmoosmoor n sphagnum bog
Torfmudde f muck, dy
Torfmuddeboden m muck soil, black fen
Torfmulch m peat mulch
Torfmull m peat powder (mould, dust), sphagnum [moss] peat
Torfquelltopf m, **Torfquelltöpfchen** n swell-up pot, Jiffy pot (for plantlet raising)
Torfschicht f peat bed
Torfschlamm m muck, dy
Torf-Stallmist-Kompost m peat manure compost
Torfstechen n peat cutting (digging)
Torfstechschaufel f turf spade (spud)
Torfstich m peatery, pea bank
Torfstreu f peat (moss) litter
Torfstück n turf
Torfteer m peat tar
Torftopf m peat pot (block)
Torftopfpresse f peat blocking machine
Torftopfstreifen m peat pot strip
ToRFV s. Tomatenringfleckenvirus
Torfwand f peat wall, vertical garden
~/blühende flowering peat wall
Toringoapfel m toringo crab-apple, Malus sieboldii
Torisker m Tori (horse breed)
Torlader m, **Torladewagen** m (forest) straddle carrier (truck), timber carrier (cart)
Torpedogras n torpedo grass, panic rampant, Panicum repens
Torpedoteiler m torpedo (cone-shaped) divider (of cutter bar)
Torpfosten m gate post
Torpidität f, **Torpor** m (zoo) torpor
Torquatusfasan m ring-neck[ed] pheasant, Phasianus colchicus torquatus
Torrente m s. Wildbach
Torsion f torsion
Torsionsscherversuch m (soil) torsional shear test
Tortikollis m (vet) torticollis
Torulahefe f torula yeast

Torula[hefe]pilz *m (bot)* torula, Torulopsis utilis
Torus *m* [pit] torus *(wood anatomy)*
Torybon *n* alarm pheromone (substance)
ToSRV *s.* Tomatenschwarzringvirus
Totalernte *f* once-over harvest[ing] *(e.g. of strawberries)*
Totalherbizid *n* total (non-selective) herbicide, soil sterilant
Totalitätsnutzung *f (forest)* salvage felling, salvaging
Toteggen *n* dead-harrowing
töten to kill, to deaden; to put down *(esp. an old or injured animal)*
~/durch Elektroschock *(slaught)* to electrocute
~/schmerzlos to euthanize
Totengräber *m* burying (sexton) beetle *(genus Necrophorus)*
Totenkopf *m* death's head [hawk-]moth, Acherontia atropos
Totenstarre *f* rigor mortis
Totenuhr *f s.* Rotscheckiger Klopfkäfer
totgeboren stillborn
Totgeburt *f* still birth
totharzen *(forest)* to tap to death, to tap with killing
totipotent *(bot, zoo)* totipotent
Totipotenz *f* totipotency
Totraum *m[/respiratorischer]* dead space *(animal physiology)*
Totraumventilation *f* dead-space ventilation
totreif dead ripe
Totreife *f* dead ripeness
totschwefeln to overstum *(must)*; to deslime *(wine)*
Totsignal *n (hunt)* mort
Totsonnen *n* solar heat method *(of bark-beetle control)*
Totstellreaktion *f* akinesia *(animal behaviour)*
Tötung *f* kill[ing]
~ durch elektrischen Strom electrocution
~/schmerzlose euthanasia
Totvakzine *f (vet)* dead (inactivated, killed) vaccine
Totwasser *n* still water
Totweiche *f* dead steep, oversteeping *(malting)*
Toulouser Gans *f* Toulouse *(breed of geese)*
Townsend's Schlickgras *n* [Townsend's] cordgrass, Spartina townsendii
Toxalbumin *n* toxalbumin
Toxämie *f (vet)* toxaemia
~ der Küken/alimentäre chick oedema disease, toxic fat disease, congestive heart failure, water belly
~ und Septikämie f/puerperale *(vet)* MAA syndrome *(of pigs)*
Toxaphen *n* toxaphene, camphechlor *(insecticide, rodenticide)*
toxigen toxi[co]genic
Toxigeni[zi]tät *f* toxigenicity
Toxikämie *f s.* Toxämie
Toxikant *n s.* Toxikum

Toxikogenetik *f* toxicogenetics
Toxikokinetik *f* toxicokinetics
Toxikologe *m* toxicologist
Toxikologie *f* toxicology
toxikologisch toxicologic[al]
Toxikose *f* toxicosis
Toxikum *n* toxicant, toxic [substance], poison *(for compounds s. under Gift)*
Toxin *n* toxin • **Toxine erzeugend** toxi[co]genic
~/phytopathogenes phytotoxin
Toxinämie *f (vet)* toxaemia
toxisch toxic[al], poisonous, virulent; venenate
Toxizität *f* toxicity, poisonousness
~/akute acute toxicity
~ gegenüber Fischen fish toxicity
~ gegenüber Pflanzen phytotoxicity
~ gegenüber Pilzen fungitoxicity
~ gegenüber Säugetieren mammalian toxicity
~ gegenüber Vögeln avian toxicity
Toxizitätsbereich *m* toxicity range
Toxizitätsnachweis *m*, **Toxizitätsprüfung** *f* toxicity test[ing]
toxogen toxi[co]genic
Toxoid *n* toxoid
Toxonose *f* toxicosis
Toxoplasmose *f (vet)* toxoplasmosis
ToZBV *s.* Tomatenzwergbuschvirus
TR *s.* Trächtigkeitsrate
Trab *m* trot, jog • **im langsamen ~** ajog • **in ~ versetzen** to trot
~/flotter middle trot
~/kurzer (langsamer) short (slow, collected) trot
~/starker strong (prompt) trot
Trabekel *f (bot, zoo)* trabecula
traben to trot
~/flott to spank
~ lassen to trot
Traber *m* trotter, trotting (harness) horse
Traberderby *n* trotting Derby
Traberkrankheit *f (vet)* scrapie *(of sheep)*
Traberkrankheitsvirus *n* scrapie agent
Trabgang *m s.* Trab
Trabrennen *n* trotting (harness) racing
Trabrennpferd *n s.* Traber
Tracer *m* tracer
Tracermethode *f*, **Tracertechnik** *f* tracer technique
Trachea *f* trachea, windpipe *(animal anatomy)*
tracheal tracheal, tracheary, tracheate
Tracheal... *s. a.* Luftröhren... *and* Tracheo...
Trachealtubus *m (vet)* tracheal tube
Tracheal- und Bronchialschleimhautentzündung *f* Tracheobronchitis
Trachee *f (bot, zoo)* trachea, vessel, vas
tracheenlos atracheate
Tracheensystem *n* tracheal system
tracheidal *(bot)* tracheidal
Tracheide *f* tracheid

Tracheide

~/dünnwandige thin-walled tracheid, early-wood tracheid
~/gefächerte (gekammerte) septate tracheid
Tracheitis f (vet) tracheitis
Tracheo... s. a. Luftröhren...
Tracheobronchitis f (vet) tracheobronchitis
~ der Küken/ansteckende avian infectious bronchitis
~ des Hundes/infektiöse contagious respiratory disease of dogs, kennel cough
Tracheomykose f (phyt) tracheomycosis
Tracheotomie f (vet) tracheotomy
Tracht f 1. honey-bee forage; 2. s. Trachtenwand; 3. (ecol) life form
Trachtbiene f foraging (harvesting, field) bee, flying [honey-]bee, forager
Trachtenwand f quarter (of hoof or claw)
Trachtenwand[horn]spalte f (vet) quarter crack
Trachtenzwinger m (vet) prolapse harness
Trachtflug m (api) foraging trip
trächtig pregnant, impregnate, gravid, heavy, in (with) young; in (with) foal (mare); in (with) farrow (sow) • ~ sein to bear; to be in fawn (red deer) • ~ werden to conceive, to settle
~/nicht non-pregnant, barren, fallow, open, empty
Trächtigkeit f pregnancy, gravidity, gestation
Trächtigkeitsabbruch m pregnancy termination
Trächtigkeitsdauer f pregnancy duration, duration of pregnancy
Trächtigkeitsdiagnose f, Trächtigkeitsfeststellung f pregnancy diagnosis, P.D., pregnancy checking (detection)
Trächtigkeitshormon n pregnancy hormone
Trächtigkeitskalender m pregnancy calendar (table), gestation table
Trächtigkeitskomplikation f pregnancy complication
Trächtigkeitsmeßgerät n pregnancy tester (for sows)
Trächtigkeitsrate f pregnancy rate
Trächtigkeitsstadium n stage of pregnancy
Trächtigkeitsstörung f pregnancy complication
Trächtigkeitstoxämie f pregnancy toxaemia (disease); twin-lamb disease
Trächtigkeitstoxikose f gestational toxicosis
Trächtigkeitsuntersuchung f pregnancy examination
Trächtigkeitstest m pregnancy test
Trächtigkeitszeit f gestation [length, period]
Trachtpflanze f (api) honey (bee) plant
Trachyt m trachyte (soil-forming rock)
Tradeskantie f spiderwort, tradescantia (genus Tradescantia)
Tragant m 1. milk-vetch, loco[-weed], astragalus, tragacanth (genus Astragalus); 2. gum dragon (plant gum)
Tragast m fruiting branch
träge inert (e.g. a soil)
Tragedauer f s. Trächtigkeitsdauer
Tragefläche f s. Tragrand
tragen to carry (e.g. a load); to support; to bear (fruits)
~/Blüten to flower
~/Ernte to crop
~/Frucht (Früchte) to fruit, to crop
~/Samen to seed
~/Zapfen to cone
~/zu reich (stark) to overbear
Tragen n bearing
~/zweijährliches biennial bearing (fruiting), bienniality (orcharding)
tragend 1. (bot) bearing; 2. s. trächtig
Träger m 1. carrier, bearer; 2. atlas (animal anatomy)
Trägerbaum m support tree (e.g. for epiphytes)
Trägergel n gel carrier (in fluid drilling)
Trägermatrix f matrix (cell fixation)
Trägerprotein n carrier protein
Trägerstoff m carrier, vehicle
Tragezeit f s. Trächtigkeitszeit
Tragfähigkeit f [load-]bearing capacity
Trägheitsbaumschüttler m inertial trunk shaker (orcharding)
Tragholz n fruit-bearing wood
Tragjahr n fruit-bearing year
Tragknospe f flower (blossom, fruit) bud
Tragkorb m pannier, basket
~ mit Henkel hamper
Tragkraft f s. Tragfähigkeit
Tragluft[dach]gewächshaus n inflated-roof greenhouse
Tragrand m bearing surface (of hoof or horseshoe)
Tragsackvorfall m s. Gebärmuttervorfall
Tragsattel m pack-saddle
Tragschicht f road base, base course
Tragseil n bearing (carrier) cable, burden (track) cable, skyline (e.g. of a forest cableway)
~/absenkbares slacking line, slack [sky]line
~/verankertes tight [sky]line
Trägspinner m vapourer moth, tussock [moth] (family Lymantriidae)
Tragtier n pack-animal
Tragtraktor m (forest) forwarder
Tragzapfen m clevis (of a three-point hitch)
Tragzapfenhalterung f clevis mounting
trainieren to train
Training n training
Trait du Nord m Trait du Nord (horse breed)
Trakehner m, Trakehner Warmblutpferd n Trakehnen (horse breed)
Traktion f traction, drawing; tractive force
Traktometer m tractometer
Traktor m tractor
~ mit hoher Bodenfreiheit high-clearance [straddle-type] tractor
~ mit Knicklenkung articulated tractor
~ mit Schiebeschild front-mounted tractor scraper

~/mittelschwerer medium tractor
Traktorabgas *n* tractor exhaust
Traktoranbaugerät *n* tractor-mounted implement
Traktor-Anhänger-Kombination *f* rig
Traktoranhängevorrichtung *f* tractor hitch
Traktordrillmaschine *f* tractor[-drawn seed] drill
Traktorenabgas *n* tractor exhaust
Traktorenanhänger *m* tractor trailer
Traktorenbaureihe *f* tractor range
Traktoreneinsatz *m* tractor use
Traktorengarage *f* tractor store
Traktorenkerosin *n* tractor vaporizing oil
Traktorenkraftstoff *m* tractor fuel
Traktorenöl *n* tractor vaporizing oil
Traktorenpark *m* fleet of tractors
Traktorenschuppen *m* tractor shed
Traktorensitz *m* tractor seat
Traktorfahrer *m* tractor driver
Traktorfahrschwingung *f* tractor rid vibration
Traktorfrontanbauvorrichtung *f* tractor front mounting
Traktorgrubber *m* tractor-drawn cultivator
Traktorhacke *f* tractor hoe
Traktorkabine *f* tractor cab
Traktorlader *m* tractor[-mounted] loader
Traktorleistung *f* tractor performance (power)
Traktorleistungsmeßgerät *n* tractor performance monitor
Traktormotor *m* tractor engine
Traktorpflug *m* tractor-plough
Traktorreifen *m* tractor tyre
Traktorrückung *f* *(forest)* tractor skidding
Traktorscharfpflug *m* tractor mould-board plough
Traktorscheibenegge *f* tractor-drawn disk [harrow]
Traktorstunde *f* tractor hour
Traktorwinde *f* tractor winch
Traktorzug *m* tractor haulage
Trampeltier *n* Bactrian (two-humped) camel, Camelus bactrianus
Tran *m* train (fish) oil
tranchieren to carve *(meat)*
Tränenapparat *m* lachrymal (lacrimal) apparatus *(animal anatomy)*
Tränenbein *n* lachrymal bone
Tränender Hausschwamm *m* house (dry-rot) fungus, Serpula (Merulius) lacrymans
Tränendes Herz *n* *(bot)* bleeding heart, Dicentra spectabilis
Tränendrüse *f* lachrymal gland
Tränendrüsensekret *n*, **Tränenflüssigkeit** *f* lachrymal fluid
Tränenkiefer *f* Himalayan (blue, Bhutan) pine, Pinus wallichiana
Tränennasengang *m*, **Tränennasenkanal** *m* tearduct, [naso]lachrymal duct
Tränenträufeln *n* *(vet)* epiphora
Tränkbecken *n* drinking trough (bowl)
Tränke *f* 1. drinking (watering) place; 2. drinker, waterer • **zur ~ gehen** to water *(game)*

Tränkeimer *m* feeding bucket
tränken 1. to water; 2. to soak, to impregnate; to saturate; to drench
~/mit Creosotöl to creosote *(wood)*
Tränkewagen *m* mobile waterer
Tränkkalb *n* bucket-reared calf
Tränknippel *m* drinking nipple
Tränkplatz *m*, **Tränkstelle** *f* drinking (watering) place
Tränktrog *m* water[ing] trough, drinker, waterer
Tränkvorrichtung *f* watering device
Tränkwasser *n* drinking water
Tränkwasserhärte *f* drinking water hardness
Tränkwasserstelle *f* *s*. Tränkplatz
Tranquilizer *m* tranquilizer, neuroleptic
Transaldolase *f* transaldolase *(enzyme)*
Transaminase *f* transaminase, aminotransferase *(enzyme)*
~ B branched-chain-amino-acid aminotransferase
Transaminierung *f* transamination
Transcobalamin *n* transcobalamin, vitamin B_{12} binding substance
Transduktion *f* *(gen)* transduction
Transekt[profil] *n* *(ecol)* transect, bisect
Transfektion *f* transformation *(genetic engineering)*
Transfer *m* transfer
Transferase *f* transferase *(enzyme)*
Transfer-Ribonucleinsäure *f* transfer (soluble) RNA, transfer ribonucleic acid
Transferrin *n* transferrin, siderophilin *(blood-plasma protein)*
Transformation *f* transformation
Transfusion *f* *(vet)* [blood] transfusion
transgen transgenic
Transglycosylase *f* glycosyl transferase *(enzyme)*
Transgression *f* *(gen)* transgression, transgressive segregation (variation)
transgressiv transgressive
transhumant transhumant
Transhumanz *f* transhumance *(method of pasturage)*
Transhydrogenase *f* $NAD(P)^+$ transhydrogenase, pyridine nucleotide transhydrogenase *(enzyme)*
Transketolase *f* transketolase *(enzyme)*
Transkriptase *f*/**Reverse** reverse transcriptase *(enzyme)*
Transkription *f* *(gen)* transcription
Transkriptionsregulation *f* transcriptional control
transkutan transcutaneous, percutaneous
Translation *f* *(gen)* translation
Translationskontrolle *f* translational control
translokal systemic *(pesticide)*
Translokation *f* translocation
Translokationsheterozygote *m* *(gen)* translocation heterozygote
translozieren to translocate
Translozierung *f* translocation
transluzent, transluzid translucent

Transmethylierung

Transmethylierung f transmethylation
Transmission f transmission
Transmissionselektronenmikroskop n transmission electron microscope
transmittieren to transmit
Transmutation f (gen) transmutation
transparent transparent
Transpiration f (bot) transpiration; (zoo) transpiration, perspiration
Transpirationsgeschwindigkeit f s. Transpirationsrate
Transpirationsintensität f transpiration intensity
Transpirationskoeffizient m transpiration coefficient (ratio)
transpirationsmindernd antitranspirant
Transpirationsrate f transpiration rate, rate of transpiration
Transpirationsstrom m transpiration (sap) stream (plant physiology)
Transpirationswiderstand m transpiration resistance
transpiratorisch transpiratory
transpirieren (bot) to transpire; (zoo) to transpire, to perspire
Transplantat n transplant (esp. organs); graft (esp. tissue, skin)
Transplantatabstoßung f graft rejection
Transplantat-gegen-Empfänger-Reaktion f graft-versus-host reaction
Transplantation f transplantation; grafting, graft
Transplantationsimmunität f graft incompatibility
transplantieren to transplant; to graft
transplazental transplacental
Transponder m transponder (automatic livestock identification)
Transport m transport, haulage, handling, (Am) transportation
~/aktiver active transport (biochemistry)
~/innerbetrieblicher in-plant handling
~ mit Zugtieren carting
~/zwischenbetrieblicher intrafarm transport
Transportanlage f transport facility
Transportbehälter m, **Transportcontainer** m [transport, shipping] container
Transporteinrichtung f transport facility
Transportentfernung f transport (hauling) distance
Transporterosion f transportation erosion
Transportfahrzeug n transport vehicle
~/landwirtschaftliches farm transport vehicle
Transporthubschrauber m helitack
transportieren to transport, to haul, to forward
Transportkiste f transport box
Transportmittel npl means of transport, handling machinery (equipment)
Transportnetz n/**forstliches** forest transport[ation] network
Transportprotein n transport protein
Transportstreß m shipping stress

Transportsubstanz f s. Trägerstoff
Transporttetanie f (vet) transport staggers, transit tetany
Transportverlust m handling loss
Transportwesen n transport system, (Am) transportation
Transportwirt m carrier (migratory) host, vector
Transposition f transposition
Transthermie f (vet) diathermy
Transvasierverfahren n transfer method (of making sparkling wine)
Transversalfraktur f (vet) transverse fracture
Transversallage f transverse (trunk) presentation (animal birth)
trapezförmig (bot) trapeziform, trapezoid[al], trapezium-shaped
Trappe f bustard (genus Otis)
Trapper m trapper
Trappistenkäse m trappist cheese
Traube f 1. (bot) raceme (an inflorescence); cluster, bunch (of fruit); 2. [wine] grape, bunch (cluster) of grapes
Träubel n s. Traubenhyazinthe
Traubenabbeermaschine f stemmer, stalk separator
traubenähnlich, traubenartig racemiform, racemose, botryoidal, botryose, cluster-like
Traubenbohne f cluster bean, guar, Cyamopsis tetragonoloba (psoraloides)
Traubeneiche f sessile (stalkless-flowered) oak, durmast [oak], Quercus petraea (sessiliflora)
Traubenerntemaschine f grape harvester
traubenförmig clustered, acinose, acinous; corymbiform
Traubengamander m (bot) cut-leaved germander, Teucrium botrys
Traubengewächshaus n grapery
Traubenhafer m (bot) danthonia (Danthonia)
Traubenholunder m red-berried elder, cut-leaved elder, Sambucus racemosa
Traubenhyazinthe f grape hyacinth (genus Muscari)
Traubenkamm m s. Traubenstiel
Traubenkernöl n grape-seed oil, raisin-seed oil
Traubenkirsche f [European] bird cherry, cluster cherry, Prunus padus, Padus avium
Traubenkirschengespinstmotte f small ermine [moth], Yponomeuta padellus
Traubenkirschen[hafer]laus f bird cherry[-oat] aphid, oat aphis, Rhopalosiphum padi
Traubenkokke f s. Staphylokokkus
Traubenkrankheit f (api, vet) clustering disease
Traubenkur f ampelotherapy
Traubenlager- und -verteilbehälter m grape storage and distribution hopper
Traubenlese f vintage
Traubenmaische f crushed grape
Traubenmost m grape must, unfermented grape-juice, stum
Traubenmühle f grape crusher

~ **mit Abbeermaschine** crusher and stalk separator
Traubenpresse f grape press, winepress, winefat
Traubenpreßkuchen m s. Traubentrester
Traubenpumpe f grape pump
Traubenquetsche f s. Traubenpresse
Traubenrebe f bunch grape, Vitis munsoniana
traubenreich corymbose
Traubenrohsaft m s. Traubenmost
Traubensaft m grape-juice
Traubensaftkonzentrat n concentrated juice from grapes
Traubenschere f grape-scissors
Traubensekt m champagne
Traubensortenkunde f ampelography
Traubenstiel m grape-stalk, cluster stem
traubentragend racemiferous
Traubentrespe f bald brome[-grass], Bromus racemosus
Traubentrester pl grape marc, grape [press] cake, grape husks and seeds
Traubentresterkompost m grape residue compost
Traubenwein m grape wine
Traubenwickler m (ent) 1. grape[-berry] moth, Polychrosia viteana; 2. grape leaf folder (roller), Desmia funeralis
Traubenzucker m grape-sugar, D-glucose, dextrose
Traubenzuckeragar m glucose agar
traubig s. traubenähnlich
Traueraspe f s. Trauerespe
Trauerbaum m 1. night jasmin[e] (genus Nyctanthes); 2. night jasmin[e], tree of sadness, Nyctanthes arbor-tristis
Trauerbuche f [green] weeping beech, Fagus sylvatica cv. pendula
Trauerespe f weeping aspen, Populus tremula cv. pendula
Trauermücke f sciarid fly (family Lycoriidae = Sciaridae)
Trauerulme f weeping elm, Ulmus glabra cv. pendula
Trauerweide f 1. weeping willow, Salix babylonica; 2. weeping (mourning) willow, Salix alba var. tristis
Trauerzypresse f funeral cypress, Chamaecyparis (Cupressus) funebris
Trauf m (forest) windbelt, [stand] border • **den** ~ **aufreißen** to tear open the wind mantle
Träufelspitze f drip trip (of tropical leaf blades)
Traufschutz m (forest) border protection
Trauma n trauma
Traumatin n s. Wundhormon
traumatisch traumatic
Traumatotropismus m (bot) traumatotropism
Treber pl spent grains, brewer's (distiller's) grains (s. a. Trester)
α,α-**Trehalase** f α,α-trehalase (enzyme)
Trehalose f trehalose (disaccharide)

Treibanbau m forced cultivation, forcing
Treibbaumart f (forest) nurse-tree species
Treibbeet n forcing bed (s. a. Frühbeet)
Treibdünger m fertilizer for plant forcing
treiben 1. to drive, to run (livestock); (hunt) to chase, to drive, to beat up; 2. to force (plants); to germinate; 3. s. flößen; 4. s. betreiben
~/**Äste** to branch [out]
~/**aus dem Bau** to unearth (fox or rabbit)
~/**Blätter** to leaf [out]
~/**Blüten** to blossom, to bloom, to flower
~/**den Blattkeim** to acrospire
~/**in den Stall** to cot (esp. sheep)
~/**in eine Koppel** to paddock (livestock)
~/**in einen Pferch** to corral
~/**mit dem Viehtreibstock** to goad
~/**Raubbau** to overcrop
~/**Rinder** (Am) to wrangle
~/**Schosser** to tiller, to sucker
~/**Vieh auf die Weide** to pasture
~/**Vieh über weite Strecken** to overland (Australia)
~/**Wurzeln** to strike roots
~/**Wurzelsprosse** to sucker
treibend/Wurzelsprosse soboliferous
Treiber m (hunt) beater
Treiberei f forced cultivation, forcing
~ **im Warmhaus** hothouse forcing
Treiberlinie f (hunt) line of beaters
Treiberwehr f (hunt) stops
Treibgatter n herd assembling gate
Treibgemüse f [hotbed-]forced vegetable
Treibgewächs n forcing crop
Treibglied n drive link (of a saw chain)
Treibhaus n forcing [green]house, glasshouse, [glass] greenhouse, growing house, conservatory (for compounds s. under Gewächshaus)
Treibholz n drift-wood, [loose-]floated timber
Treibholzart f s. Treibbaumart
Treibjagd f battue [shooting], beat, (Am) drive
~ **im Felde** (Am) field drive
Treibkasten m forcing frame (pit)
Treibkiste f flat
Treibkultur f forced (forcing) crop
Treibmist f liquid manure
Treibmistkanal m slurry channel
Treibnetz n drift net
Treibrad n driving (drive) wheel
Treibradreifen m traction tyre
Treibreis m floating (deep-water) rice
Treibsand m s. Triebsand
Treibschnee m drifting snow
Treibstoff m fuel
Treibstofftank m fuel tank
Treibstoffverbrauch m fuel consumption
Trematode f trematode [worm], fluke (class Trematoda)
Trematodenvernichtungsmittel n flukicide
Tremor m (vet) tremor

Tremor

~/epidemischer avian encephalomyelitis
Trenbolon n trenbolone (anabolic agent)
Trennanalyse f (biom) discriminant (discriminatory) analysis
Trennart f (ecol) differential species
Trennbaum m bail (in stables)
Trenneinrichtung f separating device, separator
Trenngewebe n s. Trennschicht
Trenngitter n separating lattice, partition (e.g. in animal houses)
Trennkraft f separation (removal) force (fruit picking)
Trennkultur f barrier crop
Trennsäge f (slaught) carcass splitting saw
Trennschicht f (bot) separation (abscission) layer
Trennschleuder f centrifuge
Trennungshieb m (forest) severance felling
Trense f snaffle, bridoon, bit • **die ~ anlegen** to snaffle
Trensengebiß n snaffle-bit
~/ungebrochenes bar snaffle bit
Trensenring m snaffle (cheek) ring, cheekpiece
Trensenzaum m snaffle
Trensenzügel m snaffle rein
Trepanation f (vet) trepanation
Treppenstellage f stepped shelving (greenhouse installation)
Trespe f brome[-grass] (genus Bromus)
Trespenbrand m head smut of grasses (caused by Ustilago bullata)
Trespenfederschwingel m barren fescue, Vulpia bromoides
Trespenmosaikvirus n brome mosaic virus
Trester pl marc, pomace, rape (s. a. Treber)
Tresterbranntwein m marc, eau-de-vie de marc
Trestergeschmack m stem-like taste (defect of wine)
Tresterkuchen m marc cake
Tresterschleuder f marc crumbler (disintegrator), pomace breaker (crusher, mill)
Tresterwein m marc [wine], rape wine
Tretamin n tretamine (chemosterilant, herbicide)
treten s. bespringen
Tretmühle f treadmill, tread-wheel (e.g. for exercising horses)
Treue f 1. trueness (of wool fibre); 2. fidelity (plant ecology)
TRFV s. Tabakringfleckenvirus
TRH s. Thyreotropin-Releasinghormon
Trh s. Traktorstunde
Triacontanol n triacontanol (growth regulator)
Triacylglycerid n s. Triglycerid
Triacylglycerollipase f [triacylglycerol] lipase, glycerol ester hydrolase, tributyrase (enzyme)
Triadimefon n triadimefon (fungicide)
Triadimenol n triadimenol (fungicide)
Triallat n triallate (herbicide)
Triamiphos n triamiphos (fungicide)

Triammoniumphosphat n triammonium phosphate
Triammoniumpyrophosphat n triammonium pyrophosphate
Triangulation f 1. triangulation, notch grafting; crown grafting by inlaying; 2. triangulation (terrestrial survey)
Triangulationspunkt m triangulation point, trigonometric[al] point
Triangulierung f s. Triangulation
Triarimol n triarimol (fungicide)
Triazbutyl n triazbutyl (fungicide)
Triazin n triazine (herbicide)
Triazophos n triazophos (insecticide, nematicide)
Tribromsalan n, **3,4',5-Tribromsalicylanilid** n tribromsalan (anthelmintic)
Tribus m tribe (taxonomy)
Tributylphosphat n tributyl phosphate
Tributylphosphoniumchlorid n tributyl phosphonium chloride
Tributylzinn n tributyltin (molluscicide)
Tributylzinnoxid n tributyltin oxide (fungicide)
Tributyrin n tributyrin (glyceride)
Tricalciumphosphat n tricalcium phosphate
Tricarbonsäure f tricarboxylic acid
Tricarbonsäurezyklus m tricarboxylic (citric) acid cycle, TCA cycle, Krebs cycle (biochemistry)
Trichiasis f (vet) trichiasis
Trichine[lle] f (zoo) trichina (genus Trichinella)
Trichinellose f s. Trichinose
trichinenhaltig s. trichinös
Trichinenkrankheit f s. Trichinose
Trichinenschau f (vet) trichinoscopy
trichinös (vet) trichinous, measly
Trichinose f (vet) trichinosis, trichinellosis, trichiniasis
Trichinoskopie f (vet) trichinoscopy
Trichloressigsäure f, **Trichlorethansäure** f trichloroacetic acid
Trichlorfon n trichlorfon, trichlorphon, chlorophos, chlorofos (insecticide)
Trichlormethan n trichloromethane, chloroform
Trichlormethylphosphonat n trichloromethyl phosphonate
Trichloronat n trichloronate (insecticide)
Trichlorophen n trichlorophen (anthelmintic)
Trichobezoar m (vet) trichobezoar
Trichodermin n trichodermin (mycotoxin)
Trichom n trichome, plant hair
Trichomonade f (zoo) trichomonad (genus Trichomonas)
Trichomonadenseuche f, **Trichomonose** f (vet) trichomoniasis, trichomonosis
Trichophagie f trichophagy, fur-eating
Trichophytie f (vet) trichophytosis, ringworm, tinea
Trichopilarmuskel m arrector pili muscle
Trichostrongylose f, **Trichostrongylusinfektion** f (vet) trichostrongylosis
Trichothecen n trichothecene (mycotoxin)

Trichothecin n trichothecin (antibiotic)
Trichothecium-Fäule f [des Kernobstes] pink rot [of pome fruit] (caused by Trichothecium roseum)
trichotomisch (bot) trichotomous
Trichter m funnel; hopper (for delivering materials)
Trichterfalle f funnel trap
Trichterfarn m ostrich fern, Matteuccia struthiopteris
trichterförmig infundibular, infundibulate
Trichterling m (bot) clitocybe (genus Clitocybe)
Trichtermalve f 1. malope (genus Malope); 2. three cleft mallow-wort, Malope trifida
Trichterrohr m funnel tube
Trichterzitze f inverted nipple
Trichuriasis f, **Trichurose** f (vet) trichuriasis, trichocephaliasis
Triclopyr n triclopyr (herbicide)
Tricyclazol n tricyclazole (fungicide)
Tridecansäure f tridecanoic acid (fatty acid)
Tridemorph n tridemorph (fungicide)
Tridermom n s. Teratom
Tridimenol n tridimenol (fungicide)
Tridymit m tridymite (non-clay mineral)
Trieb m 1. (bot) shoot, sprout; 2. drive • **Triebe ablegen (absenken)** to layer • **~ entfernen** to deshoot
~/einjähriger annual shoot; feather (of woody fruit plants)
~/einmalig tragender cane (e.g. of raspberry or grape)
~/junger young shoot
~/kleiner twig
~/mittellanger medium-sized shoot
~/vorzeitiger precocious shoot; feather (of woody fruit plants)
Triebabschluß m cessation of shoot growth
Triebachsenanhänger m shaft-driven trailer
Triebausreifung f shoot lignification
Triebbiegsamkeit f shoot flexibility
Triebbleichung f stem blanching
Triebkraft f germinating (germinative) power, vigour
Triebproliferation f shoot proliferation
Triebrad n drive wheel
Triebsand m drift (shifting, travelling) sand, quicksand
Triebschwellungsvirus n **des Kakaobaumes** cacao swollen shoot virus
Triebspitze f shoot tip (apex), terminal
Triebstecherlarve f (ent) leaf-roller (genus Rhynchites)
Triebstumpf m stub, stump
Triebverholzung f shoot lignification
Triebwelke f shoot wilting
Triebwickler m shoot (tip) moth (genus Evetria)
Triel m 1. dewlap, jowl (of oxen); 2. muffcock, Burhinus oedicnemus
Trietazin n trietazine (herbicide)
Triethylamin n triethylamine

Triethylaminmelamin n triethylaminemelamine (sterilant)
Trieur m indented cylinder seed cleaner
Trifenmorph n trifenmorph (molluscicide)
Trifenofos n trifenofos (insecticide)
Triflumuron n triflumuron (insecticide)
Trifluralin n trifluralin (herbicide)
Trifoliose f (vet) trifoliosis, clover disease
Trifop n trifop (herbicide)
Triforin n triforin[e] (fungicide)
Trift f 1. drive [alley], driveway, cattle drive (track), drove; 2. pasture
triften to drift, to drive, to float (timber)
Triften n, **Triftflößerei** f [loose] floating, river (timber, log) driving
Triftholz n drift-wood, [loose-]floated timber
~/gestrandetes stranded timber
Triftholzstau m [log-]jam, plug
Triftrecht n floating right
Triftrinnenverstopfung f, **Triftstauung** f [log-]jam, plug
Triftstraße f, **Triftweg** m 1. driftway, float road (way); 2. s. Trift 1.
Triglycerid n triglyceride, triacylglycerol
~/langkettiges long-chain triglyceride
Triglyceridhydrolase f triglyceride hydrolase (enzyme)
Trigonellin n trigonelline (alkaloid)
Trigonmelkstand m triangle (trigon) milking parlour
1,3,5-Trihydroxybenzen n phloroglucin[ol]
3,4,5-Trihydroxybenzoesäure f 3,4,5-trihydroxybenzoic acid, gallic acid
3,4,5-Trihydroxycyclohexen-1-carbonsäure f shikimic acid (phytohormone, growth regulator)
Triiodthyronin n triiodothyronine (thyroid hormone)
Trikosan n tricosane (carbohydrate)
Trilaurin n trilaurin (triglyceride)
Trimedlure n trimedlure (insect attractant)
trimer (bot) trimerous
Trimethoprim n trimethoprim (antiinfective agent)
Trimethylamin n trimethylamine
2-Trimethylammonio-ethanol n choline (phospholipid)
6,7,9-Trimethylisoalloxazin n lumiflavine
Trimethylphosphat n trimethyl phosphate
Trimeturon n trimeturon (herbicide)
trimmen to trim (e.g. dogs)
Trimmer m (forest) trimmer, trimming machine
trimorph trimorphic
Trimorphamid n trimorphamide (fungicide)
Trimorphismus m trimorphism
Trinidadkrankheit f (vet) paralytic rabies
Trinkmilch f liquid milk, drinking (fluid) milk
Trinksauermilch f cultured buttermilk
Trinkverhalten n drinking behaviour (habits)
Trinkwasser n drinking water; municipal (city) water

Trinkwassereinzugsgebiet 642

Trinkwassereinzugsgebiet *n* public (municipal) watershed
Trinkwasserhärte *f* drinking water hardness
Triolein *n* triolein *(triglyceride)*
Triose *f* triose *(monosaccharide)*
Triosephosphatdehydrogenase *f* glyceraldehyde-3-phosphate dehydrogenase *(enzyme)*
Triosephosphatisomerase *f* triose-phosphate isomerase *(enzyme)*
1,3,5-Trioxybenzen *n* phloroglucin[ol]
triözisch *(bot)* trioecious
Tripeptid *n* tripeptide
Triphenylzinnacetat *n* triphenyltin acetate, fentin-acetate *(fungicide)*
Triple[super]phosphat *n* triple superphosphate *(fertilizer)*
Triplett *n* triplet
triploid *(gen)* triploid
Triploide *m* triploid
Triploidie *f* triploidy
Tripmadam *f* *(bot)* tripmadam, Sedum reflexum
Tripren *n* triprene *(insecticide)*
Tripropindan *n* tripropindan *(herbicide)*
Trisaccharid *n* trisaccharide
Trisein *n* trisein *(antibiotic)*
trisom *(gen)* trisomic
Trisomie *f* trisomy
Tristearin *n* tristearin
tristich *(bot)* tristichous
Triterpen *n* triterpene
Triterpensäure *f* triterpene acid
Triticale *m* triticale, wheat-rye hybrid, rye x wheat
Tritome *f* *(bot)* 1. red-hot poker, kniphofia, tritoma *(genus Kniphofia)*; 2. torch lily, Kniphofia uvaria
Tritonymphe *f* tritonymph *(of mites)*
Trittfestigkeit *f* resistance to poaching (trampling), bearing capacity *(of a pasture or lawn)*
Trittplatte *f* stepping stone *(e.g. in gardening)*
Trittschaden *m* trampling damage
Triumphtulpe *f* triumph tulip *(group of cultivars)*
Trivalent *n* trivalent *(of meiotically paired chromosomes)*
Trivialname *m* vernacular name
Trizeps *m* triceps [muscle]
TrMV *s.* Trespenmosaikvirus
Trobicin *n s.* Spectinomycin
Trochanter *m* *(zoo, ent)* trochanter
trocken 1. dry, moisture-free *(e.g. substances)*; seasoned *(wood)*; 2. droughty, dry, arid, barren, jejune *(as soil)*; xeric *(e.g. a habitat)*; 3. dry, withered *(e.g. leaves)*; 4. dry, brut, sec, austere *(wine)*; 5. *s.* trockenstehend • ~ **werden** to dehydrate
~/absolut oven-dry, oven-dried, bone-dry
~ zur Verschiffung surface-dry *(timber)*
Trockenast *m* dead branch; dead (encased) knot
trockenasten *(forest)* to brush through (up)
Trockenastung *f* dry (low) pruning
Trockenbeizapparat *m* dry powder treater

Trockenbeizen *n* dry dressing (disinfection), dust treatment
Trockenbeizmaschine *f* powder dresser
Trockenblume *f* immortelle, everlasting *(comprehensive term)*
Trockenbodensalzigkeit *f*, **Trockenbodenversalzung** *f* dry-land salinity
Trockenbohne *f s.* Gartenbohne
Trockendestillation *f* dry distillation
Trockenei *n* dried (powdered) egg, egg powder
Trockeneis *n* dry ice
Trockeneiweiß *n* ovalbumin
Trockenerbse *f* dry (dried) pea, haricot pea
Trockenfarm *f* dry farm
Trockenfarmerei *f* dry[-land] farming, rain-fed farming • ~ **betreiben** to dry-farm
Trockenfäule *f* *(phyt)* (hard) rot
~ der Gladiole fusarium corm rot of gladiolus *(caused by Fusarium oxysporum f.sp. gladioli)*
Trockenfeldbau *m s.* Trockenfarmerei
Trockenfleisch *n* dried meat
Trockenfutter *n* 1. dry (dehydrated) feed; provender *(for pets)*; 2. *s.* Trockengrobfutter
Trockenfutterautomat *m* automatic dry-meal feeder, dry feeder
Trockenfutterhefe *f* fodder (food, mineral) yeast
Trockenfuttermittel *n s.* Trockenfutter
Trockenfütterung *f* dry feeding • **durch ~ mästen** to stall[-feed]
Trockengebiet *n* dry area
Trockengehölz *n* dry woodland
Trockengerüst *n s.* Trockengestell
Trockengeschwindigkeit *f* rate of drying, drying rate
Trockengestell *n* hack, tray, flake, crib
Trockengewicht *n* dry weight
Trockengewitter *n* dry storm
Trockengras *n* dryland grass
Trockengrobfutter *n* dry roughage, dehydrated fodder
Trockengrün[futter] *n* dried grass (green crop)
Trockengut *n* 1. dry product, material being dried; 2. *s.* Trocknungsgut
Trockenhärte *f* drought hardness
Trockenhärtung *f* drought-hardening
trockenhäutig *(bot)* scarious
Trockenhefe *f* dry (dried brewer's) yeast
Trockenheit *f* 1. dryness, aridity, aridness, drought *(of land or climate)*; 2. drought, dryness period; 3. *(vet)* xerosis
~/atmosphärische air drought
~ der Haut/abnorme *(vet)* xeroderm[i]a
~/physiologische physiological drought (dryness)
trockenheitsanfällig drought-sensitive, drought-susceptible
Trockenheitsanfälligkeit *f* drought sensitivity (susceptibility)
Trockenheitsindex *m* drought index, index of aridity

trockenheitsliebend aridophilous, xerophytic, xerophilous
trockenheitsresistent drought-resistant
Trockenheitsresistenz *f* drought resistance
trockenheitstolerant drought-tolerant, xerotolerant
Trockenheitstoleranz *f* drought tolerance
Trockenholz *n* dry wood; dead wood
~/liegendes down timber, fallen dead wood
~/stehendes dead-standing tree
Trockenhorde *f s.* Trockengestell
Trockenkalkung *f* dry liming *(sugar manufacture)*
Trockenkammer *f* drying chamber (room), [seasoning] kiln
Trockenkonservat *n* dried preserve
trockenlegen to drain, to dewater
Trockenlegung *f* drainage *(s. a. under* Dränung*)*
~ von Wäldern forest draining
Trockenluft *f* drying air
Trockenmagermilch *f* dried skim milk, skim-milk powder
Trockenmasse *f* 1. dry weight; 2. *s.* Trockensubstanz
Trockenmassebestimmung *f* dry weight determination
Trockenmauer *f* [dry] stone wall *(gardening)*
Trockenmauerpflanze *f* wall plant
Trockenmilch *f* dried (dry, powdered) milk, milk-powder
Trockenmilchanlage *f* milk drying plant
Trockenmilcherzeugnis *n* dried milk product
Trockenmolke *f* dried (dry) whey, powdered whey
Trockenmüllerei *f* dry milling
Trockenmuser *m* dry masher
Trockennährboden *m* dehydrated medium
Trockenobst *n* dried (evaporated) fruit
Trockenperiode *f* 1. dry period *(of dairy cattle)*; 2. drought, dryness period
Trockenpflanze *f* xerophyte
~ mit wasserspeicherndem Gewebe *s.* Sukkulente
Trockenpilze *mpl* dried mushrooms
trockenpökeln to dry-cure, to dry-salt
Trockenpyramide *f* tripod
Trockenquark *m* dry quarg, acid curd from skim milk
Trockenraum *m s.* Trockenkammer
Trockenreis *m* dry-land (rain-fed) rice, mountain (upland) rice
Trockenresistenz *f* drought resistance
Trockenriese *f (forest)* dry chute (slide)
Trockenriß *m* drought crack, seasoning check *(in timber)*; sun-crack
Trockenrohdichte *f* [dry-]bulk density, dry density *(of soil)*
Trockenrübe *f* dried beet
Trockenrückstand *m* dry residue
Trockenrupfmaschine *f* dry plucker *(poultry processing)*
Trockenrutsche *f s.* Trockenriese

Trockensahne *f* dried cream
Trockensalzen *n* dry salting *(cheese-making)*
Trockensäule *f* tower dryer
Trockensavanne *f* dry savanna[h], arid savanna[h]
Trockenscheibenkupplung *f* dry disk (plate) clutch
Trockenscheune *f* drying barn
Trockenschlempe *f* distiller's dried solubles
Trockenschnitzel *npl* dried [beet] pulp, dried sugar-beet chips
~/melassierte dried molassed beet pulp
Trockenschrank *m* oven • **im ~ trocknen** to oven-dry
trockenschrankgetrocknet oven-dry, oven-dried
Trockenschrankmethode *f* oven methode *(for moisture determination)*
Trockenschroten *n*, **Trockenschrotverfahren** *n* dry grinding (milling) *(malting)*
Trockenschuppen *m* crib
Trockenschuppenlagerung *f* crib storage
Trockenspeisebohne *f* dry [edible] bean, haricot [bean]
Trockenspeiseerbse *f* dry (dried) pea
Trockenstarterfutter *n* dry starter feed
trockenstehend *pr (dairy cattle)*
Trockenstehperiode *f* dry period *(of dairy cattle)*
trockenstellen to dry off *(a cow)*
Trockensterilisator *m* hot-air sterilizer
Trockenstoff *m s.* Trocknungsmittel
Trockenstrauchformation *f* maquis *(of mediterranean areas)*
Trockenstreß *m* drought stress
Trockensubstanz *f* dry matter (substance), DM, solids
~/fettfreie [milk] solids-not-fat, SNF, non-fat solids
~/verdauliche digestible dry matter
Trockensubstanzakkumulation *f* dry matter accumulation
Trockensubstanzaufnahme *f* dry matter intake
Trockensubstanzbildung *f* dry matter production
Trockensubstanzdichte *f* dry matter density
Trockensubstanzgehalt *m* dry matter content
Trockensubstanzspeicherung *f* dry matter storage
Trockensubstanzverzehr *m* dry matter consumption
Trockentoleranz *f* drought tolerance
Trockentreber *pl* dried brewer's grains
Trockentrommel *f s.* Trommeltrockner
Trockenturm *m* drying tower
Trockenvakzine *f (vet)* desiccated vaccine
Trockenvermahlung *f* dry milling
Trockenvollmilch *f* dried whole milk, whole milk powder
Trockenwald *m* dry forest
Trockenwalze *f* roller dryer
Trockenwiese *f* dry meadow
Trockenzeit *f* dry season *(in the tropics)*

trockenzuckern

trockenzuckern to chaptalize *(wine)*
Trockenzuckerung *f* chaptalization
Trockenzwiebel *f* annual onion
trocknen to dry, to dehydrate, to desiccate; to season *(e.g. wood)*; to cure *(e.g. tobacco)*
~/**an der Luft** to air-dry; to air-cure *(e.g. tobacco)*
~/**an der Sonne** to sun[-dry], to sun-cure
~/**auf einem Gestell** to hack
~/**im Trockenschrank** to oven-dry
~/**künstlich (technisch)** to kiln-dry, to dehydrate
~/**übermäßig** to overdry
Trockner *m* 1. dryer, drier, drying plant (facility), dehydrating plant, kiln; 2. *s.* Trocknungsmittel
~/**kontinuierlich arbeitender** progressive kiln
~/**pneumatischer** pneumatic dryer
Trockneraufgabegut *n s.* Trocknungsgut
Trocknisschaden *m (forest)* drought injury
Trocknung *f* drying, dehydration, desiccation; seasoning; curing
~ **der Blattspreite** colour-setting stage *(of tobacco curing)*
~ **durch Sonnenenergie** solar drying
~ **mittels Lösungsmittel** solvent drying
Trocknungsanlage *f s.* Trockner 1.
Trocknungscharge *f* kiln load
Trocknungseinrichtung *f s.* Trockner 1.
Trocknungsfahrplan *m* drying schedule, kiln (seasoning) schedule
Trocknungsfehler *m* seasoning defect *(wood)*
Trocknungsgeschwindigkeit *f* speed (rate) of drying, drying rate
Trocknungsgut *n* product (material) to be dried
Trocknungsluft *f* drying air
Trocknungsmaschine *f* mechanical dryer
Trocknungsmittel *n* drier, desiccant, dehydration (drying) agent
Trocknungsplan *m s.* Trocknungsfahrplan
Trocknungsplatz *m (forest)* seasoning (drying) yard
Trocknungsscheune *f*, **Trocknungsschuppen** *m* drying (curing) barn
Trocknungsspannung *f* drying stress *(in timber)*
Trocknungstafel *f s.* Trocknungsfahrplan
Trocknungstemperatur *f* drying temperature
Trocknungsverlust *m* loss on drying
Trocknungsverwerfung *f*, **Trocknungsverziehung** *f* warping during seasoning, seasoning set *(of timber)*
Troddelblume *f (bot)* soldanella *(genus Soldanella)*
Trog *m* trough, manger, vat, tub
Trogbeet *n* trough bed
Trogentrinder *m (forest)* pocket (bag) barker
Trogfläche *f* trough space
Trogförderer *m* pan conveyor
Trogfutter *n* trough food
Trogfütterung *f* trough (manger) feeding
Trogkettenförderer *m* trough [and] chain conveyor, pan conveyor; rigid-arm elevator

Troglänge *f* manger length
Trograum *m* trough space
Trogtränke *f* trough-type waterer, water[ing] trough
Troika *f* troika *(equestrian sport)*
Trokar *m (vet)* troc[h]ar
Trollblume *f* 1. globe-flower *(genus Trollius)*; 2. [mountain] globe-flower, Trollius europaeus
Trombidiose *f* trombidiasis *(anthropozoonosis)*
Trommelbremse *f* drum brake
Trommelbrüter *m* drum incubator
Trommelentrinder *m*, **Trommelentrindungsmaschine** *f* drum [de]barker
Trommelentsafter *m* cylinder-type juice separator
Trommelextrakteur *m*, **Trommelextraktionsanlage** *f* rotary drum diffusion apparatus *(sugar manufacture)*
Trommelfeldhäcksler *m* pick-up cylinder hopper
Trommelfell *n* tympanic membrane *(animal anatomy)*
Trommelgrasmäher *m* drum-type hay mower
Trommelhacker *m*, **Trommelhackmaschine** *f* drum chipper
Trommelhäcksler *m* cylinder-type chopper
Trommelkartoffelsortierer *m* rotary potato sorter
Trommelmähmaschine *f*, **Trommelmähwerk** *n* drum (cylinder) mower
Trommelmälzerei *f* drum malting
Trommelrasenmäher *m* cylinder lawn mower
Trommelrechen *m* side[-delivery] rake
Trommelrechwender *m* rotary haymaker, combined side rake and tedder
Trommelrupfer *m* drum picking machine
Trommelsaugfilter *n* rotary drum [vacuum] filter, vacuum drum filter
~/**zellenloses** non-cellular rotary drum [vacuum] filter
Trommelschnitzelmaschine *f* drum slicer (cutter) *(sugar-beet processing)*
Trommelseilwinde *f (forest)* yarding donkey, yarder
Trommelsiebmaschine *f* drum sifting device; rubble reel *(seed processing)*
Trommeltrockner *m* [rotary] drum dryer, cylinder (tumble) dryer; granulator *(sugar manufacture)*
Trommelwaschmaschine *f* rotary drum washer *(e.g. for root crops)*
Trommelwinde *f* drum winch
Trommelzetter *m* cylinder hay tedder
Trompetenbaum *m (bot)* catalpa *(genus Catalpa)*
Trompetenblume *f* trumpet creeper (vine, flower), Campsis (Tecoma) radicans
Trompetennarzisse *f* daffodil, Lent lily, trumpet narcissus, Narcissus pseudonarcissus
Trompetenzunge *f (bot)* painted tongue, salpiglossis, Salpiglossis sinuata
Tronchudakohl *m* Portuguese cabbage (kale), Brassica oleracea convar. capitata var. costata
Tropa[n]alkaloid *n* tropane alkaloid
Tropen *pl* [the] tropics

Tropenforstwirtschaft f exotic forestry
Tropengewächshaus n tropical [green]house
Tropengürtel m tropical belt
Tropenholz n tropical wood (timber), exotic timber
Tropenholzart f exotic tree species
Tropenklima n tropical climate
Tropenlandwirtschaft f tropical agriculture
Tropenobst n tropical fruit
Tropenwald m tropical forest, jungle
Tropenwaldwirtschaft f exotic forestry
Tropfbewässerung f drip (droplet, trickle) irrigation, daily-flow (high-frequency) irrigation; spaghetti irrigation *(of potted plants)*
Tröpfchenapplikation f droplet application *(plant protection)*
~/gesteuerte controlled droplet application (technique), CDA
Tröpfchenbewässerung f s. Tropfbewässserung
Tröpfchengröße f droplet size
Tröpfcheninfektion f *(vet)* droplet (airborne, aerator) infection
Tröpfchenspektrum n droplet spectrum
Tröpfchenverteilung f droplet distribution
Tropfdüse f [rain]drop nozzle
Tröpfelschlauch m trickle (drip) hose
Tropfeninfiltrometer n drip infiltrometer
Tropfenspektrum n drop spectrum
Tropfer m s. Tropfkörper
Tropfinfusion f *(vet)* drop infusion
Tropfkörper m, **Tröpfler** m dripper, [water] emitter
Tropfmilch f drip milk, milk drainings
Tropfrinne f gutter *(resin-tapping)*
Trophäe f *(hunt)* trophy
Trophallaxis f *(ent)* trophallaxis
Trophie f trophy
trophisch trophic
Trophoblast m *(zoo)* trophoblast
tropisch tropical
Tropische Piroplasmose f *(vet)* tropical piroplasmosis (gonderiosis, theileriosis), Egyptian fever, Mediterranean [coast] fever *(caused by Theileria annulata)*
~ Rattenmilbe f rat mite, Ornithonyssus (Bdellonyssus) bacoti
~ Speichermotte f chocolate moth, dried fig (currant) moth, Ephestia cautella
Tropischer Rattenfloh m [tropical] rat flea, Xenopsylla cheopis
Tropismus m tropism
Tropokollagen n tropocollagen
Tropomyosin n tropomyosin *(muscle protein)*
Troponin n troponin *(muscle protein)*
Tropopause f tropopause
Tropophyt m trophophyte
Troposphäre f troposphere
Troposphärenobergrenze f tropopause
Trosse f cable; hawser
Trp s. Tryptophan

Trub m sediment; trub, coagulum, coagulate, sludge *(brewing)*; lees, dregs, draff, emptings, deposit from must *(wine-making)*
trübe hazy
Trübe f slurry *(in filtration)*
Trubfilter n lees filter
Trübheit f turbidity, haziness
Trübstoff m suspended matter
Trübung f turbidity, haze
~/biologische biological haze *(e.g. of beer)*
~/kolloidale (kolloide) colloidal haze
~/milchige milkiness
Trübungsmesser m haze meter
Trübungsmessung f turbidimetry, turbidity measurement
Trubwürze f first runnings *(brewing)*
Trüffel f truffle, earth ball *(genus Tuber)*
Trüffelboden m truffle soil
Trüffelhund m truffle-dog
Trüffelschwein n truffle-pig
Trugdolde f *(bot)* cyme
trugdoldig cymose
Trugwirtel m *(bot)* false whorl
Trümmerfraktur f *(vet)* comminuted (multiple) fracture
Trunkelbeere f 1. black crowberry, Empetrum nigrum; 2. s. Rauschbeere
Trupp m herd *(of red deer)*
Truthahn m turkeycock, tom turkey, he-turkey, gobbler, bubbly-jock
Truthenne f turkey hen
Truthuhn n 1. turkey *(genus Meleagris)*; 2. turkey, Meleagris domesticus; 3. wild turkey, Meleagris gallo-pavo
Trutzfärbung f s. Warnfärbung
Trypanblau n trypan blue *(dye)*
Trypanosoma n *(zoo)* trypanosome *(genus Trypanosoma)*
trypanosomenabtötend trypanocidal
trypanosomentolerant trypanotolerant
Trypanosomose f trypanosomiasis, nagana, fly-disease *(of ruminants, caused by numerous Trypanosomatidae)*
trypanozid trypanocidal
Trypsin n trypsin *(enzyme)*
Trypsinhemmstoff m trypsin inhibitor, antitrypsin [substance]
Trypsinogen n trypsinogen *(trypsin precursor)*
Trypsinverdauung f trypsin digestion
Tryptamin n tryptamine
Tryptophan n tryptophan[e] *(amino-acid)*
Tryptophanase f tryptophanase *(enzyme)*
Tryptophandecarboxylase f aromatic-L-amino-acid decarboxylase, tryptophan decarboxylase *(enzyme)*
Tryptophan-2,3-Dioxygenase f tryptophan 2,3-dioxygenase, tryptophan oxygenase (pyrrolase) *(enzyme)*

Tryptophan-5-Monooxygenase

Tryptophan-5-Monooxygenase *f* tryptophan 5-monooxygenase *(enzyme)*
Tryptophansynthase *f* tryptophan synthase *(enzyme)*
Tryptophan-tRNA-Ligase *f* tryptophan-tRNA ligase *(enzyme)*
TS *s.* Trockensubstanz
Tschernosjom *m(n)* chernozem, black earth (soil)
tschilpen to chirp
Tsetsefliege *f* tsetse [fly] *(genus Glossina)*
Tsetsekrankheit *f s.* Trypanosomose
TSH *s.* Thyreotropin
TS[i]V *s.* Tabakstrichelvirus
t-Test *m (biom)* t-test, Student's [t-]test
Tubargravidität *f* oviductal (tubal, Fallopian) pregnancy
Tubawurzel *f* derris (tuba) root, Derris elliptica
Tuberkel *m(f)* tubercle
Tuberkelbakterium *n* tubercle bacillus
tuberkelbildend, tuberkular tubercular, tuberculate[d]
Tuberkulin *n* tuberculin
tuberkulingeprüft tuberculin-tested, TT
Tuberkulinisierung *f*, **Tuberkulinprobe** *f* tuberculin test
Tuberkulinspritze *f* tuberculin syringe
tuberkulös tuberculous
Tuberkulose *f* tuberculosis, TB, phthisis, consumption
Tuberkuloseknötchen *n* tubercle
tuberos tuberous, tuberose
Tuberose *f (bot)* tuberose, Polianthes tuberosa
Tubocin *n* rifampicin *(antibiotic)*
Tubocurarin *n* tubocurarine *(alkaloid)*
TuBSV *s.* Tulpenbuntstreifigkeitsvirus
tubulär, tubulös tubular
Tuff *m (soil)* tuff *(of volcanic origin)*; tufa, tophus *(of sedimentary origin)*
~/blühender flourishing clump
tuffartig tuffaceous
Tuffboden *m* tuff soil
Tufferde *f* tufaceous earth
TuHNV *s.* Hofnekrosevirus der Tulpe
Tularämie *f (vet)* tularaemia, rabbit fever *(caused by Francisella tularensis)*
Tulpe *f* tulip *(genus Tulipa)*
Tulpenbaum *m* 1. yellow poplar *(genus Liriodendron)*; 2. yellow poplar, tulip-tree, *(Am)* poplar, Liriodendron tulipifera; 2. African (red) tulip-tree, Spathodea campanulata
Tulpenbuntstreifigkeit *f* tulip breaking *(virosis)*
Tulpenbuntstreifigkeitsvirus *n* tulip breaking virus
Tulpenfeuer *n* fire (botrytis blight) of tulip *(caused by Botrytis tulipae)*
Tulpengallmilbe *f* wheat curl mite, Eriophyes tulipae
Tulpenköpfer *m* tulip topper
Tulpenkrätze *f s.* Tulpenzwiebeldermatitis

Tulpenmagnolie *f* Chinese magnolia, Magnolia x soulangiana
Tulpenmohn *m* tulip poppy, Papaver glaucum
Tulpenweißstreifigkeitsvirus *n* tulip white streak virus
Tulpenzüchter *m* tulipist
Tulpenzwiebel *f* tulip bulb
Tulpenzwiebeldermatitis *f* tulip finger (nails)
Tulpenzwiebellaus *f* tulip bulb aphid, Dysaphis tulipae
Tulsipflanze *f* holy (sacred) basil, holy herb, Ocimum tenuiflorum (sanctum)
Tümmlertaube *f* tumbler-pigeon *(group of breeds)*
Tumor *m (phyt, vet)* tumour
~/durch Pilze hervorgerufener *(phyt)* mycetoma
Tumorantigen *n* tumour antigen
Tumorbildung *f* oncogenesis
tumorerzeugend oncogenic, oncogenous
tumorös tumorous
Tumorvirus *n* tumour (oncogenic) virus
Tuna *f* tuna *(edible fruit of Opuntia spp.)*
Tünche *f* whitewash
tünchen to whitewash
Tundra *f* tundra
Tundraboden *m* tundra soil
Tungbaum *m* tung [tree] *(genus Aleurites)*
Tungöl *n* tung (Chinese wood) oil, Chinawood oil *(esp. from Aleurites fordii)*
Tungölbaum *m* Chinese wood-oil tree, tung[-oil] tree, Aleurites fordii
Tunica *f (bot, zoo)* tunic
tunicat *(bot, zoo)* tunicate[d]
Tunneltrockner *m* tunnel dryer (kiln), drying tunnel, progressive kiln
Tunneltrocknung *f* tunnel drying
Tupelobaum *m* tupelo [gum], gum-tree, pepperidge *(genus Nyssa)*
Tüpfel *m(n) (bot)* pit
~/behöfter bordered pit
~/blinder blind (air) pit
~/einfacher simple pit
~/skulpturierter (verzierter) vestured pit
Tüpfelfarn *m (bot)* polypody *(genus Polypodium)*
Tüpfelfeld *n* pit field
~/primäres primary pit-field, primordial pit
Tüpfelfleckenkrankheit *f* [der Kartoffel], **Tüpfelfleckigkeit** *f* skin spot [of potato] *(caused by Polyscytalum pustulans)*
Tüpfelhartheu *n* [common] St. John's wort, Hypericum perforatum
Tüpfelhöhle *f* pit cavity
Tüpfelkammer *f* pit chamber
Tüpfelkanal *m* pit canal
Tüpfelmembran *f* pit membrane
Tüpfelöffnung *f* pit aperture
~/überlappende extended pit aperture
Tüpfelpaar *n* pit pair
~/einseitig verschlossenes aspirated pit pair
Tüpfelsaat *f* sowing in pits

Tüpfelschließhaut f pit membrane
Tüpfelung f 1. pitting; 2. *(phyt)* speck[l]ing, stippling
~/gegenüberstehende (opponierte) opposite pitting
Tüpfelwucherung f lenticel *(e.g. of a potato tuber)*
Tüpfelwulst f pit border
Tupfen m blur *(e.g. on fruits)*
Tupfer m swab
Turbankürbis m turban squash, Cucurbita maxima ssp. maxima convar. turbaniformis
Turbidimetrie f turbidimetry, turbidity measurement
Turbinenmilchkühler m turbine milk cooler
Turbinenpumpe f turbo pump
Turbinenregner m turbine sprinkler
Turbinentrockner m turbine dryer
Turboaufladung f turbocharging
Turbogetriebe n torque converter
Turboheuer m rotary tedder
Turbolader m turbocharger
Turboschneidmaschine f centrifugal slicer *(sugarbeet processing)*
Turbulenz f turbulence
Turf m [the] turf *(equestrian sport)*
turgeszent turgescent
Turgeszenz f turgescence, turgidity
Turgor[druck] m turgor [pressure]
Turgorgelenk n *(bot)* pulvinus
Turibaum m *(bot)* agati [sesbania], Sesbania grandiflora
Turimycin n turimycin *(antibiotic)*
Turio[ne] f *(bot)* turio[n], hibernacle, hibernaculum
Türkenbundlilie f Turk's cap, martagon [lily], purple martagon lily, Lilium martagon
Türkenmohn m s. Türkischer Riesenmohn
Türkische Baumhasel f Turkish filbert (hazel), tree hazel, cluster nut, Corylus colurna
~ Melisse f s. Türkischer Drachenkopf
Türkischer Drachenkopf m *(bot)* Moldavian dragon's head, Dracocephalum moldavica (moldavicum)
~ Riesenmohn m oriental (great garlet) poppy, Papaver orientale (bracteatum)
Türkischrot n madder *(plant dye)*
Turmextraktionsanlage f tower extraction (diffusion) plant *(sugar manufacture)*
Turmfalke f kestrel, staniel, windhover, Falco tinnunculus
turmförmig *(bot)* turriform
Turmgewächshaus n tower glasshouse
Turmkühler m cooling tower
Turmmälzerei f tower malting
Turmsilo m tower (upright) silo
Turner-Syndrom n *(vet)* Turner syndrome
Turnip f s. Wasserrübe
Turnover m turnover
Turteltaube f turtle-dove, Streptopelia turtur
Tüten n piping *(of queen bee)*

TuWSV s. Tulpenweißstreifigkeitsvirus
t-Verteilung f *(biom)* [Student's] t distribution
T-Wert m *(soil)* [cation] exchange capacity
Tylan n, **Tylon** n s. Tylosin
Tylose f 1. *(bot)* tylosis; 2. s. Tylosis
Tylosin n tylosin *(antibiotic)*
Tylosis f *(vet)* tylosis
Tympanie f *(vet)* tympanites, tympany, bloat, meteorism, hoven
~ [mit schaumiger Durchmischungsgärung]/akute ruminal tympanites, frothy bloat
Typ m type
~ des Ertragsverhaltens bearing pattern *(orcharding)*
Typ-B-Hühnerpest f *(vet)* Newcastle disease, ND, pseudo poultry plague
Typenkarte f *(soil)* type map
Typhasterol n typhasterol *(growth regulator)*
Typhlitis f *(vet)* typhlitis
Typhlohepatitis f histomoniasis *(of poultry, caused by Histomonas meleagridis)*
Typhula-Fäule f snow rot *(of cereals, caused by Typhula spp.)*
Typus m s. Typ
Tyr s. Tyrosin
Tyramin n tyramine
Tyraminase f, **Tyraminoxidase** f amine oxidase, flavin-containing, adrenaline oxidase, tyraminase, tyramine oxidase *(enzyme)*
Tyrase f s. Tyrosinammoniumlyase
Tyrosamin n tyramine
Tyrosin n tyrosine *(amino-acid)*
Tyrosinaminotransferase f tyrosine aminotransferase *(enzyme)*
Tyrosinammoniumlyase f tyrosine ammonia lyase *(enzyme)*
Tyrosinase f 1. catechol oxidase, tyrosinase *(enzyme)*; 2. monophenol monooxygenase, tyrosinase *(enzyme)*
Tyrosindecarboxylase f tyrosine decarboxylase *(enzyme)*
Tyrosin-3-Monooxygenase f tyrosine 3-monooxygenase, tyrosine 3-hydroxylase *(enzyme)*
Tyrosinphenollyase f tyrosine phenol-lyase *(enzyme)*
T-Zelle f s. T-Lymphozyt

U

übelriechend ill-smelling, evil-smelling, nosy, *(vet)* malodorous
Überalkalität f over-alkalinity
überaltert 1. overmature; 2. senile
Überalterung f 1. overmaturity; 2. senility
Überazidität f over-acidity
überbearbeiten to overwork
Überbefruchtung f *(zoo)* superfecundation

Überbesatz

Überbesatz *m* overstock[ing], superabundance *(e.g. of game)*
überbestockt overstocked, overdense *(forest stand)*
Überbestockung *f* overstocking *(forest stand)*
Überbewässerung *f* overirrigation
überbeweiden to overgraze
Überbeweidung *f* overgrazing
Überbiß *m s.* Unterkieferverkürzung
Überblume *f (bot)* pseudanthium
Überbrennen *n* burning *(forest fire control)*
~/leichtes light (fuel-reduction) burning
~/nochmaliges reburning
Überbrücken *n* bridge grafting
Überbrückung[sveredelung] *f* bridge graft
überdauern to [out]last, to survive
überdauernd *(bot, zoo)* lasting *(s. a.* ausdauernd*)*
~/den Winter hibernal
Überdauerung *f* survival
überdeckend *(gen)* dominant
überdeckt *(gen)* recessive
überdominant *(gen)* overdominant, superdominant
Überdominanz *f* overdominance, superdominance
Überdominanzhypothese *f* overdominance hypothesis
Überdosierung *f* overdosage
Überdosis *f* overdose
Überdrehkupplung *f s.* Überholkupplung
überdüngen to overfertilize, to overmanure
Überdüngung *f* overfertilization
übereinandergreifend *(bot, zoo)* imbricated
überempfindlich hypersensitive
Überempfindlichkeit *f* hypersensitivity; anaphylaxis; allergy
Überempfindlichkeitsreaktion *f* hypersensitivity response
Überentwicklung *f* hyperplasia *(e.g. of tissues)*
Überernährung *f* overnutrition, hypernutrition
Übererregbarkeit *f* hyperexcitability
übererregt nervous
Überfamilie *f* superfamily *(taxonomy)*
Überfermentation *f* overfermentation
überfett overfat
Überfettung *f* overfatness
Überflurbewässerung *f* surface irrigation
Überflurhydrant *m* overground hydrant
Überflurtrockner *m* floor dryer
Überfluß *m (ecol)* abundance
überfluten to flood, to inundate, to flush
Überflutung *f* flood, inundation
Überflutungsdeich *m* overflow dike
überfressen/sich to overfeed, to overeat
überfrieren to freeze over *(soil)*
Überfrucht *f* cover (nurse) crop
Überfruchtung *f* superfoetation
Überführungszeitraum *m (forest)* period of conversion
Überfunktion *f* hyperfunction
überfüttern to overfeed

Überfütterung *f* overfeeding, hyperalimentation
Übergangsboden *m* transitional (intergrade) soil
Übergangsgebiet *n (ecol)* ecotone
Übergangsgesellschaft *f (ecol)* transitional community
Übergangshorizont *m (soil)* transition horizon
Übergangsknospe *f* transitional (intermediate) bud
Übergangsmoor *n* transitional bog, oligotrophic moor
Übergangsprofil *n (soil)* intergrade profile
Übergangsquote *f,* **Übergangsrate** *f* turnover *(game management)*
Übergangsröhre *f* junction tile *(drainage)*
Übergangsschnitt *m* transitory pruning *(orcharding)*
übergehen/bei Überreife in Zersetzung to blet *(fruit)*
Überhaar *n* kemp *(wool defect)*
überhaarig kempy
Überhalt *m (forest)* reserving (maintenance) of standards
Überhaltbaum *m (forest)* reserved tree, residual (remnant) tree, veteran [tree], hold-over, standrel, standard, teller
Überhaltbetrieb *m (forest)* seed-tree cutting method (system), high-forest-with-standards system, reserve cutting
überhalten *(forest)* to reserve, to hold over, to leave standing
Überhälter *m s.* Überhaltbaum
Überhieb *m (forest)* excessive felling, overcut[ting]
Überhitzer *m* superheater *(sugar manufacture)*
Überholkupplung *f* overrun[ning] clutch
überhüten to fold off
überjährig overmature *(e.g. a tree)*
Überjährigkeit *f* overmaturity
überkalken to overlime *(soil)*
Überkalkung *f* overliming
Überkehr *f* returns, tailings *(in threshing)*
Überkehrelevator *m,* **Überkehrschnecke** *f* returns auger (elevator) *(of a combine harvester)*
Überklasse *f* superclass *(taxonomy)*
Überkopfberegnung *f* overhead sprinkling (watering, irrigation)
Überkopfregner *m* overhead sprinkler
Überkreuzvererbung *f* criss-cross inheritance
Überkronenberegnung *f* overtree irrigation (sprinkling) *(s. a.* Überkopfberegnung*)*
Überkronenerntemaschine *f* straddle-harvester *(orcharding)*
überlandbrennen *(forest)* to burn broadcast
Überlastkupplung *f* overload clutch
Überlastschutz *m* overload protection
Überlastsicherheitskupplung *f* overload safety clutch
Überlastsicherung *f* safeguard against overload
~/automatische automatic trip *(of a plough body)*
Überlaufdeich *m* overflow dike

Überläufer *m* 1. hogget, hogg, singler *(of wild boars)*; 2. *s.* Überläuferkeiler
Überläuferkeiler *m* two-year-old boar
Überlaufhandlung *f* overflow action *(animal behaviour)*
überleben to survive
Überleben *n* survival
Überlebensfähigkeit *f* survival ability
Überlebensrate *f* survival rate
Überliegen *n (zoo, ent)* hold-over, diapause
Übermikroskop *n s.* Ultramikroskop
übernutzen to over-use; *(forest)* to overexploit
Übernutzung *f* over-use, over-utilization; *(forest)* overexploitation, excessive felling (cutting)
Überordnung *f* superorder *(taxonomy)*
Überpflanze *f* epiphyte, aerophyte
überpflanzen *(vet)* to transplant, to graft *(esp. tissues)*
Überpflanzenberegnung *f s.* Überkopfberegnung
Überpflanzung *f (vet)* transplantation, grafting
überpflücken to pick over
überreif overripe, overmature, hypermature; dead ripe *(esp. said of corn)*
Überreife *f* overmaturity, dead ripeness
Überrollpflug *m* roll-over plough
Überrollschutz[aufbau] *m* roll-over protection [structure], ROPS, antiroll structure *(e.g. on tractors)*
Überrollunfall *m* roll-over accident (crash)
Überrollunkrautbekämpfungsmaschine *f* roll-on weed-killer
Übersättigung *f*, **Übersaturation** *f* supersaturation *(sugar manufacture)*
überschatten to shade out *(e.g. weed)*
überschirmen *(forest)* to shelter
Überschirmung *f (forest)* shelter, canopy cover
Überschirmungsfläche *f* area under canopy (crown cover)
Überschirmungsgrad *m* canopy (crown, shade) density
Überschlagschutz *m s.* Überrollschutz[aufbau]
überschönt overfined *(wine)*
überschreitend transgressive
Überschreitung *f (gen)* transgression, transgressive segregation (variation)
Überschreitungsintervall *n (biom)* exceedance interval
Überschußkalkung *f* heavy liming
Überschußproduktion *f*/**landwirtschaftliche** farm surpluses
überschwemmen to flood, to inundate
Überschwemmung *f* flood, inundation
Überschwemmungsgebiet *n* flood plain
Überschwemmungsgrasland *n* flooded grassland
Überschwemmungssavanne *f* inundation savanna[h]
Überschwemmungsschaden *m* flood damage
Überschwemmungssumpf *m* inundation swamp
überschwer extra-heavy *(e.g. a field-tool)*

Übersetzungsgetriebe *n* transmission
übersommern to aestivate, to oversummer
Übersommerung *f* aestivation
übersponnen kempy *(wool)*
Überspringen *n*, **Übersprung** *m* hopover *(e.g. of a forest fire)*
Übersprungshandlung *f* displacement activity *(animal behaviour)*
Überständer *m s.* Überhaltbaum
überständig overripe, overmature, decadent *(stand)*; declining, doddered *(tree)*
Überständigkeit *f* overmaturity
Überstaubewässerung *f* flood (basin) irrigation
Überstauen *n* flooding; submergence
~/freies wild flooding
~ mit temporärer Eindämmung surface flooding
Überstauwiese *f* overflow (inundated) meadow
Übertopf *m* decorative [outer] pot *(for potted plants)*
übertragbar transmissible, transmittable, communicable *(a disease)*
Übertragbarkeit *f* transmissibility, communicability
übertragen to transmit, to transfer, to communicate; to carry, to vector *(e.g. a pathogen)*
übertragen/durch die Luft airborne
~/durch Insekten insect-borne
~/durch Nematoden nematode-borne *(e.g. viruses)*
Überträger *m (phyt, vet)* vector, carrier
Überträgerstoff *m* transmitter substance
Überträgerwirt *m* carrier host
Übertragung *f* transmission, transfer
~ durch Samen seed-transmission
~ von Methylgruppen methylation
Übertragungsstadium *n* carrier state *(epidemiology)*
übertreffen/im Ertrag to outyield
Übertrocknung *f* overdrying
Übervölkerung *f* overpopulation
überwachsen to overgrow
Überwachung *f* 1. monitoring, supervision, surveillance; 2. *s.* Überwachungsschnitt
~ aus der Luft aerial surveillance (observation)
~/biologische biomonitoring
Überwachungsschnitt *m* regulated pruning *(orcharding)*
Überwachungssystem *n* monitoring system
überwallen to occlude, to heal [over, up] *(a branch stub)*
Überwallung *f* occlusion, overgrowth
Überwärmung *f (vet)* hyperthermia
Überweiche *f*, **Überweichen** *n* oversteeping *(malting)*
Überwinden *n* **der Keimruhe** breaking of dormancy *(e.g. of seed)*
überwintern to hibernate, to [over]winter; to hog *(young sheep)*
~/im Freien to outwinter
~ lassen/im Freien to outwinter

Überwinterung

Überwinterung *f* hibernation, overwintering, winter survival
Überwinterungs[gewächs]haus *n* overwintering house
Überwinterungsknospe *f (bot)* hibernacle, hibernaculum
Überwinterungskokon *m* hibernation cocoon
Überwinterungsteich *m (pisc)* overwintering (hibernating) pond
Überwinterungswirt *m (phyt)* overwintering host
überwuchern to overgrow, to grow over
Überwucherung *f* overgrowth
Überzähligkeit *f* **von Zehen** polydactylism, polydactyly
überziehen/mit Propolis to propolize
~/mit Wachs to wax
überzüchtet overbred
Überzug *m* [**über Bodengefügekörpern**] *(soil)* cutan
Ubichinon *n* ubiquinone, coenzyme Q
Ubichromenol *n* ubichromenol *(component of mitochondria)*
UDP-Glucosedehydrogenase *f* UDPglucose dehydrogenase *(enzyme)*
UDP-Glucoseglycogenglycosyltransferase *f* glycogen (starch) synthase, UDPglucose-glycogen glucosyltransferase *(enzyme)*
UDP-Glucosyltransferase *f* phenol-ß-glucosyltransferase *(enzyme)*
UFB *s.* Unterflurbewässerung
Ufer *n* bank
Uferbefestigung *f* 1. bank stabilization *(e.g. by planting)*; 2. embankment
Uferböschung *f* embankment
Uferehrenpreis *m* water speedwell, Veronica anagallis-aquatica
Ufererosion *f* bank erosion
Uferrebe *f* frost (riverbank) grape, Vitis riparia
Uferriedgras *n s.* Ufersegge
Uferschutz *m* bank protection
Uferschutzwald *m* bank protection forest
Ufersegge *f* stream-bank sedge, Carex riparia
Uferspitzklette *f* sea burdock, Xanthium albinum [ssp. riparium], Xanthium italicum
Ufervegetation *f* riparian vegetation
Uferwald *m* riparian forest
Uferzone *f* li[t]toral
Ugni *f (bot)* Chilean guava, Ugni molinae
Uhr *f/***biologische (innere)** biological clock
UHT *s.* Ultrahocherhitzung
Uhu *m* 1. eagle-owl *(genus Bubo)*; 2. eagle-owl, stockowl, Bubo bubo
UK *s.* Umtauschkapazität
Ukrainisches Graues Steppenrind *n* Ukrainian Grey [Steppe] *(cattle breed)*
Ulexin *n* ulexine *(alkaloid)*
Ulkus *n (vet)* ulcer, sore, canker • **ein ~ bilden** to ulcerate
~/peptisches peptic ulcer

ULM *s.* Ultraleichtflugzeug
Ulme *f* elm *(genus Ulmus)*
Ulmenbeutelgallenblattlaus *f* woolly pear aphid, Eryosoma pyricola, Schizoneura lanuginosa
Ulmenblattkäfer *m* elm leaf-beetle, Gabrucella luteola
ulmenblättrig ulmifolious
Ulmenholz *n* elm
Ulmenkrankheit *f (phyt)* [Dutch] elm disease *(caused by Ceratocystis ulmi)*
Ulmenmaser *f* elm burr
ulmenreich elmy
Ulmenscheckungsvirus *n* elm mottle virus, ElMV
Ulmenspierstrauch *m (bot)* germander spiraea, Spiraea chamaedryfolia
Ulmensplintkäfer *m* elm bark-beetle, Dutch elm beetle, Scolytus destructor (scolytus), Eccoptogaster multistriatus
Ulmensterben *n s.* Ulmenkrankheit
Ulmenwollschildlaus *f* European elm scale, oyster-shell scale, Lepidosaphes ulmi
Ulna *f s.* Elle
ult *s.* Ultisol
Ultisol *m (soil)* ultisol
Ultrafilter *n* ultrafilter
Ultrafiltration *f* ultrafiltration
Ultrahocherhitzung *f (dairy)* ultra-high temperature preservation (sterilization), uperization
Ultraleichtflugzeug *n* micro-light, motorwing
Ultramikroskop *n* ultramicroscope
Ultramikroskopie *f* ultramicroscopy
ultramikroskopisch ultramicroscopic
Ultramikrotom *n* ultramicrotome
Ultrapasteurisierung *f s.* Ultrahocherhitzung
Ultrapen *n s.* Propicillin
ultrarot *s.* infrarot
Ultraschall *m* ultrasound
Ultraschallgerät *n* ultrasonic equipment (scanner)
~ zur Speckdickenmessung ultrasonic fat meter, ultrasonic backfat measuring device
Ultraschallpasteurisator *m* ultrasonic pasteurizer
Ultraschallwellen *fpl* ultrasonic (supersonic) waves
Ultrastruktur *f* ultrastructure
Ultraviolett... *s. a.* UV-...
Ultraviolettabsorptionsspektrometrie *f* ultraviolet absorption spectrometry
Ultraviolettglas *n* vita-glass
Ultraviolettmikroskop *n* ultraviolet microscope
Ultraviolettmikroskopie *f* ultraviolet microscopy
Ultraviolettspektroskopie *f* ultraviolet spectroscopy
Ultrazentrifugation *f* ultracentrifugation
Ultrazentrifuge *f* ultracentrifuge
ULV-Verfahren *n* ULV (ultra-low volume) spraying *(plant protection)*
Ulzeration *f (vet)* ulceration, ulcer formation
ulzerativ ulcerative, ulcerous
ulzerieren to ulcerate, to undergo ulceration

ulzerierend s. ulzerativ
ulzerös ulcerous
Umbellifere f (bot) umbellifer (family Umbelliferae = Apiaceae)
Umbildung f metamorphosis
~/blumenblattartige (bot) petalody
Umbilicus m umbilicus, navel
Umbinden n binding, banding (e.g. of tree-trunks)
Umblattabak m [für Zigarren] cigar binder tobacco
Umbocken n repeat breeding (of female sheep)
umbrechen to plough (dig) up, to turn [about], to break (a field); to root (game the soil)
Umbrellaform f umbrella form (esp. of fruit-trees)
Umbruchpflug m breaker plough
Umbullen n repeat breeding (of cow)
Umfallen n **der Treibhyazinthen** stem topple of hyacinth (non-parasitic disease)
~ der Tulpen waterneck (stem topple, wet stem) of tulips
Umfallkrankheit f (phyt) damping-off [disease], fogging-off
~ des Kohls cabbage blackleg (caused by Phoma lingam)
Umfang m **des Kreisflächenmittelstammes** mean girth (timber mensuration)
~ über Wurzelanlauf girth above buttress (timber mensuration)
Umfangsklasse f girth class
Umfangsklassengrenze f girth[-class] limit
~/kostendeckende economic girth limit
Umfangsmeßband n **auf Hoppus-Fuß-Basis** quarter-girth tape
Umfangszuwachs m girth increment
Umfassungsstreifen m isolation strip, guard area, buffer strip (surround) (e.g. of a trial plot)
Umformung f transformation
umgeben/mit einer Hecke to hedge
Umgebung f environment; surroundings
Umgebungsfeuchtigkeit f ambient humidity
Umgebungsluft f environmental air
Umgebungstemperatur f environmental (ambient) temperature
Umgebungswärmebedarf m environmental heat demand
umgeschlagen (bot) replicate
Umgestaltung f **der Natur** remaking of nature
umgestürzt prostrate (tree)
umgewendet (bot, zoo) reflexed, anatropous
umgraben to dig [up], to turn up [the soil]
~/mit einem Spaten to spade, to dig up with a spade
~/spatentief to spit
Umgraben n digging
~/flaches single digging
~/zwei Spatenstiche tiefes double-digging, bastard trenching
Umhacken n hoeing up
umhüllt (bot, zoo) tunicate

Umkehrlufttrocknung f reversed-direction airflow drying
Umkehrosmose f reverse osmosis
Umkehrtranscriptase f reverse transcriptase (enzyme)
Umkehrwetterlage f temperature inversion
umkleidet s. umhüllt
Umkolo m Kei (Kai) apple, Dovyalis (Doryalis) caffra
umlagern to translocate
Umlagerung f translocation
Umlagewirtschaft f shifting agriculture (cultivation), swidden cropping, shag (in the tropics)
Umlarven n (api) grafting
Umlauf m 1. (vet) panaritium; 2. bout (e.g. of field machines)
Umlaufgetriebe n epicyclic gear
Umlaufsprüher m recirculating sprayer
Umlaufstern m sprocket (roller) nose (of a chain-saw)
Umlaufszeit f (forest) felling circle
Umlaufverdampfer m circulation evaporator (sugar manufacture)
Umleitungsgraben m by-pass trench
Umlenkrolle f sprocket (roller) nose (of a chain-saw)
~ des Rückholseils haul-back block (of timber cableway)
Umlichtung f **der Krone** (forest) setting free of the crown
Umnetzungsmaschine f netting machine
umpflanzen to transplant, to replant, to replace [plants]; to prick [off, out]
Umpflanzmaschine f transplanter, transplanting machine
Umpflanzschock m transplanting shock
umpflügen to plough [up], to break [up]
umpfropfen to regraft, to top-graft, to rework
Umpfropfen n regrafting, top grafting
Umrauschen n repeat breeding (of sow)
Umrechnungsfaktor m, **Umrechnungszahl** f conversion factor
Umrinderer m repeat-breeder cow
Umrindern n repeat breeding (of cow)
Umrossen n repeat breeding (of mare)
Umrüstzeit f change-over time (for machines)
Umsatz m s. Stoffumsatz
umsäumt (bot, zoo) marginate[d]
umschaufeln to shovel over
Umschlag m 1. goods handling (transshipment); 2. (vet) compress
Umschlagplatz m transfer site (e.g. for timber)
Umschlagseinrichtungen fpl handling machinery (equipment)
Umschlagverlust m handling loss
umschneiden to excise
Umschneidung f excision
umschulen to transplant (seedlings)
Umsetzbarkeit f metabolizability (of nutrients)

umsetzen

umsetzen to transplant; to reset *(e.g. an equipment)*
~/im Stoffwechsel to metabolize
Umsetzung *f*/biologische bioconversion
Umstülpung *f (vet)* inversion
Umtauschkapazität *f (soil)* exchange capacity
umtopfen to repot, to pot [out]
Umtopfmaschine *f* repot machine
Umtrieb *m* 1. *(forest)* rotation [cycle]; 2. pasture rotation
~ der höchsten Waldrente rotation of the highest interest on forest capital
~ der höchsten Wertleistung rotation of the highest income
~ des höchsten Bodenreinertrages rotation of the highest soil rent, financial rotation
~ des höchsten Ertrages rotation of the highest income
~ des höchsten Massenertrages (Volumenertrages) rotation of the maximum volume production, volume rotation
~/finanzieller financial rotation
~/latenter latent rotation
~/physischer physical (silvicultural) rotation
~/technischer technical rotation
Umtriebsalter *n* rotation (exploitable) age
Umtriebsweide *f* rotational (portional, cyclic) grazing, paddock (controlled) grazing
Umtriebszeit *f* circulation (rotation) period
umveredeln *s.* umpfropfen
Umwälzpumpe *f* circulation pump
Umwälzventilator *m* air-mixing fan
umwandeln 1. to convert; 2. to metamorphose
~/ein Gel in ein Sol to peptize
~/in Dextrin to dextrinize
~/in ein Dickicht to coppice
~/in Ozon to ozonize
~/Stärke in Zucker to saccharify
Umwandlung *f* 1. conversion; 2. metamorphosis
~/biologische bioconversion
Umwandlungsbestand *m (forest)* conversion stand, subsidiary crop
Umwandlungsbetrieb *m (forest)* conversion system
Umwandlungsgestein *n* metamorphic rock
Umwandlungszeitraum *m* period of conversion
umweiseln *(api)* to requeen
Umwelt *f* environment
~/ländliche rural environment
Umweltabweichung *f* environmental variance (variation)
Umweltansprüche *mpl* environmental requirements
Umweltanzeiger *m* habitat indicator
umweltbedingt environmental; ecologic
Umweltbedingungen *fpl* environmental conditions
umweltbeeinflußt affected by environmental conditions

Umweltbeeinträchtigung *f* environmental deterioration (impact)
Umweltbelastbarkeit *f* ecological capacity
umweltbelastet environmentally stressed
Umweltbelastung *f* environmental stress; environmental deterioration
umweltbewußt environment-conscious, environmentally minded (conscious)
Umweltbewußtsein *n* ecological awareness
Umweltchemie *f* environmental chemistry
Umweltchemikalie *f* environmental chemical
Umwelteinfluß *m* environmental influence
Umwelterhaltung *f* environmental conservation
Umweltfaktor *m* environmental factor
umweltfeindlich ecologically undesirable (harmful)
Umweltforscher *m* environmental scientist
Umweltforschung *f* environmental science (research)
umweltfreundlich environmentally acceptable (beneficial), proenvironmental, ecologically safe (desirable); non-polluting
Umweltfreundlichkeit *f* environmental friendliness
Umweltgefährdung *f* environmental hazard
Umweltgeochemie *f* environmental geochemistry
Umweltgeologie *f* environmental geology
umweltgeschädigt affected by environmental conditions
Umweltgesetzgebung *f* environmental legislation
Umweltgestaltung *f* environmental management (engineering)
Umweltgift *n* environmental poison
Umwelthygiene *f* environmental hygiene
Umweltkapazität *f (ecol)* carrying capacity
Umweltkatastrophe *f* environmental catastrophe, ecocatastrophe
Umweltkontrolle *f* environmental control
Umweltkorrelation *f* environmental correlation *(breeding)*
Umweltlehre *f* ecology, bionomics, bionomy
Umweltmastitis *f (vet)* environmental mastitis
Umweltministerium *n* Department of the Environment
Umweltmonitoring *n* environmental monitoring
Umweltmutagen *n* environmental mutagen
Umweltpflege *f* environmental management
Umweltpolitik *f* environmental policy
Umweltschadstoff *m*, Umweltschmutzstoff *m* environmental pollutant
umweltschonend gentle for environment
Umweltschutz *m* environmental protection (control)
Umweltschutzbewegung *f* environmentalism
Umweltschützer *m* environmentalist, environmental protectionist (conservationist)
Umweltschutzmaßnahme *f* environmental-protection measure, environmental action
Umweltschutzministerium *n* Department of the Environment
Umweltschutzpolitik *f* environmental policy

Umweltstabilität *f* environmental stability
Umweltstreß *m* environmental stress
Umweltüberwachung *f* environmental monitoring
Umweltvarianz *f* environmental variance (variation)
umweltvernichtend ecocidal
Umweltverschmutzer *m* environmental pollutant
Umweltverschmutzung *f* environmental pollution (contamination)
umweltverträglich environmentally compatible (acceptable)
Umweltverträglichkeit *f* environmental compatibility
Umweltwiderstand *m* environmental resistance
Umweltwissenschaft *f* environmental science
umzäunen to fence [in], to enclose, to inclose, to paddock
Umzäunung *f* fence, paling
Unabhängigkeitsregel *f (gen)* law of independent assortment, Mendel's third law
unansehnlich *(bot, zoo)* inconspicuous
unauffällig *(bot, zoo)* inconspicuous
unausgedroschen unthreshed
unbearbeitbar unworkable *(s. a. unbebaubar)*
unbearbeitet unworked, unprocessed, natural
unbebaubar untillable, uncultivable *(soil)*
unbebaut untilled, uncropped, bare of crop, barren, fallow, jejune, *(Am)* raw
unbefiedert featherless, bald, callow
unbefruchtet unfertilized, non-pregnant
unbegrannt awnless, beardless
unbehaart bald, glabrous, hairless
unbehandelt untreated
unbelaubt leafless, bare
unbelebt inanimate
unbelegt unserved, maiden, open *(female animal)*
unberegnet unirrigated, non-irrigated
unbesäumt unedged *(timber)*
unbeschlagen unshod *(hoof or claw)*
unbespelzt hull-less
unbestäubt unpollinated
unbestellbar *s.* unbebaubar
unbestockt *(forest)* non-stocked, unstocked, bare
unbewachsen bare *(land)*
unbewaldet bare
unbewässert unirrigated, non-irrigated
unbeweglich immobile, non-mobile; *(zoo)* sedentary
Unbewehrte Pistazie *f* large terebinth, Pistacia atlantica
unbeweidet ungrazed
unbeweiselt *(api)* queenless
unbewirtschaftet unimproved *(land)*; unmanaged *(forest)*
unbewölkt cloudless
unbewurzelt unrooted, rootless
undurchdringlich impermeable
undurchforstet unthinned
undurchlässig impermeable
uneben rugged, *(bot, zoo)* asperous

Unebenheit *f* ruggedness
Unechte Formzahl *f* artificial form factor, $f_{1,3}$ *(timber mensuration)*
Unechter Formquotient *m* artificial form quotient *(timber mensuration)*
~ **Gänsefuß** *m* maple-leaved goosefoot, Chenopodium hybridum
Unechtes Lanzenholz *n (bot)* wild cachiman, Rollinia mucosa
~ **Tännelkraut** *n (bot)* female fluellin, Kickxia spuria
uneingezäunt unfenced
unempfänglich immune • ~ **machen** to immunize
Unempfänglichkeit *f* immunity
unempfindlich insensitive
~/**photoperiodisch** *(bot)* day-neutral
Unempfindlichkeit *f* insensitivity
unentbehrlich essential
Unentbehrlichkeit *f* essentiality (e.g. of aminoacids)
unentwickelt undeveloped; juvenescent • ~ **bleiben** *(bot, phyt)* to abort
unergiebig 1. poor, barren, hungry, jejune *(land)*; 2. low, little *(rainfall)*
Unfall *m* accident
~ **im Landwirtschaftsbetrieb/tödlicher** farm death
~ **in der Forstwirtschaft** silviculture accident
~ **in der Landwirtschaft** farm accident
Unfallverhütung *f* accident prevention, prevention of accidents
unfruchtbar 1. *(bot, zoo)* infertile, unfertile, sterile, fruitless; *(zoo)* fruitless, unfruitful, infructuose, infructuous, barren; addle[d] *(egg)*; 2. barren, poor, hungry, jejune *(land)* • ~ **machen** to sterilize
Unfruchtbarkeit *f* 1. infertility, sterility, fruitlessness; 2. poorness *(of land)*
Unfruchtbarmachung *f* sterilization
Ungarische Rauke *f* tall rocket, *(Am)* tumbling (jim-hill) mustard, Sisymbrium altissimum
~ **Trespe** *f* awnless brome[-grass], smooth brome[-grass], Bromus inermis
~ **Wicke** *f* Hungarian vetch, Vicia pannonica
Ungarischer Flieder *m* Hungarian lilac, Syringa josikaea
~ **Klee** *m* Hungarian clover, Trifolium pannonicum
Ungarisches Gelbmosaikvirus *n* [der Weinrebe] [grape-vine] Hungarian chrome mosaic virus, HCMV
~ **Weißes Fleischschwein** *n* Hungarian white *(pig breed)*
Ungastlichkeit *f* axeny *(parasitology)*
ungebeizt undressed *(seed)*
ungeboren unborn
ungedeckt unserved, maiden, open *(female animal)*
ungedroschen unthreshed
ungedüngt unfertilized, unmanured
ungefiedert featherless, bald, callow

ungeflügelt

ungeflügelt wingless, apterous
Ungehorsam *m* disobedience *(animal behaviour)*
ungekeimt ungerminated
ungemahlen unmilled, unground
ungemulcht unmulched
ungenießbar inedible, uneatable *(s. a.* unschmackhaft*)*
Ungenießbarkeit *f* inedibility
ungenutzt unimproved, uncultivated *(land)*
ungepaart unpaired, azygous
ungepflegt unmanaged *(e.g. a forest)*
ungepreßt unpressed
ungereinigt greasy, in the grease *(wool)*
ungesalzen unsalted
ungesattelt bareback[ed] *(horse)*
ungesättigt unsaturated *(fatty acid)*
~/einfach monounsaturated
~/mehrfach polyunsaturated
ungesäuert unleavened *(bread)*
ungeschält unpeeled, unhulled, unhusked, undecorticated
ungeschichtet unstratified
ungeschlachtet on the hoof
ungeschlechtlich asexual, vegetative
Ungeschlechtlichkeit *f* asexuality
ungestielt 1. *(bot, zoo)* sessile; 2. *(bot)* acaulescent, acaulous
~/fast subsessile
ungesüßt brut *(wine)*
ungeteilt undivided, entire *(e.g. a leaf)*
Ungeteilte Keulenlilie *f (bot)* blue dracaena, Cordyline indivisa
ungetrocknet undried, unseasoned, green *(e.g. timber)*
ungetrübt limpid *(wine)*
Ungewißheit *f* uncertainty *(statistics)*
ungezähmt untamed, wild, feral
Ungeziefer *n* vermin, pest • **~ bekämpfen (vernichten)** to disinfest
Ungezieferbefall *m* vermin infestation, attack by vermin
ungezieferbefallen verminous
Ungezieferbekämpfung *f* vermin (pest) control, vermin destruction (eradication)
ungeziefergeschützt vermin-proof
ungeziefersicher vermin-proof
Ungeziefervernichtungsmittel *n* disinfestant
ungiftig non-toxic, atoxic
ungleichaltrig uneven-aged; all-aged, all-staged, storeyed, *(Am)* storied *(forest stand)*
Ungleichaltrigkeit *f* uneven-aged state
ungleichartig heterogeneous, different
Ungleichartigkeit *f* heterogeneity
ungleichblättrig *(bot)* anisophyllous
Ungleichblättrigkeit *f (bot)* anisophylly
Ungleicher Holzbohrer (Holzborkenkäfer) *m* [fruit-tree] shot-hole borer, pear blight beetle, dissimilar bark-beetle, Xyleborus (Anisandrus) dispar

Ungleichflügler *m (ent)* heteropteran, bug *(order* Heteroptera*)*
ungleichförmig irregular
Ungleichgewicht *n* disequilibrium
Ungras *n* obnoxious (weed) grass, grass[y] weed
Ungräserbekämpfungsmittel *n* gramicide
Unguentum *n* unguent, ointment, salve
Ungulat *m s.* Huftier
unheilbar incurable
Unholz *n* 1. *(forest)* undesirable tree species, secondary (inferior) species; 2. woody weed, weed tree
unhygienisch unhygienic
uniform uniform
Uniformitätsgrad *m* degree of uniformity *(breeding)*
Uniformitätsregel *f (gen)* law of dominance, Mendel's first law
unilоculär unilocular, uniloculate
uniparental uniparental
unisexuell *(bot)* unisexual
Universaldrillmaschine *f* standard drill, universal (all-crop) seed drill, multipurpose (general-purpose) drill
Universalexzenterhaspel *f* general-purpose excentric reel
Universalförderer *m* general-purpose elevator
Universalfördergebläse *n* universal blower
Universalfutter[lade]wagen *m* all-purpose forage wagon
Universalgelenk *n* ball[-and-socket] joint
Universalsäge *f* variety saw
Universalschlepper *m* all-purpose tractor
univoltin *(ent)* univoltine, monovoltine
univor *(ecol)* monophagous
Univorie *f (ecol)* monophagy
unkastriert uncastrated, entire
unkoordiniert *(vet)* ataxic *(motion)*
Unkraut *n* weed [pest] • **~ beseitigen** to weed
~/ausläuferbildendes rhizomatous weed
~/breitblättriges (dikotyles) broad-leaved weed
~/einjähriges annual weed
~/einkeimblättriges *s.* Ungras
~/holziges *s.* Unholz 2.
~/zweikeimblättriges broad-leaved weed
unkrautartig weedy
Unkrautbefall *m* weed infestation
unkrautbefallen weed-infested, weed-grown
Unkrautbekämpfung *f* weed control, weeding
~/aviotechnische aerial weed control
~/biologische biological weed control
~/chemische chemical weed control, chemical weeding
~/mechanische cultural weed control
~/zwischenreihige inter-row weed control
Unkrautbekämpfungsmittel *n* herbicide, weedkiller, weedicide
Unkrautbekämpfungsspektrum *n* weed control spectrum

Unkrautbesatz *m* weed content
Unkrautbeseitigung *f s.* Unkrautbekämpfung
unkrautbewachsen weed-grown
Unkrautbiologie *f* weed biology
Unkrautegge *f s.* Unkrautstriegel
Unkrautflora *f* weed flora
unkrautfrei weed-free, weedless
Unkrautgemeinschaft *f* weed community (association)
Unkrauthirse *f (Am)* crab-grass *(esp. genera Digitaria and Setaria)*
Unkrautkonkurrenz *f* weed competition
Unkrautkunde *f* weed science
Unkrautökologie *f* weed ecology
Unkrautpflanze *f* weed plant
Unkrautpflug *m* shim
Unkrautsamen *m* weed seed
Unkrautspritze *f* weed sprayer
Unkrautstreicher *m* weed wiper
Unkrautstriegel *m* weed[er] harrow, weeder; spike-tooth harrow, chain harrow
Unkrautunterdrücker *m* smother crop
Unkrautunterdrückung *f* weed suppression
unkrautvernichtend herbicidal
Unkrautvernichtung *f* weed destruction
Unkrautvernichtungsmittel *n s.* Unkrautbekämpfungsmittel
unkultiviert *s.* unbebaut
Unland *n* waste land (ground), barren [land], badland, wild land
unlöslich insoluble
Unlöslichkeit *f* insolubility
Unordnung *f* disorder
unpaar azygous
Unpaarhufer *m* odd-toed animal (ungulate), perissodactyl[e] *(order Perissodactyla)*
unpaarhufig odd-toed, perissodactyl[e]
unpaarig azygous
~ gefiedert *(bot)* odd-pinnate[d], unequally pinnate[d], imparipinnate[d]
unphysiologisch unphysiologic[al]
unraffiniert unrefined
unregelmäßig irregular
unreif unripe, immature; in the blade *(cereals)*
Unreife *f* unripeness, immaturity
unrhythmisch arrhythmic
unruhig restless; fidgety, flighty *(e.g. fowl)*
unschädlich innocuous
Unschlitt *n* mutton tallow
unschmackhaft unpalatable, distasteful
unschnürig many-sided *(tree-trunk)*
unseptiert non-septate, coenocytic
unsortiert unsorted
Unstetdränung *f* non-steady drainage
untätig inert *(soil)*
Untenentnahme *f* bottom unloading
Untenentnahmefräse *f*, **Untenentnahmevorrichtung** *f* bottom [silo] unloader

Unterabteilung *f* 1. *(forest)* subcompartment; 2. subphylum, subdivision *(taxonomy)*
Unterarm *m* forearm, arm
Unterart *f* subspecies *(taxonomy)*
Unterbau *m* 1. foundation *(road construction)*; 2. *(forest)* planting under cover, underplanting
Unterbauch *m*, **Unterbauchgegend** *f* hypogastrium
unterbauen *(forest)* to underplant
Unterbaupflanze *f* underplant
Unterbesatz *m* understocking
Unterbestand *m (forest)* underwood, understorey, second growth
unterbestockt understocked *(forest stand)*
Unterbestockung *f* understocking *(forest stand)*
Unterbettungsschicht *f* sub-base *(road construction)*
unterbeweiden to undergraze
Unterbeweidung *f* undergrazing
Unterblatt *n (bot)* bottom leaf
Unterblattspritzgerät *n* under-leaf sprayer
Unterblattspritzung *f* under-leaf spraying
Unterboden *m* subsoil, undersoil • **den ~ lockern** to subsoil
Unterbodenazidität *f* subsoil acidity
Unterbodendüngerstreuer *m* deep-down fertilizer distributor
Unterbodendüngung *f* fertilization of subsoil
Unterbodenheizung *f* subsoil heating
Unterbodenhorizont *m* subsoil horizon, enrichment (illuvial) horizon, B-horizon, accumulate layer
Unterbodenlockerer *m* subsoiler, subsoil (chisel) plough
Unterbodenlockerung *f* subsoiling, subsoil loosening (tillage)
Unterbodenpflug *m* undersoil plough
Unterbodensprüher *m* subsoil sprayer *(soil disinfection)*
Unterbodenverdichtung *f* subsoil compaction, hard pan
Unterbrand *m* underfeed *(heating of greenhouses)*
Unterbrandbeschickung[seinrichtung] *f* underfeed stoker
unterbringen/für den Winter to in-winter *(e.g. animals)*
~/Rinder im Viehhof to yard
Unterbrust *f* chest floor *(of animal body)*
Unterdachlagerung *f* indoor storage
Unterdachsilo *m* indoor silo
Unterdachtrocknung *f* barn curing *(e.g. of tobacco)*
Unterdrehpflug *m* Scandinavian (turn-wrest) plough
Unterdrucklagerung *f* low-pressure storage, LPS, hypobaric storage *(e.g. of fruits)*
unterdrücken to suppress *(e.g. plant growth)*
~/im Anfangsstadium *(vet)* to abort *(a disease)*
~/Immunreaktionen to immunosuppress

unterdrückt

unterdrückt suppressed, choked, blind *(plant growth)*; overtopped, subordinate *(tree)*
unterempfindlich hyposensitive
Unterempfindlichkeit f hyposensitivity
Unterentwicklung f hypoplasia *(e.g. of tissues)*
~ der Geschlechtsorgane infantilism
unterernähren to underfeed
unterernährt undernourished, underfed, scraggy, hypotrophic
Unterernährung f undernutrition, undernourishment, hypotrophy
Unterfamilie f subfamily *(taxonomy)*
Unterfermentation f underfermentation
Unterfläche f *(forest)* subplot
Unterflurbelüftung f below-ground ventilation
Unterflurbelüftungsanlage f floor-ventilated bin
Unterflurbewässerung f subirrigation, subsurface irrigation, bottom watering, subbing
Unterflurbewässerungsanlage f subirrigation (bottom watering) system
Unterflurdrän m subsurface drain
Unterflurdränung f subsurface (subsoil, covered) drainage, under-drainage
Unterflurentmistung f below-floor dung cleaning
Unterflurhydrant m underground hydrant
Unterflurmelkanlage f under-level milking installation
Unterflurrohrdränung f subsurface pipe drainage
Unterflurtank m underfloor tank
Unterflurtropf[en]bewässerung f subsurface (underground) trickle irrigation
Unterform f subform *(taxonomy)*
Unterfunktion f hypofunction
~ der Nebenschilddrüse *(vet)* hypoparathyroidism
Unterfußdüngung f side dressing
Untergärung f bottom fermentation
Untergattung f subgenus *(taxonomy)*
untergipfelständig *(bot)* subterminal
Unterglasanbau m greenhouse (protected) cropping, cultivation (growing) under glass
Unterglaskultur f 1. greenhouse (protected) crop; 2. s. Unterglasanbau
untergraben to dig in
Untergras n bottom (close-growing) grass
Untergriff m share pitch (suction), body pitch, vertical (down) suction *(of plough)*
Untergriffverstell[einricht]ung f plough alignment control
Untergrößenabscheider f, **Untergrößentrenneinrichtung** f cull eliminator, undersize separator
Untergrund m 1. subgrade *(road construction)*; 2. s. Unterboden
Untergrundbewässerung f s. Unterflurbewässerung
Untergrundpacker m land (undersoil) packer, cultipacker
Untergrundwärmespeicher m underground heat storage

Unterhaar n underhair, fur hair *(of mammals)*
unterhalten/Gräben to ditch
Unterhaut f *(zoo)* subcutis, hypodermis, subcutaneous tissue, superficial fascia
Unterhautfett[gewebe] n subcutaneous fat
Unterhefe f bottom[-fermentation] yeast
Unterholz n undergrowth, underwood, undershrub, coppice[-wood], copsewood, brush[wood], bush, scrub, boscage
Unterholzbekämpfungsmittel n brush-killer
unterirdisch subterranean, subterraneous
Unterirdischer Klee m subterranean clover, subclover, Trifolium subterraneum
Unterkiefer m mandible, [lower] jaw; maxilla *(of insects and crustaceans)*
Unterkieferdrüse f mandibular gland
Unterkieferknochen m jaw-bone
Unterkieferspeicheldrüse f mandibular gland
Unterkieferverkürzung f *(vet)* undershot jaw, parrot mouth, fish face
Unterklasse f subclass *(taxonomy)*
Unterkronenberegnung f undertree sprinkling; below-the-crop sprinkling
unterkühlen to supercool, to undercool
Unterkühlung f supercooling, undercooling; *(vet)* hypothermia
Unterkultur f undercrop
Unterlage f 1. root-stock, [body] stock, *(Am)* understock *(orcharding)*; 2. substrate
~/mittelschwachwachsende semidwarfing root-stock
~/schwache (schwachwachsende) weak (low-vigour) root-stock
~/sehr schwach wachsende true dwarfing [root-] stock
~/starkwachsende invigorating root-stock
~/verschulte lined-out stock, lining-out stock
~/wuchshemmende growth-restricting (size-controlling) root-stock, dwarfing root-stock
Unterlagenbaumschule f stock nursery
Unterlagenroder m fruit-tree root-stock digger
Unterlagenvermehrung f root-stock propagation
Unterlagenverträglichkeit f root-stock compatibility
Unterlagenwirkung f influence of [the] root-stock
Unterlagenzüchtung f root-stock breeding (selection)
Unterlage-Sorten-Kombination f root-stock-scion combination
Unterlagsholz n root-stock wood (cane)
Unterlastschaltung f on-the-go shift
Unterleib m *(zoo)* abdomen
Unterlenker m lower [draft] link *(three-point hitch)*
Unterlenkerregelung f, **Unterlenkerverstellung** f lower link control
Unterlippe f lower lip
untermäßig under-sized
Unternehmen n/**landwirtschaftliches** farm enterprise

Unterordnung f suborder *(taxonomy)*
Unterpflanzenbestand m bottom crop
Unterpflanzung f bottom crop; under-tree planting
unterpflügen to plough (turn) under, to plough back (down, in), *(Am)* to plow under
Unterrasse f sub-race
Unterreich n subkingdom *(taxonomy)*
Untersaat f undersowing, undersown crop, additional sowing
untersäen to undersow, to underseed
Unterschenkel m shank, second thigh, true leg; gaskin *(of horse)*
Unterschied m/**signifikanter** *(biom)* significant difference
Unterschneidegerät n undercutter
unterschneiden to undercut; to subsoil *(nursery stock)*
Untersektion f subsection *(taxonomy)*
Unterserie f subseries *(taxonomy)*
untersetzt stocky, squat *(plant, animal)*
Untersieb n bottom (grain) sieve *(of thresher)*
Unterstamm m s. Unterabteilung 2.
Unterstand m s. Unterbestand
unterständig 1. *(bot)* inferior; 2. understorey *(tree growth)*; 3. standing under *(forelimb or hindlimb)*
Unterstärke f diameter at foot *(timber mensuration)*
Untersuchung f examination, exploration
~/rektale rectal examination
Untersuchungsparzelle f research plot
Untertemperatur f *(vet)* hypothermia
Untertischheizung f bottom heating, under-bench heating system *(in greenhouses)*
Untervarietät f subvariety *(taxonomy)*
Unterwärme f bottom heat
Unterwasserpumpe f submersible (immersion) pump
Unterwassersäge f submarine saw
Unterwuchs m s. Unterholz
Unterzungen[speichel]drüse f sublingual gland
Untugend f vice *(of animals)*
Unveränderlichkeit f constancy
unverarbeitet unprocessed, natural
unverdaulich indigestible
Unverdaulichkeit f indigestibility, indigestibleness
unverdaut undigested
unverdünnt neat *(e.g. wine)*
unveredelt ungrafted, own-root[ed]
unvergoren unfermented
unvermahlen unmilled, unground
unvermischt unmixed *(s. a. unverdünnt)*
unverpackt unpacked, loose
unverschult untransplanted *(seedling)*
unverseifbar unsaponifiable
Unverträglichkeitsgruppe f intersterility group
unverwitterbar unweatherable
Unverzerrtheit f *(biom)* unbiasedness, accuracy
unverzweigt unbranched, foxtail

unwirtschaftlich uneconomic, inefficient, unprofitable; uneconomical, wasteful; unthrifty
Unwirtschaftlichkeit f [economic] inefficiency, unprofitableness; wastefulness; unthriftiness
Unzinariose f *(vet)* uncinariasis *(caused by Uncinaria spp.)*
unzugänglich inaccessible *(e.g. a forest)*; unavailable *(e.g. nutrients)*
Upasbaum m upas[-tree], antiar, Antiaris toxicaria
Upland-Baumwolle f upland cotton, American long-staple cotton, Gossypium hirsutum [var. hirsutum]
üppig [gedeihend] luxuriant, lush *(vegetation)*
Üppigkeit f luxuriance
Ur m urus, aurochs, Bos taurus primigenius
Urachus m urachus *(animal anatomy)*
Uracil n uracil *(pyrimidine base)*
Uracil-4-carbonsäure f orotic (uracil-4-carboxylic) acid
Urämie f *(vet)* uraemia
Uratoxidase f urate oxidase *(enzyme)*
urbar arable • ~ **machen** to reclaim, to break, to cultivate; to assart *(woodland)*
Urbarmachung f reclamation, land clearance (clearing), cultivation; assartment
Urbarmachungskrankheit f reclamation disease, yellow (wither) tip *(of cereals due to copper deficiency)*
Urbild n type
Urdarm m primitive gut
Urdbohne f urd [bean], mung bean, black (green) gram, woolly pyrol, Phaseolus (Vigna) mungo
Urea f s. Harnstoff
Ureaform f urea-form *(fertilizer)*
Urease f urease *(enzyme)*
Ureasehemmstoff m urease inhibitor
Uredium n uredinium
Uredospore f ured[ini]ospore, urediospore *(of rust fungi)*
Uredosporenlager n uredinium
Ureidovaleriansäure f citrulline *(amino-acid)*
ureingesessen indigenous, autochthonal, autochthonous
Ureolyse f ureolysis
ureolytisch ureolytic
Ureter m ureter *(animal anatomy)*
Urethan n urethane, carbamate *(anaesthetic)*
Urethra f urethra *(animal anatomy)*
uretisch diuretic
Urgroßmutter f great grand dam *(animal breeding)*
Urgroßvater m great grand sire *(animal breeding)*
Urhahn m mountain cock
Uricase f s. Uratoxidase
Uridin n uridine *(nucleoside)*
Uridinkinase f uridine kinase *(enzyme)*
Uridinnucleosidase f uridine nucleosidase *(enzyme)*
Urin m urine, stale *(esp. of beef and horse)*

urinieren 658

urinieren to urinate, to micturate, to stale *(esp. beef and horse)*
Urinieren *n* urination
Urkeimzelle *f (zoo)* oogonium, ovogonium
~/männliche *s.* Ursamenzelle
Urmeristem *n (bot)* promeristem
urnenförmig *(bot)* urceolate
urnentragend *(bot)* urnigerous
Urnierengang *m* mesonephric (Wolffian) duct
Urocanase *f*, **Urocanathydratase** *f* urocanate hydratase, urocanase *(enzyme)*
Urocaninsäure *f* urocanic acid
Urogastron *n* urogastrone *(hormone)*
Urogenitalöffnung *f* genital pore *(e.g. of fishes)*
Urogenitalorgane *npl*, **Urogenitalsystem** *n* urogenital system
Urogomph *m (ent)* cornicle
Urokinase *f* urokinase *(enzyme)*
Urolith *m (vet)* urolith, cystolith, bladder stone
Urolithiasis *f (vet)* urolithiasis
Uronan *n* polyuronid[e] *(polysaccharide)*
Uronsäure *f* uronic acid
Uropepsin[ogen] *n* uropepsin *(enzyme)*
Uropoese *f* uropoiesis
Urrasse *f* primitive (primary) breed
Ursamenzelle *f* gonocyt, spermatogonium
Ursprungsgebiet *n (ecol)* provenance, provenience
ursprungsgleich homologous
ursprungsnah proximal
Ursprungszentrum *n* centre of origin (domestication) *(of cultivated plants)*
Urstele *f (bot)* protostele
Urtier[chen] *n* protozoon, protozoan *(subkingdom Protozoa)*
Urtikaria *f (vet)* urticaria, nettle-rash
Urwald *m* prim[a]eval (virgin, undisturbed) forest, primordial (primary, original) forest, bush; jungle *(in the tropics)*
Urwaldfolgebestand *m* second growth, regrowth
urwüchsig original
Usambaraveilchen *n* 1. African violet, saintpaulia *(genus Saintpaulia)*; 2. African violet, saintpaulia, Saintpaulia ionantha
Ussuripflaume *f* Ussurian plum, Prunus ussuriensis
USV *s.* Ulmenscheckungsvirus
uterin uterine
Uterinmilch *f* uterine fluid
Uteritis *f (vet)* uterine inflammation, metritis
Uteroferrin *n* purple protein *(glycoprotein)*
Uteroglobin *n* blastokinin *(glycoprotein)*
Uterus *m* uterus, womb
Uterus... *s. a.* Gebärmutter...
Uterusbiopsie *f (vet)* uterine biopsy
Uterushals *m* uterine neck, cervix
Uterushorn *n* uterine horn
Uterusmotorik *f* uterine motility
Uterusspülung *f* intra-uterine irrigation

UTP-Hexose-1-Phosphaturidylyltransferase *f* UTP-hexose-1-phosphate uridylyltransferase *(enzyme)*
UTP-Xylose-1-Phosphaturidylyltransferase *f* UTP-xylose-1-phosphate uridylyltransferase *(enzyme)*
utriculat *(bot, zoo)* utricular, utriculate
UULV-Verfahren *n* ultra-ultra-low volume spraying *(plant protection)*
UV-... *s. a.* Ultraviolett...
UV-Bestrahlung *f* ultraviolet irradiation
UV-Lichtfalle *f* blacklight trap
Uvea *f* uvea *(of the eye)*
Uveitis *f (vet)* iridochoroiditis
Uviolglas *n* vita-glass
UV-Strahlung *f* ultraviolet radiation

V

Vagina *f* vagina; *(bot)* [leaf] sheath • **innerhalb der ~** intravaginal
~/künstliche artificial vagina, AV *(for semen collection)*
vaginal vaginal
Vaginal... *s. a.* Scheiden...
Vaginalabstrich *m* vaginal smear
Vaginalplatte *f* sterigma *(of Lepidoptera)*
Vaginalprolaps *m (vet)* vaginal prolapse, colpoptosis
Vaginitis *f (vet)* vaginitis, colpitis
Vaginoskop *n (vet)* colposcope
Vagus[nerv] *m* vagus nerve
Vagusstoff *m* acetylcholine *(amino compound, neurotransmitter)*
Vakuole *f* vacuole
~/autophage cytolysosome
Vakuolenmembran *f (bot)* tonoplast
Vakuom *n* vacuome
Vakuum *n* vacuum
Vakuumbegasung *f* vacuum fumigation
Vakuum-Druck-Verfahren *n* vacuum-pressure process *(wood preservation)*
Vakuumfilter *m* vacuum filter
Vakuumfiltration *f* vacuum filtration
Vakuumfüllen *n* vacuum filling *(e.g. of milk bottles)*
Vakuumfütterungsanlage *f* vacuum feeding plant
Vakuumfütterungsautomat *m* vacuum feeding plant
Vakuumkühler *m* vacuum cooler
Vakuumkühlung *f* vacuum cooling
Vakuumlagerung *f* vacuum storage
Vakuumleitung *f* vacuum line
Vakuumpumpe *f* vacuum pump
Vakuumregelventil *n*, **Vakuumregler** *m* vacuum controller
Vakuumsägerät *n* vacuum seeder
Vakuumsilo *m* vacuum silo

Vakuumstabilisierungsgerät n vacuum stabilizer (of a pipeline milking installation)
Vakuumtank m vacuum tank
Vakuumtankanhänger m vacuum tank trailer
Vakuumtrennanlage f vacuum separator
Vakuumtrockner m vacuum dryer
Vakuumtrocknung f vacuum drying (seasoning)
Vakuumverdampfer m vacuum evaporator
Vakuumverdampfung f vacuum evaporation
Vakuumverfahren n vacuum process (wood preservation)
vakzinal (vet) vaccinal
Vakzination f (vet) vaccination
~/prophylaktische preventive vaccination
Vakzinationsprogramm n vaccination programme (schedule)
Vakzine f (vet) vaccine
~/assoziierte associated vaccine
~ aus inaktivierten Erregern inactivated (dead) vaccine
~/heterologe heterologous vaccine
~/lapinisierte lapinized vaccine
~/polyvalente polyvalent vaccine
Vakzinetherapie f vaccinotherapy
vakzinieren to vaccinate
Vakzinierung f s. Vakzination
Val s. Valin
Valencia-Erdnuß f Valencia peanut, Arachis hypogaea ssp. fastigiata var. fastigiata
Valeriansäure f valeric (pentanoic) acid
Validamycin n validamycin, (Am) validacin (antibiotic, fungicide)
Valin n valine (amino-acid)
Valinomycin n valinomycin (antibiotic)
Valsakrankheit f valsa [canker] (of pome and stone fruit, caused by Leucostoma cincta = Valsa leucostoma)
valvat (bot) valvate (with or resembling valves)
Vamidothion n vamidothion (insecticide)
Vampirfledermaus f 1. vampire [bat] (family Desmodontidae); 2. vampire [bat], Desmodus rotundus
Vanadiumdüngemittel n vanadium fertilizer
Vanda f (bot) vanda (genus Vanda)
Vandamosaikvirus n vanda mosaic virus, VMV
Vanhoutte-Spierstrauch m (bot) Vanhoutte spiraea, Spiraea x vanhouttei
Vanille f (bot) vanilla (genus Vanilla)
Vanillegras n vanilla (holy) grass, Hierochloe odorata
Vanillekapsel f, **Vanilleschote** f vanilla [bean, pod]
Vanillin n vanillin (flavour compound)
Vanillinmandelsäure f vanillomandelic acid
Vanillinsäure f vanillic acid
Vapam n metham-sodium (fungicide, herbicide, nematicide)
Vapor m s. Dampf
Vaporisation f s. Verdunstung

Variabilität f variability
~/genetische genetic variability
Variable f variable
~/stochastische (zufällige) stochastic variable
Variante f variant
Varianz f variance, dispersion
~/additive genetische additive genetic variance, genic variance, lush
~/genetische (genotypische) genetic (hereditary) variance
~/phänotypische phenotypic variance
Varianzanalyse f variance analysis, analysis of variance
~/mehrdimensionale (mehrfache) multivariate analysis of variance
Varianzkomponente f variance component
Varianz-Kovarianz-Matrix f variance-covariance matrix
Varianzquotiententest m variance-ratio test
Varianzquotientenverteilung f variance-ratio distribution
Variate f s. Zufallsvariable
Variation f variation
~/blastogene blastovariation
Variationsbreite f (biom) range [of variation]
Variationsgelenk n (bot) pulvinus
Variationsintervall n s. Variationsbreite
Variationskoeffizient m (biom) coefficient of variation
Variationsstatistik f statistics
Variationsursache f (biom) source of variation
Variator m variator
Variegation f variegation (a diversity of colours as in flowers, leaves)
Varietät f variety
Varietätenidentifikation f variety identification
Varikozele f (vet) varicocele
Variscit m variscite (non-clay mineral)
Varro[at]ose f (vet) varroasis (of honey-bees, caused by Varroa jacobsoni)
Varzea f varzea (flood-plain forest of the Amazon region)
Vase f [flower-]vase
Vasektomie f (vet) vasectomy
vasektomieren to vasectomize
Vasenform f vase shape, cup form (of fruit-trees)
vasenförmig (bot) olliform
vaskular, vaskulär vascular
Vaskularisation f vascularization
Vaskulitis f (vet) vasculitis, angiitis
Vasodilatans n s. Vasodilatator
Vasodilatation f vasodilation
Vasodilatator m vasodilator [agent]
Vasographie f (vet) angiography
Vasokonstriktion f vasoconstriction
Vasokonstriktor m vasoconstrictor [agent]
Vasomotor m vasomotor
Vasomotorensystem n vasomotor system
vasomotorisch vasomotor

Vasoneurose

Vasoneurose f (vet) vasoneurosis
Vasopressin n vasopressin, antidiuretic hormone, ADH
Vasoresektion f (vet) vasectomy
Vasospasmus m (vet) vasospasm
Vasotocin n vasotocin (peptide)
Vasotomie f (vet) vasotomy
väterlich paternal
Vaterrasse f sire breed
Vaterschaft f paternity
Vaterschaftsbestimmung f, **Vaterschaftsnachweis** m paternity test
Vatertier n sire
~/gekörtes (zuchtwertgeprüftes, zugelassenes) proved (proven) sire
Vatertierauslese f sire selection
Vatertierbewertung f sire evaluation
Vatertierhalter m sire owner
Vatertierhaltung f sire keeping
Vatertierschätzung f sire evaluation
Vatertierselektion f sire selection
Vater[tier]vergleich m sire comparison
~/direkter direct sire comparison
VEE s. Venezolanische Pferdeenzephalomyelitis
VEEV s. Venezolanisches Pferdeenzephalomyelitisvirus
Vega f brown warp soil
vegetabil[isch] vegetable
Vegetation f vegetation
Vegetationsaufnahme f vegetation survey
Vegetationschorologie f vegetation chorology
Vegetationsdecke f vegetation (plant) cover, vegetable cover
Vegetationsdynamik f vegetation dynamics
Vegetationsfolge f vegetational change (fluctuation)
Vegetationsgeographie f vegetation geography
Vegetationsgliederung f division of vegetational cover
Vegetationsheizung f vegetation heating [system] (horticulture)
Vegetationskartierung f vegetation mapping, mapping of vegetation
Vegetationskegel m s. Vegetationspunkt
Vegetationsklassifizierung f vegetation classification
Vegetationskunde f vegetation science, phytosociology, phytocoenology
vegetationskundlich phytosociological
Vegetationslandschaft f vegetated landscape
vegetationslos vegetation-free, barren
Vegetationsperiode f vegetative (growing) period, growing season
~/frostfreie frost-free growing period (season)
Vegetationsprofil n vegetation (vegetable) profile, bisect
Vegetationspunkt m apical (growing) point, apical (vegetation) cone, vegetative point (plant anatomy) • **keinen ~ habend** blind

Vegetationsring m annual ring, annual growth layer
Vegetationsruhe f dormant period
Vegetationsschichtung f vegetation stratification
Vegetationsstruktur f vegetation structure
Vegetationsstufe f vegetation belt, stage
Vegetationstranssekt n s. Vegetationsprofil
Vegetationstyp m vegetation type
Vegetationstypenentwicklung f phytocoenogenesis
Vegetationszeit f growing season (period)
Vegetationszone f vegetation zone
vegetativ vegetative
Vehikel n vehicle
Veilchen n violet, viola (genus Viola)
Veilchengewächse npl violet family (family Violaceae) • **die ~ betreffend** violaceous
Veilchenholz n (bot) gidgee, Acacia homalophylla
Veilchentabak m common tobacco, Nicotiana rustica
Veitch-Tanne f Veitch fir, Abies veitchii
Veitstanz m (vet) chorea
Vektor m (phyt, vet) vector, carrier; carrier host
Vektorbeziehung f vector relationship
Vektorenbekämpfung f vector control
Vektorinsekt n insect vector
Vektorspezifität f vector specificity
Veldziekte f (vet) heart water disease
Velum n (bot, zoo) velum, veil
Vene f vein • **in die ~ hinein** intravenous • **innerhalb einer ~** intravenous
~/kleine venule
Venenanordnung f venation
Venenentzündung f (vet) phlebitis
Veneneröffnung f (vet) phlebotomy
Venengeflecht n venous plexus
venenreich (zoo) venose
Venenthrombose f (vet) phlebothrombosis
Venenum n venom, animal poison
Venezolanische Pferdeenzephalomyelitis f (vet) Venezuelan equine encephalomyelitis, VEE
Venezolanisches Pferdeenzephalomyelitisvirus n Venezuelan equine encephalomyelitis virus, VEEV
Venezuela-Sandelholz n balsam torchwood, Amyris balsamifera
Venlo-Gewächshaus n venlo [glass]house
Venole f (zoo) venule
venös venous
Ventil n valve
Ventilation f ventilation
Ventilator m ventilator
ventilieren to ventilate, to vent
Ventiltränksystem n valve drinking system
ventral ventral
Ventraltubus m (ent) collophore
Ventrikel m ventricle (animal anatomy)
ventrikular, ventrikulär ventricular
Venula f (zoo) venule

Venusfliegenfalle f (bot) Venus['s] fly-trap, Dionaea muscipula
Venuskamm m (bot) shepherd's needle, Venus's comb, Scandix pecten-veneris
Venusschuh m slipper orchid (genus Paphiopedilum)
verabreichen to apply, to administer (e.g. a medicament)
Verabreichung f application, administration
~/örtlich begrenzte topical application
Verabreichungsmenge f dose (for compounds s. under Dosis)
Verabreichungszeitpunkt m application date
veränderlich variable, changeable; mutable
Veränderliche Lupine f pearl lupin[e], tarwi, Lupinus mutabilis
Veränderlicher Scheibenbock m (ent) tanbark borer, Phymatodes testaceus
Veränderlichkeit f variability, changeability; mutability
Verangerung f overgrowing with weeds
Verankerung f anchorage (e.g. of trees)
Veranlagung f (phyt, vet) [pre]disposition, tendency
verarbeiten to process (e.g. agricultural products)
~/zu Graupen to pearl
~/zu Marmelade to jam
~/zu Pellets to pelletize
~/zu Perlgraupen to pearl
Verarbeiter m processor
Verarbeitung f processing
Verarbeitungsanlage f processing plant (facility)
Verarbeitungsausbeute f processing yield
Verarbeitungsbetrieb m s. Verarbeitungsanlage
Verarbeitungseignung f processing potential (e.g. of fruits)
Verarbeitungsertrag m processing yield
Verarbeitungsindustrie f processing industry
Verarbeitungsqualität f processing quality
Verarbeitungsreife f processing maturity; canning maturity
Verarbeitungsrückstand m processing residue, residue of processing
Verarbeitungsverlust m processing loss
verarmen to become impoverished (poor) (e.g. a soil); to become depleted (e.g. a flora)
~/an Mineral[stoff]en to become demineralized
Verarmung f impoverishment; depletion
~ an Mineral[stoff]en demineralization
veraschen to ash, to burn (reduce) to ashes, to incinerate
Veraschen n, **Veraschung** f ashing, incineration
verästeln/sich (bot, zoo) to ramify, to branch [out]
verästelnd/sich (bot) deliquescent
verästelt branched, ramified, ramiform, dendritic
Verästelung f branching, ramification
Veratridin n veratridine (alkaloid)
Veratrin n veratrine (alkaloid)

verätzen (phyt) to etch, to scorch; (vet) to cauterize, to etch
Verätzung f (phyt) etching, scorch; (vet) cautery, cauterization
Verband m 1. (vet) dressing; bandage; 2. (ecol) alliance
Verbänderung f (bot, phyt) fasciation
Verbandsmaterial n tie material (for grafts)
verbauen to dam (waters)
Verbauung f damming (s. a. Lawinenverbauung)
verbeißen to browse, to crop (game)
~/übermäßig to overbrowse
Verbeißen n s. Verbiß
verbellen (hunt) to bay (the dog for announcing dead game)
Verbene f verbena, holy herb (genus Verbena)
Verbergungstracht f (zoo, bot) mimesis
verbessern/den Boden to ameliorate
~/durch Verdrängungskreuzung to upgrade, to grade up
Verbindung f/antitrypsinwirksame antitrypsin [substance]
~/anorganische inorganic [compound]
~/organische organic [compound]
~/oxidationshemmende antioxidant
~/phosphororganische organophosphorous compound, organophosphate
~/terpenartige terpenoid
Verbindungen fpl/organomineralische organomineral (colloidal) complex, organo-clay complex, clay-humus complex
Verbindungsgewebe n conjunctive tissue
Verbindungspunkt m tie point (photogrammetry)
Verbiß m browse, browsing [by game]
~/schädigender overbrowsing
Verbißgehölz n (forest) browsing coppice
Verbißgrad m browsing rate
Verbißintensität f browsing intensity
Verbißobergrenze f (forest) browse (grazing) line, browsing level
Verbißpflanzen fpl browse
Verbißschaden m browsing damage
Verbißschutzmittel n deer repellent, antigame protective agent
Verbißstelle f, **Verbißwunde** f browsing wound
verblasen (hunt) to sound death
verblauen to blue (timber)
verblaut blued, blue-stained (timber)
Verblauung f blu[e]ing, blue [sap-]stain (of timber due to fungal attack)
verblühen to fade, to wither, to cease blooming, to decay
verbluten to bleed to death, to exsanguinate
Verblutung f (vet) exsanguination
verborgenhodig cryptorchid
Verborgenhodigkeit f cryptorchidism
Verbraucherschutz m consumer protection
Verbraucherverpackung f consumer pack[age]
Verbraunung f (soil) brunification

Verbräunung

Verbräunung f *(phyt)* browning
~/innere internal browning, IB
Verbreitung f *(ecol)* distribution, dissemination, dispersal; spread[ing] *(e.g. of a disease)*
~ durch Ameisen myrmecochory
~ durch Wind anemochory
Verbreitungsbarriere f barrier to dispersal
Verbreitungsgebiet n range
~/geographisches geographic range
~/natürliches natural range
Verbreitungsgrenze f distribution limit
verbrennbar combustible
verbrennen 1. to burn *(material)*; to combust *(e.g. fuel)*; to burn, to undergo combustion; 2. to burn, to scorch *(plant tissue e.g. by overfertilization)*
Verbrennung f burn[ing]; combustion; scorch *(esp. of plant tissues)*
~ dritten Grades *(vet)* third-degree burn
~/fortschreitende *(forest)* progressive burning, swamper (forced) burning *(of slash)*
~ frischen Schlagabraums *(forest)* live burning
Verbrennungskraftmaschine f, **Verbrennungsmotor** m internal combustion engine
verbrühen to scald
Verbrühung f *(vet)* scald
verbunden *(bot, zoo)* conjugate
~/miteinander anastomose
~/paarweise conjugate
Verbundfolie f sandwich-type plastic film
Verbundstein m interlocking stone
Verbundsteinpflaster n pavement with interlocking flags
Verbundwirtschaft f mixed farming
Verbuschung f shrub invasion
verbuttern to churn [to butter]
Verdampfanlage f evaporation plant *(sugar manufacture)*
Verdampfapparat m evaporation apparatus, evaporator
verdampfen to evaporate, to vaporize, to volatilize
Verdampfer m evaporator
Verdampfstation f s. Verdampfanlage
Verdampfung f evaporation, vaporization
~/vierstufige quadruple effect evaporation *(sugar manufacture)*
Verdampfungskristallisation f boiling *(sugar manufacture)*
Verdampfungskristallisator m boiling apparatus
verdauen to digest
verdaulich digestible
Verdaulichkeit f digestibility
~ der Energie energy digestibility
~ des Futters feed digestibility
~/scheinbare apparent digestibility
~/wahre true digestibility
Verdaulichkeitsbestimmung f digestibility trial
Verdaulichkeitsgrad m degree of digestibility
Verdaulichkeitsversuch m digestibility trial
Verdauung f digestion

Verdauungsapparat m digestive (alimentary) system
Verdauungsdepression f digestion depression
Verdauungsdrüse f *(bot)* digestive gland
Verdauungsenzym n digestive enzyme
verdauungsfördernd digestive, peptic
Verdauungshormon n digestive hormone
Verdauungskanal m s. Verdauungstrakt[us]
Verdauungskoeffizient m digestion coefficient, coefficient of digestibility, digestibility value, D-value
Verdauungsorgan n digestive (alimentary) organ
Verdauungsorgane npl digestive system
Verdauungsphysiologie f digestive physiology
Verdauungsprodukt n digest
Verdauungsprozeß m digestive process
Verdauungsquotient m s. Verdauungskoeffizient
Verdauungssaft m digestive juice
Verdauungsstörung f digestive disorder (disturbance, upset), indigestion, maldigestion, dyspepsia
~ infolge Phytobezoars phytobezoariasis
Verdauungssystem n digestive system
Verdauungstätigkeit f digestion
~ des Pansens rumen digestion
Verdauungstrakt[us] m digestive tract, alimentary tract (canal)
Verdauungsversuch m digestion experiment
verdeckeln *(api)* to seal [over]
Verderb m decay, deterioration, spoilage, breakdown
~/bakterieller bacterial spoilage
verderben to decay, to deteriorate, to spoil, to break down, to perish, to nip
verderblich perishable
Verderblichkeit f perishability
Verdichtbarkeit f compressibility *(e.g. of a soil)*
verdichten to compress, to compact, to densify, to condense
Verdichterstation f compressor station
Verdichtung f compression, compaction, densification, condensation
~ durch Bodendruck von Traktoren tractor-induced compaction
Verdichtungsgrad m degree of compaction
Verdickung[sleiste] f/schraubige spiral thickening *(wood anatomy)*
Verdopp[e]lung f des Chromosomensatzes *(gen)* diploidization
~/identische replication *(of DNA molecules)*
verdorren to wither, to dry up, to blast, to wilt
verdrängen to crowd out, to displace
~/durch Konkurrenzwirkung to outcompete *(e.g. weeds)*
Verdrängung f crowding-out, displacement
Verdrängungskreuzung f displacement (replacement) crossing, grade breeding, grading-up
• **durch ~ verbessern** to upgrade, to grade up
• **eine ~ vornehmen** to grade

Verdrehung *f* torsion
verdunkeln to darken, to black out *(e.g. a greenhouse)*
Verdunkelungsanlage *f*, **Verdunkelungseinrichtung** *f* darkening installation, blackout system
verdünnen to dilute, to thin
Verdünnen *n* dilution, thinning
Verdünner *m* diluent, diluting agent
Verdünnung *f* 1. dilution; 2. *s.* Verdünnungsmittel
Verdünnungsendpunkt *m* dilution end-point *(virology)*
Verdünnungsmittel *n* diluent, diluting agent
verdunsten to evaporate, to vaporize, to volatilize
~ **lassen** to evaporate, to vaporize
Verdunstung *f* evaporation, vaporization
~/**potentielle** *s.* Verdunstungsvermögen
Verdunstungsanspruch *m* evaporative demand *(of the atmosphere)*
Verdunstungsfeuchtemesser *m* psychrometer
Verdunstungsgeschwindigkeit *f* evaporation rate
verdunstungshemmend evaporation-suppressive
Verdunstungskühler *m* evaporative cooler
Verdunstungskühlung *f* evaporative cooling
Verdunstungsmesser *m* evaporimeter, evaporometer, atmometer; psychrometer
Verdunstungs[meß]schreiber *m* evaporograph
Verdunstungsverlust *m* evaporation loss
Verdunstungsvermögen *n* potential evaporation, evaporating capacity, evaporitivity
Verdunstungswärmestrom *m* evaporative heat flow
Veredeler *m* grafter
veredeln to graft; to work *(esp. woody plants)*
~/**durch Okulation** to inoculate
~/**in die Krone** to top-graft, to top-work
Veredeln *n* grafting
Veredelung *f* 1. graftage; 2. graft [union], [bud] union
~/**einjährige** whip
~/**unvollkommen verwachsene** imperfectly joined graft
Veredelungsband *n* grafting tape; bud[ding] strip
Veredelungshülse *f* grafting sheath *(grape-vine graftage)*
Veredelungsmesser *n* bill[hook], grafter
Veredelungsreis *n* grafting scion (twig), graft
Veredelungsrute *f* bud stick
Veredelungsstelle *f* graft [union], [bud] union
Veredelungsteil *m*/**wuchshemmender** dwarfing medium
Veredelungsunterlage *f* [root, body] stock, *(Am)* understock
Veredelungsverband *m* wrapping
Veredelungsverfahren *n* grafting
Veredelungswunde *f* graft
Veredlung *f s.* Veredelung
vereidigt sworn *(e.g. a timber grader)*
Vereinigen *n (api)* uniting
Vereinigung *f*/**bäuerliche** farmer union

vereintkelchblättrig *(bot)* synsepalous
vereinzeln to single
~/**Sämlinge** to prick [off, out]
Vereinzeln *n* singling, singulation
~/**manuelles** hand singling
~ **mit der Hacke** hoe singling
vereinzelt solitary
Vereinzelung *f s.* Vereinzeln
Vereinzelungsabstand *m* singling distance
Vereinzelungsplatz *m* shedder *(of a livestock handling facility)*
Vereisung *f (vet)* refrigeration anaesthesia
verenden to die, to perish
Verengung *f (vet)* stenosis *(of a hollow organ)*
~/**starke** stricture
vererbbar [in]heritable
Vererbbarkeit *f* heritability
vererben to inherit
Vererber *m* inheritor
vererbt hereditary
Vererbung *f* inheritance, heredity
~/**autosomale** autosomal inheritance
~ **erworbener Eigenschaften** inheritance of acquired characters
~/**extrachromosomale** extrachromosomal (cytoplasmic, plasmatic) inheritance, extranuclear heredity (inheritance)
~/**geschlechtsbegrenzte** sex-limited inheritance
~/**geschlechtsgekoppelte** sex-linked inheritance
~/**holandrische** holandric inheritance
~/**karyotische** chromosomal inheritance
~/**matrokline** matroclinal inheritance
~/**mendelnde** Mendelian (qualitative) inheritance
~/**monogene** monogenic inheritance
~/**nichtadditive** non-additive inheritance
~/**nichtchromosomale (nichtmendelnde, plasmatische)** *s.* ~/extrachromosomale
~/**polygene (polygenische)** polygenic inheritance, polygeny
~/**qualitative** qualitative (Mendelian) inheritance
~/**quantitative** quantitative inheritance
~/**Y-chromosomale** holandric inheritance
~/**zytoplasmatische** *s.* ~/extrachromosomale
Vererbungsgesetz *n* law of inheritance
Vererbungslehre *f* genetics
~/**Mendelsche** Mendelian (particulate) inheritance, Mendelism
Vererbungsmuster *n* inheritance pattern
Vererbungsregel *f* law of inheritance
Vererbungsschema *n* inheritance pattern
Vererbungstheorie *f* **nach [Gregor] Mendel** Mendelian theory
Vererbungswissenschaft *f* genetics
Vererbungszytologie *f* cytogenetics
Veresterung *f* esterification
Verfahren *n* process; method, technique, procedure
~/**experimentelles** experimental procedure
Verfall *m* deterioration; *(phyt)* decline

verfallen

verfallen to deteriorate; to decline
verfälschen to adulterate, to dose *(e.g. wine)*
verfälscht adulterate
Verfälschung *f* adulteration
verfärben/sich to discolour, to change colour, to stain; to turn *(leafage)*; to change hair *(game)*
Verfärbung *f* discolo[u]ration; stain *(of timber)*
~/mineralische mineral stain *(of timber)*
~/schwache light stain *(of timber)*
verfärbungsfrei bright *(timber)*
Verfassung *f* condition *(e.g. of an animal)*
~/körperliche body condition, disposition
verfaulen to rot [away, down], to putrefy, to fester, to decay
~ lassen to rot
Verfaulen *n* rotting, rot, decay
verfaulend putrescent
verfault rotten, putrid
verfestigen to compact, to consolidate, to solidify
~/sich to compact, to consolidate, to solidify
Verfestigung *f* compaction, consolidation, solidification
verfettet overfat, obese
Verfettung *f* fatness, obesity, adiposity, steatosis
~/degenerative fatty degeneration
Verfilzen *n* des Felles matting of fur
verfilzt matted
Verfilzung *f* matting
verflochten *(bot)* implexous
verflüchtigen/sich to volatilize
Verflüchtigung *f* volatilization
verfolgen/eine Fährte (Spur) *(hunt)* to track, to trail, to spoor, to scent, to pursue, to quest
Verformbarkeit *f* plasticity
Verformung *f* deformation, strain
~/bleibende permanent deformation, unrecovered strain *(e.g. of wood)*
Verfrachtung *f (ecol)* passive dispersal
verfrühen to advance, to force *(plants)*
verfügbar 1. available; 2. at (in) stud *(stallion)*
~/nicht unavailable
Verfügbarkeit *f* availability
~/biologische bioavailability
verfüttern *s.* füttern
Vergabelung *f*, Vergabelungspunkt *m* jorquette *(of Theobroma cacao)*
vergällen to denaturate, to denaturize
Vergällung *f* denaturation
Vergällungsmittel *n* denaturant
vergänglich *(bot)* fugacious
vergärbar fermentable
Vergärbarkeit *f* fermentability
vergären to ferment
Vergärung *f* fermentation; attenuation *(of wort)*
Vergärungsgrad *m* degree of fermentation; degree of attenuation *(of wort)*
vergeilen to etiolate
vergeilt etiolated, spindly, leggy
Vergeilung *f* etiolation *(of plants due to light deficiency)*
Vergesellschaftung *f (ecol)* association
vergießen to overwater
vergiften to poison, to intoxicate
~/mit Gas to gas
Vergiftung *f* 1. poisoning, intoxication; 2. poisoning, intoxication, toxicosis
~/alimentäre alimentary intoxication
vergiftungsbedingt toxi[co]genic
vergilben to yellow
Vergilben *n* yellowing; yellowing stage *(tobacco curing)*
Vergilbung *f s.* 1. Vergilben; 2. Vergilbungskrankheit
Vergilbungskrankheit *f (phyt)* yellows [disease], YD
~ der Gladiole fusarium corm rot of gladiolus *(caused by Fusarium oxysporum f.sp. gladioli)*
~ der Rübe beet yellows *(virosis)*
~/virusbedingte virus yellows
Vergilbungsvirus *n* yellows virus *(comprehensive term)*
Vergißmeinnicht *n* forget-me-not, mouse-ear, scorpion-grass, myosote, myosotis *(genus Myosotis)*
verglasen to glaze
Verglasung *f* glazing
~/kittlose puttyless glazing
Vergleichsfläche *f* check area *(field experimentation)*
Vergleichsparzelle *f* control plot *(field experimentation)*
Vergleichssorte *f* check cultivar
Vergleichsvariante *f* control *(experimentation)*
Vergleyen *n (soil)* gleying
Vergleyung *f (soil)* gleyification, *(Am)* gleization
vergraben to bury
vergrast grass-covered, overgrown with grass
vergrößert/kropfartig strumose
vergrünen to green
Vergrünung *f* greening, virescence
Vergrünungskrankheit *f* bei Citrus [citrus] greening disease *(mycoplasmosis)*
verhacken to single, to thin [out], *(Am)* to block
Verhacken *n* hoe singling
Verhalten *n* behaviour
~/abnormes abnormal behaviour
~/aggressives aggressive behaviour
~/ansteckendes social facilitation
~/soziales social behaviour
Verhaltensanomalie *f* abnormal behaviour
verhaltensbestimmt behavioural
Verhaltensdarstellung *f* ethogram
Verhaltensgenetik *f* behaviour genetics
Verhaltenskunde *f* ethology
Verhaltensmerkmal *n* behavioural feature, behaviour character
Verhaltensmuster *n* behavioural pattern

Verhaltensphysiologie f behavioural physiology
Verhaltensreaktion f behavioural response
Verhaltensstörung f behavioural disorder, vice
Verhaltenssystem n behaviour system
Verhaltenswissenschaft f behavioural science
Verhältnis n **von Haspelumfangsgeschwindigkeit zu Fahrgeschwindigkeit** reel-speed ratio
~ **von Wurzelmasse zu oberirdischer Pflanzenmasse** root-to-top ratio
Verhaltung f retention
verharren to persist
Verhärtung f s. Sklerose
verharzt s. verkient
Verhauen n hoe singling
verheilen to heal [over, up]
verhoffen und aufwerfen to be on the alert (game)
verholzen to lignify, to run to wood, to convert into wood
verholzend lignescent
verholzt woody, ligneous, lignose, xyloid
Verholzung f lignification
Verhornung f hornification
~/**übermäßige** keratinization, keratosis
verhungern to starve [to death]
~ **lassen** to starve [to death], to famish
Verhungern n starvation
verhütend preventive
Verhütung f prevention
verimpfen to inoculate
verjüngen to rejuvenate; (forest) to regenerate
~/**sich** to rejuvenate; to regenerate
Verjüngung f 1. rejuvenation; (forest) regeneration; 2. s. Verjüngungsschnitt
~ **durch Luftableger** air (pot) layering, marcottage, marcotting
~ **durch Samen** regeneration by seed
~ **durch Wurzelausschlag (Wurzelbrut)** regeneration from root suckers
~/**ergänzende** supplementary regeneration
~/**generative** regeneration by seed
~/**horst- und gruppenweise** regeneration by groups
~/**horstweise** regeneration by patches
~/**künstliche** artificial regeneration (reproduction)
~/**natürliche** natural regeneration, volunteer growth
~/**schlagweise** compartment method
~/**streifen- und saumweise** regeneration by strips
Verjüngungsart f form of regeneration
Verjüngungsbestand m stand due for regeneration
Verjüngungsblock m regeneration block
Verjüngungsfläche f regeneration area, area under regeneration
Verjüngungshieb m regeneration felling, reproduction cutting
Verjüngungsperiode f reproduction period, period of natural regeneration

Verjüngungssaum m belt under regeneration
Verjüngungsschlag m 1. compartment under regeneration; 2. s. Verjüngungshieb
Verjüngungsschnitt m rejuvenation (regenerative) pruning, dehorning
Verjüngungsverfahren n regeneration method
Verjüngungszeitraum m s. Verjüngungsperiode
Verjüngungsziel n reproduction goal
Verkahlen n, **Verkahlung** f branch denudation, denudation of lateral branches (of woody plants)
Verkalben n/**seuchenhaftes, Verkalbeseuche** f contagious abortion in cattle (caused by Brucella abortus)
Verkalkung f calcification
verkappen to hood (falconry)
verkarsten (soil) to karstify
verkarstet karstic
Verkauf m **an Selbstpflücker** pick-your-own sale (of fruit)
~ **auf dem Stamm (Stock)** (forest) sale on the stump, sale of standing trees, standing (stumpage) sale
~ **nach Ausformung** (forest) sale after conversion
~ **von stehendem Holz** s. ~ **auf dem Stamm**
verkaufsfähig saleable, marketable
~/**nicht** unmarketable
Verkaufsfrucht f cash (sale, commercial) crop
Verkaufsfruchtanbau m cash (sale) cropping
Verkaufsgemüse n (Am) truck
Verkaufspackung f market pack (e.g. of potted plants)
Verkaufssortiment n merchantable assortment (e.g. of timber)
Verkaufsverpackung f market package, consumer pack[age]
verkehrt herzförmig (bot) obcordate
~ **kegelförmig** (bot, zoo) obconical
~ **lanzettlich** (bot) oblanceolate[d]
Verkernung f heartwood formation, duramin[iz]ation
verkettet (bot, zoo) catenulate
verkient resinous, resin-soaked, impregnated with resin, fat
Verkienung f resinification, resinosis, resin soak[ing]
Verkieselung f (soil) silicification, silicatization
verkitten (soil) to aggregate
Verklebung f adhesion
Verkleisterung f gelatinization (of starch granules)
verklumpen to clot, to agglutinate
verknöchern to ossify
Verknöcherung f ossification
verknorpeln to chondrify
Verknorpelung f chondrification
verknoten to knot
Verknüpfungsstelle f cross-link
verkochen to boil
~/**auf Korn** to boil to grain (sugar)
verkohlen to char, to carbonize (wood)

Verkohlung

Verkohlung f charcoal burning, carbonization
verkorken to cork [up]
~/sich *(bot)* to suberize, to cork
Verkorkung f suberization, suberification
verkosten to degust, to taste
Verkoster m taster, panelist
Verkostergremium n, **Verkosterjury** f taste panel
Verkostung f degustation
Verkostungsglas n dock-glass *(for wine)*
verkrampft *(vet)* spastic, spasmodic, cramped
Verkrautung f s. Verunkrautung
Verkrehlen n short-hoe singling
verkrümmt crooked, distorted
Verkrümmung f crookedness, distortion
verkrüppeln to cripple; to become crippled
verkrusten to crust, to cap; to scab *(blood)*
Verkrustung f crust
verkümmern to become stunted, to decline, to dwarf, to grow sickly, to abort
~ **lassen** to stunt
verkümmert stunted, rudimentary, abortive
Verkümmerung f *(phyt)* stuntedness, decline
Verladeausleger m **[für Schüttgüter]** bulk boom
Verladebrücke f loading bridge
Verladeelevator m loading (delivery) elevator
Verladegerät n loading machine
Verladerampe f loading platform (ramp, dock)
Verladereiniger m cleaner-loader
verladetrocken shipping-dry, surface-dry, SD *(timber)*
Verlagerung f dislocation, translocation
verlängert *(bot, zoo)* elongate[d]
Verlängerte Segge f, **Verlängertes Riedgras** n elongated sedge, Carex elongata
Verlängerung f elongation
Verlaubung f *(phyt)* phyllody, frondescence, virescence
Verlaufen n **der Säge** saw wandering, running out [of saw-blades]
verlaufend/tödlich pernicious
verlaust lousy, pedicular, pediculous
Verlegenheitsbewegung f displacement activity *(animal behaviour)*
Verleiten n distraction display *(animal behaviour)*
Verleseband n sorting belt (conveyor), picking belt, inspection belt (conveyor)
verlesen to sort [out], to pick, to cull *(e.g. peas)*
Verlesen n sorting, picking
Verlesetisch m sorting (picking) table
Verletzung f *(phyt, vet)* lesion, injury, trauma
Verlichtung f *(forest)* opening-up
verlieren/die Fährte to lose the trail (scent)
~/ein Hufeisen to cast a horseshoe
Verlust m loss, deprivation
Verluste mpl/**unbestimmte** undetermined losses *(sugar manufacture)*
verlustfrei loss-free
Verlustkontrollgerät n grain loss indicator (monitor), seed loss monitoring instrument *(combining)*

verlustlos loss-free, without losses
Verlustmeßgerät n loss meter
Verlustwärme f lost heat
Verlustzeit f unproductive time
vermahlbar millable
Vermahlbarkeit f millability
vermahlen to mill, to grind, to disintegrate
~/grob to crush, to kibble
~/zu Mehl to flour
Vermahlung f milling, grinding, disintegration
Vermahlungsabfälle mpl miller's offals
Vermahlungsausbeute f milling yield
Vermahlungsdiagramm n mill diagram
Vermahlungseigenschaft f milling characteristic (property)
Vermahlungsmaschine f miller
Vermahlungsnebenprodukt n milling by-product
Vermahlungsprodukt n mill product
Vermahlungsqualität f milling quality
Vermahlungsrückstand m mill[ing] residue
Vermännlichung f masculinization
vermarken to demarcate
vermarkten to market
~/lebend to sell on the hoof *(livestock)*
~/tot to sell on the hook
Vermarktung f marketing
~ **landwirtschaftlicher Erzeugnisse** agricultural marketing
Vermarktungseignung f marketability
Vermarktungseinheit f market pack *(e.g. of potted plants)*
vermarktungsfähig marketable
~/nicht unmarketable
Vermarktungsfähigkeit f marketability
Vermarktungshalle f packing house (shed, station)
Vermarktungsschwein n market hog
vermehren to multiply, to propagate, to reproduce
~/durch Ableger (Absenker) to layer
~/im Mutterbeet to stool
~/sich to propagate, to breed
~/sich durch Knospung to pullulate
~/ungeschlechtlich to propagate vegetatively (asexually), to clone
Vermehrung f multiplication, propagation, reproduction *(s. a. under Fortpflanzung)*
~ **der Amnionflüssigkeit** *(vet)* hydramnios
~ **durch Ableger** [propagation by] layering
~ **durch Abrisse** mound-layering *(esp. of fruitwood root-stocks)*
~ **durch Absenker** s. ~ **durch Ableger**
~ **durch Ausläufer** propagating by runners, runnering
~ **durch Knospen** pullulation
~ **durch Luftableger** air (pot) layering, marcottage, marcotting
~ **durch Samen** propagating by seed
~ **durch Schnittlinge (Stecklinge)** cuttage

Verschäumen

~ **durch Zwiebeldoppelschalen** propagation by twin-scaling
~ **durch Zwiebelschnittstücke** propagating by chippings
~/**generative** generative (sexual) propagation
~ **im Mutterbeet** [propagation by] stooling
~ **unter Sprühnebel** fogging propagation
~/**vegetative** vegetative (asexual) propagation
Vermehrungsbeet *n* propagation bed (bench)
Vermehrungsbetrieb *m* seed-growing firm
Vermehrungsgut *n* reproductive material
Vermehrungshaus *n* propagating [glass]house, nursery greenhouse, propagator
Vermehrungsherde *f* multiplier herd
Vermehrungsholz *n* propagation wood
Vermehrungsindex *m* index of reproduction capacity
Vermehrungskasten *m* propagating frame, propagator
Vermehrungskoeffizient *m* propagation coefficient, multiplication (reproductivity) coefficient
Vermehrungsmaterial *n* propagating material
~/**pathogenfreies** pathogen-free propagating material
Vermehrungsmethode *f* method of propagation
Vermehrungspotential *n* propagation potential, reproductive potential (capacity), breeding (biotic) potential, gross biological capacity
Vermehrungsrate *f* breeding rate
Vermehrungssaatgut *n* multiplication seed, seed for propagation
Vermehrungssubstrat *n* propagation medium
Vermeidung *f* *(ecol)* avoidance
vermengen to blend; to mix
vermessen *(forest)* to measure (mark) off, to lay off; to survey *(land)*
Vermiculit *m* vermiculite *(clay mineral)*
vermifug vermifugal
vermischen to mix; to blend
Vermizid *n* vermicide
vermodern to mould[er], to decay, to rot
Vermoderung *f* mouldering, decay
Vermoderungshorizont *m* *(soil)* fermentation layer, F-layer
Vermorschung *f* crumbling, decaying *(of wood)*
Vernageln *n* pricking during nailing (shoeing)
Vernalisation *f* vernalization
vernalisieren to vernalize
vernarben to scar, to cicatrize
Vernarbung *f* cicatrization
vernässen to waterlog
vernäßt waterlogged, soggy, imperfectly drained *(soil)*
Vernässung *f* waterlogging
Vernation *f* *(bot)* vernation, foliation
vernebeln to nebulize, to fog, to atomize
Vernebeln *n* nebulization, fogging, atomization
vernichten/durch Brand *(phyt)* to blight
~/**Ratten** to rat

~/**Ungeziefer** to disinfest
Vernichtung *f* eradication, destruction *(e.g. of pests)*
Vernichtungsmittel *n* eradicant
Vernin *n* vernin[e] *(alkaloid)*
Vernolat *n* vernolate *(herbicide)*
Verödung *f* 1. *(ecol)* devastation; 2. *(vet)* obliteration
Veronika *f* speedwell, veronica *(genus Veronica)*
verpaaren to pair up, to mate
Verpaarung *f* pairing, mating
~/**disruptive** disruptive mating
~/**gerichtete (lineare)** directional mating
~/**zentrifugale** *s.* ~/disruptive
Verpaarungssystem *n* mating system
verpachten to lease, to let, to farm out
verpacken to pack up, to package
~/**in Ballen** to ball
~/**in Körbe** to basket
~/**in Säcke** to sack
verpflanzbar transplantable
verpflanzen to transplant; to plant out, to bed [out]; to pot [out]
~/**Gewebe** to graft
~/**Sämlinge** to prick [off, out]
Verpflanzschock *m* transplanting shock
Verpflanztisch *m* bench
Verpflanzung *f* transplantation
verpichen to pitch
verpilzt mouldy
verpuppen/sich to pupate
Verpuppung *f* pupation
verregnen to sprinkle
~/**Abwasser** to sewage
Verrenkung *f* *(vet)* luxation
Verrierpalmette *f* Verrier palmette *(orcharding)*
verrosten to rust, to get rusty
verrotten to rot [away, down], to putrefy, to fester; to ret[t] *(hay)*
Verrotten *n* rotting
verrottungsfest rotproof
Verrottungsfestigkeit *f* rotproofness
Verrottungsschutzmittel *n* rotproofing agent
versalzen to salinize
Versalzung *f* salinization • **durch** ~ **gekennzeichnet** *(soil)* halomorphic
Versalzungsgrad *m* salinity *(e.g. of a soil)*
versammeln to collect *(equitation)*
Versammlungspheromon *n* aggregation pheromone
Versandkäfig *m* mailing cage
Versandstreß *m* shipping stress
versauern to acidify, to make acid *(soil as by overfertilization)*; to sour, to become acid *(soil)*
Versauerung *f* 1. acidification; souring; 2. overacidity
Verschalung *f* case-hardening *(timber drying defect)*
Verschäumen *n* foaming

verscheuchen to chase away, to frighten off
Verschiebewelle f shifting shaft
Verschiebung f/meiotische meiotic drive
verschiedenblättrig (bot) heterophyllous, diversifolious
Verschiedenblättriger Schwingel m shade fescue, Festuca heterophylla
Verschiedenblättrigkeit f heterophylly
verschiedenfarbig varicoloured, heterochromatic
Verschiedenfarbige Dahlie f common dahlia, Dahlia pinnata
verschiedenfrüchtig (bot) heterocarpous
verschiedengestaltig heteromorphic
Verschiedengestaltigkeit f heteromorphism
verschiedengriffelig (bot) heterostyled, heterostylous
Verschiedengriffeligkeit f heterostyly
verschiedenstachelig (bot, zoo) heteracanth
verschiedenwirtig heteroxenous
Verschiedenwirtigkeit f heteroxenia
verschiedenzähnig (bot, zoo) heterodont
verschimmeln to mould, to become mouldy (as bread, fruit); to mildew (as materials)
Verschimmeln n moulding
verschimmelt mouldy; mildewed, mildewy
verschlammen, verschlämmen to silt [up], to cap, to puddle (soil)
Verschlammen n silting [up], capping, puddling, mudding up
verschlammt silty
Verschlammung f, **Verschlämmung** f upsilting, siltation
Verschleiß m wear
Verschleißschicht f surface dressing (road construction)
Verschleißteil n wearing part
Verschleppung f (ecol) passive dispersal
~ **durch Ameisen** myrmecochory (of fruits or seeds)
verschlingen to devour, to gulp
verschlucken to swallow
verschluffen to silt [up]
Verschluffung f siltation
verschlungen (bot, zoo) convolute
Verschmelzung f fusion
verschmutzen to soil; to pollute (the environment); to contaminate (esp. with poisonous substances); to become (get) polluted (e.g. a river)
Verschmutzung f soiling; pollution; contamination
verschneiden 1. to geld, to castrate, to emasculate; 2. to clip, to trim, to prune, to pare (e.g. a hedge); 3. to blend, to dose, to adulterate, to water down (e.g. wine)
~/**quer** to bang (the forelock of a horse)
Verschnittank m blending tank
Verschnittmittel n adulterant
Verschnittwein m blend wine
verschorfen (vet) to slough
verschrumpeln to shrivel, to shrink (e.g. apples)

Verschulalter n (forest) planting-stock age
Verschulapparat m lining-out machine
Verschulbeet n transplant bed
Verschulbrett n transplanting (lining-out) board
Verschulcontainer m transplant box
Verschuldung f **von Landwirtschaftsbetrieben** farm indebtedness
verschulen to line out, to transplant, to prick [off, out], to replant, to replace [plants]
Verschulholz n transplanting dibble
Verschulkamp m (forest) transplant (lining-out) nursery
Verschullatte f s. Verschulbrett
Verschulmaschine f lining-out machine
Verschulmesser n transplanting dagger
Verschulpflanze f [nursery] transplant
Verschulpflug m transplanting (lining-out) plough
Verschulquartier n (forest) transplant section
Verschulrabatte f transplant bed
Verschulrechen m transplanting rake
Verschulschock m transplanting shock
verseifbar saponifiable
Verseifung f saponification
Verseifungszahl f saponification number (value)
versengen to singe, to scorch
Versenkhydrant m underground hydrant
Versenkregner m underground (pop-up) sprinkler
versetzen/in Trab to trot
~/**ins Freiland** to reset (plantlets)
verseuchen to infest
Verseuchung f infestation
~/**radioaktive** [radioactive] contamination
Versicherung f insurance
~ **für Ernte[gut]erzeugnisse** crop insurance
~ **von betrieblichen Grundmitteln** farm property insurance
versickern to seep [away], to percolate
Versickerung f seepage
versiegeln to seal
Versommerung f s. Vernalisation
versorgen 1. to supply; 2. to care, to tend, to groom; (vet) to dress
~/**mit Brennstoff** to fuel
~/**mit Futter** to forage
~/**mit Kraftstoff** to fuel
~/**mit Streu** to bed, to litter down
~/**mit Stroh** to straw
Versorgungslager n (forest) logging depot
Versorgungstank m supply tank
verspätet (bot) serotine, serotinous
verspillern s. vergeilen
versprühen to spray, to atomize
Versprühen n spraying, atomization
verspunden to bung
Verstärkerhengst m outside sire
verstäuben to dust (e.g. pesticides)
Verstäuben n dusting
~/**aviotechnisches** aerator dusting
Verstäuber m duster, dusting appliance

verstauchen *(vet)* to sprain, to distort
Verstauchung *f (vet)* sprain, distortion
Versteck *n* lie *(of animals)*
Versteckblüte *f (bot)* earth-star *(genus Cryptanthus)*
Versteckthodigkeit *f (vet)* cryptorchidism
versteinert petrified, fossil
Versteinerung *f* 1. petrifaction, fossilization; 2. petrifact, fossil
verstellbar adjustable
verstellen to adjust
Versteppung *f* steppe formation, steppization
Verstocken *n*, **Verstockung** *f* incipient decay (deterioration), dote *(e.g. of hardwood)*
verstopfen/mit Propolis to propolize
Verstopfung *f (vet)* constipation
~ **der Kloakenöffnung** pasting *(in chicks)*
~ **der Triftrinne** *(forest)* log-jam
Verstrauchung *f* shrubbing, shrub invasion
verstreuen to scatter, to disseminate
Verstrichmittel *n* grafting-clay, graft sealant
Versuch *m* experiment, trial, test
~/**faktorieller** factorial experiment
~/**gemischter faktorieller** mixed factorial experiment
Versuchsanbau *m* experimental planting
Versuchsangaben *fpl* experimental data
Versuchsanlage *f* experiment[al] design
~ **mit unvollständigen Blocks** incomplete block design
~/**systematische** systematic design
Versuchsanstalt *f* experimental station
Versuchsausrüstung *f* experimental equipment
Versuchsbedingungen *fpl* experimental conditions
Versuchsbetrieb *m* [/**landwirtschaftlicher**] experimental (pilot) farm
Versuchsdurchführung *f* experimental procedure
Versuchseinheit *f* plot
Versuchsergebnisse *npl* experimental evidence, test results
Versuchserntemaschine *f* experimental harvester
Versuchsfarm *f s.* Versuchsbetrieb
Versuchsfehler *m* experimental error
Versuchsfeld *n* experimental field
Versuchsfeldboden *m* plot soil
Versuchsfischteich *m* experimental fish pond
Versuchsfläche *f* experimental (research) area
~/**forstliche** forest sample plot
~/**wissenschaftliche** *(Am, forest)* research natural area
Versuchsforst *m* experimental forest
Versuchsgefäß *n* experimental pot
Versuchsglied *n* treatment, variant
Versuchsjahr *n* trial year
Versuchsmethode *f* experimental method (procedure)
Versuchsmethodik *f* methods of experimentation
Versuchsparzelle *f* experimental (research) plot

Versuchsplan *m* experiment design
Versuchsreihe *f* trial series
Versuchsrevier *n* experimental forest district
Versuchsschema *n* experimental design
Versuchsserie *f* trial series
Versuchsstand *m* experimental rig
Versuchsstandort *m* experimental (test) site
Versuchsstation *f* experiment[al] station
~/**forstliche** forest experiment[al] station
~/**land- und hauswirtschaftliche** *(Am)* agriculture and home economics experiment station
~/**landwirtschaftliche** agricultural experiment station
Versuchstechniker *m* research technician
Versuchsteich *m* experimental [fish] pond
Versuchsteilstück *n* experimental plot
Versuchstier *n* experimental (laboratory) animal
Versuchstierkunde *f* experimental (laboratory) animal science
Versuchswaldung *f* experimental forest
Versuchswesen *n* experimentation
~/**forstliches** experimental forestry
~/**landwirtschaftliches** agricultural experimentation
Versuchszeitraum *m* experimental period
versumpfen to get marshy, to become boggy, to paludify
versumpft marshy, boggy
Versumpfung *f* bogging, paludification
Vertebra *f s.* Wirbel
Vertebrat *m* vertebrate *(subphylum Vertebrata)*
Verteidigung *f (animal behaviour)*
~ **des Volkes** *(api)* colony defence
Verteidigungsreaktion *f* defence reaction
Verteilband *n* dispensing belt
Verteileinrichtung *f* dispensing equipment, distributor, distributing device
Verteilergetriebe *n s.* Zapfgetriebe
Verteilermaische *f s.* Zentrifugenvorlauftrog
Verteilung *f* distribution; dispersal *(population dynamics)*; *(gen)* segregation
~/**gestutzte** *(biom)* truncated distribution
~/**symmetrische** *(biom)* symmetrical distribution
~ **von Landschaftsgliedern/räumliche** *(ecol)* mosaic
~/**zufällige (zufallsweise)** *(biom)* random distribution
verteilungsfrei non-parametric
Verteilungsfunktion *f* distribution function
Verteilungskurve *f* distribution curve
Verteilungsmuster *n (ecol)* dispersion
Verteilvorrichtung *f* dispenser
Verticillium-Braunflecken *mpl (phyt)* cap-spotting *(caused by Verticillium fungicola var. aleophilum)*
Verticilliumkrankheit *f* **des Kulturchampignons** verticillium disease of mushrooms, dry bubble of mushroom *(caused by Verticillium fungicola)*
Verticilliumwelke *f (phyt)* verticillium wilt

Verticilliumwelke

~ der Nelke carnation wilt *(caused by Phialophora cinerescens)*
Verticillose *f s.* Verticilliumwelke
vertieft *(bot, zoo)* lacunose
Vertigo *f (vet)* vertigo
Vertikaldränung *f* well drainage
Vertikalparallaxe *f* Y-parallax, vertical parallax *(surveying)*
Vertikalversetzung *f* von Luftmassen convection
Vertikutieren *n* verticuting *(lawn care)*
Vertikutierer *m*, Vertikutiermaschine *f* verticutor
vertilgen to exterminate
Vertilgung *f* extermination
Vertisol *m (soil)* vertisol, ert
vertopfen to pot [out], to prick [off, out]
Vertorfung *f* peatification
verträglich compatible; *(bot)* self-compatible
Verträglichkeit *f* compatibility
Verträglichkeitsrate *f* compatibility rate
Vertragsanbau *m* contract growing
Vertrauensbereich *m (biom)* confidence interval
Vertrauensgrenze *f (biom)* confidence limit
Vertrauensintervall *n (biom)* confidence interval
Vertrauenswert *m (biom)* confidence level
vertreiben to frighten off *(e.g. game)*
Vertriebserlaubnis *f* label clearance *(e.g. of a plant protectant)*
vertrocknen to dry up (away) *(s. a. verwelken)*
~ lassen to desiccate
verunkrautet weeded, weedy, weed-infested, weed-grown
Verunkrautung *f* 1. weed infestation, weedage; 2. weediness
verunreinigen to soil; to pollute *(the environment)*; to contaminate *(esp. with poisonous substances)*; to become (get) polluted *(e.g. a river)*
Verunreinigung *f* 1. soiling; pollution; contamination; 2. *s.* Verunreinigungsstoff
Verunreinigungsstoff *m* pollutant; contaminant; impurity
Verunstaltung *f* deformity
verwachsen 1. to coalesce, to grow together; 2. to heal [over, up]
~/zu Dickicht to coppice
verwachsen *(bot, zoo)* adnate, adherent; intergrown, blind *(knot)*
verwachsenkronblättrig *(bot)* sympetalous
Verwachsensein *n* adherence
Verwachsung *f* coalescence; adnation; symphysis *(of bones)*
Verwachsungslinie *f* suture *(esp. of bones)*
Verwachsungsnaht *f (zoo)* raphe
Verwahrbulle *m* in-waiting bull
verwandlungslos *(ent)* ametabolic
verwandt related, akin
~/nicht [miteinander] unrelated
Verwandtschaft *f* relationship *(breeding)*
~/direkte direct relationship
Verwandtschaftsgrad *m* degree of relationship

Verwandtschaftskoeffizient *m* percentage of relationship (blood)
Verwandtschaftskreuzung *f* consanguineous mating
Verwandtschaftszucht *f* close [in]breeding
verwässern to water
Verwechselte Trespe *f* meadow brome[-grass], hairy brome, Bromus commutatus
Verwehung *f* drift
verweigern to refuse *(equitation)*
Verweilkatheter *m (vet)* indwelling catheter
verwelken to wilt, to wither, to fade, to blast
~ lassen to wilt
verwerfen 1. to abort, to slink; 2. to reject; to condemn *(e.g. inedible meat)*
Verwerfen *n* 1. abortion; 2. condemnation; 3. winding, twisting *(e.g. of seasoned timber)*
~/ansteckendes (seuchenhaftes) contagious abortion
Verwertungskoeffizient *m* utilization coefficient
verwesen to putrefy, to decompose, to undergo decomposition, to decay, to rot
Verwesung *f* putrefaction, putrescence, decomposition, decay
verwildern 1. to become (run) wild *(plant, animal)*; 2. to overgrow, to go wild *(e.g. a garden)*
verwildert 1. [run] wild *(plant, animal)*; feral *(animal)*; 2. overgrown, [gone] wild *(garden)*; out of cultivation *(land)*
verwittern *(soil)* to weather, to decay, to disintegrate
Verwitterung *f (soil)* weathering, decay, disintegration
Verwitterungsboden *m* weathered (residual, primary) soil, regolith
Verwitterungskrume *f* mantle rock, rock mantle
Verwitterungsmaterial *n* weathered material
Verwitterungsprodukt *n* weathering product
Verwitterungsschutt *m* eluvium, residual detritus
verwunden to wound; to screef *(a forest soil)*
~/durch ein Geschoß *(hunt)* to wound by a shot
Verzascaziege *f* Verzasca goat *(breed)*
verzehrbar eatable, edible
Verzehrbarkeit *f* eatability, edibility
verzehren to eat
Verzehrgeschwindigkeit *f* eating rate
Verzehrgewohnheit *f* dietary custom
Verzehrgewohnheiten *fpl* eating habits
Verzehrqualität *f* eating (dessert) quality
Verzehrrate *f* feeding rate
Verzehrreife *f* eating maturity
verziehen to thin [out], to bed [out] *(plantlets)*
Verziehen *n* 1. bedding [out]; hand singling *(beet growing)*; 2. *s.* Verwerfen 3.
Verzögerungseffekt *m* retarding effect
verzuckern to saccharify
Verzuckerung *f* saccharification
verzweigen/sich *(bot, zoo)* to branch [out], to ramify

verzweigend/sich *(bot, zoo)* branching, deliquescent
verzweigt branchy, branched, branching, ramified, ramiform; dendritic
~/dreiteilig *(bot)* trichotomous
Verzweigung *f* branching, ramification
Verzweigungsdichte *f* branching (ramification) density, density of branches
verzwergen to dwarf
verzwergt dwarfed, dwarfish
Verzwergung *f* dwarfishness, dwarfing, nanization
~ **der Erdbeere** *(phyt)* strawberry dwarfishness *(virosis)*
~ **der Himbeere** *(phyt)* rubus stunt *(mycoplasmosis)*
~ **von Kükenembryonen** *(vet)* baby chick effect
Verzwergungseffekt *m* dwarfing effect
Verzwergungsgen *n* dwarfing gene
Vesika *f* vesica, bladder
vesikal vesical
Vesikel *f* vesicle
vesikulär vesicular
Vesikulardrüse *f* vesicular gland
Vestibularsyndrom *n* **der Katze/idiopathisches** idiopathic feline vestibular syndrome
Vestibulum *n* vestibule *(animal anatomy)*
veterinär *s.* veterinärmedizinisch
Veterinär *m s.* Veterinärmediziner
Veterinäranatom *m* veterinary anatomist
Veterinäranatomie *f* veterinary anatomy
Veterinärbakteriologe *m* veterinary bacteriologist
Veterinärbakteriologie *f* veterinary bacteriology
Veterinärchemiker *m* veterinary chemist
Veterinärchirurg *m* veterinary surgeon, VS
Veterinärchirurgie *f* veterinary (animal) surgery
Veterinärdietetik *f* veterinary dietetics
Veterinärepidemiologie *f* veterinary epidemiology
Veterinärforschung *f* veterinary research
Veterinärhelfer *m* animal nursing auxiliary, ANA, veterinary attendant
~/staatlich zugelassener registered animal nursing auxiliary, RANA
Veterinärhelminthologie *f* veterinary helminthology
Veterinärhygiene *f* veterinary hygiene (sanitation)
veterinärhygienisch veterinary-sanitary, zoo-sanitary
Veterinärimmunologie *f* veterinary immunology
Veterinäringenieur *m* veterinary attendant
Veterinärinspektor *m* veterinary inspector (officer)
Veterinärmedizin *f* veterinary (animal) medicine
~/gerichtliche forensic veterinary medicine
~/innere veterinary internal medicine
Veterinärmediziner *m* veterinarian, veterinary [surgeon], animal doctor, vet
veterinärmedizinisch veterinary
Veterinärmikrobiologie *f* veterinary microbiology
Veterinärparasitologie *f* veterinary parasitology
Veterinärpathologie *f* veterinary (animal) pathology

Veterinärtechniker *m* veterinary attendant
Veterinärtherapie *f* veterinary therapy
Veterinärtoxikologie *f* veterinary toxicology
Veterinärvirologie *f* veterinary virology
Veterinärwesen *n* veterinary (animal) medicine
Veterinärwissenschaft *f* veterinary science
Veterinärwissenschaftler *m* veterinary research worker
Vetivergras *n (bot)* vetiver, Vetiveria zizanioides, Andropogon muricatus
Vetivergraswurzel *f* vetiver
Vetiveröl *n* vetiver oil, cuscus, khus-khus *(from Vetivera zizanioides)*
Vexiernelke *f* mullein pink, rose campion, Lychnis coronaria
VHS *s.* Septikämie der Forelle/virale hämorrhagische
Vi-Antigen *n* virulence antigen *(bacteriology)*
Viatkapferd *n* Vyatka *(horse breed)*
Vibramycin *n* doxycyclin *(antibiotic)*
Vibration *f* vibration; *(vet)* fremitus
Vibrationsegge *f* vibrating cultivator
Vibrationsroder *m* vibratory digger
Vibrio *m (zoo)* vibrio[n] *(genus Vibrio)*
Vibrionenabort *m (vet)* vibriosis
Vibrionencholera (Vibrionenhepatitis) *f* **des Huhnes** avian vibrionic (infectious) hepatitis
Vibriose *f (vet)* 1. vibriosis; 2. vibriosis of fish *(caused by Vibrio anguillarum)*
Vibrissae *fpl (zoo)* vibrissae
Vicia-cryptic-Virus *n* vicia cryptic virus, VCV
Vicilin *n* vicilin *(storage protein of legumes)*
Victoria-Brandkrankheit *f* **des Hafers** Victoria blight of oat[s] *(caused by Helminthosporium victoriae)*
Victorin *n* victorin *(mycotoxin)*
Vieh *n* [live]stock, cattle, head • **mit ~ besetzen** to stock • **~ treiben** to wrangle • **~ über weite Strecken treiben** to overland *(Australia)* • **wieder mit ~ besetzen** to restock *(a pasture)*
~/aufgetriebenes drive
~/ausgemästetes fatstock
~/minderwertiges runt
~/schlachtreifes fatstock
~/zusammengetriebenes drive
Vieh... *s. a.* Tier...
Viehauktion *f* livestock (cattle) auction
Viehauktionator *m* livestock auctioneer
Viehausstellung *f* [live]stock (cattle) show
Viehbademittel *n* stock dip *(against parasites)*
Viehbehandlungsstand *m* cattle handler
Viehbesatz *m* livestock number, stock[ing] • **mit zu geringem ~** understocked • **mit zu hohem ~** overstocked
Viehbesitzer *m (Am)* stockman
Viehbesprühung *f* cattle spraying
Viehbestand *m* [live]stock • **einen ~ ergänzen** to restock
~/anerkannt krankheitsfreier attested cattle

Viehdiebstahl

Viehdiebstahl *m* cattle-lifting, abigeat
Viehdrift *f* [cattle] drive
Vieheigner *m (Am)* stockman
Vieheinheit *f* livestock (animal) unit
Viehfarm *f* [live]stock farm, *(Am)* [cattle] ranch
Viehfarmer *m s.* Viehzüchter
Viehfliege *f* horse-fly, breeze [fly], cleg, tabanid *(family Tabanidae)*
Viehfutter[mittel] *n* forage, fodder, [livestock, stock] feed, [animal] feed-stuff
Viehfütterung *f* [live]stock feeding
Viehgatter *n* cattle-pen
Viehhalter *m* stockman, herdsman, herder *(s. a.* Viehzüchter*)*
Viehhaltung *f* animal (livestock) husbandry, [live-]stock farming, livestock (cattle) raising, keeping of cattle
Viehhändler *m* cattle-dealer, drover, *(Am)* cattle broker
Viehhänger *m* livestock (cattle) trailer
Viehherde *f* herd, *(Am)* band
~/getriebene drove
~/zusammengetriebene roundup
Viehhirt *m* herder, herd[sman]
~/berittener cowboy, wrangler, cowpuncher *(North America)*, stockrider *(Australia)*
Viehhof *m* [stock]yard • **[Rinder] im ~ unterbringen** to yard
Viehhürde *f* cattle-pen, pinfold, pound
Viehladerampe *f* livestock loading ramp
Viehmangold *m* fodder (feeding) beet, Beta vulgaris var. alba (crassa)
Viehmarkierungszange *f* cattle ear marker, cattle punch plier
Viehmäster *m* [stock, cattle] feeder, fattener
Viehpeitsche *f* stock-whip
Viehpflege *f* animal care
Viehpfleger *m* animal caretaker, herdsman, herder, stockman, stableman
Viehputzer *m*, **Viehputzgerät** *n* cattle cleaner, grooming machine
Viehsalz *n* cattle salt, fodder salt
Viehschermaschine *f* cattle clipper
viehsicher stock-proof *(e. g. a fence)*
Viehsperre *f* cattle-stop, cattle guard (grid)
Viehstall *m* animal house (shelter), cattle shed (shelter, building), cattle (stock) barn *(s. a.* Stall*)*
Viehstall... *s.* Stall...
Viehstrick *m* stock rope
Viehtränke *f* stock waterer
Viehtransport *m* transport of animals
Viehtransportanhänger *m* livestock (cattle) trailer
Viehtransporter *m* livestock transporter, cattle-lorry
Viehtransport-Lkw *m* cattle-truck, livestock van
Viehtransportschiff *n* cattle ship
Viehtransportwagen *m* cattle-lorry
~ der Eisenbahn *s.* Viehwaggon

Viehtreiber *m* drover
Viehtreibstock *m* goad
Viehtrieb *m* [cattle] drive
Viehtrift *f* cattle track, driveway
Viehvergiftung *f* stock poisoning
Viehverladerampe *f* livestock loading ramp
Viehversicherung *f* cattle insurance
Viehversteigerung *f s.* Viehauktion
Viehwaage *f* cattle weigher (scale)
Viehwagen *m* cattle-lorry, cattle-box; cattle-truck
Viehwaggon *m* cattle wagon, *(Am)* stock-car
Viehwaschmittel *n s.* Viehbademittel
Viehweide *f* cattle-range, cattle-run, cattle-ranch, animal graze
Viehwirtschaft *f* livestock management (husbandry), animal agriculture, stock farming
Viehwirtschaftsbetrieb *m* livestock operation (enterprise)
Viehwirtschaftssystem *n* livestock management system
Viehzählung *f* livestock census, census of cattle
Viehzaun *m* cattle-grid, cattle-guard
Viehzucht *f* stock (cattle) breeding, animal breeding • **betreiben** *(Am)* to ranch
Viehzuchtbetrieb *m* [live]stock farm, *(Am)* [cattle] ranch
Viehzüchter *m* [live]stock breeder, animal (cattle) breeder, stock raiser, stock (cattle) farmer, grazier, *(Am)* rancher
Viehzuchtgebiet *n* stock-rearing area
vielährig *(bot)* multiple-eared, polystachyous
Vielartengemisch *n* multispecies mixture
vielblättrig *(bot)* polyphyllous, multifoliate, plurifoliate
Vielblättrige Lupine *f* large-leaved lupin[e], Lupinus polyphyllus
Vielblättrigkeit *f* polyphylly
vielblütig *(bot)* multiflowered, polyanthous, pluriflorous
Vielblütige Felsenbirne *f* Pacific service-berry, Amelanchier florida
~ Ölweide *f* cherry elaeagnus, Elaeagnus multiflora
~ Rose *f* bramble rose, Rosa multiflora
vielfach *(bot, zoo)* multifid
Vielfachgerät *n* multipurpose equipment (implement)
~/landwirtschaftliches multiple farming machine
vielfarbig many-coloured, polychromatic
vielfingerig polydactyl
Vielfraß *m (zoo)* glutton, Gulo gulo
vielfrüchtig *(bot)* polycarpic, polycarpous
Vielfüßer *m* myriapod, myriopod *(group Myriapoda)*
vielfüßig *(zoo)* polypod
vielgestaltig polymorphous, polymorphic, ple[i]omorphic
Vielgestaltigkeit *f* polymorphism, pleomorphism
vielkernig multinuclear, multinucleate, polynuclear

Vielkernigkeit f multinuclearity
vielköpfig (bot) polycephalous
Vielliniensorte f multiline cultivar (variety)
vielpaarig (bot) multijugate, multijugous
vielreihig (bot) multiseriate
vielrippig (bot, zoo) multicostate
vielsamig (bot) polyspermous, polyspermatous
Vielsamiger Gänsefuß m all-seed, Chenopodium polyspermum
Vielscheibenschälpflug m polydisk (harrow) plough
Vielseitigkeitspferd n military horse
Vielseitigkeitsprüfung f military, three-day events
Vielseitigkeitssattel m all-purpose saddle, general-purpose saddle
Vielstammentrinder m multiple-stem barker
vielstengelig (bot) multicaulin, multicaulis
vielstrahlig (bot) multiradiate
vielteilig (bot, zoo) polymerous, multifid
vielwurzelig (bot) polyrhizous
vielzellig multicellular
Vielzweckforstwirtschaft f multiple-use (multiple-purpose) forestry
Vielzweckreitpferd n hack[ney]
vierblättrig (bot) quadrifoliate, tetraphyllous
Vierblättrige Einbeere f herb Paris, one-berry, true-love, Paris quadrifolia
Vierblattstadium n four-[true-]leaf stage
vierblütig (bot) quadriflorous
viereckig tetragonal
Viereckregner m square-area sprinkler
Viererverbindung f s. Quadrivalent
Vierfachimpfstoff m (vet) tetravaccine
Vierfleckiger Bohnenkäfer m southern cowpea weevil, Callosobruchus maculatus
vierflügelig (bot) tetrapterous
Vierflügeliger Schneeglöckchenbaum m snowdrop tree, Halesia carolina (tetraptera)
Vierfüß[l]er m quadruped [animal], tetrapod
viergeteilt (bot) quadripartite
viergliedrig (bot) tetramerous
viergriffelig (bot) tetragynous
Vierhornkäfer m broad-horned flour beetle, Gnathocerus cornutus
vierkronblättrig (bot) quadripetalous
Vierlinge mpl quadruplets, quads
Vierling-Gabelwuchs m fourfold division of the bole
viermächtig (bot) tetradynamous
Vierradantrieb m four-wheel drive, f.w.d.
Vierradschlepper m, **Vierradtraktor** m four-wheel[ed] tractor
viersamig (bot) tetraspermous
Viersamige Wicke f four-seed vetch, smooth tare, Vicia tetrasperma
vierteilig (bot) tetramerous
Viertelfettkäse m quarter-fat cheese
Viertelgemelk n quarter milk
Viertelgemelkprobe f quarter milk sample

Viertelmorgen m rood
Viertelscheffel m peck, pk
Viertelstamm m quarter-standard tree (orcharding)
Viertelumfangsmessung f quarter-girth measuring (timber mensuration)
Vierwegkreuzung f four-way cross (breeding)
Vierzeilige Gerste f four-rowed barley, bear, bere, big[g], Hordeum vulgare convar. tetrastichon
Vigor m s. Vitalität
Vikariant m (ecol) vicarious species
vikariierend vicarious
Viktualien fpl victuals
villös (bot, zoo) villose, villous
Villus m s. Zotte
Vinclozolin n vinclozolin (fungicide)
Vinifizierung f s. Weinbereitung
Vinylcarbonsäure f acrylic acid
Vinyl[kunststoff]folienabdeckung f vinyl [plastic] covering
Viola-Wittrockiana-Hybride f s. Stiefmütterchen
Violaxanthin n violaxanthin (plant dye)
Violette Königskerze f (bot) purple mullein, Verbascum phoenicum
~ **Petunie** f violet-flowered petunia, Petunia violacea
~ **Strandnelke** f common lavender, Limonium vulgare
Violetter Porling m (bot) purple conk, Polyporus abietinus
~ **Ritterling (Rötelritterling)** m amethyst agaric, wood blewits, Lepista nuda
~ **Wurzeltöter** m violet root rot, copper web (of potato, caused by Helicobasidium purpureum)
VIP s. Intestinalpeptid/vasoaktives
Viper f viper, adder (family Viperidae)
viral viral
Virelur[e] n virelure (insect attractant)
viren[ab]tötend virucidal
Vireszenz f virescence, greening (of plant parts)
Virginia-Eiche f encina, Quercus virginiana
Virginia-Erdnuß f Virginia peanut, Arachis hypogaea ssp. hypogaea var. hypogaea
Virginiahirsch m white-tailed deer, Virginia (red) deer, Odocoileus virginianus
Virginiamycin n virginiamycin (antibiotic)
Virginiatabak m common (Virginian) tobacco, Nicotiana tabacum
Virginische Erdbeere f Virginian strawberry, Fragaria virginiana ssp. virginiana
~ **Gelenkblume** f false dragonhead, obedient plant, obedience, Physostegia virginiana
~ **Hopfenbuche** f [American] hop hornbeam, Ostrya virginiana
~ **Kresse** f poor-man's pepper, Lepidium virginicum
~ **Mertensie** f (bot) Virginia[n] cowslip (bluebells), Mertensia virginica
~ **Traubenkirsche** f [common] choke-cherry, Prunus (Padus) virginiana
~ **Zaubernuß** f wych-hazel, Hamamelis virginiana

Virginischer

Virginischer Tabak *m s.* Virginiatabak
~ Wacholder *m* red juniper, savin[e], Juniperus virginiana
Virgo *f (ent)* virgin
Virilisierung *f* masculinization
Virion *n* virion
virizid virucidal
Virizid *n* virucide, viricide, antiviral agent
virobakteriell virobacterial
Viroid *n* viroid, pathogenic (infectious) RNA
Viroidnachweis *m* viroid detection
Virologe *m* virologist
Virologie *f* virology
virologisch virological
virös virose
Virose *f* virosis, virus (viral) disease
Viröse Blattadernverdickung *f* **des Salats** *(phyt)* big vein disease
Virosom *n* virosome
virulent virulent, contagious, infectious
Virulenz *f* virulence
Virulenzabschwächung *f* attenuation
Virulenzantigen *n* virulence antigen *(bacteriology)*
Virulenzgen *n* virulence gene
virulenzlos avirulent
Virus *n(m)* virus
~/defektes defective virus
~ der Blauverzwergung des Hafers oat blue dwarf virus
~ der Fruchtringberostung des Apfels apple russet ring virus
~ der Frühen Verbräunung der Erbse pea early browning virus, PEBV
~ der Gelben Kräuselblättrigkeit der Tomate tomato yellow leaf curl virus, TYLCV
~ der Getreidebestockungskrankheit cereal tillering disease virus
~ der Grünen Ringscheckung der Kirsche cherry green ring mottle virus
~ der Infektiösen Bursitis des Huhnes infectious bursal disease virus, IBV, infectious bursal agent
~ der Infektiösen Pankreasnekrose der Salmoniden trout infectious pancreatitis virus
~ der Nekrotischen Rostfleckigkeit der Kirsche cherry necrotic rusty mottle virus
~ der Rauhverzwergung des Maises maize rough-dwarf virus
~ der Scheckigen Verzwergung der Eierfrucht egg-plant mottled dwarf virus, EMDV
~ der Scheckigen Verzwergung der Luzerne lucerne mottly dwarf virus
~ der Sterilen Verzwergung des Hafers oat sterile dwarf virus, OSDV
~ der Virösen Fleckigkeit der Rübe beet virus spot virus
~ des Gelben Streifenmosaiks der Gerste barley yellow striate mosaic virus
~/geschwulstauslösendes (geschwulsterzeugendes) oncogenic virus
~/inaktives defective virus
~/inkomplettes defective virus
~/nematodenübertragenes nematode-vectored virus
~/onkogenes oncogenic virus
~/persistentes persistent (circulative) virus
~/propagatives (sich im Vektor vermehrendes) propagative virus
~/vermehrungsunfähiges defective virus
~/zirkulierendes *s.* ~/persistentes
Virusabort *m (vet)* virus (viral) abortion
~ der Stuten equine virus abortion
Virusausbreitung *f* virus spread
Virusbiologie *f* virus biology
Virusdiagnose *f* virus diagnosis
Virusdiarrhöe/Mucosal-disease *f* **der Rinder** bovine mucosal disease
Virusdiarrhöe/Mucosal-disease-Virus *n* bovine diarrhoea virus
Virusenteritis *f* **der Enten** duck plague
~ der Nerze mink virus enteritis, Fort-Williams-disease
virusfrei virus-free *(e.g. seed)*
Virushemmstoff *m* virus inhibitor
Virushepatitis *f* **der Ente** duck virus (viral) hepatitis
Virusimpfstoff *m* viral vaccine
Virusinfektion *f* virus infection
Virusinhibitor *m* virus inhibitor
Virusinterferenz *f* viral interference
viruskrank virose
Virus-N-Krankheit *f* avian cell inclusion disease
Viruspartikel *n* virus particle
~/reifes virion
Viruspersistenz *f* virus persistency
Viruspneumonie *f (vet)* viral pneumonia
Virusprotein *n* virus protein
virusresistent virus-resistant
Virusresistenz *f* virus resistance
Virusschnupfen *m* **der Katze** feline viral rhinotracheitis, FVR, cat influenza
Virusträger *m* virus carrier
virusübertragend viruliferous
Virusübertragung *f* virus transmission
Virusvakzine *f* viral vaccine
Virusvektor *m* virus vector
Virusvergilbung *f (phyt)* virus yellows
visieren to sight [at]
Visiergerät *n* sighting device
Visierlinie *f* line of sight, sighting line
Viskoelastizität *f* viscoelasticity
viskos, viskös viscous, gummy
Viskose *f* viscose
Viskosimeter *n* visco[si]meter
Viskosimetrie *f* viscometry
Viskosität *f* viscosity
Viskositätsmessung *f* viscometry
Visna-Maedi-Erkrankung *f* maedivisna, Montana sheep disease, Marsh's pneumonia, laikipia lung disease, Graaf-Reinert-disease

Visna-[Maedi-]Virus *n* visna maedi virus
Viszera *pl s.* Eingeweide
viszeral visceral
Vitalfärbung *f* vital staining *(e.g. of cells)*
Vitalität *f* vitality, vigour
Vitalitätsrückgang *m* vigour decline *(heterosis breeding)*
Vitalkapazität *f* vital capacity *(of lungs)*
Vitalpen *n s.* Phenethicillin
Vitamin *n* vitamin • **mit Vitaminen anreichern** to vitaminize
~ **A** vitamin A, axerophthol
~ **A₁** retinol
~ **B₁** vitamin B₁, aneurin, thiamine
~ **B₂** vitamin B₂, riboflavin
~ **B₆** vitamin B₆, pyridoxine, adermin
~ **B₁₂** vitamin B₁₂, [cyano]cobalamin, animal protein factor, APF, extrinsic factor
~ **BT** carnitine
~ **C** vitamin C, ascorbic acid, antiscorbutic vitamin
~ **D** vitamin D, calciferol
~ **D₂** vitamin D₂, ergocalciferol
~ **D₃** vitamin D₃, cholecalciferol
~ **E** vitamin E, [α-]tocopherol
~ **H** vitamin H, biotin, coenzyme R
~ **K** vitamin K, antihaemorrhagic vitamin
~ **K₁** phylloquinone
~ **K₃** menadione, menaquinone
~ **P** vitamin P
Vitamin-A-Aldehyd *m* vitamin A aldehyde, retinaldehyde
Vitaminantagonist *m* vitamin antagonist, antivitamin
Vitamin-A-Säure *f* vitamin A acid, retinoic acid
Vitaminbedarf *m* vitamin requirement
Vitamin-B-Komplex *m* vitamin B-complex
Vitamin-B₂-Mangelkrankheit *f (vet)* ariboflavinosis
Vitamingehalt *m* vitamin content
Vitamin-H-Mangel *m (vet)* biotin deficiency, abiotinosis
vitaminisieren to vitaminize
Vitaminisierung *f* vitaminization
Vitaminmangel *m* vitamin deficiency, poverty in vitamins
Vitaminmangelkrankheit *f (vet)* hypovitaminosis, avitaminosis
Vitaminmehl *n* vitamin flour *(from conifer needles)*
Vitaminsynthese *f* vitamin synthesis
Vitaminüberschußkrankheit *f (vet)* hypervitaminosis
Vitaminvorstufe *f* provitamin
Vitellin *n* vitellin *(egg-yolk constituent)*
Vitellinmembran *f* vitellin membrane
Vitellus *m* vitellus, [egg-]yolk
Vitexin *n* vitexin *(glucoside)*
Vitrifizierung *f* vitrification
Vivianit *m* vivianite *(non-clay mineral)*
vivipar *(bot, zoo)* viviparous

Viviparie *f* viviparity, viviparousness
Vivisektion *f* vivisection
vivisezieren to vivisect
VK *s.* Verdauungskoeffizient
VL *s.* Deutsches Veredeltes Landschwein
Vlies *n* fleece, wool cover, fell
Vliesdichte *f* fleece density
Vliesfäule *f (vet)* fleece rot
Vliesmasse *f* fleece weight
Vliesqualität *f* fleece quality
Vlieswolle *f* wool in the grease
Vogel *m* bird *(class Aves)* • **vom ~ abstammend** avian
~/**jagdbarer** game-bird, wildfowl, feathered game
~/**sich mausernder** moulter
Vogelabschreckmittel *n* bird repellent
Vogelabtötungsmittel *n* avicide
Vogelabwehr *f* bird control
Vogelabwehrvorrichtung *f* anti-bird device
Vogelbeerbaum *m* rowan[-tree], [European] mountain-ash, Sorbus aucuparia
Vogelbeere *f* rowan-berry, service-berry
vogelblütig *(bot)* ornithophilous
Vogeldunst *m (hunt)* bird (small) shot
Vogelerythroblastose *f (vet)* avian erythroblastosis, erythroblastic form of transmissible fowl leucosis
Vogelfang *m* bird-catching, fowling
Vogelfänger *m* fowler
Vogelfauna *f* avifauna
Vogelfeder *f* [bird's] feather
Vogelflinte *f* fowling piece
Vogelfraß *m* bird feeding
vogelfraßresistent bird-resistant
Vogelfraßschäden *mpl* peck marks
Vogelgarn *n* net for bird-catching
Vogelgrippe *f (vet)* avian influenza, duck flu
Vogelhaus *n s.* Voliere
Vogelhirse *f* foxtail (Italian) millet, Setaria italica
Vogelkasten *m s.* Vogelnistkasten
Vogelkirsche *f* mazard [cherry], mazzard, sweet (wild) cherry, Prunus avium
Vogelknöterich *m* knot (goose) grass, knotweed, hogweed, bird weed, *(Am)* doorweed, prostrate, Polygonum aviculare
Vogelkunde *f* ornithology
Vogelkundler *m* ornithologist
vogelkundlich ornithological
Vogelleim *m* birdlime
Vogelleukämie *f (vet)* avian leucosis
vogelliebend *(bot)* ornithophilous
Vogelmiere *f* [common] chickweed, Stellaria media
Vogelnest *n* 1. bird's nest; 2. *s.* Nestwurz
~/**eßbares** edible bird's nest *(from Collocalia spp.)*
Vogelnestfarn *m* bird's nest fern, Asplenium nidus
Vogelnistkasten *m* bird box (house)
Vogelpest *f (vet)* fowl pest (plague)
Vogelpocken *pl (vet)* fowl (bird) pox, avian diphtheria, sorehead

Vogelrepellent

Vogelrepellent *n* bird repellent
Vogelruf *m* bird-call
Vogelsamen *m* birdseed
Vogelschädling *m* bird pest
Vogelscheuche *f* scarecrow, bogle
Vogelschreckapparat *m* bird scarer
Vogelschrot *m (hunt)* bird (small) shot
Vogelschutz *m* bird protection
Vogelschutzgebiet *n* bird sanctuary
Vogelschwarm *m* flock [of birds], flush
Vogelsitzstange *f* perch
Vogelsteller *m* fowler
Vogelsternmiere *f* [common] chickweed, Stellaria media
Vogeltoxizität *f* bird toxicity *(e.g. of pesticides)*
Vogeltuberkulose *f* avian tuberculosis
Vogelwelt *f* avifauna
Vogelwicke *f* bird (tufted, cow) vetch, bird's tare, Vicia cracca
Voges-Proskauer-Reaktion *f* Voges-Proskauer reaction (test) *(microbiology)*
volar volar
volatil volatile
Voliere *f* aviary, volery, volary
Volk *n* 1. *(api)* colony; 2. covey *(of partridges)*
Volksname *m* vernacular name
Volkspark *m* public park
voll [im Geschmack] *s.* vollmundig
Vollanalyse *f* complete analysis
Vollbestand *m* full stand; closed forest
Vollbestandesfaktor *m (forest)* stocking degree
vollbestockt fully-stocked
Vollbestockung *f (forest)* full (ideal, optimum) stocking; normal stocking
Vollbier *n* vollbier
Vollblut *n s.* Vollblüter
Vollblüte *f* full flower (bloom)
Vollblüter *m* blood horse, thoroughbred
vollblütig 1. *(zoo)* thoroughbred, full-blooded; 2. *(bot)* double
Vollblutpferde *npl* bloodstock
Vollblutpferdezucht *f* thoroughbred breeding
Volldränung *f* full (systematic) drainage, parallel system of drainage
Volldrehpflug *m* reversible Brabant plough
Volldünger *m* complete [mixed] fertilizer, all-nutrient fertilizer, NPK fertilizer
Volldüngung *f* complete fertilization, NPK fertilization
Vollei *n* whole egg
vollentrinden to clean-bark, to bark and bast
Vollentsalzung *f* complete demineralization *(sugar manufacture)*
vollentwickelt fully developed, mature
Vollerntemaschine *f* complete (combine) harvester; *(forest)* feller-processor
Vollertrag *m* full bearing *(orcharding)*
Vollertragsphase *f*, **Vollertragsstadium** *n* mature stage, main bearing period *(orcharding)*

Vollerwerbsgartenbau *m* commercial gardening (horticulture)
Vollerwerbslandwirt *m* full-time farmer
Vollerwerbslandwirtschaft *f* full-time farming
Vollfeldfräse *f* full-width rotary cultivator
vollfett full fat (cream)
Vollfettkäse *m* whole (full-fat, full-cream) cheese
Vollfinne *f* plerocercoid *(of tapeworms)*
Vollgeschwister *n* full-sib *(animal breeding)*
Vollgeschwisterselektion *f* full-sib selection
Vollhandmelken *n* whole-hand (dry fist) milking
vollholzig non-tapering, full-boled, full-bodied, cylindrical *(tree-trunk)*
Vollholzigkeit *f* fullness of bole
Vollhuf *m (vet)* dropped sole
Vollinsekt *n*, **Vollkerf** *m (ent)* imago, adult
vollkernig all-heart *(timber)*
Vollkernigkeit *f* **von Samen** fullness of seeds
Vollkluppung *f (forest)* complete (full) enumeration
~/streifenweise strip enumeration
Vollkorn *n* filled (whole) grain, plump kernel, full seed
Vollkörnigkeit *f* grain plumpness *(of cereals)*
Vollkornmehl *n* wholemeal, whole-meal (straight-run) flour
Vollkornschrot *m* coarse whole meal with germs
Vollmantelgeschoß *n (hunt)* hard-nose
Vollmechanisierung *f* full (total, complete) mechanization
Vollmilch *f* whole (rich) milk, full-cream milk
~/eingedickte condensed whole milk
Vollmilchpulver *n* whole-milk powder, dried whole milk
vollmundig full-bodied *(wine)*
vollreif full ripe *(fruit, cereal)*
Vollreife *f* full ripeness (maturity)
Vollschmarotzer *m* holoparasite, true parasite
Vollschurwolle *f* single-clip wool
Vollseillinie *f (forest)* cable profile when loaded
Vollsichtkabine *f* all-round visibility cab
Vollspaltenboden *m* [fully-]slatted floor
Vollspaltenbodenstall *m* slatted-floor shed
Volltier *n s.* Vollinsekt
Vollumbruch *m (forest)* full cultivation
Vollzählung *f s.* Vollkluppung
Volte *f* volt[e] *(equitation)*
volt[ig]ieren to volt
Voltigierleine *f* lunge, longe
Volumen *n* volume
Volumenbestimmung *f*, **Volumenermittlung** *f* volume determination, calculation of volume *(e.g. of timber)*
Volumenformel *f* volume formula
Volumenleistung *f (forest)* volume production
Volumenmaß *n* volume measure *(timber mensuration)*
~/tatsächliches true volume measure, round measure
Volumenprozente *npl* percentage by volume

Volumenregelung f (forest) volume regulation (control)
Volumenschwankungsaufzeichnung f s. Plethysmographie
Volumenschwindmaß n volume (volumetric) shrinkage (of wood)
Volumentafel f (forest) [log] volume table, log rule, outturn table
~ **für eine Eingangsgröße** single-entry volume table
~ **für Einzelstämme** tree volume table
~ **für mehrere Eingangsgrößen** multiple-entry volume table
~/**lokale** local (regional) volume table, local yield table
Volumentarif m (forest) volume tariff
Volumenzuwachs m (forest) volume increment (growth)
Volumenzuwachsprozent n volume increment percent
Volva f volva (membranous covering about the base of numerous gill fungi)
Volvulus m (vet) volvulus
Vomer m vomer (animal anatomy)
Vomitoxin n vomitoxin (mycotoxin)
Vondozeb n vondozeb (fungicide)
Voranbau m (forest) advance planting, planting in advance, underplanting
Voranpassung f (gen) preadaptation
Vorarbeiten fpl [**der Harzgewinnung**] setting-up, cupping (resin-tapping)
Vorarm m forearm
Vorauflaufbehandlung f pre-emergence treatment
Vorauflaufherbizid n pre-emergence herbicide
Vorauflaufspritzung f pre-emergence spraying
Vorausdüngung f advance fertilization
Voraussaatbehandlung f presowing (preplant) treatment
Voraussage f/**beste lineare unverzerrte** best linear unbiased prediction, BLUP (animal breeding)
Vorazität f voracity
Vorbau m s. Voranbau
vorbehandeln to pretreat (e.g. seed); to condition
Vorbehandlung f pretreatment
Vorbereitungsfütterung f steaming up (of dry cows)
Vorbereitungshieb m, **Vorbereitungsschlag** m (forest) preparatory (advance) felling
Vorbereitungsstadium n (phyt, vet) prodromal period (stage)
Vorbestand m (forest) advance (pioneer, nurse) crop
vorbeugend preventive; prophylactic
Vorbeugung f prevention; prophylaxis
vorbiegig over in the knees (forelimb conformation)
Vorbiegigkeit f bucked-knee conformation, bucked knees

Vorbiß m (vet) parrot mouth
Vorblatt n (bot) bracteole
Vorblütespritzung f prebloom spray
Vorblütestadium n preflowering stage
Vorbrecher m crusher (sugar-cane processing)
Vorbrunst f prooestrus
Vorbrüter m setter
Vorderbein n 1. s. Vordergliedmaße; 2. hand (of pig carcass)
Vorderbrust f brisket; (ent) prothorax
Vorderdarm m fore-gut
Vorderendlage f cephalic (normal) presentation (veterinary obstetrics)
Vorderextremität f s. Vordergliedmaße
Vorderflanke f fore-flank (of animal body)
Vorderflügel m (ent) fore-wing
Vorderfuß m forefoot, hand
Vorderfußwurzel f carpus, knee
Vorderfußwurzelknochen m carpal bone
Vordergliedmaße f foreleg, forelimb, front leg, thoracic limb, arm
Vorderhaxe f (slaught) foreshin (of pig)
Vorderhesse f (slaught) fore-shank, foreshin, shin of beef
Vorderhirn n forebrain, prosencephalon
Vorderkopf m sinciput
Vordermast m (forest) head spar, home (main) spar (cable logging)
Vorderpfote f fore-paw
Vorderradantrieb m front-wheel drive, f.w.d.
Vorderradlenkung f front-wheel steering
Vorderröhre f shin (animal body)
Vorderschinken m ham (of pig)
Vorderstück n (slaught) rack
Vorderviertel n (slaught) forequarter
Vorderwälder Rind n Vorderwald (cattle breed)
Vorderwandhornspalte f (vet) toe crack
Vorderwürze f first wort (brewing)
Voreignung f (gen) preadaptation
Voreilung f cutter bar lead (of mounted mower)
Vorende n s. Vorgewende
Vorerkundung f (forest) preliminary reconnaissance
Vorerntefruchtfall m preharvest fruit drop (orcharding)
Vorernteschätzung f preharvest estimation
Vorerntespritzung f preharvest spray[ing]
Vorerntetrocknung f preharvest desiccation
Vorernteverlust m preharvest (precut) loss
Vorertrag m s. Vornutzungsertrag
Vorfahr m ancestor, progenitor
Vorfahren mpl ancestry
Vorfall m (vet) prolapse
Vorfallbandage f, **Vorfallgeschirr** n prolapse harness
Vorfeuer n backfire, backburn (forest fire control)
• **ein ~ anlegen** to backfire
Vorfiltration f coarse filtration

Vorfinne 678

Vorfinne f procercoid *(of tapeworms)*
Vorflut f confluence
Vorfluter m receiving body, discharge, outlet *(s. a.* Vorflutgraben*)*
~/künstlicher drainage outlet
Vorflutgraben m outlet channel (ditch), outfall channel
Vorfrucht f previous (preliminary, preceding) crop, forecrop
Vorfruchtrückstände mpl previous-crop residues
vorführen *(forest)* to skid, to haul, *(Am)* to log
Vorführen n skidding, hauling, *(Am)* logging
Vorführring m show ring
Vorgarten m front garden, *(Am)* front yard
Vorgebirgslage f foothill area
vorgeburtlich prenatal
vorgehauen undercut *(tree-trunk)*
Vorgelegewelle f layshaft
Vorgeschichte f eines Krankheitsfalles anamnesis
vorgestreckt camped in front *(forelimb conformation)*
Vorgewende n headland, turn land
Vorgewendemarkierung f headland mark
Vorgriffshauung f, **Vorgriffshieb** m *(forest)* advance (preparatory) felling
Vorhand f forehand, forebody *(s. a.* Vordergliedmaße*)*
Vorhaut f foreskin, prepuce *(animal anatomy)*
Vorhautbutter f smegma
Vorhautdrüse f preputial gland
Vorhautentzündung f *(vet)* posthitis
Vorhautsack m preputial sac
Vorhauttalg m smegma
Vorhautverengung f *(vet)* phimosis
vorherrschen to [pre]dominate
vorherrschend predominant, prevalent
Vorhieb m s. Vorgriffshauung
Vorhof m vestibule; atrium *(animal anatomy)*
Vorhoffenster n vestibular window *(of the ear)*
Vorholz n *(forest)* nurse crop
Vorinkubationskeimzahl f *(dairy)* preliminary incubation count
Vorkalkungstrübe f predefecation juice *(sugar manufacture)*
Vorkeim m *(bot)* prothallium, prothallus
Vorkeimbehälter m chitting container
vorkeimen to pregerminate; to chit *(potatoes)*
Vorkeimhaus n chitting house
Vorkeimkiste f, **Vorkeimsteige** f [potato] chitting tray
Vorkeimung f pregermination, advance germination
Vorkern m pronucleus
vorkochen to parboil
vorkommend/lokal (regional) begrenzt *(ecol)* endemic
Vorkühlapparat m precooling equipment

Vorkühler m precooler
Vorkühlung f precooling, prechilling
Vorkühlvorrichtung f precooling equipment
Vorkultur f s. Voranbau
Vorlagerungsbehandlung f prestorage treatment
Vorland n foreland; piedmont
Vorläufer m precursor
Vorleittrommel f feeder beater *(of thresher)*
Vorliefern n *(forest)* preskidding
Vormagen m fore-stomach, proventriculus *(of birds)*; proventriculus, gizzard *(of chewing insects)*
Vormagenbeweglichkeit f, **Vormagenmotilität** f fore-stomach motility
Vormagenverdauung f fore-stomach digestion
Vormaischapparat m masher
vormaischen to cook, to digest *(brewing)*
vormännlich f *(bot, zoo)* prot[er]androus
Vormännlichkeit f *(bot, zoo)* proterandry
Vormelkbecher m, **Vormelkschale** f foremilk (strip) cup
Vormilch f first (early, colostral) milk, colostrum, beastings
Vormischfutter n premix
Vormischung f premix, preblend
vornehmen/den ersten Hiebseingriff to make a first felling
~/eine Reisveredelung to [en]graft, to ingraft
~/eine Selbstung to self
~/eine Verdrängungskreuzung to grade
Vornutzung f s. Vornutzungsertrag
Vornutzungsertrag m *(forest)* produce from thinnings, intermediate [harvest] yield
~/mittlerer [jährlicher] periodic mean annual intermediate yield, periodic stand depletion
Vornutzungsetat m s. Vornutzungshiebssatz
Vornutzungsfärse f once-bred heifer
Vornutzungshieb m *(forest)* intermediate felling
Vornutzungshiebssatz m allowable intermediate cut, allowable cut of improvement cuttings, intermittent yield
Vornutzungsholz n timber from intermediate fellings
Vornutzungsplanung f *(forest)* planning of intermediate fellings
Vornutzungsprozent n *(forest)* thinning percent, relative thinning intensity
Vorpflanzbehandlung f preplant treatment
Vorpreßwalze f precompacting roller
Vorpuppe f *(ent)* prepupa, pronymph
Vorrahmen m fore-frame
Vorrat m store, stock, supply • **auf ~** in stock
~ an stehendem Holz forest crop, [total] standing volume, stumpage
~/stehender s. ~ an stehendem Holz
vorrätig in stock
Vorratsaufnahme f *(forest)* growing-stock inventory, survey of standing crop

Vorratsbehälter m reservoir, storage container (tank), [storage] bin
Vorratsbewässerung f preirrigation, preliminary (charge) watering, advance (replenishment) irrigation
Vorratsbunker m hopper *(of a seed drill)*
Vorratsdünger m slow-release fertilizer, slow-acting fertilizer
Vorratsdüngung f advance (stock, reserve) fertilization
Vorratsforschung f stored products research
Vorratshaltung f stockpiling • ~ **treiben** to stock
Vorratsinventur f s. **Vorratsaufnahme**
Vorratskalkung f heavy liming
Vorratsmethode f *(forest)* method of regulating yield by comparing actual with normal crop
Vorratsmilbe f acarid *(family Acaridae)*
Vorratsplanung f *(forest)* planning of growing stock
Vorratsraum m store-room
Vorratsroder m grubbing (digging and riddling) machine, potato grubber
Vorratsschädling m storage (stored-products) pest
Vorratsschädlingsbekämpfung f stored-products pest control
Vorratsschadmilbe f storage mite
Vorratsschutz m protection of stored products, stock protection
Vorratstrichter m storage hopper
Vorräumung f *(forest)* prelogging
vorreinigen to preclean
Vorreiniger m, **Vorreinigungsmaschine** f precleaner, aspirator
Vorreinigungssieb n precleaning sieve
Vorsaatanwendung f presowing application *(of herbicides)*
Vorsaatausbringung f preplant application *(e.g. of pesticides)*
Vorsaatbehandlung f presowing treatment
Vorsaatdünger m preplant fertilizer
Vorsaatherbizid n presowing (preplant) herbicide
Vorsaatkältebehandlung f presowing chill treatment *(of seed)*
Vorschäler m skim [coulter], skimmer, coulter, jointer *(of a share plough)*
Vorschmelzware f cheese melt, precooked cheese
Vorschneider m s. **Vorschäler**
Vorschnittsägemaschine f timber mill
Vorschwarm m *(api)* first (prime) swarm
Vorsekret n **[des Ejakulates]** presperm fraction
vorsortieren to presort, to presize, to screen
Vorspann geben to inarch *(orcharding)*
Vorspelze f *(bot)* outer pale, palea
Vorspiel n **[/sexuelles]** foreplay, premating (courtship) behaviour
vorständig camped in front *(forelimb conformation)*

vorstehen 1. to protrude; 2. to point [at], to stand, to set *(hunting dog)*
Vorsteherdrüse f prostata [gland]
Vorsteherdrüsenentzündung f *(vet)* prostatitis
Vorstehhund m pointer, *(Am)* bird dog
Vorstreckteich m *(pisc)* brood pond
Vortier n leader
Vortransport m *(Am, forest)* logging
Vortreibung f protrusion
vortrocknen to predry
Vortrockner m predryer
Vortrocknung f predrying
Vortrocknungskammer f predryer
vorübergehend ephemeral
vorverdauen to predigest
Vorverdauung f predigestion, preliminary digestion
Vorverjüngung f *(forest)* advance reproduction, natural regeneration obtained from advance growth
vorverpacken to prepack
Vorverpackung f prepackage
Vorwald m *(forest)* pioneer (nurse) crop
Vorwartehof m assembly (collecting) yard *(of a milking parlour)*
vorwärts gekehrt *(bot)* antrorse
Vorwärtseinschneideverfahren n cross bearing *(forest fire control)*
Vorwärtsmutation f forward (direct) mutation
Vorwegberegnung f advance irrigation
Vorwegbewässerung f advance irrigation
vorweiblich *(bot, zoo)* prot[er]ogynous
Vorweiblichkeit f *(bot, zoo)* proterogyny
vorweichen to presoak; to steep *(wood chippings)*
vorwelken to [pre]wilt
~ lassen to [pre]wilt
Vorwelksilage f [pre]wilted silage, low-moisture silage
Vorwerk n hamlet
Vorwuchs m *(forest)* advance (volunteer) growth
vorwüchsig leading in growth
Vorzeichenrangtest m *(biom)* Wilcoxon's matched pair rank test, signed rank test
Vorzeichentest m *(biom)* sign test
vorzeitig precocious *(e.g. blooming, fruiting)*
Vorzeitigkeit f precociousness, precocity
Vorzug m *(ecol, phyt)* preference
Vorzugsmilch f certified (attested) milk
VPR s. Voges-Proskauer-Reaktion
Vriesee f *(bot)* flaming sword, Vriesea splendens
vRP s. Rohprotein/verdauliches
VSK s. Schweinekrankheit/vesikuläre
Vulkanascheboden m volcanic ash soil
vulkanisch volcanic
Vulva f vulva *(animal anatomy)*
vulvar vulval, vulvar
Vulvitis f *(vet)* vulvitis
Vulvovaginitis f *(vet)* vulvovaginitis
~ /infektiöse pustulöse infectious pustular vulvovaginitis, coital exanthema *(in cattle)*

V-Wert

V-Wert *m (soil)* base saturation percentage, degree of base saturation
VZ *s.* Verseifungszahl

W

W *s.* Watt
Waage *f* balance, [pair of] scales; steelyard
Waagschale *f* scale [pan]
Waagstock *m (api)* scale hive
Wabe *f* [honey]comb
~/ausgebaute drawn comb
~/honigfeuchte wet comb
Wabenbau *m* comb building
Wabenfäule *f* pocket rot, peckiness *(of wood)*; honeycomb rot *(of oak heartwood)*
Wabengrind *m (vet)* favus
Wabenhonig *m* comb honey, chunk [comb] honey
Wabenrähmchen *n* frame
Wabentrester *pl (api)* slumgum, wax residue
Wabenzange *f* frame tongs
Wabenzelle *f* alveolus, cell
Wabigwerden *n* honeycombing, hollow-horning, internal check[ing], collapse check *(timber defect)*
Wachhund *m* guard (watch) dog, house-dog
Wacholder *m* 1. juniper *(genus Juniperus)*; 2. common juniper, Juniperus communis
Wacholderbeere *f* juniper berry
Wacholderbranntwein *m* gin
Wacholderdrossel *f* fieldfare, fieldpore, Turdus pilaris
Wacholdermistel *f* 1. dwarf mistletoe *(genus Arceuthobium)*; 2. juniper-mistletoe, Arceuthobium oxycedri
Wacholderöl *n* oil of juniper
Wachs *n* wax • **mit ~ überziehen** to wax
~/pflanzliches plant wax
~/tierisches animal wax
wachsartig waxy
Wachsblume *f* 1. wax plant, hoya *(genus Hoya)*; 2. wax flower, Hoya carnosa
Wachsbohne *f* wax (butter) bean *(cultivar of Phaseolus vulgaris)*
Wachsdrüse *f* wax gland *(of honey-bee)*
wachsen 1. to grow; 2. to wax *(e.g. fruits)*
~/buschartig to bush
~/in die Breite und Höhe to accrue
~/kohlkopfartig to cabbage
~/kräftig to flourish
~/strauchartig to bush
~/vegetativ to vegetate
~/wild *(bot)* to volunteer
Wachsen *n s.* Wachstum
wachsend growing
~/am oberen Stengelteil *(bot)* cauline
~/an Wegrändern ruderal
~/auf feuchten Standorten hygrophilous
~/auf Rinde corticole
~/auf Sandboden arenaceous
~/auf Schutt ruderal
~/auf sumpfigen Standorten *(bot)* uliginose, uliginous
~/außerhalb der Zellen ectotrophic
~/bei durchschnittlichen Feuchtigkeitsbedingungen mesophytic, mesic
~/büschelartig clustery
~/dicht über der Erde epigeal, epigeous
~/horstartig c[a]espitose, caespitous
~/im Freiland open-growing, free-growing
~/in Büscheln *s.* ~/horstartig
~/in den Alpen Alpine
~/in dichten Büscheln iteroparous
~/in Haufen acervate
~/mit freier Krone free-growing, open-growing *(tree)*
~/unterirdisch *(bot)* hypogeal, hypogean
~/üppig rank, rampant
wächsern waxy
Wachskürbis *m* wax (white, ash) gourd, ash pumpkin, Chinese preserving (water) melon, Benincasa hispida (cerifera)
Wachsmais *m* waxy maize, *(Am)* wax corn, Zea may convar. ceratina
Wachsmotte *f* wax moth *(genus Galleria)*
Wachspalme *f* carnauba [palm], Copernicia prunifera (cerifera)
Wachsreife *f* wax ripeness
Wachsreifestadium *n* waxy stage, hard (stiff) dough stage *(of cereals)*
Wachsschmelzer *m (api)* wax melter
Wachsschuppe *f* wax scale (flake)
wachstragend ceriferous
Wachstum *n* growth, growing • **im ~ hemmen** to stunt • **im ~ stocken** to arrest in growth, to check
~ der Seitenäste lateral growth
~/embryonales embryonic growth
~/exponentielles exponential growth
~/exzentrisches eccentric growth *(of timber)*
~/fetales foetal growth
~/interkalares *(bot)* intercalary growth
~/kompensatorisches compensatory growth
~/kräftiges thrift
~/logarithmisches exponential growth
~/luxurierendes luxuriance
~/meristematisches *(bot)* embryonic growth
~/oberirdisches top growth
~/übermäßiges overgrowth
~/ungehindertes (unkontrolliertes) unchecked growth
~/üppiges flush
Wachstums... *s. a.* Wuchs...
Wachstumsanalyse *f* growth analysis
Wachstumsbedingung *f* growing condition
Wachstumsbeeinträchtigung *f* check
wachstumsbeschleunigend growth-accelerating

Wachstumsbeschleunigung f growth acceleration
Wachstumsbewegung f (bot) nutation
~/kreisende circumnutation
Wachstumsfaktor m growth factor
wachstumsfördernd growth-promoting, growth-stimulating
Wachstumsförderung f growth promotion
Wachstumsfunktion f growth function
Wachstumsgeschwindigkeit f growth rate, rate of growth
~/relative relative growth rate, RGR (of plants)
Wachstumsgrößen fpl (forest) mean stand details
wachstumshemmend growth-inhibiting, growth-restricting
Wachstumshemmstoff m growth inhibitor
Wachstumshemmung f growth inhibition, stunting
Wachstumshormon n growth hormone, GH, metabolic hormone, somatotropin
Wachstumshormon-Releaser-Hemmfaktor m growth-hormone release inhibiting factor
Wachstumsindex m s. Proteinwirkungsverhältnis
Wachstumsinhibition f s. Wachstumshemmung
Wachstumsintensität f growth intensity
Wachstumskapazität f growth capacity
Wachstumskegel m/apikaler (bot) apical (vegetation) cone
Wachstumskoeffizient m growth coefficient
Wachstumskonstante f growth constant; relative growth rate, RGR (of plants)
Wachstumskurve f growth curve
Wachstumsmedium n growth (growing) medium
Wachstumsperiode f growth period
Wachstumsphase f growth phase
~/logarithmische log[arithmic] phase
Wachstumsphysiologie f growth physiology
Wachstumspotential n growth potential
Wachstumsprozeß m process of growth
Wachstumspunkt m (bot) growing (apical) point
Wachstumsrate f growth rate
~/relative relative growth rate, RGR (of plants)
Wachstumsregulation f growth regulation
Wachstumsregulator m [plant] growth regulator, [plant] growth substance
Wachstumsretardans n s. Wachstumsverzögerer
Wachstumsrhythmus m growth rhythm
Wachstumsrückstand m retard in growth
Wachstumsskala f growth [stage] scale
Wachstumsstadium n growth stage, GS, stage of growth
Wachstumsstimulans n growth promoter (stimulant), growth-promoting agent
Wachstumsstimulation f growth promotion (stimulation)
Wachstumsstörung f growth disorder (disturbance), dyschondroplasia
Wachstumsverhalten n growth behaviour
Wachstumsverlauf m course of growth
Wachstumsverzögerer m growth retardant

Wachstumsverzögerung f growth retardation, retard in growth, stunt[ing]
Wachstumszone f growth zone
Wachtel f 1. quail (genus Coturnix); 2. quail, Coturnix coturnix
Wachtelbroiler m quail broiler
Wachtelbronchitis f (vet) quail bronchitis
Wachtelbronchitisvirus n quail bronchitis virus
Wachtelei n quail egg
Wachtelente f common teal, Anas crecca
Wachtelkönig m s. Wiesenralle
Wachtelkrankheit f quail disease, avian ulcerated enteritis, ulcerative enteritis of birds
Wachtelleukose f (vet) quail leucosis, T virus infection
Wachtelweizen m cow-wheat, Melampyrum arvense
Wächterin f guard honey-bee
Wackelgelenk n amphiarthrosis
Wackelsitzhypothese f (gen) wobble hypothesis
Wade f (pisc) seine[-net], drag net, trawl[-net]
Wadenbein n fibula
Wadenfischerei f seining, trawling • ~ betreiben to seine, to trawl
Wadenstecher m biting house-fly, stable (dog) fly, Stomoxys calcitrans
waf s. wasser- und aschefrei
Wägekäfig m weigh-crate
Wägelysimeter n weighing lysimeter
wägen to weigh
Wagen m cart, truck; wagon, waggon
Wagenladung f cart-load; wagonload
Wagenpferd n cart (harness) horse, carriage (cab) horse
Wagenrad n cart-wheel
Wagenrunge f pin bar
Waggon m wagon, waggon
Wagner m cart-wright
Wägungsfaktor m (biom) weighting coefficient
Wahlstamm m (forest) choice log (stem, tree)
Wahnkante f wane [edge] (of timber)
wahnkantig waney, unedged
Wahrscheinlichkeit f (biom) probability, P
Wahrscheinlichkeitsdichte f probability density
Wahrscheinlichkeitsverteilung f probability distribution, random distribution
Waid m woad, dyer's weed, Isatis tinctoria
Waidmann m s. Weidmann
WaKV s. Wasserrübenkräuselvirus
Wald m forest, wood, silva
~/angepflanzter cultivated forest
~ aus Kernwüchsen seedling forest, forest of seedling origin
~/beweideter grazed (pastured) forest
~/bewirtschafteter forest in use
~/brandgeschädigter fire-damaged forest
~ der zweiten Generation secondary forest, second growth [forest]
~/geplenterter culled forest

Wald

~/geschützter protected forest
~/halbimmergrüner semievergreen forest
~/hydroperiodischer seasonal forest
~ im mittleren Baumholzalter forest approaching maturity
~/immergrüner evergreen forest
~/laubabwerfender deciduous forest
~/lichter open woodland
~ mit geschlossenem Kronendach closed forest
~/montaner montane forest
~/nach dem Nachhaltigkeitsprinzip bewirtschafteter sustained-yield forest
~/nicht eingerichteter bush
~/regengrüner seasonal forest
~/sich selbst erneuernder (verjüngender) self-renewing forest
~/stadtnaher suburban forest
~/unbehandelter (ursprünglicher) primeval (primary, original) forest
~/vom Menschen begründeter man-made forest
~ zur Brennholzgewinnung fuel wood forest
Wald... s. a. Forst...
Waldabfälle mpl forest refuse
Waldabschätzung f forest estimation (assessment)
waldähnlich silvan
Waldameisenhege f forest ant-keeping
Waldanbau m forestry planting
Waldanemone f wood anemone, snowdrop [anemone], Anemone sylvestris
Waldanflug m self-sown crop
Waldangelika f s. Waldbrustwurz
Waldanpflanzung f forestry planting
Waldarbeiter m forest[ry] worker, forester, lumberman, lumberjack
Waldarbeiterlager n logging camp
Waldarbeiterschule f forest worker school
waldarm thinly (poorly) forested, sparsely wooded
Waldarrondierung f consolidation of forest areas (holdings)
Waldassoziation f forest association (community)
Waldaufschluß m opening-up
Waldausformungsplatz m forest [log] depot, upper landing (depot), (Am) bank
Waldbach m woodland stream
Waldbär m, Waldbart m sloven, beard, tombstone, barber's chair (tree-felling)
Waldbau m silviculture, forestry
Waldbauer m, Waldbaufachmann m silviculturist
waldbaulich silvicultural
Waldbaum m forest-tree
Waldbaumbewässerungsprogramm n forest-tree irrigation programme
Waldbaumläufer m (zoo) tree creeper, Certhia familiaris
Waldbaumzüchter m tree breeder
Waldbaumzüchtung f forest-tree breeding
Waldbauplanung f silvicultural planning
Waldbausystem n silvicultural system

waldbedeckt s. waldbestanden
Waldbegang m forest inspection
Waldbergminze f (bot) wood calamint, Calamintha sylvatica
Waldbeschädigung f forest damage
Waldbesitz m 1. forest ownership; 2. forest property (estate)
Waldbesitzer m forest owner (proprietor)
Waldbestand m forest stand (land), [forest] crop, silva
~/durch Pflanzung begründeter forest plantation, forestry planting
waldbestanden wooded, woody, forested, treed, silvan
Wald[bestands]bewertung f forest stand [e]valuation, forest valuation
Waldbewirtschaftung f forest management
waldbewohnend silvicolous
Waldbewohner m inhabitant of a forest, forester, sylvan
Waldbienenweide f forest bee pasture
Waldbienenwirtschaft f s. Zeidelwirtschaft
Waldbild n forest picture
Waldbildung f silvigenesis
Waldbingelkraut n (bot) dog's mercury (cole), ground elder, Mercurialis perennis
Waldbinse f wood club-rush, Scirpus sylvaticus
Waldbläue f log blue [stain]
Waldblöße f s. Waldlichtung
Waldboden m forest[ed] soil
~/absoluter absolute forest soil
~/Brauner brown forest soil, brown earth
~/unbedingter s. ~/absoluter
Waldbodenbonitierung f s. Waldbodenschätzung
Waldbodenkartierung f forest soil mapping
Waldbodenschätzung f assessment (evaluation) of forest soils
Waldbrand m forest fire; bush fire
~/durch Brandstiftung entstandener actionable [forest] fire
~/unbekämpfter uncontrolled fire, wildfire
~/zu bekämpfender wildfire
Waldbrand... s. a. Brand...
Waldbrandabwehr f s. Waldbrandbekämpfung
Waldbrandbekämpfung f forest fire control, wildfire suppression
~ an den Flanken flanking fire suppression
~ aus der Luft aerial forest fire control
Waldbrandbekämpfungsbezirk m division
Waldbrandbekämpfungsplan m forest fire control plan
Waldbrandbeobachter m fire watcher (spotter), look-out [man], towerman; fire guard (patrol), prevention patrolman
Waldbrandbeobachtungspunkt m look-out point
Waldbrandeinsatzkarte f forest fire operations map
Waldbrandfallschirmspringer m smoke jumper

Waldbrandfläche f forest fire area, burned area, burn
~ **nach nochmaligem Überbrennen** reburn
~/**zulässige** allowable burned area, acceptable burn
Waldbrandgefahr f forest fire danger (hazard)
Waldbrandgefahrmesser m fire-danger meter
Waldbrandhäufigkeit f [forest] fire occurrence
Waldbrandhäufigkeitskarte f fire occurrence map
Waldbrandkarte f fire plotting map
Waldbrandkennziffer f fire-danger index
Waldbrandkunde f forest pyrology
Waldbrandorientierungskarte f fire-finder map
Waldbrandperiode f fire season
Waldbrandposten m s. Waldbrandbeobachter
Waldbrandriegel m firè break (trace)
~/**aufgeforsteter** evergreen fire break, greenbreak
Waldbrandsaison f fire season
Waldbrandschaden m [forest] fire damage
Waldbrandüberwachung f forest fire surveillance
Waldbrandverhütung f forest fire prevention
Waldbrandversicherung f forest fire insurance
Waldbrandwächter m s. Waldbrandbeobachter
Waldbrandwarnstation f fire-danger station
Waldbrandwehr f forest fire brigade
Waldbrandwetterstation f fire-weather station
Waldbrandwettervoraussage f fire-weather forecast
Waldbrustwurz f (bot) wild angelica, ground elder, Angelica sylvestris
Wäldchen n small wood, grove, shaw
Walddattel f wild date palm, Phoenix sylvestris
Walddevastation f forest destruction (devastation)
Walddüngung f forest fertilization
Waldeigentum n forest ownership
Waldeigentümer m forest owner (proprietor)
Waldeinteilung f division of a forest
Waldeisenbahn f forest (logging) railway
Waldentstehung f silvigenesis
Waldentwässerung f forest draining
Walderdbeere f wood (wild) strawberry, Fragaria vesca
Walderhaltung f forest conservation
Walderkrankung f forest disease (disorder)
Walderkundung f forest reconnaissance
Walderneuerung f forest renewal, reforestation, restocking, woodland regeneration
Walderneuerungsbrigade f planting crew
Walderschließung f opening-up
Waldertrag m forest yield
Waldertragskunde f, **Waldertragslehre** f forest yield science
Walderwartungswert m forest (land) expectation value, capital value
Waldexploitation f forest exploitation
Waldfarm f tree farm
Waldfauna f forest fauna
Waldfeldbau m im **Hochwald** high forest with field crops

~ im **Niederwald** [system of] coppice with field crops
Waldfeuerwehr f forest fire brigade
Waldfläche f forest area (land), [area of] woodland
~ je **Kopf der Bevölkerung** per capita forest area
~/**sich wieder verjüngende** regenerating (restocking) forest land
~/**unbestockte** non-stocked forest land, fail-place, blank
Waldflattergras n wood millet[-grass], Milium effusum
Waldflora f forest flora
Waldflurbereinigung f consolidation of forest areas (holdings), forest holding consolidation
Waldfonds m forest fund
Waldformation f forest formation
waldfrisch fresh, green, verdant (timber)
Waldfrosch m wood frog, Rana sylvatica
Waldfrostspanner m northern winter moth, Operophthera (Cheimatobia) fagata
Waldfunktion f forest function
Waldfunktionskartierung f forest function mapping
Waldgamander m (bot) wood germander, Teucrium scorodonia
Waldgärtner m pine beetle, Tomicus (Blastophagus, Myelophilus) piniperda
Waldgebiet n forest region, tract (stretch) of forest, forestry, timberland, woodland
Waldgefügetyp m forest structure type
Waldgegend f s. Waldgebiet
Waldgeißbart m (bot) goat's-beard, Aruncus dioicus
Waldgeißblatt n common honeysuckle, [woodbine] honeysuckle, Lonicera periclymenum
Waldgerste f European dune wild rye, Elymus (Leymus) arenarius
Waldgesellschaft f forest community (association)
Waldgrenze f forest (tree, timber) line
~/**alpine** tree line
~/**polare** timber limit
Waldgrenzstandort m tree-line site
Waldgürtel m forest belt
Waldhainsimse f woodrush, glow-worm grass, Luzula sylvatica
Waldhammer m marking hammer
Waldhammermarke f, **Waldhammerzeichen** n [end] mark, blaze, brand
Waldhöhenstufe f altitudinal forest zone, forest belt
Waldhorn n bugle[-horn]
Waldhuhn n grouse (family Tetraonidae)
Waldhumus m forest humus
Waldhüter m forest warden (guard, keeper)
Waldhygiene f forest hygiene
waldig forested, wooded, woody, silvan, bosky
Waldimker m s. Zeidler
Waldinsel f forest outlier
Waldkante f s. Wahnkante

Waldkarte

Waldkarte *f* forest map
Waldkartierung *f* forest mapping
Waldkataster *m* forest cadastre (cadastral register)
Waldkauz *m* tawny (wood) owl, Strix aluco
Waldkerbel *m* wild chervil, cow-parsley, Anthriscus sylvestris
Waldklassifikation *f* forest classification
Waldklima *n* forest climate
Waldlabkraut *n* wood bedstraw, Scotch mist, Galium sylvaticum
Waldland *n* forest[ed] land, woodland • ~ **urbar machen** to assart
Waldlandschaft *f* forest landscape, boscage, boskage
Waldlaubsänger *m* wood-warbler, Phylloscopus sibilatrix
Waldlauch *m* ramson[s], wild garlic, Allium ursinum
Waldlichtung *f* clearing, glade, [forest] opening
~/lange vista
Waldlilie *f* 1. wood lily, three-leaved nightshade, *(Am)* wake-robin, trillium *(genus Trillium)*; 2. wood lily, Lilium philadelphicum
waldlos destitute of forests
Waldlosigkeit *f* absence of forests
Waldmaikäfer *m* chestnut chafer, Melolontha hippocastani
Waldmassiv *n* forest massiv
Waldmast *f*, **Waldmastfutter** *n* pannage
Waldmaus *f* [European] wood mouse, long-tailed [field] mouse, Apodemus sylvaticus
Waldmeister *m* [sweet] woodruff, Galium odoratum, Asperula odorata
Waldmoor *n* wooded swamp
Waldnaßtorf *m* wet forest humus
Waldnutzungsrecht *n* forest right
Waldohreule *f* long-eared owl, Asio otus
Waldökologie *f* forest ecology
Waldökosystem *n* forest ecosystem
Waldparzelle *f s.* Waldstück
Waldpfad *m* forest path
Waldpflege *f* forest tending
Waldpilz *m* forest mushroom, woodland fungus
Waldplatterbse *f* flat pea [vine], wood vetch[ling], wood pea, Lathyrus sylvestris
Waldprimel *f (bot)* [bardfield] oxlip, five-finger, Primula elatior
Waldrand *m* forest edge (border), forest margin (fringe)
Waldrebe *f (bot)* 1. clematis, virgin's bower *(genus Clematis)*; 2. lady's-bower, old man's beard, traveller's joy, Clematis vitalba
Waldreglement *n* forest regulation
waldreich well-wooded, well-timbered, rich in wood[land]s, silvan
Waldreichtum *m* forest wealth, richness in woodland
Waldreinertrag *m*, **Waldrente** *f* forest rent[al]

Waldressourcen *fpl* forest resources (growing stock)
Waldriedgras *n s.* Waldsegge
Waldrodung *f* forest clearance
Waldrose *f* downy-leaved dog rose, tomentose rose, Rosa tomentosa
Waldsäge *f* felling (cross-cutting) saw
Waldsämaschine *f* tree seed drill
Waldsanikel *m (bot)* wood sanicle, Sanicula europaea
Waldsauerklee *m* wood sorrel, stubwort, Oxalis acetosella
Waldsaum *m s.* Waldrand
Waldsavanne *f* derived savanna[h]
Waldschachtelhalm *m* wood (silvan) equisetum, Equisetum sylvaticum
Waldschaden *m* forest damage
Waldschadenserhebung *f*, **Waldschadensinventur** *f* forest damage inventory
waldschälen to bark partially
Waldschlüsselblume *f s.* Waldprimel
Waldschneise *f* aisle, forest glade (lane), ride
Waldschnepfe *f* woodcock, Scolopax rusticola
Waldschutzgebiet *n* forest protection area, forest reserve
Waldsee *m* forest lake
Waldsegge *f* wood sedge, Carex sylvatica
Waldsimse *f s.* Waldbinse
Waldsoziologie *f* forest sociology
Waldspitzmaus *f* common shrew, Sorex araneus [castaneus]
Waldspringkraut *n (bot)* touch-me-not, Impatiens noli-tangere
Waldstandort *m* forest site
Waldstandorttyp *m* forest type
Waldsteig *m s.* Waldweg
Waldsteppe *f* forest (woodland, timbered) steppe
Waldsteppenboden *m* forest-steppe soil
Waldsteppenschwarzerde *f* forest-steppe chernozem
Waldsteppenzone *f* forest-steppe zone
Waldsterben *n* forest decay (decline), death of the forest
Waldstreu *f* [forest, wood] litter
Waldstück *n* forest (wood) plot, *(Am)* woodlot
~/urbar gemachtes assart
Waldtal *n* forested valley
~/kleines dell
~/tiefes dean
Waldtaube *f* ring-dove, wood-pigeon, queest, Columba palumbus
Waldtaxation *f* forest estimation
Waldteich *m* forest pond
Waldtorf *m* forest peat
Waldtransportnetz *n* forest transportation network
waldtrocken dried in the forest *(timber)*
Waldtundra *f* forest-tundra
Waldtyp *m* forest type
~ mit feuchter Moosdecke mossy forest type

~/sekundärer secondary forest type
Waldtypenkarte f stock map
Waldtypenklassifikation f forest type classification
Waldtypenlehre f, **Waldtypologie** f forest typology (type science)
Waldüberschußgebiet n timber-surplus region
Waldumwelt f forest environment
Waldung f forest [land], wooded area, woodland, silva
Waldvegetation f forest vegetation, silva
~ der Erde world forest vegetation
Waldverjüngung f woodland regeneration
Waldvernichtung f forest destruction (devastation)
Waldversicherung f insurance of growing timber
Waldvogel m woodland (forest) bird
Waldvögelein n (bot) helleborine (genus Cephalanthera)
Waldvorräte mpl forest resources (growing stock)
Waldwachstum n forest growth
Waldwärter m forest guard (warden, keeper), forester, (Am) forest ranger
Waldwärterbezirk m forester's (ranger) district
Waldweg m forest path, woodland walk
~/befestigter forest road
Waldwegebau m forest road construction, wood road making
Waldwegekarte f map of forest roads
Waldweide f forest pasture (grazing), wood[land] pasture
Waldweidebetrieb m forest pasturage
Waldweidegang m forest grazing
Waldweidenröschen n rose-bay, blooming willow, Epilobium (Chamaenerion) angustifolium
Waldweidenutzung f forest pasturage
Waldweidewirtschaft f forest pasturage
Waldwert m forest value
Waldwertrechnung f forest valuation
Waldwiese f forest meadow, [forest, grassy] glade, grass clearing
Waldwindröschen n snowdrop [anemone], Anemone sylvestris
Waldwirkung f forest influence
Waldwühlmaus f bank (wood) vole, Clethrionomys glareolus
Waldzeichen n end mark, blaze, brand
Waldziest m hedge nettle, Stachys sylvatica
Waldzone f forest zone
Waldzusammenlegung f consolidation of forest areas (holdings)
Waldzustand m forest condition
Waldzustandserfassung f forest inventory
Waldzwenke f slender false brome[-grass], Brachypodium sylvaticum
Wales-Pony n s. Welsh-Pony
Walfleischmehl n whale meat meal (feed-stuff)
Walhauttopf m whalehide pot (for raising woody ornamentals)
Walker m (ent) scarred melolontha, Polyphylla fullo

Walk[er]erde f fuller's earth
Wallach m castrated horse, gelding, g.
wallachen to castrate, to emasculate, to geld
Waller m s. Wels
Walliser Schwarzhalsziege f Valais Blackneck [goat] (breed)
~ Schwarznasenschaf n Valais Blacknose (sheep breed)
Walloneneiche f Valonia oak, Quercus macrolepsis (aegilops)
Walnuß f 1. walnut; 2. s. Walnußbaum
Walnußbaum m 1. walnut [tree] (genus Juglans); 2. common (English) walnut, Juglans regia
Walnußblattlaus f walnut aphid, Chromaphis juglandicola
Walnußkamm m walnut (raspberry) comb, cushion (strawberry) comb (of fowl)
Walnußkern m walnut kernel
Walnußringfleckenvirus n walnut ring spot virus
Walnußschalenfliege f walnut husk fly, Rhagoletis completa
Walrat m(n) spermaceti
Walze f roll[er]; cylinder
~/geriffelte fluted roll[er]
Wälzegge f rotary [cross] harrow, rolling harrow
walzen to roll
wälzen/sich to wallow, to welter (animal behaviour)
Walzenegge f roller harrow
Walzenentkörnungsmaschine f, **Walzengin** m roller gin (cotton processing)
walzenförmig (bot, zoo) terete
Walzenknicker m hay crusher (bruiser), roller crimper (conditioner)
Walzenmühle f roller (rolling) mill
Walzenquetscher m s. Walzenknicker
Walzenschrotmühle f, **Walzenstuhl** m s. Walzenmühle
Walzentrockner m roller (drum) dryer
Walzentrocknung f roller (contact) drying
Walzenwolfsmilch f (bot) myrtle euphorbia, Euphorbia myrsinites
Walzmaschine f [zur Sägeblattbehandlung] stretching rolls
Wambergsche Spatoperation f (vet) Wamberg modification of cunean tenectomy for bone spavin
WaMiVV s. Mildes Wasserrübenvergilbungsvirus
Wamme f jowl (of pig); dewlap (of oxen and dog)
Wand f/lose (vet) seedy toe (of hoof or claw)
Wandelklee m tick clover (trefoil) (genus Desmodium)
Wandelröschen n (bot) 1. lantana (genus Lantana); 2. lantana, Lantana camara
Wandentlüfter m wall-mounted fan
Wanderackerbau m shifting agriculture (cultivation), swidden agriculture (cropping), shag (in the tropics)
Wanderackerbauer m shifting cultivator

Wanderarbeiter

Wanderarbeiter *m* migrant worker, *(Am)* okie
Wanderbewegung *f* migratory movement
Wanderdüne *f* shifting (drifting) dune, moving (mobile, travelling) dune
Wanderer *m* migrant
Wanderfalke *m* peregrine [falcon], *(Am)* passenger falcon, game hawk, Falco peregrinus
Wanderfeldbauer *m* shifting cultivator
Wanderhaufen *m* wanderhaufen *(malting)*
Wanderherde *f* wandering (migratory) herd
Wanderheuschrecke *f* migratory locust *(comprehensive term)*
Wanderimkerei *f* migratory bee-keeping, mobile apiculture
Wanderkamp *m (forest)* shifting (flying) nursery, temporary (field) nursery
Wanderkasten *m* mobile frame *(horticulture)*
Wanderlaus *m (ent)* migrant
wandern to migrate; to drift *(game)*
wandernd migratory
Wanderniere *f (vet)* float kidney
Wanderpfad *m* hiking path
Wanderratte *f* common rat, [common] brown rat, Norway (cellar, Hanover) rat, sewer rat, Rattus norvegicus
Wanderreiten *n* trail-riding, pony-trekking
Wandertier *n (zoo)* migrant
Wanderung *f* migration; drift *(of game)*
Wanderweg *m* hiking path
Wanderweidewirtschaft *f* nomadic pastoralism
Wander[weide]zaun *m* movable (forward) fence
Wandgewächshaus *n* lean-to glasshouse
Wandlederhaut *f* laminar corium *(of hoof or claw)*
Wandluftheizer *m* wall-mounted air heater
Wange *f* cheek, chap
Wangenbein *n* cheek (zygomatic) bone, malar (jugal) bone
Wanze *f* bug, heteropteran *(order Heteroptera)*
Wanzenblume *f* tickseed *(genus Coreopsis)*
Wapiti *m* wapiti, Cervus elaphus canadiensis
Wappenträger *m* buff-tip[ped moth], Phalera bucephala
Warburg-Horecker-Dickens-Weg *m* pentose phosphate cycle *(biochemistry)*
Warburgsches Atmungsferment *n* cytochrome-c oxidase *(enzyme)*
Warfarin *n* warfarin *(rodenticide)*
warm warm, hot
Warmabfüllen *n*, **Warmabfüllung** *f* hot filling *(of wine)*
Warmbau *m (api)* warm-way hive
Warmbelüftung *f* hot-air ventilation
Warmbeschlag *m* hot shoeing
Warmblut *n s.* Warmblutpferd
Warmblüter *m* 1. warm-blooded animal, homoiotherm, endotherm; 2. *s.* Warmblutpferd
warmblütig warm-blooded, hot-blooded, homoiothermic

Warmblutpferd *n* warm-blooded (hot-blooded) horse, light horse
Wärme *f* heat
~/spezifische specific heat, thermal capacity
Wärme... *s. a.* Hitze...
Wärmeabgabe *f* heat output (dissipation)
Wärmeabgabemechanismus *m* heat-dissipating mechanism
wärmeabgebend exothermal
Wärmeableitung *f* heat dissipation
Wärmeaustausch *m* heat exchange
Wärmebedarf *m* heat (temperature) requirement
Wärmebehandlung *f* temperature (heat) treatment
wärmebeständig heat-resistant, thermostable, thermoduric
~/nicht thermolabile
Wärmebeständigkeit *f* heat resistance, thermostability
Wärmebilanz *f s.* Wärmehaushalt
Wärmebildung *f* thermogenesis
Wärmedämmschirm *m* thermal screen (blanket), heat curtain *(in greenhouses)*
Wärmedämmung *f* thermal insulation
Wärmedurchdringung *f (vet)* diathermy
Wärmedurchgang *m* heat transfer
Wärmedurchgangskoeffizient *m* heat transfer coefficient
Wärmedurchgangswert *m* heat transfer value
Wärmedurchgangszahl *f* heat transfer coefficient
Wärmedyspnoe *f* thermal hyperpnoea, second-phase panting *(animal physiology)*
wärmeempfindlich thermosensitive
Wärmeenergie *f* heat energy
Wärmeenergietransport *m* [durch bewegte Teilchen] convection
Wärmefluß *m* heat flow (flux)
wärmefreisetzend exothermal
Wärmefreisetzung *f* heat release
Wärmegefälle *n* temperature gradient
Wärmegewitter *n* heat thunderstorm
Wärmehaushalt *m* heat (thermal) balance, heat household (budget)
~ des Bodens soil thermal regime
Wärmehaushaltsgleichung *f* heat household equation
Wärmehecheln *n* thermal panting (polypnoea) *(animal physiology)*
Wärmekapazität *f* heat (thermal) capacity, volume heat
Wärmekonservierungsmechanismus *m* heat-conserving mechanism
Wärmeleitfähigkeit *f* heat conductivity
Wärmeleitfähigkeitsmesser *m* katharometer
Wärmeleitung *f* heat conduction
wärmeliebend warm-loving, thermophile, thermophilic
Wärmemessung *f* thermometry
Wärmepolypnoe *f s.* Wärmehecheln
Wärmeproduktion *f* heat production

Wärmepumpanlage f heat pump installation
Wärmepumpe f heat pump
Wärmequelle f heat source
Wärmeregulation f heat (temperature) regulation, thermoregulation
~/soziale social thermoregulation
Wärmerezeptor m warm receptor
Wärmerückgewinnung f heat recycling (recovery)
Wärmerückgewinnungsanlage f heat recycling equipment
Wärmeschirm m s. Wärmedämmschirm
Wärmeschutz m s. Wärmedämmung
Wärmespeicherung f heat storage
Wärmestau m accumulation of heat
Wärmestrahlung f thermal (heat) radiation, thermoradiation
Wärmestrahlungsaustausch m thermal-radiant exchange
Wärmestrom m heat flow (flux, stream)
Wärmesumme f heat (temperature) sum, accumulated temperature
Wärmesummenmethode f heat sum method
Wärmesummenregel f rule of temperature summation, Blunck's rule
Wärmetauscher m heat exchanger, economizer
Wärmetherapie f (phyt, vet) thermotherapy
Wärmetransport m heat transport, convection
Wärmetod m heat death
Wärmetoleranz f heat tolerance
Wärmetoleranzkoeffizient m heat-tolerance index
Wärmeübergang m heat transfer
Wärmeverbrauch m heat consumption
Wärmeverlust m heat loss (leakage)
Wärmeverteilung f heat distribution
Wärmevorhang m heat curtain (in greenhouses)
Wärmezufuhr f heat supply
Warmfermentierung f hot fermentation (wine-making)
Warmfront f warm front (meteorology)
Warmgärung f warm fermentation
Warmhaus n hothouse, warmhouse, heated greenhouse, stove • **im ~ [an]ziehen** to hothouse, to stove
Warmhauspflanze f hothouse (stove) plant
Warmluft f hot air
Warmluftkultur f hot-air culture
Warmlufttrockner m hot-air dryer, warm-air dryer
Warmlufttrocknung f hot-air drying, heated-air drying
Warmluftverteilung f hot-air distribution
Warmmasse f **des Schlachtkörpers** hot carcass weight
Warmstall m warm confinement (animal house)
Warmstallhaltung f warm indoor housing
Warmstratifikation f warm stratification (of seed)
Warmvergärung f hot fermentation
Warmwasserbehandlung f warm-water treatment
Warmwasserbrüter m hot-water brooder (incubator)
Warmwasserdauerbad n single-bath treatment (of seed)
Warmwasserdruckreinigungsgerät n hot-water pressure cleaner
Warmzeit f interglacial
Warnblinkleuchte f warning flash lamp
Warneinrichtung f monitoring device
warnen to warn, to alert
Warnfalle f (forest) warning trap
Warnfärbung f warning colo[u]ration (of animals)
Warnruf m warning call, alert (of game)
Warnsystem n monitoring system
Warntracht f (zoo) mimicry
Wartehof m corral
Wartepferch m waiting (holding) pen
Wartewirt m paratenic host
Wartezeit f waiting time (period); preharvest interval
Wartung f maintenance, servicing
wartungsfrei maintenance-free
Wartungsvorschrift f servicing schedule
Warze f (zoo) wart, verruca, papilla
warzenartig warty, verrucose, verrucous, papillary, papillate, papillose
Warzenente f Muscovy (musk) duck, Cairina moschata
Warzengeschwulst f (vet) papilloma
Warzenkaktus m nipple (pincushion) cactus (genus Mammillaria)
Warzenkiefer f knob-cone pine, Pinus attenuata
Warzenkrankheit f **des Pfirsichs** (phyt) peach wart (virosis)
Warzenkrankheitsvirus n **der Luzerne** lucern[e] papillosity virus
Warzenspindelbaum m, **Warzenspindelstrauch** m warted spindle tree, Euonymus verrucosus
warzentragend papilliferous
Warzenvirus n papilloma virus
warzig s. warzenartig
Waschanlage f washing installation
Waschbär m ra[c]coon, coon, Procyon lotor
Waschbetonplatte f washed gravel flag
Waschbetonstein m washed concrete stone
Wascher m scrubber
Wasser n water • **~ entziehen** to dewater, to dehydrate
~/destilliertes distilled water
~/fließendes running water
~/freies free water (moisture)
~/gebundenes bound (bonded) water
~/hygroskopisches (soil) hygroscopic moisture
~/nutzbares available water
~/pflanzenverfügbares plant-available, free water (moisture)
~/stehendes standing (stagnant) water
~/tellurisches (soil) telluric water
~/tritiiertes tritiated water
~/ungebundenes s. ~/freies
~/verfügbares available water

Wasser

~ **zur Bewässerung** irrigation water
Wasserabfluß *m* [water] runoff
Wasserabgabe *f* water excretion
Wasserablauf *m* [water] runoff
Wasserabscheider *m* water separator *(sugar manufacture)*
wasserabsorbierend water-absorbing, hygroscopic
Wasserabsorption *f* water absorption
wasserabstoßend, wasserabweisend water-repellent, hydrophobic, hydrophobe
Wasserähre *f* water hawthorn *(genus Aponogeton)*
Wasseranlagerung *f* hydration
wasseranziehend water-attractant, hygroscopic, hydrophilic
Wasseraufnahme *f* water uptake, uptake of water; water absorption
Wasseraufnahmevermögen *n* hygroscopicity
wasseraufnehmend water-absorbing, hygroscopic
wasseraufsaugend hygroscopic
Wasseraufstieg *m*/**kapillarer** *(soil)* capillary rise
Wasseräugigkeit *f (vet)* hydrophthalmia
Wasserausscheidung *f* water excretion
Wasserausschöpfung *f* water depletion
Wasserbad *n* water-bath
Wasserbassin *n* basin
Wasserbedarf *m* water requirement (need)
Wasserbehälter *m* water reservoir
Wasserbereitstellung *f* water supply
Wasserbewirtschaftung *f* water management
wasserbewohnend aquatic
Wasserbilanz *f* water balance
Wasserbindungsvermögen *n* water-binding capacity
Wasserblüte *f* water bloom
Wasserbrotwurzel *f* dasheen, coco yam, Colocasia esculenta
Wasserbruch *m (vet)* hydrocele
Wasserdampf *m* water vapour, steam • ~ **abgeben** to transpire • **mit ~ behandeln** to steam
Wasserdampfabgabe *f* transpiration
Wasserdampfbewegung *f* water vapour movement
Wasserdampfdestillation *f* steam distillation
Wasserdarreichung *f* water service
Wasserdecke *f* water washing *(sugar manufacture)*
~ **der Zentrifuge** centrifuge water washing
Wasserdefizit *n* water deficit
~ **der Atmosphäre** saturation deficit
wasserdruckgetrieben water-driven
Wasserdrüse *f (bot)* hydathode
Wasserdüngung *f* pond fertilization
Wasserdurchlaß *m* culvert
wasserdurchtränkt soggy
Wassereiche *f* water oak, Quercus nigra
Wassereinzugsgebiet *n* [water] catchment, catchment area (basin), gathering ground, watershed
Wasserenthärtung *f* water softening

Wasserentnahmerecht *n* water extraction right
Wasserentziehung *f*, **Wasserentzug** *m* water deprivation; dehydration
Wassererosion *f* water erosion
Wassererschöpfung *f* water depletion
Wasserfall *m* waterfall
Wasserfalle *f* water trap
Wasserfeinverteilung *f* **[in der Butter]** water dispersion value
Wasserfenchel *m* hemlock water-dropwort, Oenanthe crocata
Wasserfilter *n* water filter
Wasserfloh *m* water-flea *(family Daphnidae)*
wasserfrei water-free, moisture-free
Wasserfreiraum *m* water-free space, WFS *(of plant tissue)*
wasserführend water-bearing
Wasserführung *f* stream flow (discharge) *(in waters)*
Wasserfurche *f* water furrow
Wassergabe *f* water application
Wassergamander *m (bot)* water germander, Teucrium scordium
Wassergarten *m* 1. *(forest)* mill-pond; log harbour, rafting reservoir; sorting boom *(roundwood sorting)*; 2. water garden *(horticulture)*
Wassergeflügel *n* water-fowl
Wassergehalt *m* water (moisture) content
~/**relativer** relative water content, RWC
Wassergesetz *n* water law
Wassergewinnungsgebiet *n* water-supply zone
Wasserglas *n*, **Wasserglaslösung** *f* water-glass *(solution of sodium or potassium silicate)*
Wassergraben *m* lead; water-jump *(obstacle)*
Wassergreiskraut *n* marsh ragwort, Senecio aquaticus
Wassergüte *f* water quality
wasserhaltefähig [water-]retentive *(e.g. a soil)*
Wasserhaltefähigkeit *f s.* 1. Wasserhaltungsvermögen; 2. Wasserkapazität
wasserhaltig aqueous
Wasserhaltungsvermögen *n* water-holding capacity (power), water-binding capacity
Wasserhanf *m* water hemp, hemp agrimony, hempweed, Eupatorium cannabinum
Wasserhärte *f* water hardness
Wasserhaushalt *m* water budget (economy), water balance (regime), water metabolism
Wasserhaushaltsgleichung *f* hydrologic equation
Wasserhaushaltsstörung *f* water metabolism disorder
Wasserhaut *f* amnion, caul *(animal anatomy)*
Wasserherbizid *n* water herbicide
Wasserhof *m s.* Wassergarten 1.
Wasserhuhn *n* coot *(genus Fulica)*
Wasserhülle *f* **der Erde** hydrosphere
Wasserhund *m* water dog
Wasserhyazinthe *f* water hyacinth, Eichhornia crassipes

Wasser-in-Öl-Emulsion f water-in-oil emulsion, mayonnaise (e.g. of plant protectants)
Wasseriris f yellow[flag] iris, Iris pseudacorus
Wasserjungfer f dragon-fly (order Odonata)
Wasserkapazität f (soil) water [retention] capacity, moisture [retention] capacity, field [moisture] capacity, FC (s. a. Wasserhaltungsvermögen)
~/nutzbare available water capacity, AWC
Wasserkern m wetwood, water core (heart) (of timber)
Wasserknappheit f s. Wassermangel
Wasserknöterich m water Lady's-thumb, amphibious bistort, willow grass, Polygonum amphibium
Wasserkopf m (vet) hydrocephalus
Wasserkraft f water-power
Wasserkreislauf m water (hydrologic) cycle
Wasserkresse f great yellow cress, Rorippa amphibia
Wasserkühlung f hydrocooling (e.g. of vegetables)
Wasserkultur[methode] f water culture, hydroponics; water-tank gardening
Wasserkulturversuch m water culture experiment
Wasserlager n, **Wasserlagerplatz** m s. Wassergarten 1.
wasserlässig leaky (butter)
Wasserlauf m watercourse
Wasserlaufband n water treadmill, aquaciser (for exercising horses)
Wasserlebewesen n aquatic organism
Wasserleitfähigkeit f water conductivity
~/vertikale water-raising capacity (of a soil)
Wasserleitung f 1. water conduction; 2. water pipe; water distributing system, water main
Wasserlinse f duckweed (genus Lemna)
Wasserlinsengewächs n duckweed, duckmeat (family Lemnaceae)
wasserlöslich water-soluble
Wassermangel m water (moisture) deficiency; water famine (s. a. Wasserstreß)
Wassermelone f [water-]melon, Citrullus lanatus var. caffer
Wassermelonenvirus n 1 water-melon mosaic virus 1, WMV 1
Wassermenge f eines Teiches pondage
Wasserminze f water mint, Mentha aquatica var. aquatica
wässern to water
~/mit dem Schlauch to hose
Wassernabel m (bot) pennywort (genus Hydrocotyle)
Wassernatter f s. Ringelnatter
Wassernuß f 1. water chestnut (caltrop) (genus Trapa); 2. water chestnut (caltrop), Trapa natans
Wassernutzung f water use
Wasserpermeabilität f water permeability, hydraulic conductivity (plant physiology)
Wasserpest f (bot) elodea (genus Elodea)

Wasserpfeffer m water pepper, lakeweed, smartweed, Polygonum hydropiper
Wasserpflanze f water plant, aquatic [plant], hydrophyte
Wasserpflanzenbekämpfung f aquatic plant control
Wasserpflanzenerntemaschine f aquatic plant harvester
Wasserpflanzenmäher m water-weed cutter
Wasserporenvolumen n (soil) water porosity
Wasserpotential n water potential
Wasserqualität f water quality
Wasserquelle f water source (spring)
Wasserratte f common rat, [common] brown rat, Norway (cellar, Hanover) rat, sewer rat, Rattus norvegicus
Wasserrecht[e] n[npl] water rights
Wasserregime n water regime
wasserreich rich in water
Wasserreinigung f water purification
Wasserreis m paddy [rice], wet[land] rice, swamp (lowland) rice
Wasserreis n s. 1. Wasserschößling; 2. Wasserschoß
Wasserreisanbau m wet rice growing
Wasserreisboden m paddy (wetland rice) soil
Wasserreisfeld n paddy[-field]
Wasserreismähdrescher m wet rice combine harvester
Wasserressourcen fpl water resources
Wasserretention f water retention
Wasserretentionskurve f (soil) water retention curve, moisture characteristic
Wasserriese f (forest) wet chute, [water] flume, water slide
Wasserrinne f 1. gullet (tree-felling); 2. s. Wasserriese
Wasserrübe f [stubble] turnip, neep, Brassica rapa var. rapa
Wasserrübengelbmosaikvirus n turnip yellow mosaic virus, TuYMV, Newcastle turnip virus
Wasserrübenkräuselvirus n turnip crinkle virus, TuCV
Wasserrübenmosaikvirus n turnip mosaic virus, TuMV
Wasserrübenrosettenvirus n turnip rosette virus
Wassersalat m water lettuce, Pistia stratiotes
Wassersättigung f water saturation
Wassersättigungsdefizit n water saturation deficit, WSD
Wassersegge f water sedge, Carex aquatica (aquatilis)
Wasserschadstoff m water pollutant
Wasserscheide f watershed, [water] divide, water parting, interfluve
~/oberirdische topographic divide
Wasserscheu f hydrophobia
Wasserschierling m water (poison) hemlock, cowbane, Cicuta virosa

Wasserschlag

Wasserschlag *m* water-hammer
Wasserschnecke *f s.* Schraubenpumpe
Wasserschoß *m* water shoot (sprout), sucker
Wasserschößling *m* epicormic [shoot, branch], secondary growth, bole sprout *(wood defect)*
Wasserschutzwald *m* water conservation (regulating) forest
Wasserschutzzone *f* water conservation (protection) zone
Wasserschwaden *m* reed sweet grass, brook grass, water poa, Glyceria maxima (aquatica)
Wasserschwein *n (zoo)* capybara, Hydrochoerus capybara (hydrochoeris)
Wasserspalte *f (bot)* hydathode
Wasserspaltung *f/photooxidative* biophotolysis *(photosynthesis)*
Wasserspannung *f (soil)* moisture tension
Wasserspannungskurve *f s.* Wasserretentionskurve
Wasserspeicherung *f* water storage
Wasserspeicherungsvermögen *n (soil)* water [storage] capacity
Wasserspiegel *m* water table; water level
Wasserspiegelabsenkung *f* water-table drawdown
Wasserspitzmaus *f* water shrew, Neomys (Crossopus) fodiens
Wasserstand *m* water-level
Wasserstau *m* impounding
Wasserstaubdüsenregner *m* mist nozzle sprinkler
Wasserstoff *m* hydrogen
Wasserstoffanlagerung *f* hydrogenation
Wasserstoffionenexponent *m* pH [value]
Wasserstoffionenkonzentration *f* hydrogen-ion concentration
Wasserstoff[su]peroxid *n* hydrogen peroxide *(disinfectant)*
Wasserstoffzahl *f s.* Wasserstoffionenkonzentration
Wasserstrahlentrinder *m* hydraulic [de]barker, jet (stream) barker
Wasserstrahlentrindung *f* hydraulic barking, jet (stream) barking
Wasserstreß *m* water stress (strain)
Wassersucht *f (vet)* hydrops, dropsy
Wassersumpfkresse *f* great yellow cress, Rorippa amphibia
Wassertank *m* water tank
Wassertaro *m (bot)* dasheen, coco yam, Colocasia esculenta
Wassertransport *m* water transport
Wassertrense *f* jointed snaffle
Wassertretmühle *f s.* Wasserlaufband
Wassertrieb *m s.* Wasserschoß
Wassertupelobaum *m* water tupelo, Nyssa aquatica
wasser- und aschefrei moisture-and-ash-free, maf
Wasserunkraut *n* water (aquatic) weed

wasserunlöslich insoluble in water
Wasserverbrauch *m* water consumption (use)
Wasserverbrauchseffektivität *f* water-use efficiency, consumptive-use efficiency
Wasserverdunstung *f* water evaporation
Wasserverfügbarkeit *f* water availability
Wasserverhältnisse *npl* water relations (status)
Wasserverlagerung *f* water transfer *(e.g. in plants)*
Wasserverlust *m* water loss
Wasserverschmutzung *f* water pollution
Wasserversorgung *f* water supply (service)
Wasserverunreinigung *f* water pollution
Wasserverwendung *f* water use
Wasservorrat *m* water supply
Wasservorwärmer *m/rauchgasbeheizter* economizer
Wasserwild *n* water-fowl
Wasserwirtschaft *f* water management [and engineering]
Wasseryams *n* water (ten-months) yam, Dioscorea alata
Wasserzeichenkrankheit *f* watermark disease *(of willow, caused by Erwinia salicis)*
Wasserzustand *m* water status
wäßrig aqueous
Wäßrige Jambuse *f* water[y] rose-apple, Syzygium aqueum
watscheln to waddle
Watsonie *f (bot)* watsonia *(genus Watsonia)*
Watt *n* watt *(SI unit of power)*
Wattboden *m* tidal marsh
Watte *f* cotton wool
Wattetupfer *m (vet)* swab
Watvogel *m* wading bird, wader
WBMV *s.* Bodenbürtiges Weizenmosaikvirus
W-Chromosom *n* W chromosome
WdSV *s.* Weidelgrasscheckungsvirus
Webb's Weißtanne *f* Himalayan silver fir, Abies spectabilis
Weberdistel *f*, **Weberkarde** *f* common teasel, Dipsacus sativus (fullonum)
Weberknecht *m (zoo)* harvestman, weaver *(group Opiliones)*
Webervogel *m* weaver[-bird] *(family Ploceidae)*
Wechsel *m s.* Wildwechsel
Wechselblatthartriegel *m* alternate-leaf dogwood, Cornus alternifolia
wechselblütig *(bot)* alterniflorous
Wechselblättriges Zypergras *n* umbrella plant, Cyperus alternifolius
Wechseldrehwuchs *m* alternating spiral grain, interlocked fibre (grain), interwoven grain, changing twisted growth *(of wood)*
Wechselfestigkeit *f* thixotropy *(e.g. of soil aggregates)*
wechselfeucht periodically wet *(site)*
Wechselfieber *n (vet)* malaria

Wechselfurchenbewässerung f alternate-furrow irrigation
Wechselgrasland n temporary grassland, ley, lea
wechselgrün *(bot)* deciduous
Wechselgrünland n s. Wechselgrasland
Wechselkreuzung f criss-crossing
Wechselkreuzungszüchtung f criss-cross breeding
Wechsellagerungsschichtsilicat n *(soil)* mixed-layer mineral
wechseln/das Federkleid to moult
~/das Haar to change hair *(game)*
Wechselnutzung f alternate husbandry
Wechselpflug m alternate (alternative) plough
Wechselsieb n interchangeable (grain) sieve *(of combine harvester)*
Wechselspatenpflug m alternating spading plough
wechselständig *(bot)* alternate
Wechseltaktmelkmaschine f alternating stroke milking machine
Wechseltierchen n amoeba *(order Amoebina)*
wechselwarm *(zoo)* poikilothermic
Wechselwarmblüter m poikilotherm
Wechselweide f cropland pasture
Wechselweizen m semiwinter (facultative) wheat
Wechselwiese f arable meadow
Wechselwild n migratory game
Wechselwirkung f interaction
~ höherer Ordnung *(biom)* high-order interaction
Wechselwirtschaft f alternate husbandry, mixed farming
Wechselzahn m milk (deciduous) tooth
Weddellit m weddellite *(non-clay mineral)*
Wedel m 1. *(bot)* [foliage] frond; 2. scut, single *(of red deer)*
WEE s. Westliche Pferdeenzephalomyelitis
Weender Futtermittelanalyse f Weende [feed] analysis
WeFBV s. Weinrebenfächerblättrigkeitsvirus
Weg m/**befestigter** hard (made-up) road
~/photorespiratorischer photorespiratory pathway *(plant physiology)*
~/unbefestigter earth road
wegbeißen to bite away *(animal behaviour)*
Wegdistel f plumeless thistle, Carduus acanthoides
Wegebau m road building (construction)
Wegebelag m, **Wegedecke** f road surface
Wegekörper-Querprofil n road cross-section
Wegekraut n *(bot)* galium *(genus Galium)*
Wegelosigkeit f absence of roads
Wegenetz n road network
~/forstliches forest road network
~/landwirtschaftliches farm roads
Wegeprofil n road cross section
Wegerecht n right-of-way
Wegerich m *(bot)* plantain *(genus Plantago)*

Wegerichgemswurz f *(bot)* leopard's-bane, Doronicum plantagineum
Wegezeit f travel time
wegfliegen to fly off *(wildfowl)*
wegführen to abduct *(a limb)*
Wegführung f abduction
Wegmalve f common mallow, Malva neglecta
wegpicken to pick away *(animal behaviour)*
Wegrandpflanze f ruderal [plant]
Wegrandspritze f roadside sprayer
Wegrauke f hedge mustard, Sisymbrium officinale
Wegriese f *(forest)* road slide
Wegtaube f s. Turteltaube
Wegwarte f 1. chic[k]ory, succory *(genus Cichorium)*; 2. chic[k]ory, succory, blue sailors, Cichorium intybus
Wegwerfschar n disposable (expendable) share, one-way share
Wegzapfwelle f ground speed power take-off
wegzüchten to breed out
Wehe f 1. drift *(of snow, sand)*; 2. s. Wehen
Wehen fpl, **Wehenschmerz** m pains, labour
Wehr n weir, dam
Wehr f s. Treiberwehr
Wehrlose Trespe f smooth brome[-grass], awnless brome[-grass], Bromus inermis
Weibchen n female, jenny, she; hen *(of fowl)*
weiblich female, feminine
Weiblicher Waldfarn m female shield-fern, Athyrium (Asplenium) filix-femina
Weiblichkeit f femininity
Weibull-Berntrop-Methode f Weibull-Berntrop method *(of milk fat determination)*
weich soft; mellow *(e.g. fruits)* • **~ werden** to soften; to mellow *(e.g. fruits)*
Weichbast m soft bark
Weiche f 1. flank *(of animal's body)*; 2. steep tank, steeper *(fermentation)*
Weiche Erle f speckled alder, Alnus rugosa
~ Kirsche f heart-cherry, Prunus avium var. juliana
~ Trespe f soft brome[-grass], tender brome[-grass], lop-grass, *(Am)* soft chess, Bromus hordaceus ssp. hordaceus
weichen to liquor, to steep *(brewer's barley, malt)*
~/wiederholt to resteep
Weichenbein n hip (innominate) bone
Weiches Honiggras n creeping soft-grass, Holcus mollis
Weichfaser f soft fibre
Weichfäule f *(phyt)* soft (wet) rot
~ der Batate slime *(of batata, caused by Rhizopus nigricans)*
~ der Möhren carrot [bacterial] soft rot *(caused by Erwinia carotovora)*
~ des Kulturchampignons wet bubble [of mushrooms] *(caused by Mycogone perniciosa)*
weichfleischig soft-fleshed
Weichfutter n soft feed

Weichgrad

Weichgrad *m* degree of steeping *(malting)*
weichhaarig *(bot)* pilose, pilous
Weichhaarige Apfelrose *f* soft-leaved round-fruited rose, Rosa mollis
~ **Zaubernuß** *f* Chinese wych-hazel, Hamamelis mollis
Weichhautmilbe *f* tarsonemid [mite] *(family Tarsonemidae)*
Weichheit *f* poachiness *(of soil)*
Weichholz *n* softwood, coniferous wood (timber)
Weichholzaushieb *m (forest)* assistance felling
Weichhorn *n* soft horn *(of the hoof)*
Weichkäse *m* soft (cream) cheese
Weichkot *m* soft (night) pellets, caecotrophe *(of rabbits)*
Weichkotfressen *n* caecotrophy *(of rabbits)*
Weichlaubbaumart *f* softwooded broad-leaved species, softwood
Weichlaubholz *n* softwood
Weichmais *m* soft maize, *(Am)* flour corn, Zea mays convar. amylacea
Weichobst *n* soft fruit
Weichobsterntemaschine *f* soft fruit harvester
Weichordnung *f* air-water steep *(malting)*
Weichsel *f*, **Weichsel[kirsch]baum** *m* sour (tart) cherry, Prunus cerasus
Weichselrohr *n s.* Steinweichsel
Weichwanze *f (ent)* capsid [bug], mirid *(family Miridae)*
Weichweizen *m* [common, bread, soft] wheat, Triticum aestivum (vulgare)
Weichweizenmittelmehl *n (Am)* farina
Weichweizenstärke *f (Am)* farina
Weichwerden *n* **einer Frucht** fruit softening
Weide *f* 1. pasture, grazing, grass; range, run; 2. willow, osier *(genus Salix)* • **als ~ [be]nutzen** to pasture
Weideaufwuchs *m* pasture growth
Weideaustrieb *m* turnout, turning out *(of livestock)*
Weidebeifutter *n* pasture supplement
Weideberechtigter *m* agister
Weideberechtigung *f* agistment
Weideberegnung *f* pasture irrigation
Weidebewässerung *f* pasture irrigation
Weidebewirtschaftung *f* range (grazing) management
Weideblindheit *f (vet)* pink-eye *(of cattle)*
~ **des Rindes/infektiöse** *(vet)* infectious bovine keratoconjunctivitis
Weidedauer *f* grazing duration
Weidedegradierung *f* pasture degradation
Weideerneuerung *f* pasture renovation
Weideertrag *m* pasture yield
Weideetablierung *f* pasture establishment
Weidefläche *f* pasture, ranging ground, grazing [area], camp, acreage
Weidefruchtfolge *f* pasture rotation
Weideführung *f* grazing control (management)
Weidefutter *n* pasture [forage], herbage, feed

Weidefutterpflanze *f* herbage plant
Weidefütterung *f* pasture (outdoor) feeding
Weidegang *m* pasturage, grazing
Weidegebiet *n* pasture-land, grazing ground (area)
• **[jahreszeitabhängig] das ~ wechselnd** transhumant
Weidegemisch *n* pasture mixture
Weidegenossenschaft *f* grazing co-operative
Weidegras *n* pasture [grass], keep
Weidegräsergemisch *n* pasture mixture
Weidegrund *m s.* Weidefläche
Weidehaltung *f* grazing
Weideherde *f* grazing herd
Weidekalender *m* grazing calendar
Weidekuh *f s.* Weidemilchkuh
Weidelamm *n s.* Weidemastlamm
Weideland *n* pasture[-land], grazing [land], grass; range [land], run
~/**extensiv genutztes** extensive pasture
~/**natürliches** natural pasture, rough grazing
Weidelandboden *m* pasture soil
Weideleguminose *f* pasture legume
Weideleistung *f* pasture performance, grazing efficiency
Weidelgras *n (bot)* darnel, lolium *(genus Lolium)*
Weidelgrasscheckungsvirus *n* lolium mottle virus
Weidemähwerk *n* pasture topper
Weidemast *f* range (grass) fattening, fattening by grazing
Weidemastitis *f (vet)* summer mastitis *(caused by Corynebacterium pyogenes)*
Weidemastlamm *n* grass fat spring lamb, grass-fed lamb, grazer
Weidemelkanlage *f* pasture milking plant
Weidemelken *n* pasture milking
Weidemelkstand *m* pasture milking parlour, field (outdoor milking) bail
Weidemilchkuh *f* pasture (grazing) dairy cow
Weidemischung *f* pasture mixture
weiden to [de]pasture, to graze, to crop
~ **lassen** to [de]pasture, to graze, *(Am)* to grass, to run
~ **lassen/auf Wintergras** to fog
Weiden *n* grazing
~/**periodisches** periodic grazing
weidenblättrig willow-leaved
Weidenblättriger Spierstrauch *m* willow-leaf spiraea, Spiraea salicifolia
Weidenblättrigkeit *f* **der Pflaume** prune dwarf *(virosis)*
Weidenblättrigkeitsvirus *n* **der Pflaume** prune dwarf virus
Weidenbohrer *m* [European] goat moth, Cossus cossus
Weideneiche *f* [swamp] willow oak, peach oak, Quercus phellos
Weidengabelschwanz *m* puss moth, Cerura vinula

Weidengallenblattwespe *f* bean-gall saw-fly of willows, Pontania proxima (capraea)
Weidengerte *f s.* Weidenrute
Weidenheger *m s.* Weidenpflanzung
Weidenholz *n* willow, sallow
Weidenholzgallmücke *f* European willow wood [gall-]midge, Rhabdophaga saliciperda
Weidenkahneule *f,* **Weidenkahnspinner** *m (ent)* cream-bordered green pea, Earias (Halias) chlorana
Weidenkätzchen *n* [willow-]catkin, *(Am)* puss willow
Weidenkorb *m* wicker basket, skep, prickle
Weidenpflanzung *f* osier bed (ground), willow grove (plantation, holt)
Weidenröschen *n* rose-bay, willow-herb, blooming willow, fireweed, Epilobium (Chamaenerion) angustifolium
Weidenrute *f* whithe, whithy, willow rod (twig), osier, wand
Weidenschildlaus *f* willow (poplar) scale, Chionaspis (Aspidiotus) salicis
Weidenspringrüßler *m (ent)* poplar leaf-miner, Orchestes populi
Weidenstecklung *m* set
Weidenutzung *f* range use (utilization), pasture usage; grazing management
Weidenutzungseinheit *f* grazing unit, paddock
Weidenutzungsgebühr *f* pasture rental
Weidenutzungsrecht *n s.* Weiderecht
Weidenutzungssystem *n* grazing system
Weidenutzungsverfahren *n* grazing method
Weidepacht *f* grazing tenancy
Weideperiode *f* grazing period (season)
Weidepflanze *f* pasture (meadow) plant
Weidepflege *f* pasture maintenance, grazing management
Weidepflock *m* picket [pin]
Weidepumpe *f* pasture pump
Weiderecht *n* grazing right, pasturage, herbage
Weiderest *m* pasture grass leavings
Weiderich *m (bot)* loosestrife *(genus Lythrum)*
Weiderindvieh *n* range cattle
Weiderohrmelkanlage *f* pipeline pasture milking parlour
Weiderot *n (vet)* red-water [disease], babesiasis, babesiosis
Weiderotation *f* pasture rotation
Weidesaftfutter *n* succulent pasture
Weideschädling *m* pasture pest
Weideschaf *n* range sheep
Weideschwein *n* German Pasture, Hildesheim, Hanover-Brunswick *(pig breed)*
Weidesystem *n* grazing system
Weidetetanie *f* grass tetany (staggers), Hereford disease *(of ruminants)*
Weidetier *n* grazing animal, grazer
~ **ohne Brandzeichen** *(Am)* maverick, cleanskin *(Australia)*

Weidetierhalter *m* pastoralist
Weideunkraut *n* pasture weed
Weideverfahren *n* grazing method
Weideverhalten *n* grazing behaviour
Weideverschlechterung *f* pasture degradation
Weideversuch *m* pasture experiment, grazing trial
Weidevieh *n* grazing [live]stock, grazing animals; range cattle
Weideviehfutter *n s.* Weidefutter
Weideviehzüchter *m* pastoralist, grazier
Weidewaldung *f* pastured forest; grazing woodland
Weidewart *m* grazier
Weidewirkung *f* grazing effect
Weidewirtschaft *f* grazing (range) management, pasture farming, pastoral farming (husbandry), pastoralism
Weidezaun *m* pasture fence
Weidezeit[spanne] *f* grazing period (season, time)
Weidezusammensetzung *f* pasture composition
Weidgenosse *m* fellow huntsman
weidgerecht sportsmanlike, sportsmanly
Weidgerechtigkeit *f* sportsmanship
Weidloch *n* anus *(of game)*
Weidmann *m* hunter, huntsman, sportsman, nimrod
weidmännisch huntsmanlike *(s. a. weidgerecht)*
Weidmannsheil! good sport[s]! good hunting!
Weidmannssprache *f* hunter's language (slang)
Weidwerk *n* field (blood) sports, huntsman's craft (pursuit), woodcraft, hunting, chase, venery
• ~ **betreiben** to hunt
weidwund wounded in the bowels, shot in the intestines
Weih *f*/**lange** ropy milk
Weiher *m* pond, pool
Weihnachtsbaumpflanzung *f* Christmas tree planting
Weihnachtsbaumzucht *f* Christmas tree farming (growing)
Weihnachtskaktus *m* 1. Christmas cactus *(genus Epiphyllum)*; 2. Christmas (thanksgiving, crab) cactus, Schlumbergera truncata, Zygocactus truncatus
Weihnachtsstern *m* Christmas star, poinsettia, Euphorbia pulcherrima
Weihrauch *m* olibanum, frankincense *(gum resin from Boswellia spp.)*
Weihrauchbaum *m* 1. incense tree *(genus Boswellia)*; 2. Bible frankincense, Boswellia sacra (carteri)
Weihrauchkiefer *f* loblolly (frankincense) pine, short-leaf pine, foxtail (bull, slash) pine, Pinus taeda
Weihrauchrose *f* yellow rose, Rosa foetida
weihrauchtragend *(bot)* thuriferous
Weihrauchwacholder *m* Spanish juniper, Juniperus thurifera
Weiler *m* hamlet

Weimaraner

Weimaraner *m* Weimaraner *(dog breed)*
Wein *m* wine • **~ bereiten** to vinify, to vint
~/abgelagerter *s.* ~/ausgebauter
~/alkoholisierter fortified wine
~/aromatisierter aromatized wine
~/ausgebauter (geschulter) settled (crushed) wine
~/gespriteter fortified wine
~/gestreckter watered wine
~/herber rough wine
~/junger young wine
~/kohlendioxidfreier still wine
~/leichter light wine
~/medizinischer medicine wine
~/opalisierender hazy wine
~/rappiger rough wine
~/restsüßer sweet wine
~/schimmernder hazy wine
~/süßer sweet wine
~ vom Faß pipe-wine
Weinahorn *m* vine maple, Acer circinatum
Weinapfel *m* cider apple
Weinballon *m* demijohn
Weinbau *m* wine-growing, grape-growing, viticulture, viniculture
Weinbauer *m* wine (grape) grower, viticulturist, vineyardist, vine-dresser, vintager
Weinbaufläche *f* grape acreage, vineyard
Weinbaukooperative *f* viticulture co-operative
weinbaulich viticultural
Weinbautraktor *m s.* Weinbergschlepper
Weinbeere *f* grape [berry]
Weinbehälter *m* wine vat
Weinbereitung *f* wine-making, vinification
Weinberg *m* vineyard, domaine, viner
Weinberghackmaschine *f* vineyard hoe
Weinberglauch *m* crow garlic (onion), wild garlic (onion), Allium vineale
Weinbergpflug *m* vineyard plough
Weinbergraupe *f* vineyard tracklayer
Weinbergscheibenegge *f* vineyard disk harrow
Weinbergschlepper *m*, **Weinbergtraktor** *m* vineyard tractor
Weinbergschnecke *f* grape-wine snail, Helix pomatia
Weinbergspritze *f* vineyard sprayer
Weinbukett *n* bouquet
Weinbütte *f* dosser
Weindestillat *n* wine distillate
Weinernte *f s.* Weinlese
Weinertrag *m* vintage
Weinessig *m* wine (grape) vinegar
Weinetikett *n* wine label
Weinfachmann *m* oenologist, sommelier
Weinfaß *n* wine cask (barrel)
~/großes pipe
Weinflasche *f* winebottle
Weingärbehälter *m* wine-making vat

Weingarten *m* vineyard, grapery
Weingegend *f* wine-growing region, wine-making area
Weingeist *m* spirit[s] of wine, ethyl alcohol
Weingut *n* wine estate
Weinhändler *m* vintner, wine-merchant, viner
Weinhefe *f*, **Weinhefepilz** *m* wine yeast, Saccharomyces ellipsoideus
Weinherstellung *f s.* Weinbereitung
weinig win[e]y, vinous
Weinjahrgang *m* vintage
Weinkeller *m* [wine-]cellar, wine-vault
Weinkelterei *f* winery
Weinkelterung *f* wine-making, vinification
Weinknospenstecher *m* grape bud beetle, Glyptoscelis squamulata
Weinküfer *m* cellarer, cellarman, cellarmaster, wine dresser
Weinkunde *f* oenology, vinology
Weinkundiger *m* oenologist, sommelier
weinkundlich oenological
Weinlager *n s.* Weinkeller
Weinlese *f* grape picking, vintage
Weinleser *m* vintager
Weinprobe *f* wine-tasting
Weinraute *f* [common] rue, herb [of] grace, Ruta graveolens var. vulgaris
Weinrebe *f* [grape] vine, grape tree *(genus Vitis)*
Weinreben... *s. a.* Reben...
Weinrebenfächerblättrigkeitsvirus *n* grape-vine fan leaf virus
Weinrebengelbmosaikvirus *n* grape-vine chrome mosaic virus
Weinrose *f* sweet-brier, eglantine, Rosa rubiginosa (eglantaria)
Weinsäure *f* tartaric acid
Weinschönung *f* wine fining
Weinschwefelung *f* sulphuration
Weinstein *m* wine-stone, tartar, fur
Weinsteinsäure *f* L-tartaric acid
Weinstock *m* [grape-]vine, grape tree *(genus Vitis)*
Weintank *m* wine vat
Weintraube *f* [wine] grape, bunch (cluster) of grapes
Weintrauben... *s. a.* Trauben...
Weintraubenkernöl *n* raisin-seed oil
Weinverkoster *m* wine-taster
Weinverkostung *f* wine-tasting
Weinwaage *f* wine gauge, oenometer
Weinwirtschaft *f* wine trade
Weisel *f* queen [bee], colony queen
Weiselaufzucht *f* queen rearing (breeding)
Weiselbecher *m* cell cup
Weiselfänger *m* queen-excluder
Weiselfuttersaft *m* royal (queen bee's nutrient) jelly
Weiselkäfig *m* queen cage
weisellos queenless

Weisellosigkeit f queenlessness
weiselrichtig queenright
Weiselrichtigkeit f queenrightness
Weiselsaft m s. Weiselfuttersaft
Weiselstoff m queen substance (pheromone)
Weiselzelle f queen cell
Weiselzucht f queen breeding (rearing)
Weiserbaumart f (forest) key species
Weiserbestand m (forest) indicator stand
Weiserfläche f (forest) indicator plot
Weiserformel f (forest) indicating formula
Weiserprozent n indicating percent, current annual forest percent
Weißährigkeit f (phyt) silver-top[s]
Weißalkaliboden m white alkali soil, solonchak
Weißbier n weiss [beer]
Weißbirke f white (silver, weeping) birch, Swedish (European) birch, Betula pendula (alba, verrucosa)
weißblättrig (bot) leucophyllous
weißblütig (bot) albiflorous
Weißblütigkeit f (vet) leukaemia, leucosis
Weißbuche f 1. hornbeam, white (water) beech (genus Carpinus); 2. [European] hornbeam, white (horn, hurst) beech, yoke elm, Carpinus betulus
Weißbuchenholz n hornbeam
Weißdorn m 1. haw[thorn], whitethorn, may (genus Crataegus); 2. English hawthorn, one-seed (single-seed) hawthorn, haw, hedge-row thorn, Crataegus monogyna
Weißdornakazie f allthorn acacia, Acacia karoo (horrida)
Weißdornblättrige Himbeere f hawthorn raspberry, Rubus crataegifolius
Weißdornfrucht f haw
Weißdornhecke f quickset
Weißdornsteckling m quickset
Weiße Akazie f white acacia, Faidherbia (Acacia) albida
~ **Ameise** f white ant, termite (order Isoptera)
~ **Beltsville-Pute** f Beltsville Small White [turkey] (breed)
~ **Berberitze** f pale-leaf barberry, Berberis candidula
~ **Fetthenne** f English stonecrop, worm grass, Sedum album
~ **Fliege** f 1. white fly (family Aleurodiade); 2. [glasshouse] white fly, Trialeurodes vaporariorum; 3. cabbage white fly, Aleyrodes brassicae (proletella)
~ **Himbeere** f white raspberry, Rubus eriocarpus
~ **Johannisbeere** f white currant, Ribes rubrum
~ **Kohlrübe** f white-fleshed swede, Brassica napus var. napobrassica
~ **Lichtnelke** f white campion, (Am) white cockle, Silene alba, Melandrium album
~ **Lupine** f Egyptian lupin[e], Lupinus albus (termis)
~ **Maulbeere** f s. Weißer Maulbeerbaum

~ **Minze** f white peppermint, Mentha x piperita var. piperita f. pallescens
~ **Nachtnelke** f s. ~ Lichtnelke
~ **Nieswurz** f European white hellebore, false hellebore, Veratrum album
~ **Pestwurz** f white butterbur, Petasites albus
~ **Ramie** (bot) white ramie, Boehmeria nivea ssp. nivea
~ **Reseda** f white upright mignonette, Reseda alba
~ **Rose** f white cottage rose, Rosa x alba
~ **Rübe** f s. Wasserrübe
~ **Sapote** f (bot) white sapote, Casimiroa edulis
~ **Schleifenblume** f rock[et] candytuft, flowered candytuft, Iberis amara
~ **Seerose** f common white water lily, Nymphaea alba
~ **Sommerhyazinthe** f summer hyacinth, Galtonia candicans
~ **Taubnessel** f white dead nettle, flowering nettle, Lamium album
~ **Wucherblume** f [moon-]daisy, moon-flower, Chrysanthemum leucanthemum
~ **Wurzelfäule** f white root disease (esp. of Hevea brasiliensis, caused by Rigidoporus lignosus)
~ **Zaunrübe** f white bryony, Bryonia alba
Weißei n egg-white, [egg] albumen, egg albumin, glair[e]
Weißeiche f [American] white oak, chestnut (stave) oak, tanbark (Quebec) oak, Quercus alba
weißen to whitewash
Weißer Ackerkohl m (Am) hare's-ear [mustard], Conringia orientalis
~ **Affodil** m branching (branched) asphodel, Asphodelus albus
~ **Amur** m grass carp, white amur, Ctenopharyngodon idella
~ **Anischampignon** m horse-mushroom, Agaricus arvensis
~ **Bärenspinner** m (ent) fall web-worm, Hyphantria cunea
~ **Chrysanthemenrost** m white rust of chrysanthemum (caused by Puccinia horiana)
~ **Diptam** m dittany, fraxinella, (Am) burning bush, Dictamnus albus (fraxinella)
~ **Fuchsschwanz** m white pigweed, Amaranthus albus
~ **Gänsefuß** m white goose-foot, fat-hen, (Am) lamb's-quarters, Chenopodium album
~ **Germer** m false (European white) hellebore, Veratrum album
~ **Hartriegel** m 1. red osier [dogwood], Cornus sericea (stolonifera); 2. s. Tatarischer Hartriegel
~ **Hickory** m shagbark [hickory], bigbud (shellbark) hickory, scalebark, Carya ovata (alba)
~ **Jura** m (soil) malm
~ **Kamm** m (vet) white comb, fowl favus (caused by Trichophyton spp.)
~ **Kartoffelnematode** m s. Weißes Kartoffelzystenälchen

Weißer

~ **Kürbis** *m s.* Wachskürbis
~ **Maulbeerbaum** *m* white mulberry, Morus alba
~ **Rost** *m (phyt)* white rust *(caused by Albugo = Cystopus spp.)*
~ **Saxaul** *m (bot)* white saxoul, Haloxylon persicum
~ **Senf** *m* white mustard, Sinapis (Brassica) alba ssp. alba
~ **Sisal** *m* [white] henequen, Yucatan sisal, Agave fourcroydes
~ **Steinklee** *m* white sweet clover, white melilot, honey lotus, Melilotus alba
~ **Wau** *m s.* Weiße Reseda
~ **Weidenspinner** *m* willow (satin) moth, Leucoma (Stilpnotia) salicis
~ **Wiener** *m* Vienna White [rabbit] *(breed)*
Weißerle *f* [Norwegian] grey alder, speckled alder, Alnus incana
Weißes Bilsenkraut *n (bot)* white henbane, Hyoscyamus albus
~ **Kartoffelzystenälchen** *n* pale nematode of potato, Globodera (Heterodera) pallida
~ **Leghorn** *n* [White] Leghorn *(breed of fowl)*
~ **Neuseeländer Kaninchen** *n* New Zealand White [rabbit] *(breed)*
~ **Plymouth Rock** *n s.* White Rock
~ **Rhodeländer** *n* Rhode Island White *(breed of fowl)*
~ **Straußgras** *n* 1. fiorin[-grass], white bent[-grass], *(Am)* redtop, Agrostis gigantea; 2. creeping bent[-grass], Agrostis stolonifera (palustris)
~ **Yams** *n* white (eight months) Guinea yam, Dioscorea rotundata
Weißesche *f* white (American, Canadian) ash, Fraxinus americana
Weiße-Shorthorn-Krankheit *f s.* Weißfärsenkrankheit
Weißfärsenkrankheit *f (vet)* white heifer disease
Weißfäule *f (phyt)* white rot *(comprehensive term)*
~ **der Kartoffel** fusarium dry rot of potatoes *(caused by Fusarium spp.)*
~ **der Speisezwiebel (Zwiebel)** onion (bulb) white rot, white rot of onion *(caused by Sclerotium cepivorum)*
~ **der Zuckerrübe** white root rot [of sugar-beet] *(caused by Rosellinia necatrix)*
Weißfichte *f* [eastern] Canadian spruce, white spruce, Picea glauca (alba)
Weißfisch *m* white fish *(family Cyprinidae)*
Weißfischmehl *n* white fish meal *(feed-stuff)*
Weißfleckenkrankheit *f* **der Birne** leaf spot of pear *(caused by Mycosphaerella sentina)*
~ **der Erdbeere** strawberry leaf spot *(caused by Mycosphaerella fragariae)*
weißfleischig white-fleshed
Weißgegürtelte Rosenblattwespe *f* banded (curled) rose saw-fly, Allantus (Emphytus) cinctus
Weißgesichtsfuchs *m* white-face fox *(colour mutant)*

Weißgraue Strauchmelde *f* four-wing saltbush, Atriplex cana
Weißgummibaum *m (bot)* bursera *(genus Bursea)*
Weißhafer *m* white oat[s]
Weißherbst *m* pink wine
Weißholz *n* tension wood
Weißklee *m* white (Dutch, honeysuckle) clover, shamrock, Trifolium repens
Weißklee-Enationenvirus *n* white clover enation virus
Weißkleemosaikvirus *n* white clover mosaic virus, WCMV
Weißknospigkeit *f (phyt)* white bud
Weißkohl *m* white cabbage, Brassica oleracea [convar. capitata] var. capitata f. alba
Weißköpfiges Fleischschaf *n* German White-headed Mutton, White-headed German *(sheep breed)*
Weißkraut *m s.* Weißkohl
weißlich [werdend] *(bot, zoo)* albescent
Weißliche Akazie *f* silver wattle, silvergreen wattle [acacia], Acacia dealbata
Weißling *m* 1. albino; 2. *(ent)* pierid *(family Pieridae)*
Weißlupine *f* white lupin[e], Egyptian lupin[e], Lupinus albus (termis)
Weißmais *m* white maize
Weißmoosheide *f* moss-lichen pinery, Pinetum cladinosum
Weißmuskelkrankheit *f (vet)* white muscle disease, nutritional muscular dystrophy
Weißpappel *f* white (silver-leaf) poplar, abele, Populus alba
Weißrispigkeit *f (phyt)* silver-top[s]
Weißrost *m (phyt)* 1. white rust *(caused by Albugo = Cystopus spp.)*; 2. white blister *(caused by Albugo candida)*
weißschälen *(forest)* to clean-bark, to bark and bast
Weißschälen *n* barking in full
weißschnitzen *s.* weißschälen
Weißseuche *f* reclamation disease, yellow tip *(of cereals due to copper deficiency)*
Weißsirup *m* high-wash syrup *(sugar manufacture)*
Weißstammzirbe *f* Alpine white-bark pine, Pinus albicaulis
Weißtanne *f* silver fir, Abies alba (pectinata)
Weißtannenholz *n* whitewood
Weißtannenrüßler *m* fir weevil, Pissodes piceae
Weißtannenstammlaus *f* balsam woolly aphid, Dreyfusia piceae
Weißtannentrieblaus *f* silver fir aphid, balsam twig aphid, Mindarus abietinus
Weißtannentriebwickler *m (ent)* silver fir shoot tortricid, silver fir leaf-roller, Cacoecia murinana
Weißtorf *m* white (younger) peat
Weißulme *f* American (soft) elm, white (grey) elm, Ulmus americana

Weißwedelhirsch *m* white-tailed deer, Virginia (red) deer, Odocoileus virginianus
Weißweide *f* common (white) willow, Salix alba
Weißwein *m* white wine
~/geharzter [griechischer] retsina
Weißweizen *m* white wheat
weißwerdend albescent
Weißwurzeliger Diptam *m s.* Weißer Diptam
Weißzucker *m* refined sugar
~/granulierter table sugar
weitervermehren to grow on *(seed)*
weiterwachsend accrescent
weitmaschig wide-meshed
weitringig wide-ringed, open-grained, broad-zoned *(wood)*
weitständig sparse *(plant stand)*
Weitstrahlregner *m* large rainer, wide-range sprinkler
Weitverband *m (forest)* wide [plant] spacing
Weizen *m* wheat, corn *(genus Triticum)* • **aus ~ [hergestellt]** wheaten
~ für die Teigwarenherstellung pasta wheat
~/glasiger vitreous wheat
~/hartkörniger [glutenreicher] hard wheat
~ mit hohem Klebergehalt strong wheat
Weizenähre *f* cob
Weizenälchen *n* wheat nematode, ear cockle [eelworm], seed (flower) gall nematode, Anguina tritici
Weizenanbaubetrieb *m* wheat farm
Weizenbackschrot *m* coarse wheat meal
Weizenbier *n* wheat beer
Weizen-Brache-System *n* wheat-fallow system
Weizenbraunrost *m* brown rust of wheat, wheat leaf rust *(caused by Puccinia recondita = P. tritícina)*
Weizendunst *m* dunst *(milling)*
Weizeneule *f* white-line dart moth, Agrotis (Euxoa) tritici
Weizenfarm *f* wheat farm
Weizenflugbrand *m* loose smut of wheat, brown loose smut *(caused by Ustilago nuda)*
Weizenfuttermehl *n* wheatfeed flour, middlings
Weizengicht *f (phyt)* gout
Weizengluten *n* wheat gluten
Weizengrobmehl *n* corn meal
Weizengürtel *m*, **Weizenhauptanbaugebiet** *n* wheat belt
Weizenhirse *f* barnyard millet (grass), prickly (billion dollar) grass, Echinochloa crus-galli
Weizenkeim *m* wheat germ
Weizenkeimöl *n* wheat germ oil
Weizenkleber *m* wheat gluten
Weizenkleberprotein *n* wheat gluten protein
Weizenkleie *f* wheat bran, shorts
Weizenkorn *n* wheat [grain, kernel]
Weizenmalz *n* wheat malt, malted wheat
Weizenmalzmehl *n* wheat malt flour
Weizenmehl *n* [wheat] flour, corn meal

Weizenprotein *n* wheat protein
Weizenproteinkonzentrat *n* wheat protein concentrate
Weizenpülpe *f* wheat pulp
Weizen-Roggen-Bastard *m* wheat-rye hybrid, wheat x rye, triticale
Weizenrost *m* wheat rust *(comprehensive term)*
Weizenrostpilz *m* wheat rust [fungus]
Weizenschwarzrost *m* wheat stem rust, red robin [of wheat] *(caused by Puccinia graminis f.sp. tritici)*
Weizenstärke *f* wheat starch
Weizensteinbrand *m*, **Weizenstinkbrand** *m (phyt)* wheat bunt *(caused by Tilletia spp.)*
Weizenstrichelmosaikvirus *n* wheat streak mosaic virus, WSkMV
Weizenstroh *n* wheat straw
Weizenstrohlignin *n* wheat straw lignin
Weizenvermahlungsrückstand *m* wheat offal[s], wheatfeed
Weizenverzwergungsvirus *n* wheat dwarf virus
Weizenvollmehl *n* whole wheat meal
Welfe *m s.* Welpe
welk wilted, flaccid • **~ werden** *s.* welken • **~ werden lassen** to wilt
Welke *f s.* Welkekrankheit
Welkebereich *m* wilting range
Welkefeuchte *f*, **Welkefeuchtigkeit** *f* wilting moisture
Welkekrankheit *f (phyt)* wilt [disease], wilting
~ des Salates lettuce drop *(caused by Sclerotinia sclerotiorum)*
welken to wilt, to fade, to wither, to blast
Welken *n* wilting • **zum ~ bringen** to wilt
~ der Nelkenblüten/vorzeitiges sleepiness of carnation *(injurious effect of ethylene)*
~/permanentes permanent wilting
Welkepunkt *m* wilting point (coefficient)
~/permanenter permanent wilting percentage (point), PWP
Welketod *m* ultimate wilting
Welkfutter *n* wilted forage
Welkgrassilage *f* wilted-grass silage
Welkguttrockner *m* barn hay dryer
Welkguttrocknung *f* barn hay drying
Welksilage *f* [pre]wilted silage, low-moisture silage
Wellblattfunkie *f* plantain lily, Hosta undulata
Wellblechgetreidesilo *n* corrugated grain bin
Welldränrohr *n* corrugated drain-pipe
Welle *f* 1. wave; 2. arbor, shaft; 3. *s.* Wellengebinde
Wellenbinder *m*, **Wellenbock** *m* faggot-binder
Wellengebinde *n*, **Wellengebund** *n* faggot, bavin, bundle of copse (twigs), brushwood in bundles
Wellenkupplung *f* clutch
Wellenwuchs *m* wavy grain *(of wood)*
~/unregelmäßiger interrupted wavy grain
wellenwüchsig wavy-grown
wellig *(bot, zoo)* undate

Welliger

Welliger Fingerhut *m* Grecian foxglove, Digitalis lanata
Wellingtonia *f s.* Sequoie
Welpe *m* whelp, pup, cub, [hound-]puppy; fox-cub, young fox, kit[ten]
Wels *m* 1. catfish *(suborder Siluroides)*; 2. sheatfish, wels, Silurus glanis
Welsche Mispel *f (bot)* azarole, Crataegus azarolus
Welscher Lavendel *m* Arabian lavender, Lavandula stoechas
~ **Walnußbaum** *m* Persian walnut, Madeira nut, Juglans regia ssp. regia
~ **Weizen** *m* poulard (English) wheat, rivet [wheat], cone (turgid) wheat, Triticum turgidum
Welsches Weidelgras *n* [Italian] rye-grass, Lolium multiflorum
Welschkohl *m* savoy [cabbage], Brassica oleracea var. sabauda
Welsh Black *n* Welsh Black *(cattle breed)*
~ **Cob** *n* Welsh Cob *(horse breed)*
~ **Corgi Cardigan** *m* [Cardigan Welsh] corgi *(dog breed)*
~ **Corgi Pembroke** *m* Pembroke [Welsh corgi], corgi *(dog breed)*
~ **Halfbred[-Schaf]** *n* Welsh Halfbred *(cross between Border Leicester and Welsh Mountain)*
~ **Mountain** *n* Welsh [Mountain] *(sheep breed)*
~ **Mountain-Pony** *n* Welsh Mountain pony *(breed)*
~ **Pony** *n* Welsh pony *(breed)*
~ **Springer Spaniel** *m* Welsh springer [spaniel] *(dog breed)*
~ **Terrier** *m* Welsh terrier *(dog breed)*
Welternährungssituation *f* world food situation
Weltforstatlas *m* world forestry atlas
Weltgetreideerzeugung *f* world grain production
Weltgetreidehandel *m* world grain trade
Weltgetreidemarkt *m* world grain market
Weltlandwirtschaft *f* world agriculture
Weltverbrauch *m* world consumption
Wendeaxt *f* double[-bitted] axe, double-bladed axe
Wendeblume *f* Persian clover, Trifolium resupinatum
Wendehaken *m (forest)* cant-hook, cant-dog, *(Am)* peav[e]y, peavie
Wendekreis *m* turning cycle
wenden to turn [about] *(e.g. hay)*
Wendener Drehkrankheit *f* X disease *(of cattle after uptaking chlorated naphthalenes)*
Wenderadius *m* turning radius
Wendezeit *f* turning time
Wendung *f*/**kreisförmige** volt[e] *(equitation)*
wenigblättrig *(bot)* oligophyllous, paucifolious
wenigblühend *(bot)* rariflorous
wenigblütig *(bot)* pauciflorous
wenigfrüchtig *(bot)* oligocarpous
wenigfüßig *(zoo)* oligopod
Wensleydale[schaf] *n* Wensleydale *(sheep breed)*
werben/Heu to [make] hay, to win

Werbeverhalten *n*, **Werbung** *f* courtship behaviour *(of animals)*
werfen 1. to throw, to cast; 2. to bring forth, to give birth; to drop; to cub *(game)*; to kindle *(rabbit, hare)*; to kitten; to fawn *(red deer)*; to whelp, to litter, to pup *(bitch)*; to farrow [down], to pig *(sow)*
Werftbohrkäfer *m (ent)* wharf borer, Nacerda melanura
Werkmilch *f* processing (manufacturing) milk
Werkstattwagen *m* maintenance (workshop) truck
Werkzeugrahmen *m* tool frame
Werkzeugschiene *f* tool-bar
Werkzeugschuppen *m* tool shed
Werkzeugträger *m s.* Werkzeugschiene
Wermut *m* 1. [common] wormwood, Artemisia absinthium; 2. *s.* Wermutwein
Wermutblättrige Ambrosie *f* common ragweed, Ambrosia artemisiifolia
Wermutessenz *f* absinth
Wermutöl *n* wormwood oil
Wermutwein *m* vermouth
~/**italienischer** it
~/**weißer** vermouth
Wert *m*/**energetischer** energy value *(e.g. of a feed)*
~/**kalorischer** caloric (calorific) value
~/**osmotischer** osmotic value
Wertastung *f (forest)* pruning for quality
Wertentwicklung *f s.* Wertzuwachs
Wertholz *n* high-grade timber, primary (superior) timber, fine wood, showwood
Wertholzerziehung *f s.* Wertholzzucht
Wertholzzucht *f* production of high-grade timber
~ **bei Buche** silviculture of high-quality beech
Wertleistung *f (forest)* value (quality) production
Wertminderung *f* depreciation
Wertzuwachs *m (forest)* value increment
WESMV s. Europäisches Streifiges Mosaikvirus des Weizens
Wespe *f* wasp *(genus Vespa)*
Wespennest *n* vespiary
Wesselbron-Krankheit *f* Wesselbron disease *(sheep virosis)*
Wessex-Saddleback *n* Wessex [Saddleback], Sheeted *(pig breed)*
West Highland White Terrier *m* West Highland white terrier *(dog breed)*
Westamerikanische Hemlocktanne *f* 1. western hemlock (spruce), Pacific hemlock, West Coast hemlock, Tsuga heterophylla; 2. mountain (black) hemlock, weeping spruce, Tsuga mertensiana
~ **Lärche** *f* western larch (tamarack), Larix occidentalis
~ **Pflaume** *f* Klamath (Pacific) plum, Prunus subcordata
Westerwoldisches Weidelgras *n* Westerwolds (annual, Swiss) rye-grass, Lolium multiflorum var. westerwoldicum

Westindische Haselnuß f sword bean, Entada phaseoloides (scandens)
~ **Kirsche** f Barbados cherry, acerola, Malpighia glabra
~ **Zeder** f Honduras (bastard Barbados) cedar, Cedrela odorata (mexicana)
Westindischer Brotnußbaum m bread-nut [tree], Brosimum alicastrum
~ **Indigo** m West Indian indigo, anil indigo, Indigofera suffruticosa
Westliche Balsampappel f black cottonwood, Populus trichocarpa
~ **Pferdeenzephalomyelitis** f (vet) western equine encephalomyelitis
~ **Platane** f eastern sycamore, Platanus occidentalis
Westliches Rübenvergilbungsvirus n beet western yellow virus, BWYV
Wetter n weather
Wetterbeeinflussung f weather modification
Wetterbeobachtung f weather observation
Wetterbeobachtungssatellit m weather satellite
Wetterbericht m weather report
Wetterdatenerfassung f weather record
Wetterdienst m weather service
wetterfest weather-resistant
Wetterfestigkeit f weather resistance
Wetterfront f front
Wetterhütte f weather-instrument shelter, weather observation hut
Wetterkarte f weather chart (map)
Wetterkunde f meteorology
Wetterlage f weather pattern, meteorological conditions
Wetterleuchten n sheet-lightning, summer lightning
Wetterprognose f s. Wettervorhersage
Wetterstation f weather station
Wetterverhältnisse pl weather conditions
Wettervorhersage f weather (meteorological) forecast, weather prediction
~/**kurzfristige** short-term weather forecast
~/**langfristige** long-range weather forecast
Wetterschaden m weather damage
Wetterschicht f troposphere (of atmosphere)
Wetterwarte f weather observatory
Wetterwechsel m weather fluctuation, change in the weather
Wetzstein m whetstone, [scythe] stone; grindstone
• **mit dem ~ schärfen** to stone
WeUGMV s. Ungarisches Gelbmosaikvirus der Weinrebe
Weymouthskiefer f [eastern] white pine, Weymouth (yellow, Quebec) pine, Pinus strobus
Weymouthskiefernblasenrost m [white pine] blister rust (caused by Cronartium ribicola)
Weymouthskiefernrindenlaus f pine bark adelges (aphid), Pineus strobi
wf s. wasserfrei

WFS s. Wasserfreiraum
Whewellit m whewellite (non-clay mineral)
Whippet m whippet (dog breed)
Whiptail-Erkrankung f s. Peitschenstielerkrankung
Whirlpool m whirlpool (brewing)
Whisky m whisk[e]y
White Rock n White [Plymouth] Rock (breed of fowl)
Whiteside-Test m Whiteside test (of mastitis detection)
Whitten-Effekt m Whitten effect (of pheromons on oestrous cycle)
Wichte f density
Wichtungskoeffizient m s. Wägungsfaktor
Wicke f vetch (genus Vicia)
Wickel m (bot) scorpioid cyme
Wickelballen m round bale
Wickelballenauflösegerät n bale unroller
Wickelballenpresse f round (roll) baler, roto-baler
Wickenlaus f vetch aphid, Megoura viciae
Wickgras n vetch grass (fodder mixture)
Wickheu n vetch hay
Wickler m leaf-roller [moth], tortricid [moth], tortrix [moth] (family Tortricidae)
Wicklerlarve f budworm, leaf-roller
Wicklinse f one-flowered vetch, Vicia articulata
Widder m ram, tup
~/**hydraulischer** [hydraulic] ram
~/**kastrierter** wether
Widderlamm n ram lamb
Widderwolle f ram's wool
Widerhäkchen n (bot) glochidium
widerhakig glochiate
Widerrist m withers
Widerristfistel f (vet) fistulous withers
Widerristhöhe f withers height, height at withers
Widersacher m antagonist
Widersachertum n (ecol) antibiosis, opponency, antagonism
widersetzlich restive, intractable, obstreperous, refractory
Widersetzlichkeit f restiveness, vice
widerspenstig s. widersetzlich
Widerstandserwärmung f resistance heating (e.g. for timber drying)
widerstandsfähig resistant (e.g. to temperature, to infection); robust (e.g. body condition); hardy (e.g. plants) • ~ **machen** to harden
Widerstandsfähigkeit f resistance; robustness; hardiness
~ **gegenüber Chemikalien** chemical resistance
~ **gegenüber Termiten** termite resistance
Widerstandspsychrometer n resistance psychrometer
Widerstandsthermometer n resistance thermometer
Widerstoß m [common] sea lavender, statice, Limonium vulgare

Widerton

Widerton *m s.* Haarmoos
Wiedehopfhaue *f (forest)* planting hatchet, axe-mattock
wiederanstecken *(phyt, vet)* to reinfect
Wiederansteckung *f* reinfection
wiederaufblühen to reflourish
Wiederaufblühen *n* reflorescence
wiederaufforsten to re[af]forest, to restock
Wiederaufforstung *f* re[af]forestation, forest restoration, restocking
Wiederauffütterung *f* realimentation
Wiederaufsaugung *f* reabsorption
Wiederauftreten *n (phyt, vet)* recurrence, recurrency
Wiederaufwuchs *m* regrowth, flush
Wiederaufwuchsbekämpfung *f* regrowth control
Wiederaustrieb *m* [late-season] regrowth
Wiederbefall *m* reinfestation
wiederbegründen to re-establish *(e.g. a forest stand)*
Wiederbegrünung *f* revegetation
wiederbesiedeln to recolonize
wiederbestocken, wiederbewalden *s.* wiederaufforsten
wiederblühend *(bot)* remontant
Wiedereinbürgerung *f* reintroduction, repatriation, reacclimatization *(e.g. of game)*
Wiedererkrankung *f (phyt, vet)* recurrence, recurrency
Wiedergewinnung *f* recovery
Wiederherstellung *f* regeneration, restitution
Wiederholbarkeit *f (biom)* repeatability
Wiederholbarkeitskoeffizient *m* repeatability coefficient, coefficient of repeatability
Wiederholung *f* replication, repetition, repeat *(experimentation)*
~/teilweise fractional replication
Wiederholungsanzahl *f* number of replications (repetitions)
Wiederholungsbesamung *f* repeat insemination
wiederholungsfrei *(biom)* unreplicated
Wiederholungsimpfung *f (vet)* revaccination
Wiederholungskoeffizient *m (biom)* repeatability coefficient
Wiederholungstrieb *m (bot)* paraclade
Wiederkauakt *m* rumination
wiederkäuen to ruminate, to chew the cud
Wiederkäuen *n* rumination, cudding
wiederkäuend ruminant
Wiederkäuer *m* ruminant [animal] *(suborder Ruminantia)*
Wiederkäuerernährung *f* ruminant nutrition
Wiederkäuerfütterung *f* ruminant feeding
Wiederkäuermagen *m* ruminant stomach
Wiederurbarmachung *f* reclamation
wiegen to weigh
wiehern to neigh, to nicker, to whinny
Wiehern *n* neigh, nicker
Wielkopolska *m* Wielkopolski *(horse breed)*

Wiese *f* meadow
~/einschürige one-cut meadow
~/künstliche artificial (sown) meadow
~/natürliche native meadow
~/zweischürige two-cuts meadow
Wiesenampfer *m (bot)* sorrel, Rumex acetosa
wiesenartig meadowy
Wiesenbau *m* meadow cultivation
Wiesenbocksbart *m* [yellow] goat's-beard, meadow salsify, Tragopogon pratensis
Wiesenboden *m* meadow (grassland) soil, gley [soil], glei
Wiesenchampignon *m* [common field] mushroom, champignon, Agaricus campester (campestris, arvensis)
Wiesenegge *f* grass (pasture) harrow
Wiesenflockenblume *f* meadow (brown, black) knapweed, Centaurea jacea
Wiesenfuchsschwanz *m* meadow foxtail[-grass], common foxtail, Alopecurus pratensis
Wiesengerste *f* meadow barley grass, Hordeum secalinum
Wiesenhafer *m* meadow oat[-grass], perennial oat[s], Avenula pratensis, Helictotrichon pratense
Wiesenheu *n* meadow (grass) hay
Wiesenkalk *m* meadow limestone, bog lime
Wiesenkammgras *n (bot)* crested dog's-tail, Cynosurus cristatus
Wiesenkerbel *m* wild (cow) chervil, hare's (cow) parsley, Anthriscus sylvestris
Wiesenkerbelvergilbungsvirus *n* anthriscus yellows virus
Wiesenklee *m* red clover, Trifolium pratense
Wiesenknopf *m (bot)* burnet *(genus Sanguisorba)*
Wiesenknöterich *m* snake-weed, bistort, Polygonum bistorta
Wiesenkohl *m* cabbage thistle, Cirsium oleraceum
Wiesenkümmel *m* caraway, Carum carvi
Wiesenlabkraut *n* hedge (white) bedstraw, Galium mollugo
Wiesenlieschgras *n* timothy [grass], hurd's grass, Phleum pratense
Wiesenmargerite *f* marguerite, ox-eye [daisy], white ox-eye, moon flower (daisy), whiteweed, horse gowan, Chrysanthemum leucanthemum
Wiesennarbe *f* meadow sward
Wiesenobstanlage *f* meadow orchard
Wiesenpflanze *f* meadow plant
Wiesenpflug *m* meadow plough
Wiesenpflugkörper *m* grassland (ley, match) body
Wiesenpippau *f (bot)* rough hawk's-beard, Crepis biennis
Wiesenplatterbse *f* meadow vetchling, Lathyrus pratensis
Wiesenralle *f (zoo)* corncrake, landrail, Crex crex (pratensis)
Wiesenraute *f* meadow rue *(genus Thalictrum)*
Wiesenrispe *f*, **Wiesenrispengras** *n* smooth-stalked meadow grass, *(Am)* [Kentucky] blue grass, Poa pratensis

Wiesenritzer *m* pasture ripper
Wiesenroßkümmel *m* pepper saxifrage, Silaum silaus
Wiesenrotklee *m* wild red clover, Trifolium pratense var. spontaneum subvar. perenne
Wiesensalbei *m* meadow clary (sage), Salvia pratensis
Wiesensauerampfer *m (bot)* sorrel, Rumex acetosa
Wiesenschaumkraut *n* cuckoo flower, hairy bittercress, Canterbury-bell[s], lady-smock, Cardamine pratensis
Wiesenschaumzikade *f* meadow spittle bug, Philaenus spumarius
Wiesenschleppe *f* pasture scraper-leveller
Wiesenschnake *f* [marsh, common] crane-fly, Tipula paludosa
Wiesenschwarzerde *f* chernozem meadow soil
Wiesenschwingel *m* meadow fescue [grass], randall grass, Festuca pratensis
Wiesenstorchschnabel *m* meadow geranium (crane's-bill), Geranium pratense
Wiesensumpfhuhn *n s.* Wiesenralle
Wiesentrespe *f* upright brome[-grass], erect brome[-grass], meadow brome[-grass], Bromus erectus
Wiesenumbruchverfahren *n* meadow-kill treatment
Wiesenwalze *f* grassland roller
Wiesenwanze *f* tarnish[ed] plant bug, Lygus pratensis
Wiesenwurm *m (ent)* crane-fly grub, leather-jacket
WiKVV *s.* Wiesenkerbelvergilbungsvirus
Wilcoxon-Test *m* **für gepaarte Stichproben** *(biom)* Wilcoxon's matched pair rank test, signed rank test
wild 1. wild, uncultivated *(plant)*; wild, feral, undomesticated, untamed *(animal)*; 2. wild, savage, fierce *(animal)*
Wild *n* game, wildlife, venery • **nach ~ riechend** gam[e]y • **nach ~ schmeckend** gam[e]y
~/gejagtes chase
~/jagdbares fair (warrantable) game, fur and feather, beast [of chase]
~/nichtjagdbares non-game wildlife
~/paarhufiges hoofed game
Wildacker *m* cultivated deer pasture, food patch
Wildallel *n (gen)* wild-type allele
Wildapfel[baum] *m* crab[-apple], wild apple, Malus sylvestris ssp. sylvestris
Wildart *f* wild species
wildartig gam[e]y
Wildäsungsfläche *f* game pasture
Wildaurikel *f (bot)* bear's ear, Primula auricula
Wildbach *m* [mountain, hill] torrent, burn
Wildbachschlucht *f* ravine
Wildbachverbauung *f* torrent training (control), regulation (damming) of a torrent
Wildbahn *f* hunting-ground • **in freier ~** in the wild, in the open

Wildbesatz *m* stock of game
Wildbestand *m* game population, wildlife, stock of game
Wildbestandsermittlung *f* game survey
Wildbete *f* sea beet, Beta vulgaris ssp. maritima
Wildbewirtschaftung *f* game management
Wildbiologie *f* game biology
Wildbiotopbewirtschaftung *f* wildlife habitat management
Wildbirne *f* 1. wild pear, pearl wood, Pyrus pyraster ssp. pyraster; 2. wild pear, Pyrus pyraster ssp. achras
Wildbret *n* venison, game [meat]
wildbretartig gam[e]y
Wildbretproduktion *f* **je Flächeneinheit** area-kill
Wilddieb *m* poacher
Wilddieberei *f* poaching • **~ treiben** to poach
Wilde Blasenkirsche *f* Chinese-lantern [plant], Physalis alkekengi
~ Möhre *f* [wild] carrot, Queen Anne's lace, Daucus carota
~ Mohrenhirse *f* Aleppo (Johnson, Tunis) grass, Sorghum halepense
~ Olive *f s.* Wilder Ölbaum
~ Runkelrübe *f* sea beet, Beta vulgaris ssp. maritima
~ Tamarinde *f (bot)* white popinac, leucaena, Leucaena leucocephala
~ Zichorie *f* wild chic[k]ory, Cichorium intybus var. intybus
Wildeinkorn *n*, **Wildeinkornweizen** *m* wild einkorn [wheat], Triticum boeoticum
Wildemmer *m s.* Wilder Emmer
Wildente *f* wild duck *(comprehensive term)*
~/junge flapper
Wilder Dost *m* common origanum (marjoram), wild (perennial) marjoram, Origanum vulgare
~ Emmer *m* [common] wild emmer, Triticum dicoccoides
~ Fenchel *m* sweet anise, Foeniculum vulgare var. vulgare
~ Hafer *m* slender [wild] oat, Avena barbata
~ Lattich *m* prickly (common wild) lettuce, Lactuca serriola (scariola)
~ Majoran *m s.* Wilder Dost
~ Ölbaum *m* oleaster, wild olive, Olea europaea ssp. sylvestris
~ Roter Reis *m* red rice, Oryza rufipogon
~ Senf *m* [yellow] charlock, wild mustard, field kale, Sinapis arvensis
~ Spinat *m* Good King Henry, allgood, fat-hen, Chenopodium bonus-henricus
~ Strauchkohl *m s.* Wildkohl
~ Wein *m* woodbine, woodbind, wild honeysuckle, American ivy, *(Am)* Virginia creeper, Parthenocissus quinquefolia
Wilderer *m* poacher
wildern to poach
Wildes Stiefmütterchen *n* pansy, *(Am)* Johnny-jump-up, Viola tricolor

Wildes

~ **Zuckerrohr** *n* wild cane, Saccharum spontaneum
Wildfarm *f* game farm
Wildfauna *f* wild fauna, wildlife
Wildfeuer *n* wildfire
Wildfeuererkrankung *f* **des Tabaks** 1. angular leaf spot of tobacco, blackfire *(caused by Pseudomonas angulata)*; 2. wildfire, bacterial leaf spot of tobacco *(caused by Pseudomonas tabaci)*
Wildform *f* wild form; original *(of a breed)*
~/**pflanzliche** *s.* Wildpflanze
Wildfraßschaden *m* game damage
Wildfutterpflanze *f* browse plant
Wildfütterung *f* wildlife feeding
Wildgans *f* wild goose *(comprehensive term)*
Wildgatter *n* fencing, enclosure, holding paddock
Wildgebiet *n* wildlife area
Wildgeflügel *n* wildfowl, feathered game, wing[ed] game, game-birds
Wildgehölz *n* wild woody plant
Wildhafer *m* wild oat[s] *(comprehensive term)*
Wildhege *f* gamekeeping, game conservation (preserving)
Wildheger *m* gamekeeper
Wildhopfen *m* wild hop
Wildhüter *m* gamekeeper
Wildkalb *n* fawn, young deer
Wildkaninchen *n* [wild] rabbit, con[e]y, Oryctolagus cuniculus
Wildkarpfen *m* wild carp
Wildkatze *f* wild cat, Felis sylvestris
Wildkohl *m* wild cabbage, collard, Brassica oleracea convar. oleracea var. oleracea
Wildkunde *f* game science
wildlebend wild
Wildling *m s.* Wildpflanze
Wildnis *f* wilderness
Wildpark *m* game-preserve, wildlife (game) park
Wildpastinak *m* wild parsnip *(wild form of Pastinaca sativa)*
Wildpferd *n* wild horse; brumby, warrigal *(Australia)*
Wildpflanze *f* wild plant (stock), wild[l]ing; *(forest)* non-lined-out plant
Wildpopulation *f* game population
Wildpute *f* wild turkey, Meleagris gallo-pavo
wildreich gam[e]y, abounding in game
Wildreis *m* [American, small-seeded] wild rice, Indian (Tuscarora) rice, Zizania aquatica
Wildreservat *n* wildlife refuge (reserve), game reserve (sanctuary)
Wildrind *n* wild ox (cattle) *(comprehensive term)*
Wildsau *f* wild sow
Wildschaden *m* game damage, damage by game
Wildschadenbewertung *f* game damage evaluation
Wildschadenverhütung *f* prevention of game damage
Wildschaf *n* moufflon ewe
Wildschongebiet *n s.* Wildschutzgebiet
Wildschutz *m* wildlife conservation
Wildschutzbeauftragter *m* game commissioner
Wildschutzgebiet *n* game reserve (sanctuary), sanctuary
Wildschwein *n* wild boar (hog), Sus scrofa ssp. scrofa
~/**junges** wild piglet
Wildtier *n* wild animal, wild[l]ing, beast, brute
Wildtierbestand *m s.* Wildbestand
Wildtierfarm *f* game farm
Wildtierpark *m s.* Wildpark
Wildtrieb *m* wild shoot
Wildtyp *m* wild type
Wildtypallel *n (gen)* wild-type allele
Wildverbiß *m* browsing [by game]
Wildverbiß... *s.* Verbiß...
Wildvogel *m* wild (game) bird
wildwachsend [growing] wild, volunteer, natural, spontaneous
Wildwechsel *m* game crossing, pass, run[way], travel lane, trace
Wildwirtschaft *f* wildlife (game) management
Wildzaun *m* deer fence
Wildziege *f* wild goat
Wilson-Blair-Agar *m* bismuth sulphite agar
Wilsonsche Krankheit *f (vet)* Wilson's disease, hepatolenticular degeneration
Wiltshire Horn *n* Wiltshire Horn *(sheep breed)*
Wimmerwuchs *m* wavy grain *(of timber)*
~/**unregelmäßiger** interrupted wavy grain, finger roll
Wimper *f* cilium
Wimperlarve *f* miracidium *(of flukes)*
Wimpertierchen *n* ciliate *(class Ciliata)*
Wind *m* wind • **durch ~ erzeugt** wind-borne • **vom ~ geworfen** wind-thrown *(tree)*
~/**lokaler** local wind
~/**starker** strong breeze
~/**steifer** moderate gale
~/**stürmischer** fresh gale
Windabsatzboden *m* aeolian soil
Windausbreitung *f s.* Windverbreitung
Windbelastung *f* wind loading
windbeständig wind-resistant
Windbeständigkeit *f* wind resistance
windbestäubt *(bot)* wind-pollinated, anemophilous, anemogamous
Windbestäubung *f* wind pollination, anemophily
windblütig *s.* windbestäubt
Windbruch *m (forest)* 1. windbreak[age], windthrow, windblow, blowdown; 2. *s.* Windbruchholz
Windbruchfläche *f* windfall
Windbruchholz *n* wind-fallen wood, rolled timber (lumber), blowdowns
windbrüchig wind-fallen
windbruchsicher windfirm, wind-resistant
Winddruck *m* wind pressure

Winde f 1. bindweed, convolvulus, *(Am)* morning glory *(genus Convolvulus)*; 2. winch; hoist; capstan
Windei n wind-egg, mole
Windel f *(api)* floorboard
winden 1. *(hunter's language)* to scent, to wind *(game)*; 2. to bind, to make [up] *(flowers into a wreath)*
~/sich to [en]twine, to wind *(e.g. a plant)*
Windende Osterluzei f *(bot)* [common] Dutchman's pipe, Aristolochia macrophylla (durior)
Windenergie f wind energy
Windengewächse npl morning glory family *(family Convolvulaceae)*
Windenknöterich m black (field, ivy) bindweed, wild buckwheat, creeping jenny, dull-seed cornbind, Fallopia (Polygonum) convolvulus
Windepflanze f creeping plant, creeper
Winderosion f wind erosion, deflation, aeolation
Windfahne f wind vane
Windfall m s. Windbruch
Windfege f s. Windsichter
windfest windfirm, wind-resistant
Windfestigkeit f wind resistance
Windgalle f *(vet)* wind gall (puff)
windgepeitscht wind-whipped
Windgeschwindigkeit f wind speed (velocity)
Windgeschwindigkeitsmesser m anemometer
Windgeschwindigkeitsschreiber m anemograph
Windhafer m [common] wild oat[s], Avena fatua
Windhalm m wind (corn) grass, [loose] silky-bent, Apera spica-venti
Windhund m greyhound *(breed)*
Windhündin f greybitch
windig windy
Windkanter m *(soil)* ventifact
Windkraft f wind power
Windkraftanlage f wind machine, windmill
Windkraftgenerator windmill generator
Windkraftpumpe f wind-driven pump
Windmantel m s. Windschutzschirm
Windmaschine f wind machine *(e.g. for frost protection in orchards)*
Windmesser m, **Windmeßgerät** n wind-gauge, anemometer
Windmessung f wind measurement, anemometry
Windmühle f windmill
~/holländische smock-mill
Windmulde f blow-out *(in loose soil)*
Windrad n wind generator; fan-wheel
Windrichtung f wind direction
Windriß m wind (cup) shake, ring shake (failure) *(timber defect)*
Windröschen n wind-flower, anemone, anemony *(genus Anemone)*
Windschaden m wind damage (injury, blast)
Windschiefe f winding *(e.g. of seasoned timber)*
Windschirm m s. Windschutzschirm

Windschliff m *(soil)* corrasion
Windschnappen n wind-sucking *(vice of horses)*
Windschnapper m wind-sucker
Windschreiber m anemograph
Windschutz m 1. wind protection; 2. s. Windschutzschirm
windschützend wind-protective
Windschutzpflanzung f wind-break, *(Am)* windbreaker
Windschutzschirm m *(forest)* wind mantle (screen, break)
Windschutzstreifen m shelter-belt, protective belt (forest strip), wind-break, breakwind *(Australia)*
Windsediment n *(soil)* wind (aeolian) deposit
Windseite f weather side
Windseparator m s. Windsichter
Windsichter m air sifter (sifting machine), air separator (classifier), pneumatic deduster; [grain] winnower, winnowing seed cleaner
Windsichtung f air sifting (separation, classification), air floating (elutriation)
Windsiebsichter m fanning mill, air-screen cleaner, air-and-screen machine
Windsortierung f s. Windsichtung
Windstärke f wind-force, wind strength (intensity)
windstill calm, windless
Windstille f calm
~/völlige dead calm
Windstoß m gust, squall
windverbreitet *(bot)* anemochorous
Windverbreitung f anemochory
Windverstellung f fan speed variator, fan control, wind adjustment *(of thresher)*
Windweg m run of the wind
Windwiderstand m wind resistance
Windwurf m s. Windbruch
Winkeldrehpflug m quarter-turn plough
Winkel[hack]messer m L-blade
Winkelmessersech n knee coulter
winkelnervig *(bot)* angulinerved
Winkelpflanzung f *(forest)* angle planting, T-notching
Winkelplanierer m angledozer
Winkelprisma n prismatic (optical) square
Winkelriedgras n remote sedge, Carex remota
Winkelschar n angle blade, half shovel (sweep); share with a cheek
Winkelschlagleiste f angle bar *(of thresher)*
Winkelspiegel m s. Winkelprisma
Winkelzählprisma n prism wedge *(for timber mensuration)*
Winkelzählprobe f *(forest)* prism-count method, [Bitterlich] angle-count method, Bitterlich method [of cruising], variable-radius method, enumeration sweep
Winter m winter • **den ~ überdauernd** hibernal • **für den ~ unterbringen** to in-winter *(e.g. animals)* • **über den ~ bringen** to winter; to hog *(young sheep)* • **über den ~ kommen** to

Winteranbauzeit

[over]winter, to pass the winter *(s. a.* über-wintern*)*
Winteranbauzeit *f* rabi *(in India)*
winterannuell winter annual
Winterannuelle *f* winter (hardy) annual
Winteraster *f* chrysanth[emum], Chrysanthemum indicum
Winterblüte *f* winter flower, Chimonanthus praecox
Winterbohnenkraut *n* winter (perennial) savory, Satureja montana
Winterbrache *f* winter fallow
Winterbrand *m (phyt)* hold-over canker
Winterbutter *f* winter (hay) butter
Winterei *n* winter egg
Wintereiche *f* durmast [oak], sessile (stalkless-flowered) oak, Quercus petraea (sessiliflora)
wintereinjährig *s.* winterannuell
Wintereinfütterung *f (api)* autumn feeding
Wintereinstand *m* winter range *(of game)*; deer yard • **den ~ aufsuchen** to yard
Winterendivie *f* [winter] endive, escarole, Cichorium endivia
Winterfederkleid *n* winter (wintry) plumage
winterfest *s.* winterhart
Winterflughafer *m* winter wild oat, Avena sterilis [ssp. ludoviciana]
Winterfrost *m* winter frost
Winterfrucht *f* winter-planted crop; rabi *(in India)*
Winterfurche *f* winter furrow
Winterfutter *n* winter feed (fodder, forage)
Winterfuttergetreide *n* winter feed grain
Winterfütterung *f* winter feeding
Wintergarten *m* winter garden, conservatory
Wintergemüse *n* winter vegetable[s]
Wintergerste *f* winter barley
Wintergetreide *n* winter cereal (grain, corn), autumn[-sown] cereal
Wintergetreideart *f* winter cereal (grain)
Wintergras *n* fog • **~ stehen lassen** to fog
wintergrün evergreen
Wintergrün *n (bot)* 1. wintergreen, pyrola *(genus Pyrola)*; 2. wintergreen, mountain tea, Gaultheria procumbens
Wintergrünöl *n* sweet birch oil *(fungicide)*
Winterhaarkleid *n* winter [hair] coat, winter hair covering
Winterhafer *m* winter oat[s]
winterhart winter-hardy, cold-resistant, [cold] hardy
~/nicht tender
Winterhärte *f* winter hardiness, cold resistance
Winterjasmin *m* winter jasmin[e], Jasminum nudiflorum
Winterkalbung *f* winter calving
Winterkleid *n s.* 1. Winterhaarkleid; 2. Winterfederkleid
Winterkohl *m* winter cabbage, Brassica oleracea var. acephala

Winterkresse *f* winter (rocket) cress, yellow rocket, scurvy-grass, Barbarea vulgaris
Winterkultur *f* winter crop
Winterlagerung *f* overwintering (winter cold) storage *(e.g. of seedlings)*
Winterlammung *f* winter lambing
Winterlauch *m* 1. leek, Allium porrum; 2. *s.* Winterzwiebel
Winterlieb *n (bot)* pipsissewa *(genus Chimaphila)*
Winterlinde *f* small-leaved lime (linden), lime, little-leaf linden, Tilia cordata (parvifolia)
Winterling *m (bot)* 1. winter aconite *(genus Eranthis)*; 2. winter aconite, Eranthis hyemalis
Wintermast *f* winter fattening
Wintermelone *f* winter melon, Cucumis melo con-var. zard
Wintermilch *f* winter milk
Winterniederschlag *m* winter precipitation
Winterpelz *m* winter fur
Winterpilz *m s.* Winterrübling
Winterquartier *n (zoo)* hibernacle, hibernaculum
Winterrahm *m* winter cream
Winterraps *m* winter [oil-seed] rape
Winterrauhfutter *n* winter fodder (forage)
Winterrebe *f* 1. chicken (frost) grape, Vitis vulpina (cordifolia); 2. Spanish grape, Vitis berlandieri
Winterrettich *m s.* Rettich 2.
Winterrinde *f (bot)* Winter's bark, Drimys winteri
Winterrindenbrand *m* winter bark scorch
Winterroggen *m* winter (autumn) rye, *(Am)* fall rye
Winterrübling *m* velvet-stemmed agaric, winter mushroom, Flammulina velutipes
Winterruhe *f* winter dormancy, winter rest [period]
Wintersaat *f* winter-planted crop
Wintersaateule *f* turnip (common dart) moth, Scotia (Agrotis) segetum
Wintersaateulenraupe *f* turnip moth cutworm
Winterschachtelhalm *m* scouring-rush, scrub (shave) grass, Equisetum hyemale
Winterschlaf *m* winter sleep, hibernation • **~ halten** to hibernate • **~ haltend** dormant
Winterschläfer *m* hibernator, sleeper
Winterschneeheide *f* Irish heath, Erica erigena (mediterranea)
Winterschnitt *m* winter (dormant) pruning *(orcharding)*
Winterschur *f* winter shearing
Winterschutz *m* winter protection *(e.g. for woody ornamentals)*
Wintersonnenwende *f* winter solstice
Winterspargel *m (bot)* black salsify, scorzonera, Scorzonera hispanica
Winterspore *f (bot)* winter spore, teliospore, teleutospore
Winterspritzmittel *n* winter wash, dormant spray
~/öliges dormant oil spray
Winterspritzprogramm *n* dormant application programme *(orcharding)*
Winterspritzung *f* dormant spray[ing]

Winterstallhaltung f winter housing
Winterstallmast f winter fattening
Winterteich m *(pisc)* hibernating pond
Wintertraube f *(api)* winter cluster
Wintertreiberei f winter forcing
Wintertrocknis f parch blight *(plant physiology)*
Winterung f *s.* Wintersaat
Winterveredelung f winter (bench) grafting
Wintervorrat m winter stock
Winterweide f, **Winterweidegang** m winter grazing, foggage [grazing]
Winterweizen m winter wheat
Winterwicke f 1. winter vetch *(comprehensive term)*; 2. fodder vetch, Vicia villosa
Winterwirt m *(phyt)* overwintering (winter) host
Winterzwiebel f Japanese [bunching] onion, Welsh (bunching) onion, Japanese (stone) leek, Allium fistulosum
Winterzwischenfrucht f winter catch crop
Winzer m wine (grape) grower, viticulturist, vineyardist, wine-dresser, vintager
Winzergenossenschaft f viticulture co-operative
Wipfel m [tree-]top, head, tip
~/trockener spike-top
Wipfelbruch m topbreak
wipfeldürr stag-headed, spike-topped, dry-topped, top-dry
Wipfeldürre f stag-headedness, top drying; *(phyt)* die back • **an** ~ **kranken** to die back
Wipfelfäule f [plant-]top rot
Wipfelfeuer n crown fire
Wipfelhöhe f [tree-]top height, stand height
Wipfelholz n topwood; top (head) log
Wipfelkrankheit f polyhedral (wilt) disease, polyhedrosis *(insect virosis)*
Wipfelsproß m, **Wipfeltrieb** m top shoot
wipfeltrocken *s.* wipfeldürr
Wipphebelregner m rocker jet sprinkler
Wippschar[unter]bodenlockerer m vibrating subsoiler
Wirbel m vertebra
Wirbelarterie f vertebral artery
Wirbelbetttrockner m fluid[ized]-bed dryer
Wirbelbildung f turbulence
Wirbeldüse f vortical nozzle
Wirbelegge f whirl (swirl) harrow
Wirbelkanal m vertebral canal
Wirbelkegelstrahl m cone-shaped spray
Wirbelkörper m body of vertebra
Wirbelloch n vertebral foramen
wirbellos invertebrate
Wirbelloser m invertebrate
Wirbelsäule f vertebral column, backbone, chine, vertebrae
Wirbelschichttrockenkammer f, **Wirbelschichttrockner** m fluosolids kiln
Wirbeltier n vertebrate *(subphylum Vertebrata)*
Wirbelwind m whirlwind
wirkend/tödlich lethal

Wirksamkeit f effectiveness, efficiency, activity *(s. a. under* Wirkung*)*
~/fungizide fungicidal activity (efficiency)
~/herbizide herbicidal activity (efficiency)
Wirkstoff m active ingredient, a.i., active principle (substance); agent
~/antibiotischer antibiotic [agent]
~/organismenabtötender [chemischer] biocide
~/viren[ab]tötender virucide, viricide
Wirkstoffabbau m **in der ersten Leberpassage/metabolischer** first pass hepatic metabolism
Wirkstoffnebel m aerosol
Wirksubstanz f *s.* Wirkstoff
Wirkung f action; effect *(s. a. under* Wirksamkeit*)*
~/fungistatische fungistasis, fungistatic action
~/insektizide insecticidal action (power)
~/protektive protective effect
Wirkungsbereich m range of activity *(e.g. of pesticides)*
Wirkungsbreite f spectrum (range) of activity, action spectrum *(e.g. of pesticides)*
~/umfassende all-round efficiency
Wirkungsdauer f period of effectiveness *(e.g. of fertilizers)*
Wirkungsfläche f response surface *(for presenting test results)*
Wirkungsgesetz n **der Wachstumsfaktoren** law of diminishing returns, law of effectivity of growth factors
Wirkungskraft f strength
Wirkungskurve f response curve
Wirkungsspektrum n action spectrum, spectrum of activity *(e.g. of antibiotics)*
Wirkungssteigerung f, **Wirkungsverstärkung** f potentiation, fortification
Wirkungsweise f mode of action
Wirkungswert m action (effect) value
Wirrstroh n entangled straw
Wirsing[kohl] m savoy [cabbage], Brassica oleracea var. sabauda
Wirt m host [organism]
~/paratenischer paratenic host
Wirtel m *(bot)* whorl, verticil; branch whorl • **ungleichzählige** ~ **tragend** heterocyclic
Wirtelborstenhirse f, **Wirtelfennich** m *(bot)* bristly foxtail, Setaria verticillata
wirtelig whorled, verticillate
Wirt-Erreger-Verhältnis n host-pathogen interaction (relationship), pest-host interaction (relationship)
Wirt-Parasit-Verhältnis n host-parasite interaction (relationship)
Wirtsbereich m host range
wirtschaftlich 1. economic *(relating to economy)*; 2. economical, economically efficient, profitable
Wirtschaftlichkeit f **der Landwirtschaft** agricultural economy (economics)

Wirtschaftsbaumart

Wirtschaftsbaumart f commercial tree (timber) species
Wirtschaftsbuch n records of forest operations
Wirtschaftsdünger m organic [fertilizer], organic manure
Wirtschaftsevidenz f s. Wirtschaftsbuch
Wirtschaftsfutter n farm-produced fodder
Wirtschaftsgarten m market garden
Wirtschaftsgebäude n farm building (structure), agricultural building
Wirtschaftsgeflügel n commercial poultry
Wirtschaftsgrundsatz m forest rule
Wirtschaftshof m farmyard, barnyard
Wirtschaftsholzart f s. Wirtschaftsbaumart
Wirtschaftskarte f (forest) management map
Wirtschaftsregel f forest rule
Wirtschaftssorte f commercial variety
Wirtschaftswald m commercial (production) forest, managed (merchantable) forest, forest in use
Wirtschaftsweg m farm road
Wirtschaftszeitraum m (forest) management period
Wirtserkennung f host recognition
Wirtsfindung f host finding
Wirtsfindungsverhalten n host finding behaviour
Wirtsfutterpflanze f host food plant
Wirtsimmunität f host immunity
Wirtskreis m host range
Wirtsorganismus m host [organism]
Wirtspflanze f host [plant]
Wirtspflanzenpopulation f host plant population
Wirtspflanzenresistenz f host plant resistance
wirtsresistent host-resistant
Wirtsresistenz f host resistance
Wirtsselektion f host selection
Wirtssorte f host cultivar
Wirtsspektrum n host range • **mit weitem ~** euryxenous (parasite)
Wirtsspezialisierung f host specialization
wirtsspezifisch host-specific, host-selective
Wirtsspezifität f host specificity
Wirtssuche f host-seeking
Wirtstier n host [animal]
wirtstreu autoecious, autoicous
Wirtstreue f autoecism
Wirtsunkraut n host weed
Wirtswahl f host selection
Wirtswahlregel f host selection principle
Wirtswechsel m host alternation; heteroecism • **mit obligatem ~** heteroecious • **ohne ~** s. wirtstreu
~/obligater heteroecism
wirtswechselnd heteroecious
Wirtszelle f host cell
Wirtszellenreaktivierung f host cell reactivation (virology)
WisAMV s. Wistarienadernmosaikvirus
Wisent m wisent, [European] bison, aurochs, Bison bonasus
Wisp m wisp (grooming)
Wissenschaft f/biologische bioscience
Wistarie f (bot) 1. wisteria (genus Wisteria); 2. Chinese wisteria, Wisteria sinensis; 3. Japanese wisteria, Wisteria floribunda
Wistarienadernmosaikvirus n wisteria vein mosaic virus
wittern to scent, to wind
Witterung f 1. weather; 2. scent, wind, trail, drag • **~ [auf]nehmen** to scent, to wind • **einer ~ folgen** to road (hunting dog) • **ohne ~** scentless
Witterungsbedingungen fpl weather (atmospheric) conditions
Witterungsdaten pl weather data
Witterungseinfluß m atmospheric influence
Witterungsfaktor m meteorological factor
Witterungsschaden m weather damage
Witterungsschwankung f weather fluctuation
Witterungsunbeständigkeit f weather uncertainty
Witterungsverhältnisse npl atmospheric conditions
Witwenblume f field scabious, Knautia arvensis
WK s. Wasserkapazität
WkEV s. Weißklee-Enationenvirus
WkMV s. Weißkleemosaikvirus
Wladimir-Traktorenpferd n Vladimir Draft, Ivanovo Clydesdale (horse breed)
WmAMV s. Allgemeines Wassermelonenmosaikvirus
WN s. Weißes Neuseeländer Kaninchen
Wobble-Hypothese f (gen) wobble hypothesis
Wobbler-Syndrom n (vet) wobbler syndrome, wobbles
~ der Fohlen wobbles of foals, equine sensory ataxia
Wochenendgarten m weekend garden
Wohlfahrtswirkung f des Waldes/landeskulturelle welfare function of forest, indirect forest effect, non-wood beneficial effect
Wohlgeruch m fragrance
wohlriechend fragrant, sweet-scented, nosy
Wohlriechende Himbeere f flowering raspberry (mulberry), Rubus odoratus
~ Flockenblume (Kornblume) f (bot) [sweet] sultan, Amberboa (Centaurea) moschata
~ Reseda f mignonette, peaches and cream, Reseda odorata
~ Wicke f sweet pea, Lathyrus odoratus
Wohlriechendes Veilchen n violet, Viola odorata
wohlschmeckend tasty, pleasant-tasting
Wohlverleih m (bot) arnica (genus Arnica)
Wohnen n/ländliches rural housing
Wohnunterkunft f für Holzfäller logging camp
~ für Waldbrandwächter look-out (towerman's) cabin
Woilach m shabrack, rug
Wolf m 1. wolf, Canis lupus; 2. mincer, meat grinder; 3. s. Protz

wölfen to whelp, to bring forth *(esp. used of dog and wolf)*
Wölfin *f* bitch wolf, she-wolf
Wolfsauge *n (bot)* [small] bugloss, Anchusa (Lycopsis) arvensis
Wolfsbohne *f* lupin[e] *(genus Lupinus)*
Wolfseisenhut *m (bot)* wolfsbane, goatsbane, aconite, Aconitum vulparia (lycoctonum)
Wolfshund *m* wolfhound
Wolfskraut *n* birthwort, Aristolochia clematis
Wolfsmilch *f (bot)* spurge, wolf's-milk, euphorbia *(genus Euphorbia)*
Wolfsmilchgewächs *n* spurge, wolf's-milk *(family Euphorbiaceae)*
Wolfsschwertel *n (bot)* snake's-head, Hermodactylus tuberosus
Wolfstrapp *m* bugleweed, gypsywort *(genus Lycopus)*
Wolfszahn *m* wolf-tooth *(of horse)*
Wolkenbildung *f* cloud development
Wolkenbruch *m* cloudburst, rainstorm, torrential rain
Wolkendecke *f* cloud cover
Wolkenimpfung *f* cloud seeding
wolkenlos cloudless
Wolkenlosigkeit *f* cloudlessness
wolkig cloudy
Wollafter *m (ent)* small eggar (egger), Eriogaster (Bombyx) lanestris
Wollager *n* wool shed
Wollagerhaus *n* wool store
Wollart *f* wool type
Wollastonit *m* wollastonite *(non-clay mineral)*
Wollaus *f* mealy-bug, mealbug *(family Pseudococcidae)*
Wollbaum *m* kapok tree, Ceiba pentandra
Wollbeurteilung *f* wool grading
Wollblindheit *f* wool-blindness *(of sheep due to head wool covering the eyes)*
Wollbonitierung *f* wool grading
Wolle *f* wool
~/**abgesetzte** broken wool
~/**geschorene** fleece
~/**im Herbst geschorene** *(Am)* fall wool
~/**klettenhaltige** burry wool
~/**verkotete** dag
Wollbündel *n* [/**einzelnes**] *s.* Wollstapel
Wollefressen *n* trichophagy
Wollertrag *m* wool yield
Wollerzeugung *f* wool production
Wollfaser *f* wool fibre
Wollfeinheit *f* fineness of wool
Wollfett *n* wool fat, [wool] grease
~/**rohes** Yorkshire grease
Wollfilz *m* wool felt
Wollfollikel *m* wool follicle
Wollgras *n* cotton-grass *(genus Eriophorum)*
Wollgrasmoor *n* cotton-grass swamp
wollig woolly, lanate[d]

Wollige Napfschildlaus *f* cottony maple scale, Pulvinaria vitis (betulae)
Wolliger Schneeball *m* wayfaring-tree, *(Am)* cotton tree, Viburnum lantana
Wolliges Fingergras *n* woolly finger grass, Digitaria pentzii
~ **Honiggras** *n* [Yorkshire] fog, woolly soft grass, *(Am)* velvet grass, Holcus lanatus
Wollkaninchen *n* 1. wool-producing rabbit; 2. angora rabbit *(breed)*
Wollklassierung *f* wool grading
Wollkleid *n* wool cover, fleece
wollköpfig woolly-faced *(sheep)*
Wollkraut *n (bot)* mulle[i]n *(genus Verbascum)*
Wollkrautblütenkäfer *m* variegated carpet beetle, Anthrenus verbasci
Wollmaus *f* chinchilla *(genus Chinchilla)*
Wollmehl *n* wool meal
Wollproduktion *f* wool production
Wollprotein *n* wool protein
Wollrasse *f* wool breed
Wollsalbei *m* Mediterranean sage, Salvia aethiopis
Wollschaf *n* wool[-type] sheep
Wollschafrasse *f* wool breed
Wollschafzucht *f* breeding of wool sheep
Wollschafzüchter *m* wool-grower
Wollschuppen *m* wool shed
Wollschweiß *m* grease, suint, wool oil, yolk
Wollsorte *f* wool type
Wollsortierung *f* wool sorting
Wollspinner *m s.* Trägspinner
Wollstapel *m* wool staple
Wolltyp *m* wool type
Wollverarbeitung *f* wool-processing
Wollvlies *n* sheep fleece
Wollwachs *n* wool wax
Wollwachstum *n* wool growth
Wollwäsche *f* wool scouring
Wollwaschmaschine *f* wool washer
Wollziest *m (bot)* lamb's-ear, Stachys byzantina (lanata)
worfeln to win[now], to fan *(grain)*
Wright-Reaktion *f (vet)* Wright's test
WRMV *s.* Russisches Winterweizenmosaikvirus
Wruke *f s.* Steckrübe
WSD *s.* Wassersättigungsdefizit
WSiMV *s.* Weizenstrichelmosaikvirus
Wucherblume *f* 1. chrysanth[emum] *(genus Chrysanthemum)*; 2. *s.* Wiesenmargerite
wuchern to ramp, to accrue, to ramble, to proliferate, to grow prolifically (rampant), to straggle
wuchernd rampant
Wucherung *f* 1. proliferation; 2. *(phyt, vet)* excrescence; tumour
Wuchs *m* 1. *s.* Wachstum; 2. habit, build, stature
~/**ausladender** spreading habit
~/**gestauchter** stunted growth, stunt

Wuchs

~/kompakter compact habit
Wuchs... *s. a.* Wachstums...
Wuchsdepression *f* growth depression
Wuchsdichte *f* density of growth
Wuchsdistrikt *m* growth district *(plant ecology)*
Wuchsdynamik *f* growth dynamics
Wuchseigenschaft *f* growth characteristic
Wuchsfehler *m* defect in growth
Wuchsform *f*, **Wuchshabitus** *m* growth form, growth habit, physiognomy
Wuchshöhe *f* growth height, height of growth
Wuchshormon *n* growth hormone, GW
wüchsig thrifty, growthy
Wüchsigkeit *f* thriftiness, vigour
Wuchsklasse *f (forest)* developmental stage
Wuchskraft *f* growth potential, growing power
Wuchsleistung *f* growth performance (production) *(e.g. of a tree)*
Wuchsmerkmal *n* growth characteristic
Wuchsraum *m* growing space *(e.g. of a tree)*
Wuchsraumquotient *m (forest)* growing-space ratio
Wuchsring *m* growth ring, annual ring (growth layer)
Wuchsstärke *f* growth potential, vigour
Wuchsstockung *f* growth retardation, check
Wuchsstoff *m* growth substance (promoter)
~/hormonaler growth-promoting hormone
~/nicht identifizierter unidentified growth factor, UGF *(animal nutrition)*
~/pflanzlicher phytohormone
~/selektiver selective growth promoter
Wuchsstoffherbizid *n*, **Wuchsstoffmittel** *n* growth regulator herbicide, hormone (auxin) herbicide, translocated (translocatory) herbicide
Wuchstyp *m* type of growth
Wühlgrubber *m* soil-loosening cultivator, subsoil cultivator
Wühlmaus *f* [water-]vole, [black] water rat, Arvicola terrestris (amphibius)
Wühlratte *f s.* Wühlmaus
Wühlschar *n* loosening share
Wühlspaten *m* screefing spade
Wulstige Nemesie *f (bot)* pouched nemesia, Nemesia strumosa
Wulstkamm *m* walnut (raspberry) comb, cushion comb *(of fowl)*
Wundbehandlung *f* wound treatment
~ von Rückeschäden *(forest)* treatment of skidding wounds
Wundbett *n* couch *(of game)*
Wunde *f (phyt, vet)* wound, trauma
~/eiternde fester
Wunderapfel *m* balsam apple, Momordica balsamina
Wunderbeere *f* miraculous berry (fruit), sweet berry, Synsepalum dulcificum
Wunderblume *f (bot)* 1. four-o'clock *(genus Mirabilis)*; 2. four-o'clock, marvel of Peru, Mirabilis jalapa

Wundergeschwulst *f s.* Teratom
Wundergras *n* Delhi grass, Dichanthium annulatum
Wunderreis *m* miracle rice
Wunderstrauch *m* Bombay laurel, croton, Codiaeum variegatum
Wundfährte *f (hunt)* red track
Wundfäule *f (phyt)* wound rot (decay)
Wundgewebe *n s.* Wundkallus
Wundgummi *n*, **Wundharz** *n* wound gum
Wundharzkanal *m* wound duct, traumatic [resin] duct
Wundheilung *f* wound healing
Wundheilungsperiode *f* wound healing period
Wundheilungsprozeß *m* wound healing process
Wundholz *n* wound wood
Wundhormon *n* wound hormone, necrohormone
Wundinfektion *f* wound infection
Wundinfektions[erreger]bekämpfung *f (vet)* antisepsis
Wundkallus *m (phyt)* callus, wound tissue
Wundkern *m*, **Wundkernholz** *n* wound (traumatic) heartwood
Wundklammer *f (vet)* wound clip
Wundklee *m* 1. kidney-vetch *(genus Anthyllis)*; 2. kidney-vetch, woundwort, Lady's finger, Anthyllis vulneraria
Wundkork *m* wound cork • **~ ausbilden** to cork, to suberize
Wundkorkbildung *f* wound cork formation, suberization, suberification
Wundmyiasis *f (vet)* [blowfly] strike *(esp. of sheep)*
Wundparasit *m* wound parasite
Wundparenchym *n* wound (traumatic) parenchyma
Wundperiderm *n (bot)* wound periderm
Wundsalbe *f (vet)* dressing
Wundschock *m (vet)* wound shock
Wundstarrkrampf *m (vet)* tetanus *(caused by Clostridium tetani)*
Wundstreifen *m* mineralized strip, fire line, fuel break *(forest fire control)*
~ an Eisenbahnlinien railway safety strip
Wundstreifenpflug *m* fire plough
Wundtumorenvirus *n (phyt)* wound tumour virus
Wundverband *m* [wound] dressing
Wundverfärbung *f* wound stain *(of timber)*
Wundverschlußmittel *n* grafting-clay, graft sealant
Wünschelrute *f* divining (dowsing) rod
Wurf *m* 1. litter, fall *(of newborn animals)*; farrow; 2. snout *(of wild boar)*
Würfelpresse *f* cuber
Würfelpressen *n* **aus dem Schwad** field cubing *(hay-making)*
Würfelzucker *m* cube (lump) sugar
Wurfergebnis *n* farrowing result
Wurffessel *f* jess *(falconry)*
Wurfförderung *f* reciprocating plate feeding
Wurfgebläse *f* impeller fan, throw blower

Wurfgeschwister *n* litter-mate
Wurfgröße *f* litter size
Wurfhöhe *f* pitch *(of a chopper blower)*; height of jet *(of a sprinkler)*
Wurfkasten *m* nest box *(rabbit keeping)*
Wurfleistung *f* litter performance
Wurfmasse *f* litter weight
Wurfnetz *n (pisc)* cast-net
Wurfradrechwender *m* reel-type side rake
Würgebohrung *f* chokebore *(of a sporting gun)*
Würgekette *f* binding (binder) chain
Würgen *n (vet)* choke syndrome *(of racing horses)*
Würgepflanze *f* strangler
Würger *m (bot)* broomrape *(genus Orobanche)*
Würgfalke *m* saker [falcon], Falco cherrug
Wurm *m* worm
wurmartig wormy
Wurmbefall *m* worm attack (infestation)
Wurmbekämpfung *f* worm control
Wurmbronchitis *f (vet)* verminous bronchitis, husk
Wurmei *n* worm egg
Wurmfarn *m* male [shield] fern, shield-fern, buckler [fern], Dryopteris filix-mas
wurmförmig vermiform
Wurmfraßloch *n* worm-hole, grub-hole, pin-hole
wurmig *s.* wurmstichig
Wurmkrankheit *f (vet)* helminthiasis, helminthosis
Wurmkultur *f* vermiculture
Wurmkur *f (vet)* deworming
Wurmloch *n s.* Wurmfraßloch
Wurmmittel *n* worm remedy, wormer, helminthicide, anthelmint[h]ic, vermicide, vermifuge
Wurmröhre *f* worm burrow
Wurmsalat *m (bot)* bristly ox-tongue, Picris echioides
Wurmsame[n] *m* 1. wormseed *(comprehensive term)*; 2. wormseed, Chenopodium ambrosioides var. anthelminticum; 3. wormseed, Artemisia cina
Wurmstich *m* worm-hole, grub-hole, pin-hole
wurmstichig worm-eaten, wormy, vermiculate[d], maggoty
wurm[ver]treibend anthelmint[h]ic, vermifugal
wurstähnlich *(bot)* allantoid
wurstförmig *(bot)* allantoid
Wursthülle *f* sausage casing
Wurstkraut *n* [common, garden] thyme, [sweet] marjoram, Origanum majorana, Majorana hortensis
Württemberger Pferd (Warmblutpferd) *n* Wurttemberg *(horse breed)*
Würzagar *m* beer-wort agar
Würze *f* 1. [beer] wort; gyle; 2. *s.* Gewürz
~/gehopfte hop[ped] wort
~/ungehopfte unhopped (sweet) wort
Würzeagar *m* wort agar
Würzeanalyse *f* wort analysis
Würzeaufbereitungsanlage *f* wort treatment equipment
Würzebelüfter *m* wort aeration equipment

Würzebelüftung *f* wort aeration
Würzefarbe *f* wort colour
Würzeherstellung *f* wort production
Würzekochen *n* wort boiling
Würzekonzentrat *n* wort concentrate
Würzekühler *m* wort cooler
Würzekühlung *f* wort cooling
Wurzel *f* root • **auf eigener ~ [stehend]** self-rooted • **aus eigener ~ gewachsen** own-root[ed], ungrafted • **~ fassen (schlagen)** to root, to strike (take) roots • **zur ~ gehörend** radicular • **Wurzeln bilden** to root
~/knollige tuberous root
~/sproßbürtige adventitious root
Wurzelableger *m* root shoot (sucker)
Wurzelabscheidung *f* root diffusate
Wurzelabschlußgewebe *n* exodermis
Wurzelabsorption *f* root absorption
Wurzelabtötung *f* root kill
Wurzelälchen *n* root [eel]worm, root (soil) nematode
Wurzelanlauf *m* [root] collar, root crown (swelling) • **mit starkem ~** swell-butted, buttressed
~/spannrückiger [root] buttress
~/starker butt swelling, swollen butt
Wurzelarchitektur *f* root architecture
wurzelartig rooty, rhizoid, rhizomorphous
Wurzelatmung *f* root respiration
Wurzelausscheidung *f* root excretion
Wurzelausschlag *m* root shoot (sucker), wild shoot, sprout
Wurzelballen *m* root ball, ball [of earth]
Wurzelballenbewässerung *f* ball watering
Wurzelbärtigkeitsvirus *n* **der Zuckerrübe** beet necrotic yellow vein virus, BNYVV
wurzelbefallend root-infesting
Wurzelbereich *m* root area (space)
Wurzelbesiedelung *f* root colonization
Wurzelbett *n* root-bed
Wurzelbildung *f* root formation, rhizogenesis
Wurzelbiologie *f* root biology
wurzelblütig radiciflorous
Wurzelbohrer *m* swift moth *(family Hepialidae)*
Wurzelbrand *m (phyt)* damping-off [disease], fogging-off, blackleg [disease], seedling blight
~ der Rübe blackleg (root rot) of beet, beet damping-off *(mycosis)*
~ des Tabaks black root rot of tobacco *(caused by Thielaviopsis basicola)*
Wurzelbräune *f s.* Wurzelbrand
Wurzelbraunfäule *f* **der Tomate** tomato brown [root] rot *(caused by Pyrenochaeta lycopersici)*
Wurzelbrüchigkeit *f* root brittleness
Wurzelbrut *f* [root] suckers
Wurzelbulbille *f* root bulbil
Wurzelbürste *f* water brush
Würzelchen *n* rootlet
Wurzeldichte *f* root density
Wurzeldiffusat *n* root diffusate

Wurzeldroge

Wurzeldroge f root drug
Wurzeldruck m root pressure
Wurzeldüngung f plant-root fertilization
wurzelecht self-rooted, own-root[ed], ungrafted
Wurzeleinschlag m rooting bed
Wurzelentwicklung f s. Wurzelbildung
Wurzelerkrankung f root disease
Wurzelexkretion f root excretion
Wurzelexsudat n root exudate
Wurzelfaser f root fibril, rooty fibre
Wurzelfäule f (phyt) 1. root rot *(comprehensive term)*; 2. mushroom root rot *(esp. caused by Armillaria mellea)*
~ **der Erbse** pea root rot *(caused by Fusarium solani f. pisi)*
~ **der Zuckerrübe** black root of sugar-beet
Wurzelfäuleerreger m root rót pathogen
Wurzelfilz m s. Wurzelgeflecht
Wurzelfliege f root-fly *(comprehensive term)*
Wurzelfliegenlarve f root maggot *(comprehensive term)*
Wurzelform f root shape
wurzelförmig rhizomorphous, rhizoid
Wurzelfresser m root feeder
Wurzelfrucht f root [crop]
wurzelfrüchtig rhizocarpous
Wurzelgalle f (phyt) root gall (knot)
Wurzelgallenälchen n root-knot nematode *(genus Meloidogyne)*
Wurzelgallenbildung f root galling
Wurzelgallennematode m s. Wurzelgallenälchen
Wurzelgeflecht n root mat (network), interlaced roots, matting of roots
Wurzelgemüse n root [crop] vegetable
Wurzelgemüseerntemaschine f root vegetable harvester
Wurzelgemüsereiniger m root cleaner
Wurzelhaar n root hair
Wurzelhaarspitze f root hair tip
Wurzelhaarzone f root hair zone
Wurzelhäcksler m root shredder
Wurzelhals m root neck (collar), root crown (swelling), collum
Wurzelhalsfäule f collar rot (girdle) *(of stone fruit, caused by Phytophthora cactorum)*
~ **des Salats** bottom rot of lettuce *(caused by Rhizoctonia solani)*
Wurzelhalsgalle f, **Wurzelhalstumor** m crown gall *(caused by Agrobacterium tumefaciens)*
Wurzelhalt m roothold
Wurzelharz n (Am) wood rosin
Wurzelhaube f root cap, pileorhiza
Wurzelheizung f root zone heating *(in glasshouses)*
Wurzelherbizid n soil[-acting] herbicide, soil-applied herbicide
Wurzelholz n root wood
Wurzelinterzeption f root interception

Wurzelkanal m root channel
Wurzelkappe f s. Wurzelhaube
Wurzelkeim m rootlet
Wurzelkletterer m root climber
Wurzelknöllchen n root nodule, [root] tubercle
Wurzelknöllchenbakterium n root-nodule bacterium
Wurzelknöllchenbildung f root nodulation
Wurzelknolle f [root, radical] tuber, tuberous root
Wurzelknospe f root bud
Wurzelkolophonium n (Am) wood rosin
Wurzelkonkurrenz f root competition
Wurzelkrankheit f root disease
Wurzelkrone f root crown
Wurzelkropf m crown gall *(caused by Agrobacterium tumefaciens)*
~ **des Kernobstes** burr knot of pome fruits *(caused by Agrobacterium tumefaciens)*
Wurzelkropfbakterium n crown gall bacterium, Agrobacterium tumefaciens
Wurzelkultur f root culture
Wurzellänge f root length
Wurzelläsionsnematode m root lesion nematode *(genus Pratylenchus)*
wurzellos rootless, unrooted, arrhizal, arrhizous
Wurzelmaser f burr, burl
Wurzelmeristem n root meristem
Wurzelmesser n root cutter
Wurzelmilbe f bulb mite, Rhizoglyphus echinopus
Wurzelminierer m (ent) root-miner
Wurzelmorphologie f root morphology
wurzeln to root, to take (strike) roots
wurzelnackt bare-root[ed]
Wurzelnematode m soil nematode, root [eel]worm
~/**gallenbildender** root-knot nematode *(genus Meloidogyne)*
~/**wandernder** migratory root nematode, root lesion nematode *(esp. genus Pratylenchus)*
Wurzeloberfläche f rhizoplane
Wurzelparasit m root parasite
wurzelparasitär root-parasitic
Wurzelpathogen n root pathogen
Wurzelpetersilie f turnip-rooted parsley, Petroselinum crispum ssp. tuberosum
Wurzelpfropfung f root grafting
Wurzelranken fpl root tendrils • **mit** ~ sarmentose, sarmentous
Wurzelreichtum m rootiness
Wurzelreiniger m root cleaner
Wurzelrinde f root cortex
Wurzelrissigkeit f collar crack *(esp. of tea plants, caused by Armillaria mellea)*
Wurzelrodegerät n, **Wurzelroder** m root lifter (rake), [up]rooter
Wurzelrückstand m root residue
Wurzelrüsselkäfer m, **Wurzelrüßler** m root weevil (borer) *(comprehensive term)*
Wurzelschädling m root pest

Wurzelscheide f root sheath, coleorhiza
Wurzelscheitel m root tip
Wurzelschleim m root slime
Wurzelschneidemaschine f, **Wurzelschneider** m root cutter (cutting machine), root breaker (bruiser); root pruner
Wurzelschnitt m 1. root cut; 2. root cutting (pruning), wrenching
~/horizontaler undercutting
~/vertikaler side (lateral) cutting
Wurzelschnittling m root cutting
Wurzelschnittmesser n root-pruning knife
Wurzelschoß m layer-stool
Wurzelschößling m s. Wurzelsproß
Wurzelschwamm m (phyt) root rot
Wurzelsellerie m celeriac, turnip-rooted celery, Apium graveolens var. rapaceum
Wurzelspitze f root tip
Wurzelspitzengalle f (phyt) root tip gall
Wurzelsproß m [root] sucker, root shoot, runner
• **Wurzelsprosse entfernen** to sucker • **Wurzelsprosse treiben** to sucker • **Wurzelsprosse treibend** soboliferous
Wurzelsproßachse f root-shoot axis
Wurzelsproßpflanze f sucker plant
Wurzel-Sproß-Verhältnis n root-shoot ratio
Wurzelsteckling m root cutting
Wurzelstock m root-stock, rhizome, stem-tuber; pip (esp. of Convallaria majalis)
Wurzelstock... s. a. Rhizom...
Wurzelstockabschnitt m (forest) butt log, bottom log (piece)
Wurzelstreckung f root extension
Wurzelsystem n root system (s. a. Wurzelwerk)
Wurzelteilung f root division (for propagation)
Wurzeltiefgang m rooting depth
Wurzeltöterkrankheit f (phyt) black scurf (speck), scurfy root, rhizoctonia canker, potato black scurf (caused by Rhizoctonia solani)
~ des Salats bottom rot of lettuce (caused by Rhizoctonia solani)
Wurzeltrieb m s. Wurzelsproß
Wurzeltrockenmasse f, **Wurzeltrockensubstanz** f root dry matter
Wurzelumgebung f rhizosphere
Wurzel- und Stengelfäule f des Rhabarbers violet root rot [of rhubarb] (caused by Rhizoctonia crocorum)
Wurzel- und Stengelgrundfäule f bei Viola-Arten (phyt) pansy sickness (caused by Phytium violae)
Wurzelunkraut n root-stock weed
Wurzelverästelung f root branching
Wurzelveredelung f root grafting
Wurzelverteilung f root distribution
Wurzelverwachsung f natural root-grafting
Wurzelverzweigung f root branching
Wurzelwachstum n root growth

Wurzelwasserpotential n root water potential
Wurzelwerk n interlaced (tangled) roots, root network, rootage
Wurzelwiderstand m root resistance
Wurzelzichorie f common (large-rooted) chic[k]ory, coffee chic[k]ory, Cichorium intybus var. sativum
Wurzelzone f root[ing] zone, root space (range)
Wurzelzonenerwärmung f root zone warming
Wurzelzonenheizung f root zone heating (in glasshouses)
Wurzelzonentemperatur f root zone temperature
Wurzelzystenälchen n, **Wurzelzystennematode** m cyst-forming root eelworm, cyst nematode (genera Heterodera, Globodera and Punctodera)
würzen/mit Hopfen to hop (brewing)
Würzepfanne f [wort] copper, wort tub, kettle, gyle
Würzeseparator m wort separator
Würzezentrifugierung f wort centrifugation
Würzezusammensetzung f wort composition
würzig aromatic; spiced
Würzkraut n [pot-]herb, seasoning (aromatic) herb
Würzmittel n, **Würzstoff** m seasoning, condiment
Wüste f desert
Wüstenbildung f desertification
Wüstenboden m desert soil
Wüstenfauna f desert fauna
Wüstenheuschrecke f s. Wüstenwanderheuschrecke
Wüstenklima n desert climate
Wüstenpflanze f desert plant, eremophyte
Wüstenpflaster n desert pavement
Wüstenschaf n desert sheep
Wüstenwanderheuschrecke f desert locust, Schistocerca gregaria
Wut f s. Tollwut
WVzV s. Weizenverzwergungsvirus
Wyandotte n(f) wyandotte (breed of fowl)
WZP s. Winkelzählprobe

X

Xanthin n xanthine
Xanthindehydrogenase f xanthine dehydrogenase (enzyme)
Xanthinoxidase f [hypo]xanthine oxidase, Schardinger's enzyme
Xanthocillin n xanthocillin (antibiotic)
Xanthom n (vet) xanthoma
Xanthomatose f (vet) xanthomatosis
Xanthomegnin n xanthomegnin (mycotoxin)
Xanthomzellengeschwulst f (vet) xanthoma
Xanthon n xanthone (pigment)
Xanthophyll n xanthophyll, phylloxanthin
Xanthophyllzyklus m xanthophyll cycle (of photosynthesis)
Xanthose f (phyt) xanthosis

Xanthosome

Xanthosome *f (bot)* yautia[s] *(genus Xanthosoma)*
Xanthoxin *n* xanthoxin *(precursor of abscisic acid)*
Xanthurensäure *f* xanthurenic acid
X-beinig knock-kneed
X-Beinigkeit *f* knock knees, knee-narrow conformation
X-Chromatin *n* Barr body *(of female somatic cells)*
X-Chromosom *n* X chromosome *(sex chromosome)*
~/am Zentromer zusammengeklebtes attached X chromosome
Xenie *f (bot, gen)* xenia, metaxenia
Xenobiotikum *n* xenobiotic
xenogam *(bot)* xenogamous, allogamous
Xenogamie *f (bot)* xenogamy, allogamy, cross-pollination
xerisch xeric, dry *(e.g. a site)*
Xerodermie *f (vet)* xeroderm[i]a
xeromorph *(bot)* xeromorphic
Xeromorphie *f (bot)* xeromorphy
xerophil xerophilous, xerophile, aridophilous
Xerophthalmie *f (vet)* xerophthalmia *(symptom of vitamin deficiency)*
Xerophyt *m* xerophyte, xerophile
xerophytisch xerophytic
Xerose *f s.* Xerosis
Xeroserie *f* xerosere *(plant ecology)*
Xerosis *f (vet)* xerosis
X-Krankheit *f* X disease *(of cattle after uptaking chlorated naphthalenes)*
~ des Steinobstes *(phyt)* X disease, albino (small bitter) cherry, western X little cherry, buckskin *(mycoplasmosis)*
X-Parallaxe *f* X-parallax, absolute parallax *(surveying)*
X-Virus-Mosaik *n* **der Kartoffel** *(phyt)* potato mild (simple) mosaic
Xylan *n* xylan, wood gum *(polysaccharide)*
Xylanase *f*, **Xylanendo-1,3-ß-Xylosidase** *f* xylan endo-1,3-ß-xylosidase *(enzyme)*
Xylan-1,4-ß-Xylosidase *f* xylan-1,4-ß-xylosidase *(enzyme)*
Xylem *n (bot)* xylem
~/primäres primary xylem (wood)
~/sekundäres secondary xylem (wood)
Xylemmutterzelle *f* xylem mother cell
Xylemparenchym *n* xylem (wood) parenchyma
Xylemsaft *m* xylem sap
Xylemwasserpotential *n* xylem water potential
Xylit *n* 1. lignite; 2. *s.* Xylitol
Xylitol *n* xylitol *(sugar alcohol)*
Xylobiase *f* xylan-1,4-ß-xylosidase *(enzyme)*
Xylo-Hexulose *f* sorbose *(monosaccharide)*
Xylol *n* xylene
Xylometer *n* xylometer
xylophag xylophagous, lignivorous, wood-eating, wood-feeding
Xylophage *m* xylophage
Xylose *f* xylose, wood sugar *(pentose)*

Xyloseisomerase *f* xylose isomerase *(enzyme)*
Xylulokinase *f* xylulokinase *(enzyme)*

Y

Yacon *f* yacon strawberry, Polymnia sonchifolia (edulis)
Yak *m* yak, grunting ox, Bos grunniens
Yakut *m* Yakut *(horse breed)*
Yam *m s.* Yams
Yams *n* 1. yam *(genus Dioscorea)*; 2. Chinese yam, Chinese [sweet] potato, cinnamon vine, Dioscorea opposita (batatas)
Yamsbohne *f* 1. yam bean *(genus Pachyrrhizus)*; 2. yam (potato) bean, jicama, jiquima, Pachyrrhizus tuberosus; 3. yam bean, Pachyrrhizus erosus
Yamskäfer *m* yam beetle *(name esp. for Heterolygus meles, H. appius, Prionoryctes canaliculus, P. rufopiceus, Galerucida bicolor)*
Yamswurzel[knolle] *f* yam
Y-Chromosom *n* Y-chromosome *(sex chromosome)*
Yedofichte *f* Hondo (Yezo) spruce, Picea jezoensis
Yerba *f* maté, mate *(tea, beverage)*
Yersin-Bazillus *m* plague bacterium, Yersinia pestis
Ylang-Ylang *n*, **Ylang-Ylang-Pflanze** *f (bot)* ylang-ylang, Macassar oil, Cananga odorata
Yoghurt *m(n)* yoghurt, yogurt, mazun
Yohimbin *n* yohimbine *(alkaloid)*
Yorkshire Terrier *m* Yorkshire terrier *(dog breed)*
Yorkshireschwein *n* Large White [English, Yorkshire], Large York (English), [Grand] Yorkshire *(pig breed)*
Y-Parallaxe *f* Y-parallax, vertical parallax *(surveying)*
Ypsiloneule *f (ent)* greasy cutworm, Agrotis ipsilon
Ysander *m (bot)* pachysandra *(genus Pachysandra)*
Ysop *m (bot)* hyssop *(genus Hyssopus)*
Yucca *f (bot)* yucca *(genus Yucca)*
Yukatansisal *m* henequen
Yulanmagnolie *f* yulan, lily tree, Magnolia denudata
Y-Virus-Mosaik *n* **[der Kartoffel]** rugose mosaic, stipple (leaf drop) streak of potato *(virosis)*

Z

Zachunbaum *m* Egyptian (desert) date, bito [tree], Balanites aegyptiaca (roxburghii)
Zachunöl *n* zachun oil *(from Balanites aegyptiaca)*
Zackelschaf *n* Zackel [sheep], Prong (Twisted) Horn *(breed)*

Zackenrad *n* metering wheel *(of a pick-up baler)*
Zackenscheibenegge *f* bush and bog harrow
Zadoks-Code *m* Zadoks [decimal] code *(of development of cereal plants)*
zäh tough, tenacious; viscous; rop[e]y *(wine)*
zähflüssig viscous, semiliquid, ropy
Zähflüssigkeit *f* viscosity, ropiness, thickness
Zähigkeit *f* toughness, tenacity
Zähigkeitswert *m* toughness value *(of wood)*
Zahl f/Jaccardsche *(ecol)* Jaccard's index, coefficient of community
~/Köttsdorfer saponification number (value) *(fatty acid determination)*
~/phagozytische *(vet)* opsonin index
Zähling *m (bot)* scaly lentinus, Lentinus squamosus
zahm tame, domesticated • **~ werden** to tame
zähmbar tameable, tamable
Zähmbarkeit *f* tameability
Zahme Eberesche *f* service-tree, true service, sorb, Sorbus domestica
zähmen to tame, to break [in]; to domesticate, to reclaim
Zahn *m* 1. tooth; 2. *s.* Zinke
~/bleibender permanent (adult) tooth
Zahnabstand *m s.* Zahnteilung
Zahnalveole *f s.* Zahnfach
Zahnbein *n* dentine
Zahnbogen *m* dental arch
Zahnbürstenbaum *m* tooth-brush tree, Salvadora persica
Zahndach *n* top plate *(of the chain-saw tooth)*
Zahndachschnittwinkel *m* top-plate cutting angle, top filing (face) angle
Zahndurchbruch *m s.* Zahnen
zahnen to teethe
Zahnen *n* teething, tooth eruption, dentition
Zahnfach *n* tooth-socket, alveolus
Zahnfäule *f (vet)* [teeth, dental] caries
Zahnflachriemen *m* positive-drive belt, timing belt
Zahnflachriementrieb *m* positive-belt drive
Zahnfleisch *n* gum[s], gingiva
Zahnfleischabszeß *m (vet)* gumboil
Zahnfleischentzündung *f (vet)* gingivitis
Zahnfleischwucherung *f (vet)* epulis
Zahnform *f* tooth shape
Zahnformel *f* dental formula
Zahnfraß *m s.* Zahnfäule
Zahnhöhe *f* tooth height, gullet depth *(of a saw)*
Zahnhöhle *f* dental cavity
Zähniger Lavendel *m* toothed lavender, Lavandula dentata
Zahnkopflinie *f* tooth line *(of a saw)*
Zahnkrone *f* tooth-crown
Zahnlilie *f* dog's-tooth [violet], trout lily (flower) *(genus Erythronium)*
zahnlos toothless, edentate; gummy *(esp. said of sheep)*
Zahnlücke *f* throat *(of a saw)*

Zahnmais *m* dent maize, Zea mays convar. dentiformis
Zahnmark *n s.* Zahnpulpa
Zahnmarkentzündung *f (vet)* pulpitis
Zahnpulpa *f* [tooth] pulp
Zahnradgetriebe *n* gear drive
Zahnradmotor *m* gear engine
Zahnradpumpe *f* gear pump
Zahnriementrieb *m* positive-belt drive
Zahnrücken *m* tooth back
Zahnschmelz *m* [dental] enamel
Zahnspitzenlinie *f s.* Zahnkopflinie
Zahnspitzenwinkel *m* tooth top angle *(of a saw)*
Zahnstangengetriebe *n* rack-and-pinion gear
Zahnstaucher *m* swaging die
Zahnstein *m* dental calculus, tartar, tophus
Zahnstocherkraut *n (bot)* bisnaga, Ammi visnaga
Zahnteilung *f* tooth pitch (spacing), saw pitch
Zahnung *f s.* Zahnen
Zähnung *f* dentition *(e.g. of a leaf)*
Zahnwehholz *n* [common] prickly-ash, Zanthoxylum fraxineum (americanum)
Zahnwurz *f* toothwort *(genus Dentaria)*
Zahnwurzel *f* fang
Zahnzement *m* cement
Zahnzunge *f (bot)* odontoglossum *(genus Odontoglossum)*
zäkektomieren *(vet)* to caecectomize
Zäkum *c[a]ecum, typhlon, blind gut
ZaMV *s.* Zaunrübenmosaikvirus
Zander *m* pike-perch, *(Am)* zander, Stizostedion lucioperca
Zange *f* 1. pliers, tongs; *(vet)* forceps; 2. *s.* Meßkluppe
Zangendüse *f* tong nozzle
Zangen[rücke]traktor *m (forest)* grapple skidder
Zantedeschie *f* 1. calla lily *(genus Zantedeschia)*; 2. arum lily, white calla, Zantedeschia (Calla) aethiopica
Zäpfchen *n* 1. uvula *(animal anatomy)*; 2. *(vet)* suppository
zapfen to tap
Zapfen *m* 1. *(bot)* cone, conelet, strobile, strobilus; plug; 2. retinal cone; 3. snag *(in grafting)* • **~ tragen** to cone
zapfenartig strobilaceous, strobiloid
zapfenbildend strobilaceous, strobiliferous
Zapfenbohrer *m (ent)* cone borer *(comprehensive term)*
Zapfendarre *f (forest)* cone-dryer, seed-extraction plant, seed extractory, [seed] kiln
Zapfenernte *f* cone harvest[ing], cone collection
Zapfen[ernte]ertrag *m* cone crop
zapfenförmig strobiliform
Zapfenkreuz *n* yoke journal assembly *(of a cardan shaft)*
Zapfenpflücker *m* cone collector
Zapfenschnitt *m* removal of the snag *(grafting)*
Zapfenschuppe *f* cone scale

Zapfenschüttelmaschine

Zapfenschüttelmaschine f cone shaker
Zapfenspeicher m cone-curing shed
zapfentragend coniferous, strobiliferous
Zapfentränke f nipple (push-type tap) drinker
Zapfentrockenschuppen m cone-curing shed
Zapfentrocknung f cone drying
Zapfenzelle f [retinal] cone *(of the eye)*
Zapfenziehen n s. Zapfenschnitt
Zapfgetriebe n p.t.o. (power take-off) gear
Zapfloch n bung-hole
Zapfwelle f power take-off, p.t.o., power shaft
Zapfwellenanschluß m p.t.o. connection
Zapfwellenantrieb m p.t.o. drive
Zapfwellendrehzahl f p.t.o. speed
zapfwellengetrieben p.t.o.-driven
Zapfwellenkraftheber m p.t.o.-driven hydraulic lift
Zapfwellenkupplung f p.t.o. coupling
Zapfwellenleistung f p.t.o. power
Zapfwellenluftpumpe f p.t.o.-driven air compressor
Zapfwellenmähdrescher m p.t.o. combine
Zapfwellenschalthebel m p.t.o. selector lever
Zarge f super *(of beehive)*
zart tender *(e.g. meat)* • **~ machen** to tenderize
Zartheit f tenderness
Zaubernuß f wych-hazel, witch-hazel, hamamelis *(genus Hamamelis)*
Zaum m bridle • **an den ~ gewöhnen** to bit
zäumen to bridle, to bit, to rein
Zaumzeug n bridle; headgear, head harness (collar)
Zaun m fence
~/elektrischer electric [wire] fence
~/stationärer permanent fence
Zaunbau m fence building
Zaundraht m fence wire
Zaunladegerät n fencer
Zaunlatte f pale
Zaunpfahl m fence (fencing) post
Zaunriegel m fencing rail
Zaunrübe f *(bot)* bryony *(genus Bryonia)*
Zaunrübenmosaikvirus n white bryony mosaic virus
Zaunwicke f hedge (bush) vetch, Vicia sepium
Zaunwinde f hedge (great) bindweed, bearwind, bellbine, Calystegia sepium
Z-Chromosom n Z-chromosome *(sex chromosome)*
ZcMV s. Zimmercallamosaikvirus
Zearalenon n zearalenone *(mycotoxin)*
Zeatin n zeatin *(phytohormone, cytokinin)*
Zeatinribosid n zeatin riboside *(cytokinin)*
Zeaxanthin n zeaxanthin *(xanthophyll)*
Zebra n zebra, Equus zebra
Zebrafink m zebra finch, Taeniophygia (Poephila) guttata
Zebratradeskantie f inch plant, wandering Jew, Zebrina pendula, Tradescantia zebrina

Zebu n(m) zebu, Indian ox, humped cattle, Bos indicus
Zecke f tick *(superfamily Ixodoidea)*
Zeckenbefall m tick infestation
Zeckenbekämpfung f tick control
Zeckenbekämpfungsmittel n ixocide
Zeckenenzephalitis f *(vet)* tick-borne encephalitis
Zeckenfieber n *(vet)* tick fever
~ des Geflügels *(vet)* avian spirochaetosis *(caused by Borrelia anserina)*
Zeckenlähme f s. Zeckenparalyse
Zeckenlarve f seed tick
Zeckenparalyse f *(vet)* tick paralysis
Zeckentoxikose f *(vet)* tick toxicosis
zeckenübertragen tick-borne
Zeder f cedar *(genus Cedrus)*
Zedernfrucht f citron
Zedernholz n cedar[wood]
Zedern[holz]öl n cedarwood oil, alchitran
Zederwacholder m prickly juniper (cedar), Juniperus oxycedrus [ssp. oxycedrus]
Zedrachbaum m China tree, chinaberry, Persian lilac, Melia azedarach
Zedratzitrone f s. Zitronatzitrone
Zehe f 1. toe, digit; 2. clove *(of garlic)*
~/erste (hintere) hind-claw *(of fowl)*
Zehenballen m footpad
zeheneng toe-in, pigeon-toed *(limb conformation)*
Zehenknochen m knuckle, phalanx
Zehenkralle f toe-nail
Zehenkrallenkupierer m detoer
Zehenpicken n toe pecking *(of chickens)*
Zehenstrecksehne f digital extensor tendon
Zehenverkrümmung f [des Geflügels] crooked toe deformity
Zehnender m hart of ten
Zehn-Monate-Yams n ten-months yam, water (greater) yam, Dioscorea alata
Zehntenscheune f tithe barn
Zehrwespe f chalcid wasp *(family Chalcididae)*
Zeichentest m *(biom)* sign test
Zeichenwurz f *(bot)* jack-in-the-pulpit *(genus Arisaema)*
Zeichnung f [des Holzes] figure, grain [of wood]
~/geriegelte ripple[-mark], fiddleback [figure], cross grain
~/streifige stripe (ribbon) figure
Zeidelbaum m bee tree
Zeidelweide f forest bee pasture
Zeidelwirtschaft f forest bee-keeping
Zeidler m forest bee-keeper
Zeidlerei f s. Zeidelwirtschaft
Zeigerpflanze f indicator plant, plant indicator
Zeilkarpfen m mirror carp
Zein n zein *(maize prolamin, storage protein)*
Zeinfaser f zein staple
Zeit f/unproduktive unproductive time
Zeitgeber m timegiver, zeitgeber, synchronizer
Zeitgedächtnis n time sense

Zeitgefährtinnenvergleich *m* contemporatory comparison, CC *(animal breeding)*
zeitgerecht timely
Zeitgliederung *f s.* Zeitstudie
Zeitlose *f* autumn crocus, colchicum *(genus Colchicum)*
Zeitmischung *f (forest)* temporary mixture
Zeitraum *m* **des Durchwachsens einer Durchmesserklasse** *(forest)* time of passage
Zeitreihe *f (biom)* time series
Zeitschalter *m* time clock
Zeitsinn *m* time sense
Zeitstudie *f* time study
Zeit- und Bewegungsstudie *f* time and motion study
Zeitzuordnung *f* time allocation
Zell... *s. a.* Zyto...
Zellalterung *f* cell senescence
Zellatmung *f* cell respiration
zellauflösend cytolytic
Zellauflösung *f* cytolysis
zellbildend cytogenic, cytogenous
Zellchemie *f* cytochemistry
Zelldifferentiation *f*, **Zelldifferenzierung** *f* cell differentiation
Zelle *f* 1. *(bot, zoo)* cell; 2. *(api)* cell, alveolus; 3. compartment *(of a silo)* • **außerhalb der ~** extracellular • **innerhalb der ~** intracellular
~/chromaffine chromaffin cell
~/durch Sprossung entstandene bud cell
~/motorische motor cell *(plant anatomy)*
~/pflanzliche plant cell
~/phäochrome chromaffin cell
~/Sertolische Sertoli cell *(animal anatomy)*
Zelleib *m s.* Zytoplasma
Zelleinbruch *m s.* Zellkollaps
Zelleinschluß *m* cell (cytoplasmic) inclusion
Zelleinschlußkrankheit *f* **des Geflügels** avian cell inclusion disease
zellenartig cellular
Zellenausleser *m* indented cylinder seed cleaner
Zellenbandeinzelkornsämaschine *f* perforated belt spacing drill
Zellenlehre *f* cytology
zellenlos acellular
Zellenrad *n* cell-wheel
Zellenraddrillmaschine *f* plate feed drill, plate seeder (planter)
Zellenradsägerät *n* cell feed [wheel] mechanism, cell-wheel feed mechanism
Zellenradschleuse *f* cell-wheel injector
Zellenradzuteiler *m* cell-wheel
Zellensärad *n s.* Zellenradsägerät
Zellentrommelfilter *n* rotary drum cell filter *(sugar manufacture)*
Zellentwicklung *f* [cell] differentiation
Zellfaser *f* cellular fibre
zellfrei cell-free, acellular
Zellfusion *f* cell fusion

Zelltransformation

Zellgehalt *m* cell-count *(e.g. of milk)*
Zellgewebe *n* [cellular] tissue
Zellgift *n* cytotoxin
zellgiftig cytotoxic
Zellhohlraum *m* **[/flüssigkeitsgefüllter]** vacuole
Zellhybridisierung *f* cell fusion
zellig cellular
Zellinhalt *m* cell content
Zellkern *m* [cell] nucleus, karyon, cytoblast • **mit echtem ~** eukaryotic • **ohne echten ~** prokaryotic
Zellkernauflösung *f* karyolysis
Zellkernbestandteil *m* cell nucleus constituent
Zellkernkörperchen *n* nucleolus
~ der Eizelle germ spot
Zellkernkunde *f* karyology
Zellkernmembran *f* nuclear membrane
Zellkernplasma *n* nucleoplasm, karyoplasm
Zellkernsaft *m* karyolymph, nuclear sap
Zellkernschrumpfung *f* pycnosis
Zellkernteilung *f* nuclear division *(s. a.* Zellteilung*)*
Zellkernverschmelzung *f* karyogamy
~ bei der Befruchtung amphimixis
Zellkollaps *m* ribbing, collapse *(timber drying defect)*
Zellkolonie *f* coenobium
Zellkörper *m* cell body
Zellkultur *f* cell culture
~/stationäre batch culture
Zellmasse *f* cell mass
Zellmembran *f* cell membrane, plasmalemma
Zellmembranpotential *n* cell membrane potential
Zellorganell *n* organelle
zellpathogen cytopathogenic
Zellphysiologie *f* cell physiology
Zellproliferation *f* cell proliferation
Zellsaft *m* cell sap
Zellschicht *f* stratum
Zellstoff *m* [chemical] pulp; cellulose
~/gebleichter bleached pulp
Zellstoffaufschluß *m* chemical pulping
Zellstoffharz *n* pitch
Zellstoffholz *n* pulpwood
Zellstoffindustrie *f* pulp industry
Zellstoffwechsel *m* cell metabolism
Zellstreckung *f* cell elongation
Zellstruktur *f* cell structure
Zellsuspension *f* cell suspension
Zellsuspensionskultur *f* cell suspension culture
Zellteilung *f* cell division, cytokinesis, fission
~/äquale binary fission
~/erbgleiche *s.* **~/mitotische**
~/erbungleiche *s.* **~/meiotische**
~/meiotische meiosis, meiotic (reduction) division
~/mitotische mitosis, mitotic division, equation[al] division
~/normale binary fission
Zelltod *m* necrosis
Zelltransformation *f* cell transformation

Zelltrümmer

Zelltrümmer *pl* detritus
zellular, zellulär cellular
Zellularpathologie *f* cellular pathology
zellulolytisch cellulolytic
Zellulose *f* *s.* Cellulose
Zellverband *m*/**mehrkerniger** syncytium
Zellvergrößerung *f* hypertrophy
Zellvermehrung *f* hyperplasia
Zellverschmelzung *f* cell fusion, plasmogamy
Zellwachstum *n* cell growth
zellwachstumshemmend cytostatic
Zellwand *f* cell wall
Zellwandbestandteil *m* cell wall component
Zellwucherung *f* cell proliferation
Zellzahlbestimmung *f*, **Zellzählung** *f* cell counting
Zeltbegasung *f* tent fumigation
Zelter *m* ambler, pacer
Zeltergang *m* amble, pace, running walk
Zenkersche Degeneration (Muskeldegeneration) *f* *(vet)* Zenker's degeneration [of muscles]
Zenti-Morgan *n* *(gen)* Morgan (crossover) unit
Zentifolie *f* [moss] cabbage-rose, Provence rose, Rosa centifolia
Zentnerkürbis *s.* Riesenkürbis
Zentrale *f* milk claw, claw-piece
Zentralhydrant *m* central hydrant
Zentralkörperchen *n* centriole *(organelle)*
Zentralmark *n* central pith
Zentralnervensystem *n* central nervous system, CNS
Zentralzylinder *m* *(bot)* stele
Zentrifugaldrillmaschine *f* centrifugal [seed, feed] drill
Zentrifugaldüngerstreuer *m* centrifugal [fertilizer] distributor, centrifugal [spinner] broadcaster, centrifugal spreader
Zentrifugalemulgator *m* *(dairy)* centrifugal emulsifier
Zentrifugalentkeimung *f* *(dairy)* bactofugation
Zentrifugalpumpe *f* centrifugal pump
Zentrifugalsaatgutreinigungsmaschine *f* centrifugal seed cleaner
Zentrifugalschnitzelmaschine *f* centrifugal slicer
Zentrifugalselektion *f* disruptive selection *(breeding)*
Zentrifugalstreuer *m* *s.* Zentrifugaldüngerstreuer
Zentrifugaltraubenmühle *f* centrifugal grape mill
Zentrifuge *f* centrifuge, separator; *(api)* extractor
Zentrifugenschlamm *m* *(dairy)* separator (clarifier) slime
Zentrifugenvorlauftrog *m* centrifuge feeding trough, centrifuge mixer *(sugar manufacture)*
Zentrifugieren *n*, **Zentrifugierung** *f* centrifugation
Zentriol *n* centriole *(organelle)*
Zentromer *n* centromere *(portion of a chromosome)* • **ohne ~** acentric
Zentrosom *n* centrosome *(centriole-containing region of cytoplasm)*
Zentrosphäre *f* centrosphere *(cell division)*

Zeolith *m* zeolite *(non-clay mineral)*
Zephirblume *f* zephyr lily, flower of the west wind *(genus Zephyranthes)*
Zerealien *pl* cereals, white straw crops
zerebellär cerebellar
Zerebellum *n* cerebellum
zerebral cerebral
Zerebrom *n* *(vet)* encephaloma
Zerebrospinalflüssigkeit *f* cerebrospinal fluid, CSF
Zerebrum *n* cerebrum
Zerfall *m* decay; decomposition; disintegration
zerfallen to decay; to decompose; to disintegrate
~/geschwürig *(vet)* to ulcerate, to undergo ulceration
Zerfallsteilung *f* schizogony
Zerfaserer *m* defibrator, disintegrator; wood grinder
zerfasern to defiberize, to disintegrate
Zerfaserung *f* defibration, disintegration
zerfließend deliquescent
zergehend deliquescent
zerhacken to chop; to hog
~/zu Hackschnitzeln to chip, to hog
Zerkarie *f* cercaria *(larva of flukes)*
Zerkleinerer *m* disintegrator
zerkleinern to disintegrate; to cut up; to chop; to comminute
~/Schlagbraum *(forest)* to lop [off]
Zerkleinerung *f* disintegration, size reduction; comminution
zerklüftet rugged, jagged
zerkrümeln to crumble
zerlegbar decomposable
Zerlegbarkeit *f* decomposability
zerlegen to disassemble, to dismount *(as machines)*; to cut [up] *(e.g. a carcass)*; to break up *(game)*; to carve, to cut *(meat)*; to decompose, to dissociate, to break down *(chemically)*
~/anatomisch to dissect
Zerlegungsvorrichtung *f* *(slaught)* cutting facility
zermahlen to grind
zernagen to [be]gnaw
zerquetschen to crush, to bruise
Zerreibsel *n* *(soil)* detritus
Zerreiche *f* wainscot oak, Adriatic (Turkey, Austrian) oak, Quercus cerris
Zerreißfestigkeit *f* tensile strength
Zerreißmaschine *f* macerator
Zerreißung *f* *(vet)* rupture, laceration
zerren to strain *(a muscle)*
zersägen to saw [in]to pieces, to buck
~/in Blöcke to log
Zersatzzone *f* *(soil)* decomposition zone
zerschleifen to grind
Zerschluchtung *f* *(soil)* gully erosion, gullying
zerschmelzen to melt
zerschmelzend deliquescent

zerschroten to rough-grind, to kibble
zersetzbar decomposable
Zersetzbarkeit *f* decomposability
zersetzen to decompose, to disintegrate
~/sich to decompose, to disintegrate, to decay; to rot
Zersetzer *m* decomposer
Zersetzung *f* decomposition, disintegration, decay, breakdown • **bei Überreife in ~ übergehen** to blet *(fruit)*
~/photolytische photolytic degradation, photolysis
~/thermische thermal decomposition, pyrolysis
Zersetzungsprodukt *n* decomposition product, decay
Zersetzungstorf *m* *(soil)* disintegrated peat
Zerspaner *m* chipper, flaker, hogger
zerstäuben to atomize
Zerstäuber *m* atomizer
Zerstäuberdüse *f* atomizing jet (nozzle), atomizer
Zerstäubung *f* atomization
Zerstäubungsapparat *m* atomizer
Zerstäubungsmittel *n* atomizing agent
zerstören/die Hornknospe to disbud, to dishorn
~/die Pansenfauna to defaunate
Zerstörung *f* destruction
~ durch Pilze fungal decay
zerstreut *(bot, zoo)* sparse
zerstreutporig diffuse-porous *(wood)*
Zerstreuung *f* dispersion
zerstückelt disjunctive
Zertation *f* sperm competition
zerteilt *(bot)* laciniate[d]
Zertifikat *n* certificate
Zertifikation *f* certification
zertreten to trample, to poach *(a turf or soil)*
Zeruloplasmin *n* ceruloplasmin *(alpha-globulin)*
Zerumen *n* cerumen
zervikal cervical
Zervikalkanal *m* cervical canal
Zervikalschleim *m* cervical mucus
zervin cervine
Zervix *f* 1. cervix, neck; 2. cervix, uterine neck
Zervixkanal *m* s. Zervikalkanal
Zervizitis *f* *(vet)* cervicitis
zerwirken *(hunt)* to carve, to disjoint, to eviscerate
Zerwirkplatz *m* carcass place
Zestode *m* tapeworm, cestode [worm], cestoid *(class Cestoda)*
Zestodose *f* *(vet)* cestodiasis
zetten to ted
Zetter *m* [hay-]tedder, tedding machine
~/zweireihiger two-row tedder
Zettwender *m* tedder-and-turner
Zeug *n* *(hunt)* toils
zeugen[/Nachkommen] to generate, to sire
Zeugung *f* generation
zeugungsfähig potent, generative
Zeugungsfähigkeit *f* potence, potency
zeugungsunfähig impotent

Zeugungsunfähigkeit *f* impotence, impotency
Zezidie *f* *(phyt)* [plant] gall, gallnut
ZGE *s.* Zuchtgartenelitesaatgut
ZGSV *s.* Zwiebelgelbstreifenvirus
Zhmud *m* Zemaitukai *(horse breed)*
Zibbe *f* 1. maiden (yearling) ewe; gimmer, gimber; 2. rabbit doe; doe-hare
~/tragende in-kindle rabbit
Zibbenlamm *n* ewe lamb
~/einsömmeriges chilver
Zibetbaum *m* *(bot)* durian, Durio zibethinus
Zichorie *f* chic[k]ory, succory, blue sailors, Cichorium intybus
Zichorienwurzel *f* chic[k]ory root
Zicke *f* she-goat, goat doe, nanny[-goat]
Zickel *n* goatling, [goat] kid
zickeln to kid
Zicklein *n* s. Zickel
Zickzackegge *f* zigzag harrow
Zickzackhecke *f* zigzag hedgerow
Zickzack-Klee *m* zigzag clover, cow-grass, Trifolium medium
Zickzackpflanzung *f* zigzag planting *(vegetable growing)*
Zickzackverteilung *f* alternative distribution *(of chromosomes during meiosis)*
Zickzackwuchs *m* *(phyt)* zigzag growth
Zider *m* cider, fruit wine
Ziege *f* goat *(genus Capra)*
~/weibliche s. Zicke
Ziegeldränung *f* tile drainage
Ziegelgrustest *m* brick-grit test
Ziegelkäse *m* brick cheese
ziegelrot *(bot, zoo)* testaceous
Ziegenbock *m* he-goat, goat buck, billy[-goat]
Ziegenbocklamm *n* buckling
Ziegenbutter *f* goat butter
Ziegenfeige *f* caprifig, wild fig [tree], Ficus carica var. sylvestris
Ziegenfleisch *n* goat meat
Ziegenfütterung *f* goat feeding
Ziegenhaar *n* goat hair
Ziegenhaarling *m* goat biting louse, Bovicola (Damalinia) caprae
Ziegenhaltung *f* goat husbandry (keeping)
Ziegenhaut *f* goatskin
Ziegenherde *f* goat flock
Ziegenhirt *m* goatherd
Ziegenkäse *m* goat cheese
Ziegenlamm *n* goatling, [goat] kid
Ziegenlaus *f* goat-sucking louse, sucking goat louse, Linognathus stenopsis
Ziegenleder *n* goatskin leather
Ziegenmilch *f* goat milk
Ziegenmilchbutter *f* goat butter
Ziegenmilchkäse *m* goat cheese
Ziegenrasse *f* goat breed
Ziegenstall *m* goat house

Ziegenweide

Ziegenweide *f* goat willow, [common] sallow, Salix caprea
Ziegenwolle *f* goat hair
Ziegenzucht *f* goat breeding
Zieger *m* whey (milk serum) protein
Ziehbrunnen *m* draw-well
ziehen 1. to drift *(grazing animals)*; to trail; 2. to drag *(e.g. timber)*; 3. to train *(plantlets)*; 4. *s.* anbauen
~/im Frühbeet to hotbed
~/im Spalier to espalier, to trellis
~/im Warmhaus to hothouse, to stove
Ziehhacke *f* draw-hoe, drag fork (hoe), scuffle, bow draught hoe • **mit der ~ hacken** to scuffle
Ziehklinge *f s.* Ziehmesser
Ziehl-Neelsen-Färbung *f* Ziehl-Neelsen staining *(microbiology)*
Ziehmesser *n (forest)* draw knife, [draw] shave, scraper
Ziehroden *n* **von Stöcken (Stubben)** *(forest)* stump pulling (extraction)
Zielfernrohr *n* gunsight
Zielfindung *f (forest)* goal identification
Zielfläche *f* target area *(e.g. in pesticide application)*
Zielstamm *m (forest)* chosen (growing-stock) tree, [final] crop tree, tiller
Zielstammwirtschaft *f* chosen tree system
Zielvorrat *m (forest)* growing-stock goal (target), timber target, prescribed growing stock
Ziemer *m* pizzle
Zierapfel[baum] *m* flowering crab[-apple] *(Malus spp.)*
Zierbaum *m* ornamental tree
Zierblattpflanze *f* ornamental foliage plant
Zierfisch *m* ornamental fish
Ziergarten *m s.* Zierpflanzengarten
Ziergeflügel *n* ornamental fowl
Ziergehölz *n* woody (hardy) ornamental, ornamental (decorative) shrub
Ziergehölzanbau *m* arboriculture
Ziergehölzbaumschule *f* ornamental nursery
Ziergeschirr *n* trappings
Ziergras *n* ornamental grass
Ziergrün *n* greens
Zierkürbis *m* ornamental gourd, Cucurbita pepo ssp. pepo convar. microcarpina
Zierlauch *m* ornamental onion (garlic) *(Allium spp.)*
Zierliche Clarkie *f (bot)* clarkia, Clarkia unguiculata (elegans)
Zierlichste Fingeraralie *f (bot)* false aralia, Dizygotheca elegantissima
Ziermelone *f* mango (orange) melon, Queen Anne's pocket melon, Cucumis melo ssp. dudaim (chito)
Zierpalme *f* ornamental palm
Zierpaprika *m* ornamental pepper
Zierpflanze *f* ornamental [plant], adornment plant
~/baumförmig gezogene tree-form plant
~/einjährige annual ornamental
Zierpflanzenbau *m* ornamental horticulture, floriculture
~ unter Glas glasshouse floriculture
Zierpflanzenbehälter *m* planter
Zierpflanzengarten *m* ornamental (decorative) garden
Zierpflanzengärtner *m* ornamental horticulturist, floriculturist
Zierpflanzengärtnerei *f* ornamental nursery
Zierpflanzenindustrie *f* floricultural (floriculture) industry
Zierpflanzentopf *m* ornamental pot
Zierpflanzenzüchter *m s.* Zierpflanzengärtner
Zierpflanzenzwiebel *f* ornamental bulb
Zierquitte *f* Japanese quince, japonica, Chaenomeles japonica
Zierrasen *m* decorative lawn, fine turf
Zierrasse *f* ornamental (fancy) breed
Zierrassenzüchter *m* fancy breeder, fancier
Zierreisig *n* ornamental branches
Zierspargel *m* 1. asparagus (plumosa) fern, Asparagus setaceus (plumosus); 2. asparagus [fern], emerald feather, Asparagus densiflorus (sprengeri)
Zierstrauch *m* ornamental (decorative) shrub
Ziertabak *m* flowering tobacco, nicotiana *(Nicotiana spp.)*
Ziertaube *f* ornamental (show) pigeon
Ziertopf *m* ornamental pot
Ziervogel *m* ornamental bird
Ziest *m* hedge nettle, woundwort *(genus Stachys)*
Zigarrengestör *n* cigar-shaped raft *(timber floating)*
Zigarrenmacher *m (ent)* vine leaf-roller, Byctiscus betulae
Zigarettenblümchen *n* Mexican cigar plant, firecracker plant, Cuphaea ignea (platycentra)
Zigarettentabak *m* cigarette tobacco
Ziger *s.* Zieger
Zikade *f (ent)* 1. cicada, cicala, cigala, balm-cricket, *(Am)* locust *(genus Tettigia)*; 2. *s.* Singzikade
Ziliarkörper *m* ciliary body *(of the eye)*
Ziliate *f (zoo)* ciliate *(class Ciliata)*
Zimbelkraut *n* Kenilworth ivy, ivy-leaved toadflax, mother-of-thousands, Cymbalaria muralis, Linaria cymbalaria
Zimmerahorn *m (bot)* abutilon *(genus Abutilon)*
Zimmeraralie *f (bot)* Japanese fatsia (aralia), Fatsia japonica
Zimmerbonsai *m* indoor bonsai
Zimmercalla *f* 1. calla lily *(genus Zantedeschia)*; 2. arum lily, white calla, Zantedeschia aethiopica
Zimmercallamosaikvirus *n* dasheen mosaic virus
Zimmergießkanne *f* indoor watering can
Zimmerhopfen *m (bot)* 1. beloperone *(genus Beloperone)*; 2. shrimp plant, Beloperone guttata
Zimmerlinde *f* African hemp, sparmannia, Sparmannia africana

Zimmerpflanze f indoor (house) plant
Zimmerpflanzenschädling m house-plant pest
Zimmertanne f 1. araucaria *(genus Araucaria)*; 2. Norfolk Island pine, Araucaria heterophylla (excelsa)
Zimt m cinnamon *(spice)*
Zimtalkohol m cinnamyl alcohol *(lignin precursor)*
Zimtbaum m cinnamon *(genus Cinnamomum)*
Zimterdbeere f hautbois strawberry, Fragaria moschata (elatior)
Zimtfarn m cinnamon fern, Osmunda cinnamomea
Zimtkassie f Chinese cinnamon (cassia), cassia bark tree, Cinnamomum aromaticum (cassia)
Zimtöl n cinnamon oil
Zimtrinde f cinnamon [bark]
Zimtrose f cinnamon rose, burnet (Scotch) rose, Rosa majalis (cinnamomea)
Zimtsäure f cinnamic acid
Zimtsäure-4-Hydroxylase f cinnamic acid 4-hydroxylase *(enzyme)*
Zineb n zineb *(fungicide, herbicide)*
Zinkblende f zinc blende, sphalerite *(non-clay mineral)*
Zinkdüngemittel n zinc fertilizer
Zinke f tine, spike, tooth
Zinkenegge f spiked (tine) harrow, spike[-tooth] harrow
Zinkengerät n tined implement
Zinkengrubber m tine[d] cultivator
Zinkenhalter m tine clamp
Zinkenhaspel f tine-type reel
Zinkeninjektor m tine injector
Zinkentuch n tined canvas
Zinkentuchaufnehmer m tined canvas pick-up
Zinkenwälzegge f pitchpole harrow
Zinkmalabsorptionssyndrom n *(vet)* zinc malabsorption syndrome
Zinkmangel m zinc deficiency
Zinkphosphid n zinc phosphide *(rodenticide)*
Zinksalbe f *(vet)* zinc ointment
Zinksulfat n zinc sulphate
Zinktoxizität f zinc toxicity
Zinn n tin
Zinnie f *(bot)* 1. zinnia *(genus Zinnia)*; 2. youth-and-old-age, Zinnia elegans
Zinniol n zinniol *(phytotoxin)*
Zipfel m *(bot, zoo)* cusp
Zipfelklappe f atrioventricular valve *(of the heart)*
zipflig *(bot, zoo)* cuspidate
Zipolle f s. Zwiebel 2.
Zippe f s. Zibbe
Ziram n ziram *(fungicide)*
Zirbe[l] f s. Zirbelkiefer
Zirbeldrüse f epiphysis, pineal body (gland, organ)
Zirbeldrüsen... s. Epiphysen...
Zirbelkiefer f cembra[n] pine, arolla [pine], Swiss (stone) pine, Pinus cembra
Zirbelnuß f cembra (cedar) nut
Zirkulationsstörung f circulatory disorder

Zirkumnutation f *(bot)* circumnutation
Zirpe f s. Zikade
zirpen to chirp, to stridulate
Zirrhose f *(vet)* cirrhosis
Zirrokumulus m cirrocumulus *(cloud formation)*
Zirrostratus m cirrostratus *(cloud formation)*
Zirrus m cirrus *(cloud)*
Zisterne f [udder] cistern[a] • **innerhalb einer ~** intracisternal
Zisternenpunktion f *(vet)* cisternal puncture
Zistrose f rock (sun) rose, cistus *(genus Cistus)*
Zitrin m citrine *(non-clay mineral)*
Zitronat n candied lemon peel
Zitronatzitrone f, **Zitronatzitronenbaum** m citron, stock melon, Citrus medica
Zitrone f 1. lemon; 2. s. Zitronenbaum
Zitronellgras n 1. [Ceylon] citronella grass, nard grass, Cymbopogon nardus [var. nardus]; 2. karnkusa (khavi) grass, Cymbopogon iwarancusa
Zitronellöl n citronella
Zitronenbaum m lemon, Citrus limon
Zitronenextrakt m lemon extract
Zitronengras n lemon grass, Cymbopogon citratus
Zitronenmahagoni n dita bark, devil's-tree, Alstonia scholaris
Zitronenmelisse f [lemon] balm, common (garden, bee) balm, Melissa officinalis
Zitronenpelargonie f nutmeg[-scented] geranium, Pelargonium odoratissimum
Zitronenquendel m s. Zitronenthymian
Zitronensaft m lemon-juice
Zitronensäure f s. Citronensäure
Zitronenschale f lemon peel
Zitronenstrauch m lemon verbena, Aloysia (Lippia) triphylla, Lippia citriodora
Zitronenthymian m lemon (citron) thyme, Thymus x citriodorus
Zitrus f, **Zitrusbaum** m citrus *(genus Citrus)*
Zitrusblasenfuß m *(ent)* citrus thrips *(esp. Scirtothrips citri and S. aurantii)*
Zitruseichelfrüchtigkeit f citrus stubborn, stubborn disease of citrus
Zitruserntemaschine f citrus harvester
Zitrusfrucht f citrus [fruit]
Zitrusfruchtfleisch n citrus pulp
Zitruskommalaus f citrus mussel scale, Lepidosaphes (Mytilococcus) beckii
Zitrusöl n citrus oil
Zitrusplantage f citrus orchard
Zitruspulpe f citrus pulp
Zitrussaft m citrus juice
Zitrusschale f citrus peel
Zitrusschmierlaus f citrus (common) mealy-bug, Pseudococcus (Planococcus) citri
Zittergras n quaking (dodder) grass *(genus Briza)*
Zitterkrampf m **der Ferkel** *(vet)* congenital tremor [of piglets]

Zitterkrankheit

Zitterkrankheit *f* **der Küken** *(vet)* avian encephalomyelitis, jittery
~/enzootische border disease *(of newborn lambs)*
Zittern *n* 1. trembling, shivering *(e.g. with cold)*; 2. *(vet)* tremor
Zitterpappel *f* trembling poplar, [European, Swedish] aspen, Populus tremula
Zitwer *m (bot)* 1. zeodary, Curcuma zeodaria; 2. *s.* Zitwersamen
Zitwersamen *m* wormseed, Artemisia cina
Zitwerwurzel *f s.* Zitwer 1.
Zitze *f* teat, nipple, dug, mamilla
~/nicht milchführende blind teat
~/überzählige supernumerary teat
Zitzenanordnung *f* teat position
Zitzenbecher *m* [milking] teat cup
Zitzendesinfektionsmittel *n* teat dip
Zitzenform *f* teat shape
Zitzengummi *m* teat [cup] liner
Zitzenkanal *m* teat canal (duct)
Zitzenkanüle *f (vet)* udder cannula
Zitzenläsion *f* teat lesion
Zitzennekrose *f (vet)* teat necrosis
Zitzenöffnung *f* teat orifice
Zitzentauchbad *n* teat dip
Zitzentauchen *n* teat-dipping
Zitzenzahl *f* teat number
Zitzenzisterne *f* teat cistern, cavity of the teat
ZKZ *s.* Zwischenkalbezeit
ZMV *s.* Zwiebelmosaikvirus
ZNS *s.* Zentralnervensystem
Zobel *m* sable, Martes zibellina
Zobelfell *n* sable
Zobelpelz *m* sable
zoidiogam *(bot)* zoidiogamous
Zoidiogamie *f (bot)* zoidiogamy
Zoidiophilie *f s.* Zoophilie
Zökum *n s.* Zäkum
zöliakal coeliac
zonal zonal
Zonalität *f* zonality
Zonalpelargonie *f* zonal geranium (pelargonium), horseshoe (fish) geranium, Pelargonium zonale
zonar zonal
Zonation *f s.* Zonierung
Zone *f*/**embryonale** cell enlargement area *(in shoot or root tips)*
~/gemäßigte temperate region (zone)
~/thermisch neutrale thermoneutral (thermal-comfort) zone
Zonenelektrophorese *f* zonal electrophoresis
Zonierung *f* zonation *(geobotany)*
Zönobium *n* coenobium
zönokarp *(bot)* syncarpous
Zönose *f (ecol)* coenosis, community
Zönospezies *f (gen)* coenospecies
zönotisch coenotic
Zönotyp *m (ecol)* coenotype
zönozytisch *(bot)* coenocytic

Zönurose *f* coenurosis, circling disease, sturdy, gid, goggle *(of sheep, caused by Coenurus cerebralis)* • **an ~ erkrankt** sturdied
Zönurus *m* coenurus
Zoo *m* zoo, zoological garden
Zoo... *s. a.* Tier...
Zooanthroponose *f* zoonosis
Zoobenthos *n (ecol)* zoobenthos
Zoochorie *f (bot)* zoochory
Zoologe *m* zoologist
Zoologie *f* zoology, animal biology (science)
zoologisch zoological
Zoomorphologie *f* zoomorphology
Zoonose *f* zoonosis
zoonotisch zoonotic
Zooparasitologie *f* zooparasitology
zoophag carnivorous, flesh-eating
Zoophage *m* carnivore, flesh-eater
Zoophilie *f (bot)* zoophily
Zooplankton *n* zooplankton
Zoosporangium *n (bot)* zoosporangium
Zoospore *f* zoospore, swarm spore (cell)
Zoosporogenese *f* zoosporogenesis
Zoosterin *n s.* Zoosterol
Zoosterol *n* zoosterol, animal sterol
Zootechnik *f* zootechny
Zootechniker *m* zootechnician, animal technician
zootechnisch zootechnic[al]
Zootier *n* zoo animal
Zootiermedizin *f* zoo animal medicine
Zootomie *f* zootomy, animal anatomy
Zootoxin *n* zootoxin, animal poison
Zoozönose *f (ecol)* zoocoenosis
Zopf *m* head [log], top [log], crown, tip *(of tree)*
Zopfdurchmesser *m* small-end diameter, top diameter, diameter at the top (smaller end) *(timber mensuration)*
zopfen *(forest)* to top [off], to behead, to stop
Zopfende *n* top end, small[er] end *(of a trunk)* • **mit dem ~ voran** top end first
Zopfholz *n* topwood, tops
Zopfmaß *n* top measure
Zopfstärke *f s.* Zopfdurchmesser
Zopfstück *n* head (top) log
zopftrocken stag-headed, spike-topped, dry-topped, top-dry *(tree)*
Zopftrockenheit *f*, **Zopftrocknis** *f* stag-headedness
Zopfumfang *m* top girth
Zopfware *f s.* Zopfholz
Zotte *f* villus
Zottelwicke *f* hairy (fodder, Russian) vetch, Vicia villosa
Zottenatrophie *f (vet)* villus atrophy
zottenförmig villiform
Zottenhaut *f* chorion
Zottenpolyp *m (vet)* papilloma
zottenreich *(zoo)* frondose
zottentragend villiferous

zottig *(bot, zoo)* villose, villous, hirsute
~/einseitig *(bot)* heteromallous
Zottige Lupine *f* blue lupin[e], Lupinus micranthus (hirsutus)
Zottiger Flieder *m* late lilac, Syringa villosa
~ Kohl *m* villous cabbage, Brassica rupestris ssp. villosa
Zottiges Weidenröschen *n* great hairy willow-herb, codlins-and-cream, Epilobium hirsutum
ZP *s.* Zündwarenholz
Z-Rübe *f* Z-type sugar-beet, high-sugar beet
Z-Stamm *m s.* Zielstamm
Zubringer *m* feeder; packer *(of a pick-up baler)*
Zubringerband *n* feeder belt
Zubringerweg *m (forest)* feeder road, spar (spur) road
Zubringerzinke *f* packer finger *(of a pick-up baler)*
Zucchini *pl*, **Zucchino** *m* zucchini, summer squash, courgette, bush-type vegetable marrow, Cucurbita pepo ssp. pepo var. styriaca convar. giromontiina
Zucht *f* 1. breed; culture *(s. a. Rasse)*; 2. *s.* Züchtung 1.
Zucht... *s. a.* Züchtungs...
Zuchtalter *n* breeding age
Zuchtarbeit *f* breeding work
Zuchtberater *m* breeding advisor
Zuchtbetrieb *m* breeding enterprise
Zuchtbock *m* stud ram
Zuchtbuch *n* herd (stud) book
~/geschlossenes closed herd book
Zuchtbuchvieh *n* registered breeding stock
Zuchtbulle *m* stud (breeding) bull
Zuchtchampignon *m* [cultivated] mushroom, Agaricus bisporus
Zuchteber *m* breeding (service) boar
~/kastrierter brawner, stag, castrated [breeding] boar
züchten to breed, to cultivate *(plants)*; to culture *(bacteria)*; to breed, to raise, to rear *(animals)*
~/auf Zwergwuchs to dwarf
~/durch Kreuzung to cross-breed, to interbreed
Züchter *m* breeder, raiser, culturist
Zuchtergebnis *n s.* Zucht 1.
Züchtergemeinschaft *f* breeder co-operative
Züchterrecht *n* plant breeder's right
Züchterschutz *m* protection of breeders, breeder's rights
Züchterverein *m*, **Züchtervereinigung** *f* breeder's association
Zuchtexperiment *n* breeding experiment
Zuchtfähigkeit *f* breeding ability
Zuchtfähigkeitsdauer *f* breeding life
Zuchtfische *mpl* broodstock
Zuchtforelle *f* farmed trout
Zuchtfortschritt *m* genetic gain (improvement)
Zuchtgarten *m* nursery
Zuchtgartenelitesaatgut *n* foundation seed
Zuchtgebiet *n* breeding district
Zuchtgebrauch *m* breeding use
Zuchtgeflügel *n* breeding poultry
Zuchtgemeinschaft *f* breeding company, breed association (society)
Zuchthäsin *f* breeding doe
Zuchthengst *m* breeding stallion
Zuchtherde *f* breeding herd; breeding flock, breeder (brood) flock
Zuchthygiene *f* breeding hygiene
Zuchtjunghahn *m* breeder cockerel
Zuchtkälte *f* frigidity
Zuchtkarpfen *m* [pond] carp, Cyprinus carpio
Zuchtkondition *f* breeding condition
Zuchtlähme *f* **der Pferde** equine syphilis, covering disease *(caused by Trypanosoma equiperdum)*
Zuchtleiter *m* breeding manager
Zuchtlinie *f* [breeding] line, strain
Zuchtmaterial *n* breeding material (stock)
Zuchtmerkmal *n* breeding characteristic, [breeding] trait
Zuchtpferd *n* breeding horse
Zuchtplan *m* breeding plan
Zuchtpopulation *f* breeding population
Zuchtrasse *f* breed; pedigree race
Zuchtraum *m* brood chamber *(for mass rearing of insects)*
Zuchtrinder *npl* breeding cattle
Zuchtsau *f* brood (breeding) sow
Zuchtsorte *f* [bred] variety, [select] cultivar
Zuchtstall *m* breeding house (barn)
Zuchtstamm *m* pedigree race
Zuchtstammsaatgut *n* breeder (basic) seed
Zuchtstation *f* breeding station
Zuchtstute *f* breeding (brood) mare, stud (stock) mare
Zuchtsystem *n* breeding system
zuchttauglich at (in) stud
Zuchttauglichkeit *f* breeding suitability (soundness)
Zuchttauglichkeitsuntersuchung *f* breeding soundness examination, BSE
Zuchtteich *m* breeding [fish] pond
Zuchttier *n* breeding animal
Zuchttierbestand *m* breeding stock
Züchtung *f* 1. breeding, cultivation *(esp. of plants)*; breeding, rearing, raising *(esp. of animals)*; 2. *s.* Zucht 1.
~ auf Widerstandsfähigkeit resistance breeding
Züchtungs... *s. a.* Zucht...
Züchtungsempfehlung *f* breeding recommendation
Züchtungsforschung *f* breeding research
Züchtungsgeschichte *f* breeding history
Züchtungskunde *f* thremmatology
Züchtungsmethode *f* breeding method
Züchtungsprogramm *n* breeding programme
Züchtungsschema *n* breeding scheme
Züchtungsstrategie *f* breeding strategy
Züchtungssystem *n* breeding system

Züchtungstechnik

Züchtungstechnik f breeding technique
Züchtungsüberwachung f breeding control
Züchtungsverfahren n breeding method
Züchtungsversuch m breeding experiment
Zuchtverfahren n breeding procedure
~/diskontinuierliches discontinuous crossing
~/kontinuierliches continuous crossing
zuchtverwendungsfähig s. zuchttauglich
Zuchtvieh n breeding (pedigree) cattle, breeding stock
Zuchtwahl f selection
~/natürliche natural selection
Zuchtwart m breeding manager
Zuchtwert m breeding value (worth), genic value
~/relativer relative breeding value
Zuchtwertklasse f breeding class
Zuchtwertschätzung f estimation of breeding value, breeding-value appraisal (estimation)
Zuchtwertschätzungsverfahren n breeding-value estimation procedure
Zuchtwertverhältnis n breeding-value ratio
Zuchtwidder m stud ram
Zuchtzentrum n breeding centre
Zuchtziel n breeding objective (goal), breeding target (aim)
Zuchtzielrasse f breed
Zucker m sugar, saccharum • **Stärke in ~ umwandeln** to saccharify
~/affinierter affinated (affination) sugar, washed raw sugar
~/einfacher simple sugar
~/reduzierender reducing sugar
~/seltener unusual sugar
~/unvergärbarer non-fermentable sugar
Zuckerahorn m sugar-maple, Canadian (rock) maple, blister (bird's-eye) maple, Acer saccharum
Zuckerahornpflanzung f sugar orchard, sugar-bush
Zuckeralkohol m sugar alcohol, alditol
Zuckerapfel m s. Rahmapfel
Zuckerausbeute f sugar yield
Zuckerbestimmung f sugar determination
Zuckerbirke f sweet birch, Betula lenta
Zuckercouleur f caramel, sugar colouring
Zuckererbse f sugar-pea, snow (edible-podded) pea, mange-tout [pea], Pisum sativum convar. axiphium
Zuckerertrag m sugar yield
zuckererzeugend sugar-producing, sacchariferous
Zuckerextraktionsqualität f sugar extraction quality
Zuckerfabrik f beet-sugar (sugar-beet) factory, sugar factory (mill, plant)
Zuckerfutterrübe f fodder [sugar-]beet, Beta vulgaris var. alba (crassa)
Zuckergast m (ent) silver fish, slicker, Lepisma saccharina
Zuckergehalt m sugar content
~ des Blutes[/normaler] glycaemia

Zuckergehaltsbestimmung f saccharimetry
Zuckergewinnung f sugar manufacture
zuckerhaltig sacchariferous, saccharine, sugary
Zuckerharnruhr f s. Zuckerkrankheit
Zuckerhaus n sugar-house (of a sugar factory)
Zuckerherstellung f sugar manufacture
Zuckerhirse f 1. sweet (sugar) sorghum, Sorghum dochna (vulgare var. saccharatum); 2. s. Zuckersorghum
Zuckerhut m sugar loaf
zuckerig sugary, saccharine
Zuckerindustrie f sugar industry
Zuckerkandis m [sugar-]candy
Zuckerkiefer f sugar pine, Lambert's (gigantic) pine, Pinus lambertiana
Zuckerkrankheit f (vet) diabetes (for compounds s. under Diabetes)
Zuckerkristall m crystal of sugar
zuckerliefernd sacchariferous
Zuckerlösung f sugar solution; priming solution (brewing)
Zuckermais m (Am) sweet (sugar) corn, Zea mays convar. saccharata (var. rugosa)
Zuckermelone f [musk-]melon, musky gourd (pumpkin), honeydew melon, cantaloup[e], Cucumis melo
Zuckermelonengelbstauchevirus n musk-melon yellow stunt virus, MYSV
Zuckermetabolismus m s. Zuckerstoffwechsel
zuckern to sugar; to chaptalize (wine)
Zuckerpalme f [true] sugar palm, Arenga pinnata (sacchariferα)
Zuckerpflanze f sugar plant
Zuckerraffinerie f sugar-refinery
zuckerreich high-sugar
Zuckerrohr n 1. sugar-cane, [noble] cane, saccharum (genus Saccharum); 2. sugar-cane, Saccharum officinarum
~/mehrjährig genutztes ratoon [cane, crop]
~ vom ersten Wuchs plant cane
Zuckerrohrabfälle mpl cane-trash
Zuckerrohrbohrer m (ent) sugar-cane [shoot] borer, Diatraea saccharalis
Zuckerrohrbrand m (phyt) sugar-cane smut (caused by Ustilago scitaminea)
Zuckerrohrerntemaschine f sugar-cane harvester
Zuckerrohrhirse f sorgo, forage (sweet, roxorange) sorghum, shattercane, Sorghum bicolor (vulgare)
Zuckerrohrkarre f sugar-cane trailer
Zuckerrohrlader m [sugar-]cane loader
Zuckerrohrmark n sugar-cane pith
Zuckerrohrmelasse f cane molasses
Zuckerrohrmosaikvirus n sugar-cane mosaic virus
Zuckerrohrpflanzmaschine f sugar-cane planter
Zuckerrohrpflug m sugar-cane plough
Zuckerrohrrechen m sugar-cane rake
Zuckerrohrsaft m sugar-cane juice

Zugleistung

Zuckerrohrsilage f sugar-cane silage
Zuckerrohrsteckling m set[t]
Zuckerrohrstroh n sugar-cane straw
Zuckerrohrwachs n sugar-cane wax
Zuckerrübe f sugar-beet, [high-sugar-]beet, Beta vulgaris var. altissima
~/**normale** normal beet
~/**zuckerreiche** high-sugar beet, Z-type sugar-beet
Zuckerrüben... s. a. Rüben...
Zuckerrübenanbau m [sugar-]beet growing
Zuckerrübenanbauer m [sugar-]beet grower
Zuckerrübenanbaugebiet n beet-growing area
Zuckerrübenernte sugar-beet harvest
Zuckerrübenerntemaschine f sugar-beet harvester
Zuckerrübenköpfer m sugar-beet topper
Zuckerrübenroder m sugar-beet lifter
Zuckerrübensaatgut n sugar-beet seed
Zuckerrübensaft m sugar-beet juice
Zuckerrübenschnitzel npl [beet] cossettes, beet slices, sugar-beet chips, shreds
~/**ausgelaugte** leached cossettes, beet pulp
~/**eingesäuerte (silierte)** fermented (siloed) beet pulp
~/**vollwertige** dried sugar-beet cossettes
Zuckerrübensteckling m sugar-beet steckling
Zuckerrübentrockenschnitzel npl dried beet pulp
Zuckerrübenverarbeitung f sugar-beet processing
Zuckerrübenwurzellaus f sugar-beet root aphid, Pemphigus betae
Zuckersäure f sugar (glucaric) acid
Zucker-Säure-Verhältnis n sugar-acidity ratio *(in fruits)*
Zuckerschnitzel npl dried sugar-beet cossettes
Zuckersorghum n sugar sorghum *(comprehensive term)*
Zuckerstange f ingot of sugar
Zuckerstoffwechsel m sugar metabolism
Zuckerstrauch m 1. honeypot sugarbush, protea *(genus Protea)*; 2. Protea repens
zuckersüß sugary
Zuckertang m *(bot)* kelp, Laminaria japonica (saccharina)
Zuckertechnologie f sugar technology
Zuckerung f chaptalization *(of wine)*
Zuckerwirtschaft f sugar industry
Zuckerwurz[el] f *(bot)* chervin, skirret, Sium sisarum
Zuckmücke f midge *(family Chironomidae)*
zudecken to cover *(e.g. seed)*
~/**mit Erde** to earth [over, up]
Zudeckscheibe f covering disk *(of a seeder)*
Zuerwerbsbetrieb m part-time farm
Zufallbringen n bringing down, rolling-off *(tree-felling)*
zufällig accidental, incidental; adventitious
Zufälligkeit f randomness
Zufallsauswahl f random sampling

Zufallsfehler m *(biom)* random error
zufallsgepaart *(gen)* panmictic
Zufallsgröße f s. Zufallsvariable
Zufallsnutzung f *(forest)* extraordinary felling
Zufallspaarung f random mating, panmixia, panmixis
Zufallsstichprobe f random sample
Zufallsstichprobenverfahren n random sampling
Zufallsvariable f *(biom)* random variable, stochastic (chance) variable, variate
~/**kontinuierliche** continuous variate
zufallsverteilt randomly [distributed]
Zufallsverteilung f *(biom, ecol)* random distribution
zufallsweise randomly
Zufallswirt m *(phyt, vet)* accidental (casual) host
Zufallszahl f *(biom)* random number
Zufallszahlentafel f random number table
Zufallszuteilung f randomization
Zuflucht f shelter
Zufluchtsort m escape-cover[t] *(of game)*
Zufluß m inlet
Zuflußöffnung f inlet
Zuführen n joining *(animal breeding)*
Zuführschnecke f feeding auger
Zuführungsband n feed belt
Zuführungsrohr n delivery tube
Zugarbeit f haulage [work], tractive (draught) work
Zugast m sap drawer
Zugbeanspruchung f tensile stress
Zügel m rein, ribbon • **mit dem ~ lenken** to rein
Zügelleder n line leather
zügeln to rein, to bridle, to bit, to pull in
Zügelorchis f *(bot)* rein orchis *(genus Habenaria)*
Zügelring m rein ring
zugespitzt *(bot, zoo)* apiculate[d], spicular, spiculate, acuminate
zugewachsen overgrown
zugfest tenacious
Zugfestigkeit f tensile strength
Zughacke f draw-hoe, drag fork
Zughaken m [draw] hook, drawbar
Zughakenleistung f drawbar (hitch) power, tractive performance
Zughalsband n choke (check) collar, choke chain *(for dogs)*
Zugholz n tension wood
Zugkraft f draught (pull) power, tractive force, traction; tensile force
~/**effektive** drawbar pull
~/**tierische** [draught] animal power
Zugkraftbedarf m draught requirement, traction (pull power) requirements
Zugkraftregelung f draught control *(of a tractor)*
Zugkraftsensor m draught sensor
Zugkrampe f hame *(of a horse collar)*
Zugleine f *(pisc)* warp
Zugleistung f s. Zughakenleistung

Zugleitungsregneranlage

Zugleitungsregneranlage *f* tow-line sprinkler system, hose drag system of sprinkler irrigation
Zugluft *f* draught
Zugmaschine *f s.* Traktor
Zugnetz *n (pisc)* drag (haul) net, trawl[-net], seine[-net]
Zugpendel *n* swinging drawbar (hitch bar)
Zugpferd *n* draught-horse, cart (carriage) horse, dobbin
Zugpferderasse *f* draught breed
zugrunde gehen to die off
Zugrundegehen *n* dying-off
Zugsäge *f* drag saw
Zugsägeblatt *n* web saw
Zugscheit *n* swingletree, swingle-bar, whippletree, *(Am)* whiffletree
Zugschiene *f* drawbar, hitch bar, drag rail
Zugseil *n (forest)* drag-line, haulage cable (line), traction cable (line), main (yarding) line; skidder (skidding) line
Zugseilumlenkrolle *f* bull block
Zugspannung *f* tensile stress
Zugstrang *m* trace *(of a harness)*
Zugstraße *f* travel corridor *(of game)*; migration route *(esp. of birds)*
Zugstrick *m* calving rope
Zugtier *n* draught (fraught) animal, beast of draught
Zugtierbetrieb *m* animal traction
Zugtraktor *m* haulage (truck) tractor, utility (general-purpose) tractor
Zugtrense *f* tow snaffle[s]
Zugtrosse *f* hawser *(s. a.* Zugseil*)*
Zugvermögen *n* tractive performance
Zugvieh *n* draught cattle, work stock
Zugvogel *m* migratory bird, bird of passage
Zugvolumen *n* inspiratory volume
zuheilen to heal [over, up]
Zukauffutter[mittel] *n* purchased feed[-stuff], bought-in feed-stuff
Zukaufkalb *n* bought-in calf
Zukunftsbaum *m*, **Zukunftsstamm** *m (forest)* chosen (growing-stock) tree, elite stem (tree), [final] crop tree, tiller
Zukunftsstammwirtschaft *f* chosen-tree system
zulassen to approve *(e.g. plant cultivars, agrochemicals)*
~/zum Anbau to release
Zulassung *f* approval, admission; label clearance
Zulassungsverfahren *n* admission procedure
Zuleitungsgraben *m* feeding ditch
Zuleitungsrohr *n* feed pipe (tube)
Zulieferindustrie *f* supporting industry
Zuluft *f* ingoing air
Zumaischstoff *m* adjunct *(brewing)*
zumessen to meter, to dose
~/Abstände to space
Zumessung *f* dosage
Zunahme *f* 1. increase; gain *(in body weight)*; 2. rise *(e.g. of temperature)*; 3. *s.* Zuwachs

Zunder *m* tinder, punk *(s. a.* Zunderschwamm*)*
Zunderschwamm *m* 1. agaric *(esp. genus* Fomes*)*; 2. tinder fungus, Fomes (Polyporus) fomentarius
Zündpunkt *m* ignition temperature
zundrig tindery, punky
Zündtemperatur *f* ignition temperature
Zündversager *m* misfire
Zündwarenholz *n* matchwood
zunehmen to increase; to gain (put on) weight; to rise; to accrete
Zunge *f* tongue
Zungenbein *n* tongue-bone, hyoid apparatus (bone)
Zungenblatt *n (bot)* tongue-leaf *(genus* Glottiphyllum*)*
Zungenblättriger Mäusedorn *m (bot)* double tongue, Ruscus hypoglossum
Zungenblüte *f* ligulate ray flower
Zungenentzündung *f (vet)* glossitis
zungenförmig *(bot, zoo)* linguiform
Zungenvene *f* lingual vein
Zungenwurm *m* tongue worm, Linguatula serrata
Zungenwurzel *f* root of the tongue
Zünsler *m* pyralid [moth], pyralidan, snout moth *(family* Pyralidae*)*
Zünslerraupe *f* leaf-tier, leaf tyer, web-worm
Zuordnung *f/zufällige* randomization
zurechtschneiden, zurechtstutzen to trim, to clip
zureiten to break [in], to rough, to exercise
Zureiter *m* horse-breaker, rough-rider, [bronco]buster
Zürgelbaum *m* nettle tree, hackberry *(genus* Celtis*)*
Zürgelbeere *f* hackberry
zurichten to dress
Zurichtung *f* dressing
zurückbilden *(bot, phyt)* to abort
zurückbleiben to lag [behind]
zurückgebildet abortive; rudimentary
zurückgeblieben backward
zurückgebogen *(bot, zoo)* reflexed, retroflex[ed], reclinate
Zurückgebogener Fuchsschwanz *m* green (common) amaranth, *(Am)* redroot [pigweed], Amaranthus retroflexus
zurückgekrümmt *(bot)* recurvate
zurückgerollt *(bot)* revolute
zurückschneiden to cut back [to stump]; to prune down (back), to shorten
Zurückschneiden *n* cutting back; pruning back
~ unerwünschter Vegetation *(forest)* slashing
zurückstutzen to head [back, down]
zurückwiegen to reweigh
Zusammenarbeit *f* co-operation
zusammenbacken to cake *(e.g. fertilizer)*
zusammenballen/sich to agglutinate, to clump
Zusammenballung *f* agglutination, clump *(e.g. of bacteria)*; aggregation *(e.g. of soil particles)*

zusammenbinden to bundle
~/zu einem Floß to raft
zusammenbrechen to break down, to collapse
Zusammenbruch *m* breakdown, collapse
zusammendrängen to crush together *(animals)*
~/sich to huddle [together]
zusammenfließen to coalesce
Zusammenfließen *n* coalescence
zusammenfließend coalescent
zusammengeballt convolute
Zusammengerechte *n* raking *(hay or straw)*
zusammengerollt rolled up, convolute
zusammengeschlossen *(bot, zoo)* aggregate
zusammengeschwemmt *(soil)* colluvial
zusammengesetzt *(bot, zoo)* composite
~/doppelt decomposite
zusammenhängend coherent
zusammenharken to rake together
zusammenhäufen to cock *(hay)*
Zusammenleben *n* [**/parabiotisches**] parabiosis
zusammennehmen to collect *(a horse)*
Zusammenpflügen *n* gathering
zusammenrechen to rake together
zusammenrollen/sich to hunch *(animal)*
Zusammenschlag *m* 1. back furrow; 2. *s.* Zusammenpflügen
zusammenschlagen to backfurrow
Zusammenschluß *m* aggregation *(e.g. of soil particles)*
zusammenschütten to bulk
Zusammenschwemmung *f* colluvium
Zusammensetzung *f* 1. composition, make-up *(e.g. of a compound)*; 2. structure
~/altersmäßige age structure
~/konfektionierte formulation *(e.g. of a plant protectant)*
~ nach Arten species composition
zusammentreiben to round up, to muster *(cattle)*
Zusammentreiben *n* round-up, drive *(of cattle)*
zusammenwachsen to grow together; to accrete; to coalesce
Zusammenwachsen *n* *(forest)* accretion; concrescence
zusammenwachsend coalescent
Zusammenwirken *n* synergism, synergy
zusammenwirkend synergistic, synerg[et]ic
Zusammenziehung *f* contraction; *(vet)* syneresis
Zusatz *m* additive, admixture
~/staubverhindernder antidust [agent]
Zusatzbeleuchtung *f*, **Zusatzbelichtung** *f* supplementary lighting
Zusatzbelüftung *f* supplemental aeration
Zusatzberegnung *f* supplemental (extra) irrigation
Zusatzbewässerung *f* supplemental (extra) irrigation
Zusatzdüngung *f* complementary fertilization
Zusatzfutter *n* extra feed
Zusatzfutterfläche *f* supplementary forage area

Zusatzheizung *f* 1. supplemental heating; 2. booster heater *(e.g. in greenhouses)*
Zusatzlachte *f* back-face *(resin-tapping)*
Zusatzlicht *n* supplementary light
Zusatzmittel *n* *s.* Zusatzstoff
Zusatzstoff *m* additive, admixture; adjunct *(brewing)*
~/qualitätsmindernder (verfälschender) adulterant
Zusatzwasser *n* supplemental water
Zusatzwasserbedarf *m* irrigation requirement (need)
Zusatzwassergabe *f* irrigation (water) application
Zusatzwein *m* blend wine
Zusatzwerkzeug *n* **am Pflug** auxiliary plough working element
Zusatzwirt *m* accessory host
Zuschlag[stoff] *m* load
zuschneiden to trim
Zuschnittsägemaschine *f* stripper
zusetzen to admix, to add
~/Hefe to pitch *(brewing)*
Zusetzen *n* *(api)* adding, allocation
Zustand *m* status
Zustreicher *m* drag share, coverer *(of planters)*
zuteilen to dispense, to dose; to allowance, to ration *(e.g. food)*
~/zufallsweise to randomize
Zuteiler *m* *s.* Zuteilvorrichtung
Zuteilung *f* allowance
Zuteilvorrichtung *f* dispenser, dosing apparatus; *(api)* feeder
zutreiben *(hunt)* to chase, to beat up
Zutreter *m* draught ewe
Zuwachs *m* *(forest)* [growth] increment, accretion, ingrowth, recruitment
~/durchschnittlicher mean increment
~/laufender current increment
~/laufender jährlicher current annual increment, c.a.i.
~/periodischer periodic increment
Zuwachsberechnung *f* increment determination
Zuwachsbohrer *m* increment (accretion) borer
Zuwachsbohrung *f* increment boring
zuwachsen 1. to begome overgrown, to overgrow *(e.g. a road)*; to close up *(e.g. a hedge)*; 2. to heal [over, up], to occlude *(e.g. a wound)*
Zuwachsermittlung *f* increment determination
Zuwachshammer *m* increment hammer
Zuwachskurve *f* increment curve
Zuwachsmantel *m* growth (growing) layer *(of a tree)*
Zuwachsmittelstamm *m* increment mean stem
Zuwachsprognose *f* growth prediction
Zuwachsprozent *n* increment percent[age], growth percent
Zuwachsrate *f* rate of increment (growth)
Zuwachsring *m* annual ring (growth layer) *(of wood)*

Zuwachsringgrenze *f* growth-ring boundary
Zuwachstafel *f* increment table
Zuwachszone *f* increment (accretion) zone; growth ring *(in tropical woods)*
Zuwanderung *f (ecol)* immigration
zw *s.* zwischenständig
Zwanghuf *m (vet)* contracted heel
Zwangsbelüftung *f* forced (induced) ventilation
Zwangseinschlag *m (forest)* compulsory felling
Zwangsfütterung *f* forced feeding, force-feeding
Zwangshieb *m s.* Zwangseinschlag
Zwangslüftung *f s.* Zwangsbelüftung
Zwangsmauser *f* force-moult, induced moulting
Zwangsmittel *n* restraining device *(esp. for handling large animals)*
Zwangspferch *m* forcing pen
Zwangsstand *m* bale
Zwangsumlaufverdampfer *m* forced-circulation evaporator *(sugar manufacture)*
Zweiachsschlepper *m*, **Zweiachstraktor** *m* four-wheel[ed] tractor
zweibäuchig digastric *(muscle)*
Zweibindiger Pilzschwarzkäfer *m* two-banded fungus beetle, Alphitophagus bifasciatus
zweiblättrig *(bot)* bifoliate, diphyllous
Zweiblättriger Blaustern *m (bot)* two-leaved squill, Scilla bifolia
Zweiblattstadium *n* two-leaf stage
zweiblütig *(bot)* geminiflorous
Zweiblütige Helmbohne *f (bot)* horse gram, Dolichos biflorus
Zweibrücker Pferd *n* Zweibrucken *(horse breed)*
zweieiig dizygotic
zweietagig two-storeyed *(resin blaze)*
Zweifachkupplung *f* two-stage clutch
Zweifachzucker *m* disaccharide
zweifarbig bicoloured
Zweifarbige Eiche *f* swamp white oak, Quercus bicolor
~ Rhoeopflanze *f* Moses-in-a-boat, Moses-in-the-cradle, oyster-plant, Rhoeo spathacea (discolor)
Zweifarbiger Buschklee *m (bot)* bicolour lespedeza, Lespedeza bicolor
Zweifelderwirtschaft *f* two-field rotation (system)
zweiflügelig *(bot)* dipterous
Zweiflügler *m* two-winged fly, dipteran *(order Diptera)*
Zweifrucht[an]bau *m* double cropping
Zweifurchenpflug *m s.* Zweischar[beet]pflug
Zweig *m* twig, branch, stick • **Zweige ausbilden** to branch [out] • **Zweige tragend** branching, branchy
~/kleiner branchlet, sprig
~/überhängender hanger
Zweigabplattung *f (phyt)* branch flattening
Zweigattersägewerk *n* twin-frame sawmill
Zweigbildung *f* branch formation
zweigblütig *(bot)* ramiflorous

Zweigbohrer *m (ent)* twig girdler *(comprehensive term)*
Zweigbrand *m* twig blight *(of pome fruit, caused by Erwinia amylovora)*
Zweigdichte *f* density of branches
zweigeschlechtlich bisexual, hermaphroditic[al], hermaphrodite, digenous; *(bot)* monoclinous
Zweigeschlechtlichkeit *f* bisexuality, hermaphroditism
zweigestaltig dimorphic
Zweigestaltigkeit *f* dimorphism
zweigeteilt *(bot, zoo)* dichotomous
Zweiggrind *m* **der Birne** *(phyt)* pear scab *(caused by Venturia pirina)*
zweigig *(bot)* ramate
Zweigknoten *m* branch node
Zweigkrankheit *f* **des Flieders** phytophthora disease of lilac *(caused by Phytophthora syringae)*
Zweigkrebs *m* **der Süßkirsche** cherry detrimental canker *(virosis)*
Zweiglein *n* branchlet, sprig
Zweigminierer *m s.* Zweigbohrer
Zweigranke *f* branch tendril
Zweigriffliger Weißdorn *m* quickthorn, [common, midland] hawthorn, Crataegus laevigata (oxyacantha)
Zweigspitze *f* branch tip
Zweigsteckling *m* branch cutting; hardwood cutting
Zweigsterben *n (phyt)* twig die back
Zweigsucht *f (phyt)* witches' broom, fasciculation
Zweigtreiberei *f* cut twigs forcing
Zweihand[baum]schere *f* lopper
zweihäusig *(bot)* dioecious
Zweihäusige Zaunrübe *f* red[-berry] bryony, Bryonia [cretica ssp.] dioica
Zweihäusiges Katzenpfötchen *n (bot)* [common] pussy-toes, Antennaria dioica
Zweihäusigkeit *f (bot)* dioecism, dioecy
zweihiebig two-storeyed *(forest stand)*
Zweihöckeriges Kamel *n* [Bactrian] camel, Camelus bactrianus
zweihodig diorchic
Zweihordendarre *f* double floor kiln, two-floor kiln *(malting)*
zweihüllig *(bot)* di[plo]chlamydeous
Zweijahrespflanze *f* biennial [plant]
zweijährig biennial
Zweijährige Pippau *f (bot)* rough hawk's-beard, Crepis biennis
Zweijähriger Frühklee *m* broad[-leaved] red clover, medium (double-cut) red clover, Trifolium pratense var. sativum subvar. praecox
zweikeimblättrig dicotyledonous
Zweikorn *n* emmer [wheat], Triticum dicoccon
zweilappig *(bot, zoo)* bilobate, bilobed
zweilippig *(bot)* bilabial, bilabiate
Zweimaischverfahren *n* two-mash method *(brewing)*

Zweimannblattsäge f, **Zweimannhandsäge** f double-handed saw, two-man hand saw
zweinadelig two-needled *(conifer)*
Zweinährstoffdünger m binary fertilizer
Zweinutzungskuh f dual-purpose cow
Zweinutzungsrasse f dual-purpose breed, two-way breed
Zweinutzungsrind n dual-purpose cattle
Zweiphasendrusch m two-stage threshing
Zweiphasenernte f two-phase harvest, two-stage harvest
Zweiphasenkompostierung f two-phase composting
Zweipflanzencontainer m two-plant container
Zweipunktige Wiesenwanze f *(ent)* potato capsid, Calocoris norvegicus
Zweipunktiger Eichenprachtkäfer m *(Am, ent)* oak burncow, Coraebus (Agrilus) bifasciatus
Zweipunktkäfer m *(ent)* two-spotted ladybird, Adalia (Coccinella) bipunctata
Zweiradantrieb m two-wheel drive
Zweirad-Einachstraktor m two-wheeled walking tractor
Zweirassenwechselkreuzung f two-breed crisscross *(animal breeding)*
Zweireihenpflanzmaschine f two-row planter
Zweirichtungsselektion f bidirectional selection
Zweischar[beet]pflug m two-furrow plough
Zweischichtenpflug m double-deck plough, two-level plough, double-cut plough, double[-dig] plough
Zweischichtentiefpflug m two-level digger plough
zweischichtig two-storeyed *(e.g. a forest stand)*
Zweischichtmineral n *(soil)* two-layer mineral
zweischneidig *(bot)* ancipital, ancipitous
Zweischnittwiese f two-cuts meadow
zweischnürig straight *(tree-trunk)*
Zweiseitenkippanhänger m two-way tipping trailer
Zweiseitenkipper m two-way tipper
zweispaltig *(bot)* bifid
zweispännig two-horse
Zweisporiger Egerling m cultivated mushroom, Agaricus bisporus
zweistrahlig diarch *(root)*
Zweistufenselektion f two-stage selection *(breeding)*
zweistufig two-storeyed *(forest stand)*
zweiteilig *(bot)* dimerous, binate, bipartite
Zweiteinrichtung f *(forest)* second inventory
Zweitfrucht f second crop
Zweitfruchtfutterbau m second-crop forage production
Zweitinfektion f *(phyt, vet)* secondary infection
Zweitrommel[seil]winde f double-drum winch
Zweitschnitt m aftermath, aftergrass, aftercrop, *(Am)* rowen
Zweitwuchs m second growth, regrowth, aftergrowth
Zweitwuchsbestand m second-growth stand

Zweitwuchsholz n *(forest)* second-growth wood
zweiwirtig two-host
zweizackig *(bot)* bifurcate
zweizählig *(bot)* dimerous
Zweizahn m cuckold, bur marigold, sticktight *(genus Bidens)*
zweizähnig *(bot, zoo)* bidentate
Zweizähniger Kiefernborkenkäfer m two-toothed [pine] bark-beetle, small pine tree bark-beetle, Pityogenes bidentatus
zweizeilig *(bot)* distichous
Zweizeilige Gerste f two-rowed barley, Hordeum vulgare convar. distichon
~ **Sumpfeibe** f swamp cypress, Taxodium distichum
Zwenke f false brome[-grass] *(genus Brachypodium)*
Zwerchfell n diaphragm, midriff; *(slaught)* skirt
Zwerchfellatmung f diaphragmatic respiration
Zwerchfellbruch m, **Zwerchfellhernie** f *(vet)* diaphragmatic hernia
Zwerchfellnerv m phrenic nerve
Zwerchfellschlagader f phrenic artery
Zwerg m s. Zwergmutante
Zwergbanane f dwarf [Cavendish] banana, Cavendish (Canary) banana, Musa acuminata (cavendishii)
Zwergbaum m dwarf tree, arbuscle; bonsai
zwergbaumartig arbuscular
Zwergbirke f dwarf (Arctic) birch, Betula nana
Zwergblauschwingel m dwarf blue fescue, Festuca valesiaca
Zwergbuschkrankheit f *(phyt)* bushy dwarf, BD *(virosis)*
~ **der Himbeere** raspberry bushy dwarf
Zwergfadenwurmbefall m *(vet)* strongyloidiasis, strongyloidosis
Zwergfalke m merlin, Falco columbarius [aesalon]
Zwergfüßer m *(zoo)* symphylid *(subclass Symphyla)*
Zwergginster m dwarf broom *(genus Chamaecytisus)*
Zwerghalbstrauch m dwarf semishrub
Zwerghirschkäfer m little stag-beetle, Dorcus parallelopipedus
Zwerghirse f Abyssinian love grass, teff [grass], Eragrostis tef (abyssinica)
Zwergholunder m dwarf (ground) elder, danewort, Sambucus ebulus
Zwerghonigbiene f little bee, Apis florea
Zwerghuhn n miniature chicken, bantam
Zwergkaktus m crown cactus *(genus Rebutia)*
Zwergkastanie f *(bot)* Allegheny chinkapin, chinquapin, Castanea pumila
Zwergkiefer f dwarf Siberian pine, Pinus pumila
Zwergkirsche f Chinese fruiting cherry, Prunus (Padus) pseudocerasus
Zwergkräuselkrankheit f *(phyt)* curly dwarf disease, CD *(virosis)*

Zwerglaus

Zwerglaus f *(ent)* phylloxera *(family Phylloxeridae)*
Zwergmandel f [dwarf] Russian almond, Prunus tenella
Zwergmehlbeere f dwarf medlar, Sorbus chamaemespilus
Zwergmispel f *(bot)* cotoneaster *(genus Cotoneaster)*
Zwergmutante f *(gen)* dwarf [mutant]
Zwergpalme f dwarf fan palm, palmetto, Chamaerops humilis
Zwergpfeffer m *(bot)* peperomia *(genus Peperomia)*
Zwergpferd n pony, nag, galloway
Zwergpinscher m miniature pinscher *(dog breed)*
Zwergpudel m miniature poodle *(dog breed)*
Zwergrind n runt
Zwergrose f miniature (pot) rose
Zwergrost m der Gerste dwarf leaf rust of barley, barley brown rust *(caused by Puccinia hordei)*
Zwergschnauzer m miniature schnauzer *(dog breed)*
Zwergschneckenklee m little bur clover, small medic[k], Medicago minima
Zwergschnepfe f jack-snipe, Lymnocryptes minima
Zwergsorte f dwarf cultivar
Zwergspitzmaus f pygmy shrew, Sorex minutus
Zwergsteinbrand m des Weizens dwarf bunt [of wheat] *(caused by Tilletia contraversa)*
Zwergstrauch m dwarf shrub, low-bush
Zwergstrauchhalbwüste f low-bush semi-desert
Zwergstrauchheide f dwarf shrub heath
Zwergstrauchtundra f dwarf shrub tundra, low-bush tundra
Zwergtrappe f little bustard, Tetrax tetrax
Zwergvogelbeere f [red] chokeberry, Aronia arbutifolia
Zwergwacholder m dwarf juniper, Juniperus communis ssp. alpina
Zwergwasserlinse f *(bot)* water-meal, Wolffia arrhiza
Zwergweichsel f *(Am)* ground-cherry, Prunus (Cerasus) fruticosa
Zwergweizen m 1. dwarf wheat *(comprehensive term)*; 2. club wheat, Triticum aestivum ssp. compactum
Zwergwuchs m dwarfism, dwarf (stunted) growth, dwarf[ish]ness, nanism, nanosomia • auf ~ züchten to dwarf
~/chondrodystrophischer *(vet)* chondrodystrophy
zwergwüchsig dwarfed, dwarfish
Zwergwüchsigkeit f 1. dwarf stature; 2. *s.* Zwergwuchs
Zwergziege f dwarf goat
Zwergzikade f *(ent)* leaf-hopper, jassid *(family Jassidae)*
Zwetsche f *s.* Zwetschge
Zwetschge f [common, garden] plum, Prunus domestica [ssp. domestica]
Zwetschgennapfschildlaus f European fruit lecanium (scale), European peach scale, brown elm scale, Parthenolecanium (Eulecanium, Lecanium) corni
Zwicke f freemartin *(a usually sterile cow-calf twinborn with a bull-calf)*
Zwickenbildung f freemartinism
Zwiebel f 1. *(bot, zoo)* bulb; 2. onion, boll, Allium cepa [var. cepa]; 3. *s.* Brutzwiebel • **Zwiebeln bilden** to bulb
zwiebelartig *(bot, zoo)* bulbous; *(bot)* cepaceous
Zwiebelblasenfuß m *(ent)* onion thrips (louse), Thrips tabaci
Zwiebelboden m basal plate of bulb
Zwiebelbrand m *(phyt)* onion smut *(caused by Urocystis cepulae)*
Zwiebeldeckblatt n wrapper scale
Zwiebelerntemaschine f onion harvester
Zwiebelfäule f der Narzisse basal (fusarium) rot of narcissus *(caused by Fusarium oxysporum f.sp. narcissus)*
Zwiebelfliege f onion (bulb) fly, Hylemyia (Delia) antiqua
Zwiebelfliegenlarve f onion maggot
Zwiebelgelbstreifenvirus n onion yellow dwarf virus, OYDV
Zwiebelgemüse n bulb crops
Zwiebelgewächs n bulbous plant, bulb
Zwiebelgraufäule f der Tulpe grey bulb rot of tulip *(caused by Rhizoctonia tuliparum)*
Zwiebelhähnchen n *(ent)* onion leaf beetle, Lilioceris merdigera
Zwiebeliris f Dutch iris, Iris-Hollandica hybrid
Zwiebeljäter m onion weeder
Zwiebelknolle f onion, bulbo tuber, button
Zwiebelknospe f bulbil, bulbel, bulblet, brood bud
Zwiebelköpfer m onion topper
Zwiebellauch m onion green
Zwiebellaus f shallot aphid, Myzus ascalonicus
Zwiebelmehltau m onion downy mildew *(caused by Peronospora destructor = P. schleidenii)*
Zwiebelmondfliege f small narcissus fly, Eumerus strigatus
Zwiebelmosaikvirus n onion mosaic virus, OMV
Zwiebelmotte f leek moth, Acrolepia (Acrolepiopsis) assectella
Zwiebelöl n onion oil
Zwiebelpflanze f bulbous plant, bulb
Zwiebelring m onion ring
Zwiebelrost m onion (leek) rust *(caused by Puccinia porri)*
Zwiebelschale f onion-skin, bulb scale
Zwiebelschalenexplantat n bulb-scale explant
Zwiebelschalenvermehrung f *s.* Zwiebelschuppenvermehrung
Zwiebelscheibe f basal plate of bulb
Zwiebelschuppe f bulb scale
Zwiebelschuppenvermehrung f scaling *(e.g. of lilies)*

Zwiebelsegment *n* clove
Zwiebelsortierung *f* onion grading
zwiebeltragend bulbiferous, bulbous
Zwiebelzopf *m* onion string
Zwiebrache *f* double ploughing
Zwiehuhn *n* dual-purpose fowl
Zwiesel f(m) crotch, crutch, fork; forked branch; forked tree; double leader *(in young fruit-trees)*
Zwieselbaum *m* forked tree
Zwieselbildung *f* forking, bifurcation, forked growth
zwieselig bifurcated, forked
zwieseln to bifurcate
Zwieselstamm *m* forked (twin) stem
Zwieselung *f s.* Zwieselbildung
Zwiewuchs *m (phyt)* second growth *(e.g. of potato)*
Zwille *f s.* Zwieselbaum
Zwilling *m* 1. twin; 2. double-barrel[ed gun] • **Zwillinge gebären** to twin
Zwillinge mpl/zweieiige dizygotic (dioval) twins, biovular (fraternal) twins
Zwillingsdüsenregner *m* twin-nozzle sprinkler
Zwillingsfelge *f* twin wheel rim
Zwillingsgeburt *f* twin birth
Zwillingsgeburtenrate *f* twinning rate
Zwillingslamm *n* twin lamb
Zwillingsovulation *f* twin ovulation
Zwillingsräder *npl* twin (dual) wheels
Zwillingsreifen *m* dual tyre
Zwillingsträchtigkeit *f* twin pregnancy
Zwinger *m* kennel
Zwingerhusten *m* kennel cough, infectious tracheobronchitis of dogs, contagious respiratory disease of dogs
Zwischenachsdrillmaschine *f* mid-mounted seed drill
Zwischenachsgeräteträger *m* mid-mounted toolbar
Zwischenachshackrahmen *m* mid-mounted hoe
Zwischenachsmotor *m* mid-mounted engine
Zwischenachszapfwelle *f* under-belly p.t.o. (power take-off)
Zwischenadernmosaik *n (phyt)* interveinal mosaic *(virosis)*
~ der Johannisbeere interveinal white mosaic
Zwischenadernvergilbung *f (phyt)* intervenous yellowing
zwischenartlich interspecific
zwischenelterlich *(gen)* intermediate, intermediary
Zwischenernte *f* intermediate crop
Zwischenertrag *m s.* Zwischennutzungsertrag
Zwischenfohlzeit *f* foaling interval
Zwischenfrucht *f* intermediate (catch) crop
Zwischenfrucht[an]bau *m* catch cropping
Zwischenhäutungsstadium *n (ent)* instar
Zwischenhirn *n* diencephalon
Zwischenkalbezeit *f* calving interval (index)
Zwischenkiefer[knochen] *m* incisive bone

Zwischenknochenarterie *f* interosseous artery
Zwischenkultur *f* catch crop
Zwischenlager *n* **an der Feuerfront** line camp *(forest fire control)*
Zwischenlagerung *f* intermediate storage
Zwischenmast *m* intermediate support spar *(of cableway)*
Zwischenmelkzeit *f* milking interval
Zwischenmoor *n* transitional bog (moor, peatland)
Zwischenneuron *n* intercalated (connector) neuron, interneuron
Zwischennutzung *f (forest)* intermediate felling
~/landwirtschaftliche intermediate agricultural utilization *(esp. of forest land)*
Zwischennutzungsertrag *m (forest)* intermediate [harvest] yield, produce from thinnings
~/mittlerer jährlicher periodic mean annual intermediate yield, periodic stand depletion
zwischenpflanzen to interplant
Zwischenpflanzung *f* intercrop
Zwischenprodukt *n* intermediate [product], in-process material
Zwischenreihe *f* inter-row, aisle
Zwischenreihenabstand *m* inter-row spacing
Zwischenreihenbearbeitung *f* inter-row cultivation, intertillage
Zwischenringtasche *f* wax pocket *(of honey-bee)*
Zwischenrinnenerosion *f (soil)* interrill erosion
Zwischenrippenarterie *f* intercostal artery
Zwischenrippenmuskel *m* intercostal muscle
Zwischenröhrchenhorn *n* intertubular horn *(of hoof or claw)*
Zwischensaat *f* cover crop *(orcharding)*
zwischensäen to interseed, to intersow
Zwischenstamm *m* intermediary stock, interstock, interstem, filler *(in grafting)*
Zwischenstammglied *n (bot)* mesocotyl
zwischenständig *(forest)* intermediate, intermediary, subdominant, dominated *(crown class)*
Zwischenstoffwechsel *m* intermediate metabolism
Zwischenstromland *n* interfluve, interstream area
Zwischenstufenboden *m* intergrade soil
Zwischenstütze *f s.* Zwischenmast
Zwischenträchtigkeitszeit *f* **bei Hase und Kaninchen** kindling-to-mating interval
Zwischenveredeln *n* intermediate grafting, intergrafting, double grafting (working)
Zwischenveredelung *f* interstock graft[ing], intermediate graft[ing]
Zwischenveredelungsbaum *m* stem piece tree
Zwischenveredelungsteil *m* interstock, interstem [piece]
Zwischenwald *m* intermediate wood, alternate forest crop
Zwischenwirbelscheibe *f* intervertebral disk
Zwischenwirt *m* intermediate (bridging) host
zwischenwüchsig *s.* zwischenständig
Zwischenwurfzeit *f* farrowing interval

Zwischenzelle 730

Zwischenzelle f/**Leydigsche** Leydig cell *(of testicles)*
Zwischenzellraum m intercellular space
zwitschern to chirp
Zwitter m hermaphrodite, bisexual
Zwitterblüte f bisexual (hermaphrodite) flower
zwitterblütig *(bot)* androgynous
Zwitterblütigkeit f *(bot)* androgyny
Zwittertanne f Cunningham pine, China fir, Cunninghamia lanceolata
Zwittertum n hermaphroditism, bisexuality
Zwitterwicke f hairy tare, Vicia hirsuta
zwittrig *(bot, zoo)* hermaphroditic[al], bisexual
~/somatisch gynandromorphic
Zwittrigkeit f s. Zwittertum
Zwölfender m royal [stag]
Zwölffingerdarm m duodenum
Zwölffingerdarmentzündung f *(vet)* duodenitis
Zwölffingerdarmgeschwür n *(vet)* duodenal ulcer
Zwölfgepunktetes Spargelhähnchen n twelve-spotted asparagus beetle, Crioceris duodecimpunctata
Zwölf-Monate-Yams n twelve-months yam, yellow Guinea yam, cut-and-come-again yam, Dioscorea cayenensis
Zwölfzähniger Kiefernborkenkäfer m stenograph bark-beetle, pine tree beetle, Ips sexdentatus
Zyanose f *(vet)* cyanosis, blue jaundice
Zyathium n *(bot)* cyathium
Zybride f s. Zytoplasmahybride
zygomorph *(bot)* zygomorphic, dorsiventral
Zygospore f *(bot)* zygospore
Zygote f zygote
zygotisch zygotic
Zyklamen n cyclamen, Persian violet *(genus Cyclamen)*
Zyklamenmilbe f cyclamen (strawberry) mite, Tarsonemus (Steneotarsonemus) pallidus
zyklisch cyclic
Zyklitis f *(vet)* cyclitis
Zyklon m 1. cyclone, cyclonic storm; 2. s. Zyklonabscheider
Zyklonabscheider m cyclone, centrifugal separator
Zyklone f s. Tiefdruckgebiet
Zyklopenbiene f cyclops honey-bee *(malformation)*
Zyklus m [oestrous] cycle • **ohne** ~ acyclic
Zyklushormon n sex hormone
Zyklussteuerung f oestrous cycle control, oestrus control
Zylinderholzschleifmaschine f drum-sander
Zylindermäher m cylinder mower
Zylinderputzer[strauch] m *(bot)* 1. bottle-brush *(genus Callistemon)*; 2. crimson bottle-brush, Callistemon citrinus
Zylinderrasenmäher m cylinder lawn mower
Zylindertrieur m indented cylinder seed cleaner, cylinder separator, cockle cylinder

Zylindertrockner m tumble dryer
Zylinderzellenausleser m s. Zylindertrieur
Zymase f zymase *(mixture of enzymes)*
zymogen zymogenic, zymogenous
Zymogen n zymogen, proenzyme, enzyme precursor
Zypergras n 1. cypress grass, flat sedge *(genus Cyperus)*; 2. yellow nutsedge, Cyperus esculentus
Zypresse f cypress *(genus Cupressus)*
Zypressenkochie f summer cypress, Kochia (Bassia) scoparia
Zypressenkraut n lavender cotton, cotton lavender, Santolina chamaecyparissus
Zypressenwolfsmilch f cypress spurge, Euphorbia cyparissias
Zyste f *(zoo, vet)* cyst • **zur ~ werden** to encyst
Zystenbildung f encystation, encystment
Zysteneinschluß m encystation, encystment
Zystennematode m s. Wurzelzystenälchen
Zystenniere f polycyclic kidney [disease]
Zystitis f *(vet)* cystitis
Zystizerkose f *(vet)* cysticercosis, measles
Zystizerkus m cysticercus *(larva of numerous tapeworms)*
Zystolith m *(bot, vet)* cystolith
Zyto... s. a. Zell... und Cyto...
Zytoarchitektonik f cytoarchitectonics
Zytobiologie f cyto[bio]logy, cellular biology
Zytoblast m cytoblast, cell nucleus, karyon
Zytoblasten... s. Zellkern...
zytochemisch cytochemical
zytogen cytogenic, cytogenous
Zytogenese f cytogenesis, cell formation, cellularization
Zytogenetik f cytogenetics
zytogenetisch cytogenetic[al]
Zytokinese f cytokinesis, cell division, fission *(for compounds s. under Zellteilung)*
zytokinetisch cytokinetic
Zytokinin n cytokinin, kinin *(phytohormone)*
Zytologie f cytology
zytologisch cytological
Zytolyse f cytolysis
Zytolysin n cytolysin
Zytolysom n, **Zytolysosom** n cytolysosome
zytolytisch cytolytic
Zytomegalievirus n cytomegalovirus
Zytomixis f cytomixis
zytopathisch cytopathic
zytopathogen cytopathogenic
Zytopempsis f cytopempsis
Zytophotometer n cytophotometer
Zytophotometrie f cytophotometry
Zytoplasma n cytoplasm, cell plasma
~ der Nervenzelle neuroplasm
Zytoplasmafortsatz m **einer Nervenzelle** dendrite
Zytoplasmahybride f cybrid

zytoplasmatisch cytoplasmic
~ **[bedingt] männlich steril** *(bot)* cytoplasmic male-sterile, cms
Zytoplasmon *n* cytoplasmon
Zytostatikum *n* cytostatic
zytostatisch cytostatic
Zytotaxonomie *f* cytotaxonomy

Zytotoxin *n* cytotoxin
zytotoxisch cytotoxic
Zytotoxizität *f* cytotoxicity
Zytozentrum *n* centrosome
Z-Zelle *f* plasm[a] cell
ZZ-Rübe *f s.* Z-Rübe